# Contents

# BRADFORD'S
# CROSSWORD
# SOLVER'S
# DICTIONARY

## ANNE R. BRADFORD

Collins

Published by Collins
An imprint of HarperCollins Publishers
Westerhill Road
Bishopbriggs
Glasgow G64 2QT

Tenth Edition 2016

10 9 8 7 6 5 4 3 2 1

© Anne R. Bradford 1986, 1993, 1997,
2000, 2003, 2005, 2007, 2009, 2012,
2013, 2015, 2016

This edition: © Anne R. Bradford 2016

The Author hereby asserts her moral rights
to be identified as the author of this work.

First edition published by Longman;
second, third and fourth editions published
by Peter Collin Publishing Ltd

ISBN 978-0-00-812171-6

Collins® is a registered trademark of
HarperCollins Publishers Limited

www.collinsdictionary.com

Typeset by Davidson Publishing Solutions,
Glasgow

Printed in Great Britain by Clays Ltd,
St Ives plc

If you would like to comment on any aspect
of this book, please contact us at the given
address or online.
E-mail: dictionaries@harpercollins.co.uk
facebook.com/collinsdictionary
@collinsdict

# Author's Preface

Word puzzles have existed nearly as long as words themselves with examples being found during archaeological excavations. In his book, *The Anatomy of the Crossword*, D.St.P. Barnard describes letter patterns in triangular or diamantine form and an ingenious word square discovered at a Roman site at Cirencester.

Word puzzles are a source of pleasure even to quite young children. I myself remember playing a game where we each had a square grid – 5×5 or 6×6 – and we took turns choosing a letter to insert in it until all the squares were occupied, scoring points for any proper words that appeared either across the grid or down.

The Victorians were fond of acrostics, usually in verse form with the initial letters of each line giving the solution. Double acrostics went a step further with both the initial and last letters of each line being employed. At first these tended to be tributes of a sort. They became quite difficult puzzles when the initial verse was turned into a definition of the answer, and the subsequent lines became clues to the acrostic part.

> We shun the light and fly by night (BAT (initial letter) OWL (final))
> 1. An interjection that may make you start                    BoO
> 2. A feathered foe may pierce you to the heart                ArroW
> 3. A tax oft levied on a horse and cart                       TolL

Many years later we were playing a simpler version (BAT is the only answer),
> My first is in cable, but not in wire,
> My second in arson, but not in fire
> My last is in lettuce, though not in bean
> My whole in daylight is rarely seen.

Spoken word games were equally popular before the age of electronics. 'I-spy' is still with us and repetitive round games are very good for the memory. For example, 'I love my love with an A because she is – adorable', to be repeated by the next player who adds 'I love my love with a B because she is – beautiful' and on through the alphabet, but ignoring X and Z for the most part.

Acrostics were followed by the earliest form of the crossword as we know it, consisting of simple grids which allowed for both across and down answers, hence 'cross' words. The USA was the first country to provide this exercise in regular print when the *New York World* introduced it in 1913. More than a decade passed before such puzzles appeared in Britain, with *The Sunday Times* being the first to publish one, in 1925. People soon became addicted and the popular postcard manufacturers were quick to bring out postcards with a crossword theme, as in this illustration:

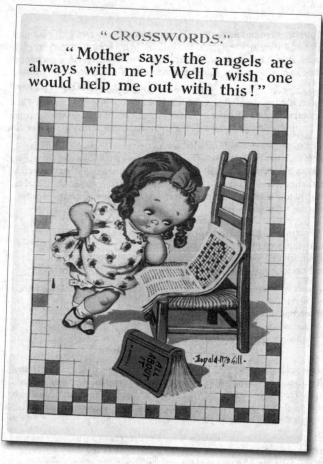

*One of the thirty-seven comic crossword designs by Donald McGill. Reproduced with consent from the Donald McGill Archive & Museum, Ryde.*

My mother and at least one of her sisters loved crosswords, so I was introduced to them at an early age. She had taught me to read and write long before I started school – entry in those days being after the 5th birthday – but although I had a passion for words I did no regular crossword puzzles until my late teens, and it was a few years more before I really took them seriously. I struggled with the weekly Ximenes puzzle in the weekend paper, learning many new words. He was particularly fond of 'lat' a form of pillar, so I started to write down a sort of memorandum. It was then that the idea came to me of a 'reverse dictionary' where headword and definition would change place. Full of enthusiasm, and by this time staying at home raising a family, I wrote to several leading dictionary publishers, none of whom were interested – possibly rightly so because when I pressed ahead with the project regardless, it was over 20 years before I had anything like enough material for a book. I analysed each crossword I completed (as I do still), selecting synonyms, cross-references, familiar adjectives and also anagram indicators. These were entered into alphabetical files and each week I worked out the percentage already included, having a target of 70% in mind in order to make a book worthy of publication. It was quite a few years before I converted to an alphabetical main file, my back-up ones being indexed by page numbers. Besides analysing puzzles I was also working my way through English dictionaries and other word books in search of further material, and barely arriving at the end of one before a new edition of another reached the market.

It was about 25 years before my labours bore fruit with the eventual appearance of *Longman's Crossword Solver's Dictionary* in 1986, but the firm was taken over by Penguin around 1990 and the reference section closed down, so I was once again seeking a publisher. A year or so later I was lucky to find Peter Collin, who published only reference works. The name *Collin's Crossword Solver's Dictionary* was unsuitable for obvious reasons, and so it became Bradford's, but might well have been Collins when this company took it on in 2002. Happily they decided my surname was sufficiently established and should remain, and as Michael, my eldest grandson, seems to have inherited my love of crosswords, he has been appointed to succeed me in due course, so that the name Bradford's will continue.

Who knows how long crosswords will survive, given our present electronic age and the advance of numerical puzzles. I am delighted to have been involved with them for most of my life, and to have made so many friends along the way. My sincere thanks to you all for your encouragement and for keeping me on my toes, and to the team at Collins who are so supportive.

Anne R. Bradford  *2015*

# Solving Crossword Clues

Crossword puzzles tend to be basically 'quick' or 'cryptic'. A 'quick' crossword usually relies on a one- or two-word clue which is a simple definition of the answer required. Many words have different meanings, so that the clue 'ball' could equally well lead to the answer 'sphere', 'orb', or 'dance'. The way to solve 'quick' crosswords is to press on until probable answers begin to interlink, which is a good sign that you are on the right track.

'Cryptic' crosswords are another matter. Here the clue usually consists of a basic definition, given at either the beginning or end of the clue, together with one or more definitions of parts of the answer. Here are some examples taken from all-time favourites recorded over the years:

1. *'Tradesman who bursts into tears'* (**Stationer**)

    *Tradesman* is a definition of stationer. *Bursts* is cleverly used as an indication of an anagram, which *into tears* is of stationer.

2. *'Sunday school tune'* (**Strain**)

    Here *Sunday* is used to define its abbreviation S, *school* is a synonym for train, and put together they give strain, which is a synonym of *tune*.

3. *'Result for everyone when head gets at bottom'* (**Ache**)
   (used as a 'down' clue)

    This is what is known as an '& lit' clue, meaning that the setter has hit on a happy composition which could literally be true. *Everyone* here is a synonym for each, move the *head* (first letter) of the word to the *bottom*, and the answer is revealed, the whole clue being the definition of the answer in this case.

4. *'Tin out East'* (**Sen**)

    In this example, *tin*, implying 'money', requires its chemical symbol Sn to go *out*(side) *East*, or its abbreviation, E, the whole clue being a definition of a currency (sen) used in the East.

5. *'Information given to communist in return for sex'* (**Gender**)

   *Information* can be defined as gen, *communist* is almost always red, *in return* indicates 'reversed', leading to gen-der, a synonym for *sex*.

6. *'Row about no enclosure of this with sardines'* (**Tin-opener**)

   *Row* is a synonym for tier, *about* indicates 'surrounding', *no enclosure* can be no pen, leading to ti-no pen-er, and another '& lit' clue.

7. *'Cake-sandwiches-meat, at Uncle Sam's party'* (**Clambake**)

   *Meat* here is lamb, *sandwiches* is used as a verb, so we have C-lamb-ake, which is a kind of party in America. *Uncle Sam* or US is often used to indicate America.

8. *'Initially passionate meeting of boy and girl could result in it'* (**Pregnancy**)

   *Initially* is usually a sign of a first letter, in this case 'p' for *passionate* + Reg (a *boy*) and Nancy (a *girl*), and another clever '& lit'.

With 'cryptic' clues the solver needs to try to analyse the parts to see what he or she is looking for – which word or words can be the straight definition, and which refer to the parts or hint at anagrams or other subterfuges. Whilst it would be unrealistic to claim total infallibility, practice has shown that in most crosswords some 90% of the answers are to be found in this work.

Anne R. Bradford

# How to Use the Dictionary

This dictionary is the result of nearly sixty years' analysis of some 475,000 crossword clues, ranging from plain 'quick' crosswords requiring only synonyms to the different level of cryptic puzzles. Therefore the words listed at each entry may be connected to the keyword in various ways, such as:

- a straightforward synonym
- a commonly-associated adjective
- an associated or proper noun
- a pun or other devious play on words

Keywords are listed alphabetically; in cases where the heading consists of more than one word, the first of these words is taken to be the keyword, and in cases where the end of a word is bracketed, the material up to the opening bracket is taken to be the keyword. Keywords marked with the symbol ▶ refer the user to other entries where additional information may be found. Keywords marked with the symbol ▷ give leads to anagrams and other ploys used by crossword setters. If the keywords found in the clue do not lead directly to the required answer, the solver should look under words given as cross-references to other entries. These are indicated by the symbol →, with the cross-referenced word shown in capitals.

Some additional entries have been divided into two parts – a general entry similar to the standard entries which appear elsewhere, and a panel entry which contains a list of more specific or encyclopedic material. So, for example, the entry 'Artist(e), Artistic' includes not only a list of general words connected with 'Artist', 'Artiste', or 'Artistic' in some way, such as 'Bohemian', 'Cubist', 'Fine', and 'Virtuoso', but also a panel with the heading 'Artists' containing a list of the names of specific artists, such as 'Bellini', 'Constable', and 'Rembrandt'. For added help, the words in these panels are arranged by length, with all three-letter words grouped together in alphabetical order, then all four-letter words, then all five-letter words, and so on.

**Publisher's Note**

All words included in this publication have been sourced from crossword puzzles published in the last sixty years, and no word is excluded on the grounds of religion, gender, or race. The presence of any word does not in any way represent the views of the author or the Publisher, HarperCollins.

# The Crossword Club

If you are interested in crosswords, you might like to consider joining the Crossword Club. Membership is open to all who enjoy tackling challenging crosswords and who appreciate the finer points of clue-writing and grid-construction. The Club's magazine, *Crossword*, contains two prize puzzles each month. A sample issue and full details are available on request.

The Crossword Club
Coombe Farm
Awbridge
Romsey, Hants.
SO51 0HN
UK

email: bh@thecrosswordclub.co.uk
website address: www.thecrosswordclub.co.uk

## About the Author

Anne Bradford's love of words began to make itself evident even in her schooldays, when, as Head Girl of her school, she instituted a novel punishment – instead of making rulebreakers write lines, she had them write out pages from a dictionary, on the grounds that this was a more useful exercise. Little did she know this was soon to be her own daily routine!

As Anne tells in her preface to this edition, she conceived the idea for the dictionary pretty well along with her first child. Over the space of 25 years, Anne continued to build on her collection of solutions, analysing every crossword clue as she solved it and adding it to her steadily growing bank of entries. This unique body of material eventually reached such proportions that she had the idea of offering it to her fellow crossword solvers as a reference book, and since then, the book has gone from strength to strength, providing valuable help to countless cruciverbalists over a number of editions.

Anne Bradford continues to devote time each day to solving crosswords, averaging some 20 a week – both quick and cryptic – and still avidly collects new solutions for her *Crossword Solver's Dictionary* at a rate of around 150 a week, compiling each solution by hand (without the use of a computer!). This latest edition therefore includes much new material, gleaned by a true crossword lover who not only solves crosswords but, as an active member of the Crossword Club, can offer the user an insight into the mind of a cunning crossword compiler.

# Aa

**A, An** Ack, Adult, Ae, Alpha, Angstrom, Are, Argon, D, Ein, Her, If, L, One, Per, They

**A1** Tiptop

**AA** Milne

**Aardvark** Ant-bear, Ant-eater, Earth-hog, Ground-hog

**Aaron's Rod** Hagtaper

**Aba, Abba** Patriarch

**Abacus** Counter, Soroban

**Abaft** Astern, Sternson

**Abalone** Ormer, Paua, Perlemoen

**Abandon(ed), Abandonment** Abdicate, Abnegate, Abort, Adrift, Aguna(h), Amoral, Apostasy, Back down, Cade, Cancel, Castaway, Cast off, Chuck, Corrupt, Decommission, Defect, Derelict, →DESERT, Desolate, Desuetude, →Dice, Discard, Disown, Dissolute, Disuse, Ditch, Drop, Dump, Elan, Evacuate, Expose, Flagrant, Forhoo(ie), Forhow, Forlend, Forsake, Gomorra, Gretel, Hansel, Homeless, Immoral, Jack(-in), Jettison, Jilt, Leave, Licentious, Lonely, Loose, Louche, Mad, Maroon, Old, Orgiastic, Profligate, Quit, Rakish, Rat, Relinquish, Renounce, Reprobate, Resign, Scrap, Scrub, Shed, Shelve, Sink, Strand, Vacate, Waive, Wanton, Wild, Yield

**Abase** Degrade, Demean, Disgrace, Eat crow, Embrute, Grovel, →HUMBLE, Kowtow, Lessen

**Abash(ed)** Daunt, Discountenance, Mortify, Shame-faced

**Abate(ment)** Allay, Appal, Decrescent, Deduction, Defervescence, Diminish, Ending, Let up, Lyse, Lysis, Moderate, Reduce, Remit, →SUBSIDE

▷ **Abate** *may indicate* a contention

**Abattoir** Knackery, Slaughterhouse

**Abbey** Abbacy, Ampleforth, Bath, Buckfast, Cloister, Downside, Fonthill, Fountains, Glastonbury, Györ, Je(r)vaulx, Medmenham, Melrose, Minster, Nightmare, Northanger, Priory, Rievaulx, Tintern, Westminster, Whitby, Woburn

**Abbot** Aelfric, Archimandrite, Brother, Eutyches, Friar

**Abbreviate, Abbreviation** Abridge, Ampersand, Compendium, Condense, Curtail, →SHORTEN, Sigla

**ABC** Absey

**Abdicate, Abdication** Cede, Demission, Disclaim, Disown, Resign

**Abdomen** Belly, C(o)eliac, Epigastrium, Gaster, Hypochondrium, Opisthosoma, Paunch, Pleon, →STOMACH, Tummy, Venter, Ventral

**Abduct(ed), Abduction** Asport, Enlèvement, Kidnap, Rapt, Ravish, Shanghai, Steal

**Aberdeen** Granite City

**Aberrant, Aberration** Abnormal, Aye-aye, Boss, Chromatic, Deviant, Idolon, Perverse, Spherical

**Abet(tor)** Aid, Back, Candle-holder, Second

**Abeyance, Abeyant** Dormant, Shelved, Sleeping, Store

**Abhor(rent)** →DETEST, Dissent, Execrable, →HATE, Loathe, Odious, Shun

**Abide (by)** Accept, Adhere, Dwell, Inhere, →LAST, Lie, Live, Observe, Remain, Stand, Tarry

**Abigail** Maid, Masham

**Ability** Acumen, Aptitude, Calibre, Capacity, Cocum, →COMPETENCE, Efficacy, ESP, Facility, Faculty, Ingine, Initiative, Instinct, Lights, Potential, Power, Prowess, Savey, Savoir-faire, Savv(e)y, Skill, Talent, Tenacity

**Abject** Base, Craven, Grovel, Humble, Servile, Slave

**Abjure** Eschew, Forswear, Recant, Renege, Reny

**Ablaze** Afire, Alow, Ardent

**Able** Ablins, Accomplished, →ADEPT, Aiblins, Apt, Can, Capable, →COMPETENT, Fere, Fit, Idiot savant, Literate, Proficient, Seaman, Streetwise, Yibbles

**Abnegate** Disown

**Abnormal(ity)** Anomalous, Aplasia, Atypical, Autism, →DEVIANT, Dysfunction, Ectopic, Erratic, Etypical, Exceptional, Freakish, Hare-lip, Malocclusion, Odd, Peloria, Phenocopy, Preternatural, →QUEER, Sport, Teras, Trisome, Unconventional, Unnatural, Varus

**Aboard** On

**Abode** Domicile, Dwelling, Habitat, →HOME, In(n), Lain, Libken, Lien, Limbo, Midgard, Remain, Seat

**Abolish, Abolition(ist)** Abrogate, Annihilate, Annul, Axe, →BAN, D, Delete, Destroy, Eradicate, Erase, Extirpate, John Brown, Nullify, Remove, Repeal, Rescind, Scrap, Tubman, Wilberforce

**Abomasum** Read

**Abominable, Abominate, Abomination** Anathema, Bane, Cursed, →HATE, Nefandous, Nefast, Revolting, Snowman, Vile, Yeti

**Aboriginal, Aborigine** Adivasi, Ainu, Aranda, Autochthon, Awakabai, Binghi, Black-fellow, Boong, Buck, Bushman, Carib, Devil's Marbles, Dharuk, Dhurga, Dieri, Diyari, Evolué, Fringe-dweller, Gin, Gurindji, Indigenous, Inuit, Jacky(-Jacky), Kamilaroi, Kipper, Koori, Lubra, Maori, Mary, Motu, Myall, Negro, Nisga'a, Nyunga(r), Pintubi, Pitjant(j)at)jara, Pre-Dravidian, Sakai, San, Sican, Siwash, Truganini, Vedda(h), Warlpiri, Wemba, Weniba, Wergaia, Wiradhui, Wiradjai, Yagara, Yupik

**Abort(ion), Abortive** Apiol, Back-street, Cancel, Chlamydial, Contagious, Ecbolic, Foeticide, Induced, Misbirth, Miscarry, Moon-calf, Slip, Sooterkin, Spontaneous, Teras, Termination

**Abound(ing)** Bristle, Copious, Enorm, Flush, Overflow, Rich, Rife, Swarm, Teem

**About** A, Almost, Anent, Around, C, Ca, Cir(c), Circa, Circiter, Concerning, Encompass, Environs, Going, Near, Of, On, Over, Re, Regarding, Round, Soon at, Upon

▷ **About** *may indicate* one word around another

**Above** Abune, Aforementioned, Aloft, Over, Overhead, Overtop, Owre, Sopra, Superior, Supra-, Suspicion, Ubi supra, Upon, Us

**Abracadabra** Cantrip, Heypass

**Abrade, Abrasive** Alumina, Carbanado, Carborundum®, Chafe, Emery, Erode, File, Garnet paper, →GRATE, Ground glass, Rub, Sand(paper), Scrape, Scrat, Scuff

**Abraham** Father of the faithful, Lincoln, Patriarch, Urite

**Abreast** Afront, Alongside, Au courant, Au fait, Beside, Level, Up

**Abridge(ment)** Audley, Compress, Condense, Contract, Cut, Digest, Dock, Edit, Epitome, Pot, Shorten, Trim

**Abroad** Afield, Away, Distant, Elsewhere, Forth, Offshore, Out, Overseas

▷ **Abroad** *may indicate* an anagram

**Abrogate** Abolish, Repeal, Replace, Rescind

**Abrupt(ly)** Bold, Brusque, Curt, Gruff, Jerky, Offhand, Premorse, Prerupt, Sharp, Short, Staccato, Terse

▷ **Abrupt** *may indicate* a shortened word

**Abscess** Gumboil, Impost(h)ume, Ulcer, Warble

**Abscond** Absquatulate, Bolt, Decamp, Desert, Elope, Escape, Flee, Jump ship, Leg-bail, Levant, Run away, Truant, Welch, Welsh

**Abseil(ing)** Dulfer, Rappel, Roping-down

**Absence, Absent(ee), Absent-minded(ness)** A, Abs, Abstracted, Away, AWOL, Distant, Distracted, Distrait, Dreamy, Drought, Exeat, Exile, Gone, Hookey, Lack, Malingerer, Missing, Mitch, No show, Oblivious, Sabbatical, Scatty, Skip, Truant, Vacuity, Vague, Void, Wanting, Wool-gathering

**Absinthe** Wormwood

**Absolute(ly)** Arrant, Bang, Complete, Dead, Deep-dyed, Downright, Fairly, Flat, Heartily, Implicit, Indeed, Ipso facto, Just, Literally, Meer, Mere, Mondo, Nominative, Not half, Okey-doke(y), Outright, Plenary, Plumb, Quite, Real, Sheer, Simply, Thorough, Total, Truly, Unadulterated, Unbounded, Unconditional, Unmitigated, Unqualified, Utter, Veritable, Very, Yeah

**Absolve, Absolution** Acquit, Assoil, Assoilzie, Clear, Exculpate, Excuse, Exonerate, Pardon, Redeem, Shrift, Shrive

**Absorb(ed), Absorbent, Absorbing, Absorption** Assimilate, Autism, Blot, Consume, Desiccant, Devour, Digest, Dope, Drink, Eat, →ENGROSS, Enrapt, Imbibe, Immerse, Ingest, Inhaust, Intent, Merge(r), Occlude, Occupy, Osmosis, Permeable, Porous, Preoccupation, Preoccupied, Rapt, Sorbefacient, Spongy, Subsume, Unputdownable, Yrapt

**Absquatulate** Skedaddle

**Abstain(er), Abstemious, Abstention, Abstinence, Abstinent** Band of Hope, Celibacy, Chastity, Continent, Desist, Eschew, Fast, Forbear, Forgo, Maigre, Nazarite, Nephalism, Pioneer, Rechab(ite), Refrain, Resist, Sober, Teetotaller, Temperate, TT, Virtue

**Abstract(ed), Abstraction** Abrege, Abridge, Academic, Appropriate, Brief, Compendium, Deduct, Digest, Discrete, Distrait, Dreamy, Epitome, Essence, Inconscient, Metaphysical, Musing, Notional, Précis, Preoccupied, Prepossessed, Prescind, Remove, Résumé, Reverie, Scatty, Stable, Steal, Subduct, Summary, Syllabus, Tachism

**Abstruse** Arcane, Deep, Esoteric, Impenetrable, Obscure, Recondite

**Absurd(ity)** Alician, Apagoge, Charade, Cockeyed, Fantastic, Farcical, Folly, Gonzo, Inept, Irrational, Laputan, Ludicrous, Madness, Nonsense, Paradox, Preposterous, Priceless, Ridiculous, Risible, Silly, Solecism, Stupid, Toshy, Whim-wham

**Abundance, Abundant** Abounding, A-gogo, Ample, Aplenty, Bounty, Copious, Corn in Egypt, Cornucopia, Cosmic, Excess, Flood, Flush, Fouth, Fowth, Fruitful, Galore, Lashings, Lavish, Liberal, Luxuriance, Manifold, Mickle, Mine, Mint, Muckle, Natural, Oodles, Oodlins, Opulent, Over, Plenitude, Plenteous, →PLENTIFUL, Plenty, Pleroma, Plethora, Plurisie, Profusion, Prolific, Relative, Replete, Rich, Rife, Rock and manger, Routh, Rowth, Sonce, Sonse, Store, Stouth and routh, Superabound, Surfeit, Tallents, Teeming, Tons, Uberous

**Abuse(r), Abusive** Assail, Becall, Billingsgate, Blackguard, Chemical, Clapperclaver, Contumely, Cruelty, Diatribe, Ear-bashing, Flak, Fustilarian, Fustil(l)irian, Hail, Hate mail, Ill-treat, Ill-use, Injury, Insolent, Insult, Invective, Jobbery, Limehouse, Malpractice, Maltreat, Miscall, →MISTREAT, Misuse, Mofo, Molest, Mud, Obloquy, Oppress, Opprobrium, Philippic, Rail, Rampallian, Rate, Rayle, Revile, Ritual, Satanic, Satire, Scarab(ee), Scurrilous, Serve, Sexual, Slang, Slate, Sledging, Snash, Solvent, Stick, Strap, Substance, Thersitical, Tirade, Torture, Traduce, Verbal, Vilify, Violate, Vituperation, Wosbird

**Abut** Adjoin, Border, Touch

**Abysm(al), Abyss** Avernus, Barathrum, Barranca, Chasm, Deep, Gulf, Swallet, Tartarean, Tartarus

**Abyssinia** Ethiopia

**AC** Current, Erk

**Acacia** Bablah, Boree, Brigalow, Eumong, Eumung, Fever tree, Gidgee, Gidjee, Koa, Mimosa, Mulga, Myall, Sallee, Shittim, Wattle

**Academic(ian)** A, Acca, Acker, Chair, Della-Cruscan, Don, Erudite, Fellow, Hypothetic(al), Immortals, Literati, Master, Pedantic, PRA, Prof(essor), RA, Reader, Rector, Scholar

**Academy, Academic** A, Athenaeum, Bookish, Dollar, Donnish, Forty, French, Learned, Loretto, Lyceum, Military, Naval, Oxbridge, Plantilla, RA, Royal, St Cyr, Sandhurst, School, Seminary, Studious, The Shop, West Point

**Acanthus** Brankursine, Ruellia

**Accede** Defer

**Accelerate, Acceleration, Accelerator** Antedate, Betatron, Bevatron, Collider, Cosmotron, Cyclotron, Festinate, G, Gal, Grav, Gun, Hasten, Increase, Linac, Linear, Rev, Signatron, Speed, Stringendo, Supercollider, Synchrotron, Throttle

**Accent(ed), Accentuate** Acute, Beat, Breve, Brogue, Bur(r), Circumflex, Cut-glass, Doric, Drawl, Enclitic, Enhance, Gammat, Grave, Hacek, Intonation, Kelvinside, Lilt, Long, Macron, Marcato, Martelé, Mockney, Morningside, Mummerset, Nasal, Orthotone, Oxford, Oxytone, Paroxytone, Perispomenon, Pitch, Primary, Proparoxytone, Rhotic, Rhythm, Rinforzando, Secondary, Sforzando, Stress, Tittle, Tone, Tonic, Twang

**Accentor** Dunnock

**Accept(able), Acceptance, Accepted, Accepting** A, Accede, Adequate, Admit, Adopt, Agree, Allow, Alright, Approbate, Bar, Believe, Buy, Can-do, Common, Compliant, Consent, Cool, Cosher, Decent, Done, Eligible, Embrace, Epenthesis, Freeload, Going, Grant, Idee recue, Include, Kosher, Meet, Nod, Obey, On, Orthodox, Pocket, Putative, Realise, Receive, Resipiscence, Satisfactory, Settle, Stand, Street cred, Suppose, Swallow, Take (on board), Tolerate, U, Valid, Wear, Widespread

**Access(ible), Accessibility, Accession** Arrival, Avenue, Blue-jacking, Card, Come-at-able, Conditional, Credit, Direct, Door, Entrée, → **ENTRY**, Fit, Gateway, Get-at-able, Hack, Ingo, Key, Log in, Log on, Manhole, Near, Open, Passe-partout, Passkey, Password, Phreaking, Ping, Random, Recourse, Remote, Sequential, Sociable, Spasm, Telnet, Wayleave

**Accessory, Accessories** Abettor, Addition, Aide, Ally, Ancillary, Appendage, Appurtenance, Attachment, Attribute, Bandanna, Bells and whistles, Cribellum, Cuff-links, Extra, Findings, Fitment, Staffage, Trappings, Trimming, Umbrella

**Accident(al)** Adventitious, Arbitrary, Bechance, Blowdown, Blunder, Calamity, → **CHANCE**, Circumstance, Contingency, Contretemps, Crash, Criticality, Dent, Disaster, Double flat, Fall, Fluke, Fortuitous, Hap, Hit and run, Inadvertent, Meltdown, Mischance, Mishap, Note, Pile up, Prang, Promiscuous, Random, Rear-ender, Shunt, Smash, Smash-up, Spill, Stramash, Unintentional, Unmeant, Wreck

**Accidie** Acedia, Sloth, Torpor

**Acclaim** Accolade, Applaud, Brava, Bravo, Cheer, Clap, Credit, Eclat, Encomium, Fame, Fanfare, Hail, Kudos, Ovation, Praise, Salute, Toast, Zindabad

**Acclimatize** Attune

**Accolade** Award, Brace, Dubbing, Honour, Palm, Token, Tribute

**Accommodate, Accommodating, Accommodation** Accustom, Adapt, Almshouse, Amenable, B and B, Bedsit, Berth, Billet, Board, Botel, Bunkhouse, Camp, Chalet, Chambers, Compromise, Crashpad, Digs, Flotel, Gaff, Gite, Grace and favour, Hall, Homestay, Hostel, Hotel, House, Humour, Lend, Loan, Lodge, Lodgement, Minshuku, Motel, → **OBLIGE**, Parador, Pension, Penthouse, Pew, Pliant, Prefab, Quarters, Rapprochement, Recurve, Room, Sheltered, Single-end, Sorehon, Stabling, Stateroom, Steerage, Storage, Tent, Timeshare, Wharepuni, Xenodochium, Youth hostel

▷ **Accommodating** *may indicate* one word inside another

**Accompany(ing), Accompanied (by), Accompaniment, Accompanist** Accessory, Alberti, And, Attach, Attend, Backing, Chaperone, Chum, Concomitant, Consort, Continuo, Descant, Duenna, Enclose, → **ESCORT**, Fixings, Harmonise, Herewith, Obbligato, Obligate, Obligato, Repetiteur, Soundtrack, Trimmings, Vamp, Wag

**Accomplice** Abettor, Aide, → **ALLY**, Bagman, Bonnet, Collaborator, Confederate, Federarie, Federary, Partner, Shill, Stale, Swagsman

**Accomplish(ed), Accomplishment** Able, → **ACHIEVE**, Arch, Attain, Clever, Complete, Consummate, Done, Doss, Effect, Expedite, Exploit, Galant, Master, Over, Perform, Polished, Prowess, Put through, Realise, Ripe, Savant, Success, Tour de force

**Accord, According(ly), According to** After, Agree, Ala, Allow, As per, Attune, Chime, Congree, Consensus, Give, Grant, Harmony, Jibe, Meech Lake, Meet, One, Per, So, Sort, Thus

**According to nature** SN

**Accordion** Bandoneary, Button, Concertina, Flutina, Piano, Squeeze-box

**Accost** Abord, Approach, Greet, Hail, Importune, Molest, Solicit, Tackle

**Account(s)** AC, Anecdote, Appropriation, Audit, Battels, Behalf, Bill, Books, Budget, Cause, Charge, Checking, Chequing, Chronicle, Control, Current, Deposit, Description, Detailed, Discretionary, Drawing, Due, Enarration, Expense, Explain, Explanation, Exposition, ISA, Joint, Lawin, Ledger, Log, Long, Memoir, Narration, Nominal, Nostro, Numbered, Overdue, Procès-verbal, Real, Reason, Recital, Record, Regest, Register, Relation, → **REPORT**, Repute, Résumé, Sake, Short, Statement, Suspense, Swindlesheet, Tab, Tale, TESSA, Thesis, Trust, Version, Viable, Vostro

**Accountable** Responsible

**Accountancy, Accountant** Auditor, Bean counter, Bookkeeper, CA, Cost, Double entry, Forensic, Hyde, Liquidator, Purser, Reckoner, Single entry, Vestry-clerk

**Accoutrement** Frontlet

**Accredit** Attribute

**Accrue** Earn, Grow

**Accumulate, Accumulation** Accrue, Adsorb, Aggregate, → **AMASS**, Augment, Backlog, Build, Collect, Drift, Gather, Hoard, Lodg(e)ment, Multiply, Oedema, Pile, Pool, Rack up, Run up, Save, Stockpile, Uplay

**Accuracy, Accurate(ly)** Bang-on, Cocker, → **CORRECT**, Dead-on, Exact, Fair, Faultless, Fidelity, Griff, Minute, Precise, Realistic, Right, Spot-on, To scale, True, Unerring, Veracious, Word-perfect

**Accursed** Argued, Blest, Blist, Damned, Sacred

**Accusation, Accuse(d)** Allege, Arraign, Asperse, Attaint, Bill, Blame, Calumny, Censure, Challenge, Charge, Criminate, Denounce, Dite, Gravamen, Impeach, Impute, Incriminate, Indictment, Information, Name, Panel, Plaint, Prosecute, Recrimination, Suspect, Tax, Threap, Threep, Traduce, Wight, Wite, Wyte

**Accustom(ed)** Acquaint, Attune, Enure, General, Habituate, Harden, Inure, Teach, Wont, Woon

**Ace(s)** Basto, Blackjack, Crabs, Crack, Demon, Dinger, → **EXPERT**, Jot, Master, Mega, Mournival, One, Quatorze, Smashing, Spadille, Spadill(i)o, Spot, Tib, Virtuoso, Whizz, Wonderful

**Acerbate** Intensify

**Acetylene** Carbide, Ethyne

**Ache, Aching** Aitch, Die, Hunger, Long, Mulligrubs, Nag, Otalgia, Pain, Sore, Stitch, Stound, Stownd, Work, Yearn, Yen

**Achieve(ment)** Accomplish, Acquisition, Attain, Big League, Come, Compass, Coup, Cum laude, → **EFFECT**, Enacture, Exploit, Feat, Fulfil, Gain, Hatchment, Masterpiece, Realise, Res gestae, Satisfice, Satisfy, Stroke, Succeed, Threepeat, Triumph, Trock, Troke, Truck

**Achilles** Heel, Tendon

**Acid(ity)** Acrimony, Corrosive, Drop, Etchant, Hydroxy, Reaction, Ribosomal, Ribozyme, Sharp, Solvent, Sour, Tart, Vinegar, Vitriol

---

**ACIDS**

| 2 letters: | 4 letters: | Amino | Mucic |
|---|---|---|---|
| PH | Acyl | Auric | Oleic |
| | Dopa | Boric | Orcin |
| 3 letters: | PABA | Caro's | Osmic |
| DNA | Pyro | Eisel | Trona |
| EPA | Uric | Fatty | |
| HCL | Wood | Folic | 6 letters: |
| LSD | | Iodic | Acetic |
| Oxo | 5 letters: | L-dopa | Adipic |
| RNA | Algin | Lewis | Bromic |
| | Amide | Malic | Capric |

Cholic
Citric
Cyanic
Domoic
Erucic
Formic
Gallic
Lactic
Lauric
Leucin
Lipoic
Lysine
Maleic
Marine
Niacin
Nitric
Oxalic
Oxygen
Pectic
Phenol
Picric
Quinic
Serine
Sialic
Sorbic
Tannic
Tiglic
Toluic
Valine

**7 letters:**
Abietic
Acrylic
Alanine
Alginic
Benzoic
Butyric
Caproic
Cerotic
Chloric
Chromic
Creatin
Cystine
Ellagic
Eugenic
Ferulic
Folacin
Fumaric
Fusidic
Glycine
Guanine
Leucine
Malonic
Meconic

Melanic
Muramic
Nitrous
Nucleic
Orcinol
Peracid
Plumbic
Proline
Prussic
Pteroic
Pyruvic
Racemic
Sebacic
Selenic
Silicic
Stannic
Stearic
Suberic
Terebic
Titanic
Valeric
Vanadic
Xanthic
Xylonic

**8 letters:**
Abscisic
Adenylic
Arginine
Ascorbic
Aspartic
Butanoic
Caprylic
Carbamic
Carbolic
Carbonic
Chlorous
Cinnamic
Creatine
Cresylic
Crotonic
Cyclamic
Cysteine
Decanoic
Ethanoic
Fulminic
Glutamic
Glyceric
Glycolic
Guanylic
Hippuric
Hydracid
Iopanoic
Itaconic

Linoleic
Lysergic
Manganic
Margaric
Molybdic
Muriatic
Myristic
Nonanoic
Palmitic
Periodic
Phthalic
Retinoic
Rhodanic
Succinic
Sulfonic
Tantalic
Tartaric
Telluric
Tungstic
Tyrosine
Uridylic
Valproic

**9 letters:**
Aqua-regia
Carnitine
Cevitamic
Citydylic
Dichromic
Glutamine
Histidine
Hydrazoic
Hydriodic
Isocyanic
Linolenic
Mefenanic
Methanoic
Nalidixic
Nicotinic
Ornithine
Panthenic
Pentanoic
Polybasic
Propanoic
Propenoic
Propionic
Saccharic
Salicylic
Sassolite
Selenious
Sulphonic
Sulphuric
Tellurous
Threonine

**10 letters:**
Aquafortis
Asparagine
Barbituric
Carboxylic
Citrulline
Dithionous
Dodecanoic
Glucuronic
Glutamatic
Glutaminic
Hyaluronic
Isoleucine
Margaritic
Methionine
Neuraminic
Orthoboric
Pelargonic
Perchloric
Phosphonic
Phosphoric
Proprionic
Pyrogallic
Ricinoleic
Thiocyanic
Thymidylic
Trans-fatty
Tryptophan

**11 letters:**
Arachidonic
Butanedioic
Decanedioic
Ethanedioic
Ferricyanic
Ferrocyanic
Gibberellic
Hydnocarpic
Hydrobromic
Hydrocyanic
Hyponitrous
Methacrylic
Octanedioic
Pantothenic
Permanganic
Phosphorous
Ribonucleic
Sarcolactic
Taurocholic
Tryptophane

**12 letters:**
Dicraboxylic
Hydrochloric

| | | | |
|---|---|---|---|
| Hydrofluoric | Pyroligneous | Pyrosulphuric | **15 letters:** |
| Hypochlorous | Terephthalic | Thiosulphuric | Orthophosphoric |
| Indoleacetic | | Transbutadoic | Paramenobenzone |
| Orthosilicic | **13 letters:** | | Pteroylglutamic |
| Persulphuric | Galactosamine | **14 letters:** | Trichloroacetic |
| Phenylalanin | Heptadecanoic | Metaphosphoric | |
| Polyadenalic | Indolebutyric | Polyphosphoric | **16 letters:** |
| Propanedioic | Phenylalanine | Pyrophosphoric | Deoxyribonucleic |
| Prostacyclin | Prostaglandin | | Triiodothyronine |

---

**Acknowledge(ment)** Accept, Admit, Agnise, Allow, Answer, Avow, Con, Confess, Credit, Grant, Greet, Mea culpa, Nod, Own, Profess, React, Receipt, Recognise, Resipiscence, Respect, Righto, Roger, Salute, Ta, Thank you, Touché, Wilco, Yo

**Acme** Apex, Apogee, Climax, Comble, Crest, Peak, Summit, Top, Zenith

**Acne** Blemish, Spots

**Acolyte** Chela, Nethinim, Novice, Server, Thurifer

**Acorn(s), Acorn-shell** Balanus, Glans, Mast, Rac(c)ahout, Valonia

**Acoustic(s)** Harmonics, Phenocamptics, Phonics, Sonics

**Acquaint(ance), Acquainted** Advise, Cognisant, Contact, Enlighten, Familiar, →INFORM, Knowledge, Nodding, Notify, Tell, Versed

**Acquiesce(nce), Acquiescent** Accede, Accept, Amenable, Bow, Comply, Conform, Resigned, Righto, Roger, Wilco, Yield

**Acquire, Acquisition, Acquisitive** Acquest, Adsorb, Cop, Earn, Ern, Gain, →GET, Glom, Grasping, Irredentist, Land, Learn, Obtain, Procure, Purchase, Rapacity, Secure, Steal, Take-over, Target, Usucap(t)ion

**Acquit(tal)** Absolve, Assoil, Cleanse, Clear, Exonerate, Free, Loose, Loste, Pardon, Vindicate

**Acre(s)** A, Area, Bigha, Hide, Rival, Rood

**Acrid, Acrimonious, Acrimony** Acid, Bitter(ness), Empyreuma, Mordant, Pungent, Resentment, Rough, Sour, Spleen, Surly, Virulent, Vitriolic

**Acrobat(s), Acrobatics** Equilibrist, Gymnast, Hot dog, Jerry-come-tumble, Ropedancer, Rope-walker, Speeler, Splits, Trampoline, Trick cyclist, Tumbler, Wing-walker

**Acropolis** Citadel, Parthenon

**Across** A, Ac, Athwart, Betwixt, O'ed, Opposite, Over, Through, Transit

**Act(ing), Action, Active, Acts** A, Actus reus, Affirmative, Afoot, Antic, Assist, Assumpsit, Atonement, Auto, Barnstorm, Barrier, Behave, Bit, Blitz, Business, Camp, Campaign, Capillary, Caretaker, Case, Caster, Catastasis, Cause, Charade, Class, Come, Conduct, Consolation, COPPA, Coup, Daff, Deal, Declaratory, →DEED, Delaying, Deputise, Detinue, Dido, Direct, Do, DORA, Double, Enabling, Enclosure, Epitasis, Evasive, Excitement, Exert, Exploit, Factory, Feat, Feign, Forthcoming, Forth-putting, Function, Habeas corpus, Histrionic, Homestead, Identic, Impersonate, Impro(visation), Improbation, Incident, Industrial, Juristic, Lance-jack, Law, Litigate, Lock-out, Locutionary, Masterstroke, Measure, Method, Mime, Movement, Mum, Mutiny, Navigation, Onstage, Overt, Partypiece, Pas, Perform(ance), Perlocutionary, Personate, Play, Positive, Pp, Practice, Pretence, Private, Procedure, Process, Public, Qua, Quia timet, Qui tam, Quiver, Rearguard, Reflex, Reform bill, Replevin, Represent, Riot, Rising, Roleplay, Routine, Sasine, Scenery, Secondary, Septennial, Serve, Settlement, Sham, Showdown, Shtick, Sick-out, Simulate, Speech, Sprightly, Stamp, Stanislavski, Statute, Steps, Strike, Stunt, Suit, Synergy, Tactic, Terminer, Test, Theatricise, Thellusson, Thing, Transitory, Treat, Trover, Truck, Turn, Twig, Uniformity, Union, Vicegerent, War, Windlass

**Actinium** Ac

**Actinon** An

**Activate** Arm, Energise, Engage, Goad, Spark, Spur, Stur, Styre, Trigger

**Active, Activist, Activity** A, Agile, Alert, Alive (and kicking), Animated, Astir, At, Athletic, Brisk, Business, Busy, Cadre, Campaigner, Deedy, DIY, Do(ing), Dynamited, Dynamo, Ecowarrior, Effectual, Energetic, Energic, Erupting, Exercise, Extra-curricular, Floruit, Fluster, Game, Go-go, Goings-on, Hum, Hyper, In play, Leish, Licht, Live, Mobile, Motile, Nimble, Nippy, Ongo, On the go, Op, Operant, Optical, Overdrive, Play, Rambunctious, Residual, Shenanigan, Sideline, Spree, Sprightly, Springe, Spry, Sthenic, Stir, Surge, Third house, Vacuum, Voice, Wick, Wimble, Working, Ya(u)ld, Zionist

**Actor(s), Actor-like** Agent, Alleyn, Artist, Ashe, Barnstormer, Benson, Betterton, Bit player, Borgnine, Brando, Burbage, Cast, Character, Company, Co-star, Diseur, Donat, Equity, Gable, Garrick, Gielgud, Guiser, Ham, Hamfatter, Heavy, Histrio(n), Impersonator, Jay, Juve(nile), Kean, Keaton, Luvvie, MacReady, Mime(ster), Mummer, Olivier, O'Toole, Pantomimist, Performer, Player, Playfair, Protagonist, RADA, Roscian, Roscius, Savoyard, Scofield, Sim, Spear-carrier, Stager, Strolling, Super, Theatrical, Thespian, Tragedian, Tree, Tritagonist, Trouper, Understudy, Utility man, Wolfit

**Actress** Bankhead, Bow, Buffa, Dietrich, Duse, Figurant, Garbo, Harlow, Ingenue, Loren, Pierrette, Siddons, Soubrette, Starlet, Swanson, Terry, West

**Actual(ity), Actually** De facto, Entelechy, Literal, Live, Material, Real, Real-life, Tangible, True, Very

**Actuate, Actuator** Suppository

**Acumen, Acuity** Insight, Nous, Sense, Shrewdness

**Acupressure** Jin shin do, Shiatsu

**Acupuncture** Moxa, Stylostixis

**Acute** Astute, Dire, Fitché, Incisive, →INTENSE, Keen, Quick-witted, Sharp

▸ **Ad** *see* ADVERT(ISE)

**Adage** Aphorism, Gnome, Maxim, Motto, Paroemia, Proverb, Saw, Saying, Truism

**Adam** Bede, Delved, Jailer

**Adamant** Firm, Inexorable, Insistent, Obdurate, Rigid, Unbending

**Adapt(er), Adaptable, Adaptation, Adaptor** Adjust, Bushing, Ecad, Evolve, Flexible, Naturalise, Persona, Pliant, Refashion, Reorient, Resilient, Tailor, Timeserver, Transform, Versatile, Version

**Add(ed), Addendum, Adder, Adding** Accrue, Adscititious, Annex, →APPENDIX, Attach, Cast, Contribute, Coopt, Death, Dub, Ech(e), Eik, Eke, Elaborate, Embroider, Enhance, Enlarge, Forthgoing, Fortify, Insert, Lace, Puff, Reckon, Reinforce, Retrofit, Score, Spike, Sum, Summate, Tack on, Top up, Tot(e), Total, Viper

**Addict(ion), Addicted, Addictive** Abuser, Acid freak, Acidhead, A colt's tooth, Alcoholic, Base head, Blunthead, Buff, Chocoholic, Couch potato, Dependency, Devotee, Dope-fiend, Dopehead, Etheromaniac, Fan, Fiend, Freak, Given, Glue-sniffing, Habit-forming, Hophead, Hound, Hype, Jones, Joypopper, Junkie, Lover, Mainliner, Mania, Narcotist, Need, Opiate, Opioid, Opium, Pillhead, Pillpopper, Pothead, Shithead, Shooter, Shopaholic, Slave, Snowbird, Space-cadet, Speedfreak, Stoner, Sybaritism, Theism, User, Vinolent, Wino, Workaholic

**Addison** Spectator

**Addition(al), Additive** Accession, Addend, Additive, Adipate, Adscititious, Adulterant, Advene, Also, And, Annexure, Antiknock, Appendage, (As an) in, Bolt-on, Braata, Carrag(h)anin, Carrageenan, Codicil, Corollary, Cyclamate, Dextran, Eik, Eke, Encore, Epexegesis, Epithesis, Etc, Excess, Extender, Extension, →EXTRA, Extramural, Footnote, →IN ADDITION, Increment, Mae, Makeweight, Mo, Monkey, New, Odd, On, On top, Other, Padding, Paragog(u)e, Parergon, Plus, Preservative, PS, Rider, Ripieno, Spare, Suffect, Suffix, Supplementary, Surcharge, Thereto, Top-up, Verandah

**Address, Address system** Accommodation, Accost, Adroit, Allocution, Apostrophe, Apostrophise, Appellation, Art, →ATLAS, Ave, Bach, Bub, Buster, Call, Cariad, Chuck, Compellation, Cousin, Dedication, Delivery, Den, Diatribe, Direction, Discourse, Effendi, Election, Epilogue, Epirrhema, Esquire, Gettysburg, Gospodin, Hail, Home, Homily, Inaugural, IP, Jimmy, Kiddo, Lala, Lecture, Letterhead, Mac, Mester, Milord, Mister,

Mush, Mynheer, Nkosi, Ode, Orate, Parabasis, Past master, Pastoral, Poste-restante, Prelection, Rig, Salute, Sermon, Sir(ree), Speech, Squire, Stance, Tact, Tannoy®, →**TITLE**, Towkay, Tuan, URL, Valedictory, Wambenger, Web, Wus, Y'all, You-all

**Adduce** Cite

**Adelphic** Adam

**Adept** Able, Adroit, Buff, Dab, Deacon, Don, →**EXPERT**, Fit, Handy, Mahatma, Master, Past master

**Adequate** Condign, Does, Due, Egal, Equal, Ere-now, Passable, Proper, →**SUFFICIENT**, Tolerable, Valid

**Adhere(nt), Adherence, Adhesive** Allegiance, Ally, Araldite®, Blutack®, Bond, Burr, Cement, Child, Cling, Conform, Cow Gum®, Dextrin, Disciple, Emplastic, Epoxy, Fidelity, Follower, Glair, Glue, Goldsize, Guebre, Gum, Hot-melt, Impact, Jain(a), Leech, Loyalist, Mixtion, Moonie, Mucilage, Nomism, Partisan, Paste, Resin, Sectator, Servitor, Stand pat, Sticker, Supporter, Synechia, Votary, Waterglass

**Adjacent, Adjoining** Bordering, Conterminous, Contiguous, Handy, Neighbouring, Nigh

**Adjective** Adnoun, Epithet, Gerundive

**Adjourn(ment)** Abeyance, Defer, Delay, Moratoria, →**POSTPONE**, Prorogate, Recess, Rise, Suspend

**Adjudicate, Adjudication, Adjudicator** Arbiter, Decide, Judge, Jury, Referee, Try, Umpire

**Adjunct** Addition, Aid, Ancillary, Rider

**Adjust(able), Adjustment, Adjuster** Accommodate, Adapt, Attune, Coapt, Dress, Ease, Fine-tune, Fit, Focus, Gang, Gauge, Gerrymander, Handicap, J'adoube, Modify, Modulate, Orientate, Prepare, Preset, Primp, Redo, Reduce, Regulate, Reorientate, Reset, Resize, Retrofit, Scantle, Scotopia, Sliding, Suit, Tailor, Temper, Toe-in, Tram, Trim, True, Tune, Tweak, Vernier

▷ **Adjust** *may indicate* an anagram

**Adjutant** Aide, Argala, Officer, Stork

**Adler** Irene

**Ad-lib** Ex tempore, Improvise, Wing it

**Administer, Administration, Administrator** Adhibit, Anele, Apply, Arrondissement, Bairiki, Bureaucrat, Control, Corridors of power, Curia, →**DIRECT**, Dispence, Dispense, Executive, Front office, Intendant, Intinction, Leadership, →**MANAGE**, MBA, Penpusher, Pepys, Provost, Raj, Regime, Registrar, Run, Secretariat, Soke, Steward, Sysop, Trustee, Whitehall

**Admirable, Admiration, Admire(d), Admirer** Beau, Clinker, Clipper, Conquest, Crichton, Envy, Esteem, Estimable, →**EXCELLENT**, Fine, Flame, Fureur, Gaze, Gem, Ho, Iconise, Idolater, Laudable, Lionise, Partisan, Popularity, Rate, Regard, Respect, Ripping, Rocking, Splendid, Stotter, Suitor, Swain, Toast, Tribute, Venerate, Wonder, Worthy, Wow

**Admiral** Adm, AF, Anson, Beatty, Beaufort, Benbow, Blake, Bligh, Boscawen, Butterfly, Byng, Byrd, Capitan, Drake, Effingham, Fisher, Hood, Hornblower, Howard, Jellicoe, Keyes, Marrowfat, Mountbatten, Navarch, Nelson, Old Grog, Raeder, Red, Rodney, Spee, Sturdee, Togo, Vanessa, Van Nieman, Van Tromp, White

**Admiralty** Sea-board

**Admission, Admit(ter), Admit(ting), Admitted, Admittance** Accept, Access, Acknowledge, Agree, Allow, Avow, Cognovit, Concede, →**CONFESS**, Enter, Entrée, Entry, Estoppel, Gateman, Give, Grant, Induct, Ingress, Initiate, Intromit, Ordain, Ordination, Owe, Own (up), Privy, Recognise, Shrift, Take, Tho(ugh), Turnstile, Yield

**Admonish, Admonition** Advice, Caution, Chide, Lecture, Moralise, Pi-jaw, Rebuke, Reprimand, →**SCOLD**, Tip, Warn

**Ado** Bother, Bustle, Fuss, Lather

**Adolescent** Bodgie, Developer, Grower, Halflin, Immature, Juvenile, Neanic, Teenager, Tweenager, Veal, Widgie, Youth

**Adonais** Keats

**Adonis** Pheasant's Eye

**Adopt(ed)** Accept, Affect, Affiliate, Allonym, Assume, Catch on, Dalt, Embrace, Espouse, Father, Foster, Latch on, Mother

**Adoration, Adore(r), Adoring** Doat, Dote, Goo-goo, Homage, Idolise, Latria, Love, Pooja(h), Puja, Revere, Venerate, Worship, Zoolater

**Adorn(ed), Adornment** Antefix, Aplustre, Attrap, Banderol, Bedeck, Bedight, Begem, Bejewel, Caparison, Clinquant, Deck, Dight, Drape, Embellish, Emblaze, Emblazon, Embroider, Enchase, Equip, Festoon, Flourish, Furnish, Garland, Garnish, Grace, Graste, Jewellery, Ornament, Riband, Story, Tassel, Tattoo, Tatu, Tinsel, Trappings

**Adrenaline** Epinephrin(e)

**Adroit(ness)** Address, Adept, Clever, Dextrous, Expert, Neat, Skilful, Slick

**Adulate, Adulation** Flatter(y), Praise, →**WORSHIP**

**Adullam** Cave

**Adult** Amadoda, Consenting, Grown-up, Imago, Man, Mature, Upgrown, X

**Adulterant, Adulterate** Cut, Debase, Impurify, Lime, Load, Mix, Multum, →**POLLUTE**, Sophisticate, Weaken

**Adulterer, Adulterous, Adultery** Avoutery, Co-respondent, Cuckold, Extra-marital, Fornication, Francesca, Lenocinium, Two-timer

**Adumbrate** Outline

**Advance(d), Advancement** A, Abord, Accelerate, Anabasis, Ante, Approach, Ascend, Assert, Better(ment), Breakthrough, Bring on, Charge, Develop, Early, Elevation, Evolué, Extreme, Far, Fast-forward, Fore, Forge, Forward, Further, Gain, Get on, Grubstake, Haut(e), Hi-tec(h), Impress, Imprest, Incede, Late, Lend, →**LOAN**, March, Mortgage, On(ward), Onrush, Outcome, Overture, Pass, Piaffe, Posit, Postulate, Precocious, Prefer, Prepone, Prest, Process, Progress, →**PROMOTE**, Propose, Propound, Push, Retainer, Ripe, Rise, Scoop, Sub, Submit, Tiptoe, Top end, Ultramodern, Upfront, Upgang, Voorskot

**Advantage(ous)** Accrual, Ad, Aid, →**ASSET**, Avail, Batten, Benefit, Bisque, Boot, Bright, Edge, Emolument, Expedient, Exploit, Favour, Fruit, Gain, Grouter, Handicap, Handle, Head-start, Help, Inside (track), Interess, Interest, Lever(age), Mess of pottage, Nonmonetary, Obvention, Odds, One-up, Oneupmanship, Oyster, Pecuniary, Percentage, Plus, Privilege, Prize, Pro, Pull, Purchase, Sake, Salutary, Serviceable, Start, Stead, Strength, Toe-hold, Trade, Trump card, Upper-hand, Upside, Upstage, Use, Van, Whiphand, Whipsaw

**Advent(ist)** Coming, Shaker

**Adventure(r), Adventuress, Adventurous** Argonaut, Assay, Aunter, Bandeirante, Buccaneer, Casanova, Condottiere, Conquistador, Dareful, Daring, Emprise, Enterprise, Escapade, →**EXPLOIT**, Filibuster, Gallant, Gest, Lark, Mata Hari, Mercenary, Merchant, Picaresque, Picaro, Picaroon, Risk, Routier, Rutter, Swashbuckler, Vamp, Viking, Voyage

**Adversary** Antagonist, Anti, Arch-enemy, Cope(s)mate, Enemy, Foe, Nemesis, Opponent

**Adverse, Adversity** Calamity, Cross, Down, Downside, Harrow, Misery, Reversal, Setback, Unfavourable, Untoward, Woe

**Advert(ise), Advertisement, Advertiser, Advertising** Above the line, Ad, Air, Allude, Attack, Banner, Bark, Bill, Blipvert, Circular, Classified, Coign(e), Coin, Commercial, Copy, Display, Dodger, Earpiece, Flier, Flyer, Flyposting, Flysheet, Hard sell, Hype, Infomercial, Jingle, Knocking copy, Madison Avenue, Mailshot, Market, Niche, Noise, →**NOTICE**, Out, Packshot, Parade, Personnel, Placard, Playbill, Plug, →**POSTER**, Proclaim, Promo, Promote, Promulgate, Prospectus, Puff, Quoin, Refer, Sandwich board, Semisolus, Shoutline, Showbill, Skyscraper, Sky-write, Splash, Sponsor, Spot, Stunt, Subliminal, Teaser, Tele-, Throwaway, Tout, Trailer, Trawl, Want(s) (ad), Wrap around

**Advice** Conseil, Counsel, →**GUIDANCE**, Guideline, Information, Invoice, Opinion, Read, Recommendation, Re(e)de, Reed, Tip (off)

**Advise(d), Adviser, Advisable** Acquaint, Apprise, Assessor, Avise(ment), Back-seat driver, Brains trust, CAB, Cabal, Camarilla, Consultant, Cornerman, Counsel, Egeria, Enjoin, Enlighten, Exhort, Expedient, Genro, Induna, Inform, Instruct, Mentor, Monitor,

Oracle, Peritus, Politic, Prudent, Ralph, → **RECOMMEND**, Starets, Staretz, Tutor, Urge, Warn, Weld, Wise

**Advocacy** Encouragement

**Advocate(d)** Agent, Argue, Attorney, Back, Counsel, Devil's, Endorse, Exponent, Gospel, Intercede, Lawyer, Move, Paraclete, Peat, Peddle, Pleader, Pragmatist, Preach, Proponent, Silk, Statist, Syndic, Urge

**Aeon** Hadean, Phanerozoic

**Aerial** Aeolian, Aery, Antenna, Beam, Clover, Clover leaf, Communal, Dipole, Directional, Dish, Ethereal, Ferrite-rod, Folded dipole, Frame, Ground-plane, Lead-in, Long-wire, Loop, Minidish, Parabolic, Rhombic, Satellite dish, Slot, Squarial, Yagi

**Aerobatics** Stunt

**Aerobics** Pilates, Step

**Aerodrome** → **AIRPORT**, Landing field, Rotor-station

**Aerodynamics** Slipstream, Spoiler

**Aerofoil** Spoiler, Trimtab

▶ **Aeroplane** *see* **AIRCRAFT**

**Aerosol** Atomiser, Ioniser, Mace®

**Aesir** Loki

**Aesthete, Aesthetic** Arty, Beautiful, Essene, Poseur, Tasteful

**Affable, Affability** Amiable, Avuncular, Benign, Bonhomie, Cordial, Gracious, Hearty, Pleasant, Suave, Urbane

**Affair(s)** Amour, Business, Carry on, Cerne, Concern, Current, Dreyfus, Effeir, Effere, Event, External, Extra-marital, Fight, Fling, Foreign, Go, Indaba, Internal, Intrigue, Liaison, Matter, Pash, Pidgin, Pi(d)geon, Ploy, Relationship, Res, Romance, Shebang, Subject, Thing

**Affect(ed), Affectation, Affection(ate), Affecting** Air, Airtsy-mairtsy, Alter, Arty, Breast, Camp, Chi-chi, Concern, Cordial, Crachach, Crazy, Distress, Effete, Emotive, Endearment, Euphuism, Foppery, Frappant, Grip, Heartstrings, High-sounding, Hit, Impress, Ladida, Lovey-dovey, Mannered, Mimmick, Minauderie, Mincing, Minnick, Minnock, Mouth-made, Mwah, Phoney, Play at, → **POSE**, Poseur, Precieuse, Preciosity, Pretence, Prick-me-dainty, Smitten, Spoilt, Stag(e)y, Storge, Stricken, Strike, Supervene, Susceptible, Sway, Sympathetic, Tender, Topophilia, Touched, Touchy-feely, Tushery, Twee, Unction, Unnatural, Upend, Vain, Warm, Yah

**Affiliate, Affiliation** Adopt, Associate, Merge, Unite

**Affinity** Bro, Kin(ship), Penchant, Rapport, Tie

**Affirm(ative), Affirmation** Assert, Attest, Avow, Maintain, Positive, Predicate, Profess, Protestation, State, Uh-huh, → **VERIFY**, Yebo

**Affix(ed)** Append, Ascribe, → **ATTACH**, Connect, Fasten, On

**Afflict(ed), Affliction** Aggrieve, Ail, Asthma, Cross, Cup, Curse, Dead leg, Disease, Furnace, Harass, Hay fever, Hurt, Lacerate, Lumbago, Molest, Nosology, Oppress, Palsy, Persecute, Pester, Plague, Scourge, Smit, Sore, → **SORROW**, Stricken, Teen, Tene, Tic, Tine, Tribulation, → **TROUBLE**, Try, Unweal, Visitation, Woe

**Affluence, Affluent** Abundance, Dinky, Ease, Fortune, Grey panther, Inflow, Moneyed, Opulence, Upmarket, Wealth

**Afford** Allow, Bear, Give, Manage, Offer, Provide, Run to, Spare, Yield

**Affray** Brawl, Fight, Fracas, Free-for-all, Mêlée, Scuffle, Skirmish

**Affront** Assault, Defy, Facer, → **INSULT**, → **OFFEND**, Outrage, Scandal, Slight, Slur

**Afghan(istan)** Bactria, Dard, Hound, Kaf(f)ir, Pakhto, Pakhtu, Pashto, Pashtu, Pathan, Pushto(o), Pushtu, Taliban

**Afloat** Aboard, Abroach, Adrift, Natant

**Afoot** Astir, Up

**Aforesaid** Above, Same

**Afraid** Adrad, Alarmed, Chicken, Fearful, Funk, Nesh, Rad, Regretful, Scared, Timorous, Windy, Yellow

**Afresh** De novo

**Africa(n)** Abyssinian, Adamawa, Akan, Algerian, Amakwerekwere, Angolan, Ashanti, Baganda, Bambara, Bantu, Barbary, Barotse, Basotho, Basuto, Bechuana, Beento, Bemba, Beninese, Berber, Biafran, Bintu, Black, Boer, Botswana(n), Bushman, Caffre, Cairene, Carthaginian, Chewa, Chichewa, Ciskei, Congo(l)ese, Cushitic, Dagomba, Damara, Dark continent, Dinka, Duala, Dyula, Efik, Eritrean, Ethiopian, Eve, Fang, Fantee, Fanti, Fingo, Flytaal, Fula(h), Gabonese, Galla, Gambian, Ganda, Gazankulu, Grikwa, Griqua, Guinean, Gullah, Hamite, Hausa, Herero, Hottentot, Hutu, Ibibio, Ibo, Igbo, Impi, Ivorian, Kabyle, Kaffer, Kaf(f)ir, Kenyan, Khoikhoi, Khoisan, Kikuyu, Kongo, Lango, Lesotho, Liberian, Libyan, Lowveld, Lozi, Luba, Luo, Maghreb, Maghrib, Malagasy, Malawi, Malian, Malinke, Mande, Mandingo, Mandinka, Masai, Mashona, Matabele, Mende, Moor, Moroccan, Mossi, Mozambican, Mswahili, Munt(u), Mzee, Nama(qua), Namibian, Ndebele, Negrillo, → **NEGRO**, Ngoni, Nguni, Nilot(e), Nubian, Nuer, Numidian, Nyanja, Oromo, Ovambo, Pedi, Pied noir, Pondo, Qwaqwa, Rastafarian, Rhodesian, Rwandan, Sahelian, San, Senegalese, Shilluk, Shluh, Shona, Somali, Songhai, Songhay, Sotho, Soweto, Sudanese, Susu, Swahili, Swazi, Tanzanian, Temne, Tiv, Togolese, Tonga, Transkei, Transvaal, Tshi, Tsonga, Tswana, Tuareg, Tunisian, Tutsi, Twi, Ugandan, Uhuru, Venda, Voltaic, Waswahili, Watu(t)si, Wolof, X(h)osa, Yoruban, Zairean, Zulu

**Afrikaan(s), Afrikaner** Cape Dutch, Crunchie, Hairyback, Mynheer, Taal, Volk, Voortrekker

**After(wards)** About, A la, At, Behind, Belated, Beyond, Eft, Epi-, → **LATER**, On, Once, Past, Post hoc, Rear, Since, Sine, Subsequent, Syne

**Afterbirth** Secundines, Sooterkin

**Afterimage** Photogene

▷ **After injury** *may indicate* an anagram

**Afterlife** Other world, The Great Beyond

**Aftermath** Consequence, Fall out, Legacy, Mow(ing), Rawing, Rawn, Rowan, Rowen, Rowing, Sequel(a), Wake

**Afternoon** A, Arvo, Ex-am, PM, Postmeridian, Undern

**Afterpiece, Afterthought** Addendum, Codicil, Epimetheus, Exode, Footnote, Note, PS, Supplement

**Aftertaste** T(w)ang

**Again** Afresh, Agen, Ancora, Anew, Back, Bis, De novo, Ditto, Do, Eft, Eftsoons, Encore, Iterum, Mair, More, Moreover, O(v)er, Re-, Recurrence, Reprise, Than, Then

**Against** A, Anent, Anti, Beside, Con, Counter, For, Gainsayer, Into, Nigh, On, One-to-one, Opposing, To, V, Versus

**Agape** Feast, Hiant, Ringent, Yawning

**Agate** Chalcedonyx, Moss, Murr(h)a, Onyx, Ruin

**Agave** Century plant, Henequen, Lily, Maenad, Maguey, Sisal

**Age(d), Ages, Aging** Absolute, Achievement, Ae, Aeon, Aet, Alcheringa, Anno domini, Antique, Archaise, Atomic, Augustan, Azilian, Bronze, Calpa, Century, Chair-days, Chellean, Coon's, Copper, Cycle, Dark, Date, Day, Discretion, Distress, Doddery, Eld, Elizabethan, Eon, Epact, Epoch(a), Era, Eternity, Generation, Gerontic, Golden, Grey, Heroic, Hoar, Hore, Ice, Information, Iron, Jazz, Jurassic, Kaliyuga, Kalpa, La Tene, Lias, Magdalenian, Maglemosian, Mature, Mental, Mesolithic, Middle, Millennium, Neolithic, New, New Stone, Of, Old, Oligocene, Paleolithic, Passé, Periclean, Period, Phanerozoic, Pre-Cambrian, Progeria, Radiometric, Reason, Reindeer, Saros, S(a)eculum, Season, Senescence, Senility, Silver, Solera, Space, Steam, Stone, Third, Villanovan, Wrinkly, Yellow, Yonks, Yug(a)

**Ageless** Evergreen

**Agency, Agent** Advertising, Agitator, Alkylating, Ambassador, Antistatic, Art, Autolysin, Bailiff, Baking soda, Bargaining, Barm, Bicarb(onate), Bond, Broker, BSI, Bureau, Buyer, Catalyst, Cat's paw, Cause, Chelating, Chemical, Child support, Commis, Commission, Complexone, Comprador(e), Confidential, Consul, Consular, Counter, Countryside, Crown, Customs, Dating, Defoaming, Del credere, Developing, Dicumaral, Disclosing, Distributor, Doer, Double, Emissary, Environment, Envoy, Enzyme, -er, Escort, Estate, Exciseman,

Executant, Executor, Factor, Fed, Finger, Flack, Forwarding, Free, Galactagogue, G-man, Go-between, Good offices, Hand, Hirudin, House, Implement, Indian, Influence, Institorial, Instrument, Intermediary, Isinglass, Itar Tass, Kinase, Law, Leavening, Legate, Literary, Magic bullet, Man, Masking, Mata Hari, Means, Medium, Melanin, Mercantile, Mitogen, Mole, Moral, Mouthwash, Mutagen, Narc, Narco, Nerve, Ninja, Nucleating, OO, Operation, -or, Orange, Order paper, Oxidizing, Parliamentaire, Parliamentary, Patent, Pathogen, Pawn, Peace corps, Penetration, Pinkerton, Press, Procurator, Provocateur, Proxy, Realtor, Reducing, Rep(resentative), Resident, Reuters, Riot, Road, Runner, Salesman, Secret (service), Setter, Shipping, Ship's husband, SIS, Sleeper, Solvent, Soman, Spook, Spy, Stock, Surfactant, Syndic, Tass, Teratogen, Third party, Ticket, Tiger team, Tool, Training, Travel, UNESCO, Vakeel, Vakil, Virino, Voice, Welfare, Wetting, Wire service

**Agenda** Business, Hidden, Order paper, Programme, Remit, Schedule

**Aggie** Agnes, Ines, Nessa, Nesta

**Aggravate** Annoy, Exacerbate, Exasperate, Harass, Inflame, Irk, Needle, Nettle, Provoke, Rankle, Try, Vex

**Aggregate, Aggregation** Ballast, Congeries, Detritus, Etaerio, Granulite, Gravel, Hard core, Manifold, Number, Omnium, Ore, Ped, Sum, Total

**Aggression, Aggressive(ly), Aggressor, Aggro** Anti-Imperialism, Arsey, Attack, Ballbreaker, Bare-knuckle, Battleaxe, Bellicose, Belligerent, Biffo, Bovver, Bullish, Butch, Defiant, Enemy, Feisty, Foe, Go-getter, Gungho, Hard-hitting, Hawk, Invader, In-your-face, Laddish, Lairy, Macho, Militant, Nasty, On-setter, Pushing, Rambo, Rampant, Road rage, Sabre-rattling, Shirty, Tooth and nail, Truculent, Violent, Wild

**Aggrieve(d)** Sore

**Agile** Acrobatic, Deft, Lissom(e), Nifty, Nimble, Quick, Spry, Supple, Swank, Twinkletoes, Wiry

**Agitate(d), Agitation, Agitator** Acathisia, Activist, Ado, Agitprop, Akathisia, Alarm, Arouse, Betoss, Boil, Bolshie, Bother, Bristling, Chartist, Churn, Commotion, Commove, Convulse, Demagogue, Discompose, Dismay, Distraught, → **DISTURB**, Doodah, Ebullient, Emotion, Euoi, Euouae, Evovae, Excite, Extremist, Fan, Fantad, Fanteeg, Fantigue, Fantod, Ferment, Firebrand, Flap, Flurry, Fluster, Flutter, Fraught, Frenzy, Fuss, Fusspot, Goad, Heat, Hectic, Het (up), Impatience, Jabble, Jumpy, Khilafat, Lather, Militant, Overwrought, Panicky, Pedetic, Perturb, Poss, Pother, Protest, Rabble-rouser, Rattle, Restless, Rouse, Ruffle, Seethed, Shake, Sod, Stew, Stir(-up), Swivet, Tailspin, Taking, Tempest, Tew, Thermal, Tizzy, Toss, Tremor, Trepidation, Trouble, Turbulent, Turmoil, Tweak, Twitchy, Twittery, Unrest, Upset, Welter, Whisk, Wrought up, Ytost

▷ **Agitate** *may indicate* an anagram

**Agley** Awry, Unevenly

**Aglow** Alight, Fervid, Tipsy

▶ **Agnes** *see* **AGGIE**

**Agnostic** Laodicean

**Ago** Lang syne, → **SINCE**

**Agog** Astir, Athirst, Eager, Excited, Keen, Pop-eyed

**Agonise, Agony** Ache, Anguish, Brood, Dread, Ecstasy, Heartache, → **PAIN**, Throe(s), Torment, Torture

**Agree(ing), Agreed, Agreement** Accede, Accept, Accord, Acquiescence, Adhere, Agt, Align, Aline, Allow, Amen, Analog(ue), Analogy, Apply, As one, Assent, Assort, Atone, Ausgleich, Aye, Bilateral, Bipartite, Bond, Camp David, Cartel, Champerty, Charterparty, Chime, Closing, Coincide, Collective, Comart, Community, Compact, Comply, Comport, Concert, Concord(at), Concordance, Concur, Condone, Conform, Congree, Congruent, Consension, Consensus, → **CONSENT**, Consist, Consonant, Contract, Contrahent, Convention, Correspond, Cotton, Covenant, Covin, Covyne, Cushty, Dayton Accords, Deal, Deffo, Deign, Determine, Done, Embrace, Entente, Equate, Escrow, Fadge, Finalise, Gatt, Gentleman's, Handfast, Harmony, Homologous, Identity, Indenture, Jibe, Knock-for-knock, League, Like-minded, Mercosur, Munich, National, Net Book, Nod,

Non-con, Nudum pactum, Okay, On, Pact(um), Pair, Placet, Plant, Plea bargaining, Predetermine, Prenuptial, Procedural, Productivity, Protocol, Rabat(te), Recognise, Reconcile, Repo, Repurchase, Right(o), Right on, Roger, Sanction, Schengen, Service, Settlement, Side, Sort(ance), Specialty, Sponsion, Square, Standstill, Substantive, Suit, Sweetheart, Sympathy, Synastry, Sync(hronise), Synesis, Syntony, Tally, Technology, Threshold, Trade, Treaty, Trucial, Uh-huh, Unanimous, Union, Unison, Unity, Unspoken, Wilco, Wukkas, Yalta, Yea, Yea-say, Yes

**Agreeable** Amene, Comfy, Harmonious, Obliging, Pleasant, Sapid, Sweet, Well-disposed, Willing, Winsome

**Agriculture, Agricultural(ist)** Arval, Ceres, Farming, Geoponic, Georgic, Inari, Moshav, Permaculture, Slash and burn, Smallholding, Tull

**Aground** Ashore, Beached, Sew, Stranded

**Ague** Dumb

▷ **Ague(ish)** *may indicate* an anagram

**Ah** Ach, Ay

**Ahead** Anterior, Before, Fast, Foreship, Forward, Frontwards, In store, Onward, Precocious, Up

**Aiblins** Perhap, Perhaps, Yibbles

**Aid(s), Aide** Accessory, ADC, Adjutant, Artificial, Assist, Audiovisual, Audiphone, Caliper, Decca, → **DEPUTY**, First, Foreign, Fresh-card, Galloper, Gift, Grant, Hearing, Help(line), Key, Legal, Lend-lease, Life-saver, Monitor, Optophone, Orthosis, PA, Realia, Relief, Satnav, Seamark, Serve, Sex, Sherpa, Stepping-stone, Subsidy, Subvention, Succour, Support, Teaching, Visual, Yeoman('s) service, Zimmer®

**AIDS** Slim

**Ail(ment), Ail(ing)** Affect, Afflict(ion), Complaint, Croup, Disease, Disorder, Enteritis, Malady, Misorder, Narks, Occupational, Pink-eye, Pip, Queasy, Sickness, Suffer, TB, Unwell

**Aim** Approach, Aspire, Bead, Bend, End, Ettle, Eye, Goal, Hub, Intent, Level, Mark, Mint, Mission, Object, Peg, Plan, Plank, Point, Point blank, Purpose, Quest, Reason, Sake, Seek, Sight(s), Target, Tee, Telos, Train, Try, View, Visie, Vizy, Vizzie, Zero-in

**Aimless** Adrift, Drifting, Erratic, Haphazard, Random, Unmotivated

**Air(s), Airer, Air-space, Airy** Aerate, Aerial, Aero, Affectation, Allure, Ambiance, Ambience, Anthem, Appearance, Aquarius, Arietta, Arioso, Atmosphere, Attitude, Aura, Bearing, Breath, Calypso, Canzona, Canzone, Cavatina, Clothes horse, Compressed, Dead, Demaine, Descant, Ditty, Draught, Dry, Emphysema, Ether(eal), Expose, Fan, Filmy, Front, Gemini, Greensleeves, Heat-island, Heaven, Horse, Inflate, Libra, Lift, Light, Liquid, Look, Lullaby, Madrigal, Maiden, Manner, Melody, Microburst, Mien, Night, Nitre, Oat, Open, Ozone, Parade, Periptery, Pneumatic, Poseur, Radio, Screen, Scuba, Serenade, Serenata, Serene, Shanty, Side, Sinus, Sky, Slipstream, Solo, Song, Strain, Swank, Thin, Tidal, Trigon, → **TUNE**, Vent, Ventilate, Vital, Wake, Wind

**Airborne** Ab, Uprisen

**Air Chief Marshal** Dowding

**Air-conditioning** Plenum system

**Aircraft, Airship** Aerodyne, Aerostat, Angels, AST, Auster, Autoflare, Autogiro, Autogyro, Aviette, Avion, Biplane, Blimp, Boeing, Brabazon, Bronco, Broomstick, Camel, Canard, Canberra, Chaser, Chopper, Coleopter, Comet, Concorde, Convertiplane, Corsair, Crate, Cropduster, Cyclogiro, Delta-wing, Dirigible, Dive-bomber, Doodlebug, Drone, Eagle, Enola Gay, Eurofighter, F, Ferret, Fixed-wing, Flivver, Flying fortress, Flying wing, Fokker, Freedom-fighter, Freighter, Galaxy, Glider, Gotha, Gyrodyne, Gyroplane, Hang-glider, Harrier, Hawkeeze, Heinkel, Helicopter, Helo, Hercules, Hunter, Hurricane, Interceptor, Intruder, Jet star, Jumbo, Jump-jet, Kite, Lancaster, Liberator, Lifting-body, Link trainer, Lysander, Messerschmitt, Microjet, Microlight, Microlite, MIG, Mirage, Monoplane, Mosquito, Moth, Multiplane, Nacelle, Nightfighter, Nightfinder, Nimrod, Oerlikon, Orion, Ornithopter, Orthopter, Parasol, Penguin, Phantom, → **PLANE**, Provider, Prowler, Pusher, Ramjet, Rigid, Rotaplane, Runabout, Scout, Scramjet, Semi-rigid, Shackleton, Skiplane,

Skyhawk, Sopwith, Sopwith Camel, Spitfire, SST, Stack, Starfighter, Starlifter, Stealth
bomber, STOL, Stratocruiser, Stratotanker, Stuka, Super Sabre, Sweptwing, Swing-wing,
Tankbuster, Taube, Taxiplane, Thunderbolt, Thunderchief, Tomcat, Tornado, Torpedo
bomber, Towplane, Tracker, Trident, Tri-jet, Triplane, Tube, Turbofan, Turbo-jet,
Turbo-prop, Turboramjet, Variable geometry, Vessel, Vigilante, Viking, Viscount, Vomit
comet, Voodoo, VTOL, War bird, Widebody, Wild weasel, Zeppelin

**Aircraftsman, Airman** AC, Aeronaut, AR, Bleriot, Co-pilot, Erk, Fokker, Kiwi, LAC,
Observer, RAF

**Aircraftswoman** Penguin, Pinguin

▸ **Airfield** *see* **AIRPORT**

**Air force** Luftwaffe

**Airless** Close, Stuffy

**Airlift** Thermal

**Airline, Airway** Aeroflot, Anthem, BAC, BEA, Bronchus, Carrier, Duct, El Al, Iberia,
JAL, Larynx, Lot, Lyric, Purple, Qantas, SAS, S(ch)norkel, Trochea, TWA, Upcast, Vent,
Weasand(-pipe), Windpipe

▸ **Airman** *see* **AIRCRAFTSMAN, FLIER**

**Airmen** Red Arrows

**Airport** Chiang Kai Shek, Drome, Dyce, Entebbe, Faro, Gander, Gatwick, Greenham
Common, Heliport, Idlewild, John Lennon, Kennedy, La Guardia, Landing strip, Le
Bourget, Lod, Luton, Lydda, Lympne, O'Hare, Orly, Prestwick, Runway, Shannon,
Stansted, Stolport, Tegal, Terminal, Vertiport, Wick

**Air-raid** Blitz, Mission

**Air-tight** Hermetic, Indisputable, Sealed

**Aisle** Catwalk, Gangway

**Aitch** Ache, Aspirate, H

**Ajar** Agee

**Ajax** Lav, Loo

**Aka** Alias

**Akin** Alike, Cognate, Congener, Kindred, Sib

**Alabaster** Oriental

**Alacrity** Readiness

**Alarm(ed), Alarming, Alarmist** Affear, Affright, Agitation, Alert, Arouse, Bell, Bleep,
Bugaboo, Caution, Concern, Dismay, Eek, False, Fire, Flap, Fricht, Fright, Frit, Ghast,
Hairy, Larum, Panic, Perturb, Radio, Rock, Rouse, Scaremonger, Siren, Smoke, Startle,
Tirrit, Tocsin, Trepidation, Unease, Unnerve, Warn, Yike(s)

**Alas** Ah, Alack, Ay, Eheu, Ha, Haro, Harrow, Io, Lackadaisy, Lackaday, O, Oh, Ohone,
O me, Ou, Sadly, Waesucks, Waly, Wel(l)away, Well-a-day, Wellanear, Woe

**Alaskan** AK, Che(e)chako, Sourdough, Tlingit, Yupik

**Alb** Sticharion

**Alban** Berg

**Albanian** Arna(o)ut

**Albatross** Alcatras, Black-footed, Golf, Gooney(-bird), Millstone, Omen, Onus,
Quaker-bird, Wandering

**Albeit** Tho(ugh)

**Albert** Chain, Chevalier, Consort, Hall, Herring, Slang

**Albion** Perfidious

**Album** Autograph, Looseleaf, LP, Photo, Record, Stamp

**Albumen, Albumin** Chalaza, Glair, Leucosin, Mucin, Myogen, Protein, Ricin, Serum,
Treadle, Treddle, White

**Alchemic, Alchemist, Alchemy** Adept, Arch-chimic, Brimstone, Cagliostro,
Faust(us), Hermetic(s), Multiplier, Orpiment, Paracelsus, Quicksilver, Sal ammoniac,
Sorcery, Spagyric, Spagyrist, Witchcraft

**Alcides** Hercules

**Alcohol(ic)** Absolute, Acrolein, Aldehyde, Amyl, Bibulous, Blue ruin, Booze, Borneol, Catechol, Cetyl, Chaptalise, Cholesterol, Choline, Citronellol, Cresol, Denatured, Diethyl, Diol, Dipsomaniac, Drinker, Ethal, Ethanol, Ethyl, Farnesol, Feni, Fenny, Firewater, Fusel-oil, Geraniol, Glycerin(e), Grain, Grog, Gut-rot, Hard, Hard stuff, Inebriate, Inositol, Isopropyl, Jakey, Jungle juice, Lauryl, Linalool, Lush, Mahua, Mahwa, Malt, Manniferous, Mannite, Mannitol, Mercaptan, Mescal, Mescalin(e), Methanol, Meths, Methyl, Moonshine, Mow(r)a, Nerol, Phytol, Pisco, Plonko, Polyol, Potato spirit, Propyl, Pyroligneous, Rotgut, Rubbing, Rubby, Scrumpy, Secondary, Snake juice, Sorbitol, Sphingosine, Spirits, Spirits of wine, Spirituous, Sterol, Taplash, Terpineol, Thiol, Tincture, Tocopherol, Triol, Wash, White lightning, Wino, Witblits, Wood, Xylitol

**Alcove** Apse, Bay, Bole, Carrel(l), Dinette, Inglenook, Lunette, Niche, Nook, Recess, Reveal, Tokonoma

**Alcyonarian** Sea-feather

**Aldehyde** Acrolein, Aldol, Vanillin

**Alder** Fothergilla

**Alderman** Bail(l)ie, CA

**Alderney** CI, Cow

**Ale, Alehouse** Audit, Barleybree, Barley-broo, Barley-broth, Barley wine, Beer, Brown, Bummock, CAMRA, Church, Draught, Feast, Four, Heather, Humming, Humpty-dumpty, Keg, Lager, Lamb's wool, Light, Mild, Morocco, Nappy, Nog, Nogg, October, Pale, Plain, Porter, Purl, Real, Small, Stout, Swats, Tiddleywink, Tipper, White, Whitsun, Wort, Yard, Yill, Yorkshire stingo

**Alert** Agog, Amber, Arrect, Astir, Astute, Attentive, Aware, Bleep, Conscious, Gleg, Gogo, Intelligent, Open-eyed, Presential, Qui vive, Red, Scramble, Sharp, Sprack, Sprag, Stand-to, Tentie, Up and coming, Vigilant, Volable, Warm, Wary, Watchful, Wide-awake, Yellow

**Alewife** Barkeeper, Gaspereau

**Alexander, Alexandrine** Alex, Arius, Macedonian, Pope, Sandy, Sasha, Sawn(e)y, Selkirk, Senarius

**Alfalfa** Lucern(e), Luzern

**Alfred** Dreyfus, Garnet, Jingle

**Alfresco** Barbecue, Plein-air

**Alga(e)** Anabaena, Blanketweed, Chlorella, Chlorophyte, Conferva, Desmid, Diatom, Dulse, Heterocontae, Isokont, Jelly, Nostoc, Periphyton, Phycology, Pleuston, Pond scum, Prokaryon, Protococcus, Red, Rhodophyte, Scum, Sea-lace, Seaweed, Spirogyra, Star-jelly, Stonewort, Ulothrix, Ulotrichales, Valonia, Volvox, Witches' butter, Yellow-green, Zooxanthella

**Algebra** Boolean, Linear, Quadratics

**Algeria(n)** .dz, Kabyle, Nimidian, Pied noir

**Algonquin** Innu, Wampanoag

**Alias** Aka, Byname, Epithet, Moni(c)ker, Nick(name), Pen-name, Pseudonym

**Alibi** Excuse, Watertight

**Alien(ate), Alienation** A-effect, Amortise, Devest, Disaffect, Drop-out, Ecstasy, Erotic, Estrange, ET, Exotic, External, Foreign, Forinsecal, Fremd, Hostile, Little green man, Martian, Metic, Outlandish, Outsider, Philistine, Repugnant, Strange(r), Vulcan

**Alight** Alowe, Avail(e), Avale, Detrain, Disembark, Dismount, Flambe, In, Lambent, Land, Lit, Perch, Pitch, Rest, Settle

**Align** Arrange, Associate, Collimate, Dress, Juxtapose, Marshal, Orient, Straighten, Synchronize

▶ **Alike** *see* LIKE(NESS)

**Alimentary** Oesophagus, Pharynx

**Aliquot** Submultiple

**Alive** Alert, Animated, Breathing, Extant, Quick, Teeming

**Alkali(ne), Alkaloid** Antacid, Apomorphine, Atropine, Base, Bebeerine, Berberine, Betaine, Borax, Brak, Brucine, Caffein(e), Capsaicin, Chaconine, Choline, Cinchon(id)ine,

Codeine, Colchicine, Corydaline, Curarine, Emetin(e), Ephedrine, Ergotamine, Gelsemin(in)e, Guanidine, Harmalin(e), Harmin(e), Hydrastine, Hyoscine, Hyoscyamine, Ibogaine, Kali, Limewater, Lixivium, Lobeline, Lye, Mescalin, Narceen, Narceine, Nicotine, Papaverine, Physostigmine, Pilocarpin(e), Piperine, Potash, Potass, Quinine, Reserpine, Rhoeadine, Scopaline, Scopolamine, Soda, Solanine, Sparteine, Stramonium, Thebaine, Theine, Theobromine, Theophylline, Totaquine, Tropine, Tubocurarine, Veratridine, Veratrin(e), Vinblastine, Vinca, Vincristine, Volatile, White, Yohimbine

**Alkane** Hexane

**All** A, En bloc, →**ENTIRE**, Entity, Every man Jack, Finis, Omni, Pan, Quite, Sum, →**TOTAL**, Toto, Tutti, Whole

**Allah** Bismillah, God

**All at once** Holus-bolus, Per saltum, Suddenly

**Allay** Alleviate, Calm, Disarm, Lessen, Quieten, Solace, Soothe

**Allegation, Allege(d)** Accuse, Assert, Aver, Claim, Declare, Mud, Obtend, Plead, Purport, Represent, Smear, So-called

**Allegiance** Faith, Foy, Loyalty, Tribalism

**Allegory, Allegorical** Apologue, Fable, Mystic, Myth, Parable

**All-embracing** Eclectic

**Allergy** Atopy, Aversion, Bagassosis, Hay fever, Hives

**Alleviate** Allay, Alleg(g)e, Calm, Mitigate, Mollify, Palliate, →**RELIEVE**, Temper

**Alley** Aisle, Blind, Bonce, Bowling, Corridor, Ennog, Ginnel, Lane, Laura, Marble, Passage, Rope-walk, Silicon, Tin Pan, Twitten, Vennel, Walk, Wynd

**Alliance** Agnation, Axis, Bloc, Cartel, Coalition, Combine, Compact, Confederation, Dreibund, Dual, Entente, Federacy, →**LEAGUE**, Marriage, NATO, Quadruple, Syndicate, Triple, Union

**Alligator** Al(l)igarta, Avocado, Caiman, Cayman

**Alliteration** Cynghanedd, Head-rhyme

**Allocate, Allocation** Allot, Apportion(ment), Assign, Designate, Distribute, Earmark, Placement, Priorate, Ration, Share, Soum, Zone

**Allot(ment), Allow(ance), Allowed, Allowing** Abear, Admit, Affect, Alimony, Allocation, Although, Aret(t), Assign, Attendance, Award, Batta, Beteem(e), Brook, Budget, Bug, Cap, Cater, Charter, Cloff, Confess, Cor(r)ody, Countenance, Diet, Discount, Dole, Down, Draft, Empower, Enable, Entitle, Excuse, Expenses, Feod, Field, Fya, Give, Grant, House-bote, Husbandage, Indulge, Jobseekers', Latitude, Legit(imate), Let, License, Licit, Luit(en), Machining, Mag, Mete, Mobility, Okay, Palimony, Parcel, Pension, Percentage, →**PERMIT**, Personal, Pin-money, Pittance, Plot, Portion, Prebend, Privy purse, Quarterage, Quota, Ratio, Ration, Rebate, Rood, Salt-money, Sanction, Separation, Sequel, Share(-out), Shrinkage, Sizings, Stint, Stipend, Subsistence, Suffer, Table money, Tare, Tax, Teene, Though, Tolerance, Tolerate, Tret, Viaticum, Vouchsafe, Weighting, Whack, Yield

**Allotment-holder** Cleruch

▶ **Allow(ance)** *see* **ALLOT(MENT)**

**Alloy** Albata, Alnico®, Amalgam, Babbitt, Bell-metal, Billon, Blend, Brass, Britannia metal, Bronze, Cermet, Chrome(l), Compound, Constantan, Cupronickel, Duralumin®, Dutch leaf, Electron, Electrum, Eutectoid, Ferrochrome, Ferrosilicon, Gunmetal, Invar®, Iridosmine, Kamacite, Latten, Magnalium, Magnox, Manganin®, Marmem, Mischmetal, Mix, Monel®, Nichrome®, Nickel-silver, Nicrosilal, Nimonic, Nitinol, Occamy, Oreide, Orichalc, Ormolu, Oroide, Osmiridium, Paktong, Pewter, Pinchbeck, Platinoid, Porous, Potin, Pot metal, Prince's metal, Shakudo, Shibuichi, Similor, Solder, Speculum, Spelter, Steel, Stellite®, Tambac, Terne, Tombac, Tombak, Tutenag, White metal, Y, Zircal(l)oy, Zircoloy

▷ **Alloy** *may indicate* an anagram

**Allright** A1, Assuredly, Fit, Hale, Hunky(-dory), Jake, OK, Safe, Tickety-boo, Well

**All-round(er)** Generalist, Overhead, Versatile

**All-seeing** Panoptic

**Allspice** Jamaica pepper, Pim(i)ento

**All the same** Even so, Nath(e)less, Nevertheless

**Allude, Allusion** Cite, Hint, Imply, Innuendo, Mention, Refer, Reference, Suggest

**Allure, Alluring** Agaçant(e), Charm, Circe, Decoy, Delilah, Entice, Femme fatale, Glam, Glamour, Houri, Inviting, It, Magnet(ic), SA, Seduce, Seductive, Siren, Tempt, Trap, Trepan, Vamp

**Alluvium** Carse, Deposit

**Ally, Allied** Accomplice, Agnate, Aide, Alley, Alliance, Ami, Backer, Belamy, Co-belligerent, Cognate, Colleague, Compadre, Dual, Foederatus, German(e), Holy, Marble, Marmoreal, Pal, Partner, Plonker, Related, Taw, Unholy, Unite

**Almanac** Calendar, Clog, Ephemeris, Morrison, Nautical, Nostradamus, Whitaker's, Wisden, Zadkiel

**Almighty** Creator, Deity, Dollar, God, Jehovah, Omnipotent

**Almond** Amygdal, Burnt, Emulsion, Jordan, Marchpane, Marzipan, Orgeat, Praline, Ratafia, Sugared, Valencia

**Almost** Anear, Anigh, Close on, Most, Near(ly), Nigh(ly), Practically, Ripe, Une(a)th, Virtually, Well-nigh, Welly

**Alms, Alms-giving** Awmous, Charity, Dole, Eleemosynary, Handout, Zakat

**Aloe** Agave, Pita

**Aloft** Aheight

**Alone** Dernful, Eremite, Hat, Hermit, Jack, Lee-lane, Onely, Pat, Secco, Separate, Single, Singly, Sola, Solo, Solus, Tod, Unaccompanied, Unaided, Unattended, Unholpen

**Along, Alongside** Abeam, Aboard, Abreast, Apposed, Beside, By, Parallel, Synchronous

**Aloof** Abeigh, Apart, Asocial, Chilly, Cool, Detached, Distant, Frosty, Hou inch, Indrawn, Insular, Mugwump, Offish, Remote, Reserved, Reticent, Skeigh, Snooty, Stand-offish, Taciturn, Toffee-nosed, Unapproachable

**Alpaca** Paco

**Alpha** A, Male

**Alphabet** ABC, Absey, Augmented Roman, Black-out, Brahmi, Braille, Chalcidian, Christcross, Cyrillic, Deaf, Devanagari, Estrang(h)elo, Finger, Futhark, Futhorc, Futhork, Glagol, Glagolitic, Glossic, Grantha, Hangul, Horn-book, International, IPA, ITA, Kana, Kanji, Katakana, Kufic, Latin, Manual, Nagari, Og(h)am, Pangram, Phonetic, Pinyin, Romaji, Roman, Runic, Signary, Slavonic, Syllabary

**Alpine, Alps** Australian, Bernese, Cottian, Dinaric, Eiger, Gentian, Graian, Julian, Laburnum, Lepontine, Maritime, Matterhorn, Ortles, Pennine, Rhaetian, Rock plant, Savoy, Southern, Transylvanian, Tyrol, Western

**Also** Add, And, Eke, Item, Likewise, Moreover, Plus, Too, Und, Withal

**Also-ran** Loser

**Altar, Altar-cloth, Altarpiece** Butsudan, Diptych, Dossal, Dossel, Family, High, Polyptych, Retable, Shrine, Tabula, Triptych

**Alter, Alteration** Adapt, Adjust, Airbrush, Bushel, Change, Changeover, Chop and change, Convert, Cook, Correct, Customise, Distort, Evolve, Falsify, Lib, Material, Modify, Modulate, Munge, Mutate, Recast, Refashion, Revise, Transient, Transmogrify, Transpose, Up-end, Variance, → **VARY**

▷ **Alter(native)** *may indicate* an anagram

**Altercation** Barney, Brawl, Fracas, Quarrel, Row, Words, Wrangle

**Alternate, Alternating, Alternation, Alternative** Aka, Boustrophedon, Bypass, Exchange, Instead, Intercut, Metagenesis, → **OPTION**, Or else, Ossia, Other, Rotate, Second best, Second string, Solidus, Staggered, Stop-go, Systaltic, Tertian, Variant, Vicissitude

▷ **Alternately** *may indicate* every other letter

**Althaea** Mallow, Malva

**Although** Admitting, Albe(e), All-be, But, Even, Howsoever, Howsomever, Whereas, While, Whilst

**Altitude** Elevation, Height, Meridian, Pressure, Rated, Snowline

**Alto** Countertenor

**Altogether** Algate(s), All-to-one, Bare, Completely, En bloc, Entirely, Holus-bolus, Idea, In all, Lock, stock and barrel, Naked, Nuddy, Nude, Nudity, Overall, Purely, Slick, Tout (ensemble), Uncut, Wholly

▷ **Altogether** *may indicate* words to be joined

**Altruistic, Altruism** Heroic, Humane, Philanthropic, Selfless(ness), Unselfish

**Alum** Potash

**Aluminium, Alumino-silicate** Al, Allanite, Bauxite, Cryolite, Euclase, Gibbsite, Sillimanite, Stilbite, Tinfoil

**Alumnus** Graduate, OB

**Alveolus** Air-sac

**Always** Algate(s), Ay(e), Constant, E'er, Eternal, Ever(more), Forever, For keeps, I, Immer, Semper, Sempre, Still

**Amalgamate** Coalesce, Consolidate, Fuse, Merge, Unite

**Amalthea** Cornucopia

**Amanuensis** Tironian

**Amarylli(d)s** Leocojum, Lily, Polianthes

**Amass** Accumulate, Assemble, Collect, Gather, Heap, Hoard, Pile, Upheap

**Amateur(s)** A, AA, Armchair, Beginner, Corinthian, Dabbler, Dilettante, DIY, Enthusiast, Hacker, Ham, Inexpert, L, Laic, Lay(man), Neophyte, Newbie, Novice, Prosumer, Sunday painter, Tiro, Tyro

**Amatory** Eros, Erotic, Fervent

**Amaze(d), Amazement, Amazing** Agape, Agog, Astonish, Astound, Awe, Awhape, Bewilder, Cor, Criv(v)ens, Dum(b)found, Far out, Flabbergast, Gasser, Gee-whiz, Gobsmack, Goodnow, Grace, Incredible, Jesus wept, Magical, Monumental, O, Open-eyed, Open-mouthed, Perplex, Poleaxe, Pop-eyed, Prodigious, Stagger, Strewth, Stupefaction, Stupendous, Thunderstruck, Unreal, Wow

**Amazon(ian)** Ant, ATS, Brimstone, Britannia, Dragon, Hippolyta, Hoyden, Jivaro, Orellana, Penthesilea, Pirai, Shield-maid, Shield-may, Thalestris, Tupi, Virago

**Ambassador** At-large, Diplomat, Elchee, Elchi, Eltchi, Envoy, Extraordinary, Fetial, HE, Internuncio, Leaguer, Ledger, Legate, Leidger, Leiger, Lieger, Minister, Nuncio, Plenipo, Plenipotentiary, Pronuncio

**Amber** Colophony, Electric, Lammer, Ligure, Resin, Retinite, Succinum

**Ambience** Atmosphere, Aura, Milieu, Setting

**Ambiguous, Ambiguity** Amphibology, Cryptic, Delphic, Double, Double entendre, Elusive, Enigmatic, Epicene, Equivocal, Gnomic, Inexactness, Loophole, Oracular, Weasel words

**Ambit** Scope

**Ambition, Ambitious** Adventurer, Aim, Arrivisme, Aspiring, Careerism, Dream, Drive, Emulate, Go-ahead, Goal, Go-getter, Grail, High-flier, Holy Grail, Keen, Office-hunter, Purpose, Pushy, Rome-runner, Thrusting, Type A

**Amble** Meander, Mosey, Pace, Poddle, Pootle, Saunter, Single-foot, Stroll, Traipse

**Ambrose** Emrys

**Ambrosia(l)** Amreeta, Amrita, Beebread, Fragrant, Odorant, Ragweed, Savoury

**Ambulance, Ambulanceman** Badger, Blood-wagon, Field, Meat wagon, Pannier, Paramedic, Van, Yellow-flag, Zambu(c)k

**Ambulatory** Stoa

**Ambush(ed)** Ambuscade, Belay, Bushwhack, Emboscata, Embusque, Forelay, Forestall, Latitant, Lie in wait, Lurch, Perdu(e), Trap, Watch, Waylay

**Amelia** Bloomer

**Ameliorate** Amend, Ease, Improve, Lenify, Remedy

**Amen** Ammon, Approval, Inshallah, Verify

**Amenable** Putty

**Amend(ment)** Alter, Change, Correct, Edit, Expiate, Expurgate, Fifth, Insertion, Protocol, Redress, Reform, Repair, Restore, → REVISE, Satisfy

▷ **Amend** *may indicate* an anagram

**Amenity** Facility

**Ament** Catkin, Idiot

**America(n)** A, Algonki(a)n, Algonqu(i)an, Am, Angeleno, Basket Maker, Caddo, Cajun, Canadian, Carib, Chicano, Chickasaw, Chinook, Copperskin, Digger, Doughface, Down-easter, Federalist, Flathead, Fox, Geechee, Gringo, Gullah, Guyanese, Huron, Interior, Joe, Jonathan, Latino, Miskito, Mission Indian, Mistec, Mixtec, Mound builder, Native, New World, Norteno, Olmec, Paisano, Redneck, Salish, Stateside, Statesman, Statist, Tar-heel, Tico, Tupi, Uncle Sam, US(A), WASP, Yankee (Doodle), Yanqui

**Americium** Am

**Amethyst** Oriental

**Amiable, Amicable** Friendly, Genial, Gentle, Inquiline, Mungo, Peaceful, Sweet, Warm

**Amid(st)** Among, Atween, Between, Inter, Twixt

**Amide** Asparagine

**Amine** Putrescine, Spermine

**Amino-acid** Dopa, Tyrosine, Valine

**Amiss** Awry, Ill, Up, Wrong

**Amity** Concord, Peatship

**Ammonia(c)** Amide, Amine, Choline, Ethylamine, Hartshorn, Imide, Oshac

**Ammonite** Serpent-stone

**Ammunition** Ammo, Bandoleer, Bandolier, Birdshot, Buckshot, Bullets, Chain-shot, Dum-dum, Grape(shot), Grenade, Round, Shot, Slug, Tracer

**Amnesia** Anterograde, Fugal, Fugue, Lethe, Retrograde

**Amnesty** Oblivion, Pardon

**Amoeba** Melboean, Rhizopoda

**Amok** Rampaging

**Among** Amid(st), In, Inter al, Within

**Amorous(ly)** Casanova, Erotic, Fervent, Lustful, Nutty, Romantic, Sheep's eyes, Smickly, Spoony, Warm

**Amorphous** Formless, Guanine, Nuclein, Shapeless, Vague

**Amount** Come, Degree, Dose, Element, Figure, Glob, Gobbet, Handful, Lashings, Levy, Lot, Measure, Nip, Number, Ocean, Offset, Outage, Plethora, Pot(s), Premium, Price, Quantity, Quantum, Shedload, Span, Stack, Stint, Sum, Throughput, Trace, Volume, Whale, Wheel

**Amour** Affair(e), Intrigue, Love

**Ampersand** Tironian sign

**Amphetamine** Benny, Benzedrine, Speed

**Amphibian(s), Amphibious** Amb(l)ystoma, Amtrack, Anura, Axolotl, Batrachian, Caecilia, Caecilian, Desman, Eft, Frog, Guana, Hassar, Herpetology, Horned toad, Labyrinthodont, Mermaid, Mudpuppy, Newt, Olm, Ophiomorph, Proteus, Rana, Salamander, Salientia, Seal, Siren, Tadpole, Toad, Tree frog, Urodela(n), Urodele, Weasel

**Amphipod** Sand-screw, Shrimp

**Amphitheatre** Arena, Bowl, Circus Maximus, Coliseum, Colosseum, Ring, Stage

**Ample, Amplitude** Bellyful, Copious, Enough, Generous, Good, Large, Much, Opulent, Profuse, Rich, Roomy, Round, Sawtooth, Spacious, Uberous, Voluminous

**Amplifier, Amplify** Booster, Double, Eke, Enlarge, Hailer, Laser, Loud hailer, Maser, Megaphone, Push-pull, Solion, Soundboard, Tannoy®, Transistor, Treble

**Amputate** Sever, Transfix

**Amulet** Abraxas, Charm, Churinga, Fetish, Greegree, Grigri, Grisgris, Haemon, Pentacle, Periapt, Phylactery, Sea-bean, Talisman, Telesm, Tiki, Toadstone, Token

**Amuse(ment), Amusing(ly)** Account, Caution, Cottabus, Disport, Diversion, Divert, Divertimento, Divertissement, Drole, Droll, Entertain, Game, Gas, Giocoso, Glee, Hoke,

Hoot, Jocular, Killing, Laughter, Levity, Light, Occupy, Pantheon, Pleasure, Popjoy, Priceless, Regale, Rich, Riot, Scream, Slay, Solace, → **SPORT**, Tickle, Titillate, Wacky

**Amy** Johnson, Robsart

▸ **An** *see* **A**

**Ana(s)** Story, Teal

**Anabaptist** Abecedarian, Dipper, Dopper, Hutterite, Knipperdolling

**Anableps** Four-eyes

**Anachronism, Anachronistic** Archaism, Solecism, Unhistorical

**Anaconda** Water boa

**Anacreon** Te(i)an

**Anaemia, Anaemic** Aplastic, Cooley's, Diamond-blackfan, Fanconi's, Favism, Haemolytic, Megaloblastic, Miner's, Pallid, Pernicious, Sallow, Sickle-cell, Sicklemia, Thalassaemia

**Anaesthetic, Anaesthetise(d), Anaesthetist** Analgesic, Apgar, Avertin®, Basal, Benzocaine, Bupivacaine, Caudal, Chloralose, Chloroform, Cocaine, Endotracheal, Epidural, Ether, Eucain(e), Fluothane, Freeze, Gas, General, Halothane, Hibernation, Infiltrate, Intravenous, Jabber, Ketamine, Lidocaine, Lignocaine, Local, Metopryl, Morphia, Novocaine, Number, Opium, Orthocaine, Pentothal, Phenacaine, Phencyclidine, Procaine, Rhigolene, Special K, Spinal, Stovaine, Topical, Trike, Twilight sleep, Under, Urethan(e)

**Anagram** Jumble

**Anal, Anus** Back passage, Poepol, Proctal, Ring, Tewel

**Analgesic** Aspirin, Bute, Codeine, Diclofenac, Disprin, Fentanyl, Ketamine, Menthol, Meperidine, Methadone, Morphia, Moxa, Opium, Painkiller, Paracetamol, Pethidine, Phenacetin, Phencyclidine, Quina, Relief, Salicin(e), Sedative

**Analogous, Analogy** Akin, Corresponding, Like, Parallel, Similar

**Analyse(r), Analysis** Alligate, Anagoge, Anatomy, Assay, Assess, Blot, Breakdown, Combinatorial, Conformational, Construe, Critique, Diagnosis, Dimensional, Discourse, Dissect, Emic, E-nose, Esda, Eudiometer, Examine, Explication, Factor, Force-field, Fourier, Gap, Gravimetric, Harmonic, Input-output, Job, Kicksorter, Lexical, Linguistic, Logical, Miscue, Numerical, Parse, Pollen, Post-mortem, Process, Psych out, Qualitative, Quant, Quantitative, Reductionism, Resolution, Risk, Rundown, Sabermetrics, Scan(sion), Semantics, Sift, Spectral, Spectroscopic, Spectrum, Statistician, → **SWOT**, Systems, Test, Transactional, Unpick, Volumetric

▹ **Analysis** *may indicate* an anagram

**Analyst** Alienist, Investment, Jung, Lay, Psychiatrist, Quant(ative), Researcher, Shrink, Systems, Trick cyclist

**Anarchist, Anarchy** Bakunin, Black Bloc(k), Black Hand, Bolshevist, Chaos, Kropotkin, Lawless, Nihilism, Provo, Punk, Rebel, Revolutionary, Riotous, Trotskyite, Unrule

**Anathema** Ban, Curse, Execration, Maranatha, Oath, Warling

**Anatole, Anatolia(n)** Asia minor, France, Hittite, Ionian, Turk

**Anatomy, Anatomist** Bones, Cuvier, De Graaf, Dubois, Framework, Henle, Herophilus, Histology, Hunter, Malpighi, Meibom, Morbid, Osteology, Pacini, Prosector, Puccini, Schneider, Spiegel, Topology, Worm

**Ancestor, Ancestral, Ancestry** Adam, Avital, Dawn man, Descent, Elder, Extraction, For(e)bear, Forefather, Gastraea, Hereditary, Humanoid, Kachina, Lin(e)age, Parent, Parentage, Pedigree, Predecessor, Primogenitor, Proband, Profectitious, Progenitor, Propositus, Roots, Sire, Tipuna, Tree, Tupina

**Anchor(age)** Atrip, Berth, Bower, Cell, Deadman, Drag, Drift, Drogue, Eremite, Grapnel, Hawse, Hermit, Host, Kedge, Kedger, Killick, Killock, Laura, Moor, Mud-hook, Mushroom, Nail, Presenter, Ride, Roads(tead), Rode, Root, Scapa Flow, Sea, Sheet, Spithead, Stock, Stream, Toehold, Waist, Weather

**Anchorite** Recluse

**Anchovy** Fish, Pear

**Ancient** Antediluvian, Archaic, Auld-warld, Bygone, Early, Gonfanoner, Historic, Hoary, Iago, Immemorial, Lights, Neanderthal, Neolithic, Ogygian, → **OLD(ER)**, Old-world, Primeval, Primitive, Pristine, Ur, Veteran

**Ancient city** Carthage, Ur

**Ancillary** Adjunct, Secondary, Subservient

**And** Als(o), Ampassy, Ampersand, Amperzand, Ampussyand, Besides, Et, Furthermore, Item, 'n', Plus, Tironian sign, Und

**Andalusite** Macle

**Andiron** Chenet, Dog, Firedog

**Andrew(es)** Aguecheek, Lancelot, Merry

**Androgynous** Epicene

**Android** Automaton, Golem, Replicant, Robot

**Anecdote(s)** Ana, Exemplum, Personalia, Story, Tale, Yarn

**Anemometer** Wind-sleeve, Windsock

**Anemone** Actinia, Pasque-flower, Windflower

**Anew** De integro, De novo

**Angel(s)** Abdiel, Adramelech, Apollyon, Archangel, Ariel, Arioch, Asmadai, Azrael, Backer, Banker, Beelzebub, Belial, Benefactor, Cake, Cherub, Clare, Destroying, Deva, Dominion, Dust, Eblis, Fallen, Falls, Fuzzy-wuzzy, Gabriel, Guardian, Heavenly host, Hierarchy, Host, Iblis, Investor, Israfel, Ithuriel, Lucifer, Michael, Nurse, Power, Principality, Raphael, Recording, Rimmon, Saint, St, Seraph, Spirit, Throne, Uriel, Uzziel, Virtue, Watcher, Zadkiel, Zephiel

**Angela** Brazil

**Angelica** Archangel

**Angel's wings** Begonia

**Anger, Angry** → **ANNOY**, Apeshit, Bate, Berserk, Bile, Black, Boiling, Bristle, Choler(ic), Conniption, Cross, Dander, Disgruntled, Displeased, Dudgeon, Enrage, Exasperation, Face, Fiery, Fired up, Fuff, Fury, Gnar, Gram, Hacked off, Heat, Het up, Horn-mad, Huff, Incense, Inflame, Infuriate, Iracund, Irascible, Ire, Kippage, Livid, Mad, Monkey, Moody, Nettle, Pique, Provoke, Radge, Rage, Rampant, Ratty, Renfierst, Rile, Roil, Rouse, Sore, Spleen, Steam, Stroppy, Tamping, Tantrum, Tarnation, Teed off, Teen(e), Temper, Tene, Tooshie, Vex, Vies, Warm, Waspish, Waxy, Worked-up, Wound up, Wrath, Wroth, Yond

**Angina** Sternalgia, Vincent's

**Angle(d), Angler, Angular, Angles, Angling** Acute, Aglee, Argument, Aspect, Attitude, Axil, Azimuthal, Baiter, Canthus, Cast, Catch, Chiliagon, Coign, Complementary, Conjugate, Contrapposto, Corner, Cos, Critical, Diedral, Diedre, Dihedral, Elbow, Elevation, Ell, Exterior, Facial, Fish, Fish-hook, Fork, Geometry, Gonion, Hade, Hip, Hour, Hyzer, In, Incidence, Interior, L, Laggen, Laggin, Latitude, Loft, Longitude, Mitre, Mung, Negative, Nook, Oblique, Obtuse, Parallax, Pediculate, Perigon, Peterman, Phase, Piend, Piscator, Pitch, Pitch-cone, Plan, Plane, Polyhedral, Position, Positive, Quoin, Radian, Rake, Re-entrant, Reflex, Right, Rod(ster), Rod(s)man, Round, Salient, Sally, Saltchucker, Sine, Sinical, Slip, Solid, Spherical, Stalling, Steeve, Steradian, Straight, Supplementary, Sweepback, The gentle craft, Trotline, Vertical, Viewpoint, Visual, Walton, Waltonian, Washin, Weather, Wide-gab

**Anglesey** Mona

**Anglican(s)** CE-men, Conformist, Episcopal

**Anglo-Catholic** High-church, Spire

**Anglo-Indian** Qui-hi, Qui-hye, Topi-wallah

**Anglo-Saxon** Hereward

**Angora** Goat, Mohair, Rabbit

**Angostura** Cusparia bark

**Angst** Dread

**Anguish(ed)** Agony, Distress, Gip, Grief, Gyp, Hag-ridden, Heartache, Misery, → **PAIN**, Pang, Sorrow, Throes, → **TORMENT**, Torture, Woe

**Angus** Aberdeen

**Animal(s)** Acrita, Anoa, Armadillo, Atoc, Bag, Bandog, Barbastel, Beast, Bestial, Brute, Cariacou, Carnal, Chalicothere, Cleanskin, Coati, Creature, Criollo, Critter, Ethology, Fauna, Felis, Feral, Gerbil, Guanaco, Herd, Huanaco, Ichneumon, Jacchus, Jerboa, Kinkajou, Klipdas, Mammal, Marmoset, Marmot, Meiofauna, Menagerie, Moose, Morken, Noctule, Oribi, Pack, Parazoon, Party, Pet, Political, Protozoa, Pudu, Pygarg, Quadruped, Quagga, Rac(c)oon, Rhesus, Rotifer, Sensual, Sloth, Stud, Symphile, Tarsier, Teledu, Urson, Waler, Xenurus, Yale, Yapock, Zerda, Zoo

**Animal-catcher** Utricularia

**Animate(d), Animation** Activate, Actuate, Alive, Arouse, Biophor, Cartoon, Ensoul, Excite, Fire, Frankenstein, Frisky, Heat, Hortatory, Hot, Inspire, Lit, Live, Morph, Mosso, Perky, Pixil(l)ation, Rouse, Spark, Spiritoso, Spritely, Stop-motion, Suspended, Toon, Verve, Vivacity, Vivify

**Animosity** Enmity, Friction, Hostility, Ill-will, Malevolence, Malice, Pique, Rancour, Strife

**Aniseed** Pernod

**Ankle** Coot, Cuit, Cute, Hock, Hucklebone, Knee, Malleolus, Talus

**Ankle(t), Ankle covering** Cootikin, Cuitikin, Cutikin, Gaiter, Jess

**Anna, Anne, Annie** Boleyn, Hathaway, Laurie, Oakley, Page, Pavlova, Pice, Sewell, Sister

**Annal(s)** Acta, Archives, Chronicles, Register

**Annatto** Roucou

**Annex(e)** Acquire, Add, Affiliate, Attach, Codicil, Extension, Lean-to, Subjoin

**Annie** Laurie, Orphan

**Annihilate** Abolish, Destroy, Erase, Exterminate, Obliterate, Slay, Unbe

**Anniversary** Birthday, Feast, Jubilee, Obit, Triennial, Wedding, Yahrzeit

**Annotate, Annotator** Comment, Interpret, Note, Postil, Scholiast

**Announce(r), Announcement** Banns, Bellman, Bill(ing), Blazon, Bulletin, Communiqué, Crier, Declare, Decree, Disclose, Divulgate, Flash, Gazette, Herald, Hermes, Impart, Inform, Intimate, Meld, Name and shame, Newsflash, Noise, Notice, Oracle, Post, Preconise, Press release, Proclaim, Profess, Promulgate, Pronunciamente, Publish, Release, → REPORT, Rescript, Speaker(ine), State, Statement, Tannoy, Toastmaster, Town crier, Trumpet

**Annoy(ance), Annoyed, Annoying** Aggravate, Aggrieve, Anger, Antagonise, Badger, Bane, Blight, Bother, Bug, Bugbear, Chafe, Chagrin, Choleric, Contrary, Cross, Deuce(d), Displeasance, Displeasure, Disturb, Doggone, Doh, Drag, Drat, Fash, Fleabite, Frab, Fumed, Gall, Gatvol, Get, Gordon Bennett, Hack off, Hang, Harass, Hatter, Hector, Hip, Hoots, Huff, Hump, Humph, Incense, Irk, → IRRITATE, Mickey-taking, Miff, Mischief, Molest, Moryah, Nag, Nark, Needle, Nettle, Niggle, Noisome, Noy(ance), Peeve, Perisher, Pesky, Pester, Pipsqueak, Pique, Plague, Provoke, Rankle, Rats, Ratty, Resentful, Ride, Rile, Roil, Rub, Shirty, Sting, Testy, Tiresome, Tracasserie, Troublesome, Try, Vex, Wazzock

**Annual, Annuity** Almanac, Bedder, Book, Consolidated, Contingent, Deferred, Etesian, → FLOWER, Half-hardy, Hardy, Immediate, Life, Pension, Perpetuity, → PLANT, Rente, Tontine, Yearbook, Yearly

**Annul(ment)** Abolish, Abrogate, Cashier, Cassation, Dissolution, Invalidate, Irritate, Negate, Recision, Repeal, Rescind, Reversal, Revoke, Vacate, Vacatur, Vacuate, → VOID

**Annular** Toric

▶ **Annunciation** *see* ANNOUNCE(R)

**Anodyne** Balm, Narcotic, Paregoric, Sedative

**Anoint(ing)** Anele, Cerate, Chris(o)m, Consecrate, Embrocate, Grease, Hallow, Nard, Smear

**Anomaly** Aberration, Eccentric, Gravity, Magnetic, Mean, True

▷ **Anomaly** *may indicate* an anagram

**Anon** Again, Anew, Erelong, Later, Soon

**Anonymous** Adespota, Anon, A.N.Other, Faceless, Grey, Impersonal, Nameless, Somebody, Unknown, Unnamed, Valentine

**Anorak** Geek, Nerd, Trainspotter, Wonk

**Another** Extra, Fresh, Per pro

**Answer(ing), Answer(s)** A, Account, Acknowledge, Amoebaean, Ans, Antiphon, Because, Comeback, Crib (sheet), Defence, Dusty, Echo, Key, Lemon, Light, No, Oracle, Rebuttal, Rebutter, Rein, Rejoin(der), Repartee, Reply, Rescript, Respond, Response, Responsum, Retort, Return, Riposte, Serve, Sol, Solution, Solve, Verdict, Yes

**Ant(s), Anthill** Amazon, Army, Bull(dog), Carpenter, Colony, Driver, Dulosis, Emmet, Ergataner, Ergates, Ergatogyne, Ergatomorph, Fire, Formic, Formicary, Leafcutter, Legionary, Myrmecoid, Myrmidon, Nasute, Neuter, Pharaoh, Pismire, Red, Sauba, Slave, Slave-maker, Soldier, Termite, Thief, Umbrella, Velvet, White, Wood

**Antacid** Limewater, Magnesia, Peptic

**Antagonist(ic), Antagonise** Adverse, Enemy, Estrange, Hostile, Oppugnant, Peare, Peer

**Antarctica** Adelie Land, Byrd Land, Graham Land, Marie Byrd Land, Wilkes Land

**Ant-bear** Tamanoir

**Ante** Bet, Punt, Stake

**Ant-eater** Aardvark, Banded, Echidna, Edental, Giant, Manis, Numbat, Pangolin, Scaly, S(e)ladang, Spiny, Tamandu, Tamandua, Tapir

**Antelope** Addax, Antilope, Blackbuck, Blaubok, Blesbok, Bloubok, Bluebuck, Bongo, Bontebok, Bubal(is), Bushbuck, Cabric, Chamois, Chikara, Chiru, Dikdik, Duiker, Duyker, Dzeren, Eland, Elk, Gazelle, Gemsbok, Gerenuk, Gnu, Goa, Goral, Grysbok, Harnessed, Hartbees, Hartebeest, Impala, Inyala, Kaama, Kid, Klipspringer, Kob, Kongoni, Koodoo, Kudu, Lechwe, Madoqua, Marshbuck, Mhorr, Mohr, Nagor, Nilgai, Nilgau, Nyala, Nylghau, Oribi, Oryx, Ourebi, Ox, Pale-buck, Pallah, Prongbuck, Pronghorn, Pronk, Puku, Pygarg, Reebok, Reedbuck, Rhebok, Sable, Saiga, Sasin, Sassaby, Serow, Sitatunga, Situtunga, Springbok, Steenbok, Steinbock, Stemback, Stembok, Suni, Takin, Thar, Topi, Tragelaph, Tsessebe, Waterbuck, Wildebeest

**Antenatal** Labour

**Antenna** Aerial, Dipole, Dish, Feeler, Horn, Rabbit's ears, Sensillum, Squarial, TVRO

**Anterior** Anticous, Earlier, Front, Prior

**Anteroom** Foyer, Voiding-lobby

**Anthelmintic** Worm

**Anthem** Chant, Die Stem, Hymn, Introit, Isodica, Marseillaise, Motet(t), National, Offertory, Psalm, Red Flag, Responsory, Song, Star Spangled Banner, Stem, Theme, Tract, Troparion

**Anthology** Album, Ana, Chrestomathy, Digest, Divan, Florilegium, Garland, Pick, Spicilege

**Anthony** Absolute, Adverse, Runt, Trollope

**Anthracite** Blind-coal

**Anthrax** Sang, Splenic fever, Woolsorter's disease

**Anthropo(i)d** Peripatus, Sivapithecus

**Anthropologist, Anthropology** Ethnography, Heyerdahl, Levi-Strauss, Mead, Somatology, Strathern, Strehlow, Verchow

**Anti** Against, Agin, Averse, Con, Gainst, Hostile

**Anti-abortion** Right to life

**Anti-aircraft** AA

**Anti-bacterial, Antibiotic** Aclarubicin, Actinomycin, Allicin, Amoxicillin, Ampicillin, Aureomycin®, Avoparcin, Bacitracin, Bacteriostat, Carbenicillin, Cecropin, Cephalosporin, Cipro®, Ciprofloxacin, Cloxacillin, Colistin, Cortisone, Co-trimoxazole, Cycloserine, Doxorubicin, Doxycycline, Drug, Erythromycin, Gentamicin, Gramicidin, Griseofulvin, Interferon, Interleukin, Kanamycin, Lincomycin, Macrolide, Magainin, Methicillin, Mitomycin, Neomycin, Nystatin, Opsonin, Oxacillin, Oxytetracycline, Penicillin, Polymyxin, Puromycin, Quinolone, Rifampicin, Rifamycin, Spectinomycin, Streptokinase, Streptomycin, Streptothricin, Terramycin®, Tetracycline, Tyrocidine, Tyrothricin, Vancomycin, Virginiamycin, Wide-spectrum

**Antibody** Agglutinin, Alemtuzumab, Amboceptor, Antitoxin, Blocker, Catuximab, H(a)emolysin, Hybroid, IgA/E/G/M/O, Isoagglutinin, Lysin, Monoclonal, Opsonin, Precipitin, Reagin, Retuximab, Trastuzumab

**Antic(s)** Caper, Dido, Frolic, Gambado, Hay, Prank, Shenanigan, Stunt

**Anti-carlist** Queenite

**Antichrist** The Man of Sin

**Anticipate, Anticipation** Against, Antedate, Augur, Await, Dread, Drool, Envisage, →EXPECT, Forecast, Foresee, Foresight, Forestall, Foretaste, Forethought, Hope, Intuition, Pre-empt, Preparation, Prevenancy, Prolepsis, Prospect, Second-guess, Type

**Anticlimax** Bathos, Comedown, Damp squib, Deflation, Disappointment, Letdown

**Anticline** Upwrap

**Anticlockwise** Dextrorse, Laevorotatory, Widdershins, Withershins

**Anticoagulant** C(o)umarin, Heparin, Hirudin, Prostacyclin, Warfarin

**Anticommunist** John Birch(er), McCarthyism

**Anticyclone** High

**Antidepressant** Prozac

**Antidote** Adder's wort, Alexipharmic, Angelica, Antivenin, Arrowroot, Bezoar, Contrayerva, Cure, Dimercaprol, Emetic, Guaco, Interleukin, Mithridate, Nostrum, Orvietan, Picrotoxin, Remedy, Ribavirin, Senega, Theriac(a), (Venice-)Treacle

**Anti-feminist** Traditional

**Anti-freeze** Glycerol, Lagging

**Anti-fur** PETA

**Antigen** Agglutinogen, Hapten(e)

**Antihistamine** Dimenhydrinate, Quercetin

**Anti-imperialist** Guelf, Guelph

**Antimacassar** Tidy

**Anti-monarchist** Republican

**Antimonopoly** Trust buster

**Antimony** Kohl, Sb, Speiss, Stibium, Tartar emetic

**Antinuclear** CND

**Antioxidant** Lycopene

**Anti-parliamentarian** Poujadist

**Antipasto** Caponata

**Antipathy** Allergy, Animosity, Aversion, Detest, →DISLIKE, Enmity, Intolerance, Repugnance

**Anti-perfectionist** Cobden

**Antiphon** The Reproaches

**Antipodean** Abo, Antarctic, Antichthon, Aussie, Enzed, Underworld

**Antipope** Novatian(us)

**Anti-protectionist** Cobden

**Antiquated, Antique, Antiquarian** Ancient, Archaic, A(u)stringer, Bibelot, Curio, Dryasdust, Egyptian, Egyptologist, FAS, Fogram(ite), Fog(e)y, Fossil, Moth-eaten, Old-fangled, Ostreger, Relic

**Anti-reformer** Obscurant

**Anti-revolutionary** Vendean, White

**Anti-Roman** Ghibel(l)ine

**Anti-royalist** Puritan, Whig

**Anti-Semitic** Pamyat

**Antiseptic** Acriflavine, Borax, Carbolic, Cassareep, Creosote, Cresol, Dettol®, Disinfectant, Eupad, Eusol, Formaldehyde, Formalin, Formol, Germicide, Guaiacol, Iodine, Lister, Lysol®, Merbromin, Phenol, Sterile, Tar, Thymol, Tutty

**Anti-slavery** Free-soil, Wilberforce

**Anti-smoker** ASH, Misocapnic

**Antisocial** Aggro, Hoodie, Hostile, Ishmaelitish, Litterbug, Litter-lout, Loner, Misanthropic, Oik, Psychopath, Standoffish

**Antithesis** Contrary, Converse, Opposite
**Anti-three** Noetian
**Antitoxin** Antibody, Antivenin, Guaco, Serum, Vaccine
**Anti-union** Secesher
**Antiviral** Rebavirin
**Antivitamin** Pyrithiamine
**Antler(s)** Bosset, Crown, Horn, Palm, Rights, Staghorn, Surroyal, Tine
**Ant-proof** Bilian
▶ **Anus** *see* ANAL
**Anvil** Bick-iron, Block, Incus, Stiddie, Stithy
**Anxiety, Anxious** Abdabs, Angst, Brood, Care(ful), Cark, Concern, Disquiet, Dreading,
    Dysthymia, Eager, Edgy, Fanteeg, Fantigue, Fantod, Fear, Fraught, Fretting, Grave,
    Habdabs, Heebie-jeebies, Hung-up, Hypochondria, Impatient, Inquietude, Itching,
    Jimjams, Jumpy, Keen, Nerviness, Panic, Reck, Restless, Scruple, Separation, Shpilkes,
    Solicitous, Stewing, Stress, Suspense, Sweat, Tension, Toey, Trepidation, Twitchy, Unease,
    Unquiet, Upset, Uptight, White-knuckle, Willies, Worriment, Worryguts, Worrywort
**Any** Arrow, Ary, Some
**Anybody, Anyone** Everyman, One, Whoso, You
**Anyhow, Anyway** Anyroad(s), However, Leastways, Leastwise, Regardless
**Anything** Aught, Diddly-squat, Oucht, Ought, Owt, Whatnot
▷ **Anyway** *may indicate* an anagram
**Apache** Arizona, AZ, Geronimo
**Apart** Aloof, Aside, Asunder, Atwain, Beside, Separate
**Apartheid** Racism, Segregation, Verkrampte
**Apartment** Atrium, Ben, Condo(minium), Cubicle, Digs, Duplex, Efficiency, Flat, Insula,
    Mansion, Pad, Paradise, Penthouse, Pied-a-terre, Quarters, Room, Simplex, Solitude,
    State, Suite, Tenement, Unit, Walk-up
**Apathetic, Apathy** Accidie, Acedia, Incurious, Indifferent, Inertia, Languid, Lethargic,
    Listless, Lobotomized, Lukewarm, Mopish, Pococurante, Stoical, Torpid, Unenthusiastic
**Ape(-like), Apeman** Anthropoid, Barbary, Big-foot, Bonobo, Catarrhine, Copy,
    Dryopithecine, Gelada, Gibbon, Gorilla, → IMITATE, Magot, Mimic, → MONKEY, Naked,
    Orang, Paranthropus, Parrot, Pithecoid, Pongid, Pongo, → PRIMATE, Proconsul,
    Replicate, Sacred, Simian, Simulate, Troglodyte, Yowie
**Aperient** Cascara, Laxative, Senna
**Aperitif** Campari, → DRINK, Pernod®
**Aperture** Balistraria, Chink, Fenestella, Hole, Keyhole, Opening, Orifice, Osculum,
    Peephole, Pinhole, Porta, Punctum, Relative, Spiracle, Swallow, Window
**Apex** Acme, Culmen, Gonion, Keystone, Knoll, Knowe, Solar, Summit, Vertex
**Aphid** Ant-cow, Blackfly, Greenfly, Phylloxera
**Aphorism** Adage, Epigram, Gnome, Maxim, Pensée, Proverb, Sutra
**Aphrodisiac, Aphrodite** Cytherean, Erotic, Idalian, Paphian, Philter, Philtre, Spanish
    fly, Urania, Yohimbine
**Aplomb** Assurance, Cool, Equanimity, Poise, Sangfroid, Serenity
**Apocryphal** Spurious, Tobit
**Apograph** Roneo®
**Apollo** Belvedere, Moonshot, Pythian, Sun
**Apologetic, Apologist, Apology** Advocate, Ashamed, Cut up, Excuse, Justifier,
    Mockery, My bad, Oops, Pardon, Scuse, Sir-reverence
**Apostate** Citer, → HERETIC, Pervert, Rat, Recreant, Renegade, Runagate, Turncoat
**Apostle, Apostolic** Cuthbert, → DISCIPLE, Evangelist, Johannine, Jude, Matthew,
    Pauline, Spoon, Thad(d)eus, Thomas, Twelve
**Apostrophe, Apostrophise** Elision, O(h), Soliloquy, Tuism
**Apothecary** Chemist, Dispenser, Druggist, LSA, Pharmacist, Pottingar
**Apothegm** Dictum, Maxim, Motto

**Appal(ling)** Abhorrent, Abysmal, Affear(e), Aghast, Dire, Dismay, Egregious, Execrable, Frighten, Horrify, Piacular, Shock, Tragic

▷ **Appallingly** *may indicate* an anagram

**Apparatus** Absorptiometer, Aerator, Alembic, Alkalimeter, Appliance, Aqualung, Aspirator, Autoclave, Block and tackle, Breeches buoy, Bridgerama, Caisson, Calorimeter, Chemostat, Churn, Clinostat, Codec, Coherer, Colorimeter, Commutator, Condenser, Converter, Convertor, Cosmotron, Critical, Cryostat, Cyclotron, Davis, Decoy, Defibrillator, Desiccator, → **DEVICE**, Digester, Ebullioscope, Effusiometer, Egg, Electrograph, Electrophorus, Electroscope, Elutriator, Enlarger, Eprouvette, Equipment, Eudiometer, Exciter, Fixings, Gadget, Gasogene, Gazogene, Generator, Giant('s) stride, Golgi, Graith, Gyroscope, Heater, Heliograph, Helioscope, Hemocytometer, Hodoscope, Holophote, Horse, Hydrophone, Hygrostat, Incubator, Inhalator, Injector, Inspirator, Installation, Instrument, Iron lung, Isotron, Jacquard, Kipp's, Kymograph, Langmuir-trough, Lease-rod, Life-preserver, Loom, Masora(h), Microreader, Mimeograph, Mine-detector, Multi-gym, Nephoscope, Nitrometer, Oscillator, Oscillograph, Oxygenator, Pasteuriser, Peat-seeker, Percolator, Phon(o)meter, Photophone, Photostat®, Phytotron, Plate-warmer, Plethysmograph, Plumber's snake, Pommel horse, Potometer, Projector, Proto®, Pulmotor®, Push-pull, Radiator, Radiosonde, Rattlebag, Rattletrap, Rectifier, Replenisher, Resistor, Respirator, Respirometer, Resuscitator, Retort, Rotisserie, Rounce, Scintiscanner, Scrubber, Scuba, Searchlight, Seeder, Semaphore, Set, Skimmer, Slide rest, Smoker, Snake, Sniffer, Snorkel, Snowbox, Soundboard, Spectrometer, Sphygmograph, Spirophore, Starter, Steamer, Stellarator, Steriliser, Still, Substage, Switchgear, Tackle, Tackling, Talk-you-down, Telecine, Teleprinter, Teleseme, Tellurian, Thermopile, Tokamak, Transformer, Transmitter, Tribometer, Tromp(e), Tuner, Ventouse, Wheatstone's bridge, Whip-and-derry, ZETA

**Apparel** Attire, Besee, → **COSTUME**, Garb, Raiment, Wardrobe, Wardrop

**Apparent(ly)** Ap, Clear, Detectable, Evident, Manifest, Open, Ostensible, Outward, Overt, Palpable, Plain, Prima facie, Seeming, Semblance, Visible

▷ **Apparent** *may indicate* a hidden word

**Apparition** Avatar, Dream, Eidolon, Fetch, Ghost, Hallucination, → **ILLUSION**, Phantom, Shade, Spectre, Vision, Visitant, Wraith

**Appeal(ing)** Ad, Attract, Beg, Cachet, Call, Catchpenny, Charisma, Charm, Cri de coeur, Cry, Dreamy, Entreat, Entreaty, Epirrhema, Exhort, Eye-catching, Fetching, Glamorous, Howzat, Intil, Invocation, It, Mediagenic, Miserere, O, Oath, Oomph, Plead, Popular, SA, Screeve, Sex(iness), Solicit, SOS, Suit, Yummy

**Appear(ance)** Advent, Air, Apport, Arise, Arrival, Aspect, Broo, Brow, Burst, Cameo, Cast, Colour, Compear, Debut, Effeir, Effere, Emerge, Enter, Entrance, Exterior, Eye, Facade, Fa(s)cia, Facies, Far(r)and, Farrant, Feature, Figure, Format, Garb, Guise, Habitus, Hue, Image, Kithe, Kythe, Looks, Loom, Manifestation, → **MANNER**, Materialise, Mien, Occur, Ostensibly, Ostent, Outward, Person, Phase, Phenomenon, Physiognomy, Pop-up, Presence, Prosopon, Represent, Rig, Rise, Seem, Semblance, Show, Species, Spectre, Spring, Superficies, Theophany, Veneer, View, Visitation, Vraisemblance, Whistle-stop, Wraith

**Appease(ment)** Allay, Alleviate, Atone, Calm, Conciliation, Danegeld, Mitigate, → **MOLLIFY**, Munichism, Pacify, Placate, Propitiate, Relieve, Satisfy, Soothe, Sop, Sweeten

**Appellant, Appellation** Nomen, Roe

**Append(age)** Addition, Adjunct, Affix, Aglet, Allantois, Annex, Antennule, Aril, Arista, Cercus, Chelicera, Codpiece, Ctene, Fang, Flagellum, Hanger-on, Lobe, Lug, Nose-leaf, Palp(us), Paraglossa, Parapodium, Pedipalp, Pendicle, Postfix, Proboscis, Stipel, Stipule, Suffix, Swimmeret, Tail, Tailpiece, Tentacle, Ugly, Uropod, Uvula

**Appendix** Addendum, Apocrypha, Codicil, Grumbling, Label, Pendant, Pendent, Rider, Schedule, Vermiform

**Appertain** Belong

**Appetite, Appetitive, Appetise(r), Appetize(r)** Amuse-bouche, Amuse-gueule, Angels on horseback, Antepast, Antipasto, Aperitif, Appestat, Bhagee, Bhajee, Bulimia, Bulimy, Canapé, Concupiscence, Concupy, Crudités, Desire, Dim-sum, Entremes(se), Entremets, Flesh, Hunger, Inner man, Limosis, Malacia, Meze, Mezze, Nacho, Orectic, Orexis, Passion, Pica, Polyphagia, Relish, Tapa(s), Titillate, Twist, Ventripotent, Whet, Yerd-hunger, Yird-hunger

**Applaud, Applause** Acclaim, Bravo, →**CHEER**, Clap, Claque, Eclat, Encore, Extol, Hum, Kentish fire, Olé, Ovation, Praise, Root, Ruff, Tribute

**Apple** Adam's, Alligator, Bad, Baldwin, Balsam, Biffin, Blenheim orange, Braeburn, Bramley, Cashew, Charlotte, Codlin(g), Cooker, Costard, Crab, Custard, Dead Sea, Discord, Eater, Granny Smith, Greening, Jenneting, John, Jonathan, Kangaroo, Leather-coat, Love, Mammee, May, McIntosh (red), Medlar, Nonpareil, Oak, Pacific Rose, Pearmain, Pippin, Pomace, Pome(roy), Pomroy, Pom(e)water, Potato, Punic, Pupil, Pyrus, Quarantine, Quarenden, Quar(r)ender, Quarrington, Queening, Quodlin, Redstreak, Reinette, Rennet, Ribston(e), Ripstone, Rotten, Royal gala, Ruddock, Russet, Seek-no-further, Snow, Sops-in-wine, Sorb, Sturmer (Pippin), Sugar, Sweeting, Thorn, Toffee, Windfall, Winesap

**Apple juice** Malic

**Apple-picker** Atalanta

**Applicant** Candidate, Ordinand, Postulant

**Application, Applicable, Apply, Appliance(s)** Address, Adhibit, Appeal, Appose, Assiduity, Astringent, Barrage, Blender, Concentration, Devote, Diligence, Dispose, Dressing, Exercise, Exert, Foment, Fridge, Gadget, Germane, Give, Implement, Impress, Inlay, Juicer, Kettle, Lay, Liquidiser, Lotion, Machine, Mixer, Ointment, Opodeldoc, Pertinent, Petition, Plaster, Poultice, Put, Request, Resort, Respirator, Rub, Sinapism, Stupe, Talon, Toggle, Truss, →**USE**, Vice, White goods

**Appliqué** Hawaiian

**Appoint(ee), Appointment** Advowson, Assign, Berth, Co-opt, Date, Delegate, Depute, Designate, Dew, Due, Executor, Induction, Installation, Make, Name, →**NOMINATE**, Nominee, Office, Ordain, Place, Position, Post, Posting, Rendezvous, Room, Set, Tryst

▷ **Appointed** *may indicate* an anagram

**Apportion(ment)** Allocate, Allot, Distribute, Entail, Mete, Parcel, Ration, Share, Weigh

**Apposite** Apt, Cogent, Germane, Pat, Pertinent, Relevant, Suitable

**Appraise, Appraisal** Analyse, →**EVALUATE**, Eye-up, Gauge, Guesstimate, Judge, Once-over, Review, Tape, Valuate, →**VALUE**, Vet

**Appreciate, Appreciation** Accrue, Acknowledgement, Admire, Cherish, Clap, Comprehensible, Dig, Empathy, Endear, Esteem, Feel, Grasp, Gratefulness, Gratitude, Increase, Phwoar, Prize, Realise, Recognise, Regard, Relish, Rise, Sense, Stock, Taste, Thank you, Treasure, →**VALUE**, Welcome

**Apprehend(ing), Apprehension** Afears, Alarm, Anticipate, Arrest, Attuent, Awestruck, →**CATCH**, Collar, Fear, Foreboding, Grasp, Insecure, Insight, Intuit, Noesis, Perceive, Presentiment, Quailing, See, Suspense, Take, Toey, Trepidation, Uh-oh, Unease, Uptake

**Apprehensive** Jumpy, Nervous, Uneasy

**Apprentice(ship)** Article, Commis, Cub, Devil, Garzone, Improver, Indent(ure), Jockey, L, Learner, Lehrjahre, Novice, Noviciate, Novitiate, Printer's devil, Pupillage, Snob, Tiro, Trainee, Turnover, Tyro(ne)

**Apprise** Enlighten

**Approach(ing), Approachable** Abord, Access, Accost, Advance, Affable, Anear, Angle, Anigh, Appropinquate, Appulse, Asymptotic, Avenue, Close, Coast, Come, Converge, Cost(e), Draw nigh, Drive, Driveway, Fairway, Feeler, Gate, Imminent, Ingoing, Line, Near, Nie, Open, Overture, Pitch, Procedure, Road, Run-in, Run-up, Stealth, Strategy, Towards, Verge, Warm

**Appropriate(ly), Appropriateness** Abduct, Abstract, Annex, Applicable, Apposite, Apt, Aright, Arrogate, Asport, Assign, Bag, Befitting, Borrow, Collar, Commandeer, Commensurate, Condign, Confiscate, Congruous, Convenient, Decent, Due, Element, Eligible, Embezzle, Expedient, Fit, Germane, Good, Happy, Hijack, Hog, Impound, In keeping, Jump, Just, Meet, Nick, Pertinent, Pilfer, Plagiarise, Pocket, Pre-empt, Proper, Propriety, Purloin, Relevant, Right, Seise, Seize, Sequester, Sink, Snaffle, Steal, Suit(ed), Swipe, Take, Timely, Trouser, Usurp

**Approval, Approve(d), Approbation** Accolade, Accredit, Admire, Adopt, Allow, Amen, Applaud, Assent, Attaboy, Aye, Blessing, Bravo, Brownie points, Change, Cheer, Clap, → COUNTENANCE, Credit, Cushty, Dig, Endorse, Favour, For, Green light, Hear hear, Homologate, Hubba-hubba, Hurra(h), Imprimatur, Initial, Kitemark, Know, Laud, Nod, Official, Okay, Olé, Orthodox, Pass, Plaudit, Praise, Rah, Ratify, Recognise, Recommend, Right-on, Rubber-stamp, Sanction, Stotter, Thumbs-up, Tick, Tribute, Vivat, Voice, Warm to, Yay, Yes, Zindabad

**Approximate(ly), Approximation** Almost, Around, Ballpark, Circa, Close, Coarse, Estimate, Guess, Imprecise, Near, Rough and ready, Roughly

**Apricot** Mebos

**April, April fool** Apr, Huntiegowk, Hunt-the-gowk

**Apron** Airside, Barm-cloth, Bib, Blacktop, Brat, Bunt, Canvas, Dick(e)y, Ephod, Fig-leaf, Gremial, Ice, Napron, Pinafore, Pinner, Pinny, Placket, Rim, Stage, Tablier, Tier, Waist

**Apse** Concha, Exedra, Niche, Recess, Tribune

**Apt(ly)** Apposite, Appropriate, Apropos, Ben trovato, Capable, Evincive, Fit, Gleg, Happy, Inclined, Liable, Pat, Prone, Suitable, Tends

**Aptitude** Ability, Bent, Ear, Eye, Faculty, Feel, Flair, Gift, Knack, Know-how, Nose, Skill, Talent, Taste, Tendency, Touch, Viability

**Aqua(tic)** Euglena, Flustra, Lentic, Lotic, Regia, Rotifera, Zizania

**Aqualung** Rebreather, Scuba

**Aquamarine** Bice, Madagascar

**Aquarium** Oceanarium

**Aqueduct** Canal, Channel, Conduit, Hadrome, Xylem

**Arab(ian), Arabia, Arabic** Abdul, Adeni, Adnan, Algorism, Ali (Baba), Baathist, Bahraini, Bahrein, Bedouin, Bedu, Druse, Druz(e), Effendi, Fedayee(n), Gamin, Geber, Hani, Hashemite, Hassaniya, Himyarite, Horse, Iraqi, Jawi, Kuwaiti, Lawrence, Moor, Mudlark, Nabat(a)ean, Nas(s)eem, Nes(h)ki, Omani, Omar, PLO, Qatari, Rag(head), Saba, Sab(a)ean, Saracen, Saudi, Seleucid, Semitic, Sheikh, Street, Syrian, UAR, Urchin, Yemen(i)

**Arabis** Cress

**Arachnid** Mite, Podogona, Ricinulei, Scorpion, Solpuga, → SPIDER

**Arbitrary** Despotic, Haphazard, Peculiar, Random, Wanton, Whim

**Arbitrate, Arbitration, Arbitrator, Arbiter** ACAS, Censor, Daysman, Judge, Negotiator, Ombudsman, Pendulum, Prud'homme, Ref(eree), Umpire

**Arboreal, Arbour** Bower, Dendroid, Pergola, Trellis

**Arc** Azimuth, Bow, Carbon, → CURVE, Dink, Flashover, Fogbow, Foil, Halo, Hance, Haunch, Island, Limb, Mercury, Octant, Quadrant, Rainbow, Reflex, Seadog, Semicircle, Trajectory, White rainbow

**Arcade** Amusement, Burlington, Cloister, Gallery, Loggia, Mall, Penny, Triforium, Video

**Arcadia(n)** Idyllic, Nemoral, Sylvan

**Arcane** Esoteric, Mystic, Obscure, Occult, Orphism, Recherché, Rune, Secret

**Arch(ed), Arching** Acute, Admiralty, Alveolar, Arblaster, Arcade, Arcature, Archivolt, Arcuate, Camber, Chief, Coom, Counterfort, Crafty, Cross-rib, Crown-green, Ctesiphon, → CUNNING, Curve, Discharging, Elfin, Embow, Espiegle, Eyebrow, Fallen, Flying buttress, Fog-bow, Fornicate, Fornix, Gill, Gothic, Hance, Haunch, Hog, Horseshoe, Instep, Intrados, Inverted, Keel, Keystone, Knowing, Lancet, Leery, Lierne, Limb-girdle, Marble, Neural, Norman, Ogee, Ogive, Opistholomos, Order, Parthian, Pectoral, Pelvic, Plantar, Pointed, Portal, Proscenium, Recessed, Relieving, Roach, Roguish, Roman,

Saddlebow, Safety, Saucy, Segmental, Shouldered, Skew, Sly, Soffit, Span, Squinch, Stilted, Trajan, Triumphal, Vault, Zygoma

**Archaeological, Archaeologist, Archaeology** Bell, Carter, Childe, Dater, Dig, Evans, Industrial, Layard, Leakey, Mallowan, Mycenae, Petrie, Pothunter, Qumran, Schliemann, Sutton Hoo, Type-site, Wheeler, Winckelmann, Woolley

**Archaic** Dated

**Archangel** Azrael, Gabriel, Israfeel, Israfel, Israfil, Jerahmeel, Michael, Raguel, Raphael, Sariel, Satan, Uriel, Yellow

**Arch-binder** Voussoir

**Archbishop** Anselm, Augustine, Cosmo, Cranmer, Davidson, Dunstan, Ebor, Elector, Hatto, Lambeth, Lanfranc, Lang, Langton, Laud, Metropolitan, Morton, Primate, Scroop, Temple, Trench, Tutu, Whitgift

**Archdeacon** Rev, Ven(erable)

**Archduke** Trio

**Archer(y)** Acestes, Bow-boy, → BOWMAN, Cupid, Eros, Hood, Petticoat, Philoctetes, Sagittary, Tell, Toxophilite

**Archetype** Avatar, Form, Model, Pattern

**Archibald, Archie, Archy** Ack-ack, Cockroach, Oerlikon, Rice, Roach

**Archilochian** Epode

**Archimandrite** Eutyches

**Archimedes** Screw

**Archipelago** Alexander, Antarctic, Azores, Bismarck, Camaguey, Dhivehi, East Indian, Fiji, Franz Josef Land, Gulag, Japan, Kerguelen, Malay, Maldives, Marquesas, Mergui, Novaya Zemlya, Orkney, Palmer, Paumotu, St Pierre and Miquelon, Severnaya Zemlya, Spitsbergen, Sulu, Svalbard, Tierra del Fuego, Tonga, Tuamoto, West Indies

**Architect(ure), Architectural** Arcology, Baroque, Bauhaus, Bricolage, Brutalism, Byzantine, Cartouche, Churrigueresque, Community, Composite, Computer, Corinthian, Creator, Data-flow, Decorated, Decorated style, Designer, Domestic, Doric, Early English, Elizabethan, Entablature, Federation, Flamboyant, Georgian, Gothic, Greek Revival, Ionic, Italian, Jacobean, Landscape, Listed, Lombard, Maker, Mission, Moderne, Moorish, Moresque, Mudejar, Naval, Neoclassical, Neo-gothic, Norman, Palladian, Pelasgian, Perpendicular, Picnostyle, Planner, Plateresque, Prostyle, Queen Anne, Romanesque, Saracenic, Saxon, Spandrel, Spandril, Tectonic, Tudor, Tudorbethan, Tuscan, Vitruvian

---

## ARCHITECTS

| 3 letters: | | | |
|---|---|---|---|
| Cox | Hooke | Repton | Neumann |
| Pei | Horta | Romano | Percier |
| | Inigo | Spence | Seidler |
| **4 letters:** | Nervi | Street | Venturi |
| Adam | Pugin | Voysey | Vignola |
| Kent | Scott | Wright | |
| Loos | Soane | | **8 letters:** |
| Nash | Speer | **7 letters:** | Bramante |
| Shaw | Utzon | Alberti | Chalgrin |
| Webb | Wyatt | Behrens | Fontaine |
| Wood | | Bernini | Greenway |
| Wren | **6 letters:** | Blacket | Niemeyer |
| | Breuer | Columbo | Palladio |
| **5 letters:** | Casson | Erskine | Piranesi |
| Barry | Foster | Griffin | Saarinen |
| Gaudi | Lasdun | Gropius | Stirling |
| | Nissen | Lutyens | Vanbrugh |

| **9 letters:** | **10 letters:** | **11 letters:** | **12 letters:** |
|---|---|---|---|
| Borromini | Inigo Jones | Abercrombie | Brunelleschi |
| Hawksmoor | Mackintosh | Butterfield | |
| Mackmurdo | Tange Kenzo | Churrighera | **15 letters:** |
| Macquarie | Trophonius | Le Corbusier | Vitruvius Pollio |
| Vitruvius | Van der Rohe | | |
| | Waterhouse | | |

**Architrave** Epistyle, Platband

**Archive(s)** Backfile, Morgue, Muniment, PRO, Records, Register

**Archon** Draco

**Arch-villain** Ringleader

**Arctic** Estotiland, Frigid, Hyperborean, In(n)uit, Inupiat, Polar, Tundra

**Ardent, Ardour** Aflame, Aglow, Boil, Broiling, Burning, Enthusiasm, Fervent, Fervid, Fiery, Fire, Flagrant, Flaming, Gusto, Heat, Het, → **HOT**, Hot-brained, In, Mettled, Mettlesome, Passion(ate), Perfervid, Rage, Spiritous, Vehement, Warm-blooded, Zealous, Zeloso

**Arduous** Laborious, Steep, Trying, Uphill

**Are** A, Exist, 're

**Area** Acre, Aleolar, Apron, Arctogaea, Are, Assisted, Bailiwick, Beat, Belt, Bovate, Broca's, Built-up, Carucate, Catchment, Centare, Centiare, Centre, Chill-out, Clearing, Conurbation, Courtyard, Craton, Curtilage, Dec(i)are, Dedans, Depressed, Dessiatine, Development, Disaster, District, Docklands, Domain, Downtown, Endemic, Eruv, Extent, Farthingland, Forecourt, Gau, Goal, Grey, Growth, Heartland, Hectare, Henge, Hide, Hinterland, Hotspot, Husbandland, Imperium, Input, Karst, Landmass, Lathe, Latitude, Lek, Locale, Locality, Lodg(e)ment, Manor, Metroplex, Milieu, Mofussil, Morgen, Mush, Neogaea, Nidderdale, No-go, No-man's-land, Notogaea, Orb, Oxgang, Oxgate, Oxland, Pale, Parish, Patch, Penalty, Place, Pleasance, Plot, Precinct, Province, Purlieu, Quad, Quadrat, Quarter (section), Range, Redevelopment, Refugium, → **REGION**, Renosterveld, Res(ervation), Reserve, Rest, Restricted, Retrochoir, Riding, Rood, Rule, Sector, Service, Shire, Site, Slurb, Special, Staging, Sterling, Subtopia, Sun belt, Support, Surface, Target, Tartary, Technical, Terra, Terrain, Territory, Theatre, Tie, Tract, Tundra, Tye, Uptown, Urban, Ure, Weald, White, Wilderness, Work station, Yard, Zone

**Arena** Battleground, Centre court, Circus, Cockpit, Dohyo, Field, Lists, Maidan, Olympia, → **RING**, Rink, Snowdome, Stadium, Tiltyard, Velodrome, Venue

**Argal** Ergo

**Argent** Ag, Silver

**Argentina** RA

**Argon** Ar

**Argonaut** Acastus, Jason, Lynceus, Meleager, Nautilus, Paper-sailor

**Argot** Flash, Idiom, Jargon, Lingo, Scamto, Shelta

**Argue, Argument(ative)** Altercation, Antistrophon, Argie-bargie, Argle-bargle, Argy-bargy, Bandy, Barney, Beef, Bicker, Blue, Brush, Cangle, Case, Casuism, Choplogic, Conflict, Contend, Contest, Contra, Cosmological, Debate, Deprecate, Diallage, Difference, Dilemma, Ding-dong, Dispute, Dissent, Elenchus, Elenctic, Enthusiasm, Enthymeme, Eristic, Exchange, Expostulate, Forensic, Fray, Free-for-all, Generalisation, Hysteron proteron, Logic, Logomachy, Mexican standoff, Moot, Ob and soller, Object, Odds, Ontological, Paralogism, Patter, Pettifog, Plead, Polemic, Polylemma, Premiss, Propound, Pros and cons, Quarrel, Quibble, Quodlibet, Rammy, Ratiocinate, → **REASON**, Rebut, Remonstrate, Row, Run-in, Scene, Sequacious, Socratise, Sophism, Sophistry, Sorites, Spar, Spat, Stickle, Straw man, Stroppy, Stushie, Summation, Syllogism, Teleological, Theme, Thetic, Third man, Tiff, Transcendental, Trilemma, Verbal, Vociferate, Words, Wrangle, Wrestle, Yike

**Argyle** Argathelian, Gravy-boat, Sock

**Aria** Ballad, Cabaletta, Cantata, Cavatina, Melody, Nessun dorma, Song

**Arid** Dry, Parched, Sere, Siccity

**Ariel** Pen

**Aris** Arse, → BOTTOM, Can

**Arise** Appear, Be, Develop, Emanate, Emerge, Stem, Upgo, Wax

**Aristocracy, Aristocrat(ic)** Blood, Blue blood, Boyar, Buckeen, Classy, Debrett, Duc, Elite, Eupatrid, Gentle, Gentry, Grandee, High-hat, Junker, Milord, Nob, Noble, Optimate, Passage, Patrician, Thane, Thegn, Toff, Tony, U-men, Upper-crust, Viscount, Well-born

**Aristotle** Peripatetic, Stagirite, Stagyrite

**Arithmetic(ian)** Algorism, Algorith, Arsmetrick, Cocker, Euclid, Logistic, Modular, Quadrivium, Sums

**Ark(wright)** Chest, Noah, Zoo

**Arly** Thicket

**Arm(ed), Arms** Akimbo, Arsenal, Bearing, Brachial, Branch, Bundooks, Canting, Cove, Crest, Cross bow, Embattle, Equip, Escutcheon, Estoc, Fin, Firth, Frith, Gnomon, Halbert, Hatchment, Heel, Heraldic, Inlet, Jib, Krupp, Limb, Loch, Long, Member, Munitions, Musket, Olecranon, Pick-up, Quillon, Radius, Rail, Ramous, Rocker, Rotor, SAA, Secular, Shield, Shotgun, Side, Small, Smooth-bore, Spiral, Tappet, Tentacle, Timer, Tone, Tooled-up, Transept, Tremolo, Ulnar, Water pistol, → WEAPON, Whip

▷ **Arm** *may indicate* an army regiment, etc.

**Armada** Spanish

**Armadillo** Dasypod, Dasypus, Fairy, Giant, Pangolin, Peba, Pichiciego, Tatou(ay), Xenurus

**Armature** Keeper, Shuttle

**Armband** Torc, Torque

**Armchair** Bergere, Carver

**Armenian** Haikh, Yezedi

**Armhole** Scye

**Armistice** Still-stand, Truce

**Armless** Inermous

**Armour(ed), Armoury** Ailette, Armature, Armet, Barbette, Beaver, Besagew, Bevor, Brasset, Breastplate, Brigandine, Buckler, Byrnie, Camail, Cannon, Casemate, Casspir, Cataphract, Chaffron, Chain, Chamfrain, Chamfron, Character, Chausses, Corium, Cors(e)let, Couter, Cuirass, Cuish, Cuisse, Culet, Curat, Curiet, Cush, Defence, Fauld, Garderobe, Garniture, Gear, Genouillère, Gere, Gorget, Greave, Habergeon, Hauberk, Hoplology, Jack, Jambe, Jambeau, Jazerant, Jesserant, Lamboys, Loricate, Mail, Male, Mentonnière, Mesail, Mezail, Nasal, Nosepiece, Palette, Panoply, Panzer, Pauldron, Petta, Placcat, Placket, Plastron, Plate, Poitrel, Poleyn, Pouldron, Rerebrace, Rest, Roundel, Sabaton, Scale, Secret, → SHIELD, Solleret, Spaudler, Splint, Stand, Tace, Tank, Taslet, Tasse(t), Thorax, Tonlet, Tuille, Vambrace, Vantbrass, Ventail, Visor, Voider, Weed

**Armpit** Axilla, Oxter

**Armstrong** Louis, Neil, Satchmo

**Army** Arrière-ban, Arrière-garde, BEF, Blue Ribbon, Church, Colours, Confederate, Crowd, Federal, Field, Fyrd, Golden (Horde), Horde, Host, IRA, Junior Service, Land, Landwehr, Lashkar, Legion, Line, Military, Militia, Mobile Command, Multitude, New Model, Para-military, Red, SA, Sabaoth, Sally, Salvation, SAS, Sena, Service, Soldiers, Squad, Standing, Stratonic, Swarm, TA, Tartan, Terracotta, Territorial, Thin red line, Volunteer, War, Wehrmacht

▷ **Army** *may indicate* having arms

**Aroma(tic)** Allspice, Aniseed, Aryl, Balmy, Camphor, Coriander, Fenugreek, Fragrant, Nose, Odorous, Pomander, Spicy, Stilbene, Vanillin, Wintergreen

**Around** About, Ambient, Circa, Near, Peri-, Skirt, Tour

▷ **Around** *may indicate* one word around another

**Arouse(d), Arousal** Alarm, Displease, → **EXCITE**, Fan, Fire, Goad, Incite, Indignant, Inflame, Inspire, Must(h), Needle, Provoke, Stimulate, Stole, Suscitate, Touch up, Urolagnia, Waken, Whet

**Arpad** ELO

**Arrange(r), Arrangement** Adjust, Array, Attune, Ausgleich, Bandobast, Bank, Bundobust, Cohabitation, Collate, Concert, Concinnity, Configuration, Coordinate, Design, Display, Dispose, Do, Drape, Dress, Echelon, Edit, Engineer, Finger, Fix, Foreordain, Format, Formation, Formwork, Grade, Ikebana, Layout, Lineation, Marshal, Modus vivendi, Neaten, Orchestrate, Orchestration, Ordain, → **ORDER**, Ordonnance, Organise, Pack, Pattern, Perm, Permutation, Plan, Position, Prepare, Prepense, Quincunx, Redactor, Regulate, Run, Rustle up, Schedule, Schema, Scheme, Score, Set(ting) (up), Settle, Sort, Spacing, Stack, Stage-manage, Stereoisomerism, Stow, Straighten, Structure, Style, Syntax, System, Tabulate, Tactic, Taxis, Tidy, Timeshare, Transcribe, Vertical

▷ **Arrange** *may indicate* an anagram

**Arras** Tapestry

**Array(ed)** Attire, Bedight, Caparison, Deck, Herse, Logic, Marshal, Matrice, Muster, Panoply, Phased, Seismic, Ula

**Arrear(s)** Aft, Ahint, Backlog, Behind, Debt, Owing

**Arrest(ed), Arresting** Abort, Alguacil, Alguazil, Ament, Apprehend, Attach, Attract, Blin, Book, Bust, Caption, Capture, Cardiac, Catch, Cessation, Check, Citizen's, Collar, Detain, False, Furthcoming, Hold, House, Infangthief, Knock, Lag, Lift, Lightning, Nab, Nail, Nick, Nip, Nobble, Pinch, Pull in, Restrain, Retard, Riveting, Round-up, Run-in, Salient, Sease, Seize, Snaffle, Snatch, Spellbind, Stasis, Stop, Sus(s), Turn in

**Arris** Groin

**Arrival, Arrive, Arriving, Arriviste** Accede, Advent, Attain, Come, Entrance, Get, Happen, Hit, Inbound, Influx, Johnny-come-lately, Land, Latecomer, Natal, Nativity, Newcomer, Parvenu, Pitch up, Reach, Roll up, Show, Strike

**Arrogance, Arrogant** Assumption, Boastful, Bold, Bravado, Bumptious, Cavalier, Cocksure, Cocky, Contemptuous, Disdain, Dogmatic, Effrontery, Haughty, Haut(eur), High, High and mighty, High-handed, High-hat, Hogen-mogen, Hoity-toity, Hubris, Imperious, Jumped up, Lordly, Morgue, Overweening, Presumption, Pretentious, Proud, Proud-stomached, Prussianism, Side, Snobbish, Stuck-up, Surquedry, Surquedy, Toploftical, Topping, Turkeycock, Uppish, Uppity, Upstart, Yuppy

**Arrogate** Appropriate, Assume, Claim, Impute, Usurp

**Arrow, Arrow-head** Acestes, Any, Ary, Blunt, Bolt, Broad(head), Cloth-yard shaft, Dart, Dogbolt, Filter, Flechette, Flight, Missile, Pheon, Pointer, Quarrel, Reed, Sagittate, Shaft, Sheaf, Straight

**Arrow-maker** Fletcher

**Arrowroot** Kuzu, Maranta, Pia

**Arse** → **BOTTOM**, Khyber (pass)

**Arsenal** Ammo, Armo(u)ry, Depot, Fire-arms, Magazine, Side, Toulon

**Arsenate, Arsenic(al), Arsenide** As, Erythrite, Realgar, Resalgar, Rosaker, Salvarsan, Scorodite, Skutterudite, Smaltite, Speiss, Zarnich

**Arson(ist)** Firebug, Pyromania, Torching

**Art(s), Arty, Art movement, Art school, Art style** Abstract, Alla prima, Applied, Ars, Arte Povera, Bauhaus, Bloomsbury, Bonsai, Britart, Brut, Chiaroscuro, Clair-obscure, Clare-obscure, Click, Clip, Cobra, Collage, Commercial, Conceptual, Constructivism, Contrapposto, Craft, Cubism, Culture vulture, Cunning, Curious, Dada, Daedal(e), Deco, Decorative, Dedal, De Stijl, Die Brucke, Diptych, Divisionism, Earth, Ekphrasis, Enamel(ling), Environmental, Es, Expressionism, Fauvism, Feat, Fine, Finesse, Flemish, Folk, Fugue, Futurism, Genre, Graphic, Grisaille, Guile, High Renaissance, Humanities, Ikebana, Impressionist, Jugendstil, Kakemono, Kano, Ka pai, Kinetic, Kirigami, Kitsch, Knack, Lacquerware, Land, Liberal, Mandorla, Mannerism, Martial, Masterwork, Mehndi, Minimal, Modern(e), Montage, Motivated, Music, Mystery, Nabis, Nazarene,

Neoclassical, Neo-impressionism, New Wave, Nihonga, Noli-me-tangere, Norwich, Nouveau, Objets trouves, Optical, Origami, Orphic Cubism, Orphism, Outsider, Pastiche, Performance, Performing, Perigordian, Plastic, Pointillism, Pop, Postimpressionism, Postmodern, Practical, Pre-Raphaelite, Primitive, Psychedelic, Public, Purism, Quadratura, Quadrivium, Relievo, Repousse, Sienese, → SKILL, Social realism, Stained glass, Still-life, Suprematism, Surrealism, Synchronism, Tachism(e), Tactics, Tatum, Tenebrism, Tessera, Toreutics, Trecento, Triptych, Trivium, Trompe l'oeil, Trouvé, Tsutsumu, Ukiyo-e, Useful, Verism, Virtu, Visual, Vorticism

▷ **Art** *may indicate* an -est ending

**Artefact(s)** Neolith, Palaeolith, Tartanalia, Tartanry, Xoanon

▷ **Artefact** *may indicate* an anagram

**Artemis** Selene

**Artemus** Ward

**Artery** Aorta, Brachial, Carotid, Coronary, Duct, Femoral, Frontal, Iliac, Innominate, $M_1$, Maxillary, Phrenic, Pulmonary, Radial, Route, Spermatic, Temporal

**Artful** Cute, Dodger, Foxy, Ingenious, Quirky, Shifty, Sly, Subtle, Tactician, Wily

**Arthropod** Insecta, Limulus, Peripatus, Prototracheata, Sea-slater, Tardigrade, Trilobite, Water-bear

**Artichoke** Cardoon, Jerusalem

**Article(s)** A, An, Apprentice, Artefact, Clause, Column, Commodity, Cutting, Definite, Doctrine, Feature, Feuilleton, Five, Gadget, Indefinite, Indenture, Item, Leader, Leading, Object, Op-ed, Paper, Part, Piece, Pot-boiler, Report, Shipping, Sidebar, Specify, The, Thing, Thinkpiece, Thirty-nine, Treatise, Turnover, Utensil, Ware

**Articulation, Articulate(d)** Clear, Coherent, Coudé, Diarthrosis, Distinct, Eloquent, Enounce, Express, Fluent, Fortis, Gimmal, Gomphosis, Hinged, Intonate, Jointed, Jymold, Lenis, Limbed, Lisp, Pretty-spoken, Pronounce, Schindylesis, Single-tongue, Tipping, Tonguing, Trapezial, Utter, Verbalise, Vertebrae, Vocal, Voice, Wrist

**Artifice(r), Artificial** Bogus, Chouse, Contrived, Davenport-trick, Dodge, Ersatz, Factitious, False, Feint, Finesse, Guile, Hoax, Inauthentic, In vitro, Logodaedaly, Made, Man-made, Mannered, Opificer, Phoney, Postiche, Pretence, Prosthetic, Pseudo, Reach, Ruse, Sell, Set, Sham, Spurious, Stratagem, → STRATEGY, Synroc, Synthetic, Theatric, → TRICK, Unnatural, Wile, Wright

**Artificial respiration** Kiss of life, Schafer's method

**Artillery(man)** Battery, Cannon(ier), Cohorn(e), Field, Fougade, Fougasse, Guns, Mortar, Ordnance, Pyroballogy, RA, Rafale, Ramose, Ramus, Train

**Artiodactyl** Camel, Chevrotain, Deerlet

**Artisan** Craftsman, Decorator, Joiner, Journeyman, Mechanic, Peon, Pioneer, Pioner, Pyoner, Shipwright, Weaver, Workman

**Artist(e), Artistic** Aesthetic, Animator, Blaue Reiter, Bohemian, Cartoonist, Colourist, Cubist, Dadaist, Daedal(e), Deccie, Decorator, Die Brucke, Enameller, Escape, Etcher, Fauve, Fine, Foley, Gentle, Gilder, Graffiti, ICA, Illustrator, Impressionist, Landscapist, Left Bank, Limner, Linear, Maestro, Make-up, Master, Mime, Miniaturist, → MUSICIAN, Nabis, Nazarene, Oeuvre, Orphism, → PAINTER, Pavement, Paysagist, Perspectivist, Piss, Plein-airist, Pre-Raphaelite, Primitive, Quick-change, RA, Rap, Screever, → SCULPTOR, Sideman, Sien(n)ese, Stripper, Surrealist, Tachisme, Tagger, Tap dancer, Touch, Trapeze, Trecentist, Virtuose, Virtuoso, Water-colourist

---

## ARTISTS

| 3 letters: | 4 letters: | Dadd | Emin |
|---|---|---|---|
| Arp | Bell | Dali | Etty |
| Cox | Chia | Done | Goya |
| Dix | Cole | Doré | Gris |
| Ono | Cuyp | Dufy | Hals |

John
Klee
Lely
Long
Miró
Nash
Opie
Phiz
Rees
West

*5 letters:*
Aiken
Appel
Bacon
Bakst
Balla
Blake
Bosch
Brown
Buren
Burra
Corot
Crane
Crome
Danby
David
Degas
Dulac
Dürer
Ensor
Ernst
Gelée
Grosz
Herge
Hirst
Hoare
Homer
Hooch
Johns
Klimt
Kline
Leech
Léger
Lippi
Lotto
Lowry
Makar
Manet
Monet
Moses
Munch
Nolan
Olley

Olsen
Orpen
Poons
Redon
Riley
Rodin
Seago
Steen
Steer
Tatum
Watts

*6 letters:*
Albers
Boudin
Braque
Bratby
Brucke
Calder
Callot
Claude
Clouet
Cotman
Derain
De Wint
Dobell
D'Orsay
Eakins
Escher
Fabrio
Fuseli
Gilles
Giotto
Greuze
Guardi
Haydon
Herman
Hopper
Ingres
Knight
Le Nain
Man Ray
Massys
Millet
Moreau
Morris
Newman
Oliver
Renoir
Ribera
Rivera
Romano
Romney
Rothko

Rubens
Sendak
Seurat
Signac
Sisley
Strang
Stubbs
Tissot
Titian
Turner
Vasari
Warhol
Zeuxis

*7 letters:*
Acconci
Allston
Apelles
Audubon
Bellini
Bernini
Bonnard
Borduas
Boucher
Bruegel
Cassall
Cellini
Cézanne
Chagall
Chardin
Chirico
Christo
Cimabue
Collier
Courbet
Cranach
Daumier
Da Vinci
Duchamp
El Greco
Epstein
Gauguin
Hobbema
Hockney
Hogarth
Hokusai
Holbein
Hoppner
Kneller
Lepicie
Lorrain
Martens
Martini
Matisse

Meldrum
Memling
Millais
Morisot
Morland
Murillo
Nattier
O'Keeffe
Parrish
Picabia
Picasso
Popover
Poussin
Preston
Prudhon
Pucelle
Rackham
Raeburn
Raphael
Rouault
Russolo
Sargent
Schiele
Sickert
Spencer
Tiepolo
Uccello
Utamaro
Utrillo
Van Dyke
Van Eyck
Van Gogh
Vermeer
Watteau
Zeuxian
Zoffany

*8 letters:*
Annigoni
Auerbach
Barbizon
Baselitz
Beckmann
Boccioni
Bronzino
Carracci
Clemente
Daguerre
Daubigny
Drysdale
Eastlake
Giordana
Kauffman
Kaufmann

| | | | |
|---|---|---|---|
| Kirchner | Whistler | Le Lorrain | Tintoretto |
| Landseer | Whiteley | Mitsunobo | Van der Goes |
| Leonardo | | Nicholson | Waterhouse |
| Magritte | **9 letters:** | Oldenburg | |
| Malevich | Beardsley | Rembrandt | **11 letters:** |
| Mantegna | Bonington | Thornhill | Fairweather |
| Masaccio | Canaletto | Velasquez | Fra Angelico |
| Mondrian | Carpaccio | | Gentileschi |
| Munnings | Constable | **10 letters:** | |
| Nevinson | Correggio | Alma-Tadema | **12 letters:** |
| Passmore | De Chirico | Botticelli | Fantin-Latour |
| Perceval | De Kooning | Burne-Jones | Gainsborough |
| Perugino | Delacroix | Caravaggio | Lichtenstein |
| Piranesi | Delaroche | Fiorentino | Michelangelo |
| Pissarro | Delauncey | Giacometti | Rauschenberg |
| Pontormo | Donatello | Guillaumin | Winterhalter |
| Reynolds | Fragonard | Holman Hunt | |
| Rockwell | Francesca | Madox Brown | **14 letters:** |
| Rossetti | Gericault | Modigliani | Jackson Pollock |
| Rousseau | Giorgione | Motherwell | |
| Severini | Grunewald | Rowlandson | **15 letters:** |
| Thorburn | Hiroshige | Schwitters | Hieronymus Bosch |
| Topolski | Kandinsky | Signorelli | Toulouse-Lautrec |
| Veronese | Kokoschka | Sutherland | |

**Artless** Candid, Homespun, Ingenuous, Innocent, Naive, Open, Seely, Simple

**Art nouveau** Jugendstil

**Arturo** Toscanini

**Arum** Acorus, Green-dragon, Lily, Taro

**As** Aesir, Als, Arsenic, Coin, Eg, Forasmuch, Kame, Qua, Ridge, 's, Since, So, Thus, Ut, While

**As above** US, Ut supra

**Asafoetida** Hing

**As before** Anew, Ditto, Do, Stet

**Asbestos** Amiant(h)us, Amosite, Chrysolite, Crocidolite, Earthflax, Fireproof, Rockwood

**Ascend(ant), Ascent, Ascension** Anabasis, Climb, Dominant, Escalate, Gradient, Lift, Pull, Ramp, Right, Rise, Sclim, Sklim, Slope, Up, Upgang, Uphill, Uprise, Zoom

**Ascertain** Determine, Discover, →ESTABLISH, Prove

**Ascetic(ism)** Agapetae, Anchor(et), Anchorite, Ancress, Ashramite, Austere, Dervish, Diogenes, Encratite, Eremital, Essene, Fakir, Faquir, Gymnosophist, Hermit, Jain(ite), Monk, Nazarite, Nazirite, Nun's flesh, Sad(d)hu, Self-denial, Simeon Stylites, Stylite, Sufic, Therapeutae, Yogi(n)

**Ascidian** Chordate, Urochordate

**Asclepiad** Stapelia

**Ascribe** Assign, →ATTRIBUTE, Blame, Credit, Imply, Impute

**Asdic** Sonar

**As far as** Quoad

**As good as** Equal, Tantamount

**Ash(es), Ashen, Ashy** Aesc, Aizle, Bone, Breeze, Cinders, Cinereal, Clinker(s), Easle, Embers, Fly, Fraxinas, Griseous, Kali, Lahar, Pallor, Pearl, Pozz(u)olana, Prickly, Rowan, Ruins, Soda, Sorb, Spodo-, Stinking, Tephra, Urn, Varec, Volcanic, Wednesday, Weeping, White, Witchen, Yg(g)drasil(l)

**Ashamed** Abashed, Embarrassed, Hangdog, Mortified, Repentant, Sheepish, Shent

**Ashore** Aland, Beached, Coast, Grounded, Stranded

**Ash-pan** Backet
**Ashram** Haven
**Asia(n), Asiatic** Afghan, Altaic, Angaraland, Armenian, Azari, Azerbaijani, Balinese,
  Bangladeshi, Bengali, Bithynia, Cambodian, Cantonese, Desi, E, Evenki, Ewenki, Gook,
  Harijan, Harsha, Hun, Hyksos, Indian, Indonesian, Jordanian, Karen(ni), Kashmir,
  Kazakh, Kirghiz, Korean, Kurd, Kyrgyz, Lao, Lydian, Malay, Medea, Media, Mongol,
  Naga, Negrito, Nepalese, Pasht(o)um, Pathan, Phrygian, Punjabi, Pushtu, Samo(y)ed,
  Saudi, Shan, Siamese, Sindi, Sogdian, Sri Lankan, Tamil, Tartar, Tatar, Tibetan,
  Tocharian, Tokharian, Turanian, Turk(o)man, Uzbeg, Uzbek, Vietnamese
**Asia Minor** Anatolia, Ionic
**Aside** Apart, By, Despite, Private, Separate, Shelved, Sotto voce, Stage whisper
**Asinine** Crass, Dull, Idiotic, Puerile, Stupid
**Ask** Bed, Beg, Beseech, Bid, Cadge, Charge, Demand, Desire, Eft, Enquire, Entreat,
  Evet, Implore, Intreat, Invite, Lobby, Newt, Petition, Pray, Prithee, Pump, Query, Quiz,
  Request, Require, Rogation, Seek, Solicit, Speer, Speir, Touch
**Askance** Asconce, Askew, Oblique, Sideways
**Askew** Agee, Aglee, Agley, Ajee, Aslant, Awry, Crooked, Skivie
**Aslant** Skew
**Asleep** Dormant, Dove, Inactive, Napping
**As needed** Ad hoc
**As often as** Toties quoties
**Asparagus** Asperge, Sparrow-grass, Spear, Sprew, Sprue, Yard-long bean
**Aspect** Angle, Bearing, Brow, Face, Facet, Facies, Feature, Hue, Look, Mien, Nature,
  Outlook, Perfective, Perspective, Phase, Sextile, Side, → VIEW, Visage, Vista
**Aspen** Trembling poplar
**Aspersion, Asperse** Calumny, Defame, Innuendo, Libel, Slander, Slur, Smear, Traduce
**Asphalt** Bitumen, Blacktop, Gilsonite®, Jew's pitch, Pitch, Pitch Lake, Uinta(h)ite
**Asphyxia** Apn(o)ea
**Aspirant, Aspirate, Aspiration, Aspire** Ambition, Breath, Buckeen, Challenger,
  Desire, Dream, Endeavour, Ettle, Goal, H, Hope(ful), Pretend, Pursue, Rough, Spiritus,
  Wannabe(e), Would be, Yearn, Yuppie
**Ass(es)** Buridan's, Burnell, Burro, Cardophagus, Chigetai, Clot, Couscous, Cuddie,
  Dawcock, Denarius, Dick(e)y, Donkey, Dziggetai, Funnel, Golden, Hemione, Hemionus,
  Hinny, Jack, Jenny, Jerusalem pony, Kiang, Kourbash, Kourmiss, Kouskous, K(o)ulan,
  Kumiss, Kurbash, Kyang, Liripipe, Liripoop, Moke, Neddy, Nitwit, Onager, Quagga,
  Sesterce, Simp, → STUPID PERSON
**Assail(ant)** Afflict, Assault, Attack, Batter, Bego, Belabour, Bepelt, Beset, Bombard, Foe,
  Harry, Impugn, Onsetter, Oppugn, Pillory, Ply, Revile
**Assassin(ate), Assassination** Attentat, Booth, Brave, Bravo, Brutus, Casca, Cassius,
  Character, Corday, Cut-throat, Dallas, Frag, Gar(r)otte, Gunman, Highbinder, Hitman, Hit
  squad, Killer, Ninja, Oswald, Sword, Sworder, Thuggee, Triggerman, Tyrannicide
**Assault** ABH, Assail, Assay, Attack, Battery, Bombard, GBH, Hamesucken, Head-butt,
  Indecent, Invasion, Knee, Maul, Molest, Mug, Push, → RAID, Scalade, Stoor, Storm,
  Stour, Stowre, Work over
**Assay(ing)** Cupel, Docimasy, Examine, Proof, Test, Wet
**As seen** Voetstoots
**Assemble(d), Assembly** Aggregate, Agora, Amass, Audience, Ball, Band, Bevy,
  Bottom-hole, Brood, Bundestag, Chapter, Chatuaqua, Cho(u)ltry, Church, Clutch,
  Co, Collation, → COLLECTION, Comitia, Company, Conclave, Concourse, Congeries,
  Congregate, Congress, Consistory, Constituent, Convene, Conventicle, Convention,
  Convocation, Convoke, Corroboree, Cortes, Council, Court, Covey, Curia, Dail Eireann,
  Dewain, Diet (of Worms), Divan, Donnybrook, D(o)uma, Ecclesia, Eisteddfod, Erect,
  Feis(anna), Fit, Flotilla, Folkmoot, Folkmote, Force, Forgather, Fuel, Gather(ing),
  Gemot(e), General, Gorsedd, Group, Headstock, Hoi polloi, House, Jirga, Kgotla, Knesset,

Landtag, Legislative, Lekgotla, Levee, Loya jirga, Majlis, Make, Mass, Meet, →**MEETING**, Mejlis, Moot, Murder, Muster, National, Nide, Oireachtas, Panegyry, Panoply, Parishad, Parliament, Patron, Pattern, Plenum, Pnyx, Powwow, Prefabrication, Presence, Primary, Quorum, Rally, Rallying-point, Rechate, Recheate, Reichstag, Relie, Repair, Resort, Riksdag, Rodeo, Roll up, Sanghat, Sanhedrin, Sanhedron, School, Scratch, Sedge, Sejm, Senate, Senedd, Sheaf, Skupshtina, Sobranje, Soc, Society, Squadron, Stort(h)ing, String, Student, Synagogue, Synedrion, Synod, T(h)ing, Tribunal, Troop, Troupe, Turn out, Unlawful, Vidhan Sabha, Volksraad, Wapens(c)haw, Wapins(c)haw, Wappens(c)haw, Wardmote, Weapon-s(c)haw, Witan, Witenagemot, Zemstvo

**Assent** Accede, Acquiesce, Agree, Amen, Aye, Comply, Concur, Jokol, Nod, Placet, Royal, Sanction, Viceregal, Yea, Yield

**Assert(ing), Assertion, Assertive** Affirm, Allege, Bumptious, Claim, Constate, Contend, →**DECLARE**, Dogmatic, Forceful, Ipse-dixit, →**MAINTAIN**, Pose, Predicate, Proclaim, Pronounce, Protest, Pushing, Pushy, Rumour, Swear (blind), Thetical

**Assess(ment), Assessor** Affeer, Appraise, Audition, Cense, Consider, Critique, Eleven-plus, Estimate, Evaluate, Formative, Gauge, Guesstimate, Inspect, →**JUDGE**, Levy, Means test, Measure, Perspective, Rating, Referee, Report, Risk, Scot and lot, Size up, Special, Stent, Stocktake, Summative, Tax, Value, Weigh

**Asset(s)** Advantage, Capital, Chargeable, Chattel, Current, Fixed, Floating, Goodwill, Intangible, Inventory, Liquid, Net, Plant, Property, Resource, Seed corn, Talent, Tangible, Virtue, Wasting

**Assiduous** Attentive, Busy, Constant, Diligent, Studious, Thorough

**Assign(ation), Assignment** Allocate, →**ALLOT**, Apply, Appoint, Aret, Ascribe, Attentat, Attribute, Award, Date, Dedicate, Depute, Detach, Detail, Duty, Entrust, Errand, Fix, Give, Grant, Impute, Mission, Ordain, Point, Quota, Refer, Sort, Tak(e), Tryst

**Assimilate(d)** Absorb, Blend, Digest, Esculent, Fuse, Imbibe, Incorporate, Merge, Osmose

**Assist(ance), Assistant** Acolyte, Adjunct, Adviser, Aid(e), Aide-de-camp, Ally, Alms, Attaché, Attend, Au pair, Batman, Befriend, Best boy, Busboy, Cad, Chainman, Collaborate, Counterhand, Counter-jumper, Deputy, Dresser, Ex parte, Facilitate, Factotum, Famulus, Feldschar, Felds(c)her, Girl Friday, Gofer, →**HAND**, Handlanger, Help, Henchman, Legal aid, Matross, Mentor, National, Nipper, Number two, Offsider, Omnibus, Orderly, Proproctor, Public, Reinforce, Relief, Second, Secretary, Server, Service, Servitor, Shill, Sidekick, Sidesman, Smallboy, Social, Stead, Subeditor, Subsidiary, Subsidy, Suffragan, Supernumerary, →**SUPPORT**, Tawny Owl, Underling, Usher, Whipper-in

**Assize** Botley, Circuit, Court, Maiden, Oyer

**Associate(d), Association** Accomplice, Affiliate, Alliance, Amphictyony, Ass, Attach, Bedfellow, Brotherhood, Cartel, Chapel, Chum, Clang, Club, Cohort, Colleague, Combine, Comecon, Community, Company, Compeer, Complice, Comrade, Concomitant, Confrère, →**CONNECT**, Consort(ium), Contact, Co-partner, Correlate, Crony, Enclisis, Familiar, Fellow, Fraternise, Fraternity, Free, Gesellschaft, Goose club, Guild, Hobnob, Housing, Identify, Inquiline, Intime, Join, Kabele, Kebele, Kindred, League, Liaison, Link, Lloyds, Mell, Member, MENSA, Mess, Mix, Moshav, Oddfellows, Pal, Parent teacher, Partner(ship), Phoresy, Press, Probus, Professional, Relate, Residents', Ring, Round Table, Samit(h)i, Sangh(at), Sidekick, Sodality, Stablemate, Staff, Symbiosis, Syndicate, Synonymous, Tenants', Toc H, Toenadering, Trade, UN(A), Union, Verein, Whiteboy, Wiener Werkstatte, Word, Yoke-fellow, Yoke-mate

**Assort(ed), Assortment** Choice, Congeries, Etc, Medley, Paraphernalia, Pick-'n'-mix, Ragbag, Various

▷ **Assorted** *may indicate* an anagram

**Assuage** Allay, Appease, Beet, Calm, Ease, Mease, Mitigate, Mollify, Relieve, Slake, Soften, Soothe

**As such** Qua

**Assume(d), Assuming, Assumption** Adopt, Affect, Arrogate, Artificial, Attire, Axiom, Believe, Don, Donné(e), Feign, Gather, Hypothesis, Lemma, Occam's Razor, Posit, Postulate, Preconception, Premise, Premiss, Presuppose, Pretend, Pretentious, Principle, Putative, Saltus, Say, Side, Simulate, Suppose, Surmise, Take

▷ **Assumption** *may indicate* 'attire'

**Assure(d), Assurance** Aplomb, Aver, Avouch, Belief, Calm, → CERTAIN, Comfort, Confidence, Confirm, Earnest, Gall, Guarantee, Knowing, Life, Pledge, Poise, Promise, Secure, Self-confidence, Term, Thoughten, Warranty

**Assuredly** Indeed, Perdie, Verily, Yea

**Assyrian** Sennacherib

**Astatine** At

**Aster** Starwort

**Astern** Abaft, Apoop, Rear

**Asteroid** Ceres, Eros, Eros 433, Hermes, Hygiea, Icarus, Juno, Minor planet, Pallas, Phaethon, Pholus, Planetoid, Sea-star, Star, Starfish, Trojan, Vesta

**Astir** Afoot, Agate, Agog

**Astonish(ed), Astonishing, Astonishment, Astound** Abash, Admiraunce, Amaze, Banjax, Bewilder, Bowl over, Confound, Corker, Crikey, Daze, Donnert, Dumbstruck, Dum(b)found, Eye-popping, Flabbergast, Gobsmack, Heavens, Mind-boggling, Open-eyed, Open-mouthed, Phew, Pop-eyed, Prodigious, Rouse, Shake, Singular, Stagger, Startle, Stun, Stupefaction, Stupefy, Stupendous, Surprise, Thunderstruck, Wide-eyed, Wow

**Astray** Abord, Amiss, Errant, Lost, Will, Wull

**Astride** Athwart, En cavalier, Spanning, Straddle-back

**Astringent** Acerbic, Alum, Catechu, Dhak, Gambi(e)r, Harsh, Kino, Krameria, Myrobalan, Obstruent, Puckery, Rhatany, Sept-foil, Severe, Sour, Stypsis, Styptic, Tormentil, Witch-hazel

**Astrologer, Astrology, Astrological** Archgenethliac, Chaldean, Culpeper, Faust, Figure-caster, Genethliac, Judicial, Lilly, Magus, Midheaven, Moore, Nostradamus, Soothsayer, Starmonger, Zadkiel

**Astronaut** Aldrin, Cosmonaut, Gagarin, Glenn, Lunarnaut, Spaceman, Spacer, Taikonaut

**Astronomer, Astronomy, Astronomical** Airy, Almagest, Aristarchus, Azimuth, Barnard, Bessel, Bliss, Bradley, Brahe, Callipic, Cassegrain, Cassini, Celsius, Christie, Coal sack, Copernicus, Dyson, Eddington, Encke, Eratosthenes, Eudoxus, Flamsteed, Galileo, Gamma-ray, Graham-Smith, Hale, Halley, Herschel, Hertzsprung, Hewish, Hipparchus, Hoyle, Hubble, Huggins, Infra red, Jeans, Kepler, Lagrange, Laplace, Leverrier, Lockyer, Lovell, Maskelyne, Meton, Moore, Neutrino, Olbers, Omar Khayyam, Oort, Physical, Planetesimal, Planetology, Pond, Ptolemy, Quadrivium, Radar, Radio, Reber, Rees, Roche, Roemer, Russell, Ryle, Schwarzschild, Selenography, Selenology, Seyfert, Sosigenes, Spencer-Jones, Stargazer, Star read, Telescopy, Tycho Brahe, Ultraviolet, Urania, Uranic, Uranography, Wolfendale, Woolley, X-ray, Zwicky

**Astrophel** Penthia

**Astrophysicist** Seifert

**Astute** Acute, Canny, Crafty, Cunning, Downy, Perspicacious, Shrewd, Subtle, Wide, Wily

**As usual** Solito

**As well** Additionally, Also, Both, Eke, Even, Forby, To boot, Too

**Asylum** Bedlam, Bin, Bughouse, Frithsoken, Funny-farm, Girth, Grith, Haven, Institution, Loony bin, Lunatic, Madhouse, Magdalene, Nuthouse, Political, Rathouse, Refuge, Retreat, Sanctuary, Shelter, Snake-pit

**Asylum-seeker** Refugee

**Asymmetric(al)** Contrapposto, Lopsided, Skew

**At** Astatine, In, Kip, To, Up-bye

**Atahualpa** Inca

**At all** Ava, Ever, Oughtlings

**At all events** Algate
**Atavistic** Reversion, Throw-back
**At first** Erst
**Atheist** Doubter, Godless, Infidel, Irreligious, Sceptic
**Athenian, Athene** Attic, Cleruch, Pallas, Pericles, Solon, Timon
**Athlete, Athletic(s)** Agile, Agonist, Blue, Coe, Discobolus, Field, Gymnast, Hurdler, Jock, Leish, Miler, Milo, Nurmi, Olympian, Owens, Pacemaker, Quarter-miler, Runner, Sexual, Shamateur, Shot-putter, Sportsman, Sprinter, Track, Track and field, Triple jump
**Athodyd** Ram-jet
**Athwart** Across, Awry, Oblique, Traverse
**Atlantic** Millpond, Pond
**Atlas** Dialect, Linguistic, Maps, Range, Silk, Telamon
▷ **At last** *may indicate* a cobbler
**Atmosphere** Aeropause, Afterdamp, Air, Ambience, Aura, Chemosphere, Climate, E-layer, Elements, Epedaphic, E-region, Ether, Exosphere, F-layer, Fug, Geocorona, Ionosphere, Lid, Magnetosphere, Mesosphere, Meteorology, Miasma, Mood, Ozone, Standard, Stratosphere, Thermosphere, Tropopause, Troposphere, Upper, Vibe(s), Vibrations
**At most** Al piu
**Atoll** Bikini, Enewetak, Eniwetok, Funafuti, Kwajalein, Male, Motu, Tarawa
**Atom(ic), Atoms, Atomism** Boson, Chromophore, Dimer, Electron, Excimer, Free, Fusion, Gram, Ion, Iota, Isobare, Isotone, Isotope, Labelled, Ligand, Logical, Molecule, Monad, Monovalent, Muonic, Nematic, Nuclide, Odoriphore, Particle, Pile, Primeval, Radionuclide, Recoil, Sellafield, Side-chain, Species, Steric, Stripped, Substituent, Tagged, Windscale, Xylyl
**Atomiser** Airbrush, Nebuliser
**At once** Directly, Ek dum, Holus-bolus, Immediate, Instanter, Presto, Statim, Straight away, Swith, Tight, Tit(e), Titely, Tout de suite, Tyte
**At one** Agreed
**Atone(ment)** Aby(e), Acceptilation, Appease, Assoil, Expiate, Penance, Purge, Redeem, Redemption, Yom Kippur
**Atop** Upon
▷ **At random** *may indicate* an anagram
**Atrocious, Atrocity** Abominable, Brutal, Diabolical, Enorm, Flagitious, Heinous, Horrible, Massacre, Monstrous, Outrage, Piacular, Terrible, Vile
**Atrophy** Degeneration, Marasmus, Sudeck's, Sweeny, Wasting
▷ **At sea** *may indicate* an anagram
**Attach(ed), Attachment** Accessory, Accrete, Adhesion, Adhibition, Adnate, Adnation, Adscript, Affix, Allonge, Annexe, Bolt, Bro, Byssus, Cleat, Covermount, Curtilage, Devotement, Devotion, Distrain, Dobby, Extra, Eyehook, Feller, Fixation, Garnish, Glom, Glue, →**JOIN**, Menge, Moor, Netsuke, Obconic, Piggyback, Pin, Reticle, Sew, Sidecar, Snell, Stick, Tack on, Tendon, Tendril, Tie, Weld
**Attack(ing), Attacker** Access, Affect, Aggression, Airstrike, Alert, Ambuscade, Ambush, Anti, Apoplexy, Asperse, Assail, Assault, Assiege, At, Banzai, Batter, Bego, Belabour, Beset, Bestorm, Blitz(krieg), Bodrag(ing), Bombard, Bordraging, Bout, Broadside, Brutalise, Bushwhack, Calumny, Camisade, Camisado, Campaign, Cannonade, Carte, Charge, Clobber, Club, Counteroffensive, Coup de main, Denounce, Depredation, Descent, Diatribe, Discomfit, Excoriate, Feint, Fit, Flèche, Foray, Fork, Forward, Gas, Get, Glass, Handbag, Happy-slapping, Harry, Hatchet job, Headbutt, Heart, Heckle, Iconoclast, Ictus, Impingement, Impugn, Incursion, Infestation, Inroad, Invade, Inveigh, Jump, Knee, Lampoon, Lash out, Lese-majesty, Let fly, Maraud, Molest, Mug, Offence, Offensive, Onding, Onfall, Onrush, Onset, Onslaught, Oppugn, Outflank, Panic, Philippic, Pillage, Pin, Poke, Polemic, Pounce, Predacious, Pre-emptive, Push, Quart(e), Raid, Rally, Rough, Sail, Sandbag, Savage, Second strike, Seizure, Sic(k), Siege,

Skitch, Slam, Snipe, Sortie, Spasm, Storm, Strafe, Straff, Strike, Swoop, Thrust, Tilt, Vilify, Vituperate, Wage, Warison, Warray, Wolf-pack, Zap

**Attain(ment)** Accomplish, Achieve, Arrive, Earn, Fruition, Get, Land, Reach

**Attempt** Attentat, Bash, Bid, Burl, Crack, Debut, Effort, Egma, Endeavour, Essay, Go, Mint, Nisus, Offer, Potshot, Seek, Shot, Show, Shy, Spell baker, Stab, Strive, Tackle, Trial, → TRY, Venture, Whack, Whirl

**Attend(ance), Attendant** Accompany, Acolyte, Aide, Appearance, Apple-squire, Await, Batman, Bearer, Be at, Behold, Bell-hop, Bower woman, Bulldog, Caddy, Cavass, Chaperone, Chasseur, Checker, Commissionaire, Corybant, Courtier, Cuadrilla, Cupbearer, Custrel, Doula, Dresser, Entourage, Equerry, Escort, Esquire, Famulus, Footman, Gate(-keeper), G(h)illie, Gilly, Hand-maiden, Harken, Hear, → HEED, Hello, Holla, Iras, Jack, Janitor, Kavass, Keeper, Led captain, → LISTEN, Loblolly-boy, Maenad, Marshal, Mute, Note, Orderly, Outrider, Outrunner, Page, Panisc, Panisk, Paranymph, People, Pew-opener, Presence, Pursuivant, Respect, Roll-up, Satellite, Second, Server, S(a)ice, Sort, Sowar, Steward, Syce, Therapeutic, Trainbearer, Trolleydolly, Turn-out, Up at, Usher, Valet, Varlet(to), Visit, Wait, Watch, Whiffler, Zambuck

**Attention, Attentive** Achtung, Alert, Assiduity, Care(ful), Concentration, Court, Coverage, Dutiful, Ear, Eye, Focus, Gallant, Gaum, Gorm, Hark, Heed, Interest, Mind, Note, Notice, Observant, Present, Ps(s)t, Punctilious, Qui vive, → REGARD, Respect, Selective, Solicitous, Spellbound, Spotlight, Tentie, Tenty, Thorough, Thought, Uxorious, Voila

**Attenuate, Attenuation** Lessen, Neper, Rarefy, Thin, Weaken

**Attest** Affirm, Certify, Depose, Guarantee, Notarise, Swear, → WITNESS

**Attic** Bee-bird, Cockloft, Garret, Greek, Koine, Loft, Mansard, Muse, Salt, Sky parlour, Solar, Soler, Sollar, Soller, Tallat, Tallet, Tallot

**Attila** Etzel, Hun

**Attire** Accoutre, Adorn, Apparel, Clobber, Clothe, Clothing, → DRESS, Garb, Habit, Slacks

**Attitude** Air, Aspect, Behaviour, Demeanour, Light, → MANNER, Mindset, Nimby, Outlook, Pose, Position, Possie, Posture, Propositional, Scalogram, Sense, Song, Spirit, Stance, Tone, Uppity, Viewpoint

**Attorney** Advocate, Counsellor, DA, District, Lawyer, Private, Proctor, Prosecutor, Public

**Attract(ion), Attractive(ness), Attractor** Attrahent, Bait, Barrie, Beauté du diable, Becoming, Bedworthy, Bewitch, Bonnie, Bonny, Bootylicious, Catchy, Charisma, → CHARM, Cheesecake, Clou, Comely, Crowd puller, Cute, Cynosure, Dinky, Dipolar, Dish(y), Draught, → DRAW, Dreamboat, Duende, Engaging, Entice, Epigamic, Eye candy, Eye-catching, Eyeful, Fanciable, Fascinate, Feature, Fetching, Fox(y), Goodly, Gravity, Great, Groovy, Heartthrob, Himbo, Hot, Hot stuff, Hotty, Hunky, Inducement, Inviting, It, Jolie laide, Loadstone, Lodestone, Looker, Lovable, Lovely, Lure, Luscious, Magnes, Magnet(ism), Mecca, Mediagenic, Meretricious, Nubile, Ornamental, Pack in, Personable, Pheromone, Photogenic, Picture postcard, Picturesque, Plum, Popsy, Prepossessing, Pretty, Pull, Seduce, Sematic, Sexpot, Shagtastic, Sideshow, Sightly, Slick, Smasher, Snazzy, Soote, Speciosity, Spunk, Stotter, Striking, Studmuffin, Stunner, Taking, Taky, Tasteful, Tasty, Tempt, Theme-park, Toothsome, Tottie, Totty, Triff(ic), Va-va-voom, Weber, Winning, Winsome, Zaftig, Zoftig, Zoophilia

**Attribute, Attribution** Accredit, Allot, Ap(p)anage, Ascribe, Asset, By, Credit, Gift, Impute, Lay, Metonym, Owe, Proprium, Quality, Refer, Resource, Shtick, Strength

**Attune** Accord, Adapt, Temper

**Atypical** Aberrant, Anomalous, Singular, Uncommon

**Aubergine** Brinjal, Brown jolly, Egg-apple, Egg-plant, Mad-apple

**Aubrey** Beardsley

**Auburn** Abram, Chestnut, Copper, Titian, Vill(age)

**Auction(eer)** Barter, Bridge, Cant, Dutch, Hammer, Knock out, Outcry, Outro(o)per, Roup, Sale, Subhastation, Tattersall, Trade sale, Vendue, Warrant sale

**Audacious, Audacity** Bald-headed, Bold, Brash, Cheek, Chutspah, Chutzpah, Cool, Der-doing, Devil-may-care, Effrontery, Face, Hardihood, Indiscreet, Insolence, Intrepid, Neck, Nerve, Rash, Sauce

**Audible** Out loud

**Audience, Auditorium** Assembly, Court, Durbar, Gate, Hearing, House, Interview, Pit, Sphendone, Theatre, Tribunal

**Audiovisual** AV

**Audit(or)** Accountant, Check, Ear, Environmental, Examine, Green, Inspect, Listener, Medical, Position, Vet

**Audition** Apply, Cattle-call, Hearing, Screen-test

**Auditory** Acoustic, Oral

**Audrey** Hoyden

**Auger** Miser

**Aught** Anything

**Augment(ed)** Boost, Eche, Eke, Grow, Ich, Increase, Pad, Supplement, Swell, Tritone

**Augur(y)** Bode, → DIVINATION, Ornithoscopy, Portend

**August** Awe-inspiring, Exalted, Grand, Imperial, Imposing, Lammas, Majestic, Noble, Royal, Solemn, Stately, Stern, Strindberg

**Augustine, Augustus** Austin, Hippo, John

**Auk** Guillemot, Ice-bird, Puffin, Roch, Rotch(e)

**Aunt(ie)** Agony, Augusta, BBC, Beeb, Giddy, Maiden, Naunt, Sainted, Tia, Welsh

**Aura** Aroma, Emanation, Halo, Mystique, Nimbus, Odour, Vibe(s), Vibrations

**Aureole** Coronary, Halo, Nimbus

**Auricle** Ear, Otic

**Aurora** Australis, Borealis, Eos, Leigh, Matutinal, Merry dancers, Northern lights, Southern (lights)

**Auspice(s)** Aegis, Patronage

**Auster** S-wind

**Austere, Austerity** Ascetic, Astringent, Bleak, Dantean, Dervish, Dour, Hard, → HARSH, Moral, Plain, Rigour, Self-disciplined, Severe, Spartan, Stern, Stoic, Stoor, Strict, Vaudois, Waldensian

**Austin** Friar

**Australia(n)** A, Alf, Antichthone, Antipodean, .au, Aussie, Balt, Banana-bender, Bananalander, Billjim, Bodgie, Canecutter, Cobber, Coon, Currency, Current, Darwinian, Digger, Gin, Godzone, Gumsucker, Gurindji, Jackie, Jacky, Koori, Larrikin, Lucky Country, Murree, Murri, Myall, Norm, Ocker, Ossie, Outbacker, Oz(zie), Pintupi, Roy, Sandgroper, Strine, Sydneysider, Wallaby, Yarra-yabbies

**Austrian** Cisleithan, Tyrolean

**Authentic(ate), Authentication** Certify, Des(h)i, Echt, Genuine, Honest, Notarise, Official, Probate, Ratify, Real, Sign, Simon-pure, Test, True, Validate

**Author(ess)** Anarch, Architect, Auctorial, Biographer, Chronicler, Hand, Inventor, Me, Parent, Penman, Playwright, Rhymer, Scenarist, Volumist, Wordsmith, → WRITER

▷ **Author** *may refer to* author of puzzle

**Authorise(d), Authorisation** Accredit, Chit, Clearance, Command, Consent, Countersign, Delegate, Depute, Empower, Enable, Entitle, Exequatur, ID card, Imprimatur, Initial, Legal(ise), Legit, → LICENCE, Licit, Mandate, Official, OK, Passport, → PERMIT, Plenipotentiary, Proxy, Ratify, Retainer, Rubber-stamp, Sanction, Sign, Signature, Stamp, Undersign, Warrant

**Authority, Authoritarian, Authoritative** Ascetic, Canon, Chair, Charter, Circar, Cocker, Commission, Commune, Crisp, Curule, Definitive, Domination, Domineering, Dominion, Establishment, Ex cathedra, Expert, Fascist, Free hand, Gravitas, Hegemony, Inquirendo, Jackboot, Leadership, Licence, License, Light, Local, Magisterial, Mana, Mandate, Mantle, Mastery, Name, Omnipotence, Oracle, Permit, PLA, Potency, → POWER, Prefect, Prestige, Pundit, Regime, Remit, Right, Rod, Savant, Say-so, Sceptre,

Sircar, Sirkar, Source, Supremacy, Supremo, Sway, Top-brass, Tyrannous, Unitary, Warrant

**Autobiography** Memoir

**Autochthonous** Aboriginal

**Autocrat(ic)** Absolute, Caesar, Cham, Despot, Khan, Neronian, Tenno, Tsar, Tyrant

**Autocue** Teleprompter

**Autogenous** Self-made

**Autograph** Signature

**Autolycus** Scrapman

**Automatic, Automaton** Android, Aut, Browning, Deskill, Instinctive, Knee-jerk, Machine, Mechanical, Pistol, Quarter-boy, Quarter-jack, Reflex, Robot, RUR, Zombi

**Autonomous** Independent

**Auto-pilot** George

**Autopsy** Necropsy

**Auto-suggestion** Coueism

**Autumn(al)** Fall, Filemot, Leaf-fall, Libra, Philamot

**Auxiliary** Adjunct, Adjuvant, Adminicle, Aide, Ancillary, Be, Feldsher, Foederatus, Have, Helper, Ido, Modal, Subsidiary

**Avail(able)** Abounded, Benefit, Dow, Eligible, Going, Handy, In season, Off-the-shelf, On, On call, On hand, On tap, Open, Out, Pickings, Potluck, → **READY**, Serve, To hand, Up for grabs, Use, Utilise, Worth

**Avalanche** Bergfall, Deluge, Icefall, Landfall, Landslide, Landslip, Lauwine, Rockfall, Slide, Slip, Snowdrop

**Avant-garde** Advanced, Modernistic, Progressive, Spearhead, Ultramodern

**Avarice, Avaricious** Cupidity, Gimmes, Golddigger, Greed, Money-grubbing, Pleonexia, Predatory, Shylock, Sordid

**Avatar** Epiphany, Incarnation, Rama

**Avaunt** Away, Go

**Avenge(r)** Alecta, Eriny(e)s, Eumenides, Goel, Kuraitcha, Megaera, Nemesis, Nightrider, Punish, Redress, Requite, → **REVENGE**, Steed, Tisiphone, Wreak

**Avenue** Allee, Alley, Approach, Arcade, Boulevard, Channel, Corso, Cradle-walk, Hall, Madison, Mall, Midway, Passage, Vista, Way, Xyst(us)

**Aver** Affirm, Assert, Asseverate, Declare, Depose, State, Swear, Vouch

**Average** Adjustment, Av, Batting, Dow Jones, Everyman, Fair, Mean, Mediocre, Middle-brow, Middling, Moderate, Moving, Norm, Par, Particular, Run, Run-of-the-mill, Soso, Standard, Usual, Weighted

**Averse, Aversion, Avert** Against, Antipathy, Apositia, Disgust, Dislike, Distaste, Hatred, Horror, Opposed, Pet, Phengephobia, Phobic, Photophobia, Risk, Scunner, Sit(i)ophobia, Stave off

**Avert** Avoid, → **DEFLECT**, Forfend, Parry, Ward

**Aviary** Volary, Volery

**Aviator** Airman, Alcock, Bleriot, Brown, Byrd, Co-pilot, De Havilland, Earhart, Flier, Hinkler, Icarus, Johnson, Lindbergh, Pilot, Red Baron, Richthofen, Yeager

**Avid** Agog, Athirst, → **EAGER**, Greedy, Keen

**Avifauna** Ornis

**Avignon** Pont

**Avocado** Aguacate, Alligator pear, Guac(h)amole, Pear

**Avocet** Scooper

**Avoid(er), Avoidance** Abstain, Ba(u)lk, Boycott, Buck, Bypass, Cop-out, Cut, Dodge, Duck, Elude, Escape, Eschew, Evade, Evitate, Evite, Fly, Forbear, Gallio, Hedge, Miss, Needless, Obviate, Parry, Prevaricate, Save, Scape, Scutage, Secede, Shelve, Shirk, Shun, Sidestep, Skirt, Skive, Spare, Spurn, Tergiversate, Waive

**Avoirdupois** Size, Weight

**Avow(ed)** Acknowledged, Affirm, Declare, Own, Swear

**Await(ed)** Abide, Bide, Expect, Godot, Tarry

**Awake(ning)** Aware, Conscious, Conversion, Fly, Rouse, Vigilant

**Award** Academy, Accolade, Acquisitive, Addeem, Addoom, Allot, Alpha, Apple, Arbitrament, Aret(t), Bafta, Bar, Bestow, Bursary, Cap, Charter Mark, Clasp, Clio, Compensation, Crown, Degree, Emmy, Exhibition, Genie, Gold disc, Golden handshake, Golden Raspberry, Golden Starfish, Grammy, Grant, Honours, Juno, Logie, Lourie, Medal, Meed, Mete, MOBO, Oscar, Padma Shri, Palatinate, Palme d'Or, Premium, Present(ation), Prix Goncourt, → **PRIZE**, Purse, Queen's, Razzie, Rosette, Scholarship, Tony, Trophy, Vir Chakra, Yuko

**Aware(ness)** Alert, Aware, C(o)enesthesis, Coconscious, Cognisant, Conscious, Conversant, Enlightenment, ESP, Est, Hep, Hip, Informed, Knowing, Liminal, Mindshare, Onto, Open-eyed, Panaesthesia, Prajna, Presentiment, Samadhi, Scienter, Sensible, Sensile, Sensitive, Sentience, Streetwise, Switched on, Vigilant, Weet, Wit, Wot

**Away** Abaxial, Absent, Afield, Apage, Aroint, Avaunt, Beyond, By, For-, Forth, Fro(m), Go, Hence, Off, Out, Past

▷ **Away** *may indicate* a word to be omitted

**Awe(d)** Dread, D(o)ulia, Fear, Intimidate, Loch, Overcome, Popeyed, Regard, Respect, Reverent, Scare, Solemn, Wonderment

**Awe-inspiring, Awesome** Mega, Numinous

**Awesome** Breathtaking, Terrific

**Awful(ly)** Alas, Appalling, Deare, Dere, Dire, Fearful, Horrendous, Lamentable, Nasty, O so, Piacular, Rotten, Terrible, Third rate, Unspeakable

▷ **Awfully** *may indicate* an anagram

**Awkward(ness)** All thumbs, Angular, Blate, Bolshy, Bumpkin, Cack-handed, Clumble-fisted, Clumsy, Complicated, Contrary, Corner, Crabby, Cubbish, Cumbersome, Cussed, Disconcerting, Dub, Embarrassing, Farouche, Fiddly, Fix, Gangly, Gauche, Gawky, Graceless, Handless, Hobbledehoy, Howdy-do, Inconvenient, Inelegant, Inept, Jam(pot), Kittle-cattle, Knotty, Lanky, Loutish, Lurdan(e), Lurden, Maladdress, Mauther, Mawr, Naff, Nasty, Nonconformist, Ornery, Perverse, Refractory, Slouch, Slummock, So-and-so, Spot, Sticky, Stiff, Stroppy, Stumblebum, Swainish, Ticklish, Twiddley, Uncoordinated, Uncouth, Uneasy, Ungainly, Ungraceful, Unhandy, Unwieldy, Wooden, Wry

**Awl(-shaped)** Brog, Els(h)in, Nail, Stob, Subulate

**Awn(ing)** Barb, Beard, Canopy, Ear, Shade, Shamiana(h), Sunblind, Velarium

**Awry** Agley, Amiss, Askent, Askew, Athwart, Cam, Haywire, Kam(me), Pear-shaped, Wonky

**Axe(s)** Abolish, Adz(e), Bardiche, Bill, Celt, Chop(per), Cleaver, Curtal, Ditch, Eatche, Gisarme, Gurlet, Halberd, Halbert, Hatchet, Hew, Holing, Ice, Jeddart staff, Jethart-staff, Labrys, Lochaber, Mattock, Palstaff, Palstave, Partisan, Piolet, Retrench, Sax, Scrub, Slate, Sparth(e), Sperthe, Spontoon, Stone, Thunderbolt, Tomahawk, Twibill, X, Y, Z

**Axeman** Bassist, Guitarist, Hendrix

**Axe-shaped** Securiform

**Axiom** Adage, Motto, Peano's, Proverb, Saw, Saying

**Axis** Alliance, Anorthic, Anticous, Axle, Caulome, Chital, Cob, Columella, Deer, Epaxial, Henge, Hinge, Major, Minor, Modiolus, Myelon, Neutral, Optic, Pivot, Polar, Precess, Principal, Rachis, Radical, Spindle, Stem, Sympodium, Visual, X, Y, Z, Zone

**Axle, Axle-shoulder** Arbor, Axis, Driving, Fulcrum, Hurter, Journal, Live, Mandrel, Mandril, Pivot, Spindle, Stub

**Ay** Ever, I, Indeed

**Aye** Always, Eer, Ever, Yea, Yes

**Ayesha** She

**Azo-dye** Para-red

**Aztec** Nahuatl

# Bb

**B** Bachelor, Black, Book, Born, Boron, Bowled, Bravo, Flipside
**Babble(r)** Blather, Brook, Chatter, Gibber, Haver, Jabber, Lallation, Lurry, Prate, Prattle, Psycho, Runnel, Tonguester, Tonguework, Twattle, Waffle, Witer
**Babe** Cutie
**Babel** Charivari, Confusion, Din, Dovercourt, Medley
**Baboon** Ape, Bobbejaan, Chacma, Cynocephalus, Dog-ape, Drill, Gelada, Hamadryas, Mandrill, Sphinx
**Baby** Bairn, Band-Aid®, Blue, Bub, Bunting, Changeling, Coddle, Designer, Duck, Grand, Infant, Jelly, Litter, Neonate, Nursling, Pamper, Papoose, Plunket, Preverbal, Rhesus, Rugrat, Sis, Small, Sook, Spoil, Suckling, Tar, Test tube, Thalidomide, Tot, War, Wean
**Babylonian** Mandaean, Semiramis, Sumerian
**Baby-sitter** Minder
**Bacchanalian, Bacchus** Ivied, Upsee, Ups(e)y
**Bacchantes** Maenads
**Bachelor** Alumnus, BA, Bach, Benedict, Budge, Celibate, En garçon, Knight, Pantagamy, Parti, Seal, Single, Stag, Wifeless
**Bacillus** Comma, Germ, Klebs-Loffler, Micrococcus, Tubercle, Virus
**Back(er), Backing, Back out, Back up, Backward** Abet, Accompany, Addorse, Aft, Again, Ago, Aid, Anticlockwise, Antimacassar, Arear, Arrear, Arrière, Assist, Baccare, Backare, Bankroll, Behind, Buckram, Champion, Chorus, Consent, Countenance, Croup, Cry off, Culet, Defender, Donor, Dorsal, Dorse, Dorsum, Dos, Ebb, Empatron, Encourage, Endorse, Fakie, Finance, Frae, Fro, Full, Fund(er), Gaff, Grubstake, Half, Help, Hind, Historic, Incremental, La-la, Late, Notaeum, Notal, Notum, On, Patronise, Pendu, Poop, Pronotum, Punt, Rear(most), Rearwards, Reinforce, Reinforcement, Reticent, Retral, Retro(grade), Retrogress, Retrorse, Retrospective, Return, Rev, Reverse, Ridge, Root, Running, Scenery, Shy, Spinal, Sponsor, Standby, Stern, Sternboard, Sternway, → SUPPORT, Sweeper, Syndicate, Tail, Telson, Tergum, Third, Thrae, Three-quarter, Tonneau, Ulu, Uphold, Verso, Vie, Vo, Wager, Watteau
▷ **Back(ing)** *may indicate* a word spelt backwards
**Back and forth** Boustrophedon
**Backbiter, Backbiting** Catty, Defame, Detract, Libel, Molar, Slander, Tooth
**Backbone** Atlas, Chine, Grit, Guts, Mettle, Spina, Spine
**Backchat** Lip, Mouth, Sass
**Backcloth, Backdrop** Cyclorama, Scenery
**Backer** Angel, Benefactor, Funder, Patron, Punter, Seconder, Sponsor
**Backfire, Backlash** Billabong, Boomerang, Reaction
**Backgammon** Acey-deucy, Blot, Lurch, Tick-tack, Trick-track, Tric-trac, Verquere
**Background** Antecedence, Chromakey, Cyclorama, Field, Fond, History, Horizon, Microwave, Muzak, Natural, Retrally, Setting, Ulterior
**Backhander** Bribe, Palm grease, Payola, Reverso, Sweetener
**Back number** Has-been
**Back problem** Kyphosis, Lumbago, Osteoporosis, Scolioma, Scoliosis
**Backroom** Boffin, Boy, Moor
**Backslide(r), Backsliding** Apostate, Lapse, Regress, Relapse, Revert
**Back-stabber** Epidural

**Backwash** Rift

**Backwater** Bogan, Ebb, Logan, Retreat, Slough, Wake

**Backwoods(man)** Boondocks, Boonies, Hinterland, Rowdy

**Backyard** Court, Patio

**Bacon** Bard, Canadian, Collar, Danish, Essayist, Flitch, Francis, Gammon, Green, Lardo(o)n, Pancetta, Pig(meat), Pork, Rasher, Roger, Smoked, Spec(k), Streaky, Verulam

**Bacteria, Bacteriologist, Bacterium** Acidophilus, Actinomycete, Aerobe, Amphitricha, Bacilli, Bacteriological, Baregin, Botulinum, →BUG, Campylobacter, Chlamydia, Clostridia, Cocci, Coliform, Culture, Detritivore, Diplococcus, E-coli, Enterococcus, Escherichia, Foul-brood, →GERM, Gonococcus, Gram-negative, Gram-positive, Hib, Intestinal flora, Klebsiella, Koch, Legionella, Listeria, Lysogen, Meningococcus, Microbe, Micrococcus, Microphyte, Mother, MRSA, Mycoplasma, Nitrifying, Nitrite, Nitrous, Nostoc, Operon, Packet, Pasteur, Pasteurella, Pathogen, Peritrich(a), Petri, Pneumococcus, Probiotic, Prokaryote, Proteus, Pseudomonas, Pus, Ray-fungus, Rhizobium, Rickettsia, Salmonella, Schizomycete, Septic, Serogroup, Serotype, Serum, Shigella, Spirilla, Spirochaete, Spirulina, Spore, Staph, Staphylococcus, Strep(tococcus), Streptobacillus, Streptomyces, Sulphur, Superbug, Thermophil(e), Treponemata, Vibrio, Vincent's angina, Vinegar-plant, Yersinia, Zoogloea

**Bad(die), Badness** Abysmal, Addled, Chronic, Crook, Defective, Degenerate, Diabolic, Drastic, Dud, Duff, Dystopia, Egregious, Evildoer, Execrable, Faulty, Fearful, Fourth-rate, God-awful, Half-pie, Heinous, Ill (timed), Immoral, Inferior, Injurious, Lither, Lulu, Mal(vu), Naughty, Nefandrous, Nefarious, Nice, Off, Ominous, Oncus, Onkus, Parlous, Piacular, Poor, Rancid, Rank, Reprobate, Ropy, Scampish, Scoundrel, Shocking, Sinful, Spoiled, The pits, Turpitude, Undesirable, Unspeakable, Useless, Wack, Wick, →WICKED

▷ **Bad(ly)** *may indicate* an anagram

**Badge** Brassard, Brooch, Button, Chevron, Cockade, Cockleshell, Comm, Cordon, Crest, Eagle, Emblem, Ensign, Epaulet, Episemon, Fáinne, Film, Flash, Garter, Gorget, ID, Insigne, Insignia, Kikumon, Mark, Mon, Numerals, Orange, Pilgrim's sign, Pin, Rondel, Rosette, Scallop(-shell), Shield, Shouldermark, →SIGN, Symbol, Tiger, Token, Totem, Vernicle, Vine branch, Vine-rod, Wings

**Badger** →ANNOY, Bait, Bedevil, Beset, Brock, Browbeat, Bug, Bullyrag, Cete, Dassi(e), Ferret, Gray, Grey, →HARASS, Harry, Hassle, Heckle, Hog, Honey, Hound, Nag, Pester, Plague, Provoke, Ratel, Ride, Roil, Sand, Sow, Stinking, Teledu, Wisconsin

**Bad habit** Cacoethes, Vice

**Badinage** Banter, Chaff, Raillery

**Bad luck** Ambs-ace, Ames-ace, Deuce-ace, Hard cheese, Hard lines, Hoodoo, Jinx, Jonah, Shame, Voodoo

**Bad-tempered** Carnaptious, Crabby, Curmudgeon, Curnaptious, Curst, Grouchy, Grum(py), Irritable, Marabunta, Moody, Nowty, Patch, Scratchy, Shirty, Sour, Splenetic, Stroppy

**Bad woman** Harridan, Loose, Mort

**Baffle(d), Baffling** Anan, Balk, Bemuse, Bewilder, Confound, Confuse, Elude, Evade, Floor, Flummox, Foil, Fox, Get, Hush-kit, Mate, Muse, Mystify, Nark, Nonplus, Perplex, Pose, Puzzle, Stump, Throw, Thwart

**Bag(gage), Bags** Acquire, Air, Albatross, Alforja, Allantois, Amaut, Amowt, Ascus, Ballonet, Bedroll, Besom, Bin-liner, Bladder, Blue, Body, Bounty, Briefcase, Bulse, Bum, Buoyancy, Caba(s), Cachet, Caecum, Callet, Capture, Carpet, Carrier, Carryall, Case, Cecum, Claim, Clutch, Cly, Cod, Colostomy, Cool(er), Corduroy, Crone, Crumenal, Cyst, Daypack, Dilli, Dilly, Dime, Diplomatic, Ditty, Doggy, Dorothy, Douche, Duffel, Dunnage, →EFFECTS, Emery, Excess, Fanny pack, Fishwife, Flannels, Flotation, Follicle, Galligaskins, Game, →GEAR, Gladstone, Goody, Grab, Green, Grip, Gripsack, Grow, Haversack, Holdall, Ice, Impedimenta, Jelly, Jiffy®, Kill, Knapsack, Ladies' companion, Lavender, Lithocyst, Loose, Marsupium, Materiel, Meal-poke, Messenger, Minx, Mixed, Money, Monkey, Moon, Mummy, Musette, Musk, Muzzle, Mystery, Nap, Necessaire, Net, Nunny, Organiser, Overnight, Overnighter, Oxford, Packsack, Pantaloons, Plastic,

Plus fours, Pochette, Pock(et), Pocketbook, Pockmanky, Pockmantie, Poke, Politzer's, Poly(thene), Port(manteau), Portmantle, Portmantua, Post, Pot, Pouch, Pounce, Pudding, Punch, Purse, Rake, Red, Reticule, Ridicule, Rucksack, Sabretache, Sac(cule), Sachet, Sack, Saddle, Sag, Satchel, Scent, School, Scrip, Scrotum, Sea, Shapeless, Shopper, Sick, Slattern, Sleeping, Specialty, Sponge, Sporran, Stacks, Steal, Strossers, Sugar, Survival, Tea, Toilet, Tool, Tote, →**TRAP**, Trews, Trollop, Trouse(r), Tucker (box), Udder, Unmentionables, Utricle, Valise, Vanity, Viaticals, Waist, Wallet, Water, Weekend, Win, Woolpack, Work, Wrap, Wrapping, Ziplock

**Bagatelle** Bauble, Fico, Trifle, Trinket

**Bagpipe** Biniou, Chanter, Chorus, Cornemuse, Drone, Gaita, Musette, Pibroch, Piffero, Skirl, Sourdeline, Uillean, Zampogna

**Bahama(s), Bahamian** BS, Conch

**Bail(er), Bailment** Bond, Ladle, Mainpernor, Mainprise, Mutuum, Remand, Replevin, Replevy, Scoop

**Bailey** Bridge, Castle wall, Ward

**Bailiff** Adam, Bandog, Beagle, Bum, Factor, Foud, Grieve, Huissier, Hundreder, Hundredor, Land-agent, Nuthook, Philistine, Reeve, Shoulder-clapper, Shoulder-knot, Steward, Tipstaff, Water

**Bairn** Baby, →**CHILD**, Infant, Wean

**Bait** Angleworm, Badger, Bait, Berley, Brandling, Burley, Capelin, Chum, Dap, Decoy, Entice, Gentle, Gudgeon, Harass, Hellgram(m)ite, Incentive, Lobworm, Lug(worm), Lure, Mawk, →**RAG**, Ragworm, Sandworm, Sledge, Teagle, Tease, Tempt, Tole, Toll

**Bake(r), Baked, Baking** Alaska, Batch, Baxter, Coctile, →**COOK**, Fire, Icer, Kiln-dry, Mr Bun, Oven, Pieman, Roast, Scorch, Shir(r)

**Baker's daughter** Own

**Baker Street** Irregular

**Bakery** Patisserie

**Balance(d)** Account, Beam, Compensation, Counterpoise, Countervail, Counterweight, Equate, Equilibrium, Equipoise, Equiponderate, Even, Fixed, Funambulate, Gyroscope, Gyrostat, Horn, Hydrostatic, Invisible, Isostasy, Launce, Level-headed, Libra, Librate, Meet, Otocyst, Otolith, Pease, Peise, Perch, Peyse, Poise, →**REMAINDER**, Remnant, Residual, Rest, Running, Scale, Sea-legs, Spring, Stability, Stand, Steelyard, Symmetry, Together, Torsion, →**TOTAL**, Trade, Trial, Trim, Tron(e), Unicycle, Visible

**Balcony** Circle, Gallery, Loggia, Mirador, Moucharaby, Pew, Porch, Quarter-gallery, Sundeck, Tarras, Terrace, Veranda(h)

**Bald, Baldness** Alopecia, Apterium, Awnless, Barren, Calvities, Coot, Crude, Egghead, Fox-evil, Glabrous, Hairless, Madarosis, Open, Peelgarlic, Pilgarlic(k), Pollard, Psilosis, Slaphead, Smoothpate, Stark, Tonsured

**Balderdash** Drivel, Flapdoodle, Nonsense, Poppycock, Rot

**Baldmoney** Emeu, Meu, Spignel

**Bale** Bl, Bundle, Evil, Lave, Pack, Sero(o)n, Truss

**Baleful** Evil, Malefic, Malignant

▶ **Balk** *see* **BAULK**

**Balkan** Albanian, Bosnian, Bulgarian, Croat, Macedon, Rumanian, Serb, Slavonic, Vlach

**Ball(s)** Aelopile, Aelopyle, Aeolipile, Aeolipyle, Agglomerate, Alley, Ally, Ammo, Aniseed, Apple, Beach, Bead, Beamer, Bearings, Birthing, Bobble, Boll, Bolus, Bosey, Bosie, Bouncer, Bowl, Break, Buckshot, Buzzer, Caltrap, Caltrop, Camphor, Cap, Cherry, Chin, Chinaman, Chopper, Clew, Clue, Condylar, Condyle, Cotill(i)on, Cramp, Creeper, Croquette, Crystal, Cue, Curve, Daisy-cutter, →**DANCE**, Delivery, Dink, Dodge, Dollydrop, Doosra, Dot, Dribbler, Eight, Ensphere, Eolipile, Eolipyle, Eolopile, Eolopyle, Falafel, Felafel, Full-pitch, Full-toss, Fungo, Gazunder, →**GLOBE**, Glomerate, Gobstopper, Googly, Goolies, Gool(e)ys, Grounder, Grub(ber), Grubhunter, Gutta, Gutter, Gutty, Hank, Hop, Hummer, Hunt, Inswinger, Ivory, Jinglet, Jump, Knob, Knur(r), Leather, Leg-break, Leg-cutter, Lob, Long-hop, Marble, Masked, Masque(rade), Matzo, Medicine, Minié,

Mirror, Moth, Nur(r), O, Object, Off-break, Off-cutter, Off-spin, Orb, Outswinger, Over, Overarm, Pakora, Parrel truck, Pea, Pellet, Pill, Poi, Pomander, Pompom, Pompon, Prom, Puck, Punch, Quenelle, Rabbit, Rissole, Root, Round, Rover, Rundle, Seamer, Shooter, Shot, Sliotar, Sneak, Sphere, Spinner, Stress, Strike, Swinger, Swiss, Taw, Tea, Testes, Thenar, Three, Tice, Time, Track(er), Witches, Wood, Wrecker's, Wrecking, Yorker, Zorb®

**Ballad** Bab, Bothy, Broadside, Bush, Calypso, Carol, Fanzone, Folk-song, Forebitter, Lay, Lillibullero, Lilliburlero, Mento, Reading Gaol, Singsong, → **SONG**, Torch-song

**Ballast** Kentledge, Makeweight, Stabiliser, Trim, Weight

**Ball-boy** Dry-bob

**Ballerina** Coryphee, Dancer, Pavlova, Prima

**Ballet, Ballet movement, Ballet-system** Arabesque, Assemblé, Balancé, Ballon, Battement, Bharat Natyam, Bolshoi, Brisé, Cabriole, Cambré, Chainé, Changement, Checkmate, Cinderella, Daphnis and Chloe, Développé, Don Pasquale, Écarté, Echappé, Enchainement, Entrechat, Firebird, Fouette, Giselle, Jeté, Kirov, Laban, Labanotation, Leg business, Mayerling, Nutcracker, Pas de basque, Pas de bourrée, Pas de chat, Petit battement, Petrushka, Pirouette, Plastique, Plie, Pointe, Pointer, Port de bras, Relevé, Saut, Swan Lake

**Ballet-interlude** Divertimento

**Ballista** Scorpion

**Ballistic** Wildfire

**Balloon(ist)** Aeronaut, Aerostat, Airship, Bag, Barrage, Billow, Blimp, Bloat, Dirigible, Distend, Dumont, Enlarge, Fumetto, Glass, Hot air, Lead, Montgolfier, Pilot, Rawinsonde, Sonde, Swell, Trial, Weather, Zeppelin

**Ballot** Butterfly, Election, Mulligan, → **POLL**, Referendum, Second, Secret, Suffrage, Ticket, Vote

**Ballot-box** Urn

**Ballpoint** Bic®, Biro®

**Ballyhoo** Racket

**Balm(y)** Anetic, Arnica, Balsam, Calamint, Emollient, Fragrant, Garjan, Gilead, Gurjun, Lemon, Lenitive, Lotion, → **MILD**, Mirbane, Myrbane, Nard, Oil, Opobalsam, Ottar, Redolent, Remedy, Soothe, Spikenard, Tiger, Tolu, Unguent

**Balmoral** Bonnet, Cap, Castle

**Baloney** Bunk, Hooey, Nonsense

**Balsam** Canada, Copaiba, Copaiva, Friar's, Nard, Noli-me-tangere, Peruvian, Resin, Spikenard, Tamanu, Tolu(ic), Touch-me-not, Tous-les-mois, Turpentine

**Balt** Esth, Lett

**Baltic** Estonian, Lettic

**Bamboo** Cane, Grass, Kendo, Split cane, Tabasheer, Whangee

**Bamboozle(d)** Cheat, Dupe, Flummox, Hoodwink, Horn-swoggle, Mystify, Nose-led, Perplex, Trick

**Ban(ned)** Abolish, Accurse, Anathema, Black(ing), Censor, Curfew, Debar, D-notice, Embargo, Estop, Exclude, Excommunicate, Forbid, For(e)say, For(e)speak, Gag, Gate, Green, Moratorium, No, Outlaw, Prohibit, Proscribe, Suppress, Taboo, Tabu, Test, Verboten, Veto

**Banal** Anorak, Corny, Dreary, Flat, Hackneyed, Jejune, Mundane, Ordinary, Platitudinous, → **TRITE**, Trivial

**Banana(s)** Abaca, Hand, Loco, → **MAD**, Matoke, Musa, Plantain, Raving, Scitamineae, Split, Strelitzia, Top, Zany

**Band(ed), Bands** Absorption, Alice, Ambulacrum, Anadem, Anklet, Armlet, Barrulet, Belt, Border, Braid, Brake, Brass, Brassard, Brassart, Caravan, CB, Channel, Chevron, Chinstrap, Chromosome, Cingulum, Circlet, Citizens', Clarain, Closet, Cohort, Collar, Collet, Combo, Company, Conduction, Corslet, Coterie, Crape, Crepe, Crew, Deely boppers, Dog collar, Elastic, ELO, Endorse, Energy, Enomoty, Facia, Falling, Fascia,

Fasciole, Ferret, Ferrule, Fess, Filament, Fillet, Fourchette, Fraternity, Frequency, Frieze, Frog, Frontlet, Galloon, Gamelan, →**GANG**, Garage, Garland, Garter, Gasket, Gaskin, Geneva, German, Gird, Girr, Girth, Group, Guard, →**HOOP**, Hope, Iron, Jazz, Jug, Kara, Kitchen, Label, Laticlave, Lytta, Macnamara's, Maniple, Mariachi, Massed, Military, Mourning, Myrmidon, Noise, Obi, One-man, Orchestra, Orchestrina, Pack, Parral, Parrel, Parsal, Parsel, Pass, Patte, Pipe, Plinth, Property, Purfle, Puttee, Retinaculum, Rib, Ribbon, Ridge, Rigwiddie, Rigwoodie, Rim, Ring, Robbers, Round, Rubber, Rymme, Sash, Scarf, Screed, Scrunchie, Scrunchy, Sect, Shadow, Shallal, Shash, Sheet, Shoe, Snood, Speckled, Steel, Strake, Strand, Strap, Stratum, String, Stripe, Succinctory, Swath(e), Sweat, Tambu-bambu, Tape, Tendon, Thecla, Thoroughbrace, Throat-latch, Tie, Tippet, Torques, Tourniquet, Train, Trangle, Tribute, Troop, Troupe, Tumpline, Turm, Tyre, Unite, Valence, Vinculum, Virl, Vitrain, Vitta, Wanty, Wedding, Weed, Weeper, Welt, Wings, With(e), Wristlet, Zona, Zone, Zonule

**Bandage** Bind, Blindfold, Capeline, Dressing, Fillet, Gauze, Ligature, Lint, Living, Pledget, Roller, Scapular, Sling, Spica, Suspensor, Swaddle, Swathe, T, Tape, Truss, Tubigrip®, Wadding

**Bandicoot** Bilby, Pig-rat

**Bandit** Apache, Bravo, Brigand, Desperado, Fruit-machine, Gunslinger, Ishmael, Klepht, Moss-trooper, Outlaw, Pirate, Rapparee, →**ROBBER**, Slot machine, Squeegee, Turpin

**Bandsman, Band-leader** Alexander, Bugler, Conductor, Maestro, Miller, Wait

**Bandstand** Kiosk, Stage

**Bandy** Bow, Exchange, Revie, Toss, Vie

**Bane** Curse, Dioxin, Evil, Harm, Nemesis, Poison

**Bang(er)** Amorce, Andouillette, Beat, Big, Cap, Chipolata, Clap, Cracker, Crock, Explode, Firecracker, Flivver, Fringe, Haircut, Heap, Implode, Jalopy, Jammy, Maroon, Pep(p)eroni, Rattletrap, Report, Sausage, Sizzler, Slam, Sonic, Thrill, →**TNT**, Wham, Wurst

**Bangladesh** .bd

**Bangle** Anklet, Armlet, Bracelet, Kara

**Banish(ment)** Ban, Debar, Deport, Depose, Dispel, Excommunicate, Exile, Expatriate, Expel, Extradition, Forsay, Maroon, Ostracise, →**OUTLAW**, Relegate, Rusticate

**Banjo** Ukulele

**Bank(ing), Bank on** An(n)icut, Asar, Backs, Bar, Bay, Beneficiary, Bet, Bk, Blood, Bluff, Bottle, Brae, Brim, Bund, Camber, Cay, Central, Chesil, Clearing (house), Cloud, Commercial, Cooperative, Data, Depend, Deposit, Dogger, Down, Drawee, Drift, Dune, Dyke, Earthwork, Escarp, Fog, Gene, Giro, Glacis, Gradient, Gradin(e), Hack, Hele, Hill(side), Home, Incline, Jodrell, Kaim, Kame, Land, Left, Lender, Levee, Link, Lombard Street, Memory, Merchant, Mound, Nap, National, Needle, Nore, Overslaugh, Oyster, Parapet, Penny, Piggy, Pot, Private, Rake, Ramp, Rampart, RBS, Reef, →**RELY**, Reserve, Retail, Ridge, Rivage, Riverside, Rodham, Row, Sandbar, Savings, Seed, Shallow, Shelf, Side, Slope, Soil, Sperm, Spit, Staithe, State, Sunk, Telephone, Terrace, Terreplein, Tier, Treasury, Trust, Vault, Wells Fargo, West, World

**Banker** Agent, Aileron, Cert(ainty), Financial, Fugger, Gnome, Lender, Lombard, Medici, →**RIVER**, Rothschild, Shroff, Teller

▷ **Banker** *may indicate* a river

**Banknote(s)** Flimsy, Greenback, Snuff-paper

**Bankrupt(cy)** Break, Broke, Bung, Bust, Cadaver, Carey Street, Chapter-eleven, Crash, Debtor, Deplete, Duck, Dyvour, Fail, Fold, Insolvent, Lame duck, Notour, Penniless, Receivership, Ruin, Rump, Scat, Sequestration, Skatt, Smash

▷ **Bankrupt** *may indicate* 'red' around another word

**Bank system** Giro

**Bann(s)** Out-ask

**Banner** Banderol(e), Bandrol, Bannerol, Blue blanket, →**FLAG**, Gumphion, Labarum, Oriflamme, Sign, Standard, Streamer

**Banquet** Beanfeast, Dine, Feast, Junket, Nosh-up, Spread

**Banquette** Firestep

**Bant** Diet, Reduce

**Bantam** Dandy-cock, Dandy-hen

**Banter** Backchat, Badinage, Borak, Borax, Chaff, Dicacity, Dieter, Jest, →**JOKE**, Josh, Persiflage, Picong, Rag, →**RAILLERY**, Rally, Repartee, Ribaldry, Roast, Rot, Tease

**Bantu** Bosotho, Gazankulu, Herero, Kaffir, Lebowa, Qwaqwa, Shangaan, Sotho, Swahili, Transkei, Tutsi, X(h)osa

**Bap** Bread, Roll, Tommy

**Baptise(d), Baptism, Baptist** Affusion, Amrit, Christen, Clinical, Conditional, Dip, Dipper, Dopper, Dunker, Hypothetical, Illuminati, Immersion, John, Mandaean, Mersion, Palingenesis, Private, Sabbatarian, Sprinkle, Tinker

**Bar(s)** Address, Angle-iron, Anti-roll, Apartheid, Astragal, Asymmetric, Axletree, Bail, Ban, Barrelhouse, Baulk, Beam, Bierkeller, Bilboes, Billet, Bistro, Blackball, Blacklist, Block(ade), Bloom, Bolt, Boom, Bottega, Brasserie, Buffet, Bull, Bullion, Bumper, But, Buvette, Café(-chantant), Café-concert, →**CAGE**, Cake, Came, Candy, Cantina, Capo, Capstan, Channel, Clasp, Clip joint, Cocktail, Coffee, Colour, Counter, Cramp(on), Cross(head), Crow, Crush, Currency, Dive, Doggery, Double, Double-tree, Draw, Drift, Dumbbell, Efficiency, Espresso, Estaminet, Estop(pel), Except, Exchange, Exclude, Fern, Fid, Flinders, Fonda, Forbid, Foreclose, Forestall, Fret, Gad, Gastropub, Gemel, Gin palace, Glazing, Grate, Grid, Grog-shop, Gunshop, Hame, Handrail, Handspike, Heck, Hershey, →**HINDRANCE**, Horizontal, Hound, Hyphen, Impediment, Ingoes, Ingot, Ingowes, Inn, Inner, Judder, Juice, Karaoke, Keeper, Kickstand, Knuckleduster, Latch, Let, Lever, Limbo, Line, Lingot, Local, Lock out, Lounge, Macron, Mandrel, Mandril, Measure, Menu, Merchant, Milk, Mousing, Muesli, Mullion, Nail, Nanaimo, Navigation, Nineteenth hole, No-go, Norman, Obstacle, Obstruct, Omerta, Onely, Orgue, Outer, Overslaugh, Oxygen, Parallel, Perch, Pile, Pinch, Pole, Posada, Prescription, Prevent, Private, Prohibit, Pub, Public, Putlog, Rack, Raddle, Rail, Ramrod, Rance, Randle-balk, Randle-perch, Randle-tree, Raw, Reach, Restrict, Rib, Risp, Rod, Roll, Roo, Rung, Saddle, Salad, Saloon, Sand, Sans, Save, Saving, Scroll, Semantron, Shaft, Shanty, Shet, Shut, Singles, Skewer, Slice, Slot, Snack, Snug, Soap, Spacer, Spar, Speakeasy, Sperre, Spina, Spit, Splinter, Spoke, Sprag, Stancher, Stanchion, Status, Stave, Stemmer, Sternson, Stick, Stirre, Stretcher, Stripe, Strut, Suspend, Sway, Swee, T, Tael, Tap(-room), Tapas, Taphouse, Task, Tavern(a), Temple, Tiki, Title, Toll, Tombolo, Tommy, Tool, Torsion, Tow, Trace, Trangle, Transom, Trapeze, Triblet, Trundle, Type, U-bolt, Vinculum, Wall, Ward, Wet, Whisker, Window, Wine, Wire, Wrecking, Z, Zed, Zygon

**Barabbas** Robber

**Barb(ed)** Bur(r), Cutter, Fluke, Harl, Herl, →**HOOK**, Jag(g), Jibe, Pheon, Prickle, Ramus, Tang, Thorn, Vexillum

**Barbados, Barbadian** Bajan, Bim(m)

**Barbara** Allen, Major

**Barbarian, Barbaric** Boor, Crude, Fifteen, Foreigner, Goth, Heathen, Hottentot, Hun, Inhuman, Lowbrow, Outlandish, Philistine, Rude, Savage, Tartar, Tatar(ic), Vandal

**Barbary** Ape, Roan

**Barbecue** Braai(vleis), Chargrill, Cook-out, Flame-grill, Grill, Hangi, Hibachi, Roast, Spit

**Barbel** Beard

**Barber** Epilate, Figaro, Hair, Scrape(r), Shaver, Strap, Todd, Tonsor, Trimmer

**Barbiturate** Goofball

**Bard(ic)** Ariosto, Druid, Gorsedd, Griot, Heine, Meat, Minstrel, Muse, Ossian, Ovate, Scald, Scop, Skald, Taliesin

**Bare, Bare-headed** Adamic, Aphyllous, Bald, Barren, Blank, Bodkin, Cere, Décolleté, Denude, Hush, Lewd, Marginal, Mere, Moon, →**NAKED**, Nude, Open, Plain, Scablands, Scant, Sear, Stark, Timber line, Topless, Uncase, Uncover, Unfurnished, Unpainted, Unveil

**Bareback** Godiva

**Barefoot** Discalced, Unshod

**Barely** At a pinch, At a stretch, Hand-to-mouth, Hardly, Just, Merely, Scarcely, Scrimp

**Bargain(ing)** Agreement, Bargoon, Barter, Bon marche, Braata, Chaffer, Champerty, →CHEAP, Cheapo, Collective, Compact, Compromise, Contract, Coup, Deal, Dicker, Distributive, Effort, Find, Go, Haggle, Higgle, Horse-trade, Huckster, Indent, Integrative, Negotiate, Option, →PACT, Plea, Productivity, Scoop, Snip, Steal, Supersaver, Time, Trade, Trock, Troke, Truck, Wanworth, Wheeler-dealing

**Barge** Birlinn, Bucentaur, Budgero(w), Butty, Casco, Elbow, Gabbard, Gabbart, Galley-foist, Gloriana, Hopper, Intrude, Jostle, Keel, Lighter, Nudge, Obtrude, Pra(a)m, Ram, Scow, →SHIP, Thrust, Trow, Wherry

▷ **Barge** *may indicate* an anagram

**Bargee, Bargeman** Hobbler, Keeler, Keelman, Legger, Lighterman, Ram, Trow

**Barium** Ba, Witherite

**Bark** Angostura, Ayelp, Azedarach, Bass, Bast, Bay, Bowwow, Calisaya, Cambium, Canella, Caribbee, Cascara, Cascara sagrada, Cascarilla, Cassia, China, Cinchona, Cinnamon, Cork, Cortex, Cusparia, Hack, Honduras, Jamaica, Jesuits', Kina, Kinakina, Latration, Liber, Mezereon, Mezereum, Myrica, Parchment, Peel, Pereira, Peruvian, Phloem, Quebracho, Quest, Quill, Quillai, Quina, Quinquina, Red, Rind, Sagrada, Salian, Sassafras, Scrape, Scurf, Shag, →SHIP, Skin, Slippery elm, Tan, Tap(p)a, Totaquine, Waff, Waugh, Winter's, Woof, Wow, Yaff, →YAP, Yellow, Yelp, Yip

**Bar-keep(er), Barmaid, Barman, Bartender** Advocate, Ale-wife, Barista, Bencher, Curate, Hebe, Luckie, Lucky, Portia, Tapster, Underskinker

**Barley (water)** Awn, Bear, Bere, Bigg, Hordeum, Malt, Orgeat, Pearl, Pot, Scotch, Truce, Tsamba

**Barm(y)** Yeast

**Barmecide, Barmecidal** Imaginary

**Barn** Bank, Byre, Cowshed, Dutch, Farm, Grange, Mow, Perchery, Skipper, Tithe

**Barnaby** Rudge

**Barnacle** Acorn, Cirriped(e), Cypris, Goose(neck), Limpet, Sticker

**Barometer** Aneroid, Glass, Orometer, Pierglass, Statoscope, Sympiesometer, Torricellian tube, Weatherglass

**Baron** B, Corvo, Drug, Magnate, Munchausen, Noble, Robber, Thyssen, Tycoon

**Baronet** Bart

**Baronne Dudevant** Sand

**Baroque** Fancy, Gothic, Ornate, Rococo

▷ **Baroque** *may indicate* an anagram

**Barrack(s), Barracking** Asteism, Boo, Cantonment, Casern(e), Cat-call, Garrison, Glasshouse, Heckle, Irony, Jeer, Quarters

**Barrage** Balloon, Boom, Broadside, Fusillade, Heat, Salvo, Shellfire

**Barred** Banned, Edh, Trabeculated

**Barrel** Bbl, Bl, Butt, Cade, Capstan, Cascabel, Cask, Chase, Clavie, Croze, Cylinder, Drum, Hogshead, Keg, Kibble, Morris-tube, Oak, Oildrum, Organ, Pièce, Pork, Run(d)let, Tan-vat, Thrall, Tierce, Tun, Vat, Water, Wood

**Barrel-organ** Apollonicon, Hurdy-gurdy, Street piano

**Barren** Addle, Arid, Badlands, Bleak, Blind, Blunt, Clear, Dry, Eild, →EMPTY, Farrow, Fruitless, Hardscrabble, Hi(r)stie, Jejune, Sterile, Unbearing, Unfruitful, Waste, Wasteland, Wilderness, Yeld, Yell

**Barrier** Baffle, Bail, Barrage, Barricade, Bayle, Block, Boom, Breakwater, Cauld, Checkrail, Cheval de frise, Chicane, Cordon (sanitaire), Crash, Crush, →DAM, Defence, Deterrent, Drawgate, Dyke, Fence, Floodgate, Fraise, Gate, Guard rail, Ha-ha, Handicap, Heat, Hedge, Hindrance, Hurdle, Mach, Obstruct, Pain, Paling, Potential, Rail(-fence), Rampart, Restraint, Revetment, Ring fence, Roadblock, Rope, Sandbag, Screen, Skreen, Sonic, Sound, Spina, Stockade, Thames, Thermal, Tollgate, Trade, Transonic, Traverse, Turnpike, Turnstile, Vapour, →WALL

**Barrister** Advocate, Attorney, Brief, Counsel, Devil, Lawyer, Recorder, Revising, Rumpole, Sergeant (at law), Serjeant(-at-law), Silk, SL, Templar, Utter

**Barrow** Applecart, Clyde, Dolly, Handcart, Henge, How, Hurley, Kurgan, Molehill, Mound, Pushcart, Tram, Trolley, Truck, Tumulus

**Barrow-boy** Coster, Trader

**Bar-tail** Scamel, Staniel, Stannel

**Barter** Chaffer, Chop, Coup, Dicker, → EXCHANGE, Haggle, Hawk, Niffer, Permutate, Sco(u)rse, Swap, → TRADE, Traffic, Truck

**Basalt** Diabase, Melaphyre, Tachylite, Tephrite, Toadstone, Trap(pean), Traprock, Wacke

**Base** Adenine, Aggregate, Air, Airhead, Alkali, Bag, Bed, Beggarly, Billon, Board, Bottom, Brest, Caitiff, Camp, Choline, Codon, Cytosine, Degenerate, Degraded, Diethyl, Dog, Down, E, Erinite, → ESTABLISH, First, Floor, Fond, Foot, Foothold, Footstall, Fort Knox, Found, Foundation, Fundus, Guanine, Harlot, Histamine, Hydroxide, Ignoble, Ignominious, Imidazole, Indamine, Infamous, Iniquitous, Install, Knowledge, La Spezia, Leuco, Lewis, Litmus, → LOW, → MEAN, Nefarious, Nook, Oasis®, Octal, Parasaniline, Partite, Patten, Platform, Plinth, Podium, Predella, Premise, Ptomaine, Purin(e), Pyrimidine, Pyrrolidine, Raca, Radix, Rascally, Ratty, Rests, Ribald, Root, Rosaniline, Roux, Rude, Scapa Flow, Schiff, Servile, Shameful, Shand, Sheeny, Snide, Socle, Soda, Sordid, Spaceport, Springing, Staddle, → STAND, Station, Substrate, Ten, Tetracid, Thymine, Torus, Triacid, Turpitude, Unworthy, Uracil, Vile

**Baseball** Apple, Nine, Twi-night

**Baseless** Idle, Invalid, Unfounded, Ungrounded

**Base-line** Datum

**Basement** Bargain, Below stairs, Cellar, Crypt

**Bash** Attempt, Belt, Bonk, Clout, Dint, Go, Hit, Rave, Shot, Slog, Strike, Swat, Swipe

**Bashful** Awed, Blate, Coy, Diffident, Modest, Prudish, Retiring, Shamefast, Sheep-faced, Sheepish, → SHY

**Basic(s), Basically, Basis** ABC, Abcee, Abecedarian, Alkaline, Aquamanale, Aquamanile, At bottom, At heart, Bare, Bedrock, Brass tacks, Cardinal, Crude, Elemental, → ESSENTIAL, Fiducial, Fond, Foundation, Fundamental, Ground(work), Gut, In essence, Integral, Intrinsic, Logic, Meat and potatoes, Need-to-know, Nitty-gritty, No-frills, No-nonsense, Nuts and bolts, One-horse, Ontology, Pou sto, Presumption, Primordial, Principle, Protoplasm, Radical, Rudimentary, Spit-and-sawdust, Staple, Substance, Substratum, Underlying, Unsophisticated, Uracil

**Basil** Pot-herb

**Basilica** St Peter's

**Basilisk** Cannon, Lizard

**Basin** Aquamanale, Aquamanile, Artesian, Aspergillum, Aspersorium, Benitier, Bidet, Bowl, Brazil, Canning, Catch, Catchment, Chott, Cirque, Corrie, Cwm, Dish, Dock, Doline, Donets, Drainage, Foxe, Geosyncline, Great, Impluvium, Kuzbass, Kuznetsk, Lavabo, Laver, Minas, Monteith, Ocean, Okavango, Pan, Park, Piscina, Playa, Porringer, Pudding, Reservoir, River, Scapa Flow, Sink, Slop(-bowl), Stoop, Stoup, Sugar, Tank, Tarim, Tidal, Washhand

**Bask** Apricate, Revel, Sun, Sunbathe, → WALLOW

**Basket, Basket-work** Baalam, Bass, Bassinet, Bread, Buck, Cabas, Calathus, Canasta, Canephorus, Car, Cesta, Chip, Cob, Coop, Corbeil(le), Corbicula, Corf, Creel, Cresset, Dosser, Fan, Flasket, Flax kit, Frail, Gabian, Goal, Hamper, Hask, Junket, Kago, Kajawah, Kipe, Kit, Kite, Leap, Litter, Maund, Mocock, Mocuck, Moses, Murlain, Murlan, Murlin, Osiery, Pannier, Ped, Petara, Pitara(h), Plate, Pollen, Pottle, Punnet, Rip, Round file, Scull, Scuttle, Seed-lip, Skep, Skull, Trolley, Trout, Trug, Van, Wagger-pagger(-bagger), Waste(-paper), Wattlework, Whisket, Wicker(-work), Will(e), Wisket, Work

**Basketball** Tip-off

**Basket-bearer** Canephor(a), Canephore, Canephorus

**Basket-maker** Alfa, Cane, Halfa, Wicker

**Basque** Biscayan, Bodice, Euskarian, Jacket
**Bass** Alberti, Ale, Alfie, B, Black, Continuo, Deep, Double, El-a-mi, Figured, Fish, Ground, Largemouth, Low, Ostinato, Serran, Smallmouth, String, Thorough, Walking
**Bassoon** Fagotto, Sausage
**Bast** Liber
**Bastard, Bastard-wing** Alula, Base, Basket, By-blow, Filius nullius, Git, Haram(za)da, Illegitimate, Mamzer, Misborn, Momzer, Mongrel, Sassaby, Side-slip, Slink, Sod, Spuriae, Spurious, Whoreson
▷ **Bastard** *may indicate* an anagram
**Baste** Enlard, Sew, Stitch, Tack
**Bastion** Citadel, Lunette, Moineau
**Bat(sman), Bat's wing, Batter, Batting, Batty** Aliped, Ames, Assail, Barbastelle, Baton, Belfry, Blink, Chiroptera, Close, Club, Cosh, Crackers, Crease, Cudgel, Dad, Die Fledermaus, Eyelid, False vampire, Flittermouse, Flutter, Flying fox, Fruit, Fungo, Grace, Hammerhead, Hatter, Haywire, Hit, Hobbs, Hook, Horseshoe, In, Ink mouse, Insectivorous, Kalong, Knock, Language, Lara, Leisler, Man, Mastiff, Maul, May, Mormops, Mouse-eared, Myopic, Nictate, Nictitate, Night, Nightwatchman, Noctilio, Nora, Nurdle, Opener, Paddle, Patagium, Pinch-hit, Pipistrel(le), Poke, Pummel, Rabbit, Racket, Racquet, Ram, Rearmouse, Reremice, Reremouse, Roussette, Ruin, Sauch, Saugh, Scorer, Scotch hand, Serotine, Sledge, Spectre, Stick, Stonewall, Straight, Striker, Swat, Switch hitter, Tail(ender), Trap-stick, Trunnion, Vampire, Vespertilionid, Viv, Whacky, Willow, Wood
**Batch** Bake, Bunch, Clutch, Crop, Tranche
**Bath(room), Bath-house** Aerotone, Aeson's, Aquae sulis, Bagnio, Bain-marie, Balneotherapy, Banya, Bed, Bidet, Blanket, Blood, Bubble, Caldarium, Cor, Dip, En suite, Epha, Foam, Hammam, Hip, Hummaum, Hummum, Jacuzzi®, Lav, Laver, Mik vah, Mud, Mustard, Oil, Oliver, Piscina, Plunge, Salt, Sauna, Shower, Sitz, Slipper, Soak, Spa, Sponge, Steam, Stew, Stop, Sudarium, Tepidarium, Therm, Tub, Turkish, Tye, Vapour, Whirlpool, Wife
**Bathe(r), Bathing** Archimedes, Balneal, Balneation, Balneology, Balneotherapy, Bay(e), Beath, Bogey, Bogie, Dip, Dook, Douk, Embay, Foment, Immerse, Lave, Lip, Skinny-dip, Souse, Splash, Stupe, → SWIM, Tub, → WASH
**Bathos** Anticlimax
**Bathrobe** Peignoir
**Batman** Valet
**Baton** Mace, Rod, Sceptre, Staff, Truncheon, Wand
**Batrachian** Frog, Toad
▷ **Bats, Batting** *may indicate* an anagram
**Battalion** Bn, Corps, Troop
**Batten** Bar, Dropper, Fasten, Tie
**Batter(ed)** Bombard, Bruise, Buffet, Decrepit, Pound, Thump
**Battery** Accumulator, Artillery, Button-cell, Cannonade, Drycell, Field, Galvanic, Heliac, Henhouse, Li(thium)-ion, Masked, Nicad, Nickel cadmium, NIMH, Penlight, Pra(a)m, Primary, Solar, Storage, Transducer, Troop, Voltaic, Waffle, Water
**Battle(s), Battleground** Action, Affair, Ben, Campaign, Clash, Cockpit, Combat, → CONFLICT, Darraign, Deraign, Encounter, Engagement, Field, → FIGHT, Fray, Front, Hosting, Joust, Maiden, Martian, Pitched, Royal, Running, Sarah, Sciamachy, Skiamachy, Spurs, Stoor, Stour, Stowre, Theatre, Theomachy, Wage, → WAR, Wargame

**BATTLES**

| 3 letters: | 4 letters: | Jena | Mons |
|---|---|---|---|
| Kut | Alma | Laon | Nile |
| Ulm | Chad | Lodi | Zama |
| | Ivry | Loos | |

**5 letters:**
Accra
Alamo
Allia
Arcot
Arras
Boyne
Bulge
Crecy
Ipsus
Issus
Lewes
Lissa
Marne
Mylae
Nancy
Parma
Pavia
Pydna
Sedan
Somme
Tours
Valmy
Ypres

**6 letters:**
Actium
Arbela
Arcola
Argyle
Arnhem
Barnet
Camlan
Cannae
Cressy
Crimea
Imphal
Kosovo
Lutzen
Maldon
Midway
Mohacs
Mycale
Naseby
Sadowa
Senlac
Shiloh
Tobruk
Towton
Varese
Verdun
Vigrid
Wagram
Wipers

**7 letters:**
Aboukir
Alamein
Almanza
Argonne
Bautzen
Beaches
Britain
Bull Run
Cambrai
Carrhae
Chalons
Colenso
Coronel
Corunna
Deorham
Dunkirk
Evesham
Flodden
Flowers
Glencoe
Iwo Jima
Jericho
Jutland
Legnano
Lepanto
Leuctra
Magenta
Marengo
Nations
Newbury
Nineveh
Okinawa
Orleans
Panipat
Picardy
Plassey
Plataea
Poltava
Pultowa
Salamis
Sempach
Vimelro
Vitoria
Warburg

**8 letters:**
Antietam
Ardennes
Ayacucho
Blenheim
Borodino
Bosworth
Chioggia

Clontarf
Culloden
Custozza
Edgehill
Erzurium
Flanders
Fontenay
Hastings
Hydaspes
Inkerman
Jemappes
Kulikova
Le Cateau
Lechfeld
Manassas
Marathon
Mehawand
Metaurus
Montreal
Naumachy
Navarino
Normandy
Omdurman
Palo Alto
Philippi
Poitiers
Ragnarok
Rossbach
Saratoga
Solomons
Spion Kop
St Albans
Syracuse
Talavera
Toulouse
Waterloo
Yorktown

**9 letters:**
Agincourt
Balaclava
Caporetto
Castilion
Chaeronea
El Alamein
Gallipoli
Ladysmith
Moerkirch
Nicopolis
Otterburn
Oudenarde
Pharsalus
Princeton
Ramillies

Sedgemoor
Solferino
St Vincent
The Saints
Trafalgar
Vercellae
Wandewash
Worcester

**10 letters:**
Adrianople
Armageddon
Austerlitz
Beneventum
Bennington
Brunanburh
Bunker Hill
Camperdown
Ferhbellin
Gettysburg
Lundy's Lane
Majuba Hill
Malplaquet
Mount Badon
Petersburg
Quatre Bras
River Plate
Shipka Pass
Stalingrad
Steenkerke
Tannenberg
Tewkesbury

**11 letters:**
Aegospotami
Aljubarrota
Armentières
Aubers Ridge
Bannockburn
Belleau Wood
Bismarck Sea
Chapultepec
Chattanooga
Hohenlinden
Marston Moor
Philiphaugh
Prestonpans
Rorke's Drift
Thermopylae
Wounded Knee

**12 letters:**
Flodden Field
Mons Graupius

| | | | |
|---|---|---|---|
| Monte Cassino | Little Bighorn | *14 letters:* | Plains of Abraham |
| Roncesvalles | Neuve-Chapelle | Castlebar Races | Teutoberger Wald |
| | Neville's Cross | Stamford Bridge | |
| *13 letters:* | Passchendaele | | *16 letters:* |
| Alcazar-Quivir | Spanish Armada | *15 letters:* | Las Navas de |
| Bosworth Field | | Missionary Ridge | Tolosa |

---

**Battle-axe** Amazon, Bill, Gorgon, Halberd, Ogress, Sparth(e), Termagant, Termagent, Turmagant, Turmagent

**Battlement** Barmkin, Crenellate, Merlon, Rampart

**Battle-order** Phalanx

**Battleship** Carrier, Destroyer, Dreadnought, Gunboat, Man-o'-war, Pocket, Potemkin, Repulse

**Bauble** Bagatelle, Gaud, Gewgaw, Trifle

**Bauhaus** Gropius

**Baulk** Demur, Gib, Hen, Impede, Jib, Reest, Reist, Shy, Thwart

**Bavardage** Fadaise

**Bawd(y)** Hare, Raunchy, Risque, Sculdudd(e)ry, Skulduddery

**Bawl** Bellow, Gollar, Howl, Weep

**Bay** Ab(o)ukir, Aere, Arm, Baffin, Bantry, Bark, Bell, Bengal, Bez, Bight, Biscay, Bonny, Botany, Broken, Brown, Byron, Cape Cod, Cardigan, Chesapeake, Cienfuegos, Classis, Cleveland, Colwyn, Corpus Christi, Cove, Covelet, Creek, Cubicle, Daphne, Delagoa, Delaware, Discovery, Dublin, Dundalk, Dvina, False, Famagusta, Fleet, Freshwater, Frobisher, Fundy, Galway, Gdansk, Georgian, Gibraltar, Glace, Golden, Great Australian Bight, Green, Guanabara, Guantanamo, Gulf, Hangzhou, Harbour, Hawke's, Herne, Hervey, Horse, →**HOWL**, Hudson, Inhambane, Inlet, Ise, Islands, James, Jervis, Jiazhou, Kavalla, Kuskokwim, Laura, Laurel, Layby, Loading, Lobito, Loblolly, Lutzow-Holm, MA, Magdalena, Manila, Massachusetts, Montego, Moreton, Narragansett, New York, Niche, Oleander, Omaha, Oriel, Passamaquoddy, Pegasus, Pigs, Plenty, Plymouth, Port Phillip, Poverty, Recess, Red, Roan, St Austell, St Michel, San Francisco, San Pedro, Santiago, Scene, Setubal, Shark, Sick, Sligo, Stall, Suvla, Swansea, Table, Tampa, Tasman, The Wash, Thunder, Tor, Toyama, Tralee, Trincomalee, Ungava, Vae, Vigo, Vlore, Voe, Vyborg, Waff, Walfish, Walvis, Wash, Whitley, Wick, Yowl

**Bayonet** Jab, Skewer, Stab, Sword

**Bazaar** Alcaiceria, Emporium, Fair, Fete, Market, Pantechnicon, Sale, Sook, Souk

**BBC** Auntie

**Be** Exist, Live, Occur

**Beach(head)** Anzio, Bikini, Bondi, Chesil, Coast, Daytona, Ground, Hard, Lido, Littoral, Machair, Miami, Myrtle, Omaha, Palm, Plage, Raised, Sand, Sea-coast, Seashore, Seaside, Shingle, Shore(line), Storm, Strand, Waikiki

**Beachcomber** Arenaria

**Beachwear** Thong

**Beacon** Belisha, Brecon, Fanal, Landing, Lantern, Lighthouse, Lightship, Need-fire, Pharos, Racon, Radar, Radio, Robot, Signal

**Bead(s), Beaded** Adderstone, Aggri, Aggry, Astragal, Baily's, Ballotini, Bauble, Blob, Bugle, Cabling, Chaplet, Crab's-eyes, Crab-stones, Dewdrop, Drop, Droplet, Gadroon, Gaud, Job's tears, Kumbaloi, Love, Mala, Moniliform, Nurl, Ojime, Passament, Passement, Paternoster, Poppet, Poppit, Prayer, Rosary, Sabha, St Cuthbert's, Se(a)wan, Spacer, Spacer plate, Subha, Sweat, Taktite, Tasbih, Tear, Wampum(peag), Worry

**Beadle** Apparitor, Bederal, Bedral, Bumble, Herald, Paritor, Shammash, Shammes, Verger

**Beagle** Snoopy, Spy

**Beak** AMA, Bailie, Bill, Cad, Cere, Coronoid, Egg-tooth, Gar, JP, Kip(p), Magistrate, Master, Metagnathous, Mittimus, Nasute, Neb, Nose, Pecker, Prow, Ram, Rectal, Rostellum, Rostrum, Shovel

**Beaker** Bell, Cup, Goblet, Mug
**Beakless** Erostrate
**Beak-shaped** Coracoid
**Beam(ing)** Arbor, Balance, Ba(u)lk, Bar, Binder, Boom, Bowstring, Box, Breastsummer, Bressummer, Broadcast, Bum(p)kin, Cantilever, Carline, Carling, Cathead, Collar, Crossbar, Crosshead, Crosspiece, Deck, Effulge, Electron, Girder, Grin, Hammer, Hatch, Herisson, Holophote, I, Irradiate, Joist, Ke(e)lson, Landing, Laser, Lentel, Lintel, Manteltree, Maser, Molecular, Moonlight, Needle, Outrigger, Particle, Pencil, Principal, Proton, Purlin, Putlock, Putlog, Radiant, Radio, → **RAFTER**, → **RAY**, Rayon, Refulgent, Rident, Ridgepole, Rood, Roof-tree, Sandwich, Scale, Scantling, Sealed, Searchlight, Shaft, Shine, Shore, Sleeper, Smile, Soffit, Solive, Spar, Stanchion, Stemson, Sternpost, Sternson, Straining, Streamer, Stringer, Stringpiece, Summer, Sunlight, Support, Tailing, Tie, Timber, Trabeate, Trabecula, Transom, Trave, Trimmer, Truss, Universal, Viga, Walking, Weigh-bauk, Yard, Yardarm
**Beamish** Galumphing, Nephew
**Bean** Abrus, Adsuki, Aduki, Adzuki, Arabica, Asparagus pea, Baked, Berry, Black, Black-eye, Borlotti, Broad, Bush, Butter, Cacao, Calabar, Castor, Cluster, Cocoa, Coffee, Cow-pea, Dwarf, Edamame, Fabaceous, Fava, Flageolet, French, Frijol(e), Garbanzo, Goa, Gram, Green, Haricot, Harmala, Head, Horse, Hyacinth, Jack, Jelly, Jequirity, Jumping, Kachang putch, Kidney, Lablab, Legume, Lentil, Lima, Locust, Molucca, Moong, Moth, Mung, Nelumbo, Nib, Noddle, Ordeal, Pichurim, Pinto, Pulse, Runner, St Ignatius's, Scarlet, Scarlet runner, Shell, Silverskin, Snap, Snuffbox, Soy(a), String, Sugar, Sword, Tepary, Tonga, Tonka, Tonquin, Urd, Wax, Winged, Yard-long
**Beanfeast** → **PARTY**, Spree, Wayzgoose
**Bear(er), Bear lover** Abide, Abrooke, Andean, Arctic, Arctophile, Aurora, Baloo, Balu, Barley, Beer, Bigg, Breed, Brook, Brown, Bruin, Brunt, → **CARRY**, Cave, Churl, Cinnamon, Coati-mondi, Coati-mundi, Cub, Demean, Dree, Ean, → **ENDURE**, Engender, Exert, Fur-seal, Gest(e), Gonfalonier, Great, Grizzly, Hack, Ham(m)al, Harbinger, Have, Hod, Hold, Honey, Humf, Hump(h), Jampanee, Jampani, Keb, Kinkajou, Koala, Kodiak, Koolah, Lioncel(le), Lionel, Lug, Mother, Nandi, Nanook, Owe, Paddington, Panda, Pertain, Polar, Pooh, Produce, Rac(c)oon, Roller, Rupert, Russia, Sackerson, Seller, Shoulder, Sit, Sloth, Spectacled, Stand, Stay, Stomach, → **SUFFER**, Sun, Sunbear, Sustain, Targeteer, Teddy, Teem, Thole, Throw, Tolerate, Tote, Transport, Undergo, Upstay, Ursine, Water, Whelp, White, Wield, Withstand, Wombat, Woolly, Yean, Yield, Yogi
**Bearberry** Manzanita, Uva-ursi
**Beard(ed)** Aaron, Alfalfa, Anchor, Arista, Assyrian, Aureole, Awn, Balaclava, Barb, Barbiche, Beaver, Belgrave, Cadiz, Cathedral, Charley, Charlie, Confront, Defy, Ducktail, Escort, Face, Five o'clock shadow, Forked, Fungus, Goatee, Hair(ie), Hairy, Hear(ie), Imperial, Jewish, Kesh, Lincolnesque, Mephistopheles, Newgate frill, Newgate fringe, Old Dutch, Olympian, Outface, Peak, Pencil, Raleigh, Rivet, Roman T, Screw, Shenandoah, Spade, Stibble, Stiletto, Stubble, Swallowtail, Tackle, Tile, Trojan, Tuft, Uncle Sam, Vandyke, Whiskerando, Whiskery, Ziff
**Beardless** Callow, Clean, Tahr, Tehr
▷ **Bearhug** *may indicate* Teddy or similar around a word
**Bearing(s)** Air, Allure, Amenaunce, Armorial, Aspect, Azimuth, Babbitt, Ball, Behaviour, Billet, Bush, Carriage, Deportment, Direction, E, Endurance, Gait, Germane, Gest, Gudgeon, Hatchment, Haviour, Heading, → **HERALDIC**, Hugger-mugger, Lioncel(le), Lionel, Manner, Martlet, Mascle, Middy, Mien, N, Needle, Nor, Pall, Pheon, Port, Presence, Reference, Relevant, Roller, S, Seme(e), Subordinary, Teeming, Tenue, Thrust, W, Yielding
▷ **Bearing** *may indicate* compass points
**Beast(ly)** → **ANIMAL**, Arna, Behemoth, Brute, Caliban, Caribou, Chimera, → **CREATURE**, Dieb, Dragon, Dzeren, Fatstock, Gargoyle, Gayal, Genet, Godzilla, Grampus, Hippogriff, Hodog, Hog, Hydra, Hy(a)ena, Jumart, Kinkajou, Lion, Mammoth, Marmot, Mastodon,

Mhorr, Monoceros, Narwhal, Ogre, Oliphant, Opinicus, Oryx, Panda, Potto, Quagga,
Queen's, Rac(c)oon, Rhytina, Rother, Rumptifusel, Sassaby, Steer, Sumpter, Swinish,
Tarand, Teg, Theroid, Triceratops, Triton, Wart-hog, Whangam, Yahoo, Yak, Yale, Zizel

**Beat(ing), Beaten, Beater** Anoint, Arsis, Athrob, Bandy, Bang, Baste, Bastinado,
Batter, Battue, Battuta, Beetle, Belabour, Belt, Bepat, Best, Blatter, Bless, Bo Diddley,
Bubble, Cadence, Cane, Cat, Chastise, Clobber, Club, Clump, Cob, Conquer, Cream,
Cudgel, Cuff, Curry, Debel, → DEFEAT, Ding, Donder, Dress, Drub, Drum, Duff up, Dunt,
Elude, Excel, Fatigue, Faze, Feague, Feeze, Fibbed, Firk, Flagellate, Flail, Flam, Flap,
Float, Flog, Floor, Flush, Fly, Fustigate, Hammer, Hiding, Hipster, Hollow, Horsewhip,
Ictus, Inteneration, Jole, Joll, Joule, Jowl, Knock, Knubble, Lace, Laidie, Laidy,
Lambast(e), Larrup, Lash, Lather, Latin, Laveer, Lay, Lick, Lilt, Lounder, Mall, Malleate,
Manor, Mell, Mersey, Mullah, Muller, Nubble, Onceover, Outclass, Outdo, Outflank,
Outshine, Outstrip, Outstroke, Overwhelm, Paik, Palpitate, Pandy, Paradiddle, Pash,
Paste, Pelt, Pip, Ploat, Pommel, Pound, Prat, Pug, Pulsate, Pulsatile, Pulse, Pulsedge,
Pummel, Pun, Quop, Raddle, Ram, Ratten, Resolve, Retreat, Rhythm, Ribroast, Rope's
end, Round, Rout, Rowstow, Ruff(le), Scourge, Scutch, Slat, Slipper, Smight, Smite,
Soak, Sock, Sort, Strap, Strap-oil, Strike, Surpass, Swinge, Swingle, Syncopation, Systole,
Taber, Tabor, Tabrere, Tachycardia, Tact, Tala, Tan, Tattoo, Thesis, Thrash, Thresh,
Throb, Thud, Thump, Thwack, Tick, Time, Tired, Top, Torture, Tricrotic, Trounce,
Tuck, Tund, Verberate, Vibrate, Wallop, Wappend, Weary, Welt, Wham, Whip, Whisk,
Whitewash, Whup, Wraught, Ybet, Yerk, Yirk

▷ **Beaten-up** *may indicate* an anagram

**Beat it** Skedaddle, Vamo(o)se

**Beatitude** Macarism

**Beau** Admirer, Blade, Brummel, Cat, Damoiseau, Dandy, Flame, Geste, Lair, Lover,
Masher, Nash, Spark, Suitor, Tibbs

**Beaufort** Scale, Windscale

**Beaut(y), Beautiful, Beautify** Advantage, Angelic, Astrid, Bathing, Belle, Bellibone,
Bombshell, Bonny, Bright, Camberwell, Charmer, Colleen, Comeliness, Comely, Corker,
Cracker, Dish, Doll, Embellish, Enhance, Exquisite, Eye candy, Eyeful, Fair, Fairness,
Fine, Glamour (puss), Glorious, Glory, Gorgeous, Grace, Helen, Houri, Hyperion,
Junoesque, Kanta, Lana, Looks, Monism, Ornament, Peri, Picture, Pink, Pride,
Pulchritude, Purler, Radiant, Scenic, Sheen, Smasher(oo), Smicker, Specious, Stunner,
Sublime, To kalon

**Beautician** Glamoriser

**Beauty spot** Patch, Tempe, Tika

**Beaver** Beard, Castor, Eager, Grind, Mountain, Oregon, Rodent, Sewellel

**Because (of)** As, Forasmuch, Forwhy, Hence, In (that), Inasmuch, Ipso facto, Sens, Since

**Beckon** Gesture, Nod, Summons, Waft, Wave, Wheft

**Become, Becoming** Apt, Besort, Decent, Decorous, Dignified, Enter, Fall, Fit, Flatter,
Get, Go, Grow, Happen, Occur, Seemly, Suit, Wax, Worth

**Bed(s), Bedding, Bedstead** Air, Allotment, Amenity, Apple-pie, Arroyo, Bacteria, Base,
Bassinet, → BEDCOVER, Berth, Border, Bottom, Bottomset, Box, Bundle, Bunk, Caliche,
Camp, Capillary, Carrycot, Channel, Charpoy, Cill, Cot(t), Couch(ette), Counterpane,
Couvade, Coverlet, Cradle, Crib, Cross, Cul(t)ch, Day, Divan, Doona, Doss, Duvet, Erf,
False, Feather, Filter, Flock, Fluidized, Flying, Form, Four-poster, Futon, Gault, Greensand,
Hammock, Inlay, Kago, Kang, Kingsize, Kip, Knot, Knot garden, Lay(er), Lazy, Lilo®,
Linen, Litter, Marriage, Mat, Matrix, Mattress, Mosquito net, Murphy, Naked, Nap, Nest,
Nookie, Oyster, Pad, Paillasse, Pallet, Palliasse, Pan, Parterre, Passage, Patch, Pavement,
Pay, Pig, Pit, Plank, Plant, Plot, Procrustean, Puff, Queensize, Quilt, Retire, River,
Rollaway, Roost, Rota, Sack, Scalp, Settle, Shakedown, Sill, Sitter, Sleep, Sofa, Spawning,
Standing, Stratum, Stretcher, Sun, T(h)alweg, Tanning, Test, The downy, Thill, Trough,
Truckle, Trundle, Twin, Wadi, Wady, Ware, Water, Wealden, Wedding

**Bedaub** Cake, Deck, Smear

**Bed-bug** B, B flat, Chinch, Flea, Louse, Vermin

**Bedchamber, Bedroom** Boudoir, Bower, Br, Chamber, Cubicle, Dorm(itory), Dormer, Dorter, Ruelle, Ward

**Bedcover** Palampore, Palempore, Puff

**Bedeck** Adonise, Adorn, Array, Festoon

▷ **Bedevilled** *may indicate* an anagram

**Bedjacket** Nightingale

**Bedlam** Asylum, Chaos, Furore, Madness, Nuthouse, Tumult, Uproar

**Bed-rest** Dutch-wife

**Bedrock** Costean

**Bedsit** Pad

**Bedwetting** Enuresis

**Bee** Afrikanised, Athenia, Bike, Bumble, Carpenter, Cuckoo, Deborah, Debra, Deseret, Dog, Drone, Drumbledor, Dumbledore, Group, Hiver, Honey, Humble, Husking, Killer, King, Lapidary, Leaf-cutter, Mason, Melissa, Mining, Nurse, Pollinator, Queen, Quilting, Raising, Solitary, Spell, Spell-down, Spelling, Swarm, Trixie, Worker, Working

**Beech** Antarctic, Copper, Fagus, Hornbeam, Mast, Taw(h)ai, Tree

**Bee-eater** Merops, Rainbow-bird

**Beef(y)** Aitchbone, Baron, Bleat, Brawny, Bresaola, Bull(y), Bullock, Carp, Carpaccio, Charqui, Chateaubriand, Chuck, Clod, Complain, Corned, Filet mignon, Flank, Gripe, Groan, Grouch, Grouse, Hough, Jerk, Keema, Kobe, Liebig, Mart, Mice, Moan, Mousepiece, Muscle, Neat, Ox, Pastrami, Peeve, Plate, Porterhouse, Rother, Salt-horse, Salt-junk, Sauerbraten, Sey, Shin, Silverside, Sirloin, Stolid, Stroganoff, Topside, Tournedos, Tranche, Undercut, Vaccine, Wagyu, Wellington, Whine

**Beefeater** Billman, Exon, Gin, Oxpecker, Warder, Yeoman

**Bee-glue** Propolis

**Beehive** Alveary, Apiary, Ball, Dioptric, Gum, Skep

**Beekeeping** Apiculture

**Beelzebub** Devil

**Been** Bin

**Beer** Ale, Alegar, Amber fluid, Amber liquid, Bantu, Barley sandwich, Bitter, Black, Bock, Chaser, Coldie, Draught, Drink, Dry, Entire, Export, Gill, Ginger, Granny, Grog, Guest, Heavy, Herb, Home-brew, Kaffir, Keg, Kvass, Lager, Lambic, Lite, Lush, Malt, March, Middy, Mild, Milk stout, Mum, Near, Nog, October, Pils(e)ner, Pint, Pony, Porter, Real, Real ale, Rice, Root, Round, Saki, Scoobs, Sherbet, Six-pack, Skeechan, Slip, Small, Spruce, Stingo, Stout, Stubby, Suds, Swankie, Swanky, Swats, Swipes, Switchel, Table, Taplash, Tinnie, Tipper, Tshwala, Tube, Turps, Wallop, Wheat, Zythum

**Beer garden** Brasserie

**Bee's nest** Bink

**Beet** Blite, Chard, Fat-hen, Goosefoot, Mangel(wurzel), Seakale, Silver, Spinach, Sugar

**Beethoven** WoO

**Beetle** Ambrosia, Anobiid, Argos tortoise, Asiatic, Bacon, Bark, Batler, Bee, Blister, Bloody-nosed, Boll weevil, Bombardier, Bruchid, Bug, Bum-clock, Buprestidae, Buprestus, Burying, Bustle, Buzzard-clock, Cabinet, Cadelle, Cane, Cantharis, Carabid, Cardinal, Carpet, Carrion, Chafer, Christmas, Churchyard, Cicindela, Click, Clock, Cockchafer, Cockroach, Coleoptera, Coleopterous, Colorado, Coprophagan, Curculio, Darkling, Deathwatch, Dermestid, Devil's coach-horse, Diamond, Diving, Dor(r), Dor-fly, Dumbledore, Dung, Dyticus, Dytiscus, Elater, Elmbark, Elytron, Elytrum, Firefly, Flea, Furniture, Glow-worm, Gold(smith), Goliath, Gregor, Ground, Hammer, Hangover, Hercules, Hop-flea, Hornbug, Huhu, Humbuzz, Impend, Japanese, Jewel, June, Khapra, Ladybird, Ladybug, Lamellicorn, Larder, Leaf, Leather, Longhorned, Longicorn, Mall(et), Maul, May-bug, Meloid, Minotaur, Museum, Musk, Oakpruner, Oil, Overhang, Pill, Pinchbuck, Pine, Pine-chafer, Potato, Project, Protrude, Race(-bug), Rhinoceros, Rhynchophora, Roach, Rosechafer, Rove, Sacred, Saw palmetto, Scamper, Scarab(ee), Scavenger, Scolytus, Scurry, Sexton, Shard,

Skelter, Sledge(-hammer), Snapping, Snout, Soldier, Spanish fly, Spider, Spring, Squirr, Stag, Tenebrio, Tiger, Toktokkie, Tortoise, Tumble-bug, Tumble-dung, Turnip-flea, Typographer, Vedalia, VW, Water, Weevil, Whew, Whirligig, Wireworm, Woodborer, Wood-engraver

**Beetle-crushers** Cops

**Befall** Happen, Occur

**Before(hand)** A, Advance, Already, An, Ante, Avant, By, Coram, Earlier, Early, Ere, Erst(while), First, →**FORMER**, Or (e'er), Parava(u)nt, Pre, Previously, Prior, Pro, Sooner, Till, To, Until, Van, Zeroth

**Before food** Ac

**Befriend** Assist, Cotton, Fraternise, Support

**Befuddle(ment)** Bemuse, Dwaal, Inebriate, Stupefy

**Beg(gar), Beggarly, Begging** Abr(ah)am-man, Ask, Badgeman, Beseech, Besognio, Bey, Bezonian, Blighter, Blue-gown, Cadge, Calendar, Clapper-dudgeon, Crave, Down and outer, →**ENTREAT**, Exoration, Flagitate, Fleech, Gaberlunzie, Gangrel, Hallan-shaker, Implore, Impoverish, Irus, Jarkman, Lackall, Lazar(us), Lazzarone, Limitary, Lumpenproletariat, Maund, Mendicant, Montem, Mooch, Mouch, Mump, Niggardly, Obtest, Palliard, Panhandle, Pauper, Penelophon, Penniless, →**PLEAD**, Pled, Pray, Prig, Procreate, Prog, Ptochocracy, Rag, Randie, Randy, Ruffler, Ruin(ate), Sadhu, Schnorr(er), Screeve, Scrounge, Shool(e), Skelder, Skell, Solicit, Standpad, Sue, Suppliant, Supplicate, Thig(ger), Toe-rag, Touch, Undo, Uprightman, Whipjack

**Beget** Gender, Kind, Procreate

**Beggar rule** Ptochocracy

**Begging bowl** Clackdish, Clapdish

**Begin(ner), Beginning** Ab initio, Ab ovo, Alpha, Alphabetarian, Author, B, Babyhood, Black, Cause, Che(e)chako, Clapdash, Commence, Daw, Dawn, Deb, Debut, Embryo, Enter, Exordium, Fall-to, Fledgling, Found, Fountainhead, Genesis, Germ, Get at, Go, Greenhorn, Inaugural, Inception, Inchoate, Incipient, Incipit, Initial, Initiate, Intro, Johnny-raw, L, Launch, Lead, Learn, Learner, Logos, Nascent, Neophyte, Noob, →**NOVICE**, Oncome, Onset, Ope(n), Ord, →**ORIGIN**, Outbreak, Outset, Pose, Prelim(inary), Presidium, Primer, Rookie, Seed, Set, Set forth, Shoot, →**START**, Startup, Strike up, Takeoff, Tenderfoot, Threshold, Tiro, To-fall, Tyro(ne), Yearn

**Begone** Aroint, Aroynt, Avaunt, Scram, Shoo, Vamo(o)se

**Begonia** Elephant's-ear(s)

**Begorrah** Bedad, Musha

**Begrudge** Envy, Resent

**Beguile(r), Beguiled** Amuse, Bewitch, Charm, Coax, Distract, Divert, Enchant, Ensnare, Entice, Eprise, Flatter, Gull, Intrigue, Jack-a-lantern, Tice, Trick, Wile

**Behalf** Ex parte, For, Part, Sake

**Behave(d), Behaviour, Behaving** Abear, Accepted, Acquired, Act, Appeasement, Attitude, Carriage, Conduct, Consummatory, Convenance, Decorum, Demean, Deportment, Do, Effrontery, Epimeletic, Etepimeletic, Ethics, Ethology, Form, Freak out, Goings-on, Guise, Horme, Life style, →**MANNER**, Meme, Nature, Netiquette, Noblesse oblige, Obey, Orientation, Practice, Praxeology, Quit, React, Response, Ruly, Satisficing, Strong meat, Tribalism, Unreasonable

**Behead** Decapitate, Decollate, Guillotine

**Behind(hand)** Abaft, Aft(er), Ahent, Ahind, Ahint, Apoop, Arear, Arere, Arrear, Arse, Astern, Backside, Beneath, Bottom, Bum, Buttocks, Can, Croup, Derrière, Fud, Fundus, Late, Overdue, Post, Prat, →**REAR**, Rump, Slow, Tardy, Tushie

**Behold(en)** Affine, Ecce, Eye, Grateful, Here's, Indebted, La, Lo, Look, Observe, See, View, Voilà

**Beige** Buff, Greige, Neutral, Suede, Tan

**Being** Cratur, Creature, Critter, Ens, Entia, Entity, Esse, Essence, Existence, Human, Man, Metaphysics, Mode, Nature, Omneity, Ontology, Organism, →**PERSON**, Saul, Soul, Subsistent, Substance, Supreme, Ubiety, Wight

**Bejabers** Arrah
**Bejewel** Enchase, Stud
**Belated** Hindsight
**Belch** Boak, Boke, Brash, Burp, Emit, Eruct, Erupt, Rift, Spew, Toby, Yex
**Belcher** Foulard, Handkerchief, Hanky, Toby
**Beldam(e)** Crone, Hag, Harridan, Scold
**Belfry** Campanile, Tower
**Belgian** Flemish, Walloon
**Belief, Believe, Believed, Believer, Believing** Accept, Accredit, Adam and Eve,
  Anata, Ativism, Bigot, Buy, Capernaite, Catechism, Chiliasm, Christian, Conviction,
  Creationism, Credence, Credit, Creed, Cult, Culture, Deem, Deist, Di(o)physite,
  Doctrine, Doxastic, Doxy, Dukkha, Dyophysite, Evangelical, Faith, Formulism, Gnostic,
  Guess, Heresy, Heterodoxy, Hold, Holist, Idea, Ideology, Idolater, Imagine, Islam,
  Ism, Latitudinarian, Lore, Ludism, Manichaeism, Mechanist, Meme, Messianist,
  Methink, Monotheist, Mysticism, Notion, Opine, →OPINION, Orthopraxy, Ovist,
  Pacifism, Pantheism, Pelagianism, Persuasion, Physicism, Pluralism, Postmillenarian,
  Presumption, Rasta, Religion, Reputed, Revelationist, S(h)aivism, Second Coming,
  Secularism, Seeing, Shema, Solfidian, Solipsism, Superstition, Supremacist, Suspect,
  Swallow, Tenet, Test, Tetratheism, Thanatism, Theist, Theosophy, Think, Threap,
  Threep, Traducianism, Transcendentalism, Trinitarian, Triphysite, Trow, Trust,
  Ubiquitarianism, Umma(h), Unitarian, Universalism, Wear, Ween, Wis(t)
**Belittle** Cheapen, Cry down, Decry, Demean, Depreciate, Derogate, Detract, Diminish,
  Discredit, Disparage, Downgrade, Humble, Pooh-pooh, Slight
**Bell(s)** Acton, Agogo, Angelus, Ben, Big Ben, Bob, Bow, Bronte, Cachecope, Canterbury,
  Carillon, Chime, Chinese pavilion, Clanger, Crotal, Curfew, Currer, Daisy, Diving,
  Division, Ellis, Gong, Grandsire, Inventor, Jar, Knell, Liberty, Low, Lutine, Market, Mass,
  Minute, Mort, Muffin, Pancake, Passing, Pavilion, Peal, Peter, Pinger, Pudding, Ring,
  Roar, Sacring, Sanctus, Shark, Sleigh, Tailor, Tantony, Tenor, Tent, Tintinnabulum,
  Tocsin, Toll, Tom, Triple, Tubular, Vair, Vaire, Verr(e)y, Vesper, Wind
**Belladonna** Nightshade
**Bell-bird** Arapunga, Campanero
**Belle** Bathing, Beauty, Brighton, Starr, Toast, Venus
**Bell-founder** Belleter
**Bellicose, Belligerence, Belligerent** Chippy, Combatant, Gung-ho, Hostile, Ire,
  Jingoist, Martial, Militant, Truculent, Warmonger
**Bellow(s)** Buller, Holla, Holler, Moo, Rant, Rave, Roar, Rout, Saul, Thunder, Troat,
  Tromp(e), Trumpet, Windbag
**Bell-ringer, Bell-ringing** Bob, Campanology, Changes, Clapper, Course, Grandsire,
  Handstroke, Hunting, Maximus, Quasimodo, Rope, Sally, Tintinnabulation, Tocsin, Toller
**Belly** Abdomen, Alvine, Bag, Beer, Beer-gut, Boep, Bunt, Calipee, Celiac, Coeliac, Gut, Kite,
  Kyte, Paunch, Pod, →STOMACH, Swell, Tum(my), Venter, Wame, Weamb, Wem(b), Womb
**Belong, Belonging(s)** Appertain, Apply, Appurtenant, Chattels, Effects, Incident,
  Inhere, Intrinsic, Our, Paraphernalia, Pertain, →PROPERTY, Relate, Roots, Things, Traps
**Beloved** Acushla, Alder-lief(est), Amy, Boyfriend, David, Dear, Doy, Esme, Inamorata,
  Joy, Leve, Lief, Loor, Morna, Pet, Popular, Precious
**Below** Beneath, Inf(erior), Infra, Nether, Sub, Subjacent, Under, Unneath
**Belt(ed)** Baldric(k), Band, Bandoleer, Bandolier, Baudric(k), Bible, Black, Cartridge,
  Chastity, Cholera, Clitellum, Clobber, Clock, Clout, Commuter, Conveyor, Copper,
  Cotton, Crios, Demolition, Equator, Fan, Flog, Fold and thrust, Galvanic, Garter, Gird(le),
  Girt, Great, Green, Hip, Hydraulic, Inertial, Judoka, Kuiper, Lap, Larrup, Life, Lonsdale,
  Mitre, Money, Muesli, Orion's, Orogenic, Polt, Pound, Radiation, Roller, Roll-on, Rust,
  Safety, Sahel, Sam Browne, Sanitary, Sash, Seat, Slug, Speed, Stockbroker, Storm, Strap,
  Stratosphere, Sun, Surcingle, Suspender, Swipe, Sword, Taiga, Tawse, Tear, Thump,
  Tore, Tract, Van Allen, Wampum, Wanty, Webbing, Wing, Zodiac, Zone, Zonulet, Zoster

**Belt up** Sh

**Belvedere** Gazebo, Mirador

**Bemoan** →LAMENT, Mourn, Rue, Sigh, Wail

**Bemuse** Infatuate, Stonn(e), Stun, Stupefy, Throw

**Ben** Battle, Craig, Hur, Jonson, Mountain, Nevis, Spence

**Bench** Banc, Banker, Bink, Bleachers, Counter, Court, Cross, Exedra, Form, Front, King's, Knifeboard, Magistrates, Opposition, Optical, Pew, Queen's, Rout seat, Rusbank, →SEAT, Settle, Siege, Stillage, Thoft, Thwart, Treasury, Trestle, Widow's

**Benchmark** Criteria, Standard, Yardstick

**Bend(er), Bending, Bends** Angle, Arc, Arch, Articular, Becket, Bight, Binge, Bow, Buck(le), Bust, Camber, Carrick, Chicane, Circumflect, Contort, Corner, Crank(le), Crimp, Cringe, →CROOK, Crouch, Curl, Curve, Diffraction, Dog-leg, Double up, Elbow, Engouled, Epinasty, Es(s), Expansion, Falcate, Fawn, Flex(ural), Flexion, Flexure, Fold, Geller, Geniculate, Genu, Genuflect, Grecian, Hairpin, Hinge, Hook, Horseshoe, Hunch, Incline, Inflect, Jag, Kink, Knee(cap), Kneel, Knot, Kowtow, Meander, Mould, Nutant, Orgy, Ox-bow, Pitch, Plash, Pliant, Plié, Ply, Recline, Reflex, Retorsion, Retortion, Retroflex, Riband, S, Sag, Scarp, Sheet, Souse, Spree, Spring, Stave, Stoop, Swan-neck, Trend, Twist, U, Ups(e)y, Uri, Wale, Warp, →YIELD, Z

▷ **Bendy** *may indicate* an anagram

**Beneath** Below, Sub, Under, Unworthy

**Benedict(ine)** Black Monk, Cluniac, Cluny, Dom, Eggs, Maurist, Olivetan, OSB, Tironensian, Tyronensian

**Benediction** Ben(t)sh, Blessing, God-speed

**Benefactor, Benefactress** Angel, Backer, Barmecide, Carnegie, Donor, Fairy Godmother, Maecenas, →PATRON, Philanthropist, Promoter

**Beneficial, Beneficiary, Benefit, Benefice, Beneficent** Advantage, →AID, Alms, Ameliorate, Asset, Avail, Behalf, Behoof, Behove, Bespeak, Bonus, Boon, Boot, Charity, Collature, Commendam, Commensal, Conferee, Devisee, Disablement, Dole, Donee, Endorsee, Enjoy, Enure, FIS, For, Fringe, Fund-raiser, Gain, Grandisonian, Grantee, Healthful, Housing, Incapacity, Incumbent, Inheritor, Injury, Interest, Inure, Invalidity, Legal aid, Living, Manna, Maternity, Ménage, Mileage, Neckverse, Pay, Perk, Perquisite, Plenarty, Plus, Portioner, Postulate, Prebend, Profit, Sake, Salutary, Sanative, Serve, Service, Sickness, Sinecure, Spin-off, Stipend, Supplementary, Symbiotic, Trickle down, UB40, Unalist, Unemployment, Use, Usufruct, Va(u)ntage, Well-being, Wholesome, Wonderful, Workfare

**Benevolence, Benevolent** Charitable, Clement, Dobbie, Dobby, Goodwill, Humanitarian, Kind, Liberal, Nis(se), Pecksniffian, Philanthropy, Pickwickian, Sprite

**Bengali** Oriya

**Benighted** Ignorant

**Benign** Affable, Altruistic, Gracious, Innocuous, Kindly, Trinal

**Benin** DY

**Benito** Duce, Mussolini

**Benjamin** Franklin

**Bennett** Alan, Phil

**Bent** Akimbo, Bowed, Brae, Concave, Coudé, Counterfeit, Courb, Criminal, Crooked, Curb, Determined, Dorsiflex, Falcate, Fiorin, Flair, Geniculate, Habit, Heath, Inclination, Ingenium, Intent, Inverted, Leant, Out, Peccant, Penchant, Ply, Predisposition, Reclinate, Redtop, Round-shouldered, Scoliotic, Stooped, Swayed, Talent, Taste, Twisted

▷ **Bent** *may indicate* an anagram

**Bent grass** Fiorin, Redtop

**Bentham** Utilitarian

**Benzine** Kinone, Phene, Toluene, Toluol

**Bequeath, Bequest** Bestow, Chantr(e)y, Demise, Endow, Heirloom, →LEAVE, Legacy, Mortification, Pass down, Pittance, Testament, Transmit, Will

**Berate(d)** Censure, Chastise, Chide, Jaw, Reproach, Scold, Shent, Slate, Vilify

**Berber** Almoravide, Kabyle, Moor, Rif(i), Riff, Shluh, Tuareg
**Bereave(d), Bereavement** Deprive, Loss, Mourning, Orb, Sorrow, Strip, Widow
**Beret** Green
**Berg** Alban, Floe, Kopje
**Berk** Clot
**Bermuda** Shorts
**Bernard** Levin, Shaw
**Bernini** Baroque
**Berry** Acai, Allspice, Bacca, Blackcurrant, Cow, Cubeb, Fruit, Goji, Goosegog, Haw, Hound's, Konini, Miracle, Mistletoe, Pea, Pepo, Peppercorn, Persian, Pigeon, Pimento, Poke, Pottage, Quinsy, Raccoon, Rhein, Rhine, Rowan, Sal(l)al, Salmonberry, Slae, Sloe, Snow, Sop, Sun, Tay, Tomatillo, Winter, Wolf
**Berserk** Amok, Ape-shit, Baresark, Frantic, Frenzy, Gungho, Rage
**Berth** Anchorage, Bunk, Cabin, Couchette, Dock, Marina, Moor, Seat, Space
**Beryl** Aquamarine, Emerald, Heliodor, Morganite, Silica
**Beryllium** Be
**Beseech** Beg, Crave, Entreat, Implore, Invoke, Obsecrate
**Beset** Amidst, Assail, Assiege, Badger, Bego, Embattled, Environ, Harry, Obsess, Perplex, Scabrid, Siege
**Beside(s)** Adjacent, Alone, And, At, Au reste, By, Else, Forby(e), Further(more), Moreover, Next, On, To, Withal, Yet
**Besiege(d)** Beset, Best(ed), Blockade, Gherao, Girt, Invest, Obsess, Plague, Poliorcetic, Surround
▷ **Besiege** *may indicate* one word around another
**Besmirch(ed)** Bloody, Bludie, Smear, Soil, Spoil, Sully
**Besom** Cow, Kow
**Besot(ted)** Dotard, Infatuate, Intoxicate, Lovesick, Smitten, Stupefy
**Bespangle** Adorn, Gem
**Bespeak, Bespoken** Address, Bee, Beta, Engage, Hint
**Best** A1, Ace, All-time, Aristocrat, Beat, Bonzer, Cap, Cat's whiskers, Champ(ion), Choice, Conquer, Cream, Creme, Damnedest, Defeat, Deluxe, Elite, Every, Eximious, Finest, First, Flagship, Flower, Foremost, Greatest, Highlight, Ideal, Nicest, Optima, Outdo, Outwit, Overcome, Peak, Peerless, Pick, Pièce de résistance, Pink, Plum, Purler, Quintessence, Ream, Sunday, Super, Supreme, The, The tops, Tiptop, Top (flight), Topper, Transcend, Ultimate, Utopian, Vanquish, Wale, World-class
**Bestial** Atrocious
**Bestiality** Zoophalia
**Bestiary** Physiologus
**Best man** Paranymph
**Bestow(al)** Accord, Bequeath, Confer, Donate, Endow, → **GIVE**, Grant, Impart, Investiture, Present
**Bestride** Cross
**Bet(ting), Betting System** Accumulator, A cheval, Ante, Antepost, Back, Banco, Banker, Chance, Daily double, Dice, Double, Each way, Fixed odds, Flutter, Gaff, Gamble, Go, Hedge, Impone, Lay, Long shot, Martingale, Mise, Note, Pari-mutuel, Parlay, Perfecta, Pip, Place, Pot, Punt, Quadrella, Quinella, Ring, Risk, Roll up, Roulette, Saver, Set, SP, Spec, Sport, Spread, Stake, Superfecta, Take, Tattersalls, Tatts, Totalisator, Totalise, Tote, Treble, Treble chance, Triella, Trifecta, → **WAGER**, Win, Yankee
**Betel** Catechu, Paan, Pan, Pawn, Siri(h)
**Betimes** Anon, Early, Soon
**Betise** Solecism
**Betoken** Portend
**Betray(al), Betrayed, Betrayer** Abandon, Abuse, Belewe, Bewray, Breach, Cornuto, Cuckold, Desert, Disclose, Divulge, Dob, Dobbin, Double-cross, Gethsemane, Giveaway,

Grass, Judas, Proditor, Renegade, Renege, Rumble, Sell, Sellout, Shop, Sing, Sinon, Split on, Stab, Telltale, Traditor, Trahison, Traitor, Treachery, Treason, Turncoat

**Betroth(ed), Betrothal** Affiance, Affy, Assure, Engage, Ensure, Espouse, Fiancé(e), Handfasting, Pledge, Promise, Sponsalia, Subarr(h)ation

**Better** Abler, Ameliorate, Amend, Apter, Bigger, Buck, Cap, Comparative, Convalescent, Cured, Edify, Fairer, Finer, Gambler, Gamester, Imponent, Improve, Layer, Master, Meliorate, Mend, Mitigate, Outdo, Outpeer, Outpoint, Outshine, Outsmart, Outstrip, Outwit, Piker, Preponderate, Punter, Race-goer, Reform, Score off, Superior, Surpass, Throw, Top, Turfite, Work, Worst

**Between** Amid, Bet, Betwixt, Inter, Interjacent, Linking, Mesne, Twixt

**Bevel** Angle, Cant, Chamfer, Oblique, Slope, Splay

**Beverage** Ale, Cocoa, Coffee, Cordial, Cup, →**DRINK**, Hydromel, Mobbie, Mobby, Nectar, Tea

**Bevy** Flock, Group, Herd, Host

**Beware** Cave, Fore, Heed, Look out, Mind, Mistrust, Pas op, Tut

**Bewilder(ed), Bewildering, Bewilderment** Amaze, Astound, At sea, Baffle, Buffalo, Confound, Confuse, Consternation, Daze, Distract, Flummox, Mate, Maze, Mind-boggling, Mystify, Obfuscate, Perplex, Stun, Taivert, Tutulbay, Wander, Will, Wull

**Bewitch(ed), Bewitching** Charm, Delight, Elf-shot, Enchant, Ensorcell, Enthral, Glam(orous), Hex, Hoodoo, Hypnotise, Jinx, Obeah, Obiah, Sirenise, Strike

**Beyond** Above, Ayont, Besides, Farther, Outwith, Over, Past, Thule, Trans, Ulterior, Ultra

**Bezique** Royal marriage

**Bias(ed)** Angle, Aslant, Bent, Chauvinism, Colour, Discriminatory, Forward, Grid, Imbalance, Loaded, One-sided, Partial, Parti pris, Partisan, Penchant, Preconception, Predilection, →**PREJUDICE**, Prepossess, Set, Sexism, Skew, Slant, Slope, Spin, Tendency, Unjust, Warp

**Bib, Bibulous** Apron, Beery, Feeder, Pout, Tope, Tucker

**Bibelot** Objet d'art

**Bible, Biblical** Adulterous, Alcoran, Alkoran, Antilegomena, Apocrypha, ASV, Authority, AV, Avesta, Bamberg, Book, Breeches, Bug, Coverdale, Cranmer, Cromwell, Douai, Douay, Family, Ferrara, Fool, Forgotten sins, Gemara, Geneva, Gideon, Good book, Goose, Gospel, Gutenberg, Haggada, Hagiographa, Helachah, Heptateuch, Hermeneutic, Hexapla, Hexateuch, Holy, Idle, Isagogic, Itala, Italic, King James (version), Leda, Matthew Parker, Mazarin(e), Midrash, Missal, Murderer, New English, NT, Omasum, Ostrog, OT, Pentateuch, Peshito, Peshitta, Peshitto, Polyglot, Psalter, Revised Version, RSV, RV, Scriptures, Septuagint, Stomach, Talmud, Tanach, Tantra, Targum, Taverner, Taverners, Text, Thirty-six-line, Treacle, Tyndale, Unrighteous, Vinegar, Vulgate, Whig, Wicked, Wife-hater, Wyclif(fe), Zurich

**Biblical scholar** Rechabite, USPG, Wycliffe

**Bibliophagist, Bibliophile** Bookworm

**Bicarb** Saleratus

**Bicker(ing)** Argue, Bowl, Brawl, Coggie, Dispute, Spat, Tiff, Wrangle

**Bi-coloured** Dichroism

**Bicycle, Bike(r)** All-terrain, Bambi, Bee, Bone-shaker, Chopper, Coaster, Crog(gy), Dandy-horse, Dirt, Draisene, Draisine, Exercise, Fixed-wheel, Hell's angels, Hobby, Hobbyhorse, Kangaroo, Mixte, Moped, Mount, Mountain, Multicycle, Ordinary, Pedal, Penny-farthing, Quad, Racer, Raleigh®, Recumbent, Roadster, Rocker, Safety, Scooter, Ski-bob, Solo, Spin, Stationary, Swarm, Tandem, Trail, Tree, UCI, Velocipede

**Bid(der), Bidding (system)** Abundance, Acol, Apply, Blackwood, Call, Canape, Command, Contract, Cue, Declare, Double, Forcing, Gone, Hostile, INT, Invite, Jump, Misère, Nod, NT, →**OFFER**, Order, Pass, →**PRE-EMPT(IVE)**, Proposal, Psychic, Puffer, Redouble, Rescue, Shut-out, Summon, Take-out, Take-over, Tell, Tender, Vied, White bonnet

**Biddy** Crone, Gaimmer, Hen

**Biennial** Trieteric

**Bier** Hearse, Litter

**Bifurcate** Fork

**Big** Altruistic, Beamy, Bulky, Bumper, Burly, Capacious, Cob, Corpulent, Enormous, Fat, Ginormous, Gross, →**LARGE**, Loud, Mansize, Massive, Mighty, Obese, Roomy, Skookum, Slockdoliger, Slockdologer, Soc(k)dologer, Sogdolager, Sogdoliger, Stonker, Strapping, Substantial, Swopper, Thumping, Tidy, Vast, Whacker, Whopper

**Bigamy, Bigamist, Bigamous** Bluebeard, Diandrous

**Bighead(ed)** Besserwisser, Ego, Uppity

**Bight** Canterbury, Great Australian, Heligoland, Karamea, South Taranaki

**Bigmouth** Boaster

**Bigot(ed)** Chauvinist, Dogmatist, Fanatic, Hide-bound, Intolerant, Narrow-minded, Racialist, Racist, Redneck, Sexist, Wowser, Zealot

**Bigshot, Bigwig** Cheese, Law lord, Nib, Nob, Oner, Oneyer, Oneyre, Swell, Titan, Toff, →**VIP**

**Bijou** Doll-like

▶ **Bike** *see* **BICYCLE**

**Bikini** Atoll, Tanga

**Bile, Bilious(ness)** Cholaemia, Choler, Gall, Icteric, Melancholy, Scholaemia, Venom, Yellow

**Bilge** Leak, Pump, Rhubarb, Rot, Waste

**Bilingual** Diglot

**Bilious** Irascible

**Bilk** Default

**Bill(ed), Billy** Ac(c), Accommodation, Accompt, Account, Act, Ad, Addition, Allonge, Appropriation, Barnacle, Beak, Becke, Budd, Buffalo, Bunter, Can, Caress, Carte, Charge, Cheque, Chit(ty), Cody, Coo, Coronoid, Cross(-bencher), Debt, Demand, Dixy, Docket, Double, Due, Egg-tooth, Enabling, Exactment, Fee, Fin, Finance, Foreign, Gates, Goat, Hybrid, Inland, Invoice, Kaiser, →**LAW**, Lawin(g), Legislation, Liam, Liar, Line-up, List, Measure, Menu, Nail, Neb, Ness, Nib, →**NOTE**, Notice, Paper, Petition, Platypus, Police, Pork barrel, Portland, Poster, Private, Programme, Pruning, Public, Puffing, Reckoning, Reform, Remanet, Rhamphotheca, Rostral, Rostrum, Score, Selsey, Short, Shot, Show, Sickle, Silly, Sparth(e), Sperthe, Spoon, Sticker, Tab, Tariff, Tenner, Tenuirostral, Tomium, Trade, Treasury, True, Twin, Victualling, Watch, Willy

**Billet** Berth, Casern, Cess, Chit, Coupon, Note, Quarter

**Billet doux** Capon, Valentine

**Billiards, Billiards player, Billiards stroke** Bar, Cannon-game, Cueist, Jenny, Lagging, Long jenny, Massé, Nursery cannon, Pills, Pocket, Pool, Potter, Pyramids, Short jenny, Snooker, String, Whitechapel

**Billion** Gillion, Milliard, Tera

**Bill of sale** Bs

**Billow** Roil, Roller, Rule, Surge, Swell, Wave

▶ **Billy** *see* **BILL(ED)**

**Bimbo** Twinkle

**Bin** Bing, Box, Chilly, Container, Crib, Crock, Discard, Dump, Hell, Litter, Loony, Receptacle, Sin, Snake-pit, Stall, Throw away, Wagger-pagger, Wheelie, Wheely

**Binary** ASCII, Contact, Semidetached

**Bind(er), Binding** Adherent, Adhesive, Akedah, Alligate, Apprentice, Astrict, Astringent, Bale, Bandage, Bandeau, Bandster, Bias, Bibliopegist, Boyer, Brail, Burst, Calf, Cement, Cerlox®, Chain, Cinch, Circuit, Clamp, Colligate, Complain, Cord, Cramp-iron, Cummerbund, Dam, Deligation, De Vigneaud, Drag, Edge, Embale, Enchain, Engage, Enslave, Enwind, →**FASTEN**, Fetter, Final, Galloon, Gird, Girdle, Grolier, Half-calf, Half-leather, Haworth, Hay-wire, Hold, Hole, Hopkins, Incumbent, Indenture, Iron, Keckle, Krebs, Lash(er), Law-calf, Leash, Ligament, Ligature, Mail, Marl, Marry, Martin, Meyerhof, Morocco, Muslin, Obi, Obligate, Oblige, Oop, Organdie, Oup, Parpen,

Paste grain, Perfect, Pinion, Porter, Quarter, Raffia, Red Tape, Restrict, Ring, →**ROPE**, Roxburghe, Seize, Sheaf, Spiral, Strap, Stringent, Stygian, Swathe, Syndesis, Tape, Tether, Thirl, Thong, Three-quarter, Tie, Tree-calf, Truss, Twine, Unsewn, Valid, Whip, Withe, Yapp, Yerk, Yoke

**Bindweed**  Bearbine, Convolvulus, With(y)wind

**Bing**  Crosby, Go, Heap

**Binge, Binging**  Bat, Beano, Bend(er), Blind, Carouse, Dipsomania, →**DRINK**, Drinking-bout, Engorge, Gorge, Party, Pig out, Riot, Soak, Souse, Splore, Spree, Toot, Tout

**Bingo**  Beano, Housey-housey, Keno, Lotto, Tombola

**Binocular(s)**  Glasses, Jumelle, OO, Stereoscope

**Biochemical, Biochemist(ry)**  Ames, Boyer, Chain, Dam, De Vigneaud, DNA, Haworth, Hopkins, Krebs, Martin, Meyerhof, Porter, Proteomics

**Biographer, Biography**  Boswell, CV, Hagiography, History, Life, Memoir, Plutarch, Potted, Profile, Prosopography, Strachey, Suetonius, Vita

**Biology, Biologist**  Algology, Berg, Bordet, Carrel, Cladistics, Cohen, Dawkins, Delbruck, Genetics, Haller, Kendrew, Kinsey, Mendel, Molecular, Morphology, Phenetics, Photodynamics, Shatten, Somatology, Stoechiology, Stoich(e)iology, Taxonomy, Teratology, Transgenics, Weismann

**Bionomics**  Ecology

**Bioscope**  Kinema

**Biped**  Man, Yahoo

**Birch**  Betula, Birk, Cane, Cow, Flog, Hazel, Kow, Larch, Larrup, Reis, Rice, Rod, Silver, Swish, Thrash, Twig, Weeping, Whip, White, Withe

**Bird(s)**  Al(l)erion, Altricial, Aves, Avian, Bertram, Brood, Damsel, Dawn chorus, Doll, Early, Flier, Fowl, Gal, →**GIRL**, Grip, Hen, Jail, Layer, Left, Limicoline, Nestling, Ornis, Ornithology, Pecker, Pen, Perching, Poultry, Praecoces, Prison, Quod, Raptor, Rare, Roaster, Sentence, Sis, Skirt, Stretch, Time, Visitant, Warbler

---

## BIRDS

| 2 letters: | Roc | Gnow | Monk |
|---|---|---|---|
| Ka | Ruc | Guan | Myna |
| Oi | Tit | Guga | Nene |
| | Tui | Gull | Otis |
| 3 letters: | | Hawk | Pavo |
| Ani | 4 letters: | Hern | Pawn |
| Auk | Barb | Huia | Pern |
| Boo | Chat | Huma | Piet |
| Cob | Cirl | Ibis | Pink |
| Emu | Cobb | Iynx | Pown |
| Fum | Cock | Jynx | Pyat |
| Jay | Coly | Kagu | Pyot |
| Kae | Coot | Kaka | Rail |
| Kea | Crax | Kite | Rhea |
| Mag | Crow | Kiwi | Roch |
| Maw | Dodo | Knot | Rook |
| Mew | Dove | Koel | Ruff |
| Moa | →DUCK | Kora | Ruru |
| Nun | Emeu | Lark | Rype |
| Owl | Erne | Loom | Shag |
| Pea | Eyas | Loon | Skua |
| Pie | Fung | Lory | Smee |
| Ree | Gled | Mina | Sora |

Swan
Taha
Tara
Teal
Tern
Tick
Tody
Tuli
Weka
Wren
Xema
Yale
Yite

**5 letters:**
Agami
Ardea
Ariel
Bennu
Booby
Bosun
Buteo
Cahow
Capon
Colin
Colly
Crake
Crane
Diver
Eagle
Egret
Eider
Finch
Fleet
Friar
Galah
Glede
Goose
Goura
Grebe
Heron
Hobby
Homer
Isaac
Junco
Kawau
Kight
Liver
Lowan
Macaw
Madge
Manch
Mavis
Merle

Mimus
Mohua
Monal
Murre
Mynah
Nandu
Nelly
Noddy
Ousel
Ox-eye
Peggy
Pekan
Pewit
Picus
Pilot
Piper
Pipit
Pitta
Poaka
Poker
Potoo
Prion
Quail
Quest
Quist
Raven
Reeve
Robin
Rotch
Ryper
Saker
Satin
Scape
Scart
Scaup
Scops
Scray
Scrub
Serin
Shama
Sitta
Skart
Snipe
Solan
Soree
Spink
Sprug
Squab
Stare
Stilt
Stint
Stork
Swift
Sylph

Terek
Tewit
Topaz
Twite
Umber
Umbre
Urubu
Veery
Vireo
Wader
Whaup
Widow
Wonga
Yaffa

**6 letters:**
Aquila
Avocet
Avoset
Bantam
Barbet
Bishop
Bittor
Bittur
Bonxie
Boubou
Brolga
Bulbul
Caille
Canary
Chough
Chukar
Condor
Corbie
Coucal
Cuckoo
Curlew
Cushat
Darter
Dikkop
Dipper
Drongo
Duiker
Dunlin
Duyker
Elanet
Evejar
Falcon
Fulmar
Gambet
Gander
Gannet
Garuda
Gentle

Gentoo
Go-away
Godwit
Gooney
Goslet
Grakle
Grouse
Hagden
Hagdon
Haglet
Hermit
Hoopoe
Houdan
Jabiru
Jacana
Jaeger
Jubjub
Kakapo
Kotare
Kotuku
Lanner
Leipoa
Linnet
Lintie
Locust
Loerie
Loriot
Lourie
Lungie
Magpie
Martin
Matata
Menura
Merlin
Merops
Missel
Mistle
Monaul
Mopoke
Mossie
Motmot
Musket
Mutton
Nandoo
Nhandu
Oriole
Oscine
Osprey
Oxbird
Parrot
Parson
Pavone
Peahen
Peeper

Peewee
Peewit
Pernis
Petrel
Phoebe
Pigeon
Piopio
Plover
Pouter
Progne
Puffin
Pukeko
Pullet
Queest
Quelea
Quoist
Redcap
Redleg
Reeler
Roller
Rotche
Scamel
Scarth
Scaury
Scoter
Scraye
Sea-cob
Sea-mew
Seapie
Shrike
Simara
Simorg
Simurg
Siskin
Skarth
Smeath
Smeeth
Soland
Sorage
Strich
Sultan
Sylvia
Tailor
Takahe
Tarcel
Tassel
Tewhit
Thrush
Tom-tit
Toucan
Towhee
Trogon
Turaco
Turbit

Turkey
Tyrant
Tystie
Verdin
Walker
Waxeye
Weaver
Whidah
Whydah
Willet
Woosel
Yaffle
Ynambu
Yucker
Zoozoo

**7 letters:**
Amokura
Anhinga
Antbird
Apteryx
Axebird
Babbler
Bécasse
Bee-kite
Bittern
Bittour
Bluecap
Blue-eye
Blue jay
Bluetit
Boobook
Bullbat
Bunting
Buphaga
Bush-tit
Bustard
Buzzard
Cacique
Cariama
Cheeper
Chewink
Chicken
Coal-tit
Cole-tit
Colibri
Corella
Cotinga
Courlan
Courser
Cow-bird
Creeper
Crombec
Cropper

Diamond
Dinorus
Dottrel
Dovekie
Dunnock
Emu-wren
Estrich
Fantail
Fern-owl
Figbird
Finfoot
Flicker
Frigate
Gleerie
Gobbler
Goburra
Gorcrow
Goshawk
Grackle
Grallae
Grey jay
Hacklet
Hadedah
Hagbolt
Hagdown
Halcyon
Harrier
Hemipod
Hoatzin
Horn owl
Humming
Ice-bird
Jacamar
Jackdaw
Kahawai
Kamichi
Kestrel
Killdee
Kinglet
Koekoea
Lapwing
Leghorn
Limpkin
Manakin
Marabou
Martlet
Mesites
Minivet
Moorhen
Mudlark
Oilbird
Ortolan
Oscines
Ostrich

Oven-tit
Pandion
Peacock
Peafowl
Pelican
Penguin
Phoenix
Pickmaw
Piculet
Pinnock
Pintado
Pintail
Pochard
Pockard
Poe-bird
Poussin
Poy-bird
Quetzal
Rainbow
Rasores
Ratitae
Redpoll
Redwing
Regulus
Rooster
Rosella
Rotchie
Ruddock
Sakeret
Sawbill
Scooper
Scourie
Sea-dove
Seaduck
Seagull
Sea-lark
Sea-mell
Seriema
Simurgh
Sirgang
Sitella
Skimmer
Skylark
Snow-cap
Spadger
Sparrow
Squacco
Staniel
Stinker
Sturnus
Sunbird
Swallow
Tanager
Tanagra

Tarrock
Tattler
Teacher
Teuchat
Tiercel
Tinamou
Titanis
Titlark
Titling
Tokahea
Totanus
Touraco
Tumbler
Tweeter
Vulture
Vulturn
Wagtail
Waxbill
Waxwing
Whooper
Widgeon
Wimbrel
Witwall
Woosell
Wren-tit
Wrybill
Wryneck
Yang-win

**8 letters:**

Aasvogel
Accentor
Adjutant
Aigrette
Alcatras
Altrices
Amadavat
Aquiline
Araponga
Arapunga
Arenaria
Avadavat
Barnacle
Bateleur
Bee-eater
Bellbird
Blackcap
Bluebird
Blue-wing
Boatbill
Boattail
Bobolink
Bob-white
Buln-buln

Caracara
Cardinal
Cargoose
Cheewink
Chirn-owl
Cockatoo
Cockerel
Coquette
Curassow
Dabchick
Didapper
Dip-chick
Dobchick
Dotterel
Estridge
Fauvette
Fernbird
Fish-hawk
Flamingo
Gambetta
Gang-gang
Garefowl
Garganey
Gnatwren
Greenlet
Grosbeak
Guacharo
Hackbolt
Hangbird
Hangnest
Hawfinch
Hazelhen
Heath-hen
Hemipode
Hernshaw
Hickwall
Hoactzin
Hornbill
Killdeer
Kingbird
King crow
Kiskadee
Landrail
Lanneret
Laverock
Longspur
Lorikeet
Lyrebird
Macaroni
Magotpie
Man-of-war
Marabout
Marsh-tit
Megapode

Mire-drum
Miromiro
Moorcock
Moorfowl
Morepork
Murrelet
Nightjar
Notornis
Nuthatch
Ovenbird
Oxpecker
Paradise
Parakeet
Peesweep
Peetweet
Percolin
Petchary
Phaethon
Pheasant
Philomel
Pihoihoi
Podargus
Poorwill
Prunella
Puffbird
Quarrian
Quarrion
Rainbird
Rallidae
Redshank
Redstart
Reedling
Reed-wren
Rice-bird
Ring-dove
Ringtail
Riroriro
Rocketer
Rock-lark
Rose-comb
Sandlark
Sandpeep
Scolopar
Screamer
Sea-eagle
Shake-bag
Shelduck
Shoebill
Shoveler
Silktail
Sittella
Skua-gull
Snowbird
Snowy owl

Stanniel
Starling
Struthio
Surfbird
Swiftlet
Tantalus
Tapacolo
Tapaculo
Teru-tero
Thrasher
Thresher
Throstle
Tickbird
Ticklace
Titmouse
Tom-noddy
Toucanet
Tragopan
Trembler
Troopial
Troupial
Tubenose
Umbrella
Umbrette
Waldropp
Water-hen
Wheatear
Whimbrel
Whinchat
Whipbird
Whitecap
White-eye
Wildfowl
Wirebird
Woodchat
Woodcock
Woodlark
Woodwale
Wood wren
Xanthura
Yoldring
Zopilote

**9 letters:**

Accipiter
Aepyornis
Albatross
Aylesbury
Bald eagle
Baldicoot
Baltimore
Beccaccia
Beccafico
Beefeater

Bergander
Blackbird
Blackhead
Blackpoll
Blood bird
Bower-bird
Brambling
Broadbill
Bullfinch
Campanero
Cassowary
Chaffinch
Chatterer
Chickadee
Coachwhip
Cockatiel
Cormorant
Corncrake
Crocodile
Cross-bill
Currawong
Dove prion
Dowitcher
Eider duck
Estreldid
Fieldfare
Fig-pecker
Fire-crest
Fledgling
Francolin
Friarbird
Frogmouth
Gallinule
Gerfalcon
Gier-eagle
Goldcrest
Goldfinch
Goosander
Grassquit
Grenadier
Guillemot
Hammerkop
Happy Jack
Helldiver
Heronshaw
Hornywink
Icteridae
Impundulu
Jack-snipe
Kittiwake
Lintwhite
Little auk
Little owl
Mallemuck

Merganser
Mistletoe
Mollymawk
Mousebird
Night-hawk
Nutjobber
Nutpecker
Olive-back
Organ-bird
Ossifraga
Ossifrage
Owl-parrot
Paddy bird
Pardalote
Partridge
Peaseweep
Peregrine
Phalarope
Pictarnie
Pine finch
Porphyrio
Ptarmigan
Razorbill
Redbreast
Red siskin
Riflebird
Rosy-finch
Sabrewing
Salangane
Sandpiper
Sapsucker
Satinbird
Scansores
Sea-turtle
Secretary
Sedge-wren
Seedeater
Sheldrake
Shoveller
Silver eye
Skunk-bird
Solitaire
Sooty tern
Spoonbill
Standgale
Stonechat
Stormbird
Storm-cock
Sugarbird
Swart-back
Sword-bill
Talegalla
Thickhead
Thick-knee

Thornbill
Tiercelet
Trochilus
Trumpeter
Turnstone
Volucrine
Water cock
Waterfowl
Water-rail
Willowtit
Wind-hover
Woodshock
Woodspite
Xanthoura

**10 letters:**
Aberdevine
Arctic tern
Bananaquit
Bearded tit
Bluebreast
Bluethroat
Brain-fever
Bubbly-jock
Budgerigar
Butter-bump
Cape pigeon
Chiff-chaff
Crested tit
Demoiselle
Dickcissel
Didunculus
Dive-dapper
Dollarbird
Dung-hunter
Ember-goose
Eyas-musket
Fallow-chat
Fly-catcher
Four o'clock
Fringillid
Goatsucker
Gobemouche
Gooney-bird
Grassfinch
Greenfinch
Greenshank
Guinea fowl
Hen-harrier
Herald-duck
Honey-eater
Honey guide
Hooded crow
Kingfisher

Kookaburra
Locust-bird
Mallee fowl
Marsh-robin
Meadowlark
Night-churr
Night heron
Noisy miner
Nutcracker
Peckerwood
Pettichaps
Pettychaps
Pick-cheese
Pratincole
Quaker-bird
Racket-tail
Rafter-bird
Rain-plover
Ramphastos
Regent-bird
Rhinoceros
Roadrunner
Ruby-throat
Saddleback
Saddlebill
Sanderling
Sandgrouse
Sea swallow
Shearwater
Sheathbill
Sicklebill
Silverbill
Silver gull
Snowy egret
Spatchcock
Stone-snipe
Sun bittern
Tanagridae
Tropicbird
Turtledove
Wattlebird
Weasel coot
Weaver bird
Whisky-jack
Whisky-john
Wonga-wonga
Woodpecker
Woodpigeon
Wood shrike
Wood thrush
Yaffingale
Yellowbird
Yellowhead
Yellowlegs

Yellowyite

Scissorbill
Scissortail

**11 letters:**
Apostlebird
Bokmakierie
Bristlebird
Butcherbird
Canada goose
Cape sparrow
Carrion crow
Cooper's hawk
Coppersmith
Fallow-finch
Fringilline
Gnatcatcher
Gobe-mouches
Golden eagle
Grallatores
Happy-family
Honey-sucker
House martin
Humming-bird
Ichthyornis
Java sparrow
Leatherhead
Little grebe
Mockingbird
Moor-buzzard
Moss-bluiter
Moss-cheeper
Nightingale
Pied wagtail
Plantcutter
Purple finch
Pyrrhuloxia
Reed bunting
Reed-sparrow
Reed-warbler

Snowbunting
Sparrow-hawk
Stilt-plover
Stone-curlew
Stormpetrel
Stymphalian
Swallowtail
Thunderbird
Tree-creeper
Tree-sparrow
Wall creeper
Water-thrush
Weaver-finch
Whitethroat
Wishtonwish
Woodcreeper
Woodswallow
Woodwarbler
Yellow-ammer

**12 letters:**
Bronze-pigeon
Collared dove
Drongo-cuckoo
Drongo-shrike
Flowerpecker
Hedge-warbler
Honey creeper
Missel-thrush
Mosquito-hawk
Peppershrike
Ring-dotterel
Sage-thrasher
Sandwich tern
Sedge-warbler
Serpent-eater

Spotted crake
Standard-wing
Stonechatter
Stormy petrel
Tangle-picker
Throstle-cock
Water-wagtail
Whippoorwill
Willy wagtail
Yellow-hammer
Yellowthroat
Yellow-yowley

**13 letters:**
Archaeopteryx
Babblingbrook
Bermuda petrel
Cetti's warbler
Chaparral cock
Cock-of-the-rock
Indigo bunting
Mocking thrush
Owlet nightjar
Oyster-catcher
Pintado petrel
Pipiwharauroa
Plantain-eater
Turkey buzzard
Whistling duck
Willow-wagtail
Willow warbler
Wilson's petrel

**14 letters:**
Manx shearwater
Pied Flycatcher
Tawny frogmouth
Welcome swallow

Woodchat shrike

**15 letters:**
Baltimore oriole
Chipping sparrow
Chuck-will's-widow
Green woodpecker
Montagu's harrier
Purple gallinule
Rainbow lorikeet
Rough-legged hawk

**16 letters:**
Loggerhead shrike
Roseate spoonbill
Tyrant flycatcher
White-fronted tern

**17 letters:**
Pectoral sandpiper
Spotted flycatcher

**18 letters:**
Paradise flycatcher
Rough-legged
   buzzard

**19 letters:**
White-crowned
   sparrow

**20 letters:**
Mother Carey's
   chickens
Rose-breasted
   grosbeak

---

▷ **Bird** *may indicate* a prison sentence
**Bird-catcher** Avicularia, Fowler, Papageno
**Bird-like** Hirundine, Sturnine
**Bird's nest(ing)** Caliology, Monotropa, Soup
**Bird-watcher** Augur, Twitcher
**Birkenhead** F.E.Smith
**Birmingham** Brum(magem)
**Birth** Burden, Congenital, Delivery, Drop, Extraction, Genesis, Geniture, Happy event,
   Jataka, Lineage, Multiple, Nativity, Natural, Origin, Parage, Parity, Parthenogenesis,
   Parturition, Virgin, Water, Whelp(ing)
**Birthday** Anniversary, Genethliac, Prophet's
**Birthmark** Blemish, Mole, Mother-spot, Naevus, Port wine stain, Stigmata, Strawberry
**Birthright** Heritage, Mess, Patrimony
**Birthwort** Aristolochia
**Bis** Again, Anew

**Biscuit** Abernethy, Amaretto, Bake, Bath-oliver, Biscotto, Bourbon, Brandysnap, Brown George, Butterbake, Captain's, Charcoal, Cookie, Cracker, Cracknel, Crispbread, Custard cream, Dandyfunk, Digestive, Dog, Dunderfunk, Fairing, Flapjack, Florentine, Fly cemetery, Fortune cookie, Four-by-two, Garibaldi, Ginger nut, Gingersnap, Hardtack, Jammy dodger, Jumbal, Kiss, Langue de chat, Lavash, Lebkuchen, Macaroon, Marie, Mattress, Matza(h), Matzo(h), Nut, Oatcake, Oliver, Osborne, Parkin, Perkin, Petit four, Petticoat tail, Pig's ear, Pilot, Poppadom, Poppadum, Pretzel, Puff, Ratafia, Rice, Rusk, Rye-roll, Sea, Ship's, Shortbread, Snap, Soda, Sponge finger, Sweetmeal, Tack, Tan, Tararua, Tea, Teiglach, Tollhouse cookie, Wafer, Water, Wine, Zwieback

**Bisexual** AC/DC, Freemartin, Switch-hitter

**Bishop(ric)** Aaronic, Abba, Aberdeen, Aidan, Ambrose, Apollinaris, Bench, Berkeley, Bp, Cambrensis, Cantuar, Chad, Chorepiscopal, Coadjutor, Coverdale, Cranmer, Diocesan, Dunelm, Ebor, Ely, Eparch, Episcopate, Eusebian, Exarch, Exon, Golias, Hatto, Henson, Jansen, Latimer, Lord, Magpie, Man, Metropolitan, Missionary, Norvic, Odo, Ordainer, Patriarch, Peter, Petriburg, Piece, Polycarp, Pontiff, Prelate, Priest, Primate, Primus, Proudie, Ridley, Roffen, RR, St Swithin, Sarum, Sleeve, Sodor and Man, Suffragan, The purple, Titular, Tulchan, Weaver, Weed, Winton, Wrexham

**Bismarck** Otto

**Bismuth** Bi

**Bison** Bonas(s)us, Buffalo, Ox, Wisent

**Bit** Ate, Baud, Byte, Cantle(t), Centre, Chad, Cheesecake, Chip, Chunk, Coin, Crumb, Curb, Curn, Dash, Degree, Drib, Excerpt, Fleck, Flibbert, Fraction, Fraise, Gag, Haet, Hait, Hate, Ion, Iota, Jaw, Jot, Leptum, Mite, Modicum, Morsel, Mote, Mu, Nit, Ort, Ounce, Pelham, Peni, Penny, → PIECE, Pinch, Port, Rap, Rare, Ratherish, Rowel, Scintilla, Scrap, Section, Shaving, Shiver, Shrapnel, Shred, Smattering, Smidge(n), Smidgeon, Smidgin, Snaffle, Snatch, Snippet, Some, Soupcon, Spale, Speck(le), Splinter, Spot, Spudding, Stop, Suspicion, Tad, Tait, Tate, Threepenny, Trace, Unce, Vestige, What, Whit

**Bite(r), Biting, Bitten** Astringent, Begnaw, Canapé, Caustic, Champ, Chelicera, Chew, Cold, Eat, Engouled, Erose, Etch, Gnash, Gnat, Gnaw, Hickey, Hickie, Incisor, Knap, Masticate, Midge, Molar, Mordacious, Mordant, Morsel, Morsure, Nacho, Nibble, Nip(py), Occlude, Peck, Pium, Pointed, Premorse, Rabid, Raw, Sarcastic, Sharp, Shrewd, Snack, Snap, Sound, Spammie, Tart, Teeth

**Bitter(ness), Bitters** Absinth, Acerb, Acid, Acrid, Acrimonious, Ale, Aloe, Angostura, Astringent, Bile, Cassareep, Caustic, Eager, Edge, Envenomed, Ers, Fell, Gall, Heated, Jaundiced, Keen, Keg, Marah, Maror, Myrrh, Picamar, Pique, Radicchio, Rancorous, Rankle, Resentful, Sarcastic, Sardonic, Snell, Sore, Spleen, Tannin, Tart(aric), Venom, Verjuice, Virulent, Vitriolic, Wersh, Wormwood, Wry

**Bitter end** At outrance

**Bittern** Boomer, Bull-of the-bog, Butterbump, Heron, Mossbluiter, Sedge, Siege

**Bittersweet** Dulcamara, Poignant, Staff-tree

**Bitumen** Albertite, Asphalt, Blacktop, Elaterite, Gilsonite®, Maltha, Mineral tar, Pissasphalt, Pitch, Slime, Tar, Tarseal, Uintaite

**Bivalve** Clam, Cockle, Lamellibranch, Mollusc, Muscle, Mussel, Oyster, Pelecypod, Piddock, Razorshell, Scallop, Tuatua, Whelk

**Bivouac** Camp

**Bizarre** Antic, Curious, Eccentric, Exotic, Fantastic, Far-out, Freaky, Gonzo, Grotesque, Kafkaesque, Odd, Offbeat, Off-the-wall, Outlandish, Outré, Pythonesque, Queer, Strange, Surreal, Weird

▷ **Bizarre** *may indicate* an anagram

**Blab** Babble, Gossip, Prate, Squeal

**Black(en), Blackness, Black-out** Afro-American, Amadoda, Asperse, Atramental, B, Ban, BB, Bess, Blae, Boong, Boycott, Cape Coloured, Carbon, Char, Charcoal, Cilla, Coal, Coloured, Coon, Cypress, Darkie, Darky, Death, Debar, Demonise, Denigrate, Dinge, Dwale, Ebon(y), Eclipse, Ethiop, Evil, Fuzzy-wuzzy, Geechee, Gladwellise, Graphite,

Grime, Heben, Hole, Ink(y), Ivory, Japan, Jeat, Jet, Jim Crow, Kohl, Lepidomelane, Malign, Market, Melanic, Melano, Moke, Moor, Muntu, Myall, Negritude, Negro, Niello, Niger, Nigrescent, Nigritude, Obliterate, Obscure, Outage, Oxford, Piceous, Pitch, Platinum, Pongo, Prince, Pudding, Puke, Quashee, Quashie, Raven, Sable, Sambo, Scab, School, Scorch, Sericon, Sheep, Slae, Sloe, Snowball, Sodium, Solvent, Sombre, Soot, Sooterkin, Soul brother, Soul sister, Spade, Spook, Starless, Stygian, Swart(y), Swarth(y), Tar, Thick-lips, Uncle Tom, Weeds

**Black art** Necromancy, Nigromancy
**Blackball** Ban, Debar, Exclude, Ostracise, Pill, Pip, Reject
**Blackberry** Acini, Bramble, Mooch, Mouch
**Blackbird** Collybird, Crow, Jackdaw, Merl(e), Ousel, Raven, Woosel
**Blackcurrant** Quinsy-berry
**Black eye(d)** Half-mourning, Keeker, Mouse, Shiner, Susan
**Blackguard** Heel, Leg, Nithing, Raff, Revile, Rotter, Scoundrel, Sweep
**Blackhead** Comedo
**Black hole** Collapsar
**Blackjack** Billie, Billy, Cosh, Flag, Sphalerite, Tankard, Truncheon, Vingt(-et)-un
**Blackleg** Fink, Rat, Scab, Snob
**Black-letter** Gothic
**Black magic** Goety
**Blackmail(er)** Bleed, Chantage, Chout, Exact, Extort, Greenmail, Honey-trap, Ransom, Shakedown, Strike, Vampire
**Blackout** ARP, Eclipse, Faint, Power cut, Shallow water, Swoon, Syncope
**Black Sea** Pontic, Pontus Euxinus
**Black sheep** Neer-do-well, Reprobate
**Blacksmith** Brontes, Burn-the-wind, Farrier, Forger, Harmonious, Plater, Shoer, Vulcan
**Blackthorn** Sloe
**Bladder(wort)** Air, Balloon, Blister, Cholecyst, Cyst, Gall, Hydatid, Isinglass, Popweed, Sac, Sound, Swim, Urinary, Utricle, Varec(h), Vesica, Vesicle
**Blade(s)** Acrospire, Andrew Ferrara, Bilbo, Brand, Brown Bill, Catling, Cleaver, Co(u)lter, Cutlass, Dandy, Espada, Faible, Foible, Forte, Froe, Gleave, Gouge, Guillotine, Hydrofoil, Knife, Kris, Lance, Lawnmower, Leaf, Man, Mouldboard, Oar, Omoplate, Paddle, Palmetto, Peel, Propeller, Rachilla, Rapier, Razor, Rip, Rotor, Scalpel, Scapula, Scimitar, Scull, Scythe, Skate, Spade-, Spatula, Spatule, Spear, Spoon, Stiletto, Stock, Strigil, Sweep, Switch, →**SWORD**, Symitar, Toledo, Turbine, Vane, Vorpal, Wash, Web
**Blair** Eric, Lionel, Orwell, Tony
**Blame(worthy)** Accuse, Censure, Condemn, Confound, Culpable, Decry, Dirdam, Dirdum, Dispraise, Fault, Guilt, Incriminate, Inculpate, Odium, Rap, Reprehensible, Reproach, Reprove, Stick, Thank, Twit, Wight, Wite, Wyte
**Blameless** Innocent, Irreproachable, Lily-white, Unimpeachable
**Blanch** Bleach, Etiolate, Scaud, Whiten
**Blancmange** Carrageen, Flummery, Mould, Shape, Timbale
**Bland** Anodyne, Flavourless, Glop, Insipid, Mild, Neutral, Pigling, Sleek, Smooth, Spammy, Suave, Tame, Tasteless, Unctuous
**Blandish(ment)** Agremens, Agrement, Cajole, →**COAX**, Flatter, Treacle, Wheedle
**Blank** Burr, Cartridge, Deadpan, Empty, Erase, Flan, Flyleaf, Ignore, Lacuna, Mistigris, Planchet, Shot, Space, Tabula rasa, →**VACANT**, Vacuous
**Blanket** Across the board, Afghan, All-over, Bluey, Chilkat, Comprehensive, Counterpane, Cover, Electric, Envelop, Fire, General, Hudson's Bay, Kaross, Mackinaw, Manta, Obscure, Overall, Overlay, Poncho, Quilt, Rug, Saddle, Sarape, Security, Serape, Shabrack, Smog, Space, Stroud, Umbrella, Wagga, Wet, Whittle
**Blare** Horn, Trumpet
**Blarney** Cajolery, Flattery, Nonsense, Sawder, Sleeveen, Taffy
**Blasé** Bored, Worldly

**Blaspheme, Blasphemous** Abuse, →CURSE, Defame, Profanity, Revile, Sacrilege

**Blast(ed), Blasting** Blight, Blore, Blow, Bombard, Dang, Darn, Dee, Drat, Dynamite, Expletive, Explode, Fanfare, Flaming, Flurry, Fo(e)hn, Gale, Grit, Gust, Hell, Noser, Oath, Pan, Parp, Planet-struck, Pryse, Rats, Ruddy, Scarth, Scath(e), Sere, Shot, Sideration, Skarth, Sneeze, Stormer, Tantara, Toot, Tout, Tromp(e), Trump(et), Volley

**Blatant** Conspicuous, Flagrant, Hard-core, Noticeable, Open, Strident, Unashamed, Vulgar

**Blather** Baloney, Gabble, Gibber, Waffle

**Blaze(r), Blazing** Afire, Beacon, Bonfire, Burn, Cannel, Conflagration, Firestorm, →FLAME, Flare, Glare, Inferno, Jacket, Low(e), Lunt, Palatinate, Race, Ratch, Sati, Star, Sun, Tead(e)

**Bleach(er)** Agene, Blanch, Chemic, Chloride, Decolorate, Etiolate, Fade, Frost, Janola®, Keir, Kier, Peroxide, Whiten, Whitster

**Bleak** Ablet, Bare, Barren, Blay, Bley, Cheerless, Dour, Dreary, Dreich, Gaunt, Midwinter, Raw, Soulless, Wintry

**Bleary** Blurred, Smudged

**Bleat** Baa, Blat, Bluster, Maa

**Bleed(er), Bleeding** Breakthrough, Cup, Diapedesis, Ecchymosis, Emulge, Epistaxis, Extort, Extravasate, Fleam, Haemorrhage, Leech, Menorrhagia, Menorrh(o)ea, Metrorrhagia, Milk, Purpura, Rhinorrhagia, Root-pressure

**Bleep** Earcon, Pager

**Blefuscudian** Big-endian, Little-endian

**Blemish** Birthmark, Blot, Blotch, Blur, Botch, Defect, Eyesore, Flaw, Imperfection, Lepra, Mackle, Mark, Milium, Mote, Naevus, Scar, Smirch, Smudge, Spot, Stain, Sully, Taint, Tash, Verruca, Vice, Wart, Wen

**Blench** Flinch, Recoil, Wince

**Blend(ing)** Amalgam, Coalesce, Commix, Contemper, Contrapuntal, Counterpoint, Electrum, Fit, Fuse, Go, Harmonize, Hydrate, Interfuse, Interlace, Intermix, Liquidise, Meld, Melt, →MERGE, Mingle, Mix, Osmose, Portmanteau, Scumble, Sfumato, Stir, Synalepha

▷ **Blend** *may indicate* an anagram

**Blenny** Eel-pout, Gunnel, Shanny

**Bless(ing), Blessed(ness)** Amen, Anoint, Approval, Asset, Beatitude, Benedicite, Benediction, Benison, Benitier, Bensh, Bismillah, Bonus, Boon, Brachah, Brocho, Charmed, Consecrate, Cup, Damosel, Darshan, Elysium, Ethereal, Felicity, Gesundheit, Giver, Godsend, Grace, Gwyneth, Hallow, Holy (dam), Kiddush, Luck, Macarise, Mercy, Mixed, Sain, Saint, Sanctify, Sanctity, Sheva Brachoth, Sheva Brochos, Sneeze, Toronto, Urbi et orbi, Xenium

**Bless me** Lawk(s)

**Blight** Afflict, Ague, American, Apple, Bespot, Blast, Destroy, Early, Eyesore, Fire, Late, Planning, Potato, Rot, →RUIN, Rust, Sandy, Shadow, Viticide, Waldersterben, Wither

**Blighter** Cuss, Perisher, Varment, Varmint

**Blimey** Coo, Cor, Crimini, Crumbs, O'Riley, Strewth

**Blimp** Airship, Colonel

**Blind(ness), Blind spot** Amaurosis, Amblyopia, Artifice, Austrian, Bedazzle, Beesome, Binge, Bisson, Blend, Blotto, Camouflage, Carousal, Cecity, Chi(c)k, Cog, Colour, Concealed, Dazzle, Drop serene, Drunk, Eyeless, Feint, Festoon, Flash, Gravel, Hemeralopia, Homer, Hood, Invisible, Jalousie, Legless, Meropia, Mole, Night, Nyctalopia, Onchocerciasis, Persian, Persiennes, Pew, Pickled, Prestriction, Rash, River, Roller, Roman, Sand, Scotoma, Seel, Shade, Shutter, Sightless, Slat, Snow, Stimie, Stimy, Stymie, Sun, Swear, Teichopsia, Typhlology, Venetian, Visually challenged, Window, Word, Yblent

**Blindfish** Amblyopsis

**Blindfold** Bandage, Hood, Hoodwink, Muffle, Seal, Wimple

**Blindworm** Anguis

**Bling** Tsatske

**Blink, Blinker(s), Blinkered, Blinking** Bat, Blepharism, Blinders, Bluff, Broken, Eye-flap, Flash, Haw, Idiot, Insular, Nictate, Owl-eyed, Owly, Twink, Wapper, Water, Wink

**Bliss(ful)** Beatitude, Bouyan, Cheer, Composer, Delight, → ECSTASY, Eden, Elysium, Glee, Happy, Heaven, Idyll, Ignorance, Joy, Married, Millenium, Nirvana, Paradise, Rapture, Seventh heaven, Sion, Tir-na-nog, Utopia, Valhalla, Walhalla, Wedded

**Blister(ed), Blistering** Blab, Blain, Bleb, Bubble, Bullate, Cantharidine, Cold sore, Epispastic, Fever, Herpes, Measle, Overgall, Pemphigus, Phlyct(a)ena, Scorching, Tetter, Vesicant, Vesicle, Visicate, Water

**Blitz** Attack, Bombard, Onslaught, Raid

**Blizzard** Buran, Gale, Snowstorm, Whiteout

**Bloat(ed), Bloater** Buckling, Gross, Puff, Strout, Swell, Swollen, Tumefy, Tumid, Turgid, Two-eyed steak, Yarmouth

**Blob** Bead, Bioblast, Dollop, Drop, Globule, O, Pick, Spot, Tear

**Bloc** Alliance, Cabal, Cartel, Party

**Block(er), Blockage, Blocked, Blocking** Altar, Anvil, Ashlar, Atresia, → BAR, Barber's, Barracks, Barricade, Barrier, Battle-axe, Brake, Breeze, Brick, Briquet(te), Building, Bung, Bunt, Capital, Cavity, Chinese, Choke, Chunk, Cinder, Cleat, Clint, Clog, Clot, Cloy, Compass, Condo(minium), Congest, Constipated, Cut-off, Cyclopean, Cylinder, Dado, → DAM, Dead-eye, Debar, Defect, Delete, Dentel, Dentil, Die, Dit, Domino, Eclipse, Electrotint, Embolism, Emphractic, Encompass, Erratic, Euphroe, Fiddle, Filibuster, Fipple, Frog, Gypsum, Hack-log, Head off, Heart, High-rise, Hunk, Ice, Ileus, Impasse, Impede, Impost, Ingot, Input, Insula, Interclude, Interrupt, Investment, Ischaemia, Jam, Licence, Lifestyle, Line, Lingot, Lodgment, Log-jam, Lump, Mental, Ministroke, Mitre, Monkey, Mounting, Mutule, Nerve, Nifedipine, Nog, Notepad, Oasis®, Obstacle, → OBSTRUCT, Occlude, Office, Opossum, Oppilate, Pad, Page, Parry, Perched, Pile-cap, Pile-up, Pillow, Planer, Plinth, Plummer, Power, Pre-empt, Prevent, Process, Psychological, Quad, Ram, Saddle, Scotch, Seal, Sett, Siege, Snatch, Snooker, Stalemate, Stap, Starting, Stenosis, Stimie, Stimy, Stone, Stonewall, Stop, Stumbling, Stymie, Sun(screen), Swage, Tamp, Tetrapod, Thwart, Tint, Tower, Tranche, Trig, Triglyph, Truck, Uphroe, Upping-stock, Veto, Vibropac®, Wedge, Wig, Wood(cut), Wrest, Writer's, Zinco, Zugzwang

**Blockbuster** Epic

**Blockhead** Jolterhead, Mome, Nitwit, Noodle, Pig sconce, Stupid

**Blockhouse** Igloo

**Bloke** Beggar, Chap, Codger, Cove, Fellow, Geezer, Gent, Man, Oik

**Blond(e)** Ash, Bombshell, Cendré, Fair, Flaxen, Goldilocks, Nordic, Peroxide, Platinised, Platinum, Strawberry, Tallent, Tow-haired, Towhead

**Blood(y), Blood-letter, Blood-letting** A, Ancestry, B, Bad, Bally, Blue, Bluggy, Blut, Buck, Butchery, Claret, Clot, Cold, Cruor, Cup, Dutch pink, Ecchymosis, Ensanguine, Epigons, Factor, Family, First, Full, → GORE, H(a)emal, Haematoma, Haemorrhage, Ichor, Internecine, Introduce, Kin, Kinship, Knut, Leech, Menses, Microcyte, New, Nut, O, Opsonin, Parentage, Penny dreadful, Persue, Phlebotomist, Pigeon's, Plasma, Platelet, Plurry, Properdin, Pup, Purple, Race, Rare, Red, Rh negative, Rh positive, Ruby, Sang, Sangrado, Schistosoma, Serum, Show, Stroma, Thrombin, Toff, Type, Venisection, Welter, Whole, Young

**Blood disease, Blood disorder, Blood-poisoning** Acidosis, Agranulocytosis, Haematuria, Hypinosis, Isch(a)emia, Leukemia, Lipaemia, Oligaemia, Purpura, Pyaemia, Sapraemia, Septicemia, Spanaemia, Thalassemia, Thrombocytopenia, Toxaemia, Uraemia

**Bloodhound** Lime, Lyam, Lym, Rach(e), Ratch, Sleuth, Spartan, Tracker

**Bloodless** Anaemic, Isch(a)emic, Wan, White

**Blood money** Eric

▶ **Blood-poisoning** *see* **BLOOD DISEASE**

**Blood-pressure** Hypertension, Hypotension, Normotensive

**Bloodshot** Red-eyed

**Blood-sport** Hunting, Shooting, Venery

**Blood-sucker** Anoplura, Asp, Bed bug, Dracula, Flea, Gnat, Ked, Leech, Louse, Mosquito, Parasite, Reduviid, Soucouyant, Sponger, Tick, Vampire(-bat)

**Bloodthirsty** Lurid, Tiger

**Blood vessel** Artery, Vein, Venule

**Bloom(er), Blooming** Anthesis, Bally, Blossom, Blow, Blush, Boner, Bread, Clanger, Cobalt, Dew, Dratted, Effloresce, Error, Film, Flipping, Florence, Florescent, Flourish, Flowery, Flush, Full-blown, Gaffe, Glaucous, Heyday, Howler, Knickers, Loaf, Miscalculation, Nickel, Out, Peach, → **PLANT**, Pruina, Rationals, Reh, Remontant, Rosy, Ruddy, Thrive, Underwear

▷ **Bloomer** *may indicate* a flower

**Bloop(er)** Outtake

**Blossom** Blow, Burgeon, Catkin, Develop, Festoon, Flourish, Flower, Marybud, May, Orange, Pip, Springtime

**Blot (out)** Atomy, Blob, Cartel, Delete, Disgrace, Dry, Eclipse, Eyesore, Obliterate, Obscure, Pad, Smear, Smudge, Southern, Splodge, Splotch

**Blotch(y)** Blemish, Giraffe, Monk, Mottle(d), Spot, Stain

**Blotto** Legless

**Blouse** Choli, Garibaldi, Gimp, Guimpe, Kerbaya, Middy, Pneumonia, Sailor, Shell, Shirtwaist, Smock, Tunic, Waist(er), Windjammer

**Blow(er), Blown** Appel, Bang, Bash, Bat, Bellows, Biff, Billow, Blip, Bloom, Body, Box, Brag, Breeze, Buckhorse, Buffet, Bump, Burst, Buster, Calamity, Chop, Clap, Clat, Claut, Clip, Clout, Clump, Conk, Coup, Cuff, Dad, Daud, Dawd, Dev(v)el, Dinnyhayser, Dint, Dod, Douse, Dowse, Estramacon, Etesian, Exsufflate, Facer, Fan, Fillip, Finisher, Fisticuffs, Fuse, Gale, Grampus, Gust, Hammer, Hander, Haymaker, Headwind, Hit, Hook, Hurricane, Ictus, Impact, Insufflate, Karate, Kibosh, Knuckle sandwich, KO, Lame, Lander, Left-hander, Lick, Lounder, Montant(o), Muff, Muzzler, Neck-herring, Northerly, Noser, Oner, One-two, Paddywhack, Paik, Pash, Peise, Peyse, Phone, Piledriver, Plague, Plug, Plump(er), Polt, Pow, Puff, Punch, Purler, Raft, Rats, Rattler, Rib-roaster, Roundhouse, Sas(s)arara, Scat, Settler, Short, Sideswipe, Side-winder, Sis(s)erary, Skiff, Skite, Skyte, Slat, Slog, Slug, Smack, Snell, Snot, Sock, Sockdolager, Sockdologer, Southwester, Spanking, Spat, Spout, Squall, Squander, Squelcher, Stripe, Stroke, Strooke, Stunning, Sufflate, Supercharger, Swash, Swat, Swinger, Swipe, Tap, Telephone, Thump, Thwack, Tingler, Tootle, Triple whammy, Trump(et), Tuck, Twister, Undercut, Upper-cut, Waft, Wallop, Wap, Waste, Welt, Whammy, Whample, Whang, Whap, Wheeze, Wherret, Whiffle, Whirret, Whistle, → **WIND**, Winder, Windswept, Wipe, Wuther

**Blown-up** Elated, Enlarged, Exploded

**Blow-out** Binge, Bloat, Blowhole, Exhale, Feast, Feed, Flat, Fulminate, Lava, Nosh-up, Snuff, Spiracle, → **SPREAD**

**Blowpipe** Hod, Peashooter, Sarbacane, Sumpit(an)

**Blub(ber)** Cry, Fat, Snotter, Sob, Speck, → **WEEP**, Whimper

**Bludge** Sinecure

**Bludgeon** Bulldoze, Bully, Club, Cosh, Cudgel, Life-preserver, Sap

**Blue(s), Bluesman** Abattu, Accablé, Adult, Anil, Aqua, Aquamarine, Azure, Azurn, Beard, Berlin, Bice, Bleuâtre, Blow, Boogie, Bottle, Butterfly, C, Caesious, Cafard, Cambridge, Cantab, Celeste, Cerulean, City, Clair de lune, Classic, Cobalt, Coomassie, Copenhagen, Cornflower, Country, Coventry, Cyan, Danish, Danube, Dejected, Dirty, Disconsolate, Doldrums, → **DOWN**, Duck-egg, Eatanswill, Eggshell, Electric, Erotica, Facetiae, Firmament, Fritter, Gentian, Germander, Glaucous, Glum, Hauyne, Heliotrope, Hump, Ice, Indecent, Indigo, Indol(e), Iron, Isatin(e), Lapis lazuli, Lavender, Leadbelly,

Lewd, Lionel, Low, Mazarine, Methylene, Midnight, Monastral®, Mope, Morose, Murder, Nattier, Naughty, Navy, Nile, Obscene, Ocean, Off-colour, Oxford, Peacock, Periwinkle, Perse, Petrol, Phycocyan, Porn, Powder, Prussian, Rabbi, Racy, Ribald, Riband, Right, Ripe, Robin's egg, Royal, Sad, Sapphire, Saxe, Saxon(y), Scurrilous, → **SEA**, Shocking, → **SKY-TINCTURED**, Slate, Smalt(o), Smutty, Sordid, Spirit, Splurge, Squander, Stafford, Steel, Stocking, Teal, Thenard's, Tony, Top shelf, Tory, Trist, True, Trypan, Turnbull's, Turquoise, Ultramarine, Unhappy, Urban, Verditer, Washing, Watchet, Wedgwood®, Welkin, Woad, Zaffer, Zaffre

▷ **Blue** *may indicate* an anagram

**Bluebell** Blawort, Blewart, Campanula, Harebell, Hyacinth

**Bluebottle** Blawort, Blewart, Blowfly, Blowie, Brommer, Brummer, Cop, Cornflower, Fly, Officer, Policeman

▶ **Blue-legged** *see* **BLUESTOCKING**

**Blueprint** Cyanotype, Design, Draft, Drawing, Plan, Recipe

**Bluestocking, Blue-legged** Basbleu, Carter, Erudite, Femme savante, Hamburg(h), Mrs Montagu, Précieuse, Sheba

**Bluff(ing)** Blunt, Cle(e)ve, Cliff, Clift, Crag, Double, Escarpment, Fake, Flannel, Four-flush, Frank, Hal, Headland, Height, Hoodwink, Kidology, Pose, Precipice, Scarp, Steep, Trick

**Blunder(er), Blundering** Barry (Crocker), Betise, Bévue, Bish, Bloomer, Blooper, Boner, Boob, Break, Bull, Bumble, Bungle, Clanger, Clinker, Cock-up, Crass, Err, Fault, Faux pas, Floater, Flub, Fluff, Gaff(e), Goof, Howler, Inexactitude, Inexpert, Irish, Josser, Malapropism, → **MISTAKE**, Muddle, Mumpsimus, OG, Oversight, Ricket, Slip, Slip up, Solecism, Stumble, Trip

**Blunt(ed), Bluntly** Abrupt, Alleviate, Bald, Bate, Bayt, Brash, Brusque, Candid, Deaden, Disedge, Downright, Dull, Explicit, Forthright, Frank, Hebetate, Home truth, Mole, Morned, Obtund, Obtuse, Outspoken, Plainspoken, Pointblank, Pointless, Rebate, Retund, Retuse, Roundly, Snub, Straight-out, Stubby

**Blur(red), Blurring, Blurry** Cloud, Confuse, Daze, Fog, Fuzz, Halation, Mackle, Macule, Muzzy, Pixilation, → **SMUDGE**, Stump, Tortillon, Unfocussed

**Blurb** Ad, Puff

**Blush(ing)** Colour, Cramoisy, Crimson, Erubescent, Erythema, Incarnadine, Mantle, → **REDDEN**, Rosy, Rouge, Rubescent, Ruby, Rufescent, Rutilant

**Bluster(ing), Blusterer, Blustery** Arrogance, Bellow, Blore, Brag, Fanfaronade, Hector, Huff-cap, Rage, Rant, Rodomontade, Roister, Sabre-rattler, Squally, Squash, Swagger, Swashbuckler, Vapour, Windbag, Wuthering

**Boa** Fur, Ophidian

**Boadicea** Charioteer

**Boar** Barrow, Calydonian, Erymanthian, Hog, Pentheus, Sanglier, Sounder, Tusker, Wild

**Board(s), Boarding** Abat-voix, Admiralty, Aquaplane, Baffle, Banker, Barge, Bd, Beaver, Billet, Bristol, Bulletin, Catchment, Centre, Cheese, Chevron, Circuit, Collegium, Committee, Contignation, Counter, Cribbage, Dagger, Dam, Dart, Daughter, Deal, Directors, Diving, Draft, Draining, Drawing, Duck, Embark, Embus, Emery, Enter, Entrain, Expansion, Fa(s)cia, Fare, Farm out, Featheredge, Fibro, Fibrolite®, Flannelgraph, Food, Full, Gib(raltar), Groaning, Gunwale, Gutter, Hack, Half, Half-royal, Hawk, Hoarding, Idiot, Instrument, Insulating, Ironing, Kip, Lag, Lap, Leader, Ledger, Lee, Lodge, Magnetic, Malibu, Management, Marketing, Masonite®, Match, Message, Mill, Monkey, Mortar, Moulding, Muft(i)at, Notch, Notice, Otter, Ouija, Paddle, Palette, Pallet, Panel, Paper, Parochial, Particle, Patch, Pedal, Peg(board), Pension, Planch(ette), Plank, Plug, Ply(wood), Punch, Quango, Ribbon-strip, Roof, Running, Sandwich, Sarking, Scale, Scaleboard, School, Score, Scraper, Scratch, Screen, Sheathing, Shelf, Shifting, Shingle, Shooting, Side-table, Sign, Skim, Skirting, Sleeve, SMART®, Smoke, Snow, Sounding, Splasher, Spring, Stage, Stretcher, Strickle, Stringboard, Supervisory, Surf, Switch, → **TABLE**, Teeter(-totter), Telegraph, Thatch, Theatre, Timber, Tray, Trencher, Tribunal, Verge, Wainscot, Wobble, Wokka, Wood chip

▷ **Board** *may refer to* chess or draughts
**Boarder** Interne, Pensioner, PG, Roomer
**Boarding house** Digs, Kip, Lodgings, Pension
**Boast(er), Boastful, Boasting** Bigmouth, Big-note, Blew, Blow, Blowhard, Bluster, Bobadil, Bounce, Brag, Braggadocio, Bravado, Breeze, Bull, Cock-a-hoop, Crake, Crow, Fanfaronade, Gas, Gascon(nade), Glory, Hot air, Jact(it)ation, Line, Loudmouth, Ostent(atious), Prate, Rodomontade, Scaramouch, Self-glorious, Show-off, Skite, Spread-eagle, Swagger, Swank, Tall, Thrasonic, Vainglory, Vapour, Vaunt, Yelp
**Boat(s)** Ark, Barge, Bark, Cat, Flagship, Fly(ing), Fore-and-after, Goldie, Isis, Keel, Kit, Lugger, She, → SHIP, → VESSEL

## BOATS

| 1 letter: | Sauce | Wangun | Mosquito |
|---|---|---|---|
| Q | Skiff | Wherry | Pleasure |
| | Sloop | | Skipjack |
| 2 letters: | Smack | 7 letters: | Surfboat |
| PT | Stake | Coaster | |
| | Swing | Cruiser | 9 letters: |
| 4 letters: | Wager | Curragh | Destroyer |
| Cock | Waist | Dredger | Lapstrake |
| Cott | Whiff | Four-oar | Lap streak |
| Four | | Drifter | Outrigger |
| Junk | 6 letters: | Foyboat | Oysterman |
| Lake | Advice | Galliot | Vaporetto |
| Long | Bawley | Liberty | Weekender |
| Pont | Caique | Lighter | Whaleback |
| Proa | Cobble | Lymphad | Whaleboat |
| Saic | Codder | Pair-oar | |
| Scow | Cutter | Pearler | 10 letters: |
| Tilt | Dragon | Scooter | Hydroplane |
| Trow | Galiot | Sculler | Purse seine |
| Yawl | Galley | Shallop | Track-scout |
| | Hooker | Sharpie | Trekschuit |
| 5 letters: | Howker | Slogger | |
| Canal | Monkey | Sounder | 11 letters: |
| Coble | Launch | Vedette | Cockleshell |
| Eight | Narrow | Vidette | Double scull |
| Ferry | Packet | Wanigan | Sidewheeler |
| Funny | Pedalo | | |
| Gravy | Puffer | 8 letters: | 12 letters: |
| Gulet | Pulwar | Billyboy | Clinker-built |
| Hatch | Sailer | Corvette | Sternwheeler |
| Jolly | Sea Dog® | Faltboat | Tangle-netter |
| Kaiak | Tanker | Flatbbat | |
| Kayak | Tender | Foldboat | 13 letters: |
| Motor | Torpid | Gallivat | Black skipjack |
| Power | Trek-ox | Mackinaw | Paddle steamer |
| Pucan | Wangan | Monohull | Revenue cutter |

**Boater** → HAT, Punter, Straw
**Boatman** Bargee, Charon, Cockswain, Coxswain, George, Gondolier, Harris, Hoveller, Legger, Noah, Phaon, Punter, Voyageur, Waterman, Wet-bob
**Boat population** Tank(i)a

**Boat-shaped** Carina, Scaphoid

**Boatswain** Bosun, Serang, Smee

**Bob** Acres, Beck, Curtsey, Deaner, Dip, Dock, Dop, Duck, Dylan, Eton crop, Float, Haircut, Hairdo, Hod, Hog, Jerk, Major, Maximus, Minor, Nod, Page-boy, Peal, Plain, Plumb, Plummet, Popple, Rob, Royal, S, Shingle, Skeleton, Skip, Sled(ge), Sleigh

**Bobbin** Quill, Reel, Shuttle, Spindle, Spool

**Bobble** Pompom

**Bobby** Bluebottle, Busy, Copper, Flatfoot, Patrolman, Peeler, Pig, → **POLICEMAN**, Rosser, Wolly

**Bobby-dazzler** Dinger, Stunner

**Bock** Stein

**Bode** Augur

**Bodgie** Aussie, Ted

**Bodice** Basque, Bolero, Bustier, Chemise, Chemisette, Choli, Corsage, Gilet, Halter, Jirkinet, Liberty, Plastron, Polonie, Polony, Spencer, Tucker, Waist, Watteau

**Bodkin** Eyeleteer, Needle, Poniard, Stilet(to)

**Body, Bodies, Bodily** Administration, Amount, Anatomic, Astral, Barr, Board, Bouk, Buik, Buke, Bulk, Cadaver, Cadre, Carcase, Carcass, Carnal, Caucas, Centrosome, Chapel, Chapter, Chassis, Chondriosome, Ciliary, Clay, Coachwork, Coccolite, Cohort, Column, Comet, Committee, Contingent, Cormus, Corpora, Corpor(e)al, Corps, Corpse, Corpus, Corse, Cytode, Detail, Earth, Elaiosome, Establishment, Flesh, Food, Frame, Fuselage, Gate, Gazo(o)n, Golgi, Goner, Grey, → **GROUP**, Heavenly, Hull, Immune, Incarnate, Inclusion, Kenning, Ketone, Lewy, Lich, Lifting, Like, Lithites, Malpighian, → **MASS**, Militia, Mitochondrion, Moit, Mote, Mummy, Nacelle, Nave, Nucleole, Nucleolus, Olivary, Orb, Order, Pack, Personal, Phalanx, Pineal, Plant, Platelet, Platoon, Polar, Politic, Posse, Purview, Quango, Relic(t), Remains, Review, Ruck, Satellite, Sect, Senate, Shaft, Solid, Soma(tic), Soredium, Sound-box, Soyle, Spinar, Spore, Squadron, Square, Staff, Statoblast, Stiff, Strobila, Syndicate, Systemic, Tagma, Testis, Thallus, Torse, Torso, Trunk, Turm, Ulema, Uvula, Vase, Vitreous, Wolffian, X

▷ **Body** *may indicate* an anagram

**Body builder** Expander, He-man, Muscleman, Steroid

**Bodyguard** Amulet, Beefeater, → **ESCORT**, Gentleman-at-arms, House-carl, Minder, Praetorian, Protector, Retinue, Schutzstaffel, → **SHIELD**, SS, Sun cream, Switzer, Triggerman, Varangian, Yeomen

**Body segment** Arthromere, Genome, Metamere

**Bodysnatcher** Burke, Hare

**Boer** Afrikaner, Kruger, Van der Merwe

**Boffin** Brain, Egghead, Expert

**Bog(e)y, Bogeyman** Boggart, Bug(aboo), Bugbear, Chimera, Colonel, Eagle, Gremlin, Mumbo jumbo, Nis(se), Ogre, Par, Poker, Rawhead, Scarer, Siege, Spectre, Troll

**Bog(gy)** Allen, Blanket, Can, Carr, Clabber, Fen, Gents, Glaur, Hag, Lair, Latrine, Lerna, Lerne, Letch, Loo, Machair, Marish, Marsh, Merse, Mire, Moory, Morass, Moss(-flow), Moss-hag, Mud, Muskeg, Peat, Petary, Quag, Raised, Serbonian, Slack, Slade, Slough, Spew, Spouty, Stodge, Sump, Swampland, Urinal, Vlei, Washroom, WC, Yarfa, Yarpha

**Boggle** Astonish, Bungle, Demur, Hesitate, Perplex, Shy

**Bogie** Trolley

**Bog-trotter** Tory

**Bogus** Assumed, Counterfeit, Ersatz, Fake, False, Faux, Histrionic, Phoney, → **SHAM**, Snide, Snobbish, Spoof, Spurious

**Bohemian** Arty, Beatnik, Boho, Calixtin(e), Demi-monde, Gypsy, Hippy, Hussite, Mimi, Offbeat, Taborite, Trustafarian, Zingara, Zingaro

**Boil(er), Boiled, Boiling (point)** Aleppo, Angry, Anthrax, Blain, Botch, Brew, Bubble, C, Carbuncle, Coction, Cook, Copper, Cree, Dartre, Decoct, Ebullient, Foam, Furuncle, Gas-fired, Gathering, Hen, Herpes, Hijinks, Kettle, Laddish, Leep, Ligroin, Pimple,

Pinswell, Poach, Poule, Rage, Reflux, Rowdy, Samovar, Seethe, Set pot, Simmer, Sod, Sore, Steam, Stew, Stye, Tea-kettle, Water tube

**Boisterous(ly), Boisterousness** Ariot, Gilp(e)y, Goustrous, Gusty, Hoo, Knockabout, Ladette, Noisy, Rambunctious, Randy, Riotous, Rollicking, Rorty, Rough, Rounceval, Splurge, Stormy, Strepitoso, Tearer, Termagant, Tomboy, Turbulent, Wild

**Bold(ly), Boldness** Assumptive, Audacious, Brash, Brass, Bravado, Bravery, Bravura, Brazen, Brussen, Caleb, Confident, Crust, Daredevil, Dauntless, Defiant, Derring-do, Diastaltic, Familiar, Forward, Free, Gallus, Gutsy, Hard-edge, Hardihood, Heroics, High-spirited, Impudent, Intrepid, Malapert, Manful, Mature, Mettle, Minx, Outspoken, Parrhesia, Pert, Plucky, Presumptive, Rash, Risoluto, Sassy, Stout, Temerity, Unabashed, Unshrinking, Valiant

**Bole** Niche, Stem, Trunk

**Bolivar** Liberator

**Bollard** Cone, Kevel

**Bolshevik, Bolshie** Agitator, Anarchist, Communist, Maximalist, Mutinous, Rebel, Soviet, Stroppy

**Bolster** Cushion, Dutch wife, Pillow, →**PROP**, Support

**Bolt** Arrow, Captive, Carriage, Coach, Cuphead, Dash, Dead, Do a runner, Eat, Elope, Expansion, Explosive, Fasten, Fish, Flee, Gobble, Gollop, Gorge, Gulp, Hurtle, Latch, Levant, Levin, Lightning, Lock, Machine, Missile, Panic, Pig, Pintle, Ragbolt, Rivet, Roll, Scoff, Slot, Snib, Sperre, Stud, Tap, Through, Thunder, Toggle, U, Wing, Wolf, Wring

**Bolus** Ball

**Bomb(ed), Bomber, Bombing, Bombshell** Atom, Attack, B, Benny, Blast, Blitz, Blockbuster, Borer, Bunkerbuster, Buzz, Candle, Car, Carpet, Cluster, Cobalt, Daisycutter, Depth charge, Deterrent, Dirty, Doodlebug, Drogue, Egg, Fission, Flop, Flying, Flying Fortress, Fragmentation, Fusion, Glide, Greek fire, Grenade, H, Hand grenade, Harris, Homicide, Hydrogen, Lancaster, Land-mine, Letter, Liberator, Loft, Logic, Mail, Megaton, Millennium, Mills, Minnie, Mint, Molotov cocktail, Mortar, Nail, Napalm, Necklace, Neutron, Nuclear, Nuke, Packet, Parcel, Petar, Petard, Petrol, Pineapple, Pipe, Plaster, Plastic, Prang, Precision, Radium, Ransom, Robot, Sex, Shell, Skip, Smart, Smash, Smoke, Sneak-raid, Stealth, Stick, Stink, Stratofortress, Stuka, Suicide, Tactical, Tank, Terrorist, Thermonuclear, Thunderbolt, Time, Torpedo, Turkey, V1, Volcanic, Vulcan, Walleye

**Bombard(ment)** Attack, Battery, Blitz, Cannonade, Crossfire, Drum-fire, Mortar, Pelt, Shell(fire), Stone, Stonk, Strafe, Straff

**Bombardon** Tuba

**Bombast(ic)** Ampullosity, Euphuism, Fustian, Grandiloquent, Grandiose, Hot air, Magniloquence, Orotund, Pomp, Rant, Swol(le)n, Timid, Tumid, Turgent

**Bombay** Nasik

**Bombay duck** Bum(m)alo

▶ **Bomber** *see* **BOMB(ED)**

**Bona fide** Echt, Genuine

**Bonanza** Luck, Windfall

**Bonaparte** Boney, →**NAPOLEON**, Plon-plon

**Bond(s), Bondage, Bonding, Bondsman** Adhesive, Affinity, Afrikander, Agent, Assignat, Baby, Bail, Bearer, Cedula, Cement, Chain, Chemical, Compact, Connect, Consols, Coordinate, Copula, Corporate, Covalent, Covenant, Daimyo, Dative, Debenture, Deep-discount, Double, Duty, Electrovalent, English, Enslave, Ernie, Escrow, Esne, Fetter, Fleming, Flemish, Geasa, Gilt, Glue, Granny, Heart, Herringbone, Hydrogen, Hyphen, Income, Investment, Ionic, James, Junk, Knot, Liaise, Ligament, Ligature, Link(age), Long, Manacle, Managed, Metallic, Mortar, Multicentre, Municipal, Nexus, Noose, Obligation, Pair, Peptide, Performance, →**PLEDGE**, Post-obit, Premium, Property, Rapport, Recognisance, Relationship, Revenue, Running, Samurai, Savings, Security, Semipolar, Serf, Servitude, Shackle, Shogun, Single, Singlet, Sinter, Slave,

Solder, Stacked, Starr, Subjection, Superglue, Surety, Thete, Thral(l)dom, Three-per-cent, →TIE, Tiger, TIGR, Treasury, Triple, Trivalent, Tusking, Valence, Valency, Vassal, Vinculum, Yearling, Yoke, Zebra

**Bone(s), Bony** Acromion, Anableps, Angular, Apatite, Astragalus, Atlas, Axis, Baculum, Busk, Calcaneus, Caluarium, Cannon, Capitate, Capitellum, Carina, Carpal, Carpus, Cartilage, Catacomb, Centrum, Chine, Chordate, Clavicle, Cly, Coccyx, Coffin, Columella, Concha, Condyle, Coracoid, Coral, Costa, Coxa, Crane, Cranium, Cuboid, Cuneiform, Cuttlefish, Dentary, Diaphysis, Dib, Dice, Diploe, Doctor, Dolos, Endosteal, Ethmoid, Femur, Fetter, Fibula, Fillet, Fossil, Frontal, Funny, Ganoid, Gaunt, Hamate, Hammer, Haunch, Hause-bane, Horn, Humerus, Hyoid, Ilium, Incus, Innominate, Interclavicle, Involucrum, Ischium, Ivory, Jugal, Kneecap, Knuckle, Lacrimal, Lamella, Long, Luez, Lunate, Luz, Malar, Malleolus, Malleus, Mandible, Manubrium, Marrow, Mastoid, Maxilla, Medulla, Membrane, Metacarpal, Metatarsal, Napier's, Nasal, Navicular, Occipital, Olecranon, Omoplate, Orthopaedics, Os, Ossicle, Osteo-, Palatine, Parasphenoid, Parietal, Patella, Pecten, Pectoral, Pedal, Pelvis, Pen, Percoid, Perone, Petrous, Phalanx, Pisiform, Ploughshare, Premaxilla, Prenasal, Pterygoid, Pubis, Pygostyle, Quadrate, Rack, Radiale, Radialia, Radius, Relic, Rib, Rump-post, Sacrum, Scaphoid, Scapula, Sclere, Sepium, Sequestrum, Sesamoid, Share, Shin, Skeleton, Skull, Spade, Sphenoid, Splint, Splinter, Spur, Squamosal, Stapes, →STEAL, Sternebra, Sternum, Stifle, Stirrup, Suboperculum, T, Talus, Tarsometatarsus, Tarsus, Temporal, Tibia, Tibiotarsus, Tot, Trapezium, Triquetral, Trochanter, Trochlea, True-rib, Turbinate, Tympanic, Ulna, Vertebrae, Vomer, Whirl, Wish, Wormian, Zygomatic

**Bonehead(ed)** Capitellum, Capitulum, Obtuse

**Bonehouse** Charnel house, Ossuary

**Boneshaker** Dandy-horse, Draisene, Draisine, Velocipede

**Bonfire** Bale-fire, Beltane, Blaze, Chumping, Clavie, Feu de joie, Pyre

**Boniface** Inn-keeper, Landlord, Taverner

**Bonne-bouche** Cate

**Bonnet** Balmoral, Bongrace, Cap, Cornette, Cowl, Easter, Glengarry, Hood, Hummel, Hummle, Kiss-me(-quick), Mobcap, Mutch, Poke, Scotch, Sun, Tam(my), Toorie, Tourie, War

**Bonny** Blithe, Gay, Merry, Sonsy, Weelfar'd

**Bonsai** Saikei

**Bonus** Bisque, Bounty, Braata, Bye, Christmas box, Danger money, Dividend, Escalator, Extra, Hand-out, Icing, Lagniappe, No-claim, →PREMIUM, Reversionary, Reward, Scrip, Signing, Spin-off, Windfall

**Boo** Barrack, Explode

**Boob** Gaffe, Nork, Simpleton, Stumer

**Booby** Dunce, Gremial, Hick, Patch, Patchcocke, Patchoke, →STUPID, Wooden spoon

**Booby trap** Infernal machine

**Boojum** Snark

**Book(s), Bookish, Bookwork** Abcee, Absey, Academic, Adversaria, Album, Antilegomena, Antiphonary, Appointment, Audio, B, Backlist, Bedside, Bestiary, Bestseller, Black, Block, Blockbuster, Blotter, Blue, Cash, Chick, Chrestomathy, Classic, Closed, Codex, Coffee-table, Diary, Digest, Directory, Diurnal, Eightvo, Ench(e)iridion, Engage(ment), Enter, Erudite, Exercise, Facetiae, Folio, Fortune, Garland, Good, Gradual, Gradus, Guide, Hardback, Hymnal, Imprint, Index, Issue, Lectionary, Ledger, Lib, Liber, Literary, Livraison, Manual, Memorandum, Missal, Monograph, Muster, Octavo, Octodecimo, Office, Open, Order, Page-turner, Paperback, Pass, Pedantic, Peerage, Phrase, Pica, Plug, Polyglot, Potboiler, Pseudepigrapha, Publication, Puzzle prize, Quair, Quarto, Quire, →RESERVE, Road, Roman-a-clef, Script, Sealed, Sext, Sexto, Sextodecimo, Sixmo, Sixteenmo, Sketch, Softback, Source, Spelling, Spine-chiller, Statute, Studious, Study, Style, Swatch, Symbolical, Table, Tablet, Talking, Tall copy, Te igitur, Text(ual), Thirty-twomo, Thriller, Title, Titule, Tome, Trade, Transfer, Twelvemo, Twenty-fourmo, Unputdownable, Visiting, Visitor's, Vol(ume), Waste, White, Whodunit, Work, Year

## BOOKS

**2 letters:**
Ex
NT
OT

**3 letters:**
Dan
Eph
Gal
Hab
Hag
Jud
Lam
Log
Rag
Red
Rom
Sir
Sus
Tit

**4 letters:**
Acts
Amos
Blad
Edda
Ezek
Ezra
Joel
John
Jude
Luke
Macc
Mark
Mook
Obad
Ruth
Veda

**5 letters:**
Atlas
Bible
Chron
Hosea
James
Kells
Kings
Manga

Micah
Nahum
Pop-up
Snobs
Sutra
Titus
To-bit

**6 letters:**
Aeneid
Baruch
Caxton
Course
Daniel
Eccles
Esdras
Esther
Exeter
Exodus
Haggai
Herbal
I Ching
Isaiah
Jashar
Jasher
Joshua
Judges
Prayer
Primer
Prompt
Psalms
Ration
Reader
Romans
Scroll
Tanach
Tanack

**7 letters:**
Chumash
Cookery
Ezekiel
Genesis
Grolier
Hebrews
Malachi
Martyrs
Matthew

Numbers
Obadiah
Octapla
Omnibus
Orarium
Ordinal
Psalter
Susanna
Timothy

**8 letters:**
Breviary
Clarissa
Domesday
Doomsday
Georgics
Grimoire
Habakkuk
Haggadah
Haggadoh
Hermetic
Libretto
Megillah
Nehemiah
Ordinary
Philemon
Porteous
Portesse
Prophets
Proverbs
Triodion
Vercelli
Vesperal

**9 letters:**
Apocrypha
Ephesians
Formulary
Galatians
Gazetteer
Kama Sutra
Leviticus
Maccabees
Portolano
Reference
Remainder
Satyricon
Sibylline

Sybilline
Telephone
Tripitaka
Vade-mecum
Zephadiah

**10 letters:**
Apocalypse
Chronicles
Colossians
Compendium
Cyclopedia
Dictionary
Heptameron
Heptateuch
Hitopadesa
Incunabula
Passionary
Persuasion
Teratology

**11 letters:**
Commonplace
Concordance
Corinthians
Deuteronomy
Evangeliary
Hagiographa
Nomenclator
Philippians
Revelations

**12 letters:**
Bodice-ripper
Ecclesiastes
Encyclopedia
Lamentations
Panchatantra
Paralipomena
Processional
Responsorial
Twelve Tables

**13 letters:**
Penny dreadful
Pharmacopoeia
Thessalonians

**Bookbinder, Bookbinding** Fanfare, Grolier, Mutton-thumper, Organdie
**Book-case** Credenza, Press, Satchel

**Bookie(s), Bookmaker** Binder, John, Layer, Librettist, Luke, Mark, Matthew, Printer, Ringman, Roget, To-bit, Turf accountant

**Booking** Gig, Reservation, Ticket

**Bookkeeper, Bookkeeping** Clerk, Double entry, Librarian, Posting, Recorder, Satchel, Single-entry

**Booklet** B, Brochure, Folder, Inlay, Pamphlet

**Book-like** Solander

**Book-lover** Incunabulist

**Bookmark, Bookplate** Ex libris, Flag, Tassel

**Book-scorpion** Chelifer

**Bookseller, Bookshop** Bibliopole, Colporteur, Conger, Librair(i)e, Sibyl, Stallman

**Bookworm** Reader, Sap, Scholar

**Boom(ing)** Baby, Beam, Boost, Bowsprit, Bump, Fishpole, Gaff, Increase, Jib, Loud, Orotund, Plangent, Prosper, Resonance, Resound, Roar, Sonic, Spar, Supersonic, Swinging, Thrive, Thunder, Torpedo, Wishbone

**Boomer** Bittern, Bull-of-the-bog, Butter-bump, Kangaroo, Mire-drum

**Boomerang** Backfire, Kiley, Kyley, Kylie, Recoil, Ricochet, Throwstick, Woomera

**Boon** Asset, Bene, Benefit, Blessing, Bounty, Cumshaw, Gift, Godsend, Mills, Mitzvah, Prayer, Windfall

**Boor(ish)** Borel, Bosthoon, Chuffy, Churl, Clodhopper, Crass, Curmudgeon, Goth, Grobian, Hog, Ill-bred, Jack, Jungli, Keelie, Kern(e), Kernish, Kill-courtesy, Lob, Lout, Lumpen, Lumpkin, Ocker, Oik, Peasant, Philistine, Pleb, Trog, Uncouth, Unmannerly, Yahoo, Yob, Yokel

**Boost(er)** Adrenalin, Afterburner, Amplify, Augment, Bolster, Ego, Eik, Eke, Elevate, Encourage, Fillip, Help, Hoist, Impetus, Increase, Injection, Invigorate, Lift, Perk up, Promote, Raise, Rap, Reheat, Reinforce, Reinvigorate, Spike, Steal, Step up, Steroid, Supercharge, Tonic, Wrap

**Boot(s)** Addition, Adelaide, Ankle-jack, Avail, Balmoral, Beetle-crushers, Benefit, Blucher, Bottine, Bovver, Brogan, Brogue, Buskin, Cerne, Chelsea, Chukka, Cockers, Cold, Combat, Concern, Cothurn(us), Cowboy, Cracowe, Crowboot, Daisy roots, Denver, Derby, Desert, Dismiss, Field, Finn(e)sko, Finsko, Fire, Football, Galage, Galosh, Gambado, Go-go, Granny, Gum, Heave-ho, Hessian, High shoe, Hip, Jack, Jemima, Jodhpur, Kamik, Kick-start, Kinky, Kletterschuh, Lace-up, Larrigan, Last, Mitten, Moon, Muchie, Muc(k)luc(k), Mukluk, Pac, Para, Profit, Riding, Rock, Russian, Sabot, →**SACK**, Seven league, →**SHOE**, Shoepac(k), Skivvy, Stogy, Surgical, Tackety, Thigh, Toe, Tonneau, Tops, Trunk, Ugg, Vibram®, Vibs, Wader, Walking, Warm, Weller, Wellie, Wellington, Welly

**Booth** Assassin, Crame, Cubicle, Kiosk, Polling, Stall, Stand, Telephone, Tolsel, Tolsey, Voting

**Bootleg(ger)** Cooper, Coper, Pirate, Runner

**Bootless** Futile, Idle, Unprofitable, Vain

**Booty** Creach, Creagh, Haul, Loot, Prey, Prize, Rump, Spoil(s), Spolia optima, Swag

**Booze(r)** →**DRINK**, Inn, Liquor, Pub, Spree, Tipple

**Bora** Rite, Wind

**Borage** Bugloss, Comfrey, Gromwell, Myosote, Viper's gloss

**Borax** Tincal

**Bordeaux** Claret

**Border(s), Borderland, Borderline** Abut, Adjoin, Apron, Bed, Bind, Bound, Boundary, Braid, Brush, Checkpoint, Coast, Cot(t)ise, Dado, Dentelle, →**EDGE**, Enclose, Engrail, Fimbria, Frieze, Fringe, Frontier, Furbelow, Guilloche, Head-rig, Hedgerow, Hem, Herbaceous, Impale, Kerb, Lambrequin, Limb, Limbate, Limbo, Limen, Limes, Limit, Limitrophe, Line, Lip, List, March, Marchland, →**MARGIN**, Mat, Mattoid, Meith, Mete, Mount, Neighbour, Orle, Outskirts, Pale, Pand, Pelmet, Penumbra, Perimeter, Purfle, Purlieu, Rand, Rim, Rio Grande, Roadside, Roon, Royne, Rubicon, Rund,

Rymme, Scottish, Screed, Selvage, Selvedge, Side, Skirt, Skirting, Splenium, Strand, Strip, Surround, Swage, T(h)alweg, The Marches, Trench, Tressure, Valance, Valence, →**VERGE**, Wayside

▷ **Borders** *may indicate* first and last letters

**Bore(d), Boredom, Borer, Boring** Aiguille, Airshaft, Anobium, Anorak, Apathy, Aspergillum, Aspergillus, Aspersoir, Auger, Awl, Beetle, Bind, Bit, Blasé, Broach, Brog, Bromide, Calibre, Cataclysm, Chamber, Chokebore, Deadly, Def(fed), Drag, →**DRILL**, Dry, Dullsville, Dusty, Dweeb, Eagre, Eat, Eger, Elshin, Elsin, Endured, Ennui, Ennuye, Fag, Flat, Foozle, Gasbag, Gim(b)let, Gouge, Gribble, Grind, Had, Heigh-ho, Ho-hum, Irk, Jack, Jumper, Land, Listless, Longicorn, Longueur, Meh, Menial, Mind-numbing, Miser, Mole, Mopoke, Motormouth, Nerd, Noyance, Nudni(c)k, Nuisance, Nyaff, Operose, Pain, Pall, Penetrate, Perforate, Pest, Pholas, Pierce, Pill, Platitude, Possessed, Probe, Prosaic, Prosy, Punch, Ream(ingbit), Rifle, Rime, Saddo, Sat, Schmoe, Scolytus, Screw, Severn, Shothole, Snooze, Snore, Sondage, Spleen, Spod, Spudding-un, Sting, Stob, Stupid, Tediosity, Tedious, Tedisome, Tedium, Tedy, Terebra, Teredo, Termes, Termite, Thirl, Tidal wave, Tire, Trepan, Trocar, Tunnel, Turn-off, Underwent, Uninterested, Vapid, →**WEARY**, Well, Wimble, Windbag, Wonk, Woodworm, Workaday, Worldweary, Xylophaga, Yawn

**Borgia** Cesare, Lucretia

**Boric** Sassolin, Sassolite

**Born** B, Begun, Free, Great, Nascent, Nat(us), Né(e)

**Borneo** Dyak, Kalimantan, Sabahan

**Boron** B

**Borough** Borgo, Brooklyn, Close, Pocket, Port, Quarter, Queens, Rotten, Township, Wick

**Borrow(ed), Borrowing** Adopt, Appropriate, Cadge, Copy, Derivative, Eclectic, George, Hum, Leverage, Scrounge, Scunge, Stooze, Straunge, →**TAKE**, Touch

**Borsch** Beetroot

**Bosh** Humbug, Nonsense, Rot

**Bosom** Abraham's, Breast, Bristols, Bust, Close, Gremial, Heart, Inarm, Intimate, Poitrine

**Boson** Gauge, Squark

**Boss(ed), Bossy** Alder(man), Big White Chief, Blooper, Burr, Cacique, Capo, Cazique, Cow, Dictate, Director, Dominate, Domineer, Gadroon, Gaffer, Governor, Guv, Headman, Honcho, Hump, Inian, Inion, Jewel, Kingpin, Knob, Knop, Knot, Leader, Maestro, →**MANAGER**, Massa, MD, →**MISTAKE**, Mistress, Netsuke, Niggerhead, Noop, Nose-led, Omphalos, Oubaas, Overlord, Overseer, Owner, Padrone, Pannikin, Pellet, Protuberance, Ruler, Run, Sherang, Straw, Stud, Superintendent, Superior, Supervisor, Supremo, Taskmaster, Top banana, Umbo(nate)

**Boston** Hub

**Bot** Oestrus

**Botany, Botanist** Banks, Bryology, Candolle, Carpology, Cockayne, Darwin, Dendrologist, Frees, Garden, Godet, Graminology, Herbist, Jungermann, Linnaeus, Marchant, Mendel, Mycology, Phytogenesis, Phytology, Pteridology, Tradescant, Weigel

**Botch(ed)** Bungle, Clamper, Cock-up, Flub, Fudge, Mismanage, Mux, Pig's ear, Spoil, Tink

**Both** Couple, Together, Two

**Bother(some)** Ado, Aggro, Annoy, Brush, Care, Deave, Deeve, Disturb, Drat, Fash, Fluster, Fracas, Fuss, Get, Harassment, Harry, Hassle, Hector, Hoot-toot, Incommode, Irk, Irritate, Moither, Nag, Nark, Nonplus, Nuisance, Palaver, Perturb, Pesky, Pest(er), Pickle, Reke, Rile, Shtuck, Todo, →**TROUBLE**, Vex

**Bottle(s)** Ampul(la), Bacbuc, Balthasar, Balthazar, Belshazzar, Blackjack, Borachio, Bravado, Bundle, Carafe, Carboy, Case, Chapine, Cock, Cork, Costrel, Courage, Cruet, Cruse, Cucurbital, Cutter, Dead-man, Decanter, Demijohn, Fearlessness, Feeding, Fiasco, Filette, Flacket, Flacon, Flagon, Flask, Glass can, Goatskin, Gourd, Grit, Guts, Half-jack, Hen, Imperial, Jeroboam, Junk, Klein, Lachrymal, Lagena, Magnetic, Magnum,

Marie-Jeanne, Matrass, Medicine, Melchior, Methuselah, Mettle, Mickey, Middy, Nansen, Nebuchadnezzar, →**NERVE**, Nursing, Phial, Pig, Pilgrim, Pitcher, Pooter, Pycnometer, Rehoboam, Resource, Retort, Salmanaser, Salmanazar, Scent, Screwtop, Siphon, Smelling, Split, Squeeze, Squeezy, Stubby, Sucking, Tear, Tube, Twenty-sixer, Vial, Vinaigret(te), Wad, Wallop, Water, Water bouget, Weighing, Winchester, Wine, Woulfe

▷ **Bottle(d)** *may indicate* an anagram or a hidden word

**Bottom** Anus, Aris, Arse, Ass, Base, Batty, Beauty, Bed, Benthos, Bilge, Booty, Breech, Bum, Butt, Buttocks, Coit, Croup(e), Croupon, Demersal, Derrière, Doup, Dowp, Duff, End, Fanny, Floor, Foot, Foundation, Fud, Fundus, Ground, Haunches, Hunkers, Hurdies, Jacksy, Keel(son), Kick, Lumbar, Minimus, Nadir, Nates, Planning, Podex, Posterior, Pottle-deep, Prat, Pyramus, Quark, Rear, Rock, Root, Rump, Seat, Ship, Sill, Sole, Staddle, Stamina, Tail, Tush, Weaver

**Bottom drawer** Glory box

**Bottomless** Subjacent

**Botulism** Limberneck

**Boudoir** Bower, Room

**Bouffant** Pouf

**Bough** Branch, Limb, Roughie, Roughy

**Bought** Coft

**Boulder** Erratic, Gibber, Niggerhead, Rock, Sarsen, →**STONE**

**Boule** Senate

**Bounce(r), Bouncing, Bouncy** Ananias, Ball, Bang, Blague, Bound, Bumper, Caper, Convention, Dandle, Dap, Dead-cat, Doorman, Dop, Dud, Eject, Evict, Fib, Jounce, Keepy-uppy, Kite, Lie, Lilt, Muscleman, Resilient, Ricochet, Spiccato, Spring, Stot, Tale, Tamp, Tigger, Trampoline, Valve, Verve, Vitality, Yorker, Yump

▷ **Bouncing** *may indicate* an anagram

**Bound(er), Boundary** Adipose, Apprenticed, Articled, Bad, Barrier, Beholden, Border, Bourn(e), Bubalis, Cad, Cavort, Certain, Circumference, Curvet, Dart, Decreed, Demarcation, Demarkation, Divide, Dool, Dule, Duty, End, Engirt, Entrechat, Erub, Eruv, Event horizon, Exciton, Extent, Fence, Finite, Four, Frape, Frontier, Galumph, Gambado, Gambol, Girt, Goal, Harestane, Hedge, Heel, Held, Hoarstone, Hops, Hourstone, Ibex, Interface, Izard, Jump, Kangaroo, K/T, →**LEAP**, Liable, Limes, Limit, Linch, Lollop, Lope, March-stone, Mason-Dixon line, Meare, Meer, Meith, Mere, Merestone, Mete, Milestone, Moho, Muscle, Obliged, Ourebi, Outedge, Outfield, Outward, Pale, Parameter, Perimeter, Periphery, Plate, Prance, Precinct, Prometheus, Purlieu, Quickset, Redound, Ring-fence, Roller, Roo, Roped, Rubicon, Scoundrel, Scoup, Scowp, Serf, Side, Sideline, Six(er), Skelp, Skip, Spang, Spring, Sten(d), Stoit, Stylolite, Sure, T(h)alweg, Terminator, Tide, Tied, Touchline, Tramline, Upstart, Vault, Verge, Wallaby, Wound

**Boundless** Illimited, Unlimited, Vast

▷ **Bounds** *may indicate* outside letters

**Bounty, Bountiful** Aid, Bligh, Boon, Christian, Generosity, →**GIFT**, Goodness, Grant, Head money, Honorarium, Largess(e), Lavish, Philanthropy, Queen Anne's, Queen's, Reward

**Bouquet** Aroma, Attar, Aura, Compliment, Congratulations, Corsage, Fragrancy, Garni, Nose, Nosegay, Odour, Perfume, Plaudit, Posy, Pot pourri, Scent, Spiritual, Spray

**Bourbon** Alfonso, Biscuit

**Bourgeois(ie)** Biedermeier, Common, Middle class, Pleb(eian), Pooter(ish)

**Bout** Bender, Binge, Bust, Contest, Dose, Go, Jag, Match, Spell, Spree, Turn, Venery, Venewe, Venue

**Boutique** Shop

**Bovine** Stolid

**Bow(ing), Bower, Bowman** Accede, Alcove, Arbour, Arc, Arch, →**ARCHER**, Arco, Arson, Bandy, Beck, Bend, Boudoir, Buckle, Butterfly, Capitulate, Cellist, Clara, Congé(e), Crescent, Crook, Cupid, →**CURVE**, Defer, Dicky, Drail, Droop, Duck, East end, Echelles,

Eros, Eugh, Eyes, Fiddle(r), Fiddlestick, Foredeck, Halse, Hawse, Headgear, Honour, Incline, Inswing(er), Jook, Jouk, Kneel, Kotow, Laval(l)ière, Lean, Londoner, Long, Loof, Lout, Lowt, Luff, Martellato, Menuhin, Moulinet, Namaste, Nameste, Nock, Nod, Nutate, Oar, Obeisance, Obtemper, Outswing, Paganini, Pergola, Prore, Quarrel, Reverence, Salaam, Seamer, Shelter, Slope, Sound, Spiccato, Staccato, Stick, →**SUBMIT**, Swing, Throw, Tie, Torrent, Tureen, Weather, Yew, Yield

**Bowdler(ize)** Comstockery, Edit(or), Water

**Bowels** Entrails, Guts, Innards, Melaena, Viscera

▷ **Bower** *may indicate* using a bow

**Bowl(ing), Bowler, Bowl over, Bowls** B, Basin, Begging, Bicker, Bocce, Bocci(a), Boccie, Bodyline, Bool, Bosey, Bouncer, Cage-cup, Calabash, Caldera, Candlepins, Cap, Carpet, Caup, Chalice, Cheese, Chinaman, Christie, Christy, Cog(g)ie, Concave, Coolamon, Crater, Cup, Deliver, Derby, →**DISH**, Dismiss, Dome, Doosra, Drake, Dumbfound, Dust, Ecuelle, End, Finger, Fivepin, Font, Goblet, Goldfish, Googly, Grail, Grub, Headgear, Hog, Hoop, Inswing(er), Jack, Jéroboam, Jorum, Kegler, Krater, Lavabo, Laver, Leg-spin, Lightweight, Lob, Locke, Mazer, Monteith, Night, Offbreak, Off-cutter, Old, Outswing, Over-arm, Overpitch, Pace(man), Pan, Pétanque, Piggin, Pitch, Porringer, Pot-hat, Pottinger, Punch, Raku, Rice, Rink, Roll, Roundarm, Seam(er), Skip, Skittle(s), Spare, Speed, Spinner, Spofforth, Stadium, Stagger, Stummel, Sucrier, Super, Swing, Ten-pin, Throw, Tom, Tureen, Underarm, Underhand, Underwood, Voce, Washbasin, Wassail, Wood, York(er)

**Box(ing)** ABA, Alert, Ark, Baignoire, Ballot, Bandbox, Bareknuckle, Bento, Bijou, Bimble, Binnacle, Black, Blow, Blue, Bonk, Booth, Buist, Bunk, Bush, Caddy, Call, Camera, Canister, Cardboard, Case, Cash, Casket, Cassette, Cassolette, Chest, Chinese, Chocolate, Christmas, Ciborium, Clog, Coach, Coffer, Coffin, Coffret, Coin, Commentary, Compartment, Confessional, Cool, Crash, Crate, Cuff, Dabba, Dead-letter, Deed, Dialog(ue), Dispatch, Ditty, Dog, Drawer, Earpiece, Egg, Encase, Enclose, Etui, →**FIGHT**, File, Fist, Fund, Fuse, Fuzz, Gear, Glory, Glove, Go-kart, Grass, Hat, Hay, Hedge, Hive, Honesty, Horse, Humidor, Hutch, Ice, Idiot, Inherce, Inro, Inter, Jewel, Journal, Juke, Junction, Jury, Keister, Kick, Kiosk, Kite, Knevell, Knowledge, Ladle, Letter, Light, Live, Locker, Lodge, Loge, Loose, Lug, Lunch, Match, Message, Mill, Mitre, Mocock, Mocuck, Money, Musical, Nest(ing), Noble art, Noble science, Omnibus, Orgone, Out, Package, Packing, Paint, Pandora's, Papeterie, Patch, Pattress, Peepshow, Peg, Pen, Penalty (area), Petara, Pew, Phylactery, Piggybank, Pill, Pillar, Pitara, Pix, Poor, Post, Pounce(t), Powder, Press, Prize fight, Prompt, Protector, Puff, Pugilism, Punnet, Pyxis, Red, Register, Resonance, Ring, Rope-a-dope, Royal, Safe-deposit, Saggar(d), Sagger, Sand, Savate, Scent, Scrap, Scrine, Seggar, Sentry, Set-top, Shadow, Shoe, Shooting, Side, Signal, Skinner, Skip(pet), Slipcase, Smudge, Sneeshin-mull, Sneeze, Soap, Solander, Sound, Sound body, →**SPAR**, Spice, Spit, Spring, Squawk, Squeeze, Stock, Strong, Stuffing, Swell, Tabernacle, Tee, Tefillin, Telephone, Telly, Thai, Tick, Tin, Tinder, Tivo, Tool, Touch, Trunk, Tube, Tuck, TV, Urn, Vanity, Vasculum, Vinaigrette, Voice, Weather, Window, Wine, Witness, Yakhdan

**Boxer(s)** Ali, Amycus, Babyweight, Bantamweight, Bruiser, Bruno, Canine, Carnera, Carpentier, Carthorse, Chinaman, Cooper, Corbett, Crater, Cruiserweight, Darcy, Dempsey, Dog, Eryx, Farr, Featherweight, Flyweight, Foreman, Ham, Heavyweight, Lightweight, McCoy, Middleweight, Mosquito-weight, Pandora, Pollux, Pug, Pugil(ist), Rebellion, Rocky, Shadow, Shorts, Southpaw, Sparrer, Strawweight, Sugar Ray Robinson, Welterweight, Wilde

**Boxing-glove** Hurlbat, Muffle, Whirlbat, Whorlbat

**Boy(s)** Amoretto, Anchor, Apprentice, Ball, Bevin, Blue-eyed, Bovver, Bub(by), Cabin, Callant, Catamite, Champagne, Chiel(d), →**CHILD**, Chokra, Chummy, Cub, Cupid, Dandiprat, Errant, Galopin, Garçon, Gorsoon, Gossoon, Green Mountain, Groom, Grummet, Ha, Hansel, I say, Jack, Kid, Klonkie, Knave, Knave-bairn, Kwedien, Lackbeard, →**LAD**, Loblolly, Loon(ie), Minstrel, Nibs, Nipper, Office, Page, Poster, Pot, Prentice, Principal, Putto, Rent, Roaring, Rude, Shaver, Ship's, Son, Spalpeen, Sprig, Stripling, Swain, Tad, Tar, Ted(dy), Tiger, Toxic, Toy, Urchin, Whipping, Wide, →**YOUTH**

▷ **Boy** *may indicate* an abbreviated name

**Boycott** Avoid, Ban, Bat, Black, Blacklist, Exclude, Geoff(rey), Hartal, Isolate, Ostracise, Shun, Swadeshi

**Boyfriend** Beau, Date, Fella, Fellow, Squeeze, Steady

**Boyle** Juno

**Bp** Bishop, DD, RR

**Brace(s), Bracing** Accolade, Clamp, Couple, Crosstree, Fortify, Gallace, Gallows, Gallus(es), Gird, Hound, Invigorate, Ozone, Pair, Pr, Rear-arch, Rere-arch, Sea air, Skeg, Spider, Splint, Stage, Steady, Stiffener, Strut, → **SUPPORT**, Suspenders, Tauten, Thorough, Tone, Tonic, Two(-hander)

**Bracelet** Armil(lla), Armlet, Bangle, Cuff, Darbies, Handcuff, Identity, Manacle, Manilla

**Brachiopod** Ecardines, Lamp-shell, Spirifer

**Bracken** Brake, Fern, Pteridium, Tara

**Bracket** Ancon, Angle-iron, Bibb, Brace, Cantilever, Console, Corbel, Couple, Cripple, Gusset, Hanger, Lance rest, Misericord(e), Modillion, Mutule, Parenthesis, Potence, Pylon, Rigger, Round, Sconce, Square, Straddle, Strata, → **STRUT**, Trivet, Truss

**Brackish** Stagnant

**Bract** Glume(lla), Hypsophyll, Involucel, Involucre, Job's tears, Leaf, Lemma, Palea, Palet, Phyllary, Spathe

**Brad** Nail, Pin, Rivet, Sprig

**Brae** Hillside

**Brag(gart), Bragging** Basilisco, Birkie, Bluster, Boast, Bobadil, Boister, Bombastic, Braggadocio, Bull, Cockalorum, Crow, Falstaff, Fanfaronade, Gab, Gascon, Hot-air, Loudmouth, Mouth off, Parolles, Puckfist, Puff, Rodomontader, Skite, Slam, Swagger, Thrason, Thrasonic, Tongue-doubtie, Tongue-doughty, Upstart, Vainglorious, Vapour, Vaunt

**Brahma(n)** San(n)yasi(n)

**Braid** A(i)glet, Aiguillette, Enlace, Fishbone, French, Frog, Galloon, Lacet, Plait, Plat, Rickrack, Ricrac, Scrambled eggs, Seaming-lace, Sennet, Sennit, Sinnet, Soutache, Tress, Trim, Twist, Weave

**Braille (system)** Moon

**Brain(box), Brain disease, Brain-power, Brain problem, Brains, Brainstorm, Brainy** Amygdala, Appestat, Bean, Boffin, Bright, Brilliant, Cerebellum, Cerebrum, Contravene, Cortex, Crane, Cranium, Diencephalon, Dura mater, Egghead, Encephalon, Epencephalon, Fornix, Genius, Gliosis, Grey matter, Gyrus, Harn(s), Head, Headpiece, Hippocampus, Hydrocephalus, Hypothalamus, Inspiration, Insula, Intelligence, IQ, Kuru, Left, Limbic, Loaf, Lobe, Lobule, Mastermind, Mater, Medulla, Medulla oblongata, Metencephalon, Mind, Noddle, Noesis, Nous, Peduncle, Pericranium, Pia mater, Pons, Pontile, Prosencephalon, Quick, Rhinencephalon, Rhombencephalon, Ringleader, Sconce, Sense, Sensorium, Smarty pants, Striatum, Subcortex, Sulcus, Tapagnosia, Tectum, Telencephalon, Thalamencephalon, Thalamus, Upper stor(e)y, Vermis, Vortex, Wetware

▷ **Brain(s)** *may indicate* an anagram

**Brainless** Anencephaly, Bimbo, Stupid, Thick

**Brainwash(ing)** Indoctrinate, Menticide, Persuade, Propaganda

**Brake, Braking** ABS, Adiantum, Aerodynamic, Air, Anchors, Antilock, Bracken, Centrifugal, Curb, Disc, Dive, Drag, Drum, Estate car, Fern, Fly, Foot, Grove, Hand, Hub, Hydraulic, Nemoral, Overrun, Ratchet, Rein, Rim, Shoe, Shooting, → **SLOW**, Spinney, Sprag, Tara, Thicket, Vacuum, Westinghouse

**Bramble, Brambly** Batology, Blackberry, Boysenberry, Brier, Cloudberry, Rubus, Thorn, Wait-a-bit, Youngberry

**Bran** Cereal, Chesil, Chisel, Oats, Pollard

**Branch(ed), Branches, Branching, Branch office** Affiliate, Antler, Arm, BO, Bough, Chapel, Cladode, Cow, Dendron, Dept, Diversify, Diverticulum, Divide, Filiate, Fork, Grain, Jump, Kow, Lateral, Leaf-trace, Limb, Lobe, Lobus, Loop, Lye, Lylum,

Offshoot, Olive, Patulous, Phylloclade, Prong, Rachilla, Raguly, Ramate, Ramulus, Reis, Rice, Shroud, Special, Spray(ey), Sprig, Spur, Stirpes, Tributary, Turning, Turn-off, Twig, Wattle, Whip, Yard

**Branch-rib** Lierne

**Brand(ing)** Broadsword, Buist, Burn, Cauterise, Chop, Class, Dealer, Denounce, Earmark, Ember, Excalibur, Falchion, Faulchin, Faulchion, Flambeau, Home, Idiograph, Ilk, Inust, Iron, Label, Line, → **MARK**, Marque, Name, Neckverse, Own, Power, Sear, Sere, Stigma, Sweard, Sword, Torch, Trade name, Wipe

**Brandish** Bless, Flaunt, Flourish, Hurtle, Waffle, Wampish, Wave

**Brandy** Aguardiente, Applejack, Apricot, Aqua vitae, Armagnac, Bingo, Calvados, Cape smoke, Cherry bounce, Cognac, Cold without, Dop, Eau de vie, Fine, Fine champagne, Framboise, Grappa, Kirsch, Mampoer, Marc, Mirabelle, Mobbie, Mobby, Nantes, Nantz, Napoleon, Palinka, Peach, Quetsch, Slivovic(a), Slivovitz, Smoke, VSOP

**Bras** Arms

**Brash** Cocky, Flashy, Impudent, Jack-the-lad, Jumped-up, Pushy, Rain, Rash, Uppity

**Brass(y), Brassware** Alpha-beta, Althorn, Benares, Brazen, Bugle, Cheek, Club, Corinthian, Cornet, Cornopean, Dinanderie, Effrontery, Face, Front, Harsh, High, Horn, Horse, Latten, Lip, Lolly, Loot, Lota(h), Loud, Matrix, → **MONEY**, Moola(h), Oof, Oricalche, Orichalc, Palimpsest, Pyrites, Sass, Snash, Sopranino, Talus, Top, Trombone, Tuba, White, Wood, Yellow metal

**Brassard** Armlet

**Brass hat** Brig

**Brassica** Brussels (sprout), → **CABBAGE**, Colza, Turnip

**Brassière** Gay deceiver

**Brat** Bairn, Bra(t)chet, Enfant terrible, Gait(t), Gamin, Geit, Get, Git, Gyte, Horror, Imp, Lad, Perisher, Terror, Tyke, Urchin

**Braun** Eva

**Bravado, Brave(ry)** Amerind, Apache, Bold, Conan, Corragio, Courage, Creek, Dare, → **DEFY**, Derring-do, Doughty, Dress, Face, Fearless, Gallant, Game, Gamy, Gutsy, Hardy, Heroism, Impavid, Indian, Injun, Intrepid, → **LION**, Lion-hearted, Lionly, Manful, Manly, → **MEXICAN**, Nannup, → **NORTH AMERICAN**, Plucky, Prow(ess), Redskin, Russian roulette, Sannup, Skookum, → **SOUTH AMERICAN**, Spunk, Stalwart, Stout, Uncas, Valiant, Valour, Venturesome, Wight, Withstand, Yeoman

**Bravo** Acclaim, B, Bandit, Bully, Desperado, Euge, Murderer, Olé, Shabash, Spadassin, Villain

**Brawl(er)** Affray, Bagarre, Bicker, Brabble, Donnybrook, Dust, Dust-up, Fight, Flite, Flyte, Fracas, Fratch, Fray, Free-for-all, Melee, Prawl, Punch up, Rammy, Roarer, Roughhouse, Row, Ruck, Scold, Scrap, Scuffle, Set-to, Shindig, Slugfest, Stoush, Tar, Troublesome, Wrangle

**Brawn** Beef, Burliness, Headcheese, He-man, Might, Muscle, Power, Rillettes, Sinew

**Bray** Cry, Heehaw, Stamp, Vicar, Whinny

**Brazen** Blatant, Bold, Brash, Brassy, Flagrant, Forward, Impudent, Shameless, Unabashed

**Brazier** Brasero, Fire, Hibachi, Mangal, Scaldino

**Brazil(ian)** Caboclo, Carioca, Cream-nut, Para, Yanomami, Yanomamo

**Breach** Affray, Assault, Break, Chasm, Cleft, Foul, Gap(e), Great schism, Gulf, Infraction, Redan, Rift, Rupture, Saltus, Schism, Solecism, Solution, Trespass, Violate

**Bread, Bread crumbs** Afikomen, Azym(e), Bagel, Baguette, Bannock, Bap, Barmbrack, Barm cake, Batch, Baton, Black, Bloomer, Brewis, Brioche, Brown, Brownie, Bun, Cash, Chal(l)ah, Chametz, Chapati, Cheat, Ciabatta, Cob, Coburg, Compone, Corn (pone), Corsned, Croissant, Crostini, Croute, Crouton, Crumpet, Crust, Currency, Damper, Dibs, Dika, Doorstep, Elephant's-foot, Eucharist, Eulogia, Fancy, Flatbread, Focaccia, Fougasse, French (stick), Funds, Garlic, Gluten, Graham, Granary, Grissini, Guarana, Hallah, Hametz, Hometz, Horse, Host, Indian, Injera, Jannock, Johnny-cake, Kaffir, Lavash, Laver, Leavened, Loaf, Long tin, Manchet, Maori, Matzo, Milk loaf, Milk-sop, → **MONEY**, Monkey,

Na(a)n, Pain, Panada, Panary, Pane, Paneity, Panini, Panko, Paratha, Pay, Petit pain, Pikelet, Pit(t)a, Pone, Poori, Popover, Poppadom, Poultice, Prozymite, Pumpernickel, Puree, Puri, Quick, Raspings, Ravel, Roll, Rooty, Roti, Round, Rusk, Rye, Sally Lunn, Schnecken, Shewbread, Shive, Simnel, Sippet, Smor(re)brod, Soda, Soft-tommy, Sop, Sourdough, Split tin, Staff of life, Standard, Stollen, Stottie, Sugar, Sweet, Tartine, Tea, Tommy, Tortoise-plant, Twist, Wastel, White, Wrap, Zakuski, Zwieback

**Breadfruit** Ja(c)k

**Breadwinner** Earner, Pa

**Break, Break-down, Break down, Break-in, Break-up, Break up, Broken** Adjourn, Analyse, Apn(o)ea, Aposiopesis, Bait, Biodegrade, Breach, Breather, Burst, Bust, Caesura, Caesure, Cantle, Career, Cark, Cesure, Chance, Chinaman, Chip, Cleave, Coffee, Comb, Comma, Commercial, Comminute, Compost, Compurgatory, Conk, Contravene, Crack, Crock, Crumble, Dash, Deave, Debacle, Decompose, Deeve, Demob, Destroy, Detach, Diaresis, Diffract, Disband, Disintegrate, Disperse, Disrupt, Dissect, Duvet day, Elevenses, Erumpent, Erupt, Exeat, Fast, Fault, Flaw, Four, → **FRACTURE**, Fragment, Fritter, Frush, Gaffe, Gap, Give, Greenstick, Haematolysis, Half-term, Half-time, Harm, Hernia, Hiatus, Holiday, Hydrolyse, Infringe, Interim, Interlude, Intermission, Interrupt, Interspace, → **INTERVAL**, Irrupt, Kark, Knap, Knickpoint, Lacuna, Lapse, Layover, Leave, Lysis, Moratorium, Natural, Nickpoint, Nooner, Outage, Parse, Part, Pause, Phreak, Playtime, Poach, Polarise, Price, Reave, Recess, Recrudescent, Relief, Rend, Resolve, Resorption, Respite, Rest, Rift, Rise, Ruin, Rupture, Saltus, Schism(a), Secede, Service, Shatter, Shear, Shiver, Smash, Smokeho, Smoko, Snap, Split, Start, Stave, Stop, Stop-over, Stove, Sunder, Take five, Take ten, Tame, Tea-ho, Tear, Tenderise, Time-out, Torn, Transgress, Truce, Twist, Vacation, Violate, Watergate, Weekend

**Breakable** Brittle, Delicate, Fissile, Fragile, Frail, Friable

**Breakdown** Abruption, Analyse, Autolysis, Cataclasm, Collapse, Conk, Crack-up, Glitch, Glycolosis, Glycolysis, Haematolysis, Histolysis, Hydrolysis, Lyse, Lysis, Nervous, Ruin

**Breaker** Billow, Circuit, Comber, Ice, Roller, Smasher, Surf

**Breakfast** B, Brunch, Chota-hazri, Continental, Deskfast, Disjune, English, Kipper, Petit déjeuner, Power, Wedding

**Breakneck** Headlong

**Breakthrough** Discovery, Quantum leap

**Breakwater** Groyne, Jetty, Mole, Pier, Tetrapod

**Bream** Fish, Porgy, Sar(gus), Sea, Silver, Tai, White

**Breast(s), Breastbone, Breastwork** Bazuma, Boob, Bosom, Brave, Brisket, Bristols, Bust, Chimney, Clean, Counter, Diddy, Duddy, Dug, Falsies, Garbonza, Gazunga, Heart-spoon, Jubbies, Jugs, Knockers, Norg, Nork, Pigeon, Rampart, Redan, Sangar, Stem, Sternum, Stroke, Sungar, Supreme, Tit, Xiphisternum

**Breastplate** Armour, Byrnie, Curat, Curiet, Pectoral, Plastron, Rational, Rest, Shield, Thorax, Xiphiplastron

**Breath(e), Breathing, Breather** Aerobe, Air-sac, Apneusis, Aqualung, Aspirate, Bated, Branchia, Buteyko method, Caesural, Cheyne-Stokes, Circular, Cypress-knee, Eupnoea, Exhalation, Expiration, Flatus, Gasp, Gill, H, Halitosis, Hauriant, Haurient, Hobday, Hypernoea, Hyperventilation, Hypopnoea, Inhale, Inspiration, Interval, Knee, Lenticellate, Lung, Nares, Nostril, Orthopnoea, Oxygenator, Pant, Plosion, Pneuma, Prana, Pulmo, Rale, Respire, Respite, Rest, Rhonchus, Rough, Scuba, Sigh, Smooth, Snore, Snorkel, Snortmast, Snotter, Snuffle, Souffle, Spiracle, Spirit, Spiritus, Stertor, Stridor, Suspire, Tachypnoea, Trachea, Vent, Wheeze, Whiff, Whift, Whisper, Whist, Wind, Windpipe

**Breathless(ness)** Anhelation, Apnoea, Asthma, Dyspnoea, Emphysema, Orthopnoea, Puffed-out, Purfled, Tachypnoea, Wheezing

**Breathtaking** Amazing, Asphyxia, Awesome, Throttling

**Breech(es)** Bible, Buckskin, Chaps, Chausses, Flog, Galligaskins, Hose, Jodhpurs, Kneecords, Knickerbockers, Pantaloons, Petticoat, Plushes, Riding, Smallclothes, Smalls, Trews, Trouse(rs), Trunk hose, Trusses

**Breed(er), Breeding(-place)** Bear, Beget, Cleck, Digoneutic, Endogamous, Engender, Engend(r)ure, Eugenics, Fancier, Fast, Generation, Gentilesse, Gentility, Gentrice, Hetero, Hotbed, In-and-in, Line, Lineage, →MANNERS, Origin, Panmixia, Procreate, Propagate, Pullulate, Race, Raise, Rear, Savoir vivre, Seminary, Sire, Species, Stirpiculture, Stock, Strain, Stud, Telegony, Thremmatology, Tribe, Voltinism

**Breeze, Breezy** Air, Breath, Brisk, Cakewalk, Catspaw, Chipper, Doctor, Draught, Fresh, Gentle, Gust, Land, Light, Mackerel, Moderate, Piece of cake, Pushover, Sea, Slant, Sniffler, Snifter, Strong, Tiff, Zephyr

**Brethren** Bohemian, Close, Darbyite, Elder, Exclusive, Herrnhuter, Ignorantine, Kin, Open, Plymouth, Trinity

**Breton** Armoric, Brezonek

**Breve** Minim, Note, O

**Breviary** Portesse, Portous

▶ **Brevity** *see* BRIEF(S)

**Brew(ery), Brewer, Brewing** Afoot, Ale, Billycan, Boutique, Brose, Browst, Bummock, →CONCOCT, Contrive, Dictionary, Distillery, Elixir, Ferment, Infusion, Liquor, Malt, Percolate, Perk, Potion, Scald, Steep, Witches', Yeast, Yill, Zymurgy

**Briar** Bramble, Canker, Lawyer

**Bribe(ry)** Backhander, Barratry, Barretry, Bonus, Boodle, Bung, Buy, Carrot, Dash, Douceur, Embracery, Get at, Gift, Graft, Grease, Hamper, Hush-money, Insult, Kickback, Lubricate, Oil, Palm, Palm-grease, Palm-oil, Payola, Schmear, Slush, Soap, Sop, Square, Straightener, Suborn, Sweeten(er), Tamper, Tempt, Tenderloin, Vail, Vales

**Bric-a-brac** Bibelot, Curio, Rattle-trap, Smytrie, Tatt, Virtu

**Brick(s), Brickwork** Adobe, Air, Bat, Bath, Bonder, Bondstone, Boob, Breeze(-block), Bristol, Bullnose, Bur(r), Clanger, Clinker, Closer, Course, Dutch clinker, Fletton, Gaffe, Gault, Gold, Good egg, Hard stocks, Header, Ingot, Klinker, Lateritious, Lego®, Malm, Nog(ging), Opus latericium, Red, Rubber, Rubble, Soldier, Spawn, Sport, Stalwart, Stretcher, Terra-cotta, Testaceous, Tile, Trojan, Trump

**Brickbat** Flak, Missile

**Bricklayer** Churchill

**Bride(s)** Bartered, Danaides, Ellen, Hen, Mail-order, Newlywed, Spouse, War, Wife, Ximena

**Bridesmaid** Paranymph

**Bridge(head), Bridge player** Acol, Air, Al Sirat, Aqueduct, Auction, Australian, Avignon, Ba(u)ck, Bailey, Balance, Barre, Bascule, Bestride, Bifrost, Biritch, Board, Bridle-chord, Brig, Brooklyn, Cable-stayed, Cantilever, Capo, Capodastro, Capotasto, Catwalk, Chevalet, Chicago, Chicane, Clapper, Clifton, Contract, Counterpoise, Cross, Cut-throat, Deck, Declarer, Drawbridge, Duplicate, Flying, Flyover, Foot, Forth, Four-deal, Gangplank, Gangway, Gantry, Girder, Golden Gate, Hog's back, Humber, Humpback, Humpbacked, Ice, Irish, Jigger, Land, Lattice, Leaf, Lifting, Ligger, Link, London, Menai, Millau, Millennium, Murray, Nasion, Overpass, Pivot, Plafond, Ponceau, Pons, Ponticello, Pontifice, Pont levis, Pontoon, Raft, Rainbow, Rialto, Rubber, Severn, Sighs, Sinvat, Skew, Snow, →SPAN, Spanner, Stamford, Straddle, Suspension, Swing, Tay, Temper, Tête-de-pont, Through, Tide over, Transporter, Traversing, Trestle, Truss, Turn, Vertical lift, Viaduct, Vint, Waterloo, Weigh, Wheatstone, Wire

**Bridge pair** EW, NS, SN, WE

**Bridge protector** Ice-apron

**Bridge system** Acol

**Bridie** Onion

**Bridle** Bit, Branks, Bridoon, Bristle, Browband, Crownpiece, Curb, Double, Hackamore, Halter, Headstall, Musrol, Noseband, Rein, Scold's

**Bridle path** Orbit, Track

**Brief(s), Briefing, Briefly, Brevity** Acquaint, Advocate, Aphoristic, Attorney, Awhile, Barristerial, Bluette, Brachyology, Breviate, Cape, Compact, →CONCISE, Conspectus,

Counsel, Crisp, Curt, Dossier, Ephemeral, Fill in, Fleeting, In a word, Inform, Instruct, King's, Laconic, Lawyer, Legal eagle, Nearly, Nutshell, Pants, Papal, Pennorth, Pithy, Precise, Prime, Scant, → **SHORT(EN)**, Short-term, Short-winded, Sitrep, Sparse, Succinct, Summing, Tanga, Terse, Transient, Undershorts, Undies, Update, Watching

**Brig** Br, Hermaphrodite, Jail, Nancy Bell, → **SHIP**, Snow

**Brigade** Anchor Boys, Boys', Corps, Fire, Fur, Girls', Green-ink, International, Naval, Red, Troop

**Brigand** Bandit, Bandolero, Cateran, Haidu(c)k, Heiduc, Heyduck, Klepht, Pillager, Pirate, → **ROBBER**, Rob Roy, Trailbaston

**Bright(ness)** Afterglow, Alert, Ashine, Bertha, Brainbox, Brainy, Breezy, Brilliant, Brisk, Cheery, Chiarezza, Chipper, Clara, Cla(i)re, Clear, Clever, Cuthbert, Danio, Effulgent, Eileen, Elaine, Ellie, Facula, Fair, Floodlit, Florid, Garish, Gay, Glad, Glary, Glow, Helen, Hono(u)r, Hubert, Light, Lit, Loud, Lucent, Lucid, Luculent, Luminous, Lustre, Net(t), Nit, Nitid, Radiant, Roarie, Rorie, Ro(a)ry, Rosy, Scintillating, Sematic, Sharp, Sheeny, Sheer, Shere, Skyre, Smart, Spark(y), Splendour, Starry, Stilb, Sunlit, Sunny, Vive, Vivid, White, Zara

**Bright spot** Facula

**Brilliant, Brilliance** Ace, Aine, Blaze, Brainy, Bravura, Bright, Def, Effulgent, Eurian, Fantastic, Flashy, Galaxy, Gay, Gemmy, Gifted, Glitter, Glossy, High flyer, Humdinger, Inspired, Irradiance, Lambent, Leam, Lucent, Lustre, Masterstroke, Mega-, Meteoric, Nitid, Pear, → **RADIANT**, Refulgent, Resplendent, Shiny, Spangle, Splendid, Splendour, Star, Superb, Virtuoso, → **VIVID**, Water

**Brim** Edge, Lip, Rim, Ugly

**Brimstone** Hellfire, S, Sulphur

**Brindisi** Skolion, Toast

**Brindled** Piebald, Tabby, Tawny

**Brine** Muriatic, Ozone, Pickle, Saline, Salt

**Bring** Afferent, Bear, Carry, Cause, Conduct, Convey, Deploy, Earn, Evoke, Fet, Fetch, Foist, Hatch, Induce, Land, Precipitate, Produce, Wreak, Yield

**Bring up** Breed, Educate, Exhume, Foster, Nurture, Raise, → **REAR**

**Brink** → **EDGE**, Eve, Lip, Rim, Shore, → **VERGE**

**Brio** Elan, Panache

**Brisk(ly), Briskness** Active, Alacrity, Alert, Allegro, Breezy, Busy, Cant, Chipper, Con moto, Crank, Crisp, Crouse, Fresh, Gaillard, Galliard, Jaunty, Kedge, Kedgy, Kidge, Lively, Nippy, Peart, Perk, Pert, Rattling, Roaring, Scherzo, Sharp, Skelp, Smacking, Smart, Snappy, Spanking, Spirited, Sprightly, Vivace, Yare, Zippy

**Bristle, Bristling, Bristly** Aciculum, Arista, Awn, Barb, Bewhiskered, Birse, Bridle, Campodeiform, Chaeta, En brosse, Flurry, Fraught, Frenulum, Glochidium, Gooseflesh, Hackles, Hair, Hérissé, Hispid, Horrent, Horripilation, Nereid, Polychaete, Seta, Setose, Striga, Strigose, Stubble, Styloid, Vibraculum, Villus, Whisker

**Bristle-tail** Campodea

**Brit(ish), Briton(s)** All-red, Anglo, Herring, Iceni, Insular, Isles, Kipper, Limey, Pict, Pom, Rooinek, Rosbif, Saxon, Silt, Silurian, UK

**Britain** Alban(y), Albion, GB, Old Dart

**Britannia (metal)** Tutania

**Brittany** Armorica

**Brittle** Bruckle, Crackly, Crimp, Crisp, Delicate, Edgy, → **FRAGILE**, Frangible, Frush, Hot-short, Redsear, Red-share, Red-shire, Redshort, Shivery, Spall, Spalt

▷ **Brittle** *may indicate* an anagram

**Broach** Approach, Open, Raise, Spit, Suggest, Tap, Widen

**Broad(ly)** Beamy, Cheesy, Crumpet, Dame, Doll, Doxy, Drab, Eclectic, Gaping, General, Generic, Hippy, Largo, Latitudinous, Loose, Outspoken, Ovate, Pro, Roomy, Spatulate, Tart, Thick, Tolerant, Wide, Woman

**Broad-beaked** Latirostrate

**Broadcast(er), Broadcasting** Ad(vertise), Air, Announce, Beam, Breaker, Broadband, CB, Disclose, Disperse, Disseminate, DJ, Downlink, Emission, Ham, IBA, Joyce, Monophonic, Multicast, Narrowband, Network, Newscast, OB, On, Outside, Pirate, Programme, Promulgate, Public address, Put out, Radiate, Radio, Reith, Relay, RTE, Run, Satellite, →SCATTER, Scattershot, Screen(ed), SECAM, Seed, Send, Simulcast, Sky, Sow, Sperse, Sportscast, Spread, Sprinkle, Stereophonic, Telebridge, Telethon, Transmission, Veejay, Ventilate, Wavelength, Wireless

**Broad-nosed** Platyrrhine

**Broadside** Barrage, Criticism, Salvo, Tire

**Broadway** Boulevard, Esplanade, Great White Way, Motorway

**Brocade** Arrasene, Baldachin, Baldaquin, Baudekin, Bawdkin, Kincob, Zari

**Brochure** Booklet, Leaflet, Pamphlet, Programme, Prospectus, Throwaway, Tract, Travelogue

**Brogue** Accent, →SHOE

**Broke(n)** Badly off, Bankrupt, Boracic, Bust(ed), Duff, Evans, Fragmentary, Fritz, Impoverished, Insolvent, Kaput, On the rocks, Puckeroo, Shattered, Skint, Stony, Stove, Strapped

▷ **Broken** *may indicate* an anagram

**Broken off** Prerupt

**Broker** Agent, Banian, Banyan, Discount, Go-between, Government, Insurer, Jobber, Mediator, →MERCHANT, Power, Shadchan, Uncle

**Bromide** Halide, Haloid, Platitude, Truism

**Bromine** Br

**Bronchitis, Bronchitic** Chesty, Husk

**Bronte(s)** Bell, Cyclops

**Brontosaurus** Apatosaurus

**Bronze(d), Bronze age** Aeneous, Aluminium, Bell, Bras(s), Brown, Corinthian, Eugubine, Gunmetal, Hallstatt(ian), Helladic, Kamakura, Manganese, Minoan, Mycenean, Ormolu, Phosphor, Schillerspar, Sextans, Suntanned, Talos, Tan, Third, Torso

**Brooch** Breastpin, Cameo, Clasp, Fibula, Luckenbooth, Ouch, Owche, Pin, Plaque, Preen, Prop, Spang, Sunburst

**Brood(y)** Clecking, Clock, Clucky, Clutch, Cogitate, Contemplate, Cour, Cover, Covey, Dwell (on), Eyas, Eye, Eyrie, Hatch, Hover, Incubate, Introspect, Kindle, Litter, Meditate, Mill, Mope, Mull, Nest, Nid, Nyas, Perch, Pet, →PONDER, Repine, Roost, Sit, Sulk, Team

**Brook** Abide, Babbling, Becher's, Beck, Branch, Burn, Countenance, Creek, Endure, Ghyll, Gill, Kerith, Kill, Pirl, Purl, Rill(et), River, Rivulet, Runlet, Runnel, Springlet, Stand, Stomach, Stream, Suffer, Thole, Tolerate, Wear

**Broom** Besom, Brush, Butcher's, Cow, Cytisus, Genista, Gorse, Greenweed, Hog, Knee-holly, Kow, New, Orobranche, Plantagenet, Retama, Spart, Sweeper, Whisk

**Brose** Atholl, Pease

**Broth** Bouillon, Bree, Brew(is), Court bouillon, Cullis, Dashi, Gruel, Kail, Kale, Muslin-kale, Pot liquor, Pottage, Ramen, Scotch, Skilly, →SOUP, Stock

**Brothel** Bagnio, Bawdy-house, Bordel(lo), Cathouse, Corinth, Crib, Den, Flash-house, Honkytonk, Hothouse, Kip, Knocking shop, Leaping-house, Red-light, Seraglio, Sporting house, Stew, Vaulting-house

**Brother(s), Brotherhood** Ally, Bhai, Billie, Billy, Blood, Boet, Brer, Brethren, Bro, Bud, Comrade, Félibre, Fellow, Fra, Freemason, Grimm, Guild, Lay, Marx, →MONK, Moose, My, Plymouth, Pre-Raphaelite, Sib(ling), Theatine, Trappist, Worker

**Brought (back)** Redux

**Brow** Crest, Forehead, Glabella, Knitted, Ridge, Sinciput, Superciliary, Tump-line

**Browbeat(en)** Badger, Bully, Butt, Cow, Hangdog, Hector, Nut

**Brown(ed)** Abram, Adust, Amber, Apricate, Auburn, Au gratin, Bay, Biscuit, Bisque, Bister, Bistre, Bole, Br, Braise, Brindle, Bronzed, Brunette, Bruno, Burnet, Burnt umber, Camel, Capability, Caramel, Caromel, Centennial, Chamois, Chocolate, Cinnamon,

Cocoa, Cook, Coromandel, Drab, Dun, Duncan, Fallow, Filemot, Fulvous, Fusc(ous), Grill, Hazel, Infuscate, Ivor, John, Khaki, Liver, March, Meadow, Mocha, Mousy, Mulatto, Mushroom, Nut, Oatmeal, Ochre, Olive, Oxblood, Philamot, Pygmalion, Rufous, Rugbeian, Russet, Rust, Sallow, Sand, Scorch, Seal, Sepia, Sienna, Snuff, Soare, Sore, Sorrel, Spadiceous, Tan, Tawny, Tenné, Tenny, Terracotta, Testaceous, Toast, Tom, Umber, Vandyke, Wallflower, Walnut, Wholemeal, Windsor

**Browne** Sam

**Brownian movement** Agitation, Pedesis

**Brownie** Dobbie, Dobby, Dobie, Goblin, Hob, Kobold, Leprechaun, Nis(se), Rosebud, Sprite

**Browse(r)** Eland, Graze, Mouch, Netscape®, Pasture, Read, Scan, Stall-read, Surf, Tapir

**Bruce** Robert

**Bruise** Black eye, Clour, Contund, Contuse, Crush, Damage, Ding, Ecchymosis, Frush, Golp(e), Haematoma, Hurt, Intuse, Livedo, Lividity, Mark, Mouse, Pound, Purpure, Rainbow, Shiner, Ston(n), Stun, Surbate, Vibex

**Brummagem** Tatty

**Brunette** Dark, Latin

**Brush (off), Brushed, Brushwood** Bavin, Bottle, Brake, Broom, Carbon, Caudate, Chaparral, Clash, Clothes, Dandy, Dismiss, Dust, Encounter, Fan, Filbert, Filecard, Firth, Fitch, Foxtail, Frith, Grainer, Hag, Hagg, Hair-pencil, Hog, Kiss, Liner, Lip, Loofa(h), Mop, Paint, Pallet, Pig, Pope's head, Putois, Rebuff, Rice, Rigger, Sable, Scrap, Scrub, Scuff, Shaving, Skim, Skirmish, Striper, Sweep, Tail, Thicket, Touch, Undergrowth, Whisk, Wipe, Wire

**Brusque** Abrupt, Blunt, Brief, Curt, Downright, Offhand, Pithy, Short

**Brussels** Carpet, Lace

**Brutal(ity), Brute** Animal, Atrocity, Barbaric, Beast, Bestial, Bête, Caesar, Caliban, Cruel, Down and dirty, Gorilla, Hun, Iguanodon, Inhuman, Nazi, Nero, Ostrogoth, Pitiless, Quagga, Rambo, Rottweiler, Roughshod, Ruffian, Stupid, Thresher-whale, Torture, Yahoo

**Brutus** Wig

**Bryophyte** Moss, Musci, Tree-moss

**Bubble(s), Bubbly** Aeration, Air-bell, Air-lock, Air pocket, Barmy, Bead(ed), Bell, Bleb, Blister, Boil, Bright, Buller, Cavitate, Champagne, Champers, Cissing, Ebullition, Effervesce, Embolus, Enthuse, Espumoso, Fizz, Foam, → **FROTH**, Gassy, Globule, Gloop, Gurgle, Head, Magnetic, Mantle, Mississippi, Moet, Perrier, Popple, Rale, Reputation, Roundel, Rowndell, Seed, Seethe, Simmer, Soap, South Sea, Vesicle, Widow

**Bubble and squeak** Colcannon

**Buccaneer** Corsair, Dampier, Drake, Freebooter, Morgan, Picaroon, Pirate

**Buck (up)** Bongo, Brace, Cheer, Dandy, Deer, Dollar, Elate, Encheer, Hart, Jerk, Leash, Male, Ourebi, Pitch, Pricket, Ram, Rusa, Sore, Sorel(l), Sorrel, Spade, Spay(a)d, → **STAG**, Staggard, Stud, Water, Wheel

**Buckaroo** Cowboy, Cowpoke

**Bucket(s)** Bail, Bale, Clamshell, Dipper, Ice, Jacob's ladder, Kibble, Ladle, Noria, Pail, Pelt, Piggin, Rain, Rust, Scuttle, Situla, Slop, Stoop(e), Stope, Stoup, Tub

**Buckeye** Ohio

**Buckle** Artois, Bend, Clasp, Contort, Crumple, Deform, Dent, Fasten, Give, Warp

▷ **Buckle** *may indicate* an anagram

**Buckle-beggar** Patrico

**Buckler** Ancile, Rondache, → **SHIELD**, Targe

▷ **Bucks** *may indicate* an anagram

**Buckshee** Free

**Buckthorn** Cascara, Rhineberry, Wahoo

**Buckwheat** Brank, Polygonium, Sarrasin, Sarrazin

**Bucolic** Aeglogue, Eglogue, Idyllic, Pastoral, Rural, Rustic

**Bud(ding), Buddy** Botoné, Bottony, Bulbil, Burgeon, Cacotopia, Caper, Clove, Cobber, Deb, Eye, Gem(ma), Germinate, Hibernaculum, Holly, Knop, Knosp, Knot, Nascent, Pal, Scion, Serial, Shoot, Sprout, Statoblast, Taste, Turion

**Buddha, Buddhism, Buddhist** Abhidhamma, Ahimsa, Amitabha, Anata, Anatta, Anicca, Arhat, Asoka, Bardo, Bodhisattva, Dalai Lama, Dukkha, Esoteric, Foism, Gautama, Hinayana, Jain, Jataka, Jodo, Kagyu, Mahatma, Mahayana, Maitreya, Maya, Nichiren, Pali, Pitaka, Pure Land, Rinzai, Ryobu, Sakya-muni, Sangha, Satori, Shinto, Siddhartha Gautama, Sila, Sima, Soka Gakkai, Soto, Sutra, Tantric, Theravada, Tripitaka, Triratna, Vajrayana, Zen(o)

**Budge** Jee, Move, Shift, Stir, Submit

**Budgerigar** Shell parrakeet, Shell parrot

**Budget(ary)** Allocation, Allot, Cheap, Estimate, Fiscal, Operating, Plan, Programme, Rudder, Save, Shoestring

**Buff** Altogether, Beige, Birthday suit, Blind man's, Cineaste, Eatanswill, Expert, Fan, Fawn, Maven, Mavin, Nankeen, Natural, Nude, Nut, Polish, →**RUB**, Streak

**Buffalo** African, Anoa, Arna, Asiatic, Bison, Bonasus, Bugle, Cap, Cape, Carabao, Obstinacy, Ox, Perplex, Takin, Tamarao, Tamarau, Timarau, Water, Zamouse

**Buffer** Bootblack, Cofferdam, Cutwater, Fender, Sleek-stone

**Buffet** Bang, Blow, Box, Carvery, Counter, Cuff, Finger-food, Fork luncheon, Fork-supper, Hit, Lam, Maltreat, Meal, Perpendicular, Shove, Sideboard, Smorgasborg, Strike, Strook(e), Thwack

**Buffoon(ery)** Antic, Clown, Comedian, Droll, Fool, Goliard, Harlequin, Horseplay, Iniquity, Jack pudding, Jester, Mime(r), Mome, Mountebank, Mummer, Nutter, Pantagruel, Pantaloon(ery), Pickle-herring, Pierrot, Punchinello, Scaramouch, Schmoe, Scogan, Scoggin, Scurril(e), Slouch, Tomfool, Vice, Wag, Zany

**Bug(s)** Ambush, Annoy, Anoplura, Antagonise, Arthropod, Assassin, Bacteria, Bedevil, Beetle, Berry, Bishop's mitre, Bunny, Cabbage, Capsid, Chinch, Cicada, Cimex, Coccidae, Cockchafer, Corixid, Creepy-crawly, Croton, Damsel, Debris, Demon, Dictograph®, Eavesdrop, E-coli, Entomology, Error, Exasperate, Flea, Germ, Get at, Gremlin, Ground, Harlequin, Hassle, Hemiptera, →**INSECT**, Irritate, Jitter, June, Kissing, Lace, Lightning, Listeria, Maori, May, Mealy, Micrococcus, Microphone, Midge, Mike, Milkweed, Millennium, Mite, Nark, Nettle, Pest(er), Pill, Reduviid, Rhododendron, Rile, Shield, Skeeter, Sow, Squash, Tap, Termite, Vex, Virus, Water-measurer, Wheel, Wiretap

**Bugbear** Anathema, Bargest, Bête noire, Bogey, Bogle, Bogy, Eten, Ettin, Poker, Rawhead

**Buggy** Beach, Car, Cart, Inside-car, Pushchair, Shay, Tipcart, Trap

**Bughouse** Fleapit, Loco

**Bugle, Bugle call** Boots and saddles, Chamade, Clarion, Cornet, Flugelhorn, Hallali, Kent, Last post, Ox, Reveille, Taps, →**TRUMPET**, Urus

**Build (up), Building(s), Building site, Build-up** Accrue, Aggrade, Anabolism, Ar(a)eostyle, Assemble, Barn, Basilica, Bathhouse, Bhavan, Big, Boathouse, Brick-laying, Bricks and mortar, Capitol, Chapterhouse, Cob, Colosseum, Commons, Construction, Containment, Corncrib, Cot, →**CREATE**, Cruck, Curia, Days' house, Develop, Dipteros, Dome, Drystone, Duplex, Ectomorph, Edifice, Edify, Endomorph, Erect, Exchange, Fabric, Gain, Gatehouse, Gazebo, Granary, Guildhall, Hangar, Heapstead, High-rise, Hut, Infill, Insula, Kaaba, Ken, Linhay, Listed, Lodge, Low-rise, Lyceum, Malting, Mansion, Mesomorph, Minaret, Monopteron, Mosque, Mould, Observatory, Odeon, Odeum, Outhouse, Palace, Palazzo, Pataka, Pavilion, Pentagon, Pentastyle, Phalanstery, Phalanx, Physique, Pile, Plaque, Portakabin®, Premises, Prytaneum, Quonset®, Raise, Rectory, Ribbon, Rotunda, Shippen, Skyscraper, Somatotype, Squat, Stance, Statehouse, Stature, Structure, Summerhouse, Suspension, Synthesis, System, Systyle, Tectonic, Telecottage, Temple, Tenement, Terrapin®, Tholos, Tower, Tower block, Town hall, Triplex®, Whata, Wheelhouse

**Builder** Bob, Brick(layer), Cheops, Constructor, Engineer, Entrepreneur, Mason, Millwright, Spiderman, Stonemason, Waller

▷ **Building** *may indicate* an anagram

**Built-up** Urban

**Bulb** Camas(h), Camass, Chive, Cive, Corm, Flash, Garlic, Globe, Lamp, Light, Olfactory, Pearl, Rupert's drop, Scallion, Set, Shallot, Squill

**Bulgaria** BG

**Bulge, Bulging** Astrut, Bag, Bias, Biconvex, Bug, Bulbous, Bunchy, Cockle, Entasis, Expand, Exsert, Inion, Node, Prolate, Protrude, Protuberant, Relievo, Rotund, Shoulder, Strout, Strut, →SWELL, Torose, Tumid

**Bulk(y)** Aggregate, Ample, Big, Body, Bouk, Coerce, Corpulent, Density, Domineer, Edict, Extent, Gross, Hull, Immensity, Lofty, Massive, Peak, Pester, Preponderance, Roughage, Scalar, →SIZE, Stout, Threaten, Vol(ume), Voluminous, Weight

**Bull(s), Bullock, Bully(ing)** Abuser, Anoa, Apis, Bakha, Beef, Blarney, Bludgeon, Bluster, Bouncer, Bovine, Brag, Brave, Browbeat, Buchis, Bucko, Centre, Cuttle, Despot, Dragoon, Drawcansir, Encierro, Englishman, Eretrian, Fancyman, Farnese, Flashman, Flatter, Gold, Gosh, Hapi, Harass, Hawcubite, Haze(r), Hector, Hibernicism, Hogwash, Hoodlum, Huff, Intimidate, Investor, Iricism, Irish(ism), John, Killcow, Lambast, Maltreat, Menace, Merwer, Mick(e)(y), Mistake, Mithraism, Mohock, Nandi, Neat, Oppressor, Ox, Pamplona, Papal, Pennalism, Piker, Pistol, Placet, Poler, Pussy-whip, Railroad, Rhodian, Roarer, Rot, Ruffian, Sitting, Souteneur, Stag, Stale, Strong-arm, Swash-buckler, Taurine, Taurus, Toitoi, Tommy-rot, Tosh, Trash, Tripe, Twaddle, Tyran(ne), Tyrannise, Tyrant, Unigenitus, Victimise, Winged, Zo(bo)

**Bulldog** Marshal, Tenacious

**Bulldoze(r)** Angledozer, Coerce, Earthmover, Flatten, Leveller, Overturn, Raze

**Bullet** Ammo, Balata, Ball, Baton round, Biscayan, Blank, Dumdum, Fusillade, Lead towel, Magic, Minié, Minié ball, Missile, Pellet, Percussio, Plastic, Round, Rubber, Shot, Slug, Soft-nosed, Tracer

**Bulletin** All points, Memo, Message, Newscast, Newsletter, News sheet, Report, Summary, Update

**Bull-fight(er), Bull-fighting** Banderillero, Banderillo, Corrida, Cuadrilla, Encierro, Escamillo, Faena, Mano a mano, Matador, Picador, Rejoneador, Tauromachy, Toreador, Torero

**Bullfinch** Monk

**Bull-head** Cottoid, Father-lasher, Pogge, Sea-poacher

**Bull-rider** Europa

**Bull-roarer** Rhombos, Tu(r)ndun

**Bull's eye** Carton, Focus, Gold, Humbug, Prick, Target

**Bullshit** BS

▶ **Bully** *see* BULL(S)

**Bulrush** Pandanaceous, Raupo, Reed, Reed-mace, Tule

**Bulwark** Bastion, Defence, Rampart, Resistor

**Bum** Ass, Beg, Beggar, Cadge, Deadbeat, Prat, Scrounge, Sponge, Thumb, Tramp, Vagabond

**Bumble** Beadle, Bedel(l)

▷ **Bumble** *may indicate* an anagram

**Bumboat woman** Buttercup

**Bumf** Spam

**Bump(er), Bumps, Bumpy** Barge, Big, Blow, Bouncer, Bradyseism, Bucket, Bustle, Cannon, Clour, Collide, Dunch, Encephalocele, Fender, Hillock, Immense, Impact, Inian, Inion, Jo(u)le, Joll, Jolt, Jostle, Jowl, Keltie, Kelty, Knar, Knock, Large, Mamilla, Mogul, Nudge, Organ, Overrider®, Phrenology, Reveille, Rouse, Speed, Supernaculum, Thump, Twitter, Uneven

**Bumph** Loo-roll

**Bumpkin** Bucolic, Bushwhacker, Clodhopper, Hawbuck, Hayseed, Hick, Jock, Lout, Oaf, Peasant, Put(t), Rube, Rustic, Yokel, Zany

**Bumptious** Arrogant, Brash, Randie, Randy, Uppity

**Bun** Barmbrack, Bath, Black, Chelsea, Chignon, Chou, Cookie, Currant, Devonshire split, Hot-cross, Huffkin, Mosbolletjie, Roll, Teacake, Toorie, Wad

**Bunch** Acinus, Anthology, Bob, Botryoid, Bouquet, Byndle, Cluster, Fascicle, Finial, Flock, Gang, →GROUP, Hand, Handful, Ilk, Lot, Lump, Nosegay, Panicle, Posy, Raceme, Spray, Staphyline, Tassel, Tee, Truss, Tuft, Tussie-mussie, Tussock

**Bundle(d)** Axoneme, Bale, Bavin, Bluey, Bottle, Byssus, Desmoid, Dorlach, Drum, Fag(g)ot, Fascicle, Fasciculate, Fascine, Fibre, Fibrovascular, Kemple, Knitch, Lemniscus, Matilda, →PACK(AGE), Parcel, Sack, Sheaf, Shiralee, Shock, Shook, Stela, Stook, Swag, Tie, Top, Trousseau, Truss, Vascular, Wad, Wadge, Wap, Yealm

**Bung** Cork, Dook, Obturate, Plug, Stopgap, Stopper

**Bungalow** Dak

**Bungle(r), Bungled, Bungling** Awkward, Blunder, Blunk, Bodge, Boob, Boss shot, Botch, Bumble, Bummle, Dub, Duff, Fluff, Foozle, Foul, Foul up, Goof, Gum up, Maladroit, Mash, Mess, Mis(h)guggle, Muddle, Muff, Mull, Prat, Screw, Spoil, Tinker

**Bunk(er), Bunk off, Bunkum** Abscond, Absquatulate, Balderdash, Baloney, Berth, Blah, Bolt, Casemate, Claptrap, Clio, Decamp, Entrap, Flit, Guff, Guy, Hazard, History, Hogwash, Hokum, Hooey, Humbug, Malarky, Moonlight flit, Moonshine, Nonsense, Rot, Sandtrap, Scuttle, Skive, Stokehold, Tommy-rot, Tosh, Trap, Tripe, Truant, Twaddle

**Bunter** Billy, Owl

**Bunthorne** Aesthete, Poet

**Bunting** Bird, Cirl, Flag, Fringilline, Ortolan, Pennant, Snow, Streamer, Tanager, Towhee, Yellow-hammer, Yowley

**Buoy (up)** Bell, Breeches, Can, Dan, Daymark, Dolphin, Float, Life, Marker, Nun, Raft, Reassure, Ring, Seamark, Sonar, Sonobuoy, Spar, Sustain, Wreck

**Buoyancy, Buoyant** Afloat, Blithe, Floaty, Mae West, Resilient

**Burble** Blat, Gibber

**Burbot** Eel-pout

**Burden** Albatross, Beare, Bob, Brunt, Cargo, Cark, Chant, Chorus, Cross, Cumber, Deadweight, Drone, Droore, Encumber, Encumbrance, Fa-la, Fardel, Folderol, Fraught, Freight, Gist, Handicap, Hardship, Hum, Lade, →LOAD, Lumber, Millstone, Monkey, Oercome, Onus, Oppress, Payload, Put-upon, Refrain, Rumbelow, Saddle, Servitude, Shanty, Substance, Task, Tax, Tenor, Theme, Torch, Tote, Trouble, Weight, White man's, Woe, Yoke

**Burdensome** Deere, Irksome, Onerous, Oppressive, Weighty

**Burdock** Clote(-bar), Clothur, Cockle-bar, Gobo, Hardoke, Weed

**Bureau** Agency, Agitprop, Breakfront, Cominform, Davenport, Desk, Interpol, Kominform, Marriage, →OFFICE, Volunteer, Weather

**Bureaucracy, Bureaucrat(ic)** Apparatchik, Bean-counter, Bumbledom, CS, Functionary, Impersonal, Jack-in-office, Mandarin, Red tape, Tapist, Technocrat, Wallah

**Burgeon(ing)** Asprout, Blossom, Bud, Grow, Sprout, Swell

**Burgess, Burgher** Citizen, Freeman, Portman

**Burgh** Burrowstown, Parliamentary, Police, Royal

**Burglar(y), Burgle** Aggravated, Area-sneak, Break-in, Cat, Crack(sman), House-breaker, Intruder, Peterman, Picklock, Raffles, Robber, Screw, Thief, Yegg

**Burgundy** Macon, Vin

**Burial (place)** Catacomb, Charnel, Committal, Crypt, Cubiculum, Darga(h), Funeral, God's acre, Golgotha, Grave, Green, Interment, Kurgan, Lair, Last rites, Pyramid, Sepulchre, Sepulture, Speos, Tholos, Tomb, Tumulus, Vault, Vivisepulture, Zoothapsis

**Burin** Graver

**Burlesque** Caricatura, Caricature, Comedy, Farce, Heroicomical, Hudibrastic(s), Hurlo-thrumbo, Lampoon, Macaronic, Parody, Satire, Skimmington, Skit, Spoof, Travesty

**Burlington** RA

**Burly** Bluff, Stout, Strapping

**Burma, Burmese** Karen(ni), Mon(-Khmer), Myanmar, Naga, Shan

**Burn(ed), Burner, Burning, Burnt** Ablaze, Adust, Afire, Alow(e), Ardent, Argand, Arson, Ash, Auto-da-fé, Back, Bake, Bats-wing, Beck, Bishop, Blaze, Blister, Blowlamp, Blowtorch, Blush, Brand, Brazier, Bren(ne), Brent, Brook(let), Bunsen, Causalgia, Caustic, Cauterise, Char, Chark, Chinese, Cinder, Clavie, Coal, Coke, Combust, Conflagration, Cremate, Crozzled, Crucial, Deflagrate, Destruct, Effigy, Eilding, Ember, Emboil, Empyreuma, Fervid, Fircone, →**FIRE**, First degree, Fishtail, Flagrant, Flambe, Flare, Flash, Frazzle, Fresh(et), Gleed, Gut, Holocaust, Ignite, In, Incendiary, Incense, Incinerate, Intense, Inure, Inust(ion), Itch, Kill, Lean, Live, Lunt, Moorburn, Muirburn, Offering, On, Oxidise, Oxyacetylene, Phlogiston, Pilot, Plo(a)t, Powder, Pyric, Pyromania, Raster, Rill, Runnel, Sati, Scald, Scaud, Scorch, Scouther, Scowder, Scowther, Sear, Sienna, Sike, Singe, Sizzle, Smart, Smoulder, Sore, Stake, Suttee, Swale, Third-degree, Thurible, Torch, Umber, Urent, Ustion, Ustulation, Weeke, Welsbach, Wick, Ybrent

**Burning bush** Wahoo

**Burp** Belch, Eruct

**Burr(ing)** Brei, Brey, Clote, Croup, Dialect, Knob, Rhotacism

**Burrow(er), Burrowing** Dig, Earth, Earthworm, Fossorial, Gopher, Groundhog, Hole, Holt, How, Howk, Mine, Mole, Nuzzle, Root, Sett, Terricole, Tunnel, Viscacha, Warren, Wombat, Worm

**Bursar(y)** Camerlengo, Camerlingo, Coffers, Grant, Purser, Scholarship, Tertiary, Treasurer

**Bursitis** Beat

**Burst(ing), Bursts** Blowout, Bout, Brast, Break, Dehisce, Disrupt, Dissilient, Ebullient, Erumpent, Erupt, →**EXPLODE**, Fits and starts, Flare-up, Fly, Gust, Implode, Pop, Salvo, Sforzato, Shatter, Spasm, Spirt, Split, Sprint, Spurt, Stave, Tetterous

**Burundi** RU

**Bury** Conceal, Cover, Eard, Earth, Embowel, Engrave, Enhearse, Entomb, Graff, Graft, Imbed, Inearth, Inhearse, Inherce, Inhume, Inter, Inurn, Landfill, Repress, Sepulture, Sink, Ye(a)rd, Yird

**Bus** Aero, Bandwagon, Car, Charabanc, Coach, Crew, Double-decker, Greyhound, Highway, Hondey, Hopper, ISA, Jitney, Mammy-wagon, Purdah, Rattletrap, Single-decker, Tramcar, Trolley, Trunk, Walking

**Bus conductor** Cad, Clippy

**Bush(es), Bush-man, Bushy** Aloe, Bitou, Bramble, Brier, Bullace, Busket, Calico, Clump, Cotton, Creosote, Dumose, Firethorn, Furze, Glib, Greasewood, Hawthorn, Hedge, Hibiscus, Ivy-tod, Jaborandi, Kapok, Kiekie, Mallee, Matagouri, Mulberry, Outback, Pachysandra, Poinsettia, Poly-poly, President, Prostanthera, Sallee, San, Scrog, Shepherd, Shrub, Sloe, Sloethorn, Sugar, Thicket, Tire, Tod(de), Tumatakuru

**Bush-baby** Durukuli, Galago, Nagapie, Night-ape

**Bushel** Ardeb, Bu, Co(o)mb, Cor, Ephah, Fou, Homer, Peck, Weight, Wey

**Bushwalker** Hoon

**Business** Affair, Agency, Biz, Bricks and clicks, Brokerage, Bus, Cahoot, Cartel, Cerne, Chaebol(s), Co, Commerce, Company, Concern, Conglomerate, Corporate, Craft, Custom, Dealership, Duty, Enterprise, Ergon, Establishment, Exchange, Fasti, Field, Firm, Funny, Game, Gear, Goings on, Hong, Industry, Kaizen, Lifestyle, Line, Métier, Monkey, Office, Palaver, Pidgin, Pi(d)geon, Practice, Professional, Racket, Shebang, Shop, Show, Thick, To-do, Trade, Traffic, Transaction, Tread, Turnover, Unincorporated, Vocation, Wall Street, Zaibatsu, Zaikai

**Businesslike** Orderly

**Businessman** Babbitt, Baron, Capitalist, City, Dealer, Entrepreneur, Fat-cat, Financier, Realtor, Taipan, Trader, Tycoon

**Busk(er)** Bodice, Corset, Entertainer, German-band

**Buskin(s)** Brod(e)kin, Cothurn(us), Shoe

**Buss** Kiss, Osculate, Smack
**Bussu** Troelie, Troely, Troolie
**Bust** Beano, Boob, Brast, Break, Chest, Dollarless, Falsies, Figurehead, Fold, Herm(a), Insolvent, Kaput, Mamma, Penurious, Raid, Rupture, Sculp, Shatter(ed), Skint, Spree, Statue, Swoop, Term(inus), To-tear, To-torne, Ups(e)y
▷ **Bust** *may indicate* an anagram
**Bustard** Bird, Otis, Turkey
**Buster** Keaton
**Bustle** Ado, Beetle, Do, Dress-improver, Flap, Fuss, Pad, Scurry, → **STIR**, Swarm, To-do, Tournure, Whew
**Busy** Active, At (it), Deedy, → **DETECTIVE**, Dick, Doing, Eident, Employ, Engaged, Ergate, Eventful, Eye, Goer, Hectic, Hive, Hot spot, Humming, Manic, Occupied, Operose, Ornate, Prodnose, Stir, Stirabout, Tec, Throng, Worksome
**Busybody** Bee, Bustler, Meddler, Noser, Pantopragmatic, Pragmatic, Snooper, Trout, Yenta
**But** Aber, Algates, Bar, Except, However, Keg, Merely, Nay, Only, Save, Sed, Simply, Tun, Without, Yet
**Butch** He-man, Macho
**Butcher(s), Butchery** Cumberland, Decko, Dekko, Eyeful, Flesher, Gander, Glimpse, Ice, Kill, Killcow, Look, Looksee, Mangle, Massacre, Ovicide, Peek, Sever, Shambles, Shochet, Shufti, Slaughter, Slay, Slink
**Butler** Bedivere, Bread-chipper, Crichton, Jeeves, Khansama(h), Major-domo, RAB, Rhett, Samuel, Servant, Sewer, Sommelier, Steward
**Butt (in)** April fool, Aris, Arse, Ass, Barrel, Bumper, Buns, Bunt, Clara, Dimp, Dout, Dowt, Dunch, Enter, Geck, Glasgow kiss, Goat, Header, Horn, Interject, Jesting-stock, Laughing-stock, Mark, Nut, Outspeckle, Pantaloon, Pipe, Push, Ram, Roach, Scapegoat, Snipe, Stompie, → **STOOGE**, Straight man, Stump, Target, Tun, Ups
**Butter** Adulation, Apple, Beurre, Billy, Blandish, Brandy, Butyric, Cacao, Cocoa, Coconut, Drawn, Flatter, Galam, Garcinia, Ghee, Ghi, Goa, Goat, Illipi, Illupi, Kokum, Mahua, Mahwa, Maitre d'hotel, Mow(r)a, Nut, Nutter, Palm, Pat, Peanut, Print, Ram, Rum, Scrape, Shea, Spread, Vegetable
▷ **Butter** *may indicate* a goat or such
**Buttercup** Bumboat woman, Crowfoot, Crow-toe, Goldilocks, Ranunculus, Reate, Thalictrum
**Butterfingers** Muff
**Butterfish** Nine-eyes
**Butterflies, Butterfly** Apollo, Argus, Birdwing, Blue, Brimstone, Brown, Cabbage white, Camberwell beauty, Cardinal, Chequered skipper, Cleopatra, Clouded yellow, Collywobbles, Comma, Common blue, Copper, Dilettante, Eclosion, Elfin, Emperor, Fritillary, Gate-keeper, Gatemen, Grayling, Hair-streak, Heath, Hesperid, Imaginal, Kaleidoscope, Kallima, Large copper, Large white, Leaf, Lycaena, Marbled-white, Meadow brown, Metalmark, Milk-weed, Monarch, Morpho, Mountain ringlet, Mourning-cloak, Nerves, Nymphalid, Nymphean, Orange-tip, Owl, Painted lady, Papilionidae, Peacock, Pieris, Psyche, Purple emperor, Red admiral, Rhopalocera, Ringlet, Satyr(idae), Satyrinae, Scotch argus, Silverspot, Skipper, Small white, Snake's head, Speckled wood, Stamper, Stroke, Sulphur, Swallow-tail, Thecla, Thistle, Tiger swallowtail, Tortoiseshell, Two-tailed pasha, Umber, Vanessa, Wall brown, White admiral
**Buttermilk** Bland, Lassi
**Butternut** Souari
**Butter-tree** Mahua, Mahwa, Mow(r)a
**Buttocks** Aristotle, Arse, Ass, Bahookie, Booty, Bottom, Buns, Can, Cheeks, Coit, Derrière, Doup, Duff, Fanny, Fud, Fundament, Gluteus maximus, Heinie, Hinder-end, Hinderlan(d)s, Hunkers, Hurdies, Jacksie, Jacksy, Keester, Keister, Mooning, Nache, Nates, Posterior, Prat, Quatch, Quoit, Seat, Tush

**Button(s)** Barrel, Bellboy, Buzzer, Fastener, Frog, Hold, Hot, Knob, Mescal, Mouse, Mute, Netsuke, Olivet, Page(boy), Panic, Pause, Pearl, Press, Push, Snooze, Stud, Switch, Toggle, Toolbar

**Buttonhole** Accost, Boutonniere, Carnation, Detain, Doorstep, Eye, Flower

**Buttress** Brace, Counterfort, Flying, Hanging, Pier, Prop, Reinforce, Stay, Support, Tambour

**Butty** Chum, Oppo

**Buxom** Bonnie, Busty, Plump, Rolypoly, Sonsy, Well-endowed, Wench

**Buy(ing), Buyer, Buy off** Accept, Believe, Bribe, Coemption, Coff, Corner, Customer, Emption, Engross, Impulse, Monopsonist, Munich, Oligopsony, Panic, Purchase, Redeem, Regrate, Shop, Shout, Spend, Take, Trade, Treat, Vendee

▷ **Buyer** *may indicate* money

**Buzz(er)** Bee, Birr, Bombilate, Bombinate, Button, Drone, Fly, Hum, Kazoo, Kick, Rumour, Scram, Whirr, Whisper, Zed, Zing, Zoom

**Buzzard** Bee-kite, Bird, Buteo, Hawk, Honey, Pern, Puttock, Turkey, Vulture

**By** Alongside, At, Beside, Gin, Gone, In, Near, Neighbouring, Nigh, Of, On, Past, Per, Through, With, X

**Bye** Extra

**Bye-bye** Adieu, Farewell, Tata

**By far** Out and away

**Bygone** B.C., Dead, Departed, Past, Yore

**By Jove** Egad

**Bypass** Avoid, Beltway, Circuit, Coronary, → DETOUR, Dodge, Evade, Ignore, Omit, Ring-road, Shunt, Skirt

**By-product** Epiphenomenon, Spill-over, Spin-off

**Byre** Cowshed, Manger, Stable, Trough

**By so much** The

**Bystander** Looker-on, Observer

**Byte** Nybble

**By the way** Apropos, Incidentally, Ob(iter)

**Byway** Alley, Lane, Path

**Byword** Ayword, Nayword, Phrase, Proverb, Slogan

**Byzantine** Catapan, Comnenus, Complicated, Exarch, Intricate, Intrince, Theme

▷ **Byzantine** *may indicate* an anagram

# Cc

**C** Around, Caught, Celsius, Cent, Centigrade, Charlie, Conservative, San

**Cab** Boneshaker, Crawler, Drosky, Fiacre, Four-wheeler, Growler, Gurney, Hackney, Hansom, Mini, Noddy, Taxi, Vettura

**Cab(b)alistic** Abraxis, Gematria, Mystic, Notarikon, Occult

**Cabal(ler)** Arlington, Ashley, Buckingham, Clifford, Clique, Conspiracy, Coterie, Faction, Junto, Lauderdale, Party, Plot

**Cabaret** Burlesque, Floorshow, Moulin Rouge

**Cabbage(-head), Cabbage soup** Black, Bok choy, Borecole, Brassica, Castock, Cauliflower, Cavalo nero, Chinese (leaf), Chinese leaves, Chou, Choucroute, Cole, Collard, Crout, Custock, Drumhead, Gobi, Kerguelen, Kohlrabi, Kraut, Loaf, Loave, Mibuna, Mizuna, Pak-choi, Pamphrey, Pe-tsai, St Patrick's, Sauerkraut, Savoy, Sea-kale, Shchi, Shtchi, Skunk, Thieve, Turnip, Wild, Wort

**Caber** Fir, Janker, Log, Sting

**Cabin** Berth, Bibby, Bothy, Box, Cabana, Caboose, Camboose, Coach, Cottage, Crannog, Crib, Cuddy, Den, Gondola, Hovel, Hut, Izba, Lodge, Loghouse, Long-house, Pod, Pressure, Room, Roundhouse, Saloon, Shack, Shanty, Signal box, Stateroom, Trunk

**Cabin-boy** Grummet

**Cabinet** Armoire, Bahut, Cabale, Case, Cellaret, Chiffonier, Chill(er), Closet, Commode, Console, Cupboard, Display, Encoignure, Filing, Kitchen, Locker, Ministry, Nest, Official family, Repository, Secretaire, Shadow, Shrinal, Unit, Vitrine

**Cabinet maker** Banting, Chippendale, Ebeniste, Garret-master, Hepplewhite, Joiner, PM

**Cable(way), Cable-car** Arrester, Choucroute, Coax(ial), Extension, Flex, Halser, Hawser, Jumper, Jump leads, Junk, Kissagram, Landline, Lead, Lead-in, Lifeline, Null-modern, Oil-filled, Outhaul, Outhauler, Rope, Shroud, Slatch, Snake, Téléférique, → **TELEGRAM**, Telegraph, Telepherique, Telpher(age), Topping lift, Towrope, Trunking, Vine, Wire, Yoke

**Cache** Deposit, Hidlin(g)s, → **HOARD**, Inter, Stash, Store, Treasure

**Cachet** Prestige

**Cack-handed** Awkward

**Cackle** Cluck, Gaggle, Gas, Haw, Horse laugh, Snicker, Titter

**Cacography** Scrawl

**Cacophony** Babel, Caterwaul, Charivari, Discord, Hubbub, Jangle

**Cactus, Cactus-like** Alhagi, Barel, Cereus, Cholla, Christmas, Dildo, Easter, Echino-, Hedgehog, Jointed, Jojoba, Maguey, Mescal, Mistletoe, Nopal, Ocotillo, Ombrophobe, Opuntia, Organ-pipe, Peyote, Pita(ha)ya, Prickly pear, Retama, Saguaro, Schlumbergera, Stapelia, Star, Strawberry, Torch-thistle, Tuna, Xerophytic

**Cad** Base, Boor, Bounder, Churl, Cocoa, Heel, Oik, Rascal, Rotter, Skunk, Varlet

**Cadaver(ous)** Body, Corpse, Deathly, Emaciated, Ghastly, Goner, Haggard, Stiff

**Caddy** Porter, Tea, Teapoy

**Cadence** Authentic, Beat, Close, Euouae, Evovae, Fa-do, Flow, Interrupted, Lilt, Meter, Perfect, Plagal, Rhythm

**Cadenza** Fireworks

**Cadet(s)** Junior, OTC, Plebe, Recruit, Rookie, Scion, Snooker, Space, Syen, Trainee, Younger

**Cadge(r)** Beg, Bludge, Bot, Bum, Impose, Mutch, Ponce, → **SCROUNGE**, Sponge

**Cadmium** Cd

**Caesar** Despot, Julian, Nero

**Caesium** Cs

**Café, Cafeteria** Automat, Bistro, Brasserie, Buvette, Canteen, Carvery, Commissary, Cybercafe, Diner, Dinette, Donko, Eatery, Estaminet, Filtré, Greasy spoon, Hashhouse, Internet, Juke joint, Netcafé, Noshery, Pizzeria, Pull-in, Snackbar, Tearoom, Tea-shop, Transport, Truckstop

**Cag(e)y** Chary

**Cage** Aviary, Bar, Battery, Box, Cavie, Confine, Coop, Corf, Dray, Drey, Enmew, Faraday, Fold, Frame, Grate, Hutch, Keavie, Mew, Mortsafe, Pen, → **PRISON**, Roll, Safety, Squirrel, Trave

**Cahoots** Hugger-mugger

**Cairn** Barp, Clearance, Dog, Horned, Man, Mound, Raise

**Caisson** Bends

**Caitiff** Meanie

**Cajole(ry)** Beflum, Beguile, Blandish, Blarney, Carn(e)y, → **COAX**, Cuittle, Humbug, Inveigle, Jolly, Persuade, Wheedle, Whillywha(w), Wiles

**Cake** Agnus dei, Angel, Baba, Babka, Baklava, Banbury, Bannock, Bara brith, Barm(brack), Battenberg, Bhaji, Biffin, Birthday, Black bun, Brandy snap, Brioche, Brownie, Buckwheat, Bun, Carcake, Cattle, Chapat(t)i, Chillada, Chupati, Chupattie, Chupatty, Clapbread, Clot, Coburg, Cookie, Corn dodger, Cotton, Croquante, Croquette, Cruller, Crumpet, Currant, Dainty, Devil's food, Drizzle, Dundee, Eccles, Eclair, Falafel, Fancy, Farl(e), Filter, Fish, Flapjack, Frangipane, Frangipani, Fritter, Galette, Gateaux, Genoa, Gingerbread, Girdle, Griddle, → **HARDEN**, Hockey, Hoe, Idli, Jaffa, Jannock, Johnny, Jumbal, Jumbles, Koeksister, Kruller, Kuchen, Kueh, Lady's finger, Lamington, Lardy, Latke, Layer, Linseed, Macaroon, Madeira, Madeleine, Maid of honour, Marble, Meringue, Millefeuille, Moon, Mooncake, Mud, Muffin, Napoleon, Nut, Oatmeal, Oil, Pan, Panettone, Paratha, Parkin, Parliament, Pastry, Pat, Patty, Pavlova, Pepper, Petit four, Pikelet, → **PLASTER**, Pomfret, Pone, Pontefract, Poori, Popover, Potato, Pound, Profiterole, Puff, Puftaloon(a), Puri, Queencake, Ratafia, Ready-mix, Religieuse, Rice, Rock, Rosti, Roti, Rout, Rum baba, Rusk, Sachertorte, Saffron, Sally Lunn, Salt, Sandwich, Savarin, Scone, Seed, Set, Simnel, Singing-hinny, Slab, Slapjack, Soap, Soul, Spawn, Spice, Sponge, Stollen, Stottie, Sushi, Swiss roll, Tablet, Tansy, Tea(bread), Tipsy, Torte, Tortilla, Twelfth, Upside down, Vetkoek, Wad, Wafer, Waffle, Wedding, Wonder, Yeast, Yule log

▷ **Cake** *may indicate* an anagram

**Cake-shaped** Placentiform

**Cakestand** Curate

**Cakewalk** Doddle

**Calaboose** Jail, Loghouse

**Calamitous, Calamity** Blow, Catastrophe, Dire, → **DISASTER**, Distress, Fatal, Ill, Jane, Ruth, Storm, Tragic, Unlucky, Visitation, Woe

**Calcareous** Ganoin, Lithite

**Calcium** Ca, Colemanite, Dogger, Dripstone, Flowstone, Otolith, Quicklime, Scawtite, Whewellite, Wollastonite

**Calculate(d), Calculation, Calculator** Abacus, Actuary, Arithmetic, Comptometer, Compute(r), Cost, Design, Estimate, Extrapolate, Four-function, Log, Napier's bones, Number-crunch, Prorate, Quip(p)u, Rate, → **RECKON**, Slide-rule, Sofar, Soroban, Tactical, Tell

**Calculus** Cholelith, Differential, Functional, Infinitesimal, Integral, Lambda, Lith, Lithiasis, Predicate, Propositional, Science, Sentential, Sialolith, Stone, Tartar, Urolith

**Caldera** Crater

**Caledonian** Kanak

**Calendar** Advent, Agenda, Almanac, Chinese, Diary, Dies fasti, Fasti, Gregorian, Hebrew, Intercalary, Jewish, Journal, Julian, Luach, Lunisolar, Menology, Newgate, New Style, Ordo, Perpetual, Planner, Revolutionary, Roman, Sothic

**Calender(ing)** Dervish, Mangle, Swissing

**Calf** Ass, Bobby, Box, Cf, Deacon, Divinity, Dogie, Dogy, Fatted, Freemartin, Golden, Law, Leg, Maverick, Mottled, Poddy, Sleeper, Slink, Smooth, Stirk, Sural, Tollie, Tolly, Tree, Veal, Vitular

**Caliban** Moon-calf

**Calibrate, Calibre** Bore, Capacity, Graduate, Mark, →QUALITY, Text

**California(n)** Fresno, Golden State

**Californium** Cf

**Caliph** Abbasid(e), Omar, Vathek

**Call(ed), Call (for), Calling, Call on, Call up** Adhan, Ahoy, Alew, Appeal, Arraign, Art, Awaken, Azan, Banco, Bawl, Beck(on), Behote, Bevy, Bid, Boots and saddles, Bugle, Business, Buzz, Career, Chamade, Cite, Claim, Clang, Clarion, Cleep, Clepe, Close, Cold, Conference, Conscript, Convene, Convoke, Coo, Cooee, Cry, Curtain, Denominate, Dial, Drift, Dub, Duty, Effectual, Entail, Evoke, First post, Game, Go, Hail, Hallali, Halloa, Halloo, Haro, Heads, Heave-ho, Hech, Heckle, Hete, Hey, Hight, Ho, Hot(e), Howzat, Huddup, Hurra(h), Invocation, Job, Junk, Last (post), Levy, Line, Local, Look in, Margin, Métier, Misère, Mobilise, Mot, Name, Nap, Need, Nemn, Nempt, Niche, Nominate, No trumps, Nuisance, Olé, Page, Peter, Phone, Photo, Pop in, Post, Profession, Proo, Pruh, Pursuit, Rechate, Recheat, Retreat, Reveille, Ring, Roll, Rort, Rouse, Route, Sa-sa, Scream, See, Sennet, →SHOUT, Shut-out, Slam, Slander, Slogan, Soho, Sola, SOS, STD, Style, Subpoena, Summon(s), Tails, Tally ho, Tantivy, Taps, Telephone, Term, Toho, Toll, Trumpet, Trunk, Turn, Tweet, Visit, Vocation, Waken, Wake-up, War cry, Whoa-ho-ho, Wo ha ho, Yell, Yo, Yodel, Yodle, Yo-ho(-ho), Yoicks, Yoo-hoo

**Calla(s)** Aroid, Lily, Maria

**Caller** Fresh, Guest, Herring, Inspector, Muezzin, Rep, Traveller, →VISITOR

**Calligraphy** Grass style, Kakemono

**Callipers** Odd legs

**Callisthenics** T'ai chi (ch'uan)

**Call off** Abort

**Callosity, Call(o)us** Bunion, Cold(-hearted), Corn, Hard, Horny, Obtuse, Ringbone, Seg, Thylose, Tough, Tylosis, Unfeeling

**Callow** Crude, Green, Immature, Jejune

**Calm** Abate, Alegge, Aleye, Allay, Allege, Appease, Assuage, Ataraxy, Composed, Cool, Dead-wind, Dispassionate, Doldrums, Easy, Easygoing, Easy-osy, Eevn, Equable, Equanimity, Even, Eye, Flat, Glassy, Halcyon, Level, Loun(d), Lown(d), Lull, Mellow, Mild, Milden, Millpond, Mollify, Nonchalant, Pacify, Patient, Peaceable, Peaceful, Philosophical, Phlegmatic, Placate, Placid, Quell, Quiet, Raise, Relax(ed), Repose, Restful, Restrained, Sedate, Self-possessed, Seraphic, Serena, Serene, Settle, Simmer down, Sleek, Sober, →SOOTHE, Sopite, Steady, Still(ness), Stilly, Subside, Supercool, Tame, Tranquil(lise), Unruffled, Unturbid, Windless

**Calorie** Gram, Kilogram

**Calumniate, Calumny** Abuse, Aspersion, Backbite, Defame, Libel, Malign, Sclaunder, Slander, Slur

**Calvary** Golgotha

**Calvin(ist), Calvinism** Accusative, Coolidge, Genevan, Hopkins, Huguenot, Infralapsarian, Perseverance of saints, Predestination, Sublapsarian, Supralapsarian

**Calydonian** Boar

**Calypso** Ogygia, Siren, Soca, Sokah, →SONG

**Cam** Cog, Dwell, River, Snail, Tappet

**Camaraderie** Fellowship, Rapport, Team spirit

**Camber** Hog, Slope

**Cambium** Phellogen

**Cambodia(n)** K, Kampuchean, Khmer (Rouge), Montagnard, Pol Pot

**Cambria(n)** Menevian, Wales

**Cambric** Lawn
**Cambridge** Blue, Cantab, Squat, Uni
**Came** Arrived
**Camel, Camel train** Aeroplane, Arabian, Artiodactyla, Bactrian, Beige, Caisson, Colt, Dromedary, Kafila, Llama, Oont, Sopwith, Tulu
**Camelopard** Giraffe
**Cameo** Anaglyph, Camaieu, Carving
**Camera, Camera man** All-round, Box, Brownie®, Camcorder, Candid, Chambers, Cine, Compact, Digicam, Digital, Disc, Dolly, Electron, Flash, Gamma, Gatso®, Grip(s), Iconoscope, Image orthicon, Imager, Instant, Kodak®, Lucida, Miniature, Minicam, Movie, Nannycam, Obscura, Orthicon, Palmcorder, Panoramic, Pantoscope, Periphery, Phone-cam, Pinhole, Point and shoot, Polaroid®, Process, Programmed, Projectionist, Reflex, Retina, Schmidt, SLR, Somascope, Speed, Spycam, Steadicam®, Stop-frame, Subminiature, Swing-back, Video, Vidicon, Viewfinder, Webcam
**Camouflage(d)** Battledress, Conceal, →**DISGUISE**, Mark, Maskirovka, Secret, Unnoticeable, War-dress
▷ **Camouflaged** *may indicate* an anagram
**Camp(er)** Affectation, Aldershot, Auschwitz, Banal, Base, Belsen, Bivouac, Boma, Boot, Buchenwald, Caerleon, Cantonment, Castral, Colditz, Concentration, Coterie, Dachau, David, Death, Depot, D(o)uar, Dumdum, Epicene, Faction, Fat, Flaunt, Gay, Gulag, Happy, Health, High, Holiday, Labour, Laer, La(a)ger, Lashkar, Leaguer, Low, Manyat(t)a, Motor, Nudist, Oflag, Outlie, Peace, Prison, Sect, Side, Site, Siwash, Stagey, Stalag, Stative, Summer, Swagman, Tent, Theatrical, Transit, Treblinka, Valley Forge, Work, Zare(e)ba, Zariba, Zereba, Zeriba
**Campaign(er)** Activist, Agitate, Barnstorm, Battle, Blitz, Blitzkrieg, Canvass, Crusade, Doorknock, Drive, Enterprise, Field, Gallipoli, Hustings, Jihad, Lobby, Mission, Offensive, Pankhurst, Promotion, Real Ale, Roadshow, Run, Satyagraha, Smear, Stint, Stopes, Strategist, Suffragette, The stump, Tree-hugger, Vendetta, Venture, Veteran, War, War horse, Warray, Warrey, Whispering, Whistle-stop, Witchhunt, Women's Lib
**Campanula** Rampion
**Campeador** Chief, Cid
**Camp-follower** Lascar, Leaguer-lady, Leaguer-lass, Sutler
**Camphor** Carvacrol, Menthol
**Campion** Knap-bottle, Lychnis, Ragged robin, Silene
▷ **Camptown** *may indicate* de-
**Can(s)** Able, Aerosol, Billy, Bin, Bog, Capable, Churn, Cooler, Dow, Dyke, Gaol, Garbage, Gents, Headphones, Is able, Jail, Jerry, John, Jug, Karsy, Kazi, Lav(atory), Loo, May, Nick, Pail, Pitcher, Pot, Preserve, →**PRISON**, Privy, Six-pack, Stir, Tank, Tin, Trash, Tube, Watering
**Canada, Canadian** Abenaki, Acadian, Bella Bella, Bella Coola, Beothuk, Bois-brûlé, .ca, Canuck, Che(e)chako, Comox, Coureur de bois, Dakotan, Dene, Dogrib, Habitans, Hare, Heiltsuk, Herring choker, Inuit, Johnny Canuck, Joual, Maliseet, Manitoban, Metis, Micmac, Montagnais, Naskapi, Nuxalk, Péquiste, Quebeccer, Quebecker, Québecois, Salishan, Salteaux, Saulteaux, Slavey, Stoney, Tsimshian, Ungava, Yukon
**Canal** Alimentary, Ampul, Anal, Birth, Caledonian, Channel, Conduit, Corinth, Cruiseway, Da Yunhe, Duct, Duodenum, Ea, Ear, Enteron, Erie, Foss(e), Gota, Grand (Trunk), Grande Terre, Grand Union, Groove, Gut, Haversian, Houston Ship, Kiel, Klong, Labyrinth, Lode, Manchester Ship, Meatus, Midi, Mittelland, Moscow, Navigation, New York State Barge, Oesophagus, Panama, Pharynx, Pipe, Pound, Regent's, Resin, Rhine-Herne, Ring, Root, Sault Sainte Marie, Scala, Schlemm's, Semi-circular, Ship, Shipway, Soo, Spinal, Stone, Suez, Suo, Urethra, Vagina, Vertebral, Waterway, Welland, Zanja
**Canal-boat** Barge, Fly-boat, Gondola, Vaporetto
**Canapé** Cate, Chesterfield, Crostini, Snack, →**SOFA**, Titbit
**Canary** Bird, Grass, Prisoner, Roller, Serin, Singer, Yellow

**Cancel(led)** Abort, Abrogate, Adeem, Annul, Axe, Counteract, Countermand, Cross, Delete, Destroy, Erase, Kill, Negate, Nix, Nullify, Obliterate, Override, Rained off, Red line, Remit, Repeal, Rescind, Retract, Retrait, Revoke, Scratch, Scrub, Undo, Unmake, Void, Wipe, Write off

**Cancer(ian), Cancerous** Big C, Carcinoma, Crab, Curse, Hepatoma, Kaposi's sarcoma, Leukaemia, Lymphoma, Marek's disease, Moon child, Oat-cell, Oncogenic, Tropic, Tumour, Wolf

**Candela** Cd

▸ **Candelabra** *see* CANDLE(STICK)

**Candid, Candour** Albedo, Blunt, Camera, Forthright, Franchise, Frank, Honesty, Ingenuous, Man-to-man, Open, Outspoken, Plain(-spoken), Round, Straight, Upfront

**Candida** Fungus

**Candidate(s)** Agrege, Applicant, Aspirant, Contestant, Entrant, Field, Literate, Maybe, Nomenklatura, Nominee, Office-seeker, Ordinand, Postulant, Running mate, Short list, Slate, Spoiler, Stalking-horse, Testee

**Candied, Candy** Angelica, Caramel, Cotton, Eryngo, Eye, Glace, Maple, Rock, Snow, Succade, Sucket, Sugar, →SWEET

**Candle(stick), Candelabra, Candles** Amandine, Bougie, C(i)erge, Chanukiah, Corpse, Dip, Fetch, Girandole, Hanukiah, International, Jesse, Lampadary, Light, Long-sixes, Menorah, Mould, New, Padella, Paschal, Pricket, Roman, Rushlight, Sconce, Serge, Shammash, Shammes, Shammosim, Shortsix, Slut, Sperm, Standard, Tace, Tallow, Tallow-dip, Taper, Tea-light, Torchère, Tricerion, Vigil light, Wax, Waxlight

**Candlefish** Eulachon, Oolakon, Oulachon, Oulakon, Ulic(h)an, Ulic(h)on, Ulikon

▸ **Candy** *see* CANDIED

**Cane, Caning** Arrow, Baculine, Bamboo, Baste, Beat, Birk, Crabstick, Dari, Dhurra, Doura, Dur(r)a, Ferula, Ferule, Goor, Gur, Jambee, Malacca, Narthex, Penang-lawyer, Pointer, Raspberry, Rat(t)an, Rod, Six of the best, Split, Stick, Sugar, Swagger-stick, Swish, Switch, Sword, Swordstick, Tan, Tickler, Vare, Wand, Whangee, Wicker(-work)

**Canine** Biter, C, Dhole, Dog, Eye-tooth

**Canker** Corrosion, Curse, Lesion, Ulcer

**Cannabis** Benj, Bhang, Bifter, Blow, Boneset, Durban poison, Ganja, Ganny, Grass, Hash, Hemp, Henry, Louie, Number, Pot, Skunk, Wacky baccy, Zol

**Cannibal** Anthropophagus, Heathen, Long pig, Man-eater, Ogre, Thyestean, Wendigo

**Cannon** Amusette, Barrage, Basilisk, Bombard, Breechloader, Carom, Carronade, Cascabel, Chaser, Collide, Criterion, Culverin, Demi-culverin, Drake, Drop, Falcon, Gun, Howitzer, Kiss, Long-tom, Loose, Monkey, Mons Meg, Nursery, Oerlikon, Saker, Stern-chaser, Trunnion, Water, Zamboorak, Zomboruk, Zumbooru(c)k

**Cannot** Canna, Cant, Downa(e), Downay

**Canny** Careful, Frugal, Prudent, Scot, Shrewd, Slee, Sly, Thrifty, Wice, Wily, Wise

**Canoe(ist)** Bidarka, Bidarkee, Canader, Canadian, Dugout, Faltboat, Kayak, Log, Mokoro, Monoxylon, Montaria, Oomiack, Paddler, Peterborough, Piragua, Pirogue, Rob Roy, Surf, Waka, Woodskin

**Canon(ise)** Austin, Besaint, Brocard, Camera, Cancrizens, Chapter, Chasuble, Code, Crab, Criterion, Decree, Honorary, Infinite, Isidorian, →LAW, Line, Mathurin(e), Minor, Nocturn, Norbertine, Nursery, Pitaka, Polyphony, Prebendary, Precentor, Precept, Premonstrant, Premonstratensian, Regular, Residential, Retrograde, Rota, Round, Rule, Secular, Square, Squier, Squire, Standard, Tenet, Unity, Vice-dean, White

**Canopy** Awning, Baldachin, Baldaquin, Chuppah, Ciborium, Clamshell, Dais, Gore, He(a)rse, Huppah, Majesty, Marquee, Marquise, Parapente, Pavilion, Shamiana(h), State, Tabernacle, Tent, Tester, Veranda(h), Virando

**Cant** Argot, Bevel, Doublespeak, Heel, Incline, Jargon, Mummery, Outrope, Patois, Patter, Rogue's Latin, Shelta, Slang, Slope, Snivel, Snuffle, Tip

**Cantankerous** Cussed, Disputative, Fire-eater, Ornery, Perverse, Querulous, Testy, Tetchy

**Cantata** Kinderspiel, Motet, Tobacco

**Canteen** Chuck-wagon, Cutlery, Dry, Mess, Munga, Naafi, Soup kitchen, Wet

**Canter** Amble, Hypocrite, Jog, Lope, Run, Tit(t)up, Tripple

**Canticle** Benedictus, Carol, Nunc dimittis

**Canto** Air, Duan, Fit(te), Fitt, Fytte, Melody, Verse

**Canton(ese)** Aargau, Appenzell, Basil, Basle, District, Eyalet, Fribourg, Glarus, Graubunden, Jura, Lucerne, Neuchatel, Quarter, St Gall, Schaffhausen, Schwyz, Solothurn, Tanka, Thurgau, Ticino, Unterwalden, Uri, Valais, Vaud, Zug, Zurich

**Cantor** Haz(z)an

**Cantred** Commot(e)

**Canvas** Awning, Big top, Binca®, Burlap, Drab(b)ler, Fly-sheet, Found, Lug-sail, Mainsail, Maintopsail, Marquee, Oil-cloth, Paint, Raven's-duck, Reef, → **SAIL**, Square-sail, Staysail, Stuns(ai)l, Tarp(aulin), Tent(age), Trysail, Wigan, Woolpack

**Canvass(er), Canvassing** Agent, Doorstep, Drum, Electioneer, Mainstreeting, Poll, Press flesh, Solicit

▷ **Canvasser** *may indicate* a painter or a camper

**Canyon** Arroyo, Box, Canada, Coprates, Defile, Grand, Grand Coulee, Kings, Nal(l)a, Nallah, Ravine, Submarine

**Cap(ped)** Abacot, Amorce, Balaclava, Balmoral, Barret, Baseball, Bathing, Bellhop, Bendigo, Ber(r)et, Better, Biggin, Biretta, Black, Blakey, Blue, Blue-bonnet, Bonnet-rouge, Bycoket, Call, Calotte, Calpac(k), Calyptrate, Capeline, Caul, Chaco, Chape, Chapeau, Chaperon, Chapka, Charge, Chechia, Cheese-cutter, Cloth, Cockernony, Coif, College, Coonskin, Cope, Cornet, Cowl, Cradle, Crest, → **CROWN**, Czapka, Davy Crockett, Deerstalker, Dunce's, Dutch, Excel, Fatigue, Ferrule, Filler, Flat, Fool's, Forage, Gandhi, Garrison, Gimme, Glengarry, Gorblim(e)y, Grannie, Granny, → **HAT**, Havelock, Hummel bonnet, Hunting, Iceberg, International, Jockey, Juliet, Kalpak, Kepi, Kilmarnock (cowl), Kippa, Kippoth, Kipput, Kiss-me(-quick), Knee, Legal, Liberty, Lid, Maintenance, Mob, Monmouth, Monteer, Montero, Mor(r)ion, Mortar-board, Muffin, Mutch, Newsboy, Night, Old wife, Outdo, Pagri, Patella(r), Percussion, Perplex, Petrol, Phrygian, Pile, Pileus, Pinner, Polar, Puggaree, Quoif, Rate, Root, Schapska, Shacko, Shako, Skullcap, Square, Squirrel-tail, Statute, Stocking, Summit, → **SURPASS**, Taj, Tam(-o'-shanter), Thimble, Thinking, Thrum, Toe, Toorie, Top, Toque, Toy, Trenchard, Trencher, Truck, Tuque, Turk's, Watch, Wishing, Yarmulka, Yarmulke, Zuchetto

**Capable, Capability** Able, Brown, Capacity, Competent, Deft, Effectual, Efficient, Firepower, Intelligent, Qualified, Reach, Skilled, Susceptible, Up to, Viable

**Capacitance, Capacious, Capacity** Ability, Ample, Aptitude, C, Cab, Calibre, Carrying, Co(o)mb, Competence, Content, Cor, Cubic, Endowment, Full, Function, Gift, Legal, Limit, Log, Mneme, Potency, Potential, Power, Prowess, Qua, Rated, Receipt, Roomy, Scope, Size, Skinful, Tankage, Thermal, Tonnage, Valence, Vital, Volume

**Caparison** Robe, Trap(pings)

**Cape(s)** Agulhas, Almuce, Athlete, Beachy Head, Blanc(o), Bon, Burnouse, Byron, C, Calimere Point, Canaveral, Canso, Cardinal, Chelyuskin, Cloak, Cod, Comorin, Delgado, Dezhnev, Domino, Dungeness, East(ern), Fairweather, Faldetta, Fanion, Fanon, Farewell, Fear, Fichu, Finisterre, Flattery, Gallinas Point, Good Hope, Guardafui, Harp, Hatteras, Head(land), Helles, Hoe, Hogh, Hook of Holland, Horn, Inverness, Kennedy, Leeuwin, Lindesnes, Lizard, Manteel, Mantilla, Mantle, Mant(e)let, Mantua, Matapan, May, Miseno, Moz(z)etta, Muleta, Naze, Ness, Nordkyn, North, Northern, Ortegal, Palatine, Palliser, Parry, Pelerine, Peninsula, Point, Poncho, Promontory, Race, Ras, Ray, Reinga, Roca, Ruana, Runaway, Sable, St Vincent, Sandy, Scaw, Skagen, Skaw, Sontag, Southwest, Talma, Tippet, Trafalgar, Ushant, Verde, Vert, Waterproof, Western, Wrath, York

**Cape of Good Hope** Stellenbosch

**Caper(ing)** Antic, Bean, Boer, Capparis, Capriole, Cavort, Dance, Dido, Escapade, Flisk, Frisk, Frolic, Gambado, Gambol, Harmala, Harmalin(e), Harmel, Harmin(e), Jaunce, Jaunse, Pigeon-wing, Prance, Prank, Romp, Saltant, Sault, Scoup, Scowp, Skip, Tit(t)up

**Capet** Marie Antoinette
**Cape Town** SA
**Capital(s)** A1, Assets, Block, Boodle, Bravo, Bully, Cap, Chapiter, Chaptrel, Circulating,
Doric, Equity, Euge, Excellent, Fixed, Flight, Float, Floating, Fonds, Great, Helix, Human,
Initial, Ionic, Lethal, Lulu, Metropolis, Principal, Refugee, Risk, Rustic, Seat, Seed, Share,
Social, Splendid, Sport, Stellar, Stock, Super, Topping, UC, Upper case, Venture, Wealth,
Working

---

## CAPITALS

| *3 letters:* | Laon | Bonne | Lhasa |
|---|---|---|---|
| Fes | Laos | Bourg | Liege |
| Fez | Leon | Braga | Lille |
| Gap | Lima | Cairo | Lyons |
| Jos | Linz | Chiba | Macao |
| Ray | Lomé | Colon | Melun |
| Rio | Male | Cuzco | Meroe |
| Ude | Metz | Cuzev | Minna |
| Ufa | Nara | Dacca | Minsk |
| Van | Nuuk | Dakar | Monza |
| Zug | Oslo | Delhi | Namur |
| | Pegu | Dhaka | Nancy |
| *4 letters:* | Pune | Dijon | Natal |
| Aden | Riga | Dilli | Nimes |
| Agra | Rome | Dover | Nukus |
| Albi | Safi | Dutse | Oskub |
| Apia | San'a | Emisa | Palma |
| Auch | Sian | Enugu | Paris |
| Baki | Sion | Goias | Parma |
| Baku | Susa | Gotha | Patna |
| Bari | Suva | Guaco | Pella |
| Bern | Vila | Hanoi | Perth |
| Bida | Xian | Harar | Petra |
| Boac | | Hefei | Pinsk |
| Bonn | *5 letters:* | Hofei | Poona |
| Brno | Aarau | Hsian | Praha |
| Caen | Abiya | Ikeja | Praia |
| Cali | Abuja | Jambi | Quito |
| Chur | Adana | Jammu | Rabat |
| Cluj | Agana | Jinan | Rouen |
| Cork | Aijal | Kabul | Salem |
| Dili | Akita | Kandy | Sanaa |
| Doha | Akure | Karor | Scone |
| Faro | Amman | Kazan | Segou |
| Graz | Aosta | Kizyl | Seoul |
| Head | Arlon | Konia | Siena |
| Homs | Assen | Konya | Simla |
| Hums | Batum | Koror | Sofia |
| Ipoh | Beira | Kyoto | Stans |
| Jaen | Belém | Lagos | Sucré |
| Jolo | Berne | Lassa | Tepic |
| Kiel | Bisho | Laval | Terni |
| Kiev | Blois | Le Paz | Tokyo |
| Kobe | Boise | Le Puy | Trier |

Tunis
Turin
Uxmal
Vaasa
Vadso
Vaduz
Wuhan
Yanan
Yenan
Zomba

**6 letters:**
Abakan
Albany
Almaty
Andros
Angkor
Ankara
Annecy
Anyang
Asmara
Astana
Athens
Austin
Bagdad
Baguio
Bamako
Bangui
Banjul
Bassau
Bastia
Batumi
Bauchi
Beirut
Berlin
Bhopal
Bogota
Bruges
Brunei
Cahors
Canton
Chonju
Colima
Colmar
Cracow
Cucuta
Cuenca
Cuiaba
Darwin
Denver
Dessau
Dispur
Dodoma
Dublin

Edessa
Erfurt
Fuchou
Geneva
Giyani
Gondar
Grozny
Habana
Haikou
Harare
Harbin
Havana
Helena
Hobart
Hohhot
Ibadan
Iloilo
Ilorin
Imphal
Jaffna
Jaipur
Jalapa
Johore
Juneau
Kaduna
Kaunas
Kerman
Kigali
Kisumu
Kohima
Kuwait
Lahore
Lisbon
Loanda
Lokoja
London
Luanda
Lusaka
Macapá
Maceió
Madrid
Maikop
Majuro
Malabo
Manama
Manaus
Manila
Maputo
Marsan
Maseru
Mekele
Merano
Merida
Moroni

Moscow
Mumbai
Munich
Murcia
Muscat
Mutare
Nagpur
Nakuru
Namibe
Nassau
Nevers
Niamey
Nouméa
Oaxaca
Orense
Ottawa
Oviedo
Owerri
Palmas
Panaji
Panjim
Peking
Pierre
Prague
Puebla
Punaka
Quebec
Quetta
Ranchi
Recife
Regina
Rennes
Riyadh
Roseau
Ryazan
Saigon
Sardes
Sardis
Sarnen
Sendai
Skopje
Sokoto
Sparta
St Gall
St Paul
Sydney
Tabora
Taipei
Tallin
Tarawa
Tarbes
Tarsus
Tehran
Tetuan

Thebes
Thimbu
Tirana
Tobruk
Toledo
Toluca
Topeka
Ulundi
Umtata
Urumqi
Vesoul
Vienna
Warsaw
Xining
Yangon
Yaunde
Zagreb
Zurich
Zwolle

**7 letters:**
Abidjan
Ajaccio
Alençon
Algiers
Altdorf
Antioch
Atlanta
Augusta
Auxerre
Baghdad
Bangkok
Barnaul
Begawan
Beijing
Belfast
Belfort
Bien Hoa
Bijapur
Bikaner
Bishkek
Bobigny
Bologna
Calabar
Caracas
Cardiff
Cayenne
Cesenza
Cetinje
Chengdu
Chennai
Coblenz
Coimbra
Colombo

Conakry
Concord
Cordoba
Cotonou
Cremona
Cuttack
Douglas
Durango
Foochow
Funchal
Gangtok
Goiania
Guiyang
Haarlem
Halifax
Hanover
Hassett
Herisau
Honiara
Huhehot
Iqaluit
Iquique
Isfahan
Izhevsk
Jackson
Jakarta
Kaesong
Kaifeng
Kampala
Karachi
Kashmir
Katsina
Kayseri
Kharkov
Khartum
Koblenz
Konakri
Kuching
Kunming
Kwangju
Lansing
Lanzhou
Lashkar
Legaspi
Liestal
Limoges
Lincoln
Louvain
Lucerne
Lucknow
Madison
Malacca
Managua
Masbate

Mathura
Mbabane
Memphis
Messene
Morelia
Munster
Nairobi
Nalchik
Nanjing
Nanking
Nanning
Nicosia
Nineveh
Novi Sad
Olomouc
Orleans
Oshogbo
Pachuca
Palermo
Palikit
Papeete
Perugia
Phoenix
Pishpek
Plovdiv
Potenza
Potsdam
Punakha
Quimper
Raleigh
Rangoon
San José
San Juan
Santa Fe
Sao Tomé
Sapporo
Saransk
Segovia
Seville
Stanley
St John's
Taiyuan
Tallinn
Tangier
Tbilisi
Teheran
Tel Aviv
Thimphu
Tiemcen
Toronto
Trenton
Trieste
Tripoli
Umuahia

Urumshi
Valetta
Vicenza
Vilnius
Vilnyus
Vitoria
Xanthus
Yakutsk
Yaounde
Yerevan

**8 letters:**
Abeokuta
Abu Dhabi
Adelaide
Agartala
Ashgabet
Asuncion
Auckland
Bar-le-Duc
Belgrade
Belmopan
Besancon
Beyrouth
Boa Vista
Brasilia
Brisbane
Brussels
Budapest
Cagliari
Calcutta
Campeche
Canberra
Cape Town
Castries
Chambéry
Changsha
Chaumont
Cheyenne
Chisinau
Coahuila
Columbia
Columbus
Culiacan
Curitiba
Damascus
Debrecen
Dehra Dun
Denpasar
Djibouti
Dushanbe
Ecbatana
Edmonton
Eraklion

Florence
Freetown
Fribourg
Funafuti
Gaborone
Godthaab
Golconda
Hamilton
Hangzhou
Hannover
Hargeisa
Hartford
Helsinki
Honolulu
Istanbul
Jayapura
Kandahar
Katmandu
Khartoum
Kilkenny
Kinshasa
Kirkwall
Kishinev
La Spezia
Lausanne
Liaoyand
Lilongwe
Luneburg
Mandalay
Mechelen
Mexicali
Monrovia
Monterey
Nanchang
Nanching
Nanterre
Narbonne
Ndjamena
New Delhi
Pago Pago
Pamplona
Pergamum
Peshawar
Pnom-Penh
Port Said
Port-Vila
Pretoria
Pristina
Roskilde
Saltillo
Salvador
Salzburg
Santiago
Sao Paulo

Sarajevo
Seremban
Shah Alam
Shanghai
Shenyang
Shillong
Silvassa
Srinagar
Sterling
St Helier
Szczecin
Tashkent
The Hague
Thonburi
Tiaxcala
Torshavn
Toulouse
Usumbura
Valencia
Valletta
Victoria
Vladimir
Warangai
Windhoek
Winnipeg
Yinchuan
Zaragoza

**9 letters:**
Amsterdam
Annapolis
Ashkhabad
Ayutthaya
Banda Aceh
Bandar Ser
Bangalore
Benin City
Birobijan
Bucharest
Bujumbura
Cartagena
Changchun
Changshar
Chengchow
Cherkessk
Chihuahua
Darmstadt
Des Moines
Edinburgh
Fongafale
Fortaleza
Frankfort
Grand Turk
Guangzhou

Heraklion
Hyderabad
Innsbruck
Islamabad
Jalalabad
Jerusalem
Karlsruhe
Kathmandu
Kingstown
Kisangani
Knoxville
Kuch Bihar
Lamberene
Leningrad
Ljubljana
Magdeburg
Maiduguri
Marrakesh
Melbourne
Mogadishu
Montauban
Monterrey
Nashville
Nelspriut
Nuku'alofa
Perigueux
Perpignan
Phnom Penh
Podgorica
Polokwane
Port Blair
Port Louis
Porto Novo
Port Royal
Putrajaya
Pyongyang
Resources
Reykjavik
Rio Branco
Samarkand
San Merino
Singapore
Solothurn
St George's
Stockholm
Stuttgart
Thorshavn
Trebizond
Ulan Bator
Vientiane
Wad Medani
Wiesbaden
Zhengzhou

**10 letters:**
Addis Ababa
Basse-terre
Baton Rouge
Bellinzona
Birobidzan
Bratislava
Bridgetown
Campobosso
Carson City
Chandigarh
Charleston
Cienfuegos
Cochabamba
Concepcion
Cooch Behar
Copenhagen
Cuernavaca
Diyarbakir
Eisenstadt
Frauenfeld
Georgetown
Harrisburg
Heidelberg
Hermosillo
Joao Pessoa
Klagenfurt
Kota Baharu
Kragujevac
Launceston
Leeuwarden
Libreville
Little Rock
Maastricht
Mexico City
Middelburg
Mogadiscio
Montevideo
Montgomery
Montpelier
Nouakchott
Panama City
Paramaribo
Persepolis
Podgoritsa
Porto Velho
Providence
Rawalpindi
Sacramento
Trivandrum
Tskhinvali
Valladolid
Valparaiso
Washington

Wellington
Whitehorse
Willemstad
Winchester
Yashkar-Ola

**11 letters:**
Bhubaneswar
Brazzaville
Buenos Aires
Campo Grande
Carcassonne
Charlestown
Dares Salaam
Fredericton
Gandhinagar
Guadalajara
Hermoupolis
Johore Bahru
Kuala Lumpur
Montbeliard
Nakhichevan
Ouagadougou
Pandemonium
Pondicherry
Port Moresby
Porto Alegre
Port of Spain
Rio Gallegas
Saarbrucken
San Salvador
Springfield
St Peter Port
Tallahassee
Tegucigalpa
Thohoyandou
Ulaanbaatar
Vatican City
Vladikavkaz
Yellowknife

**12 letters:**
Antananarivo
Anuradhapura
Barquisimeto
Barranquilla
Bloemfontein
Chilpancingo
Fort-de-France
Indianapolis
Johannesburg
Kota Kinabalu
Mont-de-Marsan
Muzzafarabad

| | | | |
|---|---|---|---|
| Pandaemonium | Shijiazhuang | Funafuti Atoll | Puerto Princesa |
| Petrozavodsk | Sidi-bel-Abbes | Guatemala City | 's-Hertogenbosch |
| Ponta Delgada | Tenochtitian | Hertogenbosch | |
| Port-au-Prince | Ujungpandang | Jefferson City | *15 letters:* |
| Port Harcourt | Villahermosa | Udjung Pandang | Chalons-sur-Marne |
| Rio de Janeiro | Williamsburg | Yaren District | Charlotte Amalie |
| Salt Lake City | Yamoussoukro | | Clermont-Ferrand |
| San Cristobal | | *14 letters:* | Sekondi-Takoradi |
| Santo Domingo | *13 letters:* | Andorra la Vella | |
| Schaffhausen | Belo Horizonte | Constantinople | *16 letters:* |
| Schoemansdal | Charlottetown | Kuala Trengganu | Pietermaritzburg |
| Seringapatam | Florianopolis | Oaxaca de Juarez | Trixtia Gutiérrez |

**Capitalise** Carpe diem
**Capitalist** Bloated, Financier, Moneyer, Sloane
▷ **Capitalist** *may indicate* a citizen of a capital
**Capitulate** Acquiesce, Comply, Defer, Fall, →**SURRENDER**, Yield
**Capless** Bare
▷ **Capless** *may indicate* first letter missing
**Capone** Al, Scarface
▷ **Capriccioso** *may indicate* an anagram
**Caprice, Capricious** Arbitrary, Boutade, Capernoitie, Cap(p)ernoity, Conceit, Desultory,
   Eccentric, Elf(in), Erratic, Fancy, Fickle, Fitful, Freak, Humoresk, Humoresque, Irony,
   Megrim, Migraine, Mood, Perverse, Quirk, Vagary, Wayward, Whim(sy)
**Capsize** Crank, Keel, Overbalance, Overturn, Purl, Tip, Turn turtle, Upset, Whemmle,
   Whomble
▷ **Capsized** *may indicate* a word upside down
**Capstan** Sprocket, Windlass
**Capsule** Amp(o)ule, Boll, Bowman's, Cachet, Habitat, Internal, Nidamentum,
   Ootheca, Orbiter, Ovisac, Pill, Pyxidium, Space, Spacecraft, Spansule, Spermatophore,
   Suppository, Time, Urn
**Captain** Ahab, Bligh, Bobadil, Bones, Bossyboots, Brassbound, Capt, Channel, Chief, Cid,
   Commander, Condottiere, Cook, Copper, Cuttle, Flint, Group, Hardy, Hook, Hornblower,
   Kettle, Kidd, Leader, Macheath, Master, Nemo, Oates, Old man, Owner, Patron, Patroon,
   Post, Privateer, Protospatharius, Pugwash, Rittmaster, Skip(per), Standish, Subah(dar),
   Subedar, Swing, Trierarch
**Caption** Cutline, Heading, Headline, Inscription, Masthead, Roller, Sub-title, Title
**Captious** Critical, Peevish
**Captivate(d), Captivating** Beguile, Bewitch, Charm, Enamour, Enthrall, Epris(e),
   Rapt, Take, Winsome
**Captive, Captivity** Babylonish, Bonds, Chains, Duress, Hostage, POW, Prisoner, Slave,
   Thrall
**Capture** Abduct, Annex, Bag, Catch, Collar, Cop, Data, Electron, Enchain, Enthral(l),
   Entrance, Grab, Land, Motion, Nail, Net, Prize, Rush, Seize, Snabble, Snaffle, Snare,
   →**TAKE**, Trap
**Capuchin** Cebus, Monkey, Sajou
**Car(s)** Alvis, Aston Martin, Astra, Audi, Austin, Auto(matic), Banger, Beemer, Beetle,
   Benz, Berlin, Biza, BL, Bluebird, Bomb, Boneshaker, Brake, Bubble, Buffet, Bugatti,
   Buick, Bumper, Bus, Cab(riolet), Cadillac, Catafalco, Catafalque, Chariot, Chelsea-tractor,
   Chorrie, Citroen, Classic, Clunker, Coach, Compact, Company, Concept, Convertible,
   Cortina, Coupé, Courtesy, Crate, Daimler, Diesel, Diner, Dodgem®, Drag(ster),
   Drophead, Dual control, Dunger, Elf, Estate, E-type, Fastback, Ferrari, Fiat, Fleet, Flivver,
   Ford, Formula, Freight, Friday, Gas guzzler, Getaway, Ghost, Gondola, Gran turismo,
   Griddle, GT, Gyrocar, Hardtop, Hatchback, Heap, Hearse, Hillman, Horseless carriage,

Hot hatch, Hot-rod, Irish, Jaguar, Jalop(p)y, Jamjar, Jammy, Jam sandwich, Jaunting, Jim Crow, Kart, Kia, Kit, Knockabout, Lada, Lagonda, Lancia, Landaulet, Landrover, Lexus, Lift-back, Limo, Limousine, Lincoln, Merc(edes), MG, Mini, Model T, Morgan, Morris, Motor, Muscle, Nacelle, Notchback, Observation, Opel, Pace, Palace, Panda, Parlo(u)r, Patrol, Pimpmobile, Popemobile, Production, Prowl, Pullman, Racer, Ragtop, Railroad, Rattletrap, Restaurant, Roadster, Roller, Rolls (Royce), Rover, RR, Runabout, Runaround, Rust bucket, Saloon, Scout, Seat, Sedan, Service, Shooting-brake, Skoda, Sleeper, Sleeping, Soft-top, Speedster, Sports, Squad, Station wagon, Steam, Stock, Stretch-limo, Subcompact, Sunbeam, Supermini, SUV, Tank, Taxi, Telepherique, Telpher, Three-wheeler, Tin Lizzie, Tonneau, Tourer, Touring, Tram, Triumph, Trolley, Tumble, Turbo, Two-seater, Vehicle, Veteran, Vintage, Voiture, Volvo, VW, Wheeler, Wheels

**Caramel** Brûlé

**Carat** K, Point

**Caravan(ner)** Caf(f)ila, Convoy, Fleet, Kafila, Motor home, Safari, Trailer, Trailer trash, Winnebago®

**Caravanserai** Choltry, Choutry, Inn, Khan

**Caraway** Aj(o)wan, Carvy, Seed

**Car-back** Boot, Dick(e)y, Tonneau

**Carbamide** Urea

**Carbide** Silicon

**Carbine** Escopette, Gun, Musket

**Carbohydrate** Agar, Agarose, Callose, Carrageenan, Cellulose, Chitin, Dextran, Disaccharide, Glycogen, Heptose, Hexose, Inulin, Ketose, Laminarin, Mannan, Mucilage, Pectin, Pectose, Pentene, Pentose, Pentylene, Polysaccharide, Saccharide, Sorbitol, Starch, Sucrose, Sugar

**Carbolic** Orcin

**Carbon(ate)** Activated, Ankerite, Austenite, Buckminsterfullerene, Buckyball, C, Charcoal, Coke, Dialogite, Diamond, Drice, Dry ice, Flame, Flimsy, Fullerene, Gas black, Graphite, Lampblack, Martensite, Natron, Petroleum coke, Scawtite, Soot, Spode, Spodium, Urao, Witherite, Zaratite

**Carbon deficiency** Acapnia

**Carboy** Demijohn

**Carbuncle** Anthrax, Eyesore, Ruby

**Carcase, Carcass** Body, Cadaver, Carrion, Corpse, Cutter, Krang, Kreng, Morkin, Mor(t)ling

**Carcinogen** Alar

**Card(s), Cardboard, Carding** Accelerator, Access, Ace, Affinity, Amex®, Arcana, Baccarat, Basto, Bill, Birthday, Blue Peter, Boarding, Bower, Business, Calling, Canasta, Cartes, Cash, Caution, Charge, Cheque, Chicane, Cigarette, Club, Comb, Communion, Community, Compass, Court(esy), Credit, Cue, Curse of Scotland, Dance, Debit, Deck, Deuce, Devil's (picture) books, Diamond, Doffer, Donor, Drawing, Ecarté, Eccentric, Euchre, Expansion, Face, False, Flash, Flaught, Flop, Flush, Fourchette, →**GAME**, Gold, Goulash, Graphics, Green, Guide, Hand, Hard, Health, Heart, Hole, Honour, Humorist, ID, Identification, Identity, Idiot, Intelligent, Jack, Jambone, Jamboree, Joker, Kanban, Key, King, Knowing, Laser, Leading, Letter, Loo, Loyalty, Magnetic, Manille, Master, Matador, Maximum, Meishi, Meld, Memory, Menu, Mise, Mistigris, Mogul, Mournival, Natural, Notelet, Oddity, Ombre, Original, Pack, Past, Pasteboard, Payment, PC, Phone, Picture, Piquet, Placard, Place, Plastic, Playing, Postal, Proximity, Punch(ed), Quatorze, Quatre, Queen, Queer, Quiz, Race, Rail, Ration, Red, Rippler, Rove, Royal marriage, Score, Scraperboard, Scratch, Scream, Screwball, Scribble, Shade, Show, SIM, Singleton, Smart, Soda, Solo, Sound, Spade, Spadille, Squeezer, Stiffener, Store, Strawboard, Sure, Swab, Swipe, Swish, Switch, Swob, Swot, Talon, Tarok, Tarot, Tease(r), Tenace, Test, Thaumatrope, Ticket, Tiddy, Time, Top-up, Tose, Toze, Trading, Trey, Trump, Two-spot, Union, Valentine, Visa, Visiting, Wag, Warrant, Weirdie, Whitechapel, Wild, Wit, Yellow, Zener

**Cardigan** Ballet-wrap, Jacket, Lumber jacket, Wampus, Wam(m)us, Woolly
**Cardinal** Apostolic vicar, Camerlingo, Chief, College, Eight, Eminence, Eminent, Grosbeak, Hat, HE, Hume, Legate, Manning, Mazarin, Medici, Newman, Nine, Number, Pivotal, Polar, Prefect, Prelate, Radical, Red, Red-hat, Richelieu, Sacred college, Seven, Sin, Spellman, Ten, Virtue, Vital, Wolsey, Ximenes
**Card-player** Dealer, Pone
**Care(r), Caring** Attention, Befriend, Burden, Cark, Caution, Cerne, Cherish, Community, →CONCERN, Cosset, Doula, Exactitude, Grief, Guard, Heed, Intensive, Kaugh, Keep, Kiaugh, Maternal, Mind, Mother, Pains, Palliative, Parabolanus, Primary, Providence, Reck(e), Regard, Reke, Residential, Respite, Retch, Rought, Shared, Solicitude, →TEND, Tenty, Thought, Trouble, Ts(o)uris, Ward, Worry
**Careen(ing)** Parliament-heel
**Career** Course, Hurtle, Life, Line, Profession, Run, Rush, Scorch, Speed, Start, Tear, Vocation
▷ **Career** *may indicate* an anagram
**Carefree** Blithe, →CARELESS(LY), Dozy, Footloose, Happy-go-lucky, Irresponsible, →NEGLIGENT, Oops, Perfunctory, Rollicking, Thoughtless, Tinker's cuss, Tinker's damn
**Careful(ly)** Canny, Chary, Delicate, Diligent, Discreet, Gentle, Heedy, Hooly, Leery, Meticulous, Mindful, Painstaking, Penny-pinching, Penny-wise, Pernickety, Provident, Prudent, Scrimp, Scrupulous, Softly-softly, Studious, Tentie, Tenty, Thorough, Thrifty, Vigilant, Ware, Wary
**Careless(ness), Careless(ly)** Anyhow, Casual, Cavalier, Cheery, Debonair, Easy, Free-minded, Gallio, Improvident, Imprudent, Inadvertent, Inattention, Inconsiderate, Insouciance, Irresponsible, Lax, Lighthearted, Négligé, →NEGLIGENT, Nonchalant, Oops, Oversight, Perfunctory, Raffish, Rash, Remiss, Resigned, Riley, Rollicking, Slam-bang, Slapdash, Slaphappy, Slipshod, Sloppy, Sloven(ly), Slubber, Taupie, Tawpie, Thoughtless, Unguarded, Unmindful, Untenty, Unwary
▷ **Carelessly** *may indicate* an anagram
**Caress** Bill, Coy, Embrace, Feel, Fondle, Kiss, Lallygag, Lollygag, Noursle, Nursle, Pet, Straik, Stroke, Touch
**Caretaker** Acting, Charge d'affaires, Concierge, Curator, Custodian, Dvornik, Granthi, Guardian, Interim, Janitor, Nightwatchman, Sexton, Shammash, Shammes, Superintendent, Verger, Warden
**Careworn** Haggard, Lined, Tired, Weary
**Cargo** Boatload, Bulk, Burden, Fraught, Freight, Lading, Last, →LOAD, Navicert, Payload, Shipload, Shipment
**Caribbean** Belonger, Cuban, Puerto Rican, Soca, Sokah, Spanish Main, Taino, WI
**Caribou** Tuktoo, Tuktu
**Caricature, Caricaturist** Ape, Beerbohm, Burlesque, Caran d'Ache, Cartoon, Cruikshank, Doyle, Farce, Gillray, Mimicry, Rowlandson, Scarfe, Skit, Spy, Tenniel, Toon, Travesty
**Carlin** Pug
**Carmelite** Barefoot, White (Friar)
**Carmen** AA, BL, Chai, RAC
**Carnage** Bloodshed, Butchery, Massacre, Slaughter
**Carnal** Bestial, Lewd, Outward, Sensual, Sexual, Worldly
**Carnation** Clove pink, Dianthus, Gillyflower, Malmaison, Picotee, Pink
**Carnival** Fair, Fasching, Festival, Fete, Mardi Gras, Mas, Moomba, Rag, Revelry, Surf
**Carnivore, Carnivorous** Allosaur, Cacomistle, Cacomixl, Coati, Creodont, Ermelin, Fennec, Fo(u)ssa, Genet, Glutton, Grison, Hyena, Meerkat, Otter, Ratel, Stoat, Sundew, Suricate, Viverridae, Weasel, Wolverine, Zoophagan
**Carob** Algar(r)oba, Locust (tree), St John's bread
**Carol(ler)** Noel, Sing, Song, Wait, Wassail, Yodel
**Carousal, Carouse** Bend, Birl(e), Bouse, Bride-ale, Compotation, Drink, Mallemaroking, Mollie, Orge, Orgy, →REVEL, Roist, Screed, Spree, Upsee, Upsey, Upsy, Wassail

**Carp(er)** Beef, Cavil, Censure, Complain, Crab, Critic, Crucian, Crusian, Fault, Gibel, Goldfish, Gripe, Id(e), Koi, Kvetch, Mirror, Mome, Nag, Nibble, Niggle, Nitpick, Prussian, Roach, Roundfish, Scold, Snipe, Twitch, Whine, Yerk, Yirk

**Carpenter** Beveller, Bush, Cabinet-maker, Carfindo, Chippy, Chips, Fitter, Joiner, Joseph, Menuisier, Quince, Sawyer, Shipwright, Tenoner, Woodworker, Wright

▷ **Carpenter** *may indicate* an anagram

**Carpet(ing)** Admonish, Aubusson, Axminster, Beetle, Berate, Bessarabian, Body, Broadloom, Brussels, Castigate, Chide, Dhurrie, Drugget, Durrie, Dutch, Excoriation, Kali, Kelim, Khilim, Kidderminster, Kilim, Kirman, Lecture, Lino, Magic, Mat(ting), Moquette, Persian, Rate, Red, Reprimand, Reproach, Roast, Rug, Runner, Shagpile, Shark, Shiraz, Stair, Turkey, Wall-to-wall, What for, Wig, Wilton

**Carrageen** Sea-moss

**Carriage** Air, Ar(a)ba, Aroba, Bandy, Barouche, Bearing, Berlin(e), Bier, Brake, Brit(sch)ka, Britska, Britzka, Brougham, Buckboard, Buggy, Cab, Calash, Calèche, Car, Cariole, Caroche, Carriole, Carryall, Cartage, Chaise, Charabanc, Charet, Chariot, Chassis, Chay, Clarence, Coach, Coch, Composite, Conveyance, Coupé, Curricle, Demeanour, Dennet, Deportment, Désobligeante, Diner, Dormeuse, Dormitory-car, Dos-a-dos, Do-si-do, Drag, Dros(h)ky, Ekka, Equipage, Fiacre, Fly, Four-in-hand, Freight, Gait, Gig, Gladstone, Go-cart, Growler, Gun, Haulage, Herdic, Horseless, Howdah, Hurley-hacket, Jampan, Job, Landau(let), Landing, Limber, Mien, Non-smoker, Norimon, Observation-car, Phaeton, Pick-a-back, Pochaise, Pochay, Poise, Port(age), Portance, Postchaise, Posture, Poyse, Pram, Pullman, Purdah, Railcar, Railway, Randem, Rath(a), Remise, Ricksha(w), Rig, Rockaway, Set-up, Shay, Sled, Sleeper, Smoker, Sociable, Spider, Spider phaeton, Stanhope, Sulky, Surrey, Tarantas(s), Taxi, T-cart, Tender, Tenue, Tilbury, Tim-whiskey, Tonga, Trail, Trap, Van, Vetture, Victoria, Voiture, Wagonette, Waterage, Whirligig, Whisk(e)y, Whisky gig

**Carriageway** Dual

**Carrier** Aircraft, Airline, Arm, Baldric, Barkis, Barrow, Bomb-ketch, Briefcase, Bulk, Cacolet, Caddy, Cadge, Camel, Charon, Coaster, Common, Conveyor, Donkey, Escort, Fomes, Fomites, Frog, Grid, Hamper, Haversack, Hawker, Hod, Janker, Jill, Majority, Minority, Nosebag, Noyade, Obo, Omnibus, Packhorse, Personnel, Pigeon, Porter, Rucksack, Satchel, Schistosoma, Semantide, Sling, Spore, Straddle, Stretcher(-bearer), Tiffin, Tranter, → **TRAY**, Trug, TWA, Vector, Wave

**Carrion** Cadaver, Carcase, Carcass, Flesh, Ket, Stapelia

**Carrot(s)** Lure, Redhead, Seseli, Titian

**Carry(ing), Carry over** Asport, Bear, Chair, Convey, Enlevé, Escort, Ferry, Frogmarch, Hawk, Hent, Humf, Hump, Humph, Kurvey, Land, Move, Pack, Pickaback, Port, Reappropriate, Stock, Sustain, Tide over, Tote, → **TRANSPORT**, Trant, Waft, Wage, With, Yank

**Carry on** Continue, Create, Wage

**Carry out** Execute, Implement, Mastermind, Perform, Pursue

**Cart(er)** Bandy, Barrow, Bogey, Buck, Cape, Car(r)iole, Chapel, Dandy, Democrat, Democrat wagon, Dog, Dolly, Dray, Egyptologist, Float, Furphy, Gambo, Gill, Golf, Governess, Gurney, Hackery, Jag, Jill, Lead, Mail(-gig), Night, Pie, Pram, Rickshaw, Scot, Scotch, Shandry, T, Tax(ed), Telega, Trolley, Tumbrel, Tumbril, Village, Wag(g)on, Wain, Water, Wheelbarrow, Whitechapel

**Cartel** Duopoly, Firms, Ring, Syndicate, Zaibatsu

**Carthaginian** Punic

**Carthorse** Aver, Shire

**Carthusian** Bruno, DOM

**Cartilage** Antitragus, Arytenoid, Chondral, Chondrin, Chondrus, Cricoid, Darwin's tubercle, Disc, Ensiform, Epiglottis, Gristle, Hyaline, Lytta, Meniscus, Semilunar, Tendrons, Thyroid, Tragus, Worm, Xiphoid

**Cartload** Fother, Seam

**Cartographer** Cabot, Chartist, Kremer, Mercator, OS, Speed

**Carton** Box, Case, Crate, Sydney, Tub

**Cartoon(ist)** Andy Capp, Animated, Bairnsfather, Bateman, Caricature, Comic, Comic strip, Disney, Drawn, Emmet, Fougasse, Fumetto, Garland, Goldberg, Lancaster, Leech, Low, Manga, Mel, Partridge, Popeye, Robinson, Schulz, Short, Shrek, Spy, Strip, Superman, Tenniel, Thurber, Tidy, Tintin, Trog

**Cartridge** Ball, Blank, Bullet, Cartouche, Cassette, Crystal, Doppie, Live, Magazine, Magnetic, Magnum, QIC, Rim-free, Shell, Spent

**Cart-track** Rut

**Cartwheel** Handspring

**Caruncle** Aril, Carnosity, Strophiole

**Carve(d), Carver, Carving** Abated, Alcimedon, Apsaras, Armchair, Bas relief, Camaieu, Cameo, Chair, Chip, Chisel, Cilery, Crocket, Cut, Dismember, Doone, Emboss, Enchase, Engrave, Entail, Entayle, Fiddlehead, Gargoyle, Gibbons, Glyphic, Glyptic, Hew, Incise, Inscribe, Insculp, Intaglio, Knotwork, Netsuke, Nick, Petroglyph, Scrimshaw, Sculp(t), Slice, Tondo, Trophy, Truncheon, Tympanum, Whakairo, Whittle

**Caryatid** Column, Telamon

**Casanova** Heartbreaker, Leman, Philanderer, Playboy, Womaniser

**Cascade** Cataract, Fall, Lin(n), Stream, Waterfall

**Cascara** Amarga, Buckthorn, Honduras bark, Rhamnus, Sagrada, Wahoo

**Case(s), Casing** Abessive, Ablative, Accusative, Action, Adessive, Allative, Altered, Appeal, Aril, Ascus, Assumpsit, Attaché, Basket, Beer, Bere, Bin, Bittacle, Blimp, Box, Brief, Bundwall, Burr, Burse, C, Ca, Cabinet, Cachet, Calyx, Canister, Canterbury, Capsule, Cartouch(e), Cartridge, Cask(et), Cause celebre, Cellaret, Chase, Chitin, Chrysalis, Cocoon, Coffin, Comitative, Compact, Crate, Croustade, Crust, Cyst, Dative, Declension, Detinue, Digi-pack, Dispatch, Dossier, Dressing, Elative, Elytron, Enallage, Enclose, Ensheath, Ergative, Essive, Etui, Etwee, Event, Example, Flan, Flapjack, Flask, Frame, Gearbox, Genitive, Grip, Hanaper, Hard, Hatbox, Helmet, Hold-all, Housewife, Hull, Humidor, Husk, Illative, Imperial, →**IN CASE**, Index, Indusium, Inessive, Instance, Kalamdan, Keg, Keister, Locative, Locket, Lorica, Manche, Matchbox, Matter, Mermaid's purse, Mezuzah, Music, Nacelle, Nominative, Non-suit, Nutshell, Objective, Oblique, Ochrea, Ocrea, Outpatient, Packing, Pair, Papeterie, Patient, Peapod, Pencil, Penner, Phylactery, Plight, Plummer-block, Pod, Port, Portfolio, Possessive, Prima facie, Puparium, Quiver, Recce, Reconnoitre, Red box, Sabretache, Sad, Scabbard, Seashell, Sheath(e), Shell, Situation, Six-pack, Sleeve, Sporocyst, Sporran, Stead, Sted, Straitjacket, Subjective, Suit, Tantalus, Tea-chest, Telium, Test, Theca, Tichborne, Toolbox, Trial, Trunk, Valise, Vanity bag, Vasculum, Vitrine, Vocative, Volva, Walise, Walking, Wallet, Wardian, Wing, Worst, Writing

**Case-harden** Nitrode

**Casein** Curd

**Casement** Frame, Roger, Sash, Window

**Cash** Blunt, Bonus, Bounty, Bread, Change, Coin, Digital, Dosh, Dot, Float, Funds, Hard, Idle money, Imprest, Liquid, Lolly, →**MONEY**, Needful, Ochre, Oof, Oscar, Pence, Petty, Ready, Realise, Redeem, Rhino, Spondulicks, Spot, Stumpy, Tender, Tin, Wampum, Wherewithal

**Cashew** Hog-plum

**Cashier, Cash machine** Annul, ATM, Break, Depose, Disbar, Dismiss, Displace, Oust, Teller, Treasurer

**Cashmere** Circassienne

**Casino** Monte Carlo

**Cask(et)** Armet, Barrel, Barrico, Bas(i)net, Box, Breaker, Butt, Cade, Casque, Cassette, Drum, Firkin, Galeate, Harness, Heaume, Hogshead, Keg, Leaguer, Octave, Pin, Pipe, Puncheon, Pyxis, Run(d)let, Salade, Sallet, Sarcophagus, Scuttlebutt, Shook, Shrine, Solera, Tierce, Tun, Wine

**Cask-stand** Stillion

**Cassava** Manioc, Tapioca, Yuc(c)a

**Casserole** Diable, Hotpot, Osso bucco, Pot, Salmi, Terrine, Tzimmes
**Cassette** Cartridge, Tape, Video
**Cassia** Cleanser, Senna
**Cassio** Lieutenant
**Cassiterite** Needle-tin, Tinstone
**Cassock** Gown, Soutane, Subucula
**Cast (down, off, out), Casting** Abattu, Actors, Add, Angle, Appearance, Bung, Cire perdue, Dash, Death mask, Die, Discard, Ecdysis, Ectype, Eject, Emit, Endocranial, Exorcise, Exuviae, Exuvial, Fling, Form, Found, Fusil, Grape, Hawk, Heave, Hob, Horoscope, Hue, Hurl, Impression, Ingo(w)es, Keb, Look, Lose, Lost wax, Mew, Mo(u)lt, Moulage, Mould, Pick, Plaster(stone), Plastisol®, Players, Print, Put, Reject, Sand, Sculptured, Sent, Shed, Shoot, Shy, Sling, Slive, Slough, Spoil, Stamp, Stookie, Swarm, Tailstock, Terracotta, → **THROW**, Toss, Tot, Warp, Wax, Worm, Ytost
▷ **Cast** *may indicate* an anagram or a piece of a word missing
**Castanet** Crotal(um), Knackers
**Castaway** Adrift, Crusoe, Gunn, Left, Man Friday, Outcast, Robinson, Selkirk, Stranded, Weft
▷ **Cast by** *may indicate* surrounded by
**Caste** Brahmin, Burakumin, Class, Dalit, Group, Harijan, Hova, Kshatriya, Rajpoot, Rajpout, Rajput, Rank, Scheduled, Sect, Shudra, Sudra, Untouchable, Vaisya, Varna
**Caster** Truckle
**Castigate** Berate, Chasten, Chastise, Criticise, Denounce, Keelhaul, Lash, Punish, Rate, Scold
**Cast-iron** Spiegeleisen
**Castle(d)** Barbara, Bouncy, Broch, C, Casbah, Chateau, Citadel, Fastness, Fort, Kasba(h), Maiden, Man, Mot(t)e, Motte and bailey, Move, Palace, Rook, Stronghold, Villa

---

## CASTLES

| | | | |
|---|---|---|---|
| **4 letters:** | Amboise | Carbonek | Edinburgh |
| Sand | Arundel | Chepstow | Lancaster |
| Trim | Belvoir | Crotchet | Restormel |
| | Blarney | Doubting | Rochester |
| **5 letters:** | Braemar | Egremont | Sherborne |
| Blair | Calzean | Elephant | Trausnitz |
| Blois | Canossa | Elsinore | |
| Conwy | Chillon | Inverary | **10 letters:** |
| Corfe | Colditz | Kronberg | Caerphilly |
| Hever | Cooling | Malperdy | Kenilworth |
| Leeds | Culzean | Pembroke | Pontefract |
| Spain | Despair | Perilous | |
| Upnor | Harlech | Rackrent | **11 letters:** |
| | Lincoln | Reculver | Carisbrooke |
| **6 letters:** | Otranto | Richmond | Chateauroux |
| Cawdor | Schloss | Stirling | Eilean Donan |
| Forfar | Skipton | Stokesay | Gormenghast |
| Glamis | Warwick | Stormont | |
| Howard | Windsor | Tintagel | **12 letters:** |
| Ludlow | | Urquhart | Fotheringhay |
| Raglan | **8 letters:** | Wartburg | Herstmonceux |
| Wemyss | Balmoral | | Sissinghurst |
| | Bamburgh | **9 letters:** | |
| **7 letters:** | Bastille | Dangerous | **13 letters:** |
| Adamant | Berkeley | Dunsinane | Carrickfergus |

**Castor** Muffineer
**Castor-oil** Ricinus
**Castrate(d), Castrato** Alter, Cut, Doctor, Emasculate, Eunuch, Evirate, Farinelli, Geld, Glib, Lib, Manzuoli, Moreschi, Mutilate, Neuter, Senesino, Spado, Spay, Swig, Wethers
**Castro** Fidel
**Casual(ly), Casuals** Accidental, Adventitious, Airy(-fairy), Blasé, Chance, Chav(ette), Flippant, Grass, Haphazard, Idle, Incidental, Informal, Jaunty, Lackadaisical, Leisurewear, Nonchalant, Odd(ment), Odd-jobber, Offhand, Off-the-cuff, Orra, Overly, Passing, Promiscuous, Random, Scratch, Shoe, Slaphappy, Slipshod, Sporadic, Stray, Temp, Throwaway
**Casualty** Blue on blue, Caduac, Chance-medley, ER, →**VICTIM**
**Casuist** Jesuit
**Cat** Ailuro-, Barf, Boat, Boke, Bush, Catamount, Dandy, Domestic, Egurgitate, Fat, Felid, Feline, Flog, Foss, Garfield, Glaring, Gossip, Grimalkin, Gus, Hipster, Jazzer, Lair, Lash, Mewer, Mog, Native, Neuter, Nib, Oriental, Painter, Palm, Pardal, Practical, Puss, Queen, Regurgitate, Sacred, Scourge, Sick, Singed, Spew, Spue, Swinger, Top, Vomit, Whip

---

## CATS

**3 letters:**
Gib
Kit
Rex
Tom

**4 letters:**
Eyra
Lion
Lynx
Manx
Musk
Pard
Puma

**5 letters:**
Alley
Civet
Felix
Fossa
Genet
Hodge
Korat
Manul
Ounce
Quoll
Rasse
Rumpy
Tabby
Tiger
Tigon
Zibet

**6 letters:**
Angora

Birman
Bobcat
Cougar
Foussa
Jaguar
La Perm
Malkin
Margay
Mouser
Musang
Ocelot
Ocicat
Serval
Somali
Sphynx
Tibert
Tybalt
Weasel
Zibeth

**7 letters:**
Burmese
Caracal
Cheetah
Clowder
Dasyure
Foumart
Genette
Leopard
Linsang
Lioncel
Maltese
Nandine
Pallas's
Panther

Persian
Pharaoh
Polecat
Ragdoll
Siamese
Tiffany
Tigress
Viverra

**8 letters:**
Balinese
Baudrons
Cacomixl
Cheshire
Devon Rex
Kilkenny
Long-hair
Mountain
Munchkin
Ringtail
Snowshoe
Tiffanie

**9 letters:**
Asparagus
Binturong
Bluepoint
Chantilly
Chartreux
Delundung
Himalayan
Lioncelle
Maine Coon
Marmalade
Mehitabel

Niebelung
Sealpoint
Shorthair
Tobermory
Tonkinese

**10 letters:**
Abyssinian
Cacomistle
Cornish Rex
Jaguarondi
Jaguarundi
Ring-tailed
Selkirk Rex
Turkish Van

**11 letters:**
Colourpoint
Egyptian Mau
Havana Brown
Russian Blue
Tongkingese

**12 letters:**
American Curl
Scottish Fold

**13 letters:**
Tortoise-shell
Turkish Angora

**14 letters:**
Asian Shorthair
Australian Mist
Siberian Forest

| *15 letters:* | *16 letters:* | *17 letters:* | *19 letters:* |
|---|---|---|---|
| Norwegian Forest | American Wirehair | American Shorthair | Californian Spangled |

**Cataclysm(ic)** Apocalypse, Dire
**Catacomb** Cemetery, Crypt, Hypogeum, Vault
**Catalepsy** Catatony, Trance
**Catalogue(r)** Categorise, Cattle dog, Dewey, Dictionary, Durchkomponi(e)rt, Index, Inventory, Itemise, K(ochel), List, Litany, Magalog, MARC, Messier, Ragman, Ragment, Raisonné, Record, Register, Roll, Specialogue, Star, Subject, Table, Tabulate, Thematic, Union
**Catalyst** Accelerator, Agent, Aldol, Chemical, Enzyme, Erepsin, Impetus, Influence, Kryptonite, Stereospecific, Unicase, Ziegler
**Catamite** Gunsel, Ingle, Pathic
**Catapult** Ballista, Ging, Launch, Mangon(el), Perrier, Petrary, Propel, Scorpion, Shanghai, Sling, Slingshot, Stone-bow, Tormentum, Trebuchet, Wye, Y
**Cataract** Cascade, Film, Overfall, Pearl, Pearl-eye, Torrent, Waterfall, Web and pin
**Catarrh** Coryza, Rheum
**Catastrophe, Catastrophic** Apocalypse, Calamity, Damoclean, →**DISASTER**, Doom, Epitasis, Fiasco, Meltdown, Ruinous, Tragedy
**Catatonia** Stupor
**Cat-call** Boo, Jeer, Mew, Miaow, Miaul, Razz, Wawl, Whistle, Wrawl
**Catch(y), Catcher, Catching, Caught** Air, Apprehend, Arrest, Attract, Backstop, Bag, Benet, Bone, C, Capture, Chape, Clasp, Cog, Collar, Conquest, Contagious, Contract, Cop, Corner, Cotton on, Ct, Deprehend, Detent, Dolly, Engage, Enmesh, Ensnare, Entoil, Entrap, Fang, Fastener, Field, Fish, Fumble, Gaper, Get, Glee(some), Grasp, Had, Hank, Haud, Haul, Hear, Hitch, Hold, Hook, Inmesh, Keddah, Keight, Kep(pit), Kheda, Kill, Land, Lapse, Lasso, Latch, Lazo, Lime, Lock, Morse, Nab, Nail, Net, Nick, Nim, Nobble, Noose, Overhear, Overhent, Overtake, Parti, Pawl, Rap, Release, Rope, Round, Rub, Safety, Save, Sean, Sear, See(n), Seize, →**SNAG**, Snap, Snare, Snib, Snig(gle), →**SONG**, Stop, Surprise, Swindle, Tack, Taen, Take, Tane, Tickle, Trammel, Trap, Trawl, Trick, Tripwire, Troll, Twenty two, Twig, Understand, Wrestle
**Catchword** Motto, Shibboleth, Slogan, Tag
**Catechism** Carritch, Shorter, Test
**Categorise, Categories, Category** →**CLASS**, Classify, Etic, Genera, Genre, Genus, Infraclass, Infraorder, Label, Order, Pigeonhole, Range, Specie, Stereotype, Taxon, Triage, Type
**Cater(er)** Acatour, Cellarer, Feed, Manciple, →**PROVIDE**, Purveyor, Serve, Steward, Supply, Victualler, Vivandière
**Caterpillar** Army worm, Aweto, Boll worm, Cabbageworm, Cotton-worm, Cutworm, Eruciform, Geometer, Gooseberry, Grub, Hop-dog, Hornworm, Inchworm, Larva, Looper, Osmeterium, Palmer, Silkworm, Tent, Webworm, Woolly-bear
**Caterwaul** Meow, Wrawl
**Catfish** Hassar, Woof
**Cathartic** Turbeth
**Cathedral** Amiens, Basilica, Birmingham, Burgos, Chartres, Chester, →**CHURCH**, Cologne, Cortona, Dome, Duomo, Durham, Ely, Evreux, Exeter, Gloucester, Guildford, Hereford, Hertford, Huesca, Kirkwall, Lateran, Lichfield, Lincoln, Lugo, Minster, Mullingar, Notre Dame, Rheims, Ripon, Rochester, St Albans, St Davids, St Paul's, Salisbury, Santiago de Compostela, Sens, Teruel, Up(p)sala, Viseu, Wakefield, Wells, Westminster, Winchester, Worcester, York
**Catherine** Braganza, Parr
**Catherine-wheel** Girandole
**Cathode** Electrode, Filament, Ray

**Catholic** Assumptionist, Broad, Christian Socialism, Comprehensive, Defenders, Doolan, Eclectic, Ecumenical, Fenian, General, German, Irvingism, Jebusite, Latin, Lazarist, Left-footer, Liberal, Marian, Old, Opus Dei, Ostiary, Papalist, Papaprelatist, Papist, Passionist, Recusant, Redemptionist, Roman, Romish, Salesian, Spike, Taig, Te(a)gue, Teigue, Theatine, Thomist, Tike, Tory, Tridentine, Tyke, Uniat, Universal, Ursuline, Waldenses, Wide

**Catkin** Amentum, Chat, Lamb's tail, Pussy-willow, Salicaceous

**Cat-lover** Ailurophile

**Catmint** Nep, Nepeta, Nip

**Cato** Porcian, Uticensis

**Cats-eye** Chatoyant, Cymophane

**Catsmeat** Lights

**Catspaw** Pawn, Property, Tool

**Cat's tail** Reed-mace, Typha

**Cat's whiskers** Vibrissa

**Cattle(pen)** Aberdeen Angus, Africander, Ankole, Aver, Ayrshire, Beefalo, Belgian Blue, Belted Galloway, Bestial, Black, Brahman, British White, Buffalo, Carabao, Charbray, Charolais, Chillingham, Dexter, Drove, Durham, Fee, Friesian, Friesland, Galloway, Gaur, Gayal, Guernsey, Gyal, Heard, Herd, Hereford, Highland, Holstein (Friesian), Illawarra, Jersey, Kerry, Kine, Kouprey, Kraal, Ky(e), Kyloe, Lairage, Limousin, Lincoln, Longhorn, Luing, Neat, Nout, Nowt, Owsen, Oxen, Piemontese, Rabble, Redpoll, Rother, Santa Gertrudis, Shorthorn, Simment(h)al, Soum, South Devon, Sowm, Steer, Stock, Store, Stot, Sussex, Tamarao, Tamarau, Teeswater, Wagyu, Welsh Black

**Cattle disease** Actinobacillosis, Actinomycosis, Anthrax, Black water, Dry-bible, Footrot, Gallsickness, Heart-water, Hoove, Johne's, Listeriosis, Lumpy jaw, Mange, Mastitis, Milk lameness, Moorill, New Forest, Quarter-ill, Red-water, Rinderpest, Scours, Scrapie, Texas fever, Wire-heel, Woody-tongue

**Cattle food** Fodder, Poonac, Silage

**Cattleman** Cowboy, Herder, Maverick, Puncher, Rancher, Ringer, Stock-rider

**Catty** Kin, Spiteful

**Caucasian** Aryan, Azabaijani, Azeri, Cherkess, European, Georgian, Iberian, Kabardian, Melanochroi, Paleface, Semite, Shemite, White, Yezdi, Yezidee, Zezidee

**Caucus** Assembly, Cabal, Cell, Gathering, Race

▶ **Caught** *see* CATCH(Y)

**Caul** Baby-hood, Kell, Membrane, Sillyhow

**Cauldron** Kettle, Pot

**Cauliflower** Curd, Ear, Floret, Gobi

**Caulk** Fill, Pay, Pitch, Snooze

**Causation, Cause(d), Causes** Aetiology, Agent, Bandwagon, Beget, Breed, Bring, Célèbre, Common, Compel, Create, Crusade, Determinant, Due, Effect, Efficient, Encheason, Engender, Entail, Evoke, Expedite, Factor, Final, First, Flag-day, Formal, Gar(re), Generate, Ideal, Incur, Induce, Inspire, Lead, Lost, Make, Material, Motive, Movement, Natural, → OCCASION, Parent, Pathogen, Precipitate, Probable, Prompt, Provoke, Proximate, Reason, Root, Sake, Secondary, Show, Source, Teleology, Topic, Trigger, Ultimate, Wreak

**Causeway** Giant's, Tombolo

**Caustic** Acid, Acrimonious, Alkaline, Burning, Common, Erodent, Escharotic, Lime, Lunar, Moxa, Potash, Pungent, Sarcastic, Scathing, Seare, Soda, Tart, Vitriol, Waspish, Withering

**Cauterise, Cauterisation** Brand, Burn, Disinfect, Inustion, Moxibustion, Sear

**Caution, Cautious (person)** Achitophel, Admonish, Ahithophel, Alert, Amber, Awarn, Beware, Cagey, Card, Care, Cave, Caveat, Chary, Circumspect, Credence, Cure, Defensive, Deliberate, Discretion, Fabian, Forewarn, Gingerly, Guard(ed), Hedger, Heedful, Leery, Prudent, Rum, Scream, Skite, Tentative, Timorous, Vigilant, Ware, → WARN, Wary, Yellow card

**Cavalcade** Pageant, Parade, Procession, Sowarree, Sowarry

**Cavalier** Brusque, Careless, Cicisbeo, Devil-may-care, Gallant, Lively, Malignant, Monarchist, Offhand, Peart, Rider, Royalist

▷ **Cavalier** *may indicate* an anagram

**Cavalry(man)** Blues, Car(a)bineer, Car(a)binier, Cornet, Cossack, Dragoon, Equites, Heavies, Horse, Horse Guards, Household, Hussar, Ironsides, Knights, Lancers, Life Guards, Light-horse, Plunger, Ressaldar, Risaldar, Rough-rider, Rutter, Sabres, Sabreur, Silladar, Spahee, Spahi, Uhlan, Yeomanry

**Cave(rn), Caves, Cave-dwelling, Cave in, Cavernous** Acherusia, Aladdin's, Alert, Altamira, Antar, Antre, Beware, Bone, Capitulate, Cellar, Cheddar, Collapse, Corycian, Deep, Den, Domdaniel, Erebus, Fingal's, Fore, Grot(to), Hollow, Jenolan, Lascaux, Look-out, Lupercal, Mammoth, Mind out, Nix, Pot-hole, Proteus, Sepulchre, Snow, Spel(a)ean, Speleology, Spelunker, Speos, Tassili, Trophonian, Vault, Waitomo, Ware, Weem, Wookey Hole

**Cave-dweller** Pict, Troglodyte, Troll

**Caveman** Adullam, Aladdin, Fingal, Neanderthal, Primitive, Troglodyte, Troll

**Caviare** Beluga, Osietra, Roe, Sevruga, Sturgeon

**Cavil** Carp, Haggle, Quibble

**Cavity** Acetabulum, Amygdale, Amygdule, Androclinium, Antrum, Archenteron, Atrial, Atrium, Body, Camera, Camouflet, Celom, Chamber, Cisterna, Clinandrium, Coelenteron, Coelom(e), Conceptacle, Concha, Countermark, Crater, Crypt, Cyst, Dent, Domatium, Druse, Enteron, Follicle, Foss, Gap, Geode, Glenoid, Gloryhole, Hold, Hole, Lacuna, Locule, Mediastinum, Mialoritic, Orbita, Orifice, Pelvis, Pleural, Pocket, Pothole, Pulp, Resonant, Segmentation, Sinus, Stomod(a)eum, Tartarus, Tear, Thunderegg, Tympanum, Vacuole, Vein, Ventricle, Vesicle, Vitta, Vomica, Vug, Vugg, Vugh, Well

**Cavort(ing)** Dance, Gambol, Jag, Scamper

**Cavy** Agouti, Capybara, Hograt, Paca

**Cayman Islands** Tax haven

**Cease(fire)** Abate, Blin, Cut, Desist, Devall, Die, Disappear, Halt, Ho, Intermit, Leese, Lin, Lose, Pass, Refrain, Remit, Sessa, →**STOP**, Truce

**Ceaseless** Eternal, Incessant, Perpetual

**Cecil** Rhodes

**Cedar(wood)** Arolla, Atlas, Barbados, Cryptomeria, Deodar, Incense, Jamaica, Japanese, Toon

**Cede** Grant, Yield

**Ceiling** Absolute, Barrel, Coffered, Cove, Cupola, Dome, Glass, Lacunar, Laquearia, Limit, Plafond, Roof, Service, Silver, Soffit, Stained glass

**Celebrate(d), Celebration, Celebrity** Ale, A-list, All-star, Beanfeast, Beano, Besung, Big name, Bigwig, Binge, B-list, Brat-packer, Carnival, Cel, Chant, Commemorate, Distinguished, Do, Eclat, Emblazon, Encaenia, Epithalamion, Epithalamium, Fame, Feast, Fest(al), Festivity, Fete, Fiesta, First-footing, Gala, Gaudeamus, Gaudy, Glitterati, Glorify, Grog-up, Harvest home, Headliner, Hold, Holiday, Honour, Hoop-la, Jamboree, Jol, Jollifications, Jollities, Joncanoe, Jubilee, Junkanoo, Keep, Large it, Laud, Legend, Limelight, Lion, Loosing, Lowsening, Maffick, Mardi Gras, Mass, Mawlid al-Nabi, Megastar, Monstre sacre, Name, Noted, Nuptials, Observe, Occasion, Orgy, Panathenaea, Party, Personage, Personality, Pinata, Praise, Randan, Rave-up, Record, Rejoice, Renown, Repute, Revel, Rite, Roister, Sangeet, Saturnalia, See in, Sex symbol, Shindig, Sing, Spree, Star, Storied, Sung, Supermodel, Superstar, Tet, Treat, Triumph, Wassail, Wet, Whoopee

**Celerity** Dispatch, Haste, Speed, Velocity

**Celery** Alexanders, Smallage, Stick

**Celestial** Chinese, Cosmic, Divine, Ethereal, Heavenly, Supernal, Uranic

**Celibate, Celibacy** Bachelor, Chaste, Nun, Paterin(e), Priest, Rappist, Rappite, Shakers, Single, Spinster

**Cell(s), Cellular** Amyloidal, Battery, Black hole, Bullpen, Cadre, Chamber, Chapel, Condemned, Crypt, Cubicle, Death, Dungeon, Group, Laura, Lock up, Padded, Peter, Priesthole, → **PRISON**, Proviral, Safety, Strip, Tank, Unit

## CELLS

*1 letter:*
T

*3 letters:*
Dry
Egg
Pec
Sex
Wet

*4 letters:*
Axon
Comb
Cone
Cyte
Fuel
Germ
Hair
HeLa
Mast
Oxum
Soma
Stem
Zeta

*5 letters:*
Ascus
Basal
Canal
Clark
Cyton
Flame
Giant
Gland
Guard
Islet
Linin
Lymph
Nerve
Nicad
Solar
Sperm
Spore
Stone
Swarm
Water
White
X-body

*6 letters:*
Button
Censor
Collar
Cybrid
Cytoid
Diaxon
Gamete
Goblet
Hadley
Helper
Killer
Morula
Mother
Neuron
Oocyte
Plasma
Sensor
Sickle
Somite
Target
Thread
Zygote

*7 letters:*
Bimorph
Cadmium
Cambium
Cathode
Conical
Daniell
Energid
Euploid
Gemmule
Gravity
Helper T
Initial
Lithite
Myotome
Myotube
Neurite
Neurone
Neutron
Plastid
Primary
Purinje
Schwann
Sertoli

Sleeper
Somatic
Spindle
Spireme
Sporule
Storage
Tapetum
Vesicle
Voltaic

*8 letters:*
Akaryote
Auxocyte
Basidium
Basophil
Blasteme
Blastula
Congenic
Cytology
Daughter
Defensin
Ectomere
Endoderm
Endosarc
Ependyma
Epiblast
Eukaryon
Galvanic
Gonidium
Gonocyte
Hapteron
Hemocyte
Meiocyte
Meristem
Monocyte
Myoblast
Neoblast
Palisade
Parietal
Platelet
Purkinje
Receptor
Retinula
Schizont
Selenium
Seredium
Squamous
Standard

Sweatbox
Symplast
Synergid
Tracheid
Unipolar
Zoosperm
Zoospore

*9 letters:*
Adipocyte
Antipodal
Astrocyte
Athrocyte
Auxospore
Basophile
Coenocyte
Companion
Corpuscle
Desmosome
Ectoplasm
Embryo-sac
Fibrocyte
Haemocyte
Honeycomb
Hybridoma
Idioblast
Internode
Iridocyte
Karyology
Laticifer
Leclanché
Leucocyte
Leukocyte
Macromere
Merozoite
Microcyte
Micromere
Myelocyte
Myofibril
Notochord
Organelle
Periplasm
Periplast
Phagocyte
Phellogen
Proembryo
Satellite
Secondary

Spermatid
Sporocyte
Suspensor
Syncytium
Synkaryon
Thymocyte
Trabecula
Tracheide

*10 letters:*
Ameloblast
Archespore
Blastoderm
Blastomere
Centrosome
Choanocyte
Chromaffin
Chromosome
Cnidoblast
Eosinophil
Epithelium
Fibroblast
Gametocyte
Histiocyte
Leucoblast

Leukoblast
Lymphocyte
Macrophage
Melanocyte
Mesenchyme
Microphage
Multipolar
Myeloblast
Neuroblast
Neutrophil
Normoblast
Osteoblast
Osteoclast
Perikaryon
Phelloderm
Protoplast
Spermatium
Spherocyte
Suppressor
Totipotent
White-blood

*11 letters:*
Aplanospore
Arthrospore

Calyptrogen
Endothelium
Erythrocyte
Granulocyte
Interneuron
Kinetoplast
Lymphoblast
Megaloblast
Melanoblast
Microgamete
Microvillus
Motor neuron
Odontoblast
Poikilocyte
Propoceptor
Schistocyte
Spheroplast
Suppressor T
Trophoblast

*12 letters:*
Aplanogamete
Chondroblast
Cytogenetics
Electrolytic

Erythroblast
Gametrangium
Haematoblast
Interstitial
Paraphysisis
Photovoltaic
Reticulocyte
Spermatocyte
Spermatozoid
Spermatozoon
Spongioblast

*13 letters:*
Chromatophore
Mitochondroin
Photoelectric
Photoreceptor
Sustentacular

*14 letters:*
Spermatogonium
Weston standard

---

**Cellar** Basement, Bodega, Coalhole, Dunny, Hypogeum, Ratskeller, Salt, Shaker, Storm, Vault, Vaultage, Vaut, Wine

**Cell division** Amitosis

**Cellist, Cello** Casals, Du Pré, Hermit, Prisoner, Tortelier

**Celluloid, Cellulose** Acetate, Cel, Viscose, Xylonite

**Celt(ic)** Archdruid, Belgic, Breton, Brython, Cornish, Druid, Gadhel, Gael(dom), Goidel, Helvetii, Kelt, La Tène, Manx, P, Q, Taffy, Welsh

**Cement** Araldite®, Asbestos, Blast-furnace, Compo, Concrete, Fix, Flaunch, Glue, Granolithic, Grout, Gunite, High-alumina, Hydraulic, Lute, Luting, Maltha, Mastic, Mastich, Mortar, Paste, Pointing, Porcelain, Portland, Putty, Rice-glue, Roman, Rubber, Screed, Slurry, → STICK, Trass, Water

**Cemetery** Aceldama, Arenarium, Arlington, Boneyard, Boot Hill, Campo santo, Catacomb, Churchyard, God's Acre, Golgotha, Graveyard, Musall, Necropolis, Père Lachaise, Potter's field, Saqqara, Urnfield

**Cenotaph** Monument

**Censer** Cassolette, Navicula, Thurible

**Censor(ious), Censorship, Censure** Abridge, Accuse, Admonition, AD notice, Airbrush, Animadvert, Appeach, Ban, Banner, Berate, Blame, Blue-pencil, Bowdler, Braid, Cato, Chasten, Comstockery, → CONDEMN, Critical, Criticise, Cut, Damn, Dang, Decry, Dispraise, Edit, Excommunicate, Excoriate, Expurgate, Gag, Obloquy, Opprobrium, Rap, Rebuke, Redact, Repress, Reprimand, Reproach, Reprobate, Reprove, Satirise, Scold, Scrub, Slam, Slate, Stricture, Suppress, Tax, Tear into, Tirade, Traduce, Wig

**Census, Census taker** Count, Head-count, Numerator, Poll

**Cent(s)** Bean, Coin, Ct, Penny, Red, Zack

**Centaur** Ch(e)iron, Horseman, Nessus, Sagittary, Therianthropic

**Centenary, Centennial** Anniversary, Colorado

**Centipede** Chilopoda, Earwig, Pauropod, Polypod, Scolopendra, Scutiger

**Central(ly), Centre** Active, Amid, Assessment, Attendance, Axis, Battlebus, Broca's, Bunt, Call, Cardinal, Chakra, Civic, Community, Contact, Core, Cost, Crisis, Day, Daycare, Dead, Design, Detention, Detoxification, Deuteron, Deuton, Downtown, Drop-in, Epergne, Eye, Field, Focus, Foyer, Frontal, Garden, Health, Heart, Heritage, Hotbed, Hothouse, Hub, Incident, Inmost, Inner, Internal, Interpretive, Juvenile, Juvie, Kernel, Kingpin, Law, Leisure, Lincoln, Live, Main, Mecca, Median, Medulla, Mid(st), Midpoint, Midway, Mission, Music, Nave, Navel, Nerve, Nucleus, Omphalus, Pompidou, Profit, Property, Reception, Rehabilitation, Remand, Respiratory, Service, Shopping, Social Education, Storm, Teachers', Trauma, Visitor, Waist, Weather, Youth custody

**Central American** Mangue, Miskito, Olmec, Otomi, Pueblo, Totomac, Zapotec

**Central heating** Cen, CH

▷ **Centre** *may indicate* middle letters

**Centrepiece** Epergne

**Century** Age, C, Eon, Era, Magdeburg, Period, Siècle, Ton

**Cephalopod** Ammonite, Calamary, Cuttle, Loligo, Nautilus, Octopus, Sepia, Squid

**Ceramic(s)** Agateware, Arcanist, Cermet, China, Earthen, Ferrite, Ferronneries, Porcelain, Pottery, Sialon, Syalon®, Tiles

**Cerberus** Hellhound

**Cereal** Amelcorn, Barley, Blé, Bran, Bread-basket, Buckwheat, Bulgar, Bulg(h)ur, Cassava, Corn, Cornflakes, Couscous, Emmer, Farina, Gnocchi, Grain, Granola, Groats, Hominy, Maize, Mandioc(a), Mandiocca, Manihot, Mani(h)oc, Mealie, Millet, Muesli, Oats, Paddy, Popcorn, Rye(corn), Sago, Samp, Sarassin, Seed, Semolina, Sorghum, Spelt, Tapioca, Tef(f), Triticale, Triticum, Wheat, Zea

**Cerebral** Sensoria

**Cerebrate, Cerebration** Pore, Thought

**Ceremonial, Ceremony** Aarti, Amrit, Asperges, Baptism, Barmitzvah, Chado, Chanoyu, Commemoration, Common Riding, Coronation, Dedication, Doseh, Durbar, Encaenia, Enthronement, Etiquette, Eucharist, Flypast, Form(al), Formality, Function, Gongyo, Habdalah, Havdalah, Havdoloh, Heraldry, Investiture, Koto(w), Matsuri, Maundy, Mummery, Nipter, Observance, Occasion, Official, Ordination, Pageantry, Parade, Pomp, Powwow, Protocol, Rite, Rite of passage, Ritual, Sacrament, Sado, Seder, Service, State, Sun dance, Tea, Topping-out, Trooping (the Colour), Unveiling, Usage

**Cerium** Ce

**Cert(ain), Certainty** Absolute, Actual, Assured, Banker, Bound, Cast-iron, Cinch, Cocksure, Confident, Conviction, Convinced, Decided, Definite, Doubtless, Exact, Fact, Fate, Foolproof, Indubitable, Inevitable, Infallible, Keen, Lock, Monte, Moral, Nap, Needly, One, Positive, Poz, Precise, Racing, Red-hot, Shoo-in, Siccar, Sicker, Snip, Some, Stiff, →SURE, Sure-fire, Truth, Type, Unerring, Yes

**Certainly** Agreed, And how, Ay, Aye-aye, Certes, Fegs, Forsooth, Indeed, Iwis, Jokol, OK, Oke, Pardi(e), Pardy, Perdie, Siccar, Sicker, →SURE, Truly, Verily, Well, Yea, Yes, Yokul, Ywis

**Certificate, Certified, Certify** Accredit, Affirm, Assure, Attest, Bene decessit, Birth, Bond, Chit, Cocket, Confirm, Credential, Death, Debenture, Depose, Diploma, Docket, Document, End-user, Enseal, Gold, Guarantee, Landscrip, Licence, Lines, Medical, MOT, Notarise, Paper, Patent, Proven, Savings, School, Scrip, Scripophily, Security, Share, Smart-ticket, Stamp note, Stock, Sworn, Talon, Testamur, Testimonial, Treasury, U, Unruly, Voucher, Warrant

**Cesare** Borgia

**Cesspit** Bog, Dungmere, Jawhole, Sinkhole, Slurry

**Cetacean** Dolphin, Porpoise, Whale

**Cete(acean)** Badger

**Ceylon(ese)** Serendip, Vedda(h)

**Chad** Dimpled, Swinging

**Chafe(r), Chafing** Chunter, Fray, Fret, Gall, Harass, Intertrigo, Irritate, Pan, Rankle, →RUB, Scuff, Seethe, Worry

**Chaff(y)** Badinage, Banter, Bran, Chip, Cornhusk, Dross, Have on, Hay, Husk, Rag, Raillery, Rally, Ramentum, Refuse, Roast, Rot, Tease, Twit

**Chaffer(ing)** Bandy, Bargain, Haggle, Higgle, Hucksterage, Traffic

**Chaffinch** Wheatbird, Whitewing

**Chagrin** Annoyance, Envy, Mortify, Spite, Vexation

**Chain(s), Chained** Acre's-breadth, Albert, Anklet, Band, Bicycle, Bind, Bond, Bracelet, Branched, Bucket, Cable, Catena, Chatelaine, Check, Choke, Cistron, Closed, Cordillera, Cyclic, Daisy, Decca, Dixie, Drive, Duplex, Dynasty, Engineer's, Esses, Fanfarona, Fetter, Fob, Food, Furlong, Gleipnir, Golden, Grand, Gunter's, Gyve, Heavy, Human, Learner's, Light, Line, Lockaway, Markov, Mayor, Micella(r), Micelle, →**MOUNTAIN**, Noria, Open, Pennine, Pitch, Range, Rockies, Rode, Roller, Safety, Seal, →**SERIES**, Shackle, Side, Sierra, Slang, Snigging, Snow, Span, Sprocket, Straight, String, Strobila, Supply, Surveyor's, Suspensor, Team, Trace, Tug, Voluntary, Watch

**Chain-gang** Coffle

**Chair** Balloon-back, Basket, Bath, Bench, Bentwood, Berbice, Bergère, Birthing, Bosun's, Butterfly, Camp, Cane, Captain's, Carver, Club, Cromwellian, Curule, Deck, Dining, Director's, Easy, Elbow, Electric, Emeritus, Estate, Fauteuil, Fiddle-back, Folding, Frithstool, Garden, Gestatorial, Guérite, High, Jampan, Jampanee, Jampani, Ladder-back, Lounger, Love-seat, Lug, Merlin, Morris, Musical, Nursing, Personal, Pew, Preside, Professorate, Reader, Recliner, Rocker, Ruckseat, Rush-bottomed, →**SEAT**, Sedan, Settee, Steamer, Stool, Straight, Sugan, Swivel, Throne, Wainscot, Wheel, Windsor, Wing

**Chair-back** Ladder, Splat

**Chairman** Convener, Emeritus, Humph, Landammann, Mao, MC, Pr(a)eses, Prof, Prolocutor, Sheraton, Speaker

**Chalaza** Albumen, Treadle, Treddle

**Chalcedony** Enhydros

**Chaldean** Babylonian, Ur

**Chalet** Cabana, Cot, Skio

**Chalice** Calyx, Poisoned

**Chalk(y)** Black, Calcareous, Cauk, Cawk, Crayon, Credit, Cretaceous, Dentin, French, Senonian, Soapstone, Spanish, Steatite, Tailor's, White(n), Whit(en)ing

**Challenge(r), Challenging** Accost, Acock, Assay, Call, Cartel, Champion, Charge, Claim, Confront, Contradict, Contest, Dare, Daur, Defy, Dispute, Face, Gage, Gainsay, Gauntlet, Glove, Hazard, Hen(ner), Iconoclasm, Impugn, Insubordinate, Opponent, Oppose, Oppugn, Provoke, Query, Question, Recuse, Remonstrate, Rival, Sconce, Shuttle, Tackle, Taker, Tall order, Tank, Threat, Tongue-twister, Vie, Wero, Whynot

**Chamber(s)** Airlock, Anteroom, Atrium, Auricle, Bladder, Bubble, Camarilla, Camera, Casemate, Cavern, Cavitation, Cavity, Cell(a), Chanty, Close-stool, Cloud, Cofferdam, Columbarian, Combustion, Commons, Cubicle, Decompression, Dene-hole, Dolmen, Echo, Float, Fogou, Fumatorium, Fume, Gas, Gazunder, Gilded, Hall, Hopper, Horrors, Hyperbaric, Hypogea, Inspection, Ionization, Jerry, Jordan, Kiva, Lavatory, Lethal, Locule, Lok Sabha, Lower, Magma, Manhole, Manifold, Mattamore, Mesoscaphe, Naos, Plenum, Po(t), Presence, Priest('s)-hole, Privy, Reaction, Resonance-box, Room, Roum, Second, Serdab, Silo, Spark, Star, Stateroom, Steam-chest, Swell-box, Synod, Thalamus, Undercroft, Upper, Utricle, Vault, Ventricle, Wilson cloud, Zeta

**Chamberlain** Camerlengo, Camerlingo, Censor

**Chameleon** Adaptor, American, Anole, Ethiopian, Floating voter, Lizard, Tarand

**Chamfer** Bevel, Groove

**Chamois** Ibex, Izard, Shammy

**Champ(er), Champers** Bite, Chafe, Chew, Chomp, Eat, Fume, Gnash, Gnaw, Hero, Ivories, Mash, Morsure, Munch

**Champagne** Boy, Brut, Bubbly, Charlie, Fizz, Gigglewater, Krug, Mumm, Pop, Sillery, Simkin, Simpkin, Stillery, Troyes, Widow

**Champion(s)** Ace, Adopt, Ali, Apologist, Apostle, Artegal, Assert, Back, Belt, Brill(iant), Campeador, Cid, Cock, Crusader, Cupholder, Defend, Don Quixote, Doucepere, Douzeper, Dymoke, Endorse, Enoch, Espouse, Gladiator, Gun, Harry, →**HERO**, Herodotus, Horse, Kemp, Kemper(yman), King, Knight, Maestro, Maintain, Matchless, Messiah, Messias, Neil, Paladin, Palmerin, Partisan, Peerless, Perseus, Promachos, Proponent, Protagonist, Roland, St Anthony, St David, St Denis, St George, St James, St Patrick, Seven, Spiffing, Spokesman, Star, Support, Tiro, Title-holder, Torch-bearer, Tribune, Upholder, Victor, Wardog, →**WINNER**, World-beater, Yokozuna

**Championship** Five Nations, Open, Seven, Six Nations, Super Bowl, Title, Tri-nations

**Chance (upon), Chancy** Accident, Adventitious, Aleatory, Aunter, Bet, Break, Buckley's, Cast, Casual, Cavel, Coincidence, Contingent, Dice, Earthly, Even, Fat, →**FATE**, Fighting, First refusal, Fluke, Fortuitous, Fortuity, Fortune, →**GAMBLE**, Game, Hap, Happenstance, Hit and miss, Hobnob, Iffy, Kevel, Light, Loaves and fishes, Look-in, Lot, →**LOTTERY**, Luck, Main, Meet, Mercy, Occasion, Occur, Odds, Odds-on, Opening, Opportunity, Outside, Peradventure, Posse, Potluck, Prayer, Probability, Prospect, Random, Rise, Risk, Run into, Russian roulette, Serendipity, Shot, Slant, Snip, Spec, Sporting, Stake, Stochastic, Stray, Sweep, Toss-up, Treble, Turn, Tychism, Ventre, Venture, Wager, Wild card

**Chancel** Adytum, Bema, Nave

**Chancellor** Adolf, Bismarck, Brandt, Dollfuss, Kohl, Logothete, Minister, More, Schmidt, Vicar-general, Wolsey

**Chancery** Court, Hanaper

**Chandelier** Candlestick, Corona, Drop, Electrolier, Gasolier, Girandole, Lustre, Pendant

**Chandler** Acater, Acatour, Raymond, Tallow

**Chaney** Lon

**Change(able), Changes, Changing** About-face, Adapt, Adjust, Agio, Aleatoric, →**ALTER**, Amendment, Amoeba, Attorn, Backtrack, Barter, Become, Bob-major, Budge, Capricious, Cash, Catalysis, Cent, Chameleon, Channel-hop, Chop, Chump, Climacteric, Climate, Cline, Codicil, Commute, Convert, Coppers, Covary, Cut, Denature, Departure, Development, Diachrony, Differentiate, Dissolve, Diversion, Ectopia, Edit, Embellish, Emend, Enallage, Esterify, Eustatic, Evolution, Evolve, Exchange, Fickle, Find, Flighty, Float, Fluctuate, Fluid, Flux, Gradate, Grandsire, Guard, Gybe, Histogen, Holiday, Inflect, Innovate, Instead, Kaleidoscope, Kembla, Killcrop, Labile, Loose, Make-over, Menopause, Mercurial, Metabolic, Metabolise, Metamorphose, Metamorphosis, Metathesise, Mew, Mobile, Modify, Modulate, Morph, Mutable, Mutalis mutandis, Mutanda, Mutation, Ontogeny, Parallax, Paraphrase, Peal, Pejoration, Peripet(e)ia, Permute, Port, Primp, Prisere, Prophase, Protean, Quantum leap, Quarter, Rat, Realise, Recant, Reconstruct, Rectify, Redact, Redo, Refine, Reform, Refraction, Regeneration, Regime, Rejig, Reset, Reshuffle, Resipiscence, Rest, Reverse, Revise, Revolutionise, Rework, Sandhi, Scourse, Sd, Sea, Seasonal, Seesaw, Sere, Sex, Shake-out, Shake-up, Shift, Shrapnel, Shuffle, Silver, Small, Sublimation, Substitute, Supervene, Swap, Sweeping, Swing, Switch, Tempolabile, Toggle, Tolsel, Tolsey, Tolzey, Transfer, Transfiguration, Transform, Transition, Translate, Transmogrify, Transmute, Transpose, Transubstantial, Triple, Turn (about), Tweak, Uncertain, Upheaval, U-turn, Vagary, Variant, Variation, Vary, Veer, Versatile, Vicissitude, Volatile, Volte-face, Wankle, Washers, Waver, Weathercock, Wheel, Wow

▷ **Change(d)** *may indicate* an anagram

**Changeling** Auf, Killcrop, Oaf, Turncoat

**Channel** Access, Aflaj, Airwave, Al Jazeera, Aqueduct, Artery, Beagle, Bed, Billabong, Binaural, Bristol, Canal, Canaliculus, Chimb, Chime, Chine, Chute, Conduit, Course, Creek, Culvert, Cut, Cutting, Datagram, Distribution, Ditch, Drain, Duct, Dyke, Ea, Eau, English, Estuary, Euripus, Fairway, Falaj, Feeder, Floodway, Flume, Foss, Funnel, Furrow, Gat, Gate, Geo, Gio, Glyph, Groove, Grough, Gully, Gut, Gutter, Head-race, Ingate, Katabothron, Katavothron, Khor, Kill, Kos, Kyle, Lake, La Manche, Lane, Latch, Leat,

Lee-lane, Leet, Limber, Major, Meatus, Medium, Minch, Moat, Mozambique, Multiplex, Narrows, North, Nulla(h), Offtake, Penstock, Pentland Firth, Pescadores, Pipeline, Qanat, Race, Raceway, Rean, Rebate, Rigol(l), Rigolets, Rivulet, Run, St George's, Sea-gate, Seaway, Sewer, Shatt-el-Arab, Shunt, Side, Sinus, Sky, Sloot, Sluice, Sluit, Sny(e), Solent, Solway Firth, Sound, Source, Sow, Spillway, Sprue, Strait, Suez, Sure, Swash, Tailrace, Tideway, Tracheole, Trough, Ureter, Vallecula, Vein, Wasteweir, Watercourse, Waterspout, Wireway, Yucatan

**Channel swimmer** Webb

**Chant** Anthem, Antiphon, Canticle, Cantillate, Cantus, Chaunt, Daimoku, Decantate, Euouae, Evovae, Gregorian, Haka, Harambee, Hymn, Incantation, Intone, Introit, Mantra(m), Motet, Pennillion-singing, Plainsong, Proper, Psalm, Sing, Slogan, Te Deum, The Reproaches, Yell

**Chantilly** Cream, Lace

**Chaos, Chaotic** Abyss, Anarchy, Confusion, Disorder, Disorganised, Fitna, Fractal, Goat fuck, Havoc, Helter-skelter, Hun-tun, Jumble, Maelstrom, Mayhem, Mess, Mixter-maxter, Muddle, Muss, Pandemonium, Shambles, Shambolic, Snafu, Tohu bohu, Turmoil

▷ **Chaotic** *may indicate* an anagram

**Chap(s)** Beezer, Bloke, Bo, Bod, Bor, Buffer, Cat, Chafe, Cheek, Chilblain, Chop, Cleft, Cod, Codger, Cove, Crack, Customer, Dog, Fella, Feller, Fellow, Flews, Genal, Gent, Gink, Guy, Hack, Johnnie, Joll, Jowl, Kibe, Lad, → **MAN**, Maxilla, Mouth, Mum, Ocker, Person, Rent, Rime, Spray, Spreathe, Spreaze, Spreethe, Spreeze, Wang

**Chapel** Alamo, Bethel, Bethesda, Beulah, Cha(u)ntry, Chevet, Ebenezer, Feretory, Galilee, Lady, Oratory, Parabema, Proprietary, Prothesis, Sacellum, Sistine

**Chaperon(e)** Beard, Cap, Cicerone, Duenna, Escort, Gooseberry, Griffin, Griffon, Gryphon, Muffin

**Chaplain(cy)** CF, Ordinary, Padre, Priest, Scarf, Skypilot, Slope

**Chaplet** Anadem, Coronet, Fillet, Garland, Wreath

▷ **Chaps** *may indicate* an anagram

**Chapter** Accidents, C, Canon, Cap, Capitular, Ch, Chap, Cr, Division, Episode, Lodge, Phase, Section, Social, Sura(h), Verse

**Char(woman)** Adust, Barbecue, Burn, Cleaner, Coal, Daily, Duster, Mop(p), Mrs Mop(p), Rosie Lee, Scorch, Sear, Singe, Smoulder, Toast, Togue, Torgoch

**Charabanc** Bus, Chara, Coach

**Character(s)** Aesc, Agma, Alphabet, Ampersand, Ampussyand, Antihero, Atmosphere, Aura, Backbone, Backslash, Brand, Calibre, Case, Cipher, Clef, Cliff, Climate, Coloration, Complexion, Contour, Credit, Delimiter, Deuteragonist, Devanagari, Digamma, Digit, Domino, Dramatis personae, Emoticon, Ess, Essence, Eta, Ethos, → **FEATURE**, Fibre, Fish, Fist, Form, Grain, Graphics, Grass, Grit, Hair, Heart, Her, Hieroglyphic, Him, Homophone, Hue, Ideogram, Ideograph, Italic, Kanji, Kern, Kind, La(m)bda, Letter, Logogram, Make-up, Mark, Mettle, Mu, Nagari, → **NATURE**, Non-person, Nu, Ogam, Ogham, Pahlavi, Pantaloon, Part, Pehlevi, Person(a), Personage, → **PERSONALITY**, Phonogram, Physiognomy, Pi, Polyphone, Protagonist, Psi, Raisonneur, Reference, Reference-mark, Repute, Rho, Role, Rune, Runic, Sampi, San, Script, Sel(f), Sigma, Sign, Sirvente, Slash, Sonancy, Sort, Space, Sphenogram, Stamp, Subscript, Superhero, Superscript(ion), Swung dash, Syllabary, Symbol, Tab, Temperament, Testimonial, Ton(e), Trait, Uncial, Unit, Vav, Vee, Waw, Wen, Wild card, Wyn(n), Yogh, Zeta

**Characterise(d), Characterism, Characteristic(s)** Acquired, Attribute, Aura, Cast, Colour, Distinctive, Earmark, Ethos, Example, Facies, Feature, Hair, Hallmark, Has, Headmark, Idiomatic, Idiosyncrasy, Jizz, Keystroke, Lineament, Mark, Metamorphism, Mien, Nature, Notate, Note, Peculiar, Persona, Phenotype, Point, Property, Quality, Signature, Stigma, Strangeness, Streak, Style, Trademark, → **TRAIT**, Transfer, Typical, Vein, Way

**Characterless** Anon, Impersonal, Inane, Wet

**Charade** Enigma, Pretence, Riddle

**Charcoal** Activated, Carbon, Coke, Fusain, Sugar

**Charge(s), Charged, Charger** Access, Accusal, Accuse, Aerate, Agist, Allege, Anchorage, Anion, Annulet, Arraign, Ascribe, Assault, Baton, Battery, Bear, Behest, Blame, Book, Brassage, Brush, Buckshot, Bum rap, Burden, Care, Carrying, Cathexis, Cellarage, Command, Commission, Community, Complaint, Congestion, Corkage, Cost, Count, Cover, Criminate, Damage, Debit, Delate, Delf, Delph, Demurrage, Depth, Depute, Directive, Dittay, Dockage, Due, Duty, Dynamise, Electric, Electron, Entrust, Entry, Exit, Expense, Fare, Fee, Fill, Fixed, Flag fall, Fleur-de-lis, Floating, Flock, Freight, Fullage, Fuse, Fusil, Fuze, Gazump, Giron, Gravamen, Gyron, → **HERALDIC**, Horse, Hot, Hypothec, Impeach, Impute, Incriminate, Indict, Inescutcheon, Inform, Instinct, Ion, Isoelectric, Laid, Last, Levy, Lien, Lioncel(le), Lionel, Live, Load, Lozenge, Mandate, Metage, Mine, Mob, Mount, Mulct, Nuclear, Objure, Obtest, Onrush, Onslaught, Onus, Ordinary, Orle, Overhead, Pastoral, Pervade, Pew-rent, Plaint, Positive, Postage, Premium, Prime, Prix fixe, Q, Quayage, Rack-rent, Rampage, Rap, Rate, Recrimination, Red-dog, Rent, Report, Reprise, Reverse, Roundel, Run, → **RUSH**, Saddle, Service, Specific, Stampede, Steed, Storm, Supplement, Tariff, Tax(ation), Tear, Terms, Tilt, Toll, Tonnage, → **TRAY**, Tressure, Trickle, Trust, Tutorage, Upfill, Vaire, Vairy, Verdoy, Vigorish, Ward, Warhead, Warhorse, Wharfage, Yardage

**Chariot(eer)** Auriga, Automedon, Biga, Cart, Charet, Curricle, Ekka, Hur, Phaethon, Quadriga, Rath(a), Vimana, Wagon, Wain

**Charisma(tic)** Oomph, Pentecostal, Personality, Stardust

**Charitable, Charity** Aid, Alms, Alms-deed, Awmous, Benign, Breadline, Caritas, Cause, Chugger, Dole, Dorcas, Eleemosynary, Glove money, Good works, Kiwanis, Largesse, Leniency, Liberal, Lion, Love, Mercy, Oddfellow, Openhanded, Outreach, Oxfam, Pelican, Philanthropic, Rotarian, Samaritan, Zakat

**Charivari** Rough music, Uproar

**Charlatan** Cheat, Crocus, Empiric, Escroc, Faker, Imposter, Katerfelto, Mountebank, Poseur, Quack(salver), Saltimbanco

**Charlemagne** Carlovingian

**Charles, Charley, Charlie(s)** Beard, C, Car, Champagne, Chan, Chaplin, Checkpoint, Chuck, Darwin, Dimwit, Elia, Fox, Half-wit, Lamb, Mug, (Old) Rowley, Pretender, Ray, Reynard, Rug-gown, Sap, Schmoe, Snow, Tail-end, Twit, Watchman

**Charles de Gaulle** Airport

**Charlock** Runch

**Charlotte** Bronte, Russe, Yonge

**Charm(er), Charmed, Charming** Abracadabra, Abrasax, Abraxas, Agacerie, Allure, Amulet, Appeal, Aroma, Attraction, Bangle, Beguile, Bewitch, Bracelet, Captivate, Charisma, Chocolate box, Circe, Comether, Cramp-bone, Cute, Cutie, Debonair, Delectable, Delight(ful), Emerods, Enamour, Enchant, Engaging, Ensorcell, → **ENTRANCE**, Fascinate, Fay, Fetching, Fetish, Grace, Greegree, Gri(s)gris, Hand of glory, Horseshoe, Houri, Incantation, Juju, Magnetic, Mascot, Mojo, Nice, Obeah, Obi(a), Periapt, Personal, Phylactery, Porte-bonheur, Pretty, Prince, Pull, Purty, Quaint, Quark, Ravish, Siren, Smoothie, Spellbind, Suave, Sweetness, Taking, Talisman, Tefillah, Telesm, Temptress, Tephillah, Tiki, Trinket, Unction, Voodoo, Winning, Winsome

▷ **Charming** *may indicate* an anagram

**Chart(ed), Charting** Abac, Alignment, Bar, Breakeven, Card, Control, Diagram, Draw, Eye, Flip, Flow, Gantt, Graph, Histogram, Histograph, Horoscope, Hydrography, Isogram, Isopleth, List, Log, Magna Carta, → **MAP**, Mappemond, Movement, Nomogram, Organisation, Pie, Plane, Plot, Portolano, Rating, Ringelmann, Run, Snellen, Social, Sociogram, Table, Test, Timetable, Waggoner, Weather, Z

**Charta, Charter** Atlantic, Book, Citizen's, Covenant, Freedom, Hire, Lease, Let, Novodamus, Rent, Social (Chapter), Tenants', Time, Voyage

**Chary** Cagey, Careful, Cautious, Frugal, Shy, Wary

**Charybdis** Maelstrom, Whirlpool

**Chase(d), Chaser, Chasing** Cannock, Chace, Chevy, Chivy, Ciseleur, Ciselure, Course, Cranbome, Decorate, Drink, Game, Harass, Hound, →**HUNT**, Inlaid, Inscribe, Jumper, Oxo, Pursuit, Race, Scorse, Sic(k), Snag, Steeple, Sue, Suit, Toreutic, Venery, Wild-goose

**Chasm** Abyss, Crevasse, Fissure, Gap, Gorge, Gulf, Hiatus, Ravine, Rent, Schism, Yawn

**Chaste, Chastity** Aggie, Agnes, Attic, Celibate, Classic, Clean, Continent, Fatima, Florimell, Ines, Innocent, Modesty, Nessa, Nunlike, Platonic, →**PURE**, Vestal, Virginal, Virtue

**Chasten(ed), Chastise(d), Chastisement** Beat, Contrite, Correct, Deflate, Discipline, Disple, Lash, Punish, Rib-roast, Rollicking, Scold, Scourge, Shame-faced, Spank, Strap, Whip

**Chat, Chatter(box), Chatterer** Babble, Bavardage, Bird, Blab(ber), Blatherskite, Blether, Campanero, Causerie, Chelp, Chew the fat, Chinwag, Clack, Clishmaclaver, Confab(ulate), Converse, Cosher, Coze, Crack, Dialogue, Froth, Gab(ble), Gas, Gibble-gabble, Gossip, Gup, Hobnob, Jabber, Jargon, Jaw, Kilfud, Liaise, Madge, Mag(pie), Nashgab, Natter, Patter, Pie, Pourparler, Prate, Prattle, Rabbit, Rabble, Rap, Rattle, Schmooze, Scuttlebutt, Shmoose, Shoot the breeze, Stone, Talk, Talkee-talkee, Talky-talky, Tattle, Tongue-work, Twattle, Waffle, Whin, Windbag, Witter, Wongi, Yacketyyak, Yad(d)a-yad(d)a-yad(d)a, Yak, Yap, Yarn, Yatter, Yellow-breasted, Yoking

**Chateau** Castle, Cru, Fontainebleau, Malmaison, Rambouillet, Schloss

**Chateaubriand** René

**Chattel** Asset, Chose, Deodand, Effects

**Chaucer(ian)** Dan, OE

**Chauffeur** Cabby, Coachy, Driver, Sice, Syce

**Chauvinist** Alf, Bigot, Jingo, MCP, Partisan, Patriot, Racist, Sexist

**Cheap** A bon marché, Bargain, Base, Budget, Catchpenny, Cheesy, Chintzy, Cut-price, Downmarket, Gimcrack, Giveaway, Ignoble, Jitney, Kitsch, Knockdown, Low, Off-peak, Poor, Sacrifice, Shoddy, Steerage, Stingy, Tarty, Tatty, Tawdry, Ticky-tacky, Tinhorn, Tinpot, Tinselly, Trashy, Trivial, Tuppenny, Two-bit, Twopenny, Twopenny-halfpenny, Undear, Vile

▷ **Cheap** *may indicate* a d- or p- start to a word

**Cheapside** Bow

**Cheat(ers), Cheating** Bam, Bamboozle, Bedswerver, Beguile, Bilk, Bite(r), Bob, Bonnet, Bubble, Bucket, Bullock, Bunce, Burn, Cabbage, Cardsharp(er), Charlatan, Chiaus, Chicane(ry), Chisel, Chouse, Clip, Cod, Cog(ger), Colt, Con, Cony-catcher, Cozen, Crib, Cross, Cross-bite(r), Cuckold, Cully, Defraud, Delude, Diddle, Dingo, Dish, Do, Do down, Doublecross, Double-dealer, Duckshove, Dupe, Escroc, Faitor, Fiddle, Finagle, Fix, Flam, Flanker, Fleece, Fob, Foister, Fox, Fraud, Gaff, Gamesmanship, Gip, Glasses, Gudgeon, Gull(-catcher), Gum, Gyp, Hoax, Hocus, Hoodwink, Hornswoggle, Horse, Intake, Jockey, Leg, Magsman, Mulct, Mump, Nick, Nobble, Pasteboard, Picaro(on), Plagiarist, Poop, Queer, Rib, Rig, Rogue, Rook, Rush, Scam, Screw, Screw over, Sell, Shaft, Sharper, Sharpie, Sharp practice, Short-change, Slur, Smouch, Snap, Specs, Stack, Stiff, Sting, Swindle, Take-in, Thimble-rigging, Trepan, Trick(ster), Trim, Twister, Two-time, Welch, Welsh, Wheedle

**Check(ed)** Abort, Anchor, Arrest, Audit, Ba(u)lk, Bauk, Bill, Block, Bridle, Collate, Compesce, Confirm, Control, Count, Counterroll, Cramp, Cross-index, Curb, Dam, Damp, Detain, Detent, Discovered, Ditch, Dogs-tooth, Examine, Foil, Forestall, Frisk, Frustrate, Gingham, Halt, Hamper, Hobble, Houndstooth, Inhibit, Inspect, Jerk, Jerque, Let, Limit(ation), Mate, Measure, Medical, Meter, Monitor, Nip, Observe, Obstacle, Overhaul, Parity, Perpetual, Prevent, Rain, Reality, Rebuff, Rebuke, Rein, Repress, Reprime, Repulse, Reread, Resist, →**RESTRAIN**, Retard, Revoke, Saccade, Screen, Service, Setback, Shepherd's, Shorten, Sit-upon, Sneap, Sneb, Snib, Snub, Sound, Spongebag, Spot, Standard, Std, →**STEM**, Stent, Stint, Stocktake, Stop(-go), Stunt, Style, Subdue, Suppress, Tab, Tally, Tartan, Tattersall, Test, Thwart, Tick, Trash, Verify, Vet

**Checkers** Chinese, Piece

**Check-out** Till

**Cheddar** Cheese, Gorge

**Cheek(y)** Alforja, Audacity, Brash, Brass-neck, Buccal, Chap, Chit, Chollers, Chutzpah, Cool, Crust, Cub, Flippant, Fresh, Gall, Gena(l), Gobby, Gum, Hard-faced, Hussy, Impertinent, Impudent, Insult, Irreverent, Jackanapes, Joll, Jowl, Lip, Malapert, Malar, Masseter, Neck, Nerve, Noma, Pert, Presumption, Quean, Sass, Sauce, Sideburns, Uppity, Upstart, Wang, Whippersnapper, Yankie, Zygoma

**Cheep** Chirp, Chirrup, Peep

**Cheer(s), Cheerful(ness), Cheering** Acclaim, Agrin, Applaud, Arrivederci, Banzai, Barrack, Blithe, Bonnie, Bravo, Bright, Bronx, Bubbly, Buck, Buoy(ant), Cadgy, Canty, Carefree, Cherry, Chin-chin, Chipper, Chirpy, Chirrupy, →COMFORT, Consolate, Console, Convivial, Crouse, Debonair, Drink, Ease, Elate, Elevate, Encourage, Enliven, Exhilarate, Exuberant, Festive, Genial, Gladden, Goodbye, Happy-go-lucky, Hearten, Hilarity, Holiday, Hooch, Hoorah, Hurra(h), Huzzah, Insouciance, Joco, Jocund, Jovial, Kia-ora, L'allegro, Light-hearted, Lightsome, Lively, Meal, Olé, Optimistic, Ovate, Peart, Perky, Please, Praise, Prosit, Rah, Riant, Rivo, Roar, Root, Rosy, Rumbustious, Shout, Sko(a)l, Slainte, Smiley, Sonsie, Sunny, Ta, Tata, Thanks, Three, Tiger, Tiggerish, Toodle-oo, Up, Upbeat, Uplift, Warm, Winsome, Yell

**Cheerless** Bleak, Dismal, Drab, Drear, Gloomy, Glum, Wint(e)ry

**Cheese, Cheesy** American, Amsterdam, Appenzell, Asiago, Au gratin, Bel Paese, Blue, Blue vein, Boc(c)oncini, Boursin, Brie, Caboc, Caerphilly, Cambazola, Camembert, Cantal, Casein, Caseous, Cheddar, Cheshire, Chessel, Chèvre, Colby, Comte, Cottage, Coulommiers, Cream, Crowdie, Curd, Damson, Danish blue, Derby, Dolcelatte, Double Gloucester, Dunlop, Dutch, Edam, Emmental(er), Emmenthal(er), Ermite, Esrom, Ewe, Fet(a), Fontina, Fromage frais, Fynbo, Gloucester, Goat, Gorgonzola, Gouda, Grana Padano, Grand Panjandrum, Green, Gruyère, Halloumi, Hard, Havarti, Huntsman, Ilchester, Islay, Jarlsberg®, Junket, Kebbock, Kebbuck, Kenno, Killarney, Lancashire, Leicester, Lemon, Limburg(er), Lymeswold®, Macaroni, Manchego, Mascarpone, Monterey Jack, Mousetrap, Mozzarella, Mu(e)nster, Mycella, Neufchatel, Numero uno, Oka, Orkney, Paneer, Parmesan, Pecorino, Pont l'Eveque, Port Salut, Pot, Provolone, Quark, Raclette, Rarebit, Reblochon, Red Leicester, Rennet, Ricotta, Romano, Roquefort, Sage Derby, Samso, Sapsago, Skyr, Stilton®, Stone, Stracchino, Swiss, Taleggio, Tilsit, Tofu, Truckle, Vacherin, VIP, Wensleydale, Whey, Yarg

**Cheesecake** Pin-up, Talmouse

**Cheese-scoop** Pale

**Cheetah** Coalition

**Chef** Commis, Escoffier, Oliver, Ramsay

**Chekhov** Anton

**Chelsea** Bun, Pensioner, Tractor

**Chemical** Acanthin, Acid, Acrolein, Adrenalin®, Agent Orange, Alar, Aldehyde, Alkali, Allomone, Alum(ina), Amide, Amino-group, Anabolic, Avertin, Barilla, Bradykinin, Bromic, Bute, Camphene, Camphor, Carbide, Carnallite, Caseose, Catalyst, Cephalin, Cerebroside, Coal tar, Co-factor, Depside, Developer, Dopamine, Encephalin, Enkephalin(e), Enol, Ethanal, Ethoxy, Ethyl, Fixer, Fluoride, Formyl, Freon, Fungicide, Furosemide, Gamone, Gibbsite, Glutamine, Glycol, Halide, Halon, Harmin, Heavy, Hecogenin, Heptane, Hexylene, Hexylresorcinol, Histamine, Hormone, Hypo, ICI, Imine, Imipramine, Indican, Inositol, Interleukin, Larvicide, Lewisite, Limonene, Lipid, Masking-agent, Massicot, Morphactin, Naioxone, Napalm, Naphtha, Natron, Neurotransmitter, Nitre, Nitroluene, Nonylphenol, Oestrogen, Olefin, Olein, Oxide, Oxysalt, Paraben, Pentane, Pentene, Pentyl, Peptide, Periclase, Phenol, Phenyl, Pheromone, Potash, Potassa, Psoralen, Ptomaine, Reagent, Resorcin, Resorcinol, Restrainer, Sequestrant, Serotonin, Soman, Soup, Stearate, Steroid, Strontia, Styrene, Sulphide, Terpene, Thio-salt, Toluol, Toner, Trimer, Tritide, Urethane, Weedicide, Weedkiller, Xylol

**Chemise** Cymar, Sark, Serk, Shift, Shirt, Simar(re), Smock, Symar

**Chemist** Analyst, Apothecary, Dispenser, Druggist, Drugstore, FPS, Pharmacist, Pothecary

## CHEMISTS

| 3 letters: | Kroto | Fischer | Backeland |
|---|---|---|---|
| FCS | Nobel | Helmont | Berzelius |
| LSA | Prout | Hodgkin | Butenandt |
| MPS | Soddy | Macadam | Cavendish |
| RIC | | Pasteur | Lavoisier |
| | 6 letters: | Pauling | Leclanche |
| 4 letters: | Baeyer | Smalley | Pelletier |
| Bohn | Bunsen | Ziegler | Priestley |
| Curl | Hevesy | | Strassman |
| Davy | Liebig | 8 letters: | |
| Gahn | Muller | Lipscomb | 10 letters: |
| Hahn | Nernst | Mulliken | Mendeleyev |
| Todd | Proust | Newlands | Paracelsus |
| Urey | Sanger | Sabatier | |
| | Schiff | Smithson | 11 letters: |
| 5 letters: | Wohler | Weizmann | Hinshelwood |
| Curie | | Welsbach | Le Chatelier |
| Debye | 7 letters: | | |
| Dewar | Buchner | 9 letters: | |
| Haber | Faraday | Arrhenius | |

**Chemistry** Alchemy, Alchymy, Chemurgy, Iatrochemistry, Inorganic, Nuclear, Organic, Physical, Radiation, Spageric, Spagiric, Spagyric, Stinks, Stoecheometry, Stoechiometry, Stoich(e)iometry, Technical, Zymurgy

**Cheops** Khufu

**Cheque** Blank, Bouncer, Giro, Gregory, Open, Rubber, Stumer, Tab, Traveller's

**Chequer** Dice

**Cherish(ed)** Dear, Dote, Enshrine, Entertain, Esteem, Foment, Foster, Harbour, Inshrine, Nestle, Nurse, Nurture, Pamper, Pet, Precious, Refocillate, Treasure

**Cheroot** Cigar, Manil(l)a

**Cherry (tree)** Amarelle, Amazon, Ball, Barbados, Bigaroon, Bigarreau, Bird, Blackheart, Bladder, Cerise, Choke, Cornelian, Gean, Ground, Heart, Jerusalem, Kearton, Kermes, Kermesite, Malpighia, Marasca, Maraschino, May-duke, Maz(z)ard, Merry, Morel(lo), Prunus, Red, Sweet, Whiteheart

**Cherry-pie** Heliotrope

**Cherub** Angel, Putto, Seraph

**Chervil** Cow-parsley

**Chess (move), Chess player, Chess term** Andersson, Black, Blindfold, Cleat, Endgame, Euwe, Fianchetto, FIDE, Fischer, Fool's mate, Grandmaster, Hexagonal, J'adoube, Karpov, Kasparov, Lightning, Mate, Miranda, Patzer, Pin, Plank, Rapid transit, Shogi, Speed, White, Zugzwang, Zwischenzug

**Chessman** Bishop, Black, Castle, Cheque, Horse, King, Knight, Pawn, Pin, Queen, Rook, White

**Chest(y)** Ark, Bahut, Bosom, Box, Breast, Buist, Bunker, Bureau, Bust, Caisson, Cap-case, Case, Cassone, Chapel, Charter, Chiffonier, Coffer, Coffin, Coffret, Commode, Community, Cub, Dresser, Girnel, Hope, Hutch, Inro, Kist, Larnax, Locker, Lowboy, Meal-ark, Medicine, Ottoman, Pectoral, Pereion, Pigeon, Pleural, Ribcage, Safe, Scrine, Scryne, Sea, Shrine, Slop, Steam, Sternum, Tallboy, Tea, Thorax, Toolbox, Treasure, Trunk, Wangan, Wangun, Wanigan, War, Wind

**Chester** Deva
**Chestnut** Aesculus, Auburn, Badious, Ch, Chincapin, Chinese, Chinkapin, Chinquapin,
Cliché, Conker, Dwarf, Favel(l), Hoary, Horse, Marron, Marron glacé, Moreton Bay, Roan,
Russet, Saligot, Soare, Sorrel, Spanish, Sweet, Water
**Chest protector** →ARMOUR, Bib
**Chevalier** Bayard, Knight, Pretender
**Chevron** Dancette, Stripe, V-shape
**Chew(ing)** Bite, Champ, Chaw, Chomp, Crunch, Cud, Eat, Fletcherism, Gnaw, Gum,
Manducate, Masticate, Maul, Meditate, Moop, Mou(p), Munch, Ruminate, Siri(h),
Spearmint
**Chewink** Ground-robin
**Chiastolite** Macle
**Chic** Dapper, Debonair, Elegant, Heroin, In, Kick, Modish, Posh, Radical, Smart, Soigné,
Stylish, Swish, Tonish, Trim
**Chicago** Windy City
**Chicane(ry)** Artifice, Deception, Fraud, Wile
**Chichester** Yachtsman
**Chichi** Precious
**Chick(en)** Australorp, Battery, Biddy, Boiler, Broiler, Capon, Cheeper, Chittagong,
Chuckie, Clutch, Cochin(-China), Coronation, Coward, Cowherd, Craven, Drumstick,
Eirack, Gutless, Hen, Howtowdie, Kiev, Layer, Marengo, Minorca, Mother Carey's,
Niderling, Pavid, Poltroon, Poot, Pope's nose, Poult, Pout, Prairie, Precocial, Pullus,
Quitter, Roaster, Scaredy-cat, Spatchcock, Spring, Squab, Supreme, Sussex, Timorous,
Unheroic, Unmanly, Wimp, Windy, Wishbone, Wyandotte, Yellow
**Chickenfeed** Maize, Peanuts
**Chickenpox** Varicella
**Chickpea** Chana, Felafel, Garbanzo
**Chickweed** Snow-in-summer
**Chicory** Endive, Radiccio, Succory, Witloof
**Chide** Admonish, Berate, Dress, Objurgate, Rate, Rebuke, Reprove, Row, Scold, Tick off,
Twit, Upbraid
**Chief(tain)** Ag(h)a, Arch, Ardrigh, Ariki, Boss, Caboceer, Cacique, Calif, Caliph, Capital,
Capitan, Capitayn, Capo, Caractacus, Caradoc, Cazique, Ch, Chagan, Coriolanus,
Dat(t)o, DG, Dominant, Duke, Eleutherarch, Emir, Figurehead, Finn (MacCool), First,
Foremost, Geronimo, Grand, Haggis, →HEAD, Hereward, Jarl, Kaid, Keystone, King,
Leader, MacDuff, →MAIN, Mass, Mocuddum, Mokaddam, Mugwump, Muqaddam,
Nawab, Nizam, Nkosi, Oba, Overlord, Paramount, Pendragon, Predominant, Premier,
Primal, Prime, Principal, Provost-marshal, Quanah, Raja(h), Rajpramukh, Rangatira,
Rangatiratanga, Ratoo, Ratu, Sachem, Sagamore, Sardar, Sarpanch, Sea-king, Sheikh,
Sirdar, Staple, Sudder, Supreme, Tanist, Tank, Taxiarch, Thane, Top
**Chiffonier** Cabinet, Commode
**Chilblain** Kibe
**Child(ren), Childhood, Childish** Aerie, Alannah, Ankle biter, Auf, Babe, Baby,
Bach(ch)a, Badger, Bairn, Bambino, Bantling, Boy, Brat, Brood, Butter-print, Ch,
Changeling, Cherub, Chick, Chickabiddy, Chit, Collop, Cub, Dream, Duddie weans,
Elfin, Eyas, Feral, Foster, Foundling, Gait, Gangrel, Ge(i)t, Girl, Guttersnipe, Gyte, Heir,
Hellion, Hurcheon, Imp, Infancy, Infant, Inner, Issue, It, Jailbait, Jejune, Juvenile, Kid,
Kiddie(wink), Kiddy, Kidult, Kinder, Lad, Lambkin, Latchkey, Limb, Litter, Littlie, Littling,
Love, Mamzer, Mardy, Minion, Minor, Mite, Moppet, Munchkin, Naive, Nipper, Nursling,
Offspring, Pantywaist, Papoose, Petty, Piccaninny, Pickin, Problem, Progeny, Puerile,
Puss, Putto, Ragamuffin, Rip, Romper, Rug rat, Scion, Second, Seed, Siblings, Small fry,
Smout, Smowt, Sprog, Street arab, Subteen, Tacker, Ted, Teeny-bopper, Tike, Toddle(r),
Tot(tie), Totty, Trot, Tweenager, Tweenie, Tyke, Urchin, Waif, Wean, Weanel, Weanling,
Weeny-bopper, Whelp, Young, Youngster, Younker, Youth

**Childbearing, Childbirth** Couvade, Dystocia, Intrapartum, Lamaze, Obstetrics, Parity, Puerperal, Tocology, Tokology

**Child-eater, Child-killer** Herod, Thyestes

**Childless** Atocous, Atokous, Barren, Nullipara, Sp

**Chile(an)** CH, Mapuche

**Chill(er), Chilly** Bleak, Cauldrife, →COLD, Cool, Cryogen, Flu, Frappé, Freeze, Freon®, Frigid, Frosty, Gelid, Ice, Iciness, Laze, Mimi, Oorie, Ourie, Owrie, Parky, Raw, Refrigerate, Relax, Rigor, Scare

**Chilli** Bird's eye, Cayenne, →PEPPER, Pimentón

**Chime(s)** Agree, Bell, Clam, Cymar, Jingle, Peal, Rhime, Ring, Semantron, Tink, →TOLL, Wind

**Chimera** Geep, Graft, Illusion

**Chimney (pot), Chimney corner** Can, Cow(l), Femerall, Flare stack, Flue, Funnel, Lamp, Lug, Lum, Smokestack, Stack, Stalk, Steeplejack, Tallboy, Tunnel

**Chimney-sweep** Chummy, Snowball

**Chimp(anzee)** Ape, Bonobo, Jocko, Pygmy

**Chin, Chinwag** Chitchat, Double, Genial, Hill-man, Jaw, Jowl, Mentum

**China(man), Chinese** Ami, Amoy, Bone, Boxer, Bud(dy), Cameoware, Cantonese, Catayan, Cathay, Celestial, Ch, Chelsea, Chink(y), Chow, Coalport, Cochin, Cock, Colleague, Communist, Confucius, Crackle, Crockery, Cully, Delft, Derby, Dresden, Eggshell, Etrurian, Flowery land, Friend, Fukien, Google, Googly, Goss, Hakka, Han, Hard paste, Hizen, Hmong, Imari, Ironstone, Kanji, Kaolin, Kuo-yu, Limoges, Macanese, Manchu, Manchurian, Mandarin, Mangi, Maoist, Mate, Meissen, Middle kingdom, Min, Ming, Minton, National, Oppo, Pal, Pareoean, Pekingese, Pe-tsai, Pinyin, Porcelain, →POTTERY, Putonghua, Queensware, Quina, Red, Rockingham, Royal Worcester, Rusticware, Semiporcelain, Seric, Sèvres, Shanghai, Sinaean, Sinic, Sino-, Soft paste, Spode®, Sun Yat-sen, Tai-ping, Taiwanese, Taoist, Teng, Tocharian, Tungus, Uigur, Wal(l)y, Ware, Wedgwood®, Whiteware, Willow pattern, Willowware, Worcester, Wu, Yao, Yellow peril

**Chindit** Wingate

**Chine** Chink, Chynd, Ridge

**Chink(y)** Chinaman, Chop, Cleft, Clink, Cloff, Crack, Cranny, Crevice, Gap, Rent, Rift, Rima, Rimose, Sinic, Window

**Chintz** Kalamkari

**Chip(s)** Blitter, Blue, Bo(a)st, Carpenter, Counter, Cut, Deep-fried, EPROM, EROM, Fish, Flake, Fragment, French fry, Game, Hack, Knap, Log, Micro, →MICROCHIP, Nacho(s), Neural, Nick, Pin, Potato, Shaving, Silicon, Spale, Spall, Span, Splinter, Tease, Teraflop, Tortilla, Transputer, Virus

▷ **Chip** *may indicate* an anagram

**Chipmunk** Gopher, Hackee, Suslik, Zizel

**Chippendale** Chinese

**Chipper** Jaunty, Spry, Wedge

**Chiron** Centaur

**Chiropody** Pedicure, Podiatry

**Chiropractic** McTimoney

**Chirp(y), Chirrup** Cheep, Cherup, Chirm, Chirr, Cicada, Peep, Pip, Pipe, Pitter, Stridulate, Trill, Tweet, Twitter

**Chisel(ler), Chisel-like** Bam, Boaster, Bolster, Bur, Burin, Carve, Cheat, Clip, Drove, Firmer, Gad, →GOUGE, Half-round, Mason, Paring, Scalpriform, Scauper, Scorper, Sculpt, Slick, Socket, Sting

**Chit** Docket, Girl, Memo, Note, Voucher

**Chivalry, Chivalrous** Brave, Bushido, Courtly, Datin, Gallant, Gent, Grandisonian, Quixotic

**Chivvy** Badger, Harass, Pursue

**Chloride, Chlorine** Calomel, Muriate

**Chlorophyll** Granum, Leaf-green

**Chock** Trig

**Chocolate** Aero, Brown, Cacao, Carob, Cocoa, Dragee, Ganache, Milk, Neapolitan, Noisette, Pinole, Plain, Praline, Rolo®, Theobroma, Truffle, Vegelate, Vermicelli

**Choice, Choose, Choosy, Chosen** Adopt, Anthology, Appoint, Aryan, Ballot, Capped, Cherry-pick, Cull, Dainty, Decide, Druthers, Eclectic, Elect, Elite, Esnecy, Fine, Fork, Free will, Hercules, Hobson's, Leet, Leve, Lief, List, Multiple, Opt, Option, Or, Ossian, Peach, Peacherino, Peculiar, → PICK, Picking, Plum(p), Precious, Predilect, Prefer, Proairesis, Rare, Recherché, → SELECT, Single out, Superb, Try(e), Via media, Volition, Wale

**Choiceless** Beggar

**Choir, Choral, Chorister, Chorus** Antiphony, Antistrophe, Anvil, Apse, Bass, Burden, Chant, Choragus, Choregus, Chorister, Choryphaeus, Dawn, Decani, Faburden, Fauxbourdon, Glee, Glee club, Group, Hallelujah, Harmony, Hymeneal, Motet, Ninth, Parabasis, Precentor, Quirister, → REFRAIN, Reprise, Ritual, Schola cantorum, Serenata, Singing, Stop, Strophe, Treble, Triad, → UNISON

**Choir-master** Choragus, Choregus, Precentor

**Choke(r)** Accloy, Block, Clog, Die, Gag, Garotte, Glut, Silence, Smoor, Smore, Smother, Stap, Stifle, Stop, Strangle(hold), Strangulate, → THROTTLE, Warp

**Choky** Can, Prison

**Choler** Irascibility, Yellow bile

**Cholera** Asiatic, British, Hog

**Cholesterol** Spinacene, Squalene

**Choliamb** Scazon

▶ **Choose** see CHOICE

**Chop, Chops, Chopper(s), Choppy** Adze, Air tax, Ax(e), Cakehole, Celt, Charge, Cheek, Chump, Cleave, Côtelette, Cuff, Curtail, Cutlet, Dice, Dismissal, False teeth, Fell(er), Flew, Hack, Hash, Helicopter, Hew, Ivory, Karate, Lop, Mince, Mouth, Rotaplane, Rough, Split, Standing, Suey, Teeth, To-rend, Underhand, Wang

**Chopin** Pantoufle, Shoe

**Chopstick(s)** Waribashi

**Chord(s)** Altered, Arpeggio, Barré, Broken, Common, Diameter, Eleventh, Harmony, Intonator, Latus rectum, Neapolitan sixth, Nerve, Ninth, Picardy third, Riff, Seventh, Sixth, Submediant, Thirteenth, Triad, Vocal

**Chore** Darg, Duty, Fag, Task

**Chorea** Sydenham's

**Choreographer** Arranger, Ashton, Balanchine, Bourne, Cecchetti, Cranko, Cunningham, Dolin, Fokine, Laban, Lifar, Massine, Murphy, Tetley, Tharp

▶ **Chorus** see CHOIR

**Chosen** Elite, Korea

**Chough** Chewet

**Chow** Nosh

**Chowder** Bouillabaisse, Clam, Skink, Soup

**Christ** Ecce homo, Lamb of God, Logos, Messiah, Pantocrator, Paschal Lamb, Prince of Peace, Saviour, Son (of God), Son of man, The Good Shepherd, The Redeemer, X, Xt

**Christen(ing)** Baptise, Launch, Name-day

**Christian(ity)** Abcee, Abecedarian, Absey, Adventist, Albigenses, Anabaptist, Antioch, Baptist, Beghard, Believer, Cathar(ist), Charismatic, Colossian, Coptic, Donatist, D(o)ukhobor, Ebionite, Eucharistic, Fletcher, Galilean, Giaour, Gilbertine, Gnostic, Godsquad, Goy, Heteroousian, Holy roller, Homo(i)ousian, Hutterite, Jehovah's Witness, Lutheran, Maronite, Marrano, Melchite, Melkite, Methodist, Molinism, Monarchian, Monophysite, Moral, Mozarab, Muscular, Mutineer, Nazarene, Nestorian, Phalange, Pilgrim, Presbyterian, Protestant, Quaker, Quartodeciman, RC, Sabotier, Scientist, SCM, Shambe, Solifidian, Traditor, Uniat(e), Unitarian, Valdenses, Waldensian, Wesleyan, Xian, Zwinglian

**Christian Scientist** Eddy

**Christmas(time)** Advent, Beetle, Box, Cactus, Card, Carol, Chrissie, C(h)rimbo, Day, Dec, Island, Nativity, Noel, Nowel(l), Pudding, Stocking, Xmas, Yuletide
**Christopher** Kit, Robin, Sly, Wren
**Chromatin** Karyotin
**Chromium** Cr
**Chromosome** Aneuploid, Autosome, Barr body, Centromere, Cistron, Euchromatin, Genome, Haploid, Homologous, Id(ant), Karyotype, Lampbrush, Operon, Philadelphia, Ploid(y), Polytene, Prophage, Satellite, Sex, Telomere, Trisomy, X, Y
**Chronic** Long
**Chronicle(r)** Anglo-Saxon, Annal, Brut, Calendar, Diary, Froissart, Hall, Historiographer, History, Holinshed, Logographer, Moblog, Narrative, Paralipomena, Parian, Paris, →**RECORD**, Register, Stow
**Chrysalis** Nymph, Pupa
**Chrysanthemum** Corn-marigold, Feverfew, Korean
**Chrysolite** Olivine, Peridot
**Chub** Chavender, Cheven, Chevin, Fish
**Chubby** Butterball, Plump
**Chuck (out)** Berry, Bin, Bung, Buzz, Chook(ie), Discard, Eject, Fling, Food, Four-jaw, Grub, Independent-jaw, Lob, Pat, Pitch, Scroll, Shy, Sling, Three-jaw, Toss, Turf
**Chuckle** Chortle, Giggle, Gurgle, Laugh, Titter
**Chukka** Polo
**Chum(my)** Ally, Associate, Boet, Buddy, Cobber, Cock, Companion, Comrade, Crony, Mate, Pal, Playmate, Sociable, Sodality
**Chump** Cretin, Fool, Mug(gins), Noddle, Sap, →**STUPID PERSON**
**Chunk(y)** Boxy, Chubby, Gob, Piece, Slab, Squat, Wad, Wedge
**Church** Abbey, Armenian, Auld Licht, Autocephalous, Basilica, Bethel, Bethesda, Broad, Brood, Byzantine, →**CATHEDRAL**, CE, Ch, Chapel, Chevet, Classis, Clergy, Collegiate, Congregational, Coptic, Decanal, Delubrum, Easter (Orthodox), Eastern, EC, Ecumenical, Episcopal, Episcopalian, Established, Faith, Fold, Free, Greek, High, House, Institutional, Kirk, Lateran, Latin, Low, Lutheran, Maronite, Melchite, Methodist, Minster, Moonie, Moravian, Mormon, Mother, National, Nazarene, Nestorian, New, New Jerusalem, Notre Dame, Old Light, Oratory, Orthodox, Parish, Peculiar, Pentecostal, Preaching-house, Prebendal, Presbyterian, Ratana, RC, Reformed, Relief, Rome, Russian Orthodox, Schism house, Schism shop, Secession, Shrine, Smyrna, Station, Stave, Steeple, Steeplehouse, Tabernacle, Temple, Title, Titular, Transept, Triumphant, Unification, Unitarian, United Free, United Reformed, Visible, Wee Free, Western, Wool
**Churchgoer, Churchman, Churchwarden** Anglican, Antiburgher, Azymite, Baptist, Barnabite, Believer, Cameronian, Cantor, Classis, Clay, Cleric, Clerk, Congregation, Deacon, Dom, Dopper, Elder, Evangelist, Hatto, High, Ignorantine, Incumbent, Invisible, Knox, Lector, Lutheran, Marrowman, Methodist, Militant, Moderator, Moonie, Mormon, MU, Newman, Oncer, Parson, PE, Pew-opener, Pipe, Pontiff, Prebendary, Precentor, Predicant, Predikant, Prelate, Presbyterian, Priest, Protestant, Puritan, Racovian, Rector, Romanist, Ruridecanal, Sacrist(an), Sidesman, Sim, Simeonite, Socinian, Spike, Subchanter, Subdeacon, Succentor, Swedenborgian, Tantivy, Triumphant, Ubiquitarian, Unitarian, Verger, Vestryman, Visible, Wesleyan, Worshipper, Wren
**Church house** Deanery, Manse, Parsonage, Presbytery, Rectory, Vicarage
**Churchill** Tank, Winston
**Churchyard** God's acre, Stoke Poges
**Churl(ish)** Attercop, Boor, Crabby, Curmudgeonly, Cynical, Ethercap, Ettercap, Gruff, Ill-natured, Nabal, Peasant, Rustic, Serf, Surly
**Churn** Bubble, Kirn, Seethe, Sicken
**Chute** Flume, Runway
**Ciao** Adieu, Adios, Aloha
**CIC** Shogun, Sirdar

**Cicada** Greengrocer, Locust, Periodical, Tettix
**Cicatrix** Scar
**Cicely** Myrrh, Seseli, Sweet
**Cicero** Cic, Orator, Tully
**Cicerone** Guide
**CID** Sûreté
**Cid** Campeador, Chief, Hero
**Cider** Drink, Hard, Perry, Scrumpy, Sweet
**Ci-devant** Ex
**Cigar(ette), Cigarette cards** Beedi(e), Bidi, Biftah, Bifter, Bumper, Burn, Camberwell
  carrot, Cancer stick, Caporal, Cartophily, Cheroot, Cigarillo, Claro, Coffin nail, Conch,
  Concha, Corona, Dog-end, Doob, Durry, Fag, Filter-tip, Gasper, Giggle(-stick), Havana,
  Joint, Locofoco, Long-nine, Loosies, Low-tar, Maduro, Manilla, Number, Panatella,
  Paper-cigar, Perfecto, Puritano, Reefer, Regalia, Roach, Roll-up, Segar, Smeek, Smoke,
  Snout, Splif(f), Stogie, Stog(e)y, Stompie, Tab, Twist, Weed, Whiff, Woodbine, Zol
**C-in-C** Supremo
**Cinch** Belt, Certainty, Doddle, Duck soup, Easy, Girth, Stroll
**Cinchona** Kina, Quina
**Cinder(s)** Ash, Breeze, Clinker, Dander, Embers, Slag
**Cinderella** Drudge, Stepdaughter
**Cinema(s)** Art house, Big screen, Biograph, Bioscope, Circuit, Drive-in, Films, Fleapit,
  Flicks, Grindhouse, IMAX®, Megaplex, Movies, Multiplex, Multiscreen, Mutoscope,
  New Wave, Nickelodeon, Nouvelle Vague, Odeon, Picture palace, Pictures, Plaza, Scope,
  Silver-screen, Theatre, Tivoli
**Cinnabar** Vermilion
**Cinnamon, Cinnamon stone** Canella, Cassia (bark), Essonite, Hessonite, Saigon, Spice
**Cipher** Chi-rho, Code, Cryptogram, Enigma, Nihil, Nobody, →**NOTHING**, Number, O,
  Steganogram, Zero
**Circadian** Diurnal
**Circle** Almacantar, Almucantar, Annulet, Antarctic, Arctic, Circassian, Co, Colure,
  Company, Compass, Cordon, Corn, Corolla, Coterie, Cromlech, Crop, Cycloid, Cyclolith,
  Dip, Disc, Dress, Druidical, Eccentric, Ecliptic, Embail, Enclose, Engird, Epicyclic,
  Equant, Equator, Equinoctial, Euler's, Fairy ring, Family, Fraternity, Full, Galactic, Girdle,
  Gloriole, Great, Gyrate, Gyre, Halo, Henge, Hoop, Horizon, Hour, Hut, Inner, Inorb, Lap,
  Longitude, Loop, Magic, Malebolge, Mandala, Meridian, Mohr's, Mural, Nimbus, O, Orb,
  Orbit, Parhelic, Parquet, Parterre, Penannular, Peristalith, Pitch, Polar, Quality, Red-line,
  Rigol, →**RING**, Rondure, Rotate, Roundel, Roundlet, Seahenge, Sentencing, Set, Setting,
  Small, Sphere, Stemme, Stone, Stonehenge, Striking, Surround, Tinchel, Tondino,
  Traffic, Transit, Tropic, Turning, Umbel, Upper, Vertical, Vicious, Vienna, Virtuous, Volt,
  Wheel, Whorl
**Circuit(-board), Circuitous** Ambit, AND, Autodyne, Bridge, Bus, Bypass, Chipset,
  Closed, Comparator, Daughterboard, Diocese, Discriminator, Dolby®, Electrics,
  Equivalent, Eyre, Feedback, Gate, Gyrator, Half-adder, Highway, IC, Indirect, Integrated,
  Interface, Lap, Le Mans, Limiter, Live, Logic, Loop, Microchip, Microprocessor, Monza,
  Motherboard, NAND, NOR, NOT, Open, OR, Orbital, Perimeter, Phantom, Phase,
  Preamp, Printed, Push-pull, Quadripole, Racetrack, Reactance, Ring main, Round,
  Roundure, Rubber-chicken, Scaler, Series, Short, Silverstone, Smoothing, Sound card,
  Squelch, Stage, Three-phase, Tour, Trunk, Windlass, XNOR, XOR
**Circuit-breaker** Air gap, Fuse
**Circular** Annular, Brochure, Court, Disc(al), Endless, Flysheet, Folder, Leaflet, Mailshot,
  Orby, Round, Spiral, Unending, Vertical, Wheely
**Circulate, Circulation, Circulatory** Ambient, Astir, Bandy, Bloodstream, Cyclosis,
  Disseminate, Eddy, Flow, Gross, Gyre, Issue, Mingle, Mix, Orbit, Out and about, Pass,
  Publish, Report, Revolve, Rotate, Scope, Send round, Spread, Stir, Treadmill, Troll, Utter

▷ **Circulating** *may indicate* an anagram

**Circumcise(r), Circumcision** Bris, Brith, Brit milah, Infibulate, Milah, Mohel, Pharaonic, Sandek

**Circumference** Boundary, Girth, Perimeter, Size

**Circumflex** Perispomenon

**Circumlocution** Bafflegab, Periphrasis, Tautology

**Circumnavigation** Periplus

**Circumscribe(d)** Define, Demarcate, Enclose, Eruv, Restrain, Restrict

**Circumspect** Cagey, Canny, Chary, Discreet, Guarded, Prudential, Wary, Watchful

**Circumstance(s), Circumstantial** Case, Concept, Detail, Event, Fact, Formal, →INCIDENT, Mitigating, Precise, Shebang, Situation, Stede

**Circumvent** Bypass, Dish, Evade, Negotiate, Outflank, Outwit, Usurp

**Circus, Circus boy** Arena, Big top, Eros, Flea, Flying, Harrier, Hippodrome, Marquee, Maximus, Media, Monty Python, Oxford, Piccadilly, Ring, Sanger, Slang, Three-ring

**Cissy** Nelly

**Cistercian** Trappist

**Cistern** Feed-head, Flush-box, Sump, Tank, Tub, Vat

**Citadel** Acropolis, Alhambra, Castle, Fort(ress), Kasbah, Keep, Kremlin, Sea-girt

**Citation, Cite** Adduce, Allegation, Instance, Mensh, Mention, Name, Quote, Recall, Reference, Repeat, Sist, Summon

**Citizen(s), Citizenship** Burgess, Burgher, Civism, Cleruch, Denizen, Dicast, Ephebe, Franchise, Freeman, Jus sanguinis, Jus soli, Kane, Keelie, National, Oppidan, Patrial, People, Proletarian, Propr(a)etor, Quirites, Resident, Roman, Second-class, Senior, Snob, Subject, Townspeople, Trainband, Trierarch, Venireman, Vigilante, Voter

**Citroen** DS

**Citron, Citrous** Bergamot

**Citrus** Acid, Calamondin, Cedrate, Hesperidium, Lemon, Lime, Mandarin, Min(n)eola, Orange, Pomelo, Tangerine, Ugli

**City** Agra, Astrakhan, Athens, Atlantis, Babylon, Burgh, Cardboard, Carthage, Cosmopolis, Ctesiphon, Dodge, EC, Empire, Eternal, Forbidden, Free, Garden, Gath, Heavenly, Hilversum, Holy, Imperial, Inner, LA, Leonine, Medina, Megalopolis, Metropolis, Micropolis, Mother, Municipal, Mycenae, Nineveh, NY, Persepolis, Petra, Pompeii, Rhodes, Salem, See, Smoke, Sparta, Square mile, Tech, Teheran, The Big Smoke, Town, Ur, Urban(e), Vatican, Weltstadt, Wen, Yonkers

**Civet** Binturong, Cat, Fo(u)ssa, Genet(te), Herpestes, Linsang, Musang, Nandine, Palm, Paradoxine, Paradoxure, Rasse, Suricate, Toddy-cat, Viverra, Zibet

**Civil(ian), Civilisation, Civilised, Civility** Amenity, Amicable, Christian, Cit, Citizen, Civ(vy), Comity, Courtesy, Culture, Fertile crescent, Humane, Humanised, Indus Valley, Kultur, Maya, Minoan, Mufti, Municipal, Nok, Non-combatant, Paramilitary, Plain clothes, Polite, Politesse, Push-button, Respectful, Secular, Temporal, Urbane

**Civil Defence** ARP, CD

**Civil Service** CS

**Clacker** Crotalum

**Clad(ding)** Sarking, Weatherboard

**Clag(gy)** Stickjaw

**Claim(s)** Allege, Appeal, Arrogate, Assert, Asseverate, Bag, Challenge, Charge, Crave, Darraign(e), Darrain(e), Darrayn, Demand, Deraign, Droit, Encumbrance, Exact, Haro, Harrow, Insist, Lien, List, Maintain, Nochel, Plea, Pose, Posit, Postulate, Predicate, Pretence, Pretend, Profess, Pulture, Purport, Puture, Rank, Revendicate, Right, Set-off, Small, Sue, Title

**Claimant** Irredentist, Petitioner, Pot-waller, Pretender, Prospector, Tichborne, Usurper

**Clairvoyance, Clairvoyancy, Clairvoyant** ESP, Extrasensory, Far-sighted, Fey, Insight, Lucidity, Prophet, Psiphenomena, Psychic, Second sight, Taisch, Taish, Telegnosis, Telepathic, Tel(a)esthesia

**Clam** Bivalve, Chowder, Cohog, Geoduck, Giant, Gweduc, Hardshell, Littleneck, Mollusc, Mya, Quahang, Quahog, Razor(-shell), Round, Soft-shell, Steamer, Tridacna, Venus, Vongole

**Clamant** Vociferous

**Clamber** Climb, Crawl, Scramble, Spra(i)ckle, Sprauchle

**Clammy** Algid, Damp, Dank, Moist, Sticky, Sweaty

**Clamour(ing), Clamorous** Blatant, Brouhaha, Din, Forensis strepitus, Hubbub, Hue, Katzenjammer, Noise, Outcry, Racket, Raird, Reird, Rout, Shout, Strepitant, Uproar, Utis, Vociferate

**Clamp(er)** Beartrap, Chuck, Clinch, Coupler, Denver boot, Fasten, Grip, Haemostat, Holdfast, Jumar, Pinchcock, Potato-pit, Serrefine, Stirrup, Tread, Vice, Wheel

**Clan(sman)** Brood, Cameron, Campbell, Clique, Gens, Gentile, Group, Horde, Kiltie, Kindred, Name, Ngati, Nomen, Phratry, Phyle, Sect, Sept, Society, Stewart, Stuart, Tribe

**Clandestine** Covert, Furtive, Hedge marriage, Secret, Sneaky, Surreptitious, Underhand

**Clang(er), Clanging, Clank** Bell, Belleter, Boob, Boo-boo, Clash, Gong, Jangle, Plangent, Ring

**Clap(per), Clapping** Applaud, Blow, Castanet, Chop, Crotal, Dose, Jinglet, Peal, Plaudit(e), Stroke hands, Thunder, Tonant

**Claptrap** Bilge, Blab, Blah, Bombast, Bunkum, Eyewash, Hokum, Mumbo-jumbo, Rot, Tripe, Twaddle

**Claque(ur)** Fans, Hat, Laudator, Sycophant

**Clara** Bow, Butt

**Clare** Nun, Sister

**Claret** Blood, Loll-shraub, Loll-shrob, Vin

**Clarify, Clarified, Clarifier** Clear, Despumate, Dilucidate, Elucidate, Explain, Explicate, Fine, Finings, Ghee, Purge, Refine, Render, Simplify, Tease out

**Clarinet** Chalumeau, Reed

**Clarion** Brassy, Clear, Trumpet

**Clary** Orval, Sage

**Clash(ing)** Bang, Clangour, Clank, Claver, Coincide, Collide, Conflict, Dissonant, Friction, Gossip, → IMPACT, Incident, Irreconcilable, Jangle, Jar, Loud, Missuit, Riot, Shock, Showdown, Strike, Swash, Tilt

**Clasp(ing)** Adpress, Agraffe, Amplexus, Barrette, Brooch, Button, Catch, Chape, Clip, Embrace, Fibula, Grasp, Hasp, Hesp, Hook, Hug, Inarm, Interdigitate, Link, Morse, Netsuke, Ochreate, Ouch, Peace, Press, Slide, Tach(e), Tie, Unite

**Class(ification), Classify, Classified, Classy** Acorn, Arrange, Assort, Bourgeois(ie), Bracket, Brand, Breed, Business, Cabin, Canaille, Caste, → CATEGORY, Chattering, Cheder, Cl, Cladistics, Clan, Clerisy, Clinic, Club, Composite, Course, Criminal, Dalit, Dewey, Digest, Division, Economy, Establishment, Estate, Evening, Faction, First, Folksonomy, Form, Genera, Genre, Gentry, Genus, → GRADE, Group, Harvard, Haryan, Heder, Hubble, Ilk, Keep-fit, Kidney, Kohanga reo, League, Lesson, Life, Linn(a)ean, List, Lower, Mammal, Master, Meritocracy, Middle, Night, Number, Nursery, Order, Peasantry, Petit bourgeois, Phenetics, Phylum, Pigeon-hole, Pleb(eian), Posh, Proletariat, Proper, Race, Range, Rank, Rate, Rating, Raypoot, Raypout, Reception, Remove, Ruling, Salariat, Second, Secret, Seminar, Shell, Siege, Social, Sort(ation), Spectral, Sphere, Standard, Steerage, Stratum, Stream, Syntax, Taxonomy, Teach-in, Third, Tony, Tourist, Tribe, Tutorial, → TYPE, U, Universal, Upper, Varna, Water, Working, World, Year

**Classic(al), Classics, Classicist** Ageless, Ancient, Basic, Derby, Elzevir, Epic, Grecian, Greek, Humane, Leger, Literature, Oldie, Pliny, Purist, Roman, Standard, Traditional, Vintage

**Clatch** Blunk, Smear, Spoil

**Clatter** Bicker, Charivari, Clack, Din, Noise, Rattle

**Clause** Acceleration, Adjunct, Apodosis, Article, Basket, Complement, Condition, Conscience, Coordinate, Dependent, Disability, Endorsement, Escalator, Escape,

Exclusion, Exemption, Filioque, Four, Golden parachute, Grandfather, Independent, Main, Member, Noun, Novodamus, Object, Omnibus, Option, Poison-pill, Predicator, Principal, Protasis, Proviso, Reddendum, Relative, Reported, Reservation, Reserve, Rider, Salvo, Saving, Sentence, Subject, Subordinate, Sunset, Tenendum, Testatum, Testing, Warrandice

**Claw** Chela, Claut, Cloye, Crab, Dewclaw, Edate, Falcula, Grapple, Griff(e), Hook, Insessorial, Lark-heel, Nail, Nipper, Pounce, Scrab, Scramb, Sere, Talent, → **TALON**, Tear, Telson, Tokay, Unguis

**Clay** Ali, Allophane, Argil, Argillite, Barbotine, B(e)auxite, Bentonite, Blaes, Blaise, Blaize, Blunge, Bole, Boulder, Calm, Cam, Cassius, Caum, Ceramic, Charoset(h), China, Cimolite, Cloam, Clunch, Cob, Cornish, Earth, Engobe, Fango, Figuline, Fire, Fuller's earth, Gault, Glei, Gley, Gumbotil, Hardpan, Haroset(h), Illite, Kaolin, Kokowai, Laterite, Lithomarge, Loam, London, Lute, Malm, Marl, Meerschaum, Mire, Mortal, Mud, Oxford, Papa, Pipeclay, Pipestone, Pise, Plastic, Plastilina, Porcelain, Potter's, Pottery, Puddle, Pug, Saggar(d), Sagger, Scroddle(d), Seggar, Sepiolite, Slip, Slurry, Smectite, Terra sigillata, Thill, Till(ite), Tumphy, Varve, Warrant, Warren, Wax

**Clean(er), Cleaning, Cleanse** Abrasive, Absterge, Ammonia, Bathbrick, Besom, Bidet, Blanco, Bleach, Blue flag, Boots, Bream, Breast, Broom, Careen, Catharise, Catharsis, Chamois leather, Char(e), Chaste, Clear, Cottonbud, Daily, Debride, Decontaminate, Dentifrice, Depurate, Deterge(nt), Dhobi, Dialysis, Dicht, Dishrag, Disinfect, Do, Douche, Dredge, Dust(er), Dyson®, Eluant, Emunge, Enema, Epurate, Erase, Ethnic, Evacuant, Evacuate, Expurgate, Fay, Fettle, Fey, Floorcloth, Floss, Flush, Full, Grave, Groom, Gut, Heels, Home help, Hoover®, House-trained, Hygienic, Immaculate, Innocent, J-cloth, Kosher, Launder, Lave, Linish, Lustrum, Lye, Mouthwash, Mrs Mop(p), Mundify, Net, Nipter, Overhaul, Porge, Prophylaxis, Pull-through, Pumice, Pure, Purgative, Purge, Ramrod, Rebite, Rub, Rump, Sandblast, Sanitize, Scaffie, Scavenge, Scour, Scrub, Shampoo, Shot-blast, Snow-white, Soap, Soogee, Soogie, Soojey, Sponge, Spotless, Square, Squeaky, Squeegee, Squilgee, Sterile, Sujee, Swab, Sweep, Syringe, Tidy, Tissue, Toothpick, Turpentine, Ultrasonic, Uproot, Vac(uum), Valet, → **WASH**, Whistle, Whiter, Wipe, Zamboni

**Clear(ance), Cleared, Clearer, Clearly** Absolve, Acquit, Allow, Aloof, Apparent, Articulate, Assart, Bald, Bell, Berth, Bold, Bore, Brighten, Bus, Categorical, Clarify, Cloudless, Cogent, Comprehensive, Concise, Consomme, Crystal, Daylight, Decode, Decongest, Definite, De-ice, Delouse, Demist, Diaphanous, Disafforest, Dispel, Distinct, Downright, Earn, Eidetic, Evacuate, Evident, Exculpate, Exonerate, Explicit, Express, Fair, Five-by-five, Flagrant, Gain, Get over, Headroom, Highland, Hyaline, Intelligible, Iron, Laund, Leap, Leapfrog, Legible, Limpid, Lucid, Luculent, Manifest, Mop, Neat, Negotiate, Net(t), No brainer, → **NOT CLEAR**, Observable, Obvious, Ope(n), Overleap, Overt, Palpable, Patent, Pay, Pellucid, Perspicuous, Plain, Play, Pratique, Predy, Pure, Purge, Quit, Rack, Realise, Reap, Remble, Rid, Ripple, Serene, Sheer, Shere, Silvery, Slum, Snowplough, Specific, Stark, Straight, Strip, Succinct, Sweep, Swidden, Thro(ugh), Thwaite, Transire, Translucent, Transparent, Unambiguous, Unblock, Unclog, Uncork(ed), Unequivocal, Unstop, Vault, Vindicate, Vivid, Void, Well, Whiten, Windage, Wipe

**Clearing** Assart, Glade, Opening, Shire, Slash

**Cleat** Bitt, Wedge

**Cleave, Cleavage, Cleft** Adhere, Bisulcate, Builder's bottom, Builder's bum, Chimney, Chine, Chink, Cling, Cloff, Cohere, Cut, Divide, Division, Divorce(ment), Fissure, Gap, Ghaut, Goose-grass, Grike, Gryke, Harelip, Meroblastic, Notch, Pharynx, Rift, Riva, Scissure, Severance, Slack, Slaty, Space, Spathose, Split, Sulcus

**Clef** Soprano, Treble

**Cleft** Crevice, Fissirostral, Notch

**Clematis** Montana, Old man's beard, Traveller's joy, Virgin's-bower

**Clemenceau** Tiger

**Clemency, Clement** Ahimsa, Attlee, Grace, Lenience, Lenity, Mercy, Mildness, Quarter, Temperate

**Clench** Close, Double, Grip, Grit, Squeeze, Stiffen, Tense

**Cleopatra** Needle

**Clergy(man), Cleric(al)** Abbé, Abbot, Archdeacon, Ayatollah, Canon, Cantor, Cardinal, Chancellor, Chaplain, Chapter, Circuit rider, Cleric, Clerk, Cloth, Curate, Curé, Deacon, Dean, Ecclesiast(ic), God-botherer, Goliard, Holy Joe, Incumbent, Josser, Levite, Ministerial, Ministry, Minor canon, Non-juror, Non-usager, Notarial, Padre, Paperwork, Parson, Pastor, Pontifex, Pontiff, Preacher, Prebendary, Precentor, Prelate, Presbyter, Presenter, Priest, Primate, Prior, Proctor, Rabbi, Rector, Red-hat, Reverend, Rome-runner, Scribal, Secretarial, Secular, Shaveling, Shepherd, Sky pilot, Slope, Spin-text, Spirituality, Squarson, Subdeacon, Theologian, Vartabed, Vicar

**Clergy-hater** Misoclere

**Clerk(s)** Actuary, Articled, Baboo, Babu, Basoche, Circar, Cleric, Cratchit, Cursitor, Enumerator, Filing, Heep, Lay, Limb, Notary, Paper-pusher, Parish, Pen-driver, Penman, Penpusher, Petty Bag, Poster, Protocolist, Prot(h)onotary, Quill-driver, Recorder, St Nicholas's, Salaryman, Scribe, Secretariat, Shipping, Sircar, Sirkar, Tally, Town, Vestry, Vicar, Writer

**Clever(ness)** Able, Accomplished, Adroit, Astute, Brainy, Bright, Canny, Cool, Cunning, Cute, Daedal(e), Deep-browed, Deft, Genius, Gleg, Habile, Ingenious, Intellectual, Jackeen, Know-all, Natty, Nimblewit, Resourceful, Sage(ness), Shrewd, Skeeley, Skilful, Smart(y), Smarty-pants, Souple, Subtle

**Clevis** Becket

**Cliché** Banality, Boilerplate, Commonplace, Corn, Journalese, Platitude, Saying, Tag

**Click(er), Clicking** Castanet, Catch, Forge, Implosive, Pawl, Rale, Ratch(et), Snick, Succeed, Tchick, Ticktack

**Client** Account, Customer, End-user, Fat, Gonk, John, Patron, Thin, Trick

**Cliff(s)** Beachy Head, Bluff, Cleve, Corniche, Crag, Craig, Escarp, Lorelei, Palisade(s), Precipice, Promontory, Sca(u)r

**Cliffhanger** Mountaineer, Samphire, Serial, Thriller

**Climate** Ambience, Atmosphere, Attitude, Continental, Mood, Saharan, Sun, Temperament, Temperature, Weather

**Climax** Apex, Apogee, Catastasis, Come, Crescendo, Crest, Crisis, Culminate, Edaphic, End, Head, Height, Heyday, Moment of truth, Orgasm, Payoff, Selling, Top, Zenith

**Climb(er), Climbing** Aid, Alpinist, Aralia, Aristolochia, Artificial, Ascend, Bignonian, Bougainvillaea, Breast, Briony, Bryony, Clamber, Clematis, Clusia, Cowage, Cowhage, Cowitch, Crampon, Creeper, Cubeb, Cucumber, Dodder, Eglatere, Ers, Heart-pea, Hedera, Honeysuckle, Ibex, Ivy, Jamming, Kie-kie, Kudzu, Lawyer, Layback, Liana, Liane, →MOUNT, Munro-bagger, Pareira, Parvenu, Pea, Peg, Poison oak, Prusik, Rat(t)an, Rhoicissus, Rise, Root, Rope, Scale, Scan, Scandent, Scansores, Sclim, Scramble, Shin, Shinny, Sklim, Smilax, Social, Speel, Steeplejack, Stegophilist, Sty(e), Swarm, Timbo, Tuft-hunter, Udo, Up(hill), Uprun, Upstart, Vetch, Vine, Vitaceae, Wistaria, Wisteria, With(y)wind, Woodbine, Zoom

**Clinch** Attach, Carriwitchet, Determine, Ensure, Fix, Quibble, Rivet, Secure, Settle

**Cling(er), Clinging** Adhere, Barnacle, Bur(r), Cherish, Cleave, Embrace, Hold, Hug, Limpet, Ring, Suctorial, Tendril

**Clinic** Abortuary, Antenatal, Dental, Dispensary, Hospital, Hospitium, Mayo, Well-woman

**Clink** Gingle, Jail, Jingle, Lock up, Nick, Prison, Stir, Ting, Tinkle

**Clinker** Ash, Slag

**Clint** Limestone

**Clip(ped), Clipper, Clipping** Alberta, Banana, Barrette, Bicycle, Brash, Bulldog, Butterfly, Cartridge, Chelsea, Clasp, Crocodile, Crop-ear, Crutch, Curt, Curtail, Cut, Cutty Sark, Dag, Dock, Dod, Excerpt, Film, Fleece, Hairslide, Jubilee, Jumar, Krab, Lop, Money,

Mow, Nail, Outtake, Pace, Paper, Pare, Pedicure, Peg, Prerupt, Prune, Roach, Scissel, Secateur, Shear, Ship, Shore, Shorn, Shorten, Snip, Spring, Staccato, Terse, Tie, Tie-tack, Tinsnips, Toe, Tonsure, Topiarist, Trim, Trot

**Clippy** Cad, Conductor

**Clique** Cabal, Clan, Club, Coterie, Elite, Faction, Four Hundred, Gang, Incrowd, Junta, Ring, Sect, Set, Tribe

**Clive** Arcot

**Cloak(room), Cloaks** Aba, Abaya, Abba, Abolla, Amice, Anonymity, Bathroom, Buffalo-robe, Burnous, Capa, Cape, Capote, Caracalla, Cardinal, Cassock, Chasuble, Chimer(e), Chlamydes, Chlamys, Chuddah, Chuddar, Cocoon, Conceal, Cope, Cover, Disguise, Dissemble, Djellaba(h), Domino, Gabardine, Gaberdine, Gal(l)abea(h), Gal(l)abi(y)a(h), Gal(l)abi(y)eh, Gentlemen, Gents, Grego, Hall-robe, Heal, Hele, Himation, Hood, Inverness, Jelab, Jellaba, Joseph, Kaross, Korowai, Ladies, Manta, Manteau, Manteel, Mantle, Mant(e)let, →MASK, Mourning, Mousquetaire, Mozetta, Opera, Paenula, Paletot, Pallium, Paludamentum, Pelisse, Pilch, Poncho, Powder-room, Rail, Revestry, Rocklay, Rokelay, Roquelaure, Sagum, Sarafan, Scapular, →SCREEN, Shroud, Swathe, Talma, Toga, Vestiary, Vestry, Visite

**Clobber** Anoint, Apparel, Attire, Clothing, Do, Dress, Garb, Garment, Habiliments, Lam, Tack, Thump

**Clock** Alarm, Ammonia, Analogue, Astronomical, Atomic, Beetle, Big Ben, Biological, Blowball, Body, Bracket, Bundy, Caesium, Carriage, Cartel, Clepsydra, Cuckoo, Dandelion, Digital, Doomsday, Dutch, Floral, Grandfather, Grandmother, Hit, Knock, Long case, Meter, Paenula, Parliament, Puss, Quartz, Repeater, Sandglass, Settler's, Solarium, Speaking, Speedo, Strike, Sundial, Taximeter, Tell-tale, Time(r), Travelling, Turret, Wag at the wa', Water

**Clockmaker** Fromanteel, Graham, Harrison, Knibb, Mudge, Tompion

**Clockwise** Deasil, Deasiul, Deasoil, Deiseal, Deisheal

**Clockwork** Precision, Regular

**Clod** Clumsy, Divot, Glebe, Lump, Mool, Mould, Mug, Put(t), Scraw, Sod, Stupid, Turf

**Clog(gy)** Accloy, Ball, Block, Clam, Congest, Crowd, Dance, Fur, Galosh, Golosh, Hamper, Jam, Lump, Mire, Obstruct, Overshoe, Patten, Sabot, Stickjaw

**Cloisonné** Shippo

**Cloister** Arcade, Confine, Cortile, Immure, Monastery, Mure, Refuge, Seclude

**Clone, Cloning** Mini-me, Ramet, Replicant, Reproduce, Therapeutic

**Cloots** Worricow

**Close(d), Closing, Closure** Adjacent, Adjourn, Agree, Airless, Alongside, Anigh, Atresia, Block, Boon, By, Cadence, Cap, Clammy, Clap, Clench, Collapse, Compact, Complete, Concentration, Cone off, Court, Crown cap, Curtain, Dear, Debar, Dense, Dissolve, →END, Epilogue, Ewest, Eye to eye, Finale, Forby, Gare, Grapple, Handy, Hard, Hard by, Hot, Humid, Imminent, Inbye, Infibulate, Intent, Intimate, Local, Lock, Lucken, Marginal, Mean, Miserly, Muggy, Mure, Narre, Narrow, Near, Nearhand, Neck and neck, Neist, Next, Nie, Niggardly, Nigh, Nip and tuck, Obturate, Occlude, Occlusion, Oppressive, Parochial, Penny-pinching, Photo-finish, Placket, Precinct, Reserved, Reticent, Seal, Secret, Serre, Serried, Serry, Shet, Shut(ter), Shutdown, Silly, Slam, Snug, Stap, Sticky, Stifling, Stuffy, Sultry, Tailgate, Temenos, Terminate, Tight(knit), Uproll, Wafer, Wanr, Warm, Yard

**Close-cropped** Crewcut, Not-pated

**Close-fitting** Skintight, Slinky, Tight

**Closet** Cabinet, Confine, Cubicle, Cupboard, Dooket, Earth, Locker, Safe, Wardrobe, WC, Zeta

**Close-up** Detail, Fill, Shut, Stop, Zoom

**Closing-time** Eleven, End

**Clot(ting)** Agglutinate, Ass, Bozo, Clag, Clump, Coagulate, Congeal, Crassamentum, Cruor, Curdle, Dag, Duffer, Embolism, Embolus, Gel, Globule, Gob, Gout, Grume,

Heparin, Incrassate, Incrust, Jell, Lapper, Lopper, →**LUMP**, Mass, Moron, Prothrombin, Splatch, Stupid, Thicken, Thrombosis, Thrombus

**Clotbuster** Heparin

**Cloth** Aba, Abaya, Abba, Antependium, Bandanna, Bearing, Bib, Bribe, Carmelite, Clergy, Cloot, Clout, Communion, Corporal(e), Dishrag, Duster, →**FABRIC**, →**FELT**, Frocking, Frontal, Gremial, G-string, Habit-cloth, Interfacing, Jharan, Kerchief, Loin, Lungi, Manta, →**MATERIAL**, Mercery, Meshing, Nap, Napery, Napje, Napkin, Nappie, Neckerchief, Needlework, Netting, Pack, Painted, Pall, Pane, Pilch, Priesthood, Pull-through, Purificator, Puttee, Putty, Rag, Raiment, Roll, Roon, Runner, Sashing, Scarlet, Serviette, Sheet, Sheeting, Shirting, Shoddy, Stock, Stripe, Stuff, Stupe, Sudarium, Supper, Sweatband, Tapestry, Tea, →**TEXTILE**, Throw, Tissue, Toilet, Vernicle, Veronica, Washrag, Whole

---

**CLOTH**

*1 letter:*
J®
T

*3 letters:*
Abb
Lap®
Rep
Say
Web

*4 letters:*
Aida
Amis
Baft
Bark
Ciré
Doek
Drab
Duck
Felt
Fent
Flax
Gair
Haik
Harn
Hyke
Ikat
Jean
Kelt
Knit
Lace
Lamé
Lawn
Leno
Line
Lint
Mull
Nude
Pina

Puke
Repp
Rund
Shag
Slop
Sulu
Tapa
Tick
Wire
Wool

*5 letters:*
Atlas
Baize
Beige
Binca
Budge
Chino
Crape
Crash
Crepe
Denim
Dobby
Drill
Duroy
Fanon
Foulé
Frisé
Gauze
Gazar
Grass
Gunny
Haick
Honan
Jaspe
Kanga
Kente
Khadi
Khaki
Kikoi

Linen
Lisle
Llama
Loden
Lurex®
Lycra®
Moiré
Mongo
Monk's
Mummy
Mungo
Ninon
Nylon
Orlon®
Panel
Panne
Paper
Perse
Pilot
Piqué
Plaid
Plush
Poult
Print
Rayon
Satin
Scrim
Serge
Slops
Surah
Surat
Surge
Tabby
Tamin
Tammy
Tappa
Terry
Tibet
Toile
Towel

Tulle
Tweed
Tweel
Twill
Union
Voile
Wigan

*6 letters:*
Aertex®
Alpaca
Angora
Armure
Barège
Beaver
Bouclé
Broche
Burlap
Burnet
Burrel
Byssus
Caddis
Calico
Camlet
Camlot
Canvas
Chintz
Cilice
Cloqué
Coburg
Coutil
Covert
Crepon
Cubica
Cyprus
Dacron®
Damask
Dévoré
Dimity
Domett

Dossal
Dossel
Dowlas
Dralon®
Drapet
Duffel
Duffle
Dupion
Durrie
Etamin
Faille
Fannel
Frieze
Gloria
Greige
Gurrah
Haique
Harden
Herden
Hodden
Hoddin
Humhum
Hurden
Jersey
Kersey
Khanga
Kincob
Lampas
Madras
Medley
Melton
Merino
Mohair
Mongoe
Moreen
Muleta
Muslin
Mutton
Nankin
Nettle
Oxford
Pongee
Poplin
Rateen
Ratine
Russel
Samite
Satara
Sateen
Saxony
Sendal
Shalli
Sherpa
Sindon

Soneri
Stroud
Tactel®
Tamine
Tartan
Tencel®
Thibet
Tricot
Vellet
Velour
Velure
Velvet
Vicuna
Wadmal
Wincey
Winsey

**7 letters:**
Abattre
Acrylic
Alamode
Alepine
Baracan
Batiste
Bolting
Brocade
Cabbage
Cambric
Camelot
Challie
Challis
Cheviot
Chiffon
Crombie
Cypress
Delaine
Dhurrie
Doeskin
Domette
Dorneck
Dornick
Drabbet
Drapery
Droguet
Drugget
Duvetyn
Etamine
Faconné
Fannell
Fishnet
Flannel
Foulard
Fustian
Galatea

Genappe
Gingham
Gore-tex®
Grogram
Hessian
Holland
Hopsack
Jaconet
Jamdani
Khaddar
Kitenge
Leather
Lockram
Mockado
Nacarat
Nankeen
Oil-silk
Oilskin
Organza
Orleans
Ottoman
Paisley
Percale
Printer
Rabanna
Raploch
Raschel
Ratteen
Rattine
Ripstop
Sacking
Sagathy
Satinet
Schappe
Silesia
Sinamay
Spandex®
Stammel
Supplex®
Tabaret
Tabinet
Taffeta
Ticking
Tiffany
Trolley
Tussore
Viscose
Viyella®
Wadmaal
Webbing
Woolsey
Worsted
Zanella

**8 letters:**
Aircraft
Algerine
American
Armozeen
Armozine
Arresine
Bagheera
Barathea
Barracan
Bayadere
Bearskin
Bobbinet
Boulting
Brocatel
Cameline
Casement
Cashmere
Casimere
Celanese
Chambray
Chamelot
Chenille
Ciclaton
Corduroy
Coteline
Coutille
Cretonne
Damassin
Drabette
Duchesse
Dungaree
Duvetine
Duvetyne
Eolienne
Florence
Gambroon
Gossamer
Homespun
Jacquard
Jeanette
Lambskin
Lava-lava
Lustring
Mackinaw
Mantling
Marcella
Marocain
Mazarine
Moleskin
Moquette
Nainsook
Oilcloth
Organdie

Osnaburg
Pashmina
Plaiding
Pleather
Prunella
Rodevore
Sarcenet
Sarsenet
Sealskin
Shabrack
Shalloon
Shantung
Sicilian
Suedette
Swanskin
Tabbinet
Tarlatan
Toilinet
Velveret
Whipcord
Wild silk
Zibeline

**9 letters:**
Aeroplane
Alcantara
Astrakhan
Baldachin
Balzarine
Bengaline
Bombasine
Calamanco
Camel-hair
Cassimere
Cerecloth
Charmeuse®
Ciclatoun
Cottonade
Courtelle®

Crepoline
Crimplene®
Crinoline
Evenweave
Fabrikoid®
Farandine
Filoselle
Folk-weave
Gaberdine
Georgette
Grenadine
Grosgrain
Haircloth
Horsehair
Indiennes
Interlock
Kalamkari
Levantine
Longcloth
Mandilion
Mandylion
Marseille
Matelassé
Messaline
Moygashel
Nitro-silk
Open-weave
Organzine
Overcheck
Paramatta
Penistone
Percaline
Persienne
Petersham
Pinstripe
Polyester
Ravenduck
Sackcloth
Sailcloth

Satin jean
Sharkskin
Silkalene
Silkaline
Stockinet
Strouding
Swansdown
Tarpaulin
Tricotine
Veloutine
Velveteen
Wire gauze
Worcester
Zibelline

**10 letters:**
Balbriggan
Baldachino
Book muslin
Broadcloth
Brocatelle
Candlewick
Farrandine
Fearnought
Ferrandine
Florentine
Geotextile
Kerseymere
Lutestring
Matellasse
Mousseline
Needlecord
Parramatta
Polycotton
Ravensduck
Russel-cord
Seersucker
Shabracque
Shiveshive

Sicilienne
Tattersall
Toilinette
Tuftaffeta
Tuftaffety
Winceyette

**11 letters:**
Abercrombie
Bedford cord
Canton crepe
Cheesecloth
Cloth of gold
Dotted Swiss
Drap-de-berry
Dreadnought
Flannelette
Hammercloth
Kendal green
Marquisette
Nun's veiling
Sempiternum
Stockinette
Stretch knit
Swiss muslin

**12 letters:**
Brilliantine
Cavalry twill
Crepe de chine
Elephant cord
Leather-cloth

**13 letters:**
Gros de Londres
Linsey-woolsey

**Cloth-designing** Batik
**Clothe(s), Clothing, Clothed** Accoutrements, Ao dai, Apparel, Array, Attire, Baggies, Battledress, Besee, Bib and tucker, Cape, Casuals, Chasuble, Chino, Choli, Cits, Clad, Clericals, Clobber, Coat, Combinations, Confection, Coordinates, Costume, Cour, Cover, Croptop, Cruisewear, Culottes, Deck, Diffusion line, Dight, Don, Drag, →**DRESS**, Duds, Dungarees, Emboss, Endue, Fig leaf, Finery, Foot muff, Frippery, Garb, Garments, Gear, Gere, Get-up, Glad rags, Grave, Gymslip, Gyves, Habit, Haute couture, Hejab, Hot pants, Hug-me-tight, Innerwear, Judogi, Jump (suit), Kimono, Layette, Leathers, Lederhosen, Leisurewear, Long-togs, Menswear, Mitumba, Mocker, Muff, Nebris, Nightdress, Outfit, Overalls, Pannicle, Pantsuit, Pareu, Pea-coat, Pea-jacket, Pin-striped, Plain, Playsuit, Plus fours, Raggery, Rag trade, Raiment, Rami, Rigout, Robes, Rompers, Samfoo, Samfu, Sayon, Scapulary, Schmutter, Scrubs, Scungies, Shell suit, Shirtwaister, Shmatte, Shroud, Slops, Stomacher, Strip, Sunday best, Sundress, Sunsuit, Swaddling, Swathe, Swothling, Tackle, Things, Toggery, Togs, Tracksuit, Trappings, Trews, Trousseau, Tube top,

Tweeds, Two-piece, Unitard, Veiling, Vernicle, Vestiary, Vestiture, Vestment, Wardrobe, Watteau, Wear, Weeds, Wetsuit, Widow's weeds, Workwear, Yclad, Ycled, Y-fronts

**Clothes basket, Clothes horse** Airer, Petara, Winterhedge

**Clothier** Dresser, Dressmaker, Tailor

**Cloud(ing), Clouded, Cloudiness, Cloudy** Altocumulus, Altostratus, Banner, Benight, C, Cataract, Cirrocumulus, Cirrostratus, Cirrus, Coalsack, Coma, Contrail, Crab Nebula, Cumulonimbus, Cumulus, Dim, Dull, Emission nebula, Fog, Fractocumulus, Fractostratus, Funnel, Goat's hair, Haze, Horsehead Nebula, Infuscate, Magellanic, Mammatus, Mare's tail, Milky, Mist, Molecular, Mushroom, Nacreous, Nephele, Nephelometer, Nepho-, Nimbostratus, Nimbus, Nubecula, Nubilous, Nuée ardente, Obnubilation, Obscure, Octa, Okta, Oort, Overcast, Pall, Pother, Protostar, Rack, Roily, Smoor, Stain, Storm, Stratocumulus, Strat(o)us, Thunder(head), Turbid, Unclear, Virga, War, Water-dog, Weft, Woolpack, Zero-zero

**Cloudberry** Mountain bramble

**Cloudless** Serene

**Clough** Dale, Gorge, Ravine

**Clout** Belt, Cloth, Crown, Hit, Influence, Lap(pie), Lapje, Muscle, Power, Pull, Raddle

**Clove** Chive, Eugenia, Garlic, Rose-apple, Split, Yrent

**Cloven** Fissilingual

**Clover** Alfalfa, Alsike, Berseem, Calvary, Cinque, Cow-grass, Dutch, Four-leaf, Hare's-foot, Hop, Hop-trefoil, Japan, Ladino, Lespedeza, Medic(k), Melilot, Owl's, Pin, Rabbit-foot, Red, Serradella, Serradilla, Shamrock, Souple, Sucklers, Suckling, Sweet, Trefoil, Trilobe, Truelove, White

**Clown(ish)** Airhead, Antic, Antick, August(e), Boor, Bor(r)el, Buffoon, Carl, Chough, Chuff, Clout-shoe, Coco, →**COMEDIAN**, Comic, Costard, Daff, Feste, Froth, Girner, Gobbo, Goon, Gracioso, Grimaldi, Harlequin, Hob, Idiot, Jack-pudding, Jester, Joey, Joker, Joskin, Leno, Merry Andrew, Mountebank, Nedda, Nervo, Patch(c)ocke, Peasant, Pickle-herring, Pierrot, Put, Rustic, Slouch, Thalian, Touchstone, Trinculo, Wag, Zany

**Cloy(ing)** Choke, Clog, Glut, Pall, Satiate, Surfeit, Sweet

**Club(s), Club-like** Adelphi, Airn, Alloa, Almack's, Alpeen, Apex, Army and Navy, Arsenal, Artel, Association, Athen(a)eum, Baffy, Band(y), Basto, Bat, Bath, Beefsteak, Blackjack, Blaster, Bludgeon, Boodles, Bourdon, Brassie, Breakfast, Brook's, Bulger, C, Caman, Card, Carlton, Caterpillar, Cavalry, Chapter, Chartered, Chigiriki, Clavate, Cleek, Clip-joint, Combine, Compassion, Conservative, Constitutional, Cordeliers, Cosh, Cotton, Country, Crockford's, Cudgel, Devonshire, Disco(theque), Dive, Driver, Driving iron, Drones, Fan, Farm team, Fascio, Fellowship, Feuillant, Fleshpot, Fustigate, Garrick, Glee, Golf, Guards, Guild, Hampden, Health, Hell-fire, Hercules', Hetairia, Honky-tonk, Indian, Investment, Iron, Jacobin, Jigger, Job, Jockey, Junior Carlton, Kennel, Kierie, Kiri, Kitcat, Kiwanis, Knobkerrie, Landsdowne, Lathi, Laughter, League, Leander, Lions, Lofter, Luncheon, Mace, Mallet, Mashie, Maul, Mell, Mere, Meri, Mess, Midiron, Minor suit, Monday, National Liberal, Niblick, Night(stick), Nightspot, Niterie, Nitery, Nulla(-nulla), Oddfellows, Paris, Patu, Pitching wedge, Polt, Pregnant, Priest, Provident, Pudding, Putter, Putting-cleek, Quarterstaff, RAC, R & A, Reform, Ring, Rota, Rotarian, Rotary, Round Table, Sand wedge, Sap, Savage, Savile, Shillelagh, Slate, Society, Soroptimist, Sorority, Sorosis, Spoon, Spot, Spurs, Strike, Strip, Stunner, Suicide, Supper, Texas wedge, Thatched House, Tong, Travellers, Trefoil, Truncheon, Trunnion, Union, United Services, Variety, Waddy, Warehouse, Wedge, White's, Wood, Yacht, Youth

**Club-foot** Kyllosis, Po(u)lt-foot, Talipes, Varus

**Clubhouse** Ch

**Clubman** Member

**Club-rush** Deer-hair, Scirpus, Sedge

**Cluck** Cherup, Chirrup, Dent

**Clue** 1ac, Across, Acrostic, Anagram, Aradne, Ball, Charade, Clavis, Dabs, Down, →**HINT**, Inkling, Key, Lead, Light, Rebus, Scent, Scooby(doo), Signpost, Thread, Tip

**Clueless** Ignorant

**Clump** Cluster, Finial, Knot, Mass, Mot(te), Patch, Plump, Sock, Tread, Tuft, Tump, Tussock

▷ **Clumsily** *may indicate* an anagram

**Clumsy** Artless, Awkward, Bauchle, Blunderbuss, Bungling, Butterfingers, Cack-handed, Calf, Chuckle, Clatch, Clodhopper, Cumbersome, Dub, Dutch, Galoot, Galumphing, Gauche, Gimp, Gink, Ham(-fisted), Heavy-handed, Horse-godmother, Hulk, Inapt, Inelegant, Inept, Inexpert, Klutz, Lob, Loutish, Lubbard, Lubber, Lumbering, Lummox, Lumpish, Maladdress, Maladroit, Mauther, Mawr, Mawther, Messy, Mor, Nerd, Nurd, Oafish, Off-ox, Overhasty, Palooka, Plonking, Rough, Schlemihl, S(c)hlemiel, Spastic, Spaz(zy), Squab, Stot, Stumbledom, Swab, Swob, Taupie, Tawpie, Two-fisted, Unco, Ungain, Unskilful, Unsubtle, Unwieldy, Wooden

**Cluster** Acervate, Agglomeration, Ament, Assemble, Asterism, Bunch, Clump, Collection, Concentre, Constellate, Conurbation, Corymb, Cyme, Galactic, Gather, Gear, Globular, Glomeration, Group, Knot, Oakleaf, Packet, Plump, Raceme, Rhipidium, Sheaf, Sorus, Strap, Telium, Thyrse, Tone, Truss, Tuffe, Tuft, Umbel, Verticillaster

**Clutch(es)** Battery, Brood, Chickens, Clasp, Cling, Eggs, Friction, Glaum, Grab, →**GRASP**, Gripe, Hold, Nest, Net, Seize, Sitting, Squeeze

**Clutter** Confusion, Impedimenta, Litter, Mess, Rummage

**Coach(es)** Autodidact, Battlebus, Berlin, Bogie, Bus, Car, Carriage, Chara(banc), Clerestory, Crammer, Diligence, Dilly, Double-decker, Drag, Edifier, Fiacre, Fly, Four-in-hand, Gig, Griddle car, Groom, Hackney, Handler, Landau(let), Life, Microbus, Mourning, Phaeton, Post chaise, Pullman, Railcar, Rattler, Repetiteur, Rolling stock, Saloon, Shay, Sleeper, Slip, Sobriety, Stage, Surrey, Tally(-ho), Teach(er), Thoroughbrace, Train(er), Transport, Tutor, Voiture

**Coach-horse** Rove-beetle

**Coachman** Automedon, Bunene, Coachy, Dragsman, Jarvey, Jehu, John

**Coagulant, Coagulate, Coagulation** Cautery, Clot, Congeal, Curdle, Curds, Jell, Rennet, Run, Runnet, Set, Solidify, Thicken

**Coal** Anthracite, Bituminous, Black diamonds, Block, Brown, Burgee, Caking, Cannel, Char, Cherry, Clinker, Coking, Coom, Crow, Culm, Day, Dice, Edge, Eldin, Ember, Fusain, Gas, Gathering, Hard, Indene, Jud, Knob, Lignite, Maceral, Mineral, Nut, Open-cast, Paper, Parrot, Pea, Purse, Sapropelite, Score, Sea, Slack, Soft, Splint, Steam, Stone, Surtarbrand, Surturbrand, Vitrain, Wallsend, White, Wood

**Coalesce(nce)** Amalgamate, Blend, Concrete, Fuse, Merge, Sintery, Synaloepha, Unite

**Coalfish** Saith

**Coalition** Alliance, Bloc, Fusion, Janata, Merger, Rainbow, Tie, Union

**Coal-tar** Aniline, Cresol, Indene

**Coal-tub** Corf, Dan, Scuttle

**Coarse(ness)** Base, Bawdy, Blowzy, Bran, Broad, Chav, Common, Crude, Dowlas, Earthy, Fisherman, Foul, Gneissose, Grained, Grobian, Gross, Grossièreté, Gruff, Haggery, Ham, Illbred, Indelicate, Low-bred, Plebeian, Rabelaisian, Rank, Rappee, Raunchy, Ribald, Rough, Rudas, Rude, Russet, Sackcloth, Schlub, Semple, Slob, Sotadic, Unrefined, Vulgar, Yahoo

**Coast(al)** Barbary, Beach, Bight, Caird, Cape, Causeway, Coromandel, Costa, Dalmatian, Drift, Freewheel, Glide, Gold, Hard, Heritage, Ivory, Littoral, Longshore, Malabar, Maritime, Med, Murman(sk), Orarian, Riviera, Scrieve, Seaboard, Seafront, Seashore, Seaside, →**SHORE**, Slave, Sledge, Strand, Sunshine, Toboggan, Trucial

**Coaster** Beermat, Drog(h)er, Mat, Roller, Ship, Smack

**Coastguard** CG, Gobby

**Coastline** Shoreline, Watermark

**Coast-road** Corniche

**Coat(ed), Coating** Ab(b)a, Abaya, Achkan, Acton, Admiral, Afghan, Anarak, Anodise, Anorak, Balmacaan, Barathea, Basan, Bathrobe, Belton, Benjamin, Blazer, Bloomed,

Bolero, Box, British warm, Buff, Buff-jerkin, Calcimine, Car, Chesterfield, Cladding, Claw-hammer, Clearcole, Cloak, Clutch, Cocoon, Coolie, Cover, Covert, Creosote, Crust(a), Cutaway, Dip, Doggett's, Drape, Dress, Duffel, Duster, Electroplate, Enamel, Encrust, Envelope, Ermelin, Ermine, Exine, Extine, Fearnought, Film, Finish, Fleece, Frock, Fur, Gabardine, Galvanise, Gambeson, Ganoin, Glaze, Grego, Ground, Hair, Happi, Ha(c)queton, Icing, Impasto, Integument, Inverness, Iridise, Jack(et), Jemmy, Jerkin, Jodhpuri, Joseph, Jump, Jupon, Lacquer, Lammie, Lammy, Lanugo, Layer, Laying, Lerp, Limewash, Loden, Lounge, Mac, Mackinaw, Matinee, Metallise, Mink, Morning, Newmarket, →OVERCOAT, Paint, Paletot, Palla, Paper, Parka, Parkee, Passivate, Patina(te), Pebbledash, Pelage, Pelisse, Perfuse, Peridium, Petersham, Phosphor, Pitch, Pla(i)ster, Plate, Plumage, Polo, Pos(h)teen, Primer, Primine, Prince Albert, Raglan, Redingote, Resin, Resist, Riding, Roquelaure, Sable, Sack, Salband, Saque, Sclera, Sclerotic, Scratch, Seal, Sheepskin, Shellac, Sherardise, Sherwani, Silver, Skinwork, Spencer, Sports, Stadium, Surtout, Swagger, Swallowtail(ed), Tabard, Taglioni, Tail, Tar, Teflon, Tent, Testa, Top, Trench, Truss, Trusty, Tunic, Tuxedo, Ulster(ette), Underseal, Varnish, Veneer, Verdigris, Warm, Wash, Weasel, Whitewash, Windjammer, Wool, Wrap-rascal, Zamarra, Zamarro, Zinc

**Coat of arms** Crest, Hatchment

**Coat-tail** Flap

**Coax** Blandish, Blarney, Cajole, Carn(e)y, Collogue, Cuittle, Entice, Flatter, Lure, Persuade, Tempt, Wheedle, Whillywha(w)

**Cob** Hazel(nut), Horse

**Cobalt** Co, Zaffer, Zaffre

**Cobber** Mate

**Cobble(s), Cobbled, Cobbler(s), Cobblestone** Bunkum, Claptrap, Clicker, Coggle, Cosier, Cozier, Dessert, Guff, Mend, Patch, Pie, Rot, Snob, Soutar, Souter, Sowter, Stone, Sutor, Twaddle, Vamp

**Cobra** King, Spitting

**Cobweb(by)** Arachnoid, Araneous, Gossamer, Snare, Trap

**Cocaine** Basuco, C, Charlie, Coke, Crystal, Flake, Freebase, Moonrock, Nose candy, Number, Ready-wash, Snow(ball)

**Coccid** Wax-insect

**Cochlear** Scala

**Cock(y), Cockerel** Alectryon, Ball, Brash, Capon, Chanticleer, Chaparral, Confident, Erect, Escape, Fighting, Flip, Fowl, France, Fugie, Half, Hay, Heath, Henny, Jack-the-lad, Jaunty, Midden, Penis, Perk, Roadrunner, Robin, Rooster, Shake-bag, Snook, Strut, Sunshine, Swaggering, Tap, Tilt, Turkey, Twaddle, Vain, Valve, Vane, Weather-vane

**Cock-a-hoop** Crowing, Elated, Jubilant

**Cockaigne** Paradise

**Cockatoo** Bird, Corella, Galah, Leadbeater's, Major Mitchell, Parrot

**Cockboat** Cog

**Cockchafer** Dor-bug, Humbuzz, May beetle, Maybug

**Cock crow** Skreigh of the day

**Cocker** Blenheim, Cuiter, Spaniel

**Cockeyed** Agee, Askew, Skewwhiff

**Cockfight(ing)** By(e), Main

**Cockle(s)** Bulge, Crease, Heart, Wrinkle

▷ **Cockle(s)** *may indicate* an anagram

**Cockney** 'Arriet, 'Arry, Bow, Eastender, Londoner, Londonese

▷ **Cockney** *may indicate* a missing h

**Cockpit** Greenhouse, Office, Well

**Cockroach** Archy, Beetle, Black beetle, Croton bug, German, Oriental, Orthoptera

▶ **Cockscomb** *see* COXCOMB

**Cocktail** →DRINK, →HORSE, Melange, Mix, Prawn

## COCKTAILS

**4 letters:**
Sour

**5 letters:**
Bumbo
Fruit
Julep
Punch
Twist

**6 letters:**
Atomic
Crusta
Gibson
Gimlet
Mai-Tai
Mojito
Rickey

**7 letters:**
Bellini
Cobbler
Egg-flip
Fustian

Martini®
Molotov
Negroni
Sangria
Sazerac®
Side-car
Slammer
Stengah
Stinger
Swizzle

**8 letters:**
Aperitif
Bullshot
Cold duck
Daiquiri
Highball
Pink lady
Sangaree
Snowball
Spritzer

**9 letters:**
Alexander

Buck's fizz
Kir Royale
Manhattan
Margarita
Pisco Sour
Rusty nail
Sea Breeze
Snakebite
White-lady

**10 letters:**
Bloody Mary
Calpirinha
Dry Martini
Horse's neck
Moscow mule
Piña colada
Tom Collins

**11 letters:**
Black Velvet
Grasshopper
Screwdriver
Whiskey Sour

**12 letters:**
Black Russian
Old-fashioned
White Russian

**13 letters:**
Planter's punch
Prairie oyster

**14 letters:**
Sherry cobbler
Singapore sling
Tequila sunrise

**15 letters:**
Brandy Alexander

**16 letters:**
Between the sheets
Harvey Wallbanger

**17 letters:**
Champagne
cocktail

---

**Cocoa** Criollo, Nib(s)
**Coconut** Coco-de-mer, Coir, Copra, Head, Madafu, Poonac, Toddy-palm
**Cocoon** Dupion, Mother, Pod, Swathe, Trehala
**Cocotte** Strumpet
**Cod** Bag, Cape, Coalfish, Fish, Gade, Gadus, Haberdine, Hoax, Keeling, Kid, Lob, Man, Morrhua, Murray, Red, Saith, Saltfish, Spoof, Stockfish, Take in, Tease, Torsk, Tusk, Whiting
**Coda** End(ing), Epilogue, Rondo, Tail(piece)
**Coddle** Cosset, Molly, Nancy, Pamper, Pet, Poach, Wet-nurse
**Code, Coding, Codification** Access, Alphanumeric, Amalfitan, Area, Bar, Barred, Binary, Brevity, Bushido, Canon law, Character, Cheat, Cipher, City, Civil, Clarendon, Codex, Colour, Computing, Condition, Cookie, Country, Cryptogram, Cryptograph, Da Vinci, Dialling, Disciplinary, Dogma, Dress, DX, Easter egg, EBCDIC, Encipher, Enigma, Error, Escape, Ethics, Etiquette, Fuero, Genetic, Gray, Green Cross, Hammurabic, Highway, Hollerith, Iddy-umpty, Justinian, MAC, Machine, Morse, Napoleon(ic), National, Netiquette, Object, Omerta, Opcode, Penal, PGP, PIN, Pindaric, Postal, Price, Protocol, Reflective binary, Rulebook, Scytale, Sharia, Shulchan Aruch, Signal, Sort, Source, STD, Talmud, Time, Twelve Tables, Zip
**Code-breaker, Code-breaking** Bletchley Park, Linear B, Malpractitioner, Turing
**Codger** Buffer, Fellow
**Codicil** Addition, Label, PS, Rider, Supp(lement)
**Codon** Initiator
**Coefficient** Absorption, Correlation, Differential, Diffusion, Distribution, Modulus, Partition, Pearson's correlation, Permeability, Saturation, Spearman's rank-order, Transmission, Young's modulus
**Coelacanth** Latimeria
**Coerce, Coercion** Big stick, Bully, Compel, Dragoon, Duress, Gherao, Impress, Pressure, Railroad, Restrain, Strong-arm, Threaten

**Coffee, Coffee beans, Coffee pot** Americano, Arabica, Bean, Black, Brazil, Cafetiere, Cappuccino, Decaff, Demi-tasse, Espresso, Expresso, Filter, Frappuccino, Gaelic, Gloria, Granules, Grounds, Instant, Irish, Java, Latte, Macchiato, Mocha, Peaberry, Percolator, Robusta, Rye, Skinny latte, Tan, Triage, Turkish, White

**Coffee-house** Lloyd's

**Coffer** Ark, Box, Casket, Cassone, Chest, Lacunar, Locker

**Coffin** Bier, Box, Casket, Hearse, Kist, Larnax, Pall, Sarcophagus, Shell, Wooden kimono, Wooden overcoat

**Cog(ged)** Contrate, Mitre-wheel, Nog, Pinion, Tooth, Wheel

**Cogent** Compelling, Forceful, Good, Sound, Telling

**Cogitate** Deliberate, Mull, Muse, Ponder

**Cognate** Paronym

**Cohabit(ant)** Bed, Indwell, Room-mate, Share, SOP

**Co-heir** Parcener

**Cohere(nt)** Agglutinate, Clear, Cleave, Cling, Logical, Stick

**Cohort** Colleague, Crony, Soldier

**Coif** Calotte, Cap, Hood

**Coiffeur** Hair-stylist

**Coiffure** Hairdo, Pompadour, Tête

**Coil(s), Coiled** Armature, Bight, Bought, Choke, Choking, Circinate, Clew, Clue, Convolute(d), Convolve, Curl, Current, Fake, Fank, Field, Flemish, Furl, Hank, Helix, Ignition, Induction, Loading, Loop, Mortal, Mosquito, Moving, Primary, Resistance, Rouleau, Scorpioid, Solenoid, Spark, Spiral, Spiraster, Spire, Tesla, Tickler, Toroid, Twine, Twirl, →WIND, Wound, Wreath, Writhe, Yoke

**Coin(er)** Base, Bean, Bit, Broad(piece), Cash, Change, Coign(e), Contomiate, Copper, Create, Doctor, Dosh, Double-header, Dump(s), Fiddler's money, Fiver, Han(d)sel, Imperial, Invent, Lucky piece, Make, Mill, Mint, Mintage, →MONEY, Neologist, Neoterise, Numismatic, Nummary, Piece, Plate, Pocket-piece, Proof, Shiner, Slip, Specie, Stamp, Sterling, Strike, Subsidiary, Sum, Tenner, Thin'un, Token, Touchpiece, Unity

## COINS

| | | | |
|---|---|---|---|
| *1 letter:* | Hao | Zuz | Jack |
| D | Jun | | Jane |
| | Kip | *4 letters:* | Jiao |
| *2 letters:* | Lat | Anna | Kina |
| As | Lei | Aora | Kobo |
| DM | Lek | Baht | Kuna |
| Kr | Leu | Bani | Kyat |
| Rd | Lev | Birr | Lari |
| Xu | Lew | Buck | Lion |
| | Mil | Cedi | Lipa |
| *3 letters:* | Mna | Cent | Lira |
| Avo | Moy | Chon | Loti |
| Ban | Ore | Dibs | Luma |
| Bar | Pul | Dime | Lwei |
| Bob | Pya | Doit | Maik |
| Cob | Red | Dong | Mark |
| Dam | Sen | Dram | Merk |
| Ecu | Sol | Duro | Mina |
| Fen | Som | Euro | Mite |
| Fil | Sou | Fiat | Mule |
| Fin | Won | Fils | Obol |
| Flu | Yen | Inti | Para |

| | | | |
|---|---|---|---|
| Paul | Eagle | Rupee | Escudo |
| Peag | Eyrir | Sceat | Filler |
| Peni | Franc | Scudo | Florin |
| Peso | Fugio | Scute | Forint |
| Pice | Gazet | Semis | Gilder |
| Posh | Gerah | Sente | Gourde |
| Pula | Gopik | Shand | Guinea |
| Puli | Groat | Smelt | Gulden |
| Punt | Grosz | Soldo | Halala |
| Rand | Haler | Souon | Haleru |
| Real | Hauer | Sucre | Heller |
| Reis | Khoum | Sycee | Hryvna |
| Rial | Krona | Tenge | Jitney |
| Riel | Krone | Tetri | Kobang |
| Rock | Kroon | Thebe | Koruna |
| Ryal | Kurus | Tical | Kroner |
| Sene | Laari | Ticky | Kroona |
| Sent | Laree | Tiyin | Kruger |
| Slog | Leone | Tolar | Kwacha |
| Tael | Liang | Toman | Kwanza |
| Taka | Liard | Tyiyn | Lepton |
| Tala | Litai | Unite | Likuta |
| Tein | Litas | Zaire | Loonie |
| Toea | Livre | Zimbi | Makuta |
| Tray | Louis | Zloty | Mancus |
| Trey | Lumma | | Markka |
| Vatu | Lyart | **6 letters:** | Mawpus |
| Yuan | Maile | Agorol | Mongoe |
| Zack | Manat | Ariary | Pa'anga |
| | Maneh | Aureus | Paduan |
| **5 letters:** | Marka | Balboa | Pagoda |
| Agora | Mohur | Bawbee | Pataca |
| Angel | Mongo | Bender | Pennia |
| Asper | Mopus | Bezant | Peseta |
| Aurar | Naira | Boddle | Pesewa |
| Baiza | Nakfa | Byzant | Poisha |
| Bekah | Ngwee | Canary | Qindar |
| Belga | Noble | Centas | Qintar |
| Bodle | Obang | Colone | Rappen |
| Brown | Oscar | Copeck | Rouble |
| Butat | Paisa | Couter | Rupiah |
| Butut | Paolo | Dalasi | Santim |
| Chiao | Pence | Danace | Satang |
| Colon | Pengo | Deaner | Sceatt |
| Conto | Penie | Décime | Seniti |
| Crore | Penni | Denier | Sequin |
| Cross | Penny | Derham | Shekel |
| Crown | Plack | Dirham | Sickle |
| Daric | Pound | Dirhem | Siglos |
| Dibbs | Razoo | Dodkin | Somoni |
| Dinar | Rider | Dollar | Stater |
| Diram | Royal | Double | Stiver |
| Dobra | Rubel | Drachm | Stotin |
| Ducat | Ruble | Ekuele | Talent |

Tanner
Tester
Teston
Thaler
Tickey
Toonie
Tugrik
Turner
Vellon
Wakiki

**7 letters:**
Afghani
Austral
Bolivar
Cardecu
Carolus
Centavo
Chetrum
Cordoba
Crusado
Drachma
Ekpwele
Guarani
Guilder
Hryvnya
Jacobus
Joannes
Kopiyka
Kreuzer
Lempira
Lisente
Metical
Millime
Milreis
Moidore
Ostmark
Ouguiya

Patrick
Piastre
Piefort
Pistole
Pollard
Quarter
Quetzal
Ringgit
Ruddock
Rufiyaa
Sextans
Solidus
Spanker
Tambala
Testoon
Testril
Thick'un
Thrimsa
Thrymsa
Tughrik
Unicorn
Xerafin

**8 letters:**
Brockage
Cardecue
Cruzeiro
Denarius
Doubloon
Ducatoon
Emalengi
Farthing
Groschen
Johannes
Kreutzer
Louis d'or
Maravedi
Millieme

Napoleon
Ngultrum
Nuevo sol
Picayune
Pistolet
Planchet
Portague
Portigue
Quadrans
Renminbi
Rigmarie
Semuncia
Sesterce
Shilling
Skilling
Solidare
Spur-rial
Spur-ryal
Stotinka
Twopence
Xeraphin
Zecchino

**9 letters:**
Boliviano
Britannia
Centesimo
Dandiprat
Dandyprat
Didrachma
Dupondius
Fourpence
Half-eagle
Half-tiger
Lilangeni
Luckpenny
Maple leaf
Ninepence

Pistareen
Rix-dollar
Rose noble
Schilling
Sou marque
Sovereign
Spur-royal
Yellowboy
Zwanziger

**10 letters:**
Chervonets
Krugerrand
Portcullis
Reichsmark
Siege-piece

**11 letters:**
Bonnet-piece
Deutschmark
Double eagle
Sword-dollar
Tetradrachm

**12 letters:**
Antoninianus
Iraimbilanja
Renminbi yuan

**13 letters:**
Half-sovereign

**14 letters:**
Three-farthings

**18 letters:**
Maria Theresa
   dollar

---

**Coinage** Currency, Invention, Nonce-word, Symmetallism
**Coincide(nt), Coincidence** Accident, Agree, Chance, Consilience, Conterminous, Fit,
   Fluke, Homotaxis, Overlap, Rabat(to), Simultaneous, Synastry, Synchronise, Tally
**Coke** Chark, Coal, Cocaine, Kola
**Col** Pass, Poort, Saddle
**Colander** Sieve
**Cold(-blooded), Cold(ness)** Ague, Algid, Aloof, Apathetic, Arctic, Asocial, Asperity,
   Austere, Baltic, Biting, Bitter, Bleak, Blue, Brr(r), C, Catarrh, Cauld(rife), Charity, Chill(y),
   Clinical, Colubrine, Common, Coryza, Coy, Dead, Distant, Ectotherm, Emotionless, Fish,
   Frappé, Frem(d), Fremit, Frigid, Frost(y), Gelid, Glacial, Hiemal, Icy, Impersonal, Jeel,
   Nippy, Nirlit, Parky, Passionless, Perishing, Piercing, Poikilotherm(ic), Polar, Psychro-,
   Remote, Rheumy, Rigor, Rume, Shivery, Siberia, Snap, Snell, Sniffles, Sour, Standoffish,
   Starving, Streamer, Subzero, Taters, Unmoved, Weed, Wintry
**Cold sore** Herpes, Shiver
**Coldstream** Borderer, Guard

**Cole** Colza, King, Nat, Porter

**Colic** Batts, Bots, Botts, Gripe, Lead, Painter's, Sand, Upset, Zinc

**Collaborate, Collaborator, Collaboration** Assist, Combine, Comply, Concert, →**COOPERATE**, Keiretsu, Milice, Quisling, Synergy, Team spirit, Vichy, Vichyite, Vichyssois(e)

**Collage** Cut up, Paste up

**Collapse, Collapsing** Apoplexy, Breakdown, Buckle, Burn out, Cave, Conk, Crash, Crumble, Crumple, Debacle, Deflate, Disintegrate, Downfall, Fail(ure), Fall (in), Flake out, Fold, Founder, Give, Go phut, Implode, Inburst, Landslide, Meltdown, Phut, Purler, Rack, Rickety, Rockfall, Rot, Ruin, Scat(ter), Sink, Slump, Snap, Stroke, Subside, Sunstroke, Swoon, Telescope, Tumble, →**TUMBLEDOWN**, Wilt, Wrack, Zonk

▷ **Collapsing** *may indicate* an anagram

**Collar(ed)** Arrest, Astrakhan, Band, Bermuda, Bertha, Berthe, Bib, Bishop, Blue, Brecham, Buster, Butterfly, Button-down, Buttonhole, Capture, Carcanet, Chevesaile, Choke(r), Clerical, Collet, Dog, Esses, Eton, Falling-band, Flea, Gorget, Grandad, Hame, Head(stall), Holderbat, Horse, Jabot, Jampot, Karenni, Lapel, Mandarin, Moran, Mousquetaire, Nab, Nail, Neckband, Necklet, Ox-bow, Peter Pan, Piccadell, Piccadillo, Piccadilly, Pikadell, Pinch, Pink, Polo, Puritan, Rabaline, Rabato, Rebater, Rebato, Revers, Rollneck, Roman, Romance, Ruff, Sailor, Seize, Shawl, Steel, Storm, Tackle, Tappet, Tie-neck, Torque, Turndown, Turtleneck, Vandyke, Whisk, White, Wing, Yoke

**Collarbone** Clavicle

**Collation** Comparison, Meal, Repast

**Colleague(s)** Accomplice, Ally, Associate, Bedfellow, Co-host, Confrère, Fellow, Mate, Mentor, Oppo, Partner, Sociate, Team mate, Workmate

**Collect(ion), Collectable, Collected, Collective(ly), Collectivism, Collector** Accrue, Agglomerate, Aggregate, Album, Alms, Amass, Amildar, Ana, Anthology, Arcana, Artel, Assemble, Aumil, Bank, Bow, Budget, Bunch, Bundle, Burrell, Bygones, Caboodle, Calm, Cap, Cete, Clan, Clowder, Compendium, Compile, Composed, Congeries, Conglomerate, Cool-headed, Covey, Cull, Dossier, Dustman, Earn, Egger, Exaltation, Exordial, Eyrie, Farrago, Fest, (Fest)schrift, Fetch, Fleet, Florilegium, Gaggle, Garbo, Garner, Gather, Get, Gilbert, Glean, Glossary, Grice, Harvest, Heap, Herd, Hive, Idant, In all, Jingbang, Job lot, Kit, Kitty, Levy, Library, Loan, Magpie, Meal, Meet, Meinie, Mein(e)y, Menagerie, Menyie, Miscellany, Mish-mash, Montem, Munro-bagger, Murmuration, Museum, Muster, Nide, Offertory, Olio, Omnibus, Omnium-gatherum, Pack, Paddling, Pile, Plate, Pod, Poor box, Post, Poste restante, Prayer, Quest, Raft, Ragbag, Raise, Rammle, Recheat, Rhapsody, Rouleau, Sangfroid, Scramble, Sedge, Self-possessed, Serene, Set, Shoe, Siege, Skein, Smytrie, Sord, Sottisier, Sounder, Spring, Stand, Tahsildar, Team, Together, Toolkit, Tronc, Troop, Ujamaa, Unkindness, Uplift, Watch, Wernher, Whipround, Wisp

▷ **Collection** *may indicate* an anagram

**Collection-box** Brod, Ladle, Rammle

**Collectorate** Taluk

**College(s)** Academy, All Souls, Alma mater, Ampleforth, Balliol, Brasenose, Business, C, Caius, Campus, CAT, Cheltenham, Clare, Classical, Coed, Commercial, Community, Conservatoire, Corpus (Christi), Cow, Cranwell, Downing, Dulwich, Electoral, Emmanuel, Eton, Exeter, Foundation, Freshwater, Girton, Grande école, Hall, Heralds', Institute, Institution, Ivy League, Jail, Junior, Keble, King's, Lancing, Linacre, Lincoln, LSE, Lycée, Lyceum, Madras(s)a(h), Madressah, Magdalen(e), Marlborough, Medrese, Medresseh, Merton, Newnham, Nuffield, Open, Oriel, Pembroke, Poly, Polytechnic, Pontifical, Protonotariat, Queen's, Ruskin, Sacred, St Johns, Saliens, Sandhurst, Selwyn, Seminary, Sixth-form, Somerville, Sorbonne, Staff, Tech(nical), Technikon, Tertiary, Theologate, Training, Trinity, Tug, UMIST, Up, Village, Wadham, Winchester, Yeshiva(h)

**Collide(r), Collision** Afoul, Barge, Bird-strike, Bump, Cannon, Carom(bole), Clash, Conflict, Dash, Elastic, Fender-bender, Foul, Hadron, Head-on, Hurtle, Impact, Inelastic, Into, Kiss, Meet, Pile-up, Prang, Ram, Rencounter, Smash-up, Strike, Thwack

**Collie** Bearded, Border, Dog, Kelpie, Kelpy, Rough, Sheepdog
**Collier** Geordie, Hoastman, Miner, Necklace, Patience, Ship
**Colloid** Aerogel, Gel, Lyophil(e), Sol, Suspensoid
**Collops** Scotch
**Collude, Collusive** Abet, Cahoots, Conspire, Deceive
**Colon** Aspinwall, C(a)ecum, Sigmoid, Spastic, Transverse
**Colonel** Bird, Blimp, Bogey, Chinstrap, Col, Everard, Goldstick, Newcome, Nissen, Pride
**Colonial(ist), Colonist** Ant, Antenatal, Bee, Boer, Creole, Emigré, Goan, Oecist, Oikist, Overseas, Phoenician, Pioneer, Planter, Polyp(e), Settler, Sicel(iot), Sikel(ian), Sikeliot, Stuyvesant, Swarm, Territorial, Voter, Wasp
**Colonnade** Ar(a)eostyle, Eustyle, File, Gallery, Peristyle, Porch, Portico, Stoa
**Colony** Acadia, Aden, Bermuda, Burkina Faso, Cape, Charter, Cleruchy, Crown, Dependency, Elea, Gibraltar, Halicarnassian, Heronry, Hive, Hongkong, Kaffraria, Nudist, Penal, Plymouth, Presidio, Proprietary, Rookery, Senegal, Settlement, Swarm, Termitarium, Warren, Zambia, Zimbabwe
**Colophony** Roset, Rosin
**Colossal** →ENORMOUS, Epochal, Gigantic, Huge, Vast
**Colosseum** Amphitheatre
**Colossus** Eten, Ettin
**Colour(ed), Colouring, Colours** Achromatic, Bedye, Blanco, Blee, Blush, C, Cap, Chromatic, Chrome, Complementary, Complexion, Crayon, Criant, Cross, Distort, Dye, False, Film, Flag, Florid, Flying, Garble, Gouache, Haem, →HUE, Imbue, Ink, Irised, Kalamkari, Leer, Livor, Local, Lutein, Metif, Nankeen, Opalescence, Orpiment, Palette, Pantone®, Pastel, Pied, Pigment, Pochoir, Polychrome, Primary, Prism, Prismatic, Process, Queen's, Raddle, Reddle, Regimental, Rinse, Riot, Ruddle, Secondary, Sematic, Shade, Shot, Slant, Solid, Spectrum, Stain, Startle, Tertiary, Tie-dye, Tinc(ture), Tinctorial, Tinge, Tint, Tone, Uvea, Wash

## COLOURS

| | | | |
|---|---|---|---|
| **2 letters:** | Navy | Gules | Auburn |
| Or | Pink | Ivory | Bisque |
| | Plum | Khaki | Bister |
| **3 letters:** | Puce | Lemon | Bistre |
| Bay | Puke | Lilac | Cerise |
| Dun | Roan | Liver | Day-Glo® |
| Jet | Rose | Lovat | Isabel |
| Red | Ruby | Mauve | Madder |
| Tan | Sand | Ocher | Maroon |
| | Sloe | Ochre | Orange |
| **4 letters:** | Teal | Olive | Reseda |
| Anil | Vert | Peach | Roucou |
| Aqua | Woad | Pearl | Sienna |
| Bice | | Rouge | Sludge |
| Blue | **5 letters:** | Sepia | Titian |
| Buff | Amber | Slate | Tusser |
| Cyan | Beige | Taupe | |
| Ecru | Camel | Tenné | **7 letters:** |
| Fawn | Chica | Tenny | Annatta |
| Gold | Coral | Umber | Annatto |
| Grey | Cream | | Apricot |
| Jade | Eosin | **6 letters:** | Arnotto |
| Lake | Flame | Anatta | Caramel |
| Lime | Green | Anatto | Crimson |

| | 8 letters: | 9 letters: | Tartrazine |
|---|---|---|---|
| Emerald | Alizarin | Alizarine | Vermillion |
| Filemot | Burgundy | Anthocyan | |
| Gamboge | Cardinal | Carnation | 11 letters: |
| Indulin | Chestnut | Chocolate | Burnt sienna |
| Magenta | Cinnamon | Indigotin | Ultramarine |
| Melanin | Eau de nil | Olive drab | |
| Oatmeal | Gunmetal | Royal blue | 12 letters: |
| Old gold | Isabella | Solferino | Cappagh-brown |
| Old rose | Lavender | Turquoise | Dragon's blood |
| Oxblood | Off-white | Vermilion | |
| Saffron | Pea-green | | 19 letters: |
| Scarlet | Philamot | 10 letters: | Thunder and |
| Umbrage | Philomot | Aquamarine | Lightning |
| Vermeil | Raw umber | Burnt umber | |
| Xanthin | Santalin | French navy | |

**Colour blindness** Daltonism, Deuteranopia, Dichrom(at)ism, Monochromatic, Protanomaly, Protanopia, Protanopic, Tritanopia

▷ **Coloured** *may indicate* an anagram

**Colourful** Abloom, Brave, Exotic, Flamboyant, Flowery, Gay, Iridescent, Kaleidoscope, Opalescent, Showy, Splashy, Vivid

**Colourless** Albino, Bleak, Drab, Dull, Faded, Flat, Hyalite, Pallid, Pallor, Wan, White

**Colour-spot** Gutta

**Colt** C, Cade, Foal, Gun, Hogget, Sta(i)g, Teenager, Two-year-old

**Columbine** Aquilegia

**Column(s), Column foot** Agony, Anta, Architrave, Atlantes, Clustered, Commentary, Control, Corinthian, Correspondence, Cylinder, Decastyle, Diastyle, Distillation, Doric, Editorial, Eustyle, Fifth, File, Flying, Fractionating, Geological, Gossip, Hypostyle, Impost, Lat, Lonelyhearts, Monolith, Nelson's, Newel, Notochord, Obelisk, Pedestal, Pericycle, Peripteral, Peristyle, Persian, Personal, Pilaster, →**PILLAR**, Pilotis, Plume, Prostyle, Pycnostyle, Rachis, Rouleau, Row, Sheet pile, Short, Spina, Spinal, Spine, Stalactite, Stalagmite, Steering, Stylobate, Systyle, Tabulate, Telamone, Third, Tige, Tore, Torus, Trajan's, Vertebral

**Columnist** Advertiser, Agony aunt, Caryatid, Newsman, Stylite, Telamon, Writer

**Coma(tose)** Apoplexy, Crown, Sedated, Sleep, Torpor, Trance

**Comb(er), Combed, Combing** Afro, Alveolate, Beehive, Breaker, Card, Copple, Crest, Ctenoid, Curry, Dredge, Fine-tooth, Hackle, Heckle, Hot, Kaim, Kame, Kangha, Kemb, Noils, Parter, Pecten, Pectinal, Rake, Rat-tail, Red(d), Ripple(r), Rose, Scribble, Search, Side, Small tooth, Smooth, Tease(l), Toaze, Tose, Toze, Trawl, Tuft, Wave

**Combat(ant), Combative** Adversarial, Agonistic, Argument, Batteilant, →**BATTLE**, Bolshie, Bolshy, Bullfight, Bullring, Competitor, Conflict, Contest, Dispute, Duel, →**FIGHT**, Gladiator, Joust, Judicial, Jujitsu, Just, Karate, Kendo, Krav mega, List, Mêlée, Militant, Oppose, Paintball, Protagonist, Spear-running, Unarmed, Veteran, War

**Combe** Hope

**Combination, Combine(d), Combining** Accrete, Aggregate, Alligate, Ally, Amalgam, Associate, Axis, Bloc, Cartel, Cleave, Clique, Coalesce, Coalition, Composite, Concert, Concoction, Conflated, Conglomerate, Consolidate, Consortium, Coordinate, Crasis, Fuse, Group, Harvester, Incorporate, Integration, Interfile, Join, Junta, Kartell, League, Meld, Merge(r), Mingle, Mixture, Monogram, Motor cycle, One, Perm(utation), Piece, Pool, Quill, Ring, Solvate, Splice, Syncretize, Synthesis, Terrace, Trivalent, Trona, Unify, Unite, Valency, Wed, Zaibatsu

**Comb-like** Ctenoid, Pecten

**Combustible, Combustion** Air-gas, Ardent, Fiery, Inflammable, Phlogistic, Phlogiston, Spontaneous, Tinder, Wildfire

▷ **Combustible** *may indicate* an anagram

**Come, Coming (back), Coming out** Accrue, Advent, Anear, Anon, Appear, Approach, Ar(r), Arise, Arrive, Attend, Debouch, Derive, Emanate, Emerge, Future, Happen, Iceman, In store, Issue, Millenarian, Orgasm, Parousia, Pass, Pop, Reach, Respond, Second, Via

**Come again** Eh

**Comeback** Boomerang, Bounce, Echo, Homer, Quip, Rally, Rearise, Rebound, Recovery, Repartee, Reply, Reprisal, Response, Retort, Retour, Return, Reversion, Riposte

**Come by** Obtain

**Comedian** Benny, Buffoon, Chaplin, →CLOWN, Comic, Durante, Emery, Farceur, Gagman, Goon, Groucho, Hardy, Harpo, Hope, Joe Miller, Joker, Jokesmith, Karno, Keaton, Laurel, Leno, Punster, Quipster, Riot, Robey, Scream, Screwball, Stand-up, Starr, Tate, Tati, Tummler, Wag, Wise, Witcracker, Yell

**Comedo** Blackhead

**Comedown** Avale, Bathetic, Bathos, Crash landing, Disappointment, Drop, Letdown, Shower

**Comedy** Alternative, Black, Blackadder, Com, Custard-pie, Drama, Ealing, Errors, Farce, High, Humour, Improv(ised), Keystone, Knockabout, Lazzo, Low, Millamant, Musical, Romantic, Romcom, Screwball, Sitcom, Situation, Slapstick, Stand-up, Thalia, Travesty

**Comely, Comeliness** Beseen, Bonny, Fair, Goodly, Graceful, Jolly, Likely, Looks, Pleasing, Pretty, Proper

**Comestible(s)** Cate, Eats, Fare

**Comet** Chiron, Geminid, Halley's, Kohoutek, Meteor, Oort cloud, Reindeer, Shoemaker-Levy 9, Vomet, Xiphias

**Come through** Weather

**Come to** Cost, Wake(n)

**Come-uppance** Downfall

**Comfort(able), Comforter, Comforting, Comfy** Affluent, Amenity, Analeptic, Armchair, Balm, Bein, Bildad, Calm, Canny, Cheer, Cherish, Cherry, Clover, Cocoon, Cold, Consolation, Console, Convenience, Cose, Cosh, Cosy, Couthie, Couthy, Creature, Crumb, Cushy, Dummy, Dutch, Ease, Easy, Eliphaz, Featherbed, Gemutlich, Heeled, Homely, Homy, Hottie, Job's, Legroom, Luxury, Mumsy, Noah, Plum, Plushy, Reassure, Relaxed, Relief, Relieve, Rosewater, Rug, Scarf, Sinecure, Snug, Solace, Soothe, Stay, Succour, There, Tosh, Trig, Warm, Wealthy, Well, Well-to-do, Zofar, Zophar

**Comic(al)** Beano, Buff, Buffo(on), Bumpkin, Buster, Chaplin, Clown, →COMEDIAN, Dandy, Drag, Droll, Eagle, Emery, Facetious, Fields, →FUNNY, Gagster, Hardy, Horror, Humorist, Jester, Knock-about, Laurel, Leno, Mag, Manga, Quizzical, Rich, Robey, Stand up, Strip, Tati, Trial, Wag, Zany

**Comma** Inverted, Oxford

**Command(eer), Commanding, Commandment(s)** About face, Attention, Behest, Bid, Categorical imperative, Charge, Coerce, Control, Decalogue, Declare, Direct, Direction, Dominate, Domineer, Easy, Edict, Expertise, Fiat, Fiaunt, Fighter, Firman, Grip, Haw, Hest, High, Hijack, Imperious, Impress, Injunction, Instruction, Jussive, Lead, Magisterial, Mandate, Maritime, Mastery, Mitzvah, Mobile, Obtest, →ORDER, Peremptory, Precept, Press, Query language, Requisition, Rule, Seize, Shun, Ukase, Warn, Warrant, Will, Wish, Writ

**Commander** Admiral, Ag(h)a, Agamemnon, Ameer, Barleycorn, Bey, Bloke, Blucher, Boss, Brennus, Brig, Caliph, Centurion, Cid, Decurion, Dreyfus, Emir, Emperor, Encomendero, Exon, Field cornet, Garibaldi, Generalissimo, Hetman, Hipparch, Imperator, Killadar, Kitchener, Leader, Manager, Marshal, Master, Meer, Mir, Moore, Mr Big, Officer, Overlord, Pendragon, Polemarch, Pr(a)efect, Raglan, Seraskier, Shogun, Sirdar, Supreme, Taxiarch, Trierarch, Turcopolier, Vaivode, Voivode, Waivode, Warlord, Wing

**Commando** Chindit(s), Fedayee(n), Green Beret, Raider, Ranger, SAS

**Commemorate, Commemoration** Encaenia, Epitaph, Eulogy, Keep, Memorial, Month's mind, Monument, Plaque, Remember, Saint's day, Trophy, Year's mind

**Commence** Begin, Initiate, Open, Start

**Commend(ation)** Applaud, Approval, Approve, Belaud, Bestow, Cite, Encomium, Entrust, Epitaph, Laud, Mooi, Panegyric, → PRAISE, Roose, Tribute

**Commensal** Epizoon, Messmate

**Commensurate** Adequate, Enough, Equivalent, Relevant

**Comment(ary), Commentator** Analyst, Animadvert, Annotate, Apercu, Barb, Comm, Coryphaeus, Coverage, Critic, Critique, Descant, Discuss, Editorial, Essay, Exegete, Explain, Exposition, Expound, Fair, Footnote, Gemara, Gloss(ographer), Glossator, Glosser, Hakam, Kibitz, Margin, Marginalia, Midrash(im), Narration, Noise, Note, Obiter dictum, Observation, Par, Platitude, Play-by-play, Postil, Remark, Rider, Running, Scholiast, Scholion, Scholium, Sidenote, Voice-over, Zohar

**Commerce, Commercial** Ad, Adland, Barter, Business, Cabotage, Jingle, Marketable, Mercantile, Mercenary, Merchant, Retail, Shoppy, Simony, Tele-ad, Trade, Traffic, Wholesale

**Commercial traveller** Drummer, Rep

**Commiserate, Commiseration** Compassion, Pity, Sympathise

**Commissar** People's, Political

**Commission(er), Commissioned** Agio, Audit, Authorise, Bonus, Boundary, Brevet, Brokage, Brokerage, Charge, Charity, Competition, Contango, Contract, Countryside, Delegation, Depute, ECE, Employ, Engage, Envoy, Errand, European, Factor, Gosplan, High, Husbandage, Interpol, Job, Kickback, Law, Magistrate, Mandate, Office(r), Official, Ombudsman, Order, Oyer and terminer, Percentage, Perpetration, Place, Poundage, Price, Rake-off, Resident, Roskill, Roving, Royal, Shroffage, Task, Task force, Trust, Wreck

**Commit(tal), Committed, Commitment** Allegiance, Aret(t), Consign, Contract, Decision, Dedication, Delegate, Devotion, Devout, Do, Engage, Entrust, Enure, Impeachment, Paid up, Perpetrate, Pledge, Position, Promise, Rubicon, Staunch, Toe

**Committee** ACRE, Audit, Board, Body, Cabinet, COBR(A), Collegium, Commission, Commune, Council, Delegacy, Group, Hanging, Joint, Junta, Politburo, Presidium, Propaganda, Review body, Riding, Samiti, School, Select, Standing, Steering, Syndicate, Table, Think tank, Vigilance, Watch, Ways and means, Works

**Commode, Commodious** Ample, Closestool, Roomy, Spacious

**Commodities, Commodity** Article, Futures, Gapeseed, Goods, Item, Physicals, Soft, Staple, Ware

**Common(ly), Commoner, Commons** Alike, As per usual, Average, Cad, Cheap, Clapham, Conventional, Diet, Dirt, Doctor's, Ealing, Eatables, Enclosure, Endemic, Epicene, Everyday, Familiar, Fare, Folk, Frequent, General, Green, Greenham, Gutterblood, House, Law, Lay, Low, Lower House, Mark, Mere, MP, Mutual, Naff, Non-U, Normal, People, Pleb, Plebe(i)an, Prevalent, Prole, Public, Ragtag, Related, Rife, Roturier, Ryfe, Scran, Sense, Shared, Stock, Stray, Tarty, The mob, Tie, Tiers d'état, Trite, Tritical, Tuft, Two-a-penny, Tye, Use, → USUAL, Vile, Vul(gar), Vulgo, Vulgus, Widespread, Wimbledon, Working-class

**Commonplace** Adversarian, Banal, Copybook, Dime-a-dozen, Dreary, Everyday, Hackneyed, Homely, Humdrum, Idée reçue, Mot, Ordinary, Pedestrian, Philistine, Plain, Platitude, Prosaic, Quotidian, Trite, Truism, Workaday

**Commonsense** Gumption, Mother wit, Nous, Savoir-faire, Smeddum, Wit

**Commonwealth** Protectorate, Puerto Rico, Res publica

**Commotion** Babel, Bluster, Brouhaha, Bustle, Carfuffle, Clangour, Clatter, Curfuffle, Dirdam, Dirdum, Do, Dust, Ferment, Flap, Flurry, Fraise, Furore, Fuss, Hell, Hoo-ha(h), Hullabaloo, Hurly-burly, Hurry, Kerfuffle, Pother, Pudder, Racket, Rattlebags, Romage, Rort, Ruckus, Ruction, Rumpus, Shemozzle, Shindig, Shindy, Shivaree, Steer(y), Stir, Stirabout, Storm, Stushie, Tirrivee, Tirrivie, To-do, Toss, Tumult, Turmoil, Upheaval, Uproar, Whirl, Wroth

**Communal, Commune** Agapemone, Collective, Com, Meditate, Menage, Mir, Paris, Phalanstery, Public, Talk, Township

**Communicate, Communication** Ampex, Anastomosis, Announce, Appui, Aviso, Baud, Bluetooth, Boyau, Braille, Cable, Cellnet, Channelling, Citizen's band, Conversation, Convey, Cybernetic, E-mail, ESP, Expansive, Exude, Impart, Infobahn, Inform, Infrastructure, Intelpost, Intelsat, Internet, Liaison, Lifeline, Memoranda, Message, Mime, Multichannel, Multimedia, Nonverbal, Note, Open letter, Oracy, Oralism, Paralanguage, Prayer, Prestel®, Proxemics, Put across, Reach, Reportage, Revelation, Road, Semaphore, Semiotics, Signal, Sitrep, Syncom, Talkback, Tannoy®, Telecom, Telepathy, Telephony, Teletex, Telex, Telstar, Tieline, Transmit, Utraquist, Viewdata, Webmail, Wire, Word of mouth

**Communion** Creed, Fellowship, Host, Housel, Intinction, Lord's Supper, Species, Viaticum

**Communiqué** Announcement, Statement

**Communism, Communist** Apparat(chik), Aspheterism, Bolshevist, Brook Farm, Cadre, Castroism, Com, Comecon, Cominform, Comintern, Commo, Comsomol, Deviationist, Engels, Essene, Fourier, Fraction, Khmer Rouge, Komsomol, Leninite, Maoist, Marxist, Menshevist, Nomenklatura, Ossi, Perfectionist, Pinko, Politburo, Populist, Red (Guard), Revisionism, Second World, Soviet, Spartacist, Stalinism, Tanky, Titoist, Trot, Vietcong, Vietminh

**Communities, Community** Agapemone, Alterne, Ashram, Association, Biome, Body, Brook Farm, Brotherhood, Clachan, Climax, Closed, Coenobitism, Coenobium, Colonia, Colony, Consocies, Constituency, District, EC, Ecosystem, EEC, Enclave, Etat, Ethnic, European, Faith, Frat(e)ry, Gated, Global, Hamlet, Kahal, Kibbutz, Mesarch, Mir, Neighbourhood, Pantisocracy, People, Phalanx, Phyle, Preceptory, Public, Pueblo, Republic, Sarvodaya, Seral, Sere, Settlement, Shtetl, Sisterhood, Sociation, Society, Speech, Street, Toon, Town, Tribe, Ujamaa, Ummah, Village, Virtual, Volost, Zupa

**Commute(r)** Change, Convert, Reduce, Shuttle, Standee, Straphanger, Travel

**Como** Lake, Perry

**Compact** Accord, Agreement, Bargain, Cement, Centralise, Concise, Conglobe, Covenant, Covin, Coyne, Dense, Entente, Fast, Firm, Flapjack, Hard, Knit, League, Match, Neat, Pledge, Powder, Solid, Tamp, Terse, Tight, Treaty, Well-knit

**Companion(able)** Achates, Arm candy, Associate, Attender, Barnacle, Bedfellow, Bonhomie, Brolga, Bud(dy), Butty, CH, China, Comate, Compadre, Compeer, Compotator, Comrade, Consort, Contubernal, Crony, Cupman, Duenna, Ephesian, Escort, Feare, Felibre, → **FELLOW**, Fere, Franion, Furked, Handbook, Helpmate, Man Friday, Mate, Native, Oliver, Pal, Pard, Pheer(e), Playmate, Pot, Roland, Shadow, Sidekick, Skaines mate, Stable, Stablemate, Thane, Thegn, Trojan, Vade-mecum, Wag, Walker

**Company, Companies** Actors, Along, Artel, Ass, Assembly, Band, Bank, Battalion, Bevy, Brigade, → **BUSINESS**, Bv, Cahoot, Cartel, Cast, Cavalcade, Chartered, Chirm, CIA, Circle, City, Close, Club, Co, Conger, Consort, Cordwainers, Core, Corporation, Corps, Coy, Crew, Crowd, Crue, Decury, Dotcom, East India, Enterprise, Entourage, Faction, Finance, Fire, → **FIRM**, Flock, Free, Gang, Garrison, Ging, Guild, Haberdashers, Heap, Holding, Hudson's Bay, ICI, Inc, Indie, In-house, Intercourse, Investment, Jingbang, Joint-stock, Limited, Listed, Livery, Management, Maniple, Muster, Order, Organisation, Parent, Plc, Present, Pride, Private, Public, Public limited, Push, Quoted, Rep(ertory), Room, SA, Sedge, Set, Set out, Shell, Siege, Sort, SpA, Stationers', Stock, Studio, Subsidiary, Syndicate, Table, Team, Thiasus, Touring, Troop, Troupe, Trust, Twa, Two(some), UPS, Visitor, White, Yfere

**Compare(d), Comparable, Comparison** Analogy, Balance, Beside, Bracket, Collate, Confront, Contrast, Correspond, Cp, Equate, Liken, Match, Odious, Parallel, Relation, Similar, Simile, Synonymous, Weigh

**Compartment** Alcove, Ballonet, Bay, Booth, Box, Cab, Carriage, Casemate, Cell, Chamber, Cockpit, Cofferdam, Cubbyhole, Cubicle, Dog box, Glove, Locellate, Locker,

Loculament, Loculus, Pane, Panel, Partition, Pigeonhole, Pocket, Pod, Room(ette),
Severy, Sleeper, Smoker, Stall, Till, Trunk, Watertight, Wind chest

**Compass** Ambit, Area, Beam, Binnacle, Bounds, Bow, Dividers, Extent, Gamut,
Goniometer, Gyro, Gyromagnetic, Gyroscope, Infold, Magnetic, Mariner's, Needle, Orbit,
Pelorus, Pencil, Perimeter, Prismatic, Radio, →**RANGE**, Reach, Rhumb, Room, Scale,
Sweep, Tessitura, Trammel, Width

**Compassion(ate)** Aroha, Bleed(ing), Clemency, Commiseration, Empathy, Goodwill,
Heart, Humane, Kindliness, Kuan Yin, Kwan Yin, Loving kindness, Mercy, Pity, Remorse,
Samaritan, Sympathy, Tender, Ubuntu

**Compatible** Consistent, Fit, Harmonious

**Compatriot** National

**Compel(ling), Compelled, Compulsion, Compulsive, Compulsory** Addiction,
Coact, Coerce, Cogent, Command, Constrain, Dragoon, Driving, Duress, Enforce, Exact,
Extort, Fain, →**FORCE**, Force majeure, Gar, Habit-forming, Hypnotic, Insistent, Make,
Mandatory, Obligate, Oblige, Pathological, Steamroller, Strongarm, Tyrannise, Urge,
Walk Spanish

**Compendium** Breviate

**Compensate, Compensation** Amend(s), Balance, Boot, Bote, Comp, Consideration,
Counterbalance, Counterpoise, Damages, Demurrage, Guerdon, Indemnity, Offset,
Payment, Recoup, Redeem, Redress, Reparation, Reprisal, Requital, Restitution, Restore,
Retaliation, Salvage, Satisfaction, Solatium, Wergild, X-factor

**Compère** Disc jockey, Emcee, Host, MC, Presenter

**Compete** Contend, Dog eat dog, Emulate, Enter, Match, Outvie, Play, Rival, Run, Vie

**Competence, Competent** Ability, Able, Adequate, Can, Capable, Capacity, Dab, Dow,
Efficient, Fit, Proficient, Responsible, Sui juris, Worthy

**Competition, Competitive, Competitor** Agonist, Antitrust, Arch rival, Autotest,
Backmarker, Battle, Bee, Biathlon, Buckjumping, Candidate, Checks and balances,
Comper, Concours, Contender, Contention, Contest, Cook off, Cup, Dog eat dog, Drive,
Entrant, Entry, Event, Field, Finals, Freestyle, Gamesman, Grand prix, Gymkhana,
Head over heels, Head-to-head, Heptathlon, Imperfect, Iron woman, Judoka, Jump
off, Karateka, Keen, Knockout, Match, Match-play, Monopolistic, Olympiad, Open,
Opponent, Outsider, Pairs, Panellist, Pentathlon, Perfect, Player, Pools, Premiership,
Pro-am, Puissance, Race, Rally, Rat race, Regatta, Repechage, Rival(ise), Rodeo, Run,
Runner-up, Show-jumping, Slam, Spelldown, Sporty, Stableford, Starter, Super G,
Tenson, Test, Three-day event, Tiger, Tournament, Tourney, Track meet, Trial, Triallist,
Wap(p)enshaw, Wild card

**Compile(r), Compilation** Anthology, Arrange, Collect, Cross, Doxographer, Edit,
Prepare, Segue, Setter, Synthesis, Zadkiel

**Complacent** Babbitt, Fatuous, Joco, Pleasant, Self-satisfied, Smug

**Complain(t), Complainer** Ache, Acne, Adenoids, Affection, Affliction, Alas, Alastrim,
Alopecia, Anaemia, Angashore, Angina, Anorexia, Arthritis, Asthma, Barrack, Beef,
Bellyache, Bewail, Bitch, Bleat, BSE, Carp, Cavil, Charge, Chorea, Colic, Crab, Cramp,
Criticise, Croup, Diatribe, Disorder, Distemper, Dropsy, Epidemic, Ergot, Exanthema,
Fever, Girn, Gout, Gravamen, Grievance, Gripe, Groan, Grouch, Grouse, Growl, Grudge,
Grumble, Grutch, Harangue, Hives, Hone, Hypochondria, Ileitis, →**ILLNESS**, Jeremiad,
King's evil, Kvetch, Lament, Lumbago, Lupus, Malady, Mange, Mean(e), Mein, Mene,
Moan, Morphew, Mump(s), Murmur, Nag, Natter, Neuralgia, Ologoan, Orchitis, Peeve,
Peritonitis, Pertussis, Plica, Poor-mouth, Protest, Pule, Pyelitis, Querimony, Quibble,
Rail, Remonstrate, Repine, Report, Rhinitis, Rickets, Ringworm, Sapego, Sciatica, Scold,
Scream, Sequacious, Sigh, Silicosis, Snivel, Squawk, Squeal, Staggers, Tennis Elbow,
Thrush, Tic, Tinea, Upset, Wheenge, Whimper, Whine, Whinge, Yammer, Yaup, Yawp

**Complaisant** Agreeable, Flexible, Suave, Supple

**Complement(ary)** Alexin, Amount, Balance, Biota, Esteemed, Finish, Freebie, Gang,
Glowing, Lot, Obverse, Reciprocate

▷ **Complement** *may indicate* a hidden word

**Complete(d), Completely, Completion** Absolute, Accomplish, Achieve, All, Altogether, Arrant, Attain, Clean, Congenital, Consummate, Crashing, Crown, Dead, Do, Downright, End, Entire, Finalise, Finish, Flat, Follow through, Foregone, Fruition, Fulfil, Full, Full-blown, Head over heels, Hollow, Incept, Integral, In toto, Neck and crop, One, Ouroboros, Out, Out and out, Perfect, Plenary, Plum, Prolative, Pure, Quite, Radical, Rank, Ready, Root and branch, Rounded, Self-contained, Sew-up, Sheer, Spang, Sum, Teetotal, Thorough(going), Total, Unabridged, Unanimous, Unbroken, Uncensored, Uncut, Unequivocal, Unmitigated, Utter, Whole (hog), Wrap

**Complex(ity)** Abstruse, Advanced, Arcane, Castration, Compound, Daedal, Developed, Difficult, Electra, Fancy, Golgi, Hard, Heath Robinson, Immune, Inferiority, Intricate, Intrince, Involute, Knot, Manifold, Megalopolis, MHC, Military-industrial, Mixed, Multinucleate, Nest, Network, Obsession, Oedipus, Overwrought, Paranoid, Persecution, Phaedra, Plexiform, Ramification, Subtle, Superiority, Syndrome, System, Tangle, Thick, Web

**Complexion** Aspect, Blee, Hue, Leer, Permatan, Temper, Tint, View

**Compliance, Compliant, Comply** Abet, Agree, Amenable, Assent, Aye-aye, Conform, Deference, Docile, Follow, Hand-in-glove, Obedience, Obey, Observe, Obtemper, Orchitis, Plastic, Sequacious, Surrender, Wilco, Yield

**Complicate(d), Complication** Bewilder, Complex, Deep, Elaborate, Embroil, Entangle, Implex, Intricate, Involution, Involve, Inweave, Knot, Node, Nodus, Perplex, Ramification, Rigmarole, Sequela, Snarl, Tangle, Tirlie-wirlie, Tricky

▷ **Complicated** *may indicate* an anagram

**Compliment(s), Complimentary** Backhanded, Baisemain, Bouquet, Congratulate, Devoirs, Douceur, Encomium, Esteemed, Flatter, Flummery, Freebie, Glowing, Greetings, Left-handed, Praise, Soap, Trade-last, Tribute

**Component(s)** Base, Capacitor, Cat's whisker, Coherer, Con-rod, Constituent, Contact, CRT, Daisy-wheel, Element, Factor, Formant, Guidance, Hygristor, Impedor, Inductor, Ingredient, Item, Longeron, Member, Module, → **PART**, Partial, Piece, Pixel, Pre-amp, Profile, Pushrod, Reactance, Resistor, Subunit, Tape drive, Tensor, Touchstone, Unit

**Comportment** Behaviour

**Compose(d), Composure** Aplomb, Appeased, Arrange, Calm, Choreograph, Collected, Consist, Cool, → **CREATE**, Equable, Equanimity, Equilibrium, Even, Face, Improvise, Indite, Level-headed, Lull, Notate, Orchestrate, Patience, Pen, Phlegm, Placid, Poise, Produce, Reconcile, Sangfroid, Score, Sedate, Serenity, Settle, Soothe, Thorough, Tranquil, Unruffled, Write

**Composer** Contrapunt(al)ist, Hymnist, Inditer, Inventor, Maker, Melodist, Minimalist, Musician, Musicker, → **POET**, Psalmist, Serialist, Six, Songsmith, Songwriter, Symphonist, Triadist, Troubadour, Tunesmith, Writer

---

## COMPOSERS

| 3 letters: | Byrd | Wolf | Boyce |
|---|---|---|---|
| Bax | Cage | | Brian |
| | Dima | 5 letters: | Bruch |
| 4 letters: | Graf | Alwyn | Crumb |
| Adam | Ives | Auber | D'Indy |
| Arne | Kern | Auric | Dukas |
| Bach | Lalo | Balfe | Dupre |
| Bart | Monk | Berio | Elgar |
| Berg | Nono | Bizet | Falla |
| Blow | Orff | Bliss | Fauré |
| Brel | Peri | Bloch | Field |
| Bull | Raff | Boito | Finzi |

Glass
Gluck
Grieg
Harty
Haydn
Henze
Holst
Ibert
Lasso
Lehar
Liszt
Loewe
Lully
Nyman
Ogdon
Parry
Prout
Ravel
Reger
Rossi
Satie
Sousa
Spohr
Suppe
Tosti
Verdi
Watts
Weber
Weill
Zappa

**6 letters:**
Alfven
Arnold
Azione
Barber
Bartók
Bennet
Berlin
Boulez
Brahms
Bridge
Burney
Busoni
Chopin
Coates
Czerny
Delius
Duparc
Dvorák
Flotow
Franck
German
Glière

Glinka
Gounod
Handel
Hummel
Joplin
Kodaly
Lassus
Ligeti
Mahler
Martin
Mingus
Morley
Mozart
Ogolon
Parker
Pierne
Porter
Rameau
Rubbra
Schutz
Tallis
Varese
Wagner
Waller
Walton
Webern

**7 letters:**
Albeniz
Alberti
Allegri
Amadeus
Babbitt
Bantock
Bellini
Bennett
Berlioz
Berners
Borodin
Britten
Brubeck
Christy
Copland
Corelli
Debussy
De Falla
Delibes
Dohnany
Dowland
Durufle
Gibbons
Ireland
Janácek
Lambert

Lilburn
Mancini
Martinu
Menotti
Milhaud
Nicolai
Nielsen
Novello
Ormandy
Poulenc
Puccini
Purcell
Purnell
Quilter
Rodgers
Rodrigo
Romberg
Rossini
Roussel
Salieri
Smetana
Stainer
Strauss
Tartini
Tavener
Tippett
Vivaldi
Warlock
Xenakis
Youmans

**8 letters:**
Alaleona
Albinoni
Anderson
Boughton
Bruckner
Chabrier
Chausson
Cimarosa
Coltrane
Couperin
Elementi
Gabrieli
Gershwin
Gesualdo
Glazunov
Grainger
Granados
Honegger
Korngold
Kreutzer
Marcello
Mascagni

Massenet
Messager
Messiaen
Paganini
Respighi
Schnabel
Schubert
Schumann
Scriabin
Sessions
Sibelius
Sondheim
Stamford
Stanford
Sullivan
Taverner
Telemann
Vangelis

**9 letters:**
Bacharach
Balakirev
Beethoven
Bernstein
Boulanger
Broughton
Buxtehude
Chaminade
Cherubini
Donizetti
Dunstable
Ellington
Hindemith
Meyerbeer
Offenbach
Pachelbel
Pergolesi
Prokofiev
Scarlatti
Schnittke
Schonberg
Zemlinsky

**10 letters:**
Birtwistle
Boccherini
Buxterhude
Canteloube
Carmichael
Cole Porter
Monteverdi
Mussorgsky
Palestrina
Penderecki

| | | | |
|---|---|---|---|
| Ponchielli | **11 letters:** | Tchaikovsky | **13 letters:** |
| Rawsthorne | Charpentier | Theodorakis | Havergal Brian |
| Saint-Saëns | Frescobaldi | Wolf Ferrari | Maxwell Davies |
| Schoenberg | Humperdinck | | |
| Stravinsky | Leoncavallo | **12 letters:** | **14 letters:** |
| Villa-Lobos | Lloyd Webber | Dallapiccola | Rimsky-Korsakov |
| Waldteufel | Mendelssohn | Khachaturian | |
| Williamson | Niedermeyer | Rachmaninoff | **15 letters:** |
| | Stockhausen | Shostakovich | Vaughan Williams |

▷ **Composing** *may indicate* an anagram

**Composite** Aster, Cosmea, Costmary, Foalfoot, Gerbera, Groundsel, Hawkweed, Hemp agrimony, Hybrid, Integral, Metal, Motley, Opinicus, Racercar, Rag(weed), Sphinx, Synthesized, Thistle

**Composition, Compositor** Albumblatt, Aleatory, Azione, Bagatelle, Beaumontage, Beaumontague, Canon, Capriccio, Caprice, Cob, Concerto, Concertstuck, Concetto, Creation, Dite, Essay, Etude, Exaration, Fantasia, Fugue, Impromptu, Inditement, Ingredient, Line, Literature, Loam, Met, Montage, Morceau, Nonet(te), Nonetto, Opus, Oratorio, Organum, Part-writing, Passacaglia, Pastiche, Piece, Pieta, Poem, Polyphony, Polyrhythm, Port, Printer, Quartette, Raga, Repoussage, Rhapsody, Round, Setting, Ship, Sing, Smoot, Smout, Sonata, Sonatina, Structure, Study, Suite, Symphony, Synthesis, Terracotta, Texture, Toccata, Treatise, Trio, Typesetter, Verismo, Voluntary, Work

**Compost** Digestate, Dressing, Fertilizer, Humus, Vraic, Zoo doo

▷ **Compound(ed)** *may indicate* an anagram

**Compound (stop), Compound word** Addition, Admixture, Aggravate, Amalgam, Anti-inflammatory, Anti-knock, Blend, →**CAMP**, Composite, Constitute, Coordination, Cpd, Cutting, Derivative, Dibasic, Ethiops, Mix, Mixture, Multiply, Oxidant, Rooting, Sodaic, Synthesise, Tatpurusha, Type, Ureic

## COMPOUNDS

| **3 letters:** | Aloin | Potin | Diazin |
|---|---|---|---|
| Azo | Amide | Pyran | Diquat |
| Hex | Amino | Salol | Epimer |
| TBT | Azide | Sarin | Fluate |
| | Azine | Soman | Glycol |
| **4 letters:** | Azole | Tabun | Haemin |
| Alum | Caria | Thiol | Halide |
| Calx | Diazo | Trona | Haloid |
| Clay | Diene | Vinyl | Hexene |
| Deet | Dimer | | Hylene |
| Dopa | Diode | **6 letters:** | Iodine |
| EDTA | Erbia | Acetal | Isatin |
| Enol | Ester | Alkane | Isomer |
| Haem | Furan | Alkene | Ketone |
| Heme | Halon | Alkyne | Kinone |
| Tepa | Imide | Ammine | Lichen |
| TEPP | Imine | Arsine | Lithia |
| Urea | Indol | Baryta | Malate |
| | Lipid | Borane | Methyl |
| **5 letters:** | Nitro | Calque | Niello |
| Aldol | Olein | Cetane | Octane |
| Algin | Oxide | Chrome | Phenol |
| Allyl | Oxime | Cresol | Pinene |

Potash
Purine
Pyrene
Rennet
Retene
Silane
Speiss
Tannin
Tartar
Tetryl
Thymol
Triene
Trimer
Uranyl

**7 letters:**
Acetone
Acridin
Adenine
Aglycon
Ammonia
Argyrol®
Aspirin
Barilla
Bauxite
Benzene
Betaine
Borazon
Bromide
Caliche
Calomel
Camphor
Caprate
Carbide
Cellose
Chelate
Choline
Cinerin
Creatin
Cumarin
Cyanide
Diamine
Diazine
Diazole
Dioxide
Dvandva
Epoxide
Erinite
Ethanol
Eugenol
Excimer
Fenuron
Ferrite
Flavone

Hormone
Hydrate
Hydride
Indican
Indoxyl
Inosine
Lactate
Lactone
Menthol
Metamer
Monomer
Niobite
Nitride
Nitrile
Nitrite
Oxazine
Oxonium
Pentane
Peptide
Peptone
Polyene
Polymer
Prodrug
Protein
Quassia
Quinoid
Quinone
Realgar
Skatole
Steroid
Sulfide
Syncarp
Taurine
Terpene
Toluene
Tritide
Urethan
Uridine
Vanadic
Vitamin
Wolfram
Zymogen

**8 letters:**
Acridine
Aglycone
Aldehyde
Alizarin
Arginine
Asbestos
Astatide
Butyrate
Caffeine
Carbaryl

Catenane
Cephalin
Ceramide
Chloride
Chromene
Coenzyme
Coumarin
Creatine
Cyanogen
Datolite
Dieldrin
Dopamine
Ethoxide
Farnesol
Fluoride
Furfuran
Glycogen
Haloform
Hydroxyl
Iodoform
Isologue
Ketoxime
Lecithin
Luteolin
Massicot
Melamine
Monoxide
Oligomer
Pentosan
Peroxide
Phthalin
Piperine
Psilocin
Ptomaine
Purpurin
Pyrazole
Pyruvate
Racemate
Retinoid
Rock-alum
Rotenone
Selenate
Silicide
Siloxane
Sodamide
Stannage
Stilbene
Sulphide
Sulphone
Tautomer
Tetroxid
Thiazide
Thiazine
Thiazole

Thiophen
Thiotepa
Thiourea
Thyroxin
Titanate
Tolidine
Triazine
Triazole
Trilling
Trioxide
Tyramine
Urethane
Xanthate
Xanthine
Ytterbia
Zirconia

**9 letters:**
Aflatoxin
Alicyclic
Aliphatic
Anhydride
Auranofin
Bahuvrihi
Biguanide
Capsaicin
Carbazole
Carnitine
Caseinate
Celloidin
Cellulose
Cementite
Cetrimide
Chromogen
Copolymer
Cortisone
Deuteride
Dibromide
Dipeptide
Diplotene
Disulfram
Endorshin
Ferrocene
Flavanone
Fool's gold
Fulleride
Glycoside
Greek fire
Guanosine
Haematein
Histamine
Hydantoin
Hydrazide
Hydroxide

Imidazole
Impsonite
Ionophore
Isoniazid
Jasmonate
Limestone
Menadione
Mepacrine
Merbromin
Methoxide
Methylene
Monoamine
Organotin
Pentoxide
Perborate
Phenazine
Phenoxide
Pheromone
Phosphide
Phthalate
Piperonal
Polyamine
Porphyrin
Prussiate
Pyrethrin
Qinghaosu
Quercetus
Quercitin
Quinidine
Quinoline
Saltpetre
Salvarsan
Sapogenin
Serotonin
Sidenafil
Telluride
Tetroxide
Thiophene

Thyroxine
Valproate
Verapamil
Veratrine

*10 letters:*
Adrenaline
Agglutinin
Amphoteric
Argyrodite
Azobenzene
Bradykinin
Cellosolve®
Cytochroma
Dichloride
Dimethoate
Disulphide
Endosulfan
Enkephalin
Ethambutol
Halocarbon
Indophenon
Isocyanate
Lumisterol
Mercaptide
Nitrazepam
Nucleoside
Nucleotide
Phenacaine
Phenformin
Picrotoxin
Piperazine
Piperidine
Propionate
Putrescine
Pyrethroid
Pyrimidine
Pyrogallol

Sildenafil
Sulphonium
Tetracaine
Thimerosal
Tocopherol

*11 letters:*
Acetanilide
Amphetamine
Coprosterol
Dimercaprol
Diphosphate
Electrolyte
Fluorescein
Galantamina
Ghitathione
Hydrocarbon
Neostigmine
Nitrosamine
Resveratrol
Sesquioxide
Sphingosine
Tributyltin
Trichlorfon
Trichloride

*12 letters:*
Arsphenamine
Carbohydrate
Fleurocarbon
Formaldehyde
Haematoxylin
Hydrastinine
Hydroquinone
Mifepristone
Permanganate
Phenanthrine
Polyurethane

Quinalizarin
Sulphonamide
Testosterone
Thiosinamine
Triglyceride
Trimethadine

*13 letters:*
Catecholamine
Cycloheximide
Diphenylamine
Isoproterenol
Mercurochrome
Metronidazole
Nitroglycerin
Nortriptyline
Phenothiazine
Physostigmine
Plastoquinone
Sulphonylurea
Trinucleotide

*14 letters:*
Cyanocobalamin
Oxyhaemoglobin
Phenolphthalin
Polycarboxylic
Polyunsaturate
Sulphonmethane
Trihalomethane

*15 letters:*
Perfluorocarbon
Succinylcholine
Tribromoethanol

*17 letters:*
Pentachlorophenol

---

**Comprehend, Comprehensive** All-in, Broad-brush, Catch-all, Catholic, Compass, Compendious, Contain, Encyclopaedic, Exhaustive, Fathom, Follow, Full-scale, General, Global, Grand, Grasp, Include, Indepth, Ken, Large, Omnibus, Overall, Panoptic, Panoramic, Perceive, School, Sweeping, Thoroughgoing, Tumble, → **UNDERSTAND**, Wide

**Compress(ed), Compression, Compressor** Astrict, Astringe, Axial-flow, Bale, Coarctate, Contract, Pack, Pump, Shoehorn, Solidify, Squeeze, Stupe, Thlipsis, Tourniquet, Turbocharger

**Comprise** Contain, Embody, Embrace, Include

**Compromise, Compromising** Avoision, Brule, Commit, Concession, Endanger, Fudge, Give and take, Golden mean, Halfway house, Happy medium, Honeytrap, Involve, Middleground, Modus vivendi, Negotiate, Settlement, Time-server, Trade off, Via media

▸ **Compulsion** *see* **COMPEL(LING)**

**Compunction** Hesitation, Regret, Remorse, Scruple, Sorrow

**Computation, Compute(r)** Analog(ue), Animatronics, Apple (Mac)®, Botnet, Calcular, Desknote, Desktop, Digital, Eniac, Fifth generation, Front-end, Host, IALI,

Laptop, Mainframe, Micro, Multiuser, Network, Notebook, Notepad, Number-cruncher, Palmtop, PC, Personal, Proxy server, Reckon, TALISMAN, Turing machine, Voice response, WIMP

**Computer hardware, Computer memory** Busbar, Chip, Dataglove®, Docking station, DRAM, EAROM, EPROM, Floptical, IDE, Modem, Neurochip, Pentium®, Platform, Plug'n'play, Processor, PROM, RAM, ROM, Router, Tower, Track(er)ball

**Computer language** Acrobat®, ADA, ALGOL, APL, ASCII, Assembly, AWK, Basic, C, COBOL, COL, Computerese, CORAL, Fortran, High-level, ICL, Java®, Java script®, LISP, LOGO, Low-level, OCCAM, PASCAL, Perl, PROLOG, Python, Scratchpad, Scripting, Small-talk, SNOBOL, SQL, Visual Basic, Weblish

**Computer network, Computer systems** Arpa, ARPANET, BIOS, Cambridge ring, Darknet, ERNIE, Ethernet, Evernet, Executive, Extranet, Fileserver, Freenet, HOLMES, Hypermedia, Internet, Intranet, JANET, LAN, Linux, MARC, MIDI, Multipoint, Neural, Peer-to-peer, Stand-alone, TALISMAN, Tally, TAURUS, Telnet, Token ring, Unix, Usenet, VAN, WAN, Web, Wide-area, WIMP

**Computer program(s), Computer programmer, Computer programming, Computer software** Abandonware, Acrobat, ActiveX, Address harvester, Adware, Agent, Antivirus, App(let), Application, Assembler, Auto-responder, Autotune, Bloatware, Bootstrap, Bot, Browse, CADMAT, Cancelbot, Careware, Case, Casemix, Chatbot, Checksum, Choiceboard, Client, Closed-loop, Columbus, Courseware, Crippleware, CU See Me, Datel®, Debugger, Demo, Device-driver, Diagnostic, Dictionary, Disassembler, Emacs, Enterprise, ERP, Est, E-wallet, Extreme, Facemail, Firewall, Firmware, Flash, Formatter, Free-to-air, Freeware, Groupware, HAL, Hard card, Heuristic, Hypermedia, ITunes®, Linker, Loader, Logic bomb, Macro, Mail-merge, Malware, Middleware, Mmorpg, Module, Neural net, Object, OCR, Parser, Payware, Plug-in, Powerpoint, Relocator, Ripper, RISC, Rootkit, Screensaver, Servlet, Shareware, Shell, Shopping agent, Shovelware, Spam killer, Spellchecker, Spider, Spreadsheet, Spyware, Stiffware, Systems, TELNET, Text editor, Translator, Trialware, Uninstaller, Utility, Vaccine, Vaporware, Virus, Warez, Web browser, Webcast, Web crawler, Wiki, Windows®, Word processor, Worm

**Computer term(s)** Address bus, Alert box, Algorism, Authoring, Autosave, Backslash, Bank-switching, Bitmap, Blog(ging), Blogroll, Bookmark, Boot, Boot-virus, Bot army, Breakpoint, Broadband, Calculate, Calculus, Cascade, Chatroom, Choke route, Clickstream, Client-server, Clipboard, Cobweb site, Coder, Cold boot, Conf, Core(dump), Counter, Cron, Cuspy, Cyber(netics), Cybercafe, Cyberslacking, Dataglove, Daughterboard, Defrag(ment), Dial-up, DIF, Disk drive, Domain name, Dotcom, Earcon, Enqueue, Estimate, FAT, FIFO, Figure, Flash ROM, Floptical, GIGO, Gopher, Greybarland, Half-adder, Hardwire, Hashing, High-end, Hotlist, Hybrid, Hypertext, Inbox, Inputter, Integrator, Interface, IT, Joypad, Kludge, Linear, List serv, Logic, Mail merge, Measure, Meatspace, Memory stick, Moblog, Morphing, Motherboard, Mouseover, Mouse potato, Mung, Network, Neural, Non-volatile, Notwork, Numlock, Nybble, Nyetwork, Object, On-line, Outbox, Package, Packet sniffer, Pageview, Patch, Path name, Peer-to-peer, Pel, Permalink, Pharming, Phishing, Phreak, Pixel, Platform, Plug and play, Podcast, Podcatcher, Point and click, Poke, Popunder, Pop-up, Pseudocode, Pseudorandom, Public-key, Pushdown, Reader farm, README file, Read-out, Realtime, Reboot, Reckoner, Report program, Rogue dialler, Rogue site, Rootserver, Router, Screensaver, Screen turtle, Scriptkiddie, Search engine, Serial port, Server, Server farm, Shared logic, Shell, Shovelware, Sim, Smart, Smurfing, Soft copy, Soft return, Source, Spam, Spigot, Splog, Spreadsheet, Sprite, String, Style sheet, Subroutine, Superserver, Swap file, Systems, Tape streamer, Telecottage, Thick client, Thin client, Time slice, Toggle, Token ring, Triple, Turnkey, Turtle graphics, ULA, Unicode, Username, Utility program, Vaccine, Vlog, Vodcast, Voice response, Voxel, Wave file, Webbie, WebBoard, Webfarm, Wideband, Wi-fi, Wiki, WIMAX, Wordwrap, WORM, Wysiwyg, Yottabyte, Zettabyte, Zmodem

**Computer user(s)** Alpha geek, Anorak, Brain, Browser, Cast(er), Chiphead, Cybernaut, Cyberpunk, Cybersurfer, Digerati, Hacker, Liveware, Luser, Mouse potato, Nerd, Nethead, Netizen, Nettie, Onliner, Otaku, Pumpking, Surfer, Tiger team, Troll, Webhead, White hat

**Comrade** Achates, Ally, Buddy, Bully-rook, Butty, China, Fellow, Frater, Friend, Kamerad, Mate, Oliver, Pal, Pard, Roland, Tovarich, Tovaris(c)h

**Con(man)** Against, Anti, Bunco, Defraudment, Diddle, Dupe, Enveigle, Fleece, Gyp, Hornswoggle, Inveigle, Jacob, Lag, Learn, Peruse, Pretence, Read, Scam, Scan, Screw, Shark, Steer, Sucker, Swindle, Tweedler

**Concave** Dished, Invexed

**Conceal(ed), Concealment** Airbrush, Blanket, Blind, Closet, Clothe, Cover, Covert, Curtain, Disguise, Dissemble, Doggo, Drown, Feal, Harbour, Heal, Heel, Hele, →**HIDE**, Inner, Latent, Latescent, Misprision, Occult, Overgreen, Palm, Paper over, Perdu(e), Recondite, Screen, Scriene, Secrete, Shroud, Sleeve, Smokescreen, Smother, Snow job, Stash, Subreption, Ulterior, Veil, Whitewash, Wrap

**Concede, Concession** Acknowledge, Admit, Allow, Appeasement, Budge, Carta, Charter, Compromise, Confess, Favour, Forfeit, Franchise, Grant, Munich, Ou, Ow, Owe, Own, Privilege, Ship, Sop, Synchoresis, Yield

**Conceit(ed)** Arrogant, Bumptious, Caprice, Carriwitchet, Cat-witted, Cocky, Concetto, Crank, Crotchet, Device, Dicty, Egoist, Egomania, Fancy, Fastuous, Figjam, Flory, Fop, Fume, Hauteur, Idea, Mugwump, Notion, Podsnappery, Popinjay, Pretentious, Prig, Princock, Princox, Puppyism, Quiblin, Self-assumption, Side, Snotty, Stuck-up, Swellhead, Swollenhead, Toffee-nose, Vain(glory), Wind

**Conceive, Conceivable** Beget, Create, Credible, Imagine, Possible, Surmise

**Concentrate(d), Concentration** Abridge, Address, Aim, Apozem, Application, Attend, Attention, Bunch, Cathexis, Centre, Collect, Condense, Dephlegmate, Distil, Elliptical, Essence, Extract, Focalise, Focus, Geographical, Intense, Kurtosis, Listen, Major, Mantra, Mass, Molality, Molarity, Navel-gazing, Pithy, Pore, Potted, Reduce, Rivet, Samadhi, Strong, Thick, Titrate, Titre, Undiluted, Undivided

**Concept(ion)** Alethic, Brain, Hent, Ideal, Ideation, Image, Immaculate, K(h)arma, Mooncalf, Motif, Myth, Notion, Onomascology, Oogamous, Sortal, Stereotype, Theurgy, Weltanschauung

**Concern(ed), Concerning** About, Affair, After, Agitation, Ail, Alarm, Altruism, Anent, As to, Bother, Business, Care, Cerne, Company, Disturb, Dot com, Firm, Going, Heed, Hereof, House, Humanitarian, In re, Intéressé, Interest, Into, Involve, Lookout, →**MATTER**, Mell, Misease, Moment, Over, Part, Pidgin, Pigeon, Re, Reck, Regard, Reke, Relevant, Respect, Retch, Shake, Solicitous, Solicitude, Touch, Trouble, Versant, Wirra, Worry

▷ **Concerned** *may indicate* an anagram

**Concert (place)** Agreement, Ballad, Barbicon, Benefit, Chamber, Charivari, Cooperation, Device, Dutch, Gig, Hootanannie, Hootananny, Hootenanny, Hootnannie, Hootnanny, League, Odeon, Odeum, Open-air, Pop, Prom(enade), Recital, Singsong, Smoker, Smoking, Subscription, Symphony, The Proms, Together, Unison, Unity, Wit

**Concertina** Bandoneon, Pleat, Squeezebox, Squiffer

**Concerto** Brandenburg, Emperor, Grosso

▶ **Concession** *see* **CONCEDE**

**Conch** Seashell, Shell, Strombus

**Conchie** CO

**Concierge** Housekeeper, Porter

**Conciliate, Conciliator** Allay, Appease, Bridge builder, Calm, Disarm, Dove, Ease, Mollify, Pacify, Placate, Reconcile

**Concise** Brief, Compact, Curt, Encapsulated, Laconic, Short, Snappy, Succinct, Telegraphic, Terse, Tight

**Conclave** Assembly, Caucus, Confab, Meeting

**Conclude(d), Conclusion, Conclusive** Achieve, A fortiori, Afterword, Amen,
Binding, Button-up, Cease, Clinch, Close, Complete, Consectary, Dead, Decide, Deduce,
Demise, Diagnosis, → END, End-all, Endwise, Envoi, Epilogue, Explicit, Finality, Finding,
Fine, Finis, → FINISH, Foregone, Gather, Illation, Infer, Lastly, Limit, Non sequitur,
Omega, Outro, Over, Peroration, Point, Postlude, Punchline, Realise, Reason, Resolve,
Settle, Showdown, Summary, Terminate, Upshot, Uptie, Verdict, Wind up
**Conclusive** Cogent, Convincing, Estoppel, Final
**Concoct(ion)** Brew, Compound, Creation, Hydromal, Plan, Tisane, Trump (up)
**Concomitant** Stablemate
**Concord** Concent, Consonance, Harmony, Peace, Plane, Sympathy, Treaty, Unity
**Concorde** SST
**Concourse** Assembly, Confluence, Esplanade, Throng
**Concrete, Concretion** Actual, Aggregate, Beton, Bezoar, Breeze, Cake, Calculus,
Caprolite, Clot, Dogger, Gunite, Hairball, Hard, Laitance, Lean, Mass, Minkstone,
No-fines, Pile-cap, Positive, Prestressed, Real, Reify, Reinforced, Siporex, Solid, Tangible,
Tremie, Vacuum
**Concubine** Apple-squire, Campaspe, Harem, Hetaera, Hetaira, Madam, Mistress,
Odalisk, Sultana
**Concur** Accord, Agree, Assent, Coincide, Comply, → CONSENT, Gree
**Concurrent(ly)** Meantime
**Concuss(ion)** Clash, Shock, Stun
**Condemn(ation)** Abominate, Accuse, Beknave, Blame, Blast, Cast, Censor, Censure,
Convict, Damn, Decry, Denounce, Deprecate, Doom, Judge, Kest, Obelise, Obloquy,
Prejudge, Proscribe, Reprove, Revile, Sentence, Theta, Upbraid
**Condensation** Dewdrop
**Condense(d), Condenser** Abbe, Abbreviate, Abridge, Brief, Capacitator, Compress,
Contract, Distil, Encapsulate, Epitomise, Jet, Liebig, Précis, Rectifier, Reduce, Shorten,
Shrink, Summarise, Surface, Vernier, Vinificator
**Condescend(ing)** De haut en bas, Deign, Patronise, Snobbish, Stoop, Superior,
Vouchsafe
**Condiment** Caraway, Catsup, Cayenne, Chutney, Cum(m)in, Flavour, Horse radish,
Kava, Ketchup, Mustard, Paprika, Pepper, Relish, Salt, Sambal, Sauce, Seasoning, Spice,
Tracklement, Turmeric, Vinegar, Zedoary
**Condition(al), Conditioning** Acathisia, Akathisia, Autism, Calvities, Case, Cense,
Cinchonism, Circ(s), Circumstance, Classical, Climate, Congenital, Connote, Contingent,
Disease, Disomy, Dropsy, Experimental, Feather, Fettle, Finite, Going, Hammertoe,
Health, Hood, Hunk, If, Indoctrinate, → IN GOOD CONDITION, Kelter, Kernicterus,
Kilter, Latah, Necessary, Nick, Order, Parole, Pass, Pavlovian, Plight, Pliskie, Ply,
Point, Position, Predicament, Premise, Premiss, Prepare, Prerequisite, Presupposition,
Protasis, Proviso, Provisory, Repair, Reservation, Reserve, Rider, Ropes, Sine qua non,
Sis, Spina bifida, Standing, State (of play), Status quo, Sted, Stipulation, String, Sufficient,
Term, Tid, Tox(a)emia, Trim, Trisomy, Understanding, Unless, Vir(a)emia, Weal, White
finger
**Condom(s)** Blob, Cap, Franger, French letter, Gumboot, Johnny, Letter, Prophylactic,
Rubber, Rubber goods, Safe, Scumbag, Sheath
**Condone** Absolve, Excuse, Forgive, Overlook
**Conduct(or), Conductance, Conductress** Abbado, Accompany, Administer,
Anode, Ansermet, Antipode, Arm, Arrester, Barbirolli, Barenboim, Bearing, Beecham,
Behaviour, Bernstein, Bohm, Boult, Bulow, Bus-bar, Cad, Capellmeister, Chobdar,
Clippie, Clippy, Coil, Comport, Demean(our), Deportment, Direct, Disorderly, Drive,
Editor, Electrode, Escort, Feedthrough, Fetch, G, Goings-on, Guide, Haitink, Hallé,
Ignitron, Kappellmeister, Karajan, Kempe, Klemperer, Lark, Lead, LED, Liber, Lightning,
Mackerras, Maestro, Mantovani, Mho, Microchip, Nerve, N-type, Officiate, Ormandy,
Outer, Ozawa, Parts, Photodiode, → PILOT, Previn, Probe, Prosecute, Protocol,

Psychagogue, Psychopomp, P-type, Rattle, Safe, Sargent, Scudaller, Scudler, Shunt, Silicon, Skudler, Solicit, Solti, Stokowski, Strauss, Szell, Tao, Thermal, Thermistor, Thyristor, Toscanini, Transact, → USHER, Varactor, Varistor, Von-Karyon, Walter, Wave guide, Wire, Wood, Zener diode

▷ **Conducting** *may indicate* an '-ic' ending

**Conduit** Aqueduct, Canal, Carrier, Channel, Culvert, Duct, Main, Penstock, Pipe, Sewer, Tube, Utilidor, Wireway

**Cone(s), Conical, Cone-shaped** Alluvial, Cappie, Circular, Conoidal, Egmont, Ellipse, Female, Fir, Fusion, Ice-cream, Monticule, Moxa, Nose, Pastille, Peeoy, Pineal, Pingo, Pioy(e), Pottle, Puy, Pyramid, Pyrometric, Retinal, Seger, Shatter, Spire, Storm, Strobilus, Taper, Tee, Traffic, Volcanic, Wind, Windsock

**Coney** Daman, Doe, Hyrax

**Confection(er), Confectionery** Bonbon, Candy, Candyfloss, Caramel, Chocolate, Concoction, Conserve, Countline, Halva, Ice, Kiss, Marzipan, Meringue, Noisette, Nougat, Quiddery, Rock, Snow-cone, Sweet, Sweetmeat, Tablet

**Confederal, Confederacy, Confederate, Confederation** Accessory, Alliance, Ally, Association, Body, Bund, Bunkosteerer, Cover, Creek, Dixie, F(o)edarie, Gueux, Illinois, League, Partner, Senegambia, Union

**Confer(ence)** Bestow, Bretton Woods, Cf, Collogue, Colloqium, Colloquy, Congress, Convention, Council, Diet, Do, Dub, Fest, Forum, Grant, Huddle, Hui, Imparlance, Imperial, Indaba, Intercommune, Lambeth, Meeting, Munich, Negotiate, News, Palaver, Parley, Pawaw, Pear, Potsdam, Pourparler, Powwow, Press, Pugwash, Quadrant, Seminar, Settle, Summit, Symposium, Synod, → TALK, Teach-in, Tete-a-tete, Video, Vouchsafe, Yalta

**Confess(ion), Confessor** Acknowledge, Admit, Agnise, Avowal, Concede, Confiteor, Cough up, Declare, Disclose, Edward, Helvetic, Own, Peccavi, Recant, Shema, Shrift, Shriver, Sing, Tetrapolitan, Verbal, Whittle

**Confide(nce), Confident(ial), Confidant** Aplomb, Aside, Assertive, Assured, Authoritative, Bedpost, Belief, Bottle, Bouncy, Brash, Can do, Certitude, Chutzpah, Cocksure, Cocky, Cred, Crouse, Egoistical, Entre nous, Entrust, Extravert, Extrovert, Faith, Favourite, Fearless, Feisty, Gatepost, Hardy, Hope, Hubris, Hush-hush, Intimate, Morale, Nerve, Pack, Panache, Positive, Presumptuous, Private, Privy, QT, Reliance, Sanguine, Secret, Secure, Self-assured, Self-possessed, Self-trust, Suavity, Sub rosa, Sure, Sure-footed, Tell, Together, Top secret, Trust, Unabashed, Unbosom, Under the rose, Unselfconscious, Vaulting

**Confine(d), Confines, Confinement** Ambit, Bail, Bale, Cage, CB, Chain, Closet, Constrain, Contain, Coop, Cramp, Crib, Detain, Down-lying, Emmew, Encase, Enclose, Endemic, Enmew, Ensheath, Gaol, Gate, Gender-moon, Hem in, House arrest, Housebound, Immanacle, Immew, Immure, Impound, → IMPRISON, Incage, Incarcerate, Incommunicado, Inertial, Inhoop, Intern, Kettle, Limit, Local, Lying in, Mail, March, Mew, Mure, Narrow, Pen, Pent, Pinion, Poky, Quarantine, Restrict, Rule 43, Rules, Section, Solitary, Tether, Thirl, Trammel

**Confirm(ed), Confirmation** Addict, Approve, Ascertain, Assure, Attest, Bear (out), Certify, Check, Chris(o)m, Christen, Chronic, Clinch, Corroborate, Dyed-in-the-wool, Endorse, Homologate, Ink in, Obsign, Official, OK, Qualify, Ratify, Reassure, Sacrament, Sanction, Seal, Strengthen, Substantiate, Ten-four, Tie, True, Validate, Vouch

**Confiscate, Confiscation** Attainder, Deprive, Dispossess, Distrain, Escheat, Garnishee, Impound, Infangenethef, Raupatu, Seize, Sequestrate

**Conflagration** Blaze, Holocaust, Inferno, Wildfire

**Conflict(ing)** Agon, Ambivalence, Antinomy, Armageddon, At odds, Battle(ground), Boilover, Camp, Casus belli, Clash, Close, Contend, Contravene, Controversy, Disharmony, Diverge, Encounter, Feud, Fray, Inconsistent, Internecine, Jar, Lists, Mêlée, Muss, Off-key, Oppose, Psychomachia, Rift, Scrape, Shoot-out, Strife, → STRUGGLE, Tergiversate, War

**Conform(ist), Conformity** Accord, Adjust, Agreement, Comply, Conservative, Consistence, Correspond, Hew to, Keep step, Normalise, Obey, Observe, Procrustean, Propriety, Quadrate, Standardize, Stereotype(d), Suit, Time-server, Toe, Trimmer, Yield

**Confound(ed)** Abash, Amaze, Astound, Awhape, Baffle, Bewilder, Blamed, Blasted, Blest, Blinking, Bumbaze, Contradict, Darn, Dash, Deuce, Devastate, Dismay, Drat, Dumbfound, Elude, Floor, Jigger, Mate, Murrain, Nonplus, Perishing, Perplex, Rabbit, Spif(f)licate, Stump, Throw

▷ **Confound** *may indicate* an anagram

**Confrère** Ally

**Confront(ation)** Appose, Beard, Breast, Brush, Cross, Eyeball, Face, Face down, Head on, Head-to-head, Impasse, Incident, Loggerheads, Mau-Mau, Meet, Militance, Nose, Oppose, Outface, Showdown, Smackdown, Tackle, Toe-to-toe, War

**Confuse(d), Confusedly, Confusion** Addle, Adrift, Anarchy, Astonishment, At sea, Babel, Baffle, Bamboozle, Bazodee, Bedevil, Befog, Befuddle, Bemuse, Bewilder, Blur, Bobby-die, Burble, Bustle, Callaloo, Chaos, Cloud, Clutter, Cobweb, Complicate, Consternation, Debacle, Desorienté, Didder, Disarray, Discombobulate, Disconcert, Disorient, Distract, Dither, Dizzy, Doubting, Dudder, Dust, Dwaal, Egarement, Embrangle, Embroglio, Embroil, Entanglement, Farrago, Flap, Flat spin, Flummox, Flurry, Fluster, Fog, Fox, Fubar, Fuddle, Gaggle, Galley-west, Garble, Guddle, Hash, Havoc, Hazy, Helter-skelter, Hirdy-girdy, Hubble-bubble, Huddle, Hugger-mugger, Hurly-burly, Hurry-scurry, Hurry-skurry, Imbrangle, Imbroglio, Inchoate, Incoherent, →IN CONFUSION, Indistinct, Litter, Lost, Lurry, Maelstrom, Maffled, Maving, Mayhem, Maze, Melange, Melee, Mess, Mingle, Mish-mash, Misorder, Mither, Mixter-maxter, Mixtie-maxtie, Mix-up, Mizzle, Mizzy maze, Moider, Moither, Moonstruck, Morass, →MUDDLE, Mudge, Muss(e), Muzzy, Mystify, Obfuscate, Overset, Pellmell, Perplex, Pi(e), Pig's ear, Pose, Puzzle head, Ravel, Razzle-dazzle, Razzmatazz, Rout, Rummage, Rumpus, Scramble, S(c)hemozzle, Skimble-skamble, Snafu, Spaced out, Spin, Stump, Stupefy, Surprise, Swivet, Synchysis, Tangle, Tapsalteerie, Throw, Tizzy, Topsy-turvy, Toss, Turbulence, Turmoil, Tzimmes, Upside down, Welter, Whemmle, Whomble, Whummle, Woolly, Woozy

▷ **Confuse(d)** *may indicate* an anagram

**Confute** Confound, Contradict, Deny, Disprove, Infringe, Redargue, Refel

**Congeal** Coagulate, Freeze, Gel, Gunge, Pectise, Set, Solidify

**Congenial** Affable, Agreeable, Amiable, Compatible, Connate, Couthie, Couthy, Happy, Kindred, Simpatico, Sympathique

**Congenital** Connate, Inborn, Innate, Inveterate

**Conger** Sea-eel

**Congest(ed), Congestion** Choke, Coryza, Cram, Crowd, Engorge, Impact, Jam, Logjam, Nasal, (O)edema, Turgid

**Conglomerate, Conglomeration** Aggregate, Banket, Chaebois, Chaebol, Empire, Gather, Heap, Mass, Pudding-stone

**Congo(u)** DRC, Shaba, Tea

**Congratulate, Congratulation** Applaud, Felicitate, Laud, Mazeltov, Preen, Salute

**Congregate, Congregation(alist)** Assembly, Barnabite, Body, Brownist, Class, Community, Conclave, Ecclesia, Flock, Fold, For(e)gather, Gathering, Group, Host, Laity, Oratory, Propaganda, Synagogue

**Congress(man)** ANC, Assembly, Capitol, Conclave, Continental, Council, Eisteddfod, Intercourse, Legislature, Pan-Africanist, Rally, Senator, Solon, Synod, Vienna

**Conifer(ous)** Araucaria, Cedar, Cypress, Cyrus, Evergreen, Larch, Macrocarpa, Picea, Pine, Redwood, Retinispora, Rimu, Spruce, Taiga, Taxus, Thuja, Yew

**Conject(ure)** Augur, Fancy, Gesse, Goldbach's, Guess, Guesswork, Infer, Speculate, Surmise, Theory, View

**Conjoin** Alligate, Ally, Connect, Knit

**Conjugate, Conjugation** Couple, Hermitian, Join, Nuptial, Synopsis, Typto, Zygosis

**Conjunction** Alligation, Ampersand, And, Combination, Consort, Coordinating, Inferior, Nor, Polysyndeton, Subordinating, Superior, Synod, Syzygy, Together, Union, Unition, Unless

**Conjure(r), Conjuror** Angekkok, Charm, Contrive, Cooper, Heypass, Heypresto, Hocus-pocus, Illusionist, Imagine, Invoke, Mage, Magic, Mystery-man, Palmer, Prestidigitator, Prestigiator, Thaumaturgus

**Conk** Nose

**Connect(ed), Connection, Connector** About, Accolade, Adaptor, Affiliate, Affinity, Agnate, Ally, Anastomosis, And, Associate, Attach, Band, Bind, Bridge, Bridle, Cable, Chiasm, Clientele, Cognate, Coherent, Colligate, Conjugate, Correlate, Couple, Cross-link, Delta, DIN, Dovetail, Downlink, Drawbar, Earth, Enlink, Fishplate, Fistula, Hook-up, Hydrant, → IN CONNECTION WITH, Interlink, Interlock, Interrelation, Join, Jumper, Kinship, Liaison, Lifeline, Link(age), Linkup, Marry, Merge, Mesh, Neck, Network, Nexus, Nose, On, Online, Patch, Pons, Raphe, Rapport, Relate, Relative, Relevant, Respect, Sentence, Shank, Socket, Splice, S-R, Synapse, Syntenosis, Syssarcosis, Tendon, Through, Tie, Tie-in, Twin, Unction, Union, Y, Yoke, Zygon

**Connecticut** Ct

**Connive, Connivance** Abet, Cahoots, Collude, Condone, Conspire, Lenocinium, Plot

**Connoisseur** Aesthete, Barista, Cognoscente, Epicure, Expert, Fancier, Gourmet, Judge, Maven, Mavin, Oenophil(e)

**Connotate, Connotation** Imply, Infer, Intent, Meaning, Overtone

**Conquer(or), Conquering, Conquest** Alexander, Beat, Caesar, Conquistador, Cortes, Crush, Debel, Defeat, Genghis Khan, Hereward, → MASTER, Moor, Norman, Ostrogoth, Overcome, Overpower, Overrun, Pizarro, Saladin, Subjugate, Tame, Tamerlane, Vanquish, Victor, Vincent, Win

**Conquistador** Cortes, Cortez, Pizarro

**Conscience, Conscientious** Casuistic, Duteous, Dutiful, Heart, Inwit, Morals, Painstaking, Pang, Remorse, Scruple(s), Scrupulous, Sense, Superego, Syneidesis, Synteresis, Thorough, Twinge

**Conscious(ness)** Awake, Aware, Black, Chit, Deliberate, Limen, Mindful, On to, Persona, Sensible, Sensitivity, Sentient, Witting

**Conscript(ion)** Blood-tax, Choco, Commandeer, Draft(ee), Impress, Inductee, Landsturm, Levy, Nasho, National Service, → RECRUIT, Register

**Consecrate(d), Consecration** Anoint, Bless, Enoch, Hallow, Noint, Oint, Sacring, Sanctify, Venerate

**Consecutive** Sequential, Successive

**Consensus** Agreement, Harmony, Unanimity

**Consent** Accord, Acquiesce, Affo(o)rd, Agree, Approbate, Assent, Comply, Concur, Grant, Homologate, Informed, Permit, Ratify, Submit, Una voce, Volens, Yes-but, Yield

**Consequence(s), Consequent(ial), Consequently** After effect, Aftermath, Consectaneous, Corollary, Effect, End, Implication, Importance, Issue, Karma, Knock-on, Logical, Moment, Outcome, Out-turn, Party game, Ramification, Repercussion, → RESULT, Sequel, Thence, Thereat, Thus, Upshot

**Conservative** Blimpish, Blue, C, Cautious, Diehard, Disraeli, Fabian, Hard-hat, Hidebound, Hunker, Misoneist, Neanderthal, New Right, Old guard, Old-line, Old School, Preppy, Progressive, Reactionary, Rearguard, Redneck, Right(-wing), Safe, Square, Thatcherite, Thrifty, Tory, True blue, Unionist, Verkramp, Verkrampte, Young Fogey

**Conservatory** Hothouse, Lean-to, Orangery, Solarium

**Conserve, Conservation(ist)** Can, Comfiture, Game warden, Greenpeace, Husband(ry), Jam, Jelly, Maintain, Maintenance, Noah, NT, Protect, Save

**Consider(able), Considerate, Consideration** Ad referendum, Animadvert, Attention, Avizandum, By-end, Case, Cerebrate, Chew over, Cogitate, Contemplate, Count, Courtesy, Debate, Deem, Deliberate, Entertain, Envisage, Factor, Fair, Feel,

Forethought, Gay, Gey, Heed, Importance, Inasmuch, Judge, Kind, Many, Materially, Measure, Meditate, Much, Mull, Muse, Pay, Perpend, Poise, Ponder, Premeditate, Pretty, Priority, Pro and con, Rate, Reck, Reckon, Reflect, Regard, Respect, Scruple, See, Sensitive, Several, Shortlist, Solicitous, Song, Speculate, Steem, Study, Substantial, Think, Tidy, Vast, View, Ween, Weigh

**Consign(ment)** Allot, Award, Batch, Bequeath, Delegate, Deliver, Drop shipment, Entrust, Freight, Lading, Ship, Shipment, Transfer

**Consist(ent), Consistency** Agree, Changeless, Coherent, Comprise, Concordant, Enduring, Even, Liaison, Rely, Sound, Steady, Texture, Uniform

**Consolation, Console** Ancon, Appease, Balm, Cheer, Comfort, Games, Panel, Play, Prize, Reassure, Relief, Solace, Sop, Station

**Consolidate** Coalesce, Combine, Compact, Gel, Merge, Pun, Unify

**Consommé** Julienne, Soup

**Consonant(s)** Affricate, Agma, Agreeing, Alveolar, Cacuminal, Cerebral, Explosive, Fortis, Fricative, Harmonious, Implosive, Labial, Lateral, Lenis, Media, Mouillé, Plosive, Sonorant, Spirant, Surd, Tenuis, Velar

**Consort** Ally, Associate, Fraternise, Maik, Mate, Moop, Moup, Partner, Spouse

**Consortium** Coalition, Combine, Ring

**Conspectus** Precis

**Conspicuous** Arresting, Blatant, Bold, Clear, Eminent, Eye-catching, Glaring, Kenspeck(le), Landmark, Light, Manifest, Patent, Radiant, Salient, Shining, Showy, Signal, Striking

**Conspiracy, Conspirator, Conspire, Conspiring** Brutus, Cabal, Cartel, Casca, Cassius, Catiline, Cato St, Champerty, Cinna, Collaborate, Colleague, Collogue, Collude, Complot, Connive, Covin, Covyne, Guy, Highbinder, In cahoots, Intrigue, Oates, Omerta, → **PLOT**, Practisant, Ring, Scheme

**Constable** Beck, Catchpole, Cop, Dogberry, Dull, Elbow, Harman(-beck), Headborough, High, Hog, John, Lord High, Officer, Painter, Petty, Pointsman, → **POLICEMAN**, Posse, Special, Thirdborough, Tipstaff, Uniformed, Verges

**Constancy, Constant** Abiding, Boltzmann, C, Changeless, Chronic, Coefficient, Cosmic, Cosmological, Decay, Devotion, Dielectric, Diffusion, Dilys, Dirac, Eccentricity, Equilibrium, Eternal, Faith, Firm, Fixed, Frequent, Fundamental, G, Gas, Gravitational, H, Honesty, Hubble's, Incessant, K, Lambert, Leal(ty), Logical, Loyal, Magnetic, Nonstop, Often, Parameter, → **PERPETUAL**, Pi, Planck's, Pole star, Rate, Regular, Relentless, Resolute, Sad, Solar, Stable, Staunch, Steadfast, Steady, Time, True, Unceasing, Unfailing, Uniform, Usual

**Constellation** Andromeda, Antlia, Apus, Aquarius, Aquila, Ara, Argo, Aries, Auriga, Bootes, Caelum, Camelopardalis, Camelopardus, Canes Venatici, Canis Major, Canis Minor, Carina, Cassiopeia, Centaurus, Cepheus, Cetus, Cham(a)eleon, Circinus, Columba, Coma Berenices, Coma Cluster, Corvus, Crater, Cygnus, Cynosure, Delphinus, Delta, Dolphin, Dorado, Draco, Equuleus, Eridanus, Fornax, Galaxy, Gemini, Great Bear, Gru(i)s, Hercules, Horologium, Hydra, Hydrus, Indus, Lacerta, Leo, Leo Minor, Lepus, Libra, Little Bear, Little Dipper, Lupus, Lynx, Lyra, Mensa, Microscopium, Monoceros, Musca, Norma, Octans, Ophiuchus, Orion, Pavo, Pegasus, Perseus, Phoenix, Pictor, Piscis Austrinus, → **PLANET**, Puppis, Pyxis, Reticulum, Sagitta, Sagittarius, Scorpius, Sculptor, Scutum, Serpens, Sextans, Southern Cross, Spica, → **STAR**, Telescopium, The Rule, Triangulum (Australe), Tucana, Twins, Unicorn, Vela, Vilpecula, Virgin, Virgo, Volans, Vulpecula, Wag(g)oner, Whale, Zodiacal

**Consternation** Alarm, Dismay, Doodah, Fear, Horror, Panic

**Constipate(d), Constipation** Astrict, Bind, Block, Costive, Mawbound, Stegnotic, Stenosis

**Constituency, Constituent** Agglutinogen, Borough, Component, Element, Immediate, Part, Principle, Seat, Staple, Sub unit, Ultimate, Voter

▷ **Constituents** *may indicate* an anagram

**Constitute, Constitution(al)** Appoint, Character, Charter, Clarendon, Compose, Comprise, Congenital, Creature, Establishment, Form, Fuero, Health, Physique, Policy, Polity, Seat, State, Stroll, Synthesis, Trek, Upmake, Walk

**Constrain(ed), Constraint** Bind, Bondage, Boundary, Coerce, Confine, Coop, Curb, Dragoon, Duress(e), Force, Hard, Impel, Limit, Localise, Oblige, Pressure, Repress, Stenosis, Taboo, Tie, Trammel

**Constrict(ed), Constriction** Bottleneck, Cage, Choke, Coarctate, Contract, Cramp, Hour-glass, Impede, Isthmus, Limit, Narrow, Phimosis, Squeeze, Stegnosis, Stenosis, Stifle, Strangle, Strangulate, Thlipsis, Tighten, Venturi

**Construct(ion), Constructor, Constructive** Architect, Assemble, Build, Cast, Compile, Engineer, Erect, Fabricate, Facture, Fashion, Form, Frame, Idolum, Make, Manufacture, Meccano, Partners, Seabee, Stressed-skin, Tectonic, Weave

**Construe** Deduce, Explain, Expound, Infer

**Consul** Ambassador, Attaché, Cicero, Horse, Lucullus, Praetor

**Consult(ant), Consultation** Avisement, Confer, Deliberate, Discuss, Emparl, Holmes, Imparl, Joint, Peritus, See, Sexpert, Shark watcher, Surgery, Vide

**Consume(r), Consumption, Consumptive** Bolt, Burn, Caterpillar®, Conspicuous, Decay, Devour, Diner, Eat, End-user, Engross, Exhaust, Expend, Feed, Glutton, Hectic, Intake, Mainline, Preoccupy, Scoff, Spend, Swallow, TB, Use, Waste, Wear

**Consummate, Consummation** Achieve, Crown, Keystone, Seal

**Contact** Abut, Adpress, Contingence, Electrode, Eye, Fax, Hook-up, Lens, Liaise, Liaison, Meet, Outreach, Radio, Reach, Shoe, Taction, Telephone, → **TOUCH**, Touchy-feely, Wiper

**Contagious, Contagion** Infection, Noxious, Poison, Psora, Taint, Variola, Viral

**Contain(er)** Amphora, Ampoule, Ampulla, Aquafer, Aquifer, Ashcan, Barrel, Basket, Bass, Beaker, Bidon, Billy(-can), Bin, Boat, Bottle, Bowl, Box, Brazier, Buddle, Bunker, Butt, Butter-boat, Cachepot, Can, Canakin, Canikin, Canister, Cannikin, Cantharus, Capsule, Carafe, Carboy, Carry, Carton, Cartridge, Case, Cask, Cassette, Censer, Chase, Chest, Chilly bin, Churn, Clip, Coffer, Coffret, Comprise, Coolamon, Crate, Crater, Crib, Crucible, Cup, Cupel, Cuvette, Decanter, Dracone, Dredger, Encircle, Enclose, Encompass, Enseam, Esky®, Feretory, Flagon, Flask, Flat, Gabion, Gallipot, Gourd, Growler, → **HOLD**, House, Humidor, Igloo, Include, Incubator, Inseam, Intray, Jar, Jeroboam, Jerrican, Jerrycan, Jug, Keg, Kettle, Kirbeh, Leaguer, Lekythos, Locker, Magnox, Melting-pot, Monkey, Monstrance, Mould, Muffineer, Nosebag, Olpe, Ostensorium, Out-tray, Packet, Pail, Percolator, Pinata, Piscina, Pitcher, Pithos, Pocket, Pod, Poke, Pottle, Punnet, Pyxis, Receptacle, Reliquary, Repository, Restrain, Sac(k), Sachet, Safe, Saggar, Scrip, Scuttle, Scyphus, Shaker, Sheath, Silo, Situla, Skin, Skip, Snaptin, Solander, Spittoon, Stamnos, Stillage, Tank, Tantalus, Tea kettle, Terrarium, Tinaja, Trough, Trug, Tub, Tun, Tupperware®, Urn, Valise, Vase, Vat, Vessel, Vinaigrette, Wardian case, Wineskin, Woolpack, Workbag

**Contaminate(d), Contaminant, Contamination** Adulterate, Corrupt, Defile, Denature, Flyblown, Impure, Infect, Moit, Mysophobia, Pollute, Salmonella, Soil, Spike, Stain, Tarnish, Toxic

**Contemplate, Contemplation** Consider, Ecce, Envisage, Hesychasm, Intend, Meditate, Muse, Ponder, Reflect, Retrospection, Rue, Samadhi, Spell, Study, Think, Watch

**Contemporary** AD, Coetaneous, Coeval, Concomitant, Current, Equal, Fellow, Modern, Modish, Present, Topical, Verism

**Contempt(ible), Contemptuous** Abject, Ageism, Aha, Arsehole, Bah, Base, BEF, Blithering, Cheap, Contumely, Crud, Crumb, Crummy, Cullion, Cur, Cynical, Derision, Despisal, Diddy, Dis(s), Disdain, Dismissive, Disparaging, Disrespect, Dog-bolt, Dusty, Fico, Fig, Figo, Flouting, Foh, Git, Hangdog, Ignominious, Insect, Jive-ass, Lousy, Low, Mean, Measly, Misbegotten, Misprision, Och, Odious, Paltry, Pelting, Pfui, Pho(h), Phooey, Pipsqueak, Pish, Poof, Poxy, Pshaw, Ratfink, Rats, Razoo, Scabby, Scarab, Schlub, Scofflaw, → **SCORN**, Scumbag, Scurvy, Sdeign, Sexism, Shabby, Shitface,

Shithead, Slimeball, Sneer, Sneeze, Sniffy, Snook, Snooty, Snot, Snotty, Soldier, Sorry, Sprat, Squirt, Squit, Supercilious, Toad, Toerag, Tossy, Turd, Tush, Vilipend, Weed, Whipster, Wretched

**Contend(er)** Allege, Argue, Athlete, Candidate, Claim, Clash, Compete, Cope, Debate, Dispute, Fight, Grapple, Oppose, Rival, Stickle, →**STRIVE**, Struggle, Submit, Tussle, →**VIE**, Wrestle

**Content(ed), Contentment** Apaid, Apay, Appay, Arcadia, Blissful, Calm, Happy, Inside, Matter, Please, Raza, Reza, Satiate, Satisfy, Subject matter, Volume

▷ **Content** *may indicate* a hidden word

**Contention, Contentious** Argument, Bellicose, Cantankerous, Case, Combat, Competitive, Eristic, Hot potato, Logomachy, Match, Perverse, Polemical, Rivalry, Strife, Struggle, Sturt

**Contest(ant)** Agon, Battle (royal), Beauty, Beetle drive, Biathlon, Bout, Catchweight, Challenge, Championship, Combat, Competition, Concours, Darraign, Decathlon, Defend, Deraign, Dogfight, Duathlon, Duel(lo), Entrant, Eurovision, Event, Examinee, Finalist, Free-for-all, Fronde, Handicap, Heptathlon, Joust, Kemp, Kriegspiel, Lampadephoria, Match, Matchplay, Olympiad, Pancratium, Panel-beater, Par, Paralympics, Pentathlon, Pingle, Play-off, Prizer, Race (meeting), Rat race, Rival, Roadeo, Rodeo, Scrap, Scrum, Set-to, Skirmish, Slam, Slugfest, Strife, Struggle, Tenson, Tetrathlon, Tournament, Triathlon, Tug-of-war, Tussle, Vie, War, With

**Context** Intentional, Opaque, Transparent

**Continent(al)** Abstinent, Asia, Atlantis, Austere, Chaste, Dark, Epeirogeny, Euro, European, Gallic, Gondwanaland, Greek, Landmass, Laurasia, Lemuria, Mainland, Moderate, NA, Oceania, Pang(a)ea, Shelf, Teetotal, Temperate, Walloon

**Contingency, Contingent** Accident, Arm, Brigade, Casual, Chance, Conditional, Dependent, Event, Fluke, Group, Possibility, Prospect

**Continual(ly), Continuous** Adjoining, Anend, At a stretch, Away, Ceaseless, Chronic, Connected, Durational, Eer, Endlong, Eternal, Eterne, Ever, Forever, Frequent, Incessant, Non-stop, On(going), Perpetual, Unbroken, Unceasing

**Continue, Continuation, Continuing, Continuity** Abye, Drag on, Duration, Dure, During, Enduring, Enjamb(e)ment, Follow-on, Go on, Hold, Keep, Last, Link, Ongoing, Onward, Perpetuate, Persevere, Persist, Proceed, Prolong, Push on, Remain, Resume, Sequel, Sequence, Stand, Subsist, Survive, Sustain, Synaphe(i)a, Tenor

▷ **Continuously** *may indicate* previous words to be linked

**Contort(ion)** Deform, Gnarl, Jib, Twist, Warp, Wreathe, Wry

**Contour** Curve, Graph, Isallobar, Isobase, Isocheim, Isochime, Isogeothermal, Isohel, Isohyet, Line, Profile, Silhouette, Streamline, Tournure

**Contraband** Hot, Illicit, Prohibited, Smuggled

**Contraception, Contraceptive** Billings method, Cap, Coil, Condom, Depo-Provera®, Diaphragm, Etonogestrel, IU(C)D, Legonorgestrel, Lippes loop, Loop, Minipill, Oral, Pessary, Pill, Precautions, Prophylactic, Rubber(s), Sheath, Spermicide, Vimule®

**Contract(ion), Contractor** Abbreviate, Abrege, Abridge, Affreightment, Agreement, Appalto, Astringency, Bargain, Biceps, Binding, Bottomry, Braxton-Hicks, Bridge, Builder, Catch, Champerty, Charter (party), Clench, Clonus, Concordat, Condense, Consensual, Constringe, Contrahent, Convulsion, Covenant, Cramp, Crasis, Curtail(ment), Debt, Develop, Diastalsis, Dupuytren's, Dwindle, Engage, Entrepreneur, Escrow, Extrasystole, Fibrillation, Fitzgerald-Lorentz, Flex, Forward, Gainsay, Gooseflesh, Guarantee, Hand-promise, Hedge, Hire, Incur, Indenture, Jerk, Ketubah, Knit, Labour, Lease, Lessen, Levator, Lorentz-Fitzgerald, Make, Mandate, Miosis, Myosis, Narrow, Obligee, Outsource, Party, Peristalsis, Policy, Privilege, Promise, Pucker, Purse, Restriction, Risus (sardonicus), Service, Shrink, Shrivel, Sign, Slam, Slim, Social, Spasm, Specialty, Squinch, Steelbow, Stenosis, Stipulation, Straddle, Supplier, Swap, Sweetheart, Synaloepha, Syngraph, Systole, Taper off, Telescope, Tender, Tense, Tetanise, Tetanus, Tic, Tighten,

Time bargain, Tittle, Tonicity, Tontine, Treaty, Triceps, Trigger-finger, Trismus cynicus, Undertaker, Wrinkle, Yellow-dog, Z

▷ **Contract** *may indicate* a bridge call, e.g. 1S, 1C, 1D

**Contradict(ion), Contradictory** Ambivalent, Antilogy, Antinomy, Belie, Bull, Contrary, Counter, Dementi, Deny, Disaffirm, Disprove, Dissent, →GAINSAY, Negate, Oxymoron, Paradox, Perverse, Sot, Stultify, Sublate, Threap, Threep, Traverse

**Contralto** Clara Butt

**Contraption** Contrivance, Doodah, Scorpion

**Contrapuntal** Fugue

**Contrarily, Contrary** Adverse, A rebours, Arsy-versy, But, Captious, Converse, Counter, Counterfleury, Crosscurrent, Cross-grained, Cross-purpose, Froward, Heretic, Hostile, Inverse, Mary, Opposite, Oppugnant, Ornery, Perverse, Rebuttal, Retrograde, Wayward, Withershins

**Contrast** Chiaroscuro, Chiasmus, Clash, Colour, Compare, Differ, Foil, Relief

**Contravene** Infringe, Oppose, Thwart, Violate

**Contribute, Contribution** Abet, Add, Assist, Chip in, Conduce, Donate, Dub, Furnish, Go, Help, Input, Kick in, Mite, Offering, Share, Sub, Subscribe, Whack, Widow's mite

▷ **Contributing to** *may indicate* a hidden word

**Contrite, Contrition** Apologetic, Penance, Penitent, Remorse, Repentant, Rue, Sackcloth, →SORRY

**Contrivance, Contrive(r), Contrived** Art, Artificial, Cam, Chicaner, Contraption, Cook, Deckle, Deus ex machina, Device, Devise, Dodge, Engine, Engineer, Finesse, Frame, Gadget, Gimmick, Gin, Hatch, Hokey, Intrigue, Invention, Machinate, Manage, Manoeuvre, Page, Plan, Plot, Procure, Rest, Rowlock, Scheme, Secure, Shift, Stage, Trump, Wangle, Weave

**Control(ler), Controllable, Controlled** Ada, Aircon, Appestat, Atorvastatin, Autopilot, Ballcock, Bias, Big Brother, Birth, Boss, Boundary layer, Bridle, Cabotage, Camshaft, Chair, Check, Choke(hold), Christmas tree, Contain, Corner, Correct(ion), Corset, Curb, Cybernetics, Damage, Descendeur, Dirigible, Dirigism(e), Dominate, Dominion, Driving seat, Duopsony, Dynamic, Elevon, Etatiste, Fader, Fast-forward, Fet(ch), Finger, Flood, Fly-by-wire, Gain, Gar, George, Gerent, Govern, Ground, Gubernation, Hae, Handle, Harness, Have, Heck, Helm, Hog, Influence, Influx, Inhibitor, Interchange, Joystick, Keypad, Knee-swell, Lead, Lever, Limit, Line, →MANAGE, Martinet, Mastery, Moderate, Mouse, Nipple, Noise, Nozzled, Numerical, Operate, Override, Pacemaker, Pilot, Placebo, Police, Population, Possess, Power, Preside, Price, Process, Puppeteer, Quality, Radio, Referee, Regime(nt), Regulate, Regulo®, Rein, Remote, Rent, Repress, Restrain, Restrict, Rheostat, Ride, Ripple, Rule, Run, School, Servo, Slide(r), Snail, Solion, Spoiler, Stage-manage, Steady, Steer, Stop, Stopcock, Stranglehold, Stringent, Subdue, Subject, Subjugate, Supervise, Suzerain, Svengali, Sway, Switch, Takeover, Tame, Tap, Temperate, Thermostat, Throttle, Tie, Tiller, Tone, Traction, Umpire, Upper hand, Valve, Weld, Wield, Zapper

**Controversial, Controversy** Argument, Cause celebre, Contention, Debate, Dispute, Emotive, Eristic(al), Furore, Heretical, Hot potato, Moot point, Polemic(al), Quarrel, Tendentious, Troll

▷ **Contuse** *may indicate* an anagram

**Conundrum** Acrostic, Egma, Enigma, Puzzle, Riddle, Teaser

**Convalesce(nt), Convalescence** Anastatic, Mend, Rally, Recover, Recuperate, Rest-cure

▶ **Convene** *see* CONVOKE(R)

**Convenience, Convenient** Behoof, Commode, Cosy, Easy, Eft, Ethe, Expedient, Facility, Gain, Gents, Handsome, →HANDY, Hend, Lav, Leisure, Men's room, Near, Opportune, Pat, Privy, Public, Suitable, Toilet, Use, Well

**Convent** Abbatial, Cloister, Fratry, Friary, House, →MONASTERY, Motherhouse, Nunnery, Port-royal, Priory, Retreat

**Convention(al)** Academic, Accepted, Babbitt, Blackwood, Bourgeois, Caucus, Code, Conclave, Conformity, →**CUSTOMARY**, Decorous, Diet, Done, Formal, Geneva, Habitude, Hidebound, Iconic, Lame, Lingua franca, Mainstream, Meeting, Middlebrow, Middle-of-the-road, More, National, Nomic, Normal, Orthodox, Ossified, Pompier, Pooterish, Proper, Propriety, Readymade, Schengen, Square, Staid, Starchy, Stereotyped, Stock, Straight, Stylebook, Synod, The thing, Uptight, Usage, Warsaw

**Converge(nce)** Approach, Focus, Inrush, Meet, Overlap, Toe-in

**Conversation(al), Conversationalist, Converse, Conversant** Abreast, Antithesis, Antitype, Aware, Board, Buck, Cackle, Causerie, Chat, Chinwag, Chitchat, Colloquy, Commune, Confab, Convo, Crack, Crossfire, Crosstalk, Deipnosophist, Dialogue, Discourse, Eutrapelia, Eutrapely, Exchange, Facemail, Hobnob, Interlocution, In tune with, Jaw-jaw, Natter, Opposite, Palaver, Parley, Persiflage, Rap, Rhubarb, Shop, Shoptalk, Sidebar, Small talk, Socialise, →**TALK**, Transpose, Trialogue, Wongi, Word

**Conversion, Converter, Convert(ible)** Adapt, Alter, Assimilate, Azotobacter, Bessemer, Cabriolet, Cash, Catalytic, Catechumen, Change, Commutate, Commute, Cyanise, Damascene, Diagenesis, Disciple, Distil, Encash, Etherify, Evangelize, Exchange, Expropriate, Fixation, Goal kick, Gummosis, Hodja, Ismalise, Kho(d)ja, Landau, L-D, Liquid(ate), Marrano, Metamorphosis, Metanoia, Missionary, Neophyte, Noviciate, Novitiate, Persuade, Prill, Proselyte, Put, Ragtop, Realise, Rebirth, Reclamation, Recycle, Revamp, Romanise, Sheik(h), Soft-top, Souper, Tablet, Taw, Torque, Transduce, Transform, Transmute, Try, Vert

▷ **Conversion, Converted** *may indicate* an anagram

**Convex(ity)** Arched, Bowed, Camber, Curved, Entasis, Extrados, Gibbous, Lenticle, Nowy

**Convey(ance)** Assign, BS, Carousel, Carriage, Carry, Carrycot, Cart, Chaise, Charter, Coach, Conduct, Cycle, Deed, Deliver, Eloi(g)n, Enfeoffment, Esloyne, Exeme, Giggit, Grant, Guide, Lease, Litter, Lorry, Mailcar(t), Pirogue, Pneumatic, Re-lease, Sac, Screw, Sled, Soc, Tip, Title deed, Tote, Tram, Transfer, Transit, Transmit, Transport, Trolley, Vehicle

**Convict(ion)** Attaint, Belief, Botany Bay, Bushranger, Canary, Certitude, Cockatoo, Cogence, Crawler, Credo, Creed, Crime, Criminal, Demon, Dogma, Emancipist, Faith, Felon, Forçat, Gaolbird, Government man, Jailbird, Lag, Magwitch, Old chum, →**PERSUASION**, Plerophory, Previous, Prisoner, Record, Ring, Trusty, Vehemence, Yardbird

**Convince(d), Convincing** Assure, Certain, Cogent, Conclusive, Credible, Doubtless, Luculent, Persuade, Plausible, Satisfy, Sold, Sure

**Convivial(ity)** Boon, Bowl, Festive, Gay, Genial, Jovial, Social

**Convoke(r)** Assemble, Call, Chairman, Convene, Summon

**Convolute(d), Convolution** Coiled, Complex, Gyrus, Helical, Intricate, Maze, Spiral, Tortuous, Twisty, Whorl, Writhen

**Convolvulus** Bindweed, Dodder

**Convoy** Caravan, Column, Conduct, Escort, Fur brigade, Pilot, Train, Wagon-train

**Convulse, Convulsion(s), Convulsive** Agitate, Clonic, Clonus, Commotion, Disturb, DT, Eclampsia, →**FIT**, Galvanic, Grand mal, Paroxysm, Petit mal, Seizure, Shudder, Sob, Spasm, Throe, Tic

**Cook(s), Cooker(y), Cooking** Aga®, Babbler, Babbling brook, Bain marie, Bake, Balti, Barbecue, Beeton, Benghazi, Bhindi, Bouche, Braise, Broil, Cacciatore, Calabash, Captain, Casserole, Charbroil, Chargrill, Chef, Coction, Coddle, Concoct, Cordon bleu, Costard, Creole, Cuisine, Cuisinier, Deep-fry, Delia, Devil, Do, Doctor, Dumple, Easy over, Edit, En papillote, Escoffier, Explorer, Fake, Falsify, Fiddle, Fireless, Fix, Flambé, Forge, Fricassee, Fry, Fudge, Fusion, Gastronomy, Gratinate, Greasy, Griddle, Grill, Haute cuisine, Haybox, Hibachi, Hot plate, Jackaroo, Kiln, Lyonnaise, Marengo, Marinière, Meunière, Microwave, Mount, Nouvelle cuisine, Poach, Prepare, Pressure, Provencale, Range, Ribroast, Rig, Ring, Roast, Roger, Sauté, Short-order, Silver, Sous-chef, Spit, Steam, Stew, Stir-fry, Stove, Tandoori, Tikka, Tire, Toast

▷ **Cook** *may indicate* an anagram

**Cookie** Biscuit, Fortune, Rye-roll

**Cool(er), Coolant, Cooling, Coolness** Ace, Aloof, Aplomb, Calm, Can, Chill, Chokey, Collected, Composed, Cryogen, Cryostat, Defervescence, Desert, Dignified, Dispassionate, Distant, Esky®, Fan, Frappé, Fridge, Frigid, Frosty, Gaol, Goglet, Heat sink, Hip, Ice(box), Imperturbable, In, Jail, Jug, Keel, La Nina, Lubricating oil, Maraging, Nervy, Nonchalant, Offish, Phlegm, Poise, Prison, Quad, Quod, Radiator, Reefer, Refresh, Regenerative, Reserved, Sangfroid, Serene, Shady, Skeigh, Splat, Stir, Super-duper, Sweat, Temper(ate), Thou(sand), Trendy, Unruffled, Wint(e)ry

**Coop** Cage, Cavie, Confine, Gaol, Hutch, Mew, Pen, Rip

**Cooper** Gary, Henry, Tubman

**Cooperate, Cooperation, Cooperative** Accommodate, Ally, Artel, Bipartisan, Collaborate, Combine, Conspire, Contribute, Coop, Credit union, Give and take, Liaise, Pitch in, Play (ball), Synergy, Tame, Teamwork, Together, Worker's

**Coordinate(s), Coordinated, Coordination** Abscissa, Abscisse, Agile, Arrange, Cartesian, Del, Ensemble, Harmony, Nabla, Orchestrate, Ordonnance, Peer, Polar, Right ascension, Spherical, Synergy, Teamwork, Tight, Twistor, Waypoint, X, Y, Z

**Coot** Stupid, Sultan

**Cop(s)** Bag, Bull, Catch, Copper, Dick, Flic, Keystone, Peeler, Peon, →**POLICEMAN**, Silent

**Copal** Dammar, Resin

**Cope** Chlamys, Deal, Face, Fare, Handle, Hood, Make do, →**MANAGE**, Mantle, Meet, Negotiate, Pallium, Poncho, Scrat(ch)

**Coping (stone)** Balustrade, Capstone, Skew

**Copious** Abundant, Affluent, Ample, Fecund, Fluent, Fruitful, Fulsome, Plentiful, Profuse

**Copper(s)** As, Atacamite, Beast, Blister, Bluebottle, Bobby, Bornite, Busy, Cash, Cent, Chessylite, →**COIN**, Cu, D, Dam, Double, Enargite, Erinite, Flatfoot, Lawman, Lota(h), Malachite, Mountain-blue, Ormolu, Peacock, Pence, Penny, Pfennig, Pie, Pig, Plack, Policeman, Red, Rosser, Rozzer, S, Sen(s), Slop, Small change, Special, Traybit, Venus, Verdet, Verditer, Washer, Washtub, Wire bar

**Coppice, Copse** Thicket, Underwood

**Copulate** Boff, Intercourse, Line, Mate, Roger, Serve, Tread, Tup

**Copy(ing), Copier, Copyist, Copywriter** Adman, Aemule, Ape, Apograph, Association, Autotype, Calk, Calque, Camera-ready, Carbon, Clerk, Clone, Counterpart, Crib, Cyclostyle, Diazo, Ditto, Double, Download, Duplicate, Dyeline, Echo, Echopraxia, Ectype, Edition, Eidograph, Electro, Emulate, Engross, Estreat, Example, Facsimile, Fair, Fax, Flimsy, Forge, Hard, Hectograph, →**IMITATE**, Issue, Jellygraph, Knocking, Knockoff, Manifold, Manuscript, Match, Me-tooer, Microdot, Milline, Mimeograph®, Mimic, Mirror, MS, Offprint, Ozalid, Pantograph, Parrot, Photostat®, Pirate, Plagiarism, Polygraph, Read-out, Repeat, Replica, Reprint, Repro, Reproduce, Review, Rip, Roneo®, Scanner, Scribe, Script, Scrivener, Sedulous, Show, Simulate, Skim, Soft, Spit, Stat, Stencil, Stuff, Tall, Telautograph®, Telefax, Tenor, Tenure, Trace, Transcribe, Transume, Transumpt, Typescript, Vidimus, Xerox®

**Copyright** C, Landgrab

**Coquette** Agacerie, Flirt, Rosina, Tease, Vamp

**Cor** Bath, Crumbs, Ephah, Gosh, Homer

**Coracle** Currach, Curragh

**Coral (reef)** Alcyonaria, Aldabra, Atoll, Brain, Cup, Deadmen's fingers, Gorgonia(n), Laccadives, Madrepore, Millepore, Organ-pipe, Pink, Precious, Red, Reef, Sea fan, Sea ginger, Sea-pen, Sea whip, Seed, Staghorn, Stony, Zoothome

**Cord, Cord-like** Achilles tendon, Aiguillette, Band, Bedford, Bind, Boondoggle, Cat-gut, Chenille, Clew, Communication, Creance, Cybernaculum, Drawstring, Elephant, Flex, Fourragère, Funicle, Gasket, Heddle, Lace, Laniard, Lanyard, Ligature, Line, Moreen, Myelon, Nerve, Net, Ocnus, Picture, Piping, Quipo, Quipu, Rep(s), Restiform, Rip,

Rope, Sash, Sennit, Service, Shroudline, Sinew, Sinnet, Spermatic, Spinal, Static line, →STRING, Tendon, Tie, Tieback, Torsade, Twine, Twitch, Umbilical, Vocal, Wick

**Cordial** Amicable, Anise(ed), Anisette, Benedictine, Cassis, Drink, Elderflower, Gracious, Grenadine, Hearty, Hippocras, Kind, Neighbourly, Oporice, Orangeade, Persico(t), Pleasant, Ratafia, Rosa-solis, Roso(g)lio, Shrub, Sweets, Tar-water, Tonic, Warm

**Cordon** Band, Beltcourse, Picket, Police, Ring, Sanitaire, Surround

**Corduroy** Rep(p)

**Cordyline** Ti-tree

**Core** Barysphere, Calandria, Campana, Centre, Chog, Essence, Filament, Hard, Heart, Hub, Kernel, Magnetic, Nife, Nitty-gritty, Plerome, Quintessence, Runt, Slug

**Co-religionist** Brother

**Corfu** Corfiot(e)

**Coriander** Cilantro

**Corinthian(s)** Casuals, Caulis, Epistolaters

**Cork(ed), Corker** Balsa, Bouché, Bung, Float(er), Humdinger, Mountain, Oner, Periderm, Phellem, Phellogen, Plug, Seal, Shive, Stopper, Suber(ate)

**Corkscrew** Bore, Opening, Spiral, Twine

**Cormorant** Duiker, Duyker, Scart(h), Shag, Skart(h)

**Corn(y)** Bajr(a), Banal, Blé, Callus, Cereal, Cob, Dolly, Durra, Emmer, Epha, Flint, Gait, Graddan, Grain, Green, Grist, Guinea, Hokey, Icker, Indian, Kaffir, Kanga pirau, Mabela, Maize, Mealie, Muid, Negro, Nubbin, Pickle, Pinole, Posho, Rabi, Rye, Seed, Shock, Stitch, Straw, Sugar, Sweet, Tail ends, Thrave, Trite, Zea

**Corncrake** Landrail

**Cornel** Dogberry, Tree

**Corner** Amen, Angle, Bend, Canthus, Cantle, Canton, Chamfer, Cranny, Dangerous, Diêdre, Dominate, Elbow, Entrap, Hog, Hole, Hospital, Inglenook, Long, Lug, Monopoly, NE, Niche, Nook, NW, Penalty, Predicament, Quoin, SE, Short, Speakers', Spot, SW, Tack, Tattenham, Tight, Trap, Tree, Vertex

**Cornerstone** Coi(g)n, Encoignure, Skew-corbel, Skew-put, Skew-table

**Cornet** Cone, Cornopean, Field, Horn

**Cornice** Surbase

**Cornish(man)** Cousin Jack

**Cornstalks** Strammel, Straw, Strummel, Stubble

**Cornucopia** Amalthea, Horn

**Cornwall** SW

**Corollary** Conclusion, Dogma, Porism, Rider, Theory, Truism

**Corona** Aureole, Cigar, Halo, Larmier, Nimbus, Wreath

**Coronation** Enthronement

**Coroner** Procurator fiscal

**Corporal** Bardolph, Bodily, Bombardier, Brig(adier), Lance-pesade, Lance-prisade, Lance-prisado, Lance-speisade, Master, Naik, NCO, Nym, Pall, Physical, Trim

**Corporation** Alvine, Beer gut, Belly, Body, Breadbasket, Closed, Commune, Company, Conglomerate, Guild, Kite, Kyte, Paunch, Pot(-belly), Public, Public service, Stomach, Swag-belly, Tum, Wame, Wem

**Corps** Body, C, Cadet, Crew, Diplomatic, Marine, Peace, RAC, RE, REME, Unit

**Corpse(s)** Blob, Body, Cadaver, Carcass, Carrion, Deader, Dust, Goner, Like, Mort, Quarry, Relic, Remains, Stiff, Zombi(e)

**Corpulence, Corpulent** Adipose, Fat, Fleshy, Gross, Obese, Poddy, Stout, Thickset, Tubby

**Corpuscle** Cell, Erythrocyte, Malpighian, Meissner's, Microcyte, Neutrophil, Pacinian, Phagocyte, Porkilocyte, Tactile

**Corral** Kraal, OK

**Correct(ive), Correcting, Correctly, Correctness, Correction, Corrector** About east, Accepted, Accurate, Alexander, Align, Amend, Aright, Blue-pencil, Bodkin, Castigate, Chasten, Chastise, Check, Cheese, Comme il faut, Decorous, Diorthortic,

Discipline, Edit, Emend, Epanorthosis, Ethical, Exact, Fair, Fix, Grammatical, Kosher, Legit, Letter perfect, Mend, Orthopaedic, Politically, Precise, Preterition, Probity, Proofread, Proper, Propriety, Punctilious, Punish, Purism, Rebuke, Rectify, Rectitude, Red pencil, Redress, Reform, Remedial, Reprove, Revise, Right(en), Scold, Spinning-house, Spot-on, Straighten, Sumpsimus, Tickety-boo, Tippex®, Trew, True, Twink, U, Yep, Yes

▷ **Corrected** *may indicate* an anagram

**Correspond(ence), Correspondent, Corresponding** Accord, Agree, Analogy, Assonance, Coincident, Communicate, Congruence, Correlate, Counterpart, Cynghanedd, Epistolist, Equate, Equivalence, Eye-rhyme, Fit, Foreign, Hate mail, Homolog(ue), Identical, Isomorph, Lobby, Match, On all fours, One-one, One to one, Par, Parallel, Parity, Pen-friend, Penpal, Post(bag), Relate, Snail mail, Symmetry, Sync, Tally, Veridical, War, Write

**Corridor** Air, Aisle, Berlin, Entry, Gallery, Greenway, Lobby, Passage, Penthouse, Polish, Re-entry

**Corroborate** Confirm, Support, Underpin, Verify

**Corrode(d), Corrosion, Corrosive** Acid, Acid rain, Brinelling, Burn, Canker, Caustic, Decay, Eat, Erode, Etch, Fret, Gnaw, Hydrazine, Mordant, →**ROT**, Rubiginous, Rust, Waste

**Corrugate** Gimp, Ridge

**Corrupt(er), Corrupting, Corruption** Abuse, Adulterate, Bastardise, Bent, Bobol, Bribable, Canker, Cesspit, Contaminated, Debase, Debauch, Debosh, Decadent, Defile, Degenerate, Depravity, Dishonest, Dissolute, Dry rot, Emancipate, Embrace(o)r, Embrasor, Empoison, Enseam, Etch, Evil, Fester, Gangrene, Graft(er), Immoral, Impaired, Impure, Infect, Inquinate, Jobbery, Leprosy, Malversation, Mar, Nefarious, Obelus, Payola, Perverse, Poison, Pollute, Power, Putrefaction, Putrid, Rakery, Ret(t), Rigged, Rot, Scrofulous, Seduce, Sepsis, Septic, Sleaze, Sodom, Sophisticate, Spoil, Stench, Suborn, Taint, Tammany, Twist, Ulcered, Venal, Vice, Vitiate

**Corsage** Buttonhole, Pompadour, Posy, Spray

**Corsair** Barbary, Picaroon, Pirate, Privateer, Robber, Rover

**Corset, Corslet** Belt, Bodice, Busk, Featherbone, Girdle, Hourglass, Lorica, Roll-on, Stays, Thorax, Waspie, Whalebone

**Corsican** Napoleon

**Cortege** Parade, Retinue, Train

**Cortex** Cerebral, Renal

**Cortisone** Hecogenin

**Corundum** Emery, Sapphire

**Coruscate** Flash

**Corvo** Rolfe

**Corybant** Roisterer

**Cosh** Life preserver, Mug, Sap

**Cosmetic** Aloe vera, Beautifier, Blusher, Bronzer, Chapstick, Conditioner, Detangler, Eye-black, Eyeliner, Eye-shadow, Face-lift, Face-pack, Foundation, Fucus, Highlighter, Kohl, Lightener, Liner, Lip gloss, Lip liner, Lippie, Lipstick, Lotion, Maquillage, Mascara, Moisturizer, Mousse, Mudpack, Nail polish, Paint, Panstick, Pearl-powder, Pearl-white, Powder, Q-tip, Reface, Rouge, Talcum, Toner, Warpaint

▶ **Cosmic** *see* **COSMOS**

**Cosmonaut** Gagarin, Spaceman, Tereshkova

**Cosmopolitan** International, Urban

**Cosmos, Cosmic** Globe, Heaven, Infinite, Mundane, Nature, Universe, World

**Cossack** Ataman, Hetman, Kazak(h), Mazeppa, Russian, Tartar, Zaporogian

**Cosset** Caress, Coddle, Fondle, Nanny, Pamper

**Cost(s), Costly** Be, Bomb, Carriage, Charge, Current, Damage, Direct, Disadvantage, Earth, Escuage, Estimate, Exes, →**EXPENSE**, Factor, Fetched, Fixed, Hire, Historic(al),

Indirect, Legal, Loss, Marginal, Opportunity, Outlay, Overhead, Precious, Price, Prime, Quotation, Rate, Rent, Running, Sacrifice, Standard, Storage, Sumptuous, Tab, Toll, Unit, Upkeep, Usurious, Variable

**Costa Rica(n)** Tico

**Costermonger** Barrow-boy, Kerb-merchant, Pearly, Pearly king, Pearly queen

**Costume(s)** Apparel, Attire, Camagnole, Cossie, Dress, Ensemble, Garb, Get-up, Gi(e), Guise, Judogi, Livery, Maillot, Motley, National, Nebris, Polonaise, Rig, Ruana, Surcoat, Tanga, Togs, Trollopee, Tutu, Uniform, Wardrobe, Wear

**Cosy** Cosh, Gemutlich, Intime, Snug

**Cot** Bed(stead), Cotangent, Dovehouse, Moses basket

**Coterie** Camarilla, Cell, Cenacle, Circle, Clan, Clique, Club, Faction, Ring, Set, Society

**Cottage(r)** Bach, Batch, Bordar, Bothie, Bothy, Bower, Box, Bungalow, Cabin, Cape Cod, Chalet, Cot, Crib, Dacha, Dove, Gite, Home-croft, Hut, Lodge, Mailer, Thatched

**Cotton** Absorbent, Agree, AL, Alabama, Balbriggan, Batiste, Batting, Bengal, Calico, Candlewick, Ceiba, Chambray, Cheesecloth, Chino, Chintz, Collodion, Coutil(le), Cretonne, Denim, Dho(o)ti, Dimity, Ducks, Fustian, Galatea, Gingham, Gossypine, Gossypium, Humhum, Ihram, Jaconet, Kapok, Lavender, Lawn, Lea, Lille, Lint, Lisle, Longcloth, Madras, Manchester, Marcella, Muslin, Nainsook, Nankeen, Nankin, Nap, Osnaburg, Percale, Pongee, Sateen, Sea-island, Seersucker, Silesia, Stranded, Surat, T-cloth, Thread, Twig, Upland, Velveteen

**Cotton soil** Regar, Regur

**Cotyledon** Seed-leaf

**Couch** Bed, Casting, Davenport, Daybed, → **DIVAN**, Express, Grass, Lurk, Palanquin, Palkee, Palki, Quick, Recamier, Sedan, Settee, Sofa, Studio, Triclinium, Vis-à-vis, Winnipeg, Word

**Coué** Auto-suggestion

**Cougar** Cat, Painter, Puma

**Cough(ing)** Bark, Chin, Croup, Expectorate, Hack, Harrumph, Hawk, Hem, Hoast, Hooping, Kink, Pertussis, Phthisis, Rale, Tisick, Tussis, Ugh, Whooping

**Could** Couth, Mought

**Council (meeting), Councillor, Counsel(lor), Counselling** Achitophel, Admonish, Admonitor, Advice, Advocate, Ahithophel, Alderman, Alfred, Amphictryon, Anziani, Aread, Ar(r)e(e)de, Assembly, Attorney, Aulic, Aunt, Ayuntamiento, Board, Body, Boule, Bundesrat, Burgess, Cabal, Cabinet, Casemate, Committee, Consistory, Corporation, County, Cr, Decurion, Defending, Dergue, Devil, Dietine, Divan, Douma, Duma, Ecofin, Ecumenical, Egeria, Europe, European, Executive, Exhort, General, Great, Greenbag, Hebdomadal, Indaba, Induna, Industrial, Info, Islands, Jirga, Junta, Kabele, Kebele, King's, Kite, Landst(h)ing, Lateran, Latrocinium, Leader, Legislative, Loan, Majlis, Mentor, Nestor, Nicaean, Nicene, Panchayat, Paraclete, Parish, Powwow, Press, Privy, Prosecuting, Provincial, Queen's, Rede, Regional, Reichsrat, Relate, Robber, Runanga, Samaritan, Sanhedrim, Sanhedrin, Security, Senate, Shoora, Shura, Sobranje, Sobranye, Soviet, States, Syndicate, Synedrion, Synod, Thing, Town, Tradeboard, Trades, Trent, Tridentine, Trullan, Unitary, Vatican, Volost, Wages, Whitley, Witan, Witenagemot, Works, Zemstvo, Zila, Zila parishad, Zillah

**Count(ed), Counter(balance), Counting** Abacus, Add, Algoriam, Anti, Aristo, Balance, Bank, Bar, Basie, Blood, Buck, Buffet, Calculate, Calorie, Cavour, Census, Check, Chip, Compute, Coost, Crystal, Cuisenaire rods, Deem, Depend, Desk, Disc, Dracula, Dump, Earl, Enumerate, Fish, Geiger, Geiger-Muller, Graf(in), Grave, Itemise, Jet(t)on, Landgrave, Margrave, Marker, Matter, Meet, Merel(l), Meril, Milton work, Nobleman, Number, Numerate, Obviate, Olivia, Oppose, Outtell, Palatine, Palsgrave, Paris, Pollen, Presume, Proportional, Rebut, → **RECKON**, Refute, Rejoinder, Rely, Resist, Respond, Retaliate, Retort, Rhinegrave, Riposte, Scaler, Scintillation, Score, Shopboard, Sperm, Squail, Statistician, Stop, Sum, Table, Tally, Tell, Tiddleywink, Tolstoy, Ugolino, Walk, Weigh, Zeppelin, Zinc

**Countenance** Approve, Aspect, Brow, Endorse, Face, Favour, Mug, Sanction, Support, Visage

**Counteract(ing)** Ant-, Antidote, Cancel, Correct, Frustrate, Neutralise, Offset, Talion

**Counterbalance** Bascule, Offset, Undo, Weigh

**Counter-charge** Recrimination

**Counterclockwise** L(a)evorotatory

**Counterfeit(er)** Bastard, Belie, Bogus, Boodle, Brum, Coiner, Doctor, Duffer, Dummy, Fain, Fantasm, Fayne, Feign, Flash, Forge, Fraudster, Imitant, Paperhanger, Phantasm, Phoney, Pinchbeck, Postiche, Pseudo, Queer, Rap, Schlenter, Sham, Shan(d), Simular, Simulate, Skim, Slang, Slip, Smasher, Snide, Spurious, Stumer

**Counterfoil** Stub

**Counterglow** Gegenschein

**Counter-irritant** Seton

**Countermand** Abrogate, Annul, Cancel, Override, Overrule, Rescind, Retract, Revoke, Unorder

**Counterpart** Copy, Double, Obverse, Oppo, Parallel, Shadow, Similar, Spit(ting), Tally, Twin

**Counterpoint** Contrapuntal, Descant

**Countersign** Endorse, Password

**Counterthrust** Riposte

**Counties, County** Co, Comital, Comitatus, District, Hundred, Metropolitan, Palatine, Parish, Seat, Shire, Six

---

## COUNTIES

| *2 letters:* | Herts | Tyrone | Buteshire |
|---|---|---|---|
| NI | Hunts | | Caithness |
| Sy | Kerry | *7 letters:* | Champagne |
| | Laois | Cumbria | Cleveland |
| *3 letters:* | Louth | Donegal | Fermanagh |
| Ely | Meath | Gwynedd | Hampshire |
| Som | Moray | Kildare | Loamshire |
| | Notts | Leitrim | Roscommon |
| *4 letters:* | Omagh | Norfolk | The Mearns |
| Avon | Perth | Rutland | Tipperary |
| Beds | Powys | Suffolk | Waterford |
| Cork | Salop | Torfaen | Westmeath |
| Down | Sligo | Wexford | Yorkshire |
| Fife | Wilts | Wicklow | |
| Kent | Worcs | | *10 letters:* |
| Mayo | | *8 letters:* | Banffshire |
| Ross | *6 letters:* | Cheshire | Ceredigion |
| | Antrim | Cornwall | Derbyshire |
| *5 letters:* | Armagh | Finnmark | Devonshire |
| Angus | Barset | Kesteven | Humberside |
| Cavan | Carlow | Kilkenny | Lancashire |
| Clare | Dorset | Limerick | Merseyside |
| Clwyd | Dublin | Longford | Midlothian |
| Derry | Durham | Lothians | Nairnshire |
| Devon | Galway | Monaghan | Perthshire |
| Dyfed | Glamis | Somerset | Shropshire |
| Essex | Offaly | | Sutherland |
| Flint | Surrey | *9 letters:* | West Sussex |
| Gwent | Sussex | Berkshire | |

| | | | |
|---|---|---|---|
| *11 letters:* | Peeblesshire | West Glamorgan | *15 letters:* |
| Breconshire | Renfrewshire | West Yorkshire | Caernarvonshire |
| East Lothian | Selkirkshire | | Carmarthenshire |
| Lanarkshire | Warwickshire | *14 letters:* | Gloucestershire |
| Londonderry | West Midlands | Brecknockshire | Kincardineshire |
| Oxfordshire | Westmoreland | Dumbartonshire | Montgomeryshire |
| Radnorshire | Wigtownshire | Glamorganshire | Neath Port Talbot |
| Tyne and Wear | | Invernessshire | Ross and Cromarty |
| West Lothian | *13 letters:* | Leicestershire | Vale of Glamorgan |
| | Dumfriesshire | Merionethshire | |
| *12 letters:* | Herefordshire | Northumberland | *16 letters:* |
| Berwickshire | Monmouthshire | North Yorkshire | Clackmannanshire |
| Denbighshire | Pembrokeshire | South Glamorgan | Northamptonshire |
| Kinrossshire | Roxburghshire | South Yorkshire | |
| Lincolnshire | Staffordshire | | *18 letters:* |
| Mid-Glamorgan | Stirlingshire | | Kirkcudbrightshire |

**Countless** Infinite, Innumerable, Myriad, Umpteen, Unending, Untold

**Country(side), Countries, Countrified** Agrest(i)al, Annam, Arcadia, Bangladesh, Bolivia, Boondocks, Bucolic, Champaign, Clime, Colchis, Edom, Enchorial, Farmland, Fatherland, Georgic, Greenwood, High, Inland, Jordan, Karoo, Karroo, →**LAND**, Lea, Lee, Low, Macedonia, Mongolia, Motherland, Nation, Nature, Oman, Outback, Parish, Paysage, People, Province, Rangeland, Realm, Region, Republic, Rural, Rustic, Satellite, Scenery, Scythia, Soil, Statal, State, Sultanate, The sticks, Thrace, Tundra, Tweedy, Veld, Venezuela, Weald, Wold, Yemen

**Country girl** Amaryllis

**Country house** Hall, Manor, Quinta

**Countryman** Arcadian, Bacon, Boor, Cottager, Culchie, Hayseed, Hick, Hillbilly, Hodge, National, Native, Peasant, Ruralist, Un, Yokel

**Coup** Blow, Deal, KO, Masterstroke, Move, Putsch, Scoop, Stroke, Treason

**Coup d'etat** Putsch

**Coupé** Cabriolet, Landaulet

**Couple(r), Coupling** Acoustic, Ally, Attach, Band, Brace, Bracket, Connect, Direct, Duet, Duo, Dyad, Enlink, Fishplate, Flange, Galvanic, Gemini, Geminy, Hitch, Interlock, Item, →**JOIN**, Marrow, Marry, Mate, Meng(e), Ment, Ming, Octave, Pair, Pr, Relate, Shackle, Tenace, Tie, Tirasse, Turnbuckle, Tway, Twosome, Union, Unite, Universal, Voltaic, Wed, Yoke

**Couple of ducks** Spectacles

**Couplet** Distich, Heroic, Hudibrastic, Riding-rhyme

**Coupon(s)** Ration, Ticket, Voucher

**Courage(ous)** Balls, Ballsy, Bottle, Bravado, Bravery, Bulldog, Cojones, Daredevil, Daring, Derring-do, Dutch, Fortitude, Gallantry, Game, Gimp, Grit, Gumption, Guts, Hardihood, Hardy, Heart, Heroism, Indomitable, Lion-heart, Macho, Manful, Mettle, Moral, Moxie, Nerve, Pluck, Prowess, Resolve, Rum, Spirit, Spirited, Spunk, Stalwart, Steel, Stomach, Valiant, Valour, Wight

**Courgette** Zucchini

**Courier** Carrier pigeon, Deliveryman, Estafette, Fed-EX, Guide, Harbinger, Herald, →**MESSENGER**, Postillion, Postman

**Course(s)** Access, Afters, Aim, Aintree, Antipasto, Appetiser, Arroyo, Ascot, Assault, Atlantic, Back straight, Barge, Bearing, Beat, Belt, Campaign, Canal, Career, Channel, Chantilly, Chase, Circuit, Civics, Collision, Consommé, Conversion, Correspondence, Crash, Current, Curriculum, Cursus, Daltonism, Damp(-proof), Dessert, Diadrom, Dish, Dromic, Easting, Entrée, Epsom, Fish, →**FOOD**, Foundation, Furrow, Gleneagles, Going, Golf, Goodwood, Greats, Gut, Heat, Hippodrome, Hors d'oeuvres, Induction, Isodomon,

Lacing, Lane, Lap, Layer, Leat, Leet, Line, Lingfield, Links, Longchamp, Magnetic, Main, Meal, Meat, Mess, Mizzen, Newbury, Newmarket, Nine-hole, Northing, Nulla, Obstacle, → OF COURSE, Orbit, Orthodromic, Period, Policy, PPE, Practicum, Procedure, Process, Programme, Progress, Pursue, Quadrivium, Race, → RACETRACK, Raik, Ravioli, Refresher, Regimen, Rhumb, Ride, Ring, Rink, Road, Rota, Route, Routine, Run, Rut, Sandown, Sandwich, Semester, Seminar, Series, Slalom, Sorbet, Soup, Southing, Span, Stadium, Starter, Stearage, Steerage, Step(s), Straight, Stratum, Streak, Stream, Stretch, Stretching, String, Syllabus, Tack, Tanride, Tenor, Track, Trade, Trail, Trajectory, Trend, Troon, Vector, Via media, Water table, Way, Wearing, Wentworth, Westing

**Court(ier), Courtship, Courtyard** Ad(vantage), Address, Admiralty, Appellate, Arbitration, Arches, Areopagus, Atrium, Attention, Audience, Audiencia, Aula, Banc, Bar, Basecourt, Bench, Beth Din, Bishop's, Boondock, Caerleon, Camelot, Canoodle, Caravanserai, Cassation, Centre, Chancery, Chase, Clay, Cloister-garth, Commercial, Commissary, Commission, Conscience, Conservancy, Consistory, County, Criminal, Crown, CS, Ct, Curia, Curia Regis, Curtilage, Cutcher(r)y, Damocles, Date, Dedans, Deuce, Dicastery, Diplock, District, Divisional, Doctor's Commons, Domestic, Duchy, Durbar, Dusty Feet, En tout cas, Evora, Eyre, Faculties, Federal, Fehm(gericht), Fehmgerichte, Fiars, Fifteen, Forensic, Forest, Forum, Fronton, Galleria, Garth, Go steady, Grass, Guildenstern, Halimot(e), Hampton, Hard, High, High Commission, Hof, Holy See, Hustings, Hypaethron, Inferior, Innyadr, Intermediate, Invite, Jack, Judicatory, Justice, Juvenile, Kachahri, Kacheri, Kangaroo, Keys, King, King's Bench, Kirk Session, Knave, Law, Law Lords, Leet, Lobby, Lyon, Magistrate's, Majlis, Marshalsea, Mash, Moot, Old Bailey, Open, Osric, Palace, Parvis, Patio, Peristyle, Petty Sessions, Philander, Piepowder, Police, Porte, Praetorium, Prerogative, Presbytery, Prize, Probate, Provincial, Provost, Quad, Quarter Sessions, Queen, Queen's Bench, Racket, Request, Retinue, Romance, Rosenkrantz, Royal, St James's, Sanhedrim, Sanhedrin, Scottishland, See, Seek, Service, Session, Sheriff, Shire-moot, Shoe, Small-claims, Spoon, Stannary, Star Chamber, Sudder, Sue, Suitor, Superior, Supreme, Swanimote, Sweetheart, Synod, Thane, Thegn, Traffic, Trial, Tribunal, Vehm, Vehmgericht(e), Vestibulum, Walk out, Ward, Wardmote, Wench, Woo, World, Wow, Yard, Youth

**Courteous, Courtesy** Affable, Agreement, Bow, Chivalry, Civil, Comity, Debonair, Devoir, Etiquette, Fair, Genteel, Gentilesse, Gentility, Gracious, Hend, Obliging, Polite, Politesse, Refined, Strain, Urbanity, Well-mannered

**Courtesan** Anonyma, Aspasia, Bianca, Bona-roba, Delilah, Demi-monde, Demi-rep, Geisha, Hetaera, Lais, Lampadion, Lorette, Madam, Phryne, Plover, Pornocracy, Prostitute, Stallion, Thais

**Courtly** Aulic, Chivalrous, Cringing, Dignified, Flattering, Refined

**Court-martial** Drumhead

**Courtyard** Area, Atrium, Close, Cortile, Enceinte, Garth, Marae, Patio, Quad

**Cousin(s)** Bette, Cater, Country, Coz, Cross, First, German, Kin, Kissing, Parallel, Robin, Second, Skater

**Couthy** Bien, Nice

**Couturier** Designer, Dior, Dressmaker, Hartnell

**Cove** Abraham's, Arm, Bay, Bight, Buffer, Creek, Cure, Gink, Grot, Guy, Hithe, Hythe, Inlet, Lulworth, Nook

**Covenant(er)** Abrahamic, Alliance, Appurtenant, Bond, Contract, Hillmen, Pledge, Restrictive, Testament, Warranty, Whiggamore

**Coventry** Isolation

**Cover(ed), Coverage, Covering** Adventitia, Air, A l'abri, Amnion, Antependium, Antimacassar, Apron, Aril, Armour, Attire, Awning, Bandage, Barb, Bard(s), Bark, Bathrobe, Bed linen, Bedspread, Bestrew, Bind, Blanket, Bodice, Bonnet, Brood, Bubblewrap, Burka, Bury, Cache-sex, Camouflage, Canopy, Cap, Caparison, Cape, Capsule, Carpet, Cartonnage, Casing, Casque, Catch-all, Caul, Ceil, Ciborium, Ciel, Cladding, Clapboard, Cleithral, Clithral, Cloak, Cloche, Coat, Cocoon, Coleorhiza,

Conceal, Cope, Copyright, Cosy, Cot, Counterpane, Cour, Covert, Cowl, Crust, Curtain, Deadlight, Debruised, Deck, Deputise, Dividend, Dome, Drape(t), Dripstone, Duchesse, Dusting, Dust-sheet, Duvet, Eiderdown, Encase, Endue, Enguard, Enlace, Ensheathe, Enshroud, Envelop(e), Enwrap, Exoderm(is), Exoskeleton, Exposure, Extra, Eyelid, Eye patch, Face, Falx, Fanfare, Fascia, Felting, Fielder, Figleaf, Fingerstall, First-day, Flashing, Flown, Fother, Front, Gaiter, Gambado, Gift wrap, Gild, Glove, Gobo, Grolier, Ground, Groundsheet, G-string, Guarantee, Hap, Harl, Hat, Hatch, Havelock, Heal, Heather, Heel, Hejab, Hele, Hell, Helmet, Hide, Hijab, Hood, Housing, Hubcap, Husk, Ice, Immerse, Incase, Include, Indument, Indusium, Inmask, Insulate, Insurance, Insure, Jacket, Lag, Lambrequin, Laminate, Lampshade, Lay, Leap, Leep, Legging, Legwarmer, Lid, Ligger, Liner, Loincloth, Loose, Manche, Mantle, Mask, Mat, Membrane, Metal, Mort-cloth, Mount, Muffle, Mulch, Notum, Numnah, Obscure, OC, Occlude, On, Oose, Operculum, Orillion, Orlop, Overgrown, Overlap, Overlay, Overnet, Overwrap, Pad, Palampore, Palempore, Pall, Pand, Panoply, Parcel, Partlet, Pasties, Patch, Patent, Pave, Pavilion, Pebbledash, Pelmet, Periderm, Perigone, Pillow sham, Pinny, Plaster, Plate, Pleura, Plumage, Pod, Point, Pseudonym, Pullover, Quilt, Radome, Redingote, Regolith, Report, Riza, Robe, Roof, Roughcast, Rug, Run, Sally, Sarafan, Scabbard, Screen, Serviette, Setting, Shagpile, Sheath, Sheet, Shell, Shelter, Shield, Shower, Shrink-wrap, Shroud, Shuck, Skin, Slipcase, Smokescreen, Solleret, Span, Spat, Splashback, Spread, Stand-by, Stand-in, Stifle, Stomacher, Strew, Superfrontal, Superimpose, Surplice, Swathe, Tampian, Tampion, Tapadera, Tapis, Tarmac, Tarp(aulin), Teacosy, Tectorial, Tectum, Tegmen, Tegument, Tent, Terne, Test(a), Tester, Thatch, Thimble, Thumbstall, Tick(ing), Tidy, Tile, Tilt, Tonneau, Tinfoil, Top, Trapper, Trench, Trip, Turtleback, Twill, Twilt, Umbrella, Up, Upholster, Valance, Veale, Veil, Vele, Veneer, Ventail, Vert, Vesperal, Vest, Vestiture, Visor, Volva, Wainscot, Warrant, Waterdeck, Weeper, Whelm, Whemmle, Whitewash, Whomble, Whommle, Whummle, Wrap, Wrappage, Wrapper, Wreathe, Yapp, Yashmak

**Covert(ly)** Clandestine, Copse, Privy, →SECRET, Shy, Sidelong, Sub rosa, Surreptitious, Tectrix, Ulterior

**Covet(ed), Covetous** Avaricious, Crave, Desiderata, Desire, Eager, Envy, Greedy, Hanker, Yearn

**Cow(s)** Adaw, Alderney, Amate, Appal, Awe, Ayrshire, Belted Galloway, Boss(y), Bovine, Brahmin, Browbeat, Cash, Cattle, Charolais, Colly, Crummy, Dant(on), Daunt, Dexter, Dsomo, Dun, Friesian, Galloway, Gally, Goujal, Guernsey, Hawkey, Hawkie, Heifer, Hereford, Intimidate, Jersey, Kouprey, Kyloe, Lea(h), Mart, Milch, Milker, Mog(gie), Moggy, Mooly, Muley, Mulley, Neat, Oppress, Overawe, Ox-eyed, Redpoll, Red Sindhi, Rother(-beast), Runt, Sacred, Santa Gertrudis, Scare, Simmental, Slattern, Springing, Steer, Step on, Stirk, Subact, Subjugate, Teeswater, Threaten, Unnerve, Vaccine, Zebu, Z(h)o

**Coward(ice), Cowardly** Bessus, Cat, Chicken, Cocoa, Craven, Cuthbert, Dastard, Dingo, Dunghill, Faint-heart, Fraidy-cat, Fugie, Funk, Gutless, Hen, Hilding, Jessie, Lily-livered, Mangy, Meacock, Milk-livered, Nesh, Niddering, Nidderling, Nidering, Niderling, Niding, Nithing, Noel, Panty-waist, Poltroon, Pusillanimous, Recreant, Scaramouch(e), Scaredy cat, Sissy, Slag, Sook, Viliaco, Viliago, Villagio, Villiago, Weak-spirited, White feather, Yellow, Yellow-belly, Yellowstreak

**Cowboy, Cowgirl** Broncobuster, Buckaroo, Cowpoke, Cowpuncher, Gaucho, Inexpert, Io, Jerrybuilder, Leger, Llanero, Neatherd, Puncher, Ranchero, Ritter, Roper, Shoddy, Vaquero, Waddie, Waddy, Wrangler

**Cow-catcher** Fender, Reata

**Cower** Cringe, Croodle, Crouch, Fawn, Quail, Ruck, Skulk, Wince

**Cowl** Bonnet, Capuchin, Granny, Hood, Kilmarnock

**Cowpat** Dung, Tath

**Cowpox** Vaccinia

**Cowshed, Cowstall** Byre, Crib, Loaning, Shippen, Shippon, Stable, Stall, Staw

**Cowslip** Culver-key, Herb Peter, Pa(i)gle
**Cox** Helmsman, Steerer
**Coxcomb** Aril, Caruncle, Copple, Crest, Dandy, Dude, Fop, Jackanapes, Popinjay, Yellow-rattle
**Coy** Arch, Coquettish, Demure, Laithfu', Mim, Modest, Nice, Shamefast, →SHY, Skeigh, Skittish
**Coyote** Prairie-wolf, SD
**CPRS** Think tank
**Crab(by), Crablike, Crabwise** Apple, Attercop, Blue swimmer, Boston, Calling, Cancer, Cancroid, Cantankerous, Capernoity, Cock, Coconut, Daddy, Decapoda, Diogenes, Dog, Ethercap, Ettercap, Fiddler, Ghost, Grouch, Hard-shell, Hermit, Horseman, Horseshoe, King, Land, Limulus, Mantis, Mitten, Mud, Nebula, Ochidore, Oyster, Pagurian, Partan, Pea, Perverse, Podite, Roast, Robber, Rock, Sand, Saucepan-fish, Scrawl, Scrog, Sentinel, Sidewards, Sidle, Soft-shell, Soldier, Spectre, Spider, Std, Stone, Velvet, Velvet-fiddler, Woolly-hand, Xiphosura, Zoea
▷ **Crab** *may indicate* an anagram
**Crab-apple** Scrog-bush, Scrog-buss
**Crab-eater** Urva
**Crabs-eye** Abrus
**Crack(ed), Cracker(s), Cracking** A1, Ace, Ad-lib, Admirable, Attempt, Bananas, Beaut, Biscuit, Bonbon, Break, Cat, Catalytic, Chap, Chasm, Chat, Chink, Chip, Chop, Clap, Cleave, Cleft, Cloff, Confab, Cranny, Craquelure, Craqueture, Craze, Cream, Crepitate, Crevasse, Crevice, Crispbread, Dawn, Decipher, Decode, Def, Doom, Dunt, Elite, Excellent, Expert, Fab, Fatiscent, Fent, Firework, First-rate, Fisgig, Fissure, Fizgig, Flake, Flaw, Flip-flop, Fracture, Gem, Gibe, Go, Graham, Grike, Gryke, Gully, Hairline, Hit, Insane, Jest, Jibe, Joint, Joke, Knacker, Leak, Liar, Little-endian, Lulu, Matzo, Mot, Moulin, One-liner, Oner, Perlite, Peterman, Pleasantry, Pore, Praise, Prawn, Quarter, Quip, Rap, Report, Rhagades, Rictus, Rift, Rille, Rima, Rime, Rimous, Rive, Rock, Saltine, Sand, Seam, Shake, Shatter, Snap, Soda, Solve, Split, Spring, Squib, Sulcus, Super, Toe, Top, Try, Waterloo, Wind shake, Witticism, Yegg
**Crackerjack** Ace, Nailer, Trump
**Crackle, Crackling** Craze, Crepitation, Crepitus, Crinkle, Decrepitate, Fizz, Glaze, Rale, Skin, Static
**Crackpot** Nutter
**Cracksman** Burglar, Peterman, Raffles
**Cradle** Bassinet, Berceau, Book rest, Cat's, Cot, Crib, Cunabula, Hammock, Knife, Nestle, Newton's, Rocker
**Craft(y), Craftwork** Adroitness, Aerostat, Arch, Art, Aviette, Barbola, Batik, Boat, Canal boat, Canny, Cautel, Crochet, Cunning, Disingenuous, Expertise, Finesse, Flotilla, Fly, Foxy, Guile, Hydroplane, Ice-breaker, Insidious, Knack, Kontiki, Landing, Lifeboat, Loopy, Machiavellian, Marquetry, Mister, Mystery, Oomiack, Pedalo, Pirogue, Powerboat, Reynard, Saic, Shallop, Ship, Shrewd, Shuttle, →SKILL, Slee, Sleeveen, Slim, Slippy, Sly, Slyboots, Sneaky, State, Subdolous, Subtil(e), Subtle, Surface, Suttle, Tender, Trade, Triphibian, Umiak, Underhand, Versute, →VESSEL, Wicker, Wile, Workmanship
▷ **Craft** *may indicate* an anagram
**Craftsman** AB, Artificer, Artisan, Artist, Cabinet maker, Chippy, Coppersmith, Cutler, Ebonist, Enameller, Fabergé, Finisher, Gondolier, Guild, Hand, Joiner, Journeyman, Mason, Mechanic, Morris, Opificer, Potter, Saddler, Stonemason, Tinsmith, Wainwright, Wright
**Crag(gy)** Coralline, Eyrie, Gnarled, Height, Heuch, Heugh, Krantz, Noup, Rock, Rugged
**Craig** Ailsa
**Cram(mer), Crammed** Bag, Bone up, Candle-waster, Chock-a-block, Cluster, Craig, Fill, Gag, Gavage, Mug up, Neck, Pang, Prime, Revise, Rugged, Scar(p), Shoehorn, Spur, Stap, Stodge, Stow, Swat, Tuck

**Cramp(ed)** Agraffe, Charleyhorse, Claudication, Confine, Constrict, Crick, Hamper, Hamstring, Incommodious, Musician's, Myalgia, Narrow, Pinch, Poky, Potbound, Restrict, Rigor, Sardines, Scrivener's palsy, Squeeze, Stunt, Tenesmus, Tetany, Writer's

**Crane, Crane-driver** Adjutant-bird, Australian, Brolga, Cherry picker, Container, Davit, Deck, Demoiselle, Derrick, Dogman, Dragline, Gantry, Gooseneck, Grabbing, Herd, Heron, Hooper, Ichabod, Jenny, Jib, Jigger, Kenworthy, Luffing-jib, Native companion, Numidian, Rail, Sandhill, Sarus, Sedge, Seriema, Shears, Sheer, Siege, Stork, Stretch, Tower, Tulip, Whooper, Whooping, Winch

**Crane-fly** Daddy-long-legs, Leatherjacket, Spinning-jenny, Tipulidae

**Cranium** Harnpan

**Crank(y)** Bell, Eccentric, Grouch, Handle, Lever, Mot, Oddball, Perverse, Start, Weirdo, Whim, Wince, Winch, Wind

**Crap** Feculence

**Crash** Accident, Bingle, Collapse, Disk, Ditch, Dush, Fail, Fall, Fragor, Frush, Intrude, Linen, Meltdown, Nosedive, Pile up, Plough into, Prang, Rack, Ram, Rote, Shock, Shunt, Slam, Smash, South Sea Bubble, Thunderclap, Topple, Wham, Wrap

▷ **Crashes** *may indicate* an anagram

**Crass** Coarse, Crude, Gross, Naff, Rough, Rude

**Crate** Banger, Biplane, Box, Case, Ceroon, Crib, Hamper, Jalopy, Langrenus, Petavius, Purbach, Rustbucket, Sero(o)n, Soapbox, Tea chest, Tube

**Crater** Alphonsus, Aniakchak, Aristarchus, Aristotle, Askja, Autolycus, Bail(l)y, Blowhole, Caldera, Cavity, Cissing, Clavius, Copernicus, Dent, Fra Mauro, Grimaldi, Hipparchus, Hole, Hollow, Impact, Kepler, Kilauea, Maar, Meteor, Newton, Pit, Plato, Ptolemaeus, Pythagoras, Schickard, Sinus iridum, Theophilus, Tycho

**Cravat** Ascot, Neckatee, Neck-cloth, Oerlay, Overlay, Scarf, Soubise, Steenkirk, Steinkirk, Tie

**Crave, Craving** Appetent, Appetite, Aspire, Beg, Beseech, Covet, Desire, Entreat, Gasp, Greed, Hanker, Hunger, Itch, Libido, Long, Lust, Malacia, Methomania, Munchies, Opsomania, Orexis, Pica, Polyphagia, Sitomania, The munchies, Thirst, Yearn, Yen

**Craven** Abject, Coward, Dastard, Hen, Recreant

**Crawl(er)** All fours, Aswarm, Australian, Back, Booze up, Clamber, Creep, Cringe, Drag, Front, Grovel, Inchworm, Isopod, Jenkins, Lag, Lickspittle, Louse, Low gear, Pub, Reptile, Scramble, Scrome, Side, Skulk, Slither, Snail, Swim, Sycophant, Tantony, Termite, Trail, Truckle, Trudge(o)n, Yes-man

**Crayfish** Astacology, Gilgie, Jilgie, Marron, Yabbie, Yabby

**Crayon** Chalk, Colour, Conté®, Pastel, Pencil, Sauce

**Craze(d), Crazy** Absurd, Ape, Apeshit, Avid, Barking, Barmy, Bats, Batty, Berserk, Bonkers, Break, Cornflake, Crack(ers), Crackpot, Cult, Daffy, Dement, Derange, Dingbats, Dippy, Distraught, Doiled, Doilt, Doolally, Doolally tap, Dottle, Dotty, Fad, Flaky, Flaw, Folie, Frantic, Furious, Furore, Furshlugginer, Gaga, Geld, Gonzo, Gyte, Haywire, Headbanger, Insane, Loco, Loony, Loopy, Lunatic, Madden, Maenad(ic), Mania, Manic, Mattoid, Melomania, Meshug(g)a, Moonstruck, Nuts, Odd, Out to lunch, Porangi, Potty, Psycho(path), Rage, Ramp, Rave, Round the bend, Round the twist, Scatty, Screwball, Skivie, Slatey, Stunt, Thing, Troppo, Typomania, Unhinge, Wacko, W(h)acky, Wet, Whim, Wowf, Zany

▷ **Crazy** *may indicate* an anagram

**Creak(y)** Cry, Grate, Grind, Rheumatic, Scraich, Scraigh, Scroop, Seam, Squeak

**Cream(y)** Barrier, Bavarian, Best, Chantilly, Cherry-pick, Cleansing, Clotted, Cold, Cornish, Crème fraîche, Devonshire, Double, Elite, Flower, Foundation, Frangipane, Ganache, Glacier, Heavy, Ivory, Jollop, Lanolin, Liniment, Lotion, Mousse, Off-white, Ointment, Opal, Paragon, Pastry, Peppermint, Pick, Ream, Rich, Salad, Salve, Shaving, Sillabub, Single, Skim, Smitane, Sour, Sun(screen), Syllabub, Unguent, Vanishing, Whipped, Whipping

**Crease(d)** Bowling, Crinkle, Crumple, → **FOLD**, Goal, Lined, Lirk, Pitch, Pleat, Ply, Popping, Return, Ridge, Ruck(le), Ruga, Rugose, Wreathe, Wrinkle

**Create, Creation, Creative** Art(s)y, Brainstorm, Build, Cause, Coin, Compose, Continuous, Craft, Devise, Dreamtime, Engender, Establish, Fabricate, Forgetive, Form, Found, Generate, Genesis, Godhead, Hexa(h)emeron, Ideate, Imaginative, →INVENT, Kittle, Knit, Nature, Omnific, Oratorio, Originate, Produce, Promethean, Shape, Synthesis, Universe

**Creator** Ahura Mazda, Author, Demiurge, Demiurgus, God, Inventor, Maker, Ormazd, Ormuzd

**Creature** Animal, Ankole, Basilisk, Beast, Being, Bigfoot, Chevrotain, Cratur, Critter, Crittur, Indri, Mammal, Man, Moner(on), Nekton, Organism, Saprobe, Sasquatch, Sphinx, Whiskey, Wight, Zoon

**Credence, Credential(s)** Certificate, Document, Papers, Qualifications, Shelf, Testimonial

**Credibility, Credible, Credit(or), Credits** Ascribe, Attribute, Belief, Billboard, Brownie points, Byline, Carbon, Catholic, Crawl, Easy terms, Esteem, Extended, Family, Ghetto, Honour, HP, Kite, Kudos, LC, Lender, Mense, Never-never, On the nod, Post-war, Probable, Reliable, Renown, Repute, Revolving, Shylock, Social, Strap, Street, Tally, Tax, Tick, Title, Trust, Weight, Youth

**Credulous** Charlie, Gobe-mouches, Green, Gullible, Naive, Simple, Superstitious, Trusting

**Creed** Apostles', Athanasian, Belief, Doctrine, Faith, Ideology, Islam, Ism, Nicene, Ophism, Outworn, Persuasion, Sect, Tenet

**Creek** Antietam, Bay, Breaches, Cooper, Cove, Crick, Dawson, Estuary, Fleet, Geo, Gio, Goe, Indian, Inlet, Kill, Pow, Slough, Vae, Voe, Wick

**Creel** Basket, Hask, Scull, Skull

**Creep(er), Creeping, Creeps, Creepy** Ai, Ampelopsis, Arbutus, Aseismic, Boston ivy, Cleavers, Crawl, Eery, Function, Grew, Grovel, Grue, Heebie-jeebies, Heeby-jeebies, Herpetic, Honey, Inch, Insect, Ivy, Mission, Nerd, Nuthatch, Periwinkle, Pussyfoot, Repent, Reptant, Sarmentous, Sidle, Silverweed, Sinister, Sittine, Skulk, Slink, Snake, Sneak(sby), Sobole(s), Soil, Speedwell, Steal, Toad, Tropaeolum, Truckle, Uncanny, Vinca, Vine, Virginia, Wickthing, Willies

**Creeping Jenny** Moneywort

**Cremate, Cremation, Crematorium** Burn, Char, Cinerarium, Ghat, Ghaut, Incinerate, Pyre, Sati, Suttee, Ustrinium

**Creole** Gullah, Haitian, Kriol, Papiamento, Tok Pisin

**Crepe** Blini, Blintz(e), Canton, Pancake

**Crescent** Barchan(e), Bark(h)an, Fertile, Growing, Lune(tte), Lunulate, Lunule, Meniscus, Moon, Red, Sickle, Waxing

**Cress** Cardamine, Garden, Hoary, Isatis, Pepperwort, Swine's, Thale, Wart, Water, Yellow

**Crest(ed)** Acme, Brow, Chine, Cimier, Cockscomb, Comb, Copple, Cornice, Crista, Height, Kirimon, Knap, Mon, Peak, Pileate, Pinnacle, Plume, Ridge, Rig, Summit, Tappit, Tee, →TOP, Tufty, Wreath

**Cretaceous** Chalky, Senonian, The Chalk

**Cretan** Candiot(e), Minoan, Teucer

**Crevasse** Bergschrund, Chasm, Gorge, Rimaye

**Crevice** Chine, Cranny, Fissure, Interstice, Ravine, Vallecula

**Crew** Boasted, Company, Complement, Co-pilot, Core, Deckhand, Eight, Equipage, Four, Ground, Lot, Manners, Men, Oars, Prize, Sailors, Salts, Seamen, Ship men, Team, Teme, Torpid

**Crew-cut** Not(t)

**Crib** Aid, Cheat, Cot, Cowhouse, Cradle, Cratch, Filch, Horse, →KEY, Manger, Pony, Purloin, Putz, Shack, Stall, Steal, Trot

**Crick** Cramp, Kink, Spasm

**Cricket(er)** All-rounder, Balm, Bat, Bosanquet, Botham, Bowler, Bradman, CC, Cicada, Dry-bob, Extra cover, Fly slip, French, Gentleman, Gower, Grace, Grasshopper, Grig,

Hobbs, Hopper, Jerusalem, Katydid, Keeper, Knott, Lara, Larwood, Leg, Long-leg, Long-off, Long-on, Longstop, March, May, Mid-on, Mole, Muggleton, Nightwatchman, Nurdle, Off-spinner, Opener, Overs, Packer, Player, Point, Pyjama, Shield, Single-wicket, Slip, Sobers, Spin bowler, Stool, Stridulate, Tate, Test, Tettix, Tip and run, Vigoro, Warner, Wart-biter, Windball, Windies, Wisden, XI (gent), Yahoo

**Cricket ground** Edgbaston, Lords, The Oval

**Crier** Bellman, Herald, Muezzin, Niobe, Outrooper

**Crikey** Argh, Gosh, I say

**Crime** ABH, Attentat, Barratry, Bias, Caper, Car jack, Chantage, Chaud-mellé, Computer, Corpus delicti, Ecocide, Embracery, Fact, Felony, Fraud, GBH, Graft, Hate, Heist, Iniquity, Inside job, Insider trading, Malefaction, Malfeasance, Mayhem, Misdeed, Misdemeanour, →OFFENCE, Organised, Ovicide, Peccadillo, Perjury, Pilferage, Public wrong, Ram raid, Rap, Rape, Rebellion, →SIN, Snaffling-lay, Stranger, Theft, Thievery, Tort, Transgression, Treason, Victimless, Villa(i)ny, War, White-collar, Wrong

**Crimea** Balaclava

**Criminal** Accessory, Arsonist, Bandit, Bent, Bigamist, Bushranger, Chain gang, Chummy, Con, Cosa Nostra, Counterfeiter, Crack-rope, →CROOK, Culpable, Culprit, Delinquent, Desperado, Escroc, Fagin, Felon, Flagitious, Forensic, Fraudulent, Gangster, Goombah, Hard men, Heavy, Heinous, Highbinder, Highwayman, Hitman, Hood(lum), Illegal, Jailbird, Ladrone, Lag, Larcener, Lifer, Looter, Lowlife, Maf(f)ia, Malefactor, Maleficent, Malfeasant, Mens rea, Miscreant, Mob(ster), Molester, Ndrangheta, Nefarious, Nefast, Offender, Outlaw, Peculator, Pentito, Perp(etrator), Peterman, Prohibited, Racketeer, Ram raider, Receiver, Recidivist, Reprehensible, Rogue, Rustler, Safe blower, Sinner, Snakehead, Terrorist, Thief, Thug, Triad, Triggerman, Underworld, Villain, Wicked, Wire, Yakuza, Yardie, Yegg

▷ **Criminal** *may indicate* an anagram

**Criminologist** Lombroso

**Crimp** Pleat, Quill

**Crimson** Carmine, Incarnadine, Modena, Red, Scarlet

**Cringe, Cringing** Cower, Creep, Crouch, Cultural, Fawn, Grovel, Recoil, Shrink, Sneaksby, Sycophantic, Truckle, Wince

**Crinkle, Crinkly** Corrugated, Rugate, Rugose

**Crinoline** Farthingale, Hoop

**Cripple(d)** Damage, Debilitate, Disable, Game, Hamstring, Handicap, Injure, →LAME, Lameter, Lamiter, Maim, Paralyse, Polio, Scotch, Spoil

**Crisis** Acme, Craunch, Crunch, Drama, Emergency, Exigency, Fastigium, Fit, Flap, Head, Identity, Make or break, Midlife, Panic, Pass, Quarterlife, Shake-out, Solution, Suez, Test, Turn, Turning-point

**Crisp(ness)** Brisk, Clear, Crimp, Crunchy, Fire-edge, Fresh, Potato, Sharp, Short, Succinct, Terse

**Crispin** Sutor(ial)

**Criss-cross** Alternate, Fret, Interchange, Lattice, Vein

**Criteria, Criterion** Benchmark, Gauge, Koch's postulates, Measure, Precedent, Proof, Rayleigh, Rule, Shibboleth, →STANDARD, Test, Touchstone

**Critic(al), Criticise, Criticism** Acute, Agate, Agee, Animadversion, Archer, Aristarch, Armchair, Arnold, Attack, Backbite, Badmouth, Bagehot, Barrack, Belabour, Bellettrist, Berate, Bird, Blame, Boileau, Boo, Bottom line, Brickbat, Bucket, Captious, Carp, Castigate, Cavil, Censor(ious), →CENSURE, Climacteric, Clobber, Comment, Condemn, Connoisseur, Crab, Criticaster, Crossroads, →CRUCIAL, Crunch, Dangle, Decisive, Denigrate, Denounce, Deprecate, Desperate, Diatribe, Diss, Do down, Dress down, Dutch uncle, Earful, Etain, Exacting, Excoriate, Exegesis, Fastidious, Fateful, Fault-finder, Feuilleton, Flak, Flay, Fulminous, Gosse, Hammer, Harrumph, Hatchet job, Higher, Iconoclast, Ideal, Important, Impugn, Inge, Inveigh, Judge, Judgemental, Judicial, Knife-edge, Knock(er), Lambast, Lash, Leavis, Lecture, Life and death, Literary,

Lower, Masora(h), Mas(s)orete, Mordacious, Nag, Nasute, Nibble, Nice, Niggle, Nitpicker, Obloquy, Overseer, Pan, Pater, Peck, Potshot, Puff, Pundit, Quibble, Rap, Rebuke, Reprehend, Reproach, Review(er), Rip, Roast, Ruskin, Savage, Scalp, Scarify, Scathe, Scorn, Second guess, Serious, Severe, Sharp-tongued, Shaw, Sideswipe, Slag, Slam, Slashing, Slate, Slaughter, Sneer, Snipe, Spray, Stick, Stricture, Strop, Swipe, Tense, Textual, Thersitic, Threap, Tipping-point, Touch and go, Trash, Turning-point, Ultracrepidate, Upbraid, Urgent, Vet, Vital, Vitriol, Vituperation, Vivisect, Watershed, Zoilean, Zoilism

**Croak(er), Croaky** Caw, Creak, Crow, Die, Grumble, Gutturalise, Hoarse, Perish, Sciaena

**Croatia(n)** Cravates, Glagolitic, HR, Serb

**Crochet** Lace, Weave

**Crock** Chorrie, Crate, Jar, Mug, Pig, Pitcher, Pot, Potshard, Potshare, Potsherd, Stean(e)

**Crockery** Ceramics, China, Dishes, Earthenware, Oddment, Service, Sunbeam, Ware

▷ **Crocks** *may indicate* an anagram

**Crocodile** Bask, Cayman, Dundee, File, Flat dog, Garial, Gavial, Gharial, Gotcha lizard, Line, Mud gecko, Mugger, River-dragon, Saltie, Saltwater, Sebek, Teleosaur(ian)

**Crocus** Autumn, Meadow saffron, Naked boys, Naked lady, Prairie, Quack doctor, Saffron

**Croesus** Lydia

**Croft** Bareland, Pightle

**Cromwell** Antimonarchist, Ironside, Lord Protector, Noll, Oliver, Protector, Richard, Roundhead

**Crone(s)** Beldam(e), Ewe, Graeae, Hag, Mawkin, Ribibe, Rudas, Sibyl, Sybil, Trot, Trout, →WITCH

**Crony** Anile, Chum, Intimate, Mate, Pal, Sidekick

**Crook(ed), Crookedness** Adunc, Ajee, Angle, Aslant, Asymmetric, Awry, Bad, Bend, Bow, Cam, Camsheugh, Camsho(ch), Cock-eyed, Criminal, Cromb, Crome, Crosier, Crummack, Crummock, Crump, Curve, Dishonest, Elbow, Flex, Fraud, Heister, Hook, Ill, Indirect, Kam(me), Kebbie, Lituus, Lowlife, Malpractitioner, Obliquity, Operator, Shank, Sheep-hook, Shyster, Sick, Skew(whiff), Slick(er), Squint, Staff, Swindler, Thraward, Thrawart, Thrawn, Twister, Wonky, Wrong'un, Wry, Yeggman

▷ **Crooked** *may indicate* an anagram

**Croon(er), Crooning** Bing, Como, Lament, Lull, Monody, Murmur, Sing

**Crop(ped), Cropping, Crops, Crop up** Abridge, Basset, Befall, Browse, Cash, Catch, Cereal, Clip, Cover, Craw, Cut, Distress, Dock, Emblements, Emerge, Energy, Epilate, Eton, Foison, Forage, Grain, Graze, →HAIRCUT, Harvest, Hog, Ingluvies, Kharif, Ladino, Lop, Milo, Not(t), Plant, Poll, Produce, Prune, Rabi, Rawn, Reap, Riding, Rod, Root, Scythe, Shave, Shear, Shingle, Silage, Sithe, Standing, Stow, Strip, Subsistence, Succession, Top, Trim, Truncate, →VEGETABLE, White

**Cropper** Downfall, Header, Purler

**Croquet (term)** Pall Mall, Peel, Rover, Wire

**Croquette** Kromesky, Quenelle, Rissole

**Cross(ing), Crossbred, Crossbreed** Angry, Ankh, Ansate, Archiepiscopal, Banbury, Bandog, Basta(a)rd, Baster, Beefalo, Bestride, Bois-brule, Boton(n)e, Brent, Bridge, Bristling, Buddhist, Burden, Calvary, Cancel, Cantankerous, Canterbury, Capital, Capuchin, Cat(t)alo, Cattabus, Celtic, Channel, Charing, Chi, Chiasm(a), Choleric, Cleche, Clover-leaf, Cocktail, Compital, Constantine, Crosslet, Crosswalk, Crotchety, Crucifix, Crux, Cut, Decussate, Demi-wolf, Dihybrid, Double, Dso(mo), Dzobo, Eleanor, Encolpion, Faun, Fiery, Fitché, Fleury, Foil, Footbridge, Ford, Frabbit, Fractious, Frampold, Franzy, Funnel, Fylfot, Geneva, George, Grade, Greek, Hinny, Holy rood, Humette, Hybrid, Ill, Imp, Indignant, Interbreed, Intersect, Intervein, Iona, Iracund, Irascible, Irate, Irked, Iron, Jersian, Jerusalem, Jomo, Jumart, King's, Kiss, Krest, Ladino, Latin, Level, Liger, Lorraine, Lurcher, Maltese, Mameluco, Market, Mermaid, Military, Misfortune, Mix, Moline, Mongrel, Mule, Narky, Nattery, Node, Norman, Northern, Nuisance, Oblique,

Obverse, Ordinary, Orthodox, Overpass, Overthwart, Papal, Pass, Patonce, Patriarchal, Pattée, Pectoral, Pedestrian, Pelican, Percolin, Perverse, Plumcot, Plus, Pommé, Potence, Potent, Preaching, Puffin, Quadrate, Railway, Ratty, Reciprocal, Red, Riled, Roman, Rood, Rose, Rosy, Rouen, Rouge, Rubicon, Ruthwell, Sain, St Andrew's, St Anthony's, St George's, St Patrick's, St Peter's, Saltier, Saltire, Sambo, Satyr, Shirty, Sign, Snappy, Southern, Span, Splenetic, Strid, Svastika, Swastika, T, Tangelo, Tau, Tayberry, Ten, Testy, Thraw, Thwart, Tiglon, Tigon, Times, Toucan, Transit, Transom, Transverse, Traverse, Tree, Unknown, Urdé, Vexed, Vext, Victoria, →**VOTE**, Weeping, Whippet, Wholphin, Wry, X, Yakow, Zambo, Zebra(ss), Zebrinny, Zebroid, Zebrula, Zebrule, Zedonk, Zhomo, Z(h)o, Zobu
▷ **Cross** *may indicate* an anagram
▶ **Cross-bar** *see* CROSSPIECE
▶ **Crossbeam** *see* CROSSPIECE
 **Cross-bearer** Crucifer
 **Cross-bill** Metagnathous
 **Cross-bones** Marrowbones
 **Cross-bow** Arbalest, Bal(l)ista
 **Cross-country** Langlauf, Overland
 **Cross-dress(er), Cross-dressing** En travesti, Eonism, Gender-bender
 **Cross-examination, Cross-examine** Elenctic, Grill, Interrogate, Question, Targe
 **Cross-eyed** Skelly(-eyed), Squint
 **Crossfertilisation** Allogamy, Heterosis, Hybrid vigour, Xenogamy
 **Cross-grained** Ill-haired, Mashlam, Mashlim, Mashlock, Mashlum, Mas(h)lin, Stubborn
 **Crosspiece, Cross-bar, Crossbeam, Cross-timber** Bail, Bar, Cancelli, Fingerground, Footrail, Inter-tie, Lierne, Phillipsite, Putlock, Putlog, Quillon, Serif, Seriph, Stempel, Stemple, Stretcher, Stull, Swingle-tree, Toggle, Transom, Trave, Whiffle-tree, Whipple-tree, Yoke
 **Crossroads** Carfax, Carfox, Carrefour, Compital, Junction, Soap
 **Crossword** Cruciverbal, Cryptic, Grid, Puzzle, Quickie
 **Crotchet(y)** Eccentric, Fad, Fancy, Grouch, Kink, Liverish, Quarter-note, Toy
 **Crouch** Bend, Cower, Cringe, Falcade, Fancy, Lordosis, Ruck, Set, Squat, Squinch
 **Croup** Angina, Cough, Kink, Rump
 **Crow** Big-note, Bluster, Boast, Brag, Carrion, Chewet, Chough, Corbie, Corvus, Crake, Currawong, Daw, Flute-bird, Gab, Gloat, Gorcrow, Hooded, Hoodie, Huia, Jackdaw, Jim(my), Ka(e), Murder, Piping, Raven, Rook, Saddleback, Scald, Skite, Squawk, Swagger, Vaunt
 **Crowbar** Gavelock, James, Jemmy, Lever
 **Crowd(ed)** Abound, Army, Bike, Boodle, Bumper, Bunch, Busy, Byke, Caboodle, Clutter, Compress, Concourse, Congest(ed), Cram, Cramp, Crush, Crwth, Dedans, Dense, Doughnut, Drove, Fill, Flock, Galere, Gang, Gate, Gathering, Herd, Horde, →**HOST**, Huddle, Hustle, Jam, Jam-packed, Lot, Many, Meinie, Mein(e)y, Melee, Menyie, Mob, Mong, Multitude, Ochlo-, Pack, Pang, Populace, Prease, Press, Rabble, Raft, Ragtag, Ram, Ratpack, Ring, Roll-up, Rout, Ruck, Scrooge, Scrouge, Scrowdge, Scrum, Serr(é), Shoal, Shove, Slew, Slue, Squash, Squeeze, Stuff, Swarm, Swell, Thick, Thrang, Three, Throng, Trinity, Varletry
 **Crowfoot** Gilcup, Reate
 **Crown** Acme, Apex, Apogee, Bays, Bull, Camp, Cantle, Cap, Capernoity, Cidaris, Civic, Coma, Corona, Cr, Diadem, Ecu, Engarland, Enthrone, Fillet, Garland, Gloria, Haku, Head, Headdress, Instal, Iron, Ivy, Krans, Krantz, Laurel, Monarch, Mural, Naval, Nole, Noll, Northern, Noul(e), Nowl, Olive, Optical, Ore, Ovation, Pate, Peak, Pediment, Pschent, Sconce, Stephen's, Summit, Taj, Thick'un, Tiar(a), →**TOP**, Treetop, Triple, Triumphal, Trophy, Vallary, Vertex
 **Crucial** Acute, Bottom line, Critical, Decider, Essential, Indispensable, Key, Kingpin, Linchpin, Momentous, Paramount, Pivotal, Quintessential, Vital, Watershed

**Crucible** Cruset, Melting-pot, Vessel

**Crucifix(ion), Crucify** Calvary, Cross, Golgotha, Mortify, Rood, Torment, Torture

**Crud** Red snow

**Crude(ness)** Bald, Brash, Brute, Coarse, Earthy, Halfbaked, Ill-bred, Immature, Incondite, Lewd, No tech, Oil, Primitive, Rabelaisian, Raunch, Raw, Rough, Rough and ready, Rough-hewn, Rough-wrought, Tutty, Uncouth, Unrefined, Vulgar, Yahoo

**Cruel(ty)** Barbarous, Bloody, Brutal, Cold-blooded, Cut-throat, Dastardly, De Sade, Draconian, Fell, Fiendish, Flinty, Hard, Heartless, Immane, Inhuman(e), Machiavellian, Mental, Neronic, Pitiless, Raw, Remorseless, Sadistic, Stern, Tiger, Tormentor, Tyranny, Unmerciful, Vicious, Violence, Wanton

▷ **Cruel** *may indicate* an anagram

**Cruet** Ampulla, Condiments, Decanter

**Cruise(r)** Booze, Busk, Cabin, Coast, Nuke, Orientation, Prowl, Rove, Sail, Sashay, Search, Ship, Tom, Travel, Trip, Voyager

**Crumb(le), Crumbly, Crumbs** Coo, Cor, Decay, Derelict, Disintegrate, Ee, Fragment, Friable, Fritter, Golly, Law, Leavings, Moulder, Mull, Murl, Nesh, Nirl, Ort, Panko, Particle, Ped, Pulverise, Raspings, Rot, Rotter, Tumbledown

**Crumpet** Dish, Girl, Muffin, Nooky, Pash, Pikelet

**Crumple** Buckle, Collapse, Crease, Crunkle, Crush, Raffle, Scrunch, Wrinkle

**Crunch(y), Crunching** Abdominal, Acid test, Chew, Craunch, Credit, Crisis, Crisp, Gnash, Graunch, Grind, Munch, Number, Occlude, Scranch, Shoot-out

**Crusade(r)** Baldwin, Campaign, Caped, Cause, Lionheart, Pilgrim, Tancred, Templar

**Crush(ed), Crusher, Crushing** Acis, Anaconda, Annihilate, Beetle, Bow, Breakback, Careworn, Champ, Comminute, Conquer, Contuse, Cram(p), Cranch, Crunch, Defeat, Demoralise, Destroy, Graunch, Grind, Hug, Humble, Jam, Knapper, Levigate, Liquidise, Litholapaxy, Mangle, Mash, Mill, Molar, Mortify, Nib, Oppress, Overcome, Overpower, Overwhelm, Pash, Policeman, Pound, Press, Pulp, Pulverise, Quash, Quell, Ruin, Schwarmerei, Scotch, Scrum, Scrumple, Scrunch, Smash, Squabash, Squash, Squeeze, Squelch, Squidger, Squish, Stamp, Stave, Steam-roll, Step on, Stove, Stramp, Suppress, Swot, Telescope, Trample, Tread, Vanquish

**Crusoe** Robinson, Selkirk

**Crust(y)** Argol, Beeswing, Cake, Caliche, Coating, Coffin, Continental, Cover, Crabby, Craton, Fur, Geogeny, Geosphere, Gratin, Heel, Horst, Ice fern, Kissing, Kraton, Lithosphere, Oceanic, Orogen, Osteocolla, Pie, Reh, Rind, Rine, Sal, Salband, Scab, Scale, Shell, Sial, Sima, Sinter, Sordes, Surly, Tartar, Teachie, Tectonics, Terrane, Tetchy, Upper, Wine-stone

**Crustacea(n)** Acorn-shell, Amphipod, Barnacle, Brachyuran, Branchiopoda, Camaron, Cirriped, Cirripede, Cirripid, Cladoceran, Copepod, Crab, Crayfish, Cumacean, Cyclops, Cyprid, Cypris, Daphnia, Decapod(a), Entomostraca, Euphausia, Fishlouse, Foot-jaw, Gribble, Isopod, Krill, Langoustine, Limulus, Lobster, Macrura, Malacostracan, Marine borer, Maron, Nauplius, Nephrops, Oniscus, Ostracoda, Pagurian, Phyllopod, Prawn, Red seed, Rhizocephalan, Sand flea, Sand-hopper, Sand-skipper, Scampi, Scampo, Schizopod, Sea slater, Shellfish, Shrimp, Slater, Squilla, Stomatopod, Woodlouse, Yabbie, Yabby

**Crutch** Morton's, Potent

**Crux** Essence, Nub

**Cry(ing)** Aha, Alalagmus, Alew, Baa, Banzai, Bark, Battle, Bawl, Bay, Bell, Bemoan, Bill, Bingo, Blat, Bleat, Bleb, Blub(ber), Boo, Boohoo, Boom, Bray, Bump, Caramba, Caw, Cheer, Chevy, Chirm, Chivy, Clang, Cooee, Crake, Croak, Crow, Dire, Euoi, Eureka, Evoe, Evoke, Exclaim, Eye-water, Fall, Field-holler, Gardyloo, Gathering, Geronimo, Gowl, Greet, Halloo, Harambee, Haro, Harrow, Havoc, Heave-ho, Heigh, Hemitrope, Herald, Hey presto, Hinny, Hoicks, Holler, Honk, Hoo, Hoop, Hosanna, Hout(s)-tout(s), Howl, Howzat, Humph, Hunt's up, Hurra(h), Io, Kaw, Low, Mewl, Miaou, Miau(l), Miserere, Mourn, Night-shriek, Nix, O(c)hone, Oi, Olé, Ow, Pugh, Rabbito(h), Rallying, Rivo, Sab, Scape, Scream, Screech, Sell, Sese(y), Sessa, →**SHOUT**, Shriek, Slogan, Snivel, Snotter,

Sob, Soho, Sola, Squall, Squawk, Street, Sursum corda, Tally-ho, Tantivy, Umph, Vagitus, View-halloo, Vivat, Vociferate, Wail, War, War whoop, Watchword, Waterworks, Waul, Wawl, Weep, Westward ho, Whammo, Whee(ple), Whimper, Whine, Whinny, Whoa, Whoop, Winge, Wolf, Yammer, Yawl, Yelp, Yicker, Yikker, Yip, Yippee, Yodel, Yo-heave-ho, Yo-ho-ho, Yoick, Yoop, Yowl

**Crypt(ic)** Catacomb, Cavern, Chamber, Crowde, Encoded, Enigmatic, Esoteric, Favissa, Grotto, Hidden, Mystic, Obscure, Occult, Secret, Sepulchre, Short, Steganographic, Tomb, Unclear, Undercroft, Vault

**Cryptaesthesia** ESP

**Cryptogam** Acotyledon, Acrogen, Fern(-ally), Moss, Pteridophyte, Steganograph

**Cryptogram, Cryptographer, Cryptography** Decoder, Public-key, Steganograph, Ventris

**Crystal(s), Crystal-gazer, Crystalline, Crystallise** Allotriomorphic, Axinite, Baccara(t), Beryl, Candy, Citrine, Clathrate, Clear, Cleveite, Copperas, Coumarin, Cumarin, Cut-glass, Dendrite, Druse, Effloresce, Elaterin, Enantiomorph, Epitaxy, Erionite, Form, Fuchsin(e), Geode, Glass, Hemihedron, Hemimorphic, Hemitrope, Ice-stone, Ideal, Imazadole, Jarosite, Lase, Lead, Liquid, Lithium, Love-arrow, Macle, Macro-axis, Melamine, Mixed, Needle, Nematic, Niacin, Nicol, Orthogonal, Orthorhombic, Palace, Pellucid, Penninite, Pericline, Phenocryst, Piezo, Piezoelectric, Pinacoid, Pinakoid, Prism, Pseudomorph, Purin(e), Quartz, R(h)aphide, R(h)aphis, Rhinestone, Rock, Rotenone, Rubicelle, Scawtite, Scryer, Shoot, Silica, Skatole, Skryer, Smectic, Snowflake, Sorbitol, Spar, Spherulite, Spicule, Table, Tina, Tolan(e), Trichite, Triclinic, Trilling, Twin(ned), Wafer, Watch-glass, Xanthene, Xenocryst, Yag

**Cub(s)** Baby, Kit, Lionet, Novice, Pup, Sic, Whelp, Wolf, Youth

**Cuba(n)** C, Castro

**Cube, Cubic, Cubist** Bath, Braque, Cu, Dice, Die, Magic, Necker, Nosean, Quadrate, Rubik's®, Serac, Smalto, Snub, Solid, Stere, Stock, Tesseract

**Cubicle** Alcove, Booth, Carrel(l), Compartment, Stall

**Cuckold** Actaeon, Cornute, Graft, Homer, Lenocinium, Mari complaisant, Two-time, Vulcan's badge, Wittol

**Cuckoo** Ament, Ani, April fool, Bird, Brain-fever bird, Chaparral cock, Dotty, Gouk, Gowk, Inquiline, Insane, Koekoea, Koel, →MAD, Mental, Piet-my-vrou, Rabid, Stupid, Zany

▷ **Cuckoo** *may indicate* an anagram

**Cuckoopint** Arum

**Cucumber** Bitter-apple, Choko, Colocynth, Coloquintida, Dill, Elaterium, Gherkin, Pickle, Sea-slug, Squirting, Trepang, Wolly

**Cuddle, Cuddly** Canoodle, Caress, Clinch, Embrace, Fondle, Hug, Inarm, Nooky, Pet, Smooch, Smuggle, Snog, Snuggle, Spoon, Zaftig

**Cudgel** Alpeen, Ballow, Bludgeon, Brain, Club, Cosh, Drub, Fustigate, Oaken towel, Plant, Rack, Rung, Shillelagh, Souple, Stick, Swipple, Tan, Towel, Truncheon

**Cue** Billiard, Cannonade, Catchword, Feed, Feed-line, Half-butt, Hint, Mace, Pool, →PROMPT, Reminder, Rod, Sign, Signal, Wink

**Cuff** Box, Buffet, Clout, French, Gauntlet, Iron, Muffettee, Rotator, Storm, Strike, Swat

**Cuirass** Armour, Corselet, Lorica

**Cuisine** Balti, Bourgeoise, Cookery, Food, Lean, Menu, Minceur, Nouvelle, Tex-Mex

**Cul-de-sac** Blind (alley), Dead-end, Impasse, Loke

**Cull** Gather, Pick, Reap, Select, Thin, Weed

**Culminate, Culmination** Apogean, Apogee, Climax, Conclusion, Crest, End, Head, Orgasm

**Culpable** Blameworthy, Faulty, Guilty

**Culprit** Offender

**Cult** Aum Shinrikyo, Cabiri, Candomble, Cargo, Creed, Fertility, Flower power, Macumba, Moony, New Age, Personality, Rastafarian, Sect, Shango, Shinto, Snake, Voodoo, Wicca, Worship

**Cultivate(d), Cultivation, Cultivator** Agronomy, Arty, Breed, Civilise, Developed, Dig, Dress, Ear, Ere, Farm, Garden, Genteel, Grow, Hoe, Hydroponics, Improve, Labour, Plough(man), Polytunnel, Pursue, Raise, Reclaim, Refine, Sative, Sophisticated, Tame, Tasteful, Till, Tilth, Wainage, Woo, Work

**Culture(d), Cultural** Abbevillean, Acheulean, Acheulian, Agar, Art(y), Aurignacian, Azilian, Bacterian, Bel esprit, Brahmin, Broth, Canteen, Capsian, Civil(isation), Clactonian, Club, Compensation, Corporate, Dependency, Enterprise, Ethnic, Experiment, Explant, Fine arts, Folsom, Gel, Gravettian, Grecian, Halafian, Hallstatt, Hip-hop, Humanism, Intelligentsia, Kultur(kreis), La Tène, Learning, Levallois, Madelenian, Magdalenian, Maglemosean, Maglemosian, Meristem, Minimalism, Minoan, Monolayer, Mousterian, New Age, Organisational, Perigordian, Polish, Polite, Pure, Refinement, Solutrean, Sophisticated, Starter, Strepyan, Suspension, Tardenoisian, Tissue, Villanovan, Water, Well-read

**Cumbersome** Clumsy, Heavy, Lumbering, →**UNWIELDY**

**Cunctator** Dilatory

**Cuneiform** Wedge(d)

**Cunning** Arch, Art, Artifice, Astute, Cautel, Craft(y), Deceit, Deep, Devious, Down, Finesse, Foxy, Guile, Insidious, Knacky, Leary, Leery, Machiavellian, Quaint, Ruse, Scheming, Skill, Slee(kit), Sleight, Slim, Sly(boots), Smart, Sneaky, Stratagem, Subtle, Vulpine, Wheeze, Wile, Wily

**Cup(s), Cupped** Aecidium, America's, Beaker, Bledisloe, Calcutta, Calix, Calyculus, Cantharus, Ca(u)p, Chalice, Claret, Communion, Cotyle, Cruse, Cupule, Cyathus, Cylix, Davis, Demitasse, Deoch-an-doruis, Deuch-an-doris, Dish, Doch-an-dorach, Dop, Egg, European, Eyebath, FA, Fairs, Final, Fingan, Finjan, Fruit, Gemma, Glenoid, Goblet, Grace, Grease, Gripe's egg, Hanap, Horn, Kylix, Loving, Melbourne, Merry, Monstrance, Moustache, Mug, Noggin, Nut, Optic, Pannikin, Paper, Parting, Planchet, Plate, Poley, Posset, Pot, Procoelous, Quaff, Quaich, Quaigh, Rhyton, Rider, Ryder, Sangrado, Scyphus, Sippy, Stem, Stirrup, Suction, Tantalus, Tass(ie), Tastevin, Tazza, Tea-dish, Tig, Tot, →**TROPHY**, Tyg, UEFA, Volva, Waterloo, World

▷ **Cup** *may indicate* a bra size

**Cup-bearer** Ganymede, Hebe

**Cupboard** Airing, Almery, Almirah, A(u)mbry, Armoire, Beauf(f)et, Cabinet, Chiffonier, Chiff(o)robe, Closet, Coolgardie safe, Court, Credenza, Dresser, Encoignure, Fume, Livery, Locker, Meat-safe, Press, Unit, Walk-in

**Cup-holder** Bra, Hanaper, Hebe, Plinth, Saucer, Zarf, Zurf

**Cupid** Amoretto, Amorino, Archer, Blind, Bow-boy, Cherub, Dan, Eros, Love, Putto

**Cupola** Belfry, Dome, Tholos

**Cup-shaped** Glenoid, Poculiform

**Cur** Caitiff, Cowardice, Dog, Hound, Messan, Mongrel, Mutt, Pi-dog, Scab, Scoundrel, Whelp, Wretch, Yap

**Curare, Curari** Ourali, Poison, Wourali

**Curassow** Crax

**Curate** Barman, Minister, Nathaniel, Padré, Perpetual, Priest

**Curator** Aquarist

**Curb** Bit, Brake, Bridle, Check, Clamp, Coaming, Constraint, Dam, Edge, Puteal, Rein, Restrain, Restringe, Rim, Snub, Stifle, Well

**Curd(s)** Bean, Cheese, Junket, Lapper(ed)-milk, Lemon, Skyr, Tofu

**Curdle** Clot, Congeal, Earn, Erne, Grue, Lopper, Posset, Ren, Rennet, Run, Set, Sour, →**TURN**, Whig, Yearn

**Cure(d), Curative** Ameliorate, Amend, Antidote, Antirachitic, Bloater, Cold turkey, Dry-salt, Dun, Euphrasy, Faith, Fix, Flue, Ginseng, Heal, Heal-all, Heat treatment, Hobday, Hydropathy, Jadeite, Jerk, Kipper, Laetrile, Magic bullet, Medicinal, Nature, Nostrum, Panacea, Park-leaves, Pickle, Posset, Prairie oyster, →**PRESERVE**, Reast, Reck, Recover, Recower, Reest, Relief, Remede, Remedy, Re(i)st, Restore, Salt, Salve,

Save, Serum, Smoke, Smoke-dry, Snakeroot, Tan, →**TREATMENT**, Tutsan, Water

▷ **Cure** *may indicate* an anagram

**Curfew** Bell, Gate, Prohibit, Proscribe

**Curie** Ci

**Curio, Curiosity, Curious** Agog, Bibelot, Bric a brac, Collector's item, Esoteric, Ferly, Freak, Inquisitive, Interesting, Into, Meddlesome, Nos(e)y, Objet d'art, Objet de vertu, Oddity, Peculiar, Prurience, Quaint, Rarity, Rum, Spectacle, →**STRANGE**, Wondering

▷ **Curious(ly)** *may indicate* an anagram

**Curium** Cm

**Curl(s), Curler, Curling, Curly** Ailes de pigeon, Bev, Bonspiel, Cirrus, Cockle, Coil, Crimp, Crimple, Crinkle, Crisp, Crocket, Dildo, Earlock, Eddy, Favourite, Frisette, Friz(z), Frizzle, Heart-breaker, Hog, Inwick, Kiss, Leaf, Loop, Love-lock, Outwick, Perm, Pigeon's wing, Pin, Quiff, Repenter, Ringlet, Roll, Roulette, Scroll, Shaving, Spiral, Spit, Tong, Tress, Trunk, Twiddle, →**TWIST**, Ulotrichous, Undée, Wave, Wind

**Curlew** Bird, Thick knee, Whaup, Whimbrel

**Curmudgeon** Boor, Churl, Crosspatch, Grouch, Route, Runt, Skinflint

**Currant** Berry, Flowering, Raisin, Rizard, Rizzar(t), Rizzer

**Currency** Cash, Circulation, →**COIN**, Coinage, Decimal, Euro(sterling), Finance, Fractional, Hard, Jiao, Kip, Koruna, Managed, Monetary, →**MONEY**, Petrodollar, Prevalence, Reserve, Soft, Tender

▷ **Currency** *may indicate* a river

**Current** Abroad, AC, Actual, Alternating, Amp(ere), Amperage, California, Canary, Contemporaneous, Cromwell, Dark, DC, Direct, Draught, Drift, Dynamo, Ebbtide, Eddy, Electric, El Nino, Emission, Equatorial, Euripus, Existent, Faradic, Flow, Foucault, Galvanic(al), Going, Gyre, Headstream, Hot button, Humboldt, Hummock, I, Immediate, Inst, Intermittent, In vogue, Japan, Jet stream, Kuroshio, Labrador, Live, Maelstrom, Millrace, Modern, Newsy, North Atlantic, Now, Ongoing, Output, Peru, Present, Present day, Prevalent, Pulsating, Race, Rapid, Recent, Rife, Rip, Roost, Running, Ryfe, Stream, Thames, Thermal, Thermionic, Tide, Tideway, Topical, Torrent, Turbidity, Underset, Undertow, Updraught, Up-to-date

**Curriculum** Core, Cursal, National, Programme, Syllabus

**Curry** Bhuna, Brush, Comb, Cuittle, Dhansak, Dress, Favour, Fawn, Groom, Ingratiate, Korma, Madras, Ruby (Murray), Skater, Spice, Tan, Tandoori, Turmeric, Vindaloo

**Curse(d)** Abuse, Anathema, Badmouth, Ban, Bane, Beshrew, →**BLASPHEME**, Blast, Bless, Chide, Dam(me), Damn, Dee, Drat, Ecod, Egad, Evil, Excommunicate, Execrate, Heck, Hex, Hoodoo, Imprecate, Jinx, Malediction, Malgre, Malison, Maranatha, Mau(l)gré, Mockers, Moz(z), Mozzle, Nine (of diamonds), Oath, Paterson's, Pize, Plague, Rant, Rats, Scourge, 'Snails, Spell, Star-crossed, Swear, Tarnation, Upbraid, Vengeance, Vituperate, Wanion, Weary, Winze, Wo(e)

**Cursive** Estrang(h)elo, Run

**Cursor** Mouse, Turtle

**Cursorily, Cursory** Casual, Hasty, Lax, Obiter, Passing, Perfunctory, Sketchy, Speedy, Superficial

**Curt** Abrupt, Blunt, Crusty, Laconic, Monosyllabic, Offhand, Short, Snappy, Stern, Terse, Uncivil

**Curtail(ment)** Abate, Abridge, Apocope, Crop, Cut, Reduce, Shorten

**Curtain(s), Curtain raiser, Curtain-rod** Air, Arras, Backdrop, Bamboo, Café, Canopy, Casement, Caudle, Cloth, Cyclorama, Death, Demise, Drape, Drop, Dropcloth, Dropscene, Fatal, Hanging, Iron, Lever de rideau, Louvre, Net, Pall, Portière, Purdah, Rag, Safety, Scene, Screen, Scrim, Shower, Swag, Tab, Tableau, Tormentor, Tringle, Upholstery, Vail, Valance, Veil, Vitrage, Window

**Curtsey** Bob, Bow, Dip, Dop, Honour

**Curve(d), Curvaceous, Curvature, Curving, Curvy** Adiabatic, Aduncate, Anticlastic, Apophyge, Arc, Arch, Archivolt, Assurgent, Axoid, Bend, Bezier, Bight, Bow,

Brachistochrone, Camber, Cardioid, Catacaustic, Catenary, Caustic, Characteristic, Chordee, Cissoid, Conchoid, Contrapposto, Crescent, Cycloid, Demand, Diacaustic, Dogleg, Dowager's hump, Ellipse, Entasis, Epicycloid, Epinastic, Epitrochoid, Ess, Evolute, Exponential, Extrados, Felloe, Felly, Folium, Freezing point, French, Gaussian, Geodesic, Gooseneck, Growth, Hance, Harmonogram, Helix, Hodograph, Hollow-back, Hook, Hyperbola, Hypocycloid, Inswing, Intrados, Invected, Isochor, J, Jordan, Kyphosis, Laffer, Learning, Lemniscate, Limacon, Linkage, Liquidus, Lissajous figure, Lituus, Lordosis, Loxodrome, Meniscus, Normal, Nowy, Ogee, Parabola, Phillips, Pothook, Pott's disease, Pulvinate, Reclinate, Record, Rhumb, RIAA, Roach, Rondure, Rotundate, Scolioma, Scoliosis, Sheer, Sigmoid flexure, Sinuate, Sinusoid, Slice, Sonsie, Spiral, Spiric, Strophoid, Supply, Survival, Swayback, Synclastic, Tautochrone, Tie, Tractrix, Trajectory, Trisectrix, Trochoid, Tumble-home, Twist, Undulose, U-turn, Volute, Witch (of Agnesi)

**Cushion(s)** Air, Allege, Bank, Beanbag, Bolster, Buffer, Bustle, Frog, Ham, Hassock, King's, Kneeler, → **PAD**, Pillow, Pin, Pouf(fe), Pulvinus, Scatter, Soften, Squab, Tyre, Upholster, Whoopee

**Cushy** Easy, Sinecure

**Cusp** Horn, Spinode, Tine

**Custard (apple)** Crème brulee, Crème caramel, Flam(m), Flan, Flaune, Flawn, Flummery, Pa(w)paw, Pastry, Zabaglione

**Custodial, Custodian, Custody** Care, Claviger, Curator, Guard, Hold, Incarceration, Janitor, Keeping, Protective, Retention, Sacrist, Steward, Trust, Ward, Wardship

**Custom(ised), Customs (officer), Customs house, Customary** Agriology, Chophouse, Coast-waiters, Cocket, Consuetude, Conventional, Couvade, Culture, Dedicated, De règle, Dhamma, Dharma, Douane, Exciseman, Familiar, Fashion, Folklore, → **HABIT**, Land-waiter, Lore, Manner, Montem, Mores, Nomic, Obsequy, Octroi, Ordinary, Perfunctory, Practice, Praxis, Protocol, Regular, Relic, Rite, Routine, Rule, Set, Sororate, Spanish, Sunna, Tax, Thew, Tidesman, Tide-waiter, Tikanga, Time-honoured, Tradition, Trait, Unwritten, Usance, Used, Usual, Won, Wont, Woon, Zollverein

**Customer(s)** Client, Cove, End user, Footfall, Gate, Patron, Prospect, Punter, Purchaser, Shillaber, Shopper, Smooth, Stiff, Trade, Trick, Ugly, User, Vendee

**Cut(ter), Cutdown, Cutting** Abate, Abbreviate, Abjoint, Ablate, Abridge, Abscission, Abscond, Acute, Adeem, Adze, Aftermath, Ali Baba, Amputate, Apocopate, Apocope, Axe, Bang, Bisect, Bit, Bite, Bowdlerise, Boycott, Brilliant, Broach, Caesarean, Caique, Canal, Cantle, Caper, Carver, Castrate, Caustic, Censor, Chap, Cheese, Chisel, Chopper, Chynd, Circumscribe, Cleaver, Clinker-built, Clip, Clod, Colter, Commission, Concise, Coppice, Coulter, Coupé, Crew, Crop, Cruel, Cube, Culebra, Curtail, Deadhead, Decrease, Dedekind, Diamond, Dicer, Die, Diminish, Director's, Discide, Discount, Disengage, Dismember, Dissect, Division, Divorce, Dock, Dod, Edge, Edit, Emarginate, Embankment, Engraver, Entail, Entayle, Entrecote, Epistolary, Epitomise, Escalope, Eschew, Estrepe, Etch, Excalibur, Excide, Excise, Exscind, Exsect, Exude, Fashion, Fell, Filet mignon, Fillet, Flench, Flense, Flinch, Flymo®, Form, Framp, Froe, Frow, Gaillard, Garb, Gash, Go-down, Grater, Graven, Gride, Groove, Gryde, Hack, Hairdo, Handsaw, Harvest, Hew(er), Ignore, Incision, Incisor, Indent, Insult, Intersect, Jigsaw, Joint, Junk, Kerf, Kern, Kirn, Lacerate, Lance, Lase(r), Leat, Lesion, Limit, Lin, Lop, Math, Medaillon, Medallion, Microtome, Milling, Minimise, Minish, Mohel, Mordant, Mortice, Mortise, Mower, Nache, Nick, Not, Notch, Nott, Occlude, Omit, Open, Operate, Osteotome, Oxyacetylene, Padsaw, Pare, Pink, Plant, Pliers, Ploughshare, Poll, Pollard, Pone, Power, Precisive, Press, Proin, Quota, Race, Rake off, Rase, Razee, Razor, Reap, Rebate, Reduction, Re-enter, Resect, Retrench, Revenue, Ring, Ripsaw, Roach, Rose, Rout, Saddle, Sarcastic, Sarky, Saw(n), Saw-tooth, Scaloppine, Scarf, Scarify, Scathing, Scion, Scission, Scissor, Score, Scrap, Sculpt, Scye, Scythe, Secant, Secateurs, Sect, Section, Set, Sever, Sey, Share (out), Shaver, Shears, Shingle, Ship, Shive, Shorn, Short, Shred, Shun, Sickle, Side, Sirloin, Skin, Skip, Slane, Slash, Slice(r), Slight, Slip, Slit, Sloop, Sned,

Snee, Snib, Snick, Snip, Snippet, Snub, Spade, Speedy, Spin, Spud, Stall, Steak, Stencil, Stereotomy, Stir, Stramac, Stramazon, Strim, Strimmer®, Style, Sunder, Surgeon, Swath(e), Tailor(ess), Tap, Tart, Tenderloin, Tenotomy, Tomial, Tomium, Tonsure, Tooth, Topside, Tournedo, Transect, Trash, Trench, Trenchant, Trepan, Trim, Truant, Truncate, Urchin, Vivisection, Whang, Whittle, Winey

▷ **Cut** *may indicate* an anagram

▷ **Cutback** *may indicate* a reversed word

**Cute** Ankle, Canny, Dinky, Perspicacious, Pert, Pretty, Taking

**Cuticle** Epidermis, Eponychium, Periplast, Pleuron, Skin

**Cut in** Interpose, Interrupt

**Cutlass** Machete, Sword

**Cutlery** Canteen, Eating irons, Flatware, Fork, Knife, Service, Setting, Silver, Spoon, Spork, Sunbeam, Tableware, Trifid

**Cutlet** Chop, Schnitzel

**Cut off** Elide, Enisle, Estrange, Inisle, Insulate, Intercept, →ISOLATE, Lop, Ostracise, Prune

**Cut-throat** Razor, Ruinous, Sweeney Todd

**Cuttlebone, Cuttlefish** Octopus, Pen, Polyp(e)s, Polypus, Sea-grape, Sea-sleeve, Sepia, Sepiost(aire), Sepium, Squid

**CV** Biodata, Resume

**Cyanide** Acrylonitrile, Nitrile, Potassium, Prussiate

**Cyborg** Replicant

**Cycad** Coontie, Coonty

**Cyclades** Thera

**Cyclamen** Sow-bread

**Cycle, Cyclist, Cycling** Anicca, Arthurian, Bike, Biorhythm, Biospheric, Born-Haber, Business, Cal(l)ippic, Calvin, Carbon, Carnot, Cell, Circadian, Citric acid, Closed, Daisy, Diesel, Eon, Era, Fairy, Four-stroke, Freewheel, Frequency, Geological, Gigahertz, Heterogony, Hydrologic, Indiction, Keirin, Ko, Krebs, Life, Light-year, Lunar, Lytic, Madison, Metonic, Minibike, Moped, Natural, Nitrogen, Oestrus, Operating, Orb(it), Otto, Pedal, Peloton, Period, Product life, Rankine, Repulp, Revolution, Ride, Roadman, Roadster, Rock, Rota, Round, Samsara, Saros, Scorch, Series, Sheng, Solar, Song, Sonnet, Sothic, Spin, Sunspot, TCA, Trade, Trick, Trike, Turn, UCI, Urea, Vicious, Water, Wheeler, Wheelman, Wu

**Cyclone** Cockeye(d) bob, Storm, Tornado, Tropical, Typhoon, Willy-willy

**Cyclops** Arges, Arimasp(i), Brontes, Polyphemus, Steropes

**Cylinder, Cylindrical** Air, Capstan, Clave, Column, Dandy-roll, Drum, Licker-in, Magic, Master, Nanotube, Pipe, Pitch, Roll, Rotor, Siphonostele, Slave, Spool, Steal, Stele, Swift, Terete, Torose, Treadmill, Tube, Vascular

**Cymbal(s)** High-hat, Hi-hat, Zel, Zill

**Cynic(al)** Crab, Diogenes, Doubter, Hard-bitten, Hard-boiled, Menippus, Misanthropist, Pessimist, Sardonic, Sceptic, Thersites, Timon, Worldly-wise, World-weary

**Cynosure** Centre, Focus

**Cynthia** Artemis, Moon

**Cypress** Bald, Lawson's, Leyland(ii), Monterey, Retinospora, Swamp, Tree

**Cypriot** Enosis, Eoka

**Cyst** Atheroma, Bag, Blister, Chalazion, Dermoid, Ganglion, Hydatid, Impost(h)ume, Meibomian, Ranula, Sac, Sebaceous, Vesicle, Wen

**Cytogenesis** Amoebic

**Czar** Despot, Nicholas

**Czech(oslovakia), Czechoslovakian** CZ, Moravian, Ruthenian, Sudetenland

# Dd

**D** Daughter, Delta, Died, Edh, Eth, Penny

**Dab(s)** Bit, Blob, Daub, Fish, Flounder, Lemon, Pat, Print, Ringer, Smear, Smooth, Spot, Stupe, Whorl

**Dabble(r)** Amateur, Clatch, Dally, Dilettante, Plouter, Plowter, Potter, Smatter, Splash, Stipple, Trifle

**Dachshund** Badger-dog, Sausage-dog, Teckel

**Dactyl** Anapaest

**Dad(dy)** Blow, Dev(v)el, Father, Generator, Hit, Male, Pa(pa), Pater, Polt, Pop, Slam, Sugar, Thump

**Daddy-longlegs** Crane-fly, Jennyspinner, Leather-jacket, Spinning-jenny, Tipula

**Daffodil** Asphodel, Jonquil, Lent-lily, Narcissus

**Daft** Absurd, Crazy, Potty, Ridiculous, Silly, Simple, Stupid

**Dag** Jag, Pierce, Pistol, Prick, Stab, Tag, Wool

**Dagga** Cape, Red, True

**Dagger(s)** An(e)lace, Ataghan, Baselard, Bayonet, Bodkin, Crease, Creese, Da(h), Diesis, Dirk, Double, Dudgeon, Hanger, Han(d)jar, Jambiya(h), Katar, Khanjar, Kindjahl, Kirpan, Kreese, Kris, Lath, Misericord(e), Obelisk, Obelus, Poi(g)nado, Poniard, Pugio, Puncheon, Pusser's, Quillon, Rondel, Sgian-dubh, Shank, Skean, Skene(-occle), Spanish, Stiletto, Swordbreaker, Whiniard, Whinyard, W(h)inger, Yatag(h)an, Yuc(c)a

**Dahlia** Cosmea, Pompom

**Daily** Adays, Broadsheet, Char(lady), Circadian, Cleaner, Diurnal, Domestic, Guardian, Help, Journal, Le Monde, Mail, Mirror, Mrs Mopp, → **NEWSPAPER**, Paper, Per diem, Quotidian, Rag, Regular, Scotsman, Sun, Tabloid

**Dainty, Daintiness** Cate(s), Cute, Delicacy, Dinky, Elegant, Elfin, Entremesse, Entremets, Exquisite, Genty, Junket, Lickerish, Liquorish, Mignon(ne), Minikin, → **MORSEL**, Neat, Nice, Particular, Petite, Precious, Prettyism, Pussy, Sunket, Titbit, Twee

**Dairy** Creamery, Days' house, Loan, Parlour, Springhouse

**Dairymaid, Dairyman** Cowfeeder, Dey, Patience

**Dais** Estrade, Machan, Platform, Podium, Pulpit, Rostrum, Stage, Tribune

**Daisy** African, Aster, Barberton, Bell, Boneset, Cineraria, Felicia, Gerbera, Gowan, Groundsel, Hardheads, Hen and chickens, Livingstone, Marguerite, Marigold, Michaelmas, Moon, Ox-eye, Ragweed, Saw-wort, Shasta, Transvaal, Vegetable sheep

**Dale(s)** Dell, Dene, Diarist, Dingle, Glen, Nidder, Ribbles, Swale, Vale, Valley, Wensley, Wharfe, Yorkshire

**Dally** Coquet(te), Dawdle, Dilatory, Finger, Flirt, Linger, Philander, Play, Spoon, Sport, Tick and toy, Toy, Trifle, Wait

**Dalmatian** Spotted dog

**Dam** An(n)icut, Arch, Aswan, Aswan High, Bar, Barrage, Barrier, Block, Boulder, Bund, Cabora Bassa, Cauld, Check, Dental, Grand Coulee, Grande Dixence, Gravity, Hoover, Kariba, Kielder, Ma, Mangla, Mater, Nile, Obstacle, Obstruct, Pen, Sennar, Stank, → **STEM**, Sudd, Tank, Three Gorges, Turkey nest, Volta River, Weir, Yangtze

**Damage(d), Damages, Damaging** Accidental, Appair, Bane, Banjax, Blight, Bloody, Blunk, Bruise, Buckle, Burn, Charge, Chip, Collateral, Contuse, Cost, Cripple, Defame, Dent, Desecrate, Detriment, Devastate, Devastavit, Discredit, Distress, Estrepe, Exemplary, Expense, Fault, Flea-bite, Foobar, Fubar, Fuck up, Harm, Havoc, Hedonic,

Hit, Hole, Hurt, Impair, Injury, Insidious, Lacerate, Lesion, Loss, Mar, Mayhem, Moth-eaten, Mutilate, Nobble, Opgefok, Pair(e), Prang, Price, Punitive, Ratten, Ravage, Reparation, Retree, Ruin, Sabotage, Scaith, Scath(e), Scotch, Scratch, Shop-soiled, Skaith, Smirch, Solatium, →**SPOIL**, Tangle, Tear, Tigger, Toll, Toxic, Unsound, Value, Vandalise, Violate, Wear and tear, Wing, Wound, Wreak, Wreck, Write off

▷ **Damage(d)** *may indicate* an anagram

**Dambuster** Ondatra

**Dame** Crone, Dowager, Edna (Everage), Gammer, Lady, Matron, Nature, Naunt, Partlet, Peacherino, Sis, Title(d), Trot, Woman

**Damn(ation), Damnable, Damned** Accurst, Attack, Blame, Blast, Blinking, Censure, Condemn, Cotton-picking, Curse, Cuss, D, Darn, Dee, Doggone, Drat, Execrate, Faust, Heck, Hell, Hoot, Jigger, Malgre, Perdition, Predoom, Ruddy, Sink, Swear, Tarnal, Tarnation, Tinker's, Very

**Damp(en), Damping, Dampness** Aslake, Black, Blight, Blunt, Check, Choke, Clam(my), Dank, Dewy, Fousty, Fusty, Humid(ity), Hydric, Mesarch, Moch, Moist(ure), Muggy, Raw, Retund, Rheumy, Rising, Roric, Soggy, Sordo, Sultry, Unaired, Viscous, →**WET**, White

**Damper** Barrier, Check, Dashpot, Killjoy, Mute, Register-plate, Sordino, Sourdine

**Damsel** Girl, Lass, Maiden, Wench

**Damson** Plumdamas

**Dan** Box, Cupid, Dare, Leno, Martial artist, Olivetan, Scuttle, Tribe

**Dance(r), Dancing** Alma(in), Astaire, Avignon, Baladin(e), Balanchine, Ballabile, Ballant, Ballerina, Ballroom, Baryshnikov, Bayadère, Bob, Body-popping, Bump and grind, Caper, Ceili(dh), Chorus-girl, Comprimario, Contredanse, Corp de ballet, Corybant, Coryphee, Dervish, De Valois, Diaghilev, Dinner, Dolin, Exotic, Figurant, Figure, Fooling, Foot, Foot-it, Gandy, Gigolo, Groove, Hetaera, Hetaira, Hoofer, Isadora Duncan, Kick-up, Knees-up, Leap, Lope, Maenad, Majorette, Markova, Matachina, Modern, Nautch-girl, Night, Nijinsky, Nod, Number, Nureyev, Oberek, Old-time, Orchesis, Partner, Pavlova, Peeler, Petipa, Pierette, Prom(enade), Pyrrhic, Rambert, Raver, Reindeer, Ring, Romp, St Vitus, Salome, Saltant, Saltatorious, Shearer, Skank, Skipper, Slammer, Spring, Step(per), Strut, Table, Tea, Terpsichore, Thé dansant, Tread, Trip(pant), Vogue(ing), Whirl, Wire-walker

## DANCES

| 3 letters: | Barn | Lion | 5 letters: |
|---|---|---|---|
| Bop | Bull | Loup | Bamba |
| Fan | Clog | Mosh | B and S |
| Gig | Dump | Nach | Belly |
| Hay | Fado | Pogo | Bogle |
| Hey | Folk | Polo | Brawl |
| Hop | Fris | Punk | Break |
| Ice | Frug | Rain | Carol |
| Jig | Giga | Reel | Ceroc® |
| Lap | Go-go | Rope | Conga |
| Pas | Haka | Sand | Disco |
| Poi | Hora | Shag | Fling |
| Sun | Hula | Slam | Furry |
| Tap | Jive | Spin | Galop |
| Toe | Jota | Spot | Ghost |
| War | Juba | Stag | Gigue |
| | Juke | Taxi | Glide |
| 4 letters: | Kolo | Wire | Gopak |
| Ball | Line | | Horah |

Limbo
Loure
Mambo
Mooch
Natch
Paspy
Pavan
Paven
Pavin
Polka
Ragga
Robot
Round
Rueda
Rumba
Salsa
Samba
Shake
Skirt
Snake
Stomp
Sword
Tango
Torch
Truck
Twist
Valse
Volta
Waltz

**6 letters:**
Apache
Ballet
Bolero
Boogie
Boston
Branle
Bubble
Canary
Can-can
Cha-cha
Fading
Floral
Friska
German
Hustle
Jump-up
Kathak
Lavolt
Maxixe
Minuet
Morris
Pavane
Redowa

Shadow
Shimmy
Smooch
Square
Trophe
Valeta
Veleta
Waggle
Watusi

**7 letters:**
Bambuca
Beguine
Bourrée
Bransle
Brantle
Cantico
Capuera
Carioca
Coranto
Cossack
Country
Courant
Csardas
Farruca
Forlana
Foxtrot
Furlana
Gavotte
Halling
Hoe-down
Lambada
Lancers
Landler
Lavolta
Macabre
Maypole
Mazurka
Measure
Moresco
Morisco
Morrice
Moshing
Musette
One-step
Pericon
Planxty
Polacca
Ridotto
Ringlet
Romaika
Roundel
Roundle
Routine

Sardana
Sashaya
Shuffle
Tanagra
Tordion
Toyi-toy
Trenise
Trip-hop
Two-step
Watutsi
Ziganka

**8 letters:**
Alegrias
Boogaloo
Bunnyhop
Bunnyhug
Cachucha
Cakewalk
Canticoy
Capoeira
Chaconne
Cotillon
Courante
Egg-dance
Excuse-me
Fandango
Flamenco
Flip-flop
Galliard
Guimbard
Habanera
Hay-de-guy
Haymaker
Headbang
Hey-de-guy
Heythrop
Hoolican
Hornpipe
Hula-hula
Irish jig
Joncanoe
Junkanoo
Kantikoy
Kapa haka
Kazachok
Kazatzka
Krumping
Lindy hop
Macarena
Marinera
Matachin
Matelote
Medicine

Merengue
Moonwalk
Murciana
Rigadoon
Robotics
Ronggeng
Saraband
Snowball
Soft-shoe
Taglioni
Toyi-toyi
Trucking

**9 letters:**
Allemande
Bergamask
Bergomask
Bossanova
Caballero
Cha-cha-cha
Chipaneca
Cotillion
Ecossaise
Eightsome
Farandole
Formation
Gallopade
Hoolachan
Jitterbug
Kathakali
Malaguena
Pas de deux
Paso doble
Passepied
Paul Jones
Polonaise
Poussette
Quadrille
Quickstep
Ring-shout
Roundelay
Sarabande
Siciliana
Siciliano
Sink-a-pace
Sugarfoot
Tambourin
Tripudium
Variation
Zapateado

**10 letters:**
Antimasque
Breakdance

Carmagnole
Charleston
Cinderella
Cinque-pace
Corroboree
Gay Gordon's
Hay-de-guise
Hay-de-guyes
Hey-de-guise
Hey-de-guyes
Hokey-cokey
Passamezzo
Petronella
Rug-cutting
Saltarello
Seguidilla
Sicilienne

Sinke-a-pace
Strathspey
Tarantella
Tripudiate
Turkey trot
Tyrolienne
Walk-around

**11 letters:**
Antistrophe
Black bottom
Buck and wing
Cracovienne
Eurhythmics
Lambeth walk
Palais glide
Passacaglia

Pastourelle
Progressive
Schottische
Shimmy-shake
Varsovienne

**12 letters:**
Bharat Natyam
Labanotation
Passemeasure
Passy-measure
Virginia reel

**13 letters:**
Highland fling
Virginian reel

**14 letters:**
Divertissement
Jack-in-the-green

**15 letters:**
Soft shoe shuffle

**16 letters:**
Circassian circle

**18 letters:**
Sir Roger de
Coverley

**Dance hall** Disco, Juke-joint, Palais
**Dance movement** Arabesque, Balancé, Battement, Batterie, Benesh, Bourree, Brisé, Chaine, Chassé, Dos-à-dos, Dosido, Entrechat, Fishtail, Fouetté, Glissade, Jeté, Lassu, Pantalon, Pas de basque, Pas de chat, Pas seul, Pigeonwing, Pirouette, Plastique, Plié, Poule, Poussette, Promenade, Routine, Sauté, Step, Telemark, Twinkle
**Dance tune** Toy
▷ **Dancing** *may indicate* an anagram
**Dancing party** Ball, Ridotto
**Dandelion** Cat's ear, Hawkbit, Kok-saghyz, Piss-a-bed, Scorzonera, Taraxacum
**Dander** Anger, Gee, Passion, Saunter, Temper
**Dandle** Dance, Doodle, Fondle, Pet
**Dandruff** Furfur, Scurf
**Dandy** Adonis, Beau, Beau Brummell, Blood, Boulevardier, Buck(een), Cat, Cockscomb, Coxcomb, Dapper, → **DUDE**, Exquisite, Fancy, Fantastico, Fop, Gem, Jay, Jessamy, Johnny, Kiddy, Knut, Lair, Macaroni, Masher, Modist, Monarcho, Muscadin, Nash, Nut, Onegin, Posh, Puss-gentleman, Roy, Smart, Spark, Spiff, Swell, Ted, Toff, U, Yankee-doodle
**Dandy-horse** Draisene, Draisine
**Dane(s)** Clemence, Dansker, Ogier, Ostmen
**Danger(ous)** Apperil, Black spot, Breakneck, Chancy, Crisis, Critical, Dic(e)y, Dire, Dodgy, Emprise, Fear, Hairy, Hazard, Hearie, Hero, High-risk, Hot, Hotspot, Icy, Insecure, Jeopardy, Lethal, Menace, Mine, Minefield, Nettle, Nocuous, Objective, Parlous, Periculous, → **PERIL**, Pitfall, Plight, Precarious, Quicksand, Risk, Rock, Serious, Severe, Sicko, Snag, Snare, Tight, Tight spot, Trap, Treacherous, Ugly, Wonchancy
**Dangle** A(i)glet, Aiguillette, Critic, Flourish, Hang, Loll, Swing
**Daniel** Dan, Defoe, Deronda, Lion-tamer, Portia, Quilp
**Dank** Clammy, Damp, Humid, Moist, Wet, Wormy
**Daphne** Agalloch, Agila, Eaglewood, Lace-bark, Laura, Laurel, Mezereon
**Dapper** Dressy, Natty, Neat, Smart, Spiff, Sprauncy, Spruce, Sprush, Spry, → **TRIM**
**Dappled** Piebald
**Darbies** Cuffs, Irons, Snaps
**Dare, Dare-devil, Daring** Adventure, Audacious, Aweless, Bold, Brave, Bravura, Challenge, Courage, Dan, Da(u)nton, Defy, Durst, Emprise, Face, Foolhardy, Gallant, Gallus, Groundbreaking, Hardihood, Hazard, Hen, Intrepid, Moxie, Neck, Prowess, Racy, Risk, Stuntman, Swashbuckler, Taunt, Venture
**Dark(en), Darkie, Darkness** Aphelia, Aphotic, Apophis, Black(out), Blind, Byronic, Caliginous, Cimmerian, Cloud, Colly, Crepuscular, Depth, Dim, Dingy, Dirk(e),

Dour, Dusky, Eclipse, Egyptian, Embrown, Erebus, Evil, Gloom, Glum, Grim, Inky, Inumbrate, Jet, Kieran, Low-key, Mare, Maria, Melanous, Mirk, Mulatto, Murk(y), Negro, Night(time), Obfuscate, Obnubilation, Obscure, Obsidian, Ominous, Ousel, Ouzel, Overcast, Pall, Phaeic, Pitch-black, Pit-mirk, Rooky, Sable, Sad, Saturnine, Secret, Shades, Shady, Shuttered, Sinister, Solein, Sombre, Sooty, Sphacelate, Starless, Stygian, Sullen, Sunless, Swarthy, Tar, Tenebrose, Tenebr(i)ous, Unfair, Unlit, Wog, Woosel, Yellowboy, Yellowgirl

**Darling** Acushla, Alannah, Asthore, Beloved, Charlie, Cher, Chéri(e), Chick-a-biddy, Chick-a-diddle, Chuck-a-diddle, Dear, Dilling, Do(a)ting-piece, Duck(s), Favourite, Grace, Honey, Idol, Jarta, Jo(e), Lal, Love, Luv, Mavourneen, Mavournin, Minikin, Minion, Oarswoman, Own, Peat, Pet, Poppet, Precious, Squeeze, Sugar, Sweetheart, Sweeting, Yarta, Yarto

**Darn** Begorra, Blow, Doggone, Hang, Mend, Repair, Sew

**Dart(s), Darter** Abaris, Arrow, Banderilla, Beetle, Dace, Dash, Deadener, Dodge, Fleat, Fléchette, Flirt, Flit, Harpoon, Javelin, Launch, Leap, Lunger, Pheon, Race, Scoot, Shanghai, Skrim, Speck, Spiculum, Sprint, Strike, Thrust, Wheech

**Darwin** Charles, Evolutionist

**Dash(ing), Dashed** Backhander, Bally, Blade, Blight, Blow, Bribe, Buck, Charge, Collide, Cut, Dad, Dah, Damn, Dapper, Dart(le), Daud, Dawd, Debonair, Ding, Dod, Doggy, Elan, Em (rule), En (rule), Fa(s)cia, Flair, Fly, Gallop, Go-ahead, Hang, Hurl, →**HURRY**, Hustle, Hyphen, Impetuous, Jabble, Jaw, Jigger, Lace, Leg it, Line, Minus, Modicum, Morse, Natty, Nip, Panache, Pebble, Race, Raffish, Rakish, Ramp, Rash, Rule, Run, Rush, Sally, Scamp(er), Scapa, Scarper, Scart, Scoot, Scrattle, Scurry, Scuttle, Shatter, Showy, Skitter, Skuttle, Souse, Spang, Speed, Splash, Splatter, Sprint, Strack, Streak, Strike, Stroke, →**STYLE**, Swashbuckling, Swung, Throw, Tinge, Touch, Treacherous, Ugly, Viretot

**Dashboard** Fascia, Panel

**Dashwood** Hell-fire club

**Dastard(ly)** Base, Coward, Craven, Nid(d)erling, Poltroon

**Data(base), Datum** Archie, Cyberspace, Donne(e), Evidence, Factoid, Facts, Fiche, File, Floating-point, Garbage, Gen, Griff, Hard copy, HOLMES, Info, Input, IT, Material, Matrix, Newlyn, News, Ordnance, Read-out, Soft copy, Statistic, Table, Triple

**Date(d), Dates, Dating** AD, Age, AH, Almanac, Appointment, Blind, Boyfriend, Calendar, Carbon, Carbon-14, Computer, Court(ship), Deadline, Engagement, Epoch, Equinox, Era, Escort, Exergue, Expiry, Fission-track, Fixture, Gig, Girlfriend, Ides, Julian, Meet, Obsolescent, Outmoded, →**OUT OF DATE**, Passé, Past, Radioactive, Radio-carbon, Radiometric, Rubidium-strontium, See, Speed, System, Target, →**TRYST**, Ult(imo), Uranium-lead, Value

**Daub** Begrime, Blob, Dab, Gaum, Mess, Moil, Noint, Plaister, Plaster, Slaister, →**SMEAR**, Smudge, Splodge, Teer, Wattle

**Daughter (in law)** Child, D, Elect, Girl, Imogen, Jephthah's, Niece, Offspring, Skevington's

**Daunt** Adaw, Amate, Awe, Deter, Dishearten, Intimidate, Overawe, Quail, Stun, Stupefy, Subdue

**Dauphin** Delphin

**David** Camp, Dai, Psalmist

**Davit** Crane, Derrick, Hoist

**Davy** Crockett, Jones

**Daw** Bird, Kae, Magpie, Margery

**Dawdle(r)** Dally, Draggle, Drawl, Idle, Lag(gard), →**LOITER**, Malinger, Potter, Shirk, Slowcoach, Snail, Tarry, Troke, Truck

**Dawn(ing)** Aurora, Cockcrow, Daw, Daybreak, Daylight, Day-peep, Dayspring, Early, Enlightenment, Eoan, Eos, False, French, Half-light, Light, Morning, Morrow, Occur, Prime, Roxane, Sparrowfart, Spring, Start, Sunrise, Sun up, Ushas

**Day(s)** Account, Ahemeral, All Fools', All Hallows', All Saints', All Souls', Anniversary, Annunciation, Anzac, April Fool's, Arbor, Armistice, Ascension, Australia, Bad hair, Baker, Banian, Banyan, Barnaby, Bastille, Borrowing, Box, Boxing, Broad, Calendar, Calends, Calpa, Canada, Canicular, Childermas, Civil, Columbus, Commonwealth, Contango, Continental, Continuation, D, Daft, Date, Decoration, Degree, Derby, Der Tag, Dismal, Distaff, Dog, Dominion, Double, Dress down, Dressed, Duvet, Early, Ember, Empire, Epact, Fast, Fasti, Father's, Feast, Ferial, Field, Fiesta, Flag, Fri, Gang, Gaudy, Glory, Groundhog, Guy Fawkes', Halcyon, Hey, High, Hogmanay, Holocaust, Holy, Holy Innocents', Holy-rood, Hundred, Ides, Inauguration, Independence, Intercalary, Jour, Judgment, Juridical, Kalends, Kalpa, Labo(u)r, Lady, Laetare, Lammas, Last, Law(ful), Lay, Leap, Mardi, Market, May, Memorial, Michaelmas, Midsummer, Mon, Morrow, Mother's, Muck-up, Mufti, Mumping, Name, Ne'erday, New Year's, Nones, Nychthemeron, Oak-apple, Octave, Off, Open, Orangeman's, Palmy, Pancake, Paper, Pay, Poppy, Post, Pound, Present, Press(ed), Primrose, Pulvering, Quarter, Rag, Rainy, Red-letter, Remembrance, Rent, Rest, Robin, Rock, Rogation, Rood(-mas), Rosh Chodesh, Sabbath, St John's, Saint's, St Swithin's, St Thomas's, St Valentine's, Salad, Sansculotterie, Sat, Scambling, Settling, Sexagesima, Shick-shack, Show, Sidereal, Snow, Solar, Solstice, Speech, Sports, Station, Sun, Supply, Tag, Term, Thanksgiving, Thurs, Ticket, Time, Transfer, Trial, Triduum, Tues, Twelfth, Utas, Valentine's, Varnishing, VE, Vernissage, Veterans', Victoria, Visiting, VJ, Waitangi, Wash, Wed, Wedding, Working
**Daybreak** Cockcrow, Cockleert, Skreigh of day
**Daydream(er), Daydreaming** Brown study, Castle(s) in the air, Dwam, Dwaum, Fancy, Imagine, Lose oneself, Muse, Reverie, Rêveur, Walter Mitty, Woolgathering
**Daylight** Artificial, Dawn, Living, Robbery, Space, Sun
**Daze(d)** Amaze, Bemuse, Confuse, Dwaal, Gally, Muddle, Muzzy, Petrify, Punch drunk, Reeling, Spaced out, →STUN, Stupefy, Stupor, Trance
**Dazzle(d), Dazzler, Dazzling** Bewilder, Blend, Blind, Bobby, Eclipse, Foudroyant, Glare, Larking glass, Meteoric, Outshine, Radiance, Resplendent, Splendour, Yblent
**Deacon** Cleric, Doctor, Minister, Permanent
**Deactivate** Unarm
**Dead(en)** Abrupt, Accurate, Alamort, Asgard, Asleep, Bang, Blunt, Brown bread, Bung, Cert, Cold, Complete, D, Deceased, Defunct, Dodo, Doggo, Expired, Extinct, Flatliner, Gone(r), Inert, Infarct, Late, Lifeless, Morkin, Muffle, Mute, Napoo, Niflheim, Numb, Obsolete, Obtund, Ringer, Sequestrum, She'ol, Slain, Smother, Stillborn, True, Under hatches, Utter, Waned
**Dead end, Deadlock** Blind alley, Cut-off, Dilemma, Impasse, Logjam, Stalemate, Stoppage
**Dead-leaf colour** Filemot, Philamot, Philomot
**Deadline** Date, Epitaph, Limit
**Deadlock** Impasse, Stalemate, Stand-off, Sticking-point
**Deadly** Baleful, Dull, Exact, Fell, Funest, Internecine, →LETHAL, Malign, Monkshood, Mortal, Mortific, No more, Pestilent, Stone, Thanatoid, Unerring, Venomous
**Deadly nightshade** Belladonna, Dwale
**Deadpan** Expressionless
**Dead reckoning** Dr
**Dead tree** Rampick, Rampike
**Deaf(en), Deafening, Deafness** Adder, Asonia, Deave, Deeve, Dunny, Heedless, Paracusis, Presbyac(o)usis, Presbyc(o)usis, Surd(ity)
**Deal(er), Dealership, Dealing(s), Deal with** Act, Address, Agent, Agreement, Allot(ment), Arb, Arbitrageur, Bargain, Biz, Breadhead, Brinjarry, Broker, Bulk, Business, Cambist, Candyman, Chandler, Chapman, Clocker, Commerce, Connection, Contract, Cope, Coup, Cover, Croupier, Dispense, Distributor, Do, Dole, Done, East, Eggler, Exchange, Fir, Franchise, Fripper, Front-running, Goulash, Hack, Hand(le), Help, Inflict, Insider, Interbroker, Jiggery-pokery, Jobber, Lashing, Lay on, Lay out, Loads, Lot,

Manage, Mercer, Merchandise, Merchant, Mickle, Middleman, Monger, Mort, Negotiate, New, North, Operator, Package, Pine, Plain, Post, Productivity, Pusher, Racketeer, Raft, Raw, Red, Relations, Sale, Scrap merchant, See to, Serve, Side, Sight, Simoniac, Slanger, Sort, South, Spicer, Spiv, Square, Stapler, Stockbroker, Stockist, Stockjobber, Takeover, Tape, Timber, Totter, Tout(er), →TRADE, Trade in, Trade off, Tradesman, Traffic, Traffick, Transaction, Treat, Truck, West, Wheeler, White, Wholesaler, Wield, Woolstapler, Yarborough, Yardie

**Dean** Acheson, Arabin, Colet, Decani, Den, Doyen, Forest, Head, Inge, Nellie, Provost, RD, Rural, Rusk, Skater, Slade, Spooner, Swift, Vale, Vicar-forane, V rev

**Dear(er), Dearest, Dear me** Ay, Bach, Beloved, Cara, Caro, Cher(e), Cherie, Chou, Chuckie, Darling, Duck(s), Expensive, High, Honey(bun), Joy, Lamb, Leve, Lief, Lieve, Loor, Love, Machree, Mouse, My, Pet, Pigsney, Pigsnie, Pigsny, Soote, Steep, Sugar, Sweet, Sweetie, Sweeting, Toots(ie), Unreasonable, Up

**Dearth** Famine, Lack, Paucity, Scantity, Scarcity, →SHORTAGE

**Deaspiration** Psilosis

**Death(ly)** Abraham's bosom, Auto-da-fe, Bane, Bargaist, Barg(h)est, Biolysis, Black, Carnage, Cataplexis, Charnel, Clinical, Commorientes, Cot, Curtains, Cypress, Demise, Deodand, Departure, Dormition, End, Eschatology, Euthanasia, Exit, Expiry, Extinction, Fatality, Fey, Funeral, Fusillation, Gangrene, Grim Reaper, Hallal, Heat, Infarction, Jordan, Karoshi, King of Terrors, Lead colic, Lethee, Leveller, Living, Loss, Mors, Mortality, Napoo, Necrosis, Nemesis, Night, Obit, Passing, Quietus, Reaper, Sati, Sergeant, SIDS, Small-back, Sorry end, Strae, Sudden, Suttee, Terminal, Thanatism, Thanatology, Thanatopsis, Thanatos, Yama

**Death-flood** Styx

**Deathless(ness)** Athanasy, Eternal, Eterne, Immortal, Struldberg, Timeless, Undying

**Debacle** Cataclysm, Collapse, Disaster, Fiasco

**Debag** Dack, Unbreech

**Debar** Black, Deny, Deprive, Exclude, Forbid, Preclude, →PREVENT, Prohibit

**Debase(d)** Adulterate, Allay, Bemean, Cheapen, Corrupt, Demean, Depreciate, Dialectician, Dirty, Grotesque, Hedge, Lower, Pervert, Traduce, Vitiate

**Debate(r)** Adjournment, Argue, Casuist, Combat, Contention, Contest, Controversy, Deliberate, Dialectic, Discept, Discourse, Discuss(ion), →DISPUTE, Flyte, Forensics, Full-dress, Moot, Paving, Polemics, Powwow, Reason, Teach-in, Warsle, Wrangle, Wrestle

**Debauch(ed), Debauchee, Debauchery** Corrupt, Decadent, Defile, Degenerate, Dissipate, Dissolute, Heliogabalus, Hellbender, Libertine, Licence, Orgy, Profligate, Raddled, Rake-hell, Riot, Roist, Roué, Royst, Seduce, Spree, Stuprate, Wet, Whore

**Debenture** Bond, Security

**Debilitate(d), Debility** Asthenia, Atonic, Cachexia, Feeble, Languid, Weak

**Debit** Charge, Debt, Direct

**Debonair** Cavalier, Chipper, Gay, Gracious, Jaunty

**Debrief** Wash up, Wind up

**Debris** Bahada, Bajada, Detritus, Eluvium, Flotsam, Jetsam, Moraine, Moslings, Pyroclastics, Refuse, →RUBBLE, Ruins, Sawdust, Shrapnel, Tel, Tephra, Waste, Wreckage

▷ **Debris** *may indicate* an anagram

**Debt(or)** Abbey-laird, Alsatia, Arrears, Arrestee, Bankrupt, Bonded, Dr, Due, Floating, Funded, Insolvent, IOU, Liability, Moratoria, National, Obligation, Obligor, Outstanding, Oxygen, Poultice, Public, Queer Street, Red, Score, Senior, Subordinated, Tick, Tie, Unfunded

**Debt-collector** Bailiff, Forfaiter, Remembrancer

**Debut** Launch, Opening, Outset, Presentation

**Debutante** Bud, Deb

**Decade** Rosary, Ten

**Decadence, Decadent** Babylonian, Decaying, Degeneration, Dissolute, Effete, Fin-de-siècle, Libertine

**Decamp** Abscond, Absquatulate, Bolt, Bunk, Depart, Flee, Guy, Levant, Mizzle, Slide, Slope, Vamoose, Welch

**Decant(er)** Carafe, Pour, Unload

**Decapitate, Decapitation** Aphesis, → BEHEAD, Guillotine

▷ **Decapitated** *may indicate* first letter removed

**Decay(ed), Decaying** Alpha, Appair, Beta, Biodegrade, Blet, Canker, Caries, Caseation, Consenescence, Crumble, Decadent, Declension, Decline, Decompose, Decrepit, Dieback, Disintegrate, Dissolution, Doat, Doddard, Doddered, Dote, Dricksie, Druxy, Dry rot, Ebb, Fail, F(o)etid, Forfair, Gamma, Gangrene, Heart-rot, Impair, Moulder, Pair(e), Perish, Plaque, Ptomaine, Putrefy, Radioactive, Ret, Rot, Rust, Saprogenic, Sap-rot, Seedy, Senility, Sepsis, Spoil, Tabes, Thoron, Time-worn, Wet-rot

**Decease(d)** Death, Decedent, Demise, Die, Stiff

**Deceit(ful), Deceive(r)** Abuse, Ananias, Artifice, Bamboozle, Barrat, Befool, Bitten, Blag, Blind, Bluff, Braide, → CHEAT, Chicane, Chouse, Con, Cozen, Cuckold, Decoy, Defraud, Deke (out), Delude, Diddle, Dissemble, Do brown, Double-cross, Double-dealing, Double-tongued, Dupe, Duplicity, False(r), Fastie, Fast-talk, Fiddle, Fineer, Flam, Fool, Four-flusher, Fox, Fraud, Gag, Gerrymander, Gloze, Guile, Gull, Hoax, Hoodwink, Hornswoggle, Humbug, Hype, Hypocritical, Illusion, Imposition, Inveigle, Invention, Jacob, Jiggery-pokery, Kid, Lead on, Liar, Malengine, Mamaguy, Mata Hari, Mendacious, Misinform, Mislead, Mislippen, Patter, Perfidy, Phenakism, Poop, Poupe, Pretence, Prevaricate, Punic, Rig, Ruse, Sell, Sham, Shifty, Sinon, Sleekit, Snow job, Spruce, Stall, Stratagem, String along, Subreption, Swindle, Swizzle, Take in, Tregetour, Trick, Trump, Trumped up, Two-faced, Two-time, Weasel, Wile

**Decency, Decent** Chaste, Decorum, Fitting, Godly, Healsome, Honest, Honourable, Kind, Mensch, Modest, Moral, Passable, Presentable, Respectable, Salubrious, Seemly, Sporting, Straight, Wholesome, Wise-like

**Decentralise** Disperse

**Deception, Deceptive** Abusion, Artifice, Bluff, Catchpenny, Catchy, Cheat, Chicanery, Codology, → DECEIT, Decoy, Disguise, Dupe, Duplicity, Elusive, Eyewash, Fallacious, False, Feigned, Fineer, Flam, Fraud, Fubbery, Gag, Gammon, Guile, Gullery, Have-on, Hocus-pocus, Hokey-pokey, Hum, Hunt-the-gowks, Hype, Ignes-fatui, Ignis-fatuus, Illusion, Insidious, Jiggery-pokery, Kidology, Legerdemain, Lie, Mamaguy, Moodies, Phantasmal, Runaround, Ruse, Scam, Sciolism, Sell, Sleight, Smoke and mirrors, Specious, Sting, The moodies, Thimblerig, → TRICK, Trompe l'oeil, Two-timing, Underhand

**Decide(r), Decided, Decisive** Addeem, Adjudge, Agree, Arbitrate, Ar(r)e(e)de, Ballot, Barrage, Bottom-line, Call, Cast, Clinch, Conclude, Conclusive, → DECISION, Deem, Definite, Determine, Distinct, Draw lots, Effectual, Engrenage, Fatal, Firm, Fix, Foregone, Jump-off, Mediate, Opt, Parti, Predestination, Pronounced, Rescript, Resolute, → RESOLVE, Result, Rule, Run-off, Seal, See, Settle, Split, Sudden death, Sure, Tiebreaker, Try

**Decimal** Mantissa, Recurring, Repeating, Terminating

**Decimate** Destroy, Lessen, Tithe, Weaken

▷ **Decipher(ed)** *may indicate* an 'o' removed

**Decipher(ing)** Cryptanalysis, Decode, Decrypt, Descramble, Discover, Explain, Interpret

**Decision** Arbitrium, Arrêt, Bottom line, Crossroads, Crunch, Crux, Decree, Engrenage, Fatwa, Fetwa, Firman, Judg(e)ment, Parti, Placit(um), Referendum, Resolution, Resolve, Responsa, Ruling, Sentence, Split, Sudden death, Verdict

**Decisive** Climactic, Clincher, Crisis, Critical, Crux, Definite, Final, Pivotal

**Deck** Adonise, Adorn, Angled, Array, Attrap, Bejewel, Boat, Canted, Cards, Clad, Clothe, Daiker, Daub, Decorate, Dizen, Embellish, Equip, Flight, Focsle, Forecastle, Garland, Hang, Helideck, Hurricane, Lower, Main, Mess, Monkey poop, Orlop, Ornament, Pack,

Pedestrian, Platform, Poop, Prim, Promenade, Quarter, Saloon, Spar, Sun, Tape, Upper, Void, Weather, Well

**Declare, Declaration, Declaim, Decree** Absolute, A(r)e(e)de, Affidavit, Affirm, Air, Allege, Announce, Annunciate, Aread, Assert, Asseverate, Aver, Avow, Balfour, Bann(s), Bayyan, Breda, Call, Canon, Dictum, Diktat, Doom, Edict, Elocute, Emit, Enact, Fatwa(h), Fiat, Firman, Go, Grace, Harangue, Hatti-sherif, Improbation, Independence, Indiction, Indulgence, Insist, Interlocutory, Irade, Law, Mandate, Manifesto, Mecklenburg, Meld, Motu proprio, Mou(th), Nisi, Noncupate, Novel(la), Nullity, Nuncupate, Orate, Ordain, Order, Ordinance, Parlando, Petition of Right, Pontificate, Predicate, Present, Proclaim, Profess, Promulgate, Pronounce, Protest, Psephism, Publish, Rant, Read, Recite, Remark, Rescript, Resolve, Restatement, Rights, Rule, Ruling, Saw, SC, Sed, Senatus consultum, Senecan, Shahada, Signify, Speak, Spout, Statement, Statutory, Swear, Testament-dative, Testify, Testimony, UDI, Ukase, Ultimatum, Unilateral, Vie, Voice, Vouch, Will, Word

▷ **Declaring** *may indicate* a word beginning 'Im'

**Decline, Declination, Declining** Abate, Abstain, Age, Ail, Atrophy, Catabasis, Comedown, Decadent, Degeneration, Degringoler, Deny, Descend, Deteriorate, Devall, Die, Diminish, Dip, Dissent, Downhill, Downtrend, Downturn, Droop, Drop, Dwindle, Ebb, Elapse, Escarpment, Fade, Fall, Flag, Forbear, Lapse, Magnetic, Opt out, Paracme, Pejoration, Peter, Plummet, Quail, Recede, Recession, Reflow, Refuse, Relapse, Retrogression, Rot, Ruin, Rust, Sag, Senile, Set, Sink, Slide, Slump, Slumpflation, Stoop, Subside, Sunset, Tumble, Twilight, Wane, Welke, → **WILT**, Withdraw, Wither

**Decoct(ion)** Apozem, Cook, Devise, Ptisan, Tisane

**Decode(d)** Analyse, En clair

**Decolleté** Low, Neckline

**Decompose, Decomposition** Biodegradable, Crumble, Decay, Degrade, Disintegrate, Electrolysis, Fermentation, Hydrolysis, Mor, Pyrolysis, Rot, Wither

**Decompression** Bends

**Decongestant** Inhalant

**Deconstruct(ion)** Iconoclasm

**Decor** Background, Scenery

**Decorate(d), Decoration, Decorative** Adorn, Aiguilette, Angelica, Aogai, Applique, Arpillera, Attrap, Award, Bard, Bargeboard, Baroque, Bauble, Beaux-arts, Bedeck, Bedizen, Bells and whistles, Biedermeier, Bordure, Braid, Brattishing, Braze, Breastpin, Brooch, Cartouche, Centrepiece, Chain, Chambranle, Champlevé, Chinoiserie, Christingle, Cinquefoil, Cloissoné, Coffer, Cresting, Crocket, Croix de guerre, Cul-de-lampe, Daiker, Decoupage, Dentelle, Dentil, Diamante, Distemper, Doodad, Doodah, Do over, Dragée, Dragging, Emblazon, Emboss, Embrave, Engrail, Enrich, Epaulet, Epergne, Etch, Fancy, Festoon, Filigree, Fillet, Finery, Finial, Fleuret(te), Fleuron, Floriated, Flushwork, Fluting, Fob, Fourragère, Frieze, Frill, Frog, Frost, Furbish, Gadroon, Gammadion, Garniture, Gaud, Gild, Gilt, Glitter, Godroon, Goffer, Gradino, Grecque key, Grotesque, Guilloche, Historiated, Ice, Illuminate, Impearl, Inlay, Intarsia, Intarsio, Interior, Jabot, Jari, Kalambari, Knotwork, Leglet, Linen-fold, Linen-scroll, Marquetry, MC, Medal(lion), Mola, Motif, Moulding, Oath, OBE, Ogee, Openwork, Order, → **ORNAMENT**, Ornate, Orphrey, Overglaze, Ovolo, Paint, Paper, Parament, Pâté-sur-pâté, Pattern, Photomural, Pinata, Pipe, Pokerwork, Polychromy, Pompom, Prettify, Prink, Purfle, Purple heart, Quilling, Rag-rolling, Rangoli, Repoussé, Ribbon, Rich, Ric(k)-rac(k), Rosemaling, Ruche, Scallop, Schwarzlot, Scrimshander, Scrimshaw, Serif, Set-off, Sgraffito, Skeuomorph, Soutache, Spangle, Staffage, Stipple, Stomacher, Storiated, Strapwork, Stucco, Studwork, Tailpiece, Tart up, Tassel, Tattoo, TD, Titivate, Tool, Topiary, Tracery, Trim, Trinket, Veneer, Vergeboard, Wallpaper, Well-dressing, Wirework, Zari

**Decorous, Decorum** Becoming, Demure, Etiquette, Fitness, Modest, Parliamentary, Prim, → **PROPER**, Propriety, Sedate, Seemlihe(a)d, → **SEEMLY**, Staid, Tasteful

**Decoy** Allure, Attract, Bait, Bonnet, Button, Call-bird, Coach, Crimp, Entice, Lure, Piper, Q-ship, Roper, Ruse, Shill, Stale, Stalking-horse, Stall, Stoolie, Stool-pigeon, Tame cheater, Tice, Tole, Toll, Trap, Trepan

**Decrease** Cut back, Decrew, Diminish, Dwindle, Fall, Iron, Lessen, Press, Ramp down, Reduce, Rollback, Slim, Step-down, Subside, Wane, Wanze

**Decree** →DECLARE

**Decrepit** Dilapidated, Doddery, Doitit, Failing, Feeble, Frail, Moth-eaten, Spavined, Time-worn, Tumbledown, Warby, Weak

**Decriminalise** Launder

**Decry** Condemn, Crab, Denounce, Derogate, Detract, Downgrade

**Dedicate(d), Dedication** Allot, Corban, Determination, Devote, Dinah, Endoss, Hallow, Inscribe, Oblate, Patriotism, Pious, Sacred, Single-minded, Votive, Work ethic

**Deduce, Deduction, Deductive** Allowance, A priori, Assume, Conclude, Consectary, Corollary, Derive, Discount, Dockage, Draw, Gather, Illation, Infer(ence), Natural, Obvert, Off-reckoning, Reason, Rebate, Recoup, Reprise, Stoppage, Surmise, Syllogism

**Deed(s)** Achievement, Act(ion), Atweel, Backbond, Back letter, Charta, Charter, Defeasance, Derring-do, Disposition, Escrol(l), Escrow, Exploit, Fact(um), Feat, Indeed, Indenture, Manoeuvre, Mitzvah, Muniments, Premises, Settlement, Specialty, Starr, →TITLE, Trust, Work

**Deem** Consider, Judge, Opine, Ordain, Proclaim, Repute, Think

**Deep(en), Deeply** Abstruse, Abysmal, Bass(o), Brine, Briny, Enhance, Excavate, Grum, Gulf, Hadal, Intense, Low, Mindanao, Mysterious, →OCEAN, Profound, Re-enter, Rich, Sea, Sonorous, Sunk(en), Throaty, Upsee, Ups(e)y

**Deep-rooted** Inveterate

**Deer(-like)** Axis, Bambi, Barasing(h)a, Barking, Blacktail, Brocket, Buck, Cariacou, Caribou, Carjacou, Cervine, Chevrotain, Chital, Doe, Elaphine, Elk, Fallow, Gazelle, Hart, Hog, Irish elk, Jumping, Moose, Mouse, Mule, Muntjac, Muntjak, Musk, Père David's, Pricket, Pudu, Pygarg, Red, Rein, Roe, Rusa, Sambar, Sambur, Selenodont, Sika, Sorel(l), Spade, Spay(d), Spayad, Spitter, Spottie, Stag(gard), Tragule, Ungulate, Virginia, Wapiti, Water, White-tailed

**Deer-hunter** Tinchel

**Deface** Disfigure, Spoil

▷ **Defaced** *may indicate* first letter missing

**Defame, Defamatory, Defamation** Abase, Bad mouth, Blacken, Calumny, Cloud, Denigrate, Detract, Dishonour, Impugn, In rixa, Libel, Malign, Mud, Mudslinging, Obloquy, Sclaunder, Scurrilous, Slander, Smear, Stigmatise, Traduce, Vilify

**Default(er)** Absentee, Bilk, Dando, Delinquent, Flit, Levant, Neglect, Omission, Renegue, Waddle, Welsh

**Defeat(ed), Defeatist** Beat, Best, Bowed, Caning, Capot, Cast, Checkmate, Clobber, Codille, Conquer, Counteract, Cream, Debel, Defeasance, Demolish, Destroy, Discomfit, Dish, Ditch, Donkey-lick, Drub, Fatalist, Floor, Foil, Foyle, Hammer, Hiding, Kippered, Laipse, Lick, Loss, Lurch, Marmelize, Master, Mate, Moral, Negative, Out, Outclass, Outdo, Outfight, Outfox, Outgeneral, Outgun, Outplay, Outvote, Outwit, →OVERCOME, Overmarch, Overpower, Overreach, Overthrow, Overwhelm, Pip, Plaster, Pulverise, Quitter, Rebuff, Repulse, Reverse, Rout, Rubicon, Scupper, Set, Shellacking, Sisera, Skunk, Squabash, Stump, Tank, Thrash, Thwart, Toast, Tonk, Trounce, Undo, Vanquish, War, Waterloo, Whap, Whip, Whitewash, Whop, Whup, Wipe-out, Worst

**Defecate, Defecation** Encopresis, Horse, Mute, Poop, Scumber, Shit, Skummer, Tenesmus

**Defect(ion), Defective, Defector** Abandon, Amateur, Apostasy, Blemish, Bug, Coma, Crack, Crawling, Deficient, Desert, Dud, Failing, Faulty, Flaw, →FORSAKE, Frenkel, Halt, Hamartia, Hiatus, Kink, Low, Manky, Mass, Mote, Natural, Paralexia, Point, Psellism, Rachischisis, Renegade, Renegate, Ridgel, Ridgil, Rig, Rogue, Runagate, Schottky,

Shortcoming, Spina bifida, Stammer, Substandard, Terrace, Treason, Trick, Want, Wanting, Weakness, Wreath

**Defence, Defended, Defend(er), Defensible, Defensive** Abat(t)is, Advocate, Alexander, Alibi, Antibody, Antidote, Antigenic, Antihistamine, Anti-predator, Apologia, Apologist, Arm, Back, Back four, Bailey, Barbican, Barmkin, Barricade, Bastion, Battery, Battlement, Berm, Bestride, Bodyguard, Bridgehead, Bulwark, Calt(h)rop, Castling, Catenaccio, CD, Champion, Chapparal, Civil, Counter-measure, Curtain, Demibastion, Ditch, Embrasure, Enguard, Estacade, Goalie, Guard, Hedgehog, Herisson, Hold, Immunity, J(i)u-jitsu, Justify, Kaim, Keeper, Kraal, Laager, Laer, Last-ditch, Libero, Linebacker, Maginot-minded, Mail, Maintain, Martello tower, MIDAS, Moat, Motte and bailey, Muniment, Outwork, Palisade, Parapet, Pentagon, Perceptual, Propugnation, Protect, Quinte, Rampart, Redan, Redoubt, Refute, Resist, Ringwall, Roman wall, Sandbag, Sangar, Scarecrow, Seawall, →**SHELTER**, Shield(wall), Sicilian, Stonewall, Strategic, Support, Sweeper, Tenable, Tenail(le), Testudo, Tower, Trench, Trou-de-loup, Uphold, Vallation, Vallum, Vindicate, Wall, Warran(t), Zonal

**Defenceless** Helpless, Inerm, Insecure, Naked, Sitting duck, Vulnerable

**Defendant** Accused, Apologist, Respondent, Richard Roe

**Defer(ence), Deferential, Deferring** Bow, Complaisance, Curtsey, Delay, Dutiful, Homage, Moratory, Morigerous, Obeisant, Pace, Polite, Postpone, Procrastinate, Protocol, Respect, Roll over, Shelve, Spaniel, Stay, Submit, Suspend, Waive, Yield

**Defiance, Defiant, Defy** Acock, Bite the thumb, Bold, Brave, Brazen, Cock a snook, Contumacy, Dare, Daring, Disregard, Do or die, Flaunt, Insubordinate, Kembo, Kimbo, Outbrave, Outdare, Rebellion, Recalcitrant, Recusant, Resist, Scab, Stubborn, Titanism, Truculent, Unruly, Yahboo

**Deficiency, Deficient** Absence, Acapnia, ADA, Anaemia, Anoxia, Aplasia, Beriberi, Dearth, Defect, Failing, Hypinosis, Inadequate, Incomplete, Kwashiorkor, Lack, Osteomalacia, Scant, Scarcity, SCID, Shortage, Shortfall, Spanaemia, Want

▷ **Deficient** *may indicate* an anagram

**Deficit** Anaplerotic, Arrears, Defective, Gap, Ischemia, Loss, Overdraft, Poor, Shortfall

**Defile(ment)** Abuse, Array, Barranca, Barranco, Besmear, Col, Conspurcation, Desecrate, Dishonour, Donga, Enseam, →**FOUL**, Gate, Gorge, Gully, Inquinate, Inseem, Kloof, Moil, Pass, Pollute, Poort, Ravine, Ray, Roncesvalles, Smear, Spoil, →**SULLY**, Taint

**Define(d), Definition, Definitive** Classic, Clear-cut, Decide, Demarcate, Determine, Diorism, Distinct, Explain, Fix, Limit, Parameter, Pinpoint, Set, Sharp, Specific, Tangible, Term

**Definite(ly)** Categorically, Cert(ainty), Classic, Clear (cut), Concrete, Deffo, Emphatic, Firm, Hard, Indeed, Pos, Positive, Precise, Sans-appel, Specific, Sure, Tangible, Unquestionably, Yes

**Deflate** Burst, Collapse, Flatten, Lower, Prick, Puncture, Squeeze

**Deflect(or), Deflection** Avert, Back-scatter, Bend, Detour, Diverge, Divert, Glance, Head off, Holophote, Otter, Paravane, Parry, Refract, Snick, Swerve, Throw, Trochotron, Veer, Windage

**Deform(ed), Deformity** Anamorphosis, Blemish, Boutonniere, Contracture, Crooked, Disfigure, Distort, Freemartin, Gammy, Hammer-toe, Harelip, Misborn, Miscreated, Misfeature, Mishapt, Mooncalf, Mutilate, Phocomelia, Phocomely, Polt-foot, Saddle-nose, Splay feet, Stenosed, Talipes, Valgus, Varus, Warp

▷ **Deformed** *may indicate* an anagram

**Defraud** Bilk, Cheat, Cozen, Gull, Gyp, Lurch, Mulct, Shoulder, Skin, Sting, Swindle, Trick

**Defray** Bear, Cover, Meet

**Defrost** Thaw

**Deft** Adept, Agile, Dab, Dexterous, Elegant, Handy, Nimble

**Defunct** Deceased, Extinct, Obsolete

▸ **Defy** *see* **DEFIANCE**

**Degauss** Demagnetise

**Degenerate, Degeneration, Degenerative** Acorn-shell, Ascidian, Atrophy, Backslide, Balanus, Base, Cirrhipedea, Cirrhipedia, Cirrhipod(a), Cirripedea, Cirripedia, Decadent, Deprave, Descend, Deteriorate, Eburnation, Effete, Fatty, Kaliyuga, Necrobiosis, Pejorate, Pervert, Rakehell, Relapse, Retrogress, Rot, Salp, Stentosis, Tunicate

**Degrade, Degradation** Abase, Brutalise, Cheapen, Culvertage, Debase, Demission, Demote, Depose, Diminish, Disennoble, Embase, Humble, Imbase, Imbrute, Lessen, Lower, →**SHAME**, Sink, Waterloo

**Degree(s)** Aegrotat, As, Attila (the Hun), Azimuthal, BA, Baccalaureate, BCom, BD, Bearing, B es S, C, Carat, Class, D, Desmond (Tutu), Doctoral, Double first, Douglas (Hurd), Engler, Extent, External, F, First, Forbidden, Foundation, Geoff (Hurst), German, Gradation, Grade, Grece, Gree(s), Greece, Gre(e)se, Grice, Griece, Grize, →**IN A HIGH DEGREE**, Incept, Incidence, K, Lambeth, Latitude, Letters, Level, Levitical, Licentiate, Longitude, MA, Master's, Measure, Mediant, Nth, Nuance, Order, Ordinary, Pass, Peg, PhD, Pin, Poll, Rate, Reaumur, Remove, Second, Stage, Status, Step, Submediant, Subtonic, Supertonic, Third, Trevor (Nunn), Water

**Dehiscence** Suture

**Dehydrate(d)** Exsiccate, Thirsty

**Deification, Deify** Apotheosis

**Deign** Condescend, Stoop

**Deity** Alpha and omega, Avatar, Cabiri, Demogorgon, Divine, Faun, →**GOD**, →**GODDESS**, Idolise, Immortalise, Krishna, Lar, Numen, Pan, Satyr, Zombi(e)

**Déjà vu** Flashback

**Deject(ed), Dejection** Abase, Abattu, Alamort, Amort, Blue, Cast down, Chap-fallen, Chopfallen, Crab, Crestfallen, Despondent, Discouraged, Dismay, Dispirited, Down, Downcast, Gloomy, Hangdog, Humble, Low, Melancholy, Spiritless, Wae

**Delaware** DE(L)

**Delay(ed), Delaying** Adjourn(ment), After-effect, Ambage, Avizandum, Await, Backlog, Behindhand, Belated, Bottleneck, Check, Cunctator, Dawdle, Defer, Demurrage, Detention, Dilatory, Fabian, Filibuster, Forsloe, For(e)slow, Frist, Hangfire, Hesitate, Hinder, Hitch, Hold up, Hysteresis, Impede, Laches, Lag, Late, Laten, Let, Linger, Loiter, Mora(torium), Obstruct, Pause, Procrastinate, Prolong, Prorogue, Remanet, Reprieve, Respite, Retard, Rollover, Setback, Slippage, Sloth, Slow, →**STALL**, Stand-over, Stay, Stonewall, Suspend, Tarry, Temporise, Time-lag, Wait

**Delectable** Delicious, Luscious, Tasty

**Delegate, Delegation** Agent, Amphictyon, Apostolic, Appoint, Assign, Commissary, Decentralise, Depute, Devolution, Mission, Nuncio, Offload, Outsource, Representative, Secondary, Transfer, Vicarial, Walking

**Delete** Adeem, Annul, Axe, Cancel, Cut, Erase, Excise, Expunge, Purge, Rase, Scratch, Scrub, Strike, Twink out

**Deliberate(ly), Deliberation** Adagio, Calculated, Conscious, Consider, Debate, Intentional, Measured, Meditate, Moderate, Muse, On purpose, Overt, Plonking, Pointedly, Ponder, Prepensely, Purposely, Ruminate, Studied, Thought, Voulu, Weigh, Witting

**Delicacy, Delicate** Airy-fairy, Beccafico, Blini, Canape, Cate, Caviare, Dainty, Difficult, Discreet, Dorty, Ectomorph, Eggshell, Elfin, Escargot, Ethereal, Fairy, Fastidious, Filigree, Fine, Finespun, Finesse, Flimsy, Foie-gras, Fragile, →**FRAIL**, Friand, Gentle, Goody, Gossamer, Guga, Hothouse, Inconie, Incony, Kickshaw, Kidglove, Lac(e)y, Ladylike, Light, Lobster, Morbidezza, Nesh, Nicety, Niminy-piminy, Ortolan, Oyster, Pastel, Reedy, Roe, Sensitive, Slight, Soft(ly-softly), Subtle(ty), Sunket, Sweetmeat, Tactful, Taste, Tender, Tenuous, Ticklish, Tidbit, Titbit, Trotter, Truffle, Wispy

**Delicatessen** Charcuterie

**Delicious** Ambrosia, Delectable, Exquisite, Fragrant, Goloptious, Goluptious, Gorgeous, Lekker, Lip-smacking, Mor(e)ish, Mouthwatering, Savoury, Scrummy, Scrumptious, Tasty, Toothsome, Yummo, Yummy, Yum-yum

**Delight(ed), Delightful** Bewitch, Bliss, Charm, Chuff, Coo, Delice, Dreamy, Ecstasy, Edna, Elated, Elysian, Enamour, Enchant, Enjoyable, Enrapture, Exhilarate, Exuberant, Exultation, Felicity, Fetching, Frabjous, Gas, Glad, Glee, Glorious, Gorgeous, Gratify, Honey, Joy, Lap up, Love, Nice, Overjoy, Over the moon, Please, Pleasure, Precious, →RAPTURE, Regale, Rejoice, Revel, Scrummy, Super, Sweet, Taking, Tickle, Turkish, Whacko, Whee, Whoopee, Wizard, Yippee, Yum-yum

▷ **Delight** *may indicate* 'darken'

**Delilah** Temptress

**Delineate** Draft, Outline, Prosciutto, Sketch, Trace

**Delinquent** Bodgie, Criminal, Halbstarker, Hoody, Juvenile, Law-breaker, Negligent, Offender, Ted

**Delirious, Delirium** Deranged, DT, Fever, Frenetic, Frenzy, Insanity, Jimjams, Mania, Phrenetic, Phrenitis, Rambling, Spaced out, Spazz, Wild

**Deliver(ance), Delivered, Deliverer, Delivery(man)** Accouchement, Air-drop, Air-lift, Bailment, Ball, Birth, Born, Bowl, Breech, Caesarean, Consign, Convey, Courier, Deal, Doosra, Drop, Elocution, Escape, Exorcise, Express, Extradition, Give, Googly, Jail, Lead, Leg-spin, Liberate, Lob, Mail drop, Messiah, Midwifery, Orate, Over, Pronounce, Punch-line, Ransom, Receipt, Recorded, Redeem, Refer, Release, Relieve, Render, Rendition, →RESCUE, Rid, Round(sman), Salvation, Save, Say, Seamer, Sell, Service, Shipment, Soliloquy, Speak, Special, Spell, Tice, Transfer, Underarm, Underhand, UPS, Utter, Ventouse extraction, Wide, Yorker

**Dell** Dale, Dargle, Dene, Dimble, Dingle, Dingl(e)y, Glen, Valley

**Delphic** Pythian

**Delphinium** Larkspur

**Delta** Camargue, D, Del, Flood-plain, Kronecker, Nabla, Nile, Oil Rivers, Triangle

**Delude, Delusion** Bilk, Cheat, Deceive, Dupe, Fallacy, Fool, Hoax, Megalomania, →MISLEAD, Myth, Paranoia, Schizothymia, Trick, Zoanthropy

**Deluge** Avalanche, Cascade, Flood, Ogygian, Saturate, Submerge, →SWAMP

**De luxe** Extra, Plush, Special

**Delve** Burrow, Dig, Excavate, Exhume, Explore, Mine, Probe, Rummage, Search

**Demagogue** Agitator, Fanariot, Leader, Mobsman, Phanariot, Speaker, Tribune

**Demand(ing), Demanded** Appetite, Ball-buster, Call, Choosy, Claim, Cry, De rigueur, Derived, Difficult, Dun, Exact, Excess, Exigent, Fastidious, Final, Gruelling, Heavy, Herculean, Hest, →INSIST, Mandate, Market, Necessitate, Need, Onerous, Order, Postulate, Pressure, Pushy, Ransom, Request, Requisition, Rigorous, Rush, Sale, Severe, Stern, Stipulate, Stringent, Summon, Tax, Ultimatum, Want

**Demean(ing)** Belittle, Comport, Debase, Degrade, Humble, Infra dig, Lower, Maltreat

**Demeanour** Air, Bearing, Carriage, Conduct, Expression, Front, Gravitas, Mien, Port, Presence

**Dement(ed)** Crazy, Frenetic, Hysterical, Insane, Mad, Possessed, Wacko

**Demi-god** Aitu, Daemon, Garuda, Hero

**Demi-mondaine** Cocotte, →LOOSE WOMAN, Prostitute

**Demise** Death(-damp), Decease, Finish

**Demo** March, Parade, Protest, Rally, Sit-in

**Democracy, Democrat, Democratic** D, Hunker, Industrial, Liberal, Locofoco, Menshevik, Montagnard, People's, Popular, Republic, Sansculotte, Social, Tammany

**Demoiselle** Crane, Damselfish, Odonata

**Demolish, Demolition** Bulldoze, Devastate, Devour, Dismantle, Floor, KO, Level, Rack, Rase, →RAZE, Smash, Tear down, Wreck

▶ **Demon** *see* DEVIL(ISH)

**Demoness** Lilith

**Demonstrate, Demonstration, Demonstrator** Agitate, Barrack, Dharma, Display, Endeictic, Évènement, Evince, Explain, Gesture, Hunger march, Maffick, Manifest, March, Morcha, Ostensive, Peterloo, Portray, Present, Proof, Protest, Prove, Provo, Send-off, →**SHOW**, Sit-in, Touchy-feely, Verify, Vigil

**Demoralise, Demoralisation** Bewilder, Corrupt, Depths, Destroy, Dishearten, Shatter, Unman, Weaken

**Demos, Demotic** Greek

**Demote, Demotion** Comedown, Degrade, Disbench, Disrate, Embace, Embase, Reduce, Relegate, Stellenbosch

**Demotic** Enchorial

**Demur** Hesitate, Jib, Object

**Demure** Coy, Mim, Modest, Prenzie, Primsie, Sedate, Shy

**Den** Dive, Domdaniel, Earth, Hell, Hide-away, Holt, Home, Lair, Lie, Lodge, Opium, Room, Shebeen, Spieler, Study, Sty, Wurley

**Denial, Deny, Denier** Abnegate, Antinomian, Aspheterism, Bar, Belie, Contradict, Controvert, Démenti, Disavow, Disclaim, Disenfranchise, Disown, Forswear, →**GAINSAY**, Nay, Negate, Nick, Nihilism, Protest, Refuse, Refute, Renague, Renay, Reneg(e), Renegue, Reney, Renig, Renounce, Reny, Repudiate, Sublate, Traverse, Withhold

**Denigrate** Besmirch, Blacken, Defame, Libel, Slander, Tar

**Denim** Jeans

**Denizen** Diehard, Inhabitant, Resident

**Denomination** Category, Cult, Sect, Variety

**Denote** Import, Indicate, Mean, Signify

**Denouement** Anagnorisis, Catastrophe, Climax, Coda, Exposure, Outcome, Showdown

**Denounce, Denunciation** Ban, Commination, Condemn, Criticise, Decry, Delate, Diatribe, Execrate, Fulminate, Hatchet job, Hereticate, Proclaim, Proscribe, Rail, Shop, Stigmatise, Thunder, Upbraid

**Denry** Card

**Dense, Density** B, Buoyant, Charge, Compact, Critical, Current, D, Double, Firm, Flux, Intense, Neutral, Opaque, Optical, Packing, Rank, Reflection, Relative, Single, Solid, Spissitude, Tesla, Thick, Transmission, Vapour, Woofy

**Dent(ed)** Batter, Concave, Dancette, Depress, Dimple, Dinge, Dint, Nock, Punctate, Punt, V

**Dental (problem), Dentist(ry)** DDS, Entodontics, Extractor, Kindhart, LDS, Malocclusion, Odontic, Paedodontics, Periodontic, Toothy

**Dentures** Biteplate, Bridge, Bridgework, False teeth, Plate, Prosthodontia, Store teeth, Wallies

**Denude** Erode, Strip

▶ **Deny** *see* **DENIAL**

**Deodorant** Anti-perspirant, Cachou, Roll-on

**Deoxidise** Outgas, Reduce

**Depart(ed), Departing, Departure** Abscond, Absquatulate, Apage, Bunk, D, Dead, Death, Decamp, Decession, Defunct, Demise, Die, Digress, Divergence, Egress, Exception, Exit, Exodus, Expire, Flight, French leave, →**GO**, Imshi, Late, Leave, Lucky, Moonlight flit, Obiter dicta, Outbound, Rack off, Remue, Scat, Send-off, Swan off, Vacate, Vade, Vamoose, Walkout

**Department** Achaea, Ain, Aisne, Allier, Alpes de Provence, Alpes-Maritimes, Angers, Arcadia, Ardeche, Ardennes, Argo, Argolis, Ariege, Arrondissement, Arta, Attica, Aube, Aude, Aveyron, Bas-Rhin, Belfort, Bell-chamber, Beziers, Bouches-du-Rhône, Branch, Bureau, Calvados, Cantal, Casualty, Charente, Charente-Maritime, Cher, Cleansing, Commissariat, Corrèze, Cote d'Or, Cotes d'Armor, Cotes du Nord, Creuse, DEFRA, Deme, Deuxième Bureau, Deux-Sevres, Division, Domain, Dordogne, Doubs, Drôme, El(e)ia, Essonne, Eure, Eure-et-Loir, Extramural, Faculty, Finistere, Fire, FO, Foggy Bottom, Gard, Gers, Gironde, Greencloth, Guadeloupe, Gulag, Haberdashery,

Hanaper, Haute-Garonne, Haute-Loire, Haute-Marne, Haute-Normandie, Hautes-Alpes, Haute-Saône, Haute Savoie, Hautes-Pyrenees, Haute-Vienne, Haut-Rhin, Hauts-de-Seine, Helpdesk, Herault, Home, Ille-et-Vilaine, Indre, Indre-et-Loire, Inspectorate, Isere, Jura, Landes, Loire, Loiret, Loir-et-Cher, Lot, Lot-et-Garonne, Lozere, Maine-et-Loire, Manche, Marne, Martinique, Mayenne, Menswear, Meurthe-et-Moselle, Meuse, Ministry, Morbihan, Moselle, Nièvre, Nome, Nomos, Nord, Office, Oise, Ordnance, Orne, Pas-de-Calais, Portfolio, Province, Puy de Dôme, Pyrénées(-Atlantique), Pyrénées-Orientales, Region, Rehabilitation, Rhône, Sanjak, Saône-et-Loire, Sarthe, Savoie, Secretariat(e), Section, Seine-et-Marne, Seine Maritime, Seine St Denis, Somme, Sphere, State, Tarn(-et-Garonne), Treasury, Tuscany, Unit, Val de Marne, Val d'Oise, Var, Vaucluse, Vendée, Vienne, Voiotia, War, Wardrobe, Yonne, Yvelines

**Depend(ant), Dependence, Dependency, Dependent** Addicted, Child, Client, Colony, Conditional, Contingent, Count, Dangle, E, Fief, Habit, Hang, Hinge, Icicle, Lean, Lie, Lippen, Minion, Pensioner, Relier, Rely, Retainer, Ross, Sponge, Stalactite, Statistical, Subject, Subordinate, Trust, Turn on, Vassal, Virgin Islands, Ward

**Dependable** Empirical, Reliable, Reliant, Rock, Safe, Secure, Sheet-anchor, Solid, Sound, Staunch, Stolid, Sure, → **TRUSTWORTHY**

**Depict** Bepoint, Delineate, Describe, Display, Draw, Limn, Paint, Portray, Present, Represent

**Depilate, Depilation, Depilatory** Electrolysis, Grain, Rusma, Slate

**Deplete** Depauperate, Diminish, Drain, Exhaust, Reduce, Sap

**Deplorable, Deplore** Base, Bemoan, Chronic, Complain, Criminal, Deprecate, Dolorous, Execrate, Grieve, Lament, Mourn, Pathetic, Piteous, Regret, Rue, Sad, Shocking, Woeful

**Deploy(ment)** Extend, Field, Herse, Unfold, Use

▷ **Deploy(ment)** *may indicate* an anagram

**Depopulate** Deracinate

**Deport(ation), Deportment** Address, Air, Banish, → **BEARING**, Carriage, Demeanour, Dressage, Exile, Extradite, Mien, Renvoi, Renvoy, Repatriation

**Depose, Deposition** Affirm, Banish, Dethrone(ment), Displace, Dispossess, Hoard, Inqueen, Overthrow, Pieta, Testify

**Deposit(s), Depository** Aeolian, Alluvial, Alluvium, Aquifer, Arcus, Argol, Arles, Atheroma, Bank, Bathybius, Bergmehl, Calc-sinter, Calc-tuff, Caliche, Cave-earth, Coral, Crag, Crystolith, Delta, Depone, Diatomite, Diluvium, Drift, Dust, Evaporite, Fan, File, Firn, Fort Knox, Fur, Glacial, Gyttja, Hoard, Icing, Illuvium, Kieselguhr, Land, Laterite, Lava, Lay, Lay away, Lay-by, Laydown, Lead tree, Limescale, Limonite, Lode, Lodge(ment), Loess, Löss, Measure, Moraine, Natron, Outwatch, Park, Pay dirt, Pay in, Phosphorite, Placer, Plank, Plaque, Precipitate, Put, Repose, Residuum, Saburra, Salamander, Sandbank, Saprolite, Saturn's tree, Scale, Sea dust, → **SEDIMENT**, Silt, Sinter, Sludge, Soot, Speleothem, Stalagmite, Stockwork, Storeroom, Stratum, Surety, Tartar, Terramara, Terramare, Till, Time, Tophus, Tripoli, Turbidite, Warehouse

**Depot** Barracoon, Base, Camp, Coach station, Depository, Etape, Station, Terminus, Treasure-city, Warehouse

**Deprave(d), Depravity** Bestial, Cachexia, Cachexy, Caligulism, → **CORRUPT**, Dissolute, Evil, Immoral, Low, Outrage, Reprobate, Rotten, Sodom, Subhuman, Total, Turpitude, Ugly, Unholy, Vice, Vicious, Vile

**Deprecate** Censure, Deplore, Expostulate, Reproach

**Depreciate** Abase, Belittle, Derogate, Detract, Discount

**Depredate, Depredation** Pillage, Plunder, Rob

**Depress(ed), Depressing, Depression** Accablé, Agitated, Alamort, Alveolus, Amort, Astrobleme, Attrist, Black dog, Blight, Blue devils, Blues, Cafard, Caldron, Canada, Canyon, Cheerless, Chill, Col, Combe, Couch, Crab, Crush, Cyclone, Dampen, Deject, Dell, Demission, Dene, Dent, Despair, Dimble, → **DIMPLE**, Dip, Dismal, Dispirit, Ditch, Doldrums, Dolina, Doline, Doomy, Downlifting, Drear, Drere, Dumpish, Endogenous, Exanimate, Flatten, Fonticulus, Foss(ula), Fossa, Fovea, Frog,

Geosyncline, Ghilgai, Gilgai, Gilgie, Glen, Gloom, Graben, Grinch, Ha-ha, Hammer, Heart-spoon, Hilar, Hilum, Hilus, Hollow, Howe, Hyp, Hypothymia, Indentation, Joes, Kettle, Kick(-up), Lacuna, Leaden, Low(ness), Low-spirited, Megrims, Melancholy, Mood, Moping, Morose, Neck, Ocean basin, Pan, Pit, Polje, Postnatal, Postpartum, Pothole, Prostrate, Punt, Qattara, Recession, Re-entrant, Retuse, Sad, Saddle, Sag, Salt-cellar, Salt-pan, Scrobicule, Sink, Sinkhole, Sinus, Sitzmark, Slot, Slough, → **SLUMP**, Slumpflation, Soakaway, Spiritless, Stomodaeum, Sump, Swag, Swale, Swallowhole, Trench, Trough, Umbilication, Vale, Vallecula, Valley, Wallow, Weigh down, Wet blanket

**Deprivation, Deprive(d)** Amerce, Bereft, Deny, Disenfranchise, Disfrock, Dispossess, Disseise, Disseize, Expropriate, Famine, Foreclose, Geld, Ghetto, Have-not, Hunger, Reduce, Remove, Rob, Sensory, Starve, Strip, Withhold

**Depth** Draught, Draw, F, Fathom, Gravity, Intensity, Isobath, Pit, Profundity

**Deputise, Deputy** Act, Agent, Aide, Assistant, Commis(sary), Delegate, Legate, Lieutenant, Locum, Loot, Mate, Number two, Prior, Pro-chancellor, Proxy, Represent, Secondary, Sidekick, Standby, Stand-in, Sub, Subchanter, Substitute, Succentor, Surmistress, Surrogate, Tanaiste, Vicar, Vice, Viceregent, Vidame

**Derange(d), Derangement** Craze, Détraqué, Disturb, Flipped, Insane, Loopy, Manic, Skivie, Trophesy, Troppo, Unhinge, Unsettle

**Derby** Boot, Demolition, Donkey, Eponym, Hat, Kentucky, Kiplingcotes, Local, Race, Roller

**Derek** Bo

**Derelict** Abandoned, Broken-down, → **DECREPIT**, Deserted, Disused, Negligent, Outcast, Ramshackle, Tramp

**Deride, Derision, Derisive** Contempt, Gup, Guy, Hiss, Ho-ho, Hoot, Jeer, Jibe, Mock, Nominal, Pigs, Raspberry, → **RIDICULE**, Sardonic, Scoff, Scorn, Sneer, Snifty, Snort, Ya(h)boo (sucks), Yah

**Derive, Derivation, Derivative** Amine, Ancestry, Apiol, Creosote, Deduce, Descend, Extract, Get, Kinone, Of, Offshoot, Origin, Pedigree, Picoline, Saponin, Secondary, Taurine, Tyramine

▸ **Dermatitis** *see* **SKIN DISEASE**

**Derogate, Derogatory** Aspersion, Belittle, Decry, Defamatory, Demeaning, Detract, Diatribe, Discredit, Libellous, Pejorative, Personal, Slanderous, Slighting, Snide, Tushing

**Deronda** Daniel

**Derrick** Crane, Davit, Hoist, Jib, Spar, Steeve

**Dervish** Calender, Doseh, Mawlawi, Mevlevi, Revolver, Santon, Whirling

**Descant** Comment, Discourse, Faburden, Melody, Song

**Descartes** René

**Descend(ant), Descent** Abseil, Ancestry, Avail, Avale, Bathos, Blood, Cadency, Catabasis, Chute, Cion, Decline, Degenerate, Dégringoler, Derive, Dismount, Dive, Drop, Epigon, Extraction, Heir, Heraclid, → **LINEAGE**, Offspring, Pedigree, Posterity, Progeny, Prone, Purler, Rappel, Said, Say(y)id, Scarp, Scion, Seed, Shelve, Sien(t), Sink, Spearside, Stock, Syen, Vest, Volplane

**Describe, Describing, Description, Descriptive** Account, Blazon, Blurb, Define, Delineate, Depict, Designate, Draw, Epithet, Exposition, Expound, Graphic, Job, Label, Liken, Narrate, Outline, Paint, Portray, Rapportage, Recount, Relate, Report, Sea-letter, Semantic, Signalment, Sketch, Specification, Sum up, Synopsis, Term, Thumbnail, Trace, Vignette, Write-up

▷ **Describing** *may indicate* 'around'

**Descry** Behold, Discern, Get, Notice, Perceive

**Desecrate, Desecration** Abuse, Defile, Dishallow, Profane, Sacrilege, Unhallow

▷ **Desecrated** *may indicate* an anagram

**Desensitise** Inure

**Desert(er), Deserted, Deserts** Abandon, Absquatulate, Apostasy, Arabian, Arid, Ar Rimal, Arunta, Atacama, AWOL, Badland, Barren, Bledowska, Bug, Bunk, Colorado,

Come-uppance, D, Dahna, Defect, Desolate, Dissident, Ditch, Drop, Due, Empty, Eremic, Etosha Pan, Factious, Fail, Fezzan, Foresay, Forhoo, Forhow, Forlorn, Forsake, Forsay, Frondeur, Garagum, Gibson, Gila, Gobi, Great Basin, Great Indian, Great Sandy, Great Victoria, Heterodox, Indian, Jump ship, Kalahari, Kara Kum, Karma, Kavir, Kyzyl Kum, Libyan, Lurch, Meeds, Merit, Mohave, Mojave, Nafud, Namib, Negev, Nubian, Ogaden, Painted, Patagonian, Pindan, Rat, Refus(e)nik, Reg, → RENEGADE, Reward, Rub'al-Khali, Run, Runaway, Sahara(n), Sahel, Sands, Secede, Sertao, Shamo, Simpson, Sinai, Sonoran, Sturt, Syrian, Tacna-Arica, Tergiversate, Thar, Turncoat, Ust(y)urt, Victoria, Void, Wadi, Waste(land), Western Sahara, Wild, Wilderness, Worthiness

**Deserve(d)** Condign, Earn, → MERIT, Rate, Well-earned, Worthy

**Desiccate(d)** Dry, Sere

**Design(er)** Adam, Aim, Amies, Arabesque, Architect(ure), Argyle, Armani, Ashley, Batik, Between-subjects, Broider, Cable stitch, Calligram(me), Cameo, Cardin, Cartoon, Castrametation, Chequer, Chop, Cloisonné, Courreges, Couturier, Create, Cul de lampe, Damascene, Decal(comania), Decor, Deep, Depict, Device, Devise, Dévoré, Dior, Draft, Eiffel, Embroidery, End, Engender, Engine(r), Engineer, Erté, Etch, Fashion, Feng-shui, Flanch, Format, Former, Fretwork, Hepplewhite, Hitech, Iconic, Imagineer, Impresa, Imprese, Industrial, Inlay, Intaglio, Intend(ment), Intent(ion), Interior, Invent, Issigonis, Klein, Layout, Le Corbusier, Limit-state, Linocut, Logo, Marquetry, Mascle, Matched pairs, McCartney, Mean, Meander, Mehndi, Millefleurs, Modiste, Monogram, Morris, Mosaic, Motif, Multifoil, Nailhead, Nissen, Paisley, Pattern, → PLAN, Plot, Propose, Prostyle, Pyrography, Quant, Retro, Ruse, Schema, Scheme, Schiaparelli, Seal, Sheraton, Sketch, Sopwith, Spatterwork, Specification, Sprig, Stencil, Stubble, Stylist, Sunburst, Tatow, Tattoo, Tattow, Tatu, Think, Tooling, Townscape, Trigram, Tupelov, Versace, Vignette, Watermark, Weiner, Werkstalte, Whittle, Within-subjects

**Designate** Appoint, Destine, Earmark, List, Mark, Name, Note, Style, Title

**Desirable, Desire, Desirous** Ambition, Aphrodisia, Appetite, Aspire, Avid, Best, Cama, Conation, Concupiscence, Covet, Crave, Cupidity, Des, Dreamboat, Earn, Eligible, Epithymetic, Esurience, Fancy, Gasp, Greed, Hanker, Hope, Hots, Hunger, Impulse, Itch, Kama(deva), Le(t)ch, Libido, List, Long, Luscious, Lust, Mania, Month's mind, Notion, Nymphomania, Orectic, Owlcar, Pica, Pleasure, Plum, Provocative, Reak, Reck, Request, Residence, Salt, Slaver, Spiffing, Streetcar, Thirst, Urge, Velleity, Vote, Wanderlust, Want, Whim, Will, Wish, Yearn, Yen

**Desist** Abandon, Cease, Curb, Pretermit, Quit, Stop

**Desk** Almemar, Ambo, Bonheur-du-jour, Bureau, Carrel(l), Cash, Check-in, Cheveret, City, Copy, Davenport, Desse, Devonport, E(s)critoire, Enquiry, Faldstool, Lectern, Lettern, Litany, Pay, Pedestal, Prie-dieu, Pulpit, Reading, Roll-top, Scrutoire, Secretaire, Vargueno, Writing

**Desman** Pyrenean

**Desolate, Desolation** Bare, Barren, Desert, Devastate, Disconsolate, Forlorn, Gaunt, Godforsaken, Gousty, Lonesome, Moonscape, Stark, Waste, Woebegone

**Despair, Desperate, Desperation** Acharne, Anomy, Dan, De profundis, Despond, Dire, Dismay, Drastic, Extreme, Forlorn hope, Frantic, Gagging, Giant, Gloom, Hairless, Headlong, Hopelessness, Last-ditch, Last-gasp, Life and death, Reckless, Unhopeful, Urgent, Wanhope

▶ **Despatch** *see* DISPATCH

**Desperado** Bandit, Bravo, Outlaw, Ruffian, Terrorist

**Despicable** Abject, Base, Bleeder, Caitiff, Cheap, Churl, Contemptible, Heel, Heinous, Ignoble, Ignominious, Low-down, Mean, Moer, Poep(ol), Puke, Ratbag, Ratfink, Scumbag, Shabby, Snip, Snot, Toerag, Vermin(ous), Vile, Worm, Wretched, Yellow dog

**Despise(d)** Condemn, Conspire, Contemn, Forhow, Futz, Hate, Ignore, Scorn, Spurn, Vilify, Vilipend

**Despite** For, Malgré, Notwithstanding, Pace, Though, Venom

**Despoil** Bezzle, Mar, Rape, Ravage, Vandalise

**Despondent** Dejected, Downcast, Forlorn, Gloomy, Lacklustre, Sad

**Despot(ism)** Autarchy, Autocrat, Bonaparte, Caesar, Darius, Dictator, Little Hitler, Martinet, Monocrat, Napoleon, Nero, Satrap, Soldan, Stratocrat, Tsar, Tyrant, Tzar

**Dessert** Afters, Apple charlotte, Baclava, Baked Alaska, Baklava, Banana split, Bavarian cream, Bavarois, Blancmange, Bombe, Cannoli, Charlotte, Charlotte russe, Cheesecake, Clafoutis, Cobbler, Compote, Coupe, Cranachan, Cream, Crème brulée, Crème caramel, Crepe Suzette, Dulce de leche, Entremets, Eve's pudding, Floating Island, Flummery, Fool, Granita, Jelly, Junket, Kissel, Knickerbocker glory, Kulfi, Marquise, Melba, Mousse, Mud pie, Nesselrode, Pannacotta, Parfait, Pashka, Pavlova, Peach Melba, → PUDDING, Rasmalai, Roulade, Rum baba, Sabayon, Sawine, Semifreddo, Shoofly pie, Sorbet, Split, Spumone, Strudel, Sundae, Syllabub, Tapioca, Tart, Tarte tatin, Tartufo, Tiramisu, Tortoni, Trifle, Vacherin, Whip, Zabaglione

**Destabilise** Unbalance

**Destine(d), Destination** Born, Design, End, Fate, Foredoom, Goal, Gole, Home, Intend, Joss, Meant, Port, Purpose, Vector, Weird

**Destiny** Doom, → FATE, Karma, Kismet, Lachesis, Lot, Manifest, Moira, Portion, Yang, Yin

**Destitute, Destitution** Bankrupt, Bare, Bereft, Broke, Devoid, Dirt-poor, Down and out, Helpless, Impoverished, Indigent, Necessitous, Needy, Penniless, Poor, Poverty, Sterile, Stony broke, Void, Waif and stray

**Destress** Anneal

**Destroy(er)** Annihilate, Antineutrino, Antineutron, Antiparticle, Apollyon, Atomise, Blight, Bulldoze, Can, Canker, Crush, D, Decimate, Deep-six, Deface, Delete, Demolish, Demyelinate, Denature, Destruct, Devastate, Dish, Dismember, Dissolve, Eat, Efface, End, Eradicate, Erase, Estrepe, Exterminate, Extirpate, Flivver, Fordo, Graunch, Harry, Iconoclast, Incinerate, Invalidate, → KILL, KO, Lay waste, Locust, Murder, Obliterate, Overkill, Perish, Predator, Pulverize, Q-ship, Ravage, Raze, Ruin, Saboteur, Sack, Scuttle, Siva, Slash, Smash, Spif(f)licate, Spoil, Sterilize, Stew-can, Stonker, Stultify, Subvert, Trash, Undo, Uproot, Vandal, Vitiate, Waste, Whelm, Wreck, Zap

**Destruction, Destructive** Adverse, Autolysis, Bane, Can, Catabolism, Collapse, Deathblow, Deleterious, Desecration, Devastation, Doom, Downfall, Ecocide, End, Götterdämmerung, Grave, Havoc, Holocaust, Hunnish, Iconoclasm, Insidious, Internecine, Kali, Lethal, Loss, Maelstrom, Maleficent, Malignant, Moorburn, Nihilistic, Pernicious, Pestilential, Pogrom, Quelea, Rack, Ragnarok, Ravage, Ruination, Sabotage, Speciocide, Stroy, Wrack, Wreckage

**Desultory** Aimless, Cursory, Fitful, Idle

**Detach(ed), Detachment** Abeigh, Abstract, Alienate, Aloof, Apart, Body, Calve, Clinical, Cut, Detail, Discrete, Disinterested, Dispassionate, Distinct, Garrison, Insular, Isle, Isolate, Loose, Outlying, Outpost, Patrol, Picket, Picquet, Separate, Sever, Staccato, Stoic, Unfasten, Unhinge, Unit, Unpick, Withdrawn

**Detached work** Ravelin

**Detail(s), Detailed** Annotate, Circumstances, Depict, Dock, Elaborate, Embroider, Expatiate, Explicit, Exploded, Expound, Instance, Intricate, → ITEM, Itemise, Minutiae, Narrate, Nicety, Nitty-gritty, Nuts and bolts, Particular(ise), Pedantry, Point, Recite, Recount, Relate, Respect, Send, Spec, Special, Specific, Specification, Technicality, Touch

▷ **Detailed** *may indicate* last letter missing

**Detain(ee), Detention (centre)** Arrest, Buttonhole, Collar, Custody, Delay, Demurrage, Detinue, Gate, Glasshouse, Hinder, Imprison, Intern, Juvie, Keep, POW, Preventive, Retard, Sin bin, Stay, → WITHHOLD

**Detect(or), Detective** Agent, Armchair, Arsène, Asdic, Bergerac, Bloodhound, Brown, Bucket, Busy, Catch, Chan, Chlorometer, CIB, CID, Cuff, Det, Dick, Discern, Discover, Divine, Doodlebug, Dupin, Enquiry agent, Espy, Eye, Father Brown, Fed, Find, Flambeau, Flic, Fortune, French, Galvanoscope, Geigercounter, Geophone, G-man, Gumshoe, Hanaud, Hercule, Holmes, Interpol, Investigator, Jack, Lecoq, Lupin, Maigret, Metal,

Methanometer, Microwave, Mine, Minitrack®, Morse, Nail, Nose, Peeper, PI, Pinkerton, Plant, Poirot, Private, Private eye, Prodnose, Radar, Reagent, Retinula, Rumble, Scent, Scerne, Sense, Sensor, Shadow, Shamus, Sherlock, → **SLEUTH**, Sleuth-hound, Smell out, Snooper, Sofar, Solver, Sonar, Sonobuoy, Spot, Store, Tabaret, Take, Tec, Thorndyke, Toff, Trace, Trent, Vance, Wimsey, Yard(man)

**Detent** Pawl, Trigger

**Deter(rent)** Block, Check, Daunt, Dehort, Delay, Disincentive, Dissuade, Faze, Prevent, Restrain, Scare, Trident, Turn-off, Ultimate

**Detergent** Cationic, Clean(s)er, Non-ionizing, Solvent, Sujee, Surfactant, Syndet, Tepol, Whitener

**Deteriorate, Deterioration** Decadence, Degenerate, Derogate, Entropy, Go to pot, Pejoration, Perish, Relapse, Retrograde, Rust, Worsen

▷ **Deterioration** *may indicate* an anagram

▷ **Determination** *may indicate* 'last letter'

**Determine(d), Determination** Adamant, All-out, Appoint, Arbitrament, Ardent, Ascertain, Assign, Assoil, Bent, Causal, Choose, Condition, Dead-set, → **DECIDE**, Define, Dictate, Doctrinaire, Dogged, Do-or-die, Dour, Drive, Earnest, Fix, Govern, Granite, Grim, Grit(ty), Headstrong, Hell-bent, Indomitable, Influence, Intent, Ironclad, Judgement, Law, Liquidate, Orient, Out, Point, Pre-ordain, Purpose, Quantify, → **RESOLUTE**, Resolve, Rigwiddie, Rigwoodie, Self-will, Set, Settle, Set upon, Shape, Single-minded, Soum, Sowm, Stalwart, Steely, Stout, Tenacious, Type, Valiant, Weigh

**Detest(able), Detested** Abhor, Abominate, Anathema, Despise, Execrable, Execrate, Hate, Loathsome, Pestful, Vile

**Detonate, Detonator** Blast, Explode, Fire, Fuse, Fuze, Ignite, Kindle, Plunger, Primer, Saucisse, Saucisson, Spring, Tetryl, Trip-wire

**Detour** Bypass, Deviate, Divert

**Detract** Belittle, Decry, Diminish, Discount, Disparage

**Detriment(al)** Adverse, Damage, Harm, Injury, Loss, Mischief

**Detroit** Motown

**Deuce** Dickens, Old Harry, Twoer

**Deuteron** Diplon

**Devalue** Cheapen, Debase, Impair, Reduce, Undermine

**Devastate, Devastation** Demolish, Destroy, Ground zero, Gut, Lay waste, Overwhelm, Ravage, Ruin, Sack, Traumatise, Waste, Wrack, Wreck

**Develop(er), Developed, Developing, Development** Advance, Age, Agile, Amidol®, Aplasia, Apotheosis, Arise, Breakthrough, Breed, Bud, Build, Burgeon, Catechol, Creep, Cutting edge, Dark room, Educe, Elaborate, Enlarge, Epigenetic, Escalate, Evolve, Expand, Expatriate, Fixer, Foetus, Full-fledged, Fulminant, Genesis, Germinate, Gestate, Grow, Hatch, Hothouse, Hydroquinone, Hypo, Imago, Immature, Improve, Incipient, Incubate, Lamarckism, Larva, Mature, Metamorphose, Metol, Morphogenesis, Morphosis, Mushroom, Nascent, Nurture, Offshoot, Oidium, Ongoing, Ontogenesis, Pathogeny, Pullulate, Pupa, Pyro, Pyrogallol, Quinol, Ribbon, Ripe(n), Sarvodaya, Sensorimeter, Separate, Shape, Soup, Speciation, Sprawl, Subtopia, Technography, Teens, Tone, Twist, Unfold, Upgrow

▷ **Develop** *may indicate* an anagram

**Deviant, Deviate, Deviation** Aberrance, Abnormal, Anomaly, Average, Blip, Brisure, Deflect, Deflexure, Depart, Derogate, Detour, Digress, Discrepant, Diverge, Divert, Drift, Error, Fade, Kinky, Kurtosis, List, Masochist, Mean, Pervert, Quartile, Sadist, Sheer, Solecism, Sport, Standard, Stray, Swerve, Transvestite, → **TURN**, Valgus, Varus, Veer, Wander, Wend, Yaw

**Device** Allegory, → **APPARATUS**, Appliance, Artifice, Bush, Contraption, Contrivance, Deus ex machina, Dodge, Emblem, Expedient, Gadget, Gimmick, Gismo, Gubbins, Instrument, Logo, Mnemonic, Motto, Plan, Pointing, Ruse, Safeguard, → **STRATAGEM**, Subterfuge, Tactic, Tag, Thing, Tool, Trademark, Trick, Wile

# DEVICES

*3 letters:*
Bug
FET
LED
Mux
Pad
Pig
POP
Set
Van
Zip

*4 letters:*
Capo
Drag
Fret
Fuse
Gobo
Grab
Head
Orle
Plug
Rest
Shoe
Skid
Spur
Stop
Tram
Trap

*5 letters:*
Audio
Balun
Chaff
Choke
Chuck
Clamp
Cleat
Codec
Combi
Conch
Corer
Cramp
Crank
Diode
E-nose
Flare
Frame
Gatso®
Gizmo
Gland
Input

Laser
Lidar
Maser
Meter
Mixer
Modem
Mouli
Mouse
Optic®
Otter
Pager
Petar
Prism
Probe
Quipu
Relay
Rotor
Saser
Scale
Scart
Servo
Shear
Sieve
Siren
Snare
Sonde
Spool
Sprag
SQUID
Stent
Taser®
Timer
Tromp
Truss
Turbo
Valve
V-chip
Waldo
Winch

*6 letters:*
Analog
Atlatl
Balise
Beeper
Biodot
Blower
Bungee
Buzzer
Charge
Chowri
Chowry

Clevis
Cotter
Cursor
Cut-off
Cut-out
Dasher
Deckle
De-icer
Detent
Dimmer
Dongle
Elevon
Engine
Etalon
Euouae
Evovae
Faller
Feeder
Filter
Friend®
Grater
Heddle
Imager
Jigger
Joypad
Keeper
Kludge
Logger
Masker
Nanite
Packer
Peeler
Petard
Pick-up
Pinger®
Possum
Pre-amp
Preset
Quippu
Rabble
Reheat
Remote
Reverb
Rocker
Roller
Router
Selsyn
Sensor
Server
Shaker
Shower
Socket

Stocks
Stoner
Switch
Swivel
Tablet
Tamper
Temple
Tipple
Tracer
Tremie
Triode
Trompe
Turtle
Tympan
Viewer
Wafter
Walker
Widget
Zapper

*7 letters:*
Adaptor
Air-trap
Bearing
Bendlet
Bleeper
Charger
Chopper
Clapper
Cleaver
Clicker
Coherer
Compass
Counter
Coupler
Crampon
Dashpot
Denture
Digibox®
Divider
Doubler
E-reader
Flip-top
Fuzzbox
Gas mask
Genlock
Gimbals
Grapnel
Hushkit
Imprese
Inhaler
Isotron

Jetpack
Krytron
Lighter
Limiter
Machine
Minicom
Monitor
Netsuke
Padlock
Pelorus
Pessary
Pickoff
Pillory
Plunger
Ratchet
Reactor
Roll-bar
Rotator
Rowlock
Scanner
Shopbot
Shut-off
Shutter
Shuttle
Simcard
Slipper
Sniffer
Snorkel
Snubber
Snuffer
Sordino
Sounder
Spoiler
Stapler
Starter
Stinger
Storage
Sundial
Swatter
Synchro
Toaster
Tokamak
Tonepad
Vernier
Vocoder

**8 letters:**
Airscoop
Alcolock
Analogue
Anti-icer
Atomiser
Autodial
Ballcock

Barostat
Betatron
Bootjack
Calutron
Commutor
Conveyor
Coupling
Cryostat
Cyberpet
Demister
Detector
Diagraph
Diestock
Earphone
Ecraseur
Eggtimer
Enlarger
Episcope
Episemon
Expander
Fairlead
Firework
Flashgun
Flywheel
Forklift
Geophone
Gunsight
Heat pump
Holdback
Hotplate
Ignitron
Keyboard
Launcher
Light-pen
Monogram
Nailhead
Occluder
Odograph
Odometer
Orthosis
Ozoniser
Paravane
Playback
Plectrum
Pullback
Pulsator
Pushback
Push-pull
Pyrostat
Radar gun
Radiator
Repeater
Resister
Rheostat

Robotics
Shoehorn
Shredder
Silencer
Slip ring
Snow-eyes
Snowshoe
Solenoid
Splitter
Spray gun
Spreader
Squeegee
Sweatbox
Swellbox
Teleport
Terminal
Thin-film
Touch pad
Trembler
Varactor
Varistor
Vibrator
Windlass

**9 letters:**
Amplifier
Aspirator
Autometer
Autotimer
Capacitor
Compasses
Condenser
Convector
Converter
Corkscrew
Decoherer
Deflector
Defroster
Delayline
Detonator
Dispenser
Dynamotor
Eccentric
Equalizer
Excelsior
Exerciser
Extractor
Fetoscope
Gear-lever
Gear-shift
Gearstick
Generator
Gyroscope
Headstock

Heliscoop
Hendiadys
Hodoscope
Hydrofoil
Hydrostat
Hygrostat
Indicator
Insulator
Jack screw
Keylogger
Konimeter
Kymograph
Megaphone
Mekometer
Metronome
Milometer
Modulator
Nebuliser
Octophone
Optophone
Overdrive
Pacemaker
Parachute
Patent log
Pedometer
Periscope
Phonopore
Photocell
Pitchbend
Polariser
Polygraph
Powerpack
Propeller
Rectifier
Regulator
Remontoir
Resonator
Responsor
Retractor
Rheotrope
Rotachute
Rotameter®
Satellite
Scrambler
Separator
Sequencer
Simulator
Smokejack
Sonograph
Spaceband
Spindryer
Spinhaler
Sprinkler
Stairlift

Standpipe
Steadicam
Stretcher
Tabulator
Tape drive
Tape punch
Tasimeter
Telegraph
Telemeter
Telepoint
Thermette
Thyristor
Tonometer
Tormentor
Trackball
Tremulant
Well sweep

*10 letters:*
Acetometer
Anemoscope
Applicator
Attenuator
Autowinder
Blackberry®
Calculator
Ceilometer
Centrifuge
Chaingrate
Chronotron
Clapometer
Commutator
Comparator
Compressor
Copyholder
Cyclometer
Cyclostyle
Daisy-wheel
Databogger
Derailleur
Descendeur
Eprouvette
Fairleader
Foetoscope
Groundprox
Humidistat
Hygroscope
Integrator
Jawbreaker
Jaws of Life
Jellygraph
Kicksorter
Lactometer
Mason's mark

Metrostyle
Microphone
Microprobe
Microscope
Mileometer
Moulinette
Nephograph
Nightscope
Noisemaker
Otter-board
Peripheral
Phonoscope
Planometer
Radiometer
Remontoire
Respirator
Self-feeder
Siderostat
Snowplough
Solid state
Spirograph
Stabiliser
Stimpmeter
Suppressor
Switchgear
Tachograph
Tachometer
Tape reader
Telewriter
Theodolite
Thermistor
Thermopile
Thermostat
Tourniquet
Transducer
Transistor
Turbulator
Turnbuckle
Ventilator
Vertoscope®
Videophone
Viewfinder
Viscometer
Water-wheel
Zener diode

*11 letters:*
Afterburner
Annunciator
Answerphone
Autochanger
Baffle-plate
Carburettor
Collet chuck

Compass rose
Conformator
Distributor
Echo-sounder
Epidiascope
Floor turtle
Fluoroscope
Helping hand
Immobilizer
Insufflator
Intoximeter
Lie detector
Link trainer
Manipulator
Microfitter
Microreader
Microwriter
Morton's fork
Moving-coils
Multiplexer
Paper cutter
Recuperator
Self-starter
Smokerlyzer
Snickometer
Solarimeter
Space heater
Spectograph
Speedometer
Stuffing-box
Swingometer
Telestrator
Thermoscope
Trackerball
Transceiver
Transformer
Transmitter
Transponder
Weather vane

*12 letters:*
Breathalyser
Concentrator
Desert cooler
Ebulliometer
Effusiometer
Electrometer
Evaporograph
Extensometer
Extinguisher
Galvanometer
Intrauterine
Lithotripter
Magnetometer

Make and break
Micro-circuit
Mine-detector
Object finder
Oscillograph
Oscilloscope
Picturephone
Sensitometer
Snooperscope
Speaking tube
Spectrometer
Spectroscope
Supercharger
Tape streamer
Telautograph
Teleprompter
Tellurometer
Thermocouple
Turbidimeter
Viscosimeter

*13 letters:*
Accelerometer
Aetherioscope
Baton-sinister
Contraceptive
Dead man's pedal
Electromagnet
Electrophorus
Metal detector
Morton's crutch
Phonendoscope
Potentiometer
Rack and pinion
Read-write head
Scintiscanner
Shock-absorber
Smoke detector

*14 letters:*
Anamorphoscope
Dead man's handle
Interferometer
Intervalometer
Peltier element
Plethysmograph
Retroreflector
Scintillometer
Spinthariscope
Surge protector
Trickle charger

*15 letters:*
Radiogoniometer

**Devil(ish), Demon** Abaddon, Afreet, Afrit, Ahriman, Amaimon, Apollyon, Archfiend, Asmodeus, Atua, Auld Hornie, Azazel, Barbason, Beelzebub, Belial, Buckra, Cacodemon, Cartesian, Clootie, Cloots, Dasyure, Davy Jones, Deev, Deil, Demogorgon, Demon, Deuce, Devling, Diable, Diabolic, Dickens, Div, Drudge, Duende, Dust, Eblis, Falin, Familiar, Fend, Fiend, Fient, Ghoul, Goodman, Goodyear, Grill, Hangie, Hornie, Iblis, Imp, Incubus, Infernal, Knave, Lamia, Legion, Lilith, Lord of the Flies, Lori, Lucifer, Mahoun(d), Man of Sin, Manta, Mara, Maxwell's, Mazikeen, Mephisto(pheles), Mischief, Nick, Nickie-ben, Old Bendy, Old Nick, Old One, Old Pandemonium, Old Poker, Old Roger, Old Split-foot, Old Toast, Printer's, Ragamuffin, Ragman, Rahu, Ralph, Satan, Satan(h)as, Satyr, Scour, Scratch, Screwtape, Season, Setebos, Shaitan, Shedeem, Snow, Sorra, Succubine, Succubus, Tailard, Tasmanian, Tempter, Titivil, Tutivillus, Unholy, Wendigo, Wicked, Wicked One, Wirricow, Worricow, Worrycow, Zernebock

**Devil-may-care** Rakish

**Devious** Braide, Cunning, Deep, Eel(y), Erroneous, Evasive, Heel, Implex, Indirect, Insincere, Meandering, Scheming, Shifty, Sly, Sneaky, Stealthy, Subtle, Tortuous, Tricky, Twisting, Two-faced

**Devise(d)** Arrange, Coin, Comment, Concoct, Contrive, Cook up, Decoct, Hatch, Hit-on, Imagine, Invenit, Invent, Plan, Plot, Thermette

**Devitrified** Ambitty

**Devoid** Barren, Destitute, Empty, Vacant, Wanting

**Devolution** West Lothian question

**Devolve** Occur, Result, Transmit

**Devote(e), Devotion(al), Devoted** Addiction, Adherent, Aficionado, Âme damnée, Angelus, Attached, Bhakti, Buff, Bunny, Commitment, Consecrate, Consign, Corban, Dedicate, Employ, Enthusiast, Fan, Fervid, Fetishism, Fidelity, Fiend, Gallantry, Grebo, Holy, Hound, Lapdog, Loyalty, Mariolate, Novena, Nut, Ophism, Partisan, Passion, Piety, Pious, Puja, Religioso, Sacred, Saivite, S(h)akta, Sanctity, Savoyard, Sea-green incorruptible, Sivaite, Solemn, Sworn, True, Voteen, Zealous

**Devour(ing)** Consume, Eat, Engorge, Engulf, Manducate, Moth-eat, Scarf, Scoff, Snarf, →SWALLOW, Vorant

▷ **Devour** *may indicate* one word inside another

**Devout** God-fearing, Holy, Pia, Pious, Religiose, Reverent, Sant, Sincere, Solemn

**Dew(y)** Bloom, Gory, Moist, Mountain, Rime, Roral, Roric, Rorid, Roscid, Serein, Serene, Tranter

**Dexterity, Dexterous** Adept, Adroit, Aptitude, Cleverness, Craft, Deft, Feat(e)ous, Featuous, →HANDY, Knack, Shrewd, Sleight, Slick

**Diabolic(al)** Cruel, →DEVILISH, Infernal, Inhuman, Satanic

**Diacritic (mark)** Acute, Angstrom, Cedilla, Circumflex, Diaresis, Eth, Grave, Háček, Thorn, Tilde, Umlaut

**Diadem** Coronet, Fillet, Garland, Tiara

**Diagnose, Diagnosis, Diagnostic** Amniocentesis, Fetal, Findings, Identify, Iridology, Pulse, Radionics, Scan, Scintigraphy, X-ray

**Diagonal(ly)** Bend(wise), Bias, Cater(-corner), Catty-cornered, Counter, Oblique, Principal, Slant, Solidus, Speed, Twill

**Diagram** Argand, Bar chart, Bar graph, Block, Butterfly, Chart, Chromaticity, Cladogram, Compass rose, Decision tree, Dendrogram, Drawing, Fault-tree, Feynman, Figure, Flow, Graph, Graphics, Grid, Hertzsprung-Russell, Indicator, Logic, Map, Phase, Plan, Plat, Run-chart, Scatter, Schema, Schematic, Scintigram, Stem-and-leaf, Stemma, Stereogram, Tephigram, Topo, Tree, Venn, Wind rose

**Dial(ling)** Card, Face, Mug, Phiz, Phone, Pulse, Ring, Speed, STD, Visage

**Dialect** Acadian, Accent, Aeolic, Alemannic, Amoy, Anglican, Arcadic, Attic, Basuto, Burr, Castilian, Damara, Doric, Eldin, Eolic, Epic, Erse, Eye, Franconian, Friulian, Galician, Gallo-Romance, Gascon, Geechee, Geordie, Greenlander, Hassaniya, Hegelian, Idiom, Ionic, Isogloss, Jargon, Jockney, Joual, Khalka, Koine, Konkani, Ladin, Lallans,

Landsmaal, Langobardic, Langue d'oc, Langue d'oil, Langue d'oui, Ledden, Lingo, Low German, Mackem, Min, Norman, Norn, Occitan, Old Icelandic, Old North French, Parsee, Parsi, Patavinity, Patois, Pedi, Picard, Prakrit, Rhaeto-Romance, Rhotic, Riffian, Rock English, Romans(c)h, Ruthenian, Salish, Savoyard, Scouse, Sesotho, Syriac, Taal, Tadzhik, Ta(d)jik, Talkee-talkee, Talky-talky, Tongue, Tshi, Tuscan, Twi, Tyrolese, Umbrian, Vaudois, Vernacular, Walloon, West Saxon, Wu, Yealdon, Yenglish, Yinglish

**Dialogue** Colloquy, Conversation, Critias, Discussion, Exchange, Imparl, Interlocution, Lazzo, Pastourelle, Repartee, Speech, Stichomythia, Talk, Upspeak

**Dialysis** Kidney, Peritoneal

**Diameter** Breadth, Calibre, Gauge, Systyle, Tactical, Width

**Diamond(s), Diamond-shaped** Adamant, Black, Boart, Brilliant, Bristol, Carbon, Carbonado, Cullinan, D, DE, Delaware, Eustace, False, Florentine, Hope, Ice, Industrial, Isomer, Jewel, Jim, Koh-i-Noor, Lasque, Lattice, Lozenge, Minor suit, Off-colour(ed), Paragon, Pick, Pitch, Pitt, Quarry, Reef, Rhinestone, Rhomb, Rock, Rose-cut, Rosser, Rough, Rustre, Sancy, Solitaire, Spark, Sparklers, Squarial, Suit

**Diana** Artemis, Di, Dors

**Diapason** Normal, Open, Ottava, Stopped

**Diaphanous** Clear, Sheer, Translucent

**Diaphoretic** Sweater

**Diaphragm** Cap, Iris, Mid-riff, Phrenic, Stop

**Diaresis** Trema

▸ **Diarist** *see* **DIARY**

**Diarrhoea** Collywobbles, Delhi belly, Gippy tummy, Lientery, Montezuma's revenge, Runs, Scours, Squitters, The shits, Trots, Verbal, Weaning-brash, Wood-evil

**Diary, Diarist** Adrian Mole, Blogger, Burney, Chronicle, Crossman, Dale, Day-book, Evelyn, Frank, Hickey, Journal, Journal intime, Kilvert, Log, Mole, Nobody, Noctuary, Pepys, Personal organiser, Planner, Pooter, Record, Video

**Diaspora** Exodus, Galuth

**Diatribe** Harangue, Invective, Philippic, Rant, Tirade

**Dibble(r)** Marsupial, Theria

**Dice(r), Dicey** Aleatory, Astragals, Bale, Bones, Chop, Craps, Cube, Doctor, Dodgy, Fulham, Fullams, Fullans, Gourd(s), Hash, Highman, Jeff, Mandoline, Mince, Novum, Poker, Shoot, Smalto, Snake-eyes, Tallmen

**Dichotomy** Split

**Dick(y), Dickey** Clever, Deadeye, Front, Ill, Laid up, Moby, OED, Policeman, Private eye, Rumble, Shaky, Shirt, Spotted, Tec, Tonneau, Tucker, Tumbledown, Unstable, Wankle, Weak, Whittington

▷ **Dick** *may indicate* a dictionary

**Dickens** Boz, Deuce, Devil, Mephistopheles

**Dicker** Bargain, Barter, Haggle, Trade

▷ **Dicky** *may indicate* an anagram

**Dictate, Dictator(ial)** Amin, Authoritarian, Autocrat, Big Brother, Bonaparte, Caesar, Castro, Cham, Command, Czar, Decree, Demagogue, Despot, Duce, Franco, Fu(e)hrer, Gaddafi, Gauleiter, Hitler, Idi, Impose, Indite, Lenin, Mussolini, Ordain, Overbearing, Peremptory, Peron, Pol Pot, Salazar, Shogun, Stalin, Tell, Tito, Totalitarian, Trujillo, Tsar, Tyrant, Tzar

**Diction** Language, Lexis, Palavinity, Speech, Style

**Dictionary** Alveary, Calepin, Chambers, Data, Etymologicon, Fowler, Gazetteer, Glossary, Gradus, Hobson-Jobson, Idioticon, Johnson's, Larousse, Lexicon, Lexis, OED, Onomasticon, Thesaurus, Vocabulary, Webster, Wordbook

**Dictum** Maxim, Obiter, Saw, Say-so

**Did** Began, Couth, Fec(it), Gan

**Didactic** Sermonical

**Diddle** Cheat, Con, Hoax

**Dido** Antic, Caper, Carthaginian, Elissa

**Die(d), Dying** Ache, Buy the farm, Calando, Cark, Choke, Conk out, Crater, Croak, Cube, D, Decadent, Desire, End, Evanish, Exit, Expire, Fade, Fail, Flatline, Forfair, Fulham, Fulhan, Fullam, Go, Go west, Hallmark, Hang, Highman, Hop, Hop the twig, Infarct, Kark, Long, Morendo, Moribund, Ob(iit), Orb, Pass, Peg out, Perdendosi, Perish, Peter, Pop off, Pop one's clogs, Slip the cable, Snuff, Snuff it, Solidum, Sphacelation, Stagheaded, Stamp, Sterve, Succumb, Suffer, Swage, Swelt, Terminal, Tessera, Tine, Touch, Wane

**Diehard** Blimp, Fanatic, Intransigent, Reactionary, Standpatter, Zealot

**Diesel** Red

**Diet(er), Dieting** Assembly, Atkins, Augsburg, Bant(ing), Cacotrophy, Congress, Council, Dail, Eat, Fare, Feed, Hay, Intake, Kashrut(h), Ketogenic, Knesset, Landtag, Lent, Macrobiotic, Parliament, Pleading, Reduce, Regimen, Reichstag, Short commons, Slim, Solid, Sprat, Staple, Strict, Tynwald, Vegan, Vegetarian, Weightwatcher, Worms, Yo-yo

**Dietetics** Sit(i)ology

**Differ(ence), Differing, Different(ly)** Afresh, Allo, Alterity, Anew, Barney, Change, Cline, Contrast, Contretemps, Deviant, Diacritic, Diesis, Disagree, Discord, Discrepant, Disparate, Dispute, Dissent, Dissimilitude, Distinct, Diverge, Diverse, Else, Elsewise, Epact, Exotic, Gulf, Heterodox, Loggerheads, Nonconformist, Nuance, Omnifarious, Other, Othergates, Otherguess, Otherness, Otherwise, Poles apart, Potential, Quantum, Separate, Several, Spat, Special, Symmetric, Tiff, Unlike, Variform, Various, Vary

**Differential, Differentiate, Differentiation** Calculus, Del, Distinguish, Nabla, Product, Secern, Segregate, Separate, Taxeme, Wage

**Difficult(y), Difficult person** Abstruseness, Ado, Adversity, Aggro, Aporia, Arduous, Augean, Badass, Balky, Ballbuster, Bitter, Block, Bolshie, Bother, Cantankerous, Catch, Choosy, Complex, Complication, Contretemps, Corner, Cough drop, Crisis, Crotchety, Deep, Delphic, Depth, Dysphagia, Embarrassment, Enigma, Extreme, Fiddly, Formidable, Gnomic, Gordian, →**HARD**, Hassle, Hazard, Hiccough, Hiccup, Hobble, Hole, Hoor, Hump, Ill, Impasse, Inconvenient, Indocile, Inscrutable, Intractable, Intransigent, Jam, Jawbreaker, Kink, Kittle, Knot, Lob's pound, Lurch, Matter, Mulish, Net, Nodus, Obdurate, Obstacle, Parlous, Perverse, Pig, Pitfall, Plight, Predicament, Pretty pass, Quandary, Queer St, Recalcitrant, Rough, Rub, Scabrous, Scrape, Scrub, Scruple, Setaceous, Shlep, Snag, Soup, Steep, Stey, Stick, Sticky, Stiff, Stinker, Strait, Stubborn, Stymie, Swine, Tall order, Testing, Thorny, Ticklish, Tight spot, Tough, Trial, Tricky, Troublous, Trying, Une(a)th, Unwieldy, Uphill, Via dolorosa, Woe

**Diffident** Bashful, Hesitant, Meek, Modest, Reserved, Retiring, Shy

**Diffuse, Diffusion** Barophoresis, Disperse, Disseminate, Endosmosis, Exude, Osmosis, Permeate, Pervade, Radiate, Run, Sperse, Spread, Thermal, Winnow

**Dig(s), Digger, Digging, Dig up** Admire, Antipodean, Australian, Backhoe, Barb, Beadle, Bed(e)ral, Bedsit, Billet, Bore, Bot, Burrow, Costean, Delve, Deracinate, Enjoy, Excavate, Flea-bag, Flophouse, Fork, Fossorial, Gaulter, Get, Gibe, Gird, Graft, Graip, Grub, Hoe, Howk, Into, Jab, Kip, Lair, Like, Lodgings, Luxor, Mine, Navvy, Nervy, Nudge, Pad, Pioneer, Probe, Prod, Prospect(ing), Raddleman, Resurrect, Root(le), Ruddleman, Sap, See, Sneer, Spade, Spit, Spud, Star-nose, Taunt, Till, Tonnell, Trench, Tunnel, Undermine, Unearth

**Digest(ible), Digestion, Digestive** Abridgement, Absorb, Abstract, Aperçu, Archenteron, Assimilate, Beeda, Bile, Bradypeptic, Brief, Codify, Concoct, Endue, Epitome, Eupepsia, Eupepsy, Fletcherism, Gastric, Indew, Indue, Insalivate, Light, Pandect, Pem(m)ican, Pepsin(e), Peptic, Précis, Salt-cat, Steatolysis, →**SUMMARY**

**Digit(s)** Binary, Bit, Byte, Check, Dactyl, Figure, Finger, Hallux, Mantissa, Number, Pollex, Prehallux, Significant, Thumb, Toe

**Digitiser** Scanner

**Dignified, Dignify** August, Elevate, Ennoble, Exalt, Grace, Handsome, Honour, Imposing, Lordly, Maestoso, Majestic, Manly, Proud, Solemn, Stately, Statuesque

**Dignitary** Alderman, Big cheese, Bigwig, Dean, Eminence, Monsignor, Name, Personage, Provost, →**VIP**

**Dignity** Aplomb, Bearing, Cathedra, Decorum, Face, Glory, Grandeur, Gravitas, High horse, Maestoso, Majesty, Nobility, Poise, Pontificate, Presence, Scarf, Tiara

**Digraph** Ash, Eng, Ng

**Digress(ion)** Apostrophe, Aside, Deviate, Diverge, Ecbole, Episode, Excurse, Excursus, Maunder, Sidetrack, Vagary, Veer, Wander

**Dike** Bank, Channel, Cludgie, Dam, Ditch, →**DYKE**, Embank(ment), Estacade, Lav(atory), Lesbian, Levee, Wall

**Dilapidated, Dilapidation** Clapped out, Clunker, Decrepit, Derelict, Desolate, Disrepair, Eroded, Rickle, Ruined, Rust bucket, Shoddy, Tumbledown

**Dilate, Dilation, Dilatation, Dilator** Amplify, Develop, Diastole, Ecstasis, Enlarge, Expand, Increase, Mydriasis, Nitro, Sinus, Swell, Telangiectasia, Tent, Varix

**Dilatory** Protracting, Slow, Sluggish, Tardy

**Dilemma** Casuistry, Choice, Cleft(stick), Double-bend, Dulcarnon, Fix, Horn, Jam, Predicament, Quandary, Stymie, Teaser, Why-not

**Dilettante** Aesthete, Amateur, Butterfly, Dabbler, Playboy

**Diligence, Diligent** Active, Application, Assiduous, Coach, Conscience, Eident, Hard-working, Industry, Intent, Painstaking, Sedulous, Studious

**Dill** Anise, Pickle

**Dilute(d), Dilution** Adulterate, Allay, Cut, Deglaze, Delay, Diluent, Lavage, Qualify, Simpson, Thin, Water, Weaken, Wishy-washy

**Dim(ness), Dimming, Dimwit(ted)** Becloud, Blear, Blur, Brownout, Caligo, Clueless, Crepuscular, Dense, Dumbo, Dusk, Eclipse, Fade, Faint, Feint, Fozy, Gormless, Ill-lit, Indefinable, Indistinct, Mist, Nebulous, Ninny, Obliterate, Obscure, Overcast, Owl, Pale, Purblind, Shadow, Stupid, Unclear, Unsmart

**Dimension(s)** Area, Breadth, Extent, Fourth, Height, Length, Linear, Measure, New, Scantling, Size, Space, Third, Volume, Width

**Dimer** Cystine

**Diminish(ed), Diminishing, Diminuendo, Diminution, Diminutive** Abatement, Allay, Assuage, Attenuate, Baby, Bate, Calando, Contract, Cot(t)ise, Deactivate, Decline, Decrease, Détente, Detract, Disparage, Dissipate, Dwarf, Dwindle, Erode, Fourth, Hypocorism(a), Impair, Lessen, Lilliputian, Little, Minify, Minus, Mitigate, Petite, Pigmy, Ritardando, Scarp, Small, Stultify, Subside, Taper, Toy, Trangle, Wane, Whittle

**Dimple(d)** Dent, Depression, Hollow, Orange-peel

**Din** Babel, Charivary, Chirm, Commotion, Deen, Discord, Gunga, Hubbub, →**NOISE**, Racket, Raird, Randan, Reel, Reird, Uproar, Utis

**Dine(r), Dining** Aristology, Bistro, Café, Eat, Feast, Mess, Refect, Sup, Trat(toria)

**Ding(h)y** Cott, Inflatable, Pram, Shallop, Ship, Skiff

**Dingbat** Doodad, Weirdo

**Dingo** Warrigal

**Dingy** Crummy, Dark, Dirty, Drear, Dun, Fleapit, Fusc(ous), Grimy, Isabel(la), Isabelline, Lurid, Oorie, Ourie, Owrie, Shabby, Smoky

**Dining-room** Cafeteria, Cenacle, Commons, Frater, Hall, Langar, Mess hall, Refectory, Restaurant, Triclinium

**Dinky** Twee

**Dinmont** Ram, Sheep

**Dinner** Banquet, Collation, Feast, Hall, Kail, Kale, Meal, Prandial, Progressive, Repast, Spread

**Dinner jacket** Penguin suit

**Dinosaur** Aepyornis, Allosaurus, Ankylosaur, Apatosaurus, Archosaur, Atlantosaurus, Baryonyx, Brachiosaurus, Brontosaurus, Ceratopsian, Ceratosaurus, Ceteosaurus, Chalicothere, Coelurosaur, Compsognathus, Cotylosaur, Cynodont, Dinothere,

Diplodocus, Dolichosaurus, Duck-billed, Elasmosaur, Galeopithecus, Glyptodon, Hadrosaur, Ichthyosaur(us), Iguanodon, Megalosaur, Microraptor, Mosasaur, Odontornithes, Ornithischian, Ornithopod, Ornithosaur, Oviraptor, Pachycephalosaur, Pelycosaur, Perissodactyl, Placoderm, Plesiosaur, Pliosaur, Prehistoric, Prosauropod, Pteranodon, Pterodactyl, Pterosaur, Pythonomorpha, Raptor, Rhynchocephalian, Saurischian, Sauropod, Sauropterygian, Smilodon, Square, Stegodon(t), Stegosaur, Teleosaurus, Theropod, Titanosaurus, Titanothere, T-rex, Triceratops, Tyrannosaurus, Uintothere, Velociraptor

**Dint** Brunt, Dent, Depression, Force, Means, Power

**Diocese** Bishopric, District, Eparchate, Eparchy, See

**Diode** Esaki, Tunnel, Zener

**Diogenes** Cynic

**Dionysian** Boozy

**Dioxide** Cassiterite, Needle-tin

**Dip(per), Dippy** Bagna cauda, Baptise, Basin, Bathe, Bob, Brantub, Dabble, Dap, Dean, Dib, Diver, Dop, Double, Duck, Dunk, Fatuous, Foveola, Geosyncline, Guacamole, Houmous, H(o)ummus, Humus, Immerge, Immerse, Intinction, Ladle, Lucky, Magnetic, Ousel, Ouzel, Paddle, Plough, Rinse, Rollercoaster, Sag, Salute, Sheep-wash, Star, Submerge, Tapenade, Taramasalata, Tzatziki, Ursa

**Diphthong** Crasis, Synaeresis, Synaloepha, Synizesis

**Diploma** Bac, Cert(ificate), Charter, Parchment, Qualification, Scroll, Sheepskin

**Diplomacy, Diplomat(ic)** Alternat, Ambassador, Attaché, Career, CD, Chargé d'affaires, Chateaubriand, Cheque-book, Consul, DA, Dean, Discretion, Dollar, Doyen, El(t)chi, Emissary, Envoy, Fanariot, Fetial, Finesse, Gunboat, Legation, Lei(d)ger, Megaphone, Metternich, Negotiator, Phanariot, Plenipotentiary, Shuttle, Suave, →TACT

▷ **Dippy** *may indicate* a bather

**Dipsomania** Lush, Oenomania

**Dipstick** Dunce, →STUPID PERSON

**Dire** Dreadful, Fatal, Fell, Grim, Hateful, Ominous, Urgent

**Direct(or), Directed, Directly** Ad hominem, Administer, Advert, Agonothetes, Aim, Airt, Air-to-air, Auteur, Aventre, Beeline, Board, Boss, Cann, Cast, Chairperson, Channel, Charge, Chorus-master, Command, Compere, Con(n), Conduct, Control, Cox, Dead, Due, Dunstable road, Enjoin, Executive, Explicit, Face to face, Fair, Fast-track, First-hand, Forthright, Frontal, Full, Guide, Helm, Immediate, Impresario, Instruct, Intendant, Kapellmeister, Lead, Manager, Mastermind, Navigate, Nonexecutive, Outright, Oversee, Person to person, Pilot, Plain-spoken, Play, Point-blank, Ready, Refer, Régisseur, Regulate, Rudder, Send, Set, Signpost, Slap-bang, Stear, →STEER, Straight, Superintend, Supervise, Teach, Telic, Tell, Train, Unvarnished, Vector

## DIRECTORS

| 3 letters: | Weir | Noyce | Godard |
|---|---|---|---|
| Ray | | Orson | Herzog |
| | 5 letters: | Parer | Huston |
| 4 letters: | Brook | Vidor | Jarman |
| Coen | Clair | Wajda | Ophuls |
| Ford | Fosse | | Pagnol |
| Hall | Hawks | 6 letters: | Powell |
| Lang | Joffe | Brooks | Renoir |
| Lean | Kazan | Bunuel | Welles |
| Meno | Korda | Curtiz | Wilder |
| Reed | Losey | De Sica | |
| Roeg | Lucas | De Vito | 7 letters: |
| Tati | Mamet | Dreyer | Bergman |

| Berkoff | **8 letters:** | Hitchcock | Zeffirelli |
|---------|----------------|-----------|------------|
| Bresson | Cousteau | Peckinpah | |
| Campion | Griffith | Preminger | **11 letters:** |
| Chabrol | Kurosawa | Spielberg | Orson Welles |
| Coppola | Merchant | Tarantino | Pressburger |
| Fellini | Pasolini | Tarkovsky | Riefenstahl |
| Guthrie | Scorsese | | Von Stroheim |
| Kaufman | Truffaut | **10 letters:** | |
| Kubrick | Visconti | Eisenstein | **12 letters:** |
| Rivette | | Littlewood | Stanislavski |
| Russell | **9 letters:** | Passbinder | Van Sternberg |
| Sennett | Antonioni | Rossellini | |

**Direction, Directive** Address, Aim, Airt, Arrow, Astern, Bearings, Course, Cross-reference, E, End-on, Guidance, Guide, Heading, Keblah, L, Line, N, Orders, Orientation, Passim, Quarter, R, Recipe, Route, Rubric, S, Sanction, Send, Sense, Side, Slap, Sub-heading, Tacet, Tack, Tenor, Thataway, Tre corde, Trend, W, Way, Wedelns

**Direction-finder** Asdic, Compass, Decca, Quadrant, Radar, Sextant, Sonar

**Directory** Crockford, Data, Debrett, Encyclop(a)edia, Folder, French, Herbal, Kelly, List, Red book, Register, Root, Search, Web, Yellow Pages®

**Dirge** Ballant, Coronach, Dirige, Epicedium, Knell, Monody, Requiem, Song, Threnody

**Dirigible** Airship, Balloon, Blimp, Zeppelin

**Dirk** Anelace, Dagger, Skean, Whiniard, Whinyard

**Dirt(y)** Augean, Bed(r)aggled, Begrime, Bemoil, Cacky, Chatty, Clag, Clarty, Colly, Contaminate, Coom, Crock, Crud, Defile, Distain, Draggle, Dung, Dust, Earth, Festy, Filth, Foul, Gen, Gore, Grime, Grubby, Grufted, Grungy, Impure, Manky, Moit, Mote, Muck, Obscene, Ordure, Pay, Pick, Pollute, Ray, Scandal, Scody, Sculdudd(e)ry, Scum, Scungy, Scuttlebutt, Scuzzy, Skanky, Skulduddery, Slattery, Smirch, Smut(ch), Soil, Sooty, Sordes, Sordor, Squalid, Squalor, Stain, Stuff, Substrata, Sully, Tidemark, Trash, Unclean, Unsatisfactory, Unwashed, Warb, Yucky, Yukky

**Dis** Hades, Hell

**Disability, Disable(d)** Cripple, Crock, Gimp, Handicapped, Hors de combat, Incapacitate, Invalid, Kayo, Lame, Maim, Paralyse, Scissor-leg, Scotch, Scupper, Supercrip, Wreck

**Disabuse** Unteach

**Disadvantage** Detriment, Disamenity, Downside, Drawback, Flipside, Handicap, Mischief, Out, Own goal, Penalise, Penalty, Prejudice, Shortcoming, Snag, Supercherie, Upstage, Wrongfoot, Zugswang

**Disaffected, Disaffection** Ennui, Malcontent

**Disagree(ing), Disagreeable, Disagreement** Altercation, Argue, Argy-bargy, Bad, Clash, Conflict, Contest, Contradict, Debate, Demur, Differ, Discrepant, Dispute, Dissent, Dissonant, Evil, Fiddlesticks, Flak, Friction, Heterodoxy, Inharmonious, Onkus, Pace, Plagu(e)y, Rank, Rift, Testy, Troll, Uh-uh, Uncongenial, Unpleasing, Vary

**Disallow(ed)** Forbid, No ball, Overrule, Surcharge

**Disappear(ing)** Cook, Dispel, Evanesce, Evanish, Evaporate, Fade, Fizzle out, Kook, Latescent, Melt, Occult, Pass, Skedaddle, Slope, →**VANISH**

**Disappoint(ment), Disappointed, Disappointing** Anticlimax, Balk, Baulk, Blow, Bombshell, Bummer, Chagrin, Choked, Comedown, Crestfallen, Delude, Disgruntle, Fizzer, Frustrate, Gutted, Heartsick, Lemon, Letdown, Mislippen, Off, Regret, Sell, Setback, Shucks, Sick, Suck-in, Sucks, Swiz(zle), Thwart, Tsk, Underwhelm

**Disapproval, Disapprove(d)** Ach, Animadvert, Boo, Catcall, Censure, Condemn, Deplore, Deprecate, Discountenance, Expostulate, Fie, Frown, Harrumph, Hiss, Mal vu, Napoo, Object, Pejorative, Po-faced, Pshaw, Raspberry, Razz, Reject, Reproach, Reprobate, Slow handclap, Squint, Tush, Tut, Tut-tut, Umph, Veto, Whiss

**Disarm(ament), Disarming** Bluff, Defuse, Demobilise, Mutilate, Nuclear, Winsome

**Disarrange** Disturb, Muddle, Ruffle, Tousle, Unsettle

**Disarray** Disorder, Mess, Rifle, Tash, Tousle, Undress

**Disaster, Disastrous** Accident, Adversity, Apocalypse, Bale, Calamity, Cataclysm(ic), Catastrophe, Chernobyl, Crash, Crisis, Debacle, Dire, Doom, Evil, Fatal, Fiasco, Flop, Impostor, Meltdown, Mishap, Pandemic, Pitfall, Providence, Quake, Rout, Ruin, Screw-up, Seism, Shipwreck, Titanic, Tragedy, Train wreck, Wipeout

**Disavow** Abjure, Deny, Disclaim, Recant, Retract

**Disband** Demob(ilise)

**Disbelief, Disbelieve(r)** Acosmism, Agnosticism, Anythingarian, Atheism, Cor, Doubt, Gawp, Huh, Incredulity, Mistrust, Nothingarianism, Occamist, Pfui, Phew, Phooey, Puh-lease, Puh-leeze, Question, Sceptic, Shoot, Stroll on, Voetsak

**Disburse** Distribute, Expend, Outlay, Spend

**Disc, Disk** Accretion, Bursting, Button, CD, Chart-buster, Cheese, Clay pigeon, Compact, Coulter, Counter, Diaphragm, Dogtag, EP, Epiphragm, Fla(w)n, Flexible, Floppy, Frisbee®, Gold, Gong, Granum, Grindstone, Hard, Hard card, Harrow, Impeller, Intervertebral, Laser, LP, Magnetic, Mono, O, Optic(al), Parking, Paten, Patin, Planchet, Plate, Platinum, Platter, Puck, RAID, RAM, Rayleigh, Record, Reflector, Rosette, Roundel, Roundlet, Rowel, Rundle, Sealed unit, Silver, Slipped, Slug, Stereo, Stylopodium, Sun, Swash plate, System, Tax, Thylacoid, Tiddl(e)ywink, Token, Video, Wafer, Wharve, Whorl, Winchester, Wink, WORM, Zip®

**Discard(ed)** Abandon, Burn, Crib, Defy, Dele, Jettison, Kill, Leave, Minimise, Obsolete, Off, Offload, Oust, Outtake, → **REJECT**, Scrap, Shed, Shuck, Slough, Sluff, Supersede, Throw over, Trash

**Discern(ing), Discernment** Acumen, Acute, Astute, Clear-eyed, Descry, Detect, Discrimination, Eagle-eyed, Flair, Insight, Intuition, Perceive, Percipient, Perspicacity, Quick-sighted, Realise, Sapient, Scry, See, Skry, → **TASTE**, Tell, Wate, Wise

**Discharge** Absolve, Acquit, Arc, Assoil, Blennorrhoea, Blow off, Boot, Brush, Cashier, Catamenia, Catarrh, Conditional, Conge, Corona, Corposant, Dejecta, Deliver, Demob, Depose, Disembogue, Disgorge, Dishono(u)rable, Dismiss, Disruptive, Drain(age), Dump, Efflux, Effusion, Egest, Ejaculate, Eject, Embogue, Emission, Emit, Encopresis, Enfilade, Evacuate, Excrete, Execute, Exemption, Expectorate, Expel, Expulsion, Exude, Fire, Flashover, Flower, Flux, Frass, Free, Fusillade, Gleet, Glow, Honourable, Issue, Jaculatory, Lava, Lay off, Leak, Let off, Leucorrhoea, Liberate, Lochia, Loose, Maturate, Menses, Mitimus, Muster out, Mute, Offload, Otorrhoea, Oust, Outfall, Ozaena, Pass, Pay, Perform, Period, Planuria, Pour, Purulence, Pus, Pyorrhoea, Quietus, Redeem, Release, Rheum, Rhinorrhoeal, Run, Sack, Salvo, Sanies, Secretion, Seepage, Show, Shrive, Smegma, Snarler, Spark, Spill(age), Static, Suppurate, Teem, Unload, Unloose, Vacuate, Vent, Void, Water, Whites

**Disciple(s)** Adherent, Apostle, Babi, Baruch, Catechumen, Chela, Dorcas, Follower, John, Judas, Luke, Mark, Matthew, Peter, Simon, Son, Student, The Seventy, Thomist, Votary

**Disciplinarian, Disciplinary, Discipline(d)** Apollonian, Ascesis, Chasten, Chastise, Constrain, Correct, Despot, Dressage, Drill, Exercise, Feng shui, Inure, Judo, Martinet, Mathesis, Penal, Phonetics, Punish, Punitive, Ramrod, Regimentation, Regulate, Sadhana, School, Science, Sergeant major, Spartan, Stickler, Subject, Taskmaster, Train, Tutor, Yoga

▸ **Disc jockey** *see* DJ

**Disclaim(er)** Deny, Disown, No(t)chel, Recant, Renounce, → **REPUDIATE**, Voetstoots

**Disclose, Disclosure** Apocalypse, Confess, Divulge, Expose, Impart, Leak, Manifest, Open, Propale, → **PUBLISH**, Report, Reveal, Showdown, Spill, Tell, Unheal, Unhele, Unrip, Unveil

**Discoloration, Discolour(ed)** Acrocyanosis, Black and blue, Bloodstain, Blotchy, Bruise, Cyanosis, Dyschroa, Ecchymosis, Fox, Livedo, Livid, Livor, Stain, Streak, Tarnish, Tinge, Weather

**Discomfit(ure)** Abash, Confuse, Disconcert, Disturb, Frustrate, Lurch, Shend

**Discomfort(ed), Discompose** Ache, All-overish, Angst, Dysphoria, Gyp, Heartburn, Pain, Purgatory, Ravel, Unease, Wedgie

▷ **Disconcert(ed)** *may indicate* an anagram

**Disconcert(ing), Disconcerted** Abash, Astound, Confuse, Disturb, Embarrass, Faze, Feeze, Flurry, Fluster, Nonplus, Off-putting, Phase, Pheese, Pheeze, Phese, Put off, → RATTLE, Red-faced, Shatter, Startle, Tease, Throw, Unnerve, Upset, Wrong-foot

**Disconnect(ed)** Asynartete, Decouple, Detach, Disassociate, Disjointed, Off-line, Segregate, Sever, Staccato, Trip, Uncouple, Undo, Ungear, Unplug

**Disconsolate** Desolate, Doleful, Downcast, → GLOOMY

**Discontent(ed)** Disquiet, Dissatisfied, Humph, Repined, Sour, Umph, Unrest

**Discontinue, Discontinuance, Discontinuity** Abandon, Break off, Cease, Desist, Desuetude, Drop, Moho, Prorogue, Stop, Terminate

**Discord(ant)** Absonant, Ajar, Charivari, Conflict, Din, Dispute, Division, Eris, Faction, Hoarse, Inharmonious, Jangle, Jar(ring), Raucous, Ruction, Strife

▷ **Discord(ant)** *may indicate* an anagram

**Discount** Agio, Cashback, Cut-rate, Deduct, Disregard, Forfaiting, Invalidate, Leave, Quantity, → REBATE, Trade

**Discountenance** Disfavour, Efface, Embarrass

**Discourage(ment)** Caution, Chill, Dampen, Dash, Daunt, Deject, Demoralise, Deter, Dishearten, Disincentive, Dismay, Dispirit, Dissuade, Enervate, Frustrate, Intimidate, Opposition, Stifle, Unman

**Discourse** Address, Argument, Colloquy, Conversation, Descant, Diatribe, Dissertate, Eulogy, Expound, Homily, Lecture, Lucubrate, Orate, Philippic, Preach, Recount, Relate, Rigmarole, Sermon, Wash

**Discourteous, Discourtesy** Disrespect, Impolite, Insult, Rude, Slight, Uncivil, Unmannerly

**Discover(y), Discoverer** Amundsen, Anagnorisis, Ascertain, Betray, Breakthrough, Columbus, Cook, Descry, Detect, Determine, Discern, Discure, Esery, Espy, Eureka, Expiscate, → FIND, Heureka, Heuristic, Hit on, Learn, Locate, Manifest, Moresby, Protegé, Rumble, Serendip, Serendipity, Spy, Sus, Tasman, Trace, Treasure trove, Trouvaille, Unearth, Unhale, Unmask, Unveil

▷ **Discovered in** *may indicate* an anagram or a hidden word

**Discredit(able)** Debunk, Decry, Disbelieve, Disgrace, Explode, Infamy, Negate, Scandal, Slur, Smear, Stigmatise, Unworthy

**Discreet, Discretion** Cautious, Circumspect, Finesse, Freedom, Judicious, Option, Polite, Politic, Prudence, Prudent, Trait, Unobtrusive, Wise

**Discrepancy** Difference, Gap, Lack, Shortfall, Variance

**Discrete** Distinct, Separate, Unrelated

**Discriminate, Discriminating, Discrimination** Ag(e)ism, Colour bar, Diacritic, Differentiate, Discern, Distinguish, Elitism, Fastidious, Handism, Invidious, Lookism, Nasute, Racism, Rankism, Reverse, Secern, Segregate, Select, Sexism, Siz(e)ism, Speciesism, Subtle, Taste

**Discursive** Roving

**Discuss(ed), Discussion** Agitate, Air, Bandy, Bat around, Canvass, Commune, Confer(ence), Consult, Corridor work, Debate, Deliberate, Dialectic, Dialog(ue), Dicker, Disquisition, Emparl, En l'air, Examine, Excursus, Expatiate, Gabfest, Handle, Heart-to-heart, Hob and nob, Imparl, Interlocution, Interplead, Issue, Kick-about, Korero, Moot, Negotiation, Over, Palaver, Parley, Pourparler, Prolegomenon, Quodlibet, Rap, Re, Round table, Symposium, Talk, Talkathon, Talkboard, Tapis, Treatment, Trialogue, Ventilate, Vex, Words

**Disdain(ful)** Belittle, Contempt, Coy, Deride, Despise, Geck, Poof, Pooh-pooh, Pugh, Puh, Rats, Sassy, Scoffer, → SCORN, Scout, Sdei(g)n, Sneering, Sniffy, Sour grapes, Spurn, Stuffy, Supercilious, Ugh

**Disease(d)** Affection, Ailment, Bug, Communicable, Comorbid, Complaint, Deficiency, Defluxion, Dunt, Epidemic, Epidemiology, Fever, Functional, Industrial, Infection, Influenza, Malady, Noso-, Nosocomial, Notifiable, Occupational, Organic, Pest(ilence), Rot, Scourge, Sickness, Wildfire

## DISEASES

*2 letters:*
CD
MD
ME
MS
TB
VD

*3 letters:*
ALS
BSE
Flu
Haw
MND
Pip
Pox
Sod
→STD
TSE
Wog

*4 letters:*
Aids
Boba
Bunt
Clap
Conk
Gout
Keel
Kuru
Loco
Lues
Lyme
Roup
Wind
Yaws

*5 letters:*
Bang's
Black
Borna
Brand
Dread
Dutch
Ebola
Edema
Ergot

Favus
Fifth
Gapes
Grape
Hoove
Kwok's
Lupus
Lurgi
Lurgy
Mesel
Mumps
Ngana
Palsy
Pinta
Polio
Pott's
Rabid
Scall
Sprue
Surra
Tinea
Virus
Weil's
Worms

*6 letters:*
Anbury
Aphtha
Blight
Blotch
Border
Cancer
Canker
Chagas'
Chorea
Cowpox
Crohn's
Cruels
Dartre
Dengue
Eczema
Farcin
Graves'
Herpes
Income
Johne's
Mad cow

Marek's
Meazel
Mildew
Morbus
Mosaic
Nagana
Oedema
Paget's
Parrot
Rabies
Sapego
Scurvy
Social
Still's
Thrush
Tunnel
Typhus
Ulitis
Urosis
Yuppie
Zoster

*7 letters:*
Anthrax
Ascites
Batten's
Bird flu
Blue-ear
Bright's
British
Caisson
Cholera
Coeliac
Crewels
Crinkle
Dieback
Dourine
Endemic
English
Eyespot
Frogeye
Frounce
Gum rash
Hansen's
Hardpad
Hydatid
Icterus

Kissing
Leprosy
Lockjaw
Maidism
Malaria
Marburg
Miller's
Mimesis
Mooneye
Moor-ill
Murrain
Mycosis
Myiasis
Pébrine
Podagra
Purples
Pyaemia
Quittor
Redfoot
Rickets
Ring rot
Rosacea
Rubella
Rosette
Scabies
Scrapie
Sequela
Serpigo
Tetanus
Tetters
Typhoid
Variola
Wilson's
Zymosis

*8 letters:*
Addison's
Alastrim
Aujesky's
Basedow's
Beri-beri
Blackleg
Black-rot
Bornholm
Bullnose
Club root
Crown rot

Curly top
Cushing's
Cynanche
Diabetes
Dutch elm
Economo's
Epilepsy
Fishskin
Fowl pest
Gape-worm
Gaucher's
Glanders
Glaucoma
Goujeers
Gummosis
Hodgkin's
Hookworm
Impetigo
Jaundice
Kala-azar
Kawasaki
Leaf-roll
Leaf-spot
Liver-rot
Loose-cut
Menière's
Minamata
Mycetoma
Myopathy
Myxedema
Nosology
Pandemic
Pathogen
Pellagra
Phthisis
Phytosis
Porrigro
Progeria
Pullorum
Rachitis
Raynaud's
Red water
Ringworm
Rose-rash
Scaly leg
Scrofula
Shingles
Slimmers'
Smallpox
Soft sore
Suppeago
Swayback
Swinepox
Syphilis

Tay-Sachs
The bends
Time-zone
Trembles
Uteritis
Venereal
Vincent's
Zoonosis

**9 letters:**
Arthrosis
Bilharzia
Blackhead
Black knot
Black-lung
Brown lung
Chancroid
Chloracne
Chlorosis
Christmas
Cirrhosis
Contagion
Cytopathy
Diathesis
Distemper
Dysentery
Ear-cockle
Enteritis
Exanthema
Filanders
Gonorrhea
Idiopathy
Influenza
Ixodiasis
Kawasaki's
King's evil
Lathyrism
Leucaemia
Leukaemia
Listeria
Loose smut
Myxoedema
Navicular
Nephritis
Nephrosis
Newcastle
New Forest
Pellagrin
Pemphigus
Phossy-jaw
Porphyria
Seborrhea
Siderosis
Silicosis

Toxicosis
Trichosis
Tularemia
Tulip root
Yuppie flu

**10 letters:**
Acromegaly
Alzheimer's
Amoebiasis
Asbestosis
Autoimmune
Babesiosis
Bagassosis
Black death
Bluetongue
Byssinosis
Chickenpox
Damping off
Dandy-fever
Diphtheria
Erysipelas
Filariasis
Fire-blight
Fowl plague
Framboesia
Giardiasis
Gonorrhoea
Heartwater
Hemophilia
Iatrogenic
Ichthyosis
Impaludism
Lassa fever
Leuchaemia
Limber-neck
Lou Gehrig's
Louping ill
Moniliasis
Muscardine
Myasthenia
Neuropathy
Nosography
Nosophobia
Ornithosis
Parkinson's
Quarter-ill
Scarlatina
Seborrhoea
Texas fever
Topagnosia
Tularaemia

**11 letters:**
Anthracosis
Berylliosis
Brittle-bone
Cardiopathy
Coccidiosis
Consumption
Farmer's lung
Green monkey
Haemophilia
Hebephrenia
Huntington's
Isle of Wight
Kwashiorkor
Listeriosis
Myxomatosis
Parasitosis
Paratyphoid
Psittacosis
Rickettsial
Sarcoidosis
Scleroderma
Scrub typhus
Septicaemia
Thalassemia
Tonsillitis
Trench mouth
Trichinosis
Waldsterben
Woolsorter's
Yellow-fever

**12 letters:**
Alkaptonuria
Avitaminosis
Black quarter
Cor Pulmonate
Ehrlichiosis
Enterobiasis
Fascioliasis
Finger and toe
Foot and mouth
Furunculosis
Hoof and mouth
Legionnaires'
Molybdenosis
Motor neurone
Osteomalacia
Osteoporosis
Scheuermann's
Shaking palsy
Slapped cheek
Thalassaemia
Tuberculosis

| | | | |
|---|---|---|---|
| Uncinariasis | Tsutsugamushi | Sporotrichosis | **16 letters:** |
| | Whooping cough | St Anthony's Fire | Pneumonoconiosis |
| **13 letters:** | | Trichomoniasis | Sleeping sickness |
| Elephantiasis | **14 letters:** | Trichophytosis | Strongyloidiasis |
| Leichmaniasis | Coalminer's lung | Vincent's angina | Sweating sickness |
| Leptospirosis | Cystic fibrosis | | |
| Osteomyelitis | Histoplasmosis | **15 letters:** | **17 letters:** |
| Panleucopenia | Leucodystrophy | Graft-versus-host | Friedreich's ataxia |
| Poliomyelitis | Onchocerciasis | Schistosomiasis | Montezuma's |
| Salmonellosis | Pasteurellosis | Sydenham's chorea | revenge |
| Sclerodermata | Pneumoconiosis | Trypanosomiasis | Multiple sclerosis |
| Syringomyelia | Psillid yellows | | |
| Toxoplasmosis | River blindness | | |

▷ **Diseased** *may indicate* an anagram

**Disembark** Alight, Detrain, Land

**Disembarrass** Extricate, Rid, Unthread

**Disembowel** Eviscerate, Exenterate, Gralloch, Gut, Viscerate

**Disenchant** Disabuse, Disillusion, Dismay, Embitter

**Disencumber** Free, Rid, Unburden

**Disengage(d), Disengagement** Breach of promise, Clear, Detach, Divorce, Liberate, Loosen, Neutral, Release, Untie

**Disentangle** Debarrass, Extricate, Red(d), Simplify, Solve, Unravel, Unsnarl

**Disestablishmentarian** Cosmist

**Disfavour** Doghouse, Maugre

**Disfigure(ment), Disfigured** Agrise, Agryze, Camsho, Club-foot, Deface, Deform, Goitre, Mangle, Mutilate, Scar, Spoil, Tash, Ugly

▷ **Disfigured** *may indicate* an anagram

**Disgorge** Discharge, Eject, Spew, Spill, Vent, Void

**Disgrace, Disgraceful** Atimy, Attaint, Baffle, Blot, Contempt, Contumely, Degrade, Diabolical, Discredit, Dishonour, Dog-house, Embace, Embase, Fie, Ignoble, Ignominious, Ignominy, Indign, Indignity, Infamous, Infamy, Mean, Notorious, Obloquy, Opprobrium, Pity, Reprehensible, Scandal, Scandalous, Shame, Shameful, Shend, Slur, Soil, Stain, Stigma, Turpitude, Yshend

**Disgruntled** Brassed off, Hacked off, Malcontent, Narked, Resentful, Sore

▷ **Disgruntled** *may indicate* an anagram

**Disguise(d)** Alias, Belie, Blessing, Camouflage, Cloak, Colour, Conceal, Cover, Covert, Dissemble, Hide, Hood, Incog(nito), Mantle, Mask, Masquerade, Obscure, Peruke, Pretence, Pseudonym, Ring, Shades, Stalking-horse, Travesty, Veil, Vele, Veneer, Visagiste, Visor, Vizard

▷ **Disguised** *may indicate* an anagram

**Disgust(ing)** Ach-y-fi, Ad nauseam, Aversion, Aw, Bah, Cloy, Discomfort, Execrable, Faugh, Fie, Foh, Fulsome, Grisly, Grody, Icky, Irk, Loathsome, Manky, Mawkish, Minging, Nauseous, Noisome, Obscene, Odium, Offputting, Oughly, Ouglie, Pah, Pho(h), Pip, Pish, Pshaw, Pugh, Repel, Repugnant, Repulse, → **REVOLT**, Revulsion, Scomfish, Scumfish, Scunner, Scuzz, → **SICKEN**, Sir-reverence, Si(e)s, Slimeball, Slimy, Squalid, Turn off, Tush, Ugh, Ugly, Ugsome, Vile, Yech, Yucko, Yu(c)k, Yukky

**Dish(y), Dish out** Adonis, Allot, Apollo, Ashet, Basin, Belle, Bowl, Butterboat, Chafing, Charger, Cocotte, Compotier, Concoction, Cook-up, Crockery, Cutie, Dent, Diable, Dole, Dreamboat, Epergne, Flasket, Flatware, Grail, Kitchen, Laggen, Laggin, Lanx, Looker, Luggie, Menu, Muffineer, Ovenware, Pan, Pannikin, Paten, Patera, Patin(e), Pay, Petri, Plate, Platter, Popsy, Porringer, Ramekin, Ramequin, Receptacle, Rechauffé, Remove, Rout, Sangraal, Sangrail, Sangreal, Satellite, Saucer, Scorifier, Scupper, Scuttle, Serve, Service, Sexpot, Side (order), Smasher, Special(ty), Stunner, Toll, Watchglass, Woodenware

# DISHES

**3 letters:**
Poi

**4 letters:**
Flan
Fool
Giro
Hova
Kiev
Melt
Mess
Meze
Milt
Olla
Puri
Sate
Soss
Taco
Tian

**5 letters:**
Adobo
Balti
Bhaji
Bhuna
Bitok
Boxty
Brose
Champ
Crepe
Crout
Curry
Daube
Dolma
Gomer
Gruel
Kasha
Kebab
Keema
Kibbe
Kofta
Korma
Laksa
Maror
Perog
Pilaf
Pilau
Pilow
Pizza
Poori
Raita
Ramen

Rosti
Sabji
Salad
Salmi
Satay
Split
Sushi
Tamal
Tikka
Tripe

**6 letters:**
Bhagee
Bharta
Bhoona
Bridie
Chilli
Confit
Cou-cou
Cuscus
Entrée
Fajita
Fondue
Gratin
Haggis
Hotpot
Junket
Kimchi
Kishke
Kissel
Masale
Mornay
Mousse
Muesli
Nachos
Paella
Pakora
Panada
Pirogi
Quiche
Ragout
Regale
Roesti
Salmis
Sea-pie
Sowans
Sowens
Subgum
Surimi
Tamale
Tsamba

**7 letters:**
Biriani
Bobotie
Burrito
Calzone
Cannoli
Cassava
Ceviche
Chowder
Comport
Compote
Crowdie
Crubeen
Crumble
Custard
Cuvette
Dariole
Dhansak
Dopiaza
Egg roll
Fajitas
Fal-a-fel
Fel-a-fel
Foo yung
Friture
Gravlax
Haroset
Marengo
Mousaka
Padella
Pad thai
Pavlova
Piccata
Pierogi
Poutine
Rarebit
Ravioli
Risotto
Roulade
Sasatie
Sashimi
Scallop
Seviche
Sosatie
Soufflé
Spag bol
Stir-fry
Stovies
Supreme
Tartare
Tempura
Terrine

Timbale
Tostada
Zampone

**8 letters:**
Bhelpuri
Brandade
Bresaola
Calabash
Caponata
Chasseur
Chop suey
Chow mein
Coolamon
Coq au vin
Coquille
Couscous
Crostini
Dog's-body
Dolmades
Entremes
Feijoada
Flummery
Frittata
Furmenty
Gado-gado
Grillade
Halloumi
Handroll
Haroseth
Jalfrezi
Kedgeree
Keftedes
Kickshaw
Kouskous
Kreplach
Linguini
Mahi-mahi
Matelote
Mazarine
McCallum
Meat loaf
Meunière
Moussaka
Pandowdy
Pastrami
Poor John
Porridge
Pot-au-feu
Pot-roast
Raclette
Scrapple

Shashlik
Sillabub
Souvlaki
Squarial
Sukiyaki
Syllabub
Teriyaki
Tzatziki
Vindaloo
White-pot
Yakimono
Yakitori

**9 letters:**
Carbonara
Carpaccio
Cevapcici
Clafoutis
Colcannon
Egg-fo-yang
Enchilada
Entremets
Escabeche
Fricassee
Galantine
Gravad lax
Guacamole
Howtowdie
Jambalaya
Lobscouse
Lyonnaise
Manicotti
Marinière
Matelotte

Nut cutlet
Pastitsio
Pepper-pot
Reistafel
Rijstafel
Rillettes
Rogan josh
Scotch egg
Shashlick
Souvlakia
Succotash
Surf 'n' turf
Thermidor
Turducken

**10 letters:**
Blanquette
Bombay duck
Cacciatore
Cottage pie
Coulibiaca
Couscousou
Doner kebab
Egg custard
Egg-foo-yung
Jugged hare
Koulibiaca
Mousseline
Nasi goreng
Parmigiana
Pease brose
Plat du jour
Provençale
Quesadilla

Rijsttafel
Salmagundi
Sauerkraut
Scaloppine
Shish kebab
Spankopita
Spitchcock
Spring roll
Steak diane
Stroganoff
Teppan-yaki
Zabaglione

**11 letters:**
Banana split
Buck-rarebit
Chicken Kiev
Chimichanga
Crappit-head
Crème brulee
French toast
Fritto misto
Ratatouille
Saltimbocca
Sauerbraten
Smorgasbord
Spanakopita
Surf and turf
Welsh rabbit

**12 letters:**
Buffalo wings
Eggs Benedict
Parmigianino

Plum Porridge
Shepherd's pie
Solomon Gundy
Steak tartare
Sweet and sour
Taramasalata
Welsh rarebit

**13 letters:**
Fish and brewis
Rumbledethump
Salade nicoise
Skirl in the pan
Toad-in-the-hole

**14 letters:**
Beef stroganoff
Beef Wellington
Chilli con carne
Rumbledethumps
Scotch woodcock

**15 letters:**
Bubble and squeak
Chicken Maryland
Eggs in moonshine

**16 letters:**
Moules marinieres
Potatoes and point

**17 letters:**
Cauliflower cheese

**Dishabille** Disarray, Négligé, Undress
**Disharmony** Distune
**Dishearten** Appal, Core(r), Cow, Daunt, Depress, Deter, Discourage, Dispirit, Ettle
**Dishevel(led)** Bedraggled, Blowsy, Blowzy, Daggy, Mess, Rumpled, Scraggly, Touse, Tousle, Touzle, Towse, Tumble, Uncombed, Unkempt, Untidy, Windswept
**Dishonest(y)** Bent, Crooked, Cross, Dodgy, False, Fraud, Graft, Hooky, Hot, Ill-gotten, Improbity, Jiggery-pokery, Knavery, Light-fingered, Malpractice, Malversation, Maverick, Ringer, Rort, Shonky, Sleazy, Snide, Stink, Twister, Underhand, Venal, Wrong'un
**Dishonour(able)** Abatement, Caddish, Defile, Disgrace, Disparage, Ignom(in)y, Indignity, Infame, Scandal, Seduce, →**SHAME**, Violate, Wrong
**Disillusion(ment)** Awakening, Disenchant, Sour
**Disincline(d), Disinclination** Apathy, Averse, Loth, Off, Reluctant
**Disinfect(ant)** Acriflavin(e), Carbolic, Carvacrol, Cineol(e), Cleanse, Cresol, Dip, Eucalyptole, Formalin, Formol, Fuchsine, Fumigate, Lysol®, Orcein, Phenol, Purify, Sheep-dip, Sheep-wash, TCP, Terebene
**Disinformation** Agitprop
**Disingenuous** Insincere, Mask, Oblique, Two-faced
**Disinherit** Deprive, Dispossess

**Disintegrate, Disintegration** Break, Collapse, Crumble, Decay, Dialysis, Erode, Fragment, Lyse, Lysis, Osteoclasis, Rd, Rutherford

**Disinter** Exhume, Unearth

**Disinterested** Apathetic, Impartial, Incurious, Mugwump, Unbiased, Yawning

**Disjoint(ed)** Bitty, Dismember, Incoherent, Rambling, Scrappy

**Disjunction** Exclusive, Inclusive

▸ **Disk** see DISC

**Dislike(d)** Abhor, Allergy, Animosity, Animus, Antipathy, Aversion, Bete noire, Derry, Detest, Disesteem, Displeasure, Distaste, Gross out, Hate, Lump, Mind, Needle, Odium, Resent, Scunner, Ug(h), Warling

**Dislocate, Dislocation** Break, Diastasis, Displace, Fault, Luxate, Slip, Subluxate

**Dislodge** Budge, Displace, Evict, Expel, Luxate, Oust, Rear, Shift, Tuft, Unship, Untenant, Uproot

**Disloyal(ty)** Blue, False, Recreant, Renegade, Treacherous, Treason, Unfaithful, Untrue

**Dismal** Black, Bleak, Blue, Cheerless, Dark, Dowie, Dowly, Drack, Dreary, Funereal, →GLOOMY, Grey, Grim, Long-faced, Morne, Obital, Sepulchral, Sombre, Sullen, Trist(e), Wae, Woebegone, Wormy

**Dismantle(d), Dismantling** Decommission, Derig, Divest, Get-out, Sheer-hulk, Strike, Strip, Unpin, Unrig

**Dismast** Unstep

**Dismay(ed)** Aargh, Aghast, Alarm, Amate, Appal, Caramba, Confound, Consternation, Coo, Criv(v)ens, Daunt, Discourage, Dispirit, Dread, Fear, Fie, Ha, Hah, Horrify, Lordy, Lumme, Nonplus, Qualms, Strewth, Uh-oh

**Dismember** Quarter

**Dismiss(al), Dismissive** Airy, Annul, Ax, Banish, Boot, Bounce, Bowl(er), Brush off, Bum's rush, Can, Cancel, Cashier, Catch, Chuck, Congé, Constructive, Daff, Discard, Discharge, Dooced, Eject, Expulsion, Fire, Forget, Golden bowler, Heave-ho, Kiss-off, Lay off, License, Marching orders, Mitten, Och, Oust, Pink-slip, Pooh-pooh, Prorogue, Push, Recall, Red card, Reform, Reject, Remove, R.O., Road, Sack, Scorn, Scout, Send, Shoo, Shrug off, Skittle out, Spit, Spurn, Stump, Suka wena, Turn out, Via, Voetsak, Walking papers, Wicket, York

**Dismount** Alight, Hecht

**Disobedience, Disobedient, Disobey** Contumacy, Defy, Flout, Insubordination, Rebel, Sit-in, Unruly, Wayward

**Disobliging** Unaccommodating

▷ **Disorder(ed)** may indicate an anagram

**Disorder(ly), Disordered** Acidosis, Affective, Ague, Ailment, Anarchy, Ariot, Asthma, Ataxia, Bear garden, Betumbler, Catatonia, Chaos, Chlorosis, Clutter, Collywobbles, Conduct, Confuse, Consumption, Contracture, Conversion, Defuse, Derange, Deray, Diabetes, Dishevel, Dissociative, DT's, Dyslexia, Dysthymic, Dystrophy, Echolalia, Entropy, Epilepsy, Farrago, Folie a deux, Greensickness, Grippe, Haemophilia, Hallucinosis, Heartburn, Huntingdon's chorea, Hypallage, Inordinate, Irregular, Mange, Mare's nest, ME, Mental, Mess, Misrule, Mistemper, →MUDDLE, Muss(y), Neurosis, Oncus, Onkus, Overset, Pandemonium, Panic, Para-, Pell-mell, Personality, Phenylketonuria, Porphyria, Priapus, Psychomatic, Psychoneurosis, Psychopathic, Psychosis, Ragmatical, Rile, Roughhouse, Rowdy, Rumple, SAD, St Vitus' Dance, Schizophrenia, Schizothymia, Seborrh(o)ea, Shambolic, Shell-shock, Sickness, Slovenly, Snafu, Sydenham's chorea, Tarantism, Thalass(a)emia, Thought, Tobacco-heart, Tousle, Turbulence, Turmoil, Ulcer, Unhinge, Unrest, Unruly, Upheaval, Uproar, Upset, Virilism

**Disorganise(d)** At sea, Deranged, Disarray, Disorderly, Haphazard, Haywire, Higgledy-piggledy, Ragtag, Ramshackle, Scatterbrain, Scatty, Shambolic, Structureless

**Disorientation** Jet lag

**Disown** Abnegate, Deny, Disclaim, Disinherit, Renig, Renounce, Repudiate, Unget

**Disparage, Disparaging** Abuse, Belittle, Decry, Defame, Denigrate, Depreciate, Derogate, Detract, Discredit, Lessen, Pejorative, Poor mouth, Racist, Run down, Sell short, →SLANDER, Slur, Snide, Traduce, Vilify

**Disparate** Motley

**Disparity** Gap

**Dispassionate** Calm, Clinical, Composed, Cool, Impartial, Objective, Serene

**Dispatch** Bowl, Celerity, Consign, Destroy, Dismiss, Epistle, Expede, Expedite, Export, Express, Gazette, Kibosh, Kill, Letter, Message, Missive, Note, Post, Pronto, Remit, Report, →SEND, Shank, Ship, Slaughter, Slay, Special

**Dispel** Disperse, Scatter

**Dispensation, Dispense(r), Dispense with** Absolve, Administer, Aerosol, Apothecary, Automat, Ax(e), Cashpoint, Chemist, Chop, Container, Distribute, Dose, Dropper, Exempt, Fountain, Handout, Hole in the wall, Indult, Inhaler, MPS, Optic, Pour, Scrap, Siphon, Soda fountain, Spinneret, Vendor, Visitation

**Disperse, Dispersible, Dispersion** Deflocculate, Diaspora, Diffract, Diffuse, Disband, Dissolve, Distribute, Evaporate, Lyophil(e), Mode, Scail, Scale, →SCATTER, Skail, Sow, Spread, Strew

**Dispirit(ed), Dispiriting** Amort, Chapfallen, Crestfallen, Dampen, Dash, Daunt, Depress, Discourage, Dishearten, Exorcism, Gloomy, Listless, Sackless

**Displace(ment), Displaced** Antevert, Blueshift, Chandler's wobble, Depose, Dethrone, Disturb, Ectopia, Ectopy, Evacuee, Fault, Heterotopia, Lateroversion, Load, Luxate, Move, Oust, Proptosis, Ptosis, Reffo, Shift, Stir, Subluxation, Unseat, Unsettle, Uproot, Upthrow, Valgus, Varus, Volumetric

**Display, Display ground** Air, Array, Blaze, Blazon, Brandish, Bravura, Dangle, Depict, Eclat, Epideictic, Etagere, Etalage, Evidence, Evince, Exhibition, Exposition, Express, Extend, Extravaganza, Exude, Fanfare, Fireworks, Flash, Flaunt, Float, Flypast, Gala, Glitz, Gondola, Hang, Head-down, Head-up, Heroics, HUD, Iconic, Lay out, LCD, LED, Lek, Liquid crystal, Manifest, Motorcade, Mount, Muster, Ostentation, Outlay, Overdress, Pageant, Parade, Paraf(f)le, Peepshow, Pixel, Pomp, Post, Present(ation), Propale, Pyrotechnics, Rode, Rodeo, Roll-out, Ruffle, Scene, Screensaver, Scroll, Set piece, Shaw, →SHOW, Showcase, Sideshow, Sight, Spectacle, Splash, Splurge, Sport, Spree, State, Stunt, Swank, Tableau, Tattoo, Tournament, Turn out, Up, Vaunt, Wear, Window dressing

**Displease(d), Displeasure** Anger, Dischuffed, Humph, Irritate, Provoke, Umbrage

**Disport** Amuse, Divert, Play

**Dispose(d), Disposal, Disposition** Apt, Arrange, Bestow, Bin, Cast, Despatch, Dump, Eighty-six, Ethos, Incline, Kibosh, Kybosh, Lay(-out), Mood, Ordonnance, Prone, Riddance, Sale, Sell, Service, Settle, Spirit, Stagger, Throwaway, Will

▷ **Disposed, Disposition** *may indicate an anagram*

**Disposition** Affectation, Attitude, Bent, Bias, Humour, Inclination, Kidney, Lie, Nature, Penchant, Propensity, Talent, Temper(ament), Trim

**Dispossess(ed)** Abate, Attaint, Bereft, Depose, Deprive, Disseise, Evict, Oust

**Disproportion(ate)** Asymmetric, Extreme, Imbalance, Incommensurate, Unequal

**Disprove, Disproof, Disproval** Debunk, Discredit, Invalidate, Negate, Rebut, Rebuttal, Redargue, Reductio ad absurdum, Refel, Refute

**Dispute(d), Disputant** Altercation, Argue, Argy-bargy, At odds, Barney, Brangle, Brawl, Cangle, Case, Chaffer, Challenge, Chorizont(ist), Contend, Contest, Contravene, Contretemps, Controversy, Debate, Demarcation, Deny, Differ, Discept, Discuss, Eristic, Feud, Fracas, Fray, Gainsay, Haggle, Issue, Kilfud-yoking, Lock-out, Loggerheads, Militate, Moot, Ob and soller, Odds, Oppugn, Plea, Polemic, Pro-and-con, Quarrel, Query, →QUESTION, Quibble, Rag, Resist, Run in, Skirmish, Slanging-match, Spar, Spat, Stickle, Stoush, Threap(it), Threep(it), Tiff, Tissue, Tug-of-love, Variance, Vendetta, Wrangle

**Disqualify** Debar, Incapacitate, Recuse, Reject, Unfit

**Disquiet(ed), Disquieting** Agitate, Concern, Discomboberate, Discombobulate, →**DISTURB**, Pain, Perturb(ation), Sinister, Solicit, Turmoil, Ugly, Uneasy, Unnerve, Unrest, Vex

**Disraeli** Dizzy, Tancred

**Disregard(ed)** Anomie, Anomy, Contempt, Defy, Disfavour, Flout, Forget, Ignore, Neglect, Oblivion, Omit, Overlook, Oversee, Pass, Pretermit, Slight, Spare, Violate, Waive

**Disrepair** Dilapidation, Fritz, Ruin

**Disreputable, Disrepute** Base, Black sheep, Bowsie, Disgrace, Grubby, Ill fame, Ken, Louche, Low, Lowlife, Notorious, Raffish, Ragamuffin, Ratbag, Reprobate, Rip, Scuzz(ball), Scuzzbag, Scuzzbucket, Seamy, Seamy side, Shady, Shameful, Shy, Shyster, Sleazy

**Disrespect(ful)** Contempt, Derogatory, Discourtesy, Flip(pant), Impiety, Impolite, Irreverent, Levity, Naughty, Profane, Sacrilege, Slight, Uncivil, Violate

**Disrupt(ion)** Breach, Cataclasm, Dislocate, Disorder, Distract, Hamper, Hiatus, Interrupt, Jetlag, Mayhem, Perturb, Quonk, Ruffle, Sabotage, Screw, Upheaval

▷ **Disruption** *may indicate* an anagram

**Dissatisfaction** Displeasure, Distaste, Humph, Umph

**Dissect(ion)** Analyse, Dismember, Examine, Necrotomy, Zootomy

**Dissemble(r)** Conceal, Feign, Fox, Hypocrite, Impostor, Misinform, Pecksniff

**Disseminate** Radiate

**Dissent(er), Dissension, Dissenting** Contend, Demur, Differ, Disagree, Discord, Dissident, Divisiveness, Faction, Flak, Friction, Heretic, Holmes, Jain, Leveller, Lollard, Maverick, Methodist, Negation, Noes, Non-CE, Non-con(formist), Occasional conformist, Old Believer, Pantile, Protest, Raskolnik, Recusant, Remonstrant, Sectary, Separat(ion)ist, Splinter group, →**STRIFE**, Vary, Wesleyan

**Dissertation** Essay, Excursus, Lecture, Paper, Thesis, Treatise

**Dissidence** →**DESERTER**, Schism

**Dissident** →**DESERTER**, Objector

**Dissimilar** Different, Diverse, Heterogeneous, Unlike

**Dissipate(d)** Debauch, Decadent, Diffuse, Dispell, Disperse, Dissolute, Gay, Revel, Scatter, Shatter, Squander, Waste

▷ **Dissipated** *may indicate* an anagram

**Dissociate** Separate, Sever, Withdraw

**Dissolute** Decadent, Degenerate, Demirep, Falstaffian, Hell, Immoral, Lax, Libertine, Licentious, Loose, Rake-helly, Rakish, Rip, Roué, Wanton

▷ **Dissolute** *may indicate* an anagram

**Dissolution** Dismissal, Divorce, End, Repeal, Separation

**Dissolve** Deliquesce, Digest, Disband, Disunite, Lap, Liquesce, Melt, Repeal, Terminate, Thaw

**Dissonance** Wolf

**Dissuade** Dehort, Deter, Discourage

**Distaff** Clotho, Female, Lady, Rock, Stick

**Distance** Absciss(a), Afield, Apothem, Apse, Apsos, Breadth, Coss, Declination, Eloi(g)n, Elongation, Farness, Focal, Foot, Headreach, Height, Hyperfocal, Ice, Intercalumniation, Interval, Klick, Kos(s), Latitude, League, Length, Long-haul, Maintenance, Mean, Mean free path, Middle, Mileage, Northing, Ordinate, Outland, Parasang, Parsec, Range, Reserve, Rod, Skip, Span, Spitting, Stade, Step, Striking, Way, Yardage, Yojan, Zenith

**Distant** Aloof, Chilly, Cold, Far, Frosty, Hyperfocal, Icy, Long, Northing, Offish, Outland, Outremer, Polar, Remote, Tele-, Timbuctoo, Timbuktu, Unfriendly, Yonder

**Distaste(ful)** Dégoût, Gory, Grimace, Gross-out, Repellent, Repugnant, Ropy, Scunner, Sour, Unpalatable, Unpleasant, Unsavoury

**Distemper** Ailment, Colourwash, Emulsion, Equine, Hard-pad, Paint, Panleucopenia, Pip, Tempera

**Distend(ed), Distension** Bloat, Dilate, Ectasia, Emphysema, Expand, Hoove, Inflate, Meteorism, →**STRETCH**, Swell, Turgid, Tympanites, Varicocele, Varicose

**Distil(late), Distillation, Distiller, Distilling** Alcohol, Alembic, Anthracine, Azeotrope, Brew, Cohobate, Condense, Destructive, Drip, Essence, Ethanol, Extract, Fractional, Naphtha, Paraffin wax, Pelican, Pyrene, Pyroligneous, Rosin, Turps, Vacuum, Vapour

▷ **Distillation** *may indicate* an anagram

**Distinct(ive)** Apparent, Beside, Characteristic, Clear, Determinate, Different, Discrete, Evident, Grand, Idiosyncratic, Individual, Peculiar, Plain, Separate, Several, Signal, → SPECIAL, Stylistic, Trenchant, Vivid

**Distinction** Beaut(y), Blue, Cachet, Class, Credit, Diacritic, Difference, Dignity, Diorism, Disparity, Division, Double-first, Eclat, Eminence, Entelechy, Honour, Laurels, Lustre, Mark, Mystique, Nicety, Note, Nuance, OM, Prominence, Quiddity, Rank, Renown, Speciality, Style, Title

**Distinguish(ed), Distinguishable, Distinguishing** Classify, Contrast, Demarcate, Denote, Diacritic, Different(iate), Discern, Discriminate, Distinct, Divide, Elevate, Eminent, Ennoble, Especial, Eximious, Mark, Nameworthy, Notable, Perceive, Pick out, Prestigious, Prominent, Rare, Renowned, Scerne, Secern, Signal, Special, Stamp, Tell, VIP

▷ **Distort(ed)** *may indicate* an anagram

**Distort(ion), Distorted** Anamorphosis, Bend, Bias, Caricature, Colour, Contort, Deface, Deform, Dent, Foreshorten, Fudge, Garble, Harmonic, Helium speech, Jaundiced, Mangle, Misshapen, Pervert, Rubato, Skew, Stretch, Thraw, Time-warp, Travesty, Twist, → WARP, Wow, Wrest, Wring, Writhe, Wry

**Distract(ed), Distraction** Absent, Agitate, Amuse, Avocation, Bewilder, Divert, Embroil, Éperdu, Forhaile, Frenetic, Loon, Lost, Madden, Mental, Nepenthe, Perplex, Red herring, Scatty, Sidetrack, Sledge, Upstage

▷ **Distract(ed)** *may indicate* an anagram

**Distrain(t)** Na(a)m, Poind, Sequestrate, Stress

**Distraught** Deranged, Elfish, Elvan, Frantic, Mad, Troubled, Unstrung

**Distress(ed), Distressing** Afflict, Aggrieve, Agony, Ail, Alack, Alopecia, Anger, Anguish, Antique, Crise, Cut up, Desperation, Distraint, Dolour, Exigence, Extremity, Fraught, Fret, Gnaw, Grieve, Harass, Hardship, Harrow, Heartbreak, Hurt, Ill, → IN DISTRESS, Irk, Misease, Misfortune, Need, Oppress, Pain, Poignant, Prey, Privation, Sad, Shorn, Sore, SOS, Straiten, Straits, Suffering, Tole, Torment, Tragic, Traumatic, Tribulation, → TROUBLE, Une(a)th, Unstrung, Upset, Wound

▷ **Distress** *may indicate* a haircut

**Distribute(d), Distribution, Distributor** Allocate, Allot, Binomial, Busbar, Carve, Chi-square, Circulate, Colportage, Deal, Deliver(y), Deploy, Dish, Dispense, Dispose, Dissemination, Exponential, F, Frequency, Gamma, Gaussian, Geographical, Geometric, Issue, Ladle out, Lie, Lot, Mete, Normal, Out(let), Pattern, Poisson, Prorate, Renter, Repartition, Send out, Serve, Share, Strew

▷ **Distributed** *may indicate* an anagram

**District** Alsatia, Amhara, Arcadia, Ards, Area, Arrondissement, Attica, Bail(l)iwick, Banat, Banate, Bannat, Barrio, Belt, Canton, Cantred, Circar, Classis, Community, Congressional, Diocese, Encomienda, End, Exurb, Falernian, Federal, Fitzrovia, Gaeltacht, Gau, Ghetto, Hundred, Land, Lathe, Liberty, Locality, Loin, Manor, Metropolitan, Nasik, → NEIGHBOURHOOD, Oblast, Pachalic, Pale, Pargana, Parish(en), Paroch, Pashalik, Patch, Peak, Pergunnah, Phocis, Precinct, Province, Quarter, Quartier, Rape, → REGION, Reserve, Ride, Riding, Ruhr, Rural, Sanjak, Section, Sheading, Sircar, Sirkar, Soc, Soke(n), Stake, Stannary, Suburb, Sucken, Talooka, Taluk, Tenderloin, Township, Urban, Venue, Vicinage, Visne, Walk, Wapentake, Ward, Way, Wealden, Zila, Zillah, Zone

**Distrust(ful)** Caution, Doubt, Misanthropic, Misfaith, Suspect, Wariness

**Disturb(ance), Disturbed, Disturbing** Ado, Aerate, Affray, Aggrieve, Agitate, Alarm, Atmospherics, Autism, Betoss, Brabble, Brainstorm, Brash, Brawl, Broil,

Carfuffle, Choppy, Clatter, Collieshangie, Concuss, Delirium, Dementia, Derange, Desecrate, Disconcert, Disquiet, Dust, Dysfunction, Eat, Feeze, Firestorm, Fracas, Fray, Fret, Harass, Hoopla, Incident, Incommode, Infest, Interference, Interrupt, Intrude, Jee, Kerfuffle, Kick-up, Kurfuffle, Macabre, Molest, Muss, Neurosis, Outbreak, Perturb(ation), Prabble, Rammy, Ramp, Riot, Ripple, Rock, Roil, Romage, Roughhouse, Rouse, Ruckus, Ruction, Ruffle, Rumpus, Shake, Shellshock, Shindig, Shindy, Shook-up, Stashie, Static, Steer, Stir, Stress, Sturt, Tremor, Troppo, Trouble, Turbulent, Turmoil, Unquiet, Unrest, Unsettle, Upheaval, Uproot, →UPSET, Vex, Whistler

▷ **Disturb(ed)** *may indicate* an anagram

**Disunite** Alienate, Dissever, Divide, Divorce, Split

**Disuse** Abandon, Abeyance, Atrophy, Desuetude, Discard, Lapse

**Ditch** Abandon, Abolish, Barathron, Barathrum, Cast aside, Channel, Chuck, Crash-land, Cunette, Delf, Delph, Dike, Discard, Donga, Drainage, Drop, Dyke, Eliminate, Euripus, Foss(e), Graft, Grip, Gully, Ha(w)-ha(w), Jettison, Khor, Last, Level, Lode, Moat, Nal(l)a(h), Nulla(h), Rean, Reen, Rhine, Rid, Sea, Sheuch, Sheugh, Sike, Sloot, Sluit, Spruit, Stank, Sunk-fence, Syke, Tenail(le), Trench

**Dither(ing)** Agitato, Bother, Dally, Dicker, Faff, Flap, Flat spin, Haver, Haw, Hesitate, Hum, Indecisive, Irresolute, Pusillanimous, Pussyfoot, Twitter, Vacillate

**Dittany** Gas-plant

**Ditty, Ditties** Air, Arietta, Canzonet, Departmental, Jingle, Lay, Song

**Diuretic** Frusemide, Furosemide, Pipsissewa, Spironolactone, Thazide, Theobromine, Zea

**Diva** Callas, Patti, Singer

**Divan** Compilement, Congress, Couch, Council, Ottoman, Settee, Sofa

**Dive, Diver(s), Diving** Armstand, Backflip, Belly-flop, Crash, Dart, Den, Didapper, Duck, Embergoose, File, Flop, Free-fall, Frogman, Full-gainer, Gainer, Grebe, Guillemot, Half-gainer, Header, Honkytonk, Jackknife, Joint, Ken, Loom, Loon, Lungie, Merganser, Night club, Nitery, Nose, Pass, Pearl, Pickpocket, Pike, Plong(e), Plummet, Plunge, Plutocrat, Pochard, Poker, Power, Puffin, Saturation, Sawbill, Scoter, Scuba, Skin, Snake-bird, Sound, Speakeasy, Stage, Step-to, Stoop, Submerge, Swallow, Swan, Swoop, Tailspin, Urinant, Urinator, Zoom

**Diverge(nce), Divergent** Branch, Deviate, Divaricate, Heterochrony, Spread, Swerve, Variant, Veer

**Divers(e), Diversify** Alter, Branch out, Chequer, Dapple, Different, Eclectic, Interlard, Intersperse, Manifold, Many, Miscellaneous, Mixed, Motley, Multifarious, Separate, Some, Sundry, Variegate, Various, Vary

**Diversion, Divert(ing)** Amuse, Avocation, Beguile, Cone, Deflect, Detour, Disport, Dissuade, Distract, Droll, Entertain, Game, Hare, Hijack, Hive off, Hobby, Interlude, Pastime, Pleasure, Prolepsis, Ramp, Red-herring, Reflect, Refract, Reroute, Ruse, Shunt, Sideline, Sideshow, Sidetrack, Siphon, Smokescreen, Sport, Stalking-horse, Steer, Stratagem, Sublimation, Sway, Switch, Syphon, Tickle, Upstage, Yaw, Zany

▷ **Diverting** *may indicate* an anagram

**Divest** Denude, Rid, Strip, Undeck, Undress

**Divide(d), Divider, Dividing, Division** Abkhazia, Adzharia, Apportion, Balk, Balkanise, Band, Bifurcate, Bipartite, Bisect, Branch, Cantle, Chancery, Cleave, Cleft, Comminute, Commot(e), Continental, Counter-pale, Cusp, Cut, Deal, Demerge, Digital, Dimidiate, Discide, Dismember, Dissever, Estrange, Fork, Furcate, Great, Indent, Isere, Lot, Montgomery, Parcel, Part, Partite, Partition, Partitive, Party wall, Pentomic, Plebs, Polarise, Potential, Precisive, Quotient, Ramify, Rend, Rift, Sectionalise, Separate, Sever, Share, →SPLIT, Stanza, Sunder, Transect, Tribalism, Trisect, Twixt, Utgard, Voltage, Watershed, Zone

**Dividend** Bonus, Contango, Div, Interim, Into, Numerator, Peace, Share

**Divination, Diviner** Anthroposcopy, Arithmancy, Augury, Auspices, Axinomancy, Belomancy, Bibliomancy, Botanomancy, Capnomancy, Cartomancy, Ceromancy,

Chiromancy, Cleromancy, Coscinomancy, Crithomancy, Crystal-gazing, Crystallomancy, Doodlebug, Dowser, Empyromancy, Gastromancy, Geloscopy, Geomancy, Gyromancy, Hariolation, Haruspex, Hepatoscopy, Hieromancy, Hieroscopy, Hydromancy, I Ching, Intuition, Lampadomancy, Leconomancy, Lithomancy, Magic, Mantic, Myomancy, Omphalomancy, Oneiromancy, Onphalomancy, Onychomancy, Ornithomancy, Ornithoscopy, Osteomancy, Palmistry, Pegomancy, Pessomancy, Pyromancy, Radiesthesia, Rhabdomancy, Scapulimancy, Scapulomancy, Sciomancy, Seer, Sibyl, Sideromancy, Sortes, Sortilege, Spae(man), Spodomancy, Taghairm, Tais(c)h, Tephromancy, Theomancy, Tripudiary, Vaticanator, Xylomancy, Zoomancy

**Divine, Divine presence, Divinity** Acoemeti, Aitu, Ambrose, Atman, Avatar, Beatific, Blessed, Celestial, Chaplain, Clergyman, Conjecture, Curate, DD, Deduce, Deific, Deity, Douse, Dowse, Ecclesiastic, Empyreal, Forecast, Foretell, Fuller, →GOD, →GODDESS, Godhead, Godlike, Guess, Hallowed, Hariolate, Heavenly, Holy, Hulse, Immortal, Inge, Isiac, Kami, Mantic, Numen, Numinous, Olympian, Pontiff, Predestinate, Predict, Presage, Priest, Prophesy, RE, Rector, RI, Rimmon, Scry, Sense, Seraphic, Shechinah, Shekinah, Spae, Superhuman, Supernal, Theandric, Theanthropic, Theologise, Theology, Triune

**Division, Divisible** Amitosis, Angiosperm, Arcana, Arm, Arrondissement, Bajocian, Banat(e), Bannet, Bar, Bizone, Branch, Brome, Caesura, Canto, Canton, Cantred, Cantref, Cassini's, Caste, Category, Cell, Champart, Chapter, Classification, Cleft, Cloison, Clove, Comitatus, Commot(e), Commune, Compartment, Coralline Crag, Corps, County, Crevasse, Curia, Department, Dichotomy, Disagreement, Disunity, Div, Duan, Eyalet, Family, Farren, Fissile, Fork, Fragmentation, Glires, Grisons, Guberniya, Gulf, Gulph, Hapu, Hedge, Hide, Holland, Hotchpot, Hundred, Inning, Isogloss, Keuper, Kim(m)eridgian, Lathe, Leet, Legion, Lindsey, List, Lobe, Long, Mannion, Maturation, M(e)iosis, Mitosis, Mofussil, Nome, Oblast, Over, Pachytene, Pargana, Part, Partition, Passus, Pergunnah, Period, Phratry, Phyle, Phylum, Pipe, Pitaka, Platoon, Polarisation, Presidency, Province, Quartering, Queen's Bench, Quotition, Rape, Red Crag, Reduction, Region, Replum, Reservation, Riding, Sanjak, Schism, Section, Sector, Segment, Semeion, Sept(ate), Sever, Share, Sheading, Shed, Shire, Short, Stage, Stake, Subheading, Suborder, Tahsil, Tanach, Taxis, Telophase, Tepal, Thanet, Theme, Trichotomy, Trio, Trivium, Troop, Tuath, Unit, Vilayet, Volost, Wapentake, Ward, Watershed

**Divisor** Aliquant, Aliquot

**Divorce(d)** Alienate, Apart, Diffarreation, Disaffiliate, Dissolution, Dissolve, Disunion, Div, Estrange, Get(t), Isolate, Part, Put away, Reno, Separate, Sequester, →SUNDER, Talak, Talaq, Unhitch

**Divot** Clod, Sod, Turf

**Divulge** Confess, Disclose, Expose, Publish, Reveal, Split, Tell, Unveil, Utter

**DIY** Flatpack

**Dizziness, Dizzy** Beaconsfield, Ben, Blonde, Capricious, Dinic, Disraeli, Giddy, Giglot, Lightheaded, Mazey, Mirligoes, Scotodinia, Scotomania, Swimming, Vertiginous, →VERTIGO, Woozy

**DJ** Deejay, Jock, Mixmaster, Monkey-suit, Penguin suit, Presenter, Selecta, Shockjock, Tuxedo, Veejay

**DNA** Adenine, Antisense, Centromere, Chromatin, Cistron, Codon, Complementary, Cytosine, Double helix, Exon, Gene, Heteroduplex, Homopolymer, Intron, Junk, Microsatellite, Mitochondrial, Muton, Nucleosome, Nucleotide, Operator, Palindrome, Papovavirus, Plasmid, Polyoma, Poxvirus, Procaryote, Profiling, Prokaryote, Pseudogene, Purine, Recombinant, Replication fork, Replicon, Retrotransposon, Ribosome, RNA, Satellite, Selfish, Southern blot, Synthetic, Telomere, Thymidine, Transcript(ion), Transfection, Transfer, Translation, Transposon, Vector, Watson-Crick model

**Do(es), Doing** Accomplish, Achieve, Act, Anent, Banquet, Barbecue, Bash, Beano, Begin, Blow-out, Char, Cheat, Chisel, Cod, Con, Cozen, Deed, Defraud, Dich, Diddle,

Dish, Div, Doobrie, Doth, Dupe, Effectuate, Enact, Event, Execute, Fare, Fleece, Function, Fuss, Gull, Handiwork, Hoax, Imitate, Jamboree, Measure up, Mill, Occasion, Perform, Perpetrate, Provide, Rip off, Rook, Same, Serve, Settle, Shindig, Soiree, Spif(f)licate, Suffice, Swindle, Thrash, Thrive, Tonic, Up to, Ut

▷ **Do** *may indicate* an anagram

**Do away** Abolish, Banish, Demolish, Kill

**Dobbie** Elf, Fairy

**Docile** Agreeable, Amenable, Biddable, Dutiful, Facile, Meek, Obedient, Placid, Submissive, Tame, Tractable, Yielding

**Dock(er), Docked, Docks** Abridge, Barber, Basin, Bistort, Bob, Camber, Canaigre, Clip, Crop, Curta(i)l, Cut, Deduct, De-tail, Dry, Floating, Grapetree, Graving, Knotweed, Lay-up, Longshoreman, Lop, Lumper, Marina, Monk's rhubarb, Moor, Off-end, Pare, Patience, Pen, Pier, Quay, Rhubarb, Rumex, Rump, Scene, Seagull, Shorten, Snakeweed, Sorrel, Sourock, Stevedore, Tilbury, Watersider, Wet, Wharf, Wharfie, Yard

**Docket** Bordereau, Invoice, Label, Tag

**Dockyard** Arsenal, Chatham, Naval, Rosyth, Sheerness

▷ **Doctor(ed)** *may indicate* an anagram

**Doctor(s)** Allopath, Alter, Arnold, Asclepiad, Barefoot, Barnardo, Bleeder, BMA, Bones, Breeze, Bright, Brighton, Brown, Caius, Castrate, Chapitalize, Clinician, Cook, Crocus, Cup(per), Cure(r), Dale, Death, Diagnose, Dolittle, Dr, Dryasdust, Erasmus, Extern(e), Fake, Falsify, Family, Faustus, Feldsher, Fell, Fiddle, Finlay, Flying, Foster, Fu manchu, Fundholder, Galen, Geriatrician, Geropiga, GP, Guillotin(e), Hakeem, Hakim, Healer, Homeopath, Houseman, Hyde, Imhotep, Intern, Internist, Jekyll, Jenner, Johnson, Juris utriusque, Kildare, Lace, Leach, Leech, Linacre, Load, Locum, Luke, Manette, Manipulate, Massage, MB, MD, Medicate, Medico, Mganga, Middleton, Mindererus, Minister, Misrepresent, MO, MOH, Molla(h), Moreau, Mulla(h), Myologist, Neuter, No, Ollamh, Ollav, Paean, Paediatrician, Panel, Pangloss, Paracelsus, Paramedic, Pedro, PhD, Physician, Pill(s), Practitioner, Quack, Quacksalver, Rabbi, RAMC, Registrar, Resident, Rhinologist, Rig, Rorschach, Salk, Sangrado, Saw, Sawbones, School, Script, Seraphic, Seuss, Shaman, Slammer, Slop, Spay, Spin, Stum, Surgeon, Syn, Syntax, Therapist, Thorne, Treat, Vaidya, Vet, Water, Watson, Who, Wind, Witch

**Doctrine** Adamitism, Adoptianism, Adoptionism, Antinomian, Apollinarian, Archology, Arianism, Averr(h)oism, Blairism, Bonism, Brezhnev, Cab(b)ala, Cacodoxy, Calvanism, Catastrophism, Chiliasm, Consubstantiation, Credo, Creed, Determinism, Diabology, Ditheism, Ditheletism, Divine right, Docetism, Dogma, Doxie, Doxy, Dualism, Dysteleology, Encratism, Eschatology, Esotery, Eutychian, Evangel, Febronianism, Federalism, Fideism, Finalism, Functionalism, Gnosticism, Gospel, Henotheism, Hesychasm, Holism, Idealism, Illuminism, Immaterialism, Immersionism, Indeterminism, Infralapsarianism, Islam, Ism, Jansenism, Krypsis, Laches, Lore, Machtpolitik, Malthusian, Manich(a)eism, Materialism, Metempsychosis, Modalism, Molinism, Monadism, Monergism, Monism, Monothel(et)ism, Monroe, Neomonianism, Nestorianism, Neutral monism, Nihilism, Panentheism, Pantheism, Pelagianism, Personalism, Physiocracy, Pluralism, Pragmatism, Predestination, Premillennialism, Preterition, Probabilism, Psilanthropism, Pythagorean(ism), Quietism, Real presence, Reformism, Satyagrahi, Scotism, Secularism, Sharia, Sheria, Shibboleth, Solidism, Soteriology, Strong meat, Subjectivism, Sublapsarianism, Subpanation, Substantialism, Swedenborgianism, Syndicalism, Synergism, System, Teleology, →**TENET**, Terminism, Theory, Theravada, Thomism, Transubstantiation, Trialism, Tridentine, Tutiorism, Universalism, Utilitarianism, Voluntarism, Wasm, Weismannism, Whiteboyism, Zoism, Zwinglian

**Document(s), Documentary** Archive, Blog, Brevet, Bumf, Bumph, Carta, Certificate, Charge sheet, Charter, Chop, Contract, Conveyance, Copy, Covenant, Daftar, Deed, Diploma, Docket, Doco, Dompass, Dossier, E-journal, Elegit, Escrol(l), Escrow, Fiat, Fieri Facias, Fly-on-the-wall, Form, Grand Remonstrance, Green paper, Holograph, Indenture, Latitat, Logbook, Mandamus, Offer, Papers, Permit, Policy, Precept,

Production, Pro forma, Public, Ragman, Ragment, Record, Resort, Roll, Roul(e), Screed, Scroll, Sea brief, Source, Stamp note, Statute, Voucher, Warrant, Waybill, Weblog, Webpage, White paper, Writ, Write up

**Dod** Pet, Poll

**Dodder(y)** Old, Shake, Stagger, Strangleweed, Totter, Tremble

**Doddle** Easy

**Dodge(r), Dodgy** Artful, Avoid, Bell-ringing, Column, Elude, Evade, Evasion, Evite, Idler, Iffy, Jink, Jook, Jouk, Malinger, Racket, Ruse, Scam, Shirk, Sidestep, Skip, Slalom, Slinter, Tip, Trick, Twist, Urchin, Weave, Welsh, Wheeze, Wire, Wrinkle

**Doe(s)** Deer, Faun, Hind

**Doff** Avail(e), Avale, Remove, Rouse, Shed, Tip

**Dog(s), Doglike** Assistance, Attack, Bowwow, Canes, Canidae, Canine, Cynic, Dropper, Feet, Fire, Fog, Hearing, Hot, Huntaway, Hunter, Isle, Kennel, Leading, Native, Nodding, Pursue, Ranger, Ratter, Sea, Search, Seeing-eye, Shadow, Sleeve, Sleuthhound, Sniffer, Spotted, Stalk, Strong-eye, Sun, Tag, Tail, Therapy, Top, Toto, Tracker, Trail, Truffle, Tumbler, Wammul, Water, Water dog, Working, Yellow

## DOGS

**3 letters:** Cur, Eye, Gun, Pig, Pom, Pug, Rab, Yap

**4 letters:** Barb, Bird, Brak, Bran, Bush, Cant, Chow, Dane, Fido, Heel, Iron, Kuri, Kuta, Kuti, Leam, Lyam, Mutt, Oath, Peke, Puli, Rach, Sled, Stag, Tike

Toby, Tosa, Tray, Tyke, Wolf

**5 letters:** Akita, Alans, Apsos, Argos, Boots, Boxer, Brach, Cairn, Coach, Corgi, Dhole, Dingo, Guard, Guide, Haunt, Hound, Husky, Hyena, Kurre, Laika, Lorel, Luath, Merle, Moera, Pidog, Pluto, Pooch, Rache

Ratch, Rover, Shock, Spitz, Spoor, Whelp, Zorro

**6 letters:** Afghan, Bandog, Barbet, Barker, Basset, Beagle, Bitser, Blanch, Borzoi, Bounce, Bowler, Briard, Caesar, Canaan, Chenet, Cocker, Collie, Coyote, Dangle, Eskimo, Gelert, Goorie, Heeler, Jackal, Katmir, Kelpie

Kennet, Ketmir, Kratim, Lassie, Mauthe, Messan, Moppet, Pariah, Piedog, Police, Poodle, Pye-dog, Saluki, Setter, Shaggy, Shough, Sirius, Sothic, Talbot, Teckel, Touser, Towser, Vizsla, Westie, Yapper, Yorkie

**7 letters:** Andiron, Basenji, Bobbery, Boerbul, Bouvier, Brachet, Bulldog

Coondog
Courser
Griffon
Harrier
Iceland
Lowchen
Lurcher
Maltese
Maremma
Mastiff
Mongrel
Orthrus
Pointer
Prairie
Raccoon
Reynard
Samoyed
Sapling
Sausage
Shar-Pei
Sheltie
Shih tzu
Showghe
Sloughi
Spaniel
Starter
→TERRIER
Volpino
Whiffet
Whippet
Yapster

**8 letters:**
Aardwolf
Aberdeen
Airedale
Alsatian
Blenheim
Bouvrier
Bratchet
Brittany
Carriage
Cerberus
Chow-chow
Doberman
Elkhound
Hovawart

Kangaroo
Keeshond
Komondor
Labrador
Landseer
Malamute
Malemute
Papillon
Pekinese
Pembroke
Pinscher
Samoyede
Sealyham
Sheepdog
Springer
Turnspit
Warragal
Warrigal

**9 letters:**
Blue merle
Buckhound
Chihuahua
Coonhound
Dachshund
Dalmatian
Deerhound
Dobermann
Draghound
Gazehound
Great Dane
Greyhound
Harlequin
Kerry blue
Lhasa apso
Molossian
Pekingese
Red setter
Retriever
Rin-tin-tin
Schnauzer
Staghound
Wolfhound

**10 letters:**
Bedlington
Bloodhound

Blueheeler
Fox terrier
Otterhound
Pomeranian
Rottweiler
Schipperke
Shin-barker
Tripehound
Weimaraner

**11 letters:**
Bichon frise
Irish setter
Jack Russell
Labradoodle
Montmorency
Skye terrier
Tibetan apso
Trendle-tail
Trindle-tail
Trundle-tail
Wishtonwish

**12 letters:**
Border collie
Gazelle hound
Japanese chin
Newfoundland
Saint Bernard
Water spaniel
Welsh terrier
West Highland

**13 letters:**
Affenpinscher
Cocker spaniel
Dandie Dinmont
English setter
Scotch terrier
Sussex spaniel

**14 letters:**
German shepherd
Italian spinone
Norwich terrier
Pit bull terrier
Tibetan mastiff

Tibetan spaniel
Tibetan terrier

**15 letters:**
Bernese mountain
Brussels griffon
Estreia mountain
Golden retriever
Hamilton stovare
Mexican hairless
Norwegian buhund
Portuguese water
Swedish vallhund

**16 letters:**
Australian cattle
Doberman-
  pinscher
Lancashire heeler
Pyrenean mountain
Russian wolfhound
Shetland sheepdog
Yorkshire terrier

**17 letters:**
Anatolian Shepherd
Dobermann-
  pinscher
Labrador retriever

**18 letters:**
Large
  Munsterlander
Old English
  sheepdog
Rhodesian
  ridgeback

**20 letters:**
Landseer
  Newfoundland

**21 letters:**
Polish Lowland
  sheepdog

**Dog-bane** Apocynum
**Doge** Dandolo
**Dog-end** Stub, Tail
**Dogfish** Huss, Rigg, Rock salmon
**Dogged** Determined, Die-hard, Dour, Indefatigable, Persistent, Pertinacious, Relentless, Stubborn, Sullen, Tenacious

**Doggerel** Cramboclink, Crambo-jingle, Laisse, Rat-rhyme

**Dog letter** R

**Dogma(tic), Dogmatist** Assertive, Belief, Bigot, Bigotry, Conviction, Creed, Doctrinal, En tété, Ewe, Fundamental, Ideology, Ipse dixit, Literal, Opinionative, Pedagogic, Peremptory, Pontifical, Positive, →**TENET**

**Do-gooder** Lady Bountiful, Piarist, Reformer, Salvationist, Samaritan, Scout

**Dogsbody** Bottle-washer, Gofer, Skivvy

**Dog star** Canicula, Lassie, Sirius, Sothic

**Do it** Dich

**Dolce** Stop, Sweet

**Dole** Alms, Batta, B(u)roo, Give, Grief, Maundy, Mete, Payment, Pittance, Pog(e)y, Ration, →**SHARE**, Tichborne, UB, Vail, Vales

**Doleful** Sombre

**Doll(y)** Barbie®, Bimbo, Bobblehead, Common, Corn, Creeper, Crumpet, Dress, Dutch, Ewe, Girly, Golliwog, Kachina, Kewpie®, Maiden, Marionette, Matryoshka, Maumet, Mommet, Moppet, Mummet, Ookpik®, Ornament, Paris, Parton, Pean, Peen, Peggy, Pein, Pene, Poppet, Puppet, Ragdoll, Russian, Sindy®, Sis(ter), Sitter, Tearsheet, Toy, Trolley, Varden, Washboard, Wax

**Dollar(s)** Balboa, Boliviano, Buck, Cob, Cob money, Euro, Fin, Greenback, Iron man, Peso, Petrol, Piastre, Pink, S, Sand, Sawbuck, Sawhorse, Scrip, Smacker, Spin, Sword, Top, Wheel

**Dollop** Glob, Helping, Share

▷ **Dolly** *may indicate* an anagram

**Dolly-bird** Dish

**Dolly Varden** Hat

**Dolour, Dolorous** Anguished, Grief, Pain, Sorrow

**Dolphin** Amazon, Arion, Beluga, Bottlenose, Cetacean, Coryphene, Delphinus, Grampus, Lampuka, Lampuki, Mahi-mahi, Meer-swine, Porpess(e), Porpoise, Risso's, River, Sea-pig

**Dolt** Ass, Blockhead, Clodhopper, Mooncalf, Noodle, Oaf, Ouph(e), Owl, →**STUPID**

**DOM** Lewdsby

**Domain** Archaea, Archduchy, Bacteria, Bourn(e), Demain, Demesne, Eminent, Emirate, Empire, Estate, Eukarya, Kingdom, Manor, Net, Predicant, Public, Rain, Realm, Region, Reign, Starosty

**Dome(-shaped)** Al-Aqsa, Bubble, Cap, Cupola, Cupula, Dagoba, Geodesic, Head, Imperial, Louvre, Millennium, Onion, Periclinal, Pleasure, Rotunda, Salt, Stupa, Tee, Tholobate, Tholos, Tholus, Tope, Vault, Xanadu

**Domestic(ate)** Char, Cinderella, Cleaner, Dom, Esne, Familiar, Fireside, Homebody, Home-keeping, Homely, House, Housetrain, Humanise, In-service, Interior, Internal, Intestine, Maid, Menial, →**SERVANT**, Swadeshi, Tame, Woman

**Domicile** Abode, Dwelling, Hearth, Home, Ménage

**Dominate, Dominance, Dominant, Domination** Alpha, Ascendancy, Baasskap, Ballbreaker, Bethrall, Boss, Clou, Coerce, Control, Enslave, Hegemony, Henpeck, Maisterdome, Master, Mesmerise, Momism, Monopolise, O(v)ergang, Overmaster, Override, Overshadow, Power, Preponderant, Preside, Rule, Soh, →**SUBDUE**, Subjugate, Top dog, Tower

**Domineer(ing)** Authoritarian, Autocratic, Battleaxe, Boss, Henpeck, Imperious, Lord, Officious, Possessive, Ride, Swagger, Tyrannize

**Dominica(n)** Jacobite, Monk, OP, Preaching friar, Predicant, Savonarola, WD

**Dominie** Maister, Master, Pastor, Sampson, Schoolmaster

**Dominion** Canada, Dom, Empire, Khanate, NZ, Realm, Reame, Reign, →**RULE**, Supremacy, Sway, Territory

**Domino(es)** Card, Fats, Mask, Matador

**Don(s)** Academic, Address, Assume, Caballero, Camorrist, Capo, Endue, Faculty, Fellow, Garb, Giovanni, Grandee, Indew, Juan, Lecturer, Mafia, Prof, Quixote, Reader, Señor, Spaniard, Tutor, Wear

**Dona(h)** Duckie, Love

**Donate, Donation** Aid, Bestow, Contribution, Gift, Give, Offertory, Peter's pence, Present, Tribute, Wakf, Waqf

**Done** Achieved, Complete, Crisp, Ended, Executed, Had, Over, Spitcher, Tired, Weary

**Donjon** Dungeon, Keep

**Donkey** Ass, Burro, Cardophagus, Cuddie, Cuddy, Dapple, Dick(e)y, Dunce, Eeyore, Engine, Funnel, Fussock, Genet(te), Ignoramus, Jackass, Jacket, Jennet, Jenny, Jerusalem pony, Kulan, Modestine, Moke, Mule, Neddy, Nodding, Onager, Stupid, Years

**Donor** Benefactor, Bestower, Blood, Settlor, Universal

**Doo** Dove

**Doodle(r)** Scribble, Yankee

**Doodlebug** Antlion, Larva, V1

**Doofer** Thingumabob

**Doom(ed)** Condemned, Damnation, Date, Destine, Destiny, →FATE, Fay, Fey, Fie, Goner, Ill-fated, Ill-omened, Ill-starred, Lot, Predestine, Preordain, Ragnarok, Ruined, Sentence, Spitcher, Star-crossed, Weird

**Doone** Carver, Lorna

**Door(s), Doorstep, Doorway** Aperture, Communicating, Damnation, Drecksill, Dutch, Elephant, Entry, Exit, Fire, Folding, French, Front, Gull-wing, Haik, Hake, Hatch, Heck, Ingress, Jib, Lintel, Louver, Louvre, Muntin, Oak, Open, Overhead, Patio, Portal, Postern, Revolving, Rory, Screen, Sliding, Stable, Stage, Storm, Street, Swing, Tailgate, Trap, Up and over, Vomitory, Wicket, Yett

**Doorkeeper, Doorman** Bouncer, Commissionaire, Concierge, Dvornik, Guardian, Janitor, Nab, Ostiary, Porter, Tiler, Tyler, Usher

**Doormat** Subservient, Weakling, Wuss

**Doorpost** Architrave, Dern, Durn, Jamb, Yate, Yett

**Dope** Acid, Amulet, Bang, Coke, Crack, Datum, →DRUG, Dunderhead, Facts, Fuss, Gen, Goose, Info, Latest, Lowdown, Narcotic, Nitwit, Nobble, Rutin, Sedate, Soup, →STUPID PERSON, Tea

**Doppelganger** Double, Look-alike, Ringer

**Dorcas** Gazelle, Needle, Shepherdess

**Dorian, Doric** Metope, Mutule

**Doris** Day, Lessing, Mollusc

**Dormant** Abed, Comatose, Hibernating, Idle, Inactive, Inert, Joist, Latent, Latitant, Quiescent, Resting, →SLEEPING, Torpescent

**Dormer** Luthern

**Dormitory** Barrack, Bunkhouse, Dorter, Dortour, Hall, Hostel, Quarters

**Dormouse** Loir

**Dorothy** Bag, Dot, Sayers

**Dorsal** Back, Neural, Notal

**Dory** Fish, John

**Dosage, Dose** Absorbed, Acute, Administer, Aperient, Booster, Cascara, Cumulative, Drachm, Draught, Drench, Drug, Fix, Hit, Kilogray, Lethal, →MEASURE, Permissible, Physic, Posology, Potion, Powder, Rem, Standing off, Threshold, Tolerance

**Doss (house), Dosser** Dharmsala, Dharmshala, Kip, Layabout, Padding-ken, Spike

**Dossier** File, Record

**Dot(s), Dotted, Dotty** Absurd, Bind(h)i, Blip, Bullet (point), Centred, Criblé, Dieresis, Dit, Dower, Dowry, Ellipsis, Engrailed, Intersperse, Leader, Lentiginous, Limp, Micro, Morse, Occult, Or, Particle, Pinpoint, Pixel, →POINT, Pointillé, Polka, Precise, Punctuate, Punctulate, Punctum, Schwa, Semé(e), Set, Speck, Spot, Sprinkle, Stigme, Stipple, Stud, Tap, Tittle, Tocher, Trema, Umlaut

**Dote, Dotage, Doting, Dotard** Adore, Anile, Anility, Cocker, Dobbie, Idolise, Imbecile, Pet, Prize, Senile, Spoon(e)y, Tendre, Twichild

**Double(s)** Alter-ego, Amphibious, Ancipital, Bi-, Bifold, Binate, Clone, Counterpart, Crease, Dimeric, Doppel-ganger, Doppio, Dual, Duo, Duple(x), Duplicate, Equivocal, Fetch, Fold, Foursome, Geminate, Gimp, Image, Ingeminate, Ka, Look-alike, Loop, Martingale, Pair, Parlay, Polyseme, Reflex, Replica, Ringer, Run, Similitude, Spit, Stuntman, Trot, Turnback, Twae, →TWIN, Two(fold), Two-ply

**Double-barrelled** Tautonym

**Double-cross, Double dealer, Double dealing** Ambidext(e)rous, Knavish, Traitor, Two-time

**Double-entendre** Polyseme, Polysemy

**Doublet** Peascod, Pourpoint, TT

**Doubt(s), Doubter, Doubtful** Agnostic, Ambiguous, Aporia, Askance, But, Debatable, Discredit, Distrust, Dubiety, Dubitate, Erm, Hesitate, Hum, Iffy, Incertitude, Misgiving, Mistrust, →NO DOUBT, Or, Precarious, Qualm, Query, →QUESTION, Rack, Reservation, Scepsis, Sceptic, Scruple, Second thoughts, Shady, Shy, Sic, Skepsis, Sus, Suspect, Suspicious, Suss, Thomas, Thos, Umph, Uncertain, Unsure, Waver

**Doubtless** Certain, Iwis, Probably, Sure, Truly, Undisputed, Ywis

**Douceur** Bonus, Sop, Sweetener

**Douche** Bath, Gush, Rinse, Shower, Wash

**Dough(y)** Boodle, Cake, Calzone, Cash, Duff, Dumpling, Gnocchi, Hush-puppy, Knish, Loot, Magma, Masa, Money, Pasta, Paste, Polenta, Pop(p)adum, Ready, Sad, Sour, Spondulicks, Strudel

**Doughboy** Dumpling, Soldier

**Doughnut** Bagel, Beavertail®, Cruller, Fried cake, Knish, Koeksister, Olycook, Olykoek, Sinker, Torus

**Doughty** Brave, Intrepid, Resolute, Stalwart, Valiant

**Dour** Glum, Hard, Mirthless, Morose, Reest, Reist, Sinister, Sullen, Taciturn

**Douse** Dip, Drench, Extinguish, Snuff, Splash

**Dove** Collared, Columbine, Culver, Cushat, Diamond, Doo, Ground, Ice-bird, Mourning, Pacifist, →PIGEON, Queest, Quoist, Ring, Rock, Stock, Turtle

**Dove-cot(e)** Columbarium, Columbary, Louver, Louvre, Lover

**Dovetail** Fit, Interosculate, Lewis(son), Mortise, Tally, Tenon

**Dowager** Elder, Widow

**Dowdy** Frumpish, Mopsy, Mums(e)y, Plain Jane, Shabby, Sloppy, Slovenly

**Dowel** Peg, Pin

**Down(s), Downbeat, Downsize, Downward, Downy** A bas, Abase, Abattu, Alow, Amort, Bank, Below, Berkshire, Blue, Cast, Catabasis, Chapfallen, Comous, Cottony, Crouch, Darling, Dejected, Demoralised, Descent, Disconsolate, Dowl(e), Drink, Duck, Epsom, Feather, Fledge, Floccus, Flue, Fluff, Fly, Fuzz, Glum, Goonhilly, Ground, Hair, Hangdog, Hill, Humble, Humiliate, Jeff, Kennet, Lanate, Lanugo, Latitant, Losing, Low, Lower, Miserable, Moxa, Nap, Neck, North Wessex, Oose, Ooze, Owing, Pappus, Pennae, Pile, Plumage, Powder, Quark, Quash, Repress, Scuttle, Sebum, Slim, Sussex, Swallow, Thesis, Thistle, Tomentum, Under, Unserviceable, Urinant, Vail, Watership, Wold, Wretched

**Downcast** Abject, Chapfallen, Dejected, Despondent, Disconsolate, Dumpish, Glum, Hangdog, Hopeless, Melancholy, Woebegone

**Downfall, Downpour** Brash, Cataract, Collapse, Deluge, Doom, Fate, Flood, Hail, Onding, Overthrow, Plash, Rain, Rainstorm, Ruin, Shower, Soak, Thunder-plump, Torrent, Undoing, Waterspout

**Downgrade(d)** Déclassé, Deskill, Disrate, Relegate

**Downmarket** Naff

**Downright** Absolute, Arrant, Bluff, Candid, Clear, Complete, Flat, Plumb, Plump, Pure, Rank, Sheer, Stark, Utter

**Downstairs** Below

**Downstream** Tail

**Down-trodden** Oppressed, Underfoot

**Downturn** Decrease, Recession, Slump

**Downwind** Leeward

**Dowry** Dot, Dower, Lobola, Lobolo, Merchet, Portion, Settlement, Tocher

**Dowse(r), Dowsing** Divine, Enew, Fireman, Radionics, Rhabdomancy, Water-witch

**Doxology** Gloria, Glory

**Doxy** Harlot, Loose woman, Opinion, Wench

**Doyen** Dean, Senior

**Doze, Dozy** Ca(u)lk, Catnap, Dove(r), Nap, Nod, Semi-coma, Sleep, Sleepyhead, Slip, Slumber

**Dozen(s)** Baker's, Daily, Dz, Long, Round, Thr(e)ave, Twal, Twelve

**Dr** Debtor, Doctor, Dram

**Drab** Ash-grey, Cloth, Dell, Dingy, Dowdy, Dreary, Dull, Dun, Ecru, Hussy, Isabel(line), Lifeless, Livor, Mumsy, Olive, Prosaic, Pussel, Quaker-colour, Rig, Road, Scarlet woman, Slattern, Sloven, Strumpet, Subfusc, Tart, Taupe, Trull, Wanton, Whore

**Drabble** Bemoil, Draggle

**Draconian** Harsh

**Dracula** Bat, Count, Vampire

**Draft** Bank, Bill, Cheque, Conscript, Draw, Ebauche, Essay, Landsturm, Minute, MS, Outline, Paste up, Plan, Press, Project, Protocol, Recruit, Rough, Scheme, Scroll, Scrowle, →SKETCH

**Drag** Car, Cigarette, Clothing, Drail, Dredge, Drogue, Elicit, Eonism, Epicene, Extort, Fiscal, Form, Gender-bender, Hale, Hang, Harl, →HAUL, Induced, Keelhaul, La Rue, Liability, Lug, Nuisance, Parasite, Pressure, Profile, Puff, Pull, Rash, Sag, Schlep, Shockstall, Shoe, Skidpan, Sled, Snake, Snig, Sweep, Toke, Tote, Tow, Trail, Trailing vortex, Train, Travail, Travois, Trawl, Treck, Trek, Tug, Tump, Vortex

**Draggle** Drail, Lag, Straggle

**Dragon** Aroid, Basilisk, Bel, Bellemère, Chaperon(e), Chindit, Draco, Drake, Fafnir, Fire-drake, Gargouille, Komodo, Kung-kung, Ladon, Lindworm, Opinicus, Peist, Puk, Python, Rouge, Safat, Serpent, Shrew, Typhoeus, Wantley, Wivern, Worm, Wyvern, Yacht

**Dragonfly** Aeschna, Demoiselle, Devil's darning needle, Nymph, Odonata

**Dragon's teeth** Cadmus, Spartae, Sparti

**Dragoon** Coerce, Force, Press, Rope-in, Trooper

**Drain(ed), Drainage, Drainer, Draining, Drainpipe** Bleed, Brain, Buzz, Can(n)ula, Catchment, Catchwater, Channel, Cloaca, Colander, Condie, Culvert, Cundy, Cunette, Delf, Delph, Dewater, Ditch, Dry, Ea(u), →EMPTY, Emulge(nt), Enervate, Exhaust, Field, Fleet, Gargoyle, Grating, Grip, Gully, Gutter, Ketavothron, Kotabothron, Lade, Leach, Leech, Limber, Lose, Lymphatic, Milk, Mole, Nala, Nalla(h), Nulla(h), Penrose, Pump, Rack, Rone, Sanitation, Sap, Scalpins, Scupper, Seton, Sew(er), Sheuch, Sheugh, Shore, Silver, Sink, Siver, Sluice, Sluse, Small-trap, Soakaway, Sough, Spend, Spunge, Stank, Storm, Suck, Sump, Sure, Syver, Tile, Trench, Trocar, Unwater, Ureter, U-trap, Weary, Well

**Drainpipe(s)** Downspout, →TROUSERS

**Dram** Drink, Drop, Nipperkin, Nobbler, Portion, Snifter, Tickler, Tiff, Tot, Wet

**Drama(tic), Drama school** Auto, Azione, Catastasis, Charade, Closet, Comedy, Costume, Drastic, Epic, ER, Eumenides, Farce, Heroic, Histrionic, Kabuki, Kathakali, Kitchen sink, Legit, Legitimate, Mask, Masque, Mime, Moralities, Music, No, Nogaku, Noh, Oresteia, Piece, Play, RADA, Sangeet, Scenic, Screenplay, Sensational, Serial, Singspiel, Soap, Spinto, Stagy, Striking, Sudser, Tetralogy, Theatric, The Birds, Thespian, Tragedy, Unities, Wagnerian, Wild

**Dramatist** Adamov, Aeschylus, Albee, Anouilh, Aristophanes, Arrabal, Barrie, Beaumarchais, Beaumont, Beckett, Beddoes, Bleasdale, Brecht, Bridie, Calderon,

Centlivre, Chapman, Congreve, Corneille, Coward, Dekker, Drinkwater, Ennius, Euripides, Farquhar, Feydeau, Fletcher, Frisch, Fry, Gay, Genet, Gogol, Goldoni, Havel, Heywood, Ibsen, Ionesco, Jarry, Kaiser, Kyd, Lorca, Lyly, Mamet, Marlowe, Massinger, Menander, Middleton, Molière, Odets, O'Neill, Orton, Osborne, Otway, Pinero, Pinter, Pirandello, Plautus, → **PLAYWRIGHT**, Racine, Rostand, Rowe, Rowley, Schiller, Seneca, Shadwell, Shaffer, Sherriff, Sophocles, Stoppard, Strindberg, Synge, Terence, Thespis, Udall, Vanbrugh, Voltaire, Von Klinger, Webster, Wedekind, Wesker, Wilde, Wilder, Will, → **WRITER**, Yeats

**Dram-shop** Bar, Boozingken, Bousingken

**Drape(ry)** Adorn, Coverlet, Coverlid, Curtain, Festoon, Fold, Hang, Lambrequin, Mantling, Swag, Swathe, Valance, Veil, Vest

**Draper** Clothier, Gilpin, Haberdasher, Hosier, Mercer, Outfitter, Ruth, Scotch cuddy, Tailor

**Drastic** Dire, Dramatic, Extreme, Harsh, Purge, Senna, → **SEVERE**, Swingeing, Violent

**Drat** Bother, Dang, Darn

**Draught(s), Draughtsman(ship)** Aloetic, Apozem, Aver, Breeze, Checkers, Chequer, Dam, Dams, Design, Dose, Drench, Drink, Fish, Gulp, Gust, Haal, Hippocrene, King, Line, Men, Nightcap, Outline, Plan, Potation, Potion, Puff, Pull, Quaff, Sketch, Sleeping, Slug, Swig, Tracer, Up-current, Veronal, Waft, Waucht, Waught, Williewaught, Wind

▷ **Draught** *may refer to* fishing

**Draught-board** Dam-board, Dambrod

**Dravidian** Tamil

**Draw (off), Drawer(s), Drawing, Drawn** Adduct, Allure, Attract, Attrahent, Bleed, Blueprint, Bottom, Cartoon, Charcoal, Cityscape, Cock, Crayon, Dead-heat, Delineate, Dentistry, Derivation, Describe, Detail, Diagram, Dis(em)bowel, Doodle, Dr, Draft, Drag, Dress, Educe, Elevation, Elicit, Elongate, Entice, Equalise, Escribe, Evaginate, Even-steven, Eviscerate, Extract, Fet(ch), Freehand, Fusain, Gather, Gaunt, Glorybox, Goalless, Graffiti, Graphics, Gravitate, Gut, Haggard, Hale, Halve, Haul, Identikit, Indraft, Induce, Indue, Inhale, Isometric, Lead, Lengthen, Limn, Line, Longbow, Lots, Lottery, Magnet, Mechanical, Monotint, No-score, Orthograph, Pantalet(te)s, Panty, Pastel(list), Pen and ink, Perpetual check, Petroglyph, Profile, Protract, Pull, RA, Rack, Raffle, Realize, Reel, Remark, Scenography, Scent, Score, Seductive, Sepia, Sesquipedalian, Shottle, Shuttle, Silverpoint, Siphon, Sketch, Slub, Snig, Spin, Stalemate, Stretch, Study, Stumps, Sweepstake, Syphon, Tap, Taut, Technical, Tempera, Tempt, Tenniel, Tie, Till, Toke, Tole, Tombola, Top, Tose, Tow(age), Toze, Trace, Traction, Trice, Troll, Tug, Unsheathe, Uplift, Visual, Wash, Working

▷ **Draw** *may indicate* something to smoke

**Drawback** Catch, Downside, Ebb, Handicap, Impediment, → **OBSTACLE**, Rebate, Retraction, Shortcoming, Shrink, Snag

**Drawbridge** Bascule, Pontlevis

**Drawl** Dra(u)nt, Haw, Slur, Twang

▷ **Drawn** *may indicate* an anagram

**Drawn up** Atrip, Drafted

**Dray** Cart, Lorry, Wagon

**Dread(ed), Dreadful** Angst, Anxiety, Awe, Awful, Chronic, Dearn, Dern, Dire, Fear, Formidable, Funk, Ghastly, Horrendous, → **HORROR**, Nightmare, Nosophobia, Penny, Rasta, Redoubt, Shocking, Sorry, Terrible, Thing, Tragic, Unholy, Willies

**Dreadnought** Battleship

**Dream(er), Dream home, Dreamland, Dreamlike, Dream state, Dreamy** Absent, Aisling, Alchera, Alcheringa, Ambitious, American, Aspire, Castle, Desire, Drowsy, Dwalm, Dwa(u)m, Fantast, Fantasy, Faraway, Fugue, Gerontius, Idealise, Illusion, Imagine, Joseph, Languor, Long, Mare, Mirth, Moon, Morpheus, Muse, Nightmare, On(e)iric, Pensive, Phantasmagoria, Phantom, Pipe, → **REVERIE**, Rêveur, Romantic, Somniate, Spac(e)y, Stargazer, Surreal, Sweven, Trance, Trauma, Utopia, Vague, Vision, Walter Mitty, Wet, Wool-gathering

**Dreary** Bleak, Desolate, Dismal, Doleful, Dreich, Dull, Gloom, Gousty, Gray, Grey, Oorie, Ourie, Owrie, Sad
**Dredge(r)** Caster, Deepen, Scoop, Unearth
**Dreg(s)** Bottom, Draff, Dunder, F(a)eces, Fecula, Gr(e)aves, Grounds, Lag(s), Lees, Legge, Mother, Mud, Residue, Riffraff, Scaff, Sediment, Settlings, Silt, Snuff, Ullage
**Dreikanter** Ventifact
**Drench** Dowse, Sluice, Sluse, Soak, Souse, Steep, Submerge
**Dress(ing), Dressed** Accoutre, Adjust, Adorn, Aguise, Align, Apparel, Array, Attire, Attrap, Bandage, Bandoline, Bedizen, Boast, Boun, Bowne, Brilliantine, Busk, Cataplasm, Charpie, Clad, →**CLOTHING**, Comb, Compost, Compress, Curry, Dandify, Decent, Deck, Deshabille, Dight, Dink, Dizen, Doll, Don, Dub, Dubbin, Elastoplast®, Endue, Enrobe, Fertiliser, French, Frou-frou, Full, Gamgee tissue, Garnish, Gauze, Get-up, Girt, Graith, Guise, Gussy up, →**HABIT**, Immantle, Italian, Jaconet, Ketchup, Line, Lint, Livery, Marie Rose, Mayonnaise, Mineral, Mulch, Oil, Ore, Pad, Patch, Plaster, Pledget, Pomade, Potash, Poultice, Prank, Preen, Prepare, Ranch, Rational, Ray, Rehearsal, Rémoulade, Rig, Russian, Rybat, Salad, Salad cream, Sartorial, Sauce, Scutch, Seloso, Sterile, Stupe, Tartare, Taw, Tenue, Tew, Thousand Island, Tiff, Tire, Toilet, Tonic, Treat, Trick, Trim, Vinaigrette, Wear, Well, Wig, Window, Yclad, Ycled

## DRESSES

**3 letters:** Fig, Mob, Rag, Tog, Top
**4 letters:** Coat, Drag, Garb, Gown, Kilt, Maxi, Midi, Robe, Sack, Sari, Suit, Tent, Toga, Tuck, Vest
**5 letters:** Ao dai, Brale, Cimar, Court, Cymar, Fancy, Frock, Ihram, Kanga, Mufti, Power, Samfu, Shift, Shirt, Simar, Smock, Stole, Symar, Talar, Tasar, Tunic
**6 letters:** Bodice, Caftan, Chimer, Corset, Dirndl, Dolman, Empire, Finery, Kaftan, Khanga, Kimono, Kirtle, Muu-muu, Peplos, Russet, Sacque, Samfoo, Sarong, Sheath, Tartan, Tussah, Tusser, Tuxedo
**7 letters:** Bloomer, Blouson, Corsage, Costume, Dashiki, Evening, Gymslip, Kitenge, Lounger, Morning, Plumage, Raiment, Simarre, Subfusc, Subfusk, Tea-gown, Tussore, Uniform, Wedding
**8 letters:** Academic, Black-tie, Cocktail, Fatigues, Flamenco, Highland, National, Pantsuit, Pinafore, Princess, Sundress, White-tie
**9 letters:** Cheongsam, Clericals, Farandine, Polonaise, Separates, Trollopee
**10 letters:** Farrandine, Ferrandine, Shirtwaist
**11 letters:** Dolly Varden, Farthingale
**12 letters:** Merveilleuse, Princess line, Shirtwaister
**13 letters:** Mother Hubbard

**Dressage** Caracol(e), Demivolt(e), Manège, Passade, Passage, Pesade, Piaffe

▷ **Dressed up, Dressing** *may indicate* an anagram

**Dresser** Adze, Almery, Bureau, Chest, Costumier, Couturier, Deuddarn, Dior, Lady's
maid, Lair, Lowboy, Sideboard, Transvestite, Tridarn, Welsh

**Dressing-gown** Bathrobe, Negligée, Peignoir

**Dressing-room** Apodyterium, Vestiary, Vestry

**Dressmaker** Costumier, Dorcas, Modiste, Seamstress, Tailor

**Drew** Steeld, Stelled

**Dribble** Drip, Drivel, Drop, Seep, Slaver, Slobber, Slop, Trickle

**Dried fish** Bum(m)alo, Bummaloti, Haberdine, Speld(r)in(g), Stockfish

▶ **Dried fruit** *see* **DRY FRUIT**

**Drift(ing), Drifter** Becalmed, Continental, Crab, Cruise, Current, Digress, Diluvium,
Drumlin, Float, Flow, Genetic, Heap, Impulse, Longshore, Maunder, Natant, Nomad,
North Atlantic, Plankton, Purport, Rorke, Sail, Slide, Swan, Tendence, Tendency,
→**TENOR**, Tramp, Waft, Wander, Zooplankton

**Drill(ing)** Appraisal, Archimedean, Auger, Bore, Burr, Close order, Directional, Educate,
Exercise, Fire, Form, Hammer, Inculcate, Jackhammer, Jerks, Kelly, Kerb, Monkey,
Pack, PE, Pierce, Pneumatic, Power, PT, Radial, Reamer, Ridge, Rig, Rimer, Rock, Rope,
Seeder, Sow, Square-bashing, Teach, Train, Twill, Twist, Usage, Wildcat

**Drink(er), Drinking, Drunk(enness)** AA, Absorb, Adrian Quist, Alkie, Alky, A pip
out, Babalas, Bacchian, Barfly, Bat, Bender, Beverage, Bev(v)y, Bezzle, Bib(ite), Bibber,
Binge, Birl(e), Bladdered, Bland, Blatted, Blind, Blitzed, Bloat, Blootered, Blotto, Bombed,
Boose, Booze, Borachio, Bosky, Bottled, Bouse, Bowl, Bowsey, Bowsie, Bracer, Brahms
and Liszt, Brandy, Brew, Bucket, Bumper, Burst, CAMRA, Capernoitie, Cap(p)ernoity,
Carafe, Carousal, Cat-lap, Chaser, Chota peg, Compotation, →**CORDIAL**, Corked, Cot
case, Crapulent, Crapulous, Cratur, Crocked, Cuppa, Cut, Demitasse, Digestif, Dionysian,
Dipsomaniac, Discombobulated, Double, Down, Drain, Draught, Drop, Ebriate, Ebriose,
Elixir, Energy, Entire, Eye-opener, Feni, Feny, Finger, Fleein', Flush, Flying, Fou, Fuddle-cap,
Fuddled, Full, Glug, Gnat's piss, Grog, Half-cut, Half-seas-over, Happy, Heart-starter,
Heavy wet, High, Hobnob, Hogshead, Honkers, Hooker, Hophead, Imbibe, In-cups,
Indulge, Infusion, Inhaust, Inked, In liquor, Insulse, Intemperate, Irrigate, Ivresse, Jag,
Jakey, Jar, Juice, Juicehead, Kaylied, Knock back, Lager lout, Langered, Lap, Legless,
Lethean, Libation, →**LIQUOR**, Lit, Loaded, Lord, Lower, Lush(y), Maggoty, Mallemaroking,
Maltworm, Maudlin, Mellow, Merry, Methomania, Methysis, Mixer, Moon-eyed,
Moony, Mops and brooms, Mortal, Mug, Mullered, Neck, Nog(gin), Obfuscated, Ocean,
Oenomania, Oiled, On, One, Oppignorate, Overshot, Paid, Paint, Paralytic, Partake,
Particular, Peg, Pickled, Pick-me-up, Pie-eyed, Pint(a), Piss-artist, Pissed, Pisshead,
Pisspot, Piss-up, Pixil(l)ated, Pledge, Plonk(o), Potation, Poteen, Potion, Primed, Quaff,
Quencher, Quickie, Rat-arsed, Ratted, Refreshment, Roaring, Rolling, Rotten, Round,
Rouse, Rumfustian, Rummer, St Martin's evil, Screamer, Screwed, Sea, Shebeen, Shicker,
Shotover, Silenus, Sink, Sip(ple), Skinned, Slake, Slewed, Sloshed, Slued, Slug, Slurp,
Smashed, Smoothie, Snort, Soak, Soused, Sozzled, Sponge, Spongy, Spunge, Squiffy,
Steaming, Stewed, Stimulant, Stinko, Stocious, Stoned, Stonkered, Stotious, Stukkend,
Stuporous, Sucker, Suckle, Suiplap, Sup, Swacked, Swallow, Swig, Swill, Tank, Tanked up,
Tape, Temulence, Tiddl(e)y, Tiff, Tift, Tight, Tincture, Tipper, Tipple, Tipsy, Tope, Toss,
Tossicated, Tost, Tot, Two-pot, Two-pot screamer, Under the weather, Upsey Dutch,
Up the pole, Usual, Wash, Wat, Wauch, Waught, Well away, Well-oiled, Wet, Whiffled,
Williewaught, Winebag, Wine bibber, Wino, Wish-wash, Woozy, Wrecked, Zonked

## DRINKS

| 2 *letters:* | 3 *letters:* | Bub | Dop |
|---|---|---|---|
| It | Ale | Cha | Fap |
| | Ava | Cup | Gin |

G&T
Hom
Kir
L&P
Mum
Pop
Red
Rum
Rye
Sec
Tea
Vin

**4 letters:**
Arak
Asti
Beer
Bock
Bull
Cava
Chai
Chug
Coke®
Flip
Half
Hock
Homa
Kava
Kola
Malt
Marc
Mate
Mead
Mild
Nipa
Ouzo
Port
Purl
Rack
Raki
Rosé
Sack
Sake
Saki
Soda
Soft
Soma
Sour
Sura
Tass
Tent
Wine
Yill

**5 letters:**
Assai
Bingo
Bombo
Bumbo
Cider
Cocoa
Copus
Crush
Doris
Float
Glogg
Haoma
Hogan
Hooch
Joram
Jorum
Julep
Kefir
Kelty
Kvass
Lager
Lassi
Mâcon
Malwa
Mauby
Meath
Medoc
Meths
Mobby
Moppy
Morat
Mosel
Mulse
Nappy
Negus
Pekoe
Pepsi®
Perry
Pimms
Polly
Pombe
Punch
Rakee
Rakia
Rumbo
Rummy
Sarsa
Sarza
Shake
Short
Shrub
Skink
Sling

Smile
Stout
Toddy
Tonic
Totty
Turps
Twist
Vodka
White
Xeres

**6 letters:**
Amrita
Apozem
Arrack
Bishop
Bitter
Bubbly
Burton
Busera
Cassis
Caudle
Cauker
Chasse
Claret
Coffee
Cognac
Cooler
Cooper
Doctor
Eggnog
Enzian
Frappe
Geneva
Gimlet
Grappa
Graves
Gutrot
Hootch
Kalied
Keltie
Kephir
Kirsch
Kumiss
Kümmel
Maotai
Meathe
Mescal
Mickey
Mobbie
Muscat
Nectar
Obarni
Old Tom

Oolong
Orgeat
Oulong
Oxymel
Pastis
Pernod®
Plotty
Porter
Posset
Pulque
Red-eye
Rickey
Rotgut
Saloop
Samshu
Scoosh
Shandy
Sherry
Skoosh
Smiler
Squash
Stingo
Strega
Strunt
Taffia
Tisane
Waragi
Whisky
Yaqona
Zythum

**7 letters:**
Absinth
Akvavit
Alcopop
Amoroso
Aniseed
Aquavit
Bacardi®
Bastard
Bitters
Cachaca
Campari®
Caribou
Catawba
Chablis
Chianti
Cobbler
Curaçao
Curaçoa
Daquiri
Eggflip
Fairish
Fustian

Gin fizz
Guarana
Instant
Italian
Koumiss
Limeade
Madeira
Malmsey
Marsala
Martini
Mineral
Nobbler
Oenomel
Oloroso
Orvieto
Persico
Philter
Philtre
Pilsner
Pink gin
Plottie
Quetsch
Ratafia
Reviver
Rosiner
Rosolio
Samshoo
Sangria
Sazerac
Screech
Scrumpy
Sherbet
Sherris
Sloe gin
Snifter
Soda pop
Stengah
Swizzle
Tequila
Tio Pepe®
Wassail
Whiskey

**8 letters:**
Absinthe
Aleberry
Ambrosia
Anisette
Aperitif
Armagnac
Babbelas
Bordeaux
Brown cow

Burgundy
Calvados
Champers
Charneco
Ciderkin
Club soda
Coca-cola®
Cocktail
Cold duck
Daiquiri
Dog's nose
Dubonnet®
Eau de vie
Geropiga
Gin sling
Gluhwein
Highball
Hollands
Homebrew
Hydromel
Lemonade
Light ale
Log juice
Mahogany
Nepenthe
Nightcap
Persicot
Pilsener
Pinotage
Ragmaker
Red biddy
Regmaker
Resinata
Resinate
Rice beer
Riesling
Root beer
Rosoglio
Saketini
Sangaree
Schnapps
Skokiaan
Snowball
Spritzer
Spumante
Switchel
Tequilla
Vermouth
Witblits

**9 letters:**
Applejack
Aqua libra®

Aqua vitae
Ayahuasca
Ayahuasco
Badminton
Buck's fizz
Burnt sack
Calabogus
Champagne
Chocolate
Claret cup
Cream soda
Cuba libre
Eccoccino
Febrifuge
Firewater
Ginger ale
Ginger pop
Grenadine
Hippocras
Lambswool
Manhattan
Metheglin
Milk punch
Milkshake
Mint julep
Mirabelle
Moonshine
Moose milk
Nipperkin
Orangeade
Pinot noir
Refresher
Rosa-solis
Sauternes
Slivovica
Slivovitz
Snakebite
Soda water
Stiffener
Sundowner
The cratur
Whisky mac

**10 letters:**
Blackstone
Bloody Mary
Buttermilk
Chartreuse®
Ginger beer
Ginger wine
Hippomanes
Hop bitters
Lolly water

Maraschino
Mickey Finn
Mochaccino
Piña colada
Poppy water
Pousse-café
Shandygaff
Tanglefoot
Tom Collins

**11 letters:**
Aguardiente
Amontillado
Athole Brose
Benedictine
Bitter lemon
Black and tan
Black velvet
Boiler-maker
Doch-an-doris
Frappuccino
Half-and-half
Niersteiner
Screwdriver
Soapolallie
Tom and Jerry
Whiskey sour
Whisky toddy

**12 letters:**
Bloody Caesar
Brandy pawnee
Cherry bounce
Deoch-an-doris
Doch-an-dorach
Doch-an-doruis
Humpty-dumpty
Jimmy Woodser
Marcobrunner
Old-fashioned
Sarsaparilla

**13 letters:**
Cobbler's punch
Deoch-an-doruis
Ginger cordial
Liebfraumilch
Mild and bitter
Planter's punch
Prairie oyster

**14 letters:**
John Barleycorn

**Drink store** Cellar, Grog shop

**Drip** Bore, Dew-drop, Dribble, Drop, Gloop, Gutter, IV, Leak, Milksop, Post-nasal, Saline, Seep, Splatter, Stillicide, Trickle, Wimp

**Dripstone** Label, Larmier

**Drive(r), Driving, Drive out** AA, Acquired, Actuate, Amber gambler, Ambition, Aroint, Automatic, Backseat, Banish, Battue, Beetle, Belt, Bullocky, Ca', Cabby, Campaign, Carman, Carriage, Chain, Charioteer, Chauffeur, Coachee, Coachy, Coact, Coerce, Countershaft, Crankshaft, Crew, Crowd, Designated, Disk, Dislodge, Dr, Drover, Drum, Dynamic, Economy, Eject, Emboss, Energy, Enew, Enforce, Engine, Exorcise, Expatriate, Faze, Feeze, Ferret, Fire, Firk, Flash, Flexible, Fluid, Force, Four-stroke, Four-wheel, Front-wheel, Fuel, Gadsman, Goad, Golfer, Hack, Hammer, Haste, Heard, Helmsman, Herd, Hie, Hish, Hiss, Hoon, Hoosh, Hot-rod, Hoy, Hunt, Hurl, Hydrostatic, Impact, Impel, Impetus, Impinge, Impulse, Instinct, Jarvey, Jehu, Jockey, Juggernaut, Key(ring), Lash, Libido, Locoman, Lunge, Mahout, Make, Mall, M(a)cGuffin, Micro, Miz(z)en, Motor, Motorman, Muleteer, Offensive, Oomph, Overland, Peg, Penetrate, Phase, Piston, Pocket, Power, Powertrain, P-plater, Propel, Puncher, Push, Put, Quill, RAC, Rack, Rally(e), Ram, Rear-wheel, Rebut, Reinsman, Ride, Road, Roadhog, Run, Sales, Scorch, Screw, Scud, Senna, Sex, Shepherd, Shoo, Shover, Spank, Spin, Spur, Start, Steer, Stroke, Sumpter-horse, Sunday, Sweep, Swift, Tape, Task-master, Teamster, Tee, Test, Testosterone, Thrust, Thumb, Toad, Toe and heel, Tool, Tootle, Torrential, Trot, Trucker, Truckie, Truckman, Tup, Turn, Twoccer, Two-stroke, Urge, Urgence, USB, Vetturino, Wagoner, Warp, Whist, Wood, Wreak, Zest

**Drivel** Balderdash, Blather, Blether(skate), Drip, Drool, Humbug, Maunder, Nonsense, Pabulum, Pap, Rot, Salivate, Slabber, Slaver, Trash

**Driving club** AA, Iron, RAC

**Drizzle** Dew, Drow, Haze, Mist, Mizzle, Roke, Scotch mist, Scouther, Scowther, Serein, Skiffle, Smir(r), Smur, Spit, Sprinkle

**Droll** Amusing, Bizarre, Comic, Funny, Humorous, Jocular, Queer, Waggish

**Drone** Air strike, Bagpipe, Bee, Buzz, Dog-bee, Doodle, Dor(r), Drant, Draunt, Drawl, Grind, Hanger-on, Hooray Henry, Hum, Idler, Parasite, Reedy, Tamboura, Thrum, Windbag, Wooster

**Drool** Dribble, Drivel, Gibber, Salivate, Slaver, Spawl

**Droop(y), Drooping** Cernuous, Decline, Epinasty, Flabby, Flaccid, Flag, Jowled, Languish, Lill, Limp, Lob, Loll, Lop, Nutate, Oorie, Ourie, Owrie, Peak, Pendulous, Ptosis, →SAG, Slink, Slouch, Slump, Weeping, Welk(e), Wilt, Wither

**Drop(s), Dropping** Acid, Airlift, Apraxia, Asperge, Bag, Bead, Beres, Blob, Butter, Cadence, Calve, Cascade, Cast, Chocolate, Cowpat, Dap, Decrease, Delayed, Descent, Deselect, Dew, Dink, Dip, Downturn, Drappie, Drib(let), Ean, Ease, Ebb, Escarp(ment), Fall, Floor, Flop, Fruit, Fumet, Gallows, Glob(ule), Gout(te), Guano, Gutta, Guttate, Ha-ha, Heel-tap, Instil, Knockout, Land, Lapse, Minim, Modicum, Muff, Mute, Omit, Pilot, Plap, Plonk, Plop, Plummet, Plump, Plunge, Plunk, Precepit, Precipice, (Prince) Rupert's, Rain, Relegate, Scat, Scrap, Scrub, Shed, Sip, Skat, Slurry, Spat, Spill, Splash, Spraint, Stilliform, Tass, Taste, Tear, Thud, Trapdoor, Turd, Virga, Wrist

**Drop-out** Beatnik, Hippie, Hippy

**Drop-shot** Dink

**Dropsy** Anasarca, Ascites, Edema, Oedema

**Dross** Chaff, Dirt, Dregs, Recrement, Scoria, Scorious, Scum, Sinter, Slack, Slag, Waste

**Drought** Dearth, Drouth, Lack, Thirst

**Drove(r)** Band, Crowd, Flock, Herd, Host, Masses, Mob, Overlander, Puncher

**Drown(ed), Drowning** Drench, Drent, Drook, Drouk, Engulf, Inundate, Noyade, Overcome, Sorrows, Submerge

**Drowse, Drowsiness, Drowsy** Blet, Comatose, Doze, Hypnagogic, Hypnopompic, Lethargic, Nap, Narcolepsy, Narcosis, Nod, Snooze, Somnolent

**Drub** Anoint, Thrash

**Drudge(ry)** Boswell, Devil, Dogsbody, Donkey-work, Fag, Grind, Hack, Hackwork, Hireling, Jackal, Johnson, Menial, Plod, Scrub, Slave(y), Snake, Spadework, Stooge, Sweat, Swink, Thraldom, Toil, Trauchle, Treadmill

**Drug(ged)** Acaricide, ACE inhibitor, Anorectic, Antabuse®, Antarthritic, Anti-depressant, Antimetabolite, Antipyrine, Antiviral, Bag, Barbiturate, Base, Blow, Blue devil, Bolus, Bomber, Boo, Botanical, Cathartic, Chalybeate, Cholagogue, Clofibrate, Clot buster, Contraceptive, Corrigent, Custom, Dadah, Deck, Depot, Depressant, Designer, DET, Diuretic, Dope, Dose, Downer, E, Ecbolic, Ecphractic, Elixir, Emmenagogue, Errhine, Euphoriant, Fantasy, Fertility, Fig, Galenical, Gateway, Gear, Generic, Hallucinogen, Hard, High, Hocus, Homeopathy, Hypnotic, Immunosuppressant, Indinavir, Joint, Knockout drops, Largactic, Lifestyle, Line, Load, Mainline, Medicine, Mercurial, Mind-expanding, Miracle, Modified release, Monged, Nervine, Nobble, Nootropic, Obstruent, OD, Opiate, Orphan, Painkiller, Paregoric, Parenteral, Peace, Pharmaceutics, Pharmacology, Pharmacopoeia, Poison, Popper, Prophylactic, Proprietary, Psychedelic, Psychoactive, Psychodelic, Purgative, Recreational, Scag, Sedate, Sedative, Shit, Shot, Sialogogue, Skin-pop, Smart, Snort, Soft, Soporific, Sorbefacient, Specific, Speedball, Spermicide, Spike, Stimulant, Stone(d), Street name, Stupefacient, Stupefy, Styptic, Substance, Sudorific, Suppressant, Synthetic, Toot, Tout, Tranquiliser, Truth, Upper, Vasoconstrictor, Vasodilator, Vermicide, Vermifuge, Weed, White stuff, Wonder, Wrap, Zeolitic, Zonked

---

## DRUGS

| | | | |
|---|---|---|---|
| **1 letter:** | Hash | Quina | Pituri |
| H | Hemp | Rutin | Prozac® |
| Q | Junk | Salep | Roofie |
| | Khat | Salop | Saloop |
| **3 letters:** | Leaf | Senna | Statin |
| AZT | Sida | Smack | Sulpha |
| Dex | Snow | Speed | Valium® |
| EPO | Soma | Splay | Viagra® |
| Eve | SSRI | Sugar | Zantac® |
| GHB | Tina | Sulfa | |
| Hop | Trip | Taxol | **7 letters:** |
| Ice | Whiz | Whizz | Alcohol |
| INH | | Zyban® | Aricept® |
| Kat | **5 letters:** | | Atabrin |
| Kif | Aloes | **6 letters:** | Atebrin® |
| LSD | Benny | Amulet | Botanic |
| PCP® | Bhang | Amytal® | Cascara |
| Qat | Candy | Ativan® | Charlie |
| STP | Coxib | Basuco | Churrus |
| Tab | Crank | Bindle | Cocaine |
| Tea | Dagga | Charas | Codeine |
| | Dexie | Curare | Damiana |
| **4 letters:** | Ganja | Dragée | Dapsone |
| Acid | Grass | Heroin | Diconal® |
| Adam | Hop-up | Inulin | Ecstasy |
| Aloe | Intal® | Joypop | Eserine |
| Ara-A | L-dopa | Lariam® | Eucaine |
| Bang | Meths | Mescla | Guarana |
| Bute | Mummy | Mummia | Hashish |
| Coca | Opium | Nubain® | Henbane |
| Dopa | Picra | Peyote | Hypnone |

Insulin
Jellies
Librium®
Metopon
Miltown®
Mogadon®
Morphia
Nurofen®
Pareira
Patulin
Quinine
Relenza®
Ritalin®
Seconal®
Septrin®
Seroxat®
Steroid
Suramin
Tacrine
Tamiflu
Trional
Triptan
Turpeth
Veronal®
Xenical®

**8 letters:**
Adjuvant
Ataraxic
Atenolol
Banthine
Benadryl®
Curarine
Diazepam
Doxapram
Fentanyl
Goofball
Hyoscine
Ketamine
Laetrile
Laudanum
Mersalyl
Mescalin
Methadon
Miticide
Moonrock
Morphine
Naloxone
Naproxen
Narcotic
Nembutal
Nepenthe
Nystatin
Orlistat

Oxytocic
Procaine
Psilocin
Quaalude®
Retrovir®
Rifampin
Roborant
Rohypnol®
Scopolia
Serevent®
Snowball
Special K
Tetronal
Thiazide
Varidase®
Veratrin
Viricide
Warfarin
Zerumbet
Zolpidem

**9 letters:**
Acyclovir
Analeptic
Angel-dust
Anovulant
Antrycide
Augmentin
Barbitone
Biguanide
Bupropion
Busulphan
Captopril
Carbachol
Celecoxib
Cisplatin
Clonidine
Clozapine
Compound Q
Corticoid
Cyclizine
Cytotoxin
Dexedrine®
Digitalis
Donepezil
Dramamine®
Electuary
Ephedrine
Foscarnet
Frusemide
Herceptin®
Ibuprofen
Iprindole
Isoniazid

Jaborandi
Largactil®
Lidocaine
Lorazepam
Marijuana
Meloxicam
Mepacrine
Methadone
Minoxidil
Modafinil
Mydriasis
Naltrexol
Novocaine
Nux vomica
Oxycodone
Oxycontin®
Paludrine®
Pethidine
Phenytoin
Practolol
Quinidine
Quinquina
Reserpine
Ritonavir
Synergist
Tamoxifen
Temazepam
Teniacide
Totaquine
Tretinoin
Trinitrum
Verapamil
Veratrine
Wobbly egg
Zanamivir

**10 letters:**
Acedapsone
Amantadine
Ampicillin
Antagonist
Anxiolytic
Atracurium
Belladonna
Benzedrine
Bufotenine
Cimetidine
Clomiphene
Clonazepam
Colestipol
Disulfiram
Endostatin®
Ergotamine
Etanercept

Ethambutol
Fluoxetine
Formestane
Furosemide
Gabapentim
Hiera-picra
Imipramine
Indapamide
Iproniazid
Irinotecan
Isoaminile
Isoniazide
Ivermectin
Ketoprofen
Lofexidine
Mandragora
Mefloquine
Methidrine
Methyldopa
Mickey Finn
Nalbuphine
Natorphine
Nifedipine
Nitrazepam
Olanzapine
Omeprazole®
Papaverine
Paroxetine
Penicillin
Pentaquine
Phenacetin
Prednisone
Primaquine
Probenecid
Psilocybin
Quinacrine
Raloxifine
Rifampicin
Salbutamol
Saquinavir
Selegiline
Stramonium
Sucralfate
Tacrolimus
Taeniacide
Taeniafuge
Vagotropic
Vancomycin
Worm-powder
Zidovudine

**11 letters:**
Acamprosate
Aldesleukin

Alendronate
Allopurinol
Aminobutene
Amoxycillin
Amphetamine
Anastrozole
Beta-blocker
Butazolidin®
Carbimazole
Carminative
Chloroquine
Ciclosporin
Cinnarizine
Clenbuterol
Clindamycin
Clopidogrel
Cyclosporin
Deserpidine
Distalgesic
Finasteride
Fluconazole
Fluvoxamine
Galantamine
Ganciclovir
Gemcitabene
Gemcitabine
Gemfibrozil
Haloperidol
Hydralazine
Idoxuridine
Indometacin
Ipratropium
Isoxsuprine
Magic bullet
Meprobamate
Methicillin
Neostigmine

Nikethamide
Ondansetron
Oseltamivir
Paracetamol
Pentamidine
Pentazocine
Phentermine
Pravastatin
Propranolol
Purple heart
Risperidone
Simvastatin
Succedaneum
Sulfadoxine
Terfenadine
Thalidomide
Theobromine
Tolbutamide
Tous-les-mois
Tropomyosin
Tumorigenic
Varenicline
Varicomycin
Vinblastine
Vincristine

*12 letters:*
Alpha-blocker
Anistreplace
Anthelmintic
Antiperiodic
Arsphenamine
Atorvastatin
Azathioprine
Capecitabine
Chlorambucil
Clomipramine

Clotrimazole
Cyclandelate
Dipyridamole
Eflornithine
Fenfluramine
Fluorouracil
Fluphenazine
Glanciclover
Gonadotropin
Guanethidine
Indomethacin
Isoprenaline
Isotretinoin
Lansoprazole
Mecamylamine
Methaqualone
Methotrexate
Mifepristone
Noradrenalin
Perphenazine
Physotigmine
Promethazine
Revastigmine
Salicylamide
Streptomycin
Sulfadiazine
Temozolomide
Trimethoprim

*13 letters:*
Amitriptyline
Anthelminthic
Antihistamine
Carbamazepine
Depressometer
Flunitrazepam
Materia medica

Metronidazole
Nitroglycerin
Nortriptyline
Penicillamine
Phencyclidine
Pyrimethamine
Spectinomycin
Sulfadimidine
Sulfathiazole
Sulphadiazine
Suxamethonium
Thiabendazole
Triamcinolone

*14 letters:*
Bendrofluozide
Bisphosphonate
Butyrhophenone
Combretastatin
Cyclobarbitone
Cyclopentolate
Cyproheptadine
Discodermolide
Flucloxacillin
Norethisterone
Pentobarbitone
Phenacyclidine
Phenobarbitone
Phenylbutazone
Spironolactone
Sulphanilamide

*15 letters:*
Sympathomimetic

*17 letters:*
Sildenafil citrate

---

**Druid** Gorsedd
**Drum(mer), Drumming, Drumbeat** Arête, Atabal, Barrel, Bass, Beatbox,
Bodhran, Bongo, Brake, Carousel, Chamade, Conga, Cylinder, Cymograph, Daiko,
Dash-wheel, Devil's tattoo, Dhol, Djembe, Dr, Droome, Drub, Ear, Flam, Gran cassa,
Kettle, Kymograph, Lambeg, Mridamgam, Mridang(a), Mridangam, Myringa, Naker,
Ngoma, Oil, Pan, Paradiddle, Percussion, Rappel, Rataplan, Reel, Rep, Ridge, Rigger,
Ringo, Roll, Ruff, Ruffle, Salesman, Side, Skin, Snare, Steel, Tabla, Tabour, Tabret, Taiko,
Tambour, Tambourin(e), Tam-tam, Tap, Tattoo, Tenor, Thrum, Timbal, Timp(ano),
Tom-tom, Touk, Traps, Traveller, Tuck, Tymbal, Tympanist, Tympano, Whim, Winding,
Work
**Drum-belly** Hoven
**Drumstick** Attorney, Leg, Rute, Tampon
▸ **Drunk(ard)** *see* DRINK(ER)
▷ **Drunken** *may indicate* an anagram
**Drupe(l)** Etaerio, Tryma
**Druse** Crystal

**Dry(ing), Drier, Dryness** Abstinent, Air, Anhydrous, Arefaction, Arefy, Arid, Blot, Bone, Brut, Corpse, Crine, Dehydrate, Demist, Desiccate, Detox, Drain, Droll, Dull, Eild, Ensear, Evaporate, Exsiccator, Firlot, Fork, Harmattan, Hasky, Hi(r)stie, Humidor, Hydrate, Jejune, Jerk, Juiceless, Khor, Kiln, Mummify, Oast, →**PARCH**, Plate rack, Prosaic, Reast, Rehab, Reist, Rizzar, Rizzer, Rizzor, Scarious, Sciroc, Scorch, Sear, Season, Sec(co), Seco, Sere, Shrivel, Siccative, Silical gel, Siroc(co), Sober, Sponge, Squeegee, Squeeze, Steme, Sterile, Stove, Ted, Teetotal, Thirsty, Thristy, Toasted, Torrefy, Torrid, Towel, Tribble, Trocken, TT, Tumbler, Turgid, Unsod, Unwatery, Watertight, Welt, Wilt, Win(n), Windrow, Wipe, Wither, Wizened, Wring, Wry, Xeransis, Xerasia, Xero(sis), Xeroderma, Xerophthalmia, Xerostomia

**Dryad** Eurydice, Nymph

**Dry fruit, Dried fruit** Achene, Akene, Cubeb, Currant, Mebos, Prune, Raisin, Samara, Silicula, Siliqua, Silique, Sultana

**Dry mouth** Xerostoma

**DT's** Dingbats, Hallucinations, Zooscopic

**Dual** Double, Twin, Twofold

**Dub** Array, →**CALL**, Ennoble, Entitle, Hete, Knight, Name

**Dubious** Arguable, Backscratching, Doubtful, Elliptic, Equivocal, Fishy, Fly-by-night, Hesitant, Iffy, Improbable, Left-handed, Questionable, Scepsis, Sceptical, Sesey, Sessa, →**SHADY**, Shifty, Shonky, Suspect, Touch and go, Trumped up, Unclear, Unlikely, Unsure

▷ **Dubious** *may indicate* an anagram

**Dubliner** Jackeen

**Duce** Leader, Musso(lini)

**Duchess** Anastasia, Camilla, Her Grace, Malfi, Peeress, Titled, Wife

**Duchy** Anhalt, Brabant, Brunswick, Cornwall, Dukedom, Franconia, Grand, Hesse, Holstein, Limburg, Lorraine, Luxembourg, Nassu, Normandy, Omnium, Realm, Savoy, Swabia, Valois, Westphalian

**Duck(ling), Ducked** Amphibian, Avoid, Aylesbury, Bald-pate, Bargander, Bathe, Bergander, Blob, Blue, Bluebill, Bob, Bombay, Broadbill, Bufflehead, Bum(m)alo, Burrow, Butterball, Canard, Canvasback, →**COUPLE OF DUCKS**, Dead, Dearie, Decoy, Dip, Diving, Dodge, Dodo, Douse, Drook, Drouk, Dunk(er), Eider, Elude, Enew, Escape, Evade, Ferruginous, Flapper, Gadwall, Garganey, Garrot, Golden-eye, Goosander, Greenhead, Hareld, Harlequin, Heads, Herald, Immerse, Indian runner, Jook, Jouk, King-pair, Lame, Long-tailed, Mallard, Mandarin, Muscovy, Musk, Nil, Nodding, Nun, O, Oldsquaw, Old Tom, Orpington, Paddling, Pair of spectacles, Palmated, Paradise, Pekin(g), Pintail, Plunge, Pochard, Poker, Putangitangi, Redhead, Ring-bill, Ruddy, Runner, Rush, St Cuthbert's, Scaup, Scoter, Sheld(d)uck, Shieldrake, Shirk, Shovel(l)er, Shun, Sitting, Smeath, Smee(th), Smew, Sord, Souse, Sowse, Spatula, Spirit, Sprigtail, Steamer, Surf(scoter), Teal, Team, Tufted, Tunker, Ugly, Velvet scoter, Whio, Whistling, Whitewing, Widgeon, Wigeon, Wild, Wood, Zero

**Duckbill** Ornithorhynchus, Platypus

**Duckwalk** Waddle

**Duckweed** Lemna

**Ducky** Sweet, Twee

**Duct** Bile, Canal(iculus), Channel, Conduit, Diffuser, Diffusor, Emunctory, Epididymus, Fistula, Flue, Gland, Lachrymal, Lacrimal, Laticifer, Lumen, Mesonephric, Pancreatic, Parotid, Passage, Pipe, Tear, Thoracic, Tube, Ureter, Vas deferens, Wolffian

**Dud** Bouncer, Failure, Flop, Non-starter, Shan(d), Stumer

**Dude** Cat, Clothes horse, Coxcomb, Dandy, Fop, Lair, Macaroni, Popinjay, Roy

**Dudgeon** Anger, Hilt, Huff, Pique

**Due(s)** Accrued, Adequate, Annates, Arrearage, Attributable, Claim, Debt, Deserts, Expected, Fit(ment), Forinsec, Geld, Heriot, Inheritance, Just, Lot, Mature, Needful, Offerings, Offload, Owing, Reddendo, Rent, Right, →**SUITABLE**, Thereanent, Toll, Tribute, Worthy

**Duel(list)** Delope, Mensur, Monomachy, Principal, Tilt

**Duenna** Chaperone, Dragon, Governess

**Duff** Bum, Bungle, Dough, Nelly, NG, Plum, Pudding, Rustle

**Duffer** Bungler, Rabbit, Shmo, Useless

**Dug** Pap, Ploughed, Teat, Titty, Udder

**Dugong** Halicore, Sea-cow, Sea-pig, Sirenian

**Dug-out** Abri, Canoe, Piragua, Pirogue, Shelter, Trench, Trough

**Duke(dom)** Albany, Alva, Chandos, Clarence, D, Duc, Ellington, Fist, Iron, Milan, Orsino, Peer, Prospero, Rohan, Wellington

**Dulcimer** Cembalo, Citole, Cymbalo, Santir, Sant(o)ur

**Dull(ard), Dullness** Anodyne, Anorak, Bald, Banal, Barren, Beef-witted, Besot, Blah, Bland, Blear, Blockish, Blunt, Boeotian, Boring, Cabbage, Cloudy, Colourless, Commonplace, Dead (and alive), Deadhead, Dense, Dim, Dinge, Dingy, Ditchwater, Doldrums, Dowf, Dowie, Drab, Drear, Dreich, Dry, Dunce, Faded, Fadeur, Flat, Fozy, Gray, Grey, Heavy, Hebetate, Hebetude, Himbo, Ho-hum, Humdrum, Illustrious, Insipid, Insulse, Jejune, Lacklustre, Lifeless, Log(y), Lowlight, Mat(t), Matte, Monochrome, Monotonous, Mopish, Mull, Mundane, Nondescript, Obtund, Obtuse, Opacity, Opiate, Ordinary, Overcast, Owlish, Pall, Pedestrian, Perstringe, Plodder, Podunk, Prosaic, Prose, Prosy, Rebate, Rust, Saddo, Slow, Solein, Sopite, Staid, Stick, Stodger, Stodgy, Stolid, Stuffy, Stultify, → **STUPID**, Sunless, Tame, Tarnish, Tedious, Ticky-tacky, Toneless, Torpor, Treadmill, Trite, Tubby, Unimaginative, Unresponsive, Vapid, Witless, Wonk, Wooden, Zoid

**Dumb(ness)** Alalia, Aphonic, Blonde, Crambo, Hobbididance, Inarticulate, Mute, Mutism, Shtum, Silent, Speechless, Stumm, Stupid, Thunderstruck

**Dumbfound(ed)** Amaze, Astound, Flabbergast, Floor, Stun, Stupefy, Stupent

**Dumb ox** Aquinas

**Dummy** Clot, Comforter, Copy, Effigy, Fathead, Flathead, Lummox, Mannequin, Mannikin, Meatball, Mock-up, Model, Pacifier, Quintain, Soother, Table, Teat, Waxwork

**Dump(ing), Dumps** Abandon, Ammunition, Blue, Core, Dejection, Dispirited, Ditch, Doldrums, Empty, Eyesore, Fly-tipping, Hole, Jettison, Jilt, Junk, Laystall, Mine, Offload, Pigsty, Scrap, Scrapyard, Screen, Shed, Shoot, Store(house), Thud, Tip, Toom, Unlade, Unload

**Dumpling(s)** Clootie, Dim sum, Dough(boy), Gnocchi, Gyoza, Knaidel, Knaidloch, Kneidlach, Knish, Kreplach, Matzoball, Norfolk, Perogi, Pi(e)rogi, Quenelle, Ribaude, Suet, Won ton

**Dumpy** Pudgy, Squat

**Dun** Annoy, Cow, Importune, Pester, → **SUE**, Tan

**Duncan** Isadora

**Dunce** Analphabet, Booby, Clod, Dolt, Donkey, Dullard, Fathead, Schmo, Schmuck, Schnook, Stupid

**Dune** Areg, Bar, Barchan(e), Bark(h)an, Erg, Sandbank, Seif, Star, Whaleback

**Dung(hill)** Album Graecum, Argol, Buffalo chips, Buttons, Chip, Cock, Coprolite, Cowpat, Droppings, Fewmet, Fumet, Fumiculous, Guano, Hing, Manure, Midden, Mixen, Mute, Night soil, Ordure, Puer, Pure, Scat, Scumber, Shairn, Shard, Sharn, Siege, Skat, Skummer, Sombrerite, Sombrero, Spawn brick, Spraint, Stercoraceous, Tath

**Dungarees** Overalls

**Dung-eating** Merdiverous

**Dungeon** Bastille, Cell, Confine, Donjon, Durance, Keep, Oubliette, Souterrain

**Dunk** Immerse, Sop, Steep, Submerge

**Dunnock** Accentor

**Duo** Couple, Pair, Twosome

**Dupe** Catspaw, Chiaus, Chouse, Cony, Cull(y), Delude, Easy game, Easy mark, Easy meat, Geck, Gull, Hoax, Hoodwink, Mug, Pawn, Pigeon, Plover, Sitter, Soft mark, Sucker, Swindle, → **TRICK**, Victim

**Duplex** Twofold

**Duplicate, Duplication, Duplicator** Clone, Copy, Counterpart, Cyclostyle, Double, Echo, Facsimile, Match, Ozalid®, Paginal, Replica, Reproduce, Roneo®, Spare, Spit(ting)

**Durable, Durability** Enduring, Eternal, Eterne, Hardy, Lasting, Permanent, Stamina, Stout, Tough

**Duralumin®** Y-alloy

**Duration** Extent, Lifetime, Limit, Period, Span, Timescale

**Duress** Coercion, Pressure, Restraint

**Durham** Palatine

**During** Amid, Dia-, For, In, Live, Over, Throughout, While, Whilst

**Dusk(y)** Dark, Dewfall, Dun, Eve, Eventide, Gloaming, Gloom, Half-light, Owl-light, Phaeic, Puliginous, Twilight, Umbrose

**Dust(y)** Arid, Ash, Bo(a)rt, Calima, Clean, Coom, Cosmic, Culm, Derris, Devil, Dicht, Duff, Earth, Fuss, Gold, Khak(i), Lemel, Limail, Limit, Lo(e)ss, Miller, Nebula, Pellum, Pollen, Pother, Pouder, Poudre, Powder, Pozz(u)olana, Pudder, Rouge, Sea, Seed, Shaitan, Slack, Springfield, Stour, Talc, Timescale, Volcanic, Wipe

▷ **Dusted** *may indicate* an anagram

**Duster** Cloth, Feather, Red, Talcum, Torchon

**Dustman** Doolittle, Garbo(logist), Refuse collector, Scaffie, Trashman

**Dust measure** Konimeter, Koniscope

**Dust-up** Fracas

**Dutch(man), Dutchwoman** Batavian, Boor, Butterbox, Cape, Courage, D(u), Double, Elm, Erasmus, Flying, Fri(e)sian, Frow, German, Kitchen, Knickerbocker, Meneer, Middle, Missis, Missus, Mynheer, Parnell shout, Patron, Pennsylvania, Sooterkin, Taal, Vrouw, Wife

**Dutiful, Duty** Active, Ahimsa, Allegiance, Attentive, Average, Blench, Bond, Charge, Corvee, Countervailing, Customs, Death, Debt, Deontology, Detail, Devoir, Docile, Drow, Due, Duplicand, End, Estate, Excise, Export, Fatigue, Feu, Filial, Function, Heriot, Homage, Import, Imposition, Impost, Incumbent, Lastage, Legacy, Likin, Mission, Mistery, Mystery, Obedient, Obligation, Octroi, Office, Onus, Pia, Picket, Pious, Point, Preferential, Prisage, Probate, Rota, Sentry-go, Shift, Stamp, Stillicide, Stint, Succession, Tariff, → **TASK**, Tax, Toll, Transit, Trap, Trow, Watch, Zabeta

**Duvet** Doona, Quilt

**Dwarf(ism)** Achondroplasia, Agate, Alberich, Andvari, Ateleiosis, Bashful, Belittle, Bes, Black, Bonsai, Brown, Doc, Dopey, Droich, Drow, Durgan, Elf, Gnome, Grumpy, Happy, Hobbit, Homuncule, Hop o' my thumb, Knurl, Laurin, Leetle, Little man, Man(n)ikin, → **MIDGET**, Mime, Minikin, Minim, Nanism, Nectabanus, Ni(e)belung, Nurl, Outshine, Overshadow, Pacolet, Pigmy, Pipsqueak, Pygmy, Red, Regin, Ront, Rumpelstiltskin, Runt, Skrimp, Sleepy, Sneezy, → **STUNT**, Tiddler, Titch, Tokoloshe, Tom Thumb, Toy, Troll, Trow, White

**Dwell(er), Dwelling** Abide, Aweto, Be, Bungalow, Cabin, Cell, Cot(tage), Descant, Discourse, Domicile, Habitation, Harp, Heteroscian, Hogan, House, Hut, Ice colours, Igloo, Laura, Lavra, Live, Lodge, Longhouse, Maison(n)ette, Mansion, Messuage, Midgard, Midgarth, Mithgarthr, Palafitte, Pied-à-terre, Place, Pueblo, Reside, Roof, Shanty, Single-end, Stress, Sty, Tenement, Tepee, Terramara, Tipi, Two-by-four, Weem, Wigwam, Won(ing), Wonning, Woon

**Dwindle** Decline, Diminish, Fade, Fail, Lessen, Peter, Shrink, Wane

**Dye(ing), Dyestuff, Dye-seller** Acid, Alkanet, Amaranth, Anil, Anthracene, Anthraquinone, Archil, Arnotto, Aweto, Azo(benzine), Azurine, Bat(t)ik, Benzidine, Brazil(e)in, Burnt umber, Camwood, Canthaxanthin, Carthamine, Catechin, Chay(a), Chica, Chicha, Chico, Choy, Cinnabar, Cobalt, Cochineal, Colour, Congo, Coomassie blue, Corkir, Crocein, Crotal, Crottle, Cudbear, Dinitrobenzene, Direct, Embrue, Engrain, Envermeil, Eosin, Flavin(e), Fluoxene, Fuchsin(e), Fustet, Fustic, Fustoc, Gambi(e)r, Gentian violet, Grain, Haematoxylin, Henna, Hue, Ice colours, Ikat, Imbrue, Imbue,

Incarnadine, Indamine, Indican, Indigo, Indigocarmine, Indigotin, Indirubin, Indoxyl, Indulin(e), Ingrain, Kalamkari, Kamala, Kermes, Kohl, Korkir, Lightfast, Madder, Magenta, Mauvein(e), Mauvin(e), Methyl violet, Murex, Myrobalan, Nigrosin(e), Orcein, Orchel(la), Orchil, Orseille, Para-red, Phenolphthalein, Phthalein, → **PIGMENT**, Ponceau, Primuline, Puccoon, Purple, Purpurin, Pyronine, Quercitron, Quinoline, Raddle, Resorcinol, Rhodamine, Rosanilin(e), Safranin(e), Salter, Shaya, → **STAIN**, Stilbene, Stone-rag, Stone-raw, Sumac(h), Sunfast, Tannin, Tartrazine, Tie-dye, Tinct, Tint, Tropaeolin, Trypan blue, Turmeric, Turnsole, Ultramarine, Valonia, Vat, Wald, Weld, Woad, Woald, Wold, Xanthium, Xylidine

▶ **Dying** *see* DIE(D)

**Dyke** Aboideau, Aboiteau, Bund, Devil's, → **DIKE**, Ditch, Gall, Offa's, Ring, Sea-wall

**Dynamic(s)** Ballistics, Ball of fire, Driving, Energetic, Forceful, Gogo, High-powered, Kinetics, Potent, Vibrant, Whizz kid

**Dynamite** Blast, Explode, Gelignite, Giant powder, TNT, Trotyl

**Dynamo** Alternator, Armature, Tiger

**Dynasty** Abbasid(e), Angevin, Bourbon, Capetian, Carolingian, Chen, Chin(g), Ch'ing, Chou, Era, Fatimid, Frankish, Gupta, Habsburg, Han, Hanoverian, Hapsburg, Holkar, Honan, House(hold), Hyksos, Khan, Manchu, Maurya, Merovingian, Ming, Omayyad, Osman, Pahlavi, Plantagenet, Ptolemy, Qajar, Q'in(g), Rameses, Romanov, Rule, Safavid, Saga, Sassanid, Seleucid, Seljuk, Shang, Song, Sui, Sung, Tai-ping, Tang, Tudor, Umayyad, Wei, Yi, Yuan, Zhou

**Dysentery** Amoebic, Bloody flux, Shigellosis

**Dysfunction** Kernicterus

**Dyslexia** Strephosymbolia

**Dyspeptic** Cacogastric

**Dysprosium** Dy

**Dystrophy** Duchenne's, Muscular

# Ee

**E** Boat, East, Echo, Energy, English, Spain

**Each** All, Apiece, A pop, Ea, → **EVERY**, Ilka, Per (capita), Respective, Severally

**Eager(ly)** Agog, Animated, Antsy, Ardent, Avid, Beaver, Bore, Bright-eyed, Dying, Earnest, Enthusiastic, Fain, Fervent, Fervid, Fidge, Frack, Game, Greedy, Gung-ho, Hot, Intent, → **KEEN**, Motivated, Perfervid, Prone, Race, Raring, Rath(e), Ready, Roost, Sharp-set, Sore, Spoiling, Thirsty, Toey, Wishing, Yare, Zealous

**Eagle(s)** Al(l)erion, Altair, American, Aquila, Bald, Bateleur, Berghaan, Bird, Convocation, Double, Eddy, Ensign, Erne, Ethon, Fish, Gier, Golden, Harpy, Hawk, Legal, Lettern, Nisus, Ossifrage, Sea, Spread, Tawny, Wedge-tailed

**Ear(drum), Ear problem** Ant(i)helix, Attention, Audience, Auricle, Barotitis, Cauliflower, Cochlea, Concha, Conchitis, Deafness, Dionysius, Dolichotus, External, Glue, Hearing, Helix, Icker, Incus, Inner, Internal, Jenkins, Kieselguhr, Labyrinth, Labyrinthitis, Listen, Locusta, Lop, Lug, Malleus, Middle, Modiolus, Myringa, Myringitis, Nubbin, Otalgia, Otalgy, Otic, Otocyst, Paracusis, Paramastoid, Parotic, Pavilion, Periotic, Petrosal, Phonic, Pinna, Presby(a)c(o)usis, Prootic, Shell-like, Souse, Spike, Spikelet, Stapes, Thick, Tin, Tragus, Tympanitis, Utricle

**Earl(dom)** Belted, Leofric, Mar, Peer, Sandwich

**Earlier, Early** Above, Ago, Ahead, Alsoon, AM, Antelucan, Auld, Betimes, Cockcrow, Daybreak, Ere-now, Ex, Foretaste, Germinal, In advance, Incipient, Matin, Matutinal, Or, Preceding, Precocious, Precursor, Prehistoric, Premature, Premie, Prevernal, Previous, Primeur, Primeval, Primordial, Prior, Rath(e), Rath(e)ripe, Rear, Rough, Rudimentary, Small hours, Soon, Timely, Tim(e)ous

▷ **Early** *may indicate* belonging to an earl

**Early man** Eoanthropus, Flat-earther

▷ **Early stages of** *may indicate* first one or two letters of the words following

**Earmark** Allocate, Bag, Book, Characteristic, Flag, → **RESERVE**, Tag, Target, Ticket

**Earn(er), Earning(s)** Achieve, Addle, Breadwinner, Cash cow, Curdle, Deserts, Deserve, Digerati, Ern, Gain, Income, Invisible, Make, Merit, O.T.E., Pay packet, Reap, Rennet, Runnet, Win, Yearn

**Earnest(ly)** Agood, Ardent, Arle(s)(-penny), Deposit, Devout, Fervent, Imprest, Intent, Promise, Serious, Sincere, Token, Wistly, Zealous

**Earring** Drop, Ear bob, Hoop, Keeper, Pendant, Sleeper, Snap, Stud

**Earshot** Hail, Hearing

**Earth(y), Earthling** Alkaline, Antichthon, Art, Asthenosphere, Barbados, Brown, Bury, Capricorn, Carnal, Clay, Cloam, Clod, Cologne, Craton, Den, Diatomite, Dirt, Drey, Dust, E, Eard, Edaphic, Epigene, Foxhole, Friable, Fuller's, Gaea, Gaia, Gault, Ge, Globe, Green, Ground, Heavy, Horst, Infusiorial, Kadi, Lair, Leaf-mould, Lemnian, Lithosphere, Loam, Malm, Mankind, Mantle, Mools, Mould, Mouls, Papa, Pise, Planet, Podsol, Rabelaisian, Racy, Rare, Raunchy, Red, Samian, Seat, Sett, Sod, → **SOIL**, Subsoil, Surcharge, Taurus, Telluric, Tellus, Terra, Terrain, Terramara, Terran, Terra rossa, Terrene, Tilth, Topsoil, Tripoli, Virgo, Wad, Yellow, Ye(a)rd, Yird

**Earth-bound** Chthonian, Mundane

**Earthenware** Arretine, Biscuit, Ceramic, Creamware, Crock(ery), Delf(t), Della-robbia, Delph, Faience, Figuline, Graniteware, Maiolica, Majolica, Pig, Pot, Queen's ware, Raku, Samian, Sanitary, Terracotta, Terra sigillata

**Earthman** Terran

**Earthquake** Aftershock, Aseismic, Bradyseism, Foreshock, Mercalli, Richter, Seism, Shake, Shock, Temblor, Trembler, Tremor

**Earth's surface** Sal, Sial

**Earthwork** Agger, Bank, Cursus, Gazon, Parados, Rampart, Remblai, Vallum

**Earthworm** Angledug, Angletwitch, Angleworm, Annelid, Bait, Night-crawler

**Earwig** Clipshear(s), Eavesdrop, Forkit-tail, Forky-tail, Listen

**Ease, Easing, Easygoing** Alleviate, Assuage, Carefree, Clear, Clover, Comfort, Content, Defuse, Deregulate, Détente, Easy-osy, Facility, Genial, Hands down, Informal, Laid back, Lax, Lenify, Mellow, Mid(dy), Mitigate, Otiosity, Palliate, Peace, Pococurante, Quiet, Relieve, Reposal, Repose, Resilient, Soothe

**East(erly), Eastward** Anglia, Asia, Chevet, E, Eassel, Eassil, Eothen, Eurus, Far, Levant, Middle, Morning-land, Near, Orient, Ost, Sunrise

**Easter** Festival, Island, Pace, Pasch(al), Pasque

**Eastern(er), Eastern language** Asian, Kolarian, Oriental, Ostman, Virginian

**East European** Lettic, Slovene

**East German** Ossi

**Easy, Easily** ABC, Amenable, Approachable, Breeze, Cakewalk, Carefree, Child's play, Cinch, Comfortable, Comfy, Crispy, Cushy, Degage, Doddle, Doss, Duck soup, Eath(e), Effortless, Ethe, Facile, Fluent, Free, Gift, Glib, Gravy train, Hands down, Independent, Jammy, Kid's stuff, Lax, Light, Midshipman, Natural, Nimps, No-brainer, Oldster, Picnic, Pie, Plain sailing, Pushover, Romp, Scoosh, Simple, Sitter, Skoosh, Snap, Snotty, Soft, Spoon fed, Tolerant, Turkey shoot, User-friendly, Walk-over, Well, Yare

▷ **Easy** *may indicate* an anagram

**Easy-care** Non-iron

**Eat(able), Eater, Eating** Bite, Bolt, Break bread, Champ, Chomp, Chop, Commensal, Consume, Corrode, Cram, Devour, Dig in, Dine, Edible, Edite, Endew, Endue, Erode, Esculent, Etch, Fare, Feast, →**FEED**, Fret, Gastronome, Gnaw, Go, Gobble, Gourmand, Gourmet, Graze, Grub, Guts, Have, Hoe into, Hog, Hyperorexia, Hyperphagia, Ingest, Manducate, Mess, Muckamuck, Munch, Nosh, Nutritive, Omnivore, Partake, Phagomania, Phagophobia, Predate, Refect, Scoff, Slurp, Snack, Stuff, Sup, Swallow, Syssitia, Take, Taste, Trencherman, Trophesy, Tuck away, Tuck into, Twist, Whale

**Eating problem** Anorexia, Bulimia, Cachexia

**Eavesdrop(per)** Cowan, Detectophone, Earwig, Icicle, Listen, Overhear, Pry, Snoop, Spy, Stillicide, Tab-hang, Tap, Wiretap

**Ebb(ing)** Abate, Decline, Recede, Refluent, Sink, →**WANE**

**Ebonite** Hard rubber

**Ebony** Black, Cocus-wood, Coromandel, Hebenon, Jamaican

**Ebullient** Brash, Effervescent, Effusive, Exuberant, Fervid, Gushing

**Eccentric** Abnormal, Antic, Atypical, Cam, Card, Character, Crackpot, Crank, Curious, Daffy, Dag, Deviant, Dingbat, Ditsy, Ditzy, E, Farouche, Fay, Fey, Fie, Flaky, Freak, Fruitcake, Geek, Gonzo, Iffish, Irregular, Kinky, Kook(y), Loon, Madcap, Mattoid, Monstre sacré, Nutcase, Nutter, Odd(ball), Offbeat, Off-centre, Off the rails, Off the wall, Original, Outré, →**PECULIAR**, Phantasime, Pixil(l)ated, Queer, Quirky, Quiz, Rake, Raky, Recondite, Rum, Scatty, Screwball, Screwy, Spac(e)y, Squirrelly, Wack(y), W(h)acko, Way-out, Weird(o), Weirdie

▷ **Eccentric** *may indicate* an anagram

**Ecclesiast(es), Ecclesiasticus, Ecclesiastical** Abbé, Clergyman, Clerical, Lector, Secular, Sir(ach), Theologian, The Preacher, Vatican

**Echelon** Formation

**Echinoderm** Asteroidea, Basket-star, Brittle-star, Comatulid, Crinoid, Heart-urchin, Ophiurid, Sea-egg, Sea-lily, Sea-urchin, Starfish

**Echo, Echoing, Echo-sounder** Angel, Answer, Ditto, E, Fathometer®, Imitate, Iterate, Mirror, Phonocamptic, Rebound, Recreate, Repeat, Repercussion, Reply,

Resemble, Resonant, → **RESOUND**, Respeak, Reverb(erate), Revoice, Ring, Rote, Sonar, Tape

**Eclat** Flourish, Glory, Prestige, Renown

**Eclectic** Babist, Broad, Complex, Diverse, Liberal

**Eclipse** Annular, Block, Cloud, Deliquium, Excel, Hide, Lunar, Obscure, Occultation, Outjump, Outmatch, Outshine, Outweigh, Overshadow, Partial, Penumbra, Rahu, Solar, Total, Transcend, Upstage

**Eclogue** Bucolic, Idyll, Pastoral

**Eco-community** Seral

**Eco-friendly** Biodegradable

**Ecology, Ecological** Bionomics, Seral

**Economise** Budget, Conserve, Eke, Entrench, Finance, Husband, Intrench, Pinch, Retrench, Scrimp, Skimp, Spare, → **STINT**, Whip the cat

**Economist** Angell, Bentham, Chrematist, Cole, Coombs, Friedman, Galbraith, Giffen, Keynes, Laffer, Malthus, Marginalist, Marx, Meade, Mill, Monetarist, Nugget, Pareto, Physiocrat, Rathenau, Ricardo, Schumacher, Schumpeter, Singh, Smith, Tinbergen, Tobin, Toynbee, Veblen, Webb, Weber

**Economy, Economic(al), Economics** Agflation, Agronomy, Autarky, Black, Brevity, Careful, Cheap rate, Chrematistics, Cliometrics, Command, Conversation, Cut, Dismal science, Domestic, Frugal, Hidden, Home, Husband(ry), Informal, Knowledge, Lean-burn, LSE, Market, Mitumba, Mixed, Neat, New, Parsimony, Planned, Political, Provident, Pusser's logic, Retrenchment, Shadow, Shoestring, Siege, Sparing, Stagflation, Stakeholder, Stumpflation, Supply-side, Thrift, Tiger, Token, Welfare

**Ecstasy, Ecstatic** Bliss, Delight, Delirious, Dove, E, Enrapt, Exultant, Joy, Liquid, Lyrical, Nympholepsy, Pythic, Rapture, Rhapsodic, Sent, Trance, Transport, Utopia

**Ecumenical** Catholic, Lateran

**Eczema** Pompholyx, Salt rheum, Tetter

**Edda** Elder, Legend, Prose, Younger

**Eddo** Taro

**Eddy** Backset, Curl, Duane, Gurge, Maelstrom, Nelson, Pirl, Purl, Rotor, Sousehole, Swelchie, Swirl, Vortex, Weel, Well, Whirlpool, Wiel

**Eden** Bliss, Fall, Heaven, Paradise, PM, Utopia

**Edentate** Ant-eater, Armadillo, Peba, Sloth, Tatou, Xenarthra

**Edge, Edging, Edgy** Advantage, Arris, Bleeding, Border, Bordure, Brim, Brink, Brittle, Brown, Burr, Chamfer, Chimb, Chime, Chine, Coaming, Costa, Creston, Cutting, Dag, Deckle, Ease, End, Flange, Flounce, Frill, Fringe, Frontier, Furbelow, Gunnel, Gunwale, Hem, Hone, Inch, Inside, Kerb, Knife, Leading, Leech, Limb(ate), Limbus, Limit, Lip, List, Lute, Marge(nt), Margin, Neckline, Nosing, Orle, Outside, Parapet, Periphery, Picot, Pikadell, Piping, Rand, Reeding, Rim, Rund, Rymme, Selvage, Selvedge, Side, Sidle, Skirt, Strand, Surbed, Tense, Tomium, Trailing, Trim, Twitchy, Tyre, Uneasy, Uptight, Verge, Wear, Whet

▶ **Edible** *see* **EAT(ABLE)**

**Edict(s)** Ban, Bull, Clementines, Decree, Decretal, Extravagantes, Fatwa, Firman, Interim, Irade, Nantes, Notice, Order, Pragmatic, Proclamation, Pronouncement, Pronunciamento, Rescript, Sext, Ukase

**Edifice** Booth, Building, Lighthouse, Structure, Stupa, Superstructure

**Edify(ing), Edification** Didactic, Enlighten(ment), Instruct, Teach

**Edinburgh** Auld Reekie

**Edit(or), Editorial** Abridge, Amend, Article, City, Copy (read), Cut, Dele, Desk, Dramaturg(e), Ed, Emend, Expurgate, Footsteps, Garble, Leader, Manipulate, Overseer, Prepare, Recense, Redact, Revise, Reword, Rewrite, Seaman, Tweak

▷ **Edited** *may indicate* an anagram

**Edith** Sitwell

**Edition** Aldine, Bulldog, Bullpup, Ed, Extra, Facsimile, Ghost, Hexapla(r), Impression, Issue, Library, Limited, Number, Omnibus, Re-issue, Trade, Variorum, Version

**Edmond, Edmund** Burke, Gosse, Ironside(s), Rostand, Spenser
**Educate(d)** Academic, Baboo, Babu, Cultured, Enlighten, Evolué, Informed, Instruct, Learned, Lettered, Literati, Nourish, Noursle, Nousell, Nousle, Nurture, Nuzzle, Polymath, Preppy, Progressive, Scholarly, School, →TEACH, Train, Yuppie
**Education(alist)** Adult, Basic, B.Ed, Classical, Conductive, D.Ed, Didactics, Estyn, Froebel, Further, Heurism, Learning, Literate, Mainstream, Montessori, Oxbridge, Paedotrophy, Pedagogue, Pestalozzi, Physical, Piarist, Primary, Schooling, Special, Steiner, Teacher, Tertiary, Tutelage, Upbringing
**Educe** Elicit, Evoke, Extract, Infer
**Edward** Confessor, Ed, Elder, Lear, Longshanks, Martyr, Ned, Ted
**Eel** Conger, Congo, Electric, Elver, Glass, Grig, Gulper, Gunnel, Hagfish, Kingklip, Lamper, Lamprey, Lant, Launce, Leptocephalus, Moray, Murray, Murr(e)y, Olm, Paste, Salt, Sand(ling), Silver belly, Snake, Snig, Spitchcock, Tuna, Vinegar, Wheat, Wolf
**Eerie** Creepy, Spooky, Uncanny, Unked, Weird
**Efface** Cancel, Delete, Dislimn, →ERASE, Expunge, Obliterate
**Effect(s), Effective(ness), Effectual** Able, Achieve, Acid trip, Acting, Alienation, Auger, Babinski, Bags, Barkhausen, Barnstorming, Belongings, Binaural, Bit, Bite, Bohr, Border, Border edge, Bricolage, Butterfly, Bystander, Causal, C(h)erenkov, Chromakey, Coanda, Coastline, Competent, Compton, Consequence, Coriolis, Do, Domino, Doppler, Dr(y)ice, Eclat, Edge, Efficacious, Electro-optical, Enact, End, Enforce, Estate, Execute, Experimenter, Fet, Foley, Fringe, Functional, Fungibles, Furnishing(s), Fx, Gangbuster, Gear, General, Goods, Greenhouse, Ground, Gunn, Hall, Halo, Hangover, Hawthorne, Home, Horns and halo, Impact, Implement(al), Impression, Influence, Introgenic, Josephson, Joule(-Thomson), Kerr, Keystone, Knock-on, Magneto-optical, Magnus, Meissner, Militate, Moire, Mossbauer, Mutual, Neat, Net, Nifty, Nisi, Notch, Operant, Optical, Outcome, Ovshinsky, Oxygen, Parallax, Peltier, Perficient, Personal, Phi, Photoelectric, Photovoltaic, Piezoelectric, Piezomagnetic, Pinch, Placebo, Pogo, Position, Potent, Practical, Prevailing, Primary, Promulgate, Punchy, Raman, Ratchet, Reaction, Recency, Redound, Repercussion, →RESULT, Ripple, Schottky, Seebeck, Shadow, Shore, Side, Skin, Slash-dot, Sound, Sovereign, Special, Spectrum, Spin-off, Stage, Stark, Striking, Stroop, Submarine, Subsidiary, Tableau, Teeth, Telling, Therapeutic, Thermoelectric, Thomson, Toxic, Tunnel, Tyndall, Upshot, Valid, Viable, Virtual, Well, Whammy, Win, Withdrawal, Work, Zeeman
**Effeminate** Airtsy-mairtsy, Camp, Carpet-knight, Carpet-monger, Cissy, Coddle, Cookie-pusher, Dildo, Epicene, Female, Gussie, Jessie, Milksop, Minty, (Miss) Nancy, Molly(coddle), Nellie, Nelly, Pansy, Panty-waist, Poovy, Pretty, Prissy, Punce, Queenie, Sissy, Swish, Tender, Tenderling, Tonk, Unman, Wuss(y)
**Effervescence, Effervescent** Bubbling, Ebullient, Fizz, Frizzante, Pétillant, Soda
▷ **Effervescent** *may indicate an anagram*
**Effete** Camp, Epicene, Epigon(e)
**Efficacious, Efficacy** Effective, Operative, Potent, Sovereign, Valid, Value
**Efficiency, Efficient** Able, Businesslike, Capable, Competent, Current, Despatch, Ecological, Electrode, Ergonomics, Expeditious, High-powered, Lean, Luminous, Productivity, Quantum, Smart, Spectral luminous, Streamlined, Strong, Thermal, Volumetric
**Effigy** Buddha, Figure, Guy, Idol, Image, Statua, Statue
**Efflorescence** Bloom, Blossom, Reh
**Effluence, Effluent, Effluvia, Effluvium** Air, Aura, Billabong, Discharge, Fume, Gas, Halitus, Miasma, Odour, Outflow, Outrush, Reek
**Effort** Achievement, All-out, Attempt, Best, Conatus, Concerted, Damnedest, Drive, Endeavour, Essay, Exertion, Fit, Frame, Hardscrabble, Herculean, Joint, Labour, Legwork, Molimen, Nisus, Pains, Pull, Rally, Shy, Spurt, Stab, Strain, Struggle, Team, Travail, →TRY, Work, Yo
**Effortless** Lenis, Low-impact, Low maintenance, Spoonfed
**Effrontery** Audacity, Backchat, Brass, Cheek, Face, Gall, Neck, Nerve, Temerity

**Effulgent** Bright, Radiant, Shining

**Effuse, Effusion, Effusive** Emanate, Exuberant, Exude, Gush, Lyric, Ode, Outburst, Prattle, Rhapsody, Sanies, Screed, Spill

**Eft** After

**Eg** As, Example

**Egalitarian** Democratic, Equaliser

**Egest** Eliminate, Evacuate, Excrete, Void

**Egg(s), Egg on** Abet, Addled, Benedict, Berry, Blow, Bomb, Caviar(e), Cavier, Chalaza, Cheer, Cleidoic, Clutch, Cockney, Collop, Coral, Curate's, Darning, Easter, Edge, Encourage, Fabergé, Fetus, Flyblow, Foetus, Free-range, Glair(e), Goad, Goog, Graine, Hoy, Incite, Instigate, Isolecithal, Layings, Mine, Nest, Nidamentum, Nit, Oocyte, Oophoron, Ostrich, Ova, Ovum, Pace, Pasch, Plover's, Prairie oyster, Press, Prod, Raun, Roe, Rumble-tumble, Scotch, Scrambled, Seed, Setting, Spat, Spawn, Spur(ne), Tar(re), Tempt, Thunder, Tooth, Tread(le), Urge, Whore's, Wind, Yelk, Yolk, Zygote

**Egg-case** Eggshell, Pod

**Egghead** Brainbox, Don, Highbrow, Intellectual, Mensa, Pedant

**Eggnog** Flip

**Egg-plant** Aubergine, Brinjal

**Egg-producer** Gametophyte, Hen, Ovipositor

**Egg-shaped** Obovate, Oval, Ovate

**Eggshell** China, Fragile

**Egg-white** Albumen, Glair

**Ego(ism), Egoist, Egotist(ical)** Che, Conceit, I, Narcissism, Not-I, Pride, Self, Self-seeker, Solipsism, Tin god, Ubu, Vanity

**Egocentric** Solipsistic

**Egregious** Eminent, Flagrant, Glaring, Shocking

**Egret** Snowy

**Egypt(ian), Egyptologist** Arab, Cairene, Carter, Cheops, Chephren, Cleopatra, Copt(ic), ET, Gippo, Goshen, Gyppo, Imhotep, Nasser, Nefertiti, Nilote, Nitrian, Old Kingdom, Osiris, Potiphar, Ptolemy, Rameses, Syene, Theban, UAR, Wafd, Wog

**Eiderdown** Bedspread, Duvet, Quilt

**Eight(h), Eighth day** Acht, Byte, Crew, Cube, Isis, Middle, Nundine, Oars, Octa, Octad, Octal, Octant, Octastrophic, Octave, Octet, Octonary, Octuor, Ogdoad, Okta, Ottava, Ure, Utas

**Eighteen** Majority

**Eighty** Fourscore, R

**Einsteinium** Es

**Either** Also, Both, O(u)ther, Such

**Ejaculate** Blurt, Discharge, Emit, Exclaim

**Eject** Belch, Bounce, Defenestrate, Disgorge, Dismiss, Emit, Erupt, Evict, Expel, Oust, Propel, Spew, Spit, Spue, Turf out, Vent, Void

**Eke** Augment, Eche, Enlarge, Husband, Supplement

**Elaborate** Baroque, Creation, Detail, Develop, Dressy, Embroider, Enlarge, Evolve, Fancy, Flesh out, Florid, Imago, Improve, Intricate, Magnificent, Opulent, Ornate, Rich, Spectacular, Stretch

**Elan** Dash, Drive, Esprit, → **FLAIR**, Gusto, Lotus, Panache, Spirit, Style, Vigour

**Elapse** Glide, Intervene, Overpass, Pass

**Elastic(ity)** Adaptable, Bungee, Buoyant, Dopplerite, Elater, Flexible, Give, Lithe(some), Resilient, Rubber, Scrunchie, Scrunchy, Spandex®, Springy, Stretchy, Tone, Tonus

**Elastomer** Adiprene®

**Elate(d), Elation** Cheer, Cock-a-hoop, Euphoric, Exalt, Exhilarate, Gladden, Hault, High, Lift, Rapture, Ruff(e), Uplift

**Elbow, Elbow tip** Akimbo, Ancon, Angle, Bender, Cubital, Hustle, Joint, Jolt, Jostle, Justle, Kimbo, Noop, Nudge, Olecranon, Tennis

**Elbow room** Leeway
**El Cid** Diaz
**Elder(ly), Eldest** Ainé(e), Ancestor, Ancient, Bourtree, Chief, Classis, Coffin dodger, Eigne, Geriatric, Greying, Guru, Kaumatua, Kuia, OAP, Presbyter, → SENIOR, Sire, Susanna, Wallwort
**Eldorado** Ophir
**Eleanor(a)** Bron, Duse, Nora(h)
**Elect(ed), Election(eer), Elective, Elector(al)** Ballot, Choice, Choose, Chosen, Constituent, Co-opt, Eatanswill, Elite, General, Gerrymander, Hustings, In, Israelite, Khaki, Member, Off-year, Opt, Optional, Pick, PR, Predetermine, Primary, Psephology, Rectorial, Return, Select, Stump, Vote in
**Electric** Live
**Electrical discharge** Corposant, Ion, Zwitterion
**Electrical instrument** Battery, Charger, Galvaniser, Magneto, Mains, Resistor, Rheostat, Shoe
**Electrical unit** Amp(ere), Coulomb, Farad, Kilowatt, Ohm, Volt, Watt
**Electric eye** Pec
**Electrician** Gaffer, Lineman, Ohm, Siemens, Sparks, Tesla
**Electricity** Galvanism, Grid, HT, Inductance, Juice, Mains, Negative, Positive, Power, Static, Utility, Vitreous
**Electrify** Astonish, Fire, Galvanise, Startle, Stir, Thrill
**Electrode** Anode, Cathode, Dynode, Element, Photocathode
**Electrolyte** Ampholyte
**Electromagnet(ic)** Abampere, Armature, Oersted, Solenoid, Weber
**Electron(ic), Electronics, Electronic device** Cooper pairs, E-book, Exciton, FET, Fly-by-wire, Linac, Lone pair, Martenot, Mole(cular), Polaron, Possum®, Quantum, Smart, Tetrode, Thermionics, Valence, Valency
**Elegance, Elegant** Artistic, Bijou, Chic, Chichi, Classy, Concinnity, Dainty, Daynt, Debonair, Dressy, Fancy, Feat, Finesse, Gainly, Galant, Grace, Jimp, Luxurious, Natty, Neat, Poise, Polished, Recherché, Refined, Ritzy, → SMART, Soigné(e), Style, Suave, Svelte, Swish, Tall, Tasteful, Urbane
**Elegy** Dirge, Lament, Poem
**Element(s), Elementary** Abcee, Abecedarian, Absey, Barebones, Chromosome, → COMPONENT, Detail, → ESSENCE, Essential, Ether, Factor, Feature, Fuel, Heating, Hot-plate, Ideal, Identity, Insertion, Logical, M(a)cGuffin, Milieu, Non-metal, Peltier, Pixel, Primary, Principle, Radio, Rare earth, Rudimental, Sieve, Simple, Simplex, Stabial, Strand, Superheavy, Trace(r), Tramp, Transition, Transuranic, Weather

## ELEMENTS

**3 letters:**
Air
Tin (Sn)

**4 letters:**
Atom
Fire
Gold (Au)
Iron (Fe)
Lead (Pb)
Neon (Ne)
Ylem
Zinc (Zn)

**5 letters:**
Alloy
Argon (Ar)
Boron (B)
Earth
Morph(eme)
Niton
Radon (Rn)
Terra
Water
Xenon (Xe)

**6 letters:**
Barium (Ba)

Carbon (C)
Cerium (Ce)
Cesium
Cobalt (Co)
Copper (Cu)
Curium (Cm)
Erbium (Er)
Helium (He)
Indium (In)
Iodine (I)
Nickel (Ni)
Osmium (Os)
Oxygen (O)
Radium (Ra)

Silver (Ag)
Sodium (Na)

**7 letters:**
Arsenic (As)
Bismuth (Bi)
Bohrium (Bh)
Bromine (Br)
Cadmium (Cd)
Caesium (Cs)
Calcium (Ca)
Dubnium (Db)
Fermium (Fm)
Gallium (Ga)

Hafnium (Hf)
Hahnium (Hn)
Halogen
Hassium (Hs)
Holmium (Ho)
Iridium (Ir)
Isotope
Krypton (Kr)
Lithium (Li)
Mercury (Hg)
Natrium
Niobium (Nb)
Rhenium (Re)
Rhodium (Rh)
Silicon (Si)
Sulphur (S)
Terbium (Tb)
Thorium (Th)
Thulium (Tm)
Uranide
Uranium (U)
Wolfram
Yttrium (Y)

Chromium (Cr)
Columbic
Didymium
Europium (Eu)
Fluorine (F)
Francium (Fr)
Hydrogen (H)
Illinium
Inchoate
Lutetium (Lu)
Masurium
Nebulium
Nitrogen (N)
Nobelium (No)
Platinum (Pt)
Polonium (Po)
Rubidium (Rb)
Samarium (Sm)
Scandium (Sc)
Selenium (Se)
Tantalum (Ta)
Thallium (Tl)
Titanium (Ti)
Tungsten (W)
Vanadium (V)

Berkelium (Bk)
Beryllium (Be)
Brimstone
Columbium (Cb)
Flerovium (Fl)
Germanium (Ge)
Joliotium
Lanthanum (La)
Magnesium (Mg)
Manganese (Mn)
Metalloid
Neodymium (Nd)
Neptunium (Np)
Palladium (Pd)
Plutonium (Pu)
Potassium (K)
Ruthenium (Ru)
Strontian
Strontium (Sr)
Tellurium (Te)
Virginium
Ytterbium (Yb)
Zirconium (Zr)

Molybdenum (Mo)
Phlogiston
Phosphorus (P)
Promethium (Pm)
Seaborgium (Sg)
Technetium (Tc)

**11 letters:**
Californium (Cf)
Copernicium (Cn)
Einsteinium (Es)
Livermorium (Lv)
Mendelevium (Md)
Quicksilver
Roentgenium (Rg)

**12 letters:**
Darmstadtium
Kurchatovium
Nielsbohrium
Praseodymium (Pr)
Protactinium (Pa)

**13 letters:**
Rutherfordium (Rf)
Transactinide
Unnilquadium
(Unq)

**8 letters:**
Actinide
Actinium (Ac)
Antimony (Sb)
Astatine (At)
Chlorine (Cl)

**9 letters:**
Alabamine
Aluminium (Al)
Americium (Am)

**10 letters:**
Dysprosium (D)
Gadolinium (Gd)
Lanthanide
Lawrencium (Lr)
Meitnerium (Mt)

---

**Elephant(ine)** African, Babar, Bull, Calf, Cow, Hathi, Indian, Jumbo, Kheda, Mammoth, Mastodon, Oliphant, Pachyderm, Pad, Pink, Proboscidean, Rogue, Stegodon, Subungulata, Trumpeter, Tusker, White

**Elephant-headed** Ganesa

**Elephant's ears** Begonia

**Elevate(d), Elevation, Elevator** Aerial, Agger, Aggrandise, Attitude, Aweight, Bank, Cheer, Colliculus, El, Eminence, Ennoble, Euphuism, Foothill, Glabella, Grain, Haute, Heighten, Hoist, Jack, Lift, Lob, Lofty, Machan, Montic(u)le, Monticulus, Pitch, Promote, →RAISE, Random, Relievo, Ridge, Rise, Steeve, Sublimate, Up(lift), Uplying, Upraise, Wallclimber

**Eleven** Elf, Hendeca-, Legs, O, Side, Tail-ender, Team, XI

**Elf(in), Elves** Alfar, Chiricaune, Dobbie, Dobby, Fairy, Fey, Fie, Goblin, Imp, Kobold, Ouph, Pigwiggen, Pixie, Ribhus, Sprite, Urchin

**Elicit** Evoke, Extract, Toase, Toaze, Tose, Toze

**Eligible** Available, Catch, Fit, Nubile, Parti, Qualified, Worthy

**Eliminate, Elimination** Cull, Cure, Deep-six, Delete, Discard, Exclude, Execute, Extirpate, Heat, Knock out, Liquidate, Omit, Preclude, Purge, Red-line, Rid, Separate, Slay, Void, Weed out, Zap

**Elision** Apocope, Synal(o)epha, Syncope

**Elite** Best, Choice, Crachach, Crack, →CREAM, Crème (de la crème), Egalitarian, Elect, Flower, Gentry, Liberal, Meritocracy, Plutocracy, Ton, Top drawer, Twelve pitch, U, Zaibatsu

**Elixir** Amrita, Arcanum, Bufo, Cordial, Cure-all, Daffy, Essence, Medicine, Panacea, Philosopher's stone, Quintessence, Tinct

**Elizabeth** Bess(ie), Gloriana, Oriano

**Elk** Deer, Gang, Irish, Moose

**Elkoshite** Nahum

**Ellipse, Elliptic** Conic, Oblong, Oval

**Elm** Dutch, Nettle-tree, Rock, Slippery, Wahoo, Weeping, Wich, Winged, Wych

**Elmer** Gantry

**Elongate** Extend, Lengthen, Protract, Stretch

**Elope** Abscond, Decamp

**Eloquence, Eloquent** Articulate, Blarney stone, Demosthenic, Facundity, Fluent, Honey-tongued, Oracy, Oratory, Rhetoric, Silver-tongued, Speaking, Vocal

**Else(where)** Absent, Alibi, Aliunde, Et al, Other

**Elucidate** Explain, Expose, Interpret, Simplify

**Elude, Elusion, Elusive** Avoid, Dodge, Eel, Escape, → EVADE, Evasive, Foil, Intangible, Jink, Pimpernel, Sliddery, Slippy, Subt(i)le, Will o' the wisp

▸ **Elves** *see* ELF(IN)

**Elysium** Tir-nan-Og

**Em** Mut(ton), Pica

**Emaciated, Emaciation** Atrophy, Erasmus, Gaunt, Haggard, Lean, Skeleton, Skinny, Sweeny, Tabid, Thin, Wanthriven, Wasted

**Email** Flame, Online, Spam, Spim

**Emanate, Emanation** Arise, Aura, Derive, Discharge, Ectoplasm, Exude, Issue, Miasma, Radiate, Spring

**Emancipate(d), Emancipation** Catholic, Deliver, Forisfamiliate, Free, → LIBERATE, Manumission, Uhuru

**Emasculate** Bobbitt, Castrate, Debilitate, Evirate, Geld, Unsex

**Embalm** Anele, Anoint, Cere, Mummify, Preserve

**Embankment** Berm, Bund, Causeway, Dam, Dyke, Earthwork, Levee, Mattress, Mound, Rampart, Remblai, Sconce, Staith(e), Stopbank, Terreplein

**Embargo** → BAN, Blockade, Boycott, Edict, Restraint

**Embark** Begin, Board, Enter, Inship, Launch, Sail

**Embarrass(ed), Embarrassing, Embarrassment** Abash, Ablush, Ashamed, Awkward, Barro, Besti, Buttock-clenching, Chagrin, Cheap, Colour, Crimson, Cringe-making, Cringe-worthy, Disconcert, Discountenance, Encumber, Gêne, Haw, Mess, Mortify, Plethora, Pose, Predicament, Scundered, Scunnered, Shame, Sheepish, Squirming, Straitened, Toe-curling, Tongue-tied, Upset, Whoopsie, Writhing

▷ **Embarrassed** *may indicate* an anagram

**Embassy** Chancery, Consulate, Embassade, Legation, Mission

**Embed(ded)** Fix, Immerse, Implant, Inlaid, Set

**Embellish(ed), Embellishment** Adorn, Beautify, Bedeck, Curlicue, Deck, Decór(ate), Dress, Embroider, Enrich, Fioritura, Frill, Garnish, Garniture, Grace note, Melisma(ta), Mordent, → ORNAMENT, Ornate, Overwrought, Prank, Prettify, Rel(l)ish, Roulade, Story, Turn, Twist

**Ember(s)** Ash, Cinder, Clinker, Gleed

**Embezzle(ment)** Defalcate, Malversation, Misappropriate, Peculate, Purloin, Shoulder, → STEAL

**Embitter(ed)** Acerbate, Aggravate, Enfested, Exacerbate, Fester, Malevolent, Rankle, Sour

**Emblem(atic)** Badge, Bear, Colophon, Daffodil, Device, Figure, Fleur-de-lis, Golp(e), Hammer and sickle, Ichthys, Impresa, Insignia, Kikumon, Leek, Lis, Logo, Maple leaf, Mon, Oak, Pip, Rose, Roundel, Shamrock, Sign, Spear-thistle, → SYMBOL, Tau-cross, Thistle, Token, Totem(ic), Triskelion, Wattle, Wheel

**Embody, Embodied, Embodiment** Epitome, Fuse, Impanation, Incarnation, Incorporate, Personify, Quintessence, Version

**Embolism** Clot, Infarct

**Embosom(ed)** In gremio

**Emboss(ed)** Adorn, Chase, Cloqué, Engrave, Matelassé, Pounce, Raise, Repoussé, Toreutic

**Embrace(d)** Abrazo, Accolade, Arm, Bear hug, Canoodle, Clasp, Clinch, Clip, Coll, Complect, Comprise, Cuddle, Embosom, Encircle, Enclasp, Enclose, Enfold, Enlacement, Envelop, Espouse, Fold, Grab, Grip, Halse, Haulst, Hause, Hesp, Hug, Imbrast, Inarm, Inclasp, Inclip, Include, Inlace, Kiss, Lasso, Neck, Overarch, Press, Snog, Snug(gle), Stemme, Twine, Welcome, Wrap

▷ **Embraces, Embracing** *may indicate* a hidden word

**Embrocate, Embrocation** Anoint, Arnica, Liniment, Lotion

**Embroider(y)** Add, Appliqué, Arpillera, Arrasene, Assisi, Battalia-pie, Braid, Brede, Colour, Couching, Crewellery, Crewel-work, Cross-stitch, Cutwork, Drawn threadwork, Embellish, Exaggerate, Eyelet, Fag(g)oting, Fancywork, Featherstitch, Filet, Framework, Gros point, Handiwork, Knotting, Lace(t), Laid work, Mola, Needlecraft, Needlepoint, Needlework, Open-work, Opus anglicanum, Orfray, Ornament, Orphrey, Orris, Petit point, Pinwork, Pulled threadwork, Purl, Queen-stitch, Sampler, Sew, Smocking, Spider-wheel, Stitch, Stitchery, Stumpwork, Tambour, Tent, Wrap, Zari

**Embroideress** Mimi

**Embroil** Confuse, Entangle, Involve, Trouble

**Embryo(nic), Embryologist** Anlage, Archenteron, Blastocyst, Blastospore, Blastula, Conceptus, Egg, Epicotyl, Fo(e)tus, Gastrula, Germ, Mesoblast, Morula, Nepionic, Neurula, Origin, Rudiment, Undeveloped, Wolff

**Emend** Adjust, Alter, Edit, Reform

**Emerald** Beryl, Gem, Green, Oriental, Smaragd, Uralian

**Emerge(ncy), Emerging** Anadyomene, Arise, Craunch, Crise, Crisis, Crunch, Debouch, Eclose, Emanate, Enation, Erupt, Exigency, Flashpoint, Hard-shoulder, Issue, Lash-up, Last-ditch, Loom, Need, Outcrop, Pinch, SOS, Spare, Spring, Stand-by, Stand-in, Strait, Surface

▷ **Emerge from** *may indicate* an anagram or a hidden word

**Emeritus** Retired

**Emerson** Waldo

**Emetic** Apomorphine, Cacoon, Evacuant, Ipecac(uanha), Puke, Sanguinaria, Stavesacre, Tartar, Vomitory

**Emigrant, Emigration, Émigré** Chozrim, Colonist, Exile, Italiot, Jordim, Redemptioner, Settler, When-we, Yordim

**Emile** Zola

**Emily** Ellis

**Eminence, Eminent** Alp, Altitude, Cardinal, Celebrity, Distinguished, Eximious, Grand, Greatness, Height, Hill, Hywel, Illustrious, Inselberg, Knoll, Light, Lion, Lofty, Luminary, Noble, →**NOTABLE**, Note, Palatine, Prominence, Red hat, Renown, Repute, Stardom, Stature, Tor, Trochanter, →**VIP**, Wallah

**Emirate** Abu Dhabi, Dubai, Qatar, Sharjah

**Emissary** Agent, Envoy, Legate, Marco Polo

**Emission, Emit** Discharge, Emanate, Field, Give, Issue, Radiate, Spallation, Thermionic, Utter, Vent

**Emmer** Amelcorn, Wheat

**Emollient** Paregoric

**Emolument** Income, Perk, Remuneration, Salary, Stipend, Tip, Wages

**Emotion(s), Emotional** Affection, Anger, Anoesis, Atmosphere, Breast, Cathartic, Chord, Ecstasy, Empathy, Excitable, Feeling, Flare up, Freak-out, Gushing, Gusty, Gut-wrenching, Hate, Heartstrings, Hippocampus, Histrionics, Hoo, Hysteria, Intense, Joy, Limbic, Maenad, Nostalgia, Nympholepsy, Passion, Poignant, Reins, Rhapsodic, Roar, Sensibility, Sensitive, Sentiment, Soulful, Spirit, Stormy, Teary, Theopathy, Torrid, Transport, Weepy, Wigged out

**Emotionless** Deadpan, Glassy

**Empathy** Identifying, Rapport, Rapprochement, Sympathy

**Emperor** Agramant(e), Akbar, Akihito, Antoninus, Augustus, Aurelian, Babur, Bao Dai, Barbarossa, Bonaparte, Caesar, Caligula, Caracalla, Charlemagne, Claudius, Commodus, Concerto, Constantine, Diocletian, Domitian, Ferdinand, Flavian, Gaius, Galba, Genghis Khan, Gratian, Great Mogul, Hadrian, Haile Selassie, Heraclius, Hirohito, HRE, Imp, Imperator, Inca, Jimmu, Justinian, Kaiser, Keasar, Kesar, King, Kubla(h) Khan, Manuel I Comnenus, Maximilian, Meiji, Menelik, Mikado, Ming, Mogul, Montezuma, Mpret, Napoleon, Negus, Nero, Nerva, Otho, Otto, Penguin, Peter the Great, Purple, Pu-yi, Rastafari, Rex, Rosco, Ruler, Severus, Shah Jahan, Shang, Sovereign, Sultan, Tenno, Theodore, Theodosius, Tiberius, Titus, Trajan, Tsar, Valens, Valentinian, Valerian, Vespasian, Vitellius, Wenceslaus

**Emphasis(e), Emphasize, Emphatic(ally)** Accent, Birr, Bold, Dramatise, Ek se, Forcible, Foreground, Forzando, Forzato, Hendiadys, Highlight, In spades, Italic, Marcato, Point up, Positive, Resounding, Risoluto, Sforzando, Sforzato, →**STRESS**, Sublineate, Underline, Underscore, Vehement

**Empire** Assyria, British, Byzantine, Celestial, Chain, Chinese, Domain, Empery, First, French, Georgia, Holy Roman, Indian, Kingdom, Latin, NY, Osmanli, Ottoman, Parthia, Persian, Principate, Realm, Reich, Roman, Russian, Second, Turkish, Western

**Empiricism** Positivism

**Emplacement** Battery, Platform

**Employ(ment)** Appoint, Bestow, Business, Calling, Designated, Engage, Exercitation, Hire, Occupy, Pay, Place, Portfolio, Post, Practice, Pursuit, Retain, Service, Shiftwork, Task, Trade, Usage, Use, Using, Utilise, Vocation

**Employee(s)** Barista, Casual, Clock-watcher, Earner, Factotum, Full-timer, Hand, Help, Hireling, Intrapreneur, Minion, Munchkin, Networker, Part-timer, Payroll, Pennyboy, Personnel, Rainmaker, Salariat, Servant, Staff, Staffer, Valet, Walla(h), Worker, Workforce, Workpeople

**Employer** Baas, Boss, Governor, Guv, Malik, Master, Melik, Padrone, Taskmaster, User

▷ **Employs** *may indicate* an anagram

**Emporium** Bazaar, Shop, Store

**Empower** Authorise, Enable, Entitle, License, Permit

**Empress** Eugenie, Josephine, Matilda, Messalina, Queen, Sultana, Tsarina, VIR

**Empty** Addle, Bare, Barren, Blank, Boss, Buzz, Claptrap, Clear, Deplete, Deserted, Devoid, Disembowel, Drain, Evacuate, Exhaust, Expel, Forsaken, Futile, Gousty, Gut, Hent, Hollow, Inane, Jejune, Lade, Lave, Meaningless, Null, Phrasy, Pump, Shallow, Space, Teem, Toom, Tum(e), Unfurnished, Uninhabited, Unlade, Unoccupied, Unpeople, Vacant, Vacate, Vacuous, Vain, Viduous, →**VOID**

▷ **Empty** *may indicate* an 'o' in the word or an anagram

**Empty-headed** Vain

**Emulate** Ape, Copy, Envy, Equal, Imitate, Match

**Emulsion** Nuclear, Pseudosolution, Tempera

**Enable** Authorise, Capacitate, Empower, Permit, Potentiate, Qualify, Sanction

**Enact** Adopt, Effect, Ordain, Personate, Portray

**Enamel(led), Enamel work** Aumail, Champlevé, Cloisonné, Della-robbia, Dentine, Fabergé, Ganoin(e), Lacquer, Mottled, Nail, Polish, Porcelain, Schwarzlot, Shippo, Smalto, Stoved, Vitreous

**Encampment** Bivouac, Castrametation, Douar, Dowar, Duar, Laager, Laer, Settlement

**Encase(d), Encasement** Box, Crate, Emboîtement, Encapsulate, Enclose, Obtect, Sheathe

**Enchant(ing), Enchanted, Enchantment** Bewitch, Captivate, Charm, Delight, Gramary(e), Incantation, Magic, Necromancy, Orphean, Rapt, Sirenize, Sorcery, Spellbind, Thrill

**Enchanter, Enchantress** Archimage, Archimago, Armida, Circe, Comus, Faerie, Fairy, Houri, Lorelei, Magician, Medea, Mermaid, Prospero, Reim-kennar, Sorcerer, Vivien, Witch

**Encircle(d), Encirclement** Belt, Besiege, Enclose, Encompass, Enlace, Entrold, Gird, Hoop (la), Inorb, Introld, Orbit, Pale, Ring, Siege, Stemme, →**SURROUND**, Wreathe

**Enclave** Cabinda, Ceuta, →**ENCLOSURE**, Melilla, Pocket, San Marino

**Enclose(d), Enclosing, Enclosure** Aviary, Bawn, Beset, Boma, Bower, Box, Bullring, Cage, Carol, Carrel, Case, Circumscribe, Cockpit, Common, Compound, Corral, Court, Cubicle, Embale, Embowel, Embower, Embrace, Enceinte, Enchase, Encircle, Enclave, Engirt, Enhearse, Enlock, Enshrine, Fence, Fold, Forecourt, Garth, Haggard, Haining, Haw, Hem, Henge, Hope, Impound, In, Incapsulate, Inchase, Include, Infibulate, Inhoop, Inlock, Insert, Interclude, Interlude, Lairage, Obvolute, Paddock, Pale, Parrock, Peel, Pele, Pen(t), Petavius, Pightle, Pin, Pinfold, Pit, Playpen, Plenum, Pocket, Radome, Rail, Rath, Recluse, Ree(d), Ring, Run, Saddling, Saleyard, Seal, Sekos, Sept, Seraglio, Serail, Several, Sin bin, Steeld, Stell, Stive, Stockade, Sty, →**SURROUND**, Tatt(ersall)s, Terrarium, Tine, Unsaddling, Vibarium, Ward, Winner's, Wrap, Yard, Zareba

**Encode** Cipher, Scramble

**Encomium** Eulogy, Praise, Sanction, Tribute

**Encompass** Bathe, Begird, Beset, Cover, Environ, Include, Surround

**Encore** Again, Agen, Ancora, Bis, Ditto, Do, Iterum, Leitmotiv, Recall, Repeat, Reprise

**Encounter** Battle, Brush, Close, Combat, Contend, Cope, Dogfight, Experience, Face, Hit, Incur, Intersect, Interview, →**MEET**, One-one, Rencontre, Ruffle, Skirmish, Tilt

**Encourage(ment), Encouraging** Abet, Acco(u)rage, Alley-oop, Animate, Attaboy, Barrack, Bolster, Boost, Brighten, Buck, Cheer, Chivy, Clap, Coax, Cohortative, Come-on, Comfort, Commend, Countenance, Dangle, Egg, Elate, Embolden, Empatron, Exhort, Fillip, Fire, Fortify, Foster, Fuel, Gee, Hearten, Heigh, Help, Heuristic, Hope, Hortatory, Incite, Inspire, Inspirit, Invite, Lift, Nourish, Nurture, Ole, Pat, Patronise, Pep talk, Proceleusmatic, Prod, Promote, Protreptic, Push, Reassure, Root, Seed, Spur, Steel, Stimulate, Stoke, Support, Tally-ho, Train, Upcheer, Uplift, Urge, Wean, Yay, Yo, Yoicks

**Encroach(ment)** Eat out, Impinge, Infringe, Inroad, Intrude, Invade, Overlap, Overstep, Poach, Purpresture, Trample, Trespass, Usurp

**Encrusted** Barnacled

**Encrypt(ion)** Coding, Public key

**Encumber, Encumbrance** Accloy, Burden, Charge, Clog, Dead weight, Deadwood, Dependent, Embarrass, →**HANDICAP**, Impede, Liability, Load, Obstruct, Saddle

**Encyclopaedia, Encyclopaedic** Compendium, Comprehensive, Diderot, Extensive, Universal, Vast

**End(ing)** Abolish, Abort, Abrogate, Abut, Aim, Ambition, Amen, Anus, Arse, Big, Bitter, Bourn(e), Butt, Cease, Cessation, Cesser, Climax, Close, Closure, Cloture, Coda, Conclude, Crust, Culminate, Curtain, Curtains, Cut off, Dead, Death, Decease, Demise, Denouement, Desinence, Desistance, Destroy, Determine, Dissolve, Domino, Effect, Envoi, Envoy, Epilogue, Exigent, Expire, Explicit, Extremity, Fade, Fatal, Fattrels, Feminine, Ferrule, Fin, Final(e), Fine, Finis, →**FINISH**, Finite, Gable, Grave, Heel, Ice, Ish, Izzard, Izzet, Kill, Kybosh, Lapse, Last, Let up, Limit, Little, Loose, Masculine, Mill, Nirvana, No side, Ort, Out, Outrance, Outro, Period, Peter, Pine, Point, Pole, Purpose, Quench, Receiving, Remnant, Rescind, Result, Roach, Round off, Runback, Scotch, Scrag, Shank, Slaughter, Sopite, Split, Sticky, Stub, Supernaculum, Surcease, Swansong, Tag, Tail, Tailpiece, Telesis, Telic, Telos, Term, Terminal, Terminate, Terminus, Thrum, Tip, Toe, Top, Ultimate, Up, Upshot, Utterance, West, Z

**Endanger** Hazard, Imperil, Periclitate, Risk, Threaten

**Endear(ing), Endearment** Adorable, Affection, Alannah, Asthore, Bach, Caress, Cariad, Chuck, Cute, Darling, Dear, Ducks, Ducky, Enamour, Hinny, Honey(-bunch), Honey-chile, Ingratiate, Jarta, Lovey, Luv, Machree, Mavourneen, Peat, Pet, Pigsnie, Pigsn(e)y, Sweetie, Sweet nothings

**Endeavour** Aim, Attempt, Effort, Enterprise, Essay, Morse, Strain, Strive, Struggle, Try, Venture

**Endemic** Local, Prevalent

**Endive** Escarole

**Endless** Aeonian, Continuous, Cornucopia, Ecaudate, Eternal, Eterne, Infinite, Interminable, Perpetual, Undated

▷ **Endlessly** *may indicate* a last letter missing

**End of the world** Doomsday, Ragnarok

**Endorse(ment)** Adopt, Affirm, Allonge, Approve, Assurance, Back, Certify, Confirmation, Docket, Initial, Okay, Oke, Ratify, Rubber stamp, Sanction, Second, Sign, Subscript, →**SUPPORT**, Underwrite, Visa

**Endow(ment)** Assign, Bequeath, Bestow, Bless, Cha(u)ntry, Dot, Dotation, Enrich, Foundation, Gift, Leave, Patrimony, State, Vest, Wakf, Waqf

**Endurance, Endure(d), Enduring** Abide, Abought, Aby(e), Bear, Bide, Brook, Dree, Dure, Face, Fortitude, Granite, Have, Hold, →**LAST**, Livelong, Lump, Marathon, Patience, Perseverance, Persist, Pluck, Ride, Stamina, Stand, Stay, Stomach, Stout, Substantial, Support, Sustain, Swallow, Tether, Thole, Timeless, Tolerance, Undergo, Wear, Weather

**Endymion** Bluebell

**Enema** Barium, Catharsis, Clyster, Purge

**Enemy** Adversary, Antagonist, Boer, Devil, Fifth column, Foe(n), Fone, Opponent, Public, Time

**Energetic, Energise, Energy** Active, Alternative, Amp, Animation, Arduous, Atomic, Barnstorming, Battery, Binding, Bond, Brisk, Cathexis, Chakra, Chi, Dark, Dash, Doer, Drive, Dynamic, Dynamo, E, Enthalpy, Entropy, EV, Feng shui, Fermi, Fireball, Firebrand, Firecracker, Force, Fossil, Free, Fructan, Fuel, Fusion, Geothermal, Ginger, Gism, Go, Go ahead, Goer, Graviton, Hartree, H.D.R., Hearty, Horme, Hustle, Hyper, Input, Instress, Internal, Isotonic, →**JET**, Jism, Jissom, Joie de vivre, Joule, Kerma, Kinetic, Kundalini, Lattice, Libido, Life, Live wire, Lossy, Luminous, Magnon, Moxie, Nuclear, Orgone, Pep, Phonon, Pithy, Pizzazz, Potency, Potential, →**POWER**, Powerhouse, Prana, QI, Quantum, Quasar, Rad, Radiant, Radiatory, Renewable, Roton, Rydberg, S(h)akti, Sappy, Second-wind, Solar, Stamina, Steam, Sthenic, Stingo, Thermodynamics, Tidal, Trans-uranic, Vehement, Verve, Vibrancy, Vibrational, Vigour, Vim, Vital, Vivo, Wave, Whammo, Whirlwind, Wind(-farm), Zappy, Zealous, Zero point, Zestful, Zing, Zip

**Enervate** Exhaust

**Enfold** Clasp, Embrace, Envelop, Hug, Stemme, Swathe, Wrap

**Enforce(ment)** Administer, Coerce, Control, Exact, Implement, Impose

**Eng** Agma

**Engage(d), Engagement, Engaging** Absorb, Accept, Adorable, Appointment, At, Attach, Battle, Bespoken, Betrothal, Bind, Book, Busy, Contract, Courtship, Date, Embark, Employ, Engross, Enlist, Enmesh, Ensure, Enter, Fascinate, Fiance(e), Fight, Gear, Gig, Hire, Hold, In gear, Interest, Interlock, Lock, Mesh, Met, Occupy, Pledge, Promise, Prosecute, Rapt, Reserve, Residency, Rope in, Sapid, Skirmish, Sponsal, Sponsion, Spousal, Sprocket, Trip, Wage, Winsome

▷ **Engagement** *may indicate* a battle

**Engender** Beget, Breed, Cause, Occasion, Produce, Spawn

**Engine, Engine part** Air, Analytical, Appliance, Athodyd, Atmospheric, Banker, Banking, Beam, Booster, Bricole, Bypass, Carburettor, Catapult, Compound, Dashpot, Diesel, Dividing, Donkey, Dynamo, Fan-jet, Fire, Four-cycle, Four-stroke, Gas, Gin, Heat, Humdinger, ICE, Internal combustion, Ion, Iron horse, Ivor, Jet, Lean-burn, Light, Little-end, Loco(motive), Machine, Mangonel, Mogul, →**MOTOR**, Nacelle, Oil, Onager, Orbital, Otto, Outboard, Overhead valve, Petard, Petrary, Petrol, Petter, Pilot, Plasma, Podded, Pony, Puffer, Pug, Pulp, Pulsejet, Push-pull, Put-put, Radial, Ramjet, Reaction, Reciprocating, Retrorocket, Rocket, Rose, Rotary, RR, Scorpion, Scramjet, Search, Side-valve, Sleeve valve, Stationary, Steam, Stirling, Sustainer, Tank, Terebra, Testudo, Thermometer, Thruster, Top-end, Traction, Trompe, Turbine, Turbofan, Turbojet, Turboprop, Turbo-ram-jet, Two-handed, Two-stroke, V, Vernier, V-type, Wankel, Warwolf, Water, Wildcat, Winch, Winding

**Engineer(ing), Engineer(s)** Aeronautical, AEU, Arrange, Badge, BE, CE, Chartered, Concurrent, Contrive, Genetic, Greaser, Ground, Human, Interactive, Knowledge, Liability, Manhattan District, Manoeuvre, Marine, Mastermind, Mechanical, Mechatronics, Military, Mime, Operator, Organise, Paper, Planner, Process, RE, Repairman, Reverse, Rig, Sales, Sanitary, Sapper, Scheme, Social, Software, Sound, Stage, Systems, Traffic, Usability, Wangle

## ENGINEERS

| 4 letters: | Eiffel | Rogallo | Stirling |
|---|---|---|---|
| Ader | Fokker | Siemens | Von Braun |
| Arup | Karman | Smeaton | |
| Otto | McAdam | Strauss | 9 letters: |
| Watt | Savery | Telford | Armstrong |
| | Wankel | Whittle | Cockerell |
| | | | De Lessops |
| 5 letters: | 7 letters: | 8 letters: | Whitworth |
| Baird | Brinell | Bessemer | |
| Royce | Heinkel | Brindley | 10 letters: |
| Tesla | Junkers | Ferranti | Stephenson |
| | Marconi | Kennelly | Trevithick |
| 6 letters: | Parsons | Samarski | |
| Austin | Porsche | Sikorsky | 12 letters: |
| Brunel | Rankine | Sinclair | Barnes Wallis |
| Diesel | | | |

▷ **Engineer** *may indicate* an anagram

**England** Albany, Albion, Blighty, Demi-paradise, Eden, John Bull, Merrie, Merry, Middle, The Old Dart

**English(man)** Ang(le), Anglican, Anglice, Baboo, Babu, Basic, Brit, Bro talk, Canajan, Choom, E, Ebonics, Eng, Estuary, Gringo, Hawaiian, Hiberno, Hong Kong, Indian, Irish, Jackeroo, John Bull, King's, Kipper, Limey, Middle, Mister, Modern, Morningside, Newspeak, New Zealand, Nigerian, Norman, Officialese, Old, Oxford, Philippine, Pidgin, Plain, Pom(my), Pommie, Pongo, Pork-pudding, Queen's, Qui-hi, Qui-hye, Rock, Rooinek, Rosbif, Sassenach, Saxon, Scotic, Scottish, Seaspeak, Shopkeeper, Side, Singapore, Singlish, South African, South Asian, Southron, Southroun, Spanglish, Standard, Strine, Wardour Street, Whingeing Pom, Woodbine, World, Yanqui, Yinglish

**Engorge** Devour, Glut, Swallow

**Engraft** Inset

**Engrave(r), Engraving** Aquatint, Blake, Bury, Carve, Cerography, Cerotype, Chalcography, Character, Chase, Cut, Die-sinker, Dry-point, Durer, Enchase, Eng, Etch, Glyptic, Glyptograph, Heliogravure, Hogarth, Impress, Inchase, Inciser, Inscribe, Insculp, Intagliate, Inter, Lapidary, Line, Mezzotint, Niello, Photoglyphic, Photogravure, Plate, Scalp, Scrimshander, Scrimshandy, Scrimshaw, Steel, Stillet, Stipple, Stylet, Stylography, Toreutics, Turn, Wood, Xylographer

**Engross(ed)** Absorb, Engage, Enwrap, Immerse, Inwrap, Monopolise, → **OCCUPY**, Preoccupy, Prepossess, Rapt, Rivet, Sink, Thrill, Transfix, Writ large

**Engulf** Overwhelm, Swamp, Whelm

**Enhance(r)** Add, Augment, Better, Catalyst, Elevate, Embellish, Exalt, Heighten, Improve, Intensify, Supplement

**Enigma(tic)** Charade, Conundrum, Cryptic, Dilemma, Gioconda, Gnomic, Mystery, Oracle, Poser, Problem, → **PUZZLE**, Quandary, Question, Rebus, Recondite, Riddle, Secret, Sphinxlike, Teaser

**Enjoin** Command, Direct, Impose, Prohibit, Require

**Enjoy(able), Enjoyment** Apolaustic, Appreciate, Ball, Brook, Delectation, Delight, Fruition, Glee, Groove, Gusto, Have, High jinks, Lap up, Lekker, Like, Own, Palate, Pleasance, Pleasing, Possess, Relish, Ripping, Sair, Savour, Stonking, Taste, Wallow

**Enlarge(ment), Enlarger** Accrue, Acromegaly, Add, Aneurism, Aneurysm, Augment, Blow-up, Diagraph, Dilate, Exostosis, Expand, Expatiate, Explain, Hypertrophy, Increase, Jumboise, →MAGNIFY, Pan, Piece, Ream, Rebore, Sensationalize, Spavin, Swell, Telescope, Tumefy, Upbuild, Varicosity, Zoom

**Enlighten(ed), Enlightenment** Aha, Aufklarung, Awareness, Bodhisattva, Dewali, Disabuse, Divali, Edify, Educate, Explain, Haskalah, Illumine, Instruct, Liberal, Luce, Nirvana, Relume, Revelation, Satori, Verlig(te)

**Enlist** Attest, Conscript, Draft, Engage, Enrol, Induct, Join, Levy, Muster, Prest, Recruit, Rope in, Roster, Sign on, Volunteer

**Enliven(ed)** Animate, Arouse, Brighten, Cheer, Comfort, Exhilarate, Ginger, Invigorate, Juice, Merry, Pep, Refresh, Warm

**Enmity** Animosity, Aversion, Bad blood, Feud, Hatred, Malice, Nee(d)le, Rancour, Spite

**Ennoble(ment)** Dub, Elevate, Ermine, Exalt, Honour, Raise

**Ennui** Boredom, Tedium

**Enormous** Colossal, Exorbitant, Gargantuan, Giant, Gigantic, Googol, Hellacious, Huge, Humongous, Humungous, →IMMENSE, Jumbo, Mammoth, Mega, Plonking, Untold, Vast, Walloper, Walloping

**Enough** Adequate, →AMPLE, Anow, Appreciable, Basta, Belay, Do(eth), Enow, Fill, Geyan, Nuff, Pax, Plenty, Qs, Sate, Satis, Sese, Sessa, Suffice, Sufficient, Via, When

**Enounce** Affirm, Declare, State

**Enquire, Enquiring, Enquiry** Ask, Case, Check, Curious, Eh, Examine, Inquest, Inquire, Organon, Probe, Public, Request, Research, Scan, See, Steward's, Trial

**Enrage(d)** Bemad, Emboss, Enfelon, Imboss, →INCENSE, Inflame, Infuriate, Irate, Livid, Madden, Wild

**Enrapture(d)** Enchant, Eprise, Ravish, Sent, Spellbound, Transport

**Enrich** Adorn, Endow, Enhance, Fortify, Fructify, Oxygenate

**Enrol(ment)** Attest, Conscribe, Conscript, Empanel, Enlist, Enter, Incept, →JOIN, List, Matriculate, Muster, Recruit, Register

**Ensconce(d)** Establish, Niche, Settle, Shelter, Snug

**Ensemble** Band, Gamelan, Octet(te), Orchestra, Outfit, Ripieno, Set, Tout, Whole

**Enshrine** Cherish, Sanctify

**Ensign** Ancient, Badge, Banner, Duster, Ens, →FLAG, Gonfalon, Officer, Pennon, Pistol, Red, White

**Enslave(ment)** Addiction, Bondage, Captivate, Chain, Enthral, Thrall, Yoke

**Ensnare** Illaqueate, →TRAP

**Ensue, Ensuing** Et sequens, Follow, Result, Succeed, Supervene, Transpire

**Ensure** Check, Guarantee

**Entail** Involve, Necessitate, Require

**Entangle(ment)** Amour, Ball, Cot, Elf, Embrangle, Embroil, Encumber, Ensnarl, Entrail, Fankle, Hank, Implicate, →KNOT, Liaison, Mat, Ravel, Retiarius, Taigle, Trammel

**Enter, Entry** Admit, Board, Broach, Come, Enrol, Field, Infiltrate, Ingo, Inscribe, Insert, Intromit, Invade, Item, Key in, Lodge, Log, Penetrate, Pierce, Post, Record, Run, Slate, Submit, Table, Wild card

**Enterprise, Enterprising** Adventure, Ambition, Aunter, Cash cow, Dash, Emprise, Forlorn hope, Free, Go ahead, Goey, Go-getter, Gumption, Indie, Industry, Initiative, Minefield, Plan, Private, Project, Public, Push, Spirit, Starship, Stunt, Up and coming, Venture

**Entertain(er), Entertaining, Entertainment** Accourt, Acrobat, Afterpiece, All-dayer, All-nighter, Amphitryon, Amuse, Apres ski, Balladeer, Ballet, Barnum, Beguile, Belly dancer, Bread and circuses, Bright lights, Burlesque, Busk, Cabaret, Carnival, Cater, Charade, Cheer, Chout, Circus, Comedian, Comic, Concert (party), Conjure, Consider, Cottabus, Crack, Craic, Cuddy, Diseur, Diseuse, Distract, Divert, Divertissement, ENSA,

Extravaganza, Fairground, Fete (champetre), Fleshpots, Floorshow, Foy, Friendly lead, Fun, Gaff, Gala, Gas, Gaudy, Geisha, Gig, Harbour, Harlequin, Have, Hospitality, Host(ess), Houdini, Impresario, Impressionist, Infotainment, Interest, Interlude, Intermezzo, Jester, Juggler, Karaoke, Kidult, Kursaal, Lap-dancer, Lauder, Leg-show, Levee, Liberace, Light, Masque, Melodrama, Mind candy, Minstrel, Movieoke, Musical, Music hall, Niterie, Olio, Opera, Palladium, Panto, Pap, Party, Peepshow, Performer, Piece, Pierrot, Play, Pop singer, Raree-show, Reception, Recreation, Redcoat, Regale, Review, Revue, Rice, Ridotto, Rinky-dink, Roadshow, Rodeo, Rush, Serenade, Showbiz, Showgirl, Sideshow, Simulcast, Singer, Sitcom, Slapstick, Snake-charmer, Soirée, Son et lumière, Street theatre, Striptease, Table, Tamasha, Tattoo, Treat, Tumbler, Tummler, Variety, Vaudeville, Ventriloquist, Wattle

**Enthral(l)** Agog, Bewitch, Bond (servant), Charm, Enchant, Enslave, Rivet, Spellbind, Transport

**Enthuse, Enthusiasm, Enthusiast(ic)** Acclamatory, Addict, Aficionado, Amateur, Ardent, Ardour, Avid, Boy, Buff, Bug, Buzz, Cat, Cheerleader, Crazy, Crusader, Delirium, Demon, Devotee, Eager, Ebullience, Ecstatic, Effusive, Empresse, Energy, Estro, Exuberant, Faddist, Fanatic, Fancier, Fandom, Fashionista, Fervid, Fiend, Fire, Flame, Freak, Furor(e), Geek, Get-up-and-go, Glowing, Gung-ho, Gusto, Hacker, Hearty, Hype, Into, Keen, Live wire, Lyrical, Mad, Mane, Mania, Motivated, Muso, Nethead, Nut, Nympholept, Oomph, Outpour, Overboard, Passion, Perfervid, Petrolhead, Preoccupation, Rah-rah, Raring, Rave, Relish, Rhapsodise, Schwärmerei, Sold, Spirit, Teeny-bopper, Thing, Turfite, Verve, Warmth, Whacko, Whole-hearted, Wonk, Young gun, Zealot, Zest, Zing

**Entice(ment), Enticing** Allure, Angle, Cajole, Carrot, Dangle, Decoy, Draw, Lure, Persuade, Seductive, →**TEMPT**, Tole, Toll, Trap, Trepan

**Entire(ly), Entirety** Absolute, All, Bag and baggage, Clean, Complete, Full Monty, Genuine, Holistic, Inly, Intact, Integral, In toto, Jingbang, Livelong, Lot, Purely, Root and branch, Systemic, Thorough, Total, Tout, Undivided, →**WHOLE**

**Entitle(ment)** Birthright, Credentials, Empower, Enable, Folk-right, Legitim, Name, Peerage, Right, Surname

**Entity** Being, Body, Existence, Holon, Monad, Tao, Tensor, Thing, Transfinite, Virino

**Entomb** Inter

**Entomologist** Fabré

**Entourage** Cortège, Retinue

**Entrail(s)** Bowels, Chawdron, Giblets, Gralloch, Guts, Ha(r)slet, Humbles, Lights, Numbles, Offal, Quarry, Tripe, Umbles, Viscera

**Entrance(d), Entrant, Entry** Access, Adit, Admission, Anteroom, Arch, Atrium, Attract, Avernus, Bewitch, Cat flap, Charm, Closehead, Contestant, Door, Doorstop, Double, Dromos, Eye, Fascinate, Foyer, Frawbridge, Gate(way), Ghat, Hypnotise, Illegal, In-door, Infare, Inflow, Ingate, Ingress, Inlet, Introitus, Item, Jawhole, Jaws, Jib-door, Mesmerise, Mouth, Narthex, Pend, Porch, Porogamy, Portal, Porte-cochère, Postern, Propylaeum, Propylon, Ravish, Reception, Record, Regest, Registration, Single, Spellbound, Starter, Stem, Stoa, Stoma, Stulm, Throat, Torii

**Entrap** Decoy

**Entreat(y)** Appeal, Ask, Beg, Beseech, Flagitate, Impetrate, →**IMPLORE**, Orison, Petition, Plead, Pray, Precatory, Prevail, Prig, Rogation, Solicit, Sue, Supplicate

**Entrée** Access, Dish, Entry, Ingate

**Entrench(ment)** Coupure, Encroach, Fortify, Trespass

**Entrepreneur** Branson, Businessman, E-tailer, Executor, Impresario, Wheeler-dealer, Yettie

**Entropy** S

**Entrust** Aret(t), Charge, Confide, Consign, Delegate, Give

▶ **Entry** *see* **ENTRANCE(D)**

**Entwine** Complect, Impleach, Intervolve, Lace, Twist, Weave

**Enumerate, Enumeration** Catalogue, Count, Detail, Fansi, List, Tell

**Enunciate, Enunciation** Articulate, Declare, Deliver, Diction, Elocution, Proclaim
**Envelop(e), Enveloping** Arachnoid, Bangtail, Chorion, Corolla, Corona, Cover(ing), Cuma, Enclose, Enshroud, Entire, First day cover, Flight, Floral, Flown cover, Invest, Involucre, Jiffy(bag)®, Muffle, Mulready, Nuclear, Perianth, Round, Sachet, Sae, Serosa, Shroud, Skin, Smother, Surround, Swathe, Window, Wrap
**Environment(s), Environmental(ist)** ACRE, Ambience, Cyberspace, Druid, Ecofreak, Ecology, Econut, Eco-warrior, Element, Entourage, Ergonomics, F of E, Green(ie), Greenpeace, Habitat, Hotbed, Hothouse, Milieu, Realo, SEPA, Setting, Sphere, Surroundings, Umwelt, Vicinity
**Envisage** Contemplate, Imagine, Suppose
**Envoi** Farewell, RIP
**Envoy** Agent, Diplomat, Elchee, El(t)chi, Hermes, Legate, Missioner, Plenipo(tentiary)
**Envy, Enviable, Envious** Begrudge, Covet, Jaundiced, Jealousy, Penis, Plum, Resentful

## ENZYMES

*3 letters:*
ACE
PSA

*5 letters:*
DNase
ELISA
Lyase
Lysin
Renin
RNase

*6 letters:*
Cytase
DNAase
Kinase
Ligase
Lipase
Mutase
Papain
Pepsin
Rennin
Zymase

*7 letters:*
Amylase
Apyrase
Caspase
Cyclase
Emulsin
Enolase
Erepsin
Guanase
Hydrase
Inulase
Lactase
Maltase
Oxidase

Pectase
Pepsine
Plasmin
Ptyalin
Sirtuin
Sucrase
Trypsin
Uricase

*8 letters:*
Aldolase
Allozyme
Arginase
Bromelin
Catalase
Diastase
Elastase
Esterase
Lysozyme
Nuclease
Permease
Protease
Steapsin
Synthase
Thrombin

*9 letters:*
Amylopsin
Autolysin
Bromelain
Cathepsin
Cellulase
Coagulase
Deaminase
DNAligase
Hydrolase
Inducible
Invertase

Isomerase
Oxygenase
Peptidase
Reductase
Sulfatase
Synaptase
Trehalase
Urokinase

*10 letters:*
Allosteric
Hexokinase
Kallikrein
Luciferase
Peroxidase
Peroxisome
Polymerase
Proteinase
Rancreatin
Saccharase
Subtilisin
Sulphatase
Telomerase
Tyrosinase

*11 letters:*
Calcineurin
Carboxylase
Chymopapain
Collagenase
Dipeptidase
Glucosidase
Histaminase
Lecithinase
Phosphatase
Restriction
Transferase
Transposase

*12 letters:*
Asparaginase
Carbohydrase
Chymotrypsin
Constitutive
Enterokinase
Fibrinolysin
Flavoprotein
Ribonuclease
Transaminase

*13 letters:*
Decarboxylase
Dehydrogenase
DNApolymerase
Galactosidase
Hyaluronidase
Neuraminidase
Oxdoreductase
Penicillinase
Phosphorylase
Streptokinase
Thrombokinase
Topoisomerase
Transcriptase

*14 letters:*
Cholinesterase
Creatine kinase
Pectinesterase
Streptodornase
Thromboplastin

*17 letters:*
Carbonic anhydrase

**Eon** Arch(a)ean, Cenozoic, Epoch, Mesozoic, Phanerozoic, Proterozoic

**Epaminondas** Theban

**Epaulette** Swab

**Ephemera(l)** Brief, Day, Drake, Fungous, Mayfly, Momentary, Passing, Transient, Transitory, Trappings

**Epic** Aeneid, Ben Hur, Beowulf, Blockbuster, Calliope, Colossal, Dunciad, Edda, Epopee, Epyllion, Eyeliad, Gilgamesh, Heroic, Homeric, Iliad, Kalevala, Lusiad(s), Mahabharata, Mock-heroic, Nibelungenlied, Odyssey, Ramayana, Rhapsody, Saga

**Epicene** Hermaphrodite

**Epicure(an)** Apicius, Apolaustic, Connoisseur, Friand(e), Gastronome, Gastrosopher, Glutton, → **GOURMAND**, Gourmet, Hedonist, Sybarite

**Epidemic** Asian flu, Enzootic, Outbreak, Pandemic, Pestilence, Plague, Prevalent, Rampant, Rash, Rife

**Epigram** Adage, Apophthegm, Gnomic, Mot, Proverb

**Epigraph** Citation, Inscription, RIP

**Epilepsy, Epileptic** Clonic, Eclampsia, Falling evil, Falling sickness, Fit, Grand mal, Petit mal, Turn

**Epilogue** Appendix, Coda, End, Postlude, Postscript

**Epiphany** Twelfthtide

**Epiphenomenon** ESP

**Epiphyte** Air-plant

**Episcopalian** PE, Prelatic

**Episode(s), Episodic** Bipolar, Chapter, Incident, Instalment, Microsleep, Page, Picaresque, Scene, Serial

**Epistle(s)** Catholic, Dispatch, General, Lesson, Letter, Missive, Pastoral, Titus

**Epitaph** Ci-git, Hic jacet, Inscription, RIP

**Epithet** Adj(ective), Antonomasia, Apathaton, Byword, Curse, Expletive, Panomphaean, → **TERM**, Title

**Epitome, Epitomise** Abridge, Abstract, Avowal, Digest, Exemplar, Image, Model, Summary, Typify

**Epoch** Age, Eocene, Era, Holocene, Magnetic, Miocene, Neogene, Oligocene, Palaeocene, Palaeolithic, Perigordian, Period, Pleistocene, Pl(e)iocene

**Epsom salts** Kieserite

**Equable, Equably** Calm, Just, Pari passu, Placid, Smooth, Tranquil

**Equal(ly), Equality, Equal quantities** A(n)a, Across the board, Alike, All square, As, Balanced, Commensurate, Compeer, Co-partner, Egal(ity), Emulate, Equinox, Equiparate, Equity, Even, Even-steven, Ex aequo, Fair, Feer, Fe(a)re, Fiere, Fifty-fifty, For, Identical, Identity, Is, Iso-, Isocracy, Isonomy, Level, Level-pegging, Maik, Make, Match, Mate, Owelty, Par, Parage, Parallel, Parametric, Pari passu, Parity, → **PEER**, Peregal, Pheer(e), Rise, Rival, → **SO**, Square, Upsides, Wyoming, Ylike

**Equanimity** Aplomb, Balance, Poise, Serenity

**Equate, Equation(s)** Arrhenius, Balance, Chemical, Cubic, Defective, Differential, Diophantine, Dirac, Exponential, Gas, Identity, Linear, Logistic, Maxwell, Nernst, Parametric, Personal, Polar, Quadratic, Reduce, Relate, Rhizic, Schrödinger, Simultaneous, Van der Waals', Wave

**Equator(ial)** Celestial, Galactic, Line, Magnetic, Thermal, Tropical

**Equerry** Courtier, Officer, Page

**Equestrian** Dressage, Eventer, Turfite

**Equilibrium** Balance, Composure, Homeostasis, Instable, Isostasy, Poise, Punctuated, Stable, Stasis, Steady state, Tautomerism, Thermodynamic

**Equine** Hinny

**Equinox** Autumnal, Vernal

**Equip(ment), Equipage, Equipped** Accoutrement, Accustrement, Adorn, Aguise, Aguize, Apparatus, Apparel, Appliance, Arm, Armament, Array, Attire, Blender, Carriage,

Chequerboard, Clobber, Clothe, Codec, Deadstock, Deck, Dight, Expertise, Fortify, →**FURNISH**, Gear, Gere, Get-up, Graith, Habilitate, Hamper, Hand-me-up, Hardware, Headset, Hi-tech, Impedimenta, Implement, Incubator, iPod®, Kit, Lie-detector, Log-reel, Material, Matériel, Mechanise, Monitor, Muniments, Outfit, Paraphernalia, Pile-driver, Plant, Projector, Receiver, Refit, Retinue, Rig, Scrambler, Sonar, Sonobuoy, Spikes, Stapler, Stereo, Stock, Stuff, Tabulator, Tack(le), Tenderiser, Tool, Trampet(te), Trampoline, Transformer, Turn-out, Vision-mixer, Wakeboard, Webcam, Well-appointed

**Equitable** Even-handed, Fair, Just

**Equity** Actors, Egalitarian, Equality, Justice, Law, Negative, Owner's, Union

**Equivalence, Equivalent** Akin, Amounting to, Correspondent, Counterpart, Dose, Equal, Equipollent, Ewe, Formal, In-kind, Same, Tantamount, Version

**Equivocal** Ambiguous, Dubious, Evasive, Fishy, Oracular, Vague

**Equivocate** Flannel, Lie, Palter, Prevaricate, Quibble, Tergiversate, Waffle, Weasel

**Er** Um

**Era** Age, Archaean, C(a)enozoic, Christian, Common, Cretaceous, Cryptozoic, Decade, Dynasty, Ediocaron, Eozoic, Epoch, Hadean, Hegira, Hej(i)ra, Hijra, Jurassic, Lias, Mesozoic, Oligocene, Palaeozoic, Period, Precambrian, Proterozoic, Republican, Torridonian, Vulgar

**Eradicate, Erase** Abolish, Delete, Demolish, Destroy, Dislimn, Efface, Expunge, Exterminate, Extirp, Obliterate, Purge, Root, Scrat, Scratch, Stamp-out, Strike off, Strike out, Uproot, Uptear, Wipe

**Erasmus** Humanist

**Eratosthenes** Sieve

**Erbium** Er

**Ere** Coram

**Erect(ion), Erector** Attolent, Boner, Build, Construct(ion), Elevate, Exalt, Hard-on, Henge, Horn, Perpendicular, Priapism, Prick, Rear, Rigger, Stiffy, Straight-pight, Tentigo, Upend, Upright, Vertical, Wall

**Ergo** Argal, Hence, Therefore

**Erica** Heather, Ling

**Ermine** Fur, Minever, Miniver, Stoat

**Ernie** Bondsman

**Erode, Erosion** Ablate, Abrade, Appair, Corrasion, Degrade, Denude, Destroy, Deteriorate, Detrition, Etch, Fret, Hush, Peneplain, Planation, Spark, Wash, Wear, Yardang

**Eros, Erotic(a)** Amatory, Amorino, Amorous, Aphrodisiac, Carnal, Cupid, Curiosa, Lascivious, Philtre, Prurient, Salacious, Steamy

**Err(or), Errant** Aliasing, Anachronism, Bish, Blip, Blooper, Blunder, Boner, Boob(oo), Botch, Bug, Clanger, Comedy, Corrigendum, EE, Execution, Fat-finger, Fault, Fluff, Glaring, Heresy, Hickey, Howler, Human, Inaccuracy, Inherited, Jeofail, K'thibh, Lapse, Lapsus, Literal, Mackle, Mesprise, Mesprize, Misgo, Misprint, Misprise, Misprize, Misstep, →**MISTAKE**, Mumpsimus, Out, Paladin, Parachronism, Probable, Recoverable, Rounding, Rove, Runtime, Sampling, Semantic, Sin, Slip, Slip-up, Solecism, Standard, Stray, Trip, Truncation, Type I, Type II, Typo, Typographical, Unforced, Wander

**Errand** Ance, Chore, Commission, Fool's, Message, Mission, Once, Sleeveless, Task, Yince

**Errand-boy** Cad, Galopin, Page

**Erratic** Haywire, Planetary, Spasmodic, Temperamental, Unstable, Vagary, Vagrant, Wayward, Whimsical

**Erroneous** False, Inaccurate, Mistaken, Non-sequitur, Untrue

**Ersatz** Artificial, Pseudo, Synthetic

**Erstwhile** Quondam

**Erudite, Erudition** Academic, Didactic, Learned, Literosity, Savant, Scholar, Well-bred, Well-read, Wisdom

**Erupt(ion), Erupture** Belch, Brash, Burst, Ecthyma, Eject, Emit, Emphlysis, Exanthem(a), Exanthemata, → **EXPLODE**, Fissure, Flare, Fumarole, Hives, Hornito, Lichen, Mal(l)ander, Mallender, Morphew, Outbreak, Outburst, Papilla, Paroxysm, Plinian, Pompholyx, Pustule, Quat, Rash, Rose-drop, Scissure, Sneeze

**Escalate, Escalator** Accrescence, Expand, Granary, Grow, Lift, Snowball, Travolator

**Escape(e), Escapade, Escapist** Abscond, Adventure, Atride, Avoid, Bale out, Bolt, Bolthole, Breakout, Caper, Close call, Eject, Elope, Elude, Elusion, Esc, Eschewal, Evade, Exit, Fire, Flee, Flight, Fredaine, Frolic, Fugacity, Gaolbreak, Get-out, Hole, Hoot, Houdini, Houdini act, Hout, Lam, Lark, Leakage, Leg-it, Let-off, Levant, Lifeline, Loop(-hole), Meuse, Mews, Miss, Muse, Narrow, Near thing, Outlet, Prank, Refuge, Rollick, Runaway, Sauve qui peut, Scapa, Scarper, Seep(age), Shave, Slip, Splore, Squeak, Stunt, Vent, Walter Mitty, Wilding, Wriggle

**Escapement** Anchor, Dead-beat, Foliot, Recoil

**Eschew** Abandon, Avoid, For(e)go, Ignore, → **SHUN**

**Escort** Accompany, Arm candy, Attend, Beard, Beau, Bodyguard, Bring, Chaperone, Comitatus, Conduct, Convoy, Cortège, Corvette, Date, Destroyer, Entourage, Frigate, Gallant, Gigolo, Guard, Guide, Lead, Outrider, Protector, Retinue, See, Send, Set, Squire, Take, Tend, Usher, Walker

**Escutcheon** Achievement, Crest, Shield

**Esker** OS

**Eskimo** Aleut, Caribou, Husky, In(n)uit, Inuk, Inukitut, Thule, Yupik

**Esoteric** Abstruse, Acroamatic, Arcane, Hermetic, Inner, Mystic, Occult, Orphic, Private, Rarefied, Recondite, Secret

**ESP** Psi, Retrocognition

**Especial(ly)** Chiefly, Esp, Espec, Outstanding, Particular

**Esperanto** Ido, Zamenhof

**Espionage** Industrial, Spying, Surveillance

**Esplanade** Promenade, Walk

**Esprit** Cameraderie, Insight, Spirit, Understanding, Wit

**Esquire** Armiger(o), Esq, Gent

**Essay(s)** Article, Attempt, Causerie, Critique, Dabble, Disquisition, Dissertation, Endeavour, Festschrift, Go, Paper, Prolusion, Sketch, Stab, Study, Theme, Thesis, Tractate, Treatise, Try

**Essayist** Addison, Bacon, Carlyle, Columnist, De Quincey, Elia, Ellis, Emerson, Hazlitt, Holmes, Hunt, Huxley, Lamb, Locke, Montaigne, Pater, Prolusion, Ruskin, Scribe, Steele, Temple, Tzara, → **WRITER**

**Essence** Alma, Atman, Attar, Aura, Being, Bergamot, Core, Crux, Element, Entia, Esse, Extract, Fizzen, Flavouring, Flower, Foison, Gist, Heart, Hom(e)ousian, Inbeing, Inscape, Kernel, Marrow, Mauri, Mirbane, Myrbane, Nature, Nub, Nutshell, Oil, Ottar, Otto, Perfume, Per-se, Petrol, Pith, Quiddity, Ratafia, Saul, Soul, Substance, Sum, Ylang-ylang

**Essential(ly), Essentials** Arabin, At heart, Bare, Basic, Central, Crucial, Entia, Formal, Fundamental, Imperative, In, Inbred, Indispensable, Inherent, In se, Integral, Intrinsic, Kernel, Key, Lifeblood, Linch-pin, Main, Marrow, Material, Mun, Must, Necessary, Need, Nitty-gritty, Nub, Nuts and bolts, Part-parcel, Per-se, Pith, Prana, Prerequisite, Quintessence, Radical, Requisite, Sine qua non, Skeleton, Soul, Vital, Whatness

**Essex** Roseland

**Establish(ed)** Abide, Anchor, Appoint, Ascertain, Base, Bred-in-the-bone, Build, Chronic, Confirm, Conform, Conventional, Create, Deep-seated, Deploy, Embed, Enact, Endemic, Engrain, Ensconce, Entrench, Erect, Evidence, Evince, Fix, → **FOUND**, Haft, Honoured, Imbed, Ingrain, Instal(l), Instate, Instil, Institute, Inveterate, Legislate, Ordain, Pitch, Pre-set, Prove, Radicate, Raise, Redintegrate, Root(ed), Secure, Set, Stable, Standing, State, Stell, Substantiate, Trad(itional), Trite, Valorise, Verify

**Establishment** Building, Business, CE, Church, Co, Concern, Conformation, Creation, Hacienda, Household, Instauration, Institution, Lodge, Proving ground, Salon, School, Seat, Succursal, System, Traditional

**Estate, Estate-holder** Acres, Allod(ium), Alod, Assets, Campus, Car, Commons, Dais, Demesne, Domain, Dominant, Dowry, Est, Estancia, Fazenda, Fee-simple, Fee-tail, Fen, First, Fourth, General, Hacienda, Hagh, Haugh, Having, Hay, Housing, Industrial, Jointure, Land-living, Latifundium, Legitim, Life, Longleat, Manor, Messuage, Odal, Patrimony, Pen, Personal(ity), Plantation, Press, Princedom, → **PROPERTY**, Real, Runrig, Second, Situation, Spiritual, Standing, Talooka, Taluk(a), Temporal, Termer, Termor, Thanage, Third, Trading, Trust, Udal, Zamindari, Zemindari

**Estate agent** Realtor

**Esteem(ed), Estimable** Account, Admiration, Appreciation, Count, Credited, Have, Honour, Izzat, Los, Precious, Prestige, Price, Pride, Prize, Rate, → **REGARD**, Reputation, Respect, Revere, Store, Value, Venerate, Wonder, Worthy

**Ester** Benzocaine, C(o)umarin, Depside, Glyceride, Lactone, Olein, Palmitin, Phthalate, Psilocybin, Succinate, Triglyceride, Urethan(e)

▶ **Estimable** *see* **ESTEEM(ED)**

**Estimate, Estimation** Appraise, Assess, Calculate, Carat, Conceit, Cost, Esteem, Extrapolation, Figure, Forecast, Gauge, Guess(timate), Inexact, Interval, Measure, Opinion, Point, Projection, Quotation, Rate, Rating, Reckon, Regard, Sight, Value, Weigh

**Estrange** Alienate, Disunite, Wean

**Estuary** Bay, Clyde, Creek, Dee, Delta, Firth, Gironde, Humber, Inlet, Mouth, Orwell, Ostial, Para, Rio de la Plata, Tay

**Esurient** Arid, Insatiable

**Etc(etera)** Et al(ia), So on

**Etch(ing)** Aquafortis, Aquatint(a), Bite, → **ENGRAVE**, Erode, Incise, Inscribe

**Eternal(ly), Eternity** Aeonian, Ageless, All-time, Amarantine, Endless, Everlasting, Evermore, Eviternal, Ewigkeit, Forever, Immortal, Infinity, Never-ending, Perdurable, Perpetual, Sempiternal, Tarnal, Timeless, Triangle, Unending

**Ethanol** Alcohol

**Ether** Air, Atmosphere, Ch'i, Crown, Gas, Petroleum, Sky, Yang, Yin

**Ethereal** Airy, Delicate, Fragile, Heavenly, Nymph

**Ethic(al), Ethics** Deontics, Ideals, Marcionite, Moral, Principles, Situation, Work

**Ethiopia(n)** African, Amharic, Asmara, Cushitic, Falasha, Galla, Geez, Kabele, Kebele, Ogaden

**Ethnic** Racial, Roots

**Ethyl** ET

**Etiquette** Code, Conduct, Decorum, Kawa, → **MANNERS**, Politesse, Propriety, Protocol, Ps and Qs, Punctilious, Table manners

**Etna** Empedocles, Vessel, Volcano

**Etonian** Oppidan, Victim

**Etrier** Rope ladder

**Etruscan** Tyrrhenian

**Etymologist, Etymology** Hobson-Jobson, Isodore

**Eucalyptus** Blackbutt, Bloodwood, Cadaga, Cadagi, Coolabah, Gum-tree, Ironbark, Jarrah, Mallee, Marri, Morrell, Red gum, Sallee, Sally, Stringybark, Sugar gum, Tallow wood, Tewart, Tooart, Tuart, Wandoo, White gum, Woolly butt, Yate

**Eucharist** Azymite, Communion, Housel, Mass, Prozymite, Supper, Viaticum

**Euchre** Jambone

**Euclid** Geometer

**Eugene** Aram, Onegin

**Eugenia** Jambal, Jambolan(a), Jambu(l)

**Eulogistic, Eulogy** Encomium, Epaenetic, Epainetic, Laudatory, Panegyric, Praise, Tribute

**Eunuch** Ridg(e)ling, Rig

**Euphausia** Krill, Shrimp

**Euphemism** Fib, Gosh, Gracious, Heck, Hypocorism, Sir-reverence

**Euphonic** Tuneful

**Euphoria, Euphoric** Buzz, Cock-a-hoop, Ecstasy, Elation, High, Jubilation, Mindfuck, Nirvana, Rapture, Rush

**Euphrasia** Eyebright

**Eurasian** Chee-chee, Chi-chi

**Europe(an)** Andorran, Aryan, Balt, Bohunk, Bosnian, Catalan, Community, Continent, Croat, E, Esth, Estonian, Faringee, Faringhi, Feringhee, Fleming, Hungarian, Hunky, Icelander, Japhetic, Lapp, Lett, Lithuanian, Magyar, Maltese, Monagesque, Palagi, Polack, Ruthene, Ruthenian, Serb, Slavonian, Slovak, Slovene, Topi-wallah, Transleithan, Tyrolean, Ugrian, Vlach, Wessi, Yugoslav

**Europium** Eu

**Eustace** Diamonds

**Euthanasia** Exit

**Evacuate, Evacuation** Dunkirk, Escape, Excrete, Expel, Getter, Medevac, Movement, Planuria, Planury, Retreat, Scramble, Stercorate, Stool, Vent, Void, Withdraw

**Evade, Evasion, Evasive** Abscond, Ambages, Avoid, Circumvent, Cop-out, Coy, Dodge, Duck, Elude, Equivocate, Escape, Fence, Fudge, Hedge, Jink, Loophole, Mealymouthed, Parry, Prevaricate, Quibble, Quillet, Quirk, Salvo, Scrimshank, Shack, Shifty, Shirk, Shuffling, Sidestep, Skive, Skrimshank, Slippy, Stall, Subterfuge, Tergiversate, Waive, Weasel, Weasel out, Whiffler

**Evaluate, Evaluation** Appraise, Assess, Estimate, Gauge, Job, Measure, Ponder, Rate, Review, Try, Waid(e), Weigh

**Evanesce, Evanescent** Cursory, Fade, Fleeting, Fugacious

**Evangelical, Evangelist(ical)** Bible-thumper, Buchman, Clappy-doo, Converter, Crusader, Fisher, Godsquad, Gospeller, Graham, Happy-clappy, Hot gospeller, Jansen, Jesus freak, John, Luke, Marist, Mark, Matthew, Missioner, Moody, Morisonian, Peculiar, Preacher, Propagandist, Revivalist, Salvationist, Salvo, Sankey, Sim(eonite), Stundist, Wild

**Evaporate, Evaporation** Angel's share, Condense, Dehydrate, Desorb, Disappear, Dry, Exhale, Steam, Steme, Ullage, Vaporise

**Eve(ning)** All Hallow's, First lady, First mate, Nightfall, Postmeridian, St Agnes's, Soirée, Subfusk, Sunset, Tib(b)s, Twilight, Vesperal, Vespertinal, Vigil, Watch night, Yester

**Evelyn** Diarist, Hope

**Even(ly), Evenness** Aid, Albe(e), Albeit, All, Average, Balanced, Clean, Drawn, Dusk, Een, Ene, Equable, Equal, Erev, Fair, Fair play, Flush, Forenight, Gradual, Iron, J'ouvert, Level, Level-pegging, Meet, Nay, Pair, Par, Parallel, Plain, Plane, Plateau, Quits, Rib, Smooth, Square, Standardise, Still, Temperate, Tie(d), Toss-up, Uniform, Well-balanced, Yet

**Even-handed** Ambidextrous, Impartial

**Evening flight** Ro(a)ding

**Evensong** Vespers

**Event(ing)** All-nighter, Bash, Case, Circumstance, Contingency, Cross-country, Discus, Dressage, Encaenia, Episode, Fest, Field, Fiesta, Function, Grand prix, Gymkhana, Happening, Happy, Heat, Incident, Iron man, Landmark, Leg, Liquidity, Media, Meeting, Milestone, Occasion, Occurrence, Ongoing, Outcome, Pass, Rag-day, Regatta, Result, Shot put, Show-jumping, Soirée, Stick-on, Telethon, Three-day, Three-ring circus, Time trial, Tour de France, Track, Triple

**Eventful** Action-packed

**Even-toed** Artiodactyl

**Eventual(ity), Eventually** Case, Contingent, Finally, Future, In time, Later, Nd, Sooner or later, Ultimate

**Ever** Always, Ay(e), Constantly, Eternal, Eviternity

**Everglade** Vlei

**Evergreen** Abies, Ageless, Arbutus, Cembra, Cypress, Fir, Gaultheria, Golden lie, Holly, Ivy, Myrtle, Oleander, Olearia, Periwinkle, Pinaster, Privet, Thuja, Thuya, Washington, Winterberry, Yacca

**Everlasting** Cat's ear, Changeless, Enduring, Eternal, Immortal, Immortelle, Perdurable, Perennial, Recurrent, Tarnal, Undying

**Every(one), Everything** All, Apiece, A'thing, Catch-all, Complete, Each, Et al, Existence, Full Monty, Ilk(a), In toto, Monty, Sub chiz, Sum, The full monty, The works, To a man, Tout, Tout le monde, Universal, Varsal

**Everyday** Banal, Informal, Mundane, Natural, Ordinary, Plain, Routine, Year round

**Everywhere** Ambient, Omnipresent, Passim, Rife, Throughout, Thru, Ubique, Ubiquity, World

**Evict(ion), Evict(or)** Clearance, Dislodge, Disnest, Disseisor, Eject, Expel, Oust

**Evidence, Evident(ly)** Adminicle, Apparent, Argument, Axiomatic, Circumstantial, Clear, Compurgation, Confessed, Credentials, Deposition, Direct, Distinct, DNA, Document, Empirical, Exemplar, Flagrant, Forensic, Hearsay, Indicate, Internal, King's, Manifest, Marked, Material, Naked, Obvious, Ostensibly, Overt, → **PATENT**, Plain, Premise, Prima facie, Probable, Proof, Queen's, Record, Sign, Smoking gun, State's, Surrebuttal, Tangible, Testimony, Understandable

**Evil** Ahriman, Alastor, Amiss, Bad, Badmash, Bale, Beelzebub, Budmash, Corrupt, Curse, Depraved, Eale, Falling, Guilty, Harm, Heinous, Hydra, Ill, Immoral, Iniquity, King's, Loki, Malefic, Malign, Mare, Mischief, Monstrous, Nasty, Necessary, Night, Perfidious, Pestilence, Rakshas(a), Satanic, Shrewd, Sin, → **SINISTER**, Theodicy, Turpitude, Vice, Villainy, Wicked

**Evil eye** Jettatura

**Evince** Disclose, Exhibit, Indicate, → **MANIFEST**, Show

**Eviscerate(d)** Debilitate, Disembowel, Drawn, Gralloch

**Evoke** Arouse, Awaken, Elicit, Move, Stir

**Evolution(ary)** Clade, Convergent, Countermarch, Darwin, Development, Emergent, Growth, Holism, Lamarck, Lysenkoism, Moner(on), Neo-Lamarckism, Orthogenesis, Phylogeny, Social, Spencerman, Stellar, Transformism, Turning

▷ **Evolution** *may indicate* an anagram

**Evolve** Speciate

**Ewe** Crone, Gimmer, Keb, Rachel, Sheep, Teg, Theave

**Ewer** Aquamanale, Aquamanile, → **JUG**

**Ex** Former, Late, Old flame, Quondam, Ten

**Exacerbate** Aggravate, Embitter, Exasperate, Inflame, Irritate, Needle

**Exact(ing), Exactitude, Exactly** Accurate, Authentic, Bang on, Careful, Dead, Definite, Due, Elicit, Estreat, Even, Exigent, Extort, Fine, Formal, It, Jump, Literal, Literatim, Mathematical, Meticulous, Minute, Nice(ty), On the nail, Pat, Plumb, Point-device, → **PRECISE**, Require, Slap-bang, Spang, Specific, Spot-on, Strict, Stringent, Sweat, T, To a 't', Verbatim

**Exaction** Blackmail, Extortion, Impost, Montem, Sorelion, Tax

**Exaggerate(d), Exaggeration** Agonistic, Amplify, Ballyhoo, Boast, Brag, Camp, Caricature, Colour, Distend, Dramatise, → **EMBROIDER**, Exalted, Goliathise, Hoke, Hype, Hyperbole, Inflate, Lie, Line-shoot, Magnify, Munch(h)ausen, Mythomania, Overdo, Overdraw, Overegg, Overpaint, Overpitch, Overplay, Overrate, Oversell, Overstate, Overstretch, Over-the-top, Play up, Romance, Shoot a line, Steep, Stretch, Tall, Theatrical, Writ large

**Exalt(ed), Exaltation** Attitudes, Deify, Dignify, Elation, Enhance, Ennoble, Ensky, Enthrone, Erect, Extol, Glorify, High, Jubilation, Larks, Laud, Lofty, Magnific, → **PRAISE**, Raise, Rapture, Ruff(e), Sama, Sublime, Supernal, Throne

**Exam(ination), Examine, Examinee, Examiner** Agrégé, A-level, Alnage, Analyse, Analyst, Anatomise, Appose, Assess, Audit, Audition, Auscultation, Autopsy, Baccalauréat, Biopsy, Case, Check-out, Check-up, Cognosce, Collate, Comb, Common Entrance, Concours, Consideration, Cross-question, CSE, Deposal, Depose, Disquisition, Dissect, Docimasy, Edexcel, Eleven plus, Endoscopy, Entrance, Expiscate, Explore, Eyeball, Finals, GCE, GCSE, Going-over, Grade(s), Great-go, Greats, Gulf, Haruspex,

Hearing, Higher, Inspect, Inter, Interrogate, Interview, Introspection, Jerque, Jury, Laparoscopy, Little-go, Local, Look, Mark, Matriculation, Medical, Mocks, Mod(erations), Moderator, Mods, Mug, Multiple choice, O-level, Once-over, Oral, Ordalian, Ordeal, Overhaul, Palp(ate), Paper, Peruse, Physical, Post-mortem, Prelims, Probe, Professional, Pry, Psychoanalyse, Pump, →QUESTION, Quiz, Ransack, Recce, Reconnaissance, Resit, Responsions, Review, Sayer, Scan, Schools, Scope, Screen, Scrutator, Scrutineer, Scrutinise, Search, Seek, Shroff, Sift, Sit, Smalls, Strip search, Study, Survey, Sus(s), Test, Trial, Tripos, Try, Unseen, Vet, Viva, Vivisection, Voir dire

**Example** Apotheosis, Assay-piece, Byword, Epitome, Erotema, Foretaste, →FOR EXAMPLE, Illustration, Instance, Lead, Lesson, Model, Monument, Paradigm, Paragon, →PATTERN, Praxis, Precedent, Prototype, Quintessence, Role model, Say, Shining, Showpiece, Specimen, Standard, Stormer, Such as, Touchstone, Type, Typify

**Exasperate, Exasperating, Exasperation** Anger, Brass off, Embitter, Exulcerate, Galling, Irk, Irritate, Nettle, Provoke

**Excavate, Excavation, Excavator** Armadillo, Bore, Burrow, Catacomb, Crater, Cutting, Delf, Delph, →DIG, Dike, Disinter, Ditch(er), Dragline, Dredge, Drift, Drive, Earthwork, Gaulter, Graft, Heuch, Heugh, Hollow, JCB, Mine, Moat, Pichiciago, Pioneer, Pioner, Power shovel, Pyoner, Quarry, Shaft, Sink, Sondage, Spade, Steam-shovel, Stope, Well

**Exceed, Exceeding(ly)** Amain, Not half, Outdo, Outnumber, Outstrip, Overshoot, Overstep, Preponderate, Surpass, Transcend, Very

**Excel(lence), Excellency, Excellent** A1, Ace, Admirable (Crichton), A-per-se, Assay-piece, Awesome, Bangin(g), Bang on, Beat, Beaut, Beezer, Better, Bitchin', Blinder, Bodacious, Boffo, Bonzer, Booshit, Boss, Bottler, Bravo, Brill, Bully, Capital, Castor, Champion, Cheese, Choice, Class(y), Classical, Cool, Copacetic, Copesettic, Copybook, Corking, Crack, Crackajack, Crackerjack, Crucial, Cushty, Daisy, Def, Dic(k)ty, Dilly, Dominate, Doozy, Dope, Elegant, Excelsior, Exemplary, Eximious, Exo, Exquisite, Extraordinaire, Fab, Fabulous, Fantastic, First-class, First rate, Five-star, Goodly, Goodness, Great, Grit, Grouse, HE, Hellacious, High, Humdinger, Hunky(-dory), Inimitable, Jake, Jammy, Jim-dandy, Kiff, Knockout, Lal(l)a palooza, Laudable, Lollapalooza, Lummy, Matchless, Mean, Mega-, Merit, Neat, Noble, Nonesuch, Olé, Out and outer, Outbrag, Outdo, Outgeneral, Outrank, Outstanding, Outstrip, Outtop, Overdo, Overpeer, Overtop, Paragon, Peachy, Peerless, Perfection, Phat, Prime, Pure, Quality, Rad, Rare, Rattling, Ring, Rinsin', Ripping, Ripsnorter, Say-piece, Shagtastic, →SHINE, Shit-hot, Sick-dog, Sik, Slammin(g), Socko, Sound, Spanking, Spiffing, Stellar, Stonking, Stupendous, Sublime, Superb, Super-duper, Superior, Supernal, Supreme, Surpass, Swell, Terrific, Tip-top, Top flight, Top-hole, Topnotch, Topping, Tops, Transcend, Transcendent, Triff, Virtue, Virtuoso, Wal(l)y, War, Way-out, Whizzo, Whizzy, Wicked, Worth

**Except(ion)** Bar, But, Else, Exc, Nobbut, Omit, Save, Than, Then, Unless

**Exceptional** Abnormal, Anomaly, Cracker, Doozy, Egregious, Especial, Ever so, Extraordinary, Extreme, Gas, Inimitable, Odd, Rara avis, Rare, Ripsnorter, Select, Singular, Spanking, Special, Super(normal), Unco(mmon), Unusual, Zinger

**Excerpt(s)** Digest, Extract, Passage, Scrap

**Excess(ive), Excessively** All-fired, Almighty, Basinful, Binge, De trop, Epact, Exaggeration, Exorbitant, Extortionate, Extravagant, Flood, Fulsome, Glut, Hard, Indulgence, Inordinate, Intense, Lake, →LAVISH, Mountain, Needless, Nimiety, OD, Old, OTT, Outrage, Over, Overabundance, Overage, Overblown, Overcome, Overdose, Over-indulgence, Overkill, Overmuch, Overspill, Oversupply, Over-the-top, Owercome, Plethora, Preponderance, Profuse, Salt, Satiety, Spate, Spilth, Staw, Steep, Superabundant, Superfluity, Superplus, Surfeit, Surplus, Terrific, Thundering, Too, Troppo, Ultra, Undue, Unequal, Unnecessary, Woundily

**Exchange** Baltic, Bandy, Banter, Barter, Bourse, Cambist, Cash, Catallactic, Change, Chop, Commodity, Commute, Confab, Contango, Convert, Cope, Corn, Crossfire,

Ding-dong, Discourse, Employment, Enallage, Excambion, Foreign, Gematria, Global, Inosculate, Intercooler, Interplay, Ion, Job centre, Labour, Logroll, → **MARKET**, Mart, Needle, Niffer, Paraphrase, PBX, Post, Quid pro quo, Rally, Rate, RE, Recourse, Redeem, Rialto, Royal, Scorse, Scourse, Sister-chromated, Spoonerism, Stock, Swap, Switch, Switchboard, Swop (shop), Telephone, Tolsel, Tolsey, Tolzey, → **TRADE**, Trade in, Traffic, Transfusion, Transpose, Trophallaxis, Truck

**Exchequer** Remembrancer

**Excise(man), Excise district** Ablate, Bobbitt, Crop, Expunge, Gauger, Resect, Ride, Tax

▷ **Excite(d)** *may indicate* an anagram

**Excite(ment), Excitable, Excitability, Excited, Exciting** Ablaze, Aboil, Abuzz, Action-packed, Aerate, Aflutter, Agitate, Agog, Amove, Amp, Animate, Apeshit, Aphrodisiac, Arouse, Athrill, Atwitter, Awaken, Brouhaha, Bubbly, Buck-fever, Buzzing, Climactic, Combustible, Commotion, Delirium, Dither, Electrify, Emove, Enthuse, Erethism, Eventful, Feisty, Fever, Fire, Flap, Flat spin, Frantic, Frenzy, Frisson, Furore, Fuss, Galvanise, Gas, Grip, Headiness, Heat, Hectic, Het, Hey-go-mad, Highly-strung, Hilarity, Hobson-Jobson, Hoopla, Hothead, Hyped, Hyper, Hypomania, Hysterical, Impel, Incite, Inebriate, Inflame, Intoxicate, Jimjams, Kick, Kindle, Liven, Maenad, Mania, Metastable, Must, Nappy, Nervous, Neurotic, Oestrus, On fire, Orgasm, Overheat, Overwrought, Panic, Passion, Pride, Prime, Provoke, Psyched up, Racy, Radge, Red-hot, Rile, Roil, → **ROUSE**, Rousement, Ruff(e), Rut, Salutation, Send, Sexy, Shivering, Spin, Splash, Spur, Startle, Stimulate, Stir(e), Suscitate, Suspense, Swashbuckling, Temperamental, Tense, Tetanoid, Tetany, Tew, Thrill, Tickle, Titillate, Turn-on, Twitter, Upraise, Va-va-voom, Waken, Whee, Whet, Whoopee, Work up, Yahoo, Yerk, Yippee, Yirk, Yoicks, Zest

**Exclaim, Exclamation (mark)** Ahem, Arrah, Aue, Begorra, Bliksem, Blurt, Bo, Ceas(e), Crikey, Criv(v)ens, Dammit, Ecphonesis, Eina, Eish, Ejaculate, Epiphonema, Eureka, Expletive, Fen(s), Good-now, Hadaway, Haith, Halleluiah, Hallelujah, Heigh-ho, Hem, Hip, Hookey Walker, Hosanna, Inshallah, Interjection, Moryah, Omigod, Oof, Oops, Phew, Pish, Pling, Pow, Protest, Pshaw, Push, Sasa, Screamer, Sese(y), Sessa, Strewth, Uh-oh, Uh-uh, Unberufen, Vociferate, Voila, Walker, Whau, Whoopee, Whoops, Wirra, Wow, Yay, Yeehaw, Yippee, Yo-ho-ho, Yummy, Zounds

**Exclave** Cabinda

**Exclude, Excluding, Exclusion** Ban, Banish, Bar, Berufsverbot, Block, Competitive, Corner, Debar, Deforcement, Disbar, Drop, Eliminate, Ex, Except, Excommunicate, Freeze out, Ice out, Omit, Ostracise, Outbar, Outwith, Pauli, Proscribe, Rule out, Shut out, Social, Upmarket

**Exclusive** Cliquish, Closed-shop, Complete, Debarment, Elect, Elite, Esoteric, In-group, Monopoly, Narrow, Particular, Pure, Rare, Scoop, Select, Single, Sole, Unique

**Excommunicate** Curse

**Excoriate** Flay, Slam

**Excrement, Excretion, Excretory** Cystinuria, Dirt, Doo-doo, Dung, Emunctory, Faeces, Fecula, Flyspeck, Frass, Jobbie, Keech, Meconium, Oliguria, Ordure, Pat, Poo(p), Poo-poo, Puer, Pure, Refuse, Scatology, Shit(e), Sir-reverence, Stercoraceous, Stool, Strangury, Turd, Urea, Waste, Whoopsie

**Excrescence** Aril, Carnosity, Caruncle, Enate, Gall, Growth, Knob, Knurl, Lump, Nurl, Pimple, Pin, Spavin(e), Strophiole, Talpa, Twitter(-bone), Wart

**Excruciate, Excruciating** Acute, Agonising, Rack, Torment, Torture

**Exculpate** Acquit, Clear, Forgive

**Excursion** Airing, Alarum, Cruise, Dart, Day tour, Day trip, Digression, Jaunt, Junket, Outing, Pleasure-trip, Railtour, Road, Sally, Sashay, Sortie, Tour, Trip, Vagary

**Excuse, Excusable** Absolve, Alibi, Amnesty, Bunbury, Condone, Cop-out, Essoin, Essoyne, Evasion, Exempt, Exonerate, Explain, Faik, Forgive, Gold brick, Hook, Justify, Let off, Mitigate, Occasion, Off come, Out, Overlook, Palliate, → **PARDON**, Plea, Pretext, Release, Salvo, Venial, Viable, Whitewash

**Execrate, Execration** Abhor, Ban, Boo, Curse, Odium

**Execute(d), Executioner, Executive, Executor** Abhorson, Accomplish, Account, Administrate, Behead, Carnifex, Deathsman, Despatch, Discharge, Dispatch, Exor, Finish, Fry, Gan, Gar(r)otte, Gin, Guardian, Hang, Headsman, Implement, Ketch, Kill, Koko, Literary, Lynch, Management, Martyr, Monsieur de Paris, Noyade, Official, Perform, Perpetrate, Pierrepoint, Politburo, Scamp, Top, Tower Hill, Trustee, Tyburn

**Exemplar(y)** Byword, Classic, Impeccable, Laudable, Model, Paragon, Perfect, Role model, St, Warning

**Exemplify** Cite, Epitomise, Illustrate, Instantiate, Satisfy

**Exempt(ion)** Aegrotat, Dispensation, Exclude, Exeem, Fainites, Fains, Free, Immune, Impunity, Indemnity, Indulgence, Overslaugh, Privilege, Quarter, Spare, Tyburn ticket, Vains

▷ **Exercise(d)** *may indicate* an anagram

**Exercise(s)** Aerobics, Air, Antic, Apply, Athletics, Bench press, Burpee, Buteyko method, Cal(l)isthenics, Callanetics®, Chi kung, Chin-up, Circuit training, Cloze, Constitutional, Dancercise, Drill, Employ, Enure, Eurhythmics, Exert, Falun dafa, Falun gong, Fartlek, Feldenkrais method, Five-finger, Floor, Gradus, Gymnastics, Hatha yoga, Inure, Isometrics, Kata, Keepy-uppy, Kegel, Krav Maga, Lat spread, Lesson, Limber, Manual, Medau, Op, Operation, PE, Physical jerks, Pilates, Ply, Plyometrics, Popmobility, Practice, Practise, Preacher curl, Press-up, Problem, Prolusion, PT, Pull-up, Pump iron, Push-up, Qigong, Sadhana, Scales, Shintaido, Sit-up, Solfege, Solfeggi(o), Step (aerobics), Stretch, Tae-Bo®, Tai chi (ch'uan), Task, Thema, Theme, Thesis, Train, Trampoline, Treadmill, Trunk curl, Use, Vocalism, Warm-down, Warm-up, Wield, Work, Work-out, Xyst(us), Yogalates, Yomp

**Exert(ion)** Conatus, →**EFFORT**, Exercise, Labour, Operate, Strain, Strive, Struggle, Trouble, Wield

**Ex-European** Japhetic

**Exhalation, Exhale** Breath, Fume, Miasma, Reek, Sigh, Smell, Steam, Transpire, Vapour

**Exhaust(ed), Exhausting, Exhaustion, Exhaustive** All-in, Backbreaking, Beaten, Beggar, Bore, Bugger(ed), Burn, Burn-out, Bushed, Clapped out, Collapse, Consume, Deadbeat, Debility, Deplete, Detailed, Dissipate, Do, Done, Drain, Eduction, Effete, Emission, Empty, End, Enervate, Euchred, Fatigue, Finish, Flue, Fordo, Forfeuchen, Forfochen, Forfoughen, Forfoughten, Forjaskit, Forjeskit, Forspent, Forswink, Frazzle, Gruelling, Haggard, Heat, Heatstroke, Inanition, Jet-lagged, Jet-stream, Jiggered, Knacker, Mate, Milk, Out, Outspent, Outwear, Overtax, Peter, Play out, Poop, Powfagged, Prostrate, Puckerood, Puggled, Rag, Ramfeezle, Rundown, Sap, Sell out, Shatter, Shot, Shotten, Spend, Spent, Stonkered, Tailpipe, Tax, Tedious, Tire, Trauchled, Up, Use (up), Used up, Wabbit, Wappend, Warby, Washed-up, Wasted, Waygone, Weak, →**WEARY**, Wind, Worn, Zonked

**Exhibition (centre), Exhibit(ing), Exhibitioner, Exhibitionism, Exhibitionist** Aquashow, Bench, Circus, Concours, Demo, Demonstrate, Demy, Diorama, Discover, Display, Earl's Court, ENC, Endeictic, Evince, Expo, Expose, Extrovert, Fair, Hang, Indicate, Installation, Lady Godiva, →**MANIFEST**, NEC, Olympia, Pageant, Panopticon, Parade, Poseur, Present, Retrospective, Rodeo, Salon, Scene, Set forth, Show(piece), Showcase, Showman, Show-off, Showplace, Sideshow, Sight, Spectacle, Sport, Stand, Streaker, Viewing, Waxworks, Zoo

**Exhilarate(d)** Bubble, Cheer, Elate, Enliven

**Exhort(ation)** Admonish, Allocution, Caution, Counsel, Harangue, Incite, Lecture, Par(a)enesis, Persuade, Protreptic, Urge

**Exhume** Delve, Disinter, Resurrect, Unearth

**Exigency, Exigent** Demanding, Emergency, Pressing, Taxing, Urgent, Vital

**Exile** Adam, Babylon, Ban, Banish, Deport, Deportee, Eject, Emigré, Eve, Expatriate, Exul, Galut(h), Ostracise, Outlaw, Relegate, Siberia, Tax, Wretch

**Exist(ence), Existing** Be(ing), Corporeity, Dwell, Enhypostasia, Entelechy, Esse, Extant, Haeccity, Identity, Inbeing, In esse, Inherent, Life, Lifespan, Live, Ontology, Perseity, Solipsism, Status quo, Substantial, Ubiety

**Existentialist** Camus, Sartre

**Exit** Débouché, Door, Egress, Emergency, Exhaust, Gate, Leave, Log off, Log out, Outgate, Outlet, Swansong, Trapdoor, Vent, Vomitory

**Exodus** Book, Departure, Flight, Hegira, Hejira, Passover

**Ex-official** Outler

**Exogamous** Outbred

**Exonerate(d)** Absolve, Acquit, Clear, Discharge, Excuse, Exempt, Shriven

**Exorbitant** Excessive, Expensive, Nimiety, Slug, Steep, Tall, Undue

**Exorcise, Exorcist** Benet, Dispirit, Lay

**Exordium** Opening, Preface, Prelude

**Exotic** Alien, Chinoiserie, Ethnic, Fancy, Foreign, Free, Outlandish, Strange

**Expand(able), Expanse, Expansion** Acreage, Amplify, Boom, Branch out, Bulking, Develop, Diastole, Dilate, Distend, Ectasis, Elaborate, →**ENLARGE**, Escalate, Flesh out, Grow, Increase, Inflate, Magnify, Ocean, Outspread, Outstretch, Sheet, Snowball, Sprawl, Spread, Stretch, Swell, Tensile, Vastitude, Wax, Wire-draw

**Expatiate** Amplify, Descant, Dwell, Enlarge, Perorate

**Expatriate** Banish, Colonial, Emigrate, Émigré, Exile, Outcast

**Expect(ant), Expectation, Expected, Expecting** Agog, Anticipate, Ask, Await, Due, En l'air, Foresee, Gravid, Hope, Imminent, Intend, Lippen, Look, Natural, On cue, Par, Pip, Predict, Pregnant, Presume, Prim, Probable, Prognosis, Prospect, Require, →**SUPPOSE**, Tendance, Think, Thought, Up the duff, Usual, Ween

**Expectorant, Expectorate** Expel, Guaiacol, Hawk, Spit

**Expedient** Advisable, Artifice, Contrivance, Dodge, Fend, Make-do, Makeshift, Measure, Politic, Resort, Resource, Salvo, Shift, Stopgap, Suitable, Wise

**Expedite, Expedition, Expeditious** Advance, Alacrity, Anabasis, Celerity, Crusade, Dispatch, Excursion, Fastness, Field trip, Hasten, Hurry, Kon-Tiki, Mission, Pilgrimage, Post-haste, Quest, Rapidity, Safari, Short cut, Speed, Trek, Trip, Turn out, Voyage, Warpath

**Expel** Amove, Blow, Deport, Dispossess, Drum out, Egest, Evacuate, Evict, Excommunicate, Excrete, Exile, Exorcize, Hoof, Oust, Out(cast), Read out, Spit, Suspend, Turn forth, Void

**Expend(iture)** Budget, Consume, Cost, Dues, Gavel, Goings-out, Mise, Occupy, Oncost, Outgo(ing), Outlay, Poll, Squander, Tithe, Toll, Use, Waste

**Expendable** Cannon-fodder

**Expense(s)** Boodle, Charge, Cost, Current, Exes, Fee, Housekeeping, Law, Oncost, Outgoing, Outlay, Overhead, Price, Sumptuary

**Expensive** Chargeful, Costly, Dear, Executive, High, Precious, Pricey, Ruinous, Salt, Steep, Top dollar, Upmarket, Valuable

**Experience(d)** Accomplished, A posteriori, Assay, Blasé, Come up, Dab (hand), Discovery, Dree, Empiric, Encounter, Expert, →**FEEL**, Felt, Find, Foretaste, Freak-out, Gust, Hands-on, Hard way, Have, Incur, Know, Learn, Level, Live, Mature, Meet, Mneme, Near-death, Occlude, Old hand, Old-stager, Ordeal, Out-of-body, Pass, Plumb, Seasoned, See, Senior, Sense, Sensory, Sophisticated, Spin, Stager, Stand, Street-smart, Streetwise, Taste, Transference, Trial, Trip, Trocinium, Try, Undergo, Versed, Veteran, Work, Worldly wise

**Experiment(al)** Attempt, Aufgabe, Avant-garde, Ballon d'assai, Control, Double blind, Empirical, Essay, Gedanken, →**JET**, Michelson-Morley, Peirastic, Pilot, Sample, Shy, Single-blind, Taste, Tentative, →**TRIAL**, Trial balloon, Try, Venture, Vivisection

**Expert(ise), Experts** Able, Accomplished, Ace, Adept, Adroit, Arch, Artistry, Astacologist, Au fait, Authority, Boffin, Buff, Cambist, Cocker, Cognoscente, Competent, Connoisseur, Crack, Craft, Dab(ster), Dab hand, Dan, Deft, Demon, Diagnostician,

Digerati, Don, Egghead, Fancier, Finesse, Fundi, Gourmet, Grand master, Gun, Guru,
Hotshot, Karateka, Know-all, Know-how, Learned, Luminary, Maestro, Masterly,
Mastery, Maven, Mavin, Meister, Nark, Nohow, Old hand, Oner, Oneyer, Oneyre, Oracle,
Past master, Peritus, Practised, Pro, Proficient, Pundit, Ringer, Rubrician, Savant, Savvy,
Science, Shroff, Skill(y), Sly, Specialist, Techie, Technique, Technocrat, Technofreak,
Technophile, Think tank, Tipster, Troubleshooter, Ulema, Used, Whizz, Wireman,
Wisard, W(h)iz, Wizard, Wonk

**Expiate, Expiation, Expiatory** Amends, Atone, Penance, Piacular

**Expire(d), Expiry** Blow, Collapse, Croak, → **DIE**, End, Exhaust(ed), Exhale, Go, Invalid,
Ish, Lapse, Neese, Pant, → **PERISH**, Sneeze, Terminate

**Explain(able), Explanation** Account, Annotate, Aperçu, Appendix, Aread, Arede,
Arreede, Clarify, Conster, Construe, Decline, Define, Describe, Eclaircissement, Elucidate,
Epexegesis, Explicate, Exponible, Expose, Expound, Extenuate, Gloss, Glossary, Gloze,
Justify, Outline, Parabolize, Salve, Solve, Tell, Upknit, Why

**Explanation, Explanatory** Apology, Commentary, Definition, Exegesis, Exegetic,
Exposition, Farse, Gloss, Gloze, Hypothesis, Interpret, Key, Note, Preface, Rationalise,
Reading, Rigmarole, Solution, Theory, Translate

**Expletive** Arrah, Darn, Exclamation, Oath, Ruddy, Sapperment

**Explicit** Clean-cut, Clear(-cut), Definite, Express, Frank, Full-on, Graphic, Open,
Outspoken, → **PRECISE**, Specific, Unequivocal

**Explode, Explosion, Explosive** Aerobomb, Agene, Airburst, Amatol, Ammonal,
ANFO, Antimatter, Aquafortis, Atishoo, Backfire, Ballistic, Bang(er), Bangalore torpedo,
Big bang, Blast, Blow-out, Booby-trap, Burst, C4, Cap, Cheddite, Chug, Clap, Controlled,
Cordite, Cramp, Crump, Cyclonite, Debunk, Demolitions, Depth bomb, Detonate, Dualin,
Dunnite, Dust, Egg, Erupt, Euchloric, Euchlorine, Fiery, Fireball, Firecracker, Firedamp,
Firework, Flip, Fulminant, Fulminate, Gasohol, Gelatine, Gelignite, Glottal stop,
Grenade, Guncotton, Gunpaper, Gunpowder, Hand grenade, HE, High, Initiator, Iracund,
Jelly, Landmine, Low, Lyddite, Megaton, Melinite, Mine, Nail-bomb, Napalm, Nitre,
Nitro(glycerine), Nitrobenzene, Nitrocotton, Outburst, Ozonide, Paravane, Payload,
Petar(d), Petre, Phreatic, Phut, Plastic, Plastique, Pluff, Pop, Population, Pow, Priming,
Propellant, Ptarmic, Pustular, Report, Roburite, SAM, Saucisse, Semtex®, Sheet,
Shrapnel, Snake, Sneeze, Soup, Squib, Supernova, TATP, Tetryl, Thermite, Thunderflash,
Tinderbox, TNT, Tonite, Trident, Trinitrobenzene, Trotyl, Volatile, Volcanic, Warhead,
Xyloidin(e)

**Exploit(ation), Exploited, Exploiter, Exploiting, Exploits** Act, Adventure,
Arbitrage, Coup, Coyote, Deed, Develop, Downtrodden, Escapade, Feat, Freeloader, Gest,
Geste, Harness, Ill-use, Impose, Kulak, Manoeuvre, Milk, Mine, Mission, Misuse, Parlay,
Play on, Predatory, Profit, Rachmanism, Ramp, Res gestae, Rip-off, Shark, Stunt, Sweat,
Tap, Use, Utilise

**Explore(r), Exploration** Bandeirante, Caver, Chart, Discover, Dredge, Examine, Feel,
Field trip, Investigate, Map, Navigator, Oceanaut, Pathfinder, Pioneer, Potholer, Probe,
Prospect, Research, Scout, Search, Spaceship, Voyageur

---

**EXPLORERS**

| 3 letters: | Eyre | Boone | Parry |
|---|---|---|---|
| Fox | Grey | Burke | Peary |
| | Park | Cabot | Ponce |
| 4 letters: | Polo | Clark | Scott |
| Byrd | Ross | David | Speke |
| Cook | | Drake | Sturt |
| Dias | 5 letters: | Fuchs | Wills |
| Diaz | Baker | Giles | |
| Eric | Banks | Oates | |

| 6 letters: | Tasman | Cousteau | Vancouver |
|---|---|---|---|
| Baffin | | Eriksson | Wentworth |
| Balboa | 7 letters: | Flinders | |
| Bering | Amerigo | Franklin | 10 letters: |
| Burton | Barents | Hargrave | Przewalski |
| Cabral | Cartier | Humboldt | Shackleton |
| Cortes | Cordoba | Magellan | |
| Da Gama | Dampier | Mitchell | 11 letters: |
| Darwin | Fiennes | Vespucci | Leif Ericson |
| De Soto | Hillary | | Livingstone |
| Lawson | Raleigh | 9 letters: | Vasco da Gama |
| Nansen | Stanley | Champlain | |
| Ralegh | | Frobisher | 14 letters: |
| Rhodes | 8 letters: | Mackenzie | Bellingshausen |
| Sabine | Amundsen | Marco Polo | |
| Stuart | Columbus | Mungo Park | |

▷ **Explosive**  *may indicate* an anagram

**Exponent** Advocate, Example, Index, Interpreter, Logarithm

**Export(s)** Despatch, Émigré, Frustrated, Invisible, Klondike, Klondyke, Ship, Visible

**Expose(d), Exposure** Adamic, Air, Anagogic, Apparent, Bare, Bleak, Blot, Blow, Burn, Crucify, Debag, Debunk, Denounce, Denude, Desert, Disclose, Double, Endanger, En prise, Exhibit, Flashing, Glareal, Imperil, Indecent, Insolate, In the buff, Liable, Moon, Nail, Naked, Nude, Object, Open, Out, Over, Paramo, Propale, Reveal, Showdown, Snapshot, Starkers, Streak, Strip, Subject, Sun, Time, Uncover, Unmask, Unrip, Unshroud, Whistle-blow, Windburn, Windswept

**Exposition** Aperçu

**Expostulate, Expostulation** Argue, Arrah, Protest, Remonstrate

**Expound(er)** Discourse, Discuss, Exegete, Explain, Open, Prelict, Red, Scribe, Ulema

**Express(ed), Expression, Expressionism, Expressive** Abstract, Air, Alas, APT, Arrah, Articulate, Aspect, Breathe, Cacophemism, Circumbendimus, Cliché, Colloquialism, Conceive, Concetto, Couch, Countenance, Crumbs, Declare, Denote, Desorb, Diction, Eloquent, Embodiment, Epithet, Estafette, Explicit, Face, Fargo, Flying Scotsman, Formulate, Frown, Function, Gesticulate(d), Godspeed, Good-luck, Gotcha, Graphic, Gup, Hang-dog, Hech, Heck, Hell's bells, Idiom, Isit, Limited, Locution, Lyrical, Manifest, Metonym, Mien, Mot (juste), Neologism, Non-stop, Orient, Paraphrase, Phrase, Pleonasm, Pony, Precise, Pronouncement, Pronto, Put, Quep, Rapid, Register, Rhetoric, Say(ne), Shade, Show, Sigh, Soulful, →SPEAK, State, Strain, Succus, Sumpsimus, Taxeme, Term, Token, Tone, Topos, Trope, Utterance, Vent, →VOICE, V-sign

**Expressionless** Aphasia, Blank, Boot-faced, Deadpan, Glassy, Impassive, Inscrutable, Po(ker)-faced, Vacant, Wooden

**Expressman** Fargo

**Expropriate** Dispossess, Pirate, Seize, Usurp

**Expulsion** Abjection, Discharge, Eccrisis, Ejection, Eviction, Exile, Pride's Purge, Removal, Sacking, Synaeresis

**Expunge** Cancel, Delete, Efface, Erase, Obliterate

**Expurgate** Bowdlerize, Castrate, Censor, Purge

**Exquisite** Beautiful, Choice, Ethereal, Fine, Fop, Intense, Lair, Macaroni, Pink, Princox, Refined, Soigné(e), Too-too

**Ex-serviceman** Vet

**Extempore, Extemporise(d)** Ad lib, Autoschediasm, Improvise, Pong

**Extend(ed), Extension** Add, Aggrandise, Annexe, Aspread, Augment, Conservative, Cremaster, Dendrite, Draw, Drop-leaf, Ecarté, Eke, Elapse, Ell, Elongate, Enlarge,

Escalate, Expand, Exsert, Extrapolation, Fermata, Grow, Increase, Jumboise, Lanai, Leaf, Length, Long, Long-range, Long-stay, Long-term, Offer, Outgrowth, Outspread, Overbite, Overlap, Pong, Porrect, Proffer, Prolong, Propagate, Protract, Reach, Renew, Retrochoir, Span, Spread, Steso, Stilt, → **STRETCH**, Substantial, Vert, Widen, Widespread, Yonks

**Extensive, Extent** Acre, Ambit, Area, Capacious, Catch-all, Compass, Comprehensive, Degree, Distance, Duration, Far-reaching, Large, Latitude, Length, Limit, → **MAGNITUDE**, Measure, Outspread, Panoramic, Range, Reach, Scale, Scope, Size, Spacious, Span, Spread-eagle, Sweeping, Wholesale, Wide, Widespread

**Extenuate** Diminish, Lessen, Mitigate, Palliate

**Exterior** Aspect, Crust, Derm, Exoteric, Facade, Outer, → **OUTSIDE**, Shell, Surface, Veneer

**Exterminate, Extermination** Abolish, Annihilate, Destroy, Ethnocide, Holocaust, The final solution, Uproot

**External** Exoteric, Exterior, Extraneous, Foreign, Outer, Outward

**Extinct(ion)** Archaeopteryx, Bucardo, Bygone, Chalicothere, Creodont, Dead, Death, Defunct, D(e)inothere, Dodo, Glyptodon, Mastodon, Oblivion, Obsolete, Ostracoderm, Placoderm, Quagga, Quietus, Rasure, Rhytina, Saururae, Theodont, Ulmin

**Extinguish(er)** Douse, Dout, Dowse, Dowt, Extirpate, Obscure, Quash, Quell, Quench, Slake, Slo(c)ken, Smother, Snuff, Sprinkler, Stamp out, Stifle, Suppress

**Extirpate** End, Erase, Excise, Obliterate, Root, Uproot

**Extol** Commend, Enhance, Eulogise, Exalt, Laud, Praise, Puff

**Extort(ion), Extortionate, Extortioner** Barathrum, Blackmail, Bleed, Bloodsucker, Chantage, Chout, Churn, Compel, Exact, Force, Gombeen, Malversation, Montem, Outwrest, Rachman, Rack, Racketeer, Ransom, Rapacious, Screw, Shank, Sokaiya, Squeeze, Sweat, Urge, Vampire, Wrest, Wring

**Extra** Accessory, Addendum, Additament, Addition(al), Additive, Adjunct, And, Annexe, Appendix, Attachment, Bisque, Bonus, By(e), Codicil, Debauchery, Else, Encore, Etcetera, Frill, Further, Gash, Lagniappe, Left-over, Leg bye, Make-weight, Mo, More, Nimiety, No ball, Odd, Optional, Out, Over, Overtime, Perk, Plus, Plusage, Reserve, Ripieno, → **SPARE**, Spilth, Staffage, Sundry, Super, Superadd, Supernumerary, Supplementary, Suppletive, Surcharge, Surplus, Top up, Trop, Undue, Walking-gentleman, Walking-lady, Wide, Woundy

**Extract(ion), Extractor** Apozem, Bleed, Breeding, Catechu, Clip, Corkscrew, Decoction, Derive, Descent, Distil, Draw, Educe, Elicit, Emulsin, Enucleate, Episode, Essence, Estreat, Excerpt, Exodontics, Extort, Formyl, Gist, Gobbet, Insulin, Ionone, Kino, Liebig, Liver, Malta, Milk, Mine, Oust, Parentage, Passage, Pericope, Pick, Piece, Pituitary, Prize, Pry, Pyrene, Pyrethrin, Quintessence, Quotation, Render, Retour, Retrieve, Smelt, Snippet, Soundbite, Squeeze, Stope, Succus, Suck, Summary, Tap, Tincture, Trie, Try, Vanilla, Vegemite®, Ventouse, Winkle, Withdraw, Worm, Wrest, Wring, Yohimbine

**Extradition** Renvoi

**Extraneous** Extrinsic, Foreign, Irrelevant, Outlying, Spurious

**Extraordinary** Amazing, By-ordinar, Case, Curious, Egregious, Fabulous, Humdinger, Important, Non(e)such, Phenomenal, Preternatural, Rare, Remarkable, Signal, Singular, Sorter, Startling, Stellar, Strange, Unusual

**Extrasensory** Clairaudience, Clairvoyance, → **ESP**

**Extra time** Lean

**Extravagance, Extravagant, Extravaganza** Bizarre, Bombastic, Dissipation, Elaborate, Enthusiasm, Excessive, Fancy, Feerie, Flamboyant, Glitzy, Grotesque, Heroic, High-flown, High roller, Hyperbole, Immoderate, Lavish, Lush, Luxury, OTT, Outré, Prodigal, Profligate, Profuse, Rampant, Reckless, Riotise, Romantic, Splash, Splurge, Squander, Sumptuous, Superfluous, Waste, Wasterfulness

**Extreme(s), Extremely, Extremist, Extremity** Acute, All-fired, Almighty, Bourn(e), Butt, Crisis, Deep-dyed, Desperate, Die-hard, Digit, Drastic, Edge, Ending, Exceptional,

Farthermost, Fascist, Finger(-tip), Gross, In spades, →**INTENSE**, Jacobin, Leveller, Limb, Major, Maximum, Mega-, Merveilleux, Militant, Minimum, Mondo, Much, National Front, Nazi, Not half, Opposite, OTT, Outrance, Over the top, Parlous, Pole, Pretty, Radical, Remote, Root and branch, So, Solstice, Steep, Sublime, Tendency, Terminal, Terrorist, The last cast, Thule, Tip, Toe, Too, Tremendous, Ultimate, Ultima thule, Ultra, Unco, Utmost, Utter(ance), →**VERY**, Violent, Vitally, Wing

▷ **Extreme** *may indicate* a first or last letter

**Extricate** Liberate, Loose, Outwind, Rescue, Untangle

**Extrinsic** Aliunde, External, Irrelevant, Outward

**Extrovert** Lad, Outgoing

**Extrude** Debar, Eject, Project

**Exuberance, Exuberant** Abundant, Brio, Bushy, Copious, Ebullient, Effusive, Feisty, Flamboyant, Gleeful, Gusto, Hearty, Joie de vivre, Lavish, Mad, Overflowing, Profuse, Rambunctious, Skippy, Streamered

**Exudation, Exude** Bleed, Ectoplasm, Emit, Extravasate, Guttate, Ooze, Perspire, Secrete, Still, Sweat, Swelter, Ulmin, Weep

**Exult(ant), Exultation** Cock-a-hoop, Crow, Elated, →**GLOAT**, Glorify, Glory be, Jubilant, Paeonic, Rejoice, Tripudiate, Triumphant, Whoop

**Eye(d), Eyes, Eye-ball, Eyeful, Eye movement, Eyepiece** Aperture, Beady, Canthus, Compound, Cringle, Deepset, Detective, Eagle, Ee, Eine, Electric, Emmetropia, Evil, Glad, Glass, Glim, Glom, Goggles, Hurricane, Huygen's, Iridal, Iris, Jack, Keek, Klieg, Lamp, Lazy, Leer, Lens, London, Magic, Many, Mincepie, Mind's, Mongoloid, Naked, →**OBSERVE**, Ocellar, Ocular, Ogle, Ommateum, Ommatidium, Optic, Orb, Pedicel, Peeper, PI, Pigsnie, Pigsn(e)y, Pineal, Private, Public, Pupil, Regard, Retina, Rhabdom, Roving, Saccade, Saucer, Sclera, Screw, Seeing, Sheep's, Shufti, Shufty, Sight, Spy, Stemma, Storm-centre, Tec, Third, Tiger, Uvea, Watch, Water-pump, Weather, Whally, Windows, Winker

**Eyebright** Euphrasy

**Eyebrow** Bree, Brent-hill, Glib, Penthouse, Superciliary

**Eyeglass** Loupe

**Eyelash** Cilium, Winker

**Eyelet** Cringle, Grommet, Hole

**Eyelid** Canthus, Ectropion, Haw, Palpebral, Winker

**Eye-opener, Eye-opening** Alarm, Revelatory

**Eye-rod** Rhabdom

**Eye-shadow** Kohl

**Eyesore** Blot, Carbuncle, Disfigurement, Sty(e)

**Eye-stalk** Ommatophore, Stipes

**Eye trouble, Eye-problem** Albugo, Amblyopia, Ametropia, Anirida, Aniseikonia, Anisomatropia, Aphakia, Asthenopia, Astigmatism, Caligo, Cataract, Ceratitis, Coloboma, Comae, Conjunctivitis, Cycloplegia, Detached retina, Diplopia, Ectropion, Ectropium, Entropion, Erythropsia, Exophthalmus, Glaucoma, Gravel-blind, Hemeralopia, Hemi(an)op(s)ia, Heterotropia, Hypermetropia, Hyperopia, Iritis, Keratitis, Lazy eye, Leucoma, Lippitude, Micropsia, Miosis, Monoblepsis, Muscae volitantes, Mydriasis, Myosis, Nebula, Nyctalopia, Nystagmus, Ommateum, Palinop(s)ia, Pearl eye, Photophobia, Photopsia, Pin and web, Pink-eye, Presbyopia, Proptosis, Ptosis, Retinitis, Retinoblastoma, Sandy blight, Scotoma(ta), Shiner, Stigmatism, Strabismus, Strephosymbolia, Strong, Stye, Synechia, Teichopsia, Thylose, Thylosis, Trachoma, Trichiasis, Tritanopia, Tylosis, Wall-eye, Xeroma, Xerophthalmia

**Eye-wash** Collyrium

**Eye-witness** Passer-by

**Eyrie** Nest

**Ezra** Pound

# Ff

**F** Fahrenheit, Fellow, Feminine, Fluorine, Following, Force, Foxtrot

**Fab** Super

**Fabian, Fabius** Dilatory, Washington, Webb

**Fable(s)** Aesop, Allegory, Apologue, Exemplum, Fiction, Hitopadesa, La Fontaine, Legend, Lie, Marchen, Milesian, Myth, Panchatantra, Parable, Romance, Tale, Tarand

**Fabric** Acetate, Cheesecloth, →CLOTH, Contexture, Dévoré, Evenweave, Felt, Framework, Hessian, Interfacing, Interlining, Interlock, Lycra, Orlon®, Plissé, Ratteen, Ripstop, Spandex, Stretch-knit, Textile, Velour

**Fabricate, Fabrication** Artefact, Concoct, Confabulate, Construct, Contrive, Cook, Fake, Fangle, Figment, Forge, →INVENT, Lie, Make up, Porky, Trump, Weave, Web

**Fabulous (beast), Fabulous place** Ace, Apocryphal, Apologue, Atlantis, Chichevache, Chimera, Cockatrice, Eldorado, Fictitious, Fung, Gear, Griffin, Hippogriff, Hippogryph, Huma, Incredible, Jabberwock(y), Kylin, Legendary, Magic, Manticora, Manticore, Merman, Monoceros, Mythical, Opinicus, Orc, Phoenix, Roc, Romantic, Simorg, Simurg(h), Snark, Sphinx, Tarand, Tragelaph, Unicorn, Unreal, Utopia, Wivern, Wyvern, Yale

**Facade** Front(age), Frontal, Mask, Persona, Pretence, Surface

**Face, Facing** Abide, Affront, Ashlar, Ashler, Aspect, Audacity, Beard, Bide, Bold, Brave, Brazen, Caboched, Caboched, Cheek, Chiv(v)y, Cliff, Coal, Confront, Countenance, Culet, Dalle, Dare, Dartle, Daur, Deadpan, Dial, Eek, Elevation, Encounter, Expression, Facade, Fat, Favour, Features, Fineer, Fortune, →FRONT, Gardant, Girn, Gonium, Grid, Groof, Groue, Grouf, Grufe, Gurn, Hatchet, Head-on, Jib, Kisser, Light, Lining, Look, Lore, Map, Mascaron, Meet, Metope, Moe, Mug, Mush, Obverse, Oppose, Opposite, Outstare, Outward, Pan, Paper tiger, Pavilion, Phisnomy, Phiz(og), Physiognomy, Poker, Puss, Revet, Revetment, Roughcast, Rud, Rybat, Side, Snoot, Socle, Straight, Stucco, Tallow, Three-quarter, Times Roman, Type, Veneer, Vis(age), Visnomy, Wall, Withstand, Zocco(lo)

**Face-ache** Noli-me-tangere

**Face-lift** Rhytidectomy, Transformation

**Face-saving** Redeeming, Salvo

**Facet(ed)** Angle, Aspect, Bezel, Culet, Face, Pavilion, Polyhedron

**Facetious** Frivolous, Jocose, Jocular, Waggish, Witty

**Facile** Able, Adept, Complaisant, Ductile, Easy, Fluent, Glib, Trite

**Facilitate, Facilities, Facility** Agrement, Amenity, Assist, Benefit, Bent, Capability, Committed, →EASE, Expedite, Fluency, Gift, ISO, Knack, Lavatory, Loo, Provision, Skill

**Facsimile** Copy, Electro, Electrotype, Photostat®, Replica, Repro

**Fact(s), Factual** Actual, Brass tacks, Case, Corpus delicti, Correct, Data, Datum, Detail, Eo ipso, Evidence, French, Gospel, Griff, In esse, Info, Information, Literal, Mainor, Material, Nay, Poop, Really, Stat, Statistics, Truism, Truth, Veridical, Yes

**Faction** Bloc, Cabal, Camp, Caucus, Clique, Contingent, Gang of four, Ghibelline, Group(let), Guelph, Junta, Junto, Party, Red Army, Schism, Sect, Tendency, Wing

**Factor(s)** Agent, Aliquot, Amildar, Broker, Cause, Chill, Clotting, Coagulation, Co-efficient, Common, →COMPONENT, Divisor, Edaphic, Element, F, Feedback, Feel-bad, Feel-good, Fertility, Growth, House, Imponderabilia, Institorial, Intrinsic, Judicial, Load, Modulus, Moment, Multiple, Power, Pull, Q, Quality, Reflection,

Representative, Rh, Rhesus, Risk, Safety, Sex, Steward, Transfer, Unit, Utilization, Wind chill, X

**Factory** Ashery, Bakery, Brickworks, Cannery, Creamery, Etruria, Gasworks, Glassworks, Hacienda, Ironworks, Maquiladora, Mill, Plant, Refinery, Sawmill, Shot tower, Steelworks, Sugarhouse, Sweatshop, Tanyard, Tinworks, Wireworks, Works, Workshop

**Factory-owner** Industrialist

**Factotum** Circar, Do-all, Handyman, Servant, Sircar, Sirkar

**Faculty** Aptitude, Arts, Capacity, Department, Ear, Ease, Flair, Hearing, Indult, Knack, Lavatory, Loo, Moral, Power, School, Sense, Speech, →**TALENT**, Teachers, Uni(versity), Wits

**Fad(dish)** Crank, Craze, Cult, Fashion, Foible, Ismy, Thing, Vogue, Whim

**Fade(d), Fading** Blanch, Decrescendo, Die, Diminuendo, Dinge, Disperse, Dwindle, Elapsion, Etiolate, Evanescent, Fall, Filemot, Fizzle, Lessen, Mancando, Miffy, Pale, Passé, Perdendo(si), Peter, Pine, Smorzando, Smorzato, Stonewashed, Vade, Vanish, Wallow, Wilt, Wither

**Faeces** Cesspit, Dingleberry, Dung, Kak, Meconium, Motion, Mute, Number two, Scybalum, Skatole, Stercoraceous, Stools

**Faff** Bother

**Fag(g)ot(s)** Bavin, Bundle, Fascine, Firewood, Homosexual, Kid, Knitch, Twigs

**Fag(ging)** Chore, Cigarette, Drag, Drudge, Fatigue, Gasper, Homosexual, Inconvenience, Menial, Pennalism, Quean, Reefer, Snout, Tire, Toil, Weary

**Fag-end** Ash, Butt, Dout, Lag, Snipe, Stub

**Faience** Trema

**Fail(ing), Failure** Achalasia, Ademption, Anile, Anuria, Awry, Backfire, Bankruptcy, Blemish, Blow, Bomb, Bummer, Burst-up, Cark, Chicken, →**COLLAPSE**, Common-mode, Conk, Crack up, Crash, Cropper, Damp squib, Debacle, Decline, Defalcation, Default, Defeat, Defect, Demerit, Demise, Die, Disaster, Dog, Down the tubes, Dry, Dud, Fatigue, Fault, Feal, Fiasco, Fink out, Flame out, Flivver, Flop, Flow, Flunk, Fold, Footfault, Founder, Frost, Futility, Glitch, Goner, Go phut, Gutser, Impotent, Infraction, Isn't, Lapse, Lemon, Lose, Lossage, Malfunction, Manqué, Meltdown, Mis-, Miscarry, Misfire, Misprision, Miss, Muff, Nerd, No-hoper, No-no, No-show, Omission, Omit, Outage, Oversight, Pip, Plough, Plow, Pluck, Pratfall, Reciprocity, Refer, Refusal, Relapse, Respiratory, Shambles, Short(coming), Short circuit, Shortfall, Sink, Slippage, Smash, Spin, Stumer, Tank, Turkey, Vice, Wash-out, Waterloo, Weakness, White elephant, Wilt, Wipeout

**Fain** Lief

**Faineant** Gallio

**Faint(ness)** Black-out, Conk, Darkle, Dim, Dizzy, Dwalm, Fade, Giddy, Lassitude, Pale, Stanck, Subtle, Swarf, Swarve, Swelt, Swerf, Swerve, Swoon, Swound, Syncope, Unclear, Wan, Whitish

**Faint-heart** Boneless, Coward, Craven, Eery, Hen, Timid, Wet

**Fair, Fairground** Adequate, Aefauld, Aefwld, A(e)fald, Barnet, Bartholomew, Bazaar, Beauteous, Beautiful, Belle, Big dipper, Blond, Bon(n)ie, Bonny, Brigg, Clean, Clement, Decent, Dishy, Donnybrook, Eirian, Equal, Equitable, Evenhanded, Exhibition, Expo(sition), Fancy, Feeing-market, →**FESTIVAL**, Fête, Fine, Fiona, Funfair, Gaff, Gala, Gay, Gey, Goose, Gwyn, Handsome, Hiring, Honest, Hopping, Isle, Isold(e), →**JUST**, Kermess, Kermis, Kirmess, Light, Market, Mart, Mediocre, Mela, Mop, Nundinal, Objective, OK, Paddington, Passable, Play, Pro rata, Rag, Rosamond, Sabrina, Second rate, So-so, Sporting, Sportsmanlike, Square, Statute, Steeple, Straight, Tavistock, Tidy, Tolerable, Tow-headed, Trade, Tryst, Unbias(s)ed, Vanity, Wake, Widdicombe, Xanthe

**Fair-buttocked** Callipygean

**Fairing** Ornament, Spat

**Fairly** Clearly, Enough, Evenly, Midway, Moderately, Pari passu, Pretty, Properly, Quite, Ratherish, So-so

**Fairway** Dog-leg, Pretties

**Fairy, Fairies** Banshee, Befana, Brownie, Cobweb, Dobbie, Dobby, Elf(in), Fay, Gloriana, Good neighbour, Good people, Hob, Hop o' my thumb, Leprechaun, Lilian, Little people, Mab, Morgane(tta), Morgan le Fay, Moth, Mustardseed, Nis, Oberon, Peri, Pigwidgin, Pigwiggen, Pisky, Pixie, Pouf, Puck, Punce, Queen Mab, Sandman, Seelie, Sidhe, Spirit, Sprite, Sugar-plum, Tink(erbell), Titania, Tooth, Unseelie, Urchin-shows

**Faith(ful)** Accurate, Achates, Adam, Belief, Constant, Creed, Cupboard, Devoted, Doctrine, Faix, Fay, Feal, Fegs, Fideism, Fiducial, Haith, Implicit, Islam, Lay, Liege, Loyal, Pantheism, Plerophory, Punic, Puritanism, Quaker, Reliance, Religion, Shahada, Shema, Solifidian, Staunch, Strict, Troth, →**TRUE**, True-blue, Trust, Truth, Umma(h), Vera

**Faithless** Atheist, Disloyal, False, Giaour, Hollow, Infidel, Nullifidian, Perfidious, Punic

**Fake(d), Faker, Faking** Bodgie, Bogus, Charlatan, Cod, Copy, Counterfeit, Duff(er), Ersatz, False, Feign, Fold, Forgery, Fraud, Fudge, Imitation, Imposter, Impostor, Inauthentic, Paste, Phoney, Pirate(d), Postiche, Pretend, Pseudo, Quack, Sham, Spurious, Straw man, Toy, Trucage, Trumped up, Truquage, Truqueur, Unreal, Untrue

**Falcon** Cast, Gentle, Hawk, Hobby, Iceland, Kestrel, Lanner(et), Merlin, Nankeen kestrel, Nyas, Peregrine, Prairie, Saker, Sakeret, Spar-hawk, Sparrow-hawk, Stallion, Staniel, Stannel, Stanyel, Stone, Tassel-gentle, Tassell-gent, Tercel-gentle, Tercel-jerkin

**Falklander** Kelper

**Fall(s), Fallen, Falling, Fall out** Abate, Accrue, Alopecia, Angel, Anticlimax, Arches, Astart, Autumn, Boyoma, Cadence, Caducous, Cascade, Cataract, Churchill, Chute, Collapse, Crash, Cropper, Cross press, Declasse, Declension, Decrease, Degenerate, Deluge, Descent, Dip, Domino effect, Douse, Downpour, Downswing, Dowse, →**DROP**, Ebb, End, Firn, Flag, Flop, Flump, Folding press, Free, Grabble, Grand, Gutser, Gutzer, Horseshoe, Idaho, Iguaçu, Incidence, Kabalega, Kaieteur, Keel over, Lag, Landslide, Lapse, Lin(n), Montmorency, Mtarazi, Niagara, Oct(ober), Onding, Overbalance, Owen, Perish, Plonk, Plummet, Plump, Plunge, Precipitance, Prolapse, Ptosis, Purl(er), Rain, Reaction, Relapse, Ruin, Season, Sheet, Sin, Sleet, Slide, Slip, Snow, Soss, Spill, Stanley, Sutherland, Swallow, Tailor, Takakkau, Teem, Topple, Toss, Trip, Tugela, Tumble, Victoria, Voluntary, Wipeout, Yellowstone, Yosemite

**Fallacious, Fallacy** Elench(us), Error, Gamblers', Idolon, Idolum, Ignoratio elenchi, Illogical, Illusion, Material, Naturalistic, Pathetic, Sophism, Specious, Unsound

**Fallible** Human, Imperfect

▷ **Falling** *may indicate* an anagram or a word backwards

**Fallow** Barren, Lea, Tan, Uncared, Uncultivated, Untilled

**False, Falsify, Falsification, Falsehood** Adulterate, Assumed, Bastard, Bodgie, Bogus, Braide, Bricking, Bum, Calumny, Canard, Cavil, Charlatan, Cook, Counterfeit, Deceitful, Disloyal, Dissemble, Doctor, Façade, Fake, Faux, Feigned, Fiddle, Forge, Illusory, Inexact, Insincere, Knave, Leasing, Lying, Masquerade, Meretricious, Misconception, Misrepresented, Misstatement, Mock, Mooncalf, Mooncall, Myth, Obreption, Perjury, Phoney, Pinchbeck, Postiche, Pretence, Prosthesis, Pseudo, Rap, Refute, Roorback, Sham, Specious, Spoof, Spurious, Strumpet, Suspect, Treacherous, Trumped-up, Two-faced, Untrue, Veneer

**False notions** Idola

**Falter** Hesitate, Limp, Lurch, Stoiter, Totter, Waver

**Fame, Famous** A-list, All-star, Bruit, Cause célèbre, Celebrity, Distinguished, Eminent, Five, Glitterati, Gloire, Glory, Greatness, History, Humour, Illustrious, Known, Kudos, Legendary, Luminary, Luminous, Lustre, Megastar, Mononym, Name, Noted, Notorious, Prestige, Reclamé, Renown, Repute, Robert, Rumour, Splendent, Spotlight, Spur, Stardom, Word

**Familiar(ise), Familiarity** Accustom, Acquaint, Assuefaction, Au fait, Auld, Chummy, Comrade, Consuetude, Conversant, Couth, Crony, Dear, Demon, Easy, Free, Fresh, Friend, Habitual, Hailfellow, Homely, Homey, Incubus, Intimate, Known, Liberty, Maty, Old, Old-hat, Privy, Public, Python, Streetwise, Used, Versant, Versed, Warhorse

**Family** Ainga, Ancestry, Bairn-team, Blood, Breed, Brood, Clan, Class, Close-knit, Cognate, Consanguine, County, Descent, Dynasty, Extended, Eye, Hapsburg, House(hold), Issue, Kin, Kind, Kindred, Line, Mafia, Medici, Name, Nuclear, One-parent, Orange, People, Phratry, Progeny, Quiverful, Race, Roots, Sept, Sib(b), Sibship, Single-parent, Stem, Stirps, Storge, Strain, Sub-order, Syndyasmian, Taffy, Talbot, Totem, Tribe, Whanau

**Family tree** Pedigree, Stemma

**Famine** Dearth, Lack, Scarcity

**Famish(ed)** Esurient, Hungry, Ravenous, Starving

▷ **Famished** *may indicate* an 'o' in the middle of a word

**Fan(s), Fan-like** Addict, Adherent, Admirer, Aficionado, Alligator, Alluvial, Arouse, Bajada, Barmy-army, B-boy, Blow, Cat, Cheer-leader, Clapper, Claque, Colmar, Cone, Cool, Cuscus, Devotee, Diadrom, Dryer, Ducted, Enthusiast, Extractor, Fiend, Flabellum, Following, Goth, Grebo, Groupie, Groupy, Headbanger, Hepcat, Khuskhus, Muso, Nut, Outspread, Partisan, Popette, Propellor, Public, Punka(h), Radiate, Rhipidate, Ringsider, Rooter, Rotary, Sail, Spectator, Splay, Spread, Supporter, Tail, Tartan army, Teenybopper, Tifosi, Trekkie, Ventilate, Votary, Voteen, Washingtonia, Wind machine, Wing, Winnow, Zealot, Zelant

▷ **Fan** *may indicate* an anagram

**Fanatic(al)** Bigot, Boatie, Devotee, Energumen, Enthusiastic, Extremist, Fiend, Frenetic, Glutton, Idolater, Mad, Maniac, Nut, Partisan, Phrenetic, Picard, Rabid, Santon, Ultra, Workaholic, Wowser, Zealot

**Fancy, Fancies, Fanciful** Adore, Caprice, Chim(a)era, Conceit, Concetto, Crotchet, Daydream, Dream, Dudish, Elaborate, Embellishment, Fangle, Fantasy, Fit, Flam, Flash, Florid, Flowery, Frilly, Frothy, Guess, Hallo, Idea(te), Idolon, →IMAGINE, Inclination, I say, Itch, Lacy, Liking, Maggot, Maya, Metaphysical, Mind, Mirage, Moonshine, My, Nap, Notion, Opine, Ornamental, Ornate, Passing, Petit four, Picture, Pipe dream, Predilection, Preference, Reverie, Rococo, Romanticise, Suppose, Thought, Unreal, Urge, Vagary, Visionary, Ween, Whigmaleerie, Whigmaleery, Whim(sy), Woolgather

▷ **Fancy** *may indicate* an anagram

**Fane** Banner, Pronaos

**Fanfare** Flourish, Sennet, Show, Tantara, Trump, Tucket

**Fang** Tooth, Tusk

**Fanny** Adams, Bottom, Gas-lit, Price

**Fantasist, Fantasy, Fantastic** Absurd, Amazing, Antic, Bizarre, Brilliant, Caprice, Centaur, Chimera, Cloud-cuckoo land, Cockaigne, Cockayne, Daydream, Dream world, Escapism, Fab, Fanciful, First class, Grotesque, Hallucination, Idol, Idola, Illusion, Kickshaw(s), Lucio, Make believe, Mega, Myth, Outré, Phantasmagoria, Pipe-dream, Queer, Reverie, Romance, Schizoid, Surreal, Transcendent, Unreal, Untrue, Walter Mitty, Wannabe(e), →WHIM, Whimsical, Wild, Wishful thinking, Wonderland, Wuxia

**Far** Apogean, Away, Distal, Distant, Eloi(g)n, Extreme, Outlying, Remote, Thether, Thither

**Farce(ur), Farcical** Burletta, Charade, Comedy, Exode, Feydeau, Lazzo, Mime, Mockery, Nonsense, Pantomime, Risible, Rix, Screaming, Sham, Travesty

**Fare** Apex, Charge, Cheer, Commons, Do, Eat, Excess, Excursion, →FOOD, Go, Passage, Passage money, Passenger, Rate, Saver, Table, Traveller

**Farewell** Adieu, Adios, Aloha, Apopemptic, Bye, Cheerio, Departure, Godspeed, →GOODBYE, Leave, Prosper, Sayonara, Send off, So long, Toodle-oo, Toodle-pip, Totsiens, Vale, Valediction

**Far-fetched** Fanciful, Improbable, Recherché

**Farm(ing), Farmhouse** Agronomy, Animal, Arable, Bender, Bocage, Bowery, City, Cold Comfort, Collective, Cooperative, Croft, Cultivate, Dairy, Deep-litter, Dry, Emmerdale, Estancia, Extensive, Factory, Fat, Fish(ery), Funny, Geoponical, Grange, Grow, Hacienda, Health, Home, Homestead, Husbandry, Intensive, Kibbutz, Kolkhoz, Land, Ley, Loaf, Location, Mailing, Mains, Mas, Mixed, No-tillage, Onstead, Orley, Oyster, Pen, Plaas,

Plough, Poultry, Ranch, Render, Rent, Set-aside, Sewage, Shamba, Sheep run, Sheep station, Smallholding, Sovkhoz, Station, Stead(ing), Sted(d), Stedde, Steed, Stock, Store, Stud, Stump, Subsistence, Tank, Till, Toon, Toun, Town, Trash, Tree, Trout, Truck, Wick, Wind

**Farmer** Blockie, Boer, Campesino, Carl, Cockatoo, Cocklaird, Cocky, Collins Street, Colon, Cow cocky, Crofter, Dairy, Estanciero, Gebur, Gentleman, George, Giles, Hick, Hobby, Husbandman, Macdonald, Metayer, Nester, NFU, Peasant, Pitt Street, Publican, Queen St, Rancher(o), Reaper, Ryot, Share-cropper, Smallholder, Sodbuster, Squatter, Stubble-jumper, Tax, Tenant, Tiller, Whiteboy, Yeoman, Zeminda(r)

**Farmhand** Cadet, Churl, Cottar, Cotter, Cottier, Cowman, Ditcher, Goat herd, Hand, Harvester, He(a)rdsman, Hind, Land girl, Neat herd, Orraman, Peon, Ploughman, Ranchero, Redneck, Rouseabout, Roustabout, Shearer, Sheepo, Stockman, Swineherd, Thresher, Vaquero

▸ **Farmhouse** *see* FARM(ING)

**Farmyard, Farm buildings** Barton, Henhouse, Hennery, Homestall, Villatic

**Faroe Islands** FO

**Farouche** Awkward, Blate, Shy, Sullen

**Farrago** Hotch-potch, Jumble, Medley, Mélange

**Farrier** Marshal, Smith

**Farrow** Litter, Mia, Sow

**Far-sighted** Clairvoyant, Presbyte

**Fart** Poep, Trump

**Farthing** Brass, F, Fadge, Har(r)ington, Mite, Q, Quadragesimal, Rag

**Fascia** Band, Fillet, Platband

**Fascinate(d), Fascinating, Fascinator** Allure, Attract, Bewitch, →CHARM, Dare, Enchant, Engross, Enrapt, Ensorcell, Enthral(l), Fetching, Hypnotise, Inthral, Into, Intrigue, Jolie laide, Kill, Mesmeric, Rapt, Rivet, Sexy, Siren, Sirenic, Spellbounding, Witch

**Fascist** Blackshirt, Blue shirt, Brownshirt, Dictator, Falange, Falangist, Iron Guard, Lictor, National Front, Nazi, Neo-Nazi, NF, Phalangist, Rexist, Sinarchist, Sinarquist

**Fashion(able), Fashioned, Fashion house** Adapt, Aguise, À la (mode), Alta moda, Armani, Bristol, Build, Chic, Construct, Convention, Cool, Corinthian, Craze, Create, Cult, Custom, Cut, Dernier cri, Design, Directoire, Du jour, Elegant, Entail, Fabricate, Fad, Fantoosh, Feat, Feign, Fly, Forge, Form, Garb, Genteel, Go, Hew, High, Hip, Hot, In, Invent, Kick, Kitsch, Look, →MAKE, Man-about-town, Manière, Manners, Method, Mode, Mondain(e), Mould, Newgate, New Look, Pink, Prada, Preppy, Rage, Rag trade, Rate, Roy, Sc, Shape, Sloane, Smart, Smith, Snappy, Snazzy, Soigne, Stile, Stylar, Style, Swish, Tailor, Ton, Tonish, Ton(e)y, →TREND(Y), Trendsetter, Turn, Twig, U, Vogue, Waif, Way, Wear, Wise, With-it, Work, Wrought

**Fast(ing), Faster** Abstain, Apace, Ashura, Breakneck, Brisk, Citigrade, Clappers, Clem, Clinging, Cracking, Daring, Dharna, Dhurna, Double-quick, Elaphine, Express, Fizzer, Fleet, Hypersonic, Immobile, Lent, Lightning, Loyal, Maigre, Meteoric, Moharram, Muharram, Muharrem, Nippy, Pac(e)y, Posthaste, Presto, Promiscuous, Pronto, Quadragesimal, Quick, Raffish, Raking, Ramadan, Ramadhan, Rash, Rathe, Relay, Sehri, Siyam, Smart, Spanking, Speedy, Stretta, Stretto, Stuck, Supersonic, Sure, Swift, Tachyon, Thick, Tied, Tight, Tisha b'Av, TishaBov, Tishah-Baav, Tishah-b(e)Ab, Tishah-b(e)Av, Whistle-stop, Xerophagy, Yarer, Yom Kippur, Zippy

**Fast and loose** Fickle, Prick-the-garter, Strap-game

**Fasten(er), Fastening** Anchor, Attach, Bar, Belay, Belt, Bind, Bolt, Buckle, Button, Chain, Clamp, Clasp, Click, Clinch, Clip, Cramp, Cufflink, Dead-eye, Diamond-hitch, Dome, Espagnolette, Eye-bolt, Frog, Gammon, Hasp, Hesp, Hitch, Hook, Infibulation, Lace, Latch, Lock, Moor, Morse, Nail, Netsuke, Nip, Nut, Padlock, Parral, Patent, Pectoral, Pin, Preen, Press stud, Reeve, Rivet, Rope, Rove, Safety pin, Screw, Seal, →SECURE, Sew up, Shut, Spar, Sprig, Staple, Steek, Stitch, Strap, Stud, Suspender,

Swift(er), Tach(e), Tag, Tape, Tassel, Tether, Thong, Tintack, Toggle, Twist-tie, U-bolt, Velcro®, Wedge, Zip

**Fastidious** Chary, Choosy, Critical, Dainty, Delicate, Fusspot, Fussy, Neat, Nice, Overnice, Particular, Picky, Precieuse, Precious, Purism, Quaint, Queasy, Quiddler, Rosewater, Squeamish

**Fastness** Bastille

**Fat(s), Fatted, Fatten, Fatty** Adipic, Adipocere, Adipose, Aldermanly, Aliphatic, Arcus, Atheroma, Bard, Batten, Battle, Beefy, Blubber, Brown, Bunter, Butter, Calf, Calipash, Calipee, Cellulite, Cholesterol, Chubbed, Chubby, Corpulent, Creesh, Curd, Degras, Deutoplasm, Dika-oil, Dosh, Dripping, Embonpoint, Enarm, Endomorph, Ester, Flab, Flesh, Flick, Fozy, Frank, Fubsy, Galam-butter, Grease, Gross, Keech, Kitchen-fee, Lanolin, Lard, Lard-ass, Leaf, Lipaemia, Lipid, Lipoma, Love handles, Margarine, Marge, Marrow, Mart, Moti, Motu, Obese, Oil, Olein, Oleomargarine, Olestra, OS, Palmitin, Pinguid, Plump, Poddy, Podgy, Polyunsaturated, Portly, Pudgy, Puppy, Pursy, Rich, Rolypoly, Rotund, Saddlebags, Saginate, Saim, Saturated, Schmal(t)z, Seam(e), Sebacic, Sebum, Shortening, Soil, Spare tyre, Spe(c)k, Squab, Stearic, Steatopygia, Steatorrhea, Steatosis, Suberin, Suet, Tallow, Tin, Tomalley, Trans, Triglyceride, Tub, Unsaturated, Vanaspati, Waller, Well-padded, Wool

**Fatal(ism), Fatality, Fate(s), Fated, Fateful** Apnoea, Atropos, Cavel, Chance, Clotho, Deadly, Death (blow), Decuma, Destiny, Doom, End, Fay, Fell, Joss, Karma, Kismet, Lachesis, Lethal, Lethiferous, Loss, Lot, Meant, Moera(e), Moira, Morta, Mortal, Mortiferous, Nemesis, Nona, Norn(a), Parca, Pernicious, Portion, Predestination, Pre-ordain, Skuld, Urd, Verdande, Waterloo, Weird, Weird sisters

**Father(s), Fatherly** Abba, Abbot, Abuna, Adopt, Agnation, Apostolic, Bapu, Begetter, Breadwinner, Brown, City, Conscript, Curé, Da, Dad, Engender, Foster, Founding, Fr, Generator, Genitor, Getter, Gov, Governor, Guv, Male, NASCAR dad, Pa, Padre, Papa, Pappy, Parent, Pater(nal), Paterfamilias, Patriarch, Patroclinic, Père, Pilgrim, Pop(pa), Popper, Priest, Rev, Seraphic, Sire, Stud, Thames, Tiber, William

**Father-lasher** Sea-scorpion

**Fathom** Delve, Depth, Dig, F, Plumb, Plummet, Understand

**Fatigue(d)** Battle, Bonk, Chore, Combat, Compassion, Exhaust, Fag, Jade, Jet lag, ME, Metal, Neurasthenia, Overdo, Overwatch, Swinked, Time-zone, Tire, Weariness, Weary

**Fatuous** Gaga, Idiotic, Inane, Silly, Stupid

**Faucet** Cock, Spigot, Tap

**Fault(y), Fault-finding** Arraign, Bad, Beam, Blame(worthy), Blunder, Bug, Cacology, Captious, Carp, Compound, Culpa, Culpable, Defect, Demerit, Dip, Dip-slip, Down to, Drop-out, Dud, Duff, →**ERROR**, Expostulate, Failing, Flaw, Foot, Frailty, Gall, Glitch, Gravity, Henpeck, Hitch, Impeach, Imperfect, Knock, Literal, Massif, →**MISTAKE**, Mortal sin, Nag, Nibble, Niggle, Nit-pick, Oblique, Oblique-slip, Out, Outcrop, Overthrust, Pan, Para, Peccadillo, Pre-echo, Quibble, Rate, Red eye, Reprehend, Rift, Rupes Recta, San Andreas, Sclaff, Set-off, Short, Slip, Snag, Step, Strike, Strike-slip, Technical, Thrust, Trap, Trough, Underthrust, Upbraid, Vice

**Faultless** Immaculate, Impeccable, Lily-white, Perfect

**Fauna** Benthos, Mesobenthos, Wild life

**Fauvist** Matisse

**Faux pas** Blunder, Boner, Conversation stopper, Gaffe, Leglen-girth, Solecism

**Favour(able), Favoured, Favourite, Favouritism** Advance, Advantage(ous), Aggrace, Agraste, Alder-liefest, Anne, Approval, Auspicious, Aye, Back, Befriend, Behalf, Benefit, Benign, Bias, Bless, Blue-eyed, Boon, Bribe, Cert, Chosen, Cockade, Condescend, Conducive, Countenance, Curry, Darling, Elitist, Ewe lamb, Ex gratia, Fancy, Favonian, Firm, Form horse, Front runner, Good turn, Grace, Gracioso, Graste, Gratify, Gree, Hackle, Hot, In, Indulge, Intend, Kickback, Lean, Minion, Nepotism, Nod, Odour, Optimal, Particular, Peat, Persona grata, Pet, Pettle, Popular, →**PREFER**, Promising,

Propitious, Resemble, Rib(b)and, Roseate, Rose-knot, Rosette, Side, Smile, Successful, Toast, Token, White boy, White-headed, Win-win

**Fawn(er), Fawning** Adulate, Bambi, Beige, Blandish, Brown-nose, Camel, Crawl, Creep, Cringe, Deer, Ecru, Elaine, Flatter, Fleech, Footlick, Grovel, Ko(w)tow, Lickspittle, Obsequious, Servile, Slavish, Smarm, Smoo(d)ge, Subservient, Sycophant, Tasar, Toady, Truckle, Tussah, Tusseh, Tusser, Tussore

**Fax** Replica

**Fay** Fairy, Korrigan, Peri

**Faze** Unman, Unnerve

**FBI** G-men

**Fear** Aichmophobia, Angst, Apprehension, Astra(po)phobia, Awe, Bathophobia, Bête noire, Bugbear, Claustrophobia, Cold sweat, Crap, Creeps, Cyberphobia, Dismay, Doubt, Drad, Dread, Dromophobia, Ecophobia, Foreboding, → FOR FEAR, Fright, Funk, Genophobia, Hang-up, Horripilation, Horror, Kenophobia, Monophobia, Mysophobia, Nostopathy, Nyctophobia, Ochlophobia, Panic, → PHOBIA, Photophobia, Redoubt, Revere, Taphephobia, Taphophobia, Terror, Thalassophobia, Trepidation, Willies

**Fearful** Afraid, Cowardly, Cowering, Dire, Horrific, Nervous, Pavid, Rad, Redoubtable, Sinister, Timorous, Tremulous, Windy

**Fearless** Bold, Brave, Courageous, Daring, Gallant, Impavid, Intrepid, Proud, Unafraid

**Fearsome** Alarming, Dire, Formidable, Redoubtable

**Feasible** Goer, Likely, On, Possible, Practical, Probable, Viable

**Feast(s)** Adonia, Agape, Assumption, Banquet, Barmecide, Beano, Belshazzar's, Blow-out, Candlemas, Carousal, Celebration, Convive, Dine, Do, Double, Eat, Encaenia, Epiphany, Epulation, Festival, Fleshpots, Folly, Fool's, Gaudeamus, Gaudy, Hakari, Halloween, Hallowmas, Heortology, Hockey, Hogmanay, Holy Innocents, Id-al-Adha, Id-al-Fitr, Immaculate Conception, Ingathering, Isodia, Junket, Kai-kai, Lady Day, Lamb-ale, Lammas, Love, Luau, Lucullus, Martinmas, Michaelmas, Midnight, Movable, Name days, Noel, Passover, Pentecost, Pesach, Pig, Potlatch, Purim, Regale, Repast, Revel, Roodmas, Seder, Shavuot(h), Shindig, Spread, Succoth, Sukkot(h), Tabernacles, Trumpets, Tuck-in, Wake, Wayzgoose, Weeks, Yule, Zagmuk

**Feast-day** Mass

**Feat** Achievement, Deed, Effort, Exploit, Gambado, Handspring, Heroic, Stunt, Tour de force, Trick

**Feather(s), Feathered, Feather-star** Aigrette, Alula, Barbicel, Boa, Braccate, Cock, Contour, Covert, Crinoid, Crissum, Down, Duster, Egret, Eiderdown, Filoplume, Flags, Fledged, Fletch, Flight, Gemmule, Hackle, Harl, Hatchel, Herl, Lei, Lure, Macaroni, Manual, Oar, Ostrich, Pen(na), Pin, Pinna, Pith, Plumage, Plume, Plumule, Prince's, Pteryla, Ptilosis, → QUILL, Rectrix, Remex, Remiges, Rocket-tail, Rotate, Saddle-hackle, Scapular, Scapus, Secondary, Semiplume, Shaft, Shag, Sickle, Standard, Stipa, Swansdown, Tail covert, Tectrix, Tertial, Tippet, Tuft, Vibrissa, White, Wing covert

**Feather-pate** Man-milliner

**Feather-worker** Plumassier

**Feature(s)** Acoustic, Amenity, Appurtenance, Article, Aspect, Attribute, Brow, Character, Chin, Contour, Depict, Double, Eye, Eyebrow, Face, Facet, Figure, Fronton, Gable(t), Hallmark, Highlight, Item, Jizz, Landmark, Lineament, Neotery, Nose, Nucleus, Overfold, Phiz(og), Physiognomy, Signature, Snoot, Spandrel, Star, Temple, Topography, Touch, Trait, Underlip

**Featureless** Flat, Nondescript

**Febrifuge** Atabrin, Atebrin®, Mepacrine, Quina

**February** Fill-dyke

**Feckless** Deadbeat

**Fecund(ity)** Fertile, Fruitful, Prolific, Uberty

**Fed** Agent, G-man

**Federal, Federation** Alliance, Axis, Bund, Commonwealth, Interstate, League, Russian, Solidarity, Statal, Union

**Fee(s)** Appearance money, Base, Bench, Capitation, Charge, Chummage, Commitment, Common, Conditional, Consideration, Consultation, Contingency, Corkage, Corporation, Drop-dead, Dues, Duty, Emolument, Entrance, Entry, Faldage, Fine, Great, Groundage, Hir(e)age, Hire, Honorarium, Interchange, Kill, Kitchen, Mortuary, Mouter, Multure, Obvention, Pay, Pierage, Premium, Ransom, Refresher, Retainer, Search, Sub, Subscription, Transfer, Tribute

**Feeble(ness)** Banal, Characterless, Daidling, Debile, Decrepit, Dotage, Droob, Effete, Faint, Feckless, Fizzenless, Flabby, Flaccid, Foisonless, Footling, Fragile, Fus(h)ionless, Geld, Ineffective, Infirm, Jessie, Lame, Limp, Milk and water, Mimsy, Namby-pamby, Pale, Pathetic, Puny, Rickety, Sassy, Sickly, Silly, Sissy, Slender, Slight, Soppy, Tailor, Tame, Thin, Tootle, Unmanly, Wallydrag, Wallydraigle, Wan, Washy, Wastrel, Weak, Weak-kneed, Weak-minded, Weed, Weedy, Wersh, Wet, Wimpish, Worn

**Feed(er), Feeding** Battle, Bib, Break, Browse, Cake, Cater, Chicken, Cibation, Clover, Cowfeteria, Cram, Cue, Demand, Diet, Dine, Dressing, Drip, →EAT, Fatten, Filter, Fire, Fishmeal, Flushing, Fodder, Food, Force, Gavage, Graze, Hay, Input, Intravenous, Line, Lunch, Meal, Munch, Nourish, Nurse, Paid, Pecten, Picnic, Provender, Refect, Repast, Sate, Soil, Stoke, Stooge, Storer, Stover, Stuff, Suckle, Sustain, Tire, Tractor, Wean, Wet nurse

**Feedback** Negative, Positive

**Feel(ingly), Feeling(s)** Aesthesia, Affetuoso, Afterglow, Algesis, Angst, Animus, Ardour, Artificial, À tâtons, Atmosphere, Ballottement, Compassion, Conscience, Darshan, Déjà vu, →EMOTION, Empathy, Empfindung, Euphoria, →EXPERIENCE, Fellow, Finger, Flaw, Frisk, Fumble, Grope, Groundswell, Handle, Hard, Heart, Heartstrings, Hunch, Intuit, Knock, Know, Mondayish, Mood, Palp(ate), Passible, Passion, Phatic, Pity, Premonition, Presentiment, Probe, Realise, Sensate, Sensation, →SENSE, Sensible, Sensitive, Sentiency, Sentiment, Somesthesis, Spirit, Sprachgefühl, Tactual, Tingle, Touch, Turn, Undercurrent, Vehemence, Vibes, Vibrations, Zeal

**Feeler** Antenna, Ballon d'essai, Barbel, Exploratory, Fingertip, Overture, Palp, Sensillum, Tentacle, Trial balloon

▶ **Feet** see FOOT(ING)

**Feign** Act, Affect, Assume, Colour, Fake, Malinger, Mime, Mock, →PRETEND, Sham, Simulate

**Feint** Deke, Disguise, Dodge, Faint, Fake, False move, Spoof, Trick

**Feisty** Game, Tigerish

**Fel(d)spar** Adularia, Albite, Amazon-stone, Anorthite, Bytownite, Gneiss, Hyalophane, Labradorite, Microcline, Moonstone, Orthoclase, Peristerite, Petuntse, Petuntze, Plagioclase, Sanidine, Saussurite, Sun-stone

**Felicity** Bliss, Happiness, Joy, Relevance

▶ **Feline** see CAT

**Fell** Axe, Chop, Cruel, Cut down, Deadly, Dire, Dread, Fen, Fierce, Floor, Heath, Hew, Hide, Hill, Inhuman, Knock-down, KO, Lethal, Lit, Log, Malign, Moor, Pelt, Poleaxe, Ruthless, Sca, Shap, Skittle

**Fellow(s), Fellowship** Academic, Associate, Bawcock, Birkie, Bloke, Bo, Bro, Buck(o), Buffer, Callan(t), Carlot, Cat, Chal, Chap(pie), Chi, China, Chum, Co, Cock, Cod(ger), Collaborator, Colleague, Co-mate, Communion, Companion, Compatriot, Comrade, Confrère, Cove, Cully, Cuss, Dandy, Dean, Dog, Don, Dude, Equal, F, Fogey, Fop, Gadgie, Gadje, Gaudgie, Gauje, Gink, Guy, Housemate, Joe, Joker, Josser, Kerel, Lad, Like, M, Mall, Man, Match, Mate, Member, Mister, Mun, Odd, Partner, Peare, Peer, Professor, Rival, Seniority, Sister, Skate, Sociate, Society, Sodality, Stablemate, Swab, Teaching, Twin, Waghalter, Wallah, Workmate

**Felon(y)** Baddy, Bandit, Convict, Crime, Gangster, Offence, Villain

**Felt** Baize, Bat(t), Drugget, Knew, Met, Numdah, Numnah, Pannose, Roofing, Sensed, Tactile, Underlay, Velour

**Female (bodies), Feminine, Feminist** Anima, Bint, Bit, Dame, Distaff, Doe, F, Fair sex, Filly, Girl(y), Greer, Harem, Hen, Her, Kermes, Lady(like), Libber, Maiden, Muliebrity, Pen, Petticoated, Pistillate, Riot girl, Sakti, Shakti, She, Sheila, Shidder, Soft, Spindle, Thelytoky, -trix, →WOMAN, Womens' libber, Yin

▷ **Female, Feminine** *may indicate* an -ess ending

**Fen** Bog, Carr, Chiao, Coin, Ea, Jiao, Marsh, Morass, Silicon, Swamp, Wash, Yuan

**Fence(r), Fencing (position)** Appel, Balestra, Bar, Barrier, Botte, Carte, Croisé, Cyclone®, Deer, Derobement, Dogleg, Electric, Encase, Enclose, Épée, Feint, Fight, Flanconade, Flèche, Foils, Fraise, Froissement, Haha, Hay, Hedge, Hot, Hurdle, Iaido, Imbroccata, Inquartata, Kendo, Kittle, Line, Link, Mensur, Molinello, Montant, Netting, Obstacle, Ox, Oxer, Pale, Paling, Palisade, Palisado, Parry, Passado, Pen, Picket, Post and rail, Quart(e), Quinte, Rabbit-fence, Rabbit-proof, Raddle, Rail, Rasper, Receiver, Reset, Ring, Scrimure, Seconde, Sepiment, Sept(um), Septime, Singlestick, Sixte, Snake, Snow, Stacket, Stockade, Stramac, Stramazon, Sunk, Swordplay, Tac-au-tac, Tierce, Touché, Trellis, Virginia, Wattle, Wear, Weir, Weldmesh®, Wire, Worm, Zigzag

**Fend(er), Fend off** Buffer, Bumper, Cowcatcher, Curb, Mudguard, Parry, Provide, Resist, Skid, Stiff-arm, Ward, Wing

**Fennel** Finnochio, Finoc(c)hio, Florence, Herb, Love-in-a-mist, Narthex, Ragged lady

**Fent** Offcut, Remnant, Slit

**Feral** Brutal, Fierce, Savage, Wild

**Ferdinand** Archduke, Bull

**Ferment(ation)** Barm, Brew, Enzym(e), Leaven, Mowburn, Must, Protease, Ptyalin, Seethe, Solera, Storm, Stum, Trypsin, Turn, Vinify, Working, Ye(a)st, Zyme, Zymo-, Zymology, Zymolysis, Zymosis, Zymotic, Zymurgy

**Fermium** Fm

**Fern** Acrogenous, Adder's-tongue, Adiantum, Archegonial, Asparagus, Aspidium, Asplenium, Azolla, Barometz, Beech, Bird's nest, Bladder, Bracken, Brake, Bristle, Buckler, Bungwall, Ceterach, Cinnamon, Coral, Cryptogam, Cyathea, Cycad, Dicksonia, Door, Elkhorn, Fairy moss, Filicales, Filices, Filmy, Fishbone, Grape, Hard, Hart's-tongue, Holly, Ice, Isoetes, Lacy, Lady, Maidenhair, Male, Man, Mangemange, Marattia, Marsh, Marsilea, Marsilia, Meadow, Miha, Moonwort, Mosquito, Mulewort, Nardoo, Nephrolepis, Northern, Oak, Ophioglossum, Osmunda, Para, Parsley, Peppergrass, Pepperwort, Pig, Pillwort, Polypody, Polystichum, Ponga, Pteridology, Pteris, Punga, Rachilla, Rhizocarp, Rockbrake, Royal, Rusty-back, Salvinia, Scale, Schizaea, Scolopendrium, Seed, Shield, Silver, Snowbrake, Soft tree, Spleenwort, Staghorn, Sweet, Sword, Tara, Tree, Venus's hair, Walking, Wall rue, Water, Whisk, Woodsia

**Ferocious** Brutal, Cruel, Fell, Predatory, Rambunctious, Savage, Tiger, Violent, Wild

**Ferret** Albin, Black-footed, Business, Fesnyng, Gill, Hob, Jill, Nose, Polecat, Ribbon, Rootle, Snoop, Trace, Unearth

**Ferry(man)** Charon, Convey, Flying bridge, Harper's, Hovercraft, Passage, Plier, Pont, Roll-on, RORO, Sea-cat, Sealink, Shuttle, Soyuz, Train, Traject, Tranect

**Fertile, Fertility (symbol), Fertilisation** Arable, Ashtoreth, Battle, Cleistogamy, Fat, Fecund, Fruitful, Green, Linga, Oasis, Priapus, Productive, Prolific, Rhiannon, Rich, Uberous

**Fertilise(r), Fertilisation** Ammonia, Auxin, Bee, Bone-ash, Bone-earth, Bone-meal, Caliche, Caprify, Compost, Cross, Dress, Fishmeal, Guano, Heterosis, Humogen, Humus, In-vitro, IVF, Kainite, Krilium®, Lime, Manure, Marl, Night soil, Nitrate, Nitre, Nitro-chalk, Pearl-ash, Phallus, Phosphate, Pollen, Pollinator, Potash, Potassa, Seaware, Self, Sham, Side dressing, Stamen, Superfetation, Superphosphate, Tankage, Top dressing, Treat

**Fervent, Fervid, Fervour** Ardent, Burning, Earnest, Gusto, Heartfelt, Heat, Hot, Hwyl, Intense, Into, Keen, Passionate, White-hot, Zeal, Zeloso

**Fester** Beal, Putrefy, Rankle, Rot, Suppurate

**Festival, Festive, Festivity** Anniversary, Beano, Carnival, Celebration, Commemoration, Convivial, En fête, →FAIR, Feast, Feis, Fête, Fête-champêtre, Gaff,

→ GALA, Gaudy, High day, → HOLIDAY, Lemural, Let-off, Play, Revel, Rush-bearing, Semi-double, Wake, Wassail

## FESTIVALS

**3 letters:**
Ale
Bon
Mod
Pop
Tet

**4 letters:**
Holi
Lent
Mela
Noel
Obon
Puja
Tide
Utas
Yule

**5 letters:**
Doseh
Druid
Hosay
Miraj
Pasch
Pesah
Pooja
Purim
Seder
Vesak
Wesak

**6 letters:**
Adonia
Ashura
Bairam
Dewali
Divali
Diwali
Easter
Fiesta
Fleadh
Fringe
Hosein

Judica
Lammas
Mawlid
Mayday
Moomba
Pardon
Pesach
Pongal
Poojah
Shrove
Yom Tob
Yomtov

**7 letters:**
Al Hijra
Baisaki
Beltane
Greater
Harvest
Holy-ale
J'ouvert
Kermess
Kermiss
Kirmess
Kwanzaa
Lady-Day
Lemuria
Matsuri
Palilia
Potlach
Samhain
Vinalia
Yuan Tan

**8 letters:**
Al Hijrah
Baisakhi
Bayreuth
Biennale
Cerealia
Chanukah
Dassehra
Day of awe

Dionysia
Encaenia
Epiphany
Fête-Dieu
Hanukkah
Hock-tide
Hogmanay
Id-al-fitr
Lag b'Omer
Passover
Salzburg
Shabuath
Shavuath
Slugfest
Tanabata
Yuletide

**9 letters:**
Aldeburgh
Candlemas
Chanukkah
Christmas
Church-ale
Crouchmas
Hallowmas
Kumbh Mela
Martinmas
Navaratra
Navaratri
Pentecost
Thargelia
Up-Helly-Aa
Woodstock
Yom Arafat

**10 letters:**
Ambarvalia
Assumption
Childermas
Corroboree
Eisteddfod
Lughnasadh
Lupercalia

Merry-night
Michaelmas
Quirinalia
Saturnalia
Shrovetide
Terminalia
Visitation
Vulcanalia

**11 letters:**
Anthesteria
Fête-galante
Glastonbury
Harvest home

**12 letters:**
All Saints' Day
Circumcision
Feast of weeks
Glyndebourne
Lailat-ul-Qadr
Lesser Bairam
Panathenaean
Plough Monday
Rosh Hashanah
Simchas Torah
Simchat Torah
Thesmophoria

**13 letters:**
Corpus Christi
Greater Bairam
Laylat-al-Miraj
Simchath Torah

**14 letters:**
Shemini Atseres

**15 letters:**
Transfiguration

**Festoon** Deck, Decorate, Encarpus, Garland, Swag, Wreathe
**Fetch(ing), Fetch up** Arrive, Attract, Bring, Charming, Fet(t), Get, Gofer, Net, Realise, Recover, Spew, Winsome
**Fête** Bazaar, Champêtre, Entertain, → FESTIVITY, Gala, Honour, Mela, Tattoo
**Fetish(ist)** Charm, Compulsion, Gimp, Idol, Ju-ju, Obeah, Obi(a), Talisman, Totem, Voodoo

**Fetter** Anklet, Basil, Bilboes, Chain, Gyve, Hamshackle, Hobble, Hopple, Iron, Leg-iron, Manacle, Shackle

**Fettle** Arrange, Condition, Frig, Potter, Repair

**Feu** Tenure

**Feud** Affray, Blood, Clash, Dissidence, Feoff, Fief, Quarrel, Strife, →**VENDETTA**

**Feudal (service), Feudalism** Arriage, Auld-farrant, Fief, Forinsec, Old, Vassalage

**Fever(ish)** African coast, Ague, Beaver, Biliary, Blackwater, Brain, Breakbone, Buck, Cabin, Calenture, Camp, Cat-scratch, Cerebrospinal, Childbed, Dandy, Dengue, East coast, Enteric, Febrile, Ferment, Fog, Frenetic, Gastric, Gate, Glandular, Haemorrhagic, Hay, Heatstroke, Hectic, Hyperpyretic, Insolation, Intense, Intermittent, Jail, Japanese river, Jungle, Kala-azar, Kissing disease, Lassa, Malaria, Malta, Marsh, Mediterranean, Miliary, Milk, Mono, Mud, Paratyphoid, Parrot, Parturient, Passion, Phrenitis, Puerperal, Putrid, Pyretic, Pyrexia, Pyrogenic, Q, Quartan, Quintan, Quotidian, Rabbit, Ratbite, Recurrent, Relapsing, Remittent, Rheumatic, Rift Valley, Rock, Rocky Mountain spotted, Roseola, Sandfly, Scarlatina, Scarlet, Sextan, Ship, Splenic, Spotted, Spring, Stage, Sunstroke, Swamp, Swine, Tap, Temperature, Tertian, Texas, Tick, Trench, Typhoid, Typhus, Undulant, Valley, Verruga, Vomito, Weed, West Nile, Whot, Worm, Yellow(jack)

**Few(er)** Handful, Infrequent, →**LESS**, Limited, RAF, Scarce, Several, Some, Wheen

**Fey** Clairvoyant, Eccentric, Elfin, Weird

**Fez** Tarboosh, Tarboush, Tarbush

**Fiancé(e)** Betrothed, Intended, Promised

**Fiasco** Bomb, Debacle, Disaster, Failure, Flask, Flop, Lash-up, Turkey, Wash-out

**Fiat** Command, Decree, Dictum, Edict, Order, Ukase

**Fib** Gag, →**LIE**, Prevaricate, Story, Taradiddle, Untruth

**Fibre, Fibrous** Abaca, Abroma, Acrilan®, Acrylic, Aramid, Arghan, Backbone, Bass, Bast, Beta, Buaze, Bwazi, Cantala, Carbon, Cellulose, Coir, Constitution, Corpus Callosum, Cotton, Courtelle®, Crimple, Cuscus, Desmosome, Dietary, Dralon®, Elastane, Elastin, Filament, Filasse, Flax, Funicle, Giant, Glass, Gore-Tex®, Graded-index, Guncotton, Hair, Harl, Hemp, Henequen, Henequin, Herl, Hypha, Ispaghula, Istle, Ixtle, Jipyapa, Jute, Kapok, Kenaf, Kevlar®, Kittul, Laps, Lemniscus, Ligament, Maguey, Manilla, Monkey-grass, Monofil, Monomode, Moorva, Moral, Multimode, Mungo, Murva, Muscle, Myotube, Nap, Natural, Nerve, Noil(s), Nub, Nylon, Oakum, Olefin(e), Optic(al), Orlon®, Peduncle, Piassaba, Piassava, Pina, Pine-wool, Pita, Polyarch, Pons, Pontine, Pulu, Raffia, Ramee, Rami, Ramie, Rayon, Rhea, Rock-cork, Roughage, Rove, Shoddy, Sida, Silk, Sinew, Sisal, Slagwool, Sleave, Slub(b), Spandex, Spherulite, Splenium, Staple, Stepped-index, Sterculia, Strand, Strick, Sunn-hemp, Tampico, Tencel®, Toquilla, Tow, Towy, Uralite, Viver, Vulcanized, Wallboard, Watap, Whisker, Wood pulp

**Fibula** Bone, Brooch, Perone

**Fickle(ness)** Capricious, Change, False, Flibbertigibbet, Inconsistent, Inconstant, Kittle, Light, Mutable, Protean, Shifty, Varying, Volage, Volatile, Wind-changing

**Fiction(al), Fictitious** Airport, Bogus, Chick-lit, Cyberpunk, Fable, Fabrication, Legal, Myth, Pap, Phoney, Picaresque, Pulp, Romance, Science, Sex and shopping, Slash, Speculative, Splatterpunk, →**STORY**, Sword and sorcery, Transgressive, Whole cloth

**Fiddle(r), Fiddlesticks, Fiddlestring, Fiddling** Amati, Bow, Calling-crab, Cello, Cheat, Con, Crab, Cremona, Croud, Crouth, Crowd, Crwth, Do, Fidget, Fix, Gju, Ground, Gu(e), Gut-scraper, Jerrymander, Kit, Launder, Nero, Peculate, Petty, Potter, Racket, Rebec(k), Rig, Rote, Sarangi, Saw, Sawah, Scam, Scotch, Scrape, Scrapegut, Second, Sharp practice, Short change, Spiel, Strad, Sultana, →**TAMPER**, Thimblerig, Tinker, Toy, Trifle, Tweedle(-dee), Twiddle, Viola, →**VIOLIN**, Wangle

**Fiddle-faddle** Nipperty-tipperty

**Fidelity** Accuracy, Faith, Fealty, Loyalty, Troth, Trust

**Fidget(y)** Fantad, Fanteeg, Fantigue, Fantod, Fike, Fuss, Fyke, Hirsle, Hotch, Impatient, Jimjams, Jittery, Niggle, Restive, Trifle, Twiddle, Twitch, Uneasy

**Fiduciary** Trustee

**Fief** Benefice, Fee

**Field(er), Fielding, Fields(man)** Aalu, Aaru, Abroad, Aceldama, Aerodrome, Agrestic, Airstrip, Area, Arena, Arish, Arpent, Arrish, Bailiwick, Baseman, Battleground, Bocage, Campestral, Campestrian, Catch, Champ(s), Chief, Close, Colour, Coulomb, Cover, Cover-point, Diamond, Discipline, Domain, Electric, Electromagnetic, Electrostatic, Elysian, Entry, Extra cover, Fid, Fine leg, Flodden, Flying, Force, Forte, Fylde, Glebe, Gracie, Gravitational, Grid(iron), Gull(e)y, Hop-yard, Ice, Keep wicket, Killing, Land, Landing, Lare, Lay, Lea(-rig), Leg slip, Ley, Line, Long leg, Long-off, Long-on, Longstop, Lords, Magnetic, Mead(ow), Mid-off, Mid-on, Mid-wicket, Mine, Oil, Padang, Paddock, Paddy, Parrock, Pasture, Peloton, Pitch, Playing, Point, Potter's, Province, Quintessence, Realm, Reame, Runners, Salting, Sawah, Scarecrow, Scope, Scout, Shamba, Short leg, Short stop, Silly, Slip, Sphere, Square leg, Stage, Stray, Stubble, Territory, Third man, Tract, Unified, Vector, Visual, W.C., World

▷ **Field** *may indicate* cricket

**Field marshal** Allenby, Bulow, French, Haig, Ironside, Kesselring, Kitchener, Montgomery, Roberts, Robertson, Rommel, Slim, Wavell

**Fieldwork** Lunette, Ravelin, Redan, Redoubt, Tenaillon

**Fiend** Barbason, Buff, Demon, →**DEVIL**, Enthusiast, Flibbertigibbet, Frateretto, Fresh air, Hellhound, Hellion, Hobbidīdance, Mahn, Modo, Obidicut, Smulkin, Succubus

**Fierce(ly)** Amain, Billyo, Breem, Breme, Cruel, Draconic, Dragon, Fell, Grim, Hard-fought, Intense, Lorcan, Ogreish, Rampant, Renfierst, →**SAVAGE**, Severe, Tigerish, Tigrish, Tranchant, Violent, Wild, Wood, Wrathy, Wud

**Fiery** Abednego, Ardent, Argand, Aries, Con fuoco, Dry, Eithna, Fervent, Flambeau, Hot, Hotspur, Idris, Igneous, Impassioned, Leo, Mettlesome, Phlogiston, Piri-piri, Sagittarius, Salamander, Zealous

**Fiesta** Carnival, Festival, Fête, Gala, Holiday

**Fife** Piffero

**Fifteen(th)** Crystal

▷ **Fifteen** *may indicate* a rugby team

**Fifth** Column, Diapente, Hemiol(i)a, Nones, Perfect, Quentin, Quint(ile), Sesquialtera, Sextans

**Fifth columnist** Traitor

**Fifty** Bull, Demi-c, Jubilee, L

**Fig** Bania, Banyan, Benjamin-tree, Caprifig, Fico, Figo, Footra, Fouter, Foutra, Foutre, Hottentot, Indian, Moreton Bay, Mouldy, Sycamore, Sycomium, Sycomore, Trifle

**Fight(er), Fighting** Achilles, Action, Affray, Agonistics, Aikido, Alpino, Altercate, Arms, Bandy, Bare-knuckle, Barney, →**BATTLE**, Battle royal, Bicker, Biffo, Blue, Bout, Box, Brave, Brawl, Bruiser, Bundeswehr, Bush-whack, Camp, Campaign, Chaud-mellé, Chetnik, Chindit, Combat, Compete, Conflict, Contest, Contra, Crusader, Cuirassier, Defender, Digladiation, Ding-dong, Dog, Donnybrook, Dreadnought, Duel, Ecowarrior, Encounter, Engagement, Extremes, F, Faction, Fecht, Fence, Fisticuffs, Flyting, Fray, Freedom, Free-for-all, Fund, Gamecock, Garibaldi, Ghazi, Gladiator, Grap(p)le, Green beret, Grudge, Guerilla, Gunslinger, Gurkha, Handicuffs, Hurricane, J(o)ust, Karate, Kendo, Kite, Kumite, Lapith, Maquis, Marine, Med(d)le, Medley, Mêlée, Mercenary, MIG, Militate, Mill, Mujahed(d)in, Mujahideen, Mujahidin, Naumachy, Night, Ninja, Partisan, Pellmell, Pillow, PLO, Prawle, Press, Pugilist, Pugnacity, Punch up, Rammy, Rapparee, Rejoneo, Repugn, Resist, Ring, Rough and tumble, Ruck, Ruction, Rumble, Run-in, Running, Savate, Sciamachy, Scold, Scrap, Scrape, Scrimmage, Scuffle, Set-to, Shadow, Shine, Shoot-out, Skiamachy, Skirmish, Slam, Slugger, Soldado, Soldier, Spar, Spat, Spitfire, Squabble, Stealth, Stoush, Straight, Strife, Struggle, Sumo, Swordsman, Tar, Tatar, Terrier, Thersites, Tilt, Toreador, Torero, Tornado, Tuilyie, Tuilzie, Tussle, Ultimate, Umbrella, War(-dog), War-horse, War-man, Warplane, Warrior, Wrangle, Wraxle, Wrestle, Yike, Zero

**Figment** Delusion, Fiction, Invention
**Figure(d), Figures, Figurine, Figurative** Action, Allegoric, Arabic, Aumail,
Bas-relief, Body, Build, Caganer, Canephorus, Cartouche, Caryatid, Cast, Chladni,
Cinque, Cipher, Cone, Cube, Cypher, Decahedron, Digit, Ecorché, Effigy, Eight, Ellipse,
Enneagon, Enneahedron, Epanadiplosis, Equiangular, Escher, Father, →**FORM**, Fret,
Fusil, Gammadion, Giosphinx, Girth, Gnomon, Graph, Heptagon, Hexagon, Hexagram,
Hour-glass, Icon, Icosahedron, Idol, Ikon, Image, Impossible, Insect, Intaglio, Integer,
Interference, Lay, Lissajous, Magot, Manaia, Mandala, Matchstick, Moai, Monogram,
Motif, Nonagon, Number, Numeral, Numerator, Numeric, Octagon, Octahedron, Orant,
Ornate, Outline, Ovoid, Parallelepiped, Parallelogram, Pentacle, Pentalpha, Plane,
Polygon, Polyhedron, Poussette, Prism, Puppet, Pyramid, Reckon, Repetend, Repoussoir,
Rhomboid, Rhombus, Sector, See, →**SHAPE**, Sheela-na-gig, Significant, Simplex, Solid,
Sonorous, Staffage, Stat(istic)s, Statue(tte), Stick, String, Table, Tableau, Tanagra,
Telamon, Tetragon, Tetrahedron, Topical, Torus, Triangle, Trigon, Trihedron, Triskele,
Triskelion, Trisoctahedron, Tropology, Undecagon, Ushabti, Waxwork
**Figure of speech** Abscission, Allegory, Alliteration, Analogy, Antimask, Antimasque,
Antimetabole, Antithesis, Antithet, Antonomasia, Assonance, Asyndeton, Catachresis,
Cataphora, Chiasmus, Deixis, Diallage, Ellipsis, Euphemism, Hendiadys, Hypallage,
Hyperbaton, Hyperbole, Hysteron proteron, Irony, Litotes, Meiosis, Metalepsis,
Metaphor, Metonymy, Onomatopoeia, Oxymoron, Paral(e)ipsis, Prolepsis, Prosopopoeia,
Siddhuism, Simile, Solecism, Syllepsis, Synecdoche, Taxeme, Tmesis, Trope, Tropology,
Zeugma
**Figure study** Arithmetic, Mathematics, Numeration
**Figure-weaver** Draw-boy
**Filament** Barbule, Byssus, Cirrus, Fibre, Fibrilla, Fimbria, Floss, Gossamer, Hair,
Hormogonium, Hypha, Mycor(r)hiza, Myofibril, Paraphysis, Protonema, Stand,
→**THREAD**, Whisker, Wreath
**Filch** Appropriate, Drib, Pilfer, Pinch, Prig, Purloin, Smouch, →**STEAL**
**File(s), Filing(s)** Abrade, Archive, Back up, Bastard, Batch, Binary, Binder, Box, Burr,
Circular, Clyfaker, Coffle, Croc(odile), Crosscut, Database, Data set, Dead-smooth,
Directory, Disc, Disk, Dossier, Download, Enter, Floatcut, Folder, Generation,
Half-round, In-box, Index, Indian, Lemel, Lever-arch, Limail, Limation, Line, Lodge,
Nail, Out-box, Packed, Pickpocket, Pigeon-hole, Podcast, Pollute, Quannet, Rank, Rasp,
Rat-tail, README, Riffler, Risp, Rolodex®, Row, Scalprum, Scratch, Signature, Single,
Single-cut, String, Swap, Swarf, Text, Tickler, TIF(F)
**Filial generation** F1
**Filibuster** Freebooter, Hinder, Obstruct, Pirate, Run on, Stonewall
**Filigree** Delicate, Fretwork, Sheer
**Filipino** Igorot, Moro, →**PHILIPPINE(S)**, Tagalog
**Fill(ing), Filler** Anaplerosis, Balaam, Banoffee, Banoffi, Beaumontag(u)e,
Beaumontique, Billow, Bishop, Bloat, Brick-nog, Brim, Bump, Caulk, Centre, Charge,
Cram, Debone, Fat-lute, Ganache, Gather, Gorge, Heart, Imbue, Implete, Impregn(ate),
Inlay, Inspirit, Instill, Jampack, Line, Load, Magma, Mastic, Mincemeat, Nagging,
Occupy, Pabulous, Packing, Permeate, Plug, Replenish, Repletive, Salpicon, Sate,
Satisfy, Sealant, Shim, Slush, Stack, Stock, Stocking, Stopgap, Stopping, →**STUFF**, Tales,
Tampon, Tank-up, Teem, Top up, Ullage
**Fillet(s)** Anadem, Annulet, Band, Bandeau, Bandelet, Bone, Cloisonné, Flaunching, Fret,
Goujons, Grenadine, Headband, Infula, Label, Lemniscus, List(el), Mitre, Moulding,
Reglet, Regula, Ribbon, Rollmop, Slice, Snood, Sphendone, Stria, Striga, Taeniate, Tape,
Teniate, Tilting, Tournedos, Vitta
**Fillip** Boost, Kick, Snap, Stimulus, Tonic
**Filly** Colt, Foal, She
**Film(s), Filmmaker, Filmy, Filming** Acetate, Actioner, Amnion, Animatronics,
Anime, Biopic, Blaxploitation, Blockbuster, Bollywood, Bubble, Buddy, Carry On, Cartoon,

Casablanca, Caul, Cel, Chick-flick, Chiller, Chopsocky, Cine, Cinéma vérité, Cinerama®, Circlorama®, Cliffhanger, Cling, Clip, Coat, Colour, Compilation, Conjunctiva, Creature feature, Deepie, Dew, Diorama, Docudrama, Documentary, Dogme, Dramedy, Dust, Epic, ET, Exposure, Fantasia, Feature, Featurette, Fiche, Flick, Floaty, Footage, Gauze, Genevieve, Gigi, Gossamer, Hammer, Haze, Hollywood, Horror, Horse opera, Ident, Infomercial, Jaws, Kell, Kidult, Lacquer, Lamella, Layer, Limelight, Loid, Machinima, Mask, Membrane, Microfiche, Mist, Molecular, Monochrome, Montage, Movie, Mylar®, Neo-noir, Newsreel, Noddy, Noir, Non-flam, Oater, Omnimax®, Outtake, Ozacling®, Panchromatic, Pathé, Patina, Pellicle, Photo, Pilot, Plaque, Prequel, Projection, Psycho, Quickie, Quota-quickie, Reel, Release, Reversal, Rockumentary, Roll, Romcom, Rush, Safety, Scale, Scenario, Scent-scale, Screen, Scum, Sepmag, Sheet, Shoot-'em-up, Short, Shot, Silent, Skin, Skin flick, Slasher-movie, Slashfest, Slick, Slo-mo, Snuff, Spaghetti western, Splatter, Star Wars, Studio, Super 8, Suspensor, Sword and sandal, Take, Talkie, Tear-jerker, Technicolor, Technothriller, Titanic, Toon, Trailer, Travelogue, Trippy, Two-shot, Ultrafiche, Ultra-rapid, Varnish, Vertigo, Vicenzi, Video, Videogram, Video-nasty, Vitaphone®, Wardour St, Web, Weepie, Weepy, Weft, Western, Wuxia

**Filmgoer** Cineaste

**Film star** Extra, Monroe, Vedette

**Filter(ing)** Band-pass, Bo(u)lt, Clarify, Colour, Dialysis, Dichroic, High-pass, Leach, Low-pass, Luxiviation, Percolate, Perk, Polarizing, Refine, Seep, Sieve, → SIFT, Sile, Skylight, Strain, Trickle

**Filth(y)** Addle, Augean, Bilge, Bogging, Colluvies, Crock, Crud, Defile, Dirt, Dung, Feculent, Foul, Grime, Hard core, Litter, Lucre, Mire, Muck, Nasty, Obscene, Ordure, Pythogenic, Refuse, Sewage, Slime, Smut(ch), Soil, Squalor, Stercoral, Sullage, Unwashed, Yuck

**Fin** Adipose, Anal, Caudal, Crack, Ctene, Dollars, Dorsal, Fiver, Fluke, Pectoral, Pelvic, Pinna, Pinnule, Rib, Skeg, Skegg, Stabiliser, Ventral

**Final(e), Finalise, Finally** Absolute, Apogee, At last, Closing, Closure, Coda, Conclusive, Cup, Decider, Denouement, End, End-all, Epilogue, Eventual, Exam, Extreme, Grand, Last, Last gap, Last resort, Net(t), Peremptory, Sew up, Swansong, Tailpiece, Terminal, Ultimate, Utter

**Finance, Financial, Financier** Ad crumenam, Angel, Back, Banian, Banker, Bankroll, Banyan, Bay Street, Bottomry, Cambism, Chrematistic, City (man), Equity, Exchequer, Fiscal, Forfaiting, Gnome, Grubstake, Mezzanine, Monetary, Moneyman, Patronise, Revenue, Sponsor, Subsidise, Treasurer, Underwrite, Wall Street

**Finback** Sei, Whale

**Finch** Bird, Brambling, Bunting, Canary, Cardinal bird, Charm, Chewink, Conirostral, Crossbill, Darwin's, Fringillid, Gouldian, Grosbeak, Linnet, Marsh-robin, Peter, Redpoll, Rosy, Serin, Siskin, Spink, Twite, Weaver-bird, Zebra

**Find(er), Finding** Ascertain, Come across, Detect, Dig up, Direction, Discover(y), Get, Gobind, Govind, Hit, Inquest, → LOCATE, Meet, Minitrack®, Provide, Rake up, Rarity, Rumble, Trace, Track down, Trouvaille, Unearth, Verdict

**Fine, Fine words** A1, Admirable, Amende, Amerce(ment), Amerciament, Arts, Assess, Bawcock, Beau(t), Bender, Blood-wit(e), Bonny, Boshta, Boshter, Boss, Brandy, Brave, Braw, Bully, Buttock-mail, Capital, Champion, Clear, Clement, Cloudless, Cobweb(by), Dainty, Dandy, Dick, Donzie, Dry, End, Eriach, Eric(k), Estreat, F, Fair, Famous, Forfeit, Gate, Godly, Good(ly), Gossamer, Gradely, Graithly, Grand, Grassum, Hair, Hairline, Handsome, Heriot, Hunkydory, Ideal, Idle, Immense, Impalpable, Inconie, Incony, Infangthief, Issue, Keen, Leirwite, Log, Maritage, Merchet, Mooi, Mulct, Nice, Nifty, Niminy-piminy, Noble, OK, Okay, Oke, Okey-doke(y), Outfangthief, Penalise, → PENALTY, Phat, Precise, Pretty, Pure, Relief, Righto, Safe, Sconce, Scratch, Sheer, Sicker, Slender, Smart, Spanking, Subtle, Summery, Super, Sure, Take, Tax, Terrific, Thin, Ticket(t)y-boo, Tiptop, Topping, Transmission, Triff, Unlaw, Wally, Waly, Well, Wer(e)gild, Wispy

**Fine-collector** Cheater

**Finery** Braws, Caparison, Fallal, Frills, Frippery, Gaudery, Glad rags, Ornament, Trinket, Wally, Warpaint

**Finesse** Adroitness, Artifice, Artistry, Delicacy, Skill, Strategy

**Fine-weather** All-hallond, All-hallow(e)n, All-hollown

**Finger(s), Fingernail** Annular, Dactyl, Digit, Fork, Green, Handle, Idle worms, Index, Lunula, Medius, Name, Nip, Piggy, Pinky, Pointer, Potato, Prepollex, Pusher, Ring(man), Shop, Sponge, Talaunt, Talon, Tot, Trigger, White

**Finger-hole** Lill, Ring

**Fingerprint(ing)** Arch, Dabs, Dactylogram, DNA, Genetic, Loop, Whorl

**Fingerstall** Hutkin

**Finial** Bunch, Knob, Ornament, Tee

**Finical, Finicky** Faddy, Fastidious, Fussy, Particular, Pernickety, Precise

**Finish(ed), Finishing (touch), Finish off** Arch, Blanket, Cadenza, Calendar, Close, Coating, Coda, Complete, →CONCLUDE, Crown, Dénouement, Die, Dish, Do, Dope, Dress, Eggshell, →END, Epilog(ue), Epiphenomena, Eradicate, Exact, Fine, Full, Gloss, Grandstand, Ice, Intonaco, Kibosh, Lacquer, Log off, Mat(t), Mirror, Napoo, Neat, Outgo, Outwork, Pebbledash, Peg out, Perfect, Photo, Picking, Polish off, Refine, Ripe, Round, Satin, Settle, Shellac, Shot, Spitcher, Surface, Terminate, Through, Top out, Up (tie), Varnish, Veneer, Washed-up, Wau(l)k, Wind-up, Wrap (up)

**Finite** Bounded, Limited

**Finland, Finn(ish)** Esth, Esthonian, Huck(leberry), Karelian, Lapp, Mickey, Mordvin, Suomic, Udmurt, Votyak

**Finn** Huckleberry

**Fiord** Bay, Hardanger, Inlet, Oslo, Randers, Trondheim

**Fir** Abies, Balsam, Douglas, Larch, Oregon, Scotch, Scots, Silver, Spruce, Umbrella

**Fire(side), Firing** Accend, Agni, Aidan, Aiden, Animate, Anneal, Ardour, Arouse, Arson, Atar, Awaken, Axe, Bake, Bale, Barbecue, Barrage, Beacon, Behram, Belting, Biscuit, Blaze, Boot, Brand, Brazier, Brush, Burn, Bush, Cashier, Central, Chassé, Conflagration, Corposant, Counterbattery, Covering, Cremate, Delope, Discharge, Dismiss, Élan, Electric, Element, Embolden, Ena, Energy, Enfilade, Enkindle, Enthuse, Flak, Flame, Friendly, Furnace, Glost, Greek, Gun, Hearth, Heater, Hob, Ignite, Inferno, Ingle, Inspire, Kentish, Kiln, Kindle, Launch, Let go, Let off, Light, Liquid, Lowe, Oust, Pop, Prime, Prometheus, Pull, Pyre, Pyromancy, Quick, Radiator, Rake, Rapid, Red, Red cock, Sack, St Anthony's, St Elmo's, Salvo, Scorch, Shell, Shoot, Smudge, Spark, Spirit, Spunk, Stoke, Stove, Strafe, Torch, Tracer, Trial, Trigger, Wake, Watch, Wisp, Zeal, Zip

▸ **Firearm** *see* GUN(FIRE)

**Fireback** Reredos

**Fireball** Bolide

**Firebird** Phoenix

**Fire-break** Epaulement, Greenstrip

**Firedamp** Blower

**Fire-dog** Andiron

**Fire engine** Green Goddess

**Fire-extinguisher** Halon, Hell-bender, Salamander

**Firefly** Glow-worm, Lightning-bug, Luciferin, Pyrophorus

**Fire-guard** Fender

**Firelighter** Arsonist, Spill

**Fireman** Abednego, Adair, Brigade, Deputy, Prometheus, Stoker, Visiting

**Fire-opal** Girasol

**Fireplace** Camboose, Chiminea, Chimney, Grate, Hearth, Hob, Ingle, Loop-hole, Range

**Fireplug** H, Hydrant

**Fireproof** Abednego, Asbestos, Incombustible, Inflammable, Meshach, Salamander, Shadrach, Uralite

**Firewalker** Abednego, Salamander
**Firewood** Billet, Faggot, Kindling, Knitch, Tinder
**Firework(s)** Banger, Bengal-light, Bunger, Catherine wheel, Cherry bomb, Cracker, Devil, Feu d'artifice, Firedrake, Fisgig, Fizgig, Flip-flop, Fountain, Gerbe, Girandole, Golden rain, Indian fire, Iron sand, Jumping jack, Maroon, Pastille, Peeoy, Petard, Pharaoh's serpent, Pinwheel, Pioy(e), Pyrotechnics, Realgar, Rocket, Roman candle, Serpent, Set piece, Skyrocket, Slap-bang, Sparkler, Tantrum, Throwdown, Tourbill(i)on, Volcano, Waterloo cracker, Wheel, Whizzbang
**Fire-worshipper** Parsee
**Firing** Baking, Counterbattery, Fusillade, Mitten, Salvo, Touchpaper, Trigger
**Firm, Firmness** Adamant, Agency, Al dente, Binding, Business, Collected, Compact, Company, Concern, Concrete, Conglomerate, Consistency, Constant, Crisp, Decided, Definite, Determined, Duro, Establishment, Faithful, Fast, Fixed, Hard, House, Inc, Inelastic, Insistent, Loyal, Marginal, Oaky, Obdurate, Obstinate, Partnership, Persistent, →RESOLUTE, Robust, Sclerotal, Secure, Set, Siccar, Sicker, →SOLID, Sound, Stable, Stalwart, Staunch, Steady, Ste(a)dfast, Steely, Steeve, Stern, Stieve, Stiff, Strict, Sturdy, Sure, Tenacious, Tight, Tough, Unflinching, Unshakeable, Well-knit
**Firmament** Canopy, Empyrean, Heaven, Sky
**First** 1st, Ab initio, Alpha, Arch, Archetype, Best, Calends, Champion, Chief, Curtain raiser, Earliest, Eldest, E(a)rst, Foremost, Former, Front, Head, I, Ideal, Imprimis, Initial, Kalends, Led, Maiden, No 1, One, Opener, Or, Ordinal, Original, Pioneer, Pole, Pole position, Premier, Première, Prima, Primal, Prime, Primo, Primordial, Principal, Priority, Prototype, Rudimentary, Scoop, Senior, Starters, Top, Uppermost, Victor, Yama
**First-aid(ers)** Zambu(c)k
**First born** Ariki, Cain, Eigne, Eldest, Heir, Major, Primogeniture, Senior
**First class, First rate** A1, Capital, Crack, Plump, Prime, Pukka, Slap up, Super-duper, Supreme, Tiptop, Top(notch)
**First day** Calends
**First fruits** Annat, Arles, Primitiae, Windfalls
**First man** Adam, Ask, Gayomart, Premier, President, Yama, Ymer, Ymir
**First offender** Eve, Probationer
▶ **First rate** *see* FIRST CLASS
**First woman** Embla, Eve, Pandora, Premier
**Firth** Dornoch, Estuary, Forth, Inlet, Moray, Pentland, Solway, Tay
**Fiscal** Monetary
**Fish(ing)** Angle, Bob, Bottom, Cast, Catch, Chowder, Coarse, Counter, Cran, Creel, Deep-sea, Dib, Dredge, Dry, Dry-fly, Episcate, Fly, Flying, Frozen, Fry, Game, Gefilte, Gefulte, Goujons, Guddle, Halieutics, Haul, Hen, Inshore, Ledger, Mess, Net, Odd, Offshore, Oily, Otterboard, Overnet, Piscary, Piscine, Poisson, Queer, Roe, Rough, Runner, Sacred, Sashimi, Shoal, Skitter, Sleeper, Snigger, Sniggle, Spin, Spot, Surfcasting, Surimi, Trawl, Troll, Trotline, Tub, Walking, Wet, White

---

**FISH**

| 2 letters: | But | Hag | Sar |
|---|---|---|---|
| Ai | Cat | Ide | Tai |
| Id | Cod | Koi | Top |
| | Cow | Lax | |
| 3 letters: | Dab | Lob | 4 letters: |
| Ahi | Dap | Mud | Barb |
| Aua | Dog | Par | Bass |
| Ayu | Eel | Pod | Blay |
| Bar | Gar | Ray | Bley |
| Bib | Ged | Rig | Brit |

Butt
Carp
Cero
Chad
Char
Chub
Chum
Coho
Cray
Cusk
Dace
Dare
Dart
Dory
Drum
Fugu
Gade
Goby
Gump
Hake
Harl
Hoka
Hoki
Huso
Huss
Ikan
Jack
Kelt
Keta
Lant
Leaf
Ling
Luce
Lump
Lung
Maid
Masu
Maze
Moki
Mola
Mort
Opah
Orfe
Parr
Peal
Peel
Penk
Pike
Pink
Poll
Pope
Pout
Raun
Rawn

Rigg
Rudd
Ruff
Scad
Scar
Scat
Scup
Seer
Seir
Shad
Sild
Slip
Snig
Sole
Star
Tope
Trot
Tuna
Tusk
Wels
Woof

**5 letters:**
Ablet
Ahuru
Allis
Angel
Apode
Aspro-
Basse
Belta
Blain
Bleak
Bream
Brill
Bully
Capon
Charr
Cisco
Clown
Cobia
Cohoe
Coley
Cuddy
Danio
Dorad
Doras
Doree
Dorse
Elops
Elver
Fluke
Gadus
Gibel

Grunt
Jewie
Jurel
Koura
Laker
Lance
Loach
Lythe
Maise
Maize
Manta
Masus
Mease
Molly
Murre
Murry
Nerka
Nurse
Padle
Perai
Perca
Perch
Pilot
Piper
Pirai
Platy
Pogge
Powan
Prawn
Roach
Roker
Royal
Ruffe
Saith
Sargo
Saury
Scrod
Sewen
Sewin
Shark
Sheat
Skate
Slope
Smelt
Smolt
Snoek
Snook
Solen
Speck
Sprat
Sprod
Squid
Tench
Tetra

Tiger
Togue
Torsk
Trout
Tunny
Umber
Wahoo
Whiff
Wirra
Witch
Yabby
Zebra

**6 letters:**
Alevin
Allice
Anabas
Angler
Archer
Ballan
Barbel
Belone
Beluga
Bichir
Big-eye
Blenny
Bonito
Bounce
Bowfin
Braise
Braize
Bumalo
Burbot
Callop
Caplin
Caranx
Caribe
Cheven
Clupea
Cockle
Comber
Conger
Conner
Cottus
Cudden
Cuddie
Cuddin
Cunner
Cuttle
Darter
Dentex
Diodon
Dipnoi
Discus

Doctor
Dorado
Dun-cow
Ellops
Espada
Finnac
Finnan
Fogash
Fumado
Gadoid
Garvie
Gilgie
Goboid
Goramy
Grilse
Groper
Gulper
Gunnel
Gurami
Gurnet
Haddie
Hapuka
Hassar
Inanga
Jerker
Jilgie
Kipper
Kokiri
Labrus
Lancet
Launce
Lizard
Louvar
Lunker
Mad Tom
Mahsir
Maigre
Marari
Marlin
Matjes
Meagre
Medaka
Medusa
Megrim
Milter
Minnow
Morgay
Mudcat
Mullet
Murena
Nerite
Oyster
Paddle
Paidle

Pakoko
Parore
Parrot
Patiki
Pholas
Piraya
Plaice
Podley
Pollan
Porgie
Puffer
Redfin
Remora
Rewaru
Rizzar
Rizzer
Rizzor
Robalo
Roughy
Saithe
Salmon
Samlet
Sander
Sardel
Sargus
Sauger
Saurel
Scampi
Scarus
Sea-bat
Sea-owl
Seeder
Serran
Shanny
Sheath
Shiner
Skelly
Sparid
Splake
Sucker
Tailor
Tarpon
Tautog
Tinker
Toitoi
Tomcod
Trygon
Turbot
Twaite
Ulicon
Ulikon
Vendis
Weever
Wirrah

Wrasse
Yabbie
Zander
Zingel

*7 letters:*
Ale-wife
Anchovy
Anemone
Anhinga
Asterid
Azurine
Batfish
Bellows
Bergylt
Birchir
Bloater
Bluecap
Boxfish
Brassie
Buffalo
Bumallo
Bummalo
Cabezon
Candiru
Capelin
Catfish
Cavalla
Cavally
Ceviche
Cichlid
Codfish
Copepod
Corvina
Cottoid
Crappie
Croaker
Crucian
Crusian
Cutlass
Dipnoan
Dogfish
Eelfare
Eel-pout
Escolar
Fantail
Findram
Finnack
Finnock
Flattie
Garfish
Garoupa
Garpike
Garvock

Geelbek
Gemfish
Goldeye
Gourami
Grouper
Growler
Grunion
Gudgeon
Gurnard
Gwiniad
Gwyniad
Haddock
Hagdown
Hagfish
Halibut
Herling
Herring
Hirling
Hogfish
Homelyn
Houting
Icefish
Ichthys
Inconnu
Jewfish
Kahawai
Keeling
Koi carp
Kokanee
Lampern
Lamprey
Lampuki
Lantern
Lingcod
Lobster
Lubfish
Lyomeri
Maatjes
Mahseer
Matelot
Medacca
Merling
Mojarra
Moon-eye
Morwong
Muraena
Oarfish
Old-wife
Oolakan
Opaleye
Osseter
Oulakan
Oulicon
Panchax

Pandora
Peacock
Pegasus
Pigfish
Pinfish
Piranha
Pollack
Pomfret
Pompano
Pupfish
Ragfish
Rasbora
Ratfish
Rat-tail
Redfish
Rorqual
Roughie
Sand dab
Sand-eel
Sardine
Scalare
Scallop
Schelly
Sculpin
Sea-bass
Sea-cock
Sea-dace
Sea-moth
Sea-pike
Sea-star
Sea-wife
Sevruga
Sillock
Silurid
Skegger
Skipper
Snapper
Sock-eye
Sparoid
Speldin
Sterlet
Sunfish
Sunstar
Surgeon
Teleost
Tiddler
Tilapia
Titling
Torgoch
Torpedo
Tubfish
Ulichon
Vendace
Vendiss

Wall-eye
Whipray
Whistle
Whiting
Wide-gab

**8 letters:**
Albacore
Albicore
Anableps
Arapaima
Asteroid
Atherine
Billfish
Blennius
Bloodfin
Blowfish
Blueback
Bluefish
Bluegill
Boarfish
Brisling
Bullhead
Bullhorn
Bummallo
Cabezone
Cabrilla
Carangid
Cardinal
Cavefish
Characid
Characin
Chimaera
Coalfish
Corkwing
Cow-pilot
Cucumber
Cyprinid
Dealfish
Dragonet
Drumfish
Eagle-ray
Elephant
Escallop
Eulachon
Fallfish
Fighting
Filefish
Flathead
Flounder
Four-eyes
Frogfish
Gambusia
Ganoidei

Gillaroo
Gilthead
Goatfish
Gobiidae
Graining
Grayling
Greeneye
Hackbolt
Hair-tail
Half-beak
Hard-head
Holostei
Hornbeak
Hornpout
Jackfish
Kabeljou
Killfish
Kingfish
Kingklip
Kukukuma
Lemon dab
Lionfish
Luderick
Lumpfish
Lungfish
Mackerel
Mahi-mahi
Mata Hari
Menhaden
Milkfish
Millions
Monkfish
Moonfish
Moray eel
Mosquito
Mulloway
Nannygai
Nennigai
Nine-eyes
Oulachon
Paradise
Patutuki
Pickerel
Pilchard
Pipefish
Pirarucu
Poor-john
Rascasse
Redbelly
Red roman
Reperepe
Rock-cook
Rockfish
Rockling

Roncador
Rosefish
Saibling
Sailfish
Saltfish
Sardelle
Scabbard
Scaridae
Sciaenid
Scorpion
Scuppaug
Sea-bream
Sea-devil
Seahorse
Sea-lemon
Sea-raven
Sea-robin
Sergeant
Serranid
Serranus
Skipjack
Smear-dab
Snake-eel
Sparidae
Sparling
Spelding
Speldrin
Stenlock
Sting-ray
Stonecat
Sturgeon
Surffish
Tarakihi
Tarwhine
Teraglin
Terakihi
Tile-fish
Toadfish
Trevally
Tropical
Tubenose
Tullibee
Weakfish
Whitling
Wolffish

**9 letters:**
Ahuruhuru
Amberjack
Anabantid
Anchoveta
Argentine
Barracuda
Blackfish

Bummaloti
Butterfly
Carangoid
Cascadura
Ceratodus
Chaetodon
Chavender
Clingfish
Clupeidae
Coregonus
Coryphene
Cyprinoid
Devilfish
Gaspereau
Glassfish
Globefish
Goldfinny
Goldsinny
Golomynka
Goosefish
Grass carp
Greenbone
Greenling
Grenadier
Haberdine
Hornyhead
Hottentot
Houndfish
Ichthyoid
Jacksmelt
Jewelfish
Kabeljouw
Killifish
Labyrinth
Latimeria
Matelotte
Menominee
Mudhopper
Neon tetra
Pikeperch
Porbeagle
Porcupine
Queenfish
Quillback
Roussette
Scaldfish
Scalefish
Schnapper
Scorpaena
Selachian
Shubunkin
Siluridae
Slickhead
Snailfish

Snakefish
Snakehead
Snipefish
Solenette
Spadefish
Spearfish
Speldring
Stargazer
Steenbras
Stingaree
Stockfish
Stonefish
Surfperch
Surmullet
Sweetfish
Sweetlips
Swellfish
Swinefish
Swordfish
Sword-tail
Thornback
Threadfin
Tittlebat
Tommy ruff
Topminnow
Trachinus
Troutfish
Troutling
Trumpeter
Trunkfish
Whitebait
White-bass
Wreckfish
Yellowfin

**10 letters:**

Amblyopsis
Barracoota
Barracouta
Barramundi
Bitterling
Bombay duck
Bottlehead
Butterfish
Candlefish
Cockabully
Cofferfish
Cornetfish
Cyclostome
Damselfish
Demoiselle
Dollarfish
Etheostoma
Fingerling

Flutemouth
Groundling
Guitarfish
Horned pout
Lake-lawyer
Largemouth
Lumpsucker
Maskalonge
Maskanonge
Maskinonge
Midshipman
Mossbunker
Mudskipper
Needlefish
Nurse-hound
Paddlefish
Pakirikiri
Rabbitfish
Red emperor
Red-snapper
Ribbonfish
Rudderfish
Sandsucker
Scopelidae
Sea-poacher
Sea-surgeon
Serrasalmo
Sheepshead
Ship-holder
Shovelnose
Silverside
Small mouth
Springfish
Squeteague
Teleostome
Titarakura
Tommy rough
Trailperch
Tripletail
White cloud
White perch
Yellowtail

**11 letters:**

Cephalis pie
Chondrostei
Cyprinodont
Dolly Varden
Istiophorus
Lapidosteus
Lepidosiren
Lophobranch
Maskallonge
Moorish idol

Muskellunge
Ostracoderm
Oxyrhynchus
Plagiostome
Plectognath
Pumpkinseed
Scolopendra
Seventy-four
Snail darter
Soldierfish
Stickleback
Stoneroller
Surgeonfish
Triggerfish
Trumpetfish
Water souchy
White martin
Yellowbelly

**12 letters:**

Ballan-wrasse
Elasmobranch
Father-lasher
Heterosomata
Histiophorus
Jack crevalle
Mangrove Jack
Miller's thumb
Mouthbreeder
Mouthbrooder
Orange roughy
Plectognathi
Rainbow-trout
Silver dollar
Squirrelfish

**13 letters:**

Burnett salmon
Leatherjacket
Musselcracker
Perennibranch
Rainbow runner
Sailor's choice
Sergeant Baker

**14 letters:**

Smallmouth-bass
Snaggle-toothed
Walking catfish
Winter flounder

**15 letters:**

Crossopterygian

**Fish and chips** Greasies
**Fish-basket** Creel, Hask, Kipe
**Fish disease** Argulus
**Fisher(man)** Ahab, Andrew, Angler, Black cat, Caper, Codder, Dragman, Heron, Herringer, High-liner, Liner, Pedro, Peter (grimes), Piscator, Rodster, Sharesman, Walton
▶ **Fisherwoman** *see* FISH-SELLER
**Fish-hawk** Osprey
**Fishing-ground** Haaf
**Fishing-line** G(u)imp, Gymp, Paternoster
**Fishpond** Ocean, Stew, Vivarium
**Fish-seller, Fisherwoman** Fishwife, Molly Malone, Ripp(i)er, Shawley, Shawlie
**Fishy** Botargo, Dodgy, Suspicious, Vacant
**Fission** Multiple, Nuclear
**Fissure** Chasm, Cleft, Crack, Crevasse, Crevice, Gap, Grike, Gryke, Lode, Rent, Rift, Rille, Rolando, Sand-crack, Scam, Swallet, Swallow hole, Sylvian, Sylvius, Vallecula, Vein, Zygon
**Fist** Clench, Dukes, Hand, Iron, Join-hand, Mailed, Neaf(f)e, Neif, Neive, Nief, Nieve, Pud, Punch, Thump, Writing
**Fit(s), Fitful, Fitter, Fitting(s), Fitness** Able(-bodied), Access, Adapt, Ague, Align, Aline, Apoplexy, Appointment, Apposite, Appropriate, Apropos, Apt(itude), A salti, Athletic, Attack, Babbitt, Bayonet, Becoming, Belong, Beseemly, Bout, Canto, Capable, Cataleptic, Cataplexy, Click, Competent, Concinnous, Condign, Congruous, Conniption, Convulsion, Culver-tail, Darwinian, Decent, Decorous, Desultory, Dod, Dove-tail, Due, Eclampsia, Egal, Eligible, Ensconce, Epilepsy, Equip, Exies, Expedient, Fairing, Fay, Fiddle, Form, Furniment, Furnishing, Fytte, Gee, Germane, Glove, Gusty, Habile, Hale, Handsome, Hang, Health, Hinge, Hissy, Huff, Hysterics, Ictus, Inclusive, In-form, Interference, Intermittent, In trim, Jactitation, Jag, Just, Kashrut(h), Like, Lune, Marry, Mate, Meet, Mood, Nest, Opportune, Paroxysm, Passus, Pertinent, Pet, Prepared, Press, →PROPER, Queme, Ready, Relevant, Rig, Rightful, Rind, Ripe, Roadworthy, Rynd, Seemly, Seizure, Serving, Set, Shrink, Sit, Sliding, Slot, Snit, Snotter, Snug, Sort, Sound, Spasm, Spell, Start, Stroke, Suit(able), Syncope, Tailor, Tantrum, Tenoner, Throe, Tide, To prepon, Tref(a), Treif, Trim, Turn, Unit, Up to, Well, Wobbler, Wobbly, Worthy, Wrath
▷ **Fit(ting)** *may indicate* a 't'
**Fitment** Adaptor, Unit
**Fitzgerald** Edward, Ella, Scott
**Fitzwilliam** Darcy
**Five(s), Fiver** Cinque, Flim, Mashie, Pallone, Pedro, Pentad, Quinary, Quincunx, Quintet, Sextan, Towns, V
**Five hundred** D, Monkey
**Five years** Lustre, Lustrum
**Fix(ation), Fixed, Fixer, Fixative** Affeer, Anchor, Appoint, Appraise, →ARRANGE, Assess, Assign, Attach, Bed, Bind, Brand, Cement, Clamp, Clew, Clue, Confirm, Constant, Corking-pin, Cure, Decide, Destinate, Destine, Determine, Do, Embed, Empight, Encastré, Engrain, Establish, Fast, Fasten, Fiddle, Firm, Fit, Freeze, Gammon, Hard and fast, Hold, Hypo(sulphite), Immutable, Impaction, Impasse, Imprint, Inculcate, Inextensible, Ingrain, Iron on, Jag, Jam, Locate, Lodge, Mend, Mount, Nail, Name, Narcotic, Nitrogen, Nobble, Odd-job man, Orientate, Peen, Peg, Permanent, Persistent, Pin, Place, Point, Quantify, Repair, Resolute, Rig, Rigid, Rivet, Rove, Rut, Scrape, Screw, Seat, Seize, Set, Settle, Ship, Shoo, Skatole, Skewer, Splice, Square, Stable, Stage, Staple, Static, Steadfast, Steady, Stell, Step, Stereotype, Stew, Stuck, Swig, Swing, Tie, To, Toe, Unchangeable, Valorize, Weld
**Fixture** Attachment, Away (game), Event, Home, Match, Permanence, Rawlplug®, Unit
**Fizz(ed), Fizzy** Bubbles, Buck's, Effervesce, Gas, Hiss, Pop, Sherbet, Sod, Soda
**Fizzle** Failure, Flop, Hiss, Washout

▶ **Fjord** *see* **FIORD**

**Flab(by)** Flaccid, Lank, Lax, Limp, Pendulous, Saggy, Tubby

**Flabbergast(ed)** Amaze, Astound, Floor, Thunderstruck

**Flaccid** Flabby, Lank, Lax, Limp, Soft

**Flag(gy), Flagging, Flags** Acorus, Ancient, Ashlar, Banderol, Banner, Black, Blackjack, Blue (Ensign), Blue Peter, Bunting, Burgee, Calamus, Chequered, Colour(s), Dan(n)ebrog, Decline, Droop, Duster, Ensign, Fail, Faint, Falter, Fane, Fanion, Field colours, Gladdon, Gonfalon, Green, Guidon, Hail, Hoist, House, Irideal, Iris, Jack, Jade, Jolly Roger, Kerbstone, Languish, Lis, Maple leaf, Old Glory, Orris, Pave(ment), Pavilion, Paviour, Pencel, Pennant, Pennon, Penoncel(le), Pensel, Pensil, Peter, Pilot, Pin, Prayer, Quarantine, Rag, Rainbow, Red, Red Duster, Red Ensign, Repeater, Royal standard, Sag, Sedge, Semaphore, Sett, Sick, Sink, Slab(stone), Slack, Stand, Standard, Stars and Bars, Stars and Stripes, Streamer, Substitute, Sweet, Tire, Tricolour, Union (Jack), Vane, Vexillology, Waft, Wasting, Weaken, Whiff, Whift, White (ensign), Wilt, Wither, Yellow (Jack)

**Flagday** Tagday

**Flagellate** Beat, Euglena, Flog, Mastigophora, Scourge, Trypanosome, Whip

**Flageolet** Penny whistle

**Flagon** Bottle, Carafe, Ewer, Jug, Pitcher, Stoop, Stoup, Vessel

**Flagpole** Pin, Staff

**Flagrant** Blatant, Egregious, Glaring, Gross, Heinous, Patent, Rank, Shameless, Wanton

**Flagship** Admiral, Barge, Victory

**Flag-waving** Jingoism

**Flail** Beat, Drub, Swingle, Swip(p)le, Threshel

**Flair** Art, Artistic, Bent, Élan, Gift, Instinct, Knack, Nose, Panache, Style, → **TALENT**

**Flak** AA, Attack, Barrage, Criticism

**Flake** Chip, Flame, Flaught, Flaw, Floccule, Flocculus, Fragment, Peel, Scale, Smut, Snow, Spark

**Flam** Impose

**Flamboyant** Baroque, Brilliant, Flame-tree, Florid, Garish, Grandiose, Jazzy, Loud, Ornate, Ostentatious, Panache, Paz(z)azz, Piz(z)azz, Pzazz, Showoff, Swash-buckler

**Flame, Flaming** Ardent, Blaze, Fire, Flake, Flambé, Flammule, Flareback, Glow, Kindle, Leman, Lover, Lowe, Musical, Naked, Olympic, Oxyacetylene, Reducing, Sensitive, Sweetheart

**Flan** Pastry, Quiche, Tart

**Flanders** Mare, Moll

**Flange** Border, Collar, Collet, Lip, Rim

**Flank(s)** Accompany, Anta, Flange, Flitch, Ilia, Lisk, Loin, Side, Spur

**Flannel** Blather, Canton, Cloth, Cotton, Face, Flatter, Outing, Soft-soap, Waffle, Washrag, Zephyr

**Flap(ped), Flapper, Flapping** Ado, Agnail, Aileron, Alar, Alarm(ist), Aventail(e), Bate, Beat, Bird, Bobbysoxer, Bustle, Chit, Deerstalker, Dither, Earcap, Elevon, Epiglottis, Epiploon, Fipple, Flacker, Flaff, Flag, Flaught, Flutter, Fly, Fuss, Giglet, Giglot, Hover, → **IN A FLAP**, Labium, Labrum, Lapel, Loma, Loppet, Louvre, Luff, Lug, Omentum, Operculum, Panic, Shirt-tail, Spin, Spoiler, State, Tab, Tag, Tailboard, Tailgate, Tiswas, To-do, Tongue, TRAM, Volucrine, Wave, Whisk

**Flare(d), Flares, Flare up** Bell, Bell-bottoms, Fishtail, Flame, Flanch, Flaunch, Godet, Magnesium, Scene, Signal, Skymarker, Solar, Spread, Spunk, Ver(e)y (light), Widen

**Flash(y), Flasher, Flashpoint** Bling, Bluette, Brainstorm, Brash, Bulletin, Coruscate, Cursor, Electronic, Emicant, Essex Man, Exposure, Fire-flag, Flare, Flaught, Fulgid, Fulgural, Garish, Gaudy, Glaik, Gleam, Glent, Glint, Glisten, Glitter, Glitzy, Green, Green ray, Helium, Indicate, Instant, Jay, Lairy, Levin, Lightning, Loud, Lurex, Magnesium, Meretricious, Mo, Moment, Nanosecond, News, Ostentatious, Photopsy, Pyrotechnic, Raffish, Rakish, Ribbon, Ring, Roary, Scintillation, Sec(ond), Sequin, Showboater, Showy,

Sluice, Snazzy, Spark, Sparkle, Sport, Streak, Strobe, Swank(e)y, Thunderbolt, Tick, Tigrish, Trice, Tulip, Twinkle, Vivid, Wink, Wire

▷ **Flashing** *may indicate* an anagram

**Flask(-shaped)** Ampulla, Aryballos, Bottle, Canteen, Carafe, Cask, Coffin, Conceptacle, Costrel, Cucurbit, Decanter, Dewar, Erlenmeyer, Fiasco, Flacket, Flacon, Florence, Goatskin, Hip, Lekythos, Livery pot, Matrass, Mick(e)y, Moon, Pocket-pistol, Powder, Pycnidium, Reform, Retort, Thermos®, Vacuum, Vial

**Flat(s), Flatness, Flatten(ed), Flattener** Adobe, Alkali, Amaze, Ancipital, Apartment, Bachelor, Bald, Banal, Beat, Bed-sit, Blow-out, Bulldoze, Callow, Cape, Complanate, Compress, Condominium, Corymb(ose), Cottage, Coulisse, Court, Dead, Demolish, Diageotropic, Dorsiventral, Double, Dress, Dry, Dull, Even, Feeble, Flew, Floor, Flue, Fool, Gaff, Garden, Granny, Guyot, Haugh, High-rise, Homaloid, Home-unit, Horizontal, Insipid, Ironed, Jacent, Key, KO, Law, Lay, Level, Lifeless, Llano, Lodge, Maderised, Maison(n)ette, Marsh, Monotonous, Mud, Nitwit, Norfolk, Obcompressed, Oblate, Ownership, Pad, Pancake, Pedestrian, Peneplain, Peneplane, Penthouse, Pentice, Pied-à-terre, Plain, Planar, Plane, Planish, Plap, Plat, Plateau, Platitude, Press, Prone, Prostrate, Puncture, Recumbent, Rooms, Salt, Scenery, Service, Smooth, Splayfoot, Spread-edged, Squash, Stale, Studio, Tableland, Tabular, Tame, Tasteless, Tedious, Tenement, Time-share, Trample, True, Uniform, Unimaginative, Unsensational, Vapid, Walk-up

**Flat-chested** Cithara

**Flat-faced** Socle

**Flat-foot(ed)** Policeman, Splay

**Flat-nosed** Camus

**Flatter(er), Flattering, Flattery** Adulate, Becoming, Beslaver, Blandish, Blarney, Bootlick, Butter, Cajole, Candied, Carn(e)y, Claw(back), Complimentary, Comprabatio, Court-dresser, Damocles, Earwiggy, En beau, Eyewash, Fawn, Fillibrush, Flannel, Flannen, Fleech, Flummery, Foot-licker, Fulsome, Gloze, Gnathonic(al), Grease, Honey, Imitation, Lip-salve, Moody, Palaver, Palp, Phrase, Poodle-faker, Proneur, Puffery, Sawder, Smarm, Snow job, Soap, Soft soap, Soother, Souk, Spaniel, Stroke, Sugar, Sweet talk, Sycophant, Taffy, Toady, Treacle, Unction, Wheedle, Word

**Flatulence, Flatulent** Belch, Borborygmus, Burp, Carminative, Colic, Gas, Tympanites, Ventose, Wind, Wind dropsy

**Flaunt** Brandish, Flourish, Gibe, Parade, Skyre, Sport, Strout, Strut, Wave

**Flavour(ed), Flavouring, Flavoursome** Absinth(e), Alecost, Amaracus, Anethole, Angostura, Anise, Aniseed, Aroma, Benne, Bergamot, Body, Bold, Borage, Bouquet garni, Chil(l)i, Clove, Coriander, Cumin, Dill, Essence, Eucalyptol, Fenugreek, Flor, Garlic, Garni, Gingili, Marinate, Mint, Orgeat, Piperonal, Potherb, Quark, Race, Ratafia, Relish, Rocambole, Sair, Sapor, Sassafras, Season, Sesame, Spearmint, Spice, Tack, Tang, Tarragon, → **TASTE**, Til, Tincture, Twang, Umami, Vanilla, Yummy

**Flaw(ed)** Blemish, Brack, Bug, Chip, Crack, Defect, Fallacy, → **FAULT**, Gall, Hamartia, Imperfection, Infirmity, Kink, Knar, Knothole, Lophole, Misspent, Nick, Red-eye, Rima, Spot, Stain, Taint, Tear, Thief, Tragic, Windshake

**Flawless** Impeccable, Intact, Perfect

**Flax(en)** Allseed, Blonde, Codilla, Harakeke, Harden, Hards, Herden, Herl, Hurden, Line, Linseed, Lint, Lint-white, Linum, Mill-mountain, Poi, Tow

**Flay** Excoriate, Fleece, Flense, Scourge, Skin, Strip, Uncase, Whip

**Flea** Aphaniptera, Chigger, Chigoe, Chigre, Daphnid, Hopper, Itch-mite, Lop, Pulex, Sand, Turnip, Water

**Flea-bane** Erigeron

**Fleabite** Denier

**Fleck** Dash, Freak, Spot, Streak

**Fledgling** Aerie, Eyas, Sorage

**Flee(ing)** Abscond, Bolt, Decamp, Escape, Eschew, Fly, Fugacity, Lam, Loup, Run, Scapa, Scarper, Scram

**Fleece(d), Fleecy** Bilk, Bleed, Coat, Con, Despoil, Flocculent, Golden, Jib, Lambskin, Lambswool, Lanose, Nubia, Overcharge, Pash(i)m, Pashmina, Plo(a)t, Pluck, Rifte, Ring, Rob, Rook, Shave, Shear, Sheepskin, Shorn, Skin, Skirtings, Sting, →**SWINDLE**, Toison, Wool

**Fleer** Ogle

**Fleet(ing)** Armada, Brief, Camilla, Caravan, Convoy, Ephemeral, Evanescent, Fast, First, Flit, Flota, Flotilla, Fugacious, Fugitive, Glimpse, Hasty, Hollow, Lightfoot, Navy, Pacy, Passing, Prison, Spry, Street, Swift, Transient, Velocipede, Volatile

**Flemish** Flamingant

**Flesh(y)** Beefy, Body, Carnal, Carneous, Carrion, Corporeal, Corpulent, Creatic, Dead-meat, Digastric, Finish, Goose, Gum, Hypersarcoma, Joint, Jowl, Ket, Long pig, Love handles, Lush, Meat, Mole, Mons, Muffin top, Mummy, Muscle, Mutton, Proud, Pulp, Quick, Sarcous, Spare tyre, Succulent, Tissue, Wattle

**Flesh-eating** Cannibalism, Carnassial, Creophagus, Omophagic

**Fleshless** Dry, Maigre, Pem(m)ican

**Flex(ible), Flexibility** Adaptable, Bend(y), Compliant, Double-jointed, Elastic, Genu, Leeway, Limber, Lissom(e), Lithe, Pliant, →**RESILIENT**, Rubato, Rubbery, Springy, Squeezy, Supple, Tensile, Tolerant, Tonus, Tractile, Versatile, Wieldy, Willing, Willowy, Wiry

▷ **Flexible, Flexuous** *may indicate* an anagram

**Flick(er), Flicks** Bioscope, Cinema, Fillip, Film, Flip, Flirt, Flutter, Glimmer, Gutter, Kinema, Kinema, Movie, Movy, Riffle, Snap, Snow, Spang-cockle, Spark, Switch, Talkie, Twinkle, Waver, Wink, Zap

**Flickertail** ND

**Flier** Aerostat, Airman, Alcock, Amy, Aviator, →**BIRD**, Bleriot, Blimp, Brown, Crow, Daedalus, Erk, Fur, George, Gotha, Handout, Icarus, Insert, Leaflet, Lindbergh, Montgolfier, Pegasus, Pilot, RAF, Scotsman, Spec, Speedy

**Flight(y), Flight path** Aeronautical, Aerospace, Air corridor, Backfisch, Birdbrain, Bolt, Bubble-headed, Capricious, Charter, Contact, Dart, Dash, Departure, Escalate, Escalier, Escape, Exaltation, Exodus, Fast, Fickle, Flapper, Flaught, Flibbertigibbet, Flip, Flock, Flyby, Fly-past, Free, Fugue, Getaway, Giddy, Grece, Grese, Gris(e), Guy, Hegira, Hejira, Hejra, Hellicat, Hijra, Lam, Loup-the-dyke, Mercy, Milk-run, Mission, Moonshot, Open-jaw, Pair, Parabola, Proving, Redeye, R(a)iser, Rode, Ro(a)ding, Rout, Runaway, Skein, Sortie, Stairs, →**STAMPEDE**, Stayre, Steps, Swarm, Test, Top, Tower, Trap, Vol(age), Volageous, Volatile, Volley, Whisky-frisky, Wing

**Flightless** Kakapo, Nandoo, Ostrich, Rhea, Struthious

▷ **Flighty** *may indicate* an anagram

**Flimsy** Airy-fairy, Delicate, Finespun, Fragile, Gimcrack, Gossamer, Jimcrack, Lacy, Paper thin, Sleazy, Sleezy, Tenuous, Thin, Weak, Wispy

**Flinch** Blench, Cringe, Funk, Quail, Recoil, Shrink, Shudder, Start, Wince

**Fling** Affair, Amour, Dance, Flounce, Heave, Highland, Hurl, Lance, Pitch, Shy, Slat, Slug, Slump, Spanghew, Spree, Throw, →**TOSS**

**Flint** Chert, Eolite, Firestone, Granite, Hag-stone, Hornstone, Microlith, Mischmetal, Optical, Pirate, Rock, Silex, Silica, Stone, Touchstone, Tranchet

**Flip(pant), Flippancy, Flipping** Airy, Bally, Brash, Cocky, Facetious, Flick, Frivolous, Go postal, Impudent, Jerk, Nog, Overturn, Persiflage, Pert, Purl, Ruddy, Sassy, Saucy, Toss, Turn, Upend

**Flipper(s)** Fin-toed, Paddle, Pinniped(e)

**Flirt(ation), Flirtatious, Flirting** Bill, Buaya, Carve, Chippy, Cockteaser, Come-hither, Come-on, Coquet(te), Dalliance, Demivierge, Fizgig, Footsie, Gallivant, Heart-breaker, Kittenish, Lumber, Mash, Minx, Neck, Philander(er), Pickeer, Prick-teaser, Prink, Rig, Spark, Toy, Trifle, Vamp, Wow

**Flit** Dart, Decamp, Flicker, Flutter, Moonlight, Scoot

**Float(er), Floating, Flotation** Ark, Balsa, Bidarka, Bob, Bubble, Buoy(ant), Caisson, Camel, Carley, Clanger, Drift, Fleet, Flotsam, Flutterboard, Froth, Fucus, Jetsam, Jetson,

Levitate, Lifebuoy, Milk, Natant, Neuston, Oropesa, Outrigger, Paddle, Planula, Pontoon, Pram, Quill, Raft, Ride, Sail, Skim, Sponson, Stick, Trimmer, Vacillate, Waft, Waggler, Waterwings, Weightless

**Floating garden** Chinampa

**Flock(s)** Assemble, Bevy, Charm, Chirm, Company, Congregation, Dopping, Drove, Flight, Fold, Forgather, Gaggle, Gather, Gregatim, Herd, Mob, Paddling, Parishioners, Rally, Rout, School, Sedge, Sord, Spring, Trip, Troop, Tuft, Vulgar, Walk, Wing, Wisp, Wool

**Flog(ger), Flogging** Baculine, Beat, Birch, Breech, Cane, Cat, Clobber, Exert, Flay, Hawk, Hide, Horsewhip, Knout, Lace, Lambast, Larrup, Lash, Lather, Lick, Orbilius, Retail, Rope's end, Scourge, Sell, Strap, Tan, Tat, Taw, → **THRASH**, Thwack, Tout, Vapulate, Welt, Whip, Whipping-cheer

**Flood(ed)** Avalanche, Awash, Bore, Cataclysm, Deluge, Deucalion's, Diffuse, Diluvium, Drown, Dump, Eger, Flash, Freshet, Gush, Inundate, Irrigate, Noachic, Ogygian deluge, Outpouring, Overflow, Overswell, Overwhelm, Pour, Rage, Smurf, Spate, Speat, Suffuse, Swamp, Tide, → **TORRENT**, Undam, Washland, Waterlog

**Floodgate** St(a)unch

**Floodlight** Ashcan, Blond(e), One-key

**Floor(ing)** Area, Astonish, Astound, Baffle, Barbecue, Beat, Bemuse, Benthos, Chess, Deck(ing), Dev(v)el, Down, Entresol, Étage, Fell, Flags(tone), Flatten, Flight, Gravel, Ground, Kayo, KO, Mezzanine, Mould loft, Orlop, Paralimnion, Parquet, Pelvic, Piano nobile, Pit, Planch, Platform, Puncheon, Screed, Shop, Siege, Sole, Stage, Stagger, Story, Stump, Terrazzo, Tessella, Tessera, Thill, Throw, Trading, Woodblock

**Floozie** Broad, Scarlet woman

**Flop(py)** Belly-landing, Bomb(shell), Collapse, Dud, Failure, Fizzer, Fosbury, Limp, Lollop, Mare's-nest, Misgo, Phut, Plump, Purler, Turkey, Washout, Whap, Whitewash

**Flora** Benthos, Biota, Cybele, Flowers, Intestinal

**Florence, Florentine** Medici, Tuscan

**Florid** Asian, Baroque, Coloratura, Cultism, Flamboyant, Fresh, Gongorism, High, Red, Rococo, Rubicund, Ruddy, Taffeta

**Florida** Fa

**Florin** Scotchman

**Florist** Spry

**Floss(y)** Dental, Flashy, Florence, Ornate, Silk

▶ **Flotation** *see* **FLOAT(ER)**

**Flotilla** Armada, Escadrille

**Flotsam** Detritus, Driftwood, Flotage, Waift, Waveson, Weft, Wreckage

**Flounce** Falbala, Frill, Furbelow, Huff, Prance, Ruffle, Sashay, Toss

**Flounder** Blunder, Flail, Fluke, Pitch, Reel, Sandsucker, Slosh, Struggle, Stumble, Tolter, Toss, Wallop, Wallow

**Flour** Buckwheat, Cassava, Couscous(ou), Cribble, Crible, Farina, Graham, Gram, Kouskous, Meal, Middlings, Pinole, Plain, Powder, Red-dog, Rice, Rock, Rye, Self-raising, Soy(a), Strong, Wheatmeal, White, Wholegrain, Wholemeal, Wholewheat, Wood

**Flourish(ed), Flourishing** Blague, Bless, Bloom, Blossom, Boast, Boom, Brandish, Bravura, Burgeon, Cadenza, Dow well, Epiphonema, Fanfare, Fiorita, Fl, Flare, Floreat, Florescent, Green, Grow, Kicking, Lick, Lush, Melisma, Mort, Omar, Palmy, Paraph, Pert, Prosper, Rubric, Ruderal, Scroll, Serif, Swash, Tantara, Thrive, Tucket, Veronica, Vigorous, Wampish, Wave, Welfare

**Flout** Defy, Disdain, Disobey, Insult, Malign, Mock, Profane, Scorn, Scout

**Flow(ing)** Abound, Afflux, Cantabile, Cantilena, Cash, Circumference, Current, Cursive, Cusec, Data, Distil, Ebb, Emanate, Estrang(h)elo, Fleet, Fluent, Fluid, Flush, Flux, Freeform, Gene, Gush, Indraft, Issue, Knickpoint, Lahar, Laminar, Liquid, Loose-bodied, Mane, Nappe, Nickpoint, Obsequent, Onrush, Ooze, Popple, Pour, Purl, Rail(e), Rayle,

Rill, Rin, Run, Rush, Scapa, Seamless, Seep, Seton, Setter, Slip, Slur, Spate, Spurt, Stream, Streamline, Teem, Tidal, Torrent, Trickle, Turbulent, Viscous, Wash, Well

**Flower (part), Flowering, Flowers, Flower bed** Best, Bloom, Bloosme, Blossom, Composite, Cream, Develop, Disc, Ecblastesis, Efflorescence, Elite, Fiori, Imperfect, Inflorescence, Parterre, Passion, Pick, Plant, Pre-vernal, Prime, Quatrefeuille, Quatrefoil, Remontant, → **RIVER**, Rogation, Serotine, Spray, Square, Stalked, Stream, Thyrse, Trefoil, Trumpet, Verdoy, Vernal, Wreath

## FLOWERS

*3 letters:*
May
Mum
Rue

*4 letters:*
Aloe
Arum
Cyme
Disa
Flag
Gold
Gool
Gule
Irid
Iris
Knot
Lily
Pink
Rose
Wald
Weld

*5 letters:*
Agave
Aster
Brook
Bugle
Camas
Canna
Daisy
Enemy
Erica
Hosta
Lotus
Lupin
Orris
Oxlip
Padma
Pansy
Phlox
Poppy
Spink
Stock

Tansy
Toran
Tulip
Tyrse
Umbel
Viola
Yulan

*6 letters:*
Adonis
Annona
Arabis
Camash
Camass
Corymb
Cosmos
Crants
Dahlia
Gollan
Henbit
Lupine
Madder
Maguey
Mallow
Mimosa
Nuphar
Onagra
Orchid
Oxslip
Paeony
Pompom
Pompon
Protea
Scilla
Sesame
Silene
Smilax
Spadix
Tassel
Thrift
Torana
Wasabi
Yarrow

*7 letters:*
Aconite
Alyssum
Amarant
Anemone
Astilbe
Bugloss
Campion
Cowslip
Freesia
Fuchsia
Fumaria
Gentian
Gilt-cup
Glacier
Gladdon
Godetia
Golland
Gowland
Hawkbit
Ipomoea
Jonquil
Kikumon
Lobelia
Melilot
Mimulus
Nosegay
Petunia
Picotee
Primula
Quamash
Rampion
Statice
Sulphur
Tellima
Verbena

*8 letters:*
Abutilon
Amaranth
Argemone
Asphodel
Bindi-eye
Bluebell

Bullhoof
Carolina
Clematis
Cyclamen
Daffodil
Floscule
Foxglove
Gardenia
Geranium
Gillyvor
Gladioli
Glory-pea
Hepatica
Hesperis
Hibiscus
Kok-sagyz
Larkspur
Leucojum
Magnolia
Marigold
Myosotis
Oleander
Primrose
Samphire
Scabious
Stapelia
Trollius
Tuberose
Turnsole
Valerian

*9 letters:*
Bald-money
Belamoure
Buttercup
Cineraria
Columbine
Edelweiss
Eglantine
Galingale
Gessamine
Golden rod
Hellebore
Hollyhock

| | | | |
|---|---|---|---|
| Hydrangea | Buttonhole | Stavesacre | *12 letters:* |
| Jessamine | Coronation | Tibouchine | Hortus siccus |
| Melampode | Fraxinella | Touch-me-not | None-so-pretty |
| Pimpernel | Granadilla | | Pasqueflower |
| Pyrethrum | Heliotrope | *11 letters:* | Pheasant's eye |
| Rudbeckia | Immortelle | Boutonniere | Tradescantia |
| Santonica | Nasturtium | Bur-marigold | |
| Saxifrage | Pentstemon | Gillyflower | *13 letters:* |
| Speedwell | Poached egg | Loose-strife | Flannelflower |
| Strobilus | Poinsettia | Meadow-sweet | |
| Tiger lily | Polyanthus | Red hot poker | *14 letters:* |
| | Pulsatilla | Saintpaulia | Transvaal daisy |
| *10 letters:* | Quinsy-wort | | |
| Bellamoure | Snapdragon | | |

▷ **Flower** *may indicate* a river

**Flower arrangement, Flower work** Barbola, Ikebana, Lei

**Flowery** Anthea, Anthemia, Damassin, Orchideous, →ORNATE, Pseudocarp, Verbose

**Flu** Bird, Fujian, Gas(tric), →INFLUENZA, ME, Wog, Yuppie

**Fluctuate(r), Fluctuating, Fluctuation** Ambivalence, Balance, Irregular, Seasonal, Seiche, Trimmer, Unsteady, Vacillate, Vary, Waver, Yo-yo

**Flue** Chimney, Duct, Funnel, Pipe, Recuperator, Tewel, Uptake, Vent

**Fluent(ly)** Eloquent, Facile, Flowing, Glib, Liquid, Oracy, Verbose, Voluble

**Fluff(y)** Blow, Bungle, Candyfloss, Dowl(e), Down, Dust, Dust bunny, Feathery, Fleecy, Flocculent, Floss, Flue, Fug, Fuzz, Girl, Lint, Mess-up, Muff, Noil, Oose, Ooze, Plot, Thistledown

**Fluid** Aldehyde, Amniotic, Anasarca, Ascites, Bile, Broo, Chyle, Cisterna, Colostrum, Condy's, Coolant, Correcting, Dewdrop, Edema, Enema, Erf, Fixative, Fl, Glycerin, Humoral, Humour, Joint-oil, Juice, Latex, →LIQUID, Lymph, Movable, Mucus, Oedema, Perfect, Perilymph, Plasma, Pus, Sap, Seminal, Serous, Serum, Shifting, Spermatic, Spittle, Succus, Synovia, Transudate, Vitreum, Vril, Water

▷ **Fluid** *may indicate* an anagram

**Fluke** Accident, Anchor, Chance, Fan, Flounder, Ga(u)nch, Grapnel, Killock, Liver, Lobe, Redia, Schistosome, Scratch, Spud, Trematoid, Upcast

**Flume** Chute

**Flummery** BS, Pudding

**Flummox** Baffle, Bamboozle, Floor, Nonplus

**Flunk** Fail

**Flunk(e)y** Chasseur, Clawback, Haiduck, Heyduck, Jeames, Lackey, Minion, Servant, Toady

**Fluorescence, Fluorescent** Bloom, Day-glo, Epipolism, Glow, Phosphorescence, Uranin

**Fluorine, Fluoride** F, Hexene

**Flurry** Bustle, Fluster, Haste, Hoo-ha, Shower

**Flush(ed)** Affluent, Beat, Bloom, Busted, Crimson, Even, Ferret, Florid, Flow, Gild, Hectic, Heyday, Hot, Level, Red, Rolling, Rose, Royal, Rud, Scour, Sluice, Spaniel, Start, Straight, Sypher, Thrill, Tierce, Vigour, Wash, Wealthy, Well-heeled

**Fluster(ed)** Befuddle, Confuse, Disconcert, Faze, Flap, Jittery, Panic, Pother, Pudder, Rattle, Shake

**Flute (player)** Bellows-mender, Bohm, Channel, Claribel(la), Crimp, English, Fife, Fipple, Flageolet, German, Glass, Glyph, Groove, Kaval, Marsyas, Nose, Ocarina, Octave, Piccolo, Pipe, Poogye(e), Quena, Shakuhachi, Sulcus, Thisbe, Tibia, Toot, Transverse, Whistle, Wineglass, Zuf(f)olo

**Flutter** Bat, Bet, Fan, Fibrillate, Flacker, Flaffer, Flap, Flaught, Flichter, Flicker, Flitter, Fly, →GAMBLE, Hover, Palpitate, Pitapat, Play, Pulse, Sensation, Twitter, Waft, Wave, Winnow

**Flux** B, D, Electric, Flow, Fusion, Luminous, Magnetic, Maxwell, Melt, Neutron, Panta rhei, Radiant, Tesla, Weber

**Fly(ing), Flies** Abscond, Agaric, Airborne, Alder, Alert, Antlion, Arch, Assassin, Astute, Aviation, Awake, Aware, A-wing, Baker, Bedstead, Bee, Black, Blister, Blowfly, Blue-arsed, Bluebottle, Bolt, Bot, Breese, Breeze, Brize, Brommer, Bulb, Bush, Cab, Caddis, Canny, Carriage, Carrot, Cecidomyia, Chalcid, Cheesehopper, Cheese skipper, Cleg, Cluster, Cock-a-bondy, Crane, Cuckoo, →CUNNING, Damsel, Dash, Decamp, Deer, Diptera, Dobson, Doctor, Dolphin, Doodlebug, Dragon, Drake, Drone, Drosophila, Dry, Dung, Dutchman, Escape, Face, Fiacre, Flee, Flesh, Flit, Fox, Frit, Fruit, Gad, Glide, Glossina, Gnat, Goutfly, Grannom, Greenbottle, Greenhead, Hackle, Hairy Mary, Harl, Harvest, Hedge-hop, Herl, Hessian, Homoptera, Hop, Horn, Horse, Hover, Hurtle, Ichneumon, Instrument, Jenny-spinner, Jock Scott, Lace-wing, Lamp, Lantern, Laputan, March brown, Midge, Mosquito, Mossie, Moth, Motuca, Murragh, Musca, Mutuca, Namu, Needle, New Forest, Nymph, Onion, Opening, Ox-warble, Palmer, Para, Pilot, Pium, Plecopteran, Pomace, Race, Rapid, Robber, Sacrifice, Saucer, Sciaridae, Sciurus, Scorpion, Scotsman, Screwworm, Scud, Sedge, Sheep ked, Silverhorn, Simulium, Smart, Smother, Snake, Snipe, Soar, Spanish, Speed, Spinner, Stable, Stone, Stream, Streetwise, Syrphidae, Tabanid, Tachina, Tag, Tail, Tear, Thrips, Tipula, Trichopteran, Tsetse, Tube, Turkey brown, Turnip, Vamoose, Vinegar, Volatic, Volitate, Warble, Watchet, Water, Welshman's button, Wet, Wheat, Wide-awake, Willow, Wily, Wing (over), Yellow Sally, Yogic, Zebub, Zimb, Zipper, Zoom

**Fly-by-night** Moth, Owl

**Fly-catcher** Attercop, Clamatorial, Cobweb, Darlingtonia, Dionaea, King-bird, Phoebe, Spider, Tanrec, Tentacle, Tyrant, Yellowhead

**Flying-fox** Fruit-bat, Kalong

**Flying saucer** UFO

**Fly-killer** Chowri, Chowry, DDT, Empusa, Swat

**Flyover** Overpass

**Foam(ing)** Aerogel, Barm, Bubble, Froth, Head, Lather, Mousse, Oasis®, Polystyrene, Ream, Scum, Seethe, Spindrift, Spooming, Spume, Sud(s), Surf, Wake, Wild water, Yeast, Yest

**Fob** Chain, Defer, Fub, Pocket, Slang

**Focal, Focus(sed)** Anal, Centre, Centrepiece, Clou, Concentrate, Converge, Eoicentre, Fix, Hinge, Hub, Narrow, Nub, Pinpoint, Pivot, Point, Pressure point, Prime, Principal, Real, Spotlight, Train, Zoom

**Fodder** Alfalfa, Browsing, Buckwheat, Cannon, Clover, Eatage, Emmer, Ensilage, Fescue, Foon, Forage, Gama-grass, Grama, Guar, Hay, Lucerne, Maize, Mangle, Mangold, Oats, Oilcake, Pasture, Provender, Rye-grass, Sainfoin, Silage, Soilage, Stover, Straw, Ti-tree, Vetch, Yarran

**Foe** Anti, Arch, Contender, →ENEMY, Opponent, Rival

**Foetus** Embryo

**Fog** Aerosol, Blur, Brume, Cloud, Damp, Fret, Haar, (London) Particular, Miasm(a), Mist, Murk, Obscure, Pea-soup(er), Roke, Sea-fret, Sea-haar, Smog, Smoke, Soup, Thick, Vapour, Yorkshire

**Fog(e)y, Fogie** Die-hard, Dinosaur, Dodo, Graybeard, Square

**Fogg** Phileas, Solicitor

**Foible** Failing, Flaw, Idiosyncrasy, Quirk, Weakness

**Foil(ed)** Ba(u)lk, Chaff, Counterpoint, Cross, Dupe, Epée, Fleuret(te), Frustrate, Gold, Gold leaf, Lametta, Leaf, Offset, Paillon, Pip, Scotch, Scupper, Silver, Stime, Stooge, Stump, Stymie, Sword, Tain, Thwart, Tinsel, Touché

**Foist** Fob, Insert, Insinuate, Suborn, Wish

**Fold(er), Folding, Folded, Folds** Anticline, Bend, Binder, Camp bed, Close, Collapse, Concertina, Convolution, Corrugate, Cote, Crash, Crease, Crimp, Crinkle, Cristate, Crunkle, Diapir, Diptych, Dog-ear, Double, Duo-tang®, Epicanthus, Epiploon, Fake, Fan, File, Fourchette, Fr(a)enum, Frill, Furl, Gather, Geanticline, Groin, Gyrus, Inflexure, Intussuscept, Jacket, Jack-knife, Lap, Lapel, Lap(p)et, Lirk, Mantle, Mesentery, Mitre, Monocline, Nappe, Nympha, Obvolute, Octuple, Omentum, Origami, Pastigium, Pen, Pericline, Pintuck, Pleach, → **PLEAT**, Plica, Plunging, Ply, Pound, Prancke, Pran(c)k, Ptyxis, Recumbent, Ruck(le), Ruga, Sheep-pen, Syncline, Triptych, Tuck, Vocal, Wrap

**Foliage** Canopy, Coma, Finial, Frond, Frondescence, Greenery, Leafage, Leaves

**Folio(s)** Crown, Elephant, F(f), File, Foolscap, Imperial, Percy, Royal

**Folk(sy)** Beaker, Homespun, Kin, Nation, People, Public

**Follicle** Graafian

**Follow(er), Following** Acolyte, Acolyth, Adhere, Admirer, After, Agree, Amoret, And, Anthony, Attend(ant), Believer, Chase, Clientele, Consequence, Copy, Dangle, Disciple, Dog, Echo, Ensew, Ensue, Entourage, Epigon(e), Equipage, F, Fan, Groupie, Heel(er), Henchman, Hereon, Hunt, Imitate, Jacob, Man, Merry men, Mimic, Minion, Muggletonian, Myrmidon, Neist, Next, Obey, Pan, Post, Prosecute, Pursue, Rake, Retinue, Road, Run, Satellite, School, Sectary, Secundum, Seewing, Segue, Sequel, Sequential, Seriation, Servitor, Shadow, Sheep, Sidekick, S(h)ivaite, So, Stag, Stalk, Stear, Steer, Subsequent, Succeed, Sue, Suivez, Supervene, Tag, Tail, Tantony, Trace, Track, Trail, Train, Use, Vocation, Votary, Yesman

▷ **Follower** *may indicate* B

**Folly** Absurd, Antic, Bêtise, Idiocy, Idiotcy, Imprudence, Inanity, Lunacy, Madness, Mistake, Moria, Niaiserie, Stupidity, Unwisdom, Vanity

**Foment(ation)** Arouse, Brew, Embrocation, Excite, Incite, Poultice, Stupe

**Fond(ness)** Amatory, Ardour, Attachment, Dote, Keen, Loving, Partial, Penchant, Tender, Tendre

**Fondant** Ice, Sweet

**Fondle** Canoodle, Caress, Dandle, Grope, Hug, Nurse, Pet, Snuggle, Stroke

**Font** Aspersorium, Bénitier, Bitmap, Delubrum, Ennage, Outline, Print, Proportional, Raster, Scalable, Source, True-type, Vector

**Food** Aliment, Ambrosia, Bait, Bakemeat, Balti, Batten, Battill, Battle, Bellytimber, Bento, Board, Bolus, Bord, Broth, Browse, Bully, Burger, Bush-tucker, Canape, Carry-out, Cate, Cereal, Chametz, Cheer, Cheese, Chometz, Chop, Chow (mein), Chuck, Chyme, Clio, Cocoyam, Collation, Comestible, Comfort, Commons, Convenience, Cook-chill, Course, Crab, Cud, Curd, Deutoplasm, Dietetics, → **DISH**, Dog's body, Doner kebab, Dunderfunk, Eatage, Eats, Esculents, Eutrophy, Falafel, Famine, Fare, Fast, Fast casual, Felafel, Fodder, Forage, Formula, Franken(stein), Freedom, Fritter, Fuel, Functional, Giffengood, Gobi, Grillade, Grub, Gruel, Hamburger, Hangi, Hometz, Incaparina, Ingesta, Jootha, Jorts, Junk, Kai, Keep, Langar, Lasagne, Leben, Lerp, Long-pig, Maigre, Makan, Maki, Manna, Mato(o)ke, Matzoon, Meal, Meat (loaf), Muckamuck, Nacho, Nardoo, Nosebag, Nosh, Nourishment, Nourriture, Oats, Obento, Opsonium, Ort, Oven-ready, Pabulum, Pannage, Pap, Parev(e), Parve, Pasta, Pasture, Peck, Pemmican, Pilaf, Pilau, Pizza, Prog, Provand, Provender, Provision, Pu(l)ture, Ration(s), Real, Refreshment, Risotto, Roughage, Royal jelly, Rysttafel, Sambal, Samosa, Sandwich, Sap, Sashimi, Scaff, Schri, Scoff, Scran, Scroggin, Sitology, Sizings, Skin, Skran, Slow, Snack, Soft meat, Soil, Soul, Square meal, Staple, Stir fry, Stodge, Sushi, Swill, Table, Tack, Takeaway, Tamale, Taro, Tempeh, Tempura, Teriyake, Tex-Mex, Tofu, Trimmings, Tripe, Trophallaxis, Tsamba, Tuck(er), Vegeburger, Veggie-burger, Viand, Victuals, Vivers, Vivres, Waffle, Yantia, Yittles, Yog(h)urt

**Foodie** Epicure, Gourmet

**Food-plant** Laser, Silphium

**Foodstore** Delicatessen, Grocery, Larder, Pantry, Silo

**Fool(hardy), Fooling, Foolish(ness)** Air-head, Anserine, April, Asinico, Asinine, Assot, Baloney, Beef-witted, Berk, BF, Blithering, Bob, Booby, Bottom, Brainless, Brash, Buffoon, Cake, Capocchia, Chump, Clot, Clown, Cockeyed, Cockscomb, Con, Coney, Coof, Coxcomb, Cuif, Cully, Daft, Dagonet, Daw, Delude, Desipience, Dessert, Dilly, Dipstick, Divvy, Doat, Doilt, Dote, Dummy, Dunce, Dweeb, Empty, Etourdi, Fatuous, Feste, Flannel(led), Folly, Fon, Fond, Fox, Gaby, Gaga, Galah, Git, Glaikit, Goat, Gobbo, Goon, Goose, Gooseberry, Gormless, Groserts, Gubbins, Gull, Gullible, Halfwit, Hanky-panky, Hare-brained, Have, Haverel, Highland, Hoax, Horseplay, Huntiegowk, Hunt-the-gowk, Idiotic, Imbecile, Inane, Ineptitude, Injudicious, Insensate, Jest, Jester, Joke, Kid, Kissel, Lark, Loon, Madcap, Maffin, Mamba, Misguide, Mislead, Mome, Moron, Muggins, Nelly, Nerk, Niaiserie, Ni(n)compoop, Nignog, Ninny, Nong, Noodle, Nose-led, Nut, Nutmeg, Oanshagh, Omadhaun, Patch, Pea-brained, Poop, Poupe, Prat, Preposterous, Punk, Rash, Rhubarb, Sawney, Scogan, Scoggin, Senseless, Shallow, S(c)hmo, Silly billy, Simpleton, Snipe, Soft, Sot, Spoony, Stultify, →STUPID, Sucker, Sweet, Thicko, Tom (noddy), Trifle, Turkey, Unredy, Unwitty, Vacuous, Vice, Wantwit, Yap, Yorick, Yoyo, Zany

**Foolproof** Fail-safe

**Fool's gold** Mundic, Pyrites

**Foot(ing), Footwork, Feet** Amphibrach, Amphimacer, Anap(a)est, Antibacchius, Antispast, Athlete's, Bacchius, Ball, Base, Board, Choliamb, Choree, Choreus, Choriamb, Club, Cold, Cretic, Dactyl, Dance, Dipody, Dochmii, Dochmius, Epitrite, F, Flat, Ft, Hephthemimer, Hoof, Hoppus, Iamb(us), Immersion, Infantry, Ionic, Molossus, Ockodols, One-two, Pad, Paeon, Palama, Pastern, Paw, Pay, Pedal, Pedate, Pedicure, Penthemimer, Pes, Pettitoes, Plates, Podiatry, Podium, Proceleusmatic, Pyrrhic, Roothold, Scazon, Semeia, Serif, Shanks's mare, Shanks's pony, Socle, Spade, Splay, Spondee, Standing, Syzygy, Tarsus, Terms, Tootsie, Tootsy, Tootsy-wootsy, Tread, Trench, Tribrach, Trilbies, Triseme, Trochee, Trotter, Tube, Ungula, Verse, Wrong, Zocco(le)

**Football(er), Football club** Aerial pingpong, American, Association, Australian Rules, Back, Banyana-banyana, Barbarian, Ba'spiel, Best, Camp, Canadian, Centre, Double header, Dynamo, Fantasy, FIFA, Five-a-side, Flanker(back), Fly-half, Futsal, Gaelic, Gazza, Goalie, Gridder, Half, Hooker, Juventus, Keeper, Kicker, League, Libero, Linebacker, Lineman, Lock, Midfield, Moore, National code, Nickelback, Pack, Pele, Pigskin, Ranger, RU, Rugby, Rugger, Rules, Safety, Seven-a-side, Sevens, Soccer(oos), Sport, Stand-off, Striker, Subbuteo®, Superbowl, Sweeper, Table, Tight-end, Togger, Total, Touch(back), Wallgame, Wing, Wingman

**Footboard** Stretcher

**Foot-fault** Bunion, Corn, Hammer-toe, Talipes, Verruca

**Foothills** Submontane

**Foothold** Lodgement, Purchase, Stirrup

**Footlights** Floats

**Footling** Trivial

**Footloose** Peripatetic

**Footman** Attendant, Flunkey, Hiker, Lackey, Ped(estrian), Pompey, Valet de chambre, Yellowplush

**Footnote** Addendum, Cross-reference, Passim, PS

**Footpad** Land-rat, Mugger, Robber

**Footpath, Footway** Banquette, Catwalk, Causeway, Clapper, Track

**Footplate** Horseshoe

**Footprint** Carbon, Ecological, Electronic, Ichnite, Ichnolite, Ornithichnite, Pad, Prick, Pug, Seal, Slot, Trace, Track, Tread, Vestige

**Footrest, Footstool** Coaster, Cricket, Hassock, Pouffe, Stirrup, Stool, Tramp

**Footrot, Footsore** Blister, Bunion, Corn, Halt, Surbate, Surbet, Weary, Wire-heel

**Footslogger** Infantryman

**Footwashing** Maundy, Nipter

**Footwear** Espadrille, Gumboot, Jackboot, Sandshoe, →**SHOE**, Slipper, Sock, Spats, Stocking

**Fop(pish)** Apery, Barbermonger, Beau, Buck, Cat, Coxcomb, Dandy, Dude, Exquisite, Fallal, Fangled, Fantastico, Finical, La-di-da, Macaroni, Monarcho, Muscadin, Petit maître, Popinjay, Skipjack, Swell, Toff

**For** Ayes, Because, Concerning, Cos, Pro, Since, To

**Forage** Alfalfa, Etape, Fodder, Graze, Greenfeed, Ladino, Lucern(e), Pickeer, Prog, Raid, Rummage, Sainfoin, Scavenge, Search

**Foray** Attack, Creach, Creagh, Raid, Sortie, Spreagh

**Forbear(ance), Forbearing** Abstain, Clement, Endure, Indulgent, Lenience, Lineage, Longanimity, Mercy, Overgo, Pardon, Parent, Patient, Quarter, →**REFRAIN**, Suffer, Tolerant, Withhold

**Forbid(den), Forbidding** Aversive, Ban, Bar, City, Denied, Don't, Dour, Enjoin, For(e)speak, Gaunt, Grim, Haram, Hostile, Illicit, Loury, NL, Prohibit, Proscribe, Sinister, Stern, Taboo, Tabu, Tapu, Tref(a), Verboten, Veto

**Force(d), Forceful(ly), Forces, Forcible, Forcing** Activist, Agency, Air-arm, Armada, Army, Assertive, Back emf, Barge, Bind, Birr, Bludgeon, Body, Bounce, Brigade, Bring, Brunt, Brute, Bulldoze, Cadre, Capillary, Cascade, Centrifugal, Centripetal, Chi, Coerce, Coercive, Cogency, Commando, Compel, Con brio, Conscript, Constabulary, Constrain, Contingent, Cops, Coriolis, Cram, Delta, Detachment, Dint, Domineer, Downflow, Dragoon, Drive, Duress(e), Dynamic, Dyne, E, Edge, Electromotive, Emphatic, Energetic, Equilibrant, Erdgeist, Erg, Exact, Exchange, Expeditionary, Extort, Extrude, F, Farci, Fifth, Fire brigade, Foot-pound, Foot-ton, Foss, Frogmarch, Full-line, G, Gar, Garrison, Gendarmerie, Gilbert, Gism, Gouge, Gravitational, Great Attractor, Hale, High-powered, Host, Hunter-killer, Hurricane, Impetus, Impose, Impress, Impulsion, Inertial, Instress, Intense, Interpol, Irgun, Irrupt, Jism, Juggernaut, Kinetic, Kundalini, Labour, Land, Landsturm, Landwehr, Lashkar, Legion, Leverage, Life, Lift, Lin(n), Live load, Lorentz, Magnetomotive, Magnus, Make, Mana, Manpower, Market, Met, Militia, Moment, Momentum, Muscle, Nature-god, Navy, Newton, Numen, Oblige, Od, Odyl(e), OGPU, Old Contemptibles, Orgone, Orotund, Personnel, Phrenism, Physical, Pierce, Pigs, Pion, Pithy, Plastic, Police, Polis, Posse, Potent, Pound, Poundal, Power, Prana, Press(gang), Pressure, Prise, Procrustean, Propel, Psyche, Psychic, Pull, Punchy, Pushy, Put, Qi, Railroad, Ram, Rape, Ravish, Reave, Red Army, Regular, Require, Restem, Robust, Route, Rush, SAS, Sforzando, Shear, Shoehorn, Snorting, Spent, Spetsnaz, Squad, Squeeze, Squirt, Steam(roller), Steem, Stick, Stiction, Sting and ling, Strained, Strength, →**STRESS**, Strong-arm, Subject, Sword, TA, Task, Teeth, Telergy, Telling, Territorial, The Bill, The Great Attractor, Thrust, Torque, Tractive, Troops, Upthrust, Van der Waals', Vehement, Vigorous, Vim, Violence, Vires, Vis, Vis major, Vis visa, Vital, Vively, Vociferous, Vril, Weak, Wedge, Wrench, Wrest, Wring, Zap

▷ **Force(d)** *may indicate* an anagram

**Forced labour** Begar

**Force-feeding** Gavage

**Forceps** Bulldog, Capsule, Crow(s)bill, Hemostatic, Mosquito, Obstetrical, Pedicellaria, Pincers, Rongeur, Tenaculum, Thumb, Vulsella

**Ford** Anglia, Anna, Capri, Car, Crossing, Drift, Escort, Industrialist, Irish bridge, Sierra, Strid, Tin Lizzy, Wade

**Forearm** Cubital, Radius, Ulna

▸ **Forebear** *see* **FORBEAR(ANCE)**

**Foreboding** Anxiety, Augury, Cloudage, Croak, Feeling, Freet, Hoodoo, →**OMEN**, Ominous, Premonition, Presage, Presentient, Presentiment, Sinister, Zoomantic

**Forecast(er), Forecasting** Aeromancy, Augury, Auspice, Divine, Estimate, Extrapolation, Glass, Horoscope, Long-range, Metcast, Metman, Numerical, Omen, Perm, Portend, Precurse, Predicate, Predict, Presage, Prescience, Prevision, Prognosis,

Prognosticate, Projection, Prophesy, Quant, Rainbird, Scry, Shipping, Skry, Soothsay, Spae, Tip, Weather

**Foreclose** Bar, Block, Obstruct, Preclude

**Forefather(s)** Ancestor, Elder, Forebear, Parent, Rude

**Forefront** Van, Vaward

**Foreground** Repoussage, Repoussoir

**Forehead** Brow, Front(let), Frontal, Glabella(r), Metopic, Nasion, Sincipitum, Temple

**Foreign(er)** Adventitious, Alien, Amakwerekwere, Arab, Auslander, Barbarian, Easterling, Ecdemic, Eleanor, Ethnic, Étranger, Exclave, Exotic, External, Extraneous, Extrinsic, Forane, Forinsecal, Forren, Fraim, Fremit, Gaijin, German, Gringo, Gweilo, Malihini, Metic, Moit, Mote, Outlander, Outlandish, Outside, Oversea, Peregrine, Remote, →STRANGE, Stranger, Taipan, Tramontane, Uitlander, Unfamiliar, Wog

▷ **Foreign** *may indicate* an anagram

**Foreign Office** FO, Quai d'Orsay

**Foreknowledge** Prescience

**Foreman** Baas, Boss, Bosun, Chancellor, Clicker, Gaffer, Ganger, Manager, Overseer, Steward, Straw boss, Superintendent, Supervisor, Tool pusher, Topsman, Walla(h)

**Foremost** First, Front, Leading, Number one, Primary, Prime, Salient, Supreme, Upfront, Van

▷ **Foremost** *may indicate* first letters of words following

**Forenoon** Undern

**Forepart** Cutwater, Front

**Forerunner** Augury, Harbinger, Herald, Messenger, Omen, Pioneer, Precurrer, Precursor, Prequel, Trailer, Vaunt-courier

**Foresee** Anticipate, Divine, Preview, Prophesy, Scry

**Foreshadow** Adumbrate, Augur, Bode, Forebode, Hint, Portend, Pre-echo, Prefigure, Presage, Type

**Foreshow** Betoken, Bode, Signify

**Foresight** Ganesa, Prescience, Prophecy, Prospect, Providence, Prudence, Taish, Vision

**Foreskin** Prepuce

**Forest(ry), Forested** Arboreal, Arden, Ardennes, Argonne, Ashdown, Black, Bohemian, Bracknell, Brush, Bush, Caatinga, Charnwood, Chase, Cloud, Cranborne Chase, Dean, Deer, Elfin, Epping, Firth, Fontainebleau, Gallery, Gapo, Glade, Greenwood, Igapo, Jungle, Katyn, Managed, Monte, Nandi, Nemoral, New, Nottingham, Petrified, Rain, Savernake, Selva, Sherwood, Silviculture, Taiga, Teutoburg, Thuringian, Urman, Virgin, Waltham, Wealden, →WOOD, Woodcraft, Woodland

**Forestall** Anticipate, Head-off, Obviate, Pip, Pre-empt, Prevent, Queer, Scoop

**Forester** Foster, Kangaroo, Lumberjack, Verderer, Waldgrave, Walker, Woodman, Woodward

**Foretaste** Antepast, Antipasto, Appetiser, Avant-goût, Pregustation, Prelibation, Preview, Sample, Trailer

**Foretell(ing), Forewarn** Augur, Bode, Caution, Divine, Fatidic, Forecast, Portend, Predict, Premonish, Presage, Previse, Prognosticate, Prophecy, Soothsay, Spae, Weird

**Forethought** Anticipation, Caution, Prometheus, Provision, Prudence

**Forever** All-time, Always, Amber, Ay(e), Constant, Eternal, Evermore, Keeps, Permanent

▶ **Forewarn** *see* FORETELL(ING)

**Foreword** Introduction, Preamble, Preface, Proem, Prologue

**For example** Eg, Say, Vg, ZB

**For fear** Lest

**Forfeit(ed)** Confiscated, Deodand, Fine, Forgo, →PENALTY, Phillepina, Phillepine, Philop(o)ena, Relinquish, Rue-bargain, Sconce

**Forge(d), Forger(y)** Blacksmith, Copy, Counterfeisance, Counterfeit, Drop(-hammer), Dud, Excudit, Fabricate, Fake, Falsify, Fashion, Foundry, Hammer, Heater, Horseshoe, Ireland, Ironsmith, Lauder, Mint, Nailery, Paper-hanger, Pigott, Proceed, Progress,

Rivet head, Rivet-hearth, Smith(y), Smithery, Spurious, Stiddie, Stiff, Stithy, Stumer, Tilt, Trucage, Truquage, Utter, Valley, Vermeer, Vulcan, Weld

**Forget(ful), Forget-me-not, Forgetting** Amnesia, Dry, Fluff, Infonesia, Lethe, Lotus, Myosotis, Neglect, Oblivious, Omit, Overlook, Senior moment, Unlearn, Wipe, Write off

**Forgive(ness), Forgiving** Absolution, Amnesty, Clement, Condone, Divine, Excuse, Lenity, Merciful, Overlook, Pardon, Placable, Remission, Remittal, Reprieve, Tolerant

**Forgo(ne)** Abstain, Cut and dried, Expected, Refrain, Renounce, Waive

**Forgotten** Bygone, Lost, Missed, Sad

**For instance** As

**Forjeskit** Overscutched

**Fork(ed), Fork out** Angle, Bifurcate, Biramous, Branch, Caudine, Cleft, Crotch, Crutch, Divaricate, Forficate, Fourchette, Grain, Graip, Morton's, Osmeterium, Pastry, Pay, Pickle, Prong, Replication, Runcible, Slave, Split, Sucket, Tine, Toaster, Toasting, Tormenter, Tormentor, Trident, Trifid, Tuner, Tuning, Y

**Forlorn(ness)** Abject, Aidless, Desolate, Destitute, Drearisome, Godforsaken, Lonely, Miserable, Nightingale, Sad, Woebegone

**Form(s)** Allotropic, Alumni, Archetypal, Bench, Body, Bumf, Cast, Ceremonial, Charterparty, Class(room), Clipped, Constitute, Coupon, Create, Document, Draw up, Dress, Etiquette, Experience, Fashion, Feature, Fig, → FIGURE, Formula, Frame, Free, Game, Generate, Gestalt, Group, Hare, Idea, Image, Inscape, Keto, Lexicalise, Life, Logical, Mode, Mood, Morph(ic), Morphology, Mould, Nucleate, Order, Originate, → OUT OF FORM, P45, Penitent, Physique, Protocol, Questionnaire, Redia, Remove, Rite, Ritual, Schedule, Sculpt, Shape, Shell, Sonata, Song, Stage, Stamp, State, Stem, Stereotype, Structure, Style, Symmetry, Talon, Ternary, Version

▷ **Form** *may indicate* a hare's bed

**Formal, Formality** Amylum, Black tie, Ceremonious, Ceremony, Conventional, Dignified, Dressy, Dry, Exact, Fit, Ice, Literal, Mannered, Methodic, Official, Pedantic, Pedantry, Perfunctory, Pomp, Precise, Prim, Protocol, Punctilio, Reserved, Routine, Set, Solemn, Starch, Starched, Starchy, Stiff, Stiff-necked, Stodgy, Stuffed shirt, Tails, Uptight, White tie

**Formation** Battalion, Brown, Catenaccio, Configuration, Diapyesis, Echelon, Eocene, Fours, Growth, Layout, Line (out), Manufacture, Origin, Pattern, Phalanx, Potence, Prophase, Reaction, Reticular, Riss, Series, Serried, Shotgun, Testudo, Wedge

**Former(ly)** Ance, Auld, Before, Ci-devant, Earlier, Ere-now, Erst(while), Ex, Late, Maker, Matrix, Old(en), Once, One-time, Past, Previous, Prior, Pristine, Quondam, Sometime, Then, Umquhile, Umwhile, Whilere, Whilom, Yesterday

▷ **Former** *may indicate* something that forms

**Formidable** Alarming, Armipotent, Battleaxe, Fearful, Forbidding, Gorgon, Grande dame, Powerful, Redoubtable, Shrewd, Stoor, Stour, Stowre, Sture, Tall order, Terrible, Tiger

**Formless** Amorphous, Invertebrate, Nebulous, Shapeless

▷ **Form of, Forming** *may indicate* an anagram

**Formosan** Tai

**Formula(te)** Conceive, Define, Devise, Doctrine, Empirical, Equation, Frame, Graphic, Incantation, Invent, Kekule, Lurry, Molecular, Paternoster, Prescription, Protocol, Prunes and prisms, → RECIPE, Reduction, Rite, Ritual, Spell, Stirling's, Structural

**For now** Interim, Meanwhile

**Forsake** Abandon, Desert, Quit, Renounce

**Forsooth** Certes, Certy, Even, Marry, Quotha

**For sure** Pukka

**Forswear** Abandon, Abjure, Disavow, Renounce, Reny

**Forsyte** Fleur, Saga, Soames

**Fort(ification), Fortress** Abatis, Acropolis, Alamo, Alhambra, Balclutha, Bastel-house, Bastide, Bastille, Bastion, Battlement, Bawn, Berchtesgaden, Blockhouse, Bonnet,

Breastwork, Bridgehead, Burg, Casbah, Castellated, Castellum, Castle, Citadel, Contravallation, Counterscarp, Crémaillère, Demilune, Deva, Dun, Earthwork, Edinburgh, Enceinte, Epaule, Escarpment, Fastness, Fieldwork, Flanker, Flèche, Fortalice, Fortilage, Fortlet, Fraise, Ft, Gabion(ade), Garrison, Gatehouse, Golconda, Grenada, Haven, Hedgehog, Hill, Hornwork, Kaim, Kame, Kasba(h), Keep, Knox, La(a)ger, Lauderdale, Legnaga, Line, Louisbourg, Maiden, Malakoff, Mantua, Martello tower, Masada, Merlon, Mile-castle, Moat, Moineau, Motte and bailey, Orillion, Pa(h), Peel, Pele, Pentagon, Peschiera, Place, Przernysl, Rampart, Rath, Ravelin, Redan, Redoubt, Reduit, Ring, Salient, Sallyport, Sangar, Sconce, Stavropol, Stockade, Stronghold, Sumter, Talus, Tenail(le), Terreplein, Tête-de-pont, Ticonderoga, Tower, Tower of London, Trench, Vallation, Vallum, Verona, Vitrified, William, Worth

**Forte** F, Métier, Specialty, Strength

**Forth** Away, From, Hence, Out

**Forthright(ness)** Blunt, Candid, Direct, Four-square, Frank, Glasnost, Outspoken, Prompt, Vocal

**Forthwith** Anon, Directly, Eft(soons), Immediately

**Fortify** Arm, Augment, Brace, Casemate, Defend, Embattle, Lace, Munify, Soup up, Steel, → **STRENGTHEN**

**Fortitude** Endurance, Grit, Guts, Mettle, Patience, Pluck, → **STAMINA**

**Fortune, Fortunate, Fortuitous** Auspicious, Blessed, Blest, Bomb, Bonanza, Chance, Coincident, Godsend, Happy, Killing, → **LUCKY**, Madoc, Opportune, Pile, Providential, Sonce, Tyche, Up, Well, Well off

**Fortune teller, Fortune-telling** Auspicious, Bonanza, Bumby, Cartomancy, Chaldee, Cha(u)nce, Chiromancy, Destiny, Diviner, Dukkeripen, Fame, Fate, Felicity, Forecast, Genethliac, Geomancy, Hap, Hydromancy, I Ching, Lot, Luck, Mint, Motser, Motza, Oracle, Packet, Palmist, Peripety, Pile, Prescience, Pyromancy, Sibyl, Soothsayer, Sortilege, Spaewife, Success, Taroc, Tarok, Tarot, Tyche, Wealth, Windfall

**Forty, Forties** Capot, F, Hungry, Kemple, Roaring

**Forty-ninth** Parallel

**Forum** Arena, Assembly, Debate, Platform, Synod, Tribunal

**Forward (looking), Forward(s)** Accede, Advanced, Ahead, Along, Anterior, Arch, Assertive, Assuming, Avanti, Bright, Cheeky, Early, Flanker, Forrad, Forrit, Forth, Fresh, Front-row, Future, Hasten, Hooker, Immodest, Impudent, Insolent, Lock, Malapert, Minx, Number eight, On(wards), Pack, Pert, Petulant, Porrect, Precocious, Prescient, → **PROGRESS**, Promote, Prop, Readdress, Redirect, Saucy, Scrum, Send, Stem, Striker, To(ward), Van, Wing

**Fossil(ised), Fossils** Amber, Ammonite, Baculite, Belemnite, Blastoid(ea), Calamite, Ceratodus, Chondrite, Conodont, Corallian, Corallite, Cordaites, Creodont, Crinite, Derived, Dolichosauria, Encrinite, Eohippus, Eozoon, Eurypterus, Exuviae, Fairy stone, Florula, Florule, Fogy, Goniatite, Graptolite, Hipparion, Hippurite, Hominid, Ichnite, Ichnolite, Ichnology, Ichthyodurolite, Ichthyolite, Index, Jew's stone, Kenyapithecus, Lepidostrobus, Lingulella, Living, Mosasauros, Nummulite, Odontolite, Olenellus, Olenus, Oligocene, Orthoceras, Osteolepis, Ostracoderm, Oxfordian, Pal(a)eo-, Pentacrinus, Petrifaction, Phytolite, Plesiosaur, Pliohippus, Pliosaur, Psilophyton, Pteridosperm, Pterodactyl(e), Pterygotus, Pythonomorph, Relics, Reliquiae, Remanié, Reworked, Sigillaria, Sinanthropus, Sivatherium, Snakestone, Stigmaria, Stromatolite, Taphonomy, Teleosaurus, Tentaculite, Thunderegg, Titanotherium, Trace, Trilobite, Uintatherium, Wood-opal, Zinganthropus, Zone, Zoolite

**Foster (child, mother), Fostering** Adopt, Cherish, Da(u)lt, Develop, Farm out, Feed, Fornent, Further, Harbour, Incubation, Metapelet, Metaplot, Nourish, Nourse(l), Noursle, Nousell, Nurse, Nurture, Nuzzle, → **REAR**

**Foul, Foul-smelling** Base, Bastardise, Bedung, Beray, Besmirch, Besmutch, Bewray, Bungle, Contaminate, → **DEFILE**, Dirty, Dreggy, Drevill, Dunghole, Enseam, Evil, Feculent, Funky, Gross, Hassle, Hing, In-off, Mephitic, Mud, Noisome, Olid,

Osmeterium, Paw(paw), Personal, Professional, Putid, Putrid, → **RANK**, Reekie, Reeky, Rotten, Sewage, Soiled, Squalid, Stagnant, Stain, Stapelia, Technical, Unclean, Unfair, Vilde, Vile, Violation, Virose

▷ **Foul** *may indicate* an anagram

**Found(ation), Foundations** Base, Basis, Bedrock, Corset, Cribwork, Establishment, Fond, Footing, Girdle, Grillage, Ground, Grounding, Groundwork, Hard-core, Hypostasis, Infrastructure, Initiate, Institution, Matrix, Mattress, Panty girdle, Pile, Pitching, Roadbed, Rockefeller, Root, Scholarship, Stays, Stereobate, Subjacent, Substrata, Substructure, Trackbed, Underlie, Underlinen

**Found (in)** Among, Base, Bed, Bottom, Build, Cast, Caught, Constitute, Create, Emong, Endow, → **ESTABLISH**, Eureka, Institute, Introduce, Met, Occur, Plant, Recovered, Rest, Stablish, Start, Table

▷ **Foundations** *may indicate* last letters

**Founder** Author, Beginner, Bell, Collapse, Crumple, Fail, Inventor, Iron-master, Miscarry, Oecist, Oekist, Patriarch, Perish, Progenitor, Settle, Sink, Steelman, Stumble

**Fount** Aonian, Digital, Source, Springlet, Wrong

**Fountain** Acadine, Aganippe, Arethusa, Bubbler, Castalian, Cause, Conduit, Drinking, Fauwara, Forts, Gerbe, Head, Hippocrene, Jet, Pant, Pirene, Salmacis, Scuttlebutt, Soda, Spring, Trevi, Well-spring, Youth

**Fountain basin** Laver

**Four(times), Foursome, Four-yearly** Boundary, Cater, Georges, Horsemen, IV, Mess, Mournival, Penteteric, Qid, Quartet, Quaternary, Quaternion, Reel, Tessara, Tessera, Tetrad, Tetralogy, Tiddy, Warp

**Four-hundred** G

**Fourpence** Groat

**Fourteenth** Bastille, Trecento, Valentine

**Fourth** Deltaic, Estate, Fardel, Farl(e), Firlot, Forpet, Forpit, July, Martlet, Perfect, Quarter, Quartet, Quaternary, Quintan, Sesquitertia, Tritone

**Fowl** Barnyard, Biddy, Boiler, Brahma, Brissle-cock, Burrow-duck, Capon, Chicken, Chittagong, Cob, Cock, Coot, Domestic, Dorking, Duck, Ember, Gallinaceous, Gallinule, Game, Gleenie, Guinea, Hamburg(h), Heather-bleat(er), → **HEN**, Houdan, Jungle, Knob, Kora, Leghorn, Mallee, Moorhen, Orpington, Papageno, Partridge, Pheasant, Pintado, Plymouth Rock, Poultry, Pullet, Quail, Rooster, Rumkin, Rumpy, Scrub, Solan, Spanish, Spatchcock, Spitchcock, Sultan, Sussex, Teal, Turkey, Wyandotte

**Fox(y)** Alopecoid, Arctic, Baffle, Bat-eared, Bewilder, Blue, Canid, Charley, Charlie, Corsac, Crafty, Cunning, Desert, Discolour, Fennec, Floor, Flying, Fool, Friend, Fur, Grey, Kit, Lowrie(-tod), Outwit, Pug, Puzzle, Quaker, Red, Reynard, Rommel, Russel, Silver, Skulk, → **SLY**, Spot, Stump, Swift, Tod, Uffa, Uneatable, Vixen, White, Zerda, Zoril(le), Zorro

**Foxglove** Cowflop, Deadmen's bells, Digitalis, Witches'-thimble

**Foxhole** Earth

**Foxtrot** Dance, F

**Foyer** Hall, Lobby, Reception

**Fracas** Brawl, Dispute, Mêlée, Prawle, Riot, Rumpus, Scrum, Shindig, Uproar

**Fraction** Common, Complex, Compound, Continued, Decimal, Improper, Ligroin, Mantissa, Mixed, Mole, Packing, Part, Partial, Piece, Proper, Quarter, Scrap, Simple, Some, Tithe, Vulgar

**Fractious** Schismatic

**Fracture** Break, Colles, Comminuted, Complicated, Compound, Crack, Fatigue, Fault, Fissure, Gap, Greenstick, Hairline, Impacted, Incomplete, Oblique, Pathological, Platy, Pott's, Rupture, Shear, Simple, Spiral, Splintery, Split, Stress, Transverse

**Fragile** Brittle, Crisp, Delicate, Flimsy, Frail, Frangible, Nesh, Slender, Tender, Vulnerable, Weak

**Fragment(s)** Agglomerate, Atom, Bit, Bla(u)d, Brash, Breccia, Brockage, Brockram, Cantlet, Clastic, Crumb, Disjecta membra, End, Flinder, Fritter, Frust, Graile, Lapilli,

Mammock, Mite, Morceau, Morsel, Ort, →**PARTICLE**, Piece, Piecemeal, Potshard, Potsherd, Relic, Restriction, Rift, Rubble, Scrap, Scree, Segment, Shard, Shatter, Sheave, Shiver, Shrapnel, Shred, Skerrick, Sliver, Smithereens, Smithers, Snatch, Snippet, Splinter

▷ **Fragment of** *may indicate* a hidden word

**Fragrance, Fragrant** Aromatic, Attar, Balsam, Bouquet, Conima, Lavender, Nosy, Odiferous, Odour, Olent, Otto, →**PERFUME**, Pot-pourri, Redolent, →**SCENT**, Sent, Spicy, Suaveolent

**Frail** Brittle, Creaky, Delicate, Feeble, Flimsy, →**FRAGILE**, Nice, Puny, Rushen, Slight, Slimsy, Tottery, Weak

**Framboesia** Morula, Yaws

**Frame(work)** A, Adjust, Airer, Angle, Armature, Babywalker, Bail, Bayle, Bier, Body, Bow, Brickbat, Build, Bustle, Cadge, Cadre, Cage, Case, Casement, Casing, Centreing, Cent(e)ring, Chase, Chassis, Clamper, Climbing, Cloche, Coaming, Cold, Compages, Companion, Cowcatcher, Cradle, Cratch, Cribwork, Crinoline, Deckel, Deckle, Draw, Dutchwife, Easel, Entablature, Espalier, Everest pack, Fabric, Falsework, Fender, Fiddley, Fit-up, Flake, Form, Frisket, Gallows, Gambrel, Gantry, Garden, Gate, Gauntry, Grid-iron, Haik, Hake, Heck, Hem, Horse, Hovel, Hull, Husk, Incriminate, Jungle gym, Lattice, Limit, Louvre, Mantel, Mixte, Monture, Mood, Mount, Mullion, Muntin(g), Newsreel, Ossature, Outrigger, Oxford, Pack, Pannier, Pantograph, Parameter, Partners, Passe-partout, Pergola, Physique, Pillory, Plant, Plot, Plummer-block, Poppet head, Portal, Pumphead, Punchboard, Puncheon, Quilting, Rack, Rave, Reading, Redact, Retable, Rib(bing), Rim, Roof rack, Sampling, Sash, Scaffold, Screen, Scuncheon, Sect(ion), Set, Setting, Skeleton, Spider, Spring-box, Stanchion, Stand, Stern, Still(age), Stitch up, Stocking, Stocks, Straddle, Stretcher, Stretching, Stroma, →**STRUCTURE**, Studwork, Substructure, Surround, Swift, Tabernacle, Taboret, Tabouret, Tambour, Tent(er), Tepee, Time, Timeline, Trave, Trellis, Tress, Tressel, Trestle, Tribble, Trussing, Tympan, Vacuum, Victimize, Walking, Wattle, Ways, Window, Yoke, Zarf, Zimmer®

**Framley** Parsonage

**Franc** Fr, Leu, Lev, Lew

**France** Anatole, Marianne, RF, Thibault

**Franchise** Charter, Concession, Contract, Liberty, Pot-wall(op)er, Privilege, Right, Suffrage, Vote, Warrant

**Franciscan** Conventional, Custos, Greyfriars, Minorite, Observant, Salesian, Scotist, Tertiaries

**Francium** Fr

**Franck** Cesar

**Frank(ish), Frankly** Artless, Austrasia, Bluff, Blunt, Cancel, →**CANDID**, Diarist, Direct, Easy, Eye-to-eye, Forthcoming, Four square, Free, Free-spoken, Guileless, Honest, Ingenuous, Man-to-man, Merovingian, Natural, Open, Outspoken, Overt, Plain-spoken, Postage, Postmark, Raw, Ripuarian, Salian, Sinatra, Sincere, Squareshooter, Stamp, Straight, Straightforward, Sty, Upfront, Vocal

**Frankincense** Laser, Olibanum, Thus

**Frans, Franz** Hals, Lehar

**Frantic** Demoniac, Deranged, Distraught, Drissy, Frenzied, Hectic, Mad, Overwrought, Phrenetic, Rabid, Violent, Whirl(ing)

▷ **Frantic** *may indicate* an anagram

**Frappé** Iced

**Fraternise, Fraternity** Affiliate, Brotherhood, Burschenschaft, Consort, Elk, Fellowship, Lodge, Mingle, Moose, Order, Shriner, Sodality

**Fratricide** Cain

**Fraud(ulent)** Barratry, Bobol, Bogus, Bubble, Chain-letter, Charlatan, Cheat, Chisel, Collusion, Covin, Cronk, Deceit, Diddle, Dishonesty, Do, Fake, Fiddle, Fineer, Grift, Gyp, Humbug, Hypocrite, →**IMPOSTOR**, Imposture, Jiggery-pokery, Jobbery, Kite, Knavery,

Liar, Peculator, Phishing, Phon(e)y, Piltdown, Pious, Pseud(o), Put-up, Quack, Ringer, Rip-off, Roguery, Rort, Salami technique, Scam, Shoulder surfing, South Sea Bubble, Stellionate, Sting, Stumer, Supercherie, Swindle, Swiz(z), Swizzle, Tartuffe, Trick, Vishing, Wire

**Fraught** Perilous

**Fray(ed), Frayer** Bagarre, Brawl, Contest, Feaze, Frazzle, Fret, Fridge, Ravel, Raw, Riot, Scrimmage, Wigs on the green

**Frazzle** Wear down

**Freak(ish)** Bizarre, Cantrip, Caprice, Chimera, Control, Deviant, Geek, Jesus, Lusus naturae, Mooncalf, Mutant, Sport, Teras, Vagary, Weirdo, Whim, Whimsy

**Freckle** Dot, Ephelis, Fern(i)tickle, Fern(i)ticle, Heatspot, Lentigines, Lentigo, Spot, Sunspot

**Frederick** Barbarossa, Carno, Great

**Free(d), Freely** Absolve, Abstrict, Acquit, Assoil, At large, Blank, Buckshee, Candid, Canny, Church, Clear, Complimentary, Cuffo, Dead-head, Deliver, Deregulate, Detach, Devoid, Disburden, Disburthen, Disembarrass, Disembroil, Disengage, Disentangle, Eleutherian, Emancipate, Enfranchise, Enlarge, Excuse, Exeem, Exeme, Exempt, Exonerate, Extricate, Familiar, Footloose, Frank, French, Generous, Gratis, Hand, House, Idle, Immune, Indemnify, Independent, Kick, Large, Lavish, Lax, Leisure, Let, Liberal, Liberate, Loose, Manumit, Open, Parole, Pro bono, Pure, Quit(e), Range, Ransom, Redeem, →**RELEASE**, Relieve, Requiteless, Rescue, Reskew, Rick, Rid, Sciolto, Scot, Solute, Spare, Spring, Stald, Stall, Trade, Unbowed, Unhampered, Unhitch, Unlace, Unlock, Unloosen, Unmew, Unmuzzle, Unpen, Unshackle, Unsnarl, Unstick, Untangle, Untie, Untwine, Untwist, Vacant, Verse, Voluntary

▷ **Free** *may indicate* an anagram

**Freebooter** Cateran, Corsair, Franklin, Marauder, Moss-trooper, Pad, Pindaree, Pindari, Pirate, Rapparee, Rider, Snapha(u)nce, Snaphaunch, Thief, Viking

**Freedom** Abandon, Autonomy, Breadth, Carte blanche, Eleutherian, Exemption, Fear, Fling, Four, Immunity, Impunity, Independence, Laisser aller, Laisser faire, Laissez aller, Laissez faire, Latitude, Leeway, Leisure, Liberty, Licence, Magna Carta, Moksha, Play, Range, Recourse, Releasement, Speech, Uhuru, UNITA, Want, Wiggle room, Worship

**Free gift** Bonus, Charism, Perk

**Freehold(er)** Enfeoff, Franklin, Frank tenement, Odal(l)er, Seisin, Udal(ler), Yeoman

**Freelance** Eclectic, Independent, Mercenary, Stringer

**Freeload(er)** Scambler, Scrounge, Sponge

▷ **Freely** *may indicate* an anagram

**Freeman** Burgess, Ceorl, Churl, Franklin, Liveryman, Thegn, Thete, Villein

**Freemason(ry), Freemason's son** Craft, Lewis, Lodge, Moose, Templar

**Free-range** Eggs, Outler

**Free State** Orange

**Freethinker** Agnostic, Bradlaugh, Cynic, Dissenter, Libertine, Sceptic

**Free-trade(r)** Cobdenism, Wright

**Free-wheel** Coast, Idle

**Free-will** Spontaneity

**Freeze(s), Freezer, Freezing** Alcarrazo, Arctic, Benumb, Congeal, Cool, Cryogenic, Cryonics, Eutectic, Freon®, Frost, Geal, Harden, Ice, Ice cold, Lyophilize, Moratoria, Nip, Numb, Paralyse, Pause, Peg, Regelate, Riss, Stiffen, Subpolar, Tense, Wage, Zero

**Freight(liner)** Cargo, Carriage, Fraught, Goods, Goods train, Lading, Load

**French(man), Frenchwoman** Alain, Alsatian, Anton, Aristo, Basque, Breton, Cajun, Crapaud, Creole, Dawn, Dreyfus, Emil(e), Frog(-eater), Gallic(e), Gascon, Gaston, Gaul, Gombo, Grisette, Gumbo, Homme, Huguenot, Joual, Jules, M, Mamselle, Marianne, Midi, Monsieur, Mounseer, Neo-Latin, Norman, Parleyvoo, Pierre, René, Rhemish, Richelieu, Savoyard, Yves

**Frenetic** Deranged, Frantic, Manic, Overwrought

**Frenzied, Frenzy** Agitato, Amok, Berserk, Corybantic, Deliration, Delirium, Demoniac, Dionysiac, Enrage, Enrapt, Euhoe, Euoi, Evoe, Feeding, Fever, Fit, Frenetic, Fury, Hectic, Hysteric, Lune, Maenad, Mania, Must, Nympholepsy, Oestrus, Phrenetic, Rage, Tantrum, Vehement

**Frequency, Frequent(er), Frequently** Angular, Attend, Audio, Bandwidth, Channel, Common, Constant, Expected, Familiar, Forcing, Formant, FR, Fresnel, Gene, Habitué, Hang-out, Haunt, Hertz, High, Incidence, Intermediate, Kilocycle, L-band, Low, Medium, Megahertz, Mode, Natural, Often, Oft-times, Passband, Penetrance, Pulsatance, Radio, Recurrent, Regular, Relative, Resort, Spatial, Spectrum, Superhigh, Terahertz, Thick, Ultrahigh, Video, Waveband

**Fresco** Intonaco, Sinopia, Tempera

**Fresh(en), Freshness** Airy, Anew, Aurorean, Brash, Caller, Chilly, Clean, Crisp, Deodorise, Dewy, Entire, Evergreen, Fire-new, Forward, Green, Hot, Insolent, Live(ly), Maiden, Mint, Nas(s)eem, New, Novel, Quick, Rebite, Recent, Roral, Roric, Rorid, Rub up, Smart, Span-new, Spic(k), Sweet, Tangy, Uncured, Verdure, Vernal, Virent, Virescent

**Freshman, Fresher** Bajan, Beginner, Bejan(t), Fresher, Frosh, Newcomer, Pennal, Plebe, Recruit, Student

**Fret(ful)** Chafe, Filigree, Fractious, Fray, Gnaw, Grate, Grecque, Haze, Impatient, Irritate, Key, Mist, Ornament, Peevish, Repine, Rile, Ripple, Roil, Rub, Stop, Tetchy, Tracery, Whittle, Worry

**Fretwork** Lattice

**Friable** Crisp, Crumbling, Powdery

**Friar(s)** Augustinian, Austin, Bacon, Barefoot, Black, Bonaventura, Bonaventure, Brother, Bungay, Capuchin, Carmelite, Conventual, Cordelier, Crutched, Curtal, Dervish, Dominican, Fra(ter), Franciscan, Frate, Grey, Jacobin, Laurence, Limiter, Lymiter, Minim, Minor, Minorite, → **MONK**, Observant, Observantine, Preaching, Predicant, Recollect, Recollet, Redemptionist, Rush, Tuck, White

**Fricative** Rill

**Friction** Attrition, Conflict, Detrition, Dissent, Drag, Massage, Rift, Rub, Skin, Sliding, Stiction, Stridulation, Tribology, Tripsis, Wear, Windblast, Xerotripsis

**Friday** Black, Casual, Girl, Golden, Good, Holy, Man, Person, Savage

**Fridge** Esky®, Freezer, Icebox, Minibar, Rub

**Fried cake** Croquette, Cruller

**Friend(ly), Friends** Achates, Affable, Ally, Alter ego, Ami(cable), Amie, Amigo, Approachable, Associate, Avuncular, Bach, Belamy, Benign, Boet(ie), Bosom, Bra, Bro, Bru, Bud(dy), Buster, Butty, Cackermander, Cater-cousin, China, Choma, Chommie, Chum, Circle, Cobber, Cock, Cohort, Compadre, Companion, Companionable, Comrade, Confidant, Cordial, Cotton, Couthie, Couthy, Crony, Cully, Damon, Dog, Downhome, Edwin, Ehoa, En ami, Fairweather, False, Familiar, Feare, Feathered, Feer, Fere, Fiere, Folksy, Gemütlich, Gossib, Gossip, Gregarious, Hail-fellow-well-met, Homeboy, Informal, Ingle, Intimate, Inward, Jong, Kidgie, Kith, Litigation, Lover, Marrow, Mate, McKenzie, Mentor, Mucker, Mutual, Near, Next, Oppo, Outgoing, Paisano, Pal, Paranymph, Pard(ner), Pen, Penn, Pheere, Platonic, Playmate, Privado, Prochain ami, Prochein ami, Pythias, Quaker, Sidekick, Sociable, Societal, Sport, Steady, Thawing, Thick, Tillicum, Tonga, Tosh, Type B, User, Wack(er), Warm, Well-disposed, Well-wisher, Wus(s), Yaar

**Friendliness, Friendship** Amity, Bonhomie, Camaraderie, Contesseration, Entente, Goodwill, Platonic, Rapprochement, Sodality

**Frieze** Dado, Metope, Penistone, Zoophorus

**Fright(en), Frightened, Frightening, Frightful** Afear, Affear(e), Agrise, Agrize, Agryze, Alarm, Aroint, Aroynt, Ashake, Chilling, Cow, Da(u)nt, Dare, Deter, Eek, Eerie, Eery, Faceache, Fear(some), Flay, Fleg, Fleme, Fley, Flush, Gallow, Gally, Ghast, Gliff, Glift, Grim, Grisly, Hairy, Horrid, Horrific, Intimidate, Menace, Nightmare, Ordeal, Panic, Petrify, Scar, → **SCARE**, Scarre, Scaur, Schrecklich, Shocking, Sight, Skear, Skeer, Skrik,

Spine-chilling, Spook, Stage, Startle, Terrible, Terrify, Terror, Tirrit, Ugly, Unco, Unease, Unman, White-knuckle, Windy, Yitten

**Frightener** Sasquatch

**Frigid** Bleak, Cold, Dry, Frory, Frosty, Ice, Indifferent, Serac, Stiff

**Frill(y)** Armil, Armilla, Bavolet, Chidlings, Chitlings, Falbala, Flounce, Furbelow, Jabot, Lacy, Lingerie, Newgate, Oriental, Ornament, Papillote, Ruche, Ruff(le), Shirt, Tucker, Valance

▷ **Frilly** *may indicate* an anagram

**Fringe(s), Fringed** Bang, Border, Bullion, Celtic, Ciliated, Ciliolate, Edge, Fall, Fimbria, Frisette, Furbelow, Interference, Laciniate, Loma, Lunatic, Macramé, Macrami, Newgate, Pelmet, Peripheral, Robin, Ruff, Run, Thrum, Toupee, Toupit, Tsitsith, Tzitzit(h), Valance, Verge, Zizith

**Frippery** Small beer

**Frisian** Holstein

**Frisk(y)** Caper, Cavort, Curvet, Fisk, Flimp, Frolic, Gambol, Search, Skip, Skittish, Wanton

**Frisson** Shiver

**Fritillary** Snake's-head

**Fritter** Batter, Beignet, Dribble, Dwindle, Fragment, Fribble, Pakora, Piddle, Potter, Puf(f)taloon, Squander, Waste, Wonder

**Frivolity, Frivolous** Butterfly, Empty(-headed), Etourdi(e), Facetious, Featherbrain, Flighty, Flippant, Footling, Frippet, Frothy, Futile, Giddy, Idle, Inane, Levity, Light, Light-minded, Lightweight, Moth, Persiflage, Playboy, Shallow, Skittish, Trifling, Trivial

**Frizz(le), Frizzly** Afro, Crape, Crimp, Crinkle, Curly, Fry, Fuzz, Hiss

**Frock** Dress, Gown, Ordain, Robe, Smock

**Frog** Amphibian, Anoura, Anura, Arrow poison, Batrachia(n), Braid, Breton, Bullfrog, Cape nightingale, Crapaud, Depression, Flying, Fourchette, Frenchman, Frush, Goliath, Hairy, Hyla, Kermit, Leopard, Marsupial, Mounseer, Nic, Nototrema, Paddock, Paradoxical, Peeper, Pelobatid, Platanna, Puddock, Puttock, Rana, Ranidae, Spring peeper, Tree, Wood, Xenopus

**Frogman** Diver

**Frogmouth** Mo(re)poke, Podargus

**Frog spawn** Redd, Tadpole

**Frolic(some)** Bender, Bust(er), Cabriole, Caper, Cavort, Curvet, Disport, Escapade, → **FRISK(Y)**, Fun, Galravage, Galravitch, Gambol, Gammock, Gil(l)ravage, How's your father, Jink, Kittenish, Lark, Play, Pollick, Prank, Rag, Rand, Rant, Rig, Romp, Scamper, Skylark, Splore, Sport, Spree, Stooshie, Tittup, Wanton

**From** A, Against, Ex, For, Frae, Of, Off, Thrae

**Frond** Fern, Leaf, Tendril

**Front(al), Frontman** Antependium, Anterior, Bow, Brass, Brow, Cold, Cover, Dead, Dickey, Dicky, Esplanade, Facade, Face, Fore(head), Forecourt, Fore end, Foreground, Groof, Grouf, Grufe, Head, Home, Insolence, Metope, National, Newscaster, Nose, Occluded, Paravant, People's, Plastron, Polar, Popular, Pose, Preface, Presenter, Pro, Prom, Prow, Rhodesian, Sector, Sinciput, Spearhead, Stationary, Tabula, Temerity, Van, Vaward, Ventral, Warm, Western

**Frontier(sman)** Afghan, Barrier, Boon, Border, Boundary, Calamity Jane, Checkpoint, Crockett, Earp, Limit, Limitrophe, List, March, North-west, Outpost, Pathan, Wild West

**Front page** P1

**Front-ranker** Pawn

**Frost(ing), Frosty, Frostbite** Air, Alcorza, Black, Chill, Cranreuch, Cryo-, Freon®, Frigid, Frore(n), Frorne, Glacé, Ground, Hoar, Hore, Ice, Icing, Jack, Mat, Nip, Rime, Silver, Trench foot, White

**Froth(y)** Barm, Bleb, Bubble, Chiffon, Cuckoospit(tle), Despumate, Foam, Frogspit, Gas, Head, Lather, Mantle, Nappy, Off-scum, Ream, Saponin, Scum, Seethe, Shallow, Spittle, Spoom, Spoon, Spume, Sud, Toadspit, Yeasty, Yest, Zephir

**Frown** Glower, Knit, Lour, Lower, Scowl
**Froze(n)** Congealed, Froren, Frorn(e), Frory, Gealed, Gelid, Glacé, Graupel, Ice-bound, Rigid, Spellbound, Static, Tundra
**Fructification, Fructify, Fructose** Aeci(di)um, Basidium, Fertilise, Flower, Fruit, Inulin
**Frugal** Meagre, Parsimonious, Provident, Prudent, Scant, Skimpy, Spare, Spartan, Thrifty
**Fruit(ing), Fruit tree, Fruity** Accessory, Achaenocarp, Achene, Acinus, Akene, Allocarpy, Apothecium, Autocarp, Bacciform, Catapult, Cedrate, Coccus, Compot(e), Confect, Conserve, Cremocarp, Crop, Dessert, Drupe, Eater, Encarpus, Etaerio, First, Follicle, Forbidden, Fritter, Harvest, Issue, Multiple, Orchard, Output, Pericarp, Poof, Primeur, Primitiae, Product(ion), Pseudocarp, Regma(ta), Replum, Result, Return, Rich, Ripe, Schizocarp, Seed, Silicle, Siliqua, Silique, Soft, Sorosis, Stoneless, Succade, Sweetie, Sweety, Syconium, Syncarp, Utricle, Valve, Wall, Xylocarp, Yield

---

**FRUITS**

**3 letters:**
Fig, Haw, Hep, Hip, Hop, Jak, Key, Nut

**4 letters:**
Acai, Akee, Bael, Bito, Cone, Date, Gage, Gean, Jack, Kaki, Kiwi, Lime, Mast, Noni, Pear, Pepo, Plum, Pome, Sloe, Sorb, Star, Tuna, Ugli®, Yuzu

**5 letters:**
Ackee, Acorn, Anana, Anona, Apple, Assai, Berry, Bread, Carob, Choko, Genip, Gourd, Grape, Guava, Jaffa, Lemon, Lichi, Lotus, Mamey, Mango, Melon, Nancy, Naras, Nashi, Nelis, Olive, Papaw, Prune, Rowan, Whort

**6 letters:**
Almond, Ananas, Babaco, Banana, Banian, Banyan, Carica, Casaba, Cherry, Chocho, Citron, Citrus, Comice, Damson, Durian, Durion, Emblic, Feijoa, Lichee, Litchi, Longan, Lychee, Mammee, Medlar, Narras, Nelies, Oilnut, Orange, Papaya, Pawpaw, Pepino, Pomace, Pomelo, Pruine, Punica, Quince, Raisin, Rennet, Russet, Samara, Sapota, Seckel, Sharon, Squash, Tomato

**7 letters:**
Amygdal, Apricot, Avocado, Bullace, Cassaba, Chayote, Crab-nut, Currant, Cypsela, Geebung, Genipap, Gherkin, Kumquat, Leechee, Litchee, Manjack, Morello, Passion, Pimento, Pinguin, Poperin, Pumpkin, Pupunha, Rosehip, Ruddock, Satsuma, Soursop, Tangelo, Winesap

**8 letters:**
Abricock, Aguacate, Apricock, Bergamot

| | | | |
|---|---|---|---|
| Bilberry | Apple-john | Sapodilla | Watermelon |
| Blimbing | Aubergine | Saskatoon | Youngberry |
| Calabash | Bakeapple | Shadberry | |
| Caprifig | Blueberry | Sorb-apple | **11 letters:** |
| Dewberry | Butternut | Star-apple | Boysenberry |
| Fraughan | Cantaloup | Tamarillo | Chokecherry |
| Goosegog | Carambola | Tangerine | Granny Smith |
| Hagberry | Caryopsis | Tomatillo | Hesperidium |
| Hastings | Cherimoya | Victorine | Huckleberry |
| Hedgehog | Colocynth | Whimberry | Lingonberry |
| Kalumpit | Crab apple | Whinberry | Marionberry |
| Minneola | Cranberry | | Pampelmoose |
| Mirliton | Deerberry | **10 letters:** | Pampelmouse |
| Mulberry | Freestone | Blackberry | Pomegranate |
| Pearmain | Haanepoot | Calamondin | Pompelmoose |
| Physalis | Hackberry | Cantaloupe | Pompelmouse |
| Plantain | Juneberry | Cherimoyer | Salmonberry |
| Prunello | Love apple | Chinaberry | |
| Rambutan | Manzanita | Chokeberry | **12 letters:** |
| Rathripe | Melon-pear | Clementine | Blackcurrant |
| Sebesten | Mirabelle | Clingstone | Checkerberry |
| Shaddock | Musk melon | Elderberry | Custard-apple |
| Silicula | Myrobalan | Granadilla | Service-berry |
| Sunberry | Naseberry | Grenadilla | Thimbleberry |
| Sweeting | Nectarine | Jargonelle | Victoria plum |
| Sweetsop | Neesberry | Loganberry | Whortleberry |
| Tamarind | Ortanique | Mangosteen | |
| Tayberry | Persimmon | Paddymelon | **13 letters:** |
| Teaberry | Pinot noir | Pick-cheese | Bullock's heart |
| Waxberry | Plumdamas | Punicaceae | Sapodilla plum |
| | Poppering | Redcurrant | |
| **9 letters:** | Raspberry | Scaldberry | **14 letters:** |
| Algarroba | Ratheripe | Strawberry | Worcesterberry |

**Fruitcake** Dundee, Madman, Nutter

**Fruitful(ness)** Calathus, Ephraim, Fat, Fecund, Feracious, Fertile, Productive, Prolific, Teeming, Uberty, Worthwhile

**Fruitless** Bare, Fool's errand, Futile, Sisyphean, Sooterkin, Sterile, Useless, Vain

**Fruit-picker** Eve

**Frump(ish)** Dowdy, Judy, Shabby, Unkempt

**Frustrate(d), Frustration** Baffle, Ba(u)lk, Beat, Blight, Bugger, Check, Cheesed off, Confound, Countermine, Dash, Defeat, Disappoint, Discomfit, Dish, Disillusionment, Foil, Forestall, Hamper, Hogtie, Outwit, Scotch, Snooker, Spike, Stymie, Tantalise, Thwart

**Fry, Fried, Fries** Blot, Brit, Christopher, Elizabeth, French, Fricassee, Fritter, Frizzle, Parr, Sauté, Sizzle, Skirl-in-the-pan, Small, Spawn, Whippersnapper, Whitebait

**Fuddle(d)** Drunk, Fluster, Fuzzle, Maudlin, Ta(i)vert, Tosticated, Woozy

▷ **Fuddle(d)** *may indicate* an anagram

**Fudge** Cook, Doctor, Dodge, Drivel, Evade, Fiddlesticks, Nonsense, Rot, Stop-press, Sweet(meat)

**Fuel** Alternative, Anthracite, Argol, Astatki, Atomic, Avgas, Benzene, Benzine, Benzol, Biodiesel, Biogas, Borane, Briquet(te), Brown coal, Bunker, Butane, Candle-coal, Cannel, Carbonette, Charcoal, Coal, Coalite®, Coke, Derv, Diesel, Eilding, Eldin(g), Ethane, Faggot, Feed, Fire(wood), Fossil, Gasahol, Gasohol, Gasoline, Go-juice, Hexamine,

Hydrazine, Hydyne, Ignite, Jud, Kerosene, Kerosine, Kindling, Knitch, Lead-free, Lignite, Lox, Mox, Multigrade, Napalm, Naphtha, Nuclear, Oilgas, Orimulsion, Outage, Paraffin, Peat, Propane, Propellant, Smokeless, Smudge, Solid, Sterno®, Stoke, SURF, Synfuel, Tan balls, Triptane, Unleaded, Yealdon

**Fug** Frowst

**Fugitive** Absconder, Defector, Ephemeral, Escapee, Fleeting, Hideaway, Lot, Outlaw, Refugee, Runagate, Runaway, Runner, Transient, Vagabond

**Fugue** Ricercar(e), Ricercata, Stretto

**Fulcrum** Key-pin, Pivot

**Fulfil(ment), Fulfilled** Accomplish, Come true, Complete, Consummate, Fruition, Honour, Implementation, Meet, Pass, Realise, →SATISFY, Serve, Steed, Subrogation

**Fulgent** Bright, Shining

**Full(est), Fullness, Fully** Abrim, Ample, Arrant, Bouffant, Capacity, Chock-a-block, Chocker, Complete, Copious, Embonpoint, Engorged, Entire, Fairly, Fat, Fed, Flush, Fou, Frontal, German, High, Hoatching, Hotch, Jam-packed, Mill, Orotund, Plein, Plenary, Plenitude, Pleroma, Plethora, Plump, Replete, Rich, Rotund, Sated, Satiated, Thorough, Thronged, Torose, Torous, Toss, Turgid, Turgor, Ullage, Uncut, Up, Wau(l)k, Whole hog, Wholly

**Full-bodied** Amoroso

**Full-faced** Caboched, Caboshed

**Full-flavoured** Rich

**Full-grown** Seeded

**Full-throated** Goitred

**Fulminate, Fulmination** Chastise, Detonate, Explode, Levin, Lightning, Rail, Renounce, Thunder

**Fumarole** Hornito, Mofette

**Fumble** Blunder, Faff, Grope, Misfield, Muff

**Fume(s)** Bluster, Gas, Halitus, Incense, Nidor, Rage, Reech, Reek, Settle, Smoke, Stum, Vapours

**Fumigate, Fumigator** Disinfect, Pastil(le), Smoke, Smudge

**Fun(ny), Funny bone** Amusing, Antic, Boat, Buffo, Caper, Clownery, Comedy, Comic(al), Crack, Craic, Delight, Droll, Frolic, Gammock, Gas, Gig, Giocoso, Glaik, Guy, Hilarity, Hoot, Horseplay, Humerus, Humorous, Hysterical, Ill, Ironic, Jest, Jokey, Jouisance, Jouysaunce, Kicks, Killing, Kinky, Lark, Music, Play, Pleasure, Priceless, Rag, Rib-tickling, Rich, Rummy, Scream, Sidesplitting, Skylark, Slap and tickle, Sport, Strange, Suspect, Unwell, Uproarious, Weird(o), Whoopee, Wisecrack, Wit, Yell

**Funambulist** Blondin, Equilibrist, Tight-rope

**Function(al), Functioning, Functions** Act, Algebraic, Antilog, Apparatchik, Arccos, Arcsin(e), Arctan, Assignment, Behave, Bodily, Bunfight, Business, Ceremony, Characteristic, Circular, Cosec, Cosh, Cot(h), Cotangent, Dance, Density, Discriminant, Distribution, Do, Dynamic, Exponential, Gamma, Gibbs, Hamilton(ian), Helmholtz, Hyperbolic, Integral, Integrand, Inverse, Jacobian, Job, Logarithm, Map(ping), Nutracentrical, →OPERATE, Periodic, Polymorphic, Practicable, Probability, Propositional, Purpose, Quadric, Quantical, Quartic, Reception, Recursive, Role, Run, Sec(h), Secant, Sensation, Sentential, Service, Sin(e), Sinh, State, Ste(a)d, Stedde, Step, Surjection, Tan(h), Tangent, Tick, Tool bar, Transcendental, Trigonometric, Truth, Up and running, Use, Utensil, Utility, Versin(e), Vital, Wave, Wingding, →WORK

**Functionary** Notary, Official

**Functionless** Otiose

**Fund(ing), Fund raiser, Fundraising, Funds** -(a)thon, Bank, Bankroll, Barrel, Capital, Chest, Coffers, Consolidated, Emendals, Endow, Evergreen, Finance, Fisc, Fisk, Focus, Gap, Gild, Green, Hedge, Imprest, Index, Jackpot, Kail, Kale, Kitty, Lend, Maestro®, Managed, Means, Mutual, Nest-egg, Onlend, Pension, Pool, Pork-barrel, Pot, Prebend, Private, Public, Purse, Rest, Revolving, Roll-up, Sinking, Slush, Social, Sou-sou,

Stabilisation, Stock, Store, Subsidise, Sustentation, Susu, Telethon, -thon, Tracker, Treasury, Trust, Vulture, Wage(s), War chest, Wherewithal

**Fundamental(ist)** Basic(s), Bedrock, Bottom, Cardinal, Essence, Grass-roots, Hamas, Integral, Missing, Nitty-gritty, Organic, Prime, Principle, Radical, Rudimentary, Taleban, Taliba(a)n, Ultimate

**Fund-holder** Rentier

**Funeral, Funereal** Charnel, Cortege, Dismal, Exequy, Feral, Hearse, Interment, Obit, Obital, Obsequy, Sad-coloured, Solemn, Tangi

**Fungicide** Benomyl, Biphenyl, Bordeaux mixture, Burgundy mixture, Captan, Diphenyl, Ferbam, Menadione, PCP, Pentachlorophenol, Resveratrol, Thiram, Zineb

**Fungoid, Fungus** Dry rot, Endophyte, Enoki, Flor, Pest, Wet rot

---

## FUNGI

**3 letters:**
Cup
Ray

**4 letters:**
Asci
Barm
Bunt
Ceps
Conk
Gall
Gill
Pore
Rust
Scab
Smut

**5 letters:**
Black
Brand
Ergot
Favus
Honey
Hypha
Jelly
Morel
Mould
Mucor
Shelf
Slime
Spunk
Stipe
Tuber
Yeast

**6 letters:**
Aecium
Agaric
Amadou
Ascius

Elf-cup
Empusa
Ink-cap
Lichen
Mildew
Oidium
Peziza
Pileum
Torula
Wax cap
Xyloma

**7 letters:**
Amanita
Blewits
Blue-rot
Boletus
Bracket
Candida
Chytrid
Fission
Jew's ear
Milk cap
Monilia
Mycetes
Oak-wilt
Phallus
Porcino
Pythium
Russula
Tarspot
Truffle
Uredine
Yellows

**8 letters:**
Ambrosia
Basidium
Bootlace
Botrytis

Clubroot
Corn smut
Death-cap
Death-cup
Dutch elm
Erumpent
Fusarium
Fuss-ball
Fuzz-ball
Merulius
Mushroom
Mycelium
Mycology
Noble rot
Oomycete
Puccinia
Puckfist
Puffball
Rhizopus
Rhytisma
Sariodes
Stromata
Thalline
Tremella
Tuckahoe
Ustilago

**9 letters:**
Beefsteak
Bird's nest
Blackknot
Blue-mould
Coral spot
Cramp-ball
Earth-star
Eumycetes
Funnel-cap
Horsehair
Imperfect
Mucorales

Polyporus
Shaggy cap
Stinkhorn
Toadstool
Wheat rust
Zygospore

**10 letters:**
Anthersmut
Apothecium
Armillaria
Ascomycete
Bread-mould
Death angel
Gibberella
Lawyer's wig
Liberty cap
Oak-leather
Orange-peel
Prototroph
Rhizomorph
Saprophyte
Shaggy mane
Shoestring
Sooty mould
Water mould
Yellow rust
Zygomycete

**11 letters:**
Anthracnose
Aspergillus
Chantarelle
Chanterelle
Condiophore
Craterellus
Fairy butter
Ithyphallus
Penicillium
Phycomycete

Saprolegnia
Sulphur tuft
Thallophyte
Velvet shank
Witches' meat
Yellow brain

**12 letters:**
Cladosporium
Cryptococcus

Discomycetes
Flowers of tan
Hypersarcoma
Shaggy ink cap
Trichophyton
Verticillium
Wood hedgehog

**13 letters:**
Jupiter's beard

Magic mushroom
Plica polonica
Powdery mildew
Saccharomyces
Witches' butter

**14 letters:**
Wood woollyfoot

**15 letters:**
Dermatophytosis
Destroying angel

**19 letters:**
Fairy ring
champignon

---

**Fungus-eater** Mycophagist
**Funicular** Cable-car
**Funk(y)** Blue, Dodge, Dread, Fear, Phobia, Scared, Spark, Stylish
**Funnel** Buchner, Chimney, Choana, Cross, Drogue, Flue, Hopper, Infundibulum, Separating, Smokestack, Stack, Stovepipe, Tun-dish, Tunnel, Wine
**Fur(ry)** Astrakhan, Astrex, Atoc, Beaver(skin), Boa, Broadtail, Budge, Calabre, Caracul, Castor, Chinchilla, Civet, Coati, Cony-wool, Coonskin, Crimmer, Deposit, Ermelin, Ermine, Fitchew, Flix, Flue, Fun, Galyac, Galyak, Genet, Genette, Kolinsky, Krimmer, Lettice, Marten, Minever, Miniver, Mink, Mohair, Mouton, Musquash, Neckpiece, Ocelot, Otter, Palatine, Pane, Pashm, Pean, Pekan, Rac(c)oon, Roskyn, Sable, Sealskin, Sea-otter, Stole, Stone-marten, Tincture, Tippet, Vair(e), Victorine, Wolverine, Zibeline, Zorino
**Furbish** Polish, Renovate, Spruce, Vamp
**Furl** Clew up, Fold, Roll, Stow, Wrap
**Furlough** Congé, Leave
**Furnace** Arc, Athanor, Blast, Bloomery, Bosh, Breeze, Calcar, Cockle, Cremator, Cupola, Destructor, Devil, Electric, Finery, Firebox, Forge, Gas, Glory-hole, Incinerator, Kiln, Lear, Lehr, Lime-kiln, Oast, Oon, Open-hearth, Oven, Pot, Producer, Reverberatory, Scaldino, Solar, Stokehold, Stokehole, Tank, Wind
**Furnish(ing)** Appoint, Array, Deck, Decorate, Endow, Endue, Equip, Feed, Fledge, Gird, Lend, Nourish, Produce, Provision, Purvey, Soft, Stock, Suit, Supply, Tabaret, Upholster
**Furniture, Furniture designer** Armoire, Bahut, Biedermeier, Bombe, Chattels, Chippendale, Couch, Dresser, Duncan Phyfe, Encoignure, Escritoire, Etagère, Flatpack, Fyfe, Hallstand, Hatstand, Hepplewhite, Highboy, IKEA, Insight, Lowboy, Lumber, Moveable, Queen Anne, Screen, Sheraton, Sideboard, Sticks, Stoutherie, Street, Tire, Unit, Washstand, Whatnot
**Furore** Brouhaha, Commotion, Outburst, Outcry, Stink, Storm, Tempest, Uproar
**Furrier** Trapper
**Furrow(ed)** Channel, Crease, Feer, Feerin(g), Frown, Furr, Groove, Gutter, Knit, Plough, Pucker, Rabbet, Ridge, Rill(e), Rugose, Rut, Stria, Sulcus, Vallecula, Wrinkle
**Fur-seal** Seecatch(ie)
**Further(est), Furthermore, Furthest** Additional, Advance, Again, Aid, Also, Apolune, Besides, Deeper, Else, Enable, Expedite, Extend, Extra, Extreme, Fresh, Infra, Longer, Mo(e), Mow, Onwards, Other, Outermost, Promote, Serve, Speed, Subserve, Then, To boot, Yet
**Furtive(ly)** Clandestine, Covert, Cunning, Hangdog, Hole and corner, Secret, Shifty, Sly, Sneaky, Stealthy, Stowlins, Stownlins, Weaselly
**Fury, Furies, Furious** Acharné, Agitato, Alecto, →**ANGER**, Apoplexy, Atropos, Avenger, Demonic, Eriny(e)s, Eumenides, Exasperation, Frantic, Frenzied, Furor, Hairless, Hectic, Hot, Incandescent, Incensed, →**IRE**, Livid, Maenad, Manic, Megaera, Paddy, Rabid, Rage, Red, Ripsnorter, Savage, Seething, Spitting, Tisiphone, Virago, Wood, Wrath, Yond
**Furze** Gorse, Ulex, Whin
**Fuse(d), Fusion** Anchylosis, Ankylosis, Arthrodesis, Blend, Coalesce, Cohere, Colliquate, Conflate, Consolidate, Converge, Encaustic, Endosmosis, Flow, Flux,

Igniter, Integrate, Knit, Match, Melt, Merge, Merit, Nuclear, Percussion, Plasmogamy, Portfire, Proximity, Rigelation, Run, Sacralization, Safety, Saucisse, Saucisson, Short, Slow-match, Solder, Symphytic, Syncretism, Syngamy, Time, Tokamak, Union, Unite, Weld

**Fuselage** Body, Monocoque, Structure

**Fuss(y)** Ado, Agitation, Anal, Anile, Ballyho, Bobsie-die, Bother, Br(o)uhaha, Bustle, Carfuffle, Carry on, Chichi, Coil, Commotion, Complain, Cosset, Create, Cu(r)fuffle, Dust, Elaborate, Faddy, Faff, Fantad, Fantod, Fiddle-faddle, Finical, Finicky, Finikin, Folderol, Futz, Hairsplitter, Hoohah, Hoopla, Mither, Mother, Niggle, Nit-pick, Noise, Old-womanish, Ostentation, Overexact, Overnice, Overwrought, Palaver, Particular, Pedantic, Perjink, Pernickety, Picky, Pother, Precise, Prejink, Primp, Prissy, Pudder, Puristical, Racket, Raise cain, Razzmatazz, Rout, Song, Song and dance, Spoffish, Spoffy, Spruce, Stashie, Stickler, Stink, → STIR, Stishie, Stooshie, Stushie, Tamasha, To-do, Tracasserie

**Fustian** Bombast, Gas, Pompous, Rant

**Futile** Empty, Feckless, Hopeless, Idle, Inept, No-go, Nugatory, Null, Otiose, Pointless, Sleeveless, Stultified, Trivial, Useless, → VAIN

**Future(s), Futurist** Again, Avenir, Be-all, By and by, Coming, Demain, Financial, Hence, Hereafter, Horoscope, Index, Interest-rate, Later, Long-range, Offing, Ovist, Paragogic, Posterity, Prospect, To-be, To come, Tomorrow, Vista

**Fuzz(y)** Blur, Crepe, Down, Fluff, Foggy, Lint, Pig, Policeman

# Gg

**G** George, Golf, Gravity

**Gab(ble), Gabbler** Chatter, Dovercourt, Jabber, Pie, Prattle, Talkative, Yabber

**Gable** Bay, Clark, Corbie, Jerkinhead, Pediment, Pine end

**Gabriel** Angel, Walter

**Gad(about), Gadzooks** Fisk, Gallivant, Lud, Rover, Sbuddikins, Sdeath, Traipse, Trape(s), Viretot

**Gadfly** Breese, Breeze, Brize, Cleg

**Gadget** Adaptor, Appliance, Artifice, Device, Dingbat, Dingus, Doodad, Doodah, Doofer, Doohickey, Gismo, Gizmo, Gubbins, Hickey, Jiggumbob, Jimjam, Notion, Possum, Tool, Toy, Utility, Waldo, Widget

**Gadolinium** Gd

**Gadzooks** Odsbobs

**Gaekwar** Baroda

**Gael(ic)** Celt, Erse, Goidel, Irish, Scottish, Teague

**Gaff(e), Gaffer** Bêtise, Blague, Bloomer, Blunder, Error, Floater, Flub, Foreman, Gamble, Game, Old man, Overseer, Solecism, Spar, Throat, Trysail, Yokel

**Gag** Brank, Chestnut, Choke, Estoppel, Joke, Pong, Prank, Retch, Scold's bridle, Silence(r), Smother, Wheeze, Wisecrack

**Gage** Challenge, Pawn, Pledge, Plum

▶ **Gaiety** *see* GAY

**Gain(s), Gained** Acquire, Appreciate, Attain, Avail, Boodle, Boot, Bunce, Capital, Carry, Catch, Chevisance, Clean-up, Derive, Earn, Edge, Fruit, →GET, Good, Gravy, Ill-gotten, Land, Lucre, Net, Obtain, Paper, Payment, Plus, Profit, Purchase, Rake-off, Reap, Thrift, Unremittable, Use, Velvet, Wan, Win, Windfall, Winnings

**Gainsay** Contradict, Deny

**Gait** Bearing, Canter, →CHILD, Pace, Piaffer, Rack, Trot, Volt(e)

**Gaiter(s)** Cootikin, Cu(i)tikin, Gambado, Hogger, Legging(s), Puttee, Spat(s), Spattee, Spatterdash, Vamp

**Gala** Banquet, Festival, Regatta

**Galaxy, Galaxies** Active, Andromeda, Blazar, Elliptical, Great Attractor, Heaven, Irregular, Local group, Magellanic cloud, Milky Way, Radio, Regular, Seyfert, Spiral, Stars, Universe

**Galbanum** Ferula

**Gale(s)** Backfielder, Equinoctial, Fresh, Moderate, Near, Peal, Ripsnorter, Sea turn, Snorter, Squall, Storm, Strong, Tempest, Whole, Winder

**Gall, Gall bladder** Aleppo, Bedeguar, Bile, Bitterness, Brass, Canker, Cholecyst, Crown, Ellagic, Enrage, Fell, Fungus, Ink, Irritate, Mad-apple, Malice, Maugre, Maulgre, Oak(nut), Oak apple, Saddle, Sage-apple, Sandiver, →SAUCE, Tacahout, Vine

**Gallant(ry)** Admirer, Amorist, Beau, Blade, Buck, Cavalier, Chevalier, Cicisbeo, Courtliness, Lover, Prow, Romeo, Sigisbeo, Spark, Valiance

**Galleon** Galloon, Ghostly, Ship

**Gallery** Accademia, Alure, Amphitheatre, Arcade, Assommoir, Balcony, Belvedere, Brattice, Bretasche, Bretesse, Brettice, Brow, Burrell (Collection), Catacomb, Celestials, Cupola, Dedans, Fly, Gods, Hayward, Hermitage, ICA, Jube, Ladies', Loft, Loggia, Louvre, Machicolation, Mine, Minstrel, National, Organ, Pawn, Picture, Pinacotheca, Pinakothek, Pitti, Prado, Press, Public, Rogues', Scaffolding, Serpentine, Shooting, Singing,

Strangers', Tate, Terrace, Traverse, Tribune, Triforium, Uffizi, Veranda(h), Whispering, Whitechapel, Winning

**Galley** Bireme, Bucentaur, Caboose, Drake, Galliot, Kitchen, Lymphad, Penteconter, Proof, Trireme

**Gallimaufry** Duke's mixture, Macedoine, Mishmash, Stew

**Gallium** Ga

**Gallon(s)** Bushel, Cong(ius), Cran, Hin, Imperial, Pottle, Rundlet, Tierce

**Galloon** Lace, Orris

**Gallop(er)** Aide, Canter, Canterbury, Career, Lope, Trot, Wallop

**Gallows** Bough, Cheat, Drop, Dule-tree, Forks, Gibbet, Nub, Nubbing-cheat, Patibulary, Stifler, Three-legged mare, Tree, Tyburn, Tyburn-tree, Widow, Woodie

**Gallows-bird** Crack-halter, Crack-hemp, Crack-rope

**Gall-stone** Cholelith

**Galore** Abundance, À gogo, Plenty, Whisky

**Galosh** Overshoe, Rubber

**Galvanise** Activate, Buck up, Electrify, Ginger, Rouse, Zinc

**Galvanometer** Tangent

**Gam** Pod

**Gambia** WAG

**Gambit** Manoeuvre, Overture, Ploy, Stratagem

**Gamble(r), Gambling(-house), Gambling place** Adventure, Amber, Ante, Back, Bet, Bouillotte, Casino, Chance, Dice(-play), Double or quits, Flutter, Gaff, Hell, High-roller, Irish sweep, Jeff, Lotto, Martingale, Mise, Pari-mutuel, Parlay, Partingale, Piker, Plunge, Policy, Punt(er), Raffle, Reno, Risk, Roulette, School, Scratch card, Spec, Speculate, Speculator, Sweep(stake), Throw(ster), Tinhorn, Tombola, Tontine, Treble chance, Two-up, →**WAGER**, Wheeze

**Gambol** Frisk, Frolic

**Game (birds)** Bag, Colin, Covey, Fowl, Grouse, Guan, Hare, Meat, Partridge, Pheasant, Prairie chicken, Preserve, Ptarmigan, Quail, →**QUARRY**, Rype(r), Snipe, Spatchcock, Venery, Wildfowl, Woodcock

**Game(s)** Away, Caper, Circensian, Closed, Commonwealth, Computer, Console, Decider, Easy, Electronic, Elis, Exhibition, Fair, Final, Frame, Gallant, Gammy, Ground, Gutsy, High-jinks, Highland, Home, Intrepid, Isthmian, Jeu, →**LAME**, Lark, Match, Middle, Mind, MUD, Needle, Nemean, Net, Numbers, Olympic, On, Open, Panel, Paralympic, Parlour, Perfect, Platform, Play, Plaything, Ploy, Plucky, Preference, Preserve, Pythian, Raffle, Ready, Road, Role-playing, Round, Rubber, Saving, Scholar's, Secular, Sport, Square, Strategy, String, Table, Test, Tie-break, Tournament, Up for, Video, Vie, Waiting, Willing

---

## GAMES

| 2 letters: | Pit | Dibs | Palm |
|---|---|---|---|
| Eo | Put | Fa-fi | Polo |
| Go | Sim | Faro | Pool |
| PE | Swy | Goff | Putt |
| RU | Tag | Golf | Ruff |
| | Tig | Grab | Scat |
| 3 letters: | Top | I-spy | Skat |
| Cat | War | Keno | Slam |
| Hob | | Kino | Snap |
| Loo | 4 letters: | Laik | Solo |
| Maw | Base | Loto | Taws |
| Nap | Brag | Ludo | Vint |
| Nim | Bull | Main | Wall |
| Pam | Crap | Mora | Word |

**5 letters:**
Bingo
Bocce
Bowls
Cards
Cardy
Catch
Chess
Cinch
Cloak
Craps
Darts
Fives
Gleek
Goose
Halma
House
Jacks
Keeno
Lotto
Lurch
Manty
Merel
Meril
Monte
Morra
Noddy
Novum
Omber
Ombre
Pairs
Pareo
Pareu
Poker
Prime
Quino
Roque
Rummy
Shell
Shogi
Spoof
Stops
Tarok
Tarot
Touch
Trugo
Trump
Two-up
Ulama
Whisk
Whist

**6 letters:**
Ballon

Basset
Beetle
Boccia
Bo-peep
Boston
Boules
Bounce
Bridge
Casino
Chemmy
Cluedo
Clumps
Cobnut
Crambo
Ecarté
Euchre
Fantan
Footer
Gammon
Gobang
Gomoku
Hazard
Hearts
Hockey
Hoopla
Hurley
Kaluki
Kitcat
Merell
Peepbo
Pelota
Piquet
Quinze
Quoits
Shinny
Shinty
Sindon
Soccer
Socker
Squail
Squash
Sudoku
Tenpin
Tipcat
Trunks
T-shirt
Uckers
Vigoro

**7 letters:**
Balloon
Ba'spiel
Bezique
Braemar

Bunting
Camogie
Canasta
Cassino
Charade
Chicken
Codille
Conkers
Coon-can
Croquet
Curling
Diabolo
Doubles
Frisbee
Fusball
God game
Hangman
Hurling
Iceball
In-and-in
Jai alai
Jukskei
Kabaddi
Kalooki
Lottery
Mahjong
Mancala
Marbles
Matador
Muggins
Murphy's
Netball
Old maid
Pachisi
Paddler
Pallone
Passage
Patball
Peekabo
Peevers
Pharaoh
Pinball
Plafond
Pontoon
Primero
Push-pin
Pyramid
Rackets
Reversi
Ring-taw
Seven-up
Singles
Snooker
Squails

Tag ends
Tenpins
Vingt-un
Wet suit
Zero-sum

**8 letters:**
All-fives
All-fours
Baccarat
Baseball
Beat 'em up
Bob-apple
Bumpball
Buzkashi
Canfield
Cardigan
Charades
Chequers
Chouette
Conquian
Cottabus
Coverall
Cribbage
Dominoes
Draughts
Fivepins
Foosball
Football
Forfeits
Four-ball
Foursome
Fussball
Gallabea
Gin rummy
Goalball
Handball
Handicap
Hardball
Honeypot
Kalookie
Kickball
Klondike
Klondyke
Korfball
Lacrosse
Leapfrog
Mahjongg
Michigan
Monopoly®
Napoleon
Ninepins
Nintendo®
Octopush

Pachinko
Pall-mall
Parchesi
Pastance
Patience
Peekaboo
Pegboard
Penneech
Penneeck
Penuchle
Petanque
Ping-pong
Pinochle
Pintable
Pope Joan
Push-ball
Pyramids
Reversis
Rolypoly
Roulette
Rounders
Sardines
Scrabble®
Scroller
Septleva
Showdown
Skittles
Slapjack
Softball
Sphairee
Subbuteo®
Teetotum
Trap-ball
Tray-trip
Tredille
Tric-trac
Verquera
Verquere
Verquire

**9 letters:**
Acey-deucy
Aunt Sally
Badminton
Bagatelle
Billiards
Black-cock
Black-jack
Bob-cherry
Broomball
Crazy golf
Crokinole
Cutthroat
Dodgeball

Duplicate
Fillipeen
Hacky Sack®
Hopscotch
Jackstraw
Jingo-ring
Lanterloo
Level-coil
Long-whist
Matrimony
Minidress
Mistigris
Mournival
Mumchance
Newmarket
Nineholes
Paintball
Parcheesi®
Pelmanism
Punchball
Quadrille
Quidditch®
Shell game
Shoot'em-up
Simon says
Solitaire
Solo whist
Speedball
Spoilfive
Stoolball
Strap-game
Stud poker
Superbowl
Test match
Tip-and-run
Tredrille
Trick-trac
Tric-track
Twenty-one
Vingt-et-un
Water polo

**10 letters:**
Angel-beast
Backgammon
Basketball
Battledore
Boiler suit
Bouillotte
Candlepins
Cat's cradle
Cup and ball
Deck tennis
Dumb crambo

Five-stones
Flapdragon
Geocaching
Handy-dandy
Horseshoes
Hot cockles
Jackstones
Jackstraws
Knurr-spell
Kriegspiel
Lansquenet
Paddleball
Paper chase
Phillipina
Phillipine
Philopoena
Pooh sticks
Punto-banco
Put and take
Seven-a-side
Short whist
Shuffle-cap
Snapdragon
Spillikins
Strip poker
Tablanette
Tchoukball
Thimblerig
Trick-track
Troll-madam
Trou-madame
Volley-ball

**11 letters:**
Barley-brake
Barley-break
Bumble-puppy
Catch-the-ten
Chemin de fer
Family coach
Fox and geese
General post
Gerrymander
Hide and seek
Knucklebone
Kriegsspiel
Mumbletypeg
PlayStation®
Post and pair
Puncto-banco
Racquetball
Rouge et noir
Sancho-pedro
Shovelboard

Span-counter
Speculation
Table-tennis
Tick-tack-toe
Tiddlywinks
Troll-my-dame

**12 letters:**
Bar billiards
Consequences
Fast and loose
Hoodman-blind
Housey-housey
Knucklebones
Minister's cat
One-and-thirty
Pitch and putt
Pitch and toss
Shuffleboard
Span-farthing
Squash-tennis
Tiddleywinks
Troll-my-dames

**13 letters:**
Blind man's buff
Chicken-hazard
Chuck-farthing
Double or quits
French cricket
Jingling match
Kiss-in-the-ring
Musical chairs
Pass the parcel
Pitch-farthing
Postman's knock
Prisoner's base
Scavenger hunt
Space Invaders®
Spin-the-bottle
Squash rackets
Table football
Table-skittles
Tenpinbowling
Tickly-benders

**14 letters:**
British bulldog
Cops and robbers
Crown and anchor
Ducks and drakes
Fives and threes
Follow-my-leader
Hunt-the-slipper

Nievie-nick-nack
Nine men's morris
Pig-in-the-middle
Prick-the-garter
Shove-halfpenny
Snip-snap-snorum
Tenpins bowling
Three-card monte

*15 letters:*
Beach volleyball
Chinese checkers
Chinese whispers
Duplicate bridge
Fivepenny morris
King-of-the-castle
Laugh and lay down
Laugh and lie down
Ninepenny morris

Puss-in-the-corner
Russian roulette

*16 letters:*
Piggy-in-the-
middle
Scotch and English
Snakes and ladders
Trente-et-quarante

*17 letters:*
Noughts and crosses
Tom Tiddler's
ground

*20 letters:*
Kiss-me-quick-in-
the-ring
Nievie-nievie-nick-
nack

**Gamekeeper** Mellors, Velveteen, Venerer, Warrener
**Gamete** Ootid
**Gamin(e)** Hoyden
**Gaming place** Bucket-shop, Casino, Saloon, Table
**Gammerstang** Taupie, Tawpie
**Gammon** Baloney, Bilge, Hokum, Tosh
**Gamut** Compass, Range
**Gander** Airport, Glimpse, Look-see
**Gandhi** Mahatma
**Gang** Baader-Meinhof, Band(itti), Bevy, Bikers, Bing, Bunch, Cadre, Canaille, Chain,
   Coffle, Core, Crew, Crue, Droog, Elk, Go, Group, Hell's Angels, Horde, Massive, Mob,
   Mods, Nest, Outfit, Pack, Posse, Press, Push, Ratpack, Rent-a-mob, Ring, Rockers,
   Shearing, Triad, Tribulation, Troop, Tsotsi, Yardie
**Ganglia** Basal
**Gangrene** Canker, Gas, Mortified, Necrose, Noma, Phaged(a)ena, Sphacelate, Thanatosis
**Gangster** Al, Bandit, Capone, Crook, Dacoit, Dakoit, Goodfella, Hatchet-man,
   Highbinder, Home boy, Homey, Homie, Hood, Mafioso, Mobster, Ochlocrat, Scarface,
   Skinhead, Skollie, Skolly, Tsotsi, Yakuza, Yardie
**Gangway** Brow, Catwalk, Road
**Gannet** Alcatras, Booby, Guga, Solan(d)
**Gantry** Elmer
**Ganymede** Cupper
▸ **Gaol(er)** *see* JAIL(ER)
**Gap** Aperture, Belfort, Breach, Chasm, Chink, Cleavage, Credibility, Cumberland, Day,
   Deflationary, Diastema, Distance, Dollar, Embrasure, Energy, F-hole, Financing, Flaw,
   Fontanel(le), Gender, Generation, Gulf, Gulph, Hair-space, Hiatus, Hole, Inflationary,
   Interlude, Interstice, Kirkwood, Lacunae, Leaf, Leap, Lin(n), Loophole, Mews, M(e)use,
   Muset, Musit, Node of Ranvier, Opening, Ostiole, Outage, Pass, Rest, Rift, Rima,
   Shard, Sherd, Skills, Slap, →SPACE, Spark, Spread, Street, Synapse, Time lag, Trade,
   Truth-value, Vacancy, Vent, Water, Wind, Window
**Gape(r), Gaping** Comber, Dehisce, Fatiscent, Gant, Ga(u)p, Gerne, Hiant, Mya,
   Outstare, Rictal, Rictus, Ringent, Rubberneck, Stare, Yawn, Yawp
**Garage** Barn, Carport, Chopshop, Hangar, Lock-up, Muffler shop
**Garb** Apparel, Burqa, Costume, Gear, Gere, Guise, Ihram, Invest, Leotard, Raiment,
   Toilet, Uniform
**Garbage** Bunkum, Junk, Refuse, Rubbish, Trash
**Garble** Edit, Jumble, Muddle
▷ **Garble** *may indicate* an anagram
**Garcon** Waiter
**Garden(ing), Gardens** Arboretum, Arbour, Area, Babylon(ian), Bagh, Bear, Beer,
   Botanic, Chinampa, Colegarth, Container, Cottage, Covent, Cremorne, Dig, Eden,
   Erf, Floriculture, Garth, Gethsemane, Hanging, Heligan, Herb(ar), Hesperides, Hoe,
   Horticulture, Italian, Japanese, Kailyard, Kew, Kitchen, Knot, Landscape, Lyceum,

Market, Monastery, NJ, Nursery, Olitory, Orchard, Orchat, Ornamental, Paradise, Parterre, Physic, Plantie-cruive, Pleasance, Plot, Potager, Ranelagh, Rockery, Roji, Roof, Rosarium, Rosary, Rosery, Stourhead, Tea, Tilth, Topiary, Truck-farm, Tuileries, Vauxhall, Vegetable, Walled, Welwyn, Window, Winter, Yard, Zoological

**Gardener** Adam, Capability Brown, Fuchs, Hoer, Hoy, Jekyll, Landscape, Mali, Mallee, Mary, Nurseryman, Topiarist, Tradescant, Trucker

**Gargantuan** Enormous, Huge, Pantagruel, Vast

**Gargle** Gargarism, Mouthwash

**Gargoyle** Magot, Waterspout

**Garibaldi** Biscuit, Blouse, Red Shirt

**Garish** Criant, Flashy, Gaudy, Glitzy, Jazzy, Kitsch, Painty, Roary, Rorie, Rory, Technicolour

**Garland** Anadem, Anthology, Chaplet, Coronal, Crants, Festoon, Lei, Stemma, Toran(a), Vallar(y), Wreath

**Garlic** Cepaceous, Clove, Elephant, Hedge, Rams(on), Rocambole

**Garment** → DRESS, Habit, Vestment, Vesture

---

## GARMENTS

**3 letters:**
Aba
Alb
Top

**4 letters:**
Abba
Bubu
Cope
Gown
Izar
Kilt
Rail
Rami
Sari
Slop
Sulu
Toga
Togs
Weed
Wrap

**5 letters:**
Abaya
Ao dai
Boubu
Bubou
Burka
Burqa
Cardy
Cimar
Cloak
Clout
Cotta
Ephod
Fanon

Gilet
Gipon
G-suit
Hoody
Ihram
Jupon
Kanga
Kanzu
Levis
Lungi
Manty
Pareo
Pareu
Pilch
Ramée
Ramie
Ruana
Shrug
Skirt
Smock
Stola
Stole
Tanga
Thong
Tunic

**6 letters:**
Anorak
Blouse
Bodice
Bolero
Boubou
Bourka
Breeks
Burkha
Caftan

Chador
Chimer
Cilice
Corset
Dirndl
Exomis
Fleece
Jersey
Jibbah
Jilbab
Jubbah
Jumper
Kaftan
Kaross
Khanga
Kimono
Kittel
Mantle
Mantua
Nebris
Nighty
Peplos
Polony
Poncho
Reefer
Rochet
Sarong
Shroud
Sindon
Skivvy
Step-in
Sweats
Tabard
Trunks
T-shirt
Woolly

Yukata
Zephyr

**7 letters:**
Blouson
Bourkha
Burnous
Busuuti
Catsuit
Crop top
Dashiki
Djibbah
Doublet
Exomion
Jilabib
Leotard
Nightie
Paddler
Pallium
Partlet
Pelisse
Polonie
Popover
Rompers
Singlet
Soutane
Spencer
Surcoat
Tankini
Tank-top
Tunicle
Unitard
Wet suit
Woollen
Wrapper

**8 letters:**
Body suit
Cardigan
Chasuble
Chausses
Coverall
Dalmatic
Gallabea
Gambeson
Himation
Jumpsuit
Leggings
Lingerie
Monokini
Negligée
One-piece
Pannicle
Pelerine

Poloneck
Scapular
Slipover
Surplice
Swimsuit
Two-piece

**9 letters:**
Brassière
Calamanco
Cerements
Cothurnis
Cover-slut
Dishdasha
Housecoat
Mandilion
Mandylion
Minidress

Nightgown
Nightrobe
Nightwear
Outerwear
Pantihose
Pantyhose
Polonaise
Sackcloth
Sanbenito
Sweatsuit
Waistcoat

**10 letters:**
Body warmer
Boiler suit
Cote-hardie
Foundation
Habiliment

Hand-me-down
Hug-me-tight
Jeistiecor
Legwarmers
Nightdress
Salopettes
Sticharion
Sweatpants
Sweatshirt

**11 letters:**
Dreadnought
Penitential
Reach-me-down

**13 letters:**
Shalwar kameez

---

**Garnet** Alabandine, Almandine, Andradite, Carbuncle, Demantoid, Essonite, Grossular(ite), Hessonite, Melanite, Pyrenite, Pyrope, Rhodolite, Spessartite, Topazine, Topazolite, Uvarovite

**Garnish** Adorn, Attach, Cress, Crouton, Decorate, Enarm, Engild, Gremolata, Lard, Parsley, Sippet, Staffage

**Garotte(r)** Thug(gee), Ugly man

**Garret** Attic, Loft, Sol(l)ar, Sol(l)er

**Garrison** Fort, Man, Presidial

**Garrulity, Garrulous** Babbling, Gas, Gushy, Sweetiewife, Windbag

**Garter** Bowyang, Crewel, Flash, G(r)amash, Gramosh, Nicky-tam

**Gary** Glitter, Player

**Gas(sy)** Blah(-blah), Blather, Blether, Blow off, Bottle(d), Chat, Emanation, Exhaust, Fizz, Flatulence, Gabnash, Jaw, Meteorism, Prate, → TALK, Waffle, → WIND, Yackety-yak

---

## GASES

| 1 letter: | 4 letters: | Lurgi | Butane |
|---|---|---|---|
| H | Coal | Marsh | Butene |
| O | Damp | Nerve | Ethane |
|  | Flue | Noble | Ethene |
| 2 letters: | Mace® | Ozone | Ethine |
| BZ | Neon | Radon | Ethyne |
| CN | Rare | Sarin | Flatus |
| CS | Sour | Sewer | Helium |
| He | Tear | Soman | Hot-air |
| Kr | Town | Swamp | Ketene |
| Ne |  | Sweet | Napalm |
| RN | 5 letters: | Tabun | Olefin |
| VX | Argon | Therm | Oxygen |
|  | Azote | Water | Petrol |
| 3 letters: | Bloat | Xenon | Plasma |
| Air | Calor® |  | Poison |
| Nox | Ether | 6 letters: | Sewage |
| Oil | Ideal | Allene | Silane |
| War | Inert | Arsine | Thoron |

| | | | |
|---|---|---|---|
| V-agent | **8 letters:** | Flocculus | Protogalaxy |
| Vapour | Chlorine | Phosphine | |
| | Cyanogen | Propylene | **12 letters:** |
| **7 letters:** | Etherion | Protostar | Carbonic acid |
| Ammonia | Ethylene | Semiwater | Chromosphere |
| Argonon | Firedamp | Solfatara | Cyclopropane |
| Carrier | Fluorine | Synthesis | Electrolytic |
| Coal-oil | Fugacity | Whitedamp | Formaldehyde |
| Crypton | Hydrogen | | Nitrous oxide |
| Fluorin | Laughing | **10 letters:** | Oxyacetylene |
| Halitus | Lewisite | Crab nebula | Taraniki wind |
| Krypton | Nitrogen | Diphosgene | |
| Methane | North Sea | Dispersant | **14 letters:** |
| Mofette | Phosgene | Euchlorine | Chromatosphere |
| Mustard | Producer | Greenhouse | Sulphur dioxide |
| Natural | | Propellant | |
| Olefine | **9 letters:** | | **17 letters:** |
| Perfect | Acetylene | **11 letters:** | Tetrafluoroethene |
| Propane | Afterdamp | Carburetted | |
| Propene | Blue water | Methylamine | **19 letters:** |
| Stibine | Butadiene | Nitric oxide | Tetrafluoroethylene |
| Utility | Chokedamp | Non-metallic | |

**Gasbag** Airship, Blimp, Envelope, Prattler
**Gascon(ade)** Boast, Braggart, Skite
**Gash** Incise, Rift, Rip, Score, Scotch, →SLASH
**Gasket** Seal
**Gas-mask** Inhaler
**Gasp(ing)** Anhelation, Apn(o)ea, Breath, Chink, Exhale, Kink, Oh, Pant, Puff, Singult, Sob
**Gast(e)ropod** Ataata, Conch, Cowrie, Cowry, Dog-whelk, Dorididae, Doris, Euthyneura, Fusus, Glaucus, Haliotis, Harp-shell, Helmet-shell, Limpet, Mitre, Mollusc, Money cowry, Murex, Nerita, Nerite, Nudibranch, Opisthobranch, Ormer, Pelican's foot, Pennywinkle, Periwinkle, Pteropod, Purpura, Sea-ear, Sea-hare, Slug, Snail, Spindle-shell, Streptoneura, Stromb, Top, Top shell, Triton, Turbo, Turritella, Unicorn, Wentletrap, Whelk, Winkle
**Gate(s), Gateway** Alley, Arch, Attendance, Bill, Brandenburg, Caisson, Cilician, Corpse, Crowd, Decuman, Entry, Erpingham, Five-barred, Golden, Head, Iron, Ivory, Kissing, Lock, Lych, Mallee, Menin, Moon, Moravian, NOR, Payment, Pearly, Port, Portal, Portcullis, Postern, Praetorian, Propylaeum, Propylon, Pylon, Sallyport, Silver, Sluice, Starting, Tail, Taranaki, Toran(a), Torii, Traitor's, Turnout, Turnstile, Vimana, Waste, Water, Wicket, Yate, Yet(t)
**Gateau** Black Forest
**Gatecrash(er)** Interloper, Intrude, Ligger, Sorn, Unasked
**Gatehouse** Lodge
**Gatepost** Sconcheon, Scontion, Scuncheon
▷ **Gateshead** *may indicate* 'g'
**Gather(ed), Gatherer, Gathering** Accrue, Aggregate, AGM, Amass, Army, Assemble, Bee, Boil, Braemar, Ceilidh, Clambake, Cluster, Collate, →COLLECT, Colloquium, Concentration, Concourse, Conglomerate, Congregate, Convene, Conventicle, Conversazione, Corral, Corroboree, Crop, Crowd, Cull, Cut, Derive, Eve, Fester, Frill, Function, Gabfest, Galaxy, Get together, Glean, Glomerate, Hangi, Harvest, Hear, Hive, Hoard, Hootenanny, Hotchpot, Hui, Hunter, Husking, In, Infer, Jamboree, Kommers, Learn, Lek, Lirk, Love-in, Mass, Meinie, Menyie, Multitude, Pleat, Plica, Plissé, Pluck, Pucker, Purse, Raft, Raising-bee, Rake, Rally, Rave, Reap, Reef, Reunion, Round-up, Rout, Ruche, Ruck, Ruff(le), Salon, Scrump, Sheave, Shindig, Shir(r), Shoal, Shovel, Singsong, Social, Spree, Stockpile, Suppurate, Swapmeet, Take, Tuck, Vindemiate, Vintage, Wappensc(h)aw, Witches' sabbath

**Gauche** Awkward, Clumsy, Farouche, Graceless, Tactless

**Gaudy** Classy, Criant, Fantoosh, Flash, Garish, Glitz(y), Meretricious, Tacky, Tawdry, Tinsel

**Gauge** Absolute, Alidad(e), Anemometer, Assay, →**ASSESS**, Block, Bourdon, Broad, Calibre, Denier, Depth, Dial, Estimate, Etalon, Evaluate, Feeler, Hydrometer, Judge, Lee, Limit, Loading, Manometer, Marigraph, Measure, Meter, Narrow, Nilometer, Oil, Ombrometer, Oncometer, Perforation, Plug, Pressure, Rain, Rate, Ring, Scantle, Size, Slip, Standard, Steam, Strain, Tape, Template, Tonometer, Tram, Tread, Tyre, Udometer, Vacuum, Water, Weather, Wind, Wire, Yardstick

**Gauguin** Paul

**Gaul** Asterix, Cisalpine, Transalpine, Vercingetorix

**Gaunt** Cadaverous, Haggard, Lancaster, Lean, Peaked, Randletree, Ranneltree, Rannletree, Rantletree, Rawbone, →**THIN**, Wasted

**Gauntlet** C(a)estus, Gantlope

**Gauss** G

**Gautama** Buddha

**Gauze, Gauzy** Dandy-roll, Gas mantle, Gossamer, Illusion, Muslin, Sheer, Tiffany, Wire

**Gavel** Hammer

**Gawky** Clumsy, Cow, Gammerstang, Sloucher

**Gawp** Rubberneck

**Gay, Gaiety** Blithe, Bonny, Boon, Buxom, Camp, Canty, Daffing, Debonair, Fem, Festal, Frolic, Gallant, Gaudy, Gladsome, Glee, Gordon, Grisette, Inverted, Jolly, Lightsome, May, Merry, Nitid, Out, Rackety, Riant, Rorty, Tit(t)upy, Volatile

**Gaze** Moon, Pore, Regard, Stare

**Gazebo** Belvedere

**Gazelle** Ariel, Gerenuk, Goa, Mhorr, Mohr, Tabitha, Thomson's

**Gazette** London, Paper

**Gear(ing), Gearbox** Alighting, Angel, Apparatus, Arrester, Attire, Bags, Bevel, Capital, Clobber, Dérailleur, Designer, Differential, Draw, Duds, Eccentric, Engrenage, Epicyclic, Fab, Finery, Granny, G-suit, Harness, Helical, Herringbone, High, Hypoid, Idle wheel, Involute, Kit, Landing, Lay-shaft, Low, Mesh, Mess, Mitre, Neutral, Notchy, Overdrive, Planetary, Ratio, Reduction, Reverse, Rig, Riot, Rudder, Running, Spur, Steering, Stickshift, Straight, Sun and planet, Switch, Synchromesh, →**TACKLE**, Timing, Tiptronic®, Top, Trim, Tumbler, Valve, Variable, Worm(-wheel)

**Gecko** Tokay

**Gee** Horse, Hump, My, Reist, Sulk, Tout, Towt, Urge

**Geek** Creep, Nerd, Nurd, Uncool

**Geiger-counter** Scintillator

**Geisha** Maiko

**Gel** Cohere, Hair, Pectin, Pectise, Silica

**Gelatin(e), Gelatinous** Agar-agar, Blasting, Calipash, Coenchyma, Collagen, Glutinous, Isinglass, Size, Tunicin

**Geld(ing)** Castrate, Lib, Neuter, Sort, Spado

**Gelignite** Jelly

**Geller** Uri

**Gem** Intaglio, →**JEWEL**, →**STONE**

---

## GEMS

| 2 letters: | | 5 letters: | Rubin |
|---|---|---|---|
| ID | Opal | Agate | |
| | Pear | Boule | |
| | Ruby | Idaho | 6 letters: |
| 4 letters: | Sard | Pearl | Iolite |
| Jade | | Prase | Jargon |
| Onyx | | | Jasper |

Jaspis
Ligure
Morion
Plasma
Pyrope
Rubine
Scarab
Zircon

**7 letters:**
Abraxas
Asteria
Callais
Cat's eye
Diamond
Emerald
Girasol
Girosol
Jacinth
Jargoon
Kunzite
Peridot
Rose-cut
Sardius
Smaragd

**8 letters:**
Baguette
Cabochon
Diamante
Emeraude
Girasole
Hawk's eye
Heliodor
Hyacinth
Marquise
Melanite
Menilite
Peridote
Pleonast
Sapphire
Sardonyx
Sparkler
Sunstone
Wood opal

**9 letters:**
Almandine
Amazonite
Andradite
Brilliant
Briolette
Cacholong

Cairngorm
Carbuncle
Carnelian
Cornelian
Cymophane
Demantoid
Grossular
Hessonite
Hiddenite
Marcasite
Moonstone
Morganite
Moss agate
Pleonaste
Rhodolite
Rubellite
Rubicelle
Solitaire
Starstone
Tiger's eye
Turquoise
Uvarovite

**10 letters:**
Alabandine
Birthstone
Bloodstone

Chalcedony
Chrysolite
Draconites
Heliotrope
Indicolite
Lherzolite
Mocha stone
Rhinestone
Topazolite
Tourmaline

**11 letters:**
Alexandrite
Amazon stone
Chrysoberyl
Chrysoprase
Lapis lazuli
Rose-diamond
Scarabaeoid
Spessartite
Spleenstone
Verd-antique
Vesuvianite

**12 letters:**
Dumortierite
Grossularite

---

**Gemination, Gemini** Diplogenesis, Twins
**Gemma** Bud, Knosp
**Gen** Info
**Gendarme** Flic
**Gender** Form, Natural, Sex
**Gene(tics)** Allel(e), Allelomorph, Anticodon, Codominant, Codon, Complementary, Control, Creation, Designer, Disomic, Dysbindin, Episome, Exon, Factor, Gay, Genome, Hereditary, Heterogamy, Holandric, Hologynic, Homeobox, Homeotic, Intron, Jumping, Lysenkoism, Mendel, Michurinism, Molecular, Muton, Oncogene, Operon, Orthologue, Paralogue, Plasmon, Promoter, Proteome, Recessive, Regulatory, Reporter, Reverse, Selfish, STR, Structural, Suppressor, Synteny, Telegony, Terminator, Testcross, Transposon, Weismannism
**Genealogist, Genealogy** Armory, Cadency, Family, Heraldry, Line, Pedigree, Seannachie, Seannachy, Sennachie, Whakapapa
**General(ly)** At large, Average, Broad, Common, Communal, Current, Eclectic, Ecumenical, Election, Endemic, Five-star, Gen, Hoi polloi, Inspector, In the main, In the mass, Main, Omnify, On average, Overall, Overhead, Prevailing, Public, Rife, Rough, Strategist, Structural, Sweeping, Tactician, → **UNIVERSAL**, Usual, Vague, Wide

---

## GENERALS

**3 letters:**
GOC
Ike
Lee

**4 letters:**
Cato
C in C
Slim
Wade

**5 letters:**
Barca
Booth
Botha
Cleon

Clive
De Wet
Grant
Monty
Smuts

| | | | |
|---|---|---|---|
| Sulla | Raglan | Belgrano | Boulanger |
| Wolfe | Rommel | Burgoyne | Kitchener |
| | Scipio | De Gaulle | Lafayette |
| **6 letters:** | | Diadochi | Macarthur |
| Antony | **7 letters:** | Galtieri | |
| Ataman | Agrippa | Hannibal | **10 letters:** |
| Banquo | Allenby | Lysander | Alcibiades |
| Brutus | Blucher | Marshall | Clausewitz |
| Caesar | Cassius | Montcalm | Coriolanus |
| Custer | Crassus | Napoleon | Cornwallis |
| Franco | Fairfax | Pershing | Eisenhower |
| Gordon | Gamelin | Shrapnel | Holofernes |
| Joffre | Hadrian | Stilwell | Montgomery |
| Joshua | Massena | Tom Thumb | Washington |
| Leslie | Othello | Xenophon | |
| Marius | Sherman | | **16 letters:** |
| Napier | Turenne | **9 letters:** | Stonewall Jackson |
| Patton | | Agamemnon | |
| Pompey | **8 letters:** | Antigonus | |
| Powell | Agricola | Antipater | |

---

**Generate, Generation, Generator** Abiogenetic, Age, Beat, Beget, Boomerang, Breeder, Charger, Cottonwool, Create, Dynamo, Electrostatic, Epigon, Father, Fuel-cell, House, Kipp, Loin, Lost, Magneto, Me, Motor, Noise, Olds, Powerhouse, Signal, Sire, Spawn, Spontaneous, Stallion, Stonewall, Tesla coil, Turbine, Van de Graaff, Wind farm, Windmill, X, Yield

**Generosity, Generous** Ample, Benign, Bounty, Charitable, Expansive, Free-handed, Free-hearted, Handsome, Kind, Large, Largess(e), → **LAVISH**, Liberal, Magnanimous, Munificent, Noble(-minded), Open, Open-handed, Open-hearted, Philanthropic, Plump, Profuse, Public-spirited, Round, Selfless, Sporting, Tidy, Unselfish, Unstinting

**Genesis** Cause, Episome, Seed

▸ **Genetic** see **GENE(TICS)**

**Geneva(n)** Calvinist, Gin, Hollands

**Genial(ity)** Affable, Amiable, Benign, Bluff, Bonhomie, Chin, Convivial, Cordial, Expansive, Hearty, Human, Kindly, Mellow

**Genie** Djinn, Marid, Mazikeen, Shedeem

**Genipap** Lana

**Genital(s)** Ballocks, Bol(l)ix, Bollocks, Box, Cooze, Crack, Crotch, Cunt, Fanny, Fourchette, Front bottom, Labia, Lunchbox, Minge, Muff, Naff, Nympha, Private parts, Privates, Pubes, Pudendum, Puna(a)ni, Puna(a)ny, Pussy, Quim, Secrets, Snatch, Tackle, Tail, Twat, Vagina, Vulva, Wedding tackle, Yoni

**Genitive** Ethical

**Genius** Agathodaimon, Bel esprit, Brain, Daemon, Einstein, Engine, Flash, Ingine, Inspiration, Ka, Maestro, Mastermind, Michaelangelo, Numen, Prodigy, Spirit

**Genome** Prophage

**Genre** Splatterpunk, Tragedy, Variety

**Gent(leman), Gentlemanly, Gentlemen** Amateur, Baboo, Babu, Beau, Caballero, Cavalier, Cocktail, Dandy, Duni(e)wassal, Dunniewassal, Effendi, Esq(uire), Gemman, Gemmen, Herr, Hidalgo, Ja(u)nty, Knight, M, Messrs, Milord, Mister, Mr, Nob, Proteus, Ritter, Runner, Rye, Sahib, Senor, Signor, Sir, Sirra(h), Smuggler, Squire, Sri, Stalko, Stir(rah), Swell, Tea, Toff, Tuan, Valet, Von, Yeoman, Younker

**Genteel** Conish, Polite, Proper, Refined

**Gentian** European, Felwort, Violet, Yellow

**Gentile(s)** Aryan, Ethnic, Goy, Nations, Shi(c)ksa, Uncircumcised

**Gentle(ness)** Amenable, Amenage, Assuage, Bland, Clement, Delicate, Gradual, Grub, Kind, Lamb, Light, Linda, Lynda, Maggot, Mansuete, Mansuetude, Mild, Soft, Sordamente, Tame, Tender

**Gentry** County, Landed, Quality, Squir(e)age

**Gents** Bog, John, Lav, Loo, WC

**Genuflexion** Bend, Curts(e)y, Knee, Kowtow, Salaam

**Genuine** Artless, Authentic, Bona-fide, Dinkum, Dinky-di, Earnest, Echt, Entire, Fair dinkum, Frank, Heartfelt, Honest, Intrinsic, Jannock, Jonnock, Kosher, Legit(imate), McCoy, Nain, Proper, Pucka, Pukka, Pure, Pusser, → REAL, Real McCoy, Right, Simon-pure, Sincere, Square, Sterling, True, Unfeigned, Unsophisticated, Veritable

**Genus** Class, Form, -ia, Mustela

**Geode** Druse

**Geographer, Geography** Chorography, Dialect, Economic, Hakluyt, Linguistic, Mercator, Pausanias, Physical, Political, Strabo

**Geological, Geologist, Geology** Buckland, Dynamic(al), Economic, Erathem, Geodynamics, Geomagnetism, Hard-rock, Historical, Hutton, Isotope, Mineralogy, Phanerozoic, Sedgwick, Seismology, Self-rock, Structural, Tectonics, Werner

**Geometry, Geometrician, Geometer** Affine, Analytical, Conics, Coordinate, Descriptive, Differential, Elliptic, Euclid(ean), Hyperbolic, Moth, Non-Euclidean, Parabolic, Plane, Porism, Projective, Quadrivium, Riemannian, Solid, Spherics, Topologist

**Geordie** Guinea, Tynesider

**George(s)** Autopilot, Best, Borrow, Eliot, Farmer, Lloyd, Orwell, Pilot, Sand

**Georgia(n)** Abkhaz, Ga, Ge, Hanover, Iberian, Mingrel(ian)

**Geraint** Knight

**Geranium** Dove's foot, Rose, Stork's bill, Yellow

**Gerbil** Jird

**Germ(s)** Bacteria, Bug, Culture, Klebsiella, Ovule, Salmonella, Seed, Sperm, Spirilla, Staph(ylococcus), Strep, Swarm-cell, Swarm-spore, Virus, Wheat, Wog, Zyme

**German(y), Germanic** Alemannic, Al(e)main(e), Angle, Anglo-Saxon, Bavarian, Berliner, Blood-brother, Boche, Cimbri, Composer, Cousin, Denglish, Franconian, Frank, Fritz, G, Goth, Habsburg, Hans, Hapsburg, Herr, Hessian, High, Hun, Jerry, Jute, Kaiser, Kraut, Landgrave, Low, Ludwig, Lusatian, Neanderthal, Ossi, Ostrogoth, Otto, Palsgrave, Pennsylvania, Plattdeutsch, Pruce, Prussian, Rolf, Salic, Saxon, Squarehead, Tedesco, Teuton(ic), Vandal, Visigoth, Volsungs, Wessi, Wolfgang

**Germane** Apt, → PERTINENT, Relevant

**Germanium** Ge

**Germ-free** Aseptic

**Germinate** Grow, Pullulate, Sprout

**Gesticulate, Gesticulation, Gesture(s)** Air quotes, Ameslan, Backslap, Beck(on), Chirology, Ch(e)ironomy, Fico, Fig, Gest(e), Harvey Smith, Mannerism, Mime, Motion, Mudra, Nod, Pass, Salaam, Salute, → SIGN, Signal, Snook, Token, V-sign, Wave, Wink

**Get(ting), Get back, Get off, Get(ting) by, Get(ting) on, Get out** Acquire, Advance, Aggravate, Annoy, Attain, Bag, Become, Becoming, Brat, Bring, Buy, Capture, Catch on, Click, Come by, Compare, Cop, Cope, Debark, Derive, Draw, Escape, Fathom, Fet(ch), Fette, Gain, Gee, Land, Learn, Make, Manage, Milk, Net, Niggle, Noy, → OBTAIN, Pass, Peeve, Procure, Progress, Reach, Realise, Recure, Rile, Roil, Secure, See, Shift, Sire, Twig, Understand, Win

**Getaway** Disappearance, Escape, Flight, Vamoose

▷ **Getting** *may indicate* an anagram

**Getting better** Convalescing, Improving, Lysis

**Get-up** Tog(s)

**Geum** Avens

**Gewgaw** Bagatelle, Bauble, Doit, Tat, Trifle

**Geyser** Soffioni, Therm

**Ghana** .gh

**Ghanaian** Ashanti, Fantee, Fanti, Tshi, Twi

**Ghastly** Charnel, Gash, Grim, Gruesome, Hideous, Lurid, Macabre, Pallid, Spectral, Ugsome, Welladay, White

**Gherkin** Cornichon

**Ghetto** Barrio, Slum

**Ghost(ly)** Acheri, Apparition, Apport, Banquo, Caddy, Chthonic, Duende, Duppy, Eerie, Eery, Fantasm, Fetch, Gytrash, Haunt, Hint, Holy, Jumbie, Jumby, Larva(e), Lemur, Malmag, Manifestation, Marley, Masca, No'canny, Paraclete, Pepper's, Phantasm(agoria), Phantom, Poe, Revenant, Sampford, Shade, Shadow, Spectre, Spectrology, →SPIRIT, Spook, Trace, Truepenny, Umbra, Unearthly, Vision, Visitant, Waff, Wraith

**Ghoul(ish)** Fiend, Macabre

**GI** Joe, Yankee

**Giant(ess)** Alcyoneus, Alifanfaron, Anak, Antaeus, Archiloro, Argus, Ascapart, Atlas, Balan, Balor, Bellerus, Blunderbore, Bran, Briareus, Brobdingnagian, Cacus, Colbrand, Colbronde, Colossus, Coltys, Cormoran, Cottus, Cyclop(e)s, Despair, Drow, Enceladus, Ephialtes, Eten, Ettin, Ferragus, Gabbara, Galligantus, Gargantua, Géant, Gefion, Geirred, Gentle, Gigantic, Gog, Goliath, Great, Grim, Harapha, Heimdal(l), Hrungnir, Hymir, Idris, Irus, Jotun(n), Jumbo, Krasir, Large, Lestrigon, Leviathan, Magog, Mammoth, Mimir, Monster, Oak, Og, Ogre, Orion, Otus, Pallas, Pantagruel, Patagonian, Polyphemus, Pope, Red, Rounceval, Skrymir, Slaygood, Talos, Talus, Thrym, Titan, Tityus, Tregeagle, Triton, Troll, Tryphoeus, Typhon, Urizen, Utgard, Ymir, Yowie

**Gibberish** Claptrap, Double Dutch, Drivel, Greek, Jargon, Mumbo-jumbo, Scat

**Gibbet** Gallows, Patibulary, Potence, Ravenstone, Swingle-tree, Tree

**Gibbon(s)** Hoolock, Hylobate, Orlando, Siamang, Stanley, Wou-wou, Wow-wow

**Gibe** Barb, Brocard, Chaff, Fleer, Glike, Jeer, Jibe, Quip, Shy, Slant, Wisecrack

**Gibraltar** Calpe

**Giddy (girl), Giddiness** Capernoitie, Cap(p)ernoity, Dinic, Dizzy, Fisgig, Fishgig, Fizgig, Giglet, Giglot, Glaikit, Glaky, Haverel, Hellicat, Hoity-toity, Jillet, Light, Light-headed, Skipping, Staggers, Sturdy, Turn, Vertigo, Volage(ous), Wheel, Woozy

**Gift(s), Gifted** Ability, Alms, Aptitude, Bef(f)ana, Bequest, Blessing, Blest, Bonbon, Bonsel(l)a, Boon, Bounty, Cadeau, Charism(a), Congiary, Corban, Covermount, Cumshaw, Dash, Deodate, →DONATION, Endow, Etrenne, Fairing, Fidecommissum, Flair, Foy, Free, Freebie, Frumentation, Gab, Garnish, Give, Godsend, Goody-bag, Grant, Gratuity, Greek, Handout, Han(d)sel, Hogmanay, Indian, Knack, Koha, Kula, Lagniappe, Largesse, Legacy, Manna, Mystique, Ne'erday, Nuzzer, Oblation, Offering, Parting, Peace-offering, PET, Potlatch, →PRESENT, Presentation, Prezzie, Propine, Reward, Sop, Stocking-filler, Talent, Theosophy, Tip, Tongues, Treat, Tribute, Wakf, Waqf, Windfall, Xenium

**Gig** Cart, Dennet, Flapper, Hurly-hacket, Moze, Whisk(e)y

**Gigantic** Atlantean, Briarean, Colossal, Goliath, →HUGE, Immense, Mammoth, Monster, Patagonian, Rounceval, Titan, Vast

**Giggle, Giggling** Cackle, Fou rire, Ha, Ha-ha, He-he, Keckle, Simper, Snicker, Snigger, Tehee, Titter

**Gigolo** Gallant, Ladykiller, Pimp, Romeo

**Gilbert** Bab, Gb, White, WS

**Gild(ed), Gilding** Checklaton, Embellish, Enhance, Inaurate, Ormolu, S(c)hecklaton, Vermeil

**Gill(s)** Beard, Branchia, Cart, Ctenidium, Dibranchiate, Jill, Noggin, Spiracle, Trematic

**Gillman's** Aqualung

**Gilpin** Draper, John, Renowned

**Gilt** Elt, Glamour, Ormolu, Parcel, Sow

**Gimcrack** Gewgaw, Tawdry, Trangam

**Gimlet** Auger

**Gimmick** Doodad, Doodah, Hype, Novelty, Ploy, Ruse, Stunt

**Gin** Bathtub, Blue ruin, Geneva, Genever, Hollands, Illaqueable, Juniper, Lubra, Max, Mother's ruin, Noose, Old Tom, Pink, Ruin, Schiedam, Schnapp(s), Sling, Sloe, Snare, Springe, Square-face, Toil, Trap, Trepan, Twankay

**Ginger, Ginger beer** Activist, Amomum, Asarum, Californian bees, Cassumunar, Costus, Curcuma, Enliven, Galanga(l), Galengale, Galingale, Gari, Malaguetta, Nut, Pachak, Pep, Pop, Putchock, Putchuk, Race, Rase, Red(head), Root, Spice, Stem, Turmeric, Wild, Zedoary, Zingiber

**Gingerbread** D(o)um-palm, Lebkuchen, Parkin, Parliament(-cake), Pepper-cake

**Gingivitis** Ulitis

▶ **Gipsy** *see* GYPSY

**Giraffe** Browser, Camelopard, Okapi

**Gird** Accinge, Belt, Equip, Gibe, Jibe, Quip

**Girder** Beam, Binder, Box, H-beam, I-beam, Lattice, Loincloth, Spar

**Girdle** Baldric, Center, Cestus, Chastity, Cincture, Cingulum, Corset, Enzone, Equator, Hippolyte, Hoop, Mitre, Panty, Pectoral, Pelvic, Ring, Sash, Shoulder, Surcingle, Surround, Zona, Zone, Zonulet

**Girl(s), Girly** Backfisch, Ball, Bimbo, Bint, Bird, Bit, Bluebell, Blushet, Bobby-dazzler, Bobby-soxer, Bohemian, Bondmaid, Broad, Burd, Calendar, Call, Charlie, Chick, Chit, Chorus, Coed, Colleen, Cover, Crumpet, Cummer, Cutey, Cutie, Cutty, Dam(o)sel, Deb, Dell, Demoiselle, Dish, Doll, Dollybird, Essex, Filly, Fisgig, Fizgig, Flapper, Flower, Fluff, Fraulein, Frippet, Gaiety, Gal, Gammerstang, Geisha, Gibson, Gill(et), Gilp(e)y, Giselle, Good-time, Gouge, Gretel, Grisette, Hen, Hoiden, Hoyden, Hussy, It, Italian, Judy, Kimmer, Kinchinmort, Ladette, Land, Lass(ock), Lorette, Maid(en), Mauther, Mawr, Mawther, May, Midinette, Miss(y), Moppet, Mor, Mot, Mousmé, Mousmee, Muchacha, Mystery, Nautch, Niece, Number, Nymph(et), Nymphette, Oanshagh, Peach, Peacherino, Petticoat, Piece, Pigeon, Popsy, Poster, Principal, Puss, Quean, Queyn, Quin(i)e, Randy, Riot, Señorita, Sheila, Shi(c)ksa, Shi(c)kse, Sis(s), Smock, Sweater, Tabby, Taupie, Tawpie, Teddy, Teenybopper, Tiller, Tit, Tootsie, Totty, Trull, Vi, Weeny-bopper, Wench, Widgie, Wimp, Wuss

▷ **Girl** *may indicate* a female name

**Girlfriend** Baby, Chérie, Confidante, Date, Flame, Hinny, Lady, Leman, Moll, Peat, Squeeze, Steady, Wag

**Girth** Cinch, Compass, Diameter, Exploitable, Size, Surcingle

**Gismo** Diameter

**Gist** Drift, Essence, Kernel, → NUB, Pith, Substance

**Give(r), Give up, Giving** Abandon, Abstain, Accede, Accord, Administer, Afford, Award, Bend, Bestow, Buckle, Cede, Confiscate, Consign, Contribute, Dative, Dispense, Dole, → DONATE, Drop, Duck, Elasticity, Enable, Endow, Enfeoff, Forswear, Gie, Grant, Hand, Impart, Indian, Jack, Largition, Present, Provide, Render, Resign, Reward, Sacrifice, Sag, Sent, Spring, Stop, Tip, Vacate, Vouchsafe, Yeve, Yield

**Give-away** Freebie, Gift-horse

**Given** If

**Give out** Belch, Bestow, Dispense, Emit, Exude, Peter

**Give over** Cease, Lin

**Glace** Candied

**Glacial, Glaciation** Gunz, Mindel, Riss, Wurm

**Glacier** Aletsch, Crevasse, Drumline, Fox, Franz-Josef, Hanging, Iceberg, Ice-cap, Icefall, Moraine, Moulin, Muir, Rhône, Riss, Serac, Stadial, Stoss, Stoss and lee, Tasman

**Glad(ly), Gladden, Gladness** Cheer, Fain, → HAPPY, Lettice, Lief, Willing

**Glade** La(u)nd

**Gladiator** Retiarius, Samnite, Spartacus

**Glamour, Glamorise, Glamorous** Charm, Glitter(ati), Glitz, Halo, It, Prestige, Ritz, SA, Sex up, Sexy, Spell, Swanky, Tinseltown

**Glamour girl** Cheesecake, Odalisk, Odalisque, Pin-up

**Glance** Allusion, Amoret, Argentite, Blink, Browse, Carom(bole), Copper-head, Coup d'oeil, Deflect, Dekko, Draw, Eld, Eliad, Eye-beam, Galena, Glad eye, Glimpse, Illiad, Inwick, Lustre, Oeillade, Once-over, Peek, → **PEEP**, Ray, Redruthite, Ricochet, Scan, Sheep's eyes, Shufti, Shufty, Side, Silver, Skellie, Skelly, Slant, Snick, Squint, Squiz, Tip, Twire, Vision, Waff

**Gland(s)** Acinus, Adenoid, Adenoma, Adrenal, Apocrine, Bartholin's, Bulbourethral, Clitellum, Colleterial, Conarium, Cowper's, Crypt, Dart-sac, Digestive, Ductless, Duodenal, Eccrine, Endocrine, Epiphysis, Exocrine, Goitre, Green, Holocrine, Hypophysis, Hypothalamus, Ink-sac, Lachrymal, Lacrimal, Liver, Lymph, Mammary, Melbomian, Musk-sac, Nectary, Oil, Osmeterium, Ovary, Pancreas, Paranephros, Parathyroid, Parotid, Parotis, Parotoid, Perineal, Pineal, Pituitary, Pope's eye, Preen, Prostate, Prothoracic, Racemose, Salivary, Salt, Scent, Sebaceous, Sericterium, Shell, Silk, Spermary, Sublingual, Submaxillary, Suprarenal, Sweat, Sweetbread, Tarsel, Tear, Testicle, Testis, Third eye, Thymus, Thyroid, Tonsil, Udder, Uropygial, Vesicle, Vulvovaginal, Zeiss

**Glanders** Farcy

**Glandular (trouble)** Adenitis

**Glare, Glaring** Astare, Blare, Blaze, Dazzle, Egregious, Flagrant, Garish, Gleam, Glower, Gross, Holophotal, Iceblink, Lour, Low(e), Naked, Notorious, Shine, Stare, Vivid, Whally

**Glass(es), Glassware, Glassy** Amen, Ampul(la), Aneroid, Avanturine, Aventurine, Aviator, Baccara(t), Balloon, Barometer, Bell, Bifocals, Bin(ocular)s, Bock, Borosilicate, Bottle, Brimmer, Bumper, Burmese, Burning, Calcedonio, Case, Cheval, Claude Lorraine, Cloche, Cocktail, Cooler, Copita, Cordial, Coupe, Cover, Crookes, Crown, Crystal, Cullet, Cupping, Cut, Dark, Delmonico, Dildo, Diminishing, Eden, Euphon, Favrile, Fibre, Field, Flint, Float, Flute, Foam, Frigger, Frit, Fulgurite, Gauge, Glare, Goblet, Goggles, Granny, Green, Ground, Hand, Handblown, Highball, Horn-rims, Humpen, Hyaline, Iceland agate, Jar, Jena, Jigger, Keltie, Kelty, Lace, Lacy, Lalique, Laminated, Lanthanum, Larking, Latticinio, Lead, Lead crystal, Lens, Liqueur, Liquid, Log, Looking, Lorgnette, Loupe, Lozen(ge), Lunette, Magma, Magnifying, Metal, Mica, Middy, Milk, Millefiori, Minimizing, Mirror, Moldavite, Monocle, Mousseline, Multiplying, Murr(h)ine, Muscovy, Musical, Nitreous, Object, Obsidian, One-way, Opal(ine), Opera, Optical, Ovonic, Pane, Parison, Paste, Pearlite, Pebble, Peeper, Pele, Pele's hair, Perlite, Perspective, Pier, Pince-nez, Pinhole, Pinta, Pitchstone, Plate, Pocket, Pon(e)y, Pressed, Prism, Prospective, Prunt, Psyche, Pyrex®, Quarrel-pane, Quarry, Quartz, Reducing, Roemer, Ruby, Rummer, Safety, Schmelz, Schooner, Seam, Seidel, Shard, Sheet, Silex, Silica, Sleever, Slide, Sliver, Smalt(o), Snifter, Soluble, Specs, → **SPECTACLES**, Spun, Stained, Stein, Stem, Stemware, Stone, Storm, Strass, Straw, Sun, Supernaculum, Tachilite, Tachylite, Tachylyte, Tektite, Telescope, Tiffany, Tiring, Toilet, Trifocals, Triplex®, Tumbler, Uranium, Varifocals, Venetian, Venice, Vernal, Vita, Vitrail, Vitreous, Vitreous silica, Vitrescent, Vitro-di-trina, Volcanic, Watch, Water, Waterford, Weather, Window (pane), Wine, Wire, Yard of ale

**Glass-gall** Sandiver

**Glass-house** Conservatory, Orangery

**Glassite** Sandemania

**Glass-maker** Annealer, Blower, Glazier, Lalique, Pontie, Pontil, Ponty, Puntee, Punty

**Glaze(d), Glazing** Aspic, Ciré, Clair de lune, Coat, Double, Eggwash, Film, Flambé, Frit, Glost, Ice, Majolica, Peach-blow, Salt, Sancai, Slip, Tammy, Temmoku, Varnish, Velatura, Vitreous

**Gleam(ing)** Aglow, Blink, Flash, Glint, Glisten, Glitter, Gloss, Leme, Light, Lustre, Ray, Relucent, Sheen, Shimmer, → **SHINE**, Spotless

**Glean(er)** Gather, Harvest, Lease, Stibbler

**Glee** Delight, Exuberance, Hysterics, Joy, Madrigal, Mirth, Song

**Glen** Affric, Ghyll, Gill, Rushy, Silicon, Strath, Vale

**Glib** Flip, Pat, Slick, Smooth

**Glide(r), Glideaway, Gliding** Aquaplane, Aviette, Chassé, Coast, Elapse, Float, Illapse, Lapse, Luge, Microlight, Monoplane, Off, On, Parascend, Portamento, Rogallo, Sail, Sailplane, Sashay, Scorrendo, Scrieve, Skate, Ski, Skim, Skite, Skyte, Sleek, Slide, Slip, Slur, Swim, Volplane

**Glimmer(ing)** Gleam, Glent, Glint, Glow, Inkling, Light, Stime, Styme, Twinkle, Wink

**Glimpse** Aperçu, Flash, Fleeting, Glance, Gledge, Glisk, Peep, Stime, Styme, Waff, Whiff

**Glint** Flash, Shimmer, → SPARKLE, Trace, Twinkle

**Glisten(ing)** Ganoid, Glint, Sheen, Shimmer, → SHINE, Sparkle

**Glitch** Blip, Misprint

**Glitter(ing)** Asterism, Clinquant, Garish, Gemmeous, Glee, Paillon, Scintillate, Sequin, Spang(le), Sparkle, Tinsel

**Gloaming** Twilight

**Gloat(ing)** Crow, Drool, Enjoy, Exult, Schadenfreude

**Globe, Global, Globule** Artichoke, Ball, Bead, Celestial, Drop, Earth, Orb, Pandemic, Pearl, Planet, Shot, Sphear, Sphere, Tectonic, Terrestrial, Ubiquitous, World

**Globulin** Legumin, Protein

**Gloom(y)** Atrabilious, Benight, Blues, Cheerless, Cimmerian, Cloud, Crepuscular, Damp, Dark, → DESPAIR, Dingy, Dire, Disconsolate, Dismal, Dool(e), Downbeat, Drab, Drear, Drumly, Dump(s), Dyspeptic, Erebus, Feral, Funereal, Glum, Grey, Grim, Half light, Louring, Lowery, Mirk, Misery, Mopish, Morbid, Morne, Morose, Mumps, Murk(y), Night(fall), Obscurity, Overcast, Sable, Sad, Saturnine, Sepulchral, Shadow, Solein, Solemn, → SOMBRE, Sourpuss, Stygian, Subfusc, Sullen, Surly, Tenebrious, Tenebrose, Tenebrous, Unlit, Wan

**Glorification, Glorify** Aggrandise, Apotheosis, Avatar, Bless, → EXALT, Extol, Halo, Laud, Lionise, Praise, Radiance, Roose, Splendour

**Glorious, Gloria, Glory** Chorale, Crow, Crowning, Grand, Halo, Hosanna, Ichabod, Knickerbocker, Kudos, Lustre, Magnificent, Nimbus, Signal, Strut, Sublime, Twelfth

**Glory-pea** Kaka-beak, Kaka-bill, Kowhai

**Gloss(y)** Ciré, Enamel, Gild, Glacé, Interpret, Japan, Lip, Lustre, Mag, Patina, → POLISH, Postillate, Sheen, Sleek, Sleekit, Slick, Slide, Slur, Supercalendered, Veneer, Wetlook, Whitewash

**Glossary** Catalogue, Clavis, Index, K'thibh

**Gloucester** Cheese

**Glove** Boxing, Cestus, Chevron, Dannock, Gage, Gauntlet, Kid, Mermaid's, Mitten, Mousquetaire, Muffle, Oven, Rubber, Velvet

**Glow(er), Glowing, Glowworm** Aflame, Ashine, Aura, Bloom, Burn, Calescence, Candent, Candescence, Candlelight, Corona, Emanate, Fire, Firefly, Flush, Foxfire, Gegenschein, Gleam, Glimmer, Glisten, Halation, Iceblink, Incandescence, Lambent, Lamp-fly, Leam, LED, Leme, Luculent, Luminesce, Lustre, Noctilucent, Perspire, Phosphorescence, Radiant, Radiate, Reflet, Ruddy, Rushlight, Rutilant, Shine, Snowblink, Sullen, Translucent, → WARMTH

**Glucin(i)um** Gl

**Glucose, Glucoside** Aesculin, Amygdalin, Dextrose, Digitalin, Indican, Maltose, Salicin(e), Saponin, Solanine

**Glue(y)** Affix, Alkyd, Araldite®, Bee, Cement, Colloidal, Epoxy, Fish, Gelatin(e), Gunk, Hot-melt, Ichthyocolla, Isinglass, Marine, Paste, Propolis, Resin, Rice, Size, Solvent, Spetch, Uhu®

**Glum** Dour, Livery, Lugubrious, Moody, Morose, Ron, Solemn, Sombre

**Glut** Choke, Gorge, Plethora, Sate, Satiate, Saturate, Surfeit

**Gluten, Glutinous** Goo, Ropy, Seiten, Sticky, Tar, Viscid, Zymome

**Glutton(ous), Gluttony** Bellygod, Carcajou, Cormorant, Edacity, Feaster, Free-liver, Gannet, Gorb, Gourmand, Greedyguts, Gulosity, Gutser, Gutsy, Gutzer, Hog, Lurcher, Pig, Ratel, Scoffer, Sin, Trencherman, Trimalchio, Wolverine

**Glyceride, Glycerine** Ester, Olein, Palmitin

**Glycoside** Hesperidin

**Gnarl(ed)** Knot, Knuckly, Knur, Nob

**Gnash(ing)** Bruxism, Champ, Grate

**Gnat** Culex, Culicidae, Midge, Mosquito

**Gnaw(ing)** Corrode, Erode, Fret, Lagomorph, Rodent

**Gnome** Adage, Bank-man, Chad, Cobalt, Epigram, Europe, Financier, Garden, Hobbit, Kobold, Maxim, Motto, Proverb, Saw, Sprite, Zurich

**Gnostic(ism)** (A)eon, Archontic, Cainite, Mand(a)ean, Marcionism, Ophite, Sabian, Tsabian, Zabian

**Gnu** Brindled, Horned horse, White-tailed, Wildebeest

**Go, Going (after, ahead, away, back, for, off, on, through, up, etc)** Advance, Afoot, Anabasis, Animation, Apage, Ascent, Assail, Attempt, Attend, Bash, Begone, Betake, Bing, Bout, Brio, Choof, Chunter, Clamber, Comb, Continuance, Crack, Deal, Depart, Die, Do, Effort, Energy, Fare, Function, Gae, Gang, Gaun, Gee, Gonna, Green (light), Hamba, Hark, Heavy, Hence, Hie, Hup, Imshi, Imshy, Ish, Kick, → **LEAVE**, March, Match, Move, Off, OK, Path, Pee, Pep, Perpetual, Ply, Quit, Raik, Repair, Resort, Resume, Run, Satanas, Scat, Scram, Segue, Shoo, Shot, Skedaddle, Snick-up, Sour, Spank, Spell, Square, Stab, Success, Tag along, Traipse, Transitory, Travel, Trine, Try, Turn, Vamo(o)se, Vanish, Verve, Via, Viable, Vim, Wend, Work, Yead, Yede, Yeed, Zap, Zest, Zing, Zip

**Goad** Ankus, Brod, Gad, Impel, Incite, → **NEEDLE**, Prod, Provoke, Rowel, Spur, Stimulate, Stimulus, Taunt

**Goal(posts)** Aim, Ambition, Basket, Bourn(e), Cage, Decider, Destination, Dool, Dream, Drop, Dule, End, Ettle, Field, Golden, Grail, Hail, Home, Horme, Hunk, Intent, Limit, Mark, Mission, Moksha, Net, Own, Score, Silver, Tap-in, Target, Tip-in, Touch-in, Ultima Thule, Uprights

**Goalless** Idle

**Goat(-like)** Alpine, Amalthea, Angora, Antelope, Antilope, Billy, Bok, Bucardo, Buck, Caprine, Cashmere, Cilician, Gait, Gate, Giddy, Goral, Hircine, Ibex, Izard, Kashmir, Kid, Libido, Markhor, Mountain, Nan(ny), Nubian, Rocky Mountain, Roue, Ruminant, Saanen, Sassaby, Serow, Serpent-eater, Steenbok, Steinbock, Tahr, Takin, Tehr, Thar, Toggenburg

**Goatsucker** Fern-owl, Nightjar

**Gob(bet)** Bespit, Clot, Dollop, Mouth, Sailor, Spit, Tar, Yap

**Gobble** Bolt, Devour, Gorge, Gulch, Gulp, Scarf, Slubber, Wolf

**Gobbledegook** Officialese

**Gobelin** Tapestry

**Go-between** Agency, Broker, Factor, Intermediate, Link, Mediate, Middleman, Pandarus, Pander, Shuttle

**Goblet** Chalice, Grail, Hanap

**Goblin** Banshee, Bargaist, Barg(h)est, Bodach, Bogey, Bogle, Bogy, Brownie, Bucca, Bull-beggar, Croquemitaine, Empusa, Erl-king, Esprit follet, Genie, Gnome, Gremlin, Knocker, Kobold, Lob-lie-by-the-fire, Lubberfiend, Lutin, Nis(se), Phooka, Phynnodderree, Pooka, Pouke, Puca, Puck, Pug, Red-cap, Red-cowl, Shellycoat, → **SPRITE**, Troll, Trow

**Gobstopper** Everlasting, Lollipop

**Goby** Dragonet

**God(s)** All-seer, Amen, Ancient of Days, → **DEITY**, Deus, Di, Divine, First Cause, Gallery, Gracious, Holy One, Household, Immortals, Inner Light, Light, Maker, Od(d), Olympian, Prime Mover, Principle, Providence, Serpent, Shechina, Soul, Supreme Being, The Creator, Tin, Trinity, Truth, Unknown, Vanir, War, Water

## GODS

*1 letter:*
D

*2 letters:*
An
As
Ra
Re

*3 letters:*
Anu
Bel
Bes
Dis
Gad
Geb
Jah
Keb
Lar
Lir
Lug
Mab
Mot
Pan
Seb
Set
Sol
Tiu
Tiw
Tum
Tyr

*4 letters:*
Abba
Agni
Aitu
Amun
Apis
Ares
Asur
Aten
Atum
Baal
Brag
Bran
Cama
Deva
Dieu
Eros
Faun
Frey
Joss

Kama
Kami
Llyr
Loki
Lugh
Mars
Mors
Nebo
Odin
Ptah
Rama
Seth
Siva
Soma
Thor
Tyrr
Yama
Zeus

*5 letters:*
Aegir
Aesir
Allah
Ammon
Brage
Bragi
Comus
Cupid
Dagan
Dagon
Donar
Freyr
Haoma
Horus
Hymen
Indra
Janus
Khnum
Liber
Lludd
Mimir
Momus
Njord
Numen
Orcus
Orixa
Pales
Picus
Pluto
Rudra
Satyr
Sebek

Shiva
Sinis
Surya
Thoth
Titan
Wodan
Woden
Wotan
Yahve
Yahwe

*6 letters:*
Adonai
Adonis
Aeolus
Amen-ra
Amon-ra
Anubis
Apollo
Ashtar
Asshur
Avatar
Balder
Boreas
Brahma
Cabiri
Chemos
Clotho
Cronus
Delian
Elohim
Faunus
Ganesa
Ganesh
Garuda
HaShem
Helios
Hermes
Hughie
Hypnos
Kronos
Mahoun
Mammon
Marduk
Mexitl
Mextli
Mithra
Moerae
Molech
Moloch
Nereus
Njorth

Oannes
Orisha
Ormazd
Ormuzd
Osiris
Panisc
Panisk
Plutus
Rimmon
Saturn
Somnus
Tammuz
Teraph
Teshup
Thamiz
Thunor
Triton
Uranus
Varuna
Vishnu
Vulcan
Yahweh
Zombie

*7 letters:*
Alastor
Alpheus
Angus Og
Anteros
Bacchus
Bhagwan
Chemosh
Daikoku
Ganesha
Goddess
Hanuman
Heimdal
Jehovah
Jupiter
Krishna
Kuan Yin
Kwan Yin
Mahound
Mercury
Mithras
Neptune
Nisroch
Oceanus
Penates
Phoebus
Priapus
Proteus

Rameses
Sarapis
Sat Guru
Serapis
Setebos
Shamash
Silenus
Thammuz
Zagreus

**8 letters:**
Achelous
Dionysus
Heimdall
Hyperion
Kamadeva
Mahadeva

Morpheus
Mulciber
Nataraja
Pantheon
Poseidon
Quirinus
Silvanus
Sylvanus
Terminus
Thanatos
Trimurti
Wahiguru
Zephyrus

**9 letters:**
All-father
Asclepius

Fabulinus
Heimdallr
Jagganath
Promachos
Tetragram
Thunderer
Vertumnus
Zernebock

**10 letters:**
Ahura Mazda
Demogorgon
Elegabalus
Hephaestus
Hephaistos
Juggernaut
Karttikaya

Mumbo-jumbo
Prometheus
Trophonius

**11 letters:**
Adrammelech
Aesculapius
Bodhisattva

**12 letters:**
Quetzalcoati
Trismegistus

**14 letters:**
Tetragrammaton

**God-bearing** Deiparous
**Goddess(es)** Divine, Green, Muse, Sea nymph

## GODDESSES

**2 letters:**
Ge

**3 letters:**
Ate
Eos
Hel
Mut
Nox
Nut
Nyx
Ops
Pax

**4 letters:**
Dian
Eris
Gaea
Gaia
Hera
Idun
Iris
Isis
Juno
Kali
Leda
Leto
Luna
Maat
Maut

Nike
Norn
Pele

Rhea
Sita
Thea

**5 letters:**
Aruru
Ceres
Diana
Dione
Durga
Erato
Flora
Freya
Grace
Horae
Houri
Hulda
Iduna
Irene
Kotys
Moera
Moira
Pales
Tanit
Terra
Tyche
Ushas

Venus
Vesta

**6 letters:**
Aglaia
Ashnan
Athene
Aurora
Bastet
Cybele
Cyrene
Eastre
Freyja
Frigga
Graeae
Graiae
Hathor
Hecate
Hertha
Hestia
Huldar
Hyaeia
Idalia
Ishtar
Ithunn
Lucina
Pallas
Parcae
Phoebe
Pomona

Satyra
Selene
Semele
Tellus
Tethys
Thalia
Themis
Thetis

**7 letters:**
Artemis
Astarte
Astraea
Bellona
Cotytto
Cynthia
Demeter
Fortuna
Kotytto
Lakshmi
Megaera
Minerva
Nemesis
Nepthys
Parvati
Sabrina
Strenia
Victory

| **8 letters:** | Victoria | Ashtoreth | **10 letters:** |
|---|---|---|---|
| Cloacina | Walkyrie | Eumenides | Amphitrite |
| Cytherea | | Mnemosyne | Proserpina |
| Libitina | **9 letters:** | Sarasvati | Proserpine |
| Rhiannon | Aphrodite | | |
| Valkyrie | Ashtaroth | | |

---

**Godfather, Godmother** Capo, Cummer, Fairy, Gossip, Kimmer, Rama, Sponsor, Woden

**Godless** Agnostic, Atheistic, Atheous, Impious, Profane, Unholy

**Godly, Godliness** Deist, Devine, Devout, Holy, Pious, Sanctity

**Godown** Hong

**God-willing** Deo volente, DV, Inshallah, Mashallah

**Go-getter** Arriviste, Hopeful, Hustler

**Goggle(s)** Gaze, Snow-eyes, Stare

**Go-go** Alert

**Going wrong** Aglee, Agley, Misfiring

▷ **Going wrong** *may indicate* an anagram

**Goitre** Derbyshire neck, Exophthalmic, Graves' disease, Struma

**Gold(en)** Age, Amber, Apple, Ass, Au, Aureate, Auriel, Auriferous, Auriol, Aurum, Bendigo, Bough, Bull, Bullion, Bull's eye, California, Chryselephantine, Doubloon, Dutch, Eagle, Electron, Electrum, Emerods, Fairy, Fiftieth, Filigree, Filled, Fleece, Fool's, Free, Fulminating, Gate, Gilden, Gule, Handshake, Hind, Horde, Horn, Ingot, King of metals, Kolar, Leaf, Lingot, Moidore, Mosaic, Muck, Nugget, Oaker, Obang, Ochre, Ophir, Or, Oreide, Ormolu, Oroide, Pistole, Placer, Pyrites, Red, Reef, Rolled, Silence, Silver-gilt, Sol, Soneri, Standard, Stream, Stubborn, Taelbar, Talent, Talmi, Thrimsa, Tolosa, Treasury, Venice, Virgin, Wash-up, White, Witwatersrand, Xanthe, Yellow

**Gold-digger** Forty-niner, Prospector

**Golden fleece** Phrixus

**Goldfield** Rand

**Goldfinch** Charm, Chirm, Redcap

**Gold leaf** Ormolu

**Gold rush** Kalgoorlie, Klondike

**Goldsmith** Cellini, Fabergé, Hilliard, Oliver

**Golf (ball)** Best ball, Better-ball, Clock, Crazy, Four-ball, Foursome, G, Gutta, Matchplay, Medal play, Miniature, Repaint, Round, Stableford, Texas scramble

**Golfer** Alliss, Braid, Cotton, Els, Faldo, Hogan, Lyle, Pivoter, Rees, Roundsman, Seve, Snead, Teer, Texas scramble, Tiger Woods, Trevino, Wolstenholme, Yipper

**Goliath** Giant

**Golly** Cor, Crumbs, Gosh, Lummy

**Gondolier** Balloonist, Bargee, Marco

**Gone** Ago, Dead, Defunct, Deid, Extinct, Napoo, Out, Past, Ygo(e), Yod

▷ **Gone off** *may indicate* an anagram

**Gone west** Had it

**Gong** Bell, DSO, →**MEDAL**, Tam-tam, VC

**Gonorrhoea** Clap

**Goo(ey)** Gleet, Gloop, Gum, Gunge, Poise, Squidgy, Treacle, Ulmin

**Goober** Monkey nut

**Good(ness), Goody(-goody)** Agatha, Agathodaimon, Altruism, Angelic, Ascertained, Bad, Banner, Behoof, Bein, Benefit, Blesses, Blinder, Bon(ism), Bonzer, Bosker, Bounty, Braw, Brod, Budgeree, By George, Canny, Castor, Civil, Classy, Clinker, Common, Coo, Cool, Corker, Crack(ing), Credit, Crikey, Dab, Dandy, Def, Divine, Dow, Enid, Estimable, Fancy that, Fantabulous, Favourable, Finger lickin', First-class, G, Gear, Giffen, Glenda, Gold, Gosh, Guid, Holy cow, Hooray, Humdinger, Lekker, Lois, Lor, Ma foi, Mega,

Merchandise, Merit, Moral, Neat, Nobility, → **NO GOOD**, Pi, Plum, Prime, Proper, Pucka, Pukka, Purler, Rattling, Rectitude, Riddance, Right(eous), Rum, St, Sake, Salutary, Samaritan, Sanctity, Slap-up, Smashing, Sound, Spiffing, Splendid, Suitable, Super, Superb, Taut, Teacher's pet, Tollol, Topping, Valid, Virtue, Virtuous, Weal, Welfare, Whacko, Wholesome, Worthy, Wrong'un

**Goodbye** Addio, Adieu, Adios, Aloha, Apopemptic, Arrivederci, Cheerio, Cheers, Ciao, Congé, Farewell, Haere ra, Hamba kahle, Hooray, Hooroo, Later, Sayonara, See-you, So long, Tata, Toodle-oo, Toodle-pip, Vale

**Good evening** Den

**Goodfellow** Brick, Puck, Robin, Samaritan, Worthy

**Good-for-nothing** Bum, Donnat, Donnot, Dud, Idler, Layabout, Lorel, Lorrell, Losel, Napoo, Naught, Scal(l)awag, Scallywag, Scant o'grace, Sculpin, Shot-clog, Stiff, Useless, Vaurien, Waff, Waster, Wastrel

**Good Friday** Parasceve, Pasch of the Cross

**Good-humour(ed), Good-natured** Amiable, Bonhomie, Clever, Gruntled, Kind, Mellow

**Good-looking** Bon(n)ie, Bonny, Bonwie, Comely, Fair, Handsome, Personable, Pretty, Telegenic, Wally, Weel-fa(u)st

**Good news** Evangel

**Good number** Thr(e)ave

**Good order** Eutaxy, Shipshape

**Goods** Bona, Brown, Cargo, Commodities, Consumer, Disposable, Durable, Durables, Fancy, Flotsam, Freight, Futures, Gear, Hardware, Insight, Ironware, Lagan, Lay-away, Line, Luxury, Merchandise, Piece, Products, Property, Schlock, Soft, Sparterie, Stock, Truck, Wares, White

**Good time** Craic

**Goodwill** Amity, Bonhom(m)ie, Favour, Gree

**Goof** Gaffe

**Goofy** Simple-minded

**Goon** Ape, Bentine, Bluebottle, Eccles, Milligan, Secombe, Sellers

**Goop** Ooze

**Goose, Geese** Anserine, Barnacle, Bernicle, Blue, Brent, Canada, Cape Barren, Colonial, Daftie, Ember, Gaggle, Gander, Gannet, Golden, Greylag, Grope, Harvest, Hawaiian, Idiot, Iron, Juggins, MacFarlane's, Magpie, Michaelmas, Mother, Nana, Nene, Pink-footed, Pygmy, Quink, Roger, Saddleback, Silly, Simpleton, Skein, Snow, Solan, Strasbourg, Stubble, → **STUPID PERSON**, Swan, Team, Wav(e)y, Wawa, Wedge, Whitehead

**Gooseberry** Cape, Chaperon(e), Chinese, Coromandel, Detrop, Fool, Gog, Groser(t), Groset, Grossart, Grozer, Honey blob, Kiwi, Physalis, Tomato

**Gooseflesh** Horripilation

**Goosefoot** Allgood, Amarantaceae, Beet, Blite, Fat-hen, Mercury, Orache, Quinoa, Saltbush

**Gooseherd** Quill-driver

**Gopher** Camass-rat, Minnesota, Pocket

**Gordian** Knot

**Gordon** Chinese, Flash, Rioter

**Gore, Gory** Blood, Cloy, Danse macabre, Gair, Horn, Inset, Toss

**Gorge(s)** Abyss, Arroyo, Barranca, Barranco, Canyon, Carnarvon, Chasm, Cheddar, Cleft, Couloir, Cram, Defile, Donga, Flume, Gap, Ghyll, Glut, Grand Canyon, Gulch, Ironbridge, Iron Gate, Katherine, Khor, Kloof, Lin(n), Nala, Nalla(h), Nulla(h), Olduvai, Overeat, Overfeed, Pass, Pig, Ravine, Snarf, Staw, → **STUFF**, Throat, Tire, Tums, Valley, Valley of the Kings, Yosemite

**Gorgeous** Delectable, Dishy, Dreamboat, Eye-candy, Grand, Ravishing, Splendid, Superb

**Gorgon** Euryale, Medusa, Ogress, Stheno

**Gorilla** Heavy, → **MONKEY**, Silverback, Whoop

**Gorse** Broom, Furze, Gosse, Ulex, Whin

**Gosh** Begad, Begorra, Blimey, Coo, Cor, Crumbs, Ecod, Fancy, Gadzooks, Gee, Golly, Gracious, Gum, Heavens, Lor, My, Och, Odsbobs, Odso, Phew, Really, Shucks

**Gospel(s), Gospeller** Apocryphal, Creed, Diatessaron, Evangel, Fact, John, Kerygma, Luke, Mark, Matthew, Nicodemus, Prosperity, Protevangelium, Synoptic, Truth, Waldensian

**Gossamer(y)** Araneous, Byssoid, Cobwebby, Gauzy

**Gossip** Ana(s), Aunt, Backbite, Blether, Cackle, Cat, Causerie, Chat, Chin, Chitchat, Clash, Clash-me-clavers, Claver, Cleck, Clish-clash, Clishmaclaver, Clype, Confab, Cosher, Coze, Crack, Cummer, Dirt, Flibbertigibbet, Furphy, Gab(nash), Gabfest, Gas, Gash, Goster, Gup, Hearsay, Hen, Jaw, Loose-tongued, Maundrel, Moccasin telegraph, Nashgab, Natter, Newsmonger, Noise, On dit, Pal, Personalist, Prate, Prattle, Prose, Quidnunc, Reportage, Rumour(monger), Scandal(monger), Schmooze, Scuttlebutt, Shmoose, Shmooze, Sweetie-wife, Tabby(cat), Talk(er), Tattle, Tattletale, Tibby, Tittle(-tattle), Twattle, Whisper, Yak, Yatter, Yenta

**Got** Gat, Obtained, Won

**Goth(ic)** Alaric, American, International, Lurid, Moesia

**Gothamite** Abderian, New Yorker

**Gouge** Chisel, Groove, Scoop

**Gourd** Bottle, Calabash, Courgette, Dishcloth, Guiro, Hercules' club, Loofa, Maraca, Marrow, Melon, Monkeybread, Pumpkin, Squash, Zucchini

**Gourmand, Gourmet** Aesthete, Apicius, Chowhound, →EPICURE, Free-liver, Gastronome, Gastrosopher, Lickerish, Table, Trencherman, Ventripotent

**Gout(y)** Chalkstone, Chiragra, Hamarthritis, Podagra, Taste, Tophus

**Govern(or), Government** Adelantado, Administer, Ag(h)a, Agricola, Alderman, Amban, Amman, Amtman, ANC, Andocracy, Archology, Aristocracy, Autarchy, Autocrat, Autonomy, Bahram, Ban, Bashaw, Beehive, Beg, Beglerbeg, Bencher, Bey, Board, Bridler, Bureaucracy, Burgrave, Cabinet, Caciquism, Caliphate, Caretaker, Cassio, Castellan, Catapan, Cham, Circar, Classis, Clive, Coalition, Command, Commonwealth, Condominium, Congress, Consistorian, Constable, Constitution, Consulate, Cybernetic, Darogha, Democracy, Dergue, Despotism, Despotocracy, Dey, Diarchy, Dictatorship, Dinarchy, Directoire, Directory, Domain, Dominate, Dominion, Downing St, Duarchy, Dulocracy, Duumvirate, Dyarchy, Dynast, Earl, Ecclesiarchy, Eminent domain, Empery, Eparch, Ergatocracy, Escapement, Ethnarch, Exarch, Fascism, Federal, G, Gauleiter, Gerontocracy, Gov, Grieve, Gubernator, Guv, Gynarchy, Hagiarchy, Hagiocracy, Hague, Hajjaz, Hakim, Harmost, HE, Helm, Heptarchy, Hexarchy, Hierocracy, Honcho, Hospodar, Imperialism, Ins, Inspector, Isocracy, Junta, Kaimakam, Kakistocracy, Kawanatanga, Kebele, Kemalism, Khalifate, Khan, Kremlin, Legate, Local, Majlis, Majorism, Matriarchy, Monarchy, Monocracy, Mudir, Nabob, Naik, Nawab, Nomarch, Nomocracy, Ochlocracy, Oireachtas, Oligarchy, Optic®, Pa, Pacha, Padishah, Pasha, Pater, Patriarchism, Pentarch, Père, Petticoat, Physiocracy, Placemen, Plutocracy, Podesta, Politics, Polity, Polyarchy, Pontius Pilate, Porte, Power, Priest-king, Proconsul, Propraetor, Proveditor, Provedor(e), Providor, Ptochocracy, Quadrumvirate, Quirinal, Raj, Realpolitik, Rection, Rector, Rectrix, Regency, Regié, Regime(n), Regulator, Reign, Rein, Republican, Ride, →RULE, Satrap, Senate, Serkali, Shogun, Signoria, Sircar, Sirkar, Soviet, Stad(t)holder, Stakhanovism, Statecraft, Stear, Steer, Stratocracy, Subadar, Subah(dar), Sway, Technocracy, Tetrarchy, Thalassocracy, Thalattocracy, Thatcherism, Thearchy, Theocracy, Theonomy, Third Republic, Timocracy, Totalitarianism, Triarchy, Triumvirate, Tuchun, Tyranny, Vaivode, Vali, Viceregal, Viceroy, Vichy, Vichyssois(e), Voivode, Wali, Warden, Wealsman, Whitehall, White House, Witan, Woiwode

**Governess** Duenna, Eyre, Fraulein, Griffin, Mademoiselle, Prism, Vicereine

**Government revenue** Jaghir(e), Jagir

**Gown** Banian, Banyan, Djellaba(h), Dressing, Empire, Geneva, Green, Jellaba(h), Johnny, Kimono, Kirtle, Manteau, Manto, Mantua, Manty, Mazarine, Morning, Mother Hubbard, Negligee, Peignoir, Polonaise, Robe, Sack, Silk, Slammakin, Slammerkin, Slop, Stola, Stuff, Tea, Tunic, Wrap(per)

**Grab** Accost, Annexe, Areach, Bag, Clutch, Cly, Collar, Glaum, Grapnel, Hold, Holt, Nab, Rap, Reach, Seise, Seize, Snaffle, → **SNATCH**, Steal, Swipe, Usurp

**Gracchi** Jewels

**Grace(s), Graceful** Aglaia, Airy, Amazing, Amnesty, Anna, Bad, Beauty, Become, Benediction, Ben(t)sh, Bethankit, Blessing, Charis(ma), Charites, Charity, Cooperating, Darling, Dr, Elegance, Eloquent, Euphrosyne, Fluent, Gainly, Genteel, Genty, Godliness, Grazioso, Handsome, Honour, Light, Mense, Mercy, Molinism, Mordent, Omnium, Ornament, Plastique, Poise, Polish, Pralltriller, Prayer, Sacrament, Saving, Spirituelle, Streamlined, Style, Svelte, Thalia, Thanks, Thanksgiving, Tuesday, WG, Willowy

**Graceless** Gauche

**Grace note** Nachschlag

**Gracious** Benign, By George, Charismatic, Gee, Generous, Good, Handsome, Hend, Mamma mia, Merciful, Polite

**Gradation** Ablaut, Cline, Degree, Nuance, Stage

**Grade, Gradient** Alpha, Analyse, Angle, Assort, Beta, Bubs, Class(ify), Conservation, Dan, Degree, Delta, Echelon, Etat, Gamma, Geothermal, Gon, Gride, Hierarchy, Inclination, Kyu, Lapse, Measure, Order, Ordinary, Pressure, Rank, Reserve, Score, Seed, Slope, Stage, Standard, Status, Temperature, Thermocline, Tier

**Gradual** Gentle, Grail, Imperceptible, Inchmeal, Piecemeal, Slow

**Graduate, Graduation** Alumnus, BA, Bachelor, Calibrate, Capping, Classman, Incept, Laureateship, Licentiate, LlB, MA, Master, Nuance, Optime, Ovate

**Graffiti** Bomb, Doodle, Tag, Tagger

**Graft** Anaplasty, Autoplasty, Boodle, Bribery, Bud, Bypass, Cion, Cluster, Crown, Dishonesty, Ditch, Dub, Enarch, Enrace, Flap, Hard, Heteroplasty, Imp, Implant, Inarch, Inoculate, Payola, Pomato, Racket, Scion, Shoot, Sien(t), Skin, Slip, Syen, Transplant, Whip, Ympe

**Grail** Chalice, Cup, Sangraal, Sangrail, Sangreal

**Grain(y), Grains** Bajra, Bajree, Bajri, Barley(corn), Bear, Bere, Boll, Bran, Cereal, Corn, Couscous, Crop, Curn, Curn(e)y, Cuscus, Distillers', D(o)urra, Dye, Extine, Floor, Frumentation, Gr, Graddan, Granule, Grit(s), Groats, Grout, Grumose, Intine, Kaoliang, Knaveship, Malaguetta, Malt, Mashlam, Mashlin, Mashloch, Mashlum, Maslin, Mealie, Millet, Milo, Minim, Mongcorn, Oats, Orzo, Panic(k), Pannick, Pickle, Pinole, Pollen, Polynology, Popcorn, Proso, Psyllium, Puckle, Quarter, Quinoa, Rabi, Raggee, Raggy, Ragi, Rhy, Rye, Sand, Scruple, Seed, Semolina, Semsem, Sorghum, Spelt, Statolith, Tef(f), Thirlage, Tola, Touch, Wheat, Wholemeal

▷ **Grain** *may indicate* wood

**Gram** Black, Chich, Chick-pea, Green, Teen, Tene, Urd

**Grammar(ian), Grammatical** Ablative absolute, Accidence, Amphibology, Anacoluthia, Anacoluthon, Anaphora, Anastrophe, Case, Cataphora, Categorical, Causative, Deixis, Donat, Donet, Generative, Gr, Inessive, Linguistics, Montague, Paradigm, Parataxis, Paucal, Pivot, Primer, Priscianist, Priscianus, Protasis, Relational, Scholiast, Stratificational, Syndetic, Syndeton, Synectics, Synesis, Syntax, Systemics, Tagmeme, Transformational, Trivium, Typto, Universal, Valency

**Gramophone** Record player, Victrolla®

**Grampus** Orc(a), Risso's dolphin, Thresher-whale, Whale

**Granary** Barn, Girnel, Silo

**Grand(eur), Grandiose** Big, Canyon, Concert, Epical, Flugel, G, Gorgeous, Guignol, High-faluting, Hotel, Imposing, K, La(h)-di-da(h), Long, Lordly, Magnificent, Majestic, Megalomania, Noble, Overblown, Palatial, Piano(forte), Pompous, Regal, Splendid, Stately, Stoor, Stour, Stowre, Sture, Sublime, Superb, Swell, Tour

**Grandchild** Mokopuna, Niece, Oe, Oy(e)

**Grandee** Adelantado, Aristo, Don, Magnifico

**Grandfather** Ancient, Avital, Clock, Goodsire, Gramps, Gudesire, Gutcher, Luckie-dad, Oldster, Old-timer, Oupa

**Grandmother** Babushka, Beldam, Gran(nie), Granny, Luckie, Moses, Nan(a), Nokomis, Ouma

**Grandparent(al)** Aval, Avital

**Grand Prix** Race(-cup)

**Grandsire** Peal

**Grange** Moated

**Granite** Aberdeen, Chinastone, Graphic, Greisen, Luxul(l)ianite, Luxulyanite, NH, Pegmatite, Protogine

**Grannie, Granny** Cowl, Forebear, Knot, Nan(a)

**Grant(ed)** Accord, Aid, Allot, Allow, Award, Benefaction, Bestow, Beteem(e), Block, Bounty, Bursary, Carta, Cary, Cede, Charta, Charter, Concession, →**CONFER**, Cy, Datum, Endow, Enfranchise, Exhibition, Feoff, General, Give, Hugh, Land, Lend, Let, License, Munich, Obreption, Patent, President, Regium donum, Scholarship, Send, Sop, Subsidy, Subvention, Supply, Teene, Ulysses, Ure, Vouchsafe, Yeven, Yield

**Granule, Granulate(d)** Kern, Otolith, Pearl, Plastid, Pound, Prill, Saburra, Statolith, Volutin

**Grape(s)** Aligoté, Botros, Botryoid, Bullace, Cabernet, Cabernet Sauvignon, Carmenère, Catawba, Cépage, Chardonnay, Chenin blanc, Colombard, Concord, Cot, Delaware, Diamond, Fox, Gamay, Garnacha, Gewurztraminer, Grenache, Haanepoot, Hamburg(h), Hanepoot, Honeypot, Hyacinth, Lambrusco, Malbec, Malmsey, Malvasia, Malvesie, Malvoisie, Marsanne, Merlot, Montepulciano, Muscadel, Muscadine, Muscat(el), Nebbiolo, Noble rot, Oregon, Petite Syrah, Pinot, Pinotage, Pinot blanc, Pinot Chardonnay, Primitivo, Ptisan, Racemose, Raisin, Rape, Riesling, Sangiovese, Sauvignon, Scuppernong, Sémillon, Sercial, Shiraz, Sour, Staphyline, Steen, Sultana, Sweet-water, Sylvaner, Syrah, Tokay, Uva, Verdelho, Véronique, Vino, Vognier, Wineberry, Zinfandel

**Grapefruit** Pampelmoose, Pomelo, Pompelmouse, Pompelo, Pumple-nose, Shaddock, Ugli®

**Grape-grower** Vigneron, Vine-dresser

**Grapeshot** Mitraille

**Grape-sugar** Glucose

**Grapevine** Gossip, Hearsay, Mocassin telegraph, Moccasin telegraph

**Graph, Graphic(s)** Avatar, Bar, Chart, Clip art, Computer, Contour, Diagram, Histogram, Learning curve, Nomograph, Ogive, Picturesque, Pie (chart), Plot, Profile, Raster, Sine curve, Sonogram, Table, Turtle, Vivid, Waveform, Waveshape

**Graphite** Kish, Plumbago

**Grapple** Clinch, Close, Hook, Lock, Struggle, Wrestle

**Grasp(ing)** Apprehend, Catch, Clat, Claut, Claw, Clench, Clinch, →**CLUTCH**, Compass, Comprehend, Fathom, Get, Go-getting, Grab, Grapple, Greedy, Grip(e), Hend, Hold, Hug, Knowledge, Prehend, Prehensile, Purchase, Raptorial, Reach, Realise, Rumble, Seize, Sense, Snap, Snatch, Squeeze, Twig, Uptak(e)

**Grass(land), Grass roots, Grassy** Agrostology, Alang, Alfa(lfa), Arrow, Avena, Bahia, Bamboo, Bang, Barbed wire, Barley, Barnyard, Beard, Bennet, Bent, Bermuda, Betray, Bhang, Blade, Blady, Blue(-eyed), Blue moor, Bristle, Brome-grass, Bromus, Buffalo, Buffel, Bunch, Bush, Campo, Canary, Cane, Canna, Cannach, Carpet, Cat's tail, Cheat, Chess, China, Citronella, Cleavers, Clivers, Clover, Cochlearia, Cocksfoot, Cockspur, Cogon, Cord, Cortaderia, Cotton, Couch, Cow, Crab, Culm, Cuscus, Cutty, Dactylis, Danthonia, Dari, Darnel, Deergrass, Dhur(r)a, Diss, Divot, Dogstail, Dog's tooth, Dogwheat, Doob, Doura, Dura, Durra, Eddish, Eel, Eelwrack, Elephant, Emmer, Ers, Esparto, Feather, Fescue, Finger, Fiorin, Flag, Flinders, Floating, Flote, Fog, Foggage, Foxtail, Gage, Gama-grass, Ganja, Gardener's garters, Glume, Glumella, Goose, Grama, Gramineae, Green(sward), Hair, Halfa, Harestail, Hashish, Hassock, Haulm, Hay, Haycock, Heath(er), Hemp, Herbage, High veld, Holy, Indian corn, →**INFORM**, Jawar(i), Job's tears, Johnson, Jowar(i), Kangaroo, Kans, Kentucky blue, Khuskhus, Kikuyu, Knoll, Knot, Lalang, Laund, Lawn, Lay, Lea, Lee, Lemon, Llano, Locusta, Lolium, Lop,

Lucern(e), Lyme, Mabela, Machair, Maize, Manna, Marram, Marrum, Mary Jane, Mat, Materass, Matweed, Mead, Meadow(-fescue), Meadow foxtail, Mealies, Melic, Melick, Millet, Milo, Miscanthus, Monkey, Moor, Moss-crop, Nark, Nassella tussock, Nature strip, Negro-corn, Nit, Nose, Nut, Oat, Orange, Orchard, Oryza, Painted, Palet, Pamir, Pampas, Panic, Paspalum, Pasturage, Peach, Pennisetum, Pepper, Persicaria, Phleum, Pilcorn, Plume, Poa, Porcupine, Pot, Purple moor, Puszta, Quack, Quaking, Quick, Quitch, Ramee, Rami(e), Rat, Rat on, Redtop, Reed, Rescue, Rhodes, Rib, Ribbon, Rice, Rips, Roosa, Rotgrass, Rough, Rumble(r), Rusa, Rush, Rye(-brome), Sacaton, Sago, Salt, Sand, Savanna(h), Saw, Scorpion, Scraw, Scurvy, Scutch, Sea-reed, Sedge, Seg, Sesame, Shave, Sheep's fescue, Shop, Sing, Sinsemilla, Sisal, Sneak(er), Snitch, Snout, Snow, Sorghum, Sour-gourd, Sourveld, Spanish, Spear, Spelt, Spike, Spinifex, Splay, Split, Squeal, Squirrel-tail, Squitch, Stag, Star(r), Stipa, Stool-pigeon, Storm, Sudan, Sugar, Sward, Swath(e), Sword, Tape, Taramea, Tath, Tea, Tef(f), Tell, Teosinte, Timothy, Toad, Toetoe, Toitoi, Triticale, Triticum, True-love, Tuffet, Turf, Tussac, Tussock, Twitch, Veld(t), Vernal, Vetiver, Viper's, Whangee, Wheat, Wheatgrass, Whistleblower, Whitlow, Wild oat, Windlestraw, Wire, Witch, Wood melick, Worm, Yard, Yellow-eyed, Yorkshire fog, Zizania, Zostera, Zoysia

**Grasshopper** Cicada, Cricket, Grig, Katydid, Locust, Long-horned, Meadow, Reeler, Short-horned, Tettix, Wart-biter, Weta

**Grate(r), Grating** Abrade, Burr, Cancelli, Chafe, Chain, Chirk, Crepitus, Diffraction, Erosure, →**FRET**, Graticule, Gravelly, Grid, Grill, Guichet, Guttural, Hack, Haik, Hake, Harsh, Hearth, Heck, Hoarse, Ingle, Iron, Jar, Lattice, Mort-safe, Nag, Portcullis, Rasp, Risp, Rub, Ruling, Scrannel, →**SCRAPE**, Scrat, Scratchy, Scroop, Shred, Siver, Strident, Syver

**Grateful** Beholden, Cinders, Indebted, Obliged

**Gratification, Gratify(ing)** Aggrate, Hedonism, Indulge, Kick, Masochism, Narcissism, Oblige, Pleasure, Regale, Reward, Sadism, Satiate, Satisfaction, Sensuous, Venery, Yummy

**Gratin** Tian

**Gratitude** Appreciation, Debt, God 'a mercy, Ta, Thanks

**Gratuitous, Gratuity** Baksheesh, Beer-money, Bonsella, Bonus, Bounty, Cumshaw, Dash, Free, Glove-money, Gratis, Lagn(i)appe, Mag(g)s, Tip

**Grave(yard)** Accent, Arlington, Austere, Barrow, Bass, Bier, Burial, Carve, Charnel, Chase, Count, Critical, Darga, Demure, Dignified, Dust, Eorl, God's acre, Heavy, Heinous, Important, Ingroove, Kistvaen, Kurgan, Lair, Long home, Mool, Mould, Mound, Passage, Pit, Sad, Saturnine, Serious, Sober, Solemn, Sombre, Speos, Staid, Stern, Tomb, Watery

**Grave-digger** Bederal, Fossor, Inhumer, Sexton

**Gravel(ly)** Calculus, Channel, Chesil, Chisel, Eskar, Esker, Glareous, Grail(e), Grit, Hard, Hoggin(g), Murram, Nonplus, Pay, Pea, Pingo, Shingle

**Gravity** Barycentric, Downforce, G, Geotaxis, Geotropism, Great Attraction, Magnitude, Mascon, Quantum, Specific, Weight, Zero

**Gravy** Baster, Bisto®, Browning, Coin, Jus, Milk, Sauce

**Gravy-boat** Argyle, Argyll

▶ **Gray** *see* **GREY(ING)**

**Grayling** Umber

**Graze, Grazing, Grazier** Abrade, Abrasion, Agist, Bark, Brush, Crease, Crop, Feed, Glance, Gride, Gryde, Heft, Herdwick, Leasow(e), Machair, Moorburn, Muirburn, Pascual, Pastoralist, Pasture, Rake, Rangeland, Scrape, Scrawn, Scuff, Shave, Sheepwalk, Shieling, Transhumance, Zero

**Grease, Greasy** Bribe, Creesh, Dope, Dubbing, Elaeolite, Elbow, Enlard, Enseam, Glit, Lanolin, Lard, Lubricate, Oil, Ointment, Pinguid, Rich, Saim, Seam(e), Shearer, Sheep-shearer, Smarm, Smear, Suint, Unctuous

**Great Bear** Arctic

**Great deal** Mort

**Greater, Greatest, Great(ly), Greats** Alfred, Ali, A majori, Astronomical, Brilliant, Bully, Capital, Classical, Colossus, Cosmic, Enorm(ous), Ever so, Excellent, Extreme, Fantastic, Gargantuan, Gatsby, Gay, Gey, Gran(d), Grit, Gt, Guns, Hellova, Helluva, Humdinger, Immense, Immortal, Important, Intense, Jumbo, Large, Lion, Macro, Magic, Magnus, Main, Major, Massive, Mega, Mickle, Mochell, Modern, Much, Muchel(l), Muckle, No end, OS, Preponderant, Profound, Rousing, Smashing, Splendiferous, Stoor, Stour, Stupendous, Sture, Sublime, Super, Superb, Superduper, Swingeing, Synergy, Tall, Thrice, Titan(ic), Top notch, Tremendous, Unco, Untold, Utmost, Vast, Voluminous, Wide, Zenith

**Greave** Jamb

**Grebe** Cargoose

**Grecian** Bend, Nose

**Greed(y)** Avarice, Avid, Bulimia, Bulimy, Cupidity, Edacious, Esurient, Gannet, Gare, Grabby, Grip(ple), Gulosity, Guts(e)y, Harpy, Hungry, Insatiable, Killcrop, Lickerish, Liquorish, Mercenary, Money-grubbing, Piggery, Pleonexia, Rapacity, Selfish, Shark's manners, Solan, Voracity, Wolfish

**Greek(s)** Achaean, Achaian, Achilles, Aeolic, Agamemnon, Ajax, Ancient, Aonian, Arcadia, Archimedes, Argive, Aristides, Athenian, Attic, Boeotian, Byzantine, Cadmean, Cleruch, Corinthian, Cretan, Cumae, Cyzicus, Delphian, Demotic, Demotike, Ding, Diomedes, Dorian, Doric, Elea, Eoka, Eolic, Epaminondas, Ephebe, Epirus, Euclid, Evzone, Fanariot, Gr, Helladic, Hellene, Hellenic, Hesychast, Homer, Hoplite, Ionian, Isocrates, Italiot(e), Javan, Katharev(o)usa, Klepht, Koine, Laconian, Lapith, Late, Leonidas, Linear B, Locrian, Lucian, Lysander, Macedonia, Medieval, Middle, Milesian, Modern, Molossian, Momus, Nestor, Nike, Nostos, Orestes, Paestum, Patroclus, Pelasgic, Pelopid, Perseus, Phanariot, Pythagoras, Romaic, Samiot, Seminole, Spartacus, Spartan, Stagirite, Strabo, Sybarite, Tean, Teian, Theban, Thersites, Theseus, Thessal(on)ian, Thracian, Timon, Typto, Uniat, Xenophon, Zorba

**Green(ery)** Almond, Apple, Avocado, Baggy, Bice, Biliverdin, Bleaching, Bottle, Bowling, Caesious, Callow, Celadon, Cerulein, Chard, Chartreuse, Chlorophyll, Chrome, Citron, Cole, Collard, Common, Copper, Corbeau, Crown, Cyan, Dioptase, Eau de nil, Eco-, Ecofreak, Ecofriendly, Ecologic, Econut, Emerald, Emerande, Envious, Environmentalist, Erin, Fingers, Foliage, Forest, Fuchsin, Fundie, Fundy, Gaudy, Glaucous, Go, Goddess, Grass, Gretna, Gull, Herbage, Immature, Inexpert, Jade, Jungle, Kendal, Kensal, Khaki, L, Lawn, Leafage, Lime, Lincoln, Loden, Lovat, Mead, Monastral®, Moss, Moulding, Naive, Neonate, New, Nile, Oasis, Olive, Organic, Paris, Pea, Peridot, Pistachio, Porraceous, Putting, Raw, Realo, Reseda, Rifle, Rink, Rookie, Sage, Sap, Scheele's, Sea, Seasick, Shaw, Sludge, Smaragdine, Sward, Teal, Tender, Terre-vert, Tiro, Turacoverdin, Tyro, Unfledged, Uninitiated, Unripe, Unsophisticated, Untrained, Uranite, Verdant, Verd antique, Verdigris, Verdure, Vert, Virent, Vir(id)escent, Virid, Viridian, Wide-eyed, Yearn, Young

**Greenheart** Bebeeru

**Greenhorn** Baby, Dupe, Ingenue, Novice, Put(t), Rookie, Sucker

**Greenhouse** Conservatory, Cooohouse, Orangery, Phytotron, Polytunnel

**Greenland(er)** Inuit

**Greens** Broccoli, Cabbage, Calabrese, Cash, Castor, Mangetout, Sprout, Vegetable(s)

**Greet, Greeting(s)** Abrazo, Accost, Air-kiss, All hail, Aloha, Arvo, Banzai, Benedicite, Bid, Blubber, Bonsoir, Chimo, Ciao, Curtsey, Den, G'day, Glad hand, Gorillagram, Hail, Hallo, Halse, Handclasp, Handshake, Haway, Heil, Heita, Hello, Herald, Hi, High-five, Hiya, Hongi, How, How d'ye do, Howsit, Jai Hind, Jambo, Kia ora, Kiss, Kissagram, Mihi, Mwah, Namaskar, Namaste, Respects, Salaam, Salam alaikum, Salue, Salute, Salve, Save you, Sd, Shalom, Shalom aleichem, Sorry, Strippagram, Strippergram, Tena koe, Tena korua, Tena koutou, Wave, Weep, → **WELCOME**, Wellmet, Wotcha, Wotcher, Yo

**Gregarious** Outgoing, Social

**Gregorian** Chant, NS, Plagal

▶ **Gremlin** *see* **GOBLIN**

**Grenade, Grenadier** Bomb, Egg, Fragmentation, Hand, Pineapple, Rat-tail, Rifle, Stun

**Grenadine(s)** Bequia, Canounan, Mustique, Union Island

**Greta** Garbo

**Grey(ing), Gray, Greybeard** Age, Agnes, Argent, Ashen, Ashy, Battleship, Beige, Bloncket, C(a)esius, Charcoal, Cinereous, Clair de lune, Dapple, Dorian, Dove, Drab, Earl, Ecru, Elegist, Feldgrau, Field, Glaucous, Gloomy, Gr, Gridelin, Griesie, Gries(l)y, Grise, Grisy, Grizzled, Gunmetal, Gy, Hoary, Hodden, Hore, Inn, Iron, Leaden, Liard, Lipizzaner, Livid, Lloyd, Lucia, Lyart, Mouse-coloured, Neutral, Oldster, Olive drab, Oyster, Pearl, Perse, Pewter, Poliosis, Putty, Sclate, Slaty, Steel, Taupe, Zane

**Greyfriars** Bunter, Magnet

**Greyhound** Grew, Italian, Lapdog, Longtail, Ocean, Persian, Saluki, Sapling, Whippet

**Grey matter** Cinerea

**Gricer** Trainspotter

**Grid(dle), Gridiron** Bar, Barbecue, Brandreth, Cattle, Control, Dot matrix, Grate, Graticule, Grating, Lattice, National, Network, Reseau, Reticle, Roo-bar, Schema, Screen, Starting, Suppressor, Tava(h), Tawa, Windscale

**Gride** Creak, Grate

**Gridlock** Stalemate

**Grief, Grievance, Grieve, Grievous** Anguish, Axe, Bemoan, Bitter, Complaint, Condole, Cry, Dear(e), Deere, Distress, Dole, Dolour, Eyedrop, Gram(e), Gravamen, Grudge, Heartbreak, Hone, Illy, Io, Lamentation, → **MISERY**, Monody, Noyous, O(c)hone, Overset, Pain, Pathetic, Peeve, Pity, Plaint, Plangent, Rue, Score, Sore, Sorrow, Tears, Teen, Tene, Tragic, Wayment, Weeping, Woe, Wrong

**Griffin** Gripe, Grype, Novice, Pony

**Grill(er), Grilling** Barbecue, Braai, Brander, Broil, Carbonado, Crisp, Cross-examine, Devil, Gridiron, Inquisition, Interrogate, Kebab, Mixed, Pump, Question, Rack, Radiator, Reja, Siver, Yakimona

**Grim** Austere, Dire, Dour, Forbidding, Gaunt, Glum, Grysie, Gurly, Hard, Hideous, Macabre, Reaper, Stern

▷ **Grim** *may indicate* an anagram

**Grimace** Face, Girn, Moe, Mop, Moue, Mouth, Mow, Murgeon, Pout, Wince

**Grime(s), Grimy** Colly, Coom, Dirt, Grunge, Peter, Rechie, Reechie, Reechy, Soil, Sweep, Tash

**Grin** Cheesy, Fleer, Girn, Leer, Risus, Simper, Smirk, Sneer

**Grind(er), Grinding** Bray, Bruxism, Chew, Crunch, → **CRUSH**, Droil, Drudgery, Gnash, Grate, Graunch, Grit, Home, Kern, Kibble, Labour, Levigate, Mano, Metate, Mill, Mince, Molar, Muller, Offhand, Powder, Pug, Pulpstone, Pulverise, Slog, Stamp, Triturate

**Grip(ping), Gripper** Absorb, Adhesion, Arm lock, Ascendeur, Bite, Chuck, Clam, Clamp, Cleat, Clip, Clutch, Craple, Dog, Duffelbag, Embrace, Engrasp, Enthral, Foothold, Get, Grapple, → **GRASP**, Haft, Hair, Hairpin, Hand(fast), Handbag, Handhold, Headlock, Hend, Hold, Hug, Interesting, Jaw, Key, Kirby®, Lewis, Obsess, Pincer, Pinion, Pistol, Prehensile, Purchase, Raven, Rhine, Sally, Setscrew, Sipe, Strain, Streigne, Thrill, Traction, Twist, Valise, Vice, Walise, Wrestle

**Gripe(s)** Beef, Colic, Complain, Ditch, Grasp, Griffin, Ileus, Pain, Tormina, Whine

**Grisly** Gory, Macabre

**Grist** Burden

**Gristle, Gristly** Cartilage, Chondroid, Lytta, Proteoglycan, Raven's bone

**Grit(s), Gritty** Blinding, Clench, Fibre, Gnash, Granular, Grate, Guts, Hominy, Mattress, Millstone, Nerve, Pennant, Pluck, Resolution, Sabulose, Sand, Shingle, Swarf, Tenacity, Toughness, Valour, Yorkshire

**Gritty** Tacky, Ugly

**Grizzle(d)** Grey

**Groan(er), Groaning** Bewail, Bing, Moan, Overladen, Sigh, Titus

**Grocer(y)** Dairy, Epicier, Grasshopper, Jorrocks, Pepperer, Symbol
**Grog(gy)** Dazed, Queasy, Shaky
**Groin** Gnarr, Inguinal, Lisk
**Groom(ed)** Brush, Coistrel, Coistril, Comb, Curry, Dress, Fettler, Kempt, Neaten, Ostler, Palfrenier, Paranymph, Preen, Primp, Prink, S(a)ice, Smarten, Soigne, Spouse, Spruce up, Strapper, Syce, Tiger, Tracer, Train, Wrangler
▷ **Groom** *may indicate* an anagram
**Groove(d), Grooves, Groovy** Bezel, Canal, Cannelure, Chamfer, Channel, Chase, Clevis, Cool, Coulisse, Croze, Dièdre, Exarate, Fissure, Flute, Fuller, Furr, Furrow, Glyph, Gouge, Hill and dale, Kerf, Key-seat, Keyway, Lead-in, Lead-out, Nock, Notch, Oche, Pod, Quirk, Rabbet, Race(way), Raggle, Raphe, Rare, Rebate, Rif(f)le, Rifling, Rigol(l), Rout, →RUT, Scrobe, Scrobiculate, Sipe, Slot, Striate, Sulcus, Throat, Track, Trough, Vallecula
**Grope(r)** À tâtons, Feel, Fumble, Grabble, Hapuka, Ripe, Scrabble
**Gross** All-up, Coarse, Coarse-grained, Complete, Crass, Dense, Earn, Earthy, Flagrant, Frankish, Fustilugs, Giant, Gr, Loathsome, Material, Obese, Obscene, Outsize, Overweight, Pre-tax, Rank, Ribald, Rough, Stupid, Sum, Whole
▷ **Gross** *may indicate* an anagram
**Grotesque** Antic, Bizarre, Fantastic, Fright, Gargoyle, Macaroni, Magot, Mascaron, Outlandish, Rabelaisian, Rococo, Teras
**Grotto** Antre, Cave, Lupercal
**Grotty** Tacky, Ugly
**Grouchy** Irascible
**Ground(ed), Grounds** Abthane, Acreage, Arena, Astroturf, A terre, Basis, Bottom, Breeding, Campus, Cause, Chewed, Clod, Common, Criterion, Crushed, Deck, Dregs, Eard, Earth, Edgbaston, Epig(a)eal, Epig(a)ean, Epigene, Epig(a)eous, Estate, Etching, Floor, Footing, Forbidden, Gathering, Grated, Grist, Grouts, Happy hunting, Headingley, High, Home, Hunting, Justification, Lees, Leeway, Lek, Lords, Lot, Marl, Meadow, Mealed, Middle, Motive, Neutral, Occasion, Oval, Parade, Piste, Pitch, Plat, Pleasure, Plot, Policy, Proving, Quad, →REASON, Rec(reation), Réseau, Ring, Sandlot, Sediment, Slade, Soil, Solum, Sports, Stadium, Stamping, Strand, Terra, Terrain, Tiltyard, Tom Tiddler's, Touch, Tract, Turf, Udal, Vantage, Venue, Waste(land), Yard, Yird
▷ **Ground** *may indicate* an anagram
**Groundbait** Chum
**Ground-breaker** Pioneer, Van(guard)
**Ground-crew** Erk
**Grounding(s)** Rabble
**Ground-rent** Crevasse
**Groundsheet** Hutchie
**Groundsman** Greenkeeper
**Group(ie), Grouping** Abelian, Acyl, Affinity, Age, Al Fatah, Align, 'A' list, Apparat, Bananarama, Band, Batch, Battle, Beatles, Bee, Bevy, Bloc(k), Blood, Bloomsbury, Board, Body, Bracket, Bratpack, Break-out, Bruges, Bunch, Caboodle, Cadre, Camarilla, Camp, Cartel, Category, Caucus, Cave, Cell, Chain, Choir, Chordata, Circle, Clade, Clan, Class(is), Clique, Clump, Cluster, Clutch, Coachload, Cohort, Colony, Combo, Committee, Commune, Community, Complex, Concertino, Confraternity, Conglomerate, Congregation, Consort(ium), Constellation, Contact, Contingent, Control, Convoy, Coterie, Covey, Crew, Decile, Dectet, Delegation, Deme, Demi-monde, Denomination, Department, Detachment, Detail, Division, Draft, Drove, En bloc, Enclave, Encounter, Ensemble, Faction, Family, Fascio, Fauna, Fleet, Flora, Focus, Fold, Follower, Fraternity, Front, Functional, Gaggle, Galère, Gang, Gemeinschaft, Gender, Generation, Genotype, Genus, Gesellschaft, Ginger, Globe, Guild, Hapu, Hardcore, Heading, Herd, Hexad, Hirsel, House, Household, Income, In-crowd, Intake, Interest, Junction, Keiretsu, Ketone, Kit, Knob, Knot, Komsomol, League, Led Zeppelin, Lichfield, Linkage, Lobby, Local, Lot, Lumpenproletariat, Machine, Marathon, Marshal, Minority, Minyan,

Movement, Nest, Network, Nexus, Oasis, Octuor, Order, Outfit, Oxford, Pack(et), Panel, Parti, Party, Passel, Peer, Phalange, Phalanx, Phratry, Phylum, Platoon, Pleiad, PLO, Plump, Pocket, Pod, Point, Pool, Pop, Posse, Powerbase, Pressure, Prosthetic, Push, Quincunx, Raceme, Racemose, Rap, Reading, Retinue, Ring, Rush, Salon, School, Sector, Seminar, Senate, Septet, Series, Set, Several, Sex, Shoal, Shower, Social, Society, Sort, Sorus, Species, Splinter, Squad(ron), Stick, Strain, Stream, String, Study, Subclass, Subculture, Subfamily, Sub-general, Sub-order, Subphylum, Subset, Subspecies, Support, Swarm, Symbol, Syndicate, Synectics, Syntagm, System, T, Tales, Taxon, Team, Tetrad, The few, Tithing, Topological, Trainband, T-Rex, Triad, Tribe, Tribune, Trilogy, Trio, Troika, Troop, Troupe, TU, Umbrella, Undecimole, Unit, Usenet®, User, Vertical, Vigilante, Wing, Workshop, Zaibatsu, Zupa

**Grouse** Bellyache, Black, Blackcock, Bleat, Blue, Caper(caillie), Capercailzie, Covey, Game, Gorcock, Greyhen, Gripe, Growl, Grumble, Hazel-hen, Heath-cock, Heathfowl, Heath-hen, Jeremiad, Kvetch, Moan, Moorcock, Moorfowl, Moor-pout, Muir-poot, Muir-pout, Mutter, Natter, Peeve, Pintail, Prairie chicken, Prairie-hen, Ptarmigan, Red, Red game, Resent, Ruffed, Rype(r), Sage, Sharp-tailed, Snarl, Spruce, Squawk, Twelfth, Wheenge, Willow, W(h)inge

**Grout** Cement, Lees

**Grove** Academy, Arboretum, Bosk, Bosquet, Copse, Glade, Hurst, Lyceum, Motte, Nemoral, Orchard, Orchat, Silva, Tope

**Grovel** Cheese, Crawl, Creep, Fawn, Ko(w)tow, Worm

**Grow(ing), Grow out, Growth** Accrete, Accrue, Acromegaly, Adenoma, Aggrandisement, Angioma, Apophysis, Arborescence, Auxesis, Bedeguar, Boom, Braird, Breer, Burgeon, Bushiness, Carcinoma, Car(b)uncle, Chancre, Cholelith, Chondroma, Compensatory, Condyloma, Corn, Crescendo, Crescent, Crop, Culture, Cyst, Down, Dysplasia, Ectopia, Edema, Ellagic, Enate, Enchondroma, Enlarge, Epiboly, Epinasty, Epitaxy, Excrescence, Exostosis, Expansion, Fibroid, Flor, Flourish, Flush, Gain, Gall, Germinate, Get, Glareal, Goitre, Groundswell, Hair, Hepatocele, Hummie, Hyperostosis, Hypertrophy, Hyponasty, Increase, Involucrum, Keloidal, Keratosis, Knee, Knur(r), Lichen, Lipoma, Mole, Monopodial, Moss, Mushroom, Myoma, Neoplasia, Nur(r), Oak-nut, Oedema, Oncology, Osselet, Osteoma, Osteophyte, Pharming, Polyp, Polypus, Proleg, Proliferate, Rampant, Rank, Scirrhus, Scopa, Septal, Snowball, Spavin, →**SPROUT**, Stalagmite, Stand, Stipule, Sympodial, Tariff, Thigmotropism, Thrive, Trichome, →**TUMOUR**, Tylosis, Upsurge, Vegetable, Wart, Wax, Weed, Witches'-broom, Wox, Zeatin

▷ **Grow(n)** *may indicate* an anagram

**Growl(er), Growling** Fremescent, Gnar, Groin, Grr, Gurl, Iceberg, Knar, Roar(e), Roin, Royne, Snar(l)

**Grown up** Adult, Mature, Risen

**Groyne** Breakwater, Mole

**Grub(by)** Assart, Aweto, Bardie, Bardy, Bookworm, Caddis, Caterpillar, Cheer, Chow, Chrysalis, Deracinate, Dig, Eats, Fare, Fodder, →**FOOD**, Gentle, Groo-groo, Gru-gru, Larva, Leatherjacket, Maggot, Mawk, Mess, Nosh, Palmerworm, Peck, Pupa, Root(le), Rout, Rowt, Sap, Shopsoiled, Slave, Stub, Tired, Wireworm, Witchetty, Wog, Worm, Wroot

**Grudge, Grudging** Chip, Derry, Envy, Grievance, Grutch, Resent, Score, Sparse, Spite, Spleen, Sting

**Gruel** Brochan, Bross, Loblolly, Skilligalee, Skilligolee, Skilly

**Gruesome** Ghastly, Grisly, Grooly, Horror, Livid, Macaberesque, Macabre, →**MORBID**, Sick

**Gruff** Guttural, Hoarse, Surly

**Grumble** Beef, Bellyache, Bitch, Bleat, Chunter, Crab, Croak, Girn, Gripe, Grizzle, Groin, Growl, Moan, Mump, Murmur, Mutter, Nark, Natter, Repine, Rumble, Whinge, Yammer

**Grump(y)** Attercop, Bearish, Crabby, Cross, Curmudgeon, Ettercap, Grouchy, Moody, Ogre(ish), Sore-headed, Surly, Testy

**Grunt** Groin, Grumph, Humph, Oink, Pigfish, Spanish, Ugh, Wheugh

**Guano** Dung, Sombrerite

**Guanoco** Llama

**Guarantee(d)** Accredit, Assure, Attest, Avouch, Certify, Cheque card, Collateral, Ensure, Fail-safe, Gage, Hallmark, Insure, Mainprise, Money-back, Pignerate, Pignorate, →**PLEDGE**, Plight, Promise, Seal, Secure, Sponsion, Surety, Underwrite, →**VOUCHSAFE**, Warn, Warrandice, Warrant(y)

**Guard(ed), Guards** Acolouthos, Advance, Apron, Beefeaters, Blues, Bostangi, Bouncer, Bracer, Cabiri, Cage, Cag(e)y, Centinel(l), Centry, Cerberus, Chamfrain, Chaperon(e), Chary, Cheesemongers, Cherry-pickers, Coast, Coldstream, Colour, Conductor, Cordon, Crinoline, Curator, Custodian, Custos, Defend, Diehards, Dragoons, Duenna, Ensure, Equerry, Escort, Eunuch, Excubant, Exon, Fence, Fender, Gaoler, Gateman, Gauntlet, Grenadiers, Greys, Hedge, Home, Horse, INS, Insure, Irish, Iron, Jaga, Jailer, Keep, Lancers, Life, Lilywhites, Look out, Mask, Militia, Mort-safe, Muzzle, National, Nightwatch(man), Noncommital, Nutcrackers, Old, →**ON GUARD**, Out-rider, Out-sentry, Pad, Palace, Patrol, Picket, Point, Policeman, Praetorian, →**PROTECT**, Provost, Quillon, Rail, Red, Ride, Roof, Scots, Screw, Secure, Security, Sentinel, Sentry, Shadow, Shield, Shin, Shopping, Shotgun, Sky marshal, Splashback, Splashboard, Splasher, SS, Strelitz, Streltzi, Swiss, Switzer, Tapadera, Tapadero, Tile, Toecap, Tsuba, Turnkey, Vambrace, Vamplate, Varangian, Vigilante, Visor, Wage, Wait(e), Ward, Warder, Wary, Watch (and ward), Watchdog, Watchman, Wear, Weir, Wire, Yeoman

**Guardian(ship)** Agathodaimon, Altair, Angel, Argus, Caretaker, Chaperone, Curator, Custodian, Custos, Dragon, Gemini, Granthi, Griffin, Griffon, Gryfon, Gryphon, Hafiz, Janus, Julius, Miminger, Patron, Protector, Templar, Trustee, Tutelage, Tutelar(y), Tutor, Warder, Watchdog, Xerxes

**Guatemala(n)** Mam

**Gudgeon** Fish, Pin, Trunnion

**Guenon** Grivet, Vervet

**Guer(r)illa** Bushwhacker, Chetnik, Comitadji, Contra, ETA, Fedayee, Gook, Haiduk, Heyduck, Irregular, Khmer Rouge, Komitaji, Maquis, Mujahadeen, Mujahedeen, Mujahed(d)in, Mujahideen, Partisan, Phalanx, Red Brigade, Tamil Tiger, Terrorist, Tupamaro, Urban, Viet Cong, Zapata, Zapatista

**Guess** Aim, Aread, Arede, Arreede, Assume, Augur, Conjecture, Divine, Educated, Estimate, Harp, Hazard, Hunch, Imagine, Infer, Inspired, Level, Mor(r)a, Mull, Psych out, Reckon, Shot, Speculate, Stab, Suppose, Surmise, Theorise, Venture

**Guessing game** Handy-dandy, Mor(r)a, Quiz

**Guess-work** Extrapolation, Idea

**Guest(s)** Caller, Company, House-party, Inquiline, Invitee, Parasite, Paying, PG, Resident, Symbion(t), Symphile, Synoecete, Umbra, Visitant, →**VISITOR**, Xenial

**Guesthouse** B & B, Minshuku, Taverna, Xenodochium

**Guff** Bosh, Gas

**Guianian** S(a)ouari

**Guidance, Guide, Guiding, Guideline** Advice, Antibarbus, Aunt, Auspice, Baedeker, Befriend, Bradshaw, Cicerone, Clue, Code, Command, Concordance, Conduct, Counsel, Courier, Cox, Curb, Cursor, Cybrary, Director(y), Docent, Dragoman, Drive, Engineer, →**ESCORT**, Field, Form, Gillie, Graticule, Helm, Heuristic, Homing, Index, Inertial, Inspire, Itinerary, Jig, Key, Lad, Landmark, Lead, Lodestar, Mahatma, Manoeuvre, Map, Mark, Marriage, Mentor, Michelin, Missile, Mitre box, Model, Navaid, Navigate, Nose, Pelorus, Pilot, Pointer, Postil(l)ion, Principle, Providence, Queen's, Rainbow, Range, Ranger, Reference, Rein, Relate, Rudder, Rule of thumb, Sabot, Satnav, Sea Ranger, Shepherd, Sherpa, Shikaree, Shikari, Sight, Sign, Sixer, Standard, Stear, Steer, Stire, Target, Template, Templet, Terminal, Terrestrial, Tiller, Train, Travelogue, Tutelage, Usher(ette), Vocational, Voyageur, Waymark, Weise, Weize, Wise

**Guild** Artel, Basoche, Company, Freemason, Gyeld, Hanse, Hoastman, League, Mistery, Mystery, Society, Tong, Union

**Guile** Art, Cunning, Deceit, Dole, Malengine

**Guillotine** Closure, Decapitate, Louisiette, Maiden, Marianne

**Guilt(y)** Affluenza, Angst, Blame, Cognovit, Contrite, Flagitious, Hangdog, Mea culpa, Nocent, Peccavi, Proven, Redhanded, Remorse, Wicked

**Guinea(s)** Canary, Geordie, Gns, Job, Ls, Meg, Spade

**Guinea-fowl** Pintado

**Guinea-pig** Abyssinian, Agoute, Agouti, Cavie, Cavy, Paca, Subject

**Guinea-worm** Dracunculus

**Guinness** Alec

**Guise** Form, Manner, Shape

**Guitar(ist)** Acoustic, Axe(man), Bass, Bottleneck, Cithern, Cittern, Dobro®, Electric, Fender®, Fretman, Gittarone, Gittern, Guthrie, Hawaiian, Humbucker, Lute, Lyre, Pedal steel, Plankspanker, Samisen, Sancho, Sanko, Segovia, Shamisen, Sitar, Slide, Spanish, Steel, Uke, Ukulele

**Gulf** Aden, Anadyr, Aqaba, Bay, Bothnia, California, Cambay, Campeche, Carpentaria, Chasm, Chihli, Corinth, Cutch, Darien, Dvina, Exmouth, Finland, Fonseca, G, Genoa, Gonaives, Hauraki, Honduras, Iskenderun, Isthmus, Izmit, Joseph Bonaparte, Kutch, Lepanto, Leyte, Lingayen, Lions, Mannar, Martaban, Maw, Mexico, Ob, Oman, Patras, Persian, Pozzuoli, Queen Maud, Rapallo, Riga, St Lawrence, St Vincent, Salerno, Salonika, Saronic, Saros, Siam, Sidra, Spencer, Taganrog, Taranto, Thailand, Tongking, Tonkin, Trieste, Tunis, Van Diemen, Venice, Vorago

**Gull(s)** Bamboozle, Black-backed, Bonxie, Cat's paw, Cheat, Cob(b), Cod, Cony, Cozen, Cull(y), Dupe, Easy game, Fool, Geck, Glaucous, Haglet, Have, Hoodwink, Hum, Ivory, Kittiwake, Laridae, Larus, Lie to, Maw, Mew, Mollyhawk, Noodle, Pickmaw, Pigeon, Queer, Ring-billed, Rook, Sabine's, Saddleback, Scaury, Scourie, Scowrie, Sea-cob, Sea-mew, Sell, Simp, Skua, Sucker, Swart-back, Tern, Tystie, Xema

**Gullet** Crop, Enterate, Maw, Oesophagus, Throat, Weasand-pipe

**Gullible** Credulous, Green, Mug punter, Naive, Starry-eyed, Sucker

**Gulliver** Lemuel

**Gully** Couloir, Donga, Fielder, Geo, Gio, Goe, Grough, Gulch, Infielder, Pit, Rake, Ravine, Sloot, Sluit, Wadi

**Gulp** Bolt, Draught, Gollop, Quaff, Slug, Sob, →SWALLOW, Swig, Swipe, Wolf

**Gum (tree)** Acacia, Acajou, Acaroid, Agar, Algin, Angico, Arabic, Arabin, Arar, Arctic, Asafoetida, Bablah, Balata, Balm, Bandoline, Bdellium, Benjamin, Benzoin, Bloodwood, Blue, Boot, Bubble, Cerasin, Chicle, Chuddy, Chutty, Coolabah, Courbaril, Cow®, Dextrin(e), Dragon's-blood, Ee-by, Eucalyptus, Euphorbium, Flooded, Frankincense, Galbanum, Gamboge, Ghost, Gingival, →GLUE, Goat's-thorn, Gosh, Grey, Guar, Ironbark, Juniper, Karri, Kauri, Lac, La(b)danum, Lentisk, Mastic(h), Mucilage, Myrrh, Nicotine, Olibanum, Opopanax, Oshac, Red, Resin, River red, Sagapenum, Sarcocolla, Scribbly, Size, Sleep, Snow, Spearmint, Spirit, Starch, Sterculia, Stringybark, Sugar, Sweet, Tacamahac, Tragacanth, Tupelo, Ulmin, Water, White, Xanthan

**Gumbo** Okra

**Gumboil** Parulis

**Gumption** Nous, Spirit

**Gun(fire), Guns, Gunfight** Amusette, Archibald, Archie, Arquebus, Automatic, Barker, Baton, Bazooka, Beanbag, Beretta, Big Bertha, Biscayan, Blunderbuss, Bofors, Bombard, Breech(-loader), Bren, Broadside, Brown Bess, Browning, Bulldog, Bullpup, Bundook, Burp, Caliver, Cannonade, Carbine, Carronade, Cement, Chokebore, Chopper, Coehorn, Colt®, Dag, Derringer, Electron, Elephant, Escopette, Falcon(et), Field, Fieldpiece, Firearm, Fire lock, Flame, Flash, Flintlock, Four-pounder, Fowler, Fowlingpiece, Full-bore, Fusil, Garand, Gas, Gat(ling), Gingal(l), Grease, HA, Hackbut, Half-cock, Harquebus, Heater, Hired, Howitzer, Jezail, Jingal, Kalashnikov, Lewis,

Long Tom, Luger®, Machine, Magazine, Magnum, Maroon, Martini-Henry®, Matchlock, Mauser®, Maxim, Metal, Minnie, Minute, Mitrailleuse, Mons Meg, Mortar, Musket(oon), Muzzle-loader, Nail, Needle, Neutron, Noonday, Oerlikon, Ordnance, Over and under, Owen, Paderero, Paterero, Ped(e)rero, Pelican, Perrier, Persuader, Petronel, Piece, Pistol(et), Pompom, Pump (action), Punt, Purdey®, Quaker, Radar, Ray, Repeater, Rev, Revolver, Riot, Rod, Roscoe, Saker, Sarbacane, Saturday night special, Scatter, Self-cocker, Shooter, Shooting iron, Shoot-out, Sidearm, Siege, Smoothbore, Snapha(u)nce, Spear, Speed, Spray, Squirt, Staple, Starting, Sten, Sterculia, Sterling, Stern-cannon, Stern-chaser, Stun, Swivel, Taser®, Tea, Thirty eight, Thompson, Three-pounder, Tier, Time, Tire, Tommy, Tool, Tupelo, Turret, Uzi, Walther, Wesson, Wheel-lock, Young, Zip

**Gunge** Gowl, Paste

**Gunman** Ace, Assassin, Bandit, Earp, Greaser, Pistoleer, Sharpshooter, Sniper, Starter

**Gunner, Gunner's assistant** Arquebusier, Arsenal, Artillerist, Cannoneer, Cannonier, Culverineer, Gr, Matross, RA

**Gunpowder** Charcoal, Pebble-powder, Saltpetre, Saucisse, Saucisson

**Gunwale** Gunnel, Portland, Portlast, Portoise

**Guppy** Million

**Gurgle** Burble, Clunk, Glug, Gobble, Gollar, Goller, Guggle, Ruckle, Squelch

**Gurnard** Tubfish

**Guru** Bhagwan, Lifestyle, Pundit, Sadhu, Teacher, Technocrat

**Gush(er), Gushing** Blether, Effusive, →**FLOOD**, Flow, Fountain, Jet, Oil well, Outpour, Rail, Raile, Regurgitate, Rhapsodize, Scaturient, Spirt, Spout, Spurt, Surge, Too-too

**Gusset** Godet, Gore, Insert, Inset, Mitre

**Gust** Blast, Blore, Flaught, Flaw, Flurry, Puff, Sar, Squall, Waff

**Gusto** Élan, Enjoyment, Relish, Verve, Zest

**Gut(s), Gutty** Abdomen, Archenteron, Balls, Beer, Bowel(s), Chitterlings, Cloaca, Colon, Disembowel, Draw, Duodenum, Enteral, Enteron, Entrails, Fore, Gill, Hind, Ileum, Innards, Insides, Kyle, Mesaraic, Mesenteron, Mid, Minikin, Omental, Omentum, Purtenance, Remake, Sack, Sand, Snell, Stamina, Staying-power, Strip, Thairm, Tripe, Ventriculus, Viscera

**Gutta-percha** Jelutong, Pontianac, Pontianak

**Gutter(ing)** Arris, Channel, Conduit, Coulisse, Cullis, Grip, Gully, Kennel, Rhone, Rigol(l), Roan, Rone, Runlet, Runnel, Sough, Spout, Strand, Swale, Swayl, Sweal, Sweel

**Guttersnipe** Arab, Gamin, Thief

**Guttural** Faucal, Throaty

**Guy** Backstay, Bo, Burgess, Buster, Cat, Chaff, Clewline, Decamp, Deride, Dude, Effigy, Fall, Fawkes, Fellow, Gibson, Gink, Josh, Mainstay, Mannering, Parody, Rag, Rib, Ridicule, Rope, Scarecrow, Send up, Stay, Taunt, Tease, Vang, Wise

**Guzzle(d)** Gannet, Gorge, Go(u)rmandize, Overeat, Snarf

**Gwyn** Nell

**Gym(nasium), Gymnast(ic)** Acrobat, Akhara, Arena, Contortionist, Dojo, Exercise, Jungle, Korbut, Lyceum, Palaestra, PE, PT, Real, Rhythmic, Sokol, Trampolinist, Tumbler, Turner

**Gymnosophist** Yogi

**Gypsum** Alabaster, Gesso, Plaster, Satin spar, Satin-stone, Selenite, Terra alba

**Gypsy, Gipsy** Bohemian, Cagot, Caird, Caqueux, Chai, Chal, Chi, Collibert, Egyptian, Esmeralda, Faw, Gipsen, Gitana, Gitano, Hayraddin, Lavengro, Meg, Pikey, Rom(any), Rye, Scholar, Siwash, Tinker, Traveller, Travelling folk, Tsigane, Tzigane, Tzigany, Vagabond, Vlach, Walach, Wanderer, Zigan, Zigeuner, Zincala, Zincalo, Zingaro

**Gyrate** Revolve, Rotate, →**SPIN**, Twirl

# Hh

**H** Ache, Aitch, Aspirate, Height, Hospital, Hotel, Hydrant, Hydrogen, Zygal

**Haberdasher(y)** Clothier, Ferret, Hosier, Notions

**Habit(s), Habitual, Habituate, Habitué** Accustom, Addiction, Apparel, Assuefaction, Assuetude, Bent, Cacoethes, Chronic, Clothes, Coat, Consuetude, Cowl, Crystal, Custom, Dependency, Diathesis, Dress, Ephod, Frequenter, Garb, Garment, Hand-me-down, Inure, Inveterate, Motley, Mufti, Nature, Outfit, Pathological, Practice, Quirk, Raiment, Regular, Riding, Robe, Rochet, Routine, Scapular, Schema, Season, Second nature, Set, Soutane, Suit, Surplice, Toge, Trait, Trick, Tway, Usual, Way, Won, Wont, Xerotes

**Habitable, Habitat(ion)** Ecad, Element, Environment, Haunt, Home, Locality, Niche, Pueblo, Refugium, Station, Tel

**Hacienda** Ranch

**Hack(er), Hacking** Blackhat, Chip, Chop, Cough, Cut, Cypherpunk, Drudge, Garble, Gash, Ghost, Grub-Street, Hag, Hash, Hedge-writer, Heel, Hew, Horse, Ink-slinger, Jade, Journo, Mangle, Mutilate, Nag, Nerd, Notch, Pad, Paper-strainer, Penny-a-liner, Phreak, Pick, Plater, Pot-boiler, Rosinante, Script kiddie, Slash, Spurn, Steed, Tadpole, Taper, Tap into, Tiger team, Tussis, Unseam, Warchalking, White hat

**Hackle(s)** Comb, Rough

**Hackney(ed)** Banal, Cab, Cliché, Corny, Percoct, Stale, Threadbare, Tired, Trite, Twice-told, Worn

**Had (to)** Ate, Moten, Must, Obliged, Threw

**Haddock** Arbroath smokie, Findram, Finnan, Fish, Norway, Rizzered, Smoky, Speldin(g), Speldrin(g), Whitefish

**Hades** Dis, Hell, Orcus, Pit, Tartarus

**Haematite** Oligist

**Haemoglobin** Chelate, Hb

**Haemorrhoids** Farmer Giles, Piles

**Hafnium** Hf

**Hag(-like)** Anile, Beldame, Besom, Carlin(e), Crone, Harpy, Harridan, Hell-cat, Hex, Moss, Nickneven, Occasion, Rudas, Runnion, Sibyl, Trot, Underwood, Witch

**Haggard** Drawn, →GAUNT, Pale, Rider

**Haggis** Kishke

**Haggle** Argue, Badger, →BARGAIN, Barter, Chaffer, Dicker, Horse-trade, Jew, Niffer, Palter, Prig

**Ha-ha** Dike, So there, Sunk-fence

**Hahnium** Hn

**Hail(er)** Acclaim, Acco(a)st, Ahoy, Ave, Bull-horn, Cheer, Fusillade, Graupel, Greet, Gunfire, Hi, Ho, Megaphone, Salue, Salute, Shower, Signal, Skoal, Skol, Sola, Stentor, Storm, Trumpet, What ho, Whoa-ho-ho

**Hair(y), Haircut, Hairlike, Hair problem/condition, Hair style** Afro, Ailes de pigeon, Ainu, Alopecia, Angora, Backcomb, Baldy, Bang, Barnet, Beard, Beehive, Bingle, Bob, Bouffant, Braid, Brede, Bristle, Brutus, Bumfluff, Bun, Bunches, Bush, Butch, Cadogan, Camel, Capillary, Catogan, Chignon, Cilia, Cleopatra, Coat, Cockernony, Coif, Coiffure, Comal, Comate, Combings, Comb-over, Comose, Cornrow, Corymbus, Cowlick, Crepe, Crew-cut, Crinal, Criniferous, Cronet, Crop, Cue, Curlicue, DA, Dangerous,

Dicey, Dreadlocks, Dubbing, Duck's arse, Ducktail, Ear-lock, Earmuffs, Elf locks,
En brosse, Esau, Excrement, Eyelash, Feather, Feather-cut, Fetlock, Fibril, Filament,
Flat-top, Floccus, Follicle, Forelock, French pleat, French roll, Frenulum, Fringe, Fur,
Garconne, Glib(s), Glochidium, Goatee, Guard, Hackles, Heare, Heer(i)e, Hippy, Hispid,
Hog, Indumentum, Kemp, Kesh, Lanate, Lanugo, Lash, List, Lock, Lovelock, Lowlights,
Madarosis, Mane, Marcel, Mohawk, Mohican, Mop, Mophead, Mullet, Muttonchops,
Not(t), Number two, Pageboy, Pappus, Pashm, Peekabo(o), Pele(s), Pelt, Perm(anent),
Pigtail, Pika, Pile, Pilus, Pincurl, Plait, Plica, Plica Polonica, Pompadour, Ponytail, Poodle
cut, Porcupine, Pouf(fe), Pow, Precarious, Prison crop, Psilosis, Puberulent, Pubescent,
Pudding basin, Punk, Queue, Quiff, Radicle, Rat-tail, Red mullet, Rhizoid, Roach, Root,
Rug, Rush, Scaldhead, Scalp lock, Scopate, Scopula, Sericeous, Set, Shag, Shingle, Shock,
Sideburns, Sidelock, Snell, Spikes, Stinging, Strammel, Strand, Strigose, Strummel,
Switch, Sycosis, Tache, Tête, Thatch, Tomentose, Tonsure, Toorie, Topknot, Tour(ie),
Tragus, Tress, Trichoid, Trichology, Trichome, Trichosis, Trim, Ulotrichous, Updo,
Velutinous, Vibrissi, Villi, Villosity, Villus, Wedge, Whisker, Widow's peak, Wig, Wiglet,
Wisp, → **WOOL**, Xerasia
**Hair-cream, Hair-oil** Conditioner, Pomade
**Hairdresser** Barber, Coiffeur, Comb, Crimper, Friseur, Marcel, Salon, Stylist,
Trichologist
**Hairless** Bald, Callow, Glabrate, Glabrescent, Glabrous, Irate
**Hairline** Brow, Nape
**Hairnet** Kell, Snood
**Hairpiece** Frisette, Merkin, Postiche, Strand, Toupee, → **WIG**
**Hairpin** Barrette, Bobbypin, Bodkin, Clip, Slide, U, U-turn
**Hair-shirt** Ab(b)a, Cilice
**Haiti** RH
**Hal** Prince
**Halberd** Spontoon
**Halcyon** Calm, Kingfisher, Mild
**Hale(r)** Drag, Healthy, Koruna, Raucle, Robust, Well
**Half, Halved** Bifid, Demi, Dimidiate, Dirempt, Divide, Hemi, Moiety, Semi, Share, Split,
Stand-off, Term
**Half-a-dozen** Six, VI
**Half-asleep, Half-conscious** Dove, Dozy
**Half-baked** Foolish, Mediocre, Samel, Slack-bake
**Half-breed, Half-caste** Bastard, Baster, Creole, Eurasian, Griqua, Mameluco, Mestee,
Mestiza, Mestizo, Metif, Métis(se), Miscegen, Mongrel, Mulatto, Mustee, Octaroon,
Quadroon, Quarteroon, Quintero, Quintroon, Sambo, Yellow-boy, Yellow-girl, Zambo
**Half-dead** Alamort
**Half-guinea** Smelt
**Half-hearted** Reluctant, Tepid
**Half-hour** Bell
**Half-pence, Half-penny** Bawbee, Mag, Magpie, Maik, Mail(e), Make, Obolus, Patrick,
Portcullis, Posh, Rap, Wood's
**Half-time** Midhour
**Half-turn** Caracol(e), Demivolt
**Half-wit** Changeling, Mome, Numbskull, Simpleton, → **STUPID**
**Hall** Anteroom, Apadana, Assembly, Atrium, Auditorium, Aula, Bachelor's, Basilica,
Bingo, Carnegie, Casino, Chamber, Citadel, City, Concert, Concourse, Corridor, Crosby,
Dance, Divinity, Dojo, Domdaniel, Dome, Dotheboys, Ex(h)edra, Festival, Foyer, Gallen,
Guild, Hardwick, Holkham, Hostel, Ivied, Judgement, Kedleston, Liberty, Lobby,
Locksley, Megaron, Mess, Moot, Music, Narthex, Newby, Odeon, Palais, Palais de danse,
Passage, Prytaneum, Rathaus, Rideau, Salle, Saloon, Stationer's, Study, Tammany, Tara,
Tolsel, Town, Trullen, Valhalla, Vestibule, Walhall(a), Wildfell

**Hallmark(ed)** Brand, Contrôlé, Logo, Platemark, Seal, Stamp
**Hallow** Consecrate, Revere, Worship
**Halloween** Guiser
**Hallucinate, Hallucinating, Hallucination, Hallucinatory, Hallucinogen**
Autoscopy, DT's, Fantasy, Formication, Freak, Freak out, Illusion, Image, Mandrake,
Mirage, Negative, Peyote, Photism, Psilocin, Psilocybin, Psychedelic, Psychotic, Trip
**Halo** Antheolion, Areola, Aura, Aureola, Corona, Galactic, Gloria, Gloriole, Mandorla,
Nimbus, Rim, Vesica, Vesica piscis
**Halogen** Iodine
**Halt(er), Halting** Abort, Arrest, Avast, Block, Brake, Bridle, Cavesson, Cease, Cesse,
Check, Deactivate, End, Full stop, Game, Hackamore, Heave-to, Hilch, Inarticulate,
Lame(d), Limp, Moratorium, Noose, Paralyse, Prorogue, Rope, Stall, Standstill, Staw,
→**STOP**, Stopover, Suspend, Toho, Tyburn-tippet, Whoa, Widdy
**Ham(s)** Amateur, Barnstormer, Flitch, Gammon, Haunch, Hock, Hoke, Hough, Hunker,
Jambon, Jamon serrano, Jay, Mutton, Nates, Overact, Overplay, Parma, Pigmeat, Prat,
Prosciutto, Radio, Serrano, Spe(c)k, Tiro, Westphalian, York
**Hamburger** Sloppy joe
**Hamfisted** Maladroit, Unheppen
**Hamite** Berber, Nilot(e)
**Hamlet(s)** Aldea, Auburn, Cigar, Clachan, Dane, Dorp, Hero, Kraal, Stead, Thorp(e),
Tower, Vill(age), Wick
**Hammer(ed), Hammerhead, Hammering** About-sledge, Atmospheric, Ballpeen,
Ballpein, Beetle, Bone, Bully, Bush, Celt, Claw, Dolly, Drop, Excudit, Flatten, Fore, Fuller,
Gavel, Hack, Incuse, Jack, Kevel, Knap, Knapping, Kusarigama, Lump, Madge, Mall(et),
Malleate, Martel, Maul, Mjol(l)nir, Monkey, Nevel, Oliver, Ossicle, Pane, Pean, Peen,
Pein, Pene, Percussion, Percussor, Piledriver, Planish, Plessor, Plexor, Pneumatic,
Rawhide, Repoussé, Rip, Rout, Sheep's-foot, Shingle, Sledge, Steam, Stone, Strike, Tack,
Tenderizer, Tendon, Tilt, Trip, Trounce, Umbre, Water, Wippen
▷ **Hammered** *may indicate* an anagram
**Hammerthrower** Thor
**Hammock** Cott
▷ **Hammy** *may indicate* an anagram
**Hamper** Basket, Cabin, Ceroon, Cramp, Cumber, Delay, Encumber, Entrammel,
Hamstring, Handicap, Hobble, Hog-tie, Impede, Obstruct, Pad, Pannier, Ped, Pinch,
Restrict, Rub, Sero(o)n, Shackle, Tangle, Trammel, Tuck
**Hamster** Cricetus, Idea
**Hamstring, Hamstrung** Cramp, Hock, Hox, Lame, Popliteal, Powerless, Thwart
**Hand(s), Hand over, Hand down, Hand-like, Handwriting** Applause,
Assist(ance), Bananas, Bequeath, Cacography, Calligraphy, Charge, Chicane, Chirography,
Clap(ping), Claque, Club, Clutch, Copperplate, Court, Crabbed, Crew, Cursive, Dab,
Daddle, Danny, Dawk, Dead, Deal, Deck, Deliver, Devolve, Donny, Dukes, Dummy,
Extradition, Famble, Fin, Fist, Flipper, Flush, Free, Full (house), Glad, Graphology,
Half-text, Help, Helping, Hidden, Hond, Hour, Impart, Iron, Israel, Italian, Jambone,
Jamboree, Jemmy, Kana, L, Laydown, Lone, Loof, Man, Manual, Manus, Maulers,
Medieval, Minute, Mitt(en), Mutton-fist, Nap, Nes(h)ki, Niggle, Operative, Orthography,
Ovation, Pad, Palaeography, Palm(atifid), Part, Pass, Paw, Podium, Post, Present, Pud, R,
Referral, Rein (arm), Round, Royal flush, Running, Script, Second, Secretary, Signature,
Span, Spencerian, Stage, Station, Straight, Sweep, Text, Tiger, Uncial, Upper, Whip,
Widow, Worker, Yarborough
**Handbag** Caba(s), Grip, Indispensable, Pochette, Purse, Reticule, Valise
**Handbook** Baedeker, Companion, Enchiridion, Guide, Manual, Vade-mecum
**Handcart** Wheelbarrow
**Handcuff(s)** Bracelet, Darbies, Golden, Irons, Manacle, Mittens, Nippers, Shackle,
Snaps, Wristlet

**Handful** Few, Gowpen, Grip, Hank, Problem, Pugil, Rip(p), V

**Handicap** Bisque, Burden, Cambridgeshire, Disable, Ebor, Encumber, Half-one, Hamper, Hunchback, Impede, Impost, Lame, Liability, Lincolnshire, Mental, →OBSTACLE, Off, Penaliser, Physical, Restrict, Scratch, Weigh(t), Welter-race

**Handicraft** Marquetry

**Handkerchief, Hanky** Bandan(n)a, Belcher, Billy, Buffon, Clout, Curch, Fogle, Foulard, Kleenex®, Madam, Madras, Monteith, Mouchoir, Muckender, Napkin, Nose-rag, Orarium, Romal, Rumal, Sudary, Tissue, Wipe(r)

**Handle(d), Handler** Ansate, Bail, Bale, Behave, Bitstock, Brake, Broomstick, Cope, Crank, Dead man's, Deal, Doorknob, Dudgeon, Ear, Feel, Field, Finger, Forename, Gaum, Gorm, Grab, Grip, Gunstock, Haft, Helve, Hilt, Hold, Knob, Knub, Lug, →MANAGE, Manipulate, Manubrium, Maul, Moniker, Name, Nib, Palp, Paw, Pistol-grip, Pommel, Port-crayon, Process, Roadie, Rounce, Shaft, Snath(e), Snead, Sneath, Sned, Staff, Staghorn, Stale, Starting, Steal(e), Steel, Steil, Stele, Stilt, Stock, Sweep, Tiller, Title, To-name, Touch, Transact, Treat, Use, Whipstock, Wield, Winder, With(e)

**Handmaid(en)** Iras, Manicurist, Valkyrie

**Hand-out** Alms, Charity, Dole, Gift, Issue, Release, Sample

**Handshake** Golden

**Hand-signal** Beck(on), Point, Wave

**Handsome** Adonis, Apollo, Attractive, Beefcake, Bonny, Brave, Comely, Dashing, Dishy, Featuous, Fine, Gracious, Kenneth, Liberal, Lush, Resplendent, Rugged, Seemly, Shapely, Tidy

**Handspring, Handstand** Cartwheel, Diamodov

**Hand-warmer** Muff, Pome

**Hand-washer** Pilate

▶ **Handwriting** *see* HAND(S)

**Handy(man)** Accessible, Close, Convenient, Deft, Dext(e)rous, Digit, Factotum, Gemmy, Get-at-able, Jack(-of-all-trades), Jemmy, Near, Nigh, Of use, On site, Palmate, Palmist, Ready, Skilful, Spartan, Useful

**Hang(er), Hanging(s), Hang up** Append, Arras, Aweigh, Chick, Chik, Coat, Curtain, Dangle, Darn, Depend, Dewitt, Dorser, Dossal, Dossel, Dosser, Drape, Droop, Execute, Exhibit, Frontal, Gobelin, Hinge, Hoove, Hove(r), Icicle, Kakemono, Kilt, Lime, Lobed, Loll, Lop, Lynch, Mooch, Noose, Nub, Obsession, Oudenarde, Overarch, Pend(ant), Pothook, Preoccupation, Sag, Scenery, Scrag, Set, Sit, Sling, String up, Suspend, Suspercollate, Swag, Swing, Tapestry, Tapet, Tapis, The rope, Toran(a)

**Hanger-on** Bur(r), Camp-follower, Dewdrop, Lackey, Leech, Limpet, Liripoop, Parasite, Satellite, Sponge(r), Sycophant, Tassel, Toady

**Hangman, Hangmen** Bull, Calcraft, Dennis, Derrick, Executor, Gregory, Ketch, Lockman, Marwood, Nubbing-cove, Pierrepoint, Topsman, Word game

**Hangnail** Agnail

**Hangover** Canopy, Cornice, Crapulence, Drape, DT's, Eaves, Executer, Head, Hot coppers, Katzenjammer, Mistletoe, Relic, Remnant, Tester, Valance

**Hank** Bobbin, Coil, Fake, Lock, Skein

**Hanker(ing)** Desire, Envy, Hunger, Itch, Long, Yearn, Yen

**Hanky-panky** Funny business, Nooky

**Hannibal** Carthaginian, Lecter, Punic

**Hansard** Minutes

**Haphazard** Aimless, Anyhow, Casual, Chance, Helter-skelter, Higgledy-piggledy, Hit and miss, Hitty-missy, Promiscuous, →RANDOM, Rough and tumble, Scattershot, Slapdash, Willy-nilly

**Happen(ing), Happen to** Afoot, Are, Be, Befall, Befortune, Betide, Chance, Come, Crop up, Event(uate), Fall-out, Incident, Materialise, →OCCUR, Pan, Pass, Phenomenon, Prove, Subvene, Thing, Tide, Transpire, Worth

**Happiness, Happy** Apposite, Ave, Beatific, Beatitude, Blessed, Bliss, Bluebird, Bonny, Carefree, Cheery, Chirpy, Chuffed, Cloud nine, Cock-a-hoop, Content, Dwarf, Ecstatic,

Elated, Eud(a)emony, Exhilarated, Felicity, Felix, Fool's paradise, Fortunate, Glad(some), Gleeful, Golden, Goshen, Gruntled, Halcyon, Half-cut, Hedonism, High-feather, Inebriated, Jovial, Joy, Jubilant, Kvell, Larry, Light-hearted, Mellow, Merry, Opportune, Radiant, Rapture, Sandboy, Seal, Seel, Sele, Serendipity, Serene, Slap, Squiffy, Sunny, Tiddl(e)y, Tipsy, Trigger, Warrior

**Happy medium** Juste milieu

**Hara-kiri** Eventration, Seppuku, Suicide

**Harangue** Declaim, Diatribe, Earwigging, Laisse, Lecture, Oration, Perorate, Philippic, Sermon, Speech, Spruik, Tirade

**Harass(ed)** Afflict, Annoy, Badger, Bait, Bego, Beleaguer, Beset, Bother, Chivvy, Distract, Dun, Gall, Grill, Grind, Grounden, Hassle, Haze, Heckle, Hector, Henpeck, Hound, Importune, Irritate, Molest, Needle, Nettle, Overdo, Persecute, Pester, Pingle, Plague, Press, Sekuhara, Stalk, Tailgate, Thwart, Torment, Trash, Vex

**Harbinger** Herald, Omen, Precursor, Usher

**Harbour(ed)** Alee, Anchorage, Basin, Brest, Cherish, Deep water, Dock, Entertain, Foster, Gosport, Haven, Heard, Herd, Hide, Hythe, Incubate, Kaipara, Lodge, Macquarie, Manukau, Marina, Mole, Mulberry, Nurse, Pearl, PLA, Poole, Port, Quay, Reset, Scapa Flow, Seaport, → SHELTER, Waitemata, Waterfront, Wellington

**Hard(en), Hardened, Hardness** Abstruse, Adamant(ine), Adularia, Arduous, Armour-plated, Augean, Austere, Billy-o, Bony, Brindell, Brinell, Brittle, Bronze, Cake, Calcify, Callous, Caramel, Cast-iron, Chitin, Compact, Concrete, Cornute, Crusty, Dentin(e), Diamond, Difficult, Dour, Draconian, Ebonite, Emery, Endure, Enure, Exacting, Fiery, Firm, Flint(y), Geal, Granite, Gruelling, H, Hawkish, Hellish, Herculean, HH, Horny, Indurate, Inure, Inveterate, Iron(y), Jasper, Knotty, Liparite, Lithoid, Metallic, Metally, Mohs, Mohs' scale, Murder, Nails, Obdurate, Obdure, Osseous, Ossify, Permafrost, Permanent, Petrify, Picrite, Raw, Rugged, Ruthless, Schist, Scirrhus, Scleral, Set, Severe, Solid, Sore, Steel(y), Steep, Stereo, Stern, Sticky, Stiff, Stoic, Stony, Strongly, Teak, Temper, Temporary, Tough, Uneasy, Unyielding, Wooden

**Hardback** Case-bound

**Hardboard** Masonite®

**Hard-boiled** Cynical

**Hard-core** Riprap, Scalpins

**Hard-headed** Obdurate, Stegocephalian

**Harding** Warden

**Hardliner** Hawk

**Hardly** Borderline, Ill, Just, Scarcely, Uneath(es), Unnethes

**Hard-pressed** Strait, Taxed

**Hardship** Adversity, Affliction, Austerity, Grief, Mill, Mishap, Ordeal, Penance, Privation, Rigour, Trial, Trouble

**Hard-top** Carapace, Shell

**Hardware** → COMPUTER HARDWARE, Gear, Ironmongery

**Hard-working** Studious

**Hardy** Brave, Dour, Durable, Gritty, Manful, Oliver, Ollie, Rugged, Spartan, Sturdy, Thomas

**Hare** Arctic, Baud(rons), Bawd, Belgian, Body-snatcher, Dash, Doe, Dolicholis, Down, Electric, Husk, Jack-rabbit, Jugged, Jumping, Lam, Leporine, Malkin, Mara, March, Mawkin, Mountain, Mouse, Ochotona, Pika, Piping, Puss, Scut, Snowshoe, Spring, Wat

**Harebell** Blawort

**Hare-brained** Giddy, Madcap, Scatty

**Harem, Harem lady** Gynaeceum, Gynoecium, Odalisque, Seraglio, Serai(l), Zenana

**Hark(en)** Ear, Hear, List(en)

**Harlequin** Chequered, Columbine, Pantaloon

**Harlot** Blue gown, Drab, Hussy, Loon, Loose, Lown, Paramour, Plover, Pusle, Pussel, Quail, Rahab, Scrubber, Slut, Strumpet, Whore

**Harm(ed), Harmful** Aggrieve, Bane, Blight, Damage, Deleterious, Dere, Detriment, Discredit, Disfigure, E-coli, Endamage, Evil, Hip, Hurt, Hyp, Inimical, Injury, Insidious, Maim, Maleficent, Malignant, Maltreat, Mischief, Nocuous, Noisome, Noxious, Pernicious, Scathe, Sinister, Spoil, Unwholesome, Wroken, Wrong

**Harmless** Benign, Canny, Drudge, Informidable, Innocent, Innocuous, Innoxious, Inoffensive

**Harmonica** Harp, Orpheus

**Harmonious, Harmonise, Harmonist, Harmony** Accord, Agree(ment), Alan, Allan, Allen, Alternation, Assort, Atone, Attune, Balanced, Barbershop, Blend, Chord, Close, Community, Concent, Concentus, Concert, Concinnity, Concord, Congruous, Consonant, Consort, Coordinate, Correspondence, Counterpoint, Descant, Détente, Diapason, Diatessaron, Doo-wop, Euphony, Eur(h)ythmy, Faburden, Feng-shui, Go, In step, Integrate, Jibe, Keeping, Key, Match, Melody, Mesh, Musical, Overblow, Overtone, Rappite, Rapport, Salve, Solidarity, Suit, Symmetry, Sympathy, Symphonious, Sync, Thorough-bass, Tone, Tune, Unanimity, Union, Unison, Unity

**Harmotome** Cross-stone

**Harness(maker)** Breeching, Bricole, Bridle, Cinch, D-ring, Equipage, Frenum, Gear, Gere, Girth, Hitch, Inspan, Lorimer, Loriner, Pad-tree, Partnership, Swingletree, Tack(le), Team, Teme, Throat-stop, Tie, Trace, Trappings, Tug, Whippletree, Yoke

**Harp(sichord)** Aeolian, Cembalo, Clairschach, Clarsach, Clavier, Drone, Dwell, Irish, Jew's, Kora, Lyre, Nebel, Trigon, Triple, Virginal, Welsh, Wind, Zither

**Harpagon** L'avare, Miser

**Harpoon(er)** Bart, Fis(h)gig, Fizgig, Grain, Iron, Lily iron, Peg, Spear, Specktioneer, Toggle iron, Toggler, Tow-iron, Trident

**Harpy** Aello, Celeno, Eagle, Ocypete

**Harridan** Hag, Harpy, Shrew, Termagant, Xantippe, Zantippe, Zentippe

**Harrier** Hen, Jet, Montagu's

**Harriet** Hetty, Martineau

**Harris** Boatman, Cloth, Island, Isle, Rolf

**Harrow(ing)** Alas, Appal, Brake, Disc, Distress, Drag, Frighten, Herse, Lacerant, Pitch-pole, Plough, Rake, Rend, Shock, Welaway, Welladay, Wellanear, Wellaway, Wring

**Harry** Aggravate, Badger, Bother, Champion, Chase, Chivvy, Coppernose, Dog, Dragoon, Flash, Fret, Hal, Harass, Hassle, Hector, Herry, Houdini, Hound, Lauder, Lime, Maraud, Molest, Nag, Pester, Plague, Rag, Ravage, Reave, Reive, Rieve, Rile, Tate, Tchick, Torment

▷ **Harry** *may indicate* an anagram

**Harsh(ness)** Abrasive, Acerbic, Asperity, Austere, Barbaric, Biting, Brassy, Cacophonous, Coarse, Cruel, Desolate, Discordant, Dissonant, Draconian, Extreme, Glary, Grating, Gravelly, Grim, Gruff, Guttural, Hard, Hoarse, Inclement, Oppressive, Raucid, Raucle, Raucous, Raw, Rigour, Risp, Rude, Ruthless, Scabrid, Scrannel, Screechy, →SEVERE, Sharp, Spartan, Stark, Stern, Stoor, Stour, Stowre, Strict, Strident, Unkind

**Hart** Deer, Spade, Spay, Spay(a)d, Venison

**Harte** Bret

**Hartebeest** Bubal, Kaama, Kongoni, Sassaby, Tsessebe

**Harum-scarum** Bayard, Chaotic, Madcap, Rantipole

**Harvest(er), Harvest home** Combine, Crop, Cull, Fruit, →GATHER, Glean, Hairst, Hawkey, Hay(sel), Hockey, Horkey, In(ning), Ingather, Kirn, Lease, Nutting, Pick, Produce, Rabi, Random, Reap, Seed-time, Shock, Spatlese, Spider, Tattie-howking, Thresh, Vendage, Vendange

**Has** Habet, Hath, Owns, 's

**Has-been** Effete, Ex, Outmoded

**Hash(ish)** Benj, Bungle, Charas, Discuss, Garble, Garboil, Hachis, Lobscouse, Mess, Mince, Pi(e), Ragout

▷ **Hashed** *may indicate* an anagram

**Hasn't** Hant, Nas

**Hassle** Aggro, Bother, Harry, M(o)ither, Moider, Strife

**Hassock** Kneeler, Pouf(fe), Stool, Tuffet

**Haste(n), Hastening, Hastily, Hasty** Amain, Cursory, Despatch, Elan, Expedite, Express, Festinately, Fly, Hare, Headlong, Helter-skelter, Hie, Hotfoot, → **HURRY**, Hurry-scurry, Impetuous, Precipitant, Race, Ramstam, Rash, Run, Rush, Scuttle, Speed, Spur, Stringendo, Subitaneous, Subito, Sudden, Tear, Tilt, Urge, Whistle-stop

**Hastings** Banda, Bustles, Senlac, Warren

**Hat** Broad-brim, → **CAP**, Cocked, → **HEADDRESS**, Head-rig, Lid, Lum, Nab, Red, Scarlet, Tit(fer)

---

## HATS

**3 letters:**
Fez
Tam
Tin
Top

**4 letters:**
Chip
Hard
Kepi
Pith
Plug
Poke
Silk
Sola
Tall
Tile
Topi
Ugly

**5 letters:**
Ascot
Beany
Beret
Brass
Bronx
Busby
Chaco
Crush
Derby
Gibus
Gimme
Mitre
Opera
Pagri
Pixie
Shako
Solah
Straw
Terai

Topee
Toque

**6 letters:**
Akubra®
Basher
Beanie
Beaver
Bicorn
Boater
Bobble
Bonnet
Bowler
Breton
Castor
Claque
Cloche
Coolie
Cowboy
Fedora
Gaucho
Hennin
Mob-cap
Panama
Safari
Sailor
Shacko
Shovel
Slouch
Sunhat
Toorie
Topper
Trilby
Turban
Witch's

**7 letters:**
Biretta
Chapeau
Christy

Cossack
Flat-cap
Hattock
Homburg
Leghorn
Matador
Petasus
Picture
Pill-box
Plateau
Pork-pie
Puritan
Skimmer
Stetson®
Sundown
Tarbush
Tricorn

**8 letters:**
Balmoral
Bearskin
Bongrace
Capotain
Christie
Mountie's
Mushroom
Planter's
Puggaree
Ramilies
Runcible
Skull-cap
Snap-brim
Sola-topi
Sombrero
Tarboosh
Tarboush
Thrummed
Tricorne
Tyrolean
Watch cap

**9 letters:**
Astrakhan
Billycock
Cartwheel
Cockle-hat
Dunstable
Glengarry
Lamington
Ramillies
Souwester
Stovepipe
Sugarloaf
Sunbonnet
Tarpaulin
Ten-gallon
Wide-awake

**10 letters:**
Balibuntal
Bluebonnet
Chimneypot
Poke-bonnet
Sola-helmet

**11 letters:**
Cabbage tree
Deerstalker
Dolly Varden
Kamelaukion
Mortarboard
Tam o'Shanter

**12 letters:**
Cheese-cutter
Fore-and-after
Steeple-crown

---

**Hat-band** Weeper

**Hatch(ment), Hatching** Achievement, Altricial, Booby, Breed, Brew, Brood, Cleck,

Clutch, Companion, Concoct, Conspire, Cover, Devise, Eclosion, Emerge, Escape, Incubate, Serving, Set, Trap-door

**Hatchet(-shaped)** Axe, Bill, Chopper, Claw, Cleaver, Dolabriform, Tomahawk

▷ **Hatching** *may indicate* an anagram

**Hatchway (surround)** Companionway, Fiddley, Guichet, Porthole, Scuttle, Service

**Hate(d), Hateful, Hatred** Abhor, Abominable, Abominate, Animus, Antipathetic, Aversion, Bugbear, Cursed, Detest, Enmity, Haterent, Loathe, Misogyny, Odium, Pet, Phobia, Racism, Resent, Sacred, Spite, Toad, Ug(h), Vitriol

**Hatless** Bareheaded, Unbeavered

**Hat-plant** S(h)ola

**Hatter** Mad

**Hat-trick** Threepeat

**Hatty** Etta

**Haughty, Haughtiness** Aloof, Aristocratic, Arrogant, Bashaw, Cavalier, Disdainful, Dorty, Fastuous, High, Hogen-mogen, Hoity-toity, Hye, Imperious, Lofty, Morgue, Orgillous, Orgulous, Paughty, → **PROUD**, Scornful, Sdeignful, Sniffy, Stiff-necked, Toffee-nosed, Toplofty, Upstage

**Haul(age), Haulier** Bag, Bouse, Bowse, Brail, Capstan, Carry, Cart, Catch, Drag, Heave, Hove, Kedge, Long, Loot, Plunder, Pull, Rug, Sally, Scoop, Snake, Snig, TIR, Tote, Touse, Touze, Tow(se), Towze, Transporter, Trice, Winch, Yank

**Haunch** Hance, Hip, Huckle, Hunkers, Quarter

**Haunt(s), Haunting** Catchy, Den, Dive, Evocative, Frequent, Ghost, Hang-out, Honky-tonk, Houf(f), Howf(f), Infest, Obsess, Possession, Purlieu, Resort, Spot, Spright

**Hauteur** Bashawism, Height, Morgue, Vanity

**Havana** Cigar

**Have, Having** Bear, Ha(e), Han, Hoax, Hold, Hoodwink, Know, Of, → **OWN**, Possess, Sell, With

**Haven** Asylum, Harbour, Hithe, Hythe, Nature reserve, Oasis, Port, Refuge, Refugium, Retreat, Safe, Sekos, Shelter, Tax

**Haver(s)** Blether, Clanjamfray, Dither, Gibber, Nigel, Owner

▶ **Haversack** *see* **RUCKSACK**

**Havoc** Desolation, Devastation, Hell, Mayhem, Ravage, Waste

▷ **Havoc** *may indicate* an anagram

**Haw** Drawl, Hip, Sloe

**Hawaiian** Kanaka

**Hawk(er), Hawkish** Accipitrine, Auceps, Austringer, Badger, Bastard, Buzzard, Cadger, Camelot, Caracara, Cast, Cheapjack, Cooper's, Cry, Duck, Eagle, Elanet, Eyas, Falcon, Fish, Gerfalcon, Goshawk, Haggard, Hardliner, Harrier, Harrumph, Hobby, Honey-buzzard, Keelie, Kestrel, Kight, Kite, Lammergeier, Lanner(et), Marsh, Merlin, Molla(h), Monger, Moolah, Mosquito, Mullah, Musket, Night, Nyas, Osprey, Ossifrage, Passage(r), Pearlie, Pearly, Peddle, Pedlar, Peregrine, Pigeon, Privet, Ringtail, Sacre(t), Sell, Slab, Slanger, Soar(e), Sorage, Sore(-eagle), Sparrow, Spiv, Staniel, Stone, Sutler, Tallyman, Tarsal, Tarsel(l), Tassel, Tercel(et), Tiercel, Tote, Tout, Trant(er), Trucker, Warlike, Warmonger

**Hawkeye** IA, Iowa

**Hawk-keeper** Austringer, Ostreger

**Hawser** Cable, Line, Rope

**Hawthorn** Albespine, Albespyne, May(flower), Quickset, Quickthorn

**Hay(cock), Hey, Haybox** Antic, Bale, Cock, Contra-dance, Fodder, Goaf, Hi, Kemple, Math, Mow, Norwegian nest, Norwegian oven, Pleach, Pook, Salt, Stack, Straw, Truss, Windrow

**Hayfever** Pollenosis, Pollinosis

**Haymaker** Blow, Slog

**Hayseed** Chaw-bacon, Hodge, Joskin, Rustic

**Hazard(ous)** Bet, Booby trap, Breakneck, Bunker, Chance, Danger, Dare, Die, Dye, Estimate, Game, Gremlin, Guess, Hero, Hornet's nest, Ice, Imperil, In-off, Jeopardy, Losing, Main, Minefield, Mist, Moral, Nice, Niffer, Occupational, Perdu(e), Peril, Pitfall, Play, Pothole, Queasy, Razor-edge, →**RISK**, Risque, Stake, Thread, Trap, Venture, Vigia, Wage, Winning

**Haze, Hazy** Blear, Cloud, Filmy, Fog, →**MIST**, Mock, Muzzy, Nebulous, Pea-souper, Smaze, Smog, Tease

▷ **Haze** *may indicate* an anagram

**Hazel(wort)** Amenta, Asarabacca, Catkin, Cob, Corylus, Filbert, Lambs' tails

**HC** Encomia, Encomium

**He, HE** A, Cestui, Helium, Tag, Tig, →**TNT**, Tom

**Head(s), Head for, Heading, Headman, Head shaped, Heady** Abuna, Aim, Apex, Ard-ri(gh), Beachy, Bean, Behead, Bill, Block, Bonce, Boss, Bound, Brain, Brainpan, Bregma, Brow, But(t), Byline, Cabbage, Caboceer, Can, Cape, Capitani, Capitate, Capitulum, Capo, Captain, Caption, Caput, Caudillo, Cauliflower, Cephalic, Chaton, Chief, Chump, Coarb, Coconut, Coma, Comarb, Commander, Conk, Cop, Coppin, Costard, Cranium, Crest, Crisis, Crown, Crumpet, Crust, Cylinder, Dateline, Dean, Director, Dome, Dummy, Each, Ear, Exarch, Figure, Flamborough, Foam, Foreland, Froth, General, Glomerate, Grand Mufti, Hegumen(os), Herm(a), Hoe, Hogh, Huff-cap, Inion, Jowl, Karmapa, Keyword, Knob, Knowledge-box, Lead(er), Lemma, Lid, Lizard, Loaf, Loave, Loo, Lore, Malik, Manager, Mayor, Maz(z)ard, Melik, Mocuddum, Mogul, Mokaddam, Morne, Mr Big, Mull, Muqaddam, Nab, Nana, Napper, Nappy, Ness, Nob, Noddle, Noggin, Noll, Noup, Nowl, Nut, Obelion, Obverse, Occiput, Onion, Panicle, Panorama, Parietal, Pash, Pate, Pater(familias), Patriarch, Pick-up, Point, Poll, Pow, Prefect, President, Pressure, Principal, Promontory, Provost, Ras, Read-write, Ream, Rector, Repair, Ringleader, Rubric, Sarpanch, Scalp, Scaup, Scaw, Scholarch, Scolex, Sconce, Short, Sinciput, Skaw, Skull, Sound, Source, Spume, Squeers, Stad(t)holder, Starosta, Strapline, Subject, Superior, Supervisor, Taipan, Talking, Tanadar, Tete, Thanadar, Throne, Tight, Tintagel, Tip, Title, Toilet, Top, Topic, Tsantsa, Twopenny, Upperworks, Vaivode, Velocity, Voivode, Yorick, Zero in, Zupan

▷ **Head** *may indicate* the first letter of a word

**Headache** Cephalalgia, Encephalalgia, Hangover, Hemicrania, Megrim, Migraine, Neuralgia, Red out, Scotodinia, Splitter

**Headband** Blindfold, Diadem, Fillet, Garland, Infula, Sphendone, T(a)enia

**Headbanger** Grebo, Nutcase

**Head cover, Headdress, Head gear** Aigrette, Alice band, Ampyx, Balaclava, Bandeau, Bas(i)net, Bearskin, Bonnet, Bridle, Burnous(e), Busby, Calotte, Caul, Chaplet, Circlet, Comb, Commode, Cor(o)net, Cowl, Coxcomb, Crownet, Curch, Diadem, Doek, Dopatta, Dupatta, Fascinator, Feather bonnet, Fontange, Fool's cap, Frontlet, Hat(tock), Helm(et), Joncanoe, Juliet cap, Kaffiyeh, Kell, Kepi, Kerchief, Kuffiyeh, Kufiah, Kufiya(h), Madras, Mantilla, Mitre, Mobcap, Modius, Mortarboard, Nubia, Periwig, Pill-box, Plug-hat, Porrenger, Porringer, Quoif, Romal, Rumal, Sakkos, Ship-tire, Silly-how, Skid lid, Skullcap, Sphendone, Stephane, Taj, Tarbush, Tiara, Tire-vallant, Topi, Tower, Tulban, Turban, War bonnet, Wig, Wimple, Wreath

**Header** Bonder, Brick, Dive, Fall, Rowlock

**Headhunter** Naga

**Headland** Beachy Head, Bill, Cape, Cape Horn, Dungeness, Finisterre, Foreland, Head-rig, Hoe, Hogh, Land's End, Morro, Naze, Ness, Noup, Point, →**PROMONTORY**, Ras, Ross, St Vincent, Scaw, Skaw

**Headless** Acephalous

**Headlight(s)** Beam, Brights, Dip, Halo, Sealed-beam

**Headline** Banner, Caption, Drophead, Frown, Kicker, Majuscular, Ribbon, Scare-head, Screamer, Splash, Strapline, Streamer, Title

**Headlock** Chancery

**Headlong** Breakneck, Helter-skelter, Pell-mell, Plummet, Precipitate, Ramstam, Reckless, Steep, Sudden, Tantivy, Tearaway

▸ **Headman** *see* HEAD(S)

**Headmaster** Arnold, Principal, Squeers

**Headphone(s)** Cans, Earpiece, Walkman®

**Headquarters** Base, Command, Command post, Depot, Guardhouse, Guildhall, Pentagon, Praetorium, SHAEF, SHAPE, Station, Torshavn, Valley Forge

▷ **Heads** *may indicate* a lavatory

**Headset** Can

**Headsman** Executioner

**Headstrong** Obstinate, Rash, Stubborn, Unruly, Wayward, Wilful

**Head-to-tail** Tête-bêche

**Headway** Advancement, Headroom, Progress

**Head-word** Lemma

**Heal(ing)** Absent, Aesculapian, Ayurveda, Balsam, Chiropractic, Cicatrise, Cleanse, Curative, Cure, Distant, Esculapian, G(u)arish, Hele, Hippocratise, Intention, Knit, Mend, Mental, Naturopathy, New Thought, Olosis, Osteopathy, Recuperation, Restore, Sain, Salve, Sanative, Sanitary, Spiritual, Styptic, Therapeutic, Time, Vulnerary

**Healer** Althea, Asa, Doctor, Homeopath, Medicine man, Naturopath, Osteopath, Sangoma, Shaman, Time

**Health(y)** Aglow, Aseptic, Bottoms up, Bouncing, Bracing, Cheerio, Chin-chin, Constitution, Cosy, Doer, Environmental, Fat-free, Fit(ness), Flourishing, Gesundheit, Hail, Hale, Hartie-hale, Heart, Holism, Hygeian, Kia-ora, L'chaim, Lustique, Lusty, Medicaid, Medicare, Piert, Pink, Prosit, Public, Robust, Rosy, Ruddy, Salubrious, Sane, Slainte, Sound, Toast, Tope, Valentine, Valetudinarian, Vigour, Welfare, Well, Wellbeing, WHO, Wholesome

**Heap(ed), Heaps** Acervate, Agglomerate, Amass, Bing, Boneshaker, Bulk, Car, Clamp, Coacervate, Cock, Compost, Congeries, Cumulus, Drift, Hog, Jalopy, Lot, Molehill, Pile, Pyre, Raff, Raft, Rattletrap, Rick(le), Ruck, Scads, Scrap, Shell, Slag, Stash, Tass, Toorie, Up-piled

**Hear(ing), Hearing problem** Acoustic, Attend, Audience, Audile, Avizandum, Captain's mast, Catch, Clairaudience, Dirdum, Ear, Glue ear, Harken, Learn, List(en), Oyer, Oyez, Panel, Paracusis, Pick up, Session, Subpoena, Tin ear, Tinnitus, Try

▷ **Hear(say)** *may indicate* a word sounding like one given

**Hearsay** Account, Anecdotal, Gossip, Report, Rumour, Second-hand, Surmise

**Hearse** Bier, Catafalco, Catafalque, Meat wagon, Shillibeer

**Heart(en), Heartily, Hearty, Heart-shaped** AB, Agood, Auricle, Backslapping, Beater, Bleeding, Bluff, Bosom, Bradycardia, Buoy, Cant, Cardiac, Centre, Cheer, Cockles, Columella, Cordate, Cordial, Core, Courage, Crossed, Daddock, Embolden, Encourage, Essence, Fatty, Floating, Gist, H, Hale, Herz, Hub, Inmost, Jarta, Kernel, Lepid, Lonely, Lusty, Memoriter, Mesial, Mid(st), Middle, Nub, Nucleus, Obcordate, Pericardium, Pith, Purple, Reassure, Robust, Root, Sacred, Sailor, Seafarer, Seaman, Sinoatrial, Staunch, Tachycardia, Tar, Ticker, Tweedy, Yarta, Yarto

**Heart-break** Crève-coeur, Grief, Sorrow

**Heartfelt** Deep, Genuine, Real, Sincere, Soulful, Triste

**Hearth** Cupel, Finery, Fireside, Home, Ingle, Killogie

**Heartless** Callous, Cored, Cruel, Inhumane, Three-suited

**Heart's ease** Pansy

**Heart-throb** Idol, Ladies' man, Valentino

**Heart trouble, Heartburn** Bradycardia, Brash, Cardialgia, Fallot's tetralogy, Fibrillation, Murmur, Pyrosis, Tachycardia

**Heat(ed), Heater, Heating** Anneal, Ardour, Arousal, Atomic, Background, Bainite, Barrage, Beath, Blood, Brazier, Calcine, Calescence, Califont, Caloric, Calorifier, Central, Chafe, Chip, Convector, Dead, Decay, Dielectric, Dudgeon, Eccaleobion, Element,

Eliminator, Emotion, Endothermic, Enthalpy, Estrus, Etna, Excite, Exothermic, Fan, Ferment, Fever, Fire, Fluster, Fug, Furnace, Gat, Gleed, Gun, Het, Hibachi, Hyperthermia, Hypocaust, Immersion, Incalescence, Induction, J, Kettle, Kindle, Latent, Liquate, Lust, Mowburn, Moxibustion, Normalise, Oestrus, Panel, Passion, Prelim, Pre-warm, Prickly, Pyrolysis, Q, Quartz, Radiant, Radiator, Rankine, Recalescence, Red, Render, Repechage, Rut, Salamandrian, Salt, Scald, Sinter, Sizzle, Smelt, Solar, Space, Specific, Spice, Stew, Storage, Stove, Swelter, Teend, Temperature, Thermotics, Tind, Tine, Torrefy, Total, Tynd(e), Underfloor, Verve, Warming-pan, Warmth, White, Zip®

**Heath(land)** Bearberry, Bent, Briar, Brier, Egdon, Epacrid, Erica, Geest, Lande, Manoao, Manzanita, Moor, Muir, Stead, Ted

**Heathen(s)** Ethnic, Gentile, Godless, Idolator, Infidel, Litholatrous, Nations, Pagan, Pa(i)nim, Paynim, Philistine, Primitive, Profane, Proselyte of the gate, Ungodly

**Heather(y)** Bell, Broom, Calluna, Epacrid, Erica, Ericoid, Foxberry, Ling, Rhodora, Sprig

▷ **Heating** *may indicate* an anagram

**Heat stroke** Calenture

**Heave(d), Heaving** Cast, Emesis, Fling, Frost, Heeze, Hoise, Hoist, Hump, Hurl, Popple, Retch, Shy, Sigh, Vomit

▷ **Heave** *may indicate* 'discard'

**Heaven(s), Heavenly** Air, Aloft, Ama, Ambrosial, Arcady, Asgard, Bliss, Celestial, Celia, Divine, Ecstasy, Elysian, Elysium, Empyrean, Ethereal, Euphoria, Fiddler's Green, Firmament, Hereafter, Himmel, Hog, Holy, Hookey Walker, Land o' the Leal, Lift, Mackerel, New Jerusalem, Olympus, On high, Paradise, Pole, Rapture, Seventh, Shangri-la, Sion, Sky, Sublime, Supermundane, Supernal, Svarga, Swarga, Swerga, Tir na n'Og, Upper region, Uranian, Utopia, Welkin, Zion

**Heavy(weight), Heavily, Heaviness** Ali, Biased, Bodyguard, Bouncer, Close, Clumpy, Dutch, Elephantine, Embonpoint, Endomorph, Gorilla, Gothic, Grave, Hefty, Last, Leaden, Lumpish, Muscleman, Onerous, Osmium, Pesante, Ponderous, Roughneck, Sad, Scelerate, Stodgy, Stout, Top, Torrential, Upsee, Ups(e)y, Weighty, Wicked

**Hebe** Barmaid

**Hebrew** Aramaic, Eli, Heb, Jesse, Karaism, Levi, Mishnayoth, Modern, Rabbinical, Yid

**Hebrides, Hebridean** Harris, Western Isles

**Heck** Doggone

**Heckle** Badger, Gibe, Harass, Hatchel, Jeer, Needle, Spruik

**Hectic** Ding-dong, Feverish, Frenetic, Rat race

**Hector** Badger, Belabour, Bluster, Browbeat, Bully, → **HARASS**, Nag

**Hedge, Hedging** Box, Bullfinch, Enclosure, Equivocate, Evade, Haw, Hay, Lay off, Meuse, Mews, Muse, Ox-fence, Pleach, Prevaricate, Privet, Pussyfoot, Quickset, Raddle, Sepiment, Shield, Stall, Stonewall, Temporise, Texas, Thicket, Waffle

**Hedgehog** Erinaceous, Gymnure, Hérisson, Tenrec, Tiggywinkle, Urchin

**Hedge-hop** Fly low

**Hedge-parson** Bucklebeggar, Patercove

**Hedge-sparrow** Accentor

**Hedonist** Cyreniac, Epicurean, Playboy, Sybarite

**Heed(ed), Heedful** Attend, Cavendo tutus, Gaum, Gorm, Listen, → **MIND**, Notice, Obey, Observe, Rear, Reck, Regard(ant), Reke, Respect, Rought, Tent, Tinker's cuss

**Heedless** Blithe, Careless, Inattentive, Incautious, Rash, Scapegrace, Scatterbrain, Unaware

**Heehaw** Bray

**Heel** Achilles, Cad, Calcaneum, Cant, Careen, Cuban, Dogbolt, Foot, French, Incline, Kitten, List, Louse, Parliament, Rat, Rogue, Seel, Spike, Stacked, Stiletto, Tilt, Wedge, Wedgie

**Heel-tap** Snuff

**Hefty** Brawny, Heavy, Solid, Weighty

**Heifer** Freemartin, Io, Quey, Stirk

**Height(en), Heights** Abraham, Altitude, Cairngorm, Ceiling, Dimension, Elevation, Embroider, Eminence, Enhance, Eye-level, Giddy, Golan, H, Hem, Hill, Ht, Hypsometry, Level, Might, Mount, Peak, Procerity, Roof, Shap, Spot, Stature, Stud, Sum, → SUMMIT, Tallness, Tor, X, Zenith

**Heinous** Abominable, Atrocious, Flagrant

**Heir** Alienee, Atheling, Claimant, Coparcener, Dauphin, Devisee, Distributee, Eigne, H(a)eres, Institute, Intitule, Legatee, Parcener, Scion, Sprig, Successor, Tanist

**Heirless** Escheat, Intestate

**Held** Captive, Hostage, Sostenuto, Ten(uto)

▷ **Held by** *may indicate* a hidden word

**Helen** Elaine, Nell(y)

**Helicopter (crew), Heliport** Airstop, Chopper, Egg-beater, Gunship, Hover, Iroquois, Medevac, Rotodyne, Sea Cobra, Sea King, Sea Knight, Sea Sprite, Sea Stallion, Sikorsky, Sky-hook, Whirlybird, Winchman

**Helios** Hyperion

**Heliotrope** Cherry-pie

**Helium** He

**Helix** Alpha, Coil, Double, Parastichy, Spiral

**Hell(ish)** Abaddon, Abyss, Ades, Agony, Amenthes, Annw(yf)n, Avernus, Below, Blazes, Bottomless pit, Chthonic, Dis, Erebus, Furnace, Gehenna, Hades, Heck, Inferno, Jahannam, Lower regions, Malebolge, Naraka, Netherworld, Orcus, Pandemonium, Perditious, Pit, Ruin, Sheol, Stygian, Tartar(ean), Tartaric, Tartarus, Tophet, Torment

**Hellbender** Menopome, Mud-puppy

**Hellebore** Bear's foot, Itchweed, Melampode, Setterwort

**Hellenic** Dorian

**Hellespont** Dardanelles

**Hello, Hallo, Hullo** Aloha, Chin-chin, Ciao, Dumela, G'day, Golden, Hi, Ho(a), Hoh, Howdy, Howzit, Wotcha, Wotcher, Yoo-hoo

**Helm(sman)** Cox, Navigator, Pilot, Steer, Tiller, Timon(eer)

**Helmet** Armet, Balaclava, Basinet, Bearskin, Beaver, Brain bucket, Burganet, Burgonet, Cask, Casque, Comb, Crash, Galea, Gas, Hard hat, Heaume, Knapscal, Knapscull, Knapskull, Montero, Mor(r)ion, Nasal, Pickelhaube, Pith, Plumed, Pot, Pressure, Salade, Sal(l)et, Shako, Skid-lid, Smoke, Tin hat, Topee, Topi

**Helot** Esne, Slave

**Help(er), Helping, Helpful** Abet, Accommodate, Accomplice, Adjuvant, Advantage, Aid(ance), Aidant, Aide, Alexis, Alleviate, Ally, Asset, → ASSIST, Avail, Back, Beet-master, Beet-mister, Befriend, Benefit, Bestead, Boon, Brownie, Carer, Char(woman), Charity, Coadjutor, Collaborate, Complice, Conducive, Daily, Dollop, Dose, Ezra, Forward, Further(some), Go, Godsend, Hand, Handyman, Henchman, Hint, Home, Hyphen, Instrumental, Intercede, Kind, Leg-up, Life-saver, Maid, Mayday, Monitor, Obliging, Ophelia, Order, Patronage, Pitch in, Promote, Prompt, Quantity, Ration, Recourse, Relieve, Samaritan, Servant, Serve, Service, Slice, SOS, Stead, Sted, Subserve, Subvention, Succour, Taste, Therapeutic, Use

**Helpless(ness)** Adynamia, Anomie, Downa-do, Feeble, High and dry, Impotent, Incapable, Incapacity, Paralytic, Prostrate, Useless

**Helpmate** Consort

**Hem** Border, Fringe, Hoop, List

**He-man** Adonis, Hunk, Jock, Macho

**Hemisphere, Hemispherical** Antichthon, Cupular, Dominant, Magdeburg, Rose-cut, Western

**Hemlock** Conia, Cowbane, Insane root, Tsuga

**Hemp** Abaca, Bhang, Boneset, Bowstring, Carl(ot), Choke-weed, Codilla, Crotalaria, Dagga, Fimble, Ganja, Hards, Henequen, Hiniquin, Indian, Kef, K(a)if, Love-drug, Manil(l)a, Mauritius, Moorva, Murva, Neckweed, Pita, Sida, Sisal, Sunn, Tat, Tow

**Hen(s)** Ancona, Andalusian, Australorp, Biddy, Buff Orpington, Chock, Clocker, Cochin, Deep litter, Dorking, Eirack, Fowl, Grig, Houdan, Langshan, Layer, Leghorn, Maori, Marsh, Mother, Mud, Orpington, Partlet, Pertelote, Plymouth Rock, Poulard, Poultry, Pullet, Ree(ve), Rhode Island red, Sitter, Spanish fowl, Speckled, Sultan, Tappit, Welsummer, Wyandotte

**Hence** Apage, Avaunt, Ergo, Go, Hinc, Scram, So, Therefore, Thus

**Henchman** Abetter, Attendant, Follower, Led captain, Myrmidon, Satellite

**Hen-house** Battery, Eggery

**Henna** Camphire

**Hennery** Run

**Hen-party** Kitchen tea

**Hen-pecked** Pussy-whipped, Spineless, Woman-tired

**Henry** Eighth, H, Hal, Hank, Hooray, Hy, James, Navigator, O

**Hep** Bacca, Berry, Hip, Wise

**Hepatic** Scale-moss

**Hepatitis** Favism, Jaundice

**Herald(ic), Heraldry** Crier, Earl Marshal, Hermes, Messenger

---

## HERALDRIES

**2 letters:**
Or

**3 letters:**
Lis
Vol

**4 letters:**
Bars
Bend
Coue
Fess
File
Golp
Lyon
Nowy
Pale
Paly
Pile
Posé
Vair
Vert
Yale

**5 letters:**
Azure
Cabré
Chief
Crest
Fesse
Flory
Golpe
Gules
Morné

Nowed
Pheon
Sable
Scarp
Scrog
Tenné
Trick
Usher
Vairé

**6 letters:**
Albany
Argent
Armory
Bagwyn
Billet
Checky
Cleché
Coupee
Erased
Fecial
Fetial
Flanch
Garter
Lionel
Lodged
Moline
Mullet
Naiant
Nebulé
Nebuly
Norroy
Pallet
Potent

Sea dog
Sejant
Verdoy
Verrey
Voided
Volant
Vorant
Wivern
Wreath
Wyvern

**7 letters:**
Alerion
Armiger
Bearing
Bordure
Chevron
Compone
Compony
Dormant
Endorse
Enfiled
Fracted
Gardant
Gironny
Gyronny
Herissé
Issuant
Manchet
Martlet
Nascent
Nombril
Passant
Portate

Portend
Purpure
Rampant
Red Hand
Roundel
Roundle
Rousant
Salient
Sea lion
Sejeant
Statant
Stentor
Trangle
Trundle
Urinant

**8 letters:**
Allerion
Bendwise
Blazonry
Caboched
Cicerone
Couchant
Dancette
Degraded
Dragonné
Emblazon
Hauriant
Herisson
Naissant
Opinicus
Ordinary
Proclaim
Sanglier

Segreant
Tressure
Trippant
Umbrated
Woodwose

**9 letters:**
Abatement
Debruised
Dimidiate
Displayed
Eightfoil
Enveloped

Precursor
Regardant
Supporter
Woodhouse

**10 letters:**
Bloody Hand
Blue Mantle
Cinquefoil
Clarenceux
Cockatrice
Difference
Fetterlock

Forerunner
King-of-arms
Portcullis
Pursuivant
Quartering
Rouge Croix
Sans nombre

**11 letters:**
Clarencieux
Honour-point
Rouge Dragon
Subordinary

**12 letters:**
Bend sinister
Interfretted
Vaunt-courier

**13 letters:**
Baton sinister
Calygreyhound
Undifferenced

**14 letters:**
Counter-passant
Lyon King of Arms

---

**Herb(aceous), Herbs** Bouquet garni, Garnish, Maror, Salad, Seasoning, Simple, Suffruticose, Weed

---

## HERBS

**3 letters:**
Bay
Oca
Pia
Rue

**4 letters:**
Aloe
Balm
Cive
Dill
Forb
Mint
Moly
Sage
Wort

**5 letters:**
Anise
Avens
Basil
Chive
Clary
Cumin
Eruca
Fitch
Inula
Medic
Orval
Senna
Tansy
Thyme
Typha
Vetch
Yerba

**6 letters:**
Ajowan
Bennet
Betony
Borage
Capers
Cicely
Cohosh
Cummin
Fennel
Ferula
Garlic
Hyssop
Lovage
Madder
Orache
Origan
Purpie
Saloop
Salvia
Savory
Sesame
Sorrel
Willow
Yarrow
Za'atar

**7 letters:**
Aconite
Alecost
Aniseed
Arugula
Boneset
Caraway
Catmint

Chervil
Chicory
Comfrey
Dittany
Felicia
Fuller's
Gentian
Gunnera
Hemlock
Lewisia
Madwort
Mustard
Oregano
Origane
Paprika
Parsley
Phlomis
Saffron
Salsify
Vervain

**8 letters:**
Agrimony
Allspice
Angelica
Bergamot
Camomile
Cardamom
Centaury
Cilantro
Costmary
Estragon
Feverfew
Fireweed
Fluellin

Knapweed
Mandrake
Marjoram
Origanum
Plantain
Purslane
Reed-mace
Rosemary
Soapwort
Staragen
Tarragon
Turmeric
Valerian
Veronica
Wormwood

**9 letters:**
Chamomile
Colic root
Coriander
Echinacea
Eyebright
Fenugreek
Germander
Haworthia
Kalanchoe
Lamb's ears
Laserwort
Parakelia
Pennyroyal
Pussytoes
Rhizocarp
Rodgersia
Spearmint
Tormentil

## Herbalist | 374

| 10 letters: | 11 letters: | 12 letters: | 13 letters: |
|---|---|---|---|
| Lemon grass | Laserpicium | Aristolochia | Good-King-Henry |
| Oleraceous | Rupturewort | Mountain flax | |
| Parakeelya | Sweet cicely | Ornithogalum | 14 letters: |
| Pipsissewa | | Skunk cabbage | Paterson's curse |
| Rest-harrow | | Southernwood | |

**Herbalist** Simplist
**Herbarium** Hortus siccus
**Herbert** Alan, AP(H), Lom, Spencer
**Herbicide** Agent Orange, Atrazine, Defoliant, Diquat, Glufosinate, Picloram, Simazine
**Herbivore** Iguanodon, Sauropod
**Hercules** Alcides, Huge, Rustam, Rustem
**Herd(er), Herding, Herdsman** Band, Buffalo, Byreman, Corral, Cowpuncher, Drive, Drover, Flock, Gang, Lowing, Marshal, Meinie, Mein(e)y, Menyie, Mob, Pod, Rabble, Raggle-taggle, Round-up, Shepherd, Tail, Tinchel, Vaquero, Wrangling
**Here** Adsum, Hi, Hic, Hither, Kilroy, Local, Now, Oy, Present
**Hereafter** Eternity, Other world
**Hereditary, Heredity** Ancestry, Blood, Breeding, Codon, Dynastic, Eugenics, Exon, Genetics, Id(ant), Idioplasm, Inborn, Mendelism, Panagenesis
▷ **Herein** *may indicate* a hidden word
**Here is laid** HS
**Heresiarch** Nestor
**Heresy, Heretic(al)** Agnoitae, Albi, Albigensian, Apollinaris, Apostasy, Arian, Arius, Bab, Bogomil, Bugger, Cathar, Cerinthus, Docete, Donatist, Dulcinist, Encratite, Errant, Eudoxian, Giaour, Gnosticism, Heresearch, Heterodoxy, Lollard, Manichaean, Montanism, Nestorian, Non-believer, Nonconformist, Origen, Patarin(e), Pelagius, Phrygian, Racovian, Rebel, Revisionist, Unitarian, Zendik
**Heritage** Birthright, Due, NT, Odette, Ottilie, Patrimony
**Hermaphrodite** Androgynous, Bi-, Gynandromorph, Monochinous, Monoecious, Prot(er)andry, Protogyny
**Hermes (rod)** Caduceus, Mercury
**Hermetic** Alchemist, Sealed
**Hermit(age), Hermit-like** Anchoret, Anchorite, Ascetic, Ashram(a), Augustinian, Austin, Cell, Cloister, Crab, Eremite, Grandmontine, Hieronymite, Loner, Marabout, Monk, Museum, Nitrian, Pagurid, Peter, Recluse, Retreat, Robber-crab, Sannyasi, Soldier-crab, Solitary, Troglodyte
**Hernia** Bubonocele, Cystocoele, Diverticulum, Enterocele, Eventration, Hiatal, Hiatus, Inguinal, Rectocele, Rupture
**Hero(es), Heroic** Asgard, Brave, Champ(ion), Couplet, Derring-do, Eidola, Epic, Eponym, Folk, God, Goody, Great, Icon, Ideal, Idol, Lion, Noble, Olitory, Priestess, Principal, Resolute, Tragic, Valiant, VC, White knight

## HEROES

| 3 letters: | Tell | Orion | Batman |
|---|---|---|---|
| Cid | | Rambo | Bunyan |
| | 5 letters: | Raven | Cyrano |
| 4 letters: | Bader | Sheik | Fingal |
| Aitu | Drake | Zorro | Gideon |
| Ajax | El Cid | | Hector |
| Eric | Faust | 6 letters: | Kaleva |
| Finn | Jason | Aeneas | Nelson |
| Kami | Orfeo | Amadis | Nestor |

| | | | |
|---|---|---|---|
| Oliver | Ivanhoe | Everyman | Lochinvar |
| Onegin | Lothair | Glooscap | Lord Byron |
| Orsino | Marmion | Heracles | Owleglass |
| Ossian | Oedipus | Hercules | Owspiegle |
| Revere | Paladin | Hiawatha | Siegfried |
| Roland | Perseus | Leonidas | Spiderman |
| Rustem | Rinaldo | Meleager | |
| Rustum | Saladin | Odysseus | *10 letters:* |
| Samson | Tancred | Owlglass | Cuchullain |
| Shandy | Theseus | Parsifal | Howleglass |
| Sigurd | Tristam | Pericles | Owlspiegle |
| Tarzan | Tristan | Roderego | |
| Virago | Ulysses | Roderick | *11 letters:* |
| | Volsung | Superman | Bellerophon |
| *7 letters:* | Werther | Tristram | Finn MacCool |
| Alcides | | | Hudibrastic |
| Asterix | *8 letters:* | *9 letters:* | Philoctetes |
| Beowulf | Achilles | Agamemnon | Ramachandra |
| Dan Dare | Argonaut | Cuchulain | Tam o' Shanter |
| Demigod | Balarama | Dambuster | |
| Gluscap | Cisco Kid | Garibaldi | *13 letters:* |
| Gluskap | Crockett | John Henry | Vercingetorix |

**Herod** Agrippa, Antipas

**Heroin** Chase-the-dragon, Diamorphine, Dogfood, Doojie, Dynamite, Gumball, H, Harry, Henry, Horse, Jack, Junk, Scag, Schmeck, Shit, Skag, Smack, Snow, Snowball, Speedball, Sugar, White stuff

**Heroine** Andromeda, Ariadne, Candida, Cleopatra, Darling, Demigoddess, Electra, Eurydice, Hedda, Heidi, Imogen, Isolde, Judith, Juliet, Leda, Leonora, Lulu, Manon, Mimi, Nana, Norma, Pamela, Star, Tess, Tosca, Una

**Heron(s)** Ardea, Bird, Bittern, Boat-billed, Butter-bump, Egret, Green, Handsaw, Kotuko, Screamer, Sedge, Siege, Squacco, Winnard

**Herpes** Cold sore, Dartre, Shingles, Shiver

**Herring** Bismarck, Bloater, Brisling, Brit, Buckling, Caller, Cisco, Clupea, Digby chick(en), Gaspereau, Glasgow magistrate, Kipper, Lake, Maise, Maize, Ma(a)tjes, Mattie, Maze, Mease, Menhaden, Norfolk capon, Ox eye, Rabbitfish, Red, Rollmop, Sea-stick, Shotten, Sild, Silt, Sparling, Teleost, Whitebait

**Herringbone** Sloping

**Hesitant, Hesitate, Hesitation** Balance, Boggle, Cunctation, Delay, Demur, Dicker, Dither, Doubtful, Dubitate, Dwell, Er, Erm, Falter, Halting, Haver, Haw, Irresolute, Mammer, Mealy-mouthed, →PAUSE, Qualm, Scruple, Shillyshally, Shrink, Stagger, Stammer, Stutter, Swither, Tarrow, Teeter, Tentative, Think twice, Um, Um and ah, Ur, Vacillate, Wait, Waver

**Hesperus** Vesper

**Hessian** Burlap, Hireling

**Heterodoxy** Heresy

**Heterogeneous** Diverse, Motley, Piebald

**Heterosexual** Hasbian, Straight

**Hew(er)** Ax, Chop, Cut, Gideon, Hack, Sever

**Hex** Bewitch, Jinx, Voodoo

**Hexameter** Dolichurus, Miurus

▸ **Hey** *see* HAY(COCK)

**Heyday** Prime, Summer

**Hi** Cooee, Hello, Howdie

**Hiatus** Caesura, Entr'acte, Gap, Hernia, Interact, Interregnum, Interval, Lacuna, Lull, Respite

**Hibernal, Hibernate, Hibernating** Estivate, Hiemal, Hole up, Latitant, Sleep, Winter

**Hibernian** Irish

**Hibiscus** Okra, Roselle, Rozelle

**Hiccup** Blip, Glitch, Hitch, Singultus, Snag, Spasm, Yex

**Hick** Jake, Oaf, Podunk, Rube, Yokel

**Hickory** Black, Jackson, Mockernut, Pecan, Scaly-bark, Shagbark

**Hidden** Buried, Cabalistic, Covert, Cryptic, Delitescent, De(a)rn, Doggo, Eclipsed, Healed, Hooded, Latent, Obscure, Occult, Pentimento, Recondite, Screened, Secret, Shuttered, Sly, Subterranean, Ulterior, Unseen, Veiled, Wrapped

▷ **Hidden** *may indicate* a concealed word

**Hide, Hiding (place)** Abscond, Babiche, Basan, Befog, Bield(y), Blind, Box-calf, Burrow, Bury, Butt, Cache, Camouflage, Cane, Ceroon, Coat, →CONCEAL, Coonskin, Cootch, Cordwain, Couch, Cour, Crop, Curtain, Cwtch, Dea(r)n, Deerskin, Derm, Dissemble, Doggo, Earth, Eclipse, Encave, Ensconce, Enshroud, Envelop, Epidermis, Fell, Flaught, Flay, Fur, Gloss over, Harbour, Heal, Heel, Hele, Hell, Hibernate, Hole-up, Hoodwink, Incave, Inter, Kip, Kipskin, Lair, Leather, Lie doggo, Mai-mai, Mask, Mew, Mobble, Morocco, Nebris, →OBSCURE, Paper over, Parfleche, Pell, Pelt, Plank, Plant, Priest's hole, Repress, Robe, Saffian, Screen, Secrete, Sequester, Shadow, Shellac(k), Shroud, Skin, Smuggle, Spetch, Squirrel, Stash, Strap-oil, Tappice, Thong, Thrashing, Trove, Veil, Wallop, Whang, Wrap

**Hidebound** Narrow

**Hideous(ness)** Deform(ed), Enormity, Gash, Ghastly, Grotesque, Horrible, Monstrous, Odious, Ugly, Ugsome

**Hie** Dash

**Hierarchic, Hierarchy** Byzantine, Echelon, Elite, Pecking order, Theocracy

**Hieroglyph** Cipher, Pictogram

**Hi-fi, High-fidelity** Ambisonics®, Ghetto blaster

**Higgledy-piggledy** Mixtie-maxtie

**High(er), Highly, Highness** Alt(a), Altesse, Alteza, Altissimo, Altitudinous, Apogee, Atop, Brent, Climax, Culminant, Doped, Drugged, E-la, Elation, Elevated, Eminent, Euphoria, Exalted, Excelsior, Exhilarated, Five, Frequency, Gamy, Half seas over, Haut(e), Intoxicated, Jinks, Lofty, Maggotty, Mind-blowing, Orthian, Prime, Rancid, Ripe, School, Senior, Sent, Shrill, So, Spaced out, Steep, Stenchy, Stoned, Stratospheric, String-out, Strong, Superior, Swollen, Tall, Tension, Tipsy, Top-lofty, Topmost, Treble, Turned on, Ultrasonic, Up(per), Very, Wired, Zonked

▷ **High** *may indicate* an anagram

**High and mighty, High-handed** Arrogant, Haughty, Hogen-mogen, Lordly

**Highball** Drink, Lob, Loft, Skier, Skyer, Sling

**Highbrow** Brain, Egghead, Intelligentsia, Long-hair, Third programme

**High-class** Best, Pedigree, Superior, U

**High-crowned** Copataine

**Highest** Apotheosis, Best, Cacumen, Climax, Culminant, Maximum, Mostwhat, Ne plus ultra, Progressive, Supreme

**Highest note** E-la

**High-flier, High-flown** Astronaut, Bombastic, Euphuism, Icarus

**Highland(er), Highlands** Black Forest, Blue-bonnet, Blue-cap, Cameron, Cat(h)eran, Down, Dun(n)i(e)wassal, Duniwassal, Gael, Gaelic, Irish Scot, Karoo, Kiltie, Masai, Nainsel(l), Nepalese, Plaid(man), Redshank, Riff, Scot, Seaforth, Shire, Teuchter

**Highlight** Accent, Beacon, Chandelier, Feature, Focus, Heighten, Spotlight, Stress

▶ **High-pitched** *see* HIGH(ER)

**High-spirited** Extravert, Extrovert

**High tension** HT

**Highway** Alaska, Alcan, Autobahn, Autopista, Autostrada, Bus, Camino Real, Divided, Flyover, Freeway, Information, Interstate, King's, Motorway, Overpass, Parkway, Pass, Queen's, Road, Rode, Tarseal, Thoroughfare, Tightrope, Tollway, Watling St

**Highwayman, Highway robber(y)** Bandit, Bandolero, Duval, Footpad, Fraternity, Gilderoy, Jack Sheppard, Land-pirate, Land-rat, Latrocinium, MacHeath, Motorist, Rank-rider, Road-agent, Scamp, Skyjacker, Toby, Tobyman, Turpin, Twitcher, Wheel

**Hijack(er)** Abduct, Pirate

**Hike(r)** Backpack, Bushbash, Bushwalk, Raise, Rambler, Ramp, Rise, Traipse, Tramp, Trape(s), Up(raise)

**Hilarious, Hilarity** Gaiety, Hoot, Hysterical, Jollity, Mirth, Riot, Side-splitting

**Hilary** Term

**Hill(ock), Hills, Hillside** Ant, Antidine, Arafar, Areopagus, Aventine, Barrow, Beacon, Ben, Bent, Berg, Beverly, Black, Blackdown, Bluff, Bombay, Brae, Breed's, Brew, Broken, Bunker, Butte, Caelian, Calvary, Capitol(ine), Cheviots, Chiltern, Chin, Cleve, Coast, Cone, Coolin, Coteau, Cotswolds, Crag-and-tail, Crest, Cuillin, Damon, Djebel, Drumlin, Dun(e), Dunsinane, Eminence, Esquiline, Fell, Flodden, Gebel, Golan Heights, Golgotha, Gradient, Grampians, Hammock, Height, Helvellyn, Highgate, Holt, Horst, How, Howe, Hummock, Incline, Inselberg, Janiculum, Jebel, Kip(p), Knap, Knoll, Knot, Kop(je), Koppie, Lammermuir, Lavender, Law, Loma, Low, Ludgate, Majubar, Malvern, Mamelon, Man, Marilyn, Matopo, Mendip, Merrick, Mesa, Monadnock, Monte Cassino, Monticule, Morro, Mound, Mount Lofty Ranges, Nab, Naga, Nanatak, Nilgiri(s), North Downs, Otway Ranges, Palatine, Pap, Pennines, Pike, Pingo, Pnyx, Quantocks, Quirinal, Rand, Range, Saddleback, Savoy, Scaur, Seven, Silbury, Sion, Steep, Stoss, Strawberry, Tara, Tel(l), Toft, Toot, Tor, Toss, Tump, Tweedsmuir, Valdai, Vatican, Viminal, Wolds, Wrekin, Zion

**Hillbilly** Yap

**Hill-dweller** Ant

**Hillman** Areopagite, Nepalese

**Hilltop** Crest, Knoll, Nab

**Hilt** Basket, Coquille, Haft, Handle, Hasp, Shaft

**Him(self)** He, Ipse, Un

**Himalaya(n)** Nepali, Panda, Sherpa, Tibetan

**Hind(er), Hindering, Hindrance, Hindsight** Back, Bar, Block, Check, Counteract, Cramp, Crimp, Cumber, Debar, → DELAY, Deter, Encumber, Estop, Hamper, Handicap, Harass, Hitch, Holdback, Imbar, Impeach, Impede, Inconvenience, Inhibit, Liability, Obstacle, Obstruct, Overslaugh, Porlock, Posterior, Preclusion, Pull-back, Rear, Rein, Remora, Retard, Retral, Retrospect, Rump, Rumple, Set back, Shackle, Slow, Stonewall, Stop, Stunt, Stymie, Taigle, Thwart, Trammel

**Hind(most)** Back, Deer, Lag, Rear, Starn, Stern

**Hindi, Hindu(ism)** Arya Samaj, Babu, Bania(n), Banyan, Brahman, Brahmin, Dalit, Gentoo, Gurkha, Harijan, Jain(a), Kshatriya, Maharishi, Nagari, Pundit, Rajpoot, Rajput, Rama, Sad(d)hu, Saiva, S(h)akta, Saktas, Sanatana Dharma, Sankhya, Shaiva, Sheik(h), Shiv Sena, Shudra, Sivaite, Smriti, Sudra, Swami, Swinger, Trimurti, Untouchable, Urdu, Vaishnava, Vais(h)ya, Varna, Vedanta, Vedism

**Hindquarters** Backside, Crupper, Haunches

**Hinge(d)** Axis, Butt, Cardinal, Cross-garnet, Drop-leaf, Garnet, Gemel, Gimmer, Ginglymus, Gullwing, Joint, Knee, Mount, Parliament, Piano, Pivot, Stamp, Strap

▷ **Hinge(s)** *may indicate* a word reversal

**Hingeless** Ecardinate

**Hinny** Ass, Donkey, Joe

**Hint** Allude, Clew, Clue, Cue, Echo, Element, Gleam, Hunch, Idea, Imply, Inkle, Inkling, Innuendo, Insinuate, Intimate, Key, Mint, Nod, Nuance, Office, Overtone, Pointer, Preview, Ray, Reminder, Scintilla, Shadow, Soupçon, → SUGGEST, Tang, Tip, Touch, Trace, Trick, Wind, Wink, Wisp, Word, Wrinkle

▷ **Hint** *may indicate* a first letter

**Hip(pie), Hippy, Hips** Beatnik, Cafard, Cheer, Coxa(l), Drop-out, Flower-power, Huck(le), Hucklebone, Hunkers, Ilium, In, Informed, Ischium, Pubis, Sciatic, Tonish

**Hippopotamus** Behemoth, Bloat, River-horse, Sea-cow, Sea horse

**Hire(d), Hiring** Affreightment, Charter, Employ, Engage, Fee, Freightage, Job, Lease, Merc(enary), Never-never, Pensionary, Rent, Shape-up, Ticca, Wage

**Hirsute** Hairy, Pilose, Shaggy

▷ **His** *may indicate* greetings

**Hispanic** Latino

**Hiss(ing)** Boo, Fizzle, Goose, Hish, Sibilant, Siffle, Sizzle, Static, Swish

**Historian** Acton, Adams, Antiquary, Archivist, Arrian, Asellio, Bede, Biographer, Bryant, Buckle, Camden, Carlyle, Centuriator, Chronicler, Du Bois, Etain, Eusebius, Froude, Genealogist, Gibbon, Gildas, Green, Griot, Herodotus, Knickerbocker, Livy, Macaulay, Oman, Paris, Pliny, Plutarch, Ponsonby, Procopius, Read, Renan, Roper, Rowse, Sallust, Spengler, Starkey, Strabo, Strachey, Suetonius, Tacitus, Taylor, Thiers, Thucydides, Toynbee, Trevelyan, Wells, Xenophon

**History, Historic(al)** Account, Age, Anamnesis, Ancient, Annal, Bunk, Case, Chronicle, Clio, Diachronic, Epoch(a), Epoch-making, Ere-now, Ever, Heredity, Heritage, Legend, Life, Living, Meiji, Mesolithic, Modern, Natural, Ontogency, Oral, Past, Record, Relie, Renaissance, Retroactive, Story, Track record, Yesterday

**Histrionic** Operatic, Theatrical

**Hit** Attain, Bang, Bash, Baste, Bat, Bean, Belt, Bepat, Best seller, Blip, Blockbuster, Bloop, Blow, Bludgeon, Boast, Bolo, Bonk, Bump, Bunt, Catch, Chip, Clip, Clobber, Clock, Clout, Club, Collide, Cuff, Dot, Flail, Flick, Flip, Foul, Fourpenny-one, Fungo, Fustigate, Get, Hay, Head-butt, Home(-thrust), Ice-man, Impact, Inner, Knock, Lam, Lob, Magpie, Mug, Outer, Pandy, Paste, Pepper, Pinch, Pistol-whip, Polt, Prang, Punto dritto, Ram, Roundhouse, Sacrifice, Score, Sensation, Six, Skier, Sky, Slam, Slap, Slosh, Smash(eroo), Smit(e), Sock, Spank, Spike, Stoush, Straik, Stricken, Strike, Strook, Struck, → **SUCCESS**, Swat, Switch, Thwack, Time-thrust, Tip, Tonk, Touché, Twat, Undercut, Venewe, Venue, Volley, Wallop, Whack, Wham, Wing, Ythundered, Zap, Zonk

**Hitch(ed)** Catch, Cat's paw, Clove, Contretemps, Edge, Espouse, Harness, Hike, Hirsle, Hoi(c)k, Hotch, Jerk, Kink, Knot, Lorry-hop, Rope, Rub, Setback, Sheepshank, Sheet bend, Shrug, Snag, Technical, Thumb, Wed

**Hitherto** Before, Yet

**Hitman** Assassin, Eliminator, Gun

**Hittite** Uriah

**HIV** Viral load

**Hive(s)** Colony, Nettlerash, Skep, Spread, Swarm, Wheal

**Hoar(y)** Ashen(-grey), Canescent, Froren, Frost, Gaudy-day, Grizzled, Rime

**Hoard(ing)** Accumulate, Amass, Bill, Billboard, Cache, Coffer, Eke, Heap, Hog, Hoord, Husband, Hutch, Mucker, Plant, Pose, Salt away, Save, Sciurine, Snudge, Squirrel, Stash, Stock, Stockpile, Store, Stow, Treasure

**Hoarse(ness)** Croupy, Frog, Grating, Gruff, Husky, Raucous, Roar(er), Roopit, Roopy, Roup, Throaty

**Hoax** April-fish, Bam, Canard, Cod, Do, Doff, Fub, Fun, Gag, Gammon, Gowk, Gull, Have on, Hum, Huntie-gowk, Josh, Kid, Leg-pull, Piltdown, Put-on, Quiz, Sell, Sham, Skit, Spoof, String, Stuff, Supercherie, → **TRICK**

**Hob** Ceramic, Cooktop, Ferret, Goblin, Lout

**Hobble, Hobbling** Enfetter, Game, Hamshackle, Hilch, Hitch, Impair, Lame, Limp, Pastern, Picket, Shackle, Spancel, Stagger, Tether

**Hobby** Avocation, Fad, Falcon, Interest, Pastance, → **PASTIME**, Predator, Pursuit, Recreation, Scrimshaw

**Hobby-horse** Dada, Obsession, Play-mare

**Hobgoblin** Bog(e)y, Bull-beggar, Puck, Worriecow

**Hobnail** Clinker, Tacket
**Hobnob** Chat, Fraternise, Mingle
**Hobo** Bum, Drifter, → TRAMP, Vagrant
**Hock** Cambrel, Dip, Gambrel, Gambril, Gammon, Ham, Heel, Hough, Hypothecate, Pawn, Pledge, Rhenish, Wine
**Hockey** Field, Goal, Grass, Hurling, Ice, Pond, Shinny, Shinty, Street
**Hod** Carrier, Tray
**Hodge** Peasant, Rustic, Yokel
**Hoe** Claut, Draw, Dutch, Grub, Grubbing, Jembe, Nab, Pecker, Prong, Rake, Scuffle, Thrust, Weed
**Hog** Babiroussa, Babirussa, Boar, Glutton, Guttle, Mexican, Peccary, Pig, Porker, Puck, Road, Shoat, Shott, Whole
**Hogmanay** Ne'erday
**Hog-rat** Hutia
**Hogshead** Butt, Cask, Muid
**Hogwash** Bull, Nonsense, Swill, Twaddle
**Hoi-polloi** Oik, Prole(tariat), Rabble
**Hoist(ing)** Boom, Bouse, Bunk-up, Crane, Davit, Derrick, Garnet, Gin, Heave, Heft, Hills, Jack, Lewis, Lift, Raise, Shearlegs, Shears, Sheerlegs, Sheers, Sway, Teagle, Trice, Whip-and-derry, Wince, Winch, Windas, Windlass
**Hold(er), Holding, Hold back, out, up, etc** Absorb, Airlock, Allege, Alow, Anchor, Apply, Argue, Asset, Backbreaker, Belay, Believe, Boston crab, Cachepot, Caesura, Canister, Cease, Cement, Cinch, Clamp, Clasp, Cling, Clip, Clutch, Contain, Corral, Cotland, Cresset, Defer, Delay, Detain, Display, Document, Dog, Embrace, Engage, Engross, Er, Facebar, Farm, Fast, Fief, Fistful, Frog, Full nelson, Garter, → GRASP, Grip, Grovet, Half-nelson, Hammerlock, Handle, Haud, Have, Headlock, Heft, Heist, Hiccup, Hinder, Hitch, Ho(a), Hoh, Hoy, Hug, Impedance, Impede, Impediment, Impound, In chancery, Incumbent, Inhibit, Intern, Intray, Japanese stranglehold, Keep, Keepnet, Lease, Lifebelt, Maintain, Manure, Nef, Nelson, Nurse, Oasis, Obstacle, Occupant, Own, Port, Proffer, Purchase, Rack, Reach, Reckon, Reluct, Reserve, Restrain, Retain, Rivet, Rob, Rundale, Runrig, Save, Scissors, Shelve, Shore, Sleeve, Sostenuto, Stand, Stock, Suplex, Suspend, Take, Tenancy, Tenement, Tenure, Territory, Toehold, Toft, Tray, Tripod, Trivet, Wait, → WRESTLING, Wristlock, Zarf, Zurf
**Hole(s), Holed, Holey** Ace, Agloo, Aglu, Albatross, Antrum, Aperture, Aubrey, Beam, Birdie, Black, Bogey, Bolt, Bullet, Burrow, Cat, Cave, Cavern, Cavity, Cenote, Cissing, Coal, Coalsack, Collapsar, Cove, Crater, Cubby, Cup, Dell, Den, Dene, Dog-leg, Dolina, Doline, Dormie, Dormy, Dreamhole, Dry, Dugout, Eagle, Earth, Ethmoid, Eye(let), Faveolate, Finger, Foramen, Funk, Gap, Geat, Glory, Gnamma, Gore, Gutta, Hag(g), Hideout, Kettle, Knot, Lenticel, Lill, Limber, Loop, Loup, Lubber's, Lumina, Maar, Mortise, Moulin, Namma, Nineteenth, Oillet, → OPENING, Orifex, Orifice, Ozone, Perforate, Pierce, Pigeon, Pinprick, Pit, Pocket, Pore, Port, Pot, Potato, Priest's, Punctuate, Punctum, Puncture, Rabbet, Rivet, Rove, Rowport, Sallyport, Scupper, Scuttle, Scye, Sinus, Situation, Slot, Snag, Snow, Soakaway, Socket, Sound, Spandrel, Spider, Spiraculum, Starting, Stead, Stew, Stop, Stove, Swallow, Tear, Thirl, Thumb, Tight spot, Touch, Trema, Vent, Ventage, Ventige, Voided, Vug, Watering, Weep(er), Well, White, Wookey
**Holiday(s), Holiday maker** Away, Bank, Benjo, Break, Busman's, Camper, Carnival, Childermas, Days of Awe, Easter, Ecotour, Ferial, Festa(l), → FESTIVAL, Fête, Fiesta, Fly-drive, French leave, Furlough, Gala, Half(term), High, Honeymoon, Kwanzaa, Lag b'Omer, Laik, Leasure, Leave, Legal, Leisure, Long, Minibreak, Off-day, Off-time, Outing, Pace, Packaged, Pink-eye, Play-day, Playtime, Public, Purim, Recess, Repose, Rest, Roman, Schoolie, Seaside, Shabuoth, Shavuot, Sojourn, Statutory, Stay, Sunday, Tax, Time off, Trip, → VACATION, Villeggiatura, Wake(s), Weekend, Whitsun, Xmas
**Holinshed** Chronicler
**Holland(s)** Batavia, Genevese, Gin, Hogen-mogen, Netherlands, NL

**Hollow(ed)** Acetabulum, Aeolipile, Alveary, Antar, Antre, Antrum, Armpit, Axilla, Blastula, Boss, Bowl, Cave(rn), Cavity, Chasm, Chott, Cirque, Cleché, Comb(e), Concave, Coomb, Corrie, Crater, Cup(mark), Cwm, Deaf, Dean, Dell, Delve, Den(e), Dent, Dimple, Dingle, Dip, Dish(ing), Dolina, Doline, Empty, Fossette, Frost, Gilgai, Glenoid, Gnamma-hole, Gowpen, Groove, Grot(to), Hole, How, Howe, Igloo, Incavo, Insincere, Intaglio, Keck(sy), Kettle(hole), Kex, Khud, Lap, Lip-deep, Mortise, Namma-hole, Niche, Omphaloid, Orbita, Pan, Philtrum, Pit, Playa, Punchbowl, Punt, Redd, Rout, Rut, Scoop, Shott, Sinus, Slade, Sleepy, Slot, Slough, Socket, Swire, Thank-you-ma'am, Trematic, Trough, Vacuous, Ventricle, Vesicle, Vlei, Vola, Wame, Wem

**Holly** Aquifoliaceae, Eryngo, Holm, Ilex, Mate, Winterberry, Yaupon

**Hollyhock** Althaea, Malva, Rose mallow

**Hollywood** Bowl, Tinseltown

**Holm** Isle

**Holmes** Sherlock, Wendell

**Holmium** Ho

**Holocaust** Churban, Fire, Shoah

**Holocene** Recency

**Hologram, Holograph** Laser, MS

**Holothurian** Trepang

**Holster** Sheath

**Holy(man), Holiness** Adytum, Alliance, Ariadne, Blessed, → **DIVINE**, Godly, Grail, Halidom, Hallowed, Helga, Hery, Inner sanctum, Khalif, Loch, Mountain, Olga, Orders, Pan(h)agia, Pious, Sacred, Sacrosanct, Sad(d)hu, Saintdom, Saintly, Sanctitude, Sannayasi(n), Santon, Sekos, Sepulchre, Shrine, Starets, Staretz, SV, Tirthankara, War

**Holy books, Holy writing** Adigranth, Atharvaveda, Bible, Gemara, Granth, Hadith, Hagiographa, Koran, Mishnah, NT, OT, Pia, Purana, Rigveda, Sama-Veda, → **SCRIPTURE**, Shaster, Shastra, Smriti, Sura(h), Tanach, Writ, Yajur-Veda

**Holy building, Holy city, Holy place** Chapel, Church, Kaaba, Kirk, Mashhad, Mecca, Medina, Meshed, Najaf, Penetralia, Sanctum, Station, Synagogue, Temenos, Temple

**Holy Ghost** Paraclete

**Holy water** Amrit

**Homage** Bow, Cense, Honour, Kneel, Manred, Obeisance, Tribute, Vail

**Home(land), Homeward** Abode, Apartment, Base, Blighty, Bro, Broken, Burrow, Cheshire, Chez, Clinic, Community, Convalescent, Crib, Domal, Domicile, Dwelling, Earth, Eventide, Family, Fireside, Flat, Funeral, Gaff, Goal, Habitat, Harvest, Heame, Hearth, Heme, Hospice, House, In, Lair, Libken, Lockwood, Lodge, Maisonette, Mental, Mobile, Montacute, Motor, Nest, Nursing, Old sod, Orphanage, Pad, Penny-gaff, Pied à terre, Pile, Pit dwelling, Plas Newydd, Remand, Res(idence), Rest, Semi, Starter, Stately, Tepee, Turangawaewae, Up-along, Villa, Warren

**Homecoming** Nostos

**Home counties** SE

**Homeless** Arab, Bag lady, Evicted, Gangrel, Nomadic, Outler, Rootless, Skell, Waif

**Homer(ic)** Comatose, Cor, Epic(ist), Maeonides, Nod, Pigeon, Simpson, Somnolent

**Home-rule** Parnellism, Swaraj

**Homesick(ness)** Heimweh, Mal du pays

**Homespun** Cracker-barrel, Folksy, Plain, Raploch, Russet, Simple

**Homestead** Ranch, Toft

**Homework** → **DIY**, Prep, Preparation

**Homicidal, Homicide** Chance-medley, Justifiable, Killing, Manslaughter

**Homily** Lecture, Midrash, Pi, Postil, Prone, Sermon, Tract

▷ **Homing** *may indicate* coming back

**Hominid** Oreopitheous

**Homogeneous** Indiscrete

**Homogram, Homograph** Abac, Heteronym

**Homosexual(ity)** Arse bandit, Auntie man, Bardash, Batty boy, Bender, Bent, Buftie, Bufty, Camp, Cat, Catamite, Closet queen, Cocksucker, Cottaging, Dike, Dyke, Fag(got), Fairy, Friend of Dorothy, Fruit, Gay, Gaydar, Ginger, Homophile, Invert, Lesbian, Meatrack, Minty, Moffie, Muscle Mary, Pederast, Ponce, Poof(tah), Poofter, Poove, Pouf(fe), Poufter, Puff, Punk, Quean, Queer, Queercore, Quiff, Rough trade, Shirt-lifter, Slash, Swish(y), Tonk, Tribade, Twinkle, Uranism, Urning, Woofter

**Hone** Grind, →SHARPEN, Whet

**Honest(y), Honestly** Aboveboard, Afauld, Afawld, Amin, Candour, Clean, Fair dinkum, Faith, Four square, Frank, Genuine, Incorruptible, Injun, Jake, Jannock, Jonnock, Legitimate, Lunaria, Lunary, Mensch, Open-faced, Penny, Probity, Realtie, Rectitude, Reputable, Righteous, Round, Sincere, Soothfast, Square, Squareshooter, Straight, Straight-arrow, Straightforward, Straight-out, Trojan, →TRUE, Truepenny, Upfront, Upright, Upstanding

**Honey(ed)** Comb, Flattery, Hybla(ean), Hymettus, Mel, Melliferous, Mellifluous, Nectar, Oenomel, Oxymel, Palm, Peach, Popsy-wopsy, Sis, Sugar, Sweetheart, Sweetie (pie), Virgin, Wild, Wood

**Honeycomb(ed)** Cellular, Faveolate, Favose, Favous, Smock, Waxwork

**Honeydew** Mildew

**Honey-eater** Bear, Blue-eye, Pooh

**Honeypot** Haanepoot

**Honeysuckle** Abelia, Anthemion, Caprifoil, Caprifole, Lonicera, Rewa rewa, Suckling, Twinflower, Woodbind, Woodbine

**Hong Kong** .hk

**Honk** Hoot, Puke

**Honour(able), Honorary, Honoured, Honorific, Honours** A, Acclaim, Accolade, Ace, Adore, Adward, Birthday, Blue, Bow, CBE, Commemorate, Credit, Crown, Curtsey, Dan, Elate, Emeritus, Ennoble, →ESTEEM, Ethic, Face-card, Fame, Fête, Gloire, Glory, Grace, Greats, Homage, Insignia, Invest, Izzat, J, Jack, K, King, Knave, Knight, Kudos, Laudation, Laureate, Laurels, MBE, Mensch, Mention, Military, OBE, Optime, Order, Pundonor, Q, Queen, Regius, Remember, Repute, Respect, Revere, Reward, Salute, Straight, Ten, Tenace, Titular, Tribute, Tripos, Venerate, White, Worship, Wranglers

**Honourable companion** CH

**Honourless** Yarborough

**Hooch** Hogan, Hogen, Moonshine

**Hood(ed)** Almuce, Amaut, Amice, Amowt, Apache, Balaclava, Bashlik, Biggin, Blindfold, Calash, Calèche, Calyptra, Capeline, Capuccio, Capuche, Chaperon(e), Coif, Cope, Cowl, Cucullate(d), Faldetta, Fume, Gangster, Headdress, Jacobin, Kennel, Lens, Liripipe, Liripoop, Mantle, Mazarine, Nithsdale, Pixie, Robin, Rowdy, Snood, Trot-cosey, Trot-cozy, Visor

**Hoodlum** Gangster, Mobster, Roughneck, Thug, Wanksta

**Hoodoo** Jonah, Moz(z)

**Hoodwink(ed)** Blear, Bluff, Cheat, →DECEIVE, Gull, Hoax, Mislead, Nose-led, Seel

**Hoof(ed)** Artiodactyla, Cloot, Coffin, Frog, Trotter, Ungula

**Hooha(h)** Carry on, Fracas, Humdudgeon

**Hook(ed), Hooker, Hooks** Addict, Adunc, Aduncous, Aquiline, Arrester, Barb(icel), Barbule, Becket, Butcher's, Cant(dog), Catch, Chape, Claw, Cleek, Clip, Clove, Cocotte, Corvus, Crampon, Cromb, Crome, Crook, Crotchet, Cup, Drail, Duck, Fifi, Fish, Floozy, Fluke, Fly, Gab, Gaff, Gig, Grap(p)le, Grapnel, Grappling, Gripple, Hamate, Hamose, Hamulus, Hanger, Heel, Hitch, Inveigle, Kype, Meat, Picture, Pot, Prostitute, Pruning, Punch, Retinaculum, Sickle, Sister, Snare, Snell, Sniggle, Solicit, Swivel, Tala(u)nt, Tart, Tenaculum, Tenter, Tie, Trip, Uncus, Wanton, Welsh

**Hookah** Bong, Chillum, Hubble-bubble, Kalian, Narghil(l)y, Narg(h)ile, Nargileh, Nargil(l)y, Pipe

**Hooligan** Apache, Bogan, Casual, Desperado, Droog, Goonda, Hobbledehoy, Hoon, Keelie, Larrikin, Lout, Ned, Rough(neck), Ruffian, Skollie, Skolly, Tearaway, Ted, Tityre-tu, Tough, Tsotsi, Vandal, Yahoo, Yob(bo)

**Hoop(s)** Bail, Band, Circle, Farthingale, Garth, Gird, Girr, Hula®, O, Pannier, →RING, Sleeper, Tire, Trochus, Trundle

**Hooray** Whoopee, Yippee

**Hoot(er)** Conk, Deride, Honk, Madge, Nose, Owl, Riot, Screech-owl, Siren, Ululate

**Hoover** Consume, Dam, Vacuum

**Hop(per)** An(o)ura, Ball, Bin, Cuscus, Dance, Flight, Jeté, Jump, Kangaroo, Leap, Lilt, Long, Opium, Pogo, Roo, Saltate, Scotch, Skip, Spring, Tremié, Vine

**Hope(ful)** Anticipate, Aspirant, Auspicious, Bob, Combe, Comer, Contender, Daydream, Desire, Dream, Esperance, Evelyn, Expectancy, Forlorn, Gleam, Good, Great white, Inshallah, Pipe-dream, Pray, Promising, Prospect, Ray, Roseate, Rosy, Sanguine, Trust, Upbeat, Valley, Wannabe, White, Wish

**Hopeless(ness), Hopeless quest** Abattu, Anomie, Anomy, Black, Buckley's chance, Dead duck, Despair, Despondent, Forlorn, Gloom, Goner, Lost cause, Non-starter, No win, Perdu, Pessimist

**Hophead** Drinker, Lush, Sot

**Hopscotch** Peevers

**Horace** Flaccus, Ode, Satirist

**Horatio** Nelson

**Horatius** Cocles

**Horde** Crowd, Golden, Many, Mass, Mob, Swarm

**Horizon** A, Apparent, Artificial, B, C, Celestial, Event, Gyro, Rational, Scope, Sea-line, Sensible, Skyline, Visible

**Horizontal** Advection, Flat, Level, Prone, Prostrate, Supine, Tabular

**Hormone** Growth, Indoleacetic, Plant, Sex

---

## HORMONES

| 3 letters: | Autacoid | Prolactin | 12 letters: |
|---|---|---|---|
| FSH | Bursicon | Secretion | Androsterone |
| IAA | Ecdysone | Serotonin | Antidiuretic |
| TSH | Estrogen | Thyroxine | Biosynthesis |
| | Florigen | | Gonadotropin |
| 4 letters: | Glucagon | 10 letters: | Luteotrophic |
| ACTH | Juvenile | Adrenaline | Noradrenalin |
| | Oestriol | Calcitonin | Pancreozymin |
| 5 letters: | Oestrone | Folliculin | Progesterone |
| Auxin | Oxytocin | Intermedin | Secretagogue |
| Kinin | Resistin | Lipotropin | Somatostatin |
| | Secretin | Oestradiol | Somatotropin |
| 7 letters: | Thymosin | | Stilboestrol |
| Gastrin | | 11 letters: | Testosterone |
| Ghrelin | 9 letters: | Aldosterone | Thyrotrophin |
| Inhibin | Adrenalin® | Angiotensin | |
| Insulin | Corticoid | Gibberellin | 13 letters: |
| Relaxin | Cortisone | Luteinizing | Catecholamine |
| Steroid | Cytokinin | Parathyroid | Gonadotrophic |
| Thyroid | Endocrine | Progestogen | Gonadotrophin |
| | Melatonin | Somatomedin | Melanotropine |
| 8 letters: | Oestrogen | Thyrotropin | Noradrenaline |
| Abscisin | Pituitrin | Vasopressin | Prostaglandin |
| Androgen | Progestin | | Somatotrophin |

| 14 letters: | Levonorgestral | 16 letters: |
|---|---|---|
| Corticosteroid | Norepinephrine | Triiodothyronine |
| Corticosterone | | |
| Erythropoietin | 15 letters: | 17 letters: |
| Hydrocortisone | Cholecystokinin | Mineralocorticoid |

---

**Horn(s), Horny** Acoustic, Advancer, Amalthea, Antenna(e), Antler, Baleen, Basset, Beeper, Bez, Brass, Buck, Bugle, Bur(r), Cape, Ceratoid, Cor, Cornet, Cornett, Cornopean, Cornu(a), Cornucopia, Cromorna, Cromorne, Cusp, Dilemma, English, Exponential, Flugel-horn, French, Frog, Gemshorn, Golden, Gore, Hooter, → **HORNBLOWER**, Hunting, Ivory, Keratin, Klaxon, Lur, Morsing, Mot, Oliphant, Parp, Periostracum, Plenty, Post, Powder, Pryse, Ram's, Saddle, Scur, Shoe, Shofar, Shophor, Spongin, Tenderling, Trey, Trez, Trumpet, Tusk, Vulcan's badge, Waldhorn

**Hornblende** Syntagmatite

**Hornblower** Brain, Horatio, Peel, Triton, Trumpeter

**Hornbook** Battledoor, Battledore

**Horned (sheep)** Cabrié, Cabrit, Cornute, Hamate, Lunate, Mouflon, Muflon

**Hornet** Stinger

**Hornless** Doddy, Humbel, Humlie, Hummel, Mooly, Mul(l)ey, Poley, Polled

**Hornpipe** Matelote

**Horoscope** Figure, Future, Prophecy, Star-map

**Horrendous** Fearsome

**Horrible, Horror** Appalling, Aw(e)some, Beastly, Brat, Creepy, Dire, Distaste, Dread(ful), Execrable, Gashful, Ghastly, Grand Guignol, Grisly, Grooly, Gruesome, Grysie, Hideous, Loathsome, Minging, Nightmare, Odious, Panic, Rascal, Shock, Shudder, Stupefaction, Terror, The creeps, Ugh, Vile

**Horrid, Horrific, Horrified, Horrify(ing)** Aghast, Agrise, Appal, Chill, Dire, Dismay, Dreadful, Frightful, Ghastly, Gothic, Grim, Grisly, H, Loathy, Odious, Shock, Spine-chilling, Spiteful, Ugly

**Hors d'oeuvres** Antipasto, Canapé, Carpaccio, Ceviche, Hoummos, Houmus, Hummus, Mez(z)e, Pâté, Smor(re)brod, Smorgasbord, Starter, Tapas, Zak(o)uski

**Horse(s)** Abasta, Airer, Bidet, Bloodstock, Carriage, Cut, Cutting, Dark, Doer, Dray, Drier, Drug, Equine, Eye-necked, Form, H, → **HEROIN**, High, Hobby, Iron, Knight, Kt, Light, Lot, Maiden, Malt, Non-starter, Outsider, Pack, Pantomime, Plug, Ride, Rocking, Sawbuck, Scag, Screen, Selling-plater, Sense, Stable, Stalking, Standard-bred, Starter, Stayer, Steeplechaser, Stiff, Stock, Teaser, Trestle, Vanner, Vaulting, White, Willing, Wooden

---

## HORSES

| 2 letters: | 4 letters: | Pony | Bevis |
|---|---|---|---|
| GG | Arab | Post | Borer |
| | Aver | Prad | Caple |
| 3 letters: | Barb | Roan | Capul |
| Ass | Buck | Snow | Favel |
| Bay | Cert | Span | Filly |
| Cob | Colt | Stud | Genet |
| Dun | Crib | Taki | Morel |
| Gee | Dale | Trot | Mount |
| Nag | Fell | Yale | Neddy |
| Pad | Foal | Yaud | Pacer |
| Pot | Hack | | Paint |
| Rip | Jade | 5 letters: | Pinto |
| Tit | Mare | Arion | Poler |
| | Pole | Arkle | Punch |

Rogue
Screw
Seian
Shire
Stage
Steed
Tacky
Takhi
Trace
Troop
Waler
Wheel
Zebra

**6 letters:**
Alfana
Ambler
Bayard
Bronco
Brumby
Calico
Canuck
Cayuse
Chaser
Cooser
Crollo
Curtal
Cusser
Dobbin
Entire
Exmoor
Favell
Ganger
Garran
Garron
Gennet
Hogget
Hunter
Jennet
Kanuck
Keffel
Lampos
Livery
Morgan
Mudder
Novice
Pad-nag
Plater
Pommel
Poster
Quagga

Randem
Remuda
Roarer
Rouncy
Runner
Sabino
Saddle
Shoo-in
Sorrel
String
Stumer
Summer
Tandem
Tarpan
Tracer
Trojan

**7 letters:**
Bobtail
Breaker
Caballo
Cavalry
Centaur
Charger
Clipper
Coacher
Courser
Cuisser
Dappled
Draught
Eclipse
Eventer
Gelding
Hackney
Hobbler
Liberty
Marengo
Marocco
Morocco
Mustang
Palfrey
Pegasus
Piebald
Pointer
Quarter
Remount
Saddler
Sheltie
Spanker
Sumpter
Swallow

Swinger
Trigger
Trooper
Trotter
Walking
Wheeler
Xanthos
Xanthus

**8 letters:**
Aquiline
Bangtail
Bathorse
Boerperd
Buckskin
Camargue
Chestnut
Clay-bank
Cocktail
Dartmoor
Destrier
Eohippus
Friesian
Galloway
Highland
Holstein
Hyperion
Kochlani
Lusitano
Palomino
Schimmel
Shetland
Skewbald
Sleipnir
Springer
Stallion
Stibbler
Trippler
Warragal
Warragle
Warragul
Warrigal
Welsh cob
Whistler
Yarraman
Yearling

**9 letters:**
Appaloosa
Black Bess
Caballine

Clavileno
Coldblood
Connemara
Dapple bay
Gringolet
Houyhnhnm
Icelandic
Incitatus
Knabstrup
Percheron
Rosinante
Rozinante
Warmblood

**10 letters:**
Andalusian
Bucephalus
Buckjumper
Buttermilk
Clydesdale
Copenhagen
Dapple-grey
Lipizzaner
Lippizaner
Pliohippus
Przewalski
Showjumper
Stagecoach
Svadilfari
Wheelhorse

**11 letters:**
Daisy-cutter
High-stepper
Przewalski's

**12 letters:**
Cleveland Bay
Hambletonian
Suffolk Punch
Thoroughbred

**13 letters:**
Perissodactyl

**14 letters:**
Strawberry roan

**16 letters:**
Tennessee Walking

---

**Horseback** Croup
**Horse-box** Stable, Stall

**Horse-chestnut** Aesculus, Conker

**Horse collar** Brecham, Hame

**Horse complaint, Horse disease, Horse problem, Horse trouble** Blind staggers, Blood spavin, Bogspavin, Bot(t)s, Broken wind, Canker, Capel(l)et, Cracked heels, Cratches, Curb, Deer-neck, Dourine, Drepance, Equinia, Eweneck, Farcin, Farcy, Fives, Founder, Frush, Glanders, Gourdy, Grape, Grass-sickness, Head staggers, Heaves, Hippiatric, Hoof rot, Knee spavin, Laminitis, Lampas, Lampers, Malander, Mallander, Mallender, Megrims, Miller's disease, Moon blindness, Mooneye, Mud fever, N(a)gana, Parrot mouth, Poll-evil, Quartercrack, Quitter, Quittor, Ringbone, Roaring, Sallenders, Sand crack, Scratches, Seedy-toe, Shaft, Spavie, Spavin, Springhalt, Staggers, Strangles, Stringhalt, Summer sores, Surra, Sway-back, Sween(e)y, Thorough-pin, Thrush, Toe-crack, Tread, Vives, Weed, Weid, Whistling, Windgall, Wind-sucking, Wire-heel, Yellows

**Horse-dealer** Buster, Coper

**Horsefly** Cleg, Tabanid

**Horse-lover** Philip

**Horseman** Ataman, Caballero, Cavalry, Centaur, Conquest, Cossack, Cowboy, Death, Dragman, Famine, Farrier, Hobbler, Hussar, Knight, Lancer, Nessus, Ostler, Parthian, Picador, Pricker, Quadrille, Revere, →**RIDER**, Slaughter, Spahi, Stradiot, Tracer, Wrangler

**Horsemanship** Manège

**Horseplay** Caper, Chukka, Knockabout, Polo, Rag, Rant, Romp

**Horsepower** Hp, Indicated, Ps

**Horseradish** Ben, Moringa

**Horseshoe(-shaped)** Henge, Hippocrepian, King-crab, Lophophorate, Lunette, Manilla, Oxbow, Plate

**Horsetail** Equisetum

**Horse thief** Blanco, Rustler

**Horticultural, Horticulture, Horticulturist** Grower, Pomology, RHS

**Hose** Chausses, Fishnet, Galligaskins, Gaskins, Hydrant, Lisle, Netherstock(ing), Nylons, Panty, Sock, Sox, Stockings, Tabi, Tights, Trunk, Tube, Wet

**Hospice, Hospital** Almshouse, Ambulance, Asylum, Barts, Base, Bedlam, Booby hatch, Bughouse, Clinic, Cottage, Day, Dressing station, ENT, Field, Foundation, General, Guest-house, Guys, H, Home, Hospice, Hôtel dieu, Imaret, Infirmary, Isolation, Karitane, Lambarene, Lazaretto, Leprosarium, Leprosery, Lock, Loony bin, Lying-in, MASH, Mental, Nosocomial, Nuthouse, Nuttery, Ozzie, Pest-house, Polyclinic, Rathouse, San, Scutari, Sick bay, Snake-pit, Special, Spital, Spittle, Teaching, Trauma centre, Trust, UCH

**Hospitable, Hospitality** Cadgy, Convivial, Corporate, Entertainment, Euxine, Kidgie, Lucullan, Open house, Philoxenia, Social, Xenial

**Host(s), Hostess** Alternate, Amphitryon, Anchorman, Army, Barmecide, Bunny girl, Chatelaine, Commerce, Compere, Crowd, Definitive, Emcee, Entertainer, Eucharist, Geisha, Heavenly, Hirsel, Hotelier, Innkeeper, Intermediate, Inviter, Laban, Landlady, Landlord, Legend, Legion, Licensee, Lion-hunter, Lot, Maitre d', Mass, Mavin, MC, Number, Presenter, Publican, Quickly, Quizmaster, Sabaoth, Speakerine, Swarm, Taverner, Throng, Torrent, Trimalchio, Wafer, Winfrey

**Hostage** Gherao, Pawn, Pledge, POW

**Hostel(ry)** Asylum, Auberge, Dharms(h)ala, Dorm, Dormitory, Entry, Halfway house, Inn, Y(MCA), YHA, Youth

**Hostile, Hostility** Adverse, Aggressive, Alien, Anger, Animus, Anti, Arms, Aversion, Bad blood, Bellicose, Bitter, Chilly, Currish, Diatribe, Enemy, Feud, Forbidding, Hating, Ho, Icy, Ill, Ill-will, Inimical, Inveterate, Opposed, Oppugnant, Pugnacity, Unfriendly, Virulent, Vitriolic, War

**Hot(spot), Hot (tempered)** Aboil, Aetnean, Aflame, Ardent, Baking, Big, Blistering, Breem, Breme, Cajun, Calid, Candent, Cayenne, Chilli, Dog days, Enthusiastic, Erotic(al), Etnaen, Facula, Fervid, Feverish, Fiery, Fuggy, Gospeller, Het, In, Incandescent, Irascible, Ireful, Latest, Lewd, Live, Mafted, Mirchi, Mustard, Nightclub, Pepper, Piping, Potato,

Quick, Randy, Red, Roaster, Scalding, Scorcher, Sexpot, Sexy, Sizzling, Spicy, Spitfire, Steamy, Stewy, Stifling, Stolen, Sultry, Sweaty, Sweltering, Sweltry, Tabasco®, Thermidor, Torrid, Toustie, Tropical, Zealful

**Hotchpotch** Bricolage, Farrago, Mish-mash, Pot pourri, Powsowdy, Welter

**Hotel, Hotelkeeper** Bo(a)tel, Boutique, Commercial, Fleabag, Flophouse, Gasthaus, Gasthof, H, Hilton, Host, Hydro, Inn, Internet, Khan, Military, Motel, Parador, Patron(ne), Pension, Posada, Private, Ritz, Roadhouse, Savoy, Tavern, Telco, Temperance, Trust, Waldorf, Watergate

**Hothead(ed)** Impetuous, Madcap, Rash, Spitfire, Volcano

**Hot-house** Conservatory, Forcing-house, Nursery, Orangery, Vinery

**Hot plate** Griddle, Salamander

**Hot rod** Dragster

**Hotshot** Whiz

**Hotspot** Bricolage, Farrago, Mish-mash, Powsowdy, Suntrap, Welter

**Hotspur** Harry, Hothead, Percy, Rantipole

**Hottentot** Griqua, Khoikhoi, Strandloper

**Hot water** Soup, Therm

**Hound(s)** Afghan, Badger, Basset, Beagle, Bellman, Brach, Cad, Canine, Cry, →**DOG**, Entry, Gabriel's, Gaze, Hamiltonstovare, Harass, Harrier, Hen-harrier, Ibizan, Importune, Javel, Kennet, Lurcher, Lyam, Lym(e), Mute, Otter, Pack, Persecute, Pharaoh, Pursue, Rache, Ranter, Reporter, Saluki, Scoundrel, Talbot, True, Tufter

**Hound's bane** Palay

**Hour(s)** Canonical, Complin(e), Daylight, Elders', Eleventh, Flexitime, Golden, H, Happy, Holy, Hr, Literacy, Little, Lunch, None(s), Office, Orthros, Peak, Prime, Rush, Sext, Sidereal, Small, Staggered, Terce, Tide, Time, Undern, Unearthly, Unsocial, Vespers, Visiting, Witching, Working, Zero

**Hourglass** Meniscoid

**House(s), Housing, Household(er)** Abode, Accepting, Adobe, Aerie, Aery, Astrology, Audience, Auditorium, B, Bach, Bastide, Beehive, Beth, Bhavan, Bhawan, Biggin, Billet, Bingo, Black, Block, Boarding, Bondage, Brick veneer, Broadcasting, Broiler, Brownstone, Bundestag, Casa, Chalet, Chamber, Chapter, Charnel, Château, Chattel, Chez, Cinema, Clan, Clapboard, Clearing, Co, Coffee, Commercial, Concern, Convent, Cote, Cottage (orné), Council, Counting, Country, Crankcase, Crib, Custom(s), Dacha, Dail, Death, Demain, Demesne, Derry, Des res, Discount, Disorderly, Domal, Domestic, Domicile, Donga, Door, Dower, Drostdy, Drum, Duplex, Dwelling, Dynasty, Edifice, Entertain, Establishment, Estate, Este, Eyrie, Familial, Fashion, Fibro(cement), Finance, Firm, Forcing, Frame, Fraternity, Free, Frontager, Full, Gaff, Gambling, Garage, Gazebo, Gemini, Gite, Government, Grace and favour, Guest, Habitat, Habitation, Hacienda, Halfway, Hall, Harbour, Hearth, HK, Ho, Home, Homestead, Ice, Igloo, Infill, Inn, Inner, Insula, Issuing, Joss, Ken, Libken, Lodge, Lofted, Loose, Lot(t)o, Maison(ette), Malting, Manor, Manse, Mansion, Mas, Meeting, Meiney, Meinie, Meiny, Ménage, Menyie, Messuage, Mobility, Monastery, Montagne, Nacelle, Node, Open(-plan), Opera, Outer, Pad, Parliament, Pent, Picts, Picture, Pilot, Pleasure, Pole, Pondokkie, Post, Prefab, Printing, Public, Quinta, Radome, Ranch, Ratepayer, Register, Residence, Rooming, Root, Rough, Sacrament, Safe, Saltbox, Satis, Schloss, School, Seat, Semi, Shanty, Sheltered, Show, Sign, Social, Software, Spec-built, Sporting, Stable, State, Station, Steeple, Storey, Succession, Tavern, Tea, Tenement, Terrace, Theatre, Third, Tied, Toft, Tombola, Tower, Town, Tract, Treasure, Tree, Trust, Try, Upby, Vaulting, Vicarage, Villa(-home), Wash, Watch, Weather, Weatherboard, Weigh, Wendy, Whare, Wheel, Work, Zero, Zodiac

## HOUSES

| 3 letters: | 4 letters: | Keys | Syon |
|---|---|---|---|
| Leo | Bush | Riad | York |

**5 letters:**
Lords
Scala
Tudor
Upper
Usher
White

**6 letters:**
Grange
Orange
Queen's
Seanad
Stuart
Wilton

**7 letters:**
Althing

Althorp
Bourbon
Commons
Hanover
Kenwood
Knesset
Lodging
Osborne
Stewart
Trinity
Windsor

**8 letters:**
Burghley
Chequers
Hapsburg
Harewood
Hatfield

Holyrood
Lagthing
Longleat
Petworth
Somerset

**9 letters:**
Admiralty
Chartwell
Knebworth
Lancaster
Number Ten
Odelsting

**10 letters:**
Chatsworth
Heartbreak
Kirribilli

Odelsthing

**11 letters:**
Plantagenet
Russborough
Sandringham

**12 letters:**
Lockwood Home

**13 letters:**
Seanad Eireann

**15 letters:**
Representatives

---

**House-boat** Wan(i)gan, Wangun
**House-builder** Jack
**House-keeper** Chatelaine, Go(u)vernante, Matron, Publican
**House-leek** Sengreen
**Housemaid's knee** Bursa
**Houseman** Betty, Doctor, Intern, Peer
**Housemate** Co-tenant
**House-warming** Infare
**Housewife** Etui, Frau, Needlecase, WI
**Housework** Chore, DIY
**Housing** Case, Crankcase, Shabrack, Shelter, Slum, Tenement
**Hova** Malagash
**Hove** Plim, Swell
**Hovel** Cru(i)ve, Den, Pigsty, Shack, Shanty
**Hover** Hang, Levitate, Lurk, Poise
**Hovercraft** Air-car
**How** Hello, Hill, Hollow, What
**How'dyedo, How d'ye do** Hallo, Pass, Salve
**However** Although, As, But, Even-so, Leastwise, Sed, Still, Though, Yet
**Howitzer** Gun
**Howl(er)** Banshee, Bawl, Bay, Bloop, Clanger, Hue, Mycetes, Slip up, Squawk, Tornado, Ululate, War whoop, Wow, Yawl, Yowl
**How much** The
**Hoy** Bilander, Ship
**HP** Never-never
**HQ** Centre, Headquarters, Horse Guards, SHAPE
**Hub** Boss, Boston, Centre, Focus, Hob, Nave, Nucleus, Pivot, Tee
**Hubbub** Charivari, Chirm, Coil, Din, Level-coil, Palaver, Racket, Row, Stir
**Hubris** Pride
**Huckster** Hawker, Kidd(i)er, Pedlar
**Huddle** Cringe, Gather, Hunch, Nestle, Ruck, Shrink
**Hudson** River, Rock
**Hue** Chrome, Colour, Dye, Outcry, Proscription, Steven, Tincture, Tinge, Umbrage, Utis
**Huff** Dudgeon, Hector, Pant, Pet, Pique, Snuff, Strunt, Umbrage, Vex
**Hug** Bear, Caress, Coll, Cuddle, Embosom, →**EMBRACE**, Snuggle, Squeeze

**Huge (number)** Astronomical, Brobdingnag, Colossal, Elephantine, Enorm(ous), Epic, Gargantuan, Giant, →**GIGANTIC**, Gillion, Ginormous, Humongous, Humungous, Immane, Immense, Leviathan, Lulu, Mega-, Milliard, Monolithic, Monster, Monumental, Octillion, Prodigious, Socking, Stupendous, Tall, Thumping, Titanian, Tremendous, Vast, Voluminous, Whacking, Whopping

**Hugo** Victor

**Huguenot** Camisard

**Hulk** Lout, Ruin, Shale, Shell, Ship

**Hull** Bottom, Framework, Husk, Inboard, Monocoque, Pod, Sheal, Sheel, Shell, Shiel, Shill, Shiplap

**Hullabaloo** Outcry, Raz(z)mataz(z), Razzamatazz

▶ **Hullo** *see* **HELLO**

**Hum(ming)** BO, Bombilate, Bombinate, Bum, Buzz, Chirm, Chirr, Drone, Eident, Lilt, Moan, Murmur, Nos(e)y, Odorate, Odorous, Pong, Ponk, Rank, Reek, Sough, Sowf(f), Sowth, Stench, Stink, Stir, Whir(r), Zing

**Human(e), Humanist, Humanitarian, Humanity, Humanoid** Anthropoid, Anthropology, Bang, Colet, Earthling, Earthman, Erasmus, Hominid, Homunculi, Incarnate, Kindness, Mandom, Meatbot, Merciful, Mortal, Philanthropic, Species, Sympathy, Ubuntu, Unpaid, Virtual, Wight

**Humble** Abase, Abash, Afflict, Baseborn, Chasten, Conquer, Cow, Degrade, Demean, Demiss(ly), Grovel, Lower, Lowly, Mean, Mean-born, →**MEEK**, Modest, Morigerate, Obscure, Poor, Rude, Small, Snub, Truckle

**Humbug** Berley, Blague, Blarney, Buncombe, Bunk(um), Burley, Cant, Claptrap, Con, Delude, Eyewash, Flam, Flummery, Fraud, Fudge, Gaff, Gammon, Gas, Guff, Gum, Hoax, Hoodwink, Hookey-walker, Kibosh, Liar, Maw-worm, Nonsense, Prig, Shenanigan, Tosh, Wind

**Humdinger** Cracker, Lulu

**Humdrum** Banal, Boredom, Bourgeois, Monotonous, Mundane, Ordinary, Prosaic, Routine, Tedious, Uninspiring

**Humid(ity)** Clammy, Damp, Dank, Hydrometry, Machie, Machy, Moch, Moist, Muggy, Saturation, Steam, Sticky, Sultry, Tropical

**Humiliate(d), Humiliation, Humility** Abase(ment), Abash, Baseness, Comedown, Debag, Degrade, Disbench, Eating crow, Fast, Indignity, Laughing stock, Lose face, Lowlihead, Mortify, Put-down, →**SHAME**, Skeleton, Take-down, Wither

**Humming-bird** Colibri, Hermit, Racket-tail, Rainbow, Rubythroat, Sabre-wing, Sapphire-wing, Sappho, Sawbill, Sylph, Thornbill, Topaz, Trochilus

**Hummock** Tump

**Humorist** Cartoonist, Comedian, Jester, Leacock, Lear, Punster, Thurber, Twain, Wodehouse

**Humour, Humorous** Aqueous, Bile, Blood, Bonhomie, Caprice, Cardinal, Chaff, Choler, Coax, Cocker, Coddle, Cosher, Cuiter, Cuittle, Custard-pie, Daut, Dawt, Droll, Dry, Facetious, Fun, Gallows, Ichor, Indulge, Irony, Jocose, Jocular, Juice, Kidney, Lavatorial, Levity, Light, Melancholy, →**MOOD**, Observe, One-liner, Pamper, Phlegm, Pun, Pythonesque, Ribaldry, Salt, Satire, Serum, Sick, Temper, Trim, Vein, Vitreous, Vitreum, Wetness, Whim, Whimsy, Wit, Wry

**Humourless** Dry, Po(-faced)

**Hump(ed), Humping** Boy, Bulge, Dorts, Dowager's, Gibbose, Gibbous, Hog, Huff, Hummock, Hunch, Middelmannetjie, Pip, Protrusion, Ramp, Road, Sex, Sleeping policeman, Speed bump, Tussock

▶ **Humpback** *see* **HUNCH(ED)**

**Humphrey** Bogart

**Humus** Compost, Leafmould, Moder, Mor, Mull

**Hun** Alaric, Atli, Attila, Fritz, German

**Hunch(ed), Hunchback** Camel, Chum, Crookback, Gobbo, Hump, Intuition, Kyphosis, Premonition, Presentiment, Quasimodo, Roundback, Sense, Squat, Urchin

**Hundred(s), Hundredfold, Hundredth** Burnham, C, Cantred, Cantref, Cent, Centesimal, Centum, Centuple, Century, Chiltern, Commot, Days, Desborough, Great, Host, →IN A HUNDRED, Long, Northstead, Old, Shire, Stoke, Tiyin, Ton, Tyiyn, Wapentake
**Hundred and fifty** CL, Y
**Hundred and sixty** T
**Hundred thousand** C
**Hundredweight** Centner, Long, Metric, Quintal, Short
**Hung** Displayed, Executed, Framed, High
**Hungarian, Hungary** Bohunk, Cheremis(s), Csardas, Magyar, Nagy, Szekely, Tzigane, Ugric, Vogul
**Hunger (strike), Hungry** Appestat, Appetite, Bulimia, Bulimy, Clem, →CRAVE, Desire, Edacity, Emaciated, Empty, Esurient, Famine, Famish, Fast, Hanker, Hunter, Insatiate, Itch, Orectic, Pant, Peckish, Pine, Pyne, Rapacious, Raven, Ravin, Sharp-set, Starve, Unfed, Unfuelled, Yaup, Yearn
▷ **Hungry** *may indicate* an 'o' in another word
**Hunk(s)** Beefcake, Chunk, Dry-fist, He-man, Miser(ly), Slab, Wedge
**Hunker** Squat
**Hunt(er), Hunting, Huntress, Huntsman** Actaeon, Alew, Archer, Artemis, Atalanta, Battue, Beachcomb, Beagle, Bellman, Blood sport, Bounty, Bushman, Calydon, Chace, Chase(r), Chasseur, Chevy, Chiv(vy), Comb, Cool, Corner, Coursing, Crockett, Cynegetic, Dog, Drag(net), Esau, Ferret, Fox, Free-shot, Gun, Halloo, Herne, Horse, Hound, Jager, Kennet, Lamping, Leigh, Letterbox, Lurcher, Montero, Mouser, National, Nimrod, Orion, Peel, Pig-sticking, Poacher, Poot, Pout, Predator, Prowl, Pursue, Quest, Quorn, Rabbit, Rach(e), Rake, Ran, Rancel, Ranzel, Ride, Rummage, Run, Safari, San, Scavenge(r), Scorse, Scout, Sealer, →SEARCH, Seek, Shikar(ee), Shikari, Skirter, Slipper, Stag, Stalk, Sticker, Still, Swiler, Terrier, Thimble, Ticker, Tinchel, Tower, Trail, Trap, Treasure, Venatic, Venator, Venerer, Venery, →WATCH, Whip, Whipper-in, Witch, Wolfer, Woodman, Woodsman, Yager
**Hunting-call** Rechate, Recheat, Tally-ho, View-halloo
**Hunting-ground** Forestation, Walk
**Hurdle(r)** Barrier, Doll, Fence, Flake, Gate, Hemery, Jump, Obstacle, Raddle, Snag, Sticks, Wattle
**Hurdy (gurdy)** Barrel-organ, Hainch, Haunch, Vielle
**Hurl(ing)** Camogie, Cast, Dash, →FLING, Heave, Put(t), Sling, Throw, →TOSS
**Hurly-burly** Furore, Noise
**Hurrah** Bravo, Cheers, Huzza, Io, Whee
**Hurricane** Baguio, Cyclone, Tornade, Tornado, Typhoon, →WIND
**Hurry, Hurried** Belt, Bustle, Chivvy, Chop-chop, Dart, Dash, Drive, Expedite, Festinate, Fisk, Frisk, Gad, Gallop, Giddap, Giddup, Giddy-up, Hadaway, Hare, Haste, Hie, Hightail, Induce, Mosey, Pop, Post-haste, Press (on), Push, Race, Railroad, →RUSH, Scamper, Scoot, Scramble, Scur(ry), Scutter, Scuttle, Skelter, Skurry, Spank, Speed, Streak, Sudden, Tear, Whirr, Zip
**Hurt(ful)** Abuse, Ache, Adverse, Aggrieve, Ake, Bruise, Cutting, Damage, De(a)re, Detriment, Disservice, Harm, Harrow, Hit, →INJURE, Lesion, Maim, Nocent, Nocuous, Noisome, Noxious, Noyous, Offend, Pain, Pang, Prick(le), Scaith, Spite, Sting, Trauma, Wound, Wring
**Hurtle** Rush, Spin, Streak, Streek
**Husband(ry), Husbands** Add, Baron, Betty, Breadwinner, Conserve, Consort, Darby, Ear, Eche, Economy, Eke, Ere, Farm, Gander(-mooner), Georgic, Goodman, Groom, H, Hoddy-doddy, Hodmandod, Hubby, Ideal, Lord and master, Man, Manage, Mate, Partner, Polyandry, Reserve, Retrench, Save, Scrape, Scrimp, Spouse, Squirrel, →STORE, Tillage
**Hush(-hush)** Bestill, Gag, St, Sh, Silent, Smug, Tace, Wheesh(t), Whisht
**Husk(s), Husky** Acerose, Bran, Draff, Eskimo, Gruff, Hoarse, Hull, Malemute, Seed, Sheal, Shiel, Shuck, Throaty

**Hussar** Cherry-picker, Cherubim
**Hussite** Calixtin(e), Taborite
**Hussy** Besom, Hen, Jezebel, Limmer, Loose, Minx, Vamp, Wench
**Hustle(r)** Fast talk, Frogmarch, Jostle, Pro, Push, Railroad, Shoulder, Shove, Skelp
**Hut(s)** Banda, Booth, Bothie, Bothy, Bustee, Cabin, Caboose, Chalet, Choltry, Gazebo, Gunyah, Hogan, Humpy, Igloo, Mia-mia, Nissen, Pondok(kie), Quonset®, Rancheria, Rancho, Rondavel, Shack, Shanty, Sheal(ing), Shebang, Shed, Shiel(ing), Skeo, Skio, Succah, Sukkah, Tilt, Tolsel, Tolsey, Tolzey, Tramping, Wan(n)igan, Whare, Wigwam, Wi(c)kiup, Wil(t)ja, Wurley, Wurlie
**Hutch** Buddle, Crate, Pen, Rabbit
**Hyacinth** Bluebell, Cape, Grape, Starch, Wild
**Hybrid** Amerasian, Bigener, Bois-brûlé, Cama, Catalo, Centaur, Chamois, Chichi, Chimera, Citrange, Cockatrice, Cross, Dso, Funnel, Geep, Graft, Hippogriff, Hircocervus, Incross, Interbred, Jersian, Jomo, Jumart, Lurcher, Mameluco, Mermaid, Merman, Metif, Métis, Mongrel, Mule, Mutation, Noisette, Onocentaur, Opinicus, Ortanique, Ox(s)lip, Percolin, Plumcot, Pomato, Ringed, Single-cross, Tangelo, Tiglon, Tigon, Topaz, Ugli, Werewolf, Zedonk, Zho(mo)
▷ **Hybrid** *may indicate* an anagram
**Hydra** Polyp
**Hydrant** Fireplug, H
**Hydrocarbon** Acetylene, Aldrin, Alkane, Alkene, Alkyl, Alkyne, Amylene, Arene, Asphaltite, Benzene, Butadiene, Butane, Butene, Camphane, Camphene, Carotene, Cetane, Cubane, Cumene, Cycloalkane, Cyclohexane, Cyclopropane, Cymogene, Decane, Diene, Dioxin, Diphenyl, Ethane, Ethylene, Gutta, Halon, Hatchettite, Heavy oil, Hemiterpene, Heptane, Hexane, Hexene, Hexyl(ene), Indene, Isobutane, Isoprene, Ligroin, Limonene, Mesitylene, Methane, Naphtha, Naphthalene, Naphthalin(e), Nonane, Octane, Olefin(e), Paraffin, Pentane, Pentene, Pentylene, Phenanthrene, Phene, Picene, Pinene, Polyene, Propane, Pyrene, Pyridine, Pyrimidine, Retene, Squalene, Stilbene, Styrene, Terpene, Toluene, Triptane, Wax, Xylene, Xylol
**Hydrogen** Deut(er)on, Diplon, Ethene, H, Heavy, Muonium, Protium, Replaceable, Tritium
**Hydroid** Sea-fir
**Hydrolysis** Saponification
**Hydrometer** Salinometer
**Hydrophobia, Hydrophobic** Rabid, St Hubert's disease
**Hydroplane** Skid
**Hydroponic** Soil
**Hydrozoa(n)** Campanularia, Millepore, Physalia, Portuguese man-of-war, Siphonophore
**Hyena** Aard-wolf, Cackle, Earthwolf, Laughing, Nandi bear, Spotted, Strand-wolf, Tiger-wolf
**Hygiene, Hygienic** Aseptic, Clean, Dental, Godly, Oral, Sanitary, Sepsis, Sleep
**Hymen** Maidenhead
**Hymn(s)** Amazing Grace, Anthem, Benedictine, Bhajan, Canticle, Carol, Cathisma, Choral(e), Coronach, Dies Irae, Dithyramb, Doxology, Epithalamia, Gloria, Hallel, Introit(us), Ithyphallic, Lay, Magnificat, Mantra, Marseillaise, Nunc Dimittis, Ode, P(a)ean, Praise, Processional, Psalm, Psalmody, Recessional, Rigveda, Sanctus, Secular, Sequence, Stabat Mater, Sticheron, Tantum Ergo, Te Deum, Trisagion, Troparion, Veda
**Hymnographer, Hymnologist** Cowper, David, Faber, Heber, Moody, Neale, Parry, Sankey, Watts
**Hype(d)** Aflutter, Ballyhoo, Blurb
**Hyperactive** Frenetic
**Hyperbola** Rectangular
**Hyperbole, Hyperbolic** Auxesis, Exaggeration, Sech

**Hypercritical** Fastidious

**Hyperion** Titan

**Hypersensitive, Hypersensitivity** Allergic, Atopy, Idiosyncratic

**Hypha(e)** Conidiophore, Stroma

**Hyphen(ated)** Dash, Parasyntheton, Soft

**Hypnosis, Hypnotise, Hypnotic, Hypnotism, Hypnotist** Braidism, Chloral, Codeine, Enthral, Entrance, Fluence, Hypotonia, Magnetic, Magnetise, Meprobamate, Mesmerism, Psychognosis, Svengali

**Hypochondria(c)** Atrabilious, Hyp, Nosophobia, Phrenesiac, Valetudinarian

**Hypocrisy, Hypocrite, Hypocritical** Archimago, Bigot, Byends, Cant, Carper, Chadband, Creeping Jesus, Deceit, Dissembler, Dissimulating, Double standards, False-faced, Heep, Holy Willie, Humbug, Insincere, Janus-faced, Mucker, Nitouche, Pecksniff, Pharisaic, Pharisee, Piety, Plaster saint, Prig, Sanctimony, Self-pious, Sepulchre, Tartuf(f)e, Two-faced, Whited sepulchre

**Hypothesis, Hypothesize, Hypothetic, Hypothetical** Avogadro, Biophor, Conditional, Continuum, Gaia, Gluon, Graviton, Micella, Nebular, Nostratic, Notional, Null, Planetesimal, Sapir-Whorf, Suppose, Suppositious, Theory, Virtual, Whorf, Working

**Hyrax** Cony, Daman, Dassie, Klipdas, Rock rabbit

**Hysteria, Hysteric(al)** Achiria, Astasia, Conniption, Crazy, Delirium, Frenzy, Meemie, Mother, Panic

# Ii

**I** A, Ch, Cham, Che, Dotted, Ego, Element, Ich, Indeed, India, Iodine, Italy, J, Je, Me, Muggins, Myself, One, Self, Yours truly

**Iambus** Scazon

**Ian** Scot

**Iberian** Celtiberian

**Ibex** Izard

**Ibis** Hadedah, Sacred, Waldrapp

**Ice(d), Ice-cream, Icing, Icy** A la mode, Alcorza, Anchor, Arctic, Ballicatter, Banana split, Berg, Black, Brainstorm, Brash, Camphor, Cassata, Coconut, Cone, Cool, Cornet, Coupe, Cream, Crystal, Diamonds, Drift, Dry, Field, Floe, Frappé, Frazil, Freeze, Frigid, Frore, Frosting, Frosty, Gelato, Gelid, Gems, Glacé, Glacial, Glacier, Glare, Glaze, Glib, Granita, Graupel, Ground, Growler, Hailstone, Hok(e)y-pok(e)y, Hommock, Hummock, Intention, Kitty-benders, Knickerbocker glory, Kulfi, Lolly, Macallum, Marzipan, Neapolitan, Neve, Oaky, Pack, Pancake, Pingo, Polar, Popsicle®, Rime, Rink, Rivière, Ross, Royal, Sconce, Serac, Shelf, Sherbet, Slay, Slider, Slob, Sludge, Slush, Sorbet, Spumone, Spumoni, Stream, Sugar, Sundae, Theme, Tickly-benders, Topping, Tortoni, Tutti-frutti, Verglas, Virga, Wafer, Water, Wintry

**Ice-axe** Piolet

**Iceberg** Calf, Floe, Growler, Lettuce

**Ice-box** Cooler, Freezer, Fridge, Frig, Yakhdan

▶ **Ice-cream** *see* ICE(D)

**Icefloe** Pan

**Iceland** IS

**Ice-skating** Choctaw, Figure, Glide

**Ichneumon** Herpestes

**Icicle** Tangle

**Icon** Avatar, Fashion, Idol, Image, Madonna, Shrine, Sprite, Toolbar

**Icterus** Jaundice

**ID** Dog-tag, Microchip, PIN

**Id(e)** Ego, Fish, Orfe

**Idea(s)** Archetype, Brainchild, Brainstorm, Brainwave, Clou, Clue, Conceit, Concept, Fancy, Figment, Fixed, Germ, Hunch, Idée fixe, Idolum, Image, Inkling, Inspiration, Intention, Interpretation, Keynote, Light, Meme, Motif, → **NOTION**, Obsession, Plan, Plank, Rationale, Recept, Theme, Theory, Thought, Whimsy, Zeitgeist

**Ideal(ise)** A1, Abstract, Apotheosis, At best, Bee's knees, Cat's pyjamas, Cat's whiskers, Dream, Eden, Ego, Erewhon, Goal, Halo, Hero, Model, Monist, Mr Right, Nirvana, Notional, Paragon, Pattern, → **PERFECT**, Perfet, Prince Charming, Role-model, Romantic, Rose, Siddhi, Sidha, Sublimate, Transcendental, Utopian, Vision

**Idealism, Idealist(ic)** Dreamer, Martyr, More, Perfectionist, Quixotic, Romantic, Storybook, Transcendental, Utopian, Visionary

**Identical** Alike, Carbon copy, Clone, Congruent, Double, Equal, Indistinguishable, Menechmian, One, Same, Selfsame, Verbatim, Very

**Identification, Identify** Armband, Bertillonage, Codeword, Cookie, Credentials, Designate, Detect, Diagnosis, Differentiate, Discern, Document, Dog-tag, Earmark, E-fit, Empathy, Espy, Finger(print), ID, Identikit®, Know, Label, Mark, Monomark,

Name, Nameplate, Name-tape, Password, Photofit®, Pin, Pinpoint, Place, Point up, Recognise, Registration, Reg(g)o, Secern, Specify, Spot, Swan-hopping, Swan-upping, Verify

**Identikit®** E-fit, Videokit

**Identity** Alias, Appearance, Corporate, Credentials, Ego, Equalness, Likeness, Mistaken, Numerical, Oneness, Personal, Qualitative, Seity, Self, Selfhood

**Ideology, Ideologue** Credo, Hard-liner, Ism, Stalinism

**Idiom** Americanism, Argot, Britishism, Cant, Dialect, Expression, Idioticon, Jargon, Language, Pahlavi, Parlance, Pehlevi, Persism, Scotticism, Slavism, Syri(a)cism, Syrism

**Idiosyncrasy, Idiosyncratic** Fad, Foible, Mannerism, Nature, Quirk, Way, Zany

**Idiot(ic), Idiocy** Airhead, Congenital, Dingbat, Dipstick, Dolt, Dotard, Dumbo, Eejit, Fatuity, Fool, Git, Goose, Half-wit, Headbanger, Imbecile, Inane, Klutz, Maniac, Moron, Nana, Natural, Nerk, Nidget, Noncom, Numpty, Oaf, Ouph(e), Stupe, →STUPID, Tony, Twit, Village, Whacko, Zany

**Idle(ness), Idler** Beachcomber, Bludger, Boondoggle, Bum, Bumble, Bummle, Cockaigne, Couch potato, Dally, Deadbeat, Diddle, Dilly-dally, Dole-bludger, Donnat, Donnot, Do-nothingism, Drone, Eric, Fainéant, Fallow, Farnarkel, Fester, Flaneur, Flim-flam, Footle, Frivolous, Gold brick, Groundless, Hawm, Inaction, Indolent, Inert, Lackadaisical, Laesie, Lallygag, Layabout, Laze, Lazy, Lead-swinger, Lie, Lig, Light, Limer, Linger, Loaf, Loll, Lollard, Lollop, Lollygag, Lotophagus, Lounge, Lusk, Micawber, Mike, Mollusc, Mooch, Mouch, Neet, Otiose, Otium, Patagonian, Piddle, Potato, Ride, Scapegrace, Shiftless, Skive, Slob, Sloth, Sluggard, Spiv, Stagnate, Stalko, Stock-still, Stooge, Stroam, Sweirt, Tarry, Tick over, Transcendental, Trifle, Trock, Troke, Truant, Truck, Twiddle, Unbusy, Unemployed, Unoccupied, Vacuity, Vain, Vegetate, Veg out, Wait, Waste, Whip the cat, Workshy

**Idol(ise)** Adore, Adulate, Baal(im), Baphomet, Bel, Crush, Eikon, E(i)luned, Fetich(e), Fetish, God, Graven image, Heartthrob, Hero, Icon, Image, Joss, Juggernaut, Lion, Mammet, Manito, Manitou, Matinee, Maumet, Mawmet, Molech, Moloch, Mommet, Moorish, Mumbo-jumbo, Pagoda, Stotter, Swami, Teraph(im), Termagant, Vision, Wood, Worship

**Idyll(ic)** Arcady, Eclogue, Eden, Paradise, Pastoral, Peneian, Xanadu

**Ie** Sc

**If, If it** Albeit, All-be, An('t), Condition, Gif, Gin, In case, Kipling, Pot, Provided, Sobeit, Whether

**Igloo** Snowden

**Igneous** Pyrogenic

**Ignis-fatuus** Elf-fire, Fire-dragon, Fire-drake, Friar's lanthorn, Wildfire

**Ignite, Ignition** Coil, Electronic, Flare, Flash-point, Glow plug, Kindle, Lightning, Spark, Spontaneous, Starter

**Ignoble** Base, Inferior, Mean, Vile

**Ignominious, Ignominy** Base, Dishonour, Fiasco, Humiliation, Infamous, Scandal, →SHAME

**Ignorance, Ignorant** 404, Agnoiology, Analphabet, Anan, Artless, Benighted, Blind, Clueless, Darkness, Green, Hick, Illiterate, Inerudite, Ingram, Ingrum, Inscient, Irony, Know-nothing, Lewd, Lumpen, Misken, Nescience, Night, Oblivious, Oik, Philistine, Purblind, Red-neck, Unaware, Uneducated, Unlessoned, Unlettered, Unread, Unschooled, Untold, Unversed, Unwist

**Ignore(d)** Alienate, Ba(u)lk, Blink, Bypass, Connive, Cut, Discount, Disregard, Forget, Leave, Neglect, Omit, Overlook, Override, Overslaugh, Pass, Pass up, Rump, Scrub round, Slight, Snub, Tune out, Unheeded

**Igor** Prince

**Iguana** Chuckwalla

**I know** Iwis, Ywis

**Iliad** Homeric

**Ill(ness)** Access, Adverse, All-overish, Awrong, Bad, Bilious, Cronk, Crook, Disorder, Evil, Gout, Grotty, Inauspicious, Income, Indisposed, Infection, Labyrinthitis, Laid up, Lovesick, Misorder, Off-colour, Poorly, Pox, Queer, Ropy, Rough, Rubella, SARS, Schistosomiasis, Scrofula, Sea-sick, → SICK, Strongylosis, Strung out, Unpropitious, Unweal, Unwell, Valetudinarian, Vomito, Wog, Wrong, Yuppie flu

▷ **Ill** *may indicate* an anagram

**Ill-adjusted** Sad sack

**Ill-advised** Foolish, Imprudent, Redeless

**Ill-balanced** Lop-sided

**Ill-bred** Carl, Churlish, Plebeian, Uncouth, Unmannerly

▷ **Ill-composed** *may indicate* an anagram

**Ill-defined** Diagnosis, Grey (area), Hazy, Mongrel, Unclear, Vague

**Ill-disposed** Antagonistic, Baleful

**Ill-dressed** Frumpish

**Illegal, Illicit** Adulterine, Black, Bootleg, Breach, Contraband, Furtive, Ill-gotten, Malfeasance, Misbegotten, Pirated, Shonky, Unlawful, Wrong(ous)

**Illegitimate** Baseborn, Bastard, By-blow, Come-o'-will, Fitz, Irregular, Love-child, Lucky-piece, Mamzer, Misbegotten, Misborn, Misfortunate, Momzer, Natural, Scarp, Slink, Spurious, Unlawful, Unlineal

**Ill-fated** Inauspicious, Unlucky

**Ill-favoured** Lean, Offensive, Thin, Ugly

**Ill-feeling, Ill-humour, Ill-will** Acrimony, Animosity, Bad blood, Bile, Complaint, Curt, Dudgeon, Enmity, Gall, Glum, Grudge, Hate, Hostility, Malice, Maltalent, Mau(l)gre, Miff, Peevish, Pique, Rheum(atic), Spite, Spleen, Tantrum

**Illiberal** Insular, Redneck, Skinflint, Strict

▶ **Illicit** *see* ILLEGAL

**Illiterate** Analphabet, Ignoramus, Letterless, Unlettered, Unread

**Ill-looking** Peaky, Poorly

**Ill-luck** Ambs-ace, Ames-ace, Bad trot, Deuce-ace, Fate, Misfortune

**Ill-mannered, Ill-natured, Ill-tempered** Acid, Attercop, Bitchy, Cad, Coarse, Crabby, Crotchety, Curst, Ethercap, Ettercap, Gnarly, Goop, Gurrier, Guttersnipe, Huffy, Lout, Mean, Splenetic, Stingy, Sullen, Surly, Ugly, Uncouth, Unkind

**Illness** Aids, Ailment, Attack, Autism, Brucellosis, Chill, Complaint, Croup, Death-bed, Diabetes, Disease, DS, Dwalm, Dwaum, Dyscrasia, Eale, Eclampsia, Grippe, Hangover, Hypochondria, Lockjaw, Malady, ME, SAD, Scarlatina, Sickness, Terminal, Toxaemia, Urosis, Weed, Weid, Wog

**Ill-nourished** Emaciated

**Illogical** Absurd, Inconsequent, Non-sequitur

**Ill repute** Discredit, Infamy

**Ill-sighted** Owl, Purblind

**Ill-smelling** F(o)etid, High, Hing, Miasmic, Stinking

▶ **Ill-tempered** *see* ILL-MANNERED

**Ill-timed** Inopportune, Unseasonable

**Ill-treat** Harm, Hurt, Shaft

**Illuminate(d), Illumination, Illuminating** Ambient, Aperçu, Brighten, Bright-field, Candlelight, Clarify, Cul-de-lampe, Daylight, Decorate, Educative, Enlighten, Floodlit, Lamplight, Langley, Lantern, Light, Limbourg, Limelight, Limn, Miniate, Moonlight, Nernst, Phot, Pixel, Radiate, Rushlight, Spotlight, Starlight

**Illusion(ary), Illusionist, Illusory, Illusive** Air, Apparition, Barmecide, Chimera, Deception, Déjà vu, Escher, Fallacy, Fancy, Fantasy, Fata morgana, Hallucination, Ignis-fatuus, Indian rope trick, Mare's-nest, Maya, Mirage, Muller-Lyer, Optical, Phantasmal, Phantom, Phi-phenomenon, Size-weight, Specious, Transcendental, Trompe l'oeil, Unreality, Will o'the wisp

**Illustrate(d), Illustration, Illustrator** Artwork, Attwell, Bleed, Case, Centrefold, Collotype, Demonstrate, Dore, Drawing, Eg, Elucidate, Epitomise, Exemplify, Explain, Figure, Frontispiece, Grangerize, Graphic, Half-tone, Heath Robinson, Hors texte, Illume, Illumin(at)e, Instance, Instantiate, Keyline, Limner, Line-engraver, Lithograph, Pictorial, Plate, Rackham, Rockwell, Show, Sidelight, Spotlight, Tenniel, Vignette, Visual, Woodcut

**Illustrious** Bright, Celebrated, Distinguished, Famous, Legendary, Noble, Noted, Renowned, Roshan

▶ **Ill-will** *see* ILL-FEELING

**I'm** I'se

**Image(s), Imaging** Atman, Blip, Brand, Corporate, Dead ringer, Discus, Effigy, E-fit, Eidetic, Eidolon, Eikon, Eiluned, Emoticon, Emotion, Enantiomorph, Favicon, Fine-grain, Gift, Graphic, Graven, Hologram, Hypnagogic, Icon, Iconograph, Ident(ikit), Idol, Invultuation, Joss, Latent, Likeness, Litho, Matte, Mirror, Morph, Murti, Paranthelium, Paraselene, Pentimento, Persona, Phantasmagoria, Photogram, Photograph, Pic(ture), Pieta, Pixel(l)ated, Pixil(l)ated, Poetic, Print, Profile, Public, Radionuclide, Real, Recept, Reflectogram, Reflectograph, Representation, Scintigram, Search, Shadowgraph, Shrine, Simulacrum, Sonogram, Species, Spectrum, Spitting, Split, Stereotype, Symbol, Teraph(im), Thermal, Thermogram, Thumbnail, Tiki, Tomogram, Totem, Vectograph, Venogram, Video, Virtual, Waxwork, Xoanon

**Imagine(d), Imaginary (land), Imagination, Imaginative** Assume, Bandywallop, Believe, Boojum, Bullamakanka, Cloud-cuckoo-land, Cockaigne, Cockayne, Conceive, Conjure, Create, Cyborg, Dystopia, Envisage, Erewhon, Esemplasy, Faery, Faine, Fancy, Feign, Fictional, Fictitious, Fictor, Figment, Figure, Hallucinate, Hobbit, Ideate, Invent, Mind's eye, Moral, Narnia, Never-never-land, Non-existent, Notional, Otherworldly, Oz, Picture, Poetical, Prefigure, Pretend, Propose, Recapture, Replicant, Scotch mist, Snark, Straw, →SUPPOSE, Surmise, Think, Tricorn, Tulpa, Unreal, Vicarious, Vision, Visualise, Whangam, Wonderland

**Imam** Ismail

**Imbecile** Anile, Fool, Idiot, →STUPID

▷ **Imbecile** *may indicate* an anagram

**Imbibe** Absorb, Drink, Lap, Quaff, Suck, Swallow

**Imbricate** Overlie

**Imbroglio** Complication, Maze

**Imbrue, Imbue** Colour, Impregnate, Indoctrinate, Infuse, Inoculate, Permeate, Revitalise, Soak, Steep

**Imitate, Imitation, Imitator** Act, Ape, Burlesque, Caricature, Clone, Copy(cat), Counterfeit, Crib, Dud, Echo, Echopraxia, Emulate, Epigon(e), Ersatz, Facsimile, Fake, False, Faux, Follow, Hit off, Marinist, Me-too, Mime, Mimesis, Mimetic, Mimic(ry), Mini-me, Mockery, Monkey, Onomatopoeia, Parody, Parrot, Paste, Paste grain, Pastiche, Pinchbeck, Potichomania, Recreate, Repro, Rhinestone, Rip-off, Sham, Simulate, Skeuomorphism, Stumer, Take-off, Travesty, Unreal

**Immaculate** Conception, Flawless, Impeccable, Lily-white, Perfect, Pristine, Spotless, Virgin

**Immanentist** Pantheist

**Immaterial** Academic, Insignificant, Spiritual, Trifling

**Immature(ly), Immaturity** Adolescent, Babyish, Beardless, Blast, Callow, Childish, Crude, Embryo, Ergate(s), Green, Imago, Inchoate, Larval, Neotenic, Non-age, Nymph, Peter Pan, Puberal, Puberulent, Pupa, Raw, Rudimentary, Sophomoric, Tender, Unbaked, Underage, Unformed, Unripe, Young

▷ **Immature** *may indicate* a word not completed

**Immediate(ly)** Alsoon, Anon, At once, B(e)live, Direct, Eftsoons, Ekdum, First-time, Forthwith, Go on, Imminent, Incontinent, Instantaneous, Instanter, Lickety-split, Near, Next, →NOW, Now-now, On the knocker, Outright, Posthaste, Present, Pronto, Ready, Right-off, Short-term, Slapbang, Spontaneous, Stat, Statim, Straight, Straight off, Sudden, Then, Thereupon, Tout de suite

**Immense** Astronomical, Brobdingnag, Cosmic, Enormous, →**GIGANTIC**, Huge, Vast, Wide

**Immerse** Baptise, Demerge, Demerse, Drench, Embathe, Emplonge, Enew, Engage, Imbathe, Plunge, Soak, Steep, Submerge

**Immigrant, Immigration, Immigrate** Aliya(h), Aussiedler, Brain gain, Carpet-bagger, Cayun, Chalutz, Choom, Freshie, Gastarbeiter, Greener, Greenhorn, Halutz, Illegal, Incomer, Issei, Jimmy Grant, Merino, Metic, New chum, Nisei, Non-quota, Olim, Outsider, Overstayer, Pilgrim, Pommy, Quota, Redemption(er), Reffo, Sanei, Sansei, Settler, Wetback, Whenwe

**Imminent** Approaching, Close, Forthcoming, Immediate, Pending

**Immobility, Immobile, Immobilise(r)** Akinesia, Cataplexy, Catatonia, Ecstasis, Hamstring, Hog-tie, Inertia, Pinion, Rigidity, Taser, Tether

**Immoderate** Excessive, Extreme, Inordinate, Intemperate, Lavish, Undue, Unreasonable, Violent

**Immodest(y)** Brash, Brazen, Forward, Impudicity, Indelicate, Unchaste

**Immolation** Sacrifice, Sati, Suttee

**Immoral(ity)** Corrupt, Degenerate, Dissolute, Evil, Lax, Libertine, Licentious, Loose, Misconduct, Nefarious, Peccable, Reprobate, Scarlet, Sleazebag, Sleazeball, Sleazy, Turpitude, Unchaste, Unclean, Unholy, Unprincipled, Unsavoury, Vice, Vicious, Wanton

**Immortal(ity)** Agelong, Amarant(h), Amarantin, Amritattva, Athanasy, Deathless, →**DIVINE**, Endless, Enoch, Eternal, Ever-living, Famous, Godlike, Hera, Memory, Sin, Struldbrug, Timeless, Undying

**Immovable** Fast, Firm, Gomphosis, Obdurate, Rigid, Rock solid, Stable, Stolid, Stubborn

**Immune, Immunisation, Immunise(r), Immunity** Acquired, Active, Amboceptor, Anamnestic, Anergy, Antiserum, Bar, Cree, Diplomatic, Dispensation, Exempt, Free, Humoral, Inoculate, Klendusic, Natural, Non-specific, Passive, Pasteurism, Pax, Premunition, Properdin, Serum, Tachyphylaxis, Vaccine

**Immure** Confine, Encloister, Imprison

**Imp(ish)** Devilet, Elf, Flibbertigibbet, Gamin(e), Gremlin, Hobgoblin, Leprechaun, Limb, Lincoln, Litherly, Monkey, Nickum, Nis(se), Puck, Ralph, Rascal, Spright, Sprite

**Impact** Astrobleme, Bearing, Brunt, Bump, Chase, Clash, Collision, Feeze, Glance, Head-on, High, Impinge, Imprint, Jar, Jolt, Pack, Percuss, Pow, Slam, Souse, Strike home, Tell, Weight, Wham, Whammo

**Impair(ed), Impairment** Appair, Cripple, Damage, Disease, Enfeeble, →**HARM**, Injure, Lame, Mar, Mental, Odd, Pair(e), Paralogia, Stale, Vitiate

**Impala** Pallah

**Impale** Elance, Ga(u)nch, Gore, Skewer, Spike, Transfix

**Impart** Bestow, Convey, Divulge, Give, Impute, Infect, Inform, Shed, Tell

**Impartial(ity)** Candid, Detached, Disinterest, Dispassionate, Equitable, Equity, Even-handed, Fair, Just, Neutral, Unbiased

**Impasse, Impassable** Deadlock, Dilemma, Invious, Jam, Log jam, Mexican standoff, Snooker, Stalemate, Stand off, Zugzwang

**Impassioned** Earnest, Emotional, Fervid, Fiery, Heated, Zealous

**Impassive** Apathetic, Bland, Deadpan, Poker-faced, Stoical, Stolid, Unemotional

**Impatience, Impatient** Agog, Chafing, Champ, Chut, Dysphoria, Dysthesia, Eager, Fiddle-de-dee, Fiddlesticks, Fidgety, Fretful, Hasty, Hoot(s), Irritable, Och, Peevish, Peremptory, Petulant, Pish, Pshaw, Restless, Tilly-fally, Till(e)y-vall(e)y, Tut

**Impeach** Accuse, Challenge, Charge, Delate, Indict

**Impeccable** Faultless, Novice

**Impecunious** Land-poor, Penniless, Poor, Short

**Impedance, Impede, Impediment** Block, Burr, Clog, Dam, Diriment, Encumber, Halt, Hamper, Hamstring, Handicap, →**HINDER**, Hog-tie, Let, Log, Obstacle, Obstruct, Reactance, Rub, Shackle, Slur, Snag, Speed bump, Stammer, Stymie, Tongue-tie, Trammel, Veto, Z

**Impel(led), Impelling** Actuate, Coerce, Drave, Drive, Drove, Goad, Inspire, Projectile,
→**URGE**

**Impend(ing)** Imminent, Looming, Toward

**Impenetrable** Adamantine, Air-tight, Dense, Hard, Impervious, Proof, Watertight

**Imperative** Categorical, Dire, Hypothetical, Jussive, Mood, Need-be, Pressing, Vital

**Imperceptible, Imperceptive** Blind Freddie, Intangible, Invisible, Latent, Minimal,
Subtle

**Imperfect(ion)** Aplasia, Aplastic, Blotch, Defect, Deficient, Faulty, Feathering, Flawed,
Half-pie, Kink, Kinkle, Lame, Poor, Rough, Second, Unideal

**Imperial(ist), Imperious** Adroit, Beard, C(a)esarian, Commanding, Dictatorial,
Flag-waver, Haughty, Lordly, Majestic, Masterful, Mint, Peremptory, Regal, Rhodes,
Royal, Tuft

**Imperil** Endanger, Risk

**Imperishable** Eternal, Immarcescible, Immortal, Indestructible

**Impermeable** Airtight, Athermanous, Proof, Resistant

**Impersonal** Abstract, Cold, Dehumanised, Detached, Inhuman, Institutional

**Impersonate(d), Impersonation, Impersonator** Amphitryon, Ape, As, Double,
Drag queen, Echo, Imitate, Imposter, Impostor, Impression, Mimic, Pose, Spoof

**Impertinence, Impertinent** Backchat, Crust, Flip(pant), Fresh, Impudent, Irrelevant,
Nos(e)y, Rude, Sass, Sauce

**Imperturbable** Cool, Placid, Stoic, Tranquil, Unruffable

**Impervious(ness)** Athermancy, Callous, Hardened, Obdurate, Proof, Tight

**Impetigo** Scrumpox

**Impetuous, Impetuosity** Birr, Brash, Bullheaded, Careless, Élan, Harum-scarum,
→**HASTY**, Headstrong, Heady, Hothead, Impulsive, Rash, Rees, Rhys, Tearaway,
Vehement, Violent, Young Turk

**Impetus** Birr, Drift, Drive, Incentive, MacGuffin, Momentum, Propulsion, Slancio,
Steam, Swing

**Impious** Blasphemous, Godless, Irreverent, Unholy

**Implacable** Deadly

**Implant(ation)** AID, Cochlear, Embed, Engraft, Enrace, Enroot, Graft, Inset, Instil,
Microchip, Nidation, Silicone, Sow, Stent

**Implausible** Far-fetched, Lame, Off-the-wall

**Implement** Agent, Apply, Backscratcher, Biffer, Breast plough, Caman, Celt, Cultivator,
Curette, Disgorger, Do, Enforce, Eolith, Execute, Flail, Follow out, Fork, Fulfil, Grater,
Grubber, Hacksaw, Harrow, Hayfork, Mezzaluna, Mop, Muller, Neolith, Pin, Pitchfork,
Plectrum, Plough, Pruning-bill, Pusher, Rest, Ricker, Ripple, Scarifier, Scuffler, Scythe,
Seed drill, Shoehorn, Sickle, Snuffer, Spatula, Splayd®, Spork, Squeegee, Straw-cutter,
Strickle, Sucket fork, Sucket spoon, Tongs, →**TOOL**, Toothpick, Tribrach, Utensil,
Wheelbrace

**Implicate, Implication** Accuse, Concern, Connotation, Drift, Embroil, Incriminate,
Innuendo, →**INVOLVE**, Material, Overtone

**Implore** Beg, Beseech, Crave, →**ENTREAT**, Obsecrate, Petition, Plead, Pray

**Imply, Implied** Connote, Hint, Insinuate, Intimate, Involve, Predicate, Signify,
→**SUGGEST**, Tacit, Unstated, Unwritten

**Impolite** Abrupt, Ill-bred, Ripe, Rude, Uncivil

**Import(s)** Convey, Denote, Drift, Invisible, Mean, Moment, Parallel, Sense, Signify, Spell,
Visible

**Importance, Important (person)** Account, Acute, A-list, Big, Big cheese, Big pot,
Big-time, Big wheel, Billing, Calibre, Capital, Cardinal, Central, Cheese, Chief, Cob,
Coming, Consequence, Considerable, Core, Cornerstone, Count, Critical, Crucial, Crux,
Earth-shaking, Earth-shattering, Ego-trip, Eminent, Epochal, Essential, Flagship,
Focal, Grandeur, Grave, Gravitas, Gravity, Greatness, Heavy, High, High-muck-a-muck,
High-profile, His nibs, Historic, Honcho, Hotshot, Huzoor, Indispensable, Instrumental,

Key, Keystone, Leading, Life and death, Macher, Magnitude, Main, Major, Material, Matters, Megastar, Mighty, Milestone, Moment(ous), Nabob, Nawab, Nib, Note, Numero uno, Obbligato, Outbalance, Overriding, Paramount, Personage, Pivotal, Pot, Preponderate, Prime, Principal, Red-carpet, Red-letter, Salient, Seismic, Seminal, Senior, Serious, Signal, Significant, Something, Special, Stature, Status, Stress, Substantive, Supreme, Tuft, Urgent, VIP, Visiting fireman, Vital, Weight, Weighty, Worth

**Importune, Importunate** Beg, Coax, Flagitate, Pester, Press(ing), Pressgang, Prig, Solicit, Urgent

**Impose(r), Imposing, Imposition** Allocate, Assess, August, Burden, Charge, Cheat, Diktat, Dread, Enforce, Enjoin, Epic, Fine, Flam, Foist, Fraud, Grand(iose), Handsome, Hidage, Homeric, Hum, Impot, Inflict, Kid, Lay, Levy, Lofty, Lumber, Majestic, Noble, Obtrude, Penance, Pensum, Pole, Scot, Sponge, Stately, Statuesque, Stonehand, Sublime, Titan, Try-on, Whillywhaw

**Impossible** Can't, Hopeless, Inconceivable, Incorrigible, Insoluble, Insurmountable, Irreparable, No can do, No-go, No-no, Unacceptable, Unachievable

**Impost** Excise, Levy, Tax, Toll

**Imposter, Impostor** Bunyip, Charlatan, Disaster, Faitor, Faitour, →**FAKE**, Fraud, Idol, Phantasm, Pretender, Ringer, Sham, Triumph, Warbeck

**Impotent** Barren, Helpless, Powerless, Spado, Sterile, Weak

**Impound(er)** Appropriate, Bond, Confiscate, Incarcerate, Intern, Pen, Pinder, Poind

**Impoverish(ed)** Bankrupt, Bare, Beggar, Exhaust, Indigent, Needy, Poor, Skint, Straiten

**Impractical** Abstract, Absurd, Academic, Blue-sky, Chim(a)era, Crackpot, Dreamer, Idealist, Inoperable, Laputan, Non-starter, Not on, Other-worldly, Quixotic, Theoretic, Useless

**Imprecation** Drat, Oath, Pize, Rat(s), 'Slife

**Imprecise** Approximate, Inaccurate, Indeterminate, Intangible, Loose, Nebulous, Rough, Sloppy, Vague

**Impregnable, Impregnate** Conceive, Embalm, Enwomb, Imbue, Inexpugnable, Inseminate, Milt, Permeate, Resinate, Virtue-proof, Watertight

**Impresario** Maestro, Manager, Producer, Showman

**Impress(ive), Impression(able)** Affect, Air, Appearance, Astonish, August, Awe(struck), Blur, Blurb, Bowl over, Brand, Class act, Cliché, Commanding, Conscript, Crimp, Deboss, Dent, Description, Draft, Dramatic, Edition, Effect, Engrain, Engram(ma), Engrave, Enstamp, Epic, Etch, Eye-catching, Feel(ing), Fingerprint, Fossil, Frank, Gas, Glorious, Grab, Grandiose, Grandstand, Greeking, Heroic, Homeric, Idea, Idée, Imitation, Impact, Impinge, Imposing, Imprint, Incuse, Indent, Ingrain, Intaglio, Kick ass, Knock, Let, Magnificent, Majestic, Mould, Name-drop, Niello, Noble, Note, Palimpsest, Pit, Plastic, Plate, Pliable, Powerful, Prent, Presence, Press(gang), Print, Prodigious, Proof, Recruit, Register, Repute, Resplendent, Responsive, Ripsnorter, Rotund, Seal, Seize, Sense, Shanghai, Signet, Slay, Smite, Soft, Spectacular, Stamp, Stately, Stereotype, Stonker, Strike, Stunning, Stupendous, Susceptible, Sway, Tableau, Take, Touch, Type, Vibrant, Watermark, Weal, Weighty, Whale, Woodcut, Wow

**Impressionist** Caxton, Cézanne, Impersonator, Liebermann, Lumin(ar)ist, Manet, Matisse, Monet, Morisot, Renoir

**Imprint** Edition, Engrave, Etch, Stamp

**Imprison(ment)** Cage, Cape, Committal, Confine, Constrain, Custody, Durance, Emmew, False, Gherao, Hitch, Immure, Incarcerate, Inside, Intern, Jail, Lock-up, Penal servitude, Quad, Quod, Stretch, Time

**Improbable** Buckley's chance, Buckley's hope, Dubious, Far-fetched, Unlikely

**Impromptu** Ad lib(itum), Extempore, Improvised, Offhand, Pong, Spontaneous, Sudden, Unrehearsed

**Improper, Impropriety** Abnormal, Blue, Demirep, False, Illegitimate, Indecent, Indecorum, Naughty, Outré, Prurient, Solecism, Undue, Unmeet, Unseemly, Untoward

▷ **Improperly** *may indicate* an anagram

**Improve(ment), Improver, Improving** Advance, Airbrush, Ameliorate, Amend, Beat, Benefit, Bete, Better, Boost, Break, Buck, Cap, Chasten, Conditioner, Convalesce, Cultivate, Defrag, Détente, Didactic, DIY, Ease, Edify, Edutainment, Embellish, Embroider, Emend, Enhance, Enrich, Eugenic, Euthenics, File, Gentrify, J-curve, Kaizen, Meliorate, Mend, Modernise, Polish, Potentiate, Progress, Promote, Rally, Refine, Reform, Resipiscence, Retouch, Revamp, Sarvodaya, Slim, Streamline, Surpass, Tart, Tatt, Titivate, Top, Touch-up, Turn round, Tweak, Upgrade, Upswing, Uptrend, Upturn, Vernissage

**Improvident** Feckless, Micawber, Poor-white, Wasteful

**Improvise(d), Improvisation** Ad hoc, Adlib, Break, Busk it, Contrive, Devise, Drumhead, Extemporise, Gorgia, Invent, Jury-rig, Knock-up, Lash-up, Noodle, On the fly, Play by ear, Pong, Ride, Scat, Scratch, Sodain, Stopgap, Sudden, Tweedle, Unscripted, Vamp, Wing it

**Imprudent** Foolhardy, Foolish, Impetuous, Impolitic, Indiscreet, Injudicious, Rash, Reckless, Unadvised, Unguarded, Unwary, Unwise

**Impudence, Impudent** Audacious, Backchat, Bardy, Barefaced, Bold, Brash, Brassy, Brazen, Cheeky, Cool, Crust, Effrontery, Forward, Gall, Gallus, Gobby, Hussy, Impertinent, Insolent, Jackanapes, Jack-sauce, Lip, Malapert, Neck, → **NERVE**, Pert, Sass(y), Sauce, Saucebox, Saucy, Skipjack, Slack-jaw, Temerity, Whippersnapper, Yankie

**Impugn** Censure, Challenge, Defame, Impeach, Malign

**Impulse, Impulsive** Acte gratuit, Beat, Compelling, Conatus, Dictate, Drive, Efferent, Flighty, Foolhardy, Headlong, Horme, Ideopraxist, Impetus, Instigation, → **INSTINCT**, Libido, Madcap, Nerve, Nisus, Precipitant, Premature, Premotion, Send, Signal, Snap, Specific, Spontaneous, Tearaway, Tendency, Thrust, Tic, Urge, Whim

**Impure, Impurity** Adulterated, Contaminated, Donor, Faints, Feints, Indecent, Lees, Lewd, Regulus, Scum, Unchaste, Unclean

**Imputation, Impute** Ascribe, Attribute, Charge, Scandal, Slander, Slur

**In** A, Amid, Amidst, Amongst, At, Batting, Chic, Current, Fashionable, Hip, Home, Hostel, I', Indium, Inn, Intil, Occupying, On, Pop(ular), Pub, Trendy, Within

**Inability** Agnosia, Anosmia, Aphagia, Aphasia, Apraxia, Ataxy, Prosopagnosia

**Inaccessible** Abaton, Eyrie, Impervious, Remote, Unattainable, Uncom(e)atable

**Inaccurate** Distorted, Erroneous, Faulty, Imprecise, Inexact, Misquote, Out, Overestimate, Rough, Slipshod, Unfaithful

**Inactive, Inaction, Inactivity** Acedia, Anestrum, Anoestrus, Cabbage, Canicular day, Comatose, Dead, Dormant, Extinct, Fallow, Hibernate, Idle, Inert, Languor, Lotus-eater, Masterly, Moratorium, Non-term, Passive, Quiescent, Racemic, Recess, Rusty, Sedentary, Sluggish, Stagnation, Stasis, Torpid, Vacancy, Veg(etate)

**In addition** Eke, Else, Further, Moreover, Plus, Thereto, To boot, Too, Yet

**Inadequate, Inadequacy** Derisory, Feeble, Hopeless, Inapt, Inferior, Joke, Lean, Meagre, Measly, Pathetic, Poor, Ropy, Scanty, Slender, Slight, Thin, Unable, Unequal, Want

**Inadvertent(ly)** Accidental, Careless, Chance, Unwitting

▷ **In a flap** *may indicate* an anagram

**In a high degree** So

**In a hundred** Percent

**Inane** Empty, Fatuous, Foolish, Imbecile, Silly, Vacant

**Inanimate** Abiotic, Lifeless

**Inappropriate** Amiss, Ill-timed, Incongrous, Infelicitous, Malapropos, Off-key, Out of place, Pretentious, Unapt, Unbecoming, Undue, Unmeet, Unsuitable, Untoward

**Inapt** Maladroit, Unsuitable

**Inarticulate(ness)** Indistinct, Mumbling, Psellism

**Inartistic** Artless, Crude

**Inattentive, Inattention** Absent, Abstracted, Asleep, Careless, Deaf, Distrait, Dwaal, Dwa(l)m, Dwaum, Heedless, Listless, Loose, Slack, Unheeding, Unobservant

**Inaudible** Infrasonic, Silent, Superhet

**Inaugurate** Dedicate, Han(d)sel, Initiate, Install, Introduce, Swear in

**Inauspicious** Adverse, Ominous, Sinister

▷ **In a whirl** *may indicate* an anagram

▷ **In a word** *may indicate* two clue words linked to form one

**Inborn, Inbred** Homogamy, Inherent, Innate, Native, Selfed, Sib

**Inca** Quechua, Quichua

**Incalculable** Endless, Unpredictable, Untold

**Incandescent** Alight, Bright, Brilliant, Excited, Radiant

**Incantation** Chant, Charm, Magic, Mantra, Spell

**Incapable** Blotto, Can't, Downa-do, Powerless, Unable, Useless

**Incapacitate** Disable, Paralyse

**Incarcerate** Intern

**Incarnation** Advent, Avatar, Embodiment, Fleshing, Hyperion, Krishna, Rama, Ramachandra

**In case** Lest, So

**Incautious** Cavalier, Foolhardy, Rash, Reckless, Unwary

**Incendiary** Arsonist, Combustible, Firebug, Fire-lighter, Fireship, Greek fire, Napalm, Thermite

**Incense(d), Incenser** Anger, Aroma, Elemi, Enfelon, Enrage, Homage, Hot, →**INFLAME**, Infuriate, Irate, Joss-stick, Mosquito coil, Navicula, Onycha, Outrage, Pastil(le), Provoke, Stacte, Thurible, Thus, Vex, Wrathful

**Incentive** Carrot, Carrot and stick, Feather-bed, Fillip, Impetus, Inducement, Motive, Premium, Spur, Stakhanovism, Stimulus, Wage

**Incessant** Constant, Endless, Unremitting

**Incest** Backcross, Spiritual

**Inch(es)** Ait, Column, Edge, Isle(t), Mil, Miner's, Sidle, Tenpenny, Uncial

**Inchoate** Formless, Immature, Incipient

**Incident(al)** Affair, Baur, Bawr, Byplay, Carry-on, Case, Chance, Circumstance, Episode, Event, Facultative, Handbags, Negligible, Occasion, Occurrent, Page, Peripheral, Scene, Throwaway

**Incinerate, Incinerator** Burn, Combust, Cremate, Destructor

**Incipient** Beginning, Germinal, Inchoate, Nascent

**Incise(d), Incision, Incisive(ness)** Bite, Cut, Edge, Engrave, Enterotomy, Episiotomy, Incavo, Intaglio, Lobotomy, McBurney's, Mordant, Notch, Phlebotomy, Pleurotomy, Punchy, Pungent, Rhizotamy, Scarf, Scribe, Slit, Surgical, Thoracotomy, Tracheotomy, Trenchant

**Incisor** Foretooth

**Incite(ment)** Abet, Agitate, Drive, Egg, Enrage, Fillip, Goad, Hortative, Hoy, Impassion, Inflame, Instigate, Kindle, Motivate, Onsetting, Prod, Prompt, Provoke, Put, Rabble-rouse, Rouse, Sa sa, Sedition, Set, Sic(k), Sool, →**SPUR**, Stimulus, Sting, Suborn, Suggest, Tar, Urge

**Incline(d), Inclination** Acclivity, Angle, Aslant, Aslope, Atilt, Bank, Batter, Bent, Bevel, Bias, Bow, Camber, Cant, Clinamen, Cock, Crossfall, Declivity, Dip, Disposed, Drift, Enclitic, Escarpment, Glacis, →**GRADIENT**, Grain, Habitus, Hade, Heel, Hill, Italic, Kant, Kip, Lean, Liable, Liking, List, Maw, Minded, Nod, On, Partial, Partisan, Peck, Penchant, Proclivity, Prone, Propensity, Rake, Ramp, Ready, Rollway, Set, Sheer, Shelve, Slant, →**SLOPE**, Steep, Steeve, Stomach, Supine, Sway, Tend, Tilt, Tip, Trend, Upgrade, Uptilt, Velleity, Verge, Weathering, Will

**Include(d), Inclusion, Inclusive** Add, All-told, Bracket, Compass, Comprise, Connotate, Contain, Cover, Embody, Embrace, Enclose, Encompass, Involve, Short-list, Social, Subsume, Therein

**Incognito** Anonymous, Disguised, Faceless, Secret, Unnamed, Unobserved

**Incoherent** Confused, Delirious, Disconnected, Disjointed, Gabbling, Garbled, Inarticulate, Rambling, Skimble-skamble, Spluttering

**Incombustible** Clinker

**Income** Annates, Annuity, Benefice, Discretionary, Disposable, Dividend, Earned, Entry, Fixed, Franked, Livelihood, Living, Meal-ticket, Milch cow, National, Notional, OTE, Penny-rent, Prebend, Primitiae, Private, Proceeds, Rent(al), Rente, Rent-roll, Returns, Revenue, Salary, Stipend, Take, Unearned, Unfranked, Wages

**Incomeless** E

**Incommunicado** Isolated, Silent

**Incomparable** Disparate, Par excellence, Supreme, Unequalled, Unique, Unlike, Unmatched

**Incompatible, Incompatibility** Clashing, Contradictory, Dyspathy, Incongruous, Inconsistent, Mismatched, Unsuited

**Incompetent(ly)** Blind Freddie, Bungler, Deadhead, Helpless, Hopeless, Ill, Inefficient, Inept, Nebbich, Not for nuts, Palooka, Rabbit, Shlepper, Shower, Slouch, Unable, Unfit, Useless

**Incomplete** Broadbrush, Cagmag, Catalectic, Deficient, Inchoate, Lacking, Partial, Pendent, Rough, Sketchy, Unfinished

**Incomprehensible, Incomprehension** Acatalepsy, Acatamathesia, Double Dutch, Hard, Obscure, Recondite, Unbelievable

**Inconceivable** Impossible, Incredible

▷ **In confusion** *may indicate* an anagram

**Incongruous, Incongruity** Absurd, Discordant, Heterogenous, Irish, Ironic, Sharawadgi, Sharawaggi, Solecism

**In connection with** Re

**Inconsequential** Light

**Inconsiderable** Light, Slight

**Inconsiderate** Asocial, High-handed, Hog, Lairy, Light-minded, Petty, Presumptuous, Roughshod, Thoughtless, Unkind, Unthinking

**Inconsistency, Inconsistent** Alien, Anacoluthon, Anomaly, Clashing, Contradictory, Discrepant, Fitful, Illogical, Jar(ring), Oxymoronic, Paradoxical, Patchy, Unequal, Unsteady, Variance

**Inconsolable** Heartbroken, Niobe

**Inconspicuous** Background, Obscure, Small, Unobtrusive

**Inconstant** Chameleon, Desultory, Fickle, Light, Moony, Mutable, →**VARIABLE**

**Incontrovertible** Evident

**Inconvenience, Inconvenient** Awkward, Bother(some), Disadvantageous, Discommode, Fleabite, Incommodious, Inopportune, Put out, →**TROUBLE**, Ungain(ly), Unseemly, Untoward

**Incorporate(d), Incorporation** Absorb, Embody, Hard wire, Inc(lude), Inorb, Integrate, Introgression, Introject, Join, Merge, Subsume

**Incorporeal** Aery, Airy, Spiritual

**Incorrect** Catachresis, Erroneous, False, Improper, Invalid, Naughty, Wrong

**Incorrigible** Hopeless, Obstinate

**Incorruptible** Copper-bottomed, Honest, Immortal, Pure, Robespierre, Sea-green

**Increase(s), Increasing** Accelerando, Accelerate, Accession, Accretion, Accrew, Accrue, Add, Additur, Aggrandise, Amplify, Amp up, Appreciate, Approve, Augment, Auxetic, Bolster, Boost, Build up, Bulge, Burgeon, Charge, Crank up, Crescendo, Crescent, Crescive, Cumulate, Deepen, Dilate, Double, Ech(e), Eech, Eik, Eke, Enhance, Enlarge, Enliven, Escalate, →**EXPAND**, Explosion, Extend, Gain, Gather, Greaten, →**GROW**, Heighten, Hike, Ich, Increment, Interbreed, Irrupt, Jack, Jack up, Joseph, Lengthen, Lift, Magnify, Mark up, Mount, Multiply, Plus, Proliferate, Prolong, Propagate, Ramp up, Redshift, Reflation, Regrate, Resurgence, Rise, Snowball, Speed up, Supercharger, Surge, Swell, Thrive, Up, Upload, Upsize, Upswell, Upswing, Up the ante, Wax, Write up

**Incredible** Amazing, Astonishing, Cockamamie, Extraordinary, Fantastic, Preposterous, Staggering, Steep, Stey, Tall, Theeing, Unbelievable, Unreal

**Incredulity, Incredulous** As if, Distrust, Infidel, Sceptic, Suspicion, Thunderstruck, Unbelief

**Increment** Accrual, Augment, Growth, Increase, Unearned

**Incriminate** Accuse, Implicate, Inculpate, Stitch up

**Incrustation** Sordes, Zaratite

**Incubate, Incubator** Brooder, Develop, Eccaleobion, Hatch, Ovisac

**Incubus** Demon, Load, Nightmare

**Inculcate** Implant, Infuse, Instil

**Incumbent** Lying, Obligatory, Occupier, Official, Resident

**Incur** Assume, Earn, Involve, Run up

**Incursion** Foray, Inroad, Invasion, Raid, Razzia

**Indecent** Bare, Blue, Fescennine, Free, Immodest, Immoral, Improper, Indelicate, Lewd, Obscene, Rabelaisian, Racy, Scurril(e), Sotadic, Spicy, Sultry, Uncomely, Unnatural, Unproper, Unseem(ly), X-rated

**Indecision, Indecisive** Demur, Dithery, Doubt, Hamlet, Havering, Hesitation, Hung jury, Inconclusive, Irresolute, Shilly-shally, Suspense, Swither, Weakkneed, Wishy-washy

**Indeclinable** Aptote

**Indecorous** Graceless, Immodest, Outré, Unbecoming, Unseemly

**Indeed** Absolutely, Atweel, Ay, Aye, Begorra(h), Da, Een, Even, Faith, Haith, I, Insooth, Ja wohl, La, Marry, Quotha, Soothly, Truly, Verily, Yah, Yea

**Indefensible** Implausible, Inexcusable, Untenable, Vincible

**Indefinable** Je ne sais quoi

**Indefinite(ly)** A, An, Any, Evermore, Hazy, Nth, Sine die, Some, Uncertain, Undecided, Vague

**Indelible** Fast, Permanent

**Indelicate** Broad, Coarse, Improper, Sultry, Vulgar, Warm

**Indemnify, Indemnification, Indemnity** Assythement, Compensation, Double, Insurance, Voetstoots

**Indent(ed), Indentation** Apprentice, Contract, Crenellate, Dancetty, Dimple, Impress, Niche, Notch, Order, Philtrum, Prophet's thumbmarks, Subentire

**Independence, Independent** Apart, Autocephalous, Autogenous, Autonomy, Crossbencher, Detached, Extraneous, Free(dom), Free-lance, Free spirit, Freethinker, I, Individual, Liberty, Mana motuhake, Maverick, Mugwump, Perseity, Self-contained, Self-sufficient, Separate, Separatist, Sui juris, Swaraj, Udal, UDI, Uhuru, Viscosity

**Indescribable** Incredible, Ineffable, Je ne sais quoi

**Indestructible** Enduring, Impenetrable, Inextirpable

**Indeterminate** Borderline, Formless, Incalculable, Open-ended, Unknown

**Index** Alidad(e), All-Ordinaries, Catalogue, Cephalic, Colour, Concordance, Cranial, Cross, DAX, Dial, Dow Jones, Exponent, Facial, Finger, Fist, Fog, Footsie, Forefinger, FTSE, Gazetteer, Glycaemic, Hang Seng, Kwic, Librorum Prohibitorum, Margin, Misery, Mitotic, Nasal, Nikkei, Opsonic, Power, Price, Refractive, → REGISTER, Rotary, Share, Stroke, Table, Therapeutic, Thumb, TPI, UV, Verborum, Zonal

**India(n)** Adivisi, Apache, Asian, Assamese, Ayah, Baboo, Babu, Bharat(i), Bihari, Canarese, Carib, Chin, Crazy Horse, Dard, Dravidian, East, File, Gandhi, Goanese, Gond(wanaland), Gujarati, Harijan, Harsha, Hindu, .in, Indic, Ink, Jain, Jat, Jemadar, Jewel in the crown, Kafir, Kanarese, Kannada, Khalsa, Kisan, Kolarian, Kshatriyas, Lepcha, Mahatma, Maratha, Ma(h)ratta, Maya, Mazhbi, → MEXICAN, Mishmi, Mission, Mofussil, Mogul, Mulki, Munda, Munshi, Naga, Nagari, Nair, Nasik, Nation, Nayar, → NORTH AMERICAN, Nuri, Ocean, Oriya, Pali, Panjabi, Pargana, Parsee, Parsi, Pathan, Peshwa, Plains, Poppadom, Prakrit, Punja(u)bee, Punjabi, Ravi, Red, Redskin, Sanskrit, Sepoy, Shri, Sikh, Sind(h), → SOUTH AMERICAN, Sowar, Subcontinent, Summer, Swadeshi, Taino, Tamil, Telegu, Treaty, Vakeel, Vakil, West, Ynd

**Indiaman** Clive

**Indiana, Indianian** Hoosier

**Indicate, Indication, Indicative, Indicator** Adumbrate, Allude, Argue, Barcode, Bespeak, Betoken, Blinker, Cite, Clue, Convey, Cursor, → **DENOTE**, Design, Designate, Desine, Dial, Dial gauge, Endeixis, Evidence, Evince, Extort, Finger, Fluorescein, Gesture, Gnomon, Guideline, Hint, Imply, Litmus, Manifest, Mean, Mood, Nod, Notation, Performance, Pinpoint, Plan-position, Point, Portend, Proof, Ray, Register, Remarque, Representative, Reveal, Show, → **SIGN**, Signal, Signboard, Signify, Specify, Speedo, Spell, Symptom, Tip, Token, Trace, Trafficator, Trait, Winker

**Indictment** Accusation, Arraign, Caption, Charge, Dittay, Reproach, Trounce

**Indifference, Indifferent** Adiaphoron, Aloof, Apathetic, Apathy, Blasé, Blithe, Callous, Cauld, Cavalier, Cold, Cool(th), Dead, Deaf, Detached, Disdain, Easy-osy, Empty, Fico, Incurious, Insouciant, Jack easy, Lax, Lukewarm, Mediocre, Neutral, Nonchalant, Perfunctory, Phlegm, Pococurante, Sangfroid, So-so, Stoical, Supercilious, Supine, Tepid, Thick-skinned, Third-rate, Unconcerned

**Indigence, Indigent** Need, Pauper, Penury, Poverty, Want

**Indigenous** Aboriginal, Endemic, Native

▷ **Indi-gent** *may indicate* Baboo or Babu

**Indigestion** Apepsia, Apepsy, Dyspepsia, Heartburn, Stomach-ache

**Indignant, Indignation** Anger, Annoyed, Bridling, Incensed, Irate, Outrage, Pique, Resentful, Steamed up, Umbrage, Wrathful

**Indignity** Affront, Outrage

**Indigo** Anil, Blue, Bunting, Carmine, Indole, Isatin(e), Wild

**Indirect** Aside, Back-handed, By(e), Bypath, Circumlocution, Devious, Evasive, Implicit, Mediate, Oblique, Remote, Roundabout, Second-hand, Sidelong, Sly, Subtle, Vicarious, Zig-zag

**Indiscreet, Indiscretion** Blabbermouth, Folly, Gaffe, Imprudence, Indelicate, Injudicious, Lapse, Loose cannon, Rash, Tactless, Unguarded, Wild oats

**Indiscriminate** Haphazard, Random, Scattershot, Sweeping, Wholesale

**Indispensable** Basic, Essential, King-pin, Linch-pin, Necessary, Requisite, Sine qua non, Vital

**Indispose(d), Indisposition** Adverse, Disincline, Ill, Incapacitate, Loth, Reluctant, Sick, Unwell

**Indisputable** Evident, Watertight

**Indistinct** Ambiguous, Bleary, Blur, Bumble, Bummle, Faint, Filmy, Fuzzy, Grainy, Hazy, Misty, Mumbling, Mush-mouthed, Nebulous, Neutral, Nondescript, Pale, Sfumato, S(c)hwa, Slurred, Smudged, Unincorporate, → **VAGUE**

**Indistinguishable** Nondescript

▷ **In distress** *may indicate* an anagram

**Indite** Compose, Pen, Write

**Indium** In

**Individual(ist), Individuality** Apiece, Being, Discrete, Exclusive, Free spirit, Gemma, Haecceity, Hand-crafted, Identity, Ka, Libertarian, Loner, Man, Man-jack, Morph, One-to-one, Original, Own, Particular, Person(al), Poll, Respective, Seity, Self, Separate, Single, Singular, Solo, Soul, Special, Unique, Unit, Zoon

**Indoctrinate** Brainwash, Discipline, Instruct

**Indo-European** Aryan, Jat(s)

**Indolence, Indolent** Bone idle, Fainéance, Inactive, Languid, Lazy, Lentor, Lotus-eater, Otiose, Purposeless, Shiftless, Sloth, Sluggish, Supine

**Indomitable** Brave, Dauntless, Invincible

**Indonesia(n)** Batavian, .id, Javanese, Nesiot, RI

**Indoor(s)** Within

**Indubitably** Certainly, Certes, Manifestly, Surely

**Induce(ment)** Bribe, Carrot, Cause, Coax, Draw, Encourage, Entice, Evoke, Get, Inveigle, Invite, Lead, Motivate, → **PERSUADE**, Prevail, Suasion, Suborn, Tempt, Urge

**Induct(ion), Inductance** Epagoge, Henry, Inaugurate, Initiate, Install, L, Logic, Mutual, Ordain, Prelude, Remanence

**Indulge(nce), Indulgent** Absolution, Aristippus, Binge, Coddle, Cosset, Debauchery, Dissipation, Drink, Favour, Fond, Gentle, Gratify, Humour, Law, Lie-in, Luxuriate, Oblige, Orgy, Pamper, Pander, Pardon, Partake, Permissive, Pet, Pettle, Pig-out, Please, Plenary, → SATISFY, Splurge, Spoil, Spoonfeed, Spree, Surfeit, Sybarite, Tolerant, Venery, Voluptuous, Wallow

**Industrial, Industrious, Industry** Appliance, Application, Basic, Black Country, Business, Busy, Commerce, Cottage, Deedy, Diligence, Eident, Energetic, Growth, Heavy, Heritage, Labour, Legwork, Millicent, Ocnus, Operose, Process, Ruhr, Service, Smokestack, Sunrise, Technical, Technics, Tertiary, Tourism, Zaibatsu

▸ **Inebriate** *see* **INTOXICATE(D)**

**Inedible** Inesculent, Noisome, Rotten

**In effect** Actual

**Ineffective, Ineffectual** Chinless wonder, Clumsy, Deadhead, Drippy, Droob, Dud, Empty, Eunuch, Fainéant, Feeble, Fruitless, Futile, Idle, Ill, Impotent, Invalid, Lame, Mickey Mouse, Milksop, Neuter, Neutralised, Null, Otiose, Powerless, Resty, Sterile, Stumbledown, Toothless, Unable, → USELESS, Void, Weak, Weenie, Wet, Wimp

**Inefficient** Clumsy, Incompetent, Lame, Shiftless, Slack, Slouch

**Inelegant** Awkward, Inconcinnity, Stiff, Turgid, Unneat

**Ineligible** Unqualified

**Inept** Absurd, Amateurish, Anorak, Cack-handed, Farouche, Flaky, Fumbler, Galoot, Loser, Maladjusted, Nerd, Otaku, Plonker, Sad sack, Schlimazel, Schmo, Unskilled, Wet

**Inequality** Anomaly, Chebyshev's, Disparity, Evection, Imparity, Injustice, Odds, Tchebyshev's

**Inert(ia)** Catatonia, Comatose, Dead, Dull, Excipient, Inactive, Krypton, Languid, Leaden, Mollusc, Motionless, Neon, Oblomovism, Potato, Rigor, Sluggish, Stagnant, Stagnation, Thowless, Torpid, Turgid

**Inescapable** Act of God

**Inestimable** Incalculable, Invaluable, Priceless

**Inevitable, Inevitably** Automatic, Certain, Fateful, Inescapable, Inexorable, Infallible, Necessary, Needs, Perforce, TINA, Unavoidable

**Inexact(itude)** Cretism, Imprecise, Incorrect, Terminological, Wrong

**Inexcusable** Untenable

**Inexhaustible** Infinite, Tireless

**Inexorable** Relentless

**Inexpedient** Impolitic, Imprudent, Unwise

**Inexpensive** Bargain, Cheap, Dirt-cheap, Economic

**Inexperience(d), Inexpert** Amateur, Awkward, Callow, Colt, Crude, Fledgling, Fresh, → GREEN, Greenhorn, Ham, Ingénue, Jejune, Newbie, Put(t), Raw, Rookie, Rude, Tender, Unconversant, Unseasoned, Unseen, Untried, Unversed, Waister, Wide-eyed, Yardbird, Youthful

**Inexplicable** Magical, Mysterious, Paranormal, Supernatural, Unaccountable

**In fact** Insooth

**Infallible** Foolproof, Oracle, Right, Sure-fire, Unerring

**Infamous, Infamy** Base, Ignominious, Notorious, Opprobrium, Shameful, Villainy

**Infant, Infancy** Babe, Baby, Innocent, Lamb, Minor, Nurs(e)ling, Oral, Rug rat, The cradle

**Infantry(man)** Buff, Foot, Grunt, Jaeger, Phalanx, Pultan, Pulto(o)n, Pultun, → SOLDIER, Tercio, Turco, Twenty, Voetganger, Zouave

▷ **Infantry** *may refer to* babies

**Infatuate(d), Infatuating, Infatuation** Assot, Besot, Circean, Crush, Enamoured, Engou(e)ment, Entêté, Epris, Fanatic, Foolish, Lovesick, Mash, → OBSESSION, Pash, Rave, Turn

**Infect(ed), Infecting, Infection, Infectious** Adenoviral, Angina, Anthrax, Babesiasis, Babesiosis, Candidiasis, Canker, Carrier, Catching, Catchy, Cholera, Communicable, Contagious, Contaminate, Corrupt, Cowpox, Cryptococcosis, Cryptosporidiosis, Dermatophytosis, Diseased, E-coli, Fascioliasis, Fester, Focal, Fomes, Giardiasis, Gonorrhoea, Herpes, Impetigo, Leishmaniasis, Listeria, Lockjaw, Mycetoma, NSU, Opportunistic, Orf, Overrun, Poison, Polio(myelitis), → **POLLUTE**, Py(a)emia, Pyoderma, Quittor, Rife, Ringworm, Roseola, Roup, Salmonella, Sarcoid, SARS, Scabies, Secondary, Septic, Shingles, Smit(tle), Strep throat, Strongyloidiasis, Strongylosis, Taint, Taking, Tetanus, Thrush, Tinea, Toxocariasis, Toxoplasmosis, Transfection, Trichuriasis, Tryp, Typhoid, Typhus, Varroa, Vincent's angina, Viral pneumonia, Virion, Virulent, Whitlow, Wog, Yersiniosis, Zoonosis, Zymosis

**Infeftment** Sasine, Seisin

**Infer(ence), Inferred** Conclude, Conjecture, Construe, Deduce, Divine, Educe, Extrapolate, Generalise, Guess, Illation, Imply, Judge, Obversion, Putative, Surmise, Syllogism

▷ **Infer** *may indicate* 'fer' around another word

**Inferior** Base, Bodgier, Cheap-jack, Cheesy, Coarse, Crummy, Degenerate, Dog, Epigon, Ersatz, Gimcrack, Grody, Grub-Street, Impair, Indifferent, Infra, Jerkwater, Less, Lo-fi, Lousy, Lower, Low-grade, Mediocre, Minor, Naff, Nether, One-horse, Ornery, Paravail, Petty, Poor, Rop(e)y, Schlock, Second, Second-best, Shilpit, Shlock, Shoddy, Shonky, Slopwork, Sprew, Sprue, Subjacent, Subordinate, Substandard, Surat, Tatty, Third-rate, Tinpot, Trashy, Under(man), Underdog, Underneath, Understrapper, Untermensch, Waste, Worse

**Infernal** All-fired, Cotton-picking, Demogorgon, Diabolic, Hellish, Phitonian, Tartarean, Unholy

**Inferno** Hellfire

**Infertile, Infertility** Barren, Farrow, GIFT, Sterile

**Infest(ed), Infestation** Acariasis, Acrawl, Beset, Blight, Dog, Hoatching, Overrun, Pediculosis, Phthiriasis, → **PLAGUE**, Stylopised, Swamp, Swarm, Taeniasis, Torment, Trombiculiasis, Trombidiasis, Trypanosomiasis, Uncinariasis

**Infidel** Atheist, Caffre, Giaour, Heathen, Heretic, Kafir, Miscreant, Pagan, Paynim, Saracen

**Infield** Intown

**Infiltrate(d), Infiltration, Infiltrator** Encroach, Enter, Entryist, Fifth columnist, Gatecrash, Instil, Intrude, Mole, Pervade, Trojan horse

**Infinite, Infinity** Cosmic, Endless, Eternal, N

**Infinitive** Split

**Infirm(ity)** Decrepit, Doddery, Feeble, Frail, Frailness, Lame, Shaky, Sick

▷ **Infirm** *may indicate* 'co' around another word

**Infirmary** Hospital, Sick bay

**Inflame(d), Inflammable, Inflammation** Afire, Anger, → **AROUSE**, Bloodshot, Enamoured, Enchafe, Enfire, Enkindle, Fever, Fire, Founder, Gleet, Ignite, Impassion, Incense, Infection, Ire, Kindle, Methane, Napalm, Naphtha, → **RED**, Rouse, Stimulate, Swelling, Touchwood

---

## INFLAMMATIONS

| *3 letters:* | *5 letters:* | Canker | Ulitis |
|---|---|---|---|
| Sty | Croup | Coryza | |
| | Felon | Eczema | *7 letters:* |
| *4 letters:* | | Garget | Bubonic |
| Acne | *6 letters:* | Iritis | Catarrh |
| Gout | Ancome | Otitis | Cecitis |
| Noma | Angina | Quinsy | Colitis |
| Stye | Bunion | Thrush | Ecthyma |

Ignatis
Ileitis
Onychia
Pinkeye
Prurigo
Rosacea
Sunburn
Sycosis
Tylosis
Uveitis
Whitlow

**8 letters:**
Adenitis
Aortisis
Bursitis
Carditis
Colpitis
Cystisis
Fibrosis
Hyalitis
Mastitis
Metritis
Mycetoma
Myelitis
Myositis
Neuritis
Orchitis
Osteitis
Ovaritis
Phlegmon
Pleurisy
Pyelitis
Rachitis
Rectitis
Rhinitis
Thylosis
Uvulitis
Vulvitis
Windburn

**9 letters:**
Arteritis
Arthritis
Balanitis
Barotitis
Carbuncle
Cheilitis
Chilblain
Cloacitis
Dysentery

Enteritis
Fasciitis
Frostbite
Gastritis
Glossitis
Keratitis
Laminitis
Nephritis
Onychitis
Parotitis
Phlebitis
Phrenitis
Pneumonia
Proctitis
Pyorrhoea
Retinitis
Scleritis
Sinusitis
Splenitis
Strumitis
Synovitis
Typhlitis
Vaginitis
Vent gleet

**10 letters:**
Asbestosis
Bronchitis
Cellulitis
Cephalitis
Cerebritis
Cervicitis
Dermatitis
Duodenitis
Erysipelas
Fibrositis
Gingivitis
Hepatitis A
Hepatitis B
Hysteritis
Intertrigo
Laryngitis
Meningitis
Oophoritis
Ophthalmia
Papillitis
Paronychia
Phlegmasia
Phlogistic
Stomatitis
Tendinitis

Tendonitis
Thrombosis
Tracheitis
Tympanitis
Urethritis
Valvulitis
Vasculitis

**11 letters:**
Blepharitis
Farmer's lung
Mad staggers
Mastoiditis
Myocarditis
Parotiditis
Peritonitis
Pharyngitis
Pneumonitis
Prostatitis
Salpingitis
Sandy blight
Sclerotitis
Shin splints
Spondylitis
Staphylitis
Tennis elbow
Thoroughpin
Thyroiditis
Tonsillitis
Trenchmouth
Utriculitis
Woody-tongue

**12 letters:**
Appendicitis
Crystallitis
Encephalitis
Endocarditis
Endometritis
Folliculitis
Golfer's elbow
Lymphangitis
Lympodenitis
Mesenteritis
Ophthalmitis
Osteoporosis
Panarthritis
Pancreatitis
Pericarditis
Polymyositis
Polyneuritis

Sacroillitis
Swimmer's itch
Vestibulitis

**13 letters:**
Cholecystitis
Enterocolitis
Epicondylitis
Jogger's nipple
Labyrinthitis
Lymphadenitis
Osteomyelitis
Perihepatitis
Perinephritis
Periodontisis
Perityphlitis
Tenosynovitis
Tenovaginitis
Thrombophilia

**14 letters:**
Clergyman's knee
Conjunctivitis
Diverticulitis
Osteoarthritis
Pyelonephritis
Sleepy staggers
Tendovaginitis
Trichomoniasis
Vincent's angina

**15 letters:**
Gastroenteritis
Pachymeningitis
Panophthalmitis

**16 letters:**
Bronchopneumonia
Rhinopharyngitis
Thrombophlebitis

**17 letters:**
Encephalomyelitis
Meningocephalitis

**19 letters:**
St Louis
   encephalitis

---

**Inflate(d), Inflation** Aerate, Aggrandise, Balloon, Bloat, Bombastic, Bracket-creep,
   Cost-push, Demand-pull, Dilate, Distend, Distent, Exaggerate, Grade, Increase,

Pneumatic, Pompous, Pump, Raise, Remonetise, RPI, Spiral, Stagflation, Stagnation, Swell, Wage-push

**Inflect(ion)** Accidence, Cadence, Conjugation, Tone

**Inflexible, Inflexibility** Adamant(ine), Authoritarian, Byzantine, Doctrinaire, Hard-ass, Hard-liner, Iron, Obstinate, Ossified, Ramrod, Relentless, Resolute, Rigid, Rigour, Set, Staid, Steely, Stiff, Stubborn, Unbending

**Inflict(ion)** Deal, Force, Give, Impose, Subject, Trouble, Visit, Wreak

**Inflorescence** Bostryx, Catkin, Ci(n)cinnus, Drepanium, Glomerule, Monochasium, Panicle, Pleiochasium, Polychasium, Raceme, R(h)achis, Umbel, Verticillaster

**Inflow** Affluence, Influx

**Influence(d), Influential** Act, Affect, After, Amenable, Backstairs, Bias, Brainwash, Catalyse, Charm, Clamour, Clout, Colour, Credit, Determine, Dominant, Drag, Earwig, Eclectic, Embracery, Éminence grise, Factor, Force, Get at, Govern, Guide, Hegemony, Hold, Hypnotise, Impact, Impinge, Impress, Incubus, Inspire, Interfere, Jinx, Lead, Leverage, Lobby, Macher, Mastery, Militate, Mogul, Mould, Nobble, Octopus, Operation, Outreach, Outweigh, Panjandrum, Power, Preponderant, Pressure, Prestige, →**PULL**, Push, Reach, Rust, Say, Securocrat, Seminal, Significant, Star, Star-blasting, Stimulus, String-pulling, Suggest, Svengali, Sway, Swing, Telegony, Thrall, Undue, Weigh with, Will, Work, Wull

**Influenza** Asian, Equine, Flu, Gastric, Grippe, Lurgi, Spanish, Wog, Yuppie

**Influx** Inbreak

**Infold(ing)** Invagination

**Inform(ation), Informant, Informed, Informer** Acquaint, Advise, Agitprop, Apprise, Arise, Au fait, Aware, Beagle, Bit, Blow, Briefing, Burst, Callboard, Canary, Ceefax®, Clype, Contact, Cookie, Database, Datum, Debriefing, Deep throat, Delate, Diane, Dicker, Dob(ber), Dobber-in, Dope, Download, Education, Exposition, Facts, Fact sheet, FAQs, Feedback, Fink, Fisgig, Fiz(z)gig, Gen, Genome, Good oil, Grapevine, Grass, Griff, Gunsel, Hep, Hip, Immersive, Input, Inside, Instruct, Izvesti(y)a, Light, Literate, Little bird, Lowdown, Media, Metadata, Microdot, Moiser, Nark, Nepit, News, Nit, Nose, Notify, Occasion, Oracle®, Output, Peach, Pem(m)ican, Pentito, Pimp, Pointer, Poop, Post, Prestel®, Prime, Printout, Promoter, Propaganda, Prospectus, Rat, Read-out, Relator, Report, Revelation, Rheme, Rumble, Shelf, Shop, Sidelight, Sing, Sneak, Snitch, Snout, SP, Squeak, Squeal, Stag, Stoolie, Stool-pigeon, Supergrass, Sycophant, Teletext®, Tell, Throughput, Tidings, Tip-off, Up, Up to speed, Videotext®, Viewdata®, Whistle(-blower), Wire, Witting

**Informal** Bat, Casual, Cosy, Free and easy, Go-as-you-please, Intimate, Irregular, Outgoing, Rough and ready, Unofficial

**Infra** Under

**Infra dig** Ignominious

**Infrequent** Casual, Occasional, Rare, Scant, Seldom, Sparse

**Infringe(ment)** Contravene, Piracy, Transgression, Violate

**Infuriate(d)** Anger, Apoplectic, Bemad, Bepester, Enrage, Exasperate, Gall, Incense, Livid, Madden, Pester, Provoke

**Infuse(r), Infusion** Brew, Distill, Gallise, Instil, Mash, Ooze, Saloop, Saturate, Steep, Tea, Tea-ball, Tea-egg, Tisane, Toddy, Uva-ursi

**Ingenious, Ingenuity** Acumen, Adept, Adroit, Art, Artificial, Clever, Cunning, Cute, Inventive, Natty, Neat, Resourceful, Smart, Subtle, Trick(s)y, Wit

**Ingenuous** Artless, Candid, Green, Innocent, Naive, Open, Transparent

**Ingest** Eat, Endue, Incept, Indue, Swallow

**Ingle** Bardash, Hearth, Nook

**In good condition** Fit, Shipshape, Taut, Trim

**Ingot** Bar, Billet, Bullion, Lingot, Sycee, Wedge

**Ingrain(ed)** Deep-seated, Fix, Impregnate, Train

**Ingrate** Thankless, Viper

**Ingratiate, Ingratiating** Bootlick, Butter, Court, Flatter, Greasy, Oily, Pick-thank, Silken, Smarm(y)

**Ingredient(s)** Additive, Admixture, Asafoetida, Basis, Content, Element, Factor, Formula, Makings, Mincemeat, Staple

**Ingrowing, Ingrowth** Onychocryptosis, T(h)ylosis

**Inhabit(ant), Inhabitants** Affect, Children, Denizen, Dweller, Indweller, Inholder, Inmate, Live, Native, Occupant, People, Populate, Population, Populous, Resident, Towny

**Inhale(r), Inhalation** Aspirate, Breath(e), Draw, Gas, Inbreathe, Inspire, Intal, Sniff, Snort, Snuff, Take, Toot, Tout

**Inharmonious** Out, Patchy

**Inherent** Characteristic, Essential, Immanent, Inbred, Innate, Native

**Inherit(ance), Inherited, Inheritor** Accede, Ancestral, Birthright, Borough-English, Congenital, Esnecy, Feoffee, Gene, Genom, Heirloom, Heritage, Inborn, Legacy, Legitim, Meek, Mendelism, Particulate, Patrimony, Portion, Reversion, Succeed, Tichborne, Ultimogenitive

**Inhibit(ing), Inhibition, Inhibitor** ACE, Antihistamine, Anuria, Captopril, Chalone, Chalonic, Deter, Donepezil, Enalapril, Etanercept, Feedback, Finasteride, Forbid, Hang-up, Indinavir, Protease, Restrain, Retard, Retroactive, Stunt, Suppress, Tightass

**Inhuman** Barbarous, Brutal, Merciless, Robotic

**Inimical** Adverse, Harmful, Hostile

**Iniquity, Iniquitous** Damnable, Diabolical, Evil, Offence, Sin, Vice

**Initial** Acronym, First, Inaugural, Letter, Monogram, Paraph, Prelim(inary), Primary, Rubric

▷ **Initially** *may indicate* first letters

**Initiate(d), Initiating, Initiation, Initiative** Baptism, Begin, Bejesuit, Blood, Bora, Bring, Ceremony, Debut, Démarche, Enter, Enterprise, Epopt, Esoteric, Gumption, Induct, Instigate, Instruct, →**LAUNCH**, Neophyte, Nous, Onset, Open, Proactive, Spark, →**START**, Tyro

**Inject(or), Injection** Antiserum, Bang, Blast, Bolus, Booster, Collagen, Direct, Enema, Epidural, Epipen®, Fuel, Hypo, Immit, Implant, Innerve, Inoculation, Instil, Introduce, Jab, Jack up, Jag, Lidocaine, Mainline, Pop, Reheat, Serum, Shoot, Shoot up, Skin-pop, Solid, Spike, Syringe, Transfuse, Venipuncture

**Injudicious** Misguided

**Injunction** Command, Embargo, Freezing, Mandate, Mareva, Quia timet, Swear, Writ

**Injure(d), Injury, Injurious, Injustice** ABH, Abuse, Accloy, Aggrieve, Bale, Barotrauma, Bled, Bruise, Casualty, Concuss, Contrecoup, Contuse, Crick, Damage, De(a)re, Disservice, Forslack, Frostbite, Gash, GBH, Harm, →**HURT**, Ill-turn, Impair, Industrial, Iniquity, Lesion, Malign, Mar, Mayhem, Mistreat, Mutilate, NAI, Needlestick, Nobble, Nocuous, Non-accidental, Noxal, Nuisance, Occupational, Oppression, Outrage, Packet, Paire, Prejudice, Rifle, RSI, Scaith, Scald, Scath(e), Scotch, Shend, Shiner, Sore, Sprain, Teen(e), Tene, Tort, Trauma, Umbrage, Whiplash, Wound, Wrong

▶ **Injury** *see* **AFTER INJURY**

**Ink(y), Inker** Atramental, Black, Bray, China, Chinese, Copying, Cyan, Gall, Gold, Indian, Invisible, Magnetic, Marking, Monk, Printer's, Printing, Sepia, Stained, Sympathetic, Tattooist, Toner, Tusche

**Inkling** Clue, Glimpse, Hint, Idea

**Inkpot** Standish

**Inlaid, Inlay(er)** Boulle, Buhl, Clear, Compurgation, Crustae, Damascene, Emblemata, Empaestic, Enamel, Enchase, Incrust, Intarsia, Intarsio, Koftgar(i), Marquetrie, Marquetry, Pietra-dura, Piqué, Set, Tarsia, Unsuspecting, Veneer

**Inland** Hinterland, Interior, Up, Upcountry

**Inlet** Arm, Bay, Bohai, Cook, Cove, Creek, Entry, Estuary, Fiord, Firth, Fjord, Fleet, Flow, Geo, Gio, Golden Horn, Gulf, Gusset, Hope, Infall, Ingate, Jervis Bay, Loch, McMurdo

Sound, Moray Firth, Pamlico Sound, Pearl Harbor, Plymouth Sound, Pohai, Port Jackson, Port Phillip Bay, Puget Sound, Ria, Rio de la Plata, Sogne Fjord, Solway Firth, Strait, Sullom Voe, Table Bay, The Wash, Tor Bay, Zuyder Zee

▷ **Inlet** *may indicate* 'let' around another word

**Inmate** Intern(e), Lodger, Patient, Prisoner, Resident

**Inn(s), Innkeeper** Albergo, Alehouse, Auberge, Barnard's, Boniface, Caravanserai, Chancery, Change-house, Coaching, Court, Gastropub, Gray's, Halfway-house, Host(ry), Hostelry, Hotel(ier), House, Imaret, In, Inner Temple, Jamaica, Khan, Kneipe, Ladin(ity), Law, Licensee, Lincoln's, Lodging, Luckie, Lucky, Maypole, Middle Temple, Motel, Padrone, Parador, Patron, Porterhouse, Posada, Posthouse, Pothouse, Publican, Roadhouse, Ryokan, Serai, Stabler, Tabard, Taphouse, Tavern(er), Victualler

▷ **Inn** *may refer to* the law

**Innards** Entrails, Giblets, Gizzard, Guts, Harigals, Harslet, Haslet, Omasa, Rein, Viscera

**Innate** Congenital, Essential, Inborn, Inbred, Inbuilt, Ingenerate, Ingrown, Instinctive, Natural, Original

**Inner(most)** Bencher, Esoteric, Home, Internal, Intima, Intimate, Lining, Man, Marrow, Medulla, Private, Red, Woman

**Innings** Chance, Knock, Turn

▶ **Innkeeper** *see* INN(S)

**Innocent** Absolved, Angelic, Arcadian, Babe, Blameless, Canny, Chaste, Cherub, Childlike, Clean, Clear, Compurgation, Dewy-eyed, Doddypoll, Dodipoll, Dove, Encyclical, Green, Guileless, Idyllic, Inadvertent, Ingenue, Lamb, Lily-white, Maiden, Naive, Opsimath, Pope, Prelapsarian, → PURE, Sackless, St, Seely, Simple, Unsuspecting, Unwitting, White

**Innocuous** Harmless, Innocent

**Innovate, Innovative, Innovation, Innovator** Alteration, Avant garde, Cutting edge, Departure, Ground-breaking, Modernise, Newell, Novelty, Novity, Pioneer, Promethean, Radical, Trendsetter, Wrinkle

**Inn-sign** Bush

**Innu** Naskapi

**Innuendo** Hint, Insinuation, Overtone, Slur

**Innumerable** Countless, Infinite, Myriad, N

**Inoculate, Inoculation** Engraft, Immunise, Jab, Protect, Vaccine, Variolate

**Inoffensive** Anodyne, Harmless, Mild, Neutral, Pleasant

**Inoperative** Futile, Nugatory, Silent, Void

**Inopportune** Disadvantageous, Inconvenient, Intempestive, Untimely

**Inordinate** Excessive, Irregular, Undue

▷ **Inordinately** *may indicate* an anagram

**Inorganic** Mineral

**In place of** For, Qua, Vice, Vise, With

**Input** Direct, OCR

**Inquest** Debriefing, Hearing, Inquiry, Investigation

**Inquire, Inquiring, Inquiry** Ask, Demand, Investigation, Maieutic, Nose, Organon, Probe, Public, Query, Question, See, Speer, Speir

**Inquisition, Inquisitive, Inquisitor** Curious, Interrogation, Meddlesome, Nosy, Prying, Rubberneck, Snooper, Spanish, Stickybeak, Torquemada

▷ **In revolt, In revolution** *may indicate* an anagram

**Inroad(s)** Breach, Encroachment, Honeycomb, Infall, Invasion

**Insane, Insanity** Absurd, Batty, Berserk, Crack-brained, Crazy, Dementia, Deranged, Headcase, Hebephrenia, Loco, Looniness, Lune, Mad, Manic, Mattoid, Mental, Nutso, Paranoia, Pellagra, Psycho, Schizo, Troppo, Yarra

**Insatiable** Greedy, Ravenous, Voracious

**Insatiate child** Killcrop

**Inscribe(d), Inscription** Chisel, Chronogram, Colophon, Dedicate, Emblazon, Endoss, Engrave, Enter, Epigraph, Epitaph, Exergue, Graffiti, Hic jacet, Hierograph, Lapidary, Legend, Lettering, Neum(e), Ogham, Pen, Posy, Writ
**Inscrutable** Deadpan, Esoteric, Mysterious, Sphinx
**Insect(s)** Entomic, Nonentity, Non-person, Stridulator, Wax

## INSECTS

| | | | |
|---|---|---|---|
| **3 letters:** | Botfly | Chalcid | Firebrat |
| Ant | Breese | Chigger | Fruit fly |
| Bee | Breeze | Corixid | Gall-wasp |
| Bot | Capsid | Cornfly | Glossina |
| Bug | Chigoe | Cricket | Goatmoth |
| Fly | Cicada | Culicid | Greenfly |
| Ked | Cicala | Cutworm | Horntail |
| Lac | Coccid | Daphnid | Horsefly |
| Nit | Day-fly | Ergates | Isoptera |
| Wog | Earwig | Firefly | Itchmite |
| | Elater | Gallfly | Lacewing |
| **4 letters:** | Gadfly | Girdler | Ladybird |
| Flea | Hopper | Gordius | Lygus bug |
| Gnat | Hornet | Goutfly | Mealybug |
| Grig | Instar | Grayfly | Metabola |
| Lice | Locust | Hexapod | Milliped |
| Luna | Maggot | Hive-bee | Mosquito |
| Mite | Mantid | Humbuzz | Myriapod |
| Moth | Mantis | Katydid | Oak-egged |
| Pium | Mayfly | Ladybug | Onion-fly |
| Pupa | Medfly | Ladycow | Pauropod |
| Tick | Noctua | Ladyfly | Pillworm |
| Wasp | Phasma | Odonata | Puss-moth |
| Weta | Podura | Oestrus | Reduviid |
| Zimb | Psocid | Oniscus | Ruby-tail |
| | Psylla | Phasmid | Scarabee |
| **5 letters:** | Punkie | Pill-bug | Silkworm |
| Aphis | Redbug | Pyralis | Snowflea |
| Borer | Sawfly | Sandfly | Stinkbug |
| Brise | Scarab | Spectre | Stonefly |
| Cimex | Slater | Spittle | Symphile |
| Culex | Spider | Stylops | Waterbug |
| Emmet | Tettix | Tabanus | Wheelbug |
| Gogga | Thrips | Termite | Whitefly |
| Imago | Vespid | | Wireworm |
| Louse | Walker | **8 letters:** | Woodworm |
| Midge | Weevil | Alderfly | |
| Nymph | | Blackfly | **9 letters:** |
| Ox-bot | **7 letters:** | Bookworm | Ametabola |
| Roach | Aeschna | Cercopid | Booklouse |
| Scale | Antlion | Circutio | Butterfly |
| Stick | Bee moth | Coccidae | Caddis-fly |
| Zebub | Bristle | Crane-fly | Campodeid |
| | Bushfly | Dipteras | Centipede |
| **6 letters:** | Buzzard | Dust mite | Cochineal |
| Acarid | Carabid | Ephemera | Cockroach |

Damselfly
Dobsonfly
Dor-beetle
Dragonfly
Ephemerid
Ergataner
Grass moth
Hawstreak
Hemiptera
Homoptera
Leaf-miner
May beetle
Mecoptera
Millepede
Millipede
Notonecta
Nut weevil
Oil beetle
Rearhorse
Robber-fly
Songololo
Squash bug
Synoekete
Tabanidae
Thysanura
Tiger-moth
Woodlouse
Xylophage

**10 letters:**
Apterygota
Bark mantis
Bluebottle
Casebearer
Cecidomyia
Chironomid
Cockchafer
Coleoptera
Collembola
Fan-cricket
Fen-cricket
Froghopper
Greendrake
Harvestman
Leaf-cutter
Leafhopper
Mallophaga
Orthoptera
Phylloxera
Plant-louse
Plecoptera
Pond-skater
Psocoptera
Rhipiptera
Rice weevil
Silverfish
Spider-mite

Spittlebug
Springtail
Thysanuran
Treehopper
Waterstick
Web spinner

**11 letters:**
Bristletail
Collembolan
Dermapteran
Grasshopper
Greenbottle
Heteroptera
Hymenoptera
Mole-cricket
Neuropteran
Plectoptera
Rhopalocera
Tiger-beetle
Trichoptera
Vine-fretter

**12 letters:**
Bishop's mitre
Creepy-crawly
Dictyopteran
Groundhopper

Heteropteran
Neuropterous
Notonectidae
Orthopterous
Rhipidoptera
San Jose scale
Strepsiptera
Thousand-legs
Thysanoptera
Water boatman

**13 letters:**
Cotton stainer
Daddy-long-legs
Jenny-longlegs
Leatherjacket
Pine-leaf scale
Praying mantis
Staphylinidae
Water scorpion

**14 letters:**
Strepsipterous

**19 letters:**
Cottony-cushion
scale

**Insecticide** Aldrin, Allethrin, Aphicide, Carbaryl, Carbofuran, Chlordan(e), Chromene, Cube, DDT, Deet, Derris, Diazinon, Dieldrin, Endosulfan, Endrin, Flycatcher, Gammexane®, Ivermectin, Lindane®, Malathion®, Menazon, Methoxychlor, Miticide, Naphthalene, Parathion, Paris green, Piperazine, Pulicide, Pyrethrin, Pyrethrum, Repellent, Rotenone, Spray, Systemic, Timbo, Toxaphene, Zineb

**Insectivore** Agouta, Desman, Donaea, Drongo, Drosera, Hedgehog, Jacamar, Nepenthaceae, Otter-shrew, Sarracenia, Shrew, Tanrec, Tenrec(idae), Tupaia, Venus flytrap, Zalambdodont

**Insecure** Infirm, →LOOSE, Needy, Precarious, Shaky, Unsafe, Unstable, Unsteady, Vulnerable

**Insensible** Iron-witted

**Insensitive, Insensitivity** Analgesia, Blunt, Callous, Crass, Dead, Indurate, Log, Numb, Obtuse, Pachyderm, Stolid, Tactless, Thick-skinned

**Inseparable** Indiscrete, Indivisible, One, Simultaneous, United

**Insert(ed), Insertion, Inset** Anaptyxis, Cue, Empiecement, Enchase, Enter, Entry, Epenthesis, Foist, Fudge, Godet, Gore, Graft, Gusset, Immit, Imp, Implant, Inchase, Inject, Inlay, Input, Intercalar, Interject, Interpolate, Interpose, Intersperse, Introduce, Intromit, Intubate, Lexical, Mitre, Pin, Plant, Punctuate, Sandwich

**Inside(r)** Content, Core, Entrails, Gaol, Giblets, Heart, Indoors, Interior, Internal, Interne, Inward, Inwith, Mole, Tum, →WITHIN

**Insidious** Artful, Crafty, Sly

**Insight** Acumen, Anagoge, Aperçu, Enlightenment, Hunch, Inkling, Intuition, Parascience, →PERCEPTION, Profundity, Tais(c)h

**Insignia** Armour, Arms, Badger, Charge, Chevron, Club tie, Crest, Eagle, Mark, Order, Regalia, Ribbon, Roundel, Tab

**Insignificant (person)** Bobkes, Bubkis, Bupkes, Bupkis, Chickenfeed, Cog, Dandiprat, Fico, Fiddling, Flea-bite, Fractional, Gnat, Inconsiderable, Insect, Jerkwater, Mickey Mouse, Minimus, Miniscule, Minnow, Nebbich, Nickel and dime, Nobody, Nominal, Nondescript, Nonentity, Non-event, Non-person, No one, One-eyed, Paltry, Peanuts, Petit, Petty, Piddling, Pipsqueak, Pissant, Quat, Rabbit, Scoot, Scout, Scrub, Shrimp, Slight, Small beer, Small potatoes, Small-time, Squirt, Squit, Tenuous, Trifling, Trivial, Two-bit, Unimportant, Venial, Warb, Whiffet, Whippersnapper, Wind

**Insincere, Insincerity** Affected, Artificial, Barmecide, Cant, Crocodile tears, Disingenuous, Double, Double-faced, Duplicity, Empty, Factitious, Faithless, False, Forced, Glib, Greenwash, Hollow, Janus-faced, Lip service, Mealy-mouthed, Meretricious, Mouth-made, Pseudo, Shallow, Superficial, Synthetic, Tongue-in-cheek, Two-faced, Unnatural

**Insinuate, Insinuating, Insinuation** Allude, Foist, Hint, Imply, Innuendo, Intimate, Sleek, Slur, Sneck-draw

**Insipid** Banal, Blab, Bland, Drippy, Fade, Flat, Insulse, Jejune, Lash, Mawkish, Milk and water, Shilpit, Spiritless, Tame, Tasteless, Vapid, Weak, Wearish, Wersh

**Insist(ent)** Adamant, Assert, Clamant, Demand, Dogmatic, Exact, Press, Require, Stickler, →STIPULATE, Stress, Swear, Threap, Threep, Urge

**Insolence, Insolent** Attitude, Audacity, Bardy, Brassy, Cheek, Contumely, Cub, Effrontery, Gum, Hectoring, Hubris, Hybris, Impudence, Lairy, Lip, Mouth, Rude, Snash, Snide, Stroppy, Wanton

**Insoluble** Cerasin, Hard, Irresolvable, Mysterious

**Insolvent** Bankrupt, Broke, Destitute, Penniless

**Insomnia** Agrypnotic, Sleeplessness, Wakefulness, White night

**Insouciant** Carefree, Careless, Cavalier

**Inspect(ion), Inspector** Ale-conner, Alnage(r), Auditor, Case, Check(er), Comb, Conner, Cook's tour, Darogha, Examine, Exarch, Go-over, Government, Investigator, Jerque, Keeker, Lestrade, Look over, Look-see, Maigret, Morse, Muster, Once-over, Peep, Perlustrate, Proveditor, Rag-fair, Recce, Review, Sanitary, School, Scrutinise, Searcher, Shufti, Spot check, Supervisor, Survey, Test, Vet, Vidimus, Visitation

**Inspire(d), Inspiration, Inspiring** Actuate, Aerate, Afflatus, Aganippe, Animate, Brainstorm, Brainwave, Breath(e), Castalian, Draw, Duende, Elate, Encourage, Estro, Exalt, Fire, Flash, Geist, Hearten, Hunch, Hwyl, Idea, Illuminate, Imbue, Impress, Impulse, Indrawn, Induce, Inflatus, Infuse, Inhale, Invention, Kindle, Messianic, Motivate, Move, Muse, Pegasus, Pig's whisper, Plenary, Prompt, Prophetic, Reassurance, Satori, Sniff(le), Stimulus, Stoke, Taghairm, Theopnautic, Theopneust(y), Uplift, Vatic, Verbal

**In spite of** Malgrado, Malgré, Maugre, Maulgre

**Instability** Anomie, Anomy

**Install(ation)** Elect, Enchase, Enthrone, Inaugurate, Induction, Infrastructure, Insert, Invest, Put (in)

**Instalment** Call, Episode, Fascicle, Fascicule, Heft, Insert, Livraison, Never-never, Part, Piecemeal, Serial, Tranche

**Instance, Instant(aneous)** As, Case, Chronon, Example, Flash, Jiffy, Moment, Present, Say, Shake, Snappy, Spur, Tick, Trice, Twinkling, Urgent, Yocto-second

**Instead (of)** Deputy, For, Lieu, Locum, Vice

**Instigate, Instigating, Instigator** Arouse, Foment, Impel, Incite, Proactive, Prompt, Ringleader, Spur

**Instil(l)** Implant, Inculcate, Infuse, Inspire, Teach, Transfuse

**Instinct(ive)** Automatic, Conation, Flair, Gut, Herd, Id, Impulse, Inbred, Ingenerate, Innate, Intuition, Knee-jerk, Life, Nature, Nose, Pleasure principle, Prim(a)eval, Reflex, Second nature, Sense, Talent, Tendency, Visceral

**Institute, Institution** Academy, Activate, Asylum, Bank, Begin, Bring, Broadmoor, Centre, Charity, College, Collegiate, Create, Erect, Found(ation), Halls of ivy, Hospital, I,

Impose, Inaugurate, Mechanical, Mechanics, MORI, Organise, Orphanage, Poorhouse, Protectory, Raise, Redbrick, Retraict, Retrait(e), Retreat, Royal, Smithsonian, Start, Technical, University, Varsity, WI, Women's, Workhouse

**Instruct(ed), Instruction, Instructor** ADI, Advice, Algorithm, Apprenticeship, Brief, CAI, Catechism, Chautauquan, Clinic, Coach, Course, Didactic, Direct(ive), Document, Drill, Edify, Educate, Enjoin, Ground(ing), Guide, How-to, Inform, Lesson, Loop, Macro, Maharishi, Mandate, Manual, Master class, Mentor, MIPS, Mystagogue, Mystagogus, Notify, Order, Patch, Pedagogue, Precept, Prescription, Program, RE, Recipe, RI, Rubric, Script, Sensei, Statement, Stet, Swami, → **TEACH**, Train, Tutelage, Tutorial, Up

**Instrument(al)** Ablative, Act, Agent, Dash(board), Helpful, Kit, Mean(s), Measure, Mechanical, → **MUSICAL INSTRUMENT**, Negotiable, → **RESPONSIBLE**, → **TOOL**, Transit, Transposing, → **UTENSIL**, Weapon

---

## INSTRUMENTS

**3 letters:**
Fan
Gad

**4 letters:**
Celt
Clam
Dupe
Fork
Mike
Prog
Rasp
Rote
Tram

**5 letters:**
Brake
Chuck
Curet
Fleam
Float
Gadge
Groma
Lance
Meter
Miser
Organ
Probe
Sonde
Tongs
Wecht

**6 letters:**
Bougie
Broach
Etalon
Grater
Megger®
Octant

Opener
Pallet
Peeler
Pestle

Reamer
Ripple
Scythe
Sector
Seeker
Speedo
Spline
Strobe
Trocar
Wimble
Xyster

**7 letters:**
Alidade
Cadrans
Caliper
Caltrop
Cautery
Compass
Curette
Dilator
Diopter
Flesher
Forceps
Grapple
Monitor
Organic
Pelican
Plogger
Plotter
Pointel
Pricker
Probang
Scalpel
Scanner

Scriber
Scummer
Sextant
Shuttle
Snuffer
Sounder
Spatula
Stapler
Strigil
Swatter
Swazzle
Swingle
Swozzle
Syringe
Trammel
Trimmer
Vocoder
Walkman

**8 letters:**
Barnacle
Boothook
Burdizzo
Calutron
Diagraph
Dividers
Ecraseur
Enlarger
Geophone
Iriscope
Luxmeter
Myograph
Nailfile
Odometer
Ohmmeter
Otoscope
Oximeter
Picklock
Quadrant

Repeater
Rheostat
Scalprum
Scissors
Snuffler
Speculum
Stiletto
Strickle
Trephine
Tweezers
Viameter
Vuvuzela
Waywiser

**9 letters:**
Algometer
Alphonsin
Arcograph
Areometer
Astrolabe
Atmometer
Auriscope
Auxometer
Barometer
Baryscope
Bolometer
Cauterant
Coelostat
Crows-bill
Cryoprobe
Cryoscope
Cymograph
Depressor
Dermatome
Dip-circle
Dosemeter
Dosimeter
Dropsonde
Eidograph

Endoscope
Ergograph
Ergometer
Eriometer
Extractor
Fadometer
Fetoscope
Flowmeter
Fluxmeter
Focimeter
Graduator
Haemostat
Heliostat
Hodometer
Hourglass
Konimeter
Kymograph
Lysimeter
Machmeter
Manometer
Marigraph
Megaphone
Megascope
Metronome
Microlith
Microtome
Milometer
Monochord
Nocturnal
Nut-wrench
Oedometer
Oncometer
Ondograph
Optometer
Optophone
Osmometer
Osteotome
Pedometer
Periscope
Pintadera
Polygraph
Potometer
Pyrometer
Pyroscope
Rain gauge
Raspatory
Refractor
Repositor
Retractor
Rheometer
Salometer
Scalprium
Set square
Skiascope

Somascope
Sonograph
Tasimeter
Telemeter
Telescope
Tellurian
Tellurion
Tenaculum
Tonometer
Toothpick
Tripmeter
Try square
Voltmeter
Volumeter
Wattmeter
Wavemeter
Xylometer
Zymometer

**10 letters:**
Acidimeter
Almacantar
Almucantar
Altazimuth
Anemograph
Anemometer
Araeometer
Buttonhook
Ceilometer
Clinometer
Colposcope
Comparator
Cross-staff
Cryophorus
Cultivator
Cyanometer
Cyclograph
Cystoscope
Declinator
Densimeter
Dictograph
Drosometer
Eudiometer
Fathometer
Fibrescope
Gaussmeter
Geodimeter®
Goniometer
Gonioscope
Gradienter
Gravimeter
Heliograph
Heliometer
Hydrometer

Hydroscope
Hygrograph
Hygrometer
Hygroscope
Hypsometer
Iconometer
Integrator
Lactometer
Lactoscope
Light organ
Lithoclast
Micrograph
Micrometer
Microphone
Microscope
Mileometer
Milliprobe
Multimeter
Nephograph
Nephoscope
Nitrometer
Opisometer
Orthoscope
Oscillator
Osteoclast
Pachymeter
Pantograph
Photometer
Piezometer
Pilliwinks
Plane table
Planigraph
Planimeter
Protractor
Pulsimeter
Pulsometer
Pycnometer
Radiometer
Radiophone
Radioscope
Radiosonde
Rhinoscope
Scotometer
Siderostat
Spirograph®
Spirometer
Tachograph
Tachometer
Telewriter
Tensimeter
Theodolite
Thermopile
Thermostat
Tintometer

Transputer
Tromometer
Tuning fork
Urinometer
Variometer
Viscometer
Voltameter

**11 letters:**
Actinometer
Auxanometer
Cardiograph
Chronograph
Chronometer
Chronoscope
Coercimeter
Colonoscope
Colorimeter
Coronagraph
Craniometer
Crescograph
Dendrometer
Dilatometer
Fluorometer
Fluoroscope
Fugitometer
Gastroscope
Gradiometer
Helicograph
Intoximeter
Jacob's staff
Keratometer
Laparoscope
Nephroscope
Odontograph
Opeidoscope
Pinnywinkle
Pitchometer
Planetarium
Plastometer
Plessimeter
Polarimeter
Polariscope
Proctoscope
Psychograph
Pyranometer
Pyrgeometer
Quantometer
Ragman Rolls
Rangefinder
Retinoscope
Rocketsonde
Salinometer
Sclerometer

Screwdriver
Seismograph
Seismometer
Seismoscope
Solarimeter
Spherometer
Stactometer
Stadiometer
Stauroscope
Stereometer
Stereoscope
Stethoscope
Stroboscope
Synthesizer
Tacheometer
Tensiometer
Thermograph
Thermometer
Thermoscope
Torsiograph
Trochometer
Vaporimeter
Vectorscope
Velocimeter
Voltammeter
Volumometer

**12 letters:**
Aethrioscope
Astrocompass
Averruncator
Bronchoscope
Camera lucide
Cathetometer
Cephalometer

Declinometer
Densitometer
Electrometer
Electroscope
Ellipsograph
Extensimeter
Extensometer
Galactometer
Galvanometer
Galvanoscope
Harmonograph
Harmonometer
Inclinometer
Isoteniscope
Kaleidoscope
Katharometer
Keraunograph
Laryngoscope
Magnetograph
Meteorograph
Methanometer
Monkey wrench
Myringoscope
Nephelometer
Oscilloscope
Penetrometer
Pinniewinkle
Psychrometer
Resectoscope
Respirometer
Scarificator
Scintillator
Sensitometer
Snooperscope
Spectrometer

Spectroscope
Sphygmograph
Sphygmometer
Sphygmophone
Sphygmoscope
Synchroscope
Tellurometer
Thoracoscope
Turbidimeter
Urethroscope
Zenith-sector

**13 letters:**
Accelerometer
Alcoholometer
Backscratcher
Diaphanometer
Dipleidoscope
Electrophorus
Inclinatorium
Opthalmometer
Perpendicular
Pharyngoscope
Phonendoscope
Pneumatograph
Pneumatometer
Potentiometer
Pyrheliometer
Reflectometer
Refractometer
Saccharometer
Scatterometer
Sigmoidoscope
Stalagmometer
Tachistoscope

Weatherometer

**14 letters:**
Circumferentor
Diffractometer
Dividing engine
Glove-stretcher
Interferometer
Kinetheodolite
Oesophagoscope
Ophthalmometer
Ophthalmoscope
Phosphoroscope
Pyrophotometer
Scintillascope
Scintilloscope
Spinthariscope
Synchronoscope

**15 letters:**
Electromyograph
Phenakestoscope
Radiogoniometer
Telestereoscope

**16 letters:**
Photopolarimeter
Sphygmomanometer
Telespectroscope

**17 letters:**
Spectrophotometer
Transit theodolite

**Insubordinate** Contumacious, Faction, Mutinous, Rebel, Refractory
**Insubstantial** Airy, Brief, Flimsy, Frail, Frothy, Illusory, Jackstraw, Light, Scotch mist, Slender, Slight, Spectre, Syllabub, Thin, Wispy, Ye(a)sty
**Insufferable** Egregious
**Insufficient** Exiguous, Inadequate, Poor, Scant, Shortfall, Too few
**Insular** Isolated, Little Englander, Moated, Narrow, Sectarian, Xenophobe
**Insulate, Insulation, Insulator** Biotite, Bushing, Corkboard, Dielectric, Electret, Enwind, Fibrefill, Grommet, Haybox, Inwind, Lagging, Mica, Muscovite, Non-conductor, Padding, Pugging, Sleeving, Standoff, Tog
**Insulin** Hormone
**Insult(ing)** Abuse, Affront, Aspersion, Barb, Becall, Charientism, Contumely, Cut, Derogatory, Diatribe, Dyslogistic, Effrontery, Embarrass, Facer, Fig, Gibe, Injurious, Lese-majesty, Mud, Mud-pie, Offend, Opprobrious, Rip on, Ronyion, Runnion, Scurrilous, Skit, Slagging, Sledge, Slight, Slur, Snub, Trample, Trauma, Uncomplimentary, Verbal, Wazzock, Yenta, Yente
**Insure(r), Insurance** Abandonee, Accident, Actuarial, Comprehensive, Cover, Coverage, Death futures, Endowment, Fidelity, Fire, Group, Guarantee, Hedge, Indemnity, Knock-for-knock, Life, Lloyds, Marine, Medibank, Medicaid, Medicare,

Mutual, Name, National, Participating, Pluvius, Policy, Public liability, Reversion, Safety net, Security, Social, Term, Third party, Tontine, Travel, Underwrite, Whole-life

**Insurgent, Insurrect(ion)** Cade, Jacquerie, Mutiny, Outbreak, Pandy, Rebel, Revolt, Riot, Rising, Sedition, Terrorist, Uprising, Whisky

▷ **Insurgent** *may indicate* 'reversed'

**Intact** Complete, Entire, Inviolate, Unused, Whole

**Intaglio, Intagliate** Diaglyph, Incavo

**Intake** Absorption, Entry, Fuel

**Intangible** Unreal

**Integer, Integral** Component, Definite, Entire, Improper, Inbuilt, Indefinite, Needful, Number, Organic, Unital, Unitary

**Integrate(d), Integration** Amalgamate, Assimilate, Combine, Coordinate, Fuse, Harmonious, Holistic, Large-scale, Mainstream, Merge, Postural, Synergism, Tightknit, Vertical

**Integrity** Honesty, Honour, Principle, Probity, Rectitude, Strength, Uprightness, Whole, Worth

**Integument** Coat, Primine, Secundine, Sheath, Skin, Velum

**Intellect, Intellectual(s)** Academic, Aptitude, Belligerati, Brain (box), Cerebral, Chattering class, Cultural, Dianoetic, Egghead, Eggmass, Erudite, Far-out, Genius, Grey matter, Highbrow, Intelligent, Intelligentsia, -ist, Learned, Literati, Luminary, Mastermind, Mental(ity), Mind, Noesis, Noetic, Noology, Nous, Pointy-headed, Profound, Reason, Sublime, Titan

**Intelligence, Intelligent** Advice, Artificial, Boss, Brainiac, Brain-power, Brains, Bright, Cerebral, CIA, Discerning, Dope, Eggmass, Emotional, Esprit, G, Gifted, Grey matter, GRU, Guile, Humint, Info, Ingenious, IQ, Knowledgeable, Machiavellian, Machine, MI, Mossad, Mother wit, News, Pate, Perspicacity, Pointy-headed, Rational, Sconce, Sense, Sharp(-witted), Shrewd, Smart, Spetsnaz, Spetznaz, Tidings, Wit

**Intelligible** Exoteric, Ungarbled

**Intemperance** Acrasia, Crapulent, Excess, Gluttony, Immoderation

**Intend(ed), Intending** Allot, Betrothed, Contemplate, Deliberate, Design, Destine, Ettle, Fiancé(e), Going, → **MEAN**, Meditate, Planned, Propose, Purpose, Think

**Intense, Intensify, Intensity, Intensive** Acute, Aggravate, Ardent, Compound, Crash, Crescendo, Deep, Depth, Earnest, Earthquake, Edgy, Emotional, Enhance, Escalate, Estro, Excess, Extreme, Fervent, Fully, Hot up, Keen, Luminous, Might, Profound, Radiant, Redouble, Saturation, Sharpen, Strong, Towering, Vehement, Vivid, Warmth

**Intent, Intention(al)** À dessein, Aim, Animus, Deliberate, Design, Dole, Earmark, Earnest, Ettle, Hellbent, Manifesto, Mens rea, Mind, Paradoxical, Prepense, Purpose, Rapt, Resolute, Set, Special, Studious, Systematic, Thought, Tire, Wilful, Witting, Yrapt

**Inter** Amid, Bury, Earth, Entomb

**Interaction** Chemistry, Enantiodromia, Solvation, Symbiosis, Synergy

**Interbreed(ing)** Cross, Miscegenation

**Intercalation** Embolism

**Intercede, Intercession** Mediate, Negotiate, Plead, Prayer

**Intercept** Absciss(a), Abscisse, Check, Hack, Meet, Tackle, Waylay

**Interchange(d)** Altercation, Alternate, Clover-leaf, Crossing, Equivalent, Junction, Mutual, Permute, Reciprocate, Substitute, Transpose

**Intercom** Entryphone®

**Intercourse** Arse, Ball, Bang, Bed, Blow job, Boff, Bone, Bonk, Buggery, Bukkake, Bump, Coition, Coitus, Commerce, Commixture, Congress, Connection, Consummation, Converse, Copulation, Cottaging, Coupling, Cover, Cunnilingus, Deflowering, Diddling, Enjoy, Fluff, Fornication, Gam, Gamahuche, Gamaruche, Gangbang, Green gown, Greens, Hochmagandy, Houghmagandie, How's your father, Hump, Incest, Jass, Jazz, Jiggy, Jiggy-jiggy, Jig(-a)-jig, Jump, Knee-trembler, Knock, Know(ledge), Koap, Laying,

Leg-over, Lie with, Make, Marriage bed, Mell, Mix, Nail, Naughty, Necrophilia, Nookie, Nooky, Nooner, Oats, One-night-stand, On the job, Plough, Poke, Poontang, Pussy, Quickie, Ride, Rim, Roger, Roll, Root, Rump, Rumpy(-pumpy), Satyriasis, Score, Screw, Sexual, Shaft, Shag, Shtup, Sixty-nine, Sociality, Sodomy, Soixante-neuf, Stuff, Swive, Tail, Teledildonics, The other, Tie, Trade, Tribadism, Trock, Troilism, Truck, Tumble, Venereal, Whoredom

**Interdict** Ban, Forbid, Prohibit, Taboo, Veto

**Interest(ed), Interesting** Amusive, APR, Attention, Behalf, Benefit, Care, Clou, Compound, Concern, Contango, Controlling, Coupon, Dividend, Double-bubble, Ear-grabbing, Engage, Engross, Enthusiasm, Fad, Fascinate, Fee-simple, Fee-tail, Grab, Hot, Human, Import, Income, Insurable, Int(o), Intrigue, Juicy, Landed, Life, Line, Meaty, Negative, Newsworthy, Nibble, Part, Partisan, Percentage, Public, Readable, Rente, Respect, Return, Revenue, Reversion, Riba, Riding, Scene, Sepid, Share, Side, Sideline, Simple, Spice, Stake, Tasty, Tickle, Titillate, Topical, Usage, Usance, Use, Usure, Usury, Vested, Vig(orish), Warm

**Interface** Centronics, Modium, Spigot

**Interfere(r), Interference** Atmospherics, Busybody, Clutter, Crackle, Disrupt, Disturb, Hamper, Hinder, Hiss, Intrude, Mar, →**MEDDLE**, Molest, Noise, Nose, Officious, Pry, Radio, Shash, Shot noise, Static, Tamper, Teratogen

**Interferometer** Etalon

**Intergrowth** Perthite

**Interim** Break, Meantime, Meanwhile, Temporary

**Interior** Backblocks, Cyclorama, Domestic, Innards, Innate, Inner, Inside, Outback, Plain, Up-country, Vitals

**Interject(ion)** Ahem, Begorra(h), Chime-in, Doh, Duh, Gertcha, Haith, Hoo-oo, Interpolate, Lackaday, Lumme, Nation, Sese(y), Sessa, 'Sheart, 'Slid, Tarnation, Tush

**Interlace** Mingle, Pleach, Weave, Wreathe

**Interlink** Entangle

**Interlock** Dovetail, Engage, Knit, Mesh, Tangle

**Interlocutor** Elihu, MC, Questioner

**Interloper** Cowan, Gate-crasher, Intruder, Trespasser

**Interlude** Antimask, Antimasque, Divertimento, Entr'acte, Interruption, Kyogen, Lunch-hour, Meantime, Pause, Verset

**Intermediary, Intermediate, Intermediatory** Agent, Bardo, Between, Bytownite, Cat's paw, Comprador(e), Contact man, Go-between, Hypabyssal, In-between, Instar, Mean, Medial, Mesne, Mezzanine, Middleman, Middle-of-the-road, Negotiant, Thirdsman, Transitional

**Interminable** Endless, Infinite, Unending

**Intermission** Apyrexia, Break, Interval, Pause, Recess

**Intermittent** Broken, Episodic, Fitful, Off-on, Periodic, Random, Spasmic, Spasmodic, Sporadic

**Intermix, Intermingle** Lace, Melting pot

**Intern(e)** Confine, Doctor, Impound, Restrict, Trainee

**Internal** Domestic, Inner, Internecine, Inward, Within

**International** Cap, Cosmopolitan, Fourth, Lion, Second, Test, Trotskyist, UN, Universal

**Internet** Blogosphere, Dotco(m), e, Infobahn, URL, Web, Wi-fi, WWW

**Interplay** Counterpoint

**Interpolate(r), Interpolation** Diaskeuast, Insert, Intercalate, Interrupt, Spatchcock, Tmesis

**Interpose** Butt in, Horn in, Interject, Interlay, Interprone, Intervene, Spatchcock, Stickle

**Interpret(er)** Aread, Ar(r)e(e)de, Conster, Construe, Decipher, Decode, Dobhash, Dragoman, Exegete, Explain, Exponent, Expositor, Expound, Glossator, Hermeneutist, Hierophant, Jehovist, Latiner, Lingster, Linguistic, Linkster, Lipreader, Medium, Moonshee, Moonshi, Moralise, Munshi, Oneirocritic, Oneiroscopist, Origenist, Polyglot,

Prophet, Rabbi, Rationalise, Read, Rede, Reed(e), Render, Represent, Spokesman, Subjectivity, Textualist, →**TRANSLATE**, Truchman, Ulema

**Interpretation** Anagoge, Anagogy, Analysis, Cabbala(h), Construction, Copenhagen, Diagnosis, Dittology, Eisegesis, Euhemerism, Exegesis, Exegete, Gematria, Gloss(ary), Gospel, Halacha(h), Halakah, Hermeneutics, Kabbala(h), Midrash, Oneirocriticism, Portray, Reading, Rede, Rendition, Spin, Targum, Translation, Tropology, Zohar

**Interrogate, Interrogation, Interrogator** Catechism, Corkscrew, Cross-question, Debrief(ing), Enquire, Examine, Grill, Inquisitor, Maieutic, Pump, →**QUESTION**, Quiz, Quiz-master

**Interrupt(ion), Interrupter** Ahem, Aposiopesis, Blip, Break, Butt, Chequer, Chip in, Cut in, Disturb, Entr'acte, Heckle, Hiatus, Intercept, Interfere, Interject, Interlard, Interpellate, Interpolate, Interpose, Interregnum, Intrusion, Overtalk, Pause, Portage, Punctuate, Rheotome, Stop, Suspend, Time-out, Tmesis, Waylay

**Intersect(ion), Intersecting** Carfax, Carfox, Carrefour, Chiasm(a), Clover-leaf, Compital, Cross, Crunode, Cut, Decussate, Divide, Groin, Metacentre, Node, Orthocentre, Quadrivium, Trace, Vertex

**Intersperse** Dot, Interlard, Interpose, Scatter, Sprinkle

**Interstice** Areole, Interlude, Pore, Space

**Intertwine** Braid, Impleach, Knit, Lace, Plait, Splice, Twist, Wreathe, Writhe

**Interval** Between, Break, Breather, Class, Closed, Comma, Confidence, Contour, Diapente, Diastaltic, Diatesseron, Diesis, Distance, Ditone, Duodecimo, Entr'acte, Episodic, Fifth, Gap, Half-step, Half-time, Harmonic, Hiatus, Hourly, Imperfect, Interim, Interlude, Interregnum, Interruption, Interspace, Interstice, Leap, Limma, Lucid, Lull, Lunitidal, Meantime, Meantone, Meanwhile, Melodic, Microtone, Minor third, Ninth, Octave, Open, Ottava, Parenthesis, Perfect, Pycnon, QT, Regular, Respite, Rest, Schisma, Semitone, Seventh, Sixth, Space, Span, Spell, Third, Thirteenth, Time lag, Tritone, Twelfth, Unison, Wait

**Intervene, Intervening, Intervention** Agency, Arbitrate, Expromission, Hypothetical, Interfere, Interjacent, Interrupt, Intromit, Mediate, Mesne, Reprieve, Step in, Theurgy, Up

**Interview** Audience, Audition, Beeper, Conference, Debriefing, Doorstep, Examine, Hearing, Oral, Press conference, See, Vox pop

**Interweave, Interwoven, Interwove** Complect, Entwine, Interlace, Monogram, Pirnit, Plait, Plash, Pleach, Raddle, Splice, Wreathed

**Intestate** Heirless, Unwilling

**Intestinal, Intestine(s)** Bowel, Chit(ter)lings, Derma, Duodenum, Enteric, Entrails, Gastric, Guts, Harigals, Innards, Jejunum, Kishke, Large, Mesenteron, Omenta, Rectum, Small, Splanchnic, Thairm, Tripes, Viscera

**In the club** Gravid, Pregnant, Up the spout

**In this year** HA

**Intimacy, Intimate(ly)** Achates, À deux, Arm-in-arm, Boon, Bosom, Close, Communion, Confidante, Connote, Familiar, Far ben, Friend, Heart-to-heart, Hint, Imply, Inmost, Innuendo, Intrigue, Nearness, Opine, Pack, Private, Signal, Special, Thick, Throng, Warm, Well

**Intimation** Clue, Hint, Implication, Inkling, Innuendo, Notice, Si quis

**Intimidate, Intimidating** Awe, Browbeat, Bulldoze, Bully, Cow, Daunt, Dragon, Harass, Hector, Menace, Niramiai, Overawe, Psych, Scare, Threaten, Tyrannise, Unnerve

**Into** At, Intil, Within

**Intolerant, Intolerable** Allergic, Bigotry, Egregious, Excessive, Illiberal, Impatient, Impossible, Insupportable, Ombrophobe, Redneck, Self-righteous

**Intone, Intonation** Cadence, Chant, Just, Twang

**In touch** Au fait

**Intoxicate(d), Intoxicant, Intoxicating, Intoxication** Alcoholic, Areca-nut, Benj, Bhang, Blasted, Coca, Corn, Crink, Cup, Disguise, Ethanol, Fuddle, Ganja, Half-cut,

Heady, → **HIGH**, Hocus, Hou high, Incite, Inebriate, Ivresse, Jag, Krunk, La-la land, Merry, Mescal, Methystic, Narcotise, Nitrogen narcosis, Peyote, Pixil(l)ated, Potent, Rapture of the deep, Rumbullion, Shroom, Slewed, Soma, Sozzle, Spirituous, Swacked, Temulent, The narks, Trolleyed, Whiskeyfied, Whiskified, Zonked

**Intractable** Disobedient, Kittle, Mulish, Obdurate, Perverse, Surly, Unruly, Wilful

**Intransigent** Adamant, Inflexible, Rigid, Uncompromising

**Intransitive** Neuter, Objectless

**Intravenous** IV

**Intrepid(ity)** Aweless, Bold, Bottle, Brave, Dauntless, Doughty, Fearless, Firm, Gallant, Plucky, → **RESOLUTE**, Stout, Unafraid, Undaunted, Valiant

**Intricate** Complex, Crinkum-crankum, Daedal(ian), Daedale, Dedal, Gordian, Intrince, Involute, Knotty, Parquetry, Pernickety, Sinuous, Tirlie-wirlie, Tricky, Vitruvian

**Intrigue(r), Intriguing** Affaire, Artifice, Brigue, Cabal, Camarilla, Cloak and dagger, Collogue, Conspiracy, Fascinate, Hotbed, Ignatian, Interest, Jesuit, Jobbery, Liaison, Machinate, Plot, Politic, Rat, → **SCHEME**, Stairwork, Strategy, Traffic, Trinketer, Web

**Intrinsic(ally)** Basically, Essential, Genuine, Inherent, Innate, Inner, Per se

▷ **Intrinsically** *may indicate* something within a word

**Introduce(r), Introduction, Introductory** Acquaint, Alap, Anacrusis, Cataphoresis, Code name, Curtain-raiser, Debut, Emcee, Enseam, Entrée, Exordial, Foreword, Immit, Import, Induct, Initiate, Inject, Insert, Instil(l), Institutes, Intercalate, Interpolate, Intrada, Introit, Isagogic, Lead-in, Lead up, Opening, Overture, Phase in, Plant, Preamble, Precede, Preface, Preliminary, Prelude, Prelusory, Preparatory, Present, Presentment, Primer, Proem, Prolegomena, Prolegomenon, Prolog, Prologue, Prooemium, Proponent, Raise, Referral, Standfirst, Start, Usher

▷ **Introduction** *may indicate* a first letter

**Intromission** Vicious

**Introspective, Introspection** Indrawn, Musing, Navel-gazing, Reflex, Ruminant, Thoughtful

▷ **In trouble** *may indicate* an anagram

**Introvert(ed)** Cerebrotonic, Ingrow, In-toed, Invaginate, Reserved, Shy, Withdrawn

**Intrude(r), Intrusion, Intrusive** Abate, Aggress, Annoy, Bother, Burglar, Derby dog, Disturb, → **ENCROACH**, Gatecrash, Hacker, Impinge, Inroad, Interloper, Invade, Lopolith, Meddle, Nosey, Personal, Porlocking, Presume, Raid, Sorn, Trespass

**In truth** En verite

**Intuition, Intuitive** Apercu, Belief, ESP, Hunch, Insight, Instinct, Inwit, Noumenon, Premonition, Presentiment, Seat-of-the-pants, Sixth sense, Telepathy, Theosophy, Visceral

**Inturn(ing)** Trichiasis

▷ **In two words** *may indicate* a word to be split

**Inuit** Caribou, Eskimo, Inuk, Inupiat, Yupik

**Inundate(d), Inundation** Awash, Engulf, Flood, Overflow, Overwhelm, Submerge, Swamp

**Inure** Acclimatise, Accustom, Harden, Season, Steel

**Invade(r), Invasion** Aggressor, Angle, Attack, Attila, Cortes, Dane, Descent, Encroach, Goth, Hacker, Hengist, Horsa, Hun, Incursion, Infest, Inroad, Intruder, Irrupt, Jute, Lombard, Martian, Norman, Norsemen, Occupation, Ostrogoth, Overlord, Overrun, Permeate, Pict, Raid, Trespass, Vandal, Viking, Visigoth

**In vain** No go

**Invalid(ate), Invalidation** Annul(led), Bad, Bogus, Bunbury, Cancel, Chronic, Clinic, Defunct, Diriment, Erroneous, Expired, False, Inauthentic, Inform, Inoperative, Irritate, Lapsed, Negate, Nugatory, Null, Nullify, Overturn, Quash, Refute, Shut-in, Terminate, Valetudinarian, Vitiate, Void

**Invaluable** Essential, Excellent, Precious, Useful

**Invariable, Invariably** Always, Consistent, Constant, Eternal, Habitual, Perpetual, Steady, Uniform

**Invective** Abuse, Billingsgate, Diatribe, Philippic, Reproach, Ribaldry, Tirade
**Inveigh** Declaim, Denounce, Marprelate, Protest, Rail
**Inveigle** Charm, Coax, Entice, Persuade, Subtrude
**Invent(ion), Inventive** Adroit, Babe, Baby, Brainchild, Chimera, Coin, Concept, Contrive, Cook up, →CREATE, Creed, Daedal, Design, Device, Dream up, Embroider, Excogitate, Fabricate, Fain, Fantasia, Feign, Fiction, Figment, Imaginary, Improvise, Independent, Ingenuity, Make up, Mint, Myth, Originate, Patent, Plateau, Pretence, Resourceful, Synectics, Trump up, Whittle, Wit
**Inventor** Artificer, Author, Coiner, Creator, Designer, Engineer, Idea-hamster, Mint-master, Patentee

## INVENTORS

| 3 letters: | 6 letters: | Daimler | 9 letters: |
|---|---|---|---|
| Kay | | Eastman | Arkwright |
| Sax | | Galileo | Cockerell |
| | | Hartley | Macintosh |
| 4 letters: | | Marconi | |
| Bell | Bramah | Pullman | 10 letters: |
| Biro | Dunlop | Schmidt | Archimedes |
| Boys | Duryea | Siemens | Cartwright |
| Brix | Edison | Unaipon | Hargreaves |
| Hero | Geiger | Whitney | Lilienthal |
| Moon | Hansom | Whittle | Torricelli |
| Otis | McAdam | | Trevithick |
| Tull | Nernst | 8 letters: | Wheatstone |
| Watt | Pearse | Crompton | |
| | Savery | Daedalus | 11 letters: |
| 5 letters: | Singer | Goodyear | Montgolfier |
| Baird | Solvay | Martenot | |
| Clegg | Sutton | Mercator | 12 letters: |
| Dyson | Wright | Newcomen | Frankenstein |
| Jubal | | Sinclair | Prince Rupert |
| Maxim | 7 letters: | Zworykin | |
| Mills | Babbage | | |
| Minié | Celsius | | |

Also in the 3-letters column: Morse, Nobel, Tesla.

**Inventory** Account, Index, Itemise, List, Perpetual, Personality, Record, Register, Scroll, Steelbow, Stock, Terrier
**Inverse, Inversion, Invert(ed)** Anastrophe, Antimetabole, Antimetathesis, Arch, Back to front, Capsize, Chiasmus, Entropion, Entropium, First, Homosexuality, Lid, Opposite, Overset, Reciprocal, Resupinate, Retrograde, Reverse, Second, Tête-bêche, Turn, Upset, Upside down
**Invertebrate** Acanthocephalan, Annelida, Anthozoan, Arrowworm, Arthropod, Brachiopod, Chaetognath, Cnidarian, Coelenterate, Crinoid, Ctenophore, Decapod, Echinoderm, Echinoid, Entoprocta, Euripterid, Feather star, Gast(e)ropod, Globigerina, Holothurian, Hydrozoan, Lobopod, Mollusc, Nacre, Onychophoran, Parazoan, Pauropod, Peritrich, Platyhelminth, Polyp, Poriferan, Protostome, Rotifer, Roundworm, Scyphozoan, Sea-cucumber, Sea-lily, →SHELLFISH, Slug, Spineless, Sponge, Spoonworm, Starfish, Tardigrade, Trepang, Trochelminth, Trochophore, Unio, Water bear, Worm, Zoophyte
**Invest(or), Investment** Agamemnon, Ambient, Angel, Assiege, Bate, Beleaguer, Beset, Besiege, Bet, Blockade, Blue-chip, Bond, Bottom-fisher, Capitalist, Clothe, Collins Street farmer, Contrarian, Debenture, Dignify, Dub, Embark, Empanoply, Enclothe, Endow,

Endue, Enrobe, Ethical, Financier, Flutter, Gilt, Girt, Gross, Holding, Infeft, Install, Inward, On, Pannicle, Panniculus, Parlay, Place, Portfolio, Put, Retiracy, Ring, Robe, Saver, Share, Siege, Sink, Smart money, Spec, Speculation, Stag, Stake, Stock, Surround, Tessa, Tie up, Trochophore, Trojan War, Trust, Trustee, Venture (capital), With profits, Zaitech

▷ **Invest** *may indicate* one word surrounding another

**Investigate, Investigation, Investigative, Investigator** Analyse, Audit, Canvass, Case, Chart, CID, Delve, DI, Enquire, Examine, Explore, Fact-find, Fed, Ferret, Fieldwork, Going over, Go into, Gumshoe, Heuristic, Hunt, Inquest, Inquirendo, Inquiry, Inquisition, Kinsey, McCarthyism, Nose, Organon, Organum, Probe, Prodnose, Pry, Quester, Rapporteur, Recce, Research, Scan, Scout, Screen, Scrutinise, Search, Sleuth, Snoop, Study, Suss, Tec, Test, T-man, Track, Try, Zetetic

**Investiture** Award, Inauguration

**Inveterate** Chronic, Double-dyed, Dyed-in-the-wool, Engrained, Habitual, Hardened

**Invidious** Harmful, Hostile, Malign

**Invigilator** Proctor

**Invigorate, Invigorating, Invigoration** Analeptic, Animate, Brace, Brisk, Cheer, Crispy, Elixir, Energise, Enliven, Exhilarate, Fortify, Insinew, Inspirit, Pep, Refresh, Renew, Stimulate, Tonic, Vital

**Invincible** Almighty, Brave, Stalwart, Valiant

**Inviolatable, Inviolate, Inviolable** Intemerate, Sacred (cow), Sacrosanct

**Invisible** Blind, Hidden, Imageless, Infra-red, Secret, Tusche, Unseen

**Invite, Invitation, Inviting** Ask, Attract, Bid, Call, Card, Overture, → REQUEST, Solicit, Stiffie, Summons, Tempt, Toothsome, Woo

**Invocation, Invoke** Appeal, Begorra, Call, Conjure, Curse, Entreat, Epiclesis, Imprecate, Solicit, White rabbits

**Invoice** Account, Bill, Docket, Itemise, Manifest, Pro forma

**Involuntary** Automatic, Instinctive, Unwitting

**Involve(d), Involvement** Active, Close knit, Commitment, Complicate, Complicit, Concern, Deep, Embroil, Engage, Enlace, Entail, Entangle, Envelop, Imbroglio, Immerse, → IMPLICATE, Include, Intervene, Into, Intricate, Knee-deep, Meet, Necessitate, Participate, Tangle, Tortuous, Tricksy

▷ **Involved** *may indicate* an anagram

**Inward(s)** Afferent, Centripuntal, Homefelt, Introrse, Mental, Private, Varus, Within

**Iodine** I, Kelp, Thyroxin(e)

**Iolanthe** Peri

**Ion** Ammonium, Anion, Carbanion, Carborium, Hydrogen, Hydronium, Hydroxyl, Isomer, Onium, Zwitterion

**Ionian** Iastic, Te(i)an

**Ionic** Electrovalent

**Iota** Atom, Jot, Subscript, Whit

**IOU** Cedula, Market, PN, Shinplaster, Vowels

**IOW** Vectis

**IQ** Mensa

**IRA** Provisional, Provo

**Iran(ian)** Babist, Kurd, Mede, Osset, Pahlavi, Parsee, Pehlevi, Persic, Tadzhik, Ta(d)jik

**Irascible** Choleric, Crusty, Fiery, Grouchy, Peevish, Quick-tempered, Short-tempered, Snappy, Tetchy, Toustie

**Irate** Angry, Cross, Infuriated, Wrathful

**Ire** Anger, Bait, Cholera, Fury, Rage, Wrath

**Ireland** Blarney-land, Composer, Deirdre, Gaeltacht, Hibernia, .ie, Innisfail, Irena, IRL, Iverna, Ould Sod, ROI, Twenty-six counties

**Irenic** Peaceful

**Iridescence, Iridescent** Chatoyant, Flambé, Opaline, Reflet, Shimmering, Shot, Water-gall

**Iridium** Ir

**Iris** Areola, Eye, Flag, Fleur-de-lis, Florence, Gladdon, Gladioli, Ixia, Lily, Lis, Orris, Rainbow, Roast-beef plant, Sedge, Seg, Stinking, Sunbow, Triandria, Uvea, Water flag

**Irish(man)** Bark, Bog-trotter, Boy, Bucko, Celt(ic), Clan-na-gael, Declan, Defender, Dermot, Dubliner, Eamon(n), Eirann, Eoin, Erse, Feargal, Fenian, Fionn, Gael, Gaeltacht, Goidel, Greek, Hibernian, Jackeen, Keltic, Kern(e), Mick(e)(y), Middle, Milesian, Mulligan, Neil, Ogamic, Orange(man), Ostmen, Paddy(-whack), Partholon, Pat(rick), Rapparee, Redshank, Reilly, Riley, Rory, Ryan, Sean, Shoneen, Teague, Temper, UDA, Ultonian, Whiteboy, Wildgeese

**Irk(some)** Annoy, Bother, Fardel, Irritate, Needle, Tedious

**Iron(s), Ironstone, Ironwork(s)** Airn, Alpha, Angle, Barking, Beta, Bloom, Branding, Carron, Cast, Cautery, Chains, Chalybeate, Chancellor, Channel, Climbing, Coquimbite, Corrugated, Cramp(on), Crimp, Cross, Curling, Curtain, Delta, Derringer, Dogger, Dogs, Driving, Eagle-stone, Even, Fayalite, Fe, Ferredoxin, Ferrite, Fetter, Fiddley, Flatten, Flip-dog, Galvanised, Gamma, Gem, Golfclub, Goose, Grappling, Grim, Grozing, →**GUN**, Gyve, Haematite, Horse, Ingot, Italian, Kamacite, Laterite, Lily, Lofty, Long, Maiden, Malleable, Marcasite, Mars, Martensite, Mashie, Mashy, Merchant, Meteoric, Mitis (metal), Pea, Pig, Pinking, →**PRESS**, Pro-metal, Rabble, Rations, Rod, Sad, Scrap, Shooting, Short, Smoother, Soft, Soldering, Spathic, Specular, Speeler, Spiegeleisen, Steam, Stirrup, Stretching, Strong, Taconite, Taggers, Terne, Tin terne, Toggle, Tow, Turfing, Wafer, Waffle, Wear, Wedge, White, Wrought

**Iron age** Latene, Villanovan

**Ironic, Irony** Antiphrasis, Asteism, Dramatic, Ferrous, Meiosis, Metal, Ridicule, Sarcasm, Satire, Socratic, Tongue-in-cheek, Tragic, Trope, Wry

**Ironside** Edmund

**Ironwood** Pyengadu

▸ **Ironwork(s)** *see* **IRON(S)**

**Irrational** Absurd, Brute, Delirious, Doolally, Foolish, Illogical, Number, Pi, Squirrelly, Superstitious, Surd, Wild, Zany

**Irreconcilable** Poles apart

**Irrefutable** Cast-iron, Evident, Positive, Undeniable

**Irregular(ity)** Abnormal, Alloiostrophus, Anomaly, Aperiodic, A salti, Asymmetric, Atypical, Bashi-bazouk, Blotchy, Carlylean, Casual, Crazy, Eccentric, Ectopic, Episodic, Erratic, Evection, Fitful, Flawed, Formless, Free-form, Glitch, Guerilla, Heteroclitic, Higgledy-piggledy, Incondite, Inordinate, Intermittent, Jitter, Kink, Occasional, Orthotone, Para-military, Partisan, Patchy, Rambling, Random, Rough, Scalene, Scraggy, Scrawl, Sebundy, Sharawadgi, Sharawaggi, Snatchy, Solecism, Spasmodic, Sporadic, Strange, TA, Turbulence, Uneven, Unorthodox, Unsteady, Unwonted, Variable, Wayward, Zigzag

▹ **Irregular** *may indicate* an anagram

**Irrelevant** Academic, Digression, Extraneous, Gratuitous, Immaterial, Inapplicable, Inconsequent, Inept, Non sequitur, Pointless, Ungermane, Unrelated

**Irreligious** Antinomian, Heathen, Impious, Pagan, Profane, Secular

**Irremedial** Hopeless, Incurable, Laches

**Irrepressible** Resilient

**Irreproachable** Blameless, Spotless, Stainless

**Irresistible** Almighty, Endearing, Inevitable, Mesmeric, Overwhelming

**Irresolute, Irresolution** Aboulia, Cliffhanger, Doubtful, Faltering, Hesitant, Timid, Unsure, Wavery, Weak-willed

**Irresponsible** Capricious, Feckless, Flighty, Fly-by-night, Free spirit, Gallio, Reckless, Skittish, Slap-happy, Strawen, Trigger-happy, Wanton, Wildcat

**Irretrievable** Black hole

**Irreverent, Irreverence** Blasphemous, Disrespectful, Godless, Impious, Profane, Sacrilege

**Irrigate, Irrigation** Canalise, Colonic, Douche, Drip, Enema, Flood, Get, Water
**Irritable, Irritability, Irritant, Irritate(d), Irritation** Abrasive, Acerbate, Anger,
Annoy, Antagonise, Bête noire, Bile, Blister, Bother, Bug, Chafe, Chauff, Chippy, Chocker,
Choleric, Crabbit, Crabby, Cross-grained, Crosspatch, Crotchety, Crusty, Dod, Dyspeptic,
Eat, Eczema, Edgy, Emboil, Enchafe, Erethism, Ewk, Exasperate, Eyestrain, Fantod,
Feverish, Fiery, Fleabite, Frabbit, Fractious, Fraught, Fretful, Gall, Get (to), Gnat, Goad,
Grate, Gravel, Hasty, Heck, Hoots, Humpy, Impatience, Intertrigo, Irk, Itch, Jangle, Jar,
Livery, Mardy, Molest, Narky, Needle, Nerk, Nettle, Niggly, Nudnik, Ornery, Peckish,
Peevish, Peppery, Pesky, Pestilent(ial), Pet, Petulance, Pinprick, Pique, Prickly, Provoke,
Rag'd, Ragde, Rankle, Rash, Rasp, Rattle, Ratty, Rile, Riley, Roil, Rub, Ruffle, Savin(e),
Scratchy, Shirty, Smart, Snappy, Snit, Snitchy, Sore, Splenetic, Sting, Tease, Techy,
Testy, Tetchy, Thorn, Tickle, Tiff, Tift, Tingle, Tiresome, Toey, Touchy, Uptight, →**VEX**,
Waspish, Waxy, Windburn, Wind-up, Yuke
▷ **Irritated** *may indicate* an anagram
**Irving** Actor, Berlin
**Is** Est, Exists, Ist
**Isaiah** Is
**Isinglass** Carlock, Fish-glue, Mica, Sturgeon
**Islam(ic)** Al Q(u)aeda, Crescent, Druse, Druz(e), Hamas, Kurd(ish), Muezzing, Pillars,
Salafism, Sanusi, Senus(si), Sheriat, Shia(h), Shiite, Sufism, Sunni(te), Taleban, Taliban,
Wah(h)abi
**Island, Isle(t)** Ait, Archipelago, Atoll, Cay, Char, Desert, Eyot, Floating, Heat, Holm, I,
Inch, Is, Key, Lagoon, Motu, Refuge, Traffic

---

## ISLANDS

| **2 letters:** | Cook | Muck | Bioko |
| --- | --- | --- | --- |
| TT | Cuba | Mull | Bohol |
| | Dogs | Niue | Bonin |
| **3 letters:** | Dunk | Oahu | Canna |
| Aru | Eigg | Rona | Capri |
| Cos | Elba | Ross | Ceram |
| Diu | Erin | Saba | Cheju |
| Fyn | Fair | Sark | Chios |
| Hoy | Fiji | Skye | Clare |
| Kos | Goat | Soay | Cocos |
| Man | Gozo | Spud | Coney |
| May | Guam | Thas | Coral |
| Rat | Herm | Truk | Corfu |
| Rum | Holy | Uist | Crete |
| Sea | Hova | Unst | Delos |
| Yap | Idse | Wake | Disko |
| | Iona | Yell | Ellis |
| **4 letters:** | Java | | Faial |
| Amoy | Jolo | **5 letters:** | Farne |
| Aran | Jura | Aland | Faroe |
| Arru | Keos | Apple | Fayal |
| Attu | King | Arran | Funen |
| Bali | Line | Aruba | Haiti |
| Biak | Long | Banka | Hondo |
| Bute | Mahe | Banks | Ibiza |
| Calf | Maui | Barra | Islay |
| Cebu | Mazu | Batan | Isola |
| Coll | Mona | Belle | Iviza |

| | | | |
|---|---|---|---|
| Jerba | Zante | Kurile | Tobago |
| Kauai | | Kvaley | Tresco |
| Kiska | **6 letters:** | Kyushu | Tubuai |
| Koror | Achill | Labuan | Tuvalu |
| Kuril | Aegean | Laputa | Unimak |
| Kyoto | Aegina | Lemnos | Ushant |
| Lanai | Amager | Lesbos | Veneti |
| Lewis | Andros | Leucas | Virgin |
| Leyte | Aurora | Leukas | |
| Lundy | Avalon | Levkas | **7 letters:** |
| Luzon | Azores | Lipari | Aeolian |
| Maewo | Baffin | Lizard | Aldabra |
| Malta | Banaba | Lombok | Amboina |
| Matsu | Bangka | Madura | Andaman |
| Melos | Barrow | Majuro | Antigua |
| Nauru | Bedloe | Marajo | Ashmore |
| Naxos | Bequia | Mercer | Austral |
| Nevis | Bikini | Midway | Bahamas |
| North | Borneo | Negros | Baranof |
| Ocean | Bounty | Ogygia | Barbuda |
| Oland | Bryher | Orkney | Basilan |
| Ormuz | Butung | Paphos | Batavia |
| Palau | Caicos | Patmos | Battery |
| Panay | Caldey | Penang | Bedloe's |
| Papua | Cancun | Pharos | Bermuda |
| Paros | Canvey | Philae | Bonaire |
| Pelew | Cayman | Phuket | Cartier |
| Pemba | Ceylon | Pladdy | Celebes |
| Pines | Chiloe | Quemoy | Channel |
| Qeshm | Cyprus | Ramsey | Chatham |
| Qishm | Devil's | Rhodes | Cipango |
| Reil's | Diomed | Rialto | Corsica |
| Rhode | Djerba | Robben | Crannog |
| Samar | Easter | Royale | Curacao |
| Samoa | Eelpie | Ryukyu | Cythera |
| Samos | Ellice | Safety | Diomede |
| Saria | Euboea | Saipan | Eivissa |
| Seram | Flores | Savage | Emerald |
| South | Fraser | Savaii | Eriskay |
| Spice | Hainan | Scilly | Faeroes |
| Sumba | Harris | Sicily | Falster |
| Sunda | Hawaii | Skerry | Frisian |
| Thass | Hobart | Skomer | Fur Seal |
| Thera | Honshu | Skyros | Gambier |
| Thule | Hormuz | Snares | Gilbert |
| Timor | Icaria | Soemba | Gotland |
| Tiree | Imbros | Soenda | Grenada |
| Tonga | Indies | Staffa | Hawaiki |
| Union | Insula | Staten | Howland |
| Upolu | Ionian | St Mary | Ireland |
| Whale | Ischia | Tahiti | Iwo Jima |
| White | Ithaca | Taiwan | Jamaica |
| Wight | Jersey | Thanet | Keeling |
| Youth | Kodiak | Thasos | Laaland |

| | | | |
|---|---|---|---|
| Ladrone | Tortola | Hong Kong | Trinidad |
| La Palma | Tortuga | Jan Mayen | Tsushima |
| Leeward | Tutuila | Kangaroo | Unalaska |
| Liberty | Vanuatu | Kermadec | Venetian |
| Lofoten | Visayan | Key Largo | Victoria |
| Lolland | Volcano | Kiribati | Viti Levu |
| Madeira | Waihake | Ladrones | Windward |
| Majorca | Watling | Lilliput | Zanzibar |
| Mariana | Western | Lord Howe | |
| Masbate | Wrangel | Luggnagg | **9 letters:** |
| Mayotte | Zealand | Mackinac | Admiralty |
| Mindoro | Zetland | Mainland | Alexander |
| Minicoy | | Maldives | Andreanof |
| Minorca | **8 letters:** | Mallorca | Anticosti |
| Molokai | Alcatraz | Malvinas | Antipodes |
| Moreton | Alderney | Marianas | Ascension |
| Mykonos | Aleutian | Marquesa | Barataria |
| Nicobar | Amindiva | Marshall | Belle Isle |
| Norfolk | Anglesey | Mauna Loa | Benbecula |
| Oceania | Anguilla | Melville | Chichagof |
| Okinawa | Antilles | Mindanao | Christmas |
| Orcades | Atlantis | Miquelon | Elephanta |
| Orkneys | Auckland | Moluccas | Ellesmere |
| Pacific | Balearic | Mustique | Falklands |
| Palawan | Barbados | Njazidja | Fortunate |
| Palmyra | Bass Rock | Northern | Galapagos |
| Paracel | Bathurst | Pelagian | Governors |
| Phoenix | Billiton | Pitcairn | Greenland |
| Purbeck | Blefuscu | Pleasant | Guadalupe |
| Rathlin | Bora-Bora | Portland | Hainan Tao |
| Reunion | Bornholm | Pribilof | Halmahera |
| Roanoke | Brownsea | Principe | Innisfree |
| Rockall | Campbell | Sakhalin | Jamestown |
| Salamis | Canaries | Sandwich | Kerguelen |
| San Juan | Canounan | Sardinia | Laccadive |
| Sheppey | Caroline | Schouten | Lampedusa |
| Shikoku | Catalina | Shetland | Lanzarote |
| Society | Choiseul | Soembawa | Macquarie |
| Socotra | Colonsay | Somerset | Manhattan |
| Sokotra | Cyclades | South Sea | Margarita |
| Solomon | Dominica | Sporades | Marquesas |
| Spratly | Falkland | Sri Lanka | Mascarene |
| St Agnes | Farquhar | St Helena | Mauritius |
| St Croix | Flinders | St Helier | Melanesia |
| Stewart | Foulness | St Martin | Nantucket |
| St Kilda | Friendly | St Thomas | New Guinea |
| St Kitts | Gothland | Sulawesi | Polynesia |
| St Lucia | Gottland | Svalbard | Rangitoto |
| Sumatra | Guernsey | Sverdrup | Rarotonga |
| Sumbawa | Hamilton | Tasmania | Runnymede |
| Suqutra | Hatteras | Tenerife | Saghalien |
| Surtsey | Hebrides | Terceira | Santorini |
| Tenedos | Hokkaido | Thousand | Sao Miguel |
| Tokelau | Holyhead | Thursday | Shetlands |

Sjaelland
St Martin's
Stromboli
St Vincent
Teneriffe
Three Mile
Tongatapu
Trobriand
Vancouver
Vanua Levu
Walcheren
Zakinthos

*10 letters:*
Ailsa Craig
Basse-Terre
Bermoothes
Campobello
Cape Barren
Cape Breton
Cephalonia
Corregidor
Dirk Hartog
Dodecanese
Formentera
Grand Manan
Grenadines
Heligoland
Hispaniola
Isle Royale
Kiritimati
Langerhans
Madagascar
Manitoulin
Marinduque

Martinique
Micronesia
Montserrat
Mornington
New Britain
New Georgia
New Ireland
Pescadores
Puerto Rico
Sahghalien
Samothrace
Sandalwood
Seychelles
Three Kings
Vesteralen
West Indies
Whitsunday

*11 letters:*
Austronesia
Dry Tortugas
Florida Keys
Glubdubdrib
Gran Canaria
Grand Bahama
Grand Canary
Grande-Terre
Guadalcanal
Lakshadweep
Lesser Sunda
Lindisfarne
Mount Desert
New Siberian
Pantelleria
Philippines

Poor Knights
San Salvador
Southampton
South Orkney
Spitsbergen

*12 letters:*
Bougainville
Cassiterides
Ellef Ringnes
Glubbdubdrib
Greater Sunda
Hinchinbrook
Marie Galante
New Caledonia
Newfoundland
Nusa Tenggara
Prince Edward
San Cristobal
Santa Barbara
Seringapatam
South Georgia
Torres Strait

*13 letters:*
Espiritu Santo
Fuerteventura
Furneaux Group
Groote Eylandt
Juan Fernandez
Little Barrier
New Providence
Outer Hebrides
Prince Charles
Prince of Wales

Santa Catalina
South Shetland

*14 letters:*
Amboina oceanic
D'Entrecasteaux
Lesser Antilles
Papua New Guinea
Queen Charlotte
Queen Elizabeth
Tristan da Cunha
Turks and Caicos
Vestmannaeyjar

*15 letters:*
Greater Antilles
Martha's Vineyard
Mont-Saint-Michel
Northern Mariana
North Stradbroke
Wallis and Futuna

*16 letters:*
Heard and
  McDonald

*17 letters:*
British West Indies
Fernando de
  Noronha

*19 letters:*
Netherlands
  Antilles

**Islander** Bermudan, Chian, Cretan, D(a)yak, Filipino, Kanaka, Kelper, Laputan, Madeiran, Maltese, Mauritian, Minoan, Native, Nesiot, Newfie, Orcadian, Parian, Rhodian, Samiot, Scillonian, Sican, Singalese, Taiwanese
**Isle of Wight** Vectis
**Isn't** Aint, Nis, Nys
**Isolate(d), Isolation** Alienate, Ancress, Apart, Backwater, Cleidoic, Cone off, Cut off, Desolate, Dissociate, Enclave, Enisle, Exclude, Incommunicado, Inisle, In vacuo, Island, Lone, Lonely, Maroon, Outlying, Pocket, Quarantine, Sea-girt, Seclude, Secret, Segregate, Separate, Sequester, Sequestration, Set apart, Siege, Six-finger country, Solitary, Sporadic, Stray
**Isomer(ic)** Carotene, Carotin, Carvacrol, Geranial, Neral, Octane, Pinene, Pyran, Theophylline, Tolidine
**Isopod** Gribble
**Isosceles** Triangle
**Isotope** Actinon, Cobalt-60, Deuterium, Iodine-131, Muonium, Protium, Radiothorium, Strontium-90, Thoron, Tritium
**Israel(i)** Beulah, IL, Meir, Sabra, Zion
**Issue(s)** Army, Bonus, Capitalization, Children, Come, Crux, Daughter, Debouch,

Denouement, Derive, Disclose, Dispense, Edition, Effluence, Egress, → EMANATE, Embryo, Emerge, Emission, Emit, Escape, Exit, Exodus, Family, Feigned, Fiduciary, Flotation, Fungible, General, Government, Gush, Handout, Hiccup, Immaterial, Ish, Litter, Material, Matter, Mise, Number, Offspring, Outcome, Outflow, Part, Point, Privatization, Proof, Publish, Release, Result, Rights, Sally, Scion, Scrip, Seed, Share, Side, Son, Spawn, Special, Spring, Stream, Subject, Topic, Turn, Utter, Yearbook

**Istanbul** Byzantium, Constantinople

**Isthmus** Darien, Karelian, Kra, Neck, Panama, San Blas, Suez, Tehuantepec

**It** A, Chic, Hep, Hip, Id, Italian, Oomph, SA, Same, Sex appeal, 't, Vermouth

**Italian, Italy** Alpini, Ausonian, Bolognese, Calabrian, Chian, Dago, Ding, Este, Etnean, Etrurian, Etruscan, Eyeti(e), Eytie, Faliscan, Florentine, Garibaldi, Genoese, Ghibelline, Guelf, Guelph, Hesperia, Irredentist, It, Latian, Latin, Lombard, Marconi, Medici, Mezzogiorno, Milanese, Moro, Neapolitan, Oscan, Paduan, Patarin(e), Rocco, Roman, Sabine, Samnite, Sicel, Sienese, Signor(i), Sikel, Spag, Tuscan, Umbrian, Venetian, Vermouth, Volscian, Wop

**Italic** Swash

**Itch(ing), Itchiness** Acariasis, Annoy, Burn, Cacoethes, Dhobi, Euk, Ewk, Hanker, Heat rash, Hives, Jock, Miliaria, Photopsy, Prickle, Prickly heat, Prurience, Prurigo, Pruritis, Psora, Scabies, Scrapie, Seven-year, Swimmer's, Tickle, → URGE, Urtication, Yen, Yeuk, Youk, Yuck, Yuke

**Item(ise)** Also, Article, Bulletin, Couple, Detail, Entry, Equipment, Exhibit, Flash, Line, List, Note, Number, Pair, Particular, Piece, Point, Product, Spot, Talking point, Too, Topic, Twosome, Unit

**Iterate** Repeat

**Itinerant, Itinerary** Ambulant, Didakai, Didakei, Did(d)icoy, Dusty Feet, Gipsy, Gypsy, Hobo, Journey, Log, Pedlar, Peripatetic, Pie-powder, Roadman, Roamer, Romany, Rootless, Route, Stroller, Traveller, Vagrom, Wayfarer

**Itself** Aseity, In se, Ipso, Per se, Sui

**Ivan** Russian, Terrible

**Ivory (tower)** Black, Bone, Chryselephantine, Dentine, Distant, Eburnean, Impractical, Incisor, Key, Molar, Solitude, Teeth, Tower, Tusk, Vegetable, Whale's bone

**Ivy** Ale-hoof, Angelica-tree, Aralia, Boston, Bush, Cat's-foot, Climber, Creeper, Evergreen, Gill, Grape, Ground, Hedera, Helix, Japanese, Panax, Poison, Rhoicissus, Shield, Sumac, Sweetheart, Udo, Weeping

**Izzard** Z

# Jj

**J** Curve, Juliet, Pen

**Ja(c)ques** Melancholy, Tati

**Jab(ber)** Chatter, Foin, Gabble, Immunise, Immunologist, Inject, Jaw, Jook, Lunge, Nudge, One-two, Peck, Poke, Prattle, Prod, Proke, Punch, Puncture, Sook, Sputter, Stab, Stick, Thrust, Venepuncture, Yak

**Jack(s)** AB, Apple, Artocarpus, Ass, Ball, Boot, Bower, Bowl(s), Boy, Cade, Card, Cheap, Coatcard, Crevalle, Deckhand, Dibs(tones), Five stones, Flag, Frost, Giant-killer, Hoist, Honour, Hopper, Horner, Hydraulic, Idle, J, Jock, Jumping, Ketch, Kitty, Knave, Knucklebones, Lazy, London, Loord, Lout, Lumber, Maker, Mark, Matlow, Mistress, Nob, Noddy, Pilot, Point, Pot, Pur, Rabbit, Raise, Rating, Ripper, Roasting, Robinson, Russell, Sailor, Salt, Screw, Sea-dog, Seafarer, Seaman, Shaun, Sprat, Spring-heeled, Springtail, Steeple, Sticker, Straw, Tar, Tee, Tradesman, Turnspit, Union, Uplift, Wood, Yellow

**Jackal** Anubis, Dieb, Hack, Lion's provider, Stooge

**Jackass** Aliboron, Goburra, Kookaburra, Stupid

**Jackdaw** Bird, Chawk, Chough, Daw, Kae, Raven, Rheims, Thief

**Jacket** Acton, Afghanistan, Air, Amauti(k), Anorak, Atigi, Bainin, Baju, Bania(n), Banyan, Barbour®, Basque, Battle, Bawneen, Bed, Bellhop, Biker, Blazer, Blouse, Blouson, Body-warmer, Bolero, Bomber, Brigandine, Bumfreezer, Bush, Cagoul(e), Camisole, Can, Caraco, Cardigan, Carmagnole, Casing, →COAT, Combat, Cosy, Cover, Dinner, Dolman, Donkey, Doublet, Drape, Dressing, Dressing-sack, Duffel coat, Duffle coat, Dust-cover, Dustwrapper, Duvet, Fearnought, Flak, Fleece, Gambeson, Gendarme, Grego, Habergeon, Hacking, Half-kirtle, Ha(c)queton, Hoodie, Hug-me-tight, Jerkin, Jupon, Kagool, Kaross, Life, Life preserver, Lumber, Mackinaw, Mae West, Mandarin, Mandilion, Mao, Matinée, Mess, Monkey, Nehru, Newmarket, Norfolk, Parka, Pea, Petenlair, Pierrot, Pilot, Polka, Potato, Pyjama, Railly, Reefer, Roundabout, Sackcoat, Safari, Sayon, Shearling, Shell, Shooting, Shortgown, Simar(re), Sleeve, Slip-cover, Smoking, Spencer, Sports, Steam, Strait, Sweatshirt, Tabard, Tailcoat, Toreador, Tunic, Tux(edo), Tweed, Vareuse, Waistcoat, Wampus, Wam(m)us, Water, Waxed, Windbreaker®, Windcheater, Windjammer, Wrapper, Zouave

**Jackknife** Dive, Fold, Jockteleg, Pike

**Jackpot** Cornucopia, Kitty, Pool

**Jackson** Old Hickory, Stonewall

**Jackstraw** Spellican, Spil(l)ikin

**Jacob** Epstein, Ladder, Sheep

**Jacobite(s)** Non-compounder, Non juror, Wild Geese

**Jacquard** Matelasse

**Jacuzzi** Hot tub

**Jade(d)** Axe-stone, Bidet, Cayuse, Cloy, Crock, Disjaskit, Exhaust, Fatigue, Greenstone, Hack, Hag, Horse, Hussy, Limmer, Minx, Nag, Nephrite, Passe, Pounamu, Rip, Rosinante, Sate, Screw, Slut, Spleenstone, Stale, Tired, Trite, Weary, Yaud, Yu(-stone)

**Jaeger** Skua

**Jag(ged)** Barbed, Cart, Drinking, Erose, Gimp, Hackly, Injection, Laciniate, Ragde, Ragged, Sawtooth, Serrate, Snag, Spree, Spur, Tooth

**Jagger** Mick, Pedlar

**Jaguar** American tiger, Car, Caracal, Cat, E-type, Ounce, Tiger

**Jail(er)** Adam, Alcaide, Alcatraz, Bastille, Bedford, Bin, Bridewell, Can, Clink, Commit, Cooler, Gaol, Hoosegow, Imprison, Incarcerate, Jug, Keeper, Kitty, Limbo, Lockup, Marshalsea, Newgate, Nick, Pen, Pokey, Porridge, → **PRISON**, Screw, Shop, Slammer, Spandau, Stir, Strangeways, Tronk, Turnkey, Warder

**Jailbird** Con, Lag, Lifer, Life server, Trusty

**Jain(ism)** Mahavira

**Jakarta** Batavia

**Jake** Honest, Hunkydory, OK, Rube

**Jalopy** Banger, Boneshaker, Buggy, Car, Crate, Heap, Shandry(dan), Stock-car

**Jam(my)** Apple butter, Block, Bottleneck, Choke, Clog, Confiture, Crowd, Crush, Cushy, Damson, Dilemma, Extra, Fix, Gridlock, Hold-up, Hole, How d'ye do, Imbroglio, Improvise, Jeelie, Jeely, Lock, Log, Pack, Paper, Pickle, Plight, → **PREDICAMENT**, Preserve, Press, Quince, Rat run, Rush hour, Seize, Snarl-up, Spot, Squeeze, Stall, Standstill, Stick, Tailback, Tangle, Traffic, Vice, Vise, Wedge

**Jamaica(n)** Inn, Rasta(farian), Rastaman, Yardie

**Jamb** Doorpost, Durn, Sconcheon, Scontion, Scuncheon, Upright

**Jamboree** Gala

**James** Agee, Bond, Bothwell, Henry, Jacobite, Jemmy, Jesse, Jim, Joyce, Pretender, Screw, Seamus, Seumas, Sid, Watt

**Jane** Austen, Calamity, Eyre, Seymour, Shore, Sian

**Jangle** Clank, Clapperclaw, Clash, Rattle, Wrangle

**Janitor** Caretaker, Concierge, Doorman, Porter, Servitor, Sweeper, Tiler

**Jankers** KP

**Jansky** Jy

**Janus** Two-faced

**Japan(ese), Japanese drama** Ainu, Burakumin, Daimio, Eta, Finish, Geisha, Genro, Gloss, Gook, Haiku, Heian, Hondo, Honshu, Issei, Japlish, Kabuki, Kami, Kana, Kirimon, Lacquer, Mandarin, Meiji, Mikado, Mousmé, Mousmee, Nihon, Nip, Nippon, Nisei, No(h), Resin, Sansei, Satsuma, Shinto, Shogun, Taisho, Togo, Tycoon, Yamato, Yellow peril

**Jape** Jeer, Joke, Prank, Trick

**Jar(ring)** Albarello, Amphora, Bell, Canopus, Churr, Clash, Crock, Cruet, Din, Dissonant, Distune, Dolium, Enrough, Gallipot, Gas, Grate, Greybeard, Gride, Grind, Gryde, Humidor, Hydria, → **JOLT**, Kalpis, Kang, Kilner®, Leyden, Mason, Monkey, Off-key, Olla, Pint, Pithos, Pot(iche), Quarrel, Rasp, Rock, Screwtop, Shake, Shelta, Shock, Stamnos, Start, Stave, Stean, Steen, Stein, Tankard, Terrarium, Tinaja, Turn, Untune, Vessel, Water-monkey

**Jargon** Argot, Babble, Baragouin, Beach-la-mar, Buzzword, Cant, Chinese, Chinook, Cyberspeak, Eurobabble, Eurospeak, Geekspeak, Gobbledegook, Gobbledygook, Greenspeak, Jive, Kennick, Legalese, Lingo, Lingoa geral, Lingua franca, Mumbo-jumbo, Netspeak, Newspeak, Officialese, Parlance, Patois, Patter, Patter-flash, Psychobabble, Shelta, Shoptalk, → **SLANG**, Sociologese, Technobabble, Technospeak, Telegraphese, Vernacular

**Jargoon** Chinook

**Jasmine** Cape, Frangipani, Gelsemine, Gelsemium, Gessamine, Jessamy, Madagascar, Olea, Red

**Jason** Argonaut

**Jasper** Basanite, Bloodstone, Egyptian, Porcelain, Touchstone

**Jaundice(d)** Cholestasis, Cynical, Icterus, Prejudiced, Sallow, Yellow

**Jaunt** Journey, Outing, Sally, Stroll, Swan, Trip

**Jaunty** Airy, Akimbo, Chipper, Debonair, Perky, Rakish

▷ **Jaunty** *may indicate* an anagram

**Java(man)** Pithecanthropus, Sundanese

**Javelin** Dart, Gavelock, Harpoon, Jereed, Jerid, Pile, Pilum, Spear

**Jaw(s), Jawbone** Blab, Chaft, Chap, Chat, Chaw, Cheek, Chide, Chin, Confab, Entry, Gills, Glass, Gnathic, Gnathite, Gonion, Hypognathous, Imparl, Jabber, Jobe, Kype, Lantern, Lumpy, Mandible, Masseter, Maw, Maxilla, Mesial, Muzzle, Mylohyoid, Natter, Opisthognathous, Overbite, Overshot, Phossy, Pi, Premaxillary, Prognathous, Ramus, Rubber, Shark, Stylet, Underhung, Undershot, Wapper-jaw, Ya(c)kety-Ya(c)k

**Jay** Bird, Grey, J, Sirgang, Whisky-jack, Whisky-john

**Jazz(er), Jazzman** Acid, Afro-Cuban, Barber, Barrelhouse, Basie, Bebop, Blues, Boogie, Boogie-woogie, Bop, Cat, Coleman, Cool, Count Basie, Dixieland, Enliven, Free, Funky, Gig, Gutbucket, Hardbop, High life, Hipster, Jam, Jive, Kansas City, Latin, Lick, Mainstream, Modern, New Orleans, New Wave, Nouvelle Vague, Progressive, Ragtime, Riff, Scat, Skiffle, Slap base, Stomp, Stride, Swinger, Tailgate, Trad, Traditional, Waller, West Coast

**Jealous(y)** Envious, Green(-eyed), Green-eyed monster, Grudging, Zelotypia

**Jean(s)** Chinos, Denims, Levis®, Pants, Trousers, Wranglers®

**Jeer(ing)** Ballyrag, Barrack, Belittle, Birl, Boo, Burl, Deride, Digs, Fleer, Flout, Frump, Gird, Heckle, Hoot, Jape, Jibe, → MOCK, Rail, Razz, Ridicule, Scoff, Sling off, Sneer, Taunt, Twit, Yah

**Jeeves** Valet

**Jehovah** God, Lord, Yahve(h), Yahwe(h)

**Jehovah's Witness** Russellite

**Jehu** Charioteer, Driver

**Jejune** Arid, Barren, Dry, Insipid, Juvenile

**Jell(y)** Acaleph(a), Acalephe, Agar(-agar), Aspic, Brawn, Calf's foot, Chaudfroid, Comb, Cow-heel, Cranberry, → EXPLOSIVE, Flummery, Gel, Isinglass, Jam, Kanten, K-Y®, Liquid paraffin, Macedoine, Meat, Medusa, Mineral, Mould, Napalm, Neat's foot, Petrolatum, Petroleum, Quiddany, Royal, Set, Shape, Sterno®, Tunicin, Vaseline®, Vitreous humour

▷ **Jelly** *may indicate* an anagram

**Jellyfish** Acaleph(a), Acalephe, Aurelia, Blubber, Box, Cnidaria, Discomedusae, Discophora, Hydromedusa, Hydrozoa, Irukandji, Medusa, Mesogloea, Nettlefish, Physalia, Planoblast, Portuguese man-of-war, Quarl, Scyphistoma, Scyphozoan, Sea-blubber, Sea-nettle, Sea-wasp, Strobila

**Jemmy** Betty, Crowbar, Lever

**Jenkins** Ear, Roy, Up

**Jenny** Ass, Lind, Long, Mule, Short, Spinner, Spinning, Spinster, Wren

**Jeopardise, Jeopardy** Danger, Double, Expose, Hazard, Imperil, Peril, Risk

**Jerboa** Desert rat

**Jeremiad** Lament, Tragedy, Woe

**Jeremy** Fisher, Irons, Jerry

**Jerk(y), Jerkily, Jerking, Jerks** Aerobics, A salti, Bob, Braid, Bump, Cant, Diddle, Ebrillade, Flirt, Flounce, Gym(nastics), Half-wit, Hike, Hitch, Hoi(c)k, Idiot, Jigger, Jolt, Jut, Kant, Knee, PE, Peck, Physical, Saccade, Shove, Shrug, Spasm, Start, Strobe, Surge, Switch, Sydenham's chorea, Tic, Toss(en), Tweak, → TWITCH, Wrench, Yank

**Jerkin** Body warmer, Jacket, Tabard

**Jerome** Hieronymic, Kern, Vulgate

**Jerry, Jerry-built** Boche, Flimsy, Fritz, Hun, Kraut, Lego, Mouse, Po(t), Slop-built

**Jersey(s)** Bailiwick, CI, Cow, Football, Frock, Gansey, Guernsey, Kine, Lily, Maillot, Polo, Potato, Roll-neck, Rugby, Singlet, → SWEATER, Sweatshirt, V-neck, Yellow, Zephyr

**Jerusalem** Ariel, Hierosolymitan, Sion, Zion

**Jess(e)** James, Strap

**Jest(er), Jesting** Badinage, Barm, Baur, Bawr, Bourd(er), Buffoon, Clown, Cod, Comic, Droll, Gleek, Goliard, Humorist, Inficete, Jape, Jig, Joculator, Joker, Josh, Merryman, Miller, Mot, Motley, Patch, Quip, Raillery, Ribaldry, Ribaudry, Rigoletto, Scogan, Scoggin, Sport, Toy, Trinculo, Wag, Waggery, Wit, Yorick

**Jesuit** Bollandist, De Molina, Ignatius, Loyola, Sanchez, Scholastic, SJ

**Jesus** →CHRIST, Emmanuel, IHS, Immanuel, INRI, Isa, Jabers, Lord

**Jet, Jet lag** Airbus®, Aircraft, Beadblast, Black, Bubble, Burner, Chirt, Douche, Executive, Fountain, Geat, Harrier, Ink, Jumbo, Plane, Pump, Sable, Sandblast, Sloe, Soffione, Spirt, Spout, Spray, Spurt, Squirt, Stream, Time-zone disease, Time-zone fatigue, Turbine, Turbo, Vapour, Water

**Jettison** Discard, Dump, Flotsam, Jetsam, Lagan, Ligan, Offload

**Jetty** Groin, Mole, Pier, Wharf

**Jew(ish), Jews** Ashkenazi, Chas(s)id, Diaspora, Essene, Falasha, Grecian, Greek, Has(s)id, Haskala(h), Hebraic, Hebrew, Hellenist, Hemerobaptist, Kahal, Karaite, Kike, Ladino, Landsman, Levite, Lubavitch, Maccabee, Marrano, Misnaged, Mitnag(g)ed, Nazarite, Neturei Karta, Nicodemus, Peculiar People, Pharisee, Refusenik, Sabra, Sadducee, Semite, Sephardim, Sheeny, Shemite, Shtetl, Smouch, Smouse, Tobit, Wandering, Yid(dish), Zealot

**Jeweller(y), Jewel(s)** Agate, Aigrette, Almandine, Artwear, Beryl, Bijou(terie), Bling(-bling), Brilliant, Cameo, Cartier, Chrysoprase, Cloisonné, Coral, Cornelian, Costume, Crown, Diamond, Earbob, Ear-drop, Emerald, Ewe-lamb, Fabergé, Fashion, Ferron(n)ière, Finery, Garnet, →GEM, Girandole, Gracchi, Jade, Junk, Lherzolite, Locket, Marcasite, Medallion, Navette, Olivine, Opal, Parure, Paste, Pavé, Pearl, Pendant, Peridot, Rivière, Rock, Rubin(e), Ruby, Sapphire, Sard, Scarab, Showpiece, Smaragd, Solitaire, Stone, Sunburst, Taonga, Tiara, Tiffany, Tom, Tomfoolery, Topaz, Torc, Treasure, Trinket, Zircon

**Jezebel** Harlot, Loose, Whore

**Jib** Ba(u)lk, Boggle, Boom, →DEMUR, Face, Flying, Foresail, Genoa, Milk, Reest, Reist, Sideswipe, Stay-sail, Storm

**Jibe** Barb, Bob, Correspond, Crack, Dig, Fling, Gleek, →JEER, Mock, Quip, Sarcasm, Slant, Taunt

**Jiffy** Mo, Pronto, Twinkling, Whiff

**Jig(gle)** Bob, Bounce, Dance, Fling, Frisk, Hornpipe, Jog, Juggle, Morris, Shake

**Jigger(ed)** Beat, Chigoe, Jolley, Ruin

**Jill** Ferret

**Jilt(ed)** Abandon, Discard, Lorn, Reject, Shed, Throw-over

**Jim(my)** Crow, Diamond, Dismal, Jas, Lucky, Pee, Piddle, Riddle

**Jingle(r)** Clerihew, Clink, Ditty, Doggerel, Rhyme, Tambourine, Tinkle

**Jingo(ism), Jingoist** Chauvin, Flag waver, Gung-ho, Odzooks, Patriot, Sabre-rattling, Warmonger, War-rant

**Jink** Elude

**Jinn(i)** Afreet, Eblis, Genie, Jann, Marid, Spirit

**Jinx(ed)** Curse, Hex, Hoodoo, Jonah, Kibosh, Moz(z), Spoil, Unlucky, Voodoo, Whammy

**Jitter(s), Jittery** Coggly, DT, Fidgets, Funk, Jumpy, Nervous, Willies

▷ **Jitter(s)** *may indicate* an anagram

**Jo** →LOVER, Sweetheart

**Job(bing), Jobs** Agiotage, Appointment, Assignment, Berth, Calling, Career, Chore, Comforter, Crib, Darg, Desk, Duty, Earner, Errand, Gig, Gut, Hatchet, Homer, Inside, Line, Métier, Mission, Nixer, Occupation, Oratorio, Paint, Parergon, Patient, Pensum, Place(ment), Plum, Position, Post, Problem, Pursuit, Put-up, Role, Sinecure, Situation, Snow, Spot, Steady, →TASK, Ticket, Trade, Trotter, Truck, Undertaking, Work

▷ **Job** *may indicate* the biblical character

**Jock** Deejay, DJ, Mac, Sawn(e)y, Scot

**Jockey** Carr, Cheat, Diddle, Disc, Eddery, Horseman, Jostle, Jump, Lester, Manoeuvre, Mouse, Piggott, Rider, Steve, Suicide, Swindle, Trick, Video, Vie, Winter

▷ **Jockey** *may indicate* an anagram

**Jocose, Jocular(ity), Jocund** Badinage, Cheerful, Debonair, Facete, Facetious, Jesting, Lepid, Scurril(e), Waggish

**Joe(y), Joseph** Addison, Dogsbody, GI, Kangaroo, Pal, Public, Roo, Sloppy, Stalin, Surface, Trey

**Jog(ger), Joggle, Jog-trot** Arouse, Canter, Dog-trot, Dunch, Dunsh, Heich-how, Heigh-ho, Hod, Jiggle, Jolt, Jostle, Memo, Mnemonic, Mosey, Nudge, Piaffe, Prompt, Ranke, Refresh, Remind, Road-runner, Run, Shake, Shog, Tickle, Trot, Whig

**Johannesburg** Jozi

**John(ny)** Ajax, Augustus, Barleycorn, Beatle, Bog, Bright, Brown, Bull, Bunyan, Can, Cloaca, Collins, Dee, Doc, Doree, Dory, Dunny, Elsan®, Elton, Evan, Gaunt, Gents, Gilpin, Groats, Halifax, Ia(i)n, Ivan, Lackland, Lat(rine), Latecomer, Lav, Lennon, Little, Loo, Peel, Po(t), Prester, Privy, Stage-door, Throne, Toot, Tout, WC

**Johnny-come-lately** Upstart

**Johnson** Cham, Doctor, Idler

**Join(er), Joined, Joining** Abut, Accede, Accompany, Add, Affix, Alligate, Ally, Amalgamate, And, Annex, Associate, Attach, Bond, Brad, Braze, Butt-end, Cabinet-maker, Carpentry, Cement, Cleave, Club, Cold-well, Combine, Conflate, Confluent, Conglutinate, Conjugate, Conjunct, Connect, Converge, Cope, → COUPLE, Dovetail, Engraft, Enlist, Enrol, Enter, Entrant, Entrist, Fay, Federate, Fuse, Glue, Graft, Hasp, Hitch, Hyphen, Include, Inosculate, Interconnect, Jugate, Knit, Link, Marry, Meet, Member, Menuisier, Merge, Mix, Mortar, Oop, Oup, Overlaunch, Piece, Piecen, Pin, Push fit, Rabbet, Regelation, Rivet, Scarf, Seam, Se-tenant, Sew, Siamize, Snug, Solder, Splice, Spot-weld, Squirrel, Staple, Stick, Stitch, Stylolite, Tack-weld, Tenon, Toenail, Together, Unite, Wed, Weld, Wire, Yoke

**Joint(ed)** Ancon, Ankle, Arthrosis, Articular, Ball and socket, Bar, Baron, Butt, Capillary, Cardan, Carpus, Chine, Clip, Co, Cogging, Collaborative, Collar, Colonial goose, Commissure, Compression, Conjunction, Coursing, Cuit, Cup and ball, Cut, Dive, Dovetail, Drumstick, Elbow, Enarthrosis, Entrecôte, Expansion, False, Fetlock, First, Fish, Flitch, Gambrel, Genu, Gigot, Gimmal, Gimmer, Ginglymus, Hainch, Haunch, Heel, Hinge, Hip, Hough, Housing, Huck, Hunker, Inseam, J, Joggle, Jolly, Junction, Knee, Knuckle, Lap(ped), Lith, Loin, Marijuana, Meat, Mitre, Mortise, Mouse (buttock), Mouse-piece, Mutton, Mutual, Node, Phalange, Phalanx, Pin, Popliteal, Psoas, Push-fit, Rabbet, Rack, Raphe, Reducer, Reefer, Rhaphe, Ribroast, Roast, Saddle, Scarf, Scarph, Schindylesis, Seam, Second, Shoulder, Silverside, Sirloin, Soaker, Splice, Spliff, Stifle, Straight, Strip, Symphysis, Synchondrosis, Syndesmosis, T, Tarsus, T-bone, Teamwork, Temperomandibular, Tenon, Together, Toggle, Tongue and groove, Topside, Trochanter, Trochite, Undercut, Union, Universal, Vertebra, Water, Wedging, Weld, Wrist

**Joist** Accouplement, Bar, Beam, Dormant, Ground plate, Groundsill, H-beam, I-beam, Rib, Rolled-steel, Sleeper, Solive, String, Trimmer

**Joke(r), Joke-book, Joking** Banter, Bar, Baur, Bawr, Boff, Booby-trap, Bourdon, Card, Chaff, Chestnut, → CLOWN, Cod, Comedian, Comic, Corn, Crack, Cut-up, Facete, Farceur, Farceuse, Fool, Fun, Funster, Gab, Gag(ster), Gamester, Gleek, Glike, Guy, Have-on, Hazer, Hoax, Hum, Humorist, In fun, Jape, Jest, Jig, Jocular, Josh, Knock-knock, Lark, Legpull, Merry-andrew, Merryman, Mistigris, One, One-liner, Pleasantry, Practical, Prank(ster), Pun, Punchline, Pundigrion, Quip, Rag, Raillery, Rib-tickler, Rot, Sally, Scherzo, Scogan, Scoggin, Scream, Sick, Skylark, Sottisier, Squib, Standing, Throwaway, Tongue-in-cheek, Wag, Wheeze, Wild, Wisecrack, Wit

**Jollity, Jolly, Jollification** 'Arryish, Bally, Beano, Bright, Cheerful, Convivial, Cordial, Dashed, Do, Festive, Galoot, Gaucie, Gaucy, Gawcy, Gawsy, Gay, Hilarious, Jocose, Jovial, Marine, Mirth, Rag, Revel, RM, Roger, Sandboy, Sight, Tar, Trip, Very

**Jolly Roger** Death's head, Flag

**Jolt(ing)** Bump, Jar, Jig-a jig, Jog(gle), Jostle, Jounce, Jumble, Shake, Shog, Start

**Jonah** Hoodoo, Jinx, Moz(z)

**Jones** Davy, Dow, Emperor, Inigo

**Jordan(ian)** Moabite, Pot, Urinal

**Joris** Horseman

▶ **Joseph** *see* JOE(Y)

**Josh** Chaff, Kid, Rib, Tease

**Josiah** Stamp, Wedgwood

**Joss** Incense, Luck, Stick

**Jostle** Barge, Bump, Compete, Elbow, Hog-shouther, Hustle, Jockey, Push, Shoulder, →SHOVE, Throng

**Jot(ter), Jotting(s)** Ace, Fig, Iota, Memo, Mite, Note, Notebook, Notelet, Pad, Stime, Styme, Tittle, Whit

**Journal** Band(e), Blog, Chronicle, Daily, Daybook, Diary, Ephemeris, E-zine, Gazette, Hansard, Lancet, Log, Mag, Noctuary, Organ, Paper, Periodical, Pictorial, Punch, Rag, Record, Reuter, TES, TLS, Trade, Waste book, Weblog, Webzine

**Journalism, Journalist** Cheque-book, Columnist, Commentariat, Contributor, Diarist, Diurnalist, Ed, Fleet St, Freelance, (GA) Sala, Gazetteer, Gonzo, Grub Street, Hack, Hackery, Hackette, Hatchetman, Inkslinger, Interviewer, Investigative, Keyhole, Leader-writer, Lobby, Marat, Muckraker, Newshound, Newsman, Northcliffe, NUJ, Penny-a-liner, Pepys, Press(man), Reporter, Reviewer, Scribe, Sob sister, Stead, Stringer, Wireman, →WRITER, Yellow

**Journey** Bummel, Circuit, Cruise, Errand, Expedition, Eyre, Foray, Grand Tour, Hadj, Hop, Jaunce, Jaunse, Jaunt, Lift, Long haul, Mush, Nestos, Odyssey, Passage, Peregrination, Periegesis, Pilgrimage, Ply, Raik, Rake, Red-eye, Ride, Round trip, Route, Run, Sabbath-day's, Sentimental, Soup run, Step, Swag, Tour, Travel, Trek, Trip, Viatical, Voyage, Walkabout, Wend

**Journeyman** Artisan, Commuter, Craftsman, Sterne, Trekker, Yeoman

**Joust** Giust, Pas d'armes, Tilt, Tiltyard, Tournament, Tourney

**Jove** Egad, Gad, Igad, Jupiter, Thunderbearer, Thunderer

**Jovial** Bacchic, Boon, Convivial, Cordial, Festive, Genial, Jolly, Merry

**Jowl(s)** Cheek, Chollers, Chops, Jaw

**Joy(ful), Joyous** Ah, Beatific, Bliss, Blithe, Charmian, Cheer, →DELIGHT, Dream, Ecstasy, Elation, Exhilaration, Exulting, Fain, Felicity, Festal, Frabjous, Glad, Glee, Gloat, Groove, Hah, Happy, Hey, Joie de vivre, Jubilant, Nirvana, Rapture, Schadenfreude, Sele, Tra-la, Transport, Treat, Yahoo, Yay, Yippee

**Joyce** Haw Haw, Traitor

**Joyrider** Twoccer

**JP** Beak, Queer cuffin, Quorum

**Jubilant, Jubilation, Jubilee** Celebration, Cock-a-hoop, Diamond, Ecstatic, Elated, Exultant, Holiday, Joy, Triumphant

**Judaism** Semitism

**Judas** Double-crosser, Iscariot, Traitor, Tree

**Judder** Put-put, Shake, Vibrate

**Jude** Obscure

**Judge(ment), Judges** Absolute, Addoom, Adjudicator, Agonothetes, Alacus, Alcalde, Appraise, Arbiter, Arbitrate, Areopagite, Aret(t), Arrêt, Assess, Assize, Auto-da-fé, Avizandum, Award, Banc, Believe, Bench, Brehon, Cadi, Calculate, Censure, Centumvirus, Chancellor, Chief Justice, Circuit(eer), Commonsense, Common Serjeant, Comparative, Connoisseur, Consider, Coroner, Court, Criterion, Critic(ise), Daniel, Dayan, Daysman, Deborah, Decern(e), Decide, Decision, Decreet, Deem(ster), Dempster, Depth, Determine, Dicast, Dies irae, Dies non, Differential, Dikast, Discern(ment), District, Doom(ster), Ephor, Ermined, Esteem, Estimate, Evaluate, Faisal, Faysal, Gauge, Gesse, Gideon, Good-sense, Guess, Hakeem, Hakim, Hearing, Hold, Honour, Inky-smudge, Interlocutor, J, Jeffreys, Jephthah, Justice, Justiciar, Kadi, Last, Line, Lord Chief Justice, Lud, Lynch, Minos, Mufti, Non prosequitur, Nonsuit, Official Referee, Old Fury, Opine, Opinion, Ordinary, Outfangthief, Panel, Paris, Podesta, Providence, Provisional, Puisne, Puny, Ragnarok, Rate, Reckon(ing), Recorder, Ref(eree), Regard, Rhadamanthus, Ruler, Samson, Samuel, Sapience, Scan, Second guess, See, Sentence,

Sentiment, Shallow, Sheriff, Sizer, Sober, Solomon, Sound, Stipendiary, Suppose, Surrogate, Syndic, Tact, Think, Touch, Trior, Try, Umpire, Value, Verdict, Ween, Weigh up, Wig, Wik, Wine-taster, Wisdom, Worship

**Judicious** Critical, Diplomatic, Discreet, Politic, Rational, Sage, Sensible, Shrewd, Sound

**Judo, Judo costume** Dan, Dojo, Gi(e), Kyu, Shiai, Waza-ari

**Jug(s)** Amphora, Aquamanale, Aquamanile, Bellarmine, Bird, Blackjack, Bombard, Breasts, Can, Cooler, Cream(er), Crock, Enghalskrug, Ewer, Flagon, Gaol, Gotch, Greybeard, Growler, Jar, John Roberts, Malling, Measuring, Olpe, Pitcher, Pound, Pourer, Pourie, → **PRISON**, Quad, Quod, Sauceboat, Shop, Slammer, Stir, Tits, Toby, Urceolus

**Juggle(r), Jugglery** Conjuror, Cook, Escamotage, Fake, Fire-eater, Hocus-pocus

**Juice, Juicy** Aloe vera, Bacca, Cassareep, Cassaripe, Cremor, Current, Fluid, Fruity, Gastric, Hypocist, Ichor, Jungle, La(b)danum, Laser, Latex, Lush, Moist, Must, Nectar, Oil, Pancreatic, Perry, Petrol, Ptisan, Rare, Sap, Snake, Soma, Spanish, Stum, Succulent, Succ(o)us, Tarantula, Thridace, Vril, Walnut, Zest

**Juju** Charm, Fetish

**Jujube** Christ's thorn, Lotus, Nabk, Padma, Sweet

**Jukebox** Nickelodeon

**Julian** Apostate

**Juliet** J

**July** Dogdays

**Jumble** Cast offs, Chaos, Conglomeration, Farrago, Gallimawfry, Garble, Hodge-podge, Huddle, Jabble, Lumber, Mass, Medley, Mingle-mangle, Mish-mash, Mixter-maxter, Mixtie-maxtie, Mixture, Mix(t)y-max(t)y, Pasticcio, Pastiche, Praiseach, Printer's pie, Raffle, Ragbag, Scramble, Shuffle, Wuzzle

▷ **Jumbled** *may indicate* an anagram

**Jumbo** Aircraft, Colossal, Elephant, Huge, Jet, Large-scale, Mammoth, OS, Plane, Vast

**Jump(er), Jumping, Jumpy** Ambush, Antelope, Aran, Assemble, Axel, Base, Batterie, Bean, Boomer, Bound, Broad, Bungee, Bungy, Bunny-hop, Caper, Capriole, Cicada, Cicata, Crew-neck, Cricket, Croupade, Daffy, Desultory, Entrechat, Euro, Eventer, Flea, Fosbury flop, Frog, Gansey, Gazump, Gelande(sprung), Grasshopper, Guernsey, Halma, Handspring, Helicopter, High, Hurdle, Impala, Itchy, Jersey, Joey, Jolly, Kangaroo, Katydid, Kickflip, Knight, Lammie, Lammy, Leap(frog), Lep, Long, Loop, Lope, Lutz, Nervous, Nervy, Ollie, Pallah, Para, Parachute(r), Pig, Pogo, Polo-neck, Pounce, Prance, Prank, Pronking, Puissance, Quantum, Quersprung, Rap, Roo, Salchow, Saltatory, Saltigrade, Saltus, Scissors, Scoup, Scowp, Shy, Skip, Skipjack, Skydiver, → **SPRING**, Star, Start, Steeplechaser, Straddle, Sweater, Tanktop, Toe(-loop), Trampoline, Triple, Turtle-neck, Vau(l)t, V-neck, Volatile, Water, Western roll

**Jumping jack** Pantine

**Junction** Abutment, Alloyed, Angle, Box, Bregma, Carfax, Circus, Clapham, Close, Clover-leaf, Connection, Crewe, Crossroads, Diffused, Gap, Intersection, Joint, Josephson, Knitting, Meeting, Node, P-n, Point, Raphe, Rhaphe, Roundabout, Spaghetti, Stage, Suture, Synapse, T, Tight, Turn off, Union

**Juneberry** Saskatoon, Shadbush

**Jungle** Asphalt, Blackboard, Boondocks, Bush, Concrete, Forest, Maze, Shola, Tangle

**Junior** Cadet, Chota, Cion, Dogsbody, Filius, Fils, Gofer, Minor, Name-son, Office, Petty, Puisne, Scion, Second fiddle, Sub(ordinate), Underling, Understrapper, Younger

**Juniper** Cade, Pencil-cedar, Red-cedar, Savin(e)

**Junk(ie), Junkshop** Addict, Bric-à-brac, Chuck in, Fiddle-de-dee, Glory hole, Glue-sniffer, Jettison, Litter, Lorcha, Lumber, Refuse, Schmeck, Ship, Shmek, Spam, Tagareen, Tatt, Trash, Tripe, User

▷ **Junk** *may indicate* an anagram

**Junker** Aristo, Prussian

**Junket(ing)** Beano, Celebration, Creel, Custard, Feast, Picnic, Rennet, Spree

**Juno** Lucina, Moneta

**Junta** Cabal, Council

**Jupiter** Jove, Newspaper, Pluvius, Zeus

**Jurassic** Bajocian, Lias, R(h)aetic

**Jurisdiction** Authority, Bailiwick, Domain, Pashalic, Pashalik, Province, Soke(n), Sucken, Verge

**Juror(s), Jurist, Jury** Array, Assize, Blue-ribbon, Dicast, Grand, Hung, Inquest, Judges, Man, Mickleton, Old Fury, Pais, Panel, Panellist, Party, Petit, Petty, Sail, Savigny, Special, Strike, Tales, Talesman, Tribunal, Venire, Venireman, Venue

**Just(ice)** Adeel, Adil, Alcalde, All, Aristides, Astraea, Balanced, Barely, By a nose, Condign, Cupar, Deserved, E(v)en, Equal, Equity, Ethical, Even-handed, Exactly, Fair, Fair-minded, Forensic, Hardly, Honest, Impartial, Incorruptible, J, Jasper, Jeddart, Jethart, Jurat, Kangaroo, Legitimate, Mere(ly), Moral, Natural, Nemesis, Newly, Nice, Only, Palm-tree, Piso, Poetic, Precisely, Provost, Puisne, Pure and simple, Quorum, Reasonable, Recent, Restorative, Right(ful), Righteous, Rightness, Rough, Shallow, Silence, Simply, Solely, Sommer, Street, Themis, Tilt, Unbiased, Upright

**Justifiable, Justification, Justify** Apology, Autotelic, Avenge, Aver, Avowry, Clear, Darraign(e), Darrain(e), Darrayn, Defend, Deraign, Deserve, Excusable, Explain, Grounds, Merit, Pay off, Raison d'être, Rationale, Reason, Vindicate, Warrant

**Just so** Exactly, Sic, Stories

**Jut(ting)** Beetle, Bulge, Condyle, Overhang, Project, Protrude, Sail

**Jute** Burlap, China, Corchorus, Gunny, Hengist, Hessian, Horsa, Jew's mallow, Urena, Wool bale

**Juvenile** Childish, Pupa, Teenage(r), Yonkers, Young, Younkers, Youth

**Juxtaposition** Parataxis

# Kk

**K** Kelvin, Kilo, King, Kirkpatrick

**K2** Dapsang, Godwin Austen

**Kaffir** Shares, Xosa

**Kail, Kale** Borecole, Cabbage, Cole, Curly-greens, Ninepins

**Kaiser** Doorn, Wilhelm

**Kaleidoscope** Dappled, Motley, Myrioscope, Various

**Kangaroo** Bettong, Boodie-rat, Boomer, Boongary, Bounder, Brush, Cus-cus, Diprotodont, Euro, Forester, Joey, Macropodidae, Nototherium, Old man, Potoroo, Rat, Red, Steamer, Tree, Troop, Wallaby, Wallaroo

**Kansas** Sunflower

**Kaolin** Lithomarge

**Karate (costume)** Gi(e), Kung Fu, Shotokan, Wushu

**Karma** Destiny, Fate, Predestination

**Kate** Greenaway, Shrew

**Kayak** Bidarka

**Kebab** Cevapcici, Doner, Gyro, Impale, Satay, Sate, Shashli(c)k, Sosatie, Souvlakia

**Keel** Bilge, Bottom, Carina, Centreboard, Cheesecutter, Daggerboard, Even, Faint, False, Fin, List, Overturn, Skeg(g), Sliding

**Keen(ness), Keener** Acid, Acuity, Acute, Agog, Ardent, Argute, Aspiring, Astute, Athirst, Avid, Aygre, Bemoan, Bewail, Breem, Breme, Cheap, Coronach, Cutting, Dash, Devotee, Dirge, Eager, Edge, Elegy, Enthusiastic, Fanatical, Fell, Game, Gleg, Greet, Grieve, Hone, Hot, Howl, Into, Itching, Lament, Mourn, Mustard, Mute, Narrow, Nuts, Ochone, Ohone, Overfond, Partial, Peachy, Penetrating, Perceant, Persant, Pie, Raring, Razor, Ready, Red-hot, Rhapsodic, Sharp, Shrewd, Shrill, Slavering, Snell, Thirsting, Threnodic, Thrillant, Trenchant, Ululate, Wail, Whet, Zeal(ous)

**Keep(er), Keeping, Kept** Ames, Armature, Austringer, Caretaker, Castellan, Castle, Celebrate, Chatelain(e), Citadel, Conceal, Conserve, Curator, Custodian, Custody, Custos, Depositary, Depository, Detain, Donjon, Escot, Fastness, Finder, Fort, Gaoler, Goalie, Guard(ian), Harbour, Have, Hoard, → HOLD, Maintain, Nab, Net, Observe, On ice, Ostreger, Own, Park, Perpetuate, Pickle, Preserve, Retain, Safe, Safeguard, Save, Stay, Stet, Stock, Store, Stow, Stronghold, Stumper, Support, Sustain, Tower (of London), Warden, Withhold

**Keep back** Detain, Recoup, Reserve, Retard, Stave

**Keepsake** Memento, Relic, Souvenir, Token

**Keep under** Cow, Subdue, Submerge

**Keep up** Float

**Keg(s)** Barrel, Cask, Ks, Powder, Tub, Tun, Vat

**Kelly('s)** Eye, Gene, Ned

**Kelp** Varec

**Kelvin** Absolute, K

**Ken** Eyeshot, Grasp, Know(ledge), Purview, Range

**Kennel(s)** Guard, Home, House, Shelter

**Kent** Lathe, SE, Superman

**Kentuckian, Kentucky** Chicken, Corn-cracker, Derby, KY

**Kenya(n)** EAK, .ke, Luo, Masai, Mau Mau

**Kerala** Nair, Nayar

**Kerb** Edge, Gutter, Roadside

**Kerchief** Babushka, Bandan(n)a, Headcloth, Romal, Scarf

**Kernel** Copra, Core, Corn, Grain, Nucleus, Pine, Pistachio, Praline, Prawlin

**Kestrel** Bird, Hawk, Keelie, Stallion, Staniel, Stannel, Stanyel, Windhover

**Ket** Carrion, Wool

**Ketch** Jack

**Ketchup** Relish, Sauce, Tomato

**Kettle** Boiler, Caldron, Cauldron, Dixie, Dixy, Drum, Fanny, Pot, Tea, Turpin, War, Whistling

**Keuper** Trias

**Key(s), Keyhole** A, Ait, Allen, Alt, Answer, Ash, Atoll, B, Backspace, Basic, Black, C, Cardinal, Cay, Central, Chief, Chip, Church, Cipher, Claver, Clavis, Clew, Clink, Clue, Command, Control, Cornerstone, Crib, Cryptographer, D, Del(ete), Dichotomous, Digital, Dital, Dominant, E, Enter, Esc(ape), Essential, F, Flat, Florida, Fruit, Function, G, Grecque, Greek, High, Holm, Hot, Ignition, Important, Inch, Index, INS, Insert, Instrumental, Isle(t), Ivory, Kaie, King-pin, Largo, Latch, Legend, Linchpin, Locker, Low, Main, Major, Master, Minor, Natural, Note, Nut, Octachord, Opener, Open sesame, Oustiti, Outsiders, Pass(word), Passe-partout, Piano, Pipe, Pivot, Pony, Prong, Reef, Return, Semibreve, Shift, Signature, Skeleton, Space bar, Spanner, Spline, Stimulate, Subdominant, Supertonic, Swipecard, Tab, Table, Tipsy, Tonal, Tuning-hammer, Turning, Type, USB, Vital, Watch, Water, Wedge, West, White, Woodruff, Yale®

**Keyboard, Keypad** Azerty, Calliope, Console, Digitorium, Dvorak, Electronic, Manual, Martenot, Numeric(al), Piano, Pianola®, Qwerty, Spinet

**Keyholder** Chatelaine, Occupant, Resident, Tenant, Warder

**Key man** Islander, Kingpin

**Keynote** Line, Mese, Theme, Tonic

**Keystone** Cops, Crux, PA, Pennsylvania, Quoin, Sagitta, Voussoir

**Keyword** Kwic, Sesame

**Khan** Aga, Chagan, Cham, Serai, Shere

**Kibbutz** Collective

**Kick(ing)** Abandon, Back-heel, Banana, Bicycle, Boot, Buzz, Corner, Dribble, Drop, Fling, Flutter, Fly, Free, Frog, Garryowen, Goal, Grub, Hack, Heel, High, Hitch, Hoof, Lash, Nutmeg, Pause, Penalty, Pile, Place, Punce, Punt, Recalcitrate, Recoil, Recoyle, Renounce, Savate, Scissors, Shin, Sixpence, Speculator, Spice, Spot, Spur, Spurn, Squib, Stab, Tanner, Tap, Thrill, Toe, Up and under, Vigour, Volley, Wince, Yerk, Zip

**Kid(s)** Arab, Bamboozle, Befool, Billy, Brood, Chaff, Cheverel, Cheveril, Chevrette, Child, Chit, Cisco, Con, Delude, Doeskin, Fox, Giles, Goat, Hircosity, Hoax, Hocus, Hoodwink, Hum, Joke, Josh, Leather, Mag, Minor, Misguide, Nappe, Nipper, Offspring, Outwit, Pretend, Rag, Rib, Small fry, Spoof, Sprig, Suede, Sundance, → **TEASE**, Tot, Trick, Whiz(z), Wiz

**Kidnap(per), Kidnapped** Abduct, Captor, Enleve, Hijack, Nobble, Plagium, Shanghai, Snatch, Spirit, Steal

**Kidney(-shaped)** Character, Mettle, Nature, Nephron, Pronephros, Reins, Renal, Reniform, Sort, Type

**Kildare** Dr

**Kill(ed), Killer, Killing** Asp, Assassin, Attrit, Axeman, Bag, Battue, Behead, Biocidal, Boojum, Booth, Bump off, Butcher, Carnage, Carnifex, Category, Chance-medley, Choke, Comical, Coup de grâce, Croak, Crucify, Cull, Curiosity, Cut-throat, Deep six, Despatch, Destroy, Do in, Electrocute, Eradicate, Euthanasia, Execute, Exhibition, Exterminate, Extirpate, Fallen, For(e)do, Frag, Garotte, Germicide, Gun(man), Handsel, Hara kiri, Hatchet man, Hilarious, Homicide, Honour, Howitzer, Humane, Ice, Immolate, Infanticide, Insecticide, Jugulate, K, Knacker, Knock off, Liquidate, Lynch, Mactation, Matador(e), Mercy, Misadventure, Misdo, Mortify, Murder, Napoo, Necklace, Ninja, NK,

Off, Orc(a), Penalty, Pesticide, -phage, Pick off, Pip, Pogrom, Predator, Prolicide, Put down, Quell, Quietus, Regrate, Sacrifice, Serial, Settle, Shochet, Shoot up, Slaughter, Slay(er), Slew, Smite, Snuff, Spike, Stifle, Stonker, Strangle, Swat, Tailor, Take out, Thagi, Thug(gee), Top, Toreador, Total, Vandal, Vaticide, Veto, Waste, Written off, Zap

**Killjoy** Crab, Puritan, Sourpuss, Spoilsport, Trouble-mirth, Wowser

**Kiln** Lime, Oast, Oven, Queen's tobacco pipe

**Kilometre** K, Km, Verst

**Kilt** Drape, Filabeg, Fil(l)ibeg, Fustanella, Phil(l)abeg, Phil(l)ibeg, Plaid, Tartan

**Kimono** Yukata

**Kin(ship), Kin(sman)** Ally, Family, Kith, Like, Nearest, Phratry, Relation, Sib(b), Sybbe

**Kind(ly)** Akin, Amiable, Avuncular, Benefic, Benevolent, Benign, Boon, Breed, Brood, Brotherly, Category, Class, Clement, Considerate, Doucely, Favourable, Gender, Generic, Generous, Genre, Gentle, Genus, Good, Good-natured, Gracious, Human, Humane, Ilk, Indulgent, Kidney, Kin, Lenient, Manner, Merciful, Modal, Nature, Nice, Sisterly, →SORT, Species, Strain, Strene, Thoughtful, Trine, Type, Understanding, Variety, Well-disposed, Ylke

**Kindle, Kindling** Accend, Fire, Ignite, Incense, Incite, Inflame, Kitten, →LIGHT, Litter, Lunt, Spark, Stimulate, Teend, Tind, Tine, Touchwood, Tynd(e)

**Kindness** Aloha, Beau geste, Benevolence, Clemency, Favour, Humanity, Mitzvah, Ubuntu

**Kindred** Allied, Blood, Like, Related

**King(s), Kingly** Ard-ri(gh), Butcher, Card, Coatcard, Cobra, Csar, Elvis, English, ER, Evil, Face card, Highness, Hyksos, Kong, Ksar, Majesty, Monarch, Negus, Pearly, Peishwa(h), Penguin, Peshwa, Pharaoh, Philosopher, Potentate, R, Raja, Ransom, Reigner, Rex, Rial, Roi, Royalet, Ruler, Ryal, Sailor, Seven, Shah, Shepherd, Shilling, Sophy, Sovereign, Stork, Tsar, Tzar

## KINGS

| 2 letters: | Inca | Etzel | 6 letters: |
|---|---|---|---|
| GR | Jehu | Gwern | Acetes |
| Og | Knut | Gyges | Aegeus |
| Re | Lear | Herod | Alaric |
| | Loki | Hiram | Alfred |
| 3 letters: | Nudd | Idris | Alonso |
| Asa | Numa | Ixion | Amasis |
| Erl | Offa | James | Arthur |
| Ine | Olaf | Laius | Atreus |
| Lir | Otto | Lludd | Attila |
| Log | Rama | Louis | Baliol |
| Lud | Saul | Mesha | Brutus |
| Zog | Zeus | Midas | Canute |
| | | Minos | Casper |
| 4 letters: | 5 letters: | Mpret | Cheops |
| Agag | Apple | Ninus | Clovis |
| Agis | Asoka | Oscar | Daneus |
| Ahab | Balak | Osric | Darius |
| Atli | Basil | Penda | Duncan |
| Brut | Brute | Prial | Edmund |
| Ceyx | Creon | Priam | Egbert |
| Cnut | Cyrus | Rufus | Faisal |
| Cole | David | Uther | Farouk |
| Edwy | Edgar | | Fergus |
| Fahd | Edwin | | Harold |

Hassan
Hellen
Josiah
Lucomo
Ludwig
Lycaon
Memnon
Miledh
Nestor
Oberon
Ogyges
Oswald
Paphos
Peleus
Philip
Ramses
Rhesus
Robert
Rudolf
Utgard
Xerxes

**7 letters:**
Acestes
Admetus
Athamas
Baldwin
Balliol
Beowulf
Busiris
Caradoc
Casimir
Cecrops
Cepheus
Croesus
Danaiis
Diomede
Elidure
Evander
Gentius
Gordius

Gunther
Jupiter
Kenneth
Macbeth
Malcolm
Oedipus
Porsena
Ptolemy
Pyrrhus
Rameses
Regulus
Servius
Sigmund
Solomon
Stephen
Tarquin
Umberto

**8 letters:**
Abdullah
Adrastus
Aegyptus
Alberich
Alcinous
Alphonso
Cambyses
Cophetua
Diomedes
Endymion
Ethelred
Hezekiah
Jereboam
Jonathan
Leonidas
Melchior
Menander
Menelaus
Milesius
Nehemiah
Odysseus
Pentheus

Porsenna
Rehoboam
Sarpedon
Siegmund
Sisyphus
Tantalus
Thutmose
Thyestes
Tigranes
Waldener
Zedekiah

**9 letters:**
Agamemnon
Ahasuerus
Alexander
Atahualpa
Athelstan
Balthazar
Bretwalda
Brian Boru
Conchobar
Cunobelin
Cymbeline
Ethelbert
Ferdinand
Florestan
Frederick
Gambrinus
Gargantua
Gilgamesh
Idomeneus
Lionheart
Lobengula
Nabonidus
Pygmalion
Ras Tafari
Rodomonte
Sigismund
Theodoric
Tyndareus

Vortigern
Wenceslas

**10 letters:**
Artaxerxes
Belshazzar
Cadwaladar
Caractacus
Erechtheus
Maximilian
Ozymandias
Tarquinius
Wenceslaus

**11 letters:**
Charlemagne
Constantine
Hardicanute
Jehoshaphat
John Balliol
Melchizedek
Mithridates
Prester John
Sennacherib
Tutenkhamun

**12 letters:**
Ashurbanipal
Wayland Smith

**13 letters:**
Chulalongkorn

**14 letters:**
Harold Harefoot
Nebuchadnezzar
Servius Tullius
Sweyn Forkbeard
Tigrath-pileser
Uther Pendragon

**Kingdom, Kingship** An(n)am, Animal, Aragon, Arles, Armenia, Ashanti, Assyria, Austrasia, Babylonia, Barataria, Belgium, Bhutan, Bohemia, Brandenburg, Brunel, Buganda, Burgundy, Castile, Cilicia, Connacht, Connaught, Dahomey, Dalriada, Darfur, Denmark, Domain, Dominion, Edom, Elam, Fes, Fez, Fife, Galicia, Granada, Gwynedd, He(d)jaz, Heptarchy, Hijaz, Jordan, Kongo, Latin, Leon, Lesotho, Lydia, Lyonnesse, Macedon(ia), Media, Mercia, Meroe, Middle, Mineral, Moab, Morocco, Murcia, Naples, Navarre, Nepal, Netherlands, Neustria, Noricum, Northumbria, Norway, Nubia, Numidia, Parthia, Phyla, Plant, Pontic, Protista, Pruce, Prussia, Rayne, Realm, Reame, Reich, Reign, Royalty, Ruritania, Saba, Samaria, Sardinia, Saudi Arabia, Saul, Sennar, Sheba, Siam, Spain, Sphere, Swaziland, Sweden, Sweyn, Thailand, Throne, Tonga, Two Sicilies, UK, Ulster, Vegetable, Wessex, Westphalia, World
**Kingfisher** Alcyone, Halcyon, Kookaburra, Laughing jackass

**Kingmaker** Neville, Warwick
**King-of-arms** Clarenc(i)eux, Garter, Lyon, Norroy (and Ulster)
**King's evil** Crewels, Cruels, Scrofula
**Kingsley** Amis, Charles
**King's son** Dauphin, Delphin, P, Prince
**Kink(y)** Bent, Buckle, Crapy, Curl, Enmeshed, Flaw, Gasp, Knurl, Null, Nurl, Odd, Perm,
   Perverted, Quirk, SM, Twist, Wavy
▷ **Kink(y)** *may indicate* an anagram
**Kinkajou** Honey-bear, Potto
**Kiosk** Booth, Call-box, Stall, Tollbooth
**Kip(per)** At, Cure, Dosser, Doze, Limey, Nap, Nod, → SLEEPER, Sleepyhead, Smoke,
   → TIE
**Kipling** Beetle
**Kirkpatrick** K
**Kish** Rubbish, Scum, Tat
**Kismet** Destiny, Fate, Karma, Predestination
**Kiss(er), Kissing** Air, Baisemain, Buss, Butterfly, Caress, Contrecoup, Cross, Deep,
   French, Graze, Lip, Mouth, Mwah, Neck, Osculate, Pax(-board), Pax-brede, Peck, Pet,
   Plonker, Pree, Salue, Salute, Smack(er), Smooch, Smouch, Snog, Spoon, Suck face,
   Thimble, Tonsil hockey, Tonsil tennis, Trap, X, Yap
**Kit** Accoutrement, Amenity, Apparatus, Apparel, Christopher, Clobber, Clothes, Cub,
   Dress, Housewife, Hussif, Jack, Layette, Marlowe, Mess, → OUTFIT, Press, Rig, Set,
   Slops, Sportswear, Strip, Tackle, Toolbag, Uniform
**Kitchen** Caboose, Chuck-wagon, Cookhouse, Cookroom, Cuisine, Dinette, Galley,
   Percussion, Scullery, Soup, Thieves
**Kite** Belly, Bird, Box, Chil, Crate, Dragon, Elanet, Forktail, Gled(e), Hawk, Milvus, Paunch,
   Puttock, Rokkaku
**Kitsch** Naff
**Kitten(ish)** Cute, Kindle, Sexy
**Kittiwake** Bird, Gull, Hacklet, Haglet
**Kitty** Ante, Cat, Fisher, Float, Fund, Jackpot, Pool, Pot, Puss, Tronc
**Kiwi** Apteryx, Chinese gooseberry, Enzed, Erk, NZ, Ratitae
**Knack** Art, Facility, Faculty, Flair, Forte, Gift, Hang, Instinct, Nose, → TALENT, Technique,
   Trick
**Knacker** Castanet, Exhaust
**Knapsack** Kitbag, Musette
**Knapweed** Matfelon
**Knave(ry)** Bezonian, Bower, Boy, Cad, Card, Coatcard, Coistril, Coystril, Custrel, Dog,
   Drôle, Fripon, Jack(-a-napes), Jock, Loon, Makar, Maker, Nob, Noddy, One for his nob,
   Pam, Pur, Rapscallion, → RASCAL, Recreant, Ropery, Scoundrel, Skelm, Taroc, Tarot,
   Tom, Treachery, Two for his heels, Varlet, Villain
**Knead** Conche, Malax(ate), Massage, Mould, Pug, Pummel, Work
**Knee(s), Knee-cap, Knee-pan** Biscuit, Genicular, Genu, Hock, Housemaid's, Lap,
   Marrowbones, Patella, Poleyn, Popliteal, Punch, Rotula, Stifle, Whirl bone
**Knee-jerk** Unthinking
**Kneel(er)** Defer, Genuflect, Hassock, Kowtow, Prie-dieu, Truckle
**Knell** Bell, Curfew, Dirge, Peal, Ring, Toll
**Knicker(bockers), Knickers** Bloomers, Culottes, Directoire, Irving, Panties,
   Plus-fours, Rational dress, Shorts, Trousers
**Knick-knack** Bagatelle, Bibelot, Bric-à-brac, Gewgaw, Pretty(-pretty), Quip, Smytrie,
   Toy, Trangam, Trifle, Victoriana
**Knife, Knife edge** Anelace, Athame, Barlow, Barong, Bistoury, Blade, Boline, Bolo,
   Bolster, Bowie, Bread, Bush, Butterfly, Canelle, Carver, Carving, Case, Catling, Chakra,
   Chiv, Clasp, Cleaver, Couteau, Cradle, Cuttle, Cutto(e), Da(h), Dagger, Dirk, Fleam, Flick,

Fruit, Gamma, Gulley, Gully, Hay, Hunting, Jockteleg, Kard, Keratome, Kukri, Lance(t), Machete, Matchet, Moon, Near thing, Oyster, Palette, Panga, Paper, Parang, Paring, Peeler, Pen, Pigsticker, Pocket, Putty, Scalpel, Scalping, Sgian-dhu, Sgian-dubh, Sheath, Shiv, Simi, Skean-dhu, Slash, Snee, Snickersnee, Spade, Stab, Stanley, Steak, Sticker, Stiletto, Swiss army, Switchblade, Table, Toothpick, Tranchet, Trench

**Knight(hood)** Accolon, Aguecheek, Alphagus, Amfortas, Artegal, Balan, Banneret, Bayard, Bedivere, Black, Bliant, Bors, Britomart, Caballero, Calidore, Cambel, Caradoc, Carpet, Cavalier, Chevalier, Chivalry, Companion, Crusader, Douceper, Douzeper, Dub, Equites, Errant, Galahad, Gallant, Gareth, Garter, Gawain, Geraint, Giltspurs, Gladys, Grey, Guyon, Hospitaller, Jedi, Kay, KB, KBE, Kemper, KG, King's, Lamorack, La(u)ncelot, Launfal, Lionel, Lochinvar, Lohengrin, Maecenas, Malta, Mark, Medjidie, Melius, Modred, Mordred, N, Noble, Orlando, Paladin, Palmerin, Palomides, Papal, Paper, Parsifal, Perceforest, Perceval, Percival, Pharamond, Pinel, Precaptory, Preux chevalier, Queen's, Red Cross, Ritter, Round Table, St Columba, Samurai, Sir, Tannhauser, Templar, Teutonic, Tor, Trencher, Tristan, Tristram, Valvassor, Vavasour, White

**Knit(ting), Knitter, Knitwear** Aran, Cardie, Cardigan, Contract, Crochet, Double, Entwine, Fair Isle, Hosiery, Intarsia, Interlock, Intertwine, Jersey, Jumper, K, Marry, Mesh, Porosis, Pullover, Purl, Seam, Set, Stockinet, Sweater, Tricoteuse, Unite, Weave, Woolly, Wrinkle

**Knob(by)** Berry, Boll, Boss, Botoné, Bottony, Bouton, Bur(r), Cam, Caput, Cascabel, Croche, Gear, Handle, Heel, Hill, Inion, Knub, Knur(r), Mouse, Mousing, Node, Noop, Pellet, Pommel, Protuberance, Pulvinar, Push-button, Snib, Snub, Snuff, Stud, Torose, Trochanter, Tuber, Tuner, Wildfowl

**Knobless** Enodal

**Knock(er), Knockabout, Knocked, Knock(ed) down, (off, out), Knockout** Aunt Sally, Bang, Beaut, Biff, Blow, Bonk, Bump, Ca(a), Chap, Chloroform, Clash, Clour, Collide, Con, Criticise, Dad, Daud, Dawd, Degrade, Denigrate, Dent, Deride, Dev(v)el, Ding, Dinnyhauser, Dod, Elimination, Etherise, Eyeful, Floor, Grace-stroke, →HIT, Innings, KD, King-hit, Knap, KO, Lowse, Lowsit, Manhandle, Mickey Finn, Mud-slinger, Opportunity, Pan, Pink, Quietus, Rap, Rat-tat, Semi-final, Six, Skittle, Socko, Spat, Steal, Stop, Stoun, Strike, Stun(ner), Sucker punch, Tap, Technical, Thump, Tit(s), Wow

**Knock-kneed** In-kneed, Valgus

**Knot(ted), Knotty** Apollo, Baff, Band, Bend, Bind, Blackwall hitch, Bow, Bowline, Bur(r), Burl, Carrick-bend, Cat's paw, Clinch, Clove hitch, Cluster, Crochet, Diamond hitch, Englishman's, Entangle, Figure of eight, Fisherman's (bend), Flat, French, Geniculate, Gnar, →GNARL, Gordian, Granny, Half-hitch, Harness hitch, Hawser-bend, Herculean, Hitch, Interlace, Knag, Knap, Knar, Knob, Knur(r), Loop, Love(r's), Macramé, Macrami, Magnus hitch, Marriage-favour, Matthew Walker, Mouse, Nirl, Node, Nowed, Nub, Nur(r), Overhand, Peppercorn, Picot, Porter's, Problem, Prusik, Quipu, Reef, Rolling hitch, Root, Rosette, Running, Seizing, Sheepshank, Sheetbend, Shoulder, Shroud, Sleave, Slip, Slub, Spurr(e)y, Square, Stevedore's, Surgeon's, Sword, Tangle, Tat, Thumb, Tie, Timberhitch, Torose, Truelove, True lover's, Tubercle, Turk's head, Virgin, Wale, Wall, Weaver's (hitch), Windsor, Witch

**Know(how), Knowing(ly), Knowledge(able), Known** Acquaintance, Aptitude, Au fait, Autodidactic, Aware, Carnal, Cognition, Common, Compleat, Comprehend, Cred, Cum-savvy, Epistemics, Erudite, Experience, Expertise, Famous, Fly, Gnosis, Gnostic, Have, Hep, Hip, Info, Information, Insight, Intentional, Intuition, Jnana, Ken(t), Kith, Kydst, Lare, Light, Lore, Mindful, Omniscience, On, On to, Pansophy, Paragnosis, Party, Polymath, Positivism, Privity, Realise, Recherché, →RECOGNISE, Resound, Sapient, Savvy, Science, Scienter, Scilicet, Sciolism, Sciosophy, Shrewd, Smartarse, Smattering, Suss, Technology, Telegnosis, Understand(ing), Up, Versed, Wat(e), Weet(e), Well-informed, Well-read, Wis(dom), Wise(acre), Wist, Wit, Wonk, Wost, Wot

**Know-all** Arrogant, Besserwisser, Bumptious, Cognoscenti, Pansophist, Polymath, Poseur, Smart alec(k), Smart-arse, Smart-ass, Wiseacre

**Knuckle (bone)** Apply, Dolos, Fist, Hock, Joint, Ossein, Submit
**Koko** List
**Kookaburra** Laughing jackass, Settler's clock
**Kop** Berg, Spion
**Koran** Scripture, Sura(h)
**Korea(n)** Chosen, ROK
**Kosher** Approved, Genuine, Legitimate, Real
**Kowtow** Kneel
**Kremlin** Citadel, Fortress
**Kri** Masora
**Krypton** Kr
**Kudos** Credit, Glory, Praise
**Ku Klux Klan** Nightrider
**Kurd** Yezidi
**Kyanite** Disthene

# Ll

**L** Latitude, League, Learner, Left, Length, Liberal, Lima, Litre, Long, Luxembourg, Pound

**La** Indeed, My

**Label** Badge, Band, Book-plate, Brand, Care, Crowner, Designer, Docket, File, Identifier, Indie, Mark, Name tag, Own, Seal, Sticker, Style, Tab, Tag, Tally, Ticket, Trace

**Labiate** Catmint, Hoarhound, Horehound

**Laboratory** Elaboratory, Lab, Language, Skunkworks, Skylab, Space-lab, Studio, Workshop

**Labour(er), Laboured, Laborious** Aesthetic, Agonise, Apronman, Arduous, Begar, Birth, Bohunk, Carl, Casual, Childbirth, Chore, Churl, Confinement, Coolie, Cooly, Corvée, Cottager, Cottar, Culchie, Dataller, Day, Direct, Docker, Donkey work, Dwell, Effort, Emotional, Farmhand, Forced, Gandy-dancer, Ganger, Gibeonite, Grecian, Grind, Grunt, Hard, Hercules, Hod carrier, Hodge, Hodman, Ida, Indirect, Job, Journeyman, Kanaka, Katorga, Leaden, Manpower, Militant tendency, Moil, Navvy, Nemean, New, Okie, Operose, Opposition, Pain, Peon, Pioneer, Prole, Redneck, Roll, Rouseabout, Roustabout, Rouster, Seagull, Serf, Sisyphean, Slave, Spalpeen, Statute, Stertorous, Stint, Strive, Struggle, Sudra, Swagman, Sweated, Task, Tedious, The grip, The lump, Tiresome, →TOIL(S), Toss, Travail, Uphill, Vineyard, Wetback, →WORK(ER), Workforce, Workmen, Yakka

**Labrador** Innu, Retriever, Tea

**Laburnum** Golden chain

**Labyrinth** Daedalus, Maze, Mizmaze, Warren, Web

▷ **Labyrinthine** *may indicate* an anagram

**Lac** Lacquer, Lakh, Resin, Shellac, Tomans

**Lace, Lacy** Alençon, Babiche, Beat, Blonde, Bobbin, Bone, Bourdon, Brussels, Chantilly, Cluny, Colbertine, Dash, Dentelle, Drug, Duchesse, Embraid, Entwine, Filet, Galloon, Guipure, Honiton, Inweave, Irish, Jabot, Lash, Macramé, Malines, Mechlin, Mignonette, Mode, Net, Orris, Pearlin, Picot, Pillow, Point, Queen Anne's, Reseau, Reticella, Ricrac, Rosaline, Seaming, Shoestring, Shoe-tie, Spiderwork, Spike, Stay, Tat(ting), Tawdry, Thrash, Thread, Tie, Torchon, Trim, Troll(e)y, Truss, Tucker, Valenciennes, Venise, Weave, Welt, Window-bar

**Lacerate(d)** Ganch, Gash, Gaunch, Maul, Rent, Rip, Slash, Tear

**Lachrymose** Maudlin, Niobe, Tearful, Water-standing, →WEEPY

**Lack(ing), Lacks** Absence, Ab(o)ulia, Aplasia, Bereft, Catalexis, Dearth, Decadent, Devoid, Famine, Gap, Ha'n't, Insufficiency, Manqué, Meagre, Minus, →NEED, Paucity, Poor, Poverty, Privation, Remiss, Sans, Shortage, Shortfall, Shy, Sterile, Void, Want

**Lackadaisical** Languid, Listless, Torpid

**Lackaday** Haro

**Lackey** Boots, Doormat, Flunkey, Lapdog, Moth, Page, Poodle, Satellite, Skip-kennel, Stooge, Underling

**Lacklustre** Dull, Insipid, Matt

**Lack of confidence** Doubt, Scepsis

**Laconic** Blunt, Close-mouthed, Curt, Dry, Spartan, Succinct, Terse

**Lacquer** Coromandel, Enamel, Hair(spray), Japan, Shellac, →VARNISH

**Lad** Boy(o), Bucko, Callan(t), Chiel(d), Child, Geit, Gyte, Knight, Loonie, Master, Nipper, Shaver, Stableman, Stripling, Tad, Whipper-snapper

**Ladder(y)** Accommodation, Aerial, Bucket, Companion, Companionway, Etrier, Extension, Fish, Jack, Jacob's, Pompier, Potence, Rope, Run, Salmon, Scalado, Scalar, Scaling, Sea, Squash, Step, Stie, Sty, Stye, Trap, Turntable

▶ **Lade** *see* **LOAD(ED)**

**Ladle** Bail, Dipper, Divider, Punch, Scoop, Shank, Toddy

**Lady, Ladies** Baroness, Bevy, Bountiful, Burd, Chatelaine, Dame, Dark, Dinner, Don(n)a, Duenna, Female, First, Frau, Frow, Gemma, Godiva, Hen, Khanum, Lavatory, Leading, Loo, Luck, Maam, Madam(e), Martha, Memsahib, Muck, Nicotine, Palsgravina, Peeress, Powder room, Señ(h)ora, Shopping bag, Signora, Slate, Tea, WC, White, Windermere

▷ **Lady** *may indicate* an '-ess' ending

**Ladybird** Cushcow, Hen, Vedalia

▷ **Ladybird** *may indicate* a female of a bird family

**Ladykiller, Ladies' man** Bluebeard, Lothario, Masher, Poodle-faker, Wolf

**Lady of the Lake** Vivian

**Lady's fingers** Gumbo, Okra

**Lady's maid** Abigail

**Lady's tresses** Orchid

**Laevorotatory** L, Left

**Lag(gard), Lagging** Culture, Dawdle, Delay, Drag, Flag, Hysteresis, Inmate, Jailbird, Jet, Late(comer), Leng, → **LINGER**, Loiter, Prisoner, Retard, Slowcoach, Slowpoke, Straggle, Time, Tortoise, Trail

**Lager** Pils(e)ner

**Lagoon** Alexandrina, Aveiro, Barachois, Coorong, Haff, Pontchartrain, Pool, Salina, Saline, Vistula

▶ **Laic, Laid** *see* **LAY(ING)**

**Lair** Couch, Den, Earth, Haunt, Hideaway, Holt, Kennel, Lodge, Spiv, Warren

**Lake(s)** Alkali, Basin, Bayou, Carmine, Cirque, Cowal, Crater, Crimson, Cut off, L, Lacustrine, Lagoon, Lagune, Limnology, → **LOCH**, Lochan, Lode, Lough, Madder, Meer, Mere, Natron, Nyanza, Ox-bow, Poets, Pond, Pool, Pothole, Red, Reservoir, Salina, Salt, Shott, Soda, Tank, Tarn, Turlough, Vlei, Wine, Zee

---

## LAKES

| 2 letters: | Tana | Myall | Barlee |
|---|---|---|---|
| No | Thun | Nam Co | Bienne |
| | | Neagh | Bitter |
| 3 letters: | 5 letters: | Nyasa | Broads |
| Ewe | Atlin | Onega | Cayuga |
| Van | Chott | Pitch | Corrib |
| | Cowan | Playa | Edward |
| 4 letters: | Frome | Poopo | Geneva |
| Amin | Garda | Pskov | George |
| Bala | Gatun | Sevan | Kariba |
| Biel | Great | Tahoe | Kittle |
| Bled | Huron | Taupo | Ladoga |
| Chad | Ilmen | Tsana | Lugano |
| Como | Leman | Urmia | Malawi |
| Erie | Leven | Volta | Miveru |
| Erne | Lherz | | Mobutu |
| Eyre | Lower | 6 letters: | Monona |
| Kivu | Malar | Albert | Nakuru |
| Nyos | Morar | Argyle | Nam Tso |
| Pink | Mungo | Averno | Nyassa |
| Taal | Mweru | Baikal | Oneida |

Peipus
Placid
Poyang
Rudolf
Saimaa
St John
Te Anau
Tekapo
Vanern
Varese
Wanaka
Zurich

**7 letters:**
Amadeus
Aral Sea
Avernus
Axolotl
Balaton
Balqash
Bizerte
Dead Sea
Iliamna
Kara Kul
Katrine
Koko Nor
Lucerne
Managua
Mendota
Nipigon
Ontario
Red Deer
Rotorua
Sempach
Shkoder
St Clair

Toronto
Torrens
Turkana
Vattern

**8 letters:**
Balkhash
Bodensee
Carnegie
Dongting
Gairdner
Grasmere
Issyk-kul
Kinneret
Maggiore
Manitoba
Masurian
Menindee
Michigan
Naumachy
Okanagan
Onondaga
Regillus
Reindeer
Rosebery
Schwerin
Superior
Tiberias
Titicaca
Tonle Sap
Tungting
Veronica
Victoria
Wakatipu
Wanawaka
Winnipeg

**9 letters:**
Athabasca
Bangweulu
Champlain
Constance
Ennerdale
Everglade
Genfersee
Great Bear
Great Salt
Innisfree
Killarney
Macquarie
Manapouri
Maracaibo
Naumachia
Neuchatel
Nicaragua
Nipissing
Qinghai Hu
Serbonian
Thirlmere
Trasimeno
Ullswater
Wairarapa
Wast Water
Winnebago
Ysselmeer

**10 letters:**
Buttermere
Caspian Sea
Chautawqua
Clearwater
Great Slave
Hawes Water

Ijsselmeer
Malabo Pool
Miraflores
Mistassini
Of the Woods
Okeechobee
Okefenokee
Serpentine
Tanganyika
Washington
Windermere

**11 letters:**
Lesser Slave
Paralimnion
Stanley Pool

**12 letters:**
Derwentwater
Memphremagog
Waikaremoana
Winnipegosis

**13 letters:**
Bassenthwaite
Coniston Water
Crummock Water
Pontchartrain

**14 letters:**
Chiputneticook
Disappointment
Ennerdale Water

---

**Lake-dwelling** Crannog

**Lakeland** Cumbria

**Lam** Flee, Scram

**Lama** Dalai, Karmapa, Panchen, Tashi

**Lamb(skin)** Baa, Barometz, Beaver, Budge, Bummer, Cade, Canterbury, Caracul, Cosset, Ean(ling), Elia, Fat, Fell, Grit, Innocent, Keb, Larry, Noisette, Paschal, Persian, Poddy, Rack, Shearling, Target, Yean(ling)

**Lambent** Flickering, Glowing, Licking

**Lambert** Constant, L

**Lame(ness)** Accloy, Claude, Cripple, Crock, Game, Gammy, Gimp(y), Halt, Hamstring, Hirple, Hors de combat, Maim, Main, Spavined, Springhalt, Stringhalt, Useless, Weak

**Lament(able), Lamentation, Lamenter** Bemoan, Bewail, Beweep, Boo-hoo, Complain, Croon, Cry, Deplore, Dire, Dirge, Dumka, Dump, Elegy, Funest, Jeremiad, Jeremiah, Keen, Meane, Mein, Mene, Moon, Mourn, Ochone, Paltry, Piteous, Plain(t), Regret, Repine, Sigh, Sorry, Threne, Threnody, Ululate, →WAIL, Wel(l)away, Welladay, Yammer

**Lamia** Deadnettle

**Lamina(te), Laminated** Film, Flake, Folium, Formica®, Lamella, Layer, Plate, Scale, Table, Tabular, Veneer

**Lamp(s)** Aladdin's, Aldis, Anglepoise, Arc-light, Argand, Blow, Bowat, Bowet, Buat, Cru(i)sie, Crusy, Cru(i)zie, Davy, Daylight, Discharge, Diya, Eye, Eyne, Flame, Fluorescent, Fog, Gas, Geordie, Girandole, Glow, Head, Hurricane, Incandescent, Induction, Kudlik, Lampion, Lantern, Lava, Lucigen, Mercury vapour, Miner's, Moderator, Neon, Nernst, Nightlight, Padella, Pendant, Photoflood, Pilot, Platinum, Quartz, Reading, Riding, Safety, Sanctuary, Scamper, Searchlight, Signal, Sodium, Sodium-vapour, Spirit, Standard, Street, Stride, Striplight, Strobe, Stroboscope, Sun, Tail, Tantalum, Tiffany, Tilley, Torch, Torchier(e), Tungsten, Uplight(er), Veilleuse, Xenon

**Lampblack** Soot

**Lamplighter** Leerie, Spill

**Lampoon** Caricature, Parody, Pasquil, Pasquin(ade), Satire, Send-up, Skit, Spoof, Squib

**Lamprey** Hag, Lampern, Sandpride

**Lampshade** Eyelid

**Lancaster** Burt, Osbert, Red rose, War plane

**Lance** Dart, Harpoon, Impale, Morne, Pesade, Pike, Prisade, Prisado, Rejôn, Sand-eel, Spear, Speisade, Thermic, White arm

**Lancelet** Amphioxus

**Lancer** Bengal, Picador, Uhlan

**Lancet** Fleam

**Land(s), Landed** Acreage, Aina, Alight, Alluvion, Arpent, Bag, Beach, Bigha, Bovate, Brownfield, Byrd, Carse, Carucate, Cavel, Common, Conacre, Corridor, Country, Croft, Crown, Curtilage, Debatable, Demain, Demesne, Disbark, Disembark, Ditch, Doab, Dock, Earth, Edom, Enderby, Estate, Fallow, Farren, Farthingland, Fee, Feod, Feoff, Feud, Fief, Freeboard, Gair, Glebe, Gondwanaland, Gore, Graham, Greenfield, Ground, Hide, Holding, Holm, Holy, Horst, Ind, Innings, Isle, Isthmus, Kingdom, La-la, Lathe, Laurasia, Lea, Leal, Ley, Light, Link, Machair, Maidan, Manor, Marginal, Marie Byrd, Mesnalty, Métairie, Moose pasture, Morgen, Mortmain, Nation, Net, Never-never, Nod, No man's, Odal, Onshore, Oxgang, Oxgate, Pakahi, Palmer, Pangaea, Panhandle, Parcel, Pasture, Peneplain, Peneplane, Peninsula, Piste, Plot, Ploughgate, Point, Polder, Pr(a)edial, Premises, Private, Promised, Property, Public, Purlieu, Queen Maud, Real estate, Realm, Realty, Reservation, Roman candle, Run, Rundale, Runrig, Rupert's, Ruritania, Savanna(h), Seigniory, Set-aside, Settle, Several, Smallholding, Soil, Spit, Splash down, Swidden, Tack, Taluk, Tenement, Terra(e), Terra-firma, Terrain, Territory, Thwaite, Tie, Tir na n'Og, Touchdown, Turbary, Tye, Udal, Unship, Ure, Van Diemen's, Veld(t), Victoria, Wainage, Waste, Whenua, Wilkes, Yird

▶ **Landfall** *see* **LANDSLIDE**

**Landing (craft, gear, stair, system)** Autoflare, Crash, Duck, Forced, Gallipoli, Gha(u)t, Half, Halfpace, Hard, Instrument, LEM, Module, Oleo, Omaha, Pancake, Pier, Quay, Quayside, Roman candle, Soft, Solar, Sol(l)er, Sollar, Splashdown, Three-point, Three-pricker, Touchdown, Undercarriage

**Landless** Dispossessed

**Landlock** Embay

**Landlord, Land owner** Absentee, Balt, Boniface, Bonnet laird, Copyholder, Eupatrid, Fiar, Franklin, Herself, Host, Innkeeper, Junker, Laird, Lessor, Letter, Licensee, Owner, Patron, Patroon, Proprietor, Publican, Rachman, Rentier, Squatter, Squattocracy, Squire, Squirearchy, Squireen, Thane, Yeoman, Zamindar(i), Zemindar

**Landmark** Cairn, Meith, Watershed

**Landmass** Angaraland, Laurasia

**Land right** Emphyteusis

**Landscape** Karst, Paysage, Picture, Saikei, Scene, Stoss and lee, Vista

**Landslide, Landfall** Avalanche, Earthfall, Éboulement, Lahar, Scree, Slip

**Landsman** Lubber

**Land tenure** Frankalmoign, Raiyatwari, Rundale, Runrig, Ryotwari

**Lane(s)** Alley, Bikeway, Boreen, Bus, Carriageway, Corridor, Crawler, Drangway, Drury, Express, Fast, Fetter, Gut, Inside, La, Loan, Lois, Loke, Lovers', Memory, Middle, Mincing, Nearside, Offside, Outside, Overtaking, Passage, Passing, Petticoat, Pudding, Ruelle, Sea-road, Slow, Twitten, Twitting, Vennel, Wynd

**Langerhans** Insulin, Islets

**Language(s)** Argot, Armoric, Artificial, Assembly, Auxiliary, Backslang, Basic, Body, Cant, Centum, Clinic, Command, Community, Comparative, Computer, →**COMPUTER LANGUAGE**, Dead, Demotic, Descriptive, Dialect, Estem, Formal, Georgian, Gothic, Heritage, High-level, Hobson-Jobson, Humanities, Idioglossia, Idiolect, Idiom, Inclusive, Jargon, Langue, Ledden, Legalese, Lingo, Lingua franca, Macaronic, Machine code, Median, Mellowspeak, Meta-, Mixed, Mobspeak, Modern, Mother tongue, Native, Natural, Neutral, Newspeak, Novelese, Object, Officialese, Parlance, Patois, Penutian, PERL, Philology, Pidgin, Plain, Polysynthetic, Pragmatics, Private, Procedural, Programming, Prose, Query, Rabbinic, Register, Relay, Rhetoric, Satem, Sea-speak, Second, Semitic, Sign, Slanguage, Sociolect, →**SPEECH**, Strong, Style, Symbolic, Synthetic, Target, Technobabble, Telegraphese, Terms, Tone, →**TONGUE**, Tropology, Tushery, Union, Vedic, Verbiage, Vernacular, Vocabulary, Wawa, Words, World

---

## LANGUAGES

### 3 letters:

| | | | |
|---|---|---|---|
| Ada | Krio | Balti | Latin |
| Bat | Lozi | Bantu | Lubon |
| Edo | Manx | Batak | Lunda |
| Fur | Mari | Cajun | Lyele |
| Giz | Maya | Carib | Makah |
| Gur | Motu | Chewa | Malay |
| Ibo | Naga | Cobol | Mande |
| Ido | Nakh | Dogon | Maori |
| Kwa | Nord | Doric | Masai |
| Lao | Nuba | Dutch | Mayan |
| Mam | Nupe | Dyula | Munda |
| Mon | Pali | Fanti | Ngoni |
| Neo | Pedi | Farsi | Nguni |
| San | Pict | Galla | Norse |
| Tai | Shan | Ganda | Oriya |
| Tiv | Shri | Gondi | Oscan |
| Twi | Sulu | Greek | Palau |
| | Susu | Gumbo | Papua |
| | Taal | Hausa | P-Celt |
| **4 letters:** | Thai | Hindi | Ponca |
| Ainu | Tshi | Hokan | Ponka |
| Avar | Tupi | Incan | Punic |
| Cham | Urdu | Indic | Sakai |
| Dani | Veps | Joual | Sango |
| Efik | Xosa | Kafri | Saxon |
| Erse | Zulu | Koine | Shona |
| Geez | Zuni | Kriol | Shono |
| Hopi | | Kuo-yu | Shuar |
| Igbo | **5 letters:** | Kwadi | Sindi |
| Inca | Aleut | Ladin | Sinha |
| Innu | Aryan | Lamba | Sintu |
| Komi | Azeri | Lamut | Sioux |

Sotho
Suomi
Swazi
Taino
Tajik
Tamil
Temne
Te reo
Tigre
Tonga
Turki
Ugric
Uzbeg
Uzbek
Venda
Vogul
Welsh
Wolof
Xhosa
Yakut
Yuman
Yupik

**6 letters:**
Adyahe
Adygei
Adyghe
Altaic
Apache
Arabic
Aranda
Asante
Aymara
Bahasa
Baluch
Basque
Basutu
Berber
Bihari
Bokmal
Brahui
Breton
Buryat
Celtic
Chadic
Coptic
Creole
Cymric
Danish
Dardic
Divehi
Eskimo
Evenki
Fantee

Fijian
Finnic
French
Fulani
Gaelic
Gagauz
Galibi
German
Gullah
Hebrew
Herero
Inupik
Italic
Jivaro
Kafiri
Ladino
Lahnda
Lakota
Lepcha
Lu-wian
Lycian
Lydian
Macush
Macusi
Manchu
Micmac
Mishmi
Mixtec
Na-Dene
Nepali
Novial
Nubian
Nyanja
Ostyak
Pahari
Paiute
Pakhti
Panoan
Papuan
Pashto
Pashtu
Polish
Pushto
Pushtu
Quapaw
Romany
Rwanda
Salish
Samoan
Shelta
Sherpa
Sindhi
Siouan
Slovak

Somali
Strine
Svanan
Syriac
Tanoan
Tartar
Telegu
Telugu
Tigray
Tongan
Tsonga
Tswana
Tuareg
Tungus
Turkic
Udmurt
Ugrian
Uralic
Yakama
Yoruba
Zyrian

**7 letters:**
Adamawa
Amboina
Amerind
Amharic
Aramaic
Ashanti
Austric
Avestan
Baluchi
Bengali
Bislama
Cabiric
Caddoan
Catalan
Chaldee
Chechen
Chinook
Chuvash
Cushite
Dhivehi
Dzongka
Elamite
Euskara
Faroese
Flemish
Frisian
Gagauzi
Gaulish
Guajiro
Guarani
Hamitic

Hittite
Hokkien
Ingrian
Inupiaq
Italian
Janlish
Japlish
Judezmo
Kannada
Khoisan
Kikapoo
Kirundi
Kurdish
Kushite
Lallans
Laotian
Lingala
Luganda
Malayan
Maleate
Malinke
Maltese
Marathi
Mashona
Miao-Yao
Mingrel
Miskito
Mordvin
Moriori
Nahuatl
Nauruan
Ndebele
Nilotic
Nynorsk
Nyungar
Occitan
Oceanic
Ossetic
Ottoman
Pahlavi
P-Celtic
Pehlevi
Persian
Pictish
Prakrit
Punjabi
Pushtoo
Quechua
Riksmal
Romance
Romanes
Romansh
Saharan
Sahrawi

Samnite
Samoyed
Serbian
Servian
Sesotho
Shawnee
Sinhala
Sinitic
Slovene
Sogdian
Sorbian
Spanish
Sudanic
Swahili
Swedish
Tagalog
Tahitan
Tibetan
Tlingit
Turkish
Turkmen
Umbrian
Uralian
Venetic
Volapuk
Voltaic
Walloon
Wendish
Wergaia
Yerkish
Yiddish

**8 letters:**
Akkadian
Albanian
Arawakan
Assamese
Balinese
Bulgaric
Cheremis
Cherkess
Chibchan
Chichewa
Creolian
Croatian
Cushitic
Dzongkha
Ethiopic
Etrurian
Etruscan
Faliscan
Fanagalo
Filipino
Frankish

Friesian
Goidelic
Gujarati
Gujerati
Gurkhali
Hiri-Motu
Illyrian
Japanese
Japhetic
Javanese
Judezono
Jugoslav
Kashmiri
Khoikhoi
Kickapoo
Kingwana
Kolarian
Kwakiutl
Landsmal
Lusatian
Makyalam
Malagasy
Mampruli
Mandarin
Matabele
Mikasuki
Moldovan
Mongolic
Mon-Khmer
Mordvine
Netspeak
Nez Perce
Old Dutch
Ossetian
Phrygian
Pilipino
Polabian
Rhaetian
Romanian
Romansch
Rumansch
Rumonsch
Salishan
Sanscrit
Sanskrit
Scythian
Setswana
Shemitic
Shoshone
Slavonic
Sumatran
Sumerian
Tahitian
Teutonic

Thracian
Tigrinya
Tshiluba
Tucanoan
Tungusic
Turanian
Turkoman
Tuvaluan
Ugaritic
Volscian
Wakashan
Warlpiri
Yanomani
Yugoslav

**9 letters:**
Abkhazian
Afrikaans
Algonkian
Algonquin
Anatolian
Brittonic
Brythonic
Cantonese
Chari-Nile
Cheremiss
Cingalese
Diglossia
Dravidian
Esperanto
Esthonian
Euskarian
Franglais
Goidhelic
Gujarathi
Gujerathi
Hottentot
Hungarian
Inuktitut
Iroquoian
Kabardian
Kamilaroi
Kiswahili
Landsmaal
Langue d'oc
Leizghian
Makyaalam
Malayalam
Marquesan
Messapian
Mongolian
Muskogean
Nostratic
Onondagan

Provençal
Putonghua
Roumanian
Roumansch
Sabellian
Sardinian
Semi-Bantu
Sinhalese
Tocharian
Tokharian
Tokharish
Tungurian
Ukrainian
Ursprache
Varangian
Winnebago

**10 letters:**
Algonquian
Araucanian
Athabascan
Athapaskan
Azerbayani
Beach-la-Mar
Bêche-la-Mar
Caprolalia
Circassian
Diachronic
Eteocretan
Finno-Ugric
Gallo-Roman
Halkomelom
Himyaritic
Hindustani
Indonesian
Kartvelian
Langue d'oil
Langue d'oui
Lithuanian
Macedonian
Malayalaam
Melanesian
Mingrelian
Montagnais
Muskhogean
Niger-Congo
Papiamento
Phoenician
Pima-pipogo
Police Motu
Portuguese
Proto-Norse
Rajasthani
Serbo-Croat

| | | | |
|---|---|---|---|
| Singhalese | Hokan-Siouan | Tessaraglot | **13 letters:** |
| Synchronic | Interglossa | Tupi-Guarani | Neo-Melanesian |
| Ugro-Finnic | Interlingua | Yuwaalaraay | Semito-Hamitic |
| Union Shona | Kordofanian | | Serbo-Croatian |
| Ural-Altaic | Langobardic | **12 letters:** | |
| Uto-Aztecan | Micronesian | Billingsgate | **14 letters:** |
| Vietnamese | Moeso-gothic | Gallo-Romance | Palaeo-Siberian |
| Wemba-Wemba | Nilo-Saharan | Idiom neutral | Thraco-Phrygian |
| | Old Prussian | Indo-European | |
| **11 letters:** | Osco-Umbrian | Norman French | **15 letters:** |
| Azerbaijani | Oto-Manquean | Platt-deutsch | Sahaptin-Chinook |
| Belarussian | Pama-Nyungan | Proto-Romance | |
| Celtiberean | Potawatomic | Sprachgefuhl | **16 letters:** |
| Dagestanian | Sino-Tibetan | Tibeto-Burman | Malayo-Polynesian |
| Finno-Ugrian | Sranantongo | Volga-Baltaic | |

**Languid, Languish** Die, Divine, Droop, Feeble, Flagging, Listless, Lukewarm, Lydia, Melancholy, Mope, Quail, Torpid, Wilt, Wither

**Languor** Lassitude

**Langur** Simpai, Wanderoo

**Lanky** Beanpole, Gangly, Gawky, Lean(y), Spindleshanks, Windlestraw

**Lanolin** Woolfat, Wool oil, Yolk

**Lantern** Aristotle's, Bowat, Bowet, Buat, Bull's eye, Chinese, Dark(e)y, Epidiascope, Episcope, Friar's, Glim, Japanese, Jaw, Lanthorn, Magic, Sconce, Stereopticon, Storm, Turnip

**Lanthanum** La

**Laodicean** Lukewarm

**Lap** Circuit, Drink, Gremial, Leg, Lick, Lip, Luxury, Override, Pace, Sypher

**Lapdog** Messan, Shough, Showghe, Yesman

▷ **Lapdog** may indicate 'greyhound'

**Lapel** Revers

**Laplander, Lapp** Saam(e), Sabme, Sabmi, Sami

**Lappet** Infula, Jardiniere

**Lapse** Aberration, Backslide, Drop, Error, Expire, Fa', Failure, Fall, Nod, Sliding, Trip

**Lapwing** Hornywink, Peewee, Teru-tero

**Larceny** Compound, Grand, Petty, Simple

**Larch** Hackmatack, Tamarack

**Lard** Enarm, Leaf, Saim, Seam(e)

**Larder** Buttery, Pantry, Spence, Springhouse

**Large(ness), Largest** Ample, Astronomical, Big, Boomer, Bulky, Bumper, Buster, Colossus, Commodious, Considerable, Decuman, Enormous, Epical, Extensive, Gargantuan, →**GIGANTIC**, Ginormous, Gog, Great, Grit, Gross, Handsome, Hefty, Helluva, Huge, Hulking, Humdinger, Humongous, Humungous, Kingsize, L, Labour intensive, Lg, Lunker, Macrocephaly, Magog, Man-sized, Massive, Maximin, Maximum, Mega, Outsize, Plethora, Prodigious, Rotund, Rounceval, Rouncival, Scrouger, Skookum, Slew, Slue, Snorter, Sollicker, Spacious, Spanking, Stonker, Stout, Swingeing, Tidy, Titanic, Vast, Voluminous, Well-endowed, Whopping

**Large number** Centillion, Fermi, Gazillion, Giga, Gillion, Googol, Googolplex, Grillion, Infinitude, Jillion, Lac, Lakh, Legion, Mille, Myriad, Nation, Nonillion, Nth, Octillion, Quadrillion, Quintillion, Raft, Regiment, Ruck, Scads, Sea, Septillion, Sextillion, Shitload, Slather, Slew, Slue, Squillion, Toman, Trillion, Zillion

**Largess** Alms, Charity, Frumentation, Generosity

**Lariat** Lasso, Reata, Riata

**Lark** Adventure, Aunter, Caper, Dido, Dunstable, Exaltation, Fool, Gammock, Giggle, Guy, Laverock, Magpie, Mud, Pipit, Prank, Spree

**Larkspur** Delphinium, Stavesacre

**Larva** Ammacoete, Amphibiotic, Amphiblastule, Aphid lion, Apteral, Army-worm, Augerworm, Axolotl, Bagworm, Bipinnaria, Bloodworm, Bookworm, Bot(t), Budworm, Cabbage worm, Caddice, Caddis(-worm), Cankerworm, Caterpillar, Cercaria, Chigger, Chigoe, Coenurus, Corn borer, Corn earworm, Cysticercoid, Doodlebug, Glass-crab, Grub, Hellgram(m)ite, Hydatid, Indusium, Instar, Jigger, Jointworm, Leather-jacket, Leptocephalus, Maggot, Mealworm, Measle, Microfilaria, Miracidium, Muckworm, Mudeye, Naiad, Nauplius, Neoteny, Nigger, Nymph, Ox-bot, Planula, Pluteus, Polypod, Porina, Redia, Screwworm, Shade, Silkworm, Spat, Strawworm, Tadpole, Trochophore, Trochosphere, Veliger, Warble, Water penny, Wireworm, Witchetty, Witchetty grub, Woodworm, Xylophage, Zoea

**Larynx, Laryngitis** Cricoid, Croup, Hives, Voice box

**Lascar** Seacunny, Tindal

**Lascivious(ness)** Crude, Drooling, Goaty, Horny, Lewd, Lubric, Paphian, Raunch(y), Satyric, Sotadic, Tentigo, Wanton

**Laser** Argon, Zap

**Lash(ed), Lashing(s)** Cat, Cilium, Firk, Flagellum, Flay, Flog, Frap, Gammon, Gripe, Knout, Mastigophora, Mousing, Oodles, Oup, Quirt, Riem, Rope's end, Scourge, Secure, Sjambok, Stripe, Swinge, Tether, Thong, Trice, Whang, →**WHIP**, Wire

**Lass(ie)** Colleen, Damsel, Maid, Quean, Queyn, Quin(i)e

**Lassitude** Accidie, Acedie, Inanition, Languor, Lethargy

**Lasso** Lariat, Lazo, Reata, Rope

**Last(ing)** Abide, Abye, Aft(er)most, →**AT LAST**, Boot-tree, Bottom, Cargo, Chronic, Coda, Dernier, Dure, Dying, Eleventh, Endmost, Endurance, Endure, Epilogue, Exist, Extend, Extreme, →**FINAL**, Finale, Hinder, Hindmost, Hold out, In extremis, Keep, Latest, Latter, Linger, Live, Load, Long-life, Model, Nightcap, Outstay, Perdure, Permanent, Perpetuate, Persist, Rearmost, Spin, Stable, Stamina, Stand, Stay, Supper, Survive, Swan-song, Tag end, Tail-ender, Thiller, Thule, Tree, Trump, Ult(imate), Ultima, Ultimo, Utmost, Uttermost, Wear, Weight, Whipper-in, Yester, Z

**Last drop** Supernaculum

**Last minute** Eleventh hour

**Last resort** Pis aller

**Last syllable** Ultima

**Last word(s)** Amen, Envoi, Farewell, L'envoy, Ultimatum, Zythum

**Latch** Bar, Clicket, Clink, Espagnolette, Lock, Night, Sneck, Thumb, Tirling-pin

**Late(r), Latest** After(wards), Afterthought, Anon, Behindhand, Brand-new, Chit-chat, Dead, Deid, Delayed, Eventual, Ex, Former, Gen, In arrears, Infra, Lag, Lamented, Manana, New(s), Overdue, Overrunning, Owl-car, Past, PM, PS, Recent, Serotine, Sine, Slow, State-of-the-art, Stop-press, Syne, Tardive, Tardy, Top shelf, Trendy, Umquhile, Update

**Late-learner** Opsimath

**Latent** Concealed, Delitescent, Dormant, Maieutic, Potential

**Lateral** Askant, Edgeways, Sideways

**Latex** Antiar, Dental dam, Gutta-percha, Jelutong, Ule

**Lath** Lag, Splat, Sway

**Lathe** Capstan, Mandrel, Mandril, Turret

**Lather** Flap, Foam, Froth, Sapples, Suds, Tan

**Latin(ist)** Biblical, Classical, Clausula, Criollo, Dago, Dog, Erasmus, Eyeti, Greaseball, High, Humanity, Italiot, L, Late, Law, Low, Medieval, Mexican, Middle, Modern, Neapolitan, New, Pig, Quarter, Rogues', Romanic, Romish, Scattermouch, Silver, Spic, Thieves', Uruguayan, Vulgar, Wop

**Latin-American** Criollo, Tico

**Latitude** Breadth, Celestial, Ecliptic, Free hand, Horse, L, Leeway, Liberty, Licence, Meridian, Parallel, Play, Roaring forties, Scope, Tropic, Width, Wiggle room

**Latrine** Ablutions, Benchhole, Bog, Cloaca, Furphy, Garderobe, Loo, Privy, Rear

**Latter** Last, Previous

**Latter-day** Recent, Saints, Young

**Lattice** Bravais, Cancelli, Clathrate, Crystal, Espalier, Grille, Matrix, Pergola, Red, Space, Treillage, Treille, Trellis

**Lattice-leaf** Ouvirandra

**Latvian** Lett

**Laud(able), Laudation, Lauder** Commend, Encomium, Eulogist, Extol, Harry, Hery, Praise, Worthily

**Lauderdale** Caballer

**Laugh(ing), Laughable, Laughter** Belly, Boff, Cachinnate, Cackle, Canned, Chortle, Chuckle, Cod, Corpse, Democritus, Deride, Derision, Fit, Fou rire, Gas, Gelastic, Giggle, Goster, Guffaw, Ha, He-he, Ho-ho, Homeric, Hoot, Horse, Hout, Howl, Irrision, Isaac, Jackass, Jocular, Last, Lauch, Leuch, Levity, Ludicrous, →MIRTH, Mock, Nicker, Peal, Present, Riancy, Riant, Rich, Rident, Ridicule, Risus, Scream, Snigger, Snirt(le), Snort, Stitches, Tehee, Titter, Yo(c)k

**Laughing-stock** Outspeckle, Sport

**Launcelot** Gobbo

**Launch(ing), Launcher, Launch pad** Bazooka, Begin, Blast-off, Catapult, Chuck, Cosmodrome, Countdown, Debut, ELV, Fire, Float, Hurl, Initiate, Introduce, Lift-off, Moonshot, Motoscalp, Opening, Pioneer, Presentation, Release, Rolling, Roll out, Send, Shipway, Shot, Slipway, Start, Steam, →TOSS, Unstock, Upsend, VTO

**Launder, Laund(e)rette, Laundress, Laundry** Bagwash, Blanchisseuse, Clean, Clear starcher, Coin-op, Lav, Linen, Steamie, Tramp, Transfer, Wash(ery), Washhouse, Whites

**Laurel(s)** Aucuba, Bay, Camphor, Cherry, Daphne, Japan, Kalmia, Kudos, Mountain, Pichurim, Rose (bay), Sassafras, Spicebush, Spotted, Spurge, Stan, Sweet-bay, True

**Laurence** Sterne

**Lava** Aa, Block, Bomb, Coulée, Cysticercus, Dacite, Flood basalt, Lahar, Lapilli, Magma, Mud, Nuée ardente, Pahoehoe, Palagonite, Pillow, Pitchstone, Plug, Pumice, Pyroclast, Scoria, Tephra, Toadstone

**Lavatory** Ajax, Bogger, Brasco, Can, Carsey, Carzey, Cludgie, Comfort station, Convenience, Cottage, Dike, Draught, Dunnakin, Dunny, Dyke, Earth closet, Elsan®, Facilities, Forica, Furphey, Gents, Heads, Jakes, Jane, John, Kars(e)y, Karzy, K(h)azi, Kleinhuisie, Kybo, Ladies, Lat(rine), Loo, Necessary, Netty, Office, Outhouse, Pissoir, Portaloo®, Privy, Rear(s), Reredorter, Shithouse, Shouse, Siege, Smallest room, Superloo, Throne, Thunderbox, Toilet, Toot, Tout, Urinal, Washroom, WC

**Lave** Lip, Wash

**Lavender** Aspic, Plumbago, Sea, Spike

**Lavengro** Borrow

**Laver** Alga, Moabite, Nori, Ore-weed

**Lavish** Barmecidal, Copious, Excessive, Expensive, Extravagant, Exuberant, Flush, Free, Fulsome, Generous, Liberal, Lordly, Lucullan, Lush, Palatial, Prodigal, Profuse, Regal, Shower, Slap-up, Sumptuous, Unsparing, Wanton, Waste

**Law(ful), Laws** Abingdon, Act, Agrarian, Anti-trust, Ass, Association, Avogadro's, Babo's, Bar, Barratry, Bernoulli's, →BILL, Biogenetic, Blue-sky, Bode's, Bonar, Bourlaw, Boyle's, Bragg's, Brehon, Brewster's, Brocard, Buys Ballot's, Byelaw, Byrlaw, Cain, Canon, Capitulary, Case, Chancery, Charles's, Civil, Code, Combination, Common, Constitution, Corn, Coulomb's, Criminal, Cupar, Curie's, Curie-Weiss, Cy pres, Dalton's, Dead-letter, Decree, Decretals, Decretum, De Morgan's, Deodand, Dharma, Dictate, Digest, Din, Distributive, Dry, Edict, Einstein's, Enact, Excise, Fiqh, Forensic, Forest, Fuero, Fundamental, Fuzz, Game, Gas, Gay-Lussac's, Graham's, Gresham's, Grimm's, Grotian, Haeckel's, Halal, Halifax, Hardy-Weinberg, Henry's, Hess's, Homestead, Hooke's, Hubble's, Hudud, Hume's, International, Irade, Iure, Joule's, Jura, Jure, Jus, Kain,

Kashrut(h), Kepler's, Kirchhoff's, Labour, Land, Lay, Legal, Leibniz's, Lemon, Lenz's, Licit, Lien, Liquor, Lor(d), Losh, Lydford, Lynch, Magdeburg, Mariotte's, Martial, May, Megan's, Mendel's, Mercantile, Military, Mishna(h), Mishnic, Moral, Mosaic, Murphy's, Natural, Newton's, Noahide, Nomistic, Nomology, Nomothetic, Octave, Ohm's, Oral, Ordinance, Pandect, Parity, Parkinson's, Pass, Penal, Periodic, Planck's, Plebiscite, Plod, Poor, Principle, Private, Public, Rape shield, Regulation, Rhodian, Roman, Rubric, Rule, Salic, Salique, Scout, Sharia(h), Sheria(t), Shield, Shulchan Aruch, Snell's, Sod's, →STATUTE, Statute book, Stefan's, Stokes, Sumptuary, Sunna, Sus(s), Sword, Table, Talmud, Tenet, The (long) robe, Thorah, Thorndike's, Torah, Tort, Tradition, Twelve Tables, Ulema, Unwritten, Use, Valid, Verner's, Vigilante, Written

**Lawbreaker, Lawless(ness)** Anarchy, Anomie, Anomy, Antinomian, Bushranger, Desperado, Offender, Piratical, Rowdy, Ruffian, Wild and woolly

**Lawmaker, Lawman, Lawyer** Alfaqui, Ambulance chaser, Att(orney), AV, Avocat, Avvogadore, Barrack room, Barrister, Bencher, BL, Bluebottle, Bramble, Brief, Bush, Cadi, Canon, Coke, Counsel, DA, Decemvir, Deemster, Defence, Dempster, Doge, Draco, Eagle(t), Earp, Enactor, Fiscal, Greenbag, Grotius, Hammurabi, Jurisconsult, Jurist, Juvenal, Legal eagle, Legist, Mooktar, Moses, MP, Mufti, Mukhtar, Nomothete, Notary, Penang, Pettifoggers, Philadelphia, Proctor, Procurator fiscal, Prosecutor, Rabbi, Sea, Shirra, Shyster, Silk, Solicitor, Spenlow, Stratopause, Talmudist, Templar, Thesmothete, Vakil, Writer, WS

**Lawn** Cambric, Cloth, Grass, Green, Linen, Ruche, Sward, Turf

**Lawrence** DH, Ross, Shaw, TE

**Lawrencium** Lr

**Lawsuit** Action, Case, Cause, Plea, Trover

▸ **Lawyer(s), Lawman** *see* LAWMAKER

**Lax(ity)** Freedom, Inexact, Laissez-aller, Latitude, Lenience, Loose, Remiss, →SLACK, Wide, Wide-open

▹ **Lax** *may indicate* an anagram

**Laxative** Aloin, Aperitive, Cascara, Cassia, Cathartic, Eccoprotic, Elaterin, Elaterium, Glauber's salt, Gregory (powder), Hydragogue, Ispaghula, Loosener, Magnesia, Physic, Purgative, →PURGE, Saline, Senna-pod, Taraxacum

**Lay(ing), Layman, Laic, Laid, Laity** Air, Amateur, Antepost, Aria, Ballad, Bed, Bet, Blow, Chant, Christian Brothers, Civil, Ditty, Drop, Earthly, Egg, Embed, Fit, Impose, Impropriator, Lied, Lodge, Man, Minstrel, Oat, Oblate, Ode, Ordinary, Outsider, Oviparous, Oviposit, Parabolanus, Pose, Secular, Set, Sirvente, →SONG, Songsmith, Sypher, Temporalty, Tertiary, Tribal, Untrained, Wager, Warp

**Layabout** Corner boy, Deadbeat, Idler, Loafer, Lotophagus, Ne'er-do-well, Oaf, Slob, Wastrel

**Lay-by** Rest stop

**Layer(s)** Abscission, Aeuron(e), Ancona, Appleton, Battery, Bed, Boundary, Cake, Caliche, Cambium, Canopy, Chromosphere, Cladding, Coating, Crust, D, Depletion, E, Ectoplasm, Ectosarc, Ekman, Epiblast, Epilimnion, Epitaxial, Epitheca, Epithelium, Erathem, E-region, Exine, Exocarp, F, Film, Flake, Friction, Ganoin, Germ, Gossan, Gozzan, Granum, Ground, Heaviside, →HEN, Herb, Hypotheca, Intima, Inversion, Kennelly(-Heaviside), Kerf, Lamella, Lamina, Lap, Leghorn, Lenticle, Lie, Malpighian, Media, Mesoblast, Miocene, Ozone, Palisade, Pan, Patina, Paviour, Photosphere, Ply, Retina, Reversing, Rind, Scale, Scattering, Sclerite, Screed, Shrub, Skim, Skin, Skiver, Sliver, Spathic, Stratify, Stratopause, Stratum, Substratum, Tabular, Tapetum, Tier, Tremie, Trophoblast, Trophoderm, Uvea, Varve, Vein, Velamen, Veneer

**Lay-off** Dismiss, Hedge, Redundance, Suspend

**Lay-out** Ante, Design, Expend, Fell, Format, Map, Mise, Pattern, Spend, Spreadsheet, Straucht, Straught, Streak, Streek, Stretch

**Laze, Laziness, Lazy (person), Lazybones** Bed-presser, Bone idle, Bummer, Cabbage, Couch potato, Faineant, Grunge, Hallian, Hallion, Hallyon, Indolent, Inert, Lackadaisical,

Laesie, Languid, Layabout, Lie-abed, Lig(ger), Lime, Lither, Loaf, Lotus-eater, Lusk, Mollusc, Ne'er-do-well, Oblomovism, Resty, Shiftless, Sleepyhead, Sloth, Slouch, Slug(-a-bed), Sluggard, Susan, Sweer, Sweir, Timeserver, Underactive, Veg, Workshy

▷ **Lazily** *may indicate* an anagram

**Lea** Grass, Meadow

**Leach(ing)** Cheluviation, Lixivial, Ooze

**Lead(er), Leading, Leadership** Ag(h)a, Ahead, Akela, Amakosi, Anglesite, Arch, Article, Atabeg, Atabek, Ayatollah, Bab, Bear away the bell, Bellwether, Black, Bluey, Bodhisattva, Bonaparte, Brand, Cable, Cade, Calif, Caliph, Came, Capitano, Capo, Captain, Castro, Caudillo, Causal, Centre, Ceruse, Chair, Cheer, Chief, Chieftain, Chiliarch, Chin, China white, Choragus, Choregus, CO, Codder, Concert-master, Condottiere, Conducive, Conduct, Corporal, Coryphaeus, Coryphee, Czar, Dalai Lama, De Gaulle, Demagogue, Dictator, Director, Dominant, Drail, Duce, Dux, Editorial, Element, Escort, Ethnarch, Extension, Figurehead, First, Flagship, Flake-white, Floor, Foreman, Foremost, Franco, Front man, Frontrunner, Fugleman, Fu(e)hrer, Gaffer, Gandhi, Garibaldi, General, Gerent, Go, Graphite, Guide(r), Halter, Hand, Head, Headman, Headmost, Headnote, Hegemony, Heresiarch, Hero, Hetman, Hiawatha, Hierarch, Honcho, Idi, Imam, Imaum, Induna, Ink(h)osi, Inveigle, Jason, Jefe, Jeune premier(e), Jump, Juve(nile), Kabir, Kame, King, Ksar, Leam, Leash, Litharge, Livid, Loss, Lost, Lyam, Lym(e), Mahatma, Mahdi, Main, Market, Marshal, Massicot, Masticot, Mayor, Meer, Mehdi, Minium, Mir, Mussolini, Nanak, No 1, Nomarch, Nose, Numero uno, Omrah, Open, Pace car, Pacemaker, Pacesetter, Padishah, Panchen Lama, Patriarch, Pb, Petain, Pilot, Pioneer, Pit, Plumb(um), Plummet, PM, Pointer, Precede, Precentor, Premier(e), President, Price, Primo, Rangitara, Ratoo, Rebbe, Rebecca, Red, Role, Ruler, Sachem, Sagamore, Saturn, Saturn's tree, Scotlandite, Scout, Scuddaler, Scudler, Senior, Shaper, Sharif, Sheik(h), Sixer, Skipper, Skudler, Soaker, Soul, Sounding, Spearhead, Stalin, Staple, Star, Start, Sultan, Supremo, Taoiseach, Tecumseh, Tenno, Tetraethyl, Top banana, Top dog, Trail(blazer), Tribune, Tsaddik, Tsaddiq, Tsar, Tzaddik, Up, Usher, Vaivode, Van(guard), Vanadinite, Va(u)nt, Vaunt-courier, Voivode, Vozhd, Waivode, Wali, Warlord, Whip, White, Whitechapel, Wulfenite, Yeltsin, Youth, Zaddik, Zia

▷ **Lead(s), Leaders** *may indicate* first letters of words

**Leaden** Flat, Plumbeous, Saturnine

**Lead-glance** Galena

**Leading lady** Eve

**Leading to** Pre

**Leaf(y), Leaves** Acanthus, Acrospire, Amphigastrium, Amplexicaul, Ascidia, At(t)ap, Baccy, Betel, Blade, Bract, Carpel, Cataphyll, Cladode, Coca, Compound, Consent, Corolla, Costate, Cotyledon, Crocket, Dolma, Drop, Duff, Dutch, Fig, Finial, Foil, Foliage, Foliar, Folio(se), Folium, Frond, Frondose, Glume, Gold, Green, Holiday, Induviae, Jugum, K(h)at, Lattice, Lilypad, Lobe, Lobulus, Maple, Megaphyll, Microphyll, Needle, Nervate, Out, P, Pad, Page, Pan, Paper, Phyllid, Phyllode, Phyllome, Pot, Qat, Recto, Repair, Riffle, Rosula, Salad, Scale, Sclerophyll, Secede, Sepal, Sheet, Siri(h), Skim, Skip, Spathe, Sporophyll, Stipule, Succubus, Tea, Ternate, Title, Tobacco, TTL, Unicostate, Valve, Verso, Vert, Vine, Withdraw

**Leafhopper** Thrip

**Leafless** Ebracteate, Nudicaul, Scape

**Leaflet** At(t)ap, Bill, Bracteole, Circular, Dodger, Flier, Fly-sheet, Foliolose, Handbill, Hand-out, Pinna, Pinnula, Prophyll, Stipel, → TRACT

**League** Achaean, Alliance, Amphictyony, Arab, Band, Bund, Compact, Decapolis, Delian, Denominal, Entente, Federation, Gueux, Guild, Hanse(atic), Holy, Ivy, L, Land, Little, Major, Minor, Muslim, Nations, Parasang, Primrose, Redheaded, Rugby, Solemn, Super, Union, Ypres, Zollverein, Zupa

**Leak(y)** Bilge, Drip, Escape, Extravasate, Gizzen, Holed, Holey, Ooze, Pee, Porous, Run, Seepage, Sype, Transude, Trickle, Urinate, Wee, Weep, Wee-wee

**Leak-proof** Airtight

**Leamington** Spa

**Lean(ing)** Abut, Aslope, Atilt, Barren, Batter, Bend, Cant, Careen, Carneous, Carnose, Griskin, Heel, Hike out, →INCLINE, Lie, Lig(ge), List, Minceur, Partiality, Prop, Propend, Rake, Rawboned, Rely, Rest, Scraggy, Scrawny, Skinny, Spare, Stoop, Taste, Tend, Thin, Tilt, Tip, Walty, Wiry

**Leander** Abydos

**Lean-to** Skillion

**Leap(ing), Leapt** Assemblé, Bound, Brisé, Cabriole, Caper, Capriole, Cavort, Clear, Croupade, Curvet, Echappé, Entrechat, Falcade, Fishdive, Flying, Frisk, Galumph, Gambade, Gambado, Gambol, Jeté, Jump, Loup, Luppen, Ollie, Over, Pigeon-wing, Pounce, Pronk, Quantum, Sally, Salto, Somersa(u)lt, Somerset, →SPRING, Stag, Transilient, Vault, Volte

**Leap year** Bissextile, Penteteric

**Lear** Edward, King, Nonsense

**Learn(ed), Learner, Learning** Associative, Beginner, Blended, Blue, Bluestocking, Chela, Classical, Con, Cram, Culture, Discipline, Discover, Discrimination, Distance, Doctor, Don, Erudite, Erudition, Gather, Get, Glean, Greenhorn, Hear, Index, Insight, Instrumental, Kond, L, Latent, Lear(e), Leir, Lere, Letters, Lifelong, Literate, Literati, Literato, Lore, Lucubrate, Machine, Master, Memorise, Mirza, Mug up, New, →NOVICE, Open, Opsimath(y), Pandit, Polymath, Programmed, Pundit, Pupil, Rep, Rookie, Savant, Scan, Scholar(ship), Scient, See, Sleep, Starter, Student, →STUDY, Tiro, Trainee, Tutee, Tyro, Visile, Wise, Wit

**Lease(-holder)** Charter, Farm, Feu, Gavel, Hire, Let, Long, Novated, →RENT, Set(t), Sublet, Subtack, Tack, Tacksman

**Leash** Lead, Lune, Lyam, Lym(e), Slip, Tether, Three, Trash, Triplet

**Least** Barest, Minimum, Rap

**Leather(s), Leather-worker, Leathery** Aqualeather, Artificial, Bouilli, Bouilly, Box-calf, Brail, Buckskin, Buff, Cabretta, Calf, Capeskin, Chammy, Chamois, Chaps, Checklaton, Cheverel, Chevrette, Chrome, Cordovan, Cordwain, Corium, Counter, Cowhide, Crispin, Crocodile, Cuir(-bouilli), Currier, Deacon, Deerskin, Diphthera, Doeskin, Dogskin, Durant, Fair, Foxing, Goatskin, Grain, Hide, Hog-skin, Horsehide, Japanned, Kid, Kip(-skin), Labretta, Lacquered, Lamp, Levant, Marocain, Maroquin, Mocha, Morocco, Mountain, Nap(p)a, Neat, Nubuck®, Oak, Ooze, Oxhide, Paste-grain, Patent, Pigskin, Plate, Rand, Rawhide, Rexine®, Riem(pie), Roan, Rock, Rough-out, Russet, Russia, Saffian, Shagreen, Shammy, Sharkskin, Shecklaton, Sheepskin, Shoe, Skiver, Slinkskin, Snakeskin, Spetch, Split, Spruce, Spur, Spur-whang, Stirrup, Strand, Strap, Strop, Suede, Tan, Taw, Thong, Upper, Wallop, Wash, Waxed, Welt, White, Whitleather, Yuft

**Leatherneck** Marine, RM

**Leave(r), Leaving(s), Leave off** Abandon, Abiturient, Abscond, Absit, Absquatulate, Acquittal, Adieu, Annual, Avoid, Bequeath, Betake, Blessing, Blow, Broken meats, Bug, Compassionate, Congé, Congee, Days off, Debris, Decamp, Depart, Desert, Desist, Devisal, Devise, Ditch, Evacuate, Except, Exeat, Exit, Exodus, Extrude, Flit, Forego, Forget, Forgo, Forsake, French, Furlough, Gardening, Garlandage, Get out, →GO, Holiday, Inspan, Ish, Legate, Liberty, Licence, Log off, Maroon, Mass, Maternity, Mizzle, Nick, Omit, Orts, Pace, Parental, Park, Part, Paternity, →PERMISSION, Permit, →QUIT, Repair, Residue, Resign, Retire, Sabbatical, Scapa, Scat, Scram, Shore, Sick(ie), Skedaddle, Skidoo®, Stick, Strand, Vacate, Vade, Vamo(o)se, Will, Withdraw

**Leaven** Barm, Ferment, Yeast

**Lebanese, Lebanon** Druse, RL

**Lecher(ous), Lechery** Gate, Goaty, Lascivious, Libertine, Lickerish, Lustful, Profligate, Rake, Randy, Roué, Salaciousness, Satirisk, Satyr, Silen, Whoremonger, Wolf

**Lectern** Ambo, Bookstand, Desk, Eagle, Oratory

**Lecture(r), Lectures, Lecturing** Address, Aristotelian, Chalktalk, Course, Creed, Curtain, Dissert(ator), Docent, Don, Earful, Erasmus, Expound, Harangue, Homily, Hulsean, Jaw, Jawbation, Jobe, L, Lantern, Lector, Moralise, Orate, Pi-jaw, Prelect, Privatdocent, Prone, Rate, Read(er), Rede, Reith, Reprimand, Roasting, Rubber chicken circuit, Scold, Sententious, →**SERMON**, Spout, Take to task, Talk, Teacher, Teach-in, Tongue-lashing, Wigging, Yaff

**Ledge** Altar, Berm, Buttery-bar, Channel, Fillet, Gradin(e), Linch, Miserere, Misericord(e), Nut, Rake, Scarcement, Settle, →**SHELF**, Sill, Subsellium, Window (sill)

**Ledger** Book, General, Purchase, Register

**Lee(s)** Dregs, Dunder, Grout, Heeltaps, Sediment, Shelter, Ullage

**Leech** Annelid, Bleeder, Gnathobdellida, Hirudinea, Horse, Medicinal, Parasite, Rhynchobdellida

**Leek** Allium, Fouat, Fouet, Porraceous, Rocambole, Sengreen

**Leer** Eliad, Fleer, Oeillade, Ogle, Perv

**Leeway** Drift, Flexibility

**Left (hand), Left-handed, Left-hander, Left-wing(er)** Abandoned, Adrift, Avoided, Balance, Bolshy, Commie, Corrie-fisted, Dolly-push, Fellow traveller, Forsaken, Gallock, Haw, Hie, High, Inherited, L, Laeotropic, Laevorotation, Larboard, Links, Loony, Lorn, Marxist, Militant, Near(side), New, Other, Over, Pink, Pinko, Port, Portsider, Prompt side, Quit, Rad, Red (Brigade), Relic, Residuum, Resigned, Secondo, Set out, Sinister, Soc(ialist), Southpaw, Split, Stage right, Thin, Titoism, Trot, Unused, Verso, Vo, Went, West, Wind, Yet

**Left-over** Astatki, Dregs, End, Gone, Lave, Oddment, Offcut, Orra, Remains, Remanet, →**REMNANT**, Residue, Rest, Waste

**Leg(s), Leggings, Leggy, Leg-wear** Antigropelo(e)s, Bandy, Barbados, Barley-sugar, Bow, Breeches, Cabriole, Cannon, Chaparajos, Chaparejos, Chaps, Crural, Crus, Cuisse, Cush, Dib, Drumstick, Fine, Fly-sail, Gaiter, Galligaskins, Gam(b), Gamash, Gambado, Garter, Gaskin, Giambeux, Gigot, Gramash, Gramosh, Ham, Haunch, Hest, Hexapod, Hock, Jamb, Jambeau, Jambeaux, Knock-knee(d), Limb, Long, Member, Milk, Myriapod, Oleo, On(side), Peg, Peraeopod, Peroneal, Pestle, Pin, Podite, Proleg, Puttees, Pylon, Relay, Sea, Section, Shanks, Shanks's pony, Shaps, Shin, Short, Spats, Spatterdash, Spider, Spindleshanks, Square, Stage, Start up, Stifle, Stump, Thigh, Tights, White

**Legacy** Bequest, Cumulative, Demonstrative, Dowry, Endowment, Entail, General, Heirloom, Residuary, Specific, Substitutional

**Legal(ism), Legally, Legitimate** Above board, Bencher, Decriminalised, De regle, Forensic, Halacha, Halaka(h), Halakha, Lawful, Licit, Nomism, Scienter, Statutory

**Legal book** Halacha, Halaka(h), Halakha, Talmud

**Leg-armour, Leg-covering** Cootikin, Cu(i)tikin, Gambado, Jamb(e), Pad

**Legate, Legator** A latere, Ambassador, Consul, Devisor, Emissary, Envoy, Nuncio

**Legatee** Heir

**Legato** Slur

**Legend(ary)** Arthurian, Caption, Edda, Fable, Folklore, Hadith, Motto, Myth, Saga, Story, Urban, Yowie

▷ **Legend** *may indicate* leg-end, e.g. foot, talus

**Leger** Swindler

**Leghorn** Livorno

**Legible** Clear, Lucid, Plain

**Legion(ary), Legionnaire** Alauda, American, Army, Brigade, British, Cohort, Countless, Deserter, Foreign, Geste, Honour, →**HOST**, Maniple, Many, Throng, Thundering, Zillions

**Legislate, Legislation, Legislator, Legislature** Assemblyman, Backbencher, Congress, Decemvir, Decree, Delegated, Diet, MP, Nomothete, Oireachtas, →**PARLIAMENT**, Persian, Senator, Solon, Supreme soviet, Thesmothete, Zemstvo

**Legitimate** Fair game, Kosher, Loyal, Proper, Rightful, Valid
**Legless** Amelia, Blotto, Boozy, Caecilia, Drunk, Mermaid, Paralytic, Psyche
**Leg-pull** Chaff, Joke, Rise, Rot
**Legume, Leguminous** Bean, Guar, Lentil, Lomentum, Pea, Peanut, Pipi, Pod, Pulse, Vetch
**Leibniz** Monadism
**Leicester** Sheep
**Leigh** Amyas
**Leisure(ly)** Adagio, Andantino, Bytime, Ease, Lento, Liberty, Moderato, Off day, Otium, Respite, Rest, Vacation
**Leitmotif** Theme
**Lemming** Morkin
**Lemon** Answer, Cedrate, Citron, Citrus, Dud, Smear-dab, Sole, Twist, Yellow
**Lemonade** Pop
**Lemur** Angwantibo, Aye-aye, Babacoote, Bush-baby, Colugo, Cynocephalus, Galago, Half-ape, Indri(s), Loris, Macaco, Malmag, Mongoose, →**MONKEY**, Nagapie, Potto, Ringtail, Sifaka, Spectre, Tana, Tarsier
**Lend(er)** Advance, Library, Loan, Prest, Sub, Swap line, Usurer, Vaunce
**Length(y), Lengthen(ing), Lengthwise** Archine, Arsheen, Arshin(e), Aune, Barleycorn, Braccio, Cable, Chain, Cubit, Distance, Eke, Ell, →**ELONGATE**, Endways, Ennage, Epenthetic, Expand, Extensive, Focal, Foot, Footage, Furlong, Inch, Ley, Longitudinal, Mile, Nail, Parsec, Passus, Perch, Piece, Plethron, Pole, Prolate, Prolix, Prolong, Protract, Reach, Remen, Rigmarole, Rod, Rope, Slow, Span, Stadium, Toise, Vara, Verbose, Yard
**Lenient, Lenience, Leniency** Clement, Exurable, Lax, Mild, Permissive, Quarter, Soft, Soft line, Tolerant
**Lens** Achromatic, Acoustic, Anamorphic, Anastigmat, Aplanatic, Apochromat(ic), Bifocal, Bull's eye, Compound, Condenser, Contact, Corneal, Crookes, Crown, Crystalline, Dielectric, Diopter, Dioptre, Diverging, Electron, Electrostatic, Eye, Eyeglass, Eye-piece, Facet, Field, Fish-eye, Fresnel, Gas-permeable, Gravitational, Hard, Immersion, Lentil, Macro, Magnetic, Metallic, Mirror, Object(ive), Object-glass, Optic, Pantoscope, Phacoid, Piano-concave, Piano-convex, Soft, Soft-focus, Stanhope, Sunglass, Telephoto, Toric, Trifocal, Varifocal, Water, Wide-angle, Zoom
**Lent** Carême, Fast, Laetare, Out, Quadragesimal, Term
**Lentil(s)** D(h)al, Dholl, Ervalenta, Lens, Phacoid, Pulse, Puy, Revalenta
**Leonora** Overture
**Leopard** Catamountain, Clouded, Cougar, Hunting, Jaguar, Leap, Libbard, Oceloid, Ocelot, Ounce, Panther, Pard, Snow, Spots, Tiger
**Leopold** Bloom
**Leotard** Maillot
**Leper, Leprosy, Leprous** Gehazi, Hansen's disease, Lazar, Leontiasis, Lionism, Meazel, Mesel, Outcast, Pariah
**Lepidopterist** Aurelian, Moth-er, Pendleton, Treacler
**Leprechaun** Elf, Gremlin, Imp
**Lepton** Muon
**Lesbian** Boi, Bull dyke, Crunchie, Diesel, Dike, Dyke, Homophile, Lipstick, Sapphist, Tribade
**Lese-majesty** Treason
**Lesion** Cut, Gash, Pannus, Scar, Serpiginous, Sore, Ulcer, Wheal, Whelk
**Less(en), Lesser, Lessening** Abate, Alaiment, Attenuate, Bate, Comedown, Contract, Deaden, Decline, Deplete, Derogate, Dilute, →**DWINDLE**, Extenuate, Fewer, Junior, Littler, Meno, Minus, Play down, Reduce, Relax, Remission, Sen, Shrink, Subordinate, Subsidiary, Tail, Under
**Lesson** Class, Example, Lear(e), Lection, Leir, Lere, Life, Liripipe, Masterclass, Moral, Object, Parashah, Period, Sermon, Shiur, Tutorial

**Let (go, off, out), Letting** Allow, Cap, Charter, Conacre, Displode, Divulge, Enable, Entitle, Explode, Hire, Impediment, Indulge, Leak, Lease, Litten, Loot(en), Luit(en), Lutten, Net, Obstacle, Obstruct, →**PERMIT**, Rent, Reprieve, Sett, Tenancy, Unhand, Warrant
**Let down** Abseil, Betray, Lower, Sell, Vail
**Let-down** Disappointment, Non-event
**Lethal** Deadly, Fatal, Fell, Mortal
**Lethargic, Lethargy** Accidie, Apathy, Coma, Comatose, Drowsy, Ennui, Hebetude, Inactive, Inertia, Lassitude, Limp, Listless, Logy, Passive, Sleepy, Sluggish, Stagnant, Stupor, Supine, Torpid, Turgid, Weariness
**Letter(s)** Ache, Aerogram, Aesc, A(y)in, Airgraph, Aleph, Alif, Alpha, Ascender, Aspirate, Bayer, Begging, Beta, Beth, Block, Breve, Cadmean, Canine, Caph, Capital, Capon, Casket, Chain, Cheth, Chi, Chitty, Circular, Col, Collins, Consonant, Covering, Credentials, Cue, Cuneiform, Daled, Daleth, Dead, Dear John, Delta, Digamma, Digraph, Dispatch, Dog, Dominical, Edh, Ef(f), E-mail, Emma, Encyclical, Ep(isemon), Epistle, Epistolet, Epsilon, Eta, Eth, Fan, Favour, Form, Fraktur, French, Gamma, Gimel, Grapheme, He, Heth, Hieratic, Initial, Iota, Izzard, Jerusalem, Juliet, Kaph, Kappa, Koppa, Kufic, Labda, Lambda, Lamed(h), Landlady, Landlord, Lessee, Lessor, Literal, Love, Mail, Mail-shot, Majuscule, Mem, Memo, Message, Miniscule, Minuscule, Missive, Monogram, Mu, Nasal, Night, Note, Notelet, Nu, Nun, Og(h)am, Omega, Omicron, Open, Ou, Pacifical, Pahlavi, Paragoge, Paston, Pastoral, Patent, Pe(h), Pehlevi, Phi, Pi, Plosive, Poison-pen, Polyphone, Postbag, Psi, Pythagorean, Qof, Qoph, Realtor, Resh, Rho, Rhyme, Rom, Romeo, Runestave, Sad(h)e, Samekh, Samian, Sampi, San, Scarlet, Screed, Screeve, Screwtape, Script, See, Shin, Ship, Sick-note, Siglum, Sigma, Sign, Signal, Sin, Sort, Stiff, Swash, Tau, Tav, Taw, Teth, Theta, Thorn, Toc, Tsade, Typo, Uncial, Upsilon, Vau, Vav, Versal, Vowel, Waw, Wen, Wyn, Wynn, Xi, Yod(h), Yogh, Ypsilon, Zayin, Zed, Zeta
**Lettering** Cufic, Kufic
**Lettuce** Batavia, Butterhead, Cabbage, Chicon, Corn-salad, Cos, Frog's, Iceberg, Lactuca, Lamb's, Lollo rosso, Mache, Mizuna, Radicchio, Romaine, Salad, Sea, Thridace
**Leucoma** Albugo
**Levant(ine)** Abscond, Coptic, Go, Israelite, Jew, Ottamite, Ottomite
**Levee** Bank, Dyke, Embankment, Party
**Level(ler)** A, Abney, Abreast, Aclinic, Ad eundum, Aim, Awash, Bargaining, Base, Break even, Bulldoze, Champaign, Confidence, Countersink, Degree, Dumpy, Echelon, Energy, Equal, →**EVEN**, Extent, Eye, Flat, Flight, Flush, Fog, Grade, Horizontal, Impurity, Infill, Logic, Meet, O, Occupational, Ordinary, Par, Plain, Planation, Plane, Plat(eau), Point, Price, Race, Rank, Rase, Raze, Reduced, Savanna, Sea, Spirit, Split, Springing, →**SQUARE**, Status, Step, Stor(e)y, Stratum, Street, Strew, Strickle, Subsistence, Summit, Support, Surveyor's, Tear-down, Tier, Top, Trophic, True, Water, Wye, Y
**Lever(age)** Backfall, Bell-crank, Brake, Cock, Crampon, Crowbar, Dues, Gear, Handspike, Jaw, Jemmy, Joystick, Key, Knee-stop, Landsturm, Pawl, Peav(e)y, Pedal, Pinch, Prise, Prize, Pry, Purchase, Stick, Sweep, Swipe, Tappet, Throttle, Tiller, Treadle, Treddle, Tremolo arm, Trigger, Tumbler, Typebar, Whipstaff
**Leveret** Hare
**Leviathan** Whale
**Levitate, Levitation** Float, Hover, Magnetic, Rise, Yogic flying
**Levity** Flippancy, Glee, Humour, Jollity
**Levy** Capital, Estreat, Impose, Imposition, Leave, Militia, Octroi, Raise, Scutage, Stent, Talliate, Tax, Tithe, Toll
**Lewd(ness)** Bawd(r)y, Blue, Cyprian, Debauchee, Impure, Libidinous, Lubricity, Obscene, Priapism, Prurient, Raunchy, Silen(us), Tentigo, Unclean
**Lewis** Carroll, Tenon
**Lexicographer, Lexicon** Compiler, Craigie, Drudge, Etymologist, Florio, Fowler, Glossarist, Grove, Johnson(ian), Larousse, Liddell, Mental, Murray, OED, Thesaurus, Vocabulist, Webster, Words-man

**Liability, Liable** Anme, Apt, Chance, Current, Debt, Employer's, Incur, Limited, Open, Product, Prone, Subject, Susceptible, White elephant

**Liaison** Affair, Amour, Contact, Link

**Liana** Guarana

**Libel(lous)** Blasphemous, Defamatory, Malign, Sclaunder, Slander, Smear, Sully, Vilify

**Liberal(ity)** Abundant, Adullamites, Ample, Besant, Bounteous, Bountiful, Breadth, Bright, Broad, Catholic, Enlightened, Free(hander), Free-hearted, → **GENEROUS**, Giver, Grey, Grimond, Grit, Handsome, Indulgent, L, Largesse, Latitudinarian, Lavish, Limousine, Munificent, Octobrist, Open, Permissive, → **PROFUSE**, Rad(ical), Right on, Samuelite, Simonite, Spender, Steel, Tolerant, Trivium, Unstinted, Verlig, Verligte, Whig

**Liberate(d), Liberation, Liberator** Bolivar, Deliver, Dissimure, Emancipate, Fatah, → **FREE**, Gay, Inkatha, Intolerant, Messiah, Nick, PLO, Redeem, Release, Risorgimento, Save, Steal, Sucre, Unfetter, UNITA, Women's

**Liberian** Kroo, Kru

**Libertarian, Libertine** Chartered, Corinthian, Debauchee, Don Juan, Laxist, Lecher, Lothario, Lovelace, Orgiast, Playboy, Rake, Rip, Roué, Wencher, Wolf

**Liberty** Bail, Civil, Discretion, Franchise, Freedom, Hall, Ish, Latitude, Licence, Mill, Presumption, Sauce

**Libido, Libidinous** Lust, Prurient

**Libra** L

**Library, Librarian** Bibliothecary, BL, Bodleian, Bookmobile, British, Chartered, Circulating, Copyright, Cottonian, Dewey, Film, Gene, Genomic, Harleian, Laurentian, Lending, Mazarin, Mobile, Morgue, PL, Public, Radcliffe, Reference, Rental, Subscription, Tauchnitz

**Librettist** Boito, Gilbert, Hammerstein, La Ponte, Lerner, Lyricist

▶ **Lice** *see* **LOUSE (UP)**

**Licence, License** Abandon, Allow, Authorisation, Carnet, Charter, Dispensation, Driving, Enable, Exequatur, Fling, Franchise, Free(dom), Gale, Import, Imprimatur, Indult, → **LATITUDE**, Let, Marriage, Occasional, Passport, Patent, → **PERMIT**, Poetic, Pratique, Provisional, Road-fund, Rope, Slang, Special, Table, Ticket of leave

**Licentious** Artistic, Corinthian, Debauchee, Hot, Immoral, Large, Lax, Liberal, Loose, Orgiastic, Prurient, Ribald, Sensual, Wanton

**Lichen** Apothecia, Archil, Corkir, Crotal, Crottle, Cup, Epiphyte, Epiphytic, Graphis, Korkir, Lecanora, Litmus, Moss, Oakmoss, Orcein, Orchel, Orchil(la), Orcine, Orseille, Parella, Parelle, Roccella, Rock tripe, Sea-ivory, Soredium, Stone-rag, Stone-raw, Tree-moss, Usnea, Wartwort

**Lick(ing)** Bat, Beat, Deer, Felch, Lambent, Lap, Leather, Rate, Salt, Slake, Speed, Tongue, Trounce, Whip

▶ **Licorice** *see* **LIQUORICE**

**Lid(ded)** Cloche, Cover, Crust, Hat, Kid, Maximum, Opercula, Screwtop, Stegocarpus, Twist-off

**Liddell** Alice

**Lido** Beach, Pool

**Lie(s), Liar, Lying** Abed, Accubation, Accumbent, Ananias, Bam, Bare-faced, Bask, Billy, Bounce(r), Braide, Cau(l)ker, Cellier, Clipe, Clype, Concoction, Consist, Contour, Couch(ant), Cracker, Cram(mer), Cretism, Cumbent, Deception, Decubitous, Decumbent, Direct, Doggo, Fable, Fairytale, False(r), Falsehood, Falsify, Falsity, Fib, Fiction, Figment, Flam, Gag, Gonk, Hori, Incumbent, Invention, Inveracity, Kip, Lair, Leasing, Lee(ar), Lig(ge), Lurk, Mythomania, Nestle, Obreption, Oner, Perjury, Plumper, Porky (pie), Procumbent, Prone, Prostrate, Pseudologia, Recline, Recumbent, Repent, Repose, Reptant, Ride, Romance(r), Sham, Sit, Sleep, Strapper, Stretcher, Supine, Swinger, Tale, Tappice, Tar(r)adiddle, Thumper, Tissue, Try, Untruth, Whacker, Whid, White, Whopper, Yanker

**Lied** Art-song, Song

**Lie-detector** Polygraph
**Lien** Mortgage, Title
**Lieu** Locus, Place
**Lieutenant** Cassio, Flag, Loot, Lt, No 1, Sub(altern)
**Life** Age, Animation, Being, Bio, Biog(raphy), Biota, Breath, Brian, Brio, C'est la vie, Chaim, Clerihew, CV, Energy, Esse, Eva, Eve, Existence, Good, Heart, High, Mean, Memoir, Mortal coil, Nellie, Nelly, Night, Non-fiction, Pep, Plasma, Private, Public, Quick, Real, Riley, Shelf, Span, Spirit, Still, Subsistence, Time, True, Useful, Vita, Vitality, Zoe
**Life-blood** Essence, Lethee
**Lifeboat(man)** Ark, Noah
**Life-cell** Energid
**Life-cycle** Redia
**Life-force, Life-style** Chi, Mana, Od, Orgone, Port, Qi
**Lifeless(ness)** Abiosis, Algidity, Amort, Arid, Azoic, Barren, Catatonic, Cauldrife, → DEAD, Dull, Flat, Inanimate, Inert, Key-cold, Log, Mineral, Possum, Stagnant, Sterile, Stonen, Vapid, Wooden
**Lifelike** Android, Breathing, Realistic, Speaking
**Lifeline** Umbilicus
**Life-rent** Usufruct
**Life-saver** Cheesemonger, Coastguard, Lineman, Mae West, Preserver, Raft, Reelman
**Lift(ed), Lifter, Lifting** Araise, Arayse, Arsis, Attollent, Bone, Cable-car, Camel, Chair, Clean and jerk, Cly, Copy, Crane, Davit, Dead, Dumb waiter, Elate, Elevator, Enhance, Exalt, Extol, Filch, Fillip, Fireman's, Greaten, Heave, Heeze, Heezie, Heft(e), Heighten, Heist, Hitch, Hoise, Hoist, Hove, Jack, Jigger, Kleptomania, Leaven, Lefte, Lever, Lewis, Nab, Nap, Nim, Otis®, Paternoster, Pilfer, Press, Pulley, → RAISE, Ride, Rotor, Scoop, Service, Shearlegs, Ski, Sky, Snatch, Sneak, Spout, Stair, Steal, Surface, T-bar, Teagle, Theft, Thumb, Topping, Up, Winch, Windlass
**Lig** Mooch
**Ligament** Annular, Cruciate, Fr(a)enum, Paxwax, Peacock-stone, Spring, Suspensory, Tendon, Urachus
**Ligation, Ligature** Ae(sc), Ash, Bandage, Bind, Funicle, Knot, Tubal
**Light(en), Lighter, Light holder, Lighting, Lights** Aerate, Afterglow, Airglow, Airy, Albedo, Ale, Alleviate, Alow, Alpenglow, Amber, Ancient, Ans(wer), Arc, Arson, Aurora, Back-up, Barge, Batement, Batswing, Beacon, Beam, Bengal, Beshine, Bezel, Birlinn, Black, Bleach, Blond(e), Brake, Breezy, Bude, Bulb, Bull's eye, Buoyant, Calcium, Candle, Cannel, Canstick, Casco, Casement, Chandelier, Chiaroscuro, Cierge, Clue, Courtesy, Day(time), Dewali, Dewbow, Diffused, Direct, Diwali, Dormer, Dream-hole, Drop, Drummond, Earth-shine, Ease, Eddystone, Electrolier, Ethereal, Eulachon, Fair, Fairy, Fall, Fan, Fantastic, Fastnet, Feathery, Fetch-candle, Fidibus, Fill, Filter, Fire, First, Fixed, Flambeau, Flame, Flare, Flax(y), Flicker, Flimsy, Flippant, Flit(t), Floating, Flood, Fluorescent, Fog (lamp), Frothy, Fuffy, Gas-poker, Gegenschein, Glare, Gleam, Glim(mer), Glow, Gossamer, Green, Guiding, Gurney, Haggis, Halation, Hazard, Head, House, Idiot, Ignite, Illum(in)e, Incandescence, Indirect, Induction, Inner, Irradiate, Junior, Keel, Key, Kindle, Kiran, Klieg, Lamp, Lampadary, Lampion, Land, Lantern, Lanthorn, Laser, Leading, LED, Leerie, Leggiero, Lenient, Levigate, Lime, Link, Linstock, Loadstar, Lobuli, Lodestar, Lozen, Lucarne, Lucigen, Luminaire, Lumine, Luminescence, Luminous, Lunt, Lustre, Lux, Mandorla, Match, Menorah, Mercurial, Merry-dancers, Mithra(s), Moon, Naphtha, Navigate, Navigation, Neon, New, Nit, Northern, Obstruction, Od(yl), Offal, Optics, Pale, Pane, Parhelion, Pavement, Pennyweight, Phosphene, Phosphorescence, Phot(ic), Photon, Photosphere, Pilot, Pipe, Polar, Pontoon, Portable, Porthole, Pra(a)m, Producer-gas, Rainbow, Range, Rear, Red, Reflex, Relieve, Relume, Rembrandt, Reversing, Riding, Robot, Rocket, Running, Rush, Safe(ty), St Elmo's fire, Satori, Scoop, Scow, Sea-dog, Sea fire, Search, Shine, Shy, Signal, Solid-state, Southern, Southern-vigil,

Sparse, Spill, Spot, Spry, Star, Steaming, Strip, Strobe, Stroboscope, Subtle, Sun,
Sunshine, Suttle, Svelte, Tail, Tally, Taper, Taps, Tead, Threshold, Tind, Tine, Torch,
Torchère, Touchpaper, Track, Traffic, Trivial, Ultraviolet, Unchaste, Unoppressive,
UV, Ver(e)y, Vesica, Vesta, Vigil, Watch, Wax, Welsbach burner, White, Windock,
→WINDOW, Winker, Winnock, Zippo, Zodiacal
▷ **Light** *may indicate an anagram*
**Lighterman** Bargee
**Light-headed** Captious, Dizzy, Kicksin
**Light-hearted** Gay
**Lighthouse** Beacon, Caisson, Eddystone, Fanal, Fastnet, Needles, Phare, Pharos,
Sea-mark, Signal, Spurn
**Lightless** Aphotic, Dark, Obscure, Unlit
**Lightness** Buoyancy, Galant, Levity, Pallor
**Lightning** Ball, Bolt, Catequil, Chain, Dry, Éclair, Enfouldered, Fireball, Fire flag, Forked,
Fulmination, Heat, Levin, Sheet, Summer, Thunderbolt, Wildfire, Zigzag
**Lightship** Floating beacon, Nore
**Lightweight** Jack straw, Nobody, Oz, Trivial
**Lignite** Jet, Surtarbrand, Surturbrand
**Like(ness), Liking** Affinity, À la, Analogon, As, Assimilate, Attachment, Broo, Care,
Corpse, Dig, Duplicate, Effigy, Eg, Egal(ly), Enjoy, Equal, Fancy, Fellow, Guise, Lich,
Palate, Parallel, Peas, Penchant, -philus, Please, Predilection, Resemblance, Semblant,
Shine, Similar, Simile, Simulacrum, Smaak, Sort, Speaking, Taste, Tiki, Uniformity
**Likely, Likelihood** Apt, Fair, Liable, Maximum, Odds-on, Offchance, On, Plausible,
Possible, Probable, Probit, Prone, Prospective
**Likewise** Also, Ditto, Do, Egally, Eke, Item, So, Too, Tu quoque
**Lilac** French, Laylock, Mauve, Pipe-tree, Syringa
**Lilliputian** Minute
**Lilt** Swing
**Lily** African, Agapanthus, Aloe, Amaryllis, Annunciation, Arum, Asphodel, Aspidistra,
Belladonna, Blackberry, Calla, Camas(h), Camass, Canada, Candock, Chincherinchee,
Colchicum, Colocasia, Convallaria, Corn, Crinum, Dale, Day, Easter, Elaine, Endogen,
Fawn, Fleur de lys, Fritillary, Funkia, Galtonia, Guernsey, Haemanthus, Hellebore,
Hemerocallis, Herb-Paris, Jacobean, Jacob's, Jersey, Kniphofia, Laguna, Lent, Leopard,
Lote, Lotos, Lotus, Madonna, Mariposa, Martagon, Meadow, Moorva, Mount Cook,
Nelumbo, Nenuphar, Nerine, Nuphar, Nymphaea, Orange, Padma, Phormium, Pig,
Plantain, Pond, Quamash, Regal, Richardia, Sabadilla, Sansevieria, Sarsa, Scilla, Sego,
Skunk cabbage, Smilax, Solomon's seal, Spider, Star of Bethlehem, Stone, Sword, Tiger,
Trillium, Tritoma, Tuberose, Turk's cap, Vellozia, Victoria, Water, Water maize, Yucca,
Zephyr
**Lily-maid** Elaine
**Lima** L, Sugar bean
**Limb** Arm, Bough, Branch, Crural, Exapod, Flipper, Forearm, Hindleg, Imp, Leg,
Leg-end, Member, Phantom, Proleg, Pterygium, Ramus, Scion, Shin, Spald, Spall,
Spaul(d), Wing
**Limbless** Amelia
**Limbo** Bardo, Isolation, Oblivion
**Lime** Bass(wood), Beton, Bird, Calc, Calcicolous, Caustic, Lind(en), Malm, Mortar, Slaked,
Soda, Teil, Tilia, Trap, Unslaked, Viscum, Whitewash
**Limerick** Doggerel, Twiner, Verse
**Limestone** Burren, Calc-sinter, Calm, Calp, Ca(u)m, Clint, Coquina, Coral Rag,
Cornbrash, Cornstone, Dolostone, Forest Marble, Grike, Karst, Kentish rag, Kunkar,
Kunkur, Landscape marble, Magnesian, Malm, Marble, Muschelkalk, Nero-antico,
Oolite, Pisolite, Rottenstone, Scaglia, Stalagma, Stinkstone, Stylolitic, Travertin(e)
**Limey** Rooinek, Seafarer

**Limit(ation), Limited, Limiting** Ambit, Asymptote, Basebound, Bind, Border, Borné, Bound, Boundary, Bourn(e), Brink, Cap, Cash, Ceiling, Chandrasekhar, Circumscribe, Climax, Compass, Confine, Constrain, Constrict, Credit, Curb, Cut-off, Deadline, Define, Demark, Determine, Earshot, Eddington, Edge, Edition, End, Entail, Esoteric, →**EXTENT**, Extreme, Finite, Fraenum, Frontier, Gate, Goal, Gole, Height, Hourlong, Impound, Induciae, Insular, Limes, Line, Lite, Lynchet, March, Maximum, Meare, Mete, Minimum, Narrow, Nth, Outedge, Pale, Parameter, Perimeter, Periphery, Predetermine, Qualify, Range, Rate-cap, Ration, Reservation, Restrict, Rim, Roche, Roof, Saturation point, Scant, Scrimp, Shoestring, Short-term, Sky, Somedeal, Somedele, Speed, Stint, String, Sumptuary, Tail(lie), Tailye, Tailzie, Term(inus), Tether, Three-mile, Threshold, Thule, Tie, Time, Tramline, Tropic, Twelve-mile, Ultimate, Utmost, Utter, Verge

▷ **Limit** *may indicate* 'surrounding'

**Limner** RA

**Limousine** Daimler, Rolls, Stretch, Zil

**Limp** Claudication, Dot, Droopy, Flabby, Flaccid, Flaggy, Flimsy, Floppy, Gimp, Hamble, Hilch, Hirple, Hitch, Hobble, Hop, Lank, Lifeless, Spancel, Tangle, Wilting

**Limpet** Keyhole, Patella, Slipper, Streptoneura

**Limpid** Clear, Lucid, Pure

**Linch** Terrace

**Lincoln(shire)** Abe, Poacher, Yellow-belly

**Linden** Baucis, Lime, Tilia

**Line(d), Lines, Lining** Abreast, Aclinic, Agate, Agonic, Allan, Anacreontic, →**ANCESTRY**, Anent, Angle, Apothem, Arew, Asclepiadean, Assembly, Asymptote, Attention, Axis, Babbitt, Bakerloo, Bar, Barcode, Baton, Battle, Baulk, Becket, Bikini, Bluebell, Bob, Body, Bombast, Bottom, Boundary, BR, Brail, Branch, Bread, Building, Bush, By, Canal, Carolingian, Carriage, Casing, Cathetus, Ceil, Cento, Central, Ceriph, Chord, Ciel, Circle, Clew, Club, Coach, Coffle, Colour, Column, Command, Conga, Contour, Cord(on), Coseismal, Course, Crease, Credit, Crib, Crocodile, Crosshatch, Crowfoot, Crow's feet, Cunard, Curve, Cushion, Dancette, Danger, Date, Datum, Dead-ball, Decidua, Delay, Descent, DEW, Diagonal, Diameter, Diffusion, Directrix, Distaff, District, Dochmiachal, Dotted, Doublure, Downhaul, Downrigger, Dress, Dynasty, Earing, El, E-la-mi, Encase, End, Equator, Equinoctial, Equinox, Faint, Fall(s), Fathom, Fault, Feint, Fess(e), Fettle, File, Finishing, Firing, Firn, Fixed, Flex, Flight, Frame, Fraunhofer, Front, Frontier, Frost, Furr(ow), Geodesic, Geotherm, Germ, Gimp, Giron, Goal, Graph, Grass, Green, Gridiron, Gymp, Gyron, Hachure, Halyard, Hard, Hatching, Hawser, Header, Hemistich, Heptameter, Hexameter, Hexapody, High-watermark, Hindenburg, Hockey, Hogscore, Hot, House, Impot, Inbounds, Inbred, Incase, Inhaul(er), Insole, Interfluve, Intima, Isallobar, Isentrope, Isobar, Isobath, Isobront, Isocheim, Isochime, Isochron(e), Isoclinic, Isoclude, Isocryme, Isogloss, Isogonal, Isogonic, Isogram, Isohel, Isohyet, Isolex, Isomagnetic, Isometric, Isonome, Isopach(yte), Isophone, Isophote, Isopiestic, Isopleth, Isopycnic, Isopyenal, Isotach, Isothere, Isotherm, Jubilee, Kill, Knittle, L, Land, Lane, Lansker, Lap, Lariat, Lasso, Lateral, Latitude, Lead, Leash, Le(d)ger, Length, Ley, Lie, Ling, LMS, Load, Log, Longitude, Lossy, Loxodrome, Lubber, Lugger, Lye, Macron, Maginot, Main, Mainsheet, Mark, Marriage, Mason-Dixon, Median, Meridian, Mesal, Metropolitan, Miurus, Monofilament, Monorail, Multiplet, Nacre, Naman, Nazca, Nidation, Noose, Norsel, Northern, Number, Oche, Octastichon, Ode, Oder-Neisse, Og(h)am, Omentum, Onedin, Ordinate, Orphan, Orthostichy, Painter, Panty, Parallel, Parameter, Parastichy, Party, Paternoster, Path, Penalty, Pencil, Phalanx, Piccadilly, Picket, Pinstripe, Pipe, Plasterboard, Pleuron, Plimsoll, Plumb, Poetastery, Polar, Police, Policy, Popping-crease, Potichomania, Poverty, Power, Princess, Procession, Product(ion), Profession, Punch, Pure, Queue, Race, Radial, Radius, Rail, Rank, Raster, Ratlin(e), Ratling, Rattlin, Ray, Receiving, Red, Reticle, Retinue, Rew, Rhumb, Ripcord, Rope,

Route, Row, Rugose, Rugous, Rule, Ry, Sarking, Scazon, Score, Scotch, Scratch, Scrimmage, Script, Secant, Seperatrix, Serif, Seriph, Service, Set, Shielded, Shore, Shout, Shroud, Siding, Siegfried, Sield, Sight, Silver, Six-yard, Slur, Snood, Snow, Soft, Solidus, Sounding, Specialty, Spectral, Spider, Spilling, Spring, Spunyarn, Squall, SR, Staff, Stance, Stanza, Starting, Static, Stave, Stean, Steen, Stein, Stem, Stich(os), Stock, Story, Strain, Strap, Streak, Strene, Stretch mark, Striate, String, Stripe, Stuff, Subject, Subtense, Swap, Swifter, Symphysis, Syzygy, Tag, Tailback, Talweg, Tangent, Teagle, Tea lead, Terminator, Tetrameter, Thalweg, Thin blue, Thin red, Thread, Throwaway, Tidemark, Tie, Tier, Tiercet, Timber, Touch, Tow, Trade, Transmission, Transoceanic, Transversal, Tree, Trimeter, Tropic, Trot, Trunk, Try, Tudor, Twenty-five, Twenty-two, Upstroke, Variety, Verse, Victoria, Vinculum, Virgule, Wad, Wallace's, Washing, Water(shed), Waterloo, White, Widow, Windrow, Wire, World, Wrinkle, Yellow, Z, Zag, Zip, Zollner's

**Lineage** Ancestry, Descent, Extraction, Filiation, Parage, Pedigree

**Linen** Amice, Amis, Barb, Bed, Byssus, Cambric, Crash, Damask, Dornick, Dowlas, Duck, Ecru, Flax, Harn, Huckaback, Inkle, Lawn, Line, Lint, Lockram, Moygashel, Napery, Percale, Seersucker, Sendal, Silesia, Snow, Table, Toile, Undies

**Liner** Artist, Bin-bag, Eye, Ocean greyhound, RMS, Rule(r), Ship, Sleeve, Steamer, Steen, Titanic

**Linesman** Beeching, Parodist, → **POET**, Touch-judge

**Linger(ing)** Chronic, Dawdle, Dwell, Hang, Hove(r), Lag, Loaf, → **LOITER**, Straggle, Taigle, Tarry, Tie

**Lingerie** Bra, Drawers, Teddy, Undies

**Lingo** Argot, Bat, Cant, Jargon, Patter, Polglish, Speech

**Linguist(ic), Linguistics** Clitic, Comparative, Descriptive, Glottic, Historical, Onomastics, Philological, Phonemics, Polyglot, Pragmatics, Semantics, Structural, Stylistics, Syntax, Tagmemics, Taxeme

**Liniment** Balm, Camphor, Carron-oil, Embrocation, Ointment, Opodeldoc, Salve

**Link(ed), Linking, Links** Associate, Between, Bond, Bridge, Chain, Cleek, Close knit, Colligate, Concatenation, Conjunction, Connect, Copula, Couple, Course, Cross-reference, Cuff, Desmid, Drag, Draw-gear, Ess, Flambeau, Golf (course), Hookup, Hot, Hotline, Hyphen, Incatenation, Index, Interconnect, Interface, Internet, Interrelation, Intertwine, Karabiner, Krab, Ley-line, Liaise, Machair, Missing, Modem, Nexus, On-line, Pons, Preposition, Reciprocal, Relate, Ring, Tead(e), Terrestrial, → **TIE**, Tie-in, Tie-line, Torch, Twin, Unite, Weakest, Wormhole, Yoke

**Linkman** Lamplighter, Mediator

**Linnet** Finch, Lintie, Lintwhite, Twite

**Linoleum** Waxcloth

**Lint** Charpie, Dossil

**Lintel** Summer, Transom

**Lion(ess)** Androcles, Aphid, Aslan, Chindit, Elsa, Glitterati, Hero, Leo, Leopard, Literary, Maned, Mountain, Nemean, Opinicus, Personage, Pride, Simba

**Lionel** Trilling

**Lion-tamer** Androcles, Dan(iel)

**Lip(py), Lips** Backchat, Beestung, Cheek, Cupid's bow, Fat, Fipple, Flews, Hare, Helmet, Jib, Labellum, Labial, Labiate, Labret, Labrum, Ligula, Muffle, Philtrum, → **RIM**, Rubies, Sass, Sauce, Slack-jaw, Spout, Submentum

**Lipase** Steapsin

**Lipid** Ganglioside, Inositol, Sphingarine

**Lipstick** Chapstick

**Liquefy** Deliquesce, Dissolve, Fuse, Melt

**Liqueur, Liquor** Bree, Brew, Broo, Broth, Creature, Elixir, Fumet, Hard stuff, Hooch, Lap, Mother, Ooze, Pot, Potation, Stock, Stuff, Vat

## LIQUEURS

**3 letters:**
Ale
Kir
Rum

**4 letters:**
Apry
Feni
Malt
Ouzo
Raki
Rose
Tape
Tiff
Tift
Wine
Wort

**5 letters:**
Anise
Crème
Fenny
Hogan
Hogen
Kirsh
Lager
Mobby
Noyau
Pasha
Rakee
Sabra
Skink
Stout

Toddy

**6 letters:**
Cassis
Cerise
Chasse
Chicha
Eggnog
Enzian
Kahlua®
Kummel
Mastic
Midori®
Mobbie
Pastis
Pernod®
Rakija
Roiano
Rotgut
Shypoo
Stingo
Strega®
Strunt

**7 letters:**
Chococo
Curaçao
Fraises
Fustian
Persico
Ratafia
Roncoco
Sambuca

Samshoo
Sloe gin
Taplash
Tequila

**8 letters:**
Abisante
Absinthe
Advokaat
Amaretto
Anisette
Calvados
Choclair
Cocoribe
Drambuie®
Galliano
Geropiga
Kaoliang
Prunelle
Rum shrub
Schnapps
Sciarada
Tia Maria®
Witblits

**9 letters:**
Cointreau®
Framboise
Metheglin
Mirabelle
Triple sec
Van der Hum®

**10 letters:**
Almondrado
Chartreuse
Cher-suisse
Hogan-mogen
Limoncello
Maraschino
Mickey Finn
Pousse-café

**11 letters:**
Aguardiente
Benedictine
Jungle juice
Kirshwasser
Tickle-brain

**12 letters:**
Cherry brandy
Crème de cacao
Grand Marnier®
Kirschwasser
Supernaculum

**13 letters:**
Cherry Marnier®
Crème de menthe
Eau des creoles
Parfait d'amour

**14 letters:**
John Barleycorn
White lightning

---

**Liquid(ate), Liquidise(r), Liquidity, Liquids, Liquefaction** Acetal, Amortise, Annihilate, Apprize, Aqua-regia, Azeotrope, Bittern, Bouillon, Bromine, Butanal, Butanol, Butyraldehide, Butyrin, Cacodyl, Cadaverine, Cash, Cash flow, Chloramine, Cinerin, Clyster, Condenser, Court-bouillon, Creosol, Creosote, Decoction, Dispersant, Dope, Eluate, Erase, Ethanal, Ethanol, Ether, Eucalyptol, Eugenol, Flow, Fluid, Fural, Furfural, Furol, Guaiacol, Halothene, Indisputable, Ink, Isoprene, Jaw, Kakodyl, Lewisite, Limonene, Linalool, Log, Lye, Massacre, Mess, Minim, Mouillé, Nebula, Picamar, Pipe, Potion, Protoplasm, PSL, Ptisan, Purge, Pyrrole, Pyrrolidine, Quinoline, Raffinate, Rhigolene, Safrole, Semen, Serum, Smectic, Solution, Solvent, Syrup, Terebene, Thinner, Thixotropy, Titer, Titre, Triptane, Tuberculin, Tusche, Ullage, Unset, Verjuice, Washing-up, Whey, Wind up, Wort

**Liquorice** Indian, Jequirity, Nail, Nail-rod, Pomfret, Pontefract-cake, Spanish juice, Sugarallie, Sugarally, Wild

**Lis** Iris, Lily

**Lisa** Mona

**Lisp(er)** Ephraimite, Sibilance

**Lissom(e)** Agile, Lithe, Nimble, Supple, Svelte

**List(s), Listing** A, Active, Agenda, Antibarbarus, Appendix, Arena, Army, Atilt, B,

Barocco, Barrace, Bead-roll, Bibliography, Border, British, Calendar, Canon, Cant, Catalog(ue), Categorise, Catelog, Cause, Check, Choice, Civil, Class, Compile, Credits, Danger, Debrett, Docket, Empanel, Entry, Enumerate, Front, Glossary, Hark, Hearken, Heel, Hit, Hit-parade, Honours, Incline, Index, Indian, Interdiction, Inventory, Itemise, Laundry, Lean, Leet, Line-up, Linked, Litany, Lloyds, Mailing, Manifest, Menu, Navy, Notitia, Official, Panel, Paradigm, Party, Payroll, Price, Prize, Register, Repertoire, Reserved, Retired, Roin, Roll, Roon, Roster, Rota, Rund, Schedule, Script, Short, Sick, Slate, Slope, Strip, Syllabary, Syllabus (of Errors), Table, Tariff, Tick, Ticket, Tilt, Timetable, Tip, To-do, Transfer, Union, Waiting, Waybill, White, Wine, Wish

▷ **List** *may indicate* 'listen'

**Listen(er)** Attend, Auditor, Auscultate, Bug, Ear, Earwig, Eavesdropper, Gobemouche, Hark, →**HEED**, List, Lithe, Lug, Monitor, Oyez, Simon, Sithee, Stethoscope, Tune-in, Wire-tap, Yo-ho(-ho)

▷ **Listen to** *may indicate* a word sounding like another

**Lister** Plough, Surgeon

**Listless(ness)** Abulia, Accidie, Acedia, Apathetic, Atony, Dawney, Draggy, Ex-directory, Inanition, Indolent, Lackadaisical, Languor, Mooning, Mope, Mopus, Sloth, Thowless, Torpor, Upsitting, Waff

**Lit** Alight, Floodlight, Landed

▷ **Lit** *may indicate* an anagram

**Litany** Eirenicon, Lesser, Procession, Synapte

**Literacy** Emotional

**Literal(ly), Literal sense** Etymon, Misprint, Simply, Typo, Verbatim, Word for word

**Literary** Academic, Bas bleu, Booksie, Erudite, Lettered

**Literary girls** Althea, Jenny, Maud, Pippa

**Literature** Agitprop, Belles lettres, Comparative, Corpus, Edda, Fiction, Gongorism, Hagiology, Midrash, Musar, Page, Picaresque, Polite, Prose, Responsa, Samizdat, Sci-fi, Splatterpunk, Sturm und Drang, Wisdom

**Lithe** Flexible, Limber, Pliant, Sinuous, Souple, →**SUPPLE**, Svelte, Willowy

**Lithium** Li

**Litigant** Barrator, John-a-Nokes, John-a-Stiles, John Doe, Party, Richard Roe, Suer, Suitor

**Litmus** Indicator, Lacmus, Lichen, Turnsole

**Litre** L

**Litter** Bed, Brancard, Brood, Cacolet, Cat, Cubs, Debris, Deep, Doolie, Duff, Emu-bob, Farrow, Jampan, Kago, Kajawah, Kindle, Mahmal, Mor, Nest, Norimon, Palankeen, Palanquin, Palkee, Palki, Pup, →**REFUSE**, Scrap, Sedan, Stretcher, Sweepings, Team, Whelp

**Little** Bagatelle, Beans, Bijou, Billee, Brief, Chicken feed, Chota, Curn, Diddy, Dorrit, Drib, Drop, Fewtrils, Fraction, Haet, Hait, Hate, Ickle, Insect, Iota, John, Jot, Leet, Lilliputian, Limited, Lite, Lyte, Manikin, Means, Mini, Miniscule, Minnow, Minuscule, →**MINUTE**, Modicum, Morceau, Nell, Paltry, Paucity, Paul, Petite, Pink, Pittance, Ronte, Runt, Scant, Scut, Shade, Shoestring, Short, Shred, Shrimp, Slight, Sliver, Sma', →**SMALL**, Smattering, Smidge(o)n, Smidgin, Smout, Smowt, Some, Soupçon, Spot, Tad, Teensy(-weensy), Tich, Tiddly, Tine, Titch, Touch, Tyne, Unimportant, Vestige, Wee, Weedy, Whit, Women

**Littoral** Coast(al), Strand

**Liturgical, Liturgy** Divine, Doxology, Hallel, Rite, Shacharis, Versicle

**Live(d), Livelihood, Living, Liveliness, Lively, Lives** Active, Advowson, Alert, Allegretto, Allegro, Am, Animated, Animation, Animato, Are, AV, Awake, Be, Benefice, Biont, Birkie, Boisterous, Bouncy, Bread, Breezy, Brio, Brisk, Canonry, Cant(y), Capriccio(so), Cheery, Chipper, Chirpy, Cohabit, Con moto, Con spirito, Crouse, Crust, Dash, Durante vita, →**DWELL**, Dynamic, Ebullient, Entrain, Esprit, Exist, Extant, Exuberant, Feisty, Frisky, Galliard, Gamy, Gay, Giocoso, Glebe, Gracious, Grig, Hang-out, Hard, High jinks, Hijinks, Hot, Indwell, Inquiline, Is, Jazz, Kedge, Lad, Lead, Lodging,

Mercurial, Merry, Mouvementé, Organic, Outgo, Pacey, Peart, Pep, Perky, Piert, Quick, Quicksilver, Rackety, Racy, Reside, Resident, Rousing, Salt, Saut, Scherzo, Simony, Skittish, Smacking, Spanking, Sparky, Spiritoso, Spirituel(le), Sprack, Sprightly, Spry, Spunky, Subsist, Subsistence, Sustenance, Swinging, Symbiotic, Thrive, Unrecorded, Up tempo, Vibrant, Vicarage, Vigoroso, Vital, Vitality, Vivace, Vive, Vivo, → **VOLATILE**, Vyvyan, Wick, Zappy, Zingy, Zippy, Zoe

▸ **Livelihood** see **LIVE(D)**

**Liver(ish)** Foie gras, Hepar, Hepatic(al), Pate, Porta, Puce, Resident, Tomalley

**Liverpool, Liverpudlian** Scouse(r)

**Liverwort** Gemma-cup, Hepatica, Riccia

**Livery(man)** Costume, Ermine, Flunkeydom, Goldsmith, Skinner, Tiger, Uniform

**Livid** Blae, Bruised, Cross, → **FURIOUS**, Pale

▸ **Living** see **LIVE(D)**

**Living-room** Lanai

**Livingstone** Doctor, Ken

**Liza, Lizzie** Bess, Betty, Flivver, Hexam, Tin

**Lizard** Abas, Agama, American chameleon, Amphisbaena, Anguis, Anole, Basilisk, Bearded, Bearded-dragon, Blindworm, Blue-tongued, Brontosaurus, Chameleon, Chuckwalla, Dinosaur, Draco, Dragon, Eft, Evet, Fence, Flying, Frilled, Frill-necked, Galliwasp, Gecko(ne), Gila, Gila monster, Glass snake, Goanna, Gotcha, Guana, Hatteria, Hellbender, Horned, Iguana, Jew, Kabaragoya, Komodo (dragon), Lacerta, Legua(a)n, Lounge, Malayan monitor, Mastigure, Menopome, Mokomoko, Moloch, Monitor, Mosasaur(us), Mountain devil, Newt, Ngarara, Perentie, Perenty, Reptile, Rock, Sand, Sauria, Scincoid, Seps, Skink, Slow-worm, Snake, Sphenodon, Stellio(n), Sungazer, Swift, Tegu(exin), Teiid, Thorny devil, Tokay, Tuatara, Tuatera, Varan, Wall, Whiptail, Worm, Worral, Worrel, Zandoli, Zonure

**Llama** Alpaca, Alpaco, Cria, Guanaco, Huanaco, Paco, Vicuña

**Load(ed), Loader, Loading, Loads** Accommodation, Affluent, Amass, Back-end, Ballast, Base, Biased, Boot-strap, Boozy, Burden, Cargo, Charge, Cobblers, Dead weight, Disc, Dope, Drunk, Dummy, Fardel, Fork-lift, Fother, Frau(gh)tage, Freight, Front-end, Fulham, Full, Gestant, Glyc(a)emic, Heap, Input, Install, Jag, Lade, Lard, Last, Live, Onus, Opulent, Pack, Packet, Pay, Peak, Power, Prime, Raft, Rich, Scads, Seam, Shipment, Shoal, Some, Span, Stow, Super, Surcharge, → **TIGHT**, Tipsy, Tod, Traction, Ultimate, Useful, Wealthy, Weight, Wharfinger, Wing

**Loaf(er), Loaves** Baguette, Bannock, Barmbrack, Batch, Baton, Beachbum, Beachcomber, Bloomer, Bludge, Bonce, Boule, Bread, Brick, Bum, Bu(r)ster, Cad, Cob, Coburg, Cottage, Currant, Danish, Farmhouse, French stick, Hawm, Head, Hoe-cake, Idle, Layabout, → **LAZE**, Lazybones, Long tin, Lusk, Manchet, Meat, Miche, Milk, Mooch, Mouch, Pan, Pan(h)agia, Plain, Plait, Quartern, Roll, Roti, Shewbread, Shoe, Showbread, Sliced, Slosh, Split tin, Square tin, Stollen, Stotty, Sugar, Tin, Vantage, Vienna, Yob

**Loam** Clay, Loess, Loss, Malm

**Loan(s)** Advance, Balloon, Benevolence, Bottomry, Bridging, Call, Consolidation, Debenture, Demand, Droplock, Imprest, Lane, Mutuum, Omnium, Out, Prest, Respondentia, Roll-over, Soft, Start-up, Student, Sub, Time, Top-up, War

**Loathe, Loathing, Loathsome** Abhor(rent), Abominate, Carrion, Despise, Detest, Execrate, Hate, Keck, Nauseate, Odious, Reptilian, Scunner, Ug(h)

**Lob** Fungo, Loft, Sky, Underarm

**Lobby** Demo, Division, Entry, Foyer, Gun, Hall, Press, Pressure group, Urge

**Lobe(d)** Anisocercal, Fluke, Frontal, Glossa, Insula, Jugum, Lacinia, Lap, Occipital, Optic, Palmate, Paraglossate, Parietal, Pinnule, Prostomium, Runcinate, Segment, Temporal, Uvula, Vermis

**Lobster** Cock, Crawfish, Crayfish, Crustacean, Decapoda, Langouste, Macrura, Newburg, Norway, Pereion, Pot, Rock, Scampo, Spiny, Squat, Thermidor, Tomalley

**Local(ity)** Area, Boor, Bro, Close, Des(h)i, Endemic, Home, Inn, Insider, Landlord, Native, Near, Nearby, Neighbourhood, Number, Parochial, Provincial, Pub, Regional, Resident, Swadishi, Tavern, Topical, Vernacular, Vicinal

▷ **Local** *may indicate* a dialect word

**Locale** Area, Scene, Site

**Locate(d), Location** Address, Connect, Echo, Emplacement, Find, Fix, Lay, Milieu, Node, Pinpoint, Pitch, Place, Placement, Plant, Post, Put, Recess, Sat, Scene, Set-up, Site, Situate, Situation, Sofar, Spot, Theatre, Trace, Ubiety, Venue, Website, Where(abouts), Workplace, Zone

**Loch, Lough** Allen, Ashie, Awe, Derg, Earn, Eil, Erne, Etive, Fine, Gare, Garten, Glen Lyon, Holy, Hourn, Katrine, → **LAKE**, Larne, Leven, Linnhe, Lomond, Long, Moidart, Morar, More, Na Keal, Neagh, Ness, Rannoch, Ryan, Sea, Shiel, Strangford, Tay, Torridon

**Lock(ing), Locker, Locks, Lock up** Bar, Barnet, Bolt, Canal, Central, Chain, Chubb®, Clap-sill, Clinch, Combination, Cowlick, Curlicue, Davy Jones, Deadbolt, Detent, Drop, Fastener, Fermentation, Foretop, Gate, Haffet, Haffit, Handcuff, Hasp, Hold, Intern, Key, Kiss curl, Latch, Lazaretto, Man, Mane, Mortise, Percussion, Prison, Quiff, Ragbolt, Rim, Ringlet, Safety, Sasse, Scalp, Scissors, → **SECURE**, Sluice, Snap, Spring, Staircase, Sta(u)nch, Stock, Strand, Tag, Talon, Tetanus, Time, Trap, Tress, Tuft, Tumbler, Vapour, Villus, Ward, Watergate, Wheel, Wrestle, Yale®

**Locket** Lucy

**Lockjaw** Tetanus, Trismus

▷ **Lockkeeper** *may indicate* a hairnet

**Locksmith** Garret-master, Hairdresser

**Locomotive** Banker, Bogie, Bul(l)gine, Engine, Iron horse, Mobile, Mogul, Rocket, Steam, Steamer, Train

**Locum** Deputy, Relief, Stand-in, Stopgap

**Locus** Centrode, Horopter, Lemniscate, Place, Spot

**Locust, Locust tree** Acacia, Anime, Carob, Cicada, Hopper, Nymph, Robinia, Seventeen-year, Voetganger

**Lode** Comstock, Lodge, Mother, Reef, Vein

**Lodestone** Magnes, Magnet

**Lodge(r)** Bestow, Billet, Board(er), Box, Chalet, Cosher, Deposit, Dig, Doss, Encamp, Entertain, Freemason, Grange, Grove, Guest, Harbour, Host, Hunting, Inmate, Inquiline, Instal, Layer, Lie, Masonic, Nest, Orange, Parasite, PG, Porter's, Put up, Quarter, Rancho, Resident, Room(er), Roomie, Roommate, Stay, Storehouse, Stow, Sweat, Tenant, Tepee, Up-put, Wigwam

**Lodging(s)** Abode, B and B, Chummage, Dharms(h)ala, Diggings, Digs, Dosshouse, Ferm, Grange, Grove, Hospitium, Hostel, Inquiline, Kip, Minshuku, Pad, Padding-ken, Pension, Pied-à-terre, Quarters, Resiant, Rooms, Singleen, Sponging-house, Spunging-house, YHA

**Loft(iness), Lofty** Aerial, Airy, Arrogant, Attic, Celsitude, Chip, Choir, Exalted, Garret, Garryowen, Grand, Haymow, High, Hoity-toity, Jube, Lordly, Magniloquent, Noble, Olympian, Organ, Pulpitum, Rarefied, Rigging, Rood, Roost, Sky(ish), Sublime, Tallat, Tallet, Tallot

**Log(ging), Logs** Billet, Black box, Cabin, Chip, Chock, Deadhead, Diarise, Diary, Enter, Hack, Key(stroke), Ln, Lumber, Mantissa, Minutes, Nap(i)erian, Neper, Patent, Poling, Raft, → **RECORD**, Stock, Tachograph, Yule

**Logarithm** Common, Lod, Mantissa, Nap(i)erian, Natural

**Logic(al)** Alethic, Analytical, Aristotelian, Boolean, Chop, Cogent, Coherent, Deontic, Dialectic(s), Digital, Distributed, Doxastic, Elench(us), Epistemics, Formal, Fuzzy, Hardhead(ed), Heuristics, Iff, Mathematical, Modal, Organon, Philosophical, Premise, Pusser's, Ramism, Ratiocinate, Rational(e), Reason, Sane, Sequacious, Shared, Sorites, Syllogism, Symbolic, Tense, Trivium, Vienna circle

**Logo** Brand, Colophon, Monogram, Motif, Trademark

**Loin(s)** Flank, Inguinal, Lisk, Lungie, Lunyie, Reins

**Loincloth** Dhoti, Lungi, Pareu, Waist-cloth

**Loiter(ing)** Dally, Dare, Dawdle, Dilatory, Dilly-dally, Idle, Lag, Lallygag, Leng, Lime, →**LINGER**, Loaf, Lollygag, Mike, Mooch, Mouch, Potter, Saunter, Scamp, Suss, Taigle, Tarry

**Lola** Dolores

**Loll** Hawm, Lounge, Sprawl

**Lollipop, Lolly** Ice pole, Lulibub, Sucker

**Lolly** Money, Popsicle®, Sweetmeat

**London(er)** 'Arry, Big Smoke, Cockaigne, Cockney, Co(c)kayne, East-ender, Flat-cap, Jack, Port, Roseland, Smoke, Town, Troynovant, Wen

**London pride** None-so-pretty

**Lone(r), Lonely** Anchoret, Bereft, Eremite, Grass widow, Hermit, Isolated, Recluse, Remote, Rogue, Saddo, Secluded, Sole, Solitary, Unked, Unket, Unkid

**Long(er), Longing, Longs** Ache, Aitch, Ake, Appetent, Appetite, Aspire, Brame, Covet, Crave, Desire, Die, Earn, Erne, Eternal, Far, Gasp, Greed, Green, Grein, →**HANKER**, Huey, Hunger, Inveterate, Island, Itch, L, Lanky, Large, Lengthy, Longa, Lust, Macron, Marathon, Miss, More, →**NO LONGER**, Nostalgia, Option, Pant, Parsec, →**PINE**, Prolix, Sesquipedalian, Side, Sigh, Tall, Thirst, Trews, Wearisome, Weary, Wish, Wist, Yearn, Yen

**Long-eared** Spicate

**Longitude** Celestial, Ecliptic, Meridian

**Long-lashed** Mastigophora(n)

**Long live(d), Long-term** Banzai, Macrobian, Permanent, Viva, Vive, Zindabad

**Longshoreman** Hobbler, Hoveller, Wharfinger

**Long-sighted(ness)** Hypermetropia

**Long-suffering** Job, Patient, Stoical

**Long-tailed** Macrural

**Long-winded** Prolix, Rambling, Verbose, Wordy

**Loo** Ajax, Bog, Can, Chapel, Dike, Game, Gents, Jakes, John, Latrine, Privy, Toilet

**Loofah** Towel gourd

**Look(s), Look at** After-eye, Air, Aspect, Await, Behold, Belgard, Blink, Bonne-mine, Browse, Busk, Butcher's, Butcher's hook, Case, Clock, Close-up, Countenance, Crane, Daggers, Decko, Deek, Dekko, Demeanour, Ecce, Ecco, Expression, Eye, Eyeball, Eye-glance, Face, Facies, Gander, Gawp, Gaze, Geek, Glad-eye, Glance, Glare, Gleam, Gledge, Glimpse, Glom, Glower, Goggle, Good, Grin, Hallo, Hangdog, Hey, Hippocratic, Iliad, Inspect, Keek, La, Leer, Lo, Mien, New, Ogle, Old-fashioned, Peek, Peep, Peruse, Prospect, Ray, Recce, Refer, →**REGARD**, Scan, Scowl, Scrutinise, Search, See, Seek, Seem, Shade, Sheep's eyes, Shufti, Shufty, Spy, Squint, Squiz, Stare, Survey, Toot, V, Vista, Wet

**Look-out (man)** Achtung, Cockatoo, Crow's nest, Dixie, Huer, Mirador, Nit, Pas op, Picket, Prospect, Sangar, Scout, Sentinel, Sentry, Spotter, Sungar, Tentie, Toot(er), Watch, Watchtower

▷ **Look silly** *may indicate* an anagram

**Loom** Beamer, Dobby, Emerge, Impend, Jacquard, Lathe, Lease-rod, Menace, Overhang, Picker, Temple, Threaten, Tower

**Loon(y)** Airhead, Diver, Nutter

**Loop(ed), Loophole, Loopy** Articulatory, Becket, Bight, Billabong, Bouclé, Carriage, Chink, Closed, Coil, Eyelet, Eyesplice, Fake, Feedback, Frog, Frontlet, Grom(m)et, Ground, Grummet, Hank, Heddle-eye, Henle's, Hysteresis, Infinite, Kink, Knop, Lasket, Lippes, Local, Lug, Noose, Oillet, Parral, Parrel, Pearl(-edge), Picot, Prusik, Purl, Riata, Scrunchie, Squiggle, Staple, Stirrup, Swag, Tab, Terry, Toe, Twist

**Loos** Anita

**Loose(n), Loose woman** Absolve, Abstrict, Adrift, Afloat, Anonyma, Baggage, Bail, Besom, Bike, Bunter, Chippie, Chippy, Clatch, Cocotte, Cutty, Demi-mondaine, Demirep,

Demivierge, Desultory, Dissolute, Dissolve, Doxy, Draggletail, Dratchell, Drazel, Ease, Emit, Flabby, Flipperty-flopperty, Flirt-gill, Floosie, Floozie, Floozy, Floppy, Franion, Free, Gangling, Gay, Geisha, Hussy, Insecure, Jade, Jay, Jezebel, Lax, Light-heeled, Limp, Loast, Loon, Loste, Mob, Mort, Naughty pack, Painted, Pinnace, Profligate, Promiscuous, Quail, Ramp, →**RELAX**, Sandy, Scrubber, Shaky, Skanky-ho, Slack, Slag, Slapper, Slipshod, Slut, Streel, Strumpet, Tart, Tramp, Trull, Ungyve, Unhasp, Unhitch, Unknit, Unknot, Unlace, Unlash, Unleash, Unpin, Unreined, Unscrew, Unstuck, Unthread, Untie, Vague, Waistcoateer, Wappend, Whore

**Loot** Berob, Boodle, Booty, Cragh, Creach, Foray, Haul, Mainour, Oof, Peel, Pillage, Pluck, →**PLUNDER**, Ransack, Rape, Reave, Reif, Rieve, Rob, Sack, Smug, Spoils, Spoliate, Stouth(e)rie, Swag, Treasure, Waif

**Lop** Behead, Clip, Clop, Curtail, Detruncate, Droop, Shroud, Sned, Snee, Trash

**Lope** Stride

**Lop-sided** Badger-legged

**Loquacious** Chatty, Gabby, Garrulous, Rambling

**Lord(s), Lordship, Lordly** Adonai, Ahura Mazda, Anaxandron, Arrogant, Boss, Byron, Cardigan, Chatelain, Cripes, Cyril, Dieu, Dominate, Domineer, Dominical, Drug, Duc, Earl, Elgin, Gad, Gilded Chamber, God, Haw-haw, Herr, Idris, Imperious, Jim, Justice, Kami, Kitchener, Land, Landgrave, Law, Ld, Liege, Lonsdale, Losh, Lud, MCC, Meneer, Mesne, Misrule, Mynheer, Naik, Oda Nobunaga, Omrah, Ordinary, Ormazd, Ormuzd, Palsgrave, Peer, Sea, Second chamber, Seigneur, Seignior, Shaftesbury, Sire, Spiritual, Taverner, Temporal, Tuan, Ullin

**Lords and ladies** Wake-robin

**Lore** Cab(b)ala, Edda, Lair, Lare, Riem, Upanis(h)ad

**Lorelei** Siren

**Lorgnette** Starers

**Lorna** Doone

**Lorry, Lorries** Artic(ulated), Camion, Carrier, Crummy, Double-bottom, Drag, Drawbar outfit, Dropsided, Flatbed, Juggernaut, Low-loader, Rig, Road train, Tipper, Tonner, →**TRUCK**, Wagon

**Los Angeles** La-la-land

**Lose(r)** Also-ran, Decrease, Drop, Elude, Fail, Forfeit, Hesitater, Leese, Misère, Mislay, Misplace, No-no, Nowhere, Saddo, Spread, Stiff, Tank, Throw, Tine(r), Tyne, Underdog, Unsuccessful, Waste, Weeper

**Loss, Lost** Angel's share, Anosmia, Aphesis, Aphonia, Apocope, Apraxia, Astray, At sea, Attainder, Boohai, Chord, Cost, Dead, Decrease, Depreciation, Detriment, Disadvantage, Elision, Extinction, Foredamned, Forfeited, Forgotten, Forlorn, Gone, Hurtful, Lore, Lorn, Lurch, Missing, Omission, Outage, Pentimento, Perdition, Perdu, Perished, Preoccupied, Privation, Psilosis, Reliance, Shrinkage, Stray, Tine, Tinsel, Tint, Toll, Traik, Tribes, Tyne(d), Ullage, Unredeemed, Wastage, Wasted, Will, Write-off, Wull

**Loss of memory** Amnesia, Black-out, Fugue, Infonesia, Paramnesia

▷ **Lost** *may indicate* an anagram or an obsolete word

**Lot(s)** Abundant, Amount, Aret(t), Badly, Bags, Batch, Boatload, Bomb, Caboodle, Cavel, Chance, Deal, Destiny, Dole, Doom, Drove, Due, →**FATE**, Fortune, Group, Hantle, Hap, Heaps, Horde, Host, Item, Job, Kevel, Kismet, Lank, Lashings, Legion, Loads, Loadsa, Luck, Manifold, Many, Mass, Moh, Moira, Mony, Mort, Much, Myriad, Oceans, Often, Omnibus, Oodles, Oodlins, Pack, Parcel, Parking, Plenitude, Plenty, Plethora, Portion, Power, Purim, Raft, Rich, Scads, Set, Shedload, Sight, Slather, Slew, Slue, Sortilege, Sortition, Stack, Sum, Tall order, The works, Tons, Vole, Wagonload, Weird

**Loth** Averse, Circumspect, Sweer(t), Sweirt(t), Unwilling

**Lothario** Lady-killer, Libertine, Poodle-faker, Rake, Womaniser

**Lotion** After-shave, Blackwash, Calamine, Collyrium, Cream, Emollient, Eye-wash, Humectant, Setting, Suntan, Unguent, Wash, Yellow wash

**Lottery, Lotto** Art union, Ballot, Bingo, Cavel, Draw, Gamble, National, Pakapoo, Pools, Postcode, Punchboard, Raffle, Rollover, Scratchcard, Sweepstake, Tattersall's, Tombola

**Lotus (eater), Lotus land** Asana, Djerba, Lotophagus, Padmasana, White

**Louche** Rip

**Loud(ness), Loudly** Bel, Big, Blaring, Booming, Brassy, Clarion, Decibel, Ear-splitting, F, FF, Flashy, Forte, Fracas, Full-mouthed, Garish, Gaudy, Glaring, Hammerklavier, High(pitched), Jazzy, Lumpkin, Noisy, Orotund, Plangent, Raucous, Roarie, Siren, Sone, Stentor(ian), Strident, Tarty, Vocal, Vociferous, Vulgar

**Loudspeaker** Action, Boanerges, Bullhorn, Hailer, Megaphone, PA, Squawk box, Stentor, Subwoofer, Tannoy®, Tweeter, Woofer

▶ **Lough** *see* LOCH

**Louis** Baker, Roi

**Louisianian** Cajun

**Lounge(r)** Cocktail, Couch potato, Daiker, Da(c)ker, Departure, Doze, Executive, Hawm, Idle, Laze, Lie, Lizard, Loaf, Loll, Lollop, Parlour, Paul's man, Recline, Settee, Sitkamer, Slouch, Sun, Sunbed, Transit, Transitive

**Louse (up), Lousy, Lice** Acrawl, Argulus, Bolix, Bollocks, Chat, Chicken, Cootie, Crab, Crawling, Crummy, Fish, Head, Isopod(a), Kutu, Mallophaga, Nit, Oniscus, Pedicular, Phthiriasis, Plant, Psocid, Psocoptera, Psylla, Pubic, Slater, Snot, Sowbug, Sucking, Vermin, Whale

**Lout(ish)** Auf, Clod(hopper), Coof, Cuif, Galere, Hallian, Hallion, Hallyon, Hick, Hob, Hobbledehoy, Hooligan, Hoon, Jack, Jake, Keelie, Lager, Larrikin, Litter, Lob(lolly), Loord, Lubber, Lumpkin, Lycra, Oaf, Oik, Rube, Swad, Tout, Tripper, Ungallant, Yahoo, Yob(bo)

**Louvre** Shutter

**Love(d), Lovable, Lover** Abelard, Admire, Adore, Adulator, Affection, Agape, Alma, Amabel, Amanda, Amant, Amateur, Ami(e), Amoret, Amoroso, Amour, Angharad, Antony, Ardour, Ariadne, Aroha, Aucassin, Beau, Bedfellow, Bidie-in, Blob, Brotherly, Calf, Care, Casanova, Chamberer, Cicisbeo, Concubine, Coquet, Court, Courtly, Cupboard, Cupid, Dear, Dona(h), Dotard, Dote, Doxy, Duck(s), Ducky, Dulcinea, Eloise, Eloper, Emotion, Enamorado, Eros, Esme, Fan(boy), Fancy man, Flame, Frauendienst, Free, Gal(l)ant, Goose-egg, Greek, Hon(ey), Idolise, Inamorata, Inamorato, Iseult, Isolde, Item, Jo, Kama, Lad, Lancelot, Leander, Leman, Like, Lochinvar, Loe, Loo, Lurve, Man, Mistress, Nada, Nihility, Nil, Nothing, Nought, Nut, O, Pairs, Paramour, Pash, Passion, Pet, Phaedra, Philander, -phile, Philtre, Platonic, Precious, Protestant, Psychodelic, Puppy, Revere, Rhanja, Romance, Romeo, Sapphism, Sigisbeo, Smitten, Spark, Spooner, Stale, Storge, Suitor, Swain, Thisbe, Tough, Toyboy, Treasure, Tristan, Troilus, True, Turtle(-dove), Valentine, Venus, Virtu, Woman, Worship, Zap, Zeal, Zero

**Love-apple** Tomato, Wolf's-peach

**Love-bite** Hickey

**Love-child** By-blow, Come-by-chance

**Love-in-a-mist** Nigella

**Love letter** Capon

**Lovely** Adorable, Belle, Cute, Dishy, Dreamy, Exquisite, Fair, Gorgeous, Looker, Nasty, Super

**Love-making** →INTERCOURSE, Kama Sutra, Sex, Slap and tickle, Snog

**Love-sick** Smit(ten), Strephon

**Loving(ly)** Amoroso, Amorous, Fond, Tender

**Low(est), Low-born, Low-cut, Lower(ing), Low-key** Abase, Abate, Abysmal, Amort, Area, Avail(e), Avale, B, Basal, Base(-born), Bass(o), Beneath, Blue, Caddish, Calf, Canaille, Cartoonist, Cheap, Church, Cocktail, Condescend, Contralto, Couch, Cow, Crestfallen, Croon, Crude, Darken, Debase, Declass, Décolleté, Deepen, Deepmost, Degrade, Deign, Demean, Demit, Demote, Depress, Despicable, Devalue, Dim, Dip, Dishonourable, Dispirited, Doldrums, Downbeat, Downmarket, Drawdown, Drop, Early, Embase, Flat, Foot, Frown, Gazunder, Glare, Guernsey, Gurly, Gutterblood,

Hedge(-hopping), Hidalgo, Humble, Ignoble, Imbase, Inferior, Jersey, Laigh, Lallan, Law, Lessen, Light, Lite, Mass, Mean(born), Menial, Moo, Mopus, Morose, Nadir, Net, Nether, Nett, Non-U, Ornery, Ostinato, Paravail, Plebeianise, Profound, Prole, Relegate, Ribald, Rock-bottom, Sad, Scoundrel, Scowl, Secondo, Settle, Shabby, Short, Soft, Stoop, Subordinate, Subscript, Sudra, Sunken, Undermost, Unnoble, Unobtrusive, Vail, Vulgar, Weak, Wretched

**Lowbrow** Essex man, Philistine

**Low country** Flanders

**Lowdown** Dirt, Gen, Info, Stats

▷ **Lower** *may refer to* cattle

**Lowland(er)** Carse, Fen, Gallovidian, Glen, Laigh, Lallans, Merse, Mudflat, Plain, Polder, Sassenach, Vlei

**Low-lying** Callow, Epigeous, Fens, Inferior, Sump

**Low maintenance** Easy care

**Low person** Boor, Bunter, Cad, Caitiff, Cocktail, Demirep, Ratfink, Snot

**Lowry** LS

**Loyal(ty)** Adherence, Allegiant, Brand, Brick, Clanship, Dependable, Diehard, Esprit de corps, Faithful, Fast, Fealty, Fidelity, Firm, Gungho, Leal, Liegedom, Liegeman, Patriotic, Pia, Stalwart, Staunch, Tribalism, Troth, → **TRUE**, True blue, Trusty

**Loyalist** Hard core, Paisley, Patriot, Tory

**Lozenge** Cachou, Catechu, Coughdrop, Fusil, Jujube, Mascle, Pastille, Pill, Rhomb, Rustre, Tablet, Troche, Voided

**LSD** Acid, Money

**Lubber(ly), Lubbers** Booby, Clod, Clumsy, Gawky, Hulk, Landsman, Lob, Looby, Oaf, Slowback, Swab, Swads

**Lubricant, Lubricate, Lubrication** Carap-oil, Coolant, Derv, Fluid, Force-feed, Grease, Oil, Petrolatum, Sebum, Synovia, Unguent, Vaseline®, Wool-oil

**Luce** Ged

**Lucerne** Alfalfa, Fodder, Medick, Nonsuch

**Lucia** Mimi

**Lucid** Bright, Clear, Perspicuous, Sane

**Lucifer** Devil, Match, Proud, Satan, Venus

**Luck(y)** Amulet, Auspicious, Beginner's, Blessed, Bonanza, Break, Caduac, Canny, Cess, Chance, Charmed, Chaunce, Daikoku, Dip, Fat, Fate, Fluke, → **FORTUNE**, Godsend, Hap, Heather, Hit, Jam(my), Jim, Joss, Lady, Lot, Mascot, Mercy, Mozzle, Pot, Prosit, Providential, Pudding-bag, Purple passage, Purple patch, Seal, Seel, Sele, Serendipity, Sess, Sonsie, Sonsy, Spawny, Star(s), Streak, Success, Talisman, Tinny, Tough, Turn-up, White rabbits, Windfall, Wishbone, Worse

**Luckless** Hapless, Wight

**Lucrative** Earner, Money-spinner

**Lucre** Money, Pelf, Tin

**Lucy** Locket

**Lud** Gad

**Luddite** Rioter, Saboteur, Wrecker

**Ludicrous** Absurd, Bathetic, Bathos, Crackpot, Farcical, Fiasco, Inane, Irish, Jest, Laughable, Risible

**Ludo** Uckers

**Luff** Derrick

**Lug** Ear, Earflap, Haul, Sea-worm, Sowle, Tote, Tow

**Luggage** Bags, Carryon, Cases, Dunnage, Excess, Grip, Hand, Kit, Petara, Samsonite®, Suiter, Traps, Trunk

**Luggage-carrier** Grid

**Lugubrious** Dismal, Drear

**Luke-warm** Laodicean, Lew, Tepid

**Lull, Lullaby** Berceuse, Calm, Cradlesong, Hushaby, Respite, Rock, Sitzkreig, Soothe, Sopite

**Lulu** Honey, Stunner

**Lumbar** Hip

**Lumber(ing)** Clump, Galumph, Jumble, Pawn, Ponderous, Raffle, Saddle, Scamble, Timber

**Lumberjack** Bushwhacker, Feller, Logger, Logman, Rafter

**Luminance, Luminous, Luminosity, Luminescence** Aglow, Arc, Candela, Dayglo, Foxfire, Glow, Hero, Ignis-fatuus, L, Light, Meteor, Nit, Phosphorescent, Scintillon, Sea-dog, Wildfire, Will o' the wisp

**Lumme** Coo, Lor

**Lummox** Galoot

**Lump(ectomy), Lump(s), Lump(y)** Adam's apple, Aggregate, Bolus, Bubo, Bud, Bulge, Bur(r), Caruncle, Chuck, Chunk, Clat, Claut, Clod, Clot, Cob, Combine, Da(u)d, Dallop, Dollop, Enhydros, Epulis, Flocculate, Ganglion, Geode, Gnarl, Gob(bet), Goiter, Goitre, Goop, Grape, Grip, Grumose, Hunch, Hunk, Inium, Knarl, Knob, Knub, Knur(r), Knurl, Lob, Lunch, Malleolus, Mass, Mastoid, Moss-litter, Mote, Mott, Myxoma, Neuroma, Nibble, Nirl, Node, Nodule, Nodulus, Nub(bin), Nubble, Nugget, Nur(r), Nurl, Osteophyte, Plook, Plouk, Quinsy, Raguly, Sarcoma, Scybalum, Sitfast, Slub, Strophiole, Tragus, Tuber(cle), Tumour, Tylectomy, Wart, Wodge

**Lumpsucker** Sea-owl

**Lunacy, Lunatic** Bedlam, Dementia, Demonomania, Folly, Insanity, Mad(ness), Madman, Maniac, Moonstruck, Nutter, Psychosis

**Lunar** Evection, Mascon, Selenological

▷ **Lunatic** *may indicate* an anagram

**Lunch(time)** Bait, Box, Crib, Dejeune, Déjeuner, Fork, L, Liquid, Nacket, Nocket, Nuncheon, Packed, Piece, Ploughman, Pm, Power, Tiff(in), Working

**Lung(s)** Alveoli, Bellows, Book, Breather, Coalminer's, Farmer's, Green, Iron, Lights, Pleural, Pulmo, Pulmonary, Soul

**Lung disease, Lung problem** Anthracosis, Atelectasis, Barotrauma, Byssinosis, Emphysema, Farmer's lung, Pneumoconiosis, Siderosis, Silicosis, Tuberculosis

**Lunge** Breenge, Breinge, Dive, Stab, Thrust, Venue

**Lungfish** Dipnoi(an)

**Lupin** Arsene

**Lurch** Reel, Slew, Stagger, Stoit, Stumble, Swee, Toss

**Lure** Bait, Bribe, Carrot, Decoy, Devon minnow, Entice, Horn, Inveigle, Jig, Judas, Loss leader, Plug, Roper, Spinner, Spoon, Spoonbait, Spoonhook, Squid, Stale, Temptation, Tice, Tole, Toll, Train, Trepan, Wormfly

**Lurgi** Illness

**Lurid** Gruesome, Purple, Sensational

**Lurk(ing)** Dare, Latitant, Skulk, Slink, Snoke, Snook, Snowk

**Lusatia(n)** Wend(ic), Wendish

**Luscious** Succulent, Sweet

**Lush** Alcoholic, Alkie, Alky, Dipso(maniac), Drunk, Fertile, Green, Juicy, Lydian, Soak, Sot, Succulent, Toper, Tosspot, Verdant

**Lust(ful), Lusty** Cama, Concupiscence, Corflambo, Desire, Eros, Frack, Goatish, Greed, Kama, Lech(ery), Lewd, Libertine, Libido, Megalomania, Obidicut, Prurience, Radge, Randy, Rank, Raunchy, Salacious, Steamy, Venereous

**Lustre, Lustrous** Brilliance, Census, Chatoyant, Galena, Gaum, Gilt, Gloss, Gorm, Inaurate, Lead-glance, Lovelight, Pearlescent, Pearly, Pentad, Reflet, Satiny, Schiller, →SHEEN, Shellac, Water

**Lute, Lutist** Amphion, Chitarrone, Cither, Dichord, Orpharion, Pandora, Pandore, Pipa, Theorbo, Vielle

**Lutetium** Lu

**Lutheran** Adiaphorist, Calixtin(e), Pietist, Protestant, Ubiquitarian
**Luvvie** Theatrical
**Lux** Lx
**Luxemburg** L
**Luxuriant, Luxuriate, Luxurious, Luxury (lover)** Apician, Bask, Clover, Cockaigne, Cockayne, Comfort, Copious, Delicate, Deluxe, Dolce vita, Extravagant, Exuberant, Five-star, Fleshpots, Lavish, Lotus-eating, Lucullan, Lush, Milk and honey, Mollitious, Opulence, Ornate, Palatial, Pie, Plush(y), Posh, Rank, → **RICH**, Ritzy, Sumptuous, Sybarite, Wallow
**Lycanthropist** Werewolf
**Lydia** Languish
**Lye** Buck
▶ **Lying** *see* **LIE(S)**
**Lymph** Chyle
**Lymphoma, Lymphocyte** Burkett's, T-cell
**Lynch(ing), Lyncher** Dewitt, Hang, Necktie party, Nightrider, String up
**Lynx** Bay, Bobcat, Caracal, Desert, Rooikat
**Lyre** Box, Cithern, Harp, Psaltery, Testudo, Trigon
**Lyric(s), Lyrical, Lyricist, Lyrist** Awdl, Cavalier, Dit(t), Epode, Gilbert, Hammerstein, Melic, Ode, Orphean, Paean, Pean, Poem, Poetic, Rhapsodic, Song, Spinto, Words

# Mm

**M** Married, Member, Metre, Mike, Mile, Thousand
**Mac** Bo, Mino, Scot, Waterproof
**Macabre** Gothic, Grotesque, Morbid, Sick
**Macaque** Rhesus
**Macaroni** Beau, Blood, Cat, Dandy, Elbow, Exquisite, Fop, Jack-a-dandy, Olio, Pasta, Petitmaitre
**Macaroon** Biscuit, Signal
**Macaulay** Layman
**Macbeth** Thane
**Mace** Club, Nutmeg, Sceptre, Spice
**Mace-bearer** Beadle, Bedel(l), Poker
**Macedonian** Alexander, Philip, Stagirite, Stagyrite
**Machete** Bolo
**Machiavellian** Savvy
**Machine(ry)** Apparat(us), Appliance, Bathing, Beam-engine, Capstan, → **DEVICE**, Facsimile, Fax, Fruit, Infernal, Instrument, Life-support, One-armed bandit, Party, Plant, Propaganda, Rowing, Sausage, Sewing, Slot, Spin, Spreader, Tape, Teaching, Time, Vending, Virtual, War, Washing, Weighing

## MACHINES

| *3 letters:* | Engine | Slasher | Windmill |
|---|---|---|---|
| Gin | Enigma | Tumbler | |
| | Grader | Turbine | *9 letters:* |
| *4 letters:* | Hopper | Twin tub | Air-engine |
| Drum | Linter | Wringer | Answering |
| Haik | Ludlow | Zamboni® | Automaton |
| Heck | Planer | | Bulldozer |
| Loom | Pulper | *8 letters:* | Dynamotor |
| Mule | Seeder | Calender | Excavator |
| Wind | Slicer | Dialyser | Hummeller |
| | Tardis | Enginery | Osmometer |
| *5 letters:* | Tedder | Filatory | Perfector |
| Churn | Turing | Hot-press | Processor |
| Cycle | Willow | Linotype® | Rotavator® |
| Lathe | | Moulinet | Separator |
| Poker | *7 letters:* | Nintendo® | Stamp-mill |
| Pokie | Burster | Pulsator | Stenotype® |
| Press | Capstan | Shredder | Treadmill |
| Robot | Dredger | Spreader | Wimshurst |
| Rover | Hawk-Eye® | Symatron | |
| Stamp | Jukebox | Thresher | *10 letters:* |
| | Milling | Throstle | Beam-engine |
| *6 letters:* | Moviola® | Transfer | Centrifuge |
| Dredge | Potcher | Windlass | Clobbering |

| | | **12 letters:** | Supercalender |
|---|---|---|---|
| Earth-mover | Typewriter | | |
| Emi-scanner® | Watersnail | Lithotripter | |
| Jawbreaker | | Muckspreader | **14 letters:** |
| Liquidiser | **11 letters:** | | One-armed bandit |
| Passimeter | Comptometer® | **13 letters:** | |
| Pile-driver | Fourdrinier | Defibrillator | **16 letters:** |
| Roadroller | Weighbridge | Slipform paver | Archimedean screw |
| Rototiller | | Spinning jenny | Combine harvester |

**Macho** Defiant, Hunk, Jock, Laddish, Rambo

**Mackerel** Albacore, Amber-fish, Brack, Dory, Fish, Horse, Pacific, Pimp, Scad, Scomber, Sky, Spanish, Spotted, Tinker, Trevally

**Mackintosh** Burberry®, Mac, Mino, Oilskin, Slicker, Waterproof

**Macropus** Euro, Wallaroo

**Mad(den), Madman, Madness** Angry, Apoplectic, Balmy, Bananas, Barking, Barmy, Bedlam, Berserk, Besotted, Bonkers, Crackbrained, Crackpot, Crazy, Cuckoo, Cupcake, Daffy, Delirious, Dement, Deranged, Détraqué, Distract, Dotty, Enrage, Fay, Fey, Fie, Folie, Folly, Frantic, Frenetic(al), Fruitcake, Furioso, Fury, Gelt, Gyte, Harpic, Hatter, Idiotic, Incense, Insane, Insanie, Insanity, Into, Irate, Ireful, Irritate, Kook, Livid, Loco, Lunatic, Lycanthropy, Madbrained, Maenad, Mango, Mania, Mattoid, Mental, Meshug(g)a, Metric, Midsummer, Moonstruck, Motorway, Mullah, Nuts, Porangi, Provoke, Psycho, Rabid, Rasputin, Raving, Redwood, Redwud, Scatty, Screwy, Short-witted, Starkers, Tonto, Touched, Troppo, Unhinged, Wacko, Wood, Wowf, Wrath, Wud, Xenomania, Yond, Zany

▷ **Mad(den)** *may indicate* an anagram

**Madagascan, Madagascar** Aye-aye, Hova, Indri, Lemur, Malagash, Malagasy, RM

**Madam(e)** Baggage, Bawd, Lady, M, Memsahib, Proprietress

**Madcap** Cake, Impulsive, Tearaway

**Madder** Alizari, Alyari, Chay(a), Gardenia, Genipap, Rose, Rubia, Shaya

**Made (it)** Built, Did, Fec(it), Ff, Gart, Invented

**Made (up)** Synthesized

**Madeira** Cake

**Madge** Pie

▷ **Madly** *may indicate* an anagram

**Madonna** Lady, Lily, Mary, Pietà, Sistine, Virgin

**Madras** Chennai

**Madrigal** Ballet, Fala, Song

**Maelstrom** Voraginous, Vortex, Whirlpool

**Maenad** Devotee, Fan

**Maestro** Artist, Toscanini, Virtuoso

**Mafia, Mafioso** Camorra, Capo, Cosa Nostra, Godfather, Goombah, Mob, Ndrangheta, Omerta, Padrone, Pentito, Sicilian, The Mob, Triad

**Mag** Mail

**Magazine** Arsenal, Clip, Colliers, Contact, Cornhill, Cosmopolitan, Digizine, Economist, E-zine, Field, Girlie, Glossy, Granta, House organ, Jazz mag, Journal, Ladmag, Lady, Lancet, Life, Listener, Little, Magnet, New Yorker, Organ, Paper, Part work, Periodical, Pictorial, Playboy, Powder, Private Eye, Pulp, Punch, She, Skin, Slick, Spectator, Store, Strand, Tatler, Time, Vogue, Warehouse, Weekly, Yoof, Zine

**Magdalene** St Mary

**Maggie** Rita

**Maggot** Bot, Flyblow, Gentiles, Gentle, Grub, Larva, Mawk, Myiasis, Weevil, Whim, Worm

**Magi** Balthazar, Gaspar, Melchior

**Magic(al), Magician, Magic square** Alchemy, Archimage, Art, Baetyl, Black, Black art, Charm, Circle, Conjury, Diablerie, Diablery, Druid, Enchanting, Fabulous, Faust,

Faustus, Fetish, Genie, Goetic, Goety, Gramary(e), Grimoire, Hermetic, Hey presto, Houdini, Illusionist, Incantation, Makuto, Math, Medea, Medicine man, Merlin, Mojo, Moly, Morgan le Fay, Myal, Nasik, Natural, Necromancer, Obeah, Occult, Pawaw, Powwow, Prospero, Reim-kenner, Rhombus, Shamanism, Sorcery, Sortilege, Spell, Speller, Stardust, Supernatural, Sympathetic, Talisman, Thaumaturgics, Theurgy, Voodoo, Warlock, White, Witch-doctor, Wizard, Zendik

**Magistracy, Magistrate** Aedile, Alcalde, Amman, Amtman, Archon, Avoyer, Bailie, Bailiff, Bailli(e), Beak, Bench, Boma, Burgess, Burgomaster, Cadi, Censor, Consul, Corregidor, Curule, Decemvirate, Demiurge, Dictator, Doge(ate), Draco, Edile, Effendi, Ephor, Field cornet, Finer, Foud, Gonfalonier, JP, Judiciary, Jurat, Justice, Kotwal, Landamman(n), Landdrost, Lord Provost, Maire, Mayor, Mittimus, Novus homo, Pilate, Podesta, Portreeve, Pr(a)efect, Pr(a)etor, Prior, Proconsul, Propraetor, Provost, Qadi, Quaestor, Recorder, Reeve, Shereef, Sherif, Stad(t)holder, Stipendiary, Syndic, Tribune, Trier, Worship

**Magnanimity, Magnanimous** Altruistic, Big, Charitable, →GENEROUS, Largeness, Lofty, Noble

**Magnate** Baron, Beaverbrook, Bigwig, Industrialist, Mogul, Onassis, Randlord, Tycoon, Vanderbilt, VIP, Zillionaire

**Magnesia, Magnesium** Bitter-earth, Epsomite, Humite, Kainite, Mg, Periclase

**Magnet(ic), Magnetism** Animal, Artificial, Attraction, Bar, Charisma, Field, Gauss, Horseshoe, Induction, It, Loadstone, Lodestone, Maxwell, Od, Oersted, Oomph, Permanent, Personal, Polar, Pole, Pole piece, Poloidal, Pull, Remanence, Retentivity, Slug, Solenoid, Terrella, Terrestrial, Tesla, Tole, Weber

**Magnificence, Magnificent** Epic, Fine, Gorgeous, Grandeur, Imperial, Laurentian, Lordly, Noble, Pride, Regal, Royal, Splendid, Splendo(u)r, State, Sumptuous, Superb

**Magnifier, Magnify(ing)** Aggrandise, Augment, Binocle, →ENLARGE, Exaggerate, Extol, Increase, Loupe, Megaphone, Microscope, Praise, Teinoscope, Telescope

**Magniloquent** Bombastic, Orotund

**Magnitude** Absolute, Abundance, Amplitude, Apparent, Earthquake, Extent, First, Modulus, Muchness, Photoelectric, Photographic, Scalar, Size, Visual

**Magnolia** An(n)ona, Beaver-tree, Champac, Champak, Mississippi, Sweet bay, Umbrella-tree, Yulan

**Magpie** Bell, Bird, Bishop, Chatterer, Hoarder, Madge, Mag, Margaret, Outer, Pica, Piet, Pyat, Pyet, Pyot

**Magus** Artist

**Magyar** Hungarian, Szekei, Szekel(y), Szekler, Ugrian, Ugric

**Mahogany** Acajou, African, Carapa, Cedrela, Philippine, Toon, Wood

**Mahommedan** Dervish, Shiah

**Maid(en), Maidenly** Abigail, Aia, Amah, Biddy, Bonibell, Bonne, Bonnibell, Burd, Chamber, Chaste, Chloe, Clothes-horse, Damoisel, Dam(o)sel, Debut, Dell, Dey, Dresser, Femme de chambre, First, Girl, Guillotine, Ignis-fatuus, Imago, Inaugural, Io, Iras, Iron, Lorelei, M, Marian, May, Miss, Nerissa, Nymph, Opening, Over, Parlour, Pucelle, Racehourse, Rhian, Rhine, Scullion, Skivvy, Soubrette, Stillroom, Suivante, Tabby, Table, Thestylis, Tirewoman, Tweeny, Valkyrie, Virgin, Walkyrie, Wench, Wicket

**Maidenhair** Fern, Ginkgo

**Mail** Air, →ARMOUR, Byrnie, Cataphract, Chain, Da(w)k, Direct, E(lectronic), Epistle, Express, Fan, Gusset, Habergeon, Hate, Hauberk, Helm, Junk, Letter, Media, Metered, Panoply, Pony express, Post, Ring, Send, Snail, Spam, Surface, Tuille(tte), Voice

**Mailbag** Pouch

**Mailboat** Packet

**Maim** Cripple, Impair, Lame, Main, Mayhem, Mutilate, Vuln

**Main(s)** Atlantic, Brine, Briny, Bulk, →CENTRAL, Chief, Cockfight, Conduit, Essential, Foremost, Gala, Gas, Generally, Grid, Gross, Head, →KEY, Lead(ing), Major, Ocean, Pacific, Palmary, Predominant, Prime, Principal, Ring, →SEA, Sheer, Spanish, Staple, Star, Water

**Mainland** Continent, Pomona, Udal

**Mainstay** Backbone, Bastion, Cornerstone, Pillar, Support

**Maintain(er), Maintenance** Alimony, Allege, Ap(p)anage, Argue, Assert, Aver, Avouch, Avoure, Avow, Claim, Conserve, Contend, Continue, Defend, Escot, Insist, Keep (up), Lengthman, Preserve, Retention, Run, Serve, Service, Sustain, Upbear, Uphold, Upkeep

**Maize** Corn, Hominy, Indian, Indian corn, Mealie, Milo, Polenta, Popcorn, Samp, Silk, Stamp, Sweetcorn, Zea

**Majestic, Majesty** August, Britannic, Dignity, Eagle, Grandeur, Imperial, Maestoso, Olympian, Regal, Royal, SM, Sovereign, Stately, Sublime, Tuanku

**Major (domo)** Barbara, Drum, Great, →**IMPORTANT**, Lulu, Momentous, Pipe, PM, Read, Seneschal, Senior, Sergeant, Signal, Star, Trumpet, Wig

**Majority** Absolute, Age, Body, Eighteen, Landslide, Latchkey, Maturity, Moral, Most, Preponderance, Relative, Silent, Working

**Make(r), Make do, Making** Amass, Assemble, Brand, Build, Cause, Clear, Coerce, Coin, Compel, Compulse, Concoct, Creant, Create, Devise, Earn, Execute, Fabricate, Factive, Fashion, Faute de mieux, Fet(t), Forge, Form, Gar(re), God, Halfpenny, Increate, Mail(e), Manage, Marque, Meg, Name, Nett, Prepare, Production, Reach, Render, Shape, Sort, Temporise, Turn, Wright

▷ **Make** *may indicate* an anagram

**Make believe** Fantasy, Fictitious, Pretend, Pseudo

**Make good** Abet, Compensate, Remedy, Succeed, Ulling

**Make hay** Ted

**Make off** Bolt, Leg it, Mosey, Run, Scarper

**Makeover** Redo

**Makeshift** Bandaid, Crude, Cutcha, Expedient, Jury, Jury-rigged, Kacha, Kachcha, Kludge, Kutcha, Lash-up, Mackle, Pis-aller, Rude, Stopgap, Timenoguy

**Make up, Make-up artist** Ad lib, Compensate, Compose, Concealer, Constitute, Constitution, Cosmetics, Eye-liner, Fard, Fucus, Gaud, Gawd, Gene, Genome, Genotype, Greasepaint, Identikit®, Kohl, Liner, Lipstick, Maquillage, Mascara, Metabolism, Moistener, Orchel, Paint, Pancake, Panstick, Powder, Prime, Reconcile, Rouge, Slap, Tidivate, Titivate, Toiletry, Visagiste, War paint, White-face

**Maladroit** Awkward, Clumsy, Gauche, Graceless, Inapt, Inelegant, Inexpert, Unperfect

**Malady** Disease, Illness, Sickness

**Malagas(e)y** Hova, RM

**Malaise** Affluenza

**Malamute** Alaskan

**Malapropism** Catachresis, Slipslop

**Malaria** Ague, Falciparum, Marsh-fever, Paludism, Tap, Vivax

**Malawi(an)** Nyanja, Nyasa

**Malay(an), Malaysia(n)** Austronesian, Bahasa, Bajou, Brunei, Datin, Datuk, D(a)yak, Jawi, Madurese, Moro, .my, Sabahan, Sakai, Tagalog, Tokay, Tuan

**Male** Alpha, Arrhenotoky, Buck, Bull, Butch, Dog, Ephebe, Ephebus, Gent, Hob, John Doe, Macho, Mansize, Masculine, Patroclinous, Ram, Rogue, Spear(side), Stag, Stamened, Telamon, Tom, Worthiest of the blood

**Malediction** Curse, Cuss, Oath, Slander

**Malefactor** Criminal, Felon, Villain

**Malevolent, Malevolence** Evil, Fell, Malign, Peri, Pernicious, Sinister, Venomous

**Malformation** Parrot-mouth, Teratogenesis

**Malfunction** Act up, Glitch, Hiccup

**Mali** RMM

**Malice, Malicious** Acid, Bitchy, Catty, Cruel, Despiteous, Envy, Grudge, Hatchet job, Hatred, Ill-will, Malevolent, Malign, Mudslinger, Narquois, Prepense, Schadenfreude, Serpent, Snide, Spite, Spleen, Venom, Viperish, Virulent, Vitriol

**Malign(ant), Malignity** Asperse, Backbite, Badmouth, Baleful, Bespatter, Defame, Denigrate, Detract, Evil, Gall, Harm, Hate-rent, Hatred, Libel, Poor-mouth, Sinister, Slander, Spiteful, Swart(h)y, Toxin, Traduce, Vicious, Vilify, Vilipend, Viperous, Virulent

**Malinger(er)** Dodge, Leadswinger, Scrimshank, Shirk, Skrimshank, Truant

**Mall** Arcade, Parade

**Mallard** Duck, Sord

**Malleable** Clay, Ductile, Fictile, Pliable

▷ **Malleable** *may indicate* an anagram

**Mallet** Beetle, Club, Gavel, Hammer, Mace, Maul, Serving, Stick, Tenderizer

**Mallow** Abutilon, Dwarf, Musk, Sida, Urena

**Malodorous** Mephitic, Stenchy

**Malpractice(s)** Sculduggery, Simony, Skulduggery

**Malt** Brewer's grain, Diastase, Grains, Grist, Single, Stingo, Straik, Wort

**Maltese (cross)** Falcon, GC

**Maltreat** Abuse, Harm, Maul, Mishandle, Misuse

**Mammal** Animal, Primate

---

## MAMMALS

**3 letters:**
Bat

**4 letters:**
Anta
Arna
Bear
Hare
Lynx
Peba
Pika
Pudu
Seal
Tahr
Titi
Vole

**5 letters:**
Coati
Dhole
Hyrax
Indri
Lemur
Loris
Otter
Pekan
Rasse
Ratel
Sable
Saola
Shrew
Skunk
Sloth
Takin

Tapir
Tayra
Whale

**6 letters:**
Alpaca
Bobcat
Cervid
Colugo
Cuscus
Dugong
Fisher
Glires
Grison
Hydrax
Margay
Marten
Numbat
Olingo
Rabbit
Sea-ape
Sealch
Sealgh
Serval
Taguan
Tanrec
Tee-tee
Teledu
Tenrec
Theria
Vicuña
Weasel

**7 letters:**
Caracal
Dolphin
Echidna
Fur seal
Giraffe
Glutton
Guanaco
Leporid
Linsang
Manatee
Meerkat
Peccary
Polecat
Raccoon
Rhytina
Sea-lung
Tamandu
Therian
Tylopod
Zorilla

**8 letters:**
Aardvark
Cetacean
Creodont
Eutheria
Kinkajou
Mongoose
Pangolin
Pinniped
Platypus
Porpoise
Sirenian

Stegodon
Tamandua
Viverrid

**9 letters:**
Armadillo
Binturong
Cacomixle
Charronia
Dinothere
Glyptodon
Lagomorph
Monotreme
Musteline
Pachyderm
Pronghorn
Solenodon
Stegodont
Wolverine

**10 letters:**
Cacomistle
Chevrotain
Dermoptera
Jaguarondi
Jaguarundi
Pine marten
Springhaas
Uintathere

**11 letters:**
Artiodactyl
Chiropteran
Metatherian

| | *12 letters:* | *13 letters:* |
|---|---|---|
| Monodelphia | Chalicothere | Notocingulate |
| Pipistrelle | Prototherian | Perissodactyl |
| Titanothere | | |

**Mammon** Money, Riches, Wealth

**Mammoth** Epic, Gigantic, Huge, Jumbo, Mastodon, Whopping, Woolly

**Man(kind), Manly, Manliness** Adam, Advance, Andrew, Ask(r), Belt, Best, Betty, Bimana(l), Biped, Bloke, Bo, Boxgrove, Boy, Boyo, Bozo, Cad, Cairn, Calf, Castle, Cat, Chal, Chap, Checker, Chequer, Chiel, Cockey, Cod, Contact, Continuity, Crew, Cro-Magnon, Cuffin, Cully, Dog, Don, Draught, Dude, Emmanuel, Essex, Everyman, Family, Fancy, Fella, Feller, Fellow, Folsom, Friday, Front, G, Gayomart, Geezer, Gent, Gingerbread, Grimaldi, Guy, He, Heidelberg, Himbo, Hombre, Hominid, Homme, Homo, Homo sapiens, Inner, IOM, Iron, Isle, It, Jack, Java, Joe (Bloggs), Joe Blow, Joe Sixpack, Joe Soap, John(nie), John Doe, Josser, Limit, Link, Lollipop, M, Mac, Male, Medicine, Microcosm, Mister, Mon, Mondeo, Mr, Muffin, Mun, Neanderthal, Numbers, Nutcracker, Oreopithecus, Organisation, Ou, Paleolithic, Party, Pawn, Peking, Person, Piece, Piltdown, Pin, Pithecanthropus, Property, Raff, Ray, Remittance, Renaissance, Resurrection, Rhodesian, Right-hand, Rook, Sandwich, Servant, Servitor, Ship, Sinanthropus, Sir, Sodor, Soldier, Solo, Spear, Staff, Stag, Standover, Straw, Terran, Third, Thursday, Trinil, Twelfth, Tyke, Type, Utility, Valet, Vir(ile), Vitality, White van, Wight

**Man-about-town** Boulevardier

**Manacle** Fetter, Handcuff, Iron, Shackle

**Manage(r), Manageable, Management, Managing** Adhocracy, Administer, Agent, Amildar, Anger, Attain, Aumil, Behave, Board, Boss, Chief, Come by, Conduct, Contrive, Control, Cope, Crisis, Darogha, Direct, Docile, Eke, Exec(utive), Fare, Fend, Find, Floor, Fund, Gerent, Get by, Govern, Grieve, Handle, Head bummer, Honcho, Husband(ry), IC, Impresario, Intendant, Line, Logistical, MacReady, Maître d('hotel), Make do, Manipulate, Manoeuvre, Middle, Nomenklatura, Operate, Organise, Proctor, Procurator, Régisseur, Rig, Roadie, →RUN, Scrape, Shift, Strategy, Subsist, Succeed, Suit, Superintend, Supervisor, Swing, Sysop, Tawie, Top, Tractable, Transact, Treatment, Trustee, Wangle, Webmaster, Wield(y), Yare

**Manatee** Lamantum, Mermaid, Sea-ape

**Manchu** Fu

**Mandala** Kalachakra

**Mandarin** Bureaucrat, Chinaman, Kuo-Yu, Nodding, Satsuma, Tangerine, Yamen

**Mandate, Mandatory** Authority, Decree, De rigueur, Fiat, Incumbent, Order

**Mandela** Madiba, Nelson

**Mandrake** Springwort

**Mandrel** Triblet

**Mane(d), Manes** Crest, Encolure, Jubate, Larva(e), Shades

**Manège** Horseplay, Train

**Manganese** Diagolite, Mn, Synadelphite, Wadd

**Mange, Mangy** Sarcoptic, Scabby

**Manger** Cratch, Crib, Hack, Stall

**Mangle** Agrise, Butcher, Distort, Garble, Hack, Hackle, Haggle, Mammock, Wring(er)

▷ **Mangle** *may indicate an anagram*

**Mango** Dika

**Manhandle** Frogmarch, Maul, Mousle, Rough

**Manhater** Misanthrope

**Manhattan** Bowery

**Mania** Cacoethes, Craze, Frenzy, Lunacy, Paranoia, Passion, Rage

**Manichaean** Albi

**Manicurist** Handmaid

**Manifest(ation), Manifestly** Apparent, Arising, Attest, Avatar, Epiphany, Evident, Evince, Exhibit, Extravert, Extrovert, Feat, List, Marked, Mode, Notably, Obvious, Open, Overt, Schizothymia, Show, Sign, Undisguised, Wrath

**Manifesto** Communist, Plank, Platform, Policy, Pronunciamento

**Manifold(ness)** Many, Multeity, Multiple

**Manila** Abaca, Cheroot

**Manioc** Cassava

**Maniple** Fannel, Fanon

**Manipulate, Manipulative, Manipulator, Manipulation** Bend, Card-sharp, Chiropractor, Cog, Control, Cook, Demagogic, Diddle, Fashion, Finagle, Finesse, Gerrymander, Handle, Hellerwork, Jerrymander, Juggle, Legerdemain, Logodaedalus, Massage, Masseuse, Master-slave, McTimoney chiropractic, Milk, Osteopath, Physiotherapist, Play off, Ply, Rig, Spin, Svengali, Swing, Tong, Tweeze, Use, Wangle, →WIELD

▷ **Manipulate** *may indicate* an anagram

**Manna** Alhagi, Briancon, Food, Trehala, Turkish

**Manner(ism), Mannerly, Manners** Accent, Airs, À la, Appearance, Attitude, Bedside, Behaved, Behaviour, Bon ton, Breeding, Carriage, Comportment, Conduct, Couth, Crew, Custom, Delivery, Deportment, Ethos, Etiquette, Farand, Farrand, Farrant, Guise, Habit, How, Mien, Mister, Mode, Mood, Morality, Mores, Of, Ostent, Panache, Politesse, Presence, Presentation, P's & Q's, Quirk, Rate, Rhetoric, Side, Sort, Style, Table, Thew(s), Thewe(s), Trick, Upsee, Upsey, Upsy, Urbanity, Way, Wise

**Manoeuvre(s)** Alley-oop, Campaign, Castle, Christie, Christy, Démarche, Ebrillade, Engineer, Exercise, Faena, Fianchetto, Fork, Gambit, Grey mail, Half-board, Heimlich, Hot-dog, Jink(s), Jockey, Loop, Manipulate, Op(eration), Pendule, Pesade, Ploy, Pull out, Renversement, Ruse, Short cut, Skewer, Steer, Stickhandle, Tactic, Takeover, Telemark, Use, U-turn, Valsalva, Wear, Wheel(ie), Whipstall, Wile, Wingover, Zigzag

▷ **Manoeuvre** *may indicate* an anagram

**Man-of-war** Armada, Bluebottle, Destroyer, Ironclad, Portuguese

**Manor (house)** Area, Demain, Demesne, Estate, Hall, Kelmscott, Schloss, Vill(a), Waddesdon

**Manse** Parsonage

**Mansion** Broadlands, Burghley House, Casa, Castle Howard, Chateau, Chatworth House, Chevening, Cliveden, Knole, Luton Hoo, Mentmore, Palace, Penshurst Place, Pile, Queen's House, Seat, Stourhead, Stowe, Waddesdon Manor, Woburn Abbey

**Mantle** Asthenosphere, Authority, Blanket, Burnous(e), Capote, Caracalla, Chlamydate, Cloak, Dolman, Elijah, Gas, Lithosphere, Pall, Pallium, Paludament, Pelisse, Rochet, Shawl, Sima, Toga, Tunic, Vakas, Veil

**Mantuan** Maro, Virgil

**Manual** Blue collar, Bradshaw, Cambist, Console, Enchiridion, Great (organ), Guide, Hand, Handbook, How-to, Portolan(o), Positif, Sign

**Manufacture(r), Manufacturing** Assemble, Create, Fabricate, Forger, Industrial(ist), Kanban, Make, Produce

**Manure** Compost, Dressing, Dung, →FERTILISER, Green, Guano, Hen-pen, Lime, Mould, Muck, Sha(i)rn, Tath

**Manuscript(s)** Book of Kells, Codex, Codicology, Folio, Hand, Holograph, Longhand, Miniscule, MS, Opisthograph, Palimpsest, Papyrus, Parchment, Script, Scroll, Scrowl(e), Slush-pile, Uncial, Vellum

**Manx(man)** Cat, IOM, Kelly, Kelt

▷ **Manx** *may indicate* a last letter missing

**Many** Bags, C, CD, Countless, Crew(e), D, Hantle, Herd, Horde, Host, L, Lot, M, Manifold, Mony, Multi(tude), Multiple, Myriad, Numerous, Oodles, Power, Scad, Scores, Sight, Slew, Stacks, Tons, Umpteen, Untold

▷ **Many** *may indicate* the use of a Roman numeral letter

**Many-sided** Versatile

**Maoist** Naxalite, Red Guard

**Maori (house)** Hapu, Hauhau, Hori, Iwi, Jikanga, Kaumatua, Mallowpuff, Moa hunter, Tangata whenua, Te reo, Wahine, Whare

**Map(s), Mapping** Atlas, A-Z, Bijection, Card, Cartogram, Chart, Chorography, Choropleth, Chromosome, Cognitive, Contour, Digital, Face, Genetic, Image, Inset, Key, Loxodromic, Mappemond, Mental, Mosaic, Moving, Mud, OS, Perceptual, Plan(isphere), Plat, Plot, Portolano, Relief, Road, Sea-card, Sea-chart, Site, Star, Strip, Topography, Weather

**Maple** Acer, Bird's-eye, Box elder, Flowering, Japanese, Manitoba, Mazer, Norway, Plane, Silver, Sugar, Sycamore, Syrup

**Map-maker** Cartographer, OS, Speed

**Maquis** Queach, Underground

**Mar** Blight, Blot, Damage, Denature, Dere, Impair, Poison, Soil, Spoil, Taint

**Marabout** Sofi, Sufi

**Marathon** Comrades, Huge, London, Long, Race, Run, Two Oceans

**Maraud(er)** Amalekite, Attacker, Bandit, Hun, Pillager, Pirate, Predator, Prowler, Raid

**Marble(s), Marbling** Aeginetan, Agate, All(e)y, Arch, Arundelian, Bonce, Bonduc, Bool, Boondoggle, Bowl, Calcite, Carrara, Chequer, Cipollino, Commoney, Devil's, Dump, Elgin, Forest, Humite, Hymettus, Knicker, Languedoc, Lucullite, Marl, Marmarosis, Marmoreal, Marver, Mind, Mosaic, Mottle, Nero-antico, Nickar, Nicker, Onychite, Onyx, Ophicalcite, Paragon, Parian, Pavonazzo, Pentelic(an), Petworth, Phigalian, Plonker, Plunker, Purbeck, Rance, Ringer, Ring-taw, Ruin, Sanity, Scagliola, Spangcockle, Taw, Tolley, Variegate, Verd antique, Wits, Xanthian

**Marcel** Proust

**March(ing), Marcher** Abut, Adjoin, Advance, Alla marcia, Anabasis, Border(er), Borderland, Boundary, Colonel Bogey, Dead, Defile, Demo(nstration), Étape, File, Footslog, Forced, Freedom, Fringe, Galumph, Go, Goosestep, Grand, Hikoi, Hunger, Ides, Jarrow, Lide, Limes, Lockstep, Long, Meare, Music, → **PARADE**, Paso doble, Procession, Progress, Protest, Quick, Regimental, Rogue's, Route, Saint, Slow time, Step, Strunt, Strut, Tramp, Trio, Tromp, Troop, Wedding, Yomp

▷ **March** *may indicate* 'Little Women' character, Amy, Beth, Jo, Meg

**Marco** Il Milione, Polo

**Mardi Gras** J'ouvert

**Mare** Dam, Flanders, Horse, M, MacCurdle's, Shanks's, Spanish, Yaud

**Margaret** Anjou, Meg, Peg, Rita

**Margarine** Oleo

**Marge, Margin(al)** Andean, Annotate, Bank, Border, Borderline, Brim, Brink, Constructive, Convergent, Curb, Edge, Fimbria, Gross, Hair's breadth, Kerb, Lean, Leeway, Limit, Lip, Littoral, Neck, Nose, Periphery, Peristome, Profit, Rand, Repand, → **RIM**, Selvedge, Sideline, Spread, Tail, Term

**Marginal note** Apostil(le), K'ri, Postil

**Margosa** Melia, Nim

**Maria(nne)** France, Tia

**Marie** Dressler, Tempest

**Marigold** Calendula, Gool, Gule, Kingcup, Tagetes

**Marijuana** Alfalfa, Bhang, Camberwell carrot, Dagga, Gage, Ganja, Grass, Greens, Gungeon, Ha-ha, Hay, Hemp, Herb, J, Jimson weed, Jive, Joint, Kaif, Kef, Kif, Leaf, Lid, Locoweed, Mary-Jane, Pot, Roach, Rope, Shit, Sinsemilla, Splay, Spliff, Tea, Toke, Weed

**Marina** Wharf

**Marinade** Chermoula, Escabeche

**Marine (animal)** Aquatic, Bootie, Bootneck, Cephalopod, Chaetognath, Cnidarian, Coelenterate, Comatulid, Ctenophora, Cunjevoi, Enteropneusta, Flustra, Foram(inifer), Galoot, Graptolite, Harumfrodite, Hemichorda, Holothurian, Horse, Hydrocoral,

Hydroid, Hydromedusa, Jarhead, Jolly, Lancelet, Leatherneck, Lobster, Mercantile, Mere-swine, Mistress Roper, Oceanic, Otarine, Physalia, Pogonophoron, Pollywag, Pollywog, Rat-tail, Salpa, Sea(-soldier), Seston, Thalassian, Ultra, Venus's girdle

**Mariner** AB, Ancient, MN, Noah, RM, Sailor, Salt, Seafarer, Spacecraft, Tar

**Marionette(s)** Fantoccini, Puppet

**Marital** Conjugal

**Marjoram** Amaracus, Origan, Pot, Sweet, Wild, Winter-sweet

**Mark(ing), Marked, Marks, Marker** Accent, Aesc, Annotate, Anoint, Antony, Apostrophe, Asterisk, Astrobleme, Badge, Banker, Barcode, Bethumb, Biological, Birth, Blaze, Blot, Blotch, Bollard, Brand, Bruise, Buck, Bull, Buoy, Butt, Cachet, Cairn, Calibrate, Caract, Caret, Caste, CE, Cedilla, Celebrate, Characteristic, Chatter, Chequer, Cicatrix, Class, Clout, Colon, Comma, Coronis, Crease, Criss-cross, Cross(let), Cup (and ring), Cursor, Dash, Denote, Dent, Designate, Diacritic, Diaeresis, Dieresis, Distinction, Ditto, DM, Dot, Duckfoot quote, Dupe, Emblem, Endorsement, Enseam, Ensign, Enstamp, Exclamation, Expression, Fanion, Feer, Flag, Flash, Fleck, Fox(ing), Freckle, Genetic, Glyph, Gnomon, Gospel, Grade, Guillemet, Gybe, Hacek, Haemangioma, Hair-line, Hash, Hatch, Heed, Hickey, High water, Hoofprint, Hyphen, Impress(ion), Imprint, Indicium, Infinitive, Ink, Inscribe, Insignia, Interrogation, Inukshuk, Keel, Kite, Kumkum, Label, Lentigo, Line, Ling, Livedo, Logo, Lovebite, Low water, M, Macron, Matchmark, Mate, MB, Medical, Merk, Mint, Minute, Mottle, NB, Nick, Nota bene, Notal, Notch, Note, Notice, Obelisk, Observe, Oche, Paginate, Paragraph, Paraph, Peg, Period, Piece together, Pilcrow, Pin, Pinpoint, Pit, Plage, Plimsoll, Pling, Pock, Point(ille), Popinjay, Port wine, Post, Presa, Printer's, Proof, Punctuation, Question, Quotation, Record, Reference, Register, Regulo, Remarque, Rillmark, Ripple, Roundel, Rune, Sanction, Scar, Scorch, Score(r), Scratch, Scribe, Scuff, Section, See, Senora, Service, Shadow, Shelf, Shilling, Shoal, Sigil, Sign(ature), Smit, Smut, Smutch, Soft touch, Sordes, Speck, Splodge, Splotch, Spot, Spousage, Stain, Stamp, Stencil, Stigma(ta), Strawberry, Stress, Stretch, Stripe, Stroke, Sucker, Swan-upping, Swastika, Symbol, Tag, Target, Tarnish, Tatow, Tattoo, Tee, Theta, Thread, Tick, Tide, Tie, Tika, Tikka, Tilak, Tilde, Tittle, Token, Touchmark, Trace, Track, Trema, Trout, Tug(h)ra, Twain, Umlaut, Ure, Victim, Wand, Warchalking, Watch, Weal, Welt, Whelk

**Market(ing), Market day, Marketeer, Market place** Advergaming, Agora, Alcaiceria, Arbitrageur, Available, Baltic, Bazaar, Bear, Billingsgate, Black, Black stump, Borgo, Bull, Buyers', Capital, Captive, Car boot sale, Cattle, Change, Chowk, Cinema, Circular, Cluster, Commodity, Common, Covent Garden, Demo, Denet, Direct, Discount, Dragon, eBay®, EC, Emerging, Emporium, Errand, Exchange, Exhibition, Fair, Farmers', Feeing, Flea, Forum, Forward, Free, Grey, Growth, Insert, Internal, Kerb, Lloyds, Main, Mandi, Mart, Mass, Meat, Mercat, Money, Niche, Nundine, Obigosony, Oligopoly, Open (air), Order-driven, Outlet, Overt, Pamphlet, Perfect, Piazza, Poster, Press, Publicity, Radio, Rag fair, Reach, Relationship, Rialto, Sale, Sell, Sellers', Servqual, Share, Shop, Single, Social, Societal, Sook, Souk, Spot, Stance, Staple, Stock, Stock Exchange, Suq, Tattersall's, TECHMARK®, Terminal, Test, Third, Tiger, Trade, Tron, Tryst, USP, Vent, Viral, Wall Street, Yard sale

**Market garden** Truck-farm

**Marksman** Archer, Sharpshooter, Shootist, Shot, Sniper, Tell

**Marlborough** Blenheim, Churchill

**Marlene** Lilli

**Marmalade** Cat, Mammee-sapota, Preserve, Squish

**Marmoset** Jacchus, Mico, Midas, Monkey, Wistiti

**Marmot** Bobac, Bobak, Dassie, Groundhog, Hoary, Hyrax, Klipdas, Rodent, Whistler, Woodchuck

**Maroon** Abandon, Brown, Castaway, Enisle, Firework, Inisle, Isolate, Strand

**Marquee** Pavilion, Tent, Top

**Marquess, Marquis** de Sade, Granby, Lorne, Queensberry

**Marquetry** Boul(l)e, Buhl, Inlay

**Marriage, Marry, Married (woman)** →ALLIANCE, Ally, Amate, Arranged, Bed, Beenah, Bigamy, Bridal, Buckle, Buckle-beggar, Civil, Cleek(it), Coemption, Combine, Common law, Commuter, Companionate, Confarreation, Conjugal, Connubial, Couple, Coverture, Digamy, Endogamy, Espousal, Espouse, Exogamy, Feme covert, Forsooth, Fuse, Gandharva, Genial, Goody, Group, Hedge, Hetaerism, Hetaerism, Hitch, Hymen(eal), Indeed, Join, Jugal, Ketubah, Knit, Knot, Lavender, Levirate, M, Match, Mating, Matrilocal, Matrimony, Matron, Memsahib, Mésalliance, Ming, Missis, Missus, Mixed, Monandry, Monogamy, Morganatic, Nikah, Noose, Nuptial, Open, Pair, Pantagamy, Pardie, Patrilocal, Polygamy, Punalua, Putative, Quotha, Sacrament, Sannup, Shidduch, Shotgun, Splice, Tie, Tie the knot, Trial, Troggs, Troth, Umfazi, →UNION, Unite, W, Wed, Wedding, Wedlock, Wive

**Marriageable** Marrow, Nubile, Parti

**Marriage-broker** Shadchan

**Marrow** Courgette, Friend, Gist, Kamokamo, Medulla, Myeloid, Pith, Pumpkin, Spinal, Squash, Vegetable

**Mars** Areography, Ares, Red (planet), Syrtis major, Tharsis

**Marsh(y)** Bayou, Bog, Camargue, Chott, Corcass, Emys, Everglades, Fen(land), Hackney, Maremma, Merse, Mire, Morass, Ngaio, Paludal, Palustrine, Plashy, Pontine, Pripet, Quagmire, Rann of Kutch, Romney, Salina, Salt, Shott, Slade, Slough, Sog, Spew, Spue, Swale, Swamp, Taiga, Terai, Vlei, Wetlands

**Marshal** Arrange, Array, Commander, Earp, Foch, French, Hickok, MacMahon, Muster, Neil, Ney, Order, Pétain, Provost, Shepherd, Sky, Steward, Tedder, Usher, Vauban, Yardman

**Marshmallow** Althaea, Mallowpuff

**Marsupial** Bandicoot, Bilby, Cuscus, Dasyure, Dibbler, Didelphia, Diprotodon(t), Dunnart, Euro, Honey mouse, Honey possum, Kangaroo, Koala, Macropod, Metatheria, Notoryctes, Nototherium, Numbat, Opossum, Pademelon, Pad(d)ymelon, Petaurist, Phalanger, Pig-rat, Polyprodont, Possum, Potoroo, Pouched mouse, Pygmy glider, Quokka, Quoll, Roo, Tammar, Tasmanian devil, Theria, Thylacine, Tuan, Wallaby, Wambenger, Wombat, Yapo(c)k

**Marten** Fisher, Mustela, Pekan, Pine, Sable, Woodshock

**Martensite** Sorbite

**Martha** Vineyard

**Martial (arts)** Aikido, Bellicose, Budo, Capoeira, Capuera, Chopsocky, Dojo, Iai-do, Judo, Ju-jitsu, Karate, Kata, Kendo, Kick boxing, Krav Maga, Kumite, Kung fu, Militant, Muay thai, Ninjitsu, Ninjutsu, Sensei, Shintaido, Tae Bo®, Tae kwon do, T'ai chi (chuan), Warlike, Wushu

**Martin** Bird, Dean, Luther, Swallow

**Martinet** Captious, Ramrod, Stickler, Tyrant

**Martini®** Cocktail, Henry

**Martyr(dom), Martyrs** Alban, Alphege, Campion, Colosseum, Cranmer, Donatist, Justin, Lara, Latimer, Metric, MM, Passional, Persecute, Ridley, Sebastian, Shaheed, Shahid, Stephen, Suffer, Tolpuddle, Wishart

**Marvel(lous)** Blinder, Bodacious, Brilliant, Bully, Épatant, Fab(ulous), Fantabulous, Lulu, Magic, Marl, Miracle, Mirific, Peachy, Phenomenon, Prodigious, Selcouth, Superb, Super-duper, Swell, Terrific, Wonder

**Marx(ism), Marxist** Aspheterism, Chico, Comintern, Commie, Groucho, Gummo, Harpo, Karl, Lenin, Mao, Menshevik, Revisionism, Tanky, Tipamaro, Zeppo

**Mary** Bloody, Celeste, Contrary, Madonna, Magdalene, Moll, Morison, Our Lady, Tum(my), Typhoid, Virgin

**Marylebone** Station

**Marzipan** Frangipani, Marchpane

**Mascara** Eye-black

**Mascot** Charm, Four-leaf clover, → **TALISMAN**, Telesm, Token

**Masculine, Masculinity** Butch, He, He-man, Linga(m), M, Machismo, Macho, Male, Manly, Virile, Yang

**Maser** Laser

**Mash(er)** Beat, Beau, Beetle, Brew, Flirt, Lady-killer, Pap, Pestle, Pound, Puree, Sour, Squash

**Mask(ed)** Bird cage, Camouflage, Cloak, Cokuloris, Death, Disguise, Dissemble, Domino, Face pack, False face, Front, Gas, Gorgoneion, Hide, Larvated, Life, Loo, Loup, Mascaron, Matte, Oxygen, Persona, Respirator, Screen, Semblance, Shadow, Ski, Stalking-horse, Stocking, Stop out, Template, Veil, Visor, Vizard

**Mason(ry)** Ashlar, Ashler, Brother, Builder, Cowan, Emplecton, Isodoma, Isodomon, Isodomum, Jude, Lodge, Moellon, Monumental, Nogging, Opus, Perry, Random, Rubblework, Squinch, Stone dresser, Stylobate

**Masque(rade), Masquerader** Comus, Domino, Guisard, Mum(m), Mummery, Pose, Pretend

**Mass(es)** Aggregate, Agnus Dei, Anniversary, Atomic, Banket, Bezoar, Bike, Blob, Body, Bulk, Cake, Canon, Chaos, Clot, Compound, Congeries, Conglomeration, Consecration, Core, Crith, Critical, Crowd, Demos, Density, Dona nobis, Dozens, Flake, Floc, Flysch, Folk, Geepound, Gradual, Gramme, Gravitational, Great, Heap, Herd, High, Horde, Hulk, Inertial, Isobare, Jud, Kermesse, Kermis, Kilo(gram), Kirmess, Low, Lump, M, Magma, Majority, Missa, Missa solemnis, Mob, Molar, Month's mind, Mop, Nelson, Nest, Phalanx, Pile, Plebs, Plumb, Pontifical, Populace, Proper, Raft, Red, Requiem, Rest, Ruck, Salamon, Salmon, Sanctus, Scrum, Sea, Serac, Service, Shock, Sicilian, Size, Slub, Slug, Solar, Solemn, Solid, Stack, Stroma, Sursum Corda, Te Igitur, Tektite, Trental, Vesper, Vigil, Volume, Wad, Weight, Welter

**Massacre** Amritsar, Battue, Beziers, Blood-bath, Butcher, Carnage, Glencoe, Havock, Kanpur, Lidice, Manchester, Peterloo, Pogrom, Purge, St Bartholomew's Day, Scullabogue, Scupper, September, Sicilian vespers, Slaughter, Slay, Trounce, Wounded Knee

**Massage, Masseur** An mo, Cardiac, Chafer, Chavutti thirumal, Do-in, Effleurage, Hellerwork, → **KNEAD**, Malax, Manipulate, Osteopathy, Palp, Petrissage, Physio, Reiki, Rolf(ing), Rubber, Shampoo, Shiatsu, Stone, Stroke, Swedish, Tapotement, Thai, Tripsis, Tui na

**Massif** Makalu

**Massive** Big, Bull, Colossal, Cyclopean, Gang, Gargantuan, Heavy, Herculean, Huge, Monolithic, Monumental, Ponderous, Seismic, Strong, Titan

**Mast(ed), Masthead** Acorn, Banner, Captain's, Crosstree, Flag, Foretop, Foreyard, High top, Hounds, Jigger, Jury, M, Mizzen, Mooring, Pannage, Pole, Racahout, Royal, Ship-rigged, Spar, Top-gallant, Truck, Venetian

**Master(ly), Mastery** Ace, Adept, Artful, Baalebos, Baas, Beak, Beat, Boss, Buddha, Bwana, Captain, Careers, Checkmate, Choir, Chorus, Conquer, Control, Dan, Dominate, Dominie, Employer, Enslave, Exarch, Expert, Genius, Gov, Grand, Grip, Harbour, Herr, Himself, International, Learn, Lord, MA, Maestro, Magistral, Mas(s), Massa, Maulana, Mes(s), Nkosi, Old, Ollamh, Ollav, Oner, Oppress, Original, Overcome, Overlord, Overpower, Overseer, Passed, Past, Pedant, Question, Rabboni, Schoolman, Seed, Seigneur, Seignior, Signorino, Sir(e), Skipper, → **SUBDUE**, Subjugate, Superate, Surmount, Swami, Tame, Task, Teach, Thakin, Towkay, Tuan, Usher, Vanquish, Virtuoso

**Mastermind** Brain, Conceive, Direct, Engineer, Genius, Orchestrate, Oversee

**Masterpiece** Chef d'oeuvre, Classic, Creation, Magnum opus

**Mastersinger** Sachs

**Master-stroke** Coup, Triumph

**Mastic** Sealant

**Masturbate, Masturbation** Abuse, Blow, Frig, Gratify, Jerk off, Jock, Onanism, Self-pollution, Toss off, Tribady, Wank, Whack off

**Mat(ted), Matting** Bast, Capillary, Coaster, Coir, Doily, Dojo, Doyl(e)y, Dutch mattress, Felt, Inlace, Pad, Paunch, Place, Plat, Prayer, Rug, Rush, Surf, Table, Taggy, →TANGLE, Tat(ami), Tatty, Taut, Tautit, Tawt, Tomentose, Web, Welcome, Zarf

**Matador** Card, Espada, Ordonez, Theseus, Torero

**Match(ed), Matching** Agree, Alliance, Amate, Balance, Besort, Bonspiel, Bout, Carousel, Compare, Compeer, Congreve, Consolation, Contest, Cope, Correlate, Correspond, Counterpart, Cup tie, Doubles, Emulate, Engagement, Equal(ise), Equate, Even, Even Stevens, Exhibition, Fellow, Fit, Fixture, Four-ball, Foursome, Friction, Friendly, Fusee, Fuzee, Game, Go, Greensome, Grudge, International, Joust, Light, Locofoco, Love, Lucifer, Main, Marriage, Marrow, Marry, Meet, Mouse, Needle, ODI, Pair(s), Paragon, Parallel, Parti, Pit, Play-off, Prizefight, Promethean, Quick, Replica, Reproduce, Return, Rival, Road game, Roland, Rubber, Safety, Semifinal, Sevens, Shield, Shoo-in, Shooting, Shouting, Singles, Slanging, Slow, Slugfest, Spunk, Striker, Suit, Sync(h), →TALLY, Team, Test, Texas scramble, Tie, Tone, To scale, Twin, Twosome, Union, Venue, Vesta, Vesuvian, Wedding

**Matchbox label (collecting)** Phillumeny

**Match girl** Bride

**Match-holder** Lin(t)stock

**Matchless** Non(e)such, Orinda

**Matchmaker** Blackfoot, Broker, Pairer, Promoter, Shadchan

**Mate, Mating** Achates, Adam, Amigo, Amplexus, Assistant, Assortative, Bedfellow, Bo, Breed, Buddy, Buffer, Butty, Check, Chess, China, Chum, Cobber, Cock, Comrade, Consort, Crony, Cully, Digger, Eve, Feare, Feer, Fellow, Fere, Fiere, First, Fool's, Helper, Husband, Ilex, Inbreed, Maik, Make, Marrow, Marry, Match, Mister, Mucker, Nick, Nickar, Oldster, Oppo, →PAIR, Pal, Pangamy, Panmixia, Panmixis, Paragon, Partner, Pheer(e), Pirrauru, Running, Scholar's, Second, Serve, Sex, Skaines, Smothered, Soul, Sport, →SPOUSE, Tea, Tup, Wack, Wacker, Wed, Wife, Wus(s)

**Material(ism)** Agitprop, Appropriate, Apt, →CLOTH, Compo, Composite, Copy, Corporeal, Data, Dialectical, Documentation, Earthling, Earthly, →FABRIC, Factual, Fallout, Fertile, Fuel, Germane, Historical, Hylic, Illusion, Infill, Leading, Matter, Pertinent, Physical, Positive, Raw, Real, Reify, Relevant, Repertoire, Substance, Tangible, Thingy, Worldly

---

## MATERIALS

| 3 letters: | | 7 letters: | |
|---|---|---|---|
| Cob | Metal | Ballast | Oilcloth |
| Pug | Oasis® | Ceramic | Regolith |
| | Staff | Matting | Silicone |
| 4 letters: | Stuff | Oilskin | Skirting |
| Bole | | Phantom | 9 letters: |
| Frit | 6 letters: | Protore | Aggregate |
| Gang | Armure | Pugging | Austenite |
| Moxa | Borsic | Sagathy | Celluloid |
| Oils | Byssus | Textile | Cellulose |
| Tape | Cermet | Tinfoil | Elastomer |
| Ylem | Corfam® | | Fibrefill |
| | Fablon® | 8 letters: | Macintosh |
| 5 letters: | Gangue | Blastema | Micromesh |
| Fibro | Gypsum | Concrete | Pina-cloth |
| Fines | Raffia | Fettling | Polythene |
| Flong | Sporex® | Graphite | Sackcloth |
| Fomes | Tartan® | Illuvium | Samsonite® |
| Fritt | Tusser | Lambskin | Towelling |

| 10 letters: | 11 letters: | Polystyrene | Plasterstone |
|---|---|---|---|
| Fibreboard | Fibrocement | | |
| Fibreglass | Gutta percha | 12 letters: | 13 letters: |
| Protoplasm | Interfacing | Agalmatolite | Wattle and daub |
| Thermolite® | Papier-maché | Plasterboard | |

---

**Materialise** Appear, Apport, Click, Reify
**Materialist(ic)** Banausian, Earthling, Hylist, Hyloist, Philistine, Somatist
**Mathematician** Optime, Statistician, Wrangler

---

## MATHEMATICIANS

| 4 letters: | Euclid | Penrose | Dunstable |
|---|---|---|---|
| Hero | Fermat | Poisson | Fibonacci |
| Zeno | Gunter | Ptolemy | Friedmann |
| | Jacobi | Pytheas | Minkowski |
| 5 letters: | Jevons | Riemann | Whitehead |
| Bayes | Kaluza | Russell | |
| Boole | Mobius | | 10 letters: |
| Euler | Napier | 8 letters: | Apollonius |
| Frege | Newton | Archytas | Archimedes |
| Gauss | Pascal | Bourbaki | Diophantus |
| Godel | Turing | De Morgan | Mandelbrot |
| Julia | Walker | Goldbach | Pythagoras |
| Klein | Wiener | Hamilton | Torricelli |
| Pitts | | Lagrange | Von Neumann |
| | 7 letters: | Mercator | |
| 6 letters: | Fourier | Playfair | 11 letters: |
| Agnesi | Hawking | Poincare | Von Leibnitz |
| Bessel | Hilbert | | |
| Briggs | Laplace | 9 letters: | 12 letters: |
| Cantor | Leibniz | Bernoulli | Eratosthenes |
| Cocker | Neumann | Descartes | |

---

**Mathematics, Mathematical, Maths** Algebra, Applied, Arithmetic,
   Arsmetrick, Calculus, Combinatorics, Exact science, Geometry, Haversine,
   Higher, Logarithms, Mechanics, New, Numbers, Porism, Pure, Topology, Trig,
   Trigonometry
**Matilda** Liar, Swag, Untruthful, Waltzing
**Matinee** Coat, Idol, Show
**Mating** Pangamy
**Matins** Nocturn
**Matricide** Orestes
**Matrimony, Matrimonial** Bed, Conjugal, Marriage, Nuptial, Sacrament, Spousal,
   Wedlock
**Matrix** Active, Array, Boston, Hermitian, Jacobian, Mould, Orthogonal, Pattern,
   Scattering, Square, Symmetric, Transpose, Uterus
**Matron** Dame, Hausfrau, Lucretia, Nurse, Warden
**Matt(e)** Dense, Dingy, Dull
**Matter** Affair, Alluvium, Bioblast, Biogen, Body, Business, Concern, Condensed,
   Consequence, Content, Count, Dark, Degenerate, Ejecta, Empyema, Epithelium,
   Evidence, Flux, Front, Gear, Gluon, Go, Grey, Hyle, Ichor, Impost(h)ume, Issue, Mass,
   Material, Molecule, Multiverse, Neutrino, Phlegm, Pith, Plasma, Point, Positron,
   Premise, Protoplasm, Pulp, Pus, Quark, Reading, Reck, Reke, Scum, Sediment, Shebang,

Signify, Solid, Sputum, Stereome, Stuff, Subject, →**SUBSTANCE**, Symptom, Theme, Thing, Topic, Tousle, Touzle, Vinyl, White, Ylem

**Matter of fact** Pragmatic

**Matthew** Arnold, Levi

**Mattress** Air bed, Bed(ding), Biscuit, Dutch, Featherbed, Foam, Futon, Lilo®, Pallet, Pa(i)lliasse, Spring, Tick

**Mature, Maturity** Adult, Age, Auld, Blossom, Bold, Concoct, Develop, Fully-fledged, Grow (up), Mellow, Metaplasis, Old, Puberty, Ripe(n), Rounded, Seasoned, Upgrow(n)

**Maudlin** Fuddled, Mawkish, Sentimental, Slip-slop, Sloppy, Too-too

**Maul** Hammer, Manhandle, Paw, Rough, Savage, Tear

**Maundy** Money, Nipter, Thursday

**Mauretanian, Mauritania(n)** Moor, RIM

**Mauritius** MS

**Mausoleum** Agra, Halicarnassus, Mole, Sepulchre, Taj Mahal, Tomb

**Mauve** Lavender, Lilac, Mallow, Perkin's

**Maverick** Free agent, Loner, Misfit, Nonconformist, Rebel, Rogue, Unconventional

**Mavis** Throstle

**Maw** Crop, Gorge, Gull(et), Mouth, Oesophagus

**Mawkish** Dippy, Maudlin, Mushy, Sentimental, Sickly

**Max** Ernst

**Maxim** Adage, Aphorism, Apo(ph)thegm, Axiom, Byword, Dictum, Gnome, Gorki, Gun, Hiram, Moral, Motto, Precept, Proverb, Restaurateur, →**RULE**, Saw, Saying, Sentence, Sentiment, Watchword

**Maximum** All-out, Full, Highest, Limit, Most, Peak, Utmost

**May** Blossom, Can, Hawthorn, Merry, Might, Month, Mote(n), Quickthorn, Shall, Whitethorn

**Maybe** Happen, Mebbe, Peradventure, Percase, Perchance, Perhaps, Possibly

▷ **May become** *may indicate* an anagram

**May day** Beltane, SOS

**Mayfair** WI

**Mayfly** Ephemera, Ephemeroptera, Green-drake, Sedge

**Mayhem** Chaos, Crime, Damage, Havoc, Pandemonium, Riotry

**Mayonnaise** Aioli, Rémoulade

**Mayor** Alcaide, Burgomaster, Casterbridge, Charter, Councilman, Portreeve, Provost, Syndic, Whittington, Worship, Worthy

**Maze** Honeycomb, Labyrinth, Meander, Network, Theseus, Warren, Wilderness

**MC** Announcer, Compere, Host, Ringmaster

**MD** Doctor, Healer

**ME** Yuppie flu

**Me** I, Mi, Moi, One, Sel(f), Us

**Mead(ow)** Flood, Grass(land), Haugh, Hydromel, Inch, Ing, Lea(se), Ley, Meath(e), Metheglin, →**PASTURE**, Runnymede, Saeter, Salting, Water

**Meadowsweet** Dropwort

**Meagre** Arid, Bar, Bare, Exiguity, Exiguous, Insubstantial, Measly, Mingy, Paltry, Pittance, Scant, Scrannel, Scranny, Scrawny, Skimpy, Skinny, Slender, Spare, Sparse, Stingy, Thin

**Meal(s), Mealie, Mealy** Allseed, Banquet, Barbecue, Barium, Beanfeast, Blow-out, Board, Breakfast, Brunch, Buffet, Carry out, Cassava, Cereal, Chilled, Cholent, Chota-hazri, Collation, Corn, Cornflour, Cottoncake, Cottonseed, Cou-cou, Couscous, Cribble, Dejeune(r), Deskfast, Dinner, Drammock, Ear, Ervalenta, Fare, Farina, Feast, Feed, Flour, Food, Glacier, Grits, Grout, Hangi, High tea, Iftar, Indian, Italian, Kai, Lock, Lunch, Mandioc, Mandioc(c)a, Mani(h)oc, Matzo, Melder, Meltith, Mensal, Mess, Morning, Mush, No-cake, Nosh, Nuncheon, Ordinary, Picnic, Piece, Pizza, Plate, Ploughman's lunch, Poi, Polenta, Porridge, Prandial, Prix fixe, Rac(c)ahout, Refection, Repast, Revalenta, Rijst(t)afel, Salep, Scambling, Scoff, Seder, Sehri, Slap-up,

Smorgasbord, Snack, Sohur, Spread, Square, Suhur, Supper, Table d'hôte, Takeaway, Tamale, Tea, Thali, Tiffin, Tightener, Tousy tea, Twalhours, Undern

**Meal-ticket** LV

**Mean(ing), Meant** Aim, Arithmetic(al), Average, Base, Betoken, Bowsie, Caitiff, Cheap, Cheeseparing, Close, Connotation, Curmudgeon, Definition, Denotate, Denote, Design, Dirty, Drift, Essence, Ettle, Feck, Footy, Foul, Geometric(al), Gist, Golden, Hang, Harmonic, Humble, Hunks, Ignoble, Illiberal, Imply, Import, Inferior, Insect, Intend, Intermediate, Kunjoos, Lexical, Low(down), Mang(e)y, Marrow, Measly, Medium, Mesquin, Message, Method, Mid, Miserly, Narrow, Near, Niggardly, Nirlie, Norm, Nothing, One-horse, Ornery, Paltry, Par, Penny-pinching, Penurious, Petty, Piker, Pinch-penny, Pith, Point, Purport, → **PURPOSE**, Quadratic, Ratfink, Revenue, Ribald, Roinish, Roynish, Scall, Scrub, Scurvy, Semanteme, Semantic(s), Sememe, Sense, Shabby, Signify, Slight, Slink, Small, Sneaky, Snoep, Snot, Sordid, Sparing, Spell, Squalid, Stingy, Stink(ard), Stinty, Substance, Symbol, Thin, Threepenny, Tight-lipped, Tightwad, Two-bit, Value, Vile, Whoreson

**Meander** Fret, Ring, Sinuate, Stray, Wander, Weave, Wind

**Meaningless** Ducdame, Empty, Flummery, Hollow, Hot air, Insignificant, Nonny, Rumbelow

**Means** Agency, Ample, Dint, Income, Instrumental, Media, Method, Mode, Opulence, Organ, Private, Recourse, Resources, Staple, Substance, Tactics, Visible, Ways, Wherewithal

**Meantime, Meanwhile** Among, Emong, Greenwich, Interim, Whilst

**Measles** Morbilli, Roseola, Rose-rash, Rubella, Rubeola, Sheep

**Measure(d), Measuring, Measure(ment)** By(e)law, Calibre, Centile, Circular, Corn Law, Crackdown, Customise, → **DANCE**, Démarche, → **DIMENSION**, Dipstick, Distance, Doggerel, Dose, Dry, → **GAUGE**, Gavotte, Gross, Imperial, → **INSTRUMENT**, IQ, Limit, Linear, Liter, Litre, Meed, Metage, Moratorium, Of, Offset, Precaution, Prophylactic, Quickstep, Ration, Remen, Sanction, Sea-level, Share, Short, → **SIZE**, Sound, Standard, Statute, Step, Stichometry, Strike, Struck, Survey, Tachymetry, Timbre, Token, Triangulate, → **UNIT**, Weigh, Wine

---

**MEASUREMENTS**

| 2 letters: | Mil | Gill | Pipe |
|---|---|---|---|
| As | Rod | Hank | Pole |
| Em | Tot | Hide | Pond |
| En | Tsp | Inch | Pood |
| Mu | Wey | Koss | Ream |
| | | Last | Reau |
| 3 letters: | 4 letters: | Line | Rood |
| Are | Acre | Link | Rope |
| Bel | Aune | Maze | Rotl |
| Cab | Bath | Mete | Shot |
| Cor | Boll | Mile | Span |
| DIN | Bolt | Mole | Tape |
| Ell | Comb | Mott | Thou |
| Erg | Cord | Muid | Unit |
| Fat | Coss | Nail | Vara |
| Hin | Cran | Octa | Volt |
| Lay | Culm | Okta | Warp |
| Lea | Dram | Omer | Yard |
| Ley | Epha | Pace | |
| Log | Foot | Peck | 5 letters: |
| Lug | Gage | Pint | Anker |

Ardeb
Barye
Bekah
Bigha
Caneh
Carat
Chain
Clove
Combe
Coomb
Crore
Cubit
Cumec
Cusec
Depth
Ephah
Fermi
Float
Gauge
Grain
Groma
Hanap
Homer
Joule
Kaneh
Lento
Liang
Ligne
Lippy
Loure
Mease
Meter
Metre
Middy
Noddy
Optic®
Perch
Plumb
Quart
Romer
Ruler
Scale
Skein
Stade
Stere
Stone
Tesla
Therm
Toise
Verst
Wecht
Yojan

**6 letters:**
Albedo
Alnage
Arpent
Arshin
Barrel
Barren
Beegah
Bovate
Bushel
Chenix
Chopin
Cicero
Cubage
Degree
Denier
Double
Etalon
Exergy
Fathom
Firkin
Firlot
Gallon
Height
Hemina
Jigger
Kelvin
Kilerg
League
Lippie
Liquid
Modius
Morgan
Mutton
Noggin
Oxgang
Parsec
Pascal
Pottle
Radius
Rotolo
Runlet
Sazhen
Second
Sievert
Stadia
Thread
Tierce
Yojana

**7 letters:**
Aneroid
Arshine
Braccio

Breadth
Burette
Caliper
Candela
Chalder
Choenix
Conguis
Coulomb
Cyathus
Decibel
Drastic
Entropy
Furlong
Geodesy
Lambert
Leaguer
Pelorus
Quarter
Refract
Rundlet
Sleever
Spindle
Spondee
Venturi
Virgate

**8 letters:**
Angstrom
Calipers
Calliper
Carucate
Chaldron
Crannock
Desyatin
Diameter
Exitance
Fistmele
Foot rule
Hogshead
Kilogray
Luxmeter
Mutchkin
Odometer
Oximeter
Parasang
Poulter's
Puncheon
Quadrant
Tape-line
Teraflop
Viameter
Waywiser

**9 letters:**
Astrolabe
Atmometer
Barometer
Bolometer
Callipers
Cryometer
Decalitre
Decastere
Dosimeter
Ergometer
Eriometer
Flowmeter
Hodometer
Kilojoule
Kilometre
Konimeter
Lysimeter
Machmeter
Manometer
Mekometer
Nipperkin
Octameter
Oenometer
Pedometer
Pentapody
Potometer
Salimeter
Steradian
Tappet-hen
Tasimeter
Telemeter
Titration
Tonometer
Yardstick

**10 letters:**
Acidometer
Amphimacer
Anemometer
Barleycorn
Bathometer
Bathymeter
Centimetre
Chronotron
Coulometer
Cyclometer
Densimeter
Dessiatine
Dessyatine
Drosometer
Eudiometer
Geodimeter
Goniometer

Gravimeter
Humidistat
Hydrometer
Hygrometer
Lactometer
Lactoscope
Micrometer
Mileometer
Millimetre
Opisometer
Photometer
Piezometer
Pychometer
Resistance
Touchstone

Tromometer
Winchester

**11 letters:**
Actinometer
Auxanometer
Calorimeter
Conformator
Dioptometer
Dynamometer
Gradiometer
Intoximeter
Jacob's staff
Long Hundred
Rangefinder

Stereometer
Tacheometry
Venturi tube
Weighbridge

**12 letters:**
Breathalyzer
Cathetometer
Coulombmeter
Densitometer
Electrometer
Electronvolt
Extensimeter
Extensometer
Galactometer

Gravitometer
Katharometer
Nephelometer
Permittivity
Tellurometer
Thermocouple
Viscosimeter

**13 letters:**
Saccharometer

**15 letters:**
Katathermometer

---

**Meat(s)** Aitchbone, Bacon, Bard, Beef, Beefsteak, Biltong, Brawn, Brisket, Brown, Burger, Cabob, Carbonado, Carrion, Charcuterie, Chop, Collop, Confit, Croquette, Cut, Cutlet, Dark, Devon, Dog-roll, Doner kebab, Easy, Edgebone, Entrecôte, Escalope, Essence, Fanny Adams, Fatback, Fillet, Fleishig, Fleishik, Flesh, Flitch, Force, Galantine, Game, Gigot, Gobbet, Gosht, Griskin, Halal, Ham, Haslet, Haunch, Jerky, Joint, Junk, Kabab, Kabob, Kebab, Kebob, Lamb, Loin, Luncheon, Mart, Medaillon, Medallion, Mince, Mutton, Noisette, Offal, Olive, Oyster, Pastrami, Paupiette, Pem(m)ican, Piccata, Pith, Pope's eye, Pork, Processed, Prosciutto, Rack, Red, Rillettes, Roast, Saddle, Sasatie, Satay, Scaloppino, Schnitzel, Scran, Scrapple, Sey, Shank, Shashlik, Shishkebab, Short ribs, Side, Sirloin, Sosatie, Spam®, Spare rib, Spatchcock, Spaul(d), Steak, Strong, Tenderloin, Tiring, Tongue, Variety, Veal, Venison, Vifda, Virgate, Vivda, White, Wiener schnitzel, Wurst

**Meatball(s)** Cecils, Croquette, Faggot, Falafel, Felafel, Fricadel, Frikkadell, Goujon, Knish, Kofta, Kromesky, Quenelle, Rissole

**Meat extract** Brawn, Gravy, Juice, Stock

**Meatless** Banian, Lent, Maigre, Vegetarian

**Mecca** Centre, Honeypot, Kaaba, Keblah, Kibla(h), Omayyad, Qibla, Umayyad

**Mechanic(s)** Apron-man, Artificer, Artisan, Banausic, Barodynamics, Bottom, Card, Celestial, Classical, Dynamics, Engineer, Fitter, Fluid, Fundi, Grease monkey, Greaser, Hand, Journeyman, Kinematics, Kinesiology, Kinetics, Newtonian, Operative, Quantum, Rock, Soil, Statics, Statistical, Technician, Wave

▷ **Mechanic(al)** *may indicate* characters from 'A Midsummer Night's Dream'

**Mechanical, Mechanism** Action, Apparatus, Auto, Autodestruct, Automatic, Banausic, Bottom, Chargehand, Clockwork, Defence, Dérailleur, Escape, Escapement, Foul-safe, Gimmal, Gust-lock, Instrument, Machinery, Movement, Organical, Pulley, Pushback, Rackwork, Regulator, Rigger, Robotic, Rote, Servo, Synchroflash, Synchromesh, Traveller, Trippet, Works

**Medal(lion)(s)** Award, Bar, Bronze, Cameo, Congressional, Croix de guerre, Decoration, Dickin, DSM, GC, George, Gold, Gong, Gorget, Military, MM, Numismatic, Pan(h)agia, Purple Heart, Putty, Roundel, Silver, Tony, Touchpiece, VC, Vernicle

**Meddle(r), Meddlesome, Meddling** Busybody, Dabble, Finger, Hen-hussy, →INTERFERE, Interloper, Marplot, Mell, Monkey, Officious, Pantopragmatic, Potter, Pragmatic, Pry, Snooper, Spoilsport, Tamper, Tinker, Trifle

**Media** Fibre, Intelsat, Mass, Mixed, New, PR

**Mediate, Mediator** ACAS, Arbitrate, Conciliate, Intercede, Interpose, Intervene, Liaison, Muti, Peacemaker, Referee, Stickler, Thirdsman, Trouble-shooter

**Medic(k)** Lucern(e), Nonesuch, Snail

**Medic(o), Medicine man** Albergist, Bone-setter, Corpsman, Extern, Feldsher, Houseman, Koradji

**Medical, Medicine (chest), Medicament, Medication** Aesculapian, Algology,
Allopathy, Aloetic, Alternative, Amulet, Analgesic, Andrology, Anodyne, Antacid,
Antibiotic, Antidote, Antisepsis, Antiseptic, Arnica, Arrowroot, Asafetida, Aurum
potabile, Aviation, Ayurveda, Bariatrics, Bi, Bismuth, Blister, Brunonian, Buchu,
Bucku, Calumba, Carminative, Charm, Chinese, Chiropody, Chlorodyne, Chrysarobin,
Clinician, Complementary, Cordial, Corpsman, Cubeb, Curative, Defensive, Demulcent,
Diapente, Diascordium, Diatessaron, Discutient, Doctor's stuff, Dosage, Dose, Draught,
Drops, →DRUG, Dutch drops, Eardrop, Electuary, Elixir, Emetic, Emmenagogue,
Empirics, Enema, Epulotic, Excipient, Expectorant, Fall-trank, Febrifuge, Feldsher, Folk,
Forensic, Fringe, Functional, Galen, Galenism, Gelcap, Genitourinary, Gripe water®,
Gutta, Haematinic, Haematology, Herb, Herbal, Hesperidin, Holistic, Hom(o)eopathy,
Horse-drench, Hyssop, Iatric(al), Imhotep, Indian, Industrial, Inhalant, Inro, Internal,
Iodine, Ipecac(uanha), Iron, Ko cycle, Lariam®, Laxative, L-dopa, Leechcraft, Legal,
Lime-water, Loblolly, Lotion, Magnesia, Maqui, Menthol, Microbubbles, Mishmi,
Mixture, Moxar, Muti, Natural, Naturopathy, Nephritic, Nephrology, Nervine, Neurology,
Nosology, Nostrum, Nuclear, Nux vomica, Ob-gyn, Occupational, Officinal, Oncology,
Oporice, Orthopoedics, Osteopath, Palliative, Panacea, Paregoric, Patent, Pathology,
Pectoral, P(a)ediatrics, Pharmacy, Phlegmagogue, Physic, Physical, Pill, Placebo,
Polychrest, Polypill, Posology, Potion, Poultice, Preparation, Preventive, Proctology,
Prosthetics, Prozac®, Psionic, Psychiatry, Ptisan, Purgative, Quin(quin)a, Quinacrine,
Quinine, Qinghaosu, Radiology, Reborant, Red Crescent, Red Cross, Relaxative,
→REMEDY, Salts, Salve, Sanative, Sanguinaria, Sebesten, Senna, Serology, Simple,
Snake-oil, Space, Specific, Sports, Steel, Stomachic, Stomatology, Stramonium, Stupe,
Suppository, Synergast, Syrup, Tabasheer, Tabashir, Tablet, Tar-water, Tetracycline,
Therapeutics, Thimerosal, TIM, Tincture, Tisane, Tocology, Tonic, Totaquine, Trade,
Traditional Chinese, Traumatology, Treatment, Trichology, Troche, Valerian, Veronal,
Veterinary, Virology, Witchhazel, Wychhazel
**Medieval** Archaic, Feudal, Gothic, Med, Old, Trecento
**Mediocre** Average, Bland, Fair, Indifferent, Middle-of-the-road, Middling, Ordinary, Pap,
Poor, Respectable, Run-of-the-mill, Second-class, So-So, Undistinguished
**Meditate, Meditation, Meditator, Meditative** Brood, Chew, Cogitate,
Contemplate, Falun gong, Fifteen o's, Gymnosophy, Hesychast, Insight, Muse, Mystic,
Nirvana, Pensive, Ponder, Reflect, Reverie, Revery, Ruminate, Samadhi, Tantric,
Thanatopsis, Transcendental, Vipassana, Weigh, Yoga, Yogic flying, Zazen
**Mediterranean** Great Sea, Levant, Med, Midi, Scattermouch
**Medium** (A)ether, Agency, Air, Average, Channel, Clairvoyant, Contrast, Culture,
Dispersive, Earth, Element, Ether, Even, Fire, Happy, Home, Intermediary, Interstellar,
M, Magilp, Mean, Megilp, Midsize, Midway, Milieu, Oils, Organ, Ouija, Planchette, Press,
Radio, Regular, Shaman, Spiritist, Spiritualist, Television, Telly, TV, Vehicle, Water
**Medley** Charivari, Collection, Gallimaufry, Individual, Jumble, Macedoine, Melange,
Mishmash, Mix, Pastiche, Patchwork, Pi(e), Pot-pourri, Quodlibet, Ragbag, Salad,
Salmagundi, Series, Tat
▷ **Medley** *may indicate* an anagram
**Medusa** Jellyfish, Petrifying, Planoblast
**Meek** Docile, Griselda, Humble, Milquetoast, Patient, Sheepy, Tame
**Meerkat** Suricate
**Meerschaum** Sepiolite
**Meet(ing), Meeting place** Abide, Abutment, Achieve, AGM, Appointment, Apposite,
Apropos, Apt, Ascot, Assemblage, Assemble, Assembly, Assignation, Audience, Baraza,
Bosberaad, Briefing, Cabinet, Camporee, Caucus, Chapterhouse, Chautauqua, Clash,
Commissure, Conclave, Concourse, Concur, Confluence, Confrontation, Congress,
Connivance, Conseil d'etat, Consistory, Consult(ation), Contact, Conterminous, Convene,
Convent(icle), Convention, Converge, Conversazione, Convocation, Correspond,
Crossroads, Cybercafé, Date, Defray, Demo, EGM, Encounter, Ends, Experience, Face,

Find, Fit, For(e)gather, Forum, Fulfil, Gala, Gemot, General, Giron, Gorsedd, Greeting, Guild, Gyeld, Gymkhana, Gyron, Hall, Howf(f), Hunt, Hustings, Imbizo, Impact, Indaba, Infall, Interface, Interview, Jamboree, Join, Junction, Kgotla, Korero, Lekgotla, Liaise, Marae, Match, Moot, Mother's, Obviate, Occlusion, Occur, Oppose, Overflow, Partenariat, Pay, Plenary, Plenum, Pnyx, Pow-wow, Prayer, Prosper, Quadrivial, Quaker, Quorate, Quorum, Race, Races, Rally(ing point), Rencontre, Rencounter, Rendezvous, Replay, Reunion, Sabbat(h), Satisfy, Séance, See, Seminar, Session, Sit, Social, Sports, Suitable, Summit, Swap, Symposium, Synastry, Synaxis, Synod, Tackle, Talkfest, Talk-in, Talking-shop, Think-in, Town, Track, Tryst, Venery, Venue, Vestry, Wapinshaw, Wardmote, Wharenui, Wharepuni, Workshop

**Megalith(ic)** Sarsen, Skara Brae, Stonehenge

**Megalomaniac** Monarcho

**Megaphone** Bull-horn, Loudhailer

**Megapode** Mound-bird, Talegalla

**Meiosis** Understatement

**Meistersinger** Sachs

**Melancholy, Melancholic** Adust, Allicholy, Allycholly, Anatomy, Atrabilious, Blue, Cafard, Despond(ency), Dreary, Dump(s), Gloom, Heart-sore, Hipped, Hump, Hyp, Hypochondria, Jaques, Lienal, Lugubrious, Moper, Panophobia, Pensieroso, Pensive, Saturnine, Sombre, Spleen, Splenetic, Triste, Tristesse, Weltschmerz

**Melanese, Melanesian** Kanak, Motu

**Mêlée** Brawl, Commotion, Dogfight, Fracas, Free-for-all, Rally, Salmagundi, Scrum

**Melia** Margosa, Neem, Nim

**Mellifluent, Mellifluous** Cantabile, Melodic

**Mellow** Age, Fruity, Genial, Mature, Ripe, Smooth

**Melodrama(tic)** Bathos, Histrionic, Lurid, Sensation, Transpontine

**Melody, Melodious** Air, Arioso, Cabaletta, Canorous, Cantabile, Cantilena, Canto (fermo), Cantus, Cavatina, Chant, Chopsticks, Conductus, Counterpoint, Descant, Dulcet, Euphonic, Fading, Musical, Orphean, Part-song, Plainsong, Ranz-des-vaches, Refrain, Songful, Strain, Sweet, Theme, Tunable, →**TUNE(S)**

**Melon(like)** Cantaloup(e), Cas(s)aba, Charentais, Galia, Gourd, Honeydew, Mango, Musk, Nar(r)as, Ogen, Pepo, Persian, Rock, Spanspek, Winter

**Melt(ed), Melting** Ablate, Colliquate, →**DISSOLVE**, Eutectic, Eutexia, Flux, Found, Fuse, Fusil(e), Liquescent, Liquid, Run, Smectic, Syntexis, Thaw, Touch

**Member** Adherent, Arm, Beam, Branch, Bro(ther), Charter, Chin, Confrère, Cornice, Coulisse, Crossbeam, Crypto, Direction, Felibre, Fellow, Finger, Forearm, Forelimb, Founder, Girder, Gremial, Harpin(g)s, Insider, Keel, Leg, Limb, Lintel, Longeron, M, MBE, Montant, MP, Organ, Part, Partisan, Peer, Politicaster, Politician, Private, Rood-beam, Soroptomist, Stile, Stringer, Strut, Syndic, Tie, Toe, Upright

**Membrane, Membranous** Amnion, Arachnoid, Axilemma, Bilayer, Caul, Cell, Chorioallantois, Chorion, Choroid (plexus), Chromoplast, Conjunctiva, Cornea, Cyst, Decidua, Dissepiment, Dura (mater), Eardrum, Endocardium, Endometrium, Endosteum, Ependyma, Exine, Extine, Fell, Film, Foetal, Frenulum, Fr(a)enum, Haw, Head, Hyaloid, Hymen, Indusium, Intima, Intine, Involucre, Kell, Mater, Mediastinum, Meninx, Mesentery, Mucosa, Mucous, Neurolemma, Nictitating, Nuclear, Parchment, Patagium, Pellicle, Pericardium, Pericarp, Perichondrium, Pericranium, Periost(eum), Periton(a)eum, Pia mater, Plasma, Plasmalemma, Pleura, Putamen, Retina, Rim, Sarcolemma, Scarious, Schneiderian, Sclera, Serosa, Serous, Skin, Synovial, Tectorial, Tela, Third eyelid, Tissue, Tonoplast, Trophoblast, Tunic, Tympan(ic), Vacuolar, Velamen, Velum, Vitelline, Web, Yolk-sac

**Memento, Memoir** Keepsake, Locket, Relic, Remembrancer, Souvenir, Token, Trophy

**Memo(randum)** Bordereau, Cahier, Chit, IOU, Jot, Jurat, Minute, Note, Notepad, →**REMINDER**, Slip

**Memoirist** Casanova

**Memorable, Memorise, Memory** Associative, ATLAS, Bubble, Cache, Catchy, Collective, → **COMPUTER MEMORY**, Con, Core, DIMM, DRAM, Dynamic, Echoic, Elephantine, Engram(ma), Extended, Flash (bulb), Folk, Get, Highlight, Historic, Hypermnesia, Iconic, Immortal, Immunological, Keepsake, Kilobyte, Learn, Living, Long-term, Main, Mainstore, Memoriter, Mind, Mneme, Mnemonic, Mnemosyne, Non-volatile, Noosphere, Notable, Pelmanism, Photographic, Race, Read-write, Recall, Recollection, Recovered, Red-letter day, → **REMEMBER**, Retention, Retrospection, ROM, Ro(a)te, Samskara, Screen, Semantic, Short-term, SIMM, Souvenir, Sovenance, Special, Static, Storage, Study, Video, Virtual, Volatile, Word, Working

**Memorial** Albert, Altar tomb, Brass, Cenotaph, Cromlech, Ebenezer, Gravestone, Hatchment, Headstone, Marker, Martyr's, Mausoleum, Monument, Mount Rushmore, Obelisk, Pantheon, Plaque, Relic, Relique, Statue, Tomb(stone), Trophy, War, Wreath

▸ **Memory loss** *see* **LOSS OF MEMORY**

**Men(folk)** Amadoda, Androcentric, Chaps, Chess, Cuffins, Male, Messrs, Mortals, OR, People, Race, Troops

**Menace, Menacing** Danger, Dennis, Endanger, Foreboding, Intimidate, Jeopardise, Minatory, Ominous, Peril, Pest, Scowl, Sinister, Threat(en)

**Menagerie** Ark, Circus, Zoo

**Mend(er)** Beet, Bete, Bushel, Cobble, Correct, Cure, Darn, Fix, Heal, Improved, Mackle, Patch, Piece, Recover, Remedy, → **REPAIR**, Set, Sew, Solder, Tinker, Trouble-shoot

**Mendelevium** Md

**Mendicant** Beggar, Calender, Fakir, Franciscan, Frater, Pauper, Servite

**Menhir** Standing stone

**Menial** Bottlewasher, Dogsbody, Drudge, Drug, Eta, Fag, Flunkey, Lackey, Lowly, Scullion, Servile, Toady, Underling, Wood-and-water joey

**Meninx** (D)jerba

**Meniscus** Dome

**Menopause** Andropause, Climacteric

**Menstruation** Curse, Menarche, Menorrh(o)ea, Menses, Monthly, Period

**Mental (condition), Mental disorder, Mentality** Alienism, Barking, Bunker, Doolally, Eject, Hallucinosis, Insane, Noetic, Nut job, Nutty, Paranoia, Psychic, Siege

▷ **Mental** *may indicate* the chin

**Mention(ed)** Advert, Allusion, Bename, Benempt, Bring up, Broach, Bynempt, Citation, Drag up, Hint, Honourable, Hote, Instance, Name(-check), Notice, Quote, Refer, Same, Specify, Speech, State, Suggest, Touch

**Mentor** Advisor, Guru, Rebbe, Tutor

**Menu** Agenda, Card, Carte, Carte du jour, Cascading, Cuisine, Drop-down, Fare, List, Option, Prix fixe, Table d'hôte, Tariff

**Mercantile** Commercial, Trade

**Mercaptan** Thiol

**Mercator** Cartographer

**Mercenary** Arnaout, Condottiere, Freelance, Gallo(w)glass, Greedy, Hack, Hessian, Hired gun, Hireling, Landsknecht, Legionnaire, Mean, Money-grubbing, Pindaree, Pindari, Rutter, Sordid, Spoilsman, Swiss Guard, Switzer, Venal, Warmonger, Wildgeese

**Merchandise** Cargo, Goods, Line, Produce, Ware(s)

**Merchant(man)** Abbas, Abudah, Antonio, Argosy, Broker, Bun(n)ia, Burgher, Chandler, Chap, Commission, Crare, Crayer, Dealer, Doom, Factor, Flota, Gossip, Hoastman, Importer, Jobber, Law, Magnate, Marcantant, Mercer, Monger, Nathan, Négociant, Pedlar, Polo, Provision, Retailer, Scrap, Seller, Shipper, Speed, Squeegee, Stapler, Sutler, Trader, Vintner, Wholesaler

**Mercia** Offa

**Merciful, Mercy** Amnesty, Charity, Clement, Compassionate, Corporal, Grace, Humane, Kind, Kyrie, Lenient, Lenity, Miserere, Misericord(e), Pacable, Pity, Quarter, Ruth, Sparing, Spiritual

**Merciless** Cruel, Hard, Hard-hearted, Inclement, Pitiless, Wanton

**Mercurial, Mercuric sulphide, Mercury** Azoth, Cyllenius, Dog's, Freddie, Fulminating, Herald, Hermes, Hg, Horn, Hydrargyrum, Messenger, Proteus, Queen's yellow, Quicksilver, Red, Red-man, Spurge, Thimerosal, Tiemannite, Torr, Volatile

**Mere(ly)** Allenarly, Bare, Common, Lake, Only, Pond, Pool, Poor, Pure, Sheer, Tarn, Ullswater, Very

**Merge(r), Merging** Amalgamate, Blend, Coalesce, Coalise, Composite, Conflate, Consolidate, Die, Elide, Fusion, Incorporate, Interflow, Interpenetrate, Liquesce, Meld, Melt, Mingle, Symphysis, Syncretism, Synergy, Unify, Unite

**Meridian** Magnetic, Noonday, Prime

**Meringue** Pavlova

**Merit(ed)** CL, Condign, Deserve, Due, Earn, Found, Lustre, Meed, Rate, Virtue, Worth(iness)

**Mermaid** Dugong, Halicore, Merrow, Siren, Tavern, Undine

**Merriment, Merry** Andrew, Blithe(some), Bonny, Boon, Cant, Cherry, Chirpy, Crank, Cricket, Elated, Full, Gaudy, Gay, Gean, Glad, Gleesome, Greek, Hilarity, Jocose, Jocular, Jocund, Jolly, Joyous, L'allegro, Lively, Nitid, On, Page, Riant, Sportive, Sunny, Tipsy, Vogie, Waggery, Wassail

**Merry-andrew** Clown, Jack-pudding, Pickle-herring

**Merry-go-round** Carousel, Galloper, Whirligig

**Merry-making** Cakes and ale, Carnival, Festivity, Gaiety, Gaud, Gawd, Mardi Gras, Revel, Saturnalia, Wassail

**Merrythought** Clavicle, Collarbone, Wishbone

**Mesh** Cancellate, Chain, Entangle, Mantle, Net, Reseau, Screen

**Mesmer(ise)** Hypnotise

**Mess(y), Mess up** Anteroom, Balls-up, Bedraggled, Blotch, Boob, Boss, Botch, Canteen, Caudle, Chaos, Clamper, Clutter, Cock-up, Dining-room, Disorganise, Dog's dinner, Failure, Farrago, Fiasco, Flub, Garboil, Glop, G(l)oop, Gory, Guddle, Gunge, Gunk, Gun-room, Hash, Horlicks, Hotch-potch, Hugger-mugger, Imbroglio, Lash-up, Louse, Mash, Meal, Mismanage, Mix, Mixter-maxter, Modge, Muck, Muddle, Muff, Mullock, Muss, Mux, Pi(e), Pig's ear, Piss-up, Plight, Pollute, Pottage, Screw-up, Scungy, Shambles, Shambolic, Shemozzle, Sight, Slaister, Smudge, Snafu, Soss, Sty, Sully, Tinker, Tousle, Trifle, Untidy, Wardroom, Whoopsie, Yuck(y)

**Message(s), Messaging** Aerogram, Bull, Bulletin, Cable(gram), Caption, Contraplex, Dépêche, Despatch, Dispatch, Email, Epistle, Errand, Error, Fax, Flame, Inscription, Kissagram, Kissogram, Letter, Marconigram, Missive, News, Note, Notification, Pager, Ping, Posting, Postscript, Propaganda, PTO, Radiogram, Radio telegraph, Read-out, Rumour, Signal, Slogan, SMS, SOS, Stripagram, Strippergram, Subtext, Telco, Telegram, Telepheme, Telephone, Teletype®, Telex, Text, Tidings, Toothing, Tweet, Valentine, Voice mail, Wire, → **WORD**

**Messenger** Angel, Angela, Apostle, Azrael, Beadle, Caddie, Caddy, Carrier pigeon, Chaprassi, Chuprassy, Corbie, Courier, Culver, Despatch-rider, Emissary, Envoy, Errand boy, Forerunner, Gaga, Gillie-wetfoot, Gillie whitefoot, Hatta, Herald, Hermes, Internuncio, Iris, Ladas, Mercury, Nuncio, Page, Peon, Post, Pursuivant, Runner, Send, Seraph, Shellycoat, Valet de place, Valkyrie

**Messiah** Christ, Emmanuel, Immanuel, Mahdi, Mashiach, Prince of peace, Saviour, Shiloh, Son of man, Southcott

**Met** Constabulary, Faced, Old Bill, Opera, Weather, Weatherman

**Metabolism** Basal, Cryptobiotic

**Metal(s), Metallic, Metalware, Metalwork** Aeneous, Antifriction, Base, Death, Expanded, Filler, Fine, Fusible, Heavy, Hot, Jangling, Leaf, Mercuric, Mineral, Noble, Nonferrous, Ore, Perfect, Planchet, Precious, Prince's, Road, Scrap, Sheet(-iron), Sprue, Stannic, Thrash, Torque, Tramp, Transition, Type, White, Yellow

## METALS

| | | | |
|---|---|---|---|
| **2 letters:** | Monel | Cadmium | Platinum |
| Ag | Muntz | Gallium | Samarium |
| Al | Steel | Iridium | Scandium |
| Er | Terne | Lithium | Speculum |
| Sm | | Natrium | Tantalum |
| Sn | **6 letters:** | Protore | Thallium |
| | Aiglet | Regulus | Tinplate |
| **3 letters:** | Alkali | Rhenium | Titanium |
| Gib | Billon | Taggers | Tungsten |
| Tin | Chrome | Terbium | |
| | Cobalt | Thorium | **9 letters:** |
| **4 letters:** | Copper | Tutania | Aluminium |
| Bell | Erbium | Tutenag | Beryllium |
| Foil | Monell | Wolfram | Britannia |
| Gold | Nickel | Zorgite | Germanium |
| Iron | Niello | | Manganese |
| Slug | Ormolu | **8 letters:** | Ruthenium |
| Tole | Osmium | Actinium | Strontium |
| Zinc | Pewter | Antimony | Toreutics |
| | Silver | Babbitt's | |
| **5 letters:** | Sodium | Chromium | **10 letters:** |
| Aglet | Speiss | Europium | Dysprosium |
| Brass | Terbic | Filagree | Promethium |
| Ingot | | Filigree | |
| Invar® | **7 letters:** | Gold leaf | **11 letters:** |
| Misch | Bismuth | Kamacite | Aiguillette |

**Metallurgy** Powder

**Metal-worker** Blacksmith, Founder, Goldsmith, Lorimer, Robot, Silversmith, Smith, Spurrier, Tinsmith, Tubal Cain, Whitesmith

**Metamorphose, Metamorphosis, Metamorphism** Regional, Transfiguration, Transmogrify

▷ **Metamorphosing** *may indicate* an anagram

**Metaphor** Conceit, Figure, Image(ry), Kenning, Malonym, Mixed, Symbol, Trope, Tropical

**Metaphysics** Ontology, Scotism

**Mete** Inflict

**Meteor(ic), Meteorite** Achondrite, Aerolite, Aerosiderite, Bolide, Chondrite, Comet, Drake, Falling star, Fireball, Geminid, Iron, Leonid, Perseid, Quadrantid, Siderite, Siderolite, Star(dust), Stony(-iron), Tektite

**Meteorologist, Meteorology** Aeromancy, Weather prophet

**Meter** Alidad(e), Electric, Exposure, Flow, Gas, Light, Orifice, Parking, Postage, Postal, Torque, Torsion, Water, White

**Methamphetamine** Chalk, Ice

**Methane, Methanol** Alkane, Marsh gas, Synthesis gas

**Methedrine®** Speed

**Method(ology), Methodical** Art, Billings, Buteyko, Direct, Feldenkrais, Formal, Formula, Gram's, Historical, Hi-tec(h), How, Kenny, Kumon, Line, Manner, Mode, Modus, Modus operandi, Monte Carlo, Montessori, Neat, Orderly, Organised, Organon, Organum, Ovulation, Painstaking, Phonic, Plan, Ploy, Procedure, Process, Q, Rhythm, Schafer's, Scientific, Socratic, Stanislavski, Systematic, Tactics, Technique, Way, Withdrawal

**Methodism, Methodist** Huntingdonian, Itinerant, Jumper, Methody, Primitive, Ranter, Scientism, Sim, Soper, Southcottian, Swaddler, Wesley

**Meths** White Lady

**Methuselah** Bottle, Macrobiote

**Meticulous** Careful, Diligent, → **EXACT**, Finicky, Minute, Painstaking, Precise, Punctilious, Quiddler, Scrupulous, Thorough

**Métier** Line, Trade, Vocation

**Metonymy** Metalepsis

**Metre, Metrical** Alexandrine, Amphibrach, Amphimacer, Anapaest, Antispast, Arsis, Ballad, Cadence, Choliamb, Choree, Choriamb, Common, Dipody, Galliambic, Iambic, Ithyphallic, Long, M, Penthemimer, Prosody, Pyrrhic, Rhythm, Sapphic, Scansion, Scazon, Semeion, Service, Short, Spondee, Strophe, Tribrach, Tripody, Trochee

**Metric (system)** MKS

**Metroland** Subtopia

**Metropolis, Metropolitan** Big Apple, Eparch

**Metrosexual** Epicene

**Mettle** Ardour, Bravery, Courage, Ginger, Guts, Pith, → **PLUCK**, Pride, Smeddum, Spirit, Spunk, Steel

**Mew** Caterwaul, Cry, Miaou, Miaow, Pen, Purr, Seagull, Shed, Waul, Wrawl

**Mews** Meuse, Muse(t), Musit, Stables, Yard

**Mexican (Indian)** Atlatl, Aztec, Carib, Chicano, Chichibec, Cuna, Diaz, Greaser, Gringo, Hairless, Hispanic, Kuna, Latino, Maya, Mixe-Zoque, Mixtec, Montezuma, Nahuatl, Nortéño, Olmec, Otomi, Pachuco, Pedro, Spic, Spik, Taino, Tewa, Toltec, Wetback, Yucatan, Zapotec, Zuni

**Mezzanine** Entresol

**Mezzo-soprano** Tessa

**MG** TD

**Miasma** Fug

**Mica** Biotite, Daze, Fuchsite, Glimmer, Isinglass, Lepidolite, Lepidomelane, Muscovite, Paragonite, Phlogopite, Rubellan, Sericite, Talc, Verdite, Vermiculite

**Micawber** Wilkins

**Michael** Mick(e)y

**Mick(ey)** Greek, Mouse

**Micro** Mu

**Microbe, Microorganism** Extremophile, Germ, Lactobacillus, Nanobe, Organism, Plankton

**Microbiologist** Fleming, Sabine, Salk

**Microchip** ULA

**Micro-organism** Amoeba

**Microphone** Bug, Carbon, Crystal, Directional, Lavaliere, Lip, Mike, Phonic Ear®, Radio, Ribbon, Throat

**Microscope** Acoustic, Compound, Confocal, Darkfield, Dissecting, Electron, Engyscope, Field-ion, Lens, Optical, Phase-contrast, Phase-difference, Polarizing, Proton, Reading, Reflecting, SEM, Simple, Solar, TEM, Ultraviolet

**Microwave** Nuke

**Mid(st)** Amongst, Mongst

**Midas** Goldinger, Tamarin

**Midday** Meridian, N, Noon, Noon-tide, Noon-time

**Middle(way), Middling, Midpoint** Active, Ariston metron, Basion, Centre, Core, Crown, Enteron, Epitasis, Equidistant, Excluded, Eye, Girth, Heart, Innermost, Internal, Loins, Meat, Median, Mediocre, Medium, Meridian, Meseraic, Mesial, Mesne, Meso, Midriff, Moderate, Nasion, Noon, Passive, Turn, Twixt, Undistributed, Via media, Wa(i)st

**Middle age(d)** Forty, Grey, Menopause

**Middle-Cambrian** Menevian

**Middle class** Bourgeois, Hova, Mondeo Man

**Middle East(ern), Middle-Easterner** Arab, Iraqi, Kurdish, Mede, Omani, Persic

**Middle European** Magyar

**Middleman** Agent, Broker, Centre, Comprador(e), Diaphragm, Interlocutor, Intermediary, Jobber, Median, Navel, Regrater, Regrator

**Middlesex** Hermaphrodite

**Midge** Chironomid, Gall, Gnat

**Midget** Dwarf, Homunculus, Lilliputian, Pygmy, Shrimp

**Midianite** Prowler

**Midlander** Brummie

**Midlands** Mercia

**Midnight** G, O Am, Witching hour

▶ **Midnight** *see* **PAST MIDNIGHT**

**Midriff** Phrenic, Skirt, Waist

**Midshipman** Brass-bounder, Easy, Middy, Oldster, Reefer, Snottie, Snotty

▶ **Midst** *see* **MID(ST)**

**Midsummer** Solstice

**Mid-Westerner** Indianan

**Midwife** Accoucheur, Doula, Gran(nie), Granny, Howdie, Howdy, Lucina, Mab, Maieutic, Obstetric

**Midwinter** Solstice

**Mien** Air, Bearing, Demean, Manner

**Might(iness), Mighty** Could, Force, Main, Maud, Mote, Muscle, Nibs, Oak, Potence, →**POWER**, Prowess, Puissant, Should, Strength

**Mignon(ette)** Dyer's rocket, Fillet, Reseda, Wald, Weld

**Migraine** Megrim, Scotodinia, Teichopsia

**Migrant** Economic, Externe, Gastarbeiter, Lemming, Snowbird, Traveller

**Migrate, Migration, Migratory** Colonise, Diapedesis, Diaspora, Drift, Eelfare, Exodus, Fleet, Great Trek, Run, Tre(c)k, Volk(er)wanderung

**Mikado** Emperor, Kami, Teno

**Mike** Bug, M, Stentorphone

**Milanese** Patarine

**Mild(ly), Mildness** Balmy, Benign, Bland, Clement, Euphemism, Genial, Gentle, Lenient, Lenity, Litotes, Mansuete, Meek, →**MODERATE**, Pacific, Patient, Pussycat, Sarcenet, Sars(e)net, Temperate

**Mildew** Downy, Foxing, Fungus, Mould, Oidium, Powdery, Vine, Wheat

**Mile(r), Miles** Admiralty, Coss, Coverdale, Food, Geographical, Hour, Irish, Knot, Kos, League, Li, Mi, Milliary, Nautical, Passenger, Roman, Royal, Scots, Sea, Soldier, Square, Standish, Statute, Swedish, Train

**Milesian** Teague

**Milestone** Birthday, Milliary, MS

**Milfoil** Yarrow

**Militancy, Militant, Military** Activist, Aggressive, Battailous, Belligerent, Black Panther, Black Power, Commando, Fortinbras, Hawkish, Hezbollah, Hizbollah, Hizbullah, Hostile, Ireton, Janjaweed, Janjawid, Junta, Kshatriya, Landsturm, Landwehr, Leftist, Logistics, Lumper, Mameluke, Martial, Nahal, Naxalite, Presidio, Provisional, Provo, Soldatesque, Stratocracy, Tactical, War machine, War paint, West Point, Zealous

**Militia(-man)** Band, Fyrd, Guard, Haganah, Milice, Minuteman, Peshmerga, Reserve, Tanzim, Trainband, Yeomanry

**Milk(er), Milky** Acidophilus, Beestings, Bland, Bleed, Bonny-clabber, Bristol, Butter, Casein, Certified, Churn, Colostrum, Condensed, Creamer, Crud, Curd, Dairy, Emulge, Evaporated, Exact, Exploit, Extract, Galactic, Glacier, Goat's, Homogenised, Jib, Kefir,

Kephir, K(o)umiss, Lactation, Lacteal, Latex, Long-life, Maas, Madafu, Madzoon, Magnesia, Malted, Mamma, Matzoon, Mess, Moo-juice, Opaline, Pasteurised, Pigeon's, Pinta, Posset, Raw, Rice, Sap, Semi-skimmed, Shedder, Skim(med), Soya, Squeeze, Strip(pings), Stroke, Suckle, Town, UHT, Use, Whey, Whig, Whole, Yaourt, Yogh(o)urt

**Milking-machine, Milking parlour** Loan, Tapper

**Milking-pail** Leglan, Leglen, Leglin

**Milkless** Agalactic, Dry, Eild

**Milkmaid, Milkman** Chalker, Dey, Emulge, Kefir, Kephir, Radha, Rounder, Roundsman, Skimmed

**Milksop** Coward, Meacock, Namby-pamby, Nance, Pance, Weakling, Wimp

**Milk-vetch** Loco

**Milkweed** Asclepias

**Milkwort** Senega

**Milky Way** Via Lactea

**Mill(ing), Mills** Aswarm, Ball, Barker's, Blag, Boxing, Coffee, Crazing, Economist, Flatford, Flour, Gang, Gastric, Gig, Grind(er), Hayley, Kibble, Knurl, Lumber, Malt, Mano, Melder, Molar, Nurl, Oil, Paper, Pepper, Plunge-cut, Post, Powder, Press, Pug, Pulp, Quartz, Quern, Reave, Rob, Rolling, Rumour, Satanic, Scutcher, Smock, Spinning, Stamp, Stamping, Strip, Sucken, Sugar, Surge, Thou, Tide, Tower, Tuck, Water, Wool(len), Works

**Miller** Dusty, Glen, Grinder, Jester, Joe, Molendinar, Multurer

**Millet** Bajra, Bajree, Bajrii, Couscous, Dari, Dhurra, Doura, Dur(r)a, Grain, Miliary, Negro-corn, Pearl, Proso, Ragee, Raggee, Ragi, Whisk

**Milliner** Hatter, Modiste

**Millionaire** Astor, Carnegie, MOP, Rockefeller, Rothschild, Vanderbilt

**Millions, Millionth** Crore, Femto-, Milliard, Muckle, Pico-

**Millipede** Diplopod, Songololo

**Millstone** Ligger, Rind, Rynd

**Mim** Perjink

**Mime, Mimic(ry)** Ape, Batesian, Copycat, Echo, Farce, Imitate, Impersonate, Lipsync, Marceau, Mina, Mock, Mullerian, Mummer, Myna, Parody, Sturnine, Take-off

**Mimosa** Cacoon, Raintree, Saman

**Mince, Mincing** Cecils, Chop, Dice, Grate, Grind, Keema, Nipperty-tipperty, Prance, Rice

**Mind(er)** Agent, Aide, Baby-sitter, Beware, Bodyguard, Brain, Care, Gaum, Genius, Grasshopper, Grey matter, Handler, Head, →HEED, Herd, Id, Ideo-, Intellect, Mentality, Month's, Noology, Noosphere, Nous, One-track, Open, Phrenic, Psyche, Psychogenic, Resent, Sensorium, Tabula rasa, Tend, Thinker, View, Wit, Woundwort, Year's

**Mine, Mining** Acoustic, Antenna, Appalachia, Biomining, Bomb, Bonanza, Bord and pillar, Bottom, Bouquet, Burrow, Camouflet, Chemical, Claymore, Coalfield, Colliery, Contact, Creeping, Dane-hole, Data, Dig(gings), Drifting, Egg, Eldorado, Excavate, Explosive, Fiery, Floating, Flooder, Fougade, Fougasse, Gallery, Gob, Golconda, Gold, Gopher, Grass, Homing, Land, Limpet, Magnetic, Microbiological, Naked-light, Nostromo, Open-cast, Open-cut, Ophir, Pit, Placer, Pressure, Prospect, Rising, Sap, Set(t), Show, Silver, Sonic, Stannary, Stope, Strike, Strip, Undercut, Wheal, Win, Workings

**Mine-deflector** Otter, Paravane

**Mine-owner** Operator

**Miner, Mine-worker, Mine-working** Bevin boy, Butty-gang, Buttyman, Collier, Continuous, Corporal, Cutter, Digger, Faceworker, Forty-niner, Geordie, Leaf, Molly Maguire, Noisy, NUM, Oncost(man), Pitman, Sapper, Shot-firer, Stall, Tippler, Tributer, Tunneler, UDM, Undersawyer

**Mineral(s)** Accessory, Essential, Index, Ore, Owre

## MINERALS

*3 letters:*
YAG

*4 letters:*
Clay
Foid
Gang
Mica
Sard
Spar
Talc
Trap
Urao

*5 letters:*
Balas
Borax
Chert
Emery
Flint
Fluor
Macle
Mafic
Nitre
Prase
Topaz
Trona
Umber

*6 letters:*
Acmite
Albite
Augite
Blende
Cerite
Galena
Gangue
Garnet
Glance
Gypsum
Hauyne
Illite
Iolite
Jargon
Kermes
Lithia
Natron
Nosean
Pinite
Pyrite
Quartz
Rutile

Schorl
Silica
Sphene
Spinel
Tincal
Zircon

*7 letters:*
Alunite
Amosite
Anatase
Apatite
Axinite
Azurite
Barytes
Biotite
Bornite
Brucite
Calcite
Calomel
Catseye
Crystal
Cuprite
Cyanite
Diamond
Dysodil
Epidote
Erinite
Euclase
Eucrite
Fahlore
Felspar
Gahnite
Göthite
Gummite
Hessite
Ice spar
Jadeite
Jargoon
Kainite
Kernite
Kyanite
Leucite
Mellite
Mullite
Nacrite
Niobite
Olivine
Pennine
Peridot
Pyrites
Realgar

Rosaker
Sylvine
Sylvite
Thorite
Thulite
Tripoli
Turgite
Ulexite
Uralite
Uranite
Uranium
Zeolite
Zeuxite
Zincite
Zoisite
Zorgite

*8 letters:*
Adularia
Allanite
Analcime
Analcite
Andesine
Ankerite
Antimony
Aphanite
Asbestos
Autunite
Blue john
Boehmite
Boracite
Braunite
Bronzite
Brookite
Calamine
Cerusite
Chlorite
Chromite
Cinnabar
Cleveite
Corundum
Crocoite
Cryolite
Datolite
Dendrite
Diallage
Diaspore
Diopside
Disthene
Dolomite
Dysodile
Dysodyle

Enargite
Epsomite
Erionite
Euxenite
Fayalite
Feldspar
Flinkite
Fluorite
Galenite
Gibbsite
Goethite
Gyrolite
Hematite
Idocrase
Ilmenite
Iodyrite
Jarosite
Lazulite
Lazurite
Lewisite
Limonite
Liparite
Massicot
Meionite
Melilite
Mimetite
Monazite
Nephrite
Noselite
Orpiment
Petuntse
Picotite
Prehnite
Pyroxene
Resalgar
Rock-salt
Sanidine
Saponite
Sardonyx
Siderite
Smaltite
Smectite
Sodalite
Stannite
Stibnite
Stilbite
Sunstone
Taconite
Tenorite
Tinstone
Titanite
Troilite

Vesuvian
Xenotime
Zaratite

**9 letters:**
Alabaster
Allophane
Amazonite
Amphibole
Anglesite
Anhydrite
Anorthite
Aragonite
Argentite
Atacamite
Blackjack
Blacklead
Carnelian
Carnotite
Celestine
Celestite
Cerussite
Chabazite
Chalybite
Cheralite
Chondrule
Cobaltine
Cobaltite
Coccolite
Columbate
Columbite
Covellite
Cystolith
Dolomitic
Elaeolite
Endomorph
Enhydrite
Enstatite
Erythrite
Fibrolite®
Flowstone
Fluorspar
Fool's gold
Gehlenite
Germanite
Geyserite
Gmelinite
Goslarite
Haematite
Harmotome
Hercynite
Hiddenite
Hornstone
Kaolinite

Kermesite
Kieserite
Limestone
Magnesite
Magnetite
Malachite
Manganite
Marcasite
Margarite
Marialite
Microlite
Microlith
Millerite
Mispickel
Mizzonite
Moonstone
Muscovite
Natrolite
Nepheline
Nephelite
Niccolite
Nitratine
Olivenite
Ottrelite
Paramorph
Pargasite
Pectolite
Penninite
Periclase
Pericline
Perimorph
Phenacite
Pigeonite
Pleonaste
Polianite
Pollucite
Powellite
Proustite
Rhodonite
Rubellite
Scapolite
Scheelite
Scolecite
Sepiolite
Septarium
Spodumene
Sylvanite
Tantalite
Tremolite
Troostite
Tungstite
Uraninite
Uvarovite
Variscite

Vulpinite
Wavellite
Wernerite
Willemite
Witherite
Wulfenite
Zinkenite

**10 letters:**
Actinolite
Alabandine
Alabandite
Andalusite
Bastnasite
Calaverite
Carnallite
Chalcocite
Chessylite
Chrysolite
Colemanite
Cordierite
Crocoisite
Dyscrasite
Forsterite
Gadolinite
Garnierite
Glauconite
Halloysite
Heulandite
Honey-stone
Hornblende
Indicolite
Indigolite
Jamesonite
Laurdalite
Meerschaum
Microcline
Mirabilite
Oligoclase
Oomphacite
Orthoclase
Paragonite
Perovskite
Phosgenite
Piemontite
Polybasite
Polyhalite
Pyrolusite
Pyrrhotine
Pyrrhotite
Redruthite
Riebeckite
Ripidolite
Samarskite

Saphir d'eau
Sapphirine
Saussurite
Serpentine
Smaragdite
Sperrylite
Sphalerite
Staurolite
Tennantite
Thaumasite
Thenardite
Thorianite
Tiemannite
Torbernite
Tourmaline
Triphylite
Vanadinite
Wolframite

**11 letters:**
Alexandrite
Amblygonite
Annabergite
Apophyllite
Baddeleyite
Bastnaesite
Cassiterite
Chiastolite
Chloanthite
Chrysoberyl
Clinochlore
Crocidolite
Dendrachate
Franklinite
Greenockite
Hypersthene
Idiomorphic
Josephinite
Labradorite
Molybdenite
Pentlandite
Philogopite
Phosphorite
Piedmontite
Pitchblende
Plagioclase
Pseudomorph
Psilomelane
Pyrargyrite
Pyrrhotiner
Sal ammoniac
Sillimanite
Smithsonite
Tabular spar

Tetradymite
Vermiculite
Vesuvianite
Ythro-cerite

**12 letters:**
Adularescent
Arfvedsonite
Arsenopyrite
Babingtonite

Chalcanthite
Chalcopyrite
Cristobalite
Dumortierite
Feldspathoid
Fluorapatite
Hemimorphite
Lepidomelane
Pyromorphite
Pyrophyllite

Senarmontite
Skutterudite
Strontianite
Synadelphite
Tetrahedrite
Wollastonite

**13 letters:**
Cummingtonite
Rhodochrosite

**14 letters:**
Yttro-tantalite

**15 letters:**
Gooseberry-stone
Montmorillonite

---

**Mineralogy, Mineralogist** Haüy, Heuland, Miller-Smithson, Oryctology

**Mineral water** Apollinaris, Tonic

**Minesweeper** Oropesa, Unity

**Mingle, Mingling** Assort, Blend, Circulate, Commix, Consort, Interfuse, Intermarry, Mell, Merge, → MIX, Participate, Socialise, Theocrasy, Unite

**Mini** Cab, Car, Skirt, Teen(s)y, Teeny-weeny

**Miniature, Miniaturist** Cosway, Dwarf, Lilliputian, Microcosm, Midget, Model, Toy, Young

**Minimise, Minimum (range)** Bare, Downplay, Fewest, Floor, Gloze, Least, Neap, Pittance, Quorum, Scant, Shoestring, Stime, Styme, Threshold, Undervalue

▷ **Minimum of** *may indicate* the first letter

**Minion** Flunkey, Lackey, Pet, Subordinate, Tool, Vassal

**Minister** Ambassador, Attend, Buckle-beggar, Cabinet, Chancellor, Chaplain, Cleric, Coarb, Commissar, Curate, Deacon, Dewan, Diplomat, Divine, Dominee, Dominie, D(i)wan, Envoy, First, Foreign, Front Bench, Holy Joe, Home Secretary, Mas(s)john, Mes(s)john, Moderator, Nurse, Officiant, Ordinand, Ordinee, Padre, Parson, Pastor, Peshwa, Preacher, Predikant, Presbyter, Priest, Prime, Rector, Richelieu, Secretary, Seraskier, → SERVE, Stick, Stickit, Subdeacon, Tanaiste, Tend, Visier, Vizier, Wazir, Wizier

**Ministry** Cabinet, Cloth, Defence, Defra, Department, Dept, DoE, MOD, MOT, Orders, Service, Treasury

▷ **Ministry** *may indicate* some government department

**Mink** Kolinsky, Mutation, Vison

**Minnow** Devon, Penk, Pink, Tiddler

**Minoan** Knossus

**Minor(ity)** Child, Comprimario, Ethnic, Faction, Few, Fractional, Incidental, Infant, Junior, Less(er), Marginal, Minutia, Negligible, Nominal, Nonage, One-horse, Peripheral, Petty, Piffling, Pre-teen, Pupillage, Signed, Slight, Small-time, Sub(sidiary), Subordinate, Trivial, Ward, Weeny

**Minotaur** Bull-headed, Cretan

**Minster** York

**Minstrel** Allan-a-Dale, Ballad-monger, Bard, Blondel, Bones, Busker, Cantabank, Christy, Cornerman, Gleeman, Hamfatter, Joculator, Jongleur, Minnesinger, Nigger, Pierrot, Scop, Singer, Taillefer, Tannhauser

**Mint** Aim, Bugle-weed, Bull's eye, Catnip, Coin, Ettle, Fortune, Herb, Horse, Humbug, Labiate, Monarda, Monetise, Nep, New, Penny-royal, Pepper, Pile, Polo®, Poly, Rock, Royal, Selfheal, Spear, Stamp, Stone, Strike, Unused, Utter, Water

**Minus** Less, Nonplus

**Minute(s), Minutiae** Acta, Alto, Bijou, Degree, Detailed, Diatom, Entry, Infinitesimal, Lilliputian, Little, Mere, Micron, Mo, Mu, Nano-, New York, Pinpoint, Resume, Small, Teen(t)sy, Teeny, Tine, Tiny, Trivia, Tyne, Wee

**Minx** Hellion

**Miracle(s), Miraculous, Miracle worker** Cana, Marvel, Merel(l), Meril, Morris, Mystery, Mythism, Phenomenon, Saluter, Supernatural, Thaumatology, Thaumaturgic, Theurgy, Wirtschaftswunder, Wonder, Wonderwork

**Mirage** Delusion, Fata morgana, Illusion, Loom, Northern lights

**Mire** Bog, Glaur, Lair(y), Latch, Lerna, Lerne, Loblolly, Marsh, Mud, Mudge, Quag, Sludge, Soil

**Mirky** Dark, Dirk(e)

**Mirror(s), Mirrored** Alasnam, Antidazzle, Busybody, Cambuscan, Catoptric, Cheval, Claude Lorraine glass, Coelostat, Conde, Conjugate, Dare, Driving, Enantiomorph, Glass, Handglass, Heliostat, Image, Imitate, Keeking-glass, Lao, Magnetic, Merlin, One-way, Pierglass, Primary, Psyche, Rearview, →**REFLECT**, Reynard, Shisha, Siderostat, Sign, Specular, Speculum, Stone, Tiring-glass, Two-way, Vulcan, Wing

**Mirror-image** Perversion

**Mirth(ful)** Cheer, Dream, Festive, Glee, Hilarity, Joy, Laughter, Spleen

▷ **Misalliance** *may indicate* an anagram

**Misanthrope** Cynic, Timon

**Misapplication** Catachresis, Misuse

**Misappropriate, Misappropriation** Asport, Detinue, Embezzle, Purloin, Steal

**Miscarry** Abort, Backfire, Fail, Slink, Warp

**Miscegenation** Allocarpy

**Miscellaneous, Miscellany** Ana, Assortment, Chow, Collectanea, Diverse, Etceteras, Gallimaufry, Job lot, Misc, Odds and ends, Odds and sods, Olio, Omnium-gatherum, Paraphernalia, Pie, Potpourri, Raft, Ragbag, Sundry, Varia, Variety, Various

**Mischance** Misfare

**Mischief(-maker), Mischievous** Ate, Bale, Bane, Cantrip, Cloots, Devilment, Diablerie, Dido, Disservice, Evil, Gallus, Goings on, Gremlin, Hanky-panky, Harm, Hellery, Hellion, Hob, Imp, Injury, Jiggery-pokery, Jinks, Larky, Larrikin, Limb, Litherly, Make-bate, Malicho, Mallecho, Monkeyshines, Monkey-tricks, Nickum, Owl-spiegle, Pestilent, Pickle, Prank, Puckish, Rascal, Rogue, Scally(wag), Scamp, Scapegrace, Shenanigans, Spalpeen, Spriteful, Tricksy, Varmint, Wag, Wicked, Widgie

**Misconception** Delusion, Idol(on), Idolum, Mirage, Misunderstanding

**Misconduct** Impropriety, Incivism, Malfeasance, Malversation

**Miscreant** Bad lot, Blackguard, Reprobate, Sinner, Tortfeasor

**Misdeed** Crime, Offence, Peccadillo, Trespass, Wrong

▷ **Misdelivered** *may indicate* an anagram

**Misdemeanour** Delict, Offence, Peccadillo, Tort, Wrongdoing

**Miser(ly)** Carl, Cheapskate, Cheese-parer, Close, Curmudgeon, Flay-flint, Gare, Grasping, Harpagon, Hunks, Marner, Meanie, Mingy, Muckworm, Niggard, Nipcheese, Nipcurn, Nipfarthing, Pennyfather, Penny-pincher, Pinch-commons, Puckfist, Runt, Save-all, Scrape-good, Scrape-penny, Screw, Scrimping, Scrooge, Shylock, Skinflint, Snudge, Storer, Tightwad, Timon

**Miserable, Misery, Miserably** Abject, Angashore, Bale, Bane, Cat-lap, Crummy, Cut up, Distress, Dog's-life, Dole, Face-ache, Forlorn, Gloom, Grief, Heartache, Hell, Joyless, Killjoy, Lousy, Mean, Measly, Perdition, Punk, Sad, Saturnist, Scungy, Sorry, Sourpuss, Spoilsport, Torture, Tragic, Triste, →**UNHAPPY**, Wet blanket, Woe(begone), Wretched

**Misfire** Dud, Pink

**Misfit** Black sheep, Drop-out, Geek, Loner, Maverick, Sad sack

**Misfortune** Accident, Adversity, Affliction, Bale, Calamity, Curse, Disaster, Distress, Dole, Harm, Hex, Ill, Ill-luck, Kicker, Mis(c)hanter, Reverse, Rewth, Ruth, Wroath

**Misgiving(s)** Anxiety, Doubt, Dubiety, Qualms, Scruples

**Misguide(d)** Impolitic, Off-beam

▷ **Misguided** *may indicate* an anagram

**Mishandle** Abuse, Muff

**Mishap** Accident, Contretemps, Drere, Glitch, Misaunter, Misfortune, Pile-up, Wroath

**Misheard** Mondegreen

**Mishit, Misstroke** Crab, Draw, Edge, Fluff, Muff, Sclaff, Shank, Slice, Thin, Toe, Top

**Misinformation** Bum steer

**Misinterpret(ation)** Mondegreen, Warp, Wrest
**Misjudge(ment)** Blunder, Misween, Overrate
**Mislay** Leese, Lose
**Mislead(ing)** Blind, Bum steer, Con, Cover-up, Deceive, Delude, Dupe, Equivocate, Fallacious, False, Gag, Half-truth, Red herring, Runaround, Smoke and mirrors, Snow job
▷ **Misled** *may indicate* an anagram
**Mismanage** Blunder, Bungle, Muddle
**Mismatch** Kludge
**Misplace(ment)** Anachorism, Ectopia
**Misplay** Fluff, Whitechapel
**Misprint** Error, Literal, Literal error, Slip, Typo
**Mispronunciation** Cacoepy, Lallation, Lambdacism
**Misrepresent(ation)** Abuse, Belie, Calumny, Caricature, Colour, Distort, Falsify, Garble, Lie, Slander, Subreption, Traduce, Travesty
**Miss(ing)** Abord, Absent, Air, Astray, Avoid, AWOL, Colleen, Desiderate, Dodge, Drib, Err(or), Eschew, Fail, Forego, Gal, →GIRL, Kumari, Lack, Lass, Link, Lose, Mademoiselle, Maid, Maiden, Mile, Muff(et), Near, Need, Neglect, Negligence, Omit, Otis, Overlook, Señorita, Shy, Skip, Spinster, Stoke, Unmeet, Wanting, Whiff
▷ **Miss** *may refer to* Missouri
**Missal** Breviary, Te igitur, Triodion
**Misshapen** Crooked, Deformed, Dysmelia, Gnarled
**Missile** ABM, Air-to-air, ALCM, Ammo, Anti-ballistic, Arrow, Artillery, Atlas, Ball, Ballistic, Beam Rider, Blue streak, Bolas, Bolt, Bomb, Boomerang, Brickbat, Bullet, Condor, Cruise, Dart, Death star, Dingbat, Doodlebug, Dum-dum, Exocet®, Falcon, Fléchette, Genie, Grenade, Guided, HARM, Harpoon, Hawk, Hellfire, Hound Dog, ICBM, Interceptor, Jired, Kiley, Kyley, Kylie, Lance, Mace, MARV, Maverick, Minuteman, MIRV, Missive, Mx, Onion, Patriot, Pellet, Pershing, Phoenix, Polaris, Poseidon, Qual, Quarrel, Rocket, SAM, Scud, Sea Skimmer, Seeker, Sergeant, Shell, Shillelagh, Shot, Shrike, Side-winder, Smart bomb, Snowball, Sparrow, Spartan, Spear, Sprint, SSM, Standard Arm, Standoff, Styx, Subroc, Surface to air, Surface to surface, Talos, Tartar, Terrier, Thor, Titan, Tomahawk, Torpedo, Tracer, Trident, UAM, Warhead
**Mission(ary)** Aidan, Alamo, Antioch, Apostle, Assignment, Augustine, Barnabas, Bethel, Boniface, Caravan, Charge, Columba, Cuthbert, Cyril, Delegation, Embassage, Embassy, Errand, Evangelist, Foreign, Function, Happy-clappy, Iona, Legation, Livingstone, LMS, Message, Missiology, NASA, Neurolab, Ninian, Op, Paul, Pr(a)efect, Quest, Reclaimer, Redemptorist, Schweitzer, Silas, Task, Vocation, Xavier
**Missis, Missus, Mrs** Devi, Maam, Mrs, Wife
**Missive** Dispatch, Epistle, Letter, Message, Note
**Missouri** Mo
▶ **Misstroke** *see* MISHIT
**Mist(y)** Aerosol, Australian, Blur, Brume, Cloud, Damp, Dew, Drow, Dry-ice, Film, Fog, Fret, Haar, Haze, Hoar, Miasma, Moch, Nebular, Niflheim, Nimbus, Rack, Red, Roke, Scotch, Sea-fret, Sfumato, Smir(r), Smog, Smur, Spotted, Spray, Steam, Vapour, Veil
**Mistake(n)** Aberration, Barry (Crocker), Bish, Bloomer, Blooper, Blue, Blunder, Boner, Boob, Booboo, Boss, Botch, Bull, Category, Clanger, Clinker, Confound, Deluded, Domino, Erratum, Error, Fallacy, Fault, Floater, Flub, Fluff, Folly, Gaffe, Goof, Hash, Horlicks, Howler, Identity, Incorrect, Lapse, Malapropism, Misprision, Miss, Muff, Mutual, Nod, Off-beam, Oops, Oversight, Own goal, Plonker, Pratfall, Ricket, Screw-up, →SLIP, Slip-up, Solecism, Stumer, Trip, Typo, Wrongdoing
▷ **Mistake(n)** *may indicate* an anagram
**Mister** Babu, Effendi, Lala, Mr, Reb, Sahib, Señor, Shri, Sir, Sri, U
**Mistletoe** Album, Hemiparasite, Missel, Parasite, Sinker, Viscum
**Mistreat** Abuse, Attrite, Manhandle, Violate

**Mistress** Amie, Aspasia, Canary-bird, Chatelaine, Concubine, Courtesan, Delilah, Demimondaine, Devi, Doxy, Goodwife, Herself, Hussif, Inamorata, Instructress, Kept woman, Lady, Leman, Maintenon, Martha, Montespan, Mrs, Natural, Paramour, Querida, Stepney, Teacher, Wardrobe, Wife

**Mistrust(ful)** Askant, Doubt, Gaingiving, Suspect, Suspicion

**Misunderstand(ing)** Cross-purpose(s), Disagreement, Discord, Generation gap, Mistake

**Misuse** Abuse, Catachresis, Defalcate, Malappropriate, Malapropism, Maltreat, Perversion, Torment

**Mite** Acaridian, Acarus, Berry bug, Bit, Bulb, Cheese, Child, Dust, Flour, Forage, Fowl, Gall, Harvest, Itch, Lepton, Little, (Red) spider, Rust, Sarcoptes, Speck, Sugar, Trombiculid, Tyroglyphid, Varroa, Widow's

**Mitigate, Mitigating** Abate, Allay, Allegge, Allieve, Ameliorate, Assuage, Excuse, Extenuating, Lenitive, Lessen, Mease, Palliate, Quell, Relief, Relieve, Soften

**Mitosis** Anaphase

**Mitre** Hat, Tiar(a)

**Mitt(en), Mittens** Fist, Glove, Hand, Paw, Pockies

**Mix(ed), Mixer, Mixture, Mix-up** Allay, Alloy, Allsorts, Amalgam, Ambivalent, Associate, Assortment, Attemper, Balderdash, Bigener, Bittersweet, Bland, Blend, Blunge, Bombay, Bordeaux, Brew, Carburet, Card, Caudle, Chichi, Chow, Cocktail, Co-meddle, Compo, Compound, Conché, Conglomerate, Consort, Cross, Cut, Disperse, Diversity, Dolly, Drammock, Dukkah, Embroil, Emulsion, Eutectic, Farrago, Fold-in, Freezing, Friar's balsam, Garble, Grill, Griqua, Half-breed, Heather, Hobnob, Hodge-podge, Hotchpotch, Hybrid, Imbroglio, Immingle, Interlace, Intermingle, Isomorphous, Jumble, Lace, Lard, Lignin, Linctus, Load, Macedoine, Marketing, Matissé, Meddle, Medley, Meiny, Melange, Mell, Meng(e), Ment, Mess, Mestizo, Métis, Ming(le), Miscellaneous, Miscellany, Mishmash, Mong, Mongrel, Motley, Muddle, Muss(e), Neapolitan, Octaroon, Octoroon, Olio, Olla, Pastiche, Pi(e), Potin, Pousowdie, Powsowdy, Praiseach, Preparation, Promiscuous, Raggle-taggle, Ragtag, Salad, Scramble, Shuffle, Soda, Solution, Spatula, Stew, Stir, Temper, Through-other, Tonic, Trail, Vision, Witches' brew, Yblent

▷ **Mixed** *may indicate* an anagram

**Mixed marriage** Miscegenation

**Mizzle** Decamp, Scapa, Scarper

**Mnemonic(s)** Fleming's rules, Mafic, Memoria technica, Quipo, Quipu, Reminder

**Moab(ite)** Balak, Ruth, Wash-pot

**Moan(ing), Moaner** Beef, Bewail, Bleat, Carp, Complain, Groan, Grouse, Grumble, Hone, Keen, →**LAMENT**, Meane, Plangent, Sigh, Snivel, Sough, Wail, W(h)inge

**Moat** Dike, Ditch, Foss(e)

**Mob(ster)** Army, Assail, Canaille, Crew, Crowd, Doggery, Drove, Faex populi, Flash, Gaggle, Gang, Herd, Hoi-polloi, Hoodlum, Horde, Lynch, Many-headed beast, Mobocrat, Ochlocrat, Press, Rabble, Rabble rout, Raft, Ragtag, Ribble-rabble, Riff-raff, Rout, Scar-face, Throng

**Mobile, Mobilise, Mobility** Agile, Donna, Downward, Fluid, Horizontal, Intergenerational, Movable, Plastic, Rally, Social, Thin, Upward(ly), Vagile, Vertical

**Mob-rule** Ochlocracy

**Mocassin** Larrigan, Shoe, Snake

**Mock(ery), Mocking** Ape, Banter, Catcall, Chaff, Chyack, Cod, Cynical, Deride, Derisory, Dor, Ersatz, False, Farce, Fleer, Flout, Gab, Geck, Gibe, Gird, Guy, Imitation, Ironise, Irony, Irrisory, Jape, →**JEER**, Jibe, Lampoon, Laugh, Mimic, Narquois, Paraselene, Parody, Paste, Pillorise, Piss-taking, Rag, Rail(lery), Rally, Ridicule, Sacrilege, Sardonic, Satirise, Scorn, Scout, Send up, Serve, Sham, Simulate, Slag, Sneer, Snide, Sport, Tease, Travesty, Twit, Wry

**Mocking-bird** Mimus, Sage-thrasher

**Mode** Aeolian, Authentic, Church, Convention, Dorian, Ecclesiastical, Fashion, Form, Formal, Greek, Gregorian, Hyperdorian, Hypo(dorian), Hypolydian, Iastic, Insert, Ionian, Locrian, Lydian, Major, Manner, Material, Medieval, Minor, Mixolydian, Phrygian, Plagal, Raga, Rate, Real-time, Sleep, Step, Style, Ton

**Model(ler), Modelling** Archetype, Bozzetto, Cast, Clothes horse, Copy, Cover girl, Cutaway, Demonstration, Diorama, Doll, Dress-form, Dummy, Ecorché, Effigy, Epitome, Example, Exemplar, Exemplary, Fashionist, Fictor, Figure, Figurine, Icon, Ideal, Image, Instar, Jig, Last, Lay-figure, Layman, Madame Tussaud, Manakin, Manikin, Mannequin, Maquette, Mark, Matchstick, Mirror, Mock-up, Moulage, → MOULD, Norm, Original, Orrery, Papier-mâché, Parade, Paradigm, Paragon, Pattern, Phelloplastic, Pilot, Plasticine, Plastilina, Play-Doh®, Pose(r), Posture-maker, Precedent, Prototype, Replica, Role, Scale, Schema, Sedulous, Sitter, Specimen, Standard, Stereotype, Superwaif, T, Tellurion, Template, Templet, Terrella, Toy, Trilby, Twiggy, Type, Typify, Version, Waif, Waxwork, Working

▷ **Model(s)** *may indicate* an anagram

**Modem** Subset

**Moderate(ly), Moderation** Abate, Abbreviate, Allay, Alleviate, Assuage, Attemper, Average, Ca'canny, Centre, Chair, Chasten, Continent, Decent, Diminish, Discretion, Ease, Gentle, Girondist, Ho(a), Lessen, Lukewarm, Measure, Mediocre, Medium, Menshevik, Mezzo, Middling, Mild, Mitigate, Muscadin, OK, Politique, Pretty, Realo, Reason(able), Relent, Restraint, RR, Slake, So-so, Sparing, Subdue, Sumptuary, Temper(ate), Temperance, Tolerant, Tone, Via media, Wet

**Modern(ise)** AD, Aggiornamento, Contemporary, Fresh, Latter(-day), Millie, Neonomian, Neoterical, → NEW, New-fangled, Present-day, Progressive, Recent, Retrofit, Space age, State-of-the-art, Streamline, Swinger, Trendy, Update, Up-to-date

**Modest(y)** Aidos, Blaise, Chaste, Coy, Decent, Demure, Discreet, Fair, Humble, Humility, Ladylike, Low-key, Lowly, Maidenly, Mim, Mussorgsky, Propriety, Prudish, Pudency, Pudicity, Pure, Reserved, Reticent, Shame, Shamefaced, Shy, Simple, Slender, Unaffected, Unassuming, Unpretending, Unpretentious, Verecund

**Modicum** Dash

**Modifiable, Modification, Modified, Modifier, Modify** Adapt, Adjust, Adverb, Alter, Backpedal, Change, Enhance, Extenuate, Genetically, H, Hotrod, Leaven, Misplaced, Plastic, Qualify, Restyle, Retrofit, Sandhi, Scumble, Soup, Streamline, Temper, Top, Trim, Vary

**Modulation, Module, Modulus** Accent, Amplitude, Bulk, Cadence, Command, Distance, Element, Excursion, Frequency, Habitat, Inflexion, Lem, Lunar, Mitigate, Phase, Pulse, Service, Shear, Tune, Unit, Vary, Velocity, Young's

**Mogul** Bigwig, Magnate, Nawab, Padishah, Plutocrat, Potentate, Taipan, Tycoon, VIP

**Mohair** Moire

**Mohammed, Mohammedan (era)** Hadith, Hegira, Hejira, Hejra, Hijra, Islamite, Mahdi, Mahoun(d), Moslem, Muezzin, Mussulman, Prophet, Said, Shiite, Sunna(h)

**Mohican** Haircut

**Moist(en), Moisture** Baste, Bedew, Damp, Dank, De(a)w, Dewy, Humect, Imbue, Latch, Love-in-a-mist, Madefy, Mesarch, Mesic, Moil, Nigella, Oozy, Precipitation, Slake, Slocken, Soggy, Sponge, Wet

▷ **Moither** *may indicate* an anagram

**Molar** Cheek tooth, Grinder, Mill-tooth, Secodont, Tooth, Wang, Wisdom tooth

**Molasses** Blackstrap, Sorghum, Treacle

**Moldova** MD

**Mole(hill)** Beauty spot, Breakwater, Espionage, Fen-cricket, Golden, Groyne, Hydatidiform, Insider, Jetty, Labour, Marsupial, Miner, Mo(u)diewart, Moudi(e)wart, Mouldiwarp, Naeve, Notoryctes, Orology, Pier, Plant, Sea-wall, Shrew, Sleeper, Spot, Spy, Star-nose(d), Talpa, Want(hill), Want knap, Warp

**Molecule(s), Molecular** Acceptor, Achiral, Aptameter, Atom, Buckyball, Carbene, Cavitand, Chimera, Chiral, Chromophore, Closed chain, Cobalamin, Codon, Coenzyme, Cofactor, Dimer, DNA, Electrogen, Enantiomorph, Footballene, Fullerene, Gram, Hapten, Iota, Isomer, Kinin, Kisspeptin, Ligand, Long-chain, Metabolite, Metameric, Monomer, Nanotube, Nitryl, Oligomer, Peptide, Polymer, Polysaccharide, Quark, Replicon, Ribozyme, Semantide, Stereoisomer, Synthon, Triatonic, Trimer, Uridine, Vector

**Molendinar** Mill

**Molest(er)** Annoy, Bother, Disturb, Harass, Nonce, Scour, Touch up

**Moll(y), Mollie** Bloom, Bonnie, Carousal, Cutpurse, Flanders, Girl, Maguire, Malone, May, Sissy

**Mollify** Appease, Assuage, Fob, Mease, Mitigate, Pacify, Placate, Relax, Soften, Temper

**Mollusc(s)** Bivalve, Malacology, Opisthobranch, → SHELLFISH, Tectibranch, Univalve

---

## MOLLUSCS

**3 letters:**
Mya

**4 letters:**
Arca
Clam
Slug
Spat
Unio

**5 letters:**
Bulla
Capiz
Chank
Conch
Cowry
Doris
Gaper
Helix
Idler
Murex
Olive
Pinna
Polyp
Sepia
Snail
Solen
Spoot
Squid
Turbo
Venus
Whelk

**6 letters:**
Chiton
Cockle
Cowrie
Cuttle
Limpet
Loligo
Mussel
Nerita
Oyster
Pecten
Pholas
Poulpe
Quahog
Tellen
Tellin
Teredo
Triton
Winkle

**7 letters:**
Abalone
Octopod
Octopus
Pandore
Piddock
Quahaug
Scallop
Sea-hare
Sea-slug
Spirula
Toheroa
Trochus

Veliger
Vitrina

**8 letters:**
Ammonite
Argonaut
Ark-shell
Auricula
Nautilus
Pteropod
Saxicava
Sea-lemon
Shipworm
Strombus
Top-shell

**9 letters:**
Belemnite
Cone-shell
Dentalium
Gastropod
Goniatite
Nautiloid
Neopilina
Razor-clam
Razor-fish
Rock borer
Tusk-shell
Wing-shell
Wood-borer

**10 letters:**
Amphineura

Cephalopod
Cuttlefish
Duck mussel
Gasteropod
Heart-shell
Money cowry
Pelecypoda
Protostome
Razorshell
Scaphopoda
Venus shell
Wentletrap

**11 letters:**
Horse mussel
Marine boxer
Paper-sailor
Trochophore
Trough-shell

**12 letters:**
Heart-cockler
Pelican's-foot

**13 letters:**
Lamellibranch
Paper nautilus
Slipper limpet

**14 letters:**
Monoplacophora
Pearly nautilus
Polyplacophora

---

**Mollycoddle** Indulge, Nanny, Pamper
**Moloch** Thorn-devil
**Molten** Dissolved, Fusil, Igneous, Melted
**Molybdenum** Mo

**Moment(s), Momentous** Aha, Bending, Bit, Blonde, Brief, Dipole, Electromagnetic, Eureka, Eventful, Flash(point), Gliffing, Glift, Hogging, Import, Instant, Jiffy, Magnetic, →MINUTE, Mo, Nonce, Point, Psychological, Pun(c)to, Sagging, Sands, Sec, Senior, Shake, Stound, Stownd, Tick, Time, Trice, Twinkling, Two-ticks, Weighty, Wink

**Momentum** Angular, Impetus, L, Speed, Steam, Thrust

**Mona(s)** I, IOM

**Monaco** Grimaldi

**Mona Lisa** La Gioconda

**Monarch(y)** Absolute, Autocrat, Britain, Butterfly, Caesar, Cole, Constitutional, Crown, Dual, Emperor, HM, K, Karling, King, Kuwait, Limited, Merry, Netherlands, Norway, Oman, Potentate, Q, Queen, R, Raine, Realm, Realty, Reign, Ruler, Saudi Arabia, Sovereign, Swaziland, Sweden, Tonga, Tsar

**Monarchist** Cavalier

**Monastery, Monastic** Abbey, Abthane, Celibate, Charterhouse, Chartreuse, Cloister, Community, Gompa, Holy, Hospice, Iona, Lamaserai, Lamasery, La Trappe, Laura, Monkish, Oblate, Priory, Retreat, Sangha, Secluded, Tashi, Vihara, Wat

**Monday** Black, Collop, Handsel, J'ouvert, Meal, Oatmeal, Plough, Whit

**Mondrian** Piet

**Money, Monetary** Ackers, Akkas, Allowance, Annat, Ante, Appearance, Archer, Assignat, Banco, Batta, Beer, Blood, Blue, Blunt, Boodle, Bottle, Brass, Bread, Bread and honey, Broad, Bull's eye, Bunce, Cabbage, Capital, Cash, Caution, Century, Change, Chink, Circulating medium, Cob, Cock, →COIN, Collateral, Confetti, Conscience, Crackle, Cranborne, Crinkly, Crust, Currency, Danger, Dib(s), Dingbat, Dollar, Dosh, Dough, Dump, Dust, Earnest, Easy, Escrow, Even, Fat, Fee, Fiat, Finance, Float, Folding, Fonds, Found, Fund, Funny, Gate, Gelt, Gilt, Godiva, Gold, Grand, Grant, Gravy, Greens, Gross, Hard, Head, Heavy sugar, Hello, Hoot, Hot, Housekeeping, Hush, Idle, Ingots, Investment, Jack, Kail, Kale, Kembla, Key, Knife, L, Legal tender, Lolly, Loot, Lucre, M, Mammon, Maundy, Mazuma, Means, Mint, Monkey, Monopoly, Moola(h), Narrow, Near, Necessary, Needful, Nest-egg, Note, Nugger, Numismatic, Nummary, Oaker, Ocher, Ochre, Offertory, Oof, Option, Outlay, P, Packet, Paper, Passage, Pavarotti, Payroll, Peanuts, Pecuniary, Pelf, Petrodollar, Pin, Pine-tree, Pink, Pittance, Plastic, Plum, Pocket, Pony, Posh, Press, Prize, Proceeds, Profit, Protection, Purse, Push, Quid, Ransom, Ration, Ready, Reap silver, Rebate, Remuneration, Resources, Revenue, Rhino, Ring, Risk, Rogue, Rowdy, Salt(s), Score, Scratch, Scrip, Seed, Settlement, Shekels, Shell, Shin-plaster, Ship, Short, Siller, Silly, Silver, Sinews of war, Slush (fund), Smart, Soap, Soft, Spending, Spondulicks, Stake, Sterling, Stipend, Stuff, Subsidy, Subsistence, Sugar, Sum, Surety, Table, Take, Takings, Tea, Tender, Tin, Toea, Token, Tranche, Treaty, Tribute, Turnover, Viaticum, Wad, Wealth, Windfall, Wonga

**Money-box** Penny-pig, Piggy bank, Till

**Moneylender** Gombeen, Scrivener, Shroff, Shylock, Usurer

**Moneymaking** Cash cow, Earner, Profitable, Quaestuary

**Mongol(ian)** Bashkir, Buriat, Buryat, Calmuck, Chuvash, Epicanthic, Evenski, Genghis Khan, Golden Horde, Kalmuck, Kara-Kalpak, Kazak(h), Khalifa(h), Khalkha, Kubla(i) Khan, Kyrgyz, Lapp, Lepcha, Manchoo, Manchu, Mishmi, Mogul, Pareoean, Samoyed, Shan, Sherpa, Tamerlane, Ta(r)tar, Tungus(ic), Uig(h)ur, Ural-altaic, Uzbek

**Mongoose** Herpestes, Ichneumon, Mangouste, Meerkat, Suricate, Urva

**Mongrel** Bitser, Cross(bred), →DOG, Goorie, Goory, Hybrid, Kuri, Lurcher, Mutt, Quadroon, Tyke, Underbred, Zo

**Monitor(ing)** Dataveillance, Detect, Goanna, Iguana, Komodo dragon, Lizard, Observe, Offer, Ofgas, Ofgem, Oflot, Ofsted, Oftel, Ofwat, Oversee, Prefect, Preview, Record, Regulator, Screen, Ship, Sniffer, Speed trap, Sphygmophone, Surveillance, Tag, Track, Warship, Watchdog, Whole-body, Worral, Worrel

**Monk(s)** Anchorite, Bodhidharma, Bro, Brother, Frere, General, Order, Provincial, Religieux, Thelonious, Votary

## MONKS

**3 letters:**
Dan
Dom
Fra

**4 letters:**
Bede
Lama

**5 letters:**
Abbot
Aidan
Black
Bonze
Bruno
Frati
Friar
Minor
Prior
Roshi

**6 letters:**
Austin
Bhikhu
Culdee
Hermit

Jerome
Oblate
Palmer
Sangha

**7 letters:**
Beghard
Caedmon
Caloyer
Cluniac
Dervish
Félibre
Hegumen
Jacobin
Maurist
Recluse

**8 letters:**
Acoemeti
Angelico
Basilian
Cenobite
Jacobite
Minorite
Olivetan
Pelagian

Rakehell
Rasputin
Salesian
Sub-prior
Talapoin
Theatine
Trappist

**9 letters:**
Celestine
Cellarist
Coenobite
Dominican
Feuillant
Gyrovague
Hesychast
Recollect
Thelemite

**10 letters:**
Bernardine
Carthusian
Cistercian
Fraticelli
Hildebrand
Norbertine

Savonarola

**11 letters:**
Abbey-lubber
Augustinian
Benedictine
Bonaventura
Camaldolite
Ignorantine
Mekhitarist
Tironensian

**12 letters:**
Bethlehemite
Mechitharist
Obedientiary

**13 letters:**
Archimandrite
Crutched Friar
Possessionate
Thomas à Kempis

**14 letters:**
Simeon Stylites

**Monkey** Anger, Ape, Aye-aye, Baboon, Bandar, Bobbejaan, Bonnet, Bushbaby, Capuchin, Catar(r)hine, Cebidae, Cebus, Chacma, Coaita, Colobus, Cynomolgus, Diana, Douc, Douroucouli, Drill, Durukuli, Entellus, Galago, Gelada, Gibbon, Gorilla, Grease, Green, Grison, Grivet, Guenon, Guereza, Hanuman, Hoolock, Howler, Hylobates, Imp, Indri, Jacchus, Jackey, Jocko, Kippage, Kipunji, Langur, Leaf, Lemur, Loris, Macaco, Macaque, Magot, Malmag, Mandrill, Mangabey, Marmoset, Meddle, Meerkat, Mico, Midas, Mona, Mycetes, Nala, Nasalis, New World, Old World, Orang-utang, Ouakari, Ouistiti, Phalanger, Platyrrhine, Pongo, Powder, → PRIMATE, Proboscis, Pug, Puzzle, Rage, Ram, Rapscallion, Rascal, Rhesus, Sago(u)in, Saguin, Sai(miri), Sajou, Saki, Sapajou, Satan, Scamp, Semnopithecus, Siamang, Sifaka, Silen(us), Silverback, Simian, Simpai, Slender loris, Spider, Squirrel, Talapoin, Tamarin, Tamper, Tana, Tarsier, Tee-tee, Titi, Toque, Trip-hammer, Troop, Tup, Uakari, Urchin, Vervet, Wanderoo, White-eyelid, Wilderness, Wistiti, Wou-wou, Wow-wow, Wrath, Zati

**Monkey-nut** Earth-pea

**Monkey-puzzle** Araucaria, Bunya-bunya

**Monkshood** Aconite

**Monocle** Eye-glass, Gig-lamp, Lorgnon, Quiz(zing-glass)

**Monocot(yledon)** Araceae, Endogen, Tradescantia

**Monodon** Narwhal

**Monogram, Monograph** Chi-rho, Cipher, Study, Treatise, Tug(h)ra

**Monolith** Ayers Rock, Cenotaph, Chambers Pillar, Uluru

**Monologue** Dramatic, Interior, Patter, Rap, Recitation, Soliloquy, Speech

**Monopolise, Monopoly** Absolute, Appalto, Bloc, Bogart, Cartel, Coemption, Corner, Engross, Octroi, Régie, Trust

**Monorail** Aerobus

**Monosyllable** Proclitic

**Monotone, Monotonous, Monotony** Boring, Dull, →FLAT, Grey, Humdrum, Repetitive, Same(y), Sing-song, Soul-destroying, Tedious, Thrum

**Monsoon** Dry, Hurricane, Typhoon, Wet, →WIND

▷ **Monsoon** *may indicate* weekend: Mon soon

**Monster, Monstrous** Alecto, Apollyon, Asmodeus, Bandersnatch, Behemoth, Bugaboo, Bunyip, Caliban, Cerberus, Cete, Charybdis, Chichevache, Chim(a)era, Cockatrice, Colossal, Cyclops, Dabbat, Dalek, Deform, Dinoceras, Dismayd, Div, Dragon, Echidna, Enormous, Erebus, Erinys, Erl-king, Eten, Ettin, Evil-one, Fiend, Fire-drake, Frankenstein, Freak, Geryon, Ghost, Giant, Gila, Goblin, Godzilla, Golem, Gorgon, Green-eyed, Grendel, Harpy, Hippocampus, Hippogriff, Hippogryph, Huge, Hydra, Jabberwock, Kraken, Lamia, Leviathan, Lilith, Lusus naturae, Mastodon, Medusa, Minotaur, Misbegotten, Moloch, Mooncalf, Mylodont, Nessie, Nicker, Nightmare, Ogopogo, Ogre, Ogr(e)ish, Opinicus, Orc, Outrageous, Pongo, Prodigy, Sasquatch, Satyral, Scylla, Serra, Shadow, Simorg, Simurg(h), Siren, Skull, Snark, Spectre, Sphinx, Spook, Stegodon, Stegosaur, Succubus, Taniwha, Teras, Teratism, Teratoid, Triceratops, Triffid, Troll, Typhoeus, Typhon, Unnatural, Vampire, Vast, Wasserman, Wendego, Wendigo, Wer(e)wolf, Whale, Wivern, Wyvern, Xiphopagus, Yowie, Ziffius

**Monstrance** Ostensory

**Monteith** Bandanna

**Month(ly)** Ab, Abib, Adar, Anomalistic, April, Asadha, Asvina, August, Bhadrapada, Brumaire, Bul, Caitra, Calendar, Cheshvan, Chislev, December, Dhu-al-Hijjah, Dhu-al-Qadah, Draconic, Elul, February, Floréal, Frimaire, Fructidor, Gander, Germinal, Hes(h)van, Iy(y)ar, January, July, Jumada, June, Jyaistha, Karttika, Kisleu, Kislev, Lide, Lunar, Lunation, Magha, March, Margasirsa, May, Messidor, Mo, Moharram, Moon, Muharram, Muharrem, Nisan, Nivôse, Nodical, November, October, Ovulation, Periodical, Phalguna, Pluviôse, Prairial, Rabi(a), Rajab, Ramadan, Ramazon, Rhamadhan, Safar, Saphar, S(h)ebat, September, Sha(a)ban, Shawwal, Sidereal, Sivan, Solar, Stellar, Synodic, Tammuz, Tebeth, Thermidor, Tishri, Tisri, Tropical, Vaisakha, Veadar, Vendémiaire, Ventôse

**Monument** Ancient, Arch, Archive, Cairn, Cenotaph, Charminar, Column, Cromlech, Cross, Dolmen, Eugubine, Henge, Megalith, Memorial, Menhir, Monolith, National, Pantheon, Pyramid, Sacellum, Stele(ne), Stone, Stonehenge, Stupa, Talayot, Tombstone, Trilith, Trilithon, Urn

**Mood(y)** Active, Air, Anger, Atmosphere, Attitude, Aura, Bipolar, Capricious, Conjunctive, Dudgeon, Emoticon, Enallage, Fettle, Fit, Foulie, Glum, Grammar, Huff, Humour, Hump, Imperative, Indicative, Infinitive, Mercurial, Miff, Morale, Optative, Passive, Peat, Pet, Revivalist, Sankey, Spleen, Strop, Subjunctive, Sulky, Temper, Temperamental, Tid, Tone, Tune, Vein, Vinegar, Whim

**Moon(light), Moony** Aah, Adrastea, Alignak, Amalthea, Aningan, Apogee, Artemis, Astarte, Blue, Callisto, Calypso, Chandra, Cheese, Crescent, Cynthia, Diana, Epact, Europa, Eye, Flit, Full, Gander, Ganymede, Gibbous, Glimmer, Grimaldi, Harvest, Hecate, Hunter's, Hyperion, Iapetus, Inconstant, Io, Juliet, Leda, Lucina, Luna(r), Mani, Mascon, McFarlane's Buat, Midsummer, Mock, Month, Mooch, Mope, New, Nimbus, Nocturne, Octant, Oliver, Orb, Paddy's lantern, Paraselene, Paschal, Pasiphaë, Phobos, Phoebe, Plenilune, Proteus, Raker, Rear-view, Satellite, Selene, Set, Shepherd, Shot, Sickle, Sideline, Silvery, Sonata, Stargaze, Stone, Syzygy, Thebe, Thoth, Titan, Triton, Umbriel, Wander

**Moon god** Thoth, Trismegistus

**Moonraker** Astrogeologist, Gothamite

**Moonshine(r)** Balderdash, Gibberish, Guff, Hootch, Poteen, Rot, Shebeener, Starveling, Tosh

**Moor(ing), Moored, Moorish, Moorland** Anchor, Berth, Bodmin, Culloden, Dock, Fell, Fen, Fern land, Flow country, Girt, Grouse, Heath, Iago, Ilkley, Makefast, Marina, Marston, Moresque, Moroccan, Mudéjar, Othello, Otter, Palustrine, Roadstead, Ry(e)peck, Saracen, Secure, Sternfast, Tether, → **TIE**, Wharf, Wold

**Mop(ping)** Dwile, Flibbertigibbet, Girn, Glib, Malkin, Shag, Squeegee, Squilgee, Swab, Swob, Thatch, → **WIPE**

**Mope** Boody, Brood, Peak, Sulk

**Mor** Humus

**Moral(ity), Morals** Apologue, Austere, Deontic, Ethic(al), Ethos, Everyman, Fable, Gnomic, High-minded, Integrity, Laxity, Message, Parable, Precept, Principled, Probity, Puritanic, Righteous, Sittlichkeit, Tag, Upright, Virtuous, Well-thewed

**Morale** Ego, Mood, Spirit, Zeal

**Moralise, Moralising** Preach, Sententious

**Moralist** Aesop, Pharisee, Prig, Prude, Puritan, Whitecap

**Morass** Bog, Fen, Flow, Marsh, Moss, Quagmire, Slough

**Morbid(ity)** Anasarca, Ascites, Cachaemia, Dropsy, Ectopia, Ghoul(ish), Gruesome, Pathological, Plethora, Prurient, Religiose, Sick, Sombre, Unhealthy

**Mordant** Base, Biting, Caustic, Critic(al), Sarcastic, Tooth

**Mordent** Inverted, Lower, Pralltriller, Upper

**More** Added, Additional, Else, Extra, Increase, Intense, Less, Mae, Merrier, Mo(e), → **NO MORE**, Over, Piu, Plus, Rather, Seconds, Stump, Utopia

**Moreover** Also, Besides, Eft, Either, Eke, Further, Too, Withal, Yet

**Mores** Etiquette

**Morgan** Buccaneer, Pirate

**Moribund** Dying, Stagnant, Withered

**Mormon** Apostle, Danite, Latter-day Saint, Salt Lake City, Utah, Young

**Morning** Ack-emma, Am, Antemeridian, Dawn, Daybreak, Early, Forenoon, Levée, Matin(al), Matutinal, Morrow, Sparrowfart

**Morning-glory** Bindweed, Ipomoea, Turbith, Turpeth

**Morning-star** Morgenstern, Phosphor(us), Threshel, Venus

**Moroccan, Morocco** Agadir, French, Leather, Levant, MA, Mo(o)r, Persian, Riff, Tangerine, Venus

**Moron** Fool, Idiot, Imbecile, Schmuck, → **STUPID**

**Morose** Acid, Boody, Churlish, Crabby, Cynical, Disgruntled, Gloomy, Glum, Grum, Moody, Sour-eyed, Sullen, Surly

**Morph** Phase

**Morris** Car, Dance, Fivepenny, Merel(l), Meril, Nine Men's, Ninepenny

**Morrow** Future

**Morse** Code, Dah, Dit, Endeavour, Iddy-umpty, Inventor, Tusker, Walrus

**Morsel** Bit, Bite, Bouche, Canape, Crumb, Dainty, Morceau, Ort, Scrap, Sippet, Sop, Tidbit, Titbit

**Mortal(ity)** Averr(h)oism, Being, Deathly, → **FATAL**, Grave, Human, Lethal, Yama

**Mortar, Mortar-board** Bowl, Cannon, Cement, Co(e)horn, Compo, Grout, Gunite, Hawk, Howitzer, Life, Metate, Mine-thrower, Minnie, Moaning (Minnie), Parget, Plaster, Pot gun, Screed, Square, Squid, Toc emma, Trench(er)

**Mortgage(e)** Balloon, Bond, Cap and collar, Cedula, Chattel, Debt, Dip, Encumbrance, Endowment, First, Hypothecator, Loan, Pension, Pledge, Repayment, Reverse, Wadset(t)

**Mortification, Mortified, Mortify** Abash, Ashame, Chagrin, Crucify, Crush, Gangrene, Humble, Humiliate, Infarct, Necrose, Penance, Sick, Sphacelus, Wormwood

**Mortuary** Deadhouse

**Mosaic** Buhl, Cosmati, Impave, Inlay, Intarsia, Musive, Opus musivum, Pietra dura, Screen, Smalto, Tarsia, Terrazzo, Tessella(te), Tessera, Tobacco, Venetian

**Moscow** Dynamo

**Moses** Grandma
▶ **Moslem** *see* MUSLIM (RITUAL)
**Mosque** Dome of the Rock, El Aqsa, Jami, Masjid, Medina, Musjid
**Mosquito** Aedes, Anopheles, Culex, Culicine, Gnat, Parasite, Stegomyia
**Moss(y)** Acrogen, Agate, Bryology, Bur(r), Carrag(h)een, Ceylon, Club, Fairy, Fog,
   Fontinalis, Hag(g), Hypnum, Iceland, Irish, Lecanoram, Lichen, Litmus, Liverwort, Long,
   Lycopod, Marsh, Musci, Muscoid, Parella, Peat, Polytrichum, Protonema, Reindeer,
   Rose, Scale, Selaginella, Spanish, Sphagnum, Staghorn, Tree, Usnea, Wall, Wolf's claw
**Most(ly)** Basically, Largest, Major, Maxi(mum), Optimum
**Mot** Quip, Saying
**Mote** Atom, Particle, Speck

## MOTHS

| 2 letters: | Tiger | Leopard | Notodonta |
|---|---|---|---|
| Io | Tinea | Lobster | Pyralidae |
| | Umber | Noctuid | Saturniid |
| 3 letters: | Wheat | Old-lady | Scavenger |
| Bag | Y-moth | Pug-moth | Underwing |
| Bee | Yucca | Silver-Y | Woodborer |
| Fox | | Tortrix | |
| Nun | 6 letters: | Tussock | 10 letters: |
| Owl | Antler | Tussore | Death's head |
| Wax | Bogong | Unicorn | Gooseberry |
| | Bugong | Zygaena | Leafroller |
| 4 letters: | Burnet | | Peach-bloom |
| Arch | Carpet | 8 letters: | Peppercorn |
| Bell | Codlin | Bobowler | Pine-beauty |
| Corn | Dagger | Bombycid | Pine-carpet |
| Dart | Ermine | Cecropia | Polyphemus |
| Goat | Herald | Cinnabar | Privet hawk |
| Hawk | Kitten | Dart-moth | |
| Luna | Lackey | Drepanid | 11 letters: |
| Meal | Lappet | Geometer | Diamondback |
| Puss | Lichen | Goldtail | Hummingbird |
| Wave | Magpie | Night-fly | Lepidoptera |
| | Muslin | Oak-egger | |
| 5 letters: | Noctua | Peppered | 12 letters: |
| Atlas | Psyche | Saturnia | Cactoblastis |
| Eggar | Sphinx | Silkworm | Giant peacock |
| Egger | Turnip | Sphingid | Kentish glory |
| Flour | Tusser | Tapestry | Large emerald |
| Ghost | Veneer | Tineidae | Lymantriidae |
| Gipsy | Winter | Vapourer | Red underwing |
| Grass | | Wainscot | Sallow-kitten |
| Gypsy | 7 letters: | | |
| House | Abraxas | 9 letters: | 13 letters: |
| Imago | Buff-tip | Arctiidae | Lasiocampidae |
| Owlet | Cabbage | Brown-tail | Mother of pearl |
| Plane | Clothes | Carpenter | Mother Shipton |
| Plume | Codling | Clearwing | Processionary |
| Snout | Emerald | Corn -borer | Purple emperor |
| Swift | Emperor | Geometrid | |
| Thorn | Hook-tip | Honeycomb | |

| 15 letters: | 16 letters: | |
|---|---|---|
| Yellow underwing | Clifden nonpareil | Macrolepidoptera |
| | | Microlepidoptera |

**Mothball(s)** Abeyance, Camphor, Naphtha, Preserver
**Moth-eaten** Flea-bitten
**Mother** Abbess, Bearer, Church, Cognate, Cosset, Courage, Dam(e), Den, Dregs, Ean,
  Earth, Eoan, Eve, Fecula, Foster, Generatrix, Genetrix, Genitrix, Goose, Hubbard, Lees,
  Ma, Machree, Madre, Mam(a), Mamma, Mater, Matroclinic, Maya, Minnie, Mollycoddle,
  Mom, Multipara, Mum, Mummy, Native, Nature, Nourish, Nursing, Parent, Parity,
  Pourer, Prim(o), Primipara, Progenitress, Reverend, Shipton, Slime, Superior, Surrogate,
  Theotokos, Venter, Wit
▷ **Mother** *may indicate* a lepidopterist; moth-er
**Mother-in-law** Naomi
**Motherless** Adam, Orphan
**Motif** Anthemion, Design, Gist, Idée, Theme
**Motion** Angular, Blocking, Composite, Contrary, Direct, Diurnal, Early day, Fast,
  Free-fall, Gesture, Harmonic, Impulse, Kepler, Kinematics, Kinetic, Kipp, Link, Move,
  Oblique, Offer, Parallactic, Parallel, Peculiar, Perpetual, PL, Precession, Proper, Proposal,
  Rack and pinion, Rider, Sewel, Similar, Slow, Spasm, Tide, Wave
**Motionless** Doggo, Frozen, Immobile, Inert, Quiescent, Stagnant, Standstill, Stasis, Still,
  Stock-still
**Motive, Motivate, Motivation** Actuate, Cause, Drive, Ideal, Impel, Impetus,
  Incentive, Intention, Mainspring, Mobile, Object, → **PURPOSE**, Raison d'être, Rationale,
  Reason, Spur, Ulterior, Urge
**Motley** Jaspé, Medley, Piebald, Pied, Variegated
**Motor(boat)** Auto, Benz, Car, Dynamo, Electric, Engine, Hot rod, Hydroplane, Inboard,
  Induction, Jato, Linear, Mini, Outboard, Paint job, Rocket, Scooter, Series-wound,
  Servo, Stator, Supermini, Sustainer, Synchronous, Thruster, Turbine, Turbo, Universal,
  Vaporetto, Water
**Motorcade** Procession
**Motorcycle, Motorcyclist** Bambi, Beemer, Bikie, Chookchaser, Chopper,
  Combination, Farm-bike, Greaser, Harley Davidson, Hell's Angel, Minimoto, Moped,
  Pipsqueak, Scooter, Scramble, Tourist Trophy, Trail bike, TT, Yamaha®
**Motorist(s)** AA, Driver, Petrolhead, RAC, Road hog, Tripper
**Motorman** Austin, Benz, Ford, Morris
**Motor race, Motor sport** F1, Formula One, Rally, Scramble, TT
**Motorway** Autobahn, Autopista, Autoput, Autoroute, Autostrada, Expressway, M(1),
  Orbital, Superhighway, Throughway, Thruway
**Mottle(d)** Brindled, Chiné, Jaspé, Marbled, Marly, Mirly, Pinto, Poikilitic, Tabby
**Motto** Device, Epigraph, Excelsior, Gnome, Ich dien, Impresa, Imprese, Impress(e),
  Legend, Maxim, Mot, Poesy, Posy, Saw, Slogan
**Mou(e)** Grimace, Mim
**Mould(ed), Moulder, Mouldable, Moulding, Mouldy** Accolade, Architrave,
  Archivolt, Astragal, Baguette, Balection, Bandelet, Beading, Bend, Black, Blow,
  Blue, Bolection, Bread, Briquet(te), Cabling, Casement, Cast(ing), Cavetto, Chain,
  Chessel, Chill, Cold, Cornice, Coving, Cyma (recta), Cymatium, Dancette, Dariole, Die,
  Die-cast, Dogtooth, Doucine, Dripstone, Ductile, Echinus, Egg and dart, Emboss,
  Flong, Forge, → **FORM**, Foughty, Fousty, Fungose, Fungus, Fusarol(e), Fust, Gadroon,
  Geat, Godroon, Gorgerin, Green, Hood-mould, Hore, Humus, Injection, Iron, Jelly,
  Leaf, Machine, Matrix, Mildew, Model, Mool, Moulage, Mucedinous, Mucid, Mucor,
  Must(y), Mycetozoan, Myxomycete, Nebule, Necking, Noble rot, Ogee, Ovolo, Palmette,
  Papier-mâché, Penicillin, Phycomycete, Picture, Pig, Plasm(a), Plaster, Plastic, Plastisol,
  Plat, Platband, Plate, Prototype, Prunt, Quarter-round, Reeding, Reglet, Rhizopus,
  Rib, Rot, Rust, Sandbox, Scotia, Shape, Slime, Smut, Soil, Soot(y), Spindle, Storiated,

Stringcourse, Stucco, Surbase, Tailor, Talon, Template, Templet, Timbale, Tondino, Torus, Trochilus, Vinew, Water table

**Moult(ing)** Cast, Metecdysis, Mew, Shed

**Mound** Agger, Bank, Barp, Barrow, Berm, Cahokia, Cone, Dike, Dun, Embankment, Heap, Hillock, Hog, Knoll, Kurgan, Mogul, Molehill, Monticule, Mote, Motte, Orb, Pile, Pingo, Pome, Rampart, Rampire, Remblai, Tel(l), Teocalli, Teopan, Tuffet, Tumulus, Tussock

**Mound-bird** Leipoa, Megapode

**Mount(ed), Mounting, Mountain (peak), Mountains, Mountainside** Air, →ALPINE, Ascend, Back, Barp, Ben, Berg, Board, Breast, Butter, Chain, Charger, Cliff, Clift, →CLIMB, Colt, Cordillera, Cradle, Dew, Display, Djebel, Dolly, Eminence, Escalade, Frame, Hinge, Horse, Inselberg, Jebel, Massif, Monture, Mt, Nunatak, Orography, Orology, Passe-partout, Peak, Pike, Pile, Pin, Pownie, Quad, →RANGE, Ride, Rosinante, Saddlehorse, Saddle up, Scalado, Scale, Sclim, Set, Soar, Stage, →STEED, Stie, Strideways, Tel, Tier, Topo, Tor, Turret, Upgo, Volcano, Yaud

## MOUNTAINS

**2 letters:**
K2

**3 letters:**
Apo
Ida
Kaf
Ore

**4 letters:**
Alai
Blue
Bona
Cook
Etna
Fuji
Harz
Hoss
Jaya
Jura
Meru
Nebo
Oeta
Ossa
Rigi
Ubac
Zeil

**5 letters:**
Abora
Adams
Aldan
Altai
Amara
Andes
Aneto

Athos
Atlas
Badon
Black
Blanc
Coast
Djaja
Eiger
Ellis
Er Rif
Evans
Ghats
Green
Guyot
Hekla
Horeb
Idris
Kamet
Kenya
Logan
Munro
Ozark
Pelée
Rocky
Rydal
Sayan
Serra
Sinai
Siple
Smoky
Snowy
Table
Tabor
Tatra
Tirol
Tyree

Tyrol
Uinta
Urals
Welsh
White

**6 letters:**
Ala Dag
Alaska
Amhara
Anadyr
Arafat
Ararat
Averno
Balkan
Bogong
Carmel
Cho Oyu
Dragon
Egmont
Elbert
Elberz
Elbrus
Erebus
Gilead
Gimbal
Hermon
Hoggar
Hoosac
Katmai
Kazbek
Kunlun
Lhotse
Makalu
Mourne
Olives

Ortles
Pamirs
Pelion
Pindus
Pisgah
Pocono
Robson
Scopus
Sintra
Sorata
Steele
Tasman
Taunus
Taurus
Umbria
Vernon
Vosges
Zagros

**7 letters:**
Aetolia
Ala Dagh
Aorangi
Aragats
Arcadia
Bernina
Brocken
Buffalo
Calvary
Cariboo
Cascade
Chianti
Corbett
Dapsang
Estreia
Everest

Helicon
Kaufman
Kennedy
Khingan
Kuenlun
Lebanon
Lucania
Manaslu
Markham
Nan Shan
Olympic
Olympus
Orontes
Palomar
Perdido
Pilatus
Rainier
Rhodope
San Juan
Scafell
Selkirk
Skiddaw
Snowdon
Sperrin
Stanley
St Elias
Sudeten
Tibesti
Travers
Troglav
Whitney
Wicklow

**8 letters:**
Anapurna
Arcadian
Aspiring
Ben Nevis
Cambrian
Carstenz
Catskill
Caucasus
Cevennes
Cumbrian
Damavand
Demavend
Fujiyama
Grampian
Guerrero
Hymettus
Illimani
Jungfrau
Katahdin
Kinabalu

King Peak
Leibnitz
McKinley
Mulhacen
Ngaliema
Ouachita
Pennines
Pinatubo
Pyrenees
Rushmore
Seamount
St Helen's
Taraniki
Tian Shan
Tien Shan
Vesuvius
Victoria
Wrangell

**9 letters:**
Aconcagua
Allegheny
Annapurna
Apennines
Ben Lomond
Blackburn
Blue Ridge
Cairngorm
Carstensz
Catskills
Caucasian
Connemara
Demavrand
Dhaulagir
Dolomites
El Capitan
Grampians
Guadalupe
Helvellyn
Hercynian
Highlands
High Tatra
Himalayas
Hindu Kush
Jebel Musa
Karakoram
Lenin Peak
Longs Peak
Marmolada
Mont Blanc
Monte Rosa
Nanda Devi
Parnassus
Pikes Peak

Ruwenzori
Shivering
Sugar Loaf
Tirich Mir
Tongariro
Trans Alai
Trossachs
Tupungato
Vancouver
Venusberg
Voralberg
Weisshorn
Woodroffe
Yablonovy
Zugspitze

**10 letters:**
Altazimuth
Arakan Yoma
Armageddon
Black Hills
Cader Idris
Cantabrian
Carpathian
Delectable
Dhaulagiri
Equatorial
Erymanthus
Erzgebirge
Great Gable
Great Smoky
Harney Peak
Horselberg
Kongur Shan
Kosciuszko
Laurentian
Masharbrum
Masherbrum
Matterhorn
Monte Corno
Montserrat
Pentelicus
Pentelikon
Puncak Jaya
Puy de Sancy
Qomolangma
Sagarmatha
St Michael's
Tengri Khan
Teton Range
Vorarlberg
Washington
Waziristan
Wellington

Wetterhorn

**11 letters:**
Adirondacks
Alaska Range
Anti-Lebanon
Appalachian
Bartle Frere
Bimberi Peak
Brooks Range
Coast Ranges
Drakensberg
Fairweather
Gerlachovka
Kilimanjaro
Kinder Scout
Kirkpatrick
Kolyma Range
Machu Picchu
Nanga Parbat
Pico de Aneto
Pico de Teide
Salmon River
Scafell Pike
Sierra Madre

**12 letters:**
Albert Edward
Cascade Range
Eastern Ghats
Godwin Austen
Gran Paradiso
Ingleborough
Kanchenjunga
Monte Perdido
Ruahine Range
Sierra Morena
Sierra Nevada
Slieve Donard
Southern Alps
Tararua Range
Victoria Peak
Vindhya Range
Vinson Massif
Wasatch Range
Western Ghats

**13 letters:**
Brecon Beacons
Carrantuohill
Croagh Patrick
Flinders Range
Frenchman's Cap
Great Dividing

| | | | |
|---|---|---|---|
| Grossglockner | Hamersley Range | Teutoburger Wald | *18 letters:* |
| Humphrey's Peak | Kaikoura Ranges | | Great Dividing |
| Kangchenjunga | Kommunizma Peak | *16 letters:* | Range |
| Massif Central | Liverpool Range | Emperor | |
| Mount Klinovec | Musgrove Ranges | Seamounts | *19 letters:* |
| Petermann Peak | Queen Maud Range | Macdonnell Ranges | Macgillicuddy's |
| San Bernardino | Ruwenzori Range | Owen Stanley | Reeks |
| Stanovoi Range | Sangre de Cristo | Range | |
| Tibesti Massif | Stirling Ranges | Thabana-Ntlenyana | *20 letters:* |
| | Stzelecki Range | | Salmon River |
| *14 letters:* | Thadentsonyane | *17 letters:* | Mountains |
| Admiralty Range | Wind River Range | Continental Divide | |
| Bohemian Forest | | Transylvanian Alps | |
| Carnarvon Range | *15 letters:* | Warrumbungle | |
| Finsteraarhorn | New England Range | Range | |

**Mountain-building** Orogenesis

**Mountaineer(ing)** Aaron, Abseil, Alpinist, Arnaut, Climber, Hunt, Sherpa, Smythe, Upleader

**Mountebank** Antic(ke), Baladin(e), Charlatan, Jongleur, Quack, Saltimbanco

**Mourn(er), Mournful, Mourning** Adonia, Alack, Black, Cypress, Dirge, Dole, Elegiac, Grieve, Grone, Half-mast, Hatchment, Jamie Duff, Keen, Lament, Mute, Niobe, Omer, Ovel, Plangent, Saulie, Shibah, Shivah, Shloshim, Sorrow, Tangi, Threnetic, Threnodial, Weeds, Weep, Willow

**Mouse(like), Mousy** Black eye, Bus, Church, Deer, Dormouse, Dun(nart), Fat, Field, Flitter, Harvest, Honey, House, Icon, Jerry, Jumping, Kangaroo, Marsupial, Meadow, Mechanical, Mickey, Minnie, Mischief, Muridae, Murine, Optical, Pocket, Pouched, Rodent, Shiner, Shrew, Vermin, Waltzer, White-footed

**Mousetrap** Samson's post

**Mousse** Styling

**Moustache(d)** Algernon, Boxcar, Burnside, Charley, Charlie, Chevron, Excrement, Fu Manchu, Handlebar, Hindenburg, Horseshoe, Kaiser, Mistletoe, Pencil, Pyramid, Regent, Roman T, Ronnie, Soupstrainer, Toothbrush, Walrus, Waxed, Wings, Zapata

**Mouth(piece)** Aboral, Bazoo, Bocca, Brag, Buccal, Cakehole, Chapper, Check, Crater, Debouchure, Delta, Embouchure, Estuary, Fauces, Fipple, Gab, Gam, Geggie, Gills, Gob, Gub, Gum, Hard, Horn, Kisser, Labret, Laughing gear, Lawyer, Lip, Manubrium, Maw, Neb, Orifex, Orifice, Os, Oscule, Ostium, Outfall, Outlet, Peristome, Port, Potato trap, Rattle-trap, Speaker, Spokesman, Spout, Stoma, Swazzle, Swozzle, Teat, Trap, Trench, Uvula

**Mouthful** Bite, Canape, Gob, Gobbet, Inlet, Mealy, Morceau, Morsel, Sip, Sup, Taste

**Mouthless** Astomatous

**Mouth-organ** Harmonica, Harp, Palp, Sang

**Mouth-watering** Sialogogue

**Move(d), Mover, Movable, Moving** Act, Actuate, Affect, Andante, Astir, Aswarm, Budge, Career, Carry, Castle, Catapult, Chattel, Choreic, Circulate, Claw off, Coast, Counter-measure, Coup, Decant, Démarche, Deploy, Displace, Disturb, Ease, Eddy, Edge, Eloign, Evoke, Extrapose, False, Fidget, Flit, Flounce, Fluctuate, Forge, Fork, Forklift, Frogmarch, Galvanise, Gambit, Gee, Give and go, Glide, Go, Gravitate, Haulier, Hustle, Impress, Inch, Inspire, Instigate, Jee, Jink, Jump, Kedge, Kinetic, Knight's progress, Link, Lumber, Lunge, March, Mill, Mobile, Mosey, Motivate, Motor, Mouse, Nip, Opening, Outwin, Overcome, Pan, People, Poignant, Prime, Proceed, Progress, Progressional, Prompt, Propel, Propose, Push, Qui(t)ch, Quicken, Quinche, Rearrange, Redeploy, Relocate, Remuage, Retrocede, Roll, Rollaway, Roller-skate, Rouse, Roust, Sashay, Scamper, Scoot, Scramble, Scroll, Scurry, Scuttle, Sealed, Sell, Shift, Shog, Shoo, Shunt,

Sidle, Skelp, Skitter, Slide, Soulful, Spank, Steal, Steer, Step, Stir, Styre, Surf, Swarm, Sway, Swish, Tack, Tactic, Taxi, Teleport, Touch, Transfer, Translate, Translocate, Transplant, Transport, Transpose, Travel, Troll, Trundle, Turn, Undulate, Unstep, Up, Up sticks, Urge, Vacillate, Vagile, Veronica, Vire, Volt(e), Waft, Wag, Wapper, Whirry, Whish, Whisk, Whiz, Whoosh, Wuther, Yank, Zoom, Zwischenzug

**Movement(s)** Action, Advection, Aerotaxis, Akathisia, Al Fatah, Allegro, Allemande, Almain, Andantino, Antic, Antistrophe, Arts and crafts, Azapo, Badinerie, Bandwagon, Brisé, Brownian, Buchmanism, Cadence, Capoeira, Cause, Cell, Charismatic, Chartism, Chemonasty, Constructivism, Course, Crusade, Dadaism, Diapirism, Diaspora, Diastole, Ecumenical, Enlightenment, Eoka, Epeirogeny, Eurhythmics, Expressionism, Faction, Falange, Feint, Fianchetto, Fris(ka), Gait, Gallicanism, Geneva, Gesture, Groundswell, Heliotaxis, Hip-hop, Honde, Imagism, Indraught, Inkatha, Intermezzo, Jhala, Jor, Kata, Keplarian, Kinematics, Kinesis, Kin(a)esthetic, Kinetic, Kipp, Larghetto, Largo, Lassu, Ligne, Locomotion, Logistics, Maltese cross, Manoeuvre, Men's, Migration, Motion, Mudra, Nastic, Naturalism, Naziism, Neofascism, Neorealism, New Age, New Urbanism, New Wave, Nihilism, Official, Operation, Orchesis, Overspill, Oxford, Oxford Group, Panislamism, Pan-Slavism, Pantalon, Parallax, Pase, Passade, Passage, Pedesis, Photokinesis, Photonasty, Piaffer, Pincer, Plastique, Play, Populist, Port de bras, Poule, Poulette, Procession, Progress, Provisional, Punk, Puseyism, Reconstructionism, Reformation, Regression, REM, Renaissance, Resistance, Revivalism, Ribbonism, Risorgimento, Romantic, Rondo, Saccade, Scherzo, Scissors, Seiche, Seismic, Sinn Fein, Solifluction, Solifluxion, Spuddle, Stir(e), Strophe, Sturm und Drang, Subsidence, Swadeshi, Swing, Symbolist, Tachism, Tamil Tigers, Tantrism, Taphrogenesis, Taxis, Tectonic, Telekinesis, Thermotaxis, Thigmotaxis, Tic, Tide, Tractarianism, Transhumance, Trend, Trenise, Ultramontanism, UNITA, Verismo, Veronica, Wave, Wheel, White flight, Women's, Zionism

**Movie** Bioscope, Buddy, Cine(ma), Disaster, Film, Flick, Newsreel, Nudie, Popcorn, Road, Slasher, Snuff, Splatter, Star Wars, Talkie

**Mow(er), Mowing** Aftermath, Cut, Grimace, Lattermath, Lawn, Math, Rawing, Rawn, Reap, Rowan, Rowen, Rowing, Scytheman, Shear, Sickle, Strimmer®, Tass, Trim

**MP** Backbencher, Commoner, Deputy, Gendarme, Knight of the Shire, Member, Oncer, Politico, Provost, Redcap, Retread, Snowdrop, Stannator, Statist, TD

▶ **Mr** *see* **MISTER**

▶ **Mrs** *see* **MISSIS**

**Mrs Brown** VR

**Mrs Copperfield** Agnes, Dora

**Mrs Siddons** Tragic muse

**Mrs Simpson** Marge, Wallis

**Muc(o)us** Blennorrhoea, Booger, Catarrh, Gleet, Operculum, Phlegm, Pituate, Pituita, Salt rheum, Sleep, Snivel, Snot, Snotter, Sputum

**Much** Abundant, Considerable, Ever so, Far, Glut, Great, Lots, Mickle, Mochell, Rotten, Scad, Sore, Viel

**Mucilage** Gum, → MUC(O)US, Putty, Resin

**Muck (up), Mucky** Bungle, Dirt, Dung, Grime, Island, Lady, Leep, Manure, Midden, Mire, Rot, Sludge, Slush, Soil, Sordid, Spoil, Stercoral

**Mucker** Fall, Pal, Purler

**Mud(dy)** Adobe, Clabber, Clart, Clay, Cutcha, Dirt, Drilling, Dubs, Fango, Glaur, Glob, Gutter, Kacha, Lahar, Lairy, Limous, Lumicolous, → MIRE, Moya, Mudge, Ooze, Peloid, Pise, Poach, Red, Riley, Roily, Salse, Silt, Slab, Slake, Sleech, Slime, Slob, Slobland, Slough, Sludge, Slur(ry), Slush, Slutch, Tocky, Trouble, Turbid, Volcanic

**Muddle(d)** Addle, Befog, Bemuse, Botch, Chaos, Cock up, Confuse, Disorder, Disorient, Embrangle, Fluster, Gump, Higgledy-piggledy, Jumble, Mare's nest, Mash, Mêlée, Mess, Mess up, Mix, Mull, Pickle, Puddle, Screw up, Shemozzle, Snarl-up, Stupefy, Tangle, Ta(i)vert, Tiert

▷ **Muddled** *may indicate* an anagram

**Mudfish** Lepidosiren

**Mudguard** Splashboard, Wing

**Mudlark** Ragamuffin, Urchin

**Muesli** Granola

**Muff** Blunder, Boob, Botch, Bungle, Drop, Snoskyn

**Muffin** Bun, Mule, Popover

**Muffle(d), Muffler** Baffle, Damp, Deaden, Earplug, Envelop, Hollow, Low, Mob(b)le, Mute, Scarf, Silencer, Sourdine, Stifle

**Mug(ger), Muggy** Assault, Attack, Bash, Beaker, Bock, Can, Club, Con, Croc(odile), Cup, Dial, Do over, Dupe, Enghalskrug, Face, Fool, Footpad, Gob, Humid, Idiot, Latron, Learn, Mou, Noggin, Pan, Pot, Puss, Rob, Roll, Sandbag, Sap, Sconce, Simpleton, Steamer, Stein, Sucker, Swot, Tankard, Tax, Thief, Thug(gee), Tinnie, Tinny, Toby, Trap, Twerp, Ugly, Visage, Yap

**Mulatto** Griff(e)

**Mulberry** Artocarpus, Breadfruit, Cecropia, Contrayerva, Cow-tree, Indian, Jack, Morat, Morus, Murrey, Osage orange, Overlord, Paper, Sycamine

**Mulch** Compost

**Mulct** Fine

**Mule, Mulish** Ass, Bab(o)uche, Barren, Donkey, Fadda, Funnel, Hemionus, Hybrid, Mocassin, Moccasin, Moyl(e), Muffin, Muil, Obdurate, Pack, Rake, Shoe, Slipper, Spinning, Sumpter

**Muleteer** Arriero

**Mull** Brood, Chew, Galloway, Kintyre, Ponder, Promontory, Study

**Mullein** Aaron's rod

**Mullet** Goatfish, Hairpiece, Wig

**Mullion** Monial, Trumeau

**Multi-coloured** Kaleidoscopic, Scroddled

**Multiform** Allotropic, Diverse, Manifold

**Multiple, Multiplication, Multiplied, Multiplier, Multiply** Augment, Breed, Chorisis, Common, Double, Elixir, →INCREASE, Manifold, Modulus, Populate, Product, Proliferate, Propagate, Raise, Scalar, Severalfold, Square, Triple

**Multi-purpose** Polychrest

**Multitude** Army, Crowd, Hirsel, Horde, Host, Legion, Populace, Shoal, Sight, Throng, Zillion

**Mum(my), Mummify** Boutonné, Carton(n)age, Corpse, Egyptian, Embalm, Mamma, Mine, Mute, Peace(ful), Pharaoh, Quiet, Sh, Shtum, Silent, Tacit, Whisht, Wordless

**Mumble** Grumble, Moop, Moup, Mouth, Mump, Mushmouth, Mutter, Royne, Slur

**Mumbo jumbo** Hocus pocus, Mammet, Maumet, Mawmet, Mommet

**Mummer(y)** Actor, Guising, Mime, Scuddaler, Scudler, Skudler

**Mumps** Parotitis

**Munch** Champ, Chew, Chomp, Expressionist, Moop, Moup, Scranch

**Mundane** Banal, Common, Earthly, Nondescript, Ordinary, Prosaic, Quotidian, Routine, Secular, Subcelestial, Trite, Trivial, Workaday, Worldly

**Mungo** Park

**Municipal(ity)** Civic, Nasik

**Munificent, Munificence** Bounteous, Generous, Largesse, Liberal, Profuse

**Munition(s)** Arms, Arsenal, Artillery, Matériel, Ordnance

**Munro** Saki

**Mural(s)** Fresco, Graffiti

**Murder(er), Murderess, Murderous** Abort, Aram, Assassin, Blood guilty, Blue, Bluebeard, Bravo, Burke, Butcher, Butler, Cain, Cathedral, Crackhalter, Crippen, Crows, Cutthroat, Danaid(e)s, Dispatch, Do in, Eliminate, End, Filicide, First degree, Fratricide, Genocide, Hare, Hatchet man, Hit, Hitman, Homicide, Hyde, Internecine, Judicial,

→ **KILL**, Liquidate, Locusta, Made man, Man-queller, Massacre, Matricide, Modo, Mullah, Muller, Parricide, Patricide, Petty treason, Poison, Red, Regicide, Removal, Ripper, Ritual, Ritz, Rub out, Second degree, Sikes, Slaughter, Slay, Stiff, Strangle(r), Sweeney Todd, Take out, Thagi, Throttle, Thug(gee), Tyrannicide, Ugly man, Vaticide, Whodun(n)it

**Murk(y)** Black, Dark, Dirk(e), Gloom, Obscure, Rookish, Stygian

**Murmur(ing)** Babble, Breath, Brool, Bruit, Bur(r), Burble, Coo, Croodle, Croon, Grudge, Heart, Hum, → **MUTTER**, Purr, Repine, Rhubarb, Rumble, Rumour, Souffle, Sough, Sowf(f), Sowth, Sturnoid, Syllable, Undertone, Whisper

**Murphy** Chat, Potato, Pratie, Spud, Tater

**Muscle, Muscleman, Muscular** Abductor, Abs, Accelerator, Accessorius, Adductor, Agonist, Anconeus, Aristotle's lantern, Aryepiglottic, Arytaenoid, Athletic, Attollens, Azygous, Beef(y), Beefcake, Biceps, Bowr, Brachialus, Brawn, Buccinator, Buff, Cardiac, Ciliary, Clout, Complexus, Corrugator, Creature, Cremaster, Delt(oid), Depressor, Diaphragm, Digastric, Dilat(at)or, Duvaricator, Écorché, Effector, Elevator, Erecter, Erector, Evertor, Extensor, Eye-string, Flexor, Force, Gastrocnemius, Gemellus, Glute, Glut(a)eus, Gluteus maximus, Gracilis, Hamstring, Heavy, Hiacus, Hunky, Ideomotor, Iliacus, Intrinsic, Involuntary, Kreatine, Lat, Latissimus dorsi, Laxator, Levator, Lumbricalis, Masseter, Mesomorph, Might, Motor, Mouse, Myalgia, Mylohyoid, Myology, Myotome, Myotonia, Nasalis, Obicularis, Oblique, Occlusor, Omohyoid, Opponent, Orbicularis, Pathos, Pec(s), Pectoral, Perforans, Perforatus, Peroneus, Plantaris, Platysma, Popliteus, → **POWER**, Pronator, Protractor, Psoas, Pylorus, Quad(riceps), Quadratus, Rambo, Rectus, Retractor, Rhomboid, Rhomboideus, Ripped, Risorius, Rotator cuff, Sarcolemma, Sarcous, Sartorius, Scalene, Scalenus, Serratus, Sinew, Six-pack, Smooth, Soleus, Sphincter, Spinalis, Splenial, Sthenic, Striated, Striped, Supinator, Suspensory, Temporal, Tenaculum, Tendon, Tensor, Teres, Thenar, Thew, Tibialis, Toned, Tonus, Trapezius, Triceps, Vastus, Voluntary, Xiphihumeralis, Zygomatic

**Muscovite** Mica, Talc

**Muse(s), Muse's home, Musing** Aglaia, Aonia(n), Attic, Calliope, Clio, Cogitate, Consider, Dream, Dwell, Erato, Euphrosyne, Euterpe, Goddess, Helicon, Inspiration, IX, Laura, Melpomene, Mull, Nine, Nonet, Pensée, Pierides, Poly(hy)mnia, Ponder, → **REFLECT**, Ruminate, Study, Teian, Terpsichore, Thalia, Tragic, Urania, Wonder

**Museum** Alte-Pinakothek, Ashmolean, BM, British, Fitzwilliam, Gallery, Getty, Guggenheim, Heritage centre, Hermitage, Hunterian, Kelvingrove, Louvre, Metropolitan, National Gallery, Parnassus, Prado, Repository, Rijksmuseum, Science, Smithsonian, Tate, Te papa Tongarewa, Uffizi, VA, V and A, Waxworks

**Mush** Cree, Glop, Goo, Mess, Pop, Porridge, Puree, Schmaltz, Slop

**Mushroom** Aecidium, Aedium, Agaric, Ascomycetes, Blewits, Boletus, Burgeon, Button, Cep, Champignon, Chanterelle, Darning, Destroying angel, Enoki, Escalate, Expand, Explode, Field, Fly agaric, → **FUNGUS**, Girolle, Grisette, Gyromitra, Honey fungus, Horse, Hypha(l), Ink-cap, Liberty cap, Magic, Matsutake, Meadow, Morel, Oyster, Parasol, Penny-bun, Pixy-stool, Porcino, Reishi, Russula, Sacred, St George's, Scotch bonnet, Shaggy cap, Shaggymane, Shiitake, Shroom, Sickener, Snowball, Spread, Start-up, Straw, Truffle, Upstart, Velvet shank, Waxcap

**Music** Absolute, A-side, B-side, Classical, Colour, Indeterminate, Lesson, Light, Minstrelsy, Mood, Morceau, → **MUSICAL INSTRUMENTS**, Passage work, Phase, Piece, Popular, Programme, Quotation, Recital, Score, Sound, Table, Tremolando

## MUSIC

| 2 letters: | 3 letters: | Art | Emo |
|---|---|---|---|
| Oi | Air | Dub | Gat |
| | AOR | EMI | Jor |

Mas
MOR
Pop
Rag
Rai
Rap
Rug
Ska
Son

**4 letters:**
Alap
Chin
Coda
Duet
Folk
Funk
Go-go
Jass
Jazz
Loco
Meno
Note
Opus
Prom
Raga
Rave
Riff
Rock
Romo
Roxy
Soca
Soul
Surf
Tala
Trad
Trio
Tune
Zouk

**5 letters:**
Alaap
Alapa
Bebop
Benga
Canon
Chant
Cliff
Conga
Crunk
Cu-bop
Disco
Dream
Dumka

Early
Etude
Fugue
Funky
Gabba
House
Indie
Jhala
Krunk
Kwela
Largo
March
Motet
Muzak®
Neume
Nonet
Outro
Piped
Ragga
Rondo
Roots
Rough
Salon
Salsa
Salve
Sheet
Sokah
Staff
Suite
Swing
Thema
Tonal
Trash
Truth
Vocal
World
Zoppo

**6 letters:**
Anthem
Arioso
Aubade
Bebung
Bouree
Decani
Doo-wop
Enigma
Equali
Façade
Fugato
Fusion
Gagaku
Galant
Garage

Gospel
Gothic
Grunge
Hip-hop
Jungle
Khayal
Kirtan
Kwaito
Lounge
Lydian
Mantra
Marabi
Mashup
Medley
Melody
Motown®
New Age
Organa
Plagal
Popera
Pycnon
Ragini
Redowa
Reggae
Rhythm
Rootsy
Sextet
Skronk
Sonata
Strain
Techno
Tenuto
Thrash
Trance
Verset
Zydeco

**7 letters:**
Afropop
Allegro
Andante
Ars nova
Ballade
Baroque
Bhangra
Bluette
Bourree
Britpop
Cadenza
Calypso
Cantata
Ceilidh
Chamber
Chorale

Country
Dad rock
Electro
Europop
Euterpe
Fanfare
Gangsta
Hardbag
Introit
Klezmer
Landler
Marcato
Melisma
Messiah
Mordent
New Wave
Numbers
Nu-metal
Organum
Orphean
Partita
Passion
Pecking
Pibroch
Prelude
Qawwali
Quartet
Quintet
Ragtime
Rastrum
Requiem
Reverse
Romanza
Rondeau
Rondino
Rosalia
Roulade
Sanctus
Scherzo
Secondo
Setting
Skiffle
Soukous
Stretto
Toccata
Trip hop
Ziganka

**8 letters:**
Acid rock
Afrojazz
Afrorock
Aleatory
Bel canto

Berceuse
Blue beat
Canticle
Chaconne
Cock rock
Concerto
Concrete
Continuo
Coranach
Coronach
Elevator
Entracte
Fantasia
Flamenco
Folk rock
Glam rock
Hard core
Hard rock
High life
In nomine
Janizary
Karnatak
Lollipop
Madrigal
Maggiore
Mariachi
Mbaqanga
Medieval
Modality
Nocturne
Notation
Old-skool
Oratorio
Overture
Parlando
Partitur
Pastiche
Postlude
Post-rock
Preludio
Psalmody
Punk rock
Rhapsody
Ricercar
Romantic
Saraband
Serenade

Serenata
Sinfonia
Symphony
Synth-pop
Waltzian
Warhorse

**9 letters:**
Acid-house
Allemande
Americana
Antiphony
Arabesque
Bagatelle
Bluegrass
Breakbeat
Cantilena
Capriccio
Crossover
Dancehall
Dixieland
Drum'n'bass
Finlandia
Fioritura
Goa trance
Grandioso
Hardhouse
Hillbilly
Honky-tonk
Interlude
Klezmorim
Obbligato
Partitura
Pastorale
Pastorali
Pitchbend
Plainsong
Polonaise
Polyphony
Portabeul
Prick-song
Queercore
Quodlibet
Reggaeton
Ricercare
Rock'n'roll
Septimole

Serialist
Slow march
Spiritual
Swingbeat
Tambourin
Technopop
Toccatina
Voluntary
Wallpaper
Warehouse

**10 letters:**
Albumblatt
Anacrustic
Chopsticks
Coloratura
Death metal
Desert rock
Electronic
Gangsta rap
Gothic rock
Heavy metal
Hindustani
Humoresque
Incidental
Intermezzo
Jam session
Lovers' rock
Martellato
Mersey beat
Minimalist
New Country
Percussion
Polyhymnia
Polyrhythm
Portamento
Quadrivium
Ragamuffin
Rare groove
Ritornello
Rockabilly
Rocksteady
Seguidilla
Shoegazing
Tarantella
Toccatella
Twelve-tone

Urban blues

**11 letters:**
Boeremusiek
Concertante
Country rock
Mersey sound
Motor rhythm
Passacaglia
Psychobilly
Raggamuffin
Renaissance
Rogues' march
Sinfonietta
Solmisation
Stadium rock
Third stream
Thrash metal
Tin Pan Alley

**12 letters:**
Blue-eyed soul
Boogie-woogie
Concertstück
Contrapuntal
Divertimento
Electroclash
Late medieval
Neo-classical
Nunc Dimittis
Pralltriller
Western swing

**13 letters:**
Choral prelude
Detroit techno
Early medieval
Progressional

**14 letters:**
Durchkomponirt
Rhythm and blues

**15 letters:**
Durchkomponiert
Musique concrete
Progressive rock

**Musical** Annie, Arcadian, Azione, Brigadoon, Canorous, Carousel, Cats, Chess, Chicago, Euphonic, Evergreen, Evita, Gigi, Grease, Hair, Half a Sixpence, Harmonious, Kabuki, Kismet, Kiss Me Kate, Les Miserables, Lyric, Mame, Melodic, My Fair Lady, Oliver, →**OPERA**, Operetta, Oratorio, Orphean, Revue, Showboat, South Pacific, Top Hat, Trial by Jury, West Side Story

**Musical box** Juke-box, Polyphon(e), Stereo
**Musical chairs** Level-coil

## MUSICAL INSTRUMENTS

*2 letters:*
Ax
Gu

*3 letters:*
Axe
Gue
Kit
Oud
Qin
Saz
Uke
Zel

*4 letters:*
Buva
Chyn
Crwd
Drum
Erhu
Fife
Gong
Harp
Horn
Kora
Koto
Lure
Lute
Lyre
Moog®
Oboe
Pipa
Rate
Reed
Rote
Sang
Tuba
Vina
Viol
Whip
Zeze

*5 letters:*
Aulos
Banjo
Bugle
Cello
Clave
Cobza

Corno
Crowd
Crwth
Dobro®
Esraj
Flute
Gaita
Gazog
Guiro
Guqin
Gusla
Gusle
Gusli
Kaval
Kazoo
Labia
Mbira
Naker
Nebel
Organ
Piano
Quena
Rebec
Regal
Sanko
Sansa
Sarod
Shalm
Shawm
Sitar
Stick
Tabla
Tabor
Tenor
Tibia
Veena
Viola
Zanze
Zinke

*6 letters:*
Antara
Atabal
Biniou
Bisser
Bongos
Citole
Cornet
Cymbal

Euphon
Flugel
Guitar
Kanoon
Maraca
Poogye
Racket
Rebeck
Relish
Ribibe
Sancho
Santir
Santur
Shalme
Shofar
Sittar
Spinet
Syrinx
Tom-tom
Trigon
Vielle
Violin
Yidaki
Zither
Zufolo

*7 letters:*
Alphorn
Anklong
Bagpipe
Bandore
Bandura
Baryton
Bassoon
Bazooka
Celesta
Celeste
Cembalo
Ceol mor
Chikara
Cithara
Cittern
Clarino
Clarion
Clavier
Clogbox
Console
Cornett
Dichord

Dulcian
Fagotto
Flutina
Gamelan
Gazogka
Gittern
Hautboy
Helicon
High-hat
Kalimba
Kantela
Kantele
Kithara
Klavier
Lyricon
Mandola
Marimba
Musette
Ocarina
Pandora
Pandore
Pandura
Pianino
Pianola®
Piccolo
Poogyee
Posaune
Rackett
Rellish
Ribible
Sackbut
Sambuca
Samisen
Santour
Sarangi
Saxhorn
Saxtuba
Serpent
Symbole
Tambour
Tambura
Theorbo
Timbrel
Timpano
Trumpet
Tympany
Ukelele
Ukulele
Vihuela

Violone
Whistle
Zuffolo

**8 letters:**
Angklung
Archlute
Autoharp®
Barytone
Bass-drum
Berimbau
Bombarde
Bouzouki
Calliope
Canorous
Carillon
Charango
Cimbalom
Clarinet
Clarsach
Clavecin
Cornetto
Cornpipe
Cromorna
Cromorne
Crumhorn
Dulcimer
Gemshorn
Guarneri
Guimbard
Handbell
Hautbois
Humstrum
Jew's harp
Keyboard
Key-bugle
Langspel
Lyra-viol
Mandolin
Manzello
Martenot
Melodeon
Melodica
Melodion
Mirliton
Oliphant
Ottavino
Pan pipes
Phorminx
Pianette
Polyphon
Psaltery
Recorder
Reco-reco

Slughorn
Sourdine
Spinette
Squiffer
Sticcado
Sticcato
Surbahar
Tamboura
Tamburin
Tenoroon
Theremin
Triangle
Trichord
Trombone
Virginal
Vocalion
Zambomba
Zampogna

**9 letters:**
Accordion
Aerophone
Alpenhorn
Baby grand
Balalaika
Bandoneon
Bandurria
Banjulele
Bombardon
Chalumeau
Clarionet
Cornemuse
Decachord
Dulcitone®
Euphonium
Flageolet
Flexatone
Flute-à-bec
Gittarone
Gutbucket
Harmonica
Harmonium
Humbucker
Idiophone
Kent-bugle
Krummhorn
Langspiel
Mandoline
Mellotron®
Monochord
Mouth-harp
Nose flute
Orpharion
Pantaleon

Pastorale
Polyphone
Reed organ
Saxophone
Seraphine
Slughorne
Snare-drum
Sonometer
Sopranino
Steel drum
Stockhorn
Trompette
Vibraharp
Washboard
Welsh harp
Xylophone
Xylorimba

**10 letters:**
Arpeggione
Basset-horn
Bullroarer
Chitarrone
Clavichord
Colascione
Concertina
Contrabass
Cor anglais
Cornettini
Didgeridoo
Flugelhorn
Fortepiano
French horn
Gramophone
Hurdy-gurdy
Kettledrum
Lagerphone
Light organ
Mellophone
Nun's fiddle
Ophicleide
Orpheoreon
Pentachord
Shakuhachi
Small pipes
Sousaphone
Squeeze-box
Stylophone®
Symphonium
Tambourine
Thumb piano
Tin whistle
Vibraphone
Wokka board

**11 letters:**
Chordophone
Clairschach
Contrabasso
Harmoniphon
Harpsichord
Heckelphone
Nickelodeon
Octave flute
Orchestrina
Orchestrion
Phonofiddle
Player piano
Stock-in-horn
Straduarius
Synthesizer
Trump-marine
Viola d'amore
Violoncello
Wobble-board

**12 letters:**
Chapman stick®
Chinese block
Clavicembalo
Glockenspiel
Harmonichord
Harmoniphone
Metallophone
Penny-whistle
Sarrusophone
Stock and horn
Stradivarius
Tromba-marina
Tubular bells
Viola da gamba

**13 letters:**
American organ
Contrabassoon
Contrafagotto
Ondes Martenot
Panharmonicon
Physharmonica
Slide trombone
Swanee whistle

**14 letters:**
Clavicytherium
Glass harmonica
Hawaiian guitar
Jingling Johnny
Musical glasses
Ondes musicales

| | 15 *letters:* | 18 *letters:* |
|---|---|---|
| Piano accordion | Moog synthesiser | Chinese temple |
| Swannee whistle | | block |
| Viola da braccio | | |

**Music-hall** Alhambra, Disco, Empire, Folies Bergere, Odeon

**Musician(s), Musicologist** Accompanist, Arion, Arist, Armstrong, Ashkenazi, Bassist, Beiderbecke, Boy band, Brain, Buononcini, Busker, Carmichael, Casals, Cellist, Chanter, Clapton, Combo, →**COMPOSER**, Conductor, Crowder, Duet, Ellington, Ensemble, Executant, Flautist, Gate, Group, Grove, Guido d'Arezzo, Guslar, Handel, Jazzer, Jazzman, Joplin, Keyboardist, Klezmer, Labelmate, Luter, Lyrist, Maestro, Mahler, Mariachi, Menuhin, Minstrel, Moke, Muso, Noisenik, Nonet, Octet, Orphean, Percussionist, Peterson, Pianist, Pied Piper, Quartet, Quintet, Rapper, Reed(s)man, Répétiteur, Ripienist, Rubinstein, Satchmo, Schonberg, Septet, Serenader, Session, Sextet, Sideman, Soloist, Spohr, String, Techno, Tortelier, Troubador, Trouvère, Trumpeter, Violinist, Waits

**Music-lover** Promenader

**Musk** Civet, Mimulus, Must

**Musket** Brown Bess, Caliver, Carabine, Eyas, Flintlock, Fusil, Gingal(l), Hawk, Jezail, Jingal, Nyas, Queen's-arm, Weapon

**Musketeer** Aramis, Athos, D'Artagnan, Fusilier, Ja(e)ger, Porthos, Rifleman, Sam

**Muslim (ritual), Moslem** Alaouite, Alawite, Ali, Almohad(e), Balochi, Baluchi, Berber, Black, Caliph, Dato, Dervish, Druse, Fatimid, Ghazi, Hadji, Hafiz, Hajji, Hamas, Hezbollah, Hizbollah, Hizbullah, Iranian, Islamic, Ismaili, Karmathian, Khotbah, Khotbeh, Khutbah, Mahometan, Mawlawi, Meivievi, Mog(h)ul, Mohammedan, Moor, Morisco, Moro, Muezzin, Mufti, Mughal, Mus(s)ulman, Mutazilite, Nawab, Panislam, Paynim, Pomak, Said, Saladin, Saracen, Say(y)id, Senus(s)i, Shafiite, Shia(h), Shiite, Sofi, Sonnite, Sufi, Sulu, Sunna, Sunni(te), Tajik, Turk, Umma(h), Wahabee, Wahabi(te), Wahhabi, Whirling Dervish

**Muslin** Butter, Cloth, Coteline, Gurrah, Jamdani, Leno, Mousseline, Mull, Nainsook, Organdie, Persienne, Swiss, Tarlatan, Tiffany

**Musquash** Ondatra

**Mussel(s)** Bearded, Bivalve, Clabby-doo, Clam, Clappy-doo, Deerhorn, Duck, Edible, Horse, Modiolus, Moules marinières, Mytilus, Naiad, Niggerhead, Pearl, Scalp, Swan, Unio, Unionidae, Zebra

**Mussolini** Benini, Il Duce

**Mussorgsky** Modest

**Must(y)** Amok, Essential, Foughty, Fousty, Froughy, Frowsty, Frowy, Funky, Fust, Gotta, Man, Maun(na), Mote, Mould, Mucid, Mun, Necessary, Need(s)-be, Obbligato, Shall, Should, Stum, Vinew, Wine

▷ **Must** *may indicate* an anagram

**Mustard** Black, Brown, Charlock, Cress, Dijon, English, Erysimum, French, Garlic, Gas, Nitrogen, Praiseach, Quinacrine, Runch, Sarepta, Sauce-alone, Senvy, Treacle, Wall, White, Wild, Wintercress

**Mustard plaster** Sinapism

**Musteline** Atoc, Atok, Skunk

**Muster** Array, Assemble, Bangtail, Call up, Enrol, Mass, Peacock, Raise, Rally, Really, Recruit, Round-up, Turn out, Wappenshaw

**Mutability** Wheel

**Mutate, Mutant, Mutation** Auxotroph(ic), Change, Heterogenesis, Polybasic, Saltation, Somatic, Sport, Suppressor, Terata, Transform, Vowel

▷ **Mutation** *may indicate* an anagram

**Mute(d)** Deaden, Dumb, Harpo, Mourner, Noiseless, Saulie, Silent, Sorda, Sordino, Sordo, Sourdine, Stifle, Stop

**Mutilate(d), Mutilation** Castrate, Concise, Deface, Dismember, Distort, Garble, Hamble, Injure, Maim, Mangle, Mayhem, Obtruncate, Riglin, Tear

▷ **Mutilate(d)** *may indicate* an anagram

**Mutineer, Mutiny** Bounty, Caine, Christian, Curragh, Indian, Insurrection, Jhansi, Meerut, Nore, Pandy, Rebel, → REVOLT, Rising, Sepoy, Treason

**Mutter(ing)** Chunter, Drone, Fremescent, Grumble, Maunder, Mumble, Mump, Murmur, Mussitate, Rhubarb, Roin, Royne, Rumble, Sotto voce, Whittie-whattie, Witter

**Mutton** Braxy, Chump, Colonial goose, Em, Ewes, Fanny Adams, Gigot, Macon, Rack, Saddle, Sheep, Theave, Traik

**Mutual (aid)** Common, Complementary, Frank-pledge, Interplay, Log-roll, Reciprocal, Symbiosis

**Muzzle** Decorticate, Gag, Gunpoint, Jaw, Mouth, Mute, Restrain, Snout

**My** Begorra, Blimey, By Jove, Christ, Coo, Gad, Gee, Gemini, Golly, Gorblimey, Gosh, Great Scott, Ha, Jeepers, Lor, Lumme, M, Musha, Odso, Oh, Our, Tush

**Myna(h)** Hill, Stare, Starling

**Mynheer** Stadholder

**Myopia, Myopic** Hidebound, Mouse-sight, Narrow, Short-sighted, Thick-eyed

**Myriad** Host, Zillion

**Myriapod** Centipede

**Myristic** Nutmeg

**Myrrh** Stacte

**Myrtle** Bog, Callistemon, Crape, Creeping, Crepe, Eucalyptus, Gale, Jambolana, Tasmanian, Tooart, Trailing, Tuart

**Mysterious, Mystery** Abdabs, Abdals, Acroamatic, Arcane, Arcanum, Cabbala, Closed book, Craft, Creepy, Cryptic, Dark (horse), Deep, Delphic, Eleusinian, Enigma(tic), Esoteric, G(u)ild, Grocer, Incarnation, Inscrutable, Miracle, Mystagogue, Numinous, Occult, Original sin, Orphic, Penetralia, Recondite, Riddle, Sacrament, → SECRET, Shadowy, Shady, Spooky, Suspense, Telestic, Thriller, Trinity, UFO, Uncanny, Unearthly, Unexplained, Unknown, Whodunit

▷ **Mysterious(ly)** *may indicate* an anagram

**Mystic (word), Mystical, Mysticism** Abraxas, Agnostic, Cabbala, Cab(e)iri, Eckhart, Epopt, Fakir, Familist, Gnostic, Hesychast, Mahatma, New Age, Occultist, Quietism, Rasputin, Rosicrucian, Secret, Seer, Sofi, Sufi, Swami, Tantric, Tantrist, Theosophy, Transcendental, Zohar

**Mystify** Baffle, Bamboozle, Bewilder, Metagrabolise, Metagrobolise, Perplex, Puzzle

**Myth(ology), Mythological, Mythical (beast)** Allegory, Atlantis, Behemoth, Bunyip, Centaur, Cockatrice, Dragon, Dreamtime, Euhemerism, Fable, Fantasy, Fictitious, Folklore, Garuda, Geryon, Griffin, Hippocampus, Impundulu, Kelpie, Kylin, Legend, Leviathan, Lore, Lorelei, Lyonnesse, Otnit, Pantheon, Pegasus, Phoenix, Sasquatch, Sea horse, Sea serpent, Selkie, Solar, Speewah, Sphinx, Sun, Tarand, Therianthropic, Thunderbird, Tokoloshe, Tragelaph, Unicorn, Urban, Wivern, Wyvern, Yale, Yeti

# Nn

**N** Name, Nitrogen, Noon, North, November
**Nab** Arrest, Capture, Collar, Confiscate, Grab, Seize
**Nabob** Deputy, Nawab, Wealthy
**Nadir** Bottom, Depths, Dregs, Minimum
**Nag(ging)** Badger, Bidet, Brimstone, Callet, Cap, Captious, Complain, Fret, Fuss, Harangue, Harp, Henpeck, Horse, Jade, Jaw, Keffel, Peck, Pester, Pick on, Plague, Rosinante, Rouncy, → SCOLD, Tit, Xant(h)ippe, Yaff
**Nail(ed)** Brad, Brod, Catch, Clinker, Clout, Coffin, Fasten, Frost, Hob, Horse, Keratin, Onyx, Pin, Rivet, Screw, Secure, Seize, Shoe, Sisera, Sixpenny, Sparable, Sparrow-bill, Spick, Spike, Sprig, Staple, Stub, Stud, Tack(et), Talon, Tenpenny, Tenterhook, Thumb, Tingle, Toe, Unguis, Wire
**Naive(té)** Artless, Dewy-eyed, Green(horn), Guileless, Gullible, Ingenuous, Innocence, Open, Pollyanna, Simpliste, Simplistic, Starry-eyed, Trusting, Unsophisticated, Wide-eyed
**Naked(ness)** Adamical, Artless, Bare, Blunt, Buff, Clear, Cuerpo, Defenceless, Encuerpo, Exposed, Gymno-, Kaal gat, Nature, Nuddy, Nude, Querpo, Raw, Scud, Simple, Skyclad, Stark(ers), Uncovered
**Namby-pamby** Milksop, Nance, Sissy, Weak, Weakling, White-shoe
**Name(d), Names** Agnomen, Alias, Allonym, Anonym, Appellation, Appoint, Attribute, Badge, Baptise, Behight, Byline, Call, Celeb(rity), Christen, Cite, Cleep, Clepe, Cognomen, Day, Designate, Dinges, Dingus, Dit, Domain, Dub, Entitle, Epithet, Eponym, Exonym, Family, First, Font, Generic, Given, Handle, Hete, Hight, Hypocorism, Identify, Identity, Label, Maiden, Marque, Masthead, Mention, Metronymic, Middle, Moni(c)ker, Mud, N, Nap, Nemn, Nempt, Nom, Nomen(clature), Noun, Onomastics, Onymous, Patronymic, Pennant, Personage, Pet, Place, Praenomen, Proper, Proprietary, Pseudonym, Quote, Red(d), Repute, Scilicet, Sign, Signature, Sir, Specify, Stage, Street, Subdomain, Substantive, Tag, Tautonym, Teknonymy, Term, → TITLE, Titular, Titule, Toponymy, Trade, Trivial, User
**Name-dropper** Eponym
**Nameless** Anon, Unchrisom
**Namely** Ie, Sc, Scilicet, To-wit, Videlicet, Viz
**Namesake** Homonym
**Name unknown** Anon, A N Other, NU
**Namibian** Herero
**Nancy** Coddle, Effeminate, Milksop
**Nanny** Ayah, Cosset, Foster, Goat, Nurse, Wet-nurse
**Naos** Cell(a)
**Nap(py)** Ale, Bonaparte, Diaper, Doze, Drowse, Fluff, Forty winks, Frieze(d), Fuzz, Game, Happen, Hippin(g), Kip, Moze, Nod, Oose, Ooze, Oozy, Power, Put(t), Shag, Shuteye, Siesta, → SLEEP, Slumber, Snooze, Tease, Teasel, Teaze, Terry, Tipsy, Tuft
**Nape** Niddick, Noddle, Nucha, Scrag, Scruff, Scuff, Scuft
**Napier** Logarithm
**Napkin** Cloth, Diaper, Doily, Doyley, Linen, Muckender, Paper, Sanitary, Serviette, Table
**Napless** Threadbare
**Napoleon** Badinguet, Bonaparte, Boustrapa, Brandy, Cognac, Coin, Consul, Corporal Violet, Corsican, December, Little Corporal, Nantz, Nap, Pig, Rantipole, Solo

▷ **Napoleon** *may indicate* a pig

**Napper** Bonce, Shearman

**Narcissus, Narcissism** Echo, Egocentric, Egomania, Jonquil

**Narcotic** Ava, B(h)ang, Benj, Cannabin, Cannabis, Charas, Churrus, Coca, Codeine, Dagga, Datura, Dope, →**DRUG**, Heroin, Hop, Kava, Laudanum, Mandragon, Mandrake, Marijuana, Meconium, Methadone, Morphia, Narceen, Narceine, Nicotine, Opiate, Opium, Pituri, Sedative, Tea, Tobacco, Trional

**Nark** Grass, Inform, Irritate, Nose, Pique, Roil, Squealer, Stag

**Narrate, Narration, Narrative, Narrator** Allegory, Anecdote, Cantata, Describe, Diegesis, Fable, History, Ishmael, Oblique, Periplus, Plot, Raconteur, Récit, Recital, Recite, Recount, Saga, Sagaman, Scheherazade, Splatterpunk, Story, Tell, Thanatography, Voice-over

**Narrow(ing), Narrow-minded** Alf, Babbitt, Bigoted, Borné, Bottleneck, Close, Constringe, Cramp, Ensiform, Grundy(ism), Hairline, Hidebound, Illiberal, Insular, Knife edge, Kyle, Limited, Meagre, Nary, One-idead, Parochial, Phimosis, Pinch, Pinch-point, Po(-faced), Provincial, Prudish, Puritan, Scant, Sectarian, Shrink, Slender, Slit, Specialise, Squeak, Stenosed, Strait, Straiten, Strait-laced, Strict, Suburban, Taper, Verkramp, Wafer-thin, Waist

**Narwhal** Monodon

**Nasal** Adenoidal, Rhinolalia, Sonorant, Twang

**Nash** Beau

**Nashville** Bath

**Nastiness, Nasty** Disagreeable, Drevill, Filth, Fink, Ghastly, Lemon, Lo(a)th, Malign(ant), Noisome, Noxious, Obscene, Odious, Offensive, Ogreish, Poxy, Ribby, Scummy, Sif, Sinister, Sordid, Unholy, Vile, Virose

**Nat(haniel)** Hawthorne, Winkle

**Natal** Inborn, Native, Patrial

**Natant** Afloat, Swimming

**Nation(s), National(ist), Nationalism** Anthem, Baathist, Broederbond, Casement, Chetnik, Country, Cuban, Debt, De Valera, Eta, Federal, Five, Folk, Grand, Hindutva, Indian, INLA, IRA, Israeli, Jingoist, Kuomintang, Land, Malcolm X, Mexican, Oman, Pamyat, Parnell, Patriot, →**PEOPLE**, Plaid Cymru, Polonia, Race, Rainbow, Risorgimento, Scottish, Shiv Sena, Six, SNP, Subject, Swadeshi, Timor-Leste, Tonga, Tribespeople, Turk, United, Vanuatu, Vatican City, Verkrampte, Vietminh, Wafd, Xenophobe, Yemini, Young Ireland, Young Turk, Zionist

**Native(s)** Abo(rigin), Aborigine, African, Amerind, Annamese, Arab, Ascian, Australian, Autochthon, Aztec, Basuto, Belonging, Bengali, Boy, Bushman, Cairene, Carib, Carioca, Chaldean, Citizen, Colchester, Conch, Creole, Criollo, Domestic, Dyak, Edo, Enchorial, Endemic, Eskimo, Fleming, Fuzzy-wuzzy, Genuine, Habitual, Home-bred, Inborn, Inca, Indigene, Indigenous, Inhabitant, Intuitive, John Chinaman, Kaffir, Libyan, Local, Malay, Maori, Mary, Micronesian, Moroccan, Norwegian, Oyster, Polack, Portuguese, Scythian, Son, Spaniard, Te(i)an, Thai, Tibetan, Tribesman, Uzbeg, Uzbek, Whitstable, Yugoslav

**Nativity** Birth, Jataka, Putz

**Natron** Urao

**Natter** Chat, Gossip, Jack, Prate

**Natty** Bumppo, Chic, Dapper, Leatherstocking, Smart, Spruce

**Natural(ly), Naturalise(d), Naturalism** Altogether, Artless, Ass, Denizen, Easy, Endenizen, Genuine, Green, Gut, Homely, Idiot, Illegitimate, Inborn, Inbred, Indigenous, Ingenerate, Inherent, Innate, Instinctive, Moron, Native, Nidget, Nitwit, Nude, Ordinary, Organic, Prat, Real, Simpleton, Simpliciter, Sincere, True, Undyed, Untaught, Verism

**Naturalist** Banks, Bates, Buffon, Darwin, De Lamarck, Durrell, Wallace, White

**Nature** Adam, Akin, Character, Disposition, Esse(nce), Ethos, Haecceity, Human, Hypostasis, Inbeing, Inscape, Manhood, Mould, Quiddity, Quintessence, Root, Second, SN, Temperament

**Naught** Cypher, Failure, Nil, Nothing, Zero

**Naughty** Bad, Disobedient, Girly, Improper, Indecorous, Light, Marietta, Nineties, Nonny, Offender, Rascal, Remiss, Rudery, Spright, Sprite, Wayward

**Nausea, Nauseous** Disgust, Dwa(l)m, Dwaum, Fulsome, Malaise, Queasy, Sickness, Squeamish, Wamble, Wambly

**Nave** Aisle, Apse, Centre, Hub, Modiolus, Nef

**Navel** Belly-button, Jaffa, Naff, Nave, Omphalos, Orange, Tummy button, Umbilicus

**Navigate, Navigator** Albuquerque, Baffin, Bering, Bougainville, Cabot, Cartier, Columbus, Control, Cook, Da Gama, Davis, Dias, Direct, Drake, Eric the Red, Franklin, Frobisher, Gilbert, Hartog, Haul, Henry, Hudson, Keel, Magellan, Navvy, Neighbour, Orienteer, Pilot, Raleigh, Sail, Star-read, → **STEER**, Tasman, Traverse, Vancouver, Vespucci, Weddell

**Navigation (aid, system)** Asdic, Cabotage, Celestial, Decca, Dectra, Echosounder, Fido, Gee, Inertial, Inland, Loran, Loxodromics, Navarho, Omnirange, Portolan(o), Portulan, Radar, Satnav, Seamark, Shoran, Tacan, Teleran®, Vor

**Navvy** Workhorse

**Navy, Naval** AB, Armada, Blue, Fleet, French, Maritime, Merchant, N, Red, RN, Senior Service, Wavy, White squadron, Wren

**Nawab** Huzoor, Nabob, Viceroy

**Nazi** Brownshirt, Gauleiter, Hess, Hitler, Jackboot, SS, Stormtrooper, Third Reich, Wer(e)wolf

**NB** Niobium, Nota bene

**NCO** Bombardier, Corp(oral), Havildar, Noncom, Orderly, Pipe-major, Sergeant, SM

**Neanderthal** Mousterian

**Neap** Low, Tide

**Neapolitan** Ice

**Near(er), Nearest, Nearby, Nearly, Nearness** About, Adjacent, All-but, Almost, Anigh, Approach, Approximate, Beside, By, Close, Cy pres, Degree, Even, Ewest, Feckly, Forby, Gain, Handy, Hither, Imminent, Inby(e), Mean, Miserly, Most, Narre, Neist, Next, Nie, Niggardly, Nigh, Oncoming, Outby, Propinquity, Proximity, Short-range, Stingy, Thereabout(s), To, Upon, Warm, Well-nigh

**Neat(ly), Neatness** Bandbox, Cattle, Clean-cut, Clever, Dainty, Dapper, Deft, Dink(y), Doddy, Donsie, Elegant, Featly, Feat(e)ous, Featuous, Gayal, Genty, Gyal, Intact, Jemmy, Jimpy, Kempt, Lower, Nett, Nifty, Ninepence, Orderly, Ox(en), Perjink, Preppy, Pretty, Rother, Saola, Shipshape, Short(horn), Smug, Snod, Spick and span, Spruce, Straight, → **TIDY**, Trig, Trim, Uncluttered, Unwatered, Well-groomed

**Neb** Beak, Bill, Nose, Snout

**Nebula, Nebulous** Aeriform, Celestial, Cloudy, Dark, Emission, Gum, Hazy, Horsehead, Obscure, Planetary, Reflection, Shadowy, Vague

**Necessary, Necessarily** Bog, Cash, De rigueur, → **ESSENTIAL**, Estovers, Imperative, Important, Indispensable, Intrinsic, Loo, Money, Moolah, Needful, Ought, Perforce, Prerequisite, Requisite, Vital, Wherewithal

**Necessitate, Necessity** Ananke, Compel, Constrain, Cost, Emergency, Entail, Essential, Exigent, Fate, Indigence, Logical, Mathematical, Moral, Must, Natural, Need, Need-be, Oblige, Perforce, Require, Requisite, Staple

**Neck(ed)** Bottle, Brass, Canoodle, Cervical, Cervix, Channel, Col, Collar, Crag, Craig, Crew, Crop, Cuff, Embrace, Ewe, Gall, Gorgerin, Halse, Hause, Hawse, Inarm, Inclip, Isthmus, Kiss, Mash, Nape, Nuzzle, Pet, Polo, Rack, Rubber, Scoop, Scrag, Scruff, Smooch, Snog, Stiff, Strait, Surgical, Swan, Swire, Theorbo, Torticollis, Trachelate, Vee, Volcanic

▷ **Necking** *may indicate* one word around another

**Necklace** Afro-chain, Anodyne, Bib, Brisingamen, Chain, Choker, Collar, Corals, Hei-tiki, Laval(l)ière, Lunula, Mangalsutra, Medallion, Negligee, Pearls, Rope, Sautoir, String, Torc, Torque

**Neckline** Boat, Collar, Cowl, Crew, Décolletage, Lanyard, Palter, Plunging, Scoop, Sweetheart, Turtle, Vee

**Neck-warmer** Scarf, Snood

**Neckwear** Ascot, Barcelona, Boa, Bow, Collar, Cravat, Fur, Rail, Steenkirk, Stock, Tie

**Necromancer** Goetic, Magician, Ormandine, Osmand, Witch, Wizard

**Necrosis** Gangrene, Infarct, Sphacelus

**Nectar** Ambrosia, Amrita, Honey, Mead

**Ned(dy)** Donkey, Kelly, Ludd

**Need(ed), Needy** Absence, Ananke, Beggarly, Call, Demand, Desiderata, Egence, Egency, Essential, Exigency, Gap, Gerundive, Impecunious, Indigent, → LACK, Mister, Prerequisite, Pressing, PRN, Rainy day, Require, Special, Strait, Strapped, Want

**Needle(s)** Acerose, Acicular, Aciform, Acupuncture, Anger, Antagonise, Between, Bodkin, Cleopatra's, Darner, Darning, Dip, Dipping, Dry-point, Electric, Etching, Goad, Gramophone, Hagedorn, Hype, Hypodermic, Ice, Icicle, Inoculate, Knitting, Leucotome, Magnetic, Mainline, Miff, Monolith, Neeld, Neele, Netting, Obelisk, Packing, Pine, Pinnacle, Pique, Pointer, Prick, R(h)aphis, Sew, Sharp, Spanish, Spicule, Spike, Spine, Spud, Stylus, Tattoo, Tease, Thorn, Wire

**Needless** Undue

**Needlewoman** Cleopatra, Seamstress

**Needlework** Applique, Baste, Crewel, Drawn(-thread), Embroidery, Fag(g)oting, Fancy work, Gros point, Lacet, Mola, Patchwork, Petit point, Piqué, Plainwork, Rivière, Sampler, Smocking, Spanish, Tapestry, Tattoo, White-seam, Woolwork, Worsted-work

**Ne'er-do-well** Badmash, Budmash, Bum, Good-for-nothing, Scallywag, Scullion, Shiftless, Skellum, Waster, Wastrel

**Negation, Negative** Ambrotype, Anion, Apophatic, Cathode, Denial, Double, Downside, Enantiosis, False, Infinitant, Ne, No, Non, Nope, Nullify, Pejorative, Photograph, Refusal, Resinous, Unresponsive, Veto, Yin

**Neglect(ed), Neglectful, Negligence, Negligent** Careless, Casual, Cinderella, Contributory, Cuff, Default, Dereliction, Disregard, Disuse, Failure, Forget, Forlorn, For(e)slack, G-devant, Heedless, Inadvertence, Inattention, Incivism, Laches, Malpractice, Misprision, Omission, Oversight, Pass, Pass-up, Rack and ruin, → REMISS, Scamp, Shirk, Slight, Slipshod, Undone, Unilateral, Unnoticed, Waif, Wanton

▷ **Neglected** *may indicate* an anagram

**Negligee** Déshabillé, Manteau, Mob, Nightgown, Peignoir, Robe

**Negligible** Fig, Minimal

**Negotiate, Negotiator** Arbitrate, Arrange, Bargain, Barter, Clear, Confer, Deal, Diplomat, Haggle, Intercede, Interdeal, Intermediary, Liaise, Manoeuvre, Mediator, Parley, Petition, Talk, Trade, Transact, Treat(y), Tret, Weather

**Negro(id)** → AFRICAN, Baganda, Bambara, Barotse, Bemba, Bergdama, Bini, Black, Blackamoor, Buck, Chewa, Creole, Cuffee, Cuffy, Damara, Dinge, Duala, Dyula, Ebon(y), Edo, Efik, Ethiop, Ewe, Fang, Ga, Ganda, Gullah, Hausa, Hottentot, Hutu, Ibibio, Ibo, Igbo, Igorot, Jim Crow, Kikuyu, Kongo, Luba, Luganda, Malinke, Maninke, Mestee, Moke, Moor, Mossi, Mustee, Ndebele, Nilote, Nupe, Nyanja, Nyoro, Ovambo, Pondo, Quashee, Quashie, Sambo, Snowball, Sotho, Spade, Susu, Temne, Thick-lips, Tiv, Tonga, Tsonga, Tswana, Twi, Uncle Tom, Venda, Watu(t)si, Wolof, Xhosa, Yoruba, Zambo, Zulu

**Negus** Emperor, Rumfruction, Selassie

**Nehru** Pandit

**Neigh** Bray, Hinny, Nicker, Whicker, Whinny

**Neighbour(ly), Neighbouring, Neighbours** Abut(ter), Adjoin, Alongside, Amicable, Bor, Border, But, Friendly, Joneses, Nearby, Next-door, Vicinal

**Neighbourhood(s)** Acorn®, Area, Community, District, Environs, Locality, Precinct, Vicinage, Vicinity

**Neither** Nor

**Nell(ie), Nelly** Bly, Dean, Trent

**Nelson** Columnist, Eddy, Horatio

**Nemesis** Alastor, Avenger, Deserts, Downfall, Fate, Retribution, Revenge

**Neodymium** Nd

**Neolithic** Avebury, Halafian, Skara Brae, Stonehenge

**Neon** Ne

**Nepalese** Gurkha

**Neper** N

**Nephrite** Yu

**Nepotism** Kin, Partisan, Patronage

**Neptune** God, Planet, Poseidon

**Neptunium** Np

**Nerd** Anorak, Geek, Otaku

**Nereid** Cymodoce, Nymph, Panope

**Nerve(s), Nervous(ness), Nervure, Nerve centre, Nervy** Abdabs, Abducens, Accessory, Acoustic, Afferent, Aflutter, Afraid, Alveolar, Antsy, Appestat, Auditory, Autonomic, Axon, Baroreceptor, Bottle, Bouton, Brass neck, Buccal, Butterflies, Chord, Chutzpah, Collywobbles, Column, Commissure, Cones, Courage, Cranial, Cyton, Dendron, Depressor, Edgy, Effector, Efferent, Electrotonus, Epicritic, Excitor, Facial, Fearful, Fidgety, Gall, Ganglion, Glossopharyngeal, Grit, Guts, Habdabs, Heart-string, High, Highly-strung, Hyp, Hypoglossal, Impudence, Jitters, Jittery, Jumpy, Median, Mid-rib, Motor, Moxie, Myelon, Nappy, Neck, Neurological, Nidus, Oculomotor, Olfactory, On edge, Optic, Pavid, Perikaryon, Pons, Proprioceptor, Protopathic, Rad, Radial, Receptor, Restiform, Restless, Sacral, Sangfroid, Sass, Sauce, Sciatic, Screaming abdabs, Screaming meemies, Sensory, Shaky, Shpilkes, Solar plexus, Somatic, Splanchnic, Spunk, Squirrel(l)y, Stage fright, Steel, Strung-up, Sympathetic, Synapse, Tense, Timorous, Tizzy, Toey, Tongue-tied, Trembler, Tremulous, Trigeminal, Trochlear, Twitchy, Ulnar, Uptight, Vagus, Vapours, Vasodilator, Vestibular, Vestibulocochlear, Wandering, Willies, Windy, Wired (up), Wittery, Yips

**Nervous disease, Nervous disorder** Chorea, Epilepsy, Neuritis, Tarantism, Tetany

▷ **Nervously** *may indicate* an anagram

**Ness** Cape, Headland, Ras

**Nessus** Centaur

**Nest** Aerie, Aery, Aiery, Ayrie, Bike, Bink, Brood, Byke, Cabinet, Cage, Caliology, Clutch, Dray, Drey, Eyrie, Eyry, Guns, Hive, Lodge, Love, Nid, Nide, Nidify, Nidus, Norwegian, Sett, Termitarium, Turkey, Wurley

**Nestle** Burrow, Coorie, Cose, Courie, Cuddle, Nuzzle, Rest, Snug(gle)

**Nestor** Counsellor, Kea, King, Parrot, Sage

**Net(ting), Nets, Network(ing), Networker** Anastomosis, Bamboo, BR, Bunt, Bus, Butterfly, Cast, Casting, Catch, Caul, Clap, Clathrate, Clear, Co-ax(ial), Cobweb, →COMPUTER NETWORK, Craquelure, Crinoline, Criss-cross, Crossover, Diane, Drift, Earn, Eel-set, Enmesh, Equaliser, Fetch, File server, Filet, Final, Fish, Fisherman, Flew, Flue, Fret, Fyke, Gain, Gill, →GRID, Hammock, Heliscoop, Honeycomb, Hose, Insect, Kiddle, Lace, LAN, Land, Landing, Lattice, Leap, Line, Linin, Mains, Malines, Mattress, Maze, →MESH, Mist, Mosquito, Mycelium, Nerve, Neural, Neuropil, Old boys', PCN, Plexus, Portal system, Pound, Pout, Purse-seine, Quadripole, Reseau, Rete, Retiary, Reticle, Reticulate, Reticulum, Ring, Safety, Sagene, Scoop, Screen, Sean, Seine, Senior, Set(t), Shark, Skype®, Snood, Speed, Stake, Sweep-seine, Symplast, System, Tangle, Tela, Telex, Tissue, Toil, Torpedo, Trammel, Trap, Trawl, Trepan, Tulle, Tunnel, Wire

**Netball** Let

**Nether** Below, Inferior, Infernal, Lower, Under

**Nettle(rash)** Anger, Annoy, Day, Dead, Hemp, Hives, Horse, Irritate, Labiate, Nark, Ongaonga, Pellitory, Pique, Ramee, Rami, Ramie, Rhea, Rile, Roman, Ruffle, Sting, Urtica(ceae), Urticaria

**Neuralgia, Neuritis** Migraine, Pleurodynia, Sciatica, Tic

**Neurosis** Combat, Compulsion, Hang up, Obsessive-compulsive, Shellshock, Trichotillomania

**Neuter** Castrate, Gib, Impartial, Neutral, Sexless, Spay

**Neutral(ise)** Alkalify, Angel gear, Buffer zone, Counteract, Degauss, Grey, Impartial, Inactive, Schwa, Sheva, Shiva, Unbiased

**Neutron(s)** Delayed, Fast, Nucleon, Prompt, Slow, Thermal, Virgin

**Never(more)** As if, Nary, Nathemo(re), No more, Nowise, St Tibb's Eve

**Never-ending** Age-long

**Never mind** Nix my dolly

**Nevertheless** Algate, All the same, Anyhow, But, Even, Howbeit, However, Quand même, Still, Tout de même, Yet

**New(s), Newborn, News agency** Avant garde, Bulletin, Communique, Copy, Coranto, Dope, Euphobia, Evangel, Flash, Forest, Fresh, Fudge, Gen, Green, Griff, Info(rmation), Initiate, Innovation, Intake, Intelligence, Itar Tass, Item, Kerygma, Latest, Mint, Modern, N, Novel, Oil(s), Original, PA, Paragraph, Pastures, Pristine, Propaganda, Raw, Reborn, Recent, Report, Reuter, Scoop, Sidebar, Snippet, Span, Splash, Split, Stranger, Tass, Teletext®, Tidings, Ultramodern, Unco, Update, Usenet, Wire service, Word, Young

▷ **New** *may indicate* an anagram

**New boy** Gyte

**Newcomer** Dog, Freshman, Griffin, Immigrant, Jackaroo, Jackeroo, Jillaroo, Johnny-come-lately, L, Learner, Newbie, Novice, Parvenu, Pilgrim, Settler, Tenderfoot, Upstart

**Newfoundland** Dog, Nana, Vinland

**Newgate** Calendar

**Newly wed** Benedick, Benedict, Bride, Groom, Honeymooner, Neogamist

**Newman** Cardinal, Noggs, Paul

**New moon** Rosh Chodesh

**New Orleans** Big easy

**Newsman, News-reader** Announcer, Editor, Journalist, Legman, Press, Reporter, Sub, Sysop

**Newsmonger, News-vendor** Butcher, Gossip, Quidnunc

**Newspaper** Beast, Big Issue, Blat(t), Broadsheet, Compact, Courier, Daily, Express, Fanzine, Feuilleton, Freesheet, Gazette, Guardian, Heavy, Herald, Intelligencer, Izvestia, Journal, Jupiter, Le Monde, Mercury, National, Organ, Patent inside, Patent outside, Post, Pravda, Press, Print, Rag, Red-top, Scandal sheet, Scotsman, Sheet, Spoiler, Squeak, Sun, Tabloid, Today, Yellow Press

**Newsreel** Actualities

**Newsworthy** Topical

**Newt(s)** Ask(er), Eft, Evet, Swift, Triton, Urodela

**Newton** N

**New World** USA

**New Year** Hogmanay, Ne'er-day, Rosh Hashana(h), Tet

**New York(er)** Big Apple, Bronx, Coney Island, Gotham, Knickerbocker, Manhattan, Queens

**New Zealand(er)** Aotearoa, Diggers, Enzed, Jafa, Kiwi, Maori, Mooloo, Moriori, .nz, Pakeha, Pig Island, Ronz(er), Shagroon, Zelanian

**Next** Adjacent, Adjoining, After, Alongside, Beside, By, Following, Immediate, Later, Nearest, Neighbour, Neist, Proximate, Proximo, Sine, Subsequent, Syne, Then, Thereafter

**Nib(s)** Cocoa, J, Pen, Point, Tip

**Nibble** Bite, Brouse, Browse, Byte, Canapé, Crop, Eat, Gnaw, Knap(ple), Moop, Moup, Munch, Nag, Nepit, Nosh, Peck, Pick, Snack

**Niblick** Wedge

**Nice(ly), Nicety** Accurate, Amene, Appealing, Cool, Dainty, Fastidious, Fine, Finical, Genteel, Lepid, Mooi, Ninepence, Pat, Pleasant, Precise, Quaint, Rare, Refined, Subtil(e), Subtle, Sweet, T, To a t

**Niche** Alcove, Almehrahb, Almery, Ambry, Apse, Aumbry, Awmrie, Awmry, Columbarium, Cranny, Exedra, Fenestella, Mihrab, Recess, Slot

**Nicholas** Santa

**Nick(ed)** Appropriate, Arrest, Bin, Blag, Can, Chip, Cly, Colin, Copshop, Crib, Cut, Denay, Dent, Deny, →**DEVIL**, Erose, Groove, Hoosegow, Kitty, Knock, Nab, Nap, Nim, Nock, Notch, Pinch, Pocket, Pook, Pouk, Prison, Run in, Scratch, Serrate, Sneak, →**STEAL**, Steek, Swan-upping, Swipe, Thieve, Whip, Wirricow, Worricow, Worrycow

**Nickel (silver)** Coin, Garnierite, Jitney, Millerite, Ni, Packfong, Paktong, Zaratite

**Nicker** Bonduc, Neigh, Whinny

**Nickname** Alias, Byname, Byword, Cognomen, Monicker, So(u)briquet, To-name

**Nicotine** Tobacco, Weed

**Nifty** Smart, Stylish

**Niger** RN

**Nigeria(n)** Biafran, Cross River, Efik, Hausa, Ibibio, Ibo, Igbo, .ng, Nupe, Tiv, WAN, Yoruba

**Niggard(ly)** Dry-fist, Illiberal, Mean, Miser, Near-(be)gaun, Nippy, Nirlie, Nirlit, Parsimonious, Penny wise, Pinchcommons, Pinchgut, Pinchpenny, Scrunt, Skinflint, Tightwad

**Niggle** Carp, Gripe, Nag, Potter, Trifle

**Night(s), Nightfall** Acronical, Acronychal, Arabian, Burns, Darkling, Darkmans, First, Gaudy, Guest, Guy Fawkes, Hen, Leila, Nacht, Nicka-nan, Nutcrack, Nyx, Opening, School, Sleepover, Stag, Twelfth, Twilight, Walpurgis, Watch, White

**Night-blindness** Day-sight, Nyctalopia

**Night-cap** Biggin, Cocoa, Kilmarnock cowl, Nip, Pirnie, Sundowner

**Nightclub** Boite de nuit, Clip joint, Dive, Honkytonk, Hot spot

**Night-dew** Serein, Serene

**Nightdress** Baby doll, Wylie-coat

**Nightingale** Bulbul, Florence, Frog, Jugger, Lind, Philomel, Philomena, Scutari, Swedish, Watch

**Nightjar** Chuck-will's-widow, Churn-owl, Evejar, Fern-owl, Goatsucker, Poorwill, Potoo

**Night-light** Moonbeam

**Nightmare, Nightmarish** Cacod(a)emon, Ephialtes, Incubus, Kafkaesque, Oneirodynia, Phantasmagoria

**Night-rider** Revere

**Nightshade** Atropin(e), Belladonna, Bittersweet, Black, Circaea, Deadly, Dwale, Enchanter's, Henbane, Morel, Solanum, Woody

**Nightwatchman** Charley, Charlie, Rug-gown

**Nightwork** Lucubrate

**Nihilist** Anarchist, Red, Sceptic

**Nil** Nothing, Nought, Zero

**Nile** Albert, Blue, Luvironza, Victoria, White

**Nimble(ness), Nimbly** Active, →**AGILE**, Alert, Deft, Deliver, Fleet, Legerity, Light, Light-footed, Lissom(e), Lithe, Quiver, Sciolto, Springe, Spry, Supple, Sure-footed, Swack, Wan(d)le, Wannel, Wight, Ya(u)ld

**Nimbus** Aura, Aureole, Cloud, Gloriole, Halo

**Nimrod** Hunter

**Nincompoop** Ass, Fool, Imbecile, Moron, Ninny, Stupid

**Nine, Ninth** Choral, Ennead, Muses, Nonary, Nonet, Novenary, Pins, Sancho, Skittles, Tailors, Worthies

**Nine hundred** Sampi

**Nine of diamonds** Curse of Scotland

**Nineteen(th)** Bar, Decennoval
**Ninetieth, Ninety** N, Nonagesimal
**Ninevite** Assyrian
**Ninny (hammer)** Fool, Goose, Idiot, Stupid, Tony
**Ninon** Nan
**Niobium** Nb
**Nip(per), Nippers** Bite, Brat, Check, Chela, Chill, Claw, Cutpurse, Dip, Dram, Fang, Foil, Gook, Jack Frost, Jap, Lad, Lop, Nep, Nirl, Outsiders, Peck, Pickpocket, Pincers, Pinch, Pook, Pop, Scotch, Sneap, Susan, Tad, Talon, Taste, Tot, Tweak, Urchin, Vice, Vise
**Nipa** At(t)ap, Palm
**Nipple** Dug, Grease, Jogger's, Mastoid, Pap, Teat
**Nis** Brownie, Goblin, Kobold, Sprite
**Nit** Egg, Insect, Louse
**Nit-picking** Carping, Pedantry, Quibble
**Nitre** Saltpetre
**Nitric, Nitrogen** Azote, Azotic, Gas, N, Quinoline
**Nitroglycerine** Glonoin, Soup
**Nitwit** Ass, Flat, Fool, Scatterbrain, Simpleton, →STUPID
**No** Aikona, Denial, Na(e), Nah, Naw, Negative, Nix, Nope, Nyet, O, Refusal
**Noah** Arkite, Beery, Utnapishtim
**Nob(by)** Grandee, Parage, Prince, Swell, Toff
**Nobble** Dope, Hilch, Injure, Interfere
▷ **Nobbled** *may indicate* an anagram
**Nobelium** No
**Noble(man), Noblewoman, Nobility, Nobly** Adela, Adele, Adeline, Aneurin, Aristocrat, Atheling, Baron(et), Baroness, Baronet(ess), Baronne, Bart, Blue blood, Boyar, Brave, Bt, Burgrave, Childe, Contessa, Count, County, Cousin, Daimio, Datuk, Dauphine, Dom, Don, Doucepere, Douzeper(s), Duc, Duke, Duniwassal, Earl, Empress, Eorl, Ethel, Eupatrid, Fine, Galahad, Gent, Glorious, Graf, Grandee, Grandeur, Great, Heroic, Hidalgo, Highborn, Illustrious, Infant, Jarl, Junker, King, Landgrave, Lofty, Lord, Maestoso, Magnate, Magnificent, Magnifico, Manly, Margrave, Marquis, Mona, Nair, Nawab, Nayar, Palatine, Patrician, Patrick, Peer, Rank, Ritter, Rose, Seigneur, Seignior, Sheik(h), Stately, Sublime, Thane, Thegn, Titled, Toiseach, Toisech, Vavasour, Vicomte, Vidame, Viscount, Waldgrave
**Noble gas(es)** Argon, Helium, Krypton, Neon, Radon, Xenon
**Nobody** Diarist, Gnatling, Jack-straw, Nebbish, Nemo, None, Nonentity, Nyaff, Pipsqueak, Pooter, Quat, Schlepp, Scoot, Shlep, Zero
**Nocturnal (creature)** Bat, Galago, Moth, Night, Owl
**Nod(ding)** Agree, Assent, Beck(on), Bob, Browse, Catnap, Cernuous, Dip, Doze, Drowsy, Headbang, Mandarin, Nutant, Somnolent
**Node, Nodular, Nodule** Ascending, Boss, Descending, Enhydros, Geode, Knot, Lump, Lymph, Milium, Pea-iron, Ranvier, Root, Septarium, Swelling, Thorn, Tophus, Tubercle
**No doubt** Iwis, Ywis
**Noel** Christmas, Coward, Yule
**Nog(gin)** Ale, Cup, →DRINK, Peg
**No go** Anergia
**No good** Dud, NG, Ropy
**No-hoper** Drongo, Gone goose, Goner
**Noise, Noisy** Ambient, Babel, Bedlam, Big, Blare, Blat(t), Bleep, Blip, Blue murder, Bobbery, Boing, Boink, Bray, Bruit, Cangle, Charm, Cheep, Chellup, Clam, Clamant, Clamour, Clangour, Clash, Clatter, Clitter, Clutter, Coil, Crackle, Creak, Deen, Din, Dirdum, Discord, Euphonia, Euphony, F, Flicker, Fuss, Hewgh, Howlround, Hubbub, Hue, Hullabaloo, Hum, Hurly-burly, Knocking, Loud, Mush, Obstreperous, Phut, Ping, Pink, Plangent, Quonk, Racket, Raucous, Report, Risp, Roar, Roarie, Roary, Robustious,

Rorie, Rort, Rory, Row(dow-dow), Rowdedow, Rowdy(dow)(dy), Rucous, Rumble, Schottky, Schottky-Utis, Scream, Screech, Shindig, Shindy, Shot, Shreek, Shreik, Shriech, Shriek, Slosh, Solar, Sone, Sonorous, Sound, Strepent, Strepitation, Strepitoso, Stridor, Surface, Thermal, Thunder, Tinnitus, Top, Trumpet, Tumult, → **UPROAR**, VIP, Visual, Vociferous, Whinny, White, Whoomph, Zoom

**Noisome** Fetid, Invidious, Noxious, Offensive, Rank

**No longer** Ex, Past

**Nomad(ic)** Amalekite, Ammonites, Bedawin, Bedu, Bed(o)uin, Berber, Chal, Drifter, Edom(ite), Errant, Fula(h), Gypsy, Hottentot, Hun, Hunter-gatherer, Hyksos, Itinerant, Kurd, Kyrgyz, Lapp, Rom, Rootless, Rover, Saracen, Sarmatian, Strayer, Tsigane, Tsigany, Tuareg, Turk(o)man, Unsettled, Vagabond, Vagrant, Wanderer, Zigan

**Noman** Ta(r)tar

**No man's land** Tom Tiddler's ground

**Nome** Province

**Nomenclature** Term

**Nominal** Formal, Onomastic, Titular, Token, Trifling

**Nominate, Nomination** Appoint, Baptism, Designate, Elect, Postulate, Present, → **PROPOSE**, Slate, Specify, Term

**Nomogram** Abac

**No more** Gone, Napoo

**Nomothete** Enactor, Legislator

**Non-Aboriginal** Wudjula

**Non-attachment** Limbo

**Non-attender** Absentee, Recusant

**Non-attribute** Ens

**Non-believer** Atheist, Cynic, Infidel, Nothingarian, Sceptic

**Non-belligerent** Neutral

**Non-catalyst** Zymogen

**Nonchalance, Nonchalant** Blasé, Carefree, Casual, Cool, Debonair, Insouciant, Jaunty, Poco

**Non-Christian** New-age, Saracen

**Noncommittal** Guarded, Pussyfoot, Trimmer

**Non-communist** West

**Non-conductor** Insulatro

**Non-conformist, Non-conformity** Beatnik, Bohemian, Chapel, Deviant, Dissent(er), Dissident, Drop-out, Ebenezer, Enfant terrible, Heresiarch, Heretic, Maverick, Odd-ball, Outlaw, Pantile, Patarine, Rebel, Recusant, Renegade, Renegate, Sectarian, Wesleyan

**Nondescript** Dull, Formless, Grey, Insipid, Neutral, Nyaff

**Non-directional** Scalar

**Non-drip** Thixotropic

**None** Nada, Nary, Nil, Nought, Zero

**Nonentity** Cipher, Nebbich, Nebbish(er), Nebish, Nobody, Pipsqueak, Quat, Whippersnapper

**Non-essential** Adiaphoron, Disposable, Extrinsic, Incidental

**Nonesuch** Model, Nonpareil, Paradigm, Paragon, Rarity

**Nonetheless** Mind you

▷ **Nonetheless** *may indicate* an 'o' to be omitted

**Non-existent** Unbeing, Virtual

**Non-finite** Verbid

**Non-Gypsy** Gajo, Gorgio

**Non-interference** Laissez faire

**Non-Jewish** Gentile, Goy, Shegetz, Shi(c)ksa, Shkotzim, Sho(y)getz

**Non-juror** Usager

**Non-Maori** Tangata tiriti, Tauiwi

**Non-Muslim** Dhimmi, Raia, Rayah
**Non-observance** Breach
**No-nonsense** Hardball, Strict
**Non-orthodox** Progressive
**Non-pairing** Ameiosis
**Nonpareil** Nonesuch, Pearl, Peerless, Type, Unequal, Unique
**Nonplus(sed)** Baffle, Bewilder, Blank, Perplex, Stump
**Non-professional** Amateur, Laic
**Non-radiative** Auger
**Non-resident** Extern, Outlier
**Non-runner** Scratched, Solid
**Nonsense** Absurdity, Amphigon, Amphigory, Balderdash, Baloney, Bilge, Bizzo,
  Blague, Blah, Blarney, Blat(her), Blatherskite, Blether, Bollocks, Boloney, Bora(c)k,
  Borax, Bosh, Bs, Bull, Bulldust, Bullshit, Bull's wool, Buncombe, Bunk, Bunkum, Chaff,
  Clamjamfr(a)y, Clamjamphrie, Claptrap, Cobblers, Cock, Cockamamie, Cod, Codswallop,
  Crap, Crapola, Drivel, Dust, Eyewash, Faddle, Falderal, Fandangle, Farce, Fiddlededee,
  Fiddle-faddle, Fiddlesticks, Flannel, Flapdoodle, Flim-flam, Folderol, Footling, Fudge,
  Gaff, Galimatias, Gammon, Gas and gaiters, Get away, Gibberish, Gobbledygook,
  Guff, Gum, Hanky-panky, Haver, Hogwash, Hokum, Hooey, Hoop-la, Horsefeathers,
  Humbug, Irishism, Jabberwocky, Jazz, Jive, Kibosh, Kidstakes, Malark(e)y, Moonshine,
  Mouthwash, Mumbo-jumbo, My eye, Niaiserie, Phooey, Piffle, Pishogue, Pshaw, Pulp,
  Ratbaggery, Rats, Rawmaish, Rhubarb, Rigmarole, Rot, Rubbish, Scat, Shenanigans,
  Shit(e), Squit, Stuff, Taradiddle, Tom(foolery), Tommy-rot, Tosh, Trash, Tripe, Tush,
  Twaddle, Unreason, Waffle
**Non-sequitur** Anacoluthia, Irish bull, Irrelevant
**Non-smoker** NS
**Non-specialist** User-friendly
**Non-standard** Anomalous
**Non-starter** No-no
**Non-stick** PTFE, Teflon®, Tusche
**Non-stop** Through
**Non-transferable** Adiabatic
**Non-U** Naff
**Non-Unionist** Freerider
**Non-violence** Ahimsa, Pacificism, Satyagraha
**Non-white** Coloured, Yolk
**Noodle(s)** Capellini, Crispy, Daw, Fool, Head, Laksa, Lokshen, Manicotti, Mee, Moony,
  Ninny, Pasta, Sammy, Simpleton, Soba, Udon
**Nook** Alcove, Angle, Corner, Cranny, Niche, Recess, Rookery
**Noon** Am end, M, Midday, N, Narrowdale
**No one** Nemo, None
**Noose** Fank, Halter, Hempen caudle, Lanyard, Loop, Necktie, Rebecca, Rope, Rope's end,
  Snare, Twitch, Widdy
▶ **Nor** *see* **NOT**
**Nordic, Norse(man)** Aryan, Icelander, Norn, → **NORWEGIAN**, Scandinavian, Viking
**Norm** Canon, Criterion, Rule, Standard
**Normal** Average, Conventional, Customary, Everyday, General, Natural, Norm, Ordinary,
  Orthodox, Par, Perpendicular, Regular, Standard, Straightforward, Unexceptional,
  Usu(al)
**Normal eyes** Emmetropia
**Norman** French, Mailer, Rufus
**North(ern), Northerner** Arctic, Boreal, Cispontine, Copperhead, Dalesman,
  Doughface, Eskimo, Geographic, Hyperborean, Icelander, Magnetic, N, Norland, Runic,
  Scotia, Scotsman, Sea, Septentrion, True, Up

**North American (Indian)** Injun, Papoose, Red(skin), Scalper, Totemist, Tribe

## NORTH AMERICAN INDIANS

*3 letters:*
Fox
Sao
Ute

*4 letters:*
Crow
Dene
Erie
Hopi
Innu
Pima
Pomo
Sauk
Tewa
Tiwa
Yana
Yuma
Zuni

*5 letters:*
Brave
Cajun
Creek
Haida
Huron
Makah
Miwok
Omaha
Osage
Piute
Ponca
Sioux
Taino
Teton

*6 letters:*
Abnaki
Apache
Cayuga
Galibi
Klooch
Lakota
Micmac
Mixtec
Mohave
Mohawk
Navaho

Nootka
Oglala
Ojibwa
Oneida
Paiute
Papago
Pawnee
Pequot
Plains
Pueblo
Quapaw
Sachem
Salish
Sannup
Shasta
Siwash
Yanqui

*7 letters:*
Abenaki
Arapaho
Caddoan
Chibcha
Chinook
Choctaw
Gwich'in
Hidatsa
Kikapoo
Klootch
Kutenai
Mahican
Miskito
Mission
Mohegan
Mohican
Mugwump
Natchez
Norteno
Ojibway
Palouse
Pontiac
Senecan
Serrano
Shawnee
Shuswap
Tahitan
Tlingit
Wichita

Wyandot
Yalkama
Zapotec

*8 letters:*
Algonkin
Angeleno
Cahuilla
Cherokee
Cheyenne
Chippewa
Comanche
Delaware
Flathead
Geronimo
Hiawatha
Iroquois
Kickapoo
Kootenai
Kootenay
Kwakiutl
Menomini
Mikasuki
Mogollon
Muskogee
Nez Percé
Okanagon
Okinagan
Onondaga
Sagamore
Sahaptan
Sahaptin
Seminole
Shoshone

*9 letters:*
Algonkian
Algonquin
Blackfoot
Chichimec
Chickasaw
Chipewyan
Manhattan
Melungeon
Menominee
Mescalero
Muskogean
Potawatom

Sahaptian
Shahaptin
Suquamish
Tsimshian
Tuscarora
Wampanoag
Winnebago
Wyandotte
Yawelmani

*10 letters:*
Algonquian
Copperskin
Crazy Horse
Halkomelem
Hooded Crow
Miniconjou
Montagnais
Montagnard
Muskhogean
Pocahontas
Six Nations
Tarahumara
Uto-Aztecan

*11 letters:*
Assiniboine
Basket Maker
Five Nations
Kiowa Apache
Massachuset
Minneconjou
Narraganset
Sitting Bull

*12 letters:*
Mound Builder

*13 letters:*
Massachusetts
Northern Piute
Southern Piute
Susquehannock

*14 letters:*
Northern Paiute
Southern Paiute

**Northern Ireland** NI, Six Counties

**North star** Tyrian cynosure
**Northwestern** Aeolis
**Norway, Norwegian** Bokmal, Fortinbras, Landsma(a)l, N, Nordic, Norweyan, Nynorsk, Rollo, Scandinavian
**Nose, Nosy** A(d)jutage, Aquiline, Beak, Bergerac, Boko, Bouquet, Breather, Catarrhine, Conk, Copper, Cromwell, Curious, Desman, Droop, Fink, Flair, Gnomon, Grass, Grecian, Greek, Grog-blossom, Honker, Hooknose, Hooter, Index, Informer, Instinct, Leptorrhine, Meddle, Muffle, Muzzle, Nark, Neb, Nozzle, Nuzzle, Parker, Platyrrhine, Proboscis, Prying, Pug, Red, Retrousse, Rhinal, Roman, Scent, Schnozzle, Shove, Smelly, Sneb, Sniff, Snoot, Snout, Snub, Squeal, Stag, Stickybeak, Toffee
**Noseband** Barnacle, Cavesson, Musrol
**Nose-bleed** Epistaxis
**Nosh** Eat, Food, Nibble, Snack
**Nostalgia** Longing, Memory lane, Oldie, Retrophilia, Wistfulness, Yearning
**Nostril(s)** Blowhole, Cere, Choana, Nare
**Nostrum** Elixir, Medicine, Remede, Remedy
**Not, Nor** Aikona, Dis-, Na(e), Narrow A, Ne, Neither, Never, No, Pas, Polled, Taint
**Notable, Notability** Conspicuous, Dignitary, Distinguished, Eminent, Especial, Landmark, Large, Lion, Memorable, Personage, Signal, Striking, Unco, VIP, Worthy
**Not allowed** NL
▷ **Not allowed** *may indicate* a word to be omitted
**Notary** Apostolical, Ecclesiastical, Escribano, Scrivener
**Not at all** Au contraire
**Notation(al)** Benesh, Cantillation, Descriptive, Entry, Formalism, Hexadecimal, Infix, Memo, Octal, Polish, Positional, Postfix, Romic, Scientific, Staff, Tablature
**Notch(ed)** Crena(l), Crenel, Cut, Dent, Erode, Erose, Gain, Gap, Gimp, Indent, Insection, Jag, Kerf, Mush, Nick, Nock, Raffle, Score, Serrate, Serrulation, Sinus, Snick, Tally, Vandyke
**Not clear** Blocked, NL, Obscure, Opaque, Pearl
**Note(s), Notebook, Noted** A, Acciaccatura, Accidental, Advance, Adversaria, Advice, Agogic, Apostil(le), Apparatus, Appoggiatura, Arpeggio, Auxiliary, B, Bill(et), Bradbury, Bread and butter letter, Breve, C, Cedula, Chit(ty), Chord, Cob, Comment, Commentary, Conceit, Continental, Cover, Credit, Crotchet, Currency, D, Debit, Delivery, Demand, Dig, Dispatch, Do(h), Dominant, Double-dotted, E, E-la, Entry, F, Fa(h), False, Fame, Fiver, Five-spot, Flag up, Flat, Flim, G, Gamut, Gloss(ary), Gold, Grace, Greenback, Greeny, Gruppetto, Harmonic scale, Heed, Hemiole, Hypate, Identic, Index rerum, IOU, Iron man, Item(ise), Jot(tings), Jug(-jug), Key, Kudos, La, Large, Leading, Letter, Lichanos, Line(r), Log, Long, Longa, Lower mordent, Marginalia, Mark, Masora(h), Masoretic, Me, Mediant, Melisma, Melody, Memo(randum), Mese, Message, Mi, Minim, Minute, Missive, →**MONEY**, Mordent, Music, Muzak®, Nachschlag, Natural, NB, Nete, Neum(e), Oblong, Observe, Octave, Oncer, On record, Open, Ostmark, Outline, Parhypate, Passing, Postal, Post-it®, Pound, Promissory, Prompt, Proslambanomenos, Protocol, PS, Quarter, Quaver, Rag-money, Re, Reciting, Record, Remark, Renown, Request, Right, Root, Scholion, Scholium, Scotch catch, Scotch snap, Semibreve, Semiquaver, Semitone, Sensible, Septimole, Sextolet, Sharp, Shinplaster, Shoulder, Si, Sick, Sixteenth, Sixty-fourth, Sleeve, Smacker, Snuff-paper, So(h), Sol, Some, Stem, Strike, Subdominant, Submediant, Subtonic, Supertonic, Te, Ten(ner), Third, Thirty-second, Tierce, Tonic, Treasury, Treble, Two-spot, Undecimole, Ut, Variorum, Verbal, Wad, Warison, Whole, Wolf, Wood
**Note-case** Pochette, Purse, Wallet
▷ **Notes** *may indicate* the use of letters A–G
**Noteworthy** Eminent, Extraordinary, Memorable, Particular, Signal, Special
**Nothing, Nought** Buckshee, Bugger-all, Chargeless, Cipher, Damn-all, Devoid, Diddlysquat, Emptiness, FA, Gratis, Jack, Love, Nada, Napoo, Naught, Nihil, Niks-nie,

Nil, Nix(-nie), Noumenon, Nowt, Nuffin, Nullity, O, Ought, Rap, Rien, Small beer, Sweet FA, Void, Z, Zero, Zilch, Zip(po)

**Notice(able)** Ad(vertisement), Advance, Advice, Affiche, Apprise, Attention, Avis(o), Banns, Bill, Blurb, Bold, Bulletin, Caveat, Circular, Clock, Cognisance, Crit, D, DA, Descry, Detect, Discern, Discover, Dismissal, Enforcement, Evident, Gaum, Get, Gorm, Handbill, → **HEED**, Intimation, Marked, Mensh, Mention, Message, NB, No(t)chel, Obit(uary), Observe, Oyez, Perceptible, Placard, Plaque, Playbill, Poster, Press, Proclamation, Prominent, Pronounced, → **REMARK**, Review, See, Short, Signal, Si quis, Spot, Spy, Sticker, Tent, Warning, Whip

**Notify, Notification** Acquaint, Advise, Apprise, Aviso, Awarn, Inform, Payslip, → **TELL**, Warn

**Notion(al)** Academic, Chimera, Conceit, → **CONCEPT**, Crotchet, Fancy, Hunch, Idea, Idée, Idolum, Inkling, Opinion, Reverie, Vapour, Whim

**Notoriety, Notorious** Arrant, Byword, Crying, Egregious, Esclandre, Fame, Flagrant, Ill-fame, Infamous, Infamy, Legendary, Notour, Proverbial, Réclame, → **RENOWN**, Repute

**No trump** Laical, Lay, NT

**Notwithstanding** Albe(e), Although, Despite, Even, For, Howbeit, However, Mau(l)gre, Natheless(e), Nath(e)less, Naythles, Nevertheless, Spite

**Nougat** Montelimar, Sundae

▸ **Nought** *see* **NOTHING**

**Noughts and crosses** Tic(k)-tac(k)-to(e)

**Noumenon** Thing-in-itself

**Noun** Abstract, Agent, Agentive, Aptote, Collective, Common, Concrete, Count, Gerund, Mass, N, Proper, Seg(h)olate, Substantive, Tetraptote, Verbal, Vocative

**Nourish(ing), Nourishment** Aliment, Battill, Cherish, Cultivate, Feed, Grub, Ingesta, Manna, Meat, Nurse, Nurture, Nutrient, Promote, Repast, Replenish, Sustenance, Trophic

**Nous** Intellect, Intelligence, Reason, Sense

**Nova Scotia(n)** Acadia, Blue-nose

**Novel(ty)** Aga-saga, Airport, Bildungsroman, Bonkbuster, Book, Campus, Change, Clarissa, Different, Dime, Dissimilar, E-book, Emma, Epistolary, Erewhon, Fad, Fiction, Fresh, Gimmick, Gothic, Graphic, Historical, Horror, Idiot, Innovation, Ivanhoe, Kenilworth, Kidnapped, Kim, Middlemarch, Modern, → **NEW**, Newfangled, Novation, Original, Outside, Page-turner, Pamela, Paperback, Pendennis, Penny dreadful, Persuasion, Picaresque, Pot-boiler, Primeur, Pulp, Rebecca, River, Roman-à-clef, Romance, Roman fleuve, Saga, Scoop, Sex and shopping, She, Shilling-dreadful, Shilling-shocker, Terror, Thesis, Ulysses, Unfamiliar, Unusual, Weepie, Whodun(n)it, Yellowback

▹ **Novel** *may indicate* an anagram

▸ **Novelist** *see* **WRITE(R)**

**November** N, Nov

**Novice** Acolyte, Apprentice, Beginner, Cadet, Chela, Colt, Cub, Green(horn), Griffin, Jackaroo, Jillaroo, Johnny-raw, Kyu, L, Learner, Neophyte, New chum, Noob, Patzer, Postulant, Prentice, Rabbit, Rookie, Tenderfoot, Trainee, Tyro(ne), Unweaned

**Now(adays)** AD, Alate, Anymore, Current, Here, Immediate, Instantaneously, Instanter, Interim, Modish, Nonce, Nunc, Present, Pro tem, This

**Nowhere** Limbo

**No-win** Dead heat

**Nowt** Cattle, Cows, Ky(e), Neat, Nothing

**Noxious** Harmful, Noisome, Offensive, Poisonous, Toxic, Toxin, Venomous

**Nozzle** Aerospike, A(d)jutage, Fishtail, Nose, Nose-piece, Rose, Spout, Stroup, Syringe, Tewel, Tuyere, Tweer, Twier, Twire, Twyer(e)

**Nuance** Gradation, Nicety, Overtone, Shade

**Nub**  Crux, Gist, Knob, Lump, Point

**Nubile**  Beddable, Marriageable, Parti

**Nuclear, Nucl(e)ide, Nucleus**  Cadre, Calandria, Centre, Chernobyl, Core, Crux, Daughter, Deuteron, Eukaryon, Euratom, Even-even, Even-odd, Heartlet, Hub, Isomer, Isotone, Karyon, Kernel, Linin, Mesic, Mesonic, Mushroom, Nuke, Organelle, Pith, Prokaryon, Recoil, Sizewell, Synkaryon, Triton

▷ **Nucleus**  *may indicate* the heart of a word

**Nude, Nudism, Nudist, Nudity**  Adamite, Altogether, Aphylly, Bare, Buff, Eve, Exposed, Full-frontal, Godiva, Gymnosophy, → **NAKED**, Nuddy, Scud, Stark, Stripped, Undress

**Nudge**  Dunch, Dunsh, Elbow, Jostle, Knee, Poke, Prod

**Nudibranch**  Sea-slug

**Nugget**  Chunk, Cob, Gold, Lump

**Nuisance**  Bore, Bot, Bugbear, Chiz(z), Drag, Impediment, Inconvenience, Mischief, Pest, Plague, Public, Terror, Trial, Trouble-maker, Varment

**Null(ification), Nullify**  Abate, Cancel, Counteract, Defeasance, Destroy, Diriment, Disarm, Invalid(ate), Negate, Neutralise, Overturn, Recant, Terminate, Undo, Veto, Void

**Numb(ness)**  Asleep, Blunt, Dead(en), Stun, Stupor, Torpefy, Torpescent, Torpid, Tranquillise, Unfeeling

**Number(s)**  Abscissa, Abundant, Access(ion), Air, Aleph-null, Aleph-zero, Algebraic, Algorithm, Aliquant, Aliquot, Amiable, Amicable, Anaesthetic, Analgesic, Anthem, Antilog, Apocalyptic, Apostrophus, Army, Atomic, Augend, Avogadro, Babylonian, Binary, Box, Brinell, Calculate, Cardinal, Cetane, Chromosome, Cinque, Class, Cocaine, Coefficient, Cofactor, Complex, Composite, Concrete, Constant, Coordination, Count, Cyclic, Decillion, Decimal, Deficient, Deficit, Diapason, Digit, DIN, Drove, E, Edition, Epidural, Ether, Eucaine, Ex-directory, F, Feck, Figurate, Figure, Flock, Folio, Folksong, Fraction, Friendly, Frost(bite), Froude, Gas, Gobar, Golden, Googol, Handful, Hantle, Hash(mark), Hemlock, Host, Hyperreal, Imaginary, Include, Incomposite, Index, Infimum, Integer, Irrational, Isospin, Isotopic, Item, Kochel, Lac, Lakh, Legion(s), Lepton, Lignocaine, Livraison, Local, Mach, Magazine, Magic, Mantissa, Mass, Melodic, Milliard, Minuend, Minyan, Mixed, Mort, Muckle, Multiple, Multiplex, Multiplicity, Multitude, Myriadth, Nasik, Natural, Neutron, No(s), Nonillion, Nth, Nuclear, Nucleon, Num, Numerator, Numerical, Octane, Octillion, Opiate, Opium, Opposite, Opus, Ordinal, OT, Paginate, Par, Paucal, Peck, Perfect, Pile, PIN, Plural, Polygonal, Prime, Procaine, Production, Proton, Quantum, Quarternion, Quorum, Quota, Quotient, Radix, Raft, Random, Rational, Real, Reckon, Registration, Regulo®, Repunit, Reynold's, Root, Sampi, Scads, Serial, Shedload, Show-stopper, Sight, Slew, Slue, Some, Square, Strangeness, Strength, Subtrahend, Summand, Surd, T, Tale, Telephone, Tell, Thr(e)ave, Totient, Totitive, Transcendental, Transfinite, Troop, Turn-out, Umpteen, Umpty, Urethan(e), Verse, Wave, Whole, Wrong, Zeroth

▷ **Number**  *may indicate* a drug

**Numeral(s)**  Arabic, Chapter, Figure, Ghubar, Gobar, Integer, Number, Roman, Sheep-scoring

**Numerous(ness)**  Divers, Galore, Legion, Lots, Many, Multeity, Myriad, Teeming

**Numskull**  Blockhead, Booby, Dunce, Stupid

**Nun(nery)**  Basilian, Beguine, Bhikkhuni, Cell, Clare, Cloistress, Cluniac, Conceptionist, Dame, Deaconess, Gilbertine, Minim, Minoress, Mother Superior, Outsister, Pigeon, Poor Clare, Prioress, Religeuse, Salesian, Sister, Sister of Mercy, Top, Trappistine, Ursuline, Vestal, Visitant, Vowess, Zelator, Zelatrice, Zelatrix

▷ **Nun**  *may indicate* a biblical character, father of Joshua

**Nuptial (chamber)**  Bridal, Marital, Marriage, Thalamus

**Nurse(ry), Nursing, Nursemaid**  Aia, Alice, Amah, Angel, Ant, Au pair, Ayah, Barrier, Bonne, Caledonia, Candy-striper, Care(r), Cavell, Charge, Cherish, Consultant, Cradle, Crèche, Day, Deborah, District, Dry, EN, Flo(rence), Foster, Gamp, Glumdalclitch,

Harbour, Health visitor, Karitane, Mammy, Midwife, Minister, Mother, Mrs Gamp, Nan(n)a, Nanny, Night, Nightingale, Norland, Nourice, Nourish, Parabolanus, Phytotron, Playroom, Playschool, Plunket, Practical, Probationer, RN, School, Scrub, Seminary, SEN, Sister, Staff, Suckle, Tend, Therapist, VAD, Visiting, Wet

**Nursery(man)** Conservatory, Crèche, Garden, Hothouse, Rhyme, Seedsman, Slope

▷ **Nursing** *may indicate* one word within another

**Nurture** Breeding, Cherish, Cradle, Cultivate, Educate, Feed, Foster, Suckle, Tend

**Nut(s), Nutcase, Nutshell, Nutter, Nut tree, Nutty** Acajou, Acorn, Almond, Amygdalus, Anacardium, Aphorism, Arachis, Areca, Arnut, Babassu, Barcelona, Barking, Barmy, Bats, Beech-mast, Bertholletia, Betel, Bonce, Brazil, Briefly, Buffalo, Butterfly, Butternut, Cashew, Castle, Chock, Coal, Cob, Coco-de-mer, Coffee, Cohune, Coke, Cola, Conker, Coquilla, Coquina, Core, Cranium, Crank, Cream, Cuckoo, Dukka(h), En, Filberd, Filbert, Freak, Frog, Gelt, Gilbert, Gland, Glans, Goober, Goober-pea, Gum, Hard, Hazel, Head, Helmet, Hickory, Illipe, Ivory, Kachang puteh, Kernel, Kola, Kooky, Lichee, Li(t)chi, Litchi, Loaf, Lug, Lunatic, Lychee, Macadamia, Macahuba, Macaw-palm, Macoya, Manic, Marking, Mast, Mockernut, Monkey, Noisette, Noodle, Nucule, Oak, Oil, Pakan, Palmyra, Para, Pate, Pecan, Pekan, Philippina, Philippine, Philopoena, Physic, Pili, Pine, Pin(y)on, Pistachio, Poison, Praline, Prawlin, Quandang, Quantong, Queensland, Rhus, Sapucaia, Sassafras, Scrotum, Shell, Skull, Slack, Sleeve, Stuffing, Supari, Testicles, Thumb, Tiger, Tough, Walnut, Weirdo, Wing, Zany, Zealot

▷ **Nut** *may refer to* Egyptian god, father of Osiris

▶ **Nutcase, Nutshell** *see* NUT(S)

**Nutcracker** Cosh

**Nutmeg** Calabash, Connecticut, CT, Mace, Myristica

**Nutrient, Nutriment, Nutrition** Betacarotene, Dietetics, Eutrophy, Food, Ingesta, Protein, Sitology, Sustenance, Trace element, Trophic, Vitamin

▷ **Nuts** *may indicate* an anagram

**Nuzzle** Nose, Snoozle

**Nyasaland** Malawi

**Nymph(et)** Aegina, Aegle, Amalthea, Arethusa, Callisto, Calypso, Camenae, Carme, Clytie, Constant, Cymodoce, Daphne, Doris, Dryad, Echo, Egeria, Eurydice, Galatea, Hamadryad, Hesperides, Houri, Hyades, Ida, Insect, Larva, Liberty, Lolita, Maelid, Maia, Maiden, Mermaid, Naiad, Nereid, Oceanid, Oenone, Oread, Pupa, Rusalka, Sabrina, Satyra, Scylla, Siren, Sylph, Syrinx, Tessa, Tethys, Thetis, Water, Wood

# Oo

**O** Blob, Duck, Nought, Omega, Omicron, Oscar, Oxygen, Spangle, Tan, Zero

**Oaf** Auf, Changeling, Dolt, Fool, Lout, Mou, Ocker, Ouph(e), Sot, Stupid, Twit, Yahoo

**Oak(s)** Bog, Bur, Cerris, Classic, Cork, Desert, Dumbarton, Durmast, Flittern, Fumed, Gabriel, Herne, Holly, Holm, Honour, Ilex, Jerusalem, Kermes, Live, Major, Native, Parliament, Pedunculate, Philemon, Poison, Quercus, Red, Roble, Royal, Scrub, Sessile, Silky, Swamp, Swilcar, → TREE, Turkey, Valonia, Watch, White

**Oakley** Annie

**Oar(s), Oarsman, Oarsmen** Blade, Bow, Ctene, Eight, Galley slave, Leander, Organ, Paddle, Pair, Palm, Propel, Rower, Scull, Spoon, Stroke, Sweep

**Oasis** Biskra, Buraimi, Haven, Hotan, Hotien, Refuge, Spring, Tafilalet, Tafilelt

**Oat(meal), Oats** Ait, Athole brose, Avena, Brome-grass, Fodder, Grain, Grits, Groats, Gruel, Haver, Loblolly, Parritch, Pilcorn, Pipe, Porridge, Quaker®, Rolled, Wild

**Oatcake** Bannock, Clapbread, Farle, Flapjack, Jannock

**Oath** Affidavit, Begorrah, Blast, Blimey, Bribery, Burgess, Curse, Damn, Dang, Dash, Demme, Doggone, Drat, Ecod, Egad, Expletive, God-so, Gospel, Halidom, Hell, Hippocratic, Igad, Imprecation, Jabers, Jesus, Keech, Lumme, Lummy, Nouns, Oons, Promise, Rats, Sacrament, Sal(a)mon, Sapperment, Saucer, 'Sbodikins, Sbud(dikins), Sdeath, Sfoot, Sheart, Shoot, Slid, 'Slife, 'Slight, Snails, Sonties, Strewth, Stygian, Swear, Tarnation, Tennis-court, Voir dire, Vow, Zbud, Zounds

**Obdurate** Adamant, Cruel, Flinty, Hard, Intransigent, Stony, Stubborn, Tenacious

**Obedient, Obedience, Obey** Bent, Biddable, Bridlewise, Canonical, Comply, Dutiful, Follow, Good, Hear, Mindful, Obsequious, Observe, Obtemper, Passive, Perform, Pliant, Servant, Yielding

**Obeisance** → BOW, Salaam

**Obelisk, Obelus** Aguilla, Column, Dagger, Monument, Needle, Pillar

**Oberon** King, Merle

**Obese, Obesity** Bariatrics, Corpulent, Fat, Stout

**Obfuscation** Fudge

**Object(s), Objection(able), Objective(ness), Objector** Ah, Aim, Ambition, Argue, Artefact, Article, Artifact, Bar, Beef, But, Case, Cavil, Challenge, Clinical, Cognate, Complain(t), Conchy, Conscientious, Contest, Cow, Demur, Detached, Direct, Dissent, Doodah, End, Exception, Fetish, Found, Fuss, → GOAL, Her, Him, Ifs and buts, Impersonal, Improper, Indifferent, Indirect, Intensional, Intention, It, Item, Jib, Lion, Loathe, Mind, Moral, Near-earth, Niggle, Nimby, Nitpick, Non-ego, Non-partisan, Noumenon, Ob, Obnoxious, Offensive, Oppose, Outness, Percept, Perspective, Plan, Plot, Point, Protest, Proximate, Quasi-stellar, Question, Quibble, Quiddity, Rank, Rebarbative, Recuse, Refuse, Relation, Resent, Resist, Retained, Sake, Scruple, Sex, Subject, Sublime, Target, Thing, Transitive, Tut, Ultimate, Unbiased, Unsavoury, Virtu, Wart

▷ **Object** *may indicate* a grammatical variant

**Objectless** Intransitive

**Objet d'art** Curio

**Oblate, Oblation** Gift, Monk, Offering, Offertory, Prothesis, Sacrifice

**Oblige(d), Obliging, Obligation, Obligatory** Accommodate, Affable, Behold, Binding, Burden, Charge, Coerce, Compel, Complaisant, Compliant, Constraint, Contract, Corvée, Debt, De rigueur, Duty, Easy, Easygoing, Encumbent, Force, Giri, Gratify, Impel,

Incumbent, IOU, Mandatory, Must, Necessitate, Needed, Novation, Obruk, Obstriction, Peremptory, Promise, Recognisance, Responsibility, Sonties, Synallagmatic, Tie, Wattle

**Oblique(ly)** Askance, Askew, Asklent, Asquint, Athwart, Awry, Cross, Diagonal, Glance, Glancing, Indirect, Perverse, Plagio-, Separatrix, Sidelong, Skew, Skewwhiff, Slanting, Solidus, Squint, Virgule

▷ **Oblique** *may indicate* an anagram

**Obliterate(d)** Annul, Black out, Blot, Dele(te), Efface, Eradicate, Expunge, Exterminate, Rase, Rast, Raze, Wash away, Wipe, Zap

**Oblivion, Oblivious** Forgetful, Lethe, Limbo, Nirvana, Obscurity, Silence, Unaware

**Oblong** Rectangular

**Obloquy** Opprobrium

**Obnoxious** Eyesore, Foul, Horrid, Offensive, Pestilent, Repellent, Repugnant, Septic, Sod, Unpleasant, Wart

**Oboe** Piffero

**Obscene(ly), Obscenity** Bawdy, Blue, Fescennine, Filth, Gross, Hard-core, Indecent, Lewd, Lubricious, Paw(paw), Porn(o), Profane, Raunchy, Ribald, Salacious, Scatology, Smut, Vulgar

**Obscure, Obscurity** Abstruse, Anheires, Arcane, Becloud, Befog, Black out, Blear, Blend, Blot out, Blur, Break, Cloud, Cobweb, Conceal, Cover, Cryptic, Darken, Deep, Dim, Disguise, Eclipse, Elliptic, Encrypt, Engloom, Envelop, Esoteric, Filmy, Fog, Hermetic, Hide, Indistinct, Inky, Jude, Mantle, Mist, Murk, Mystic(al), Nebular, Night, Nubecula, Obfuscate, Obnubilate, Opaque, Oracular, Overcloud, Overshade, Overshadow, Recherché, Recondite, Shadowy, Tenebrific, Twilit, Unclear, Unobvious, →**VAGUE**, Veil, Vele, Wrap

▷ **Obscure(d)** *may indicate* an anagram

**Obsequious(ness)** Bootlicker, Brown nose, Crawler, Creeping Jesus, Fawn, Fulsome, Grovelling, Kowtowing, Menial, Oily, Parasitic, Pig, Servile, Slavish, Sleeveen, Slimy, Subservient, Suck-hole, Suck up, Sycophantic, Tantony, Toady

**Observance, Observant, Observation** Adherence, Alert, Aphorism, Attention, Comment, Custom, Empirical, Espial, Experience, Eyeful, Holy, Honour, Hour-angle, Inkhorn, Lectisternium, Mass, →**NOTICE**, Obiter dicta, Perceptive, Percipient, Practice, Quip, Ready-eyed, Recce, Remark, Right, Rite, Ritual, Use, Vising

**Observatory** Arecibo, Atalaya, Greenwich, Herstmonceux, Hide, Hurstmonceux, Jodrell Bank, Lookout, Mount Palomar, Tower

**Observe(d), Observer** Behold, Bystander, Celebrate, Commentator, Detect, Espy, Eye, Eyeball, Fly-on-the-wall, Heed, Keep, Mark, Monitor, NB, Note, Notice, Obey, Onlooker, Optic, Pharisee, Regard(er), Remark, Rite, Scry, See, Seer, Sight, Spectator, Spial, Spie, Spot, Spy, Study, Take, Twig, View, Voyeur, Watch, Witness

**Obsess(ed), Obsession(al), Obsessive** Anal, Anorak, Besot, Bug, Bugbear, Complex, Craze, Dominate, Fetish, Fixation, Hang-up, Haunt, Hobbyhorse, Hooked, Idée fixe, Infatuation, Mania, Monomania, Necrophilia, Nerd, Neurotic, One-track, Paranoic, Preoccupy, Smitten, Thing, Wonk

**Obsidian** Pe(a)rlite

**Obsolete, Obsolescence, Obsolescent** Abandoned, Antique, Archaic, Dated, Dead, Defunct, Disused, Extinct, Latescent, Obs, Outdated, Outworn, Passé, Planned

**Obstacle** Barrage, Barrier, Boyg, Cheval de frise, Chicane, Clog, Dam, Drag, Dragon's teeth, Drawback, Gate, Handicap, Hazard, Hindrance, Hitch, Hurdle, Node, Oxer, Remora, Rock, Rub, Sandbank, Snag, Stimie, Stumbling-block, Stymie, Tank-trap

**Obstetrics** Gynaecology, Midwifery, Tocology, Tokology

**Obstinacy, Obstinate** Asinine, Bigoted, Bitter-ender, Buckie, Bullheaded, Bullish, Contrarian, Contumacious, Cussed, Die-hard, Dour, Entêté, Froward, Headstrong, High-stomached, Inflexible, Intractable, Intransigent, Mule, Persistent, Perverse, Pervicacious, Piggish, Pig-headed, Recalcitrant, Refractory, Restive, Rigid, Rusty, Self-will, Stiff(-necked), Strure, Stubborn, Thraward, Thrawart, Wilful

**Obstreperous** Defiant, Noisy, Stroppy, Truculent, Undisciplined, Unruly

**Obstruct(ion)** Airlock, Bar, Barricade, Barrier, Block, Bottleneck, Caltrop, Chicane, Clog, Crab, Cross, Cumber, Dam, Delay, Embolus, Fil(l)ibuster, Gridlock, Hamper, Hand-off, Hedge, Hinder, Hurdle, Ileus, Impede, Let, Obstacle, Occlude, Oppose, Sab(otage), Sandbag, Snarl-up, Snooker, Stall, Stap, Stonewall, Stop, Stymie, Sudd, Thwart, Trammel, Trump

**Obtain** Achieve, Acquire, Borrow, Buy, Cop, Derive, Exist, Gain, Get, Land, Pan, Prevail, Procure, Realise, Secure, Succeed, Wangle, Win

**Obtrude, Obtruding, Obtrusive** Expel, Impose, King Charles' head, Loud, Prominent, Push, Sorn, Thrust

**Obtuse** Angle, Blunt, Dense, Dull, Purblind, Stolid, Stupid, Thick

**Obverse, Obversion** Complement, Cross, Equipollence, Face, Front, Head, Permutation

**Obviate** Forestall, Preclude, Prevent

**Obvious** Apparent, Axiom, Bald, Blatant, Brobdingnag, Clear, Distinct, Evident, Flagrant, Frank, Inescapable, Kenspeck(le), Manifest, Marked, Needless, Open(ness), Open and shut, Overt, Palpable, Patent, Pikestaff, Plain, Pronounced, Salient, Self-evident, Staring, Stark, Transparent, Truism, Unsubtle, Visible, Writ large

**Occasion** Call, Cause, Ceremony, Do, Encheason, Engender, Event, Fête, Field day, Nonce, →**OPPORTUNITY**, Reason, Ride, Sometime, Tide, Time, Treat, Whet

**Occasional(ly)** At times, Black tie, Casual, Cause, Chance, Daimen, Day, Episode, Ever and anon, Instance, Intermittent, Irregular, Lawful, Motive, Odd, Orra, Periodic, Scattered, Social, Sometimes, Sporadic, While, White tie

**Occident(al)** West, Western(er)

**Occlude, Occlusion** Absorb, Clog, Coronary, Embolism, Obstruct

**Occult(ist)** Angekkok, Arcane, Art, Esoteric, Gnostic, I-Ching, Magic, Mysterious, Mystic, Supernatural

**Occupant, Occupation, Occupy(ing)** Absorb, Acquire, Activity, Amuse, Avocation, Beset, Business, Busy, Career, Denizen, Dwell, Embusy, Employ, Engage, Engross, Fill, Hold, In, Incumbent, Indwell, Inhabitant, Inmate, Invade, Involve, Line, Man, Métier, Obsess, Overrun, People, Possess, Profession, Pursuit, Reserved, Residency, Resident, Runrig, Sideline, Squat, Stay, Tenancy, Tenant, Tenure, Thrift, Trade, Upon, Use, Vocation, Walk of life

**Occur(rence)** Arise, Be, Betide, Betime, Case, Contingency, Crop up, Event, Eventuate, Fall, Happen, Incident, Instance, Outbreak, Outcrop, Pass, Phenomenon

**Ocean(ic), Oceania** Abundance, Abyssal, Antarctic, Arctic, Atlantic, Blue, Deep, German, Hadal, Herring-pond, High seas, Indian, Melanesia, Micronesia, Millpond, Pacific, Panthalassa, Pelagic, Polynesia, Pond, Sea(way), Southern, Thalassic, Waves, Western

**Och aye** Troggs

**Ochre** Burnt, Keel, Lemnian ruddle, Rubric, Ruddle, Sienna

**Octave** Diapason, Diminished, Eight, Great, Ottava, Perfect, Small, Utas

**Octopus** Blue-ringed, Cephalopod, Cuero, Devilfish, Paper nautilus, Polyact, Polyp, Poulp(e), Scuttle, Squid

**Octoroon** Mestee, Mestizo, Mustee

**Od** Energy, Force

**Odd (person), Oddity** Abnormal, Anomaly, Bizarre, Card, Cure, Curio, Curious, Droll, Eccentric, Eery, Erratic, Fishy, Freaky, Gink, Gonzo, Impair, Imparity, Jimjam, Offbeat, Original, Orra, Outré, Paradox, Parity, Peculiar, Queer, Quirky, Quiz, Random, Rare, Remote, Rum, Screwball, Singular, Spooky, →**STRANGE**, Unequal, Uneven, Unmatched, Unpaired, Unusual, Weird, Whims(e)y, Zany

▷ **Odd(s)** *may indicate* an anagram or the odd letters in words

**Oddball, Oddperson** Ditz, Weirdo

**Oddfellow** OF

**Odd job man** Joey, Loppy, Orraman, Rouster, Smoot, Thronner

**Odds, Oddments** Bits, Carpet, Chance, Gubbins, Handicap, Line, Long, Price, Short, SP, Tails, Variance

**Ode** Awdl, Dit, Epicede, Epicedium, Epinicion, Epinikion, Genethliacon, Horatian, Hymn, Lay, Lyric, Monody, Paeon, Pindaric, Poem, Sapphic, Song, Stasimon, Strophe, Threne, Threnody, Verse

**Odin** One-eyed, Woden

**Odium, Odious** Comparison, Disestimation, Disgrace, Foul, Hatred, Heinous, Invidious, Ponce, Repellent, Repugnant, Stigma

**Odorous, Odour** Air, Aroma, Bad, BO, Flavour, Funk, Good, Hum, Musk, Opopanax, Perfume, Quality, Redolence, Sanctity, Scent, Smell, Stench, Waff, Waft, Whiff

**Odourless** Silent

**Odyssey** Epic, Journey, Wandering

**Oedipus, Oedipal** Complex, Laius, Parricide

**Oeillade** Glance, Leer, Ogle, Wink

**Oesophagus** Crop

**Oestrogen, Oestrus** Daidzein, Frenzy, Genistein®, Heat, Isoflavone, Mestranol, Must, Rut, Stilb(o)estrol

**Of (me)** About, Among, Aus, By, De, From, In, My, Re

▷ **Of** *may indicate* an anagram

**Of course** Certainly, Natch, Yes

**Off** Absent, Agee, Ajee, Away, Discount, Distance, Far, From, High, Inexact, Licence, Odd, Rancid, Reasty, Reesty, Relâche, Start

▷ **Off** *may indicate* an anagram

**Offal** Cagmag, Carrion, Chidlings, Chitterling, Entrails, Fry, Giblets, Gralloch, Gurry, Haggis, Ha(r)slet, Heart, Innards, Kidney, Lamb's fry, Lights, Liver, Numbles, Pig's fry, Pluck, Sweetbread, Tripe, Variety meat

**Off-beat** Zoppo

**Off-colour** Pale, Seedy, Wan

▷ **Off-colour** *may indicate* an anagram

**Offence** Affront, Attack, Crime, Delict, Delinquency, Demerit, Distaste, Fault, Huff, Hurt, Indictable, Lapse, Lese majesty, Malfeasance, Miff, Misdemeanour, Misprision, Odium, Outrage, Peccadillo, Perjury, Pip, Pique, Piracy, Praemunire, Regrate, Sedition, →SIN, Summary, Trespass, Umbrage, Violation

**Offend(ed), Offender** Affront, Anger, Annoy, Boobhead, Bridles, Criminal, Culprit, Default, Delinquent, Disoblige, Displease, Distaste, Hip, Huff, Hurt, Hyp, Infringe, Inveigh, Miffy, Miscreant, Nettle, Nonce, Nuisance, Outrage, Peeve, Perp, Provoke, Serial, Sin(ner), Sledge, Sting, Stray, Sus, Touchy, Transgress, Twoccer, Umbrage, Violate, Wrongdoer

**Offensive(ness)** Affront, Aggressive, Alien, Attack, Bombardment, Campaign, Charge, Charm, Cruel, Derisatory, Derogatory, Dysphemism, Embracery, Euphemism, Execrable, Eyesore, Forbidding, Foul, Gobby, Hedgehog, Hedgepig, Indecent, Indelicate, Inroad, Insulting, Invidious, Miasmic, Nasty, Noisome, Obnoxious, Obscene, Odious, Peccant, Personal, Pungent, Push, Putrid, Rank, Repugnant, →RUDE, Scandalous, Scurrilous, Sortie, Storm, Ugly, Unbecoming, Unsavoury, War

**Offer(ing)** Alms, Altarage, Anaphora, Approach, Bargain, Bid, Bode, Bouchée, Cadeau, Corban, Deodate, Dolly, Epanophora, Extend, Ex voto, Gift, Give, Godfather, Heave, Hold, Inferiae, Introduce, Invitation, Libation, Oblation, Overture, Peace, Peddle, Plead, Pose, Potla(t)ch, Present, Propine, →PROPOSE, Propound, Sacrifice, Shewbread, Shore, Special, S(h)raddha, Stamp, Stand, Submit, Suggestion, Tempting, Tender, Utter, Volunteer, Votive, Wave, Xenium

**Offhand** Airy, Banana, Brevi manu, Brusque, Casual, Cavalier, Currente calamo, Curt, Extempore, Impromptu, Indifferent, Snappy

**Office(s)** Abbacy, Agency, Bedelship, Benefice, Booking, Box, Branch, Broo, Bucket shop, Bureau, Buroo, Caliphate, Chair, Chancellory, Chancery, Circumlocution, Clerical,

Colonial, Commonwealth, Complin(e), Consulate, Crown, Cube farm, Cutcher(r)y, Daftar, Dataria, Dead-letter, Deanery, Decemvirate, Den, Divine, Dogate, Drostdy, Employment, Evensong, Foreign, Front, Function, Holy, Home, Job, Land, Last, Lav(atory), Left luggage, Lieutenancy, Little, Little hours, Loan, Loo, Lost property, Mayoralty, Met(eorological), Ministry, Missa, Mistery, Mudiria, Mutessarifat, Mystery, Nocturn, Nones, Obit, Oval, Palatinate, Papacy, Patent, Patriarchate, Penitentiary, Personnel, Petty Bag, Pipe, Place, Plum, Portfolio, Position, Post, Prefecture, Prelacy, Press, Prime, Printing, Provosty, Record, Regency, Register, Registry, Rite, Satrapy, Scottish, Secretarial, Secretariat, See, Seraskierate, Sext, Shogunate, Sinecure, Situation, Sorting, Speaker(ship), Stamp, Stationery, Sultanate, Tariff, Tenebrae, Terce, Tiara, Ticket, Tierce, Tol(l)booth, Tribunate, Vespers, Vicary, War, Yamen

**Officer(s)** Branch, Compliance, Counter-round, Customs, Duty, Engineer, Executive, First, Flag, Flying, Gal(l)ant, Gazetted, Group, Incumbent, Liaison, Non-commissioned, Nursing, Orderly, Peace, Petty, PO, Police, Presiding, Press, Prison, Probation, Radio, Relieving, Returning, Rodent, Safety, Scene-of-crime, Staff, Treasurer, Wardroom, Warrant, Watch

---

## OFFICERS

| | | | |
|---|---|---|---|
| *2 letters:* | Pasha | Agistor | Alguazil |
| Lt | Pilot | Bailiff | Bimbashi |
| SL | Posse | Blue Rod | Black Rod |
| SM | Sewer | Captain | Brass-hat |
| | | Colonel | Cursitor |
| *3 letters:* | *6 letters:* | Co-pilot | Decurion |
| Aga | Acater | Coroner | Familiar |
| CEO | Beatty | Darogha | Gendarme |
| Cop | Copper | Dragoon | Havildar |
| Gen | Cornet | Equerry | Hog-reeve |
| GOC | Datary | Filacer | Phylarch |
| NCO | Deacon | Filazer | Subahdar |
| Sub | Ensign | General | Tipstaff |
| | Gauger | Hayward | Woodward |
| *4 letters:* | Guidon | Jamadar | |
| Agha | Gunner | Jauntie | *9 letters:* |
| Aide | Hetman | Jemadar | Ale-conner |
| Bosn | Jaunty | Jemidar | Apparitor |
| Capt | Lictor | Marshal | Brigadier |
| CIGS | Purser | Pantler | Catchpole |
| Exon | Pusser | Prefect | Catchpoll |
| Imam | Rector | Proctor | Cellarist |
| Mate | Rosser | Provost | Centurion |
| | Sbirro | Redcoat | Commander |
| *5 letters:* | Schout | Samurai | Commodore |
| Blimp | Serang | Sea Lord | Constable |
| Bosun | Sexton | Sheriff | Exciseman |
| Gager | Tindal | Skipper | First mate |
| Imaum | Varlet | Speaker | Inspector |
| Janty | Warden | Striper | Messenger |
| Jonty | Warder | Subadar | Moderator |
| Jurat | Yeoman | Tribune | Number one |
| Macer | | | Pipe major |
| Major | *7 letters:* | *8 letters:* | President |
| Pacha | Admiral | Adjutant | Prorector |

| | | | |
|---|---|---|---|
| Select-man | Securocrat | Field Marshal | **15 letters:** |
| Subaltern | Subchanter | Group captain | Lord High Steward |
| Tahsildar | Supercargo | Remembrancer | |
| Tarpaulin | Tidewaiter | | **16 letters:** |
| Waldgrave | | **13 letters:** | Procurator fiscal |
| | **11 letters:** | Drill-sergeant | |
| **10 letters:** | Chamberlain | Lance-sergeant | **17 letters:** |
| Aide de camp | Earl Marshal | Quartermaster | Official Solicitor |
| Air-marshal | Grand Vizier | Sergeant-major | |
| Bluebottle | Infirmarian | Sublieutenant | **21 letters:** |
| Bombardier | Silver-stick | | Quartermaster- |
| Bumbailiff | | **14 letters:** | sergeant |
| Chancellor | **12 letters:** | Air vice-marshal | |
| Pursuivant | Commissioned | Provost-marshal | |
| Second mate | Commissioner | Superintendent | |

**Office-worker** Clerk, Peon, Temp, Typist
**Official(s), Officiate, Officious** Aga, Agent, Aleconner, Amban, Amtman, Apparatchik, Atabeg, Atabek, Attaché, Authorised, Beadle(dom), Borough-reeve, Bossy, Bumble, Bureaucrat, Catchpole, Censor, Chamberlain, Chancellor, Chinovnik, Claviger, Commissar, Commissioner, Consul, Convenor, Coroner, Count, Count palatine, Datary, Dean, Dignitary, Diplomat, Dockmaster, Dogberry, Ealdorman, Ephor, Equerry, Escheater, Eurocrat, Executive, Executor, Factotum, Fonctionnaire, → **FORMAL**, Fourth, Functionary, Gauleiter, Governor, Gymnasiarch, Handicapper, Hayward, Hazzan, Incumbent, Inspector, Intendant, Jack-in-office, Jobsworth, Keeper, Landdrost, Lictor, Lifeguard, Line judge, Linesman, Macebearer, Macer, Mandarin, Marplot, Marshal, Mayor, MC, Meddlesome, Mirza, Mueddin, Muezzin, Mukhtar, Nazir, Notary, Notary public, Ombudsman, Omlah, Overbusy, Palatine, Panjandrum, Paymaster, Placeman, Pleaseman, Plenipotentiary, Polemarch, Pontificate, Poohbah, Postmaster, Postulator, Praefect, Pragmatic, Prefect, Proconsul, Proctor, Procurator, Prog, Proveditor, Provedor(e), Providor, Provost, Purveyor, Recorder, Reeve, Ref(eree), Régisseur, Registrar, Remembrancer, Sachem, Scrutineer, Secretary, Shammash, Shammes, Sherpa, Silentiary, Souldan, Spoffish, Stadtholder, Staff, Standard, Steward, Subdean, Suffete, Suit, Summoner, Surveyor, Syndic, Timekeeper, Tipstaff, Touch judge, Tribune, Trier, Trior, Triumvir, Turncock, Umpire, Valid, Valuer General, Veep, Verderer, Verger, Vicar-general, Viscount, Vizier, Walla(h), Whiffler, Whip, Woodward, Yamen, Yeoman
**Off-key** Flat
**Off-limit(s)** Prohibited
**Off-load** Dump, Shed
**Offprint** Separate
**Off-putting** Deferrable, Dehortative, Discouraging, Mañana, Negative, Procrastination, Rebarbative, Red herring, Repellent, Yips
**Offset** Balance, Cancel, Compensate, Counter(act), Counterbalance, Neutralise
**Offshoot** Bough, Branch, Cion, Limb, Lye, Member, Outgrowth, Plant, Scion, Sien, Sient, Swarm, Syen
**Offspring** Boy, Brood, Burd, Chick, Children, Daughter, Descendant, Family, Fruit, Fry, Get, Girl, Heir, Litter, Procreation, Product, Progeny, Seed, Sient, Son, Spawn
**Offstage** Wings
**Off-the-cuff** Improv(isation)
**Off-white** Bone, Cream, Ecru
**Often** Frequent, Habitual, Repeated
▷ **Often** *may indicate* 'of ten'
**Ogee** Cyma, Moulding, Talon
**Ogle** Astare, Drake, Eliad, Eye, Glad eye, Glance, Leer, Oeillade, Wodewose

**Ogre(ss)** Baba Yaga, Boyg, Brute, Eten, Etten, Fiend, Giant, Monster, Orc, Shrek
**Ohio** Buckeye
**Oil(s), Oily, Oil producer** Anele, Anoint, Balm, Black gold, Bribe, Crab, Crude, Derv, Diesel, Drying, Essence, Essential, Ethereal, Fatty, Fish, Fixed, Frying, Fuel, Good, Grease, Hair, Heavy, Illupi, Joint, Lamp, Landscape, Lipid, Long, Lube, Lubricant, Macaw-tree, Midnight, Mineral, Monounsaturated, Multigrade, Oint, Oleaginous, Pellitory, Polyunsaturated, Pomade, Residual, Seed, Short, Sleek, Slick, Smalmy, Smarmy, Smeary, Sweet, Topped crude, Turps, Unction, Zest

---

## OIL PRODUCERS

*2 letters:*
BP®

*3 letters:*
Ben
Emu
Gas
Nim
Nut

*4 letters:*
Baby
Bath
Bone
Cade
Coal
Corn
Musk
Nard
Neem
Nimb
Oleo
Otto
Palm
Poon
Rape
Rock
Rose
Rusa
Slum
Tall
Tolu
Tung
Wood
Wool
Yolk

*5 letters:*
Ajwan
Argan
Attar
Benne
Benni

Clove
Colza
Copra

Fusel
Grass
Maize
Niger
Olein
Olive
Ottar
Poppy
Pulza
Rosin
Savin
Sebum
Shale
Shark
Snake
Sperm
Spike
Stand
Thyme
Train
Ulyie
Ulzie
Whale

*6 letters:*
Ajowan
Almond
Balsam
Banana
Butter
Canola
Carapa
Carron
Castor
Chrism
Cineol
Cloves
Cohune
Croton
Elaeis

Illipe
Jojoba
Magilp
Megilp
Monola®
Neroli
Oleine
Peanut
Ramtil
Savine
Semsem
Seneca
Sesame
Shamoy
Tallow
Virgin
Walnut

*7 letters:*
Aniline
Apiezon®
Arachis
Bittern
Cajeput
Cajuput
Camphor
Cineole
Coconut
Dittany
Eugenol
Gingili
Jinjili
Linalol
Linseed
Lumbang
Menthol
Mirbane
Moringa
Mustard
Myrbane
Myrrhol
Naphtha
Picamar

Pyrrole
Retinol
Ricinus
Rocktar
Saffron
Safrole
Spindle
Verbena
Vitriol
Wallaba

*8 letters:*
Bergamot
Camphire
Cod-liver
Creasote
Creosote
Flaxseed
Gingelli
Gingelly
Hazelnut
Hempseed
Kerosene
Kerosine
Lavender
Linalool
Macassar
North Sea
Oiticica
Pachouli
Paraffin
Photogen
Pristane
Rapeseed
Rosewood
Volatile

*9 letters:*
Aleuritis
Beech-mast
Candlenut
Carvacrol
Eleoptene

| | | | |
|---|---|---|---|
| Golomynka | Star-anise | Peppermint | **12 letters:** |
| Grapeseed | Sunflower | Petit grain | Benzaldehyde |
| Groundnut | Terpineol | Sandalwood | Benzonitrile |
| Neat's-foot | Vanaspati | Turpentine | Brilliantine |
| Parathion | Vegetable | Ylang-ylang | Hungary water |
| Patchouli | | | |
| Patchouly | **10 letters:** | **11 letters:** | **14 letters:** |
| Petroleum | Chaulmugra | Camphorated | Glutaraldehyde |
| Photogene | Citronella | Chaulmoogra | Parnassus grass |
| Quinoline | Cotton-seed | Chinese wood | |
| Safflower | Elaeoptene | Extra virgin | **15 letters:** |
| Sassafras | Eucalyptus | Stearoptene | Evening primrose |
| Spearmint | Guttiferae | Wintergreen | |
| Spikenard | Juniper tar | | |

**Oilcake** Poonac

**Oilcan** Pourie

**Oilcloth** American, Lino

**Oilman** Driller, Prospector, Rigger, Texan

**Oil painting** Master, Titian

**Ointment** Balm, Basilicon, Boracic, Boric, Cerate, Collyrium, Cream, Liniment, Lipsalve, Lotion, Nard, Pomade, Pomatum, Rub, Salve, Spikenard, Theriac, Tiger balm®, Unction, Unguent, Vaseline®, Zinc

**OK** Agree(d), Approve, Authorise, Clearance, Copacetic, Copesettic, Go-head, Green light, Hunky-dory, Initial, Kosher, Mooi, No sweat, Permissible, Respectable, Right(o), Roger, Sanction, Sound, U, Vet

**Okra** Bhindi, Gumbo, Lady's fingers

**Old(er), Oldest, Oldie** Ae(t), Aged, Aine(e), Ancient, Antique, Auld, Bean, Decrepit, Dutch, Earlier, Elderly, Ex, Fogram, Former, Gaffer, Geriatric, Glory, Golden, Gray, Grey, Hills, Hoary, Immemorial, Major, Mature, Methusaleh, Moore, Nestor, Nick, O, OAP, Obsolete, Off, Ogygian, One-time, Original, Outworn, Palae-, Passé, Primeval, Ripe, Rugose, Sen(escent), Senile, Senior, Shot, Signeur, Stager, Stale, Trite, Venerable, Veteran, Victorian(a), Worn

**Old boy, Old girl** Alumnae, Alumnus, Fossil, OB

**Old days** Once, Past, Yore

**Old English** OE

**Old-fashioned** Aging, Ancient, Antediluvian, Antwackie, Arch(aic), Arriéré, Back number, Bygone, Corn(y), Dated, Dodo, Dowdy, Dusty, Fogey, Fuddy-duddy, Fusty, Hidebound, Medieval, Museum piece, Neanderthal, No tech, Obsolete, Ogygian, Oldfangled, Outdated, Outmoded, Outre, Outworn, Passé, Podunk, Primeval, Quaint, Relic, Retro, Rinky-dink, Schmaltzy, Shot, Square, Square-toes, Steam, Stick-in-the-mud, Traditional, Uncool, Victorian, Vieux jeu, Vintage, Worm-eaten

**Old-hand** Stager

**Old hat** Clichéd, Outmoded

**Old maid** Biddy, Spinster

**Old man, Old woman** Anile, Aunty, Bodach, Buda, Budi, Burd, Cailleach, Carlin(e), Cicerone, Codger, Coniston, Crinkly, Crone, Crow, Crumbly, Faggot, Fantad, Fantod, Fogey, Fogramite, Fogy, Fussy, Gammer, Geezer, Gramps, Grandam, Grannam, Greybeard, Greyhen, Husband, Kangaroo, Koro, Kuia, Luckie, Lucky, Matriarch, Methuselah, Mort, Mzee, OAP, Oom, Pantaloon, Patriarch, Presbyte, Roo, Rudas, Southernwood, Tante, Tripod, Trot, Trout, Whitebeard, Wife, Wight, Woopie, Wrinkly

**Old-timer** Hourglass, Sundial, Veteran

**Oleander** Nerium, Rhododaphne

**Olid** Fetid, Foul, High, Rancid, Rank

**Olio** Hash, Medley, Mess, Potpourri, Stew

**Olive (grove), Olivine** Calamata, Cerulein, Drupe, Dunite, Gethsemane, Kalamata, Lilac, Olea(ster), Peridot, Queen, Russian

**Oliver** Bath, Cromwell, Goldsmith, Hardy, Noll, Protector, Twist

**Olympian, Olympics, Olympus** Artemis, Asgard, Athlete, Celestial, Coe, Demeter, Elis, Hera, Pantheon, Quadrennium, Summer, Winter, Zeus

**Ombudsman** Trouble shooter, Watchdog

**Omelette** Crêpe, Foo yong, Foo yung, Frittata, Fu yung, Pancake, Spanish, Tortilla

**Omen** Abodement, Absit, Augury, Auspice, Foreboding, Forewarning, Freet, Freit, Portent, Presage, Prodrome, Sign, Token, Warning

**Omentum** Caul, Epiploon

**Ominous** Alarming, Baleful, Bodeful, Dire, Dour, Forbidding, Grim, Inauspicious, Menacing, Oracular, Portentous, Sinister, Threatening, Ugly

**Omission, Omit** Aph(a)eresis, Apocope, Apospory, Apostrophe, Asyndeton, Caret, Disregard, Drop, Elide, Elision, Ellipse, Ellipsis, Exception, Failure, Haplography, Haplology, Lipography, Loophole, Miss, Neglect, Nonfeasance, Non-user, Oversight, Paral(e)ipomenon, Pass, Pretermit, Senza, Skip

**Omnibus** Anthology, Coach, Collection

**Omnipresent** Ubiquitous

**Omniscient, Omniscience** Encyclopedia, Pansophy

**Omnivorous** Pantophagous

**On (it)** Aboard, About, Agreed, Alight, An, An't, At, Atop, By, Game, Gaun, Going, Half-cut, In, Leg, O', Of, Oiled, Over, Pon, Re, Running, Tipsy, Up(on), Viable

▷ **On** *may indicate* an anagram

**On account of** Over

▷ **On board** *may indicate* chess, draughts, or 'SS' around another word

**Once(r)** Ance, As was, →**AT ONCE**, Bradbury, Earst, Erst(while), Ever, Ex, Fore, Former, Jadis, Oner, Onst, Secular, Sole, Sometime, Whilom

**One(self)** A, Ace, Ae, Alike, An(e), Any, Body, Chosen, Digit, Eeny, Ego, Ein, Formula, I, Individual, Integer, Lunchtime, Me, Monad, Per se, Person, Single(ton), Singular, Solo, Tane, Un, Unify, Unit(y), Unitary, United, Us, We, Yin, You

**One-act-er** Playlet

**One-dimensional** Linear

**One-eared** Monaural

**One-eyed** Arimasp(ian), Cyclops

**One-man band** Moke

**One o'clock** 1 am, NNE

**One-off** Ad hoc, Sui generis

**One-rayed** Monact

**Onerous** Arduous, Exacting, Taxing, Tedious, Weighty

**Ongoing** Continual

**On guard** Excubant

**Onion(s)** Allium, Bengi, Bonce, Bulb, Chibol, Chive, Cibol, Cive, Eschalot, Green, Head, Ingan, Jibbons, Leek, Lyonnaise, Moly, Pate, Pearl, Ramp, Ramson, Rocambole, Ropes, Scallion, Scilla, Shal(l)ot, Soubise, Spanish, Spring, Squill, Sybo(e), Sybow, Tree, Welsh

**Online** E

**Onlooker** Beholder, Bystander, Kibitzer, Observer, Rubberneck, Spectator, Witness

**Only** Allenarly, Anerly, But, Except, Just, Meer, Merely, Nobbut, One, Seul, Singly, Sole, Sommer, Unique

**Onset** Affret, Attack, Beginning, Charge, Dash, Ending, Rush, →**START**, Thrust

**Onslaught** Attack, Barrage, Cannonade, Dead-set, Diatribe, Onset, Raid, Spreagh, Storm, Swoop

**On the way** Agate

**On this side** Cis

**On time** Pat, Prompt, Punctual

**Onus** Burden, Charge, →DUTY, Responsibility

**Onward** Advance, Ahead, Away, Forth, Forward, Progress

**Oodles** Heaps, Lashings, Lots, Slather

**Oolite** Peastone, Pisolite, Roestone

**Oomph** Energy, It, SA, Verve

**Ooze, Oozy** Dowl, Drip, Exhale, Exude, Gleet, Globigerena, Ichorous, Mud, Percolate, Pteropod(a), Radiolarian, Seep, Sew, Sipe, Slime, Slob, Spew, Spue, Sweat, Sype, Transude, Uliginose, Uliginous

**Opal(escent)** Black, Cymophanous, Fire, Gem, Girasol, Girosol, Hyalite, Hydrophane, Liver, Menilite, Noble, Potch, Wood

**Opaque, Opacity** Cloudy, Dense, Dull, Intense, Leucoma, Milky, Obscure, Obtuse, Onycha, Onyx, Roil, Thick, Turbid

**Open(er), Opening, Openness** Adit, Aedicule, Agape, Airhole, Ajar, Antithesis, Anus, Apert(ure), Apparent, Apse, Arch, Armhole, Autopsy, Bald, Bare, Bat, Bay, Begin, Bole, Breach, Break, Broach, Buttonhole, Candid, Candour, Cardia, Cavity, Champaign, Chance, Chasm, Chink, Circumscissile, Clear, Crevasse, Crowbar, Dehisce, Deploy, Dilate, Dispark, Door(way), Drawbridge, Dup, Embrasure, Exordium, Expansive, Explicit, Eyelet, Fair, Fenestra, Fissure, Fistula, Flue, Fontanel(le), Foramen, Frank, Free, Free-for-all, Funnel, Gambit, Gap, Gaping, Gat, Gate, Give, Glasnost, Glottis, Guichet, Gullwing, Hagioscope, Hatch, Hatchback, Hatchway, Hiatus, Hilus, →HOLE, Ice-breaker, Inaugural, Intake, Interstice, Intro, Key, Kisser, Lacy, Lamp hole, Lance, Latchkey, Lead, Loid, Loophole, Loose, Machicolation, Manhole, Meatus, Micropyle, Mofette, Moongate, Mouth, Naked, Nare, Natural, Nook, Oillet, Orifice, Os, Oscule, Osculum, Ostiole, Ostium, Ouvert, Overt, Overture, Pandora, Paper knife, Passe partout, Patent, Peephole, Persuadable, Pert, Pervious, Pick(lock), Placket, Plain, Plughole, Pop, Pore, Port(age), Porta, Porthole, Preliminary, Premiere, Prise, Pro-am, Public, Pylorus, Receptive, Relaxed, Rent, Ring-pull, Riva, Room, Scuttle, Scye, Sesame, Sicilian, Sincere, Slit, Slot, Spare, Spiracle, Spirant, Squint, Start, Stenopaic, Stokehole, Stoma, Stulm, Suasible, Syrinx, Thereout, Thirl, Touchhole, Transparent, Trapdoor, Trema, Trou, Truthful, Unbar, Unbolt, Unbutton, Unclasp, Uncope, Uncork, Undo, Unfurl, Unhasp, Unlatch, Unreserved, Unscrew, Unstop, Unsubtle, Untie, Unwrap, Unzip, Upfront, Vacancy, Vent, Vulnerable, Wide, Window, Yawning

**Open air** Alfresco, Sub divo, Sub Jove

**Opera(tic), Opera house, Operetta** Aida, Ariadne, Ballad, Boris Godunov, Bouffe, Buffo, Burletta, Carmen, Comic, Comique, Das Rheingold, Der Rosenkavalier, Die Fledermaus, Die Walküre, Don Carlos, Don Giovanni, Dramma giocoso, Electra, ENO, Ernani, Euryanthe, Falstaff, Faust, Fedora, Fidelio, Glyndebourne, Grand, Hansel and Gretel, Horse, Idomeneo, Iolanthe, I Puritani, Kirov, La Bohème, La Donna e Mobile, Lakme, La Scala, Light, Lohengrin, Lulu, Macbeth, Magic Flute, Manon, Merrie England, Met, Musical, Nabucco, Norma, Oater, Oberon, Onegin, Orfeo, Otello, Owen Wingrave, Pag, Parsifal, Pastorale, Patience, Peter Grimes, Pinafore, Porgy and Bess, Rienzi, Rigoletto, Ring, Ruddigore, Rusalka, Salome, Savoy, Seria, Simon Boccanegra, Singspiel, Soap, Space, Sudsen, Tell, The Met, Threepenny, Tosca, Turandot, Verismo, Werther, Work, Zarzuela

**Opera-glasses** Jumelle, Starers

**Opera-lover** Wagnerite

**Opera-singer** Baritone, Bass, Contralto, Diva, Savoyard, Soprano

**Operate, Operating, Operation(s), Operative** Act(ion), Activate, Actuate, Afoot, Agent, Artisan, Attuition, Barbarossa, Bypass, Caesarean, Campaign, Colectomy, Combined, Conduct, Couching, Current, Desert Storm, Detective, Doffer, Exercise, Function, Game, Hobday, Holding, Hysterectomy, Jejunostomy, Keystroke, Laparotomy, Leucotomy, Liposuction, Lithotomy, Lithotripsy, Lobotomy, Logical, Manipulate, Mechanic, Mules, Nip and tuck, Nose job, Oner, Overlord, Plastic, Practice, Proceeding,

Rhytidectomy, Run, Sealion, Shirodkar's, Sortie, Splenectomy, Sting, Strabotomy, Surgery, Titration, Tummy tuck, Unit, Ure, Valid, Wertheim, Work

**Operator** Agent, Barnard, Camshaft, Conductor, Dealer, Laplace, Manipulator, Nabla, Sawbones, Sparks, Surgeon, Sysop, System

**Opiate, Opium** Buprenorphine, Dope, Drug, Hop, Laudanum, Meconin, Meconite, Meconium, Morphine, Narcotic, Paregoric, Religion, Soporific, Thebaine

**Opinion(ated), Opinionative** Advice, Attitude, Belief, Bet, Bias, Conjecture, Consensus, Cri, Deem, Diagnosis, Dictum, Dogma, Dogmatic, Doxy, Editorial, Entêté, Esteem, Estimation, Fatwa(h), Feeling, Groundswell, Guess, Heresy, Impression, Judgement, Mind, Mumpsimus, Parti pris, Pious, Prejudice, Private, Public, Pulse, Say, Second, Sense, Sentence, Sentiment, SO, Stand, Syndrome, Take, Tenet, Thought, Utterance, View, Viewpoint, Voice, Vote, Vox pop, Vox populi

**Opossum** Lie, Marmose, Phalanger, Tarsipes, Vulpine, Water, Yapo(c)k

**Oppidan** Cit, Townsman, Urban

**Opponent(s)** Adversary, Antagonist, Anti, Denier, E-N, Enemy, E-S, Foe, Gainsayer, Mitnaged, N-E, N-W, S-E, Straw-man, S-W, Tiger, W-N, W-S

**Opportune, Opportunist, Opportunity** Appropriate, Apropos, Break, Buccaneer, Carpetbagger, → CHANCE, Day, Equal, Facility, Favourable, Ganef, Ganev, Ganof, Godsend, Godslot, Go-go, Golden, Gonif, Gonof, Heaven-sent, Occasion, Opening, Pat, Photo, Providential, Room, Scope, Seal, Seel, Sele, Snatcher, Sneak thief, Tabula rasa, Tide, Timely, Timous, Vantage, Well-timed, Window

**Oppose(d), Opposer, Opposing, Opposite, Opposition** Across, Against, Agin, Anti, Antipathy, Antipodes, Antiscian, Antithesis, Antithetic, Antitype, Antonym, Argue, At, Athwart, Au contraire, Averse, Battle, Beard, Black, Breast, Buck, Collision, Colluctation, Combat, Confront, Contradict, Contrary, Converse, Counter(part), Countermove, Diametric, Dis(en)courage, Disfavour, Dissent, Dissident, Distance, E contrario, Face, Foreanent, Fornen(s)t, Gainsay, Hinder, Hostile, Impugn, Inimical, Inverse, Ironic, Meet, Militate, Mugwump, Noes, Object, Obscurant, Overthwart, Polar, Reactance, Reaction, Recalcitrate, Reluct, Repugn, Resist, Retroact, Reverse, Rival, Shadow, Subtend, Synoeciosis, Syzygy, Teeth, Terr, Them, Thereagainst, They, Thwart, Toe to toe, Toto caelo, Traverse, V, Versus, Vice versa, Vis-à-vis, Withstand

**Oppress(ion), Oppressive** Airless, Bind, Burden, Close, Crush, Dead hand, Despotic, Heavy, Holy cruel, Incubus, Jackboot, Laden, Onerous, Overbear, Overpower, Persecute, Ride, Snool, Stifling, Sultry, Tommy, Totalitarian, Tyrannise, Yoke

**Opprobrium** Disgrace, Envy, Odium, Scandal

**Oppugn** Attack, Criticise

**Opt, Option(al)** Alternative, Call, → CHOICE, Choose, Crown-jewel, Decide, Default, Double zero, Elect(ive), Facultative, Fine, Leipzig, Local, Menu, Naked, Omissible, Pick, Plump, Put, Select, Share, Soft, Swap(tion), Trade(d), Traditional, Voluntary, Votive, Wale, Zero(-zero)

**Optic(al), Optics** Active, Adaptive, Electron, Fibre, Fire, Lens, Photics, Prism, Reticle, Visual

**Optimism, Optimist(ic)** Bull, Chiliast, Elated, Expectant, Feelgood, Hopeful, Micawber, Morale, Overplay, Pangloss, Pollyanna, Rosy, Sanguine, Starry-eyed, Upbeat, Utopiast, Yea-sayer

**Opulent, Opulence** Abundant, Affluent, Luxury, Moneyed, Rich, Splendour, Wealthy

**Opus** Piece, Study, Work

**Or** Au, Either, Ere, Gold, Ossia, Otherwise, Sol

**Oracle(s), Oracular** Delphi, Dodonian, Mirror, Prophet, Pythian, Pythoness, Sage, Seer, Sibyl(line), Thummim, Trophonius, Urim, Vatic

**Oral** Acroamatic, Noncupative, Sonant, Spoken, Unwritten, Verbal, Viva, Viva voce, Vocal

**Orange** Agent, An(n)atta, An(n)atto, Apricot, Arnotto, Aurora, Bergamot, Bigarade, Bilirubin, Bitter, Blenheim, Blood, Blossom, Calamondin, Chica, Claybank, Clockwork, Croceate, Flame, Flamingo, Fulvous, Genip(ap), Jaffa, Kamala, Kamela, Kamila, Karaka, Kumquat, Mandarin,

Methyl, Mock, Naartje, Nacarat, Nartjie, Navel, Ochre, Osage, Petit grain, Pig, Roucou, Ruta, Satsuma, Seville, Shaddock, Sour, Sweet, Tangerine, Tenné, Ugli®, Ulsterman

**Orang-utan** Ape, Monkey, Satyr

**Orate, Oration, Oratory** Address, Chapel, Declaim, Declamation, Eloge, Elogium, Elogy, Eulogy, Harangue, Panegyric, Philippics, Speech

**Oratorio, Orator(y)** Boanerges, Brompton, Brougham, Cantata, Cicero, Creation, Demagogue, Demosthenes, Diction, Elijah, Hwyl, Isocrates, Lectern, Morin, Nestor, Prevaricator, Proseucha, Proseuche, Rant, Rhetor, Samson, Spellbinder, Stump, Tub-thumper, Windbag, Yarra-banker

**Orb** Ball, Eyeball, Firmament, Globe, Mound, Ocellus, Pome, Sphere

**Orbit(al)** Apolune, Apse, Apsis, Circuit, Dump, Eccentric, Ellipse, Eye, Graveyard, Lunar, Osculating, Parking, Path, Periastron, Perigee, Perihelion, Perilune, Periselenium, Polar, Revolution, Stationary, Subshell, Synchronous

**Orcadian** Hoy

**Orchard** Arbour, Grove, Holt

**Orchestra(te), Orchestration** Brass, Chamber, Charanga, Concertgebouw, Concerto, ECO, Ensemble, Gamelan, Hallé, Instrumentation, LPO, LSO, Palm Court, Percussion, Pit, Ripieno, Score, Sinfonietta, SNO, Stage-manage, String, Symphony, Woodwind

**Orchid** Adam and Eve, Adder's mouth, Arethusa, Babe-in-a-cradle, Bee, Bee-orchis, Bird's nest, Bog, Burnt-tip, Butterfly, Calanthe, Calypso, Cattleya, Cooktown, Coralroot, Coral wort, Cymbidium, Cypripedium, Disa, Epidendrum, Fly, Fly orchis, Fragrant, Fringed orchis, Frog, Helleborine, Hyacinth, Lady, Lady's slipper, Lady's tresses, Lizard, Man, Marsh, Military, Miltonia, Moccasin-flower, Monkey, Musk, Naked lady, Odontoglossum, Oncidium, Phalaenopsis, Pogonia, Purple-fringed, Puttyroot, Pyramidal, Rattlesnake plantain, Salep, Scented, Slipper, Snakemouth, Soldier, Spider, Spotted, Swamp pink, Swan, Twayblade, Vanda, Vanilla

**Ord** Beginning, Point

**Ordain** Arrange, Command, Decree, Destine, Enact, Induct, Japan, Priest

**Ordeal** Corsned, Disaster, Preeve, Test, →TRIAL, Via Dolorosa

**Order(ed), Orderly, Orders** Acoemeti, Action, Adjust, Administration, Affiliation, Alphabetical, Anton Piller, Apollonian, Apple-pie, Arrange, Array, ASBO, Attachment, Attendant, Attention, Attic, Augustine, Avast, Bade, Banker's, Bankruptcy, Bath, Batman, Battalia, Batting, Bed, Behest, Benedictine, Bernardine, Bespoke, Bid, Book, Boss, Brotherhood, Buffalo, Call, Camaldolite, Canon, Category, Caveat, CB, Chaprassi, Charter, Cheque, Chit, Chronological, Chuprassy, Class, Cluniac, Coherent, Command(ment), Committal, Compensation, Composite, Corinthian, Cosmo, Cosmos, Court, Decorum, Decree, Demand, Dictate, Diktat, Direct(ion), Directive, Dispone, Distringas, Dominican, Doric, Draft, DSO, Edict, Embargo, Enclosed, Enjoin, En règle, Errand, Established, Establishment, Eutaxy, Eviction, Exclusion, Feldsher, Fiat, Fiaunt, Firing, Firman, Form(ation), Franciscan, Fraternity, Freemason, Full, Gagging, Garnishee, Garter, Gilbertine, Ginkgo, Good, Grade, Group, Habeas corpus, Heast(e), Hecht, Hest, Holy, Hospitaller, Indent, Injunction, Insectivora, Instruct, Interdict, In turn, Ionic, Irade, Khalsa, Kilter, Knights Hospitallers, Kosmos, Language, Large, Law, Lexical, Loblolly boy, Loblolly man, Loose, Mail, Major, Mandamus, Mandate, Marching, Marist, Market, Marshal, Masonic, Medjidie, Merit, Methodical, Minor, Mittimus, Monastic, Money, Monitor, Moose, Natural, Neatness, Nunnery, OBE, Oddfellows, Official, OM, Open, Orange, Ord, Ordain, Organic, Organised, Pecking, Plot, Possession, Postal, Precedence, Precept, Premonstrant, Prepare, Prescribe, Preservation, Prioritise, Provisional, Pyragyrite, Rank, Receiving, Reception, Regiment, Règle, Regular, Regulation, Religious, Requisition, Restraining, Return, Right, Rule, Ruly, Sailing, Sarvodaya, Scale, Sealed, Search, Sequence, Seraphic, Series, Settle, Shipshape, Short, Side, Sisterhood, Sort, Standing, Starter's, State, Statutory, Stop(-loss), Straight, Stratify, Subpoena, Summons, Supersedere, Supervision, System, Tabulate, Tall, Taxis, Tell, Templar, Teutonic, Third, Thistle, Tidy, Trim, Tuscan, Ukase, Uniformity, Warison, Warrant, Word, Working, Writ

▷ **Ordering** *may indicate* an anagram

**Ordinal** Book, Number, Second, Sequence

**Ordinance** Byelaw, Capitulary, Decree, Edict, Law, Prescript, Rescript, Rite, Statute

**Ordinary** Average, Banal, Bog standard, Canton, Chevron, Comely, Common (or garden), Commonplace, Cot(t)ise, Everyday, Everyman, Exoteric, Fess(e), Flanch, Flange, Folksy, Grassroots, Hackneyed, Humdrum, Mass, Mediocre, Middling, Mundane, → **NORMAL**, O, OR, Pedestrian, Plain, Prosy, Pub, Rank and file, Routine, Ruck, Run-of-the-mill, Saltier, Saltire, Scarp, Simple, So-so, Tressure, Trite, Trivial, Undistinguished, Unexceptional, Uninspired, Usual, Vanilla, Workaday, Your

**Ordnance** Artillery, Cannon, Guns, Pelican, Supply

**Ordure** Cess, Dung, Fertiliser, Manure

**Ore** Alga, Babingtonite, Bauxite, Bornite, Braunite, Breunnerite, Calamine, Calaverite, Calx, Cerusite, Chalcocite, Chalcopyrite, Chloanthite, Coffinite, Coin, Coltan, Copper, Crocoite, Dry-bone, Element, Enargite, Galenite, Glance, Haematite, Hedyphane, Horseflesh, Ilmenite, Iridosmine, Ironstone, Kidney, Limonite, Magnetite, Mat, Melaconite, Middlings, Millhead, Milling grade, Mineral, Minestone, Morass, Niobite, Oligist, Owre, Peacock, Pencil, Phacolite, Pipe, Pitchblende, Proustite, Psilomelane, Pyrargyrite, Pyromorphite, Realgar, Red-lead, Ruby silver, Schlich, Seaweed, Siderite, Sinoptite, Slime, Slug, Smaltite, Speiss, Sphalerite, Stephanite, Stilpnosiderite, Stockwork, Stream-tin, Taconite, Tailing, Tenorite, Tetrahedrite, Tin, Wad(d), White-lead, Yellow cake

**Orfe** Ide

**Organ(s), Organic** Adjustor, Adnexa, American, Anlage, Antimere, Apollonicon, Appendix, Archegonium, Barrel, Biogenic, Biotic, Bladder, Bursa, Calliope, Carbon, Carpel, Carpogonium, Cercus, Chamber, Chemoreceptor, Choir, Chord, Claspers, Clave, Colour, Conch(a), Console, Corti's, Cribellum, Ctene, Ear, Echo, Electric, Electronic, Electroreceptor, Emunctory, End, Epinastic, Essential, Exteroceptor, Eyeball, Feeler, Fin, Flabellum, Fundus, Gall bladder, Gametangium, Gill, Glairin, Gonad, Hammond®, Hand, Hapteron, Harmonica, Harmonium, Haustorium, House, Hydathode, Hydraulos, Imine, Isomere, Kerogen, Kidney, Lien, Light, Liver, Lung-book, Lyriform, Mag(azine), Means, Mechanoreceptor, Media, Medulla, Melodion, Ministry, Modiolus, Nasal, Natural, Nectary, Nematocyst, Nephridium, Newspaper, Nose, Olfactory, Oogonia, Ovary, Ovipositor, Ovotestis, Palp, Pancreas, Paper, Parapodium, Part, Pedal, Photogen, Photophore, Photoreceptor, Physharmonics, Pipe, Pipeless, Placenta, Plastid, Portative, Positive, Procarp, Prothallus, Pudenda, Pulmones, Purtenance, Pyrophone, Radula, Receptor, Recit, Reed, Regal, Relict, Rhizoid, Sang, Saprobe, Scent, Sense, Sensillum, Serinette, Serra, Siphon, Spinneret, Spleen, Sporangium, Sporocarp, Sporophore, Stamen, Statocyst, Steam, Swell, Syrinx, Systaltic, Tentacle, Textual, Theatre, Theca, Thymus, Tongue, Tonsil, Tool, Trichocyst, Tympanum, Ureic, Uterus, Vegetative, Velum, Verset, Viscera, Viscus, Vitals, Voice, Voluntary, Wing, Womb, Wurlitzer®

**Organelle** Peroxisome

**Organise(d), Organisation, Organiser** Activate, Administer, Agency, Aggregator, Amnesty, Anatomy, Apparat, → **ARRANGE**, Association, Body, Brigade, Broederbond, Caucus, Charter, CIA, Class(ify), Codify, Collect, Comecon, Company, Compile, Configure, Constitution, Coordinate, Design, Direct, Edifice, Embody, Entrepreneur, Eoka, Fascio, Fatah, Firm, Group, Guild, Hamas, Hierarchy, Impresario, Infrastructure, Jaycee, Krewe, Ku Klux Klan, Logistics, Machine, Mafia, Marshal, Mastermind, Mobilise, Movement, NATO, Octopus, Opus Dei, Orchestrate, Orderly, Outfit, Personal, PLO, Promotor, Quango, Rally, Red Crescent, Red Cross, Regiment, Resistance, Rosicrucian, Run, Setup, Sharpbender, Social, Soroptimist, Sort, Stage, Stage manage, Stahlhelm, Steward, Sysop, System, Tidy, Together, UN, UNESCO, Viet Minh

▷ **Organise(d)** *may indicate* an anagram

**Organism(s)** Aerobe, Agamic, Alga, Archaea, Asymmetron, Auxotroph, Being, Biogenic, Biometric, Biont, Biotic, Cell, Chimeric, Chlamydia, Ciliate, Clade, Coral, Detritivore,

Diplont, Ecad, Endogenous, Endosymbiont, Entity, Eozoon, Epibenthos, Epizoite, Epizoon, Eucaryote, Euglena, Eukaryote, Eurytherm, Extremophile, Germ, Halobiont, Halophile, Haplont, Hemiparasite, Holophyte, Holoplankton, Homeotherm, Incross, Infauna, Infusoria(n), Lichen, Macrobiote, Medusa, Meiosis, Meroplankton, Metamale, Microaerophile, Microbe, Moneron, Morphology, Nekton, Neuston, Osmoconformer, Paramecium, Pathogen, Periphyton, Phenetics, Ph(a)enology, Plankter, Plankton, Pleuston, Poikilotherm, Prokaryote, Protist, Protista, Protozoan, Radiolarian, Saprobe, Saprotroph, Schizomycete, Seaslater, Sea spider, Sea squirt, Streptococcus, Symbion(t), Teratogen, Thermophile, Torula, Trypanosome, Virino, Volvox, Vorticella, Zoarium

**Organ-part, Organ-stop** Bourdon, Clarabella, Diapason, Gamba, Messiaen, Montre, Nasard, Principal, Pyramidon, Quint, Salicet, Stop, Swell

**Organ-tuner** Reed-knife

**Orgasm** Climax, Come

**Orgy** Bacchanalia(n), Binge, Blinder, Bust, Carousal, Dionysian, Feast, Revel, Saturnalia, Spree, Wassail

**Orient(al)** Adjust, Annamite, Attune, Cantonese, Chinoiserie, Dawn, Dayak, E, East(ern), Far-e(ast), Fu Manchu, Hindu, Laotian, Levant, Leyton, Malay, Mongol, Mongolian, Pareoean, Shan, Sunrise, Tatar, Thai, Tibetan, Turk(o)man

**Orientation** Tropism

**Orifice** Aperture, Blastosphere, Gap, Hole, Micropyle, Nare, Opening, Pore, Spiracle, Trema, Vent

**Origen's work** Tetrapla

**Origin(al), Originate, Originating** Abiogenesis, Abo, Adam, Arise, As per, Beginning, Big bang, Birth, Breed, Come, Cradle, Creation, Derive, Editio princeps, Elemental, Emanate, Epicentre, Etymon, Extraction, First, Firsthand, Focus, Found, Generic, Genesis, Genetical, Germ, Grow, Hatch, Imaginative, Incunabula, Ingenious, Initial, Innovate, Invent(ive), Master, Mother, Nascence, Natality, New, Novel, Ord, Parentage, Precedent, Primal, Primary, Primigenial, Primitive, Primordial, Pristine, Promethean, Protoplast, Prototype, Provenance, Provenience, Radical, Rise, Root, Seed, Seminal, Source, Spring, Start, Unborrowed, Ur, Urtext, Ylem, Zoism

**Oriole** Firebird, Hangbird

**Orion** Alnilam, Alnitak, Ballatrix, Betelgeuse, Hatsya, Lambda, Meissa, Mintaka, Rigel, Saiph

**Orison** Blessing, Prayer

**Ormer** Abalone, Haliotis

**Ornament(al), Ornamentation** Acroter(ia), Additament, Adorn, Aglet, Aiguillette, Anaglyph, Antefix, Anthemion, Aplustre, Applique, Arabesque, Bahuti, Ball-flower, Barbola, Baroque, Barrette, Bead, Bedeck, Bez(z)ant, Billet, Blister, Boss, Bracelet, Breloque, Broider, Brooch, Bugle, Bulla, Caparison, Cartouche, Charm, Chase, Clock, Cockade, Conceit, Corbeil(le), Cornice, Coromandel work, Crocket, Cross-quarters, Curin, Curlicue, Decor, Decorate, Decoration, Diamanté, Die-work, Diglyph, Dog's-tooth, Doodad, Dreamcatcher, Egg and anchor, Egg and dart, Egg and tongue, Embellish, Emblem(a), Embroider, Enrich, Epaulet(te), Epergne, Fallal, Fandangle, Festoon, Fiddlehead, Figuration, Figurine, Filagree, Filigrain, Filigree, Fillagree, Fleur de lis, Fleuret, Fleurette, Fleuron, Florid, Fret, Fretwork, Frill, Frounce, Furbelow, Furnish, Gadroon, Garnish, Gaud, Gingerbread, Gorget, Griff(e), Guilloche, Gutta, Headwork, Hei-tiki, Helix, Hip-knob, Honeysuckle, Horse-brass, Illustrate, Inlay, Japanaiserie, Knosp, Knotwork, Labret, Lambrequin, Lavalier, Leglet, Lotus, Lunette, Lunula, Macramé, Mantling, Mense, Millefleurs, Mordent, Moresque, Motif, Nail-head, Necklet, Netsuke, Nicknackery, Niello, Nose-ring, O, Okimono, Ouch, Ovolo, Palmette, Paraphernalia, Parure, Patera, Paternoster, Paua, Pawa, Pectoral, Pendant, Picot, Pipe, Piping, Plume, Pompom, Pompo(o)n, Poppyhead, Pounce, Pralltriller, Prettify, Prunt, Purfle, Quatrefoil, Rel(l)ish, Rocaille, Rococo, Rosette, Scalework, Scrollwork, Shell, Shoulder-knot, Snowdome, Snowglobe, Spangle, Spar, Stomacher, Tassel, Tettix, Tiki,

Tool, Torc, Torque, Torsade, Tracery, Trappings, Tremolo, Trill, Trimming, Trinket, Triquetra, Tsuba, Turn, Twiddle, Versal, Wally, Water-leaf, Whigmaleerie, Whigmaleery, Whim-wham

**Ornate** Baroque, Churrigueresque, Dressy, Elaborate, Fancy, Florid, Flowery

▷ **Ornate** *may indicate* an anagram

**Ornithologist** Audubon, Birdman

**Orotund** Bombastic, Grandiose, Pompous, Rhetorical, Sonant

**Orphan** Annie, Foundling, Topsy, Ward

**Orpheus** Lutenist

**Orpiment** Arsenic, Zarnec, Zarnich

**Orpington** Buff, Hen

**Ort** Bit, Crumb, Morsel, Remnant

**Orthodox** Bien-pensant, Cocker, Conventional, Fundamental, Hardshell, Proper, Sound, Standard

**Orthorhombic** Enstatite

**Ortolan** Bird, Bunting, Rail

**Oscar** Award, O, Statue, Wilde

**Oscillate, Oscillation, Oscillator** Dynatron, Excitor, Fluctuate, Librate, Local, Parasitic, Relaxation, Ripple, Rock, Seesaw, Seiche, Squeg, Surge, Swing(swang), Vibrate, Waver

**Osier** Red, Reed, Sallow, Willow

**Osmium** Os

**Osmosis** Reverse

**Osprey** Fish-hawk, Lammergeier, Ossifrage, Pandion

**Osseous** Bony, Hard, Skeletal, Spiny

**Ossuary** Urn

**Ostensibly** Apparent, External, Seeming

**Ostentation, Ostentatious** Camp, Dash, Display, Dog, Dressy, Éclat, Epideictical, Extravagant, Fantoosh, Fastuous, Flamboyant, Flash(y), Flaunt, Florid, Flourish, Garish, Gaudy, Ghetto fabulous, Highfalutin(g), Large, Parade, Pomp, Ponc(e)y, Pretence, Puff, →SHOW(ING), Showboating, Side, Splash, Swank, Tacky, Tulip

**Osteoporosis** Sudeck's atrophy

**Ostler** Stabler

**Ostracise, Ostracism** Banish, Blackball, Blacklist, Boycott, Cut, Exclude, Exile, Petalism, Potsherd, Proscribe, Snub, Taboo, Tabu

**Ostrich** Em(e)u, Estrich, Estridge, Nandoo, Nandu, Ratite, Rhea, Struthio(nes), Titanis

**Othello** Moor, Morisco

**Other(s), Otherwise** Additional, Aka, Alia, Alias, Allo-, Alternative, Besides, Different, Distinct, Else, Et al, Et alli, Etc, Excluding, Former, Further, Hanky-panky, It, Notwithstanding, Rest, Significant, Unlike

**Other things** Alia

▷ **Otherwise** *may indicate* an anagram

**Otiose** Idle, Indolent, Ineffective, Lazy, Needless, Superfluous, Useless

**Otis** Bustard

**Otologist** Aurist

**OTT** Ostentatious

**Ottawa** Bytown

**Otter** Edal, Paravane, Sea, Tarka, Waterdog

**Otto** Attar, Chypre, Mahratta

**Ottoman** Osmanli, Porte, Rayah, Rumelia, Turk

**Oubliette** Dungeon, Pit, Prison

**Ouch** Argh, Brooch, Ornament, Ow

**Ought** All, Should

**Ouida** Ramée

**Ouija** Board, Planchette

**Ounce** Cat, Fluid, Liang, Oz, Panther, Snow leopard, Tael, Trace, Uncial

**Our(selves)** Us, We

▶ **Ousel** *see* **OUZEL**

**Oust** Depose, Dislodge, Eject, Evict, Expel, Fire, Supplant, Unnest, Unseat

**Out (of)** Absent, Aglee, Agley, Al fresco, Asleep, Aus, Away, Begone, Bowl, Comatose, Dated, En ville, Exposed, External, Forth, From, Furth, Haro, Harrow, Hence, Hors, Inaccurate, In bloom, In blossom, Lent, Oust, Passe, Skittle, Striking, Stump, Taboo, Uit, Unfashionable, Up, York

▷ **Out** *may indicate* an anagram

**Out and out** Absolute, Arrant, Rank, Sheer, Stark, Teetotal, Thorough, Totally, Utter

**Outback** Backblocks, Bundu, Never-never, The mulga

**Outbreak** Ebullition, Epidemic, Eruption, Explosion, Flare-up, Plague, Putsch, Rash, Recrudescence, Spate

**Outbuilding** Garage, Shed

**Outburst** Access, Blurt, Bluster, Boutade, Brainstorm, Eruption, Evoe, Explosion, Fit, Flaw, Furore, Fusillade, Gale, Gush, Gust, Paroxysm, Passion, Philippic, Sally, Salvo, Sternutation, Storm, Tantrum, Tirade, Torrent, Tumult, Volley

**Outcast** Cagot, Discard, Eta, Exile, Exul, Ishmael, Leper, Mesel, Pariah, Robinson, Rogue

**Outcome** Aftermath, Consequence, Decision, Dénouement, Effect, Emergence, End, Event, Issue, Reflection, → **RESULT**, Sequel, Upshot, Wash-up

**Outcrop** Basset, Blossom, Crag, Creston, Inlier, Mesa, Rognon, Spur, Tarpit

**Outcry** Alew, Blue murder, Bray, → **CLAMOUR**, Halloa, Halloo, Howl, Hue, Humdudgeon, Protest, Racket, Shright, Steven, Uproar, Utas

**Outdated, Out of date** Archaic, Dinosaur, Effete, Feudal, Fossil, Horse and buggy, Obsolete, Old hat, Outmoded, Passé, Square

**Outdo** Beat, Best, Cap, Picnic, Superate, Surpass, Top, Trump, Worst

**Outdoor(s)** Alfresco, External, Garden, Open air, Outbye, Plein-air

**Outer** External, Extrogenous, Magpie, Superficial, Top

**Outfit(ter)** Accoutrement, Arm, Catsuit, Drawbar, Dress, Ensemble, Equipage, Fitout, Furnish, Get-up, Haberdasher, Habit, Kit, Layette, Rig, Samfoo, Samfu, Strip, Suit, Tackle, Team, Trousseau, Turnout, Weed(s), Whites

**Outflank** Bypass, Overlap

**Outflow** Anticyclone, Discharge, Ebb, Effluence, Eruption, Exodus, Gorge, Issue, Surge

**Outgoing** Egression, Exiting, Extrovert, Migration, Open, Rental, Retiring

**Outgrowth** Ala(te), Appendage, Aril, Bud, Caruncle, Enation, Epiphenomenon, Exostosis, Flagellum, Ligule, Offshoot, Osteophyte, Propagulum, Root-hair, Sequel, Strophiole, Trichome

**Outhouse** Conservatory, Lean to, Privy, Shed, Skilling, Skillion, Skipper, Stable

**Outing** Excursion, Hike, Jaunt, Junket, Picnic, Sortie, Spin, Spree, Treat, Trip, Wayzgoose

**Outlandish** Alien, Barbarous, Bizarre, Exotic, Foreign, Peregrine, Rum

**Outlaw** Allan-a-Dale, Attaint, Badman, Ban, Bandit(ti), Banish, Broken man, Bushranger, Desperado, Exile, Forbid, Friar Tuck, Fugitive, Hereward, Hood, Horn, Jesse James, Klepht, Maid Marian, Ned Kelly, Proscribe, Put to the horn, Robin Hood, Rob Roy, Ronin, Tory, Waive

**Outlay** Cost, Expense, Mise

**Outlet** Débouché, Drain, Egress, Escape, Estuary, Exit, Femerall, Market, Opening, Orifice, Outfall, Overflow, Sluice, Socket, Spout, Tuyere, Tweer, Twier, Twire, Twyer(e), Vent

**Outline** Adumbration, Aperçu, Circumscribe, Configuration, Contorno, Contour, Delineate, Describe, Digest, → **DRAFT**, Draught, Esquisse, Footprint, Layout, Note, Perimeter, Plan, Profile, Projet, Prospectus, Relief, Scenario, Schematic, Shape, Silhouette, Skeletal, Skeleton, Sketch, Summary, Syllabus, Synopsis, T(h)alweg, Trace

**Outlook** Aspect, Attitude, Casement, Mindset, Perspective, Prospect, View(point), Vista, Weltanschauung

**Outmanoeuvre** Upstage
**Outmoded** Wasm
▷ **Out of** *may indicate* an anagram
**Out of date** Corny, Obs, Passé, Scrap, Square, Worn
**Out of form** Amorphous, Awry
**Out of order** Fritz, Kaput
**Out of sorts** Cachectic, Nohow, Peevish, Poorly
▷ **Out of sorts** *may indicate* an anagram
**Out of tune** Discordant, Flat, Scordato, Scordatura
**Outpace** Leave standing
**Outpatient** Externe
**Outpost** Colony, Picquet, Station
**Outpour(ing)** Bavardage, Effuse, Flood, Flow, Gush, Libation, Spate, Stream, Torrent
**Output** Data, Emanation, Get, Gross, Print out, Produce, Production, Turnout, Yield
▷ **Output** *may indicate* an anagram
**Outrage(ous)** Affront, Apoplectic, Appal, Atrocity, Crime, Desecrate, Diabolical, Disgust,
Egregious, Enorm(ity), Flagitious, Flagrant, Indignation, Insult, OTT, Rich, Sacrilege,
Scandal, Shocking, Ungodly, Unholy, Violate
▷ **Outrageously** *may indicate* an anagram
**Outright** Clean, Complete, Entire, Point-blank, Utter
**Outrun** Spreadeagle
**Outset** Ab initio, Beginning, Start
**Outshine** Eclipse, Excel, Overshadow, Surpass, Upstage
**Outside** Ab extra, Crust, Derma, Enthetic, Exterior, External, Extramural, Front, Furth,
Hors, Periphery, Plein-air, Rim, Rind, Rine, Shell, Surface
**Outsider** Alien, Bolter, Bounder, Cad, Extern, Extremist, Foreigner, Incomer, Oustiti,
Palagi, Pariah, Ring-in, Roughie, Stranger, Stumer, Unseeded, Upstart
**Outsize** Capacious, Giant, Gigantic, Huge, OS
**Outskirts** Edge, Fringe, Periphery, Purlieu
**Outspoken** Bluff, Blunt, Broad, Candid, Explicit, Forthright, Frank, Plain, Rabelaisian,
Round, Vocal, Vociferous
**Outstand(ing)** Ace, Beaut(y), Belter, Billowing, Bulge, Chief, Crack, Crackerjack,
Debt, Egregious, Eminent, Especial, Exceptional, Exquisite, Extant, Extraordinaire,
First, Fugleman, Highlight, Humdinger, Impasto, Jut, Left, Lulu, Marked, Masterpiece,
Matchless, Oner, Overdue, Owing, Paragon, Paramount, Peerless, Phenom(enal), Pièce
de résistance, Pre-eminent, Prince, Prize, Prominent, Promontory, Prosilient, Protrude,
Protuberant, Proud, Purler, Red letter, Relief, Relievo, Salient, Shining light, Signal,
Special, Squarrose, Star, Stellar, Strout, Super(b), Top flight, Tour de force, Unmet,
Unpaid, Unsettled, Vocal
**Outstrip** Best, Cap, Cote, Distance, Exceed, Overtake
**Outward** Efferent, Extern(e), External, Extrinsic, Extrorse, Extrovert, Posticous,
Postliminary, Superficial
**Outweigh** Preponderate
**Outwit** Baffle, Best, Circumvent, Crossbite, Dish, Euchre, Fox, Outthink, Over-reach,
→**THWART**, Trick
**Outwork** Demilune, Jetty, Moon, Tenail(le), Tenaillon
**Outworn** Decrepit, Obsolete, Used
**Ouzel** Merle, Ring, Water
**Oval(s)** Cartouche, Cassini, Ellipse, Henge, Mandorla, Navette, Obovate, Ooidal
**Ovary** Oophoron
**Ovation** Applause, Cheer, Standing
**Oven(-like)** Aga®, Calcar, Camp, Combination, Convection, Cul-de-four, Dutch, Electric,
Fan, Furnace, Gas, Hangi, Haybox, Horn(it)o, Kiln, Lear, Leer, Lehr, Lime kiln, Maori,
Microwave, Muffle, Norwegian, Oast, Oon, Rotisserie, Stove, Umu

**Over** Above, Across, Again, Atop, C, Clear, Done, Finished, Hexad, Left, Maiden, Of, On, Ore, Ort, Owre, Past, Sopra, Spare, Superior, Surplus, Through, Uber, Wicket maiden, Yon

**Overact** Burlesque, Emote, Ham, Hell, Hoke

**Overactive** Hyper

**Overall(s)** Boiler suit, Chaps, Denims, Dungarees, Dust-coat, Fatigues, Generally, Jumper, Siren suit, Smicket, Smock, Tablier, Umbrella, Workwear

**Overbalance** Outweigh

**Overbear(ing)** Arrogant, Bossy, Dogmatic, Domineering, High-muck-a-muck, Imperious, Insolent, Lordly, Macher, Oppressive, Supercilious, Weigh down

**Overbid** Gazump

**Overcast** Cloudy, Dull, Lowering, Sew, Sombre

**Over-cautious** Old-maidish

**Overcharge** Clip, Extort, Fleece, Gazump, Gyp, OC, Rack-rent, Rook, Rush, Soak, Sting

**Overcoat** Balmacaan, Benjamin, Benny, British warm, Chesterfield, →COAT, Crombie, Dolman, Grego, Inverness, Jemmy, Joseph, Paletot, Pea-jacket, Petersham, Pos(h)teen, Prince Albert, Raglan, Redingote, Spencer, Surtout, Tabard, Taglioni, Ulster, Warm, Wooden, Wrap-rascal

**Overcome** Beat, Bested, Conquer, Convince, Dead-beat, Defeat, Expugn, Hit for six, Kill, Master, Mither, Moider, Moither, Prevail, Quell, Speechless, Stun, Subdue, Subjugate, Superate, Surmount, Survive, Swampt, Underfong, Vanquish, Win

**Overconfident, Overconfidence** Besserwisser

**Overcrowd** Congest, Jam, Pack

**Overdo(ne)** Burnt, Exceed, Ham, Hokey, Hokum, OTT, Percoct, Tire

**Overdose** OD, Surfeit

**Overdraft** Red

▷ **Overdrawn** *may indicate* 'red' outside another word

**Overdress(ing)** Dudism, Flossy, Overall

**Overdue** Behindhand, Belated, Excessive, Late, Unpaid

**Overeat(ing)** Binge, Gorge, Hypertrophy, Pig out, Satiate

**Over-elaborate** Baroque

**Over-emotional** Melodramatic

**Overemphasize** Rub in, Stress

**Over-excited** Hyper

**Overfeed(ing)** Glut, Gorge, Sate, Stuff

**Overflow(ing)** Abrim, Cornucopia, Lip, Nappe, Ooze, Outpour, Ream, Redound, Spillage, Surfeit, Teem

**Overfull** Brimming, Hept

**Overground** Subaerial

**Overgrow(n)** Ivy'd, Jungle, Ramp(ant), Rank, Rhinophyma

**Overhang(ing)** Beetle, Bulge, Cornice, →JUT, Loom, Project, Shelvy

**Overhasty** Rash

**Overhaul** Bump, Catch, Overtake, Recondition, Refit, Revision, Service, Strip

**Overhead(s)** Above, Aloft, Ceiling, Cost, Exes, Hair(s), Headgear, Oncost, Rafter, Upkeep, Zenith

**Overhear** Catch, Eavesdrop, Tap

**Overheat** Enrage

**Over here** Psst

**Overindulge(nt)** Crapulent, Crass, Dissipated, Dissolute, Pig

**Overjoy** Elate, Thrill

**Overland** Portage

**Overlap(ping)** Correspond, Equitant, Imbricate, Incubous, Kern(e), Limbous, Obvolute, Stretto, Tace, Tasse

**Overlay** Ceil, Ciel, Smother, Stucco, Superimpose, Too, Veneer

**Overlearned** Pedantic
**Overload** Burden, Plaster, Strain, Surcharge, Tax
**Overlong** Sesquipedalian
**Overlook(ed)** Condone, Disregard, Excuse, Forget, Forgive, Indulge, Miss, Neglect, Omit, Pass, Pretermit, Superintend, Unnoticed, Waive
**Overlord** Edwin, Enslaver, Excess, Invasion, Swoop
**Overlying** Incumbent, Jessant, Pressing
**Overmuch** Excessive, Surplus, Too, Undue
**Overplay** Ham, Hoke
**Overpower(ing)** Crush, Evince, Mighty, Onerous, Oppress, Outman, Overwhelm, Potent, Profound, Subdue, Surmount, Swelter, Whelm
**Overpraise** Adulate
**Overprotective** Nannyish
**Over-refined** Dainty, Nice, Pernickety, Precious
**Override, Overrule** Abrogate, Disallow, Outvote, Outweigh, Paramount, Preponderant, Reverse, Talk down, Veto
**Overrun** Exceed, Extra, Infest, Inundate, Invade, Lip, Swarm, Teem
**Overseas** Abroad, Colonial, Foreign, Outremer, Transmarine, Ultramarine
**Oversee(r)** Administer, Baas, Banksman, Boss, Captain, Care, Deputy, Direct, Eyebrow, Foreman, Forewoman, Grieve, Handle, Induna, Mediate, Moderator, Periscope, Steward, Supercargo, Superintend, Supervise, Survey(or)
**Oversentimental** Byronic, Slushy
**Overshadow(ed)** Cloud, Dominate, Dwarf, Eclipse, Obscure, Outclass, Umbraculate
**Overshoe** Arctic, Galosh, Sandal, Snowboot
**Oversight** Blunder, Care, Error, Gaffe, Inadvertence, Lapse, Neglect, Parablepsis
**Overstate(ment), Overstated** Embroider, Exaggerate, Hyperbole, Theatral, Theatrical
**Overstrained** Epitonic
**Overt** Manifest, Patent, Plain, Public
**Overtake** Catch, For(e)hent, Lap, Leapfrog, Overget, Overhaul, →**PASS**, Supersede, Usurp
**Overthrow** Dash, Defeat, Demolish, Depose, Dethrone, Down, Labefact(at)ion, Putsch, Ruin, Smite, Stonker, Subvert, Supplant, Topple, Unhorse, Unseat, Usurp, Vanquish, Whemmle, Whommle, Whummle, Worst
**Overtime** Extension
**Overtone** Harmonic
**Overture** Advance, Approach, Carnival, Concert, Egmont, French, Hebrides, Intro, Italian, Leonora, Offer, →**OPENING**, Prelude, Propose, Serenade, Sinfonia, Toccata, Toccatella, Toccatina
**Overturn(ing)** Capsize, Catastrophe, Coup, Cowp, Engulf, Keel, Quash, Rebut, Reverse, Tip, Topple, Up(set), Upend, Whemmle, Whomble, Whommle, Whummle
**Overuse(d)** Hackney(ed), RSI
**Overvalue** Exaggerate, Salt
**Overweening** Bashaw, Cocky, Excessive, Imperious, Presumptuous
**Overweight** Heavy, Lardy, Obese, Pursy, Sunk
**Overwhelm(ed), Overwhelming** Accablé, Assail, Banging, →**CRUSH**, Dearth, Defeat, Deluge, Engulf, Flabbergast, Foudroyant, Inundate, KO, Mind-boggling, Oppress, Overcome, Plough under, Scupper, Smother, Snow, Submerge, Swamp, Whup
**Overwork(ed)** Fag, Hackneyed, Ornament, Slog, Stale, Supererogation, Tax, Tire, Toil, Travail
**Overwritten** Palimpsest
**Overwrought** Frantic, Hysterical, Ore-rested, Ornate, Rococo
**Ovid** Naso
**Ovum** Egg, Oosphere, Seed, Zygote
**Owe(d), Owing** Attribute, Due, OD
**Owen** Glendower

**Owl(s)** African, Barn, Barred, Blinker, Boobook, Brown, Bubo, Bunter, Chinese, Eagle, Elegant, English, Fish, Glimmergowk, Grey, Hawk, Hoo(ter), Horned, Howlet, Jenny, Little, Long-eared, Longhorn, Madge, Moper, Mopoke, Mopus, Night, Ogle, Parliament, Ruru, Saw-whet, Scops, Screech, Sea, Snowy, Spotted, Strich, Striges, Strigiformes, Tawny, Wood

**Own(er), Owning, Ownership** Acknowledge, Admit, Agnise, Confess, Domain, Dominium, Fess, Have, Hold, Mortmain, Nain, Of, Personal, Possess, Proper, Proprietor, Recognise, Reputed, Title, Tod, Use

**Own way** More suo

**Ox(en)** Anoa, Aquinas, Aurochs, Banteng, Banting, Bison, Bonas(s)us, Buffalo, Bugle, Bullock, Cat(t)alo, Fee, Gaur, Gayal, Gyal, Kouprey, Mart, Musk, Musk-sheep, Neat, Ovibos, Rother, Saola, Sapi-utan, S(e)ladang, Steare, Steer, Stirk, Taurus, Ure, Urus, Vu quang, Water, Water buffalo, Yak, Yoke, Zebu, Z(h)o

**Oxford (group)** Blue, Buchmanism, OU, Puseyism, Shoe

**Oxhead** Aleph

**Oxidation, Oxide, Oxidise(d)** Alumina, Anatase, Ceria, Erbia, Eremacausis, Gothite, Gummite, Holmia, Kernite, Lithia, Magnesia, Nitrous, Ochre, Psilomelane, Quicklime, Rare earth, Red lead, Rust, Rutile, Samarskite, Strontia, Thoria, Zaffer, Zaffre

**Oxlip** Paigle

▷ **Oxtail** *may indicate* 'x'

**Oxygen (and lack of)** Aerobe, Anoxia, Epoxy, Liquid, Lox, Loxygen, O, Ozone, Vital air

**Oyer** Hearing, Trial

**Oyster (bed), Oyster disease, Oyster-eater** Avicula, Bivalve, Bonamia, Bush, Cul(t)ch, Kentish, Lay, Mollusc, Native, Ostrea, Ostreophage, Pandore, Pearl, Plant, Prairie, Salsify, Scallop, Scalp, Scaup, Seed(ling), Spat, Spondyl, Stew, Vegetable

**Oyster-catcher** Sea-pie

**Oyster-plant** Gromwell, Salsify

**Oz** Amos, Australia, NSW

**Ozone** Air, Atmosphere, Oxygen

# Pp

**P** Papa, Parking, Penny, Piano, Prince

**PA** Aide, Tannoy

**Pabulum** Aliment, Cheer, Food, Fuel, Nourishment

**Pace, Pacemaker** Canter, Clip, Cracking, Dog-trot, Easter, Footstep, Gait, Geometric, Heel and toe, Jog-trot, Lope, Measure, Military, Pari passu, Pioneer, Prowl, Rack, →RATE, Roman, Scout's, Single-foot, Snail's, Spank, Speed, Step, Stride, Stroll, Tempo, Tramp, Tread, Trot

**Pachyderm** Armadillo, Elephant, Hippo, Mastodon, Rhino

**Pacific, Pacify** Appease, Bromide, Calm, Conciliate, Dove, Ease, Eirenic, Imperturbable, Irenic, Lull, Mild, Moderate, Ocean, Placate, Placid, Quiet, Serene, Soothe, Subdue, Sweeten, Tranquil

**Pacifist** Anti-war, CO, Conciliator, Dove, D(o)ukhobor, Peacenik

**Pack(age), Packaging, Packed, Packing, Pack in** Back, Bale, Blister, Bobbery, Box, Bubble(wrap), Bundle, Can, Cards, Carry, Cold, Compress, Congest, Cram, Crate, Crowd, Cry, Deck, Dense, Dunnage, Embox, Entity, Everest, Excelsior, Face, Fardel, Flock, Floe, Forswear, Gasket, Gaskin, Glut, Hamper, Hooker, Hunt, Ice, Jam, Kennel, Kitbag, Knapsack, Lies, Load, Matilda, Naughty, Pair, →PARCEL, Pikau, Power, Pun, Ram, Rat, Rout, Ruck, Rucksack, Set, Shiralee, Shrink-wrap, Steeve, Stow, Suits, Sumpter, Tamp, Team, Tread, Troop, Truss, Wad, Wet, Wolf, Wrap

**Packet** Bindle, Boat, Bomb, Bundle, Cookie, Deck, Liner, Mailboat, Mailer, Mint, Parcel, Pay, Red, Roll, Sachet, Steam, Steamboat, Wage

**Pack-horse** Sumpter

**Packman** Chapman, Hawker, Hiker, Pedlar, Tinker

**Pact** Agreement, Alliance, Bargain, Bilateral, Cartel, Contract, Covenant, Entente cordiale, Locarno, Munich, Stability, Suicide, →TREATY, Warsaw

**Pad(ding)** Bachelor, Batting, Bombast, Brake, Bustle, Compress, Condo, Crash, Cushion, Dabber, Damper, Dossil, Earmuff, Enswathe, Expand, Falsies, Filler, Flat, Frog, Gumshield, Hard, Hassock, Horse, Ink, Jotter, Knee, Launch, Leg-guard, Lily, Nag, Note, Numnah, Patch, Paw, Ped, Pillow, Pincushion, Plastron, Pledget, Plumper, Porters' knot, Pouf(fe), Protract, Pudding, Puff, Pulvillus, Pulvinar, Quitting, Scratch, Shoulder, Squab, Stamp, Stuff, Sunk, Swab, Tablet, Thief, Touch, Tournure, Tylopod, Tympan, Velour(s), Velure, Wad, Waffle, Wase, Writing

**Paddington** Bear, Station

**Paddle, Paddle boat, Paddle-foot** Canoe, Dabble, Doggy, Oar, Pinniped, Row, Seal, Side-wheel, Spank, Splash, Stern-wheeler, Wade

**Paddock** Enclosure, Field, Frog, Holding, Meadow, Park, Parrock, Sacrifice

**Paddy, Paddy field** Fury, Ire, Irishman, Mick, Pat(rick), Pet, Rag, Rage, Sawah, Tantrum, Temper, Wax

**Padre** Chaplain, Cleric, Father, Monk, Priest

**Paean** Eulogy, Hymn, Ode, Praise, Psalm

**Paediatrician** Rett

**Paedophile** Nonce

**Pagan(ism)** Animist, Atheist, Baalite, Ethnic, Gentile, Gentoo, Godless, Heathen, Heretic, Idolater, Infidel, Lectisternium, Odinist, Paynim, Saracen, Sun cult, Wicca

**Page(s), Pageboy** Back, Bastard title, Beep, Bellboy, Bellhop, Bleep, Boy, Buttons, Callboy, Centrefold, Contact, Flyleaf, Fold out, Folio, Foolscap, Front, Gate-fold, Groom, Haircut, Hairdo, Henchman, Home, Hornbook, Leaf, Master, Messenger, Moth, Octavo, Op-ed, P, Pane, PP, Problem, Quarto, Ream, Recto, Ro, Servant, Sheet, Side, Splash, Squire, Tear sheet, Thirty-twomo, Tiger, Title, Varlet, Verso, Web, Yellow

**Pageant** Antic, Anticke, Antique, Cavalcade, Pomp, Spectacle, Tattoo, Triumph

**Pagoda** Anking, Anqing, Temple, To

**Pah** Pish, Tush, Umph

▶ **Paid** *see* **PAY(MASTER)**

**Pail** Bucket, Kettle, Leglan, Leglen, Leglin, Piggin, Slop

**Pain(ful), Pains** Ache, Aggrieve, Agony, Ake, Algesis, Angina, Anguish, A(a)rgh, Arthralgia, Bad, Bale, Bedsore, Bitter, Bore, Bot(t), Bother, Burn, Causalgia, Colic, Cramp, Crick, CTS, Distress, Dole, Doleur, Dolour, Dool(e), Dysmenorhoea, Dysury, Eina, Excruciating, Fash, Felon, Fibrositis, Gastralgia, Gip, Grief, Gripe, Growing, Gyp, Harrow, Heartburn, Hemialgia, → **HURT**, Ill, Kink, Laborious, Lancination, Lumbago, Mal, Mastalgia, Mastodynia, Metralgia, Migraine, Misery, Molimen, Mulligrubs, Myalgia, Neuralgia, Nociceptive, Pang, Persuant, Pest, Phantom, Pleurodynia, Prick, Pungent, Rack, Raw, Referred, Rick, Sair, Sciatica, Smart, Sore, Sorrow, Splitting, Sten(d), Sternalgia, Sting, Stitch, Strangury, Stung, Tarsalgia, Teen(e), Tene, Throe, Topalgia, Torment, Tormina, Torture, Travail, Twinge, Wo(e), Wrench, Wring

▷ **Pain** *may indicate* bread (French)

**Painkiller** Aminobutene, Analgesic, Bute, Celecoxib, Cocaine, Coxib, Distalgesic, Endorphin, Enkephalin, Jadeite, Meperidine, Metopon, Morphine, Number, Pethidine

**Painless(ness)** Analgesia, Easy

**Painstaking** Analgesic, Assiduous, Careful, Diligent, Elaborate, Exacting, Meticulous, Sedulous, Studious, Thorough

**Paint(ed), Painting** Abstract, Abstract expressionism, Acrylic, Action, Airbrush, Alla prima, Aquarelle, Arcimboldo, Art autre, Art deco, Artificial, Art nouveau, Ash Can School, Barbizon, Baroque, Battlepiece, Bice, Blottesque, Brushwork, Byzantine, Camaieu, Canvas, Cellulose, Cerograph, Chiaroscuro, Clair-obscure, Clobber, Coat, Colour, Constable, Cubiform, Cubism, Dadaism, Daub, Dayglo, Decorate, Depict, Describe, Diptych, Distemper, Duco, Eggshell, Emulsion, Enamel, Encaustic, Expressionist, Fard, Fauvism, Finery, Finger, Flatting, Flemish, Fore-edge, Fresco, Fucus, Genre, Gild, Gloss, Gothic, Gouache, Graining, Gravure, Grease, Grisaille, Guernica, Hard-edge, Historical, Icon, Impasto, Impressionism, Intimism(e), Intonaco, Intumescent, Lead, Limn, Lithochromy, Luminous, Magilp, Mannerist, Maquillage, Matt, Megilp, Mehndi, Miniate, Miniature, Modello, Mona Lisa, Monotint, Mural, Naive, Neoclassical, Neo-expressionist, Neo-Impressionism, Neo-Plasticism, Nightpiece, Nihonga, Nocturne, Non-drip, Oaker, Ochre, Oil, Old Master, Oleo(graph), Op art, Orphism, Paysage, Pentimento, Pict, Picture, Pigment, Pinxit, Plein air, Pointillism(e), Polyptych, Pop art, Portray, Poster, Post-Impressionism, Predella, Pre-Raphaelite, Primavera, Primitive, Quadratura, Raddle, Rag-rolling, Realist, Renaissance, Rococo, Romantic, Rosemaling, Roughstuff, Sand, Scenography, Scumble, Secco, Semi-gloss, Sfumato, Sien(n)ese, Skyscape, Spray, Stencil, Stereochrome, Still life, Stipple, Suprematism, Surrealist, Tablature, Tableau, Tachism(e), Tag, Tall-oil, Tanka, Tempera, Tenebrism, Thangka, Tondo, Townscape, Ukiyo-e, Umber, Umbrian, Undercoat, Underglaze, Vanitas, Veduta, Vorticism, War, Wax

**Painted woman** Courtesan, Harlot, Pict, Tart

**Painter(s)** Animalier, Aquarellist, → **ARTIST**, Ash Can School, Colourist, Cubist, Decorator, Gilder, Illusionist, Impressionist, Lazy, Limner, Little Master, Luminarist, Miniaturist, Modernist, Muralist, Nazarene, Old Master, Paysagist, Plein-airist, Primitive, Sien(n)ese, Soutine, Sunday, Vedutista

**Pair(ing)** A deux, Brace, Cooper, Couple(t), Doublet, Duad, Duo, Dyad(ic), Electron, Exciton, Fellows, Geminate, Item, Jugate, Jumelle, King, Link, Lone, Match, Mate,

Minimal, Ocrea, Pigeon, Pr, Span, Spouses, Synapsis, Syndyasmian, Syzygy, Tandem, Thummim, Twa(e), Tway, Twin, Two, Urim, Yoke

**Paisley** Ian, Orange, Shawl

**Pakistan(i)** Jat, Pathan, -.pk, Punjabi, Sind(h)i

**Pal** Ally, Amigo, Bud(dy), China, Chum, Comrade, Crony, Cully, Friend, Mate, Playmate, Roomie, Wus(s)

**Pal(a)eolithic** Acheulean, Acheulian, Azilian, Capsian, Chellean, Clactonian, Gravettian, Levallois(ian), Lower, Madelenian, Magdalenian, Middle, Neanderthal, Perigordian, Solutrean, Strepyan, Upper

**Palace** Alcazar, Alhambra, Basilica, Blenheim, Buckingham, Court, Crystal, Edo, Élysée, Escorial, Escurial, Fontainebleau, Forbidden City, Fulham, Gin, Goslar, Hampton Court, Holyrood, Holyroodhouse, Hotel, Istana, Kensington, Lambeth, Lateran, Linlithgow, Louvre, Mansion, Nonsuch, Palatine, Picture, Pitti, Pushkin, Quirinal, St James's, Sans Souci, Schloss, Seraglio, Serail, Shushan, Topkapi, Trianon, Tuileries, Valhalla, Vatican, Versailles, Winter

**Paladin** Champion, Charlemagne, Defender, Douzeper, Fièrabras, Ganelon, → **KNIGHT**, Ogier, Oliver, Orlando, Rinaldo, Roland

**Palanquin** Doolie, Kago, Litter, Palkee, Palki, Sedan

**Palatable, Palatalized, Palate** Cleft, Dainty, Hard, Mouille, Relish, Roof, Sapid, Savoury, Soft, Taste, Toothsome, Uranic, Uraniscus, Uvula, Velum

**Palatial** Alhambresque, Ornate, Splendid

**Palatinate, Palatine** Officer, Pfalz

**Palaver** Chatter, Debate, Parley, Powwow, → **TALK**

**Pale, Paling** Albino, Ashen, Blanch, Bleach, Cere, Dim, English, Etiolate(d), Fade, → **FAINT**, Fence, Ghostly, Grey, Haggard, Insipid, Jewish, Lily (white), Livid, Mealy, Ox-fence, Pallescent, Pastel, Pasty-faced, Peaky, Peelie-wally, Picket, Sallow, Shilpit, Stang, Verge, Wan, Whey-faced, White, Wishy-washy

**Paleography** Diplomatics

**Paleozoic** Hercynian, Permian, Silurian

**Palestine, Palestinian** Amorite, Fatah, Gadarene, Galilean, Gaza, Hamas, Holy Land, Intifada, Israel, Pal, Per(a)ea, Philistine, PLO, Samaria

**Palette** Board, Cokuloris

**Palindrome, Palindromic** Cancrine, Sotadic

**Palisade** Barrier, Fence, Fraise, Stacket, Stockade

**Pall** Bore, Cloy, Curtain, Damper, Glut, Hearse-cloth, Mantle, Mortcloth, Satiate, Shroud

**Palladium** Defence, Pd, Safeguard

**Pallas** Athene

**Pallet** Bed, Cot, Couch, Mattress, Tick

**Palliate, Palliative** Alleviate, Anetic, Ease, Extenuate, Lessen, Mitigate, Reduce, Relieve, Sedative

**Pallid** Anaemic, Ashen, Insipid, Pale, Wan, Waxy

**Palm** Accolade, Areca, Assai, Atap, Babassu, Bangalow, Betel, Buriti, Burrawang, Bussu, Cabbage, Calamus, Carna(h)uba, Carpentaria, Chamaerops, Chiqui-chiqui, Coco, Cohune, Conceal, Coquito, Corozo, Corypha, Cycad, Date (tree), Doom, Doum, Elaeis, Euterpe, Fan, Feather, Fob, Foist, Gomuti, Gomuto, Groo-groo, Gru-gru, Hand, Hemp, Ita, Itching, Ivory, Jip(p)i-Jap(p)a, Jipyapa, Jupati, Kentia, Kittul, Laurels, Loof, Looves, Macahuba, Macaw, Macoya, Miriti, Moriche, Nikau, Nipa, Oil, Palmyra, Paxiuba, Peach, Pupunha, Raffia, Raphia, Rat(t)an, Royal, Sabal, Sago, Saw palmetto, Sugar, Talipat, Talipot, Thatch, Thenar, Toddy, Triumph, Troelie, Troolie, Trooly, Trophy, Vola, Washingtonia, Wax, Wine, Zamia

**Palmer** Lilli, Pilgrim

**Palmerston** Pam

**Palmistry** Ch(e)irognomy

**Palm-leaf** Frond

**Palm-oil** Bribe, Payola

**Palpable** Evident, Gross, Manifest, Patent, Plain, Tangible

**Palpitate, Palpitation** Flutter, Pitpat, Pulsate, Throb, Twitter, Vibrate

**Palsy** Bell's, Cerebral, Paralysis, Scrivener's, Shakes, Shaking, Spastic paralysis

**Paltry** Bald, Cheap, Chickenfeed, Exiguous, Mean, Measly, Mere, Peanuts, Pelting, Petty, Pimping, Poor, Puny, Scald, Scalled, Shabby, Shoestring, Sorry, Thingummybob, Tin(-pot), Tinny, Trashy, Trifling, Two-bit, Vile, Waff, Whiffet

**Pamper(ed)** Baby, Cocker, Coddle, Cosher, Cosset, Cuiter, Feather-bed, Gratify, High-fed, →INDULGE, Mollycoddle, Overfeed, Pet, Pompey, Spoon-fed

**Pamphlet(eer)** Brochure, Catalogue, Chapbook, Defoe, Leaflet, Notice, Sheet, Tract

**Pan** Agree, Auld Hornie, Bainmarie, Balit, Basin, Betel(-pepper), Braincase, Chafer, Dent, Dial, Drip, Dripping, Drub, Goat-god, Goblet, God, Hard, Ice-floe, Iron, Jelly, Karahi, Knee, Ladle, Lavatory, Muffin, Nature-god, Non-stick, Oil, Pancheon, Panchion, Patella, Patina, Peter, Plate, Poacher, Preserving, Prospect, Roast, Salt, Search, Skid, Skillet, Slag, Slate, Spider, Steamer, Sweep, Tube, Vacuum, Vessel, Warming, Wo(c)k, Work

**Panacea** All-heal, Azoth, Catholicon, Cure(-all), Diacatholicon, Elixir, Ginseng, Heal-all, Parkleaves, Remedy, Tutsan

**Panache** Bravura, Crest, Dash, Elan, Flair, Paz(z)azz, Piz(z)azz, Plume, Pzazz, Show, Style, Talent

**Panama** Isthmus

**Pancake** Blin(i), Blintz(e), Burrito, Crêpe (suzette), Crumpet, Drop(ped)-scone, Flam(m), Flapjack, Flaune, Flawn, Fraise, Fritter, Froise, Galette, Latke, Pikelet, Poppadum, Potato, Quesadilla, Ro(e)sti, Scotch, Slapjack, Spring roll, Suzette, Taco, Tortilla, Tostada, Waffle

**Pancreas** Isles of Langerhans, Sweetbread

**Panda** Bear-cat, Car, Chi-chi, Chitwah, Common, Giant, Lesser, Red, Squad car

**Pandarus** Go-between

**Pandemonium** Bedlam, Chaos, Inferno, Mayhem, Uproar

**Pander** Broker, Indulge, Minister, Pimp, Procurer, Toady

**Pane** Glass, Light, Panel, Quarrel, Quarry, Sheet

**Panegyric** Encomium, Eulogy, Laudation, Praise, Tribute

**Panel(ling)** Adoption, Array, Board, Cartouche, Children's, Console, Control, Dashboard, Fa(s)cia, Gore, Hatchment, Inset, Instrument, Jury, Lacunar, Mandorla, Mimic, Mola, Orb, Patch(board), People's, Reredorse, Reredos(se), Rocker, Screen, Skreen, Solar, Stile, Stomacher, Table, Tablet, Tongue and groove, Triptych, Valance, Volet, Wainscot

**Pang** Achage, Ache, Crick, Qualm, Spasm, Stab, Stound, Travail, Twinge, Wrench

**Pangloss** Optimist

**Pangolin** Ant-eater, Manis

**Panhandle(r)** Beggar, W. Virginia

**Panic** Alar(u)m, Amaze, Blue funk, Consternation, Fear, Flap, Flat-spin, Flip, Fright, Funk, Guinea-grass, Hysteria, Lather, Millet, Raggee, Raggy, Ragi, Sauve qui peut, →SCARE, Scaremonger, Scarre, Stage fright, Stampede, Stampedo, State, Stew, Tailspin, →TERROR

**Panicle** Thyrse

**Panjandrum** Bashaw

**Pannier** Basket, Cacolet, Corbeil, Dosser, Saddlebag, Skip, Whisket

**Panoply** Armour, Array, Pomp

**Panorama, Panoramic** Cyclorama, Range, Scenery, Veduta, View, Vista

**Pan-pipes** Antara

**Pansy** Gay, Heart's-ease, Herb-trinity, Jessie, Kiss-me-quick, Love-in-idleness, Nance, Powder-puff, Queer, Viola

**Pant(s)** Bags, Boxer shorts, Breeches, Capri, Cargo, Chaps, Chinos, Culottes, Deck, Dhoti, Drawers, Fatigues, Flaff, Gasp, Gaucho, Harem, Hot, Knickers, Long johns, Longs, Parachute, Pech, Pedal-pushers, Pegh, Puff, Rot, Ski, Slacks, Smalls, Stirrup, Stovepipe, Sweat, The pits, Throb, Toreador, Training, Trews, Trousers, Trunks, Wheeze, Yearn

**Pantaloon** Columbine, Dupe, Pants

**Pantheism** Idolatry, Immanency

**Panther** Bagheera, Black, Cat, Cougar, Grey, Jaguar, Leopard, Pink

**Panties** Briefs, Knickers, Scanties, Step-ins, Undies

**Pantomime, Pantomime character** Aladdin, Charade, Cheironomy, Cinderella, Dumb-show, Farce, Galanty, Harlequinade, Pierrot, Play

**Pantry** Buttery, Closet, Larder, Spence, Stillroom

**Pap** Dug, Mealie, Mush, Nipple, Teat, Udder

**Papa** Dad, Father, P

**Papal, Papist, Papistry** Catholic, Clementine, Concordat, Guelf, Guelph, Holy See, Legation, Pontifical, RC, Roman, Tiara, Vatican

**Paper(s), Paperwork, Papery** Admin, Allonge, Antiquarian, Art, Atlas, Ballot, Baryta, Bible, Blat(t), Blotting, Bond, Brief, Broadsheet, Broadside, Bromide, Brown, Building, Bumf, Bumph, Butter, Cap, Carbon, Cartridge, Cellophane®, Chad, Chinese, Chiyogami, Cigarette, Colombier, Comic, Command, Commercial, Confetti, Corrugated, Cream-laid, Cream-wove, Credentials, Crêpe, Crown, Curl, Cutch, Daily, Deckle-edge, Decorate, Demy, Docket, Document, Dossier, Eggshell, Elephant, Emery, Emperor, Essay, Exam, File, Filter, Final, Flock, Folio, Foolscap, Form(s), Fourdrinier, FT, Funny, Furnish, Galley, Garnet, Gazette, Gem, Glass(ine), Glumaceous, Government, Grand eagle, Grand Jesus, Graph, Greaseproof, Green, Guardian, Gutter press, Hieratica, ID, Imperial, India, Japanese, Jesus, Journal, Kent cap, Kraft, Kutch, Lace, Laid, Lavatory, Legal cap, Linen, Litmus, Loo-roll, Mail, Manifold, Manil(l)a, Marble, Mercantile, Mirror, Monograph, MS, Munimenti, Music(-demy), Needle, News(print), →**NEWSPAPER**, Note, Notelet, Oil, Onion-skin, Order, Origami, Packing, Pad, Page, Papillote, Papyrus, Parchment, Pickwick, Plotting, Position, Post, Pot(t), Pravda, Press, Print, Printing, Quair, Quarto, Quire, Rag, Ramee, Rami(e), Ream, Red top, Retree, Rhea, Rice, Rolled, Rolling, Royal, Safety, Satin, Saxe, Scent, Scotsman, Scrip, Script, Scroll, Scrowl, Sheaf, Sheet, Ship's, Silver, Skin, Slipsheet, Spoilt, Stamp, Starch, State, Steamer, Sugar, Sun, Super-royal, Tabloid, Taffeta, Tap(p)a, Tar, Term, Ternion, TES, Test, Thesis, Thread, Tiger, Tissue, Today, Toilet, Torchon, Touch, Tracing, Tract, Trade, Transfer, Treatise, Treeware, Tri-chad, Turmeric, Two-name, Vellum, Velvet, Voucher, Walking, Wall, Waste, Watch, Wax(ed), Web, Whatman®, White, Willesden, Wirewove, Wood(chip), Woodfree, Worksheet, Wove, Wrapping, Writing, Zine

**Paperback** Limp(back)

**Paper-cutting, Paper-folding** Decoupage, Kirigami, Origami, Psaligraphy

**Papier-mâché** Carton-pierre, Flong

**Paprika** Spanish

**Par** Average, Equate, Equivalent, →**NORMAL**, Scratch

**Parable** Allegory, Fable, Proverb

**Parabola** Arc, Curve, Hyperbola

**Parachute, Parachutist** Aeroshell, Aigrette, Brake, Drag, Drogue, Extraction, Float, Freefall, Golden, Jump, Pack, Pappus, Para, Parabrake, Parapente, Red Devil, Ribbon, Silk, Sky-diving, Skyman, Thistledown, Umbrella

**Parade (ground)** Air, Arcade, Catwalk, Cavalcade, Ceremony, Church, Concours d'élégance, Display, Dress, Drill, Easter, Emu, Esplanade, Flaunt, Gala, Hit, Identification, Identity, Line-up, Maidan, March-past, Monkey-run, Pageantry, Passing-out, Pomp, Prance, Procession, Prom(enade), Sashay, Show, Sick, Sowarry, Stand-to, Strut, Ticker tape, Troop

**Paradise** Arcadia, Avalon, Bliss, Earthly, Eden, Elysium, Fool's, Garden, Happy-hunting-ground, Heaven, Idyll(ic), Lost, Malaguetta, Nirvana, Park, Regained, Shangri-la, Sky, Surfer's, Svarga, Swarga, Swerga, →**UTOPIA**

**Paradox(ical)** Absurdity, Cantor's, Contradiction, Dilemma, Electra, Epimenides, French, Gilbertian, Hydrostatic, Irony, Koan, Liar, Olber's, Puzzle, Russell's, Sorites, Twin, Zeno's

**Paraffin** Earthwax, Kerosene, Kerosine, Liquid, Ozocerite, Ozokerite, Photogen(e), Propane

**Paragon** Model, Non(e)such, Pattern, Pearl, Phoenix, Role model, Rose

**Paragraph (mark)** Article, Balaam, Causerie, Note, Passage, Piece, Pilcrow

**Paraguay** PY

**Parakeet** Parrot, Popinjay, Rosella

**Parallax** Annual, Daily, Diurnal, Geocentric, Heliocentric

**Parallel** Analog, Analogy, Arctic circle, Collateral, Collimate, Corresponding, Equal, Even, Forty-ninth, Like, Pattern

**Parallelogram** Rhomb

**Paralysis, Paralyse** Akinesia, Apoplexy, Benumb, Cataplexy, Catatonia, Cramp, Curarise, Cycloplegia, Diplegia, Halt, Hemiplegia, Infantile, Lithyrism, Monoplegia, Numbness, Ophthalmoplegia, Palsy, Paraplegia, Paresis, Polio, Quadriplegia, Radial, Scram, Shock, Shut, Spastic, Spina bifida, Stun, Torpefy, Transfix

**Paramedic** Ambulance-man

**Parameter** Definition

**Paramilitary** Inkatha, Phalangist, SAS, Sena, UDA

**Paramount** Chief, Dominant, Greatest, Overall, Premier, →**SUPREME**, Topless, Utmost

**Paramour** Beau, Franion, Gallant, Leman, Lover, Mistress, Potemkin, Thais

**Paranoid** Tweak

**Paranormal** Clairvoyant, ESP, Psionics, Psychic, Spiritual, Telekinesis

**Parapet (space)** Balustrade, Barbette, Bartisan, Bartizan, Battlement, Breastwork, Brisure, Bulwark, Crenel, Flèche, Machicolation, Merlon, Rampart, Redan, Surtout, Terreplein, Top, Wall

**Paraphernalia** Armamentarium, Belongings, Equipment, Gear, Trappings

**Parasite, Parasitic** Amoeba, Ascarid, Autoecious, Aweto, Babesiasis, Beech-drops, Bilharzia, Biogenous, Biotroph, Bladder-worm, Bloodsucker, Bonamia, Bot, Candida, Chalcid, Chigoe, Coccus, Conk, Copepod, Cosher, Crab-louse, Cryptosporidium, Cryptozoite, Dodder, Ectogenous, Ectophyte, Endamoeba, Endophyte, Entophyte, Entozoon, Epiphyte, Epizoon, Facultative, Filarium, Flatworm, Flea, Freeloader, Gapeworm, Giardia, Gregarinida, Guinea worm, Haematozoon, Hair-eel, Hair-worm, Heartworm, Heteroecious, Hook-worm, Ichneumon, Inquiline, Isopod, Kade, Ked, Lackey, Lamprey, Leech, Leishmania, Licktrencher, Liverfluke, Louse, Lungworm, Macdonald, Mallophagous, Measle, Mistletoe, Monogenean, Necrotroph, Nematode, Nit, Obligate, Orobanche, Phytosis, Pinworm, Plasmodium, Puccinia, Pulix, Quandong, Rafflesia, Redia, Rhipidoptera, Rickettsia, Root, Roundworm, Schistosoma, Scrounger, Shark, Smut-fungus, Sponge(r), Sporozoa(n), Strangleweed, Strepsiptera, Strongyle, Strongyloid, Stylops, Sucker, Symphile, Tachinid, Tapeworm, Tick, Toady, Toxoplasma, Trematode, Trencher-friend, Trencher-knight, Trichina, Trichomonad, Tryp(anosoma), Vampire, Viscum, Wheatworm, Whipworm, Witchweed, Worms

**Parasol** Awning, Brolly, En tout cas, Marquise, Sunshade, Umbrella

**Paratrooper** Red Devil, Skyman, Stick leader

**Parcel** Allocate, Allot, Aret, Bale, Bundle, Dak, Enwrap, Holding, Inwrap, Lot, Package, Packet, Plot, Sort, Wrap

**Parch(ed), Parching** Arid, Bake, Dry, Graddan, Hot coppers, Roast, Scorched, Sere, Thirsty, Toast, Torrefied, Torrid, Xerotes

**Parchment** Diploma, Forel, Membrane, Mezuzah, Panel, Papyrus, Pell, Pergameneous, Roll, Roule, Scroll, Scrow, Sheepskin, Vegetable, Vellum, Virgin

**Pard** Leopard, Pal, Partner

**Pardon(able), Pardoner** Absolution, Absolve, Amnesty, Anan, Assoil, Clear, Condone, Eh, Excuse, →**FORGIVE**, Grace, Mercy, Quaestionary, Quaestuary, Qu(a)estor, Release, Remission, Remit, Reprieve, Venial, What

**Pare** Chip, Flaught, Flay, Peel, Shave, Skive, Sliver, Strip, Whittle

**Parent(al)** Ancestral, Father, Forebear, Foster, Generant, Genitor, Maternal, Mother, Paternal, Rear, Single, Solo, Storge

**Parenthesis** Aside, Brackets, Innuendo
**Parhelion** Sun-dog
**Pariah** Ishmael, Leper, Outcast, Pi(e)dog, Pyedog
**Paris(ian), Parisienne** Abductor, Athene, Elle, Gai, Gay, Grisette, Lutetia (Parisiorum), Lutetian, Maillotin, Midinette, Trojan
**Parish** Charge, District, Flock, Kirkto(w)n, Parischan(e), Parishen, Parochin(e), Peculiar, Province, Title
**Parity** Equalness, Equivalence, Smithsonian
**Park(ing)** Amusement, Business, Car, Caravan, Common, Country, Domain, Enclosure, Forest, Fun, Game, Garage, Grounds, Hardstand, Industrial, Lung, Motor, National, Off-street, P, Petrified Forest, Pitch, Pleasure ground, Preserve, Rec, Safari, Sanctuary, Science, Siding, Stand, Stop, Technology, Terrain, Theme, Trailer, Valet, Valley, Water, Wildlife, Wind, Yard

## PARKS

*4 letters:*
Hyde

*5 letters:*
Dales
Green
Ibrox
Mungo
Tsavo
Upton

*6 letters:*
Etosha
Exmoor
Hwange
Jasper
Kakadu
Katmai
Kruger
Oyster
Tivoli

*7 letters:*
Central
Gardens
Nairobi
Phoenix

Regent's
Sandown

*8 letters:*
Daintree
Dartmoor
Jurassic
Osterley
Paradise
St James's
Yosemite

*9 letters:*
Algonquin
Battersea
Fiordland
Grampians
Green lung
Lamington
Mansfield
Mesa Verde
Serengeti
Snowdonia

*10 letters:*
Disneyland
Everglades

Kejimkujik
Pittie-ward

*11 letters:*
Alton Towers
Death Valley
Grand Canyon
Kobuk Valley
Mammoth Cave
Wood Buffalo
Yellowstone

*12 letters:*
Lake District
Mount Rainier
Peak District
Quttinirpaaq

*13 letters:*
Banff National
Brecon Beacons
Mount Aspiring
Mount McKinley

*14 letters:*
Egmont National
Jasper National

Kruger National
Lassen Volcanic
Northumberland
North York Moors
Riding Mountain
Yorkshire Dales

*15 letters:*
Kalahari Gemsbok
Nahanni National
Sequoia National

*16 letters:*
Gates of the Arctic

*18 letters:*
Mount Kenya
National
Prince Edward
Island
Shenandoah
National

*19 letters:*
Great Smoky
Mountains

---

**Parka** Atigi
**Parker** Dorothy, Nos(e)y
**Parkleaves** Tutsan
**Parley** Confer, Discourse, Palaver, Speak, Tret
**Parliament** Addled, Althing, Barebones, Black, Boule, Bundestag, Chamber, Commons, Congress, Cortes, Council, Cross-bench, Dail, Diet, Drunken, D(o)uma, Eduskunta, European, Folketing, House, Imperial, Knesset, Lack-learning, Lagt(h)ing, Landst(h)ing, Lawless, Legislature, Lok Sabha, Long, Lords, Majlis, Merciless, Mongrel, Odelst(h)ing, Political, Rajya Sabha, Reichsrat, Reichstag, Riksdag, Rump, St Stephens, Sanhedrin, Seanad, Seanad Éireann, Sejm, Short, Stannary, States-general, Stirthing, Stormont,

Stort(h)ing, The Beehive, Thing, Tynwald (Court), Unicameral, Unlearned, Useless, Vidhan Sabha, Volkskammer, Volksraad, Westminster

**Parliamentarian** Cabinet, De Montfort, Fairfax, Ireton, Leveller, Member, MP, Politico, Roundhead, Whip

**Parlour** Beauty, Funeral, Ice-cream, Lounge, Massage, Milking, Salon, Snug, Spence

**Parnassus** Museum, Verse

**Parochial** Insular, Narrow-minded

**Parody** Burlesque, Cod, Lampoon, Mock, Piss-take, Satire, Send-up, Skit, Spoof, Travesty

**Parole** Pledge, Promise, Trust, Word

**Paronychia** Agnail, Felon, Whitlow

**Paroxysm** Fit, Frenzy, Rapture, Spasm, Subintrant, Throe

**Parricide** Cenci

**Parrot** Amazon, Ape, Budgerigar, Cockatoo, Conure, Copy, Echo, Emulate, Flint, Green leek, Grey, Imitate, Kaka(po), Kea, Lorikeet, Lory, Lovebird, Macaw, Mimic, Nestor, Owl, Parakeet, Paroquet, Poll(y), Popinjay, Psittacine, Quarrion, Repeat, Rosella, Rote, Shell, Stri(n)gops, T(o)uraco

**Parrot-bill** Glory-pea

**Parry** Block, Counter, Defend, Dodge, Forestall, Parade, Repel, Riposte, Septime, Sixte, Tac-au-tac, Thwart, Ward

**Parsee** Zoroastrian

**Parsimonious, Parsimony** Aberdonian, Cheese-paring, Mean, Narrow, Near(ness), Niggardly, Scanty, Stingy, Thrift, Tight

**Parsley** Apiol, Cicely, Cow, Dog, Kecks, Kex, Persillade, Pot-herb

**Parsnip** Buttered, Buttery, Dill, Masterwort, Sium, Skirret

**Parson** Clergyman, Cleric, Holy Joe, Minister, Non juror, Pastor, Priest, Rector, Rev, Sky-pilot, Soul-curer, Yorick

**Parsonage** Glebe, Haworth, Manse, Rectory, Vicarage

**Part(s), Parting, Partly** Accession, Aliquot, Among, Antimere, Area, Aspect, Aught, Bad, Behalf, Bit, Bite, Bulk, Bye, Cameo, Character, Chunk, Cog, Compartment, Component, Constituent, Crack, Cue, Department, Detail, Dislink, Diverge, Divide, Dole, Element, Episode, Escapement, Farewell, Fascicle, Fork, Fraction, Good, Goodbye, Great, Half, Ill, Imaginary, Ingredient, Instalment, Integrant, Into, Lathe, Lead, Leave, Leg, Lill, Lilt, Lines, List, Livraison, Member, Meronym, Moiety, Morsel, Organ, Parcel, Passus, Percentage, → PIECE, Portion, Primo, Principal, Private, Proportion, Pt, Quit, Quota, Rape, Ratio, Real, Region, Rive, Role, Scena, Scene, Secondo, Section, Sector, Segment, Segregate, Separate, Serial, Sever, Shade, Share, Shed, Sleave, Sle(i)ded, Small, → SOME, Spare, Split, Stator, Sunder, Synthon, Tithe, To a degree, Tranche, Twin(e), Unit, Vaunt, Voice, Walking, Walk on, Wrench

**Partake(r)** Allottee, Eat, Figure, Participate, Share

**Parthenogenesis** Deuterotoky, Thelytoky

**Partial(ity), Partially** Biased, Ex-parte, Fan, Favour, Halflins, Imbalance, Incomplete, Nepotism, One-sided, Predilection, Prejudiced, Slightly, Unequal, Weakness

**Participate, Participant, Participation** Audience, Engage, Field, Join, Muck-in, Panellist, Partake, Share, Symposiast, Traceur

**Participle** Dangling, Misrelated, Past, Perfect, Present

**Particle(s)** Alpha, Anion, Antielectron, Antineutron, Antiproton, Atom, Baryon, Beta, Bit, Boson, Charmonium, Corpuscle, Cosmic dust, Curn, Dander, Delta, Deuteron, Effluvium, Electron, Elementary, Episome, Exchange, Fermion, Fleck, Floccule, Fragment, Fundamental, Gauge boson, Gemmule, Globule, Gluon, Grain, Granule, Graviton, Hadron, Heavy, Higgs, Hyperon, Ion, J, Jot, J/psi, Kaon, Laitance, Lambda, Lemail, Lemel, Lepton, Lipoplast, Liposome, Meson, Micelle, Microsome, Mite, Molecule, Monopole, Mote, Muon, Negatron, Neutralino, Neutretto, Neutrino, Neutron, Nibs, Nobiliary, Nucleon, Omega-minus, Parton, Pentaquark, Photon, Pion, Plasmagene, Plastisol, Platelet, Positon, Positron, Preon, Proton, Psi(on), Quark, Radioactivity,

Scintilla, Shives, Shower, Sigma, Singlet, Sinter, Smithereen, Spark, Speck, Strange, Subatom, Submicron, Subnuclear, Tachyon, Tardyon, Tau neutrino, Tauon, Thermion, Tittle, Virion, W, Whit, WIMP, X-hyperon, XI, Z

**Parti-coloured** Fancy, Motley, Piebald, Pied, Variegated

**Particular** Choosy, Dainty, → **DETAIL**, Endemic, Especial, Essential, Express, Faddy, Fastidious, Fiky, Fog, Fussy, Item, Itself, London fog, Minute, Nice, Niffy-naffy, Nipperty-tipperty, Nitpicker, Old-maidish, Own, Pea-souper, Peculiar, Pedant, Pernickety, Pet, Point, Prim, Prissy, Proper, → **RESPECT**, Special, Specific, Stickler, Strict, Stripe

**Partisan** Adherent, Axe, Biased, Carlist, Champion, Devotee, Factional, Fan, Irregular, Partial, Provo, Queenite, Sider, Spear, Stalwart, Supporter, Tendentious, Yorkist, Zealot

**Partition(ed)** Abjoint, Bail, Barrier, Brattice, Bretasche, Bulkhead, Cloison, Cubicle, Diaphragm, Dissepiment, Divider, Division, Hallan, Mediastinum, Parpane, Parpen(d), Parpent, Parpoint, Perpend, Perpent, Replum, → **SCREEN**, Scriene, Septum, Skreen, Tabula, Wall, With

**Partlet** Hen, Overlaid

**Partner(ship)** Accomplice, Affiliation, Alliance, Ally, Associate, Bidie-in, Butty, Cahoot(s), Coachfellow, Cohab(itee), Cohabitor, Colleague, Comrade, Confederate, Consort, Copemate, Couple, Date, Dutch, Escort, E-W, Firm, Gigolo, Husband, Limited, Mate, Moll, N-S, Offsider, Oppo, Other half, Pair, Pal, Pard, Rival, Sidekick, Significant other, Silent, Sleeping, SOP, Sparring, Spouse, Stablemate, Stand, Symbiosis, Wag, Wif(i)e

▷ **Part of** *may indicate* a hidden word

**Partridge** Bird, Chik(h)or, Chukar, Chukor, Covey, Flapper, Quail, Red-legged, Tinamou, Ynambu

**Part-timer** Semi-pro

**Party** Acid house, Advance, Aftershow, Alliance, ANC, Apparat, Apres-ski, Assembly, At-home, Ba'ath, Bachelor(ette), Bake, Ball, Band, Barbecue, Bash, Beano, Bee, Binge, Birthday, Bloc, Blowout, Boarding, Body, Bottle, Buck's, Bunfight, Bust, Caboodle, Camp, Carousal, Carouse, Caucus, Celebration, Clambake, Coach, Cocktail, Colour, Commando, Communist, Concert, Congress, Conservative, Contingent, Cookie-shine, Cooperative, Coterie, Cult, Democratic, Detail, Ding, Dinner, Disco(theque), Do, Drum, DUP, Faction, Falange, Federalist, Fest, Fête champêtre, Fête Galante, Fianna Fáil, Fiesta, Fine Gael, Firing, Foy, Function, Funfest, Gala, Galravage, Gang, Garden, Ghibel(l)ine, GOP, Green, Greenback, Grumbletonian, Guelf, Guelph, Guilty, Hen, High heels, Hoedown, Hooley, Hootenannie, Hootenanny, Hoot(a)nannie, Hoot(a)nanny, House, Housewarming, Hurricane, Inkatha, Irredentist, Jana Sangh, Janata, Jol(lities), Junket, Junto, Kegger, Kettledrum, Kitchen tea, Klat(s)ch, Knees-up, Kuomintang, L, Labour, Landing, Launch, Lawn, Levee, Lib, Liberal, Lig, Love-in, Low heels, Luau, Mallemaroking, Mollie, Movement, Musicale, National, Necking, Neck-tie, Octobrist, Opposition, Orgy, Peace, People's, Person, Petting, Plaid, Political, Populist, Posse, Progressive, Prohibition, Pyjama, Radical, Rage, Rave, Rave-up, Razzle(-dazzle), Reception, Republican, Reunion, Revel(ry), Ridotto, Roast, Rocking, Roister, Rort, Rout, Scottish Nationalist, SDP, Search, Sect, Set, Shindig, Shindy, Shine, Shivoo, Shiv Sena, Shooting, Shower, Shower tea, Side, Sinn Fein, Slumber, Small and early, Smoker, SNP, Soc(ialist), Social, Social Credit, Social Democratic, Socialise, Soirée, Spree, Squad(rone), Squadrone volante, Stag, Street, Symposium, Tailgate, Tea, Teafight, Third, Thrash, Tory, Treat, UKIP, Ultramontane, Unionist, United, Wafd, Wake, Warehouse, Whig, Whoop-de-do(o), Wine, Wingding, Working, Wrap

**Partygoer** Rager, Raver, Reveller, Socialite

**Party-piece** Solo

**Parvenu** Arriviste, Upstart

**Pascal** Blaise, Pa, Pressure

**Pash** Crush, Devotion

**Pasha** Achmed, Dey, Emir, Ismet

**Pass(ed), Passing, Pass on, Past, Pass through** Absit, Aforetime, Ago, Agon, Annie Oakley, Aorist, Approve, Arise, Arlberg, Before, Behind, Bernina, Beyond, Blow over, Boarding, Bolan, Botte, Brenner, Brief, Burgess, By (the by), Bygone, Caudine Forks, Centre, Cerro Gordo, Chal(l)an, Chilkoot, Chine, Chit(ty), Cicilian Gates, Clear, Col, Cote, Cross, Cursory, Death, Dee, Defile, Delate, Demise, Diadrom, Die, Disappear, Double, Dummy, Dunno, Elapse, Emit, Enact, End, Ensue, Ephemeral, Exceed, Exeat, Faena, Flashback, Fleeting, Fob, Foist, Forby, Forgone, Former, Forward, Gap, Gate, Gha(u)t, Give, Glencoe, Glide, Go, Go by, Gorge, Great St Bernard, Gulch, Halse, Hand, Happen, Hause, Hospital, ID, Impart, Impermanent, Interrail, Interval, In transit, Jark, Jump, Khyber, Killiecrankie, Kloof, La Cumbre, Lap, Late, Lead, Legislate, Live, Long syne, Loss, Mesmerism, Migrate, Momentary, Mont Cenis, Moravian Gate, Needle, Nek, Nine days' wonder, No bid, Nod through, Notch, Nutmeg, Nye, Occur, Oer, O grade, OK, Okay, Oke, Omit, One-time, Overhaul, Overshoot, Overslaugh, Overtake, Pa, Palm, Parade, Participle, Perish, Permeate, Permit, Perpetuate, Poll, Poort, Predicament, Preterit(e), Pretty, Proceed, Propagate, Pun(c)to, Qualify, Railcard, Ratify, Reach, Reeve, Refer, Relay, Retro, Retroactive, Retrospect, Reverse, Roncesvalles, Run, Safe conduct, St Bernard, St Gotthard, San Bernardino, Sanitation, Scissors, Sea-letter, Senile, Serve, Shangri-la, Shipka, Simplon, Since, Skim, Skip, Skirt, Slap, Sling, Small and early, Snap, Spend, Stab, State, Swipecard, Temporal, Thermopylae, Thread, Through, Thru, Ticket, Time immemorial, Tip, Transient, Transilient, Transitory, Transmit, Transpire, Transude, Travel, Triptyque, Troop, Uspallata, Veronica, Vet, Visa, Visé, Wall, Wayleave, Weather, While, Wrynose, Yesterday, Yesteryear, Ygoe

**Passable, Passible** Adequate, Fair, Navigable, Tolerable

**Passage(way), Passages** Abature, Adit, Airshaft, Airway, Aisle, Alley(way), Alure, Apostrophe, Arcade, Archway, Areaway, Arterial, Atresia, Avenue, Bank, Breezeway, Bridge, Bylane, Cadenza, Canal, Caponier(e), Career, Catwalk, Channel, Choana, Chute, Citation, Clarino, Clause, Close, Coda, Condie, Conduit, Corridor, Creep, Crossing, Crush, Cundy, Dead-end, Deambulatory, Defile, Drake, Drift, Duct, Eel-fare, Episode, Epitaph, Excerpt, Extract, Fare, Fat, Fauces, Fistula, Flat, Flight, Flue, Fogou, Gallery, Gangway, Gap, Gat, Gate, Ghat, Ginnel, Gorgia, Gully-hole, Gut, Hall, Head, Honeycomb, Inlet, Intestine, Journey, Kyle, Labyrinth, Lane, Lapse, Larynx, Lick, Lientery, Loan, Lobby, Locus, Meatus, Melisma, Meridian, Middle, Mine, Mona, Moto perpetuo, Movement, Northeast, Northwest, Para(graph), Parashah, Path, Pend, Pericope, Phrase, Pore, Port, Portion, Prelude, Presto, Prose, Purple, Race, Retournelle, Ride, Ripieno, Rite, Ritornell(o), Road, Rough, Route, Sailing, Screed, Shaft, Shunt, Sinus, Skybridge, Skywalk, Slap, Slype, Snicket, Solus, Spillway, Sprue, Strait, Street, Stretta, Stretto, Subway, Sump, Text, Thirl, Thorough(fare), Throat, Tour, Trachea, Trance, Transe, Transit(ion), Travel, Tunnel, Tutti, Undercast, Unseen, Ureter, Voyage, Walkway, Way, Windpipe, Windway

▷ **Passage of arms** *may indicate* 'sleeve'

**Passé** Corny, Dated, Ex, Obsolete, Old-fashioned

**Passenger(s)** Cad, Commuter, Fare, Parasite, Pax, Payload, Pigeon, Pillion, Rider, Slacker, Steerage, Straphanger, Transit, Traveller, Voyager, Way, Wayfarer

**Passible** Patible

▶ **Passible** *see* BAULK

**Passion(ate), Passionately** Anger, Appetite, Ardent, Ardour, Con calore, Con fuoco, Crush, Dander, Duende, Emotion, Fervour, Fire, Flame, Frampold, Fury, Gust, Gutsy, Hate, Heat, Hot, Hunger, Hwyl, Ileac, Iliac, Infatuation, Intense, Ire, Irish, Kama, Love, Lust, Mania, Messianic, Metromania, Obsession, Oestrus, Polemic, Rage, Reverent, Sizzling, Steamy, Stormy, Strong, Sultry, Torrid, Vehement, Violent, Warm, Wax, Wrath, Yen, Zeal, Zoolatria

**Passion-fruit** Water-lemon

**Passionless** Tepid

**Passion play** Oberammergau

**Passive (stage), Passivity** Apathetic, Dormant, Drifter, Inaction, Inert, Pathic, Patient, Pupa, Stolid, Supine, Vegetating, Vegetative, Yielding

**Pass out** Faint, Graduate, Swarf, Swarve, Swoon

**Passover** Agadah, Haggada, Omer, Pesach

**Passport** Access, Clearance, Congé(e), E, ID, Key, Laissez-passer, Nansen, Navicert, Sea-letter, Visa, Visitors'

**Password** Code, Countersign, Logon, Nayword, Parole, Sesame, Shibboleth, Sign, Tessera, Watchword

▶ **Past** *see* PASS(ED)

**Pasta** Agnolotti, Al dente, Anelli, Angel hair, Bucatini, Cannelloni, Cappelletti, Carbonara, Cellentani, Conchiglie, Durum, Eliche, Farfal, Farfalle, Farfel, Fedelini, Fettuc(c)ine, Fusilli, Gnocch(ett)i, Lasagna, Lasagne, Linguini, Macaroni, Maccheroncini, Manicotti, Noodles, Orecchietti, Orzo, Pappardelle, Penne, Perciatelli, Ravioli, Rigatoni, Ruote, Spaghetti, Spaghettina, Tagliarini, Tagliatelle, Tortelli(ni), Vermicelli, Ziti

**Paste, Pasty** Almond, Ashen, Batter, Beat, Berbere, Botargo, Boule, Bridie, Cerate, Clobber, Cornish, Dentifrice, Dough, E, Electuary, Empanada, Fake, Filler, Fondant, Frangipane, Gentleman's Relish®, Glue, Guarana, Hard, Harissa, Knish, Lute, Magma, Marchpane, Marzipan, Masala, Mastic, Meat, Miso, Mountant, Pale, Pallid, Panada, Pâté, Patty, Pearl-essence, Pie, Piroshki, Pirozhki, Poonac, Pulp, Punch, Putty, Rhinestone, Rillettes, Rout, Sallow, Samosa, Sham, Slip, Slurry, Soft, Spread, Strass, Tahina, Tahini, Tan, Tapenade, Taramasalata, Trounce, Wan, Wasabi

**Pastern** Hobble, Knee, Tether

**Pastiche** Cento, Collage, Medley, Patchwork, Potpourri

**Pastille** Jujube, Lozenge

**Pastime** Diversion, Game, Hobby, Interest, Recreation, Seesaw, Sport, Zeitvertreib

**Past master** Champion, Expert, Historian, Pro

**Past midnight** 1 am

**Pastor(al)** Arcadia, Bucolic, Curé, Eclogue, Endymion, Idyl(l), Minister, Priest, Rector, Rural, Shepherd, Simple

**Pastry** Apfelstrudel, Baclava, Bakemeat, Baklava, Beignet, Bouchée, Bridie, Brik, Calzone, Canape, Cannoli, Chausson, Cheese straw, Choux, Clafoutis, Coquile, Creamhorn, Cream puff, Croissant, Croustade, Cruller, Crust, Danish, Dariole, Dough, Eclair, Empanada, Feuilleté, Filo, Flaky, Flan, Frangipane, French, Gougère, Hamantasch, Millefeuille, Muffin, Phyllo, Pie, Pie-crust, Pirog, Piroshki, Pirozhki, Profiterole, Puff, Quiche, Raised, Rough-puff, Rug(g)elach, Samosa, Shortcrust, Strudel, Tart, Turnover, Vol-au-vent

**Pasture** Alp, Eadish, Eddish, Feed, Fell, Fodder, Grassland, Graze, Herbage, Kar(r)oo, Lair, Lare, Lay, Lea, Lease, Leasow(e), Leaze, Lee, Ley, Machair, Mead(ow), Moose, Outrun, Pannage, Pascual, Potrero, Raik, Rake, Sheal(ing), Shiel(ing), Soum, Sowm, Tie, Transhume, Tye

▶ **Pasty** *see* PASTE

**Pat** Apt, Bog-trotter, Butter, Chuck, Clap, Dab, Glib, Letter-perfect, Lump, On cue, Postman, Print, Prompt, Rap, Slap, Stroke, Tap

**Patch(work)** Cento, Fleck, Miscellany, Mosaic, Motley, Piecing, Pocket, Sexton, Speculum, Turf

**Patch(y)** Bed, Bit, Blotchy, Cabbage, Chloasma, Clout, Coalsack, Cobble, Cooper, Court plaster, Cover, Friar, Fudge, Knit, Manor, → MEND, Mosaic, Mottled, Nicotine, Pasty, Piebald, Piece, Plage, Plaque, Plaster, Pot, Purple, Repair, Shinplaster, Shoulder, Solder, Sunspot, Tingle, Tinker, Transdermal, Turf, Uneven, Vamp, Variegated

**Pate, Pâté** Crown, Paste, Rillettes, Taramasalata, Terrine

**Patent(ed)** Brevet d'invention, Breveté, Clear, Copyright, Evident, Letters, Licence, License, Obvious, Overt, Plain, Rolls

**Pater(nity)** Father, Filiation, Walter

**Paterfamilias** Coarb, Master

**Path(way)** Aisle, Allée, Alley, Arc, Berm, Berme, Boreen, Borstal(l), Bridle, Bridleway, Byroad, Catwalk, Causeway, Causey, Cinder, Clickstream, Corridor, Course, Cycleway, Downlink, Eclipse, Ecliptic, Eightfold, Embden-Meyerhof, Flare, Flight, Gangway, Garden, Gate, Gennel, Ginnel, Glide, Lane, Ley, Lichwake, Lichway, Locus, Lykewake, Mean-free, Metabolic, Orbit, Packway, Pad, Parabola, Pavement, Peritrack, Primrose, Ride, Ridgeway, Route, Run, Runway, Sidewalk, Slipway, Spurway, Stie, Sty(e), Swath(e), Taxiway, Tow, Track, Trail, Trajectory, Trod, Walkway, → **WAY**, Xystus

**Pathan** Pakhto, Pakhtu, Pashto, Pashtu, Pushto(o), Pushtu

**Pathetic(ally)** Abysmal, Derisory, Doloroso, Drip, Forlorn, Piss-poor, Piteous, Plaintive, Poignant, Sad, Saddo, Schlub, Schnook, Sorry, Touching, Wet

**Pathfinder** Compass, Explorer, Guide, Pioneer, Scout

**Pathogen** Virus

**Pathologic(al)** Aphony, Diseased, Gangrene, Morbid, Moria, Septic

**Pathos** Bathos, Pity, Sadness, Sob-stuff

**Patience** Calm, Endurance, Forbearance, Fortitude, Indulgence, Klondike, Klondyke, Longanimity, Monument, Operetta, Solitaire, Stoicism, Virtue

**Patient(s)** Calm, Case, Clinic, Cot-case, Forbearing, Grisel(da), Grisilda, Invalid, Job, Long-suffering, Passive, Private, Resigned, Stoic, Subject, Unprotesting, Walking case, Ward

**Patois** Argot, Cant, Dialect, Gumbo, Jargon, Jive, Lingo, Scouse

**Patriarch** Aaron, Abraham, Abuna, Asher, Catholicos, Ecumenical, Elder, Enoch, Isaac, Jesse, Job, Levi, Maron, Methuselah, Nestor, Noah, Pope, Primogenitor, Simeon, Venerable

**Patrician** Aristocrat, Noble, Senator

**Patrick** Mick, Paddy, Pat, Spens

**Patrimony** Ancestry, Estate, Heritage

**Patriot(ic), Patriotism** Cavour, Chauvinist, DAR, Emmet, Flag-waving, Flamingant, Garibaldi, Hereward, Irredentist, Jingoism, Loyalist, Maquis, Nationalist, Revere, Tell, Wallace, Zionist

**Patrol** Armilla, Beat, Coastguard, Guard, Outguard, Picket, Piquet, Prowl-car, Reconnaissance, Round, Scout, Sentinel, Sentry-go, Shark, Shore, Turm

**Patron(age), Patroness, Patronise(d), Patronising** Advowson, Aegis, Athena, Auspices, Backer, Benefactor, Business, Cavalier, Champion, Client, Condescend, Customer, Donator, Egis, Fautor, Favour, Friend, Lady Bountiful, Maecenas, Nepotic, Protector, Protégé, Provider, Shopper, → **SPONSOR**, Stoop, Stoup

**Patsy** Dupe, Fall guy, Hendren, Scapegoat, Stooge

**Patter** Backchat, Cant, Jargon, Lingo, Mag, Pitch, Rap, Sales talk, S(c)htick, Spiel

**Pattern(ed)** Agouti, Agouty, Aguti, Archetype, Argyle, Bird's eye, Blueprint, Branchwork, Broché, Candy stripe, Check, Chequer, Chiné, Chladni figure, Clock, Crisscross, Design, Dévoré, Diaper, Diffraction, Dog's tooth, Draft, Egg and dart, Epitome, Example, Exemplar, Faconné, Fiddle, Figuration, Format, Fractal, Fret, Gammadion, Gestalt, Grain, Greek key, Greque, Herringbone, Holding, Honeycomb, Hound's tooth, Ideal, Imprint, Intarsia, Intonation, Karman vortex street, Koru, Kowhaiwhai, Matel(l)asse, Matrix, Meander, → **MODEL**, Moire, Moko, Mosaic, Norm, Paisley, Paradigm, Paragon, Pinstripe, Plan, Polka-dot, Pompadour, Precedent, Prototype, Queenstitch, Quincunx, Radiation, Raster, Rat-tail, Rhythm, Ribbing, Rosette, Scansion, Shawl, Starburst, Stencil, Structure, Symmetry, Syndrome, Tala, Talea, Tangram, Tarsia, Tattersall, Template, Templet, Tessella, Tessera, Test, Tracery, Traffic, Tread, Type, Veneration, Vol, Watermark, Whorl, Willow

**Patty** Bitok, Bouchée, Fishcake, Hoecake, Pie

**Paul** Jones, Oom, Pry, Revere, Robeson, S, St

**Pauline** Day-boy, Perils

**Paunch** Beerbelly, Belly, Corporation, Gut, Kite, Kyte, Pod, Rumen, Tripe, Tum

**Pauper** Bankrupt, Beggar, Have-not, Mendicant, Penniless

**Pause** Break, Breakpoint, Breather, Caesura, Cessation, Cesura, Comma, Desist, Er,
Fermata, Hesitate, Hiatus, Interkinesis, Intermission, Interregnum, Interval, Limma,
Lull, Pitstop, Pregnant, →**RESPITE**, Rest, Selah, Semi-colon, Stop, Tacet, Time out,
Whistle-stop

**Pave(d), Pavement, Paving** Causeway, Causey, Clint, Cobble, Corsey, Crazy,
Desert, Diaper, Flagging, Flagstone, Granolith, Limestone, Moving, Path, Plainstanes,
Plainstones, Roadside, Set(t), Sidewalk, Tessellate, Travolator, Trottoir

**Pavilion** Chinese, Ear, Gazebo, Jingling Johnny, Kiosk, Marquee, Tent

**Paw** Kangaroo, Maul, Mitt, Pad, Pat, Pud, Pug, Pussyfoot

**Pawky** Dry, Humorous, Shrewd, Sly

**Pawn(shop), Pawnbroker, Pawnee** Agent, Betel, Chessman, Counter, Derby,
Dip, Fine, Gage, Gallery, Hanging, Hock, Hockshop, Hostage, Isolated, Leaving-shop,
Lumber, Lumberer, Moneylender, Mont-de-piété, Monte di pietà, Nunky, Pan, Passed,
Peacock, Piece, Pignerate, Pignorate, Pledge, Pledgee, Pop, Redeemer, Security, Sheeny,
Siri, Spout, Stalking-horse, Three balls, Tiddleywink, Tool, Tribulation, Uncle, Usurer,
Wadset, Weed

**Pax** Peace, Truce

**Pay(master), Payment, Paid, Pay off, Pay out** Aby, Advertise, Agterskot, Alimony,
Amortise, Annat, Annuity, Ante, Arles, Atone, Backhander, Balloon, Bank draft, Basic,
Batta, Blench, Bonus, Bukshee, Bukshi, Cain, Cashier, Cens, Cheque, COD, Commute,
Compensate, Consideration, Damage, Defray, Disburse, Discharge, Dividend, Down,
Dub, E, Earnest, Emolument, Endow, Equalisation, Eric, Escot, Farm, Fee, Feu-duty,
Finance, Foot, Fork out, Fund, Gale, Gate, Giro, Give, Grassum, Gratuity, Grave,
Greenmail, Guarantee, Han(d)sel, Hazard, Hire, Honorarium, Hoot(oo), HP, Imburse,
Intown multure, Kain, Kickback, Leads and lags, Lin(e)age, Lobola, Lobolo, Lump sum,
Mail, MasterCard®, Meet, Merchet, Métayage, Mise, Modus, Mortuary, Outcome,
Overtime, Palimony, Part exchange, Payola, Pension, Pittance, Pony, Posho, Prebendal,
Premium, Primage, Pro, Pro forma, Progress, Purser, Quarterage, Quit(-rent), Ransom,
Rate, Reap-silver, Rebate, Rebuttal, Redundancy, Refund, Remittance, Remuneration,
Rent, Requite, Residual, Respects, Retainer, Reward, Royalty, Salary, Satisfaction, Scot,
Screw, Scutage, Settle, Severance, Shell, Shell out, Shot, Sick, Sink, SO, Sold(e), Soul-scat,
Soul-scot, Soul-shot, →**SPEND**, Sponsor, Square, Stipend, Strike, Stump, Sub, Subscribe,
Sweetener, Table, Take-home, Tar, Tender, Tithe, Token, Tommy, Transfer, Treasure,
Treat, Tribute, Truck, Unpurse, Usance, Veer, Wage, Wardcorn, X-factor

**PC** Constable, Right on

**PE** Aerobics, Gym

**Pea(s)** Carling, Chaparral, Chickling, D(h)al, Desert, Dholl, Egyptian, Garbanzo, Goober,
Hastings, Legume, Mangetout, Marrow, Marrowfat, Mushy, Passiform, Petit pois,
Pigeon, Pulse, Rounceval, Snow, Split, String, Sturt's desert, Sugar, Sugar snap, Vetch

**Peace(ful), Peaceable, Peace-keeper, Peace organisation, Peace symbol**
Ahimsa, Antiwar, Armistice, Ataraxy, Calm, Douce, Ease, Equilibrium, Frieda, Frith,
Halcyon, Harmony, Hush, Interceder, Irenic(on), King's, Lee, Lull, Nirvana, Olive, Order,
Pacific, Pax, Pbuh, Queen's, Quiet, Repose, Rest, Rose, Roskilde, Salem, Serene, Sh,
Shalom, Siegfried, Siesta, Silence, Solomon, Soothing, Still, Tranquil, Truce, UN

**Peacemaker** ACAS, Arbitrator, Conciliator, Mediator, Trouble-shooter, Wilfred

**Peach** Blab, Cling, Clingstone, Dish, Dob, Freestone, Humdinger, Inform, Laetrile,
Malakatoone, Melba, Melocoto(o)n, Nectarine, Oner, Quandang, Shop, Sing, Sneak, Split,
Squeak, Stunner, Tattle, Tell, Victorine

**Peachum** Polly

**Peacock** Coxcomb, Dandy, Fop, Junonian, Muster, Ostentation, Paiock(e), Pajock(e),
Pavo(ne), Pawn, Payock(e), Pown, Sashay

**Peak(y)** Acme, Aiguille, Alp, Ancohuma, Apex, Ben, Cap, Chimborazo, Climax, Comble,
Communism, Cone, Crag, Crest, Darien, Drawn, Eiger, Flower, Gable, Gannett, Garmo,
Harney, Horn, Ismail Samani, Kazbek, Matterhorn, Meridian, Mons, →**MOUNTAIN**,

Nevis, Nib, Nunatak, Optimum, Pale, Petermann, Pikes, Pin, Pinnacle, Piton, Point, Pyramidal, Rainier, Sallow, Snowcap, Snowdon, Spire, Stalin, Sukarno, Top, Tor, Visor, Widow's, Zenith

**Peal** Carillon, Change, Chime, Clap, Toll, Triple

**Peanut(s)** Arnut, Chickenfeed, Goober, Groundnut, Monkey-nut, Pittance

**Pear** Aguacate, Alligator, Anchovy, Anjou, Asian, Asparagus, Avocado, Bartlett, Bergamot, Beurré, Blanquet, Carmelite, Catherine, Choke, Colmar, Comice, Conference, Cuisse-madame, Dutch admiral, Jargonelle, Muscadel, Muscatel, Musk, Nashi, Neli(e)s, Nelis, Perry, Poperin, Poppering, Poprin, Prickly, Pyrus, Queez-maddam, Sabra, Seckel, Seckle, Taylor's Gold, Warden, William

**Pearl(s), Pearly** Barocco, Barock, Baroque, Cultured, False, Gem, Imitated, Jewel, Mabe, Margaret, Margaric, Nacrous, Olivet, Onion, Orient, Prize, Rope, Seed, Simulated, String, Sulphur, Unio(n)

**Pear-shaped** Obconic, Obovate, Pyriform

**Peasant** Bogtrotter, Bonhomme, Boor, Bumpkin, Carlot, Chouan, Churl, Clodhopper, Contadino, Cossack, Cottar, Cott(i)er, Fellah(s), Fellahin, Hick, Jungli, Kern(e), Kisan, Kulak, M(o)ujik, Muzhik, Oik, Prole, Quashi(e), Raiyat, Roturier, Rustic, Ryot, Swain, Tyrolean, Volost, Whiteboy, Yokel

**Pea-shaped** Pisiform

**Peat(y)** Moss-litter, Sod, Turbary, Turbinacious, Turf, Yarfa, Yarpha

**Pebble(s), Pebbly** Banket, Bibble, Calculus, Chuck, Cobblestone, Dornick, Dreikanter, Gallet, Gooley, Gravel, Psephism, Pumie, Pumy, Scotch, Scree, Shingle, Ventifact

**Peccadillo** Mischief, Misdemeanour, Offence

**Peccary** Mexican hog, Tayassuid

**Peck** Bill, Bushel, Dab, Forpet, Forpit, Gregory, Job, Kiss, Lip, Lippie, Modius, Nibble, Pickle, Tap

**Pecksniff** Charity

**Peculiar(ity)** Abnormal, Appropriate, Bizarre, Characteristic, Curiosity, Curious, Distinct, Eccentric, Eery, Especial, Exclusive, Ferly, Funny, Idiosyncratic, Kink, Kooky, Loopy, Mannerism, Odd, Original, Own, Personal, Proper, Queer, Quirk, Royal, Singular, →SPECIAL, Specific, Strange, Unusual

▷ **Peculiar** *may indicate* an anagram

**Pedagogue** Academic, B.Ed, Teacher

**Pedal** Accelerator, Bike, Brake, Chorus, Clutch, Cycle, Damper, Lever, P, Rat-trap, Soft, Sostenuto, Sustaining, Treadle, Treddle, Wah-wah

**Pedal-coupler** Tirasse

**Pedant(ic)** Casaubon, Chop logic, Dogmatic, Don, Dryasdust, Elucubrate, Inkhorn, Intellectual, Jobsworth, Lucubrate, Nit-picking, Pedagogue, Pernickety, Pompous, Precisian, Quibbler, Scholastic, Sesquipedalian, Stickler

**Peddle, Pedlar** Bodger, Boxwallah, Camelot, Chapman, Cheapjack, Colporteur, Crier, Drummer, Duffer, Hawk, Huckster, Jagger, Packman, Pedder, Pether, Push, Sell, Smouch, Smouse(r), Sutler, Tallyman, Tink(er), Yagger

▷ **Peddling** *may indicate* an anagram

**Pedestal** Acroter(ion), Axle guard, Basis, Dado, Die, Footstall, Pillar, Support

**Pedestrian** Banal, Commonplace, Dull, Earth-bound, Ganger, Hack, Hike, Itinerant, Jaywalker, Laborious, Mediocre, Mundane, Ordinary, Ostrich, Trite, Voetganger, Walker

**Pedigree(s)** Ancestry, Blood, Breeding, Descent, Family tree, Genealogy, House, Lineage, Phylogeny, Pure-bred, Stemma(ta), Stirp(s), Studbook, Thoroughbred, Whakapapa

**Pediment** Fronton

**Peduncle** Scape, Stalk

**Peek** Eye, Glance, Glimpse, Peep

**Peel(er)** Bark, Bobby, Candied, Constable, Decorticate, Desquamate, Exfoliate, Flype, Grilse, Orange, Pare, PC, Pill, Potato, Rind, Rine, Rumbler, Scale, Sewen, Shell, Skin, →STRIP, Tirr, Zest

▷ **Peeled** *may indicate* outside letters to be removed from a word

**Peep(er), Peephole** Bo, Cheep, Cook, Crow, Glance, Gledge, Judas, Keek, Kook, Lamp, Nose, Peek, Pink, Pry, Snoop, Spy, Squeak, Squint, Stime, Styme, Voyeur

**Peer(age), Peers** Archduke, Aristocrat, Backwoodsman, Baron(et), Burke, Coequal, Coeval, Counterpart, Daimio, Debrett, Doucepere, Douzeper(s), Duke, Earl, Egal, Elevation, Equal, Eyeball, Gynt, Hereditary, Law Lord, Life, Lord, Match, Noble, Paladin, Peregal, Pink, Pry, Rank, Representative, Scry, Spiritual, Squint, Stare, Stime, Styme, Temporal, Toot, Tweer, Twire

**Peerless** Best, Matchless, Nonpareil, Supreme

**Peevish(ness)** Capernoited, Captious, Crabby, Cross, Doddy, Frabbit, Frampal, Frampold, Franzy, Fretful, Girner, Hipped, Ill, Lienal, Meldrew, Moody, Nattered, Pet, Petulant, Pindling, Protervity, Querulous, Shirty, Sour, Spleen, Teachie, Te(t)chy, Testy

**Peewit** Lapwing, Peewee

**Peg(gy)** Cheville, Cleat, Clothespin, Cotter-pin, Crawling, Die, Dowel, Drift-pin, Fix, Freeze, Jukskei, Kabaddi, Knag, Lee, Leg, Margaret, Nail, Nog, Odontoid, Pin(-leg), Piton, Shoe, Snort, Spigot, Spile, Square, Stengah, Stinger, Support, Tap, Tee, Thole, Tholepin, Thowel, Toggle, Tooth, Tot, Tuning, Vent, Woffington

**Pegboard** Solitaire

**Pegleg** Timber-toes

**Peking man** Pithecanthropus, Sinanthropus

**Pelagic** Deep-sea, Marine, Oceanic

**Pelf** Lucre, Mammon, Money, Notes, Riches

**Pelican** Alcatras, Bird, Crossing, Golden Hind, LA, Louisiana, Steganopode

**Pellagra** Maidism

**Pellet** Birdshot, Bolus, Buckshot, Bullet, Pill, Pilula, Pilule, Pithball, Prill, Shot, Slug, Snow

**Pellucid** Clear

**Pelmet** Valance

**Pelt** Assail, Clod, Fleece, Fur, Hail, Hide, Hie, Lam, Pepper, Random, Sealskin, Shower, Skin, Squail, Stone

**Peltast** Soldier, Targeteer

**Pelvis** Ilium, Pubis, Renal

**Pen** Author, Ballpoint, Bamboo, Bic®, Biro®, Cage, Calamus, Can, Cartridge, Catching, Confine, Coop, Corral, Crawl, Crib, Crow-quill, Cru(i)ve, Cub, Cyclostyle, Dabber, Data, Enclosure, Epi®, Fank, Farm, Felt(-tipped), Fold, Fountain, Gaol, Gladius, Hen, Highlighter, Hoosegow, J, →JAIL, Keddah, Kraal, Lair, Laser, Light, Magic marker, Marker, Mew, Mure, Music, Piggery, Poison, Pound, Quill(-nib), Rastrum, Ree, Reed, Ring, Rollerball, Scribe, Sheepfold, Stell, Stie, Stir, Stockade, Sty(e), Stylet, Stylo, Stylograph, Stylus, Submarine, Swan, Sweatbox, Tank, Weir, Write, →WRITER

▷ **Pen** *may indicate* a writer

**Penal(ize)** Cost, Fine, Gate, Handicap, Huff, Mulct, Punitive, Servitude

**Penalty** Abye, Amende, Card, Cost, Death, Endorsement, Eriach, Eric, Fine, Fixed, Foot-fault, Forfeit, Han(d)sel, Huff, Keltie, Kelty, Levy, Major, Pain, Price, Punishment, Rubicon, Sanction, Tap, Ticket, Wide

**Penance** Atonement, Expiation, Shrift

**Penates** Lares

**Pence** D, P, Peter's

**Penchant** Predilection

**Pencil** Beam, Ca(l)m, Caum, Charcoal, Chinagraph®, Crayon, Draft, Draw, Eyebrow, Fusain, Grease, Harmonic, Ink, Keelivine, Keelyvine, Lead, Outline, Propelling, Slate, Stub, Stump, Styptic, Tortillon

**Pend(ing)** Imminent, In fieri, On hold, Unresolved, Until

**Pendant** Albert, Chandelier, Drop, Earring, Girandole, Laval(l)ière, Medallion, Necklace, Poffle, Sautoir, Stalactite

**Pendragon** Uther
**Pendule** Poffle
**Pendulous, Pendulum** Compensation, Dewlap, Foucault's, Metronome, Noddy, One-way, Seconds, Swing, Wavering
**Penetrate, Penetrating, Penetration** Acumen, Acuminate, Bite, Bore, Bridgehead, Cut, Enpierce, Enter, Imbue, Impale, Incisive, Indent, Indepth, Infiltrate, Insight, Into, Intrant, Lance, Permeate, Pierce, Probe, Sagacious, Shear, Shrill, Strike, Thrust, Touch, X-ray
**Penguin** Adélie, Aeroplane, Anana, Auk, Blue, Emperor, Fairy, Gentoo, King, Korora, Little, Macaroni, Rock-hopper
**Penicillin** Cloxacillon, Fleming
**Peninsula** Arm, Neck, Promontory, Spit, Spur

## PENINSULAS

**4 letters:**
Alte
Ards
Cape
Eyre
Kola

**5 letters:**
Banks
Fylde
Gaspé
Gower
Kerch
Korea
Lleyn
Malay
Otago
Sinai
Upper
Yorke

**6 letters:**
Alaska
Arabia
Avalon
Balkan
Bataan

Crimea
Iberia
Istria
Palmer
Seward
Taimyr
Tasman
Taymyr
Wirral

**7 letters:**
Arabian
Boothia
Cape Bon
Cape Cod
Chukchi
Florida
Furness
Iberian
Jutland
Kintyre
Kowloon
Leizhou
Luichow
Olympic
S.W. Malay
Yucatan

**8 letters:**
Brittany
Cape York
Delmarva
East Cape
Galloway
Hispania
Labrador
Liaodong
Liaotung
Malaysia
Melville
Portland
Quiberon
S. Jutland

**9 letters:**
Antarctic
Black Isle
Cape Verde
Freycinet
Gallipoli
Indo-China
Kamchatka
Kathiawar
Northland
The Lizard

**10 letters:**
Cape Blanco
Chalcidice
Chersonese
Coromandel
Dunnet Head
Graham Land
Mornington
Nova Scotia

**11 letters:**
Lindisfarne
Peloponnese

**12 letters:**
Scandinavian

**14 letters:**
Baja California

**16 letters:**
Rhinns of Galloway

**17 letters:**
Wilson's Promontory

**Penis** Archie, Chopper, Cock, Cor(e)y, Dick, Dildo(e), Dipstick, Dong, Ferret, Giggle(stick), Horn, Jack, John Thomas, Knob, Langer, Member, Membrum virile, Mojo, Organ, Pecker, Peezle, Percy, Peter, Phallus, Pillicock, Pintle, Pisser, Pizzle, Plonker, Prick, Putz, Rod, Roger, Schlong, Schmock, Shaft, Shmock, Shmuck, Stiffy, Tallywhacker, Tockley, Todger, Tonk, Tool, W(h)ang, Weenie, Weeny, Willie, Willy, Winkle, Yard, Zeppelin
**Penitent(iary)** Calaboose, Cilice, Clink, Contrite, Gaol, Jail, Jug, Prison, Repenter, Rosary, Rueful, Stir
**Pennant, Pennon** Banner, Broad, Bunting, Fane, Flag, Guidon, Streamer
**Penniless** Bankrupt, Boracic, Broke, Bust, Impecunious, Poor, Skint, Strapped
**Penny** Bean, Cartwheel, Cent, Copper, D, Dreadful, Gild, Honest, New, P, Pretty, Sen, Sou, Sterling, Stiver, Win(n), Wing

**Penny-farthing** Bicycle, Ordinary
**Penny-pinching** Cheapskate
**Penpusher** Plumassier
**Pension(er)** Allowance, Ann(at), Annuitant, Board, Chelsea, Cod, Cor(r)ody, Full-board, Gasthaus, Gratuity, Guest-house, Half-board, Hostel, Hotel, Non-contributory, Occupational, Old-age, Oldster, Payment, Personal, Retire(e), Senior citizen, Serps, SIPP, Stakeholder, Stipend, Superannuation
**Pensive** Dreamy, Moody, Musing, Thoughtful, Triste, Wistful
**Pentameter** Elegiac, Iambic
**Pentateuch** T(h)orah
**Pentecost** Whit(sun)
**Penthouse** Cat, Lean-to, Roof, Skyhome
**Penultimate** Y
**Peon** Peasant, Serf, Slave, Ticca
**Peony** Moutan
**People(s)** Beings, Bods, Body, Chosen, Commonalty, Commons, Demos, Ecology, Electorate, Enchorial, Flower, Folk, Fraim, Gens, Grass roots, Guild, Herd, Human(kind), Inca, Indigenous, Inhabit, Janata, Kin, Land, Lapith, Lay, Man(kind), Masses, Men, Mob, Nair, Nation(s), Nayar, One, Peculiar, Personalities, Phalange, Populace, Proletariat(e), Public, Punters, Quorum, Rabble, Race, Raffle, September, Settle, Society, Souls, They, Tribe, Tuath, Tungus, Volk
**Pep** Buck, Dash, Enliven, Gism, Go, Jism, Jissom, Stamina, Verve, Vim
**Pepper(y)** Alligator, All-spice, Ancho, Ava, Betel, Bird, Black, Caper, Capsicum, Cayenne, Cherry, Chilli, Chipotle, Condiment, Cubeb, Devil, Dittander, Dittany, Ethiopian, Green, Guinea, Habanero, Jalapeno, Jamaica, Kava, Long, Malaguetta, Matico, Negro, Paprika, Pelt, Pim(i)ento, Piper, Piperine, Piquillo, Red, Riddle, Sambal, Scotch bonnet, Spice, Sprinkle, Sweet, Szechuan, Szechwan, Tabasco®, Techy, Testy, Wall, Water, White, Yaqona, Yellow
**Peppercorn** Nominal, →PAYMENT, →RENT
**Peppermint** Bull's Eye, Humbug, Pandrop
**Peptide** Cecropin, Substance P
**Per** By, Each, Through, Thru
**Perambulate, Perambulator** Buggy, Expatiate, Pedestrian, Pram, Stroller, Wagon, Walker
**Perceive, Perceptible, Perception, Perceptive** Acumen, Acute, Alert, Anschauung, Apprehend, Astute, Clairvoyance, Clear-eyed, Cryptaesthetic, Descry, Dianoia, Discern, Divine, ESP, Extrasensory, Feel, Image, Insight, Intelligence, Intuit(ion), Kinaesthesia, Noesis, Notice, Observe, Pan(a)esthesia, Remark, →SEE, Sense, Sensitive, Sentience, Shrewd, Sixth sense, Subjective, Subliminal, Tact, Taste, Telegnosis, Tel(a)esthesia, Understanding, Visual
**Percentage** Agio, Commission, Contango, Cut, Mark-up, Proportion, Rake off, Royalty, Scalage, Share, Vigorish
**Perch(ing)** Aerie, Alight, Anabis, Bass, Comber, Eyrie, Fish, Fogash, Gaper, Insessorial, Lug, Miserere, Ocean, Perca, Pole, Roost, Ruff(e), Seat, Serranid, →SIT, Wall-eye, Zingel
**Percolate, Percolation** Filter, Infiltrate, Leach, Lixiviate, Ooze, Osmosis, Permeate, Seep, Sipe, Soak, Strain, Sype
**Percussion (cap)** Amorce, Battery, Chinese temple block, Gong, Idiophone, Impact, Knee, Knock, Spoons, Thump, Timbrel, Traps
**Percy** Harry Hotspur, Shelley
**Perdition** Ades, Hades
**Peremptory** Absolute, Decisive, Haughty, Imperative, Imperious
**Perennial** Continual, Enduring, Flower, Livelong, Perpetual, Recurrent
**Perfect(ly), Perfection(ist)** Absolute, Accomplish, Accurate, Acme, Apple-pie, Bloom, Complete, Consummation, Cross-question, Dead, Develop, Edenic, Fare-thee-well,

Faultless, Finish, Flawless, Fulfil, Full, Holy, Hone, Ideal(ist), Impeccable, Intact, It, Letter, Matchless, Mature, Mint, Mr Right, Par, Paradisal, Paragon, Past, Pat, Peace, Pedant, Peerless, Point-device, Practice, Present, Pure, Quintessential, Refine, Salome, Siddha, Soma, Sound, Spotless, Spot-on, Stainless, Stickler, Sublime, The nines, Thorough, Three-pricker, To a t(ee), Unblemished, Unflawed, Unqualified, Unspoilt, Utopian, Utter, Very, Whole, Witeless

**Perfidy** Betrayal, Falsehood, Treachery, Treason

**Perforate(d), Perforation, Perforator** Cribrate, Cribrose, Drill, Eyelet, Fenestration, Hole, Leaky, → **PIERCE**, Prick, Punch, Puncture, Riddle, Trephine, Trocar

**Perforce** Necessarily, Needs

**Perform(ed), Performer, Performing** Achieve, Acrobat, Act(or), Action, Aerialist, Appear, Artist(e), Barnstorming, Basoche, Busk, Carry out, Chansonnier, Comedian, Contortionist, Discharge, Do, Duo, Effect, Enact, Entertainer, Execute, Exert, Exhibit, Extra, Fancy Dan, Fire-eater, Fulfil, Function, Geek, Hand, Headliner, Hersall, Hot dog, Houdini, Implement, Interlocutor, Lion-tamer, Majorette, Make, Mime, Minstrel, Moke, Nonet, Octet, Officiate, On, Operant, Patzer, Perpetrate, Player, Praxis, Quartet(te), Quintet, Rap artist, Recite, Render, Represent, Ripieno, Scene-stealer, Septet, Sextet, Showstopper, Soloist, Strongman, Supererogate, Svengali, Sword-swallower, Throw, Transact, Trio, Troupe, Vaudevillian, Virtuoso, Wire-dancer

**Performance** Accomplishment, Achievement, Act(ion), Auto, Blinder, Bravura, Broadcast, Chevisance, Command, Concert, Dare, Deed, Demonstration, Discharge, Division, Double act, Enactment, Entr'acte, Execution, Floorshow, Gas, Gig, Hierurgy, Holdover, Hootenanny, House, Karaoke, Masque, Master-class, Masterstroke, Matinee, Mime, Monodrama, Monologue, One-night stand, Operation, Perpetration, Practice, Première, Production, Programme, Recital, Rehearsal, Rendering, Rendition, Repeat, Repertoire, Rigmarole, Roadshow, Scene, Second house, Show (stopper), Showing, Simul, Sketch, Sneak preview, Solo, Specific, Spectacle, Stunt, Theatricals, Track record, Turn, Unicycle

**Perfume (box)** Abir, Ambergris, Angel water, Aroma, Attar, Bergamot, Cassolette, Chypre, Civet, Cologne, C(o)umarin, Eau de cologne, Eau de toilette, Enfleurage, Essence, Fragrance, Frangipani, Incense, Ionone, Lavender (water), Linalool, Millefleurs, Muscone, Muskone, Myrrh, Nose, Opopanax, Orris, Orrisroot, Otto, Patchouli, Patchouly, Pomander, Potpourri, Redolence, Rose water, → **SCENT**, Smellies, Terpineol, Toilet water, Tonka bean

**Perfunctory** Apathetic, Careless, Cursory, Indifferent, Token

**Perhaps** A(i)blins, Belike, Haply, Happen, May(be), Peradventure, Percase, Perchance, Possibly, Relative, Say, Yibbles

▷ **Perhaps** *may indicate* an anagram

**Perigee** Apsis, Epigeum

**Peril(ous)** → **DANGER**, Hazard, Jeopardy, Precarious, Risk, Threat, Yellow

**Perimeter** Boundary, Circuit, Circumference, Coastline, Limits

**Period(ic)** Abbevillian, Acheulian, AD, Aenolithic, Age, Alcher(ing)a, Andropause, Annual, Archaean, Aurignacian, Azilian, Base, Bi-weekly, Bout, Cal(l)ippic, Cambrian, Carboniferous, Chalcolithic, Chukka, Chukker, Climacteric, Comanchean, Cooling off, Cretaceous, Critical, Curse, Cycle, Day, Decad(e), Devonian, Diapause, Dot, Down, Dreamtime, → **DURATION**, Eocene, Epoch, Excerpt, Floruit, Full-stop, Gestation, Glacial, Grace, Great schism, Haute époque, Hercynian, Heyday, Holocene, Honeymoon, Horal, Incubation, Indiction, Innings, Interregnum, Jurassic, Kalpa, Latency, Latent, Lesson, Liassic, Limit, Meantime, Meanwhile, Menopause, Menses, Mesolithic, Mesozoic, Middle Kingdom, Miocene, Mississippian, Moment, Monthly, Moratorium, Neocomian, Neolithic, Neozoic, Octave, Oestrus, Olde-worlde, Oligocene, Ordovician, Palaeogene, Paleolithic, Patch, Payback, Pennsylvanian, Permian, Phanerozoic, Phase, Phoenix, Pleistocene, Pliocene, Pre-Cambrian, Proterozoic, Protohistory, QT, Quarter, Quaternary, Recurrent, Reformation, Refractory, Regency, Rent, Riss, Romantic, Saeculum, Safe,

Saros, Season, Session, Sidereal, Silurian, Span, Spasm, Spell, Stage, Stop, Stretch, Synodic, Teens, Term, Tertiary, Time, Trecento, Triassic, Triduum, Trimester, Tri-weekly, Usance, Weekly, Window

**Periodic(al)** Bi-weekly, Catamenia, Comic, Digest, Economist, Etesian, Journal, Liassic, Listener, Mag, New Yorker, Organ, Paper, Phase, Publication, Punch, Rambler, Regency, Review, Scandal sheet, Solutrean, Solutrian, Spectator, Strand, Stretch, Tatter, Tract

**Peripatetic** Ambulatory, Gadabout, Itinerant, Promenader, Travelling

**Periphery** Ambit, Bounds, Exurb, Fringe, Outskirts, Surface

**Periscope** Eye(-stalk)

**Perish(able), Perished, Perishing** Brittle, → DIE, End, Ephemeral, Expire, Fade, Forfair, Fungibles, Icy, Tine, Tint, Transitory, Tyne, Vanish

**Periwinkle** Apocynum, Blue, Madagascar, Myrtle

**Perjure(d)** Forswear, Lie, Mansworn

**Perk(s), Perky, Perk up** Bonus, Brighten, Chipper, Deadhead, Dividend, Enliven, Freebie, Freshen, Fringe benefit, Jaunty, LV, → PERQUISITE, Tronc

**Perm(anent)** Abiding, Durable, Enduring, Eternal, Everlasting, Fixed, For keeps, Full-time, Indelible, → LASTING, Marcel, Stable, Standing, Stative, Timeless, Unending, Wave

**Permeable, Permeability, Permeate** Imbue, Infiltrate, Leaven, Magnetic, Osmosis, Penetrate, Pervade, Poromeric, Porous, Seep, Transfuse

**Permission, Permissive, Permit(ted)** Allow, Authorise, By-your-leave, Carnet, Chop, Clearance, Congé(e), Consent, Copyright, Easy, Enable, Franchise, Give, Grant, Green light, Indult, Lacet, Laisser-passer, Latitude, Leave, Legal, Legitimise, Let, Liberty, Licence, License, Lief, Loan, Luit, Nihil obstat, Ok(e), Pace, Pass, Placet, Planning, Power, Pratique, Privilege, Remedy, Safe-conduct, Sanction, Stamp-note, Suffer, Ticket, Tolerate, Triptyque, Visa, Vouchsafe, Warrant, Way-leave, Wear

**Pernicious** Damnable, Evil, Fatal, Harmful, Lethal, Noisome, Noxious, Pestilent, Wicked

**Pernickety** Faddish, Fikish, Hair-splitting, Niggly

**Peroration** Pirlicue, Purlicue

**Peroxide** Bleach, Blonde, Colcothar

**Perpendicular** Aplomb, Apothem, Atrip, Cathetus, Erect, Normal, Orthogonal, Plumb, Sheer, Sine, → UPRIGHT, Vertical

**Perpetrate** Commit, Effect, Execute, Offender, Redo

**Perpetual** Constant, Eternal, Incessant, Sempiternal

**Perplex(ed), Perplexity** Anan, At a loss, Baffle, Bamboozle, Bemuse, Beset, Bewilder, Bother, Buffalo, Bumbaze, Cap, Confound, Confuse, Embarrass, Feague, Floor, Flummox, Fox, Knotty, Meander, Mystify, Nonplus, Obfuscate, Out, Pother, Pudder, Puzzle, Quizzical, Stump, Tangle, Throw, Tickle, Tostication

**Perquisite** Ap(p)anage, Emolument, Extra, Gratuity, → PERK, Tip

**Perrier** Stoner

**Perry** Mason

**Persecute, Persecution** Afflict, Annoy, Badger, Bully, Crucify, Dragon(n)ades, Harass, Haze, Intolerant, McCarthyism, Oppress, Paranoia, Pogrom, Ride, Torment, Torture, Victimise, Witch hunt

**Persevere, Perseverance** Assiduity, Continue, Fortitude, Hold on, Insist, Jusqu'auboutisme, Patience, Persist, Plug, Press on, Soldier on, Stamina, Steadfastness, Stick, Stickability, Tenacity

**Persia(n)** Achaemenid, Babee, Babi, Bahai, Cyrus, Dari, Farsi, Iran(ian), Mazdean, Mede, Middle, Pahlavi, Parasang, Parsee, Pehlevi, Pushtu, Samanid, Sassanid, Sohrab, Xerxes, Zoroaster

**Persiflage** Satire

**Persimmon** Kaki, Sharon fruit

**Persist(ence), Persistent** Adhere, Assiduity, Chronic, Constant, Continual, Diligent, Doggedness, Endure, Eternal, Hang-on, Importunate, Incessant, Keep at, Labour, Last,

Longeval, Lusting, Nag, Persevere, Press, Relentless, Sedulous, Sneaking, Stamina, Stick, Stubborn, Tenacity, Unabated, Urgent

**Person(s), Personal(ly)** Alter, Artificial, Aymaran, Being, Bird, Bod(y), Chai, Chal, Character, Chav, Chi, Cookie, Displaced, Entity, Everyman, Figure, First, Fish, Flesh, Ga(u)dgie, Gadje, Gauje, Gut, Head, Human, Individual, In propria persona, Me, Nabs, Natural, Nibs, One, Own, Party, Passer-by, Pod, Private, Quidam, Second, Selfhood, Skate, Sod, Soul, Specimen, Tales, Third, Type, Walla(h), Wight

**Personage, Personality** Alter ego, Anima, Celeb(rity), Character, Charisma, Dignitary, Ego, Godhead, Grandee, Identity, Jekyll and Hyde, Megastar, Multiple, Noble, Notability, Panjandrum, Presence, Psychopath, Sama, Schizoid, Seity, Sel, Self, Sell, Somatotonia, Split, Star, Temperament, Tycoon, Viscerotonia

**Personified, Personification, Personify** Embody, Epitome, Incarnate, Prosopop(o)eia, Represent

**Personnel** Employees, Hands, HR, Liveware, Manpower, Staff

**Perspective** Aerial, Atmosphere, Attitude, Distance, Foreshorten(ed), Linear, Point of view, Proportion, Scenography, Slant, Take, View, Vista

**Perspicacious, Perspicacity** Astute, Clear-sighted, Discerning, Insight, Keen, Shrewd

**Perspiration, Perspire, Perspiring** Aglow, Forswatt, Glow, Hidrosis, Sudor, Suint, Sweat, Swelter

**Persuade(d), Persuasion, Persuasive** Brainwash, Cajole, Carrot and stick, Coax, Cogent, Conviction, Convince, Disarm, Eloquent, Exhort, Faith, Feel, Forcible, Geed, Get, Induce, Inveigle, Lead on, Move, Plausible, → **PREVAIL**, Religion, Rhetoric, Seduce, Silver-tongued, Smooth-talking, Soft sell, Suborn, Sway, Sweet-talk, Tempt, Truckled, Wheedle, Winning

**Pert(ness)** Bold, Brisk, Cocky, Dicacity, Flippant, Forward, Fresh, Impertinent, Insolent, Jackanapes, Minx, Quean, Saucy, Tossy

**Pertain** Apply, Belong, Concern, Effeir, Effere, Relate, Touch

**Pertinacious** Dogged, Obstinate, Persistent, Stickler, Stubborn

**Pertinent** Ad rem, Apropos, Apt, Fit, Germane, Relevant, Timely

**Perturb(ation)** Aerate, Confuse, Dismay, Disturb, Dither, Faze, Pheese, State, Trouble, Upset, Worry

**Peru(vian)** Inca, PE, Quechua(n), Quichua(n)

**Peruse, Perusal** Examine, Inspect, Read, Scan, Scrutiny, → **STUDY**

**Pervade, Pervasion, Pervasive(ness)** Aroma, Atmosphere, Diffuse, Drench, Immanence, Permeate, Saturate

**Perverse, Perversion, Pervert(ed), Perversity** Aberrant, Abnormal, Algolagnia, Awkward, Awry, Balky, Cam(stairy), Camsteary, Camsteerie, Cantankerous, → **CONTRARY**, Corrupt, Crabbed, Cussed, Decadent, Deform, Deviate, Distort, Donsie, False, Froward, Gee, Kam(me), Kinky, Licentious, Misinterpret, Misuse, Nonce, Paraphilia, Protervity, Refractory, Sadist, Sicko, Stubborn, Thrawn, Traduce, Travesty, Twist, Unnatural, Untoward, Uranism, Warp(ed), Wayward, Wilful, Wrest, Wry

▷ **Perverted** *may indicate* an anagram

**Pessimism, Pessimist(ic)** Alarmist, Bear, Cassandra, Crapehanger, Crepehanger, Cynic, Defeatist, Dismal Jimmy, Doom merchant, Doomwatch, Doomy, Doubter, Downbeat, Eeyore, Fatalist, Glumbum, Jeremiah, Killjoy, Negative, Weltschmerz

**Pest(er)** Aggravate, Badger, Bedbug, Beleaguer, Besiege, Blight, Bluebottle, Bombard, Bot, → **BOTHER**, Brat, Breese, Bug, Dim, Disagreeable, Earbash, Fly, Fowl, Fruit fly, Gapeworm, Greenfly, Harass, Hassle, Irritate, Menace, Microbe, Mither, Molest, Mouse, Nag, Nudnik, Nuisance, Nun, Oestrus, Pize, Plague, Rotter, Scourge, Tease, Terror, Thysanoptera, Vermin, Weevil

**Pesticide** Benomyl, Botanic(al), DDT, Derris, Dichlorvos, Endrin, Glucocorticoid, Glucosinolate, Heptachlor, Mouser, Permethrin, Synergist, Warfarin

**Pestilence, Pestilent** Curse, Epidemic, Evil, Lues, Murrain, Murren, Noxious, Outbreak, Pernicious, Plague

**Pet** Aversion, Cade, Canoodle, Caress, Chou, Coax, Coddle, Cosset, Cuddle, Dandle, Darling, Daut(ie), Dawt(ie), Dear, Dod, Dort, Ducky, Favourite, Fondle, Glumps, Hamster, Huff, Hump, Indulge, Ire, Jarta, Jo, Lallygag, Lapdog, Messan, Miff, Mouse, Neck, Pamper, Pique, Poach, Rabbit, Smooch, Snog, Spat, Stroke, Strum, Sulk(s), Tantrum, Teacher's, Temper, Tiff, Tout, Towt, Umbrage, Virtual, Yarta

**Petal(s)** Ala, Corolla, Keels, Labellum, Leaf, Standard, Vexillum

**Petard** Firework, Squib

**Pete(r), Peter out** Aumbry, Bell, Cell, Diminish, Dwindle, End, Grimes, Hermit, Pan, Pears, Pegleg, Principle, Quince, Quint, Rabbit, Safe, Saint, Sellers, Simon, Simple, Wane, Weaken

**Petite** Dainty, Mignon, Small

**Petition(er)** Appeal, Beg, Boon, Claimant, Crave, Entreaty, Litany, Millenary, Orison, Plaintiff, Postulant, Prayer, Press, Representation, Request, Round robin, Solicit, Sue, Suit(or), Suppli(c)ant, Supplicat, Vesper

**Pet-name** Hypocorisma, Nickname, So(u)briquet

**Petrel** Bird, Mother Carey's chicken, Nelly, Prion, Procellaria, Stormbird, Stormy, Wilton's

**Petrify(ing)** Fossilise, Frighten, Lapidescent, Niobe, Numb, Ossify, Scare, Terrify

**Petrol(eum)** Avgas, Cetane, Cutting, Diesel, Esso®, Ethyl, Fuel, Gas, High-octane, High-test, Leaded, Ligroin, Maz(o)ut, Octane, Oilstone, Olein, Platforming, Refinery, Rock oil, Rock-tar, STP, Styrene, Unleaded, Vaseline®

**Petticoat** Balmoral, Basquine, Crinoline, Female, Filabeg, Fil(l)ibeg, Jupon, Kilt, Kirtle, Phil(l)abeg, Phil(l)ibeg, Placket, Sarong, Shift, Slip, Underskirt, Wylie-coat

**Pettifogger** Lawmonger

**Petty, Pettiness** Baubling, Bumbledom, Childish, Little, Mean, Minor, Narrow, Niggling, Nyaff, One-horse, Parvanimity, Picayunish, Piffling, Pimping, Puisne, Puny, Shoestring, Small, Small-minded, Small-time, Small town, Stingy, Tin, Trivial, Two-bit

**Petty officer** Cox, CPO, PO

**Petulance, Petulant** Fretful, Huff, Mardy, Moody, Peevish, Perverse, Procacity, Querulous, Sullen, Toutie, Waspish

**Pew** Box, Carrel, Chair, Perch, Seat, Stall

**Pewter** Trifle, Tutenag

**Phaeton** Spider

**Phalanger** Cus-cus, Honey-mouse, Honey possum, Opossum, Petaurist, Phascogale, Possum, Sugar glider, Tait, Tarsipes, Tuan, Wambenger

**Phalanx** Cohort, Coterie, Legion

**Phalarope** Lobe-foot

**Phallus** Linga(m), Penis, Priapus

**Phantasist, Phantasm** Apparition, Chimera, Spectre, Werewolf

**Phantom** Apparition, Bogey, Bugbear, Eidolon, Feature, Idol, Incubus, Maya, Pepper's ghost, Shade, Spectre, Tut, Wild hunt, Wraith

**Pharaoh** Akhenaton, Amenhotep, Cheops, Egyptian, Rameses, River-dragon, Theocrat, Thutmose, Tut, Tutankhamen, Tutankhamun, Tyrant

**Pharisee** Formalist, Humbug, Hypocrite, Nicodemus

**Pharmacist, Pharmacologist** Apothecary, →CHEMIST, Dispenser, Druggist, Loewi, MPS, Officinal, Preparator

**Phase** Climacteric, Coacervate, Colour, Cycle, Form, Nematic, Period, Post-boost, Primary, Quarter, REM, Schizont, Stage, State, Synchronise, Transition

**Pheasant** Argus, Bird, Fireback, Junglefowl, Mona(u)l, Nide, Nye, Pea-chick, Peacock, Pea-fowl, Pea-hen, Ring-necked, Silver, Tragopan

**Phenol** Orcine, Orcinol, Resorcinol, Xylenol

**Phenomenon** Autokinetic, Blip, Eclipse, Effect, Event, Figure ground, Flying saucer, Flysch, Geohazard, Heterography, Hormesis, Marvel, Meteor, Miracle, Mirage, Paranormal, Parascience, Phenology, Phi, Psi, Rankshift, Raynaud's, Synergy

**Phial** Bologna, Bottle, Flask

**Phil, Philip** Fluter, Macedonia, Pip

**Philander(er)** Flirt, Keeper, Libertine, Lothario, Playboy, Toyer, → **TRIFLE**, Wolf, Womaniser

**Philanthropist, Philanthropy** Altruist, Barnardo, Benefactor, Carnegie, Charity, Chisholm, Coram, Donor, Freemason, Geldof, Getty, Guggenheim, Hammer, Humanist, Humanitarian, Lever, Mayer, Nobel, Nuffield, Peabody, Rockefeller, Rowntree, Samaritan, Shaftesbury, Tate, Wilberforce

**Philately** Timbromania

**Phileas** Fogg

▶ **Philip** *see* **PHIL**

**Philippic** Diatribe, Invective, Tirade

**Philippine(s)** Bisayan, Igorot, Moro, Pangasinian, PI, RP, Tagalog, Visayan

**Philistine, Philistinism** Artless, Ashdod, Barbarian, Bigot, Foe, Gath, Gaza, Gigman, Goliath, Goth, Lowbrow, Podsnappery, Vandal

**Philology** Linguistics, Semantics, Speechcraft

**Philosopher, Philosophy** Academist, Activism, Ahimsa, Analytical, Animism, Anthrosophy, Antinomianism, Antiochian, A priorist, Atomic, Atomist, Attitude, Averr(h)oism, Cartesian, Casuist, Comtism, Conceptualism, Conservatism, Cracker-barrel, Critical, Cynic, Deipnosophist, Deontology, Eclectic, Eleatic, Empiricism, Enlightenment, Epistemology, Ethics, Existentialism, Fatalism, Gnostic, Gymnosophist, Hedonism, Hermeneutics, Hobbism, Holist, Humanism, I Ching, Idealism, Ideology, Instrumentalism, Ionic, -ism, Kaizen, Linguistic, Logical atomism, Logicism, Logos, Maieutic, Marxism, Materialism, Mechanism, Megarian, Metaphysician, Metaphysics, Metempiricism, Monism, Moral(ist), Natural, Neoplatonism, Neoteric, Nihilism, Nominalism, Occamist, Occam's razor, Ockhamist, Opinion, Panhellenism, Peripatetic, Phenomenology, Platonism, Populism, Positivism, Rationalism, Realism, Rosminian, Sage, Sankhya, Sceptic, Schoolman, Scientology, Scotism, Secular-humanism, Sensist, Shankara(-charya), Solipsism, Sophist, Stoic, Synthetic, Taoism, Theism, Theosophy, Thomist, Thought, Transcendentalism, Ultraism, Utilitarianism, Utopianism, Vedanta, Voluntarism, Weltanschauung, Whitehead, Yoga, Yogi

---

## PHILOSOPHERS

| 4 letters: | Dewey | Engels | 7 letters: |
|---|---|---|---|
| Ayer | Hegel | Farabi | Abelard |
| Hume | James | Godwin | Aquinas |
| Jedi | Locke | Herder | Barthes |
| Kant | Moore | Hobbes | Bentham |
| Mach | Paine | Lao-tzu | Bergson |
| Mill | Pater | Ockham | Bradley |
| Ryle | Plato | Olbers | Buridan |
| Weil | Quine | Ortega | Derrida |
| Wolf | Renan | Pascal | Diderot |
| Zeno | Smith | Peirce | Eckhart |
|  | Sorel | Popper | Emerson |
|  | Taine | Pyrrho | Erasmus |
| 5 letters: |  | Sartre | Erigena |
| Amiel |  | Scotus | Haldane |
| Bacon | 6 letters: | Seneca | Herbart |
| Bayle | Agnesi | Tagore | Hypatia |
| Bruno | Arendt | Thales | Leibniz |
| Buber | Carnap |  | Malthus |
| Comte | Cicero |  | Marcion |
| Croce | Cousin |  |  |

Marcuse
Mencius
Meng-tse
Ptolemy
Rosmini
Russell
Schlick
Serbati
Sheffer
Spencer
Spinoza
Steiner
Tillich

**8 letters:**
Alembert
Anderson
Avicenna
Berkeley
Boethius
Cyreniac
Diogenes
Epicurus

Foucault
Hamilton
Harrison
Maritain
Menippus
Old Moore
Passmore
Plotinus
Plutarch
Rousseau
Schiller
Socrates
Xenophon

**9 letters:**
Antiochus
Aristotle
Bosanquet
Cleanthes
Confucius
Descartes
Euhemerus
Heidegger

Leucippus
Lucretius
Nietzsche
Santayana
Schelling

**10 letters:**
Anacharsis
Anaxagoras
Anaximenes
Antiochene
Apemanthus
Apollonius
Aristippus
Campanella
Chrysippus
Democritus
Empedocles
Helveticus
Heraclitus
Hutchinson
Maimonides
Paracelsus

Parmenides
Protagoras
Pythagoras
Saint Simon
Swedenborg
Von Leibniz
Xenocrates
Xenophanes

**11 letters:**
Anaximander
Antisthenes
Kierkegaard
Machiavelli
Montesquieu

**12 letters:**
Callisthenes
Merleau-Ponty
Schopenhauer
Theophrastus
Wittgenstein

**Philosophic(al)** Calm, Fatalistic, Rational, Resigned, Thoughtful, Tranquil
**Philtre** Aphrodisiac, Charm, Drug, Hippomanes, Potion
**Phlegm(atic)** Calm, Composed, Pituita(ry), Pituite, Stolid, Unperturbed, Unruffled
**Phloem** Leptome, Liber
**Phobia** Aversion, Dread, Fear, Neurosis, Thing
**Phoebe, Phoebus** Apollo, Artemis, Day-star, Deaconess, Moon, Selene, Sol, Sun
**Phoenician** Tripolitania
**Phoenix** Bird-of-wonder, Fum, Fung, Paragon, Self-begotten
**Phon(e)y** Bogus, Charlatan, Counterfeit, Ersatz, Faitor, Fake, Hokey, Impostor, Poseur, Quack, →SHAM, Specious, Spurious
**Phone** Bell, Blower, Call, Cellular, Clamshell, Dial, Dual band, Flip, Handset, Intercom, Mob(i)e, Mobile, Moby, Pay, Picture, Ring, Roam, Satellite, Saver, Skype, Smart, Talkback, Tel, →TELEPHONE, Text
**Phonetic(s)** Acoustic, Articulatory, Auditory, Interdental, Mouille, Oral, Palaeotype, Palatal, Palato-alveolar, Plosion, Spoken, Symbol, Synaeresis
▷ **Phonetically** may indicate a word sounding like another
▷ **Phony** may indicate an anagram
**Phosphate** Apatite, Monazite, Sphaerite, Torbernite, Vivianite, Wavellite, Xenotime
**Phosphor(escent), Phosphorescence, Phosphorus** Bologna, Briming, Cephalin, Foxfire, Friar's lantern, Ignis fatuus, Jack o'lantern, Luminescent, Malathion®, Noctilucent, P, Pyrosome, Sarin, Sea-fire, Tabun, Will o' the wisp
**Photo(copy), Photograph(y), Photographic, Photo finish** Ambrotype, Anaglyph, Angiogram, Beefcake, Black and white, Blow-up, Cabinet, Calotype, Clog, Close-up, Composite, Contre-jour, Daguerrotype, Diazo, Digicam, Duplicate, Dyeline, Enprint, Exposure, Ferroprint, Ferrotype, Film, Flash, Half-tone, Headshot, Heliochrome®, Heliotype, Hologram, Infra-red, Kallitype, Karyogram, Kirlian, Kodak®, Microdot, Microfilm, Microgram, Micrograph, Microprint, Monochrome, Montage, Mugshot, Negative, Nephogram, Opaline, Panel, Picture, Pinhole, Platinotype, Polaroid®, Positive, Print, Resorcin, Rotograph, Rotogravure, Schlieren, Sepia, Shoot, Shot, Shutterbug, Slide, Snap, Spirit, Still, Sun-print, Take, Talbotype, Time-lapse,

Tintype, Tomography, Topo, Trimetrogon, Vignette, Wire, Woodburytype, Xerography, X-ray

**Photographer** Bailey, Beaton, Brandt, Brassai, Cameraman, Cameron, Capa, Cartier-Bresson, Daguerre, Fox Talbot, Man Ray, Mapplethorpe, Pap(arazzo), Schlierin, Shutterbug, Snowdon, Stalkerazzi, Stannotype

**Phrase** Abject, Actant, Asyndeton, Buzzword, Cadence, Catch(word), Catchcry, Cliché, Climacteric, Comma, Expression, Hapax legomenon, Heroic, Hook, Idiophone, Laconism, Leitmotiv, Lemma, Locution, Mantra, Motto, Noun, Phr, Prepositional, Refrain, Riff, Set, Slogan, Soundbite, Tag, Term, Theme, Trope, Verb

**Phrygian** Midas

**Phthisis** Decay, TB

**Phylactery** Amulet, Talisman, Tefillin, Tephillin

**Phyllopod** Brine-shrimp

**Physic(s)** Cluster, Cryogenics, Culver's, Cure, Dose, Electronics, Electrostatics, Geostatics, Health, High-energy, Kinematics, Medicine, Nuclear, Nucleonics, Particle, Photometry, Purge, Remedy, Rheology, Science, Solid-state, Sonics, Spintronics, Statistics, Thermodynamics, Ultrasonics

**Physical** Bodily, Carnal, Corpor(e)al, Material, Natural, Tangible

**Physician** Addison, Allopath, Bach, Buteyko, Chagas, Doctor, Erastus, Eustachio, Galen, Gilbert, Graves, Guillotin, Hakim, Hansen, Harvey, Hippocrates, Internist, Jenner, Lamaze, Leech, Linacre, Lister, Medic(o), Menière, Mesmer, Mindererus, Paean, Paian, Paracelsus, Practitioner, Preceptor, Quack, Ranvier, Roget, Russell, Salk, Sézary, Spiegel, Stahl, Still, Therapist, Time, Vaidya, Wavell

**Physicist** →SCIENTIST

---

## PHYSICISTS

**3 letters:** Ohm

**4 letters:** Bohr, Born, Bose, Gold, Hahn, Kerv, Lawe, Mach, Rabi, Vafa

**5 letters:** Adams, Auger, Bondi, Bragg, Curie, Debye, Dicke, Dirac, Fermi, Gamow, Gauss

Henry, Hertz, Hooke, Hoyle, Joule, Lodge, Nambu, Pauli, Penny, Popov, Raman, Stark, Volta, Weber, Young, Zener

**6 letters:** Alfven, Ampère, Carnot, Dalton, Davies, Geiger, Giorgi, Kelvin, Landau

Morley, Nernst, Newton, Peirce, Penney, Picard, Planck, Powell, Skyrme, Teller, Wilson

**7 letters:** Alhazen, Alvarez, Bardeen, Broglie, Charles, Coulomb, Crookes, Doppler, Faraday, Feynman, Fresnel, Galileo, Gilbert, Hawking

Huygens, Laplace, Lorentz, Marconi, Maxwell, Meitner, Moseley, Nielsen, Oersted, Peebles, Penzias, Piccard, Rankine, Reaumur, Richter, Rontgen, Sievert, Tyndall, Wheeler

**8 letters:** Anderson, Angstrom, Appleton, Avogadro, Blackett, Brattain

| | | | |
|---|---|---|---|
| Brewster | Susskind | Michelson | Watson-Watt |
| Bridgman | Van Allen | Ovshinsky | |
| Cerenkov | | Robertson | **11 letters:** |
| Davisson | **9 letters:** | | Chamberlain |
| Einstein | Alanasoff | **10 letters:** | Joliot-Curie |
| Foucault | Becquerel | Archimedes | Oppenheimer |
| Millikan | Cockcroft | Bernouilli | Schrödinger |
| Oliphant | Friedmann | Fahrenheit | Van der Waals |
| Rayleigh | Heaviside | Heisenberg | |
| Roentgen | Josephson | Rutherford | |
| Schottky | Kirchhoff | Torricelli | |

**Physiognomist, Physiognomy** Face, Features, Lavater

**Physiology, Physiologist** Bernard, Bordet, Dale, Eccles, Einthoven, Loeb, Malpighi, Pavlov, Purkinje, Schafer, Wagner, Zoonomia

**Physiotherapist** Masseur

**Physique** Body, Build, Figure, Pyknic, Set-up, Somatotype

**Pi, Pious** Breast-beater, Craw-thumper, Devotional, Devout, Fraud, Gallio, God-fearing, Godly, Holy, Holy Willie, Mid-Victorian, Religiose, Reverent, Sanctimonious, Savoury, Smug, Unco guid, Wise, Zaddik

**Pi(ous)** Orant, Reverent, Saintly

**Piaffe** Spanish-walk

**Pianist** Anda, Arrau, Bernstein, Concert, Hambourg, Hess, Hofmann, Liberace, Liszt, Mingus, Morton, Ogdon, Pachmann, Paderewski, Peterson, Répétiteur, Schnabel, Tatum, Vamper, Virtuoso, Waller

**Piano** Baby grand, Bechstein, Boudoir grand, Broadwood, Celesta, Celeste, Concert grand, Cottage, Dumb, Flugel, Forte, Grand, Hammerklavier, Honkytonk, Joanna, Keyboard, Mbira, Overstrung, P, Player, Prepared, Semi-grand, Softly, Steinway, Stride, Thumb, Upright

**Piano-maker** Erard

**Picaresque** Roman à tiroirs

**Picaroon** Brigand, Corsair, Pirate, Rogue

**Picasso** Cubist

**Piccadilly** Whist

**Piccolo** Ottavino

**Pick(er), Pickaxe, Picking, Pick out, Pick up** Break, Cherry, Choice, →**CHOOSE**, Contract, Cream, Cull, Elite, Emu-bob, Evulse, Flower, Gather, Glean, Gurlet, Hack, Holing, Hopper, Mattock, Nap, Nibble, Oakum, Plectrum, Pluck, Plum, Select, Single, Sort, Steal, Strum, Tone arm, Tong, Wale

▷ **Picked** *may indicate* an anagram

**Picket** Demonstrate, Fence, Flying, Pale, Palisade, Post, Protester, Riata, Stake, Tether, Tie

**Pickings** Harvest, Profits, Scrounging, Spoils

**Pickle(r)** Achar, Beetroot, Brine, Cabbage, Caper, Chow-chow, Chutney, Corn, Corner, Cucumber, Cure, Dilemma, Dill, Eisel, Esile, Gherkin, Girkin, Imp, Jam, Kimchi, Marinade, Marinate, Mess, Mull, Olive, Onion, Peculate, Peregrine, Piccalilli, →**PLIGHT**, Relish, Rod, Samp(h)ire, Scrape, Souse, Spot, Steep, Trouble, Vinegar, Wolly

**Picklock** Oustiti, Peterman

**Pick-me-up** Bracer, Drink, Restorer, Reviver, Tonic

**Pickpocket(s)** Adept, Bung, Cly-faker, Cutpurse, Dip, Diver, Fagin, File, Nipper, Swell mob, Swellmobsman, Whizzer, Wire

**Pick-up** Arrest, Light o'love, Truck, Ute

**Picnic** Alfresco, Braaivleis, Burgoo, Clambake, Fun, Junketing, Outing, Push-over, Spread, Tailgate, Valium, Wase-goose, Wayzgoose

**Picture(s)** Anaglyph, Arpillera, Art, Bambocciades, Bitmap, B-movie, Canvas, Caricature, Cartoon, Cinema, Cloudscape, Collage, Cutaway, Cyclorama, Decoupage, Depict, Describe, Diptych, Drawing, Drypoint, Emblem, Envisage, Envision, Epitome, Etching, Film, Flick, Fresco, Gouache, Graphic, Histogram, Icon, Iconic, Identikit®, Illusion, Imagery, Inset, Kakemono, Landscape, Lenticular, Likeness, Lithograph, Montage, Mosaic, Motion, Movie, Moving, Movy, Mugshot, Myriorama, Oil, Painture, Photo, Photofit®, Photogram, Photomontage, Photomosaic, Photomural, Pin-up, Pix, Plate, Polyptych, Portrait, Predella, Prent, Presentment, Print, Represent, Retraitt, Retrate, Rhyparography, Scene, Semble, Shadowgraph, Shot, Skyscape, Slide, Snapshot, Stereochrome, Stereogram, Stereograph, Stevengraph, Still-life, Table(au), Talkie, Tapestry, Tattoo, Thermogram, Tone, Topo, Transfer, Transparency, Vanitas, Vectograph, Vignette, Vision, Votive, Vraisemblance, Word, X-ray, Zincograph
**Picturesque** Chocolate box, Idyllic, Scenic
**Pidgin** Bislama, Chinook jargon, Creole, Fanagalo, Fanakalo, Hiri Motu, Japlish, Kamtok, Mobilian, New Guinea, Police Motu, Solomon Islands, Tok Pisin
**Pie(s)** Anna, Banoffee, Battalia, Bird, Bridie, Camp, Chewet, Cinch, Cobbler, Cottage, Coulibiac, Curry puff, Custard, Deep-dish, Easy, Flan, Floater, Florentine, Hash, Humble, Koulibiaca, Madge, Meat, Mess, Mince(meat), Mud, Mystery bag, Pandowdy, Pastry, Pasty, Patty, Périgord, Pica, Piet, Pirog, Pizza, Printer's, Pyat, Pyet, Pyot, Quiche, Rappe, Resurrection, Shepherd's, Shoofly, Shred, Spoil, Squab, Stargaz(e)y, Star(ry)-gazy, Sugar, Tart, Tarte tatin, Torte, Tourtière, Turnover, Tyropitta, Umble, Vol-au-vent, Warden
▷ **Pie** *may indicate* an anagram
**Piebald** Calico, Dappled, Lacuna, Motley, Paint, Pied, Pinto, Skewbald, Tangun
**Piece(s)** Adagio, Add, Arioso, Bagatelle, Bishop, Bit, Blot, Cameo, Cannon, Cent, Charm, →**CHESSMAN**, Chip, Chunk, Coin, Companion, Component, Composition, Concerto, Conversation, Counter, Crumb, Domino, End, Entr'acte, Episode, Extract, Firearm, Fit, Flake, Flitters, Fragment, Frust, Gat, Goring, →**GUN**, Haet, Hait, Hunk, Item, Join, Mammock, Man, Médaillons, Mite, Money, Morceau, Morsel, Museum, Nip, Novelette, Nugget, Oddment, Off-cut, Ort, Part, Party, Pastiche, Patch, Pawn, Pce, Period, Peso, Pin, Pistareen, Pole, →**PORTION**, Recital, Rifle, Rook, Scliff, Scrap, Section, Sector, Set, Shard, Sherd, Skliff, Slice, Slip, Sliver, Snatch, Snippet, Soffit, Sonata, Sou, Spare part, Speck, String, Stub, Swatch, Tad, Tait, Tate, Tile, Toccata, Truncheon, →**WEAPON**, Wedge, Wodge
**Pièce de résistance** Star-turn
**Piecemeal, Piecework** Gradually, Intermittent, Jigsaw, Serial, Task, Tut
**Pie-crust** Coffin, Lid, Pastry
**Pied-à-terre** Nest, Pad
**Pieman** Pastrycook, Shepherd
**Pier(s)** Anta, Chain, Groyne, Jetty, Jutty, Landing, Mole, Plowman, Quay, Slipway, Swiss roll, Wharf, Wigan
**Pierce(d), Piercer, Piercing** Accloy, Awl, Bore, Broach, Cleave, Cribrose, Dart, Drill, Endart, Fenestrate(d), Fulminant, Gimlet, Gore, Gride, Gryde, Hull, Impale, Jag, Keen, Labret, Lance, Lancinate, Lobe, Move, Needle, Penetrate, Perforate, Pertusate, Pike, Pink, Poignant, Prince Albert, Punch, Puncture, Riddle, Rive, Shrill, Skewer, Slap, Sleeper, Spear, Spike, Spit, Stab, Steek, Stilet(to), Sting, Tap, Thirl, Thrill(ant), Transfix
**Piety** Devotion, Godliness, Purity, Sanctity
**Piffle** Bilge, Codswallop, Hogwash, Nonsense, Poppycock, Tommy-rot, Tosh, Twaddle
**Pig(s), Piggy, Pigmeat, Pigskin** Anthony, Babe, Babirusa, Baconer, Barrow, Bartholomew, Bessemer, Bland, Boar, Bonham, British Lop, Bush, Captain Cooker, Cutter, Doll, Duroc, Elt, Farrow, Fastback, Football, Gadarene, Gilt, Gloucester, Gloucester Old Spot, Glutton, Greedy guts, Grice, Grumphie, Gryce, Guffie, Guinea, Gus, Gutzer, Ham, Hampshire, Hog, Ingot, Iron, Javelina, Kentledge, Kintledge, Kunekune, Lacombe, Landrace, Land-shark, Lard, Large Black, Large White, Lingot, Long, Middle White, Napoleon, Old Spot, Peccary, Policeman, Porchetta, Pork(er), Raven, Razorback,

Rosser, Runt, Saddleback, Shoat, Shot(e), Shott, Slip, Snowball, Sounder, Sow, Squealer, Sucking, Suid(ae), Tamworth, Tayassuid, Tithe, Toe, Tootsie, Truffle, Vietnamese potbellied, Warthog, Welsh, Yelt

**Pig-disease** Bullnose

**Pigeon** Archangel, Barb, Bird, Bronze-winged, Cape, Capuchin, Carrier, Clay, Cropper, Culver, Cumulet, Danzig, Dove, Fairy Swallow, Fantail, Goura, Ground, Gull, Homer, Homing, Horseman, Jacobin, Kereru, Kuku, Lahore, Manumea, Mourning dove, New Zealand, Nun, Owl, Passenger, Peristeronic, Piwakawaka, Pouter, Ringdove, Rock(er), Roller, Ront(e), Ruff, Runt, Scandaroon, Solitaire, Spot, Squab, Squealer, Stale, Stock-dove, Stool, Stork, Swift, Talkie-talkee, Tippler, Tooth-billed, Trumpeter, Tumbler, Turbit, Wonga(-wonga), Zoozoo

**Pigeonhole** Classify, Compartment, File, Label, Postpone, Shelve, Slot, Stereotype

**Pigeon-house** Columbary, Cote, Dovecot(e)

**Pig-food** Mast, Slop, Swill

**Pig-headed** Self-willed

**Pig-iron** Kentledge, Kintledge

**Pigman** Hog-reeve

**Pigment(s), Pigmentation** Accessory, Anthoclore, Anthocyan(in), Argyria, Betacyanin, Bilirubin, Biliverdin, Bister, Bistre, Bronzing, Cappagh-brown, Carmine, Carotene, Carotenoid, Carotin, Carotinoid, Chloasma, Chlorophyll, Chrome, Chromogen, Cobalt, Colcothar, Colour, Crocus, Curcumin, Dye, Etiolin, Eumelanin, Flake-white, Flavin(e), Fucoxanthin, Gamboge, Gossypol, Green earth, Haem, Hem(e), H(a)ematin, H(a)emocyanin, H(a)emoglobin, Iodopsin, King's yellow, Lake, Lamp-black, Lipochrome, Lithopone, Liverspot, Lutein, Luteolin, Lycopene, Madder, Madder lake, Melanin, Monastral®, Mummy, Naevus, Naples yellow, Nigrosine, Oaker, Ochre, Opsin, Orpiment, Paris-green, Phthalocyanine, Phycobilin, Phycocyan, Phycoerythrin, Phycophaein, Phycoxanthin, Phytochrome, Porphyrin, Porphyropsin, Pterin, Puccoon, Quercetin, Realgar, Red lead, Respiratory, Retinene, Rhiboflavin, Rhodophane, Rhodopsin, Saffron, Scheele's green, Sepia, Sienna, Sinopia, Sinopsis, Smalt, Tapetum, Tempera, Terre-verte, Tincture, Toner, Turacoverdin, Ultramarine, Umber, Urobilin, Urochrome, Verditer, Vermilion, Viridian, Whitewash, Xanthophyll, Xanthopterin(e), Yellow ochre, Zinc white

**Pigtail** Braid, Cue, Plait, Queue

**Pi jaw** Cant

**Pike** Assegai, Crag, Dory, Fogash, Gar(fish), Ged, Gisarme, Glaive, Hie, Holostei, Javelin, Lance, Langdale, Luce, Partisan, Pickerel, Ravensbill, Scafell, Snoek, Spear, Speed, Spontoon, Vouge, Walleyed

▸ **Pilaster** *see* PILLAR(ED)

**Pilchard** Sardine

**Pile(d), Piles, Piling** Agger, Amass, Atomic, Big, Bing, Bomb, Bubkes, Camp-sheathing, Camp-shedding, Camp-sheeting, Camp-shot, Clamp, Cock, Column, Crowd, Deal, Dolphin, Down, Emerods, Farmers, Fender, Fig, Floccus, Fortune, Galvanic, Hair, Haycock, Heap, Hept, Historic, Hoard, Load, Lot, Mansion, Marleys, Mass, Moquette, Nap, Pier, Post, Pyre, Raft, Reactor, Ream(s), Rouleau, Screw, Shag, Sheaf, Sheet, Slush, → STACK, Starling, Stately home, Stilt, Toorie, Trichome, Upheap, Velvet, Voltaic, Wad, Wealth, Windrow, Wodge

**Pile-driver** Tup

**Pilfer(ing)** Crib, Filch, Finger, Maraud, Miche, Nick, Peculate, Pickery, Pickle, Pinch, Plagiarise, Plunder, Purloin, Snitch, → STEAL

**Pilgrim(age)** Aske, Childe Harold, Expedition, Fatima, Gaya, Hadj(i), Haji, Hajj(i), Karbala, Kerbela, Kum, Loreto, Lourdes, Mathura, Mecca, Nasik, Nikko, Palmer, Pardoner, Qom, Questor, Qum, Reeve, Scallop-shell, Shrine, Umra(h), Voyage, Yatra

**Pill(s)** Abortion, Ball, Beverley, Bitter, Bolus, Cachou, Caplet, Capsule, Chill, Dex, Doll, Dose, Globule, Golfball, Goofball, Lob, Medication, Medicine, Number nine, Peace, Peel,

Pellet, Pep, Pilula, Pilule, Placebo, Poison, Protoplasmal, Radio, Sleeping, Spansule, Tablet, Troche, Trochisk, Upper

**Pillage** Booty, Devastate, Plunder, Raid, Ransack, Rapine, Ravage, Razzia, Robbery, Sack, Spoil

**Pillar(ed), Pillars** Anta, Apostle, Atlantes, Baluster, Balustrade, Boaz, Canton, Caryatides, Chambers, Cippus, Columel, Column, Earth, Eustyle, Gendarme, Goal, Hercules, Herm, Impost, Islam, Jachin, Lat, Man, Modiolus, Monolith, Newel, Nilometer, Obelisk, Pedestal, Peristyle, Pier, Post, Respond, Saddle, Serac, Stack, Stalactite, Stalagmite, Stanchion, Stoop, Telamon, Tetrastyle, Trumeau

**Pill-box** Hat, Inro

**Pillion** Cushion, Pad, Rear

**Pillory** Cang(ue), Cippus, Crucify, Jougs, Little-ease, Pelt, Satirise, Slam

**Pillow(case)** Bear, Beer, Bere, Bolster, Cod, Cow, Cushion, Headrest, Hop, Lace, Pad, Pulvinar, Throw

**Pilot(s)** Ace, Airman, Auto(matic), Aviator, Bader, Biggles, Branch, Bush, Captain, → **CONDUCT**, Experimental, Flier, George, Govern, Guide, Hobbler, Hoveller, Kamikaze, Lead, Lodesman, Lodestar, Palinure, Palinurus, Pitt, Prune, Radar, Red Baron, Shipman, Steer, Test, Tiphys, Trial, Trinity House, Usher, Wingman

**Pimento** Allspice

**Pimp** Apple-squire, Bludger, Fancyman, Fleshmonger, Hoon, Lecher, Mack, Pandarus, Pander, Ponce, Procurer, Solicit, Souteneur

**Pimpernel** Bastard, Bog, Poor man's weatherglass, Scarlet, Water, Wincopipe, Wink-a-peep, Yellow

**Pimple, Pimply** Blackhead, Botch, Bubukle, Button, Goosebump, Gooseflesh, Grog-blossom, Hickey, Horripilation, Milium, Papilla, Papula, Papule, Plook, Plouk, Pock, Pustule, Quat, Rumblossom, Rum-bud, Spot, Tetter, Uredinial, Wen, Whelk, Whitehead, Zit

**Pin** Axle, Bayonet, Belaying, Bolt, Brooch, Candle, Cask, Corking, Cotter, Curling, Dowel, Drawing, Drift, End, Fasten, Fid, Firing, Fix, Gam, Gnomon, Gudgeon, Hair, Hairgrip, Hob, Hook, Joggle, Kevel, King, Leg, Nail, Needle, Nog, Panel, Peg, Pintle, Pivot, Preen, Prick, Rivet, Rolling, Saddle, Safety, Scarf, SCART, Scatter, Shear, Shirt, Skewer, Skittle, Skiver, Spike, Spindle, Split, Staple, Stick, Stump, Swivel, Taper, Tertial, Thole, Thumbtack, Tie, Tietac(k), Tre(e)nail, Trunnion, U-bolt, Woolder, Wrest, Wrist

**Pinafore** Apron, Brat, HMS, Overall, Pinny, Save-all, Tire

**Pinball** Pachinko

**Pince-nez** Nose-nippers

**Pincers** Chela, Claw, Forceps, Forfex, Nipper, Nips, Tongs, Tweezers

**Pinch(ed)** Arrest, Bit, Bone, Chack, Constrict, Cramp, Crimp, Crisis, Emergency, Gaunt, Misappropriate, Nab, Narrow, Nick, Nim, Nip, Nirlit, Peculate, Peel, Pilfer, Pocket, Pook(it), Pouk, Prig, Pugil, Raft, Raw, Rob, Save, Scrimp, Scrounge, Skimp, Smatch, Snabble, Snaffle, Sneak, Sneap, Sneeshing, Snuff, Squeeze, → **STEAL**, Swipe, Tate, Trace, Tweak, Twinge

**Pine(s), Pining** Ache, Arolla, Bristlecone, Celery, Cembra, Chile, Cluster, Cone, Conifer, Cypress, Deal, Droop, Dwine, Earn, Erne, Evergreen, Fret, Green, Ground, Hone, Hoop, Huon, Jack, Japanese umbrella, Jeffrey, Kauri, Knotty, Languish, Languor, Loblolly, Lodgepole, Long, Longleaf, Lovelorn, Lovesick, Monkey-puzzle, Monterey, Moon, Norfolk Island, Norway, Nut, Oregon, Parana, Picea, Pinaster, Pitch, Ponderosa, Radiata, Red, Scotch, Scots, Screw, Sehnsucht, Slash, Softwood, Spruce, Starve, Stone, Sugar, Tree, Umbrella, Urman, Waste, White, Yearn, Yellow

**Pineapple** Anana, Bomb, Bromelia, Grenade, Piña, Poll, Sorosis, Tillandsia

**Ping** Knock, Whir(r)

**Pinguin** Anana(s)

**Pinion** Fetter, Lantern, Penne, Pinnoed, Secure, Shackle, Wing

**Pink** Blush, Carnation, Carolina, Castory, Cheddar, Clove, Colour, Coral, Cyclamen, Dianthus, Dutch, Emperce, FT, Fuchsia, Gillyflower, Indian, Knock, Kook, Lake, Lily, Lychnis, Maiden, Moss, Mushroom, Old rose, Oyster, Peach-blow, Peak, Perce, Pierce, Pompadour, Pounce, Rose(ate), Rose-hued, Rose madder, Ruddy, Salmon, Scallop, Sea, Shell, Shocking, Shrimp, Spigelia, Spit, Stab, Tiny

**Pinkerton** Detective

**Pinnacle** Acme, Apex, Apogee, Crest, Crown, Gendarme, Height, Hoodoo, Needle, Pinnet, Summit, Zenith

**Pinniped** Seal

**Pin-point** Focus, Highlight, Identify, Isolate, Localise

**Pint(s)** Cab, Jar, Log, Reputed

**Pintail** Duck, Smeath, Smee(th)

**Pin-up** Bimbo, Cheesecake, Dish, Star, Sweater girl

**Pioneer(ing)** Alcock, Armstrong, Avant garde, Babbage, Baird, Bandeirante, Blaze, Boone, Brown, Colonist, Emigrant, Explore, Fargo, Fawkner, Fleming, Frontiersman, Ground-breaking, Harbinger, Herodotus, Innovator, Lead, Lister, Marconi, Oecist, Pathfinder, Planter, Rochdale, Sandgroper, Settler, Spearhead, Stopes, Trail-blazer, Trekker, Turing, Voortrekker, Waymaker, Wells, Yeager

▸ **Pious** *see* PI

**Pip** Ace, Acinus, Blackball, Bleep, Distemper, Heart, Hip, Hump, Lurgi, Phil, Pyrene, Seed, Star

**Pipe(s), Piper, Pipeline, Piping** Ait, Antara, Aorta, Aulos, Balance, Barrel, Blub, Boatswain's, Bong, Briar, Briarroot, Bronchus, Broseley, Bubble, Calabash, Call, Calumet, Cask, Chanter, Cheep, Cherrywood, Chibouk, Chibouque, Chillum, Churchwarden, Clay, Cob, Conduit, Corncob, Crane, Cutty, Dip, Division, Down, Downcomer, Drain, Drill, Drillstring, Drone, Dry riser, Duct, Dudeen, Dudheen, Ell, Escape, Exhaust, Faucet, Feed, Fistula, Flue, Flute, Gage, Gas main, Gedact, Gedeckt, Hawse, Hod, Hogger, Hooka(h), Hose, Hubble-bubble, Hydrant, Ice, Indian, Injection string, Irish, Jet, Kalian, Kelly, Mains, Manifold, Marsyas, Meerschaum, Mirliton, Montre, Narghile, Nargile(h), Narg(h)il(l)y, Oat(en), Oboe, Oesophagus, Organ, Ottavino, Outlet, Pan, Peace, Pepper, Pibroch, Piccolo, Pied, Pifferaro, Pitch, Poverty, Principal, Pule, Qanat, Quill, Rainwater, Recorder, Ree(d), Rise, Riser, Sack-doudling, Salicional, Sennit, Serpent, Service, Sewer, Shalm, Shawm, Sheesha, Shisha, Shoe, Shrike, Sing, Siphon, Skirl, Sluice, Soil, Spout, Squeak, Stack, Standpipe, Stopcock, Stummel, Sucker, Syrinx, Tail, Tee, Throttle, Tibia, Tootle, Trachea, Tremie, Tube, Tubule, Tweet, U-bend, Uillean(n), Union, Uptake, U-trap, U-tube, Vent, Ventiduct, Volcanic, Waste, Water(-spout), Watermain, Weasand, Whiss, Whistle, Woodcock's head, Woodnote, Worm

**Pipefish** Sea-adder

**Pipe-laying** Graft

**Pipit** Bird, Skylark, Titlark

**Pippin** Apple, Orange, Ribston

**Pipsqueak** Nobody

**Piquancy, Piquant** Heat, Pungent, Racy, Relish, Salt, Savoury, Sharp, Spicy, Tangy

**Pique** Bah, Dod, Huff, Irritation, Pride, Resentment, Titillate

**Piranha** Caribe, Characinoid, Piraya

**Pirate(s), Pirated, Piratical, Piracy** Algerine, Barbarossa, Blackbeard, Boarder, Bootleg, Brigand, Buccaneer, Buccanier, Cateran, Condottier, Conrad, Corsair, Crib, Dampier, Fil(l)ibuster, Flint, Gunn, Hijack, Hook, Kidd, Lift, Loot, Morgan, Penzance, Pew, Picaro(on), Pickaroon, Plagiarise, Plunder, Rakish, Rover, Sallee-man, Sallee-rover, Sea-dog, Sea-king, Sea-rat, Sea-robber, Sea-wolf, Silver, Skull and crossbones, Smee, Steal, Teach, Thief, Unauthorised, Viking, Water-rat, Water-thief

**Pistillate** Female

**Pistol** Air, Ancient, Automatic, Barker, Barking-iron, Captive bolt, Colt®, Dag, Derringer, Gat, →GUN, Hackbut, Horse, Iron, Luger®, Pepperbox, Petronel, Pocket, Puffer, Revolver, Rod, Saloon, Shooter, Sidearm, Starter, Starting, Very, Water, Weapon, Zip gun

**Piston** Four-stroke, Plunger, Ram, Trunk

**Pit(ted), Pitting, Pits** Abyss, Alveolus, Antrum, Bed, Bottomless, Catch, Cave, Cesspool, Chasm, Cissing, Cloaca, Coalmine, Colliery, Crater, Den, Depression, Depth, Dungmere, Ensile, Fossa, Fougasse, Fovea, Foxhole, Gehenna, Hangi, Heapstead, Heartspoon, Hell, Hillhole, Hole, Hollow, Inferno, Inspection, Khud, Lacunose, Lime, Mark, Match, Measure, →MINE, Mosh, Nadir, Orchestra, Parterre, Pip, Plague, Play, Pock-mark, Potato, Punctate, Putamen, Pyrene, Ravine, Rifle, Salt, Scrobicule, Silo, Slime, Soakaway, Solar plexus, Stone, Sump, Tar, Tartarus, Tear, Trap, Trous-de-loup, Underarm

**Pitch(ed)** Absolute, Asphalt, Atilt, Attune, Bitumen, Burgundy, Catapult, Coal-tar, Concert, Crease, Diamond, Diesis, Dive, Ela, Elect, Elevator, Encamp, Erect, Establish, Fever, Fling, Fork(ball), French, Ground, Heave, Height, International, Intonation, Key, Knuckleball, Labour, Length, Level, Lurch, Macadam, Maltha, Mineral, Nets, Neume, Outfield, Patter, Peck, Perfect, Philharmonic, Philosophical, Piceous, Pight, Pin, Plong(e), Plunge, Pop, Purl, Relative, Resin, Rock, Ruff(e), Sales, Scend, Seel, Send, Shape, Sling, Slope, Soprarino, Spiel, Spitball, Stoit, Tar, Tessitura, Tilt, Tone, Tonemic, Tonus, Tremolo, Tune, Unison, Vibrato, Wicket, Wild, Wood

**Pitchblende** Cleveite

**Pitcher(-shaped)** Aryt(a)enoid, Ascidium, Baseballer, Bowler, Cruse, Ewer, Jug, Steen, Urceolus

**Pitchfork** Hurl, Toss

**Pitchstone** Retinite

**Pitfall** Ambush, Danger, Hazard, Snare, Trap

**Pith(y)** Ambatch, Aphorism, Apo(ph)thegm, Brief, Core, Down, Essence, Gnomic, Hat-plant, Heart, Laconic, Marrow, Meaty, Medulla, Moxa, Nucleus, Rag, Sententious, Succinct, Terse

**Pithead** Broo, Brow, Minehead

**Pithless** Thowless

**Pitiless** Flint-hearted, Hard, Hard-headed, Relentless, Ruthless

**Piton** Rurp

**Pitt** Chatham

**Pittance** Peanuts

**Pity, Piteous, Pitiful, Pitiable** Ah, Alack, Alas, Commiseration, →COMPASSION, Hapless, Mercy, Pathos, Pilgarlic, Poor, Quarter, Red-leg, Rue, Ruth(ful), Seely, Shame, Sin, Sympathy, Too bad, Waefu(l), Wretched

**Pivot(al)** Ax(i)le, Central, Focal, Fulcrum, Gooseneck, Gudgeon, Kingbolt, Marker, Revolve, Rotate, Slue, →SWIVEL, Trunnion, Turn, Wheel

**Pixie** Brownie, Elf, Fairy, Gremlin, Sprite

**Pizza** Calzone, Pepperoni

**Placard** Affiche, Bill, Playbill, Poster

**Placate** Appease, Calm, Conciliate, Mollify, Pacify, Placate, Propitiate, Soothe

**Place(ment)** Ad loc, Aim, Allocate, Appoint, Area, Arena, Assisted, Berth, Bro, Decimal, Deploy, Deposit, Dispose, First, Fix, Habitat, Haunt, Hither, Howf, Identify, Impose, →IN PLACE OF, Insert, Install, Job, Joint, Juxtapose, Lay, Lieu, Locality, Locate, Locus, Niche, Parking, Pitch, Plat, Plaza, Point, Posit, →POSITION, Post, Product, Put, Realm, Region, Repose, Resting, Room, Rowme, Scene, Second, Set, Sit, Site, Situate, Situation, Slot, Spot, Station, Stead, Sted(e), Stedd(e), Stratify, Third, Toponym, Town, Vendôme

**Placebo** Snake-oil

**Placid** Cool, Easy, Easy-osy, Even-tempered, Quiet, Tame, Tranquil, Untroubled

**Plagiarise, Plagiarist** Copy, Crib, Lift, Pirate, Steal

**Plague (spot)** Ailment, Annoy, Bane, Bedevil, Black death, Boil, Bubonic, Burden, Cattle, Curse, Death, Dog, Dun, Epidemic, Frogs, Gay, Goodyear, Goujeers, Harry, Importune, Infestation, Locusts, Lues, Molest, Murrain, Murran, Murrin, Murrion, Nag, Obsess, Pest, Pester, Pox, Press, Scourge, Tease, Token, Torment, Torture, Try, Vex

**Plaid** Maud, Roon, Shepherd's, Tartan, Wales

**Plain(s)** Abraham, Archimedes, Artless, Ascetic, Au naturel, Bald, Banat, Bare, Blatant, Broad, Campagna, Campo, Campus Martius, Candid, Carse, Ceará, Chryse, Clavius, Clear, Cook, Dowdy, Downright, Dry, Esdraelon, Evident, Explicit, Flat, Flood, Girondist, Gran Chaco, Great, Homely, Homespun, Inornate, Jezreel, Kar(r)oo, Lande, Langrenus, Liverpool, Llano, Lombardy, Lowland, Maidan, Manifest, Marathon, Mare, Matter of fact, Monochrome, Nullarbor, Obvious, Ocean of Storms, Oceanus Procellarum, Olympia, →ORDINARY, Outspoken, Overt, Packstaff, Palpable, Pampa(s), Paramo, Patent, Pikestaff, Plateau, Playa, Polje, Prairie, Prose, Ptolemaeus, Purbach, Sabkha(h), Sabkha(t), Sailing, Salisbury, Savanna(h), Secco, Serengeti, Sharon, Simple, Sodom, Spoken, Staked, Steppe, Tableland, Thessaly, Tundra, Unadorned, Unremarkable, Vanilla, Vega, Veldt, Visible, Walled

**Plainchant** Canto fermo

**Plainsman** Llanero

**Plainsong** Alternatim, Ambrosian, Chant

**Plaint(ive)** Complaint, Dirge, Lacrimoso, Lagrimoso, Lament, Melancholy, Sad, Whiny

**Plaintiff** Doe, Impeacher, Litigant, Suer

**Plait** Braid, Crimp, Cue, Entwine, Frounce, Furbelow, Goffer, Intertwine, Pigtail, Plica, Plight, Queue, Ruche, Sennit, Sinnet, Splice, Tress

**Plan(s), Planned, Planner, Planning** Aim, American, Angle, Architect, Arrange, Atlas, Axonometric, Battle, Blueprint, Brew, Budget, Care, Chart, Commission, Complot, Conspire, Contingency, Contrive, Dalton, Dart, Deep-laid, Deliberate, Delors, Design, Desyne, Device, Devise, Diagram, Draft, Drawing, Elevation, Engineer, European, Family, Figure on, Five-Year, Flight, Floor, Forethought, Format, Galveston, Game, Ground, Hang, Ichnography, Idea, Idée, Initiative, Instal(l)ment, Intent, Itinerary, Lay(out), Leicester, Leicestershire, Logistics, Machinate, Manoeuvre, Map, Marshall, Master, Mastermind, Mean, Meditate, Nominal, Open, Outline, Pattern, Pipe-dream, Plat, Plot, Ploy, Policy, Premeditate, Prepense, Procedure, Programme, Project, Projet, Proposal, Prospectus, Protraction, Rapacki, Relief map, Road map, Ruse, Scenario, Schedule, Scheme, Schlieffen, Shape, Spec(ification), Stratagem, Strategy, Subterfuge, System, Tactician, Town, Trace, View, Wallchart, Wheeze

**Planck** Quantum theory

**Plane(s)** Aero(dyne), Air, →AIRCRAFT, Airliner, Airship, Axial, Bandit, Basal, Block, Boeing, Bomber, Bus, Buttock, Camel, Canard, Cartesian, Cessna, Chenar, Chinar, Comet, Concorde, Crate, Dakota, Datum, Delta-wing, Ecliptic, Even, Facet, Fault, Fillister, Flat, Float, Focal, Freighter, Galactic, Glider, Gliding, Gotha, Homaloid, Hurricane, Icosahedron, Icosohedra, Inclined, Jack, Jet, Jointer, Jumbo, Level, London, Main, MIG, Mirage, Mosquito, Moth, Octagon, Perspective, Platan(us), Polygon, Prop-jet, Pursuit, Rocket, Router, Shackleton, Shave, Shuttle, Smooth, Soar, Sole, Spitfire, Spokeshave, Spy, Stealth (bomber), STOL, Surface, Sycamore, Tail, Taube, Thrust, Tow, Trainer, Tree, Trident, Tropopause, Trying, Two-seater, Viscount

**Plane figure** Endecagon, Hendecagon

**Planet(s), Planetary** Alphonsine, Ariel, Asteroid, Body, Cabiri, Ceres, Chiron, Constellation, Dispositor, Earth, Eros, Extrasolar, Gas giant, Georgian, Giant, House, Hyleg, Inferior, Inner, Jovian, Jupiter, Lucifer, Major, Mars, Mercury, Minor, Moon, Neptune, Outer, Pallas, Pluto, Primary, Psyche, Quartile, Red, Satellitium, Saturn, Sedna, Significator, Sphere, Starry, Sun, Superior, Terra, Terrestrial, Uranus, Venus, Vista, Vulcan, World, Zog

**Plangent** Mournful

**Plank** Board, Chess, Deal, Duckboard, Garboard, Manifesto, Plonk, Sarking, Slab, Spirketting, Straik, Strake, Stringer, Weatherboard, Wood, Wrest

**Plankton** Nekton, Neuston, Noctiluca, Pelagic, Red tide, Seston, Spatfall

**Plant(s), Plant part** Acrogen, Agent, Amphidiploid, Anemochore, Annual, Anther, Aphotoic, Autophyte, Bed, Biennial, Biota, Bloomer, Bonsai, Bryophyte, CAM,

Chamaephyte, Chomophyte, Conspecific, Cotyledon, Creeper, Cropper, Cultigen, Cultivar, Dayflower, Dibble, Ecad, Eccremocarpus, Embed, Endogen, Enemy, Enrace, Epilithic, Epiphyllous, Epiphyte, Establish, Factory, Fix, Flora, Forb, Geophyte, G(u)ild, Growth, Gymnosperm, Halophyte, Halosere, Herbage, Herbarium, House, Humicole, Hydrastus, Hydrophyte, Hygrophyte, Hylophyte, Incross, Insert, Instil, Inter, Labiate, Land, Lathe, Legume, Lithophyte, Livelong, Longday, Lurgi, Machinery, Mill, Mole, Monocotyledon, Ornamental, Perennial, Phanerogam, Phloem, Pilot, Pitcher, Power, Protophyte, Psilophyte, Ramet, Resurrection, Root, Rosin, Saprophyte, Schizophyte, Sciophyte, Sclerophyll, Scrambler, Sensitive, Sere, Shortday, Shrub, Simple, Sow, Spermatophyte, Sponge, Spy, Steelworks, Stickseed, Sticktight, Strangler, Streptocarpus, Succulent, Superweed, Thallophyte, Therophyte, Thickleaf, Trailer, → TREE, Trifolium, Trillium, Tropophyte, Twining, Vascular, Vegetal, Vegetation, Washery, Wilding, Works, Zoophyte

## PLANTS

| 3 letters: | Grex | Sunn | Cress |
|---|---|---|---|
| Dal | Guar | Tare | Cubeb |
| Ers | Hebe | Taro | Cumin |
| Hom | Herb | Thea | Daisy |
| Hop | Hioi | Vine | Dwale |
| Ivy | Homa | Weld | Erica |
| Kex | Hoya | Woad | Ficus |
| Lis | Ixia | Wort | Fitch |
| Meu | Kaki | Yarr | Fouat |
| Nep | Kali | | Fouet |
| Pia | Kava | **5 letters:** | Fucus |
| Rue | Khat | Abaca | Gemma |
| Set | Lily | Agave | Glaux |
| Soy | Ling | Ajwan | Gorse |
| Til | Loco | Anise | Guaco |
| Udo | Mate | Anona | Hosta |
| Urd | Mint | Arnut | Hovea |
| Yam | More | Aroid | Inula |
| | Moss | Aster | Jalap |
| **4 letters:** | Musk | Avens | Kenaf |
| Alga | Nard | Basil | Knawe |
| Aloe | Noni | Benni | Kudzu |
| Anil | Ombu | Betel | Laser |
| Arum | Pink | Blite | Ledum |
| Balm | Pita | Bluet | Liana |
| Beet | Poly | Boree | Linum |
| Bixa | Rape | Broom | Loofa |
| Chay | Reed | Buchu | Lotus |
| Cube | Rhus | Bucku | Luffa |
| Daal | Rose | Bugle | Lupin |
| Dahl | Rush | Calla | Medic |
| Deme | Ruta | Camas | Morel |
| Dhal | Sage | Canna | Murva |
| Dill | Sego | Carex | Musci |
| Fern | Sida | Chara | Naiad |
| Flag | Silk | Chaya | Orach |
| Flax | Snow | Chufa | Orpin |
| Geum | Sola | Clary | Orris |
| Gobo | Soma | Clote | Orval |

Oshac
Osier
Oxeye
Oxlip
Panax
Pansy
Peony
Phlox
Pilea
Poppy
Reate
Sedge
Sedum
Senna
Shaya
Sotol
Spart
Spink
Stock
Tansy
Tetra
Timbo
Tulip
Urali
Urari
Urena
Vetch
Vinca
Viola
Vitex
Vitis
Xyris
Yucca
Yulan
Zamia

**6 letters:**
Abelia
Acacia
Acorus
Ajowan
Alisma
Allium
Alpine
Althea
Ambari
Ambary
Amomum
Annona
Arabis
Aralia
Arnica
Aucuba
Azalea

Bablah
Balsam
Bamboo
Bauera
Betony
Borage
Briony
Bryony
Burnet
Cactus
Caltha
Camash
Camass
Cassia
Catnep
Catnip
Celery
Cicely
Cicuta
Cissus
Cistus
Cleome
Clivia
Clover
Clusia
Cnicus
Cockle
Cohage
Cohosh
Coleus
Conium
Coonty
Cornel
Cosmea
Cosmos
Cotton
Cowpea
Crinum
Crocus
Croton
Cummin
Dahlia
Daphne
Darnel
Datura
Derris
Dodder
Echium
Endive
Eringo
Erinus
Erynga
Exacum
Exogen

Fat hen
Fennel
Ferula
Funcka
Funkia
Garlic
Gnetum
Henbit
Hoodia
Hyssop
Iberis
Jojoba
Juncus
Kentia
Kerria
Kie-kie
Knawel
Kochia
Korari
Kumara
Kumera
Lentil
Lichen
Lolium
Loofah
Lovage
Lunary
Lupine
Luzula
Madder
Maguey
Mallow
Manioc
Manoao
Medick
Mimosa
Moorva
Nerine
Nerium
Nettle
Nuphar
Onagra
Orache
Orchid
Orchis
Orpine
Ourali
Ourari
Oxalis
Oxslip
Oyster
Pachak
Paeony
Peanut

Pepino
Pepper
Pieris
Protea
Radish
Ramtil
Rattle
Reseda
Retama
Rubber
Ruscus
Salvia
Savory
Scilla
Senega
Sesame
Seseli
Silene
Smilax
Sorbus
Sorrel
Spider
Spirea
Spurge
Spurry
Squill
Styrax
Sundew
Teasel
Teazle
Thrash
Thrift
Tomato
Tulipa
Turnip
Tutsan
Violet
Viscum
Wasabi
Yacona
Yarrow
Yautia
Zinnia

**7 letters:**
Absinth
Aconite
Alkanet
All-good
Allheal
Allseed
Alyssum
Anchusa
Anemone

Arachis
Astilbe
Awlwort
Barilla
Bartsia
Bee-balm
Begonia
Bogbeam
Boneset
Brinjal
Bugbean
Bugloss
Burdock
Burweed
Calluna
Caltrap
Caltrop
Campion
Caraway
Cardoon
Carduus
Carline
Cascara
Cassava
Catechu
Catmint
Cat's ear
Celosia
Century
Chayote
Chelone
Chervil
Chicory
Clarkia
Clivers
Cocoyam
Comfrey
Compass
Coontie
Cowbane
Cowbird
Cowhage
Cowherb
Cowitch
Cowslip
Cudweed
Cumquat
Curcuma
Cushion
Dasheen
Deutzia
Diascia
Dioecia
Dittany

Dogbane
Dogwood
Drosera
Epacris
Ephedra
Erodium
Eugenia
Felicia
Felwort
Filaree
Fly-trap
Freesia
Frogbit
Fuchsia
Gazania
Genista
Gentian
Gerbera
Ginseng
Godetia
Gunnera
Haemony
Hawkbit
Heather
Hemlock
Henbane
Hogweed
Ipomoea
Isoetes
Jasmine
Jonquil
Juniper
Kingcup
Kumquat
Lantana
Lettuce
Liatris
Lobelia
Logania
Lucerne
Lychnis
Lythrum
Madwort
Mahonia
Manihot
Maranta
Matweed
Mayweed
Melilot
Mercury
Milfoil
Mimulus
Monarda
Mudwort

Mugwort
Mullein
Mustard
Nelumbo
Nemesia
Nigella
Nonsuch
Olearia
Opuntia
Palmiet
Papyrus
Pareira
Parella
Parelle
Parsley
Parsnip
Penthia
Petunia
Pigface
Pinesap
Pinguin
Potherb
Primula
Puccoon
Pumpkin
Ragwort
Rampion
Raoulia
Redroot
Rhatany
Rhodora
Rhubarb
Ribwort
Ricinus
Robinia
Romneya
Rosebay
Ruellia
Saffron
Salfern
Salsify
Salsola
Sampire
Sanicle
Sawwort
Scandix
Seakale
Sea pink
Senecio
Setwall
Skirret
Solanum
Spignel
Spinach

Spiraea
Spurrey
Squilla
Stachys
Stapela
Statice
Syringa
Tagetes
Tellima
Thallus
Tobacco
Trefoil
Triffid
Tritoma
Turbith
Turpeth
Vanilla
Verbena
Vervain
Vetiver
Weigela
Woorali
Woorara
Wourali
Yaquona
Zebrina
Zedoary

**8 letters:**
Abelmosk
Absinthe
Abutilon
Acanthus
Achillea
Ageratum
Agrimony
Agueweed
Alocasia
Aloe vera
Alumroot
Angelica
Apocynum
Arenaria
Argemone
Asphodel
Barbasco
Barometz
Bauhinia
Bear's ear
Bedstraw
Beetroot
Bellwort
Bergamot
Bergenia

| | | | |
|---|---|---|---|
| Bignonia | Dog daisy | Khuskhus | Prunella |
| Bindi-eye | Dog's bone | Knapweed | Psilotum |
| Bindweed | Dracaena | Knotweed | Psoralea |
| Bird's eye | Dropwort | Kohlrabi | Psyllium |
| Bluebell | Duckweed | Krameria | Purslane |
| Bottonia | Dumbcane | Lad's love | Putchock |
| Boxberry | Earthnut | Larkspur | Queencup |
| Brassica | Eelgrass | Lathyris | Ratooner |
| Buckbean | Erigeron | Lavatera | Ratsbane |
| Buddleia | Eucharis | Lavender | Redshank |
| Bull-hoof | Euonymus | Licorice | Rock rose |
| Buplever | Feverfew | Locoweed | Roly-poly |
| Caladium | Fireweed | Lonicera | Rosemary |
| Calamint | Flax-lily | Lungwort | Sainfoin |
| Calamite | Fleabane | Macleaya | Saltwort |
| Calathea | Fleawort | Malefern | Salvinia |
| Calthrop | Fluellin | Mandrake | Samphire |
| Camellia | Foxglove | Marigold | Sandwort |
| Camomile | Fumitory | Mariposa | Scabious |
| Canaigre | Furcraea | Marjoram | Scammony |
| Cannabis | Galangol | Martagon | Sea-blite |
| Capsicum | Galtonia | Milkweed | Sea-holly |
| Cardamom | Gardenia | Milkwort | Self-heal |
| Cardamum | Geranium | Miltonia | Sept-foil |
| Carl-hemp | Gesneria | Monstera | Shamrock |
| Catchfly | Gladioli | Moonseed | Shinleaf |
| Cat's foot | Gloriosa | Moonwort | Sidalcea |
| Centaury | Glory pea | Mosspink | Silkweed |
| Charlock | Gloxinia | Mouse-ear | Silphium |
| Chayroot | Glyceria | Myosotis | Snowdrop |
| Chenopod | Gnetales | Navicula | Soapwort |
| Chickpea | Goutweed | Nenuphar | Solidago |
| Cilantro | Grape ivy | Nepenthe | Sowbread |
| Cleavers | Gromwell | Nymphaea | Sparaxis |
| Clematis | Hag-taper | Oleander | Spergula |
| Clubrush | Harakeke | Oleaster | Stapelia |
| Coltwood | Hardhack | Oncidium | Staragen |
| Costmary | Harebell | Opopanax | Starwort |
| Cow-wheat | Hawkweed | Origanum | Suckling |
| Crowfoot | Helenium | Oxtongue | Sunberry |
| Crucifer | Henequen | Pandanus | Sundrops |
| Cucurbit | Hepatica | Paspalum | Sweet pea |
| Cumbungi | Hesperis | Phacelia | Tamarisk |
| Cunjevoi | Heuchera | Phormium | Tarragon |
| Cyclamen | Hibiscus | Physalis | Tayberry |
| Daffodil | Hippuris | Pinkroot | Tickseed |
| Damewort | Honewort | Pipewort | Tigridia |
| Dentaria | Hornwort | Plantain | Tree-lily |
| Diandria | Horokaka | Plumbago | Trigynia |
| Dianthus | Hyacinth | Pokeroot | Tritonia |
| Dicentra | Hydrilla | Pokeweed | Trollius |
| Dielytra | Hyperium | Polygata | Tuberose |
| Dipsacus | Japonica | Pondweed | Tuckahoe |
| Dogberry | Jatropha | Primrose | Turmeric |

| | | | |
|---|---|---|---|
| Turnsole | Bromeliad | Digitalis | Hypericum |
| Valerian | Brooklime | Dittander | Impatiens |
| Venidium | Brookweed | Dock-cress | Jacaranda |
| Veratrum | Broom-rape | Dog fennel | Job's tears |
| Veronica | Browallia | Dog violet | Judas tree |
| Viburnum | Buckwheat | Doronicum | Kalanchoe |
| Viscaria | Buglewood | Dulcamara | Kniphofia |
| Wait-a-bit | Burrawang | Dutch rush | Ladysmock |
| Wallwort | Butterbur | Dyer's weed | Lamb's ears |
| Water yam | Buttercup | Echeveria | Laserwort |
| Wistaria | Calcicole | Echinacea | Lespedeza |
| Wisteria | Calcifuge | Edelweiss | Liquorice |
| Withwind | Calendula | Eglantine | Lithodora |
| Woodroof | Calla lily | Epilobium | Liver-wort |
| Woodruff | Campanula | Equisetum | Lousewort |
| Woodrush | Candytuft | Erythrina | Mare's-tail |
| Wormseed | Cardamine | Euphorbia | Marijuana |
| Wormwood | Carnation | Eyebright | Marshwort |
| Xanthium | Catchweed | Fatshedra | Meadow-rue |
| | Ceanothus | Fenugreek | Mistletoe |
| **9 letters:** | Celandine | Feverwort | Mitrewort |
| Aaron's rod | Centaurea | Flame tree | Monandria |
| Achimenes | Chamomile | Forsythia | Moneywort |
| Adderwort | Cherry pie | Fourcroya | Monkshood |
| Alfilaria | Cineraria | Friar's cap | Monogynia |
| Alfileria | Claytonia | Galingale | Monotropa |
| Amaryllis | Clianthus | Gelsemium | Moon daisy |
| Anacharis | Clintonia | Germander | Moschatel |
| Andromeda | Clove pink | Gessamino | Moss plant |
| Anthurium | Cocklebur | Gladiolus | Mousetail |
| Apple mint | Cock's comb | Glasswort | Muscadine |
| Aquilegia | Colchicum | Goldenrod | Myristica |
| Archangel | Colicroot | Goosefoot | Naked lady |
| Arracacha | Colicweed | Grass tree | Narcissus |
| Arrowhead | Collinsia | Greenweed | Navelwort |
| Arrowroot | Colocasia | Grindelia | Nemophila |
| Artemisia | Colocynth | Groundnut | Nicotiana |
| Artichoke | Coltsfoot | Groundsel | Oenothera |
| Artillery | Columbine | Gypsywort | Ouviranda |
| Asclepias | Cordaites | Hardheads | Parrot jaw |
| Asparagus | Coreopsis | Heliconia | Patchouli |
| Astrantia | Coriander | Hellebore | Pearlwort |
| Aubrietia | Corydalis | Helophyte | Pellitory |
| Ayabuasca | Creamcups | Herb-Paris | Pennywort |
| Bald-money | Crocosnia | Herb Peter | Penstemon |
| Baneberry | Crosswort | Hieracium | Peperomia |
| Bear's foot | Crowberry | Hoarhound | Pimpernel |
| Beech fern | Crowsfoot | Hollyhock | Pineapple |
| Bee-orchid | Dandelion | Horehound | Pokeberry |
| Birthroot | Day nettle | Horsemint | Polygonum |
| Birthwort | Desert pea | Horse-tail | Portulaca |
| Bloodroot | Desmodium | House leek | Pyrethrum |
| Bog myrtle | Devil's bit | Houstonia | Quillwort |
| Breadroot | Didynanua | Hydrangea | Rafflesia |

Rattlebox
Riverweed
Rocambole
Rosinweed
Rudbeckia
Sabadilla
Safflower
Sagebrush
Santoline
Santonica
Saponaria
Saxifrage
Screwpine
Sea-rocket
Shoreweed
Sinningia
Snakeroot
Snakeweed
Spearmint
Spearwort
Speedwell
Spikenard
Spikerush
Sprekalia
Stargrass
Stickweed
Stinkweed
Stone-crop
Strapwort
Sunflower
Sweet flag
Sweet-gale
Taraxacum
Telegraph
Thorow-wax
Tiger lily
Titan arum
Tomatillo
Toothwort
Tormentil
Twinberry
Vaccinium
Verbascum
Vetchling
Wake-robin
Waterleaf
Water vine
Wincopipe
Witchweed
Withywind
Wolf's bane
Wood avens
Woundwort
Xanthoxyl

Xerophyte

**10 letters:**
Adder's wort
Agapanthus
Alexanders
Ampelopsis
Anacardium
Angiosperm
Artocarpus
Asarabacca
Aspidistra
Astralagus
Barrenwort
Beggarweed
Biddy-biddy
Bitter-king
Bitterweed
Bladder-nut
Bluebottle
Brugmansia
Busy Lizzie
Butterdock
Butterwort
Buttonbush
Calico-bush
Canada-lily
Candelilla
Catananche
Cat-cracker
China aster
Chionodoxa
Cinquefoil
Cloudberry
Commiphora
Coneflower
Coralberry
Corncockle
Cornflower
Cottonweed
Cow parsley
Cow parsnip
Crakeberry
Cranesbill
Crown vetch
Cuckoopint
Cupid's dart
Day-neutral
Deadnettle
Delphinium
Dog's-fennel
Dog's-tongue
Dragonhead
Dragonroot

Dyer's-broom
Earth-smoke
Easter lily
Elecampane
Epilimnion
Escallonia
Eupatorium
Five-finger
Flamboyant
Fleur-de-lis
Foamflower
Four o'clock
Frangipani
Fraxinella
Friar's cowl
Fritillary
Frog's mouth
Gaillardia
Gaultheria
Glycophate
Gnaphalium
Goat-sallow
Goatsbeard
Goat's-thorn
Goat-willow
Goldenseal
Goldilocks
Goldthread
Goose grass
Gypsophila
Hawksbeard
Heart's-ease
Heathberry
Helianthus
Heliotrope
Herb-bennet
Herb-Robert
Hobble-bush
Hop-trefoil
Hyoscyamus
Icosandria
Illecebrum
Immortelle
Indian pink
Indian pipe
Indian poke
Indian shot
Jew's mallow
Jew's-myrtle
Jimsonweed
Joe-pye weed
Joshua-tree
King's spear
Lemon grass

Loganberry
Maidenhair
Marchantia
Marguerite
Masterwort
Meconopsis
Mexican-tea
Mignonette
Montbretia
Moonflower
Motherwort
Nasturtium
Nightshade
Nipplewort
Ouvirandra
Ox-eye daisy
Painted cup
Parkleaves
Parrot-beak
Parrot-bill
Passiflora
Pennycress
Pennyroyal
Pentagynia
Pentandria
Pentstemon
Peppermint
Pepperwort
Periwinkle
Pimpinella
Pipsissewa
Plume poppy
Poinsettia
Polemonium
Polianthes
Polyanthus
Potentilla
Puschkinia
Ragged lady
Ranunculus
Rest-harrow
Rhoicissus
Rock violet
Rose laurel
Rose mallow
Salicornia
Sarracenia
Sauce-alone
Scindapsus
Scorzonera
Setterwort
Silverweed
Sinsemilla
Snake's-head

Snapdragon
Sneezewort
Spiderwort
Stavesacre
Stitchwort
Stonebreak
Storksbill
Strelitzia
Sweetbriar
Thalictrum
Thunbergia
Tibouchina
Tillandsia
Touch-me-not
Tragacanth
Tree mallow
Tropaeolum
Tropaesium
Tumbleweed
Turtlehead
Twinflower
Venus's comb
Wallflower
Watercress
Water lemon
Windflower
Woodsorrel
Yellowroot
Yellowweed
Yellowwort

**11 letters:**
Aaron's beard
Acidanthera
Adam's needle
Antirrhinum
Baby's breath
Bastard balm
Bear's-breech
Beggar's lice
Biscuit-root
Bishop's weed
Bittercress
Bittersweet
Bitter vetch
Bladderwort
Blazing star
Blood-flower
Bog asphodel
Bottlebrush
Brankursine
Bristle-fern
Bur-marigold
Burning bush

Calceolaria
Callitriche
Cheddar pink
Cheese plant
Convolvulus
Corn spurrey
Cotoneaster
Crape-myrtle
Crepe-myrtle
Dame's violet
Dragon's head
Dusty-miller
Dyer's rocket
Erythronium
Fingergrass
Flamboyante
Forget-me-not
Fothergilla
Gentianella
Gillyflower
Globeflower
Gobe-mouches
Greendragon
Hart's tongue
Helichrysum
Herb of grace
Herb-trinity
Hippeastrum
Honeysuckle
Horseradish
Hurtleberry
Incarvillea
Kangaroo paw
Kiss-me-quick
Labrador tea
Lady's finger
Lady's mantle
Lamb's tongue
Lattice-leaf
Lithotripsy
London pride
Loosestrife
Love-in-a-mist
Madonna lily
Marsh mallow
Meadowsweet
Menispermum
Monadelphia
Mountain tea
Nancy-pretty
Oysterplant
Pachysandra
Paritaniwha
Parma violet

Parrot's bill
Pelargonium
Potamogeton
Proletarian
Ragged robin
Rupturewort
Saintpaulia
Sansevieria
Schizanthus
Scurvy grass
Sea lavender
Sea milkwort
Selaginella
Shrimp plant
Slipperwort
Spanish moss
Sparaganium
Steeplebush
Stephanotis
St John's wort
Strawflower
Sulphurwort
Sweet cicely
Sweet sultan
Swiss cheese
Thimbleweed
Thoroughwax
Tiger flower
Tous-les-mois
Trumpetweed
Vallisneria
Water purple
Water violet
Welwitschia
White bryony
Wild mustard
Wintercress
Wintergreen
Xeranthemum

**12 letters:**
Adam's flannel
Adder's tongue
Alstroemeria
American aloe
Aristolochia
Autumn crocus
Bacon and eggs
Beggar's ticks
Brandy bottle
Cactus dahlia
Calico flower
Cape hyacinth
Cape primrose

Carolina pink
Checkerbloom
Cheese-rennet
Christophene
Christ's thorn
Cobblers' pegs
Corn marigold
Cuckoo flower
Cucumber tree
Darlingtonia
Devil-in-a-bush
Dragoon's head
Elephant's ear
Epacridaceae
Eschscholzia
Fennelflower
Flower delice
Flower deluce
Globe-thistle
Grapple-plant
Helianthemum
Hemp-agrimony
Hortus siccus
Hound's tongue
Iceland poppy
Indian turnip
Jacob's ladder
Lady's fingers
Lady's slipper
Lady's thistle
Lady's tresses
Lemon verbena
Leopard's bane
Lithospermum
Mariposa lily
Marvel of Peru
Midsummermen
Monkey flower
Morning glory
Mountain flax
None-so-pretty
Old man's beard
Ornithogalum
Parsley-piert
Pasqueflower
Philadelphus
Philodendron
Phytobenthos
Pickerelweed
Pitcher plant
Plantain lily
Pleurisy root
Prickly poppy
Pteridosperm

Pterydophyte
Rhododendron
Rose geranium
Rose of Sharon
Salpiglossis
Sarsaparilla
Scouring rush
Scrophularia
Sea buckthorn
Sempervivium
Service berry
Shepherd's rod
Shirley poppy
Snow-in-summer
Solomon's seal
Southernwood
Spring beauty
Stone bramble
Stone parsley
Strophanthus
Sweet alyssum
Sweet William
Tradescantia
Venus flytrap
Virgin's bower
Wandering Jew
Water-soldier
Weatherglass
Wild hyacinth
Wild williams
Zantedeschia

**13 letters:**
African violet
Alligator pear
Asparagus fern
Barbados pride
Black bindweed
Bladder cherry
Bleeding heart
Bougainvillea
Butcher's broom
Butterfly bush
Carrion-flower
Christmas rose

Cranberry bush
Creeping jenny
Creosote plant
Crown imperial
Dieffenbachia
Dutchman's pipe
Elephant's ears
Elephant's foot
Eschscholtzia
Flannel flower
Grape hyacinth
Greek valerian
Indian tobacco
Mariposa tulip
Marsh marigold
Marsh samphire
Meadow saffron
Mountain avens
Noli-me-tangere
Paschal flower
Passionflower
Rose of Jericho
Shepherd's club
Slipper orchid
Spathyphyllum
Summer cypress
Sweet woodruff
Swine's succory
Tortoise plant
Townhall clock
Traveller's joy
Venus's flytrap
Viper's bugloss
Virginia stock
Water chestnut
Water dropwort
Water hyacinth
Water plantain
Winter aconite

**14 letters:**
Alder-buckthorn
Barberton daisy
Belladonna lily
Bird of paradise

Black-eyed Susan
Bladder campion
Bougainvillaea
Canterbury bell
Cape gooseberry
Cardinal flower
Castor-oil plane
Chincherinchee
Chinese cabbage
Chinese lantern
Gold-of-pleasure
Hen and chickens
Lords and ladies
Love-in-idleness
Partridgeberry
Prince's feather
Queen Anne's lace
Shepherd's glass
Shepherd's purse
Spanish bayonet
Star-of-the-earth
Sweet horsemint
Treacle mustard
Vegetable sheep
Witches' thimble

**15 letters:**
Bird's nest orchid
Burnet saxifrage
Christmas cactus
Creeping thistle
Dog's tooth violet
Evening primrose
Golden saxifrage
Jack-in-the-pulpit
Lily-of-the-valley
Meadow saxifrage
Michaelmas daisy
Shepherd's myrtle
Star of Bethlehem
Virginia creeper
Wandering sailor

**16 letters:**
Annunciation lily

Barren strawberry
Bird's foot trefoil
Carolina allspice
Clove gillyflower
Clowgillie-flower
Deadly nightshade
Herb of repentance
Indian paintbrush
Livingstone daisy
Love-lies-bleeding
Mesembrianthemum
Poached-egg flower
Queen-of-the-
   meadow
Swiss cheese plant

**17 letters:**
Devil's bit scabious
Dutchman's
   breeches
Mother-of-
   thousands
Queen of the prairie
Sheep's bit scabious
Snow-on-the-
   mountain
Squarrose
   knapweed
St Patrick's cabbage

**18 letters:**
Mother-in-law's
   tongue
Venus's looking
   glass

**19 letters:**
Ploughman's
   spikenard

**20 letters:**
Chickweed
   wintergreen
Enchanter's
   nightshade

---

**Plantagenet** Angevin, Broom
**Plantain** Mato(o)ke, Ribwort, Waybread
**Plantation** Arboretum, Bosket, Bosquet, Estate, Fazenda, Grove, Hacienda, Pen, Pinetum, Ranch, Tara, Tope, Veticetum, Vineyard
**Plant disease** Anthracnose, Blight, Bunt, Club-root, Curl, Curlytop, Ear-cockle, Eyespot, Frogeye, Leaf curl, Leaf-roll, Leaf-spot, Psyllid yellows, Rootknot, Rosette, Shanking, Smut, Sooty mould, Streak
**Planted** In, Under

**Planter** Dibber, Farmer, Pot, Settler, Trowel
**Plaque** Calculus, Dental, Plateau, Scale, Tablet
**Plasm** Germ
**Plasma** Dextran, Sigmond
**Plaster(ed), Plaster board** Artex®, Bandage, Blister, Blotto, Butterfly clip, Cake, Cataplasm, Clam, Clatch, Compo, Court, Daub, Diachylon, Diachylum, Dressing, Drunk, Emplastrum, Fresco, Gesso, Grout, Gyprock®, Gypsum, Intonaco, Laying, Leep, Lit, Mud, Mustard, Oiled, Parge(t), Polyfilla®, Porous, Poultice, Render, Roughcast, Scratch-coat, Screed, Secco, Shellac, Sinapism, Smalm, Smarm, Smear, Sowsed, Staff, Sticking, Stookie, Stucco, Teer, Wattle and daub
**Plastic** Amex®, Bakelite®, Bubblewrap, Cel(luloid), Cling film, Ductile, Fablon®, Fibreglass, Fictile, Flexible, Fluon, Formica®, Ionomer, Laminate, Loid, Lucite®, Melamine, Mylar®, Perspex®, Plexiglass®, Pliant, Polyethylene, Polystyrene, Polythene, Polyvinyl, PVC, Reinforced, Styrene, Styrofoam®, Supple, Teflon®, Urea-formaldehyde, Vinyl, Wet-look, Xylonite, Yielding
▷ **Plastic** *may indicate* an anagram
**Plasticine** Morph
**Plastic surgeon** McIndoe
**Plastic surgery** Neoplasty, Nose job, Otoplasty, Rhinoplasty
**Plate(s), Plated, Platelet, Plating** Acierage, Ailette, Anchor, Angle, Anode, Armadillo, Armour, Ashet, Baffle, Bakestone, Baleen, Base, Batten, Brass, Butt, Chamfrain, Chape, Charger, Chrome, Coat, Coccolith, Communion, Copper, Cramper, Cribellum, Ctene, Dasypus, Deadman, Denture, Diaphragm, Dinner, Disc, Dish, Echo, Electro, Electrotype, Elytron, Elytrum, Enamel, Entoplastron, Equatorial, Escutcheon, Etching, Face, Fashion, Feet, Fine, Fish, Flatware, Foil, Frog, Frons, Frontispiece, Futtock, Glacis, Gold, Graal, Gravure, Ground, Gula, Half, Hasp, Home, Horseshoe, Hot, Hypoplastron, Illustration, Kick, L, Lame, Lamella, Lamina, Lanx, Latten, Lead, Licence, Madreporic, Mascle, Mazarine, Nail, Nef, Neural, Nickel, Notum, Number, Onycha, Ortho, Osteoderm, P, Paten, Patin(e), Patina, Pauldron, Peba, Petri, Phototype, Planometer, Plaque, Plastron, Platter, Pleximeter, Poitrel, Prescutum, Print, Pygal, Quarter, Race, Registration, Riza, Roof, Rove, Salamander, Scale, Screw, Scrim, Scutcheon, Scute, Scutum, Seg, Selling, Sheffield, Shield, Shoe, Side, Sieve, Silver, Slab, Soup, Spacer, Spoiler, Squama, Stall, Steel, Stencil, Stereo(type), Sternite, Strake, Surface, Swash, T, Tablet, Tace, Tasse(l), Tea, Tectonic, Tergite, Terne, Thali, Theoretical, Tin(ware), Torsel, Touch, Trade, Tramp, Trencher, Trivet, Trophy, Tsuba, Tuill(ett)e, Tymp, Urostegite, Vane, Vanity, Vassail, Vessail, Vessel, Wall, Water, Web, Wet, Whirtle, Whole, Wobble, Workload, Wortle, Wrap(a)round, Zincograph
**Plateau** Altiplano, Anatolian, Barkly Tableland, Central Karoo, Chota Nagpur, Darling Downs, Dartmoor, Deccan, Durango, Eifel, Ellesworth Land, Field, Fjeld, Fouta Djallon, Had(h)ramaut, Highland, Highveld, Horst, Kalahari, Kar(r)oo, Kimberleys, Kurdestan, Kurdistan, La Mancha, Lamington, Langres, Laurentian, Mat(t)o Grosso, Mesa Verde, Meseta, Najd, Nilgiris, Ozark, Paramo, Piedmont, Puna, Shan, Shillong, Shire Highlands, Tableland, The Kimberleys, Ust Urt, Ustyurt
**Platform** Accommodation, Almemar, Balcony, Bandstand, Barbette, Base, Bay, Bema, Bench, Bier, Bridge, Catafalque, Catwalk, Crane, Crow's nest, Dais, Deck, Dolly, Drilling, Emplacement, Entablement, Estrade, Exedra, Exhedra, Fighting top, Flake, Footpace, Footplate, Foretop, Gangplank, Gantry, Gauntree, Gauntry, Gravity, Hustings, Kang, Landing stage, Launch-pad, Machan, Maintop, Manifesto, Monkeyboard, Oil, Oil-rig, Pad, Paint-bridge, Pallet, Perron, Plank, Podium, Predella, Production, Programme, Pulpit, Quay, Raft, Rig, Rostrum, Round-top, Scaffold, Shoe, Skidway, Skylab, Soapbox, Space, Sponson, → **STAGE**, Stand, Stereobate, Stoep, Strandflat, Stylobate, Tee, Terminal, Thrall, Ticket, Top, Traverser, Tribunal, Tribune, Turntable, Wave-cut, Wharf
**Platinum** Pt, Ruthenium, Sperrylite, Spongy
**Platitude** Bromide, Cliché, Commonplace, Phrase, Truism

**Platocephalus** Flat-headed
**Platonic, Platonist** Academician, Ideal, Spiritual
**Platoon** Company, Squad, Team
**Platter** Charger, Dish, EP, Graal, Grail, Lanx, LP, Plate, Record, Salver, Trencher
**Platypus** Duckbill, Duck-mole, Water mole
**Plausible, Plausibility** Cogent, Credence, Credible, Fair, Glib, Likely, Logical, Oil, Probable, Proball, Sleek, Smooth, Specious
**Play(s), Playing** Accompany, Active, Amusement, Antic, Antigone, Assist, At, Brand, Busk, Candida, Caper, Charm, Chronicle, Clearance, Closet, Coriolanus, Crucible, Curtain-raiser, Dabble, Daff, Dalliance, Dandle, Docudrama, Doodle, Drama, Echo, Endgame, Epitasis, Equus, Escapade, Everyman, Extended, Fair, Finesse, Foul, Freedom, Frisk, Frolic, Fun, Gamble, Gambol, Game, Ghosts, Grand Guignol, Hamlet, Harlequinade, Harp, History, Holiday, Inside, Interlude, Jam, Jape, Jest, Jeu, Kinderspiel, Kitchen-sink, Laik, Lake, Lark, Latitude, Lear, Leeway, Licence, Lilt, Long, Loot, Macbeth, Mask, Masque, Match, May, Medal, Melodrama, Miracle, Monodrama, Morality, Mousetrap, Mummers, Mysteries, Nativity, Noh, Nurse, Oberammergau, On, One-acter, Orestaia, Othello, Parallel, Passion, Pastorale, Perform, Personate, Peter, Portray, Power, Prank, Pretend, Puppet, Recreation, Represent, Riff, Role, Rollick, Romp, Room, Rope, RUR, Satyr, Saw, Screen, Shadow, Shoot, Show, Shuffle, Sketch, Sport, Squeeze, Stage, Straight, Strain, Strike up, Stroke, Strum, Summerstock, Thrum, Thumb, Tolerance, Tonguing, Toot, Touchback, Toy, Tragedy, Tragicomedy, Trifle, Triple, Tweedle, Twiddle, Two-hander, Vamp, Vent, Whitechapel, Word
▷ **Play** *may indicate* an anagram
**Playback** Echo, Repeat, Replay
**Playboy** Adulterer, Casanova, Don Juan, Hedonist, Rake, Roué, Seducer
**Player(s)** Accompanist, Actor, Athlete, Back, Backstop, Black, Brass, Bugler, Busker, Cast, CD, Centre, Centre forward, Centre-half, Colt, Contestant, Cornerback, Cover point, Dealer, Defenceman, Disc, DVD, E, East, ENSA, Equity, Fetcher, Fiddle, Flanker, Fly-half, Flying wing, Fly-slip, Forward, Franchise, Fullback, Gary, Ghetto-blaster, Goalie, Goalkeeper, Goaltender, Gramophone, Grand master, Gridder, Guard, Half, Half-back, Half-forward, Harlequin, Hooker, Infielder, iPod®, It, Juke-box, Keg(e)ler, Kest, Kicker, Linebacker, Lineman, Lion, Lock, Long-leg, Longstop, Loose-head, Lutanist, Lutenist, Man, Marquee, Midfield, Mid-on, Mime, Muffin, Musician(er), N, Nero, Nickelback, Nightwatchman, North, Nose guard, Nose tackle, Ombre, Onside, Orpheus, Outfielder, Out(side)-half, Pagliacci, Participant, Pianola®, Pitcher, Pocket, Pone, Pro, Prop, Quarterback, Receiver, Record, Red shirt, Reliever, Reserve, Rover, S, Safetyman, Scrape, Scratch, Scrum half, Seagull, Secondo, Seed, Shamateur, Short-leg, Shortstop, Side, South, Split end, Stand-off, Stand-off half, Stereo, Striker, Strings, Strolling, Substitute, Super, Sweeper, Tabrere, Target man, Team, Thesp(ian), Tight end, Troubador, Troupe, Upright, Utility, Virtuosi, W, Walker-on, Walkman®, West, White, Wide receiver, Wing(back), Winger, Wingman
**Playfair** Code
**Playfellow** Actor, Chum, Companion
**Playful** Arch, Coy, Frisky, Gamesome, Humorous, Impish, Jocose, Kittenish, Ludic, Merry, Piacevole, Scherzo, Skittish, Sportive, Spry, Wanton
**Playgirl** Actress, Electra
**Playgoer** Groundling, Savoyard
**Playground** Adventure, Close, Garden, Park, Rec(reational), Rectangle, Theatre, Tot lot, Yard
**Playhouse** Amphitheatre, Cinema, Theatre, Wendy
**Play off** Decider
**Playsuit** Rompers
**Playwright** → DRAMATIST, Dramaturge, Dramaturgist, Scriptwriter

## PLAYWRIGHTS

| *3 letters:* | *6 letters:* | Delaney | Mortimer |
|---|---|---|---|
| Fry | Barrie | Doggett | Rattigan |
| Hay | Bellow | Feydeau | Sheridan |
| Kyd | Besier | Garrick | Stoppard |
| | Brecht | Goldoni | Vanbrugh |
| *4 letters:* | Coward | Harwood | Wedekind |
| Bolt | Dekker | Hellman | Williams |
| Bond | Dryden | Ionesco | |
| Gems | Jonson | Kaufman | *9 letters:* |
| Hare | Lerner | Marlowe | Aeschylus |
| Inge | Mercer | Marston | Ayckbourn |
| Shaw | Miller | Maugham | Bleasdale |
| Tate | Morton | Mauriac | Corneille |
| | O'Casey | Molière | Euripides |
| *5 letters:* | O'Neill | Osborne | Goldsmith |
| Albee | Pinero | Plautus | Massinger |
| Arden | Pinter | Rostand | Priestley |
| Barry | Racine | Simpson | Sophocles |
| Behan | Sartre | Terence | Wycherley |
| Frayn | Sherry | Thespis | |
| Genet | Storey | Travers | *10 letters:* |
| Gorky | Toller | Webster | Drinkwater |
| Ibsen | Wesker | | Pirandello |
| Leigh | Wilder | *8 letters:* | Strindberg |
| Odets | | Beaumont | Williamson |
| Orton | *7 letters:* | Congreve | |
| Simon | Anouilh | Etherege | *11 letters:* |
| Synge | Beckett | Fletcher | Maeterlinck |
| Wilde | Bennett | MacNeice | |
| | Chekhov | Marivaux | *12 letters:* |
| | Dario Fo | Menander | Beaumarchais |

**Plea(s)** Alford, Appeal, Claim, Common, Defence, Entreaty, Essoin, Excuse, Exoration, Nolo contendere, Orison, Petition, Placit(um), Prayer, Rebuttal, Rebutter, Rogation, Suit

**Plead(er), Pleading** Answer, Argue, Beg, Entreat, →IMPLORE, Intercede, Litigate, Moot, Placitory, Solicit, Special, Supplicant, Urge, Vakeel, Vakil

**Please(d), Pleasant, Pleasing, Pleasure(-seeker), Pleasurable** Affable, Aggrate, Agreeable, Alcina, Algolagnia, Amenable, Amene, Amiable, Amuse, Apolaustic, Appeal, Arride, Artistic, Be my guest, Beneplacito, Benign, Bitte, Braw, Cheerful, Chuffed, Comely, Comfort, Content, Cordial, Cute, Delectation, Delice, Delight, Divine, Do, Euphonic, Eye candy, Fair, Felicitous, Fit, Flatter, Fun, Genial, Glad, Gladness, Good-o, Gratify, Gusto, Harmonious, Hedonism, Jammy, Joy, Kama, Kindly, Lekker, Lepid, List, Naomi, Oblige, Piacevole, Primrose path, Prithee, Prythee, Purr, Queme, Regale, Sapid, Satisfy, Schadenfreude, Sightly, Suit, Tasty, Thrill, Tickle, Tickle pink, Toothsome, Treat, Vanity, Voluptuary, Wally, Will, Winsome, Wrapped, Xanadu List

**Pleasure-garden, Pleasure-ground** Lung, Oasis, Paradise, Park, Policy, Ranelagh, Tivoli

**Pleasure-seeker** Hedonist, Playboy

**Pleat** Accordion, Box, Crimp, Crystal, Fold, French, Frill, Goffer, Gusset, Inverted, Kick, Kilt, Knife, Plait, Pranck(e), Prank, Ruff(le), Sunburst, Sunray

**Pleb(eian)** Common, Essex Man, Homely, Laic, Low-born, Ordinary, Popular, Roturier

**Pledge(r)** Abstainer, Affidavit, Arlene, Arles, Band, Betroth, Bond, Borrow, Bottomry, Collateral, Commitment, Dedicate, Deposit, Earnest(-penny), Engage, Fine, Frithborn, Gage, Gilbert, Giselle, Guarantee, Hand, Hock, Hypothecate, Impignorate, Mortgage, Oath, Pass, Pawn, Pigenerate, Pignorate, Plight, Pop, Promise, Propine, Sacrament, Security, Sponsorship, Stake, Surety, Teetotal, Toast, Troth, Undertake, Vow, Wad, Wage(r), Wed

**Pleiades** Alcyone, Celaeno, Electra, Maia, Merope, Sterope, Taygete

**Plenitude** Stouth and routh

**Plentiful, Plenty** Abounding, Abundance, Abundant, Ample, Bags, Copious, Copy, Cornucopia, Easy, Excess, Foison, Fouth, Ful(l)ness, Fushion, Galore, Goshen, Lashings, Loads, Lots, Oodles, Pleroma, Profusion, Quantity, Riches, Rife, Routh, Rowth, Scouth, Scowth, Slue, Sonce, Sonse, Teeming, Umpteen

**Plenum** Spaceless

**Pliable, Pliant** Amenable, Docile, Flexible, Limber, Limp, Lithe, Malleable, Plastic, Sequacious, Supple, Swack, Swank, Wanle

▶ **Pliers** *see* **PLY**

**Plight** Betrothal, Case, Misdight, Peril, Pickle, Pledge, Predicament, State, Troth

**Plimsoll(s)** Dap, Gutty, Gym-shoe, Line, Mutton-dummies, Pumps, Sandshoe, Tacky

**Plinth** Acroter, Base, Block, Socle, Stand, Zocco, Zoccolo

**Plod(der)** Drudge, Ploughman, Traipse, Tramp, Trog, Trudge

**Plonk(er)** Bonce, Marble, Rotgut, Wine

**Plop** Cloop, Drop, Fall, Plap, Plump

**Plot(s)** Allotment, Area, Babington, Bed, Brew, Cabal, Carpet, Chart, Cliché, Collude, Connive, Conspiracy, Conspire, Contrive, Covin, Covyne, Croft, Device, Engineer, Erf, Erven, Frame-up, Garden, Graph, Gunpowder, Imbroglio, Intrigue, Lair, Locus, Lot, Machination, Map, Meal-tub, Odograph, Orchard, Pack, Parcel, Patch, Plan, Plat, Popish, Rye-house, Scenario, → **SCHEME**, Sect(ion), Seedbed, Shot, Site, Story, Storyline, Taluk, Terf, Turf, Web

**Plotter** Artist, Box (and whisker), Brutus, Cabal, Camarilla, Casca, Catesby, Conspirator, Device, Digital, Engineer, Incremental, Intrigant, Microfilm, Oates, Rosary, Schemer

**Plough(man), Ploughed, Ploughing** Arable, Ard, Arval, Big Dipper, Breaker, Bull tongue, Chamfer, Charles's Wain, Contour, Dipper, Disc, Drail, Drill, Ear, Earth-board, Ere, Fail, Fallow, Farmer, Feer, Flunk, Gadsman, Gang, Great Bear, Harrow, Lister, Middlebreaker, Middlebuster, Mouldboard, Piers, Pip, Pleuch, Pleugh, Plodder, Push, Rafter, Rib, Ridger, Rive, Rotary, Rove, Sand, Scooter, Septentrion(e)s, Sill, Sodbuster, Sow, Stump-jump, Swing, The Wagon, Till(er), Tractor, Trench, Triones, Wheel

**Plough-cleaner** Pattle, Pettle

**Ploughshare** Co(u)lter, Sock

**Ploughwise** Boustrophedon

**Plover** Bud, Congregation, Dott(e)rel, Lapwing, Peewit, Pratincole, Prostitute, Stand, Tewit, Wing

**Plowman** Piers

**Ploy** Brinkmanship, Dodge, Feint, Finesse, Gambit, Manoeuvre, M(a)cGuffin, Stratagem, Strike, Subterfuge, Tactic, Wile

**Pluck(ing), Plucky** Avulse, Bare, Carphology, Cock, Courage, Deplume, Epilate, Evulse, Floccillation, Gallus, Game, → **GRIT**, Guts, Loot, Mettle, Pick, Pinch, Pip, Pizzicato, Plectron, Plectrum, Ploat, Plot, Plumassier, Plunk, Pook(it), Pouk(it), Pull, Race, Scrappy, Snatch, Spin, Spirit, Spunk, Summon, Tug, Twang, Tweak, Tweeze, Vellicate, Yank

**Plug** Access eye, Ad, Adapter, Adaptor, Advocate, Banana, Block, Bung, Caulk, Chaw, Chew, Commercial, Dam, DIN, Dook, Dossil, Dottle, Douk, Fipple, Fother, Gang, Glow, Go-devil, Heater, Hype, Jack, Lam, Operculum, Pessary, Phono, Prod, Promote, Publicity, Ram, Rawlplug®, Recommendation, Safety, Salt, Scart, Sealant, Spark(ing), Spigot, Spile, Spiling, Stem, Stop(per), Stopple, Strobili, Suppository, Tampion, Tap, Tent, Tompion, Vent, Volcanic, Wage, Wall, Wander, Wedge

**Plum** Beach, Bullace, Cherry, Choice, Damask, Damson, Drupe, Gage, Greengage, Ground, Jamaica, Japanese, Java, Kaki, Mammee-sapota, Marmalade, Maroon, Mirabelle, Musk, Mussel, Myrobalan, Naseberry, Neesberry, Peach, Persimmon, Proin(e), Pruin(e), Prune(llo), Quetsch, Raisin, Sapodilla, Sebesten, Victoria, Wodehouse

**Plumage, Plume** Aigrette, Crest, Eclipse, Egret, Feather, Hackle, Mantle, Panache, Preen, Ptilosis, Quill

**Plumb(er), Plumbing** Bullet, Dredge, Fathom(eter), Lead(sman), Perpendicular, Plummet, Sheer, Sound, Test, True, U-trap, Vertical

**Plumbago** Graphite, Leadwort, Wad(d), Wadt

**Plummet** Dive, Drop, Lead, Nosedive, → PLUNGE

**Plump(er)** Bold, Bonnie, Bonny, Buxom, Choose, Chopping, Chubbed, Chubby, Cubby, Cuddly, Dumpy, Embonpoint, Endomorph, Fat, Fleshy, Flop, Fubsy, Full, Lie, Matronly, Opt, Pick, Plank, Plonk, Plop, Podgy, Portly, Pudgy, Roll-about, Rolypoly, Rotund, Round(about), Rubenesque, Sonsie, Sonsy, Soss, Souse, Squab, Squat, Stout, Swap, Swop, Tidy, Tubby, Well-covered, Well-fed, Well-padded, Well-upholstered, Zaftig, Zoftig

**Plunder(er)** Berob, Booty, Brigand, Depredate, Despoil, Devastate, Escheat, Fleece, Forage, Freebooter, Gut, Harry, Haul, Herriment, Herryment, Hership, Loot, Maraud, Peel, Pill(age), Predation, Prey, Privateer, Raid, → RANSACK, Rape, Rapparee, Raven, Ravin, Ravine, Reave, Reif, Reive, Rieve, Rifle, Rob, Rummage, Sack, Scoff, Shave, Skoff, Spoil(s), Spoliate, Sprechery, Spuilzie, Spuly(i)e, Spulzie, Swag

**Plunge(r)** Dasher, Demerge, Dive, Douse, Dowse, Duck, Enew, Immerge, Immerse, La(u)nch, Nose-dive, Plummet, Plump, Raker, Send, Sink, Souse, Swoop, Thrust

**Plural** Multiply, Pl

**Plus** Addition, And, Gain, More, Positive

**Plush(ed)** Die, Luxurious, Rich, Smart, Tint, Velour, Velvet

**Pluto(crat), Plutonic** Abyssal, Dis, Dog, Hades, Hypogene, Magnate, Nob, Pipeline, Underground

**Plutonium** Pu

**Ply, Plier(s)** Bend, Birl, Cab, Exercise, Exert, Gondoliers, Importune, Layer, Practise, Run, Trade, Wield

▷ **Plying** *may indicate* an anagram

**Plymouth Brethren** Darbyite

**PM** Addington, Afternoon, Arvo, Asquith, Attlee, Autopsy, Balfour, Bute, Cabinet-maker, Callaghan, Chamberlain, Chatham, De Valera, Disraeli, Gladstone, Major, Melbourne, Peel, Pitt, Portland, Premier, → PRIME MINISTER, Salisbury, Taoiseach, Walpole

**Pneumonia** Lobar, Lobular, Visna

**Poach** Burn-the-water, Cook, Encroach, Filch, Lag, Steal, Trespass

**Pochard** Duck, Scaup

**Pocket** Air, Appropriate, Bag, Bin, Breast, Cargo, Cavity, Cly, Cup, Enclave, Fob, Glom, Hideaway, Hip, Jenny, Misappropriate, Patch, Placket, Plaid-neuk, Pot, Pouch, Purloin, Purse, Sac, Sky, Slash, Sling, Slit, Steal, Take, Trouser, Vest, Watch, Whitechapel

**Pocketbook** Reader

**Pod(s)** Babul, Bean, Belly, Carob, Chilli, Dividivi, Engine, Gumbo, Hull, Lablab, Legume, Lomentum, Neb-neb, Okra, Pipi, Pregnant, Pudding-pipe, Seed, Senna, Siliqua, Tamarind, Vanilla, Vine

**Podgy** Gaucie, Gaucy, Gawcy, Gawsy, Roly-poly

**Poem(s), Poetry** Acmeism, Acrostic, Aeneid, Alcaic, Anthology, Art, A Shropshire Lad, Awdl, Ballad(e), Beowulf, Bestiary, Bucolic, Byliny, Caccia, Canto, Canzone, Cargoes, Cento, Choliamb, Choriamb, Cicada, Cinquain, Complaint, Concrete, Decastich, Dewan, Dit(t), Dithyramb, Divan, Dizain, Doggerel, Duan, Dub, Dunciad, Eclogue, Elegy, Elene, Endymion, Epic(ede), Epigram, Epilogue, Epithalamium, Epode, Epopee, Epopoeia, Epos, Epyllion, Erotic, Fifteener, Finlandia, Gauchesco, Georgic, Ghazal, Graveyard, Haikai, Haiku, Heptastich, Heroic, Hexastich, Hokku, Hull, Hypermeter,

Idyl(l), If, Iliad, Imagism, Inferno, Jazz, Kyrielle, Lay, Limerick, Logaoedic, London, Madrigal, Mahabharata(m), Mahabharatum, Meliboean, Melic, Metaphysical, Metre, Mock-heroic, Monostich, Monostrophe, Nostos, Ode, Odyssey, Palinode, Paracrostic, Parnassus, Pastoral, Penill(ion), Pentameter, Pentastich, Performance, Poesy, Prelude, Prose, Prothalamion, Punk, Purana, Qasida, Quatorzain, Quatrain, Quire, Ramayana, Rat-rhyme, Renga, Rhapsody, Rig-Veda, Rime, Rime riche, Rondeau, Rondel(et), Rubai(yat), Rune, Scazon (iambus), Senryu, Sestina, Sijo, Sirvente, Sixain, Song, Sonnet, Sound, Spondee, Stanza, Stornello, Symphonic, Tanka, Telestich, Temora, Tercet, Tetrastich, Thebaid, Title, Tone, Triolet, Tristich, Vers(e), Versicle, Villanelle, Völuspá, Voluspe, Waka

**Poet(s), Poetic** Acmeist, Amorist, Bard(ling), Beatnik, Cavalier, Cumberland, Cyclic, Elegist, Georgian, Iambist, Idyllist, Imagist, Lake, Laureate, Layman, Liner, Lyrist, Makar, Maker, Meistersinger, Metaphysical, Metrist, Minnesinger, Minor, Minstrel, Mistral, Monodist, Odist, Parnassian, Performance, PL, Pleiad(e), Poetaster, Rhymer, Rhymester, Rhymist, Rymer, Scald, Scop, Silurist, Skald, Smart, Sonneteer, Sound, Spasmodic, Spasmodic School, Te(i)an, Thespis, Tragic, Trench, Troubadour, Trouvère, Trouveur, Verse-monger, Verse-smith, Versifier, Vers librist(e), Water

---

## POETS

| | | | |
|---|---|---|---|
| **2 letters:** | Arion | Lucan | Butler |
| AE | Auden | Marot | Cibber |
| | Ayres | Meyer | Clarke |
| **3 letters:** | Basho | Moore | Clough |
| Gay | Bemia | Nashe | Cowley |
| Poe | Blair | Noyes | Cowper |
| | Blake | Plath | Crabbe |
| **4 letters:** | Blunt | Pound | Curnow |
| Abse | Burns | Prior | Daniel |
| Baif | Byron | Rilke | Daurat |
| Bemi | Cadou | Rishi | Davies |
| Blok | Carew | Sachs | Domett |
| Cory | Cinna | Smith | Dowson |
| Dyer | Clare | Tasso | Dryden |
| Gray | Crane | Theon | Dunbar |
| Gunn | Dante | Tzara | Ennius |
| Hogg | Donne | Vazor | Fuller |
| Hood | Eliot | Wever | George |
| Hope | Flint | Wyatt | Glycon |
| Hugo | Frost | Yeats | Goethe |
| Hunt | Gower | Young | Graves |
| Lang | Griot | | Harpur |
| Lear | Heine | **6 letters:** | Heaney |
| Omar | Hesse | Adamov | Hemans |
| Ovid | Homer | Alonso | Hesiod |
| Owen | Horne | Arnold | Horace |
| Pope | Hulme | Austin | Hughes |
| Rowe | Iqbal | Barham | Jensen |
| Rumi | Jarry | Barnes | Jonson |
| Tate | Keats | Belloc | Landor |
| Vega | Keyes | Binyon | Larkin |
| | Lewis | Borges | Lawman |
| **5 letters:** | Logue | Brecht | Lowell |
| Alley | Lorca | Brooke | Marini |

| | | | |
|---|---|---|---|
| Milton | Enright | Browning | Euripides |
| Morris | Flaccus | Campbell | Goldsmith |
| Motion | Flecker | Catullus | Henderson |
| Neruda | Herbert | Cummings | Lamartine |
| Newman | Heredia | Cynewulf | Lucretius |
| Ossian | Herrick | Davenant | Marinetti |
| Pindar | Hopkins | Day Lewis | Masefield |
| Porter | Housman | De la Mare | Quasimodo |
| Racine | Juvenal | De Musset | Shenstone |
| Sappho | Khayyam | Drummond | Simonides |
| Seaman | Layamon | Du Bellay | Sophocles |
| Shanks | Lydgate | Ginsberg | Stevenson |
| Sidney | Martial | Hamilton | Swinburne |
| Tagore | Marvell | Harrison | Wergeland |
| Thomas | Meynell | Hausmann | |
| Valery | Montale | Kynewulf | **10 letters:** |
| Vergil | Newbolt | Laforgue | Baudelaire |
| Villon | Orpheus | Langland | Chatterton |
| Virgil | Patmore | Lawrence | Drinkwater |
| Waller | Philips | Leopardi | Fitzgerald |
| Warton | Pushkin | Lovelace | La Fontaine |
| Watson | Rimbaud | Macaulay | Longfellow |
| | Ronsard | Mallarmé | McGonagall |
| **7 letters:** | Russell | Menander | Propertius |
| Addison | Sassoon | Meredith | Tannhauser |
| Alcaeus | Service | Petrarch | Theocritus |
| Alfieri | Shelley | Rossetti | Wordsworth |
| Aneirin | Sitwell | Sandberg | |
| Aretino | Skelton | Schiller | **11 letters:** |
| Ariosto | Sotades | Shadwell | Apollinaire |
| Beddoes | Southey | Stephens | Archilochus |
| Belleau | Spender | Suckling | Asclepiades |
| Blunden | Spenser | Taliesin | Bildermeier |
| Bridges | Statius | Tennyson | Castiglione |
| Bunting | Terence | Thompson | Maeterlinck |
| Caedmon | Thomson | Traherne | Pherecrates |
| Campion | Vaughan | Tyrtaeus | |
| Chapman | Whitman | Verlaine | **12 letters:** |
| Chaucer | Woolner | Voltaire | Archilochian |
| Collins | | Whittier | Aristophanes |
| Corinna | **8 letters:** | | |
| Cotteau | Akenside | **9 letters:** | **14 letters:** |
| Crashaw | Anacreon | Aeschylus | Dante Alighieri |
| Cynwulf | Banville | Alexander | |
| Doughty | Beranger | Bunthorne | **15 letters:** |
| Douglas | Berryman | Coleridge | Ettrick Shepherd |
| Drayton | Betjeman | Deschamps | |
| Emerson | Brentano | Dickinson | |

**Poetaster** Della-Cruscan
**Poetess** Ingelow, Orinda
**Poet laureate** Bridges, Motion, PL
▸ **Poetry** *see* POEM(S)
**Po-faced** Stolid

**Poignant** Acute, Biting, Haunting, Keen, Moving, Pungent, Stirring, Touching
**Point(ed), Pointer, Points** Accumulation, Ace, Acerose, Acnode, Acro-, Aculeate,
Aim, Angular, Antinode, Antler, Apex, Aphelion, Apogee, Appui, Apse, Apsis,
Arrowhead, Ascendant, Bar, Barb, Barrow, Base, Basis, Bisque, Boiling, Bradawl,
Break(ing), Brownie, Burble, Burbling, Calk, Cape, Cardinal, Cash, Catch, Centre, Choke,
Clou, Clovis, Clue, Colon, Comma, Compass, Compensation, Cone, Conic, Corner, Cover,
Crag, Crisis, Critical, Crux, Culmination, Cultrate, Curie, Cursor, Cusp, Cuss, Cutting,
Danger, Dead, Decimal, Deflater, Deflator, Degree, Descendant, Detail, Dew, Diamond,
Di(a)eresis, Direct, Dot, Dry, E, Ear, End, Entry, Epanodos, Épée, Equant, Equinoctial,
Eutectic, Exclamation, Extremity, Fang, Fastigiate, Feature, Fescue, Fesse, Fielder,
Finger(tip), Firing, Fitch(e), Five, Fixed, Flash, Focal, Focus, Foreland, Fourteen, Freezing,
Fulcrum, Gallinas, Game, Germane, Gist, Gnomon, Gold, Hastate, Head, High, Hinge,
Hint, Home-thrust, Horn, Hour hand, Icicle, Ideal, Index, Indicate, Indicator, Intercept,
Ippon, Isoelectric, Issue, Jag, Jester, Jog, Juncture, Keblah, Kiblah, Kip(p), Knub, Lace,
Lagrangian, Lance, Lanceolar, Lead, Limit, Lizard, Locate, Locus, Low, Mandelbrot set,
Mark, Match, Melting, Metacentre, Microdot, Moot, Mucro, Mull, Muricate, N, Nail,
Nasion, Near, Neb, Needle, Neel, Ness, Nib, Nocking, Node, Nodus, Nombril, Now, Nub,
Obconic, Obelion, Obelisk, Objective, Opinion, Ord, Organ, Oscillation, Particle, Peak,
Pedal, Penalty, Periapsis, Periastron, Perigee, Perihelion, Perilune, Pin, Pinch, Pinnacle,
Pixel, Place, Pour, Power, Pressure, Promontory, Prong, Prow, Punchline, Punctilio,
Punctual, Punctum, Purpose, Radix, Rallying, Ras, Reef, Respect, Rhumb, Rhumbline, S,
Sample, Saturation, Scribe, Seg(h)ol, Selling, Set, Setter, Shaft, Sharpener, Sheva, Show,
Shy, Silly, Socket, Sore, Spearhead, Specie, Spicate, Spick, Spike, Spinode, Spinulose,
Stage, Stagnation, Starting, Stationary, Steam, Sticking, Stigme, Stiletto, Sting, Stipule,
Strong, Sum, Suspension, Synapse, Tacnode, Talking, Tang, Taper, Tax, Technicality,
Tine, →**TIP**, Tongue, Trafficator, Train, Transition, Trig, Trigger, Triple, Turning,
Umlaut, Urde(e), Urdy, Use, Vane, Vanishing, Vantage, Verge, Verse, Vertex, Vowel,
Voxel, W, Waggle-dance, Weak, Yad, Yield, Yuko, Zenith
**Pointless** Blunt, Curtana, Flat, Futile, Idle, Inane, Inutile, Muticous, Otiose, Stupid, Vain
**Point of honour** Pundonor
**Poise** Aplomb, Balance, Composure, Grace, P, Serenity
**Poison(er), Poisoning, Poisonous** Bane, Contact, Contaminate, Deleterious,
Envenom, Ergotise, Food, Malevolent, Miasma, Noxious, Plumbism, Rankle, Rot,
Sausage, Systemic, Taint, Toxic, Toxicology, Toxicosis, Toxin, Toxoid, Venom(ous),
Viperous, Virose, Virous, Virulent

---

## POISONS

| 4 letters: | Timbo | Endrin | Arsenic |
|---|---|---|---|
| Cube | Urali | Hebona | Atropia |
| Fugu | Venin | Iodism | Atropin |
| Gila | | Obeism | Boletus |
| Lead | 6 letters: | Ourali | Bromism |
| Loco | Aldrin | Ourari | Brucine |
| Tutu | Antiar | Phenol | Cacodyl |
| Upas | Borgia | Pyemia | Coniine |
| | Cicuta | Septic | Cowbane |
| 5 letters: | Curara | Uremia | Cyanide |
| Abrin | Curare | V-agent | Emetine |
| Algae | Curari | Wabain | Flybane |
| Aspic | Datura | | Hebenon |
| Ricin | Dioxin | 7 letters: | Hemlock |
| Sarin | Durban | Aconite | Henbane |
| Soman | Emetin | Amanita | Lindane |

Mineral
Neurine
Neutron
Ouabain
Oxalate
Phallin
Pyaemia
Safrole
Solpuga
Stibine
Stibium
Surinam
Tanghin
Tropine
Venefic
Woorali
Woorara
Wourali

**8 letters:**
Acrolein
Adamsite
Apocynum
Atropine
Barbasco
Botulism
Cannabin
Cyanuret
Daturine
Dumbcane
Embolism
Exotoxin
Flypaper
Gossypol
Lewisite
Litharge

Lobeline
Locoweed
Mephitic
Methanol
Mezereon
Miticide
Nerve gas
Nicotine
Paraquat®
Ptomaine
Pulicide
Raphania
Ratsbane
Rhodanic
Samnitis
Santonin
Solanine
Thebaine
Toxaemia
Trembles
Urushiol
Veratrin
Warfarin

**9 letters:**
Aflatoxin
Autotoxin
Benzidine
Brominism
Bufotalin
Ciguatera
Coyotillo
Digitalin
Echidnine
Fluorosis
Gelsemine

Monkshood
Muscarine
Mycotoxin
Parathion
Sapraemia
Sassy wood
Saturnism
Saxitoxin
Sparteine
Stonefish
Tanghinin
Toxaphene
Veratrine
Wolfsbane
Yohimbine

**10 letters:**
Aqua-tofana
Belladonna
Bufotenine
Cadaverine
Colchicine
Hydrastine
Jimson weed
Limberneck
Manchineal
Mandragora
Molybdosis
Neurotoxin
Paris green
Phalloidin
Phylotoxin
Picrotoxin
Salicylism
Salmonella
Strychnine

Tetrotoxin
Thorn-apple

**11 letters:**
Calabar-bean
Dog's mercury
Gelseminine
Gila monster
Hyoscyamine
Listeriosis
Phosphorism
Pilocarpine
Scopolamine
Septicaemia
Sugar of lead
Sulphur tuft
Veratridine

**12 letters:**
Fool's parsley
Formaldehyde
Hydrargyrism
Nitromethane
Noogoora burr
Strophanthus
Tetrodotoxin

**13 letters:**
Scheele's green
Silver nitrate

**16 letters:**
Deadly nightshade

---

**Poke, Poky** Bonnet, Broddle, Chook, Dig, Garget, Itchweed, Jab, Jook, Meddle, Mock, Nousle, Nudge, Nuzzle, Ombu, Peg, Pick, Poach, Pote, Pouch, Powter, → **PRISON**, → **PROD**, Prog, Proke, Punch, Root(le), Rout, Rowt, Sporran, Stab, Thrust

**Poker (work)** Brag, Bugbear, Curate, Draw, Game, Gas, High-low, Lowball, Mistigris, Penny ante, Pyrography, Red-hot, Salamander, Strip, Stud(-horse), Texas hold'em, Tickler, Tine, Toe

**Poland, Polish** Cracovian, PL, Polack, Pomeranian, Racovian, Sarmatia, Sejm, Slav, Stefan

**Polar, Pole(s), Poler** Animal, Anode, Antarctic, Arctic, Boathook, Boom, Bowsprit, Bum(p)kin, Caber, Celestial, Clothes, Copernicus, Cowl-staff, Crossbar, Electret, Extremity, Fishgig, Fizgy, Flagstaff, Flagstick, Furlong, Gaff, Galactic, Gas, Geomagnetic, Greasy, Icy, Janker, Kent, Liberty, Lug, Magnetic, Mast, May, N, Nadir, Negative, Nib, North, Oar, Periscian, Permafrost, Po, Polack, Positive, Punt, Quant, Quarterstaff, Range, Ricker, Ridge, Ripeck, Rood, Roost, Ry(e)peck, S, Shaft, South, Spar, Spindle, Sprit, Staff, Stake, Stanchion, Stang, Starosta, Stilt, Sting, Stobie, Telegraph, Terrestrial, Thyrsos, Thyrsus, Tongue, Topmast, Totem, Utility, Vegetal, Zenith

▷ **Polar** *may indicate* with a pole

**Polaris** Lodestar, Rhodanic, Rocket, Star

**Polecat** Ferret, Fitch, Fitchet, Foulmart, Foumart, Quail, Weasel

**Polemic(al)** Argument, Controversy, Debate, Eristic(al)

**Police(man), Policewoman** Babylon, Bear, Beast, Beria, Bill, Bizzy, Black and Tans, Blue, Bluebottle, Blue heeler, Bobby, Bog(e)y, Boss, Boys in blue, Bull, Busy, Carabinero, Carabiniere, Catchpole, Centenier, Cheka, Chekist, CID, Commissioner, Constable, Cop(per), Cotwal, Crusher, Darogha, Detective, DI, Dibble, Druzhinnik, Europol, Filth, Flatfoot, Flattie, Flic, Flying Squad, Force, Fuzz, Garda, Garda Siochana, Gendarme, Gestapo, Gill, G-man, Guard, Gumshoe, Harmanbeck, Heat, Hermandad, Inspector, Interpol, Jamadar, Jawan, Jemadar, John Hop, Keystone, KGB, Kitchen, Kotwal, Lawman, Limb, Mata-mata, Met(ropolitan), Military, Mobile, Morse, Mountie, MP, Mulligan, Nabman, Nark, Ochrana, Officer, OGPU, Ovra, Patrolman, PC Plod, Peeler, Peon, Pig, Plod, Pointsman, Polis, Polizei, Porn squad, Posse (comitatus), Prefect, Provincial, Provost, Puppy-walker, Ranger, Redbreast, Redcap, Regulate, RIC, Riot, Robert, Rosser, Roundsman, Rozzer, RUC, Sbirro, SC, Secret, Securitate, Securocrat, Sepoy, Shamus, Sleeping, Slop, Smokey, Snatch squad, Sowar(ry), Special, Special Branch, Stasi, State Trooper, Super, Superintendent, Sureté, Sweeney, T(h)anadar, Texas Rangers, The Bill, The Law, Thirdborough, Thought, Traffic, Traps, Vice squad, Vigilante, Walloper, Wolly, Woodentop, Yardie squad, Zabtieh, Zaptiah, Zaptieh, Zomo

**Police car** Black Maria, Panda, Patrol, Prowl

**Police station** Copshop, Lock-up, Tana, Tanna(h), Thana(h), Thanna(h), Watchhouse

**Policy** Assurance, Ballon d'essai, Byline, CAP, Comprehensive, Course, Demesne, Endowment, Expedience, First-loss, Floating, Good neighbour, Gradualism, Insurance, Keystone, Knock for knock, Laisser-faire, Lend-lease, Line, Manifesto, Method, Open(-sky), Open door, Perestroika, Plank, Platform, Pork-barrel, Practice, Programme, Reaganism, Reaganomics, Revanchism, Scorched earth, Socred, Stop-go, Tack, Tactics, Thatcherism, Third party, Ticket, Traditional, UDI, Valued, White Australia

**Polish(ed), Polisher** Beeswax, Black(ing), Blacklead, Bob, Bruter, Buff, Bull, Burnish, Chamois, Complaisant, Edit, Elaborate, Elegant, Emend, Emery, Enamel, Finish, French, Furbish, Gentlemanly, Glass, Glaze, Gloss, Heelball, Hone, Inland, Jeweller's rouge, Lap, Lustre, Nail, Perfect, Pewter-mill, Planish, Polite, Polverine, Pumice, Refinement, Refurbish, Rottenstone, Rub, Sand, Sandblast, Sandpaper, Scour, Sheen, Shellac, Shine, Sleekstone, Slick, Slickenside, Sophistication, Supercalender, Svelte, Tutty, Urbane, Veneer, Wax

**Polite(ness)** Affable, Cabinet, Civil, Courteous, Genteel, Grandisonian, Mannered, Mannerly, Suave, Urbane, Well-bred, Well-mannered

**Politic(al), Politics** Apparat, Azapo, Body, Chartism, Civic, Diplomacy, Discreet, Dog-whistle, Expedient, Falange, Fascism, Gesture, Leftism, Neoliberalism, New Left, Party, Poujadism, Power, Practical, Public, Radicalism, Rightism, State, Statecraft, Tactful, Wise, Yuppie, Yuppy

**Politician(s)** Back bench, Bright, Carpet-bagger, Catiline, Centrist, Chancellor, Chesterfield, Christian Democrat, Congressman, Coningsby, Delegate, Demagogue, Demo(crat), Diehard, Disraeli, DUP, Eden, Euro-MP, Eurosceptic, Evita, Front bench, Gladstone, Green, Hardie, Hardliner, Incumbent, Independent, Ins, Isolationist, Laski, Left, Legislator, Liberal, Log-roller, Loony left, MEP, Minister, Moderate, MP, Nationalist, Nazi, Obstructionist, Octobrist, Paisley, Parliamentarian, Parnell, Politico, Pollie, Polly, Poujade, Powell, Puppet, Rad, Rep, Richelieu, Senator, Socialist, Statesman, Statist, Tadpole, Taper, TD, Thatcherite, Tory, Trotsky, Unionist, Veep, Warhorse, Whig, Whip, Wilberforce

**Poll(ing)** Advance, Ballot, Bean, Canvass, Count, Cut, Deed, Dod, Election, Exit, Gallup, Head, Humlie, Hummel, Lory, MORI, Nestor, Not(t), Opinion, Parrot, Pineapple, Pow, Push, Referendum, Scrutiny, Sondage, Straw, Votes

▷ **Poll** *may indicate* a first letter

**Pollack** Coalfish, Coley, Fish, Lob, Lythe, Saith(e)

**Pollard** Doddered

**Pollen, Pollinate(d), Pollination** Anemophilous, Beebread, Dust, Entomophilous, Errhine, Ex(t)ine, Farina, Fertilised, Geitonogamy, Intine, My(i)ophily, Palynology, Sternotribe, Witch-meal, Xenia

**Pollenbrush** Scopa

**Pollex** Thumb

**Pollster** Psephologist

**Pollute(d), Pollutant, Pollution** Acid rain, Adulterate, Atmosphere, Besmear, Contaminate, Defile, Dirty, Feculent, File, Fly ash, Foul, Impure, Infect, Light, Miasma, Noise, Nox, Oil slick, Rainout, Smog, Soil, Soilure, Stain, Sully, Taint, Thermal, Violate, Waldsterben

**Polly** Flinders, Parrot, Peachum

**Polo** Bicycle, Chukka, Marco, Mint, Navigator, Rink, Water

**Polonium** Po

**Poltergeist** Apport, Ghost, Spirit, Trouble-house

**Poltroon** Coward, Craven, Dastard, Scald, Scaramouch

**Polyandry** Nair

**Polygraph** Lie-detector

**Polymath** Knowall, Toynbee

**Polymer** Acrylic, Elastomer, Fructans, Isotactic, Lignin, Oligomer, Paraldehyde, Resin, Seloxane, Silicone, Sporopollenin, Tetramer, Trimer

**Polymorphic** Multiform, Proteus, Variform

**Polynesian** Moriori, Niuean, Tahitian, Tongan

**Polyp(s)** Alcyonaria, Cormidium, Gonophore, Hydra, Hydranth, Nematophore, Obelia, Sea-anemone, Tumour

**Polyphemus** Cyclops

**Polyphony** Counterpoint

**Polysaccharide** Cellulose

**Polystyrene** Expanded

**Polyzoan** Sea-mat

**Pom** Choom

**Pomander** Pounce(t)-box

**Pome** Apple

**Pomegranate** Punica, Punic apple

**Pommel** Beat, Knob, Pound, Pummel

**Pomp(ous)** Aldermanlike, Big, Bloviate, Bombastic, Budge, Ceremonial, Display, Dogberry, Euphuistic, Fustian, Grandiloquent, Grandiose, Heavy, Highfalutin(g), High-flown, High-muck-a-muck, High-sounding, Hogen-mogen, Holier than thou, Inflated, Orotund, Ostentatious, Pageantry, Panjandrum, Parade, Pontificating, Pooh-Bah, Pretentious, Self-important, Sententious, Solemn, Splendour, Starchy, State, Stilted, Stuffed shirt, Stuffy, Turgid

**Pom-pom** Ball, Tassel

**Ponce** Pander, Pimp, Solicit, Souteneur

**Poncho** Ruana

**Pond(s)** Atlantic, Curling, Dew, Dub, Flash, Hampstead, Lakelet, Lentic, Mill, Oceanarium, Pool, Pound, Puddle, Settling, Shield(ing), Slough, Stank, Stew, Tank, Turlough, Vivarium, Viver

**Ponder(ous)** Brood, Cogitate, Contemplate, Deliberate, Heavy, Laboured, Mull, Muse, Perpend, Poise, Pore, Puzzle, Reflect, Ruminate, →THINK, Vise, Volve, Weigh, Weight(y), Wonder

**Poniard** Bodkin, →DAGGER, Dirk, Stiletto

**Pontiff, Pontifical, Pontificate** Aaron, Aaronic, Antipope, Dogmatise, Papal, Spout

**Pontoon** Blackjack, Bridge, Caisson, Chess, Game, Twenty one, Vingt-et-un

**Pony** Bidet, Canuck, Cayuse, Cow, Dales, Dartmoor, Eriskay, Exmoor, Fell, Garran, Garron, Gen(n)et, GG, Griffin, Griffon, Gryfon, Gryphon, Jennet, Jerusalem, Mustang,

New Forest, One-trick, Pit, Polo, Pownie, Sable Island, Shanks', Sheltie, Shetland, Show, Tangun, Tat(too), Timor, Welsh, Welsh Mountain, Western Isles

**Ponytail** Queue

**Poodle** Barbet, Swan

**Pooh** Bah, Bear, Pish, Pugh, Tush, Winnie, Yah

**Pool(s)** Backwater, Bank, Bethesda, Billabong, Birthing, Bogey hole, Cenote, Cess, Collect, Combine, Dub, Dump, Flash, Flow, Fund, Gene, Hag, Hot, Infinity, Jackpot, Jacuzzi®, Kitty, Lasher, Lido, Lin(n), Malebo, Meer, Mere, Mickery, Mikvah, Mikveh, Millpond, Moon, Natatorium, Paddling, Piscina, Piscine, Plash, Plesh, Plunge, → POND, Reserve, Share, Siloam, Snooker, Spa, Stank, Stanley, Sump, Tank, Tarn, Treble chance, Wading, Water(ing) hole, Wave

**Poor(ly)** Abysmal, Bad, Bare, Base, Bijwoner, Breadline, Buckeen, Bywoner, Catchpenny, Cheapo, Churchmouse, Conch, Cronk, Destitute, Desuetude, Dire, Dirt, Gens de peu, Gritty, Half-pie, Hard-up, Have-nots, Hopeless, Humble, Hungry, Ill(-off), Impecunious, Indigent, Lazarus, Lean, Lo-fi, Lousy, Low, Low-downer, Low-fi, Low-paid, Lumpen, Meagre, Mean, Naff, Needy, Obolary, One-horse, Pathetic, Patzer, Pauper, Peaky, Poxy, Redleg, Roinish, Rop(e)y, Roynish, Sad, Scrub, Second rate, Shabby, Shitty, Shoddy, Sober, Sorry, Strapped, Sub, Tacky, Tatty, Thin, Third-rate, Tinpot, Trashy, Undeserving, Unwell, Useless, Wattle, Wishy-washy, Wretched

▷ **Poor** *may indicate* an anagram

**Poorhouse** Union, Workhouse

**Pooter** Nobody, Nonentity

**Pop (off), Popper, Popping** Bang, Brit, Burst, Cloop, Cream soda, Crease, Daddy, Die, → DRUG, Each, Father, Fr, Ginger ale, Gingerbeer, Hip-hop, Hock, Iggy, Insert, Lemonade, Lumber, Mineral, Nip, Number, Parent, Party, Pater, Pawn, Pledge, Population, Press-stud, Punk, Rock'n'roll, Scoosh, Sherbet, Slip, Snap fastener, Soda, Splutter, Sputter, Weasel

▷ **Pop** *may indicate* an anagram

**Pope(s)** Adrian, Alexander, Atticus, Benedict, Black, Boniface, Borgia, Clement, Dunciad, Eminence, Fish, Great Schism, Gregory, Hildebrand, Holiness, Innocent, Joan, Leo, Papa, Pius, Pontiff, Ruff(e), Schism, Sistine, Sixtius, Theocrat, Tiara, Urban, Vatican, Vicar-general of Christ, Vicar of Christ

**Pop-gun** Bourtree-gun

**Popinjay** Barbermonger, Coxcomb, Dandy, Fop, Macaroni, Parrot, Prig, Skipjack

**Poplar** Abele, Aspen, Balsam, Cottonwood, Lombardy, Trembling, Tulip, White, Yellow

**Poppet** Cutie pie, Valve

**Poppy** Argemone, Bloodroot, Blue, California, Chicalote, Coquelicot, Corn, Corydalis, Diacodin, Eschscholtzia, Field, Flanders, Horned, Iceland, Matilija, Mawseed, Opium, Papaver, Plume, Ponceau, Prickly, Puccoon, Rhoeadales, Shirley, Tall, Welsh

**Poppycock** Bosh, Nonsense, Piffle, Rubbish

**Popular(ity), Popularly** Best-seller, Common, Crowd-pleaser, Cult, Democratic, Demotic, Enchorial, Evergreen, Fashionable, General, Grass roots, Heyday, Hit, Hot ticket, In, Laic, Lay, Mass, Plebeian, Prevalent, Public, Sell-out, Street cred, Successful, Tipped, Trendy, Vogue, Vulgo

**Population, Populace** Catchment, Census, Closed, Deme, Demography, Inhabitants, Joe Public, Malthusian, Mass, Mob, Optimum, → PEOPLE, Public, Universe

**Porcelain** Arita, Artificial, Bamboo, Belleek®, Blanc-de-chine, Celadon, Chantilly, Chelsea, China, Coalport, Crackle(ware), Crouch-ware, Crown Derby, Derby, Dresden, Eggshell, Famille, Famille jaune, Famille noir, Famille rose, Famille verte, Frit, Goss, Hard-paste, Hizen, Imari, Ivory, Jasp, Jasper(ware), Kakiemon, Limoges, Lithophane, Meissen, Minton, Parian, Petuntse, Petuntze, Sèvres, Softpaste, Spode, Sung, Yuan

**Porch** Galilee, Lanai, Stoa, Stoep, Veranda(h)

**Porcupine** Hedgehog, Urson

**Pore** Browse, Hole, Hydrathode, Lenticel, Muse, Ostiole, Ostium, Outlet, Ponder, Stoma, Study

**Porgy** Braise, Scup(paug)

**Pork(y)** Bacon, Boar, Brawn, Chap, Char sui, Crackling, Cracknel, Flitch, Griskin, Ham, Lie, Pancetta, Salt, Scrapple, Scruncheon, Scrunchion, Spare-rib, Spek, Tenderloin

**Porn(ography), Pornographic** Curiosa, Erotica, Hard, Hard-core, Jazz mag, Rhyparography, Snuff-film, Soft, Soft-core, Video nasty

**Porous** Cellular, Permeable, Pumice, Sponge

**Porpoise** Bucker, Dolphin, Mereswine, Pellach, Pellack, Pellock, Phocaena, Sea pig, Sea swine

**Porridge** Berry, Bird, Brochan, Brose, Burgoo, Busera, Crowdie, Drammach, Drammock, Gaol, Grits, Grouts, Gruel, Hominy, Kasha, Mabela, Mahewu, Mealie pap, Mielie pap, Oaten, Oatmeal, Parritch, Pease-brose, Polenta, Pottage, Praiseach, Sadza, Samp, Sentence, Skilly, Stirabout, Stretch, Sup(p)awn, Time, Ugali

**Porridge stick** Thible, Thivel

**Port(s)** Beeswing, Carry, Cinque, Container (terminal), Entrepot, Free, Gate, Gateway, Geropiga, → **HARBOUR**, Haven, Hinterland, Induction, Larboard, Left, Manner, Mien, Outport, Parallel, Row, Ruby, Serial, Tawn(e)y, Treaty, USB, VSOP, Wine

---

**PORTS**

| 3 letters: | Kiel | 5 letters: | Gabes |
|---|---|---|---|
| Abo | Kiev | Akaba | Galle |
| Ayr | Kobe | Anzio | Gavie |
| Gao | Kure | Aqaba | Genoa |
| Hué | Lima | Arhus | Ghent |
| Rio | Linz | Arica | Gijon |
| Rye | Lomé | Aulis | Goole |
| Tyr | Luda | Bahia | Haifa |
| | Naha | Bahru | Hania |
| 4 letters: | Oban | Banff | Hithe |
| Acre | Omsk | Barry | Horta |
| Aden | Oran | Basra | Hythe |
| Akko | Oslo | Batum | Imari |
| Amoy | Oulu | Beira | Izmir |
| Apia | Perm | Belem | Jaffa |
| Baku | Pori | Bharu | Jambi |
| Bari | Pula | Blyth | Jedda |
| Boma | Puri | Brest | Jidda |
| Cobh | Ruse | Cadiz | Joppa |
| Cork | Safi | Cairo | Kerch |
| Deal | Said | Canea | Kochi |
| Dill | Salé | Colon | Larne |
| Doha | Sfax | Dakar | Leith |
| Eisk | Suez | Davao | Lulea |
| Elat | Susa | Derry | Mainz |
| Faro | Suva | Dilli | Malmo |
| Gary | Tang | Dover | Masan |
| Gaza | Tema | Duala | Merca |
| Gyor | Tvev | Dubai | Miami |
| Hilo | Tyre | Eilat | Mocha |
| Hull | Vigo | Elath | Mokpo |
| Icel | Wick | Emden | Narva |
| I-pin | Wuhu | Fowey | Newry |

Omaha
Ophir
Osaka
Ostia
Palma
Palos
Pisco
Ponce
Poole
Pusan
Pylos
Rabat
Rouen
Saida
Sakai
Salto
Selby
Sidon
Skien
Split
Surat
Susah
Tajik
Tampa
Tanga
Tunis
Turku
Vaasa
Varna
Visby
Vlore
Volos
Yalta
Yeisk
Yeysk
Yibin

**6 letters:**

Aarhus
Abadan
Agadir
Albany
Alborg
Amalfi
Ancona
Andong
Annaba
Aveiro
Balboa
Bastia
Batumi
Bergen
Bilbao
Bissao

Bissau
Blanca
Bombay
Bootle
Boston
Braila
Bremen
Bukavu
Burgas
Cairns
Calais
Callao
Candia
Cannes
Canton
Cavite
Chania
Chi-lin
Cochin
Cuiaba
Cuyaba
Dalian
Da Nang
Danzig
Darwin
Dieppe
Djambi
Douala
Duluth
Dunbar
Dundee
Durban
Durres
Elblag
Galata
Galati
Gdansk
Gdynia
Harbin
Havana
Hobart
Ichang
Iligan
Iloilo
Inchon
Jaffna
Jarrow
Juneau
Kalmar
Khulna
Kisumu
Lepaya
Lisbon
Lobito

Lubeck
Lushun
Macelo
Mackay
Madras
Malabo
Malaga
Manado
Manama
Manaos
Manaus
Manila
Maputo
Matadi
Melaka
Menado
Mersin
Mobile
Mumbai
Muscat
Nagano
Namibe
Nantes
Napier
Naples
Narvik
Nassau
Nelson
Newark
Ningbo
Ningpo
Nizhni
Oamaru
Odense
Odessa
Oporto
Ostend
Padang
Patras
Peoria
Pesaro
Quebec
Quincy
Rabaul
Ragusa
Recife
Rijeka
Rimini
Romney
Roseau
Rostov
Samara
Samsun
Santos

Sarnia
Sasebo
Savona
Skikda
Smyrna
Sousse
Speyer
Spires
St John
St Malo
St Paul
Suakin
Sydney
Syzran
Szeged
Tacoma
Tajiki
Thurso
Timaru
Tobruk
Toledo
Toulon
Tromso
Tyumen
Velsen
Venice
Vyborg
Weihai
Whitby
Wismar
Wonsan
Xiamen
Yangon
Yantai

**7 letters:**

Aalborg
Abidjan
Ajaccio
Alesund
Almeria
Antalya
Antibes
Antwerp
Aracaju
Astoria
Augusta
Averiro
Bamberg
Bangkok
Bayonne
Bengasi
Berbera
Bizerta

Bizerte
Bristol
Buffalo
Bushehr
Bushire
Calabar
Cam Ranh
Canopus
Cantala
Cardiff
Catania
Changde
Changte
Chicago
Chilung
Cologne
Colombo
Conakry
Corinth
Corunna
Cotonou
Derbent
Detroit
Drammen
Dunedin
Dunkirk
El Minya
Ephesus
Esbjerg
Foochow
Fukuoka
Funchal
Gauhati
Geelong
Gosport
Grimsby
Halifax
Hamburg
Hampton
Harwich
Heysham
Hodeida
Horsens
Houston
Hungnam
Incheon
Iquique
Iquitos
Kaolack
Karachi
Karumba
Kavalla
Kenitra
Kherson

Kinsale
Kolding
Konakri
Kowloon
Kuching
La Plata
Latakia
Legaspi
Le Havre
Lepanto
Liepaja
Livorno
Lorient
Makurdi
Marsala
Masbate
Massaua
Massawa
Maulman
Melilla
Memphis
Messina
Milazzo
Mits'twa
Mombasa
Moulman
Munster
Nanjing
Nanking
Nanning
Neusatz
Newport
Niigata
Niteroi
Novi Sad
Oakland
Okayama
Onitsha
Otranto
Pahsien
Palermo
Pelotas
Phocaea
Piraeus
Qingdao
Qiqihar
Randers
Rangoon
Rapallo
Ravenna
Rosario
Rostock
Runcorn
Salerno

San Remo
Sao Luis
Seattle
Sekondi
Setubal
Seville
Shantou
Shantow
Sinuiju
Stettin
St John's
St Louis
Sukhumi
Swansea
Tadzhik
Tampico
Tangier
Taranto
Trabzon
Trapani
Trieste
Tripoli
Ulan-Ude
Ushuaia
Vitebsk
Vitoria
Wanxian
Wenchou
Wenchow
Wenzhou
Whyalla
Yakutsk
Yichang
Yingkou
Yingkow

**8 letters:**
Aalesund
Abeokuta
Aberdeen
Acapulco
Alicante
Alleppey
Arbroath
Auckland
Badalona
Barletta
Batangas
Bathurst
Benghazi
Benguela
Bobruisk
Bobryusk
Bordeaux

Boulogne
Brindisi
Brisbane
Bromberg
Caesarea
Cagliari
Calcutta
Castries
Changsha
Changteh
Chaochow
Cheribon
Chimbote
Chingtao
Chongjin
Cuxhaven
Dortmund
Drogheda
Duisburg
Dunleary
El Ferrol
Elsinore
Falmouth
Flushing
Freetown
Gisborne
Gonaives
Goteborg
Greenock
Haiphong
Hakodate
Halmstad
Hamilton
Hangchow
Hangzhou
Harfleur
Hartford
Hastings
Helsinki
Holyhead
Honolulu
Iraklion
Istanbul
Jayapura
Jinjiang
Kanazawa
Kawasaki
Keflavik
Kingston
Klaipeda
La Coruna
La Guaira
La Guyara
La Spezia

Lattakia
Les Cayes
Limassol
Limerick
Luderitz
Mariupol
Matanzas
Maulmain
Mayaguez
Mazatlan
Monrovia
Montreal
Moulmein
Murmansk
Mytilene
Nagasaki
Nan-ching
Newhaven
Nha Trang
Novgorod
Nykøbing
Pago Pago
Paramibo
Pavlodar
Paysandu
Peiraeus
Penzance
Pevensey
Plymouth
Pnom Penh
Port Said
Pozzuoli
Qui Nhong
Ramsgate
Rio Bravo
Rosslare
Salvador
Samarang
Sanarang
Sandakan
San Diego
Sandwich
Santarem
Santiago
Savannah
Schiedam
Selencia
Semarang
Shanghai
Sorrento
St Helier
Stockton
Surabaja
Surabaya

Syracuse
Szczecin
Tadzhiki
Taganrog
Takoradi
Tangiers
Tarshish
Tauranga
Teresina
Tjirebon
Tsingtao
Valdivia
Valencia
Veracruz
Victoria
Wakayama
Wanganui
Weymouth
Yarmouth
Yokohama
Yokosuka
Zaanstad

**9 letters:**
Anchorage
Angostura
Annapolis
Antserana
Archangel
Balaclava
Balaklava
Baltimore
Barcelona
Bass-Terre
Bhavnagar
Bujumbura
Bydgoszcz
Carnarvon
Cartagena
Cherbourg
Chisimaio
Chongqing
Chungking
Cleveland
Constanta
Dartmouth
Den Helder
Djajapura
Dordrecht
Dubrovnik
Ellesmere
Epidaurus
Esperance
Esquimalt

Essaouira
Europoort
Famagusta
Fishguard
Fleetwood
Flensburg
Fortaleza
Fremantle
Gallipoli
Gateshead
Geraldton
Gravesend
Guayaquil
Hangchoio
Helsinger
Heraklion
Hiroshima
Immingham
Inhambane
Jasselton
Kagoshima
Kaohsiung
King's Lynn
Kingstown
Kirkcaldy
Kota Bahru
Kozhikode
Krasnodar
Kronstadt
Las Palmas
Lowestoft
Magdeburg
Mahajanga
Mangalore
Maracaibo
Mariehamn
Marseille
Matamoros
Matsuyama
Melbourne
Milwaukee
Morecambe
Newcastle
Nuku'alofa
Palembang
Peterhead
Phnom Penh
Pontianak
Port Blair
Port Louis
Port Sudan
Reykjavik
Rotterdam
Santa Cruz

Santander
Schleswig
Sheerness
Singapore
Soerabaja
Stavanger
St George's
St Nazaire
Stornoway
Stralsund
Stranraer
Sundsvall
Takamatsu
Tarragona
Toamasina
Trebizond
Trondheim
Tynemouth
Volgograd
Walvis Bay
Waterford
Weihaiwei
Whangarei
Zamboanga
Zeebrugge

**10 letters:**
Alexandria
Balikpapan
Belize City
Birkenhead
Bratislava
Bridgeport
Bridgetown
Caernarvon
Cap-Haitien
Casablanca
Charleston
Cheboksary
Chittagong
Cienfuegos
Copenhagen
Corrientes
Dzerzhinsk
East London
Felixstowe
Folkestone
Fray Bentos
Fredericia
Georgetown
Gothenburg
Hammerfest
Hartlepool
Herakleion

Iskenderun
Joao Pessoa
Karlskrona
Khabarovsk
Khota Bharu
Kitakyushu
La Rochelle
Launceston
Libreville
Los Angelos
Louisville
Matozinhos
Montevideo
Mostaganem
New Bedford
New Orleans
Norrkoping
Paramaribo
Pittsburgh
Pontevedra
Port Gentil
Portobello
Portsmouth
Port Talbot
Providence
Queenstown
Sacramento
Santa Marta
Sebastopol
Sevastopol
Strasbourg
Sunderland
Talcahuano
Thunder Bay
Townsville
Valparaiso
Whitstable

Willemstad
Wilmington
Winchelsea

*11 letters:*
Antofagusta
Antseranana
Bahia Blanca
Banjarmasin
Banjermasin
Baranquilla
Bremerhaven
Cheng-chiang
Dares Salaam
Fredrikstad
Grangemouth
Helsingborg
Hermoupolis
Kaliningrad
Makhachkala
Maryborough
New Plymouth
Newport News
Nuevo Laredo
Pointe-Noire
Port Moresby
Porto Alegre
Port of Spain
Punta Arenas
Rockhampton
San Fernando
Scarborough
Shimonoseki
Southampton
Telukbetong
Trincomalee
Vizagapatam

Vlaardingen
Vladivostok

*12 letters:*
Angtofagasta
Bandjarmasin
Bandjermasin
Barranquilla
Buenaventura
Chandemagore
Dun Laoghaire
Ho Chi Min City
Jacksonville
Kota Kinabalu
Kristiansand
Milford Haven
Philadelphia
Pointe-à-Pitre
Ponta Delgada
Port Adelaide
Port-au-Prince
Port Harcourt
Prince Rupert
Rio de Janeiro
San Francisco
San Sebastian
Santo Domingo
South Shields
St Petersburg
Tanjungpriok
Thessaloniki
Ujung Pandang
Usti nad Labem

*13 letters:*
Chandernagore
Charlottetown

Ciudad Bolivar
Corpus Christi
Florianopolis
Great Yarmouth
Ho Chi Minh City
Hook of Holland
Middlesbrough
Port Elizabeth
Tandjungpriok
Teloekbetoeng
Trois Rivières
Visakhapatnam
Wilhelmshaven

*14 letters:*
Burnie-Somerset
Mina Hassen Tani
Nizhni Novgorod
Santiago de Cuba
Vishakhapatnam

*15 letters:*
Alexandroupolis
Angra-de-
  Heroismo
Blagoveshchensk
Charlotte-Amalie
Forster-Tuncurry
Sault SaintMarie

*16 letters:*
Reggio di Calabria
Sault Sainte Marie

*18 letters:*
Castellon de la
  Plana

---

**Portable** Lapheld, Laptop, Mobile, Palmtop
**Portend, Portent(ous)** Augur, Awesome, Bode, Dire, Omen, Ominous, Ostent, Phenomenon, Presage, Solemn, → **WARN(ING)**
**Porter** Ale, Bearer, Bellboy, Bellhop, Bummaree, Caddie, Caddy, Carrier, Cole, Concierge, Coolie, Door-keeper, Doorman, Dvornik, Entire, Gatekeeper, Ham(m)al, Hamaul, Humper, Janitor, October, Ostiary, Plain, Red-cap, Skycap, Stout, Ticket
**Portfolio** Briefcase, Holding
**Portico** Colonnade, Decastyle, Distyle, Dodecastyle, Exedra, Loggia, Narthex, Parvis(e), Porch, Propylaeum, Prostyle, Stoa, Veranda(h), Xyst(us)
**Portion** Aliquot, Ann(at), Bit, Deal, Distribute, Dole, Dose, Dotation, Endowment, Fraction, Fragment, Helping, Heritage, Hunk, Instalment, Jointure, Lot, Lump, Measure, Meed, Mess, Modicum, Moiety, Nutlet, Ounce, Parcel, → **PART**, Piece, Ratio, Sample, Scantle, Scantling, Section, Segment, Serving, Share, Size, Slice, Something, Spoonful, Tait, Taste, Tate, Tittle, Tranche, Wodge
**Portland** Bill, Cement, Stone
**Portly** Ample, Corpulent, Gaucie, Gaucy, Gawcy, Gawsy, Stout

**Portmanteau, Portmanteau word** Avoision, Bag, Combination, Holdall, Valise

**Portrait(ist)** Carte de visite, Composite, Depiction, Drawing, Eikon, Icon, Identikit®, Ikon, Image, Kit-cat, Lely, Likeness, Painting, Pin-up, Retraitt, Retrate, Sketch, Vignette

**Portray(al)** Caricature, Depict, Describe, Feature, Image, Limn, Notate, Paint, Personate, Render, Represent, →**SHOW**

**Portsmouth** Pompey

**Portugal, Portuguese** Lusitania(n), Luso-, Macanese, Senhor

**Pose(r), Poseur** Aesthete, Affect(ation), Arabesque, Asana, Ask, Contrapposto, Conundrum, Dilemma, Drape, Enigma, Lotus, Man(n)ikin, Mannequin, Masquerade, Model, Place, Plastique, Posture, Pretend, Problem, Propound, Pseud, Puzzle, Sit, Stance, Sticker, Tableau vivant, Tickler

**Poseidon** Earthshaker

**Posh** Chic, Classy, Grand, Lah-di-dah, Ornate, Ritzy, Sou, Swanky, Swish, Toff, Top drawer, U

**Position** Arrange, Asana, Attitude, Bearing(s), Brace, Bridgehead, Case, Close, Codille, Delta, Ecarte, Echelon, Emplacement, Enfilade, False, F(o)etal, Fixure, Foothold, Fowler's, Grade, Honour point, Instal, Lay, Lie, Location, Locus, Lodg(e)ment, Lotus, Missionary, Mudra, Niche, Office, Open, Pass, Peak, Place, Plant, Point, Pole, Port, Possie, Post, Pozzy, Put, Rank, Recovery, Recumbent, Root, Seat, Set(ting), Sextile, Sims, Sinecure, Sit, Site, Situ, Situs, Stance, Standing, Standpoint, Station, Status, Strategic, Syzygy, Tagmeme, Thesis, Tierce, Trendelenburg's, Tuck, Viewpoint

**Positive, Positivist** Absolute, Actual, Anode, Assertive, Categorical, →**CERTAIN**, Comte, Definite, Emphatic, False, Plus, Print, Rave, Sure, Thetic, Upbeat, Upside, Utter, Veritable, Yang, Yes

**Posse** Band, Mob, Vigilantes

**Possess(ed), Possession(s), Possessive** Adverse, Apostrophe, Asset, Aver, Bedevil, Belonging(s), Demonic, Driven, Energumen, Estate, Ewe lamb, Have, Haveour, Haviour, Heirloom, His, Hogging, Know, Lares (et) penates, Mad, Obsessed, Occupation, →**OWN**, Proprietorial, Sasine, Seisin, Sprechery, Substance, Tenancy, Usucap(t)ion, Vacant, Worth

**Possible, Possibility, Possibly** Able, Attainable, Contingency, Could, Feasible, Imaginable, Likely, Maybe, Mayhap, Off-chance, On, Option(al), Oyster, Peradventure, Perchance, Perhaps, Posse, Potential, Prospect, Resort, Viable, Well, Will

▷ **Possibly** *may indicate* an anagram

**Possum** Burramys, Cataplexy, Opossum, Pygmy, Rigo(u)r, Ringtail, Sugar glider, Sugar squirrel, Tait

**Post(s), Postage** Affix, After, Airmail, Appointment, Assign, Billet, Bitt, Bollard, Carrick bitt, Column, Command, Correspondence, Cossack, Dak, Dawk, Delivery, Dragon's teeth, Durn, Emily, Excess, Finger, First(-class), Flagpole, Fly, Goal, Graded, Gradient, Guardhose, Heel, Hitching, Hovel, Hurter, Jamb, Joggle, Junk, King, Last, Laureate, Listening, Log, Mail, Mast, Newel, Observation, Outstation, Pale, Paling, Parcel, Pendant, Penny, Picket, Pigeon, Pile, Piling, Piquet, Placard, Place, Plant, Plum, Pole, Position, Presidio, Puncheon, Pylon, Queen, Quintain, Quoin, Registered, Remit, Residency, RM, Rubbing, Samson's, Seat, Second-class, Send, Sheriff's, Snubbing, Sound, Spile, Staff, Staging, Stake, Stanchion, Stand, Starting, Station, Stell, Stoop, Stoup, Stud, Studdle, Tana, Tee, Term(inal), Thanna(h), Tom, Tool, Totem pole, Trading, Troll, Upright, Vacancy, Waymark, Winning

**Postcard(s)** Deltiology, Picture

**Poster** Advertisement, Affiche, Bill, Broadsheet, Pin-up, Placard, Playbill, Sender, Showbill, Solus, Sticker

**Posterior** Behind, Bottom, Jacksie, Jacksy, Later, Lumbar, Pygal, Rear, Tail

**Post-free** Franco

**Postman, Postmaster, Postwoman** Carrier, Courier, Emily, Hill, Messenger, Nasby, Pat, Portionist, Sorter

**Postmark** Frank
**Post-modern** Po-mo
**Post mortem** Autopsy, Dissection, Enquiry, Necropsy
**Postpone(ment), Postponed** Adjourn, Backburner, Carryover, Contango, Defer, Delay, Frist, Hold over, Lay over, Long-finger, Moratorium, Mothball, Offput, On ice, Pigeon-hole, Postdate, Prorogue, Put over, Remanet, Reprieve, Respite, Roll back, Shelve, Spike, Stay, Suspend, Withhold
**Postscript** Envoi
**Postulant** Candidate, Noumenon, Novice
**Postulate(s)** Assert, Assume, Claim, Koch's, Posit, Propound
**Posture(r), Posturing** Affectation, Asana, Attitude, Birkie, Camp, Carriage, Counter-view, Decubitus, Deportment, Gesture, Mudra, Pose, Pretence, Site, Stance, Swank, Vorlage, Yoga
**Post-war** Post-bellum
**Posy** Bouquet, Buttonhole, Corsage, Nosegay, Tussiemussie, Tussle-mussle, Tuzzi-muzzy, Tuzzy-muzzy
**Pot(s), Potting, Potty** Abridge, Aludel, Ante, Bankroll, Basil, Belly, Besotted, Billycan, Cafetière, Ca(u)ldron, Cannabis, Cannikin, Casserole, Cast, Ceramic, Chamber, Chanty, Chatti, Chatty, Chimney, Close-stool, Cocotte, Coil, Commode, Crewe, Crock(ery), Crucible, Cruse(t), Cupel, Delf(t), Dixie, Doolally, Ewer, Flesh, Gaga, Gage, Gallipot, Ganja, Gazunder, Grass, Hash(ish), Helmet, Hemp, Hooped, In off, Inurn, Jardinière, Jordan, Kaif, Kef, Kettle, Kitty, Livery, Lobster, Loco, Lota(h), Maiolica, Majolica, Marijuana, Marmite, Melting, Ming, Monkey, Olla, Olpe, Pan, Papper, Pat, Piñata, Pint, Pipkin, Planter, Po, Pocket, Pool, Poot, Posnet, → **POTTERY**, Pottle, Pounce, Pout, Prize, Quart, Samovar, Shoot, Sink, Skeet, Skillet, Smudge, Steamer, Steane, Stomach, Tajine, Tea, Terrine, Test, Throw, Togine, Trivet, Tureen, Urn, Vial, Ware, Wash, Whitechapel, Wok
**Potash** Kalinite, Polverine, Potassa, Sylvine, Sylvite
**Potassium** K, Kalium, Pearl ash, Saleratus, Saltpetre
**Potation** Dram, Drink
**Potato(es)** African, Aloo, Alu, Batata, Chat, Clean, Couch, Datura, Duchesse, Early, Fluke, Hashbrowns, Hog, Hole, Hot, Irish, Jacket, Jersey, Kidney, Kumara, Lyonnaise, Maris piper, Mash, Murphy, Parmentier, Peel-and-eat, Pratie, Praty, Ro(e)sti, Rumbledethump(s), Seed, Small, Solanum, Stovies, Sweet, Tatie, Tattie, Teddy, Tuber, Ware, White, Yam
**Pot-bearer** Trivet
**Pot-bellied** Kedge, Kedgy, Kidge, Paunchy, Portly, Stout
**Potboiler** Hob
**Pot-boy** Basil, Ganymede, Scullion
**Potent(ate)** Cogent, Despot, Dynamic, Emeer, Emir, Emperor, Huzoor, Imaum, Influential, Kinglet, Mogul, Nawab, Panjandrum, Powerful, Ras, Ruler, Satrap, Squirearch, Sultan, Virile
**Potential(ly)** Action, Capability, Capacity, Chemical, Electric, Electrode, In posse, Ionization, Latent, Making(s), Manqué, Possible, Promise, Resting, Scope, Viable
▷ **Potentially** *may indicate* an anagram
**Pothole(r)** Chuckhole, Giant's kettle, Spelunker
**Pot-house** Shebeen, Tavern
**Potion** Dose, Draught, Drink, Dwale, Elixir, Love, Mixture, Philtre, Tincture
**Pot-pourri** Hotchpotch, Medley, Miscellany, Pasticcio, Salmi
**Potsherd** Ostracon, Ostrakon
**Pottage** Berry
**Potter** Amble, Cue, Dabbity, Dabble, Dacker, Daidle, Daiker, Daker, Dibble, Dilly-dally, Dodder, Etruscan, Fettle, Fictor, Fiddle, Footer, Footle, Fouter, Gamesmanship, Harry, Idle, Mess, Minton, Muck, Niggle, One-upmanship, Plouter, Plowter, Poke, Spode, Thrower, Tiddle, Tink(er), Troke, Truck, Wedgwood

▷ **Potter** *may indicate* a snooker-player

**Pottery** Agateware, Bank, Basalt, Bisque, Cameo ware, Celadon, Ceramet, Ceramic, Chelsea, China, Creamware, Crock, Crouch-ware, Dabbity, Delf(t), Dresden, Earthenware, Encaustic, Etruria(n), Faience, Flatback, Gombroon, Granitewear, Hollowware, Ironstone, Jomon, Lustreware, Maiolica, Majolica, Ming, Minton, Pebbleware, Queensware, Raku, Red-figured, Satsuma, Scroddled, Sgraffito, Slab, Slipware, Smalto, Spode, Spongeware, Stoke, Stoneware, Studio, Sung, Terra sigillata, Ware, Wedgwood®, Wemyss, Whieldon, Whiteware

**Pouch(ed)** Bag, Brood, Bum-bag, Bursa, Caecum, Cheek, Cisterna, Codpiece, Cyst, Diverticulum, Fanny pack, Gill, Jockstrap, Marsupial, Marsupium, Papoose, Pocket, Poke, Posing, Purse, Sac, Saddlebag, Scrip, Scrotum, Snood, Spleuchan, Sporran, Tobacco

**Pouffe** Humpty

**Poultice** Application, Cataplasm, Embrocation, Emollient, Epithem(a), Lenient, Plaster

**Poultry** Dorking, Fowl, Gallinaceous, Plymouth Rock, Poot, Pout, Welsummer

**Poultry disease** Keel, Scaly-leg, Vent gleet

**Pounce** Claw, Jump, Lunge, Powder, Sere, Souse, Sprinkle, Swoop, Talon

**Pound(er)** Ache, As, Bar, Bash, Batter, Battersea, Beat, Bombard, Bradbury, Bray, Broadpiece, Bruise, Catty, Clomp, Contund, Coop, Drub, Embale, Enclosure, Ezra, Fold, Green, Greenie, Greeny, Hammer, Hatter, Imagist, Intern, Iron man, Jail, Jimmy o'goblin, Kiddle, Kidel, Kin, Knevell, L, Lam, Lash, Lb, Lock, Mash, Nevel, Nicker, Oncer, One-er, Oner, Pale, Palpitate, Pen, Penfold, Pestle, Pin, Pindar, Pinfold, Pink, Powder, Pulverise, Pun, Quid, Quop, Rint, Scots, Smacker, Sov(ereign), Squid, Stalag, Stamp, Sterling, Strum, Tenderise, Throb, Thump, Tower, Troy, Weight

**Pour(ing)** Affusion, Be mother, Birl(e), Bucket, Cascade, Circumfuse, Decant, Diffuse, Disgorge, Flood, Flow, Jaw, Jirble, Libate, Rain, Seil, Shed, Sile, Skink, Spew, Stream, Teem, Trill, Turn, Vent, Weep, Well

**Pout** Bib, Blain, Brassy, Eel, Fish, Horn(ed), Mope, Mou(e), Scowl, Sulk, Tout, Towt, Whiting

**Poverty** Beggary, Dearth, Deprivation, Hardship, Illth, Indigence, →LACK, Locust years, Necessity, Need, Paucity, Pauperism, Penury, Poortith, Puirtith, Squalor, Tobacco Road, Want

**Powder(ed), Powdery** Allantoin, Alumina, Amberite, Araroba, Baking, Ballistite, Bleaching, Boracic, Calamine, Calomel, Chalk, Chilli, Cocoa, Colcothar, Condition, Cosmetic, Crocus, Culm, Curry, Custard, Cuttlefish, Dentifrice, Dover's, Dust, Dusting, Eupad, Explosive, Face, Flea, Floury, Fly, Fulminating, Giant, Glaucous, Goa, Gregory, Grind, Gun, Hair, Insect, Itching, Kohl, Levigate, Lithia, Litmus, Lupulin, Magnesia, Meal, Mepacrine, Mould-facing, Moust, Mu(i)st, Pearl, Pemoline, Percussion, Persian, Plaster of Paris, Plate, Polishing, Pollen, Pounce, Pound, Priming, Prismatic, Projecting, Pruinose, Pulver, Pulvil, Putty, Rachel, Rochelle, Rottenstone, Rouge, Saleratus, Seidlitz, Seme(e), Sherbet, Silver iodide, Sitosterol, Smeddum, Smokeless, Snuff, Soap, Spode, Spodium, Talc(um), Talcose, Thimerosal, Toner, Tooth, Triturate, Tutty, Washing, Zedoary, Zein

**Power(ful), Powers** Ability, Able, Aeon, Aggrandisement, Air, Almighty, Alpha, Amandla, Arm, Arnold, Athletic, Atomic, Attorney, Audrey, Autarchy, Authority, Axis, Beef, Big, Capability, Chakra, Cham, Charisma, Clairvoyance, Clout, Cogency, Colossus, Command, Corridor, Cube, Danger, Despotic, Diadem, Dieu, Dioptre, Dominion, Effective, Electricity, Eminence, Éminence grise, Empathy, Empery, Energy, Eon, ESP, Exponent, Facility, Faculty, Fire, Flower, Force, Force majeure, Gaddi, Gas, Generator, Geothermal, Grey, Grip, Gutty, Hands, Hefty, Hegemony, Herculean, High, Hildebrandic, Horse, Hot, Hp, Hydroelectric, Imperium, Imput, Influence, Juice, Kami, Kick, Kilowatt, King, Leccy, Leverage, Locomotion, Log, Logarithm, Lusty, Mana, Mandarin, Mandate, Mastery, Megalomania, Megawatt, Might, Mogul, Motive, Motor, Movers and shakers, Muscle, Natural, Nature, Nth, Nuclear, Od-force, Oligarch, Omnificent, Omnipotent,

Option, P, Panjandrum, People, Pester, Plenary, Plenipotency, Posse, Potency, Prepollence, Prepotent, Puissant, Punch, Purchasing, Regime, Resolving, Say-so, Sea, Siddhi, Sinew, Solar, Soup, Stamina, Staying, Steam, Steel, Stiff, Stopping, Stranglehold, Strength, →**STRONG**, Supercharge, Supreme, Suzerain, Sway, Teeth, Telling, Throne, Tidal, Titan, Tycoon, Tyranny, Tyrone, Ulric, Valency, Vertu(e), Vigour, Vis, Volt, Vroom, Water, Watt, Wattage, Wave, Weight, Welly, Wheel and axle, Whiphand, Wind, World, Yeast

**Powerless** Diriment, Downa-do, Failing, Freewheel, Hamstrung, Helpless, Impotent, Impuissant, Incapable, Inert, Numb, Unable, Unarmed, Weak

**Power station** Dungeness

**Powwow** Confab, Conference, Council, Meeting

**Pox** Chicken, Cow, French, Great, Orf, Pize, Small, Spanish

**Practical, Practicable, Practicalities** Active, Applied, Brass tacks, Doable, Down-to-earth, Easy-care, Feasible, Hands on, Hard-boiled, Joker, Logistics, Nitty-gritty, No-nonsense, Nuts and bolts, On, Pragmatic, Realist(ic), Realpolitik, Rule of thumb, Sensible, Shrewd, Technical, Useful, Utilitarian, Viable, Virtual

**Practice(s), Practise, Practitioner, Practised** Abuse, Adept, Custom, Distributed, Do, Drill, Dry run, Dummy run, Enure, Exercise, Fire, General, Graft, Group, Habit, Inure, Ism, Keep, Knock-up, Massed, Meme, Mock, Nets, Operate, Order, Ordinance, Pipe opener, Ply, Policy, Praxis, Private, Prosecution, Pursuit, Rehearsal, Rehearse, Restrictive, Rite, Rule, Rut, Sadhana, Sharp, Sighter, Spanish, System, Target, Teaching, Test-run, Trade, Tradition, Train, Trial, Try out, Ure, Usage, Use, Wage

**Pragmatic, Pragmatist** Ad hoc, Busy, Dogmatic, Humanist, Meddling, Officious, Realist, Trimmer, Unholy

**Prairie** IL, Illinois, Llano, Plain, Savanna, Steppe, Tundra, Veldt

**Prairie dog** Whippoorwill, Wishtonwish

**Praise(worthy)** Acclaim, Accolade, Adulation, Alleluia, Allow, Anthem, Applause, Beatify, Belaud, Bepuff, Bless, Blurb, Bouquet, Bravo, Butter, Carol, Citation, CL, Commend(ation), Compliment, Congratulate, Crack up, Cry up, Dulia, Ego boost, Encomium, Envy, Eulogise, Eulogium, Eulogy, Exalt, Exemplary, Extol, Flattery, Gloria, Glory, Hail, Hero-worship, Herry, Hery(e), Hosanna, Hymn, Hype, Incense, Kudos, Laud, Laurels, Lip service, Lo(o)s, Meritorious, Paean, Palmary, Palp, Panegyric, Plaudit, Puff(ery), Rap, Rave, Recommend, Roose, Talk-up, Thank, Tout, Tribute

**Pram** Buggy

**Prance** Brank, Canary, Caper, Cavort, Galumph, Gambol, Jaunce, Jaunse, Prank(le), Swagger, Tittup, Trounce

**Prang** Accident, Crash, Smash, Whale

**Prank(s)** Attrap, Bedeck, Bedizen, Caper, Dido, Escapade, Fredaine, Frolic, Gaud, Jape, Lark, Mischief, Pliskie, Rag, Reak, Reik, Rex, Rig, Spoof, Trick, Vagary, Wedgie

**Praseodymium** Pr

**Prat** Bottom, →**STUPID PERSON**

**Prate** Babble, Boast, Haver, Talk

**Prattle** Babble, Blat(her), Chatter, Gab(nash), Gas, Gibber, Gossip, Gup, Lalage, Patter, Smatter, Yap

**Prawn** Banana, Crevette, Dublin Bay, King, Scampi, School, Shrimp, Tiger

**Pray(ing)** Appeal, Bed, Beg, Beseech, Bid, Daven, →**ENTREAT**, Impetrate, Intercede, Intone, Invoke, Kneel, Mantis, Patter, Solicit, Wrestle

**Prayer(s), Prayer book, Prayer wall** Acoemeti, Act, Amidah, Angelus, Ardas, Ave (Maria), Bead, Beadswoman, Bede, Bene, Bidding, Breviary, Carmelite, Collect, Commination, Common, Confiteor, Cry, Cursus, Daven, Deus det, Devotion, Eleison, Embolism, Entreaty, Epiclesis, Euchologion, Evensong, Geullah, Grace, Habdalah, Hail Mary, Hallan-shaker, Imam, Intercession, Introit, Invocation, Kaddish, Khotbah, Khotbeh, Khutbah, Kol Nidre, Kyrie, Kyrie eleison, Lauds, Litany, Lord's, Loulat-ul-qadr, Lychnapsia, Ma'ariv, Ma(c)hzor, Maiden's, Mani, Mantis, Mat(t)ins, Mincha(h), Missal,

Morning, Musaf, Novena, Opus dei, Orant, Orarium, Orison, Our Father, Paternoster, Patter, Petition, Phylactery, Placebo, Plea, Preces, Prime, Proseucha, Proseuche, Puja, Requiem, Requiescat, Responses, Rogation, Rosary, Salat, Secret, Shema, Siddur, State, Stations of the Cross, Suffrage, Te igitur, Tenebrae, Terce, Triduum, Venite, Vesper, Vigils, Wish, Yajur-Veda, Yizkor

▷ **Prayer** *may indicate* one who begs

**Praying mantis** Rear-horse

**Preach(er)** Ainger, Boanerges, Circuit rider, Dawah, Devil-dodger, Dominican, Donne, Ecclesiastes, Evangelist, Exhort, Gospeller, Graham, Holy Roller, Itinerant, Kerygma, Knox, Lecture, Local, Mar-text, Minister, Missionary, Moody, → **MORALISE**, Patercove, Pontificate, Postillate, Predicant, Predicate, Predikant, Priest, Prophet, Pulpiteer, Rant, Revivalist, Sermonise, Soper, Spintext, Spurgeon, Teach, Televangelist, Wesley

**Preamble** Introduction, Lead-in, Preface, Proem, Prologue

**Prearrange(d)** Book, Stitch up

**Pre-Cambrian** Torridonian

**Precarious** Dangerous, Knife edge, Parlous, Perilous, Risky, Touch and go, Trickle, Uncertain, Unsteady, Unsure

**Precaution** Care, Fail-safe, Guard, In case, Prophylaxis, Safeguard, Safety net

**Precede(nce), Precedent** Antedate, Example, Forego, Forerun, Head, Herald, Pas, Predate, Preface, Prepotent, Priority, Protocol, Test case, Zeroth

**Precept(s)** Adage, Canon, Commandment, Maxim, Mishna, Motto, Saw

**Precession** Larmor

**Precinct(s)** Ambit, Area, Banlieue, Close, Courtyard, District, Environs, Pedestrian, Peribolos, Region, Shopping, Temenos, Verge, Vihara

**Precious** Adored, Chary, Chichi, Costly, Dear, Dearbought, Ewe-lamb, La-di-da, Murr(h)a, Nice, Owre, Precise, Priceless, Prissy, Rare, Twee, Valuable

**Precipice** Bluff, Cliff, Crag, Krans, Kran(t)z, Sheer

**Precipitate, Precipitation, Precipitous, Precipitator** Abrupt, Accelerate, Catalyst, Cause, Deposit, Hailstone, Hasty, Headlong, Impetuous, Launch, Lees, Pellmell, Pitchfork, Rash, Sca(u)r, Serein, Serene, Sheer, Shoot, Sleet, Snowfall, Snowflake, Start, → **STEEP**, White

**Précis** Abstract, Aperçu, Epitome, Résumé, Summary

**Precise(ly), Precisian, Precision** Absolute, Accurate, Dry, Exact, Explicit, Fine-drawn, Literal, Minute, Nice(ty), Niminy-piminy, Overnice, Particular, Perfect, Pernickety, Plumb, Point-device, Prig, Prim, Punctilious, Razor, Sharpness, Spang, Specific, Starchy, Stickler, Strict, Stringent, Succinct, Surgical, Tight, To the letter, Very

**Preclude** Bar, Debar, Estop, Foreclose, Hinder, Impede, Prevent

**Precocious(ness)** Advanced, Bratpack, Enfant terrible, Forward, Madam, Premature, Protogyny

**Preconception** Ideating

**Precursor** Avant-courier, Forerunner, Harbinger

**Predator(y)** Carnivore, Condor, Eagle, Eyas, Fox, Glede, Harpy-eagle, Honey badger, Jackal, Kestrel, Kite, Lycosa, Mantis, Marauder, Nyas, Pike, Predacious, Prey, Puma, Skua, Tanrec, Tarantula, Tenrec, Trapper, Wolf

**Pre-dawn** Antelucan, Ante lucem

**Predecessor** Ancestor, Forebear, Foregoer

**Predestined** Doomed, Fated, Tramway

**Predetermine(d)** Set

**Predicament** Box, Dilemma, Embarrassment, Embroglio, Hobble, Hole, In chancery, Jam, Pass, Peril, Pickle, Plight, Quandary, Scrape, Spot

**Predict(ion), Predictable, Predicted, Predictor** Astrologer, Augur, Belomancy, Bet, Clairvoyance, Damn, Divination, Doomsayer, Doomster, Doomwatch, Ex ante, Far-seeing, Forecast, Foreordain, Foreread, Foresay, Foresee, Foreshadow, Foreshow, Forespeak, Foretell, Formulaic, Forsay, Futurist, Geomancy, Horoscope, Jeremiah, Nap,

Necromancy, Omen, Portend, Presage, Previse, Prognosis, Project, Prophecy, Prophesy, Quant, Regular, Second-guess, Soothsayer, Spae, Tip

**Predilection** Fancy, Liking, Prejudice, Taste, Tendency

**Predisposition** Aptitude, Bent, Inclination, Parti-pris, Tendency

**Predominate, Predominance** Abound, Govern, Overshadow, Prepollency, Prevail, Reign, Ruling

**Pre-eminence, Pre-eminent** Arch, Foremost, Monarchic, Palm(ary), Paramount, Primacy, Supreme, Top dog, Topnotch, Unique

**Pre-empt(ive)** Enter

**Preen** Perk, Primp, Prink, Prune, Titivate

**Prefab(ricated)** Quonset, Terrapin®

**Preface** Avant-propos, Foreword, Herald, Intro, Preamble, Precede, Proem, Prolegomenon, Prolepsis, Usher

**Prefect** Haussmann, Pilate, Prepositor, Pr(a)eposter

**Prefer(ence), Preferred** Advance, Better, Choose, Discriminate, Druthers, Elect, Faard, Faurd, Favour, Imperial, Incline, Lean, Liquidity, Predilect(ion), Prefard, Priority, Proclivity, Promote, Rather, Select, Sooner, Stocks, Taste, Will

**Prefix** Eka, Introduce, Name

**Pregnancy, Pregnant** Big, Clucky, Cyesis, Due (to), Ectopic, Enceinte, Extrauterine, Fertile, F(o)etation, Gestation, Gravid(a), Great, Great-bellied, Heavy, Hysterical, In foal, In pig, In pup, Knocked-up, Molar, Phantom, Pseudocyesis, Pudding-club, Retirement, Significant, Stomack, Teem, Up the duff, Up the pole, Up the spout, Up the stick, With child

**Prehistoric** Ancient, Azilian, Beaker Folk, Boskop, Brontosaurus, Cambrian, Clovis, Cro-Magnon, Eocene, Folsom, Mound Builder, Ogygian, Primeval, Primitive, Pteranodon, Pterodactyl(e), Pterosaur, Saurian, Sinanthropus, Stonehenge, Titanis, Titanosaurus, Trilith(on)

**Prejudice(d)** Ageism, Bias, Bigotry, Derry, Discrimination, Down, Illiberal, Impede, Inequity, Injure, Insular, Intolerance, Partiality, Parti pris, Preoccupy, Prepossession, Racism, Sexism, Slant, Unfair

**Prelate** Archiepiscopal, Cardinal, Churchman, Exarch, Monsignor, Odo, Priest

**Preliminary** Curtain-raiser, Draft, Exploration, Heat, Initial, Introductory, Opening, Precursory, Preface, Preparatory, Previous, Prodrome, Proem, Prolusion, Propaedeutic, Rough, Title-sheet

**Prelude** Entrée, Forerunner, Intrada, Overture, Proem(ial), Ritornell(e), Ritornello, Verset

**Premature** Early, Precocious, Pre(e)mie, Premy, Pre term, Previous, Slink, Untimely, Untimeous

**Premedication** Atropia

**Premeditate** Anticipate, Foresee, Plan

**Premier** Chief, Leader, Lenin, Main, PM, → **PRIME MINISTER**, Tojo, Top (drawer)

**Premise(s)** Assumption, Datum, Epicheirema, Ground, Hypothesis, Inference, Lemma, Licensed, Major, Postulate, Property, Proposition, Reason, Syllogism, Term, Unlicensed

**Premium** Ap, Bond, Bonus, Discount, Grassum, Pm, Reward, Scarce, Share

**Premonition** Hunch, Omen, Presentiment, Prodromal, Specter, Spectre, Warning

**Preoccupation, Preoccupied, Preoccupy** Absorb, Abstracted, Distrait, Engross, Hang-up, Intent, Obsess, Self-centred, Thing

**Prepaid** Pro-forma, Sae

**Prepare(d), Preparation** Address, À la, Anticipate, Arrange, Attire, Boun, Bowne, Brilliantine, Busk, Calver, Cock, Concoct, Cook, Cooper, Countdown, Decoct, Did, Do, Dress, Edit, Extract, Forearm, Foundation, Game, Gear (up), Groom, Ground, Groundwork, Inspan, Key, Lay (out), Legwork, Limber (up), Lotion, Measure, Mobilise, Organise, Parasceve, Paste up, Pomade, Poultice, Preliminary, Prime, Procinct, Prothesis, Provide, Psych, Qualified, → **READY**, Redact, Rehearsal, Revise, Ripe, Run up, Rustle up, Scout, Scrub up, Set, Spadework, Stand-to, Suborn, Train, Trim, Truss, Tune up, Type, Up to, Warm-up, Whip up, Willing, Yare

▷ **Prepare(d)** *may indicate* an anagram

**Preponderance, Preponderant, Preponderate** Important, Majority, Outweigh, Paramount, Prevalence, Sway

**Preposition** Lemma

**Prepossessing, Prepossession** Attractive, Fetching, Predilection, Winsome

**Preposterous** Absurd, Chimeric, Exorbitant, Foolish, Grotesque, Rich, Tall order, Unreasonable

▷ **Preposterous** *may indicate* a word reversed

**Pre-Raphaelite** Rossetti, Waterhouse

**Prerequisite** Condition, Essential, Necessity, Sine qua non

**Prerogative** Faculty, Franchise, Liberty, Privilege, Right, Royal

**Presage** Abode, Foresight, Omen, Portend, Presentiment, Prophesy

**Presbyter(ian)** Berean, Blue, Cameronian, Classic, Classis, Covenanter, Elder, Knox, Macmillanite, Moderator, Sacrarium, Seceder, Secesher, Secession Church, Wee Free, Whig(gamore)

**Prescient** Clairvoyant, Fly

**Prescribe(d), Prescription** Appoint, Assign, Dictate, Enjoin, Impose, Negative, Ordain, Positive, Rule, Scrip, Set, Statutory

**Prescription** Cipher, Decree, Direction, Formula, Medicine, Placebo, R, Rec, Receipt, Ritual, Specific

**Presence** Aspect, Bearing, Closeness, Company, Debut, Face, Hereness, Imminence, Mien, Real, Shechinah, Shekinah, Spirit

**Present(ation), Presented, Presenter, Presently** Ad sum, Advowson, Anchorman, Anon, Assists, Autocutie, Award, Befaba, Bestow, Bonsela, Boon, Bounty, Box, Breech, By, By and by, Cadeau, Congiary, Coram, Current, Debut, Dee-jay, Demo, Deodate, DJ, Donate, Dotal, Douceur, Dower, Emcee, Endemic, Endew, Endow, Endue, Enow, Étrenne, Exhibit, Existent, Exposition, Fairing, Feature, Format, Free-loader, Front-man, Gie, →**GIFT**, Give, Going, Grant, Gratuity, Hand, Here, Historical, Hodiernal, Holocene, Host, Image, Immediate, Inbuilt, Inst, Introduce, Jock(ey), Largess(e), Linkman, MC, Mod, Newsreader, Nonce, Now, Nuzzer, Offering, On hand, Porrect, Pose, Potlach, Pr, Prevailing, Produce, Proffer, Pro-tem, Put, Render, Rendition, Serve-up, Show, Slice, Stage, Study, Submit, Tense, The now, There, Tip, Today, Trojan horse, Vee-jay, Window dressing, Xenium, Yeven

**Preserve(d), Preservation, Preservative, Preserver** Additive, Bottle, Burnettize, Can, Chill, Chow-chow, Cocoon, Confect, Confiture, Corn, Creosote, Cure, Damson cheese, Dehydrate, Dry, Eisel, Embalm, Enshield, Enshrine, Fixative, Formaldehyde, Formalin, Freeze, Guard, Hain, Hesperides, Index link, Jam, Jerk, Keep, Kinin, Kipper, Konfyt, Kyanise, Lay up, Life, Lifebelt, →**MAINTAIN**, Marmalade, Mothball, Mummify, National Trust, On ice, Paraben, Pectin, Peculiar, Piccalilli, Pickle, Pot, Powellise, Quince, Quinoline, Salt(petre), Salve, Saut, Season, Souse, Store, Stratify, Stuff, Sweetmeat, Tanalith, Tanalized, Tar, Tin, Vinegar, Waterglass

**Preshrunk** Sanforized®

**Preside(nt)** Abe, Adams, Allende, Arthur, Ataturk, Banda, Botha, Buchanan, Bush, Carter, Chair, Chief Barker, Childers, Chirac, Cleveland, Clinton, Coolidge, Coty, Dean, De Gaulle, Director, Eisenhower, Fillmore, Ford, Garfield, Grand Pensionary, Grant, Harding, Harrison, Hayes, Hoover, Ike, Jackson, Jefferson, Johnson, Kennedy, Kruger, Lead, Lincoln, Madison, Mitterand, Moderator, Monroe, Mugabe, Nixon, Old Hickory, P, Peron, Polk, Pompidou, Pr(a)eses, Prexy, Reagan, Roosevelt, Sa(a)dat, Speaker, Superintendent, Supervisor, Taft, Taylor, Tito, Truman, Tyler, Van Buren, Vasquez, Veep, Washington, Wilson, Yeltsin

**Press(ed), Pressing, Pressure** Acute, Aldine, Armoire, Atmospheric, Bar, Barometer, Bench, Blackmail, Blood, Bramah, Button, Cabinet, Chivvy, Cider, Clarendon, Click, Closet, Clothes, Coerce, Compact, Compression, Copying, Cram, Crease, Crimp, Critical, Crowd, Crush, Cupboard, Cylinder, Dragoon, Drill, Dun, Durable, Duress, Duresse,

Enforcement, Enslave, Exigent, Filter, Flat-bed, Fleet St, Fluid, Fly, Folding, Force, Fourth estate, Free, Full-court, Goad, Greenmail, Gutter, Hasten, Head, Heat, Herd, Hie, High, Hothouse, Hug, Hurry, Hustle, Hydraulic, Hydrostatic, Impact, Impinge, Important, Importune, Inarm, Instant, Intense, Iron, Isobar, Jam, Jostle, Knead, Leverage, Lie, Lobby, Low, Make, Mangle, Megabar, Microbar, Mill, Minerva, Newspapers, Obligate, Oil, Onus, Osmotic, PA, Palpate, Partial, Pascal, Peer, Permanent, Persist, Piezo-, Ply, Prease, Printing, Private, Psi, Pump, → **PUSH**, Racket, Ram, Ratpack, Record, Recruit, Reportage, Reporter, Ridge, Roll, Root, Rotary, Rounce, Rub, Rush, Samizdat, Sandwich, Screw, Scrooge, Scrouge, Scrowdge, Scrum, Serr(e), Sit, Speed, Spur, Squash, Squeeze, Stanhope, Static, Stop, Strain(t), Stress, Tax, Tension, Thlipsis, Threap, Three-line-whip, Threep, Throng, Throttle, Thrutch, Torr, Tourniquet, Tread, Turgor, → **URGE**, Urgence, Urgency, Vanity, Vapour, Vice, Waid(e), Wardrobe, Weight, Wine, Wring, Yellow

**Press agent** Flack, Spin doctor

**Press-gang** Crimp, Force, Impress, Shanghai

**Pressman** Bramah, Ed, Journalist, Journo, PRO, Reporter, Twicer

**Prestidigitate(r)** Conjure, Juggle, Legerdemain, Magician, Palm

**Prestige, Prestigious** Asma, Cachet, Credit, Distinguished, Fame, Influence, Izzat, Kudos, Mana, Notable, Status

**Presume, Presumably, Presumption, Presumptuous** Allege, Arrogant, Audacity, Believe, Bold, Brass, Cocksure, Cocky, Doubtless, → **EXPECT**, Familiar, Forward, Gall, Impertinent, Insolent, Liberty, Outrecuidance, Overweening, Pert, Probably, Put upon, Suppose, Uppish, Upstart, Whipper-snapper

**Pretence, Pretend(er), Pretext** Act, Affect(ation), Afflict, Assume, Blind, Bluff, Bogus, Cant, Charade, Charlatan, Claim, Claimant, Cover, Cram, Dauber(y), Dissemble, Dissimulate, Dive, Excuse, False, Feign, Feint, Gondolier, Guise, Hokum, Humbug, Hypocrisy, Impersonation, Impostor, Jactitation, Kid(stakes), Lambert Simnel, Let-on, Make-believe, Malinger, Masquerade, Obreption, Old, Ostensible, Parolles, Perkin Warbeck, Play act, Plea, Pose, Pretension, Profess, Pseud(o), Quack, Sham, Simulate, Stale, Stalking-horse, Subterfuge, Suppose, Swanking, Warbeck, Would-be, Young

**Pretentious(ness), Pretension** Arty(-farty), Bombast, Chi-chi, Fantoosh, Fustian, Gaudy, Grandiose, High-falutin(g), Kitsch, La-di-da, Lady Muck, Orotund, Ostentatious, Overblown, Paraf(f)le, Pompous, Ponc(e)y, Pseud(o), Sciolism, Show, Showy, Snob, Snobbish, Squirt, Tat, Tattie-peelin, Tinhorn, Toffee-nosed, Uppity, Upstart, Vulgar, Wanky, Whippersnapper

**Pretty** Attractive, Becoming, Bobby-dazzler, Chocolate-box, Comely, Cute, Dear, Decorate, Dish, Elegant, Fair(ish), Fairway, Fetching, Inconie, Incony, Keepsaky, Kind of, Looker, Moderately, Pass, Peach, Personable, Picturesque, Primp, Pulchritudinous, Purty, Quite, Rather, Sweet, Twee, Winsome

**Pre-Union** Antenati

**Prevail(ing)** Dominate, Endure, Go, Induce, Outweigh, Persist, Persuade, Predominant, Preponderate, Reign, Ring, Triumph, Victor, Win

**Prevalent, Prevalence** Catholic, Common, Currency, Dominant, Endemic, Epidemic, Obtaining, Rampant, Rife, Set in, Widespread

**Prevaricate, Prevarication** Equivocate, Hedge, Lie, Runaround, Stall, Whiffle, Whittie-whattie

**Prevent(ion), Prevent(at)ive** Avert, Bar, Block, Daidzein, Debar, Deter, Disallow, Disenable, Dissuade, Embar, Estop, Foil, Foreclose, Forfend, Hamper, Help, Hinder, Hold back, Impound, Inhibit, Keep, Let, Nobble, Obstruct, Obturation, Obviate, Preclude, Prophylactic, Save, Sideline, Stop, Theriac, Thwart, Trammel

**Preview** Foretaste, Sneak, Taster, Trailer, Vernissage

**Previous(ly)** Afore, Already, Antecedent, Backlog, Before, Earlier, Ere(-now), Fore, Foreran, Former, Hitherto, Old, Once, Prior, Whilom

**Prey** Booty, Currie, Curry, Feed, Kill, Pelt, Plunder, Predate, Proul, Prowl, Quarry, Raven, Ravin(e), Soyle, Spreagh, Victim

**Price(d), Pricing, Price-raising, Pricy** Appraise, Asking, Assess, Bride, Charge, Consequence, Contango, →**COST**, Cost-plus, Dearth, Due, Evens, Exercise, Expense, Factory-gate, Fare, Fee, Fiars, Hammer, Hire, Intervention, Issue, Limit, List, Lobola, Loco, Market, Mark up, Offer, Packet, Perverse, Predatory, Prestige, Purchase, Quotation, Quote, Rack, Ransom, Rate, Regrate, Reserve, Sale, Selling, Shadow, Sky high, Song, Spot, Starting, Street value, Striking, Subscription, Toll, Trade, Unit, Upset, Valorise, Value, Vincent, Weregild, Wergeld, Wergild, Worth, Yardage

**Priceless** Comic, Invaluable, Killing, Unique

**Prick(ed), Prickle, Prickly** Acanaceous, Acanthus, Accloy, Argemone, Arrect, Bearded, Brakier, Bramble, Brog, Bunya, Cactus, Cloy, Cnicus, Echinate, Goad, Gore, Gorse, Hedgehog, Hedgepig, Impel, Inject, Jab, Jag, Jaggy, Jook, Juk, Kali, Penis, Perse, Pierce, Prod, Prog, Puncture, Rowel, Rubus, Ruellia, Seta, Setose, Smart, Spicula, Spinate, Stab, Star-thistle, Stimulus, Sting, Tattoo, Tatu, Teasel, Thistle, Thorn, Tingle, Urge, Whin

**Prickly heat** Miliaria

**Prickly-pear** Opuntia, Tuna

**Pride** Arrogance, Bombast, Brag, Conceit, Elation, Esprit de corps, Glory, Hauteur, Hubris, Inordinate, Lions, London, Machismo, Plume, Preen, Purge, Triumphalism, Vainglory, Vanity

**Priest(ess), Priests** Aaron, Abaris, Abbess, Abbot, Ananias, Annas, Archimandrite, Bacchae, Bacchantes, Baptes, Becket, Bonze, Brahmin, Caiaphas, Cardinal, Celebrant, Clergyman, Cleric, Club, Cohen, Concelebrant, Corybant(es), Curé, Dalai Lama, Druid, Eli, Elisha, Exorcist, Father, Fetial, Flamen, Fr, Habacuc, Habakkuk, Hero, Hierarch, Hieratic, Hierophant, High, H(o)ungan, Io, Jethro, John, Kohen, Lack-Latin, Lama, Laocoon, Lazarist, Levite, Lucumo, Mage, Magus, Mallet, Mambo, Marabout, Mass, Mess, Metropolitan, Minister, Missionary, Monsignor, Mufti, Non-juror, Norma, Oratorian, Ordinand, P, Padre, Papa, Parish, Parson, Pastor, Patercove, Patrico, Pawaw, Père, Pontifex, Pontiff, Pope, Pope's knight, Powwow, Pr, Preacher, Prelate, Presbyter, Prior(ess), Pujari, Pythia, Pythoness, Rabbi, Rebbe, Rector, Rev, Sacerdotal, Salian, Samuel, Savonarola, Seminarian, Shaman, Shaveling, Sir John Lack-Latin, Sky pilot, Spoiled, Tohunga, Turbulent, Usager, Vestal, Vicar, Vivaldi, Worker, Zadok, Zymite

**Prig(gish)** Dandy, Fop, Humbug, Nimmer, Pilfer, Prim, Prude, Puritan

**Prim** Demure, Governessy, Mun, Neat, Old-maidish, Perjink, Preceese, Precise, Proper, Schoolma'amish, Starchy

**Prim(a)eval** Ancient, Prehistoric, Primitive

**Primacy, Primate** Angwantibo, Ape, Australopithecus, Aye-aye, Bandar, Bigfoot, Biped, Bishop, Bush baby, Cardinal, Catar(r)hine, Colobus, Ebor, Gibbon, Hanuman, Hominid, Jackanapes, King Kong, Langur, Lemur, Loris, Macaque, Magot, Mammal, Marmoset, →**MONKEY**, Orang, Pongid, Potto, Prosimian, Protohuman, Quadruman, Ramapithecus, Rhesus, Sifaka, Simian, Slender loris, Tarsier, Wanderoo, Zinjanthropus

**Prima donna** Diva, Patti, Star

**Prime(r), Primary, Priming** Arm, Basic, Bloom, Cardinal, Charging, Chief, Choice, Claircolle, Clearcole, Clerecole, Closed, Detonator, Direct, Donat, Donet, Election, Enarm, Fang, First, Flower, Heyday, Mature, Open, Original, Paint, Paramount, Peak, Principal, Radical, Remex, Sell-by-date, Supreme, Thirteen, Tip-top, Totient, Totitive, Valuable, Windac, Windas, Ylem

**Prime Minister** Aberdeen, Ahern, Asquith, Attlee, Baldwin, Balfour, Begin, Bute, Callaghan, Campbell-Bannerman, Canning, Chamberlain, Chatham, Churchill, Dewan, Diefenbaker, Disraeli, Diwan, Eden, Gladstone, Grafton, Grand Vizier, Grey, Heath, Home, Iron Duke, Leaderene, Liverpool, Lloyd George, Macdonald, Macmillan, Major, Melbourne, North, Number Ten, Palmerston, Peel, Perceval, Pitt, PM, Premier, Rockingham, Shastri, Tanaiste, Taoiseach, Thatcher, Trudeau, Walpole, Wilson, Winston

**Primitive** Aborigine, Amoeba, Antediluvian, Arabic, Archaic, Atavistic, Barbaric, Caveman, Crinoid, Crude, Early, Elemental, Eozoon, Evolué, Feather-star, Fundamental, Hunter-gatherer, Medi(a)eval, Naive, Neanderthal, Neolithic, Oidia, Old, Persian, Prim(a)eval, Primordial, Pro, Prothyl(e), Protomorphic, Protyl(e), Radical, Rudimentary, Savage, Subman, Turkish, Uncivilised, Ur, Zygote

**Primordial** Blastema, Earliest, Fundamental, Original

**Primrose, Primula** Auricula, Bear's ear, Bird's eye, Cape, Cowslip, Evening, League, Oenothera, Onagra, Ox-lip, Pa(i)gle, Rosebery, Vicar, Yellow

**Prince(ly)** Ahmed, Albert, Ameer, Amir, Amphitryon, Anchises, Arjuna, Atheling, Barmecide, Black, Cadmus, Caliph, Chagan, Charming, Crown, Czarevich, Donalbain, Elector, Emir, Equerry, Eugene, Florizel, Fortinbras, Gaekwar, Ganymede, Gospodar, Guicowar, Hal, Hamlet, Highness, Hospodar, Huzoor, Igor, Inca, Infante, Jason, Khan, Ksar, Lavish, Lucumo, Maharaja, Margrave, Meleager, Merchant, Mir, Mirza, Nawab, Nizam, Noble, Orange, Otto, P, Pantagruel, Paris, Pendragon, Pirithous, Porphyrogenite, Potentate, Rainier, Rajah, Rana, Ras, Rasselas, Ratoo, Ratu, Regal, RH, Rudolph, Rupert, Serene, Sharif, Shereef, Sherif, Siegfried, Student, Tengku, Tereus, Troilus, Tsar(evich), Tunku, Upper Roger

**Princess** Anastasia, Andromache, Andromeda, Anne, Ariadne, Begum, Creusa, Czarevna, Czarista, Danae, Di(ana), Electra, Electress, Eudocia, Europa, Grace, Helle, Hermione, Hesione, Ida, Imogen, Infanta, Isabella, Iseult, Isolde, Jezebel, Maharanee, Maharani, Medea, Palatine, Philomela, Pocahontas, Procne, Rani, Regan, Sadie, Sara(h), Tou Wan, Tsarevna, Tsarista, Turandot, Yseult

**Principal** Arch, Capital, Central, →**CHIEF**, Decuman, Especial, First, Foremost, Grand, Head, Headmaster, Leading, Lion's share, Main(stay), Major, Mass, Mistress, Protagonist, Ringleader, Special, Staple, Star, Top banana, Uppermost

**Principality** Andorra, Flanders, Liechtenstein, Moldavia, Moldova, Monaco, Muscovy, Orange, Wal(l)achia, Wales

**Principle(s), Principled** Accelerator, Animistic, Anthropic, Archimedes, Aufbau, Axiom, Basis, Bernouilli, Brocard, Canon, Carnot, Code, Contradiction, Correspondence, Cosmological, Credo, Creed, Criterion, Cui bono, Cy pres, D'Alembert's, Doctrine, Dogma, Element, Entelechy, Equivalence, Essential, Estoppel, Ethic, Exclusion, Fermat's, First, Fourier, Gause's, Geist, Generale, Germ, Greatest happiness, Ground rule, Guideline, Hard line, Heisenberg uncertainty, Hinge, Honourable, Huygen's, Ideal, Indeterminacy, Key, Law, Least time, Le Chatelier's, Lights, Logos, Methodology, Modus, Morality, Object soul, Occam's razor, Organon, Ormazd, Ormuzd, Pauli-exclusion, Peter, Plank, Platform, Pleasure, Precautionary, Precept, Prescript, Psyche, Purseyism, Rationale, Reality, Reason, Reciprocity, Relativity, Remonstrance, Right-thinking, Rudiment, Rule, Sakti, Sanction, Scrupulous, Seed, Shakti, Spirit, Standard, Summum bonum, Tenet, Theorem, Ticket, Uncertainty, Uti possidetis, Verification, Vital, Weismannism, Word, Yang, Yin

**Prink** Beautify, Bedeck, Dress

**Print(er), Printing** A la poupée, Aldine, Baskerville, Batik, Benday, Bromide, Calotype, Caveman, Caxton, Chain, Chapel, Chromo, Cibachrome, Cicero, Collotype, Compositor, Contact, Copperplate, Counter, Creed, Cyclostyle, Dab, Dot matrix, Duotone, Electrostatic, Electrothermal, Electrotint, Electrotype, Elzevir, Engrave, Etching, Ferrotype, Film set, Fine, Flexography, Font, Gravure, Gurmukhi, Gutenberg, Half-tone, Hard copy, Hectograph, Heliotype, HMSO, Image, Impact, Impress, Incunabula, India, Ink-jet, Intaglio, Italic, Jobbing, Laser, Letterpress, Letterset, Line, Line-engraving, Lino-cut, Lithograph, Logotype, Lower-case, Matrix, Metallographer, Mezzotint, Mimeograph®, Monotype®, Moon, Non-impact, Off-line, Offset, Offset litho, Old-face, Oleo, Oleograph, Opaline, Perfector, Perfect proof, Phototype, Plate, Platinotype, Positive, Press, Process, Publish, Release, Remarque, Report, Reproduction, Retroussage, Reverse, Rotogravure, Run off, Samizdat, Screen, Serigraph, Ship, Shout, Silk-screen, Small, Smoot, Splash, Spore, Stamp, Stenochrome, Stereotype, Stonehand,

Strike, Thermal, Three-colour, Thumb, Thumb mark, Trichromatic, Typesetter, Typewriter, Typography, Typothetae, Whorl, Woodburytype, Woodcut, Xerography, Xylograph, Zincograph

**Printing-press** Rounce

**Print out** Hard copy

**Prior(ity)** Abbot, Afore, Antecedent, Anterior, Aperture, Earlier, Former, Grand, Hitherto, Monk, Outweigh, Overslaugh, Pre-, Precedence, Prefard, Preference, Previous, Privilege, Shutter, Triage, Until

▸ **Prise** *see* PRIZE(S)

**Prism(s), Prismatic** Catadioptric, Iriscope, Nicol, Periaktos, Rhombohedron, Spectrum, Teinoscope, Wollaston

**Prison** Albany, Alcatraz, Bagnio, Barracoon, Bastille, Belmarsh, Big house, Bin, Bird, Boob, Bridewell, Brig, Brixton, Bullpen, Cage, Can, Carceral, Cell, Chillon, Chok(e)y, Clink, Club, College, Confine, Cooler, Coop, Counter, Dartmoor, Dispersal, Dungeon, Durance, Encage, Fleet, Fotheringhay, Gaol, Glass-house, Guardhouse, Guardroom, Gulag, Hokey, Holloway, Hoos(e)gow, Hulk(s), Internment, → JAIL, Jug, Kitty, Labour camp, Limbo, Little-ease, Lob's pound, Lock-up, Logs, Lumber, Marshalsea, Massymore, Mattamore, Maze, Newgate, Nick, Oflag, On ice, Open, Panopticon, Parkhurst, Pen, Penitentiary, Pentonville, Pit, Pok(e)y, Porridge, Pound, Princetown, Quad, Quod, Rasp-house, Reformatory, Roundhouse, Scrubs, Shop, Sing-Sing, Slammer, Spandau, Stalag, State, Stir, Strangeways, Supermax, The Leads, Tol(l)booth, Tower, Tronk, Wandsworth, Wormwood Scrubs

**Prisoner** Canary-bird, Captive, Collegian, Collegiate, Con(vict), Detainee, Detenu, Hostage, Inmate, Internee, Jailbird, Lag, Lifer, Parolee, Passman, Political, POW, Rule 43, Trustee, Trusty, Yardbird, Zek

**Pristine** Fire-new, Flawless, Fresh, New, Original, Unmarked, Unspoiled

**Private(ly), Privacy** Ain, Apart, Aside, Atkins, Auricular, Buccaneer, Byroom, Clandestine, Close, Closet, Conclave, Confidential, Enisle(d), Entre nous, Esoteric, Homefelt, Hush-hush, In camera, Individual, Inmost, Inner, Intimate, Inward, Non-com, Non-governmental, Own, Personal, Piou-piou, Poilu, Postern, Proprietary, Pte, Rank(er), Retired, Retreat, Sanctum, Sapper, Secluded, Secret, Sequestered, Several, Single soldier, → SOLDIER, Squaddie, Sub rosa, Tommy, Under the rose

**Privateer(s)** Buccaneer, Corsair, Freebooter, Marque(s), Pirate

**Privation** Hardship, Penury, Want

**Privilege(d)** Birthright, Blest, Charter, Curule, Enviable, Exempt, Favour, Franchise, Freedom, Haves, Indulgence, Insider, Letters patent, Liberty, Mozarab, Nomenklatura, Octroi, Palatine, Parliamentary, Patent, Prerogative, Pryse, Regale, Regalia, Right, Sac, Sloane

**Privy** Apprised, Can, Close-stool, Closet, In on, Intimate, Jakes, John, Loo, Necessary, Reredorter, Secret, Sedge, Siege

**Prize(s), Prizewinner, Prized** Acquest, Acquisitive, Apple, Archibald, Assess, Award, Best, Booby, Booker, Bravie, Bronze, Capture, Champion, Cherish, Consolation, Creach, Cup, Dux, Efforce, → ESTEEM, Force, Garland, Gold, Goncourt, Grice, Honour, Jackpot, Jemmy, Lever, Loot, Lot, Man Booker, Money, Nobel, Palm, Pay out, Pearl, Pewter, Pie, Plum, Plunder, Pot, Premium, Prix Goncourt, Pulitzer, Purse, Ram, Reprisal, → REWARD, Rollover, Rosette, Russell, Scalp, Ship, Silver, Spreaghery, Sprechery, Stakes, Sweepstake, Taonga, Tern, Treasure, Trophy, Turner, Value, Win, Wooden spoon

**Pro** Aye, Coach, For, Harlot, Moll, Paid, Tramp, Yea, Yes

▸ **Pro** *see* PROSTITUTE

**Probable, Probability** Apparent, Belike, Classical, Conditional, Enthymeme, Ergodic, Feasible, Likely, Marginal, Mathematical, Possible, Posterior, Prior, Proball, Verisimilar

**Probation(er)** Cadet, Novice, Novitiate, P-plater, Stibbler, Test, Trainee, Trial

**Probe** Antenna, Bore, Bougie, Canopus, Cassini, Corot, Delve, Dredge, Examine, Explore, Fathom, Feeler, Fossick, Galileo, Gene(tic), Giotto, Inquire, Investigate, Magellan,

Mariner, Mars Surveyor, Otoscope, Palpitate, Pelican, Pioneer, Poke, Pump, Ranger, →SEARCH, Seeker, Sonde, Sound, Space, Stardust, Stylet, Tent, Thrust, Tracer, Venera

**Probity** Honour, Integrity, Justice

**Problem(s), Problematic** Acrostic, Anuria, Black spot, BO, Boyg, Brainteaser, Business, Can of worms, Catch, Challenge, Conundrum, Crisis, Crux, Difficulty, Dilemma, Egma, Enigma, Facer, Fault, Glitch, Handful, Hang-up, Hassle, Headache, Hiccup, Hitch, How d'ye do, Hurdle, Indaba, Issue, Knot(ty), Koan, Mind-body, Miniature, Musive, Mystery, Net, Nuisance, Obstacle, Pons asinorum, Poser, Predicament, Quandary, Question, Re, Rebus, Retractor, Riddle, Rider, Snag, Snarl-up, Sorites, Stimy, Sum, Teaser, Teething, Thing, Thorny, Tickler, Toughie, Trilemma, Trouble, Tsuris, Weed, Yips

**Problem-solving** Synectics

**Proboscis** Haustellum, Promuscis, Snout, Trunk

**Proceed(s), Proceeding, Procedure** Acta, Afoot, Algorithm, Assets, Case, Continue, Course, Derive, Do, Drift, Drill, Emanate, Fand, Firedrill, Flow, Fond, Form, Goes, Haul, Heimlich, Issue, Machinery, March, Mechanics, Method, Mine, MO, Modal, Move, On (course), Paracentesis, Pass, Point of order, Practice, Praxis, Process, Profit, Protocol, Punctilio, Pursue, Put, Rake, Receipts, Return, Rigmarole, Rite, Ritual, Rope(s), Routine, Sap, Steps, Subroutine, System, Take, Tootle, Use, Yead(s), Yede, Yeed

**Process(ing), Procession, Processor** Acromion, Action, Additive, Ala, Ambarvalia, Anger, Axon, Ben Day, Bessemer, Bosch, Calcination, Castner, Catalysis, Cavalcade, Cibation, Coction, Concoction, Congelation, Conjunction, Corso, Cortège, Cyanide, DAP, Demo, Diagonal, Dissolution, Double, Exaltation, Exequy, Fermentation, Frack(ing), Front-end, Haber(-Bosch), Handle, Managing, Markov, Method, Moharram, Mond, Motorcade, Muharram, Multiple pounding, Multiplication, Number-crunch, Odontoid, Olecranon, Open hearth, Operation, -osis, Pageant, Parade, Parallel, Paseo, Photosynthesis, Pipeline, Planar, Pomp, Primary, Projection, Pterygoid, Puddling, Pultrusion, Purex, Putrefaction, Recycle, Ritual, Screen, Secondary, Separation, Series, Silkscreen, Single, Skimmington, Solvay, Speciation, Spinous, Sterygoid, String, Sublimation, Subtractive, Thermite, Thought, Tie and dye, Titration, Torchlight, Train, Transaction, Transverse, Treat, Trial, Turn(a)round, Unit, Vermiform, Xephisternum, Xiphoid, Zygomatic

**Proclaim, Proclamation** Announce, Annunciate, Ban, Blaze, Blazon, Boast, Broadsheet, Cry, Decree, Edict, Enounce, Enunciate, Herald, Indiction, Kerygma, Manifesto, Oyez, Preconise, Predicate, Profess, Publish, Ring, Shout, Trumpet, Ukase

**Proconsul** Ape, Hominid

**Procrastinate, Procrastinating, Procrastinator** Cunctator, Defer, Delay, Dilatory, Dilly-dally, Hang-fire, Linger, Pettifog, Postpone, Shelve, Temporise, Vacillate

**Procreate** Beget, Engender, Generate, Initiate

**Procrustean** Conformity, Stretcher

**Proctor** Agent, King's, Monitor, Prog, Proggins, Proxy, Queen's

**Procurator, Procure(r)** Achieve, Acquire, Aunt, Crimp, Earn, Get, Induce, Naunt, Obtain, Pander, Pilate, Pimp, Sort, Suborn

**Prod** Cattle, Egg, Goad, Impel, Jab, Job, Jog, Nudge, Poke, Pote, Powter

**Prodigal** Costly, Extravagant, Free, Lavish, Profligate, Scattergood, Spendall, Unthrift, Wanton, Wasteful, Waster

**Prodigious, Prodigy** Abnormal, Amazing, Huge, Immense, Infant, Little wonder, Monster, Monument, Mozart, Phenomenal, Portentous, Tremendous, Wonder, Wonderwork, Wunderkind

**Produce(r), Producing** Afford, Bear, Beget, Breed, Cause, Create, Crop, De Mille, Disney, D'Oyly Carte, Dramaturg, Ean, Edit, Effect, Engender, Entail, Evoke, Exhibit, Extend, Fabricate, Fruit, Generate, Get, Giulini, Goldwyn, Grow, Home-grown, Impresario, Ingenerate, Issue, Kind, Make, Offspring, Onstream, Originate, Output, Outturn, Propage, Propound, Puttnam, Raise, Realise, Roach, Selznick, Sloganeer, Son,

Spawn, Spielberg, Stage, Supply, Teem, Throw, Tree, Trot out, Upcome, Wares, Whelp, Yield, Zeffirelli, Ziegfeld

▷ **Produces** *may indicate* an anagram

**Product(ion), Productive(ness), Productivity** Actualities, Apport, Artefact, Ashtareth, Ashtaroth, Astarte, Autogeny, Bore, Cartesian, Coefficient, Commodity, Creation, Cross, Depside, Dot, Drama, Effectual, End, Factorial, Fecund, Fertile, Fruit, Genesis, Global, Handiwork, Harvest, Inner, Line, Mass, Net domestic, Net national, Output, Outturn, Pair, Partial, Pastiche, Power(house), Primary, Profilic, Resinoid, Result, Rich, Scalar, Secondary, Set, Show, Speiss, Substitution, Uberous, Uberty, Vector, Waste, Work, Yield

▷ **Production** *may indicate* an anagram

**Proem** Foreword, Overture, Pre, Preface

**Profane, Profanation, Profanity** Blaspheming, Coarse, Coprolalia, Desecrate, Impious, Irreverent, Sacrilege, Unholy, Violate

**Profess(ed), Professor** Absent-minded, Academic, Acknowledge, Adjoint, Admit, Artist, Aspro, Asset, Assistant, Associate, Avow, Challenger, Claim, Declare, Disney, Emeritus, Full, Higgins, Hodja, Kho(d)ja, Know-all, Ostensible, Own, Practise, Pundit, Regent, Regius, RP, STP, Visiting

**Profession(al)** Accomplished, Admission, Assurance, Avowal, Buppy, Business, Calling, Career, Creed, Expert, Métier, Practice, Practitioner, Pretence, Pursuit, Regular, Salaried, Skilled, Trade, Vocation, Yuppie

**Proffer** Give, Present, Proposition, Tender

**Proficiency, Proficient** Able, Accomplished, Adept, Alert, Dan, Expert, Forte, Master, Past master, Practised, Skill, Technique

**Profile** Analysis, Contour, Cross, Half-cheek, Half-face, High, Long, Loral, Low, Market, Outline, Silhouette, Sketch, Statant, T(h)alweg, Vignette

**Profit(able), Profiteer, Profits** Advantage, Arbitrage, Asset, Avail, Benefit, Bestead, Boon, Boot, Bunce, Cash cow, Cash in, Cere, Clear, Divi(dend), Earn, Economic, Edge, Emblements, Emoluments, Expedient, Exploit, Extortionist, Fat, Fruitful, Gain, Gelt, Graft, Gravy, Grist, Gross, Income, Increase, Increment, In pocket, Issue, Jobbery, Juicy, Landshark, Leech, Lucrative, Makings, Margin, Melon, Mesne, Milch cow, Mileage, Moneymaker, Money-spinner, Negative, Net, Overcharge, Pay(ing), Pay (off), Perk, Pickings, Plummy, Preacquisition, Productive, Quids in, Rake-off, Return, Reward, Royalty, Scalp, Spoils, Tout, Use, Usufruct, Utile, Utility, Vail, Windfall

**Profligate** Corinthian, Corrupt, Degenerate, Dissolute, Extravagant, Lech(er), Libertine, Lorel, Losel(l), Oatmeal, Rakehell, Reprobate, Roué, Spend-all, Spendthrift, Unprincipled, Wastrel

**Profound, Profundity** Abstract, Altum, Bottomless, Complete, Deep(-seated), Depth, Intense, Recondite

**Profuse, Profusion** Abounding, Abundant, Copious, Excess, Free, Galore, Lavish, Liberal, Lush, Quantity, Rank, Rich, Two-a-penny

**Progenitor, Progenitrix** Ancestor, Ma, Predecessor, Sire, Stock

**Progeny** Burd, Children, Descendants, Fruit, Issue, Offspring, Seed

**Prognosis** Forecast, Prediction

**Prognosticate, Prognostication** Augur, Foretell, Omen, Predict, Presage, Prophesy

▶ **Program(ming), Programming language, Programmer** *see* COMPUTER PROGRAM(S)

**Programme(s)** Agenda, Broadcast, Card, Chat show, Code, Community, Corrida, Countdown, Docudrama, Documentary, Docusoap, Docutainment, Double-header, Dramedy, Entitlement, Episode, Est, Event, Faction, Feature, Fly-on-the-wall, Format, Infotainment, Linear, Live show, Mastermind, Medicaid, Miniseries, Minisode, Mockumentary, Neighbours, Neurolinguistic, Newscast, Newsreel, PDL, Phone-in, Pilot, Plan, Playbill, Prank, Race card, Radiothon, RECHAR, Regimen, Report, Satellite, Schedule, Scheme, Sepmag, Serial, Shockumentary, Show, Simulcast, Sitcom, Sked,

Soap, Software, Sportscast, Sustaining, Syllabus, System, Telecast, Teleplay, Telethon, Timetable, Twelve step, Webcast, YPO

**Progress(ive), Progression** →**ADVANCE**, Afoot, Arithmetic, Arpeggio, Avant garde, Course, Endosmometric, Fabian, Flow, Forge, Forward, Forward-looking, Gain, Geometric, Get along, Go (ahead), Growth, Harmonic, Headway, Incede, Inroads, Knight's, Left, Leftist, Liberal, Move, Onwards, Paraphonia, Periegesis, Pilgrim's, Prosper, Rack, Radical, Rake's, Reformer, Roll, Run, Sequence, Series, Step, Stepping stone, Vaunce, Way, Yead, Yede, Yeed

**Prohibit(ed), Prohibition(ist)** Ban, Block, Debar, Dry, Embargo, Enjoin, Estop, Forbid, Hinder, Index, Injunct, Interdict, Noli-me-tangere, Off-limits, Preclude, Prevent, Pussyfoot, Rahui, Suppress, Taboo, Tabu, Verboten, Veto

**Project(ile), Projecting, Projection, Projector** Aim, Ammo, Antitragus, Assignment, Astral, Astrut, Axonometric, Azimuthal, Baby, Ball, Ballistic, Beetle, Bullet, Butt, Buttress, Cam, Canopy, Carina, Cast, Catapult, Channel, Cinerama®, Cog, Conceive, Condyle, Conic, Conical, Console, Corbel, Coving, Cremaster, Crossette, Cutwater, Dendron, Denticle, Diascope, Discus, Ear, Eaves, Echinus, Elance, Enterprise, Epidiascope, Episcope, Excrescence, Exsert, Extrapolate, Extrude, Fet(ter)lock, Flange, Gair, Gore, Grapeshot, Guess, Halter(e), Hangover, Helicity, Hoe, Homolosine, Housing, Human genome, Hurtle, Inion, Jut, Kern, Kinetoscope, Knob, Ledge, Lobe, Lug, Magic lantern, Malleolus, Manhattan, Map, Mercator, Mitraille, Mohole, Mollweide, Mucro, Mutule, Nab, Nose, Nunatak(er), Oblique, Olecranon, Opaque, Orillion, Orthogonal, Orthographic, Outcrop, Outjet, Outjut, Outrigger, Outshot, Overhang, Overhead, Oversail, Palmation, Peak, Peters', Pitch, Planetarium, Planisphere, Polyconic, Pork barrel, Prickle, Promontory, Prong, Propel, →**PROTRUDE**, Proud(er), Prow, Pseudopod, Quillon, Raguly, Roach, Rocket, Sail, Salient, Sally, Sanson-Flamsteed, Scaw, Scheme, Scrag, Screen, Shelf, Shot, Shrapnel, Sinusoidal, Skaw, Skeg, Slide, Sling, Snag, Snout, Spline, Sponson, Sprocket, Spur, Squarrose, Stand out, Stereopticon, Stick out, Stud, Tang, Tappet, Tenon, Thorn, Throw, Toe, Tongue, Tracer, Trimetric, Trippet, Trunnion, Turnkey, Turtleback, Tusk, Umbo, Underhung, Undertaking, Villiform, Villus, Vitascope, Whizzbang, Zenithal

**Prolapse** Procidence

**Proletarian, Proletariat** Jamahiriya, People, Plebeian, Popular

**Proliferate** Expand, Increase, Multiply, Propagate, Snowball, Teem

**Prolific** Abounding, Fecund, Fertile, Fruitful, Profuse, Teeming

**Prolix(ity)** Lengthy, Longueur, Prosaic, Rambling, Rigmarole, Verbose, Wire-draw, Wordy

**Prologue** Introduce, Preface

**Prolong(ed)** Continue, Drag out, Extend, Lengthen, Persistent, Protract, Sostenuto, Spin, Sustain

**Prom(enade)** Alameda, Boulevard, Cakewalk, Catwalk, Concert, Crush-room, Esplanade, Front, Mall, Parade, Paseo, Pier, Sea-front, Stroll, →**WALK**

**Prometheus** Fire

**Promethium** Pm

**Prominence, Prominent** Antitragus, Blatant, Bold, Colliculus, Condyle, Conspicuous, Egregious, Emphasis, Featured, Gonion, Headliner, High profile, Important, Insistent, Leading light, Luminary, Manifest, Marked, Mastoid, Noted, Obtrusive, Outstanding, Salient, Signal, Solar, Splash, Spotlight, Tall poppy, Teat, Toot, Tragus

**Promiscuous, Promiscuity** Casual, Chippie, Chippy, Demivierge, Fast, Free, Goer, Hornbag, Horny, Indiscriminate, Licentious, Light, Loose, Loslyf, Mixed, Motley, Pell-mell, Skanky(-ho), Slapper, Trollop, Wanton, Whoredom

**Promise, Promising** Accept, Agree, Assure, Augur, Auspicious, Avoure, Behest, Behight, Behote, Betrothal, Bode, Bright, Coming, Commit, Compact, Covenant, Earnest, Engagement, Foreshadow, Foretaste, Gratuitous, Guarantee, Hecht, Hest, Hete, Hight, IOU, Likely, Manifest, Oath, Parole, Pledge, Plight, Pollicitation, Potential, Pregnant, Recognisance, Recognizance, Resolution, Rosy, Sign, Sponsor, Swear, Tile, Troth, Undertake, Upbeat, Vow, Warranty, Word

**Promised land** Beulah, Canaan, Israel

**Promissory note** IOU, PN

**Promontory** Bill, Cape Sable, Cliff, Flamborough Head, Foreland, Giant's Causeway, Hatteras, →HEADLAND, Hoe, Hogh, Land's End, Mull, Mull of Galloway, Naze, Ness, Nose, Peak, Pillars of Hercules, Ras, Rock, Spit, The Lizard, Tintagel Head

**Promote(r), Promotion** Ad, Adman, Advance, Advancement, →ADVERTISE, Advocate, Aggrandise, Aid, Assist, Back, Banner ad, Blurb, Boost, Breed, Brevet, Buggins' turn, Campaign, Churn, Dog and pony show, Elevate, Encourage, Eulogy, Event, Exponent, Float, Foment, Foster, Further, Help, Hype, Incite, Increase, Kick upstairs, Leaflet, Lord of Misrule, Mailshot, Make, Market, Peddle, Plug, Pracharak, Prefer, Prelation, Promulgate, Provoke, Push, Queen, Raise, Rear, Remove, Roadshow, Run, Salutary, Sell, Sponsor, Spruik, Stage, Step (up), Subserve, Tendencious, Tendentious, Tout, Upgrade, Uplead, Uprate

**Prompt(er), Promptly, Promptness** Accelerate, Actuate, Alacrity, Autocue®, Believe, Cause, Celerity, Chop-chop, Cue, Early, Egg, Expeditious, Feed, Frack, Idiot-board, Immediate, Incite, Inspire, Instigate, Motivate, Move, On-the-nail, Opposite, Pernicious, Post-it note, Premove, Punctual, Quick, Ready, Sharp, Speed(y), Spur, Stage right, Stimulate, Stir, Sudden, Swift, Tight, Tit(e), Titely, Trigger, Tyte, Urgent

**Promulgate** Preach, Proclaim, Publish, Spread

**Prone** Apt, Groof, Grouf, Grovel, Laid back, Liable, Lying, Prostrate, Recumbent, Subject, Susceptible

**Prong** Fang, Fork, Grain, Peg, Tang, Tine

**Pronghorn** Cabrie, Cabrit

**Pronoun** Deictic, Impersonal, Itself, Oneself, Personal, Reciprocal, Relative

**Pronounce(d), Pronouncement** Adjudicate, Affirm, Agrapha, Articulate, Assert, Asseveration, Clear, Conspicuous, Declare, Definite, Dictum, Emphatic, Enunciate, Fatwa, Fiat, Indefinite, Marked, Opinion, Palatalise, Philosophise, Pontificate, Predication, Recite, Utter, Velarise, Vocal, Voice, Vote

**Pronto** PDQ

**Pronunciation** Betacism, Cacoepy, Delivery, Diction, Etacism, Itacism, Labiodental, Labionasal, Labiovelar, Lallation, Localism, Orthoepy, Phonetics, Plateasm, Proclitic, Received, Rhotacism, Sound, Syllabic, Tense

**Proof(s)** Acid test, Apagoge, Argument, Artist's, Assay, Bona fides, Confirmation, Corroboration, Direct, Evidence, Firm, Foundry, Galley, Godel's, India, Indirect, Justification, Lemma, Positive, Preif(e), Probate, Pull, Quality, Receipt, Refutation, Remarque, Reproduction, Resistant, Revision, Secure, Slip, Smoking gun, Strength, Test, Tight, Token, Trial, Upmake, Validity, Watertight

**Prop(s)** Airscrew, Becket, Bolster, Buttress, Clothes, Crutch, Dog-shore, Fulcrum, Leg, Loosehead, Misericord(e), Pit, Point d'appui, Punch(eon), Rance, Rest, Scotch, Set, Shore, Sprag, Spur, Staff, Stay, Stempel, Stemple, Stilt, Stoop, Stoup, Strut, Studdle, Stull, →SUPPORT, Tighthead, Trig, Underpin

**Propaganda, Propagandist** Agitprop, Ballyhoo, Black, Brainwashing, Chevalier, Doctrine, Exponent, Goebbels, Grey, Promotion, Psyop, Psywar, Publicity, Slogan, Spin doctor, White

**Propagate, Propagator, Propagation** Breed, Clone, Dispread, Generate, Graft, Hatch, Hotbed, Hothouse, Increase, Layering, Populate, Produce, Promulgate, Provine, Spread, Tan-bed

**Propel(ler), Propellor** Airscrew, Ca', Drive, Fin, Fling, Frogmarch, Launch, Leg, Lox, →MOVE, Oar(sman), Paddle, Pedal, Pole, Project, Push, Rotor, Row, Screw, Send, Tail rotor, Throw, Thruster, Tilt-rotor, Tractor, Twin-screw, Vane

**Propensity** Aptness, Bent, Inclination, Penchant, Tendency

**Proper(ly)** Ain, Convenance, Correct, Courteous, Decent, Decorous, Due, Eigen, En règle, Ethical, →FIT, Genteel, Governessy, Kosher, Legitimate, Maidenish, Nimity-pimity, Noun, Ought, Own, Pakka, Pathan, Prim, Pucka, Pukka, Puritanic, Real, Rightful, Seemly, Staid, Strait-laced, Suitable, Tao, Trew, True, Veritable, Well

**Property, Properties** Assets, Attribute, Aver, Belongings, Capacitance, Chattel, Chirality, Chose, Contenement, Dead-hand, Demesne, Des res, Dowry, Effects, Enclave, Enthalpy, Escheat, Escrow, Essence, Estate, Fee, Feu, Flavour, Fonds, Freehold, Goods, Haecceity, Hereditament, Heritable, Holding, Home, Hot, Hotchpot, Immoveable, Inertia, In rem, Intellectual, Jointure, Land, Leasehold, Living, Means, Mortmain, Mystique, Paraphernalia, Peculium, Personal, Personalty, Pertinent, Predicate, Premises, Private, Projective, Public, Quale, Quality, Real, Second home, Settlement, Stock, Stolen, Theft, Thixotropy, Time-share, Timocracy, Trait, Usucapion, Usucaption

**Prophesy, Prophecy, Prophesying, Prophet(s), Prophetess, Prophetic** Amos, Augur, Bab, Balaam, Calchas, Cassandra, Clairvoyant, Daniel, Deborah, Divine, Druid, Elias, Elijah, Elisha, Ezekiel, Ezra, Fatal, Fatidical, Forecast, Foretell, Former, Geomancer, Habakkuk, Haggai, Haruspex, Hosea, Is, Isa, Is(a)iah, Jeremiah, Joel, Jonah, Latter, Mahdi, Mahound, Major, Malachi, Mani, Mantic, Micah, Minor, Mohamet, Mohammed, Mopsus, Mormon, Moses, Mother Shipton, Nahum, Nathan, Necromancy, Nostradamus, Obadiah, Old Mother Shipton, Ominous, Oracle, Portend, Predictor, Prognosticate, Pythoness, Samuel, Second sight, Seer, Sibyl, Tipster, Tiresias, Vatic, Vaticinate, Völuspá, Weather, Zachariah, Zarathustra, Zechariah, Zephaniah, Zoroaster, Zwickau

**Prophylactic, Prophylaxis** Inoculation, Preventive, Serum, Vaccine, Variolation

**Propitiate** Appease, Atone, Pacify, Reconcile, Sop

**Propitious** Benign, Favourable, Lucky

**Proponent** Advocate, Backer, Partisan

**Proportion(ate)** Commensurable, Cotangent, Dimension, Fraction, Harmonic, Inverse, Percentage, Portion, Pro rata, Quantity, Quota, Ratio, Reason, Regulate, Relation, Sine, Size, Soum, Sowm, Symmetry, Tenor

**Propose(r), Proposal** Advance, Advocate, Aim at, Approach, Ask, Bid, Bill, Canvass, Eirenicon, Feeler, Fiancé, Idea, Irenicon, Mean, Motion, Move, Nominate, Offer, Overture, Plan, Pop, Premise, Proffer, Propound, Recommend, Resolution, Scheme, Slate, Submission, →SUGGEST, Table, Tender, Toast, Volunteer, Woot, Would

**Proposition** Asses' bridge, Axiom, Convertend, Corollary, Deal, Disjunction, Ergo, Hypothesis, Identical, Implicature, Lemma, Overture, Pons asinorum, Porism, Premise, Premiss, Rider, Sorites, Spec, Superaltern, Theorem, Thesis

**Propound** Advocate, Purpose, State

**Proprietor, Propriety** Bienséance, Convenance, Correctitude, Decorum, Etiquette, Grundy, Keeper, Lord, Master, Owner, Patron, Rectitude

**Prosaic** Common, Drab, Everyday, Flat, Humdrum, Matter of fact, Pedestrian, Tedious, Workaday

**Proscenium** Forestage

**Proscribe(d)** Exile, Forbid, Outlaw, Prohibit, Taboo, Tabu

**Prose, Prosy** Euphuism, Haikai, Polyphonic, Purple, Purple patch, Saga, Stich, Verbose, Version, Writing

**Prosecute, Prosecutor, Prosecution** Allege, Arraign, Avvogadore, Charge, Crown, Do, Double jeopardy, Fiscal, Furtherance, Impeach, Indict, Lord Advocate, Practise, Public, Pursue, Sue, Wage

**Proselytise(r), Proselytism** Convert, Indoctrination, Propagandism, Souper

**Prospect(or), Prospecting** Bellevue, Costean, Dowser, Explore, Forty-niner, Fossick, Future, Look-out, Mine, Opportunity, →OUTLOOK, Panorama, Perspective, Pleases, Possibility, Reefer, Scenery, Search, Sourdough, Street, Sweep-washer, View, Vista, Visto, Wildcatter

**Prospectus** Menu, Pathfinder

**Prosper(ity), Prospering, Prosperous** Aisha, Ay(e)sha, Blessed, Blossom, Boom, Do well, Fair, Fat cat, Flourish, Get ahead, Heyday, Mérimée, Opulent, Palmy, Sleek, →SUCCEED, Thee, Thrift, Thrive, Up, Warison, Wealth, Welfare, Well-heeled, Well-to-do, Well-to-live

**Prosthetic** Fals(i)e

**Prostitute, Prostitution** Brass, Broad, Bulker, Callet, Catamite, Chippie, Cockatrice, Cocotte, Comfort woman, Convertite, Debase, Dell, Demi-mondaine, Dolly-mop, Doxy, Drab, Fancy woman, Fille de joie, Floozie, Floozy, Grande cocotte, Harlot, Hetaera, Hetaira, Hierodule, Ho, Hooker, Hostess, Hustler, Jailbait, Laced mutton, Lady of the night, Loon, Loose-fish, Loose woman, Lowne, Madam, Magdalen(e), Moll, Mutton, Night-walker, Pict, Plover, Pole-cat, Poule, Pro, Public woman, Pug, Punk, Quail, Quiff, Rent-boy, Road, Rough trade, Scrubber, Shippie, Slap, Social evil, Stale, Stew, Streetwalker, Strumpet, Tart, Tramp, Trull, Venture, Wench, Whore, Working girl

**Prostrate, Prostration** Collapse, Exhausted, Fell, Flat, Flatling, Ko(w)tow, Laid, Lying, Obeisance, Overcome, Procumbent, Prone, Repent, Throw

**Protactinium** Pa

**Protagonist** Anti-hero, Leading man

**Protean** Amoebic, Fusible, Taro, Variable

**Protect(ed), Protection, Protective, Protector** Adonise, Aegis, Aircover, Alexin, Amulet, Antigropelo(e)s, Arm, Armour, Asylum, Auspice, Barbican, Bastion, Bestride, Bield, Bodyguard, Boom, Brolly, Buckler, Bullbar, Bullet-proof, Cathodic, Chaffron, Chain mail, Chamfrain, Chamfron, Charm, Cherish, Cloche, Coat, Cocoon, Coddle, Coleor(r)hiza, Conserve, Copyright, Cosset, Cover, Covert, Crash helmet, Cromwell, Curb, Cushion, Danegeld, Data, Defend, Defilade, Degauss, Diaper, Egis, Enamel, Entrenchment, Escort, Estacade, Faun, Featherbed, Fence, Fender, Firewall, Flank, Gobo, Goggle, Grill(e), Groundsheet, Guard(ian), Gumshield, Hedge, House, Hurter, Immune, Inalienable, Indemnify, Indemnity, Indusium, Insulate, Insure, Integument, Keckle, Keep, Kickback, Klendusic, Kneepad, Lag, Lee, Listed, Mac(k)intosh, Mail, Male, Mentor, Mollycoddle, Mother, Mothproof, Mouthpiece, Mudguard, Muniment, Nannyish, Napkin, Nappy, Noddy suit, Noll, Nosey, Oliver, Ombrella, Orillion, Overall, Pad, Palladium, Parados, Parapet, Patent, Patron, Pelta, Penthouse, Police, Polytunnel, Pomander, Preserve, Procrypsis, Rabbit's foot, Radome, Rampart, Raymond, Reserve, Revetment, Ride shotgun, Sacrosanct, Safeguard, Sandbag, Save, Schanse, Schan(t)ze, Screen, Scug, Security, Serviette, Shadow, Sheathing, Sheeting, Shelter, →**SHIELD**, Skug, Souteneur, Splashback, Splashboard, Splasher, Starling, Stockade, Sunscreen, Sunshade, Supermax, Talisman, Telomere, Testa, Testudo, Thimble, Thumbstall, Tower, Tribune, Tribute, Tutelar, Twilled, Umbrella, Underlay, Underseal, Vaccine, Waist-cloth, Ward(ship), Warhead, Warrant, Weatherboard, Weatherproof, Weatherstrip, Windbreaker, Windshield, Wing, Winterweight, Write

**Protectorate** Qatar

**Protégé** Godson, Pupil, Tutee, Ward, Whiteheaded boy

**Protein** Complement, Conjugated, Repressor, Simple

---

## PROTEINS

| 3 letters: | 5 letters: | 6 letters: | Myosin |
|---|---|---|---|
| PSA | Abrin | Alexin | Ossein |
| RNA | Actin | Avidin | Pepsin |
| TSP | Lysin | Capsid | Tempeh |
| TVP | Mucin | Cyclin | |
| | Opsin | Enzyme | 7 letters: |
| 4 letters: | Pharm | Fibrin | Adipsin |
| CREB | Porin | Globin | Alanine |
| Meat | Prion | Gluten | Albumen |
| Soya | Quorn® | Lectin | Albumin |
| Zein | Renin | Leptin | Aleuron |
| | Ricin | Leucin | Elastin |
| | | Myogen | Fibroin |

Gelatin
Gliadin
Histone
Hordein
Isozyme
Legumin
Leucine
Nuclein
Opsonin
Pepsine
Peptone
Sarcode
Sericin
Spongin
Tubulin

**8 letters:**
Aleurone
Allergen
Amandine
Analogon
Antibody
Collagen
Copaxone®
Cytokine
Ferritin

Gliadine
Globulin
Glutelin
Integrin
Pellicle
Permease
Prolamin
Proteose
Pyrenoid
Ribosome
Spectrin
Troponin
Vitellin

**9 letters:**
Apoenzyme
Aquaporin
Capsomere
Fibrillin
Filaggrin
Flagellin
Luciferin
Myoglobin
Ovalbumin
Phaseolin
Prolamine

Properdin
Protamine
Sclerotin
Spirulina
Ubiquitin

**10 letters:**
Actomyosin
Bradykinin
Calmodulin
Caseinogen
Conchiolin
Dystrophin
Factor VIII
Ferredoxin
Fibrinogen
Huntingtin
Incaparina
Interferon
Lewy bodies
Lymphokine
Single-cell
Thrombogen
Toxalbumin

**11 letters:**
Angiostatin
Angiotensin
Haemoglobin
Haptoglobin
Interleukin
Lactalbumin
Prothrombin
Transferrin
Tropomyosin

**12 letters:**
Fibronectina
Neurotrophin
Serum albumin

**13 letters:**
Ceruloplasmin
Lactoglobulin
Macroglobulin
Serum globulin

**14 letters:**
Immunoglobulin

---

**Protest(er)** Abhor, Andolan, Anti, Aver, Avouch, Black Bloc(k), Boycott, Clamour, Come, Complaint, Démarche, Demo, Demonstrate, Demur, Deprecate, Dharna, Dhurna, Dissent, Expostulate, Fulminate, Gherao, Go-slow, Gripe, Hartal, Inveigh, I say, Lady Godiva, Lock-out, Luddite, March, Moonlighter, Nimby, Object, Outcry, Peenge, Picket, Plea, Rail, Refus(e)nik, Remonstrate, Representation, Riot, Sit-in, Squawk, Squeak, Squeal, Stand, Suffragette, Work-to-rule

**Protestant** Amish, Anabaptist, Anglo, Arminian, Calvin, Congregationalism, Covenanter, Cranmer, Dissenter, Evangelic, Gospeller, Huguenot, Independent, Lady, Loyalist, Lutheran, Mennonite, Methodist, Moravian, Neo-Orthodoxy, Nonconformist, Oak-boy, Orangeman, Peep o' day Boys, Pentecostal, Pietism, Prod(die), Puritan, Reformed, Religioner, Right-footer, Sacramentarian, Seventh Day Adventist, Stundist, Swaddler, Waldensian, Wasp, Wesleyan

**Protocol** Agreement, Code, Convention, Etiquette, Geneva, Kyoto, Point-to-Point

**Proton** Nucleon, Quark

**Protoplasm(ic)** Biogen, Coenocyte, Coenosarc, Cytode, Plasmodium, Sarcode, Somatoplasm

**Prototype** Blueprint, Exemplar, Model, Original, Paradigm, Pattern, Pilot

**Protozoa(n)** Am(o)eba, Foraminifer, Giardia, Globigerina, Gregarine, Heliozoan, Infusoria, Leishmania, Mastigophoran, Merozoite, Moner(a), Moneron, Paramecium, Peritricha, Phagocyte, Radiolaria, Rhizopod, Sarcodinian, Sea-mat, Toxoplasm, Trichomonad, Trophozoite, Trypanosome, Volvox, Vorticella

**Protract(ed)** Delay, → EXTEND, Lengthen, Livelong, Long, Prolong

**Protrude, Protrusion** Bulge, Eventration, Exsert, Hernia, Jut, Pop, Pout, Project, Pseudopodium, Rectocele, Strout, Tel

**Protuberance, Protuberant** Apophysis, Bulge, Bump, Burl, Condyle, Crankle, Ergot, Gibbous, Hump, Inia, Knap, Knob, Malleolus, Mamelon, Node, Papillose, Papule, Spadix, Styloid, Swelling, Tragus, Tuber, Tuberosity, Venter

**Proud** Arrogant, Boaster, Cocky, Conceited, Dic(k)ty, Egotistic, Elated, Flush, Haughty, Haut, Jutting, Level, Lordly, Orgulous, Outstanding, Protruding, Superb, Vain

**Prove(d), Proving** Apod(e)ictic, Argue, Ascertain, Assay, Attest, Attribution, Authenticate, Aver, Confirm, Convince, Deictic, Establish, Evince, Justify, Probative, → **PROOF**, Quote, → **SHOW**, Substantiate, Test, Trie, Try, Turn out

**Proverb** Adage, Axiom, Byword, Gnome, Maxim, Paroemia, Saw

▷ **Proverbial** *may refer to* the biblical Proverbs

**Provide(d), Provident(ial)** Afford, Allow, Arrange, Besee, Bring, Cater, Compare, Conditional, Endow, Endue, Equip, Far-seeing, Feed, Fend, Find, Furnish, Generate, Give, Grubstake, Heaven sent, If, Lay on, Lend, Maintain, Offer, Plenish, Proviso, Purvey, Quote, Render, Serve, So, Sobeit, → **SUPPLY**, Suttle

**Province, Provincial(ism)** Area, Circar, Countrified, County, District, Eparchy, Exclave, Eyalet, Forte, Insular, Land, Mofussil, Narrow, Nomarchy, Nome, Nomos, Oblast, Palatinate, Pale, Petrographic, Realm, Regional, Rural, Sircar, Sirkar, Small-town, Subah, Suburban, Territory, Vilayet

---

## PROVINCES

| 2 letters: | Tirol | Drenthe | Chekiang |
|---|---|---|---|
| NI | Tyrol | Eritrea | Chinghai |
| | | Galilee | Connacht |
| 4 letters: | 6 letters: | Gascony | Dauphine |
| Gaul | Acadia | Gauteng | Hainault |
| Ifni | Anhwei | Granada | Helvetia |
| Jaen | Aragon | Guienne | Illyrian |
| Jaya | Artois | Guizhou | Kiaochow |
| Shoa | Basque | Guyenne | Leinster |
| Sind | Bengal | Hainaut | Liaoning |
| | Fujian | Jiangsu | Limousin |
| 5 letters: | Fukien | Jiangxi | Lorraine |
| Anhui | Gansul | Jiazhou | Lyonnais |
| Anjou | Hainan | Kiangsi | Manitoba |
| Anwei | Kosovo | Kiangsu | Maritime |
| Coorg | Marche | Kwazulu | Ninghsia |
| Gansu | Poitou | Limpopo | Normandy |
| Hebei | Pontus | Livonia | Northern |
| Hejaz | Punjab | Munster | Nuristan |
| Henan | Quebec | Ningsia | Pashalic |
| Honan | Raetia | Ontario | Pashalik |
| Hopeh | Sanjak | Picardy | Provence |
| Hopei | Shansi | Prairie | Shandong |
| Hubei | Shanxi | Qinghai | Shantung |
| Hunan | Shensi | Rhaetia | Szechuan |
| Irian | Sikang | Satrapy | Szechwan |
| Jehol | Tabasa | Shaanxi | Touraine |
| Jilin | Ulster | Sichuan | Tsinghai |
| Kansu | Yunnan | Suiyuan | Zhejiang |
| Kirin | | Tucuman | |
| Liege | 7 letters: | Utrecht | 9 letters: |
| Namur | Alberta | Western | Apeldoorn |
| Natal | Almeria | Zeeland | Aquitaine |
| Otago | Antwerp | | Bubalidar |
| Skane | Bohemia | 8 letters: | Connaught |
| Tigre | Brabant | Atlantic | Flevoland |

| | | | |
|---|---|---|---|
| Free State | *10 letters:* | Hesse-Nassau | *14 letters:* |
| Friesland | Gelderland | Kaliningrad | Eastern Rumelia |
| Groningen | Mpumalanga | Paphlagonia | Flemish Brabant |
| Guangdong | New Castile | Western Cape | Walloon Brabant |
| Hainan Tao | Nova Scotia | West Prussia | |
| Illyricum | Overijssel | | *15 letters:* |
| Kurdistan | Patavinity | *12 letters:* | British Columbia |
| Languedoc | Roussillon | Heilongjiang | Orange Free State |
| Lusitania | Wellington | New Brunswick | |
| Nivernais | Westphalia | North Brabant | *17 letters:* |
| North West | | North Holland | North West |
| Orleanais | *11 letters:* | Saskatchewan | Frontier |
| Santa Cruz | Balochistan | South Holland | |
| Sungkiang | Baluchistan | | *23 letters:* |
| Tarragona | Eastern Cape | *13 letters:* | Newfoundland and |
| Transvaal | Guelderland | Syrophoenicia | Labrador |

**Provision(s), Provisional** Acates, Ap(p)anage, Board, Budget, Contingency, Cover(age), Endowment, Entrenched, Fodder, Foresight, Groceries, Insolvency, Jointure, Larder, Lend-lease, Mart, Proggins, Scran, Skran, Stock, Stuff, Supply, Suttle, Viands, Viaticum, Victuals

**Proviso, Provisional** Caution, Caveat, Clause, Condition, Interim, Interlocutory, IRA, Makeshift, Nisi, On trial, Reservation, Salvo, Stipulation, Temporary, Tentative

**Provocation, Provocative, Provoke** Agacant, Aggro, Alluring, Anger, Bait, Challenge, Egg, Elicit, Erotic, Exacerbate, Excite, Flirty, Gar, Goad, Harass, Impassion, Incense, Incite, Incur, Induce, Inflame, Instigate, In yer face, Irk, Irritate, Kindle, Needle, Nettle, Occasion, Pique, Prompt, Raise, Red rag, Sedition, Sound, Spark, Stimulate, Stir, Sultry, Tantalise, Tar, Tarty, Tease, Urge, Vex, Wind up

**Provost** Dean, Keeper, Marshal, Warden

**Prow** Bow, Cutwater, Fore, Nose, Prore, Stem

**Pro-war** Hawk

**Prowess** Ability, Bravery, Forte, Fortitude

**Prowl(er)** Hunt, Lurch, Lurk, Mooch, Prog, Prole, Rache, Ramble, Ratch, Roam, Rove, Snoke, Snook, Snowk, Tenebrio, Tom

**Proxime accessit** Next best

**Proximity** Handiness

**Proxy** Agent, Attorn, Deputy, PP, Regent, Sub, Surrogate, Vicar, Vice

**Prude(nce), Prudent, Prudery, Prudish** Bluenose, Canny, Caution, Circumspect, Comstocker, Conservative, Discreet, Discretion, Economy, Far-sighted, Foresight, Frugal, Grundyism, Judicious, Metis, Mimsy, Mrs Grundy, Politic, Prig, Prissy, Provident, Restrained, Sage, Sensible, Sparing, Strait-laced, Strait-lacer, Thrifty, Tight-laced, Vice-nelly, Victorian, Ware, Wary, Well-advised, Wise

**Prune(r)** Bill-hook, Clip, Dehorn, Lop, Plum, Proign, Proin(e), Reduce, Reform, Secateur, Shred, Slash, Sned, Snip, Thin, Trim

**Prunella** Hedge-sparrow, Self-heal

**Prurient** Avaricious, Itchy, Lewd, Obscene

**Prussia(n)** Blue, Junker, Pruce, Spruce, Westphalian

**Pry** Ferret, Force, Lever, Meddle, Nose, Paul, Peep, Question, Search, Snoop, Stickyback, Toot

**Psalm** Anthem, Cantate, Chant, Chorale, Hallel, Hymn, Introit, Jubilate, Metrical, Miserere, Neck-verse, Paean, Penitential, Proper, Ps, Song, Tone, Tract, Tractus, Venite

**Pseud(o)** Bogus, Mock, Posy, Pretentious, Sham, Spurious

**Pseudonym** Aka, Alias, Allonym, Anonym, Pen-name, Stage-name

**Pshaw** Chut, Pooh, Tilley-valley, Tilly-fally, Tilly-vally

**Psyche** Anima, Ego, Self, Soul, Spirit, Superego

**Psychiatrist, Psychologist** Adler, Alienist, Asperger, Clare, Coué, Ellis, Freud, Headshrinker, Jung, Kraft-Ebing, Laing, Müller-Lyer, Rat-tamer, Reich, Shrink, Skinner, Trick-cyclist

**Psychic, Psychosis** Clairvoyant, ESP, Fey, Korsakoff's, Lodge, Medium, Mind-reader, Seer, Telekinesis, Telepathic

**Psychological, Psychology, Psychologist** Analytical, Behaviourism, Binet, Clinical, Comparative, Constitutional, De Bono, Depth, Development, Dynamic, Educational, Experimental, Eysenck, Gestalt, Hedonics, Humanistic, Industrial, James, Latah, Occupational, Organisational, Piaget, Skinner, Social, Structural, Windt

**Psychosis, Psychotic** Korsakoff's, Manic-depressive, Organic, Schizophrenia, Sociopath

**Psychotherapist, Psychotherapy** Coué, Laing, Rebirthing, Shen

**Ptarmigan** Rype

**Ptomaine** Neurine

**Pub(lic) house** Bar, Beerhall, Beverage room, Boozer, Brew, Chequers, Free-house, Gin-palace, Groggery, Hostelry, Houf(f), House, Howf(f), Inn, Jerry-shop, Joint, Local, Lush-house, Mughouse, PH, Pothouse, Potshop, Roadhouse, Rubbidy, Rubbity, Shanty, Tavern, Tiddlywink, Tied house, Watering-hole

**Puberty, Pubic** Adolescence, Beaver, Bush, Hebetic, Teens

**Pubescence** Tomentum

**Pubis** Sharebone

**Public** Apert, Audience, Civil(ian), Common, Demos, Estate, General, Great unwashed, Janata, Lay, Limelight, National, Open, Out, Overt, Populace, State, Vulgar, World

**Publican** Ale-keeper, Bung, Host, Landlord, Licensee, Tapster, Taverner

**Publication** Announcement, Bluebook, Book, Booklet, Broadsheet, Edition, Ephemera, Exposé, E-zine, Festschrift, Issue, →JOURNAL, Lady, Mag, Magazine, Organ, Pamphlet, Pictorial, Red-top, Samizdat, Tabloid, Tatler, Tract, Tribune, Weekly, Yearbook

**Publicise, Publicist, Publicity** Ad(vert), Airing, Announce, Ballyhoo, Billing, Build up, Coverage, Declassify, Exposure, Flack, Glare, Headline, Hype, Leakage, Limelight, Notoriety, Photocall, Plug, PR(O), Promo(te), Promotion, Promulgate, Propaganda, Réclame, Spin-doctor, Splash

**Publish(er), Published, Publishing, Publicise** Air, Blaze, Cape, Copyleft, Delator, Desktop, Disclose, Edit, Electronic, Evulgate, Gollancz, Issue, Larousse, Noise, OUP, Out, Pirate, Plug, Post, Print(er), Proclaim, Propagate, Put about, Release, Ren, Run, Stationer, Vanity, Vent, Ventilate

**Puck** Disc, Elf, Lob, Sprite, Squid

**Pucker(ed)** Bullate, Cockle, Contract, Crease, Gather, Plissé, Purse, Ruck, Shir(r), Wrinkle

**Pud** Fin, Neafe, Nief, Nieve, Paw

**Pudding** Afters, Baked Alaska, Bakewell, Black, Blancmange, Blood, Bread (and butter), Brown Betty, Cabinet, Charlotte, Christmas, Clootie dumpling, College, Crumble, Custard, →DESSERT, Dog's body, Drisheen, Duff, Dumpling, Eve's, Flummery, Fool, Fritter, Fromenty, Frumenty, Furme(n)ty, Furmity, Haggis, Hasty, Hodge, Hog's, Ice-cream, Kugel, Lokshen, Mealie, Milk, Nesselrode, Panada, Pandowdy, Panna cotta, Parfait, Pease, Plum, Plum-duff, Pockmanky, Pockmantic, Pock-pudding, Popover, Portmanteau, Queen's, Rice, Roly-poly, Sago, Savarin, Semolina, Sowens, Sponge, Spotted dick, Spotted dog, Stickjaw, Stodge, Suet, Summer, Sundae, Sweet, Tansy, Tapioca, Umbles, White, White hass, White hause, White hawse, Yorkshire, Zabaglione

**Puddle** Collect, Dub, Flush, Pant, Plash, Plouter, Plowter, Pool, Sop

**Pueblo** Aldea, Zuni

**Puff(ed), Puffer, Puffy** Advertise, Bellows, Bloat, Blouse, Blow, Blowfish, Blurb, Bouffant, Breath, Chuff, Chug, Cream, Drag, Encomist, Eulogy, Exsufflicate, Fag, Flaff, Flatus, Fluffy, Fuff, Globe-fish, Grampus, Gust, Hype, Lunt, Pech, Pegh, Pluffy, Plug,

Powder, Quilt, Recommend, Skiff, Slogan, Smoke, Steam, Swell, Toke, Twilt, Waff, Waft, Waif, Whiff, Whiffle

**Puffin** Fratercula, Rockbird, Sea-parrot, Tammie Norie, Tam Noddy

**Pug(ilist), Pugilism** Belcher, Boxer, Bruiser, Carlin, Fancy, Fistic, Monkey, Ring

**Pugnacious** Aggressive, Belligerent, Combative, Feisty, Scrappy

**Puke** Retch, Sick, Vomit

**Pukka** Authentic, Genuine, Real, True, Valid

**Pulchritude** Beauty, Cheese-cake, Grace

**Pull (up), Pull out** Adduce, Attraction, Charm, Crane, Cry off, Demand, Drag, Draw, Earn, Force, Gravity, Haul, Heave, Heeze, Hoist, Hook, →INFLUENCE, Lug, Mousle, Pluck, Pop-top, Rein, Ring, Rove, Row, Rug, Saccade, Sally, Seduce, Snatch, Sole, Sool(e), Sowl(e), Stop, Tit, Touse, Touze, Tow, Towse, Towze, Traction, Trice, Tug, Undertow, Withdraw, Wrench, Wrest, Yank

**Pulley** Block, Capstan, Fusee, Idle(r), Jack-block, Swig, Trice, Trochlea, Truckle

**Pullover** Jersey, Jumper, Roll-neck, Slip on, Sweater, Sweatshirt, Tank-top, Windcheater

**Pullulate** Teem

**Pulp** Cellulose, Chyme, Chymify, Crush, Flong, Gloop, Kenaf, Marrow, Mash, Mush, Pap, Paste, Pomace, Pound, Puree, Rot, Rubbish, Squeeze, Squidge, Wood

**Pulpit** Ambo(nes), Bully, Lectern, Mimbar, Minbar, Pew, Rostrum, Tent, Tub, Wood

**Pulsar** Geminga

**Pulsate, Pulsatory** Beat, Palpitate, Quiver, Systaltic, Throb, Thump, Vibrate

**Pulse** Adsuki, Adzuki, Alfalfa, →BEAN, Beat, Calavance, Caravance, Chickpea, Daal, D(h)al, Dholl, Dicrotic, Fava (bean), Flageolet, Garbanzo, Gram, Groundnut, Heartbeat, Ictus, Lentil, Lucerne, Pea, Rhythm, Sain(t)foin, Snow pea, Soy beans, Sphygmic, Sync, Systaltic, Systole, Throb

**Pulverise** Calcine, Comminute, Contriturate, Demolish, Grind, →POUND, Powder

**Puma** Catamount, Cougar, Mountain lion, Panther

**Pummel(ling)** Batter, Beat, Drub, Fib, Knead, Massage, Nevel, Pound, Tapotement, Thump

▷ **Pummelled** *may indicate* an anagram

**Pump(ing)** Aerator, Air, Bellows, Bicycle, Bilge, Bowser, Breast, Centrifugal, Chain, Compressor, Cross-examine, Cross-question, Diaphragm, Donkey, Drive, Electromagnetic, Elicit, Feed, Filter, Foot, Force, Fork, Geissler, Grease-gun, Grill, Heart, Heat, Hydropult, Inflate, Interrogate, Knee-swell, Lift, Monkey, Mud, Nodding-donkey, Optical, Parish, Petrol, Piston, Pulsometer, Question, Quiz, Rotary, Scavenge, Shoe, Sodium, Stirrup, Stomach, Suction, Turbine, Vacuum, Water, Wind

**Pumpernickel** Rye (bread)

**Pumphandle** Sweep

**Pumpkin** Butternut, Cashaw, Gourd, Pampoen, Quash, Queensland blue, Squash

**Pun** Calembour, Clinch, Equivoque, Jeu de mots, Paragram, Paronomasia, Quibble, Quip, Ram, Wordplay

**Punch(ed)** Antic, Bell, Biff, Blow, Boff, Bolo, Box, Bradawl, Bumbo, Card, Centre, Chad, Check, Chin, Chop, Clip, Cobbler's, Conk, Cross, Dong, Dry-beat, Fib, Fid, Fist(ic), Fourpenny one, Gang, Glogg, Haymaker, Hit, Hook, Horse, Jab, Key, Kidney, Knevell, Knobble, Knubble, KO, Lam, Lander, Mat, Milk, Nail set, Nevel, Nubble, One-er, One-two, Overhand, Perforate, Pertuse, Planter's, Plug, Poke, Polt, Pommel, Pounce, Prod, Pummel, Puppet, Rabbit, Roundhouse, Rum, Rumbo, Sangria, Slosh, Sock, Steed, Sting(o), Stoush, Stunner, Sucker, Suffolk, Sunday, Swop, Tape, Upper-cut, Wap, Wind, Zest

**Punctilious** Exact, Formal, Nice, Particular, Picked, Precise, Prim, Stickler

**Punctual(ly), Punctual(ity)** Betimes, Politesse, Prompt, Regular, Sharp

**Punctuate, Punctuation (mark)** Apostrophe, Bracket, Close, Colon, Comma, Duckfoot quote, Em-dash, Emphasize, Em-rule, Guillemet, Hyphen, Interabang, Interrobang, Interrupt, Mark, Semicolon, Tittle

**Puncture(d)** Bore, Centesis, Criblé, Cribrate, Deflate, Drill, Flat, Hole, Lance, Lumbar, Pearse, Perforate, Pierce, Pounce, Prick, Scarify, Thoracocentesis

**Pundit** Egghead, Erudite, Expert, Guru, Maven, Oracle, Sage, Savant, Swami, Teacher, Tipster

**Pungency, Pungent** Acid, Acrid, Acrolein, Alum, Ammonia, Bite, Bitter, Caustic, Hot, Mordant, Nidorous, Piquant, Poignant, Point, Racy, Sair, Salt, Spice, Sting, Tangy, Witty

**Punish(ment), Punished, Punishing** Algates, Amerce, Attainder, Baculine, Baffle, Bastinado, Beat, Birch, Brasero, Bum rap, Cane, Cang, Capital, Cart, Castigate, Chasten, Chastise, Come-uppance, Commination, Corporal, Correct, Cucking-stool, Dam(nation), Defrock, Desert(s), Detention, → **DISCIPLINE**, Execution, Fatigue, Fine, Flog, Gantlope, Gate, Gauntlet, Gruel, Hellfire, Hiding, High jump, Horsing, Hot seat, Imposition, Impot, Interdict, Jankers, Jougs, Kang, Keelhaul, Knee-capping, Knout, Laldie, Laldy, Lambast(e), Leathering, Lines, Log, Marmalise, Necklace, Nemesis, Pack-drill, Padre Pio, Pandy, Pay out, Peine forte et dure, Penalise, Penance, Penology, Pensum, Perdition, Picket, Pillory, Pine, Rap, Red card, Reprisal, Retribution, Ruler, Sanction, Scaffold, Scath, Scourge, Sentence, Serve out, Six of the best, Smack, Smite, Spank, Spif(f)licate, Stick, Stocks, Stoning, Strafe, Straff, Strap, Strappado, Swinge(ing), Talion, Tar and feather, Thick-ear, Timber-mare, Toco, Toko, Tophet, Torture, Treadmill, Trim, Tron(e), Trounce, Tumbrel, Tumbril, Vice anglais, Visit, War(r)ison, What for, Whip, Whirligig, Wild mare, Ywrake, Ywroke

▷ **Punish** *may indicate* an anagram

**Punk** Goop, Inferior, Ne'er-do-well, Nobody, Pogo, Touchwood, Worthless

**Punnet** Basket, Pottle, Thug

**Punt(er), Punting** Antepost, Back, Bet, Gamble, Gondolier, Kent, Kick, Pound, Quant, Turfite, Wager

**Puny** Frail, Inferior, Petty, Reckling, Runtish, Scram, Shilpit, Sickly, Small, Weak

**Pup(py)** Cub, Nurseling, Whelp

**Pupa** Chrysalis, Exarate, Neanic, Nymph, Obtect

**Pupil** Abiturient, Academical, Adie's, Apple, Apprentice, Bluecoat, Boarder, Cadet, Catechumen, Dayboy, Daygirl, Disciple, Etonian, Exit, Eyeball, Fag, Follower, Greycoat, Gyte, Intake, Junior, L, Monitor, Prefect, Preppy, Protégé(e), Scholar, Senior, Student, Tiro, Trainee, Tutee, Ward, Wykehamist

▷ **Pupil** *may refer to* an eye

**Puppet(s), Puppeteer** Bunraku, Creature, Doll, Dummy, Fainéant, Fantoccini, Finger, Galanty show, Glove, Guignol, Jack-a-lent, Judy, Mammet, Marionette, Mawmet, Mommet, Motion(-man), Motion generative, Pageant, Pawn, Pinocchio, Promotion, Punch(inello), Quisling, Rod, Thunderbird, Tool

**Purchase(r), Purchasing** Acquisition, Bargain, Buy, Coff, Compulsory, Earn, Emption, End-user, Gadsden, Get, Grip, Halliard, Halyard, Hold, Layaway, → **LEVERAGE**, Louisiana, Money, Offshore, Oligopsony, Parbuckle, Perquisitor, Repeat, Secure, Shop, Toehold, Traction

**Pure, Purist, Purity** Absolute, Angelic, Cando(u)r, Cathy, Chaste, Chiarezza, Clean(ly), Cleanness, Cosher, Fine, Glenys, Good, Holy, Immaculate, Incorrupt, Innocent, Intemerate, Inviolate, Kathy, Kosher, Lily, Lilywhite, Maidenhood, Meer, Me(a)re, Net(t), Precisionist, Pristine, Quintessence, Refined, Sanctity, Sheer, Simon, Simple, Sincere, Snow-white, Snowy, Stainless, Sterile, Thoroughbred, True, Unalloyed, Unapplied, Undrossy, Vertue, Virgin, Virtue, White

**Puree** Baba ghanoush, Coulis, D(h)al, Fool

**Purgative, Purge** Aloes, Aloetic, Araroba, Aryanise, Cacoon, Calomel, Cascara, Cassia, Castor-oil, Catharise, Catharsis, Cholagogue, Colquintida, Comstockery, Croton, Delete, Detox, Diacatholicon, Diarrh(o)ea, Drastic, Elaterin, Elaterium, Eliminate, Eluant, Emetic, Enos®, Erase, Evacuant, Exonerate, Expiate, Flux, Gleichschaltung, Hiera-picra, Hydragogue, Ipecacuanha, Ipomoea, Jalap, Jalop, Laxative, McCarthyism, Number nine, Physic, Picra, Pride's, Relaxant, Scour, Scur, Senna, Soil, Turbith, Turpeth, Wahoo

**Purgatory** Cacatopia

**Purification, Purifier, Purify(ing)** Absolve, Bowdlerise, Catharsis, Clay, Clean(se), Depurate, Despumate, Dialysis, Distil, Edulcorate, Eluent, Elution, Exalt, Expurgate, Filter, Fine, Gas-lime, Green vitriol, Lustre, Lustrum, Niyama, Osmosis, Refine, Retort, Reverse osmosis, Samskara, Sanctify, Sanitise, Scorify, Scrub, Smudging, Sublime, Try, Whiten

**Puritan(ical)** Ascetic, Bible belt, Bluenose, Browne, Cromwell, Digger(s), Ireton, Ironsides, Killjoy, Pi, Pilgrim, Plymouth Colony, Precisian, Prig, Prude, Prynne, Roundhead, Seeker, Strait-laced, Traskite, Waldenses, Wowser, Zealot

**Purl(er)** Cropper, Eddy, Fall, Knit, Ripple, Stream

**Purloin** Abstract, Annex, Appropriate, Lift, Nab, Pilfer, Snaffle, Sneak, Steal

**Purple** Amaranthine, Amarantin(e), Amethyst, Assai, Aubergine, Burgundy, Cassius, Chlamys, Claret, Corkir, Cudbear, Dubonnet, Eminence, Fuchsia, Golp(e), Heather, Heliotrope, Hyacinthine, Imperial, Indigo, Korkir, Lavender, Lilac, Magenta, Mallow, Mauvin(e), Mulberry, Murrey, Orcein, Orcin(e), Orcinol, Pance, Pansy, Plum, Pompadour, Pontiff, Porporate, Proin(e), Prune, Puce, Puke, Punic, Purpure, Rhodopsin, Royal, Solferino, Tyrian, Violet, Visual

**Purport** Bear, Claim, Drift, Feck, Mean, Tenor

**Purpose(ful)** Advertent, Aim, Avail, Calculated, Cause, Cautel, Cross, Design, Errand, Ettle, Function, Goal, Here-to, Idea, → INTENT, Marrow, Mean(ing), Meant, Mint, Mission, Motive, Object, Plan, Point, Raison d'être, → REASON, Resolution, Resolve, Sake, Telic, Telos, Tenor, Use, View

**Purposeless** Dysteleology, Futile, Indiscriminate, Otiose

**Purr** Curr, Rumble

**Purse** Ad crumenam, Bag, Bung, Caba, Clutch, Contract, Crease, Crumenal, Egg, Embouchure, Exchequer, Fisc, Fisk, Long Melford, Mermaid's, Pocket, Prim, Privy, Prize, Public, Pucker, Spleuchan, Sporran, Wallet, Whistle

▷ **Pursed** *may indicate* one word within another

**Purser** Mud-clerk

**Purslane** Sea, Water

**Pursue(r), Pursuing, Pursuit** After, Alecto, Business, Chase, Chivvy, Course, Dog, Follow, Follow up, Harry, Hobby, Hot-trod, Hound, Hue and cry, Hunt, Line, Pastime, Practice, Practise, Proceed, Prosecute, Quest, Scouring, Stalk, Trivial

**Pursuivant** Blue Mantle

**Purulent** Mattery

**Purvey(or)** Cater, Provide, Provisor, Sell, Supply

**Pus** Empyema, Matter, Purulence, Pyuria, Quitter, Quittor

**Push(er), Push in, Push out, Pushy** Airscrew, Astrut, Barge, Birr, Boost, Brash, Buffet, Bunt, Butt, Ca', Detrude, Drive, Dunch, Edge, Effort, Elbow, Fire, Horn, Hustle, Hyper, Impulse, Invaginate, Jostle, Motivation, Nose, Nudge, Nurdle, Obtrude, Offensive, Onrush, Pitchfork, Plod, Ply, Press, Promote, Propel, Railroad, Ram, Rush, Sell, Shog, Shoulder, → SHOVE, Snoozle, Subtrude, Thrust, Urge

**Pushchair** Baby Buggy®, Buggy, Stroller, Trundler

**Pushover** Doddle, Soda

**Pusillanimous** Coward, Timid, Weak, Weak-kneed, Wimp, Yellow

**Puss(y)** Amentum, → CAT, Catkins, Face, Feline, Galore, Hare, Malkin, Mouth, Rabbit, Septic

**Pussyfoot** Dry, Equivocate, Inch, Paw, Steal, TT

**Pustule** Blotch, Pimple, Pock

**Put (off, on, out, up)** Accommodate, Add, Alienate, Bet, Board, Cup, Daff, Defer, Dish, Do, Don, Douse, Implant, Impose, Include, Incommode, Inn, Lade, Launch, Lay, Locate, Lodge, Lump, Miff, Oust, Pit, Pitch, Place(d), Plonk, Set, Sheathe, Simulate, Sited, Smoor, Smore, Snuff, Station, Stow, Temporise

**Put away, Put by** Distance, Save, Sheathe, Store, Stow

**Put down** Abase, Degrade, Demean, Disparage, Floor, Humiliate, Land, Relegate, Repress, Reprime, Snuff, Write

▷ **Put off** *may indicate* an anagram

**Putrefaction, Putrefy(ing), Putrid** Addle, Bitter, Corrupt, Decay, Fester, Mephitic, Olid, Rot, Sepsis, Septic

**Putsch** Revolution

**Putt(ing)** Gimme, Gobble, Green, Hash, Pigeon, Sink, → **STUPID PERSON**

**Putter** Chug, Club

**Put together** Assemble, Compile, Synthesize

**Putty** Glaziers', Jewellers', Mastic, Painters', Plasterers', Polishers'

**Puzzle(r), Puzzled** Acrostic, At a loss, Baffle, Bemuse, Bewilder, Brainteaser, Chinese, Confound, Confuse, Conundrum, Crossword, Crux, Crux medicorum, Egma, Elude, Enigma, Feague, Floor, Fox, Get, Glaik, Gravel, Intrigue, Jigsaw, Jumbo, Kakuro, Kittle, Logogriph, Magic pyramid, Maze, Mind-bender, Monkey, Mystery, Mystify, Nonplus, Perplex, Ponder, Pose(r), Rebus, Riddle, Rubik's Cube®, Sorites, Sphinx, Stick(l)er, Stump, Sudoku, Tangram, Teaser, Thematic, Tickler, Wordsearch, Wordsquare

**Pygmalion** Centennial brown

**Pygmy** Atomy, Dwarf, Hop o'my thumb, Negrillo, Negrito, Pyknic, Thumbling

**Pyjamas** Baby-doll, Churidars, Jimjams

**Pyramid(s)** Cheops, Chephren, Egyptology, Frustum, Magic, Population, Stack, Teocalli

**Pyre** Bale(-fire), Bonfire, Brasero, Darga, Gha(u)t

**Pyrenean** Basque

**Pyrites** Arsenical, Cockscomb, Copper, Fool's gold, Iron, Magnetic, Mispickel, Mundic, Spear, White

**Pyrotechnics** Arson, Fireworks

**Pyroxene** Aegirine, Aegirite, Diopside

**Pyrus** Service-tree

**Pythagoras** Samian

**Pythian (seat)** Delphic, Tripod

**Python** Anaconda, Diamond, IDLE, Kaa, Monty, → **SNAKE**, Zombi(e)

# Qq

**Q** Koppa, Quebec, Question
**Qatar** Emirate
**Q-boat** Mystery ship
**QC** Silk
**Qua** As
**Quack** Charlatan, Crocus, Dulcamara, Empiric, Fake, Homeopath, →IMPOSTOR, Katerfelto, Mountebank, Pretender, Saltimbanco
**Quad(rangle)** Close, Complete, Compluvium, Court, Em, En, Horse, Oblong, Pane
**Quadrilateral** Lambeth, Tetragon, Trapezium, Trapezoid
**Quadrille** Dance, Lancers, Matador(e), Pantalon
**Quaff** Carouse, Drink, Imbibe
**Quagmire** Bog, Fen, Imbroglio, Marsh, Morass, Swamp, Wagmoire
**Quahog** Clam
**Quail** Asteria, Bevy, Bird, Blench, Bob-white, Button, Caille, Colin, Flinch, Harlot, Hen, Quake, Shrink, Tremble, Wince
**Quaint** Cute, Far(r)and, Farrant, Fie, Naive, Odd, Old-world, Picturesque, Strange, Twee, Wham, Whim(sy)
**Quake(r), Quaking** Aminadab, Broad-brim, Didder, Dither, Dodder, Fox, Friend, Fry, Hicksite, Obadiah, Palpitate, Penn, Quail, Seism, Shake(r), Shiver, →TREMBLE, Tremor, Trepid, Wamble
**Qualification, Qualified, Qualify** Able, Adapt, Adverb, Agrege, Alloy, But, Capacitate, Caveat, Competent, Condition, Credential, Degree, Diplomatic, Doctorate, Eligible, Entitle, Fit, Graduate, Habilitate, Higher Still, Meet, Moderate, Modifier, Nisi, Parenthetical, Pass, Past-master, Proviso, Quantify, Restrict, Temper, Versed
**Quality** Aroma, Attribute, Aura, Body, Calibre, Cast, Charisma, De luxe, Esse, Essence, Extra virgin, Fabric, Fame, First water, Five-star, Flavour, Grade, Inscape, Insight, It, Kite-mark, Letter, Long suit, Mystique, Nature, Phat, Pitch, Plus, Premium, Primary, Property, Q, Quale, Reception, Sanctitude, Savour, Sort, Standard, Stature, Style, Substance, Suchness, Terroir, Texture, Thew, Thisness, Timbre, Tone, Tophole, Top-notch, Total, Up-market, Vein, Vinosity, Virgin, Virtu(e), Water, Worth
**Qualm** Compunction, Fear, Misgiving, Scruple
**Quandary** Dilemma, Fix, Predicament, Trilemma
**Quantity** →AMOUNT, Analog(ue), Batch, Bundle, Capacity, Deal, Dose, Feck, Fother, Hank, Heaps, Hundredweight, Idempotent, Intake, Jag, Lion's share, Loads, Lock, Lot, Mass, Measure, Melder, Multitude, Myriad, Niblet, Nip, Nonillion, Number, Ocean(s), Omnium, Operand, Output, Parameter, Parcel, Peck, Plenty, Posology, Pottle, Qs, Qt, Quire, Quota, Quotient, Radicand, Ream, Scalar, Slather, Slew, Slue, Sum, Surd, Tret, Unknown, Vector, Wad, Warp, Whips
**Quantum** Graviton, Isospin, Magnon, Phonon, Photon, Roton
**Quarantine** Isolate, Lazarette
**Quark** Bottom, Charm(ed), Down, Flavo(u)r, Particle, Strange, Top up
**Quarrel(some), Quarreler** Affray, Aggress, Altercate, Argue, Arrow, Barney, Barratry, Barretry, Bate, Bicker, Brabble, Brattle, Brawl, Breach, Breeze, Broil, Brulyie, Brulzie, Bust-up, Cagmag, Cantankerous, Carnaptious, Cat and dog, Caterwaul, Catfight, Chance-medley, Chide, Clash, Combative, Contentious, Contretemps, Difference,

Disagree, Dispute, Domestic, Dust-up, Eristic, Estrangement, Exchange, Fall out, Feisty, Feud, Fire-eater, Fracas, Fractious, Fratch(et)y, Fray, Hassle, Issue, Jar, Loggerheads, Miff, Outcast, Outfall, Pugnacious, Ragbolt, Row, Ruction, Spat, Squabble, Tangle, Tiff, Tile, Tink, Tweedledee, Tweedledum, Vendetta, Vitilitigation, Wap, Whid, Wrangle

**Quarry, Quarry face** Chalkpit, Chase, Currie, Curry, Game, Heuch, Mark, Mine, Pit, Prey, Scabble, Scent, Stone pit, Victim

**Quart** Winchester

**Quarter(ing), Quarters** Airt, Barracks, Barrio, Billet, Camp, Canton(ment), Casbah, Casern(e), Chinatown, Chum, Clemency, Close, Coshery, District, Dorm, E, Empty, Enclave, Fardel, Farl, First, Fo'c'sle, Forecastle, Forpet, Forpit, Fourth, Ghetto, Ham(s), Harbour, Haunch, Last, Latin, Medina, →**MERCY**, N, Note, Oda, Pity, Point, Principium, Quadrant, Region, S, Season, Sector, Tail, Trimester, Two bits, W, Wardroom, Warp, Winter

**Quarter-day** LD

▷ **Quarterdeck** *may indicate* a suit of cards

**Quartermaster** Seacunny

**Quartet** Dissonance, Foursome, Mess, String, Tetrad

**Quarto** Crown, Demy, Foolscap, Imperial, Medium, Royal, Small

**Quartz** Adventurine, Agate, Amethyst, Bristol diamond, Buhrstone, Cacholong, Cairngorm, Chalcedony, Chert, Citrine, Crystal, Flint, Granophyre, Granulite, Itacolumite, Jasp(er), Love-arrow, Morion, Onyx, Plasma, Prase, Rainbow, Rose, Rubasse, Sapphire, Silex, Silica, Smoky, Spanish topaz, Stishovite, Tiger-eye, Tonalite, Whin Sill

**Quash** Abrogate, Annul, Nullify, Oppress, Quell, Rebut, Recant, Repress, Scotch, Subdue, Suppress, Terminate, Void

**Quasimodo** Bellringer, Gibbose, Hunchback

**Quaver(ing)** Shake, Tremulous, Trill, Vibrate, Warble

**Quay** Bund, Jetty, Landing, Levee, Staithe, Wharf

**Queasy** Delicate, Nauseous, Squeamish

**Quebec** Q

**Queen(ly)** Adelaide, African, Alcestis, Alexandra, Anna, Anne, Artemesia, Atossa, Balkis, Beatrix, Beauty, Bee, Begum, Bess, Boadicea, Boudicca, Brun(n)hild(e), Camilla, Candace, Card, Caroline, Cat, Chesspiece, Christina, Cleopatra, Closet, Clytemnestra, Coatcard, Dido, Drag, Drama, Eleanor(a), Ellery, Ena, ER, Esther, FD, Gertrude, Guinevere, Harvest, Hatshepset, Hatshepsut, Hecuba, Helen, Henrietta Maria, Hera, Here, Hermione, Hippolyta, HM, Isabel, Isabella, Ishtar, Isolde, Jocasta, Juliana, Juno, King, Leda, Maam, Mab, Maeve, Margaret, Marie Antoinette, Mary (Tudor), Matilda, May, Medb, Mobled, Monarch, Nance, Nefertiti, Omphale, Oriana, Pance, Pansy, Parr, Paunce, Pawnce, Pearly, Penelope, Persephone, Phaedra, Prince, Prom, Proserpina, Qu, R, Ranee, Rani, Regal, Regina(l), Sara, Semiramis, Sheba, Sultana, Titania, Vashti, Victoria, Virgin, Warrior

**Queen Anne** Mrs Morley

**Queer(ness)** Abnormal, Berdash, Bizarre, Crazy, Cure, Curious, Fey, Fie, Fifish, Fishy, Gay, Nance, Nancy, →**ODD**, Outlandish, Peculiar, Pervert, Poorly, Quaint, Rum, Spoil, Uranism, Vert

**Quell** Alegge, Allay, Calm, Quiet, Repress, Subdue, Suppress

**Quench** Assuage, Cool, Extinguish, Satisfy, Slake, Slo(c)ken, Sta(u)nch, Yslake

**Querulous** Huffy

▶ **Query** *see* **QUESTION(ING)**

**Quest** Goal, Graal, Grail, Hunt, Pursuit, Search, Venture, Vision

**Question(ing), Questioner, Questionnaire** Appose, Arraign, Ask, Bi-lateral, Burning, Catechise, Challenge, Chin, Consult, Contest, Conundrum, Cross-examine, Curious, Debrief, Dichotomous, Direct, Dispute, Dorothy Dixer, Doubt, Erotema, Eroteme, Erotesis, Examine, Fiscal, Good, Grill, Heckle, Homeric, Impeach, Impugn, Indirect, Information, Innit, Inquisitor, Interpellation, Interrogate, Interview, Investigate,

Issue, Koan, Leading, Loaded, Maieutic, Matter, Open, Oppugn, Peradventure, Point
of order, Pop, Pose, Previous, Probe, Problem, Pump, Q, Qu, Quaere, Quiz, Rapid-fire,
Refute, Rhetorical, Riddle, Socratic method, Sound, Speer, Speir, Survey, Suspect, Tag,
Teaser, Tickler, Vexed, West Lothian, WH, What, Worksheet

**Questionable** Ambiguous, Dubious, Fishy, Socratic, Unclear

**Question-master** Interrogator, Socrates, Torquemada, Ximenes

**Queue** Braid, Breadline, Cercus, Crocodile, Cue, Dog, File, Kale, → **LINE**, Line up, Pigtail,
Plait, Plat, Stack, Tail(back), Track

**Quibble(r), Quibbling** Balk, Carp, Carriwitchet, Casuist, Cavil, Chicaner, Dodge,
Elenchus, Equivocate, Haggle, Hairsplitting, Nitpick, Pedantry, Pettifoggery, Prevaricate,
Pun, Quiddity, Quillet, Quirk, Sophist

**Quiche** Flan, Tart

**Quick(en), Quickening, Quicker, Quickie, Quickly, Quickness, Quickwitted**
Accelerate, Acumen, Adroit, Agile, Alive, Allegr(ett)o, Animate, Apace, Breakneck,
Breathing, Bright, Brisk, Celerity, Chop-chop, Citigrade, Cito, Con moto, Core, Cracking,
Cuticle, Dapper, Deft, Enliven, Existent, Expeditious, Express, Fastness, Festination,
Fleet, Foothot, Gleg, Hasten, Hie, High-speed, Hotfoot, Hypersonic, Impetuous,
Impulsive, Intelligent, Jiffy, Keen, Lickety-split, Living, Mercurial, Meteoric, Mistress,
Mosso, Nailbed, Nifty, Nimble, Nippy, Nooner, Pdq, Piercing, Piu mosso, Post-haste,
Prestissimo, Presto, Prompt, Pronto, Rapid, Rath(e), Ready, Rough and ready, Schnell,
Sharp, Short cut, Skin, Slippy, Smart, Snappy, Snort, Sodain(e), Soon, Spry, Streamline,
Stretta, Stretto, Sudden, Swift, Swith, Tout de suite, Trice, Up tempo, Veloce, Vital, Vite,
Vivify, Volable, Wikiwiki, Yare

**Quicksand** Flow, Syrtis

**Quicksilver** Mercury

**Quid** Chaw, Chew, L, Nicker, Oner, Plug, Pound, Quo, Sov, Tertium, Tobacco

**Quidnunc** Gasbag

**Quid pro quo** Mutuum, Tit-for-tat

**Quiescence, Quiescent** Calm, Di(o)estrus, Inactive, Inert, Latent, Still

**Quiet(en), Quieter, Quietly** Accoy, Allay, Appease, Barnacle, Calm, Clam, Compose,
Conticent, Decrescendo, Diminuendo, Doggo, Ease, Easeful, Easy, Encalm, Entame, Gag,
Grave, Hush, Kail, Laconic, Loun(d), Low, Lown(d), Low-profile, Lull, Meek, Mezzo voce,
Millpond, Mp, Muffle, Mute, Orderly, P, Pacify, Pastel, Pauciloquent, Pause, Peace, Piano,
Pipe down, Plateau, QT, Reserved, Reticent, Sedate, Settle, Sh, Shtoom, Shtum, Silence,
Sitzkrieg, Sly, Sober, Soothe, Sotto voce, Still, Stum(m), Subact, Subdued, Tace, Taciturn,
Tranquil, Wheesht, Whish, Whisht, Whist

**Quill** Calamus, Feather, Float, Plectre, Plectron, Plectrum, Plume, Remex, Spine

**Quillwort** Isoetes

**Quilt(ed), Quilting** Comfort(er), Continental, Counterpane, Cover, Crazy, Doona®,
Duvet, Echo, Eiderdown, Futon, Kantha, Matel(l)asse, Patch(work), Puff, Trapunto

**Quince** Bael, Bel, Bengal, Bhel, Flowering, Japanese, Japonica

**Quinine** China, Crown-bark, Kina, Quina, Tonic

**Quinsy** Angina, Cynanche, Garget, Squinancy

**Quintessence, Quintessential** Classic, Heart, Pith

**Quintet** Pentad, Trout

**Quip** Carriwitchet, Crack, Epigram, Gibe, Jest, Jibe, Joke, Repartee, Taunt, Zinger

**Quirk(y)** Concert, Foible, Idiosyncrasy, Irony, Kink, Mannerism, Strange, Twist

**Quisling** Collaborator, Traitor

**Quit(s)** Abandon, Absolve, Ap(p)ay, Cease, Desert, Desist, Even(s), Go, Leave, Meet, Part,
Resign, Rid, Stash, → **STOP**, Stow, Vacate, Yield

**Quite** Actually, All, Altogether, Ap(p)ay, Clean, Dead, Enough, Enow, Fairly, Fully, Mezzo,
Precisely, Rather, Real(ly), Right, Sheer, Very, Yes

**Quiver(ing)** Ashake, Aspen, Pulsate, Quake, Shake, Sheaf, Sheath, The yips, Tremble,
Tremolo, Tremor, Tremulate, Trepid, Vibrant, Vibrate, Wobble

**Qui vive** Go-go

**Quixote, Quixotic** Don, Errant, Impractical

**Quiz** Bandalore, Banter, Bee, Catechism, Examine, Hoax, Interrogate, I-spy, Mastermind, Mockery, Oddity, Probe, Pub, Pump, Question, Smoke, Third degree, Trail, Yo-yo

**Quizzical** Askance, Curious, Derisive, Odd, Queer, Socratic

**Quod** Can, Clink, Jail, Prison

**Quoit** Disc(us), Disk, Ring

**Quondam** Once, Sometime, Whilom

**Quorum** Minyan

**Quota** Numerus clausus, Proportion, Ration, Share

**Quotation, Quote(d)** Adduce, Citation, Cite, Co(a)te, Duckfoot, Epigraph, Estimate, Evens, Excerpt, Extract, Forward, Instance, List, Locus classicus, Name, Price, Recite, Reference, Say, Scare, Soundbite, Stock, Tag, Verbatim, Wordbite

**Quoth** Co, Said

**Quotient** Achievement, Intelligence, Kerma, Quaternion, Ratio, Respiratory

# Rr

**R** Arithmetic, Canine letter, Dog letter, King, Queen, Reading, Recipe, Right, Romeo, Run, Writing

**RA** Academy, Argentina

**Rabbi** Dayan, Mashgiah, Rav, Rebbe

**Rabbit** Angora, Astrex, Blather, Brer, British Lop, Buck, Bun(ny), Bury, Chat, Chitchat, Chunter, Con(e)y, Cottontail, Daman, Dassie, Doe, Duffer, Earbash, Gas, Goon, Harp, Haver, Hyrax, Jabber, Jack, Jaw, Klipdas, Long White, Lop-eared, Marmot, Muff, Natter, Nest, Novice, Oarlap, Palaver, Patzer, Prate, Prattle, Rack, Rattle, Rex, Rock, Sage, Snowshoe, Tail-ender, Tapeti, Terricole, Waffle, Warrener, Welsh, White, Witter, Yak, Yap, Yatter

**Rabble, Rabble-rousing** Canaille, Clamjamphrie, Clanjamfray, Colluvies, Crowd, Demagoguery, Doggery, Galère, Herd, Hoi-polloi, Horde, Legge, Meinie, Mein(e)y, Menyie, Mob, Raffle, Rag-tag, Rascaille, Rascal, Riff-raff, Rout, Scaff-raff, Shower, Tag, Tagrag

**Rabelaisian** Pantagruel, Panurge

**Rabid, Rabies** Extreme, Frenzied, Hydrophobia, Lyssa, Mad, Raging, Virulent

**Raccoon** Coati(-mondi), Coati-mundi, Olingo, Panda, Procyon

**Race, Racing** Alpine, Ancestry, Arms, Autocross, Autopoint, Aztec, Bathtub, Belt, Boat, Boskop, Breed, Broose, Brouze, Bumping, Career, Car rally, Caucus, Chantilly, Chase, Claiming, Classic, Comrades, Cone, Consolation, Contest, Corso, Country, Course, Criterium, Current, Cursus, Cyclo-cross, Dash, Dogs, Double sculls, Drag, Egg and spoon, Enduro, Event, F1, Fastnet, Flapping, Flat, Flow, Formula One, Fun-run, Generation, Ginger, Half-marathon, Handicap, Hare and hounds, Harness, Herrenvolk, Hialeah, High hurdles, Human(kind), Hurdles, Hurry, Inca, Indy car, Keiren, Keirin, Kentucky Derby, Kermesse, Kind, Lampadedromy, Lampadephoria, Leat, Leet, Lick, Lignage, Line(age), Man, Marathon, Master, Mediterranean, Meets, Mile, Monza, Motocross, Nascar, Nation, → **NATIONAL**, National Hunt, Nursery, Nursery stakes, Obstacle, One-horse, Palio, Paper chase, Pattern, Picnic, Plate, Pluck, Point-to-point, Potato, Pre-Dravidian, Prep, Pursuit, Rallycross, Rallying, Rapids, Rat, Regatta, Relay, Rill, Road, Rod, Ronne, Roost, Run-off, Sack, Scramble, Scratch, Scud, Scurry, Seed, Selling(-plate), Shan, Sheep, Slalom, Slipstream, Sloot, Slot-car, Sluit, Smock, Speedway, Sprint, Stakes, Steeplechase, Stem, Stirp(s), Stirpes, Stock, Strain, Streak, Strene, Supermoto, Sweepstake, Tail, Taste, Tear, Three-legged, Tide, Torch, Torpids, Tribe, Trotting, TT, Turf, Two-horse, Volsungs, Walking, Walk-over, Waterway, Welter, Wetherby, Whid, White

**Racehorse, Racer** Arkle, Dragster, Eclipse, Filly, Go-kart, Hare, Kart, Maiden, Mudder, Neddy, Novice, Plater, Red Rum, Shergar, Snake, Steeplechaser, Trotter

**Raceme** Bunch, Corymb, Panicle

**Race meeting, Racecourse, Racetrack** Aintree, Ascot, Ayr, Brands Hatch, Cambridgeshire, Catadrome, Catterick, Cesarewitch, Derby, Doggett's Coat and Badge, Doncaster, Dromical, Dromos, Epsom, Goodwood, Grand National, Grand Prix, Guineas, Hippodrome, Imola, Indy, Kentucky Derby, Leger, Le Mans, Longchamps, Madison, National Hunt, Newmarket, Oaks, Paceway, Racino, Redcar, Regatta, St Leger, Silverstone, Super G, Thousand Guineas, Towcester, Two Thousand Guineas, Velodrome, Wetherby, Wincanton, York

**Racial (area), Racialist** Anti-semite, Apartheid, Colour, Ethnic, Ghetto, National Front, Quarter

**Rack** Agonise, Anguish, Bin, Cloud, Cratch, Drier, Flake, Frame, Hack, Hake, Heck, Pipe, Plate, Pulley, Roof, Stretcher, Toast, Torment, Torture, Touse, Towse

**Racket(eer)** Bassoon, → BAT, Battledore, Bloop, Blue murder, Brattle, Caterwaul, Charivari, Chirm, Clamour, Con, Crime, Crosse, Deen, Din, Discord, Earner, → FIDDLE, Fuss, Gyp, Hubbub, Hullaballoo, Hustle, → NOISE, Noisiness, Numbers, Protection, Ramp, Rattle, Rort, Ruction, Scam, Sokaiya, Stridor, Swindle, Tirrivee, Tumult, Uproar, Utis

▷ **Racketeer** *may indicate* a tennis or squash player

**Racy** Ethnic, Piquant, Pungent, Ribald, Salty, Spicy, Spirited

**Rad** Rem

**Radar** Acronym, Angel, AWACS, Beacon, DEW line, Doppler, Gadget, Gee, Gull, Lidar, Loran, Monopulse, Navar, Rebecca-eureka, Scanner, Shoran, Surveillance, Teleran®, Tracking

**Raddle** Hurdle, Ochre, Red

**Radial** Osteal, Quadrant, Rotula, Spoke, Tire, Tyre

**Radiance, Radiant** Actinic, Aglow, Aureola, Beamish, Brilliant, Gleam(y), Glisten(ing), Glittery, Glory, Glow, Happy, Luminous, Lustre, Refulgent, Shechina, Sheen, Shekinah

**Radiate, Radiating, Radiation, Radiator** Actinal, Adaptive, Air-colour, Annihilation, Beam, Black body, Bremsstrahlung, Cavity, C(h)erenkov, Characteristic, Disseminate, Dosimetry, Effulgence, Effuse, Emanate, Emit, Exitance, Fluorescence, Gamma, Glow, Hawking, Heater, Infrared, Insolation, Ionizing, Isohel, Laser, Microwave, Millirem, Non-ionizing, Pentact, Photon, Picowave, Pulsar, Quasar, Rem(s), Rep, Roentgen, → SHINE, Sievert, Soft, Solar, Spherics, Spoke, Stellate, Stray, SU, Sun, Synchrotron, Terrestrial, Ultra violet, UVA, UVB, Van Allen, Visible

**Radical** Acetyl, Alkyl, Allyl, Amide, Ammonium, Amyl, Aryl, Benzil, Benzoyl, Bolshevist, Bolshie, Butyl, Calumba, Carbene, Cetyl, Chartist, Dibutyl, Drastic, Dyad, Egalitarian, Elemental, Ester, Ethynyl, Extreme, Free, Fundamental, Gauchist, Genre-busting, Glyceryl, Glycosyl, Hexyl, Hydroxy, Innate, Isopropyl, Jacobin, Leftist, Leveller, Ligand, Maximalist, Methyl, Montagnard, Nitryl, Oxonium, Parsnip, Phenyl, Phosphonium, Pink, Propyl, Red, Revolutionary, Rhizocaul, Root, Rudiment, Sulfone, Sulphone, Taliban, Taproot, Trot(sky), Uranyl, Vinyl, Vinylidene, Whig, Xylyl, Yippie, Yippy, Young Turk

**Radio** Beatbox, Blooper, Bluetooth, Boom-box, Broadcasting, Cat's whisker, CB, Cellular, Citizen's band, Clock, Cognitive, Community, Crystal set, Digital, Ether, Gee, Ghetto-blaster, Ham, Local, Long wave, Loudspeaker, Marconigraph, Pirate, Receiver, Receiving-set, Rediffusion®, Reflex, Rig, Set, Short wave, Simplex, Sound, Steam, Talk, Talkback, Tranny, Transceiver, Transistor, Transmitter, Transponder, Tuner, Walkie-talkie, Walkman®, Walky-talky, Wireless

**Radioactive, Radioactivity** Actinide, Americium, Astatine, Autinite, Bohrium, Cheralite, Cobalt 60, Curie, Darmstadtium, Emanation, Fall-out, Hot, Megacurie, Niton, Nucleonics, Plutonium, Radon, Steam, Thorianite, Thorite, Thorium, Torbernite, Unstable, Uranite, Uranium

**Radiogram, Radiograph(y)** Cable, Telegram, Venography, Ventriculography, Wire

**Radiology** Interventional

**Radish** Charlock, Daikon, Mooli, Runch

**Radium** Ra

**Radius** Bone, Long, Schwarzschild, Short, Turning

**Radon** Rn

**Raffia** Rabanna

**Raffle(s)** Burglar, Draw, Lottery, Sweepstake

**Raft(ing)** Balsa, Carley float, Catamaran, Float, Kon-Tiki, Life, Log, Mohiki, Pontoon, Slew, Whitewater

**Rafter** Barge-couple, Beam, Chevron, Jack, Joist, Principal, Ridge, Spar, Timber

**Rag(ged), Ragged(ness), Rags** Bait, Bate, Clout, Coral, Daily, Deckle, Dud(s), Duddery, Duddie, Duster, Fent, Figleaf, Glad, Gutter press, Guyed, Haze, Horror, Kid, Lap(pie), Lapje, Mop, Moth-eaten, →**NEWSPAPER**, Nose, Paper, Red(top), Remnant, Revel, Rivlins, Roast, Rot, Scabrous, Scold, Scrap, S(c)hmatte, →**SHRED**, Slate, Slut, Splore, Tack, Tat(t), Tatter(demalion), Tatty, Taunt, →**TEASE**, Tiger, Tongue, Uneven

▷ **Rag(ged)** *may indicate* an anagram

**Rage, Raging** Amok, →**ANGER**, Ardour, Bait, Bate, Bayt, Boil, Chafe, Conniption, Explode, Fad, Fashion, Fierce, Fit, Fiz(z), Fume, Furibund, Furore, Fury, Gibber, Go, Irate, Ire, Madness, Mania, Mode, Monkey, Paddy(-whack), Passion, Pelt, Pet, Pique, Rabid, Rail, Ramp, Rant, Road, 'roid, See red, Snit, Storm, Tear, Temper, Ton, Trolley, Utis, Wax, Wrath

**Raglan** Sleeve

**Ragout** Blanquette, Compot, Goulash, Haricot, Stew

**Rag-picker** Bunter

**Ragwort** Yellowseed

**Raid(er)** Assail, Assault, Attack, Baedeker, Bear, Bodrag, Bust, Camisado, Chappow, Commando, Corporate, Dawn, Do, Forage, For(r)ay, Imburst, Incursion, Inroad, Inrush, Invade, Jameson, Maraud, March-treason, Mosstrooper, Pict, Pillage, Plunder, Ram, Ransel, Razzia, Reive, Rob, Sack, Scrump, Skrimp, Skrump, Smash-and-grab, Sortie, Spreagh, Storm, Swoop, Viking

**Rail(er), Railing** Abuse, Amtrack, Arm(rest), Arris, Balustrade, Ban, Banister, →**BAR**, Barre, Barrier, Bird, Bullhead, Cloak, Communion, Conductor, Coot, Corncrake, Crake, Criticise, Dado, Fender, Fiddle, Fife, Flanged, Flat-bottomed, Flite, Flow, Fulminate, Grab, Grinding, Guide, Gush, Insult, Inveigh, Light, Limpkin, Live, Metal, Monkey, Neckerchief, Notornis, Parclose, Picture, Pin, Plate, Post, Pulpit, Pushpit, Rack, Rag, Rate, Rave, Rung, Scold, Slang-whang, Slate, Slip, Snash, Sneer, Sora, Soree, Spar, T, Taffrail, Takahe, Taunt, Thersites, Third, Towel, Train, Vituperation, Weka

**Raillery** Badinage, Banter, Chaff, Persiflage, Sport

**Railroad, Railway** Aerial, Amtrak, BR, Branch line, Bulldoze, Cable, Cash, Coerce, Cog, Crémaillère, Dragoon, El, Elevated, Funicular, Gantlet, GWR, Inclined, L, Light, Lines, LMS, LNER, Loop-line, Maglev, Marine, Metro, Monorail, Mountain, Narrow-gauge, Press, Rack, Rack and pinion, Rly, Road, Rollercoaster, Ropeway, ROSCO, Ry, Scenic, Ship, Siding, SR, Stockton-Darlington, Switchback, Telpher-line, Track, Train, Tramline, Tramway, Trans-Siberian, Tube, Underground

**Railwayman** Driver, Fettler, Footplateman, Gandy dancer, Guard, Length(s)man, Locoman, NUR, Plate layer, Stephenson, Stoker, Tracklayer

**Raiment** Apparel, Clothes, Finery, Garb, Ihram

**Rain(y), Rainstorm** Acid, Blash, Deluge, Downpour, Drizzle, Flood, Hyad(e)s, Hyetal, Mistle, Mizzle, Oncome, Onding, Onfall, Pelt, Pelter, Piss, Plump, Pluviose, Pluvious, Pour, Precipitation, Right, Roke, Scat, Scotch mist, Seil, Serein, Serene, Shell, Shower, Sile, Silver thaw, Skiffle, Skit, Smir(r), Smur, Soft, Spat, Spet, Spit, Storm, Teem, Thunder-plump, Virga, Water, Weep, Wet, Yellow

**Rainbow(-maker)** Arc, Arc-en-ciel, Bifrost, Bruise, Dew-bow, Iridescence, Iris, Moon-bow, Spectroscope, Sunbow, Sundog, Torrent-bow, Trout, Water-gall, Weather-gall, White

**Raincoat, Rainproof** Burberry®, Cagoule, Gaberdine, Mac, Mino, Oils(kins), Slicker, Waterproof, Weatherboard

**Raingauge** Ombrometer, Udometer

**Rain-maker** Indra

**Rain tree** Saman

**Raise(d), Raising** Advance, Aggrade, Attollent, Aweigh, Boost, Bouse, Bowse, Broach, Build, Buoy up, Cat, Coaming, Cock, Collect, Elate, →**ELEVATE**, Emboss, Enhance, Ennoble, Erect, Escalate, Exalt, Extol, Fledge, Grow, Heave, Heezie, Heft, High(er),

Hike, Hoick, Hoist, Increase, Inflate, Jack, Key, Leaven, Levy, Lift, Mention, Overcall, Perk, Prise, Rear, Regrate, Relievo, Repoussé, Revie, Rouse, Saleratus, Siege, Sky, Snarl, Step-up, Sublimate, Take up, Up, Upgrade, Uprear, Weigh

**Rake, Raker, Rakish** Bag of bones, Bed-hopper, Buckrake, Casanova, Comb, Corinthian, Croupier, Dapper, Dissolute, Don Giovanni, Don Juan, Enfilade, Gay dog, Jaunty, Lecher, Libertine, Lothario, Raff, Reprobate, Rip, Roam, Roué, Scan, Scour, Scowerer, Scrape, Scratch, Sporty, Strafe, Straff, Stubble, Swash-buckler, Swinge-buckler, Wagons, Wolf, Womaniser

**Rale** Crepitus, Rattle

**Rally, Rallying-point** Assemble, Autocross, Autopoint, Badinage, Banter, Demo, Gather, Jamboree, Meeting, Mobilise, Monte Carlo, Morcha, Muster, Oriflamme, Persiflage, Raise, Recover, Regroup, Rely, Rest, Reunion, Revive, Risorgimento, Roast, Rouse, Scramble, Spirit, Treasure hunt

**Ralph** Imp, Nader, Rackstraw

**Ram** Aries, Battering, Buck, Bunt, Butt, Butter, Corvus, Crash, Drive, Hidder, Hydraulic, Mendes, Pound, Pun, Sheep, Stem, Tamp, Thrust, Tup, Wether

**Ramble(r), Rambling** Aberrant, Aimless, Digress, Excursive, Hike, Incoherent, Liana, Liane, Maunder, Meander, Phrasy, Rabbit, Rigmarole, Roam, Rose, Rove, Skimble-skamble, Sprawl, Stray, Stroll, Vagabond, Wander

**Rameses** Pharaoh

**Ramp** Bank, Gradient, Helicline, Incline, Linkspan, Runway, Slipway, Slope, Speed, Vert

**Rampage** Fury, Riot, Spree, Storm, Warpath

**Rampant** Lionel, Predominant, Profuse, Rearing, Rife

▷ **Rampant** *may indicate* an anagram or a reversed word

**Rampart** Abat(t)is, Brisure, Butt, Defence, Fortification, Parapet, Terreplein, Vallum, Wall

**Ramrod** Gunstick

**Ramshackle** Decrepit, Heath Robinson, Rickety, Rickle

**Ranch** Bowery, Corral, Dude, Estancia, Farm, Fazenda, Hacienda, Spread, Stump

**Rancid** Frowy, Rafty, Reast(y), Reest(y), Reist(y), Sour, Turned

**Rancour** Acrimony, Bad blood, Gall, Hate, Malgré, Malice, Resentment, Spite

**Rand** Border, R, Roon

**Random** Accidental, Ad hoc, Aleatoric, Arbitrary, →AT RANDOM, Blind, Casual, Desultory, Fitful, →HAPHAZARD, Harvest, Hit-or-miss, Hobnob, Indiscriminate, Lucky dip, Scattershot, Sporadic, Stochastic, Stray

▷ **Random(ly)** *may indicate* an anagram

**Randy** Lustful

**Range(r), Rangy** Admiralty, Aga, Align, Ambit, Andes, Atlas, AZ, Ballpark, Band, Bowshot, Bushwhack, Capsule, Carry, Cascade, Chain, Cheviot, Compass, Cotswolds, Course, Dandenong, Darling, Diapason, Dispace, Dolomites, Dynamic, Earshot, Err, →EXTENT, Eye-shot, Flinders, Forest, Game warden, Gamme, Gamut, Glasgow, Grade, Great Dividing, Gunshot, Hamersley, Harmonic, Helicon, Himalayas, Home, Interquartile, Kaikoura, Karakoram, Ken(ning), Kolyma, Ladakh, Leggy, Limit, Line, Locus, Long, MacDonnell, Massif, Middleback, →MOUNT, Musgrave, New England, Orbit, Otway, Oven, Owen Stanley, Palette, Pennine Hills, Point-blank, Prairie, Prism, Purview, Pyrenees, Radius, Rake, Reach, Register, Repertoire, Rifle, Roam, Rocket, Rove, Ruivenzori, Run, Saga, Scale, Scope, Sc(o)ur, Selection, Serra, Shooting, Short, Sierra, Sloane, Spectrum, Sphere, Stanovoi, Stanovoy, Stove, Strzelecki, Sweep, Tape, Tessitura, Teton, Texas, The Wolds, Tier, Urals, Waldgrave, Wasatch, Waveband, Woomera

**Range-finder** Radar, Telemeter

**Rank(s), Ranking** Arrant, Assort, Ayatollah, Begum, Brevet, Caste, Category, Cense, Classify, Condition, Cornet, Curule, Degree, Dignity, Downright, Earldom, Echelon, Estate, État(s), Flag, Flight sergeant, General(issimo), Grade, Graveolent, Gree, Gross,

High, Hojatoleslam, Hojatolislam, Majority, Malodorous, Olid, Parage, Percentile, Petty Officer, Place, Profuse, Queue, Rammish, Range, Rate, Reist, Rooty, Row, Seed, Seigniorage, Sergeant, Serried, Sheer, Shoulder-strap, Sort, Stance, Stand(ing), → **STATION**, Status, Substantive, Table, Taxi, Tier, → **TITLE**, Titule, Top drawer, Utter, Viscount

**Rankle** Chafe, Fester, Gall, Grate, Irritate, Nag

**Ransack** Fish, Loot, Pillage, Plunder, Rifle, Ripe, Rob, Rummage, Tot(ter)

**Ransom** King's, Redeem, Release, Rescue

**Rant(er), Ranting** Bluster, Bombast, Declaim, Fustian, Ham, Harangue, Rail, Rodomontade, Scold, Slang-whang, Sound off, Spout, Spruik, Stump, Thunder, Tirade, Tub-thump

**Rap(ped)** Blame, Censure, Chat, Clour, Gangsta, Halfpenny, Knock, Ratatat, Shand, Strike, Swapt, Tack, Tap

**Rapacious** Accipitrine, Esurient, Exorbitant, Greedy, Harpy, Kite, Predatory, Ravenous, Ravine

**Rape** Abuse, Assault, Belinda, Cole-seed, Colza, Creach, Creagh, Date, Deflower, Despoil, Gangbang, Grass(line), Hundred, Linseed, Lock, Lucretia, Navew, Oilseed, Plunder, Ravish, Statutory, Stuprate, Thack, Tow, Violate, Vitiate

**Rapid(ity), Rapidly** Chute, Dalle, Double-quick, Express, Fast, Fleet, Meteoric, Mosso, Presto, Pronto, Quick-fire, Quicksilver, Riffle, Sault, Shoot, Skyrocket, Speedy, Stickle, Swift, Tantivy, Veloce, Vibrato, Whiz(zing), Wildfire

**Rapier** Sword, Tuck

**Rappel** Abseil

**Rapport** Accord, Affinity, Agreement, Harmony

**Rapprochement** Détente, Reconciliation

**Rapt** Engrossed, Riveted

**Raptor** Eagle, Elanet, Kestrel, Osprey, Standgale, Staniel, Stannel, Stanyel, Stooper

**Rapture, Rapturous** Bliss, → **DELIGHT**, Ecstasy, Elation, Euphoria, Joy, Trance

**Rare, Rarity** Blue moon, Curio, Earth, Geason, Gold dust, Infrequent, Intemerate, Oddity, One-off, Rear, Recherché, Scarce, Seeld, Seld(om), Singular, Surpassing, Thin, → **UNCOMMON**, Uncooked, Underdone, Unusual

**Rare earth** Lu(tetium)

**Rarefied** Thin

**Rascal(ly)** Arrant, Bad hat, Cad, Cullion, Cur, Deer, Devil, Gamin, Hallian, Hallion, Hallyon, → **KNAVE**, Limner, Loon, Lorel, Losel(l), Low, Lozel(l), Nointer, Rip, Rogue, Scallywag, Scamp, Scapegrace, Schelm, Skeesicks, Skellum, Skelm, Smaik, Spalpeen, Tinker, Toe-rag, Varlet, Varmint, Villain

**Rash(ness), Rasher** Acne, Ate, Bacon, Barber's, Brash, Collop, Daredevil, Eczema, Eruption, Erysipelas, Exanthem(a), Fast, Foolhardy, Gum, Harum-scarum, → **HASTY**, Headlong, Heat, Hives, Hotbrain, Hotspur, Ill-advised, Ill-considered, Impetigo, Impetuous, Imprudent, Impulsive, Indiscreet, Lardo(o)n, Lichen, Madbrain, Madcap, Miliaria, Morphew, Nappy, Nettle, Outbreak, Overhasty, Pox, Precipitate, Purpura, Reckless, Road, Roseola, Rubella, St Anthony's fire, Sapego, Scarlatina, Serpigo, Spots, Temerity, Tetter, Thoughtless, Unheeding, Unthinking, Unwise, Urticaria

**Rasp(er)** File, Grate, Odontophore, Radula, Risp, Rub, Scrape, Scroop, Xyster

**Raspberry** Berate, Black(cap), Boo, Bronx-cheer, Etaerio, Hindberry, Razz, Wineberry

**Rastafarian** Dread

**Rat(s), Ratty** Agouta, Apostate, Bandicoot, Betray, Blackleg, Blackneb, Boodie, Brown, Bug-out, Cad, Camass, Cane, Cur, Cutting grass, Defect, Desert, Fink, Footra, Foutra, Geomyoid, Gym, Heck, Heel, Hood, Hydromys, Informer, Kangaroo, Malabar, Mall, Maori, Mole, Moon, Norway, Pack, Pig, Poppycock, Potoroo, Pouched, Pshaw, Pup(py), Renegade, Renegate, Rice, Rink, Rodent, Roland, Rot(ten), Scab, Sewer, Shirty, Squeal, Stinker, Tell, Turncoat, Vole, Water, Wharf, Whiskers, White, Wood

**Rat-catcher** Cat, Ichneumon, Mongoose, Pied Piper

**Rate(s), Rating** A, Able, Able-bodied, Apgar, Appraise, Appreciate, Assess, Base, Basic, Birth, Bit, Carpet, Castigate, Cess, Cetane, Chide, Classify, Click, Conception, Conversion, Cost, Count, Credit, Death, Deserve, Effective, ELO, Erk, Estimate, Evaluate, Exchange, Grade, Headline, Hearty, Horsepower, Hurdle, Incidence, Interest, ISO, Knot, Lapse, Leading, Lick, Mate's, Merit, Mortality, Mortgage, MPH, Mutation, Octane, Ordinary, OS, Pace, Penalty, Percentage, PG, Piece, Poor, Prime (lending), Rag, Rank, Rebuke, Red, Refresh, Reproof, Rocket, Row, Sailor, Scold, Sea-dog, → **SET**, Slew, → **SPEED**, Standing, Starting, Steerageway, Surtax, Take-up, TAM, Tariff, Tax, Tempo, Tick off, Tog, U, Upbraid, Value, Water, Wig, World-scale, X, Zero

**Rather** Affirmative, Agreed, Assez, Degree, Fairly, Gay, Gey, Instead, Kinda, Lief, Liever, Loor, More, Not half, Prefer, Pretty, Some(what), Somedele, Sooner, Yes

**Ratify** Amen, Approve, Confirm, Homologate, Pass, Sanction, Seal, Validate

**Ratio** Advance, Albedo, Aspect, Bypass, Cash, Compound, Compression, Cosine, Distinctiveness, Duplicate, Focal, Fraction, Gear, Golden, Gyromagnetic, Inverse, Liquidity, Loss, Mark space, Mass, Neper, PE, Pi, Picture, Pogson's, Poisson's, Position, Price-dividend, Price-earnings, Proportion, Protection, Quotient, Reserve, Savings, Signal-to-noise, Sin(e), Slip, Space, Tensor, Trigonometric

**Ration(s)** Allocate, Allot, Apportion, Compo, Dole, Étape, Iron, K, Quota, Restrict, Scran, Share, Short commons, Size, Stint, Whack

**Rational(ism), Rationalisation, Rationalist, Rationalize** A posteriori, Descartes, Dianoetic, Dispassionate, Free-thinker, Humanistic, Level-headed, Logical, Lucid, Matter-of-fact, Pragmatic, Reasonable, Sane, Sapient, Sensible, Sine, Sober, Tenable, Wice

**Rationale** Motive

**Ratten** Sabotage

**Rattle (box), Rattling, Rattle on** Alarm, Blather, Chatter, Clack, Clank, Clap, Clatter, Clitter, Conductor, Crescelle, Crotalaria, Death, Demoralise, Discombobulate, Discomfort, Discompose, Disconcert, Gas-bag, Hurtle, Jabber, Jangle, Jar, Maraca, Natter, Nonplus, Rale, Rap, Red, Reel, Rhonchus, Ruckle, Sabre, Shake, Sistrum, Sunn, Tirl, Upset, Vuvuzela, Yellow

**Rat-trap** Pedal

**Raucous** Discordant, Guttural, Hoarse, Loud, Strident

**Ravage** Depredation, Desecrate, Despoil, Havoc, Pillage, Prey, Ruin, Sack, Waste

**Rave, Raving** Adulate, Boil, Doiled, Enthuse, Praise, Redwood, Redwud, Storm, Ta(i)ver, Tear

**Ravel** Disentangle, Entrammel, Explain, Fray, Involve, Snarl, Tangle

**Raven(ous)** Black, Corbel, Corbie, Corvine, Croaker, Daw, Grip, Hugin, Munin, Prey, Unkindness, Wolfish

**Ravine** Arroyo, Barranca, Barranco, Canada, Canyon, Chasm, Chine, Clough, Coulée, Couloir, Dip, Flume, Ghyll, Gorge, Goyle, Grike, Gulch, Gully, Kedron, Khor, Khud, Kidron, Kloof, Lin(n), Nal(l)a, Nallah, Nulla(h), Pit, Purgatory, Wadi

**Ravish(ing)** Abduct, A ravir, Constuperate, Constuprate, Debauch, Defile, Devour, Outrage, Rape, Stuprate, Transport, Violate

**Raw** Brut, Chill, Coarse, Crude, Crudy, Damp, Fresh, Green(horn), Natural, New, Recruit, Rude, Sashimi, Uncooked, Wersh

**Raw-boned** Gaunt, Lanky, Lean, Randle-tree

**Ray(s), Rayed** Actinic, Alpha, Beam, Beta, Bivium, Canal, Cathode, Cosmic, Cramp-fish, Death, Delta, Devil, Devilfish, Diactine, Dun-cow, Eagle, Electric, Extraordinary, Fish, Gamma, Grenz, Guitarfish, Homelyn, Laser, Manta, Medullary, Monactine, Numbfish, Ordinary, Polyact, Positive, R, Radioactive, Radius, Re, Roentgen, Roker, Röntgen, Sawfish, Sea-devil, Sea-vampire, Sephen, Shaft, Skate, Starburst, Stick, Sting, Stingaree, T, Tetract, Thornback, Torpedo, UV, Vascular

**Rayon** Acetate, Faille, Viscose

**Raze** Annihilate, Bulldoze, Demolish, Destroy, Level, Slight

**Razor(-maker)** Cut-throat, Occam, Safety, Shaver, Straight

**Razorbill** Murre

**Razor-fish** Solen

**Razz** Raspberry

**RE** Sappers

**Re** About, Rhenium, Touching

**Reach(ed)** Achieve, Ar(rive), Attain, Boak, Boke, Carry, Come, Extend, Gain, Get at, Get out, Grasp, Hent, Hit, Key-bugle, Lode, Octave, Peak, Raught, Rax, Retch, Ryke, Sease, Seize, Stretch, Touch, Win

**Reach-me-downs** Slop-clothing

**React(or), Reaction(ary)** Addition, Allergy, Anaphylaxis, Answer, Backlash, Backwash, Behave, Blimp, Blowback, Boiling water, Bourbon, Breeder, Bristle, Bummer, Calendria, CANDU, Cannizzaro, Catalysis, Chain, Chemical, Converter, Convertor, Core, Counterblast, Dark, Dibasic, Diehard, Diels-Adler, Dinosaur, Double-take, Dounreay, Dyed-in-the-wool, Emotion, Endergonic, Exoergic, Falange, Fast(-breeder), Feedback, Fission, Flareback, Flehmen, Flinch, Friedel-Crafts, Furnace, Fusion, Gas-cooled, Graphite, Gut, Heavy-water, Hydrolysis, Imine, Incomplete, Insulin, Interplay, Inulase, Junker, Kickback, Knee-jerk, Light, Lightwater, Magnox, Molten salt, Neanderthal, Nuclear, Old Guard, Outcry, Oxidation, Pebble-bed, Photolysis, Pile, Polymerization, Poujade, Pressure-tube, Pressurized water, Reciprocate, Recoil, Redox, Reflex, Repercussion, Respond, Reversible, Rigid, Sensitive, Solvolysis, Spallation, Sprocket, Stereotaxis, Swing-back, Thermal, Thermonuclear, Tokamak, Topochemistry, Ultraconservative, Vaccinia, Wassermann, Water

▷ **Reactionary** *may indicate* reversed or an anagram

**Read(ing)** Abomasum, Bearing, Browse, Decipher, Decode, Devour, Exegesis, First, Gauge, Grind, Grounden, Haftarah, Haphtarah, Haphtorah, Interpret, Learn, Lection, Lesson, Lu, Maftir, Maw, Paired, Pericope, Peruse, Pore, Rad, Rennet-bag, Say, Scan, Second, See, Sight, Skim, Solve, Speed, Stomach, → STUDY, Third, Uni(versity), Vell, Version, Ycond

**Reader(s)** ABC, Academic, Alidad(e), Bookworm, Document, Editor, Epistoler, Gauge, Gentle, Homeridae, Lay, Lector, Microfilm, Phrenologist, Primer, Silas Wegg, Softa, Tape, Taster

**Readiest, Readily, Readiness, Ready** Alacrity, Alamain, Alert, Amber, Amenability, Apt, Atrip, Available, Boun, Bound, Braced, Brass, Cash, Conditional, Dosh, Dough, Eager, Early, Eftest, En garde, Fettle, Fit, Fiver, Forward, Game, Geared-up, Gelt, Go, In the wings, Keyed, Latent, Lolly, Masterman, Money, On (call), Petty cash, Predy, Prepared, Present, Prest, Primed, Procinct, Prompt, Promptitude, Ransom, Reckoner, Ripe, Running costs, Set, Soon, Spot, Tenner, To hand, Turnkey, Unhesitant, Usable, Wherewithal, Willing, Yare, Yark

**Readjust** Mend, Regulate, Retrue

**Readymade** Bought, Precast, Prepared, Prêt-à-porter, Slops, Stock, Store

**Reagent** Analytical, Benedict's, Grignard, Ninhydrin, Reactor, Schiff's, Titrant, Tollens

**Real, Reality, Realities, Really** Actual, Ah, Augmented, Bona-fide, Brass tacks, Coin, Deed, De facto, Dinkum, Dinky-di(e), Earnest, Echt, Ens, Entia, Entity, Essence, Ever so, Fact(ion), → GENUINE, Hard, Honest, Indeed, Mackay, McCoy, McKoy, Naive, Ontic, Positive, Quite, Royal, Simon Pure, Sooth, Sterling, Straight up, Substantial, Tangible, Tennis, The case, Thing(li)ness, True, Verismo, Verity, Very, Virtual

**Realgar** Rosaker, Zarnec, Zarnich

**Realise, Realisation, Realism, Realistic** Achieve, Attain, Attuite, Cash (in), Dirty, Down-to-earth, Embody, Encash, Entelechy, Fetch, Fruition, Fulfil, Hard-edged, Learn, Lifelike, Magic, Naive, Naturalism, Practical, Pragmatism, See, Sell, Sense, Social, Socialist, Suss, Understand, Verisimilitude, Verismo, Verité

▶ **Realities, Reality** *see* REAL

**Realm** Domain, Dominion, Duchy, Field, Kingdom, Land, Notogaea, Region, Special(i)ty, UK

**Ream** Bore, Foam, Froth, Paper, Printer's, Rime, Screed

**Reap(er)** Binder, Crop, Death, Earn, Gather, Glean, Harvest, Scythe, Shear, Sickleman, Solitary, Stibbler

**Reappear(ance)** Emersion, Materialise, Recrudesce

**Rear(ing)** Aft, Back(side), Background, Baft, Behind, Bottom, Breeches, Bring-up, Bunt, Butt, Cabré, Catastrophe, Derrière, Empennage, Foster, Haunch, Hind, Hindquarters, Loo, Natch, Nousell, Nurture, Podex, Poop, Prat(t), →RAISE, Rampant, Retral, Rump, Serafile, Serrefile, Stern, Sternward, Tonneau, Train

**Rearmament** Moral

**Rearrange(ment)** Adjust, Anagram, Ectopia, Permute, Reorder, Shuffle

**Reason(able), Reasoning** A fortiori, Agenda, Analytical, Apagoge, A priori, Argue, Argument, Basis, Call, Casuistry, Casus belli, Cause, Colour, Consideration, Deduce, Economical, Expostulate, Fair, Ground(s), Hypophora, Ijtihad, Inductive, Inference, Intellect, Intelligent, Ipso facto, Justification, Logic, Logical, Logistics, Logos, Metamathematics, Mind, Moderate, Motive, Noesis, Petitio principii, Plausible, Point, Practical, Pretext, Pro, Proof, Pure, Purpose, Ratiocinate, Rational(e), Sane, Sanity, Sense, Sensible, Settler, Somewhy, Sophism, Syllogism, Synthesis, Temperate, Think, Viable, What for, Why, Wit

**Reassure, Reassurance** Solace, There(-there)

**Reave** Despoil, Reif, Rob, Spoil

**Rebate** Diminish, Lessen, Refund, Repayment, Return

**Rebecca** Sharp

**Rebel(s), Rebellion, Rebellious** Aginner, Anarchist, Apostate, Arian, Beatnik, Blouson noir, Bolshy, Bounty, Boxer, Cade, Contra, Croppy, Danton, Defiance, Diehard, Disobedient, Dissident, Drop out, Easter, Emeute, Fifteen, Forty-five, Frondeur, Glendower, Green Mountain Boys, Hampden, Hereward the Wake, Hippy, Iconoclast, Insubordinate, Insurgent, Insurrection, IRA, Jacobite, Jacquerie, Kick, Luddite, Maccabee, Malignant, Mutine(er), Mutiny, Oates, Pilgrimage of Grace, Putsch, Rebecca, Recalcitrant, Recusant, Reluct, Resist, →REVOLT, Rise, Rum, Scofflaw, Sedition, Sepoy, Spartacus, Steelboy, Straw, Taiping, Ted, Titanism, Tyler, UDI, Unruly, Venner, Warbeck, Wat Tyler, Whiteboy, Young Turk, Zealot

▷ **Rebellious** *may indicate* a word reversed

**Rebirth** Palingenesis, Reincarnation, Renaissance, Revival, Samsara

**Rebound** Backfire, Bounce, Cannon, Carom, Echo, Elastic, Recoil, Repercussion, Ricochet, Snapback

**Rebuff** Censure, Check, Cold-shoulder, Earwig, Noser, Quelch, Repulse, Retort, Rubber, Setdown, Sneb, Snib, Snub

**Rebuild** Haussmannize

**Rebuke** Admonish, Berate, Check, Chide, Earful, Lecture, Neb, Objurgate, Rap, Rate, Razz, Reprimand, Reproof, Reprove, Rollick, Scold, Score, Slap, Slate, Snib, Snub, Strop, Threap, Threep, Tick off, Trim, Tut, Upbraid, Wig

**Rebut** Disprove, Elide, Refute, Repulse, Retreat

**Recalcitrant** Mulish, Obstinate, Renitent, Unruly, Wilful

**Recall(ing)** Annul, Echo, Eidetic, Encore, Evocative, Flashback, Go over, Memory, Partial, Reclaim, Recollect, Redolent, Remember, Remind, Reminisce, Repeal, Retrace, Revoke, Total, Unsay, Withdraw

**Recant(ation)** Disclaim, Palinode, Retract, Revoke

**Recap(itulate), Recapitulation** Epanodos, Palingenesis, Summarise

**Recapture** Rescue

▷ **Recast** *may indicate* an anagram

▶ **Recce** *see* RECONNAISSANCE

**Recede, Receding** Decline, Ebb, Hairline, Lessen, Regress, Retrograde, Shrink, Withdraw

**Receipt(s)** Acknowledge, Chit, Docket, Gate, Quittance, Recipe, Revenue, Take, Voucher

**Receive(d), Receiver** Accept, Accoil, Acquire, Admit, Aerial, Antenna, Assignee, Bailee, Bleeper, Cop, Dipole, Dish, Donee, Ear, Earphone, Earpiece, Fence, Get, Grantee, Greet, Hydrophone, Inherit, Intercom, Official, Pernancy, Phone, Pocket, Radio, Radiopager, Remit, Reset, Responser, Responsor, Roger, Set, Sounder, Take, Tap, Transistor, Transponder, Tuner, Wide, Wireless

**Recent(ly)** Alate, Current, Fresh, Hot, Just, Late, Low, Modern, New, New-found, Of late, Yesterday, Yestereve, Yesterweek

**Receptacle** Ash-tray, Basket, Bin, Bowl, Box, Chrismatory, Ciborium, Container, Cyst, Hell-box, Hypanthium, Locket, Loom, Monstrance, Muffle, Outtray, Portfolio, Receiver, Reliquary, Relique, Reservatory, Sacculus, Skip, Spermatheca, Spittoon, Tank, Thalamus, Tidy, Tore, Torus, Trash can

**Reception, Receptive** Acceptance, Accoil, Antechamber, At home, Bel-accoyle, Couchée, Court, Durbar, Entertainment, First-class, Ghost, Greeting, Helpdesk, Infare, Kursaal, Levée, Open, Ovation, Pervious, Ruelle, Saloon, Sensory, Soirée, Superheterodyne, Teleasthetic, Ticker-tape, Warm, Welcome

**Receptor(s)** Metabotropic, Steroid

**Recess(ion)** Alcove, Antrum, Apse, Apsidal, Apsis, Bay, Bole, Bower, Break, Breaktime, Bunk, Closet, Columbarium, Corner, Corrie, Cove, Croze, Dinette, Ebb, Embrasure, Exedra, Fireplace, Grotto, Hitch, Indent, Inglenook, Interval, Loculus, Mortise, →**NICHE**, Nook, Oriel, Outshot, Pigeonhole, Rabbet, Rebate, Respite, Rest, Slump, Toehold, Withdrawal

▷ **Recess** *may indicate* 'reversed'

**Rechabite** TT

**Réchauffé** Hachis, Hash, Salmi

**Recidivist** Relapser

▷ **Recidivist** *may indicate* 'reversed'

**Recipe** Dish, Formula, Plan, Prescription, R, Receipt, Take

**Recipient** Assignee, Beneficiary, Disponee, Donee, End user, Grantee, Heir, Legatee, Receiver, Suscipient

**Reciprocal, Reciprocate** Corresponding, Elastance, Even the score, Exchange, Inter(act), Mutual, Repay, Return, Two-way

**Recite(r), Recital, Recitation(ist)** Ave, Concert, Declaim, Diseuse, Enumerate, Incantation, Litany, Monologue, Mystic, Parlando, Quote, Reading, Reel, Relate, Rendition, Rhapsode, Say, Sing, Tell

**Reckless(ness)** Bayard, Blindfold, Careless, Catiline, Chicken, Desperado, Desperate, Devil-may-care, Gadarene, Harum-scarum, Hasty, Headfirst, Headlong, Hell-bent, Irresponsible, Jaywalker, Madcap, Perdu(e), Ramstam, Rantipole, →**RASH**, Slapdash, Tearaway, Temerity, Ton-up, Wanton, Wildcat

▷ **Reckless** *may indicate* an anagram

**Reckon(ed), Reckoner, Reckoning** Abacus, Assess, Bet, Calculate, Cast, Census, Computer, Consider, Count, Date, Doomsday, Estimate, Fancy, Figure, Guess, Impute, Number, Rate, Reputed, Settlement, Shot, Tab

**Reclaim(ed), Reclamation** Assart, Empolder, Impolder, Innings, Novalia, Polder, Recover, Redeem, Restore, Salvage, Swidden, Tame, Thwaite

**Recline, Reclining** Accubation, Accumbent, Lean, Lie, Lounge, Rest

**Recluse, Reclusive** Anchor(et), Anchorite, Ancress, Eremite, Essene, Hermit, Lone wolf, Low-profile, Monastical, Solitaire

**Recognise(d), Recognition** Accept, Accredit, Acknow(ledge), Admit, Anagnorisis, Appreciate, Apprehend, Ascetic, Character, Cit(ation), Count, Discern, Exequatur, Gaydar, Identify, Isolated, Ken, →**KNOW**, Kudos, Nod, Notice, Oust, Own, Perception, Resipiscence, Reward, Salute, Scent, Sense, Standard, Sung, Voice, Wate, Weet, Wit, Wot

**Recoil** Backlash, Bounce, Kick(back), Quail, Rebound, Redound, Repercussion, Resile, Reverberate, Shrink, Shy, Spring, Start, Whiplash

**Recollect(ion)** Anamnesis, Memory, Pelmanism, Recall, → **REMEMBER**, Reminisce
▷ **Recollection** *may indicate* an anagram
**Recommend(ation)** Advise, Advocate, Counsel, Direct, Encourage, Endorse, Exhort,
   Move, Nap, Praise, Precatory, Promote, Rider, Suggest, Testimonial, Tip, Tout, Urge
**Recompense** Cognisance, Deodand, Deserts, Eric, Expiate, Guerdon, Pay, Remunerate,
   Repayment, Requite, Restitution, Reward
**Reconcile(d), Reconciler, Reconciliation** Accord, Adapt, Adjust, Affrended, Atone,
   Bridge builder, Harmonise, Henotic, Make up, Mend, Square
**Recondite** Difficult, Esoteric, Mystic, Obscure, Occult, Profound
**Reconnaissance, Reconnoitre** Case, Investigate, Patrol, Recce, Scout, Survey
**Reconstitute, Reconstitution** Diagenesis
**Reconstruction** Dramatisation, Perestroika, Telophase
**Record(er), Recorded, Recording (company)** All-time, Blu-ray®, Book,
   Camera, Chart, Chronicle, Clock, Coat(e), Descant, Enrol, Enter, Entry, Ever, Fact, File,
   Hi-fi, Itemise, Log, Mark, Memorise, Mind, Notate, Note, Previous, Quote, Release,
   Remember, Seismograph, Set down, Somerset House, Sunshine, Take, Tally, Tallyman,
   Trace, Trip, Vote, VTR, Weigh, Write

## RECORDS

**2 letters:**
CD
EP
LP

**3 letters:**
Can
Cut
EMI
Rec
Vid
Wax

**4 letters:**
Disc
Film
Form
Gram
List
Memo
Mono
Roll
Tape
TiVo®
VERA
Wire

**5 letters:**
Album
Ampex
Annal
A-side
Aulos
B-side

Crash
Decca
Diary
Eloge
Elpee
Fiche
Flute
Indie
Meter
Notch
Promo
Quipo
Quipu
Score
Track
Video

**6 letters:**
Flight
Ledger
Memoir
Minute
Public
Regest
Single
Wisden

**7 letters:**
Account
Acetate
Archive
Daybook
Digital
Dossier

Epistle
Estreat
Filater
Hansard
History
Journal
Logbook
Memento
Platter
Podcast
Practic
Shellac

**8 letters:**
Analogue
Annalist
Black box
Bookmark
Casebook
Demo-tape
Document
Herstory
Hologram
Lap-chart
Marigram
Memorial
Miniment
Noctuary
Odometer
Open-seel
Pass book
Playback
Practick
Pratique

Pressing
Protocol
Rapsheet
Register
Studbook
Travelog

**9 letters:**
Archivist
Audiotape
Bench-mark
Cartulary
Ephemeris
Forty-five
Score card
Seven-inch
Spirogram
Statement
Stenotype®
Tachogram
Time sheet
Videogram
Videotape
Worksheet

**10 letters:**
Audit trail
Blue Riband
Dictaphone®
Dictograph®
Gramophone
Maxi-single
Memorandum
Provenance

| | | | |
|---|---|---|---|
| Quadruplex | **11 letters:** | Incremental | Seventy-eight |
| Reel-to-reel | Cardiograph | Oscillogram | |
| Scoreboard | Case history | Sphygmogram | **13 letters:** |
| Spectogram | Clickstream | Thirty-three | Congressional |
| Tachograph | Clog-almanac | | Ghetto blaster |
| Transcript | Electrogram | **12 letters:** | Quadrophonics |
| Twelve-inch | Endorsement | English flute | |
| | Helical scan | Hierogrammat | **14 letters:** |
| | Hill and dale | Remembrancer | Campbell-Stokes |

**Record-holder** Champion, Sleeve

**Record-player** DJ, Stereo

**Recount** Describe, Enumerate, → **NARRATE**, Relate, Tell

**Recourse** Access, Resort

**Recover(y)** Amend, Clawback, Comeback, Common, Convalescence, Cure, Dead cat bounce, Get over, Heal, Lysis, Over, Perk (up), Pull round, Pull through, Rally, Rebound, Reclaim, Recoup, Recuperation, Redeem, Regain, Rehab, Repaint, Replevin, Replevy, Repo(ssess), Rescript, Rescue, Resile, → **RETRIEVE**, Revanche, Salvage, Salve, Second-wind, Spontaneous, Upswing, Upturn

**Recreate, Recreation** Diversion, Hobby, Palingenesia, Pastime, Play, Pleasure, R&R, Revive, Reinvent, Sport

**Recriminate, Recrimination** Ruction

**Recruit(s)** Attestor, Bezonian, Choco, Conscript, Crimp, Draft, Employ, Engage, Enlist, Enrol, Headhunt, Hire, Intake, Muster, New blood, Nignog, Nozzer, Press, Rookie, Sprog, Volunteer, Wart, Yardbird, Yobbo

**Rectangle, Rectangular** Dimetric, Golden, Matrix, Oblong, Quad, Quadrate, Square

**Rectifier, Rectify** Adjust, Amend, Dephlegmate, Redress, Regulate, → **REMEDY**, Repair, Right, Silicon

**Recto** Ro

**Rector** R

**Rectum** Tewel

**Recumbent** Prone

**Recuperate** Convalesce, Rally, Recover

**Recur(rent), Recurring** Chronic, Ergodic, Quartan, Quintan, Recrudesce, Repeated, Repetend, Return

▷ **Recurrent** *may indicate* 'reversed'

**Recycle(r), Recycling** Freegan, Nephron, Pulp

**Red(den), Redness** Admiral, Alizarin, Anarch(ist), Angry, Archil, Arun, Ashamed, Auburn, Bashful, Beet, Bilirubin, Bloodshot, Blush, Bolshevik, Brick, Burgundy, C, Cain-coloured, Carmine, Carrot-top, Carroty, Castory, Cent, Cerise, Cherry, Chianti, Chica, Chinese, Choy-root, Chrome, Cinnabar, Claret, Coccineous, Commie, Commo, Communist, Congo, Copper, Coquelicot, Coral, Corallin(e), Corkir, Cramesy, Cremosin, Crimson, Crocoite, Cuprite, Cyanin, Damask, Debit, Dubonnet, Duster, Embarrassed, Eosin, Eric, Erik, Erythema, Ffion, Flame, Flaming, Florid, Flush, Foxy, Garnet, Geranium, Ginger, Gory, Grog-blossom, Gule(s), Hat, Henna, Herring, Incarnadine, Indian, Indigo, Inflamed, Infra, Inner, Intertrigo, Iron, Jacqueminot, Judas-coloured, Keel, Kermes, Korkir, Lac-lake, Lake, Lateritious, Left(y), Lenin, Letter, Magenta, Maoist, Maroon, Marxist, McIntosh, Medoc, Menshevik, Miniate, Minium, Modena, Mulberry, Murrey, Neaten, Orchel, Orchilla-weed, Orseille, Overdraft, Oxblood, Phenol, Pillar-box, Pinko, Plethoric, Plum, Pompeian, Ponceau, Poppy, Pyrrhous, Raddle, Radical, Raspberry, Raw, Realgar, Rhodamine, Rhodopsin, Ridinghood, Roan, Rosaker, Rose, Rot, Rouge, Roy, Rubefaction, Rubefy, Rubella, Rubescent, Rubicund, Rubric, Ruby, Ruddle, Ruddy, Rufescent, Rufus, Russ(e), Russet, Russian, Russky, Rust(y), Rutilant, Safranin(e), Sang-de-boeuf, Sanguine, Santalin, Sard, Scarlet, Sea, Sericon, Setter, Shame-faced,

Solferino, Stammel, Tape, Tidy, Tile, Titian, Trot, Trotsky, Turacin, Turkey, Tyrian, Venetian, Vermeil, Vermilion, Vermily, Vinaceous, Wallflower, Wax, Wine

▷ **Red** *may indicate* an anagram

**Redcoat** Rust, Soldier

**Redeem(er), Redemption(ist)** Cross, Liberate, Liguorian, Lowse, Mathurin, Messiah, Ransom, Retrieve, Salvation, Save

**Red-faced** Coaita, Florid, Flushed, Rubicund

**Red-handed** Bang to rights

**Redhead** Auburn, Bashful, Blue(y), Carrot-top, Carroty, Commie, Commissar, Ginger, Mao, Medoc, Rufus, Safranin(e), Sea

**Red herring** Norfolk capon, Soldier

▸ **Red Indian** *see* **NORTH AMERICAN (INDIAN)**

**Redirect** Reset, Sublimate

▷ **Rediscovered** *may indicate* an anagram

**Redistil** Cohobate

**Redolent** Aromatic, Fragrant, Reeking, Suggestive

**Redoubtable** Stalwart

**Redress** Amends, Offset, Recompense, Rectify, Regrate, Remedy, Right

**Redshank** Gambet, Totanus

**Redskin** Indian, Tomato

**Red spot** Tika

**Reduce(d), Reducer, Reduction** Abatement, Allay, Alleviate, Amortize, Asyndeton, Attenuate, Bate, Beggar, Beneficiate, Calcine, Clip, Commutation, Commute, Concession, Condense, Contract, Cull, Curtail, Cut, Cutback, Damping, Debase, Decimate, Decrease, Decrement, De-escalate, Demote, Deoxidate, Deplete, Depreciation, Detract, Devalue, Dil(ute), Diminish, Diminuendo, Discount, Downgrade, Downscale, Downsize, Draw-down, Drop, Emasculate, Epitomise, Foreshorten, Grate, Grind, Hatchet job, Jeff, Kinone, → **LESSEN**, Lite, Markdown, Miniature, Mitigate, Model, Moderate, Palliate, Pot, Proclitic, Pulp, Put, Quinol, Rarefaction, Razee, Regression, Relegate, Remission, Retrench, Rundown, Scant, Shade, Shorten, Shrinkage, Slash, Strain, Streamline, Supersaver, Taper, Telescope, Thin, Weaken, Whittle, Write-off

**Redundancy, Redundant** FIFO, Frill, Futile, Lay-off, Needless, Otiose, Pink slip, Pleonasm, Retrenchment, Superfluous, Surplus

**Redwood** Amboyna, Mahogany, Sanders, Wellingtonia

**Reed** Arundinaceous, Broken, Calamus, Double, Free, Oboe, Osier, Papyrus, Pipe, Quill, Raupo, Rush, Sedge, Seg, Sley, Spear, Sudd, Syrinx, Thatch, Twill, Whistle

**Reef** Atoll, Barrier, Bioherm, Bombora, Bommie, Cay, Coral, Fringing, Great Barrier, Key, Knot, Lido, Motu, Saddle, Sca(u)r, Skerry, Witwatersrand

**Reefer** Cigarette, Grass, Jacket, Joint

**Reek** Emit, Exude, Stench, Stink

**Reel** Bobbin, Dance, Drum, Eightsome, Hoolachan, Hoolican, Inertia, Lurch, Multiplier, News, Pirn, Spin, Spool, Stagger, Strathspey, Sway, Swift, Swim, Tirl, Totter, Virginia, Wheel, Whirl, Wince, Wintle

**Re-enlist** Re-up

**Reestablish** Redintegrate, Transplant

**Reeve** Hen

**Refectory** Frater

**Refer** Advert, Allude, Assign, Cite, Direct, Mention, Pertain, Relate, Remit, Renvoi, Renvoy, See, Submit, Touch, Trade

**Referee** Arbiter, Commissaire, Linesman, Mediate, Oddsman, Official, Ref, Umpire, Voucher, Whistler, Zebra

**Reference(s), Reference room** Allusion, Almanac, Apropos, Autocue, Biaxal, Chapter and verse, Character, Coat, Credentials, Cross, Grid, Guidebook, Index,

Innuendo, Lexicon, Mention, Morgue, Passion, Promptuary, Quote, Regard, Renvoi, Respect, Retrospect, Testimonial, Thesaurus, Thumb index, Vide

**Referendum** Mandate, Plebiscite, Vox populi

**Refill** Replenish, Top up

**Refine(d), Refinement, Refiner(y)** Alembicated, Attic, Catcracker, Couth, Cultivate, Culture, Cupellation, Cut-glass, Dainty, Distil, Distinction, Elaborate, Elegance, Ethereal, Exility, Exquisite, Genteel, Grace, Horsy, Ladify, Nice, Nicety, Polish(ed), Polite, Précieuse, Preciosity, Pure, Rare(fy), Recherché, Saltern, Sieve, Sift, Smelt, Sophisticated, Spiritualize, Spirituel, Sublimate, Subtilise, Subtlety, Tasteful, Try, U, Urbane, Veneer

**Reflect(ing), Reflection, Reflective, Reflector** Albedo, Apotheosis, Aspersion, Blame, Catoptric, Cat's eye®, Chaff, Chew, Cogitate, →**CONSIDER**, Echo, Glass, Glint, Glisten, Image, Meditate, Mirror, Muse, Narcissus, Nonspecular, Ponder, Redound, Repercuss, Ricochet, Ruminate, Spectacular, Speculum, Symmetrical, Tapetum, Thought

**Reflex(ive)** Achilles, Babinski, Bent, Cancrizans, Diving, In, Knee-jerk, Patellar, Pavlovian, Reciprocal, Re-entrant, Single-lens, Tic, Twin-lens

**Reflux** Acid

**Reform(er), Reforming, Reformist** AA, Agrarian, Amend, Apostle, Besant, Beveridge, Bloomer, Calvin, Chartism, Chastise, Convert, Correct, Counter-Reformation, Enrage, Fourier, Fry, Gandhi, Glassite, Gradualism, Howard, Hussite, Improve, Knox, Lafayette, Land, Lollard, Luther, Meiji, Melanchthon, Mend, Modify, Mucker, New Deal, Owenite, Penn, Pietism, PR, Progressionist, Protestant, Proudhon, Puritan, Rad(ical), Really, Recast, Reclaim, Reconstruction, Rectify, Regenerate, Resipiscence, Restyle, Ruskin, Satyagraha, Savonarola, Simons, Stanton, Syncretise, Tariff, Taskmaster, Transmute, Tyndale, Whig, Wilberforce, Wilkes, Worms, Wycliffe, Young Turk, Zinzendorf, Zwingli

▷ **Reform(ed)** *may indicate* an anagram

**Reformatory** Borstal, Magdalen(e)

**Refract(ion), Refractive, Refractor(y)** Anaclastic, Double, Firestone, Obstinate, Perverse, Prism, Recalcitrant, Refringe, Restive, Stubborn, Sullen, Wayward

**Refrain** Abstain, Alay, Avoid, Bob, Burden, Chorus, Desist, Epistrophe, Faburden, Fa-la, Forbear, Haunting, Hemistich, Leave, Mantra, O(v)erword, Owreword, Repetend, Resist, Ritornello, Roundel, Rumbelow, Rum(p)ti-iddity, Rum-ti-tum, Spare, Tag, Tirra-lirra, Tirra-lyra, Tra-la, Turn again, Undersong, Waive, Wheel

**Refresh(ment), Refresher** Air, Bait, Be(a)vers, Buffet, Cheer, Coffee, Elevenses, Enliven, Exhilarate, Food, Four-hours, Milk shake, Nap, New, Nourishment, Purvey, Refection, Reflect, Refocillate, Reinvigorate, Renew, Repast, Restore, Revive, Seltzer, Shire, Slake, Sorbet, Tea, Water

**Refrigerator** Chill, Chiller, Cold store, Cooler, Deep freeze, Esky®, Freezer, Freon, Fridge, Ice-box, Minibar, Reefer

**Refuel(ling)** Pit stop

**Refuge** Abri, Adytum, Ark, Asylum, Bolthole, Bothie, Bothy, Burrow, Caravanserai, Dive, Fastness, Foxhole, Funkhole, Girth, Grith, Harbour, Haven, Hideaway, Hole, Holt, Home, Hospice, Oasis, Port, Reefer, Resort, Retreat, Sanctuary, Sheet-anchor, →**SHELTER**, Soil, Stronghold, Women's

**Refugee(s)** Boat people, DP, Economic, Escapist, Fugitive, Grenzganger, Huguenot, Reffo

**Refund** Clawback, Rebate, Repayment, Surcharge

**Refurbish** New, Refit, Renew

▷ **Refurbished** *may indicate* an anagram

**Refusal, Refuse** Attle, Bagasse, Ba(u)lk, Bilge, Bin, Black, Blackball, Boycott, Bran, Brash, Breeze, Brock, Bull, Bunkum, Cane-trash, Chaff, Cinder, Clap-trap, Contumacy, Crane, Crap, Cul(t)ch, Debris, Decline, Denay, Deny, Discountenance, Disown, Draff, Drivel, Dross, Dunder, Dung, Eighty-six, Fag-end, Fenks, Fiddlesticks, Finks, First, Flock, Frass, Garbage, Gob, Guff, Hards, Hogwash, Hold-out, Hurds, Husk, Interdict,

Jews' houses, Jews' leavings, Jib, Junk, Knickknackery, Knub, Lay-stall, Leavings, Litter, Lumber, Mahmal, Marc, Megass(e), Midden, Mother, Mullock, Mush, Nay(-say), Nill, No (dice), Noser, Nould(e), Nub, Offal, Off-scum, Orts, Passup, Pellet, Pigswill, Pigwash, Potale, Punk, Radwaste, Raffle, Rags, Rape(cake), Rat(s), Rebuff, Recrement, Recusance, Red(d), Redargue, Redline, Reest, Regret, Reject, Reneg(u)e, Renig, Repudiate, Resist, Rot, → **RUBBISH**, Ruderal, Scaff, Scrap, Scree, Screenings, Scum, Sewage, Sewerage, Shant, Shell heap, Slag, Sordes, Spurn, Sullage, Sweepings, Swill, Tailings, Tinpot, Tip, Toom, Tosh, Trade, Trash, Tripe, Trock, Troke, Trumpery, Turndown, Twaddle, Unsay, Utter, Wash, Waste, Waste paper, Wastrel

▷ **Re-fused** *may indicate* an anagram

**Refutation, Refute** Deny, Disprove, Elench(us), Rebut, Rebuttal, Redargue, Refel

**Regain** Recoup, Recover, Revanche

**Regal** Maeve, Majestic, Organ

▸ **Regal** *see* **ROYAL(TY)**

**Regalia** → **CIGAR**, Livery, Mound, Orb, Sceptre

**Regard(ing)** Anent, Apropos, As to, Attention, Care, Consider, → **ESTEEM**, Eye, Gaum, Look, Observe, Odour, Pace, Rate, Re, Repute, Respect, Revere, Sake, See, Steem, Value, Vis-à-vis

**Regardless** Anyway, Despite, Heedless, In any event, Irrespective, No matter, Notwithstanding, Rash, Though, Uncaring, Unmindful, Willy-nilly

**Regatta** Head of the river, Henley

**Regenerate** Restore

**Regent** Interrex, Ruler, Viceroy

**Regent's Park** Zoo

**Reggae** Ska

**Regicide** Ireton, Macbeth

**Regime(n)** Administration, Control, Diet(etics), Method, Raj, Regency, Reich, Tyranniss

**Regiment** Black Watch, Buffs, Colour(s), Discipline, Foot, Greys, Ironsides, Life Guards, Marching, Monstrous, Nutcrackers, Organise, RA, RE, REME, Rifle, Royals, → **SAS**, Scots Greys, Tercio, Tertia

▷ **Regiment** *may indicate* an anagram

**Region(s), Regional** → **AREA**, Belt, Canton, Central, Climate, Climature, Clime, Critical, District, Domain, Enclave, End, Endemic, Locality, Offing, Part, Province, Quart(er), Realm, Sector, Side, Territory, Tract, Variable, Zone

---

## REGIONS

| *1 letter:* | Bundu | Thule | Ogaden |
|---|---|---|---|
| D | Caria | Tibet | Persis |
| E | Dacia | Tigré | Punjab |
| F | Ionia | Troas | Sparta |
|  | Loire | Weald | Thrace |
| *4 letters:* | Lycia |  | Tigray |
| Aceh | Lydia | *6 letters:* | Tundra |
| Ards | Macao | Alsace | Umbria |
| Asir | Mysia | Amhara | Ungava |
| Brie | Negeb | Canaan | Valois |
| Midi | Negev | Epirus | Veneto |
| Nejd | Nubia | Guiana |  |
| Oudh | Opher | Mallee | *7 letters:* |
| Vaud | Sahel | Mascon | Algarve |
|  | Segou | Mercia | Alsatia |
| *5 letters:* | Sumer | Molise | Bavaria |
| Attic | Tagma | Murcia | Bohemia |

| | | | |
|---|---|---|---|
| Borders | Carniola | Cantabria | Old Castile |
| Cariboo | Caucasia | Catalonia | Westphalia |
| Chaldea | Chaldaea | Circassia | |
| Chiasma | Dust bowl | Cleveland | *11 letters:* |
| Cilicia | Ethiopia | Ecosphere | Austronesia |
| Elysium | Hebrides | Holarctic | Mecklenburg |
| Hundred | La Mancha | Lusitania | Mesopotamia |
| Illyria | Lorraine | Macedonia | Namaqualand |
| Kashmir | Niflheim | Manchuria | Rhizosphere |
| Katanga | Nuristan | Molossian | Spanish Main |
| Lapland | Oriental | Mordvinia | Strathclyde |
| Lothian | Pannonia | New Quebec | Tetrarchate |
| Lusatia | Piedmont | Palestine | Ultima Thule |
| Maghreb | Provence | Patagonia | Vuelta Abajo |
| Masuria | Refugium | Pergunnah | |
| Moravia | Ruthenia | Rhineland | *12 letters:* |
| Navarre | Sarmatia | Turkestan | Low Countries |
| Neogaea | Slavonia | Turkistan | Matabeleland |
| Ossetia | Sogdiana | Val d'Aosta | Thermosphere |
| Pargana | Stannery | Vojvodina | The Trossachs |
| Scythia | Subtopia | | Transylvania |
| Siberia | Taymiria | *10 letters:* | |
| Tayside | Teesside | Appalachia | *13 letters:* |
| Teeside | Thessaly | Bessarabia | Transcaucasia |
| Tuscany | Walachia | Cappadocia | |
| | Zululand | Constantia | *14 letters:* |
| | | Hinterland | Transdniestria |
| *8 letters:* | | Ionosphere | |
| Asturias | *9 letters:* | Lacustrine | *16 letters:* |
| Auvergne | Andalusia | Mauretania | Champagne- |
| Brittany | Aquitaine | Micronesia | Ardenne |
| Calabria | Arctogaea | Midlothian | |
| Camargue | Bantustan | New Castile | |
| Carnatic | Caledonia | | |

**Register(ing), Registration, Registry** Actuarial, Almanac, Annal, Cadastral, Cadastre, Calendar, Cartulary, Cash, Census, Check-in, Child abuse, Dawn, Diptych, Docket, Enlist, Enrol, Enter, Flag out, Gross, Handicap, Index, Indicate, Inscribe, Inventory, Land, Ledger, List, Lloyd's, Log, Matricula, Menology, NAI, Net, Note, Notitia, Obituary, Parish, Park, Patent, Patent Rolls, Poll, Quotation, Read, Reception, Record, Reg(g)o, Rent-roll, Roll, Roule, Score, Shift(ing), Ship's, Sink in, Soprano, Terrier, Till, Voice

**Registrar** Actuary, Greffier, Medical, Protocolist, Recorder, Specialist, Surgical

**Regress(ion)** Backslide, Recidivism, Revert

**Regret(ful), Regrettable** Alack, Alas, Apologise, Bemoan, Deplore, Deprecate, Ewhow, Forthwink, Ichabod, If only, Lackaday, Lament, Mourn, Otis, Penitent, Pity, Remorse, Repentance, Repine, Resent, Rew, →RUE, Ruth, Sorrow, Tragic

**Regular(ity), Regularly, Regulars** By turn, Clientele, Clockwork, Constant, Custom(er), Daily, Episodic, Equilateral, Even, Giusto, Goer, Habitual, Habitude, Habitué, Hourly, Insider, Level, Methodic, Nightly, Nine-to-five, Normal, Often, Orderly, Orthodox, Patron, Peloria, Periodic, Punter, Rhythmic, Routine, Set, Smooth, Soldier, →STANDARD, Stated, Statutory, Steady, Strict, Symmetric, Uniform, Usual, Yearly

**Regulate, Regulation, Regulator** Adjust, Appestat, Ballcock, Ballonet, Bye-law, Code, Control, Correction, Curfew, Customary, Direct, Dispensation, Gibberellin, Governor, Guide, Hormone, King's, Logistics, Metrostyle, Modulate, Order, Ordinance,

Police, Prescriptive, Protocol, Queen's, Red tape, Rule, Snail, Square, Standard, Statute,
Stickle, Stopcock, Sumptuary, Thermostat, Valve

**Regulus** Matte

**Regurgitation** Merycism, Trophallaxis

**Rehab(ilitate), Rehabilitation** AA, Cure, Orthotics, Physio(therapy), Repone

**Rehearsal, Rehearse** Band-call, Dress, Drill, Dry-block, Dry-run, Dummy-run,
Practice, Practise, Preview, Recite, Repeat, Run through, Technical, Trial, Walk through

**Reichenbach** Falls, Od

**Reign(ed)** Era, Govern, Meiji, Prevail, Raine, Rang, Realm, Restoration, Ring, → **RULE**,
Sway

**Reimburse(ment)** Compensate, Indemnity, Recoup, Redress, Repay

**Rein(s)** Bearing, Caribou, Check, Control, Curb, Deer, Free, Gag, Leading strings, Long,
Lumbar, Restrain, Ribbons, Safety, Stop, Tame, Tight, Walking

**Reincarnation** Palingenesis

**Reindeer** Blitzen, Caribou, Comet, Cupid, Dancer, Dasher, Donner, Moss, Prancer,
Rudolf, Tarand, Vixen

**Reinforce(ment)** Aid, Augment, Beef up, Bolster, Boost, Brace, Buttress, Cleat,
Counterfort, Line, Negative, Partial, Plash, Pleach, Positive, Re-bar, Recruit, Reserve,
Ripieno, → **STRENGTHEN**, Support, Tenaille, Tenaillon, Tetrapod, Underline, Welt

**Reinstate** Repone, Restore

**Reinvigorate** Recruit

**Reiterate(d), Reiteration** Battology, Ding, Emphasize, Ostinato, Plug, → **REPEAT**

**Reject(ion)** Abhor, Abjure, Athetise, Bin, Blackball, Brush off, Cast, Cast off, Debar,
Deny, Dice, Disallow, Discard, Disclaim, Discount, Disdain, Disown, Diss, Elbow,
Eliminate, Export, Flout, Frass, Heave-ho, Iconoclasm, Jettison, Jilt, Kest, Kill,
Knock-back, No(t)chel, Ostracise, Oust, Outcast, Outtake, Pip, Plough, Quash, Rebuff,
Recuse, Refuse, Reny, Repel, Reprobate, Repudiate, Repulse, Retree, Scout, Scrub, Spet,
Spike, Spin, Spit, → **SPURN**, Sputum, Thumbs-down, Trash, Turndown, Veto

**Rejoice, Rejoicing** Celebrate, Exult, Festivity, Gaude, Glory, Joy, Maffick, Sing

**Rejoin(der), Rejoined** Answer, Comeback, Counter, Relide, Reply, Response, Retort,
Reunite

**Rejuvenation** Shunamitism

**Rekindle** Relume

**Relapse** Backslide, Deteriorate, Hypostrophe, Recidivism, Regress, Revert, Sink

**Relate(d), Relation(ship), Relations, Relative, Relativity** About, Account,
Affair, Affine, Affinity, Agnate, Akin, Allied, Amour, Antibiosis, Appertain, Apposition,
Associate, Blood, Blude, Bluid, Brer, Brisure, Causality, Cognate, Commensal, Commune,
Concern, Connection, Connexion, Consanguinity, Coosen, Cousin(-german), Coz,
Dalliance, Deixis, Dependent, Dispersion, Einstein, Eme, Enate, Equation, Equivalence,
External, False, Formula, German(e), Goodfather, Granny, Guanxi, Heterogeneous,
Homologous, How's your father, Impart, Inbreeding, Industrial, In-law, Internal,
International, Item, Kin, Kinsman, Labour, Liaison, Link, Love-hate, Mater, Material,
Matrix, Mutualism, Nan(n)a, Narrative, Naunt, Nooky, Object, One-to-one, Osculant,
Pertain, Phratry, Pi, Platonic, Poor, Predation, Privity, → **PROPORTION**, Pro rata,
Proxemics, Public, Race, Rapport, Rapprochement, Ratio, Reciprocity, Recite, Recount,
Rede, Refer(ence), Relevant, Respect(s), Saga, Sib(b), Sibbe, Sibling, Sine, Sybbe,
Symbiosis, Syntax, Tale, Tell, Truck, Who

**Relating to** Of

**Relax(ation), Relaxant, Relaxed** Abate, Atony, Autogenics, Calm, Casual, Chalone,
Chill (out), Com(m)odo, Contrapposto, Dégagé, Délassement, Détente, Diversion, Downbeat,
Ease, Easy-going, Flaccid, Gallamine, Icebreaker, Informal, Laid-back, Laze, Leisured, Lesh
states, Let-up, Lighten, → **LOOSEN**, Mellow (out), Mitigate, Outspan, Peace, Recline, Relent,
Relief, Remit, Rest, Settle, Sit down, Slacken, Sleep, Slump, Soma, Soothe, Toneless, Tranquil,
Unbend, Unbrace, Unclench, Unknit, Unrein, Unstiffen, Untie, Unwind, Veg out, Yoga

▷ **Relaxed** *may indicate* an anagram
**Relay(er)** Convey, Medley, OB, Race, Shift, Tell, Telstar, Torch-race, Webcast
▷ **Relay(ing)** *may indicate* an anagram
**Release** Abreact, Abrogation, Announcement, Bail, Block, Cable, Catharsis, Clear, Day, Death, Deliver(y), Desorb, Disburden, Discharge, Disclose, Disengage, Disenthral, Disimprison, Dismiss, Disorb, Emancipate, Enfree, Exclaustration, Excuse, Exeem, Exeme, Exemption, Exonerate, Extricate, Exude, Free, Handout, Happy, → **LIBERATE**, Manumit, Merciful, Moksa, Nirvana, Outrush, Parole, Press, Quietus, Quitclaim, Quittance, Relinquish, Remission, Ripcord, Soft, Spring, Tre corde, Trip, Unchain, Unconfine, Uncouple, Undo, Unhand, Unharness, Unleash, Unlock, Unloose, Unpen, Unshackle, Unsnap, Unteam, Untether, Untie
**Relegate** Banish, Consign, Demote, Exile, Marginalise, Sideline, Stellenbosch
**Relent** Bend, Mollify, Soften, Weaken, Yield
**Relentless** Cruel, Hard, Hardface, Indefatigable, Inexorable, Pitiless, Remorseless, Rigorous, Stern
**Relevance, Relevant** Ad rem, Appliable, Applicable, Apposite, Apropos, Apt, Bearing, Germane, Material, Pertinent, Point, Real world, Valid
▶ **Reliable, Reliance** *see* **RELY**
**Relic** Antique, Ark, Artefact, Fly-in-amber, Fossil, Leftover, Memento, Neolith, Remains, Sangraal, Sangrail, Sangreal, Souvenir, Survival, Vestige
**Relict** Survivor, Widow
**Relief, Relieve(d)** Aid, Air-lift, Allay, Allegeance, Alleviate, Alms, Anaglyph, Anastatic, Anodyne, Assistance, Assuage, Bas, Beet, Beste(a)d, Bete, Cameo, Catharsis, Cavo-relievo, Comfort, Contrast, Cure, Détente, Ease(ment), Emboss, Emollient, Exempt, Free, Grisaille, Help, High, Indoor, Let-up, Lighten, Linocut, Low, Lucknow, Mafeking, MIRAS, Mitigation, On the parish, Outdoor, Palliate, Phew, Photo, Pog(e)y, Reassure, Redress, Refection, Remedy, Remission, Replacement, Repoussé, Reprieve, → **RESCUE**, Respite, Retirement, Rid, Scratch, Sigh, Spare, Spell, Stand-in, Stiacciato, Succour, Taper, Tax, TENS, Thankful, Thermoform, Tondo, Toreutics, Wheugh, Whew, Woodcut
**Religion, Religious (sect)** Congregant, Creed, Cult, Denomination, Devout, Doctrine, Eremite, Faith, Godfearing, God-slot, God-squad, Hieratic, Hospital(l)er, Messeigneurs, Missionary, Missioner, Monastic, Monseigneur, Nun, Oblate, Opium, Opus Dei, Orthodox, Pagan, Pi, Russellite, Serious, Spiritual, State, Theology, Whore, Zealous

---

## RELIGIONS

| | | | |
|---|---|---|---|
| *3 letters:* | Sunna | Taoism | Sikhism |
| MAM | Wicca | The Way | Tsabian |
| | | Yezidi | |
| *4 letters:* | *6 letters:* | Zabian | *8 letters:* |
| Druz | Culdee | | Buddhism |
| Jain | Gueber | *7 letters:* | Druidism |
| | Guebre | Aaronic | Familist |
| *5 letters:* | Hadith | Animism | Lutheran |
| Baha'i | Hassid | Biblist | Manichee |
| Druse | Jesuit | Bogomil | Mathurin |
| Druze | Khalsa | Ismaili | Mazdaism |
| Hasid | Loyola | Judaism | Mazdeism |
| Islam | Maoism | Lamaism | New Church |
| Jaina | Sabian | Macumba | New Light |
| Jewry | Shaker | Mahatma | Revealed |
| Moony | Shango | Orphism | Salesian |
| Pietà | Shiism | Parsism | Santeria |
| Spike | Shinto | Piarist | Sodality |

| | | **11 letters:** | **13 letters:** |
|---|---|---|---|
| Stundism | Shintoism | Camaldolite | Redemptionist |
| Theatine | Utraquist | Hare Krishna | Sons of Freedom |
| Theravada | Voodooism | Ignorantine | Swedenborgian |
| | Zoroaster | Manichaeism | Tractarianism |
| **9 letters:** | Zwinglian | Progressive | |
| Arya Samaj | | Rastafarian | **14 letters:** |
| Candomble | **10 letters:** | Reformation | Sacramentarian |
| Cargo cult | Albigenses | Rosicrucian | |
| Celestine | Brahmanism | Ryobu Shinto | **15 letters:** |
| Coenobite | Carthusian | Sabbatarian | Christadelphian |
| Falun Gong | Cistercian | Scientology® | Jehovah's Witness |
| Jansenism | Gilbertine | Trinitarian | Resurrectionist |
| Mithraism | Gnosticism | | |
| Mormonism | Heathenism | **12 letters:** | **17 letters:** |
| Pantheist | Manicheism | Christianity | Premonstratensian |
| Parseeism | Revivalism | Confucianism | |
| Postulant | Solifidian | Zarathustric | |
| Sectarian | Triphysite | | |
| Shamanism | Zend-Avesta | | |

**Religious book** Bible, Koran, Missal, NT, OT, Sefer, Sifrei, Tantra, Targum, T(h)orah

**Relinquish** Abdicate, Cede, Demit, Discard, Drop, Forgo, Forlend, Remise, Surrender, Waive(r), Yield

**Reliquary** Chef, Encolpion, Encolpium, Simonious, Tope

**Relish(ing)** Appetite, Aspic, Botargo, Caponata, Catsup, Chakalaka, Chow-chow, Chutney, Condiment, Embellishment, Enjoy, Flavour, Gentleman's, Gout, Gust(o), Horseradish, Ketchup, Lap(-up), Lust, Opsonium, Palate, Pesto, Piccalilli, Pickle, Sapid, Sar, Sauce, Savour, Seasoning, Tang, Tooth, Worcester sauce, Zest

**Reluctant, Reluctance** Averse, Backward, Chary, Circumspect, Cockshy, Cold feet, Grudging, Half-hearted, Hesitant, Laith, Lethargy, Loath, Loth, Nolition, Prudish, Renitent, Shy, Under protest, Unwilling

**Rely, Reliance, Reliant, Reliable** Addiction, Authentic, Bank, Bread and butter, Brick, Confidence, Constant, Copper-bottomed, → **COUNT**, Dependent, Found, Honest, Hope, Inerrant, Jeeves, Leal, Lean, Loyal, Mensch, Predictable, Presume, Pukka, Rest, Robin, Safe, Secure, Solid, Sound, Sponge, Stalwart, Stand-by, Staunch, Steady, Straight, Sure, Trade on, Trump, Trustworthy, Trusty, Unfailing

**Remain(s), Remainder, Remaining** Abide, Ash(es), Balance, Bide, Carcass, Continue, Corse, Dreg(s), Dwell, Embers, Estate, Extant, Exuviae, Fag-end, Fossils, Heeltap, Kreng, Last, Late, Lave, Left, Lie, Locorestive, Manet, Nose, Oddment, Orts, Other, Outstand, Persist, Relic(ts), Reliquae, → **REMNANT**, Residue, Rest, Ruins, Rump, Scourings, Scraps, Stand, Stay, Stick, Stub, Stump, Surplus, Survive, Tag-end, Talon, Tarry, Wait, Wreck(age)

**Remark** Aside, Aspersion, Barb, Bromide, Comment(ary), Compliment, Descry, Dig, Epigram, Generalise, Mention, Noise, → **NOTE**, Notice, Obiter dictum, Observe, Personal, Platitude, Pleasantry, Quip, Reason, Sally, Say, Shot, State

**Remarkable, Remarkably** A1, Amazing, A one, Arresting, Beauty, Bodacious, Come-on, Conspicuous, Dilly, Egregious, Eminent, Extraordinary, Heliozoan, Lamentable, Legendary, Lulu, Mirable, Notable, Notandum, Noteworthy, Personal, Phenomenal, Rattling, → **SIGNAL**, Singular, Some, Striking, Tall, Unco, Uncommon, Visible

**Remedial, Remedy** Adaptogen, Aid, An mo, Antacid, Antibiotic, Antidote, Antihistamine, Antiodontalgic, Antispasmodic, Arcanum, Arnica, Azoth, Bach®, Bach Flower®, Basilicon, Bicarb, Boneset, Calomel, Catholicon, Corrective, Cortisone, → **CURE**, Cure-all, Decongestant, Dinic, Drug, Elixir, Emetic, Febrifuge, Femiter, Feverfew,

Fumitory, Ginseng, Heal, Ipecac, Leechdom, Medicate, Medicine, Moxa, Nosode, Nostrum, Palliative, Panacea, Panpharmacon, Paregoric, Poultice, Provisional, Rectify, Redress, Repair, Rescue®, Salutory, Salve, Simillimum, Simple, Solve, Sovereign, Specific, Sucralfate, Taraxacum, Therapeutic, Tonga, Treatment, Tutsan

**Remember(ed), Remembering, Remembrance** Bethink, Catchy, Commemorate, Con, Mem, Memorial, Memorise, Mention, Mneme, Poppy, Recall, Recollect, Remind, Reminisce, Retain, Rosemary, Souvenir

▷ **Remember** *may indicate* RE-member, viz. Sapper

**Remind(er)** Aftertaste, Aide-memoire, Bell ringer, Bethought, Bookmark, Evocatory, Evoke, Jog, Keepsake, Mark, Memento (mori), Memo, Mnemonic, Mnemotechnic, Monition, Nudge, Phylactery, Prod, Prompt, Shades of, Souvenir, Spur, Throwback, Token

**Reminiscence(s), Reminiscent** Ana, Evocative, Memory, Recall, Recollect, Remember, Retrospect

**Remiss** Careless, Derelict, Errant, Lax, Lazy, Negligent, Slack-handed, Tardy

**Remission** Abatement, Absolution, Acceptilation, Indulgence, Pardon, Pause, Spontaneous

**Remit** Excuse, Forgive, Forward, Pardon, Postpone

**Remnant** Butt, End, Fent, Heeltap, Leavings, Left-over, Odd-come-short, Offcut, Relic, Relict, →**REMAINDER**, Rump, Stub, Sweepings, Trace, Vestige, Witness

**Remonstrate** Argue, Complain, Expostulate, Protest, Reproach, Reprove

**Remorse(ful)** Angst, Apologetic, Ayenbite, Breast-beating, Compunction, Contrition, Had-i-wist, Pity, →**REGRET**, Repentance, Rue, Ruing, Ruth, Sorrow, Worm

**Remote(ness)** Afield, Aloof, Aphelion, Back blocks, Backveld, Backwater, Backwood, Boondocks, Bullamakanka, Bundu, Bush, →**DISTANT**, Far flung, Forane, Foreign, Inapproachable, Insular, Irrelevant, Jericho, Lonely, Long(inquity), Mystique, Nowhere, Off-the-map, Out(part), Outback, Out of the way, Reassert, Scrub, Secluded, Shut-out, Slightest, Surrealistic, Unlikely, Withdrawn, Woop Woop, Wop-wops

**Remount(s)** Remuda

**Removal, Remove(d)** Abduct, Ablation, Abstract, Airbrush, Apocope, Asport, Assuage, Banish, Blot, Circumcision, Clear, Couch, Deaccession, Debridement, Declassify, Deduct, Dele(te), Depilate, Depose, Deracinate, Detach, Dethrone, Detract, Dishelm, Dislodge, Disloign, Dismiss, Dispel, Displace, Doff, Efface, Eject, Eliminate, Eloi(g)n, Emend, Eradicate, Erase, Esloin, Esloyne, Estrange, Evacuate, Evict, Exalt, Excise, Expunge, Expurgate, Extirpate, Extradite, Extricate, Far, Fillet, Flit, Gut, Huff, Nick, Obviation, Ouster, Raise, Raze, Razee, Recuse, Redline, Remble, Rid(dance), Scratch, Sequester, Shift, Sideline, Spirit, Strip, Sublate, Subtract, Supplant, Swipe, Transfer, Transport, Unbelt, Unload, Unperson, Unseat, Unstep, Uproot, Wrest

**Remuneration, Remunerate** Pay, Return, Reward, Salary, Solde, Stipend

**Remus** Uncle

**Renaissance** Awakening, Cinquecento, Early, Erasmus, High, Quattrocento, Revival, Risorgimento

**Rend** Cleave, Harrow, Lacerate, Rip, Rive, Rupture, Tear

**Render(ing)** Construe, Deliver, Do, Gie, Give, Interpretation, Make, Melt, Pebble-dash, Plaster, Provide, Recite, Represent, Restore, Setting, Submit, Tallow, Try, Yeve, Yield

**Rendezvous** Date, Meeting, Philippi, Tryst, Venue

**Rendition** Account, Delivery, Interpretation, Translation, Version

**René** Descartes

**Renegade, Reneg(u)e** Apostate, Default, Defector, Deserter, Pike, Rat(ton), Recreant, Traitor, Turncoat, Weasel out

▷ **Renegade** *may indicate* a word reversal

**Renew(al)** Instauration, Neogenesis, Palingenesis, Refresh, Replace, Resumption, Retrace, Revival, Urban

**Rennet** Steep, Vell

**Renounce, Renunciation** Abandon, Abdicate, Abjure, Abnegate, Disclaim, Disown, Forfeit, For(e)go, Forisfamiliate, Forsake, For(e)say, Forswear, Kenosis, Outclaim, Pass up, Quitclaim, Recede, Recuse, Refuse, Relinquish, Renay, Retract, Sacrifice

**Renovate(d), Renovation** Duff, Face-lift, Instauration, Makeover, Refurbish, Renew, Repair, Restore, Revamp, Touch up, Translate

**Renown(ed)** Fame, Glory, Illustrious, Kudos, Lustre, Notoriety, Prestige, Stardom

**Rent(er), Rented, Renting** Asunder, Attorn, Broken, Charge, Cornage, Cost, Crack, Cranny, Cuddeehih, Cuddy, Division, Economic, Fair, Farm, Fee, Fissure, Gale, Gavel, Ground, → HIRE, Lease, Let, List, Mail, Market, Occupy, Opening, Pendicle, Penny(-mail), Peppercorn, Quit-rent, Rack, Rip, Rived, Riven, Screed, Seat, Slit, Split, Stallage, Subtenant, Tare, Tenant, Tithe, Tore, Torn, Tythe, White

**Reorganise** Rationalise, Realign, Shake up

▷ **Reorganised** *may indicate* an anagram

**Reorientate** Rabat

**Repair(s), Repairer, Reparation** Amend(s), Anaplasty, Assythment, Botch, Cobble, Damages, Darn, DIY, Doctor, Dry dock, Expiation, Fettle, Fitter, Fix, Garage, Go, Haro, Harrow, Heel, Jury rig, Make good, → MEND, Neoplasty, Overhaul, Patch, Piece, Point, Recompense, Recover, Redress, Refit, Reheel, Remedy, Renew, Renovate, Repoint, Resort, Restore, Retouch, Revamp, Roadworks, Running, Satisfaction, Save, Service, Stitch, Stopgap, Tenorrhaphy, Ulling, Vamp, Volery, Wright

**Repartee** Backchat, Badinage, Banter, Cross talk, Persiflage, Rejoinder, Retort, Riposte, Wit, Wordplay

**Repast** Bever, Collection, Food, Meal, Tea, Treat

**Repay(ment)** Avenge, Compensate, Perseverate, Quit, Reassert, Refund, Reimburse, Requite, Retaliate, Revenge, Reward, Satisfaction

**Repeal** Abrogate, Annul, Cancel, Rescind, Revoke

**Repeat(ed), Repeatedly, Repetition, Repetitive** Again, Alliteration, Anadiplosis, Anaphora, Ancora, Battology, Belch, Bis, Burden, Burp, Copy, Cycle, Ditto(graphy), Do, Duplicate, → ECHO, Echolalia, Encore, Epanalepsis, Epistrophe, Epizeuxis, Eruct, Facsimile, Habitual, Harp, Image, Imitate, Ingeminate, Iterate, Iterum, Leit-motiv, Merism, Ostinato, Palillogy, Parrot, Parrot-fashion, Passion, Perpetuate, Perseverate, Playback, Polysyndeton, Reassert, Recapitulate, Recite(r), Redo, Refrain, Regurgitate, Reiterate, Renew, Rep, Repetend, Reprise, Rerun, Retail, Ritual, Rondo, Rosalia, Rote, Same(y), Screed, Segno, Symploce, Tautology, Tautophony, Thrum, Trite, Verbigerate

**Repel(lent)** Aversive, Camphor, Deet, Estrange, Harsh, Offensive, Rebarbative, Reject, Repulse, Resist, Revolt, Scare, Shoo, Squalid, Turn-off, Ug(h), Ward

**Repent(ant), Repentance** Metanoia, Penitent, Regret, Rue, Sackcloth, Yamim Nora'im

**Repercussion** Backlash, Backwash, Echo, Effect, Impact, Recoil

**Repertoire, Repertory** Company, Depot, Rep, Store

▶ **Repetition** *see* REPEAT(ED)

**Replace(ment), Replaceable, Replacing** Change, Deputise, Diadochy, Euphorism, For, Instead, Novation, Overwrite, Pinch-hit, Pre-empt, Prosthesis, Raincheck, Refill, Reinstate, Relief, Renew, Replenish, Restore, Spare part, Stand-in, Substitute, Supersede, Supplant, Surrogate, Taxis, Transform, Transliterate, Understudy, Upgrade, Usurp

**Replay** Action, Instant, Iso(lated), Segno, Slo-mo

**Replenish** Refill, Refresh, Revictual, Stock, Supply, Top (up)

**Replete, Repletion** Awash, Full, Gorged, Plenitude, Plethora, Sated, Satiation

**Replica** Clone, Copy, Duplicate, Facsimile, Image, Repetition, Spit

**Reply** Accept, Answer, Churlish, Counter-attack, Duply, Echo, Over, Rejoinder, Replication, Repost, Rescript, Response, Retort, Roger, Surrebut, Surrebutter, Surrejoinder, Triply

**Report(s), Reporter** Account, Announce, Annual, Auricular, Bang, Beveridge, Blacksmith, Bruit, Bulletin, Cahier, Clap, Columnist, Comment, Commentator, Compte rendu, Correspondent, Court, Court circular, Cover, Crack, Crump, Cub, Debrief, Describe, Despatch, Disclose, Dispatch, Dissertation, Document, Explosion, Fame, Fireman, Grapevine, Gunshot, Hansard, Hearsay, Informant, Item, Jenkins, Journalist, Legman, Libel, Narrative, News, Newsflash, Newshawk, Newshound, Newsman, Noise, Notify, On dit, Paper, Pop, Powwow, Pressman, Protocol, Rapporteur, Read-out, Recount, Relate, Relay, Representation, Repute, Return, Roorback, Rumour, Shot, Sitrep, Sound(bite), Staffer, State(ment), Stringer, Survey, Tale, →TELL, Thesis, Thunder (clap), Transactions, Transcribe, Tripehound, Troop, Update, Weather, Whang, White paper, Wolfenden, Write up

▷ **Reported** *may indicate* the sound of a letter or word

**Repose** Ease, Kaif, Kef, Kif, Lie, Lig, Peace, Relax, →REST, Serenity, Slumber

**Repository** Archive, Ark, Cabinet, Cinerarium, Container, Genizah, Museum, Reservoir, Sepulchre, Vault

**Repossess(ion)** Distringas

**Reprehend, Reprehensible** Base, Blame, Blameworthy, Censure, Criticise, Ill, Paper, Rebuke, Shameful, Warn

**Represent(ation), Representative, Represented** Agent, Ambassador, Anaconic, Archetypal, Assembly-man, Caricature, Client, Commercial, Commissary, Commissioner, Cross-section, Delegate, Depict, Deputation, Describe, Display, Drawing, Drummer, Effigy, Elchee, Eltchi, Emblem, Embody, Emissary, Epitomise, Example, Figurative, Histogram, Ikon, Image, Instantiate, John Bull, Legate, Limn, Lobby, Mandala, Map, Mimesis, Model, Mouthpiece, MP, Nuncio, Personate, Personify, Piechart, Portray, Proportional, Quintessence, Rep, Resemble, Salesman, Senator, Shop steward, Simulacrum, Spokesman, Stand-in, Statua, Status, Steward, Symbolic, Syndic, Tableau, Tableau vivant, Tiki, Token, Transcription, Traveller, Typical, Vakeel, Vakil, Vernicle, Vice-consul, Visitor-general

▷ **Represented** *may indicate* an anagram

**Repress(ed)** Bottle, Check, Curb, Pent, Quell, Reprime, Sneap, Stifle, Stultify, Subjugate, Withhold

**Reprieve** Delay, Mercy, Postpone, Relief, Respite

**Reprimand** Admonish, Blast, Bounce, Carpet, Castigate, →CENSURE, Chastise, Chew out, Chide, Dressing-down, Earful, Jobe, Lace, Lambast, Lecture, Rark up, Rating, Rebuke, Reproof, Rocket, Rollicking, Scold, Slate, Strafe, Targe, Tick off, Tongue-lashing, Wig

**Reprint** Copy, Paperback, Replica

**Reprisal(s)** Marque, Recaption, Retaliation, Revenge

**Reproach** Besom, Bisom, Blame, Braid, Byword, Cataian, Catayan, Chide, Discredit, Dispraise, Exprobate, Gib, Mispraise, Odium, Opprobrium, Rebuke, Ronyon, Runnion, Scold, Shend, Sloan, Stigma, Taunt, Truant, Twat, Twit, Upbraid, Upcast, Yshend

**Reprobate** Cur, Degenerate, Libertine, Lost soul, Outcast, Rascal, Scallywag, Scamp

**Reprocess** Re-make

**Reproduce(r), Reproduction, Reproductive (organ)** Ambisonics®, Amphimixis, Ape, Apomixis, Archegonium, Arrhenotoky, Bearing, Carpel, Clone, Copy, Counterfeit, Depict, Duplicate, Ectype, Edition, Egg(s), Etch, Eugenics, Gamogenesis, Gemmate, Generation, Genitalia, Homogenesis, Isospory, Loins, Megaspore, Meristematic, Mono, Monogenesis, Monogyny, Multiply, Oogamy, Ozalid®, Parthenogenesis, Phon(e)y, Pirate, Playback, Proliferate, Propagate, Pullulation, Refer, Replica, Roneo®, S(h)akti, Schizogony, Seminal, Simulate, Spermatia, Stereo, Strobilation, Syngamy, Syngenesis, Vegetative, Viviparism

▷ **Reproduce** *may indicate* an anagram

**Reproof, Reprove** Admonish, Berate, Brickbat, Censure, Chide, Correction, Correption, Lecture, Rap, Rate, Rebuff, Rebuke, Reprehension, Scold, Sloan, Take to task, Tut, Upbraid

**Reptile, Reptilian** Agamid, Alligarta, Alligator, Base, Basilisk, Caiman, Cayman, Chameleon, Chelonian, Creeper, Crocodile, Cynodont, Diapsid, Dicynodont, Dinosaur, Galliwasp, Gecko, Goanna, Herpetology, Lacertine, Lizard, Mamba, Pelycosaur, Pit viper, Pteranodon, Pterodactyl, Pterosaur, Rhynchocephalian, Sauroid, → **SNAKE**, Sphenodon, Squamata, Synapsid, Tegu(exin), Thecodont, Therapsid, Theriodontia, Tortoise, Tuatara, Tuatera, Turtle, Worm

**Republic(s)** Banana, Federal, Fifth, First, Fourth, People's, Second, State, Third, Weimar

---

## REPUBLICS

**1 letter:**
R

**3 letters:**
RMM
UAR
USA

**4 letters:**
Chad
Cuba
Eire
Fiji
Iran
Iraq
Komi
Laos
Mali
Peru
Togo
Tuva

**5 letters:**
Adhar
Altai
Belau
Benin
Chile
China
Congo
Czech
Egypt
Gabon
Ghana
Haiti
India
Italy
Kenya
Khmer
Libya
Malta
Nauru
Nepal
Niger

Palau
Sakha
Sudan
Syria
Tatar
Yakut
Yemen
Zaire

**6 letters:**
Adygai
Adygei
Angola
Bharat
Biafra
Brazil
Bukavu
Buryat
Cyprus
France
Gambia
Greece
Guinea
Guyana
Ingush
Israel
Kalmyk
Kosovo
Latvia
Malawi
Mari-El
Mexico
Myanma
Panama
Poland
Russia
Rwanda
Serbia
Somali
Turkey
Udmurt
Uganda
Venice
Weimar

Zambia

**7 letters:**
Adharca
Albania
Algeria
Andorra
Armenia
Austria
Bashkir
Belarus
Bolivia
Burkina
Burundi
Chechen
Chuvash
Comoros
Croatia
Ecuador
Estonia
Finland
Georgia
Germany
Hungary
Iceland
Ireland
Jibouti
Kalmuck
Kalmyck
Khakass
Lebanon
Liberia
Moldova
Myanmar
Namibia
Nigeria
Romania
Senegal
Somalia
Surinam
Tunisia
Ukraine
Uruguay
Vanuatu

Vietnam
Yakutia

**8 letters:**
Abkhazid
Botswana
Bulgaria
Buryatia
Cambodia
Cameroon
Chechnya
Colombia
Dagestan
Djibouti
Dominica
Esthonia
Honduras
Karelian
Kiribati
Malagasy
Maldives
Moldavia
Mongolia
Pakistan
Paraguay
Portugal
Roumania
Sinn Fein
Slovakia
Slovenia
Sri Lanka
Suriname
Tanzania
Udmurtia
Zimbabwe

**9 letters:**
Argentina
Badakshan
Cape Verde
Costa Rica
Dominican
Guatemala
Indonesia

Kazakstan
Lithuania
Macedonia
Mauritius
Nicaragua
San Marino
Singapore
Tatarstan
Venezuela

*10 letters:*
Azerbaijan
Bangladesh
Belarussia
El Salvador
Gorno-Altai
Kara-Kalpak
Kazakhstan
Khakhassia
Kyrgyzstan
Madagascar

Mauritania
Montenegro
Mordvinian
Mozambique
North Korea
North Yemen
Seychelles
South Korea
South Yemen
Tajikistan
Ubang-Shari
United Arab
Uzbekistan
Yugoslavia

*11 letters:*
Afghanistan
Burkina-Faso
Byelorussia
Cote d'Ivoire
Nakhichevan

Philippines
Sierra Leone
South Africa
Soviet Union
Switzerland
Tadjikistan
West Germany

*12 letters:*
Guinea-Bissau
South Vietnam
Turkmenistan

*13 letters:*
Bashkortostan
North Ossetian

*14 letters:*
Czechoslovakia

*15 letters:*
Gorno-Badakhshan
Kabardino-Balkar
Marshall Islands
United Provinces

*16 letters:*
Congo-Brazzaville
Equatorial Guinea
Karachai-Cherkess
São Tomé e
Príncipe

*17 letters:*
Bosnia-
Herzegovina
Mari
El-Nakhichevan
Trinidad and
Tobago

---

**Republican** Antimonarchist, Belarussian, Democrat, Fenian, Fianna Fáil, Girondist, GOP, International Brigade, IRA, Iraqi, Leveller, Montagnard, Mugwump, Plato, Provisional, Provo, R, Red, Sansculotte, Sansculottic, Sinn Fein, Whig, Young Italy

**Repudiate** Abjure, Deny, Disaffirm, Disavow, Discard, Disclaim, Disown, Ignore, Recant, Reject, Renounce, Repel, Retract

**Repugnance, Repugnant** Abhorrent, Alien, Disgust, Distaste, Fulsome, Horror, Loathing, Nastiness, Noisome, Obscene, Odious, Revulsion

**Repulsive, Repulse** Abhorrent, Creepy, Grooly, Icky, Lo(a)th, Odious, Off-putting, Rebuff, Rebut, Refel, Refuse, Repel, Repugnant, Slimy, Squalid, Ugly, Vile

**Reputable, Reputation, Repute(d)** Bubble, Credit, Dit, Estimate, Fame, Good, Izzat, Loos, Los, Name, Note, Notoriety, Odour, Opinion, Prestige, Putative, Regard, Renown, Said, Sar, → STANDING, Stature, Status, Stink, Stock, Trustworthy

**Request** Adjure, Appeal, Application, Apply, Ask, Beg, Desire, D-notice, Entreaty, Implore, Invite, Petition, Plea, Prayer, Precatory, Solicit, Supplication, Touch

**Requiem** Agnus Dei, Mass, War

**Require(d), Requirement** Charge, Crave, De rigueur, Desideratum, Desire, Enjoin, Entail, Essential, Exact, Expect, Incumbent, Lack, Mandatory, Necessity, Need, Prerequisite, Priority, Proviso, Seek, Sine qua non, Stipulate, Then

**Requisite, Requisition** Commandeer, Due, Embargo, Essential, Indent, Necessary, Needful, Order, Press, Simplement

**Rescind** Abrogate, Annul, Recant, Remove, Repeal

**Rescue(r)** Aid, Air-sea, Bring off, Deliver, Free, Liberate, Lifeboat, Lifeline, Lifesave, Mountain, Noah, Ransom, Reclaim, Recover, Recower, Redeem, Regain, Relieve, Repatriate, Reprieve, Retrieve, Salvage, Salvation, → SAVE, White knight

**Research(er)** Audience, Boffin, Delve, Dig, Enquiry, Explore, Fieldwork, Indagator, Investigate, Legwork, Market, MORI, Motivation(al), Near-market, Operational, Opposition, Pioneer, Post-doctoral, Psychical, Quest, Res, Scientist, Sus(s), Test, Thesis, Think-tank

**Resell** Scalp

**Resemblance, Resemble, Resembling** Affinity, Apatetic, Ape, Approach, Assimilate, Assonant, Dead ringer, Homophyly, Likeness, Match, -oid, -opsis, Quasi, Replica, Similitude, Simulacrum, Simulate

**Resent(ful), Resentment** Acrimony, Anger, Bitter(ness), Bridle, Chippy, Choler, Cross, Derry, Dudgeon, Embittered, Envy, Grudge, Indignation, Ire, Jaundiced, Malic, Malign, Miff, Mind, Offence, Pique, Rancour, Rankle, Smart, Snarling, Spite, Umbrage

**Reservation, Reserve(d), Reservist(s)** Aloof, Arrière-pensée, Aside, Backlog, Bag, Bank, Bashful, Book, But, By, Capital, Caveat, Central, Cold, Condition, Coy, Demiss, Detachment, Distant, Earmark, Engage, Ersatz, Except, Fall-back, Federal, Fort Knox, Fund, General, Gold, Hold, Husband, Ice, Indian, Introvert, Landwehr, Layby, Locum, Median strip, Mental, Militiaman, Modesty, Nature, Nest-egg, Nineteenth man, Pool, Pound, Proviso, Qualification, Reddendum, Res, Rest, Restraint, Retain, Reticence, Retiring, Rez, Safari park, Salvo, Sanctuary, Save, Scenic, Scruple, Serengeti, Set aside, Shyness, Special, Spoken for, Stand-by, Stand-offishness, Starch, Stash, Stock(pile), Sub(stitute), TA (men), Taciturn, Twelfth man, Uncommunicate, Undemonstrative, Understudy, Warren, Waves, Withhold

**Reservoir** Basin, Cistern, Font, G(h)ilgai, Gilgie, Header tank, Inkholder, Lake, Oilcup, Repository, Rybinsk, Service, Stock, Sump, Tank, Water tower, Well

**Reset** Taxis

**Reside(nce), Resident(s), Residential** Abode, Address, Amban, Chequers, Commorant, Consulate, Denizen, Domicile, Dwell, Embassy, Establishment, Expatriate, Exurb(anite), Gaff, Gremial, Guest, Home, Hostel, Housemate, In, Indweller, Inholder, Inmate, Intern, Ledger, Lei(d)ger, Lieger, Liveyer(e), Lodgement, Lodger, Masonry, Metic, Native, Occupant, Pad, Parietal, Permanent, Populace, Resiant, Roost, Settle, Settlement, Sojourn, Squat, Stay, Tenant, Tenement, Up, Uptown, Vicinage, Villager, Yamen

**Residual, Residue** Ash, Astatki, Boneblack, Calx, Caput, Chaff, Cinders, Clinker, Coke, Crud, Dottle, Draff, Dregs, Expellers, Greaves, Heeltap, Leavings, Mazout, Mortuum, Pitch, Prefecture, Raffinate, Remainder, Remanent, Remnant, Scourings, Sediment, Slag, Slurry, Snuff, Soot, Vinasse

**Resign(ed), Resignation** Abandon, Abdicate, Demit, Fatalism, Heigh-ho, Leave, Meek, Patience, Philosophical, → **QUIT**, Reconcile, Step down, Stoic, Submit

**Resilience, Resilient** Bounce, Buoyant, Elastic, Flexible, Recoil, Rugged, Springy, Stamina

**Resin** Acaroid, Acrylic, Agila, Alkyd, Amber, Amine, Amino, Anime, Arar, Asaf(o)etida, Bakelite®, Bal(sa)m of Gilead, Balsam, Benjamin, Benzoin, Burgundy pitch, Bursera, Cachou, Cannabin, Cannabis, Caranna, Carauna, Catechu, Charas, Cholestyramine, Churrus, Colophony, Conima, Copai(ba), Copaiva, Copal(m), Coumarone, Courbaril, Cutch, Cymene, Dam(m)ar, Dammer, Dragon's blood, Elaterite, Elemi, Epoxy, Frankincense, Galbanum, Galipot, Gambi(e)r, Gamboge, Glyptal, Guaiacum, Gum, Hasheesh, Hashish, Hing, Jalapic, Jalapin, Kino, Labdanum, Lac, Ladanum, Lignaloes, Limonene, Lupulin, Mastic, Melamine, Methacrylate, Myrrh, Natural, Olibanum, Opopanax, Perspex®, Phenolic, Phenoxy, Plastisol, Podophyl(l)in, Polycarbonate, Polyester, Polymer, Polypropylene, Polysterene, Polyvinyl, Propolis, Retinite, Roset, Rosin, Rosit, Rozet, Rozit, Sagapenum, Sandarac(h), Saran®, Scammony, Shellac, Silicone, Storax, Styrene, Synthetic, Tacamahac, Tacmahack, Takamaka, Taxin, Thus, Urea, Vinyl, Xylenol

**Resist, Resistance, Resistant, Resistor** All-weather, Anti, Antibiotic, Barretter, Bleeder, Bristle, Buck, Ceramal, Cermet, Chetnik, Coccidiostat, Combat, Consumer, Contest, Defiance, Defy, Diehard, Drag, Element, Face, Fend, Friction, Gainstrive, Grapo, Hostile, Immunity, Impede, Impediment, Internal, Intifada, Invar, Klendusic, Klepht, Maquis, Maraging, Market, Megohm, Microhm, Negative, Obstacle, Ohm(age), Omega, Oppose, Partisan, Passive, Pat, Pull, R, Radiation, Redound, Reluct, Reluctance, Renitent, Resilient, Rheostat, Sales, Satyagraha, Shockproof, Soul-force, Specific, Stability, Stand (pat), Stonde, Stubborn, Tamil Tiger, Tough, Toughen, Voltage divider, → **WITHSTAND**

**Resolute, Resolution** Adamant, Analysis, Bold, Cast-iron, Casuistry, Closure, Courage, Decided, Decision, Denouement, Determined, Dogged, Doughty, → **FIRM**, Fortitude, Granite, Grim, Grit, Hardiness, Insist, Iron, Joint, Manful, Motion,

New Year, Pertinacity, Promotion, Rede, Reed(e), Resolve, Stable, Stalwart, Staunch, Stout(-hearted), Strength, Strong-willed, Sturdy, Telic, Tenacity, Tough, Unbending, Unmoved, Valiant, Willpower

**Resolve(d), Resolver** Aim, Analyse, Calculate, Conation, Conciliate, Decide, Declare, →**DETERMINE**, Deus ex machina, Factorise, Fix, Grit, Hellbent, Intent, Nerve, Pecker, →**PURPOSE**, Right, Settle, Sort out, Steadfast, Tenacity, Vow, Will

▷ **Resolved** *may indicate* an anagram

**Resonance, Resonant, Resonator** Canorous, Cavity, Electromer, Morphic, Orotund, Parallel, Rhumbatron, Ringing, Sonorous, Timbre, Vibrant

**Resort** Acapulco, Antibes, Arbroath, Aspen, Benidorm, Biarritz, Blackpool, Bognor, Bournemouth, Brighton, Cancun, Cannes, Centre, Chamonix, Clacton, Copacabana, Davos, Dive, Estoril, Étaples, Expedient, Frame, Frequent, Frinton, Gstaad, Haunt, Health, Herne Bay, Hove, Hydro, Invoke, Klosters, Lair, Last, Las Vegas, Llandudno, Locarno, Lowestoft, Malaga, Malibu, Margate, Menton, Miami, Minehead, Morecambe, Nassau, Nice, Orlando, Ostend, Paignton, Palm Beach, Pau, Penzance, Pis aller, Poole, Portrush, Ramsgate, Rapallo, Recourse, Redcar, Repair, Rhyl, Rimini, Riviera, St Ives, St Tropez, Seaside, Skegness, Southend, Spa(w), Stand by, Swanage, Tampa, Thredbo, Torquay, Torremolinos, Troon, Use, Utilise, Waikiki, Watering place, Weston-super-Mare, Weymouth, Whitby, Worthing, Yalta, Zermatt

▷ **Resort(ing)** *may indicate* an anagram

**Resound(ing)** Echo, Plangent, Reboant, Reboation, Reverberate, Ring, Sonorous, Ting

**Resource(s), Resourceful** Assets, Beans, Bottom, Chevisance, Clever, Enterprise, Faculty, Funds, Gumption, Human, Ingenious, Input, Inventive, Manpower, Means, Natural, Renewable, Shared, Sharp, Smeddum, Stock-in-trade, →**VERSATILE**, Ways and means, Wealth, Webliography

**Respect(ed), Respectability, Respectable, Respectful** Admire, Ahimsa, Aspect, Behalf, Bien-séance, Clean cut, Consecrate, Consider, Cred(it), Curtsey, Decent, Deference, Devoir, Douleia, Doyen(ne), Duty, Eminent, Esteem, Fear, Genteel, Gigman, Homage, →**HONOUR**, Intent, Kempt, Kowtowing, Latria, Obeisant, Officious, Pace, Particular, Polite, Preppy, Presentable, Prestige, Proper, Reference, Regard, Relation, Reputable, Revere, Sir, S(t)irrah, U, Venerate, Way, Wellborn, Well-thought-of, Wise, Worthy

**Respective** Several

**Respirator, Respire, Respiration** Artificial, Blow, Breathe, Exhale, External, Gasmask, Inhale, Iron lung, Mouth-to-mouth, Pant, Snorkel

**Respite** Break, Breather, Frist, Interval, Leisure, Let up, Pause, Reprieve, Rest, Stay, Truce

**Respond, Response, Responsive** Amenable, Answer, Antiphon, Autoreply, Backchat, Backlash, Bi, Comeback, Conditioned, Counteroffer, Duh, Echo, Feedback, Flechman, Grunt, Immune, Kneejerk, Kyrie, Litany, Meow, Nastic, Pavlovian, Photonasty, Plea, Prebuttal, Psychogalvanic, Racket, React(ion), Reagency, Rebutter, Reflex, Reply, Repost, Retort, Rheotaxis, Rheotropism, Rise, Sensitive, Stayman, Synapte, Syntonic, Tender, Thigmotropic, Tic, Tropism, Unconditioned, Voice, Warm, Wilco

**Responsibility, Responsible** Accountable, Anchor, Answerable, Baby, Behind, Blame, Buck, Charge, Collective, Culpable, Dependable, Diminished, Duty, Frankpledge, Guilty, Hot seat, Incumbent, Instrumental, Liable, Mantle, Mea culpa, Millstone, Noblesse oblige, Onus, Parental, Perpetrate, Pigeon, Sane, Solid, Stayman, Trust

**Rest(ing), Rest day** Abutment, Alt, Anchor, Avocation, Balance, Bed, Beulah, Break, Breather, Calm, Catnap, Cetera, Comma, Depend, Dormant, Dwell, Ease, Easel, Etc (etera), Fermata, Feutre, Fewter, Gallows, Gite, Half-time, Halt, Inaction, Jigger, Lance, Lave, Lay to, Lean, Leasure, Leisure, Lie, Lie-in, Light, Lodge, Loll, Lound, Lull, Lyte, Minim, Nap, Noah, Nooning, Oasis, Others, Outspan, Overlie, Pause, Quiescence, Quiet, Relâche, Relax, Rely, Remainder, Repose, Requiem, Reserve, Residue, Respite, Sabbath, Shut-eye, Sick leave, Siesta, Silence, →**SLEEP**, Slide, Sloom, Slumber, Spell, Spider, Static, Stopover, Support, Surplus, Teabreak, Time out, Waypoint, Y-level

**Re-start** Da capo, Reboot

**Restate** Reformulate

**Restaurant, Restaurateur** Automat, Beanery, Bistro, Brasserie, British, Cabaret, Café, Canteen, Carvery, Chew'n'spew, Chinkie, Chinky, Chippy, Chip-shop, Chophouse, Coffee shop, Commissary, Cook shop, Creperie, Diner, Eatery, Eating-house, Estaminet, Gastropub, Greasy spoon, Grill, Grillroom, Grub shop, Luncheonette, Maxim's, Naafi, Noshery, Padrone, Pizzeria, Porter-house, Rathskeller, Ratskeller, Raw bar, Roadhouse, Rotisserie, Slap-bang, Steakhouse, Takeaway, Taqueria, Taverna, Tea garden, Teahouse, Tearoom, Teashop, Trat(toria)

**Rest-home** Aggie, Hospice

**Resting-place** Bed, Couch, Dharmsala, Gite, Grave, Inn, Khan, Serai, She'ol, Stage

**Restitute, Restitution** Amends, Apocatastasis, Reparation, Restore, Return

**Restive, Restless(ness)** Agitato, Chafing, Chorea, Fantods, Feverish, Fidgety, Fikish, Fitful, Free-arm, Impatient, Itchy, Jactitation, Spring fever, Toey, Unsettled

▷ **Restless** *may indicate* an anagram

**Restoration, Restorative, Restore(d)** Bring to, Cure, Descramble, Graft, Heal, Mend, New, Pentimento, Pick-me-up, Postliminy, Rally, Reclaim, Recondition, Recuperate, Redeem, Redintegrate, Redress, Redux, Refresh, Refurbish, Regenerate, Rehabilitate, Reinstate, Reintegrate, Rejuvenate, Remedial, Renew, Renovate, Replenish, Replevy, Repone, Restitute, Resuscitate, Retouch, Revamp, Revive, Righten, Salvage, Stet, Tonic, Undelete, Whole

**Restrain(ed), Restraint** Abstinence, Ban, Bar, Bate, Bit, Bottle, Branks, Bridle, Cage, Censor, Chain, Chasten, → CHECK, Checks and balances, Chokehold, Coerce, Cohibit, Compesce, Confinement, Contain, Control, Cramp, Curb, Dam, Decorum, Detent, Dry, Duress, Embargo, Enfetter, Estoppel, Fetter, Freeze, Gag-rein, Gyve, Halt, Hamshackle, Handcuffs, Harness, Heft, Hinder, Hopple, Immanacle, Impound, Inhibit, Jess, Leash, Leg-iron, Lid, Low-key, Manacle, Measure, Mince, Moderation, Muzzle, Patient, Pen, Pinion, Quiet, Rein, Repress, Restrict, Ritenuto, Seat belt, Shackle, Sober, Sobriety, Spancel, Squeeze, Stay, Stent, Stint, Straitjacket, Strait-waistcoat, Tabu, Temper(ate), Tether, Tie, Tieback, Trash, Underplay

**Restrict(ed), Restriction** Band, Bar, Bind, Bit, Block, Burden, Cage, Catch, Censorship, Chain, Circumscribe, Closet, Condition, Constrain, Cord, Corset, Cramp, Curb, Curfew, DORA, Entail, Fence, Fetter, Fold, Gate, Ground, Guard, Hamper, Hamstring, Handcuff, Hedge, Hidebound, Hobble, Inhibit, Intern, Irons, Kennel, Let, → LIMIT, Localise, Lock, Mere, Narrow, Net, Nick, No-go, Oche, Pale, Parochial, Pen, Pent, Pier, Pin, Poky, Pot-bound, Private, Proscribed, Qualify, Ration, Regulate, Rein, Rent, Repression, Rope, Safety belt, Scant, Seal, Section, Selected, Shackle, Snare, Squeeze, Stenopaic, Stent, Stint, Stop, Straiten, Stunt, Swaddle, Tether, Tie

**Restructure, Restructuring** Perestroika

**Result(s)** After-effect, Aftermath, Ans(wer), Arise, Bring, Causal, Consequence, Effect, Emanate, End, End-product, Ensue, Entail, Event, Eventuate, Finding, Fruict, Fruition, Fruits, Issue, Karmic, Knock-on, Lattermath, → OUTCOME, Outturn, Pan, Pay off, Proceeds, Product, Quotient, Score-line, Sequel, Side-effect, Sum, Therefore, Upshot, Verdict, Wale

**Resume, Résumé** Continue, Pirlicue, Purlicue, Summary

**Resurrect(ion)** Anabiosis, Anastasia, Rebirth, Revive, Zomb(ie)

**Resuscitate(d), Resuscitation** Mouth-to-mouth, Quicken, Redivivus, Restore, Revive

**Retail(er)** Category killer, Chain store, Chandler, Cheesemonger, Dealer, Haberdasher, → NARRATE, Regrate, Sell, Shopkeeper, Shopman, Stockist, Superstore, Symbol, Tell

**Retain(er), Retains, Retention, Retentive** Brief, Contain, Deposit, Fee, Hold, Hold-all, Keep, Long, Memory, Panter, Pantler, Reserve, Retinue, Servant, Ur(a)emia, Vassal

**Retaliate, Retaliation** Avenge, Carousel, Counter, Lex talionis, Pay back, Pay home, Quid pro quo, Quit(e), Redress, Repay, Reprisal, Requite, Retort, Revenge, Talion, Tit for tat

**Retard(ed), Retardation** Arrest, Belate, Brake, Cretin, Encumber, Hinder, Hysteresis, Slow, Stunt

**Retch** Boak, Bock, Boke, Cowk, Gap, Heave, Keck, Reach, Vomit

**Reticence, Reticent** Boutonne, Clam, Close, Cowardly, Coy, Dark, Guarded, Introvert, Reserve, Restraint, Secretive, Shy, Taciturn

**Reticule, Reticulum** Bag, Carryall, Dragnet, Handbag, Lattice, Net

**Retina** Detached, Fovea, Macula lutea

**Retinue** Comitatus, Company, Cortège, Equipage, Following, Meiney, Meinie, Meiny, Menyie, Sowarry, Suite

**Retire(d), Retiree, Retirement, Retiring** Abed, Aloof, Asocial, Baccare, Backare, Backpedal, Blate, Bowler-hat, Bow out, Cede, Coy, Demob, Demure, Depart, Ebb, Emeritus, Essene, Former, Leave, Lonely, Modest, Mothball, Nun, Outgoing, Pension, Perfing, Private, Put out, Quit, Recede, Recluse, Reserved, Resign, Retract, Retread, Retreat, Retrocedent, Roost, Rusticate, Scratch, Sequester, Shy, Superannuate, Timid, Unassertive, Withdraw

▷ **Retirement** *may indicate* 'bed' around another word, or word reversed

**Retort** Alembic, Comeback, Courteous, Floorer, Quip, Repartee, → **REPLY**, Retaliate, Riposte, Still, Tu quoque

**Retract(ion)** Backpedal, Backtrack, Disavow, Epanorthosis, Palinode, Recall, Recant, Renounce, Revoke

**Retread** Recap

**Retreat** Abbey, About turn, Arbour, Ashram(a), Asylum, Backpedal, Backwater, Berchtesgaden, Bower, Bug, Camp David, Cell, Climb down, Cloister, Convent, Crawfish, Dacha, Departure, Donjon, Draw back, Funkhole, Girth, Grith, Growlery, Hermitage, Hibernaculum, Hideaway, Hide-out, Hole, Interstadial, Ivory-tower, Katabasis, Lair, Lama(sery), Mew, Monastery, Nest, Neuk, Nook, Nunnery, Pullback, Recede, Recoil, Recu(i)le, Redoubt, Reduit, Refuge, Retire, Retraite, Right-about, Rout, Shangri-La, Shelter, Skedaddle, Stronghold, Withdraw

**Retribution** Come-uppance, Deserts, Nemesis, Revenge, Reward, Utu, Vengeance

**Retrieve(r), Retrieval** Access, Bird-dog, Chesapeake Bay, Fetch, Field, Gundog, Labrador, Read-out, Recall, Reclaim, Recoup, Recover, Redeem, Rescue, Salvage

**Retroflex** Cacuminal

**Retrograde** Backward, Deasi(u)l, Deasoil, Decadent, Decline, Hindward, Rearward, Regrede

**Retrospect(ive)** Contemplative, Ex post facto, Hindsight, Regardant

**Return(s)** Agen, Answer, Bricole, Census, Comeback, Counter, Day, Diminishing, Dividend, Earnings, Echo, Elect, Er, Exchange, Extradite, Gain, Homecoming, Nil, Pay, Payback, Proceeds, Profit, Rebate, Rebound, Recur, Redound, Regress, Reject, Rejoin, Render, Rent, Repair, Repay, Replace, Reply, Requital, Respond, Rest, Restitution, Restoration, Restore, Retort, Retour, Revenue, Reverse, Revert, Riposte, Takings, Tax, Tit for tat, Traffic, → **YIELD**

**Reuse** Cannibalise

**Rev(ving)** Gun, Minister, Vroom

**Reveal(ing), Revelation** Acute, Admit, Advertise, Air, Apocalyptic, Bar, Bare, Betray, Bewray, Confess, Declare, Descry, Disclose, Discover, Discure, → **DIVULGE**, Epiphany, Evince, Exhibit, Explain, Expose, Eye-opener, Giveaway, Hierophantic, Impart, Indicate, Indiscreet, Ingo, Kythe, Leak, Let on, Low-cut, Manifest, Open, Out, Parade, Pentimento, Rake up, Satori, Scanty, Scry, → **SHOW**, Skimpy, Spill, Tell-tale, Unclose, Uncover, Unfold, Unheal, Unmask, Unveil

**Reveille** Raise

**Revel(ling), Revelry** Ariot, Bacchanalia, Bend, Carnival, Carouse, Comus, Dionysian, Disport, Feast, Gloat, Glory, Joy, Maffick, Merriment, On the tiles, Orgy, Rant, Rejoice,

Riot, Roister, Rollicks, Rout, Royst, Saturnalia, Splore, Swig, Upsee, Ups(e)y, Wallow, Wassail, Whoopee

**Reveller** Bacchant, Birler, Corybant, Guisard, Guiser, Maenad, Merrymaker, Orgiast, Silenus

**Revenant** Fetch, Ghost, Spectre

**Revenge(r), Revengeful** Aftergame, Avenge, Commination, Goel, Grenville, Montezuma's, Nightrider, Payback, Reprise, Requite, Retaliation, Revanche, Settlement, Tit for tat, Ultion, Utu, Vigilante, Vindictive

**Revenue** Capital, Fees, Finance, Fisc(al), Fisk, Income, Inland, Internal, Jaghire, Jag(h)ir, Prebend, Primitiae, Rent, Taille, Take, Tax, Turnover, Zamindar, Zemindar

**Reverberate, Reverberation** Echo, Reboant, Recoil, Reflect, Repercuss, Resound

**Revere(nce), Revered** Admire, Adoration, Awe, Bostonian, Dread, Dulia, Esteem, Fear, Hallow, Hero, Hery, Homage, → HONOUR, Hyperdulia, Idolise, Latria, Obeisance, Paul, Prostration, Respect, Venerate

**Reverie** Abstraction, Brown study, Daydream, Dream(iness), Fantasy, Memento

**Revers** Lap(p)el

**Reversal, Reverse, Reversing, Reversion, Reversible** Anatropy, Antithesis, Antonym, Arsy-versy, Atavism, Back(slide), B-side, Change-over, Chiasmus, Commutate, Counter(mand), Escheat, Evaginate, Exergue, Flip, Flip side, Inversion, Mirror image, Misfortune, → OPPOSITE, Overturn, Palindrome, Pile, Regress, Repeal, Retrograde, Revoke, Rheotropic, Setback, Switchback, Tails, Throwback, Transit, Turn, Turnabout, Two-faced, Un-, Undo, Upend, U-turn, Verso, Vice versa, Volte-face, Woman

**Revert** Annul, Backslide, Regress, Relapse, Resort, Retrogress, Return

**Review(er)** Appeal, Audit, Censor, Credit, Critic, Criticaster, Critique, Editor, Encomium, Feuilleton, Footlights, Glimpse, Inspect, Iso-, Judicial, Magazine, March-past, Notice, Pan, Panorama, Peer, Pick over, Pundit, Quarterly, Recapitulate, Repeat, Retrospect, Revise, Rundown, Run over, Slate, Spithead, Summary, Summing-up, Survey, Write-up

▷ **Review** *may indicate* an anagram or a reversed word

**Revile, Reviling** Abuse, Execrate, Inveigh, Rail, Rayle, Vilify, Vituperate

**Revise(r), Revision(ist)** Alter, Amend, Change, Correct, Diaskeuast, Diorthosis, Edit, Emend, Heretic, Peruse, Reappraise, Reassess, Recense, Reform, Rev, Rework, Update

▷ **Revise(d)** *may indicate* an anagram

**Revitalise** Rejuvenate, Resuscitate

**Revive(r), Revival(ist), Revivify, Reviving** Araise, Classical, Enliven, Gothic, Greek, Kiss of life, Neo-classical, Rake up, Rally, Reanimate, Reawake(n), Rebirth, Redintegrate, Redux, Refresh, Rekindle, Relive, Renaissance, Renascent, Renew, Renovate, Restore, Resurrect, Resuscitate, Risorgimento, Romantic, Romo, Rouse, Sal volatile, Smelling salts, Wake

**Revoke** Abrogate, Cancel, Countermand, Negate, → RECALL, Repeal, Rescind

**Revolt(ing), Revolution(ary)** Agitator, Agitprop, American, Anarchist, Apostasy, Appal, Barrel roll, Bloodless, Bolivar, Bolshevik, Bolshevist, Boxer, Bukharin, Bulldog, Cade, Castro, Chartist, Che, Chinese, Circle, Commune, Coup d'état, Cultural, Cycle, Danton, Defection, Dervish, Desmoulins, De Valera, Disgust, Emeute, Emmet, Engels, Enragé, February, Fenian, Foul, French, Girondin, Girondist, Glorious, Green, Grody, Guevara, Gyration, Ho Chi Minh, Icky, Industrial, Inqilab, → IN REVOLT, Insurgent, Insurrection, Intifada, IRA, Jacobin, Jacquerie, Komitaji, Lafayette, Lap, Lenin, Leninist, Mao, Marat, Marti, Marx, Marxist, Maximalist, Maypole, Minimalist, Montagnard, Mutiny, Nauseating, Nihilist, October, Orbit, Outbreak, Paine, Palace, Paris Commune, Peasants, Pilgrimage of grace, Poujadist, Putsch, Radical, → REBEL, Red, Red Guard, Red Shirt, Reformation, Reign of terror, Repellent, Riot, Rise, Robespierre, Roll, Rotation, Round, Run, Russian, Sandinista, Sansculotte(rie), Savimbi, Sedition, Septembrist, Sicilian Vespers, Spartacist, Spartacus, Spiral, Syndicalism, The Mountain, Thermidor, Titanomachy, Trot(sky), Twist, Ugly, Ultra, Unsavoury, Up(rise), → UPRISING, Upryst, Velvet, Villa, Wat Tyler, Weatherman, Whirl, Wolfe Tone, Young Turk, Zapata

▷ **Revolutionary** *may indicate* 'reversed'

**Revolve(r), Revolving** Carrier, Catherine wheel, Centrifuge, Colt®, Gat, Girandole, Grindstone, →GUN, Gyrant, Gyrate, Iron, Klinostat, Lathe, Maelstrom, Merry-go-round, Peristrephic, Pistol, Pivot, Planet, Roll, Roller, Rotate, Rotifer, Rotor, Roul, Roundabout, Run, Six-shooter, Spin, Swivel, Tone, Turn(stile), Turntable, Turret, Twiddle, Waterwheel, Wheel, Whirl(igig), Whirlpool

**Revue** Follies

**Revulsion** Abhorrence, Distaste, Goose skin, Loathing, Repugnance, The creeps, Ugh

**Reward(ing)** Albricias, Bonus, Bounty, Compensate, Consideration, Desert, Emolument, Fee, Guerdon, Head money, Jackpot, Medal, Meed, Payment, Premium, Price, Prize, Profit, Purse, Push money, Reap, Recognise, Recompense, Reguerdon, Remuneration, Repay, Requital, Requite, S, Shilling, Stipend, Tanti, Tribute, Wage, War(r)ison

**Reword** Edit, Paraphrase

**Reworking** Rifacimento

**Rex** Cornish, Devon, Priam, R

**Reynolds** Joshua, PRA

**Rhapsodic, Rhapsody** Bohemian, Ecstasy, Epic, Music, Unconnected

**Rhea** Em(e)u, Nandoo, Nandu, Nhandu, Ostrich, Ramee, Rami, Ramie

**Rhenium** Re

**Rheostat** Potentiometer

**Rhesus** Bandar, Macaque, Monkey

**Rhetoric(al)** Alliteration, Anaphora, Anastrophe, Antimetabole, Antithesis, Antostrophe, Apophasis, Aposiopesis, Assonance, Asteism, Asyndeton, Aureate, Bombast, Brachylogia, Cacophony, Catachresis, Chiasmus, Ecbole, Eloquence, Enantiosis, Epanadiplosis, Epanados, Epanalepsis, Epanorthosis, Epexegesis, Epistrophe, Epizeuxis, Erotema, Eroteme, Erotesis, Euphemism, Hendiadys, Hypallage, Hyperbole, Litotes, Metonymy, Oratory, Oxymoron, Paradox, Paral(e)ipsis, Periphrasis, Peroration, Platform, Pleonasm, Polysyndeton, Scesisonomaton, Speechcraft, Syllepsis, Synoeciosis, Trivial, Trivium, Zeugma

**Rhino** Blunt, Bread, Cash, Lolly, Loot, →MONEY, Tin

**Rhinoceros** Baluchitherium, Keitloa, Square-lipped, Sumatran, White

**Rhizome** China-root

**Rhodes, Rhodesia(n)** Cecil, Colossus, Ridgeback, Scholar, Zimbabwe

**Rhodium** Rh

**Rhomboid** Fusil

**Rhubarb** Fiddlesticks, Forced, Monk's, Pie-plant, Rhapontic, Rheum, Rot, Spat, Tripe

**Rhyme(s), Rhymer, Rhyming** Assonance, Clerihew, Closed couplet, Counting out, Couplet, Crambo, Cynghanedd, Doggerel, Double, Eye, Feminine, Head, Identical, Internal, Jingle, Macaronic, Male, Masculine, Measure, Mother Goose, Near, Nursery, Ode, Pararhyme, Perfect, Poetry, Poulter's measure, Rich, Riding, Rime riche, Rondel, Royal, Runic, Sight, Slang, Slant, Tail(ed), Tercet, Terza-rima, Thomas, Triple, →VERSE, Virelay, Vowel

**Rhythm(ic)** Agoge, Alpha, Asynartete, Backbeat, Beat, Beta, Bo Diddley beat, Breakbeat, Cadence, Circadian, Clave, Dolichurus, Dotted, Drumbeat, Duple, Euouae, Evovae, Four-four, Hemiol(i)a, Ictic, In-step, Lilt, Meter, Movement, Oompah, Ostinato, Prosody, Pulse, Pyrrhic, Rising, Rove-over, Rubato, Scotch catch, Scotch snap, Sdrucciola, Sesquialtera, Singsong, Sprung, Stride piano, Swing, Syncopation, Tala, Talea, →TEMPO, Theta, Three-four, Time, Two-four, Voltinism

**Rib(bed), Ribbing, Rib-joint** Bar, Better half, Chaff, Chiack, Chip, Chyack, Cod, Cord, Costa, Cross-springer, Dutch, Eve, False, Fin, Floating, Futtock, Groin, Intercostal, Lierne, Nervate, Nervular, Nervure, Ogive, Persiflage, Rack, Rag, Rally, Short, Spare, Springer, Subcosta, Taunt, Tease, Tierceron, Tracery, True, Wife

**Ribald(ry)** Balderdash, Bawdy, Coarse, Scurrilous, Smut, Sotadic, Vulgar

**Ribbon** Band, Bandeau, Blue, Bow, Braid, Caddis, Caddyss, Cordon, Fattrels, Ferret, Fillet, Grosgrain, Hatband, Infula, Multistrike, Pad, Petersham, Radina, Red, Rein, Riband, Rosette, Rouleau, Soutache, Taenia, Tape, Teniate, Tie, Topknot, Torsade, Yellow

**Ribless** Ecostate

**Rice (cake)** Arborio, Basmati, Bir(i)yani, Brown, Canada, Carnaroli, Elmer, Entertainer, Golden, Idli, Indian, Kedgeree, Miracle, Paddy, Patna, Pilaf, Pilau, Pilaw, Pillau, Reis, Risotto, Spanish, Sushi, Twigs, Vialone nano, Water, Wild, Zizania

**Rich(es), Richness** Abounding, Abundant, Affluent, Ample, Amusing, Bonanza, Buttery, Comfortable, Comic, Copious, Croesus, Dives, Edmund, Edwin, Fat, Feast, Fertile, Filthy, Flamboyant, Flush, Fruity, Full, Generous, Golconda, Haves, Heeled, High, Idle, Larney, Loaded, Luscious, Lush, Luxe, Luxurious, Mammon, Moneybags, Moneyed, Nabob, New, Oberous, Oofy, →**OPULENT**, Plenteous, Plush, Plutocrat, Prolific, Resonant, Rolling, Silvertail, Sumptuous, Tallent, Toff, Top hat, Treasure, Upper ten, Vulgarian, →**WEALTHY**, Well-heeled, Well off, Well-to-do

**Richard** Angevin, Burbage, Dick(y), Lionheart, Nixon, Rick, Roe

**Richthofen** Red Baron

**Rick (burning)** Goaf, Haymow, Sprain, Swingism, Twist, Wrench

**Rickets, Rickety** Dilapidated, Rachitis, Ramshackle, Rattletrap, Shaky, Unsound

▷ **Rickety** *may indicate* an anagram

**Rickshaw** Pedicab, Tuktuk

**Ricochet** Boomerang, Glance, Rebound

**Rid** Clear, Deliver, Ditch, Eliminate, Eradicate, Expulse, Expunge, Free, Obviate, Offload, Purge, Scrap, Scrub, Shot

**Riddle(r)** Boulter, Charade, Colander, Conundrum, Dilemma, Enigma, Koan, Logograph, Pepper, Perforate, Permeate, Puzzle, Screen, Searce, Search, Seil, Sieve, Sift, Sile, Siler, Sorites, Sphinx, Strain, Tems(e), Trommel, Winnow

**Ride, Riding** Annoy, Aquaplane, Bareback, Bestride, Big dipper, Bruise, Burn, Canter, Car(r)ousel, Coast, Crog(gy), Cycle, District, Division, Draisene, Draisine, Drive, Equitation, Ferris wheel, Field, Free, Galloper, Hack, Harass, Haute école, Helter-skelter, Hitchhike, Lift, Merry-go-round, Mount, Pick(-a-)back, Pickpack, Piggyback, Postil(l)ion, Rape, Revere's, Roadstead, Rollercoaster, Rural, Sit, Spin, Stang, Surf, Switchback, Third, Transport, Trot, Waltzer, Weather, Welter, Wheelie, Whip, White-knuckle

**Rider(s)** Addendum, Addition, Adjunct, Afterthought, Appendage, Attachment, Boundary, Bucket, Cavalier, Charioteer, Circuit, Clause, Coachman, Codicil, Condition, Corollary, Dispatch, Equestrian, Eventer, Freedom, Gaucho, Godiva, Guidon, Haggard, Horseman, Jockey, Lochinvar, Messenger, Peloton, Postil(l)ion, Proviso, PS, Revere, Scrub, Spurrer, Transport, Walkyrie

**Ridge(pole)** Alveolar, Annapurna, Anthelix, Antihelix, Arête, Arris, As(ar), Aseismic, Balk, Bank, Bar, Baulk, Berm, Brow, Bur(r), Carina, Chine, Clint, Costa, Coteau, Crease, Crest, Crista, Cuesta, Culmen, Darling Range, Drill, Drum(lin), Dune, Eskar, Esker, Fret, Gonys, Gyrus, Hammock, Hoe, Hogback, Hog's back, Horst, Hummock, Interfluve, Kaim, Kame, Keel, Knur(l), Ledge, Linch, List(er), Lynchet, Mid-Atlantic, Middleback, Mid-ocean, Missionary, Moraine, Nek, Nut, Oceanic, Oche, Offset, Pressure, Promontory, Ramp, Rand, Raphe, Razor-back, Reef, Rib, Riblet, Rig, Rim, Roof-tree, Sastruga, Screw-thread, Serac, Serpentine, Shoulder, Sowback, Torus, Varix, Verumontanum, Vimy, Wale, Weal, Welt, Whelp, Whorl, Windrow, Withers, Witwatersrand, Wrinkle, Yardang, Zastruga

**Ridicule, Ridiculous** Absurd, Badinage, Bathos, Chaff, Charade, Cockamamie, Debunk, Deride, Derisory, Egregious, Foolish, Gibbet, Gibe, Gird, Goad, Guy, Haze, Jeer, Jibe, Josh, Lampoon, Laughable, Ludicrous, Mimic, Mock, Paradox, Pasquin, Pillory, Pish, Pooh-pooh, Rag, Raillery, Rally, Rib, Rich, Risible, Roast, Satire, Scoff, Scout, Screwy, Send up, Sight, Silly, Skimmington, Sneer, Taunt, Travesty

**Ridinghood** Nithsdale, Red, Trot-cos(e)y

**Riding-master** RM

**Riding-school** Manège
**Rife** Abundant, Manifest, Numerous, Prevalent
**Riffle** Rapid
**Riff-raff** Canaille, Hoi polloi, Mob, Populace, Rag-tag, Rag, tag and bobtail, Scaff, Scum, Trash
**Rifle(man)** Air, Armalite®, Assault, Bone, Browning, Bundook, Burgle, Calic, Carbine, Chassepot, Enfield, Enfield musket, Escopette, Express, Ferret, Garand, →GUN, Jaeger, Kalashnikov, Lee Enfield, Loot, Magazine, Martini®, Martini-Henry, Mauser®, MI, Minié, Pea, Petronel, Pick, Pilfer, Pillage, Raid, Ransack, Reave, Reive, Remington, Repeater, Rieve, Rob, Ruger, Saloon, Shiloh, Springfield, Winchester®
**Rift** Altercation, Breach, Canyon, Chasm, Chink, Cleft, Crevasse, Fault, Fissure, Gap, Gulf, Separation, Split
**Rig(ging), Rigger** Accoutre, Apparel, Attire, Bermuda, Deadeye, Drilling, Equip, Feer, Frolic, Gaff, Get-up, Gunter, Hoax, Jack-up, Jury, Mainbrace, Manipulate, Marconi, Martingale, Oil(man), Oilwell, Outfit, Panoply, Platform, Ratline, Rattlin, Ropes, Roughneck, Schooner, Semisubmersible, Slant, Sport, Stack, Standing, Strip, Stuns'l, Swindle, Tackle, Togs, Top hamper, Trull, Wanton, Yardarm
▷ **Rigged** *may indicate* an anagram
**Right(s), Righten, Rightful, Rightness** Accurate, Advowson, Affirmative, Ancient lights, Angary, Animal, Appropriate, Appurtenance, Ay, Bang, Befit, Blue-pencil, BNP, Bote, Cabotage, Champart, Civil, Claim, Competence, Conjugal, Conservative, Copyhold, Cor(r)ody, →CORRECT, Coshery, Cuddy, Cure, Curtesy, Customer, Dead on, De jure, Dexter, Direct, Divine, Doctor, Droit, Due, Easement, Emend, Eminent domain, Emphyteusis, Entitlement, Equity, Esnecy, Estover, Ethical, Exactly, Faldage, Farren, Fascist, Feu, Fiar, Fire-bote, Fitting, Forestage, Franchise, Free-bench, Freedom, Gay, Germane, Gunter, Haybote, Hedge-bote, Human, Inalienable, Infangthief, Interest, Isonomy, Iure, Junior, Jural, Jure, Jus (mariti), Leet, Legal, Legit(imate), Letters patent, Liberty, Lien, Maritage, Maternity, Meet, Merit, Miner's, Miranda, Moral, Naam, Neo-con, New, Ninepence, Ninepins, Off, Offhand, Offside, OK, Okay, Oke, Okey-dokey, Option, Ortho-, Oughtness, Paine, Pannage, Passant, Pasturage, Pat, Patent, Paternity, Performing, Pit and gallows, Ploughbote, Pose, Postliminy, Pre-emption, Prerogative, Primogeniture, Priority, Prisage, Privilege, Proper, Property, Pukka, R, Rain, Reason, Recourse, Rectify, Rectitude, Redress, Remainder, Remedy, Repair, Ripe, Rt, Sac, Sake, Serial, Side, Slap, So, Soc, Spot-on, Squatter's, Stage, Starboard, Stillicide, Substantive, Suo jure, Suo loco, Tao, Tenants', Terce, Ticket, Tickety-boo, Title, Tory, Trivet, Trover, True, Turbary, User, Usucap(t)ion, Usufruct, Venville, Vert, Warren, Water, Women's
**Right-angle(d)** Orthogonal
**Righteous(ness)** Devout, Good, Just, Moral, Pharisee, Prig, Rectitude, Sanctimonious, Tzaddik, Virtuous
**Right-hand** Dexter, E, Far, Recto, RH, Ro
**Right-winger** Bircher, Dry, Falangist, Fascist, Hard hat, Neocon, Neo-fascist, Republican
**Rigid(ity)** Acierated, Catalepsy, Catatonic, Craton, Extreme, Fixed, Formal, Hard and fast, Hard-set, Hard-shell, Hidebound, Inflexible, Lignin, Ossified, Renitent, Rigor, Set, Slavish, Starch(y), Stern, Stiff, Stretchless, Strict, Stringent, Tense, Turgor
**Rigmarole** Jazz, Nonsense, Palaver, Paraphernalia, Protocol, Ragman, Ragment, Riddlemeree, Screed
**Rigorous, Rigo(u)r** Accurate, Austere, Cruel, Exact, Firm, Hard, Harshness, Inclement, Iron-bound, Severe, Stern, Strait, Strict, Stringent, Thorough
**Rile** Anger, Annoy, Harry, Irritate, Needle, →NETTLE, Vex
▷ **Rile(y)** *may indicate* an anagram
**Rill** Nal(la), Purl, Sike
**Rim** Atlantic, Border, Chimb, Chime, Edge, Felloe, Felly, Flange, Girdle, Kelyphitic, →LIP, Margin, Pacific, Strake, Verge

**Rime** Crust, Frost, Hoar, Rhyme, Rhythm

**Rind** Bark, Crackling, Crust, Peel, Skin

**Ring(ed), Ringer, Ringing, Rings** Anchor, Angelus, Annual, Annulus, Anthelion, Arcus, Arena, Band, Bangle, Bayreuth, Bell, Benzine, Betrothal, Boom-iron, Broch, Brogh, Call, Cambridge, Carabiner, Cartel, Cartouche, Change, Chime, Circinate, Circle, Circlet, Circlip, Circus, Claddagh, Clam, Clang, Clink, Coil, Collet, Cordon, Cornice, Corona, Corral, Corrida, Cramp, Crawl, Cricoid, Cringle, Cromlech, Cycle, Cyclic, Dead, Death's head, Dial, Dicyclic, Diffraction, Ding, Disc, Dohyo, Dong, Donut, Doorbell, Draupnir, Dress, D(o)uar, Echo, Encircle, Enclosure, Encompass, Engagement, Enhalo, Enlace, Envelop, Environ, Enzone, Eternity, Extension, Eyelet, Fainne, Fairlead(er), Fairy, Ferrule, Fisherman, Fisti(cuffs), Gas, Gimmal, Gimmer, Gird(le), Girr, Gloriole, Groin, Grom(m)et, Growth, Grummet, Guard, Gyges, Gymmal, Gyre, Halo, Hank, Hob, →**HOOP**, Hoop-la, Hound, Hula-hoop, Ideal, Image, Inner, Inorb, Involucre, Jougs, Jow, Karabiner, Kartell, Keeper, Key, Knell, Knock-out, Kraal, Lactam, Laer, Lifebelt, Link, Loop, Luned, Lute, Magpie, Manacle, Manilla, Marquise, Mourning, Napkin, Newton's, Nibelung, Nimbus, Nose, O, Oil-control, Orb, Outer, Pappus, Parral, Parrel, Peal, Pele, Pen, Phone, Ping, Piston, Potato, Price, Prize, Puteal, Quoit, Re-echo, Resonant, Resound, Retaining, Reverberate, Round, Rove, Rowel, Rundle, Runner, Rush, Sale, Scarf, Scraper, Screw eye, Scrunchy, Seal, Signet, Slinger, Slip, Snap-link, Solomon, Sound, Spell, Split, Stemma, Stemme, Stonehenge, Surround, Swivel, Syndicate, Tang, Tattersall, Teething, Terret, Territ, Thimble, Thumb, Timbre, Ting, Tingle, Tink(le), Tinnitus, Tintinnabulate, Toe, Token, Toll, Toplady, Tore, Torquate, Torques, Torret, Torus, Travelling, Tree, Trochus, Troth, Turret, Tweed, Varvel, Vervel, Vice, Vortex, Wagnerian, Washer, Wedding, Welkin, Whorl, Withe, Woggle, Zero

**Ring-dance** Carol

**Ring-dove** Que(e)st, Qu(o)ist

**Ring-leader** Bell-wether, Fugleman, Instigator

**Ringlet** Curl(icue), Lock, Tendril, Tress

**Ringmaster** Wagner

**Ringworm** Serpigo, Tinea

**Rink** Ice, Roller, Skating

**Rinse** Bathe, Blue, Cleanse, Douche, Sind, Sine, Sluice, Swill, Synd, Syne, Tint, Wash

**Riot(er), Riotous(ly), Riots** Anarchy, Brawl, Clamour, Demo, Deray, Gordon, Hilarious, Hubbub, Luddite, Medley, Mêlée, Nicker, Orgy, Pandemonium, Peterloo, Petroleur, Porteous, Profusion, Quorum, Race, Rag, Ragmatical, Rebecca, Rebel, Roaring, Roister, Rout, Rowdy, Ruction, Ruffianly, Scream, Sedition, Swing, Tumult

▷ **Rioters, Riotous** *may indicate* an anagram

**Rip(per), Ripping, Rip off** Avulse, Basket, Buller, Cur, Dilacerate, Fleece, Grand, Handful, Horse, Jack, Lacerate, Rent, Rep, Roué, Scallywag, Splendid, Tear, Tide, Topnotch, To-rend, Unseam

**Ripe, Ripen(ing)** Auspicious, Full, Geocarpy, Mature, Mellow, Rathe, Ready

**Riposte** Counterblow, Countermove, Repartee, Retaliate, Retort

**Ripple, Rippling** Bradyseism, Fret, Jabble, Overlap, Popple, Purl, Ruffle, Undulation, Wave, Wavelet, Wimple, Wrinkle

▷ **Rippling** *may indicate* an anagram

**Rise(r), Rising** Advance, Appreciate, Ascend, Aspire, Assurgent, Bull, Butte, Cause, Dry, Dutch, Easter, Eger, Elevation, Emanate, Emerge, Emerse, Émeute, Eminence, Erect, Escalate, Get up, Gradient, Hance, Hauriant, Haurient, Heave, Heliacal, Hike, Hill, Hummock, Hunt's up, Improve, Increase, Incremental, Insurgent, Intifada, Intumesce, Jibe, Knap, Knoll, Lark, Leap, Levee, Levitate, Lift, Molehill, Motte, Mount, Mutiny, Orient, Origin, Peripety, Point, Prove, Putsch, Rear, Rebel, Resurgent, Resurrection, →**REVOLT**, Riot, Rocket, Saleratus, Scarp, Sklim, Sky-rocket, Soar, Spiral, Stand, Stay, Stie, Sty, Stye, Surface, Surge, The Fifteen, Tor, Tower, Transcend, Up, Upbrast, Upburst, Upcurl, Upgo, Uprest, Upshoot, Upspear, Upsurge, Upswarm, Upturn, Well

**Risk(y)** Actuarial, Adventure, Apperil, Back, Calculated, Chance, Compromise, Counterparty, → **DANGER**, Daring, Dice, Dicy, Emprise, Endanger, Fear, Gamble, Game, Hairy, Hazard, High-wire, Iffy, Imperil, Impetuous, Jeopardy, Liability, Morass, Nap, Parlous, Peril(ous), Precarious, Security, Shoot the works, Spec, Stake, Throw, Touch and go, Touchy, Unsafe, Venture

**Risorgimento** Renaissance

**Risqué** Blue, Racy, Salty, Saucy, Scabrous, Spicy

**Rissole(s)** Cecils, Chillada, Croquette, Faggot, Falafel, Felafel, Paupiette, Quennelle, Veggieburger

**Rite(s)** Asperges, Bora, Ceremony, Eastern, Exequies, Initiation, Last offices, Liturgy, Mystery, Nagmaal, Obsequies, Powwow, Ritual, Sacral, Sacrament, Sarum use, Solemnity, Superstition, York

**Ritual** Agadah, Arti, Ceremony, Chanoyu, Cultus, Customary, Formality, Haggada, Lavabo, Liturgy, Mumbo-jumbo, Puja, Rite, Sacrament, Sacring, Seder, Social, Tantric, Telestic, Use

**Rival(ry), Rivals** Absolute, Acres, Aemule, Binocular, Challenge, Compete, Contender, Emulate, Emule, Envy, Fo(n)e, → **MATCH**, Needle, Opponent, Retinal, Touch, Vie

**River(s)** Bayou, Creek, Dalles, Ea, Eau, Estuary, Flood, Flower, Fluvial, Potamic, Potamology, R, Riverain, Runner, Stream, Tide(-way), Tributary, Waterway

---

## RIVERS

| 2 letters: | Oil | Dart | Lech |
|---|---|---|---|
| Ay | Oka | Deva | Lena |
| Ob | Ord | Doon | Liao |
| Po | Red | Dove | Luan |
| Si | San | Drin | Lune |
| Xi | Tay | Earn | Maas |
| | Tet | East | Main |
| 3 letters: | Ure | Ebbw | Meta |
| Aar | Usk | Ebro | Milk |
| Aln | Wye | Eden | Mino |
| Axe | Yeo | Eder | Mole |
| Ayr | | Elbe | Nene |
| Bug | 4 letters: | Emme | Neva |
| Cam | Abus | Erne | Nile |
| Dee | Abzu | Esla | Nith |
| Don | Acis | Eure | Oder |
| Ems | Adda | Gila | Ohio |
| Esk | Adur | Gota | Oise |
| Exe | Aire | Huon | Ouse |
| Fal | Alma | Idle | Oxus |
| Fly | Alph | Isar | Prut |
| Fox | Amur | Iser | Rock |
| Han | Aran | Isis | Ruhr |
| Hsi | Aras | Isla | Saar |
| Hué | Arno | Ivel | Sava |
| Inn | Aude | Jiul | Soar |
| Lee | Avon | Juba | Spey |
| Lot | Back | Kama | Styx |
| Luo | Beni | Kill | Swan |
| Lys | Bomu | Kura | Swat |
| Mur | Cher | Kwai | Tadi |
| Nar | Culm | Lahn | Taff |

Tana
Tarn
Tees
Teme
Test
Tone
Tyne
Uele
Ural
Uvod
Vaal
Waal
Wear
Xero
Yalu
Yare
Yate
Yser
Yuan
Yuen

**5 letters:**
Abana
Acton
Adige
Afton
Agate
Aisne
Aldan
Apure
Argun
Avoca
Benue
Boyne
Broad
Cauca
Chari
Clwyd
Clyde
Clyst
Colne
Congo
Conwy
Cross
Culbá
Dasht
Desna
Doubs
Douro
Drava
Drave
Duero
Dvina
Eblis

Ebola
Firth
Fleet
Forth
Ganga
Gogra
Green
Greta
Havel
Hotan
Indre
Indus
Isere
Ishim
James
Jumna
Juruá
Kasai
Kaven
Kefue
Kenga
Kuban
Lethe
Liard
Limay
Loire
Marne
Mbomu
Meuse
Minho
Mosel
Mulla
Mures
Namoi
Negro
Neman
Niger
Ogowe
Onega
Oreti
Peace
Pearl
Pecos
Pelly
Piave
Pison
Plate
Purus
Rainy
Rance
Rhine
Rhône
Rogue
Roper

Saône
Seine
Shari
Shire
Siang
Siret
Skien
Slave
Snake
Snowy
Somme
Spree
Staff
Stour
Swale
Tagus
Tamar
Tapti
Tarim
Teign
Terek
Tiber
Tisza
Tobol
Trent
Tweed
Volga
Volta
Warta
Weser
Xiang
Xingu
Yaqui
Yarra
Yonne
Yssel
Yukon

**6 letters:**
Allier
Amazon
Anadyr
Angara
Arzina
Atbara
Barcoo
Barrow
Bio-Bio
Broads
Buller
Calder
Canton
Chenab
Clutha

Colima
Croton
Crouch
Cydnus
Danube
Dawson
Donets
Duddon
Durack
Escaut
Finlay
Fraser
Gambia
Ganges
Glomma
Granta
Harlem
Hodder
Hsiang
Hudson
Humber
Iguacu
Ijssel
Irtish
Irtysh
Irwell
Isonzo
Itchen
Japura
Javari
Javary
Jhelum
Jordan
Kaduna
Kagera
Kaveri
Kennet
Kistna
Kolyma
Komati
Liffey
Loiret
Mamoré
Medway
Mekong
Mersey
Mindel
Mohawk
Molopo
Morava
Moskva
Murray
Neckar
Neisse

Nelson
Nyeman
Ogooue
Orange
Orwell
Ottawa
Pahang
Parana
Peneus
Platte
Pripet
Prosna
Rakaia
Ribble
Riffle
Rother
Sabine
Saluda
Sambre
Santee
Seneca
Severn
St John
Struma
Sutlej
Swanee
Tanana
Tarsus
Tevere
Teviot
Thames
Ticino
Tigris
Tugela
Tyburn
Ubangi
Ussuri
Vardar
Vienne
Vltava
Vyatka
Wabash
Wairau
Wensum
Wharfe
Wupper
Yarrow
Yellow

*7 letters:*
Acheron
Aruwimi
Bassein
Berbice

Berezua
Bermejo
Buffalo
Burnett
Caqueta
Cauvery
Chagres
Cocytus
Damodar
Darling
Derwent
Detroit
Dnieper
Dubglas
Durance
Ettrick
Fitzroy
Garonne
Genesee
Gironde
Guapore
Hari Rud
Helmand
Hooghly
Huang He
Hwangho
Iguassu
Irawadi
Kanawha
Klamath
Krishna
Lachlan
Limpopo
Lualaba
Madeira
Manning
Maranon
Maritsa
Mataura
Meander
Moselle
Narbada
Narmada
Neuquén
Niagara
Nipigon
Oceanus
Orinoco
Orontes
Parrett
Pechora
Pharpar
Potomac
Red Deer

Rubicon
Sabrina
Salinas
Salween
Salzach
Sanders
San Juan
Scheldt
Senegal
Shannon
Songhua
Spokane
St Clair
St Croix
St Johns
St Mary's
Swannee
Tapajos
Thomson
Tugaloo
Ucayali
Uruguay
Vistula
Waikato
Waitaki
Washita
Wateree
Welland
Xi Jiang
Yangtse
Yenisei
Yenisey
Zambese
Zambezi

*8 letters:*
Amu Darya
Anderson
Apurimac
Araguaia
Araguaya
Arkansas
Berezina
Blue Nile
Burdekin
Canadian
Charente
Cherwell
Cheyenne
Chindwin
Chu Kiang
Clarence
Colorado
Columbia

Congaree
Daintree
Demerara
Dneister
Dordogne
Flinders
Franklin
Gascoyne
Godavari
Granicus
Guadiana
Hamilton
Han Jiang
Illinois
Kennebec
Kentucky
Klondike
Kootenay
Maeander
Mahanadi
Manawatu
Menderes
Missouri
Mitchell
Ob 'Irtysh
Ocmulgee
Okanagan
Okavango
Okovango
Ouachita
Pactolus
Paraguay
Parnaiba
Putumayo
Rio Negro
Safid Rud
Saguenay
Savannah
Suwannee
Syr Darya
Thompson
Tonle Sap
Torridge
Toulouse
Tunguska
Van Hades
Veronezh
Victoria
Volturno
Wanganui
Windrush
Zhu Jiang

| 9 letters: | Rio Branco | San Joaquin | Susquehanna |
|---|---|---|---|
| Allegheny | Rio Grande | Schuylkill | Yellowstone |
| Ashburton | Salambria | St Lawrence | |
| Athabasca | Santa Cruz | White Volta | 12 letters: |
| Billabong | St George's | Yesil Irmak | Guadalquivir |
| Churchill | White Nile | | Murrumbidgee |
| Crocodile | Wisconsin | 11 letters: | Saõ Francisco |
| Des Moines | | Aegospotami | Saskatchewan |
| Essequibo | 10 letters: | Assiniboine | Victoria Nile |
| Euphrates | Black Volta | Brahmaputra | |
| Irrawaddy | Blackwater | Castlereagh | 13 letters: |
| Kuskokwim | Chao Phraya | Connecticut | Little Bighorn |
| Mackenzie | Courantyne | Cooper Creek | |
| Magdalena | Cumberland | Delaguadero | 14 letters: |
| Murchison | Great Slave | Guadalentin | Jacques Cartier |
| Parnahiba | Hawkesbury | Lesser Slave | |
| Perihonca | Housatonic | Madre de Dios | 17 letters: |
| Pilcomayo | Kizil Irmak | Mississauga | North |
| Porcupine | Phlegethon | Mississippi | Saskatchewan |
| Qu'Appelle | Rangitaiki | Monongahela | South |
| Rangitata | Rangitikei | Montmorency | Saskatchewan |
| Richelieu | Sacramento | Shatt-al-Arab | |

**River-bank, Riverside** Brim, Carse, Riparian
**River-bed** T(h)alweg
**River-mouth** Firth, Frith
**Rivet(ing)** Bolt, Clinch, Clink, Concentrate, Explosive, Fasten, Fix, Pean, Peen, Stud, Transfix, Unputdownable
**Rivulet** Beck, Brook, Burn, Gill, Rill, Runnel, Strand
**RMA** The Shop
**RNA** Antisense, → **DNA**, Initiator codon, Messenger, Molecule, M-RNA, Retrotransposon, Ribosomal, Ribosome, Ribozyme, Soluble, Transcribe, Transfer, Uracil, Viroid
**Ro(u)manian, Rumanian** Ro, RO, R(o)uman, Transylvanian, Vlach, Wal(l)achian
**Roach** Arch(ie), Fish, Incurve, Red-eye
**Road(s), Roadside, Road surface** A, A1, Access, Anchorage, Arterial, Asphalt, Autobahn, Autopista, Autostrada, Ave(nue), B, Beltway, Blacktop, Boulevard, Burma, Bypass, Carriageway, Causeway, Clay, Clearway, Close, Cloverleaf, Coach, Concession, Corduroy, Corniche, Course, Crossover, Crown, Cul-de-sac, Dirt, Driveway, Drove, Dunstable, Escape, Exit, Expressway, Fairway, Feeder, Fly-over, Fly-under, Foss(e) Way, Freeway, Frontage, Grid, Hampton, Hard, Highway, Horseway, Interstate, Kerb, Lane, Loan, Loke, M1, Macadam, Mall, Metal, Motorway, Off-ramp, Orbital, Overpass, Parkway, Path, Pike, Post, Private, Rat-run, Rd, Relief, Ride, Ridgeway, Ring, → **ROUTE**, Royal, Service, Shoulder, Shunpike, Side, Silk, Skid, Slip, Speedway, Spur(way), St(reet), Superhighway, Switchback, Tarmac, Tar-seal, Terrace, Thoroughfare, Throughway, Tobacco, Toby, Tollway, Track(way), Trunk, Turning, Turnpike, Unadopted, Underpass, Unmade, Verge, Via, Viaduct, Way
**Roadblock** Barrier, Cone, Jam, Sleeping policeman, Thank-you-ma'am, Toll
**Road-keeper** Way-warden
**Road-maker** Drunkard, Macadam, Navigator, Telford, Wade
**Roadstead** La Hogue
**Roam** Enrange, Extravagate, Peregrinate, Rake, Ramble, Rove, Stray, Wander, Wheel
**Roan** Barbary, Bay, Horse, Leather, Schimmel, Strawberry
**Roar(ing)** Bawl, Bell(ow), Blare, Bluster, Boom, Boys, Cry, Forties, Guffaw, Laugh, Leonine, Roin, Rote, Rout, Royne, Thunder, Tumult, Vroom, Wuther, Zoom

**Roast** Bake, Barbecue, Baste, Birsle, Brent, Cabob, Cook, Crab, Crown, Decrepitate, Excoriate, Grill, Kabob, Pan, Parch, Pot, Ridicule, Scald, Scathe, Sear, Slate, Spit, Tan, Torrefy

**Rob(bed), Robber(y)** Abactor, Abduct, Bandalero, Bandit, Barabbas, Bereave, Blag, Bonnie, Brigand, Burgle, Bust, Cabbage, Cacus, Cateran, Clyde, Dacoit, Dakoit, Daylight, Depredation, Despoil, Dispossess, Do, Drawlatch, Fake, Filch, Fleece, Flimp, Footpad, Gilderoy, Heist, Hership, Highjack, High toby, Highwayman, Hijack, Hold-up, Hustle, Job, Knock off, Kondo, Ladrone, Land-pirate, Larceny, Latrocinium, Latron, Loot, Mill, Moskonfyt, Mosstrooper, Mug, Pad, Pandoor, Pandour, Pillage, Pinch, Piracy, Pluck, Plunder, Procrustes, Ramraid, Rapine, Reave, Reft, Reive, Rieve, Rifle, Road agent, Roberdsman, Robertsman, Roll, Rover, Roy, Rubbet, Rustler, Sack, Sciron, Score, Screw, Sheppard, Short change, Sinis, Sirup, Skinner, Smash and grab, Snaphaunch, Snatch, Spoiler, Spoliation, Spring-heeled Jack, → **STEAL**, Steaming, Stick-up, Sting, Swindle, Syrup, Thief, Thug(gee), Toby, Turn-over, Turpin

**Robe(s)** Alb, Amice, Amis, Attrap, Buffalo, Camis, Camus, Canonicals, Cassock, Chimer, Chrisom(-cloth), Christom, Dalmatic, Djellabi, Dolman, → **DRESS**, Gown, Habit, Ihram, Jilbab, Kanga, Kanzu, Khalat, Khilat, Kill(a)ut, Kimono, Mantle, Night, Parament, Parliament, Pedro, Peplos, Pontificals, Purple, Regalia, Rochet, Saccos, Sanbenito, Soutane, Sticharion, Stola, Stole, Talar, Tire, Vestment, Yukata

**Robert** Bob(by), Bridges, Browning, Burns, Cop, Flic, Peel, Rab, Rob

**Robin** Adair, American, Bird, Cock, Day, Goodfellow, Hob, Hood, Puck(-hairy), Ragged, Redbreast, Reliant, Round, Ruddock, Starveling, Wake

**Robot** Android, Animatronic, Automaton, Cyborg, Dalek, Golem, Nanobot, Puppet, RUR, Telechir

**Robust** Able-bodied, Fit, Hale, Hardy, Healthy, Hearty, Iron, Lusty, Muscular, Rude, Sound, Stalwart, Sthenic, Stout, Strapping, Sturdy, Vigorous

**Roc** Bird, Ruc, Rukh

**Rock(s), Rocker, Rocking, Rocky** Acid, Ages, Agitate, Astound, Ayers, Birthstone, Cairn, Cap, Cock, Country, Cradle, Destabilise, Edinburgh, Elvis, Erratic, Extrusive, Garage, Gem, Gib(raltar), Goth, Heavy metal, Hybrid, Jounce, Jow, Lithology, Mantle, Marciano, Marlstone, Matrix, Native, Nunatak(kr), Oscillate, Pelitic, Permafrost, Petrology, Petrous, Platform, Plymouth, Progressive, Punk, Quake, Reel, Reggae, Reservoir, Rimrock, Rip-rap, Rudaceous, Sally, Scar, Scare, Scaur, Sclate, → **SHAKE**, Shoogle, Showd, Soft, Stonehenge, Stun, Sway, Swee, Swing, Ted, Teeter, Terra, Totter, Traverse, Tremble, Ultrabasic, Ultramafic, Uluru, Unstable, Unsteady, Wall, Weeping, Whin, Wind, Windsor, Wobble

---

## ROCKS

| 2 letters: | Lias | Chalk | Olgas |
|---|---|---|---|
| Aa | Noup | Chert | Peter |
| | Reef | Cliff | Scalp |
| 3 letters: | Sill | Clint | Scrae |
| Ice | Sima | Craig | Scree |
| Tor | Trap | Elvan | Shale |
| | Tufa | Emery | Slate |
| 4 letters: | Tuff | Flint | Solid |
| Bell | Zoic | Geode | Stone |
| Coal | | Glass | Trass |
| Crag | 5 letters: | Krans | Wacke |
| Gang | Arête | Loess | |
| Glam | Brash | Mafic | 6 letters: |
| Jura | Calpe | Magma | Albite |
| Lava | Chair | Nappe | Aplite |

Arkose
Banket
Basalt
Dacite
Desert
Diapir
Dogger
Dunite
Felsic
Flaser
Flysch
Fossil
Gabbro
Gangue
Garnet
Gibber
Gneiss
Gossan
Gozzan
Inlier
Kingle
Living
Marble
Masada
Norite
Oolite
Oolith
Ophite
Pelite
Pluton
Pumice
Rognon
Sarsen
Schist
Sinter
Skerry
Sklate
S. Peter
Stonen
Synroc
Tephra

**7 letters:**
Aquifer
Archean
Arenite
Boulder
Breccia
Clastic
Cuprite
Cyanean
Diamond
Diorite
Erathem

Eucrite
Fastnet
Felsite
Geofact
Granite
Greisen
Haplite
Igneous
Lignite
Lorelei
Marlite
Minette
Molasse
Moraine
Needles
Olivine
Ophites
Outcrop
Outlier
Pennant
Peridot
Picrite
Remanie
Rhaetic
Sinking
Spilite
Stadium
Syenite
Terrane
Thulite
Tripoli
Wenlock

**8 letters:**
Adularia
Aegirine
Aiguille
Andesite
Aphanite
Archaean
Asbestos
Basanite
Brockram
Burstone
Calcrete
Calc-tufa
Calc-tuff
Ciminite
Diabasic
Dolerite
Dolomite
Eclogite
Eklogite
Elvanite

Eutaxite
Fahlband
Felstone
Footwall
Ganister
Hepatite
Hornfels
Idocrase
Inchcape
Isocline
Laterite
Lenticle
Liparite
Lopolith
Mesolite
Mudstone
Mylonite
Obsidian
Oil shale
Peperino
Petuntse
Phyllite
Pisolite
Plutonic
Porphyry
Psammite
Psephite
Ragstone
Regolith
Rhyolite
Rocaille
Roe-stone
Saxatile
Saxonite
Scorpion
Sunstone
Taconite
Tarpeian
Tephrite
The Olgas
Tonalite
Trachyte
Trappean
Volcanic
Whin sill
Xenolith

**9 letters:**
Anticline
Argillite
Batholite
Batholith
Bentonite
Bluestone

Buhrstone
Caenstone
Claystone
Cockhorse
Colluvium
Cornstone
Dalradian
Diatomite
Dinantian
Dolostone
Eddystone
Evaporite
Firestone
Flagstone
Flowstone
Gannister
Goslarite
Granulite
Greensand
Greystone
Greywacke
Gritstone
Hornstone
Impactite
Intrusion
Ironstone
Laccolite
Laccolith
Lardalite
Larvikite
Limestone
Meteorite
Mica-slate
Migmatite
Monadnock
Monocline
Monzonite
Mortstone
Mugearite
Natrolite
Neocomian
Ophiolite
Ottrelite
Pegmatite
Phonolite
Phosphate
Pleonaste
Propylite
Protogine
Quartzite
Sandstone
Saprolite
Scablands
Schistose

Siltstone
Soapstone
Tachylyte
Theralite
Tinguaite
Toadstone
Travertin
Underclay
Uriconian
Variolite
Veinstone
Veinstuff
Ventifact
Vulcanite
Whinstone
White Lias
Whunstane
Zechstein

*10 letters:*
Ailsa Craig
Amygdaloid
Camptonite
Epidiorite
Foundation

Granophyre
Greenstone
Grey-wether
Hypabyssal
Ignimbrite
Kersantite
Kimberlite
Laurdalite
Laurvikite
Lherzolite
Limburgite
Mica-schist
Novaculite
Orthophyre
Palagonite
Peridotite
Phenocryst
Pitchstone
Pyroxenite
Rhinestone
Rupestrian
Schalstein
Serpentine
Sparagmite
Stinkstone

Stonebrash
Syntagmata
Teschenite
Touchstone
Travertine
Troctolite

*11 letters:*
Agglomerate
Alexandrite
Amphibolite
Annabergite
Anorthosite
Carbonatite
Geanticline
Halleflinta
Lamprophyre
Metamorphic
Monchiquite
Napoleonite
Nephelinite
Phillipsite
Pyroclastic
Sedimentary
Slickenside

Symplegades

*12 letters:*
Babingtonite
Baltic Shield
Coal Measures
Granodiorite
Grossularite
Serpentinite
Straticulate
Stromatolite
Syntagmatite
Thunderstone

*13 letters:*
Hypersthenite

*14 letters:*
Giant's Causeway
Knotenschiefer
Rhombenporphyr
Roche moutonnée

*18 letters:*
Scandinavian Shield

---

**Rock-boring** Pholas
**Rock-cress** Arabis
**Rocket** Arugula, Blue, Booster, Capsule, Carpet, Carrier, Congreve, Dame's, Delta, Drake, Dressing down, Dyer's, Earful, Engine, Eruca, Flare, Ion, Iron horse, Jato, Life, London, Missile, Multistage, Onion, Payload, Posigrade, Reprimand, Reproof, Retro, Rockoon, Rucola, Salad, SAM, Sea, Skylark, Soar, Sonde, Sounding, Space probe, Step, Stephenson, Take-off, Thruster, Tourbillion, Ullage, Upshoot, V1, Vernier, Von Braun, Wall, Warhead, Weld, Yellow, Zero stage
**Rock-living** Rupicoline, Saxatile, Saxicoline, Saxicolous
**Rock-pipit** Sea-lark
▷ **Rocky** *may indicate* an anagram
**Rococo** Baroque, Fancy, Ornate, Quaint
**Rod(-shaped), Rodlike, Rods** Aaron's, Angler, Axle, Baculiform, Bar, Barbel(l), Barre, Birch, Caduceus, Caim, Came, Camshaft, Can, Cane, Centre, Connecting, Control, Cue, Cuisenaire®, Dipstick, Divining, Dopper, Dowser, Drain, Ellwand, Emu, Fasces, Filler, Fin-ray, Firearm, Fisher, Fishing, Fly, Fuel, Gauging, Gold stick, Gun, Handspike, Jacob's staff, Kame, King, Laver, Lease, Lightning, Linchpin, Lug, Mapstick, Measure, Measuring, Mopstick, Moses, Napier's bones, Nervure, Newel, Notochord, Perch, Pin, Pistol, Piston, Pitman, Pointer, Poker, Poking-stick, Pole, Pontie, Pontil, Ponty, Probang, Puntee, Punty, Push, Raddle, Range, Regulating, Rhabdoid, Rhabdus, Riding, Rood, Scollop, Shaft, Sounding, Spindle, Spit, Stadia, Stair, Stanchion, Staple, Stave, Stay-bolt, Stick, Sticker, Strickle, Switch, Swizzle stick, Tension, Tie, Track, Triblet, Tringle, Trocar, Twig, Urochord, Ventifact, Verge, Virgate, Virgulate, Wand, Welding, Withe
**Rod-bearer** Lictor
**Rode** Raid
**Rodent** Acouchi, Acouchy, Agouty, Ag(o)uti, Bandicoot, Bangsring, Banxring, Beaver, Biscacha, Bizcacha, Bobac, Bobak, Boomer, Capybara, Cavy, Chickaree, Chincha, Chinchilla, Chipmunk, Civet, Coypu, Cricetus, Dassie, Deer-mouse, Degu, Delundung,

Dormouse, Fieldmouse, Gerbil(le), Glires, Glutton, Gnawer, Gopher, Groundhog, Guinea pig, Ham(p)ster, Hedgehog, Hog-rat, Hutia, Hyrax, Hystricomorph, Jerboa, Jird, Lemming, Loir, Mara, Marmot, Mole rat, Mouse, Murid, Mus, Musk-rat, Musquash, Nutria, Ochotona, Ondatra, Paca, Porcupine, Potoroo, Prairie dog, Rat, Ratel, Ratton, Renegade, Runagate, Sciurine, Sewellel, Shrew, Simplicidentate, Spermophile, Springhaas, Springhase, Squirrel, S(o)uslik, Taguan, Taira, Tuco-tuco, Tucu-tuco, Vermin, Viscacha, Vole, Woodchuck, Woodmouse

**Roderick** Random, Usher

**Rodomontade** Bluster, Boast, Bombast, Brag, Gas

**Roe** Avruga, Botargo, Bottarga, Caviar(e), Coral, Fry, Hard, Melt, Milt(z), Pea, Raun, Rawn, Richard, Soft

**Roger** Ascham, Bacon, Jolly, OK, Rights

**Rogue, Roguish(ness)** Aberrant, Arch, Bandit, Bounder, Charlatan, Chiseller, Crook, Drole, Dummerer, Elephant, Espiègle(rie), Ganef, Ganev, Ganof, Gonif, Gonof, Greek, Gypsy, Hedge-creeper, Heel, Hempy, Herries, Imp, Knave, Latin, Limmer, Miscreant, Monkey, Palliard, Panurge, Picaresque, Picaroon, Pollard, Poniard, Rapparee, Ra(p)scal(l)ion, Reprobate, Riderhood, Rotter, Savage, Scallywag, Scamp, Schellum, Schelm, Scoundrel, Skellum, Sleeveen, Slip-string, Sly, Swindler, Terror, Varlet, Villain, Wrong 'un

**Roil** Agitate, Annoy, Churn, Provoke, Vex

**Roin** Roar

**Roister(er), Roisterous** Blister, Carouse, Ephesian, Laddish, Revel, Rollick, Scourer, Scowrer, Skylark, Swashbuckler, Swinge-buckler

**Role** Bit, Cameo, Capacity, Function, Gender, Hat, Lead, Métier, → **PART**, Persona, Prima-donna, Stead, Title, Travesty

**Roll(ed), Roller, Roll-call, Rolling, Rolls** Absence, Bagel, Bap, Barrel, Beigel, Billow, Birmingham, Bolt, Bridge, Brioche, Bun, Butterie, Calender, Cambridge, Chamade, Comber, Convolv(ut)e, Cop, Couch, Court, Croissant, Cylinder, Dandy, Drum, Dutch, Electoral, Enswathe, Enwallow, Eskimo, Even, Fardel, Fardle, Finger, Flatten, Forward, Furl, Go, Goggle, Holy, Hotdog, Inker, Involute, Labour, List, Loaded, Lurch, Makimono, Mangle, Mano, Marver, Matricula, Morning, Motmot, Moving, Music, Muster, Notitia, Opulent, Pain au chocolat, Paradiddle, Patent, Paupiette, Pay, Petit-pain, Piano, Pigeon, Pipe, Platen, Porteous, Rafale, Ragman, Record, Reef, Reel, Register, Ren, Rent, Revolute, Revolve, Rhotacism, Rich, Ring, Road, Rob, Rolag, Roster, Rota, Rotate, Rotifer, Roul(e), Roulade, Rouleau, Row, RR, Rub-a-dub, Rumble, Run, Sausage, Schnecke(n), Skin up, Snap, Somersault, Souter's clod, Spool, Spring, Summar, Sway, Swell, Swiss, Table, Tandem, Taxi, Temple, Tent, Terrier, Thread, Toilet, Tommy, Toss, Trill, Trindle, Trundle, Tsunami, Tube, Upfurl, Valuation, Victory, Volume, Volutation, Wad, Wallow, Wamble, Waul, Wave, Wawl, Weather, Web, Well-heeled, Welter, Western, Wince, Wrap, Yaw, Zorbing

**Rollick(ing)** Frolic, Gambol, Romp, Sport

▷ **Rollicking** *may indicate* an anagram

**Roly-poly** Chubby

**Roman** Agricola, Agrippa, Aurelius, Caesar, Calpurnia, Candle, Catholic, Cato, Centurion, Consul, CR, Crassus, Dago, Decemviri, Decurion, Empire, Flavian, Galba, Holiday, Italian, Jebusite, Latin, Maecenas, Nero, Papist, Patrician, PR, Quirites, Raetic, RC, Retarius, Rhaetia, Road, Scipio, Seneca, Sulla, Tarquin, Tiberius, Trebonius, Type, Uriconian, Veneti, Volsci

**Romance, Romantic (talk)** Affair, Amoroso, Amorous, Byronic, Casanova, Catalan, Chocolate box, Dreamy, Fancy, Fantasise, Fib, Fiction, Gest(e), Gothic, Historical, Invention, Ladin(o), Ladinity, Langue d'oc(ian), Langue d'oil, Langue d'oui, Liaison, Lie, Neo-Latin, New, Novelette, Poetic, Quixotic, Rhapsodic, R(o)uman, Ruritania, Sentimental, Stardust, Sweet nothings, Tale, Tear-jerker

**Romanov** Nicholas

▶ **Romany** *see* GYPSY

**Rome** Holy See, Imperial City

**Romeo** Casanova, Montagu, R, Swain

**Romp(ing)** Carouse, Escapade, Fisgig, Fizgig, Frisk, Frolic, Hoyden, Jaunce, Randy, Rig, Rollick, Skylark, Sport, Spree

**Ron** Glum, Moody

**Rondo** Rota

**Ronnie** Biggs

**Röntgen** R, X-ray

**Roo** Joey

**Roof (edge), Roofing** Asphalt, Belfast, Bell, Broach, Ceil, Cl(e)ithral, Cover, Curb, Divot, Dome, Drip, Eaves, French, Gable, Gambrel, Hardtop, Hip(ped), Home, Housetop, Hypostyle, Imperial, Jerkin-head, Leads, M, Mansard, Monopitch, Onion dome, Palate, Pavilion, Pent, Pitched, Pop-top, Porte-cochère, Rag top, Rigging, Saddle, Saddleback, Shingle, Skillion, Skirt, Span, Sun(shine), Targa top, Tectiform, Tectum, Tegula, Thatch, Thetch, Tiling, Top, Uraniscus, Vaulting, Yealm

**Roof-climber, Roofer** Slater, Stegopholist

**Roofless** Hypaethral, Upaithric

**Rook** Bird, Builder, Castle, Cheat, Crow, Fleece, Fool, Overcharge, R, Swindle

**Rookie** Beginner, Colt, Galoot, Greenhorn, Learner, Nignog, Novice, Recruit, Tenderfoot, Tyro

**Room(y)** Capacity, Cavernous, Ceiling, Clearance, Commodious, Elbow, Latitude, Leeway, Margin, Place, Scope, Smoke-filled, → SPACE, Spacious, Standing, Tolerance, Wiggle, Zenana

## ROOMS

| *2 letters:* | Kiva | Lavra | Exedra |
|---|---|---|---|
| CC | Loft | Lodge | Family |
| Rm | Long | Music | Garret |
| | Pump | Oriel | Hostel |
| *3 letters:* | Rest | Panic | Living |
| Ben | Sale | Press | Locker |
| But | Snug | Rangy | Lounge |
| Day | Tool | Sales | Lumber |
| End | Twin | Salle | Parvis |
| Gap | Ward | Salon | Powder |
| Gun | Wash | Solar | Public |
| Lab | Work | Spare | Robing |
| Leg | Zeta | Staff | Rubber |
| Loo | | Steam | Rumpus |
| Oda | *5 letters:* | Still | School |
| Pad | Attic | Stock | Serdab |
| Sun | Berth | Study | Single |
| Tap | Bibby | Suite | Spence |
| Tea | Bower | | Street |
| | Cabin | *6 letters:* | Strong |
| *4 letters:* | Cuddy | Boiler | Studio |
| Cell | Divan | Camera | Tardis |
| Chat | Foyer | Cellar | Throne |
| Dark | Green | Closet | Tiring |
| Digs | Grill | Common | Ullage |
| Dojo | Lanai | Durbar | Vestry |
| Hall | Laura | Engine | |

| | | | |
|---|---|---|---|
| *7 letters:* | Rotunda | Sacristy | Dissecting |
| Apadana | Sanctum | Scullery | Lebensraum |
| Boudoir | Servery | Sitkamer | Misericord |
| Cabinet | Service | Solarium | Operations |
| Cenacle | Shebang | Vestiary | Penetralia |
| Chamber | Sitting | | Priesthole |
| Chaumer | Smoking | *9 letters:* | Projection |
| Control | Stowage | Apartment | Recitation |
| Cubicle | Two-pair | Boardroom | Recreation |
| Cutting | Utility | Camarilla | |
| Dinette | Waiting | Composing | *11 letters:* |
| Drawing | | Extension | Antechamber |
| Exhedra | *8 letters:* | Glory-hole | Calefactory |
| Genizah | Anteroom | Herbarium | Chancellery |
| Kursaal | Assembly | Mould-loft | Combination |
| Library | Casemate | Palm Court | Compartment |
| Megaron | Changing | Receiving | Misericorde |
| Oratory | Cockloft | Reception | Scriptorium |
| Orderly | Conclave | Single-end | |
| Parlour | Delivery | Voorkamer | *13 letters:* |
| Pentice | Dressing | | Spheristerion |
| Pentise | Incident | *10 letters:* | |
| Private | Property | Commercial | |
| Reading | Recovery | Consulting | |

**Roost(er)** Cock, Perch, Siskin, Sit
**Root(s), Rooted, Rooting, Rootstock** Aruhe, Aryl, Asarum, Beet, Buttress, Calamus, Calumba, Cassava, Celeriac, Cheer, Cocco, Contrayerva, Costus, Couscous, Cube, Culver's, Cuscus, Dasheen, Delve, Deracinate, Derivation, Derris, Dig, Eddo, Elecampane, Eradicate, Eringo, Eryngo, Etymic, Etymon, Extirpate, Fern, Fibrous, Foundation, Gelseminine, Ginseng, Grass, Grout, Grub, Heritage, Horseradish, Hurrah, Immobile, Implant, Incorrigible, Insane, Ipecac(huana), Irradicate, Jalap, Jicama, Khuskhus, Knee, Lateral, Licorice, Liquorice, Mallee, Mandrake, Mangold, Mishmee, Mishmi, Mooli, More, Myall, Navew, Nousle, Nuzzle, Origins, Orris, Pachak, Pleurisy, Pneumatophore, Poke, Prop, Pry, Putchock, Putchuk, Race, Radical, Radicate, Radicle, Radish, Radix, Repent, Rhatany, Rhizic, Rhizoid, Rhizome, Scorzonera, Senega, Sessile, Setwall, Skirret, Snuzzle, Source, Spur, Square, Stilt, Stirpes, Stock, Strike, Tap, Taro, Tuber, Tuberous, Tulip, Turbith, Turnip, Turpeth, Ventral, Vetiver, Yam, Zedoary
**Rootless** Psilotum
**Rope(s)** Abaca, Backstay, Ba(u)lk, Becket, Bind, Bobstay, Boltrope, Bracer, Brail, Breeching, Bunt-line, Cable, Cablet, Cat's paw, Colt, Cord, Cordage, Cordon, Cringle, Downhaul, Drag, Earing, Fake, Fall, Flake, Flemish coil, Fly, Foot, Fore-brace, Foresheet, Forestay, Funicular, Futtock-shroud, Gantline, Garland, Grass line, Grist, Guest, Guide, Guy, Halliard, Halser, Halter, Halyard, Hawser, Hawser-laid, Headfast, Inhaul, Jack-stay, Jeff, Jib-sheet, Jump, Kernmantel, Kickling, Knittle, Ladder, Lanyard, Lasher, Lashing, Lasso, Lazo, Leg, Lifeline, Line, Longe, Lunge, Mainbrace, Mainsheet, Manil(l)a, Marlin(e), Match-cord, Messenger, Monkey, Mooring, Nettle, Nip, Noose, Oakum, Outhaul, Painter, Parbuckle, Pastern, Prolonge, Prusik, Pudding, Rawhide, Reef point, Riata, Ridge, Ringstopper, Roband, Robbin, Rode, Runner, St Johnston's ribbon, St Johnston's tippet, Sally, Salt-eel, Seal, Selvagee, Sennit, Sheet, Shroud, Sinnet, Span, Spancel, Spun-yarn, Stay, Sternfast, Stirrup, String, Strop, Sugan, Swifter, Tackle, Tail, Tether, Tie, Timenoguy, Tippet, Tow(line), Trace, Trail, Triatic, Triatic stay, Vang, Wanty, Warp, Widdy, Wire, Yarn
**Ropework** Macrame

**Rosalind** Ganymede

**Rosary** Beads, Mala, Paternoster

**Rose(-red), Rosie, Rosy** Albertine, Alexandra, Amelanchier, Aurorean, Avens, Bear's-foot, Blooming, Bourbon, Breare, Briar, Brier, Burnet, Cabbage, Canker, Ceiling, Cherokee, China, Christmas, Compass, Corn, Crampbark, Damask, Dog, Eglantine, Eglatère, England, English, Floribunda, G(u)elder, Geum, Golden, Hellebore, Hybrid, Jack, Jacque, Jacqueminot, Lal(age), Lancaster, Lee, Monthling, Moss, Multiflora, Musk, Noisette, Opulus, Peace, Petra, Pink, Potentilla, Promising, Provence, Province, Provincial, Provins, Pyrus, Quillaia, Quillaja, Rambler, Red(dish), Remontant, Rhoda, Rhodo-, Rock, Rugosa, Scotch, Snowball, Sprinkler, Standard, Sweetbrier, Tea, Tokyo, Tudor, White, Whitethorn, York

**Rose-apple** Jamboo, Jambu

**Rose-bay** Oleander

**Roseland** SE

**Rosemary** Rosmarine

**Rosette** Buttonhole, Chou, Cockade, Favour, Patera, Rosula

**Rosin** Colophony, Resin, Roset, Rosit, Rozet, Rozit

**Rosinante** Jade

**Roster** List, Register, Scroll, Table

**Rostrum** Ambo, Bema, Lectern, Podium, Pulpit, Tribune

**Rot(ten), Rotting** Addle, Baloney, Biodegrade, Boo, Bosh, Botrytis, Brown, Bull, Caries, Carious, Corrode, Corrupt, Crown, Daddock, Decadent, → **DECAY**, Decompose, Decrepitude, Degradable, Dotage, Dricksie, Druxy, Dry, Eat, Erode, Fester, Foot, Foul, Gangrene, Halt, Kibosh, Manky, Mildew, Noble, Nonsense, Off, Poppycock, Poxy, Punk, Putid, Putrefy, Putrescent, Putrid, Rail, Rancid, Rank, Rat, Red, Ret, Rhubarb, Ring, Rust, Sapropel, Septic, Soft, Sour, Squish, Twaddle, Vrot, Wet

**Rotate, Rotating, Rotation, Rotator** Axial, Backspin, Crankshaft, Crop, Feather, Gyrate, Laevorotation, Lay-farming, Optical, Pivot, Pronate, Rabat(te), Reamer, Rebato, Revolve, Roll, Selsyn, Succession, Sway, Teres, Topspin, Trochilic, Trundle, Turn, Turntable, Twiddle, Vortex, Vorticose, Wheel, Windmill

**Rote** Heart, Memory, Recite, Routine

**Rotisserie** Spit

**Rotor** Auxiliary, Flywheel, Impeller, Squirrel cage, Tilt

▶ **Rotten** *see* ROT(TEN)

▷ **Rotten** *may indicate* an anagram

**Rotter** Bad apple, Cad, Heel, Knave, Stinker, Swine

**Rotund** Chubby, Corpulent, Plump, Round, Stout, Tubby

**Rotunda** Pantheon

**Roué** Debauchee, Decadent, Libertine, Lothario, Profligate, Rake(-shame), Rip

**Rouge** Blush, Gild, Jeweller's, Raddle, Redden, Reddle, Ruddle, Ruddy

**Rough(en), Roughly, Roughness** About, Abrasive, Approximate, Asper(ate), Blunt, Broad, Broad brush, Burr, C, Ca, Choppy, Circa, Coarse, Craggy, Craig, Crude, Draft, Exasperate, Frampler, Grained, Gross, Gruff, Guestimate, Gurly, Gusty, Hard, Harsh, Hirsute, Hispid, Hoarse, Hoodlum, Hooligan, Ill, Impolite, Imprecise, Incondite, Indecorous, Inexact, Irregular, Jagged, Karst, Keelie, Kokobeh, Muricate, Obstreperous, Of sorts, Or so, Push, Ragged, Ramgunshoch, Raspy, Raucle, Rip, Risp, Robust, Row, Rude, Rugged, Rusticate, Rusty, Sandblast, Scabrid, Scabrous, Scratchy, Sea, Shaggy, Sketchy, Some, Spray, Spreathe, Squarrose, Stab, Strong-arm, Stubbly, Swab, Tartar, Tearaway, Ted, Textured, Tiger country, Tousy, Touzy, Towsy, Towzy, Uncut, Violent, Yahoo

**Roughage** Ballast, Bran, Fodder

**Rough breathing** Asper, Rale, Wheeze

**Roughcast** Harl

▷ **Roughly** *may indicate* an anagram

**Roulette** Russian

**Round(ed), Roundness** About, Ammo, Ball, Beat, Bombe, Bout, Cartridge, Catch,
Circle, Circular, Complete, Cycle, Dance, Dome, Doorstep, Fat, Figure, Full, Geoidal,
Global, Globate, Globose, Hand, Heat, Inorb, Jump-off, Lap, Leg, Milk, O, Oblate,
Obtuse, Orb, Orbicular, Orbit, Orby, Ought, Paper, Patrol, Peri-, Pirouette, Plump, Pudsy,
Qualifying, Quarter, Quarter-final, Rev, Ring, Robin, Roly-poly, Ronde, Rondure, Rota,
Rotund, Route, Routine, Rundle, Rung, Salvo, Sandwich, Sarnie, Sellinger's, Semi-final,
Shot, Skirt, Slice, Sphaer, Sphere, Spherical, Spiral, Step, Table, Tour, Trick, Tubby, Tune,
U-turn, Walk

▷ **Round** *may indicate* a word reversed

**Roundabout** Ambages, Approximately, Bypass, Carousel, Circle, Circuit,
Circumambient, Circumbendibus, Circus, Devious, Eddy, →**INDIRECT**,
Merry-go-round, Peripheral, Rotary, Tortuous, Traffic circle, Turntable, Waltzer,
Whirligig, Windlass

▷ **Roundabout** *may indicate* an anagram

**Round building** Tholos, Tholus

**Rounders** Patball

**Round-mouth** Hag

**Round up** Bang-tail muster, Collate, Corner, Corral, Drag-net, Gather, Herd, Muster,
Rodeo, Spiral

**Roup** Auction, Croak, Pip, Roop

**Rouse(r), Rousing** Abrade, Abraid, Abray, Amo(o)ve, Animate, Awaken, Beat, Bestir,
Cheerleader, Emotive, Enkindle, Excite, Firk, Flush, Hearten, Heat, Innate, Kindle, Knock
up, Rear, Send, Shake up, Stimulate, Suscitate, Unbed, Waken, Whip

**Rousseau** Émile

**Rout** Clamour, Debacle, Defeat, Drub, Fleme, Flight, Hubbub, Hurricane, Rabble, Retreat,
Rhonchal, Snore, Thiasus, Upsee, Upsey, Upsy, Vanquish, Whoobub

**Route(s)** Arterial, Autobahn, Avenue, Byroad, Camino real, Causeway, Clearway,
Corridor, Course, Direction, Escape, Itinerary, I-way, Line, Ling, Motorway, M-way, Path,
Red, Road, Round, Sea-lane, Stock, Topo, Track, Trade, Transit, Via, Via Dolorosa, Walk,
Waterway, Way

**Routine** Automatic, Day-to-day, Drill, Everyday, Grind, Groove, Habitual, Heigh-ho,
Helch-how, Ho-hum, Jogtrot, Journeywork, Monotony, Pattern, Perfunctory, Pipe-clay,
Prosaic, Red tape, Regular, Rota, Rote, Round, Run-of-the-mill, Rut, Schtik, S(c)htick,
SOP, Stand-up, Treadmill, Workaday

**Rove(r), Roving** Car, Discursive, Enra(u)nge, Errant, Freebooter, Gad, Globetrotter,
Marauder, Nomad, Prowl(er), Ralph, Range, →**ROAM**, Slub(b), Stray, Tramp, Vagabond,
Varangarian, Viking, Wander

**Row(er)** Align, Altercation, Arew, Argue, Argument, Artillery, Bank, Barney, Bedlam,
Bobbery, Bow, Brattle, Brawl, Brulyie, Bru(i)lzie, Cacophony, Cannery, Cat fight, Clatter,
Colonnade, Crescent, Death, Debate, Deen, Din, Dispute, Dust-up, Feud, File, Fireworks,
Food, Fyle, Hoo-ha, Hullabaloo, Leander, Line(-up), Noise, Note, Oar, Octastich,
Orthostichy, Paddle, Parade, Peripteral, Pluriserial, Ply, Pull, Quarrel, Queue, Rammy,
Range, Rank, Raunge, Remigate, Reproach, Rew, Rhubarb, Rotten, Ruction, Rumpus,
Savile, Scene, Scrap, Scull, Series, Set (to), Shindig, Shindy, Shine, Skid, Spat, Splore,
Stern, Stound, Street, Stridor, Stroke, Stushie, Sweep, Terrace, Tier, Tiff, Tone, Torpid,
Twelve-tone, Vendetta, Wetbob, Wherryman

**Rowan** Ash, Quicken, Sorb

**Rowdy, Rowdiness** Boisterous, Bovver, Cougan, Hoo, Hooligan, Ladette, Loud, Noisy,
Obstreperous, Rorty, Rough, Roughhouse, Ruffian, Scourer, Scozza, Skinhead, Stroppy,
Unruly, Uproarious

**Roy** Rob

**Royal(ty), Royalist** Academy, Angevin, Basilical, Battle, Bourbon, Crowned,
Emigré, Exchange, Fee, Hanoverian, HR(H), Imperial, Imposing, Inca, Kingly,

King's man, Majestic, Malignant, Palatine, Payment, Pharaoh, Plantagenet, Prince, Princess, Purple, Queenly, Real, Regal, Regis, Regius, Regnal, Sail, Sceptred, Society, Tsarista

**Rub(bing), Rubber(y), Rub out** Abrade, Attrition, Balata, Buff, Buna®, Bungie, Bungy, Bunje(e), Bunjie, Bunjy, Butyl, Calk, Calque, Camelback, Caoutchouc, Chafe, Chloroprene, Cold, Condom, Corrade, Corrode, Cow gum®, Crepe, Cul(t)ch, Delete, Destroy, Dunlop®, Ebonite, Efface, Elastic, Elastomer, Elaterite, Embrocate, Emery, Eradicator, Erase, Factice, Factis, Fawn, Foam, Foursome, Fray, Fret, Friction, Fridge, Frottage, Frotteur, Fudge, Funtumia, Gall, Galoch, Goodyear®, Grate, Graze, Grind, Guayule, Gum elastic, Gutta-percha, Hale, Hard, Hevea, High-hysteresis, Hule, India, Inunction, Irritate, Isoprene, Jelutong, Johnnie, Lagos, Latex, Leather, Masseur, Negrohead, Neoprene, Nuzzle, Obstacle, Para, Polish, Pontianac, Pontianak, Root, Safe, Sandpaper, Scour, Scrape, Scrub, Scuff, Seringa, Silastic®, Smoked, Sorbo®, Sponge, Stroke, Synthetic, Towel, Trace, Ule, Vulcanite, Wild, Wipe, Xerotripsis

▷ **Rubbed** *may indicate* an anagram

**Rubbish** Bad mouth, Balls, Bilge, Brash, Brock, Bull, Bunkum, Cack, Chaff, Clap-trap, Cobblers, Codswallop, Culch, Debris, Detritus, Dirt, Discredit, Dre(c)k, Drivel, Dross, Eyewash, Fiddlesticks, Garbage, Grot, Grunge, Gubbins, Guff, Hogwash, Hokum, Kack, Kak, Landfill, Leavings, Litter, Mullock, Mush, Nonsense, Pan, Pants, Phooey, Piffle, Pish, Raff, Raffle, Red(d), → **REFUSE**, Riff-raff, Scrap, Sewage, Slate, Spam, Stuff, Thrash, Tinpot, Tinware, Tip, Tom(fool), Tosh, Totting, Trade, Tripe, Trouch, Truck, Trumpery, Twaddle, Urethra

**Rubbish heap** Coup, Cowp, Dump, Lay-stall, Sweepings, Toom

**Rubble** Brash, Debris, Detritus, Hard-core, Moellon, Random, Remains, Riprap, Talus

**Rubicund** Red, Ruddy

**Rubidium** Rb

**Ruby** Agate, Balas, Brazilian, Colorado, Cuprite, Oriental, Pigeon's blood, Port, Red, Spinel, Star, Starstone, Type

**Ruck** Furrow, Scrum, Wrinkle

**Rucksack** Backpack, Bergen, Pickapack, Pikau

**Ruction** Ado, Affray, Fuss, Quarrel

**Rudder** Budget, Helm, Steerer

**Ruddle** Keel, Lemnian

**Ruddy** Bally, Bloody, Flaming, Flashy, Florid, Raddled, Red, Roseate, Rubicund, Rufous, Sanguine

**Rude(ness)** Abusive, Barbaric, Bear, Bestial, Bumpkin, Callow, Carlish, Churlish, Coarse, Discourteous, Disrespect, Elemental, Goustrous, Green, Ignorant, Ill-bred, Impolite, Indecorous, Indelicate, Inficete, Ingram, Ingrum, Insolent, Ocker, Offensive, Peasant, Profane, Raw, Ribald, Risqué, Rough, Simple, Surly, Unbred, Uncivil, Uncomplimentary, Uncourtly, Unlettered, Unmannered, Vulgar, Yobbish

**Rudiment(ary), Rudiments** ABC, Absey, Anlage, Basidial, Beginning, Element, Embryo, Foundation, Germ(en), Germinal, Inchoate, Primitive, Primordial, Seminal, Vestige

**Rudolph** Hess, Reindeer

**Rue(ful)** Apologetic, Boulevard, Dittany, Goat's, Harmala, Harmel, Herb of grace, Meadow, Mourn, Poignant, Regret, Repent, Rew, Ruta, Sorry, Wall

**Ruff** Collar, Crest, Fraise, Frill, Mane, Partlet, Pope, Rabato, Rebato, Ree, Ruche, Trump

**Ruffian** Apache, Bashi-bazouk, Brute, Bully, Cut-throat, Desperado, Goon(da), Highbinder, Hoodlum, Hooligan, Keelie, Larrikin, Loord, Lout, Miscreant, Mohock, Myrmidon, Ned, Phansigar, Plug-ugly, Raff, Rowdy, Skinhead, Sweater, Tearaway, Thug, Toe-ragger, Trailbaston, Tumbler

**Ruffle(d), Ruffle(s)** Bait, Dishevel, Falbala, Flounce, Fluster, Fret, → **FRILL**, Gather, Irritate, Jabot, Peplum, Ripple, Rouse, Ruche, Rumple, Shirty, Tousle, Windswept

▷ **Ruffle** *may indicate* an anagram

**Rug** Afghan, Bearskin, Bergama, Buffalo-robe, Carpet, Drugget, Ensi, Flokati, Gabbeh, Hearth, Herez, Heriz, Kelim, K(h)ilim, Kirman, Lap robe, Mat, Maud, Numdah, Oriental, Pilch, Prayer, Rag, Runner, Rya, Scatter, Steamer, Tatami, Throw, Travelling, Wig

**Rugby (player)** Back, Fifteen, Forward, Harlequin, League, Lion, Pack, Quin, RU, Scrum, Sevens, Threequarter, Touch, Union, Wing

**Rugged** Craggy, Gnarled, Harsh, Knaggy, Rough, Strong, Uneven

**Ruin(ed), Ruination, Ruins, Ruinous** Annihilate, Banjax, Bankrupt, Blast, Blight, Blue, Butcher, Carcase, Collapse, Corrupt, Crash, Crock, Damn, Decay, Defeat, Demolish, Despoil, Destroy, Devastate, Dilapidation, Disaster, Disfigure, Dish, Disrepair, Dogs, Do in, Doom, Downcome, Downfall, Dry rot, End, Fine, Fordo, Hamstring, Heap, Hell, Insolvent, Inure, Kaput(t), Kibosh, Loss, Mar, Mockers, Mother's, Overthrow, Perdition, Perish, Petra, Pigs and whistles, Pot, Puckerood, Ravage, Reck, Relic, Rust, Scotch, Screw, Scupper, Scuttle, Shatter, Sink, Smash, Spill, → **SPOIL**, Stramash, Subvert, Undo, Unmade, Unmake, Ur, Violate, Vitiate, Whelm, Woe, Wrack, Write off

▷ **Ruined** *may indicate* an anagram

**Rule(r), Rules, Ruling** Advantage, Algorithm, Align, Aristocrat, Arrêt, Article, Bosman, Bylaw, Calliper, Canon, Chain, Club-law, Code, Commonly, Condominium, Constitution, Control, Criterion, Decree, Divine right, Dominate, Domineer, Dominion, Em, Empire, En, Establishment, Estoppel, Etiquette, Fatwa, Feint, Fetwa, Fleming's, Formation, Formula, Gag, Global, Golden, Govern, Govern-all, Ground, Gynocracy, Home, In, Institutes, Jackboot, Law, Leibniz's, Lesbian, Lex, Lindley, Liner, Majority, Markownikoff's, Mastery, Matriarchy, Maxim, McNa(u)ghten, Measure, Mede, Meteyard, Method, Ministrate, Mistress, Mobocracy, Motto, Naismith's, Netiquette, Norm(a), Oppress, Ordinal, Organon, Organum, Pantocrator, Parallel, Parallelogram, Phase, Phrase-structure, Pie, Placitum, Plumb, Precedent, Precept, Predominant, Prescript, Prevail, Principle, Proscribe, Protocol, Ptochocracy, Pye, Rafferty's, Raine, Realm, Reciprocity, Rector, Regal, Regnant, Regula, Reign, Rewrite, Ring, Routine, Rubric, Scammozzi's, Selection, Setting, Slide, Squirearchy, Standard, Statute, Straight edge, Stylebook, Sutra, Sway, Syntax, System, Ten-minute, Ten-yard, Theorem, Three, Thumb, Transformation(al), Trapezoid, T-square, Tycoon, Tyrant, Uti possidetis, Wield, Yardstick

---

## RULERS

| *1 letter:* | Imam | Herod | *6 letters:* |
|---|---|---|---|
| K | Inca | Hoyle | Atabeg |
| R | Khan | Hyleg | Atabek |
| | King | Judge | Caesar |
| *3 letters:* | Nero | Mogul | Caliph |
| Ban | Pope | Mpret | Castro |
| Bey | Rana | Mudir | Chagan |
| Dey | Ratu | Nawab | Cheops |
| Mir | Shah | Negus | Dergue |
| Oba | Tsar | Nizam | Despot |
| Raj | Vali | Octet | Dynast |
| Rex | Wali | Pasha | Exarch |
| | | Queen | Franco |
| *4 letters:* | *5 letters:* | Rajah | Führer |
| Amir | Ameer | Ratoo | Gerent |
| Cham | Ardri | Shaka | Harold |
| Czar | Creon | Sheik | Hitler |
| Doge | Dewan | Sophi | Judges |
| Duce | Diwan | Sophy | Kabaka |
| Emir | Henry | Tenno | Kaiser |

Mamluk
Manchu
Mikado
Peshwa
Prince
Rajput
Regent
Ronald
Sachem
Satrap
Sheikh
Sherif
Shogun
Sirdar
Sovran
Squier
Squire
Stalin
Sultan
Swaraj
Walter

**7 letters:**
Abbasid
Ardrigh
Autarch
Bajayet
Bajazet
Bodicea
Catapan
Chogyal
Elector

Emperor
Gaekwar
Gaikwar
Jamshid
Jamshyd
Khedive
Miranda
Monarch
Omayyad
Pharaoh
Podesta
Rajpoot
Richard
Saladin
Serkali
Souldan
Toparch
Umayyad
Viceroy
Zamorin

**8 letters:**
Archduke
Autocrat
Bismarck
Boudicca
Burgrave
Caligula
Caudillo
Cromwell
Dictator
Ethnarch

Frederic
Heptarch
Hespodar
Hierarch
Maharaja
Mamaluke
Mameluke
Napoleon
Oligarch
Overlord
Padishah
Pentarch
Pericles
Reginald
Roderick
Sagamore
Sassanid
Suleiman
Suzerain
Synarchy
Tetrarch
Thearchy
Theocrat

**9 letters:**
Alexander
Amenhotep
Bretwalda
Britannia
Cleopatra
Cosmocrat
Frederick

Montezuma
Ochlocrat
Pendragon
Plutocrat
Potentate
President
Sovereign
Tamerlane

**10 letters:**
Caractacus
Plantocrat
Principate
Rajpramukh
Stratocrat

**11 letters:**
Charlemagne
Genghis Khan
Prester John
Queensberry
Stadtholder
Tutankhamun

**12 letters:**
Chandragupta

**13 letters:**
Haile Selassie

---

**Rule-book** Code, Pie, Pye

**Rum(mer)** Abnormal, Baba, Bacardi, Bay, Cachaca, Curious, Daiquiri, Dark, Demerara, Droll, Eerie, Eery, Glass, Grog, Island, Jamaica, Kooky, Odd(er), Peculiar, Quaint, Queer, Screech, Strange, Tafia, Weird

▸ **Rumanian** see RO(U)MANIAN

**Rumble, Rumbling** Borborygmus, Brool, Curmurring, Drum-roll, Groan, Growl, Guess, Lumber, Mutter, Roll, Rumour, Thunder, Tonneau, Twig

**Ruminant, Ruminate** Antelope, Cabrie, Camel, Cavicornia, Cervid, Champ, Chew, Contemplate, Cow, Eland, Gemsbok, Gnu, Goat, Ibex, Llama, Meditate, Merycism, Muse, Nilgai, Nyala, Okapi, Oorial, Oryx, Palebuck, Pecora, Pronghorn, Reindeer, Saola, Serow

**Rummage** Delve, Ferret, Fish, Foray, Fossick, Jumble, Powter, Ransack, Rifle, Root, Rootle, Scavenge, Search, Tot

**Rummy** Canasta, Cooncan, Game, Gin, Queer

**Rumour** Breeze, Bruit, Buzz, Canard, Cry, Fame, Furphy, →GOSSIP, Grapevine, Hearsay, Kite, Kite-flying, Mail, Noise, On-dit, Pig's-whisper, Report, Repute, Roar, Say-so, Smear, Tale, Talk, Underbreath, Unfounded, Vine, Voice, Whisper, Word

**Rump** Arse, Bottom, Buttocks, Croup(e), Croupon, Crupper, Curpel, Derrière, Nates, Parliament, Podex, Prat, Pygal, Steak, Uropygium

**Rumple** Corrugate, Crease, Mess, Muss, Touse, Tousle, Touze, Towse, Towze, Wrinkle

**Rumpus** Bagarre, Commotion, Din, Noise, Rhubarb, Riot, Row, Ruction, Shemozzle, Shindig, Shindy, Shine, Storm, Stushie, Tirrivee, Uproar

**Run(ning), Run away, Run into, Run off, Runny, Runs** Admin(ister), Arpeggio, Black, Bleed, Blue, Bolt, Break, Bunk, Bye, Canter, Career, Chase, Chicken, Clip, Consider, Control, Coop, Corso, Course, Cresta, Cross-country, Current, Cursive, Cursorial, Cut, Dart, Dash, Decamp, Diarrhoea, Dinger, Direct, Dog-trot, Double, Dribble, Drive, Dry, Dummy, Enter, Escape, Execute, Extra, Fartlek, Flee, Flit, Flow, Fly, Follow, Fun, Fuse, Gad, Gallop, Gauntlet, Glissando, Go, Green, Ground, Hare, Haste(n), Hennery, Hie, Hightail, Home, Hoof, Idle, Jog, Jump bail, Ladder, Lam, Lauf, Leg(work), Leg bye, Lienteric, Liquid, Lope, Manage, Marathon, Melt, Milk, Mizzle, Mole, Molt, Monkey, Neume, Now, Offset, On, On-line, Operate, Orchestration, Pace, Pacific, Paper chase, Parkour, Pelt, Pilot, Ply, Pour, Print, Purulent, R, Race, Range, Rear end, Red, Renne, Rin, Roadwork, Romp, Root, Roulade, Rounder, Ruck, Scamper, Scapa, Scarpa, Scarper, School, Schuss, Score, Scud, Scuddle, Scutter, Scuttle, See, Sequence, Shoot, Single, Skate, Skedaddle, Ski, Skid, Skirr, Skitter, Slalom, Slide, Smuggle, Spew, Split, Spread, Sprint, Sprue, Squitters, Stampede, Straight, Streak, Stream, Superintend, Taxi, Tear, Tenor, Test drive, Tick over, Tie-breaker, Tirade, Trial, Trickle, Trill, Trot, Well, Wide
**Runaway** Drain, Easy, Escapee, Fugie, Fugitive, Refugee
**Run down** Asperse, Belie, Belittle, Calumniate, Decry, Denigrate, Derelict, Detract, Dilapidated, Infame, Knock, Low, Obsolesce(nt), Poorly, Rack, Résumé, Scud, Seedy, Synopsis, Tirade, Traduce
**Rune, Runic** Ash, Futhark, Futhorc, Futhork, Kri, Ogham, Spell, Thorn, Wen, Wyn(n)
**Rung** Crossbar, Roundel, Rundle, Spoke, Stave, Step, Tolled, Tread
**Runner(s)** Atalanta, Athlete, Bean, Blade, Bow Street, Candidate, Carpet, Chataway, Coe, Contrabandist, Courser, Dak, Deserter, Drug, Emu, Errand boy, Field, Foot, Geat, Gentleman, Gillie-wetfoot, Harrier, Hatta, Hencourt, Internuncio, Lampadist, Leg bye, Legman, Messenger, Miler, Milk, Mohr, Mousetrap, Nurmi, Oribi, Ovett, Owler, Pacemaker, Pacesetter, Policeman, Racehorse, Rhea, →RIVER, Rug, Rum, →RUN(NING), Sarmentum, Scarlet, Scud, Series, Slipe, Smuggler, Stolon, Stream, Tailskid, Trial
▷ **Running, Runny** *may indicate* an anagram
**Run of the mill** Average, Mediocre
**Runt** Anthony, Dilling, Oobit, Oubit, Reckling, Scalawag, Scrog, Scut, Smallest, Tantony, Titman, Woobut, Woubit
**Run through** Impale, Pierce, Rehearsal
**Runway** Airstrip, Drive, Slipway, Strip, Tarmac®, Trajectory
**Run wild** Lamp, Rampage
**Rupee(s)** Lac, Lakh, Re
**Rupert** Bear
**Rupture** Amniotomy, Breach, Burst, Crack, Enterocele, Hernia, Rend, Rhexis, Rift, Scissore, Split
**Rural** Agrarian, Agrestic, Backwoodsman, Boo(h)ai, Booay, Boondocks, Bucolic, Country(side), Cracker-barrel, Forane, Georgic, Hick, Mofussil, Pastoral, Platteland, Praedial, Predial, Redneck, Rustic, Sticks, The Shires, Ulu, Upland, Wop-wops
**Ruse** Artifice, Decoy, Dodge, Engine, Hoax, Pawk, Stratagem, →TRICK
**Rush(ed)** Accelerate, Barge, Bolt, Bustle, Career, Charge, Dart, Dash, Debacle, Dutch, Eriocaulon, Expedite, Fall, Faze, Feese, Feeze, Feze, Flaw, Fly, Forty-nine, Frail, Friar, Gad, Gold, Gust, Hare, Hasten, Hectic, High-tail, Horsetail, →HURRY, Hurry and Scurry, Hurtle, Jet, Juncus, Lance, Lash, Leap, Luzula, Moses, Odd-man, Onset, Palmiet, Pellmell, Phase, Pheese, Pheeze, Phese, Plunge, Pochard, Precipitate, Railroad, Rampa(u)ge, Rash, Rayle, Reed, Rip, Sally, Scamp(er), Scirpus, Scour(ing), Scramble, Scud, Scurry, Scuttle, Sedge, Shave-grass, Spate, Speed, Stampede, Star(r), Streak, Streek, Surge, Swoop, Swoosh, Tantivy, Tear, Thrash, Thresh, Tilt, Torrent, Tule, Viretot, Whoosh, Zap, Zoom
**Rusk** Zwieback
**Russell** AE, Bertrand, Jack
**Russet** Rutile

**Russia(n), Russian headman, Russian villagers** Alexei, Apparatchik, Ataman, Bashkir, Belorussian, Beria, Bolshevik, Boris, Boyar, Buryat, Byelorussian, Cesarevitch, Chechen, Chukchee, Chukchi, Circassian, Cossack, Dressing, D(o)ukhobor, Esth, Evenki, Ewenki, Igor, Ingush, Ivan, Kabardian, Kalmuk, Kalmyck, Leather, Leonid, Lett, Mari, Menshevik, Mingrel(ian), Minimalist, Mir, Misha, Muscovy, Octobrist, Old Believer, Osset(e), Putin, Red, Romanov, Rus, Russ(niak), Russki, Ruthene, Salad, Serge, Sergei, Slav, Stakhanovite, SU, Tatar, The Bear, Thistle, Udmurt, Ukrainian, Uzbeg, Uzbek, Vladimir, Vogul, White, Yakut, Yuri, Zyrian

**Rust(y)** Aeci(di)um, Blister, Brown, Corrode, Cor(ro)sive, Eat, Erode, Etch, Ferrugo, Goethite, Iron oxide, Iron-stick, Laterite, Maderise, Oxidise, Puccinia, Reddish, Rubiginous, Soare, Stem, Teleutospore, Telium, Uredine, Uredo, Verdigris, Wheat, Yellow

**Rust-fungus** Aecidiospore

**Rustic** Arcady, Bacon, Bor(r)el(l), Bucolic, Bumpkin, Carl, Carlot, Chawbacon, Churl, Clodhopper, Clown, Corydon, Countryman, Cracker-barrel, Crackle, Culchie, Damon, Doric, Forest, Georgic, Hayseed, Hick, Hillbilly, Hind, Hob, Hobbinoll, Hodge, Homespun, Idyl(l), Pastorale, Peasant, Pr(a)edial, Put(t), Rube, Rural, Silk, Strephon, Swain, Sylvan, Uplandish, Villager, Villatic, Yokel

▷ **Rustic** *may indicate* an anagram

**Rusticate** Banish, Ruralize, Seclude

**Rustle(r), Rustling** Abactor, Crackle, Crinkle, Duff, Fissle, Frou-frou, Gully-raker, Poach, Silk, Speagh(ery), Sprechery, Steal, Stir, Stocktaking, Susurration, Swish, Thief, Whig

**Rust-proof** Antioxide, Zinced

**Rut** Channel, Furrow, Groove, Heat, Routine, Sulcus, Track

**Ruth** Babe, Compassion, Mercy, Pity, Remorse, Rewth

**Ruthenium** Ru

**Rutherfordium** Rf

**Ruthless** Brutal, Cruel, Dog eat dog, Fell, Fierce, Hard, Hardball, Hard-bitten, Indomitable, Inhuman

**Rwanda(n)** Hutu, Tutsi

**Rye** Gentleman, Grain, Grass, Spelt, Whisky

# Ss

**S** Ogee, Saint, Second, Sierra, Society, South, Square

**SA** It, Lure

**Sabbatarian** Wee Free

**Sabbath** Juma, Lord's Day, Rest-day, Shabbat, Sunday, Witches'

**Sabbatical** Leave, Year off

**Sabine** Horace, Women

**Sable** American, Black, Jet, Negro, Pean, Zibel(l)ine

**Sabotage, Saboteur** Cripple, Destroy, Frame-breaker, Hacktivism, Ratten, Sab, Spoil, Treachery, Undermine, Vandalise, Worm, Wrecker

**Sabre, Sabre rattler** Jingo, Sword, Tulwar

**Sabrina** Severn

**Sac** Air, Allantois, Amnion, Aneurism, Aneurysm, Bag, Bladder, Bursa, Caecum, Castoreum, Cisterna, Cyst, Diverticulum, Embryo, Follicle, Ink, Pericardium, Peritoneum, Pneumatophore, Pod, Pollen, Scrotum, Spermatheca, Tylose, Tylosis, Utricle, Vesica, Vocal, Yolk

**Saccharine** Dulcite, Dulcose

**Sack(cloth), Sacking** Axe, Bag, Bed, Boot, Bounce, Budget, Bulse(r), Burlap, Can, Cashier, Chasse, Chop, Coal, Compression, Congé, Congee, Dash, Depose, Depredate, Despoil, Discharge, Dismissal, Doss, Fire, Growbag, Gunny, Havoc, Heave-ho, Hessian, Hop-pocket, Jute, Knap, Lay waste, Loot, Mailbag, Maraud, Marching orders, Mat, Mitten, Pillage, Plunder, Poke, Postbag, Push, Raid, Rapine, Ravage, Reave, Replace, Rieve, Rifle, Road, Rob, Sad, Sanbenito, Self-abasement, Sherris, Sherry, Spoliate, Vandalise, Walking papers

▷ **Sacks** *may indicate* an anagram

**Sacrament** Baptism, Christening, Communion, Confirmation, Eucharist, Extreme unction, Housel, Lord's Supper, Matrimony, Nagmaal, Orders, Penance, Promise, Reconciliation, Ritual, Unction, Viaticum

**Sacred (object), Sacred books, Sacred place** Adytum, Churinga, Delphi, Divine, Hallowed, Hareem, Harem, Harim, Heart, Hierurgy, → **HOLY**, Ineffable, Inner sanctum, Manito(u), Nine, Omphalos, Padma, Pietà, Purana, Sacrosanct, Sanctum, Taboo, Tapu, Temenos

**Sacrifice** Alcestic, Cenote, Corban, Cost, Forego, Gambit, Gehenna, Hecatomb, Holocaust, Immolate, Iphigenia, Isaac, Lay down, Molech, Moloch, Molochize, Oblation, → **OFFERING**, Paschal lamb, Peace offering, Relinquish, Sati, Suovetaurilia, Supreme, Surrender, Suttee, Taurobolium, Tophet, Vicarious, Victim

**Sacrilege, Sacrilegious** Blaspheme, Impiety, Profane, Violation

**Sacristan, Sacristy** Diaconicon, Sceuophylax, Sexton

**Sacrosanct** Inviolable

**Sad(den), Sadly, Sadness** Alas, Attrist, Bittersweet, Blue, Con dolore, Dejected, Depressed, Desolate, Disconsolate, Dismal, Doleful, Dolent, Dolour, Downcast, Drear, Dull, Dumpy, Elegiac, Fadeur, Forlorn, Heartache, Heart-rending, Lamentable, Lovelorn, Low, Lugubrious, Mesto, Mournful, Niobe, Oh, Plaintive, Plangent, Poignancy, Proplastid, Sorrowful, Sorry, Tabanca, Tearful, Tear-jerker, Threnody, Tragic, Triste, Tristesse, Unhappy, Wan, Weltschmerz, Wo(e)begone

**Saddle (bag, cloth, flap, girth, pad), Saddled** Alforja, Aparejo, Arson, Bicycle, Burden, Cantle, Cinch, Col, Crupper, Demipique, Kajawah, Lumber, Numnah, Oppress,

Pack, Pad, Panel, Pigskin, Pilch, Pillion, Seat, Sell(e), Shabrack, Shabracque, Side, Skirt, Stock, Tree, Unicycle, Western
**Saddle-bow** Arson
**Saddler** Whittaw(er)
**Sadie** Thompson
**Sadism, Sadist(ic)** Algolagnia, Cruel, Dominator
▷ **Sadly** *may indicate* an anagram
**Safari** Expedition, Hunt
**Safe(ty)** Active, All right, Almery, Ambry, Awmrie, Blue-chip, Cert, Coolgardie, Copper-bottomed, Deliverance, Delouse, Deposit, Fireproof, GRAS, Harmless, Hunk, Immunity, Impunity, Inviolate, Keister, Meat, Night, Passive, Peter, Proof, Reliable, Roadworthy, Sanctuary, Secure, Sheltered, Sound, Strong-box, Strongroom, Sure, Unadventurous, Whole-skinned, Worthy
**Safebreaker** Peterman, Yegg, Yeggman
**Safeguard** Air bag, Bulwark, Caution, Ensure, Fail-safe, Frithborh, Fuse, Hedge, Inoculate, Palladium, Preserve, Protection, Register, Shield, Ward
**Saffron** Bastard, Crocus, False, Meadow, Mock, Yellow
**Sag(gy)** Decline, Dip, Droop, Hang, Hogged, Lop, Slump, Swayback, Wilt
**Saga** Aga, Chronicle, Edda, Epic, Forsyte, Icelandic, Laxdale, Legend, Odyssey, Volsunga
**Sagacity, Sagacious** Astute, Commonsense, Depth, Elephant, Judgement, Sapience, Wisdom
**Sage(s)** Abaris, Aquinian, Bactrian, Bias, Carlyle, Cheronian, Chilo(n), Clary, Cleobulus, Confucius, Counsellor, Egghead, Elder, Greybeard, Hakam, Herb, Imhotep, Jerusalem, Maharishi, Mahatma, Malmesbury, Manu, Mirza, Moolvie, Ollav, Orval, Pandit, Periander, Philosopher, Pittacus, Rishi, Salvia, Savant, Seer, Seven, Solomon, Solon, Tagore, Thales, Wiseacre, Wood
**Sage-brush** Nevada
**Sago** Portland
**Saharan** Hassaniya, Sahrawi
**Sahelian** Chad, Mali, Mauritania, Niger
**Sahib** Burra, Pukka, Tippoo, Tipu
**Said** Above-named, Co, Emir, Port, Quo(th), Related, Reputed, Spoken, Stated
▷ **Said** *may indicate* 'sounding like'
**Sail(s), Sailing** Balloon, Bunt, Canvas, Circumnavigate, Cloth, Coast, Course, Cross-jack, Cruise, Drag, Drift, Fan, Fore(course), Fore-and-aft, Full, Gaff(-topsail), Gennaker, Genoa, Goose-wing, Head, Jib, Jigger, Jut, Land, Lateen, Leech, Luff, Lug, Moon, Moonraker, Muslin, Navigate, Orthodromy, Parachute spinnaker, Peak, Plain, Plane, Ply, Rag, Raven(s)-duck, Reef, Rig, Ring-tail, Royal, Sheet, Shoulder-of-mutton, Smoke, Solar, Spanker, Spencer, Spinnaker, Spritsail, Square, Staysail, Steer, Storm-jib, Studding, Stun, Stuns'l, Suit, Top(-gallant), Top-hamper, Up anchor, Van, Vela, Wardrobe, Water, Windsurf, Yard
**Sailor(s)** AB, Admiral, Anson, Argonaut, Blue-jacket, Boater, Boatman, Boatswain, Bos'n, Bos(u)n, Budd, Canvas-climber, Commodore, Crew, Deckhand, Drake, Evans, First mate, Foremastman, Freshwater, Galiongee, Gob, Greenhand, Grommet, Hand, Hat, Hearties, Helmsman, Hornblower, Hydronaut, Jack, Janty, Jauntie, Jaunty, Jonty, Khalasi, Killick, Killock, Kroo(boy), Krooman, Kru(boy), Kruman, Lascar, Leadsman, Liberty man, Limey, Loblolly (boy), Lt, Lubber, Mariner, Matelot, Matlo(w), Middy, MN, Nelson, Noah, NUS, Oceaner, Oldster, OS, Petty Officer, Pirate, Polliwog, Pollywog, Popeye, Powder monkey, Privateer, Rating, Reefer, RN, Salt, Seabee, Seacunny, Sea-dog, Seafarer, Sea-lord, → SEAMAN, Serang, Shellback, Sin(d)bad, Steward, Stowaway, Submariner, Swabber, Swabby, Tar, Tarp(aulin), Tarry-breeks, Tindal, Topman, Triton, Waister, Wandering, Water-dog, Wave, Wren, Yachtie, Yachtsman
**Saint(ly)** Canonise, Canonize, Hagiology, Hallowed, Holy, Latterday, Leger, Patron, Pi, Pillar, Plaster, St, Sunday, Templar, Thaumaturgus

## SAINTS

*1 letter:*
S

*2 letters:*
SS

*3 letters:*
Cyr

*4 letters:*
Bede
Bees
Chad
Elmo
Eloi
Hugh
Ives
John
Jude
Just
Lucy
Luke
Malo
Mark
Odyl
Olaf
Paul
Ride
Roch
Rule

*5 letters:*
Agnes
Aidan
Alban
Alvis
Asaph
Basil
David
Denis
Denys
Diego

Elvis
Enoch
Giles
Hilda
James
Kevin
Kilda
Linus
Lucia
Mungo
Peter
Ronan
Roque
Simon
Vitus

*6 letters:*
Agatha
Alexis
Andrew
Anselm
Audrey
Brigid
Canute
George
Helena
Hilary
Jerome
Joseph
Loyola
Magnus
Martha
Martin
Monica
Ninian
Oswald
Simeon
Teresa
Thecia
Thomas
Tobias
Ursula

*7 letters:*
Alphege
Ambrose
Anthony
Barbara
Bernard
Birinus
Brandan
Brendan
Bridget
Cecilia
Clement
Columba
Crispin
Dominic
Dunstan
Dymphna
Eulalie
Francis
Isidore
Leonard
Matthew
Michael
Pancras
Patrick
Quentin
Regulus
Rosalie
Severus
Stephen
Swithin
Theresa
Vincent
Walstan
Wilfred
William

*8 letters:*
Aloysius
Barnabas
Benedict
Boniface

Columban
Crispian
Cuthbert
Dorothea
Gertrude
Hilarion
Ignatius
Lawrence
Margaret
Nicholas
Paulinus
Polycarp
Veronica
Vladimir
Winifred

*9 letters:*
Augustine
Catharine
Genevieve
Hildegard
Kentigern
Sebastian
Valentine

*10 letters:*
Bernadette
Crispinian
Hieronymus
Stanislaus

*11 letters:*
Bartholomew
Christopher

*12 letters:*
Simon Zelotes

*13 letters:*
Francis Xavier

---

**Sake** Account, Behalf, Cause, Drink, Mirin
**Sal** Nitre, Salt, Volatile
**Salacious, Salacity** Fruity, Lewd, Lust, Obscene, Prurient, Scabrous
**Salad** Beetroot, Burnet, Caesar, Calaloo, Calalu, Chef's, Chicon, Coleslaw, Corn, Cos,
   Cress, Cucumber, Days, Endive, Escarole, Fennel, Finnochio, Finoc(c)hio, Frisée, Fruit,
   Greek, Guacamole, Horiatiki, Lactuca, Lamb's lettuce, Lettuce, Lollo rosso, Lovage,
   Mache, Mesclum, Mesclun, Mixture, Mizuna, Niçoise, Purslane, Radicchio, Radish,
   Rampion, Rocket, Rojak, Roquette, Russian, Salmagundi, Salmagundy, Slaw, Tabbouleh,
   Tabbouli, Tomato, Waldorf, Watercress, Word

698 | Salutation

▷ **Salad** *may indicate* an anagram

**Salamander** Axolotl, Congo eel, Ewt, Hellbender, Lizard, Menopome, Mole, Mudpuppy, Olm, Proteus, Siren, Snake, Spring-keeper, Tiger

**Salami, Salami technique** Fraud, Peperoni

**Salary** Emolument, Fee, Hire, Pay, Prebend, Screw, Stipend, →**WAGE**

**Sale(s)** Attic, Auction, Boot, Breeze up, Cant, Car-boot, Clearance, Farm-gate, Fire, Garage, Jumble, Market, Outroop, Outrope, Pitch, Raffle, Retail, Roup, Rummage, Subhastation, Trade, Turnover, Upmarket, Venal, Vend, Vendue, Vent, Voetstoets, Voetstoots, Warrant, Wash, White, Wholesale, Yard

**Saleroom** Pantechnicon

**Salesman, Saleswoman** Agent, Assistant, Bagman, Banian, Banyan, Broker, Buccaneer, Bummaree, Cheapjack, Counterhand, Counter jumper, Drummer, Huckster, Loman, Pedlar, Rep, Retailer, Tallyman, Tout, Traveller, Vendeuse, Vendor

**Salient** Coign, Jut, Projection, Prominent, Redan, Spur

**Salisbury** Cecil, Sarum

**Saliva** Dribble, Drool, Parotid, Ptyalism, Sial(oid), Slobber, Spawl, Spit(tle), Sputum

**Sallow** Adust, Pallid, Pasty, Sale, Sauch, Saugh, Wan

**Sally** Aunt, Boutade, Charge, Dash, Escape, Excursion, Flight, Foray, Issue, Jest, Mot, Pleasantry, Quip, Retort, Ride, Riposte, Sarah, Sortie, Wisecrack, Witticism

**Salmagundi** Mess

**Salmon** Alevin, Atlantic, Australian, Baggit, Blueback, Blue-cap, Boaz, Burnett, Char(r), Chinook, Chum, Cock, Coho(e), Dog, Dorado, Grav(ad)lax, Grayling, Grilse, Humpback, Kelt, Keta, King, Kipper, Kokanee, Lax, Ligger, Lox, Masu, Mort, Nerka, Oncorhynchus, Ouananiche, Par(r), Peal, Pink, Quinnat, Red, Redfish, Rock, Samlet, Shedder, Silver, Skegger, Slat, Smelt, Smolt, Smout, Smowt, Sockeye, Sparling, Spirling, Springer, Sprod, Umber

**Salon, Saloon** Barrel-house, Beauty, Car, Hair, Hall, Honkytonk, Last chance, Lounge, Nail bar, Pullman, Sedan, Shebang, Tavern

**Salt(s), Salty** AB, Acid, Alginate, Aluminate, Andalusite, Antimonite, Arseniate, Arsenite, Ascorbate, Aspartite, Attic, Aurate, Azide, Base, Bath, Benzoate, Bicarbonate, Bichromate, Boiler, Borate, Borax, Brackish, Brine, Bromate, Bromide, Capr(o)ate, Caprylate, Carbamate, Carbonate, Carboxylate, Celery, Cerusite, Chlorate, Chlorite, Chromate, Citrate, Columbate, Complex, Condiment, Corn, Cure(d), Cyanate, Cyclamate, Datolite, Deer lick, Diazonium, Dichromate, Dioptase, Dithionate, Double, Efflorescence, Enos, Eosin, Epsom, Ferricyanide, Formate, Glauber, Glutamate, Halite, Halo-, Health, Hydrochloride, Hygroscopic, Iodide, Ioduret, Isocyanide, Kosher, Lactate, Lake-basin, Linoleate, Lithate, Liver, Magnesium, Malate, Malonate, Manganate, Mariner, Matelot, Mersalyl, Microcosmic, Monohydrate, Mucate, Muriate, NaCl, Niobate, Nitrate, Nitrite, Oleate, Orthoborate, Orthosilicate, Osm(i)ate, Oxalate, Palmitate, Pandermite, Perborate, Perchlorate, Periodate, Permanganate, Phenolate, Phosphate, Phosphite, Phthalate, Picrate, Piquancy, Plumbate, Plumbite, Potassium, Powder, Propionate, Pyruvate, Rating, Reh, Resinate, Rochelle, Rock, Rosinate, Sailor, Sal ammoniac, Salicylate, Salify, Sal volatile, Saut, Sea-dog, Seafarer, Seasoned, Sebate, Selenate, Smelling, Soap, Sodium, Solar, Sorbate, Sorrel, Stannate, Stearate, Suberate, Succinate, Sulfite, Sulphate, Sulphite, Sulphonate, Table, Tannate, Tantalate, Tartrate, Tellurate, Tellurite, Thiocyanate, Thiosulphate, Titanate, Trithionate, Tungstate, Uranin, Uranylic, Urao, Urate, Vanadate, Volatile, Water-dog, Whewellite, White, Wit(ty), Xanthate

**Salt meat** Mart

**Saltpetre** Caliche, Chile, Cubic, Nitre, Norway

**Salt-water** Sea

**Salubrious** Healthy, Sanitary, Wholesome

**Salutary** Beneficial, Good, Wholesome

**Salutation, Salute** Acclaim, Address, Asalam-wa-leikum, Australian, Ave, Banzai, Barcoo, Bid, Cap, Cheer, Command, Coupé(e), Curtsey, Embrace, Feu de joie, Fly-past,

Genuflect, Greet, Hail, Hallo, Halse, Homage, Honour, Jambo, Kiss, Middle finger, Namas kar, Namaste, Present, Salaam, Salvo, Sieg Heil, Toast, Tribute, Wassail, Wave

**Salvador** Dali

**Salvage** Cannibalise, Dredge, Lagan, Ligan, Reclaim, Recover, Recycle, Rescue, Retrieve, Tot

**Salvation(ist)** Booth, Redemption, Rescue, Socinian, Soterial, Yeo

**Salve** Anele, Anoint, Assuage, Ave, Lanolin(e), Lotion, Ointment, Remedy, Saw, Tolu, Unguent, Weapon

**Salver** Dish, Platter, Tray, Waiter

**Salvo** Fusillade, Salute, Volley

**Sal volatile** Hartshorn

**Sam** Browse, Soapy, Uncle, Weller

**Samara** Ash-key

**Samaritan** Good

**Samarium** Sm

**Same(ness)** Ae, Agnatic, Congruent, Contemporaneous, Do, Egal, Ejusd(en), Equal, Equiparate, Equivalent, Ib(id), Ibidem, Id, Idem, Identical, Identity, Ilk, Iq, Like, One, Rut, Thick(y), Thilk, Uniform, Ylke

**Samovar** Urn

**Samoyed** Dog, Uralian, Uralic

**Sample, Sampling** Amniocentesis, Biopsy, Blad, Browse, Example, Extract, Fare, Foretaste, Handout, Matched, Muster, Pattern, Pree, Prospect, Quadrat, Quota, Random, Scantling, Smear, Snip, Specimen, Spread, Stratified, Swatch, Switch, → **TASTE**, Taster, Toile, Transect, Try

**Samuel** Pepys, Smiles

**Samurai** Ronin

▷ **Sam Weller** *may indicate* the use of 'v' for 'w' or vice versa

**Sanctify** Consecrate, Enhalo, Purify, Saint

**Sanctimonious, Sanctimony** Banbury, Creeping Jesus, Devout, Goody-goody, Holy, Pi, Preachy, Prig, Religiose, Righteous, Saintly

**Sanction(s), Sanctioned** Allow, Appro, Approbate, Approof, Approve, Assent, Authorise, Bar, Confirm, Countenance, Economic, Enable, Endorse, Fatwa(h), Fetwa, Fiat, Green light, Homologate, Imprimatur, Legal, Legitimate, Mandate, OK, Pass, Pragmatic, Ratify, Smart, Sustain, Upstay, Warrant

**Sanctities, Sanctity** Enhab, Halidom, Holiness, Hollidam, Sonties

**Sanctuary, Sanctum** Adytum, Ark, Asylum, By-room, Cella, Ch, Chancel, Church, Delubrum, Frithsoken, Frithstool, Girth, Grith, Haven, Holy, JCR, Kaaba, Lair, Naos, Oracle, Penetralia, Preserve, Refuge, Sacellum, Sacrarium, Salvation, SCR, → **SHELTER**, Shrine, Tabernacle, Temple

**Sand(bank), Sandbar, Sands, Sandy** Alec, Alex, Alexander, Areg, Arena(ceous), Arenose, Arkose, As, Atoll, Bar, Barchan(e), Bark(h)an, Beach, Beige, Caliche, Dene, Desert, Dogger Bank, Down, Dudevant, Dune, Dupin, Ecru, Eremic, Erg, Esker, Foundry, Gat, George, Ginger, Goodwin, Grain, Granulose, Hazard, Hurst, Light, Loess, Machair, Nore, Oil, Outwash, Overslaugh, Podsol, Podzol, Portlandian, Psammite, Rangoli, Ridge, River, Sabulous, Saburra, Sawney, Seif dune, Shelf, Shoal, Shore, Silica, Singing, Tar, Tee, Time, Tombolo

**Sandal(s)** Alpargata, Buskin, Calceamentum, Chappal, Espadrille, Flip-flop, Ganymede, Geta, Huarache, Jelly, Patten, Pump, Slip-slop, Talaria, Thong, Zori

**Sandalwood** Algum, Almug, Chypre, Pride, Santal

**Sandarac** Arar

**Sander** Pike-perch

**Sandgroper** Pioneer

**Sandhopper** Amphipod

**Sandhurst** RMA

**Sand-loving** Ammophilous, Psammophil(e)

**Sandpiper** Bird, Dunlin, Knot, Oxbird, Peetweet, Ree, Ruff, Sandpeep, Stint, Terek, Turnstone

**Sandstone** Arkose, Calciferous, Cat's brains, Dogger, Fa(i)kes, Flysch, Grey-wether, Grit, Hassock, Holystone, Itacolumite, Kingle, Molasse, New Red, Old Red, Psammite, Quartzite, Red, Sarsen, Silica

**Sandstorm** Haboob, Tebbad

**Sandwich(es), Sandwiched** Between, Bruschetta, Butty, Club, Clubhouse, Croque-monsieur, Cuban, Doorstep, Earl, Hamburger, Hoagie, Island, Jeely piece, Knuckle, Open, Panini, Piece, Roti, Round, Sanger, Sango, Sarmie, Sarney, Sarnie, Smørbrød, Smörgåsbord, Smørrebrød, Squeeze, Stottie, Sub, Submarine, Tartine, Thumber, Toastie, Toebie, Triple-decker, Twitcher, Victoria, Wad, Western, Zak(o)uski

▷ **Sandwich(es)** *may indicate* a hidden word

**Sane, Sanity** Compos mentis, Formal, Healthy, Judgement, Rational, Reason, Right-minded, Sensible, Wice

**Sangfroid** Aplomb, Cool, Poise

**Sanguine** Confident, Haemic, Hopeful, Optimistic, Roseate, Ruddy

**Sanitary, Sanitise** Disinfect, Hygienic, Salubrious, Sterile

**Sanitation** Drainage

**Sans** Sine, Without

**Sanskrit** Bhagavad-Gita, Panchatantra, Purana, Ramayana, Sutra, Upanishad, Vedic

**Santa (Claus)** Abonde, Kriss Kringle, Secret

**Sap** Attenuate, Benzoin, Bleed, Cosh, Cremor, Depress, Drain, Enervate, Entrench, Ichor, Juice, Laser, Latex, Latice, Lymph, Mine, Mug, Nuclear, Pulque, Ratten, Resin, Roset, Rosin, Rozet, Rozit, Secretion, Soma, Sucker, Sura, Swot, Undermine, Unnerve, Weaken

**Sapid** Flavoursome, Savoury, Tasty

**Sapience, Sapient** Discernment, Sage, Wisdom

**Sapling** Ash-plant, Flittern, Ground-ash, Plant, Tellar, Teller, Tiller, Youth

**Sapper(s)** Engineer, Miner, RE

**Sapphire** Star, Water, White

**Sappho** Lesbian

**Sapwood** Alburnum

**Sarah** Battle, Gamp, Sal

**Sarcasm, Sarcastic** Acidity, Antiphrasis, Biting, Caustic, Cutting, Cynical, Derision, Irony, Mordacious, Mordant, Pungent, Quip, Quotha, Sarky, Satire, Sharp, Sharp-tongued, Smartmouth, Snide, Sting, Wisecrack, Wry

**Sardine** Fish, Sard

**Sardonic** Cutting, Cynical, Ironical, Scornful, Wry

**Sargasso** Ore, Sea(weed)

**Sark** Chemise, CI, Shirt

**Sarong** Sulu

**SAS** Red Devils

**Sash** Baldric(k), Band, Belt, Burdash, Cummerbund, Fillister, French, Lungi, Obi, Scarf, Turban, Window

**Saskatchewan** .sk

**Sassaby** Tsessebe

**Sassenach** English, Lowlander, Pock-pudding

**Satan** Adversary, Apollyon, Arch-enemy, Arch-foe, Cram, →DEVIL, Eblis, Evil One, Lucifer, Prince of darkness, Shaitan, Tempter, The old serpent

**Satchel** Bag, Postbag, Scrip

**Sate(d), Satiate** Cloy, Glut, Replete, Sad, Surfeit

**Satellite** Adrastea, Ananke, Ariel, Artificial, Astra, Atlas, Attendant, Aussat, Belinda, Bianca, Bird, Callisto, Calypso, Camenae, Carme, Charon, Communications, Comsat®, Cordelia, Cosmos, Cressida, Deimos, Desdemona, Despina, Dione, Disciple, Early bird, Earth, Echo, Elara, Enceladus, Europa, Explorer, Fixed, Follower, Galatea, Galilean, Ganymede, Geostationary, Helene, Henchman, Himalia, Hipparchus, Hyperion, Iapetus,

Intelsat, Io, Janus, Lackey, Larissa, Leda, Lysithea, Meteorological, Metis, Mimas, Miranda, Moon, Mouse, Naiad, Navigation, Nereid, Oberon, Ophelia, Orbiter, Pan, Pandora, Pasiphae, Phobos, Phoebe, Planet, Portia, Prometheus, Puck, Rhea, Rosalind, Sinope, Smallset, Space probe, SPOT, Sputnik, Syncom, Telesto, Telstar, Tethys, Thalassa, Thebe, Tiros, Titan, Titania, Triton, Umbriel, Weather

▶ **Satin** *see* SILK(Y)

**Satire, Satirical, Satirist** Arbuthnot, Archilochus, Burlesque, Butler, Candide, Chaldee, Dryden, Horace, Iambographer, Juvenal, Lampoon, Lash, Lucian, Mazarinade, Menippean, Menippos, Mockery, Pantagruel, Parody, Pasquil, Pasquin(ade), Pope, Rabelais, Raillery, Sarky, Sotadic, Spoof, Squib, Swift, Travesty, Wasps

**Satisfaction, Satisfactory, Satisfy(ing), Satisfied, Satisfactorily** Adequate, Agree, Ah, Answer, Ap(p)ay, Appease, Assuage, Atone, Change, Compensation, Complacent, →CONTENT, Defrayment, Enough, Feed, Fill, Fulfil, Glut, Gratify, Happy camper, Indulge, Jake, Job, Liking, Meet, Nice, OK, Okey-dokey, Pacation, Palatable, Pay, Please, Pride, Propitiate, Qualify, Redress, Relish, Repay, Replete, Reprisal, Revenge, Sate, Satiate, Sensual, Serve, Settlement, Slake, Smug, Square, Suffice, Supply, Tickety-boo, Well

**Saturate(d)** Drench, Glut, Imbue, Impregnate, Infuse, Permeate, →SOAK, Sodden, Steep, Surcharge, Waterlog

**Saturday** Holy, Sabbatine

**Saturn** God, Kronos, Lead, Planet, Rocket

**Satyr** Faun, Lecher, Leshy, Lesiy, Libertine, Marsyas, Pan, Silen(us), Woodhouse, Woodwose

**Sauce, Saucier, Saucy** Agrodolce, Aioli, Alfredo, Allemanse, Apple, Arch, Avgolemono, Baggage, Barbecue, Béarnaise, Béchamel, Bigarade, Bold(-faced), Bolognese, Bordelaise, Bourguignonne, Bread, Brown, Caper, Carbonara, Catchup, Catsup, Chasseur, Chaudfroid, Cheek, Chef, Chilli, Chutney, Condiment, Coulis, Cranberry, Cream, Creme anglaise, Cumberland, Custard, Dapper, Dip, Dressing, Enchilada, Espagnole, Fenberry, Fondue, Fricassee, Fudge, Fu yong, Fu yung, Gall, Garum, Gravy, Hard, Hoisin, Hollandaise, Horseradish, HP®, Impudence, Jus, Ketchup, Lip, Malapert, Marinade, Marinara, Matelote, Mayo(nnaise), Melba, Meunière, Mint, Mirepoix, Mole, Monkeygland, Mornay, Mousseline, Mouth, Nam pla, Neck, Nerve, Newburg, Nuoc mam, Oxymal, Oyster, Panada, Parsley, Passata, Peart, Peking, Perky, Pert, Pesto, Piert, Piri-piri, Pistou, Pizzaiola, Ponzu, Portugaise, Puttanesca, Ragu, Ravigote, Relish, Remoulade, Rouille, Roux, Sabayon, Sal, Salad cream, Salpicon, Salsa, Salsa verde, Sambal, Sass, Satay, Shoyu, Soja, Soubise, Soy(a), Stroganoff, Sue, Sugo, Supreme, Sweet and sour, Tabasco®, Tamari, Tartar(e), Tomato, Topping, Tossy, Trimmings, Velouté, Vinaigrette, Vindaloo, White, Wine, Worcester, Worcestershire, Yakitori

**Sauceboat-shaped** Scaphocephalate

**Saucepan** Chafer, Goblet, Skillet, Steamer, Stockpot

**Saucer** Ashtray, Discobolus, Flying, Pannikin, UFO

**Sauna** Banya, Bath, Steam-bath, Steam room, Sudatorium, Sudorific

**Saunter** Amble, Dacker, Da(i)ker, Dander, Lag, Mosey, Promenade, Roam, Shool, Stroll, Toddle

**Sausage(s)** Andouille, Andouillette, Banger, Black pudding, Blood, Boerewors, Bologna, Boudin, Bratwurst, Cervelat, Cheerio, Chipolata, Chorizo, Corn dog, Cumberland, Devon, Drisheen, Frankfurter, Garlic, Hot dog, Kielbasa, Kishke, Knackwurst, Knockwurst, Liver(wurst), Lorne, Luncheon, Mortadella, Mystery bag, Pep(p)eroni, Polony, Pudding, Salami, Sav(eloy), Snag(s), Snarler, Square, String, Vienna, Weenie, Weeny, White pudding, Wiener(wurst), Wienie, Wourst, Wurst, Zampone

**Sausage-shaped** Allantoid

**Sauté** Fry

**Savage** Ape, Barbarian, Bitter, Boor, Brute, Cannibal, Cruel, Feral, Fierce, Frightful, Grim, Gubbins, Hun, Immane, Inhuman, Maul, Noble, Remorseless, Sadistic, Truculent, Vitriolic, Wild

**Savanna** Cerrado, Plain, Sahel

**Savant** Expert, Mahatma, Sage, Scholar
**Save(r), Saving(s)** Bank, Bar, Besides, But, Capital, Collect, Conserve, Cut-rate, Deposit, Economy, Except, Goalie, Hain, Hoard, Husband, Investment, ISA, Keep, Layby, National, Nest egg, Nirlie, Nirly, Not, PEPS, Post office, Preserve, Put by, Reclaim, Recycle, Redeem, Relieve, Reprieve, →**RESCUE**, Reskew, Sa', Salt (away), Salvage, SAYE, Scrape, Scrimp, Shortcut, Slate club, Soak away, Sock away, Sou-sou, Spare, Stint, Stokvel, Succour, Susu, TESSA, Unless
**Saviour** Deliverer, Jesu(s), Lifeline, Messiah, Redeemer
**Savour(ed), Savoury** Aigrette, Bouchée, Canapé, Devils-on-horseback, Essence, Fag(g)ot, Flavour, Odour, Olent, Ramekin, Rarebit, Relish, Resent, Sair, Sapid, Sar, Smack, Starter, Tang, →**TASTE**, Umami, Vol au vent
**Savoy** Cabbage, Opera
**Savvy** Sense
**Saw** Adage, Aphorism, Apothegm, Azebiki, Back, Band, Beheld, Bucksaw, Buzz, Chain, Circular, Cliché, Commonplace, Compass, Coping, Cross-cut, Crown, Cut, Dictum, Double-ender, Dovetail, Dozuki, Ensured, Flooring, Frame, Fret, Gang, Glimpsed, Gnome, Grooving, Hack, Hand, Jig, Keyhole, Legend, Log, Maxim, Met, Motto, Pad, Panel, Paroemia, Pitsaw, Proverb, Pruning, Quarter, Rabbeting, Rack, Ribbon, Rip, Ryoba, Sash, Saying, Scroll, Serra, Skil®, Skip-tooth, Slasher, Slogan, Span, Spied, Stadda, Stone, Sweep, Tenon, Trepan, Trephine, Whip, Witnessed
**Sawbill** Merganser
**Sawbones** Surgeon
**Saw-toothed** Runcinate
**Sawyer** Logger, Tom
**Saxifrage** Astilbe, Bishop's cap, Burnet, Golden, Heuchera, London pride, Mitre-wort, St Patrick's cabbage
**Saxon** Cedric, Hengist, Hereward, Wend
**Saxophone** Axe
**Say, Saying(s)** Adage, Agrapha, Allege, Aphorism, Apophthegm, Apostrophise, Articulate, Axiom, Beatitude, Bon mot, Bromide, Byword, Cant, Catchphrase, Centos, Cliché, Declare, Dict(um), Eg, Enunciate, Epigram, Expatiate, Express, Fadaise, For example, For instance, Gnome, Impute, Input, Logia, Logion, →**MAXIM**, Mean, Mot, Mouth, Observe, Phrase, Platitude, Predicate, Pronounce, Proverb, Put, Quip, Recite, Rede, Relate, Remark, Report, Repute, Saine, Saw, Sc, Sententia, →**SPEAK**, Suppose, Sutra, Talk, Utter, Voice, Word
▷ **Say, Saying(s)** *may indicate* a word sounding like another
**Scab(by)** Blackleg, Crust, Eschar, Leggism, Leprose, Mangy, Rat, Scald, Scall, Sore, Strike-breaker
**Scabbard** Frog, Pitcher, Sheath, Tsuba
**Scabies** Itch, Psora, Scotch fiddle
**Scabrous** Harsh, Rough, Thersites
**Scaffold(ing), Scaffolder** Gallows, Gantry, Hoarding, Putlock, Putlog, Rig, Spiderman, Stage, Staging
**Scald** Blanch, Burn, Leep, Ploat, Plot
**Scale(s), Scaly** Analemma, API gravity, Ascend, Balance, Baumé, Beaufort, Binet-Simon, Bismar, Brix, Bud, Burnham, Celsius, Centigrade, Ceterach, Chromatic, →**CLIMB**, Cottony-cushion, Dander, Dandruff, Desquamate, Diagonal, Diatonic, Douglas, Elo, Enharmonic(al), Escalade, Fahrenheit, Flake, Fujita, Full, Furfur, Gamme, Gamut, Ganoid, Gapped, Gauge, Gravity, Gray, Gunter's, Heptatonic, Hexachord, Humidex, Indusium, Interval, Kelvin, Krab, Ladder, Lamina, Layer, Leaf, Lepid, Lepidote, Leprose, Libra, Ligule, Likert, Lodicule, Loricate, Magnitude, Major, Mercalli, Mesel, Metric, Minor, Mohs, Munsell, Natural, Nominal, Octad, Ordinal, Oyster shell, Palea, Palet, Patagium, Peel, Pentatonic, Pholidosis, Placoid, Plate, Platform, Proportion, Ramentum, →**RANGE**, Rankine, Ratio, Réau(mur), Regulo, Richter, San Jose, Scalade, Scan, Scarious, Scent, Scincoid, Scurf, Scutellate, Shin,

Skink, Sliding, Speel, Spring, Squama, Squame(lla), Submediant, Tegmentum, Tegula, Tonal, Tridymite, Tron(e), Unified, Vernier, Wage, Weighbridge, Wentworth, Whole-tome, Wind
▷ **Scale(d)** *may indicate* a fish
**Scallion** Leek
**Scallop(ed)** Bivalve, Clam, Coquille, Crenate, Crenulate, Escalop, Frill, Gimp, Mush, Pecten, Queenie, Seashell, Vandyke
**Scallywag** Rascal, Scamp, Skeesicks, Whippersnapper
**Scalp** Cut, Scrape, Skin, Trophy
**Scalpel** Bistoury, Knife
**Scam** Con, Fast and loose, Ramp, Strap game
**Scamp** Fripon, Imp, Limb, Lorel, Lorrell, Losel, Lozell, Neglect, → **RASCAL**, Reprobate, Rip, Rogue, Scallywag, Skeesicks, Toerag
**Scamper** Gambol, Lamp, Run, Scoot, Scurry, Scutter, Skedaddle, Skelter, Skitter, Trot
**Scan(ning), Scanner** Barcode, CAT, CT, EEG, Examine, Flat-bed, Helical, Inspect, Interlaced, Iris, OCR, Optical, Oversee, Peruse, PET, Rake, Raster, Scrutinise, Sector, SEM, Sequential, SPET, Study, Survey, Tomography, Ultrasound, Vertical, Vet
**Scandal(ous), Scandalise** Belie, Canard, Commesse, Disgrace, Exposé, Gamy, -gate, Hearsay, Muck-raking, Mud, Opprobrium, Outrage, Shame, Slander, Stigma, Stink, Tattle, Watergate
**Scandalmonger** Muckraker
**Scandinavian** Dane, Finn, Gotland, Icelander, Laplander, Lapp, Nordic, Norman, Norseland, Northman, Olaf, Runic, Squarehead, Swede, Varangian, Viking
**Scandium** Sc
**Scant(y), Scantness** Bare, Brief, Exiguous, Jejune, Jimp, Low, Meagre, Oligotrophy, Parsimonious, Poor, Scrimpy, Short, Shy, Skimpy, Slender, Spare, Sparse, Stingy
**Scapegoat, Scapegrace** Butt, Fall-guy, Hazazel, Joe Soap, Martyr, Patsy, Skainesmate, Stooge, Target, Victim, Whipping-boy
**Scapula** Blade, Omoplate
**Scar(face)** Al, Blemish, Cheloid, Cicatrix, Cliff, Craig, Epulotic, Hilum, Keloid, Leucoma, Leukoma, Mark, Pockmark, Stigma, Ulosis, Wipe
**Scarab** Beetle, Gem
**Scarce(ly), Scarcity** Barely, Dear, Dearth, Famine, Few, Hardly, Ill, Lack, Paucity, Rare, Scanty, Seldom, Short, Strap, Uncommon, Want
**Scare(d), Scarify, Scaring, Scaremongering, Scary** Adaw, Afraid, Alarmist, Alert, Amaze, Aroint, Etch, Fleg, Fright, Gally, Gliff, Glift, Hair-raising, Hairy, Panic, Petrify, Skeer, Spook, Startle, Tattie-bogle, Windy
**Scarecrow** Bogle, Bugaboo, Dudder, Dudsman, Gallibagger, Gallibeggar, Gallicrow, Gallybagger, Gallybeggar, Gallycrow, Malkin, Mawkin, Potato-bogle, Ragman, S(h)ewel, Tattie-bogle
**Scarf** Babushka, Belcher, Cataract, Comforter, Cravat, Curch, Doek, Dupatta, Fascinator, Fichu, Hai(c)k, Haique, Headsquare, Hyke, Lambrequin, Madras, Mantilla, Muffettee, Muffler, Neckatee, Neckcloth, Neckerchief, Neckgear, Neckpiece, Necktie, Neckwear, Nightingale, Orarium, Pagri, Palatine, Pashmina, Patka, Pugg(a)ree, Rail, Rebozo, Sash, Screen, Shash, Stock, Stole, Tallith, Tippet, Trot-cosy, Trot-cozy, Vexillum
**Scarifier** Scuffler
**Scarlet** Cinnabar, Cochineal, Crimson, Lac, Lac-dye, Pimpernel, Pink, Ponceau, Red, Vermilion
**Scarper** Abscond, Absquatulate, Bunk, Hightail, Imshi, Run, Shoo, Welsh
**Scat** Aroint, Dropping, Vamo(o)se
**Scathe, Scathing** Caustic, Mordant, Sarcastic, Savage, Severe, Vitriolic
**Scatter(ed), Scattering** Bestrew, Broadcast, Diaspora, Disgregation, Disject, Dispel, → **DISPERSE**, Dissipate, Dot, Flurr, Inelastic, Intersperse, Litter, Rayleigh, Rout, Scail, Skail, Sow, Sparge, Sparse, Splutter, Sporadic, Sprad, Spread, Sprinkle, Squander, Straw, Strew, Strinkle
**Scatterbrain(ed)** Dippy, Ditsy, Ditz(y), Harum-scarum, Tête folie

**Scavenge(r)** Ant, Dieb, Forage, Gully-hunter, Hunt, Hy(a)ena, Jackal, Rake, Ratton, Rotten, Scaffie, Sweeper, Totter, Vulture

**Scenario** Outline, Plot, Script, Storyboard, Worst case

**Scene(ry)** Arena, Backcloth, Boscage, Cameo, Coulisse, Decor, Diorama, Episode, Flat(s), Landscape, Locale, Outtake, Periaktos, Phantasmagoria, Prop, Prospect, Riverscape, Set, Set piece, Sight, Site, Sketch, Stage, Tableau, Take, Tormenter, Tormentor, Transformation, Venue, View, Wing

**Scent** Aroma, Attar, Chypre, Civet, Cologne, Eau de cologne, Essence, Fragrance, Frangipani, Fumet(te), Gale, Moschatel, Musk, Nose, Odour, Orris, Ottar, Otto, Perfume, Pomander, Sachet, Smell, Spoor, Vent, Waft, Wind

**Scentless** Anosmia

**Sceptic, Sceptical(ly), Scepticism** Agnostic, Askant, Cynic, Disbeliever, Doubter, Europhobe, Incredulous, Infidel, Jaundiced, Nihilistic, Nullifidian, Pyrrho(nic), Sadducee, Solipsism, Thomas

**Schedule** Agenda, Calendar, Classification, Itinerary, List, Prioritise, Programme, Register, Slot, Table, Timescale, Time-sheet, Timetable

**Scheme, Schemer, Scheming** Angle, Calculate, CATS, Colour, Concoct, Connive, Conspire, Crafty, Cunning, Dare, Darien, Dart, Decoct, Décor, Design, Devisal, Diagram, Dodge, Draft, Evince, Gin, Honeytrap, Housing, Intrigue, Jezebel, Machiavellian, Machinate, Manoeuvre, Master plan, Nostrum, Pension, Pilot, → **PLAN**, Plat, Plot, Ponzi, Project, Proposition, Purpose, Put-up job, Pyramid, Racket, Rhyme, Ruse, Scam, Set-aside, Stratagem, System, Table, Top-hat, Wangle, Wheeler-dealer, Wheeze

**Schism(atic)** Antiburgher, Break, Disunion, Division, Eastern, Great, Greek, Heterodox, Rent, Secession, Split, Western

**Schizo(phrenia)** Catatonic, Dementia praecox, Hebephrenia, LSD

**Schmaltz(y)** Goo, Mush, Slush, Tear-jerker

**Schmieder** S

**Schmook** Drip

**Schmuck** Gunsel

**Schnapps** Enzian

**Scholar, Scholiast** Abelard, Academic, Alcuin, Alumni, Atticus, BA, Bookman, Boursier, Catachumen, Classicist, Clergy, Clerisy, Clerk, Commoner, Demy, Disciple, Don, Erasmus, Erudite, Etonian, Exhibitioner, Extern(e), Externat, Faculty, Goliard, Graduate, Grecian, Hafiz, Hebraist, Inkhorn, Jowett, Literate, Littérateur, MA, Mal(l)am, Masorete, Maulana, Noter, Occam Ulama, Ollamh, Ollav, Pauline, Plutarch, Polymath, Pupil, Rhodes, Sap, Savant, Saxonist, Schoolboy, Sizar, Soph, → **STUDENT**, Tabardar, Taberdar, Taberder, Tom Brown, Varro

**Scholarship** Bursary, Closed, Education, Erudition, Exhibition, Grant, Grant-in-aid, Learning, Lore, Mass, Rhodes

**School** Brainwash, Discipline, Drill, Educate, Exercise, Feeder, Peripatetic, Sciences, Scul, Scull(e), Teach, → **TRAIN**, Tutor

## SCHOOLS

| 2 letters: | Ski | Eton | RADA |
|---|---|---|---|
| GS | | Free | Real |
| | 4 letters: | High | Sect |
| 3 letters: | Coed | Home | Sink |
| Day | Cool | Kant | Song |
| Gam | Cult | Lake | Tech |
| LSE | Dada | Life | |
| Old | Dame | Play | 5 letters: |
| Pod | Dojo | Poly | Board |
| RAM | Dual | Prep | Charm |

Choir
Drama
Faith
First
Grade
Group
Heder
Hedge
Ionic
Kindy
List D
Lower
Lycée
Night
Perse
Piano
Rydal
Shoal
Slade
State
Stowe
Style
Trade
Upper

**6 letters:**
Ash Can
Beacon
Cheder
Church
Fettes
Harrow
Honour
Hostel
Infant
Junior
Kindie
Lyceum
Magnet
Middle
Normal
Oundle
Public
Ragged
Ramean
Repton

Summer
Sunday
Whales

**7 letters:**
Academy
Alleyn's
Bauhaus
Cockney
Council
Crammer
Driving
Essenes
Flemish
Grammar
Jim Crow
Lancing
Loretto
Madrasa
Nursery
Primary
Private
Rhodian
Roedean
Rossall
Sabbath
Satanic
Special
Writing
Yeshiva

**8 letters:**
Approved
Barbizon
Benenden
Bluecoat
Boarding
Business
Cranwell
Downside
Externat
Graduate
Hospital
Kailyard
Kaleyard
Language

Mahayana
Mannheim
National
Provided
Sadducee
Seminary
Separate
Tenebrum

**9 letters:**
Chartreux
Classical
Community
Composite
Finishing
Frankfurt
Gymnasien
Gymnasium
Institute
Madrassah
Palaestra
Parochial
Porpoises
Sandhurst
Secondary
Single-sex
Spasmodic
Tonbridge
Voluntary

**10 letters:**
Ampleforth
Chautauqua
Elementary
Foundation
Grange Hill
Grant-aided
Greyfriars
Historical
Industrial
Integrated
Maintained
Manchester
Parnassian
Pensionnat
Scandalous

Sole charge
Stonyhurst
St Trinian's
Wellington
Winchester

**11 letters:**
Direct grant
Giggleswick
Gordonstoun
Hypermodern
Independent
Maintaining
Marlborough
Preparatory
Reformatory
Residential

**12 letters:**
Charterhouse
Conservative
Conservatory
Intermediate
Kindergarten
Malory Towers
Progymnasium

**13 letters:**
Comprehensive
Conservatoire
Dotheboys Hall

**14 letters:**
Correspondence
Voluntary-aided

**15 letters:**
Grant-maintained
Secondary-modern

**19 letters:**
Voluntary-
 controlled

---

**Schoolboy, Schoolgirl** Alumna, Bluecoat, Carthusian, Coed, Colleger, East, Etonian, Fag, Gait, Geit, Gyte, Miss, Monitor, Oppidan, Petty, Stalky, Wykehamist
**School-leaver** Abiturient
**Schoolma'am, Schoolman, Schoolmaster, Schoolmistress, Schoolteacher**
Aram, Beak, Dominie, Duns, Holofernes, Miss, Occam, Orbilius, Pedagogue, Pedant, Servitor, Sir, Squeers, Teacher, Tutress, Ursuline
**Schooner** Glass, Hesperus, Hispaniola, Prairie, Ship, Tern

**Schubert** D

**Sciatica** Hip-gout

**Science** Aerodynamics, Anatomy, Anthropology, Applied, Art, Astrodynamics,
Astrophysics, Atmology, Avionics, Axiology, Behavioural, Biology, Biotech, Botany,
Chemistry, Christian, Cognitive, Computer, Crystallography, Cybernetics, Dismal,
Domestic, Earth, Ekistics, Electrodynamics, Entomology, Eth(n)ology, Eugenics,
Euphenics, Exact, Forensic, Gay, Geodesy, Geology, Hard, Information, Knowledge,
Life, Lithology, Macrobiotics, Materia medica, Mechanics, Metallurgy, Meteorology,
Metrology, Military, Mineralogy, Mnemonics, Natural, Noble, Nomology, Noology,
Nosology, Occult, Ology, Ontology, Optics, Optometry, Pedagogy, Penology, Phrenology,
Physical, Physics, Policy, Political, Psychics, Pure, Rocket, Rural, Semantics, Semiology,
Serology, Skill, Social, Soft, Soil, Sonics, Stinks, Stylistics, Tactics, Technics, Technology,
Tectonics, Telematics, Thermodynamics, Thremmatology, Toxicology, Tribology,
Trigonometry, Typhlology, Zootechnics

**Science fiction** Cyberpunk

**Scientist** Alchemist, Anatomist, Archimedes, Aston, Astronomer, Atomist,
Bacteriologist, Bell, →**BIOLOGIST**, Boffin, BSc, Cavendish, →**CHEMIST**, Climatologist,
Copernicus, Curie, Dalton, Darwin, Davy, Doppler, Egghead, Einstein, Euler,
Experimenter, Expert, Faraday, Fourier, FRS, Galileo, Gay-Lussac, Geodesist, Geometer,
Harvey, Heaviside, Herschel, Hooke, Hubble, Introchemist, Kennelly, Lamarck, Laplace,
Lodge, Lovell, Mach, Magnetist, Medawar, Mendeleev, Metallurgist, Newton, Oersted,
Pascal, Pasteur, Pauli, →**PHYSICIST**, Piccard, Potamologist, Réaumur, Researcher,
Rocket, Technocrat, Tesla, Theremin, Van der Waals, Volta

**Scimitar** Acinaciform, Sword

**Scintillate** Dazzle, Emicate, Gleam, Glitter, →**SPARKLE**

**Scion** Cion, Graft, Imp, Offspring, Sien(t), Slip, Sprig, Sprout, Syen

**Scissors** Clippers, Criss-cross, Cutters, Forfex, Nail, Probe, Shears

**Scoff** Belittle, Boo, Chaff, Deride, Devour, Dor, Eat, Feast, Flout, Food, Gall, Geck, Gibe,
Gird, Gobble, →**JEER**, Jest, Mock, Rail, Rib, Ridicule, Roast, Scaff, Scorn, Send up, Sneer,
Swallow, Taunt

**Scold(ing)** Admonish, Berate, Callet, Catamaran, Chastise, Chide, Clapperclaw,
Cotquean, Do, Earful, Earwig, Flite, Flyte, Fuss, Jaw(bation), Jobation, Lecture, Nag,
Objurgate, Philippic, Rag, Rant, Rate, →**REBUKE**, Reprimand, Reprove, Revile, Rollick,
Rollock, Rouse on, Row, Sas(s)arara, Sis(s)erary, Slang, Slate, Termagant, Threap, Threep,
Through-going, Tick-off, Tongue-lash, Trimmer, Upbraid, Virago, What for, Wig,
Xant(h)ippe, Yaff, Yankie, Yap

**Sconce** Candlestick, Crown, Forfeit, Head, Ice, Nole

**Scone** Drop, Girdle, Griddle cake

**Scoop** Bale, Dipper, Exclusive, Gouge, Grab, Hollow, Ladle, Lap, Pale, Rout, Shovel,
Spoon, Story, Trowel

**Scoot** Scamper

**Scooter** Vespa®

**Scope** Ambit, Bargaining, Breadth, Compass, Diapason, Domain, Elbow-room, Extent,
Freedom, Gamut, Indulgence, Ken, Latitude, Leeway, Play, Purview, Range, Remit,
Room, Rope, Scouth, Scowth, Size, Sphere

**Scorch(er)** Adust, Birsle, Blister, Brasero, →**BURN**, Char, Destroy, Frizzle, Fry, Parch,
Scouther, Scowder, Scowther, Sear, Singe, Soar, Speed, Swale, Swayl, Sweal, Sweel,
Torrefy, Torrid, Wither

**Score(s), Scoring** Aggregate, Apgar, Arrange, Behind, Bill, Birdie, Bradford, Bye, Capot,
Chalk up, Chase, Clock up, Conversion, Count, Crena, Debt, Dunk, Eagle, Etch, Full,
Gash, Goal, Groove, Hail, Honours, Incise, Ingroove, Ippon, Koka, Law, Leaderboard,
Lots, Magpie, Make, Mark, Music, Net, Nick, Notation, Notch, Nurdle, Open,
Orchestrate, Partitur(a), Peg(board), Pique, Point, Record, Repique, Rit(t), Rouge, Run,
Rut, Scotch, Scrat, Scratch, Scribe, Scrive, Set, Sheet music, Single, Spare, Stableford,

Stria, String, Sum, Tablature, →**TALLY**, TE, Touchdown, Try, Twenty, Vocal, Waza-ari, Win, Yuko

**Score-board, Score-sheet** Card, Telegraph

▷ **Scorer** *may indicate* a composer

▷ **Scoring** *may indicate* an anagram

**Scorn(ful)** Arrogant, Bah, Contemn, Contempt, Contumely, Deride, Despise, Dis(s), Disdain, Dislike, Disparagement, Flout, Geck, Haughty, Insult, Meprise, Mock, Opprobrium, Phooey, Putdown, Raillery, Rebuff, Ridicule, Sarcastic, Sardonic, Sarky, Scathing, Scoff, Scout, Sdaine, Sdeigne, Sneer, Sniffy, Spurn, Wither

**Scorpion** Arachnid, Book, Chelifer, False, Father-lasher, Pedipalp(us), Rock, Vinegarroon, Water, Whip

**Scot(sman), Scots(woman), Scottish** Alistair, Angus, Antenati, Berean, Blue-bonnet, Bluecap, Caledonian, Celt, Clansman, Covenanter, Duni(e)wassal, Dunniewassal, Erse, Fingal, Gael, Highland, Ian, Jock, Kelt, Kelvinside, Kiltie, Kitty, Knox, Laird, Lallan(s), Lot, Lowland, Luckie, Lucky, Mac, Mon, Morningside, Pecht, Peght, Pict, Ross, Sandy, Sawn(e)y, Shetlander, Stuart, Tartan, Tax, Teuchter, Torridonian

**Scotch(man)** Censor, Dish, Distiller, Foil, Glenlivet®, Nip in the bud, Notch, Score, Scratch, Stop, Thwart, Usquebaugh, Whisky

**Scot-free** Wreakless

**Scotland** Alban(y), Albion, Caledonia, Gaeltacht, Gaidhealtachd, Lallans, Lothian, NB, Norland, Scotia

**Scoundrel** Cad, Cur, Dog, Fink, Heel, Hound, Knave, Miscreant, Rat, Reprobate, Scab, Smaik, Varlet, →**VILLAIN**, Wretch

**Scour(er)** Beat, Depurate, Full, Holystone, Lant, Purge, Quarter, Scrub

▷ **Scour** *may indicate* an anagram

**Scourge** Bible-thumper, Cat, Disciplinarium, Discipline, Flagellate, Flog, Knout, Lash, Pest, →**PLAGUE**, Scorpion, Whip, Wire

**Scouse** Liver bird, Wacker

**Scout** Akela, Baden-Powell, Beaver, Bedmaker, Bird dog, Colony, Deride, Disdain, Emissary, Explorer, Flout, Guide, King's, Mock, Outrider, Pathfinder, Patrol, Pickeer, Pioneer, Queen's, Ranger, Reconnoitre, Rover, Runner, Scoff, Scorn, Scourer, Scurrier, Scurriour, Sea, Sixer, Spial, Spyal, Talent, Tenderfoot, Tonto, Track, Vedette, Venture

**Scowl(ing)** Frown, Glower, Gnar, Lour, Lower, Sullen

**Scrabble** Claw, Paw

**Scrag(gy)** Bony, Dewitt, Ewe-necked, Neck, Scrawny

**Scram** Begone, Hence, Scat, Shoo

**Scramble** Addle, Clamber, Encode, Grubble, Hurry, Maul, Mêlée, Mix, Motocross, Muss(e), Scamble, Sprattle, Sprawl, Swerve, Texas

**Scrap(s), Scrappy** Abandon, Abolish, Abrogate, Bin, →**BIT**, Brock, Cancel, Conflict, Cutting, Discard, Ditch, Dump, End, Erase, →**FIGHT**, Fisticuffs, Fragment, Fray, Iota, Jot, Junk, Leftover, Mêlée, Mellay, Morceau, Morsel, Odd, Off-cut, Ort, Ounce, Papier collé, Patch, Piece, Pig's-wash, Rag, Rase, Raze, Remnant, Rescind, Rew, Row, Ruck, Scarmoge, Scintilla, Scissel, Scissil, Scroddled, Scrub, Set-to, Shard, Sherd, Shred, Skerrick, Skirmish, Snap, Snippet, Spall, Stoush, Tait, Tate, Tatter, Titbit, Trash, Truculent, Tussle, Whit, Wisp

**Scrap book** Album, Grangerism

**Scrap box** Tidy

**Scrape(r)** Abrade, Agar, Bark, Clat, Claw, Comb, Curette, D and C, Erase, Escapade, Grate, Graze, Gride, Harl, Hoe, Hole, Jar, Kowtow, Lesion, Lute, Pick, Predicament, Racloir, Rake, Rasorial, Rasp, Rasure, Raze, Razure, Saw, Scalp, Scart, Scrat(ch), Scroop, Scuff, Shave, Skimp, Skin, Skive, Squeegee, Strake, Stridulate, Strigil, Xyster

**Scraping noise** Curr, Scroop

**Scrap merchant** Didakai, Didakei, Diddicoi, Diddicoy, Didicoi, Didicoy, Gold-end-man, Totter

**Scratch(es), Scratched, Scratching** Annul, Cancel, Cla(u)t, Claw, Cracked heels, Curry, Devil, Efface, Eradicate, Erase, Etch, Grabble, Graze, Key, Mar, Nick, Par, Periwig, Pork, Quit, Race, Rase, Rasp, Rast, Ritt, Root, Satan, Scarify, Scart, Score, Scrab(ble), Scram(b), Scrape, Scrattle, Scrawm, Scrawp, Scrooch, Scrorp, Scrub, Scuff, Spag, Streak, Striation, Tease, Teaze, Wig, Withdraw

▷ **Scratch(ed)** *may indicate* an anagram

**Scrawl** Doodle, Scratch, Scribble, Squiggle

**Scream(er)** Aargh, Amusing, Bellow, Cariama, Caterwaul, Comedian, Comic, Cry, Eek, Headline, Hern, Hoot, Kamichi, Laugh, Priceless, Primal, Riot, Scare-line, Screech, Seriema, Shriek, Skirl, Squall, Sutch, Yell

**Scree** Bahada, Bajada, Eluvium, Talus

**Screech(ing)** Cry, Hoot, Screak, Screich, Screigh, Scriech, Scritch, Skreigh, Skriech, Skriegh, Ululant, Whoot

**Screed** Blaud, Megillah, Ms, Plastered, Rat-rhyme, Tirade

**Screen(s), Screening** Abat-jour, Air, Arras, Back projection, Backstop, Blind(age), Block, Blue, Boss, Brise-soleil, Camouflage, Cervical, Chancel, Check, Chick, Cinerama®, Cloak, Comb, Cornea, Coromandel, Cover, Cribble, Curtain, Divider, Dodger, Eclipse, Eyelid, Festoon-blind, Fight, Fire, Flat, Fluorescent, Glib, Gobo, Grid, Grille, Hallan, Help, Hide, Hoard, Hoarding, Iconostas(is), Intensifying, Jube, Lattice, Long-persistence, Mantelet, Mask, Meat, Monitor, Net, Nintendo®, Nonny, Obscure, Organ, Over-cover, Overhead, Parclose, Partition, Part-off, Pella, Plasma, Pulpitum, Purdah, Radar, Radarscope, Reardos, Reredorse, Reredos(se), Retable, Riddle, Rood, Scog, Sconce, Scope, Seclude, → **SHADE**, Shelter, Shield, Shoji, Show, Sift, Sight, Silver, Skug, Small, Smoke, Split, Strain, Sunblock, Televise, Tems, Test, Testudo, TFT, Touch, Transenna, Traverse, Umbrella, VDU, Vet, Visor, Wide, Windbreak, Window, Windshield, Winnow

**Screw** Adam, Allen, Archimedes, Blot, Butterfly, Cap, Cheat, Coach, Coitus, Countersunk, Double-threaded, Dungeoner, Endless, Extort, Female, Fleece, Grub, Guard, Gyp, Ice, Interrupted, Jack, Jailer, Jailor, Lag, Lead, Levelling, Lug, Machine, Male, Mar, Micrometer, Miser, Monkey-wrench, Niggard, Pay, Perpetual, Phillips®, Prop(ellor), Pucker, Raised head, Robertson, Rotate, Ruin, Salary, Screweye, Scrunch, Skinflint, Spiral, Squinch, Swiz(zle), Thumb(i)kins, Twin, Twine, Twist, Vice, Wages, Whitworth, Worm, Wreck

**Screwdriver** Cocktail, Phillips®, Pozidriv®, Ratchet, Scrum, Stubby, Tweaker

**Scribble** Doodle, Note, Pen, Scrawl

**Scribe** Clerk, Ezra, Mallam, Scrivener, Sopherim, Tabellion, Writer, WS

**Scrimmage** Bully, Fracas, Maul, Mêlée, Rouge, Scrap, Skirmish, Struggle

**Scrimp** Economise, Pinch, Save, Scrape, Skrimp

**Script (reader)** Book, Calligraphy, Demotist, Devanagari, Gurmukhi, Hand, Hieratic, Hiragana, Italic, Jawi, Kana, Kufic, Libretto, Linear A, Linear B, Lines, Lombardic, Longhand, Miniscule, Nagari, Nashki, Nastalik, Nastaliq, Nes(h)ki, Og(h)am, Prompt book, Ronde, Scenario, Screenplay, Shooting, Shorthand, Writing

**Scriptless** Improvised

**Scripture(s), Scriptural version** Adi Granth, Agadah, Alcoran, Antilegomena, Avesta, Bible, Gemara, Gematria, Gospel, Granth (Sahib), Guru Granth, Haggada(h), Hermeneutics, Hexapla, Holy book, Holy writ, Koran, K'thibh, Lectionary, Lesson, Lotus Sutra, Mishna(h), OT, Rig-veda, Smriti, Tantra, Targum, Testament, Upanishad, Veda, Vedic, Verse, Vulgate

**Scrivener** Tabellion

**Scrofula** Crewels, Cruel(l)s, King's evil, Struma

**Scroll(-work)** Cartouche, Dead Sea, Gohonzon, Makimono, Megillah, Mezuza(h), Monkeytail, Parchment, Pell, Roll, Roul(e), Scrow, Sefer Torah, Stemma, Torah, Turbinate, Upcurl, Vitruvian, Volume, Volute

**Scrooge** Blagueur, Miser

**Scrotum** Oscheal

**Scrounge(r)** Beg, Blag, Bludge(r), Borrow, Bot, Cadge, Forage, Freegan, Freeload, Layabout, Ligger, Scunge, Sponge

**Scrub(ber), Scrubland, Scrubs** Abandon, Cancel, Chaparral, Cleanse, Dele(te), Exfoliate, Expunge, Facial, Fynbos, Gar(r)igue, Heath, Hog, Holystone, Horizontal, Loofa(h), Luffa, Mallee, Masseur, Nailbrush, Negate, Pro, Rescind, Rub, Scour, Sticks, Strim, Tart, Wormwood

▷ **Scrub** *may indicate* 'delete'

**Scruff(y)** Dog(-eared), Fleabag, Grubby, Mangy, Nape, Nucha, Raddled, Ragamuffin, Ragbag, Raggle-taggle, Scarecrow, Tatty, Uncombed, Untidy

**Scrum(mage)** Bajada, Fracas, Maul, Melée, Mob, Pack, Rouge, Ruck

**Scrummy, Scrumptious** Delectable, Delicious, Toothy, Yum-yum

**Scrunt** Carl

**Scruple(s), Scrupulous** Compunction, Conscience, Doubt, Meticulous, Nicety, Precise, Punctilious, Qualm, Queasy, Righteous, Stickle, Thorough

**Scrutinize, Scrutiny** Check, Docimasy, Examine, Inspect, Observe, Peruse, Pore, Pry, → **SCAN**, Size up, Study

**Scud** East, Scoot, Spark, Spindrift, Spoom, Spoon, Spray

**Scuff** Brush, Nape, Shuffle

**Scuffle** Bagarre, Brawl, Melee, Scarmage, Skirmish, Struggle, Tussle

▷ **Scuffle** *may indicate* an anagram

**Scull** Oar, Row

**Sculpt(ure)** Acrolith, Aeginetan, Bas-relief, Boast, Bronze, Bust, Calvary, Canephor(a), Canephore, Canephorus, Carve, Chisel, Chryselephantine, Della-robbia, Figure, Glyptics, High-relief, Kore, Kouros, Marble, Mezzo-relievo, Mezzo-rilievo, Mobile, Nude, Pergamene, Pietà, Relief, Relievo, Sc, Scabble, Scapple, Shape, Stabile, → **STATUARY**, Topiary

**Sculptor** Arp, Artist, Bartholdi, Bernini, Brancusi, Butler, Calder, Canova, Cellini, Daedalus, Della Robbia, Donatello, Dubuffet, Epstein, Flaxman, Giacometti, Gibbons, Gill, Hepworth, Klippel, Landseer, Michelangelo, Moore, Myron, Nicholson, Noguchi, Nollekens, Paolozzi, Pevsner, Phidias, Picasso, Pisano, Praxiteles, Pygmalion, Rodin, Scopas, Stevens, Tatlin, Wheeler, Woolner

**Scum, Scumbag** Confervoid, Dregs, Dross, Epistasis, Film, Glass-gall, Kish, Legge, Louse, Mantle, Mother, Pellicle, Pond, Rabble, Rat, Sandiver, Scorious, Scruff, Slag, Slime, Spume, Sullage, Vermin

**Scupper** Drain, Ruin, Scuttle, Sink

**Scurf, Scurvy** Dander, Dandriff, Dandruff, Furfur, Horson, Lepidote, Lepra, Leprose, Scabrous, Scall, Scorbutic, Whoreson, Yaws, Yaw(e)y

**Scurrilous** Cur, Fescennine, Profane, Ribald, Sotadic, Thersites, Vulgar

**Scurry** Beetle, Hurry, Scamper, Scutter, Skedaddle, Skelter, Squirr

**Scut** Fud, Tail

**Scute** Plate

**Scuttle** Abandon, Dan, Dash, Hod, Purdonium, Scamper, Scoop, Scrattle, Scupper, Scurry, Sink, Wreck

**Scythe** Bushwhacker, Cradle, Cut, Hook, Sickle, Sieth, Snath(e), Snead, Sneath, Sned

**Sea(s), Seawards** Beam, Billow, Brine, Briny, Ditch, Drink, Electron, Epicontinental, Euphotic, Euxine, Foam, Herring-pond, Main, Mare, Mare clausum, Mare liberum, Maritime, Molten, Narrow, → **OCEAN**, Offing, Offshore, Open, Out, Quantity, Strand, Tide, Tide-rip, Water

---

**SEAS**

| *3 letters:* | *4 letters:* | | *5 letters:* |
|---|---|---|---|
| Ler | Aral | Head | Banda |
| Med | Azov | High | Black |
| Red | Blue | Java | Ceram |
| Zee | Dead | Kara | China |
| | Four | Ross | Coral |
| | | Sulu | |

Cross
Great
Irish
Japan
North
Oggin
Seven
Short
South
Timor
White

**6 letters:**
Aegean
Baltic
Bering
Biscay
Celtic
Cortes
Flores
Inland
Ionian
Laptev

Tasman
Tethys
Yellow

**7 letters:**
Andaman
Arabian
Arafura
Barents
Benthos
Caspian
Celebes
Channel
Chukchi
Euripus
Galilee
Icarian
Marmara
Marmora
Okhotsk
Pelagic
Polynya
Solomon

Weddell

**8 letters:**
Adriatic
Amundsen
Beaufort
Bismarck
Bosporus
Hwang Hai
Kattegat
Labrador
Ligurian
Sargasso
Tiberias

**9 letters:**
Bosphorus
Caribbean
East China
E. Siberian
Greenland
Hudson Bay
Norwegian

Skagerrak
Thalassic
Waddenzee

**10 letters:**
Philippine
South China
Tyrrhenian

**11 letters:**
Spanish Main

**12 letters:**
Nordenskjold

**13 letters:**
Mediterranean

**14 letters:**
Bellingshausen

---

**Sea-anemone** Actinia, Zoantharia
**Sea-bear** Fur-seal, Otary, Seal, Seecatchie
**Sea-beast** Ellops, Lamp-shell, Loriciferan, Manatee
**Sea-bream** Carp, Fish, Porgie, Porgy, Tai
**Sea-cow** Dugong, Lamantin, Manatee, Rhytina, Sirenian
**Sea-cucumber** Bêche-de-mer, Trepang
**Sea-dog** Salt, Seal, Tar
**Sea-eagle** Erne
**Sea-ear** Abalone, Paua
**Sea-fight** Naumachy
**Seafood** Calamari, Crab, Crevette, →FISH, Lobster, Plankton, Prawn, Shrimp, Squid, Whelk, Winkle, Zooplankton
**Seafront, Seashore, Seaside** Beach, Coast(line), Esplanade, Littoral, Orarian, Prom(enade), Seaboard, Waterfront
**Sea-god** Neptune, Nereus, Triton
**Sea-green** Glaucous, Incorruptible, Robespierre
**Sea-horse** Hippocampus, Hippodame, Lophobranchiate, Morse, Pipefish, Tangie
**Seal(ant), Seal box, Sealed, Seals** Airtight, Appose, Atlantic, Bachelor, Bladdernose, Block(ade), Bull(a), Cachet, Cap, Caulk, Chesterfield, Chop, Clinch, Close, Cocket, Common, Consign, Cork, Crab-eater, Cylinder, Eared, Earless, Elephant, Emblem, Fisherman's ring, Fob, Fur, Gasket, Great, Greenland, Grey, Hair, Harbour, Harp, Hermetic, Hooded, Hudson, Impress, Jark, Lemnian, Leopard, Lute, Mastic, Monk, Obsign(ate), Operculum, O-ring, Otary, Phoca, Pinnipedia, Pintadera, Plug, Pod, Privy, Proof, Putty, Quarter, Ribbon, Ringed, Ronan, Rookery, Saddleback, Sea-bear, Sealch, Sea-leopard, Sealgh, Seecatch(ie), Selkie, Sigil, Signet, Silkie, Silky, Size, Skippet, Solomon's, Sphragistics, Stamp, SWALK, Tar, Vacuum-packed, Wafer, Washer, Water, Weddell, Whitecoat, Womb, Zalophus, Ziplock
**Sea-legs** Balance, Pleons
**Sea-level** Geoid
**Sea-lily** Crinoid, Palmatozoa

**Seam, Seamstress** Channel, Commissure, Dorsal suture, Fell, Felled, French, Furrow, Join, Layer, Middle-stitching, Midinette, Monk's, Sew, Suture, Thread, Welt, Zawster

**Seaman, Seamen** AB, Argonaut, Circumnavigator, Crew, Jack, Lascar, Lubber, Mariner, OD, Ordinary, PO, Rating, RN, →**SAILOR**, Salt, Swabby, Tar

**Sea-mat** Flustra, Hornwrack

**Sea-matiness** Gam

**Sea-monster** Kraken, Merman, Wasserman, Ziffius

**Sea-mouse** Bristle-worm

**Séance** Communication, Levitation, Session, Sitting

**Sea-parrot** Puffin

**Sear** Brand, Burn, Catch, Cauterise, Char, Frizzle, Parch, Scath(e), Scorch, Singe, Wither

**Search(ing)** Beat, Body, Comb, Delve, Dowse, Dragnet, Examine, Ferret, Fingertip, Fish, →**FORAGE**, Fossick, Frisk, Global, Google(-whack), Grope, Home, Hunt, Indagate, Inquire, Jerk, Jerque, Kemb, Manhunt, Perquisition, Perscrutation, Probe, Proll, Prospect, Proul, Prowl, Pursue, Quest, Rake, Rancel, Ransack, Ransel, Ranzel, Ravel, Ripe, Root, Rootle, Rummage, Scan, Scavenge, Scour, Scout, Scur, Sker, Skirr, Snoop, Strip, Surf, Sweep, Talent spotting, Thumb, Trace, Trawl, Zotetic

**Sea-rover** Norseman, Viking

**Sea-serpent, Sea-snake** Ellops, Hydrophidae, Phoca

▸ **Seaside** *see* **SEAFRONT**

**Sea-slug** Bêche-de-mer, Trepang

**Sea-snail** Neritidae

**Season(able), Seasonal, Seasoned, Seasoning** Accustom, Age, Aggrace, Autumn, Betimes, Christmas, Close, Condiment, Devil, Dress, Duxelles, Easter, Enure, Etesian, Fall, Fennel, Festive, Fines herbes, Flavour, Garlic, G(h)omasco, Growing, Heat, Hiems, High, In, Inure, Lent, Marjoram, Master, Mature, Noel, Nutmeg, Off, Open, Paprika, Peak, Pepper, Powellise, Practised, Ripen, Salt, Sar, Seal, Seel, Seil, Sele, Silly, Solstice, Spice, Spring, Summer(y), Tahini, Ticket, Tide, Time, Timeous, Weather-beaten, Whit, Winter, Xmas

**Sea-squirt** Ascidian, Cunjevoi, Salpa(e)

**Seat(ing)** Arthur's, Backside, Banc, Banquette, Barstool, Beanbag, Behind, Bench, Bleachers, Booster, Booty, Borne, Bosun's chair, Bottom, Box, Bucket, Bum, Bunker, Buttocks, Canapé, Catbird, Centre, Chair, Chaise longue, Choirstall, Coit, Couch, Country, Creepie, Croup(e), Croupon, Cushion, Davenport, Deckchair, Derrière, Dick(e)y, Dicky, Divan, Duff, Ejector, Epicentre, Faldistory, Faldstool, Foundation, Fud, Fundament, Gradin, Hall, Hassock, Home, Hot, Houdah, Howdah, Humpty, Hurdies, Inglenook, Judgement, Jump, Knifeboard, Lap, Love, Marginal, Marquise, Mercy, Miserere, Misericord, Natch, Nates, Ottoman, Palanquin, Palfrey, Passenger, Perch, Pew, Pillion, Pit, Pouffe, Ringside, Rocker, Royal box, Rumble, Rumble-tumble, Rump, Saddle, Safe, Sagbag, Sedes, Sedile, Sedilium, See, Sell, Selle, Settee, Settle, Shooting stick, Sidesaddle, Siege, Siege Perilous, Sliding, Sofa, Squab, Stall, Stand, Stool, Strapontin, Subsellium, Sunk(ie), Sunlounger, Synthronus, Tabo(u)ret, Throne, Thwart, Tip up, Tonneau, Upholstery, Window, Woolsack

**Sea-urchin** Asterias, Echinus, Pluteus, Sphaeridia, Whore's egg

**Sea-vampire** Manta

**Sea-wall** Bulwark, Dyke, Groyne

**Seaweed** Agar, Alga(e), Arame, Badderlock, Bladderwort, Bladderwrack, Carrag(h)een, Ceylon moss, Chondrus, Conferva, Coralline, Cystocarp, Desmid, Devil's apron, Diatom, Driftweed, Dulse, Enteromorpha, Florideae, Fucus, Gulfweed, Heterocontae, Hijiki, Hornwrack, Kale, Karengo, Kelp, Kilp, Kombu, Konbu, Laminaria, Laver, Lemon-weed, Maerl, Nori, Nullipore, Oarweed, Ore, Peacock's tail, Phyco-, Porphyra, Purple laver, Redware, Rockweed, Sargasso, Seabottle, Sea-furbelow, Sea-girdle, Sea-lace, Sea-lettuce, Sea-mat, Sea-moss, Sea-tangle, Seaware, Sea-whistle, Sea-wrack, Tang(le), Tetraspore, Ulva, Varec(h), Vraic, Wakame, Ware, Wrack

**Sea-wolf** Pirate

**Sea-worm** Palolo, Spunculid

**Sea-worthy** Watertight

**Sebastian** Coe

**Sec** Dry, Instant

**Secateurs** Pruners

**Secede(r), Secession(ist)** Adullamite, Antiburgher, Breakaway, Cave, Defy, Desert, Dissident, Flamingant, Separatist, Sever, Splinter, UDI

**Seclude(d), Seclusion** Cloister, Incommunicado, Isolate, Ivory tower, Maroon, Nook, Pleasance, Poke(y), Privacy, Purdah, Quarantine, Remote, Retiracy, Retreat, Secret, Sequester, Shyness, Solitude

**Second(ary), Seconds** Abet, Alternative, Another (guess), Appurtenance, Assist, Atomic, Back(er), Beta, Byplay, Chaser, Collateral, Coming, Comprimario, Congener, Cornerman, Deuteragonist, Ephemeris, Fiddle, Flash, Flip, Friend, Handler, Imperfect, Indirect, Inferior, Instant, Jiffy, Latter, Leap, Lesser, Minor, Mo(ment), Nature, Other, Pig's-whisper, Red ribbon, Redwood, Runner-up, Saybolt-Universal, Sec, Shake, Share, Side(r), Sideline, Sight, Silver, Split, Subsidiary, Subtype, Support, Tick, Tone, Trice, Twinkling, Universal, Wind

**Second-best** Worsted

▶ **Second-class** *see* SECOND-RATE

**Second coming** Parousia

**Second earth** Antichthon

**Second-hand** Flea market, Hand-me-down, Hearsay, Preloved, Reach-me-down, Re-paint, Trade in, Tralaticious, Unoriginal, Used, Vicarious

**Second-rate, Second-class** B, Inferior, Mediocre, Sub

**Second-sight** Deuteroscopy, Divination, Tais(c)h

**Second tine** Bay, Bez

**Second-year student** Semi(e)(-bajan), Sophomore

**Secrecy, Secret(s), Secretive** Apocrypha, Arcana, Arcane, Arcanum, Backstairs, Cabbalistic, Cagey, Clam, Clandestine, Classified, Closet, Code, Conference, Confidence, Conventicle, Corner, Couvert, Covert, Cranny, Cryptadia, Cryptic, Crypto, Dark, Dearn, Deep, Deep-laid, Dern, Devious, Esoteric, Furtive, Hidden, Hidling, Hidlin(g)s, Hole and corner, Hugger-mugger, Hush-hush, Hushy, In camera, Inly, Inmost, Inner, In pectore, In petto, Know-nothing, Latent, Mysterious, Mystical, Mystique, Open, Oyster, Password, Penetralia, Petto, →PRIVATE, Privity, Privy, QT, Rune, Scytale, Seal, Sensitive, Shelta, Silent, Slee, Sly, Sneaky, State, Stealth, Sub rosa, Surreptitious, Tight-lipped, Top, Trade, Unbeknown, Underboard, Undercover, Underhand, Undescried, Unknown, Unre(a)d, Unrevealed, Untold

**Secretary** Aide, Amanuensis, Chancellor, Chronicler, CIS, Desk, Desse, Famulus, Home, Minuteman, Moonshee, Munshi, Notary, Parliamentary, Permanent, Private, Prot(h)onotary, Scrive, Social, Steno(grapher), Stenotyper, Temp

**Secretary-bird** Messenger, Serpent-eater

**Secrete, Secretion** Aequorin, Aldosterone, Allomone, Apocrine, Autacoid, Cache, Castor, Chalone, Colostrum, Cuckoo-spit, Discharge, Earwax, Emanation, Exude, Gland, Hide, Honeydew, Hormone, Juice, Lac, Lactate, Lerp, Melatonin, Mucus, Musk, Nectar, Osmidrosis, Phlegm, Prostacyclin, Pruina, Ptyalin, Recrement, Renin, Resin, Rheum, Saliva, Sebum, Secern, Smegma, Spit(tle), Succus, Trypsin

**Sect(arian), Secret society** Abelite, Adamite, Ahmadiy(y)ah, Albigenses, Amish, Anabaptist, Assassin, Babee, Babi, Bahai, Bigendian, Bigot, Brahmin, Cabal, Cainite, Calixtin(e), Camorra, Campbellite, Cathar, Christadelphian, Clan, Clapham, Covenantes, Crypto, Cult, Cynic, Danite, Darbyite, Disciples of Christ, Dissenter, Docate(s), Donatist, Druse, Druze, Dunkard, Dunker, Ebionite, Encratite, Essene, Familist, Fifth monarchy, Gabar, Gheber, Ghebre, Giaour, Glassite, Gnostic, Group, Gueber, Guebre, Gymnosophist, Harmonist, Harmonite, Hassid, Hauhau, Hemerobaptist, Hesychast,

Hillmen, Holy Roller, Hutterite, Illuminati, Ismaili, Jacobite, Jansenist, Jehovah's Witness, Jodo, Karaite, Karmathian, Little-endian, Lollard, Macedonian, Macmillanite, Mandaean, Marcionite, Maronite, Mendaites, Monothelite, Montanist, Moonie, Mormon, Mucker, Muggletonian, Nasorean, Nazarine, Noetian, Ophites, Order, Partisan, Patripassian, Paulician, Perfectation, Perfectionist, Pharisee, Philadelphian, Phrygian, Picard, Pietist, Plymouth Brethren, Plymouthite, Porch, Pure Land, Ranter, Rappist, Rasta, Ribbonism, Russellite, Sabbatian, Sabian, Sadducee, S(h)aiva, Saktas, Sandeman, School, Schwenkfelder, Seekers, Senus(s)i, Seventh Day Adventist, Sex, Shafiite, Shaker, Shembe, Shia(h), Shiite, Soka Gakkai, Sons of Freedom, Taliban, Therapeutae, Tunker, Unitarian, Utraquist, Vaishnava, Valdenses, Vaudois, Wahabee, Wahabi(i)te, Waldenses, Yezdi, Yezidee, Yezidi, Zealot, Zen, Zezidee

**Section, Sector** Appendix, Area, Balkanize, Caesarian, Chapter, Classify, Compartment, Conic, Cross, Cut, Department, Directorate, Division, Edge, Ellipse, Empennage, Episode, Eyalet, Gan, Golden, Gore, Hyperbola, Length, Lith, Lune, Meridian, Metamere, Mortice, Movement, Octant, Outlier, Panel, Passus, Peraeon, → **PIECE**, Platoon, Private, Public, Pull-out, Quarter, Rhythm, Rib, S, Segment, Septum, Severy, Sextant, Shard, Sherd, Slice, Stage, Track, Ungula, Unit, Warm, Wing, Zenith, Zone

**Secular(ise)** Earthly, Laic, Non-CE, Profane, Temporal, Ungod, Worldly

**Secure(d), Security** Affix, Anchor, Assurance, Bag, Bail, Band, Bar, → **BASIC**, Batten, Belay, Bellwether, Belt and braces, Bolt, Bond, Bottomry, Buckle, Buck Rogers, Button, Calm, Cash ratio, Catch, Cement, Chain, Cheka, Cinch, Clamp, Clasp, Clench, Clinch, Close, Cocoon, Collateral, Collective, Come by, Confine, Consolidate, Consols, Cosy, Counterseal, Cushy, Debenture, Deposit, Disreputable, Doorman, Dunnage, Earn, Earthwork, Engage, Enlock, Ensure, Equity, Establishment, Fasten, Fastness, Firm, Fortify, Frap, Fungibles, Gain, Gilt, Gilt-edged, Gird, Grith, Guarantee, Guy, Heritable, Hostage, Hypothec, Immune, Impregnable, Indemnity, Inlock, In the bag, Invest(ment), Knot, Lace, Land, Lash, Latch, Lien, Listed, Lock (up), Lockaway, Lockdown, Lockfast, Long-dated, Longs, Medium-dated, Mortgage, Nail, National, Obtain, Padlock, Patte, Pin, Pledge, Pot, Pre-empt, Preference, Procure, Protect, Quad, Rope, Rug, → **SAFE**, Safety, Screw, Seal, Settle, Shutter, Snell, Snug, Social, Sound, Stable, Stanchion, Staple, Staylace, Stock, Strap, Sure(ty), Tack, Take, Tie, Tight, Trap, Trice, Tyde, Vest, Warrant, Watertight, Wedge, Win

**Sedan** Battle, Brougham, Chair, Jampan(i), Jampanee, Litter, Palanquin, Palkee, Palki, Saloon

**Sedate** Calm, Cool, Decorous, Demure, Dope, Douce, Drug, Sad, Serene, Sober(sides), Staid, Stand

**Sedative** Amytal®, Anodyne, Aspirin, Barbitone, Bromal, Bromide, Chloral, Depressant, Deserpidine, Hypnic, Laurel water, Lenitive, Lupulin(e), Meprobamate, Metopryl, Miltown, Morphia, Narcotic, Nembutal®, Opiate, Painkiller, Paraldehyde, Pethidine, Phenobarbitone, Premed(ication), Rohypnol®, Roofie, Scopolamine, Seconal®, Snuff, Soothing, Temazepam, Thridace, Valerian, Veronal®

**Sedentary** Inactive, Sessile, Stationary

**Sedge** Carex, Chufa, Cinnamon, Clubrush, Eriophorum, Grey, Seg, Xyris

**Sediment** Alluvium, Chalk, Deposit, Dregs, F(a)eces, Fecula, Flysch, Foots, Graded, Grounds, Grouts, Incrustation, Lees, Molasse, Placer, Residue, Salt, Sapropel, Silt, Sludge, Terrigenous, Till, Turbidite, Varve, Warp

**Sedition, Seditious** Incitement, Insurrection, Leasing-maker, Revolt, Riot, Treason

**Seduce(r), Seduction, Seductive** Allure, Bed, Beguilement, Betray, Bewitch, Bribe, Come-hither, Cuckold-maker, Debauch, Dishonour, Entice, Honeyed, Honied, Ixion, Jape, Lothario, Luring, Mislead, Pull, Sexpot, Sexy, Siren, Slinky, Tempt, Trepan, Undo, Vamp, Wrong

▷ **Seduce** *may indicate* one word inside another

**See(ing)** Acknow, Apostolic, Barchester, Bath and Wells, Behold, Believing, Bishopric, C, Carlisle, Consider, Date, Deek, Descry, Diocesan, Discern, Durham, Ebor, Ecce,

Ely, Episcopal, Exeter, Eye, Get, Glimpse, Holy, In as much as, La, Lo, Meet, Norwich, Notice, Observe, Papal, Perceive, Realise, Remark, Ripon, Rochester, Rubberneck, Rumble, St David's, Salisbury, Sight, Since, Sodor and Man, Spae, Spot, Spy, Truro, Twig, Understand, V, Vatican, Vid(e), View, Vision, Visit, Voilà, Witness, York

**Seed(s), Seedy** Achene, Apiol, Argan, Arilli, Arillode, Ash-key, Bean, Ben, Benne, Best, Blue, Bonduc, Cacoon, Caraway, Cardamom, Carvy, Cebadilla, Cedar-nut, Cevadilla, Chickpea, Cocoa, Colza, Coriander, Corn, Crabstone, Cum(m)in, Dragon's teeth, Embryo, Endosperm, Ergot, Favourite, Fern, Germ, Grain, Gritty, Inseminate, Issue, Ivory-nut, Kernel, Lentil, Lima, Lomentum, Mangy, Mawseed, Miliary, Mote, Nickar, Nicker, Niger, Nucellous, Nut, Oat, Offspring, Origin, Ovule, Pea, Peaky, Pinon, Pip, Pomegranate, Poorly, Poppy, Pyxis, Sabadilla, Samariform, Scuzz, Semen, Seminal, Senvy, Sesame, Shabby, Shea-nut, Silique, Sordid, Sorus, Sow, Sperm, Spore, Stane, Stone, Terminator, Thistledown, Urd, Zoosperm

**Seed-case** Aril, Bur(r), Endopleura, Husk, Pea(s)cod, Pod, Testa, Theca

**Seed-leaf** Cotyledon

**Seedsman** Driller, Nurseryman, Sower

**Seek(er), Seeking** Ask, Beg, Busk, Cap-in-hand, Chase, Court, Endeavour, Ferret out, Fish, Forage, Gun for, Pursue, Quest, Scavenge, Scur, Search, Skirr, Solicit, Suitor, Try

**Seem(ing), Seemingly** Apparent, Appear, As if, Look, Ostensible, Purport, Quasi, Think

**Seemly** Apt, Comely, Decent, Decorous, Fit, Proper, Suitable

**Seep(age)** Angel's share, Bleed, Dribble, Exude, Leak, Ooze, Osmose, Percolate, Permeate

**Seer** Augur, Auspex, Balaam, Eye, Melampus, Nahum, Nostradamus, Observer, Oculiform, Onlooker, Oracle, Prescience, Prophet, Sage, Sibyl, Soothsayer, T(e)iresias, Witness, Zoroaster

**Seesaw** Bascule, Boom and bust, Oscillate, Teeter(-totter), Teeter-board, Tilt, Vacillate, Wild mare

**Seethe(d), Seething** Aboil, Boil, Bubble, Churn, Ferment, Fume, Simmer, Smoulder, Sod

**Segment(ation)** Antimere, Arthromere, Cut, Division, Gironny, Gyronny, Intron, Joint, Lacinate, Lith, Lobe, Merogenesis, Merome, Merosome, Metamere, Metathorax, Part, Piece, Pig, Proglottis, Propodeon, Prothorax, Quadrant, Scliff, Section, Share, Shie, Skliff, Somite, Split, Sternite, Syllable, Tagma, Telson, Trochanter, Urite, Uromere

**Segregate, Segregation** Apartheid, Exile, Insulate, Intern, →**ISOLATE**, Jim Crow, Seclude, Separate

**Seidlitz** Powder, Rochelle

**Seismic, Seismography** Richter, Terremotive

**Seismograph** Tromometer

**Seize, Seizing, Seizure** Angary, Apprehend, Appropriate, Areach, Arrest, Assume, Attach(ment), Bag, Bone, Capture, Catch, Claw, Cleek, Clutch, Cly, Collar, Commandeer, Confiscate, Cop, Coup, Distrain, Distress, Extent, For(e)hent, →**GRAB**, Grip, Hend, Hi-jack, Ictus, Impound, Impress, Maverick, Nab, Na(a)m, Nap, Nim, Poind, Possess, Pot, Raid, Ravin, Replevy, Rifle, Sease, Sequestrate, Smug, Snag, Snatch, Stroke, Tackle, Trover, Usurp, Wingding, Wrest

**Seldom** Infrequent, Rare, Unoften

**Select(ion), Selecting, Selector** Adopt, Artificial, Assortment, Bla(u)d, Cap, Casting, Catalogue, Choice, Choose, Classy, Clonal, Cream, Cull, Darwinism, Discriminate, Draft, Draw, Eclectic, Edit, Elite, Excerpt, Exclusive, Extract, Favour, Garble, Handpick, Inside, K, Kin, Nap, Natural, Pericope, →**PICK**, Pot-pourri, Prefer, Recherché, Redline, Sample, Seed, Sex, Single, Sort, Stream, Tipster, Triage, UCCA, Vote

**Selenium** Se, Zorgite

**Self** Atman, Auto, Character, Ego, Person, Psyche, Seity, Sel, Soul

**Self-assertive** Arrogant, Uppish

**Self-concern** Dog-eat-dog
**Self-confident, Self-confidence, Self-willed** Aplomb, Ego, Headstrong, Jaunty
**Self-conscious** Guilty
**Self-contained** Absolute, Reticent, SC, Taciturn
**Self-contradictory** Absurd, Irish
**Self-control, Self-discipline** Abstinence, Ascesis, Encraty, Modesty, Patience,
    Restraint, Stiff upper lip, Temper(ance), Willpower
**Self-criticism** Psychogas
▶ **Self-defence** *see* MARTIAL (ARTS)
**Self-destructive** Lemming
**Self-effacing** Modest
**Self-esteem** Amour-propre, Conceit, Confidence, Egoism, Pride, Vainglory
**Self-evident** Axiom, Ipso facto, Manifest, Obvious, Patent, Truism, Truth
**Self-examination** Soul-searching
**Self-existence** Solipsism
**Self-fertilisation, Self-origination** Aseity, Autogamy
**Self-governing** Autonomy, Idior(r)hythmic, Kabele, Kebel, Puritanism, Swaraj
**Self-help** Smiles
**Self-important, Self-indulgent, Self-interested, Self-regarding** Aristippus,
    Arrogant, Bumptious, Chesty, Cocky, Conceited, Coxy, Egocentric, Hedonist,
    Immoderate, Jack-in-office, Licentious, Mugwump, Narcissistic, Pompous, Pooterish,
    Pragmatic, Primadonna, Profligate, Solipsist, Sybarite, Vainglorious
**Selfish(ness)** Avaricious, Dog eat dog, Dog-in-the-manger, Egocentric, Egoist,
    Egomaniac, Grabby, Greedy, Hedonist, Hog, Mean, Solipsism
**Selfless(ness)** Altruistic, Non-ego, Tuism
**Self-limiting** Kenotic
▶ **Self-origination** *see* SELF-FERTILISATION
**Self-pollinating** Cl(e)istogamic
**Self-possession** Aplomb, Assurance, Composure, Cool, Nonchalant, Phlegm
**Self-restraint** Reserve
**Self-righteous** Pharisee
**Self-satisfied, Self-satisfaction** Complacent, Narcissism, Smug, Tranquil
**Self-service** Automat, Buffet, Cafeteria, Supermarket
**Self-styled** Soi-disant
**Self-sufficient, Self-sufficiency** Absolute, Autarky, Complete, Hunter-gatherer
**Self-taught** Autodidact
**Sell(er), Selling** Apprize, Auction, Barter, Bear, Betray, Blackmail, Blockbuster, Cant,
    Catch, Chant, Chaunt, Cold-call, Cope, Costermonger, Direct, Dispose, Divest, Do,
    Eggler, Fancier, Fellmonger, Flog, Go, Hard, Have, Hawk, Huckster, Hustle, Inertia,
    Knock down, Market, Marketeer, Ménage, Merchant, Missionary, Oligopoly, Pardoner,
    Party, Peddle, Peddler, Pick-your-own, Purvey, Push, Pyramid, Rabbito(h), Realise,
    Rep, Retail, Ruse, Scalp, Shift, Short, Simony, Soft, Stall-man, Sugging, Switch, Tout,
    → TRADE, Trick, Vend, Vent, Wholesaler
**Selvage** Border, Edge, Roon, Rund
**Semantics** General, Generative, Interpretive, Notional, Onomasiology, Semasiology,
    Sematology
**Semaphore** Signal, Tic-tac, Wigwag
**Semblance** Appearance, Aspect, Guise, Likeness, Sign, Verisimilitude
**Semen** Jis(so)m, Milt, Spoof, Spunk
**Semi-circular** D, Hemicycle
**Semi-conductor** Diode, Germanium, LED, Thryristor
**Seminar(y)** Class, → COLLEGE, Colloquium, Group, Theologate, Tutorial, Webinar,
    Workshop, Yeshiva
**Semiotics** Syntactics

**Semi-paralysis** Dyaesthesia

**Semitic** Accadian, Akkadian, Ammonite, Amorite, Arab, Aramaic, Canaanite, Chaldean, Geez, Jewish, Phoenician

**Semitone** Pycnon

**Semolina** Couscous

**Senate** Council, Curia, Seanad (Eireann), Second chamber

**Senator** Antiani, Cicero, Concept father, Elder, Legislator, Patrician, Shadow, Solon

**Send, Sent** Consign, → DESPATCH, Disperse, Emanate, Emit, Entrance, Extradite, Issue, Launch, Mail, Order, Post, Rapt, Refer, Remit, Ship, Transmit, Transport

**Send back** Refer, Remand, Remit, Return

**Send down** Demit, Lower, Refer, Rusticate

**Send up** Chal(l)an, Lampoon, Promote

**Senegal** SN

**Senescence** Age

**Senile, Senility** Caducity, Dementia, Disoriented, Doddery, Doited, Doitit, Dotage, E(i)ld, Gaga, Nostology, Twichild

**Senior(ity)** Aîné, Doyen, Elder, Father, Grecian, Major, Majorat, Old(er), Oldie, Oldster, Oubaas, Père, Primus, Superior, Upper

**Senna** Bladder, Cassia

**Señor(a)** Caballero, Don(a), Hidalga, Hidalgo

**Sensation(al)** Acolouthite, Aftershock, Anoesis, Aura, Blood, Blood and thunder, Commotion, Drop-dead, Emotion, Empfindung, Feeling, Furore, Gas, Impression, Lurid, Melodrama, Organic, Par(a)esthesia, Phosphene, Photism, Pyrotechnic, Rush, Sensory, Shocker, Shock-horror, Showstopper, Splash, Stir, Styre, Synaesthesia, Thrill, Tingle, Vibes, Wow, Yellow

**Sense, Sensual(ist), Sensing** Acumen, Animalist, Attuite, Aura, Carnal, Coherence, Common, Conscience, Dress, Ear, ESP, Faculty, Feel, Gaydar, Gross, Gumption, Gustation, Hearing, Horse, Idea, Import, Instinct, Intelligence, Intuition, Lewd, Loaf, Logic, Marbles, Meaning, Moral, Nous, Olfactory, Palate, Perceptual, Proprioceptive, Rational, Receptor, Remote, Rumble-gumption, Rum(m)el-gumption, Rumgumption, Rum(m)le-gumption, Sanity, Satyr, Sight, Sixth, Slinky, Smell, Spirituality, Sybarite, Synesis, Taste, Taste bud, Touch, Voluptuary, Voluptuous, Wisdom, Wit

**Senseless** Absurd, Anosmia, Asinine, Illogical, Inane, Lean-witted, Mad, Numb, Silly, Stupid, Stupor, Unconscious, Unwise, Vegetal

**Sensible** Aware, Clear-headed, Dianoetic, Down to earth, Lucid, No-nonsense, Politic, Prudent, Raisonné, Rational, Realistic, Sane, Sapient, Solid, Together, Well-balanced

**Sensitive, Sensitivity** Aesthete, Algesia, Alive, Allergic, Atopy, Dainty, Delicate, Discreet, Emotive, Erethism, Erogenous, Hypaesthesia, Keen, Mimosa, Mystique, Nesh, Niceness, Nociceptive, Orthochromatic, Panchromatic, Passible, Quick, Radiesthesia, Sore, Sympathetic, Tactful, Tender, Thermaesthesia, Thin-skinned, Ticklish, Touchy(-feely), Vulnerable

**Sensor(y)** Cercus, Detector, Exteroceptor, Interoceptor, Nerve end, Palpi, Proprioceptor, Remote

**Sentence(s)** Antiphon, Assize, Bird, Carpet, Clause, Closed, Commit, Complex, Compound, Condemn, Custodial, Death, Decree(t), Deferred, Doom, Fatwah, Indeterminate, Judgement, Life, Matrix, Open, Pangram, Paragraph, Period(ic), Porridge, Predicate, Punish, Rap, Rheme, Rune, Send up, Simple, Stretch, Suspended, Swy, Tagmene, Time, Topic, Verdict, Versicle, Weigh off

**Sententious** Concise, Gnomic, Laconic, Pithy, Pompous, Terse

**Sentience** Awareness

**Sentiment(al), Sentimentality** Byronism, Chocolate box, Corn, Cornball, Drip, Emotive, Feeling, Goo, Govey, Gucky, Gush, Hokey, Icky, Lovey-dovey, Maudlin, Mawkish, Mind, Mush, Namby-pamby, Nationalism, Nostalgia, Opinion, Posy, Romantic, Rose-pink, Rosewater, Saccharin, Schmaltzy, Sloppy, Slushy, Smoochy,

Sob-stuff, Softy, Soppy, Spoony, Sugary, Swoony, Syrupy, Tear-jerker, Too-too, Traveller, Treacly, Twee, View, Weepy, Wertherian, Yucky

**Sentry, Sentinel** Caveman, Cordon sanitaire, Custodian, Guard, Jaga, Look-out, Picket, Sentinel, Vedette, Vidette, Watch

**Separate(d), Separation, Separately, Separatist** Abscise, Abstract, Analyse, Apart, Asunder, Atmolysis, Avulsion, Bulkhead, Bust up, Comma, Compartmentalise, Cull, Curdle, Cut, Decollate, Decompose, Decouple, Deduct, Deglutinate, Demarcate, Demerge, Detach, Dialyse, Diastasis, Diazeuxis, Diremption, Disaggregate, Disally, Discerp, Disconnect, Discrete, Disintegrate, Disjunction, Dissect, Dissociate, Distance, Distinct, Disunite, Divide, Division, Divorce, Eloi(g)n, Elute, Elutriate, Esloin, Estrange, ETA, Extricate, Filter, Flaky, Grade, Gulf, Heckle, Hive, Hyphenate, Insulate, Intervene, Isolate, Judicial, Laminate, Lease, Legal, Liquate, Monosy, Part, Particle, Partition, Partitive, Parturition, Peel off, Piece, Prescind, Prism, Ramify, Red(d), Rift, Sashing, Scatter, Schism, Screen, Scutch, Secern, Segregate, Sequester, Sever, Several, Shear, Shed, Shore, Shorn, Sift, Sleave, Sle(i)ded, Solitary, Sort, →SPLIT, Spread, Staccato, Steam-trap, Stream, Sunder, Sundry, Tease, Tems(e), Tmesis, Try, Twin(e), Unclasp, Unhitch, Unravel, Winnow, Wrench, Yandy

**Sepia** Cuttle, Ink

**Seppuku** Hara-kiri, Hari-kari

**Septic** Festering, Poisonous, Rotting

**Septimus** Small

**Septum** Cloison, Mediastinum

**Sepulchral, Sepulchre** Bier, Cenotaph, Charnel, Crypt, Easter, Funeral, Monument, Pyramid, Tomb, Vault, Whited

**Sequel** After-clap, Aftermath, Consequence, Effect, Offshoot, Outcome, Suite

**Sequence, Sequential** Agoge, Algorithm, Byte, Cadence, Chronological, Consecution, Consensus, Continuity, Continuum, Cycle, Escape, Fibonacci, Gene, Intervening, Intron, Line, Linear, Main, Montage, Order, Peptide, Plot, Polar, Program(me), Rotation, Routine, Run, Seriatim, Series, Shot, Signal, Sonnet, Storyboard, String, Succession, Suit, Suite, Train, Vector

**Sequester, Sequestrate** Confiscate, Esloin, Esloyne, Impound, Isolate, Retire, Seclude, Separate

**Sequin** Paillette, Zecchino, Zechin

**Sequoia** Redwood, Wellingtonia

**Seraph** Abdiel, →ANGEL

**Serb(ian)** Chetnik

**Sere** Arid, →DRY, Scorch, Wither

**Serenade(r)** Aubade, Charivari, Horning, Love song, Minstrel, Nocturne, Shivaree, Sing-song, Wait, Wake

**Serene, Serenity** Calm, Composed, Impassive, Placid, Quietude, Repose, Sangfroid, Sedate, Seraphic, Smooth, →TRANQUIL

**Serf(dom)** Adscript, Bondman, Ceorl, Churl, Helot, Manred, →SLAVE, Thete, Thrall, Vassal, Velle(i)nage, Villein

**Serge** Russian, Say

**Sergeant** Buzfuz, Chippy, Chips, Colour, Cuff, Drill, Flight, Halberdier, Havildar, Kite, Lance, Master, →NCO, Pepper, Platoon, RSM, Sarge, SL, SM, Staff, Technical, Troy

**Serial(ism)** Episode, Feuilleton, Heft, Livraison, Total

**Series** Actinide, Actinium, Arithmetical, Balmer, Battery, Catena, Chain, Concatenation, Consecution, Continuum, Course, Cycle, Cyclus, Docusoap, Electromotive, Enfilade, Engrenage, En suite, Episode, Epos, Ethylene, Exponential, Fibonacci, Fourier, Geometric, Gradation, Harmonic, Homologous, Lanthanide, Line, Links, Loop, Maclaurin's, Methane, Molasse, Neptunium, Partwork, Pedigree, Power, Process, →PROGRESSION, Radioactive, Rally, Random walk, Ranks, Rest, Rosalia, Rosary, Rounds, Routine, Rubber, Run, Sequence, Ser, Set, Sitcom, String, Succession, Suit, Taylor's, Test, Thorium, Time, Tone, Tournament, Train, Uranium, World

**Serious(ly)** Critical, Earnest, Extreme, For real, Grave, Gravitas, Harsh, Heavy, Important, In earnest, Intense, Major, Momentous, Pensive, Radical, Real, Sad, Serpentine, Sober, Solemn, Sombre, Staid, Straight(-faced), Unamused, Very

**Sermon** Address, Discourse, Gatha, Homily, Khutbah, Lecture, Preachment, Prone, Ser, Spital

**Serow** Goral, Thar

**Serpent(ine)** Adder, Amphisbaena, Anguine, Apepi, Apophis, Asp, Aspic(k), Basilisk, Bass horn, Boa, Caduceus, Cockatrice, Dipsas, Firedrake, Midgard, Nagas, Ophiolite, Ouroboros, Peridotite, Pharaoh's, Reptile, Retinalite, Sea-snake, Shesha, →**SNAKE**, Traitor, Uraeus, Verd-antique, Verde-antico, Viper, Wyvern

**Serrate(d), Serration** Diprionidian, Saw, Scallop, Serried, Tooth

**Serum** Albumin, Antiglobulin, Antilymphocyte, Antitoxin, ATS, Fluid, Globulin, Humoral, Opsonin, Senega, Truth

**Serval** Bush-cat

**Servant, Server** Aid(e), Attendant, Ayah, Bartender, Batman, Bearer, Bedder, Bedmaker, Between-maid, Bond, Boot-catcher, Boots, Boy, Busboy, Butler, Caddie, Chambermaid, Chaprassi, Chokra, Chuprassy, Civil, Columbine, Cook, Cook-general, Daily, Dogsbody, Domestic, Dromio, Drudge, Employee, Esne, Factotum, Famulus, File, Flunkey, Footboy, Footman, Friday, Gehazi, General, G(h)illie, Gip, Gorsoon, Gully, Gyp, Haiduk, Handmaid, Helot, Henchman, Heyduck, Hind, Hireling, Iras, Jack, Jack-slave, Jeames, Khansama(h), Khidmutgar, Khitmutgar, Kitchen-knave, Kitchen-maid, Knave, Lackey, Ladle, Lady's maid, Lazy Susan, Leroy, Maid, Major-domo, Man, Man Friday, Menial, Minion, Mixologist, Muchacha, Muchacho, Myrmidon, Nethinim, Obedient, Orderly, Page, Pantler, Parlourmaid, Person, Pistol, Postman, Public, Pug, Redemption, Retainer, Retinue, Scout, Scrub, Scullion, Servitor, Sewer, Skip, Skivvy, Slavey, Soldier, Soubrette, Steward, Tablespoon, Tapsman, Tendance, Theow, Thete, Tiger, Trotter, Turnspit, Tweeny, Underling, Vails, Vales, Valet, Valkyrie, Varlet, Vassal, Waiter, Wash-rag, Weller

**Serve(r), Service(s)** Acas, Ace, Act, Active, Agency, All-up, Amenity, Answer, Army, Arriage, Asperges, Assist, ATS, Attendance, Avail, Baptism, Barista, Barman, Barperson, Benediction, Breakfast, Campaign, Candlemas, Cannonball, Canteen, Ceefax®, China, Christingle, Civil, Communion, Community, Complin(e), Conscription, Corvée, Credo, Devotional, Dien, Dinnerset, Diplomatic, Dish, Divine, Do, Dollop, Dow, Drumhead, Dry, Duty, Ecosystem, Emergency, Employ, Evensong, Facility, Fault, Fee, Feudal, Fish, Foreign, Forensic, Forward, →**FUNCTION**, Funeral, Further, Go, Help, Helpline, Hour, Ibadat, Jury, Ka(e), Kol Nidre, Ladle, Lauds, Let, Line, Ling, Lip, Litany, Liturgy, Ma'ariv, Marriage, Mass, Mat(t)ins, Memorial, Memory, Mincha, Minister, Ministration, Ministry, Missa, National, Navy, Nocturn, Nones, Oblige, Offertory, Office, Oracle, Overarm, Overhaul, Pass, Pay, Personal, Pit stop, Placebo, Possum, Pottery, Pour, Prayer meeting, Prime, Proper, Public, Radio, RAF, Regular, Requiem, Rite, RN, Room, Sacrament, SAS, Satisfy, SBS, Secret, Selective, Senior, Sext, Shacharis, Shaharith, Shuttle, Silent, Silver, Skeleton, Social, Sorb(us), Stead, Sted, Sue, Tableware, Tea, Tenebrae, Tierce, Trental, Uncork, Under-arm, Use, Utility, Vespers, Wait, Waiterage, Waitron, Waitstaff, Watch-night, Wild, Worship, Yeoman('s)

**Service-book** Hymnal, Hymnary, Missal, Triodion

▷ **Serviceman** *may indicate* a churchman

**Servile, Servility** Abasement, Base, Crawling, Creep, Knee, Kowtowing, Lickspittle, Menial, Minion, Obsequious, Slavish, Slimy, Submissive, Suck-hole, Sycophantic, Tintookie, Truckle

**Serving** Helping, Heuristic, Portion, Precursory

**Servitude** Bondage, Domination, Penal, Peonage, Peonism, Slavery, Thirlage, Thrall, Vassalry, Yoke

**Sesame** Beni, Benne, Gingelly, Gingili, Grapple-plant, Jinjilli, Semsem, Tahini, Til

**Session(s)** All-nighter, Bout, Executive, Galah, Hearing, Jam, Kirk, Meeting, Nightshift, Petty, Poster, Quarter, Rap, Round, Séance, Sederunt, Settle, Sitting, Special, Term

**Set(ting) (about, aside, down, in, off, out, up)** Activate, Adjust, Apply,
Appoint, Arrange, Array, Assail, Assiege, Backdrop, Batch, Bent, Bezel, Boun, Brooch,
Cabal, Cake, Case, Cast, Chaton, Class, Claw, Clique, Cliveden, Closed, Coagulate,
Cock, Cockshy, Codomain, Collection, Collet, Comp(ositor), Companion, Compose,
Congeal, Congelation, Context, Coterie, Couvert, Crew, Crystal, Cyclorama, Data, Dead,
Decline, Decor, Detonate, Diorama, Direct, Dispose, Duchesse, Earmark, Earnest,
Earth, Enchase, Ensky, Environment, Establish, Explode, Film, Firm, Fit, Flagstone,
Flash, Flat(s), Found, Framed, F-stop, Gang, Garniture, Geal, Gel, Gelatinise, Genome,
Group, Habitat, Hairdo, Harden, Heliacal, Ilk, Inchase, Incrowd, Incut, Infinite, Inlay,
Jee, Jeel, Jell(y), Jet, Julia, Kit, Knit, Laid, Land, Lay, Layette, Leg, Locale, Locate, Lot,
Mandelbrot, Mental, Milieu, Mise en scène, Miserere, Monture, Mournival, Nail,
Nest, Occident, Open, Ordain, Ordered, Ordinate, Ossify, Ouch, Pair, Parure, Pavé,
Permanent, Physique, Pitch, Place(ment), Plant, Plaste, Ply, Point, Posed, Posit, Power,
Put, Radio, Rate, Ready, Receiver, Relay, Resolute, Rig, Rigid, Rooted, Rouse, Rubber,
Saw, Scenery, Series, Service, Settle(d), Showcase, Sink, Slate, Smart, Solidify, Solution,
Squad, Stand, Stationed, Stede, Stell, Stick, Stiffen, Still, Stream, Stud, Subscriber, Suit,
Suite, Surround, Synchronize, Tar, Tea, Team, Teeth, Televisor, Telly, The four hundred,
Theme, Tiffany, Till, Toilet, Trannie, Transistor, Trey, Trigger, Trip, Truth, Tube, TV,
Union, Universal, Venn (diagram), Weather, Wide-screen, Yplast
**Setback** Bodyblow, Checkmate, Downturn, Glitch, Hiccough, Hiccup, Jolt, Knock,
Relapse, Retard, Retreat, Reversal, Scarcement, Sickener, Tes, Vicissitude, Whammy
**Setter** Cement, Comp, Compiler, Concrete, Dog, English, Gelatin(e), Gordon, Gundog,
Hair gel, Hairspray, Irish, Pectin, Red, Smoot, Sphinx, Sun, Trend
**Settle(d), Settlement, Settler** Adjust, Agree, Alight, Ante, Appoint, Arrange,
Ascertain, Ausgleich, Avenge, Balance, Bandobast, Bed, Bench, Boer, Borghetto, Borough,
Botany Bay, Bundobust, Bustee, Camp, Clear, Clench, Clinch, Colonial, Colonise,
Colony, Compose, Compound, Compromise, Cough up, Crannog, Cut and dry, Decide,
Defray, Determine, Diktat, Discharge, Dispose, Dorp, Dowry, Ekistics, Encamp, Endow,
Ensconce, Entail, Establish, Expat, Faze, Feeze, Finalise, Fix, Foot, Foreclose, Gravitate,
Gridironer, Guilder, Habitant, Hama, Hyannis, Illegitimate, Informal, Jamestown,
Jointure, Kibbutz, Land, Ledge, Light, Lull, Lyte, Manyat(t)a, Meet, Merino, Mise,
Mission, Moreton Bay, Moshav, Nahal, Nest, Nestle, New Amsterdam, Oecist, Oikist,
Opt, Ostman, Outpost, Outstation, Over, Pa(h), Pakka, Pale, Patroon, Pay, Payment,
Peise, Penal, People, Perch, Pheazar, Pheese, Pheeze, Phese, Pilgrim, Pioneer, Placate,
Planter, Populate, Port Arthur, Port Nicholson, Presidio, Pucka, Pueblo, Pukka,
Rancheria, Rancherie, Readjust, Reckoning, Reconcile, Redditch, Reduction, Reimburse,
Remit, Repay, Reside, Resolve, Rest, Roofie, Roost, Sate, Satisfaction, Saxon, Scare, Seal,
Seat, Secure, Sedimentary, Set fair, Shagroon, Shtetl, Silt, Smoot, Snuggle, Sofa, Soldier,
Solve, Soweto, Square, Square up, State, Still, Straits, Subside, Sudden death, Taurus,
Township, Ujamaa, Undertaker, Utu, Vest(ed), Viatical, Visigoth, Voortrekker, Wrap up
▷ **Settlement** *may indicate* an anagram
▷ **Settler** *may indicate* a coin
**Set upon** Assail, Attack, Sick
**Seven(th), Seven-sided** Ages, Days, Dials, Great Bear, Hebdomad, Hepta-, Hills,
Magnificent, Nones, Pleiad(es), S, Sages, Seas, Septenary, Septilateral, Septimal, Sins,
Sisters, Sleepers, Stars, Wonders, Zeta
**Seventy** S, Ytterbium
**Seven-week** Omer
**Sever** Amputate, Cut, Detach, Divide, Sunder
**Several** Divers, Many, Multiple, Plural, Some, Sundry, Various
**Severe(ly), Severity** Acute, Astringent, Austere, Bad, Caustic, Chronic, Cruel, Dour,
Draconian, Drastic, Eager, Extreme, Grave, Grievous, Gruel(ling), Hard, →**HARSH**, Ill,
Inclement, Morose, Penal, Rhadamanthine, Rigo(u)r, Roaming, Roundly, Ruthless,
Serious, Sharp, Snell(y), Sore, Spartan, Stark, Stern, Strict, Swingeing

**Sew(ing), Sew up** Baste, Clinch, Cope, Darn, Embroider, Fell, Fine-draw, Hemstitch, Machine, Mitre, Overcast, Overlock, Run up, Seam, Seel, Stitch, Tack, Whip

**Sewage, Sewer** Bacteria, Cesspool, Cloaca, Culvert, Dorcas, → **DRAIN**, Effluence, Jaw-box, Jaw-hole, Mimi, Needle, Privy, Seamster, Shore, Soil, Sough, Soughing-tile, Sure, Waste

**Sex(ist), Sexual, Sexy** Bed-hopping, Carnal, Congress, Cottaging, Coupling, Cunnilingus, Cybersex, Erotic, Fair, Favours, Fellatio, Female, Foreplay, Fornication, French, Gam(ic), Gamahuche, Gamaruche, Gender, Greek love, Hanky-panky, Hump, Incest, Intercourse, Intimacy, Jailbait, Kind, Knee-trembler, Libidinous, Libido, Lingam, Lumber, Male, Mate, Naughty, Non-penetrative, Nookie, Oomph, Opposite, Oral, Outercourse, Paedophilia, Paraphilia, Pederasty, Phallocratic, Phat, Phone, Priapean, Prurient, Race, Randy, Raunchy, Rough trade, Rut(ish), Safe, Salacious, Screw, Sect, Six, Slinky, SM, Steamy, Stud, Sultry, Tantric, Teledildonics, Troilism, Unprotected, Unsafe, Venereal, Venery, VI, Voluptuous, Weaker

**Sex appeal** It, Oomph, SA

**Sexcentenarian** Shem

**Sexless** Agamogenetic, Atoke, Epicene, N, Neuter, Platonic

**Sextet** Over, Six

**Sexton** Blake, Fossor, Patch, Sacristan, Shammes, Warden

**Seychelles** SY

**Sh** P, Quiet

**Shabby** Base, Buckeen, Dingy, Dog-eared, Down-at-heel, Fleapit, Fusc(ous), Grotty, Grungy, Low-lived, Mangy, Mean, Moth-eaten, Old hat, Oobit, Oorie, Oubit, Ourie, Outworn, Owrie, Raunch, Scaly, Scarecrow, Scruffy, Seedy, Shoddy, Squalid, Tacky, Tatty, Tawdry, Threadbare, Unkempt, Worn, Woubit

**Shack** Fibro, Heap, Hideout, Hovel, Hut, Sheal

**Shackle(s)** Bilboes, Bind, Bracelet, Chain, Constrain, Darbies, Entrammel, Fetter(lock), Gyve, Hamper, Irons, Manacle, Restrict, Tie, Trammel, Yoke

**Shad** Allice, Allis, Fish, Twait(e)

**Shaddock** Grapefruit, Pomelo

**Shade(d), Shades, Shading, Shadow, Shady** Adumbrate, Arbour, Arcade, Awning, Blear, Blend, Blind, Bongrace, Bowery, Brise-soleil, Brocken spectre, Buff, Cast, Cerise, Chiaroscuro, Chroma, Cloche, Cloud, Colo(u)r, Corrupt, Cross-hatch, Degree, Demirep, Dis, Dog, Dubious, Eclipse, Enigma, Eye, Fawn, Five o'clock, Galanty, Gamp, Ghost, Gnomon, Gradate, Gray, Hachure, Hatch, Hell, Herbar, Hint, Hue, Inumbrate, Larva, Lee, Magnolia, Melt, Mezzotint, Modena, Nuance, Opaque, Overtone, Parasol, Pastel, Phantom, Presence, Rain, Ray-Bans®, Satellite, Screen, Shroud, Sienna, Silhouette, Silvan, Skia-, Soften, Sound, Spectre, Spirit, Stag, Sunglasses, Swale, Swaly, Tail, Tenebrious, Tinge, Tint, Titian, Tone, Track, Trail, Ugly, Ultramarine, Umbra(tile), Umbrage(ous), Umbrella, Umbrose, Underhand, Underworld, Velamen, Velar(ium), Velum, Visitant, Visor, Wraith

**Shadowless** Ascian

**Shaft(ed), Shafting** Arbor, Arrow, Axle tree, Barb, Barrow-train, Beam, Befool, Capstan, Cardan, Chimney, Collet, Column, Crank, Cue, Diaphysis, Disselboom, Dolly, Downcast, Drive, Escape, Fil(l), Flue, Fust, Gleam, Idler, Incline, Journal, Lamphole, Lay, Limber, Loom, Mandrel, Mandril, Manhole, Moon pool, Moulin, Parthian, Passage, Pile, Pit, Pitbrow, Pitch, Pithead, Pole, Propeller, Quill (drive), Ray, Rib, Rise, Scape, Scapus, Shank, Snead, Spindle, Staff, Stairwell, Stale, Steal(e), Steel, Steen, Stele, Stem, Stulm, Sunbeam, Telescopic, Thill, Tige, Tomo, Trave, Truncheon, Upcast, Well, Winning, Winze

**Shag** Cronet, Hair, Intercourse, Nap, Pile, Scart(h), Skart(h), Tire, Tobacco

**Shaggy** Ainu, Beetle-browed, Bushy, Comate, Hairy, Hearie, Hirsute, Horrid, Horror, Maned, Nappy, Rough, Rugged, Shock, Shough, Tatty, Tousy, Touzy, Towsy, Towzy, Untidy

**Shah** Abbas, Pahlavi, Ruler, Sophi, Sophy

**Shake(n), Shake off, Shakes, Shakiest, Shaky** Agitate, Ague(-fit), Astonish, Bebung, Brandish, Coggle, Concuss, Dabble, Dick(e)y, Didder, Diddle, Disconcert, Dither, Dodder, →**DT'S**, Epicentre, Feeble, Groggy, Hod, Hotch, Ictal, Jar, Jiggle, Joggle, Jolt, Jounce, Judder, Jumble, Lose, Milk, Mo, Nid-nod, Press flesh, Quake, Quiver, Quooke, Rattle, Rickety, Rickle, →**ROCK**, Rouse, Shimmer, Shimmy, Shiver, Shock, Shog, Shoogle, Shudder, Steel, Succuss(ation), Sweat, Swish, Thunderstruck, Tremble, Tremolo, Tremor, Tremulous, Trill(o), Tumbledown, Undulate, Unsteady, Vibrate, Vibrato, Wag, Waggle, Wind, Wobble, Wonky

▷ **Shake** *may indicate* an anagram

**Shakedown** Blackmail, Chantage, Pallet

**Shakespeare** Bard, Will, WS

**Shale** Blaes, Fa(i)kes, Kerogen, Kupferschiefer, Oil, Rock, Till, Torbanite

**Shall** Sal

**Shallot** C(h)ibol, Onion, Scallion, Sybo(e), Sybow

**Shallow(s)** Ebb, Flat, Fleet, Flew, Flippant, Flue, Justice, Neritic, Rattlebrain, Riffle, Sandbank, Sandbar, Shoal, Slight, Superficial

**Sham** Apocryphal, Bluff, Bogus, Braide, Charade, Counterfeit, Deceit, Fake, →**FALSE**, Hoax, Idol, Impostor, Mimic, Mock, Phony, Pinchbeck, Postiche, Potemkin, Pretence, Pseudo, Repro, Simulated, Snide, Spurious, Straw man

**Shaman** Angek(k)ok, Sorcerer

**Shamble(s)** Abattoir, Bauchle, Butchery, Mess, Scamble, Shuffle, Totter, Tripple

**Shame(ful), Shame-faced** Abash, Aidos, Atimy, Aw, Chagrin, Confusion, Contempt, Crying, Degrade, Discredit, Disgrace, Dishonour, Disrepute, Embarrass, Fi donc, Fie, Gross, Guilt, Hangdog, Honi, Humiliate, Ignominy, Infamy, Inglorious, Modesty, Mortify, Ohone, Pity, Pudency, Pudor, Pugh, Sad, Scandal, Shend, Sin, Slander, Stain, Stigma, Tsk, Vile, Yshend

**Shameless** Audacious, Barefaced, Brash, Brazen, Flagrant, Hussy, Immodest, Impudent, Ithyphallic, Jezebel, Reprobate

**Shampoo(ing)** Massage, Tripsis, Wash

**Shandy** Drink, Sterne, Tristram

**Shanghai** Abduct, Kidnap, Trick

**Shank** Leg, Shaft, Steal(e), Steel, Steil, Stele, Strike

**Shanty, Shanty town** Bidonville, Boatsong, Bothy, Bustee, Cabin, Chant, Dog-hole, Favela, Forebitter, Hutment, Lean-to, Pondok, Sea, Shack, Shypoo, Song

**Shape(d), Shapely, Shaping** Blancmange, Boast, Bruting, Cast, Contour, Cuneiform, Die-cast, Face, Fashion, Figure, Form, Format, Fractal, Geoid, Geometrical, Gnomon, Headquarters, Hew, Holohedron, Jello, Model, Morph, Morphology, →**MOULD**, Navette, Net, Octagon(al), Pendentive, Polyomine, Quadrant, Ream, Rhomb(us), Roughcast, Scabble, Scalene, Scallop, Sculpt, Spheroid, Spile, Step-cut, Tromino, Turn, Voluptuous, Whittle, Wrought, Zaftig, Zoftig

**Shapeless** Amorphous, Blob, Chaos, Dumpy, Indigest, Vague

**Shard** Fragment, Sliver, Splinter

**Share(d), Shares, Sharing** Allocation, Allotment, Allottery, Angels' cost, Apportion, Blue-chip, Bovate, Cahoots, Chop, Co, Cohabit, Coho(e), Common, Communal, Contango, Co-portion, Co-tenant, Culter, Cut, Deferred, Divi(dend), Divide, Divvy (up), Dole, Dutch, Equity, Finger, Flatmate, Founders, Golden, Grubstake, Impart, Interest, Job, Kaffer, Kaf(f)ir, Kangaroo, Law, Lay, Lion's, Market, Moiety, Mutual, Odd lot, OFEX, Ordinary, Oxgang, Oxgate, Oxland, Parcener, →**PART**, Partake, Participate, Penny, PIBS, Plough, Plough-iron, Portfolio, Portion, Prebend, Pref(erred), Preference, Pro rata, Prorate, Quarter, Quota, Rake off, Ration, Rug, Rundale, Scrip, Security, Shr, Slice, Snack, Snap, Sock, Split, Stock, Taurus, Teene, Time, Tranche, Two-way, Whack

**Shareholder** Plough, Stag

**Shark** Angel, Basking, Beagle, Blue, Bluepointer, Bonnethead, Bronze-whaler, Bull, Carpet, Cestracion, Cow, Demoiselle, Dog(fish), Flake, Fox, Great white, Gummy, Hammerhead, Houndfish, Huss, Lemonfish, Leopard catshark, Loan, Mackerel, Mako, Miller's dog, Monkfish, Noah, Nurse, Penny-dog, Plagiostomi, Porbeagle, Requiem, Reremai, Rhin(e)odon, Rigg, Rook, Sail-fish, Sand, Saw, School, Sea-ape, Sea-fox, Sea-lawyer, Sevengill, Sharp, Shortfin mako, Shovelhead, Smoothhound, Soupfin, Spotted ragged-tooth, Squaloid, Swindler, Thrasher, Thresher, Tiger, Tope, Usurer, Whale, Whaler, Wobbegong, Zygaena

**Sharkskin** Shagreen

**Sharp(er), Sharpen(er), Sharply, Sharpness** Abrupt, Accidental, Acerose, Acetic, Acidulous, Acrid, Aculeus, Acumen, Acuminate, Acutance, Acute, Alert, Angular, Arris, Astringent, Bateless, Becky, Benchstone, Bitter, Brisk, Cacuminous, Cheat, Clear, Coticular, Cutting, Dital, Edge(r), Fine, Fly, Gleg, Grind, Hone, Hot, Keen, Kurtosis, Massé, Mordant, Oilstone, Penetrant, Peracute, Piquant, Poignant, Precision, Prompt, Pronto, Pungent, Quick-witted, Razor, Rogue, Rook, Saw doctor, Set, Shrewd, Smart, Snap, Snell, Sour, Spicate, Stoccato, Strop, Swindler, Tart, Testy, Tomium, Twenty-twenty, Varment, Vivid, Volable, Vorpal, Whet

**Sharpshooter** Bersaglier, Franc-tireur, Sniper, Tirailleur, Voltigeur

**Sharp-sighted** Lynx-eyed

**Shatter(ing)** Astone, Astound, Break, Brisance, Bust, Craze, Dash, Explode, Shiver, Smash, Smithereen, Splinter, Traumatic, Unnerve

**Shave(r), Shaving(s)** Barb(er), Close, Depilation, Electric, Excelsior, Filings, Flake, Grain, Moslings, Pare, Plane, Pogonotomy, Poll, Rasure, Raze, Scrape, Skive, Sliver, Splinter, Swarf, Todd, Tonsure, Turnings, Whittle

**Shaw** Artie, Green, Spinn(e)y, Wood

**Shawl** Afghan, Buibui, Cashmere, Chuddah, Chuddar, Dopatta, Dupatta, Fichu, India, Kaffiyeh, Kashmir, Manta, Mantilla, Maud, Paisley, Partlet, Pashmina, Prayer, Serape, Sha(h)toosh, Stole, Tallis, Tallit(ot), Tallith, Tippet, Tonnag, Tozie, Tribon, Whittle, Wrap(per), Zephyr

**She** A, Hoo

**Sheaf, Sheave** Aplustre, Bee, Bundle, Clevis, Dorlach, Folder, Gait, Garb(e), Gerbe, Mow, Shock, Thr(e)ave

**Shear(er), Shearing, Shears** Clip, Cut, Fleece, Greasy, Jaws of life, Mulesing, Pinking, Poll, Pruning, Ring(er), Secateurs, Shave, Snips, Tinsnips, Trim, Wind

**Sheath(e)** Axolemma, Capsule, Case, Cocoon, Coleoptile, Coleorhiza, Condom, Cover, Encase, Epineurium, Extine, Fingerstall, Glume, Medullary, Myelin, Neurilemma, Neurolemma, Node of Ranvier, Oc(h)rea, Perineurium, Periosteum, Quiver, Retract, Rhinotheca, Root, Scabbard, Spathe, Thecal, Thumbstall, Urceolus, Vagina, Volva, Wing

**Shed(ding), Shedder** Autotomy, Barn, Byre, Cast, Cho(u)ltry, Coducity, Cootch, Cwtch, Depot, Discard, Doff, Downsize, Drop, Ecdysis, Effuse, Emit, Exuviate, Hangar, Hovel, Hut, Infuse, Lair, Lean-to, Linhay, Linn(e)y, Mew, Milking, Moult, Outbuilding, Outhouse, Pent, Potting, Salmon, Shearing, Shippen, Shippon, Shuck, Skeo, Skillion, Skio, Slough, Sow, Spend, Spent, Spill, Spit, Tilt, Tool

**Sheen** Glaze, Gloss, Luminance, Lustre, Patina, Schiller, Shine

**Sheep(ish)** Ammon, Ancon(es), Aoudad, Argali, Ashamed, Barbary, Bell(wether), Bharal, Bident, Bighorn, Black, Blackface, Blate, Border Leicester, Broadtail, Burhel, Burrel(l), Caracul, Charollais, Cheviots, Coopworth, Corriedale, Cotswold, Cotswold lion, Coy, Crone, Dall('s), Dinmont, Domestic, Dorset Down, Dorset Horn, Down, Drysdale, Embarrassed, Ewe, Exmoor, Fank, Fat-tailed, Flock, Fold, Gimmer, Hair, Hampshire, Hampshire Down, Hangdog, Herdwick, Hidder, Hirsel, Hog(g), Hogget, Jacob, Jemmy, Jumbuck, Karakul, Kent, Kerry Hill, Lamb, Lanigerous, Leicester, Lincoln, Lo(a)ghtan, Loghtyn, Long, Lonk, Marco Polo, Masham, Merino, Mor(t)ling, Mouf(f)lon, Mountain, Muflon, Mug, Mus(i)mon, Mutton, Oorial, Ovine, Oxford Down, Perendale, Portland, Ram, Rambouillet, Romeldale, Romney Marsh, Rosella, Ryeland, Scottish Blackface,

Shearling, Shetland, Shidder, Short, Shorthorn, → **SHY**, Soay, Southdown, Spanish, Stone('s), Suffolk, Sumph, Swaledale, Teeswater, Teg(g), Texel, Theave, Trip, Tup, Twinter, Two-tooth, Udad, Urial, Vegetable, Welsh Mountain, Wensleydale, Wether, Wiltshire Horn, Woollyback, Yow(e), Yowie

**Sheep disease, Sheep problem** Black, Blue tongue, Braxy, Dunt, Gid, Hoof rot, Hoove, Louping-ill, Orf, Ringwomb, Rubbers, Scabby mouth, Scrapie, Staggers, Sturdy, Swayback, Variola, Water-brain, Wildfire, Wind

**Sheepdog** Collie, Huntaway, Maremma, Polish Lowland, Puli

**Sheepfold** Fank, Pen

**Sheepskin** Basan, Caracul, Karakul, Mouton, Parchment, Roan, Wool

**Sheeptrack** Terracette

**Sheer** Absolute, Clear, Main, Mere, Peekaboo, Perpendicular, Plumb, Precipitous, Pure, See-through, Simple, Stark, Steep, Swerve, Thin, Utter

**Sheet(ing), Sheets** Balance, Cel, Cellophane, Cere-cloth, Cerement, Charge, Chart, Clean, Crime, Cutch, Diet, Dope, Expanse, Film, Flow, Fly, Folio, Foolscap, Heft, Ice, Inset, Intrusive, Lasagne, Leaf, Membrane, Nappe, Out-hauler, Page, Pane, Pot(t), Pour, Proof, Prospectus, Rap, Ream, Rope, Sail, Scandal, Scratch, Shroud, Stern, Stratus, Taggers, Tarpaulin(g), Tear, Tentorium, Terne, Thunder, Time, Title, Web, White, Winding

**Sheet-anchor** Letter-weight, Paper clip, Paperweight

**Sheet-iron** Taggers, Terne(plate)

**Sheik(dom)** Abu Dhabi, Bahrein, Dubai, Kuwait

**Shekel** Mina, Sickle

**Sheldrake** Bergander

**Shelf, Shelve(d), Shelves** Bank, Bar, Bracket, Continental, Counter, Credence, Delay, Dresser, Étagère, Gondola, Grand Banks, Hob, Ice, Ledge, Leeboard, Mantelpiece, Mantle, On ice, Overmantel, Parcel, Postpone, Rack, Retable, Rick, Ross Ice, Shunt, Sidetrack, Sill, Spinsterhood, Whatnot, Windowsill

**Shell(ed), Shellfish, Shellwork** Abalone, Acorn-shell, Admiral, Ambulacrum, Ammo, Ammonite, Argonaut, Balamnite, Balanus, Balmain bug, Barnacle, Belemnite, Bergmehl, Bivalve, Blitz, Boat, Bodywork, Bombard, Buckie, Camaron, Camera, Capiz, Capsid, Carapace, Cartridge, Casing, Chank, Chelonia, Chitin, Clam, Cleidoic, Clio, Coat-of-mail, Cochlea, Cockle, Cohog, Conch, Cone, Copepoda, Cover, Cowrie, Cowry, Crab, Cracked, Crustacea, Cuttlebone, Dariole, Deerhorn, Dentalium, Dop, Drill, Electron, Escallop, Eugarie, Foraminifer, Framework, Frustule, Gas, Geoduck, Globigerina, Haliotis, Hull, Husk, Hyoplastron, Isopoda, Kernel, Lamp, Langouste, Limacel, Limpet, Live, Lobster, Lorica, Lyre, Malacostraca, Midas's ear, Mitre, Mollusc, Money, Monocoque, Moon, Moreton Bay bug, Mother-of-pearl, Murex, Music, Mussel, Nacre, Nautilus, Olive, Ormer, Ostracod, Ostrea, Otter, Oyster, Paua, Pawa, Pea(s)cod, Peag, Peak, Pecten, Peel, Pereia, Periostracum, Periwinkle, Pilgrim's, Pipi, Pipsqueak, Plastron, Pod, Prawn, Projectile, Purple, Putamen, Quahaug, Quahog, Razor, Rocaille, Sal, Scalarium, Scallop, Scollop, Sea-ear, Sea-pen, Shale, Shard, Sheal, Sheel, Shiel, Shill, Shock, Shot, Shrapnel, Shrimp, Shuck, Sial, Smoke-ball, Snail, Spat, Spend, Spindle, Star, Stomatopod, Stonk, Straddle, Strafe, Stromb(us), Swan-mussel, Tear, Tellen, Tellin, Test(a), Thermidor, Toheroa, Tooth, Top, Torpedo, Tracer, Trivalve, Trough, Trumpet, Turbo, Turritella, Tusk, Univalve, Valency, Venus, Wakiki, Wampum, Whelk, Whiz(z)bang, Winkle, Xenophya, Yabbie, Yabby, Zimbi

▷ **Shelled** *may indicate* an anagram

**Shell money** Wakiki, Wampum, Zimbi

**Shelter(ed)** Abri, A l'abri, Anderson, Arbour, Asylum, Awn, Awning, Barn, Bay, Belee, Bender, Bield, Billet, Bivouac, Blind, Blockhouse, Booth, Bunker, Burladero, Butt, Byre, Cab, Carport, Casemate, Coop, Cot(e), Cove, Covert, Coverture, Defence, Dodger, Donga, Dovecote, Dripstone, Dug-out, Earth, Embower, Fall-out, Garage, Gunhouse, Gunyah, Harbour, Haven, Hithe, Hospice, Hostel, House, Hovel, Humpy, Hut, Hutchie,

Hwl, Igloo, Imbosom, Kipsie, Lee, Lee-gage, Loun, Lound, Lown, Lownd, Mai mai, Mission, Morrison, Nissen, Nodehouse, Palapa, Pilothouse, →**REFUGE**, Retreat, Roadstead, Roof, Sanctuary, Scog, Sconce, Scoog, Scoug, Screen, Scug, Secluded, Shed, Shiel(ing), Shroud, Skug, Snowhole, Snowshed, Stell, Storm-cellar, Succah, Sukkah, Summerhouse, Suntrap, Tax, Tent, Te(e)pee, Testudo, Tortoise, Tupik, Twigloo, Umbrage, Weather, Wheelhouse, Wickyup, Wi(c)kiup, Wil(t)ja, Windbreak, Windscreen, Windshield

**Shemozzle** Debacle

**Shenanigan(s)** Antic, Mischief

**Shepherd(ess)** Abel, Acis, Amaryllis, Amos, Bergère, Bo-peep, Bucolic, Chloe, Clorin, Conduct, Corin, Corydon, Cuddy, Daphnis, Dorcas, Drover, Endymion, Escort, Ettrick, Feeder, Flock-master, German, Good, Grubbinol, Gyges, Herdsman, Hobbinol, Lindor, Marshal, Menalcas, Padre, Pastor(al), Pastorella, Phebe, Pilot, Sheepo, Strephon, Tar-box, Thenot, Thyrsis, Tityrus

**Sherbet** Beer, Soda

**Sheriff** Bailiff, Deputy, Earp, Grieve, Land-dros(t), Lawman, Process-server, Shireman, Shire-reeve, Shirra, Shrievalty, Viscount

**Sherry** Amoroso, Bristol milk, Cobbler, Cream, Cyprus, Doctor, Dry, Fino, Gladstone, Jerez, Manzanilla, Oloroso, Palo cortado, Sack, Solera, Sweet, Whitewash, Xeres

**Sherwood** Anderson, Forest

**Shiah** Ismaili

**Shibboleth** Password

**Shield(s), Shield-shaped** Ablator, Achievement, Aegis, Ancile, Armour, Arms, Baltic, Biological, Bodyguard, Box, Brolly, Buckler, Canadian, Carapace, Cartouche, Clypeus, Defend, Dress, Escutcheon, Fence, Gobo, Guard, Gumshield, Gyron, Hatchment, Heat, Hielaman, Human, Inescutcheon, Insulate, Laurentian, Lozenge, Mant(e)let, Mask, Pavis(e), Pelta, Plastron, Protect, Randolph, Ranfurly, Riot, Rondache, Scandinavian, Screen, Scutcheon, Scute, Scutum, Sheffield, Splashboard, Sternite, Targe(t), Thyroid, Toecap, Vair, Visor, Water

**Shift(er), Shifty** Amove, Astatic, Back, Blue, Budge, Change, Chemise, Core, Cymar, Day, Devious, Displace, Dogwatch, Doppler, Dress, Dying, Einstein, Evasive, Expedient, Fend, Function, Graveyard, Great Vowel, Hedging, Jiggle(r), Lamb, Landslide, Lateral, Linen, Louche, Meve, Move, Night, Nightie, Nighty, Oil, Paradigm, Realign, Red, Relay, Remove, Rota, Ruse, Scorch, Sell, Shirt, Shovel, Shuffle, Shunt, Simar(re), Slicker, Slip(pery), Sound, Spell, Split, Stagehand, Steal, Stick, Stint, Swing, Switch, Tergiversate, Tour, Transfer, Tunic, Turn, Turnabout, Vary, Veer, Warp

▷ **Shift(ing)** *may indicate* an anagram

**Shilling** Bob, Deaner, Falkiner, Hog, King's, Queen's, S, Teston

**Shilly-shally** Whittie-whattie

**Shimmer(ing)** Aventurine, Aventurine, Chatoyant, Gleam, Glint, Glitter, Iridescence, Mona(u)l, Opalescence, Shine

▷ **Shimmering** *may indicate* an anagram

**Shin** Clamber, Climb, Cnemial, Leg, Shank, Skink, Swarm

**Shindig, Shindy** Bobbery, Row, Ruction, Rumpus, Shivoo, Uproar

**Shine(r), Shining, Shiny** Aglitter, Aglow, Beam, Bright, Buff, Burnish, Deneb, Effulge, Excel, Flash, Glaze, Gleam, Glimmer, Glisten, Glitzy, Gloss, →**GLOW**, Irradiant, Japan, →**LAMP**, Leam, Leme, Lucent, Luminous, Lustre, Micate, Mouse, Nitid, Nugget, Phoebe, Phosphoresce, Polish, Radiant, Radiator, Refulgent, Relucent, Resplend, Rutilant, Shellac, Shimmer, Skyre, Sleek, Twinkle, Varnish

**Shingle(s), Shingly** Beach, Chesil, Cut, Dartre, Dartrous, Gravel, Herpes, Herpes Zoster, Herpetic, Loose metal, Shake, Shale, Stone, Tiles, Zona, Zoster

**Shinpad** Greave

**Shinty** Caman, Camanachd

▷ **Shiny** *may indicate* a star

**Ship(ping), Shipping area, Ships** Boat, Convoy, → DISPATCH, Embark, Export, Fastnet, Flota, Her, Keel, Man, Marine, Nautical, Post, Prize, Prow, Raft, Ram, Sail, She, SS, Transport, Tub, Vessel, Victualling

## SHIPS

| *1 letter:* | Yawl | Wager | Launch |
|---|---|---|---|
| Q | Zulu | Whiff | Lorcha |
| | | Xebec | Lugger |
| *2 letters:* | *5 letters:* | Yacht | Masula |
| MV | Aviso | Zabra | Monkey |
| PT | Barge | Zebec | Mother |
| | Broke | | Nuggar |
| *3 letters:* | Camel | *6 letters:* | Packet |
| Ark | Canoe | Argosy | Pedalo |
| Cat | Cargo | Banker | Pequod |
| Cog | Coble | Barque | Pinkie |
| Dow | Coper | Bateau | Pirate |
| Fly | Crare | Bawley | Pitpan |
| Hoy | Dandy | Beagle | Pulwar |
| Kit | Dingy | Bethel | Puteli |
| Red | Drake | Bireme | Randan |
| | Ferry | Borley | Reefer |
| *4 letters:* | Funny | Bottom | Sampan |
| Argo | Jolly | Bounty | Sandal |
| Bark | Ketch | Caique | School |
| Brig | Laker | Carack | Schuit |
| Buss | Liner | Carvel | Schuyt |
| Cock | Moses | Castle | Settee |
| Cott | Oiler | Coaler | Saique |
| Dhow | Pinky | Cobble | Slaver |
| Dory | Pinto | Codder | Tanker |
| Duck | Plate | Cooper | Tartan |
| Fire | Praam | Crayer | Tender |
| Flat | Prahu | Curagh | Tonner |
| Grab | Prore | Cutter | Torpid |
| Hulk | Pucan | Decker | Trader |
| Isis | Q-boat | Dingey | Trek-ox |
| Koff | Razee | Dinghy | Triton |
| Long | Rover | Dogger | Turret |
| Nina | Sabot | Droger | Whaler |
| Pink | Saick | Dromon | Wherry |
| Pont | Scoot | Drover | Zebeck |
| Pram | Screw | Dugout | |
| Prau | Scull | Escort | *7 letters:* |
| Proa | Shell | Flying | Belfast |
| Ro-ro | Skiff | Frigot | Bidarka |
| Saic | Slave | Galiot | Bumboat |
| Scow | Sloop | Galley | Capital |
| Snow | Smack | Gay-you | Caravel |
| Tall | Tramp | Goldie | Carrack |
| Tern | Troop | Hooker | Carract |
| Trow | U-boat | Howker | Carrect |
| Yare | Umiak | Jigger | Catboat |

Clipper
Coaster
Collier
Consort
Coracle
Counter
Cruiser
Currach
Curragh
Dredger
Drifter
Drogher
Dromond
Factory
Felucca
Flattop
Flyboat
Frigate
Gabbard
Gabbart
Galleon
Galliot
Galloon
Geordie
Gondola
Gunboat
Jetfoil
Kontiki
Liberty
Lymphad
Masoola
Mistico
Monitor
Mudscow
Mystery
Oomiack
Patamar
Pelican
Pinnace
Piragua
Pirogue
Polacca
Polacre
Pontoon
Repulse
Revenge
Sculler

Shallop
Sharpie
Steamer
Stew-can
Tartane
Titanic
Trawler
Trireme
Tugboat
Vedette
Victory
Vidette
Weather

**8 letters:**
Acapulco
Bilander
Billyboy
Bylander
Cabotage
Corocore
Corocoro
Corvette
Dahabieh
Faldboat
Flagship
Flatboat
Foldboat
Galleass
Galliass
Gallivat
Hospital
Hoveller
Indiaman
Ironclad
Longboat
Longship
Mackinaw
Mary Rose
Masoolah
Merchant
Monohull
Mosquito
Pinafore
Sallyman
Savannah
Schooner

Shanghai
Showboat
Training

**9 letters:**
Bucentaur
Catamaran
Container
Cutty Sark
Dahabeeah
Dahabiyah
Dahabiyeh
Discovery
Dromedary
First-rate
Freighter
Frigatoon
Hydrofoil
Klondiker
Klondyker
Lapstrake
Lapstreak
Leviathan
Lightship
Lusitania
Mayflower
Minelayer
Monoxylon
Multihull
Outrigger
Peter-boat
Privateer
Sallee-man
Shear-hulk
Sheer-hulk
Steamboat
Submarine
Temeraire
Vaporetto
Whale-back
Whaleboat

**10 letters:**
Barkentine
Brigantine
Fourmaster
Golden Hind

Hydroplane
Icebreaker
Knockabout
Mine-hunter
Paddleboat
Quadrireme
Sandsucker
Santa Maria
Trekschuit
Triaconter
Windjammer

**11 letters:**
Barquentine
Bellerophon
Berthon-boat
Cockleshell
Dreadnought
Merchantman
Minesweeper
Penteconter
Quinquereme
Side-wheeler
Skidbladnir
Submersible
Supertanker
Three-decker
Three-master
Torpedo boat

**12 letters:**
Deepwaterman
East Indiaman
Fore-and-after
Great Eastern
Marie Celeste
Stern-wheeler
Tangle-netter

**13 letters:**
Paddle steamer

**14 letters:**
Flying Dutchman
Ocean greyhound

**Shipmate** Crew, Hearty, Sailor
**Shipment** Cargo, Transit
**Shipping line** P and O
**Ship's biscuit** Dandyfunk, Dunderfunk
**Shipshape** Apple-pie, Neat, Orderly, Tidy, Trim
**Shipwreck(ed)** Castaway, Logen, Split

**Shire** Carthorse, Comitatus, County

**Shirk(er)** Bludge, Cuthbert, Dodge, Embusqué, Evade, Funk, Gold brick, Malinger, Mike, Pike, Poler, Scrimshank, Skive, Skrimshank, Slack, Soldier

**Shirt** Aloha, Black, Boiled, Brown, Bush, Caftan, Calypso, Camese, Camise, Chemise, Choli, Cilice, Dasheki, Dashiki, Dick(e)y, Dress, Fiesta, Garibaldi, Grandad, Hair, Hawaiian, Hoodie, Jacky Howe, Kaftan, Kaross, K(h)urta, Muscle, Nessus, Non-iron, Parka, Partlet, Polo, Rash, Red, Rugby, Safari, Sark, Serk, Set, Shift, Smock, Sports, Stuffed, Subucula, Swan(n)dri®, Sweat, T, Uncle (Bert)

**Shiva** Destroyer

**Shiver(ing), Shivers, Shivery** Aguish, Aquiver, Atingle, Break, Brrr, Chitter, Crumble, Dash, Dither, Fragile, Frisson, Gooseflesh, Grew, Grue, Malaria, Matchwood, Nither, Oorie, Ourie, Owrie, Quake, Quiver, → **SHAKE**, Shatter, Shrug, Shudder, Smash, Smither, Smithereens, Splinter, Timbers, Tremble

▷ **Shiver(ed)** *may indicate* an anagram

**Shoal** Bar, Fish, Quantity, Reef, Run, Sand-bar, School, Shallows, Shelf, Tail

**Shock(ed), Shocker, Shocking** Acoustic, Aghast, Agitate, Amaze, Anaphylactic, Appal, Astone, Astony, Astound, Astun, Awful, Awhape, Bombshell, Brunt, Bunch, Consternate, Criminal, Culture, Daze, Defibrillate, Devastate, Disconcert, Disgust, Dorlach, Dreadful, Drop, Dumbfound, Earthquake, ECT, Egregious, Electric, Electrocute, Epiphenomenon, EST, Eye-opener, Fleg, Floccus, Forelock, Gait, Galvanism, Gobsmack, Hair, Haycock, Haystack, Horrify, Horror, Impact, Infamous, Insulin, Isoseismic, Jar, Jolt, Knock cold, Live, Mane, Mop, Numb, Obscene, Outrage, Poleaxe, Putrid, Recoil, Return, Revolt, Rick(er), Rigor, Scandal(ise), Seismic, Septic, Shaghaired, Shake, Sheaf, Shell, Shilling, Shog, Shook, Stagger, Start(le), Stitch, Stook, Stound, Stun, Stupor, Surgical, Tangle, Thermal, Thunderstruck, Torpedinidae, Trauma, Tremor, Turn

**Shock-absorber** Buffer, Oleo, Snubber

▷ **Shocked** *may indicate* an anagram

**Shod** Calced

**Shoddy** Cagmag, Catchpenny, Cheap, Cheapjack, Cheapo, Cloth, Cowboy, Drecky, Gimcrack, Imitation, Oorie, Ourie, Owrie, Poor, Rag-wool, Ropy, Schlock, → **SHABBY**, Slapdash, Slopwork, Tatty, Tawdry, Tinny

**Shoe(s)** Accessory, Arctic, Athletic, Ballet, Balmoral, Bauchle, Birkenstock, Blocked, Boat, Boot, Bootee, Brake, Brogan, Brogue, Brothel creepers, Buskin, Calceate, Calk(er), Calkin, Carpet slipper, Casuals, Caulker, Cawker, Charlier, Chaussures, Chopin(e), Clodhopper, Clog, Co-respondent, Court, Creeper, Dap, Deck, Espadrille, Flattie, Flip-flops, → **FOOTWEAR**, Galage, Galoche, Galosh, Gatty, Geta, Ghillie, Golosh, Gumboot, Gumshoe, Gym, High-low, High tops, Hot, Hush-puppies®, Jandal®, Jellies, Kamik, Kletterschue, Kurdaitcha, Lace up, Launch(ing), Loafer, Mary-Janes®, Mocassin, Moccasin, Muil, Mule, Open-toe, Oxford, Oxonian, Panton, Patten, Peeptoe, Pennyloafer, Pile, Plate, Plimsole, Plimsoll, Poulaine, Pump, Rivlin, Rope-soled, Rubbers, Rullion, Runner, Sabaton, Sabot, Saddle, Safety, Sandal, Sandshoe, Sannie, Scarpetto, Shauchle, Skid, Skimmer, Slingback, Slip-on, Slipper, Slip-slop, Sneaker, Snow, Sock, Soft, Solleret, Spike, Stoga, Stogy, Suede, Tabi, Tackies, Takkies, Tennis, Tie, Topboot, Track, Trainer, T-strap, Upper, Vamp(er), Veld-schoen, Veldskoen, Velskoen, Vibram®, Vibs, Wagon lock, Wedgie, Welt, Winkle-picker, Zori

**Shoeless** Barefoot, Discalced

**Shoemaker** Blacksmith, Choo, Clogger, Cobbler, Cordiner, Cordwainer, Cosier, Cozier, Crispi(a)n, Farrier, Gentle craft, Leprechaun, Sachs, Smith, Snob, Soutar, Souter, Sowter, Sutor

**Shoe-string** Cheap, Lace, Pittance

**Shoe-toe** Poulaine

**Shoo** Away, Begone, Hoosh, Off, Scat(ter), Voetsek

**Shoot(er), Shooting, Shoot out** Ack-ack, Airgun, Arrow, Bine, Bostryx, Braird, Breer, Bud, Bulbil, Burgeon, Camera, Catapult, Chit, Cion, Cyme, Dart(le), Delope,

Discharge, Drib, Elance, Enate, Eradiate, Film, Fire, Flagellum, Germ, Germain(e), Germen, Germin(ate), Glorious twelfth, →GUN, Gunsel, Head-reach, Hurl, Imp, In bud, Jet, Lateral, Layer, Lens, Limb, Loose, Marksmanship, Offset, Osier, Outgun, Pepper, Photocall, Photograph, Pip, Plink, Pluff, Plug, Poot, Pop, Pot, Pout, Ramulus, Rapids, Ratoon, Riddle, Rod, Rough, Rove, Runner, Scion, Septembriser, Shell, Showdown, Sien(t), Skeet, Snap, Snipe, Spire, Spirt, Spout, Spray, Sprout, Spurt, Spyre, Start, Stole, Stolon, Strafe, Sucker, Syen, Tellar, Teller, Tendril, Tendron, Tiller, Trap, Turion, Twelfth, Twig, Udo, Vimen, Wand, Weapon, Whiz(z), Wildfowler, Zap

**Shop(per), Shopping, Shops** Agency, Arcade, Assembly, Atelier, Automat, Bag, Betray, Betting, Body, Boutique, Bucket, Buy, Cantina, Chain, Charcuterie, Charity, Chippy, Chop, Closed, Coffee, Commissary, Cook, Co-op, Cop, Corner, Cut-price, Dairy, Delicatessen, Denounce, Dobbin, Dolly, Duddery, Duka, Duty-free, Emporium, Factory, Five and dime, Food court, Galleria, Gift, Grass, In bond, Inform, Junk, Kiosk, Luckenbooth, Machine, Mail (order), Mall, Mall crawl, Mall-rat, Market, Megastore, Mercat, Messages, Minimart, Muffler, Mystery, Naafi, Never-never, Office, Officinal, Off-licence, Off-sales, Op(portunity), Open, Outlet, Parlour, Patisserie, Personal, Pharmacy, Precinct, Print, PX, Rat on, Report, Retail, RMA, Salon, Sex, Shambles, Share, Shebang, Spaza, Squat, →STORE, Strip mall, Studio, Sundry, Superette, Supermarket, Superstore, Swap, Talking, Tally, Tea (room), Thrift, Tick, Tommy, Trade, Truck, Tuck, Union, Vintry, Warehouse, Whistle-blow, Works

**Shopkeeper** British, Butcher, Chemist, Clothier, Gombeen-man, Greengrocer, Grocer, Haberdasher, Hosier, Ironmonger, Merchant, Newsagent, Provisioner, Retailer, Stationer, Tradesman, Vendor

**Shoplift(er)** Boost, Heist

**Shore** Bank, Beach, Buttress, Coast, Coastline, Coste, Eustatic, Foreside, Landfall, Lee, Littoral, Machair, Offing, Prop, Rance, Rivage, Saxon, Seaboard, Strand, Strandline, Support

**Short(en), Shortly** Abbreviate, Abridge, Abrupt, Anon, Apocope, Brief, Brusque, Close-in, Commons, Compendious, Concise, Contract, Crisp, Cross, Curt, Curtail, Curtal, Cutty, Digest, Diminish, Drink, Eftsoons, Epitomise, Ere-long, Flying, Fubsy, Fuse, Hard up, Impolite, Inadequate, In a while, In brief, Lacking, Laconical, Light, Limited, Low, Mini, Near, Nip, Nirlie, Nutshell, Offing, Pithy, Pudsey, Punch, Pyknic, Reduce, Reef, Retrench, Scantle, Scanty, Scarce, Shrift, Shy, Skimpy, Snatch, Soon, Sparse, Spirit, Squab, Squat(ty), Staccato, Stint, Stocky, Strapped, Stubby, Succinct, Syncopate, Systole, Taciturn, Teen(s)y, Telescope, Temporal, Temporaneous, Terse, Tight, Tot, Towards, Transient, Under, Wee

**Shortage** Brevity, Dearth, Deficiency, Deficit, Drought, Famine, Lack, Need, Paucity, Scarcity, Sparsity, Ullage, Wantage

**Short circuit** Varistor

**Shortcoming** Defect, Limitation, Sin, Weakness

**Shortfall** Deficit

**Shorthand** Diphone, Gregg, Outline, Phonographic, Phraseogram, Pitman, Speedwriting®, Stenography, Stenotypy, Tachygraphy, Tironian, Tironian notes, Triphone, Weblish

**Short-headed** Brachycephal

**Short-lived, Short-term** Day to day, Ephemeral, Fragile, Meson, Transitory

**Shorts** Bermuda, Board, Boxer, Briefs, Culottes, Cycling, Hot pants, Kaccha, Lederhosen, Plus-fours, Skort, Stubbies®, Trunks

**Short-sight** Myopia, Myosis

**Short-winded** Breathless, Concise, Puffed, Purfled, Pursy, Succinct

**Shot(s)** Aim, Air, All-in, Ammo, Approach, Attempt, Backhand, Ball, Bank, Barrage, Bisque, Blank, Blast, Bricole, Bull, Bullet, Burl, Canna, Cannonball, Cartridge, Case, Catapulted, Chain, Chatoyant, Chip, Close up, Corner, Cover, Crab, Crack, Daisy cutter, Dink, Dolly, Dram, Draw, Drop, Duckhook, Dum dum, Dunk, Elt, Essay, Exhausted,

Explosion, Flew, Forehand, Fusillade, Gesse, Get, Glance, Go, Grape, Guess, Gun-stone, Hazard, Hook, In-off, Iridescent, Jab, Jump, Kill, Langrage, Langrel, Langridge, Lay-up, Longjenny, Magpie, Marksman, Maroon, Massé, Matte, Mitraille, Money, Moon-ball, Mulligan, Multi-coloured, Musket, Nip, Noddy, Opalescent, Pack, Parthian, Parting, Passing, Pelican, Pellet, Penalty, Photo, Pitch, Plant, Pluff, Pop, Pot, Puff, Push, Rake, Rid, Round, Safety, Salvo, Scratch, Shell, Shy, Sighter, Silk, Six, Slam-dunk, Slap, Slice, Slug, Slung, Smash, Snap, Snifter, Sped, Spell, Spent, Square cut, Stab, Still, Streaked, Tap in, Tee, Throw, Toepoke, Tonic, Tot, Tracking, Trial, Try, Turn, Volley, Warning, Wrist, Yahoo

**Shotgun** Sawn-off

**Should** Ought

**Shoulder(-blade)** Carry, Cold, Crossette, Epaule, Frozen, Hard, Hump, Joggle, Omohyoid, Omoplate, Pick-a-back, Roadside, Scapula, Shouther, Soft, Spald, Spall, Spaul(d), Speal, Spule, Tote, Withers

**Shout(er), Shouting** Alley-oop, Barrack, Bawl, Bellock, Bellow, Boanerges, Boo, Call, Claim, Clamour, Conclamation, Cry, Din, Exclaim, Geronimo, Heckle, Hey, Hoi(cks), Holla, Holla-ho(a), Holler, Hollo, Holloa, Hooch, Hosanna, Howzat, Hue, Och, Oi, Oy, Parnell, Rah, Rant, Rave, Roar, Root, Round, Sa sa, Storm, Treat, Trumpet, Vociferate, Whoop, Yammer, Yell(och), Yicker, Yippee, Yodel, Yoohoo, Yorp

**Shove** Barge, Birr, Elbow, Jostle, Push, Ram, Spoon, Thrust

**Shovel** Backhoe, Dustpan, Hat, Loy, Main, Peel, Power, Scoop, Shool, Spade, Steam, Trowel, Van

**Show(ing), Shown, Showy** Anonyma, Appearance, Aquacade, Bad, Bench, Betray, Branky, Broadcast, Brummagem, Burlesque, Cabaret, Cattle, Chat, Circus, Come, Con, Cruft's, Dashing, Define, Demo(nstrate), Depict, Describe, Dime museum, Diorama, Display, Do, Drama, Dramedy, Dressy, Dumb, Effeir, Effere, Endeictic, Entertainment, Epideictic, Establish, Evince, →**EXHIBIT**, Expo, Express, Extravaganza, Exude, Facade, Fair, Fangled, Farce, Fine, Flamboyant, Flash, Flaunt, Floor, Fly, Folies Bergere, Galanty, Game, Garish, Gaudy, Gay, Gig, Give, Glitter, Glitz(y), Gloss, Good, Horse, Indicate, Jazzy, Kismet, Koni, Lay bare, Light, Loud, Manifest, Matinée, Meretricious, Minstrel, Moon, Musical, Naumachy, One-man, Ostensible, Ostentatious, Pageant, Panel game, Panto(mime), Parade, Patience, Peacock, Peep, Performance, Phen(o), Phone-in, Point, Pomp, Portray, Presentation, Pretence, Preview, Pride, Procession, Prog(ramme), Project, Prominence, Prove, Pseudery, Puff, Puppet, Quiz, Raree, Razzmatazz, Reality, Register, Represent, Reveal, Revue, Road, Rodeo, Roll-out, Ruddigore, Rushes, Screen, Shaw, Sight, Singspiel, Sitcom, Slang, Soap, Son et lumière, Specious, Spectacle, Splash, Splay, Stage, Stunt, Swankpot, Talk, Tamasha, Tattoo, Tawdry, Telecast, Telethon, Theatrical, Three-man, Tinhorn, Tinsel(ly), Tulip, Unbare, Uncover, Unveil, Usher, Vain, Variety, Vaudeville, Veneer, Viewy, Wear, Wild west, Zarzuela

**Showdown** Confrontation, Crunch

**Shower** Douche, Downfall, Exhibitor, Flurry, Hail, Indicant, Indicator, Kitchen tea, Lavish, Lot, Meteor, Panoply, Party, Pelt, Pepper, Precipitation, Rain, Regale, Scat, Scouther, Scowther, Scud, Skatt, Skit, Snow, Spat, Spet, Spit, Splatter, Spray, Sprinkle, Ticker tape, Volley

▷ **Showers** *may indicate* an anagram

**Showgirl** Evita, Nanette

▷ **Showing, Shown in** *may indicate* a hidden word

**Showman** Bailey, Barnum, Buffalo Bill, Entertainer, Goon, Impresario, Lord Mayor, MC, Ringmaster, Todd

**Show-off** Coxcomb, Exhibitionist, Extrovert, Flash Harry, Jack the lad, Masher, Peacock, Piss artist, Poseur, Sport, Swagger, Swank, Tulip, Wiseacre

**Showpiece** Flagship

**Show-place** Exhibition, Olympia, Pavilion, Theatre

**Show up** Unmask

**Shrapnel** Fragment, Shell, Splinter

**Shred** Clout, Filament, Grate, Julienne, Mammock, Mince, Mummock, Rag, Screed, Swarf, Tag, Tatter, Ta(i)ver, Tear up, Thread, To-tear, Wisp

**Shrew** Bangsring, Banxring, Callet, Catamaran, Elephant, Fury, Hellcat, Kate, Marabunta, Musk, Nag, Otter, Pygmy, Show, Solenodon, Sondeli, Sorex, Spitfire, Squirrel, Tana, Termagant, Tree, Trull, Tupaia, Virago, Vixen, Water, Xant(h)ippe, Yankie, Yenta

**Shrewd(ness)** Acumen, Acute, Arch, Argute, Artful, Astucious, Astute, Callid, Canny, Clued-up, Cute, Far-sighted, File, Gnostic, Gumptious, Hard-nosed, Judicious, Knowing, Pawky, Politic, Prudent(ial), Sagacious, Sapient(al), Savvy, Sharp-sighted, Tactical, Wide boy, Wily, Wise

**Shriek** Cry, Scream, Scrike, Shright, Shrike, Shrill, Shritch, Skirl, Yell

**Shrift** Attention, Penance, Short

**Shrike** Bird, Boubou, Butcher-bird

**Shrill** Argute, High, Keen, Piping, Pipy, Reedy, Scraich, Screech(y), Sharp, Skirl, Squeaky, Treble

**Shrimp(s)** Brine, Crevette, Fairy, Freshwater, Krill, Mantis, Midge, Opossum, Potted, Prawn, Runt, Sand, Skeleton, Small, Spectre, Squill(a), Stomatopod, Tiger

**Shrine** Adytum, Alamo, Altar, Dagaba, Dagoba, Dargah, Delphi, Fatima, Feretory, Harem, Holy, Joss house, Kaaba, Lourdes, Marabout, Martyry, Memorial, Naos, Pagoda, Pilgrimage, Reliquary, Scrine, Scryne, Stupa, Tabernacle, Temple, Tope, Vimana, Walsingham

**Shrink(age), Shrink from, Shrinking, Shrunk** Abhor, Alienist, Analyst, Blanch, Blench, Boggle, Cling, Compress, Constringe, Contract, Cour, Cower, Creep, Crine, Cringe, Dare, Decrew, Depreciate, Dread, Dwindle, Flinch, Funk, Gizzen, Less, Minimise, Nirl, → **PSYCHIATRIST**, Pycnosis, Quail, Recoil, Reduce, Retract, Sanforised, Shrivel, Shrug, Shy, Sphacelate, Timid, Violet, Wane, Waste, Wince, Wither, Wizened

**Shrivel(led)** Cling, Crine, Desiccate, Dry, Dwindle, Gizzen, Nirl, Parch, Scorch, Scrump, Sear, Shrink, Skrimp, Skrump, Tabid, Welk, Wither, Wizened, Writhled

**Shropshire** Salop

**Shroud(s)** Cerecloth, Chadri, Chuddah, Chuddar, Cloak, Cloud, Conceal, Cover, Futtock, Grave-cloth, Pall, Rigging, Screen, Sheet, Sindon, Turin, Veil, Winding-sheet, Wrap

**Shrove Tuesday** Fastens, J'ouvert, Pancake

**Shrub(bery)** Arboret, Brush, → **BUSH**, Dead-finish, Horizontal, Petty whin, Plant, Undergrowth

## SHRUBS

| *3 letters:* | Ruta | Hakea | Thyme |
|---|---|---|---|
| Kat | Sunn | Hazel | Toyon |
| Qat | Titi | Henna | Wahoo |
| Rue | Tutu | Holly | Yapon |
| | Ulex | Ledum | Yupon |
| *4 letters:* | | Maqui | Zamia |
| Acer | *5 letters:* | Monte | |
| Aloe | Aalii | Mulga | *6 letters:* |
| Coca | Bosky | Nebek | Acacia |
| Cola | Brere | Peony | Alhagi |
| Dita | Briar | Pyxie | Ambach |
| Grex | Brier | Ramee | Aucuba |
| Hebe | Buaze | Ramie | Azalea |
| Kava | Buazi | Salal | Bauera |
| Nabk | Buchu | Savin | Cobaea |
| Olea | Caper | Senna | Correa |
| Rhus | Gorse | Sumac | Croton |

Crowea
Daphne
Fatsia
Feijoa
Frutex
Fustet
Fynbos
Gambir
Garrya
Jojoba
Kalmia
Laurel
Lignum
Manoao
Manuka
Maquis
Matico
Mimosa
Myrica
Myrtle
Nebbuk
Nebeck
Neinei
Paeony
Pituri
Privet
Protea
Prunus
Savine
Smilax
Sorbus
Storax
Sumach
Tutsan
Wandoo
Yaupon

**7 letters:**
Acerola
Akiharo
Ambatch
Arbutus
Bauhini
Boronia
Bullace
Cascara
Chamise
Chamiso
Cytisus
Deutzia
Dogwood
Emubush
Epacris
Ephedra

Filbert
Fuchsia
Gambier
Guayule
Hop-tree
Jasmine
Juniper
Lantana
Mahonia
Mesquit
Muntrie
Oleacea
Olearia
Phlomis
Rhatany
Romneya
Rosebay
Savanna
Shallon
Skimmia
Syringa
Tea-tree
Waratah
Weigela

**8 letters:**
Abutilon
Allspice
Balisier
Barberry
Bayberry
Berberis
Bignonia
Bilberry
Bluebush
Buddleia
Camellia
Caragana
Coprosma
Cowberry
Danewort
Euonymus
Gardenia
Hardhack
Heketara
Hibiscus
Horopito
Inkberry
Japonica
Jetbread
Koromiko
Krameria
Lavender
Leadwort

Magnolia
Mairehau
Mesquite
Mezereon
Ninebark
Ocotillo
Oleander
Oleaster
Photinia
Rangiora
Rock rose
Rosemary
Saltbush
Savannah
Shadbush
Snowbush
Sorbaria
Spekboom
Sweetsop
Tamarisk
Viburnum
Waxplant

**9 letters:**
Andromeda
Bearberry
Buckthorn
Ceanothus
Clianthus
Cordyline
Coreopsis
Coyotillo
Croqberry
Eucryphia
Firethorn
Forsythia
Gelsemium
Grevillia
Hamamelis
Hydrangea
Jaborandi
Jessamine
Kumarahou
Manzanita
Melaleuca
Mistletoe
Patchouli
Pernettya
Perovskia
Phillyria
Rauwolfia
Screw bean
Snowberry
Spicebush

Sterculia
Tree peony
Twinberry
Widow wail
Wolfberry

**10 letters:**
Aphelandra
Callicarpa
Cascarilla
Coralberry
Crossandra
Embothrium
Eriostemon
Escallonia
Fatshedera
Frangipani
Fringe tree
Gaultheria
Goat's thorn
Gooseberry
Greasewood
Holodiscus
Joshua tree
Laurustine
Marcgravia
Mock orange
Mock privet
Parkleaves
Pilocarpus
Poinsettia
Potentilla
Pyracantha
Schefflera
Supplejack
Twinflower

**11 letters:**
Beautybrush
Bottlebrush
Carpenteria
Chaenomeles
Cotoneaster
Farkleberry
Honeysuckle
Huckleberry
Japan laurel
Leatherwood
Mustard tree
Pittosporum
Postanthera
Sheep laurel
Silverberry
Staggerbush

| | | | |
|---|---|---|---|
| Steeplebush | **12 letters:** | Southernwood | **13 letters:** |
| Stephanotis | Phanerophyte | Streptosolen | Wayfaring tree |
| Wintergreen | Philadelphus | Strophanthus | Winter jasmine |
| Wintersweet | Rhododendron | | |
| Wortleberry | Serviceberry | | |

---

**Shrug** Discard, Dismiss(ive), Toss

**Shuck** Peel

**Shudder(ing)** Abhor, Ashake, Frisson, Grew, Grise, Grue, Horror, Jerk, Quake, Quiver, Shake, Spasm, Tremble, Tremor

**Shuffle(d)** Dodge, Drag, Hedge, Make, Mix, Palter, Permute, Randomise, Rearrange, Redeployment, Riffle, Scuff, Shamble, Shauchle, Soft-shoe, Stack, Waddle

▷ **Shuffle(d)** *may indicate* an anagram

**Shun** Attention, Avoid, Boycott, Eschew, Evade, Forbear, Ignore, Ostracise, Secede, →SPURN

**Shunt** Move, Prang, Shelve, Shuttle, Side-track

**Shut (down, in, out, up), Shuts** Bar, Cage, Close, Closet, Confined, Coop, Debar, Embar, Emure, Fasten, Fend, Impale, Impound, Latch, Lay-off, Lock, Occlude, Paralysis, Rid, Scram, Seal, Shet, Slam, Spar, Steek, Telescope, Tine, To

**Shutter(s)** Blind, B-setting, Damper, Dead-lights, Douser, Eyelid, Focal-plane, Jalousie, Louver, Louvre, Persiennes, Shade

**Shuttle** Alternate, Challenger, Commute, Drawer, Flute, Go-between, Navette, Orbiter, Shoot, Shunt, Space, Tat(t), Weave

**Shy** Bashful, Blate, Blench, Cast, Catapult, Chary, Clam, Coconut, Coy, Deficient, Demure, Farouche, Flinch, Funk, Go, Heave, Introvert, Jerk, Jib, Laithfu', Leery, Lob, Mim, Mims(e)y, Modest, Mousy, Rear, Recoil, Reserved, Reticent, Retiring, Sally, Sheepish, Shrinking violet, Skeigh, Sling, Start, Thraw, Throw, Timid, Tongue-tied, Toss, Try, Verecund, Wallflower, Willyard, Willyart, Withdrawn

**Shyster** Ambulance chaser

**Siamese, Siamese twins** Chang, Eng, Parabiosis, Seal-point, T(h)ai

**Siberia(n)** Chukchi, Evenki, Frozen, Ostiak, Ostyak, Samo(y)ed, Tungus, Vogul, Yakut, Yupik

**Sibilant** Hissing, Whistling

**Sibling** Brother, German, Kin, Sister

**Sibyl** Oracle, Prophetess, Seer, Seeress, Soothsayer, Voluspa, Witch

**Sicilian** Sicanian, Trinacrian

**Sick(en), Sickener, Sickening, Sickliness, Sickly, Sickness** Aegrotat, Affection, Ague, Ail, Altitude, Anaemic, Bad, Bends, Bilious, Cat, Chalky, Chunder, Cloying, Colic, Crapulence, Cringeworthy, Crook, Decompression, Delicate, Diseased, Disorder, Donsie, Emetic, Emetin(e), Gag, Green, Hacked off, Hangover, Icky, Ill, Infection, Infirm, Lazar, Leisure, Loathsome, Maid-pale, Mal, Mawkish, Milk, Morbid, Morning, Motion, Mountain, Nauseous, Off-colour, Pale, Peaky, Peelie-wallie, Peely-wally, Pestilent, Pindling, Plague, Poorly, Puly, Puna, Queachy, Queasy, Queechy, Radiation, Regorge, Repulsive, Retch, Serum, Shilpit, Sleeping, Sleepy, Soroche, Space, Spue, Squeamish, Sweating, Travel, Twee, Uncle Dick, Valetudinarian, Virus, Vomit, Wamble-cropped, Wan

**Sick bay, Sickroom** San, Ward

**Sickle(-shaped)** Ba(d)ging-hook, Falcate, Falx, Grasshook, Hook, Scythe, Shear

**Side, Sidepiece** Abeam, Airs, Ally, B, Beam, Blind, Border, Branch, Camp, Cis-, Distaff, Division, Edge, Effect, Elevation, Eleven, English, Epistle, Ex intraque parte, Facet, Flank, Flip, Gospel, Gunnel, Hand, Heavy, Hypotenuse, Iliac, Lateral, Lee(ward), Left, Long, Lore, Obverse, Off, On, OP, Pane, Part, Partisan, Party, Pleura, Port, Pretension, Profile, Prompt, Rave, Reveal, Reverse, Right, Rink, Scratch, Short, Silver, Slip, Spear, Spindle, Starboard, Swank, →TEAM, Tight, Weak, West, Wind, Windward, Wing, XI

**Sideboard(s)** Beauf(f)et, Buffet, Cellaret, Commode, Credence, Credenza, Dinner-wagon, Dresser, Whiskers
**Side by side** Appose(d)
**Side-effect, Side-issue** Fall-out, Logograph, Logogriph, Offshoot, Secondary, Spin-off
**Sidekick** Right-hand man, Satellite
**Side-line** Bay, Demote, Hobby, Lye, Siding, Spur
**Sidepost** Cheek
**Sideshoot** Offset
**Side-step** Crab, Dodge, Evade, Hedge, Maori, Volt
**Side-track** Distract, Divert, Shunt
**Sidewalk** Crab, Footpath, Pavement
**Sideways** Askance, End-on, Indirect, Laterally, Laterigrade, Oblique
**Siding** Alliance, Byway, Lie, Lye, Spur, Turnout
**Sidle** Edge, Passage
**Siege (work), Siege engine** Alamo, Antioch, Antwerp, Beleaguer, Beset, Blockade, Bog, Charleston, Gherao, Heron, Investment, Khartoum, Ladysmith, Leaguer, Mafeking, Masada, Metz, Obsidional, Perilous, Pleven, Plevna, Poliorcetic, Ravelin, Sarajevo, Surround, Verdun, Vicksburg, Warsaw, Warwolf
**Sienese** Tuscan
**Sienna** Burnt, Raw
**Sierra** Range, S
**Sierra Leone** Mende
**Siesta** Nap, Noonday, Nooning
**Sieve, Sift(ing)** Analyse, Bolt(er), Boult(er), Bunting, Colander, Coliform, Cribble, Cribrate, Cribrose, Cullender, Eratosthenes, Ethmoid, Filter, Molecular, Rice, Riddle, Screen, Searce, Search, Separate, Siler, Strain, Sye, Tamis, Tammy, Tems(e), Trommel, Try, Winnow
**Sigh** Exhale, Heave, Lackaday, Long, Moan, Sithe, Sough, Suspire, Welladay
**Sight(ed)** Aim, Barleycorn, Bead, Conspectuity, Eye(ful), Eyesore, Glimpse, Ken, Long, Oculated, Panoramic, Peep, Prospect, Range, Rear, Riflescope, Scene, Scotopia, Second, See, Short, Spectacle, Taish, Telescopic, Twenty-twenty, Vane, →VIEW, Visie, Vision, Vista, Vizy, Vizzie
**Sight-screen** Eyelid
**Sightsee(ing), Sightseer** Do, Lionise, Observer, Rubberneck, Tourist, Tripper, Viewer
**Sign(ing), Signpost, Signs** Accidental, Ache, Addition, Air, Ale-pole, Ale-stake, Ampassy, Ampersand, Ankh, Apostrophe, Aquarius, Archer, Aries, Arrow, Auspice, Autograph, Badge, Balance, Beck, Beckon, Birth, Board, Brand, Bull, Bush, Call, Cancer, Capricorn, Caract, Caret, Character, Chevron, Clue, Coronis, Crab, Cross, Cue, Dactylology, Dele, Denote, Diacritic, Di(a)eresis, Diphone, Division, Dollar, DS, Earmark, Earth, Emblem, Endeixis, Endorse, Endoss, Enlist, Enrol(l), Equals, Evidence, Exit, Fascia, Fire, Fish, Gemini, Gesture, Goat, Grammalogue, Hallmark, Hamza(h), Harbinger, Harvey Smith, Hash, Hex, Hieroglyphic, Hint, Ideogram, Indian, Indicate, Indication, Indicium, Initial, INRI, Inscribe, Ivy-bush, Leo, Lexigram, Libra, Local, Logogram, Milepost, Milestone, Minus, Motion, Mudra, Multiplication, Negative, Neume, Nod, Notice, Obelisk, Obelus, Omen, Peace, Phraseogram, Pisces, Plus, Positive, Pound, Presa, Presage, Prodrome, Prodromus, Radical, Ram, Ratify, Red lattice, Rest, Rune, Sacrament, Sagittarius, Sain, Scorpio, Segno, Semeion, Semiotics, Shingle, Shorthand, Show, Sigil, Sigla, Signal, Star, Subscribe, Subtraction, Superscribe, Symbol, Symptom, Syndrome, Tag, Taurus, Tic(k)tac(k), Tilde, Titulus, Token, Trace, Triphone, Twins, Umlaut, V, Vestige, Virgo, Vital, Warison, Warning, Water, Waymark, Word, Zodiac
**Signal(ler)** Alarm, Aldis lamp, Alert, All clear, Amber, Assemble, Baud, Beacon, Beckon, Bell, Bleep, Bugle, Busy, Buzz, Call, Chamade, Code, Compander, Compandor, Cone, Cue, Detonator, Diaphone, Distant, Distress, Duplex, Earcon, Emit, Flag, Flagman, Flare, Flash, Fog, Gantry, Gesticulate, Gesture, Gong, Griffin, Gun, Hail, Harmonic, Heliograph,

Heliostat, Herald, Heterodyne, High sign, Hooter, Horse and hattock, Icon, Important, Indicator, Input, Interrupt, Interval, Knell, Luminance, Mark, Mase, Mayday, Megafog, Message, Modem, Morse, Navar, NICAM, Notation, Noted, Output, Password, Peter, Pheromone, Pinger, Pip, Pollice verso, Prod, Pulsar, Radio, Renowned, Reveille, Robot, Salient, Semaphore, Semiology, Simplex, Singular, Smoke, Snook, Sonogram, SOS, Spoiler, Squawk, Storm, Taps, Target, Tattoo, Tchick, Telegraph, Teles(e)me, Thumb, Tic(k)-tac(k), Time, Token, Traffic, Transmit, Troop, Vehicle-actuated, Very, Video, V-sign, Waff, Waft, Wave, Wave-off, Wigwag, Wink, Word, Yeoman

**Signature** Alla breve, Allograph, Autograph, By-line, Digital, Hand, John Hancock, John Henry, Key, Mark, Onomastic, Per pro, Sculpsit, Sheet, Specimen, Subscription, Tag, Time

**Signet** Ring, Seal, Sigil, Sphragistics

**Significance, Significant** Cardinal, Consequence, Cosmic, Emblem, Epochal, Ethos, Great, Impact, Important, Indicative, Key, Landmark, Magnitude, Major, Material, Matter, M(a)cGuffin, Meaningful, Milestone, Moment(ous), Notable, Noted, Noteworthy, Operative, Other, Paramount, Pith, Pregnant, Red-letter day, Salient, Special, Telling, Totemic, Weight

**Signify** Bemean, Denote, Imply, Indicate, Intimate, Matter, →**MEAN**, Represent

**Sign language** Ameslan, Finger spelling, Makaton, Semaphore, Tic(k)tac(k)

**Sikh(ism)** Granth, Kaccha, Kangha, Kara, Kesh, Khalsa, Kirpan, Mazhbi, Mechanised, Nanak, (Ranjit) Singh

**Silage** Haylage

**Silas** Uncle, Wegg

**Silence(r), Silent** Amyclaean, Choke-pear, Clam, Clamour, Conticent, Creepmouse, Dead air, Dolby, Dumbfound, Dumbstruck, Earplug, Gag, Hesychastic, Hist, Hush, Hushkit, Mim(budget), Muffler, Mum(p), Mumchance, Mute, Obmutescent, Omertà, Quench, Quiesce, →**QUIET**, Reticence, Shtoom, Shtum, Shush, Speechless, Squelch, Still, Sulky, Tace(t), Tacit(urn), Throttle, Tight-lipped, Tongue-tied, Unvoiced, Wheesh(t), Whis(h)t

**Silhouette** Contour, Outline, Planform, Profile, Shadow figure, Shadowgraph, Shape, Skyline

**Silica(te)** Albite, Allanite, Analcite, Andalusite, Chabazite, Chert, Cristobalite, Datolite, Diopside, Dioptase, Epidote, Fayalite, Float-stone, Gadolinite, Garnierite, Harmotome, Heulandite, Hiddenite, Humite, Iolite, Kieselguhr, Kyanite, Monticellite, Montmorillonite, Natrolite, Olivine, Opal, Pectolite, Penninite, Phillipsite, Pinite, Quartz, Rhodonite, Riebeckite, Saponite, Sard, Scapolite, Silex, Spodumene, Staurolite, Stishovite, Tridymite, Tripoli, Ultrabasic, Vermiculite, Vitreosil®, Vitreous, Zeolite

**Silicon** Chip, Moore's law, Si

**Silk(y), Silk screen** Alamode, Artificial, Atlas, Barathea, Blonde-lace, Brocade, Bur(r), Charmeuse®, Chenille, Chiffon, Cocoon, Corn, Crape, Crepe, Duchesse, Dupion, Faille, Fibroin, Filature, Filoselle, Florence, Florentine, Flosh, Floss, Flox, Foulard, Gazar, Gazzatum, Georgette, Gimp, Glossy, Grosgrain, Honan, KC, Kente, Kincob, Lustrine, Lustring, Lutestring, Madras, Makimono, Malines, Marabou(t), Matelasse, Mercery, Milanese, Moiré, Near, Ninon, Oiled, Organza, Ottoman, Paduasoy, Parachute, Peau de soie, Pongee, Prunella, Prunelle, Prunello, Pulu, QC, Raw, Samite, Sars(e)net, Satin, Schappe, Seal(ch), Sendal, Seric, Sericeous, Sericite, Serigraph, Shalli, Shantung, Sien-tsan, Sleave, Sle(i)ded, Sleek, Slipper satin, Smooth, Soft, Spun, Surah, Tabaret, Tabby, Taffeta, Tasar, Thistledown, Thrown, Tiffany, Tram, Tulle, Tussah, Tusseh, Tusser, Tussore, Vegetable, Velvet, Wild

**Silkworm (eggs), Silkworm disease** Bombyx, Eria, Graine, Multivoltine, Muscardine, Sericulture, Tussore

**Sill** Ledge, Straining, Threshold, Whin

**Silly, Silliness** Absurd, Anserine, Apish, Brainless, Buffer, Childish, Crass, Cuckoo, Daffy, Daft, Dandy, Ditsy, Divvy, Dotish, Drippy, Dumb(o), Dunce, Dweeb, Fatuous,

Feather-brained, Fluffy, Folly, Fool, Foolery, Footling, Frivolous, Goopy, Goosey, Gormless, Hen-witted, Idiotic, Imbecile, Inane, Inept, Infield(er), Liminal, Mid-off, Mid-on, Mopoke, Prune, Puerile, Scatterbrain, Season, Simple, Soft(y), Sot, Spoony, →**STUPID**, Tomfoolery, Tripe, Wacky, Wally

▷ **Silly** *may indicate* relating to a sill

**Silt** Alluvium, Deposit, Dregs, Land, Lees, Loess, Residue, Sullage, Varve

**Silver(skin)** Ag, Albata, Alpac(c)a, Arg(ent), Argyria, British plate, Cardecue, Cat, Cerargyrite, Diana's tree, Electroplate, Free, Fulminating, German, Grey, Horn, Long John, Luna, Nickel, One-legged, Pa(c)kfong, Pakt(h)ong, Parcel-gilt, Pegleg, Piastre, Pirate, Plate, Plateresque, Ruby, Stephanite, Sterling, Sycee, Talent, Thaler

▷ **Silver** *may indicate* a coin

**Silversmith** Demetrius, Lamerie, Plater

**Silver-tongued** Fluent

**Simian** Apelike, Catar(r)hine

**Similar(ity)** Affinity, Akin, Analog(ue), Analogical, Corresponding, Equivalent, Etc, Homoeoneric, Homogeneous, Homoiousian, Homologous, Homonym, Isomorphism, Kindred, →**LIKE**, Likeness, Likewise, Parallel, Patristic, Resemblance, Samey, Suchlike

**Simile** Epic, Homeric

**Similitude** Parable

**Simmer** Bubble, Poach, Seethe, Stew

**Simon** Bolivar, Cellarer, Magus, Peter, Pure, Simple

**Simper** Bridle, Giggle, Smirk

**Simple(r), Simplicity, Simplify, Simply** Aefa(u)ld, Afa(w)ld, Arcadian, Artless, Austere, Bald, Bare, Basic, Bog-standard, Breeze, Chaste, Crude, Daw, Doddle, Doric, →**EASY**, Eath(e), Elegant, Elemental, ESN, Ethe, Eyebright, Facile, Fee, Folksy, Gomeral, Gotham, Green, Gullish, Herb(alist), Herborist, Homespun, Idyllic, Incomposite, Inornate, Jaap, Japie, Mere, Moner(on), Naive(té), Naked, Niaiserie, No brainer, Noddy, One-fold, Open and shut, Ordinary, Paraphrase, Pastoral, Peter, Plain, Pleon, Provincial, Pure, Reduce, Renormalise, Rustic, Saikless, Sapid, Semplice, Sheer, Silly, Simon, Spartan, Straight, Streamline, Stupid, Suave, Tout court, Uncluttered, Understated, Unicellular, Unsophisticated, Woollen

**Simpleton** Abderite, Airhead, Cokes, Cuckoo, Daw, Duffer, Flat, Fool, Gaby, Galah, Gomeral, Gomeril, Greenhorn, Johnny, Juggins, Natural, Shot-clog, Spoon, →**STUPID PERSON**, Wiseacre, Zany

**Simulate(d), Simulating** Affect, Anti, Feign, Pretend, VR

**Simultaneous** Coincidental, Coinstantaneous, Contemporaneous, Synchronous, Together, Unison

**Sin(ful), Sinfulness** Aberrant, Accidie, Acedia, Actual, Anger, Avarice, Besetting, Bigamy, Capital, Cardinal, Covetousness, Crime, Deadly, Debt, Depravity, Envy, Err, Evil, Folly, Gluttony, Guile, Hamartiology, Harm, Hate, Impious, Impure, Lapse, Lust, Misdeed, Misdoing, Mortal, →**OFFENCE**, Original, Peccadillo, Piacular, Pride, Sacrilegious, Scape, Scarlet, Shirk, Sine, Sloth, Transgress, Trespass, Unrighteous, Venial, Vice, Wicked, Wrath, Wrong

**Sinai** Horeb, Mount

**Since** Ago, As, Cos, For, Meantime, Seeing, Sens, Sine, Sinsyne, Sith(en), Syne, Whereas, Ygo(e)

**Sincere(ly), Sincerity** Bona-fide, Candour, Earnest, Entire, Frank, Genuine, Heartfelt, Heartwhole, Honest, Open, Real(ly), Realtie, Simple-hearted, True, Verity, Whole-hearted

**Sinclair** Lewis, Upton

**Sine** Coversed, Versed

**Sinecure** Bludge, Commendam

**Sinew(y)** Fibre, Ligament, Nerve, String, Tendinous, Tendon

▸ **Sinful** *see* **SIN(FUL)**

**Sing(ing)** Antiphony, Barbershop, Bel canto, Belt out, Bhajan, Carol, Chant, Cheep, Chorus, Coloratura, Community, Cough, Croon, Crow, Descant, Diaphony, Diddle, Doo-wop, Glee club, Gorgia, Gregorian, Hum, Incant, Inform, Intone, Karaoke, Kirtan, La-la, Lilt, Lyricism, Melic, Parlando, Peach, Pen(n)illion, Pipe, Plainchant, Rand, Rant, Rap, Record, Render, Scat, Second(o), Serenade, Solmization, Spinto, Sprechgesang, Sprechstimme, Squeal, Tell, Thrum, Trill, Troll, Unitary, Vocalese, Warble, Woodshedding, Yodel

**Singapore** .sg

**Singe** Burn, Char, Scorch, Swale, Swayl, Sweal, Sweel

**Singer(s)** A cappella, Alto, Baillie, Baker, Balladeer, Bard, Baritone, Bass, Beatle, Bing, →**BIRD**, Blondel, Bono, Brel, Buffo, Callas, Canary, Cantabank, Cantatrice, Cantor, Car, Carreras, Caruso, Cash, Castrato, Chaliapin, Chanteur, Chanteuse, Chantor, Chauntress, Chazan, Cher, Chorister, Coloratura, Comprimario, Countertenor, Crooner, Dawson, Diva, Dylan, Ella, Elvis, Falsetto, Folk, Gigli, Glee club, Gleemaiden, Gleeman, Gobbi, Grass, Griot, Hammond, Haz(z)an, Heldentenor, Isaac, Kettle, Lark, Lauder, Lay clerk, Lead, Lind, Lorelei, Lulu, Mathis, Meister, Melba, Melodist, Mezzo, Minstrel, Opera, Orbison, Oscine, Patti, Pavarotti, Piaf, Pitti, Precentor, Prima donna, Qawwal, Rapper, Robeson, Semi-chorus, Session, Shrike, Sinatra, Siren, Snitch, Songman, Songstress, Soprano, Soubrette, Spinto, Stoolie, Succentor, Swan, Syren, Tatiana, Tenor, Tenure, Torch, Treble, Troubador, Vocalist, Voice, Wait, Warbler

**Single, Singly** Ace, Aefa(u)ld, Aefawld, Alone, Azygous, Bachelor, Celibate, Discriminate, EP, Exclusive, Feme sole, Haplo-, Individual, Lone, Matchless, Monact, Mono, Odd, One-off, One-shot, Only, Pick, Run, Seriatim, Sole, Solitary, Solo, Spinster, Unary, Unattached, Uncoupled, Uniparous, Unique, Unwed, Versal, Yin

**Single-cell** Protista

**Single-chambered** Monothalamous

**Singlestick** Sword

**Singlet** Tunic, Vest

**Singleton** Lonely heart, Stag

▷ **Singleton** *may indicate* an old recording, e.g. Forty-five, Seventy-eight

**Singular(ity)** Curious, Especial, Exceptional, Extraordinary, Ferly, Naked, Odd, Once, One, Peculiar, Queer(er), Rare, S, Strange, →**UNIQUE**, Unusual

**Singultus** Hiccup

**Sinister** Bend, Dark, Dirke, Evil, L, Left, Lh, Louche, →**OMINOUS**, Port, Rasputin, Spooky, Svengali

**Sink(ing), Sinker, Sunk(en)** Abandon, Basin, Bidet, Bog, Cadence, Carbon, Cower, Deep-set, Delapse, Depress, Descend, Devall, Dip, Down, Drain, Draught-house, Drink, Drop, Drown, Ebb, Embog, Flag, Founder, Gravitate, Heat, Hole, Immerse, Invest, Jarbox, Kitchen, Lagan, Laigh, Lapse, Ligan, Merger, Pad, Poach, Pot, Prolapse, Put(t), Relapse, Sag, Scupper, Scuttle, Set, Settle, Shaft, Shipwreck, Slump, Steep-to, Stoop, Sty, Submerge, Subside, Swag, Swamp, Titanic

**Sinner** Evildoer, Malefactor, Offender, Reprobate, Trespasser

**Sinuous** Curvy, Eely, Ogee, Slinky, Snaky, Wavy, Winding

**Sinus** Cavity, Ethmoidal, Frontal, Maxillary, Recess, Sphenoidal

**Sioux** Dakota, Sitting Bull

**Sip(ping)** Delibate, Hap'orth, Libant, Sample, Sowp, Sup, Taste, Tiff(ing), Tift

**Siphon** Draw, Rack, Soda, Suck, Transfer

**Sir** Dan, Dom, K, Knight, Kt, Lord(ing), Milord, Sahib, Signor, Sirrah, Stir, Stirra(h), Towkay, Tuan

**Sire** Ancestor, Beget, Father, Get

**Siren** Alarm, Alert, Charmer, Delilah, Diaphone, Enchanter, Femme fatale, Hooter, Houri, Leucosia, Ligea, Lorelei, Mermaid, Oceanides, Parthenope, Salamander, Shark, Teaser, Temptress, Vamp

**Sirenian** Dugong, Lamantin, Manatee, Manati, Sea-cow

**Sirius** Sothic
**Sirloin** Backsey
**Sirree** Bo
**Sisal** Agave
**Siskin** Aberdevine, Bird, Finch
**Sister(s)** Anne, Beguine, Carmelite, Fatal, Lay, Minim, → **NUN**, Nurse, Out, Pleiades, Religeuse, Sib, Sibling, Sis, Sob, Soul, Swallow, Theatre, Titty, Ugly, Ursuline, Verse, Ward, Weak, Weird
**Sistine** Chapel, Sextus
**Sisyphean** Uphill
**Sit(ter), Sitting** All-night, Bestride, Clutch, Dharna, Duck, Gaper, Gimme, Incubate, Lime, Lit de justice, Model, MP, Perch, Pose, Reign, Represent, Roost, Séance, Sederunt, Sejeant, Sesh, Session, Squat
**Site, Siting** Area, Arpa, Brochure, Brownfield, Building, Camp, Caravan, Chat room, Cobweb, Feng shui, Gap, Greenfield, Home-page, Locality, Location, Lot, Mirror, Orphan, Pad, Place, Plot, Ramsar, Rogue, Sacred, Silo, Spot, Stance, Visie, Vizy, Vizzie, World Heritage
**Situation** Affair, Ballpark, Berth, Can of worms, Cart, Case, Catch, Catch-22, Chicken and egg, Cliff-hanger, Contretemps, Cow, Dilemma, Drama, Galère, Hole, Hornet's nest, Hot seat, Job, Knife-edge, Lie, Location, Lurch, Matrix, Mire, Nail-biter, Niche, Novel, No-win, Office, Outcome, Place, Plight, Position, Post, Scenario, Scene, Schmear, Schmeer, Seat, Set-up, Shebang, Showdown, State of play, Status quo, Sticky wicket, Strait, Stringalong, Where, Worst case
**Six(th)** Digamma, French, German, Half(-a)dozen, Hexad, Italian, Neapolitan, Prime, Sax, Senary, Sestett(e), Sextet, Sice, Size, Vau, VI
**Six counties** NI
**Six days** Hexa(e)meron
**Six feet, Six-footer** Fathom, Hornet, Insect, Miurus, Termite
**Sixpence** Bender, Kick, Mill, Slipper, Tanner, Tester(n), Testril(l), Tizzy, VID, VIP, Zack
**Sixteen** Hexadecimal, Sweet
**Sixty** Degree, Sexagesimal, Shock, Threescore
**Size(able)** Amplitude, Area, Bulk, Calibre, Clearcole, Countess, Demy, Displacement, → **EXTENT**, Format, Girth, Glair, Glue, Guar, Gum, Imperial, Measure, Particle, Party, Physique, Plus, Pot(t), Princess, Proportion, Tempera, Tidy, Trim
**Sizzle** Fry, Hiss, Scorch
**Skate(r), Skateboard(er), Skateboarding, Skating** Blade, Bob, Cheap, Choctaw, Cousins, Curry, Dean, Fakie, Figure, Fish, Free, Grommet, Half-pipe, Hot dog, In-line, Maid, Mohawk, Ollie, Overacid, Rink, Rock(er), Roller, Rollerblade®, Runner, Short-track, Sit spin, Speed, Torvill
**Skedaddle** Beat it, Scarper, Scram, Shoo, Vamoose
**Skein** Hank, Hasp
**Skeleton, Skeletal** Anatomy, Atomy, Axial, Bones, Cadaverous, Cadre, Cage, Coenosteum, Coral, Corallite, Corallum, Family, Framework, Hydrostatic, Key, Ossify, Outline, Scenario, Sclere, Tentorium
**Sketch(y)** Bozzetto, Cameo, Character, Charade, Charcoal, Croquis, Delineate, Diagram, Doodle, Draft, → **DRAW**, Ébauche, Esquisse, Illustration, Limn, Line, Map out, Maquette, Modello, Outline, Pencilling, Pen portrait, Playlet, Pochade, Précis, Profile, Representation, Rough, Skit, Study, Summary, Tenuous, Thumbnail, Trick, Vague, Vignette, Visual
**Skew** Agee, Ajee, Oblique, Sheer, Squint, Swerve, Veer
**Skewer** Brochette, En brochette, Kebab, Prong, Spear, Spit, Transfix
**Ski(er), Skiing** Aquaplane, Carving, Free ride, Glide, Glissade, Hot-dog, Langlauf, Mogul, Nordic, Schuss, Schussboomer, Super G, Telemark, Vorlage, Wedeln
**Skid** Aquaplane, Drift, Fishtail, Jackknife, Side-slip, Slew, Slide, Slip, Slither, Spinout

▷ **Skidding** *may indicate* an anagram

**Skiff** Canoe, Dinghy, Outrigger

**Skilful, Skill(ed)** Ability, Able, Accomplished, Ace, Address, Adept, Adroit, Art, Artistic, Bravura, Canny, Chic, Competence, Craft, Deacon, Deft, Demon, Dextrous, Endowment, Enoch, Expertise, Facility, Feat, Finesse, Flair, Gleg, Habile, Hand, Handicraft, Handy, Hend, Hot, Ingenious, Keepy-uppy, Knack, Know-how, Knowing, Lear(e), Leir, Lere, Masterly, Masterpiece, Mastery, Mean, Métier, Mistery, Mystery, Mystique, Practised, Proficient, Prowess, Quant, Resource, Savvy, Science, Skeely, Sleight, Soft, Speciality, Tactics, Talent, Technic, Technique, Touch, Trade, Transferable, Trick, Versed, Virtuoso, Wise, Workmanship

**Skim** Cream, Despumate, Flit, Glide, Graze, Plane, Ream, Scan, Scud, Scum, Skiff, Skitter

**Skimp** Cut corners, Restrict, Scamp, Scrimp, Stint

**Skin(s)** Ablate, Agnail, Armour, Bark, Basan, Basil, Bingo wing, Box-calf, Bronzed, Calf, Callus, Case, Cere, Chevrette, Coat, Corium, Cortex, Crackling, Cutaneous, Cuticle, Cutis, Deacon, Deer, Derm(a), Dermatome, Dermis, Dewlap, Disbark, Ectoderm, Enderon, Envelope, Epicanthus, Epicarp, Epidermis, Eschar, Excoriate, Exterior, Fell, Film, Flaught, Flay, Flench, Flense, Flinch, Forel, Fourchette, Goldbeater's, Hangnail, Hide, Integra®, Jacket, Kip, Kirbeh, Leather, Membrane, Muktuk, Nebris, Nympha, Pachyderm, Parfleche, Patagium, Peau, Peel, Pell, Pellicle, Pelt, Perinychium, Plew, Plu(e), Prepuce, Pteryla, Rack, Rape, Rind, Scalp, Scarfskin, Serosa, Shagreen, Shell, Shoder, Spetch, Strip, Swindle, Tegument, Tulchan, Veneer, Water-bouget, Wattle, Woolfell

**Skin disease, Skin problem, Skin trouble** Boba, Boil, Buba, Causalgia, Chloasma, Chloracne, Cowpox, Cradle cap, Cyanosis, Dartre, Dermatitis, Dermatosis, Dyschroa, EB, Ecthyma, Eczema, Erysipelas, Exanthem(a), Favus, Flay, Framboesia, Gum rash, Herpes, Hives, Ichthyosis, Impetigo, Leishmaniasis, Leucodermia, Lichen, Livedo, Lupus vulgaris, Maidism, Mal del pinto, Mange, Miliaria, Morphew, Morula, Patagium, Pellagra, Pemphigus, Pinta, Pityriasis, Prurigo, Pseudofolliculitis, Psoriasis, Pyoderma, Rash, Red-gum, Ringworm, Rosacea, Rose-rash, St Anthony's fire, Sapego, Scabies, Sclerodermia, Scurvy, Seborrhoea, Serpigo, Strophulus, Telangiectasia, Tetter, Tinea, Vaccinia, Verruca, Verruga, Vitiligo, Xanthoma, Xerodermia, Xerosis, Yaws, Yawy

**Skinflint** Cheapo, Dryfist, Miser, Niggard, Pinch-gut, Scrooge, Tightwad

**Skinful** Drunk, Sausage

**Skinhead** Not, Punk, Scalp

**Skink** Seps

**Skinless** Ecorché

**Skinny** Angular, Barebone, Bony, Cutaneous, Dermal, Emaciate, Lean, Scraggy, Thin, Underweight, Weed

**Skint** Broke, Ghat, Penniless, Stony

**Skip(ped), Skipper** Boss, Bound, Caper, Captain, Cavort, Drakestone, Dumpster, Elater, Frisk, Hesperian, Jump, Jumping-mouse, Lamb, Luppen, Miss, Omit, Patroon, Ricochet, Roo, Sand, Saury, Scombresox, Spring, Tittup, Trip, Trounce(r)

**Skirl** Humdudgeon, Pibroch, Pipe, Screigh

**Skirmish(er)** Brawl, Brush, Dispute, Escarmouche, Fray, Pickeer, Spar, Tirailleur, Velitation, Voltigeur

**Skirt(ing)** Bases, Bell, Border, Bouffant, Bypass, Cheongsam, Circle, Coat, Crinoline, Culotte(s), Dado, Dirndl, Edge, Fil(l)ibeg, Fringe, Fustanella, Fustanelle, Girl, Gore, Grass, Harem, Hobble, Hoop, Hug, Hula, Kilt, Lamboys, Lava-lava, Marge, Mini, Mopboard, Pareo, Pareu, Pencil, Peplum, Petticoat, Philibeg, Pinafore, Piu-piu, Plinth, Puffball, Ra-ra, Rim, Sarong, Sidestep, Stringboard, Tace, Tail, Taslet, Tasse(t), Tonlet, Tube, Tutu, Valance, Washboard, Wrapover, Wrap(a)round

**Skit** Lampoon, Parody, Sketch

**Skittish** Coy, Curvetting, Frisky, Restless, Skeigh

**Skittle(s)** Bayle, Bowl, Cheese, Kail(s), Kayle, Kingpin, Ninepin, Pin, Spare

**Skive(r)** Absentee, Laik, Malinger, Scrimshank, Shirk, Skewer, Swing the lead

**Skivvy** Drudge, Slave

**Skrimshank** Bludge, Skive

**Skua** Boatswain, Bos'n

**Skulk** Loiter, Lurk, Mooch, Shool

**Skull** Brainpan, Bregma(ta), Calvaria, Cranium, Death's head, Fontanel, Harnpan, Head,
Head case, Malar, Maz(z)ard, Obelion, Occiput, Pannikell, Phrenology, Scalp, Sinciput,
Vault, Yorick

**Skullcap** Ya(r)mulka, Yarmulke, Zucchetto

**Skunk** Atoc, Atok, Ferret, Hognosed, Polecat, Pot, Striped, Surfeit, Teledu, Zoril(lo),
Zorino

**Sky(-high), Sky-tinctured, Skywards** Air, Azure, Blue, Canopy, Carry,
Cloud-kissing, El Al, E-layer, Element, Empyrean, Ether, Firmament, Heaven, Lift, Lob,
Loft, Mackerel, Occident, Octa, Okta, Raise, Rangi, Uranus, Welkin

**Sky-diver** Para

**Skylark** Aerobatics, Bird

**Skylight** Abat-jour, Aurora, Comet, Companion, Lunette, Star

**Skyline** Horizon, Rooftops

**Sky-pilot** Chaplain, Vicar

**Slab(s)** Briquette, Bunk(er), Cake, Cap(e)stone, Chunk, Dalle, Hawk, Ledger, Marver,
Metope, Mihrab, Mud, Paver, Paving-stone, Planch, Plank, Sclate, Sheave, Slate, Slice,
Stela, Stelene, Tab, Tablet, Tile, Wood-wool

**Slack(en), Slacker, Slackness** Abate, Careless, Clock-watch, Crank, Dilatory, Dross,
Ease (off), Easy-going, Flaccid, Glen, Idle, Inanition, Languor, Lax(ity), Lazybones,
Let-up, Loose, Malinger, Nerveless, Off-peak, Off-season, Relax, Release, Remiss, Shirk,
Skive, Slatch, Slow, Surge, Unscrew, Unwind, Veer

**Slade** Dean

**Slag** Badmouth, Basic, Calx, Cinder, Dross, Foamed, Lava, Scoria, Scum, Sinter, Tap
cinder, Tart

**Slake** Abate, Cool, Quench, Refresh, Satisfy

**Slalom** Super-G

**Slam, Slammer** Cocktail, Crash, Criticise, Dad, Grand, Little, Pan(dy), Poetry, Small,
Sock, Swap, Swop, Vole, Wap

**Slander(ous)** Asperse, Backbite, Badmouth, Calumny, Defame, Derogatory, Detraction,
Disparage, Infame, Insult, Libel, Malediction, Malign, Mendacity, Missay, Mud,
Mudslinging, Obloquy, Sclaunder, Smear, Traduce, Vilify, Vilipend, Vitriol

**Slang** Abuse, Argot, Back, Berate, Blinglish, Cant, Colloquial, Ebonics, Flash, Jargon,
Lingo, Nadsat, Parlyaree, Polari, Rhyming, Slate, Tsotsitaal, Verlan, Vernacular, Zowie

**Slant(ed), Slanting** Angle, Asklent, Atilt, Bevel, Bias, Brae, Cant, Careen,
Catty-cornered, Chamfer, Clinamen, Diagonal, Escarp, Oblique, Prejudice, Rake, Slew,
→ **SLOPE**, Splay, Squint, Talus, Tilt, Virgule

**Slap(ping)** Clatch, Clout, Cuff, Daub, Happy, Make-up, Pandy, Piston, Sclaff, Scud,
Skelp, Smack, Spat, Swipe, Tape, Twank, Warpaint

**Slapdash** Careless, Hurried, Messy, Random

**Slaphead** Bald pate

**Slash(ed)** Chive, Cut, Diagonal, Gash, Hack, Jag, Lacerate, Laciniate, Leak, Oblique,
Rash, Rast, Reduce, Scorch, Scotch, Separatrix, Slice, Slit, Solidus, Stroke, Virgule,
Wee

**Slat(s)** Fish, Jalousie, Louvre, Spline, Stave

**Slate, Slaty, Slating** Alum, Berate, Blast, Calm, Cam, Caum, Countess, Credit, Criticise,
Decry, Diatribe, Double, Duchess, Duchy, Enter, Flak, Griseous, Imperial, Killas,
Knotenschiefer, Lady, List, Log, Marchioness, Ottrelite, Pan, Peggy, Polishing, Princess,
Queen, Rag(g), Rap, Roof, Run down, Schalstein, Shingle, Slat, Small, Small lady, Tabula,
Tomahawk, Viscountess

**Slater** Hellier, Insect

**Slattern** Bag, Besom, Bisom, Drab, Drazel, Frump, Mopsy, Ragbag, Ragdoll, Slammakin, Slammerkin, Sloven, Slummock, Sozzle, Traipse, Trapes, Trollop

**Slaughter(house), Slaughterer** Abattoir, Behead, Bleed, Bloodshed, Butcher, Carnage, Decimate, Hal(l)al, Holocaust, Immolation, Jhatka, Kill, Mactation, →MASSACRE, Off, Scupper, Shambles, S(c)hechita(h), Shochet, Smite, Trounce

**Slav, Slavonic** Bohunk, Bulgar, Croat, Czech, Czechic, Jack, Kulak, Lusatia, Polabian, Russian, Serb, Sorb, Toil, Wend(ic)

**Slave(ry), Slaves, Slavish** Addict, Aesop, Aida, Androcles, Barracoon, Blackbird, Bond, Bond(s)man, Bondwoman, Bordar, Boy, Caliban, Coffle, Contraband, Dogsbody, Drudge, Drug, Dulocracy, Dulosis, Enthralment, Esne, Galley, Gibeonite, Helot, Hierodule, Jack, Mameluke, Mamluk, Marmaluke, Maroon, Minion, Nativity, Odali(s)que, Odalisk, Peasant, Pr(a)edial, Rhodope, Serf, Servitude, Spartacus, Terence, Theow, Thersites, Thete, Thrall, Toil, Topsy, Vassal, Villein, Wage, Wendic, White, Yoke

**Slave-driver, Slave-owner** Assam, Sweater, Task-master

**Slaver** Bespit, Dribble, Drivel, Drool, Slabber, Slobber, Spawl, Spit

**Slay(er), Slaying** Destroy, Execute, Ghazi, →KILL, Mactation, Murder, Quell, Saul, Slaughter, Transport

**Sleazy, Sleaze** Affair, Flimsy, Red-light, Scuzzy, Seamy, Sordid, Squalid, Tack, Thin

**Sled(ge), Sleigh(-ride)** Bob, Dog train, Dray, Hurdle, Hurley-hacket, Kibitka, Komatic, Komatik, Lauf, Luge, Mud-boat, Mush, Polack, Pulk(h)(a), Pung, Rocket, Skeleton bob(sleigh), Skidoo®, Slipe, Stoneboat, Tarboggin, Toboggan, Train, Travois

**Sleek** Bright, Shine, Silky, Smarm, Smooth, Smug, Streamlined

**Sleep, Sleeper(s), Sleepiness, Sleeping, Sleepy** Beauty, Bed, Bivouac, Blet, Bundle, Bye-byes, Car, Catnap, Coma, Couchette, Crash, Cross-sill, Cross-tie, Dormant, Dormient, Dormouse, Doss, Doze, Drop off, Drowse, Earring, Endymion, Epimenides, Flop, Forty winks, Gowl, Gum, Hibernate, Hypnology, Hypnos, Kip, Land of Nod, Lassitude, Lethargic, Lie, Morpheus, Nap, Narcolepsy, Narcosis, Nod, Oscitation, Over, Paradoxical, Petal, Policeman, Pop off, Psychopannychism, REM, Repast, Repose, Rest, Rip Van Winkle, Roomette, Rough, Sandman, Seven, Shuteye, Siesta, Skipper, Sleepover, Sloom, Slumber, Snooz(l)e, Somnolent, Sopor(ose), Sownd, Spine bashing, Swone, Tie, Torpid, Twilight, Wagon-lit, Wink, Zeds, Zizz

**Sleeping place** Bed, Cot, Dormitory, Kang, Roost

**Sleeping sickness** Trypanosomiasis

**Sleepless** Wake-rife, Wauk-rife

**Sleep-walking** Noctambulation, Somnambulism

**Sleet** Graupel, Hail, Virga

**Sleeve (opening)** Arm(hole), Balloon, Batwing, Bishop's, Bush, Cap, Collet, Cover, Dolman, Gatefold, Gigot, Gland, Kimono, Lawn, Leg-o'-mutton, Liner, Magyar, Manche, Pagoda, Pudding, Querpo, Raglan, Record, Sabot, Scye, Slashed, Trunk, Turnbuckle, Wind

**Sleeveless** Exomis

▶ **Sleigh** *see* SLED(GE)

**Sleight** Artifice, Conjury, Cunning, Dodge, Legerdemain, Trick

**Slender(ness)** Asthenic, Ectomorph, Elongate, Exiguity, Exility, Fine, Flagelliform, Flimsy, Gracile, Jimp, Leptosome, Loris, Narrow, Rangy, Skinny, Slight, Slim, Small, Spindly, Stalky, Styloid, Svelte, Swank, Sylph, Tenuous, Thready, Trim, Waif

**Sleuth** Bloodhound, Detective, Dick, Eye, Holmes, Lime-hound, Lyam(-hound), Lyme(-hound), Poirot, Wimsey

**Slew** Number, Skid, Slide, Twist

**Slice** Cantle, Chip, Collop, Cut, Doorstep, Fade, Frustrum, Lop, Piece, Rasure, Round, Sector, Segment, Share, Sheave, Shive, Slab, Sliver, Spoon, Tranche, Wafer, Whang

▷ **Slice of** *may indicate* a hidden word

**Slick** Adroit, Glim, Mealy-mouthed, Oil, Sheen, Sleeveen, Smooth, Suave

**Slide** Barrette, Chute, Cursor, Diapositive, Drift, Ease, Fader, Glissando, Hair,
Helter-skelter, Hirsle, Hollow-ground, Ice-run, Illapse, Lantern, Mount, Portamento,
Pulka, Schuss, Scoop, Ski, Skid, Skite, Slip, Slippery dip, Slither, Snowboard, Tailskid,
Telescope, Transparency, Volplane

**Slight(ly)** Affront, Belittle, Cold shoulder, Cut, Detract, Disparage, Disregard, Disrespect,
Elfin, Facer, Flimsy, Fragile, Halfway, Insult, Minor, Misprise, Neglect, Nominal,
Partial, Pet, Petty, Puny, Rebuff, Remote, Scorn, → **SLENDER**, Slim, Slimsy, Slur, Small,
Smattering, Sneaking, Snub, Sparse, Stent, Subtle, Superficial, Sylphine, Tenuous, Thin,
Tiny, Trifling, Trivial, Wee, Wispy

**Slim(mer)** Attenuate, Bant, Cut, Diet, Jimp, Macerate, Reduce, Slender, Slight, Svelte,
Sylph, Tenuous, Thin, Trim, Weight-watcher

**Slime, Slimy** Glair, Glareous, Glit, Gorydew, Guck, Gunk, Mother, Muc(o)us,
Myxomycete, Oily, Ooze, Sapropel, Slabbery, Slake, Sludge, Uliginous

**Sling** Balista, Catapult, Drink, Fling, Hang, Parbuckle, Prusik, Shy, Singapore, Support,
Toss, Trebuchet

**Slink** Lurk, Proll, Prowl, Skulk, Slope

**Slip(ped), Slipping, Slips** Avalanche, Blunder, Boner, Boob, Come home, Coupon,
Cover, Cutting, Deteriorate, Disc, Docket, Drift, EE, Elapse, Elt, Engobe, Error,
Escape, Faux pas, Fielder, Form, Freudian, Glide, Glissade, Infielder, Label, Landslide,
Lapse, Lapsus linguae, Lath, Lauwine, Leash, Lingerie, Lingual, Mistake, Muff, Nod,
Overbalance, Oversight, Parapraxis, Peccadillo, Petticoat, Pink, Plant, Prolapse, Ptosis,
Quickset, Rejection, Relapse, Run, Scape, Sc(h)edule, Scoot, Set, Shim, Sin, Ski, Skid,
Skin, Skite, Slade, Slidder, Slide, Slither, Slive, Spellican, Spillican, Stumble, Surge,
Ticket, Trip, Tunicle, Underskirt, Unleash, Wage(s)

**Slipper(s)** Baboosh, Babouche, Babuche, Baffies, Banana skin, Calceolate, Carpet,
Chappal, Eel, Errorist, Japanese, Mocassin, Moccasin, Moyl, Muil, Mule, Pabouche,
Pampootie, Pantable, Pantof(f)le, Panton, Pantoufle, Pump, Rullion, Runner, Ski, Sledge,
Sneaker, Sock

**Slippery** Eely, Elusive, Errorist, Foxy, Glid, Icy, Lubric, Shady, Shifty, Skidpan, Slick, Slimy

**Slipshod** Careless, Haphazard, Hurried, Jerry, Lax, Slapdash, Slatternly, Sloppy, Slovenly,
Toboggan

▷ **Slipshod** *may indicate* an anagram

**Slit** Buttonhole, Cranny, Cut, Fent, Fissure, Fitchet, Gash, Gill, Loop, Pertus(at)e, Placket,
Placket-hole, Race, Rit, Scissure, Spare, Speld(er), Unseam, Vent

**Slithy** Tove

**Sliver** Flake, Fragment, Moslings, Rove, Shard, Shaving, Slice, Splinter, Trace

**Sloan** Snib, Snub

**Slob(ber)** Couch potato, Drool, Lout, Slaver, Smarm, Wet

**Sloe(thorn)** Blackthorn, Slae

**Slog(ger)** Drag, Grind, Logwork, Strike, Swink, Swot, Thump, Traipse, Tramp, Trape,
Trauchle, Trudge, Yacker, Yakka, Yakker

**Slogan** Amandla, Byword, Catchphrase, Catchword, Chant, Cry, Jai Hind, Jingle,
Masakhane, Mot(to), Murdabad, Nayword, Phrase, Rallying-cry, Slughorn(e), Splash,
Street cry, Tapline, Warcry, Watchword

**Sloop** Cutter, Hoy, Ship

**Slop(pily), Slops, Sloppy** Careless, Cop(per), Gardyloo, Jordeloo, Lagrimoso, Lowse,
Madid, Muck, Mushy, Policeman, Remiss, Rossers, Rozzers, Schmaltz, Schmaltzy,
Shower, Slapdash, Slipshod, Sloven, Slushy, Sop, Sozzly, Spill, Swill, Unmethodical,
Untidy, Weepie

**Slope(s), Sloping** Acclivity, Angle, Anticline, Bahada, Bajada, Bank, Batter, Bevel,
Borrow, Borstal(l), Brae, Breast, Camber, Chamfer, Cle(e)ve, Cuesta, Declivity, Delve,
Diagonal, Dip, Dry, Escarp, Escarpment, Fastigiate, Fla(u)nch, Foothill, Geanticline,
Glacis, Grade, Gradient, Heel, Hill, Hipped, Incline, Isoclinical, Kant, Lean, Natural,
Nursery, Oblique, Pediment, Pent, Periclinal, Piste, Pitch, Rake, Ramp, Rollway, Scarp,

Schuss, Scrae, Scree, Shelve, Sideling, Skewback, Slade, Slant, Slippery, Slipway, Splay, Steep, Stoss, Talus, Tilt, Verge, Versant, Weather

▷ **Sloppy** *may indicate* an anagram

**Slosh(y)** Dowse, Fist, Splash, Wet

**Slot(ted)** Expansion, God, Graveyard, Groove, Hasp, Hesp, Hole, Key, Keyway, Letterbox, Mortice, Mortise, Niche, Seat, Slit, Swanmark, Time

**Sloth(ful)** Accidie, Acedia, Ai, Bradypus, Edentate, Ground, Idle, Inaction, Indolent, Inertia, Lazy, Lie-abed, Megatherium, Mylodon, Slugabed, Sweer(t), Sweered, Sweir(t), Three-toed, Torpor, Unau

**Slot machine** One-armed bandit, Pokey, Pokie

**Slouch** Loll, Lop, Mooch, Mope, Slump

**Slough(ing)** Cast, Despond, Ecdysis, Eschar, Exfoliate, Exuviae, Lerna, Marish, Marsh, Mire, Morass, Paludine, Shed, Shorten, Shuck, Swamp

**Slovakia** .sk

**Sloven(ly)** Careless, Dag(gy), D(r)aggle-tail, Dishevelled, Down-at-heel, Frowsy, Grobian, Jack-hasty, Mawkin, Rag-doll, Ratbag, Slaister, Slammakin, Slammerkin, Slattern, Sleazy, Slipshod, Slubberdegullion, Slubberingly, Slummock, Slut, Streel, Untidy

**Slow(er), Slowing, Slowly, Slow-witted** Adagio, Allargando, Andante, Andantino, Behindhand, Brady, Brake, Broad, Calando, Calf, Crawl, Dawdle, Decelerate, Deliberate, Dilatory, Dim, Draggy, Dull, Dumka, ESN, Flag, Gradual, Halting, Hesitant, Inchmeal, Insulse, Lag, Langram, Larghetto, Largo, Lash, Lassu, Late, Lean-witted, Leisurely, Lentamente, Lentando, Lento, Lifeless, Loiter, Losing, Meno mosso, Obtuse, Pedetentous, Rall(entando), Rein, Reluctant, Retard, Ribattuta, Rit, Ritardando, Ritenuto, Roll-out, Slack, Slug, Sluggish, Snail's pace, Snaily, Solid, Stem, Tardigrade, Tardive, Tardy, Tardy-gaited, Thick

**Slowcoach** Slowpoke, Slug

**Slow-match** Portfire

**Sludge** Activated, Gunge, Mire, Muck, Sapropel, Slob

**Slug(s)** Ammo, Bêche-de-mer, Blow, Brain, Bullet, Cosh, Draught, Drink, Gast(e)ropod, Grapeshot, Knuckle sandwich, Lead, Limaces, Limax, Linotype®, Mollusc, Nerita, Pellet, Shot, Snail, Tot, Trepang

**Sluggard** Drone, Lazy, Lie-abed, Lusk, Unau

**Sluggish** Dilatory, Drumble, Idler, Inactive, Inert, Jacent, Lacklustre, Laesie, Languid, Lazy, Lentor, Lethargic, Lug, Phlegmatic, Saturnine, Sleepy, →SLOW, Stagnant, Tardy, Torpid, Unalive

**Sluice** Aboideau, Aboiteau, Drain, Floodgate, Gutter, Koker, Penstock, Rinse, Sasse

**Slum** Basti, Bustee, Busti, Cabbagetown, Cardboard city, Favela, Ghetto, Rookery, Shanty, Shantytown, Slurb, Warren

**Slumber** Doze, Drowse, Nap, Nod, Sleep, Sloom, Snooze

**Slump** Decrease, Depression, Deteriorate, Dip, Flop, Recession, Sag, Sink, Slouch, Sprawl, Stoop

**Slur(ring)** Defame, Drawl, Innuendo, Libel, Ligature, Opprobrium, Slight, Smear, Synaeresis, Tie

**Slush(y)** Bathos, Boodle, Bribe, Drip, Money, Mush, Pap, Slop, Slurry, Snow-broth, Sposh, Swash, Swashy

**Slut** Candle, Dollymop, Draggle-tail, Dratchell, Drazel, Floosie, Harlot, Pucelle, Puzzle, Slattern, Sow, Tart, Traipse, Trapes, Trollop

**Sly, Slyness** Canny, Christopher, Clandestine, Coon, Covert, Cunning, Foxy, Furtive, Guile, Leery, Peery, Reynard, Secretive, Shifty, Slee, Sleekit, Sleeveen, Slicker, Sneaky, Stallone, Stealthy, Subtle, Surreptitious, Tinker, Tod, Tricky, Weasel, Wily

▷ **Slyly** *may indicate* an anagram

**Smack(er)** Aftertaste, Buss, Cuff, Flavour, Foretaste, Fragrance, Hooker, Kiss, Klap, Lander, Lips, Pra(h)u, Relish, Salt, Saut, Skelp, Slap, Slat, Smatch, Smell, Smouch, Soupçon, Spank, Spice, Splat, Tack, →TANG, Taste, Thwack, Tincture, Trace, Twang, X, Yawl

**Small (thing), Smaller, Smallest amount** A minori, Ateleiosis, Atom, Bantam,
Beer, Bijou, Bittie, Bitty, Centesimal, Chickenfeed, Chotta, Collops, Crumb, Curn, Denier,
Diddy, Diminutive, Dinky, Dreg, Drib, Driblet, Elfin, Elfish, Endomorphic, Few, Fleabite,
Fry, Grain, Haet, Ha'it, Half-pint, Handful, Hint, Hobbit, Holding, Hole-in-the-wall,
Hyperosmia, Insect, Ion, Itsy-bitsy, Knurl, Leet, Leetle, Lepton, Lilliputian, Limited, Lite,
→ **LITTLE**, Lock, Low, Meagre, Mean, Measly, Microscopic, Midget, Mignon, Miniature,
Minikin, Minority, Minute, Mite, Modest, Modicum, Neap, Nominal, Nurl, Peerie,
Peewee, Petit(e), Petty, Pickle, Pigmean, Pigmy, Pink(ie), Pinky, Pint-size, Pittance,
Pocket, Poky, Poujadist, Puckle, Rap, Reduction, Runt, S, Santilla, Scantling, Scattering,
Scrump, Scrunt, Scruple, Scut, Shoebox, Shortarse, Shrimp, Single, Skerrick, Slight, Slim,
Smattering, Smidge(o)n, Smidgin, Smithereen, Smout, Snippet, Soupçon, Sprinkling,
Spud, Squirt, Stim, Stunted, Subminiature, Suspicion, Tad, Teenty, Thin, Tidd(l)y, Tiny,
Titch(y), Tittle, Tot(tie), Totty, Trace, Trivial, Unheroic, Wee, Weedy, Whit
**Smallest** Least, Minimal, Runt
**Smallholder, Smallholding** Croft, Nursery, Rundale, Share-cropper, Stead
**Small-minded(ness)** Parvanimity, Petty
**Smallness** Exiguity, Exility, Paucity
**Smallpox** Alastrim, Variola
**Smarm(y)** Oil, Smoothie, Unctuous
**Smart(en), Smartest, Smartness** Ache, Acute, Alec, Astute, Best, Bite, Burn, Chic,
Classy, Clever, Cute, Dandy, Dapper, Dressy, Elegant, Flash, Flip, Fly, Groom, Gussy up,
Jemmy, Kookie, Kooky, Larnery, Natty, Neat, New pin, Nifty, Nip, Nobby, Outwit, Pac(e)y,
Pacy, Pert, Posh, Preen, Primp, Prink, Pusser, Raffish, Rattling, Ritzy, Saucy, Slick, Sly,
Smoke, Smug, Snappy, Snazzy, Soigné(e), Spiff, Sprauncy, Sprightly, Spruce, Sprush, Spry,
Sting, Street cred, Stylish, Swagger, Sweat, Swish, Tiddley, Tippy, Titivate, Toff, Trendy,
U, Well-groomed, Wiseacre, Zippy
**Smash(ed), Smasher, Smashing** Atom, Bingle, Brain, Break, Cannon, Corker,
Crush, Demolish, Devastate, Dish, Drunk, Forearm, High, Jarp, Jaup, Kaput, Kill, Lulu,
Plastered, Ram, Shatter, Shiver, Slam, Squabash, Squiffy, Stave, Super, Terrific, Tight,
To-brake, → **WRECK**
▷ **Smash(ed)** *may indicate* an anagram
**Smear** Anoint, Assoil, Bedaub, Besmirch, Blur, Borm, Calumniate, Cervical, Clam, Daub,
Defile, Denigrate, Discredit, Drabble, Enarm, Gaum, Gild, Gorm, Lick, Mud, Oil, Oint,
Pap(anicolaou), Pay, Plaster, Slairg, Slaister, Slake, Slander, Slather, Slime, Slubber, Slur,
Smalm, Smarm, Smudge, Splodge, Spredd, Sully, Swipe, Teer, Traduce, Wax
**Smell(ing), Smelly** Aroma, Asafoetida, BO, Cacodyl, Caproate, Effluvium, Empyreuma,
Exhale, F(o)etid, Fetor, Fug, Funky, Gale, Gamy, Graveolent, Guff, Hing, Honk, Hum,
Ionone, Mephitis, Miasm(a), Ming, Musk, Nidor, Niff, Nose, Odour, Olent, Olfact(ory),
Osmatic, Osmeterium, Osmic, Perfume, Pong, Ponk, Pooh, Rank, Redolent, Reech, Reek,
Ripe, Sar, Savour, → **SCENT**, Sensory, Smack, Sniff, Snifty, Snoke, Snook, Snuff, Steam,
Stench, Stifle, Stink, Tang, Whiff
**Smelling salts** Ammonia, Sal volatile
**Smelt(ing)** Atherinidae, Melt, Salmon, Scoria, Sparling, Speiss, Sperling, Spirling
**Smile(s), Smiling, Smily** Agrin, Beam, Cheese, Emoticon, Favour, Gioconda, Grin,
Rictus, Samuel, Self-help, Simper, Smirk, Watch the birdie
**Smirk** Grimace, Simper
**Smite, Smitten** Assail, Bash, Enamoured, Epris(e), Hit, Strike, Strook
**Smith** Adam, Artisan, Farrier, FE, Forger, Hammerman, Mighty, Stan, Vulcan, Wayland
**Smithy** Forge, Smiddy, Stithy, Studdie
**Smock** Blouse, Chemise, Drabbet, Gather, Overall, Shift, Slop, Smicket
**Smog** Electronic, Photochemical
**Smoke(r), Smoking, Smoky** Arbroath, Blast, Bloat, Censer, Chain, Chillum, Chimera,
Chimney, → **CIGAR(ETTE)**, Cure, Drag, Exhaust, Fog, Fuliginous, Fume, Fumigate, Funk,
Gasper, Hemp, Incense, Indian hemp, Inhale, Kipper, Latakia, London ivy, Lum, Lunt,

Mainstream, Manil(l)a, Nicotian, Opium, Panatella, Passive, Peat reek, Peaty, Pother, Pudder, Puff, Reech, Reefer, Reek, Reest, Roke, Secondary, Sidestream, Smeech, Smeek, Smirting, Smoor, Smother, Smoulder, Smudge, Snout, Tear, Tobacconalian, Toke, Vapour, Viper, Water, Whiff, Wreath

**Smoke-hating** Misocapnic

**Smokestack** Funnel

**Smoking-room** Divan

**Smollett** Tobias

▸ **Smooch** *see* SMOUCH

**Smooth(er), Smoothly** Alabaster, Bald, Bland, Brent, Buff, Cantabile, Chamfer, Clean, Clockwork, Debonair, Dress, Dub, Easy, Even, Fettle, File, Flat, Fluent, Fretless, Glabrous, Glare, Glass paper, Glassy, Glib, Goose, Iron, Legato, Level, Levigate, Linish, Mealy-mouthed, Mellifluous, Mellow, Millpond, Oil, Plane, Planish, Plaster, Pumice, Rake, Roll, Rub, Sad-iron, Sand(er), Satiny, Scrape, Shiny, Sleek, Slick, Slickenslide, Slithery, Slur, Smug, Snod, Sostenuto, Straighten, Streamlined, Suave, Swimmingly, Terete, Terse, Trim, Unwrinkled, Urbane

**Smooth-haired** Lissotrichous

**Smother** Burke, Choke, Dampen, Muffle, Oppress, Overlie, Smoor, Smore, Smoulder, Stifle, Suppress

**Smouch** Cheat, Kiss, Lallygag, Lollygag, Neck

**Smoulder** Burn, Seethe

**Smudge** Blur, Dab, Offset, Slur, Smear, Smooch, Stain

**Smug** Complacent, Conceited, Gloating, Goody-goody, Goody-two-shoes, Neat, Oily, Pi, Sanctimonious, Self-satisfied, Trim

**Smuggle(d), Smuggler, Smuggling** Body-packer, Bootleg, Contraband, Contrabandist, Coyote, Donkey, Fair trade, Free trader, Gunrunning, Moonshine, Mule, Owler, Rum-runner, Run, Secrete, Sneak, Steal, Traffic

**Smut(ty)** Bawdy, Black, Blight, Blue, Brand, Burnt-ear, Coom, Crock, Filth, Grime, Racy, Soot, Speck, Stinking

**Smut-fungus** Basidia, Ustilago

**Snack** Bever, Bhaji, Bhelpuri, Bite, Blintz, Bombay mix, Breadstick, Breakfast bar, Brunch, Burger, Butty, Canapé, Chack, Choc bar, Churro, Crisps, Croque monsieur, Crudités, Doner kebab, Elevenses, Enchilada, Entremets, Finger buffet, Four-by-two, Gorp, Goujons, Hoagie, Hors (d'oeuvres), Hot dog, Knish, Meze, Munchies, Nacho, Nacket, Nibble, Nigiri, Nocket, Nooning, Nuncheon, Padkos, Pasty, Pie, Piece, Ploughman's lunch, Popcorn, Pork scratchings, Rarebit, Refreshment, Samo(o)sa, Sandwich, Sarney, Sarnie, Savoury, Scroggin, Sloppy joe, Small chop, Smorgasbord, Spring roll, Sushi, Tapa, Taste, Toast(y), Trail mix, Vada, Voidee, Wada, Wrap, Zakuska

**Snaffle** Bit, Bridoon, Grab, Purloin

**Snag** Aggro, Anoint, Catch, Contretemps, Drawback, Hindrance, Hitch, Impediment, Knob, Nog, Obstacle, Remora, Rub, Snubbe, Stub, Stumbling block, Tear

**Snail(s)** Brian, Cowrie, Cowry, Dew, Dodman, Escargot, Garden, Gasteropod, Giant African, Heliculture, Helix, Hodmandod, Limnaea, Lymnaea, Nautilus, Nerite, Planorbis, Pond, Ramshorn, Roman, Slow, Slug, Strombus, Unicorn-shell, Univalve, Wallfish, Whelk, Wing

**Snake, Snaking** Drag, Meander, →SERPENT, Slither, Wind

---

**SNAKES**

| 3 letters: | Sea | Bull | Milk |
|---|---|---|---|
| Asp | | Corn | Naga |
| Boa | 4 letters: | Habu | Naia |
| Kaa | Apod | Hoop | Naja |
| Rat | Boma | King | Pine |

Pipe
Rock
Seps
Tree
Whip
Worm

**5 letters:**
Adder
Apode
Blind
Brown
Cobra
Congo
Coral
Cribo
Elaps
Glass
Grass
Hydra
Krait
Mamba
Mulga
Racer
Tiger
Viper
Water

**6 letters:**
Anguis
Carpet

Clotho
Daboia
Dipsas
Dugite
Elaeis
Ellops
Flying
Garter
Gopher
Indigo
Karait
Python
Ratbag
Ribbon
Smooth
Taipan
Thread
Uraeus
Vasuki

**7 letters:**
Anguine
Camoodi
Coluber
Diamond
Hognose
Langaha
Rattler
Reptile

**8 letters:**
Anaconda
Cerastes
Jararaca
Jararaka
Joe Blake
Lachesis
Mocassin
Moccasin
Ophidian
Pit-viper
Plumber's
Ringhals
Ringneck
Rinkhals
Slowworm
Spitting
Squamata
Sucurujú
Surucucu
Takshaka

**9 letters:**
Berg-adder
Blue-racer
Boomslang
Coachwhip
Hamadryad
Horsewhip
King cobra
Puff-adder

River jack
Sand viper

**10 letters:**
Bandy-bandy
Blacksnake
Bush-master
Copperhead
Crotalidae
Death-adder
Dendrophis
Fer-de-lance
Homorelaps
Massasauga
Sidewinder

**11 letters:**
Aesculapian
Amphisbaena
Constrictor
Cottonmouth
Diamond-back
Horned viper
Massasauger

**13 letters:**
Russell's viper
Water moccasin

**17 letters:**
Timber rattlesnake

**Snake-charmer** Lamia
**Snake-in-the-grass** Peacher, Rat, Traitor
**Snake-root** Bistort, Senega, Snakeweed, Virginia, White
**Snap(per), Snappy, Snap up** Abrupt, Alligator, Autolycus, Bite, Break, Brittle, Camera, Click, Cold, Cold wave, Crack, Crocodile, Cross, Curt, Edgy, Fillip, Gator, Girnie, Glitch, Glom, Gnash, Grab, Hanch, Impatient, Knacker, Knap, Livery, Mugshot, Photo, Photogene, Retort, Scotch, Snack, Snatch, Spell, Still, Swift, Tetchy, Vigour
**Snare** Bait, Benet, Engine, Enmesh, Entrap, Gin, Grin, Honeytrap, Hook, Illaqueate, Inveigle, Mantrap, Net, Noose, Rat-trap, Springe, Springle, Toil, →**TRAP**, Trapen, Trepan, Web, Weel, Wire
**Snarl(ing)** Chide, Complicate, Cynic, Enmesh, Girn, Gnar(l), Gnarr, Growl, Grumble, Knar, Knot, Snap, Tangle, Yirr
**Snatch** Claucht, Claught, Excerpt, Fragment, Glom, Grab, Kidnap, Nip, Pluck, Race, Ramp, Rap, Rase, Raunch, Refrain, Snippet, Song, Spell, Steal, Strain, Take, Tweak, Wheech, Whip up, Wrap, Wrest
▷ **Snatch** *may indicate* the first letter of a word
**Snazzy** Cat
**Snead** Snath
**Sneak(y)** Area, Carry-tale, Clipe, Clype, Creep, Furtive, Infiltrate, Inform, Lurk, Mumblenews, Nim, Peak, Scratch, Scunge, Skulk, Slink, Slip, Slither, Slyboots, Snitch, Snoop, Split, Steal, Stoolie, Surreptitious, Tell(-tale), Underhand
**Sneer(ing)** Barb, Critic, Cynical, Fleer, Gibe, Jeer, Sardonic, Scoff, Smirk, Snide, Twitch

**Sneeze (at), Sneezing** Atishoo, Errhine, Neese, Neeze, Ptarmic, Scorn, Sternutation

**Snick** Click, Cut, Edge, Glance

**Snicker** Snigger, Te-hee, Titter, Whinny

**Snide** Bitchy, Shand

**Sniff, Sniffle** E-nose, Inhale, Nose, Nursle, Nuzzle, Scent, Smell, Snivel, Snort, Snuffle, Vent, Whiff

**Snifter** Noggin

**Snigger** Giggle, Laugh, Snicker, Snirtle, Titter, Whicker

**Snip(pet)** Bargain, Cert, Clip, Cut, Doddle, Piece, Sartor, Snatch, Snick, Tailor

**Snipe(r)** Backbite, Bird, Bushwhacker, Criticise, Dunlin, Franc-tireur, Gunman, Gutter, Heather-bleat(er), Heather-bluiter, Heather-blutter, Pick off, Potshot, Scape, Shoot, Walk, Wisp

**Snitch** Conk, Grass, Konk, Nose

**Snivel** Blubber, Snotter, Snuffle, Weep, Whine

**Snob(bery), Snobbish** Cobbler, Crachach, Crispin, Dic(k)ty, Genteel, High-hat, Inverted, La-di-da, Prudish, Pseud, Scab, Side, Sloane, Snooty, Snow, Soutar, Souter, Sowter, Toffee-nose, Vain, Vamp

**Snooker** Crucible, Frame, Pool, Stimie, Stimy, Stym(i)e, Thwart

**Snoop(er)** Curtain-twitcher, Eavesdrop, Meddle, Nose, Pry, Tec

**Snooty** Bashaw, Pooh Bah, Sanctimonious, Snob(bish)

**Snooze** Calk, Caulk, Dove, Dover, Doze, Nap, Nod, Siesta, Sleep

**Snore, Snoring** Rhonchus, Rout, Snort, Snuffle, Stertorous, Zz

**Snort(er)** Dram, Drink, Grunt, Nare, Nasal, Roncador, Snore, Toot

**Snot(ty)** Mucoid

**Snout** Bill, Boko, Cigar, Gasper, Gruntie, Informer, Muzzle, Nose, Nozzle, Proboscis, Schnozzle, Tinker, Tobacco, Wall

**Snow(y), Snowdrift, Snowstorm** Brig, Buran, Cocaine, Coke, Corn, Cornice, Crud, Firn, Flake, Flurry, Graupel, Half-pipe, Heroin, Horse, Marine, Mogul, Neve, Nival, Niveous, Nivose, Noise, Oncome, Onding, Powder, Red, Sastruga, Sleet, Spotless, Stall, Virga, White-out, Wintry, Wreath, Yellow, Zastruga

**Snowball** Accelerate, Cramp-bark, Cumulative, Escalate, Guelder-rose, Increase, Magnify, Opulus, Pelt, Rose

**Snowdrop** Avalanche, Eirlys, Galanthus

**Snowflake(s)** Graupel, Leucojum, St Agnes' flower

**Snow-goose** Wav(e)y

**Snowman** Abominable, Eskimo, Junkie, Sherpa, Yeti

**Snowmobile** Sno-cat

**Snowshoe** Bear paw, Racket, Racquet, Ski

**Snub** Brush off, Cut, Diss, Go-by, Lop, Pug, Put-down, Quelch, Rebuff, Reproof, Retroussé, Set-down, Short, Slap, Slight, Sloan, Sneap, Snool, Wither

**Snuff(le)** Asarabacca, Douse, Dout, Errhine, Extinguish, Maccabaw, Maccaboy, Maccoboy, Ptarmic, Pulvil, Rappee, Smother, Snaste, Sneesh(an), Sniff, Snift, Snotter, Snush, Stop, Tobacco, Vent

**Snuffbox** Anatomical, Mill, Mull, Ram's horn

**Snug(gery), Snuggle** Burrow, Comfy, Cose, →**cosy**, Couthie, Couthy, Croodle, Cubby(hole), Cuddle, Embrace, Intime, Lion, Neat, Nestle, Nuzzle, Rug, Snod, Tight, Trim

**So** Argal, Ergo, Forthy, Hence, Sae, Sic(h), Sol, Such, Therefore, This, Thus, True, Very, Yes

**Soak(ed)** Bate, Bath(e), Beath, Bewet, Bloat, Blot, Buck, Cree, Deluge, Drench, Drent, Drink, Drook, Drouk, Drown, Drunk, Duck, Dunk, Embay, Embrue, Fleece, Grog, Imbrue, Impregnate, Infuse, Inundate, Lush, Macerate, Marinate, Mop, Oncome, Permeate, Plastered, Rait, Rate, Ret(t), Rinse, Rob, Saturate, Seep, Sipe, Sog, Sop, Sorb, Souce, Souse, Sows(s)e, Steep, Sype, Thwaite, Toper, Waterlog, Wet, Wino

**Soap(y), Soap opera** Brookside, Cake, Carbolic, Castile, Cleanser, Coronation St, Dallas, Eluate, ER, Flake, Flannel, Flattery, Glass, Green, Hard, Joe, Lather, Lux®, Marine, Metallic, Moody, Mountain, Pears®, Pinguid, Saddle, Safrole, Saponaceous, Saponin, Sawder, Serial, Shaving, Slime, Soft, Spanish, Suds, Sudser, Sugar, Syndet, Tablet, Tall-oil, Tallow, The Bill, Toheroa, Toilet(ry), Washball, Windsor, Yellow

**Soapstone** French chalk, Spanish chalk, Steatite, Talc

**Soar(ing)** Ascend, Essorant, Fly, Glide, Hilum, Plane, Rise, Tower, Zoom

**Sob (stuff)** Blub(ber), Boohoo, Goo, Gulp, Lament, Singult, Singultus, Snotter, Wail, Weep, Yoop

**Sober(sides), Sobriety** Abstemious, Austere, Calm, Demure, Pensive, Sedate, Staid, Staidness, Steady, Steddy, TT

**Sobriquet** Byname, Cognomen, Nickname, To-name

**So-called** Alleged, Nominal, Soi-disant

**Soccer** Footer, Footie

**Sociable, Sociability** Affable, Cameraderie, Chummy, Clubby, Cosy, Couthie, Extravert, Extrovert, Folksy, Friendly, Genial, Gregarious, Mixer, Phatic

**Social(ise)** Apres-ski, Barn dance, Convivial, Hobnob, Hui, Interact, Mingle, Mix, Musicale, Phatic, Salon, Tea-dance, Thé dansant, Yancha

**Socialism, Socialist** Ba'(a)th, Champagne, Chartist, Dergue, Engels, Fabian, Fourierism, Guild, Hardie, ILP, International, Karmathian, Lansbury, Left(y), Marxism, Menchevik, Menchevist, Menshevik, National, Nihilism, Owen(ist), Owenite, Parlour pink, Pasok, Pinko, Red, Revisionist, St Simonist, Sandinista, Second international, Spartacist, Utopian, Webb

**Socialite** Deb, It girl, Jet set, Mingler, Silvertail, Sloane

**Social worker** Almoner

**Society** Affluent, Alternative, Association, Band of Hope, Beau monde, Benefit, Black Hand, Body, Boxer, Brahma, Brahmo, Broederbond, Building, Camorra, Carbonari, Casino, Choral, Class, Club, College, Company, Conger, Consumer, Co-op, Cooperative, Culture, Danite, Debating, Defenders, Dorcas, Duddieweans, Eleutheri, Elite, Elks, Fabian, Fashion, Fellowship, Foresters, Freemans, Freemasons, Friendly, Friends, Glee club, Grand monde, Grotian, Group, Guarantee, Guilds, Haut monde, Hetairia, High, High life, Humane, Illuminati, Institute, Invincibles, John Birch, Ku-Klux-Klan, Kyrle, Law, Linnean, Lodge, Mafia, Malone, Masonic, Mass, Mau-Mau, Ménage, Molly Maguire, National, Oddfellows, Open, Oral, Orangemen, Oratory, Order, Oxford Union, Permissive, Phi Beta Kappa, Plunket, Plural, Pop, Provident, Repertory, Ribbonism, Risk, Rosicrucian, Rotary, Royal, S, Samaj, School, Secret, Soc, Sodality, Somaj, Soroptomist, Sorority, Stakeholder, Surveillance, Tammany, Theosophical, Toc H, Ton, Tong, Triad, U, Whiteboy, World

**Sociologist** Weber

**Sock(s)** Almond, Argyle, Argyll, Biff, Bobby, Bootee, Digital, Dipso, Hose(n), Lam, Leg warmer, Punch, Rock, Slipper, Slosh, Strike, Tabi, Thwack, Trainer, Walk, Wind

**Socket** Acetabulum, Alveole, Bayonet, Budget, Eyepit, Gudgeon, Hollow, Hosel, Hot shoe, Jack, Keeper, Lampholder, Nave, Nozzle, Orbit, Ouch, Outlet, Plug, Pod, Point, Port, Power-point, Screw, Serial port, Shoe, Strike, Torulus, Whip

**Sock-eye** Nerka, Salmon

**Socle** Tube, Zocco(lo)

**Socrates, Socratic** Ironist, Maieutics, Sage

**Sod** Clump, Delf, Delph, Divot, Fail, Gazo(o)n, Mool, Mould, Mouls, Scraw, Sward, Turf

**Soda, Sodium** Acmite, Arfvedsonite, Baking, Barilla, Bicarb, Caustic, Club, Cream, Keratophyre, La(u)rvikite, Na, Natrium, Natron, Reh, Saleratus, Splash, Thenardite, Trona, Washing

**Sodomy** Vice anglais

**Sofa** Canapé, Chaise longue, Chesterfield, Couch, Daybed, Divan, Dos-à-dos, Dosi-do, Lounge, Ottoman, Settee, Squab, Tête-à-tête

**So far (as)** As, As yet, Quoad, Until, Yonder

**Soft(en), Softener, Softening, Softly** Amalgam, Anneal, Assuage, B, BB, Blet, Boodle, Calm, Casefy, Cedilla, Cottony, Cree, Cushion, Dim, Dolcemente, Doughy, Ease, Emolliate, Emollient, Flabby, Furry, Gentle, Hooly, Humanise, Intenerate, Lash, Lax, Lenient, Lenition, Limp, Low, Macerate, Malacia, Malax(ate), Malleable, Mardarse, Mardie, Mease, Mellow, Melt, Mild, Milksop, Mitigate, Modify, Modulate, Mollify, Mollities, Morendo, Mulch, Mush(y), Mute, Neale, Nesh, Option, P, Pad(ded), Palliate, Pastel, Piano, Plushy, Porous, Propitiate, Rait, Rate, Relent, Scumble, Sentimental, Silly, Slack, Soda, Spongy, Squashy, Squidgy, Squishy, Sumph, Talcose, Temper, →TENDER, Tone, Velvet, Weak, Yielding

**Softness** Lenity

▸ **Software** *see* COMPUTER PROGRAM(S)

**Sog(gy)** Goop, Sodden

**Soil(ed), Soily** Acid, Adscript, Agrology, Agronomy, Alkali(ne), Alluvium, Azonal, Backfill, Bedraggle, Begrime, Bemire, Beray, Besmirch, Blacken, Chernozem, Clay, Cohesive, Contaminate, Defile, Desecrate, Desert, Dinge, Dirt(y), Discolour, Duricrust, Eard, Earth, Edaphic, Edaphology, Frictional, Gault, Glebe, Grey, Grimy, Ground, Gumbo, Hotbed, Humus, Illuvium, Intrazonal, Lair, Land, Latosol, Lithosol, Loam, Loess, Lome, Loss, Marl, Mire, Mo(u)ld, Mool, Mud, Mulch, Mull, Night, Ordure, Peat, Ped, Pedalfer, Pedocal, Pedogenic, Pedology, Phreatic, Planosol, Podsol, Podzol, Pollute, Prairie, Pure, Regar, Regolith, Regosol, Regur, Rendzina, Rhizosphere, Root-ball, Sal, Sedentary, Smudge, Smut, Solonchak, Solonetz, Solum, Soot, Stain, Stonebrash, Sub, Sully, Tarnish, Tash, Terrain, Terricolous, Tilth, Top, Tschernosem, Udal, Umber, Virgin, Yarfa, Yarpha, Zonal

**Soirée** Drum, Levee, Musicale

**Sojourn** Abide, Respite, Stay, Tabernacle, Tarry

**Sol** G, Soh, Sun

**Solace** Cheer, Comfort, Relief

**Solar(ium)** Heliacal, Tannery

**Sold** Had

**Solder** Braze, Join, Spelter, Tin, Weld

**Soldier(s)** Ant, Chocolate, Detachment, Fighter, Gyrene, Insect, Old Bill, Persevere, Unknown, Warmonger

---

## SOLDIERS

| 2 letters: | 4 letters: | 5 letters: | Miner |
|---|---|---|---|
| GI | Army | Anzac | Nahal |
| OR | Corp | Bluff | Nizam |
| | Foot | Botha | Pandy |
| 3 letters: | Fyrd | Brave | Perdu |
| ATS | Impi | Cadet | Poilu |
| Bod | Jock | Choco | Pongo |
| Ded | Kern | Corps | Sabre |
| Inf | Levy | El Cid | Sammy |
| Joe | Line | Emmet | Sepoy |
| NCO | Merc | Fagot | Soger |
| POW | Naik | GI Joe | Sowar |
| Reb | Peon | Gippo | Sweat |
| SAS | Post | Grunt | Tommy |
| Tin | Rank | Gyppo | Turco |
| Toy | Swad | Jawan | Uhlan |
| Vet | | Kerne | Wagon |
| | | Miles | |

**6 letters:**
Alpini
Amazon
Arnaut
Askari
Atkins
Banner
Caimac
Chocko
Cohort
Cornet
Detail
Digger
Dugout
Evzone
Faggot
Galoot
Gurkha
Hussar
Knight
Lancer
Nasute
Non-com
Perdue
Rajput
Ranger
Ranker
Reiter
Rutter
Sodger
Swaddy
Tercio
Troops
Yankee
Yeoman
Zouave

**7 letters:**
Arnaout
Brigade
Bullman
Charlie
Chindit
Colonel
Colours
Cossack
Dog-face
Draftee
Dragoon
Enomoty
Federal
Flanker
General
Goorkha

Grim dig
Guardee
Hobbler
Hoplite
Jackman
Lashkar
Lobster
Maniple
Man o' war
Orderly
Palikar
Pandoor
Pandour
Peltast
Phalanx
Pikeman
Platoon
Private
Rat-tail
Redcoat
Regular
Retread
Saddler
Samurai
Sebundy
Snarler
Soldado
Sowaree
Sowarry
Squaddy
Tarheel
Templar
Terrier
Trooper
Vedette
Velites
Veteran
Warrior

**8 letters:**
Achilles
Bluecoat
Borderer
Buff-coat
Caimacam
Centinel
Centonel
Chasseur
Commando
Crusader
Doughboy
Engineer
Fugleman
Fusilier

Greycoat
Guerilla
Guerrilla
Immortal
Infantry
Iron Duke
Ironside
Janizary
Kaimakam
Linesman
Martinet
Palatine
Partisan
Piou-piou
Point man
Regiment
Rifleman
Sentinel
Serafile
Silladar
Spearman
Squaddie
Stalhelm
Strelitz
Timariot
Trencher
Warhorse
Woodbind
Woodbine
Yardbird

**9 letters:**
Battalion
Blue beret
Butter-nut
Cannoneer
Carbineer
Carbinier
Centinell
Centonell
Centurion
Desert fox
Desert rat
Fencibles
Field-gray
Field-grey
Gregarian
Grenadier
Guardsman
Irregular
Janissary
Johnny Reb
Kitchener
Legionary
Men-at-arms

Mercenary
Minuteman
Missileer
Musketeer
Paratroop
Pistoleer
Rapparree
Reformado
Reservist
Signaller
Subaltern
Targeteer
Train-band
Turcopole
Voltigeur
Volunteer
Whitecoat
Wild Geese

**10 letters:**
Bersaglier
Bombardier
Buff-jerkin
Cameronian
Campaigner
Carabineer
Carabinier
Cataphract
Contingent
Cuirassier
Foederatus
Fuzzy-wuzzy
Galloglass
Green beret
Hackbuteer
Lansquenet
Militiaman
Serviceman
Stalhelmer

**11 letters:**
Bashi-Bazouk
Bersagliere
Confederate
Continental
Forlorn-hope
Gallowglass
Imperialist
Johnny Rebel
Landsknecht
Leatherneck
Legionnaire
Rank and file
Territorial

| *12 letters:* | Old moustache | *14 letters:* | *16 letters:* |
|---|---|---|---|
| Cannon-fodder | Stormtrooper | Miles gloriosus | Old Contemptibles |

▷ **Soldiers** *may indicate* bread for boiled eggs

**Sole, Solitaire, Solitary** Alone, Anchoret, Anchorite, Antisocial, Ascetic, Asocial, Clump, Convex, Corporation, Crepe, Dover, Dropped, Eremite, Fish, Friendless, Incommunicado, Independent, Inner, Lemon, Lonesome, Meered, Megrim, Merl, Meunière, Monastical, Monkish, One, On ice, Only, Pad, Palm, Patience, Pegboard, Pelma, Planta(r), Plantigrade, Platform, Recluse, Sand, Scaldfish, Single(ton), Skate, Slip, Smear-dab, Tap, Thenar, Tread, Unique, Vibram®, Vola

**Solemn** Agelast, Austere, Devout, Earnest, Grave, Gravitas, Impressive, Majestic, Owlish, Po-faced, Sacred, Sedate, Serious, Sober, Sobersides, Sombre

**Solent** Lee

**Solicit** Accost, Approach, Ask, Attract, Bash, →BEG, Canvass, Commission, Cottage, Drum up, Importun(at)e, Plead, Ply, Proposition, Speer, Speir, Touch, Tout, Woo

**Solicitor(s)** Advocate, Attorney, Avoué, Beggar, Canvasser, Chugger, Courtier, Crown agent, Hallanshaker, Law-agent, Lawyer, Moll, Notary, Official, Side-bar, SL, Tout, Trull, Writer to the Signet, WS

**Solid(arity), Solidify, Solidity** Burly, Cake, Chunky, Clot, Clunky, Compact, Comradeship, Concrete, Cone, Congeal, Conoid, Consolidate, Cube, Cylinder, Dense, Dilitancy, Enneahedron, Esprit de corps, Ethal, Firm, Foursquare, Freeze, Frustrum, Fuchsin(e), Gel, Hard, Holosteric, Impervious, Kotahitanga, Masakhane, Merbromin, Octahedron, Pakka, Parallelepiped, Petrarchan, Platonic, Polyhedron, Prism, Pucka, Pukka, Purin(e), Robust, Rockhewn, Set, Skatole, Square, Squatly, Stable, Staunch, Stereoscopic, Stilbene, Sturdy, Sublimate, Substantial, Tetrahedron, Thick (set), Trusty, Unanimous

**Solipsism** Egotism, Panegoism

▸ **Solitary** *see* SOLE

**Solitude** Privacy, Seclusion

**Solo** Aria, Cadenza, Cavatine, Concertante, Lone, Monodrama, Monody, Ombre, One-man, Recit, Scena, Single-handed, Unaided, Variation

**Solon** Sage

**So long** Cheerio, Ciao, Goodbye, Tata, Toodle pip

**Solstice** Summer, Tropic, Winter

**Soluble** Alkaline, Consolute, Poristic, Surfactant

**Solution** Acetone, Alkali, Ammonia, Amrit, →ANSWER, Austenite, Benedict's, Brine, Collodion, Colloidal, Dakin's, Dobell's, Éclaircissement, Electrolyte, Elixir, Emulsion, Eusol, Fehling's, Final, Fix, Formalin, Hairspray, Key, Leachate, Limewater, Liquid, Lixivium, Lye, Normal, Oleoresin, Oleum, Rationale, Reducer, Remedy, Ringer's, Rinse, Rubber, Saline, Solid, Solvent, Soup, Standard, Suspensoid, Tincture, Titrate, Tone, Viscose

▷ **Solution** *may indicate* an anagram

**Solve(d), Solver** Absolve, Assoil, Calculate, Casuist, Clear, Crack, Decode, Holmes, Loast, Loose, Panacea, Read(er), Suss out, Troubleshoot, Unclew, Undo, Unriddle, Work

**Solvent** Above water, Acetaldehyde, Acetone, Afloat, Alcahest, Aldol, Alkahest, Anisole, Aqua-regia, Banana oil, Benzene, Chloroform, Cleanser, Cyclohexane, Cyclopentane, Cymene, Decalin, Denaturant, Diluent, Dioxan(e), Eleunt, Eluant, Ether, Funded, Furan, Heptane, Hexane, Ligroin, Megilp, Menstruum, Methanol, Methylal, Naphtha, Nitromethane, Paraldehyde, Picoline, Protomic, Pyridine, Sound, Stripper, Terebene, Terpineol, Terts, Tetrachloromethane, Thinner, Thiophen, Toluene, Toluol, Trike, Trilene, Turpentine, White spirit

**Somalia** .so

**Sombre** Dark, Drab, Drear, Dull, Funereal, Gloomy, Grave, Morne, Morose, Subfusc, Subfusk, Sullen, Triste

**Some** Any, Arrow, Ary, Certain, Divers, Few, One, Part, Portion, Quota, Sundry, These, They, Wheen

▷ **Some** *may indicate* a hidden word

**Somebody** Dignitary, Name, Notable, One, Person, Quidam, Someone, Tuft, → **VIP**

**Somehow** Somegate

▷ **Somehow** *may indicate* an anagram

**Somersault** Back-flip, Barani, Catherine wheel, Deltcher, Flip(-flap), Flip-flop, Handspring, Pitchpole, Pitchpoll

**Somerset** Maugham, Protector

**Something** Aliquid, Article, Chattel, Item, Matter, Object, Summat, What, Whatnot

**Sometime(s)** Erstwhile, Ex, Former, Intermittent, Occasional, Off and on, Otherwhiles, Quondam

**Somewhat** Bit, -ish, Mite, Partly, Quasi, Quite, Rather, Relatively, Slightly, Summat, To a degree, Wheen

**Somewhere** Somegate

**Somnolence** Drowsiness

**Son** Boy, Descendant, Disciple, Epigon(e), Fils, Fitz, Lad, Lewis, M(a)c, Native, Offspring, Prodigal, Progeny, Scion

**Sonata** Minuet, Moonlight, Trio, Waldstein

**Song** Air, Amoret, Anthem, Antistrophe, Aria, Ariette, Art, Aubade, Ayre, Ballad, Ballant, Ballata, Barcarol(l)e, Belter, Berceuse, Bhajan, Blues, Brindisi, Burden, Burthen, Cabaletta, Calypso, Cancionero, Cantata, Cante hondo, Cante joudo, Canticle, Canticum, Cantilena, Cantion, Canzona, Canzone, Canzonet(ta), Carmagnole, Carol, Catch, Cavatina, Chanson, Cha(u)nt, Chantey, Come-all-ye, Conductus, Corn-kister, Corroboree, Cycle, Descant, Dirge, Dithyramb, Ditty, Drinking, Duettino, Dynasty, Elegy, Epithalamion, Epithalamium, Fado, Fit, Fitt, Flamenco, Folk, Forebitter, Gaudeamus, Gita, Glee, Gorgia, Gradual, Hillbilly, Hum, Hymeneal, Hymn, Internationale, Jug(-jug), Lament, Lay, Lied(er), Lilt, Lullaby, Lyric, Madrigal, Magnificat, Marseillaise, Matin, Melic, Melisma, Melody, Mento, Minnesang, Negro spiritual, Noel, Number, Nunc dimittis, Oat, Octastichon, Paean, Pane, Part, Patter, Penillion, Plain, Plaint, Plantation, Pop, Prick, Prothalamion, Prothalamium, Psalm, Qawwali, Rap, Recitativo, Red Flag, Relish, Rhapsody, Rispetto, Roulade, Roundelay, Rune, Scat, Scolion, Sea-shanty, Secular, Serenade, Shanty, Shosholoza, Siren, Sirvente, Skolion, Solo, Sososholoza, Spiritual, Stave, Stomper, Strain, Strophe, Swan, Taps, Tenebrae, Theme, Torch, Trill, Tune, Tyrolienne, Vaudeville, Villanella, Volkslied, Waiata, War, Warble, Wassail, Waulking, Yodel, Yodle

**Songbook** Cancionero, Hymnal, Kommersbuch, Libretto, Psalter

**Songsmith, Songwriter** Balladeer, Carmichael, Dowland, Espla, Foster, Kern, Lyricist, Minot, Porter, Waitz, Zappa

**Sonnet** Amoret, Elizabethan, English, Italian, Miltonic, Petrarch(i)an, Shakespearean, Shakespearian, Spenserian

**Sonometer** Monochord

**Soon(er)** Anon, Betimes, Directly, Enow, Erelong, Imminent, Lief, Nearly, OK, Oklahoma, Presently, Shortly, Tight, Timely, Tit(ely), Tite, Tyte

**Soot(y)** Colly, Coom, Crock, Fuliginous, Gas black, Grime, Lampblack, Smut, Speck

**Soothe(r), Soothing** Accoy, Allay, Anetic, Anodyne, Appease, Assuage, Bucku, Calm, Compose, Demulcent, Dulcet, Ease, Emollient, Irenic, Lenitive, Lull, Mellifluous, Mollify, Obtundent, Pacific, Paregoric, Placate, Poultice, Quell, Rock, Stroke

**Soothsayer** Astrologer, Augur, Calchas, Chaldee, Divine, Forecaster, Haruspex, Melampus, Oracle, Picus, Prophet, Pythoness, → **SEER**, Shipton, Tiresias

**Sop(py)** Appease, Berry, Douceur, Rait, Ret, Salvo, Sashy, Sponge

**Sophist(ic)** Casuist, Elenchic, Quibbler

**Sophisticate(d)** Blasé, Boulevardier, City slicker, Civilised, Classy, Cogniscento, Cosmopolitan, Couth, Cultured, Doctor, High-end, Hitec, Patrician, Polished, Sative, Slicker, Smooth, Suave, Svelte, Urbane, Worldly

▷ **Sophoclean** *may indicate* Greek alphabet, etc.

**Sophomore** Semie

**Soporific** Barbiturate, Bromide, Drowsy, Halothane, Hypnotic, Lullaby, Narcotic, Opiate, Seconal, Sedative, Tedious

**Soppiness, Soppy** Maudlin, Salvo, Sashy, Schwärmerei, Sloppy, Slushy, Wet

**Soprano** Caballé, Callas, Castrato, Crespin, Descant, Lehmann, Lind, Patti, Treble

**Sorb** Wend

**Sorbet** Glacé, Water ice

**Sorcerer, Sorceress, Sorcery** Angek(k)ok, Ashipu, Black art, Circe, Conjury, Diablerie, Diabolist, Genie, Hoodoo, Kadaitcha, Kurdaitcha, Lamia, Mage, Magian, Magic(ian), Magus, Medea, Merlin, Morgan le Fay, Mother Shipton, Necromancer, Obi, Pishogue, Shaman, Sortilege, Venefic(ious), Voodoo, Warlock, Witch, Witch knot, Wizard

**Sordid** Base, Low-life, Miserable, Rhyparography, Scungy, Seamy, Seedy, Sleazy, Squalid, Vile

**Sore(ly), Sores** Abrasion, Anthrax, Bitter, Blain, Boil, Canker, Chancre, Chap, Chilblain, Cold, Dearnly, Felon, Gall, Impost(h)ume, Ireful, Kibe, Nasty, Noma, Pressure, Quitter, Quittor, Raw, Running, Rupia(s), Saddle, Sair, Sensitive, Shiver, Sitfast, Soft, Surbate, Tassell, Tercel, Ulcer(s), Whitlow, Wound

**Sore throat** Garget, Prunella, Quinsy, Tonsillitis

**Sorghum** Kaoliang, Mabela, Milo

**Sorrel** Common, French, Hetty, Mountain, Oca, Roman, Sheep, Soar(e), Sore, Sourock

**Sorrow(ful)** Affliction, Attrition, Deplore, Distress, Dole, Dolente, Doloroso, Dolour, Emotion, Fee-grief, →**GRIEF**, Lament, Misery, Nepenthe, Ochone, Penance, Pietà, Plaintive, Remorse, Rue, Triste, Wae, Waugh, Wirra, Woe, Yoop

**Sorry** Apologetic, Ashamed, Contrite, Eh, Miserable, Oops, Paltry, Penitent, Pitiful, Poor, Regretful, Relent, Rueful, Simple, Wan, Wretched

▷ **Sorry** *may indicate* an anagram

**Sort(ing)** Arrange, Brand, Breed, Category, Character, Classify, Collate, Drive, Genre, Grade, Kidney, →**KIND**, Nature, Permutation, Pranck(e), Prank, Sieve, Sift, Species, Stamp, Straighten, Stripe, Systemise, Tidy, Triage, Type, Variety

**Sortie** Attack, Foray, Mission, Outfall, Raid, Sally

▶ **Sorts** *see* **OUT OF SORTS**

**So-so** Average, Indifferent, Mediocre, Middling

**So to speak** Quasi

▷ **So to speak** *may indicate* 'sound of'

**Sotto voce** Murmur, Whisper

▶ **Soubriquet** *see* **SOBRIQUET**

**Sough** Rustle, Sigh

**Soul(ful)** Alma, Ame, Anima, Animist, Atman, Ba, Bardo, Bod(y), Brevity, Deep, Entelechy, Eschatology, Essence, Expressive, Heart, Inscape, Ka, Larvae, Lost, Manes, Motown, Object, Person, Pneuma, Psyche, Saul, Shade, Spirit, Traducian, Universal

**Sound(ed), Sounding, Soundness, Sound system** Accurate, Ach-laut, Acoustic, Affricate, Albemarle, Allophone, All there, Alveolar, Amphoric, Aspirate, Audio, Bay, Blare, Bleep, Blip, Bloop, Blow, Boing, Bong, Bray, Breathed, Cacophony, Chime, Chirl, Chirr(e), Chord, Chug, Clam, Clang, Clank, Clink, Cloop, Clop, Clunk, Compos, Consistent, Continuant, Copper-bottomed, Dah, Dental, Diphthong, Dit, Dive, Dolby®, Dream, Dusky, Echo, Eek, Epenthesis, Euphony, Fast, Fathom, Fere, Fettle, Fit, Flap, Flawless, Flow, Foley, Glide, Good, Hale, Harmonics, Hayle, Healthy, Hearty, Hiccup, Hi-fi, Hiss, Ich-laut, Inlet, Intact, Islay, Jura, Kalmar, Knell, Kyle, Labiodental, Lene, Lo-fi, Long Island, Low, Lucid, Mach, Madrilene, McMurdo, Mersey, Milford, Monophthong, Mouillé, Murmur, Musak, Music, Muzak®, Narrow, Nasal, Nicam, →**NOISE**, Off-glide, Onomatopoeia, Oompah, Optical, Orate, Orinasal, Orthodox, Palatal, Palato-alveolar, Pamlico, Paragog(u)e, Peal, Pectoriloquy, Pest, Phone(me), Phonetic, Phonic, Phonology, Phut, Pitter(-patter), Plap, Plink, Plonk, Plop, Plosion, Plosive,

Plumb, Plummet, Plunk, Plymouth, Probe, Pronounce, Puget, Put-put, Quadraphonic(s), Quadrophonic(s), Rale, Rational, Rat-tat, Real, Reasonable, Reliable, Ring, Roach, Robust, Rong, Rumble, Rustle, Sabin, Safe, Sandhi, Sane, Scoresby, Sensurround®, S(c)hwa, Skirl, Solid, Sonance, Sondage, Sone, Souffle, Sough, Sowne, Speech, Splat, Stereo, Stereophony, Strait, Stroke, Surround, Swish, Tamber, Tannoy®, Tchick, Tenable, Thorough, Timbre, Ting, Tone, Toneme, Trig, Trill, Triphthong, Trumpet, Twang, Ultrasonic(s), Unharmed, Uvular, Valid, Viable, Voice, Vowel, Wah-wah, Watertight, Well, Whine, Whinny, Whistle, Whole(some), Whoosh, Whump, Wolf

**Sounder** Echo, Lead(sman)

**Sounding board** Abat-voix

**Soundproof** Deaden

**Sound-track** Dubbing, Movietone®, Stripe, Sync

**Soup** Alphabet, Avgolemono, Bird's nest, Bisk, Bisque, Borsch, Bouillabaisse, Bouillon, Brewis, Broth, Burgoo, Cal(l)aloo, Chowder, Cioppino, Clam chowder, Cock-a-leekie, Cockieleekie, Cockyleeky, Consommé, Crab chowder, Cullen skink, Duck, Garbure, Gazpacho, Gomb(r)o, Gruel, Gumbo, Harira, Hoosh, Julienne, Kail, Kale, Lokshen, Madrilene, Marmite, Mess, Minestrone, Miso, Mock turtle, Mulligatawny, Oxtail, Palestine, Pea(se), Pho, Pot(t)age, Pot-au-feu, Primordial, Puree, Ramen, Rice, Rubaboo, Sancoche, Scoosh, Scotch broth, Shchi, Shtchi, Skilligalee, Skilligolee, Skilly, Skink, Stock, Tattie-claw, Toheroa, Turtle, Vichyssoise

▷ **Soup** *may indicate* an anagram

**Soupçon** Thought, Touch

**Sour(puss)** Acerb, Acescent, Acid, Acidulate, Aigre-deux, Alegar, Bitter, Citric, Crab, Eager, Esile, Ferment, Moody, Stingy, Subacid, →**TART**, Turn, Unamiable, Verjuice, Vinegarish

**Source** Authority, Basis, Bottom, Centre, Closed, Database, Derivation, Egg, Fons, Font, Fount, Fountain-head, Germ, Head-stream, Leak, Literary, Mine, Mother, Neutron, Origin, Parent, Pi, Pion, Point, Principle, Prot(h)yle, Provenance, Quarry, Reference, Rise, Riverhead, Root, Seat, Seed, Spa, Spring, Springhead, Stock, Supply, Upriver, Urn, Well, Wellhead, Wellspring, Widow's cruse, Ylem

**Sour milk** Curds, Smetana, Whey, Whig, Yogh(o)urt

**Souse** Beath, Duck, Immerse, Pickle, Plunge, Soak, Spree, Steep

**South(ern), Southerner** Austral, Confederacy, Dago, Decanal, Decani, Deep, Dixieland, Meridian, Meridional, S, Scal(l)awag, Scallywag

**South Africa(n)** Azania, Bantu, Caper, Ciskei, Grikwa, Griqua, Hottentot, Kaf(f)ir, Lebowa, Qwaqwa, SA, Soutie, Soutpiel, Springbok, Swahili, Xhosa, ZA, Zulu

**South American** Araucanian, Arawak, Argentino, Aymara, Bolivian, Carib, Chibcha, Chilean, Galibi, Guarani, Inca, Jivaro, Kechua, Latin, Llanero, Mam, Mapuchi, Mayan, Mixe-Zogue, Mixtac, Mochica, Quechua, SA, Shuar, Tapuyan, Tupi

**South-east** Home Counties, Roseland, SE

**Southpaw** Corrie-fisted

**Southwark** Boro'

**Souvenir** Goss, Keepsake, Memento, Relic, Remembrance, Scalp, Token, Trophy

**Sou'wester** Cornishman

**Sovereign(ty), Sovereign remedy** Anne, Autocrat, Bar, Condominium, Couter, Dominant, Emperor, ER, Goblin, Haemony, Harlequin, Imperial, Imperium, James, King, L, Liege, Monarch, Napoleon, Nizam, Pound, Quid, Rangatiratanga, Reign, Royalty, Ruler, Shiner, Supreme, Swaraj, Synarchy, Thick' un, Thin' un

**Soviet** Circassian, Council, Estonian, Russian, Stalin, Supreme, Volost

**Sow(ing)** Catchcrop, Elt, Foment, Gilt, Inseminate, Plant, Scatter, Seed, Sprue, Strew, Yelt

**Soya** Sitosterol, Tempe(h)

**Spa** Aachen, Baden, Baden-Baden, Bath, Buxton, Ems, Evian, Fat farm, Godesberg, Harrogate, Hydro, Kurhaus, Kursaal, Leamington, Malvern, Pump-room, Vichy

**Space, Spaced (out), Spaceman, Spacing, Spacious, Spatial** Abyss, Acre, Airy, Alley, Area, Areola, Bay, Bedsit, Bolthole, Bracket, Breathing, Bronchus, Catatonic, Cellule, C(o)elom(e), Cislunar, Clearing, Cofferdam, Compluvium, Concourse, Contline, Crawl, Crookes, Cubbyhole, Daylight, Deducted, Deep, Diastema, Distal, Distance, Elbow-room, Elliptic, Em, En, Esplanade, Ether, Exergue, Expanse, Extent, Flies, Footprint, Forecourt, Freeband, Gagarin, Gap, Glade, Glenn, Goaf, Gob, Groggy, Gutter, Hair, Hash(mark), Headroom, Hell, Homaloid, Indention, Inner, Intergalactic, Interim, Interlinear, Interplanetary, Interstellar, Interstice, Invader, Kerning, Killogie, Kneehole, Lacuna, Lair, Leading, Lebensraum, Legroom, Life, Lobby, Logie, Lumen, Lunar, Lung, Machicolation, Maidan, Manifold, Manorial, Metope, Mihrab, Minkowski, Mosh pit, MUD, Muset, Musit, Orbit, Outer, Palatial, Parking, Parvis(e), Peridrome, Personal, Plenum, Polemics, Pomoerium, Priest hole, Proportional, Proxemics, Quad, Retrochoir, Riemannian, → **ROOM**, Ruelle, Sample, Sheets, Shelf room, Sinus, Slot, Spandrel, Spandril, Sparse, Step, Steric, Storage, Third, Topological, Tympanum, Ullage, Uncluttered, Vacua, Vacuole, Vacuum, Vast, Vector, Virtual, Void, Volume, Well

**Space age** Hi-tech

**Spacecraft, Space agency, Space object, Spaceship, Space station** Apollo, Capsule, Challenger, Columbia, Columbus, Deep Space, Explorer, Galileo, Gemini, Genesis, Giotto, Lander, LEM, Luna, Lunik, Mariner, Mercury, MIR, Module, NASA, Orbiter, Pioneer, Probe, Quasar, Ranger, Rocket ship, Salyut, Shuttle, Skylab, Soyuz, Space lab, Sputnik, Starship, Tardis, Viking, Voskhod, Vostok, Voyager, Zond

**Spacer (plate)** Bead(s)

**Space walk** EVA

**Spade** Breastplough, Caschrom, Cas crom, Castrato, Detective, Flaughter, Graft, Loy, Mole, Negro, Paddle, Paddle staff, Pattle, Peat, Pettle, Pick, S, Shovel, Slane, Spit, Suit, Turf, Tus(h)kar, Tus(h)ker, Twiscar

**Spain** E, Hesperia, Iberia, Wean

**Spalpeen** Sinner

**Span** Age, Arch, Attention, Bestride, Bridge, Chip, Ctesiphon, Extent, Life, Memory, Octave, Range, Timescale

**Spangle(d)** Avanturine, Aventurine, Glitter, Instar, O, Paillette, Sequin

**Spaniard, Spanish** Alguacil, Alguazil, Andalusian, Asturian, Balearic, Barrio, Basque, Cab, Caballero, Carlist, Castilian, Catalan, Chicano, Dago, Diego, Don, Fly, Grandee, Hidalgo, Hispanic, José, Madrileno, Main, Mestizo, Mozarab, Pablo, Papiamento, Señor, Spic(k), Spik

**Spaniel** Blenheim, Cavalier, Clumber, Cocker, Crawler, Creep, Dog, Fawner, Field, Irish water, King Charles, Maltese, Papillon, Placebo, Skip-kennel, Springer, Sussex, Tibetan, Toad-eater, Toady, Toy, Water, Welsh springer

**Spank(ing)** Cob, Paddywhack, Rapid, Scud, Slap, Slipper, Sprack

**Spanner** Arc, Box, Bridge, Clapper, Key, Monkey wrench, Ring, Shifter, Shifting, Socket, Spider, Torque, Wrench

**Spar** Barite, Barytes, Blue John, Boom, Bowsprit, Box, Cauk, Cawk, Derbyshire, Fight, Gaff, Heavy, Iceland, Icestone, Jib-boom, Mainyard, Manganese, Martingale, Mast, Mizzenmast, Nail-head, Outrigger, Rafter, Rail, Ricker, Satin, Schiller, Shearleg, Sheerleg, Snotter, Spathic, Sprit, Steeve, Stile, Tabular, Triatic, Whiskerboom, Whiskerpole, Yard

**Spare, Sparing(ly)** Angular, Cast-off, Dup(licate), Economical, Fifth wheel, Free, Frugal, Galore, Gash, Gaunt, Hain, Lean, Lenten, Narrow, Other, Pardon, Relieve, Reprieve, Reserve, Rib, Save, Scant, Skimp, Skinny, Slender, Stint, Subsecive, Tape, Thin

**Spark** Animate, Arc, Beau, Blade, Bluette, Dandy, Flash, Flaught, Flicker, Flint, Funk, Ignescent, Ignite, Kindle, Life, Muriel, Quenched, Scintilla, Smoulder, Spunk, Trigger, Vital, Zest

**Sparkle(r), Sparkling** Aerated, Aventurine, Bling, Burnish, Coruscate, Crémant, Diamanté, Effervesce, Élan, Emicate, Fire, Fizz, Flicker, Frizzante, Gem, Glamour, Glint,

Glisten, Glister, Glitter, Life, Patina, Pétillant, Scintillate, Seltzer, Seltzogene, Spangle, Spirited, Spritzig, Spumante, Twinkle, Verve, Witty, Zap

**Sparrow** Bird, Cape, Chipping, Hedge, Isaac, Java, Junco, Mah-jong(g), Mossie, Passerine, Piaf, Prunella, Savanna, Song, Spadger, Speug, Sprug(gy), Titling, Tree, Vesper

**Sparrow-grass** Asparagus, Sprue

**Sparse** Meagre, Rare, Scant, Thin

**Spartan(s)** Ascetic, Austere, Basic, Enomoty, Hardy, Helot, Heraclid, Lacedaemonian, Laconian, Lysander, Menelaus, Severe, Valiant

**Spasm(s), Spasmodic** Ataxic, Blepharism, Chorea, Clonus, Convulsive, Cramp, Crick, Fit(ful), Hiccup, Hippus, Hyperkinesis, Intermittent, Irregular, →**JERK**, Kink, Laryngismus, Nystagmus, Paroxysm, Periodical, Start, Strangury, Tetany, Throe, Tonic, Tonus, Trismus, Twinge, Twitch, Vaginismus, Writer's cramp

▷ **Spasmodic** *may indicate* an anagram

**Spastic** Athetoid, Clonic, Jerky

**Spat(s)** Altercation, Bicker, Brattle, Gaiters, Legging, Quarrel, Set to, Shower, Tiff

**Spate** Flood, Gush, Sluice, Torrent

▶ **Spatial** *see* **SPACE**

**Spatter** Disject, Ja(u)p, Scatter, Splash, Splosh, Spot, Sprinkle

▷ **Spattered** *may indicate* an anagram

**Spatula** Applicator, Tongue depressor

**Spawn(ed), Spawning (place)** Anadromous, Blot, Eelfare, Fry, Progeny, Propagate, Redd, Roud, Seed, Shotten, Spat, Spet, Spit

**Speak(er), Speaking** Address, Ad lib, Articulate, Bang on, Broach, Chat, Cicero, Collocuter, Communicate, Converse, Coo, Declaim, Diction, Dilate, Discourse, Diseur, Dwell, Earphone, Effable, Elocution, Eloquent, Expatiate, Express, Extemporise, Filibuster, Intercom, Intone, Inveigh, Jabber, Jaw, Lip, Loq, Loquitur, Management, Mang, Mention, Mike, Mina, Mouth, Mouthpiece, Nark, Native, Open, Orate, Orator, Palaver, Parlance, Parley, Perorate, Pontificate, Prate, Preach, Prelector, Public, Recite, Rhetor, →**SAY**, Sayne, Soliloquize, Spout, Spruik, Squawk box, Stump, Talk, Tannoy®, Tongue, Trap, Tub-thumper, Tweeter, Utter, Voice, Waffle, Wibble, Windbag, Witter, Woofer, Word

**Speakeasy** Fluent, Shebeen

**Spear** Ash, Asparagus, Assagai, Assegai, Barry, Dart, Demi-lance, Engore, Fishgig, Fizgig, Gad, Gavelock, Gig, Glaive, Gleave, Gum digger's, Gungnir, Harpoon, Hastate, Impale, Javelin, Lance(gay), Launcegaye, Leister, Morris-pike, Partisan, Pierce, Pike, Pilum, Prong, Skewer, Spike, Trident, Trisul(a), Waster

**Spearhead** Lead

**Spear-rest** Feutre, Fewter

**Special(ly)** Ad hoc, Constable, Designer, Disparate, Distinctive, Extra, Important, Notable, Notanda, Particular, Peculiar, Red-letter, S, Specific, Strong suit, Vestigial

**Specialise, Specialist(s), Speciality** Allergist, Authority, Concentrate, Connoisseur, Consultant, ENT, Esoteric, Expert, Field, Forte, Illuminati, Internist, Logistician, Maestro, Major, Optometrist, Pomologist, Quant, Recondite, Technician

**Species** Biotype, Class, Darwin, Ecad, Ecotype, Endangered, Genera, Genre, Genus, Indicator, Infima, Kind, Opportunistic, Pioneer, Strain, Taxa

**Specific(ally), Specification, Specified, Specify** Adduce, Ad hoc, As, Ascribe, Assign, Concretize, Cure, Define, Designate, Detail, Explicit, Formula, Full-blown, Given, Itemise, Medicine, Namely, Of, Precise, Quantify, Remedy, Sp, Special, Spell out, State, Stipulate, Stylesheet, The, To wit, Trivial, Vide licit

**Specimen(s)** Archetype, Assay, Example, Exemplar, Imago, Model, Museum piece, Sample, Slide, Swab, Topotype, Type

**Specious** False, Glib, Hollow, Pageant, Plausible, Seeming, Spurious

**Speck, Speckle(d)** Atom, Bit, Dot, Fleck, Floater, Freckle, Gay, Mealy, Mote, Muscae volitantes, Particle, Peep(e), Pip, Smut, Spot, Spreckle, Stud

**Spectacle(s), Spectacled, Spectacular** Arresting, Barnacles, Bifocals, Blazers, Blinks, Bossers, Cheaters, Colourful, Epic, Escolar, Giglamps, → **GLASSES**, Goggles, Horn-rims, Lorgnette, Lorgnon, Meteoric, Nose-nippers, Oo, Optical, Outspeckle, Pageant, Pebble glasses, Phenomenon, Pince-nez, Pomp, Preserves, Raree-show, Rose-coloured, Scene, Show, Sight, Son et lumière, Staggering, Stunt, Sunglasses, Tamasha, Tattoo, Trifocal, Varifocals

**Spectate, Spectator(s)** Audience, Bystander, Dedans, Etagère, Eyer, Gallery, Gate, Groundling, Kibitzer, Observer, Onlooker, Passer-by, Ringsider, Standerby, Terrace, Wallflower, Witness

**Spectograph, Spectometer** Aston, Calutron

**Spectral, Spectre** Apparition, Bogle, Bogy, Brocken, Eidolon, Empusa, Ghost, Idola, Iridal, Larva, Malmag, Phantasm, Phantom, Phasma, Spirit, Spook, Tarsier, Walking-straw, Wraith

**Spectrum** Absorption, Action, Band, Continuous, Emission, Fission, Iris, Mass, Optical, Radio, Rainbow, Range, Sunbow, Sundog, Visible, X-ray

**Speculate, Speculative, Speculator, Speculation** Academic, Agiotage, Arb(itrage), Assume, Bear, Better, Boursier, Bull, Conjecture, Flier, Flyer, Gamble, Guess, Ideology, If, Imagine, Meditate, Notional, Operate, Pinhooker, Presume, Raider, Shark, Stag, Theoretical, Theorise, Theory, Thought, Trade, Transcendent, Wonder

**Speech, Speech element** Accents, Address, Argot, Articulation, Bat, Blah, Bunkum, Burr, Curtain, Declamation, Delivery, Dialect, Diatribe, Diction, Direct, Discourse, Dithyramb, Drawl, Éloge, Eloquence, English, Epilogue, Eulogy, Farewell, Filibuster, Free, Gab, Glossolalia, Grandiloquence, Guttural, Harangue, Helium, Idiolect, Idiom, Inaugural, Indirect, Intonation, Jargon, Keynote, King's, Lallation, → **LANGUAGE**, Lingua franca, Litany, Logopaedics, Maiden, Monologue, Morph(eme), Motherese, Musar, Oblique, Occlusive, Oral, Oration, Parabasis, Parle, Peroration, Phasis, Philippic, Phonetics, Prolocution, Prolog(ue), Queen's, Rant, Reported, Rhetoric, RP, Sandhi, Say, Scanning, Screed, Sermon, Set, Side, Slang, Soliloquy, Stemwinder, Stump, Tagmeme, Talk, Taxeme, Tirade, Toneme, Tongue, Uptalk, Vach, Verbal, Visible, Voice, Wawa, Whaikorero, Whistle-stop, Xenoglossia

**Speech defect, Speech disease** Alalia, Alogia, Aposiopesis, Dysarthria, Dysphasia, Dysphoria, Echolalia, Halt, Idioglossia, Lallation, Lisp, Palilalia, Paralalia, Paraphasia, Pararthria, Phonasthenia, Psellism, Rhinolalia, Stammer, Stutter, Word salad

**Speechless** Alogia, Dumb, Dumbstruck, Inarticulate, Mute, Silent, Tongue-tied

**Speech-writer** Logographer

**Speed(ily), Speedy** Accelerate, Alacrity, Amain, Amphetamine, ANSI, Apace, ASA, Average, Barrel, Bat, Baud, Belive, Belt, Benzedrine, Breakneck, Burn, C, Career, Cast, Celerity, Clip, Cruising, Dart, Despatch, Dictation, DIN, Dispatch, Expedite, Fang, Fast, Film, Fleet, Further, Gait, Gallop, Goer, Group, Gun, Hare, Haste, Hie, Hotfoot, Hypersonic, Induce, Instantaneous, Knot, Landing, Lick, Mach, Merchant, MPH, → **PACE**, Pelt, Phase, Pike, Post-haste, Prompt, Pronto, Race, Rapidity, Rate, Rev, RPS, Rush, Scorch, Scud, Scurr, Skirr, Soon, Spank, Split, Stringendo, Supersonic, Swift, Tach, Tear, Tempo, Teraflop, Ton up, V, Velocity, Ventre à terre, Vroom, Wave, Whid, Wing, Zoom

**Speedwell** Bird's eye, Brooklime, Fluellin, Germander, Veronica

**Spelaean** Troglodyte

**Spelk** Skelf, Splinter

**Spell(ing)** Abracadabra, Bewitch, Bout, Cantrip, Charm, Conjuration, Do, Elf-shoot, Enchantment, Entrance, Fit, Go, Gri(s)-gri(s), Hex, Incantation, Innings, Jettatura, Juju, Knock, Knur, → **MAGIC**, Mojo, Need-fire, Nomic, Open sesame, Orthography, Period, Phase, Philter, Philtre, Phonetic, Pinyin, Relieve, Ride, Romaji, Run, Rune, Scat, Shift, Shot, Signify, Sitting, Snap, Snatch, Sorcery, Sp, Span, Spasm, Splinter, Stint, Stretch, Tack, Term, Time, Tour, Trick, Turn, Weird, Whammy, Wicca, Witchcraft

**Spelling-book** ABC, Grimoire

**Spencer** Bodice, Topcoat, Tracy, Vest

**Spend(er), Spending** Anticipate, Birl, Blow, Blue, Boondoggling, Consume, Deficit, Deplete, Disburse, Exhaust, Extravagant, Fritter, Lash out, Lay out, Live, Outlay, Pass, Pay, Shopaholic, Splash, Splash out, Splurge, Squander, Squandermania, Ware

**Spendthrift** Essex Man, High-roller, Prodigal, Profligate, Profuser, Scattergood, Wastrel

**Spent** All-in, Consumed, Dead (beat), Done, Exhausted, Expended, Gone, Jaded, Stale, Tired, Used, Weak, Weary, Zonked

**Sperm** Gossypol, Seed, Semen

**Spew** Eject, Emit, Gush, Spit, Vomit

**Sphagnum** Moss, Peat

**Sphere, Spherical** Armillary, Attraction, Ball, Benthoscope, Celestial, Discipline, Earth, Element, Field, Firmament, Globe, Magic, Mound, Orb(it), Planet, Primum mobile, Prolate, Province, Realm, Schwarzschild, Theatre, Wheel

**Sphincter** Pylorus

**Sphinx** Criosphinx, Hawk-moth, Oracle, Riddler

**Spice, Spicy** Amomum, Anise, Aniseed, Aryl, Baby, Baltic, Caraway, Cardamom, Cardamon, Cardamum, Cassareep, Cassaripe, Cayenne, Chili powder, Cinnamon, Clove, Clow, Coriander, Cough drop, Cubeb, Cum(m)in, Dash, Devil, Galingale, Garam masala, Ginger, Green ginger, Jerk, Mace, Malaguetta, Marjoram, Masala, Myrrh, Nutmeg, Oregano, Paprika, Peppercorn, Picante, Pimento, Piperic, Piquant, Posh, Risque, Root ginger, Saffron, Salsa verde, Season, Sexed up, Stacte, Staragen, Tamal(e), Tamara, Tansy, Tarragon, Taste, Turmeric, Vanilla, Variety, Za'atar

**Spick** Dink, Neat, Spike, Tidy

**Spicule** Sclere, Tetract

**Spider(s)** Anancy, Ananse, Arachnid, Aranea, Araneida, Arthrapodal, Attercop, Bird, Black widow, Bobbejaan, Bolas, Cardinal, Cheesemite, Chelicerate, Citigrade, Diadem, Epeira, Epeirid, Ethercap, Ettercap, Funnel-web, Harvest(er), Harvestman, House, Hunting, Huntsman, Jumping, Katipo, Lycosa, Mite, Money, Monkey, Mygale, Orb-weaver, Pan, Phalangid, Podogona, Program, Pycnogonid, Red, Redback, Rest, Ricinulei, Saltigrade, Scorpion, Solifugae, Solpuga, Spinner, Strap, Tarantula, Telary, Trapdoor, Violin, Water, Wolf, Zebra

**Spiderwort** Tradescantia

**Spiel** Patter, Pitch, Spruik

**Spignel** Baldmoney, Meu

**Spigot** Bung, Plug, Tap

**Spike(d)** Barb, Brod, Calk, Calt(h)rop, Chape, Cloy, Crampon, Doctor, Ear, Fid, Filopodium, Foil, Gad, Gadling, Goad, Grama, Herissé, Icicle, Impale, Kebab, Lace, Locusta, Marlin(e), Nail, Needle, →PIERCE, Pin, Piton, Point, Pricket, Prong, Puseyite, Raceme, Rod, Sharp, Shod, Skewer, Spadix, Spear, Spicate, Spicule, Spire, Strobiloid, Surge, Tang, Thorn, Tine

**Spill(age)** Divulge, Drop, Fidibus, Jackstraw, Lamplighter, Leakage, Let, Lighter, Overflow, Overset, Reveal, Scail, Scale, Shed, Skail, Slart, Slop, Stillicide, Swatter, Taper, Tumble, Ullage

**Spin(ner), Spinning (wheel)** Aeroplane, Arabian, Arachne, Aswirl, Bielmann, Birl, Camel, Centrifuge, Chark(h)a, Cribellum, Cut, Dance, Day trip, Dextrorse, DJ, Eddy, Eke, Flat, Flax-wrench, Flip, Gimp, Googly, Gymp, Gyrate, Gyre, Gyroscope, Hurl, Isobaric, Isotopic, Jenny, Lachesis, Mole, Nun, Peg-top, Piecener, Piecer, Pirouette, Pivot, PR, Precess, Prolong, Purl, Reel, Rev(olve), Ride, Rotate, Royal, Screw, Side, Sinistrorse, Slant, Slide, Somersault, Spider, Stator, Strobic, Swirl, Swivel, Throstle, Tirl, Toss, Trill, Trundle, Turntable, Twirl, Twist, Wheel, Whirl, Whirligig, Work

**Spinach** Florentine, Orach(e), Popeye, Sa(a)g

**Spinal (cord), Spine(d), Spiny** Acanthoid, Acerose, Acicular, Acromion, Aculeus, Areole, Arête, Backbone, Barb, Chine, Coccyx, Column, Doorn, Dorsal, Epidural, Muricate, Myelon, Notochord, Ocotillo, Prickle, Quill, Rachial, R(h)achis, Ray, Ridge bone, Thorn, Torso, Tragacanth

**Spindle(-shanks), Spindly** Arbor, Axis, Axle, Bobbin, Capstan, Fusee, Fusiform, Fusil, Mandrel, Mandril, Pin, Scrag, Staff, Triblet

▶ **Spine** *see* SPINAL (CORD)

**Spinel** Balas, Picotite

**Spineless(ness)** Cowardice, Inerm, Invertebrate, Lily-livered, Muticous, Timid, Weak, Wimp

**Spinn(e)y** Coppice, Shaw, Thicket

**Spinning-wheel** Chark(h)a

**Spin-off** By-product, Payola

**Spinster** Discovert, Feme sole, Old maid, Tabby

**Spiral** Archimedes, Caracol, Chalaza, Cochlea, Coil, Curl, Dexiotropic, Dextrorse, Ekman, Genetic, Gyrate, Gyre, Helical, Helix, Hyperbolic, Inflationary, Logarithmic, Loxodromical, Parastichy, Ringlet, Screw, Scroll, Sinistrorse, Spin, Tailspin, Turbinate, Turnpike, Twist, Vibrio, Volute, Vortex, Whorl, Wind

**Spire(-shaped)** Broach, Flèche, Peak, Shaft, Steeple, Thyrsoid

**Spirit(s), Spirited** Afreet, Afrit, Animal, Animation, Animus, Ardent, Blithe, Bogeyman, Dash, → DRINK, Dutch courage, Élan, Element(al), Emit, Entrain, Essence, Ethereal, Etheric, Ethos, Feisty, Fettle, Fiend, Fight, Free, Game, Gasoline, Geist, Ginger, Gism, Go, Grit, Gumption, Heart, Holy, Hugh, Kindred, → LIQUOR, Lively, Mettle, Morale, Mystique, Nobody, Oversoul, Panache, Pecker, Pep, Presence, Pride, Racy, Rotgut, Scientology, Sloe gin, Soul, Spunk, Steam, Stomach, Team, Ton, Verve, Vigour, Vim, Vital, Zing

---

## SPIRITS

| | | | |
|---|---|---|---|
| **2 letters:** | Raki | Metal | Daemon |
| Ka | Ruin | Meths | Djinni |
| | Salt | Mobby | Duende |
| **3 letters:** | Saul | Numen | Dybbuk |
| Div | Wili | Party | Empusa |
| Imp | Wine | Peart | Esprit |
| Nis | Wood | Pluck | Fachan |
| Nix | | Pooka | Faints |
| Rum | **5 letters:** | Proof | Feints |
| Rye | Angel | Rakee | Fetich |
| | Ariel | Satyr | Fetish |
| **4 letters:** | Bogie | Shade | Geneva |
| Arak | Bogle | She'ol | Genius |
| Bogy | Djinn | Short | Grappa |
| Brio | Dryad | Sylph | Jinnee |
| Cant | Duppy | Tafia | Jumbie |
| Deev | Eblis | Turps | Kelpie |
| Deva | Fenny | Vodka | Kirsch |
| Feni | Genie | White | Kobold |
| Gamy | → GHOST | | Lemure |
| Ginn | Ghoul | **6 letters:** | Manito |
| Grog | Huaca | Arrack | Manitu |
| Jann | Jinni | Astral | Methyl |
| Jinn | Jumby | Brandy | Mobbie |
| Jism | Kehua | Buggan | Numina |
| Loki | Larva | Buggin | Ondine |
| Mare | Lemur | Cherub | Orenda |
| Peri | Manes | Cognac | Pernod® |
| Puck | Marid | Crouse | Petrol |

| | | | |
|---|---|---|---|
| Plucky | Aquavit | Shaitan | Paraclete |
| Pneuma | Archeus | Smeddum | Rectified |
| Potato | Asmoday | Spectre | Tokoloshe |
| Poteen | Banshee | Spright | Weltgeist |
| Psyche | Bitters | Taniwha | Zeitgeist |
| Python | Boggart | Tequila | |
| Samshu | Bravura | | **10 letters:** |
| Seraph | Buggane | **8 letters:** | Brollachan |
| Shadow | Courage | Archaeus | Glendoveer |
| Sprite | Eidolon | Creature | Methylated |
| Strunt | Erl king | Erdgeist | Mindererus |
| Tangie | Eudemon | Familiar | Rumbullion |
| Undine | Fetiche | Hollands | Turpentine |
| Voodoo | Glastig | Rakshasa | Water horse |
| Wairua | Gremlin | Schnapps | |
| Wraith | Gytrash | Surgical | **11 letters:** |
| Zephon | Incubus | Witblits | Poltergeist |
| Zombie | Indwelt | | Rosicrucian |
| | Kachina | **9 letters:** | |
| **7 letters:** | Manitou | Applejack | **12 letters:** |
| Ahriman | Mineral | Aqua vitae | Agathodaimon |
| Akvavit | Neutral | Domdaniel | Distillation |
| Alcohol | Phantom | Firewater | |
| Ammonia | Rakshas | Hartshorn | **13 letters:** |
| Apsaral | Samshoo | Nain rouge | Crème de menthe |

**Spiritless** Craven, Dowf, Inanimate, Insipid, Languid, Meek, Milksop, Poor, Tame, Vapid

**Spirit-level** Vial

**Spiritual(ism), Spiritualist, Spirituality** Aerie, Aery, Channelling, Coon-song, Ecclesiastic, Ethereous, Eyrie, Eyry, Incorporeal, Inwardness, Mystic, Negro, Planchette, Platonic, Psychic, Slate-writing, Swedenborg, Table-rapping, Table-turning, Yogi

**Spirt** Gush, Jet, Rush, → SPURT, Squirt

**Spit(ting), Spittle** Bar, Barbecue, Broach, Brochette, Chersonese, Dead ringer, Dribble, Drool, Emptysis, Eructate, Expectorate, Fuff, Gob, Golly, Gooby, Goss, Grill, Hawk, Hockle, Impale, Jack, Lookalike, Peninsula, Phlegm, Ras, Ringer, Rotisserie, Saliva, Shish kebab, Skewer, Slag, Spade(ful), Spawl, Spear, Sputter, Sputum, Tombolo, → TONGUE, Yesk, Yex

**Spite(ful)** Backbite, Bitchy, Catty, Grimalkin, Harridan, Irrespective, Malevolent, Malgrado, Malgré, Malice, Mau(l)gre, Mean, Mischievous, Nasty, Petty, Pique, Rancour, Spleen, Venom, Viperish, Waspish

**Spitfire** Cacafogo, Cacafuego, Wildcat

**Spittoon** Cuspidor(e)

**Spiv** Lair, Rorter

**Splash** Befoam, Blash, Blue, Dabble, Dash, Dog, Drip, Feature, Flouse, Fl(o)ush, Gardyloo, Jabble, Ja(u)p, Jirble, Paddle, Plap, Plop, Plowter, Sket, Slosh, Slush, Soda, Soss, Sozzle, Spairge, Spat(ter), Spectacle, Splat(ch), Splatter, Splodge, Splosh, Splotch, Spot, Spray, Spree, Squatter, Swash, Swatter, Water, Wet

▷ **Splash** *may indicate* an anagram

**Splay(ed)** Curl, Flew, Flue, Patté(e), Spread

**Spleen** Acrimony, Ague-cake, Bite, Lien, Melt, Milt(z), Pip, Stomach, Vitriol, Wrath

**Splendid, Splendour** Ah, Braw, Brilliant, Bully, Capital, Champion, Clinker, Dandy, Divine, Éclat, Effulgent, Excellent, Fine, Finery, Fulgor, Gallant, Garish, Glitterand, Glittering, Glorious, Glory, Gorgeous, Grand(eur), Grandiose, Ha, Heroic, Hunky-dory, Lavish, Lustrous, Majestic, Mooi, Noble, Palatial, Panache, Pomp, Proud, Radiant, Rich, Ripping, Royal, Stunning, Super(b), Superduper, Tophole, Wally, Zia

**Splice(d)** Braid, Eye, Join, Knit, Mainbrace, Married, Wed

▷ **Spliced** *may indicate* an anagram

**Splint** Air, Airplane, Banjo, Brace, Cal(l)iper, Splenial, Stent, T

**Splinter(s)** Bone-setter, Breakaway, Flinder, Fragment, Matchwood, Shatter, Shiver, Skelf, Sliver, Spale, Spall, Speel, Spelk, Spell, Spicula, Spill

**Split(ting)** Areolate, Axe, Banana, Bifid, Bifurcate, Bisect, Breach, Break, Broach, Burst, Chasm, Chine, Chop, Chorism, Cleave, Cleft, Clint, Clove(n), Crack, Crevasse, Cut, Decamp, Departmentalise, Disjoin, Distrix, Disunite, → **DIVIDE**, Division, Divorce, End, Estrange, Fissile, Fissure, Flake, Fork(ed), Fragment, Grass, Headache, Lacerate, Left, Maul, Partition, Red(d), Rift(e), Rip, Rive, Rupture, Russian, Ryve, Schism, Scissor, Segment, Segregate, Separate, Septemfid, Sever, Share, Skive, Slit, Sliver, Spall, Spalt, Speld, Spring, Tattle, Tmesis, Told, To-rend, To-tear, Trifurcate, Vamoose, Wedge, Xerochasy

▷ **Split** *may indicate* a word to become two; one word inside another; or a connection with Croatia (or the former Yugoslavia)

**Splodge, Splotch** Blot, Drop, Splash

**Splurge** Binge, Indulge, Lavish, Spend, Splash, Spree

**Splutter** Chug, Expectorate, Fizz, Gutter, Spray, Stammer

**Spode** Roderick

**Spoil(s), Spoiler, Spoilt** Addle, Agrise, Agrize, Agryze, Air dam, Blight, Blunk, Booty, Botch, Bribe, Coddle, Corrupt, Crool, → **DAMAGE**, Dampen, Deface, Defect, Defile, Deform, Disfigure, Dish, Fairing, Feather-bed, Foul, Gum, Hames, Harm, Impair(ed), Impoverish, Indulge, Loot, Maderise, Maltreat, Mar, Mardy, Mollycoddle, Muck, Mutilate, Mux, Pamper, Party pooper, Pet, Pickings, Pie, Pillage, Plunder, Prejudicate, Prize, Queer, Rait, Rate, Ravage, Ret, Rot, Ruin, Screw up, Scupper, Spoon-fed, Spuly(i)e, Swag, Taint, Tarnish, Turn, Vitiate, Wanton, Winnings, Wreck

▷ **Spoil(ed), Spoilt** *may indicate* an anagram

**Spoilsport** Damper, Killjoy, Marsport, Meddler, Party pooper, Wet blanket, Wowser

**Spoke(s)** Concentric, Radius, Ray, Rung, Said, Sed, Strut

**Spoken** Dixi, Said

▷ **Spoken** *may indicate* the sound of a word or letter

**Spokesman** Foreman, Mouthpiece, Orator, Prophet, Representative

**Spoliation, Spoliative** Devastation, Pillage, Plunder, Predatory, Reif

**Sponge(r), Spongy** Alcoholic, Ambatch, Angel cake, Argentine, Battenburg, Bum, Cadge, → **CAKE**, Cleanse, Diact, Diploe, Fozy, Free-loader, Glass-rope, Hexact, Hyalonema, Leech, Lig, Lithistid(a), Loofa(h), Madeira, Madeleine, Mermaid's glove, Mooch, Mop, Mouch, Mump, Parasite, Parazoa, Pentact, Platinum, Poachy, Porifera(n), Porous, Quandong, Rhabdus, Rum baba, Sarcenchyme, Scambler, Schnorrer, Scrounge, Shark, Shool(e), Shule, Siphonophora, Smell-feast, Sooner, Sop, Sucker, Swab, Sweetbriar, Sycophant, Tectratine, Tetract, Tetraxon, Tiramisu, Tylote, Vegetable, Velamen, Venus's flowerbasket, Wangle, Wipe, Zimocca, Zoophyte

**Spongewood** Sola

**Sponsor(ship)** Aegis, Angel, Auspice, Backer, Bankroll, Egis, Finance, Godfather, Godparent, Gossip, Guarantor, Lyceum, Patron, Surety, Undertaker

**Spontaneous** Aleatoric, Autonomic, Exergonic, Free, Gratuitous, Immediate, Impromptu, Improvised, Impulsive, Instant, Intuitive, Lightning, Natural, Off-the-cuff, Ultroneus, Unasked, Unpremeditated, Unprompted, Unrehearsed, Untaught

**Spoof** Chouse, Cozenage, Deception, Delusion, Fallacy, → **HOAX**, Imposture, Ramp, Swindle, Trick

**Spook(s), Spooky** CIA, Eerie, Fantom, Frightening, Ghost, Haunted, Phantom, Shade, Spectral, Uncanny

**Spool** Bobbin, Capstan, Pirn, Reel, Spit, Trundle

**Spoon(ful), Spoon-shaped** Apostle, Canoodle, Cochlear, Deflagrating, Dollop, Dose, Eucharistic, Gibby, Greasy, Horn, Labis, Ladle, Mote, Neck, Rat-tail, Runcible, Salt, Scoop, Scud, Server, Snuff, Spatula, Stir, Sucket, Trolling, Trout, Woo, Wooden

**Spoonerism** Marrowsky, Metathesis
**Spoor** Trace, Track, Trail
**Sporadic** Fitful, Isolated, Occasional, Patchy
**Spore(s), Spore case** Asexual, Conidium, Ex(t)ine, Fungus, Glomerule, Lenticel,
Palynology, Resting, Seed, Sexual, Sorus, Spreathed, Telium, Uredinium
**Sporran** Pock
**Sport(ing), Sportive, Sports, Sporty** Amusement, Bet, Blood, Breakaway, Brick,
By-form, Contact, Daff, Dalliance, Dally, Demonstration, Deviant, Extreme, Field, Freak,
Frisky, Frolic, Fun, →GAME, Gent, In, Joke, Laik, Lake, Lark, Merimake, Merry, Morph,
Mutagen, Nautics, Pal, Pastime, Recreate, Rogue, Rules, Shikar, Spectator, Tournament,
Tourney, Toy, Wear, Winter

## SPORTS

| | | | |
|---|---|---|---|
| **2 letters:** | Snooker | **10 letters:** | **12 letters:** |
| PE | Surfing | Cyclo-cross | Bar billiards |
| RU | Tailing | Drag-racing | Boardsailing |
| | | Flat-racing | Cross country |
| **3 letters:** | **8 letters:** | Heli-skiing | Heli-boarding |
| Gig | Aquatics | Kickboxing | Kite-boarding |
| | Ballgame | Monoskiing | Orienteering |
| **4 letters:** | Bonspiel | Pace-egging | Parascending |
| Polo | Climbing | Pancratium | River bugging |
| Sumo | Dressage | Parakiting | Sailboarding |
| | Eventing | Paraskiing | Snowboarding |
| **5 letters:** | Korfball | Rallycross | Speed-skating |
| Basho | Lacrosse | Real tennis | Steeplechase |
| Fives | Langlauf | Rugby Union | Tag-wrestling |
| Kendo | Natation | Sky-jumping | Trampolining |
| | Octopush | Sky-surfing | Trapshooting |
| **6 letters:** | Ringette | Street luge | Wakeboarding |
| Aikido | Skipping | Volleyball | |
| Diving | Softball | | **13 letters:** |
| Hockey | Speedway | **11 letters:** | Bungee-jumping |
| Karate | Swoffing | Bicycle Polo | Prizefighting |
| Shinny | | Coasteering | Skeet Shooting |
| Shinty | **9 letters:** | Fell walking | Ten-pin bowling |
| Squash | Abseiling | Free running | Weightlifting |
| Tennis | Athletics | Hang-gliding | |
| | Autocross | Kite-surfing | **15 letters:** |
| **7 letters:** | Autopoint | Paragliding | Extreme fighting |
| Angling | Canyoning | Paralympics | |
| Archery | Motocross | Parapenting | **16 letters:** |
| Camogie | Potholing | Parasailing | Ultimate fighting |
| Curling | Skijoring | Race-walking | |
| Fencing | Ski-kiting | Rugby League | **17 letters:** |
| Hurling | Ski-towing | Scuba-diving | Whitewater rafting |
| Netball | Skydiving | Showjumping | |
| Parkour | Speedball | Snorkelling | **18 letters:** |
| Putting | Twitching | Table tennis | White-water |
| Rackets | Wargaming | Tent-pegging | canoeing |
| Rafting | Water polo | Truck racing | |
| Shot put | Wrestling | Water-skiing | |
| Skating | | Windsurfing | |

▷ **Sport(s)** *may indicate* an anagram

**Sportsground** Rec

**Sportsman, Sportsmen** All-rounder, Amateur, Athlete, Blue, Corinthian, Half-blue, Hunter, Nimrod, Pentathlete, Pitcher, Rower, Shamateur, Shikaree, Shikari, Shot putter, Showjumper, Springbok, Varment, Varmint, Wrestler

**Sportswear** Gie, Wet suit

**Spot(s), Spotted, Spotter, Spotting, Spotty** Ace, Acne, Area, Areola, Areole, Baily's beads, Bausond, Bead, Beauty, Befoul, Bespatter, Blackhead, Blain, Blemish, Blind, Blip, Blister, Blob, Blot, Blotch(ed), Blur, Brind(l)ed, Café-au-lait, Carbuncle, Caruncle, Cash, Check, Cloud, Colon, Comedo, Corner, Curn, Cyst, Dalmatian, Dance, Dapple(-bay), Defect, Descry, Detect, Dick, Dilemma, Discern, Discover, Dot, Drop, Eruption, Espy, Eye, Facula, Flat, Flaw, Fleck, Floater, Flyspeck, Fogdog, Foxed, Freak, Freckle, Furuncle, G, Gay, Glimpse, Gout, Gräfenberg, Gricer, Guttate, High, Hot, Identify, Jam, Leaf, Lentago, Leopard, Light, Little, Liver, Locale, Location, Loran, Mackle, Macle, Macul(at)e, Mail, Meal, Measly, Microdot, Milium, Moil, Mole, Morbilli, Mote, Motty, Muscae volitantes, Naevoid, Naevus, Nightclub, Note, Notice, Ocellar, Ocellus, Paca, Papule, Paraselene, Pardal, Parhelion, Patch, Peep(e), Penalty, Perceive, Performance, Petechia, Pied, Pimple, Pin, Pip, Place, Plague, Plight, Plook, Plot, Plouk, Pock, Point, Poxy, Predicament, Punctuate, Pupil, Pustule, Quat, Radar, Rash, Recognise, Red, Rose-drop, Rubella, Scene, Scotoma, Scout, Sight, Situation, Skewbald, Smut, Soft, Soil, Speck(le), Speculum, Splodge, Spoil, Spy, Stigma, Sully, Sun, Sweet, Taint, Tar, Tight, Touch, Trace, Trouble, Venue, Weak, Whelk, Whitehead, Witness, Woodpecker, X, Yellow, Zit

**Spotless** Clean, Immaculate, Pristine, Spick and span, Virginal

**Spotlight** Ace, Baby, Bon-bon, Brute, Foreground, Maxi-brute

**Spot on** Exact, To a t

**Spouse** Better half, Companion, Consort, Dutch, Feare, Feer, F(i)ere, Hubby, Husband, Mate, Oppo, Other half, Partner, Pheer, Pirrauru, Significant other, Wife, Xant(h)ippe

**Spout(er)** Adjutage, Erupt, Gargoyle, Geyser, Grampus, Gush, Impawn, Jet, Mouth, Nozzle, Orate, Parrot, Pawn, Pourer, Raile, Rote, Spurt, Stream, Stroup, Talk, Tap, Vent

**Sprain(ed)** Crick, Rax, Reckan, Rick, Stave, Strain, Wrench, Wrick

**Sprat** Brit, Fish, Garvie, Garvock

**Sprawl** Conurbation, Grabble, Loll, Scamble, Spraddle, Sprangle, Spread, Stretch, Urban

**Spray** Aerosol, Aigrette, Airbrush, Antiperspirant, Atomiser, Bespatter, Blanket, Bouquet, Buttonhole, Chap, Corsage, Cyme, Egret, Fly, Hair, Mace®, Nasal, Nebuliser, Perse, Pesticide, Posy, Rose, Rosula, Scatter, Shower, Sparge, Spindrift, Splash, Spoondrift, Sprent, Sprig, Sprinkle, Spritz, Strinkle, Syringe, Twig, Wet

▷ **Spray** *may indicate* an anagram

**Spread(ing), Spreader** Air, Apply, Banquet, Bestrew, Beurre, Bid offer, Blow-out, Branch, Bush, Butter, Carpet, Centre, Circumfuse, Contagious, Couch, Coverlet, Coverlid, Deploy, Diffract, Diffuse, Dilate, Disperse, Dissemination, Distribute, Divulge, Double, Double-page, Drape, Dripping, Elongate, Emanate, Engarland, Expand, Extend, Fan, Feast, Flare, Guac(h)amole, Honeycomb, Infect, Jam, Lay, Mantle, Margarine, Marge, Marmite®, Meal, Metastasis, Middle-age(d), Multiply, Mushroom, Nutter, Oleo, Open, Overgrow, Palliate, Paste, Pâté, Patent, Patté, Patulous, Perfuse, Pervade, Picnic, Pour, Proliferate, Propagate, Radiant, Radiate, Rampant, Ran, Ranch, Run, Scale, Scatter, Sea-floor, Set, Sheet, Slather, Smear, Smörgåsbord, Sow, Span, Speld, Spelder, Spillover, Splay, Sprawl, Spray, Straddle, Straw, Stretch, Strew, Strow, Suffuse, Swell, Systemic, Tath, Teer, Unfold, Unfurl, Unguent, Unroll, Vegemite®, Widen, Wildfire

▷ **Spread** *may indicate* an anagram

**Spree** Bat, Batter, Beano, Bender, Binge, Bum, Bust, Buster, Carousal, Frolic, Gilravage, Jag, Jamboree, Juncate, Junket, Lark, Loose, Orgy, Randan, Rantan, Razzle(-dazzle), Revel, Rouse, Splore, Tear, Ups(e)y

**Sprig** Brad, Branch, Cion, Cyme, Nail, Scion, Sien, Sient, Spray, Syen, Twig, Youth

**Sprightly, Sprightliness** Agile, Airy, Chipper, Elfin, Esprit, Jaunty, Mercurial, Pip

**Spring(s), Springtime, Springy** Aganippe, Air, Alice, Arise, Axel, Black smoker, Bolt, Bounce, Bound, Box, Bunt, Cabriole, Caper, Capriole, Castalian, Cavort, Cee, Coil, Dance, Elastic, Emanate, Eye, Fount(ain), Free, Gambado, Germinate, Geyser, Grass, Hair, Helix, Hippocrene, Hop, Hot, Jeté, Jump, Leaf, Leap, Lent, Lep, Litt, Lollop, Low-water, May, Mineral, Originate, Persephone, Pierian, Pounce, Prance, Primavera, Prime, Resilient, Ribbon, Rise, Saddle, Season, Skip, Snap, Source, Spa, Spang, Spaw, Start, Stem, Stot, Submarine, Sulphur, Summer, Suspension, Teal, Thermae, Thermal, Trampoline, Valve, Vault, Vaute, Vawte, Vernal, Voar, Ware, Watch, Waterhole, Weeping, Well(-head), Well up, Whip, Winterbourne

▷ **Spring(y)** *may indicate* an anagram

**Springbok** Amabokoboko

**Springless** Telega

**Springtail** Apterygota

**Sprinkle(r), Sprinkling** Asperge, Aspergill(um), Bedash, Bedew, Bedrop, Bescatter, Caster, Disponge, Dispunge, Dredge, Dust, Hyssop, Lard, Papper, Pouncet, Powder, Rose, Scatter, Scouthering, Shower, Sift, Sow, Spa(i)rge, Spatter, Splash, Spray, Spritz, Strinkle

**Sprint(er)** Burst, Dash, Gallop, Race, Rash, Run, Rush, Scurry, Wells

**Sprite** Apsaras, Banshee, Croquemitaine, Dobbie, Dobby, Echo, Elf, Fairy, Fiend, Genie, Gnome, Goblin, Gremlin, Hobgoblin, Icon, Kelpie, Kelpy, Nickel, Nis(se), Oberon, Ondine, Puck, Pug, Spirit, Troll, Trow, Umbriel, Undine

**Sprocket** Whelp

**Sprout** Braird, Breer, Brussels, Bud, Burgeon, Chit, Crop, Eye, Germ(inate), Grow, Pullulate, Shoot, Spire, Tendron, Vegetate

**Spruce** Balsam, Dapper, Engelmann, Hemlock, Natty, Neat, Norway, Picea, Pitch-tree, Prink, Shipshape, Sitka, Smart, Snazzy, Spiff, Tidy, Tree, Trim, Tsuga, White

**Spry** Active, Agile, Constance, Dapper, Nimble, Volable

**Spud** Murphy, Potato, Spade, Tater, Tatie

**Spume** Eject, Foam, Froth, Lather, Spet, Spit

**Spunk** Courage, Grit, Pluck, Spark, Tinder

**Spur(s)** Accourage, Activate, Aphrodisiac, Calcar(ate), Encourage, Fame, Fire, Fuel, Galvanise, Gee, Gilded, Goad, Groyne, Heel, Incite, Limb, Lye, Needle, Offset, Prick, Prong, Rippon, Rowel, Shoot, Spica, Stimulus, Strut, Stud, Tar, Urge

**Spurge (tree)** Candelilla, Croton, Euphorbia, Kamala, Manihot, Poinsettia, Ricinus

**Spurious** Adulterine, All-to, Al-to, Apocryphal, Bogus, Counterfeit, Dog, Fake, False, Phoney, Pseudo, Sciolism, Untrue

▷ **Spurious** *may indicate* an anagram

**Spurn** Despise, Disdain, Eschew, Ignore, Jilt, Leper, Rebuff, Reject, Repudiate, Repulse, →**SCORN**, Sdayn, Shun, Snub

**Spurrey** Yarr

**Spurt** Burst, Forge, Geyser, Jet, Outburst, Pump, Spout, Start

**Sputter** Bespit, Fizzle, Spit, Splutter, Stutter

**Spy(ing), Spies** Agent, Beagle, Blunt, Burgess, Caleb, CIA, Cicero, Curtain-twitcher, Descry, Dicker, Double agent, Eavesdrop, Emissary, Espionage, Fink, Fuchs, Infiltrate, Informer, Keeker, Maclean, Mata Hari, MI, Mole, Mossad, Mouchard, Nark, Ninja, Nose, Operative, Pickeer, Pimp, Plant, Pry, Recce, Scout, See, Setter, Shadow, Sinon, Sleeper, Snoop, Spetsnaz, Spook, Tachometer, Tarpeia, Tout, Voyeur, Wait

**Spyhole** Eyelet, Judas-hole, Oillet, Peephole

**Squab** Chubby, Cushion, Obese

**Squabble** Argue, Bicker, Brabble, Quarrel, Rhubarb, Rift, Row, Scene, Scrap, Spar, Tiff

**Squad(ron)** Awkward, Band, Blue, Company, Crew, Death, Drugs, Escadrille, Fifteen, Firing, Flying, Force, Fraud, Hit, Nahal, Platoon, Porn, Red, Snatch, Vice, White, Wing

**Squalid, Squalor** Abject, Colluvies, Dickensian, Dinge, Dingy, Filth, Frowsy, Grungy, Mean, Poverty, Scuzzy, Seedy, Skid Row, Sleazy, Slum(my), Slurb, Sordid

**Squall** Blast, Blow, Chubasco, Commotion, Cry, Drow, Flaw, Flurry, Gust, Line, Rainstorm, Sumatra, Wail, White, Williwaw, Yell, Yowl

**Squander** Blow, Blue, Dissipate, Fritter, Frivol, Lash, Misspend, Mucker, Scamble, Slather, Splash, Splurge, Ware, →WASTE

**Square(d), Squares** Agree, Anta, Arrière, Ashlar, Ashler, Bandanna, Bang, Barrack, Belgrave, Berkeley, Bevel, Block, Bribe, Chequer, Compone, Compony, Corny, Cube, Deal, Dinkum, Dodo, Even(s), Fair, Fog(e)y, Forty-nine, Fossil, Four, Gobony, Grey, Grosvenor, Latin, Least, Leicester, Level, Madison, Magic, Market, Meal, Mean, Mitre, Nasik, Neandert(h)aler, Nine, Norma, Old-fashioned, Old school, Old-time, Out, Palm, Passé, Pay, Perfect, Piazza, Place, Platz, Plaza, Quad(rangle), Quadrate, Quarry, Quits, Red, Rhomboid, Rood, S, Set(t), Sloane, Solid, Squier, Squire, Stick-in-the-mud, Straight, T, Tee, Tiananmen, Times, Traditionalist, Trafalgar, Try, Uncool, Unhip

**Squash(y)** Address, Butternut, Conglomerate, Crush, Flatten, Gourd, Kia-ora®, Knead, Marrow, Mash, Obcompress, Oblate, Pattypan, Press, Pulp, Pumpkin, Rebut, Shoehorn, Silence, Slay, Slew, Slue, Soft, Squeeze, Squidge, Squidgy, Summer, Suppress, Torpedo, Winter

**Squat(ter), Squatting** Bywoner, Caganer, Crouch, Croup(e), Cubby, Dumpy, Fubby, Fubsy, Hunker, Inquilinism, Occupy, Pudsey, Pyknic, Rook, Ruck, Sawed off, Sit, Spud, Squabby, Stubby, Stumpy, Swatter, Tubby, Usucaption

**Squaw** Kloo(t)chman

**Squawk** Cackle, Complain, Cry, Scrauch, Scraugh

**Squeak(er)** Cheep, Creak, Narrow, Near, Peep, Pip, Scroop, Shoat, Squeal

**Squeal(er)** Blow, Creak, Eek, Howl, Inform, Peach, Pig, Screech, Sing, Sneak, Tell, Wee, Yelp

**Squeamish(ness)** Delicate, Disgust, Missish, Nervous, Prudish, Queasy, Reluctant

**Squeeze(r)** Bleed, Chirt, Clench, Coll, Compress, Concertina, Constrict, Cram, Cramp, Credit, Crowd, Crush, Dispunge, Embrace, Exact, Express, Extort, Extrude, Hug, Jam, Mangle, Milk, Pack, Preace, Press, Reamer, Sandwich, Sap, Scrooge, Scrouge, Scrowdge, Scruze, Shoehorn, Squash, Squish, Strangle, Sweat, Thrutch, Thumbscrew, Vice, Wring

**Squelch** Gurgle, Squash, Squish, Subdue

**Squib** Banger, Damp, Firework, Lampoon

**Squid** Calamari, Calamary, Cephalopod, Cuttlefish, Ink-fish, Loligo, Mortar, Nautilus, Octopus, Sleeve fish

**Squiffy** Drunk, Lit, Tiddley, Tipsy

▷ **Squiggle** *may indicate* an anagram

**Squill** Sea, Spring

**Squint(ing)** Boss-eyed, Cast, Cock-eye, Cross-eye, Glance, Gledge, Glee, Gley, Hagioscope, Heterophoria, Louche, Opening, Proptosis, Skellie, Skelly, Sken, Squin(n)y, Strabism, Swivel-eye, Vergence, Wall-eye

**Squire** Armiger(o), Beau, Donzel, Escort, Hardcastle, Headlong, Land-owner, Sancho Panza, Scutiger, Swain, Western, White

**Squirm(ing)** Fidget, Reptation, Twist, Worm, Wriggle, Writhe

**Squirrel, Squirrel's nest** Aye-aye, Boomer, Bun, Cage, Chickaree, Chipmuck, Chipmunk, Dray, Drey, Flickertail, Flying (-fox), Gopher, Grey, Ground, Hackee, Hoard(er), Marmot, Meerkat, Petaurist, Phalanger, Prairie dog, Red, Richardson's ground, Sciuroid, Sewellel, Skug, Spermophile, S(o)uslik, Taguan, Vair, Zizel

**Squirt(er)** Chirt, Cockalorum, Douche, Jet, Scoosh, Scoot, Skoosh, Spirt, Spout, Spritz, Urochorda, Wet, Whiffet, Whippersnapper

**Sri Lanka(n)** Ceylon, Cingalese, CL, .lk, Serendip, Sinhalese, Tamil, Vedda

**St** Saint, Street

**Stab** Bayonet, Chib, Chiv, Crease, Creese, Dag, Effort, Go, Gore, Guess, Jab, Knife, Kreese, Kris, Lancinate, Pang, Pierce, Pink, Poniard, Prick, Prong, Punch, Stick, Stiletto, Turk, Wound

**Stabilise(r), Stability** Aileron, Anchor, Balance, Ballast, Balloonet, Emulsifier, Even, Fin, Fixure, Gyroscope, Maintain, Pax Romana, Peg, Permanence, Plateau, Poise, Steadfastness, Steady, Tail panel

**Stable(s)** Adjusted, Augean, Balanced, Barn, Byre, Certain, Consistent, Constant, Durable, Equerry, Equilibrium, Firm, Livery, Loose box, Manger, Mews, Permanent, Poise, Sane, Secure, Settled, Solid, Sound, Stall, Static(al), Steadfast, Steady, Stud, Sure, Together, Well-adjusted

**Stableman** Groom, Lad, Ostler

**Stachys** Betony

**Stack(s)** Accumulate, À gogo, Chimney, Clamp, Cock, End, Funnel, Heap, Lum, Nest, → PILE, Reckan, Rick, Ruck, Shock, Sight, Smoke, Staddle

**Stadium** Anfield, Arena, Astrodome, Ballpark, Bowl, Circus, Circus Maximus, Coliseum, Headingley, Hippodrome, Murrayfield, Speedway, Trent Bridge, Velodrome, Wembley

**Staff** Aesculapius, Alpenstock, Ash-plant, Bato(o)n, Bouche, Bourdon, Bread, Burden, Caduceus, Cane, Crew, Crook, Crosier, Cross(e), Crozier, Crutch, Cudgel, Entourage, Equerry, Establishment, État-major, Faculty, Ferula, Ferule, Flagpole, General, Ground, Jacob's, Jeddart, Linstock, Lituus, Mace, Man, Office, Omlah, Pastoral, Personnel, Pike, Pole, Ragged, Rod, Rung, Runic, Sceptre, Seniority, Skeleton, Stave, Stick, Supernumerary, Taiaha, Tapsmen, Tau, Thyrsus, Token, Truncheon, Verge, Wand, Workers, Workforce, Wring

**Stag** Actaeon, Brocket, Buck, Deer, For men, Hummel, Imperial, Knobber, Line, Male, Party, Royal, Rutter, Shadow, Ten-pointer, Wapiti

**Stage** Act, Anaphase, Apron, Arena, Ashrama, Bandstand, Bardo, Bema, Boards, Catasta, Centre, Chrysalis, Committee, Diligence, Dog-leg, Estrade, Fare, Fargo, Fit-up, Gastrula, Grade, Hop, Imago, Instar, Juncture, Key, Landing, Leg, Levee, Level, Metaphase, Milestone, Moment, Mount, Napron, Oidium, Orbital, Perform, Phase, Phasis, Pier, Pin, Platform, Podium, Point, Postscenium, Present, Prophase, Proscenium, PS, Puberty, Report, Resting, Rostrum, Scene, Sensorimotor, Sound, Stadium, Step, Stepping stone, Stor(e)y, Subimago, Theatre, Theatrical, Thrust, Transition, Trek, Wells Fargo, Yuga, Zoea

**Stage-coach** Diligence, Thoroughbrace

**Stagecraft** Pinafore

**Stagehand** Flyman, Grip

**Stagger(ed), Staggering** Alternate, Amaze, Astichous, Astonish, Astound, Awhape, Daidle, Dodder, Falter, Floor, Lurch, Recoil, Reel, Rock, Sensational, Shock, Startle, Stoiter, Stot(ter), Stumble, Sway, Teeter, Thunderstricken, Thunderstruck, Titubate, Tolter, Totter, Waddle, Wamble, Wintle

▷ **Staggered** *may indicate* an anagram

**Stagirite, Stagyrite** Aristotle

**Stagnant, Stagnation** Cholestasis, Foul, Inert, Moribund, Scummy, Stasis, Static

**Staid** Decorous, Demure, Formal, Grave, Matronly, Prim, Prudish, Sad, Seemly, Sober, Stick-in-the-mud

**Stain(er)** Aniline, Bedye, Begrime, Besmirch, Blemish, Blob, Blot, Blotch, Chica, Discolour, Dishonour, Dye, Embrue, Ensanguine, Eosin, Fox, Gram-negative, Gram-positive, Gram's, Grime, Imbrue, Inkspot, Iodophile, Keel, Maculate, Mail, Meal, Mote, Portwine, Slur, Smirch, Smit, Soil, Splodge, Splotch, Stigma, Sully, Taint, Tarnish, Tinge, Tint, Vital, Woad

**Stair(case), Stairs** Apples, Apples and pears, Caracol(e), Cochlea, Companionway, Escalator, Flight, Moving, Perron, Rung, Scale (and platt), Spiral, Step, Tread, Turnpike, Vice, Wapping, Winding

**Stake(s)** Ante, Bet, Claim, Deposit, Eclipse, Extracade, Gage, Go, Holding, Impale, Impone, Interest, Lay, Loggat, Mark, Mise, Nursery, Paal, Pale, Paliform, Paling, Palisade, Peel, Peg, Pele, Picket, Pile, Play, Post, Pot, Punt, Put, Rest, Revie, Risk, Septleva, Set, Spike, Spile, Stang, Stob, Straddle, Sweep, Tether, Vie, Wager, Weir, Welter

**Stalactite** Dripstone, Dropstone, Helictite, Lansfordite, Soda straw
**Stalagmite** Onyx marble
**Stale** Aged, Banal, Chestnut, Flat, Fozy, Frowsty, Fusty, Hackneyed, Handle, Hoary, Mouldy, Musty, Old, Pretext, Rancid, Stagnant, Urine, Worn
▷ **Stale** *may indicate* an obsolete word
**Stalemate** Deadlock, Dilemma, Draw, Hindrance, Impasse, Mexican standoff, Saw-off, Standoff, Tie, Zugswang
**Stalinist** Kirov
**Stalk(er), Stalks** Anthophore, Bennet, Bun, Cane, Caulicle, Follow, Funicle, Garb(e), Gynophore, Ha(u)lm, Keck(s), Kecksey, Keksye, Kex, Ommatophore, Pedicel, Pedicle, Peduncle, Petiole, Petiolule, Phyllode, Prowler, Pursue, Reed, Rush, Scape, Seta, Shaw, Spear, Spire, Stem, Sterigma, Still-hunter, Stipe(s), Strae, Straw, Stride, Strig, Strut, Stubble, Stump, Trail, Yolk
**Stalking-horse** Stale
**Stall(s)** Arrest, Bay, Booth, Box, Bulk, Crib, → **DELAY**, Floor, Flypitch, Hedge, Horse-box, Kiosk, Loose-box, Orchestra, Pen, Pew, Prebendal, Procrastinate, Seat, Shamble, Sideshow, Stable, Stand, Starting, Stasidion, Sty, Sutlery, Temporise, Trap, Traverse, Travis, Trevis(s), Whip, Whipstall
**Stall-holder** Choirboy
**Stallion** Cooser, Cuisser, Cusser, Entire, → **HORSE**, Stag, Staig, Stonehorse, Stud
**Stalwart** Anchor-man, Buirdly, Firm, Manful, Robust, Sturdy, Trusty, Valiant
**Stamen(ed)** Androecium, Octandria, Polyandria, Synandrium
**Stamina** Endurance, Fibre, Fortitude, Guts, Last, Stamen, Stay, Steel, Vigour
**Stammer(ing)** Balbutient, Er, Hesitate, Hum, Psellism, Sputter, Stumble, → **STUTTER**, Waffle
**Stamp(s), Stamped** Albino, Appel, Cachet, Cast, Character, Coin, Date(r), Die, Dry print, Enface, Enseal, Fiscal, Frank, Gutter-pair, Health, Imperforate, Impress, Imprint, Incuse, Kind, Label, Matchmark, Mint, Mintage, Obsign, Pane, Penny black, Perfin, Philately, Pintadera, Postage, Press(ion), Print, Rubber, Seal, Seebeck, Se-tenant, Signet, Spif, Strike, Swage, Tête-bêche, Touch, Touchmark, Trading, Trample, Tread, Tromp, Type, Visa
**Stamp-collecting** Philately, Timbrology, Timbrophily
**Stampede** Debacle, Flight, Onrush, Outrush, Panic, Rampage, → **RUSH**, Sauve qui peut
**Stance** Attitude, Ecarté, En garde, Pose, Position, Posture, Quinte
**Stand(ing), Stand for, Stand up** Apron, Arraign, Attitude, Base, Bay, Be, Bear, Bide, Bier, Binnacle, Bipod, Bristle, Brook, Canterbury, Caste, Cock, Confrontation, Cradle, Crease, Dais, Degree, Desk, Dock, Dree, Dumb-waiter, Easel, Endure, Epergne, Étagère, Extant, Face, Firedog, Foothold, Freeze, Gantry, Gueridon, Hard, Hob, Importance, Insulator, Klinostat, Last, Lazy Susan, Lectern, Leg, Lime, Music, Nef, Odour, One-night, Ovation, Pedestal, Place, Plant, Podium, Pose, Position, Pou sto, Predella, Prestige, Promenade, Protest, Qua, Rack, Rank, Regent, Remain, Represent, Repute, Rise, Rouse, Shout, Stall, Statant, Station, → **STATUS**, Stay, Stillage, Stock, Stomach, Stool, Straddle, Straphang, Striddle, Stroddle, Strut, Table, Tantalus, Taxi, Teapoy, Terrace, Toe, → **TREAT**, Tree, Tripod, Trivet, Umbrella, Upright, Whatnot, Witness
**Standard(s)** Banner, Base, Baseline, Basic, Benchmark, Bog, Bogey, Bread and butter, British, Canon, CAT, Classic(al), Cocker, Code, Colour(s), Conventional, Copybook, Criterion, Double, Eagle, English, Ethics, Etiquette, Examplar, Example, Exemplar, Fiducial, Flag, Ga(u)ge, Gold, Gonfalon, Grade, Guidon, Horsetail, Ideal, Jolly Roger, Kite-marker, Labarum, Level, Living, Measure, Model, Morals, Netiquette, Norm(a), Normal, Numeraire, Old Glory, Oriflamme, Par, Parker Morris, Pennon, Principle, Rate, Regular, Rod, Rose, Routine, Royal, → **RULE**, Scruples, Silver, Spec(ification), Staple, Stereotype, Sterling, Stock, Time, Touchstone, Tricolour, Troy, Two-power, Uniform, Usual, Valuta, Vexillum, Yardstick
**Standard-bearer** Alferez, Cornet, Ensign, Vexillary

**Stand-by** Adminicle, Reserve, Substitute, Support, Twelfth man, Understudy
**Stand-in** Double, Locum, Stunt man, Sub(stitute), Surrogate, Temp, Understudy
**Standish** Miles
**Stand-off(ish)** Aloof, Half-back, Number ten, Remote, Reserved, Stalemate, Upstage
**Standpoint** Angle, Slant, View
**Standstill** Deadset, Halt, Jam, Stalemate
**Stanley** Baldwin, Knife, Rupert
**Stannic** Tin
**St Anthony's fire** Ergotism, Erysipelas
**Stanza** Antistrophe, Ballad, Elegiac, Envoi, Envoy, Heroic, Matoke, Ottava, Ottava rima, Poem, Quatrain, Sixaine, Spasm, Spenserian, Staff, Stave, Tantum ergo, Tetrastich, Troparion, Verse
**Staple** Basic, Bread, Chief, Maize, Matoke, Oats, Pin, Rice, Stock, Wool
**Star(s)** Adept, Aster(isk), Binary, Body, Celebrity, Champ, Class act, Coma Berenices, Companion, Constant, Constellation, Cushion, Cynosure, Dark, Death, Double, Esther, Exploding, Falling, Fate, Feather, Feature, Film, Fixed, Flare, Giant, Headline, Hero, Hester, Hexagram, Idol, Late type, Lead, Leading light, Lion, Main sequence, Mogen David, Movie, Mullet, Multiple, Pentacle, Personality, Phad, Pip, Plerion, Pointer, Principal, Pulsating, Red-top, Seven, Shell, Shine, Shooting, Sidereal, Solomon's seal, Spangle, Starn(ie), Stellar, Stern, Swart, (The) Pointers, Top banana, Top-liner, Ultraviolet, Valentine, Variable, Vedette

---

### STARS

| 3 letters: | Dwarf | Carina | 7 letters: |
|---|---|---|---|
| Dog | Gamma | Castor | Alnilam |
| Sol | Hyads | Cygnus | Alnitak |
| | Indus | Dorado | Antares |
| 4 letters: | Lupus | Étoile | Calaeno |
| Argo | Mensa | Fornax | Canopus |
| Beta | Merak | Galaxy | Capella |
| Grus | Mizar | Hatsya | Cepheus |
| Lode | Norma | Hyades | Chamber |
| Lyra | North | Lambda | Columba |
| Mira | Polar | Lizard | Dolphin |
| Nova | Radio | Megrez | Epsilon |
| Pavo | Rigel | Meissa | Éstoile |
| Pole | Rigil | Merope | Evening |
| Ursa | Saiph | Meteor | Gemingo |
| Vega | Spica | Octans | Lucifer |
| Vela | Theta | Phecda | Mintaka |
| Zeta | Venus | Plough | Morning |
| | Virgo | Pollux | Neutron |
| 5 letters: | Wagon | Psyche | Perseus |
| Acrux | Whale | Pulsar | Phoenix |
| Agena | | Puppis | Polaris |
| Algol | 6 letters: | Quasar | Procyon |
| Alpha | Alioth | Saturn | Proxima |
| Ceres | Alkaid | Sirius | Regulus |
| Comet | Altair | Sothis | Sabaism |
| Delta | Aquila | Uranus | Serpent |
| Deneb | Auriga | Vesper | Sterope |
| Draco | Boötes | Volans | Triones |
| Dubhe | Carbon | | Wagoner |

| 8 letters: | Scorpius | Pentagram | 11 letters: |
|---|---|---|---|
| Achernar | Synastry | Rigil-Kent | Circumpolar |
| Arcturus | Waggoner | Supernova | |
| Barnard's | | Wolf-Rayet | 12 letters: |
| Circinus | 9 letters: | | Little Dipper |
| Denebola | Aldebaran | 10 letters: | Septentrione |
| Equuleus | Andromeda | Betacrucis | |
| Eridanus | Bellatrix | Betelgeuse | 13 letters: |
| Hesperus | Big Dipper | Betelgeuze | Grande vedette |
| Magnetar | Black hole | Brown dwarf | Southern Cross |
| Mira Ceti | Centaurus | Cassiopeia | |
| Pegasean | Collapsar | Orion's Belt | 14 letters: |
| Phosphor | Delphinus | Phosphorus | Camelopardalis |
| Pleiades | Fire-drake | Supergiant | |
| Praesepe | Fomalhaut | White dwarf | 15 letters: |
| Red dwarf | Meteorite | | Proxima Centauri |
| Red giant | Ophiuchus | | |

**Starboard** Right

**Starch(y), Starch producer** Amyloid, Amylum, Animal, Arrowroot, Cassava, Ceremony, Congee, Conjee, Coontie, Coonty, Cycad, Farina, Fecula, Formal, Glycogen, Lichenin, Manioc, Maranta, Pentosan, Pyrene, Pyroid, Sago, Stamina, Statolith, Stiff, Tapioca, Tous-les-mois

**Stare** Eyeball, Fisheye, Gape, Gapeseed, Gawp, Gaze, Geek, Glare, Goggle, Gorp, Look, Ogle, Outface, Peer, Rubberneck, Scowl

**Starfish** Ambulacra, Asterid, Asteroid(ea), Bipinnaria, Brittlestar, Ophiurid, Radiata

**Star-gaze(r), Star-gazing** Astrodome, Astronomy, Copernicus

**Stark** Apparent, Austere, Bald, Bare, Bleak, Gaunt, Harsh, Naked, Nude, Sheer, Stiff, Utterly

**Starling** Bird, Gippy, Hill mynah, Murmuration, Pastor, Rosy pastor, Stare, Stuckie

**Star of Bethlehem** Chincherinchee, Chinkerinchee

**Start(ed), Starter, Starting, Starting-point** Ab ovo, Abrade, Abraid, Abray, Activate, Actuate, Baseline, Begin, Bhajee, Boggle, Boot-up, Bot, Broach, Bug, Bully off, Bump, Chance, Commence, Consommé, Course, Crank, Create, Crudités, Curtain up, Dart, Debut, Ean, Embryo, Entrée, Face-off, False, Fire, Flinch, Float, Flotation, Flush, Flying, Found, Gambit, Gan, Generate, Genesis, Getaway, Gun, Handicap, Head, Hors-d'oeuvres, Hot-wire, Impetus, Imprimis, Incept(ion), Initiate, Instigate, Institute, Intro(duce), Jar, Jerk, Judder, Jump, Jump lead, Jump-off, Kick-off, L, Lag, Launch, Lead, Melon, Nidus, Novice, Off, Offset, Onset, Ope(n), Ord, Origin, Outset, Poppadom, Potage, Preliminary, Prelude, Proband, Push, Put-up, Reboot, Resume, Roll, Roul, Rouse, Scare, Set off, Shy, Slip, Snail, Soup, Source, Spark, Spring, Springboard, Spud, String, Syndicate, Tee-off, Terminus a quo, Toehold, Wince

▷ **Start** *may indicate* an anagram or first letters

**Startle(d), Startling** Agape, Alarm, Bewilder, Disturb, Electric, Eye-opener, Flush, Frighten, How d'y(e)do, Lurid, Magical, Rock, Scare

**Starvation, Starve(d), Starving** Anorexia, Anoxic, Bant, Clem, Cold, Deprive, Diet, Famish, Foodless, Inanition, Innutrition, Macerate, Perish, Pine, Undernourished

▷ **Starving** *may indicate* an 'o' in the middle of a word

**Stash** Hide, Hoard, Secrete

**State(s), Stated, Stateside** Affirm, Alle(d)ge, Aread, Arrede, Assert, Assever, Attest, Aver, Avow, Buffer, Case, Circar, Cite, Client, Commonwealth, Condition, Confederate, Construct, Country, Critical, Cutch, Declare, Dependency, Dirigisme, Emirate, Empire, État, Explicit, Express, Federal, Fettle, Flap, Formulate, Free, Going, Habitus, Humour, Kingdom, Land, Lesh, Limbo, Maintain, Mess, Metastable, Mode, Name, Nanny,

Nation, Native, Palatinate, Papal, Para, Plateau, Plenarty, Plight, Police, Posit, Power, Predicament, Predicate, Premise, Profess, Pronounce, Protectorate, Puppet, Quantum, Realm, Republic, Rogue, Samadhi, Sanctitude, Satellite, Satori, Say, Sircar, Sirkar, Slave, Sorry, Standard, Standing, Steady, Succession, Sunbelt, Threeness, Thusness, Uncle Sam, Union, United, Welfare, Yap

## STATES

| 2 *letters:* | 5 *letters:* | Colima | Bavaria |
|---|---|---|---|
| Ga | Amapa | Dakota | Belarus |
| Ia | Assam | Greece | Benelux |
| Md | Bahia | Hawaii | Buffalo |
| Me | Benin | Indore | Chiapas |
| Mi | Benue | Jigawa | Comoros |
| NC | Bihar | Johore | Croatia |
| NY | Ceará | Kaduna | Durango |
| Pa | Dixie | Kansas | Eritrea |
| RI | Dubai | Kerala | Estonia |
| UK | Gabon | Khelat | Florida |
| US | Ghana | Kosovo | Georgia |
| Ut | Hesse | Latvia | Grenada |
| Va | Idaho | Kuwait | Gujarat |
| | Jammu | Madras | Gujerat |
| 3 *letters:* | Kalat | Malawi | Haryana |
| Ark | Kedah | Mysore | Hidalgo |
| Del | Kutch | Nevada | Indiana |
| Fla | Kwara | Oaxaca | Ireland |
| Goa | Lippe | Oregon | Jalisco |
| NSW | Lycia | Orissa | Jamaica |
| Oyo | Maine | Pahang | Jodhpur |
| USA | Malay | Parana | Kashmir |
| Wis | Mewar | Penang | Malacca |
| | Nepal | Perlis | Manipur |
| 4 *letters:* | Oshun | Puebla | Mizoram |
| Abia | Perak | Punjab | Montana |
| Acre | Piaui | Rivers | Morelos |
| Chad | Qatar | Saxony | Morocco |
| Conn | Reich | Serbia | Nayarit |
| Gulf | Sabah | Sikkim | New York |
| Iowa | Samoa | Sokoto | Nirvana |
| Kano | Texas | Sonora | Paraiba |
| Kogi | Tibet | Sparta | Pradesh |
| Laos | Tyrol | Styria | Prussia |
| Mass | | Tassie | Roraima |
| Ogun | 6 *letters:* | Tonkin | Sarawak |
| Ohio | Alaska | | Sergipe |
| Oman | Balkan | 7 *letters:* | Sinaloa |
| Ondo | Baltic | Alabama | Tabasco |
| Osun | Baroda | Alagoas | Tongkin |
| Shan | Bauchi | Algeria | Tonking |
| Swat | Belize | Anambra | Tripura |
| Togo | Bremen | Andorra | Trucial |
| Utah | Brunei | Arizona | Udaipur |
| | Cochin | Barbary | Vermont |

Vietnam
Wyoming
Yucatan

**8 letters:**
Abu Dhabi
Amazonas
Arkansas
Botswana
Campeche
Carolina
Coahuila
Colorado
Delaware
Ethiopia
Honduras
Illinois
Jharkand
Kelantan
Kentucky
Kiribati
Maranhao
Maryland
Michigan
Missouri
Nagaland
Nebraska
Oklahoma
Paraguay
Rondonia
Saarland
Sao Paulo
Selangor
Tanzania
Tasmania
Tiaxcala
Tongking

Transkei
Veracruz
Victoria
Virginia

**9 letters:**
Chihuahua
Costa Rica
Dixieland
Guatemala
Hyderabad
Indonesia
Karnataka
Louisiana
Manchukuo
Meghalaya
Michoacán
Minnesota
Nassarawa
New Jersey
New Mexico
Nuevo Léon
Queretaro
Rajasthan
Rajputana
San Marino
Singapore
St Vincent
Tamil Nadu
Tennessee
Thuringia
Tocantins
Trengganu
Venezuela
Wisconsin
Zacatecas

**10 letters:**
California
Guanajuato
Jamahiriya
Jumhouriya
Manchoukuo
Orange Free
Pernambuco
Queensland
Tamaulipas
Tanganyika
Terengganu
Travancore
Washington
West Bengal

**11 letters:**
Brandenberg
Connecticut
Jamahouriya
Maharashtra
Mecklenburg
Minas Gerais
Mississippi
North Dakota
Quintana Roo
South Dakota
Uttaranchal
Vatican City

**12 letters:**
Chhattisgarh
Madhya Bharat
New Hampshire
Pennsylvania
Saxony-Anholt
Uttar Pradesh

West Virginia

**13 letters:**
Andhra Pradesh
Madhya Pradesh
Massachusetts
Negri Sembilan
New South Wales
San Luis Potosi
Santa Catarina
South Carolina

**14 letters:**
Aguascalientes
Rio Grande do Sul
South Australia
Vindhya Pradesh

**15 letters:**
Himachal Pradesh
Schaumburg-Lippe
St Kitts and Nevis

**16 letters:**
Rio Grande do
  Norte

**17 letters:**
Schleswig-Holstein

**19 letters:**
Rhineland-
  Palatinate

**20 letters:**
North Rhine-
  Westphalia

▷ **Stated** *may indicate* a similar sounding word

**Stately, Stately home** August, Dome, Grand, Imposing, Junoesque, Majestic, Mansion, Noble, Pile, Regal, Solemn

**Statement** Accompt, Account, Affidavit, Aphorism, Assertion, Asseveration, Attestation, Avowal, Axiom, Bill, Bulletin, Case, Communiqué, Credo, Declaration, Deposition, Description, Dictum, Diktat, Encyclical, Enigma, Evidence, Expose, Factoid, Generalisation, Grand Remonstrance, Impact, Indictment, Invoice, Jurat, Manifesto, Mission, Motto, Non sequitur, Note, Outline, Paraphrase, Plaint, Pleading, Press release, Profession, Pronouncement, Pronunciamento, Proposition, Protocol, Quotation, Release, Report, Return, Sentence, Shema, Shout out, Soundbite, Sweeping, Testament, Testimony, Theologoumenon, Truism, Utterance, Verbal

**Stateroom** Bibby, Cabin

**Statesman** American, Attlee, Augustus, Botha, Brandt, Briand, Bright, Canning, Castlereagh, Cato, Chesterfield, Chirac, Cicero, Clarendon, Clemenceau, Cosgrave, De Valera, De Witt, Diefenbaker, Diplomat, Disraeli, Dollfuss, Draco, Dulles, Elder, Flaminius, Franklin, Gandhi, Genro, Georgian, Gladstone, Gracchi, Grotius, Guy,

Kissinger, Kruger, Lafayette, Lie, Mitterand, Molotov, Nasser, North, Nyerere, Palmerston, Peel, Perceval, Pericles, Peron, Pitt, Politician, Politico, Pompidou, Potemkin, Pretorius, Pym, Rockingham, Seneca, Smuts, Solon, Stein, Talleyrand, Tasmanian, Texan, Thiers, Tito, Verwoerd, Vorster, Walesa, Walpole, Walsingham, Wealsman, Yankee

**Static** Atmospherics, Becalmed, Electricity, Inert, Maginot-minded, Motionless, Sferics, Stagnant, Stationary

**Station(s)** Action, Aid, Air, Base, Berth, Birth, Camp, Caste, CCS, Channel, Charing Cross, Coaling, Comfort, Crewe, Deploy, Depot, Docking, Dressing, Earth, Euston, Filling, Fire, Garrison, Gas, Generation, Halt, Head, Hill, Hilversum, Ice, King's Cross, Lay, Location, London Bridge, Marylebone, Meridian, Mir, New Street, Nick, Outpost, Paddington, Panic, Pay, Petrol, Pitch, Place, Plant, Point, Police, Polling, Post, Power, Powerhouse, Quarter, Radio, Rank, Relay, Rowme, Seat, Service, Sheep, Sit, Situate, Space, Stance, Stand, Star, Status, Stond, Subscriber, Tana, Tanna(h), Terminus, Testing, Thana(h), Thanna(h), Tracking, Transfer, Triangulation, Vauxhall, Victoria, Waterloo, Waverley, Way, Weather, Whistlestop, Wind farm, Wireless, Work

**Stationary** At rest, Fasten, Fixed, Immobile, Parked, Sessile, Stable, Static

**Stationer(y), Stationery-case** Continuous, Multi-part, Papeterie

**Statistic(ian), Statistical, Statistics** Actuary, Bose-Einstein, Cusum, Descriptive, ERA, Fermi-Dirac, Figure, Gallup, Gradgrind, Graph, Inferential, Isotype, Lod, Nonparametric, Number, Parametric, Percentage, Quant(um), Sampling, Student's t, Vital

**Statuary, Statue(tte)** Acrolith, Bronze, Bust, Colossus (of Rhodes), Discobolus, Effigy, Eros, Figure, Figurine, Galatea, Idol, Image, Kore, Kouros, Liberty, Marmoreal, Memnon, Monolith, Monument, Oscar, Palladium, Pietà, Sculpture, Sphinx, Stonework, Stookie, Tanagra, Torso, Xoanon

**Stature** Growth, Height, Inches, Rank

**Status** Amateur, Beacon, Caste, Class, Curule, Pecking-order, Political, → POSITION, Prestige, Professional, Quo, Rank, Standing

**Statute** Act, Capitular, Chapter 11, Chapter 7, Decree, Edict, Law, Limitations, Novels, Provisors, Westminster

**Staunch** Amadou, Leal, Resolute, Steady, Stem, Stout, Styptic, Watertight

**Stave** Break, Dali, Forestall, Lag, Slat, Stanza, Ward

**Stay(ing), Stayer, Stays** Abide, Alt, Avast, Bide, Blay, Board, Bolster, Cohab(it), Continue, Corselet, Corset, Embar, Endure, Forbear, Fulcrum, Gest, Guest, Guy, Hawser, Hold, Indwell, Jump, Lie, Lig, Linger, Lodge, Manet, Moratorium, Pause, Pernoctate, Piers, Postpone, Prop, → REMAIN, Reprieve, Respite, Restrain, Rope, Settle, Sist, Sleepover, Sojourn, Stamina, Stem, Stop off, Stop-over, Strut, Sustain, Tarry, Triatic, Villeggiatura, Visit

**Stay-at-home** Indoor, Tortoise

**STD** Aids, Herpes, Telephone, VD

**Steadfast** Abiding, Changeless, Constance, Constant, Dilwyn, Firm, Immutable, Implacable, Perseverant, Resolute, Sad, Stable, Unswerving

**Steadier, Steady** Andantino, Ballast, Beau, Boyfriend, Changeless, Composer, Consistent, Constant, Even, Faithful, Fast, Firm, Girlfriend, Level-headed, Malstick, Measured, Regular, Rock, Rock-solid, Stabilise, Stable, Sustained, Unswerving

**Steak, Steakhouse** Carpet-bag, Chateaubriand, Chuck, Diane, Entrecote, Fillet, Flitch, Garni, Grill room, Mignon, Minute, Pepper, Pope's eye, Porterhouse, Ribeye, Rump, Slice, Tartare, T-bone, Tenderloin, Tournedos, Vienna

**Steal(ing), Steal away** Abstract, Bag, Bandicoot, Bone, Boost, Cabbage, Cly, Condiddle, Convey, Creep, Crib, Duff, Edge, Elope, Embezzle, Filch, Glom, Grab, Half-inch, Heist, Hotting, Joyride, Kidnap, Knap, Knock down, Knock off, Lag, Liberate, Lift, Loot, Mag(g), Mahu, Mill, Misappropriate, Naam, Nam, Nap, Nick, Nim, Nip, Nobble, Nym, Peculate, Phone-jack, Pilfer, Pillage, Pinch, Piracy, Plagiarise, Plunder, Poach, Pocket, Prig, Proll,

Purloin, Purse, Ram-raid, Remove, Rifle, Rip-off, Rob, Rustle, Scrump, Sculk, Shoplift, Skrimp, Skulk, Smug, Snaffle, Snatch, Sneak, Snitch, Souvenir, Swipe, Take, Theft, Thieve, Tiptoe, TWOC, Whip

**Stealth(y)** Art, Catlike, Covert, Cunning, Furtive, Obreption, Stolenwise, Surreptitious, Tiptoe

**Steam(ed), Steaming, Steamy** Boil, Condensation, Cushion, Dry, Fume, Gaseous, Het, Humid, Live, Livid, Mist, Porn, Radio, Roke, Sauna, Snift, Spout, Vapor, Vapour, Wet

**Steamer, Steamboat** Hummum, Kettle, Ocean tramp, Paddle, Showboat, Side-wheeler, SS, Str, Tramp, Turbine

**Steam-hammer, Steamroller** Crush, Ram

**Steam-organ** Calliope

**Steed** Avenger, Charger, Horse, Mount, Pownie

**Steel(y)** Acierate, Adamant, Bainite, Bethlehem, Blade, Blister, Bloom, Brace, Carbon, Cast, Chrome, Chromium, Cold, Concrete, Crucible, Damascus, Damask, High-carbon, High-speed, Low-carbon, Magnet, Manganese, Maraging, Martensite, Metal, Mild, Nerve, Nickel, Pearlite, Pedal, Ripon, Rolled, Shear, Silver, Sorbite, Spray, Stainless, Structural, Sword, Taggers, Terne plate, Toledo, Tool, Tungsten, Vanadium, Wootz

**Steelyard** Bismar

**Steep(ening)** Abrupt, Arduous, Bold, Brent, Buck, Cliff-face, Costly, Embay, Expensive, High-pitched, Hilly, Immerse, Krans, Krantz, Kranz, Macerate, Marinade, Marinate, Mask, Monocline, Plo(a)t, Precipice, Precipitous, Rait, Rapid, Rate, Ret, Saturate, Scarp, →SHEER, Soak, Sog, Sop, Souse, Stey, Stickle, Tan, Towery

**Steeple(jack)** Belfry, Spiderman, Spire, Turret

**Steer(er), Steering** Ackerman, Airt, Buffalo, Bullock, Bum, Cann, Castor, Con(n), Cox, Coxswain, Direct, →GUIDE, Handlebar, Helm, Navaid, Navigate, Ox, Pilot, Ply, Power, Rudder, Stot, Whipstaff, Zebu

**St Elmo's fire** Corona discharge, Corposant

**Stem** Alexanders, Arrow, Axial, Biller, Bind, Bine, Bole, Caudex, Caulicle, Caulome, Check, Cladode, Cladophyll, Confront, Corm, Culm, Dam, Eddo, Epicotyl, Floricane, Ha(u)lm, Kex, Originate, Pedicle, Peduncle, Pin, Pseudaxis, R(h)achilla, Rachis, Ram, Rhachis, Rhizome, Rise, Rod, Sarment, Scapus, Seta, Shaft, Shank, Sobole(s), Spring, Stalk, Staunch, Stipe, Stolon, Stopple, Straw, Sympodium, Tail, Tamp, Terete

**Stench** F(o)etor, Funk, Miasma, Odour, Pong, Reek, Smell, Stink, Whiff

**Stencil** Copy, Duplicate, Mimeograph®, Pochoir

**Stenographer, Stenography** Amanuensis, Secretary, Shorthand, Typist

**Step(s)** Act, Apples and pears, Balancé, Chassé, Choctaw, Companionway, Corbel, Corbie, Curtail, Dance, Degree, Démarche, Echelon, Escalate, False, Flight, Fouetté, Gain, Gait, Glissade, Goose, Grade, Grapevine, Grecian, Greece, Grees(e), Greesing, Grese, Gressing, Grice, Griece, Grise, Grize, Halfpace, Increment, Lavolt, Lock, Measure, Move, Notch, Pace, Pas, Pas de souris, Perron, Phase, Pigeon('s) wing, Quantal, Raiser, Ratlin(e), Rattlin(e), Rattling, Roundel, Roundle, Rung, Sashay, Shuffle, Slip, Stage, Stair, Stalk, Stile, Stope, Stride, Sugarfoot, Toddle, Trap, Tread, Trip, Unison, Waddle, Walk, Whole, Winder

**Step by step** Gradation

**Stephen** Martyr, Stainless

**Stepmother** Novercal

**Stepney** Spare

**Steppe** Kyrgyz, Llano, Plain

**Stereo** Ghetto blaster, IPod®, Nicam, Personal, Walkman

**Stereoscope** Pseudoscope

**Stereotype(d)** Hackney, Ritual, Spammy

**Sterile, Sterilise(r), Sterilisation, Sterility** Acarpous, Aseptic, Atocia, Autoclave, Barren, Clean, Dead, Fruitless, Impotent, Infertile, Neuter, Pasteurise, Spay, Tubal ligation, Unproductive, Vasectomy

**Sterling** Excellent, Genuine, Pound, Silver, Sound

**Stern** Aft, Austere, Back, Counter, Dour, Flinty, Grim, Hard, Implacable, Iron, Isaac, Nates, Poop, Rear, Relentless, Rugged, Stark, Strict, Tailpiece, Transom

**Steroid** Anabolic, Androsterone, Calciferol, Cortisone, Dexamethasone, Ergosterol, Fusidic, Lipid, Lumisterol, Mifepristone, Nandrolone, Predniso(lo)ne, Spironolactone, Stanozolol, Testosterone, Tetrahydrogestrinone

**Sterol** Stigmasterol

**Stertorous** Snore

**Stet** Restore

**Stethoscope** Pinard

**Stevedore** Coal-whipper, Docker, Dockhand, Lighterman, Loader, Longshoreman, Stower, Wharfinger

**Stevenson** RLS, Tusitala

**Stew(ed), Stews** Bagnio, Bath, Blanquette, Boil, Bordel(lo), Bouillabaisse, Bouilli, Bourguignon, Braise, Bredie, Broth, Brothel, Burgoo, Carbonade, Carbonnade, Casserole, Cassoulet, Cholent, Chowder, Coddle, Colcannon, Compot(e), Daube, Flap, Fricassee, Fume, Fuss, Goulash, Haricot, Hash, Hell, Hot(ch)pot(ch), Irish, Jug, Lather, Lobscouse, Maconochie, Matapan, Matelote, Mulligan, Navarin, Olla podrida, Osso bucco, Oyster, Paddy, Paella, Pepperpot, Pot-au-feu, Pot-pourri, Ragout, Ratatouille, Rubaboo, Salmi, Sass, Scouse, Seethe, Simmer, Slumgullion, Squiffy, Stie, Stove, Stovies, Sty, Succotash, Sweat, Swelter, Tajine, Tatahash, Tzimmes, Zamzawed, Zarzuela

**Steward(ess)** Bailiff, Butler, Cabin crew, Cellarer, Chamberlain, Chiltern Hundreds, Dewan, Factor, Flight attendant, Hind, Keeper, Major domo, Malvolio, Manciple, Maormor, Mormaor, Official, Oswald, Panter, Purser, Redcoat, Reeve, Seneschal, Sewer, Shop, Smallboy, Sommelier, Waiter

▷ **Stewed** *may indicate* an anagram

**St Francis** Seraphic Father

**Stibnite** Antimony, Kohl

**Stick(ing) (out), Stickiness, Sticks, Stuck, Sticky** Adhere, Affix, Agglutinant, Agglutinogen, Aground, Ash, Ashplant, Atlatl, Attach, Backwater, Baguette, Bamboo, Bastinado, Bat, Baton, Bauble, Bayonet, Beanpole, Blackthorn, Bludgeon, Bond, Boondocks, Broadside, Caman, Cambrel, Cammock, Cane, Celery, Cement, Chalk, Chapman, Clag, Clam(my), Clarty, Clave, Cleave, Cleft, Cling, Clog, Club, Cocktail, Cohere, Coinhere, Composing, Control, Crab, Crayon, Crosier, Cross(e), Crotch, Crozier, Crummack, Crummock, Cue, Distaff, Divining-rod, Dog, Dure, Endure, Execration, Exsert, Fag(g)ot, Firewood, Fix, Flak, Flypaper, Founder, Fuse, Gad(e), Gaid, Gambrel, Gelatine, Glair, Gliadin, Glit, Gloopy, Glue, Goad, Gold, Goo, Gore, Ground-ash, Gum, Gunge, Gunk, Harpoon, Hob, Hold on, Hurley, Immobile, Impale, Inhere, Isinglass, Jab, Jam, Joss, Jut, Kebbie, Kid, Kierie, Kindling, Kip, Kiri, Knife, Knitch, Knobkerrie, Ko, Lance, Lath(i), Lathee, Lentisk, Limy, Lug, Mallet, Message, Minder, Molinet, Needle, Orange, Parasitic, Paste, Penang-lawyer, Persist, Phasmid, Piceous, Pierce, Pin, Piolet, Plaster, Pogo, Poise, Pole, Posser, Pot, Protrude, Protuberant, Pugil, Q-tip, Quarterstaff, Rapier, Rash, Ratten, Resinous, Rhubarb, Rhythm, Rod, Ropy, Rural, Scouring, Seat, Shillela(g)h, Shooting, Size, Ski, Smeary, Smudge, Spanish windlass, Spear, Spillikin, Spurtle, Squail(er), Stab, Staff, Stand, Stang, Stob, Stodgy, Stubborn, Supplejack, Swagger, Switch, Swizzle, Swordstick, Tacamahac, Tack(y), Tally, Tar, Thick, Throwing, Toddy, Tokotoko, Truncheon, Trunnion, Twig, Vare, Viscid, Viscose, Viscous, Waddy, Wait, Walking, Wand, Wattle, Waxy, Wedge, White, Woolder, Woomera(ng), Yardwand

**Sticker** Araldite®, Barnacle, Bumper, Bur, Burr, Flash, Gaum, Glue, Label, Limpet, Partisan, Pin, Poster, Post-it®, Slogan, Viscose

**Stickler** Legalist, Pedant, Poser, Problem, Purist, Rigid, Rigorist, Tapist

**Stickybeak** Nosy Parker, Paul Pry

**Stiff, Stiffen(er), Stiffening, Stiffness** Anchylosis, Angular, Ankylosis, Baleen, Bandoline, Body, Brace, Buckram, Budge, Cadaver, Corpse, Corpus, Crick, Dead, Defunct,

Dilate, Expensive, Fibrositis, Firm, Formal, Frore(n), Frorn(e), Gammy, Goner, Gromet, Grommet, Grummet, Gut, Hard, Inelastic, Interfacing, Lignin, Mort, Muscle-bound, Myotonia, Petrify, Pokerish, Prim, Ramrod, Rheumatic(ky), Rigid, Rigor, Rigor mortis, Sad, Set, Shank-iron, Size, Solid, Starch, Stark, Stay, Steep, Steeve, Stieve, Stilted, Stoor, Stour, Stowre, Sture, Tarlatan, Tensive, Trubenize®, Unbending, Unyielding, Upper lip, Whalebone, Wigan, Wooden

**Stifle** Crush, Dampen, Depress, Funk, Muffle, Scomfish, Smore, Smother, Stive, Strangle

**Stigma(tise)** Blemish, Brand, Carpel, Discredit, Note, Slur, Smear, Spot, → STAIN, Wound

**Stile** Gate, Slamming, Steps, Sty

**Stiletto** Bodkin, Heel, Knife

**Still** Accoy, Airless, Alembic, Anymore, Assuage, At rest, Becalm, Breathless, Calm, Check, Current, Doggo, Ene, Even(ness), Freeze-frame, Higher, Howbe, However, Hush, Idle, Illicit, Inactive, Inanimate, Inert, Kill, Languid, Limbec(k), Lull, Motionless, Nevertheless, Nonetheless, Notwithstanding, Patent, Peaceful, Photograph, Placate, Placid, Polaroid, Posé, Pot, Practitioner, Quiescent, Quiet, Resting, Retort, Serene, Silent, Snapshot, Soothe, Stagnant, Static, Stationary, Stock, Stone, Though, Tranquil, Windless, Yet

**Stilt** Avocet, Bird, Poaka, Prop, Scatch

**Stilted** Formal, Mannered, Pedantic, Stiff, Unruffled, Wooden

**Stimulate, Stimulus, Stimulant, Stimulation** Activate, Adrenaline, Anilingus, Ankus, Antigen, Aperitif, Aphrodisiac, Arak, Arouse, Auxin, Benny, Brace, Caffeine, Cardiac, Cinder, Clomiphene, Coca, Conditioned, Coramine, Cue, Dart, Dex(edrine)®, Digitalin, Digoxin, Doxapram, Egg, Energise, Erotogenic, Evoke, Excitant, Fillip, Foreplay, Fuel, Galvanize, Ginger, Goad, Grains of Paradise, G-spot, Guinea grains, Hop up, Hormone, Incentive, Incitant, Incite, Innerve, Inspire, Irritate, Jog, K(h)at, Key, Kick, L-dopa, Mneme, Motivate, Nikethamide, Oestrus, Oxytocin, Pa(a)n, Paraphilia, Paratonic, Pemoline, Pep, Pep pill, Peyote, Philtre, Pick-me-up, Piquant, Pituitrin, Potentiate, Prod, Promote, Provoke, Psych, Qat, Rim, Ritalin®, Roborant, → ROUSE, Rowel, Rub, Sassafras, Sensuous, Somatosensory, Spark, Spur, Sting, Stir, String, Suggestive, Tannin, Tar, Theine, Tickle, Tik-tik, Titillate, Tone, Tonic, Tropism, Unconditioned, Upper, Urge, Whet(stone), Wintergreen, Winter's bark

**Sting(er), Stinging** Aculeate, Barb, Bite, Cheat, Cnida, Con, Goad, Nematocyst, Nettle(tree), Overcharge, Perceant, Piercer, Poignant, Prick, Provoke, Pungent, Rile, Scorcher, Scorpion, Sea anemone, Sephen, Smart, Spice, Stang, Stimulus, Surcharge, Tang, Tingle, Trichocyst, Urent, Urtica, Venom, Wasp

**Sting-ray** Sephen, Trygon

**Stingy** Cheeseparing, Chintzy, Close, Costive, Hard, Illiberal, Mean, Miserly, Narrow, Near, Niggardly, Nippy, Parsimonious, Save-all, Skimpy, Snippy, Snudge, Tight(wad), Tight-arse

▷ **Stingy** *may indicate something that stings*

**Stink(er), Stinking, Stinks** Abroma, Atoc, Atok, Brock, Cacodyl, Cad, Crepitate, Desman, Fetor, Foumart, Guff, Heel, Hellebore, Malodour, Mephitis, Miasma, Ming, Niff, Noisome, Pen, Polecat, Pong, Ponk, Rasse, Reek, Rich, Science, → SMELL, Sondeli, Stench, Teledu

**Stinkbird** Hoa(c)tzin

**Stint** Allot, Bout, Chore, Economise, Limit, Scamp, Scantle, Scrimp, Session, Share, Skimp, Spell

**Stipend** Ann(at), Annexure, Pay, Prebend, Remuneration, Salary, Wages

**Stipulate, Stipulation** Clause, Condition, Covenant, Insist, Provision, Proviso, Rider, Specify, String

**Stipule** Ocrea

**Stir(red), Stirrer, Stirring** Accite, Admix, Ado, Afoot, Agitate, Amo(o)ve, Animate, Annoy, Araise, Arouse, Awaken, Bird, Bother, Bustle, Buzz, Can, Churn, Cooler,

Emotional, Emotive, Evocative, Excite, Foment, Furore, Fuss, Gaol, Hectic, Impassion, Incense, Incite, Inflame, Inspire, Instigate, Insurrection, Intermix, Jee, Jog, Jug, Kitty, Limbo, Live, Makebate, →**MIX**, Molinet, Move, Newgate, Nick, Noy, Paddle, Penitentiary, Poach, Poss, Pother, →**PRISON**, Prod, Provoke, Quad, Quatch, Quetch, Qui(t)ch, Quinche, Quod, Rabble, Rear, Roil, Rouse, Roust, Rummage, Rustle, Sod, Steer, Styre, Swizzle, To-do, Touch, Upset, Upstart, Wake

▷ **Stir(red), Stirring** *may indicate* an anagram

**Stirrup (guard)** Bone, Footrest, Footstall, Gambado, Iron, Stapes, Tapadera, Tapadero

**Stitch(ing), Stitch up** Bargello, Bar tack, Basket, Baste, Blanket, Blind, Box, Buttonhole, Cable, Chain, Couching, Crewel, Crochet, Cross, Daisy, Embroider, Fancy, Feather, Fell, Flemish, Florentine, Garter, Gathering, Grospoint, Hem, Herringbone, Honeycomb, Insertion, Kettle, Knit, Lazy daisy, Lock, Machine, Middle, Monk's seam, Moss, Needle, Open, Overcast, Overlock, Pearl, Petit point, Pinwork, Plain, Purl, Queen, Rag, Railway, Rib, Rope, Running, Saddle, Satin, Screw, Sew, Slip, Smocking, Spider, Split, Stab, Stay, Steek, Stem, Stockinette, Stocking, Straight, Sutile, Suture, Tack, Tailor's tack, Tent, Topstitch, Vandyke, Wheat-ear, Whip, Whole, Zigzag

**St James** Scallop-shell

**St Jerome** Hieronymic

**St John's bread** Carob

**St Lucia** WL

**Stock(ed), Stockpile, Stocks, Stocky** Aerie, Aery, Alpha, Ambulance, Amplosome, Arsenal, Barometer, Blue-chip, Bouillon, Bree, Breech, Brompton, Buffer, But(t), Capital, Cards, Carry, Cattle, Choker, Cippus, Common, Congee, Conjee, Court-bouillon, Cravat, Crop, Dashi, Debenture, Delta, Die, Endomorph, Equip, Evening, Fumet, Fund, Gamma, Gear(e), Government, Graft, Gravy, Growth, Gun, Hackneyed, Handpiece, He(a)rd, Hilt, Hoard, Hoosh, Industrial, Intervention, Inventory, Joint, Just-in-time, Kin, Larder, Laughing, Line, Little-ease, Locuplete, Log, Night-scented, Omnium, Pigeonhole, Preferred, Pycnic, Race, Ranch, Recovery, Rep(ertory), Replenish, Reserve, Resource, Rolling, Root, Scrip, Seed, Shorts, Soup, Squat, Staple, Stash, Steale, Steelbow, Stereotype, Stirp(e)s, →**STORE**, Strain, Stubby, Supply, Surplus, Talon, Tap, Taurus, Team, Thickset, Tie, Trite, Trust(ee), Usual, Utility, Virginian, Water

**Stockade** Barrier, Eureka, Zare(e)ba, Zereba, Zeriba

**Stock Exchange** Big Board

**Stockholder** Rustler

**Stocking(s)** Bas, Body, Boot-hose, Fishnet, Hogger, Hold ups, Hose, Hosiery, Leather, Legwarmer, Legwear, Moggan, Netherlings, Netherstocking, Nylons, Popsock, Seamless, Sheer, Silk, Sock, Spattee, Support, Surgical, Tights

**Stockman, Stockbroker** Broker, Jobber, Neatherd

**Stocktaking** Rustling

**Stodge, Stodgy** Dull, Filling, Heavy

**Stoic(al)** Impassive, Job, Logos, Patient, Philosophical, Plato, Porch, Seneca(n), Spartan, Stolid, Uncomplaining, Zeno

**Stoke(r), Stokes** Bram, Chain grate, Coal-trimmer, Fire(man), Fuel, S, Shovel

**Stole(n)** Bent, Boa, Epitrachelion, Fichu, Hot, Maino(u)r, Manner, Manor, Nam, Orarion, Orarium, Reft, Scarf, Screen, Soup, Staw, Tippet, Tweedle, Waif, Wrap

**Stolid** Beefy, Deadpan, Dour, Dull, Impassive, Phlegmatic, Po(-faced), Thickset, Wooden

**Stomach(ic)** Abdomen, Abomasum, Accept, Alvine, Appetite, Belly, Bible, Bingy, Bonnet, Bread-basket, Brook, C(o)eliac, Corporation, Craw, Epigastrium, Epiploon, Face, Fardel-bag, Gaster, Gastric, Gizzard, Gut, Heart, Inner man, Jejunum, King's-hood, Kite, Kyte, Little Mary, Manyplies, Mary, Maw, Mesaraic, Midriff, Omasum, Opisthosoma, Paunch, Potbelly, Propodon, Proventriculus, Psalterium, Puku, Pylorus, Read, Rennet, Reticulum, Rumen, Stand, Stick, Swagbelly, →**SWALLOW**, Tripe, Tum, Tun-belly, Urite, Uromere, Vell, Venter, Wame, Washboard, Wem, Zingiber

**Stomach-ache** Colic, Colitis, Collywobbles, Gastralgia, Giardiasis, Gripe, Gutrot, Mulligrubs

**Stone(s), Stone age, Stoned, Stony** Blotto, Cast, Coggle, Deseed, Drake, Drunk, Foundation, →GEM, Henge, Imposing, Ink, Inukshuk, Lapideous, Lucky, Lydian, Masonry, Mort, Niobe(an), Ore, Pelt, Petrified, Precious, Putting, Rolling, Roughcast, Seeing, Sermon, Shingle, Standing, Step(ping), Through, Touch, Tusking

## STONES

*2 letters:*
St

*3 letters:*
Gem
Hog
Pip
Pit
Rag
Tin

*4 letters:*
Bath
Blue
Celt
Door
Flag
Hone
Horn
Iron
Jasp
Kerb
Lias
Lime
Lode
Onyx
Opal
Plum
Ragg
Sard
Skew
Slab
Soap
Tile
Trap

*5 letters:*
Agate
Amber
Balas
Beryl
Black
Chalk
Chert
Coade
Culch
Drupe
Flint
Gooly
Grape
Jewel
Kenne
Lapis
Logan
Menah
Metal
Mocha
Paste
Penny
Prase
Pumie
Quern
Quoin
Quoit
Rubin
Rufus
Rybat
Satin
Scone
Scree
Slate
Slick
Sneck
Stela
Stele
Topaz
Wacke
Wyman

*6 letters:*
Amazon
Arthur
Ashlar
Ashler
Baetyl
Bezoar
Brinny
Chesil
Chisel
Cobble
Coping
Cultch
Dolmen
Flusch
Fossil
Gibber
Gooley
Goolie
Gravel
Humite
Iolite
Jargon
Jasper
Kernel
Kidney
Kingle
Ligure
Lithic
Marble
Menhir
Metate
Mihrab
Mosaic
Muller
Nutlet
Oamaru
Paving
Pebble
Pencil
Pot-lid
Pumice
Pyrene
Rip-rap
Samian
Sarsen
Scarab
Summer
Tanist
Yonnie

*7 letters:*
Asteria
Avebury
Azurite
Blarney
Bologna
Boulder
Breccia
Callais
Cat's eye
Chuckie
Clinker
Curling
Girasol
Granite
Hyacine
Hyalite
Jacinth
Jargoon
Lia-fail
Lithoid
Moabite
Olivine
Parpane
Parpend
Parpent
Peacock
Pennant
Peridot
Perpend
Perpent
Petrous
Pudding
Purbeck
Putamen
Rocking
Rosetta
Rubbing
Sardine
Sardius
Sarsden
Scaglia
Schanse
Schanze
Smaragd
Staddle
Tektite
Telamon
Thunder
Trilith
Tripoli
Urolith
Zauxite

*8 letters:*
Aerolite
Aerolith
Amethyst

| | | | |
|---|---|---|---|
| Asteroid | Petrosal | Cornelian | Chalcedony |
| Baguette | Phengite | Crossette | Draconites |
| Cabochon | Pisolite | Dichroite | Enhydritic |
| Calculus | Portland | Firestone | Fieldstone |
| Cinnamon | Potstone | Gannister | Gastrolith |
| Corundum | Rollrich | Greensand | Grey-wether |
| Cromlech | Sapphire | Hessonite | Kimberlite |
| Cryolite | Sardonyx | Hoarstone | Lherzolite |
| Ebenezer | Scalpins | Lithiasis | Lithophyte |
| Elf-arrow | Schantze | Malachite | Pearlstone |
| Endocarp | Specular | Meteorite | Penny-stone |
| Essonite | Tonalite | Paleolith | Rhinestone |
| Ganister | Traprock | Pipestone | Sleekstone |
| Girasole | Voussoir | Rubicelle | Slickstone |
| Lapidate | | Scagliola | |
| Megalith | **9 letters:** | Trilithon | **11 letters:** |
| Menamber | Alabaster | Turquoise | Meteorolite |
| Monolith | Almandine | Ventifact | Pencil-stone |
| Nephrite | Asparagus | | Peristalith |
| Omphalos | Cairngorm | **10 letters:** | |
| Onychite | Carnelian | Adamantine | **12 letters:** |
| Parpoint | Cholelith | Alectorian | Carton-pierre |
| Peastone | Chondrite | Aragonites | Philosopher's |

**Stone-crop** Orpin(e), Rose-root, Sedum, Succulent
**Stone-pusher** Sisyphus
**Stone-thrower** Bal(lista), Catapult, David, Mangonel, Onager, Perrier, Sling, Trebuchet
**Stone-wall(er)** Block, Jackson, Mule, Revet
**Stoneware** Crouch-ware
**Stone-worker** Jeweller, Knapper, Sculptor
**Stooge** Butt, Cat's-paw, Feed, Joe Soap, Straight man
**Stook(s)** Sheaf, Stack, Thr(e)ave
**Stool** Bar, Buffet, Commode, Coppy, Cracket, Creepie, Cricket, Cucking, Curule, Cutty, Ducking, Faeces, Foot, Hassock, Litany, Milking, Music, Piano, Pouf(fe), Repentance, Ruckseat, Seat, Sir-reverence, Step, Stercoral, Sunkie, Taboret, Tripod, Tripos, Turd
**Stoop(ed)** Bend, Condescend, Cringe, Crouch, C(o)urb, Daine, Deign, Incline, Lout, Lowt, Porch, Round-shouldered, Slouch
**Stop(page), Stopcock, Stopper, Stopping** Abate, Abort, Adeem, Anchor, An(n)icut, Aperture, Arrest, Aspirate, Avast, Avert, Bait, Ba(u)lk, Belay, Bide, Blin, Block, Brake, Buffer, Bung, Can, Canting-coin, Carillon, → CEASE, Cessation, Chapter, Check, Checkpoint, Cheese, Cholestasis, Clarabella, Clarino, Clarion, Clog, Close, Cog, Colon, Comfort, Comma, Conclude, Conversation, Cork, Coupler, Cremo(r)na, Cremorne, Cromorna, Cut, Cut out, Deactivate, Debar, Demurral, Desist, Deter, Devall, Diapason, Diaphone, Discontinue, Discourage, Dit, Dock, Dolce, Dot, Drop, Dulciana, Echo, Embargo, Emergency, End, Enough, Expression, Extinguish, F, Fagotto, Fare stage, Field, Fifteenth, Flag, Flue, Flute, Forbid, Foreclose, Forestall, Foundation, Freeze, Fr(a)enum, Frustrate, Full, Full point, Gag, Gamba, Gemshorn, Glottal, Gong, Halt, Hamza(h), Hang, Hartal, Heave to, Hinder, Hitch, Ho, Hoa, Hoh, Hold, Hoy, Inhibit, Intermit, Ischuria, Jam, Kibosh, Kill, Lay to, Let-up, Lill, Lin, Lute, Media, Moratoria, Mutation, Nasard, Oboe, Obstruent, Obturate, Occlude, Oppilate, Organ, Outage, Outspan, Pack in, Pause, Period, Piccolo, Pit, Plug, Point, Poop, Preclude, Prevent, Principal, Prop, Prorogue, Pull-in, Pull over, Pull-up, Punctuate, Pyramidon, Quash, Quint, Quit, Racket, Red, Reed, Refrain, Register, Rein, Remain, Request, Rest, Roadblock, Salicet, Salicional, Scotch, Screw-top, Semi-colon, Sese, Sesquialtera, Sext, Silence, Sist, Sneb, Snub, Snuff out,

Sojourn, Solo, Spigot, Stall, Stanch, Standstill, Stap, Stash, Stasis, Station, Staunch, Stay, Stent, Stive, Strike, Subbase, Subbass, Suction, Supersede, Suppress, Surcease, Suspend, T, Tab, Tackle, Tamp(ion), Tap, Tea break, Tenuis, Terminate, Thwart, Toby, Toho, Truck, Trumpet, Tuba, Twelfth, Voix celeste, Vox angelica, Vox humana, Waldflute, Waldhorn, Waypoint, When, Whistle, Whoa

**Stopgap** Caretaker, Gasket, Gaskin, Interim, Makeshift, Pis aller, Temporary

**Stopwatch** Chronograph

**Storage, Store(house)** Accumulate, Archive, Armoury, Arsenal, Associative, Backing, Barn, Big box, Bin, Bookshop, Bottle, Bottom drawer, Boxroom, Buffer, Bunker, Buttery, Byte, Cache, Capacitance, Catacomb, Cell, Cellar(et), Chain, Cheek pouch, Clamp, Clipboard, Coffer, Convenience, Co-op(erative), Co-operative, Cootch, Core, Corn-crib, Cupboard, Cutch, Database, Deep freeze, Deli, Dene-hole, Dépanneur, Department(al), Depository, Depot, Dime, Discount, Dolia, Dolly-shop, Drive, EAROM, Elevator, Emporium, Ensile, Entrepot, Étape, External, Freezer, Fridge, Fund, Galleria, Garner, Gasholder, Genizah, Girnal, Glory hole, Go-down, Granary, Groceteria, Hayloft, Hive, → **HOARD**, Hog, Hold, Honeycomb, Hope chest, House, Houseroom, Humidor, Husband, Hypermarket, IKEA, Imbarn, Keep, Larder, Lastage, Lazaretto, Liquor, Locker, Lumber room, Magazine, Main, Mart, Mattamore, Meat safe, Memory, Mine, Minimart, Morgue, Mothball, Mow, Multiple, Nest-egg, Off-licence, One-step, Ottoman, Package, Pantechnicon, Pantry, Pithos, Preserve, Provision, Pumped, Rack(ing), RAM, Reel, Repertory, Reposit, ROM, Root house, Save, Sector, Shed, → **SHOP**, Silage, Silo, Sim card, Speakeasy, Spence, Spooling, Springhouse, Squirrel, Stack, Stash, Stillroom, Stock, Stockpile, Stockroom, Stow, Superbaza(a)r, Superette, Supermarket, Supply, Tack-room, Tank, Thesaurus, Tithe-barn, Tommy-shop, Trading post, Uplay, Vestiary, Vestry, Virtual, Volutin, Warehouse, Woodshed, Woodyard, Wool (shed), WORM

▸ **Storey** *see* **STORY**

**Stork** Adjutant, Antigone, Argala, Bird, Jabiru, Marabou(t), Marg, Saddlebill, Shoebill, Wader, Whale-headed, Wood, Wood ibis

**Stork's bill** Erodium

**Storm(y)** Ablow, Adad, Assail, Assault, Attack, Baguio, Blizzard, Bluster, Bourasque, Brouhaha, Buran, Calima, Charge, Cloudburst, Cockeye(d) bob, Cyclone, Devil, Dirty, Dust, Electric, Enlil, Expugn, Furore, Gale, Gusty, Haboob, Hurricane, Ice, Line, Magnetic, Monsoon, Onset, Oragious, Pelter, Rage(ful), Raid, Rain, Rampage, Rant, Rate, Rave, Red spot, Rugged, Rush, Shaitan, Snorter, Squall, Sumatra, Tea-cup, Tebbad, Tempest, Tornade, Tornado, Tropical, Turmoil, Unruly, Violent, Weather, White squall, Willy-willy, Wroth, Zu

**Stormproof** Unassailable

▹ **Stormy** *may indicate* an anagram

**Story, Storyline, Stories** Account, Actioner, Allegory, Anecdote, Apocrypha, Apologise, Arthuriana, Attic, Bar, Basement, Baur, Bawr, Bedtime, Biog, Blood and thunder, Chapbook, Chestnut, Clearstory, Clerestory, Cock and bull, Conte, Cover, Decameron, Detective, Edda, Epic, Episode, Etage, Exclusive, Exemplum, Fable, Fabliau, Fabrication, Falsehood, Feature, Fib, Fiction, Flat, Floor, Folk-lore, Folk-tale, Gag, Geste, Ghost, Glurge, Hair-raiser, Hard-luck, Heptameron, Hitopadesa, Horror, Idyll, Iliad, Jataka, Lee, Legend, Lie, Lore, Mabinogion, Märchen, Mezzanine, Myth(os), Mythus, Narrative, Nouvelle, Novel(la), Oratorio, Parable, Passus, Pentameron, Photo, Plot, Rede, Report, Roman a clef, Romance, Rumour, Saga, Scoop, Script, Serial, SF, Shaggy dog, Shocker, Short, Smoke-room, Sob, Spiel, Spine-chiller, Splash, Spoiler, Stage, Storey, Success, Tale, Tall, Thread, Thriller, Tier, Tragedy, Triforium, Upper, Version, Whodun(n)it, Yarn

**Storyteller** Aesop, Fibber, Grimm, Griot, Liar, Miller, Munchausen, Narrator, Raconteur, Sagaman, Shannachie, Tusitala, Uncle Remus

**Stoup** Benitier, Bucket, Vessel

**Stout(ness)** Ale, Beer, Black velvet, Burly, Chopping, Chubby, Cobby, Corpulent, Doughty, Embonpoint, Endomorph, Entire, Fat, Fubsy, Guinness, Hardy, Heavyset, Humpty-dumpty, Lusty, Manful, Milk, Obese, Overweight, Plump, Porter, Portly, Potbelly, Robust, Rotund, Stalwart, Stalworth, Sta(u)nch, Strong, Stuggy, Sturdy, Substantial, Tall, Tufty, Velvet

**Stove** Aga, Baseburner, Break, Calefactor, Chauff(f)er, Chiminea, Cockle, Cooker, Cooktop, Furnace, Gasfire, Hob, Oven, Potbelly, Primus®, Range, Salamander

**Stow** Cram, Flemish (down), Load, Pack, Rummage, Stack, Stash, Steeve

**St Paul's** Wren-ch

**Strabismus** Squint

**Straddle, Straddling** Bestride, Enjamb(e)ment, Strodle

**Strafe** Bombard, Shell, Shoot

**Straggle(r), Straggly** Estray, Gad, Meander, Ramble, Rat-tail, Spidery, Sprawl, Stray, Wander

**Straight(en), Straightness** Align, Bald, Beeline, Blunt, Boning, Correct, Die, Direct, Downright, Dress, Frank, Gain, Het(ero), Home, Honest, Lank, Legit, Level, Line, Narrow, Neat, Normal, Ortho-, Orthotropous, Rectilineal, Rectitude, Righten, Sheer, Slap, Tidy, True, Unbend, Unbowed, Uncoil, Uncurl, Unlay, Upright, Veracious, Virgate

**Straight edge** Lute, Ruler

**Straightfaced** Agelast

**Straightforward** Candid, Direct, Downright, Easy, Even, Forthright, Honest, Jannock, Level, Plain sailing, Pointblank, Simple, Uncomplicated

**Straight-haired** Leiotrichous

**Strain(ed), Strainer, Straining** Agonistic, Air, Ancestry, Aria, Breed, Bulk, Carol, Charleyhorse, Clarify, Colander, Distend, Drawn, Effort, Exert, Filter, Filtrate, Fit, Fitt(e), Force, Fray, Fytt(e), Intense, Kind, Lineage, Lullaby, Melody, Milsey, Minus, Molimen, Music, Nervy, Note, Overstretch, Overtask, Passus, Percolate, Plus, Pressure, Pull, Purebred, Rack, Raring, Reck(an), Repetitive, Retch, Rick, Seep, Seil(e), Set, Shear, Sieve, Sift, Sile, Stape, Start, Stirps, Stock, Streak, Stress, Stretch, Stripe, Sye, Tamis, Tammy, Taut, Tax, Tems(e), Tenesmus, Tense, Tension, Threnody, Try, Tune, Unease, Vein, Vice, Work, Wrick

**Strait(s)** Bab el Mandeb, Basilan, Bass, Bering, Bosp(h)orus, Canso, Channel, Condition, Cook, Crisis, Cut, Dardanelles, Davis, Denmark, Desperate, Dire, Dover, Drake Passage, East River, Euripus, Florida, Formosa, Foveaux, Gat, Gibraltar, Golden Gate, Great Belt, Gut, Hainan, Hormuz, Hudson, Johore, Juan de Fuca, Kattegat, Kerch, Korea, Kyle, Little Belt, Lombok, Mackinac, Magellan, Malacca, Menai, Messina, Mona Passage, Narrow, North Channel, Oresund, Otranto, Palk, Predicament, Soenda, Solent, Sound, St, Sumba, Sunda, Taiwan, Tatar, Tiran, Torres, Tsugaru, Windward Passage

**Straiten(ed)** Impecunious, Impoverish, Poor, Restrict

**Strait-laced** Blue-nosed, Narrow, Prig, Primsie, Prudish, Puritan, Stuffy

**Strand(ed)** Abandon, Aground, Bank, Beach, Castaway, Desert, Enisle, Fibre, Ground, Haugh, Hexarch, Isolate, Lock, Maroon, Neaped, Ply, Rice, Rope, Shore, Sliver, Thread, Three-ply, Tress, Twist, Wisp

**Strange(ness), Stranger** Abnormal, Alien, Aloof, Amphitryon, Bizarre, Curious, Dougal, Eccentric, Eerie, Exotic, Ferly, Foreign, Fraim, Freaky, Frem(d), Fremit, Frenne, Funny, Guest, Jimmy, Malihini, New, Novel, Odd(ball), Outlandish, Outsider, Quare, Quark, Queer, Rum, S, Screwy, Selcouth, Singular, Surreal, Tea-leaf, Uncanny, Unco, Uncommon, Unfamiliar, Unked, Unket, Unkid, Unused, Unusual, Wacky, Weird, Weyard, Wondrous

▷ **Strange** *may indicate* an anagram

**Strangle(r)** Anaconda, Bindweed, Boa, Choke, Garotte, Jugulate, Suffocate, Suppress, Throttle, Thug(gee)

**Strap(ping)** Able-bodied, Band, Barber, Beat, Bowyangs, Braces, Brail, Braw, Breeching, Browband, Cheekpiece, Crownpiece, Crupper, Cuir-bouilli, Curb, Deckle, Garter, Girth,

G-string, Halter, Harness, Holdback, Jess, Jock(ey), Kicking, Larrup, Lash, Leather, Ligule, Lorate, Lore, Manly, Martingale, Nicky-tam, Octopus, Overcheck, Palmie, Pandy, Rand, Rein, Robust, Shoulder, Sling, Spaghetti, Spider, Strop, Surcingle, Suspender, T, Tab, Taws(e), T-bar, Thong, Thoroughbrace, Throatlash, Throatlatch, Trace, Tump-line, Wallop, Watch, Watchband

**Stratagem, Strategist, Strategy** Artifice, Clausewitz, Contrivance, Coup, Deceit, Device, Dodge, Exit, Fetch, Finesse, Fraud, Game plan, Generalship, Guile, Heresthetic, Kaupapa, Lady Macbeth, Malengine, Manoeuvre, Maskirovka, Masterstroke, Maximum, Minimax, Plan, Realpolitik, Rope-a-dope, →RUSE, Salami, Scheme, Scorched earth, Sleight, Subterfuge, Tack, Tactic(s), Tactician, Trick, Wheeze, Wile

**Stratum, Strata** Bed, Coal Measures, Kar(r)oo, Layer, Neogene, Permian, Schlieren, Seam, Syncline

**Strauss** Levi

**Straw(s), Strawy** Balibuntal, Boater, Buntal, Chaff, Cheese, Crosswort, Halm, Hat, Haulm, Hay, Insubstantial, Kemple, Last, Leghorn, Monkey-pump, Nugae, Oaten, Panama, Parabuntal, Pea(se), Pedal, Rush, Short, Sipper, Stalk, Strae, Stramineous, Strammel, Strummel, Stubble, Sucker, Trifles, Truss, Wisp, Ye(a)lm

**Strawberry** Alpine, Barren, Birthmark, Fragaria, Fraise, Garden, Hautbois, Hautboy, Potentilla, Wild

**Stray(ing)** Abandoned, Aberrant, Alleycat, Chance, Depart, Deviate, Digress, Err, Excursion, Forwander, Foundling, Gamin, Maverick, Meander, Misgo, Pye-dog, Ramble, Roam, Sin, Straggle, Streel, Street arab, Traik, Unowned, Waff, Waif, Wander, Wilder

**Streak(ed), Streaker, Streaky** Archimedes, Bended, Blue, Brindle, Comet, Flambé, Flaser, Flash, Fleck, Freak, Hawked, Hawkit, Highlights, Lace, Layer, Leonid, Lowlight, Marble, Mark, Merle, Mottle, Primitive, Race, Ra(t)ch, Run, Schlieren, Seam, Shot, Splodge, Striate, Striga, Strip(e), Vein, Venose, Vibex, Waif, Wake, Wale, Yellow

**Stream** Acheron, Anabranch, Arroyo, Beam, Beck, Blast, Bogan, Bourne, Brook, Burn, Consequent, Course, Current, Driblet, Fast, Flow, Flower, Freshet, Ghyll, Gill, Gulf, Gush, Headwater, Influent, Influx, Jet, Kill, Lade, Lane, Logan, Meteor, Nala, Nalla(h), Nulla(h), Obsequent, Onflow, Pokelogan, Pour, Pow, Riffle, Rill, River, Rivulet, Rubicon, Run, Runnel, Sike, Slough, Spill, Spruit, Squirt, Star, Strand, Streel, Subsequent, Syke, The Fleet, Third, Thrutch, Tide-race, Torrent, Tributary, Trickle, Trout, Watercourse, Water-splash, Winterbourne

**Streamer** Banderol(e), Bandrol, Banner(all), Bannerol, Pennon, Pinnet, Ribbon, Tape, Tippet, Vane

**Streamline(d), Streamliner** Clean, Fair, Fairing, Simplify, Sleek, Slim

**Street** Alley, Ave(nue), Bay, Boulevard, Bowery, Broad, Broadway, Carey, Carnaby, Cato, Causey, Champs Elysées, Cheapside, Civvy, Close, Corso, Court, Crescent, Downing, Drive, Easy, Ermine, Fleet, Gate, Grub, Harley, High(way), Kármán vortex, Lane, Lombard, Main, Main drag, Meuse, Mews, One-way, Parade, Paseo, Poultry, Queer, Road, Sesame, Side, Sinister, St, Strand, Terrace, Thoroughfare, Threadneedle, Throgmorton, Two-way, Vortex, Wall, Wardour, Watling, Way, Whitehall

**Street arab** Mudlark

**Streetcar** Desire, Tram

**Street seller** Hawker, Patterer

**Streetwise** Cynical

**Strength(en), Strengthened, Strengthener, Strengthening** Afforce, Anneal, Arm, Asset, Augment, Ausforming, Bant, Beef, Brace, Brawn, Build, Confirm, Consolidate, Edify, Embattle, Enable, Energy, Field, Fish, Foison, Force, Force majeure, Forte, Fortify, Fortitude, Freshen, Fur, Fus(h)ion, Grit, Heart, Herculean, Horn, Integrity, Intensity, Invigorate, Iron, Lace, Line, Main, Man, Might, Munite, Muscle, Neal, Nerve, →POWER, Prepotence, Pre-stress, Proof, Reinforce, Roborant, Shear, Sinew, Spike, Spine, Stamina, Steel, Sthenia, Stoutness, →STRONG, Sustain, Tensile, Thews, Titration, Ultimate, Unity, Vigour, Vim, Willpower, Yield

**Strenuous** Arduous, Effort, Exhausting, Hard, Laborious, Vehement
**Strephon** Rustic, Wooer
**Stress(ed), Stressful** Accent, Actuate, Angst, Arsis, Birr, Brunt, Careworn, Creep, Drive
home, Emphasis, Highlight, Ictus, Impress, Italicise, Marcato, Nerves, Orthotonesis,
Oxidative, Oxytone, Paroxytone, Post-traumatic, Press, Primary, Proclitic, Proof, PTSD,
Rack, Ram (home), Rhythm, RSI, Secondary, Sentence, Sforzando, Shear, Strain, Taut,
Tense, →**TENSION**, Testing, Thetic, Tonic, Try, Umlaut, Underline, Underscore, Urge,
Wind shear, Word, Yield (point)
**Stretch(able), Stretched, Stretcher, Stretching** Acreage, Alength, Amplitude,
Belt, Brick, Crane, Distend, Doolie, Draw, Ectasis, Eke, Elastic, Elongate, Exaggerate,
Expanse, Extend, Extensile, Farthingale, Fib, Frame, Give, Gurney, Home, Lengthen, Lie,
Life, Limo, Litter, Narrows, Outreach, Pallet, Pandiculation, Porrect, Procrustes, Prolong,
Protend, Pull, Rack, Rax, →**REACH**, Sentence, Shiner, Span, Spell, Spread, Spreadeagle,
Strain, Streak, Taut, Tend, Tense, Tensile, Tenter, Term, Time, Tract, Tractile, Traction,
Tree, Trolley
**Stretcher-bearer** Fuzzy-wuzzy angel
**Striate** Lineolate, Vein
**Stricken** Beset, Hurt, Overcome, Shattered
**Strict(ly)** Authoritarian, De rigueur, Dour, Exacting, Fundamentalist, Hard and fast,
Harsh, Literal, Medic, Narrow, Orthodox, Penal, Proper, Puritanical, Religious, Rigid,
Rigorous, Severe, Spartan, Stern, Strait(-laced), Stringent
**Stride(s)** Gal(l)umph, Jeans, Leg, Lope, March, Pace, Piano, Stalk, Sten, Stend, Straddle,
Stroam, Strut, Stump
**Strident** Brassy, Discordant, Grinding, Harsh, Raucous, Screech, Shrill
**Strife** Bargain, Barrat, Bate(-breeding), Brigue, Colluctation, Conflict, Conteck, Contest,
Discord, Disharmony, Dissension, Feud, Food, Friction, Ignoble, Scrap(ping), Sturt
**Strike(r), Striker, Striking, Strike out** Affect, Affrap, Air, Alight, Annul, Appulse,
Arresting, Astonishing, Attitude, Backhander, Baff, Band, Bandh, Bang, Bash, Bat, Baton,
Batsman, Batter, Beat, Belabour, Better, Biff, Black, Bla(u)d, Bludgeon, Bonanza, Bop,
British disease, Buff, Buffet, Bund(h), Butt, Cane, Catch, Chime, Chip, Clap, Clash, Clatch,
Clip, Clock, Clout, Club, Cob, Collide, Conk, Constitutional, Coup, Cue, Cuff, Dad, Dele,
Dent, Dev(v)el, Ding, Dint, Dismantle, Distingué, Douse, Dowse, Dramatic, Drive, Dush,
Éclat, Effective, Emphatic, Especial, Événement, Fat, Fet(ch), Fillip, Firk, Fist, Flail, Flog,
Frap, General, Get, Gnash, Go-slow, Gowf, Hail, Handsome, Hartal, Head-butt, →**HIT**,
Horn, Hour, Hunger, Ictus, Illision, Impact, Impinge, Impress, Jarp, Jaup, Jole, Joll,
Joule, Jowl, Knock, Lam, Lambast, Laser, Lash, Lay(-off), Lightning, Match, Memorable,
Middle, Mint, Noticeable, Official, Out, Pash, Pat(ter), Pat, Pean, Peen, Pein,
Pene, Percuss, Pize, Plectrum, Pounce, Pound, Pronounced, Pummel, Punch,
Quarter-jack, Rag-out, Raid, Ram, Rap, Remarkable, Rolling, Roquet, Salient, Scrub,
Scutch, Shank, Sick out, Sideswipe, Signal, Sitdown, Sit-in, Sizzling, Slam, Slap, Slat,
Slog, Slosh, Smack, Smash, Smite, Sock, Souse, Sowce, Sowse, Spank, Stayaway,
Stop(page), Stub, Swap, Swat, Swinge, Swipe, Switch, Swop, Sympathy, Tan, Tangent,
Tapotement, Tat, Thump, Thwack, Tip, Token, Tonk, Tripper, Twat, Unconstitutional,
Unofficial, Vivid, Walk-out, Wallop, Wap, Whack, Whale, Whang, Whap, Wherret, Who
does what, Whomp, Whop, Wick, Wildcat, Wipe, Wondrous, Zap
**Strike-breaker** Blackleg, Fink, Rat, Scab
**String(s), Stringy** Anchor, Band, Bant, Beads, Bootlace, Bow, Bowyang, Cello, Chalaza,
Chanterelle, Cord, Cosmic, Creance, Cremaster, Drill, Enfilade, Fiddle, Fillis, First, Floss,
G, Glass, Gut, Henequin, Heniquin, Hypate, Idiot, Injection, Keyed, Kill, Lace, Lag,
Laisse, Leading, Lichanos, Macramé, Mese, Necklace, Nete, Nicky-tam, Oil, Paramese,
Paranete, Pledget, Production, Proviso, Purse, Quint, Ripcord, Rope, Rosary, Rough,
Second, Series, Shoe(-tie), Silly®, Sinewy, Snare, Spit, Stable, Straggle, Strand, Sultana,
Sympathetic, Team, Tendon, Thairm, Tie, Tough, Train, Trite, Twiddling-line, Viola,
Violin, Worry-beads, Wreathed

**String-course** Moulding, Table

**Stringent** Exacting, Extreme, Rigid, Severe, Strict, Urgent

**String-pulling** Cat's cradle

**Strip(ped), Stripper, Stripping, Striptease** Agent orange, Airfield, Armband, Asset, Band(eau), Bare, Bark, Batten, Belt, Bereave, Bimetallic, Blowtorch, Caprivi, Casparian, Chippendale, Comic, Cote, Defoliate, Denude, Deplume, Deprive, Derobe, Despoil, Devest, Disbark, Dismantle, Dismask, Disrobe, Divest, Doab, Dosing, Drag, Ecdysiast, Ecdysis, Écorché, Excorticate, Fannel(l), Feeler gauge, Fiche, Film, Flashing, Flaught, Flay, Fleece, Flench, Flense, Flight, Flinch, Flounce, Flype, Furring, Gaza, Goujon, Hatband, Infula, Jib, Label, Landing, Lap-dancer, Lardon, Lath, Ledge, Linter, List, Littoral, Loading, Locust, Magnetic, Mail-rod, Maniple, Median, Möbius, Nature, Nude, Paint, Panhandle, Parting, Peel, Pillage, Pluck, Pull, Puttee, Puttie, Rand, Raunch, Raw, Reglet, Reservation, Riband, Ribbon, Rifle, Ring-bark, Roon, Royne, Rumble, Rund, Runway, Scent, Screed, Scrow, Shear, Shed, Shim, Shorn, Shred, Shuck, Skin, Slat, Slit, Sliver, Spellican, Spilikin, Spill(ikin), Splat, Splent, Spline, Splint, Splinter, Spoil, Sportswear, Straik, Strake, Strap, Streak, Strop, Sugar soap, Swath(e), Sweatband, Tack, Tear, Tear-off, Tee, Thong, Tirl, Tirr, Tombolo, Tongue, Trash, Unbark, Uncase, Unclothe, Undeck, Undress, Unfrock, Unrig, Unrip, Unrobe, Unvaile, Valance, Weather, Widow, Zona, Zone

**Stripe(d)** Agate, Band, Bausond, Candy, Chevron, Cingulum, Cove, Endorse, Go-faster, Lance-jack, Lash, Laticlave, Line, List, Magnetic, →NCO, Ombré, Pale, Paly, Pin, Pirnie, Pirnit, Slash, Snip, Straik, Strake, Streak, Striation, Stroke, Tabaret, Tabby, Tiger, Tragelaph(us), Vitta, Weal, Zebroid

**Stripling** Lad

**Strive, Striving** Aim, Aspire, →ATTEMPT, Contend, Emulous, Endeavour, Enter, Kemp, Labour, Nisus, Persevere, Pingle, Press, Strain, Struggle, Toil, Try, Vie

**Stroke** Apoplex(y), Backhander, Bat, Bisque, Blow, Boast, Breast, Butterfly, Caress, Carom, Chip, Chop, Counterbuff, Coup, Coy, Crawl, Dab, Dash, Dint, Dog(gy)-paddle, Down-bow, Drear(e), Drere, Dropshot, Effleurage, Estrarnazone, Exhaust, Feat, Flick, Fondle, Foozle, Forehand, Glance, Ground, Hairline, Hand(er), Hyphen, Ictus, In-off, Inwick, Jenny, Jole, Joll, Joule, Jowl, Knell, Knock, Lash, Lightning, Like, Line, Loft, Long jenny, Loser, Massé, Master, Oarsman, Oblique, Odd, Off-drive, Outlash, Palp, Paw, Pile-driver, Pot-hook, Pull, Punto reverso, Put(t), Reverso, Ridding straik, Roquet, Rub, Scart, Scavenge, Sclaff, Scoop, Seizure, Serif, Seriph, Sheffer's, Short Jenny, Sider, Sixte, Slash, Slice, Smooth, Solidus, Spot, Strike, Stripe, Sweep, Swipe, Tact, Tittle, Touch, Touk, Trait, Trudgen, Trudgeon, Tuck, Upbow, Virgule, Wale, Whang, Wrist shot

**Stroll(er), Strolling** Amble, Ambulate, Bummel, Dander, Daun(d)er, Dawner, Flânerie, Flâneur, Frescade, Idle, Lounge, Perambulate, Ramble, Saunter, Stravaig, Stray, Toddle, Walk, Walkabout, Wander

**Strong(est)** Able, Boofy, Brawny, Buff, Cast-iron, Doughty, Durable, F, Fat, Fierce, Firm, Fit, Forceful, Forcible, Forte, Full-blown, Hale, Heady, Hercules, High-powered, Humming, Husky, Intense, Ironside, Keen, Marrowy, Mature, Mighty, Muscular, Nappy, Ox, Pithy, Pollent, Potent, Powerful, Predominant, Pronounced, Pungent, Racy, Rank, Robust, Samson, Solid, Sour, Stale, Stalwart, Stark, Steely, Sthenic, Stiff, Stout, Str, Strapping, →STRENGTH, Sturdy, Substantial, Suit, Tarzan, Tenable, Theory, Thesis, Thewy, Thickset, Tough, Trusty, Valid, Vegete, Vehement, Vigorous, Violent, Virile, Well-built, Well-set, Wight, Ya(u)ld

**Stronghold** Acropolis, Aerie, Bastion, Castle, Citadel, Eyrie, Eyry, Fastness, Fortalice, Fortress, Holt, Keep, Kremlin, Redoubt, Tower

**Strongroom** Genizah, Safe

**Strontium** Sr

**Strop(py)** Cantankerous, Leather, Sharpen, Strap

**Struck** Aghast, Raught, Smitten, Smote

**Structural, Structure** Acrosome, Allotrope, Analysis, Anatomy, Arch, Armature, Atomic, Building, Catafalque, Centriole, Chromosome, Cold frame, Compage(s), Conus, Darga(h), Data, Database, Deep, Edifice, Erection, Fabric, Fairing, Flaser, Format(ion), Formwork, Frame, Galea, Gantry, Headframe, Helictite, Heterarchy, Hut, Hyperbolic, Hyperfine, Ice-apron, Idant, Kekulé, Lantern, Lattice, Macrocosm, Malpighian, Manubrium, Mole, Organic, Ossature, Pagoda, Palmation, Parawalker, Pea-trainer, Pediment, Pergola, Phloem, Physique, Pod, Power, Prophyll, Protein, Retinaculum, Set-up, Shape, Shell, Shoring, Skeleton, Sponson, Sporocarp, Squinch, Staging, Stand, Starling, Stylobate, Surface, Syntax, System, Tectonic, Telomere, Texas, Texture, Thylakoid, Trabecula, Trilithon, Trochlea, Undercarriage

**Struggle, Struggling** Agon(ise), Agonistes, Amelia, Battle, Buckle, Camp, Chore, Class, Combat, Conflict, Contend, Contest, Cope, Debatement, Duel, Effort, Encounter, Endeavour, Exertion, Fag, Fight, Flounder, Grabble, Grapple, Hassle, Jockey, Kampf, Labour, Luctation, Maul, Mill, Pingle, Rat-race, Reluct, Resist, Scrabble, Scramble, Scrape, Scrimmage, Scrum, Scrummage, Scuffle, Slugfest, Sprangle, Strain, Strift, →**STRIVE**, Toil, Tug, Tuilyie, Tussle, Up a tree, Uphill, Vie, War(sle), Warfare, Work, Wraxle, Wrest(le)

▷ **Struggle** *may indicate* an anagram

**Strum** Thrum, Twang, Tweedle, Vamp

**Strumpet** Cocotte, Harlot, Hiren, Lorette, Paramour, Succubus, Waistcoateer, Wench

**Strut(ter), Strutting** Bracket, Brank, Bridging, Cock, Dolphin striker, Flounce, Haught(y), Jet, Kingrod, Longeron, Martingale boom, Member, Nervure, Peacock, Pown, Prance, Pronk, Prop, Scotch, Shore, Spur, Stalk, Stretcher, Strunt, Swagger, Swank, Tail-boom, Tie-beam

**Stuart** Anne, James, Pretender

**Stub(by)** Butt, Counterfoil, Dout, Dowt, Dumpy, Squat, Stob, Stocky

**Stubble** Ar(r)ish, Bristle, Designer, Hair, Ill-shaven, Stump

**Stubborn(ness)** Adamant, Bigoted, Bulldog, Bull-headed, Contumacious, Cross-grained, Cussed, Diehard, Dogged, Entêté, Hard(-nosed), Hidebound, Intransigent, Inveterate, Moyl(e), Mulish, Mumpsimus, Obdurate, Obstinate, Opinionated, Ornery, Ortus, Pertinacious, Perverse, Recalcitrant, Reesty, Refractory, Rigwiddie, Rigwoodie, Self-willed, Stiff, Stoor, Stout, Tenacious, Thrawn, Tough, Wrong-headed

**Stubbs** Una

**Stucco** Cement

**Stuck** Beached, Fast, Glued, Jammed, Lodged, Set, Stopped, Stumped, Trapped, Wedged

**Stuck-up** Chesty, Highty-tighty, Hoity-toity, La(h)-di-da(h), Proud, Sealed, Toffee-nosed, Vain

**Stud(ded)** Boss, Cooser, Cripple, Cu(i)sser, Doornail, Entire, Farm, Frost, He-man, Knob, Nail, Press, Race, Rivet, Seg, Set, Shear, Shirt, Sire, Stop

**Student(s)** Abiturient, Alphabetarian, Alumnus, Apprentice, Bajan, Bejant, Bursar, Bursch(en), Cadet, Candle-waiter, Catechumen, Class, Coed, Collegian, Commoner, Dan, Dig, Disciple, Dresser, Dux, Exchange, Exhibitioner, Extensionist, External, Form, Fresher, Freshman, Goliard, Gownsman, Graduand, Green welly, Grind, Gyte, Hafiz, Ikey, Internal, Junior, Kommers, Kyu, →**LEARNER**, Lucubrator, Magistrand, Matie, Mature, Medical, Mootman, Nomologist, NUS, Opsimath, Ordinand, Oxonian, Peking duck, Pennal, Plebe, Poll, Postgraduate, Preppy, Pupil, Reader, Rushee, Sap, →**SCHOLAR**, Self-taught, Semi, Seminar, Seminarian, Senior, Shark, Sixth former, Sizar, Sizer, Smug, Softa, Soph(omore), Sophister, Spod, Subsizar, Swat, Swot, Talibe, Templar, Tiro, Tosher, Trainee, Tuft, Tukkie, Tutee, Underclassman, Undergraduate, Wedge, Welly, Witsie, Wonk, Wooden spoon, Wooden wedge, Wrangler, Year

**Studio(s)** Atelier, Bottega, Ealing, Elstree, Film set, Gallery, Lot, Pinewood, Shepperton, Workshop

**Study, Studies, Studied, Studious, Studying** Analyse, Bionics, Bone, Brown, Carol, Carrell, Case, Classics, Comparability, Con(ne), Conscious, Consider,

Course(work), Cram, Den, Dig, Étude, Examine, Eye, Feasibility, Field, Gen up, Intramural, Isagogics, Lair, Learn, Liberal, Lucubrate, Media, Motion, Mug up, Mull, Muse, Nature, Ology, Perusal, Peruse, Pilot, Pore, Portrayal, Post-doctoral, Prep(aration), Probe, Read, Recce, Reconnoitre, Research, Reverie, Revise, Sanctum, Sap, Scan, Science, Scrutinise, Shiur, Sketch, Specialize, Stew, Swat, Swot, Take, Time and motion, Trade-off, Train, Tutorial, Typto, Voulu, Work

**Stuff(iness), Stuffing, Stuffy** Airless, Bloat, Bombast, Canvas, Close, Cloth, Cloy, Codswallop, Cram, Crap, Dimity, Equipment, Farce, Feast, Fiddlesticks, Fill, Force, Forcemeat, Formal, Frows(t)y, Frowzy, Fug, Gear, Glut, Gobble, Gorge, Gubbins, Guff, Hair, Havers, Hooey, Horsehair, Hot, Inlay, Kapok, Lard, Line, Linen, →**MATERIAL**, Matter, Musty, No-meaning, Nonsense, Overeat, Pad, Pang, Panne, Pompous, Ram, Replete, Rot, Salpicon, Sate, Satiate, Scrap, Sob, Stap, Steeve, Stew, Stifling, Substance, Surfeit, Taxidermy, Trig, Upholster, Wad, Youth

**Stultify** Repress, Ridicule, Smother

**Stumble** Blunder, Bobble, Daddle, Err, Falter, Flounder, Founder, Lurch, Peck, Snapper, Stoit, Titubate, Trip

**Stump(ed), Stumps, Stumpy** At sea, Bamboozle, Black, Bobtail, Butt, Clump, Fag-end, Floor, More, Nog, Nonplus, Orate, Peg, Runt, Scrag, Snag, Snooker, Spud, Squab, St, Staddle, Stob, Stock, Stool, Stub(ble), Tortillon, Tramp, Truncate, Wicket

**Stun(ned), Stunning** Astonish, Astound, Awhape, Bewilder, Bludgeon, Concuss, Cosh, Daze, Dazzle, Deafen, Donnard, Donnert, Dove(r), Drop-dead, Eclectic, Fantastic, Faze, Flabbergast, Glam, Gobsmack, KO, Numb, Poleaxe, Shell-shocked, Shock, Stoun, Stupefy, Taser®

**Stunner** Belle, Bobby-dazzler, Cheese, Cosh, Doozy, KO, Peach, Plastic bullet, Taser®

**Stunt(ed)** Aerobatics, Confine, Droichy, Dwarf, Escapade, Exploit, Feat, Gimmick, Hot-dog, Hype, Jehad, Jihad, Loop, Nirl, Puny, Ront(e), Runt, Ruse, Scroggy, Scrub(by), Scrunt(y), Stub, Trick, Wanthriven, Wheelie

**Stupefaction, Stupefy(ing), Stupefied** Ag(h)ast, Amaze(ment), Assot, Astonishment, Awesome, Benumb, Catatonic, Dopy, Dozen, Dumbfound, Etherise, Fuddle, Hocus, Moider, Moither, Mull, Narcoses, Numb, Stonne, Stun

**Stupendous** Mighty

**Stupid, Stupid person** Anserine, Asinine, Besotted, Blithering, Blockish, Braindead, Clay-brained, Crass, Daft, Datal, Dense, Desipient, Dim(wit), Dip, Donner(e)d, Dozy, Dull(ard), Fatuous, Flat, Foolish, Gaumless, Gross, Half-arsed, Half-baked, Hammerheaded, Hare-brained, Hatter, Hen-witted, Inane, Insensate, Insipient, Lamming, Mindless, Natural, Obtuse, Senseless, Silly, Sodden-witted, Thick, Thick-witted, Torpid, Vacuous, Witless, Wooden(head)

---

## STUPID PERSON

| 3 letters: | Oaf | Cake | Dork |
|---|---|---|---|
| Ass | Owl | Calf | Dote |
| Auf | Put | Clod | Fogy |
| Bev | Sap | Clot | Fool |
| Bob | Sot | Cony | Fozy |
| Cod | Wof | Coof | Gaby |
| Daw | Yap | Coot | Gaga |
| Div | | Dill | Geck |
| Fon | **4 letters:** | Ditz | Gelt |
| Git | Berk | Doat | Goat |
| Jay | Bete | Dodo | Goof |
| Lob | Bobb | Does | Goon |
| Log | Bozo | Dolt | Goop |
| Nit | Burk | Dorb | Gorm |

Gouk
Gowk
Gull
Gump
Hash
Jaap
Jerk
Lown
Lunk
Meff
Mome
Mong
Mook
Mutt
Nana
Nerd
Nerk
Nong
Nurd
Ouph
Poon
Poop
Prat
Putt
Putz
Rook
Simp
Slow
Stot
Tony
Tube
Twit
Warb
Yo-yo
Zany

*5 letters:*
Bevan
Blent
Bobby
Booby
Brute
Bumbo
Chick
Chump
Clunk
Cokes
Cuddy
Cully
Dicky
Diddy
Dilly
Divvy
Dorba

Dorky
Dubbo
Dumbo
Dummy
Dunce
Dweeb
Eejit
Fogey
Galah
Golem
Goofy
Goose
Hoser
Idiot
Kerky
Klutz
Looby
Loony
Lowne
Moron
Neddy
Ninny
Nitty
Noddy
Ocker
Ouphe
Patch
Plank
Prune
Quo-he
Schmo
Simon
Snipe
Spoon
Stock
Stupe
Sumph
Tonto
Twerp
Waldo
Wally
Yampy

*6 letters:*
Bampot
Barren
Bauble
Boodle
Buffer
Cretin
Cuckoo
Cuddie
Dawney
Dickey

Dodkin
Donkey
Doofus
Dottle
Drongo
Gander
Gaupus
Gunsel
Ignaro
Ingram
Ingrum
Johnny
Josser
Loonie
Lummox
Lurdan
Lurden
Muppet
Newfie
Nidget
Nig-nog
Nincum
Nitwit
Noodle
Nudnik
Numpty
Obfusc
Oxhead
Sawney
Schlep
Schmoe
Scogan
Shmock
Shmuck
Simple
Sucker
Tavert
Thicko
Tosser
Tumphy
Turkey
Turnip
Wigeon
Wommit
Zombie

*7 letters:*
Airhead
Asinico
Barmpot
Becasse
Buffoon
Charlie
Cupcake

Damfool
Dawbake
Dawcock
Dim bulb
Dingbat
Dipshit
Dizzard
Donnard
Donnart
Donnert
Fuckwit
Gomeral
Gomeril
Gubbins
Half-wit
Haverel
Insulse
Jackass
Johnnie
Juggins
Jughead
Lurdane
Mafflin
Mampara
Minnock
Muggins
Palooka
Pampven
Pillock
Pinhead
Plonker
Pot-head
Saphead
Schlepp
Schmock
Schmuck
Schnook
Scoggin
Taivert
Thickie
Tosspot
Twinkle
Want-wit
Wazzock

*8 letters:*
Abderian
Abderite
Baeotian
Boeotian
Bonehead
Boofhead
Bullhead
Clodpate

Clodpole
Clodpoll
Clueless
Crackpot
Deadhead
Dickhead
Dipstick
Dodipoll
Dotterel
Dottrell
Dumbbell
Flathead
Gobshite
Goofball
Goose-cap
Gormless
Imbecile
Knobhead
Liripipe
Liripoop
Lunkhead
Maffling
Meathead

Moon-calf
Numskull
Omadhaun
Pea-brain
Shithead
Shot-clog
Softhead
Tom-noddy
Wiseacre
Woodcock

**9 letters:**
Beccaccia
Birdbrain
Blockhead
Capocchia
Chipochia
Clarthead
Cornflake
Doddipoll
Doddypoll
Dottipoll
Dumb-cluck

Gothamite
Ignoramus
Jobernowl
Lamebrain
Malt-horse
Nicompoop
No brainer
Numbskull
Pigsconce
Schlemiel
Schlemihl
Simpleton
Thickhead
Thick-skin
Woodentop

**10 letters:**
Analphabet
Changeling
Dummelhead
Dunderhead
Dunderpate
Headbanger

Hoddy-doddy
Loggerhead
Muttonhead
Nickumpoop
Nincompoop
Sheepshead
Thickskull
Thimblewit
Touchstone

**11 letters:**
Chowderhead
Chucklehead
Featherhead
Knucklehead
Leather-head
Ninny-hammer
Simple Simon
Van der Merwe

**12 letters:**
Featherbrain
Shatterbrain

**Stupidity** Betise, Goosery, Hebetude, Oscitancy, Thickness, Torpor, Unwisdom
**Stupor** Catatony, Coma, Daze, Dwa(u)m, Fog, Lethargy, Narcosis, Trance
**Sturdy** Burly, Dunt, Gid, Hardy, Hefty, Lubbard, Lubber, Lusty, Robust, Rugged, Solid, Stalwart, Staunch, Steeve, Stieve, Stocky, Strapping, Strong, Stuffy, Thickset, Turnsick, Vigorous
**Sturgeon** Beluga, Ellops, Fish, Huso, Osseter, Sevruga, Sterlet
**Stutter(ing)** Blaise, Hesitate, Stammer
**St Vincent** WV
**Sty** Frank, Hogpen, Hovel, Pen, Piggery, Pigpen
**Stye** Eyesore, Hordeolum
**Style(s), Stylish, Stylist** Adam, À la, A-line, Anime, Art nouveau, Band, Barocco, Barock, Baroque, Bel canto, Biedermeier, Blocked, Blow-dry, Brachylogy, Burin, Call, Cantilena, Carry-on, Chic, Chi-chi, Chinoiserie, Chippendale, Class, Cultism, Cursive, Cut, Dapper, Dash, Decor, Decorated, Demotic, Diction, Directoire, Dress sense, Dub, Dude, Élan, Elegance, Empire, Entitle, Euphuism, Execution, Face, Fancy Dan, Farand, →FASHION, Fetching, Finesse, Flamboyant, Flava, Flossy, Fly, Font, Form(at), Free, Friseur, Galant, Genre, Ghetto fabulous, Glamour, Gnomon, Gongorism, Gothic, Grace, Grand, Gr(a)ecism, Greek, Groovy, Hair-do, Hand, Hepplewhite, Heroic, Heuristic, Hip, Homeric, House, International (Gothic), Intitule, Italianate, Katharev(o)usa, Lapidary, Locution, Louis quatorze, Louis quinze, Manner, Marivaudage, Metrosexual, Mock heroic, Mod(e), Modernism, Modish, Natty, New, New Look, Nib, Nifty, Novelese, Old, Panache, Pattern, Pen, Perm, Perpendicular, Personal, Phrase, Picturesque, Pistil, Plateresque, Pointel, Port, Posh, Post-modernism, Preponderant, Probe, Prose, Queen Anne, Rakish, Rank, Regency, Retro, Ritzy, Rococo, Romanesque, Rudie, Sheraton, Signature, Silk, Slap-up, Smart, Snappy, Snazzy, Soigné, Spiffy, Sporty, Street, Surname, Swish, Taste, Term, Title, Ton, Tone, Tony, Touch, Traditional, Trendsetter, Tuscan, Uncial, Unisex, Vain, Va-va-voom, Verismo, Vogue, Way
**Stylus** Needle
**Stymie** Baulk, Frustrate, Thwart
**Styptic** Alum, Amadou, Matico, Sta(u)nch

**Suave** Bland, Debonair, Oily, Smooth, Unctuous, Urbane
**Sub** Advance, Due, Fee, Journalist, Journo, Lieu, Submarine, Subordinate, U-boat, Under
**Subaltern** Loot, Lt
**Subarea** Talooka
**Sub-atomic** Mesic
**Subconscious** Inner, Instinctive, Not-I, Subliminal, Suppressed
**Sub-continent** India(n)
**Subcontract** Outsource
**Subdivision** Arm, Branch, Cohort, Commot(e), Cotyledon, Oblast, Sanjak, Section, Segment, Senonian, Sheading, Tepal, Wapentake
**Subdominant** Fah
**Subdue(d)** Abate, Adaw, Allay, Chasten, Conquer, Cow, Crush, Dampen, Dant(on), Daunt(on), Dim, Dominate, Entame, Lick, Low-key, Master, Mate, Mute, Overbear, Overpower, Quail, →QUELL, Quieten, Reduce, Refrain, Repress, Restrain, Slow, Sober, Soft pedal, Subact, Suppress, Tame, Under
**Subfusc, Subfusk** Dim, Dressy, Dusky, Evening, Sombre
**Subheading** Strapline
**Subhuman** Apeman, Bestial
**Subject(ed), Subjection, Subjectivity, Subjects, Subject to** Amenable, Art, Bethrall, Caitive, Case, Citizen, Contingent, Core, Cow, Dedicatee, Dhimmi, Donné(e), Enthrall, Foundation, Gist, Guinea pig, Hobby, Hobby-horse, Inflict, Issue, Liable, Liege(man), Matter, Metic, Motif, National, On, Oppress, Overpower, PE, People, Personalism, Poser, PPE, Rayah, RE, RI, Serf, Servient, Servitude, Sitter, Slavery, Snool, Submit, Suit, Syllabus, →THEME, Thirl, Thrall, Topic, Under, Undergo, Vassal, Villein
**Subjugate** Enslave, Master, Oppress, Overcome, Overpower, Reduce, Repress, Suppress
**Sublieutenant** Cornet
**Sub-lieutenant** Cornet
**Sublimate(r)** Aludel, Cleanse, Suppress, Transfer
**Sublime** Ali, Alice, August, Empyreal, Grand, Great, Holy, Lofty, Majestic, Outstanding, Perfect, Porte, Splendid
**Submarine(r)** Boomer, Diver, Hydronaut, Innerspace, Nautilus, Pig-boat, Polaris, Sub, U-boat, Undersea, X-craft
▷ **Submarine** *may indicate* a fish
**Submerge(d)** Dip, Dive, Drown, Embathe, Engulf, Imbathe, Impinge, Lemuria, Overwhelm, Ria, Sink, Take, Whelm
**Submissive, Submission, Submit** Acquiesce, Bow, Capitulate, Comply, Cringe, Defer, Docile, File, Folio, Gimp, Knuckle, Lapdog, Meek, Obedient, Obtemperate, Passive, Pathetic, Pliant, Propound, Refer, Render, Resign, Snool, Stepford, Stoop, Succumb, Truckle, →YIELD
**Subordinate** Adjunct, Below, Dependent, Flunky, Inferior, Junior, Minion, Myrmidon, Nether, Offsider, Postpone, Secondary, Second banana, Servient, Stooge, Subject, Subservient, Subsidiary, Surrender, Under(ling), Underman, Under-strapper, Vassal
**Subscribe(r), Subscription** Abonnement, Approve, Assent, Cedilla, Conform, Due, Endorsement, Pay, Pay TV, Sign(atory), Signature, Undersign, Underwrite
**Subsequent(ly)** Anon, Consequential, Future, Later, Next, Postliminary, Since, Then, Ulterior
**Subservient** Kneel, Obedient, Obsequious, Tame cat
**Subside, Subsidence, Subsidy** Abate, Adaw, Aid, Assuage, Bonus, Cauldron, Diminish, Ebb, Grant, Headage, Lysis, Sink, Sit, Slake, Swag
**Subsidiary, Subsidise** Anglesey, Auxiliar(y), By(e), By-end, Feather-bed, Junior, Secondary, Second banana, Side(-shoot), Sideline, Spin-off, Succursal
**Subsist(ence)** Batta, Bread-line, Dole, Keep, Live, Maintain, Rely, Survive
**Substance, Substantial** Allergen, Ambergris, Anethole, Antigen, Antithrombin, Antitoxin, Apiol, Axerophthol, Blanco, Blocky, Body, Calyx, Castoreum, Cermet, Chalone,

Chemzyne, Chitin, Chromatin, Cofactor, Colloid, Considerable, Content, Cosmin(e),
Creatine, Cytochalasin, Dense, Ectocrine, Ectoplasm, Elemi, Endorphin, Enorm(ous),
Enzyme, Essential, Ester, Ethambutol, Excipient, Extender, Exudate, Fabric, Feck,
Fixative, Flavanone, Getter, Gist, Gluten, Gossypol, Gravamen, Growth, Guanazolo,
Gutta-percha, Hearty, Hefty, Hirudin, Hylic, Imine, Indol, Inhibitor, Iodoform, Iodophor,
Isatin(e), Isomer, Kryptonite, Lase, Lecithin, Lectin, Leucotriene, Linin, Luciferin,
Material, Matter, Meaning, Meat(y), Metabolite, Metol, Mineral, Misoprostol, Mitogen,
Molal, Mole, Morphactin, Morphogen, Mucigen, Murr(h)ine, Mutagen, Myelin, Naloxone,
Neotoxin, Neurotoxin, Noselite, Nutrient, Orgone, P, Papier mâché, Particulate,
Pepsinogen, Perforine, Phlogiston, Phosphor, Pith, Polymer, Proinsulin, Promoter,
Prostaglandin, Protyl(e), Purin(e), Queen (bee), Quid, Reagent, Reality, Resin, Salacin(e),
Secretagogue, Sense, Sequestrant, Smeclic, Solid, Sorbitol, Stramonium, Stuff, Sturdy,
Suint, Sum, Sunblock, Surfactant, Sympathin, Synergist, Syntonin, Tabasheer, Tabashir,
Taeniafuge, Tangible, Terra alba, Thermoplastic, Thiouracil, Thiourea, Tocopherol,
Tusche, Viricide, Volutin, Weighty, Ylem

**Substandard** Inferior, Infra dig, Off, Poor, Schlo(c)k, Second, Small
▶ **Substantial** *see* SUBSTANCE
**Substantiate** Confirm, Flesh, Prove, Strengthen, Support
**Substantive** Direct, Noun
**Substitute, Substitution** Acting, Alternative, Carborundum®, Change, Changeling,
Commute, Creamer, Deputy, Dextran, Double, Dub, Emergency, Ersatz, -ette,
Euphemism, Eusystolism, Exchange, Fill-in, Imitation, Improvise, Instead, Lieu(tenant),
Locum, Makeshift, Metonymy, Mock, Nominee, Novation, Pinch-hit, Proxy, Regent,
Relieve, Replace, Represent, Reserve, Resolution, Ringer, Sentence, Seth, Simulacrum,
Soya, Spare, Stalking-horse, Stand-in, Stead, Step in, Stopgap, Subrogate, Succedaneum,
Supernumerary, Supply, Surrogate, Switch, Swop, Synthetic, Twelfth man, Twentieth
man, Understudy, Vicar(ial), Vicarious
**Substructure** Base, Foundation, Keelson, Platform, Podium
**Subterfuge** Artifice, Chicane, Evasion, Hole, Manoeuvre, Off-come, Ruse, Strategy, Trick
**Subterranean** Concealed, Mattamore, Sunken, Underground, Weem
**Subtle(ty)** Abstruse, Alchemist, Crafty, Delicate, Fine(spun), Finesse, Hair-splitting,
Ingenious, Innuendo, Nice(ty), Nuance, Overtone, Refinement, Sly, Subdued, Suttle,
Thin, Wily
**Subtle difference** Nuance
**Subtract(ion)** Commission, Deduct, Discount, Remove, Sum, Take, Tithe, Withdraw
**Suburb(s)** Banlieue, Dormitory, Environs, Exurbia, Faubourg, Garden, Metroland,
Outskirts, Purlieu, Subtopia, Uptown
**Subverse, Subversion, Subversive, Subvert** Agitprop, Fifth column, Overthrow,
Reverse, Sabotage, Sedition, Treasonous, Undermine, Upset
**Subway** Dive, Metro, Passage, Tube, Underground
**Succeed, Success(ful), Successfully** Accomplish, Achieve, Answer, Arrive,
Big-hitter, Bingo, Blockbuster, Boffo, Breakthrough, Chartbuster, Coast, Come off,
Contrive, Coup, Do well, Éclat, Effective, Efficacious, Ensue, Fadge, Fare, Felicity,
Flourish, Follow, Fortune, Gangbuster, Get, Go, Heyday, Highflyer, Hit, Hotshot, Inherit,
Killing, Landslide, Luck, Made, Make good, Make it, Make out, Manage, Masterstroke,
Mega, Midas touch, Offcome, Parlay, Pass, Prevail, Procure, Profitable, Promising,
Prosper, Pull off, Purple patch, Pyrrhic, Rags to riches, Reach, Replace, Result, Riot, Roll,
Score, Seal, Seel, Sele, Sell out, Soaraway, Socko, Speed, Stardom, Superstar, Sure thing,
Take, Tanistry, The bitch goddess, Thrive, Thumbs up, Triumph, Up, Up and coming,
Upstart, Vault, Victory, Weather, Well, Win, Winnitude, W(h)iz(z)kid, Wow,
Wunderkind
**Succession** Apostolic, Chain, Cognate, Dead men's shoes, Ecological, Heirdom, Indian
file, Line, Mesarch, Neum(e), Order, Parlay, Result, Reversion, Sequence, Seriatim,
Series, String, Suite

**Successor** Co(m)arb, Deluge, Descendant, Ensuite, Epigon(e), Heir, Incomer, Inheritor, Khalifa, Next, Syen

**Succinct** Brief, Cereus, Compact, Concise, Encapsulating, Houseleek, Laconic, Pithy, Short

**Succour** Aid, Assist, Help, Minister, Relieve, Rescue, Sustain

**Succulent** Agave, Aloe, Cactus, Echeveria, Hoodia, Ice-plant, Juicy, Lush, Rich, Saguaro, Sappy, Spekboom, Tender, Toothy

**Succumb** Capitulate, Fall, Go under, Surrender, Yield

**Such** Like, Sae, Sike, Similar, So, That

**Suck(er), Sucking** Absorb, Acetabular, Acetabulum, Amphistomous, Antlia, Aphid, Aphis, Aspirator, Ass, Bull's eye, Culicidae, Dracula, Drink, Dupe, Fawn, Felch, Fellatio, Gnat, Gobstopper, Graff, Graft, Greenfly, Gull, Haustellum, Haustorium, Hoove, Lamia, Lamprey, Leech, Liquorice, Lollipop, Mammal, Monotremata, Mouth, Mug, Muggins, Osculum, Patsy, Plunger, Remora, Rook, Scolex, Shoot, Siphon, Slurp, Smarm, Spire, Spyre, Straw, Surculus, Sweetmeat, Swig, Sycophant, Tellar, Teller, Tick, Tiller, Toad-eater, Turion, Vampire

**Suckle, Suckling** Feed, Infant, Mother, Nourish, Nurse, Nurture

**Suction** Adhere, Implosion, Pump, Siphon

**Sud(s)** Foam, Lather, Sapples

**Sudan(ese)** Dinka, Mahdi, Nigritian, Nilot, Nuba

**Sudden(ly)** Abrupt, Astart, Astert, Extempore, Ferly, Flash, Fleeting, Foudroyant, Fulminant, Hasty, Headlong, Impulsive, Overnight, Precipitate, Rapid, Slap (bang), Sodain, Subitaneous, Subito, Swap, Swop, Unexpected

**Sue** Apply, Ask, Beseech, Dun, Entreat, Implead, Implore, Litigate, Petition, Pray, Process, Prosecute, Woo

**Suede** Split

**Suffer(er), Suffering** Abide, Aby(e), Ache, Affliction, Agonise, Auto, Bale, Be, → **BEAR**, Brook, Calvary, Cop, Die, Distress, Dree, Dukkha, Endurance, Endure, Feel, Gethsemane, Golgotha, Grief, Hardship, Have, Hell, Incur, Indolent, Languish, Let, Luit, Mafted, Martyr, Ordeal, Pain, Passible, Passion, Passive, Patible, Patience, Pay, Pellagrin, Permit, Pine, Plague, Purgatory, Smart, Stand, Stomach, Stress, Sustain, Thole, Tolerate, Toll, Torment, Torture, Trial, Tribulation, Undergo, Use, Victim

**Suffering remnant** Macmillanite

**Suffice, Sufficiency, Sufficient** Abundance, Adequate, Ample, Basta, Do, Due, Enough, Enow, Experimental, Nuff, Run to, Satisfy, Serve

**Suffix** Enclitic

**Suffocate** Asphyxiate, Choke, Smoor, Smore, Smother, Stifle, Stive, Strangle, Throttle

**Suffrage(tte)** Ballot, Davison, Feminist, Franchise, Lucy Stoner, Manhood, Pankhurst, Vote

**Suffuse** Colour, Glow, Imbue, Saturate, Spread

**Sugar(y), Sugar cane** Aldohexose, Aldose, Amygdalin, Arabinose, Barley, Beet, Blood, Brown, Candy, Cane, Caramel, Carn(e), Cassonade, Caster, Cellobiose, Cellose, Chaptalise, Confectioner's, Cube, Daddy, Demerara, Deoxyribose, Dextrose, Disaccharide, Flattery, Fructose, Fucose, Furanose, Galactose, Gallise, Glucose, Glucosoric, Glycosuria, Goo(r), Granulated, Granulose, Grape, Gur, Heptose, Heroin, Hexose, Honeydew, Hundreds and thousands, Iced, Icing, Inulin, Invert, Jaggary, Jaggery, Jagghery, Ketose, Lactose, Laevulose, Loaf, Lump, Maltose, Manna, Mannose, Maple, Milk, Money, Monosaccharide, Muscovado, Nectar, Nucleoside, Palm, Panocha, Pentose, Penuche, Pyranose, Raffinose, Rhamnose, Ribose, Saccharine, Saccharoid, Simple, Sis, Sorbose, Sorghum, Sorg(h)o, Sparrow, Spun, Sweet, Syrup, Tetrose, Trehalose, Triose, White, Wood, Xylose

**Sugar-daddy** Lyle, Tate

**Suggest(ion), Suggestive** Advance, Advice, Advise, Blue, Breath, Connote, Counter-proposal, Cue, Float, Guess, Hint, Hypnotic, Idea, Imply, Innuendo, Insinuate,

Intimate, Kite, Mention, Modicum, Moot, Nominate, Posit, Posthypnotic, Postulate, Prompt, Proposal, Propound, Provocative, Racy, Raise, Recommend, Redolent, Reminiscent, Ring, Risqué, Savour, Scenario, Smacks, Soft core, Suspicion, Threat, Touch, Trace, Twang, Undertone, Vestige, Vote, Wind, Wrinkle

**Suicide** Felo-de-se, Hara-kiri, Hari-kari, Kamikaze, Lemming, Lethal, Sati, Seppuku, Shinju, Suttee

**Suit** Action, Adapt, Adjust, Agree, Answer, Anti-G, Apply, Appropriate, Become, Befit, Beho(o)ve, Bequest, Beseem, Besit, Birthday, Boiler, Cards, Case, Cat, Clubs, Conform, Courtship, Demob, Diamonds, Dinner, Dittos, Diving, Do, Drapes, Dress, Dry, Effeir, Effere, Etons, Exec(utive), Fadge, Fashion, Fit, G, Garb, Gee, Get on, Gree, Hearts, Hit, Jump, Lis pendens, Litigation, Long, Lounge, Major, Mao, Match, Menswear, Minor, Monkey, NBC, Noddy, Orison, Outcome, Paternity, Penguin, Petition, Pinstripe, Plaint, Play, Plea, Please, Point, Prayer, Pressure, Process, Pyjama, Quarterdeck, Queme, Res judicata, Romper(s), Safari, Sailor, Salopettes, Samfoo, Samfu, Satisfy, Serve, Shell, Siren, Skeleton, Slack, Space, Spades, Strong, Sun, Sunday, Supplicat, Sweat, Swim, Swords, Tailleur, Three-piece, Track, Trial, Trouser, Trumps, Tsotsi, Tweeds, Twin, Two-piece, Uniform, Union, Wet, Wingsuit, Zoot

**Suitable** Apposite, Appropriate, Apropos, Apt, Becoming, Capable, Competent, Congenial, Consonant, Convenance, Convenient, Decorous, Due, Eligible, Expedient, → **FIT**, Giusto, Habile, Keeping, Meet, Opportune, Pertinent, Relevant, Seasonal, Seemly, Sittlichkeit, Very, Worthy

**Suitcase** Port

**Suite** Allemande, Apartment, Chambers, Court, Dolly, Edit, Ensemble, Entourage, Hospitality, Lounge, Nutcracker, Partita, Retinue, Rooms, Serenade, Set, Skybox, Tail, Three-piece, Train, Two-piece

**Suitor** Beau, Gallant, John Doe, Lover, Petitioner, Pretendant, Pretender, Suppli(c)ant, Swain, Wooer

**Sulk(y), Sulkiness** B(r)oody, Carriage, Disgruntled, Dod, Dort, Gee, Glout(s), Glower, Glum, Grouchy, Grouty, Grumps, Gumple-foisted, Huff, Hump, Jinker, Mardy, Maungy, Moody, Mope, Mulligrubs, Mump, Pet, Petulant, Pique, Pout, Snit, Spider, Strunt, Stuffy, Stunkard, Sullen, Tout(ie), Towt, Umbrage

**Sullen** Black, Brooding, Dorty, Dour, Farouche, Glum(pish), Grim, Grumpy, Moody, Mumpish, Peevish, Po, Stunkard, Sulky, Sumph, Surly, Truculent

**Sully** Assoil, Bedye, Besmirch, Blot, Deface, Defile, Glaur(y), Smear, Smirch, Smutch, Soil(ure), Tarnish, Tar-wash

**Sulphate, Sulphide** Alum, Alunite, Blende, Bluestone, Bornite, Copperas, Coquimbite, Glance, Jarosite, Melanterite, Pyrites, Zarnec, Zarnich

**Sulphur** Baregine, Brimstone, Cysteine, Hepar, Oleum, S, Stannite, Thionic

**Sultan(a), Sultanate** Brunei, Caliph, Emir, Grand Seignoir, Grand Turk, Hen, Kalif, Murad, Nejd, Oman, Osman, Padishah, Roxane, Saladin, Soldan, Suleiman, Tippoo, Tipu, Vizier, Wadai

**Sultry** Houri, Humid, Sexy, Smouldering, Steamy, Tropical

**Sum(s), Sum up** Add(end), Aggregate, All (told), Amount, Arsmetric, Bomb, Connumerate, Encapsulate, Foot, Logical, Lump, Number, Perorate, Plumule, → **QUANTITY**, Re-cap, Refund, Remittance, Reversion, Slump, Solidum, Tidy, Total, Vector

**Summarize, Summary** Abridge, Abstract, Aperçu, Bird's eye, Breviate, Brief, Coda, Compendium, Condense, Conspectus, Digest, Docket, Epanodos, Epitome, Footnote, Gist, Headnote, Instant, Memo, Minute, Offhand, Outline, Overview, Pirlicue, Précis, Purlicue, Recap(itulate), Resume, Résumé, Round-up, Rundown, Short (shrift), Sitrep, Syllabus, Synopsis, Tabloid, Tabulate, Tabulation, Wrap-up

**Summer(time)** Abacus, Adder, Aestival, August, BST, Computer, Estival, Heyday, Indian, Lintel, Luke, Prime, St Luke's, St Martin's, Season, Sigma, Solstice, Totter

**Summerhouse** Belvedere, Chalet, Conservatory, Folly, Gazebo, Pavilion

**Summit** Acme, Acro-, Apex, Braeheid, Brow, Climax, Conference, →**CREST**, Crown, Eminence, Height, Hillcrest, Jole, Jungfrau, Mont Blanc, Peak, Pike, Pinnacle, Ridge, Spire, Vertex, Vertical, Yalta

**Summon(s)** Accite, Arraign, Arrière-ban, Azan, Beck(on), Bleep, Call, Call in, Cist, Cital, Citation, Command, Conjure, Convene, Convent, Drum, Evoke, Garnishment, Gong, Hail, Invocation, Muster, Order, Originating, Page, Post, Preconise, Rechate, Recheat, Reveille, Signal, Sist, Subpoena, Ticket, Warn, Warrant, What-ho, Whoop, Writ

**Sumo (wrestling)** Basho, Makunouchi, Niramial, →**WRESTLING**, Yokozuna

**Sump** Bilge, Cesspit, Drain, Pool, Sink

**Sumpter** Led horse, Pack-horse

**Sumptuous** De luxe, Expensive, Lavish, Luxurious, Opulent, Palatial, Rich(ly), Superb

**Sun(-god), Sunlight, Sunny, Sunshine** Albedo, Amen-Ra, Amon-Ra, Apollo, Ashine, Aten, Bright, Cheer, Combust, Daily, Day(star), Dry, Earthshine, Eye of the day, Glory, Heater, Heliacal, Helio(s), Helius, Horus, Mean, Midnight, Mock, New Mexico, Nova, Orb, Paper, Paranthelion, Parhelion, Pet-day, Phoebean, Photosphere, Ra, Radiant, Rays, Re, Rising, Shamash, Sol(ar), Soleil, Sonne, Surya, Svastika, Swastika, Tabloid, Tan, Titan, UV

**Sunbathe** Apricate, Bask, Brown, Tan

**Sunbeam** Car, Ray

**Sunblock** Parasol

**Sunburn** Bronze, Combust, Heliosis, Peeling, Tan

**Sunday** Advent, Best, Cantate, Care, Carle, Carling, Dominical, Easter, Fig, Jubilate, Judica, Laetare, Lord's Day, Lost, Low, Mid-Lent, Mothering, Orthodox, Palm, Passion, Quadragesima, Quasimodo, Quinquagesima, Refection, Refreshment, Remembrance, Rogation, Rose, Rush-bearing, S, Septuagesima, Sexagesima, Stir-up, Tap-up, Trinity, Whit

**Sunday school** SS

**Sunder** Divide, Divorce, Part, Separate, Sever, Split

**Sundew** Drosera, Eyebright

**Sundial** Analemma, Gnomon, Solarium

**Sundry** Divers, Several, Various

**Sunflower** Kansas, KS

**Sunglasses** Ray-Bans®, Shades

▸ **Sun-god** *see* SUN(-GOD)

▸ **Sunken** *see* SINK(ING)

**Sunrise, Sun-up** Aurora, Cosmical, Dawn, East

**Sunset** Acronical, Eve(ning)

**Sunshade** Awning, Bongrace, Brise-soleil, Canopy, Chi(c)k, Cloud, Parasol, Umbrella

**Sunspot** Facula, Freckle, Macula

**Sunstroke** Heliosis, Siriasis

**Sunwise** Deasi(u)l, Deasoil, Deis(h)eal, Eutropic

**Sun-worshipper** Heliolater

**Sup** Dine, Eat, Feast, Sample, Sip, Swallow

**Super** A1, Actor, Arch, Extra, Fab(ulous), Great, Grouse, Ideal, Lulu, Paramount, Superb, Terrific, Tip-top, Top-notch, Tops, Walker-on, Wizard

**Superadded** Advene

**Superb** A1, Concours, Fine, Gorgeous, Grand, Great, Majestic, Peerless, Phat, Splendid, Top-notch

**Supercilious** Aloof, Arrogant, Bashaw, Cavalier, Haughty, Lordly, Snide, Sniffy, Snooty, Snotty, Snouty, Superior, Toffee-nosed, Upstage, Withering

**Supercontinent** Pangaea

**Superficial** Cosmetic, Cursenary, Cursory, Dilettante, Exterior, Facile, Glib, One-dimensional, Outside, Outward, Overlying, Perfunctory, Shallow, Sketchy, Skindeep, Smattering, Veneer, Window-dressing

▷ **Superficial(ly)** *may indicate* a word outside another

**Superfluous, Superfluity** Appendix, Cheville, De trop, Extra, Lake, Mountain, Needless, Otiose, Pleonastic, Plethora, Redundant, Spare, Unnecessary

**Super-giant** Rigel

**Superhuman** Bionic, Herculean, Heroic, Supernatural

**Superintend(ent)** Boss, Curator, Director, Foreman, Guide, Janitor, Oversee(r), Preside, Provost, Sewer, Supercargo, Surveillant, Warden, Zanjero

**Superior(ity)** Abbess, Abbot, Abeigh, Above, Advantage, Ahead, Aloof, Ascendant, Atop, Better, Brahmin, Choice, Classy, Condescending, Custos, De luxe, Dinger, Elite, Eminent, Excellent, Exceptional, Feuar, Finer, Forinsec, Gree, Herrenvolk, High-class, High-grade, Jethro, Lake, Liege, Master race, Mastery, Morgue, Mother, Nob, Noble, Outgrown, Outstanding, Over, Overlord, Oversee, Paramount, Plum, Pooh-Bah, Posh, Predominance, Premium, Prestige, Pretentious, Prevalent, Prior, Smug, Snooty, Speciesism, Stuck up, Superordinate, Supremacy, Swell, Top(-loftical), Transcendent(al), U, Udal, Upmarket, Upper(most), Upper crust, Uppish, Upstage

**Superlative** Best, Exaggerated, Peerless, Smasheroo, Supreme, Utmost

**Superman** Batman, Bionic, Titan, Übermensch

**Supermarket** ALDI, ASDA, Co-op, Fund, GUM, Self service, Store

**Supernatural** Divine, Eerie, Endemon, Fay, Fey, Fie, Fly, Gothic, Kachina, Mana, Manito(u), Metaphysical, Occult, Paranormal, Selky, Sharp, Siddhi, Tokoloshe, Uncanny, Unearthly, Wargod, Wight

**Supernova** Plerion

**Supernumerary** Additional, Corollary, Extra, Mute, Orra

**Supersede** Replace, Stellenbosch, Supplant

**Superstition** Aberglaube, Abessa, Fable, Folk-lore, Freet, Myth, Pisheog, Pishogue, Uncertainty

**Superstructure** Mastaba(h)

**Supertonic** Ray

**Supervise(d), Supervision, Supervisor** Administer, Chaperone, Check, Direct, Engineer, Floorwalker, Foreman, Gaffer, Grieve, Handle, Honcho, Invigilate, Key grip, Manager, Marshal, Monitor, Officiate, Organise, Overman, Oversee(r), Probation, Proctor, Regulate, Seneschal, Shopwalker, Stage-manage, Steward, Symposiarch, Targe, Taskmaster, Tool pusher, Under, Walla(h)

**Supine** Inactive, Inert, Lying, Passive, Protract

**Supper** Bar, Burns, Dinner, →**DRINK(ER)**, Fork, Hawkey, Hockey, Horkey, Last, Meal, Nagmaal, Repast, Soirée

**Supplant** Displace, Exchange, Oust, Overthrow, Pre-empt, Replace, Substitute, Supersede

**Supple, Suppleness** Agile, Compliant, Leish, Limber, Lissom(e), →**LITHE**, Loose, Loose-limbed, Lythe, Malleable, Plasticity, Pliable, Sinuous, Souple, Wan(d)le, Wannel, Whippy

**Supplement(ary), Supplementing** Addend(um), Addition, Adjunct, And, Annex(e), Appendage, Appendix, As well as, Augment, Auxiliary, Bolt-on, Codicil, Colour, Eche, Eik, Eke, Extra, Footnote, Glucosamine, Incaparina, Inset, Mend, Paralipomena, Postscript, Practicum, PS, Relay, Ripienist, Ripieno, Rutin, Sports, TES, Weighting

**Supplicant, Supplicate** Beg, Entreat, Importune, Invoke, Petition, Plead, Pray, Request, Schnorr, Sue

**Supply, Supplies, Supplier** Accommodate, Advance, Afford, Amount, Cache, Cater, Commissariat, Contribute, Crop, Deal, Endue, Equip, Excess, Exempt, Feed, Fill, Find, Fit, Foison, Fund, Furnish, Give, Grant, Grist, Grubstake, Heel, Holp(en), Hydrant, Indew, Indue, Issue, Lay on, Lend, Lithely, Mains, Matériel, Ordnance, Pipeline, Plenish, Ply, Pool, →**PROVIDE**, Provision, Purvey, Push, RASC, Replenishment, Reservoir, Resource, Retailer, Serve, Source, Stake, Stock, →**STORE**, Viands, Vintner, Water, Widow's cruse, Yield

**Support(er), Supporting** Abacus, Abet, Abutment, Acco(u)rage, Adherent, Adminicle, Advocate, Aegis, Affirm, Aficionado, Aftercare, Aid, Aidance, Aide, Aliment(ative), Ally, Ammunition, Anchor, Anciliary, Andiron, Anta, Appui, Arch, Arm, Assistant, Athletic, Axle, Back(bone), Back-up, Baculum, Baluster, Banister, Bankroll, Barrack, Barre, Base, Basis, Batten, Beam, Bear, Befriend, Behind, Belt, Benefactor, Bibb, Bier, Bolster, Book end, Boom, Bouclée, Bra, Brace, Bracket, Brassiere, Breadwinner, Breast-summer, Bridge, Bridgeboard, Buttress, Carlist, Caryatid, Cavalier, Chair, Champion, Chaptrel, Cheerleader, Chenet, Cherish, Circumstantiate, Clientele, Clipboard, Colonnade, Column, Comfort, Confirm, Console, Corbel, Corbel-table, Cornerstone, Corroborate, Countenance, Cradle, Cripple, Cross-beam, Cruck, Crutch, C(ee)-spring, Dado, Diagrid, Disciple, Dog-shore, Doula, Easel, Encourage, Endorse, Endoss, Endow, Engager, Enlist, Enthusiast, Espouse, Evidence, Family, Fan, Favour, Fid, Finance, Flying buttress, Fly-rail, Footrest, Footstool, For, Foster, Friend, Fulcrum, Gamb, Gantry, Garter, Girder, Glia, Grapevine, Grass roots, Groundswell, Guy, Handrail, Hanger, Harpin(g)s, Hat-peg, Headrest, Help, Henchman, Hold with, Home help, Horse, Hound, I-beam, Idealogue, Impost, Income, Indorse, Instantiate, Ite, Jack, Jackstay, Jockstrap, Joist, Keep, Keystone, Kingpost, Knee, Knife rest, Knighthead, Lath, Learning, Lectern, Leg, Lierne, Lifebelt, Lifebuoy, Lobby, Loper, Loyalist, Mahlstick, Mailstick, Mainbrace, Mainstay, Maintain, Makefast, Mill-rind, Miserere, Misericord(e), Monial, Moral, Mortsafe, Mount, Neck, Nervure, Neuroglia, -nik, Nourish, Pack, Pack-frame, Packstaff, Paranymph, Parawalker, Partisan, Partizan, Partners, Patronage, Pedestal, Peronist, Pessary, Phalanx, Pier, Pile(-cap), Pillar, Pin, Plinth, Poppet, Post, Potent, Price, Promote, Prop, Proponent, Prop-root, PTA, Pull-for, Puncheon, Purlin(e), Purlins, Pylon, Queenite, Raft, Rally round, Rebato, Regular, Reinforce, Relieve, Respond, Rest, Rind, Rod, Roof-plate, Root, Royalist, Rynd, Samaritan, Sanction, Sarking, Sawhorse, Scaffolding, Sconce, Second, Shoetree, Shore, Skeg, Skeleton, Skewput, Skid, Sleeper, Sling, Snotter, Socle, Solidarity, Spectator, Splat, Splint, Sponson, Sponsor, Sprag, Spud, Squinch, Staddle, Staddlestone, Staff, Staging, Stake, Stalwart, Stanchion, Stand(-by), Stay, Steady, Stem(pel), Step, Stick, Stirrup, Stool, Stringer, Strut, Stull, Stylobate, Subscribe, Subsidy, Succour, Suffragist, Summer, Suppedaneum, Suspender, Sustain, Sustentacular, Sustentaculum, Sustentation, Tailskid, Tartan army, Technical, Tee, Telamon, Tendril, Third, Tie, Tige, Torsel, Trabecula, Trellis, Tress(el), Trestle, Tripod, Trivet, Trotter, Truss, Tumpline, Underlay, Underpin, Understand, Unipod, Uphold, Upkeep, Verify, Vindicate, Viva, Walker, Waterwings, Welfare, Well-wisher, Y-level, Yorkist, Zealot

**Suppose(d), Supposedly, Supposition** An, Assume, Believe, Conjecture, Daresay, Expect, Guess, Hypothetical, Idea, If, Imagine, Imply, Infer, Opine, Presume, Putative, Reputedly, Said, Say, Sepad, Theory, What if

**Suppository** Pessary

**Suppress(ion), Suppressed** Abate, Abolish, Adaw, Burke, Cancel, Censor, Check, Clampdown, Conditioned, Crackdown, Crush, Cushion, Ecthlipsis, Elide, Elision, Epistasis, Gag, Gleichschaltung, Hide, Hush-up, Inhibit, Mob(b)le, Muffle, Quash, Quell, Quench, Restrain, Silence, Sit on, Smother, Squash, Squelch, Stand on, Stifle, Strangle, Subdue, Submerge, Subreption, Throttle, Under

**Suppurate, Suppuration** Diapyesis, Discharge, Exude, Fester, Maturate, Ooze, Pus, Pyorrhoea, Rankle

**Supreme, Supremacy, Supremo** Apical, Baaskap, Best, Caudillo, Consummate, Dominant, Kronos, Leader, Napoleon, Overlord, Paramount, Peerless, Pre-eminent, Regnant, Sovereign, Sublime, Sudder, Superlative, Top, Utmost, White

**Surcharge** Addition, Extra, Tax

**Surd** Voiceless

**Sure(ly)** Assured, Ay, Bound, Cert(ain), Certes, Confident, Definite, Doubtless, Firm, Indeed, Inevitable, Infallible, Know, Pardi(e), Pardy, Perdie, Positive, Poz, Safe, Secure, Self-confident, Shoo-in, Sicker, Syker, Uh-huh, Unerring, Yeah, Yep, Yes

**Surety** Bail, Frithborth, Guarantee, Mainprise, Security, Sponsional

**Surf(er), Surfing** Breach, Breaker, Browse, Corndogging, Grommet, Internet, Lurk, Onliner, Rollers, Rote, Sea, Waxhead

**Surface** Aerofoil, Appear, Area, Arise, Astroturf®, Bitumen, Brane, Camber, Carpet, Caustic, Ceiling, Control, Crust, Cutis, Day, Dermal, Dermis, Emerge, Epigene, Exterior, External, Face, Facet, Finish, Flock, Interface, Linish, Macadam, Meniscus, Nanograss, Notaeum, Out, Outcrop, Outward, Overglaze, Paintwork, Patina, Pave, Plane, Reveal, Rise, Salband, Scarfskin, Side, Skim, Skin, Soffit, Spandrel, Superficial, Superficies, Supracrustal, Tarmac®, Tar-seal, Texture, Top, Topping, Toroid, Veneer, Wearing course, Worktop

**Surf-boat, Surfboard(er), Surfboard(ing)** Goofy-footer, Masoola(h), Masula, Shredder

**Surfeit(ed)** Blasé, Cloy, Excess, Glut, Overcloy, Plethora, Satiate, Stall, Staw

▷ **Surfer** *may indicate* programming

**Surge** Billow, Boom, Drive, Gush, Leap, Onrush, Seethe, S(c)end, Storm, Sway, Swell, Upgush, Wind

**Surgeon** Abernethy, Barber, BCh, Brain, BS, CHB, CM, Doctor, DS, Dupuytren, House, Hunter, Leech, Lister, Medic, Operator, Orthopod, Plastic, Sawbones, Staff, Tang, Tree, Vet(erinary)

**Surgery** Anaplasty, Bypass, Cordotomy, Cosmetic, Dentistry, Facelift, Hobday, Keyhole, Knife, Laparotomy, Laser, LASIK, Mammoplasty, Medicine, Nip and tuck, Nose job, Op, Open-heart, Orthop(a)edics, Osteoplasty, Plastic, Prosthetics, Reconstructive, Repair, Section, Spare-part, Stereotaxis, Ta(g)liacotian, Thoracoplasty, Tuboplasty, Zolatrics

**Surly** Bluff, Cantankerous, Chough, Chuffy, Churl(ish), Crabby, Crusty, Cynic, Glum, Gruff, Grum, Grumpy, Huffy, Rough, Snarling, Sullen, Truculent

**Surmise** Assume, Extrapolate, Guess, Imagine, Infer, Opine, Presume, Speculate, Suppose

**Surmount** Beat, Climb, Conquer, Crest, Master, Overcome, Scan, Superate, Tide, Transcend

**Surname** Cognomen, Patronymic

**Surpass(ing)** Bang, Beat, Best, Cap, Cote, Ding, Eclipse, Efface, Exceed, Excel, Frabjous, Outdo, Outfoot, Outgo, Outgun, Out-Herod, Outman, Outreach, Outshine, Outstrip, Overshadow, Overtop, Transcend, Trump

**Surplice** Cotta, Ephod, Rochet, Sark, Serk, Vakass

**Surplus** De trop, Excess, Extra, Gash, Glut, Lake, Mountain, Offcut, Out-over, Over, Overabundance, Overage, Overcome, Remainder, Residue, Rest, Spare, Superplus, Surfeit

**Surprise(d), Surprising** Ag, Alert, Amaze, Ambush, Arrah, Astonish, Aykhona wena, Bewilder, Blimey, Boilover, Bombshell, By Jove, Caramba, Catch, Confound, Coo, Cor, Crick(e)y, Crikey, Criminé, Cripes, Criv(v)ens, Crumbs, Dear, Eye-opener, Gadso, Gee, Geewhiz, Gemini, Geminy, Gemony, Gobsmacked, Godsend, Golly, Good-lack, Gorblimey, Gordon Bennett, Gosh, Gotcha, Great Scott, Ha, Hah, Hallo, Heavens, Hech, Heck, Heh, Hello, Hell's teeth, Hey, Hit for six, Ho, Holy cow, Hullo, Jeepers, Jeepers creepers, Jeez(e), Jinne, Jirre, Law, Lawks, Lor, Lordy, Lumme, Lummy, Man alive, Marry, Musha, My, Nooit, Obreption, Och, Odso, Omigod, Oops, Open-mouthed, Overtake, Phew, Pop-eyed, Really, Sheesh, Shock, Singular, Sjoe, So, Spot, Stagger, Startle, Strewth, Struth, Stun, Sudden, Treat, Turn-up, Uh, Upset, Whew, Whoops, Whoops-a-daisy, Wide-eyed, Wonderment, Wow, Wrongfoot, Yikes, Yipes, Yow, Zart, Zinger, Zowie

**Surrealist** Bizarre, Dali, Ernst, Grotesque, Magritte, Man Ray, Miró

**Surrender** Abandon, Capitulate, Cave-in, Cede, Cessio honorum, Cession, Enfeoff, Extradite, Fall, Forego, Forfeit, Handover, Hulled, Kamerad, Naam, Recreant, Release, Relinquish, Remise, Rendition, Renounce, Resign, Roll over, Strike, Submit, Succumb, Waive, → **YIELD**, Yorktown

**Surreptitious** Clandestine, Covert, Fly, Furtive, Hole and corner, Secret, Slee, Sly, Stealthy, Underhand

**Surrey** Carriage, Sy

**Surrogate** Agent, Depute, Deputy, Locum, Proxy, Wet nurse

**Surround(ed), Surrounding(s)** Ambient, Amid, Amongst, Architrave, Background, Bathe, Begirt, Bego, Beset, Besiege, Bundwall, Cinct, Circumvallate, Circumvent, Compass, Doughnutting, Ecology, Embail, Encase, → **ENCIRCLE**, Enclave, Enclose, Encompass, Enfold, Entomb, Envelop, Environ, Enwheel, Enwrap, Fence, Gherao, Gird, Girt, Hedge, Hem in, Impale, Inorb, Invest, Mid, Orb, Orle, Outflank, Outside, Perimeter, Periphery, Setting, Wall

**Surtees** Jorrocks, Sponge

**Surveillance, Survey(ing), Surveyor** Behold, Browse, Cadastre, Case, Census, Chartered, Conspectus, Dialler, Domesday, Doomwatch, Espial, Examination, Eye, Geodesy, Geological, Groma, Look-see, Map, Once-over, Ordnance, Overeye, Overview, Patrol, Poll, Prospect, Quantity, Recce, Reccy, Reconnaissance, Regard, Review, Rodman, Scan, Scrutiny, Staffman, Stakeout, Straw poll, Supervision, Terrier, Theodolite, Triangulate, Trilateration, Vigil, Watch, Y-level

**Survival, Survive, Surviving, Survivor** Bushcraft, Castaway, Cope, Die hard, Endure, Exist(ence), Extant, Finalist, Hibakusha, Last (out), Leftover, Live, Outdure, Outlast, Outlive, Outwear, Overlive, Persist, Pull through, Relic(t), Ride (out), Sole, Street-wise, Subsist, Viability, Warhorse, Weather, Withstand

**Susan** Lazy

**Susceptible, Susceptibility** Allergy, Anaphylaxis, Electrical, Impressionable, Liable, Receptive, Vulnerable

**Suspect, Suspicion, Suspicious** Askance, Assume, Breath, Cagey, Distrust, Dodgy, Doubt, Dubious, Equivocal, Fishy, Grain, Grey list, Guess, Hinky, Hint, Hunch, Hunky, Iffy, Imagine, Inkling, Jalouse, Jealous, Leery, Misdeem, Misdoubt, Misgiving, Mislippen, Mistrust, Modicum, Notion, Paranoia, Queer, Scent, Sense, Smatch, Soupçon, Stealthy, Think, Thought, Tinge, Whiff

▷ **Suspect, Suspicious** *may indicate* an anagram

**Suspend(ed), Suspender, Suspense, Suspension** Abate, Abeyance, Adjourn, Anabiosis, Anti-shock, Cliffhanger, Colloid, Dangle, Defer, Delay, Dormant, Freeze, Garter, Ground, → **HANG**, Hang-gliding, Hovering, Hydraulic, Independent, Intermit, Lay off, Mist, Moratorium, Mystery, Nailbiter, Pensile, Poise, Prorogue, Put on ice, Reprieve, Respite, Rub out, Rusticate, Sideline, Sol, Stand off, Stay, String, Swing, Table, Tension, Tenterhooks, Truce, Undercurrent, Underslung, Withhold

▷ **Suspended** *may indicate* 'ice' on ice at the end of a down light

**Sussex** Rape

**Sustain(ed), Sustaining, Sustenance** Abide, Afford, Aliment, Bear, Constant, Depend, Endure, Food, Keep, Last, Maintain, Nourish, Nutrient, Nutriment, Nutrition, Pedal, Prolong, Sostenuto, Succour, Support, Ten(uto), Upbear, Upstay

**Sutler** Vivandière

**Suture** Button, Catgut, Cobbler, Coronal, Lambda, Pterion, Purse-string, Sagittal, Stitch

**Suzanne, Suzie** Lenglen, Wong

**Svelte** Lithe, Slender, Slim

**Swab** Dossil, Dry, Mop, Pledget, Scour, Sponge, Squeegee, Stupe, Tampon, Tompon, Wipe

**Swaddle, Swaddling** Bind, Envelop, Incunabula, Swathe, Wrap

**Swag** Booty, Bundle, Encarpus, Festoon, Haul, Loot, Maino(u)r, Manner, Matilda, Shiralee, Toran(a)

**Swagger(er), Swaggering** Birkie, Bluster, Boast, Bobadil, Brag, Bragadisme, Bravado, Bucko, Cock, Cockiness, Crow, Jaunty, Matamore, Nounce, Panache, Pra(u)nce, Roist, Roll, Rollick, Roul, Royster, Ruffle, Sashay, Side, Strive, Strut, Swagman, Swank, Swash(-buckler), Tigerism

**Swain** Amoretti, Beau, Churl, Corin, Damon, Hind, Lover, Rustic, Shepherd, Strephon, Wooer

**Swallow(able), Swallowing** Absorb, Accept, Aerophagia, Ariel, Barn, Bird, Bolt, Bredit, Buy, Cliff, Consume, Credit, Deglutition, Devour, Down(flow), Drink, Eat, Endue, Englut, Engulf, Engulph, Esculent, Glug, Gobble, Gula, Gulch, Gulp, Hirundine, Incept, Ingest, Ingulf, Ingurgitate, Itys, Lap, Martin, Martlet, Neck, Progne, Quaff, Shift, Sister, Slug, Stomach, Swift, Swig, Take, Take off

**Swamp(y)** Bog, Bunyip, Cowal, Cypress, Deluge, Dismal, Drown, Engulf, Everglade, Flood, Great Dismal, Inundate, Lentic, Lerna, Lerne, Loblolly, Mar(i)sh, Morass, Muskeg, Okavango, Okefenokee, Overrun, Overwhelm, Pakihi, Paludal, Poles'ye, Pripet Marshes, Purgatory, Quagmire, Slash, Slough, Sudd, Uliginous, Urman, Vlei, Vly, Wetland

**Swan(s)** Avon, Bewick's, Bird, Black, Cob, Cygnet, Cygnus, Game, Leda, Lindor, Mute, Pen, Seven, Seward, Song, Stroll, Trumpeter, Whistling, Whooper, Whooping

**Swank(y)** Boast, Lugs, Pretentious, Side, Style

**Swansong** Finale, Last air, Last hurrah

**Swap, Swop** Alternate, →**BARTER**, Chop, Commute, Exchange, Pass, Scorse, Switch, Trade, Transpose, Truck

▷ **Swap(ped)** *may indicate* an anagram

**Sward** Grass, Green, Lawn, Sod, Turf

**Swarm(ing)** Abound, Alive, Bike, Bink, Byke, Cast, Clamber, Cloud, Crowd, Flood, Geminid, Hoatching, Host, Hotch, Hotter, Infest, Meteor, Overrun, Pullulate, Rife, Shin, Shoal, Teem, Throng

**Swarthy** Black-à-vised, Dark, Dusky, Melanotic

**Swash** Send, Swig, Swill

**Swashbuckler, Swashbuckling** Adventurer, Boaster, Braggart, Dashing, Gascon, Swordsman

**Swastika** Filfot, Fylfot, Gamma(dion), Hakenkreuz

▶ **Swat** *see* **SWOT**

**Swath(e)** Bind, Enfold, Enroll, Envelop, Swaddle, Swipe, Wrap

**Sway(ing)** Careen, Carry, Command, Diadrom, Domain, Dominion, Flap, Fluctuate, Govern, Hegemony, Influence, Lilt, Oscillate, Prevail, Reel, Reign, Rock, Roll, Rule, Sally, Shog, Shoogie, Shoogle, Swag, Swale, Swee, Swing(e), Teeter, Titter, Totter, Vacillate, Wobble

**Swear(ing), Swearer, Swear word** Asseverate, Attest, Avow, Billingsgate, Coprolalia, Curse, Cuss, Darn, Depose, Eff, Execrate, Expletive, Invective, Jurant, Juratory, Oath, Objure, Pledge, Plight, Rail, Sessa, State, Tarnal, Tarnation, Trooper, Verify, Vow

**Sweat(ing), Sweaty** Agonise, Apocrine, Beads, Clammy, Cold, Dank, Diaphoresis, Eccrine, Egest, English, Excrete, Exude, Flop, Forswatt, Glow, Hidrosis, Lather, Muck, Ooze, Osmidrosis, →**PERSPIRE**, Secretion, Slave, Stew, Sudament, Sudamina, Sudate, Suint, Swelter, Toil

**Sweater** Aran, Argyle, Circassian, Circassienne, Cowichan, Fair Isle, Gansey, Guernsey, Indian, Jersey, Polo, Pullover, Roll-neck, Siwash, Skinny-rib, Skivvy, Slip-on, Slop-pouch, Sloppy Joe, Turtleneck, V-neck, Woolly

**Swede** Brassica, Inga, Nordic, Olaf, Rutabaga, Scandinavian, Sven, Turnip

**Sweeney** Police, Todd

**Sweep(er), Sweeping(s)** Besom, Broad, Broom, Brush, Chimney, Chummy, Clean, Curve, Debris, Detritus, Expanse, Extensive, Generalisation, Lash, Libero, Lottery, Net, Oars, Pan, Phasing, Police-manure, Range, Scavenger, Scud, Sling, Snowball, Soop, Sooterkin, Spoom, Street, Stroke, Surge, Swathe, Sway, Vac(k), Vacuum, Waft, Well, Wholesale, Wide, Widespread

**Sweepstake** Draw, Gamble, Lottery, Raffle, Tattersall's, Tombola

**Sweet, Sweeten(er), Sweetmeat, Sweetness** Acesulfame-K, Afters, Aspartame, Baclava, Baklava, Bonus, Bribe, Bung, Cassata, Chaptalise, Charity, Charming, Cherubic, Cloying, Confect(ion), Confiserie, Conserve, Crème, Cute, →**DESSERT**, Douce(t), Dowset, Drop, Dulcet, Dulcie, Dulcitude, Edulcorate, FA, Flan, Flapjack, Flummery, Fool, Fragrant,

Fresh, Glucose, Glycerin, Goody, Honey(ed), Icky, Indican, Kiss, Lavender, Liqueur, Luscious, Melodious, Molasses, Money, Nectared, Nonpareil, Nothing, Pea, Pet, Pie, Pud(ding), Redolent, Romic, Saccharin(e), Seventeen, Sillabub, Sixteen, Solanine, Soot(e), Sop, Sorbet, Spice, Split, Sucrose, Sugar, Sugary, Syllabub, Syrupy, Tart(let), Thaumatin, Torte, Trifle, Twee, Uses, William, Winsome, Xylitol, Zabaglione

---

## SWEETS

**3 letters:**
Gum
Ice

**4 letters:**
Choc
Jube
Mint
Rock

**5 letters:**
Bombe
Candy
Dolce
Dolly
Fudge
Gundy
Halva
Lolly
Taffy

**6 letters:**
Aldose
Bonbon
Cachou
Choccy
Comfit
Confit
Dragée

Eringo
Eryngo
Halvah
Humbug
Jujube
Mousse
Nougat
Sucker
Tablet
Toffee

**7 letters:**
Adeline
Alcorza
Amabile
Caramel
Fondant
Gumdrop
Halavah
Lozenge
Pandrop
Praline
Swedger
Truffle
Wine-gum

**8 letters:**
Acid drop
Bull's eye

Confetti
Cracknel
Licorice
Lollipop
Marzipan
Noisette
Pastille
Peardrop
Pick'n'mix
Scroggin
Stickjaw

**9 letters:**
Bubble gum
Chocolate
Cyclamate
Jelly baby
Jelly bean
Lemon drop
Liquorice
Marchpane
Muscavado
Sugarplum

**10 letters:**
Brandyball
Candyfloss
Coconut ice
Elecampane

Fairy floss
Gob-stopper
Nanaimo Bar

**11 letters:**
Aniseed ball
Barley sugar
Marshmallow

**12 letters:**
Burnt-almonds
Butterscotch
Dolly mixture

**14 letters:**
Peppermint drop
Pontefract cake
Turkish delight

**15 letters:**
Peppermint cream

**20 letters:**
Hundreds and
thousands

---

**Sweetbread** Bur(r), Inchpin, Pancreas, Thymus

**Sweetheart** Amoret, Amour, Beau, Boyfriend, Darling, Dona(h), Dowsabel(l), Doxy, Dulcinea, Flame, Follower, Girlfriend, Honey(bunch), Honeybun, Jarta, Jo(e), Lass, Leman, Lover, Masher, Neaera, Peat, Romeo, Steady, Toots(y), True-love, Valentine, Yarta, Yarto

**Sweet-seller** Butcher, Confectioner

**Sweet talk** Taffy

**Swell(ing)** Adenomata, Ague-cake, Anasarca, Aneurysm, Apophysis, Bag, Balloon, Bellying, Berry, Billow, Blab, Blister, Bloat, Blow, Boil, Boll, Bolster, Botch, Braw, Bubo, Bulb, Bulge, Bump, Bunion, Burgeon, Capellet, Carbuncle, Carnosity, Cat, Chancre, Chilblain, Clour, Cratches, Curb, Cyst, Dandy, Desmoid, Diapason, Dilate, → DISTEND, Dom, Don, Eche, Ectasia, Edema, Eger, Elephantiasis, Encanthis, Enhance, Enlarge, Entasis, Epulis, Excellent, Farcy-bud, Frog, Gall, Gathering, Gent, Gnarl, Goiter, Goitre, Gout, Grandee, Ground, Head sea, Heave, Heighten, H(a)ematoma, Hove, Hydrocele, Hydroma, Hygroma, Increase, Inflate, Intumesce, Kibe, L, Lampas(se), Lampers, Louden, Lump, Macaroni, Milk leg, Mouse, Nodule, Odontoma, Oedema, OK, Onco-, Ox-warble,

Parotitis, Plim, Plump, Protrude, Protuberance, Proud, Pulvinus, Rise, Roil, Roller, Scirrhus, Scleriasis, Sea, Shinsplints, Splenomegaly, Strout, Struma, Stye, Stylopodium, Sudamina, Surge, Teratoma, Toff, Torose, Torulose, Tragus, Tuber(cle), Tumefaction, Tumescence, Tumour, Tympanites, Tympany, Upsurge, Varicocele, Varicose, Venter, Vesicle, Vulvitis, Vulvovaginitis, Wallow, Warble, Wen, Whelk, Windgall, Xanthoma

▷ **Swelling** *may indicate* a word reversed

**Swelter(ing)** Perspire, Roast, Stew, Sweat, Tropical

**Swerve, Swerving** Bias, Broach, Careen, Deflect, Deviate, Dodge, Lean, Sheer, Shy, Snoke, Stray, Sway, Swee, Swing, Veer, Warp, Wheel

**Swift(ly)** Apace, Bird, Dean, Dromond, Fleet, Flock, Hasty, Martlet, Newt, Nimble, Presto, Prompt, Pronto, Quick, →**RAPID**, Reel, Slick, Sodaine, Spanking, Speedy, Sudden, Velocipede, Wight

**Swig** Drink, Gulp, Nip, Scour, Swill, Tighten

**Swill** Guzzle, Leavings, Rubbish, Slosh, Swash

▷ **Swilling** *may indicate* an anagram

**Swim(ming)** Bathe, Bogey, Bogie, Crawl, Dip, Float, Freestyle, Naiant, Natant, Natatorial, Paddle, Reel, Run, Skinny-dip, Soom, Synchro(nized), Trudgen, Whim, Whirl

▷ **Swim** *may indicate* an anagram

**Swimmer** Bather, Cichlid, Copepod(a), Ctene, Duckbill, Duckmole, Dugong, Frogman, Leander, Mermaid, Pad(d)le, Paidle, Planula, Pleopod, Pobble, Salpa, Terrapin, Trochosphere, Webb

▷ **Swimmer** *may indicate* a fish

**Swimming costume** Bathers, Bikini, Cossie, Maillot, Monokini, One-piece, Tanga, Tankini, Tog, Trunks

**Swindle(r)** Beat, Bite, Bucket(-shop), Bunco, Bunkosteerer, Cajole, Champerty, →**CHEAT**, Chiz(z), Chouse, Con, Concoct, Crimp, Defraud, Diddle, Do, Escroc, Fake, Fiddle, Finagle, Fineer, Fleece, Fraud, Gazump, Gip, Gold brick, Goose-trap, Graft, Grifter, Gull, Gyp, Hocus, Hoser, Hustler, Leg, Leger, Long-firm, Magsman, Mountebank, Mulct, Nobble, Peter Funk, Plant, Ponzi scheme, Racket, Ramp, Rig, Rogue, Scam, Sell, Shaft, Shakedown, Shark, Sharper, Shicer, Shyster, Skelder, Skin, Skin game, Slicker, Sting, Stitch-up, Stumer, Suck, Swiz(z), Take, Trick, Tweedle, Twist, Two-time

**Swine(herd)** Boar, Brute, Cad, Eumaeus, Gadarene, Heel, Hog, Peccary, Pig, Porcine, Pork, Rat, Rotter, Sounder, Sow, Sybotic

**Swing(er), Swinging** Colt, Dangle, Flail, Gate, Hang, Hep, Hip, Kip(p), Lilt, Metronome, Mod, Music, Oscillate, Pendulate, Pendulum, Reverse, Rock, Rope, Shog, Shoogie, Shuggy, Slew, Slue, Swale, Sway, Swee, Sweep, Swerve, Swey, Swipe, Swivel, Trapeze, Veer, Vibratile, Voop, Wave, Western, Wheel, Whirl, Yaw

**Swipe(s)** Backhander, Beer, Haymaker, Purloin, Seize, Steal, Strike, Tap-lash

**Swirl** Eddy, Purl, Swoosh, Tourbill(i)on, Twist, Whirl

▷ **Swirling** *may indicate* an anagram

**Swish** Cane, Frou-frou, Rustle, Smart, Whir, Whisper

**Swiss** Genevese, Ladin, Roll, Tell, Vaudois

**Switch(ed), Switches, Switching** Birch, Button, Change, Churn, Convert, Crossbar, Cryotron, Dead man's handle, Dimmer, Dip, Dolly, Exchange, Gang, Hairpiece, Isolator, Knife, Legerdemain, Master, Mercury, Mercury tilt, Message, Pear, Point, Relay, Replace, Retama, Rocker, Rod, Scutch, Shift, Swits, Thyristor, Time, Toggle, Transpose, Tress, Trip, Tumbler, Twig, Wave, Zap

**Switchback** Rollercoaster

▷ **Switched** *may indicate* an anagram

**Switzerland** CH, Helvetia

**Swivel** Caster, Pivot, Root, Rotate, Spin, Terret, Territ, Torret, Turret, Wedein

**Swiz** Chiz(z)

**Swollen** Blown, Bollen, Bombe, Bulbous, Full, Gourdy, Gouty, Incrassate, Nodose, Puffy, Tumid, Turgescent, Turgid, Varicose, Ventricose, Vesiculate

**Swoon** Blackout, Collapse, Deliquium, Dover, Dwa(l)m, Dwaum, Faint, Swarf, Swerf

**Swoop** Descend, Dive, Glide, Plummet, Pounce, Souse

▸ **Swop** *see* SWAP

**Sword(-like), Swordplay** Andrew Ferrara, Anelace, Angurvadel, Anlace, Arondight, Assegai, Balisarda, Balmunc, Balmung, Bilbo, Blade, Brand, Brandiron, Broad(sword), Brondyron, Caliburn, Cemitare, Claymore, Colada, Cold steel, Court, Curtal-ax, Curtana, Curtax, Cutlass, Daisho, Damascene, Damaskin, Damocles, Dance, Dirk, Duranda(l), Durindana, Ensate, Ensiform, Epée, Espada, Estoc, Excalibur, Falchion, Faulchi(o)n, Firangi, Foil, Forte, Fox, Gladius, Glaive, Glamdring, Gleave, Glorious, Hanger, Iai-do, Jacob's staff, Joyeuse, Katana, Kendo, Khanda, Kirpan, Kreese, Kris, Kukri, Kusanagi, Machete, Mandau, Merveilleuse, Mimming, Montanto, Morglay, Nothung, Parang, Philippan, Rapier, Reverso, Rosse, Sabre, Samurai, Schiavone, Schläger, Scimitar, Semita(u)r, Shabble, Shamshir, Sharp, Sigh, Simi, Skene-dhu, Slangwhanger, Smallsword, Spadroon, Spirtle, Spit, Spurtle(blade), Steel, Tachi, Toasting-iron, Toledo, Tuck, Tulwar, Two-edged, Waster, Whinger, Whiniard, Whinyard, White-arm, Xiphoid, Yatag(h)an

**Sword-bearer, Swordsman(ship), Swordswoman** Aramis, Athos, Baldric, Blade, Brenda(n), D'Artagnan, Fencer, Frog, Gladiator, Matador, Porthos, Sai-do, Selictar, Spadassin, Spadroon, Spartacus, Swashbuckler, Zorro

**Sword-dancer** Matachin

**Swordfish** Espada, Istiophorus, Xiphias

**Sword-swallower** Samite

**Swot** Dig, Grind, Kill, Mug, Read up, Revise, Smug, Spod, Stew, Strike, Swat, Wonk

**Sybarite, Sybaritic** Aristippus, Decadent, Epicure, Hedonist, Voluptuary

▸ **Sybil** *see* SIBYL

**Sycamore** Acer, Maple, Mulberry fig, Plane, Tree

**Sycophant(ic)** Apple polisher, Brown-nose, Claqueur, Crawler, Creeper, Damocles, Fawner, Gnathonic, Groveller, Hanger-on, Lickspittle, Parasite, Pickthank, Placebo, Servile, Toad-eater, Toady, Yesman

**Syllabary** Hiragana, Kana, Katakana

**Syllable(s)** Acatalectic, Anacrusis, Aretinian, Nonsense, Om, Outride, Thesis, Tonic, Ultima

**Syllabus** Program(me), Prospectus, Résumé, Summary, Table, Timetable

**Syllogism** Argument, Conclusion, Deduction, Enthymeme, Epicheirema, Sorites

**Sylph** Ariel, Nymph

**Symbiotic** Adnascent

**Symbol(ic), Symbolism, Symbolist, Symbols** Allegory, Ampussy-and, Character, Charactery, Decadent, Del, Descriptor, Diesis, Iconography, K, Klimt, Logotype, Metaphor, Minus, Moral, Mystical, Nominal, Notation, Operator, Placeholder, Plus, Quantifier, Regalia, Semicolon, Semiotic, Sex, Shadowy, Shamrock, Slur, Status, Syllabary, Syllabogram, Synthetism, T-cross, Trisul, Type, Weather

---

## SYMBOLS

| *2 letters:* | *4 letters:* | Rose | Colon |
|---|---|---|---|
| Om | Agma | Rune | Crest |
| Pi | Ankh | Sign | Eagle |
| | Clef | Tiki | Equal |
| *3 letters:* | Hash | Yoni | Index |
| Edh | Icon | | Kanji |
| Eng | Ikon | *5 letters:* | Motif |
| One | Logo | Badge | Nabla |
| Tag | Mark | Caret | Neume |
| | Neum | Chord | Omega |

| | | | |
|---|---|---|---|
| Presa | Heitiki | Phonetic | Hieroglyph |
| Redon | Ichthus | Svastika | Kalachakra |
| Segno | Ichthys | Swastika | Length mark |
| Sigla | Mandala | Talisman | Mogen David |
| Tilde | Menorah | Triskele | Pictograph |
| Token | Mezuzah | Wild card | Triskelion |
| Totem | Thistle | | |
| | Waymark | *9 letters:* | *11 letters:* |
| *6 letters:* | | Acrophony | Apostrophus |
| Cachet | *8 letters:* | Ampersand | Christogram |
| Cipher | Aniconic | Double-axe | Grammalogue |
| Emblem | Aramanth | Fertility | Liberty Bell |
| Filfot | Asterisk | Hierogram | Phraseogram |
| Fylfot | Caduceus | Ideograph | Punctuation |
| Letter | Daffodil | Logograph | Spread eagle |
| Obelus | Emoticon | Ouroborus | Star of David |
| Smiley | Grapheme | Paragraph | |
| Uraeus | Hashmark | Phonogram | *12 letters:* |
| Wreath | Hiragana | Pictogram | Metalanguage |
| | Ideogram | Sacrament | |
| *7 letters:* | Kitemark | Trademark | *14 letters:* |
| Algebra | Lexigram | | Tetragrammaton |
| Cedilla | Logogram | *10 letters:* | |
| Dingbat | Pentacle | Choropleth | |

---

**Symmetric(al), Symmetry** Balance, Bilateral, Digonal, Diphycercal, Even, Harmony, Isobilateral, Mirror, Pseudocubic, Radial, Regular, Skew

**Sympathetic, Sympathise(r), Sympathy** Affinity, Agreeable, Approval, Commiserate, Commiseration, Compassion, Condole(nce), Condone, Congenial, Crypto, Dear-dear, Empathy, Fellow-traveller, Genial, Humane, Kind, Mediagenic, Par, Pathos, Pity, Rapport, Ruth, Side, Supportive, Understanding, Vicarious, Well-disposed

**Symphony** Alpine, Antar, Babi Yar, Bear, Clock, Concert, Drum-roll, Echo, Eroica, Farewell, Feuer, Fifth, Finlandia, Haffner, Horn-signal, Hunt, Ilya Murometz, Jupiter, Laudon, Leningrad, Linz, London, L'Ours, Manfred, Matin, Midi, Miracle, Music, New World, Ninth, Opus, Oxford, Pastoral, Prague, Queen, Resurrection, Rhenish, Sinfonia, Sinfonietta, Surprise, Tragic, Unfinished

**Symposium** Assembly, Conference, Synod

**Symptom(s)** Epiphenomenon, Feature, Indicia, Merycism, Mimesis, Prodrome, Semiotic, Sign, Syndrome, Token, Trait, Withdrawal

**Synagogue** Beit Knesset, Beth Knesseth, Shul, Temple

**Synchronise(r)** Coincide, Genlock, Interlock, Tune

**Synclinal** Basin

**Syncopated, Syncopation, Syncope** Abridged, Breakbeat, Offbeat, Revamp, Vasovagal, Zoppa, Zoppo

**Syndicate** Associate, Cartel, Combine, Mafioso, Pool, Ring, Stokvel

**Syndrome** Adams-Stokes, Alport's, Asperger's, Carpal tunnel, Cerebellar, Characteristic, China, Chinese restaurant, Chronic fatigue, Compartment, Couvade, Cri du chat, Crush, Cushing's, De Clerambault's, Down's, Economy-class, Empty nest, Erotomania, False memory, Fetal alcohol, Fragile X, Goldenhar's, Gorlin, Guillain-Barré, Gulf War, Hughes, Hutchinson-Gilford, Irritable-bowel, Jerusalem, Klinefelter's, Korsakoff's, Locked-in, Long QT, Marfan, ME, Meniéres, Metabolic, Munch(h)ausen's, Nonne's, Overuse, Parkinson's, Pattern, POS, Postviral, Prader-Willi, Premenstrual, Proteus, Reiter's, Rett's, Revolving door, Reye's, SADS, SARS, Savant, Sezary, Shaken baby, Sick building, SIDS, Sjogren's, Stevens-Johnson, Stockholm, Stokes-Adams, Sturge-Weber, Tall-poppy,

Temperomandibular, TMJ, Total allergy, Tourette's, Toxic shock, Turner's, Wag the dog, Wernicke-Korsakoff, Williams, Wobbler, XYY

**Synod** Assembly, Conference, Convocation, General, Robber, Whitby

**Synonym(ous)** Comparison, Reciprocal

**Synopsis** Abrege, Abstract, Blurb, Conspectus, Digest, Outline, Résumé, Schema, →SUMMARY

**Syntax** Grammar

**Synthesis** Amalgam, Aperture, Fusion, Merger

**Synthesizer** Moog®, Vocoder, Wind

**Synthetic** Android, Dralon, Empirical, Ersatz, Fake, False, Guanazolo, Mock, Neoprene, Plastic, Polyamide, Resin, Silicone, Spencerian, Tow, Urea

**Syphilis** Chancre, French pox, Lues, Pip, Pox, Secondary, Tertiary

**Syrian** Aramaean, Aramaic, Damascene, Druse, Druz(e), Hittite, Hurrian, Levantine, Phoenician

**Syringe(s)** Douche, Flutes, Harpoon, Hypo, Hypodermic, Needle, Reeds, Spray, Squirt, Wash, Works

**Syrphid** Hoverfly

**Syrup(y)** Capillaire, Cassareep, Cassis, Cocky's joy, Coquito, Corn, Diacodion, Diacodium, Flattery, Glycerol, Golden, Goo, Grenadine, Linctus, Maple, Molasses, Moskonfyt, Orgeat, Quiddany, Rob, Rosehip, Sorghum, Starch, Sugar, Treacle, Viscous, Wig

**System(s), Systematic** ABO, Alpha, An mo, Apartheid, Auditory, BACS, Beam, Bertillon, Binary, Black, Bordereau, Braille, Brunonian, Carboniferous, Ceefax, Centauri, Circulatory, Closed loop, Code, Colloidal, Colonial, Compander, Complexus, Continental, Copernican, Cosmos, Course, Crystal, Cybernetics, Decimal, Delsarte, Dewey (Decimal), Dianetics, Distributed, Dolby®, DOS, Early warning, Economy, Eocene, Ergodic, Establishment, Ethic, Expert, Feng Shui, Feudal, Fixed, Folksonomy, Formal, Fourierism, Froebel, Front-end, Giorgi, Grading, Harvard, Haversian, Hexagonal, HLA, Holist, Honour, Hub and spoke, Iastic, I Ching, Immune, Imperial, Imprest, Imputation, Induction loop, Inertial, ISA, Ism, Kalamazoo, Kanban, Life-support, Limbic, Lobby, Long wall, Loop, Lymphatic, Madras, Mercantile, Mereology, Merit, →METHOD, Metric, Microcosm, Midi, Minitel, Miocene, MKSA, Movable, Muschelkalk, Natural, Navigational, Neat, Nervous, Network, Nicam, Notation, Number, Octal, Operating, Order, Organon, Orphism, Orrery, Panel, Periodic, Permian, Pleiocene, Plenum, Points, Portal, Process, Ptolemaic, Public address, Purchase, Quota, Quote-driven, Raisonné, Regime, Regular, Reproductive, Respiratory, Root, Run-time, Scheme, Schmitt, Scientific, Selsyn, Servo, Sexual, SI, Sofar, Solar, Solmisation, Sonar, Sound, Spoils, Sprinkler, Squish lip, Stack(ing), Staff, Stakhanovism, Stand-alone, Stanislavski, Star, STOL, Structure, Studio, Support, Sweating, Tactic, Talk-down, Tally, Ternary, Theory, Third-rail, Tommy, Totalitarianism, Touch, Trias(sic), Truck, Turnkey, Tutorial, Two-party, Universe, Unix, Urogenital, Vestibular, VOIP, Warehousing, Water, Water vascular, Weapon, Windows

# Tt

**T** Bone, Junction, Potence, Tango, Tau-cross, Tee, Time, Toc(k)

**Tab(s)** Bill, Check, Cig(arette), Decimal, Flap, → **LABEL**, Monitor, Ring-pull, Slate, Stay-on, Tally, Trim, Trimming

**Tabby** Blabbermouth, Brindled, → **CAT**, Gossip, Mottled, Spinster, Striped, Trout

**Tabernacle** Niche

**Tabitha** Gazelle

**Table(-like), Tables** Alphonsine, Altar, Board, Bradshaw, Breakfast, Calendar, Capstan, → **CHART**, Coffee, Communion, Console, Contingency, Corbel, Counter, Credence, Credenza, Cricket, Decision, Desk, Diagram, Dinner, Dissecting, Dolmen, Draw-leaf, Draw-top, Dressing, Drop-leaf, Drum, Ephemeris, Experience, Food, Gateleg, Gate-legged, Glacier, Graph, Green-cloth, Grub, Gueridon, High, Imposing, Index, Key, Ladder, League, Life, Light, → **LIST**, Log, Lord's, Lowboy, Mahogany, Matrix, Mensa(l), Mesa, Monopode, Mortality, Multiplication, Nest, Occasional, Operating, Orientation, Pembroke, Periodic, Piecrust, Pier, Plane, Plateau, Platen, Pool, Prothesis, Pythagoras, Ready-reckoner, Reckoner, Refectory, Roll, Round, Rudolphine, Sand, Schedule, Scheme, Slab, Sofa, Spoon, Stall, Statistical, Stone, Suggest, Taboret, Tabular, Tariff, Tea, Te(a)poy, Throwing, Tide, Times, Toilet, Toning, Top, Tray(mobile), Trestle, Trolley, Truth, Twelve, Washstand, Water, Whirling, Wool, Workbench, Writing

**Tableau** Pageant, Semantic

**Tablecloth** Damask, Linen

**Table-land** Barkly, Kar(r)oo, Mesa, Plateau, Puna

**Table-list** Memo, Menu

**Tablet** Abacus, Album, Aspirin, Caplet, Cartouche, E, Eugebine, Graphics, Hatch, Hatchment, Medallion, Opisthograph, Osculatory, Ostracon, Ostrakon, → **PAD**, → **PILL**, Pilule, Plaque, Rune, Slate, Stele, Stone, Tabula, Tombstone, Torah, Triglyph, Triptych, Troche, Trochisk, Ugarit, Votive, Wax

**Table-talker** Deipnosophist

**Table-turner** Tartar

**Table-ware** China, Cutlery, Silver

**Taboo, Tabu** Ban(ned), Bar, Blackball, Forbidden, Incest, Non dit, No-no, Tapu, Unclean

**Tachograph** Spy-in-the-cab

**Tacit, Taciturn(ity)** Clam, Implicit, Laconic, Mumps, Oyster, Reticent, Silent, Understood

**Tack(y)** Adhesive, Bar, Baste, Beat, Boxhaul, Brass, Cheesy, Cinch, Clubhaul, Cobble, Gybe, Harness, Kitsch, Leg, Martingale, Nail, Noseband, Saddlery, Salt-horse, → **SEW**, Sprig, Stirrup, Tailor's, Tasteless, Veer, Wear, White-seam, Yaw, Zigzag

**Tackle** Accost, Address, Approach, Attempt, Beard, Bobstay, Burton, Cat, Chin, Claucht, Claught, Clevis, Clew-garnet, Collar, Dead-eye, Fishing, Garnet, Gear, Haliard, Halyard, Harness, Jury-rig, Kit, Ledger, Nose, Rig, Rigging, Sack, Scrag, Spear, Stick, Straight-arm, Topping-lift, Undertake

**Tact, Tactful** Delicacy, Diplomacy, Diplomatic, Discreet, Discretion, Kidglove, Politic, Savoir-faire

**Tactic(s)** Audible, Carrot and stick, Crossruff, Finesse, Hardball, Manoeuvre, Masterstroke, Plan, Ploy, Ruse, Salami, Scare, Shock, Smear, → **STRATEGY**, Strong-arm, Zwischenzug

**Tactless(ness)** Blundering, Brash, Crass, Gaffe, Gauche, Indelicate, Indiscreet, Loud mouth, Maladroit

**Tadpole** Ascidian, Polliwig, Polliwog, Pollywig, Pollywog, Porwiggle

**Taffy** Thief, Toffee, Welshman

**Tag** Aglet, Aiguillette, Cliché, Dog, Electronic, End, Epithet, → **FOLLOW**, Kabaddi, Kimball, Label, Meta, Price, Question, Quotation, Quote, Remnant, Tab, Tail end, → **TICKET**, Treasury

**Tahini** Sesame

**Tail, Tailpiece, Tailboard** All-flying, Amentum, Apocopate, → **APPENDAGE**, Bob, Brush, Bun, Caudal, Cercal, Cercus, Coda, Codetta, Colophon, Cue, Dock, Empennage, Endgate, Fan, Fee, Flag, Floccus, → **FOLLOW**, Fud, Liripoop, Parson's nose, Point, Pole, Pope's nose, PS, Queue, Rumple-bane, Scut, Seat, Shirt, Stag, Stern, Telson, → **TIP**, Train, Uro(some), Uropod, Uropygium, Women

**Tailless** Acaudal, An(o)urous, Fee-simple

**Tail-lobes** Anisocercal

**Tailor(ed)** Adapt, Bespoke, Bushel, Cabbager, Clothier, Couturier, Customise, Cutter, Darzi, Draper, Durzi, Epicene, Feeble, Flint, Form, Merchant, Nine, Outfitter, Pick-the-louse, Pricklouse, Sartor, Seamster, Snip, Starveling, Style, Whipcat, Whipstitch

▷ **Tailor** *may indicate* an anagram

**Taint(ed)** Besmirch, Blemish, Fly-blown, Foughty, High, Impure, Infect, Leper, Off, Poison, → **SPOIL**, Stain, Stale, Stigma, Tinge, Trace, Unwholesome

**Taiwan** RC

**Take(n), Take in, Taking(s), Take over, Takeover** Absorb, → **ACCEPT**, Adopt, Annex, Appropriate, Assume, Attract, Bag, Beg, Besotted, Bewitch, Bite, Bone, Borrow, Bottle, → **CAPTURE**, Catch, Charming, Claim, Cop, Coup (d'etat), Detract, Dig, Dishy, Distrain, Eat, Entr(y)ism, Epris, Exact, Expropriate, Film, Get, Grab, Greenmail, Handle, Haul, Hent, House, Howe, Huff, Impound, Incept, Ingest, Leveraged buy out, Loot, Mess, Misappropriate, Nationalise, Nick, Occupy, On, Pocket, Poison pill, Quote, R, Rec, Receipt, Receive, Recipe, Reserved, Reverse, Rob, Seise, Sequester, Ship, Smitten, Snaffle, Snatch, Sneak, Spoken for, → **STEAL**, Stomach, Subsume, Swallow, Sweet, Swipe, Toll, Trump, Turnover, Usher, Usurp, Wan, Winsome, Wrest

**Take away, Take-away, Take back, Take off** Abduct, Annex, Aph(a)eresis, Asport, Carry-out, Curry, Deduct, Destruct, Dock, Doff, Doggy bag, Dot, Esloin, Exenterate, Expropriate, Indian, Jato, Minus, Parody, Parrot, Press-gang, Recaption, Resume, Scramble, Shanghai, Skit, Spirit, Spoof, Streak, Subtract, Vertical, VTO(L)

**Take care** Guard, See, Tend, Watch

**Take down, Take up** Appropriate, Cap, Choose, Osmose, Shot, Snaffle, Unhook

▷ **Taken up** *may indicate* reversed

**Take part** Act, Engage, Side

**Taker** Recipient

**Talbot House** Toc H

**Talc** Potstone, Rensselaerite, Soapstone, Steatite, Venice

**Tale(s)** Aga-saga, Allegory, Anecdote, Blood, Boccaccio, Cautionary, Conte, Decameron, Edda, Fable, Fabliau, Fairy, Fairy story, Fiction, Folk, Gag, Geste, Hadith, Hair-raiser, Iliad, Jataka, Jeremiad, Legend, Lie, Mabinogion, Maise, Märchen, Ma(i)ze, Mease, Milesian, Narrative, Odyssey, Old wives', Pentameron, Rede, Saga, Sandabar, Score, Sinbad, Sind(a)bad, Sob-story, Spiel, → **STORY**, Teratology, Toy, Tradition, Traveller's, Weird, Yarn

**Tale-bearer, Tale-teller** Gossip, Grass, Informer, Sneak, Tattler, Tusitala

**Talent(ed)** Ability, Able, Accomplishment, Aptitude, Beefcake, Bent, Brilliance, Budding, Dower, Endowment, Faculty, Flair, Forte, Genius, Gift, Idiot savant, Ingenium, Knack, Long suit, Nous, Obol, Prodigy, Schtick, Strong point, Tottie, Versatile, Virtuoso, Whiz-kid, W(h)iz(z)

**Talion** Reprisal

**Talisman** Amulet, Charm, Luck, Mascot, Saladin, Sampo, Scarab, Telesm

**Talk(ing), Talking point, Talker, Talks** Address, Ana, Articulate, Babble, Bibble-babble, Blab, Blague(er), Blat, Blather, Blether-skate, Cant, Causerie, Chalk, Chat, Chew the fat, Chinwag, Chirp, Chitchat, Circumlocution, Colloquy, Commune, Confabulate, Confer, Contact, Converse, Coo, Cross, Descant, Dialog(ue), Diatribe, Dilate, Discourse, Diseur, Dissert, Double, Earbash, Earful, Expatiate, Express, Fast, Filibuster, Froth, Gab, Gabble, Gabnash, Gas, Gibber, Gossip, Grandiloquence, Guff, Harp, High-level, Hobnob, Hot air, Imparl, Jabber, Jargon, Jaw-jaw, Jazz, Korero, Lalage, Lalla, Lip, Logorrhoea, Macrology, Mang, Maunder, Mince, Monologue, Motormouth, Nashgab, Natter, Noise, Omniana, Palabra, Palaver, Parlance, Parley, Patter, Pawaw, Pep, Perorate, Phraser, Pidgin, Pillow, Pitch, Potter, Powwow, Prate, Prattle, Presentation, Prose, Proximity, Ramble, Rap, Rattle on, Regale, Rigmarole, Rote, Sales, SALT, Sermon, Shop, Slang(-whang), Small, Soliloquy, →**SPEAK**, Speech, Spiel, Spout, Straight, Summit, Sweet, Table, Tachylogia, Topic, Turkey, Twaddle, Twitter, Unbosom, Up(s), Utter, Vocal, Waffle, Wibble, Witter, Wongi, Wrangle, Yabber, Yack, Yad(d)a-yad(d)a-yad(d)a, Yak, Yalta, Yammer, Yap, Yatter

**Talkative** Chatty, Expansive, Fluent, Gabby, Garrulous, Gash, Glib, Loquacious, Vocular, Voluble, Windbag

**Tall** Beanpole, Etiolated, Exaggerated, Far-fetched, Hie, High, Hye, Lanky, Lathy, Leggy, Lofty, Long, Order, Procerity, Randle-tree, Rangy, Rantle-tree, Spindly, Tangle, Taunt, Tower, Towery

**Tallboy** Chest, Dresser

**Tallow** Greaves, Hatchettite, Lead-arming, Mineral, Vegetable, Wax

**Tally** Accord, →**AGREE**, Census, Correspond, Count, Match, Nickstick, Notch, Record, →**SCORE**, Stick, Stock, Tab, Tag

**Talmud** Gemara, Mishna(h)

**Talon** Claw, Ogee, Single

**Talus** Scree

**Tamarind** Assam

**Tamasha** Fuss, To-do

**Tame** Amenage, Break, Docile, Domesticate, Gentle, Lapdog, Mail, Mansuete, Meek, Mild, Safe, Snool, Subdue

**Tammany** Hall, Sachem

**Tamp, Tampon** Plug, Ram

**Tamper(ing)** Bishop, Cook, Doctor, Fake, Fiddle, Meddle, Medicate, Monkey, Nobble, Phreaking

**Tam-tam** Gong

**Tan(ned), Tanned skin, Tanning** Adust, Bablah, Babul, Bark, Basil, Beige, Bisque, Boarding, Bronze, →**BROWN**, Canaigre, Catechu, Furan, Furfuran(e), Insolate, Lambast, Leather, Neb-neb, Paste, Pipi, Puer, Pure, Spank, Sun, Sunbathe, Tenné, Umber, Valonea, Val(l)onia, Weather-beaten, Ybet

**Tandem** Duo, Random

**Tang** Relish, Smack, Taste

**Tangent** Ratio, Slope, Touching

**Tangible** Concrete, Palpable, Plain, Solid, Tactile, Tactual

**Tangle** Alga, Badderlock, Burble, Driftweed, Dulse, Embroil, Enmesh, Entwine, Fank, Fankle, Heap, Hole, Implication, Ket, →**KNOT**, Labyrinth, Laminaria, Lutin, Mat, Mess, Mix, Nest, Oarweed, Ore, Perplex, Pleach, Raffle, →**RAVEL**, Sea-girdle, Seaweed, Skean, Skein, Snarl, Taigle, Taut(it), Tawt, Thicket, Tousle, Varec

▷ **Tangled** *may indicate* an anagram

**Tango** Dance, T

**Tank(ed)** Abrams, Alligator, Amphibian, Aquarium, Back boiler, Belly, Bosh, Casspir, Centurion, Cesspool, Challenger, Chieftain, Cistern, Crusader, Dracone, Drop, Drunk,

Fail, Feedhead, Float, Flotation, Fuel, Gasholder, Gasometer, Header, Keir, Kier, Mouse, Panzer, Pod, Quiescent, →**RESERVOIR**, Ripple, Sedimentation, Septic, Sherman, Shield pond, Sponson, Sump, Surge, Think, Tiger, Valentine, Vat, Venter, Ventral, Vivarium, Weasel, Whippet

**Tankard** Blackjack, Jug, Peg, Pewter, Pot, Stein, Tappit-hen

**Tanker** Bowser, Crude carrier, Lorry, Oiler, VLCC

**Tanner(y)** Bender, Currier, Kick, Solarium, Sunbather, Sunshine, Tawery, Tester(n), 'VId', Zack

**Tannin** Catechu

**Tantalise** Entice, Tease, Tempt, Torture

**Tantalum** Ta

**Tantivy** Alew, Halloo

**Tantrum** Conniption, Hissy fit, Paddy, Pet, Rage, Scene, Snit, Tirrivee, Tirrivie, Wobbly

**Tanzania(n)** EAT, Sandawe

**Tap(ping), Taps** Accolade, Ague, Bibcock, Blip, Bob, Broach, Bug, Cock, Col legno, Dip into, Drum, Eavesdrop, Faucet, Fever, Fillip, Flick, Hack, H and C, Listen, Mag, Milk, Mixer, Monitor, Paracentesis, Pat, Patter, Percuss, Petcock, →**RAP**, Screw, Spigot, Spile, Spinal, Standpipe, Stopcock, Stroup, Tack, Tat, Tit, Touk, Tuck, Water

**Tape** Adhesive, Chrome, DAT, Demo, →**DRINK**, Duct, Ferret, Finish, Friction, Gaffer, Grip, Idiot, Incle, Inkle, Insulating, Magnetic, Masking, Measure, Metal, Narrowcast, Paper, Passe-partout, Perforated, Punched, Record, Red, Reel to reel, Scotch, Sellotape®, Shape, Stay, Sticky, Ticker, Tit, Video, Welding

**Taper(ed), Tapering** Candle, Diminish, Fastigiate, Featheredge, Flagelliform, Fusiform, Lanceolate, Morse, Narrow, Nose, Spill, Subulate, Tail

**Tapestry** Alentous, Arras(ene), Aubusson, Bayeux, Bergamot, Crewel-work, Dosser, Gobelin, Hanging, Mural, Oudenarde, Petit point, Sewing, Tapet, Weaving

**Tapeworm** Coenurus, Echinococcus, Hydatid, Measle, Scolex, Strobila, Taenia, Teniasis

**Tapioca** Cassava, Pearl, Yuca, Yucca

**Tapir** Anta, S(e)ladang

**Tar, Tar product** AB, Aniline, Bitumen, Carbazole, Coal, Creosote, Deckhand, Egg, Furan, Gas, Gladwellise, Gob, Indene, Juniper, Maltha, Matelot, Matlo, Mineral, Naphtha, Needle, OS, Parcel, Pay, Picamar, Picene, Pine, Pitch, Rating, Retene, Sailor, Salt, Uintahite, Uintaite, Wood, Wood pitch, Wren, Xylol

**Tardy** Behindhand, Dilatory, Late, →**SLOW**

**Tare** T, Tine, Vetch

**Target** Admass, →**AIM**, Ambition, Attainment, Blank, Butt, Clay, Clout, Cockshy, Dart(board), Drogue, End, Ettle, Hit, Home, Hub, Inner, Magpie, Mark, Mark-white, Motty, Nick, →**OBJECT**, Object ball, Outer, Peg, Pelta, Pin, Popinjay, Prey, Prick, Quintain, Sitter, Sitting (duck), Tee, Victim, Wand, Zero in, Zero on

**Tariff** Levy, List, Menu, Preferential, Protective, Rate, Revenue, Zabeta

**Tarnish** Asperse, Defile, Discolour, Discredit, Soil, Stain, Sully, Taint

**Taro** Arum, Coc(c)o, Dasheen, Eddo

**Tarot** Arcana

**Tarpaulin** Weathercloth

**Tarragon** Staragen

**Tarry** Bide, Bituminous, Dally, Leng, →**LINGER**, Stay, Sticky

**Tarsier** Malmag

**Tarsus** Saul

**Tart** Acetic, Acid, Bakewell, Broad, Charlotte, Cheesecake, Cocotte, Croquante, Cupid, Custard, Dariole, Deck, Doxy, Duff, Flam(m), Flan, Flawn, Frock, Harlot, Ho, Hussy, Jade, Jay, Lemony, Mirliton, Moll, Mort, Nana, Painted woman, →**PIE**, Pinnace, Piquant, Pro, Pungent, Quean, Quiche, Quine, Rate, →**SHARP**, Slag, Slapper, Slut, Snappy, Sour, Stew, Strumpet, Tatin, Tom, Tramp, Treacle, Trollop, Trull, Unsweet, Vinegary

**Tartan** Argyle, Argyll, Check, Maud, Plaid, Set(t), Trews

**Tartar** Argal, Argol, Beeswing, Calculus, Crust, Hell, Plaque, Rough, Scale, Tam(b)erlane, Zenocrate

**Tarzan** Greystoke

**Tashkent** Uzbek

**Task** Assignment, Aufgabe, →CHORE, Clat, Commission, Drudgery, Duty, Emprise, Errand, Exercise, Fag, Imposition, Legwork, Marathon, Mission, Onus, Ordeal, Pensum, Remit, Stint, Thankless, Uphill, Vulgus

**Taskmaster** Martinet

**Tasmania** Apple Isle, Van Diemen's Land

**Tassel** Fringe, Pompom, Toorie, Tourie, Tsutsith, Tuft

**Taste(ful), Taster, Tasty** Acquired, Aesthetic, Appetite, Assay, Dash, Degust, Delibate, Delicious, Discrimination, →EAT, Elegant, Excerpt, Fad, Fancy, Fashion, Flavour, Form, Gout, Gust, Gustatory, Hint, Lekker, Lick, Liking, Palate, Penchant, Pica, Pree, Refinement, Relish, →SAMPLE, Sapor, Sar, Savour, Scrummy, Seemly, Sensation, S(c)hme(c)k, Sip, Smack, Smatch, Smattering, Snack, Soupçon, Specimen, Stomach, Succulent, Tang, Titbit, Toothsome, →TRY, Umami, Vertu, Virtu, Waft, Wine

**Tasteless** Appal, Brassy, Coarse, Fade, Flat, Gaudy, Indelicate, Insipid, Insulse, Kitsch, Stale, Tacky, Tawdry, Vapid, Vulgar, Watery, Wearish, Wersh

**Tat, Tatter, Tatty** Flitter, Grot, Moth-eaten, Rag, Ribbon, Roon, Schlock, Scrap, Shabby, Shred, Tag, Tan, Ta(i)ver, Untidy

**Tattie-bogle** Scarecrow

**Tattle(r)** Blab, Chatter, Gash, →GOSSIP, Prate, Rumour, Sneak, Snitch, Totanus, Willet

**Tattoo** Devil's, Drum, Edinburgh, Moko, Pony, Rataplan, Row-dow, Tat

**Tatum** Art

**Taught** Up

**Taunt** Bait, Catcall, Dig, Fling, Gibe, Gird, →JEER, Jest, Jibe, Rag, Razz, Ridicule, Twight, Twit

**Taut** Stiff, Strained, Tense

**Tavern** Bar, Bodega, Bousing-ken, Bush, Fonda, →INN, Kiddleywink, Kneipe, Mermaid, Mitre, Mughouse, Night-house, Pothouse, Shebeen, Taphouse

**Taw** Alley, Ally, Marble

**Tawdry** Brash, Catchpenny, →CHEAP, Flashy, Gaudy, Gingerbread, Raffish, Sleazy, Tatty, Tinsey

**Tawny** Brindle, Dusky, Fawn, Fulvous, Mulatto, Port, Tan

**Tawse** Cat, Lash, Thong, Whip

**Tax(ation), Taxing** ACT, Agist, Aid, Alms-fee, Arduous, Assess, Capital gains, Capitation, Carbon, Carucage, Cense, Cess, →CHARGE, Corporation, Council, CRT, Custom, Danegeld, Death duty, Deferred, Direct, Duty, Energy, EPT, Escot, Escuage, Eurotax, Exact, Excise, Exercise, EZT, Fat, Gabelle, Geld, Gelt, Gift, Green, Head, Head money, Hearth money, Hidage, Hidden, Impose, Imposition, Impost, Impute, Indirect, Inheritance, IR, Jaghir(e), Jagir, Keelage, Land, Levy, Likin, Lot, Murage, Negative, Octroi, Operose, Overtask, Overwork, Pavage, PAYE, Peter's-pence, Poll, Poundage, Precept, Primage, Property, Proportional, PT, Punish, Purchase, Rate, Regressive, Road, Rome-pence, Sales, Scat(t), Scot (and lot), Scutage, Sess, SET, Ship money, Sin, Single, Skat, Stealth, Stent, Strain, Streetage, Stretch, Stumpage, Super, Taille, Tallage, Talliate, Tall order, Tariff, Tartan, Task, Teind, Tithe, Tobin, Toilsome, Toll, Tonnage, Tribute, Try, Turnover, Tyre, Unitary, Value-added, VAT, Wattle, Wealth, Weary, White rent, Windfall, Window, Withholding, Zakat

**Tax area** Tahsil, Talooka, Taluk(a)

**Tax-collector, Taxman** Amildar, Cheater, Exciseman, Farmer, Gabeller, Ghostbuster, Inspector, IR(S), Publican, Stento(u)r, Tidesman, Tithe-proctor, Tollman, Undertaker, Vatman, Zemindar

**Taxi(s), Taxi driver** Air, Cab, Coast, Gharri, Gharry, Hackie, Hackney, Joe baxi, Minicab, Rank, Samlor, System, Zola Budd

**Taxidermist** Venus
**Taxiway** Peritrack
▶ **Taxman** *see* TAX-COLLECTOR
**TB** Scrofula
**TE** Lawrence, Ross, Shaw
**Tea** Afternoon, Assam, Beef, Black, Bohea, Brew, Brew-up, Brick, Bubble, Bush, Cambric, Camomile, Caper, Ceylon, Cha, Chai, Chamomile, Chanoyu, Char, China, Chirping-cup, Congo(u), Cream, Cuppa, Darjeeling, Earl Grey, Grass, Green, Gunfire, Gunpowder, Herb(al), High, Hybrid, Hyson, Ice(d), Indian, Jasmine, K(h)at, Kitchen, Labrador, Lapsang, Lapsang Souchong, Leaves, Ledum, Lemon, Malt, Manuka, Marijuana, Maté, Mexican, Mint, Morning, Mountain, New Jersey, Oolong, Orange pekoe, Oulong, Paraguay, Pekoe, Post and rail, Pot, Qat, Red-root, Rooibos, Rosie Lee, Russian, Sage, Senna, Souchong, Stroupach, Stroupan, Switchel, Tay, Thea, Theophylline, Tousy, Twankay, White, Yapon, Yerba (de Maté)
**Teach(er), Teaching (material), Teachings** Academe, Academician, Acharya, Adjoint, Advisory, Agrege, AMMA, Anthroposophy, Apostle, Aristotle, AUT, Barbe, Beale, BEd, Bhagwan, Buddha, Buss, Catechist, Chalk and talk, Chalkface, → COACH, Communicate, Con(ne), Didactic, Didascalic, Docent, Doctrine, Dogma, Dominie, Dressage, Edify, → EDUCATE, Educationalist, Edutainment, EIS, ELT, Explain, Faculty, Froebel, Gerund-grinder, Gooroo, Gospel, Governess, Guru, Head, Heuristic, Hodja, Inculcate, Indoctrinate, Inform, Instil, Instruct, Ism, Kho(d)ja, Kindergart(e)ner, Kumon (Method), Lair, Lancasterian, Larn, Lear(e), Lecturer, Leir, Lere, Maam, Maggid, Magister, Maharishi, Mahavira, Mallam, Marker, Marm, Master, Maulvi, Mentor, Message, Miss, Mistress, Molla(h), Monitor, Montessorian, Moola(h), Moolvi(e), Mufti, Mullah, Munshi, Mwalimu, Mystagogue, Nuffield, NUT, Paedotribe, PAT, Pedagogue, Pedant, Peripatatic, Phonic method, Posture-master, Preceptor, Pr(a)efect, Privat-docent, Proctor, Prof, Prog, PT, Pupil, Rabbetzin, Rabbi, Rav, Realia, Rebbe, Remedial, Rhetor, Scholastic, Schoolie, Schoolman, Scribe, Sensei, Show, Sir, Smriti, Socrates, Sophist, Specialist, Staff, Starets, Staretz, Stinks, Substitute, Sufism, Sunna, Supply, Swami, Tantra, Team, Tonic sol-fa, Train(er), Tuition, Tutelage, Tutor, Tutress, Tutrix, Usher
**Teach-in** Seminar
**Teahouse** Sukiya
**Teak** African, Bastard, White
**Teal** Spring
**Team** All Blacks, Argyll, Bafana Bafana, Colts, Crew, Dream, Écurie, Eleven, Équipe, Farm, Fifteen, Hearts, Man U, Nine, Outfit, Oxen, Panel, Possibles, Probables, Proto, Relay, Scrub, Set, → SIDE, Span, Special, Spurs, Squad, Squadron, Staff, Syndicate, Tiger, Troupe, Turnout, Unicorn, Unit, United, XI
**Tea-party** Boston, Bunfight, Cookie-shine, Drum, Kettledrum, Shine
**Teapot** Billycan, Cadogan, Samovar
**Tear(s), Tearable, Tearful, Tearing** Beano, Claw, Crocodile, Dismember, Divulsion, Drop(let), Eye-drop, Eye-water, Greeting, Hurry, Lacerate, Lachrymose, Laniary, Mammock, Maudlin, Pelt, Ranch, Rash, Reave, → REND, Rheum, Rip, Rive, Rume, Scag, Screed, Shred, Snag, Split, Spree, Sprint, Tire, Vale, Waterworks, Wet, Worry, Wrench, Wrest
**Tearaway** Get, Hothead, Ned, Yahoo
**Tear-jerker** Melodrama, Onion
**Tear-pit** Crumen, Larmier
**Tease, Teaser, Teasing** Arch, Backcomb, Badinage, Bait, Ballyrag, Banter, Card, Chaff, Chap, Chiack, Chip, Chyack, Cod, Comb, Coquet, Discredit, Drag, Enigma, Grig, Guy, Hank, Imp, Ironic, Itch, Josh, Kemb, Kid, Mag, Mamaguy, Nark, Persiflage, → RAG, Raillery, Rally, Razz, Rib, Rip on, Rot, Strip, → TANTALISE, Toaze, Torment(or), Touse, Touze, Towse, Towze, Twilly, Twit, Worrit
**Teasel** Dipsacus, Valerian

**Teat** Dug, Dummy, Mamilla, Mastoid, Nipple, Pap, Soother, Tit

**Tea-time** Chat

**Teaze** Gig, Moze

**Technetium** Tc

**Technical, Technician, Technique** Adept, Alexander, Art, Artisan, Brushwork, Campimetry, College, Craftsmanship, Cusum, Delphi, Execution, Foley artist, Footsteps editor, Harmolodics, Honey-trap, Junior, Kiwi, Know-how, Layback, Manner, Metamorphic, → **METHOD**, Operative, Phasing, Phlebotomist, Pixil(l)ation, Reflectography, Salami, Sandwich, Science, Scientist, Senior, Serial, Slam-dunk, Slo-mo, Split-screen, Stop-motion, System, Toe and heel, Touch, Western blotting, Work around

**Technology, Technologian, Technological** Blue tooth, Electronics, Engineering, High, Information, Intermediate, IT, Pull, Push, Robotics, State of the art, Stealth, Telescience, Thickfilm, Thinfilm

**Ted(dy)** Bodgie, Dexter, Ducktail, Moult, Roosevelt, Underwear, Widgie, Yob

**Tedium, Tedious** Boring, Chore, Deadly, Doldrums, Drab, Drag, Dreariness, Dreich, Dull, Ennui, Foozle, Heaviness, Ho-hum, Laborious, Langueur, Long, Longspun, Longueur, Mind-numbing, Monotony, Operose, Prosy, Rigmarole, Snore, Soul-destroying, Tiresome, → **TIRING**, Twaddle, Wearisome, Yawn

**Tee** Hub, Umbrella, Wind

**Teem(ing)** Abound, Bustling, Empty, Great, Heaving, Pullulate, Swarm

**Teenage(r)** Adolescent, Bobbysoxer, Junior, Juvenile, Minor, Mod, Pubertal, Rocker, Sharpie, Skinhead, Youth

▶ **Teeth** see **TOOTH(ED)**

**Teething ring** Coral

**Teetotal(ler)** Abdar, Abstainer, Blue Ribbon, Nephalist, Rechabite, Sober, Temperate, TT, Water-drinker, Wowser

**Tegument** Seed coat

**Telecommunications** Cellnet®, Vodafone®

**Telegram, Telegraph** Bush, Cable, Ems, Facsimile, Fax, Grapevine, Greetings, International, Marconi, Message, Moccasin, Mulga wire, Overseas, Quadruplex, Radiogram, Singing, Telautograph®, Telex, Wire

**Telegu** Gentoo

**Telepathy, Telepathic** Clairvoyance, ESP, Psychic, Seer

**Telephone, Telephonist** Ameche, ATLAS, Bell, Blackberry, Blower, BT, Call, Cellphone, Centrex, Cordless, Detectophone, Dial, Dog and bone, Exchange, Freephone®, GRACE, Handset, Horn, Hotline, Intercom, Line, Lo-call®, Mercury, Mobile, Mob(e)y, Noki, Operator, Patchboard, Payphone, Pay-station, Pdq, → **PHONE**, POTS, Ring, Snitch line, Speakerphone, Squawk box, STD, Telebridge, Textphone, Tie line, Touch-tone, Utility, Vodafone®, Wire

**Teleprinter** Creed

**Telescope** Altazimuth, Astronomical, Binocle, Cassegrain(ian), Collimator, Comet finder, Coronagraph, Coronograph, Coudé, Electron, Equatorial, Finder, Galilean, Gemini, Glass, Gregorian, Heliometer, Hubble, Interferometer, Intussuscept, Meniscus, Newtonian, Night-glass, Optical, Palomar, Perspective, Prospect(ive)-glass, Radio, Reading, Reflecting, Reflector, Refractor, Schmidt, Sector, Shorten, Sniperscope, Snooperscope, Speculum, Spyglass, Stadia, Terrestrial, Tube, X-ray, Zenith

**Teletext®** Ceefax®, Oracle®

**Television, Telly** Appointment, Box, Breakfast, Cable, Closed-circuit, Confessional, Digibox®, Digital, Diorama, Docu-soap, Event, Flatscreen, Goggle box, Iconoscope, Image orthicon, Interactive, ITV, MAC, Narrowcast, PAL, Pay, Plumbicon®, Projection, Reality, RTE, Satellite, SECAM, Set, Small screen, Subscription, Terrestrial, Tree and branch, Tube, → **TV**, Video

**Tell(ing), Teller, Telltale** Acquaint, Announce, Apprise, Archer, Beads, Blab, Break, Cashier, Clipe, Clype, Compt, Confess, Direct, → **DISCLOSE**, Divulge, Effective, Fess,

Give, Grass, Impart, Influential, Inform(er), → **NARRATE**, Noise, Nose, Notify, Number, Rat, Recite, Recount, Relate, Report, Retail, Rumour, Scunge, Sing, Sneak, Snitch, Spin, Teach, Unbosom, William

**Tellurium** Te

**Temerity** Cheek, Gall, Impertinence, Imprudence, Impudence, Incaution, Rashness, Recklessness

**Temper, Temperate** Abstemious, Abstinent, Adjust, Allay, Alloy, Anneal, Assuage, Attune, Balmy, Bate, Bile, Blood, Calm, Cantankerous, Choler, Comeddle, Continent, Dander, Delay, Ease, Fireworks, Flaky, Inure, Irish, Leaven, → **MILD**, Mitigate, Moderate, Modify, → **MOOD**, Neal, Outburst, Paddy, Paddywhack, Pet, Radge, Rage, Season, Short fuse, Snit, Sober, Soften, Spitfire, Spleen, Strop, Swage, Tantrum, Techy, Teen, Teetotal, Tetchy, Tiff, Tone, Trim, Tune, Wax

**Temperament(al)** Bent, Blood, Choleric, Crasis, Cyclothymia, Disposition, Equal, Just, Kidney, Mean-tone, Melancholy, Mettle, Moody, → **NATURE**, Neel, Over-sensitive, Phlegmatic, Prima donna, Sanguine, Unstable, Up and down, Viscerotonia

**Temperance** Good Templar, Moderation, Pledge, Rechabite

**Temperature** Absolute, Black body, Celsius, Centigrade, Chambré, Colour, Core, Critical, Curie, Dew point, Eutectic, Fahrenheit, Fever, Flashpoint, Heat, Heterothermal, Hyperthermia, Ignition, Kelvin, Melting, Néel, Permissive, Regulo, Restrictive, Room, Supercritical, T, Thermodynamic, Transition, Weed, Weid

**Tempest(uous)** Bourasque, Euraquilo, Euroclydon, Gale, High, Marie, → **STORM(Y)**, Wrathy

**Template** Prototype, Stencil

**Temple, Temple gate** Abu Simbel, Abydos, Adytum, Amphiprostyle, Amritsar, Artemis, Capitol, Cella, Chapel, Church, Delphi, Delubrum, Ephesus, Erechtheum, Erechthion, Fane, Gompa, Gurdwara, Haffet, Haffit, Heroon, Inner, Josshouse, Karnak, Mandir(a), Masjid, Middle, Monopteron, Monopteros, Mosque, Museum, Naos, Nymphaeum, Pagod(a), Pantheon, Parthenon, Sacellum, Serapeum, → **SHRINE**, Shul(n), Teocalli, Teopan, Torii, Vihara, Wat

**Tempo** Agoge, Andantino, Lento, Rate, → **RHYTHM**, Rubato

**Temporal** Petrosal, Petrous

**Temporary** Acting, Caretaker, Casual, Cutcha, Ephemeral, Fleeting, Freelance(r), Hobjob, Impermanent, Interim, Jury-rigged, Kutcha, Lash-up, Locum, Makeshift, Pro tem, Provisional, Quick-fix, Scratch, Short-term, Stopgap, Temp, Transient, Transitional

**Temporise(r)** Politique

**Tempt(ation), Tempting, Tempter, Temptress** Allure, Apple, Bait, Beguile, Beset, Circe, Dalilah, Dangle, Decoy, Delilah, Draw, → **ENTICE**, Eve, Femme fatale, Groundbait, Impulse, Induce, Irresistible, Lure, Mephistopheles, Peccable, Providence, Satan, Seduce, Serpent, Sexy, Siren, Snare, Tantalise, Test, Tice, Trial, Woo

**Ten** 10, Commandments, Decad, Dectet, Decury, Denary, Googol, Iota, Long, Tera-, Tribes, X

**Tenacious, Tenacity** Adhesive, Clayey, Determined, Dogged, Drive, Fast, Grim death, Guts, Hold, Intransigent, Persevering, Persistent, Resolute, Retentive, Sticky

**Tenancy, Tenant(s)** Boarder, Censuarius, Cosherer, Cottager, Cottar, Cotter, Cottier, Dreng, Feuar, Feudatory, Gavelman, Homage, Ingo, Inhabit, Kindly, Leaseholder, Lessee, Liege, → **LODGER**, Mailer, Metayer, Occupant, Occupier, Pendicler, Periodic, Regulated, Rentaller, Renter, Secure, Shorthold, Sitting, Socager, Socman, Sokeman, Suckener, Tacksman, Valvassor, Vassal, Vavasour, Villein, Visit

**Tend(ing)** Apt, Care, Dress, Herd, Incline, Keep, Lean, Liable, Mind, Minister, Nurse, Prone, Run, Shepherd, Stoke, Verge, Volunteer

**Tendency** Apt, Bent, Bias, Central, Conatus, Disposition, Drift, Genius, Idiosyncrasy, Import, Inclination, Leaning, Militant, Orientation, Penchant, Proclivity, Propensity, Trend

**Tender(iser), Tenderly, Tenderness** Affettuoso, Amoroso, Bid, Bill, Charitable, Coin, Con amore, Crank, Dingey, Ding(h)y, Fond, Frail, Gentle, Green, Humane,

Jolly-boat, Legal, Nesh, Nurse(maid), →**OFFER**, Painful, Papain, Pinnace, Pra(a)m, Prefer, Present, Proffer, Proposal, Quotation, Red Cross, Sair, Shepherd, →**SOFT**, Sore, SRN, Submit, Sweet, Swineherd, Sympathy, Tendre

**Tenderfoot** Babe, Chechacho, Che(e)chako, Cub, Greenhorn, Innocent

**Tenderloin** Psoas, Undercut

**Tendon** Achilles, Aponeurosis, Hamstring, Kangaroo, Leader, Paxwax, Sinew, String, Vinculum, Whitleather

**Tendril(led)** Capreolate, Cirrose, Cirrus, Tentacle

**Tenement(s)** Dominant, Land, Rook, Rookery, Tack

**Tenet** Adiaphoron, Credo, Creed, →**DOCTRINE**, Dogma

**Tenfold** Decuple

**Tennis** Close, Court, Deck, Jeu de paume, Lawn, LTA, Real, Royal, Set, Short, Sphairistike, Squash, Table, Wimbledon

**Tennis court** En-Tout-Cas®

**Tennis player** Ashe, Edberg, Laver, Nastase

**Tenon** Cog, Dovetail, Lewis, Lewisson, Tusk

**Tenor** Caruso, Course, Direction, Domingo, →**DRIFT**, Effect, Even, Feck, Ferreras, Gigli, Gist, Heldentenor, Heroic, Pavarotti, Purport, Sense, Singer, T, Tide, Timbre, Trial, Vein

**Tense** Agitato, Aor, Aorist, Case, Clench, Cliffhanger, Conditional, Drawn, Edgy, Electric, Essive, Flex, Fraught, Imperfect, Keyed up, Knife-edge, Laconic, Mood(y), Nail-biting, Nervy, On edge, Overstrung, Past, Perfect, Pluperfect, Present perfect, Preterit, Preterite, Rigid, Simple, Stiff, Strained, Stressed(-out), Strict, T, →**TAUT**, Tighten, Uptight

**Tensing** Sherpa

**Tension** Creative, Dialectic, High, Isometrics, Isotonic, Meniscus, Nail-biting, Nerviness, Premenstrual, →**STRAIN**, Stress, Stretch, Surface, Tone, Tonicity, Tonus, Yips

**Tent** Bell, Bivouac, Bivvy, Cabana, Douar, Dowar, Duar, Ger, Gur, Kedar, Kibitka, Marquee, Oxygen, Pavilion, Probe, Pup, Red wine, Ridge, Shamiana(h), Shamiyanah, Shelter, Tabernacle, Teepee, Tepee, Tilt, Tipi, Top, Topek, Trailer, Tupek, Tupik, Wigwam, Wine, Y(o)urt

**Tentacle** Actinal, Cirrate, Feeler, Hectocotylus, Horn, Limb, Lophophore

**Tentative** Cautious, Empirical, Experimental, Feeler, Gingerly, Peirastic

**Tent-dweller, Tent-maker** Camper, Indian, Kedar, Omar, St Paul

**Tenth** Cohort, Disme, Submerged, Teind, Tithe

**Ten Thousand** Toman

**Tenuous** Frail, Slender, Slight, Thin, Vague

**Tenure** Blench, Burgage, Copyhold, Cottier(ism), Drengage, Fee, Fee-farm, Feu, Frankalmoi(g)n(e), Frank-fee, Gavelkind, Leasehold, Manorial, Occupation, Raiyatwari, Rundale, Runrig, Ryotwari, Socage, →**TERM**, Vavasory, Venville, Zemindar

**Tepid** Laodicean, Lew, Lukewarm

**Terbium** Tb

**Terete** Centric(al)

**Term(s), Terminal, Termly** Air, Anode, Boundary, Buffer, Buzzword, Cathode, Coast, Container, Coste, Designate, Desinent(ial), Distal, Distributed, Dub, Dumb, Easy, →**EPITHET**, Euphemism, Expression, Final, Gnomon, Goal, Half, Hilary, Inkhorn, Intelligent, Kathode, Law, Lent, Major, Michaelmas, Middle, Minor, Misnomer, Never-never, →**PERIOD**, Point-of-sale, Rail(head), Real, Remit, Removal, Sabbatical, School, Semester, Session, Smart, Spell, Stint, Stretch, Trimester, Trimestrial, Trinity, Ultimatum, Verb, Waterloo, →**WORD**, Work station, Zeroth

**Termagant** Jade, Shrew, Shrow, Spitfire, Virago, Vixen

**Terminate, Termination, Terminus** Abolish, Abort, Axe, Cease, Conclude, Depot, Desinent, Earth, →**END**, Euston, Expiry, →**FINISH**, Goal, King's Cross, Liquidate, Naricorn, Paddington, Railhead, Suffix, Waterloo

**Terminology** Jargon

**Termite** Duck-ant, White ant

**Tern** Egg-bird, Noddy, Scray(e), Sooty, Three, Trio

**Terpene** Squalene

**Terrace** Barbette, Beach, Bench, Crescent, Kop, Linch, Lynchet, Offset, Patio, Perron, River, Row house, Shelf, Stoep, Tarras, Undercliff, Veranda(h)

**Terra-cotta** Della-Robbia, Tanagra

**Terrain** Area, Hinterland, Landscape, Scablands, Tract

**Terrapin** Diamondback, Emydes, Emys, Slider, Turtle

**Terrible, Terribly** Appalling, Atrocity, Awful, Deadly, Dire, Fearsome, Fell, Fiendish, Frightful, Ghastly, Heinous, Hellacious, Horrible, Humgruffi(a)n, Ivan, Much, Odious, Very

**Terrible person** Humgruffi(a)n, Ivan, Ogre

**Terrier** Aberdeen, Airedale, Apsos, Australian, Australian silky, Bedlington, Black and tan, Border, Boston, Bull, Cairn, Catalogue, Cesky, Dandie Dinmont, Fox, Glen of Imaal, Griffon, Irish, Jack Russell, Kerry blue, Lakeland, Maltese, Manchester, Norfolk, Norwich, Pinscher, Pit bull, Ratter, Register, Schauzer, Scotch, Scottie, Scottish, Sealyham, Silky, Skye, Soft-coated wheaten, Staffordshire bull, Sydney silky, TA, Tibetan, Welsh, West Highland, West Highland white, Westie, Wheaten, Wire-haired, Yorkie, Yorkshire

**Terrific, Terrified, Terrify(ing)** Affright, Aghast, Agrise, Agrize, Agryze, Appal, Awe, Blood-curdling, Enorm, Fear, Fine, Fley, Gast, Helluva, Huge, Mega, Nightmarish, Overawe, → **PETRIFY**, Scare, Superb, Thumping, Unman, Yippee

**Territory, Territorial(ist)** Abthane, Ap(p)anage, Area, Colony, Coral Sea Islands, Doab, Domain, Dominion, Duchy, Emirate, Enclave, Exclave, Goa, Golan Heights, Indian, Irredentist, Kingdom, Latium, Lebensraum, Mandated, Manor, Margravate, No-man's-land, Northern, Northwest, Nunavut, Palatinate, Panhandle, Papua, Patch, Petsamo, Princedom, Principality, Principate, Protectorate, Province, Realm, → **REGION**, Reserve, Rupert's Land, Scheduled, Sphere, Stamping ground, Sultanate, Swazi, Ter(r), Trieste, Trust, Tuath, Union, Yukon

**Terror(s)** Blue funk, Brat, Bugaboo, Bugbear, Eek, → **FEAR**, Fright, Holy, Imp, Night, Panic, Skrik

**Terrorism, Terrorist** Alarmist, Al Fatah, Anarchist, Black Hand, Bogeyman, Bomber, Bully, Cagoulard, Consumer, Death squad, Desperado, Dynamitard, Eta, Grapo, Hijacker, Ku Klux Klan, Mau-mau, Maximalist, Mountain, Nightrider, Nihilist, OAS, Pirate, Player, PLO, Provo, Red Brigade, Robespierre, Ustashi

**Terry** Ellen, Towel

**Terse** Abrupt, Brief, Brusque, Curt, Laconic, Pithy, Precise, Succinct

**Tertiary** Cainozoic, Eocene, Miocene, Neogene, Oligocene, Palaeogene, Pliocene

**Tessellation** Mosaic

**Test(er), Testing, Tests** Achievement, Acid, Alpha, Ames, Amnio(centesis), Analyse, Apgar, Appro, Aptitude, Ashes, Assay, Audition, Barany, Bench, Bender, Benedict, Beta, Bioassay, Biopsy, Blood, Breath, Breathalyser®, Brinell, Burn-in, Candle, Canopy, Check, Chi-square, Cis-trans, Cloze, Conn(er), Coomb's, Crash, Criterion, Crosscheck, Cross-match, Crucial, Crucible, Crunch, Dick, Docimastic, Driving, Drop, Dummy-run, Éprouvette, Esda, Essay, Etudes, Exacting, Examine, Exercise, Experiment, Fehling's, Field, Finals, Flame, Frog, Hagberg, Ink-blot, Intelligence, International, Litmus, Lydian stone, Mann-Whitney, Mantoux, Match, Mazzin, Means, Medical, Mom, MOT, Mug, Neckverse, Needs, Objective, Oral, Ordalian, → **ORDEAL**, Pale, Pap, Papanicolaou, Paraffin, Patch, Paternity, Performance, Personality, PH, Pilot, Ping, Pons asinorum, Pree, Preeve, Preif, Preve, Prieve, Probative, Probe, Projective, Proof, Prove, Proving-ground, PSA, Pyx, Q-sort, Qualification, Quiz, Rally, Reagent, Reliability, Road, Rorschach, SAT, Scalogram, Scan, Schick's, Schilling, Schutz-Charlton, Scientise, Scratch, Screen, Shadow, Shibboleth, Showdown, Shroff, Sign, Signed-ranks, Significance, Sixpence, Skidpan, Skin, Slump, Smear, Smoke, Snellen, Soap, Sound, Sounding, Spinal, Stanford-Binet, Stress, Task, Tempt, Tensile, Thematic apperception, Tongue-twister, Touch, Touchstone, Trial, Trier, Trior, Try, Turing, Ultrasonic, Viva, Wassermann's, Weigh, Wilcoxon, Zack, Zohar

**Testament** Bible, Covenant, Hagographa, Heptateuch, Hexateuch, Hornolog(o)umena, Midrash, New, Old, Pentateuch, Scripture, Septuagint, Tanach, Targum, Will

**Test-drive** Trial run

**Testicle(s)** Ballocks, Balls, Bollix, Bollocks, Bush oyster, Cobblers, Cojones, Cruet, Doucets, Dowsets, Family jewels, Goolie, Gool(e)y, Knackers, Monkey-gland, Monorchid, Nads, Nuts, Orchis, Pills, Prairie oyster, Ridgel, Ridgil, Rig(gald), Rocks, Stone

**Testify(ing), Testimonial, Testimony** Attestation, Character, Chit, Declare, Depone, Deposition, → EVIDENCE, Hard, Rap, Reference, Scroll, Tribute, Viva voce, Vouch, Witness

**Testy, Tetchy** Cross, Examiner, Legal, Narky, Peevish, Ratty

**Tetanus** Lockjaw

**Tête-à-tête** A quattr' occhi, Collogue, Confab, Hobnob, Twosome

**Tether** Cord, Endurance, Hitch, Knot, Lariat, Leash, Noose, Picket, Seal, Stringhalt, → TIE

**Tetrahedrite** Fahlerz, Fahlore

**Tetrarchy** Iturea

**Tetrasyllabic** Paeon

**Tetrode** Resnatron

**Teuton(ic)** Erl-king, German, Goth, Herren, Vandal

**Texas** Lone Star, Ranger

**Text(s), Textbook, Texting** ABC, Alkoran, Apocrypha, Body, Brahmana, Church, Codex, Copy, Corpus, Donat, Ennage, Greeked, Harmony, Letterpress, Libretto, Lines, Mandaean, Mantra(m), Masoretic, Mezuzah, Minitel, Ms, Nynorsk, Octapla, Op-cit, Panegyricon, Philology, Plain, Proof, Purana, Pyramid, Quran, Responsa, Rubric, S(h)astra, Script, Sermon, Shema, SMS, → SUBJECT, Sura, Sutra, Tao Te Ching, Tefillin, Tephillin, Tetrapla, Thesis, Topic, Tripitaka, Tweet, Typography, Upanis(h)ad, Urtext, Variorum, Viewdata, Vulgate, Writing, Zohar

**Textile** Cloth, Fabric, Mercy

**Texture** Complexion, Constitution, Feel, Fiber, Fibre, Grain, Open, Set(t), Wale, Weave, Woof

**Thai(land)** Karen, Lao(s), Mon, Shan, Siam

**Thalamus** Optic

**Thallium** Tl

**Thames** Father, Tamesis

**Than** And

**Thane** Banquo, Ross

**Thank(s), Thankful, Thanksgiving** Appreciate, Collins, Deo gratias, Gloria, Grace, Gramercy, Grateful, Gratitude, Kaddish, Mercy, Roofer

**Thankless** Ingrate, Vain

**That (is), That one** As, By, Cestui, Das heisst, Dh, Exists, How, Id est, Ie, Ille, Namely, Que, Sc, Such, Thence, Thon(der), What, Which, Yon, Yonder, Yt

**Thatch(er), Thatching** At(t)ap, Daych, Hair, Heard, Hear(i)e, Hele, Hell, Lath, Mane, PM, Reed, Straw, Sway, Thack, Theek, Wig, Ye(a)lm

**Thaw** Debacle, Defreeze, Defrost, Detente, Freeze, Fresh, → MELT, Melt-water, Relax, Silver

▷ **Thaw** *may indicate* 'ice' to be removed from a word

**The** Der, Die, El, Il, La, Le, Los, T', That, Ye, Ze

**Theatre(s), Theatrical(ity)** Abbey, Absurd, Adelphi, Aldwych, Arena, Auditorium, Balcony, Broadway, Camp, Cinema, Circle, Coliseum, Criterion, Crucible, Drama, Drury Lane, Epic, Event, Everyman, Field, Folies Bergere, Fourth-wall, Fringe, Gaff, Gaiety, Globe, Grand Guignol, Grandiose, Great White Way, Hall, Haymarket, Hippodrome, Histrionic, House, Kabuki, La Scala, Legitimate, Little, Living, Lyceum, Melodramatic, Mermaid, Moulin Rouge, Musical, Music-hall, National, News, Nickelodeon, Noh, Novello, Odeon, Odeum, Off-Broadway, Off-off-Broadway, Old Vic, Operating, OUDS, Palladium, Panache, Pennygaff, Pit, Playhouse, Political, Rep(ertory), Royal Court,

Sadler's Wells, Shaftesbury, Sheldonian, Shop, Stage, Stalls, Stoll, Straw-hat, Street, Studio, Summer stock, Tivoli, Total, Touring, Vic, Windmill, Winter Garden(s), Wyndham's, Zarzuela

**Theatregoer** Circle, Gallery, Gods, Pit, Pittite, Stalls

**Theft, Thieving** Appropriation, Bluesnarfing, Burglary, Haul, Heist, Identity, Kinchinlay, Larceny, Maino(u)r, Manner, Petty larceny, Pilfery, Pillage, Piracy, Plagiarism, Plunder, Pugging, Ram-raid, Rip off, Robbery, Shrinkage, Stealth, Stouth(rief), →**THIEF**, Touch, TWOC, Walk-in

**Their** Her

**Theist** Believer, Unitarian

**Them** 'Em, Hem, Tho

**Theme** Burden, Crab canon, Donnée, Fugue, Idea, Leitmotiv, Lemma, Lemmata, →**MELODY**, Motif, Mythos, Mythus, Peg, Question, →**SUBJECT**, Subtext, Text, Topic, Topos

**Then(ce)** Already, Away, Next, Since, Sine, So, Syne, Thereupon, Tho

▷ **The northern** *may indicate* t'

**Theodolite** Diopter, Dioptre, Groma, Tacheometer, Tachymeter, Transit

**Theologian, Theologist, Theology** Abelard, Ambrose, Aquinas, Arminius, Barth, Baur, Calvin, Christology, Colet, DD, Divine, Eckhart, Erastus, Eschatology, Eusebius, Exegetics, Faustus, Fideism, Genevan, Harnack, Hase, Infralapsarian, Irenics, Isidore, Jansen, Kierkegaard, Knox, Laelius, Liberation, Luther, Moral, Mullah, Natural, Newman, Niebuhr, Origen, Paley, Pastoral, Patristics, Pectoral, Pelagius, Peritus, Pusey, Rabbi, Religious, Sacramentarian, Schoolman, Schwenkfeld, Scotus, Socinus, Softa, STP, Supralapsarian, Swedenborg, Tertullian, Thomas à Kempis, Tirso de Molina, Ulema, Universalist

**Theory, Theorem, Theoretical, Theorist** Abstract, Academic, Atomic, Attachment, Attribution, Auteur, Automata, Band, Bayes(ian), Bernouilli's, Big bang, Binomial, Bohr, Boo-hurrah, Boolean, Calorific, Catastrophe, Chaos, Communications, Complexity, Connectionism, Conspiracy, Corpuscular, Cosmogony, Creationism, Darwinian, Decision, Deduction, Dependency, Dictum, Doctrinaire, Domino, Double aspect, Dow, Einstein, Emboîtement, Empiricism, Epigenesist, Euhemerism, Exponential, Fermat's (last), Fortuitism, Gaia, Galois, Game, Gauge, Germ, Gödel's, Grand Unified, Grotian, Group, Guess, Holism, Hormic, Hypothesis, Ideal, Identity, Ideology, Information, Ism(y), James-Lange, Jordan curve, Kinetic, Kock's, Laingian, Lamarckism, Lemma, Lunar, MAD, Metaphysical, Milankovitch, Model, Monism, Mythical, Nebular, Neo-Lamarckism, Neovitalism, Nernst heat, Notion, Number, Object relations, On paper, Pancosmism, Pantologism, Perturbation, Petrinism, Pluralism, Positivism, Poynting, Probability, Proof, Pure, Pythagoras, Quantity, Quantum, Quantum field, Queueing, Random walk, Rational choice, Reception, Relativism, Relativity, Satisfaction, Set, Solipsism, Speculative, Steady state, String, Superdense, Superstring, Supersymmetry, Supposition, System, Tachyon, TOE, Traducianism, Trickle-down, Twistor, Tychism, Unified Field, Utilitarianism, Voluntarism, Vortex, Vulcanist, Wages fund, Wasm, Wave, Wholism, Wolfian

**Therapy, Therapeutic, Therapist** Analyst, Family, Fever, Insight, Non directive, Past life, Remedial, →**TREATMENT**

---

## THERAPIES

| 3 letters: | | TENS | Group |
|---|---|---|---|
| Art | Sex | X-ray | Light |
| CST | | Zone | Music |
| ECT | 4 letters: | | Narco |
| HRT | Deep | | Natal |
| MLD | Gene | 5 letters: | Radio |
| ORT | Germ | Bowen | Reiki |
| | SHEN | Drama | |

Serum
Shock
Sound
Touch

**6 letters:**
Colour
Gerson
Larval
Oxygen
Primal
Radium
Retail
Scream
Speech

**7 letters:**
Crystal
Gestalt
Natural
Pattern
Rainbow
Rolfing
Shiatsu
Shiatzu

**8 letters:**
Aura-Soma
Aversion
Cellular
Curative

Faradism
Gemstone
Germ-line
Hypnosis
Live cell
Magnetic
Movement
Physical
Polarity
Pressure
Reichian
Rogerian
Sanatory
Sitz-bath

**9 letters:**
Auricular
Behaviour
Chelation
Cognitive
Dianetics
Flotation
Implosive
Radiation
Root-canal
Theriacal
Water cure

**10 letters:**
Hellerwork
Logopedics

Looyenwork
Osteopathy
Regression
Relaxation
Supportive

**11 letters:**
Acupressure
Acupuncture
Combination
Gate control
Logopaedics
Psychodrama
Reflexology
Scientology®

**12 letters:**
Chemotherapy
Craniosacral
Curietherapy
Electroshock
Heliotherapy
Narcotherapy
Occupational
Phototherapy
Primal scream

**13 letters:**
Arsenotherapy
Brachytherapy
Client-centred

Electric shock
Immunotherapy
Speleotherapy
Thermotherapy

**14 letters:**
Crystal healing
Electrotherapy

**15 letters:**
Minimal invasive
Oral rehydration
Psychosynthesis
Röntgenotherapy
Thalassotherapy

**16 letters:**
Chavuttithirumal

**17 letters:**
Electroconvulsive

**20 letters:**
Cognitive-
  behavioural
Metamorphic
  technique

**There(after), Thereby, Thereupon** Attending, Ecco, Holla, Ipso facto, Present, Thither, Thon, Upon, With that, Y, Yonder
**Therefore** Argal, Ergo, Forthy, Hence, So, Thus, Why
**Thermodynamic** Enthalpy, Entropy
**Thermometer** Aethrioscope, Centesimal, Clinical, Cryometer, Gas, Glass, Katathermometer, Maximum and minimum, Psychrometer, Pyrometer, Resistance, Thermograph, Water, Wet and dry bulb, Wet bulb
**Thermoplastic** Cel(luloid), Resin
**Thermos** Flask
**Thesaurus** Dictionary, Lexicon, Roget, Treasury, Word-finder
**These** Thir
**Theseus** Champion
**Thesis** Argument, Dissertation, Doctorial, Theme
**Thespian** →ACTOR, Ham, Olivier, Performer, Theatrical
**Thessalonian** Lapith
**They** A
**Thick(en), Thickening, Thickener, Thickness, Thickset** Abundant, Agar-agar, Algin, Brainless, Burly, Bushy, Callosity, Callus, Clavate, Cloddy, Cruddle, Curdle, Dense, Dextrin(e), Dumb, Dumose, Engross, Fat, Grist, Grouty, Grume, Guar, Gum, Hyperostosis, In cahoots, Incrassate, Inspissate, Kuzu, Liaison, Lush, Luxuriant, Nirlie, Nuggety, Pally, Panada, Ply, Reduce, Roux, Sclerosis, →SOLID, Soupy, Spissitude, Squat, Stocky, Stumpy, →STUPID, Thieves, This, Thixotropic, Turbid, Viscous, Waulk, Wooden, Xantham

**Thick-coated** Atheromatous

**Thicket** Bosk, Brake, Brush, Cane-brake, Chamisal, Chap(paral), Coppice, Copse, Covert, Dead-finish, Fernshaw, Greve, Grove, Macchia, Maquis, Queach, Reedrand, Reedrond, Salicetum, Shola

**Thick-lipped** Labrose

**Thick-skinned** Armadillo, Call(o)us, Pachyderm, Tough

**Thief, Thieves, Thievish** Abactor, Area sneak, Autolycus, Blood, Bulker, Chummy, Coon, Corsair, Cracksman, Cutpurse, Dip, Dismas, Dysmas, Filcher, Flood, Footpad, Forty, Freebooter, Furacious, Ganef, Gestas, Gully-raker, Heist, Hotter, Huaquero, Ice-man, Jackdaw, Joyrider, Kiddy, Kondo, Larcener, Lifter, Light-fingered, Limmer, Looter, Mag, Magpie, Montith, Nip(per), Nuthook, Pad, Peculator, Pickpocket, Pilferer, Pirate, Plagiarist, Poacher, Poddy-dodger, Prig, Raffles, River-rat, → **ROBBER**, Rustler, Safeblower, Safebreaker, Safecracker, St Nicholas's clerks, Scrump, Shark, Shop-lifter, Sneak, Snowdropper, Sticky fingers, Taffy, Taker, Tarry-fingered, Tea-leaf, Thick, Twoccer

**Thigh** Femoral, Gaskin, Ham, Haunch, Hock, Meros

**Thin(ner), Thinness** Acetone, Atomy, Attenuate, Bald, Beanpole, Bony, Cadaverous, Cornstalk, Cull, Diluent, Dilute, Ectomorph, Emaciated, Enseam, Filmy, Fine, Fine-drawn, Flimsy, Gaunt, Hair('s)-breadth, Hairline, Inseem, Lanky, Lathy, Lean, Matchstick, Mawger, Narrow, Puny, Rackabones, Rangy, Rare, Rarefied, Reedy, Scant, Scraggy, Scrannel, Scrawny, Sheer, Sieve, Skeletal, Skelf, Skimpy, Skinking, Slender, Slight, Slim, Slimline, Slink, → **SPARE**, Sparse, Spindly, Stilty, Stringy, Subtle, Svelte, Taper, Tenuous, Threadbare, Turpentine, Turps, Wafer, Washy, Waste, Watch, Water(y), → **WEAK**, Wear, Weedy, Whirtle, Wiry, Wispy, Wortle, Wraith

**Thing(s)** Alia, Article, Chattel, Chose, Cratur, Craze, Doodah, Doofer, Entia, Fetish, First, Fixation, It, Item, Jingbang, Job, Last, Material, Matter, Near, Notanda, Noumenon, → **OBJECT**, Obsession, Paraphernalia, Phobia, Res, Tool, Vision, Whatnot

**Thingumabob, Thingummy** Dingbat, Dinges, Dingus, Doobrey, Doobrie, Doodad, Doodah, Doofer, Doohickey, Gubbins, Hootenanny, Hoot(a)nanny, Jigamaree, Oojah, Oojamaflip, Whatsit, Yoke

**Think(er), Thinking** Appraise, Associate, Audile, Believe, Brain, Brainstorm, Brood, Casuistry, Chew over, Cogitate, Cognition, Conjecture, Consider, Contemplant, → **CONTEMPLATE**, Deem, Deliberate, Descartes, Devise, Dianoetic, Divergent, Esteem, Fancy, Fear, Feel, Fogramite, Forward, Ghesse, Gnostic, Guess, Hegel, Hold, → **IMAGINE**, Introspection, Judge, Lateral, Meditate, Mentation, Mindset, Mull, Muse, Opine, Pensive, Philosopher, Phrontistery, Ponder, Pore, Presume, Ratiocinate, Rational(e), Reckon, Reflect, Reminisce, Ruminate, Speculate, Synectics, Trow, Vertical, Ween, Wishful

**Thin-skinned** Sensitive

**Third, Third rate** Bronze, C, Eroica, Gamma, Gooseberry, Interval, Major, Mediant, Minor, Picardy, Quartan, Tertiary, Tertius, Tierce, Trisect

**Third man** Abel, Lime

**Thirst(y)** Adry, → **CRAVE**, Dives, Drought, Drouth, Dry, Hydropic, Nadors, Pant, Polydipsia, Thrist

**Thirteen** Baker's dozen, Devil's dozen, Long dozen, Riddle, Triskaidekaphobia, Unlucky

**Thirty** Lambda

**Thirty-nine books** All-OT, OT

**This** Hic, Hoc, The, Thick, Thilk, Thir

**Thistle** Canada, Carduus, Carline, Cnicus, Creeping, Dayshell, Echinops, Milk, Musk, Rauriki, Russian, Safflower, Scotch, Sow, Spear, Star, Thrissel, Thristle

**This year** Ha

**Thomas** Aquinas, Arnold, Christadelphian, De Quincey, Didymus, Doubting, Dylan, Erastus, Hardy, Loco, Parr, Rhymer, Tompion, True, Turbulent

**Thomas Aquinas** Angelic Doctor

**Thong** Babiche, Jandal®, Lash, Latchet, Leather, Lore, Riem, Riempie, Shoe-latchet, → **STRAP**, Strop, Taws(e), Whang, Whip

**Thor** Thunderer

**Thorax** Chest, Peraeon, Pereion, Scutellum, Throat

**Thorium** Th

**Thorn(y)** Acantha, Aculeus, Bael, Bel, Bhel, Bramble, Briar, Coyotillo, Doom, Edh, Eth, Irritation, Jerusalem, Jew's, Mahonia, Mayflower, Nabk, Nar(r)as, Nebbuk, Nebe(c)k, →NEEDLE, Paloverde, Pricker, Prickle, Slae, Spine, Spinescent, Spinulate, Trial, Wagn'bietjie, Y, Ye, Zare(e)ba, Zariba, Zeriba

**Thorn-apple** Jimpson-weed

**Thornless** Inerm

**Thorough(ly), Thoroughgoing** À fond, Complete, Deep, Downright, Even-down, Firm, Fully, Good, In depth, Ingrained, Inly, Intensive, Not half, Out, Out and out, Painstaking, Pakka, Pucka, Pukka, Radical, Rigorous, Ripe, Root and branch, Searching, Sound, Strict, Total, Tout à fait, Up

**Thoroughbred** Arab, Bloodstock, Full-blooded, Pedigree, Post-vintage, Pursang

**Thoroughfare** Avenue, Broadway, Causeway, Freeway, Highway, Parkway, →ROAD, Street

**Those** Thae, Thaim, Them, Tho, Yon

**Thou** M, Mil

**Though** Albe, Albeit, All-be, Ever, Tho, Whenas

**Thought(s), Thoughtful(ness)** Avisandum, Broody, Censed, Cerebration, Charitable, Cogitation, Concept, Conscience, Considerate, Contemplation, Dianoetic, Felt, Idea, Imagination, Indrawn, Innate, Kind, Maieutic, Mind, Musing, Notion, Opinion, Pansy, Pensée, Pensive, Philosophy, Reason, Reflection, Rumination, Second, Studious

**Thoughtless** Blindfold, Careless, Goop, Heedless, Improvident, Incogitant, Inconsiderate, Pillock, →RASH, Reckless, Reflexive, Remiss, Scatter-brained, Stupid, Unintentional, Unkind, Vacant, Vain

**Thousand(s)** Chiliad, G, Gorilla, Grand, K, Lac, Lakh, M, Millenary, Millennium, Myriad, Octillion, Plum, Sextillion, Toman

**Thracian** Spartacus

**Thrall** Captive, Esne, Serf, Slave

**Thrash(ing)** →BEAT, Belabour, Belt, Bepelt, Binge, Bless, Cane, Dress, Drub, Flail, Flog, Jole, Joll, Joule, Jowl, Lace, Laidie, Laidy, Lambast, Larrup, Lather, Leather, Lick, Marmelise, Onceover, Paste, Ploat, Quilt, Rout, Slog, Smoke, Strap-oil, Swaddle, Swat, Tank, Targe, Thraiping, Towel, Trim, Trounce, Wallop, Whale, Whap, Work over, Writhe

**Thread(ed), Threadlike** Acme screw, Addenda, Ariadne, Bar, Bottom, Bride, Buttress, Chalaza, Chromatid, Chromatin, Chromosome, Clew, Clue, Cop(pin), Cord, Coventry blue, Eel-worm, End, Female, Fibre, Filament, File, Filiform, Filose, Filoselle, Float, Floss, Flourishing, Gist, Gold, Gossamer, Hair, Heddle, Ixtle, Lace, Lap, Lingel, Lingle, Link, Lisle, Lurex®, Male, Meander, Microfibre, Mycellum, Needle, Nematode, Nematoid, Organzine, Pack, Pearlin(g), Pick, Plasmodesm, Ravel, Reeve, Roon, Rope-yarn, Rove, Sacred, Screw, Sellers screw, Seton, Shoot, Silver, Single, Spider line, Spireme, Sporangiophore, Stamen, →STRAND, Stroma, Suture, Tassel, Tendril, Tenor, Theme, Thrid, Thrum, Trace, Tram, Trundle, Tussore, Twine, Twist, Two-start, Warp, Watap, Wax(ed) end, Weft, Whitworth, Whitworth screw, Wick, →WIND, Wisp, Worm, Zari

**Threadbare** Frayed, Hackneyed, Motheaten, Napless, Shabby, Worn

**Threadworm** Nemathelminth, Strongyl, Vinegar-eel

**Threat(en), Threatened, Threatening** Baleful, Black(en), Blackmail, Bluster, Brew, Brutum fulmen, Bully, Coerce, Comminate, Denounce, Discovered check, Duress, Extort, Face, Fatwa, Fraught, Greenmail, Greymail, Hazard, Impend, Imperil, Intimidate, Jeopardise, Loom, Lower, →MENACE, Minacious, Minatory, Mint, Nuclear, Omen, Ominous, Or else, Overcast, Overhang, Parlous, Peril, Portent, Ramp, Sabre-rattling, Shore, Strongarm, Ugly, Veiled, Warning, Yellow peril

**Three, Threefold, Three-wheeler, Thrice** Cheers, Graces, Har, Harpies, Jafenhar, Leash, Muses, Musketeers, Pairial, Pair-royal, Parial, Prial, Ter, Tercet, Tern(ate),

Terzetta, Thridi, Tid, T.i.d, Tierce, Tray, Trey, Triad, Trial, Tricar, Triennial, Trifid, Trigon, Trilogy, Trinal, Trine, Trinity, Trio, Triple, Triptote, Troika

**Three-D(imensional)** Cinerama, Lenticular, Spatial, Stereopsis, Vectograph

**Three-day** Triduan, Triduum

**Threehalfpence** Dandiprat, Dandyprat

**Three-handed** Cutthroat

**Three-headed** Cerberus, Geryon

**Three hundred** B, Carpet

**Three-legged** IOM, Triskele, Triskelion

**Threepence, Threepenny bit** Tickey, Tray, Trey, Treybit

**Three-quarter** Wing

**Three-year old** Staggard

**Threnody** Dirge, Epicede, →LAMENT

**Thresh(er)** Beat, Flail, Sea-ape, Separate

**Threshold** Absolute, Brink, Cill, Difference, Doorstep, Limen, Liminal, Nuclear, Sill, Tax, Verge

▶ **Thrice** see THREE

**Thrift(y)** Economy, Frugal, Husbandry, Oeconomy, Scrimping, Sea-grass, Sea-pink, Virtue, Wary

**Thrill(er), Thrilling** Atingle, Buzz, Charge, Delight, Dindle, Dinnle, Dirl, Dread, Dynamite, Electric, Emotive, →ENCHANT, Enliven, Excite, Film noir, Frisson, Gas, Jag, Kick, Page-turner, Perceant, Plangent, Pulsate, Pulse, Quiver, Sensation, Thirl, Tinglish, Titillate, Tremor, Vibrant, Whodunit, Wow(-factor), Zing

**Thrive** Batten, Blossom, Boom, Do, Fl, →FLOURISH, Flower, Grow, Mushroom, →PROSPER, Succeed, Thee

**Throat(y)** Craw, Crop, Deep, Dewlap, Fauces, Gorge, Gular, Gullet, Guttural, Hot coppers, Jugular, Laryngeal, Maw, Oropharynx, Pereion, Pharynx, Prunella, Quailpipe, Red lane, Roopit, Roopy, Strep, Swallet, Thrapple, Thropple, Throttle, Weasand, Wesand, Whistle, Windpipe

**Throb(bing)** Beat, Palpitate, Pant, Pit-a-pat, Pound, Pulsate, Quop, Stang, Tingle, Vibrato

▷ **Throbbing** *may indicate* an anagram

**Throe(s)** Agony, Pang, Paroxysm

**Thrombosis, Thrombose** Clot, Deep-vein

**Throne** Bed-of-justice, Cathedra, Episcopal, Gadi, →LAVATORY, Mercy-seat, Peacock, Rule, Seat, See, Siege, Stone of Scone, Stool, Tribune

**Throng(ing)** Crowd, Flock, Horde, Host, Multitude, Press, Resort, Swarm

**Throttle** →CHOKE, Gar(r)otte, Gun, Mug, Regulator, Scrag, Silence, Stifle, Strangle, Strangulate, Thrapple, We(a)sand

**Through, Throughout** Along, Ana, By, Dia-, During, Everywhere, Over, Passim, Per, Pr, Sempre, Sic passim, To, Trans, Up and down, Via, Yont

**Throw (up), Thrower, Throw-out** Bin, Cast-off, Chunder, Discobolus, Egesta, Eject, Emesis, Estrapade, Floor, Flummox, Flying mare, Go, Jettison, Mangonel, Pash, Puke, Reject, Slam-drunk, Spatter, Spew, Squirt, Squit, →TOSS, Ventriloquism

▶ **Throw(n)** see TOSS(ING)

**Throwback** Atavism, Echo

**Thrush** Antbird, Aphtha, Bird, Chat, Fieldfare, Hermit, Homescreetch, Mavis, Missel, Mistle, Mocking-bird, Olive-back, Pitta, Prunella, Redwing, Ring-ousel, Sprue, Turdine, Veery

**Thrust(er)** Abdominal, Aventre, Bear, Boost, Botte, Burn, Burpee, Detrude, Dig, Drive, Elbow, Engine, Exert, Extrude, Flanconade, Foin, →FORCE, Gist, Hay, Hustle, Imbroc(c)ata, Impulse, Jet, Job, Lift-off, Lunge, Montant(o), Muscle, Obtrude, Oust, Pass, Passado, Peg, Penetrate, Perk, Pitchfork, Poach, Poke, Potch(e), Pote, Probe, Prog, Propel, Pun, Punto, →PUSH, Put, Ram, Remise, Repost, Run, Shoulder, Shove,

Single-stock, Sock, Sorn, Squat, Stap, Stick, Stoccado, Stoccata, Stock, Stuck, Thrutch, Tilt, Tuck, Venue

**Thud** Bounce, Drum, Dump, Flump, Phut, Plod, Thump, Thunk, Whump

**Thug(s)** Brute, Gangster, Goon(da), Gorilla, Gurrier, Heavy, Hood(lum), Keelie, Loord, Ninja, Ockers, Phansigar, Plug-ugly, Rough(neck), SS, Strangler, Ted, Tityre-tu, Tsotsi, Yahoo

**Thule** Ultima

**Thulium** Tm

**Thumb** Bally, Gouge, Green, Hitch, Leaf, Midget, Ovolo, Pollex, Scan, Sore, Tom

**Thump(ing)** Blow, Bonk, Clobber, Cob, Crump, Da(u)d, Dawd, Ding, Dod, Drub, Dub, Enormous, Hammer, Knevell, Knock, Lamp, Nevel, Oner, Paik, Percuss, → **POUND**, Pummel, Ribroast, Slam, Slosh, Souse, Swat, Swingeing, Thud, Trounce, Tund, Whud, Whump

**Thunder(ing), Thunderstorm** Astrophobia, Bolt, Boom, Clap, Coup de foudre, Donnerwetter, Foudroyant, Foulder, Fulminate, Intonate, Lei-king, Microburst, Pil(l)an, Raiden, → **ROAR**, Rumble, Summanus, Tempest, Thor, Tonant

**Thunderbolt** Ward

**Thurible** Incense burner

**Thursday** Chare, Holy, Maundy, Sheer, Shere

**Thus** Accordingly, Ergo, Hence, Sic, So, Therefore

**Thwart** Baffle, Balk, → **CROSS**, Dash, Dish, Foil, Forestall, Frustrate, Hamstring, Hogtie, Obstruct, Outwit, Pip, Prevent, Scotch, Scupper, Snooker, Spike, Spite, Stonker, Stymie, Transverse

**Thy** Yourn

**Thyme** Basil, Lemon, Water

**Thyroid** Goitre, Myxodema

**Tiara** Cidaris, Crownet, Diadem, Triple crown

**Tiberius** Gracchus

**Tibetan** Ladakhi, Lamaist, Naga, Sherpa, Sitsang

**Tic** Spasm, Synkinesis, Twitch, Vocal

**Tick, Ticking-off, Tick off** Acarida, Acarus, Arachnid, Beat, Bloodsucker, Check, → **CHIDE**, Click, Cr, → **CREDIT**, Deer, HP, Idle, Instant, Jar, Ked, Mattress, Mile, Mo, Moment, Ricinulei, Second, Seed, Sheep, Soft, Strap, Wigging, Worm

**Ticker** Clock, Heart, Metronome, Watch

**Ticket(s)** Billet, Bone, Brief, Carnet, Commutation, Complimentary, Coupon, Day, Docket, Dream, E(lectronic), Excursion, Hot, Kangaroo, Label, Meal, One-day, One-way, Open-jaw, Parking, Pass, Pass-out, Pasteboard, Pawn, Platform, Raffle, Raincheck, Return, Round-trip, Rover, Saver, Scratchcard, Season, Single, Soup, Split, Straight, Stub, Supersaver, → **TAG**, Tempest, Tessera(l), Through, Tix, Transfer, Tyburn, Unity, Voucher, Walking, Zone

**Ticket-seller** Scalper

**Tickle, Ticklish** Amuse, Delicate, Divert, Excite, Fondle, Gratify, Gump, → **ITCH**, Kittle, Queasy, Thrill, Titillate

**Tiddler** Brit, Tom

**Tiddleywink** Counter

**Tide, Tidal** Current, Drift, Eagre, Easter, Eger, Estuary, Flood, High, High water, Lee, Low, Marigram, Neap, Red, Rising, River, Roost, Sea, Seiche, Slack water, Spring, Surge, Trend, Wave

**Tide-gate** Aboideau, Aboiteau, Weir

**Tidings** Gospel, → **NEWS**, Rumour, Word

**Tidy** Big, Comb, Considerable, Curry, Do, Fair, Fettle, Groom, Kempt, Large, Neat, Neaten, → **ORDER**, Pachyderm, Predy, Preen, Primp, Red(d), Slick, Snug, Sort, Spruce, Trim, Valet

**Tie, Tied, Tying** Ascot, Attach, Barcelona, Berth, Bind, Black, Bolo, → **BOND**, Bootlace, Bow, Bowyang, Cable, Chain, Clip-on, Cope, Cord, Cravat, Cup, Dead-heat, Drag, Draw,

Fasten, Fetter, Four-in-hand, Frap, Halter, Halve, Handicap, Harness, Hitch, Holdfast, Kipper, →**KNOT**, Lace, Lash, Level, Ligament, Ligate, Ligature, Link, Marry, Match, Moor, Neck and neck, Oblige, Obstriction, Old School, Oop, Oup, Overlay, Raffia, Relation, Restrain, Rod, Rope, Scarf, School, Score draw, Scrunchie, Semifinal, Shackle, Sheave, Shoelace, Shoestring, Sleeper, Slur, Solitaire, Soubise, Splice, Stake, Standoff, Strap, String, Tawdry-lace, Tether, Together, Trice, Truss, Unite, White, Windsor

**Tie-breaker** Decider

**Tier** Apron, Bank, Gradin(e), Knotter, Layer, Range, Rank, Row, Stage, Storey

**Tierce** Leash, Tc

**Tiff** Bicker, Contretemps, Difference, Dispute, Exchange, Feed, Feud, Huff, Miff, Skirmish, Spat, Squabble

**Tiffany** Gauze

**Tiger, Tigress** Ambush, Bengal, →**CAT**, Clemenceau, Demoiselle, Lily, Machairodont, Machairodus, Man-eater, Margay, Paper, Sabre-tooth, She-cat, Shere Khan, Smilodon, Stripes, Tamil, Tasmanian, Woods

**Tight(en), Tightness, Tights** Boozy, Bosky, Brace, Canny, Cinch, Close(-hauled), Constriction, Cote-hardie, →**DRUNK**, Fishnet, Fleshings, High, Hose, Jam, Leggings, Leotards, Lit, Loaded, Maillot, Mean(-spirited), Merry, Niggardly, Oiled, Pang, Pantihose, Phimosis, Pickled, Pinch(penny), Plastered, Prompt, Proof, Rigour, Snug, Squiffy, Stenosis, →**STINGY**, Stinko, Strict, Stringent, Swift, Swig, Taut, Tense, Tipsy, Trig, Woozy

**Tight-lipped** Shtum, Taciturn

**Tightrope(-walker)** Aerialist, Blondin, Equilibrist, Funambulist, High wire, Petauriste

**Tightwad** Cheapskate, →**MISER**, Scrooge

**Tile(s), Tiled** Antefix, Arris, Azulejo, Carpet, Chapeau, Dalle, Derby, Dutch, Encaustic, Field, →**HAT**, Hung, Imbrex, Imbricate, Lid, Lino, Mahjong(g), Ostracon, Ostrakon, Peever, Quarrel, Quarry, Rag(g), Ridge, Rooftop, Sclate, Shingle, Slat, →**SLATE**, Tegular, Tessella, Tessera, Titfer, Topper, Wall, Wally

**Till** Cashbox, Checkout, Coffer, Ear, Eulenspiegel, Farm, Hasta, Hoe, Husband, Lob, Peter, →**PLOUGH**, Rotavate, Set, Unto, Up to

**Tiller** Coxswain, Gardener, Helm, Ploughman, Rotavator, Wheel

**Tilt(ed)** Awning, Bank, Camber, Cant, Careen, Cock, Dip, Heel, Hut, Joust, Just, →**LIST**, Quintain, Rock, Tip, Trip, Unbalance, Version

**Timber** Apron, Ashlaring, Balk, Batten, Beam, Bolster, Bond, Bowsprit, Bridging, Cant-rail, Carapa, Cedarwood, Chess, Clapboard, Compass, Coulisse, Cross-tree, Cruck, Dogshores, Driftwood, Druxy, Dwang, Elmwood, Flitch, Float, Four-by-two, Futchel, Futtock, Greenheart, Groundsell, Hardwood, Harewood, Intertie, Iroko, Ironwood, Joist, Keel, Knee, Knighthead, Lauan, Ligger, Lignum, Lintel, Log, Loggerhead, Lumber, Nogging, Nothofagus, Plank-sheer, Purlin(e), Putlock, Putlog, Pyengadu, Radiata, Ramin, Rib, Ridgepole, Roseweed, Roundwood, Rung, Sandalwood, Sapele, Sapodilla, Satinwood, Scantling, Shook, Shorts, Sissoo, Skeg, Sneezewood, Softwood, Souari, Stemson, Stere, Sternpost, Sternson, Straddle, Stud, Stull, Stumpage, Summer, Swing-stock, Tilting fillet, Towing-bitts, Transom, Trestletree, Two-by-four, Wale, Wall plate, Weatherboard, Whitewood, →**WOOD**, Yang

**Timbre** Clang, Klang(farbe), Register, →**TENOR**, Tone, Tone colour

**Time(s), Timer, Timing** Access, African, Agoge, Apparent, Assymetric, Astronomical, Atlantic, Atomic, Autumn, Awhile, Bird, BST, By, Central, Chronaxy, Chronic, Chronometer, Chronon, Clock, Closing, Common, Compound, Connect, Core, Counter, Cryptozoic, Date, Day, Dead, Decade, Dimension, Double, Duple, Duration, Early, Eastern, Eastern Standard, Egg-glass, Enemy, Eon, Ephemeris, Epoch, Epocha, Epoque, Equinox, Era, EST, European, Eve(ning), Extra, Father, Fleximetime, Fold, Forelock, Four-four, Fourth dimension, Free, Full, Geological, Gest, Glide, Half, Healer, High, Horologe, Hour, Hourglass, Hr, Idle, Imprisonment, Injury, Innings, Instant, Interim, Interlude, Jiff, Juncture, Kalpa, Killing, Latent, Lay-day, Lead, Lean, Leisure, Length, Life, Lighting-up, Lilac, Local, Lowsing, Lustra, Man-day, Man-hour, Mean,

Menopause, Metronome, Mountain standard, Multiple, Needle, Nonce, Nones, Normal, Occasion, Oft, →ON TIME, Opening, Pacific, Paralysis, Part, Peak, Period, Phanerozoic, Pinger, Porridge, Post, Precambrian, Prelapsarian, Prime, Proper, Quadruple, Quality, Question, Quick, Reaction, Real, Reaper, Recovery, Released, Response, Responsum, Reverberation, Rhythm, Run(ning), Sandglass, Sands, Schedule, Seal, →SEASON, Seel, Seil, Semeion, Sentence, Serial, Session, Shelf-life, Sidereal, Sight, Simple, Sith(e), Slot, Slow, Solar, Solstice, Space, Spacious, Span, Spare, Spell, Spin, Split, Spring, Squeaky-bum, Standard, Stoppage, Stopwatch, Stound, Stownd, Stretch, Summer, Sundial, Sundown, Sync(h), Sythe, T, Tem, Tempo, Tempore, Tense, Thief, Three-four, Thunderer, Tick, Tid, Tide, Trice, Triple, True, Turnaround, Two-four, Universal, Usance, Whet, While, Winter, X, Yonks, Yukon, Zero

**Timebomb** Demographic

**Timekeeper, Timekeeping, Timepiece** Ben, Chronometer, Clock, Clockwork, Hourglass, Ref, Sand-glass, Sundial, Ticker, Tompion, Watch

**Timeless** Eternal, ND, Undying

**Timely** Appropriate, Apropos, Happy, Heaven-sent, Opportune, Pat, Periodical, Prompt, Punctual

**Time-machine** Tardis

**Timescale** Geological

**Time-server** Convict, Fence-sitter, Prisoner, Trimmer, Vicar of Bray

**Timeshare** Box and cox

**Timetable** ABC(ee), Absee, Bradshaw, →CHART, Schedule

**Time-waster** Filibuster

**Timid, Timorous** Afraid, Aspen, Bashful, Blate, Chicken, Cowardly, Eerie, Eery, Faint-hearted, Fearful, Fibreless, Hare, Hen-hearted, Meticulous, Milquetoast, Mouse, Mous(e)y, Pavid, Pigeon-hearted, Pusillanimous, Pussy, Quaking, Schnok, Shrinking, →SHY, Skeary, Sook, Tremulous, Wuss, Yellow

**Timothy** Cat's-tail, Grass, Phleum

**Tin(ned), Tinfoil, Tinny** Argentine, Block, Britannia metal, Can, Cash, Debe, Dixie, Maconochie, Mess, →MONEY, Moola(h), Ochre, Plate, Rhino, Sn, Stannary, Stannic, Stream, Tain, Tole

**Tincture** Arnica, Brown, Bufo, Chroma, Elixir, Fur, Infusion, Laudanum, Metal, Or, Sericon, Sol, Spice, Taint, Tenné, Vert

**Tinder** Amadou, Faggot, Fuel, Funk, Punk, Spark, Spunk, Touchwood

**Tine** Antler, Bay, Cusp, Grain, Prong, Snag, Spire, Surroyal, Tray, Trey

**Tinge(d)** Cast, Dye, Eye, Flavour, Gild, →HUE, Infuscate, Taint, Tincture, Tone, Touch

**Tingle, Tingling** Dinnle, Dirl, Paraesthesia, Pins and needles, Prickle, Thrill, Throb, Tinkle

**Tinker** Bell, Caird, Coster, Didakai, Didakei, Diddicoy, Didicoy, Didikoi, →FIDDLE, Gypsy, Meddle, Mender, Pedlar, Potter, Prig, Putter, Repair, Sly, Smouse, Snout, Tamper, Tramp, Traveller, Tweak

**Tinkle, Tinkling** Pink, Ring, Thin

**Tinsel(ly)** Clinquant, Gaudy, Glitter, O, Spangle, Turkey

**Tint** Colour, Grey, Henna, Hue, Pigment, →STAIN, Tinct, Tinge, Tone, Woad

**Tiny** Atto-, Baby, Chickenfeed, Diddy, Dwarf, Fleabite, Ha'it, Infinitesimal, Itsy-bitsy, Leet(le), Lilliputian, Meagre, Midget, Minikin, Minim, Mite, Negligible, Petite, Pint-sized, Pitiful, Pittance, Small, Smidge(o)n, Smidgin, Stime, Teeny, Tiddl(e)y, Tiddy, Tim, Tine, Tottie, Totty, Toy, Wee(ny)

**Tip (off), Tipping** Advice, Apex, Arrowhead, Ash-heap, Asparagus, Backshish, Baksheesh, Batta, Beer-money, B(u)onamono, Bonsel(l)a, Bonus, Cant, Capsize, Cert, Chape, Counsel, Coup, Cowp, Crown, Cue, Cumshaw, Doff, Douceur, Dump, Extremity, Fee, Felt, Ferrule, Filter, Forecast, Glans, Gratillity, Gratuity, Heel, →HINT, Hunch, Inkle, Iridise, Lagniappe, Largess(e), Lean, List, Mag(g), Mess, Middenstead, Nap, Nib, Noop, Ord, Perk, Perquisite, Point, Pointer, Pour, Pourboire, Previse, Prong, Scrapheap,

Slagheap, Straight, Suggestion, Summit, Tag, Tail, Tilt, Toom, Touch, Tronc, Upend, Upset, Vail, Vales, Warn, Whisper, Wink, Wrinkle

**Tipper** Ale

**Tippet** Cape, Fur, Scarf

**Tipple** Bib, Booze, →DRINK, Paint, Pot, Poteen

**Tipster** Prophet, Tout

**Tipsy** Askew, Bleary, Boozy, Bosky, →DRUNK, Elevated, Merry, Moony, Nappy, Oiled, On, Rocky, Screwed, Slewed, Slued, Squiffy, Stewed, Tight, Wet

▷ **Tipsy** *may indicate* an anagram

**Tiptoe** Digitigrade, Spanish, Walk

**Tiptop** Pinnacle

**Tirade** Diatribe, Invective, Jobation, Laisse, Philippic, Rand, Rant, Rave, Screed, Slang

**Tire(d), Tiredness, Tiring** All-in, Aweary, Beat, Bejade, Bleary-eyed, Blown, Bore, Brain fag, Bushed, Caparison, Cooked, Deadbeat, Dress, Drowsy, →EXHAUST, Fag, Fagged out, Fatigue, Flag, Footsore, Fordid, Fordod, Forjeskit, Frazzle, Gruel, Irk, Jack, Jade, Languor, Lassitude, Limp, ME, Overspent, Pall, Poop, Puggled, →ROBE, Rubber, Sap, Shagged, Sicken, Sleepry, Sleepy, Sloomy, Snoozy, Spent, Swinkt, Tax, Tedious, Trying, Tucker, Wabbit, Wappend, Weary, World-weary, Wrecked

**Tireless** Inexhaustible

**Tiresome** Boring, Exhausting, Humdrum, Pill, Tedious, Trying, Vexing

**Tirl** Rattle, Risp, Strip, Turn

▶ **Tiro** *see* TYRO

**Tissue** Adenoid, Adhesion, Adipose, Aerenchyma, Aponeurosis, Archesporium, Bast, Callus, Carbon, Cartilage, C(o)elom, Cementum, Chalaza, Cheloid, Chlorenchyma, Coenosarc, Collagen, Collenchyma, Commissure, Conducting, Connective, Corpus luteum, Corpus Striatum, Cortex, Dentine, Diploe, Elastic, Elastin, Endarch, Endosperm, Endosteum, Epigenesis, Epimysium, Epineurium, Epithelium, Eschar, Evocator, Fabric, Fascia, Fibroid, Filament, Flesh, Gamgee, Gauze, Gleba, Glia, Granulation, Granuloma, Gum, Handkerchief, Hankie, Heteroplasia, Histogen, Histoid, Hypoderm(is), Infarct, Interlay, Junk, Keloid, Kleenex®, Lamina, Liber, Lies, Ligament, Luteal, Lymphate, Lymphoid, Macroglia, Marrow, Matrix, Mechanical, Medulla, →MEMBRANE, Meristem, Mesenchyme, Mesophyll, Mestom(e), Mole, Muscle, Myelin(e), Myocardium, Neoplasia, Neoplasm, Neuroglia, Nucellus, Olivary, Pack, Palisade, Pannus, Paper, Papilla, Parenchyma, Periblem, Perichylous, Pericycle, Peridesmium, Perimysium, Perinephrium, Perineurium, Perisperm, Phellogen, Phloem, Pith, Placenta, Plerome, Polyarch, Pons, Primordium, Procambium, Prosenchyma, Prothallis, Pterygium, Pulp, Radula, Retina, Sarcenet, Sars(e)net, Scar, Sclerenchyma, Scleroma, Sequestrum, Sinew, Siphonostele, Siphuncle, Soft, Somatopleure, Stereome, Stroma, Submucosa, Suet, Tarsus, Tela, Tendon, Toilet, Tonsil, Trace, Tunica, Vascular, Velum, Web, Wound, Xylem, Zoograft

**Tit, Tit-bit(s)** Analecta, Canapé, Crested, Currie, Curry, Delicacy, Dug, Nag, Nipple, Nun, Pap, Quarry, Sample, Scrap, Snack, Snippet, Teat, Tug, Twitch, Willow, Wren, Zakuska

**Titan(ic), Titaness** Atlas, Colossus, Cronos, Cronus, Drone, Enormous, Giant, Ginormous, Huge, Hyperion, Kronos, Large, Leviathan, Liner, Oceanus, Phoebe, Prometheus, Rhea, Superman, Themis, Vast

**Titanium, Titanite** Rutin, Sagenite, Sphene, Ti

**Tit for tat** Deserts, Revenge, Talion

**Tithe** Disme, Dyzemas, Frankpledge, Teind, Tenth

**Titian** Abram, Auburn

**Titillate(r), Titillating, Titillation** Delight, Excite, Fluffer, Naughty, Suggestive, Tickle

**Titivate** Preen, Primp

**Title** Abbé, →ADDRESS, Ag(h)a, Agname, Antonomasia, Appellative, Bab, Bahadur, Baroness, Baronet, Bart, Bastard, Bhai, Bretwalda, Burra sahib, Calif, Caliph, Caption,

Charta, Chogyal, Claim, Conveyance, Count(ess), Courtesy, Credit, Dan, Datin, Datuk, Dauphin, Dayan, Deeds, Denominative, Devi, Dom, Don, Don(n)a, Dowager, Dub, Duchess, Duke, Earl, Effendi, Eminence, Epithet, Esquire, Excellency, Fra, Frau(lein), Ghazi, Gospodin, Grand Master, Great Mogul, Gyani, Hafiz, Handle, Header, Heading, Headline, Hereditary, Highness, Hojatoleslam, Hon, Honour, Il Duce, Imperator, Interest, Kabaka, Kalif, Kaliph, Kaur, Khan, King, Kumari, Lady, Lala, Lemma, →**LIEN**, Lord, Mal(l)am, Marchesa, Marchese, Marquess, Marquis, Master, Masthead, Maulana, Memsahib, Meneer, Mevrou, Miladi, Milady, Milord, Mirza, Mr(s), Mynheer, Name, Native, Negus, Nemn, Nickname, Nizam, Nomen, Ownership, Pacha, Padishah, Pasha, Peerage, Pir, Polemarch, Prefix, Prince(ss), Queen, →**RANK**, Reb, Reverence, Reverend, →**RIGHT**, Rubric, Running, Sahib, Sama, San, Sardar, Sayid, Senhor(a), Señor(a), Shri, Singh, Sir, Sirdar, Son, Sowbhagyawati, Sri, Stratum, Tannie, Tenno, Titule, Torrens, Tuanku, Tycoon, U, Voivode, Worship

**Title-holder** Cartouche, Champion, Landlord, Noble

**Titmouse** Bird, Hickymal, Mag, Reedling, Tit

**Tito** Gobbi

**Titter** Giggle, Snigger, Tehee

**Tittle** Jot

**Titus** Oates

**Tizz(y)** Flap, Flat spin, Pother, Spin, State, Tanner, Testril, Vld

**TNT** Explosive, Trotyl

**To(wards)** At, Beside, Inby, Intil, Oncoming, Onto, Prone, Shet, Shut, Till, Until

**Toad(y)** Bootlicker, Bufo, Bumsucker, Cane, Clawback, Cocksucker, Crapaud, Crawler, Fawn, Frog, Hanger-on, Horned, Jackal, Jenkins, Knot, Lackey, Lick-platter, Lickspittle, Midwife, Minion, Natterjack, Nototrema, Paddock, Parasite, Pick-thank, Pipa, Placebo, Platanna, Poodle, Pouch, Puddock, Queensland cane, Sook, Spade-foot, Squit, Surinam, Sycophant, Tree, Tuft-hunter, Walking, Warty, Xenopus, Yesman

**Toadstone** Lava

**Toadstool** Amanita, Death-cap, Death-cup, Destroying angel, Fly agaric, →**FUNGUS**, Grisette, Horsehair, Marasmus, Paddock-stool, Parrot, Saffron milk cap, Sickener, Sulphur tuft, Verdigris, Wax cap

**Toast(er)** Bacchus, Bell, Birsle, Brindisi, →**BROWN**, Bruschetta, Bumper, Cheers, Chin-chin, Crostini, Croute, Crouton, Drink-hail, French, Gesundheit, Grace-cup, Grill, Health, Heat, Iechyd da, Immortal memory, Kia-ora, L'chaim, Lechayim, Loyal, Melba, Pledge, Pop up, Propose, Prosit, Round, Salute, Scouther, Scowder, Scowther, Sentiment, Sippet, Skoal, Slainte, Slainte mha(i)th, Soldier, Sunbathe, Wassail, Zwieback

**Toastmaster** MC, Symposiarch

**Tobacco, Tobacco-field** Alfalfa, Bacchi, Baccy, Bird's eye, Broadleaf, Burley, Burn, Canaster, Capa, Caporal, Cavendish, Chew, Dottle, Filler, Honeydew, Indian, Killikinnick, Kinnikinick, Latakia, Mundungus, Nailrod, Navy-cut, Negro-head, Nicotian, Nicotine, Niggerhead, Perique, Pigtail, Pipe, Plug, Quid, Rapper, Régie, Returns, Shag, Sneesh, Snout, Snuff, Straight cut, Stripleaf, Turkish, Twist, Vega, Virginia, Weed, Wrapper

**To be arranged** TBA

**Toboggan** Sled(ge), Sleigh

**To boot** Furthermore

**Toby** Dog, High, Highwayman, Jug, Low

**Tocsin** Alarm, Siren

**Today** Hodiernal, Now, Present

**Toddle(r)** Baim, Gangrel, Mite, Tot, Totter, Trot, Waddle

**Toddy** Arrack, →**DRINK**, Sura, Whisky

**To-do** Sensation, Stir

**Toe(s), Toed** Dactyl, Digit, Fissiped, Hallux, Hammer, Pigeon, Piggy, Pinky, Pointe, Poulaine, Prehallux, Tootsie

**Toff** Gent, Highbrow, Nob, Nut, Snob, Swell

**Toffee** Banket, Butterscotch, Caramel, Cracknel, Gundy, Hard-bake, Hokey-pokey, Humbug, Tom-trot

**Toga** Palla

**Together** Among, At-one, Atone, Attone, Col, En bloc, En masse, Gathered, Hand-in-glove, Hand-in-hand, In concert, Infere, In mass, In step, Job lot, →**JOINT**, Juxtaposed, Pari-passu, Sam, Simultaneous, Tutti, Unison, Wed, Y, Yfere, Ysame

**Toggle** Fastener, Netsuke

**Togs** Clothes, Gear, Rig, Strip

**Toho** Halt

**Toil(s)** Drudge, Fag, Graft, Industry, →**LABOUR**, Mesh, Net, Seine, Sisyphus, Slog, Sweat, Swink, Tela, Tew, Trap, Trauchle, Travail, Tug, Web, →**WORK**, Wrest, Yacker, Yakka, Yakker

**Toilet** Can, Chemical, Coiffure, Garderobe, Gents, Head(s), John, Ladies, Lat(rine), Lavabo, →**LAVATORY**, Loo, Necessary house, Necessary place, Pan, Pot, Powder room, Restroom, Toot, WC

**Token** Abbey-counter, Abbey-piece, Buck, Check, Chip, Counter, Coupon, Disc, Double-axe, Emblem, Favour, Gift, Indication, Mark, →**MEMENTO**, Monument, Nominal, Omen, Portend, Seal, Sign, Signal, Slug, Symbol, Symptom, Tessella, Tessera, Valentine, Voucher, White flag

**Tolerable** Acceptable, Bearable, Fair(ish), Mediocre, Passable, So-so

**Tolerance, Tolerant, Tolerate(d)** Abear, Abide, Accept, Admit, →**ALLOW**, Bear, Broadminded, Brook, Countenance, Endure, Enlightened, Good-natured, Hack, Had, Immunological, Latitude, →**LENIENT**, Liberal, Long-suffering, Lump, Mercy, Permit, Stand (for), Stick, Stomach, Studden, Suffer, Support, Thole, Wear, Zero

**Toll** Chime, Chok(e)y, Customs, Due, Duty, Excise, Jole, Joll, Joule, Jow, Light-dues, Octroi, Pierage, Pike, Pontage, Rates, →**RING**, Scat, Scavage, Streetage, Tariff, Tax, Turnpike

**Toll-breaker** Rebecca

**Tom(my)** Atkins, Bell, Bowling, Bread, Brown, →**CAT**, Chimney sweep, Collins, Edgar, Gib, Grub, Gun, He-cat, Jerry, Jones, Mog(gy), Nosh, Peeping, Private, Pro(stitute), Pte, Puss, Ram-cat, Sawyer, Snout, Soldier, Stout, Thos, Thumb, Tiddler, Tucker

**Tomahawk** Hatchet

**Tomato** Beef(steak), Cherry, Gooseberry, Husk, Love-apple, Plum, Portuguese, Strawberry, Tamarillo, Tree, Wolf's peach

**Tomb(stone)** Burial, Catacomb, Catafalque, Cenotaph, Cist, Coffin, Cromlech, Dargah, Durgah, Grave, Hypogeum, Inurn, Kistvaen, Marmoreal, Mastaba, Mausoleum, Megalithic, Monument, Pyramid, Repository, →**SEPULCHRE**, Sepulture, Serdab, Shrine, Speos, Tell el Amarna, Tholos, Tholus, Through-stane, Through-stone, Treasury, Vault

**Tombola** Draw, Lottery, Raffle

**Tomboy** Gamine, Gilpey, Gilpy, Hoyden, Ladette, Ramp, Romp

**Tome** →**BOOK**, Omnibus, Volume

**Tomfoolery** Caper, Fandangle, Shenanigan

**Tomorrow** Future, Manana, Morrow, The morn

**Tompion** Watchman

**Tom Snout** Tinker

**Ton(nage)** C, Century, Chic, Displacement, Freight, Gross, Hundred, Long, Measurement, Metric, Net register, Register, Shipping, Short, T

**Tone, Tonality** Aeolian, Brace, Colour, Combination, Compound, Dialling, Difference, Differential, Engaged, Fifth, Gregorian, Harmonic, Hum, Hypate, Inflection, Key, Klang, Mediant, Minor, Ninth, Partial, Passing, Pure, Qualify, Quarter, Real, Resultant, Ring, Ringing, Side, →**SOUND**, Strain, Summational, Temper, Tenor, Timbre, Touch, Trite, Whole

**Tong(s)** Curling, Lazy, Sugar, Wafer

**Tongue, Tonguing** Brogue, Burr, Chape, Clack, Clapper, Doab, Double, Final, Flutter, Forked, Glossa, Glossolalia, Glottal, Isthmus, Jinglet, →**LANGUAGE**, Languet(te), Lap, Ligula, Lill, Lingo, Lingual, Lingulate, Lytta, Mother, Organ, Radula, Ranine, Rasp, Red rag, Single, Spit, Tab, Triple, Voice, Vulgar

**Tongue-tied** Mush-mouthed, See a wolf

**Tongue-twister** Jaw-breaker, Shibboleth

**Tonic** Booster, Bracer, C(h)amomile, Cascara, Doh, Elixir, Key, Keynote, Mease, Medicinal, Mishmee, Mishmi, Myrica, Oporice, Pareira brava, Pick-me-up, Quassia, Refresher, Roborant, Sage tea, Sarsaparilla, Solfa

▷ **Tonic** *may indicate* a musical note

**Tonsil, Tonsillitis** Almond, Amygdala, Antiaditis, Pharyngeal, Quinsy

**Tonsure(d)** Epilate, Haircut, Peel, Pield

**Tony** Bête, Chic, Classy, Fool, Smart, U

**Too** Als(o), As well, Besides, Eke, Excessive, Item, Likewise, Moreover, Oer, Over, Overly, Plus, Troppo

**Took** Naam, Nam, Set, Stole, Wan, Won

**Tool(s), Tool-maker** Flatter, →**IMPLEMENT**, →**INSTRUMENT**, Maker, Palaeolith, Penis, Percussion, Power, Property, Utensil

---

## TOOLS

*2 letters:*
Ax

*3 letters:*
Awl
Axe
Bit
Bur
Die
Fid
Gad
Hob
Hoe
Saw
Set

*4 letters:*
Adze
Brog
Burr
File
Froe
Frow
Iron
Loom
Lute
Pawn
Pick
Rasp
Rirp
Roll
Rurp
Snap

Tint
Vice

*5 letters:*
Auger
Bevel
Burin
Croze
Dolly
Drift
Drill
Drove
Edger
Elsin
Facer
Float
Graip
Hardy
Jemmy
Lewis
Miser
Piton
Plane
Prunt
Punch
Snake
Spade
Swage
Tongs

*6 letters:*
Beetle
Bodkin

Broach
Chaser
Chisel
Dibber
Dibble
Eatche
Eolith
Firmer
Former
Fraise
Fuller
Gimlet
Gnomon
Gouger
Graver
Hammer
Hopdog
Husker
Jackal
Jumper
Laster
Mallet
Muller
Pattle
Pestle
Pliers
Rabble
Rammer
Reamer
Ripple
Roller
Router
Sander

Saw set
Scutch
Scythe
Shoder
Sickle
Slater
Strike
Switch
Trowel
Wimble
Wrench

*7 letters:*
Bradawl
Carbide
Catspaw
Chopper
Crampon
Fretsaw
Go-devil
Grapnel
Icepick
Insculp
Jim Crow
Jointer
Knapper
Machine
Nail gun
Nail set
Nippers
Oustiti
Pickaxe
Plunger

| | 8 letters: | 9 letters: | 11 letters: |
|---|---|---|---|
| Pointer | Aiguille | Centre bit | Bagging-hook |
| Pricker | Airbrush | Come-along | Glass-cutter |
| Rocking | Billhook | Corkscrew | Marlinspike |
| Rounder | Calipers | Drawknife | Mitre square |
| Scalpel | Chainsaw | Drawshave | Plough-staff |
| Scalper | Clippers | Microlith | Screwdriver |
| Scauper | Driftpin | Moon-knife | Spirit-level |
| Scorper | Findings | Outsiders | Spitsticker |
| Scraper | Grattoir | Pitchfork | Steam hammer |
| Scriber | Hardware | Secateurs | |
| Seamset | Picklock | Toothpick | 12 letters: |
| Slasher | Pitching | Try square | Hedge-trimmer |
| Sleeker | Puncheon | | Marlinespike |
| Spanner | Scissors | 10 letters: | Monkey wrench |
| Spudder | Strickle | Float-stone | Sledge-hammer |
| Swingle | Strimmer® | Fore-hammer | Spell-checker |
| Swipple | Tjanting | Jackhammer | Wire-stripper |
| Terebra | Tranchet | Loggerhead | |
| Triblet | Tweezers | Spokeshave | 13 letters: |
| T-square | Vibrator | | Microkeratome |
| Twibill | | | Shooting stick |
| Upright | | | |

**Toot(er)** Blow, Horn, Parp, Trumpet
**Tooth(ed), Toothy, Teeth** Baby, Bicuspid, Bit, Buck, Bunodont, Cadmean, Canine, Carnassial, Chactodon, Cheek tooth, Chisel, Choppers, Cog, Comb, Comer, Cott's, Crena(te), Ctenoid, Cusp, Deciduous, Denticle, Dentin(e), Dentures, Egg, Eye, False, Fang, Gam, Gap, Gat, Gnashers, Grinder, Heterodont, Impacted, Incisor, Ivory, Joggle, Laniary, Milk, Mill, Molar, Nipper, Odontoid, Orthodontics, Overbite, Pawl, Pearly gates, Pectinate, Periodontics, Peristome, Permanent, Phang, Plate, Poison-fang, Pre-molar, Prong, Radula, Ratch, Ratchet, Scissor, Secodont, Sectorial, Selenodont, Serration, Set, Snaggle, Sprocket, Stomach, Store, Sweet, Trophi, Tush, Tusk, Uncinus, Upper, Wallies, Wang, Wiper, Wisdom, Wolf, Zalambdodont, Zygodont
**Toothache, Tooth troubles** Caries, Odontalgia, Odontoma, Tartar
**Toothless(ness)** Anodontia, Edentate, Gummy, Pangolin
**Toothpaste** Dentifrice
**Top (drawer, hole, line, notcher), Topper, Topping, Topmost** 1st, A1, Ace, Acme, Altissimo, Apex, Apical, Behead, Best, Better, Big, Blouse, Blouson, Boob tube, Brow, Bustier, Cacumen, Camisole, Cap, Capstone, Ceiling, Classic, Coma, Cop, Coping, Corking, Cream, →CREST, Crista, Crop, Crown, Culmen, Decapitate, De capo, Decollate, Diabolo, Dog, Dome, Dominant, Double, Drawer, Dreid(e)l, Dux, Elite, Execute, Fighting, Finial, Flip, Foremost, Gentry, Gyroscope, Halterneck, Hard, Hat, →HEAD, Height, Hummer, Humming, Imperial, Impost, Jumper, Lead, Lid, Maillot, Marzipan, Nun, One-er, Optimate, Orb, Parish, →PEAK, Pediment, Peerie, Peery, Peg, Peplos, Peplus, Pinnacle, Pitch, Quark, Replenish, Ridge, Roof, Sawyer, Screw, Secret, Shaw, Shirt, Skim, Sky, Slay, Soft, Spinning, Star, Summit, Superate, Superb, Supernal, Supreme, Supremo, Surface, Sweater, Table, Tambour, Targa, Teetotum, Texas, Tile, Trash, Trump, T-shirt, Turbinate, Unroof, Up(most), Uppermost, V, Vertex, Vest, Whipping, Whirligig, Winner
▷ **Top** may indicate first letter
**Topaz** Citrine, Colorado, Occidental, Oriental, Pycnite, Rose, Scottish, Spanish
**Topcoat** Finish, Overall, Overcoat, Ulster
**Tope(r)** Boozer, Bouser, Dagaba, Dagoba, →DRUNK, Imbibe, Sot, Tosspot
**Topic(al)** Agenda, Head, Hobbyhorse, Issue, Item, Local, Motion, Place, Shop, Subject, Text, →THEME, Timely, Up to date

**Top-knot** Tuft
**Top man** Wallah
**Topping** Grand, Icing, Meringue, Pepperoni, Piecrust, Streusel
**Topple** Depose, Dethrone, Oust, Overbalance, Overturn, Tip, Upend, →UPSET
**Topsy** Parentless
**Topsy-turvy** Careen, Cockeyed, Inverted, Summerset, Tapsalteerie, Tapsleteerie
**Torah** Maftir
**Torch** Blow, Brand, Cresset, Fire, Flambeau, Flashlight, Hards, Hurds, Lamp, Lampad, Link, Olympic, Penlight, Plasma, Roughie, Tead(e), Weld, Wisp
**Torch-bearer** Usherette
**Toreador** Escamillo, Matador, Picador, Torero
**Torment(ed), Tormentor** Agony, Anguish, Bait, Ballyrag, Bedevil, Butt, Cruciate, Crucify, Curse, Distress, Excruciate, Frab, Gehenna, Gibe, Grill, Hag-ridden, Harass, Harry, Haunt, Hell, Martyrdom, Molest, Nag, Nettle, Oppress, Pang, Pine, Plague, →RACK, Sadist, Tantalise, Tease, Wrack
**Torn** Agnail, In two, Ripped
**Tornado** Cyclone, Twister, Waterspout, Whirlwind
**Toronto** Hogtown
**Torpedo** Bangalore, Bomb, Fish, Missile, Ray, Subroc, Tin fish, Weapon
**Torpedo-guard** Crinoline
**Torpid, Torpor** Accidie, Acedia, Comatose, Dormant, Gouch, Inertia, Languid, Lethargic, Sluggish, Slumbering, Stupor
**Torquemada** Inquisitor
**Torrent** Flood, Spate
**Torrid** Amphiscian, Fiery, Hot, Sultry, Tropical
**Torsk** Cusk
**Torso** Body, Midriff, Trunk
**Tortilla** Pancake, Quesadilla, Taco, Tostada
**Tortoise** Chelonia, Emydes, Emys, Galapagos, Giant, Hic(c)atee, Kurma, Pancake, Snapping-turtle, Terrapin, Testudo, Timothy, Turtle, Water
**Tortoiseshell** Cat, Epiplastra, Hawksbill, Testudo
**Tortuous** Ambagious, Twisty, Winding
▷ **Tortuous** *may indicate* an anagram
**Torture, Torture chamber, Torture instrument** Agonise, Auto-da-fé, Bastinade, Bastinado, Boot, Bootikin, Catasta, Chinese burn, Chinese water, Crucify, Devil-on-the-neck, Engine, Excruciate, Flageolet, Fry, Gadge, Gauntlet, Gyp, Hell, Iron maiden, Knee-cap, Naraka, Peine forte et dur, Persecute, Pilliwinks, Pine, Pinniewinkle, Pinnywinkle, →RACK, Sadism, Scaphism, Scarpines, Scavenger, Scavenger's daughter, Scourge, Skeffington's daughter, Skevington's daughter, Strappado, Tantalise, Third degree, Thumb(i)kins, Thumbscrew, Torment, Treadmill, Triphook, Tumbrel, Tumbril, Water, Wheel, Wrack
▷ **Tortured** *may indicate* an anagram
**Torturer** Torquemada
**Torus** Disc, Stellarator
**Tory** Abhorrer, Blimp, Blue, C, Catholic, Opposition, Right, Taig, Tantivy, U, Unionist, Young England
**Tosh** Old bean
**Toss(ing), Throw(n)** Abject, Bandy, Birl, Bounce, Buck, Bung, Buttock, Cant, Canvass, Cast, Catapult, →CHUCK, Cottabus, Crabs, Crap, Cross-buttock, Dad, Daud, Dawd, Deal, Dink, Discomfit, Disconcert, Dod, Elance, Estrapade, Falcade, Faze, →FLING, Flip, Floor, Flump, Flutter, Flying (head)-mare, Free, Full, Gollum, Hanch, Haunch, Heave, Hipt, Hoy, →HURL, Jack, Jact(it)ation, Jaculation, Jeff, Juggle, Jump, Lance, Launch, Lob, Loft, Nick, Pash, Pick, Pitch, Purl, Put(t), Roll, Round-arm, Salad, Seamer, Shy, Slat, Sling, Squail, Unhorse, Unseat, Upcast, Wheech, Yuko

**Toss-up** Cross and pile, Heads or tails

**Tot** Add, Babe, Bairn, →**CHILD**, Dop, Dram, Infant, Mite, Moppet, Nightcap, Nip(per), Nipperkin, Slug, Snifter, Snort, Tad

**Total(ity), Totally, Toto** Absolute, Aggregate, All(-out), All told, Amount, Balance, Be-all, →**COMPLETE**, Count, Entire, Gross, In all, Lot, Mass, Ouroborus, Outright, Overall, Sum(mate), Tale, Tally, Unqualified, Uroborus, Utter, Whole

**Totalitarian** Autocrat, Despot, Étatiste, Fascist

**Tote** Bear, →**CARRY**, Yomp

**Totem** Fetish, Icon, Image, Pole

**To the point** Ad rem

**Tottenham** Hotspur

**Totter** Abacus, Daddle, Daidle, Didakai, Didakei, Didicoi, Did(d)icoy, Halt, Lurch, Ragman, Reel, Rock, Shamble, →**STAGGER**, Swag, Sway, Topple, Waver, Wobble

**Toucan** Ariel, Ramphastos

**Touch(ed), Touching, Touch up, Touchy** Abut, Accolade, Adjoin, Affect, Against, Airbrush, Anent, Apropos, Badass, Barmy, Cadge, Captious, Carambole, Caress, Carom, Common, Concern, Connivent, Contact, Contiguous, Dash, Easy, Emove, →**FEEL**, Feisty, Final, Finger, Finishing, Flick, Fondle, Glance, Handle, Haptic, Heart-warming, Huffish, Huffy, →**IN TOUCH**, Iracund, Irascible, Irritable, J'adoube, Kiss, Liaison, Libant, Loan, Loco, Meet, Midas, Miffy, Near, Nie, Nigh, Nudge, Palp, Pathetic, Paw, Potty, Re, Reach, Sense, Shade, Skiff, Soft, Sore, Spice, →**SPOT**, Tactile, Tactual, Tag, Tangible, Tap, Taste, Tat, Tetchy, Tickle, Tig, Tinderbox, Tinge, Titivate, Trace, Trait, Trifle, Tuck, Vestige

**Touchdown** Rouge

**Touchline** Tangent

**Touchstone** Basanite, Criterion, Norm, Standard

**Touch wood** Unberufen

**Touchwood** Absit omen, Monk, Punk, Spunk, Tinder

**Tough(en)** Adamantine, Anneal, Apache, Arduous, Ballsy, Bruiser, Burly, Chewy, Dab, Exacting, →**HARD**, Hardball, Hard-boiled, Hard-nosed, Hard nut, Hardy, Heavy duty, He-man, Hood, Hoodlum, Husky, Indurate, Keelie, Knotty, Leathern, Leathery, Nut, Pesky, Rambo, Resilient, Rigwiddie, Rigwoodie, Robust, Roughneck, Sinewy, Skinhead, Spartan, Steely, Stiff, Strict, String, Sturdy, Teuch, Thewed, Thug, Tityre-tu, Virile, Wiry, Withy, Yob

**Toupee** Hairpiece, Rug, Tour, →**WIG**

**Tour(er), Tourism, Tourist** Adventure, Barnstorm, Benefit, Circuit, Conducted, Cook's, Emmet, Excursion, Gig, Grand, Grockle, GT, Holiday-maker, Itinerate, →**JOURNEY**, Lionise, Mystery, Outing, Package, Parra, Posting, Pub crawl, Reality, Roadie, Road show, Rubberneck, Safari, Sightsee, Spin, Steerage, Swing, Tiki, →**TRAVEL**, Trip(per), Viator, Weather, Whistle-stop

**Tourmaline** Indicolite, Indigolite, Schorl, Zeuxite

**Tournament** American, Basho, Bonspiel, Bridge drive, Carousel, Drive, Event, Jereed, Jerid, Joust, Just, Ladder, Open, Plate, Pro-am, Pro-celebrity, Round robin, Royal, Spear-running, Super Twelve, Swiss, Tilt, Tourney, Whist drive, Wimbledon

**Tourniquet** Gar(r)otte, Garrot(e), Throttle, Torcular

**Tousle** Dishevel, Rumple

**Tout** Barker, Laud, Ply, Praise, Runner, Solicit, Spruik, Toot, Work-watcher

**Tow(ing), Towpath** Aquaplane, Button, Fibre, →**HAUL**, Hobbler, Pull, →**ROPE**, Ski, Skijoring, Stupe, Track road

▶ **Towards** *see* **TO(WARDS)**

**Towel** Dry, Jack, Nappy, Pantyliner, Roller, Rub, Sanitary, Tea, Tea-cloth, Terry, Turkish

**Tower, Tower over** AA, Aspire, Atalaya, Babel, Barbican, Bastille, Bastion, Belfry, Bell, Blackpool, Bloody, Brattice, Brettice, Brogh, Campanile, Clock, Conning, Control, Cooling, Donjon, Dungeon, Dwarf, Edifice, Eiffel, Fly, Fortress, Gantry, Garret, Gate, Giralda, Gopura(m), Guérite, Hawser, Horologium, Husky, Ivory, Keep, Leaning, Loom, Maiden,

Martello, Minar(et), Monument, Mooring, Mouse, Nuraghe, Nurhag, Overtop, Peel, Pinnacle, Pisa, Pound, Pylon, Rear, Rise, Rolandseck, Rood, Round, Sail, Sears, Shot, Signal, Sikhara, Silo, Ski-lift, Skyscraper, Space Needle, Specula, Spire, Stealth, Steeple, Swiss Re, Tête-de-pont, Texas, Tractor, Tugboat, → TURRET, Victoria, Watch, Water, Yagura, Ziggurat, Zikkurat

**Town, Township** Boom, Borgo, Borough, Bourg, Burg(h), City, Company, Conurbation, County, Deme, Dormitory, Dorp, Favella, Five, Garrison, Ghost, Ham(let), Intraurban, Market, Municipal, Nasik, One-horse, Open, Place, Podunk, Pueblo, Satellite, Shanty, Shire, Soweto, Staple, Tinsel, Tp, Twin, Urban, Whistle stop, Wick

**Townee, Townsman** Cad, Cit(izen), Dude, Freeman, Oppidan, Philister, Resident, Snob, Urbanist, Urbanite

**Town hall** Prytaneum

**Toxaemia** Eclampsia

**Toxic(ity), Toxin** Abrin, Aflatoxin, Antigen, Botox®, Botulin, Cadaverine, Cadmium, Chlorin(e), Coumarin, Curare, Deadly, Dioxan, Dioxin, Eclampsia, Fluorin(e), Lethal, Melittin, Muscarine, Nicotine, Paraquat, Phalloidin, Phenol, Phenothiazine, Pre-eclampsia, Psoralen, Ricin, Sepsis, Serology, Venin, Venomous, Virulence, Yellow rain, Zootoxin

**Toy** Babyhouse, Bauble, Bottle-imp, Bull-roarer, Cartesian devil, Cockhorse, Coral, Cyberpet, Dally, Dandle, Dinky®, Doll, Doll's house, Dreid(e)l, Executive, Faddle, Fiddle, Finger, Flirt, Frisbee®, Gewgaw, Golly, Gonk, Jack-in-the-box, Jumping-jack, Kaleidoscope, Kickshaw, Knack, Lego®, Meccano®, Newton's cradle, Noah's ark, Novelty, Paddle, Pantine, Peashooter, Pinwheel, Plaything, Pogo stick, Popgun, Praxinoscope, Quiz, Rag doll, Rattle, Russian doll, Scooter, Shoofly, Skipjack, Stroboscope, Tamagotchi, Tantalus-cup, Taste, Teddy, Thaumatrope, Top, → TRIFLE, Trinket, Tu(r)ndun, Wheel of life, Whirligig, Windmill, Yoyo, Zoetrope

**Trace** Atom, Cast, Derive, Describe, Draft, Draw, Dreg, Echo, Footprint, Ghost, Gleam, → HINT, Leaf, Limn, Mark, Memory, Outline, Relic, Relict, Remnant, Scan, Scintilla, Semblance, Sign, Smack, Soupçon, Spark, Strap, Streak, Suspicion, Tinge, → TOUCH, Track, Vestige, Whiff, Whit

**Tracery** Filigree, Frostwork

**Track(s), Tracker, Tracking, Trackman** Aintree, Aisle, Band, B-road, Caterpillar®, Cinder, Circuit, Course, Crawler, Cycleway, Dirt, Disrail, Dog, DOVAP, Drag strip, Drift, Ecliptic, El, Fast, Fettler, Flap(ping), Footing, Gandy dancer, Green road, Greenway, Groove, Hunt, Ichnite, Ichnolite, Icknield Way, Inside, Lane, Ley, Line, Loipe, Loopline, Mommy, Monitor, Monza, Orbit, Pad, → PATH, Persue, Piste, Pitlane, Pug, Pursue, Race, Raceway, Rail, Railway, Rake, Ridgeway, Riding, Route, Run, Runway, Rut, Scent, Siding, Sign, Skidway, Sleuth, Slot, Sonar, Speedway, Spoor, Stylus, Tan, Tan-ride, Taxiway, Tenure, Tideway, Title, Towpath, Trace, → TRAIL, Trajectory, Tram, Tramline, Tramroad, Tramway, Tread, Trode, Tug(boat), Twin, Wake, Wallaby, Way, Y

**Tract(able), Tracts** Area, Belt, Bench, Clime, Colporteur, Common, Dene, Digestive, Enclave, Enteral, Flysheet, Lande, Leaflet, Monte, Moor, Olfactory, → PAMPHLET, Park, Prairie, Province, Purlieu, Pusey, Pyramidal, Region, Scabland, Screed, Taluk, Tawie, Terrain, Wold

**Tractarian(ism)** Newman, Oxford movement, Pusey(ism)

**Tractor** Back hoe, Bombardier®, Bulldozer, Cat, Caterpillar®, Chelsea, Fendalton, Pedrail, Remuera, Skidder, Tower

**Tracy** Dick, Spencer

**Trade(r), Tradesman, Trading** Arb(itrageur), Art, Banian, Banyan, Bargain, Barrow boy, Barter, Bear, Bilateral, Bricks and clicks, Bull, Bun(n)ia, Burgher, Business, Cabotage, Calling, Carriage, Chaffer, Chandler, Chapman, Cheapjack, Cheesemonger, Clicks and mortar, Coaster, Comanchero, → COMMERCE, Coper, Coster, Costermonger, Crare, Crayer, Custom, Deal(er), Decorator, Dicker, Easterling, Eggler, Errand, Exchange, Exporter, Factor, Fair, Floor, Free, Galleon, Handle, Higgler, Horse, Hosier, Hot,

Importer, Indiaman, Industry, Insider, Ironmonger, Jobber, Kidder, Line, Logrolling, Matrix, Mercantile, Mercer, Merchant, Mercosur, Métier, Middleman, Milkman, Mister, Monger, Mystery, Occupy, Outfitter, Paralleling, Pitchman, Plumber, Ply, Program(me), Rag, Retailer, Roaring, Rough, Roundtripping, Salesman, Scalp, Screen, Sell, Shrivijaya, Simony, Slave, Stallenger, Stallholder, Stallinger, Stationer, Sutler, Suttle, → **SWAP**, Tailor, Traffic, Transit, Trant, Truck, Union, Vaisya, Vend, Wheeler-dealer, Wholesaler, Wind, Worker

**Trademark, Trade name** Brand, Chop, Idiograph, Label, Logo, Tm, TN

**Trade union** Amicus, ASLEF, COHSE, Equity, Local, Samiti, Solidarity, Syndicalism, UNISON, USDAW

**Trading money, Trading post** Cabotage, Fort, Wampum

**Tradition(s), Traditional(ist)** Ancestral, Classical, Convention, Custom(ary), Diehard, Eastern, Folksy, Folkway, Hadith, Heritage, Legend, Lore, Mahayana, Misoneist, Old guard, Old-line, Old-school, Orthodox, Pharisee, Pompier, Practice, Purist, Square, Suburban, Time-honoured, Trad, Tralaticious, Tralatitious, Unwritten

**Traduce** Abuse, Asperse, Defame, Impugn, Malign, Smear, Vilify

**Traffic(ker), Traffic pattern** Air, Barter, Broke, Cabotage, Clover-leaf, Commerce, Contraflow, Coyote, Deal, Export, Negotiate, Passage, Run, Sell, Slave trade, Smuggle, Tailback, Through, Trade, Truck, Vehicular, Way

**Tragedian, Tragedy, Tragic** Aeschylus, Antigone, Buskin, Calamity, Cenci, Corneille, Dire, → **DRAMA**, Euripides, Lear, Macready, Melpomene, Oedipean, Oresteia, Otway, Pathetic, Seneca, Sophoclean, Thespis

**Trail(er), Trailing** Abature, Advert, Appalachian, Audit, Bedraggle, Caravan, Condensation, Creep, Dissipation, Drag, Draggle, Fire, Follow, Forerunner, Foretaste, Horsebox, Ipomaea, Ivy, Lag, Liana, Liane, Low-loader, Nature, Oregon, Paper, Path, Persue, Preview, Prevue, Promo(tion), Pursue, Repent, Runway, Santa Fe, Scent, Shadow, Sickle-cell, Sign, Sleuth, Slot, Slowcoach, Snail, Spoor, Straggle, Stream, Streel, Tag, Tow, Trace, → **TRACK**, Trade, Traipse, Trape, Trauchle, Trayne, Troad, Vapour, Vine, Virga, Wake

**Train(er), Training** Accommodation, Advanced, Apprenticeship, APT, Autogenic, Baggage, Boot camp, BR, Break in, Breed, Brighton Belle, Bullet, Caravan, Cat, Cavalcade, Choo-choo, Circuit, Coach, Commuter, Condition, Cortège, Day release, Diesel, Direct, Discipline, Dog, Double-header, Dressage, Drill, Drive, Educate, Entourage, Enure, Epicyclic, Eurostar®, Excursion, Exercise, Express, Fartlek, Field, Flier, Flight simulator, Freightliner®, Fuse, Gear, Ghan, Ghost, Gravy, Grounding, GWR, Handle(r), HST, → **INSET**, Instruct, Intercity®, Interval, Jerkwater, Journey, Limber up, Liner, Link, LMS, LNER, Loco, Longe, Lunge, Maglev, Mailcar, Manège, Manrider, Meinie, Mein(e)y, Mentor, Milk, Mixed, Multiple unit, Nopo, Nurture, Nuzzle, Omnibus, Orient Express, Outward Bound®, Owl, Pack, Paddy, Parliamentary, Passenger, Pavlov, PE, Pendolino, Personal, Potty, Power, Practise, → **PREPARE**, Procession, PT, Puffer, Puff-puff, Push-pull, Q, Qualified, Queue, Railcar, Rattler, Rehearse, Retinue, Road, Roadwork, Rocket, Roughrider, Royal Scot, Ry, Sack, Sacque, → **SCHOOL**, Series, Shoe, Shuttle service, Siege, Simulator, Sinkansen, Skill centre, Sleeper, Sloid, Sloyd, Sneaker, Sowarree, Sowarry, Special, Square-bashing, SR, Steer, String, Suite, Tail, Tame, → **TEACH**, Through, Tire, Tirocinium, Tone up, Track shoe, Trail, Trellis, Tube, Twin bill, Wage, Wagon, Wave, Way, Whale oil

▷ **Train(ed)** *may indicate* an anagram

**Trainee** → **APPRENTICE**, AT, Cadet, Cub, Fledgling, Intern, Jackaroo, Jackeroo, Learner, Ordinand, Pupil, Rookie, Rooky, T

**Train-spotter** Gricer

**Traipse** Gad

**Trait** Characteristic, Feature, Knack, Oddity, Peculiarity, Ph(a)enotype, Sickle-cell, Strain, Thew, Trick, Vein

**Traitor** Benedict Arnold, Betrayer, Casement, Dobber-in, Fifth column, Joyce, Judas, Judas Maccabaeus, Nid(d)ering, Nid(d)erling, Nithing, Proditor, Quisling, Renegade, Reptile, Snake, Tarpeian, Traditor, Treachetour, Turncoat, Viper, Wallydraigle, Weasel

**Trajectory** Parabola, Track

**Tram, Tramcar** Tip, Trolley

▷ **Trammel** *may indicate* an anagram

**Tramp, Trample** Bog-trotter, Bum, Caird, Clochard, Clump, Crush, Deadbeat, Derelict, Derro, Dingbat, Dosser, Down and out, Drifter, Estragon, Footslog, Freighter, Gadling, Gangrel, Gook, Hike, Hobo, Knight of the road, Lumber, Meff, Override, Overrun, Pad, Piepowder, Piker, Plod, Poach, Potch(e), Prostitute, Rover, Scorn, Ship, Slog, Slut, Splodge, Sundowner, Swagman, →**TINKER**, Toe-rag(ger), Tom, Track, Traipse, Tread, Trek, Trog, Tromp, Truant, Trudge, Tub, Vagabond, Vagrant, Weary Willie, Whore

**Trampoline** Trampet(te)

**Trance** Aisling, Catalepsy, Cataplexy, Goa, Narcolepsy, Somnambulism

**Tranche** Gold, Reserve

**Tranquil(lity)** Ataraxy, Calm, Compose, Composure, Easy, Halcyon, Lee, Peace(ful), Placid, Quietude, Restful, Sedate, →**SERENE**, Still

**Tranquillise(r)** Appease, Ataractic, Ataraxic, →**CALM**, Compose, Diazepam, Downer, Hypnone, Hypnotic, Largactil®, Librium®, Lullaby, Nervine, Nitrazepam, Oxazepam, Paregoric, Placate, Satisfy, Sedative, Soothe, Still, Valium®

**Transact, Transaction(s)** Affair, Agio, Brokerage, Deal, Deed, Escrow, Ex-div, Fasti, Leaseback, Passage, Put through, Retour, Tr

**Transcend(ent), Transcendental(ist), Transcendentalism** Emerson, Excel, Mystic, Overtop, Surpass, Thoreau

**Transcribe, Transcript(ion)** Copy, Inclusive, Pinyin, Rescore, Tenor, →**TRANSLATE**, Transume

**Transfer(ence)** Alien, Alienate, →**ASSIGN**, Attorn, Bosman, Calk, Calque, Carryover, Cede, Chargeable, Communize, Consign, Convey(ance), Credit, Cross over, Crosstalk, Cutover, Dabbity, Decal(comania), Deed, Demise, Devolve, Download, Embryo, Exchange, Explant, Extradite, Ferry, Flit, Gene, Hive off, Incardinate, Iron-on, Letraset®, Make over, Mancipation, Metathesis, Mortmain, Nuclear, On-lend, Pass, Photomechanical, Print through, Provection, Reassign, Redeploy, Remit, Remove, Render, Repot, Second, Settlement, Slam, Spool, Thought, Transcribe, Transduction, Transfection, Transhume, Translocation, Uproot, Vire, Virement

▷ **Transferred** *may indicate* an anagram

**Transfix** Gore, Impale, Rivet, →**SKEWER**, Spear, Spit

**Transform(ation), Transformer** Affine, Alchemist, Alter, Apotheosis, Balun, Change, Fourier, Linear, Lorentz, Makeover, Metamorphism, Metamorphose, Metamorphosis, Metaplasia, Metastasis, Morphallaxis, Morphing, Mutate, Permute, Rectifier, Sea change, Sepalody, Tesla coil, Tinct, Toroid, Toupee, Transfigure, Transmogrify, Variation, Wig

▷ **Transform(ed)** *may indicate* an anagram

**Transfusion** Apheresis

**Transgress(ion)** Encroach, Err, Infraction, Infringe, Offend, Overstep, Peccancy, →**SIN**, Violate

**Transient, Transit(ion), Transitory** Brief, Caducity, Ecotone, Ephemeral, Evanescent, Fleeting, Fly-by-night, Forbidden, Fugacious, Hobo, Impermanent, Metabasis, Passage, Passing, Provisional, Rapid, Segue, Sfumato, T, Temporary

**Transistor** Drift, Emitter, Epitaxial, Field-effect, Junction

**Translate, Translation, Translator** Calque, Construe, Convert, Coverdale, Crib, Decipher, Decode, Decrypt, Encode, Explain, Free, Horse, Interpret, In vitro, Itala, Jerome, Key, Linguist, Loan, Machine, Metaphrase, Nick, Paraphrase, Pinyin, Polyglot, Pony, Reduce, Render, Rendition, Rhemist, Septuagint, Simultaneous, Targum, Tr, Transcribe, Transform, Trot, Tyndale, Unseen, Version(al), Vulgate, Wycliffe

▷ **Translate(d)** *may indicate* an anagram

**Transmigrate, Transmigration** Exodus, Metempsychosis, Passage, Trek

**Transmit(ter), Transmitted, Transmission** Aerial, Air, Aldis lamp, Allele, Analogue, Automatic, Band, Baseband, Beacon, Broadband, →**BROADCAST**, Cable, Carry, CB, Communicate, Compander, Compandor, Conduct, Consign, Contagion, Convection, Convey, Digital, Diplex, Facsimile, Filler, Forward, Gearbox, Gene, Heredity, Impart, Intelsat, Localizer, Manual, Mast, Mic(rophone), Modem, Nicol, Permittivity, Pipe, Propagate, Racon, Radiate, Radio (galaxy), Receiver, Responser, Send, Simplex, Simulcast, Sonabuoy, Spark, Synchronous, Tappet, Telautograph®, Telecast, Telegony, Telematics, Telemetry, Telepathy, Teleprinter, Teletex, Televise, Telex, Telstar, Tiptronic®, Tiros, Traduce, Traject, Tralaticious, Tralatitious, UART, Ultrawideband, Uplink, Upload, Walkie-talkie, WAP, Webcam, Wi-Fi®

**Transom** Reverse, Traverse

**Transparent, Transparency** Adularia, Clarity, Clear, Crystal(line), Diaphanous, Dioptric, Glassy, Glazed, Hyaloid, Iolite, Leno, Limpid, Lucid, Luminous, Patent, Pellucid, Porcelain, Sheer, Slide, Tiffany, Transpicuous

**Transpire** Happen, Occur

**Transplant** Allograft, Anaplasty, Graft, Repot, Reset(tle), Shift

**Transport(ed), Transporter, Transportation** Active, Aerotrain, Air-bus, Air-lift, Airline, Ar(a)ba, Argo, Barca, Bathorse, Beachbuggy, Bear, Bike, Black Maria, Boat, Boat-train, Broomstick, BRS, Buggy, Bus, Cable-car, Cargo, Carract, →**CARRY**, Cart, Casevac, Cat-train, Charabanc, Charm, Conductor, Convey, Cycle, Cyclo, Delight, Deliver, Dray, Ecstasy, Elation, Electron, Eloin, Enrapt, Enravish, Entrain, Esloin, Estro, Exalt, Ferriage, Ferry, Fishyback, Freight (train), Haul(age), Hearse, Helicopter, Hydrofoil, Jag, Jerrican, Jet ski, Joy, Kart, Kurvey, Landau, Lift, Lug, Maglev, Mambrane, Matatu, Medevac, Minicab, Minivan, Monorail, Motor cycle, Overjoy, Pack animal, Palanquin, Pantechnicon, Park and ride, Paytrain, Penny farthing, Pipeline, Plane, Portage, Public, Put, Q-train, Rape, Rapine, Rapture, Ravish, Rickshaw, Roadster, Ropeway, Ship, Shorthaul, Shuttle, Sidecar, Skateboard, Sledge, Sleigh, Sno-Cat, Snowmobile, Stagecoach, Supersonic, Tandem, Tanker, Tape, Tardis, Taxi, Tote, Train, Tramway, Transit, Trap, Trolley, Troopship, Tuktuk, Tumbril, Ubiquinone, Waft, Waterbus, Wheelchair, Wheels, Wireway

**Transpose, Transposition** Anagram, Commute, Convert, Invert, Metathesis, Shift, Spoonerism, Switch, Tr

▷ **Transposed** *may indicate* an anagram

**Transsexual** Invert

**Transubstantiate, Transubstantiation** Capernaite

**Transverse** Across, Crosscut, Diagonal, Obliquid, Thwart

**Transvest(it)ism, Transvestite** Berdache, Berdash, Cross-dressing, Eonist

**Tranter** Dolly

**Trap(s), Trapdoor, Trapped, Trappings** Accoutrement, Ambush, →**BAGGAGE**, Bags, Belongings, Birdlime, Booby, Buckboard, Bunker, Carriage, Catch, Catch-pit, Clapnet, Cobweb, Corner, Creel, Crevasse, Cru(i)ve, Deadfall, Death, Decoy, Dip, Dogcart, Downfall, Drain, Eelset, Emergent, Enmesh, Ensnare, Entoil, Entrain, Fall, Fit-up, Fly, Flypaper, Frame-up, Fyke, Geel, Gig, Gin, Gob, Gravel, Grin, Haaf-net, Hatch, Honey, Housings, Ice-bound, Illaqueate, Jinri(c)ksha(w), Keddah, Kettle, Kheda, Kiddle, Kidel, Kipe, Kisser, Knur(r), Light, Lime, Live, Lobster pot, →**LUGGAGE**, Lure, Mesh, Mouth, Net, Nur(r), Oil, Paraphernalia, Pitfall, Plant, Polaron, Police, Pot, Poverty, Putcheon, Putcher, Quicksand, Radar, Regalia, Sand, Scruto, Scuttle, →**SNARE**, Speed, Spell, Spider, Springe, Stake-net, Star, Steam, Stench, Sting, Stink, Sun, Tangle, Tank, Teagle, Toil, Tonga, Tourist, Trapfall, Tripwire, Trojan horse, Trou-de-loup, Two-wheeler, U, U-bend, Vampire, Waterseal, Web, Weel, Weir, Wire

**Trapezist** Leotard

**Trapper** Carson, Voyageur

**Trash(y)** Bosh, Deface, Desecrate, Dre(c)k, Garbage, Junk, Kitsch, Off-scum, Pulp, →**RUBBISH**, Schlock, Scum, Tinpot, Trailer, Trumpery, Vandalise, White, Worthless, Write off

**Trauma, Traumatise** Insult, Scar, Shell-shock, Shock

**Travel(ler), Travelling** Aeneas, Backpack, Bagman, Bushwhacker, Caird, Chapman, Columbus, Commercial, Commute, Crustie, Crusty, Drive, Drummer, Eurostar, Explorer, Fare, Fellow, Fly, Fogg, Geoffrey, Gipsen, Gipsy, Gitano, Globe-trotter, Go, Gulliver, Gypsy, Hike, Hitchhiker, Interrail, Itinerant, Jet-setter, Journey, Locomotion, Long-haul, Marco Polo, Meve, Migrant, Motor, Move, Mush, New Age, Nomad, Odysseus, Pardoner, Passenger, Passepartout, Peregrination, Peripatetic, Pilgrim, Ply, Polo, Pootle, Range, Rep, Ride, Road, Roam, Rom(any), Rove, Safari, Sail, Salesman, Samaritan, Sinbad, Sledger, Space, Spaceman, Stowaway, Teleport, Tool, →**TOUR**, Tourist, Trek, Tripper, Tsigane, Viator, Voyage, Waft, Wanderjahr, Wayfarer, Wend, Wildfire, Zigan

**Traverse** Cross, Girdle, Measure, Quest, Trace

**Travesty** Burlesque, Charade, Distortion, Parody, Show, Skit

**Trawl** Beam, Drag-net, Hose-net, Net

**Tray** Antler, Bottle-slide, Carrier, Case, Charger, Coaster, Gallery, In, Joe, Lazy Susan, Mould, Out, Plateau, →**SALVER**, Shower, Tea, Trencher, Typecase, Voider, Waiter

**Treacherous, Treachery** Bad faith, Betrayal, Deceit, Delilah, Fickle, Ganelon, Guile, Insidious, Judas-kiss, Knife, Mala fide, Medism, Perfidious, Punic, Punic faith, Quicksands, Sedition, Serpentine, Sleeky, Snaky, Sneaky, Trahison, Traitor, Trappy, →**TREASON**, Two-faced, Unleal, Viper, Weasel

**Treacle** Black(jack), Butter, Molasses, Syrup, Venice

**Tread** Clamp, Clump, Dance, Pad, Step, Stomp, Stramp, Track, Trample

**Treadle** Footboard, Pedal

**Treason** Betrayal, Constructive, High, Insurrection, Lèse-majesté, Lese-majesty, Perduellion, Petty, Sedition, →**TREACHERY**

**Treasure(r), Treasury** Aladdin's cave, Banker, Bursar, Cache, Camera, Camerlengo, Camerlingo, Cherish, Chest, Cimelia, Coffer, Ewe-lamb, Exchequer, Fisc(al), Fisk, Godolphin, Golden, Heirloom, Heritage, Hoard, Hon(ey), Montana, Nugget, Palgrave, Pork barrel, →**PRIZE**, Procurator, Purser, Quaestor, Relic, Riches, Steward, Sweetie, Taonga, Thesaurus, Trove

**Treat, Treatment** Actinotherapy, Action, Acupressure, Acupuncture, Address, Allopathy, Antidote, Antiserum, Apitherapy, Archilowe, Arenation, Aromatherapy, Arsphenamine, Balneotherapy, Beano, Beauty, Beneficiate, Besee, Body wrap, Botox®, Capitulate, Care, Chemotherapy, Chiropractic, Condition, Course, Coverage, Crymotherapy, Cryotherapy, Cupping, Cure, Deal, Detox(ification), Dialysis, Do, →**DOCTOR**, Dose, Dress, Dutch, ECT, Electrotherapy, Enantiopathy, Entertain, EST, Facial, Faith-healing, Fango, Faradism, Figuration, Finish, Foment, Frawzey, Handle, Heliotherapy, Hellerwork, Holistic, Homeopathy, HRT, Hydrotherapy, Hypnotherapy, Immunotherapy, Insulin, Intermediate, Jin shin do, Kenny, Laser, Manage, Massotherapy, Mechanotherapy, Medicament, Medicate, Mercerise, Mesotherapy, Moxibustion, Narcotherapy, Naturopathy, Negotiate, Opotherapy, Organotherapy, Orthoptics, Osteopathy, →**OUTING**, Pasteur, Pedicure, Pelotherapy, Phototherapy, Physiatrics, Physic, Physiotherapy, Pie, Poultice, Probiotics, Process, Prophylaxis, Psychoanalysis, Psychodrama, Psychotherapy, Radiotherapy, Regale, Rehab(ilitation), Rest cure, Root, Secretage, Serotherapy, Setter, Shiatsu, Shout, Shrift, Sironise, Smile, Softener, Speleotherapy, →**STAND**, Statin, Tablet, Tebilise®, TENS, Thalassotherapy, →**THERAPY**, Thermotherapy, Titbit, Traction, Turkish bath, Twelve-step, UHT, Usance, Use, Vet

▷ **Treated** *may indicate* an anagram

**Treatise** Almagest, Bestiary, Commentary, Cybele, Didache, Discourse, Dissertation, Essay, Monograph, Pandect, Prodrome, Profound, Summa, Tract(ate), Upanishad, Vedanta

**Treaty** Agreement, Alliance, Assiento, Concordat, Covenant, Entente, GATT, Jay's, Lateran, Locarno, Lunéville, Maastricht, Nijmegen, North Atlantic, → PACT, Paris, Private, Protocol, Rapallo, Rijswijk, Ryswick, San Stefano, Sovetsk, Test-ban, Utrecht, Verdun, Versailles, Westphalia, Yorktown

**Treble** Castrato, Choirboy, Chorist(er), Pairial, Soprano, → TRIPLE, Triune, Voice

**Tree(s)** Actor, → ANCESTRY, Axle, Beam, Bluff, Boom, Bosk, Chaparral, Clump, Conifer, Coppice, Corner, Covin, Cross, Daddock, Deciduous, Decision, Dendrology, Descent, Family, Fault, Fringe, Gallows, Genealogical, Greenery, Grove, Hang, Hardwood, Jesse, Nurse, Pedigree, Phanerophyte, Pole, Rood, Roof, Sawyer, Shoe, Silviculture, Softwood, Staddle, Stand, Stemma, Summer, Thicket, Timber, Tyburn, Ulmaceous, Vista, Wicopy, → WOOD

---

## TREES

| | | | |
|---|---|---|---|
| **2 letters:** | Bito | Rhus | Boree |
| Bo | Cade | Rimu | Bread |
| Ti | Coco | Sack | Bunya |
| | Cola | Shea | Butea |
| **3 letters:** | Dali | Silk | Cacao |
| Ake | Dhak | Sloe | Carap |
| Ash | Dika | Soap | Carob |
| Asp | Dita | Sorb | Cedar |
| Bay | Eugh | Tawa | Ceiba |
| Bel | Gean | Teak | China |
| Ben | Hule | Teil | Clove |
| Box | Jack | Titi | Cocoa |
| Cow | Kaki | Toon | Cocus |
| Elm | Karo | Tung | Coral |
| Fig | Kiri | Tutu | Ebony |
| Fir | Kola | Upas | Elder |
| Gum | Lead | Wych | Fagus |
| Ita | Lime | Yang | Fever |
| Jak | Lote | Yuzu | Flame |
| Koa | Mako | | Fruit |
| Mot | Meal | **5 letters:** | Gauze |
| Nim | Milk | Abele | Genip |
| Oak | Ming | Abies | Grass |
| Oil | Mira | Ackee | Guava |
| Sal | Mott | Afara | Hakea |
| Tea | Mowa | Agila | Hazel |
| Til | Neem | Alamo | Hevea |
| Ule | Nipa | Alder | Holly |
| Wax | Noni | Alnus | Iroko |
| Yew | Olea | Anona | Ivory |
| | Ombu | Areca | Jambu |
| **4 letters:** | Palm | Argan | Jarul |
| Acer | Pine | Aspen | Judas |
| Akee | Pipe | Babul | Kapok |
| Aloe | Pith | Banak | Karri |
| Amla | Plum | Bania | Kauri |
| Arar | Poon | Beech | Khaya |
| Atap | Puka | Belah | Kiaat |
| Bael | Rain | Birch | Kokum |
| Bhel | Rata | Bodhi | Larch |

| | | | |
|---|---|---|---|
| Lemon | Tsuga | Diana's | Mimosa |
| Lichi | Tuart | Dragon | Missel |
| Lilac | Tulip | Durian | Mopane |
| Lotus | Vitex | Durion | Mopani |
| Mahoe | Wahoo | Emblic | Myrtle |
| Mahua | Wenge | Eumong | Nutmeg |
| Mahwa | Wilga | Eumung | Obeche |
| Maire | Withy | Feijoa | Orange |
| Mamey | Xylem | Fustet | Orihou |
| Mango | Yacca | Fustic | Padauk |
| Mapau | Yulan | Gallus | Padouk |
| Maple | Zaman | Garjan | Pagoda |
| Marri | Zamia | Gidgee | Papaya |
| Matai | | Gidjee | Pawpaw |
| Melia | **6 letters:** | Gingko | Peepul |
| Motte | Abroma | Ginkgo | Pepper |
| Mowra | Acacia | Glinap | Platan |
| Mugga | Akeake | Gnetum | Pomelo |
| Mulga | Alerce | Gopher | Poplar |
| Mvule | Angico | Guango | Popple |
| Myall | Annona | Gurjun | Protea |
| Ngaio | Antiar | Gympie | Pumelo |
| Nikau | Arbute | Hupiro | Puriri |
| Nyssa | Arolla | Illipe | Quince |
| Olive | Babaco | Illipi | Red-bud |
| Opepe | Bablah | Illupi | Red gum |
| Osier | Balsam | Jarool | Ricker |
| Palas | Banyan | Jarrah | Roucou |
| Palay | Baobab | Joshua | Rubber |
| Panax | Bilian | Jujube | Sabicu |
| Peach | Bombax | Jupati | Sallow |
| Pecan | Bonsai | Kamahi | Samaan |
| Pinon | Bo-tree | Kamala | Sandal |
| Pipal | Bottle | Kamela | Sapele |
| Pipul | Buriti | Kapuka | Sapium |
| Pitch | Cadaga | Karaka | Sapota |
| Plane | Cadagi | Karamu | Saxaul |
| Quina | Carapa | Karite | She-oak |
| Ramin | Carica | Kentia | Sinder |
| Roble | Cashew | Kowhai | Sissoo |
| Rowan | Cembra | Laurel | Sorrel |
| Sabal | Cercis | Lebbek | Souari |
| Saman | Cerris | Linden | Spruce |
| Sassy | Chaste | Locust | Styrax |
| Scrog | Chenar | Longan | Sumach |
| Silva | Cherry | Loquat | Sunder |
| Smoke | Chinar | Lucuma | Sundra |
| Sumac | Citron | Lungah | Sundri |
| Tawai | Coffee | Macoya | Tallow |
| Taxus | Cordon | Mallee | Tamanu |
| Thorn | Cornel | Manuka | Tawhai |
| Thuja | Cornus | Mastic | Tewart |
| Thuya | Damson | Mazard | Thyine |
| Tilia | Deodar | Medlar | Titoki |

Tooart
Totara
Tupelo
Waboom
Wandoo
Wicken
Willow
Witgat
Yarran
Zamang

**7 letters:**
Ailanto
Ambatch
Amboina
Apricot
Araroba
Arbutus
Avodire
Bebeeru
Bilimbi
Bilsted
Bubinga
Buck-eye
Bursera
Cajeput
Cajuput
Calamus
Camphor
Camwood
Canella
Carbeen
Cascara
Cassava
Catalpa
Cedrela
Champac
Champak
Chayote
Chesnut
Coquito
Corylus
Corypha
Cumquat
Cypress
Dagwood
Dogwood
Dryades
Durmast
Geebung
Genipap
Gluinap
Gumtree
Hickory

Hog-plum
Holm-oak
Houhere
Jipyapa
Kumquat
Lacquer
Lagetto
Lentisk
Logwood
Lumbang
Madrono
Mahaleb
Manjack
Marasca
Margosa
Mazzard
Meranti
Mesquit
Moringa
Morrell
Mustard
Papauma
Paxiuba
Pereira
Pilinut
Pimento
Platane
Pollard
Populus
Pukatea
Quassia
Quicken
Quillai
Quinain
Radiata
Rampick
Rampike
Redwood
Rock elm
Saksaul
Sandbox
Saouari
Sapling
Saturn's
Sausage
Sequoia
Seringa
Service
Shittah
Sourgum
Soursop
Spindle
Sundari
Talipat

Talipot
Taraire
Taupata
Tawhiri
Trumpet
Varnish
Wallaba
Wirilda
Witchen
Wych-elm
Xylopia
Zelkova

**8 letters:**
Aguacate
Algaroba
Aquillia
Bangalay
Bangalow
Basswood
Benjamin
Bergamot
Berrigan
Blackboy
Blimbing
Bountree
Bourtree
Breadnut
Brigalow
Calabash
Chestnut
Cinchona
Cinnamon
Cocoplum
Coolabah
Coolibah
Corkwood
Crabwood
Cucumber
Cudgerie
Dendroid
Dracaena
Espalier
Flittern
Fraxinus
Garcinia
Ghost-gum
Gnetales
Guaiacum
Hagberry
Hawthorn
Hinahina
Hornbeam
Huon-pine

Igdrasil
Inkberry
Ironbark
Ironwood
Jelutong
Kawakawa
Kingwood
Laburnum
Lacebark
Lecythis
Loblolly
Magnolia
Mahogany
Makomako
Mangrove
Manna-ash
Mesquite
Mulberry
Ocotillo
Oiticica
Oleaceae
Oleaster
Pachouli
Palmetto
Pandanus
Parapara
Pichurim
Pinaster
Pithtree
Pyinkado
Quandang
Quandong
Quantong
Quillaia
Quillaja
Raintree
Rambutan
Rangiora
Rewa-rewa
Sago-palm
Sandarac
Santalum
Sapindus
Sapucaia
Sasswood
Sea grape
Shaddock
Shagbark
Simaruba
Snowball
Snowdrop
Soapbark
Sourwood
Standard

Stinging
Sugar gum
Sweet gum
Sweetsop
Sycamine
Sycamore
Sycomore
Tamarack
Tamarind
Tamarisk
Taxodium
Umbrella
Whitegum
Wine-palm
Ygdrasil

**9 letters:**
Agila-wood
Ailantous
Albespine
Angophora
Araucaria
Azedarach
Bilimbing
Bitternut
Blackbutt
Blackjack
Blackwood
Bloodwood
Bolletrie
Boobialla
Broadleaf
Bulletrie
Bully-tree
Bulwaddee
Burrawary
Butternut
Caliatour
Caliature
Candlenut
Canoewood
Carambola
Casuarina
Chempaduk
Cherimoya
Chincapin
Chinkapin
Coachwood
Coco-de-mer
Cordyline
Courbaril
Crab apple
Cupressus
Curryleaf

Eaglewood
Evergreen
Firewheel
Flame-leaf
Greengage
Greenwood
Grevillea
Hackberry
Ivory palm
Jacaranda
Jackfruit
Kahikatea
Krummholz
Kurrajong
Lancewood
Lemonwood
Leylandii
Macadamia
Marmalade
Melaleuca
Mirabelle
Mockernut
Monkeypot
Naseberry
Nectarine
Nux vomica
Paloverde
Paperbark
Patchouli
Patchouly
Paulownia
Persimmon
Pistachio
Pitch-pine
Poinciana
Ponderosa
Pontianac
Prickwood
Pricky ash
Primavera
Quebracho
Rauwolfia
Rose-apple
Sapodilla
Saskatoon
Sassafras
Satinwood
Shellbark
Simarouba
Soapberry
Star-anise
Star-apple
Sterculia
Stinkwood

Stone pine
Sweetwood
Tacamahac
Tamarillo
Terebinth
Toothache
Torchwood
Wagenboom
Wayfaring
Whitebeam
Whitewood
Wineberry
Wych-hazel
Yggdrasil
Zebrawood

**10 letters:**
Arbor Vitae
Axe-breaker
Bitterbark
Blackbully
Breadfruit
Bulletwood
Bunya-bunya
Buttonball
Buttonwood
Calamondin
Calliature
Candle-wood
Cannonball
Chamaerops
Chaulmugra
Cheesewood
Chinaberry
Chinquapin
Cottonwood
Cowrie-pine
Eucalyptus
Fiddlewood
Flamboyant
Flindersia
Frangipani
Ginkgoales
Green-heart
Hackmatack
Ilang-ilang
Jaboticaba
Jippi-jappa
Kaffirboom
Kotokutuku
Letter-wood
Lilly-pilly
Macrocarpa
Manchineel

Mangabeira
Mangosteen
Marblewood
Nithofagus
Palisander
Paper birch
Pepperidge
Pohutukawa
Prickly ash
Quercitron
Ribbonwood
Sandalwood
Sappanwood
Schefflera
Silk-cotton
Silverbell
Sneezewood
Spotted gum
Strawberry
Tawheowheo
Traveller's
Turpentine
Witch-hazel
Witgatboom
Woollybutt
Yellowwood
Ylang-ylang

**11 letters:**
Anchovy-pear
Appleringie
Bladderwort
Bristlecone
Bristlepine
Cabbage-palm
Chaulmoogra
Chokecherry
Copperbeech
Crack-willow
Cryptomeria
Dawn redwood
Dipterocarp
Eriodendron
Flamboyante
Fothergilla
Gingerbread
Guttapercha
Honey locust
Horseradish
Jesuit's bark
Leatherwood
Lignum vitae
Liquidambar
Loblolly bay

| | | | |
|---|---|---|---|
| Maceranduba | Shittimwood | Hercules' club | Wellingtonia |
| Metasequoia | Sitka spruce | Liriodendron | |
| Osage orange | Stringybark | Mammee-sapota | *13 letters:* |
| Pomegranate | | Masseranduba | Paper-mulberry |
| Purpleheart | *12 letters:* | Monkey-puzzle | |
| Retinispora | African tulip | Raspberry jam | *14 letters:* |
| River red gum | Haemotoxylon | Washingtonia | Western hemlock |

**Tree-climber, Tree-dweller** Monkey, Opossum, Sciurus, Squirrel, Unau

**Tree disease** Dutch elm, Oak wilt, Waldsterben

**Tree-man** Ent

**Tree-moss** Usnea

**Tree-paeony** Moutan

**Tree-pecker** Picus

**Tree-shrew** Tana

**Treetop** Canopy

**Trefoil** Bird's foot, Clover, Hop, Lotos, Lotus

**Trek(ker)** Afrikaner, Hike, Journey, Leg, Odyssey, Safari, Yomp

**Trellis** Espalier, Lattice, Pergola, Treillage, Treille

**Tremble, Trembling, Tremor** Aftershock, Aquiver, Ashake, Butterfly, Dither, Dodder, Foreshock, Fremitus, Hotter, Intention, Judder, Marsquake, Milk sickness, Moonquake, Palpitate, Quail, Quake, Quaver, Quiver, Seismal, →**SHAKE**, Shiver, Shock, Shudder, Stound, Temblor, Titubation, Trepid, Twitchy, Vibrant, Vibrate, Vibration, Vibratiuncle, Vibrato, Wobble, Wuther, Yips

**Tremendous** Big, Enormous, Extreme, Gargantuan, Howling, Immense, Marvellous, Thundering

**Tremolo** Bebung, Quaver, Trill(o)

▶ **Tremor** *see* **TREMBLE**

**Tremulous** Cranky, Dithering, Hirrient, Quaking, Quavery, Shaky, Timorous, Vibrato

**Trench(er), Trencherman** Boyau, Cunette, Cuvette, Delf, Delph, Dike(r), →**DITCH**, Dyke(r), Encroach, Fleet, Foss(e), Foxhole, Fur(r), Furrow, Grip, Gullet, Gutter, Knife and fork, Leat, Line, Mariana, Moat, Oceanic, Outwork, Passage, Rill, Rille, Ring-dyke, Robber, Salient, Sap, Shott, Slidder, Slit, Sod, Sondage

**Trenchant** Acid, Cutting

**Trend(y), Trendsetter** Bellwether, Bent, Bias, Chic, Climate, Drift, Fashion, Groovy, Hep, Hip, Hipster, In, Latest, Mainstream, Mode, Modern, New Age(r), Newfangled, Pacemaker, Pop, Poserish, Posey, Rage, Right-on, Smart, Style, Swim, Tendency, Tendenz, Tenor, Tide, Tonnish

**Trepidation** Butterflies

**Trespass(er), Trespassing** Aggravated, Encroach, Errant, Hack, Impinge, Infringe, Offend, Peccancy, Sin, Trench, Wrong(doer)

**Tress(es)** Curl, Lock, Ringlet, Switch, Tallent

**Trestle** Sawhorse

**Triad** Chord, Ternion, Three, Trey, Trimurti, Trinity

**Trial** Acid test, Adversity, Affliction, Appro, Approbation, Approval, Assize, Attempt, Bane, Bernoulli, Bout, Burden, Case, Clinical, Compurgation, Corsned, Court-martial, Cow, Cross, Dock, Drumhead, Dry run, Dummy run, Empirical, Essay, →**EXPERIMENT**, Field, Fitting, Go, Hearing, Jeddart justice, Jethart justice, Lydford law, Nuremberg, Ordeal, Pest, Pilot, Pree, Probation, Proof, Race, Rehearsal, Rigour, Salem, Scramble, Sheepdog, Show, State, Taste, Test, Test bed, Time

**Triangle(d), Triangular** Acute, Bermuda, Circular, Cosec, Deltoid, Equilateral, Eternal, Frame, Gair, Golden, Gore, Gyronny, Isosceles, Obtuse, Pascal's, Pedimental, Pendentive, Pyramid, Rack, Right-angled, Scalene, Similar, Spherical, Trigon, Triquetral, Tromino, Warning

**Trias(sic)** Bunter, Keuper, Muschelkalk, Rhaetic

**Tribe(s), Tribal, Tribesman** Amalekite, Ammonites, Angle, Ashanti, Asher, Benjamin, Celt, Cherokee, Cimmerii, Clan(nish), Cree, Creek, Crow, Dan, Dinka, D(a)yak, Dynasty, Edomites, Ephraim, Family, Gad, Gens, Gentes, Gentilic, Gond, Goth, Guarani, Hapu, Helvetii, Hittite, Horde, Hottentot, Ibo, Iceni, Israelite, Issachar, Iwi, Jat, Judah, Kaffir, Kenite, Kurd, Lashkar, Levi, Levite, Longobardi, Lost, Manasseh, Masai, Moabite, Mongol, Moro, Naga, Nair, Naphtali, Nation, Nayar, Nervii, Ngati, Ordovices, Ostrogoths, Pathan, Phyle, Picts, →RACE, Reuben, Riff, Rod, Sakai, Salian, Schedule, Senones, Senussi, Sept, Shawnee, Silures, Simeon, Strandloper, Tasaday, Teuton, Trinobantes, Ute, Vandals, Wolof, Wyandot(te), X(h)osa, Zebulun

**Tribune, Tribunal** Aeropagus, Bema, Bench, →COURT, Divan, Employment, Forum, Hague, Industrial, Leader, Platform, Rienzi, Rota, Star-chamber, Waitangi

**Tributary** Affluent, Bogan, Branch, Confluent, Creek, Fork

**Tribute** Cain, Capelline, Citation, Commemoration, Compliment, Crants, Danegeld, Dedication, Deodate, →DUE, Encomium, Epitaph, Festschrift, Floral, Gavel, Heriot, Homage, Kain, Memento, Ode, Panegyric, Peter's pence, →PRAISE, Rome-penny, Rome-scot, Scat(t), Tax, Testimonial, Toast, Toll, Wreath, Wroth

**Trice** Flash, Instant, Wink

**Trichosanthin** Q

**Trick(ed), Trickery, Tricks(ter), Tricky** Antic, Art, Artifice, Attrap, Awkward, Bamboozle, Begunk, Book, Bunco, Bunko, Cantrip, Capot, Catch, Charley pitcher, Cheat, Chicane(ry), Chouse, Claptrap, Cod(-act), Cog, Con(fidence), Coyote, Crook, Davenport, Deceit, Deception, Deck, Decoy, Deke, Delicate, Delude, Device, Dirty, →DO, →DODGE, Double, Dupe, Elf, Elfin, Elvan, Elven, Entrap, Fard, Feat, Fetch, Fiddle, Finesse, Finicky, Flam, Flim-flam, Fob, Fox, Fraud, Fun, Gambit, Game, Gammon, Gaud, Get, Gimmick, Gleek, Glike, Gowk, Guile, Had, Hanky-panky, Hey presto, Hoax, Hocus(-pocus), Hoodwink, Hornswoggle, Hot potato, Hum, Illude, Illusion, Illywhacker, Imposture, Jadery, Jape, Jockey, John, Kittle, Knack, Lark, Legerdemain, Leg pull, Magsman, Mislead, Monkey, Monkey-shine, Murphy's game, Nap, Nasruddin, Palter, Parlour, Pass, Pawk, Phish, Pleasantry, Pliskie, Prank, Prestige, Put-on, Quick, Ramp, Raven, Reak, Reik, Rex, Rig, Rope, Ropery, Roughie, Ruse, Scam, Sell, Set-up, Shanghai, Shavie, Shenanigan, Shifty, Shill, Skin-game, Skite, Skul(l)duggery, Skylark, Skyte, Slam, Sleight, Slight, Slinter, Sophism, Spoof, Stall, Stealth, Stint, Stunt, Subterfuge, Sug, Swiftie, Take in, Thimble-rig, Three-card, Ticklish, Tip, Trait, Trap, Tregetour, Trump, Turn, Tweedler, Undercraft, Underplot, Vole, Wangle, Wheeze, Wile, Wrinkle

▷ **Trick** *may indicate an anagram*

**Trickle** Drib(ble), Driblet, Drip, Dropple, Gutter, Leak, Ooze, Rill, Seep

**Trickless** Misère

**Triclinic** Anorthic

**Tricycle** Pedicab

**Trident** Fork, Plane, Trisul(a)

**Trifle(s), Trifling** Bagatelle, Banal, Baubee, Bauble, Bibelot, Birdseed, Bit, Bric-a-brac, Bubkes, Cent, Chickenfeed, Coquette, Dabble, Dalliance, →DALLY, Denier, Desipient, Dessert, Dilly-dally, Do, Doit, Faddle, Falderal, Falderol, Fallal, Fattrell, Feather, Fewtril, Fiddle, Fiddle-faddle, Fig, Fingle-fangle, Fizgig, Flamfew, Fleabite, Flirt, Folderol, Fool, Footle, Fribble, Frippery, Fritter, Frivol, Gewgaw, Idle, Inconsequential, Insignificant, Iota, Kickshaw, Knick-knack, Luck-penny, Mess, Mite, Nick-nacket, Niff-naff, Nothing, Nugae, Nugatory, Nyaff, Old song, Palter, Paltry, Peanuts, Peddle, Peppercorn, Petty, Philander, Picayune, Piddle, Piffle, Pin, Pingle, Pittance, Play, Potty, Quelquechose, Quiddity, Quiddle, Sherry, Slight, Small beer, Small wares, Smatter, Song, Sport, Stiver, Strae, Straw, Sundry, Sweet Fanny Adams, Tiddle, Tom, Toy, Trinket, Trivia, Whifflery, Whim-wham, Whit

**Trig(onometry)** Neat, Sech, Spherical, Tosh, Trim

**Trigger** Activate, Detent, Hair, Instigate, Krytron, Pawl, Precipitate, Schmitt, Set off, Spark, Start, Switch on, Touch off, Tripwire

**Trill(ed), Triller, Trilling** Burr, Churr, Hirrient, Quaver, Ribattuta, Roll, Staphyle, Trim, Twitter, Warble

**Trilobite** Olenellus, Olenus, Paradoxide

**Trim(med), Trimmer, Trimming** Abridge, Adorn, Adornment, Ballast, Barb, Bleed, Braid, Bray, Chipper, Clip, Dapper, Defat, Dinky, Dress, Ermine, Face, Falbala, Fettle, File, Froufrou, Garni, Garnish, Garniture, Gimp, Guimpe, Hog, Macramé, Macrami, Marabou, Neat, Net(t), Order, Ornament, Pare, Passament, Passement(erie), Pipe, Plight, Posh, Preen, Proign, Proyn(e), Pruin(e), Prune, Roach, Robin, Ruche, Sax, Sett, Shear, Shipshape, Smirk, Smug, Sned, Snod, Soutache, → **SPRUCE**, Straddle, Stroddle, Strodle, Stylist, Svelte, Tiddley, → **TIDY**, Time-server, Top, Torsade, Trick, Whippersnipper, Wig

**Trinidadian** Carib

**Trinity, Trinitarian** Mathurin(e), Prosopon, Triad, Trimurti, Triune, Word

**Trinket(s)** Bauble, Bibelot, Bijou(terie), Charm, Falderal, Fallal, Folderol, Knickknack, Nicknack, Toy, Trankum, Trumpery

**Trio** Catch, Graces, Magi, Randan, Randem, Skat, Terzetto, Threesome

**Trip(per)** Awayday, Cook's tour, Cruise, Dance, Day, Druggie, Ecotour, Ego, Emmet, Errand, Expedition, → **FALL**, Field, Flight, Flip, Guilt, Head, High, Hop, Joint, Jolly, Journey, Junket, Kilt, Lap, Link, Outing, Passage, Pleasure, Ply, Power, Ride, Round, Run, Sail, Sashay, Spin, Spurn, → **STUMBLE**, Tootle, Tour, Trek, Trial, Voyage

▷ **Trip** *may indicate* an anagram

**Tripe** Abracadabra, Bosh, Bull, Caen, Claptrap, Entrails, Honeycomb, Offal, Plain, Rot

**Triple, Triplet** Codon, Hemiol(i)a, Perfect, Sdrucciola, Ternal, Tiercet, Treble, Trifecta, Trilling, Trin(e), Tripling

**Tripod** Cat, Cortina, Highhat, Oracle, Triangle, Trippet, Trivet

**Triptych** Volet

**Trishaw** Cycle

**Trite** Banal, Boilerplate, Cornball, Corny, Hackneyed, Hoary, Laughable, Mickey Mouse, Novelettish, Pabulum, Platitude, Rinky-dink, Stale, Stock, Time-worn, Truism, Worn

**Triton** Eft, Evet, Ewt, Newt, Trumpet-shell

**Triumph(ant)** Cock-a-hoop, Codille, Cowabunga, Crow, Eureka, Exult, Glory, Impostor, Jubilant, Killing, Oho, Olé, Ovation, Palm, Prevail, Victorious, → **WIN**

**Triumvir** Caesar, Crassus, Pompey

**Trivet** Brandise, Tripod, Trippet

**Trivia(l), Triviality** Adiaphoron, Bagatelle, Balaam, Bald, → **BANAL**, Bathos, Footling, Frippery, Frothy, Futile, Idle, Inconsequential, Light, Minutiae, Nitpicking, No-brainer, Nonentity, Nothingism, Paltry, Pap, Peppercorn, Pettifoggery, Petty, Picayune, Piddling, Piffling, Puerile, Shallow, Small, Small beer, Small fry, Snippety, Squirt, Squit, Toy(s), Twaddle, Vegie

**Trixie** Bea

**Trochee** Choree

**Troglodyte** Ape, Caveman, Hermit, Spelean, Wren

**Trojan** Aeneas, Agamemnon, Dardan(ian), Iliac, Paris, Priam, Teucrian, Troic

**Troll** → **FISH**, Gnome, Rove, Spoon, Trawl, Warble

**Trolley** Brute, Cart, Crane, Dinner-wagon, Dolly, Gurney, Hostess, Shopping, Tea, Teacart, Traymobile, Truck, Trundler

▶ **Trollop** *see* **LOOSE(N)**

**Trombone** Bass, Posaune, Sackbut, Tenor

**Trompe l'oeil** Quadratura, Quadrature

**Troop(s), Trooper** Alpini, Anzac, Band, BEF, Brigade, Cohort, Company, Depot, Detachment, Garrison, Guard, Horde, Household, Logistics, Midianite, Milice, Militia, Monkeys, Pultan, Pulton, Pultoon, Pultun, SAS, School, Scout, Shock, → **SOLDIER**, Sowar, State, Storm, Subsidiary, Tp, Turm(e), Velites

**Troopship** Transport

**Trope** Euouae, Evovae

**Trophy** Adward, Ashes, →**AWARD**, Bag, Belt, Brush, Cup, Emmy, Jackpot, Memento, Palm, Plate, →**PRIZE**, Scalp, Schneider, Shield, Silverware, Spoils, Tourist, Triple crown, TT

**Tropic(al)** Cancer, Capricorn, Derris, Jungle, Neogaea, Sultry

**Trot(ter), Trot out** Air, Clip, Crib, Crubeen, Hag, Job, Jog, Passage, Pettitoes, Piaffe, Pony, Ranke, Red(-shirt), Rising, Tootsie, Trotskyist

**Troth** Perfay, Troggs

**Trotsky(ist)** Entr(y)ism, Leon, Militant Tendency

**Troubador** Blondel, Griot, Manrico, Minstrel, Singer, Sordello

**Trouble(s), Troublemaker, Troublesome** Ache, Ado, Affliction, Aggrieve, Aggro, Agitate, Ail, Alarm, Annoy, Assail, Bale, Barrat, Bedevil, Beset, →**BOTHER**, Bovver, Brickle, Burden, Care, Coil, Concern, Debate, Disaster, Dismay, Disquiet, Distress, Disturb, Dog, Dolour, Eat, Esclandre, Exercise, Fash, Fashious, Finger, Firebrand, Fossick, Fret, Frondeur, Fun and games, Fuss, Gram(e), Grief, Hag-ride, Harass, Harry, Hassle, Hatter, Heat, Heist, Hellion, Hot potato, Hot water, Howdyedo, Hydra, Incommode, Inconvenience, Infest, →**IN TROUBLE**, Irk, Jam, Kaugh, Kiaugh, Malcontent, Mayhem, Mess, Mixer, Moil, Molest, Noy, Onerous, Perturb, Pester, Pestiferous, Picnic, Plague, Play up, Poke, Reck, Rioter, Rub, Ruffle, Scamp, Scrape, Shake, Shtook, Shtuck, Soup, Spiny, Stir, Stirrer, Storm, Sturt, Tartar, Teen, Teething, Thorny, Tine, Toil, Trial, Tsouris, Tsuris, Turn-up, Tyne, Typhoid Mary, Unpleasant, Unrest, Unsettle, Upsetter, Varmint, Vex, →**WORRY**

**Trouble-free** Gallio

**Trouble-shooter** Ombudsman

▷ **Troublesome** *may indicate* an anagram

**Trough** Back, Backet, Bed, Buddle, Channel, Chute, Culvert, Graben, Gutter, Hod, Hutch, Langmuir, Launder, Leachtub, Manger, Pneumatic, Puerto Rico, Stock, Straik, Strake, Syncline, Troffer, Tundish, Tye, Vale, Watering

**Trounce** →**BEAT**, Hammer, Thrash, Thump

**Trouser(s)** Bags, Bell-bottoms, Bloomers, Breeches, Bumsters, Capri pants, Cargo pants, Chinos, Churidars, Clam-diggers, Combat, Continuations, Cords, Corduroys, Cossacks, Culottes, Cut-offs, Daks, Denims, Drainpipe, Drawers, Ducks, Dungarees, Eel-skins, Flannels, Flares, Galligaskins, Gaskins, Gauchos, Hip-huggers, Hipsters, Indescribables, Inexpressibles, Innominables, Jazzpants, Jeans, Jeggings, Jodhpurs, Jog-pants, Kaccha, Ke(c)ks, Knee cords, Lederhosen, Levis, Longs, Loon-pants, Loons, Moleskins, Overalls, Oxford bags, Palazzo (pants), Palazzos, Pantalet(te)s, Pantaloons, Pants, Pedal pushers, Pegtops, Plus-fours, Plus-twos, Pyjamas, Rammies, Reach-me-downs, Salopettes, Shalwar, Ski pants, Slacks, Stirrup pants, Stovepipes, Strides, Strossers, Sweatpants, Thornproofs, Trews, Trouse, Trunk-breeches, Unmentionables, Unutterables, Utterless

**Trout** Aurora, Brook, Brown, Bull, Char(r), Coral, Cutthroat, Finnac(k), Finnock, Fish, Gillaroo, Hag(fish), Herling, Hirling, Kamloops, Peal, Peel, Phinnock, Pogies, Quintet, Rainbow, Salmon, Sewen, Sewin, Speckled, Splake, Steelhead, Togue, Whitling

**Trow** Faith, Meseems

**Trowel** Float, Slicker

**Troy** Ilium, Laomedon, Sergeant, T, Weight

**Truant** Absentee, AWOL, Bunk off, Dodge, Hooky, Idler, Kip, Mich(e), Mitch, Mooch, Mouch, Skive, Wag

**Truce** Armistice, Barley, Ceasefire, Fainites, Fains, Hudna, Interlude, Keys, Pax, Stillstand, Treague, Treaty

**Truck** Bakkie, Bogie, Breakdown, Business, Cabover, Cattle, Cocopan, Dealings, Dolly, Dray, Dumper, Flatbed, Forklift, Haul, Hopper, Journey, →**LORRY**, Low-loader, Monster, Pallet, Panel, Pick-up, Road-train, Semi, Sound, Stacking, Tipper, Tommy, Tow(ie), Traffic, Tram, Trolley, Trundle, Ute, Utility, Van, Wrecker

**Truckdriver** Teamster

**Trudge** Footslog, Jog, Lumber, Pad, Plod, Stodge, Stramp, Taigle, Traipse, Trash, Trauchle, Trog, Vamp

**True** Accurate, Actual, Apodictic, Axiomatic, Candid, Constant, Correct, Exact, Factual, Faithful, Genuine, Honest, Indubitable, Leal, Literal, Loyal, Platitude, Plumb, Pure, Real, Realistic, Richt, Right, Sooth, Vera, Very

**Truffle** Tartuffe, Tuber, Tuberaceae

**Trug** Basket, Wisket

**Truly** Certainly, Certes, Fegs, Forsooth, Honestly, Indeed, Insooth, Surely, Verily, Yea

**Trump(s), Trumpet(er)** Agami, Alchemy, Alchymy, Armstrong, Bach, Bass, Blare, Blast, Bray, Buccina, Bugle(r), Call, Card, Clang, Clarion, Conch, Cornet, Corona, Crossruff, Crow, Daffodil, Ear, Elephant, Extol, Fanfare, Hallali, Honours, →**HORN**, Invent, Jew's, Last, Lituus, Long ten, Lur(e), Lurist, Manille, Marine, Megaphone, →**NO TRUMP**, Overruff, Pedro, Proclaim, Ram's-horn, Rant, Resurrect, Rogue, Ruff, Salpingian, Salpinx, Sancho, Satchmo, Sennet, Shell, Shofar, Shophar, Slug-horn, Speaking, Splash, Surpass, Swan, Tantara, Tantarara, Tar(at)antara, Theodomas, Tiddy, Triton, Triumph

**Trumpery** Fattrels, Jimcrack, Paltry, Trashy

**Truncate(d)** Abrupt, Cut, Dock, Shorten, Snub

**Truncheon** Billie, Billy, Blackjack, Cosh, Night-stick, Warder

**Trundle** Hump, Roll, Trill, Troll, Wheel

**Trunk(s)** Aorta(l), A-road, Body, Bole, Box, Bulk, Bus, But(t), Caber, Cabin, Carcase, Chest, Coffer, Hose, Imperial, Log, Nerve, Peduncle, Pollard, Portmanteau, Portmantle, Proboscis, Puncheon, Ricker, Road, Saratoga, Shorts, STD, Steamer, Stock, Stud, Suitcase, Synangium, Togs, Torso, Valise, Wardrobe

**Truss** →**BIND**, Ligate, Oop, Oup, Sheaf, Tie, Upbind

**Trust(y), Trusting, Trustworthy** Active, Affy, Apex, Authentic, Belief, Bet on, Blind, Box, Camaraderie, Care, Carnegie, Cartel, Charge, Charitable, Combine, Confide, Count on, Credit, Dependable, Dewy-eyed, Discretionary, Escrow, →**FAITH**, Fidelity, Fiduciary, Foundation, Gullible, Honest, Hope, Hospital, Investment, Leal, Lippen, Loyal, Naif, National, NT, Reliable, Reliance, Rely, Repose, Reputable, Responsible, Sound, Special, Split, Staunch, Tick, Trojan, Trow, True, Trump, Unit

**Trustee** Agent, Executor, Fiduciary, Judicial, Pensioner, Public, Tr

**Truth(ful), Truism** Accuracy, Alethic, Axiom, Bromide, Cliché, Cold turkey, Dharma, Dialectic, →**FACT**, Facticity, Forsooth, Gospel, Griff, Home, Honesty, Idea(l), Logical, Maxim, Naked, Necessary, Pravda, Principle, Reality, Sooth, Soothfast, Strength, Troggs, Veracity, Veridical, Verisimilitude, Verity, Vraisemblance

**Try(ing)** After, Aim, Approof, Arraign, Assay, Attempt, Audition, Bash, Bate, Bid, Birl, Burden, Burl, Conative, Contend, Court martial, Crack, Effort, Empiric(utic), →**ENDEAVOUR**, Essay, Examine, Experiment, Fand, Fish, Fling, Foretaste, Go, Gun for, Harass, Hard, Hear, Impeach, Importunate, Irk, Noy, Offer, Ordalium, Ordeal, Penalty, Pesky, Pop, Practise, Pree, Prieve, Prove, Push-over, →**SAMPLE**, Seek, Shot, Sip, Stab, Strain, Strive, Struggle, Tackle, Taste, Tax, Tempt, Test, Touchdown, →**TRIAL**, Whirl

**Tryst** Date, Rendezvous

**Tsar(ist)** Alexis, Boris, Drug, Emperor, Godunov, Ivan the Terrible, Octobrist, Peter the Great, Romanov, Ruler, Tyrant

**TT** Dry, Race, Rechabite, Soberside

**Tub(by), Tubbiness, Tubman, Tub-thumper** Ash-leach, Back, Bath, Boanerges, Bran, Bucket, Cooper, Corf, Cowl, Dan, Demagogue, Diogenes, Dolly, Endomorph, Firkin, Hip bath, Keeve, Kid, Kieve, Kit, Luckydip, Mashing, Meat, Pin, Podge, Pot-bellied, Powdering, Pudge, Pulpit, Rolypoly, Seasoning, Stand, Swill, Tun, Twin, Vat, Wash, Whey

**Tuba** Bombardon, Euphonium, Helicon

**Tube, Tubing, Tubular** Acorn, Arteriole, Artery, Barrel, Blowpipe, Bronchus, Buckyball, Buckytube, Burette, Calamus, Camera, Canaliculus, Can(n)ula, Capillary,

Casing, Catheter, Cathode-ray, Cave, Conduit, Crookes, Digitron, Diode, Discharge, Drain, Draw, Drift, Dropper, Duct, Electron, Endiometer, Epididymis, Eustachian, Extension, Fallopian, Fistula, Flash, Fluorescent, Fulgurite, Geissler, Germ, Glowstick, Grommet, Hawsepipe, Hose, Iconoscope, Idiot box, Image (orthicon), Inner, Kinescope, Klystron, Macaroni, Malpighian, Matrass, Metro, Morris, Nasogastric, Neural, Nixie, Optic, Orthicon, Oval, Oviduct, Pastille, Peashooter, Pentode, Picture, → **PIPE**, Pipette, Piping, Pitot(-static), Pneumatic, Pollen, Postal, Promethean, Salpinx, Saticon®, Saucisse, Saucisson, Schnorkel, Shadow-mask, Shock, Sieve, Siphon(al), Siphonet, Siphonostele, Siphuncle, Skelp, Skiatron, Sleeve, Slide, Snorkel, Spaghetti, Speaking, Spout, Staple, Static, Stem, Stent, Stone canal, Storage, Strae, Straw, Strip light, Strobotron, Subway, Sucker, Swallet, Syringe, Tele, Telescope, Teletron, Television, Telly, Terete, Test, Tetrode, Thermionic, Thyratron, Tile, Torpedo, Torricellian, Trachea, Travelling-wave, Triniscope, Trocar, Trochotron, Trunk, Tunnel, Tuppenny, TV, U, Underground, Ureter, Urethra, Vacuum, Vas, VDU, Vein, Vena, Venturi, Video, Vidicon®, Worm, X-ray

**Tuber(s)** Arnut, Arracacha, Bulb, Chufa, Coc(c)o, Dahlia, Dasheen, Earth-nut, Eddoes, Ginseng, Jicama, Mashua, Oca, Pignut, Potato, Root, Salep, Taproot, Taro, Tater, Tuckahoe, Yam, Yautia

**Tuberculosis** Consumption, Crewels, Cruel(l)s, Decline, King's evil, Lupus, Lupus vulgaris, Phthisis, Scrofula, White plague

**Tuck** Dart, Friar, Gather, Grub, Hospital corner, Kilt, Pin, Pleat, Scran, Truss, Tummy

**Tudor** Stockbrokers'

**Tuesday** Hock, Pancake, Shrove, Super

**Tuff** Schalstein

**Tuft(ed)** Aigrette, Amentum, Beard, Candlewick, Catkin, C(a)espitose, Cluster, Coma, Comb, Cowlick, Crest, Dollop, Ear, Flaught, Floccus, Flock, Goatee, Hank, Hassock, Knop, Knot, Lock, Pappus, Penicillate, Pledget, Quiff, Scopate, Shola, Tait, Tassel, Tate, Toorie, Topknot, Toupee, Tourie, Tussock, Tuzz, Whisk

**Tug** Chain, Drag, Haul, Hoick, Jerk, Lug, Pug, → **PULL**, Rive, Rug, Saccade, Ship, Sole, Soole, Sowl(e), Tit, Tow, Towboat, Yank

**Tui** Poebird

**Tuition** Grind, Masterclass, Seminal, Sleep-learning

**Tully** Cicero

**Tumble, Tumbler** Acrobat, Cartwheel, Drier, Fall, → **GLASS**, Header, Jack, Jill, Lock, Pitch, Popple, Purl, Realise, Roller-coaster, Spill, Stumble, Tailer, Topple, Touser, Towser, Trip, Twig, Voltigeur, Welter

▷ **Tumble** *may indicate* an anagram

**Tumbledown** Decrepit, Dilapidated, Ramshackle, Rickle, Ruinous

**Tumbril** Caisson

**Tummy** Belly, Colon, Mary, Paunch, Pod

**Tummy-ache** Colic, Gripe, Tormina

**Tumour** Adenoma, Anbury, Angioma, Angiosarcoma, Astroblastoma, Astrocytoma, Burkitt('s) lymphoma, Cancer, Carcinoid, Carcinoma, Carcinosarcoma, Chondroma, Condyloma, Crab(-yaws), Craniopharyngioma, Dermoid, Encanthis, Encephaloma, Enchondroma, Endothelioma, Epulis, Exostosis, Fibroid, Fibroma, Ganglion, Germinoma, Gioblastoma, Glioma, Granuloma, Grape, → **GROWTH**, Gumma, Haemangioma, Haematoma, Hepatoma, Lipoma, Lymphoma, Medulloblastoma, Melanoma, Meningioma, Mesothelioma, Metastasis, Mole, Myeloma, Myoma, Myxoma, Neoplasm, Nephroblastoma, Neuroblastoma, Neurofibroma, Neuroma, Odontoma, -oma, Oncogenesis, Oncology, Osteoclastoma, Osteoma, Osteosarcoma, Papilloma, Polypus, Retinoblastoma, Rhabdomyoma, Rous sarcoma, Sarcoma, Scirrhous, Secondary, Seminoma, Steatoma, Struma, Syphiloma, Talpa, Teratocarcinoma, Teratoma, Thymoma, Wart, Warthin's, Wen, Wilms', Windgall, Wolf, Xanthoma, Yaw

**Tumult, Tumultuous** Brattle, Brawl, Coil, Deray, Ferment, Fracas, Hirdy-girdy, Hubbub, Hurly-burly, Reird, Riot, →ROAR, Romage, Rore, Stoor, Stour, Stowre, Stramash, Tew, Tristan, Tristram, Turbulent, →UPROAR

**Tumulus** Barrow, How(e), Mote, Motte

**Tun** Cask, Keg

**Tuna** Ahi, Eel, Pear, Skipjack, Yellowfin

**Tundra** Barren Grounds, Barren Lands

**Tune(s), Tuneful, Tuner, Tuning** Adjust, Air, Aria, Ayre, Canorous, Carillon, Catch, Choral(e), Dial, Dump, Earworm, Étude, Fine, Fork, Gingle, Harmony, Hornpipe, Hunt's up, Jingle, Key, Maggot, Measure, Melisma, →MELODY, Morrice, Morris, Old Hundred, →OUT OF TUNE, Peg, Planxty, Port, Potpourri, Raga, Rant, Ranz-des-vaches, Reel, Scordatura, Signature, Snatch, Song, Spring, Strain, Sweet, Syntonise, Syntony, Temper, Temperament, Theme, Tone, Toy, Tweak

**Tungstate, Tungsten** Scheelite, W, Wolfram

**Tunic** Ao dai, Caftan, Chiton, Choroid, Cote-hardie, Dalmatic, Dashiki, Gymslip, Hauberk, Kabaya, Kaftan, Kameez, K(h)urta, Salwar kameez, →SINGLET, Surcoat, Tabard, Toga

**Tunicate** Pyrosoma, Salpa

**Tunnel(ler)** Blackwall, Bore, Channel, Chunnel, Condie, Countermine, Culvert, Cundy, Earthworm, Euro, Gallery, Head, Mine, Mole, Qanat, Rotherhithe, Sewer, Simplon, Smoke, Stope, Subway, Sure, Syrinx, Transmanche, Tube, Underpass, Warren, Water, Wind, Wormhole

**Tunny** Bonito, Tuna

**Turban** Bandanna, Hat, Mitral, Pagri, Puggaree, Puggery, Puggree, Sash, Scarf, Toque, Tulipant

**Turbid** Cloudy, Dense, Drumly, Roily

**Turbine** Francis, Gas, Impulse, Ram air, Reaction, Steam, Water, Wind

**Turbulence, Turbulent** Atmospheric, Becket, Bellicose, Buller, Factious, Fierce, Overfall, Rapids, Roil, Stormy, Unruly

▷ **Turbulent, Turbulence** *may indicate* an anagram

**Tureen** Terreen

**Turf** Caespitose, Clod, Divot, Earth, Fail, Feal, Flaught, Gazo(o)n, →GRASS, Greensward, Kerf, Peat, Racing, Scraw, →SOD, Sward, Territory

**Turk(ish)** Anatolian, Bashaw, Bashkir, Bey, Bimbashi, Bostangi, Byzantine, Caimac(am), Crescent, Effendi, Golden Horde, Grand, Gregory, Horse(tail), Irade, Kaimakam, Kazak(h), Kurd, Mameluke, Mutessarif(at), Omar, Osman(li), Ottamite, Ottoman, Ottomite, Rayah, Scanderbeg, Selim, Seljuk(ian), Seraskier, Spahi, Tartar, Tatar, Timariot, Usak, Uzbeg, Uzbek, Yakut, Young

**Turkey, Turkey-like** Anatolia, Antioch, Brush, Bubbly(-jock), Cold, Curassow, Dud, Eyalet, Flop, Gobbler, Lame brain, Lemon, Norfolk, Plain, Scrub, Sultanate, Talegalla, Talk, TR, Trabzon, Vulturn

**Turkish delight** Rahat lacoum, Trehala

**Turmeric** Curcumin(e)

**Turmoil** Ariot, Chaos, Confusion, Din, Disruption, Dust, Ferment, Maelstrom, Mess, Pother, Pudder, Stoor, Stour, Tornado, Tracasserie, Tumult, Unrest, →UPROAR, Welter

**Turn(ing), Turn(ed) away, Turn(ed) up, Turns** Acescent, Act, Adapt, Addle, Advert, Antrorse, Apostrophe, Apotropaic, Avert, Bad, Bank, Become, Bend, Blow in, Buggins, Bump, Canceleer, Cancelier, Caracol(e), Careen, Cartwheel, Cast, Chainé, Chandelle, Change, Char(e), Chore, Christiania, Christie, Christy, Churn, Coarsen, Cock, Coil, Convert, Corotate, Crank(le), Cuff, Curd(le), Curve, Defect, Deflect, Demi-volt(e), Detour, Deviate, Dig, Digress, Divert, Ear, Earn, Elbow, Evert, Evict, Fadge, Ferment, Flip, Forfend, Go, Good, Gruppetto, Gyrate, Hairpin, Handbrake, Head-off, Hie, High, Hinge, Hup, Immelmann, Influence, Innings, Intussuscept, Invert, Jar, Jink, Jump, Keel, Kick, Laeotropic, Lodging, Lot, Luff, Mohawk, Move, Nip, Number, Obvert, Parallel,

Parry, Penchant, Pivot, Plough, Pronate, Prove, PTO, Quarter, Quersprung, Rebut, Refer, Refract, Remuage, Retroflex, Retroussé, Retrovert, Rev, Revolt, Ride, Riffle, Rocker, Roll, Root, →**ROTATE**, Rote, Roulade, Rout, Routine, Screw, Secund, Sheer, →**SHOT**, Shout, Sicken, Skit, Slew, Slue, Solstice, Sour, →**SPELL**, Spin, Spot, Sprain, Star, Start, Stem, Step, Stunt, Swash, Swerve, Swing, Switch, Swivel, Telemark, Thigmotropism, Three-point, Throw, Tiptilt, Tirl, T-junction, Torque, Transpose, Trend, Trick, Trie, Trochilic, Turtle, Twiddle, Twist, Twizzle, U, Uey, U-ie, Up, Veer, Versed, Version, Vertigo, Volta, Volte-face, Volutation, Wap, Warp, Wedeln, Wend, Went, →**WHEEL**, Whelm, Whirl, Whorl, Wimple, Wind, Wrast, Wrest, Wriggle, Zigzag

▷ **Turn(ing)** *may indicate* an anagram

**Turn-coat** Apostate, Cato, Defector, Quisling, Rat, Renegade, Rottan, Tergiversate, Traitor

**Turner** Axle, Capstan, Crank, Lana, Lathe, Page, Painter, Pivot, Remueur, Rose-engine, Spanner, Tina, Worm, Wrench

**Turning point** Crisis, Crossroads, Landmark, Solstice, Watershed

**Turnip(-shaped)** Baggy, Bagie, Hunter, Indian, Jicama, Napiform, Navew, Neep, Prairie, Rutabaga, Shaw, →**STUPID PERSON**, Swede, Tumshie

▷ **Turnip** *may indicate* a watch

**Turnkey** Gaoler, Jailer, Locksman

**Turn on** Boot

**Turn-out, Turn out** Eventuate, Evict, Gathering, Product, Rig, Splay, Style, Team, Transpire, Wear

**Turn over, Turnover** Bridie, Capsize, Careen, Flip, Inversion, Mull, Production, PTO, Samosa, Somersault, TO, Up-end

**Turnpike** Highway, Toll

**Turnstile** Tourniquet

**Turntable** Racer, Rota, Rotator, Round-house

**Turpentine** Galipot, Rosin, Thinner, Turps, Venice

**Turquoise** Bone, Fossil, Ligure, Occidental, Odontolite, Oriental, Turkey stone

**Turret(ed)** Barmkin, Bartisan, Belvedere, Garret, Gazebo, Louver, Louvre, Mirador, Pepperbox, Sponson, Tank top, →**TOWER**, Turriculate

**Turtle, Turtle head** Bale, Box, Calipash, Calipee, Chelone, Cooter, Diamondback, Emys, Floor, Green, Hawk(s)bill, Inverted, Leatherback, Loggerhead, Matamata, Mossback, Mud, Musk, Painted, Ridley, Screen, Snapper, Snapping, Soft-shelled, Stinkpot, Terrapin, Thalassian

**Tuscany** Chiantishire

**Tusk** Gam, Horn, Ivory, Tooth, Tush

**Tusker** Dicynodont, Elephant, Mastodon

**Tussle** Giust, Joust, Mêlée, Scrimmage, Scrum, Scuffle, Skirmish, Touse, Touze, Towse, Towze, Tuilyie, Wrestle

**Tussock** Hassock, Niggerhead, Tuft

**Tut(-tut)** Mummy, Och, Pooh

**Tutelary** Guardian, Protector

**Tutor** Abbé, Aristotle, Ascham, Bear, →**COACH**, Crammer, Don, Edify, Instruct, Leader, Mentor, Preceptor, Répétiteur, Starets, Staretz, Supervisor, Teacher, Train

**Tuxedo** DJ

**TV** Baird, Box, Breakfast, Cable, Closed circuit, Digibox®, Digital, Docudrama, Docusoap, Flat screen, Idiot-box, Lime Grove, Mini-series, Monitor, NICAM, PAL, Pay, Reality, SECAM, Sitcom, Sky, Tele, →**TELEVISION**, Telly, Tie-in, Triniscope, Tube, Video

**Twaddle** Blether, Drivel, Fadaise, Rot, Slipslop, Tripe

**Twang** Nasal, Pluck, Plunk, Rhinolalia

**Tweak** Pinch, Pluck, Primp, Twiddle, Twist, Twitch

**Twee** Chocolate box

**Tweed(y)** Donegal, Harris®, Homespun, Lovat, Raploch

**Tweet** Cherup, Chirrup

**Twelfth, Twelve** Apostles, Dozen, Epiphany, Glorious, Grouse, Midday, Midnight, N, Night, Noon(tide), Ternion, Twal

**Twenty, Twenty-sided** Icosahedron, Score, Vicenary, Vicennial, Vicesimal, Vigesimal

**Twenty-five, Twentyfifth** Inner, Pony, Quartern, Semi-jubilee

**Twenty-four** Thr(e)ave

**Twerp** Pipsqueak

▶ **Twice** *see* TWO(SOME)

**Twice-yearly** Biennial, Equinox

**Twiddle** Fidget, Twirl

**Twig(s)** Besom, Birch, Brushwood, Cotton, Cow, Dig, Fathom, Grasp, Kow, Osier, Realise, Reis, Rice, Rod, Rumble, Sarment, See, Sprig, Stick, Sticklac, Switch, Understand, Walking, Wand, Wattle, Whip, Wicker, Withe

**Twilight** Astronomical, Civil, Cockshut, Crepuscular, Demi-jour, Dimpsy, Dusk, Gloam(ing), Götterdämmerung, Nautical, Ragnarok, Summerdim

**Twill** Cavalry, Chino, Serge

**Twin(s)** Asvins, Castor, Coetaneous, Conjoined, Couplet, Didymous, Dioscuri, Ditokous, Dizygotic, Double, Dual, Fraternal, Gemel, Geminate, Gemini, Hemitrope, Identical, Isogeny, Juxtaposition, Kindred, Kray, Look-alike, Macle, Monozygotic, Parabiotic, Pigeon-pair, Pollux, Remus, Romulus, Siamese, Thomas, Tweedledee, Tweedledum

**Twine** Binder, Braid, Coil, Cord, Inosculate, Packthread, Sisal, Snake, String, Twist, Wreathe

**Twinge** Pang, Scruple, Stab, Twang

**Twinkle, Twinkling** Glimmer, Glint, Mo(ment), → SPARKLE, Starnie, Trice

**Twirl** Spin, Swivel, Tirl, Tirlie-wirlie, Trill, Trundle, Twiddle, Twizzle, Whirl

▷ **Twirling** *may indicate* an anagram

**Twist(ed), Twister, Twisting, Twisty** Aglee, Agley, Anfractuous, Askant, Askew, Baccy, Becurl, Bought, Braid, Buckle, Card-sharper, Chisel, Coil, Contort, Convolution, Corkscrew, Crinkle, Crinkum-crankum, Crisp, Cue, Curl(icue), Curliewurlie, Cyclone, Deform, Detort, Diddle, Dishonest, Distort, → DODGE, Eddy, Embraid, Entrail, Entwine, Garrot, Helix, Imposture, Kink, Lemon peel, Loop, Mangulate, Mat, Meander, Misshapen, Möbius strip, Oliver, Pandanaceous, Plait, Quirk, Raddle, Ravel, Rick, Rogue, Rotate, Rove, Serpent, Skew, Slew, Slub(b), Slue, Snake, Snarl, Spin, Spiral, Sprain, Squiggle, Squirm, Strand, Swivel, Tendril, Thraw(n), Torc, Tornado, Torque, Torsade, Torsion, Torticollis, Tortile, Turn, Tweak, Twiddle, Twine, Twirl, Twizzle, Typhoon, Valgus, Volvulus, Wamble, Warp, Welkt, Wigwag, Wind, Wound-wrap, Wrast, Wreathe, Wrench, Wrest, Wrethe, Wrick, Wriggle, Wring, Writhe, Wry, Zigzag

▷ **Twisted, Twisting** *may indicate* an anagram

**Twit, Twitter** Airhead, Birdbrain, Chaff, Cheep, Cherup, Chirrup, Dotterel, Gear(e), Giber, → JEER, Rag, Stupid, Taunt, Tweet, Warble

**Twitch(ing), Twitchy** Athetosis, Birdwatch, Clonic, Fibrillation, Grass, Jerk, Life-blood, Saccadic, Sneer, Spasm, Start, Subsultive, Tic, Tig, Tippet, Tit, Toss, Tweak, Twinge, Vellicate, Yips

**Two(some), Twofold, Twice** Bice, Bis, Bisp, Both, Brace, Company, Couple(t), Deuce, Double, Duad, Dual, Duet, Duo, Duple, Dyad, Item, → PAIR, Snake-eyes, Swy, Tête-à-tête, Twain, Twins, Twister

**Two-edged** Ancipitous

**Two-faced** Dihedral, Dorsiventral, Hypocritical, Janus, Redan

**Two-gallon** Peck

**Two-headed** Amphisbaenic, Dicephalous, Orthos

**Two hundred** H

**Two hundred and fifty** E, K

**Two-master** Brig

**Two-piece** Bikini

**Two-pronged** Bidental
**Two-rayed** Diactinal
**Two-sided** Bilateral, Equivocatory
**Two thousand** Z
**Two-time** Cheat
**Two-tone** Shot, Trillo
**Two-up** Kip, Swy
**Two-wheeler** Bicycle, Scooter
**Tycoon** Baron, Empire-builder, Entrepreneur, Fat cat, Gates, Magnate, Mogul, Murdoch, Nabob, Onassis, Plutocrat, Shogun
**Tyke** Geit, RC
**Tympany** Castanets, Cymbal, Drum, Kitchen, Triangle, Xylophone
**Tyneside(r)** Geordie, George
**Type(s), Typify, Typing** A, Agate, Aldine, Antimony, Antique, B, Balaam, Baskerville, Bastard, Batter, Beard, Bembo, Black-letter, Block, Blood, Bodoni, Body, Bold face, Bold Roman, Bourgeois, Braille, Brand, Brevier, Brilliant, Canon, Caslon, Category, Character, Chase, Cicero, Clarendon, Class, Columbian, Condensed, Cut, Egyptian, Elite, Elzevir, Em, Emblem, Emerald, En(nage), English, Epitomise, Exemplar, Face, Font, Footer, Form(e), Founder's, Fount, Fraktur, Fudge, Garamond, Gem, Genre, Gent, Gothic, Great primer, Gutenberg, Hair, Hot metal, Ilk, Image, Kern(e), Key, Keyboard, Kidney, Kind, Late-star, Ligature, Light-faced, Logotype, Longprimer, Ludlow, Make, Mating, Melanochroi, Minion, Modern, Monospaced, Moon, Mould, Mullioned, Non-pareil, Norm, Old English, Old-face, Old Style, Paragon, Pattern, Pearl, Peculiar, Personality, Pi, Pica, Pie, Plantin, Point, Primer, Print, Quad(rat), Roman, Ronde, Ruby, Sanserif, Secretary, Semibold, Serif, Serological, Slug, →SORT, Sp, Species, Spectral, Stanhope, Style, Times, Times Roman, Tissue, Touch, Variety, Version
▷ **Type of** *may indicate* an anagram
**Typesetting** Hot metal
**Typewriter** Golfball, Portable, Stenograph, Stenotype®, Varityper®
**Typhoid, Typhus** Camp-fever, Murine, Putrid fever, Scrub, Tick-borne
**Typhoon** Cyclone, Hurricane, Monsoon, Tornado, Wind
**Typical** Average, Characteristic, Classic, Echt, Everyman, Natural, Normal, Representative, Standard, Symbolic, True-bred, Usual
**Typist** Audio, Copy, Printer, Steno(grapher), Temp
**Typo** Literal
**Tyrannise(d)** Domineer, Lord, Under
**Tyrant, Tyranny, Tyrannical** Absolutism, Autocrat, Caligula, Czar, Despot, Dictator, Dominion, Drawcansir, Gelon, Herod, Ivan the Terrible, Lordly, Nero, Oppressor, Pharaoh, Pisistratus, Sardanapalus, Satrap, Stalin, Totalitarian, Tsar, Yoke
**Tyre(s)** Balloon, Cross-ply, Cushion, Earthing, Flat, Michelin®, Pericles, Pneumatic, Radial(-ply), Recap, Remould, Retread, Shoe, Sidewall, Slick, Snow, Spare, Stepney, Toe in, Tread, Tubeless, Whitewall
**Tyro** Beginner, Ham, →NOVICE, Rabbit, Rookie, Rooky, Starter
**Tyrolese** R(h)aetian

# Uu

**U, U-type** Gent, Unicorn, Universal, Uranium
**U-bend** Airtrap, Drip trap
**Ubiquitous** Everywhere, Inescapable, Omnipresent, Wall-to-wall
**Udder** Bag, Dug
**UFO** Roswell
**Uganda(n)** Obote, .ug
**Ugly** Abhorrent, Butters, Cow, Crow, Customer, Disfigured, Eyesore, Faceache, Foul, Gorgon, Grotesque, Gruesome, Hideous, Homely, Huckery, Jolie laide, Loath, Loth, Mean, Monstrosity, Ominous, Plain, Sight, Unsightly
**Ugrian** Ostiak, Ostyak, Samo(y)ed, Vogul
**UK** GB
**Ukase** Decree
**Ukraine, Ukrainian** Russniak, Ruthene, UA
**Ulcer(ous)** Abscess, Aphtha, Bedsore, Canker, Chancre, Chancroid, Decubitus, Duodenal, Enanthema, Gastric, Helcoid, Imposthume, Mouth, Noli-me-tangere, Noma, Peptic, Phagedaena, Plague-sore, Rodent, Rupia, Sore, Varicose, Wolf
**Ulster** NI, Overcoat, Raincoat, Red hand, Ulad
**Ulterior** External, Hidden
**Ultimate(ly)** Absolute, Basic, Deterrent, Eventual, Final, Furthest, Last, Maximum, Mostest, Omega, So, Supreme, Thule, Ult
**Ultimatum** Threat
**Ultra** Drastic, Extreme, Radical
**Ultra-modern** Space age
**Ultra-republican** Leveller
**Ultrasound** Lithotripsy
**Ululate** Wail
**Ulysses** Bloom, Grant, Odysseus
**Umbellifer(ous)** Angelica, Arnut, Car(r)away, Dill, Honewort, Narthex, Pig-nut, Seseli
**Umber** Burnt, Mottled, Raw, Waved
**Umbrage** Offence, Pique, Resentment, Shade
**Umbrella(-shaped)** Brolly, Bubble, Bumbershoot, Chatta, En tout cas, Gamp, Gingham, Gloria, Mush(room), Nuclear, Parasol, Sunshade, Tee
**Umbria** Eugubine, Iguvine
**Umpire** Arb(iter), Byrlawman, Daysman, Decider, Judge, Mediate, Oddjobman, Odd(s)man, Overseer, Oversman, Referee, Rule, Stickler, Thirdsman
**Unabashed** Bare-faced, Brazen, Shameless
**Unable** Can't, Downa-do, Incapable
**Unaccented** Atonic, Proclitic
**Unacceptable** Beyond the pale, Ineligible, Non-U, Not on, Out, Repugnant, Stigmatic, Taboo
**Unaccompanied** A cappella, Alone, High-lone, Secco, Single, Solo, Solus
**Unaccustomed** Desuetude, Inusitate, New, Unwonted, Usedn't
**Unacknowledged** Covert
**Unadorned** Au naturel, Bald, Plain, Stark
**Unadulterated** Natural, Sincere

**Unadventurous** Staid, Stay-at-home
**Unaffected** Artless, Genuine, Homely, Insusceptible, Naif, Naive, Natural, Plain, Sincere, Unattached
**Unaided** Single-handed, Solo
**Unaligned** Neutral
**Unalloyed** Pure
**Unaltered** Constant, Same
**Unambiguous** Categorical, Direct, Univocal
**Unanimous** Accord, Nem con, Per curiam
**Unanswerable** Erotema, Irrefragable, Irrefutable
**Unappealing** Distasteful, Grim, Offensive, Off-putting, Rank
**Unappreciated, Unappreciative** Ingrate, Thankless
**Unapproachable** Remote
**Unapproved** Black list
**Unarguable** Erotema
**Unarmed** Inerm, →MARTIAL ARTS, Naked, Vulnerable
**Unashamed** Blatant, Brazen, Open
**Unassailable** Cast-iron
**Unassigned** Adespota, Anonymous, Vacant
**Unassisted** Naked eye
**Unassuming** Lowly, Modest
**Unattached** Disengaged, Fancy free, Freelance, Loose
**Unattractive** Demagnetised, Dowdy, Drac(k), Frump(y), Hideous, Lemon, Minger, Munter, Plain, Plug-ugly, Rebarbative, Scungy, Seamy, Skanky, Ugly
**Unattributable** Anon
**Unauthentic** Plagal
▷ **Unauthentic** *may indicate* an anagram
**Unavail(able), Unavailing** Bootless, Futile, Ineluctable, Lost, NA, No use, Off, Useless, Vain
**Unavoidable** Enforced, Ineluctable, Inevitable, Necessary, Perforce
**Unaware(ness)** Blind-side, Cloistered, Coma, Heedless, Ignorant, Incognisant, Innocent, Oblivious, Stupor
**Unbalanced** Asymmetric, Deranged, Doolalli, Doolally, Loco, Lopsided, Nutty, Out to lunch, Skewwhiff, Twisted, Uneven
**Unbearable** Bassington, Intolerable, Severe
**Unbeaten, Unbeatable** All-time, Perfect
**Unbecoming, Unbefitting** Improper, Indecent, Infra dig, Shabby, Unfitting, Unseemly, Unsuitable, Unworthy
**Unbelievable, Unbeliever** Agnostic, Atheist, Cassandra, Doubter, Giaour, Heathen, Heretic, Incredible, Infidel, Pagan, Painim, Paynim, Sceptic, Tall, Zendik
**Unbend(ing)** Relax, Relent, Strict
**Unbent** Relaxed
**Unbiased** Fair, Impartial, Independent, Just, Neutral, Non-partisan, Objective, Open-minded, Unattainted
**Unblemished** Clean, Intact, Spotless, Vestal
**Unblinking** Alert, Astare, Fearless
**Unblock(ing)** Clear, Free, Recanalization
**Unborn** Foetus, Future, Unbred
**Unbounded** Infinite
**Unbowed** In-kneed, Resolute
**Unbranded** Cleanskin
**Unbreakable** Infrangible, Inviolate
**Unbridled** Fancy free, Footloose, Lawless, Uncurbed, Unrestricted, Unshackled, Untramelled
**Unburden** Confide, Disembosom, Offload, Relieve, Unload

**Uncanny** Eerie, Eldritch, Extraordinary, Geason, Rum, Spooky, Wanchancie, Wanchancy, Weird

**Uncastrated** Stone

**Unceasing** Continuous, Open-ended

**Unceremonious** En famille, Offhand

**Uncertain(ty)** Acatalepsy, Agnostic, Blate, Broken, Chancy, Chary, Confusion, Contingent, Delicate, Dicey, Dither, Dodgy, Doubtful, Dubiety, Equivocal, Grey, Heisenberg, Hesitant, Iffy, Indeterminate, Indistinct, Irresolute, Limbo, Obscure, Parlous, Peradventure, Precarious, Queasy, Risky, Slippery, Suspense, Tentative, Vagary, Vor, Wide open

▷ **Uncertain** *may indicate* an anagram

**Unchallengeable, Unchallenge(d)** Inerrant, Irrecusable, Sackless

**Unchangeable, Unchanged, Unchanging** As is, Enduring, Eternal, Idempotent, Immutable, Intact, Monotonous, Perennial, Pristine, Read only, Semper idem, Stable, Standpat, Timeless

**Uncharacteristic** Atypical

**Uncharged** Neutral, Neutron

**Unchaste** Corrupt, Immodest, Immoral, Impure, Lewd, Light-heeled, Wanton

**Unchecked** Rampant, Raw, Unrestrained

**Unchristian** Islamic, Mean

**Uncivil(ised)** Barbaric, Benighted, Boondocks, Brutish, Discourteous, Disrespectful, Giant-rude, Goth, Heathen, Impolite, Liberty, Military, Rude, Rudesby, Short, Unmannerly

**Uncle** Abbas, Afrikaner, Arly, Bob, Dutch, Eme, Nunky, Oom, Pawnbroker, Pawnee, Pawnshop, Pledgee, Pop-shop, Remus, Sam, Silas, Tio, Tom, U, Usurer, Vanya

**Unclean** Defiled, Dirty, Impure, Obscene, Ordure, Squalid, Tabu, T(e)refa(h)

**Unclear** Ambitty, Blurred, Cloudy, Grey area, Hazy, Inexplicit, Nebulous, Obscure, Opaque, Overcast, Sketchy, Slurred

**Unclothed** Bald, Nude

**Uncloven** Soliped

**Uncoded** En clair

**Uncomfortable** Awkward, Mean, Spartan, Uneasy

**Uncommitted** Evasive, Free-floating, Laodicean

**Uncommon** Rara avis, Rare, Sparse, Strange, Unusual

▷ **Uncommon(ly)** *may indicate* an anagram

**Uncommunicative** Reserved, Tight-lipped

**Uncompanionable** Threesome

**Uncomplaining** Stoic

**Uncomplicated** Naive

**Uncomplimentary** Blunt, Critical

**Uncomprehending** Anan, Ignorant

**Uncompromising** Cutthroat, Hardline, Hardshell, Intransigent, Relentless, Rigid, Strict, Ultra, Zero tolerance

**Unconcealed** Open, Overt, Pert

**Unconcerned** Bland, Careless, Casual, Cold, Impassive, Indifferent, Insouciant, Nonchalant, Strange

**Unconditional** Absolute, Free, No strings, Pure

**Unconfident** Diffident

**Uncongenial** Icy

**Unconnected** Asyndetic, Detached, Disjointed, Enodal, Off-line

**Unconscionable** Ordinate, Ungodly

**Unconscious(ness)** Asleep, Automatic, Catalepsy, Cold, Comatose, Instinctive, Non-ego, Not-I, Subliminal, Syncope, Trance, Unaware, Under, Zonked out

**Unconsidered** Impetuous, Rash

**Unconsummated** Mariage blanc

**Uncontaminated** Axenic

**Uncontrolled** Adrift, Anarchic, Atactic, Free, Hysterical, Incontinent, Intemperate, Loose, Loose cannon, Rampant, Skid, Wild

**Uncontroversial** Anodyne

**Unconventional** Anti-hero, Avant garde, Beatnik, Bohemian, Divergent, Drop-out, Eccentric, Far-out, Freakish, Freeform, Gonzo, Heretic, Heterodox, Hippy, Informal, Irregular, Offbeat, Off-the-wall, Original, Outlandish, Outré, Out there, Raffish, Rebel, Screwball, Spac(e)y, Swinger, Unorthodox, Way-out, Wild

▷ **Unconventional** *may indicate* an anagram

**Unconverted** Neat

**Unconvinced, Unconvincing** Farfet(ched), High-flow, High-flown, Humph, Lame, Thin, Wafer-thin

**Uncooked** Rare, Raw

**Uncooperative** Bolshie, Recalcitrant, Stroppy

**Uncoordinated** Asynergia, Ataxic, Awkward, Clumsy

**Uncorrect** Stet

**Uncorrupted** Innocent

**Uncouth(ness)** Baboon, Backwoodsman, Bear, Boorish, Churlish, Crude, Gothic, Inelegant, Rough, Rube, Rude, Rugged, Slob, Sloven, Uncivil

**Uncover(ed)** Bare, Denude, Disclose, Dismask, Expose, Inoperculate, Naked, Open, Overt, Peel, Reveal, Shave, Shill, Shuck, Uncap, Unhood, Unveil

**Uncritical** Indiscriminate

**Unction, Unctuous(ness)** Anele, Balm, Chrism, Extreme, Greasy, Last rites, Oil(y), Ointment, Oleaginous, Ooze, Smarm, Soapy

**Uncultivated, Uncultured** Artless, Bundu, Fallow, Feral, Ignorant, Incult, Lowbrow, Philistine, Rude, Tramontane, Waste, Wild, Wildland, Wildwood

**Undamaged** Intact, Sound, Whole

**Undated** Sine die

**Undecided** Aboulia, Dithering, Double-minded, Doubtful, Havering, Hung, Moot, Non-committal, Open-ended, Pending, Pendulous, Torn, Uncertain, Wavering

**Undefiled** Chaste, Clean, Pure, Virgin

**Undefined** Open-ended, Vague

**Undeniable** Fact, Incontestable, Irrefutable

**Under(neath)** Aneath, Below, Beneath, Hypnotized, Hypo-, Infra, Sotto, Sub-, Unconscious, Unneath

**Underarm** Axilla, Lob

**Underbodice** Jump

**Underburnt** Samel

**Under-butler** Bread-chipper

**Undercarriage** Bogie, Chassis

**Undercoat** Base, Primer

**Undercooked** Rare, Raw, Samel

**Undercover** Cloak and dagger, Espionage, Secret, Veiled

**Undercurrent** Acheron, Riptide, Undertone, Undertow

**Underdeveloped, Underdevelopment** Aplasia, Ateleiosis, Backward, Retarded

**Underdog** Cerberus, Loser, Victim

▶ **Undergarment** *see* UNDERWEAR

**Undergo** Bear, Dree, Endure, Solvate, Sustain

**Undergraduate** Commoner, Fresher, L, Pup, Questionist, Sizar, Sophomore, Student, Subsizar, Tuft

**Underground (group)** Basement, Catacomb, Cellar, Clandestine, Erebus, Fogou, Hell, Hypogaeous, Infernal, Irgun, Kiva, Macchie, Maquis, Mattamore, Metro, Phreatic, Pict, Plutonia, Pothole, Secret, Souterrain, Subsoil, Subterranean, Subway, Tube, Tunnel, Warren, Weem

**Undergrowth** Brush, Chaparral, Firth, Frith, Scrub

**Underhand** Arch, Backstair, Dirty, Haunch, Insidious, Lob, Oblique, Scullduggery, Secret, Shady, Sinister, Sly, Sneaky, Surreptitious

**Underlease** Subtack

**Underlie, Underlying** Subjacent, Subtend, Ulterior

**Underline** Emphasise, Insist, Reinforce, Sublineation

**Underling** Bottle-washer, Cog, Inferior, Jack, Menial, Minion, Munchkin, Subordinate

**Undermine** Destabilise, Erode, Fossick, Handbag, Sap, Subvert, Tunnel, Weaken

**Undernourished** Puny, Skinny, Starveling

**Underpaid** Rat

**Underpass** Simplon, Subway

**Underside** Bed, Soffit

**Underskirt** Petticoat, Slip

**Understand(able), Understanding, Understood** Accept, Acumen, Agreement, Alliance, Apprehend, Capeesh, Catch on, Clear, Cognisable, Comprehend, Conceive, Concept, Connivance, Consideration, Cotton-on, Deal, Dig, Digest, Empathy, Enlighten, Entente, Exoteric, Fathom, Follow, Gather, Gauge, Gaum, Geddit, Get it, Gorm, Grasp, Grok, Have, Head, Heels, Hindsight, Implicit, Insight, Intelligible, Intuit, Ken, Kind, Knowhow, Latch on, Learn, Light(s), Lucid, OK, Omniscient, Pact, Perspicuous, Plumb, Prajna, Rapport, Rapprochement, Realise, Roger, Savey, Savvy, See, Sense, Sole, Subintelligitur, Substance, Tacit, Take, Tenderness, Tolerance, Treaty, Tumble, Twig, Unspoken, Unstated, Uptak(e), Wisdom, Wit

**Understate(d), Understatement** Litotes, Low-key, Minify, M(e)iosis, Subtle

▶ **Understood** *see* **UNDERSTAND(ABLE)**

**Understudy** Deputy, Double, Stand-in, Sub

**Undertake, Undertaking** Adventure, Attempt, Commitment, Contract, Covenant, Emprise, Endeavour, Enterprise, Essay, Feat, Guarantee, Misere, Pledge, Promise, Scheme, Shoulder, Tackle, Task, Venture, Warranty

**Undertaker** Editor, Entrepreneur, Mortician, Obligor, Sponsor, Upholder

**Under-ten** Unit, Yarborough

**Undertone** Murmur, Rhubarb, Sotto voce

**Undervalue** Denigrate

**Underwater** Demersal

**Underwear** Alb, Balbriggan, Balconette, Bloomers, Bodice, Body, Bodyshaper, Body stocking, Body suit, Boxers, Bra(ssiere), Briefs, Broekies, Butt bra, Camiknickers, Camisole, Chemise, Chemisette, Chuddies, Combinations, Combs, Corselet, Corset, Dainties, Drawers, (French) knickers, Frillies, Girdle, Grundies, G-string, Hosiery, Innerwear, Jump, Knick(er)s, Linen, Lingerie, Linings, Long johns, Pantalets, Pantaloons, Panties, Pantihose, Panty girdle, Petticoat, Scanties, Semmit, Shift, Shimmy, Shorts, Singlet, Skivvy, Slip, Smalls, Spencer, Stammel, Stays, Step-ins, Subucula, Suspender-belt, Suspenders, Tanga, Teddy, Thermal, Trunks, Underdaks, Undergarments, Underlinen, Underpants, Underset, Undershirt, Underthings, Undies, Unmentionables, Vest, Wyliecoat, Y-fronts®

**Underworld** All-fired, Avernus, Chthonic, Criminal, Gangland, Hades, Hell, Lowlife, Mafia, Pluto, Shades, Tartar(e), Tartarus, Tartary

**Underwrite, Underwritten** Assure, Endorse, Guarantee, Insure, Lloyds, PS

**Undeserving** Immeritous

**Undesirable** Kibitzer, Riff-raff

**Undeveloped** Ament, Backward, Depauperate, Green, Inchoate, Latent, Nubbin, Ridgel, Ridgil, Ridgling, Rig, Riggald, Riglin(g), Rudimentary, Seminal

**Undifferentiated** Thalliform, Thallus

**Undigested** Crude

**Undignified (end)** Disaster, Foot, Improper, Infra dig, Unseemly

**Undiluted** Absolute, Neat, Pure, Sheer, Straight

**Undiminished** Entire, Intact, Whole

**Undiplomatic** Brusque, Tactless
**Undisciplined** Bacchanalian, Hothead, Rule-less, Rulesse, Sloppy, Unruly, Wanton
**Undisclosed** Hidden, In petto
**Undisguised** Apert, Clear, Plain
**Undisputed** Authentic
**Undistinguished** Mediocre, Nameless, Plebeian, Run of the mill
**Undisturbed** Halcyon, Serene
**Undivided** Aseptate, Complete, Entire, Indiscrete, One
**Undo(ing)** Annul, Defeat, Destroy, Disconnect, Downfall, Dup, Poop, Poupe, Release, Rescind, Ruin, Unravel
**Undoctored** Neat
**Undone** Arrears, Left, Postponed, Ran, Ruined, Unlast
**Undoubted(ly)** Ay, Certes, Clearly, Ipso facto, Positively, Sure, To be sure
**Undress(ed)** Bare, Disarray, Disrobe, En cuerpo, Expose, Négligé, Nude, Nue, Peel, Querpo, Raw, Rough, Self-faced, Spar, Strip, Unapparelled
**Undue** Premature
**Undulate, Undulating** Billow, Nebule, Ripple, Roll, Swell, Wave
▷ **Unduly** *may indicate* an anagram
**Undyed** Greige
**Undying** Amaranthine, Eternal
**Unearth(ly)** Astral, Dig, Discover, Disentomb, Exhumate, Indagate
**Unease, Uneasiness, Uneasy** Angst, Angular, Anxious, Creeps, Discomfort, Disquiet, Inquietude, Itchy, Malaise, Qualm, Queasy, Restive, Shy, Tense, The willies, Trepidation, Uptight, Windy, Womble-cropped
**Unedifying** Idle
**Unembarrassed** Blasé, Dégagé
**Unemotional** Bland, Clinical, Cool, Frigid, Iceberg, Matter-of-fact, Phlegmatic, Poker-face, Sober, Stoic, Stolid
**Unemployed, Unemployment** Drone, Idle, Jobless, Laik, Lake, Latent, Lay-off, Neet, Redundant, Residual, Stalko, Surfie
**Unending** Chronic, Eternal, Lasting, Sempiternal
**Unenlightened** Ignorant, Nighted, Obscure
**Unenthusiastic** Cool, Damp, Desultory, Half-hearted, Lackadaisical, Listless, Tepid
**Unenveloped** Achlamydeous
**Unequal(led)** Aniso-, Disparate, Non(e)such, Scalene, Unjust
**Unequivocal** Direct
**Unerring** Dead, Exact, Precise
**Unestablished** Free
**Unethical** Amoral, Corrupt, Immoral, Sharp, Shyster
**Uneven(ness)** Accident, Blotchy, Bumpy, Erose, Erratic, Irregular, Jaggy, Lopsided, Patchy, Ragged, Rough, Scratchy, Streaky
▷ **Unevenly** *may indicate* an anagram
**Unexceptional** Ordinary, Run of the mill, Workaday
**Unexciting** Flat, Mundane, Staid, Tame
**Unexpected(ly)** Abrupt, Accidental, Adventitious, Bonus, Emergency, Fortuitous, Infra dig, Inopinate, Ironic, Snap, Sodain(e), Startling, Sudden, Turn-up, Unawares, Unforeseen, Untoward, Unware, Unwary, Windfall
**Unexperienced** Strange
**Unexplained** Mystery, Obscure
**Unexploded** Live
**Unfading** Evergreen, Immarcescible
**Unfailing** Sure
**Unfair** Bias(s)ed, Crook, Dirty, Discriminatory, Inclement, Iniquitous, Invidious, Mean, One-sided, Partial, Raw deal, Thick, Unsportsmanlike

**Unfaithful** Adulterer, Cuckold, Disloyal, Godless, Infidel, Traitor, Two-timing
**Unfamiliar** Alien, Disinure, Foreign, New, Quaint, Strange
**Unfashionable** Cube, Daggy, Demode, Dowdy, Lame, Mumsy, Obsolescent, Out(moded), Out-of-date, Passé, Square, Vieux jeu
▷ **Unfashionable** *may indicate* 'in' to be removed
**Unfasten** Undo, Untie, Untruss
**Unfathomable** Abysmal, Bottomless, Deep
**Unfavourable** Adverse, Ill, Inimical, Outsider, Poor, Untoward
**Unfeeling** Adamant, Brutish, Callous, Cold, Cruel, Dead, Empty, Hard, Inhuman(e), Insensate, Iron-witted, Numb, Robotic, Scared, Stony-hearted
**Unfeigned** Heartfelt
**Unfilled** Vacant
**Unfinished, Unfinishable** Crude, Inchoate, Incondite, Raw, Scabble, Scapple, Sisyphean, Stickit
**Unfit(ting)** Cronk, Disabled, Faulty, Ill, Impair, Inept, Outré, Seedy, Stiffie, Tre(i)f, Trefa, Unable
▷ **Unfit** *may indicate* an anagram
**Unfixed** Indeterminate, Isotropic, Loose
**Unflappable** Stoic
**Unflattering** Dowdy
**Unfledged** Gull
**Unflinching** Fast, Staunch
**Unfocused** Glazed, Grasshopper-mind, Vague
**Unfold** Deploy, Develop, Disenvelop, Display, Divulge, Evolve, Interpret, Open, Relate, Spread
**Unforced** Voluntary
**Unforeseen** Accident, Sudden, Surprising
**Unfortunate(ly)** Accursed, Alack, Alas, Catastrophic, Devil, Down and out, Hapless, Ill-omened, Ill-starred, Indecorous, Luckless, Shameless, Sorry, Star-crossed, Unlucky, Worse luck
**Unfounded** Baseless, Groundless
**Unfrequented** Lonely
**Unfriendly** Aloof, Antagonistic, Asocial, Chill(y), Cold, Cold fish, Crusty, Fraim, Fremd, Fremit, Frosty, Hostile, Icy, Inhospitable, Remote, Standoffish, Surly, Wintry
**Unfruitful** Abortive, Barren, Sterile
**Unfulfilled** Frustrated, Manqué
**Ungainly** Awkward, Gawkish, Uncouth, Weedy
**Ungenerous** Cheapskate, Illiberal, Mean, Meanies, Small
**Ungodliness, Ungodly** Impiety, Irreligious, Pagan, Perfidious, Profane, World
**Ungracious** Cold, Mesquin(e), Offhand, Rough, Rude
**Ungrammatical** Anacoluthia
**Ungrateful** Ingrate, Snaky
**Unguarded** Trusting
**Unguent** Nard, Pomade, Salve
**Ungulate** Anta, Antelope, Dinoceras, Eland, Equidae, Hoofed, Moose, Pachydermata, Rhino, Ruminantia, Takin, Tapir, Tylopoda
**Unhappily, Unhappy, Unhappiness** Blue, Dejected, Depressed, Disconsolate, Disgruntled, Dismal, Distress, Doleful, Downcast, Down-hearted, Dysphoria, Glumpish, Ill-fated, Love-lorn, Lovesick, Miserable, Sad, Sore, Tearful, Unlief, Upset
▷ **Unhappily** *may indicate* an anagram
**Unharmed, Unharmful** Innocuous, Safe, Scatheless, Spared
**Unharness** Outspan
**Unhealthy** Bad, Clinic, Diseased, Epinosic, Insalubrious, Morbid, Noxious, Peaky, Poxy, Prurient, Scrag, Sickly, Twisted

**Unheeding** Oblivious
**Unhelpful** Detrimental
**Unholy** Profane, Wicked
**Unhurried** Deliberate, Gradual, Patient
**Unhurt** Whole-skinned
**Unhygienic** Grubby
**Uniat** Maronite, Melchite
**Unicorn** Ch'i-lin, Coin, Monoceros, Moth, Myth, Narwhal, U
**Unidentified** Anon, Anonym(ous), Incognito, Ligure, Unknown
**Unification, Unify(ing)** Esemplastic, Henotic, Integrate, Risorgimento, Unite
**Uniform** Abolla, Alike, Apparel, Battledress, Consistent, Constant, Doublet, Dress, Equable, Equal, Even, Flat, Forage-cap, Homogeneous, Homomorphic, Identical, Khaki, Kit, Level, Livery, Monkey suit, Regimentals, Regular, Rig, Robe, Same, Sole, Standard, Steady, Strip, Suit, U, Unitary, Unvaried
**Unilateral** One-sided
**Unimaginative** Banausic, Cabbage, Earthbound, Literalistic, Meagre, Pedestrian, Pooter, Short-sighted, Slavish
**Unimpaired** Entire, Intact, Sound
**Unimportant** Academic, Cog, Down-the-line, Expendable, Fiddling, Folderol, Footling, Frivolous, Hot air, Idle, Immaterial, Inconsequent, Inconsiderable, Insignificant, Junior, Light, MacGuffin, Makeweight, Miniscule, Minnow, Minutiae, Negligible, Nonentity, Nugatory, Peddling, Peripheral, Petty, Piddling, Slight, Small beer, Small-time, Trifling, Trivia(l)
**Unimpressible** Cynical
**Uninformed** Ingram
**Uninhabited** Bundu, Deserted, Desolate, Lonely
**Uninhibited** Abandoned, Bold, Free spirit, Raunchy
**Uninjured** Inviolate
**Uninspired, Uninspiring** Barren, Bored, Flat, Humdrum, Nondescript, Pedestrian, Pompier, Stereotyped, Sterile, Tame
**Unintelligent** Dull, Dumb, Fuckwit, Obtuse, Quo-he, Stupid, Witless
**Unintelligible** Arcane, Code, Double Dutch, Greek, Inarticulate
**Unintentional** Inadvertent, Unwitting
**Uninterested, Uninteresting** Apathetic, Bland, Drab, Dreary, Dry, Dull, Grey, Incurious, Nondescript, Non-event
**Uninterrupted** Constant, Continuous, Incessant, Running, Steady
**Uninvited** Gatecrasher, Interloper, Intruder, Sorner, Trespasser, Umbra
**Union(ist)** Affiance, African, Agreement, Allegiance, Alliance, Amicus, Anschluss, Art, ASLEF, Association, Bed, Benelux, Bond, Brotherhood, Brussels, Civil, Close, Coalition, Combination, Company, Concert, Confederacy, Covalency, Craft, Credit, Customs, Diphthong, Economic, Enosis, Ensemble, Equity, EU, European, Fasciation, Federal, Federation, French, Frithgild, Fusion, Group, Guild, Heterogamy, Horizontal, Impanation, Industrial, Integration, Isogamy, Junction, Knight of labour, Latin, League, Liaison, Liberal, Link-up, Management, Marriage, Match, Merger, NUM, Nuptials, NUR, NUS, NUT, OILC, Pan-American, Parabiosis, Pearl, Postal, Print, RU, Rugby, Samiti, Sex, Sherman, Shop-steward, Solidarity, Soviet, Splice, Sponsal, Student, Symphysis, Syngamy, Synizesis, Synostosis, Synthesis, Syssarcosis, Teamsters, Tenorrhaphy, →**TRADE UNION**, TU, U, UNISON, USDAW, Uxorial, Verein, Vertical, Vienna, Wedding, Wedlock, Western European, Wield, Yoke, ZANU, Zollverein, Zygosis
**Unique(ness)** Alone, A-per-se, Farid, Hacceity, Inimitable, Irreplaceable, Lone, Matchless, Nonesuch, Nonpareil, Nonsuch, One-off, One(-to)-one, Onliest, Only, Peerless, Rare, Singular, Sole, Specific, Sui generis
**Unisex(ual)** Epicene, Hermaphrodite
**Unison** Chorus, Harmony, One, Sync

**Unit(s)** Bargaining, Battery, Board of Trade, Brigade, Cadre, Cell, Cohort, Commando, Commune, Control, Corps, Derived, Detachment, Division, Dyad, Ecosystem, Element, Ensuite, Feedlot, Flight, Fundamental, Home, Horsepower, Hub, Income, Item, Last, Measure, Message, Module, Monetary, Panzer, Patrol, Peninsular, Period, Peripheral, Practical, Sealed, Secure, Segment, Shed, Squad(ron), Stock, Syllable, Team, Terminal, Theme, Timocracy, Tower

## UNITS

*1 letter:*
K
X

*2 letters:*
AU
Em
En
RA
SI
TA

*3 letters:*
Ace
Amp
Bar
Bel
Bit
BTU
DIN
Dol
EMU
Erg
Fps
Gal
GeV
Ion
Lux
Mho
Mil
Mol
Nit
Ohm
Ped
Rem
Rep
Tex
Tod
Tog
Var

*4 letters:*
Acre
Barn
Base

Baud
Byte
DALY
Dyne
Gram
Grav
Gray
Hank
Hapu
Hide
Hour
Inch
Mile
Mole
Nest
Octa
Okta
Phot
Pica
Pint
Pond
Rood
Sink
Slug
Sone
Torr
Vara
Volt
Wall
Watt
Wing
Yard

*5 letters:*
Codon
Crith
Cusec
Daraf
Darcy
Debye
Ephah
Farad
Fermi
Field
Gauss

Henry
Hertz
Holon
Joule
Katal
Litre
Lumen
Metre
Monad
Mongo
Neper
Nepit
Ounce
Pixel
Point
Poise
Pound
Power
Quart
Qubit
Remen
Sabin
Stere
Stilb
Stoke
Stone
Tesla
Therm
Token
Voxel
Weber
Yrneh

*6 letters:*
Biogen
Bushel
Calory
Dalton
Degree
Denier
Dobson
Emdash
Erlang
Gallon
Jansky

Kelvin
Kilerg
League
Lexeme
Megohm
Micron
Minute
Mongoe
Morgan
Morgen
Newton
Pascal
Phyton
Probit
Radian
Reverb
Second
Sememe
Stokes
Vanity

*7 letters:*
Archine
Biophor
Calorie
Candela
Centare
Chronon
Congius
Coulomb
Dioptre
Echelon
Energid
Episome
Foot-ton
Fresnel
Gestalt
Gigabit
Gilbert
Hartree
Kiloton
Lambert
Langley
Maceral
Man-hour

| | | | |
|---|---|---|---|
| Maxwell | Chaldron | Foot-pound | Nanosecond |
| Megabit | Electron | Gigahertz | Person-hour |
| Megaton | Gigaflop | Kilderkin | Picosecond |
| Micella | Gigawatt | Kilometre | Ploughgate |
| Micelle | Glosseme | Light-year | Protoplast |
| Milline | Hogshead | Megahertz | Rutherford |
| Nephron | Kilowatt | Microinch | |
| Oersted | Magneton | Microvolt | ***11 letters:*** |
| Phoneme | Megabyte | Organelle | Centimorgan |
| Poundal | Megaflop | Singleton | Foot-lambert |
| Rontgen | Megawatt | Steradian | Pennyweight |
| Semeion | Morpheme | Strontium | |
| Siemens | Mutchkin | Tetrapody | ***12 letters:*** |
| Sievert | Parasang | Yottabyte | Archiphoneme |
| Syntagm | Petaflop | Zettabyte | Astronomical |
| Tagmeme | Roentgen | | Bohr magneton |
| Tripody | Syntagma | ***10 letters:*** | |
| | Terabyte | Ampere-hour | ***13 letters:*** |
| ***8 letters:*** | Teraflop | Centimetre | Electrostatic |
| Abampere | Therblig | Centipoise | |
| Absolute | Vanitory | Dessiatine | ***15 letters:*** |
| Acre-foot | Watt-hour | Foot-candle | Electromagnetic |
| Angstrom | | Hoppus-foot | |
| Bioblast | ***9 letters:*** | Microcurie | |
| Biophore | Becquerel | Millilitre | |
| Centiare | Degree day | Millimetre | |

**Unitarian** Arian, Paulian, Racovian, Socinian
**Unite(d), Uniting** Accrete, Band, Bind, Cement, Close-knit, Coalesce, Combine, Concordant, Connate, Connect, Consolidate, Consubstantiate, Covalent, Ecumenical, Fay, Federal, Federalise, Federate, Fuse, Gene, Graft, Harmonise, Injoint, Inosculate, Join, Joinder, Jugum, Kingdom, Knit, Lap, Link, Marry, Meint, Meng, Ment, Merge, Meynt, Ming, Nations, Oneness, Oop, Oup, Piece, Siamese, Solid, States, Tie, Tightknit, Unify, Utd, → **WED**, Weld, Yoke
**United Ireland** Fine Gael
**United Kingdom** Old Dart, UK
**Unity** Cohesion, Harmony, One, Solidarity, Sympathy, Togetherness
**Univalent** Monatomic
**Universal, Universe** All, All-embracing, Catholic, Cosmogony, Cosmos, Creation, Ecumenic(al), Emma, Expanding, General, Global, Infinite, Inflationary, Island, Macrocosm, Mandala, Microcosm, Omnify, Oscillating, Sphere, U, Via Lactea, World(wide)
**University** Academe, Academy, Alma mater, Aston, Bangor, Bath, Berkeley, Bonn, Brown, Campus, Civic, College, Columbia, Cornell, Dartmouth, Exeter, Gown, Harvard, Heidelberg, Ivy League, Keele, MIT, Open, OU, Oxbridge, Pennsylvania, Princeton, Reading, Redbrick, St Andrews, Sorbonne, Stamford, Syracuse, Varsity, Whare wanaga, Wittenberg, Witwatersrand, Yale
**Unjust(ified)** Groundless, Inequitable, Inequity, Iniquitous, Invalid, Tyrannical
**Unkempt** Bedraggled, Bushy, Dishevelled, Greaseball, Greebo, Mal soigné, Raddled, Ragged, Raggle-taggle, Scarecrow, Scody, Scraggy, Scuzzy, Shaggy, Tatty, Tousy, Touzy, Towsy, Towzy
**Unknot** Burl
**Unknown, Unknowable** Acamprosate, Agnostic, Anon, A.N. Other, Dark horse, Hidden, Ign, Incog(nito), Inconnu, Indeterminate, N, Nobody, Noumenon, Occult,

Quantity, Recondite, Secret, Soldier, Strange, Symbolic, Tertium quid, Unchartered, Untold, Warrior, X, Y

**Unlawful** Illegal, Non-licit

**Unleavened** Azymous

**Unless** Nisi, Save, Without

**Unliable** Exempt

**Unlicensed** Illicit

**Unlike(ly)** As if, Difform, Disparate, Dubious, Far-fetched, Implausible, Improbable, Inauspicious, Last, Long shot, Outsider, Remote, Tall, Unlich

**Unlimited** Almighty, Borderless, Boundless, Indefinite, Measureless, Nth, Open-ended, Pure, Universal, Vast

**Unlisted** Ex-directory

**Unload** Disburden, Discharge, Drop, Dump, Jettison, Land, Strip, Unship

**Unlock(ed)** Bald

**Unlucky** Donsie, Hapless, Ill(-starred), Ill-fated, Ill-omened, Inauspicious, Infaust, Jonah, Misadventure, Misfallen, S(c)hlimazel, Sinister, Stiff, Thirteen, Untoward, Wanchancie, Wanchancy, Wanion

**Unman, Unmanned** Castrate, Desex, Gelding

**Unmanageable** Handful, Riotous, Tartarian

**Unmannerly** Crude, Discourteous, Impolite, Low bred, Rude, Solecism

**Unmarried** Bachelor, Celibate, Common-law, Lane, Lone, Single, Spinster, Tallywoman

**Unmask** Expose, Rumble

**Unmatched** Bye, Champion, Orra, Unique

**Unmentionable(s)** Bra, Foul, No-no, Secret, → **UNDERWEAR**, Undies

**Unmindful** Heedless, Oblivious, Regardless

**Unmissable** Must see

**Unmistakable** Clear, Manifest, Plain

**Unmitigated** Absolute, Arrant, Sheer, Ultra

**Unmixed** Meer, Me(a)re, Neat, Nett, Pure, Raw, Sincere, Straight

**Unmoved, Unmoving** Adamant, Doggo, Dry-eyed, Firm, In situ, Serene, Static, Stolid

**Unnamed** Anon

**Unnatural** Abnormal, Absonant, Affected, Artificial, Cataphysical, Contrived, Eerie, Far-fetched, Flat, Geep, Irregular, Man-made, Strange, Studied, Transuranian

▷ **Unnaturally** *may indicate* an anagram

**Unnecessary** De trop, Extra, Gash, Gratuitous, Needless, Otiose, Redundant, Superfluous

**Unnerve(d), Unnerving** Creepy, Discouraging, Eerie, Faze, Rattle, Spooked

**Unobserved** Backstage, Sly, Unseen

**Unobtainable** Nemesis

**Unobtrusive** Discreet, Low profile, Quiet, Stealthy

**Unoccupied** Désouvré, Empty, Idle, Inactive, Otiose, Vacant, Void

**Unofficial** Black, Disestablish, Fringe, Wildcat

**Unopened** Sealed

**Unoriginal** Banal, Copy, Déjà vu, Derivative, Imitation, Plagiarised, Slavish, Trite

**Unorthodox** En passant, Heretic, Heterodox, Irregular, Maverick, Off-beat, Off-the-wall, Outré, Stagyrite, Unconventional

▷ **Unorthodox** *may indicate* an anagram

**Unpaid** Amateur, Brevet, Hon(orary), Outstanding, Voluntary

**Unpaired** Azygous, Bye

**Unpalatable** Acid, Bitter, Unsavoury

**Unparalleled** Sublime, Supreme, Unique

**Unpartitioned** Aseptate

**Unperturbed** Bland, Calm, Collected, Serene

**Unpigmented** Albino

**Unpinned** Legless

**Unplaced** Legless

**Unplanned** Disorganised, Happenstance, Impromptu, Improvised, Spontaneous

**Unpleasant, Unpleasant person** Cow, Creep, Drastic, Fink, Foul, God-awful, Grim, Grotty, Gruesome, Gunk, Harsh, Hoor, Horrible, Icky, Insalubrious, Invidious, Mucky, Nasty, Obnoxious, Odious, Offensive, Painful, Pejorative, Poxy, Putrid, Rank, Rebarbative, Reptile, Scrote, Shady, Shitty, Shocker, Skanky, Snarky, Snot, Sour, Sticky, Thorny, Toerag, Wart

**Unploughed** Lea-rig

**Unpolished** Coarse, Inelegant, Rough

**Unpolluted** Sterile

**Unpopular** Abhorred, Avant garde, Detested, Friendless, Hat(e)able

**Unpractical** Academic, Futile, Orra

**Unpredictable** Act of God, Aleatory, Capricious, Dicy, Erratic, Loose cannon, Maverick, Scatty, Vagary, Wayward, Wild card

**Unprepared** Ad lib, Cold, Extempore, Green, Impromptu, Improvised, Last minute, On the hop, Raw, Unready

**Unpretentious** Comely, Down home, Hole in the wall, Honest, Modest, Plain, Quiet

**Unprincipled** Amoral, Dishonest, Irregular, Opportunist, Reprobate, Unscrupulous

**Unproductive** Arid, Atokal, Atokous, Barren, Dead-head, Desert, Eild, Fallow, Futile, Infertile, Lean, Poor, Shy, Sterile, Yeld, Yell

**Unprofessional** Amateur, Laic, Malpractice

**Unprofitable** Bootless, Fruitless, Lean, Thankless, Wasted

**Unprogressive** Inert, Square

**Unpronounceable** Clitic

**Unpropitious** Bleak

**Unproportionate** Incommensurate

**Unprotected** Exposed, Nude, Vulnerable

**Unpublished** Inedited

**Unpunctual** Tardy

**Unqualified** Absolute, Arrant, Categoric, Downright, Entire, Outright, Perfect, Profound, Pure, Quack, Sheer, Straight, Thorough, Total, Tout court, Utter

**Unquestionably, Unquestioning, Unquestioned** Absolute, Axiomatic, Certain, Doubtless, Implicit

**Unravel(ling)** Construe, Denouement, Disentangle, Feaze, Fray, Solve, Undo

**Unreadable** Poker-faced

**Unready** Unripe

**Unreal(istic)** Academic, Alice-in-Wonderland, Cockamamie, Eidetic, En l'air, Escapist, Fake, Fancied, Illusory, Insubstantial, La-la-land, Mirage, Mythical, Oneiric, Phantom, Phon(e)y, Pipe dream, Planet Zog, Pseudo, Romantic, Sham, Spurious, Storybook, Virtual

**Unreasonable, Unreasoning** Absurd, Bigot, Exorbitant, Extreme, Illogical, Irrational, Misguided, Perverse, Rabid, Steep, Tall order

**Unreciprocated** One-way

**Unrecognised** Incognito, Inconnu, Invalid, Obscure, Thankless, Unnoticed, Unsung

**Unrefined** Bestial, Coarse, Common, Crude, Earthy, Gur, Impudent, Impure, Inelegant, Natural, Rude, Slob, Vul(g), Vulgar

**Unreformed** Impenitent

**Unregistered** Flapping

**Unrehearsed** Candid, Extempore, Impromptu, On sight

**Unrelenting** Implacable, Remorseless, Severe, Stern

**Unreliable** Broken reed, Chequered, Dishonest, Dodgy, Dubious, Erratic, Fair-weather, Fickle, Flibbertigibbet, Flighty, Fly-by-night, Insincere, Kludge, Misleading, Shonky, Skitter, Unstable, Wankle, Weak sister, Wonky

**Unremarkable** Nondescript

**Unremitting** Dogged, Intensive

**Unreserved** Implicit, Total
**Unresponsive** Aloof, Blank, Catatonic, Cold, Frigid, Nastic, Rigor
**Unrest** Discontent, Ferment, The Troubles
**Unrestrained** Ariot, Effusive, Extravagant, Free, Freewheeling, Hearty, Homeric, Immoderate, Incontinent, Lax, Loose, Lowsit, Orgic, Rampant, Wanton, Wild
**Unreturnable** Ace
**Unrighteousness** Adharma
**Unrivalled** Nonesuch, Peerless, Supreme
**Unromantic** Classic(al), Mundane, Prosaic
**Unruffled** Calm, Placid, Serene, Smooth, Tranquil
**Unruly** Anarchic, Bodgie, Buckie, Camstairy, Camsteary, Camsteerie, Coltish, Disruptive, Exception, Fractious, Insubordinate, Lawless, Obstreperous, Obstropalous, Ragd(e), Raged, Ragged, Rambunctious, Rampageous, Rattlebag, Refractory, Riotous, Rowdy, Tartar, Torn-down, Turbulent, Turk, Wanton, Wayward, Zoo
▷ **Unruly** *may indicate* an anagram
**Unsafe** Deathtrap, Fishy, Insecure, Perilous, Precarious, Unsound, Vulnerable
**Unsatisfactory, Unsatisfying** Bad, Disappointing, Lame, Lemon, Lousy, Meagre, Rocky, Thin, Wanting
**Unsavoury** Epinosic, On the nose
**Unsay** Recant
**Unscramble** Decode, Decrypt
**Unscripted** Ad lib
**Unscrupulous** Chancer, Immoral, Rascally, Sharp, Shyster, Slippery, Spiv
**Unseasonable, Unseasoned** Green, Hors de saison, Murken, Raw, Untimely
**Unseat** Depose, Dethrone, Oust, Overset, Overthrow, Throw
**Unseemly** Coarse, Improper, Incivil, Indecent, Indecorous, Indign, Risque, Seedy, Tasteless, Untoward
**Unseen** Masked
**Unselfish** Altruist, Generous
**Unsent** Square
**Unsentimental** Cynical, Gradgrindery, Hard-nosed
**Unserious** Flippant
**Unsettle(d)** Disconcert, Faze, Grey area, Homeless, Hunky, Inconclusive, Indecisive, Nervous, Open, Outstanding, Overdue, Owed, Queasy, Restive, Restless, Troublous
▷ **Unsettled** *may indicate* an anagram
**Unsexy** N, Neuter
**Unshakeable** Shockproof
**Unshaven** Designer stubble
**Unsheltered** Bleak, Exposed, Homeless
**Unsight(ed), Unsightly** Eyeless, Hideous, Repulsive, Ugly
**Unsinning** Impeccable, Pure
**Unskilled, Unskilful** Awkward, Dilutee, Gauche, Green, Hunky, Inexpert, Menial, Raw, Rude, Stumblebum, Talentless, Whitechapel
**Unsmiling** Agelastic
**Unsociable** Anchoretic, Grouchy, Solitary, Stay-at-home
**Unsolicited** Sponte sua
**Unsophisticated** Alf, Basic, Boondocks, Boonies, Bushie, Cornball, Corny, Cracker-barrel, Direct, Down-home, Faux-naïf, Green, Hick, Hillbilly, Homebred, Homespun, Ingenu(e), Inurbane, Jaap, Jay, Naive, Natural, Primitive, Provincial, Rough, Rube, Rustic, Verdant, Yokel
**Unsound** Barmy, Infirm, Invalid, Shaky, Specious, Wildcat, Wonky
▷ **Unsound** *may indicate* an anagram
**Unsparing** Severe
**Unspeakable** Dreadful, Ineffable, Nefandous

**Unspecific, Unspecified** Broad, General, Generic, Somehow, Such, Thingummy(jig), Umpteenth, Vague

**Unspoiled, Unspoilt** Innocent, Natural, Perfect, Pristine, Pure, Virgin

**Unspoken** Silent, Tacit

**Unspotted** Innocent

**Unstable, Unsteady** Anomic, Astatic, Bockedy, Casual, Crank(y), Dicky, Doddery, Erratic, Fitful, Flexuose, Flexuous, Flit(ting), Fluidal, Giddy, Groggy, Infirm, Insecure, Labile, Minute-jack, Quicksand, Rickety, Shaky, Shifty, Skittish, Slippy, Tickle, Top-heavy, Tottery, Totty, Vacillating, Variable, Volatile, Walty, Wambling, Wankle, Warby, Wobbly, Wonky

**Unstated** Concordat, Tacit, Unknown

▶ **Unsteady** *see* UNSTABLE

**Unstressed** Enclitic, Schwa

▷ **Unstuck** *may indicate* an anagram

**Unsubstantial** Aeriform, Airy, Flimsy, Paltry, Shadowy, Slight, Thin, Yeasty

**Unsubtle** Overt, Sledgehammer

**Unsuccessful** Abortive, Also ran, Disastrous, Duff, Futile, Joyless, Loss-maker, Manqué, Vain

**Unsuitable** Amiss, Ill-timed, Impair, Improper, Inapt, Incongruous, Inexpedient, Malapropos, Misbecoming, Unbecoming, Unfit

**Unsullied** Pristine

**Unsupported, Unsupportable** Astylar, Floating, Free-standing, Stroppy, Unfounded

**Unsure** Hesitant, Tentative, Vacillating

**Unsurpassed** All-time, Best, Nonpareil, State-of-the-art, Supreme

**Unsuspecting** Credulous, Innocent, Naive

**Unsweetened** Brut, Natural

**Unswerving** True

**Unsymmetrical** Heterauxesis(m), Irregular, Lopsided

**Unsympathetic** Short shrift

**Unsystematic** Piecemeal

**Untainted** Axenic

**Untaught** Intuitive

**Unthinking** Inadvertent, Inconsiderate, Mechanical, Not-I, Robotic, Slapdash

**Untidy** Daggy, Dishevelled, Dog's breakfast, Dog's dinner, Dowd(y), Frowzy, Frump, Guddle, Litterbug, Ragged, Ragtag, Raunchy, Scruff(y), Slipshod, Slob, Slovenly, Slut, Straggly, Tatty

▷ **Untidy** *may indicate* an anagram

**Untie** Free, Undo, Unlace

**Until** Hasta, Thereto

**Untilled** Fallow

**Untimely** Anachronism

**Untiring** Assiduous

**Unto** Intil, Until

**Untold** Secret, Umpteen, Unread, Unred, Vast

**Untouchable** Burakumin, Dalit, Harijan, Immune, Pariah, Sacred, Sacrosanct, Sealed

**Untouched** Chaste, Intact, Inviolate, Pristine, Virgin

▷ **Untrained** *may indicate* 'BR' to be removed

**Untreated** Raw

**Untried** New, Potential, Virgin

**Untroubled** Carefree, Insouciant

**Untrue, Untruth** Apocryphal, Eccentric, Fable, Fabrication, Faithless, False(hood), Lie, Lopsided, Prefabrication, Unleal

**Untrustworthy** Dishonest, Disloyal, Eel, Fickle, Fly-by-night, Mamzer, Momzer, Shifty, Sleeky, Slippery, Tricky

**Untypical** Anomalous, Etypic(al), Foreign, Isolated, Unusual

**Unused, Unusable** Impracticable, New, Over, Spare, Wasted

**Unusual(ly)** Aberration, Abnormal, Anomalous, Atypical, Departure, Different, Especial, Exceptional, Exotic, Extra(ordinary), Eye-popping, Freak, Gonzo, Kinky, New, Non-standard, Novel, Odd, Offbeat, Other, Out-of-the-way, Outré, Particular, Peculiar, Phenomenal, Quaint, Queer, Rara avis, Rare (bird), Remarkable, Singular, Special, →STRANGE, Unco, Unique, Untypical, Unwonted, Variant, Wacko

▷ **Unusual** *may indicate* an anagram

**Unutterable** Ineffable

**Unvarnished** Bald

**Unvarying** Constant, Eternal, Monotonous, Repetitive, Stable, Static, Uniform

**Unveil** Expose, Honour, Roll up

**Unvoiced** Surd

**Unwanted** Black list, De trop, Exile, Gooseberry, Nimby, Outcast, Pidog, Sorn

**Unwashed** Grubby

**Unwatered** Dry, Neat

**Unwavering** Steadfast, Steady, Thick and thin

**Unwed** Celibate, Single

**Unwelcome, Unwelcoming** Frosty, Hostile, Icy, Intruder, Lulu, Obtrusive, (Persona) Non grata, Repugnant

**Unwell** Ailing, Bedridden, Crook, Dicky, Ill, Impure, Indisposed, Poorly, Quazzy, Queasy, Rop(e)y, Rough, Seedy, Shouse, Toxic

**Unwholesome** Insalutary, Miasmous, Morbid, Noxious, Stagnant, Stinkpot

**Unwieldy** Cumbersome, Elephantine

**Unwilling(ness)** Averse, Disinclined, Intestate, Laith, Loath, Loth, Nolition, Nolo, Obdurate, Perforce, Reluctant, Shy, Tarrow

**Unwind** Descramble, Relax, Straighten, Unclew, Uncoil, Undo, Unravel, Unreave, Unreeve

▷ **Unwind** *may indicate* an anagram

**Unwinnable** Catch 22

**Unwise(ly)** Foolish, Ill-advised, Ill-judged, Impolitic, Imprudent, Inexpedient, Injudicious, Insipient, Rash

**Unwitting** Accidental, Nescient

**Unwonted** Inusitate

**Unworkable** Impossible, Inoperable

**Unworldly** Naif, Naive

**Unworried** Carefree

**Unworthy** Below, Beneath, Golden calf, Indign, Inferior, Infra dig, Substandard, Undeserving

**Unwritten** Verbal

**Unyielding** Adamant, Eild, Firm, Granite, Hardline, Inexorable, Inextensible, Intransigent, Mulish, Obdurate, Relentless, Rigid, Steadfast, Steely, Stern, Stiff, Stolid, Stubborn, Tough, Unalterable

**Unyoke** Outspan

**Up(on), Upturned, Upper, Uppermost, Uppish, Uppity** A, Acockbill, Afoot, Ahead, Antidepressant, Apical, Arrogant, Astir, Astray, Astride, Cloud-kissing, Elevated, Erect, Euphoric, Excited, Heavenward, Hep, Horsed, Incitant, Off, On, Overhead, Primo, Quark, Range, Ride, Riding, Risen, Senior, Skyward, Speed, →UPPER CLASS, Vamp, Ventral, Wart

**Up-anchor** Atrip, Weigh

**Upbeat** Anacrusis, Arsis

**Upbraid** Abuse, Berate, Rebuke, Reproach, Reprove, Scold, Storm, Twit

**Upcountry** Anabasis, Inland

**Update** Brief, Refresh, Renew, Report, Sitrep

**Upfront** Open

**Upgrade** Improve, Promote

**Upheaval** Cataclysm, Chaos, Eruption, Maelstrom, Rummage, Seismic, Shake out, Stir, Turmoil, Upturn, Volcano

▷ **Upheld** *may indicate* 'up' in another word

**Uphill** Arduous, Borstal, Sisyphean

**Uphold** Assert, Defend, Maintain, Sustain

**Upholster(ed), Upholstery** Fleshy, Lampas, Moquette, Tabaret, Trim

**Upkeep** Support

**Upland(s)** Alps, Dartmoor, Downs, Hilly, Moor, Wold

**Uplift** Boost, Edify, Elate, Elevation, Exalt, Hoist, Levitation, Sky

**Upmarket** Smart

**Upper class, Upper crust** Aristocrat, County, Crachach, Hooray Henry, Nobility, Patrician, Posh, Privileged, Sial, Top-hat, Tweedy, U

**Upright(s), Uprightness** Aclinic, Anend, Apeak, Apeek, Aplomb, Arrect, Atrip, Beanpole, Bedpost, Doorpost, Erect, Goalpost, Honest, Incorrupt, Jamb, Joanna, Merlon, Moral, Mr Clean, Mullion, Orthograde, Perpendicular, Piano, Pilaster(s), Post, Prig, Probity, Rectitude, Roman, Splat, Stanchion, Standing, Stares, Stile, Stud, Vertical, Virtuous, White

**Uprising** Incline, Insurrection, Intifada, Meerut, Naxalbari, Rebellion, Revolt, Tumulus

**Uproar(ious)** Bagarre, Ballyhoo, Bedlam, Blatancy, Brouhaha, Charivari, Clamour, Clangour, Collieshangie, Commotion, Cry, Din, Dirdam, Dirdum, Durdum, Emeute, Ferment, Flaw, Fracas, Furore, Garboil, Hell, Hooha, Hoopla, Hubbub(oo), Hullabaloo, Hurly(-burly), Imbroglio, Katzenjammer, Madhouse, Noise, Noyes, Outcry, Pandemonium, Racket, Raird, Randan, Razzmatazz, Reird, Riotous, Roister, Romage, Rough music, Rowdedow, Rowdydow(dy), Ruckus, Ruction, Rumpus, Shemozzle, Stramash, Tempest, Tumult, Turmoil, Utis, Whoobub

**Uproot** Averruncate, Deracinate, Dislodge, Eradicate, Evict, Outweed, Supplant, Weed

**Upset(ting)** Aerate, Aggrieve, Alarm, Applecart, Ate, Bother, Capsize, Catastrophe, Choked, Coup, Cowp, Crank, Derail, Derange, Dip, Disarrange, Discomboberate, Discombobulate, Discomfit, Discomfort, Discommode, Disconcert, Dismay, Disorganise, Displease, Disquiet, Distraught, Disturb, Dod, Eat, Fuss, Grieve, Gutted, Heart-rending, Inversion, Keel, Miff, Nauseative, Niggling, Offend, Overbalance, Overthrow, Overtip, Overturn, Peeve, Perturb, Pip, Pother, Purl, Rattle, Renverse, Rile, Ruffle, Rumple, Sad(den), Seel, Shake, Shatter, Shook up, Sore, Spill, Tapsalteerie, Teary, Tip, Topple, Trauma, Undo, Unsettled

▷ **Upset** *may indicate* an anagram; a word upside down; or 'tes'

**Upshot** Outcome, Result, Sequel

**Upside down** Inverted, Resupinate, Tapsie-teerie, Topsy-turvy

**Upsilon** Hyoid

**Upstart** Buckeen, Jumped-up, Mushroom, Parvenu, Vulgarian

▷ **Upstart** *may indicate* 'u'

**Upstream** Thermal

**Upsurge** Groundswell, Thrust, Waste

**Uptake** Shrewdness, Understanding, Wit

**Up to** Till, Until

**Up-to-date** Abreast, Advanced, Contemporary, Current, Gear, Hip, Mod, New-fashioned, Rad, Right-on, State-of-the-art, Swinging, Switched on, Topical, Trendy

**Upwards** Acclivious, Aloft, Antrorse, Cabré

**Uranium** Depleted, Pitchblende, U, Yellowcake

**Urban, Urbanite** Civic, Megalopolis, Municipal, Street, Town, Townsman

**Urbane, Urbanity** Civil, Debonair, Eutrapelia, Refined, Smooth, Townly

**Urchin** Arab, Asterias, Brat, Crinoid, Crossfish, Cystoid, Echinoderm, Echinoidea, Echinus, Gamin, Guttersnipe, Gutty, Heart, Hedgehog, Mudlark, Nipper, Pedicellaria,

Pluteus, Ragamuffin, Sand-dollar, Sea, Sea-egg, Spatangoidea, Spatangus, Street-arab, Township

**Urge, Urgency, Urgent** Acute, Admonish, Ca, Coax, Coerce, Constrain, Craving, Crying, Desperate, Dire, Drive, Egg, Enjoin, Exhort, Exigent, Goad, Hard, Haste, Hie, Hoick, Hunger, Hurry, Id, Immediate, Impel, Imperative, Importune, Impulse, Incense, Incite, Insist(ent), Instance, Instigate, Itch, Kick, Libido, Nag, Orexis, Peremptory, Persuade, Press(ing), Prod, Push, Scrub, Set on, Sore, Spur, Stat, Strenuous, Strident, Strong, Threapit, Threepit, Vehement, Wanderlust, Whig, Whim, Yen

▷ **Urgent** *may indicate* 'Ur-gent', *viz.* Iraqi

**Uriah** Hittite, Humble, Umble

**Urinal** Bog, John, Jordan, →**LAVATORY**, Loo, Pissoir

**Urinate(d), Urine** Chamber-lye, Emiction, Enuresis, Lant, Leak, Micturition, Number one, Oliguria, Pee, Piddle, Piss, Planuria, Relieve, Slash, Stale, Strangury, Tiddle, Uresis, Werris (Creek), Whiz(z), Widdle

**Urn(s), Urn-shaped** Canopic, Cinerarium, Ewer, Grecian, Lachrymal, Olla, Ossuary, Samovar, Storied, Tea, Urceolate, Vase

**Us** Me, Ourselves, 's, UK, Uns, We

**Usage, Use(r), Used, Utilise** Accustomed, Application, Apply, Avail, Boot, Consume, Custom, Deploy, Dow, →**EMPLOY**, End, Enure, Ex, Exercise, Exert, Expend, Exploit, Flesh, Function, Habit(uate), Hand-me-down, Inured, Loanee, Manner, Milk, Mores, Ply, Practice, Pre-owned, Sarum, Snorter, Spare, Spent, Sport, Stock, Stoner, Take, Tradition, Treat, Try, Ure, Utilisation, Wield, With, Wont

**Useful** Asset, Availing, Commodity, Convenient, Dow, Expedient, Invaluable, Practical

**Useless** Appendix, Base, Bung, Cumber, Cumber-ground, Dead duck, Dead loss, Dead-wood, Dud, Empty, Futile, Gewgaw, Grotty, Ground, Idle, Inane, Incapable, Ineffective, Inutile, Lame, Lemon, Nonstarter, Nugatory, Otiose, Plug, Pointless, Reject, Sculpin, Sterile, Swap, US, Vain, Void, Wet, White elephant

**Usher** Black Rod, Blue Rod, Chobdar, Commissionaire, Conduct(or), Doorman, Escort, Gentleman, Guide, Herald, Huissier, Macer, Marshal, Rod, Show, Steward

**Usual, Usually** Average, Common, Customary, Habit(ual), In general, In the main, Most, Natural, Normal, Ordinary, Routine, Rule, Solito, Standard, Stock, Tipple, Typical, Vanilla, Wont

**Usurer, Usury** Gombeen, Gripe, Lender, Loanshark, Moneylender, Note-shaver, Shark, Uncle

**Usurp(er)** Abator, Arrogate, Assume, Encroach, Invade

**Ut** As, Doh, Utah

**Utah** Ut

**Utensil(s)** Batterie, Battery, Cafetiere, Ca(u)ldron, Canteen, Chopsticks, Colander, Cookware, Corer, Double boiler, Egg-slice, Fish-kettle, Fork, Funnel, Gadget, Grater, Gridiron, Holloware, Implement, Instrument, Jagger, Kettle, Knife, Mandolin(e), Ricer, Scoop, Sieve, Skillet, Spatula, Spoon, Things, Tool, Whisk, Zester

▶ **Utilise** *see* **USAGE**

**Utilitarian** Benthamite, Mill, Practical, Useful

**Utility** Elec(tricity), Expected, Gas, Mains, Public, Water

**Utmost** Best, Extreme, Farthest, Maximum, Nth

**Utopia(n)** Adland, Cloud-cuckoo-land, Ideal, More, Never-never-land, Pantisocracy, Paradise, Perfect, Shangri-la

**Utter(ance), Uttered, Utterly** Absolute, Accent, Agrapha, Agraphon, Aread, Arrant, Aside, Cry, Dead, Deliver, Dictum, Dog, Downright, Ejaculate, Emit, Enunciate, Express, Extreme, Glossolalia, Issue, Judgement, Lenes, Lenis, Locution, Mint, Most, Oracle, Pass, Phonate, Pronounce, Pure, Quo(th), Rank, Rap, Rattle, Remark, Saw, →**SAY**, Sheer, Speak, Spout, Stark, State, Syllable, Tell, Thorough, Tongue, Ug, Unmitigated, Vend, Vent, Very, Voice

**Uvula** Staphyle

# Vv

**V** Anti, Bomb, Del, Five, Nabla, See, Sign, Verb, Verse, Versus, Victor(y), Volt, Volume

**Vacancy, Vacant** Blank, Empty, Glassy, Goaf, Hole, Hollow, Inane, Place, Space, To let, Vacuum, Wooden

**Vacation** Holiday, Leave, Long, Non-term, Outing, Recess, Trip, Voidance, Volunteer

**Vaccination, Vaccine** Antigen, Antiserum, Attenuated, Bacterin, Booster, Cure, HIB, Jenner, MMR, Sabin, Salk, Serum, Subunit

**Vacillate, Vacillating** Chop, Dither, Feeble, Halt, Hesitate, Shilly-shally, Teeter, Trimmer, Wabble, Wave(r), Whiffle

**Vacuous, Vacuity** Blank, Empty, Inane, Toom, Vacant, Void

**Vacuum** Blank, Cleaner, Dewar, Eiky, Emptiness, Magnetron, Nothing, Nothingness, Plenum, Thermos®, Torricellian, Ultra-high, Void

**Vade-mecum** Ench(e)iridion, Notebook

**Vagabond** Bergie, Gadling, → GYPSY, Hobo, Landlo(u)per, Outcast, Picaresque, Rapparee, Romany, Rover, Runabout, Runagate, Tramp

**Vagina** Box, Crack

**Vagrant** Beachcomber, Bum, Bummer, Caird, Crusty, Derro, Dosser, Drifter, Flotsam, Gadabout, Gangrel, Gang-there-out, Goliard, Gypsy, Hobo, Landlo(u)per, Lazzarone, Nomad, Patercove, Pikey, Rinthereout, Rogue, Romany, Rover, Scatterling, Strag, Straggle, Stroller, Swagman, Tinker, Tinkler, → TRAMP, Truant, Vagabond, Walker

**Vague(ness)** Amorphous, Bleary, Blur, Confused, Dim, Dreamy, Equivocal, Evasive, Faint, General, Hazy, Ill-defined, Ill-headed, Imprecise, Indecisive, Indefinite, Indeterminate, Indistinct, Inexact, Loose, Loste, Mist, Nebulous, Obscure, Shadowy, Sketchy, Woolly-minded

▷ **Vaguely** *may indicate* an anagram

**Vain** Bootless, Conceited, Coxcomb, Coxcomical, Dandyish, Egoistic, Empty, Fruitless, → FUTILE, Hollow, Idle, Narcissistic, Peacock, Pompous, Pown, Profitless, Proud, Strutting, Unuseful, Useless, Vogie

**Vainglory** Panache

**Valance** Pand, Pelmet

**Vale** Addio, Adieu, Aloha, Cheerio, Coomb, Dean, Dedham, Dene, Ebbw, Enna, Evesham, Glamorgan, Glen, Tara, Ta-ta, Tempé, Valley

**Valediction, Valedictory** Apopemptic, Cheerio, Farewell, Tata

**Valentine** Card, Sweetheart

**Valerian** All-heal, Cetywall, Greek, Red, Setuale, Setwale, Setwall, Spur

**Valet** Aid, Andrew, Gentleman's gentleman, Jeames, Jeeves, Lacquey, Man, Passepartout, Quint, Servant, Skip-kennel

**Valetudinarian** Hypochondriac, Invalid

**Valiant** Brave, Doughty, Heroic, Redoubtable, Resolute, Stalwart, Stouthearted, Wight

**Valid(ity), Validate** Confirm, Establish, Holding, Just, Legal, Legitimate, Probate, Rational, Right, Sound

**Valise** Bag, Case, Dorlach, Satchel

**Valkyrie** Brynhild

**Valley** Ajalon, Aosta, Argolis, Baca, Barossa, Bekaa, Beqaa, Bolson, Cleavage, Cleugh, Clough, Comb(e), Coomb, Cwm, Dale, Dargle, Dean, Death, Defile, Dell, Den, Dene, Dingle, Dip, Drowned, Dry, Emmental, Gehenna, Ghyll, Glen, Glencoe, Gleneagles, Glyn, Gorge, Graben, Great Glen, Great Rift, Griff(e), Grindelwald, Gulch, Hanging, Haugh, Heuch,

Hollow, Hope, Humiliation, Hutt, Imperial, Indus, Ladin, Lagan, Lallan, Monument, Napa, Nemea, Olympia, Po, Ravine, Rhondda, Ria, Rift, Ruhr, San Fernando, Seaton, Silicon, Slack, Slade, Sonoma, Strath(spey), Strathmore, Tempe, Tophet, Trossachs, Umbria, U-shaped, Valdarno, Vale, Vallambrosa, Vallis Alpes, Water, Water gap, Yosemite

**Valour** Bravery, Courage, Gallantry, Heroism, Merit, Prowess

**Valuable, Valuation, Value(s)** Absolute, Acid, Appraise, Appreciate, Apprize, Assess(ment), Asset, Attention, Bargain, Blue chip, Book, Break up, Calibrate, Calorific, Carbon, Checksum, Cherish, CIF, Cop, Cost, Crossover, Datum, Dear, Denomination, Entry, Equity, Esteem, Estimate, Exit, Expected, Face, Feck, Hagberg, Intrinsic, Jew's eye, Limit, Market, Merit, Modulus, Money's worth, Museum piece, Net present, Net realizable, Nominal, Nuisance, Number, Omnium, Par, PH, Place, Prairie, Precious, Premium, Present, Price, Prize, Prys, Q, Quartile, Rarity, Rate, Rateable, Rating, Regard, Residual, Respect, Rogue, Salt, Scarcity, Sentimental, Set, Snob, Steem, Stent, Store, Street, Surplus, Surrender, Taonga, Time, Treasure, Tristimulus, Truth, Utility, Valuta, →**WORTH**

**Valueless** Bum, Fig, Mare's nest, Orra, Trivial, Useless, Worthless

**Valve** Acorn, Air, Aortic, Ball(cock), Bicuspid, Bleed, Blow, Butterfly, Check, Choke, Clack, Cock, Diode, Drawgate, Dynatron, Escape, Eustachian, Exhaust, Flip-flop, Foot, Gate, Induction, Inlet, Magnetron, Mitral, Mixing, Needle, Non-return, Outlet, Pallet, Pentode, Petcock, Piston, Poppet, Pulmonary, Puppet, Radio, Resnatron, Safety, Seacock, Semilunar, Shut-off, Side, Sleeve, Slide, Sluice, Sluicegate, Snifter, Snifting, Stopcock, Suction, Tap, Tetrode, Thermionic, Throttle, Thyratron, Tricuspid, Triode, Turncock, Vacuum, Ventil, Vibrotron

**Vamoose** Abscond, Decamp, Scarper, Scat, Scram

**Vamp** Adlib, Charm, Improvise, Maneater, Rehash, Seduce, Siren, Strum, Twiddle

**Vampire** Bat, Dracula, False, Ghoul, Lamia, Lilith, Nosferatu, Pontianak, Stringes

**Van(guard)** Advance, Box-car, Brake, Breakdown, Camper, Cart, Cube, Delivery, Dormobile®, Forefront, Foremost, Freight-car, Front, Furniture, Guard's, Head, Kombi®, Lead, Leader(s), Lorry, Loudspeaker, Luggage, Meat wagon, Panel, Panel-truck, Pantechnicon, Patrol-wagon, Pick-up, Prison, Removal, Spearhead, Tartana, Truck, Ute, Wagon

**Vanadium** V

**Vandal(ise), Vandalism** Deface, Desecrate, Freebooter, Hooligan, Hun, Loot, Pillage, Ravage, Rough, Sab(oteur), Sack, Saracen, Skinhead, Slash, Smash, Trash, Wrecker

**Vandyke** Beard, Painter

**Vane(s)** Dog, Fan, Guide, Rudder, Swirl, Telltale, Vexillum, Weather(cock), Web, Wind (tee), Wing

**Vanessa** Butterfly

**Vanilla** Pinole

**Vanish(ed), Vanishing** Cease, Depart, Disappear, Disperse, Dissolve, Evanesce(nt), Evaporate, Extinct, Faint(ed), Mizzle, Slope, Transitory, Unbe

**Vanity** Amour-propre, Arrogance, Ego, Ego-trip, Esteem, Fair, Futility, Narcissism, Peacockery, Pomp, Pretension, Pride, Self-conceit, Self-esteem, Self-importance

**Vanquish, Vanquished** Beat, Conquer, Floor, Loser, Master, Overcome, Overwhelm, Rout

**Vantage (point)** Ascendancy, Coign(e), Height

**Vaporise, Vapour** Aerosol, Boil, Cloud, Contrail, Effluent, Fog, Fume, Halitus, Inhalant, Iodine, Miasma, Mist, Moisture, Reek, Roke, Skywriting, →**STEAM**, Steme, Water

▸ **Variable, Variance, Variant, Variation** *see* **VARY(ING)**

**Varicose** Haemorrhoids

▸ **Varied, Variety** *see* **VARY(ING)**

▷ **Varied** *may indicate* an anagram

**Variegate(d)** Calico, Dappled, Flecked, Fretted, Harlequin, Motley, Mottle, Pied, Rainbow, Skewbald, Tissue

▷ **Variety of** *may indicate* an anagram

**Various** Divers(e), Manifold, Multifarious, Separate, Several, Sundry
**Various years** Vy
**Varlet** Cad, Knave, Page, Rascal, Rogue
**Varnish(ing)** Arar, Bee-glue, Copal, Cowdie-gum, Dam(m)ar, Dammer, Desert, Dope,
　　Dragon's-blood, French polish, Glair, Japan, Lacquer, Lentisk, Mastic, Nail, Nibs, Oil,
　　Resin, Sandarac, Shellac, Spirit, Tung-oil, Tung-tree, Vernis martin, Vernissage
**Vary(ing), Variable, Variance, Variant, Variation, Varied, Variety, Various**
　　Ablaut, Aelotropy, Alter, Amphoteric, Assorted, Assortment, Breed, Brew, Cepheid,
　　Change, Chequered, Colour, Contrapuntal, Counterpoint, Daedal(e), Dedal, Dependent,
　　Differ, Discrepancy, Dispute, Diverse, Diversity, Dummy, Eclectic, Eclipsing, Enigma,
　　Farraginous, Fickle, Fluctuating, Form, Grid, Heterodox, Iid, Inconsistent, Inconstant,
　　Independent, Intervening, Isochor, Isopleth, Isotopy, Line, Local, Medley, Mix, Morph,
　　Morphosis, Multifarious, Multiplicity, Music hall, Mutable, Nimrod, Nuance, Nutation,
　　Odds and ends, Olio, Omniform, Orthogenesis, Parametric, Partita, Protean, Random,
　　Remedy, Response, Smörgåsbord, Sort, Species, Spice, Sport, Stirps, Stochastic, Strain,
　　String, Timeserver, Tolerance, Twistor, Uneven, Unknown, Var, Varicellar-zoster,
　　Vaudeville, Versatile, Versiform, Version, Vicissitude, Vl, Wane, Wax, X, Y, Z
**Vase** Bronteum, Canopus, Cornucopia, Diota, Hydria, Jardinière, Kalpis, Lachrymal, Lecythus,
　　Lekythos, Lustre, Moon flask, Murr(h)a, Portland, Pot, Potiche, Stamnos, Urn, Vessel
**Vasectomy** Desexing
**Vassal** Client, Daimio, Dependant, Feoffee, Lackey, Liege, Liegeman, Man, Manred,
　　Servant, Vavaso(u)r
**Vast(ness)** Big, Cosmic, Cyclopic, Enormous, Epic, Extensive, Googol, Huge(ous),
　　Immeasurable, Immense, Mighty, Monumental, Ocean, Prodigious
**Vat** Back, Barrel, Bath, Blunger, Chessel, Copper, Cowl, Cuvée, Fat, Girnel, Keir, Kier,
　　Mash tub, Pressfat, Stand, Tank, Tan-pit, Tub, Tun, Winefat
**Vatican** Rome, V
**Vaudeville** Zarzuela
**Vaughan** Silurist
**Vault(ed), Vaulting** Arch, Barrel, Cavern, Cellar, Chamber, Charnel house, Clear,
　　Cross, Crypt, Cul-de-four, Cupola, Dome, Dungeon, Fan, Firmament, Fornicate, Groin,
　　Hypogeum, Jump, Kiva, Leap(frog), Lierne, Mausoleum, Ossuary, Overarch, Palm, Pend,
　　Pendentive, Pole, Rib, Safe, Sepulchre, Serdab, Severy, Shade, Souterrain, Tholus, Tomb,
　　Tunnel, Undercroft, Underpitch, Vaut, Wagon, Weem, Wine
▷ **Vault** *may indicate* an anagram
**Vaunt** Boast, Brag, Crow, Skite
**Veal** Escalope, Fricandeau, Galantine, Scallop, Schnitzel, Vituline, Wiener schnitzel
**Vector, Vector operator** Del, Dyad, Expression, Nabla, Phasor, Polar, Radius
**Veda** Yajurveda
**Veer** Bag, Boxhaul, Broach, Clubhaul, Deviate, Draw, Gybe, Splay, Sway, Swerve, Tack,
　　Turn, Wear, Yaw
**Veg(etate), Vegetator, Vegetation** Alga, Biome, Brush, Cover, Flora, Fynbos,
　　Gar(r)igue, Greenery, Herb, Laze, Lemna, Maquis, Quadrat, Scrub, Stagnate, Sudd, Transect
**Vegan** Parev(e), Parve
**Vegetable(s)** Flora, Hastings, Inert, Jardinière, Plant, Root, Salad, Sauce, Truck

---

**VEGETABLES**

| 3 letters: | 4 letters: | Guar | Sium |
|---|---|---|---|
| Alu | Aloo | Kale | Spud |
| Oca | Bean | Leek | Taro |
| Pea | Beet | Neep | Wort |
| Udo | Cole | Okra | |
| Yam | Gobi | Okro | |

**5 letters:**
Beans
Chana
Chard
Chive
Choko
Chufa
Crout
Ingan
Mooli
Navew
Onion
Orach
Pease
Pulse
Sabji
Savoy
Sibol
Swede
Tuber

**6 letters:**
Allium
Batata
Calalu
Camote
Carrot
Catalu
Celery
Coulis
Daikon
Endive
Fennel
Frisée
Garlic
Greens
Jicama
Kumara
Lablab
Legume
Mangel
Marrow
Matoke

Mibuna
Mizuna
Orache
Pepper
Pomato
Potato
Pratie
Quinoa
Radish
Rapini
Sorrel
Squash
Tattie
Tomato
Turnip
Wakame

**7 letters:**
Brinjal
Cabbage
Calaloo
Cardoon
Castock
Cataloo
Chayote
Chicory
Cocoyam
Collard
Custock
Earlies®
Filasse
Gherkin
Legumen
Lettuce
Mangold
Matooke
Olitory
Pak-choi
Parsnip
Pimento
Pot herb
Pottage
Pumpkin

Rampion
Salsify
Shallot
Skirret
Soybean
Spinach
Spinage
Sprouts
Succory
Triffid
Witloof

**8 letters:**
Beetroot
Borecole
Brassica
Broccoli
Celeriac
Chick pea
Cucumber
Cucurbit
Eggplant
Escarole
Eschalot
Kohlrabi
Leaf-beet
Mirepoix
Mushroom
Rutabaga
Samphire
Scallion
Zucchini

**9 letters:**
Artichoke
Asparagus
Aubergine
Calabrese
Colcannon
Courgette
Finocchio
Macedoine
Mangetout

Primavera
Radicchio
Rocambole
Romanesco
Succotash
Sweet corn
Tonka-bean
Turnip top

**10 letters:**
Alexanders
Cavalo nero
Chiffonade
Runner bean
Sauerkraut
Scorzonera
String bean
Swiss chard
Tuscan kale

**11 letters:**
Bamboo shoot
Cauliflower
Chinese leaf
Haricot bean
Ratatouille
Spinach-beet
Spring onion
Sweet potato

**12 letters:**
Cherry tomato
Corn-on-the-cob
Mangel-wurzel
Marrow-squash

**14 letters:**
Globe artichoke

**18 letters:**
Jerusalem artichoke

---

**Vegetable extract** Solanine

**Vegetarian** Giraffe, Herbivore, Lactarian, Maigre, Meatless, Parev(e), Parve, Pythagorean, Tofu, Vegan, Veggie

**Vegetation** Greenery

**Vehemence, Vehement(ly)** Amain, Ardent, Fervid, Forcible, Frenzy, Heat, Hot, Intense, Violent

**Vehicle(s)** Agent, Artic, Articulated, Base, Commercial, Conveyance, Double-bottom, Fleet, Half-track, High occupancy, Hybrid, Machine, Means, Medium, Multipurpose, Offroad, Oil, Rattletrap, Recovery, Recreational, Re-entry, Space, Superload, Tempera, Tracked, Ute, Utility, Wheels, Wrecker

## VEHICLES

*3 letters:*
ATV
Bus
Cab
Car
Fly
LEM
SUV

*4 letters:*
Biga
Cart
Dray
Duck
Jeep®
Kago
Kart
Limo
MIRV
Quad
Rego
Scow
Shay
Sled
Tank
Taxi
Tram
Trap

*5 letters:*
Brake
Buggy
Crate
Cycle
Delta
Float
Go-Ped®
Lorry
Motor
Reggo
Rover
Soyuz
Sulky
Tip-up
Tonga
Truck
Turbo
Vespa®
Wagon

*6 letters:*
Boxcar
Camper

Dennet
Dodgem
Estate
Fiacre
Gharri
Gharry
Go-cart
Go-kart
Hansom
Hearse
Hummer
Humvee®
Jet-Ski
Jingle
Jinker
Jitney
Koneke
Landau
Launch
Limber
Litter
Matatu
Pick-up
Put-put
Samlor
Skibob
Skidoo®
Sledge
Sleigh
Sno-Cat®
Spider
Surrey
Tanker
Tardis
Tricar
Troika
Tuk tuk
Vahana
Weasel

*7 letters:*
Air taxi
Amtrack
Blokart
Capsule
Caravan
Casspir
Channel
Chariot
Crew cab
Dog-cart
Gritter
Growler

Jeepney
Minibus
Minicab
Minivan
Norimon
Pedicab
Phaeton
Rail bus
Ricksha
Shebang
Shuttle
Sidecar
Taxi cab
Tipcart
Tractor
Trailer
Tramcar
Trishaw
Trolley
Tumbril
Volante

*8 letters:*
Brancard
Cable car
Carry-all
Curricle
Dragster
Rickshaw
Runabout
Sport ute
Stanhope
Steam-car
Tarantas
Tricycle
Trimotor
Unicycle

*9 letters:*
Ambulance
Autocycle
Battlebus
Buckboard
Dormobile®
Dune buggy
Estate car
Gladstone
Hatchback
Land Rover®
Motorhome
Sand-yacht
Tarantass
Tumble-car

Two-seater
Wagonette
Winnebago

*10 letters:*
All-terrain
Earth-mover
Four-by-four
Four-seater
Gas-guzzler
Hovercraft
Juggernaut
Load-lugger
Mammy wagon
Roadroller
Rust-bucket
Snowmobile
Snowplough
Trolleybus
Tumble-cart
Two-wheeler
Velocipede

*11 letters:*
People-mover
Semitrailer
Transporter
Wheelbarrow

*12 letters:*
Autorickshaw
Double-decker
Micro-scooter
Pantechnicon
Perambulator
Single-decker
Space shuttle
Station wagon
Three-wheeler

*13 letters:*
Paddock-basher
Penny-farthing
People carrier

*14 letters:*
Chelsea tractor

*16 letters:*
Personnel carrier

**Veil** Burk(h)a, Calyptra, Chad(d)ar, Chador, Chuddah, Chuddar, Cloud, Cover, Curtain, Envelop, Eucharistic, Hejab, Hide, Hijab, Humeral, Kalyptra, Khimar, Kiss-me, Lambrequin, Mantilla, Mist, Nikab, Niqab, Obscure, Purdah, Sacramental, Scene, Sudarium, Veale, Volet, Weeper, Wimple, Yashmak

**Vein** Artery, Azygas, Basilic, Brachiocephalic, Coronary, Costa, Diploic, Epithermal, Fahlband, Gate, Hemiazygous, H(a)emorrhoid, Innominate, Jugular, Ledge, Lode, Mainline, Media, Midrib, Mood, Naevus, Nervure, Organic, Outcrop, Percurrent, Pipe, Portal, Postcava, Precava, Pulmonary, Radius, Rake, Reef, Rib, Saphena, Sectorial, Spur, Stockwork, Stringer, Style, Thread, Tone, Varicose, Varix, Vena, Venule, Vorticose

**Vellum** Cutch, Japanese, Kutch, Parchment

**Velocity** Angular, Circular, Escape, Mustard, Muzzle, Orbital, Parabolic, Radial, Rate, Speed, Terminal, V

**Velvet(y)** Bagheera, Chenille, Moleskin, National, Panne, Pile, Three-pile, Velour, Velure, Villose, Villous

**Venal** Corruptible, Mercenary, Sale

**Vend(or), Vending** Auctor, Automat, Emporium, E-tailor, Hawk, Peddle, Pedlar, Rep, Sammy, Sell, Sutler

**Vendetta** Feud

**Veneer** Facade, Finish, Gloss, Varnish

**Venerable** Aged, August, Augustus, Bede, Guru, Hoary, Iconic, Sacred, Sage, Vintage

**Venerate, Veneration** Adore, Awe, Douleia, Dulia, Filiopietistic, GOM, Hallow, Homage, Honour, Hyperdulia, Iconise, Idolise, Latria, Respect, Revere, Worship

**Venereal** NSU, VD

**Venery** Chase

**Venetian** Aldine, Blind, Doge, Gobbo, Polo

**Vengeance, Vengeful** Commination, Erinyes, Reprisal, Ultion, Vindictive, Wan(n)ion, Wrack, Wreak

**Venial** Base, Excusable

**Venice** La Serenissima

**Venison** Cervena, Deer

**Venom(ous)** Bitchy, Black widow, Gall, Gila, Jamestown-weed, Jim(p)son-weed, Platypus, Poison, Rancour, Solpuga, Spite, Toxic, Virus, Zootoxin

**Vent** Airway, Aperture, Belch, Chimney, Emit, Express, Fumarole, Hornito, Issue, Louver, Louvre, Ostiole, Outlet, Smoker, Solfatara, Spiracle, Undercast, Wreak

**Venter** Uterus

**Ventilate, Ventilator** Air, Air-brick, Air-hole, Discuss, Draught, Express, Louvre, Plenum, Shaft, Voice, Windsail, Windway, Winze

**Venture(d)** Ante, Assay, Bet, Callet, Chance, Dare, Daur, Durst, Enterprise, Flutter, Foray, Handsel, Hazard, Jump, Mint, Opine, Presume, Promotion, Prostitute, Risk, Spec, Strive, Throw

**Venue** Bout, Locale, Place, Showground, Stadium, Stateroom, Tryst, Visne

**Venus** Armless, Clam, Cohog, Cytherean, Hesper(us), Love, Lucifer, Morning-star, Phosphorus, Primavera, Quahaug, Quahog, Rokeby, Vesper

**Venus fly-trap** Dionaea

**Veracity, Veracious** Accurate, Factual, Sincere, Truth(ful)

**Veranda(h)** Balcony, Gallery, Lanai, Patio, Piazza, Porch, Sleep-out, Stoep, Stoop, Terrace

**Verb(al), Verbs** Active, Argy-bargy, Auxiliary, Causative, Conative, Copula, Ergative, Factitive, Finite, Infinitive, Intransitive, Irregular, Modal, Passive, Perfective, Performative, Phrasal, Preterite, Stative, Transitive, Vb, Word-of-mouth

**Verbascum** Mullein

**Verbatim** Literally

**Verbena** Vervain

**Verbose, Verbosity** Gassy, Padding, Prolix, Talkative, Wordy

**Verdant** Green, Lush

**Verdict** Decision, Epitaph, Fatwah, Formal, Judg(e)ment, Majority, Narrative, Open, Opinion, Pronouncement, Resolution, Ruling, Special

**Verdigris** Aeruginous, Patina

**Verge** Border, Brink, →EDGE, Hard shoulder, Incline, Limit, Long paddock, Rim, Roadside, Threshold

**Verger** Beadle, Pew-opener

**Verify, Verification** Accredit, Affirm, Ascertain, Check, Confirm, Constatation, Control, Crosscheck, Prove, Validate

**Verily** Yea

**Verisimilitude** Artistic, Authenticity, Credibility

**Verity** Fact, Sooth, Truth

**Vermifuge** Cow(h)age, Cowitch

**Vermilion** Cinnabar, Minium, Red

**Vermin(ous)** Carrion, Catawampus, Lice, Mice, Pest, Ratty, →RODENT, Scum

**Vermouth** Absinthiated, French, It(alian), Martini®

**Vernacular** Common, Dearnly, Dialect, Idiom, Jargon, Lingo, Native, Patois, Slang, Vulgate

**Veronica** Hebe, Hen-bit, Speedwell

**Verruca** Plantar wart, Wart

**Versatile** Adaptable, All-rounder, Flexible, Handy, Many-sided, Multipurpose, Octavalent, One man band, Protean, Resourceful

**Verse(s), Versed** Dactyl, Fluent, Free, Linked, Logaoedic, Passus, Poetry, Political, Reported, Rhophalic, →RHYME, System

---

## VERSES

| *1 letter:* | Epode | Jingle | Pythian |
|---|---|---|---|
| V | Fitte | Laisse | Rondeau |
| | Fytte | Miurus | Sapphic |
| *3 letters:* | Gazal | Octave | Sestina |
| Fit | Haiku | Pantun | Sestine |
| | Hokku | Rondel | Sixaine |
| *4 letters:* | Ionic | Scazon | Stiches |
| Awdl | Lyric | Senary | Strophe |
| Blad | Meter | Sonnet | Tiercet |
| Duan | Poesy | Stanza | Triolet |
| Epic | Renga | Strain | Tripody |
| Epos | Rubai | Tenson | |
| Fitt | Spasm | Tercet | *8 letters:* |
| Hymn | Stave | Vulgus | Cinquain |
| Line | Tanka | | Clerihew |
| Neck | Tract | *7 letters:* | Doggerel |
| Poem | Triad | Alcaics | Glyconic |
| Rime | | Couplet | Hexapody |
| Sijo | *6 letters:* | Dimeter | Kyrielle |
| Song | Adonic | Elegiac | Madrigal |
| Vers | Ballad | Epigram | Nonsense |
| | Burden | Fabliau | Pindaric |
| *5 letters:* | Ghazal | Huitain | Quatrain |
| Blank | Ghazel | Leonine | Rhopalic |
| Blaud | Gnomic | Pantoum | Rove-over |
| Canto | Haikai | Pennill | Rubaiyat |
| Comus | Heroic | Prosody | Scansion |

| | | | |
|---|---|---|---|
| Senarius | Hexameter | Fescennine | Octastichon |
| Sing-song | Macaronic | Hypermeter | Riding-rhyme |
| Sirvente | Monometer | Mock-heroic | Septenarius |
| Syllabic | Monorhyme | Ottava rima | |
| Terzetta | Monostich | Pennillion | *12 letters:* |
| Trimeter | Octameter | Pentameter | Archilochian |
| Tristich | Octastich | Rhyme-royal | Asclepiadean |
| Versicle | Saturnian | Serpentine | Hudibrastics |
| | Stornello | Tetrameter | Octosyllabic |
| *9 letters:* | Terza rima | Tetrastich | |
| Amphigory | Vers libre | Villanelle | *14 letters:* |
| Asclepiad | | | Longs and shorts |
| Beatitude | *10 letters:* | *11 letters:* | |
| Dithyramb | Asynartete | Acatalectic | *15 letters:* |
| Ditrochee | Catalectic | Alexandrine | Poulter's measure |
| Goliardic | Cynghanedd | Hudibrastic | |

▷ **Versed** *may indicate* reversed

**Versed sine** Sagitta

**Versifier, Versification** Lyricist, Poetaster, Prosody, Rhymer, Rhymester

**Version** Account, Adaptation, Authorised, Cephalic, Cover, Edition, Form, Paraphrase, Rede, Remake, Rendering, Rendition, Revised, Revision, Rhemish, Standard, Summary, Translation, Urtext, Variorum

**Vertebra(e), Vertebrate** Agnathan, Amniote, Amphioxus, Ascidian, Atlas, Axis, Bone, Centrum, Cervical, Chordae, Coccyx, Cyclostome, Dorsal, Foetus, Gnathostome, Ichthyopsida, Lamprey, Lumbar, Placoderm, Reptile, Sacral, Sauropsida, Spondyl, Tetrapod, Tunicata, Vermis

**Vertex** Apex, Crest, Crown, Summit, Zenith

**Vertical** Apeak, Apeek, Apothegm, Atrip, Erect, Lapse, Montant, Muntin(g), Ordinate, Perpendicular, Plumb, Prime, Sheer, Standing, Stemmed, Stile, Upright

**Vertigo** Dinic, Dizziness, Fainting, Giddiness, Megrim, Nausea, Staggers, Whirling

**Vertue** Visne

**Verve** Dash, Energy, Go, Gusto, Panache, Vigour

**Very (good, well)** A1, Ae, Assai, Awfully, Boffo, Bonzer, Boshta, Boshter, Dashed, Dead, Def, Ever (so), Extreme(ly), Fell, Frightfully, Full, Gey, Grouse, Heap, Hellova, Helluva, Highly, Hugely, Jolly, Keen, Light, Mighty, Molto, Much, OK, Opt, Precious, Precise, Purler, Real(ly), Right, Self same, So, Sore, Stinking, Très, Unco, Utter, V, VG, Way

**Vesicle** Ampul, Bladder

**Vespers** Evensong, Lychnic, Placebo, Sicilian

**Vessel(s)** →BOAT, Capillary, Container, Craft, Dish, Lacteal, Logistics, Motor, Pressure, Receptacle, Retia, Seed, →SHIP, Tomentum, Utensil, Vascular, Weaker

## VESSELS

| *3 letters:* | Tub | Cask | Skin |
|---|---|---|---|
| Bin | Urn | Cowl | Snow |
| Cog | Vas | Dhow | Vase |
| Cup | Vat | Etna | Vein |
| Dow | | Font | Vena |
| Fat | *4 letters:* | Grab | Vial |
| Obo | Back | Horn | Zulu |
| Pan | Bowl | Lota | |
| Pig | Brig | Olpe | *5 letters:* |
| Pyx | Buss | Raft | Aorta |

Aviso
Blood
Cogue
Crare
Crewe
Crock
Cruet
Cruse
Cupel
Dandy
Dixie
Gourd
Grail
Ketch
Laver
Liner
Lotah
Mazer
Oiler
Phial
Pokal
Quart
Round
Scoop
Shell
Sloop
Stean
Steen
Stoop
Stoup
Tazza
Varix
Xebec
Zabra

**6 letters:**
Aludel
Argyle
Argyll
Artery
Banker
Beaker
Bicker
Bouget
Bucket
Carafe
Carboy
Chatty
Copper

Crayer
Dinghy
Dogger
Dolium
Elutor
Flagon
Frigot
Galiot
Galley
Goblet
Goglet
Guglet
Humpen
Jam jar
Jet-ski
Kettle
Lorcha
Mortar
Noggin
Retort
Rumkin
Sailer
Sampan
Sconce
Settee
Shippo
Situla
Steane
Tassie
Teacup
Trough
Tureen
Urinal
Venule
Wherry

**7 letters:**
Amphora
Ampoule
Ampulla
Canteen
Chalice
Cistern
Coaster
Costrel
Creamer
Cresset
Cuvette
Cyathus

Dredger
Drifter
Felucca
Firepan
Four oar
Frigate
Gaff-rig
Galleon
Galliot
Gunboat
Gunship
Gurglet
Jugular
Mudscow
Patamar
Pinnace
Pirogue
Pitcher
Polacca
Precava
Sharpie
Steamer
Stewpot
Tankard
Terreen
Vedette
Washpot

**8 letters:**
Billycan
Calabash
Cauldron
Ciborium
Colander
Coolamon
Crucible
Cucurbit
Decanter
Figuline
Flatboat
Galleass
Galliass
Gallipot
Gallivat
Hoveller
Hydroski
Jerrican
Lifeboat
Longboat

Monteith
Pancheon
Panchion
Pannikin
Schooner
Showboat
Sinusoid
Spittoon
Stockpot
Trimaran
Workboat

**9 letters:**
Alcarraza
Autoclave
Bucentaur
Calandria
Casserole
Cullender
Destroyer
Hydrofoil
Privateer
Tappit-hen
Whaleback
Whaleboat
Wineglass

**10 letters:**
Advice-boat
Bathyscaph
Chamberpot
Deep-sinker
Icebreaker
Jardinière
Triaconter

**11 letters:**
Aspersorium
Bathyscaphe
Side-wheeler

**12 letters:**
Fore-and-after
Lachrymatory
Stern-wheeler
Sternwheeler

---

**Vest** Beset, Confer, Crop top, Gilet, Modesty, Rash, Semmit, Singlet, Spencer, Sticharion, String, Undercoat, Undershirt, Waistcoat
**Vestibule** Anteroom, Atrium, Entry, Exedra, Foyer, Hall, Lobby, Narthex, Oeil-de-boeuf, Porch, Portico, Pronaos, Tambour

**Vestige** Hint, Mark, Mention, Shadow, Sign, Trace

**Vestment** Alb, Breastplate, Canonicals, Chasuble, Chimar, Chimer(e), Cotta, Dalmatic, Ephod, Fannel, Fanon, Garb, →**GARMENT**, Maniple, Mantelletta, Omophorion, Pallium, Parament, Ph(a)elonian, Pontificals, Raiment, Rational, Rochet, Rocquet, Saccos, Sakkos, Sticharion, Stole, Superhumeral, Surplice, Tunic(le)

**Vestry** Common, Sacristy, Select

**Vet(ting), Veterinary, Vets** Censor, Check, Doc(tor), Examine, Ex-serviceman, Farrier, Herriot, Horse-doctor, Inspect, OK, Positive, Screen, Veteran, Zoiatria, Zootherapy

**Vetch** Bitter, Ers, Fitch, Kidney, Locoweed, Milk, Tare, Tine

**Veteran** BL, Expert, GAR, Master, Old-stager, Oldster, Old sweat, Old-timer, Old 'un, Retread, Seasoned, Soldier, Stager, Stalwart, Stalworth, Vet, War-horse, Warrior

▷ **Veteran** *may indicate* 'obsolete'

**Veto** Ban, Bar, Blackball, Debar, Item, Line-item, Local, Negative, Pocket, Reject, Taboo, Tabu

**Vex(ing), Vexatious, Vexed** Ail, Anger, Annoy, Bepester, Bother, Chagrin, Debate, Fret, Gall, Grieve, Harass, Haze, Irritate, Madden, Mortify, Noy, Peeve, Pester, Rankle, Rile, Sore, Spite, Tease, Torment, Trouble(some), Trying, Worrisome

**Vexation(s)** Barrator, Chagrin, Drat, Fashery, Grief, Humph, Irksome, Nuisance, Pique, Spite, Trouble, Try, Umph, Untoward

**Vexillum** Web

**Via** By, Per, Through

**Viable** Economic, Going, Healthy, Possible

**Vial** Spirit-level

**Viand** Cate

**Vibrate, Vibration(s), Vibrant** Active, Atmosphere, Chatter, Diadrom, Dinnle, Dirl, Energetic, Flutter, Free, Fremitus, Harmonogram, Hotter, Jar, Judder, Oscillate, Plangent, Pulsate, Pulse, Purr, Quake, Resonance, Resonant, Rumble, Seiche, Shimmy, Shudder, Thrill, Throb, Tingle, Tremble, Tremor, Trill, Trillo, Twinkle, Uvular, Wag, Whir(r)

**Viburnum** Opulus, Snowball

**Vicar** Apostolic, Bray, Choral, Cleric, Elton, Forane, General, Incumbent, Lay, Pastoral, Plenarty, Primrose, Rector, Rev(erend), Trimmer

**Vice** Acting, Clamp, Cramp, Crime, Deputy, Eale, Evil, Foible, Greed, Iniquity, Instead, Jaws, Regent, Second (in command), →**SIN**, Stair

**Vice-president** Croupier, Veep

**Viceroy** Khedive, Nawab, Provost, Satrap, Willingdon

**Vichy (water)** Eau, Milice

**Vicinity** Area, Environs, Hereabouts, Locality, Neighbourhood, Region, Round about

**Vicious** Brutal, Cruel, Flagitious, Hotbed, Lethal, Vitriolic

**Victim(s), Victimisation** Abel, Angel, Butt, Casualty, Currie, Curry, Dupe, Easy meat, Fall guy, Fashion, Frame, Hitlist, Host, Judenhetze, Lay-down, Mark, Martyr, Nebbich, Neb(b)ish, Pathic, Patsy, Pigeon, Prey, Quarry, Sacrifice, Scapegoat, Sitting duck, Target

**Victor(y)** Bangster, Banzai, Beater, Cadmean, Cannae, Captor, Champ(ion), Conqueror, Conquest, Epinicion, Epinikion, Eunice, Flagship, Fool's mate, Gree, Gris, Hallelujah, Hugo, Jai, Jai Hind, Kobe, Landslide, Lepanto, Ludorum, Mature, Moral, Nike, Palm, Philippi, Pyrrhic, Romper, Runaway, Scalp, Shut-out, Signal, Squeaker, Sweeping, Triumph, V, VE (day), Vee, Vic, Walk-away, Walkover, Win(ner)

**Victoria(n)** Aussie, Empress, Plum, Prig, Prude(nt), Station, Terminus

**Victualler** Caterer, Grocer, Licensed, Purveyor, Supplier, Vivandière

**Video(-tape)** Betacam®, Cassette, Digital, Full-motion, Interactive, Laser vision, Minitel, Pixelation, Promo, Quadruplex, Reverse, Scratch, Still, Vera, Webcast

**Vie** Compete, Contend, Emulate, Strive

**Vienna** Wien

**Vietcong** Charley, Charlie

**Vietnam(ese)** Cham, Tonkin, VN

**View(er)** Aim, Angle, Aspect, Attitude, Behold, Belief, Bird's eye, Cineaste, Consensus, Consider, Cosmorama, Cutaway, Dekko, Dogma, Doxy, Endoscope, Estimation, Exploded, Eye (shot), Facet, Gander, Glimpse, Grandstand, Helicopter, Heresy, Idea, Introspect, Jaundiced, Kaleidoscope, Landscape, Line, Look, Notion, Observe, Opinion, Optic, Outlook, Pan, Panorama, Parallax, Perception, Perspective, Point, Private, Profile, →**PROSPECT**, Scan, Scape, Scene(ry), Scope, See, Sight, Sightlined, Skyscape, Slant, Snapshot, Spectate, Spectre, Specular, Spyglass, Standpoint, Stereoscope, Strain, Survey, Synop(sis), Tenet, Terrain, Thanatopsis, Theory, Vantage-point, Veduta, Vista, Visto, Watch, Witness, Worm's eye

**Viewpoint** Angle, Attitude, Belvedere, Conspectus, Elevation, Eyeshot, Grandstand, Instance, Observatory, Perspective, Sight, Sightline, Tendentious, Voxpop, Watch tower

**Vigil(ance), Vigilant(e)** Awake, Aware, Baseej, Basij, Deathwatch, Eve, Guardian angel, Hawk-eyed, Lyke-wake, On guard, Pernoctate, Prudence, Wake, Wake-rife, Wary, Watch, Waukrife, Whitecap

**Vignette** Print, Profile, Sketch

**Vigorous(ly), Vigour** Aggressive, Agitato, Alive, Animation, Athletic, Bant, Bellona, Billy-o, Billy-oh, Birr, Blooming, Bouncing, Brio, Brisk, Con brio, Cracking, Drastic, Dynamic, Élan, Emphatic, Energetic, Flame, Forceful, Full-blooded, Furioso, Go, Green, Gusto, Heart(y), Heterosis, Hybrid, Lush, Lustihood, Lustique, Lusty, Manful, Moxie, P, Pep, Pith, Potency, Punchy, Pzazz, Racy, Rank, Raucle, Red-blooded, Robust, Round, Rude, Sap, Smeddum, Spirit, Sprack, Sprag, Steam, Sthenic, Stingo, Strength, Strenuous, Strong, Thews, Tireless, Tone, Tooth and nail, Trenchant, Two-fisted, Up, Vegete, Verve, Vim, Vinegar, Vitality, Vivid, Vivo, Voema, Zip

▷ **Vigorously** *may indicate* an anagram

**Viking** Dane, Leif, Norseman, Raider, Rollo, R(y)urik, Sea king, Sea wolf, Varangian

**Vile(ness)** Base, Corrupt, Depraved, Dregs, Durance, Earthly, Infamy, Infernal, Mean, Offensive, Scurvy, Vicious

**Vilify, Vilification** Denigrate, Slander, Smear

**Villa** Bastide, Chalet, Dacha, House

**Village** Aldea, Auburn, Borghetto, Burg, Clachan, Corporate, Dorp, Endship, Global, Gotham, Gram, Greenwich, Hamlet, Kaik, Kainga, Kampong, Kirkton, Kraal, Legoland, Manyat(t)a, Mir, Outlet, Outport, Pit, Pueblo, Rancheria, Rancherie, Shtetl, Skara Brae, Thorp(e), Ujamaa, Vill, Wick

**Villain(y)** Anti-hero, Baddy, Bluebeard, Bravo, Crim(inal), Crime, Dastard, Dog, Fagin, Heavy, Iago, Knave, Lawbreaker, Macaire, Miscreant, Mohock, Nefarious, Ogre, Reprobate, Rogue, Scab, Scelerat, Scoundrel, Sikes, Skelm, Steerforth, Tearaway, Traitor

**Villein** Bordar, Churl, Serf

**Vim** Energy, Go, Vigour, Vitality, Zing

**Vincent** Van Gogh

**Vindicate, Vindication** Absolve, Acquit, Apologia, Avenge, Clear, Compurgation, Darraign(e), Darrain(e), Darrayn, Defend, Deraign, Exculpate, Exonerate, Justify

**Vindictive** Bunny-boiler, Hostile, Malevolent, Repay(ing), Spiteful, Vengeful

**Vine(yard)** Akatea, Ampelopsis, Ayahuasco, Balloon, Balsam apple, Bindweed, Bine, Bush rope, Château, Clinging, Clos, Colocynth, Cross, Cru, Cubeb, Cypress, Dodder, Domaine, Grapery, Hop, Idaean, Ivy, Kangaroo, Kudzu, Lawyer, Liana, Martha's, Matrimony, Muskmelon, Naboth's, Potato, Puncture, Quinta, Russian, Sarsaparilla, Stephanotis, Supplejack, Swallowwort, Trumpet, Turpeth, Vitis, Winery, Wonga-wonga, Yam, Yquem

**Vinegar** Acetic, Acetum, Alegar, Balsam, Balsamic, Eisel(l), Esile, Malt, Oxymel, Tarragon, Wine, Wood

**Vintage** Classic, Crack, Cru, Old, Quality

**Viol(a), Violet** African, Alto, Amethyst, Archil, Crystal, Dame's, Dog, Dog's tooth, Gamba, Garden, Gentian, Gridelin, Heart's ease, Hesperis, Ianthine, Indole, Iodine,

Ionone, Kiss-me, Lilac, Lyra, Mauve, Methyl, Neapolitan, Orchil, Pansy, Parma, Prater, Quint(e), Rock, Saintpaulia, Shrinking, Sweet, Tenor, Visual, Water

**Violate, Violating, Violation** Abuse, Breach, Contravene, Defile, Desecrate, Fract, Infraction, →INFRINGE, March-treason, Outrage, Peccant, Rape, Ravish, Sacrilege, Solecism, Stuprate, Transgress, Trespass

**Violence, Violent(ly)** Acquaintance, Amain, Attentat, Bangster, Battery, Berserk, Bloody, Brutal, Brute force, Cataclysmic, Crude, Drastic, Droog, Extreme, Fierce, Flagrant, Force, Frenzied, Furious, Heady, Het, High, Hooliganism, Hot, Inbreak, Mighty, Onset, Rabid, Rage, Rampage, Rampant, Riot, Rogue, Rough, Rough stuff, Rude, Rumbustious, Savage, Severe, Shoot 'em up, Slap, Stormy, Strongarm, Ta(r)tar, Tearaway, Terrorism, Thuggery, Tinderbox, Tub-thumping, Vehement, Vie, Wild, Wrath

**Violet** Anil, Gentian, Neapolitan, Purple, →VIOLA

**Violin(ist), Violin-maker, Violin-shaped** Alto, Amati, Cremona, Fiddle, Griddle, Gu(e), Guarneri(us), Guarnieri, Heifetz, Kennedy, Kit, Kubelik, Leader, Luthier, Menuhin, Nero, Oistrakh, Paganini, Pandurate, Rebec(k), Rote, Stradivarius

**VIP** Bashaw, Bigshot, Bigwig, Brass, Cheese, Cob, Effendi, Envoy, Grandee, Imago, Kingpin, Magnate, Magnifico, Mugwump, Nabob, Nib, Nob, Pot, Snob, Someone, Swell, Tuft, Tycoon, Worthy

**Viper** Asp, Cerastes, Gaboon, Horned, Judas, Pit, Rattlesnake, River-jack, Russell's, Sand, Saw-scaled, →SNAKE, Traitor, Villain

**Virago** Amazon, Battle-axe, Beldam(e), Harpy, Randy, Shrew, Termagant

**Virgil** Maro

**Virgin(al), Virginity, Virgin Mary** Airline, Blessed, Celibate, Chaste, Cherry, Extra, Intact, Ladykin, Madonna, Maiden, Maidenhead, Maidenhood, Marian, May, New, Our lady, Pan(h)agia, Parthenos, Pietà, Pucel(l)age, Pucelle, Pure, Queen, Snood, Tarpeia, Theotokos, Untainted, Vestal, Zodiacal

**Virginia(n)** Creeper, Old Dominion, Tuckahoe, Va, Wade

**Virile, Virility** Energetic, Lusty, Machismo, Macho, Male, Manly, Red-blooded

**Virtu** Curio

**Virtue(s), Virtuous, Virtual** Angelic, Aret(h)a, Assay-piece, Attribute, Cardinal, Caritas, Charity, Chastity, Continent, Cyber, Dharma, Efficacy, Ethical, Excellent, Faith, Foison, Fortitude, Fus(h)ion, Good, Goody-goody, Grace, Honesty, Hope, Justice, Moral(ity), Natural, Patience, Plaster-saint, Practical, Principal, Prudence, Pure, Qua, Say-piece, Squeaky-clean, Straight and narrow, Temperance, Theological, Upright, Worth

**Virtuosity, Virtuoso** Artist, Bravura, Brilliance, Excellence, Executant, Maestro, Menuhin, Paganini, Savant, Whiz

**Virulent** Acrimonious, Deadly, Hostile, Malign, Noxious, Toxic, Vitriolic, Waspish

**Virus** AIDS, Antigen, Arbovirus, Bacteriophage, Boot, Capsid, Chikungunya, Computer, Contagium, Coronavirus, Coxsackie, Defective, DNA, EB, Ebola, Echo, Enterovirus, Epstein-Barr, Filovirus, Filterable, Fowlpest, Germ, Granulosis, Hantavirus, Hendra, Herpes, HIV, HIV negative, HIV positive, Lassa, Latent, Leaf-mosaic, Lentivirus, Michelangelo, Microbe, Microorganism, Norwalk, Oncogen, Oncornavirus, Parainfluenza, Parvo(virus), Pathogen, Peach-yellow, Picornavirus, Polyoma, Prophage, Reovirus, Retrovirus, Rhabdovirus, Rhinovirus, Ross River, Rotavirus, SARS, Shingles, Slow, Street, SV40, Swine flu, Tobacco mosaic, Trojan horse, Varicella, Venom, Virino, Virion, West Nile, Zoster

**Visa** Transit

**Viscera** Bowels, Entrails, Giblets, Guts, Harigal(d)s, Haslet, Innards, Omentum, Splanchnic, Umbles, Vitals

**Viscount** Vis

**Viscous (liquid), Viscosity** Absolute, Glaireous, Gleety, Gluey, Gummite, Gummy, Kinematic, Slab, Specific, Sticky, Stoke, Tacky, Tar, Thick, Thixotropic

**Visible, Visibility** Clear, Conspicuous, Evident, Explicit, Export, In sight, Obvious, Zero-zero

**Visigoth** Asaric

**Vision(ary)** Abstraction, Aery, Aisling, Apparition, Awareness, Beatific, Binocular, Bourignian, Day-dreamer, Double, Dream(er), Emmetropia, Fancy, Fantast, Fey, Foresight, Idealist, Ideologist, Illusionist, Image, Kef, Moonshine, Mouse-sight, Mystic, Ocular, Phantasm(a), Phantom, Pholism, Photism, Photopia, Rainbow-chaser, Revelation, Romantic, Seeing, Seer, Sight, Sightline, Stereo, Stereopsis, Sweven, Tunnel, Twenty-twenty, Viewy

**Visit(or)** Affliction, Alien, Away, Caller, Day-tripper, Domiciliary, ET, Event, First-foot, Frequent, Gam, Guest, Habitué, Haunt, Health, Hit, Inflict, Kursaal, Look in, Look up, Manuhiri, Pop in, Prison, See, Sightseer, Sojourn, State, Stay, Stranger, Take, Theatregoer, Tourist, Wait upon, Weekender

**Visor, Vizor** Eyeshade, Face-saver, Mesail, Mezail, Umbrel, Umbr(i)ere, Umbril, Vent(ayle)

**Vista** Enfilade, Outlook, Scene(ry), View

**Visual(ise)** Envisage, Graphical, Imagine, Ocular, Optical, Picture, See, Sketch, Visible

**Vital(ity)** Alive, Bounce, Central, Critical, Crucial, Energy, Esprit, Essential, Existent, Foison, Gusto, Indispensable, Juice, Key, Kick, Life-blood, Lifeline, Linchpin, Lung, Mites, Momentous, Necessary, Oomph, Organ, Pizzazz, Pulse, Salvation, Sap, Verve, Viable, Vigour, Zing, Zoetic

**Vitals** Numbles, Umbles, Viscera

**Vitamin(s)** A, Adermin, Aneurin, Axerophthol, B, Bioflavonoid, Biotin, C, Calciferol, Calcitriol, Citrin, Cobalamin, D, E, Ergocalciferol, Folacin, G, H, Inositol, K, Linoleic, Menadione, Menaquinone, Niacin, Niacinamide, P, Pan(to)thenol, Phylloquinone, Phytonadione, Pyridoxine, Retinene, Retinol, Riboflavin, Ribose, Thiamin(e), Tocopherol, Torulin, Tretinoin

**Vitiate(d)** Flaw(ed)

**Vitreous** Glassy, Hyaline

**Vitriol(ic)** Acid, Acrimonious, Biting, Blue, Caustic, Green, Mordant, White

**Vituperate** Abuse, Berate, Castigate, Censure, Defame, Inveigh, Lash, Rail, Scold

**Viva** Oral

**Vivacity, Vivacious** Animation, Brio, Esprit, Exuberant, Sparkle, Spirit, Sprightly, Verve

**Vivid** Bright, Brilliant, Colourful, Dramatic, Eidetic, Fresh, Graphic, Keen, Live, Lurid, Pictorial, Picturesque, Sharp, Shocking, Violent

**Vivien** Leigh

**Vixen** Catamaran, Harridan, Shrew, Virago

**Viz** Sc, Videlicet

**Vizier** Pheazar, Wazir

▶ **Vizor** *see* VISOR

**Vocabulary** Active, Glottochronology, Idiolect, Idioticon, Jargon, (Kata)kana, Lexicon, Lexis, Meta-language, Nomenclator, Passive, Wordbook

**Vocal(isation), Vocalist** Articulate, Cantilena, Doo-wop, Eloquent, Minstrel, Oral, Phonal, Schwa, Singer, Songster, Sprechgesang

**Vocation** Call, Career, Métier, Mission, Priesthood, Profession, Pursuit, Shop

**Vociferous(ly)** Clamant, Loud, Loud-mouth(ed), Ore rotundo, Strident

**Vogue** Chic, Day, →FASHION, Groovy, It, Mode, Rage, Style, Ton, Trend

**Vogul** Ugrian, Ugric

**Voice(d)** Active, Air, Alto, Ancestral, Bass, Chest, Contralto, Countertenor, Descant, Edh, Emit, Eth, Express, Falsetto, Glottis, Harp, Head, Inner, Intonate, Lyric, Mastersinger, Meistersinger, Mezzo-soprano, Middle, Mouth, Opinion, Passive, Phonic, Pipe, Presa, Quill, Say, Sonant, Soprano, Speak, Spinto, Sprechstimme, Steven, Syrinx, Tais(c)h, Tenor, Throat, Tone, →TONGUE, Treble, Utter, White

**Voiceless** Aphonia, Aphony, Dumb, Edh, Eth, Mute, Silent, Tacit

**Void** Abyss, Annul, Belch, Blank, Chasm, Counter, Defeasance, Defecate, Diriment, Empty, Erase, Evacuate, Gap, Hollow, Inane, Inoperative, Invalid, Irritate, Lapse, Negate, Nullify, Quash, Space, Vacuum

**Voila** There

**Volatile** Excitable, Explosive, Inconsistent, Latin, Live(ly), Mercurial, Skittish, Tear gas, Temperamental, Terpene, Tinderbox, Unstable

**Volcano(es), Volcanic** Agglomerate, Basalt, Black smoker, Burning mountain, Composite, Cone, Conic, Fumarole, Greystone, Hornito, Ice, Idocrase, Igneous, Ignimbrite, Monticule, Mud, Obsidian, Pele, Pelée, Plinian, Pozz(u)olana, Pumice, Puzzolana, Sandblow, Shield, Soffioni, Solfatara, Stratovolcano, Tephra, Trass, Tuff

## VOLCANOES

| 2 letters: | Semeru | 9 letters: | Pico de Teyde |
|---|---|---|---|
| Aa | Tolima | Aniakchak | |
| | | Corcovado | 12 letters: |
| 3 letters: | 7 letters: | Haleakala | Citlaltépetl |
| Aso | Aragats | Helgafell | Ixtaccahuatl |
| Puy | Comoros | Huascaran | Iztaccahuatl |
| | El Misti | Mount Fuji | National Park |
| 4 letters: | Huascan | Nevis Peak | Popocatepetl |
| Etna | Iliamna | Paricutin | |
| Fuji | Iwo Jima | Scablands | 13 letters: |
| Maui | Kilauea | Stromboli | Mount Demavend |
| Taal | Mofette | Tangariro | Mount Pinatubo |
| | Rotorua | | Mount St Helens |
| 5 letters: | Ruapehu | 10 letters: | |
| Askja | Semeroe | Chimborazo | 14 letters: |
| Hekla | St Kilda | Lassen Peak | Mount Suribachi |
| Kauai | Tambora | Montserrat | Nevada de Colima |
| Mayon | | Mount Eigon | Nevada de Toluca |
| Misti | 8 letters: | Mount Kenya | Soufrière Hills |
| Okmok | Amygdale | Mount Pelée | |
| Salse | Andesite | Nyiragongo | 17 letters: |
| Thera | Antisana | | Fernando de |
| | Cameroon | 11 letters: | Noronha |
| 6 letters: | Cotopaxi | Erciyas Dagi | Warrumbungle |
| Ararat | Jan Mayan | Kilimanjaro | Range |
| Asosan | Krakatoa | Mount Egmont | |
| Azores | Mauna Kea | Mount Erebus | 20 letters: |
| Egmont | Mauna Loa | Mount Katmai | D'Entrecasteau |
| Erebus | St Helena | Mount Kazbek | Islands |
| Ischia | St Helens | Mount Shasta | |
| Katmai | Taranaki | Nyamuragira | |
| Kazbek | Unalaska | Olympus Mons | |
| Lipari | Vesuvius | Pico de Teide | |

**Vole** Arvicola, Meadow mouse, Muskrat, Musquash, Ondatra

**Volition** Velleity, Will

**Volley** Barrage, Boom, Broadside, Platoon, Round, Salvo, Tirade, Tire

**Volt(age)** BeV, Bias, Electron, Grid bias, HT

**Voltaire** Arouet

**Volte face** Enantiodromia, U-turn, Zig

**Voluble** Fluent, Glib

**Volume** Atomic, Band, Bande, Barrel, Book, Bushel, Capacity, CC, Code(x), Content, Critical, Cubage, Gallon, Hin, Loudness, Mass, Ml, Molecular, Omnibus, Peck, Pint, Quart(o), Roll, Roul(e), Size, Space, Specific, Stere, Swept, Tidal, Tom, Tome, Ullage, Vol

**Voluntary, Volunteer** Docent, Enlist, Fencible, Free, Free-will, Honorary, Offer, Postlude, Reformado, Spontaneous, Tender, Tennessee, Terrier, TN, Ultroneous, Yeoman

**Voluptuary, Voluptuous** Carnal, Hedonist, Houri, Luscious, Sensuist, Sensuous, Sybarite

**Volute** Helix, Roll

**Vomit(ing)** Anacatharsis, Barf, Black, Boak, Boke, Cascade, Cat, Chuck up, Chunder, Disgorge, Egest, Egurgitate, Emesis, Fetch-up, Haematemesis, Honk, Keck, Kotch, Parbreak, Posset, Puke, Ralph, Regorge, Regurgitate, Retch, Rolf, Spew, Technicolour yawn, Throw up, Upchuck

**Voodoo** Charm, Jettatura, Kurdaitcha, Macumba, Mambo, Obeah, Sorcery, Zombi(e)

**Voracious, Voracity** Bulimia, Edacity, Gluttony, Greed, Man-eater, Ravenous, Serrasalmo

**Vortex** Charybdis, Eddy, Gyre, Trailing, Whirlpool

**Votary** Adherent, Cenobite, Devotee, Disciple, Fan, Nun, Swinger, Zealot

**Vote(r), Votes, Voting** Alternative, Assentor, Aye, Ballot, Ballotee, Block, Card, Casting, Choose, Colonist, Constituent, Coopt, Cross, Crossover, Cumulative, Division, Donkey, Fag(g)ot, Floating, Franchise, Free, Grey, Informal, Mandate, Nay, Negative, No, Opt, People, Placet, Plebiscite, Plump, Plural, Poll, Postal, Pot-wabbler, Pot-waller, Pot-walloner, Pot-walloper, Pot-wobbler, PR, Preferential, Proportional representation, Protest, Qualified majority, Referendum, Return, Scrutin de liste, Scrutiny, Show of hands, Side, Single transferable, Straw(-poll), Suffrage, Swinging, Sympathy, Tactical, Ten-pounder, The stump, Theta, Ticket, Token, Transferable, Voice, X, Yea, Yes

**Vote-catcher** Pork

**Vouch(er), Vouchsafe** Accredit, Assure, Attest, Beteem(e), Book token, Chit, Coupon, Credit note, Endorse, Gift, Guarantee, Luncheon, Meal-ticket, Promise, Receipt, Slip, Ticket, Token, Warrant

**Voussoir** Quoin, Wedge

**Vow** Affirm, Baptismal, Behight, Behot(e), Earnest, Ex voto, Hecht, Hest, I do, Nuncupate, →OATH, Obedience, Pledge, Plight, Promise, Simple, Solemn, Swear, Troth, Vum

**Vowel(s)** Ablaut, Anaptyxis, Aphesis, Breve, Cardinal, Diphthong, Gradation, Indeterminate, Monophthong, Murmur, Mutation, Point, Rhyme, Seg(h)ol, S(c)hwa, Svarabhakti, Triphthong

**Voyage(r)** Anson, Columbus, Course, Cruise, Launch, Maiden, Passage, Peregrinate, Salt, Sinbad, Travel

**Voyeur** Peeping Tom, Scopophiliac

**VTOL** Convertiplane

**Vulcan(ite)** Blacksmith, Ebonite, Fire, Mulciber, Spock, Wayland

**Vulgar(ian)** Banausic, Barbaric, Base, Blatant, Blue, Brassy, Buffoon, Canaille, Cheap, Cit, Coarse, Common, Crude, Demotic, Earthy, Filthy, Flash(y), Forward, Gaudy, General, Gent, Gorblim(e)y, Gross, Heel, Hussy, Ignorant, Indecent, Kitsch, Laddish, Lavatorial, Lewd, Low(-life), Naff, Obscene, Ostentatious, Pandemian, Parvenu, Plebby, Plebeian, Popular, Proletarian, Raffish, Ribald, Riff-raff, Rude, Scaff, Scurrilous, Slag, Snob, Tacky, Tarty, Tawdry, Threepenny, Tiger, Tink, Twopenny, Upstart, Vulg

**Vulnerable, Vulnerability** Achilles heel, Defenceless, Endangered, Exposed, Frangible, Open, Pregnable, Susceptible, Unguarded, Weak, Wide-open

**Vulture** Aasvogel, Bearded, Bird, Buzzard, California (condor), Condor, Culture, Falcon, Gallinazo, Gier, Griffon, Gripe, Grype, King, Lammergeier, Lammergeyer, Ossifrage, Predator, Turkey, Urubu, Zopilote

# Ww

**W** Watt, West, Whisky, Women
**Wacky** Offbeat
**Wad(ding)** Batt(ing), Lump, Pad, Pledget, Roll, Swab, Wodge
**Waddle** Toddle, Waggle
**Waddy** Club, Cowboy, Stick
**Wade(r), Wading** Antigropelo(e)s, Ardea, Crane, Curlew, Dikkop, Egret, Flamingo, Ford,
Godwit, Grallae, Grallatorial, Greenshank, Gumboot, Heron, Ibis, Jacksnipe, Lapwing,
Limpkin, Oyster-catcher, Paddle, Phalarope, Plodge, Plover, Pukeko, Ree, Sandpiper,
Sarus, Seriema, Shoebill, Snipe, Splodge, Stilt(bird), Terek, Virginia, Wellington
**Waesucks** Ewhow, O(c)hone
**Wafer** Biscuit, Cracker, Crisp, Gaufer, Gaufre, Gofer, Gopher, Host, Papad, Seal
**Waff** Flap, Flutter, Wave
**Waffle** Adlib, Blather, Cake, Equivocate, Fudge, Gas, Gaufer, Gaufre, Gofer, Gopher,
Hedge, Padding, Poppycock, Prate, Rabbit, Wibble
**Waft(ing)** Airborne, Aura, Blow, Drift, Float
**Wag(gish), Waggle** Arch, Card, Comedian, Facetious, Joker, Lick, Niddle-noddle, Nod,
Rogue, Shake, Sway, Swee, Wit(snapper), Wobble
**Wage(s)** Ante, Award, Fee, Greengage, Hire, Income, Living, Meed, Minimum, Nominal,
Pay, Portage, Practise, Prosecute, Rate, Salary, Screw, Subsistence
**Wage-earner** Breadwinner, Employee, Proletariat(e)
**Wager** Ante, Back, →**BET**, Gamble, Lay, Pascal's, Stake, Wed
**Wagon(er)** Ar(a)ba, Aroba, Boötes, Boxcar, Brake, Break, Buck, Buckboard, Buggy,
Caisson, Carriage, Cart, Cattle truck, Chuck, Coachman, Cocopan, Conestoga, Corf,
Covered, Democrat, Drag, Dray, Flatcar, Fourgon, Freight-car, Gambo, Go-cart, Hopper,
Hutch, Low-loader, Mammy, Paddy, Palabra, Patrol, Plaustral, Police, Prairie schooner,
Rave, Reefer, Rubberneck, Shandry, Stage, Station, Tank, Tartana, Telega, Tender, Trap,
Trekker, Truck, Van, Victoria, Wain, Water
**Waif** Arab, Foundling, Gamin, Jetsam, Stray, Urchin, Victoria, Wastrel, Water, Weft
**Wail(er)** Banshee, Bawl, Blubber, Howl, Keen, Lament, Moan, Skirl, Threnody, Threnos,
Ululate, Vagitus, Wah-wah, Yammer
**Wain** Cart, Dray, Wagon
**Waist(band)** Belt, Cummerbund, Girdlestead, Girth, Hour-glass, Middle, Midship, Obi,
Sash, Shash, Wasp, Zoster
**Waistcoat** Gilet, Jerkin, Lorica, MB, Pressure, Sayon, Shawl, Sleeve(d), Stabvest, Tuxedo,
Vest, Weskit
**Wait(er), Waiting** Abid(e), Ambush, Attend, Barista, Bide, Busboy, Butler, Buttle, Carhop,
Commis, Cupbearer, Dally, Delay, Estragon, Expect, Flunkey, Frist, Garçon, Hang on, Hesitate,
Hover, Interval, Khidmutgar, Lead time, Lime, Linger, Loiter, Lurch, Maître d', Maître d'hôtel,
Minority, Omnibus, Pannier, Pause, Penelope, Pozzo, Queue, Remain, Serve(r), Sommelier,
Stacking, Stay, Steward, Suspense, Taihoa, Tarry, Tend(ance), Tray, Vladimir, Wine, Won
**Waitress** Bunny girl, Hebe, Miss, Mousme(e), Nippy, Server
**Waive** Abandon, Defer, Forgo, Overlook, Postpone, Relinquish, Renounce, Suspend
**Wake(n)** Abrade, Abraid, Abray, Aftermath, Alert, American, Animate, Arouse, Astern,
Backwash, Deathwatch, Excite, Finnegan's, Hereward, Keen, Knock-up, Like, Lyke, Prod,
Rear, Revive, →**ROUSE**, Surface, Trail, Train, Wash

**Waldo** Emerson

**Wale(r)** Prop, Ridge, Weal

**Wales** Cambria, Cymru, Dyfed, Principality

**Walk(er), Walking, Walkabout, Walkway** Aisle, Alameda, Alley, Alure, Amble, Ambulate, Arcade, Berceau, Birdcage, Charity, Cloister, Clump, Constitutional, Daddle, Dander, Dauner, Emu, Esplanade, EVA, Expatiate, Festination, Flânerie, Forefoot, Frescade, Gait, Gallery, Gangplank, Ghost, Go, Gradient, Gressorial, Heel and toe, Hike, Hookey, Hump, Lambeth, Leg, Lumber, Mainstreeting, Mall, March, Mince, Mooch, Mosey, Nordic, Pace, Pad, Paddle, Pasear, Paseo, Passage, Passerby, Path, Pavement, Ped(estrianism), Perambulate, Pergola, Perp, Piaffe, Piazza, Pipe-opener, Pole, Pound, Power, Prance, Prom(enade), Rack, Ramble, Rampart, Random, Ring, Routemarch, Sashay, Scamble, Schlep, Shamble, Sidle, Slommock, Space, Spanish, Sponsored, Stalk, Step, Stoa, Striddle, Stride, Stroll, Strut, Stump, Taligrade, Terrace, Toddle, Tramp, Trash, Travolator, Tread, Trog, Truck, Trudge, Turn, Wade, Wander, Wayfare, Wend, Widow's, Xyst

**Walking-stick** Cane, Stilt

**Walk-over** Doddle, Pie, Scratch

**Wall** Antonine, Bail, Bailey, Barrier, Berlin, Berm, Cavity, Cell, Chinese, Climbing, Countermure, Crib, Curtain, Dado, Dam, Dike, Dry-stone, Enceinte, Epispore, Exine, Fail-dike, Fourth, Fronton, Frustule, Gable, Great, Groyne, Hadrian's, Hanging, Hangman, Head, Immure, Intine, Mahjongg, Mani, Merlon, Mutual, Myocardium, Non-bearing, Parapet, Parie(te)s, Parietal, Parpane, Parpen(d), Parpent, Parpoint, Partition, Party, Peribolos, Pericarp, Perpend, Perpent, Pleuron, Podium, Puteal, Qibla, Retaining, Reveal, Revet(ment), Ring, River, Roman, Roughcast, Screen, Sea, Septum, Severus, Side, Somatopleure, Spandrel, Spandril, Street, Studding, Tambour, Tariff, Trumeau, Vallation, Vallum, Video, Wa', Wailing, Western, Withe, Zooecia

**Wallaby** Brusher, Dama, Kangaroo, Pademelon, Pad(d)ymelon, Quokka, Tammar, Whiptail

**Wallah** Competition

**Wallaroo** Euro

**Wall-covering, Wallpaper** Anaglypta®, Arras, Burlap, Flock, Lincrusta, Paper, Tapestry, Tapet

**Waller** Fats, Mason

**Wallet** Billfold, Case, Flybook, Folder, Notecase, Pochette, Pocket-book, Purse, Scrip

**Wallflower** Crucifer, Dowd(y), Pariah

**Wall-game** Eton, Mahjongg

**Wallop** Axe, Bash, Baste, Batter, Beat, Biff, Clout, Cob, Gigantic, →**HIT**, Lam, Lounder, Oner, Polt, Pound, Slog, Strap, Swinge, Tan, Tat, Thud, Trounce

**Wallow(ing)** Bask, Flounder, Luxuriate, Revel, Roll, Slubber, Splash, Swelter, Tolter, Volutation, Welter

**Wall-painting** Fresco, Graffiti, Grisaille

**Wallpaper** →**WALL-COVERING**, Woodchip

**Wall-plate** Tassel, Torsel

**Wall-support** Beam, Foundation, Pier, Rear-arch, Rere-arch

**Wally** Ass, Dipstick, Moron, Nerd, Nincompoop, Prat

**Walnut** Black, Butternut, Hickory, Juglans, Satin, White

**Walrus** Morse, Moustache, Pinniped, Rosmarine, Sea-cow, Sea-horse, Tash, Ugly

**Walter** Bruno, Mitty, Pater, Raleigh, Scott

**Waltz** Anniversary, Blue Danube, Boston, Concert, Dance, Hesitation, Minute, Rotate, Valse

**Wampum** Peag(e), Shell-money

**Wan** Lurid, Pale, Pallid, Pasty, Sanguine, Sorry

**Wanchancy** Unlucky

**Wand** Baton, Caduceus, Rod, Runic, Stick, Thyrse, Thyrsus, Vara, Vare

**Wander(er), Wandering** Aberrance, Adrift, Amble, Bedouin, Berber, Bum, Caird, Daiker, Daydream, Delirious, Desultory, Deviate, Digress, Divagate, Diverge, Drift, Errant, Estray, Evagation, Excursive, Expatiate, Extravagate, Gad(about), Grope, Hobo, Itinerant, Jew, Landloper, Maunder, Meander, Meandrian, Mill, Mither, Moider, Moither, Moon, Noctivagant, Nomad(e), Odysseus, Pedder, Peregrine, Peripatetic, Polar, Prodigal, Rache, Ramble, Range, Ratch, Roamer, Romany, Room, Rove, Solivagant, Stooge, Straggle, Stravaig, Stray, Strayve, Streel, Stroam, Stroll, Swan, Ta(i)ver, Tramp, Troll, Truant, Tuareg, Vagabond, Vagile, Vagrant, Vague, Waif, Wend, Wheel, Wilder, Wolves

▷ **Wandering** *may indicate* an anagram

**Wane** Decline, Decrease, Diminish, Ebb

**Wangle** Arrange, Finagle, Trick

**Want(ing), Wants** Absence, Conative, Covet, Crave, Dearth, Defect, Deficient, Derth, Desiderata, → **DESIRE**, Destitution, Distress, Envy, For, Hardship, Indigent, Itch, Lack, Like, Long, Mental, Moldwarp, Mole, Need, Penury, Require, Scarceness, Scarcity, Shortfall, Shy, Void, Wish, Yen

**Wanton(ness)** Bona-roba, Cadgy, Chamber, Cocotte, Colt's tooth, Deliberate, Demirep, Filly, Flirt-gill, Gammerstang, Giglet, Giglot, Gillflirt, Hussy, Jay, Jezebel, Jillflirt, Lewd, Licentious, Light o' love, Loose, Nice, Protervity, Rig, Roué, Slut, Smicker, Sportive, Sybarite, Toyish, Twigger, Unchaste, Wayward

**Wap** Blow, Knock, Strike

**War(fare), Wars** American Civil, American Independence, Ares, Armageddon, Arms, Asymmetrical, Attrition, Bacteriological, Barons', Bate, Battle, Biological, Bishop, Blitz(krieg), Chemical, Civil, Clash, Class, Cod, Cold, Combat, Conflict, Crescentade, Crimean, Crusade, Culture, Electronic, Emergency, Feud, → **FIGHT**, Flagrante bello, Flame, Food, Franco-Prussian, Fray, Germ, Gigantomachy, Great, Guer(r)illa, Gulf, Holy, Hostilities, Hot, Hundred Years', Information, Internecine, Jehad, Jenkins' ear, Jihad, Jugurthine, Korean, Krieg, Limited, Mars, Mexican, Nam, Napoleonic, Nuclear, Opium, Peasants', Peloponnesian, Peninsular, Phony, Price, Private, Propaganda, Psychological, Punic, Push-button, Queen Anne's, Rebellion, Revolutionary, Roses, Russo-Japanese, Secession, Seven against Thebes, Seven Years', Shooting, Six Day, Social, Spam, Spanish-American, Spanish Civil, Star, Stoush, Sword, Terrapin, Theomachy, Thirty Years', Total, Trench, Trojan, Turf, Vietnam, Winter, World, Yom Kippur

**Warble(r)** Carol, Cetti's, Chiff-chaff, Chirl, Fauvette, Peggy, Record, Rel(l)ish, Singer, Sylvia, Trill, Vibrate, Yodel, Yodle

**War-chant, War-cry** Alalagmos, Haka, Slogan

**Ward (off)** Artemus, Averruncate, Avert, Care, Casual, Casualty, Charge, Defend, District, Fend, Guard, Hand-off, Inner, Keyhole, Marginal, Maternity, Minor, Nightingale, Oppose, Orphan, Outer, Parry, Protégé, Pupil, Soc, Soken, Thunderbolt, Vintry, Wear, Weir

**Warden** Beefeater, Caretaker, Church, Concierge, Constable, Crossing, Curator, Custodian, Game, Guardian, Keeper, Maori, Meter maid, Pear, Provost, Ranger, Septimus, Sidesman, Spooner, Steward, Traffic, Way

**Warder, Wardress** Beefeater, Gaoler, Guardian, Keeper, Matron, Provost, Screw, Turnkey, Twirl

**Wardrobe** Almirah, Armoire, Breakfront, Capsule, Closet, Clothes, Garderobe, Outfit, Vestuary

**Ware(s)** Alga, Arretine, Basalt, Beware, Biscuit, Cameo, Canton, Chelsea, China, Etruria, Fabergé, Faience, Goods, Hollow(w)are, Jasper, Lapis lazuli, Lustre, Merchandise, Palissy, Plate(d), Queen's, Samian, Sanitary, Satsuma, Shippo, Truck, Wemyss

**Warehouse** Bonded, Data, Depository, Entrepôt, Freight-shed, Go-down, Hong, Store

▶ **Warfare** *see* **WAR(FARE)**

**War-game** Kriegs(s)piel

**War-god** Ares, Mars, Tiu, Tiw, Tyr

**Warhead** Atomic, Supremo

**Warhorse** Charger, Destrier, Fighter

**Wariness, Wary** Ca'canny, Cagey, Careful, Cautel, Caution, Chary, Discreet, Distrust, Gingerly, Guarded, Leerie, Leery, Mealy-mouthed, Prudent, Sceptical, Suspicious, Tentie, Tenty, Vigilant

**Warlike** Battailous, Bellicose, Gung-ho, Lachlan, Martial, Militant

**Warlock** Sorcerer

**Warlord** Haw-haw, Kitchener, Shogun, Tuchun

**Warm(er), Warming, Warmth** Abask, Admonish, Air, Ardour, Atingle, Balmy, Bonhomie, British, Calefacient, Calid(ity), Cardigan, Chambré, Cordial, Cosy, Eager, El Nino, Empressement, Enchafe, Fervour, Flame, Foment, Gemütlich, Genial, Gladden, Global, Glow, → HEAT, Hospitable, Hot, Incalescent, Kang, Kindly, Lew, Logic, Loving, Muff, Muggy, Mull, Nuke, Radiator, Tepid, Thermal, Toast, Toasty, Tog

**Warm-blooded** Endothermic, Homothermal, Homothermic, Homothermous, Idiothermous

**Warmonger** Hawk, Merc(enary)

**Warn(ing)** Admonish, Alar(u)m, Alert, Amber, Aposematic, Apprise, Beacon, Bell, Beware, Bleep, Buoy, Caution, Cave, Caveat, Caveat emptor, Commination, Cone, Counsel, Cowbell, Detector, DEW, Document, Early, En garde, Example, Foghorn, Fore, Foreshadow, Foretoken, Gardyloo, Garnishment, Griffin, Harbinger, Hazchem, Heads up, Hoot, Horn, Illocution, Klaxon, Knell, Larum, Lesson, Light, Maroon, Minatory, Monition, Nix, Noli-me-tangere, Nota bene, Notice, Notification, Omen, Pi-jaw, Portent, Premonish, Premonitory, Presage, Prodromal, Profit, Protevangelium, Red alert, Red flag, Red light, Remind, Riot Act, Rumble strip, Scaldings, Scarborough, Sematic, Shore, Signal, Siren, Spindle, Stoplight, Storm, Tattler, Threat, Timber, Tip-off, Token, Toot, Vigla, Vor, Yellow card

**Warner** Alarm, Fore, Plum, Siren

**Warp(ed)** Bent, Bias, Buckle, Cast, Contort, Distort, Hog, Kam, Kedge, Pandation, Spring, Time, Twist, Weft, Zag

**Warpath** Rampage

▷ **Warped** *may indicate* an anagram

**Warrant(y), Warrant officer** Able, Authorise, Behight, Behote, Bench, Bosun, Capias, Caption, Certificate, Charter, Death, Deserve, Detainer, Distress, Dividend, Fiat, Fiaunt, Fugle, General, Guarantee, Justify, Merit, Mittimus, Mortgage, Peace, Permit, Precept, Reprieve, Royal, Search, Sepad, Special, Swear, Transire, Vouch, Warn, Writ

**Warren** Burrow, Colony, Hastings, Rabbit

**Warrior** Achilles, Agamemnon, Ajax, Amazon, Anzac, Arimasp, Attila, Berserk(er), Brave, Cold, Cossack, Crusader, Eorl, Fianna, Fighter, Finlay, Finley, Geronimo, Ghazi, Gurkha, Haiduk, Heimdall, Heyduck, Housecarl, Impi, Jihadi, Lewis, Louis, Myrmidon, Nestor, Rainbow, Rajpoot, Rajput, Roger, Samurai, Soldier, Tatar, Unknown, Wardog, Warhorse, Warwolf, Zulu

**Warship** Battleship, Blockship, Castle, Cog, Corvette, Cruiser, Destroyer, Drake, Dromon(d), Frigate, Galleass, Galliass, Invincible, Man-o-war, Mine-layer, Monitor, Privateer, Ram, Repulse, Wooden Walls

**Wart(y)** Anbury, Angleberry, Blemish, Genital, Keratose, Lump, Muricate, Plantar, Tuberous, Verruca, Wen

**Warthog** Boar

**Warwick** Kingmaker, Neville

▶ **Wary** *see* **WARINESS**

**Was** Erat, Existed, Lived, Past

**Wash(ed), Washer, Washing (up), Wash out** Ablution, Affusion, Alluvion, Bath, Bay(e), Bidet, Bubble-dancing, Bur(r), Calcimine, Circlip, Clean(se), Cradle, D, Dashwheel, Dele(te), Dip, Edulcorate, Elute, Elutriate, Enema, Erode, Fen, Flush, Freshen, Front-loader, Gargle, Grom(m)et, Grummet, Hose, Hush, Irrigate, Kalsomine, Lap, → LAUNDER, Lavabo, Lave, Leather, Lip, Lotion, Marsh, Maundy, Mop, Nipter,

Pan, Pigswill, Poss, Purify, Rinse, Sapple, Scrub, Shampoo, Shim, Sind, Sloosh, Sluice, Soogee, Soojee, Soojey, Squeegie, Stand-up, Stream, Sujee, Swab, Synd, Syne, Tempera, Tie, Toiletry, Toilette, Top and tail, Twin tub, Tye, Wake, Wudu, Yellow

**Washbasin, Washing machine, Washtub, Washhouse** Copper, Dash-wheel, Lavabo, Steamie

**Washerman, Washerwoman** Dhobi, Laundress

**Washington** Dinah, Wa

**Wasn't** Nas, Wasna

**Wasp(ish)** Appledrain, Bembex, Bink, Bite, Chalcid, Cuckoo-fly, Cynipidae, Cynips, Digger, European, Fig, Fretful, Gall(-fly), Gold, Hornet, Horntail, Hoverfly, Irritable, Marabunta, Mason, Miffy, Muddauber, Paper, Peevish, Pompilid, Potter, Ruby-tail, Sand, Seed, Solitary, Spider, Syrphus, Velvet ant, Vespa, Wood, Yellow jacket

▷ **Wasp** *may indicate* a rugby player

**Wasp's nest** Bike, Bink, Byke

**Wassail** Carouse, Pledge, Scolion, Toast

**Wast** Wert

**Wastage, Waste(d), Wasting, Wasteful, Wasteland, Wastepipe, Waster, Wastrel** Amyotrophy, Atrophy, Bilge, Blight, Blow, Blue, Bluer, Boondoggle(r), Cesspit, Cirrhosis, Colliquative, Consume, Contabescent, Coom(b), Cotton, Crud, Culm, Decay, Dejecta, Desert, Detritus, Devastate, Dilapidate, Dissipate, Dregs, Dross, Dung, Dwindle, Dwine, Dystrophy, Effluent, Egesta, Emaciate, Erode, Estrepe, Excrement, Exhaust, Expend, Exudate, Faeces, Flue, Forpine, Fribble, Fritter, Garbage, Gash, Gob, Grog, Guano, Gunge, Haggard, Half-cut, Havoc, Hazardous, High, High-level, Hi(r)stie, Husk, Ice-field, Idler, Inefficient, Kill, Knub, Landfill, Lavish, Lean, Loose, Lose, Loss, Low-level, Marasmus, Merino, Misspent, Moor, Moulder, Muir, Mullock, Mungo, Natural, Ne'er-do-well, Novalia, Nub, Nuclear, Offal, Offcut, Off-scouring, Oller, Ordure, Pellagra, Perish, Phthisis, Pigswill, Pine, Prodigalise, Profligate, Rack and manger, Radioactive, Rammel, Ravage, Recrement, Red mud, Red tape, → **REFUSE**, Reif, Rubble, Ruderal, Ruin, Scant o' grace, Scattergood, Schappe, Scissel, Scoria, Scrap, Scum, Sew(er)age, Skeletal, Slag, Slurry, Spend, Spend-all, Spendthrift, Spill, Spoil(age), Squander, Stalko, Sullage, Swarf, Syntexis, Tabes, Tailing, Thin, Thwaite, Toxic, Trash, Tundra, Ureal, Urine, Uropoiesis, U-trap, Vagabond, Vast, Wanze, Wear, Wilderness, Yearn

▷ **Wasted** *may indicate* an anagram

**Watch(er), Watch out** Accutron®, Analog(ue), Analogon, Argus, Await, Bark, Behold, Big brother, Bird-dog, Black, Case, Cave, Chronograph, Clock, Coastguard, Cock-crow, Digital, Dog, Eryl, Espy, Eyeball, Fob, Glom, Gregory, Guard, Half-hunter, Huer, Hunter, Kettle, Latewake, Lever, Lo, Look, Look-out, Lykewake, Middle, Monitor, Morning, Nark, Neighbourhood, Night, Nit, Note, Nuremberg egg, Observe, Overeye, Patrol, Pernoctation, Posse, Quartz, Regard, Repeater, Rolex®, Rubberneck, Scout, Sentinel, Sentry, Shadow, Snoop, Spectate, Spie, Spotter, Spy, Stake out, Stemwinder, Suicide, Surveillance, Tend, Ticker, Timekeeper, Timepiece, Timer, Tompion, Tout, Turnip, Vedette, View, → **VIGIL**, Voyeur, Wait, Wake, Ward, Weather eye, Wrist(let)

**Watch-chain** Albert, Slang

**Watch-control** Escapement

**Watchful(ness)** Alert, Aware, Care, Dragon, Ira, Jealous, Vigilant, Wakerife, Wary, Waukrife, Weather eye, Wide awake

**Watchman** Argus, Bellman, Charley, Charlie, Cho(w)kidar, Chok(e)y, Guard, Huer, Sentinel, Sentry, Speculator, Tompion, Viewer

**Watch-tower** Atalaya, Barbican, Beacon, Garret, Mirador, Sentry-go, Turret

**Watchword** Cry, Password, Shibboleth, Slogan

**Water(ed), Waters, Watery** Adam's ale, Adam's wine, Aerated, Amrit, Apollinaris, Aq(ua), Aquatic, Aqueous, Ascites, Barley, Bayou, Bedabble, Bilge, Bound, Branch, Brine, Broads, Brook, Burn, Canal, Cancer, Chlorine, Chresard, Chuck, Cold, Cologne, Compensation, Conductivity, Connate, Dead, Deaw, Deg, Demersal, Dew, Dill, Dilute,

Dribble, Drinking, Eau, Ebb, Echard, Element, Ennerdale, Epilimnion, Euphotic, Evian®, First, Flood, Ford, Fossil, Functional, Gallise, Gallize, Ganga jal, Grey, Gripe, Ground, Hard, Heavy, Hectum, Hellespont, High, Holy, Hot, Hungary, Hydatoid, Irrigate, Javel(le), Kuroshio, Kyle, Lagoon, Lagune, Lake, Lant, Laurel, Lavender, Leachate, Lentic, Light, Lime, Limnology, Lithia, Loch(an), Lode, Lotic, Lough, Low, Lubricated, Lymph, Mains, Melt, Meteoric, Mineral, Miner's inch, Moiré, Mother, Nappe, North, Oasis®, Oedema, Orange-flower, Overfall, Pani, Pawnee, Pee, Perrier®, Phreatic, Pisces, Polly, Polynia, Polynya, Poppy, Potash, Potass, Pump, Purest, Quarry, Quick, Quinine, Rain, Rapids, Rate, Reach, Rheumy, Rice, Rip, Riverine, Rose, Running, Runny, Rydal, Saltchuck, Scorpio, Sea, Seltzer, Sera, Serous, Serum, Shoal, Shower, Simpson, Skinkling, Slack, Slick, Sloshy, Sluice, Soda, Sodden, Soft, Solent, Sound, Souse, Southampton, Sprinkle, Standpipe, Steam, Stream, Surface, Tabby, Table, Tam, Tap, Tar, Tarn, Temper, Territorial, Thermocline, Thin, Tide, Toilet, Tonic, Urine, Utility, Vadose, Vichy, Viscous, Vlei, Vly, Wai, Wake, Wash(y), Weak, Wee, Whey, White, White coal, Wild, Wishy-washy

**Waterbaby** Moses, Tom
**Water-bed** Channel
**Water-boa** Anaconda
**Water-boatman** Notonecta
**Water-brash** Pyrosis
**Waterbuck** Kob
**Water-buckets** Noria
**Water-carrier** Aqueduct, Bheestie, Bheesty, Bhistee, Bhisti, Bucket, Carafe, Chatty, Drain, Furphy, Hose, Hydra, Hydria, Kirbeh, Pail, Pitcher, Rigol
**Water-chestnut** Saligot
**Water-colour** Aquarelle, Painting, Pastel, RI
**Water-course** Arroyo, Billabong, Canal, Ditch, Dyke, Falaj, Furrow, Gutter, Khor, Lead, Leat, Nala, Nalla(h), Nulla, Nullah, Rean, Rhine, Rill, River(et), Riverway, Serpentine, Shott, Spruit, Wadi, Whelm
**Watercress** Nasturtium
**Water-device** Shadoof, Shaduf
**Water-diviner** Dowser, Hydrostat
**Waterfall** Angel (Falls), Cataract, Churchill, Chute, Cuquenan, Espelands, →FALL(S), Force, Foss, Iguaçú, Kahiwa, Kaieteur, Kile, Lasher, Lin(n), Lower Mar Valley, Mardel, Montmorency, Mtarazi, Niagara, Overfall, Rapid, Salmon leap, Sault, Sutherland, Takakkaw, Tugela, Tyssestrengene, Utigord, Victoria, Yellowstone, Yosemite
**Water-fern** Marsilea, Salvinia
**Water-gate** Penstock, Sluice, Sluse
**Water-god** Aleion, Aleyin, Alpheus
**Water-hen** Gallinule
**Water-hole, Watering place** Bore, Gilgai, Mickery, Oasis, Wiesbaden
**Waterless** Arid, Dry, Neat
**Water-lily** Candock, Lotus, Nenuphar, Nuphar, Spatterdock, Victoria
**Waterlog(ged)** Saturate, Sodden
**Waterloo** Rout, Station
**Waterman** Aquarius, Bargee, Ferryman, Oarsman
**Water-monster** Nicker
**Water-nymph** Kelpie, Kelpy, Naiad, Ondine, Rusalka
**Water-parsnip** Sium, Skirret
**Water-plant** Alga, Alisma, Aquatic, Cress, Crowfoot, Elodea, Gulfweed, Lace-leaf, Lattice-leaf, Nelumbo, Nenuphar, Nuphar, Ouvirandra, Pontederia, Quillwort, Reate, Rush, Sea-lace, Sea-mat, Sedge, Seg, Stratiotes, Urtricularia, Vallisneria
**Waterproof, Water-tight** Cagoul(e), Caisson, Camlet, Caulk, Cerecloth, Cofferdam, Corfam®, Curry, Dampcourse, Dubbin(g), Groundsheet, Loden, Mac, Mino, Oilcloth,

Oilers, Oilpaper, Oilskin, Pay, Sealant, Sealskin, Seaworthy, Sta(u)nch, Stank, Suberin, Tarp, Tar-paper, Tarpaulin, Waders

**Water pump** Ee, Eye

**Water-rat** Arvicola, Musk-rat, Ratty, Vole

**Watershed** Divide, Height of land, Hilltop

**Water-spout** Gargoyle, Geyser, Hurricano

**Water-sprite** Kelpie, Kelpy, Nix(ie), Nixy, Tangie, Undine, Water-nymph

**Water supply** Dewpond, H, Hydrant, Spring, Tank, Tap

**Waterway** Aqueduct, Billabong, Canal, Channel, Creek, Culvert, Ditch, Dyke, Igarapé, Illinois, Intracoastal, Lode, River, St Lawrence Seaway, Sny(e), Sound, Straight, Suez

**Water-wheel** Noria, Overshot, Pelton, Sakia, Saki(y)eh, Tympanum, Undershot

**Watford** Gap

**Wattle(s)** Acacia, Boobialla, Boree, Dewlap, Gills, Golden, Mimosa, Mulga, Sallow, Savanna, Snot, Snotter

**Wave(s), Waved, Waveform, Wavelength, Waver, Wavy** Alfven, Alpha, Beachcomber, Beam, Beck, Beta, Billow, Bore, Bow, Brain, Brandish, Breaker, Carrier, Circular polarisation, Clapotis, Cold, Comber, Complex, Compression, Continuous, Crenulate, Crest, Crime, Crimp, Crispate, Cymotrichous, De Broglie, Decuman, Delta, Dominant, Dumper, Elastic, Electromagnetic, Feather, Finger, Flap, Flaunt, Float, Flote, Flourish, Fourier series, Gesticulate, Gesture, Gravitational, Gravity, Graybeard, Ground, Groundswell, Gyrose, Harmonic, Haystack, Head sea, Heat, Hertzian, Impulse, Internal, Ionospheric, Lee, Long, Longitudinal, Marcel, Matter, Medium, Mexican, Nebule, New, Oundy, Peristalsis, Perm(anent), Plunger, Primary, Pulse, Radar, Radiation, Radio, Rayleigh, Repand, Rip, Ripple, Roller, Rooster, Sastrugi, Scrub, Sea, Secondary, Seiche, Seismic, Shake, Shock, Short, Signal, Sine, Sinuate, Sinuous, Skipper's daughter, Sky, Skyrmion, Snaky, Soliton, Sound, Spiller, Square, Squiggle, Standing, Stationary, Stern, Stream, Supplementary, Surf, Surge, Sway, Tabby, Theta, Third, Thought, Tidal, Tidal bore, Tide, Tide rip, Train, Transverse, Travelling, Tsunami, Ultrasonic, Undate, Unde, Undertow, Undulate, Vermicular, Waffle, Waft, Wag, Waive, Wand, Wash, Waw, Wawe, Whelm, Whitecap, White-horse, Wigwag

▷ **Wave(s)** *may indicate* an anagram

**Wave-band** Channel

**Wave-detector** Coherer

**Wavelength** Band, Complementary, De Broglie, Ultrashort

**Waver(ing), Waverer** Dither, Double-minded, Falter, Flag, Gutter, Halt, Hesitate, Indecision, Oscillate, Reel, Stagger, Sway, Swither, Teeter, Trimmer, Vacillate, Waffle, Wet, Wobble, Wow

**Wax(ed), Waxing, Waxy** Adipocere, Ambergris, Appal, Bate, Bees, Bone, Brazilian, Candelilla, Carna(h)uba, Cere, Ceresin, Cerumen, Chinese, Cobbler's, Cutin, Earth, Effuse, Enseam, Enthuse, Ethal, Fury, Geraldton, Grave, Greaves, Grow, Heelball, Honeycomb, Increase, Increscent, Inseam, Ire, Japan, Kiss, Lecithin, Lipide, Livid, Lost, Lyrical, Mineral, Montan, Mummy, Myrtle, Ozocerite, Ozokerite, Paraffin, Parmacitie, Pela, Petroleum, Propolis, Pruina, Rage, Rise, Seal, Sealing, Spermaceti, Suberin, Tallow, Tantrum, Temper, Toxaphene, Vegetable, White, Yielding

**Waxwing** Cedar-bird, Icarus

**Way(s), Wayside** Access, Agate, Appian, Autobahn, Avenue, Boardwalk, Borstal(l), Budo, Bypass, Companion, Course, Crescent, Defile, Direction, Door, Draw, E, Each, Entrance, Family, Fashion, Flaminian, Foss(e), Four-foot, Gate, Greek, Habit, Hatch, Hedge, High, Hither, How, Icknield, Lane, Manner, Means, Method, Milky, MO, Mode, Modus, N, Pass, Passage, Path, Pennine, Permanent, Pilgrim's, Procedure, Railroad, Regimen, Ridge, → **ROAD**, Route, S, Sallypost, St(reet), Style, System, Taoism, Technique, Third, Thoroughfare, Thus, Trace, Trail, Troade, Turning, Turnpike, Underpass, Untrodden, Via, W, Wise

**Wayfarer** Commuter, Passer by, Piepowder, Pilgrim, Traveller, Voyager

**Waylay** Accost, Ambuscade, Ambush, Beset, Bushwhack, Buttonhole, Molest, Obstruct, Stick up

**Way-out** Advanced, Bizarre, Egress, Esoteric, Exit, Exotic, Extreme, Offbeat, Trendy

**Wayward** Capricious, Disobedient, Errant, Erratic, Loup-the-dyke, Obstreperous, Perverse, Scapegrace, Stray, Unruly, Wilful

**WC** Fields, Gents, Ladies, Lav, Loo

**We** I and I, Oo, Royal, Us

**Weak(er), Weaken(ing), Weakest, Weakness** Achilles' heel, Acrasia, Adynamia, Antimnemonic, Aphesis, Appair, Appal, Arsis, Assuage, Asthenia, Attenuate, Blot, Brickle, Brittle, Cachexia, Cataplexy, Chink, Cissy, Cripple(d), Debile, Debilitate, Decimate, Decrease, Delay, Delicate, Deplete, Dilling, Dilute, Disable, Drip, Effete, Emasculate, Embrittle, Enervate, Enfeeble, Entender, Fade, Faible, Failing, Faint, Fallible, Fatigue, Feeble, Fissile, Flag, Flaw, Flimsy, Foible, Fragile, Frail(tee), Frailty, Frontolysis, Give, Glass chin, Gone, Groggy, Ham, Hamartia, Helpless, Honeycomb, Impair, Impotence, Infirm, Knock-kneed, Labefaction, Lame, Languishing, Lassitude, Leptosomatic, Loophole, Low, Low ebb, Malaise, Meagre, Mild, Milk and water, Myasthenia, Namby-pamby, Pale, Pall, Paraparesis, Paresis, Penchant, Puny, Push-over, Pusillanimous, Reckling, Reduce, Runt, Sap, Simp, Slack, Softie, Softling, Soft spot, Spineless, Starveling, Tenuous, Thesis, Thin, Thready, Tottery, Unable, Underdog, Undermine, Unman, Unnerve, Unstable, Vapid, Velleity, Vessel, Vulnerability, W, Wane, Washy, Water(y), Weed, Weenie, Wimp, Wish(y)-wash(y), Wuss(y)

**Weakling** Dilling, Drip, Milksop, Nerd, Nisgul, Reed, Softie, Wuss

**Weal** Ridge, Stripe, Urticant, Wealth, Welfare, Welt, Whelk

**Wealth(y)** Abundance, Affluence, Bonanza, Bullion, Capital, Croesus, Digerati, Ease, Fat-cat, Fortune, Golconda, Jet-set, Klondike, Klondyke, Load(sa), Loaded, Loadsamoney, Lolly, Magnate, Mammon, Means, Mine, Mint, Moneyed, Nabob, Opulence, Ore, Pelf, Plutocrat, Privileged, Prosperous, Reich, Rich, Ritzy, Solid, Substance, Treasure, Trustafarian, Untold, Well-heeled, Well-off, Well-to-do

**Wean** Ablactation, Bairn, Spain, Spane, Spean

**Weapon(s)** Ammo, Antitank, Arm, Arsenal, Assault, Binary, Cultural, Deterrent, Greek fire, →GUN, Hoplology, Long-range, Missile, Munition, Nuclear, Nuke, Ordnance, Piece, →PISTOL, →SWORD, Theatre, Thermonuclear, Tool, Traditional

---

## WEAPONS

| 2 letters: | Club | Estoc | Vouge |
|---|---|---|---|
| Da | Cosh | Flail | |
| V1 | Dart | Knife | 6 letters: |
| | Gade | Kukri | Airgun |
| 3 letters: | Gaid | Lance | Archie |
| Axe | Kris | Lathi | Cestus |
| Bow | Mere | Maxim | Cohorn |
| Dag | Mine | Orgue | Creese |
| Gad | Pike | Panga | Cudgel |
| Gat | Spat | Pilum | Dagger |
| Rod | Sten | Rifle | Dragon |
| SAM | Tank | Sabre | Duster |
| Uzi | Tuck | Saker | Gingal |
| | | Slung | Glaive |
| 4 letters: | 5 letters: | Spear | Jingal |
| Beam | Arrow | Staff | Katana |
| Bill | Baton | Stick | Lathee |
| Bolo | Blade | Sting | Mauser® |
| Bomb | Brand | Taser® | Mortar |

| | | | |
|---|---|---|---|
| Musket | Javelin | Pea-rifle | Sword cane |
| Onager | Longbow | Petronel | Tormentum |
| Rapier | Machete | Repeater | Trebuchet |
| Sparke | Matchet | Revolver | Truncheon |
| Sparth | Petrary | Scimitar | Welsh hook |
| Sumpit | Poleaxe | Scorpion | |
| Taiaha | Poniard | Shuriken | *10 letters:* |
| Tomboc | Sandbag | Skean-dhu | Broadsword |
| Voulge | Shotgun | Skene-dhu | Knobkerrie |
| | Sidearm | Spontoon | Pea-shooter |
| *7 letters:* | Sjambok | Stiletto | Shillelagh |
| Arblast | Sticker | Stinkpot | Smallsword |
| Assagai | Swatter | Tomahawk | Swordstick |
| Assegai | Torpedo | Tommy gun | Throw-stick |
| Ataghan | Trident | Whirl-bat | |
| Bayonet | Warhead | Whorl-bat | *11 letters:* |
| Bazooka | | Yataghan | Hand grenade |
| Blowgun | *8 letters:* | | Morgenstern |
| Bondook | Alderman | *9 letters:* | Morning star |
| Caliver | Arbalest | Arquebuse | Singlestick |
| Caltrap | Armalite® | Backsword | Snickersnee |
| Caltrop | Arquebus | Battleaxe | Switchblade |
| Carbine | Ballista | Boomerang | |
| Chopper | Blowpipe | Catchpole | *12 letters:* |
| Coehorn | Bludgeon | Chainshot | Dagger of lath |
| Cutlass | Calthrop | Chainshot | Flamethrower |
| Dragoon | Catapult | Derringer | Jeddart staff |
| Enfield | Culverin | Doodlebug | Quarterstaff |
| Fougade | Elf-arrow | Escopette | |
| Gingall | Field gun | Excalibur | *13 letters:* |
| Gisarme | Fougasse | Flintlock | Knuckleduster |
| Grenade | Howitzer | Forty-five | Life-preserver |
| Halberd | Mangonel | Harquebus | Manrikigusari |
| Halbert | Nerve gas | Nunchucks | |
| Harpoon | Nunchaku | Sarbacane | *14 letters:* |
| Hatchet | Partisan | Slingshot | Nunchaku sticks |
| | | Slungshot | |

**Weapon-carrier** Frog, Holster, Quiver, Rocket-launcher, Sheath

**Wear(ing), Wear Out** Abate, Ablative, Abrade, Air, Attrition, Chafe, Clothing, Corrade, Corrode, Deteriorate, Detrition, Efface, Enfeeble, Erode, Erosion, Fashion, Fatigue, For(e)spend, Fray, Frazzle, Fret, Garb, Garni, Impair, In, Mush, Pack, Sap, Scuff, Sport, Stand, Tedy, Tolerate, Utility

▷ **Wear** *may indicate* the NE, e.g. Sunderland

**Weariness, Wearisome, Weary(ing)** Beat, Bejade, Blethered, Bore, Cloy, Deave, Dog-tired, Effete, Ennui, Ennuyé, Exhaust, Fag, Fatigate, Fatigue, Flag(ging), Harass, Hech, Heigh-ho, Irk, Jade, Lacklustre, Lassitude, Pall, Puny, Ramfeezle, Sate, Sick, Sleepy, Spent, Tire, Tiresome, Trash, Try, Tucker, Wabbit, Worn

**Weasel** Beech-marten, Cane, Delundung, Ermine, Ferret, Foumart, Glutton, Grison, Kolinsky, Marten, Mink, Mustela, Otter, Pekan, Pine-marten, Polecat, Skunk, Stoat, Taira, Tayra, Vermin, Whit(t)ret, Whitterick, Whittrick, Wolverine, Woodshock, Zorilla

**Weather, Weather forecast** Atmosphere, Climate, Cyclone, Discolour, Dreich, Ecoclimate, Elements, El Niño, Endure, Hail, La Nina, Met, Monkey's wedding, Outlive, Rain, Ride, Sky, Snow, Sprat, Stand, Survive, Synoptic, Tiros, Undergo, Withstand

**Weatherboard** Rusticating

**Weathercock** Barometer, Fane, Vane

**Weave(r), Weaves, Weaving** Arachne, Basket, Broché, Cane, Complect, Contexture, Entwine, Finch, Fishnet, Folk, Heald, Heddle, Interlace, Jacquard, Knotwork, Lace, Lease, Leno, Lion, Loom, Marner, Osiery, Penelope, Pick, Plain, Plait, Raddle, Ripstop, Rya, Satin, Shuttle, Sparrow, Spider, Splice, Stevengraph, Taha, Textorial, Texture, Throstle, Throwster, Tissue, Tweel, Twill, Twine, Wabster, Waggle, Wattle, Webster, Zigzag

**Weaver-bird** Amadavat, Avadavat, Quelea, Rice-bird, Taha

**Web(bed), Webbing, Web-footed, Web-site** Aranea, Fissipalmate, Food, Forum, Fourchette, Hit, Infomediary, Internet, Mat, Maze, Mesh(work), Network, Offset, Palama, Palmate, Palmiped, Patagium, Pinnatiped, Portal, Retiary, Skein, Snare, Spider, Tear, Tela, Tissue, Toil, Totipalmate, Vane, World Wide

**Webster** Spider, Weaver

**Wed(ding), Wedlock** Alliance, Bet, Destination, Diamond, Espousal, Golden, Hymen, Join, Knobstick, Liaison, Link, Marriage, Marry, Mate, Matrimony, Meng(e), Me(i)nt, Meynt, Ming, Monkey's, Nuptials, Pair, Penny, Ruby, Sacrament, Shotgun, Silver, Spousage, Spousal, → UNION, Unite, Wad, White, Y

**Wedge(d)** Accretionary, Canting-coin, Chock, Chunk, Cleat, Cotter, Cuneal, Doorstop, Feather, Forelock, Gad, Gagger, Gib, Impacted, Jack, Jam, Key, Lofter, Niblick, Pitching, Prop, Quoin, Sand, Scotch, Shim, Spaceband, Sphenic, Stick, Texas, Trig, Vomerine, Voussoir, Whipstock

**Wedgwood** Benn, China

**Wednesday** Ash, Midweek, Pulver, Spy

**Wee** Leak, Little, Pee, Slash, Sma(ll), Tinkle, Tiny, → URINATE, Widdle

**Weed(y)** Adderwort, Agrestal, Alga, Allseed, Anacharis, Arenaria, Bedstraw, Bell-bind, Blinks, Burdock, Buttercup, Carpetweed, Catch, Charlock, Chickweed, Chlorella, Cigar(ette), Cissy, Clotbur, Clover, Cobbler's pegs, Cockle, Cocklebur, Colonist, Coltsfoot, Corncockle, Couch, Daisy, Dallop, Dandelion, Darnel, Dock, Dollop, Dulse, Elder, Elodea, Ers, Fag, Fat hen, Femitar, Fenitar, Fluellen, Fluellin, Fork, Fucoid, Fumitory, Gangly, Goutweed, Goutwort, Ground elder, Groundsel, Helodea, Hoe, Indian, Joe-pye, Knapweed, Knawel, Knot-grass, Lanky, Lemna, Mare's-tail, Marijuana, Matfelon, Mayweed, Nard, Nettle, Nipplewort, Nostoc, Onion, Oxygen, Paterson's curse, Pearlwort, Peed, Perique, Pilewort, Pineapple, Piri-piri, Plantain, Potamogeton, Purslane, Ragi, Ragwort, Reate, Rest-harrow, Ribbon, Rib-grass, Ribwort, Ruderal, Runch, Sagittaria, Sargasso, Scal(l)awag, Scallywag, Senecio, Shrimp, Softy, Sorrel, Speedwell, Spurge, Spurrey, Stink, Sudd, Sun-spurge, Swine's-cress, Tab, Tansy, Tare, Thistle, Tine, Tobacco, Tormentil, Twitch, Ulotrichale, Ulva, Vetch, Viper's bugloss, Wartcress, Widow's, Winnow, Yarr

▷ **Weed** *may indicate* 'urinated'

**Weedkiller** Arsenic, Atrazine, Dalapon, Diquat, Diuron, Herbicide, Hoe, Paraquat®, Selective, Simazine

**Week(s), Weekly** Ember, Expectation, Great, Hebdomadary, Holy, Omer, Orientation, Ouk, Oulk, Passion, Periodical, Prophetic, Rag, Rogation, Schoolies, Sennight, Working

**Weekday** Feria

**Weekend** K, Sat, Sun

**Weep(er), Weeping, Weepy, Wept** Bawl, Blubber, Cry, Grat, Greet, Lachrymose, Lament, Leak, Loser, Maudlin, Niobe, Ooze, Pipe, Screet, Seep, Sob, Tearful, Wail, Waterworks

**Weevil** Anthonomous, Bean, Boll, Bug, Cornworm, Curculio, Diamond-beetle, Grain, Insect, Nut, Pea, Rice, Seed, Snout beetle

**Weft** Roon, Shot, Texture, Warp, Woof

**Weigh(ing), Weigh down, Weight(y)** All-up, Apothecaries', Atomic, Avoirdupois, Balance, Ballast, Bantam, Barbell, Baric, Bob, Bow, Bulk, Burden, Clout, Consider, Count, Counterpoise, Cruiser, Dead, Deliberate, Denier, Drail, Dumbbell, Emphasis, Equivalent, Feather, Formula, Grammage, Great, Gross, Handicap, Heaviness, Heft, Import, Importance, Impost, Incumbent, Journey, Kerb, Live, Load, Mark, Massive, Matter,

Metage, Metrology, Minimum, Molecular, Moment, Mouse, Nett, Onerous, One-sided, Oppress, Overpoise, Payload, Perpend, Plumb-bob, Plummet, Poise, Ponderal, Pregnant, Preponderance, Prey, Rate, Sash, Sinker, Slang, Slung-shot, Stress, Tare, Throw, Ton(nage), Tophamper, Tron(e), Troy, Trutinate, Unmoor, Welter, Wey

## WEIGHTS

*1 letter:*
G
K

*2 letters:*
As
Ct
Oz
Wt

*3 letters:*
Kat
Kin
Kip
Mna
Oke
Pud
Rod
Ser
Sit
Tod

*4 letters:*
Dram
Gram
Kati

Khat
Last
Mina
Nail
Obol
Peck
Pood
Rotl
Seer
Tael
Tola
Unce

*5 letters:*
Artal
Candy
Carat
Catty
Clove
Gerah
Grain
Kandy
Katti
Liang
Libra
Maund

Ounce
Pease
Peaze
Peise
Peize
Peyse
Pikul
Pound
Pudge
Recul
Stone
Tical
Tonne
Truss

*6 letters:*
Arroba
Candie
Cantar
Cental
Derham
Dirham
Dirhem
Drachm
Firkin
Fother

Kantar
Rotolo
Talent

*7 letters:*
Centner
Drachma
Kiloton
Lispund
Pesante
Quintal
Scruple

*8 letters:*
Decagram
Lispound
Semuncia

*9 letters:*
Micromole
Shippound

*10 letters:*
Decagramme

**Weighing machine** Bismar, Scales, Steelyard, Tron(e)
**Weightless** Agravic
**Weight-lifter** Atlas, Crane, Lewis, Windlass
**Weir** Cauld, Dam, Garth, Kiddle, Kidel, Lasher, Pen, Watergate
**Weird** Bizarre, Curious, Dree, Eerie, Eery, Eldritch, Far out, Kookie, Odd, Offbeat, Spectral, Spooky, Strange, Supernatural, Taisch, Uncanny, Unearthly, Zany
**Welch, Welsh** Abscond, Cheat, Default, Embezzle, Levant, Rat, Reneg(u)e, Renig, Skedaddle, Weasel
**Welcome, Welcoming** Acclaim, Aloha, Ave, Bel-accoyle, Ciao, Embrace, Entertain, Glad-hand, Godsend, Greet, Haeremai, Hail, Hallo, Halse, Handshake, Heil, Hello, Hi, Hospitable, How, Hullo, Karanga, Open-armed, Open house, Ovation, Powhiri, Receive, Reception, Salute, Snug, Ticker-tape, Wotcha, Wotcher, Yellow-ribbon
**Weld(ing), Welder** Arc, Butt, Cold, Explosion, Fillet, Friction, Fuse, Gas, Join, Merge, MIG, Oxyacetylene, Resistance, Seam, Sinter, Spot, Stud, Tack, TIG, Ultrasonic, Unite
**Welfare** Advantage, Alms, Benison, Common weal, Ha(y)le, Heal, Health, Sarvodaya, Social, Weal
**Welkin** Firmament, Sky
**Well (done)** Artesian, Atweel, Ave, Aweel, Bien, Bore(hole), Bravo, Carbon, Casinghead, Cenote, Chipper, Development, Discovery, Downhole, Dropping, Dry hole, Easily, Euge, Famously, Fine, Fit, Foot, Gas, Gasser, Geyser, Good, Gosh, Gusher, Hale, → **HEALTHY**,

Hot, Inkpot, Ka pai, Law, Mickery, My, Namma hole, Odso, Oh, Oil(er), Phreatic, Potential, Pour, Pump, So, Source, Spa, Spouter, Spring, Sump, Surge, Teek, Tube, Um, Upflow, Wildcat, Wishing, Worthily, Zemzem

**Wellbeing** Atweel, Bien-être, Comfort, Eudemonic, Euphoria, Euphory, Good, Health, Oomph, Welfare

**Well-born** Eugene

**Well-bred** Genteel

**Well-built** Sturdy, Tight

**Well-covered** Chubby, Padded

**Well-curb** Puteal

**Welles** Orson

**Wellington, Welly** Accelerate, Boot, Green, Gumboot, Iron Duke, Nosey

**Well-known** Famous, Iconic, Illustrious, Infamous, Notorious, Notour, Prominent

**Well-off** Affluent, Bien, Far, Rich, Wealthy

**Well part** Bucket, Shadoof, Shaduf

**Wells** Bombardier, Fargo, HG, Llandrindod, Sadler's

**Well-turned** Elegant

**Well-versed** Fluent

**Well-wisher** Friend

**Welsh(man), Welshwoman** Aled, Briton, Brittonic, Brython, Cake, Cambrian, Celtic, Cog, Crachach, Cym(ric), Cymry, Dafydd, Dai, Ebbw, Emlyn, Emrys, Enid, Evan, Fluellen, Gareth, Harp, Idris, Ifor, Ivor, Keltic, Megan, P-Celtic, P-Keltic, Rabbit, Rarebit, Rees, Rhys, Sion, Taff(y), Tudor, W, Walian

▸ **Welsh** *see* WELCH

**Wen** Cyst, Talpa, Tumour, Wart

**Wench** Blowze, Court, Girl, Gouge, Hussy, Maid, Ramp, Rig, Smock, Strumpet

**Wend** Meander, Sorb, Steer

**Wendy** Darling, House

**Went** Left, Peed, Sold, Yode

**Werewolf** Loup-garou, Lycanthrope, Nazi, Turnskin, Vampire

**Wesleyan** Epworth, Methodist

**West(ern), Westerly** Ang mo, Far, Favonian, Film, Hesperian, Mae, Middle, Movie, Oater, Occidental, Ponent, Spaghetti, Sunset, True Grit, W, Westlin, Wild

**West African** Fantee, Fanti, Kroo, Mandingo, Togolese, Wolof

▷ **West end** *may indicate* 't' *or* 'W1'

**West Indian** Carib, Creole, Jamaican, Quashee, Quashie, Taino

**Westminster** SW1

**Wet(ting), Wetland** Bedabble, Bedraggled, Clammy, Daggle, Damp, Dank, Dew, Dip, Douse, Dowse, Drench, Drip(ping), Drook, Drouk, Dunk, Embrue, Enuresis, Feeble, Foppish, Humect, Humid, Hyetal, Imbrue, Imbue, Irrigate, Irriguous, Macerate, Madefy, Madid, Marshy, Moil, Moist(en), Molly, Namby-pamby, Pee, Piddle, Pouring, Rainy, Ramsar site, Ret(t), Rheumy, Roral, Roric, Runny, Saturate, Seepy, Shower, Simp(leton), Sipe, Sissy, Sluice, →SOAK, Sodden, Sopping, Sour, Steep, Tiddle, Tipsy, Urinate, Wat, Wee, Widdle, Wimpy, Wringing

**Wetsuit** Steamer

**Whack(ed), Whacking** Astronomic, Belt, Bemaul, Biff, Deadbeat, Hefty, Jiggered, Joll, Joule, Jowl, Lambast, Lounder, Share, Swat, Swish, Thump, Weary

**Whale(meat), Whaling** Baleen, Beaked, Beluga, Black, Blower, Blubber, Blue, Bottlehead, Bottlenose, Bowhead, Bull, Cachalot, Calf, Cetacea(n), Cete, Cetology, Cow, Cowfish, Dolphin, Dorado, Fall, Fin(back), Finner, Gam, Glutton, Grampus, Greenland (right), Grey, Greyback, Humpback, Ishmael, Killer, Kreng, Leviathan, Manatee, Minke, Monodon, Mysticeti, Narwhal, Odontoceti, Orc(a), Paste, Physeter, Pilot, Pod, Porpoise, Right, River dolphin, Rorqual, School, Scrag, Sea-canary, Sea-unicorn, Sei, Social, Sperm, Spouter, Sulphur-bottom, Thrasher, Toothed, Toothless, White, Zeuglodon(t), Ziphius

▷ **Whale**  *may indicate*  an anagram

**Whalebone** Busk

**Whaler** Ahab, Harpooner, Ship, Specksioneer, Specktioneer, Waister

**Whales' meat** Clio

**Wham** Bang, Collide

**Whang** Blow, Flog, Thrash, Whack

**Wharf(inger)** Canary, Dock(er), Jetty, Key, Landing, Pier, Quay(side), Roustabout, Rouster, Staith(e)

**What, Whatever** Anan, Any, Come again, Eh, How, Owt, Pardon, Que, Regardless, Siccan, Sorry, Such, That, Which

**Whatnot, What's-its-name** Dinges, Dingus, Doings, Doobrey, Doobrie, Étagère, Gismo, Jigamaree, Jiggumbob, Thingamy, Thingumajig, Thingumbob, Thingummy, Timenoguy

**Wheat** Allergen, Amber, Amelcorn, Bald, Beard(ed), Beardless, Blé, Bulg(h)ur, Cone, Couscous, Cracked, Durum, Einkorn, Emmer, Federation, Fromenty, Frumenty, Furme(n)ty, Furmity, Grain, Hard, Mummy, Red, Rivet, Sarrasin, Sarrazin, Seiten, Semolina, Sharps, Soft, Spelt, Spring, Summer, Triticum, White, Winter

**Wheatsheaf** Bale, Gerbe, Stook

**Wheedle** Banter, Barney, Blandish, Butter up, Cajole, Coax, Cog, Cuiter, Cuittle, Flatter, Inveigle, Tweedle, Whilly(whaw)

**Wheel(er)** Balance, Bedel, Bevel, Bicycle, Big, Bogy, Breast, Bucket, Buff(ing), Caracol(e), Cart's tail, Caster, Castor, Catherine, Chain, Chark(h)a, Circle, Cistern, Count, Crown, Cycle, Daisy, Diamond, Disc, Driving, Emery, Epicycloidal, Escape, Fan, Felloe, Felly, Ferris, Fifth, Fortune, Gear, Grinding, Gyrate, Helm, Hurl, Idle(r), Jagger, Jigger, Jolley, Joy, Kick, Lantern, Magnate, Master, Medicine, Mitre, Monkey, Mortimer, Nabob, Nave, Nose, Paddle, Pattern, Pedal, Pelton, Perambulator, Persian, Pin, Pinion, Pitch, Pivot, Planet, Potter's, Prayer, Pulley, Rag, Ratchet, Rhomb, Roll, Roller, Rotate, Roulette, Rowel, Sheave, Snail, Spare, Spider, Spinning, Sprocket, Spur, Star, Steering, Stepney, Stitch, Swing, Tail, Throwing-table, Training, Tread, Treadmill, Trindle, Trochus, Trolley, Truckle, Trundle, →**TURN**, Tympan(um), Water, Web, Wharve, Whirling-table, Wire, Worm, Zoetrope

**Wheelbarrow** Hurlbarrow, Monotroch

**Wheelhouse** Caravan, Paddle-box

**Wheel-hub** Axle, Nave

**Wheelman** Croupier, Cyclist, Ixion

**Wheelwright** Spokesman

**Wheeze** Asthma, Breathe, Jape, Joke, Pant, Pech, Ploy, Rale, Reak, Reik, Rhonchus, Ruse, Stridor, Trick, Whaisle, Whaizle

**Whelk** Buckie, Limpet, Shellfish, Stromb, Triton

**Whelm** Nalla(h), Nulla(h)

**Whelp** Bear, Bra(t)chet, Pup

**When(ever)** Although, As, If, Once, Though, Time

**Where(abouts)** Location, Neighbourhood, Place, Site, Vicinity, Whaur, Whither

**Wherefore** Cause, Reason, Why

**Whereupon** So, When

**Wherewithal** Finance, Means, Money, Needful, Resources

**Wherry** Barge, Rowboat

**Whet(stone)** Coticular, Excite, Hone, Oilstone, Rubstone, Sharpen, Stimulate, Stroke

**Whether** Conditional, If

**Whey** Plasma, Serum, Whig

**Which(ever), Which is** Anyway, As, QE, Whatna, Whilk, Who

**Whiff** Breath, Cigarette, Gust, Hum, Puff, Redolence, Smatch, Sniff, Trace, Waft

**Whig** Adullamite, Jig, Rascal, Tory, Whey

**While** Although, As, Interim, Since, Space, Span, Spell, Though, Throw, Time, When, Whenas, Whereas, Yet

**Whim(s), Whimsical, Whimsy** Bizarre, Caprice, Conceit, Crotchet, Droll, Fad, Fancy, Fantastic, Fay, Fey, Fie, Flisk, Impulse, Kicksy-wicksy, Kink, Maggot, Notion, Quaint, Quirk, Tick, Toy, Vagary

**Whimper** Cry, Grizzle, Mewl, Pule, Snivel, Whine

**Whin** Furze, Gorse, Ulex

**Whine, Whinge(r)** Cant, Carp, Complain, Cry, Grumble, Kvetch, Mewl, Miaow, Moan, Peenge, Pule, Snivel, Sword, Whimper, Whinge, Yammer

**Whinny** Neigh, Nicker, Whicker

**Whip(ped), Whip out, Whipping** Beat, Braid, Brede, Bullwhack, Bullwhip, Cat, Cat o' nine tails, Chabouk, Chantilly, Chastise, Chief, Cilium, Colt, Crop, Drive, Feague, Firk, Five-line, Flagellate, Flagellum, Flay, Gad, Hide, Jambok, Knout, K(o)urbash, Larrup, →LASH, Leather, Limber, Lunge, Quirt, Rawhide, Riem, Scourge, Sjambok, Slash, Steal, Stock, Strap-oil, Swinge, Swish, Switch, Taw, Thong, Three-line, Thresh, Trounce, Welt, West Country, Whap, Whop

**Whippersnapper** Dandiprat, Dandyprat, Pup, Squirt

**Whippoorwill** Wishtonwish

**Whirl(er), Whirling** Bullroarer, Circumgyrate, Dervish, Eddy, Gyrate, →IN A WHIRL, Maelstrom, Pivot, Reel, Spin, Swing, Swirl, Vortex, Vortical, Vorticose, Vortiginous, Whirry

**Whirlpool** Eddy, Gulf, Gurge, Maelstrom, Moulin, Sea purse, Swelchie, Vorago, Vortex, Weel, Wiel

**Whirlwind** Cyclone, Dust devil, Eddy, Sand-devil, Tornado, Tourbillion, Typho(o)n, Vortex, Willy-willy

**Whirr** Birr

**Whisk** Balloon, Chowri, Chowry, Fly, Swish, Switch, Whid, Whip

**Whisk(e)y** Alcohol, Barley-bree, Barley-broo, Barley-broth, Bond, Bourbon, Canadian, Cape smoke, Chain lighting, Corn, Cratur, Crayther, Creature, Fife, Fire-water, Grain, Hard stuff, Hard tack, Highball, Hokonui, Hoo(t)ch, Irish, Islay, Malt, Monongahela, Moonshine, Morning, Mountain dew, Nip, Peat-reek, Pot(h)een, Ragwater, Red eye, Rye, Scotch, Sourmash, Southern Comfort®, Spunkie, Stirrup-dram, Tanglefoot, Tarantula juice, Tun, Usquebaugh, W, Wheech, Whiss

**Whisker(s)** Beard, Beater, Bristles, Burnsides, Cat's, Dundreary, Eggbeater, Excrement, Face fungus, Hackle, Hair, Moustache, Mutton-chop, Samuel, Satyric tuft, Side(-boards), Side-burns, Sidelevers, Stibble, Stubble, Vibrissa

▷ **Whisky** *may indicate* an anagram

**Whisper** Aside, Breath(e), Bur(r), Chinese, Hark, Hint, Innuendo, Murmur, Pig's, Round, Rumour, Rustle, Sigh, Stage, Susurrus, Tittle, Undertone, Whittie-whattie

**Whist** Dummy, Hush, Long, Mum, Progressive, Quiet, Sh, Short, Solo, Whisk and swabbers

**Whistle(r)** Blow, Boatswain's, Calliope, Catcall, Feedback, Flageolet, Flute, Hewgh, Hiss, Marmot, Pedro, Penny, Phew, Ping, Pipe, Quail-pipe, Ref, Siffle(ur), Sowf(f), Sowth, Steam, Stop, Stridor, Swab(ber), Swanee, Tin, Toot, Tweedle, Tweet, Warbler, Wheeple, Wheugh, Whew, Whiffle, Wolf

**Whistle-blower** Informer, Nark, Ref

**Whit** Atom, Doit, Figo, Haet, Hait, Hate, Iota, Jot, Particle, Pentecost, Point, Red cent, Snap, Straw

**White(n), Whitener, Whiteness, White-faced** Agene, Agenise, Alabaster, Albedo, Albescent, Albino, Albugineous, Albumen, Argent, Ashen, Au lit, Bakra, Blameless, Blanch, Blanche, Blanco, Bleach, Buckra, Cabbage, Calm, Cam, Camstone, Candid, Candida, Candour, Canescent, Canities, Caucasian, Caum, Chalk(y), Chardonnay, Chaste, China, Chinese, Christmas, Cliffs, Collar, Company, Cream, Cue ball, Dealbate, Egg, Elephant, Ermine, European, Fang, Fard, Feather, Flag, Flake, French, Glair, Gwen(da), Gwendolen, Gwyn, Hawked, Hoar(y), Hock, Honorary, Hore, House, Innocent, Ivory, Large, Leucoma, Lie, Lily, Livid, Man, Marbled, Mealy, Muscadet, Niveous, Opal,

Oyster, Pakeha, Pale(face), Pallor, Paper, Paris, Pearl(y), Poor, Pure, Redleg, Russian, Sclerotic, Selborne, Sheep, Silver, Small, Snow(y), Spanish, Taw, Vitiligo, Wan, Wedding, Wine, Wyn, Zinc

**Whitefish** Menominee

**Whitefriars** Alsatia

**Whitehall** Ministry

**Whitehead** Milium

**White horse(s)** Skipper's daughters, Wave

**White man** Anglo, Ba(c)kra, Buckra, Caucasian, Corn-cracker, Cracka, Gora, Gub(bah), Haole, Honkie, Honky, Kabloona, Larney, Mzungu, Norteno, Occidental, Ofay, Pakeha, Paleface, Redleg, Redneck, Umlungu, WASP, Wigga, Wigger

**Whitewash** Calcimine, Concealment, Excuse, Grannie, Granny, Kalsomine, Lime, Skunk, Trounce

**Whitlow** Ancome, Felon, Panaritium, Paronychia

**Whitsun** Pentecost, Pinkster, Pinxter

**Whittle** Carve, Pare, Sharpen

**Whizz** Wheech

**Who** As, Doctor, Qui

**Whodunit** Mystery

**Who knows** Quien sabe

**Whole, Wholehearted, Wholeness, Wholly** All, Cosmos, Eager, Entire(ty), Entity, Every inch, Fully, Hale, Indiscrete, Intact, Integer, Integral, Integrity, In toto, Largely, Lot, Shebang, Sound, Sum, Systemic, Thoroughly, Total, Tout à fait, Unbroken, Uncut

**Wholesale(r)** Cutprice, En bloc, Engrosser, Ingross, Jobber, Root and branch, Stockjobber, Supplier, Sweeping, Trader

**Wholesome** Clean, Good, Healthy, Physical, Pure, Salubrious, Salutary, Sound

**Whoop(er), Whooping cough** Alew, Celebrate, Chincough, Crane, Cry, Excite, Kink(cough), Kink-host, Pertussis, Swan, War

**Whoopee** Carouse, Evoe, Hey-go-mad, Roister

**Whoosh** Birr, Swish

**Whopper, Whopping** Barn, Crammer, Goliath, Huge, Immense, Jumbo, Lie, Lig, Oner, Out and outer, Plumper, Scrouger, Slapper, Slockdolager, Soc(k)dalager, Soc(k)dolager, Soc(k)doliger, Soc(k)dologer, Sogdolager, Sogdoliger, Sogdologer, Stonker, Tale, Taradiddle

**Whore** Drab, Harlot, Loose woman, Pinnace, Pro, Prostitute, Quail, Road, Strumpet, Tart

**Whorl** Corolla, Eucyclic, Spiral, Swirl, Verticil, Volute, Volution

**Why** How come, Raison d'être, Reason, Yogh

**Wick** Farm, Rush, Snaste, Snuff, Vill(age)

**Wicked(ness)** Adharma, Atrocity, →BAD, Candle, Criminal, Cru(i)sie, Crusy, Depravity, Devilish, Evil, Facinorous, Flagitious, Goaty, Godless, Heinous, High-viced, Immoral, Impious, Improbity, Iniquity, Lantern, Miscreant, Naughty, Nefarious, Night-light, Pernicious, Perverse, Ponerology, Pravity, Rush, Satanic, Scelerate, Sin(ful), Splendid, Super, Taper, Turpitude, Unchaste, Unholy, Vile

▷ **Wicked** *may indicate* containing a wick

**Wicker(work)** Basketry, Sale, Seal, Wattlework

**Wicket** Crease, Gate, Hatch, Infield, Maiden, Pitch, Square, Sticky, Stool, Stump, W, Yate

**Wicket-keeper** Gateman, Stumper

**Wide, Widen(ing), Width** Abroad, Ample, Bay, Braid, Broad, Comprehensive, Dilate, Drib, Eclectic, Expand, Extend, Far, Flanch, Flange, Flare, Flaunch, Ga(u)ge, General, Latitude, Miss, Prevalent, Roomy, Scope, Set, Spacious, Span, Spread, Sundry, Sweeping, Vast

**Wide-awake** Alert, Fly, Hat, Wary, Watchful

**Widespread** Catholic, Diffuse, Epidemic, Extensive, General, Pandemic, Panoramic, Pervasive, Prevalent, Prolate, Rife, Routh(ie), Sweeping, Universal

**Widow(ed)** Bereft, Black, Dame, Discovert, Dowager, Golf, Grass, Hempen, Jointress, Relict, Sati, Sneerwell, Suttee, Twankey, Vidual, Viduous, Whydah-bird, Widdy

**Wield** Brandish, Control, Exercise, Exert, Handle, →MANIPULATE, Ply, Sound

**Wife, Wives** Ball and chain, Better half, Bride, Common-law, Concubine, Consort, Devi, Dutch, Enid, Evadne, Feme, Feme covert, Fiere, Frau, Goody, Haram, Harem, Harim, Helpmate, Helpmeet, Hen, Her indoors, Kali, Kickie-wickie, Kicksy-wicksy, Kloo(t)chman, Lakshmi, Little woman, Mate, Memsahib, Missis, Missus, Mrs, Mummer's, Partner, Penelope, Pirrauru, Potiphar's, Rib, Seraglio, Spouse, Squaw, Stepford, Trophy, Trouble and strife, Umfazi, Ux(or), Vrou, W, Wag

**Wife-beater** (Mr) Punch

**Wig** Adonis, Bagwig, Bob(wig), Brigadier, Brutus, Buzz-wig, Cadogan, Campaign, Carpet, Cauliflower, Caxon, Chevelure, Chide, Cockernony, Dalmahoy, Fright, Full-bottomed, Gizz, Gooseberry, Gorgone, Gregorian, Hair(piece), Heare, Jas(e)y, Jazy, Jiz, Macaroni, Major, Periwig, Peruke, Postiche, Ramil(l)ie(s), Rate, Reprimand, Rug, Scold, Scratch, Sheitel, Spencer, Syrup, Targe, Tie, Toupee, Toupet, Tour

**Wiggle, Wiggly** Jiggle, Scoleciform, Wobble, Wriggle

**Wight** Man, Vectis

**Wigwam** Te(e)pee

**Wild(er), Wildness** Abandoned, Aberrant, Agitato, Agrestal, Amok, Amuck, Angry, Barbarous, Baresark, Berserk, Bundu, Bush, Chimeric, Crazy, Demented, Dionysian, Earl, Enraged, Enthusiastic, Errant, Erratic, Extravagant, Farouche, Feral, Frantic, Frenetic, Frontier, Gene, Gohardery, Haggard, Hectic, Lawless, Mad(cap), Maenadic, Manic, Meshugge, Myall, Natural, Outlaw, Rampant, Raver, Riotous, Romantic, Rumbustious, →SAVAGE, Skimble-skamble, Tearaway, Unmanageable, Unruly, Untamed, Violent, Warrigal, West, Woolly

▷ **Wild(ly)** *may indicate* an anagram

**Wild beast** Eyra, Sapi-utan, Scrubber

**Wildcat** Lion, Manul, Ocelot, Strike, Tiger

**Wilde** Marty, Oscar

**Wilderness** Bush, Desert, Negev, Outback, Ruderal, Sinai, Solitude, Waste, Wasteland

**Wild goose** Chase, Greylag

**Wild oats** Haver

**Wile, Wily** Art, Artful, Artifice, Astute, Braide, →CUNNING, Deceit, Foxy, Peery, Ruse, Shifty, Shrewd, Slee, Slippery, →SLY, Spider, Stratagem, Streetwise, Subtle, Trick, Versute, Wide

**Wilful(ly)** Deliberate, Headstrong, Heady, Obstinate, Recalcitrant, Scienter, Wayward

**Will, Willing(ly)** Alsoon, Amenable, Bard, Bequeath, Bewildered, Biddable, Bill(y), Can do, Complaisant, Compliant, Conation, Content, Desire, Devise, Fain, Force, Free, Game, General, Hay, Holographic, Leave, Legator, Leve, Lief, Lieve, Living, Mind, Nerve, Noncupative, Obedient, On, Open, Pacable, Please, Prone, Purpose, Raring, Rather, Ready, Receptive, Resolution, Scarlet, Shakespeare, Soon, Spirit, Swan, Testament, Testate, Thelma, Tolerant, Up for, Velleity, Volens, Volition, Voluntary, Volunteer, Way, Wimble, Woot

▷ **Will** *may indicate* an anagram

**William(s)** Bill(y), Conqueror, Occam, Orange, Pear, Rufus, Silent, Sweet, Tell, Tennessee

**Will o' the wisp** Fatuous fire, Fen-fire, Friar's lantern, Ignis-fatuus, Jack o'lantern, Min min, Nightfire, Rush, Spunkie, Wildfire

**Willow(ing), Willowy** Arctic, Crack, Diamond, Lissom(e), Lithe, Osier, Poplar, Port Jackson, Pussy, Sale, Salix, Sallow, Sauch, Saugh, Seal, Slender, Supple, Twilly, Weeping, Withy

**Willpower** Ab(o)uha, Determination, Resolve, Strength

**Willy-nilly** Nolens volens, Perforce

**Wilt** Decline, Droop, Fade, Flag, Sap, Shalt, Wither

**Wiltshireman** Moonraker
▶ **Wily** see **WILE**
**Wimp(ish)** Drip, Milksop, Mouse, Namby-pamby, Pantywaist, Saddo, Snool, Weed
**Wimple** Gorget, Meander, Ripple, Turn, Veil
▷ **Wimple** *may indicate* an anagram
**Win(ner), Winning** Achieve, Acquire, Adorable, Ahead, Appealing, Attain,
Backgammon, Bangster, Banker, →**BEAT**, Capot, Carry off, Cert, Champion, Charm,
Conciliate, Conquer, Cup, Cute, Decider, Disarming, Dividend, Dormie, Dormy, Earn,
Effect, Endearing, Engaging, Fetching, First, Fool's mate, Gain, Gammon, Grand slam,
Hit, Jackpot, Land(fall), Landslide, Laureate, Lead, Luck out, Medallist, Motser, Motza,
Nap hand, Nice, On a roll, Pile, Pot, Prepossessing, Prevail, Profit, Purler, Reap, Repique,
Result, Rollover, Rubicon, Scoop, Shoo-in, Slam, Snip, Success, Sweet, Take, Top dog,
→**TRIUMPH**, Up, Vellet, Velvet, Victor(y), Vole, Walk over, Wrest, Yellow jersey,
Yokozuna
**Wince** Blench, Cringe, Flinch, Recoil
**Winch** Crab, Crane, Jack, Windlass
**Winchester®** Rifle, Wykehamist
**Wind(er), Winding(s), Windy** Air, Airstream, Anabatic, Anfractuous, Backing,
Ball, Bend, Blow, Bottom, Brass, Burp, Capstan, Carminative, Chill, Coil, Colic, Crank,
Creeky, Curl, Curve, Cutter, Draught, Draw, Entwine, Entwist, Evagation, Fart, Fearful,
Flatulence, Flatus, Flaw, Gas, Gust, Katabatic, Meander, Nervous, Periodic, Ponent,
Poop, Prevailing, Purl, Quarter, Quill, Reeds, Reel, Roll, Screw, Sea, Second, Series,
Serpentine, Serpentize, Sinuous, Slant, Snake, Spiral, Spool, Surface, Swirl, Tail, Tendril,
Thread, Throw, Tortuous, Trade, Trend, Turn, Twaddle, Twine, Twisty, Veer, Veering,
Ventose, Waffle, Weave, Wiggle, Winch, Windle, Winnle, Woold, Wrap, Wreathe,
Wrest, Wuthering

## WINDS

| 4 letters: | Sough | 7 letters: | Tornado |
|---|---|---|---|
| Berg | Zonda | Aeolian | Twister |
| Bise | | Ambages | Typhoon |
| Bora | 6 letters: | Aquilon | |
| Firn | Aquilo | Bluster | 8 letters: |
| Fohn | Auster | Chinook | Apparent |
| Gale | Baguio | Cyclone | Argestes |
| Libs | Boreas | Etesian | Downwash |
| Link | Breeze | Gregale | Easterly |
| Puna | Buster | Kamseen | Favonian |
| Vayu | Ghibli | Khamsin | Favonius |
| | Haboob | Maestro | Levanter |
| 5 letters: | Heaves | Meltemi | Libeccio |
| Blore | Kamsin | Mistral | Scirocco |
| Buran | Levant | Monsoon | Taranaki |
| Chili | Samiel | Muzzler | Westerly |
| Corus | Sciroc | Noreast | Williwaw |
| Eurus | Shamal | Norther | Zephyrus |
| Foehn | Simoom | Pampero | |
| Gibli | Simoon | Shimaal | 9 letters: |
| Greco | Solano | Sirocco | Anti-trade |
| Noser | Squall | Snifter | Bourasque |
| Notus | Typhon | Snorter | Cordonazo |
| Ostro | Wester | Souther | Dust devil |
| Solar | Zephyr | Sumatra | Euraquilo |

| | | | |
|---|---|---|---|
| Harmattan | **10 letters:** | **11 letters:** | **13 letters:** |
| Hurricane | Cape doctor | Northwester | Northwesterly |
| Hurricano | Euroclydon | Norwesterly | Tehuantepecer |
| Jet stream | Rip-snorter | White squall | |
| Knee-swell | Tourbillon | | **15 letters:** |
| Libecchio | Tramontana | **12 letters:** | Southerly buster |
| Norwester | Whirlblast | Brickfielder | |
| Volturnus | Willy-willy | | |

---

**Windbag** Balloon, Bore, Chatterbox, Drogue, Prattler, Whoopee cushion, Zeppelin
**Windfall** Bonanza, Buckshee, Caduac, Fortune, Godsend, Manna
**Windflower** Anemone
**Windlass** Differential, Spanish, Whim, Winch
**Windmill** Pinwheel, Post, Smock, Whirligig
**Window(s)** Atmosphere, Bay, Bow, Casement, Catherine-wheel, Companion, Compass, Day, Deadlight, Dormer, Double-hung, Dream-hole, Entry, Eye, Eyelids, Fanlight, Fenestella, Fenestra, French, Gable, Garret, Glaze, Guichet, Jalousie, Jesse, Judas, Jut, Lancet, Lattice, Launch, Light, Loop-light, Louver, Louvre, Lozen, Lucarne, Lunette, Luthern, Lychnoscope, Marigold, Mezzanine, Mirador, Monial, Mullion, Oculus, Oeil-de-boeuf, Ogive, Opportunity, Orb, Oriel, Ox-eye, Pane, Pede, Picture, Plate glass, Pop-under, Pop-up, Porthole, Program, Quarterlight, Radio, Re-entry, Rosace, Rose, Round, Sash, Sexfoil, Shed dormer, Shop, Shot, Skylight, Spyhole, Storm, Transom, Trellis, Ventana, Weather, Wheel, Wicket, Windock, Windore, Winnock
**Window-bar, Window-fastening** Astragal, Espagnolette
**Windpipe** Bronchus, Gular, Throat, Trachea, Weasand
**Windscale** Beaufort
**Windsock** Drogue, Sleeve
**Windsor** Barbara, Castle, Knot
**Windswept** Scud
**Wind-up** End, Fright, Liquidate, Miff, Needle, Span
**Windward** Ahold, Aloof, A-weather, Laveer, Luff, Up
**Wine** Bin, Blush, Cabinet, Case, Cup, Cuvée, Doc, Espumoso, Essence, Fortified, Grand cru, Low, Mulled, Must, Piece, Pigment, Premier cru, Prisage, Rotgut, Rouge, Semi-dry, Sparkling, Steen, Tannin, Terroir, The grape, Tirage, Unoaked, Varietal, Vat, Vintage, Zymurgy

---

## WINES

| | | | |
|---|---|---|---|
| **2 letters:** | Palm | Blanc | Syrah |
| It | Pipe | Bombo | Table |
| | Port | Comet | Tavel |
| **3 letters:** | Race | Gallo | Toddy |
| Dao | Rosé | Gamay | Tokay |
| Kir | Rosy | Macon | White |
| Red | Sack | Maqui | Xeres |
| Sec | Sekt | Médoc | |
| Tun | Stum | Mirin | **6 letters:** |
| Vin | Tent | Mosel | Alsace |
| | Tutu | Negus | Barley |
| **4 letters:** | Vino | Pinot | Barolo |
| Asti | | Plonk | Barsac |
| Brut | **5 letters:** | Rhine | Beaune |
| Cava | Anjou | Rioja | Bishop |
| Hock | Anker | Soave | Bubbly |
| Mull | Biddy | Straw | Canary |

Claret
Ginger
Graves
Lisbon
Malaga
Malbec
Merlot
Muscat
Piment
Plotty
Red Ned
Sherry
Shiraz
Solera

**7 letters:**
Alicant
Amoroso
Auslese
Bastard
Catawba
Chablis
Château
Chianti
Cowslip
Currant
Demi-sec
Dessert
Eiswein
Fendant
Icewine
Madeira
Malmsey
Margaux
Marsala
Moselle
Oenomel
Orvieto
Pomerol
Pommard
Retsina
Rhenish
Sangria
Sherris
Vouvray

**8 letters:**
Bordeaux
Bucellas
Buckfast®
Burgundy
Cabernet
Champers
Charneco
Dubonnet®
Essencia
Frascati
Gluhwein
Grenache
Jerepigo
Kabinett
Log-juice
Malvasia
Malvesie
Montilla
Mountain
Muscadel
Muscadet
Muscatel
Nebbiolo
Oenology
Pinotage
Pradikat
Prosecco
Red biddy
Resinata
Rheingau
Riesling
Sancerre
Sangaree
Sauterne
Sémillon
Spätlese
Spumante
St Julien
Sylvaner
Verdelho
Vermouth
Vinsanti

**9 letters:**
Bacharach

Bardolino
Carmenère
Champagne
Colombard
Dandelion
En primeur
Falernian
Gladstone
Hermitage
Hippocras
Hoccamore
Inglenook
Lambrusco
Languedoc
Loll-shrob
Malvoisie
Meersault
Minervois
Muscadine
Ordinaire
Pinot noir
Sauvignon
St Emilion
Tafelwein
Tarragona
Vin-du-pays
Zinfandel

**10 letters:**
Beaujolais
Bull's blood
Chambertin
Chardonnay
Constantia
Elderberry
Genevrette
Hochheimer
Loll-shraub
Manzanilla
Montrachet
Muscadelle
Napa Valley
Peter-see-me
Piesporter
Sangiovese
Vinho verde

**11 letters:**
Amontillado
Dom Perignon
Niersteiner
Petite Sirah
Pouilly-Fumé
Rudesheimer
Scuppernong
Steinberger
Tempranillo

**12 letters:**
Johannisberg
Marcobrunner
Supernaculum
Valpolicella
Vin ordinaire

**13 letters:**
Beerenauslese
Entre-Deux-Mers
Liebfraumilch
Montepulciano
Pouilly-Fuissé

**14 letters:**
Gewürztraminer
Johannisberger

**15 letters:**
Lachryma Christi
Liebfrauenmilch

**16 letters:**
Chateau cardboard
London particular

**17 letters:**
Cabernet Sauvignon
Nuits Saint Georges

**20 letters:**
Trockenbeeren-
auslese

---

**Wine-cellar, Wine-shop** Bistro, Bodega, Vault, Vaut(e)
**Wine-glass** Flute
**Wine-making** Gallising, Remuage
**Wing(s), Winged, Winger, Wing-like** Aerofoil, Ala(r), Aliform, Alula, Annexe,
   Appendage, Arm, Bastard, →**BIRD**, Branch, Buffalo, Canard, Cellar, Corium, Coulisse,
   Delta, Dipteral, El(l), Elevon, Elytral, Elytriform, Elytron, Elytrum, Fan, Fender, Flap, Flew,
   Flex, Flipper, Flying, Forward, Gull, Halteres, Hurt, Left, Limb, Offstage, Parascenia,

Parascenium, Patagium, Pegasus, Pennate, Pennon, Pinero, Pinion, Pip, Pterygoid, Putto, Right, Rogallo, Sail, Samariform, Satyrid, Scent-scale, Segreant, Seraphim, Split, Standard, Sweepback, Sweptback, Sweptwing, Swift, Swingwing, Tailplane, Tectrix, Tegmen, Tormentor, Transept, Van, Vol(et), Water, Wound(ed)

**Winged sandals** Talaria

▷ **Winger** *may indicate* a bird

**Wing-footed** Aliped, Fleet, Swift

**Wingless** Apteral

**Wink (at)** Atone, Bat, Condone, Connive, Eliad, Eyelid, Flicker, Ignore, Illiad, Instant, Nap, Nictitate, Oeillade, Pink, Twinkle

**Winkle** Gastropod

**Winnie** Pooh

**Winnow** Fan, Riddle, Separate, Sift, Van, Wecht

**Winsome** Bonny, Engaging, Gay, Pleasant

**Winter, Wintry** Blackthorn, Bleak, Brumal, Cold, Dec, Fimbul, Frigid, Frore, Hibernate, Hiemal, Hiems, Hodiernal, Jack Frost, Jasmine, Nuclear, Shrovetide, Snowy, Subniveal, W

**Winter cherry** Chinese lantern

**Wintergreen** Chickweed, Pyrola, Sarcodes

**Winter pear** Nelis

**Winter-sport** Ski

**Wipe (out), Wiping** Abolish, Abrogate, Absterge, Amortise, Annihilate, Cancel, Cleanse, Demolish, Destroy, Deterge, Dicht, Dight, Efface, Eradicate, Erase, Expunge, Forget, Hanky, Kleenex®, Mop, Nose-rag, Null, Purge, Raze, Retroussage, Rub, Slorm, Sponge, Tersion, Tissue

**Wire(s), Wirework, Wiry** Aerial, Barb(ed), Cable, Cat's whiskers, Chicken, Coil, Earth, Element, Fencing, Filament, Filar, File, Filigree, Heald, Heddle, High, In on, Kirschner, Lead, Lean, Lecher, Live, Marconigram, Messenger, Mil, Nichrome®, Nipper, Number eight, Piano, Pickpocket, Razor, Sevice, Shroud, Sinewy, Snake, Solenoid, Spit, Staple, Stilet, Strand, String, Stylet, Telegram, Telegraph, Thoth, Thread, Tightrope, Trace, Trip

**Wireless (operator), Wireless part** Baffle, Set, Sparks, Tranny, Valve

**Wirral** Peninsula

**Wise(acre), Wisdom** Advisedly, Ancient, Astute, Athena, Athene, Canny, Conventional, Cracker barrel, Depth, Ernie, Ganesa, Gothamite, Gudrun, Hep, Hindsight, Horse sense, Judgement, Judicious, Knowledge, Learned, Long-headed, Lore, Manner, Mimir, Minerva, Norman, Oracle, Owl, Pearl, Penny, Philosopher, Philosophy, Politic, Polymath, Prajna, Profound, Prudence, Sagacity, Sage, Salomonic, Sapience, Savvy, Shrewd, Smartie, Solomon, Solon, Sophia, Tooth, Wice

**Wisecrack** Dig, One-liner, Quip, Sally

**Wise man** Balthazar, Caspar, Gaspar, Hakam, Heptad, Melchior, Nestor, Pandit, Sage, Sapient, Seer, Solomon, Swami, Thales, Tohunga, Worldly

**Wish(es), Wishing** Ache, Ake, Aspire, Covet, Crave, Death, Desiderate, →**DESIRE**, Envy, For, Hope, Itch, List, Long, Nill, Pant, Pleasure, Pray, Precatory, Regards, RIP, Velleity, Want, Yearn

**Wishbone** Furcula, Marriage-bone, Merrythought, Skipjack

**Wishy-washy** Bland, Feeble, Insipid, Irresolute, Milksop, Weak, Wheyey

**Wisp(y)** Cirrate, Cirrose, Frail, Scrap, Shred, Virga, Wase

**Wistful** Elegiac

**Wit(s), Witticism, Witty** Acumen, Attic, Badinage, Banter, Bon mot, Brevity, Card, Commonsense, Concetto, Cunning, Dry, Epigram, Esprit (de l'escalier), Estimation, Eutrapelia, Eutrapely, Facetious, Fantasy, Gnome, Hartford, Horse sense, Humour, Imagination, Intelligence, Irony, Jest, Jeu d'esprit, Joke, Marbles, Marinism, Memory, Mind, Mot, Mother, Native, Nous, One-liner, Oscar Wilde, Pawky, Pun, Quipster, Repartee, Rogue, Sally, Salt, Saut, Sconce, →**SENSE**, Shaft, Smart, Sparkle, Videlicet, Viz, Wag, Weet, Wisecrack, Word-play

**Witch(craft)** Beldam(e), Besom-rider, Broomstick, Cantrip, Carline, Circe, Coven, Craigfluke, Crone, Cutty Sark, Diabolism, Enchantress, Ensorcell, Galdragon, Glamour, Goety, Gramary(e), Gyre-carlin, Hag, Hecat(e), Hex, Invultuation, Lamia, Magic, Medea, Myal(ism), Necromancy, Night-hag, Obeahism, Obia, Obiism, Pishogue, Pythoness, Salem, Selim, She-devil, Sibyl, Sieve, Sorceress, Speller, Sycorax, Termagant, Trout, Valkyrie, Vaudoo, Vilia, Voodoo, Water, Weird, Wicca, Wise woman

**Witch-doctor** Animist, Boyla, Medicine man, Mganga, Obi, Pawaw, Powwow, Sangoma, Shaman

**Witch-hazel** Fothergilla, Platan(e), Winter-bloom

**Witch-hunter** McCarthy

**With** And, By, Con, Cum, Hereby, In, Mit, Of, Plus, Using, W

**Withdraw(al), Withdrawn** Abdicate, Abstract, Alienate, Aloof, Back out, Backpedal, Breakaway, Climb down, Cloistered, Cold turkey, Cry off, Deduct, Desertion, Detach, Disengage, Distrait, Enshell, Estrange, Evacuate, Extract, Hive off, Inshell, Introvert, Leave, Offish, Palinode, Phantom, Precede, Preserve, Recant, Recede, Recoil, Renegue, Repair, Rescind, Resile, Reticent, Retire, Retract(ion), Retreat, Revoke, Revulsion, Scratch, Secede, Secesh, Sequester, Shrink, Shy, Stand down, Subduce, Subduct, Subtract, Tap, Unreeve, Unsay

**Wither(ed), Withering, Withers** Arefy, Atrophy, Blast, Blight, Burn, Corky, Decadent, Die, Droop, Dry, Evanish, Fade, Forpine, Gizzen, Googie, Languish, Marcescent, Miff, Nose, Sarcastic, Scram, Sere, Shrink, Shrivel, Welk, Welt

**Withershins** Eastlin(g)s

▷ **With gaucherie** *may indicate* an anagram

**Withhold(ing), Withheld** Abstain, Conceal, Curt, Deny, Detain, Detinue, Hide, Keep, →RESERVE, Ritenuto, Trover

**Within** Enclosed, Endo-, Immanent, Indoors, Inside, Interior, Intra

**With it** Hep, Hip, Syn, Trendy, W

**Without** Bar, Beyond, Ex, Lack(ing), Less, Minus, Orb, Outdoors, Outside, Sans, Save, Sen, Senza, Sine, X

▷ **Without** *may indicate* one word surrounding another

▷ **Without restraint** *may indicate* an anagram

**Without stimulus** Nastic

**Withstand** Blight, Brave, Contest, Defy, Endure, Oppose, Resist, Weather

**Witless** Crass, →STUPID PERSON

**Witness** Attend, Attest, Behold, Bystander, Catch, Character, Compurgator, Confirm, Crown, Deponent, Depose, Endorse, Evidence, Experience, Expert, Eye, Glimpse, Hostile, Jehovah's, Mark, Martyr, Material, Muggletonian, Note, Notice, Observe, Obtest, Onlooker, Passer-by, Perceive, Proof, →SEE, Show, Sight, Sign, Spy, Stander-by, Survey, Testament, Teste, Testify, Testimony, View, Vouchee, Watch

**Witness-box** Peter, Stand

▶ **Witticism** *see* WIT(S)

**Wizard (priest)** Archimage, Awesome, Carpathian, Conjuror, Demon, Expert, Gandalf, Hex, Mage, Magician, Merlin, Obiman, Oz, Prospero, Shaman, Sorcerer, Super, Warlock, →WITCH-DOCTOR

**Wizen(ed)** Dehydrate, Dry, Sere, Shrivel, Sphacelate, Wither

**Woad** Anil, Dye, Indigo, Isatis, Pastel, Pastil

**Wobble, Wobbling, Wobbly** Chandler's, Coggle, Hissy fit, Precess, Quaver, Reel, Rock, Shimmy, Shoggle, Shoogle, Teeter, Totter, Tremble, Trillo, Unstable, Unsteady, Wag, Waggle, Walty, Waver, Wibble

**Wodehouse** Plum

**Woe(ful), Woebegone, Woeful** Agony, Alack, Alas, Bale, Bane, Distress, Dool(e), Dule, Ewhow, Execrable, Gram, Grief, Hurt, Jeremiad, Lack-a-day, Misery, Pain, Plague, →SORROW, Torment, Tribulation, Triste, Unhappy, Wailful, Wednesday's child

**Wolds** Lincoln(shire), Yorkshire

**Wolf(ish), Wolf-like** Akela, Assyrian, Bolt, Cancer, Carcajou, Casanova, Coyote, Cram, Dangler, Dasyure, Dire, Earth, Engorge, Fenrir, Fenris, Gorge, Grey, Ise(n)grim, Lobo, Lone, Lothario, Lupine, Luster, Lycanthrope, MI, Michigan, Pack, Philanderer, Prairie, Rake, Ravenous, Red, Rip, Roué, Rout, Rudolph, Rye, Scoff, Sea, Seducer, Strand, Tasmanian, Thylacine, Tiger, Timber, Wanderer, Were, Whistler

**Wolfram** Tungsten

**Wolf's bane** Aconite, Friar's-cap

**Wolseley** Sir Garnet

**Woman(hood), Women** Aguna(h), Anile, Beldam(e), Bellibone, Besom, Biddy, Bimbo, Bint, Bit, Boiler, Broad, Cailleach, Callet, Caryatid, Chai, Chap(p)ess, Chook, Citess, Cotquean, Crone, Crumpet, Cummer, Dame, Daughter, Distaff, Doe, Dona(h), Dorcas, Doris, Doyenne, Drab, Duenna, Eve, F, Fair, Fair sex, → FEMALE, Feme, Femme fatale, Flapper, Floozy, Frail, Frow, Gammer(stang), Gimmer, Gin, Girl, Gyno-, -gyny, Harpy, Harridan, Hausfrau, Hen, Her, Ho, Housewife, Inner, It, Jade, Jane, Kloo(t)chman, Lady, Liberated, Lilith, Lorette, Madam(e), Mademoiselle, Maenad, Mary, Miladi, Milady, Millie, Minge, Mob, Modicum, Mort, Ms, Muliebrity, Painted, Pandora, Peat, Petticoat, Pict, Piece, Piece of goods, Placket, Point, Popsy, Puna(a)ni, Puna(a)ny, Pussy, Quean, Queen, Ramp, Rib, Ribibe, Ronyon, Rudas, Runnion, Sabine, Sakti, Scarlet, Shakti, Shawlay, Shawlie, She, Skirt, Sloane Ranger, Sort, Squaw, Tail, Tedesca, Tib, Tiring, Tit, Tottie, Totty, Trot, Umfazi, Vahine, Wahine, Weaker sex, Wifie, Zena

**Womaniser** Casanova, Lady-killer, Poodle-faker, Wolf

**Womb** Belly, Matrix, Metritis, Side, Uterus, Ventricle

**Women's club, Women's lib** S(h)akti, Soroptimist

**Won** Chon, W

**Wonder(s)** Admire, Agape, Amazement, AR, Arkansas, Arrah, Awe, Chinless, Colossus, Ferly, Grape-seed, Hanging Gardens, Humdinger, Marle, → MARVEL, Mausoleum, Meteor, Mirabilia, Miracle, Muse, Nine-day, One-hit, Pharos, Phenomenon, Prodigy, Pyramids, Seven, Speculate, Statue of Zeus, Stupor, Suppose, Surprise, Temple of Artemis, Thaumatrope, Wheugh, Whew, Wow(ee)

**Wonderful(ly)** Amazing, Bees' knees, Bitchin(g), Chinless, Divine, Épatant, Fantastic, Far-out, Ferly, Geason, Gee-whiz, Glorious, Gramercy, Grand, Great, Heavenly, Keen, Lal(l)apalooza, Magic, Mirable, Must-see, Old, Priceless, Purely, Ripping, Smashing, Stellar, Sublime, Superb, Wicked

**Wonder-worker** Fakir, Thaumaturgist, Thaumaturgus

**Wonky** Cockeyed, Lopsided

**Wont(ed)** Accustomed, Apt, Custom, Habit, Shan't, Used, Way, Winna

**Woo(er)** Address, Beau, Carve, Chase, Court, Frog, Seduce, Serenade, Suitor, Swain

**Wood(s), Wooden, Woodland, Woody** Arboretum, Batten, Beam, Birken, Board, Boord(e), Bough, Brake, Cask, Channel, Chipboard, Chuck, Chump, Clapboard, Conductor, Dead, Deadpan, Expressionless, Fardage, Fathom, Fire, Fish, Funk, Furious, Gantry, Gauntree, Guthrie, Hanger, Hard, Hyle, Kindling, Knee, Krummholz, Late, Lath, Loggerhead, Lumber, Mad, Magnetic, Miombo, Nemoral, Nemorous, Offcut, Pallet, Pegboard, Plastic, Pulp(wood), Punk, Silvan, Slat, Spilikin, Spill, Spinney, Splat, Spline, Splint, Stolid, Sylvan, Tenon, Three-ply, Tiger, Timber, Tinder, Touch, Treen, Trees, Twiggy, Two-by-four, Vert, Xylem, Xyloid

---

**WOOD**

| 3 letters: | Red | Carr | Holt |
|---|---|---|---|
| Ash | | Cord | Iron |
| Box | 4 letters: | Cork | King |
| Cam | Beef | Deal | Lana |
| Elm | Bent | Eugh | Lima |
| Log | Bowl | Gapó | Lime |

Pine
Rata
Rock
Shaw
Soft
Spar
Teak
Wild
Yang

**5 letters:**
Afara
Agila
Algum
Almug
Balsa
Bavin
Beech
Cedar
Copse
Drive
Ebony
Elfin
Firth
Frith
Green
Grove
Heben
Hurst
Igapó
Iroko
Jarul
Joist
Kauri
Klaat
Kokra
Lance
Maple
Mazer
Myall
Opepe
Peach
Plane
Ramin
Rowan
Sapan
Spoon
Stink
Taiga
Thorn
Tulip
Wenge

Zante
Zebra

**6 letters:**
Alerce
Bamboo
Beaver
Birnam
Bocage
Brazil
Calico
Canary
Carapa
Cheese
Citron
Citrus
Deodar
Dingle
Forest
Fustet
Fustic
Fustoc
Gaboon
Gopher
Herman
Jarool
Jarrah
Letter
Lignum
Loggat
Manuka
Muntin
Obeche
Orache
Orange
Paddle
Poplar
Raddle
Sabele
Sabicu
Sandal
Sapele
Sappan
Sissoo
Sponge
Tallow
Tupelo
Violet
Waboom
Walnut
Wandoo
Yellow

**7 letters:**
Amboina
Barwood
Boscage
Brassie
Cambium
Cerrado®
Coppice
Dudgeon
Dunnage
Duramen
Gambrel
Gumwood
Hadrome
Hickory
Leopard
Meranti
Mesquit
Nutwood
Palmyra
Paranym
Pimento
Sanders
Sapwood
Shawnee
Shittim
Trumpet
Wallaba

**8 letters:**
Agalloch
Alburnum
Basswood
Bushveld
Caatinga
Coulisse
Harewood
Hornbeam
Kingwood
Laburnum
Ligneous
Mahogany
Masonite®
Mesquite
Mountain
Ovenwood
Pyengadu
Pyinkado
Rosewood
Sapucaia
Shagbark
Southern

Tamarack

**9 letters:**
Balsam fir
Briarwood
Butternut
Caliature
Campeachy
Coachwood
Cocuswood
Driftwood
Eaglewood
Fruitwood
Heartwood
Ivorywood
Matchwood
Partridge
Porcupine
Primavera
Quebracho
Satinwood
Snakewood
Torchwood

**10 letters:**
Afrormosia
Blockboard
Bulletwood
Calamander
Candlewood
Cheesewood
Chittagong
Coromandel
Fiddlewood
Greenheart
Hackmatack
Marblewood
Nettle-tree
Orangewood
Palisander
Scaleboard
Sneezewood
Springwood
Summerwood

**11 letters:**
Lignum-vitae
Sanderswood
Slippery elm

**13 letters:**
Savanna-wattle

▷ **Wood** *may indicate* an anagram in sense of mad

**Wood-carver** Bodger, Gibbons, Whittler

**Woodchuck** Bobac, Groundhog, Marmot

**Woodcock** Becasse, Beccaccia, Snipe

**Woodlouse** Isopod, Oniscus, Slater

**Woodman** Ali (Baba), Coureur de bois, Feller, Forester, Hewer, Logger, Lumberjack, Sawyer

**Woodpecker** Bird, Descent, Flicker, Hairy, Hickwall, Picalet, Picarian, Pileated, Rainbird, Sapsucker, Saurognathae, Witwall, Woodspite, Woodwale, Woody, Yaffle

**Wood-pigeon** Bird, Cushat, Que(e)st, Qu(o)ist, Torquate

**Wood-sorrel** Oca

**Wood-tar** Furan, Furfuran

**Woodwind** Bassoon, Clarinet, Cornet, Flute, Oboe, Piccolo, Pipe, Recorder, Reed

**Woodwork(er)** Carpentry, Ebonist, Forestry, Intarsia, Joinery, Marquetrie, Marquetry, Sloid, Sloyd, Tarsia, Termite

**Woodworm** Gribble, Termes

**Wookey** Stalactite

**Wool(len), Woolly (haired)** Alpaca, Angora, Aran, Ardil, Bainin, Barège, Beige, Berlin, Botany, Bouclé, Calamanco, Cardi(gan), Cashmere, Cas(s)imere, Clean, Clip, Combings, Cotton, Crutchings, Daglock, Delaine, Doeskin, Dog, Doily, Down, Doyley, Drugget, Duffel, Fadge, Fingering, Fleece, Flock, Frib, Frieze, Fuzz, Glass, Greasy, Guernsey, Hank, Hause-lock, Heather mixture, Hogget, Indumentum, Jaeger, Jersey, Kashmir, Ket, Knitwear, Lanate, Laniferous, Lanigerous, Lanose, Llama, Lock, Loden, Merino, Mineral, Mortling, Moul, Mullein, New, Noil(s), Nun's-veiling, Offsorts, Oo, Paco, Pashm, Pelage, Persian, Pine, Qiviut, Rock, Rolag, Sagathy, Saxon, Say, Shahtoosh, Shalloon, Shamina, Shetland, Shoddy, Skein, Skin, Slag, Slipe, Slip-on, Slub, Smart, Spencer, Staple, Steel, Strouding, Stuff, Swansdown, Tamise, Tammy, Tank top, Telltale, Thibet, Three-ply, Tod, Tricot, Tweed, Twin set, Ulotrichous, Vague, Vicuña, Virgin, Wire, Wood, Worcester, Yarn, Zephyr, Zibel(l)ine

**Wool-gather(er), Woolgathering** Abstraction, Argo, Dreamer, Reverie

**Wool-holder, Woolsack** Bale, Distaff

**Woolly-bear** Tiger-moth, Woubit

**Wool-oil** Yolk

**Woopie** Glam

**Wooster** Bertie

**Woozy** Drunk, Faint, Vague, Woolly

**Worcester** Wigorn

**Word(s), Wording, Wordy** Al(l)-to, Appellative, Argument, Aside, Bahuvrihi, Buzz, Cataphor(a), Catch, Cheville, Claptrap, Clipped, Clitic, Code, Coinage, Comment, Content, Dick, Dicky bird, Dit(t), Echoic, Effable, Embolalia, Enclitic, Epitaph, Epithet, Epos, Etymon, Faith, Four-letter, Function, Functor, Ghost, Grace, Hapax legomenon, Hard, Heteronym, Hint, Holophrase, Homograph, Homonym, Horseman's, Household, Hyponym, →**IN A WORD**, →**IN TWO WORDS**, Janus, Jonah, Key, Last, Lexeme, Lexicon, Lexis, Loan, Logia, Logos, Long-winded, Lyrics, Mantra, Meronym, Message, Morpheme, Mot, Neologism, News, Nonce, Nonsense, Noun, Oath, Om, Operative, Oracle, Order, Palabra, Paragram, Paranym, Parenthesis, Parlance, Parole, Paronym, Paroxytone, Particle, Perissology, Peristomenon, Phrase, Piano, Pledge, Pleonasm, Polysemen, Portmanteau, Preposition, Prolix, Promise, Pronoun, Reserved, Rhematic, Rhyme, Rumbelow, Rumour, Saying, Selah, Semantics, Signal, Soundbite, Subtitle, Surtitle, Syntagma, Talkative, Tatpurasha, Term, Tetragram, Text, Tirade, Trigger, Trope, Typewriter, Verb, Verbiage, Verbose, Vocab(ulary), Vogue, Warcry, Weasel, Winged, Wort, Written

**Word-blindness** Alexia, Dyslexia

**Wordless** Tacit

**Word-play** Charade, Paronomasia, Pun

**Wordsmith** Logodaedalus
▷ **Work** *may indicate* a book or play, etc.
**Workable** Feasible, Practical
**Workaholic, Work(er), Working(-class), Workman, Workmen, Works, Workman(ship)** Act(ivate), Aga saga, Ant, Application, Appliqué, Apronman, Artefact, Artel, Artifact, Artificer, Artisan, At it, At task, Barmaid, Beamer, Beaver, Bee, Blue-collar, Blue-singlet, Bohunk, Boon(er), Boondoggle, Brief, Bull, Business, Busy, Careerist, Casual, Char, Chare, Chargehand, Chigga, Chippy, Chore, Claim, Clock, Colon, Community, Computer, Contingent, Coolie, Cooly, Corvée, Craftsman, Crew, Cultivate, Darg, Dig, Diss(ertation), Do, Dog, Dogsbody, Donkey, Draft-mule, Droil, Drudge, Drug, Dung, Earn, Effect, Effort, Elbow grease, Em, Erg(ataner), Ergatoid, Erg-nine, Ergon, Ergonomics, Erg-ten, Eta, Everything, Evince, Exercise, Exergy, Exploit, Factotum, Facture, Fast, Fat, Ferment, Fettler, Field, Filter, Flat cap, Flex(i)time, Floruit, Fret, Fuller, →**FUNCTION**, Gae, Gastarbeiter, Gel, Girl Friday, Go, Graft, Grass, Grind, Grisette, Grunt, Guest, Hand, Harness, Hat, Hobo, Horse, Hot-desking, Hunky, Indian, Industry, Innards, Intray, Jackal, Job, Journeyman, Key, Knead, Knowledge, Kolhoznik, Labour, Laid, Leave, Luddite, Lump, Machinist, Maid, Man, Manipulate, Manpower, McJob, Mechanic(ian), Meng, Menge, Menial, Midinette, Mine, Ming, MO, Moider, Moil, Moonlight, Movement, Navvy, Neuter, Number, Oeuvre, On, On (the) job, Op, Opera(tion), Operative, Operator, Opus, Opusc(u)le, Orderly, Outreach, Outside, Ouvrier, Ox, Parergon, Part, Partisan, Passage, Peasant, Peg, Pensum, Peon, Pink-collar, Plasterer, Ply, Poker, Portfolio, Postlude, Potboiler, Practicum, Practise, Production, Project, Prole(tariat), Prud'homme, Public, Pursuit, Red-neck, Reduction, Rep, Ride, Robot, Rotovate, Roughneck, Round, Rouseabout, Roustabout, Run, Salaryman, Samiti, Sandhog, Satisfactory, Scabble, Scapple, Scullion, Secretariat, Sedentary, Servant, Serve, Service, Servile, Seven, Sewage, Shift, Shop (floor), Situation, Skanger, Slogger, Smithy, Social, Soldier, Spiderman, Staff, Stagehand, Stakhanovite, Stevedore, Stint, Strap, Straw, Strive, Support, Surface, Swaggie, Swagman, Sweat, Swink, Take, Tamper, Task, Team, Technician, Telecommuter, Temp, Tenail(le), Tenaillon, Termite, Tew, Text, Tick, Till, Toccata, Toil, Toreutic, Travail, Treatise, Trojan, TU, TUC, Turk, Tut, Tutman, Typto, Uphill, Wage plug, Walla(h), Wark, Welfare, White-collar, Wobblies, Wright, Yacker, Yakka, Yakker, Yarco
**Work-basket, Workbox** Caba(s), Nécessaire
**Workbench** Banker, Siege
**Workhouse** Casual ward, Spike, Union
▷ **Working** *may indicate* an anagram
**Working-party** Bee, Quilting-bee, Sewing-bee, Squad
**Workmate** Yokefellow
**Work out** Deduce, Figure, PE, PT
**Works, Workplace, Workshop** Atelier, Engine, Factory, Forge, Foundry, Garage, Hacienda, Hangar, Innards, Lab, Mill, Passage, Plant, Public, Shed, Sheltered, Shipyard, Shop, Skylab, Smithy, Studio, Study, Sweatshop, Tannery, Telecottage, Time, Tin, Turnery, Upper
**Workshy** Indolent, Lazy, Sweer(ed), Sweert, Sweir(t)
**World(ly), Worldwide** Adland, Carnal, Chthonic, Cosmopolitan, Cosmos, Cyberspace, Dream, Earth, First, Fleshly, Fourth, Free, Ge, Global village, Globe, Kingdom, Lay, Lower, Mappemond, Meatspace, Microcosm, Midgard, Mondaine, Mondial, Mould, Mundane, Natural, Nether, New, Old, Orb, Other, Oyster, Planet, Possible, Second, Secular, Sensual, Small, Society, Sphere, Spirit, Temporal, Terra, Terrene, Terrestrial, Third, Universe, Vale, Web, Welt, Whole
**Worm(-like), Worms, Wormy** Acorn, Angle, Anguillula, Annelid, Annulata, Apod(e), Apodous, Army, Arrow, Articulata, Ascarid, Bilharzia, Bladder, Blind, Blood, Bob, Bootlace, Brandling, Bristle, Caddis, Capeworm, Caseworm, Catworm, Cercaria, Cestode, Cestoid, Chaetopod, Clamworm, Clew, Copper, Dew, Diet, Diplozoon, Dracunculus, Edge, Enteropneust, Fan, Filander, Filaria, Flag, Flat, Flesh, Fluke,

Galley, Gape, Gilt-tail, Gordius, Gourd, Gru-gru, Guinea, Hair, Hair-eel, Hairworm, Heartworm, Helminth, Hemichordata, Hookworm, Horsehair, Idle, Inchworm, Leech, Liver-fluke, Lob, Lumbricus, Lytta, Maw, Measuring, Merosome, Miner's, Mopani, Muck, Nemathelminthes, Nematoda, Nematode, Nematodirus, Nematomorpha, Nemertean, Nemertina, Nereid, Night-crawler, Oligochaete, Onychophoran, Paddle, Palmer, Palolo, Paste-eel, Peripatus, Phoronid, Pile, Pin, Piper, Planarian, Platyhelminth, Polychaete, Ragworm, Redia, Ribbon, Rootworm, Roundworm, Sabella, Sand mason, Schistosome, Scoleciform, Scolex, Screw, Seamouse, Serpula, Servile, Ship, Sipunculacea, Sipunculoidea, Spiny-headed, Stomach, Strawworm, Strongyl(e), Taenia, Tag-tail, Taint, Tapeworm, Tenioid, Teredo, Termite, Threadworm, Tiger, Tiger tail, Tongue, Toxocara, Trematode, Trichin(ell)a, Trichinosed, Triclad, Tube, Tubifex, Turbellaria, Vermiform, Vinegar, Vinegar eel, Wheat-eel, Wheatworm, Whipworm

**Wormkiller** Anthelmintic, Santonin

**Wormwood** Absinth, Appleringie, Artemisia, Moxa, Mugwort, Santonica, Southernwood

**Worn (out)** Attrite, Bare, Decrepit, Detrition, Effete, Épuisé, Exhausted, Forfairn, Forfoughten, Forjaskit, Forjeskit, Frazzled, Gnawn, Knackered, Old, On, Passé, Raddled, Rag, Seedy, Shabby, Shopsoiled, Shot, Spent, Stale, Tatty, Threadbare, Tired, Traikit, Trite, Used, Weathered, Whacked

**Worried, Worrier, Worry** Agonise, Ail, Angst(-ridden), Annoy, Anxiety, Badger, Bait, Beset, Bother, Brood, Burden, Care(worn), Cark, Chafe, Concern, Consternate, Deave, Deeve, Distraught, Distress, Disturb, Dog, Eat, Exercise, Faze, Feeze, Frab, Frantic, Fret, Fuss, Gnaw, Harass, Harry, Headache, Hyp, Inquietude, Knag, Nag, Niggle, Perturb, Pester, Pheese, Pheeze, Phese, Pingle, Pium, Preoccupy, Rattle, Rile, Sool, Stew, Tew, Touse, Towse, Trouble, Unease, Unnerve, Unsettle, Vex, Wherrit, Worn

▷ **Worried** *may indicate* an anagram

**Worse(n)** Adversely, Aggravate, Compound, Degenerate, Deteriorate, Exacerbate, Impair, Inflame, Pejorate, Regress, Relapse, War(re), Waur, Well away

**Worship(per)** Adore, Adulation, Allostery, Ancestor, Angelolatry, Aniconism, Animist, Autolatry, Bardolatry, Bless, Churchgoer, Congregation, Cosmolatry, Cult, Deify, Devotion, Dote, Douleia, Doxology, Dulia, Elementalism, Epeolatry, Exalt, Exercise, Fetish, Glorify, Groupie, Gurdwara, Happy-clappy, Henotheism, Hero, Ibadah, Iconology, Idolatry, Idolise, Latria, Lauds, Lionise, Liturgics, Lordolatry, Mariolatry, Meeting-house, Monolatry, Odinism, Oncer, Orant, Praise, Puja, Revere, Sabaism, Sakta, Service, Shacharis, Shakta, Sun, Synaxis, Thiasus, Vaishnava, Venerate, Votary, Wodenism

**Worst** Beat, Best, Better, Conquer, Defeat, Get, Less, Nadir, Outdo, Overpower, Pessimum, Rock-bottom, Scum, Severest, The pits, Throw, Trounce

**Worsted** Caddis, Caddyss, Challis, Coburg, Crewel, Genappe, Lea, Ley, Serge, Shalli, Tamin(e), Whipcord

▷ **Worsted** *may indicate* an anagram

**Wort** Hopped, Laser, Parkleaves, Plant, Sweet, Tutsan

**Worth(while), Worthy, Worthies** Admirable, Ad valorem, Asset, Be, Cop, Cost, Cost effective, Deserving, Eligible, Estimable, Face value, Feck, → **MERIT**, Nine, Notable, Significant, Substance, Tanti, Use, Value, Venerable, Vertu, Virtu(e), Virtuous, Wealth

**Worthless (person)** Average, Bad egg, Base, Beggarly, Bilge, Blown, Bodger, Bootless, Bum, Candy floss, Catchpenny, Chaff, Cheapjack, Crumb, Cypher, Damn, Despicable, Docken, Dodkin, Doit, Doitkin, Draffish, Draffy, Dreck, Dross, Duff, Ephemeron, Fallal, Footra, Fouter, Foutre, Frippery, Gimcrack, Gingerbread, Glop, Gubbins, Hilding, Ignoble, Javel, Jimcrack, Knick-knack, Left, Light, Lorel, Lorrell, Losel, Lozell, Manky, Mare's nest, Mauvais sujet, Mud, Naughty, Nugatory, Nyaff, Obol, Ornery, Orra, Otiose, Pabulum, Paltry, Pin, Poxy, Punk, Raca, Rag, Rap, Razoo, Riffraff, Rubbishy, Rump, Scabby, Scrote, Scum, Shinkin, Shotten, Siwash, Sorry, Straw, Tawdry, Tinhorn, Tinpot, Tinsel, Tittle, Toerag, Trangam, Trashy, Tripy, Trumpery, Tuppenny, Twat, Two-bit, Twopenny, Useless, Vain, Vile, Waff, Wanworthy, Wauff, Zero

**Wotchermean** Anan

**Would be** Assumed, Pseudo, Soi-disant

**Wouldn't** Nould(e)

**Wound(ed)** Battery, Bite, Bless, Blighty, Bruise, Chagrin, Coiled, Crepance, Cut, Dere, Dunt, Engore, Entry, Exit, Flesh, Ganch, Gash, Gaunch, Gore, Harm, Hurt, Injury, Knee, Lacerate, Lesion, Maim, Maul, Molest, Mortify, Offend, Pip, Sabre-cut, Scab, Scar, Scath, Scotch, Scratch, Shoot, Snaked, Snub, Sore, Stab, Sting, Trauma, Twined, Umbrage, Vuln, Vulnerary, Walking, Wing, Wint

**Woundwort** Clown's, Marsh

**Woven** Faconne, Inwrought, Knitted, Pirnit, Textile, Wattle

**Wow** Amaze, Howl, Impress, My, Success

**Wrack** Destroy, Downfall, Kelp, Ore, Torment, Varec(h), Vengeance

**Wraith** Apparition, Fetch, Ghost, Phantom, Shadow, Spectre

**Wrangle(r), Wrangling** Altercate, Argie-bargie, →ARGUE, Bandy, Bicker, Brangle, Broil, Cample, Controvert, Dispute, Haggle, Hassle, Herder, Horse, Mathematical, Rag, Rodeo, Second, Senior, Vitilitigation

**Wrap(per), Wrapped, Wrapping, Wraparound, Wrap up** Amice, Amis, Bag, Bandage, Bathrobe, Bind, Boa, Body, Bubble, Bundle, Carton(age), Cellophane®, Cere, Clingfilm, Cloak, Clothe, Cocoon, Conclude, Cover-up, Drape, Emboss, Encase, Enfold, Enrol(l), Ensheath(e), Envelop(e), Enwind, Foil, Folio, Furl, Gladwrap®, Hap, Hem, Infold, Kimono, Kraft, Lag, Lap, Mail, Mob, Muffle, Negligee, Nori, Outsert, Package, Parcel, Plastic, Roll, Rug, Sarong, Shawl, Sheath(e), Sheet, Shrink, Shroud, Stole, Swaddle, Swathe, Throw, Tinfoil, Tsutsumu, Velamen, Wap, Wimple

**Wrasse** Conner, Cunner, Parrot-fish, Scar

**Wrath** Anger, Cape, Fury, Ire, Passion, Vengeance

**Wreak** Avenge, Indulge, Inflict

**Wreath(e)** Adorn, Anadem, Bridal, Chaplet, Civic crown, Coronal, Crown, Entwine, Festoon, Garland, Laurel, Lei, Steven, Torse, Tortile, Twist

**Wreathe(d)** Hederated

**Wreck(age), Wrecked, Wrecker** Banjax, Blight, Blotto, Crab, Debris, Demolish, Devastate, Flotsam, Founder, Goner, Hesperus, Hulk, Lagan, Ligan, Loss, Luddite, Mutilate, Nervous, Ruin(ate), Sabotage, Saboteur, Shambles, Shatter, Sink, Smash, Spif(f)licate, Stramash, Subvert, Torpedo, Trash, Vandalise, Wrack

▷ **Wrecked** *may indicate* an anagram

**Wren** Architect, Bird, Fairy, Fire-crested, Golden-crested, Hannah, Heath, Jenny, Kinglet, Rifleman-bird, Sailor, Superb blue, Willow

**Wrench** Allen, Bobbejaan, Box, Fit, Jerk, Lug, Mole, Monkey, Nut, Pin, Pipe, Pull, Rick, Screw, Socket, Spanner, Spider, Sprain, Stillson®, Strain, Strap, T-bar, Tear, Torque, Twist, Windlass, Wrest

**Wrestle(r), Wrest, Wrestling** All-in, Antaeus, Arm, Backbreaker, Basho, Bearhug, Bodycheck, Boston crab, Catch-as-catch-can, Catchweight, Clinch, Clothes line, Cross buttock, Cross press, Featherweight, Flying mare, Foil, Folding-press, Forearm smash, Freestyle, Full-nelson, Grapple, Gr(a)eco-Roman, Grovet, Half-nelson, Hammerlock, Haystacks, Headlock, Hip-lock, →HOLD, Indian, Judo, Knee-drop, Makunouchi, Milo, Monkey climb, Mud, Nelson, Niramiai, Ozeki, Palaestral, Pancratium, Pinfall, Posting, Rikishi, Sambo, Stable, Straight arm lift, Stranglehold, Struggle, Sumo, Sumotori, Suplex, Tag (team), Toehold, Tussle, Whip, Wraxle, Wristlock, Writhe, Yokozuna

**Wretch(ed)** Abject, Bally, Blackguard, Blue, Caitiff, Chap-fallen, Crumb, Cullion, Cur, Darned, Donder, Forlorn, Git, Goddamned, Hapless, Ignoble, Lorn, Low, Measly, Miscreant, Miser, Miserable, Peelgarlic, Pilgarlick, Pipsqueak, Pitiable, Poltroon, Poor, Punk, Rakeshame, Rascal, Rat, Scoundrel, Scroyle, Seely, Snake, Sorry, Toerag, Unblest, Waeful, Wo(e), Woeful

▷ **Wretched** *may indicate* an anagram

**Wriggle** Hirsle, Shimmy, Squirm, Twine, Wiggle, Writhe

**Wright** Smith

**Wring(er)** Drain, Extort, Mangle, Screw, Squeeze, Twist

**Wrinkle(d), Wrinkly** Clue, Cockle, Corrugate, Crankle, Crease, Crepy, Crimple, Crimpy, Crinkle, Crow's-foot, Crumple, Fold, Frounce, Frown, Frumple, Furrow, Gen, Groove, Headline, Hint, Idea, Knit, Line, Lirk, Plissé, Plough, Pucker, Purse, Ridge, Rimple, Rivel, Rop(e)y, Ruck(le), Rugose, Rumple, Runkle, Seamy, Shrivel, Sulcus, Time-worn, Tip, Whelk, Wizened, Wrizled

**Wrist, Wristband** Carpus, Cuff, Radialia, Shackle-bone

**Writ(s)** Attachment, Audita querela, Capias, Certiorari, Cursitor, Dedimus, Devastatit, Distringas, Elegit, Fieri facias, Filacer, Habeas corpus, Holy, Injunction, Jury process, Latitat, Law-burrows, Mandamus, Mise, Mittimus, Noverint, Praemunire, Process, Quare impedit, Quo warranto, Replevin, Scirefacias, Significat, Subpoena, Summons, Supersedeas, Supplicavit, Tolt, Venire, Venire facias, Warrant

**Write(r), Writing** Allograph, Amphigory, Annotator, Apocrypha, →**AUTHOR**, Automatic, Balladist, Ballpoint, Belles lettres, Bellet(t)rist, BIC®, Biographer, Biro®, Blog, Bloomsbury Group, Book-hand, Boustrophedon, Calligraphy, Causerie, Cento, Chalk, Charactery, Clerk, Clinquant, Collectanea, Columnist, Continuity, Copperplate, Creative, Cuneiform, Cursive, Diarist, Dissertation, Dite, Draft, →**DRAMATIST**, Elohist, Endorse, Endoss, Engross, Enrol, Epigrammatise, Epistle, →**ESSAYIST**, Expatiate, Farceur, Festschrift, Feudist, Fist, Form, Formulary, Freelance, Ghost, Gongorism, Graffiti, Grammatology, Graphite, Hack, Hairline, Hand, Haplography, Hieratic, Hieroglyphics, Hierology, Hiragana, Homiletics, Indite, Ink, Inkhorn-mate, Ink-jerker, Inkslinger, Inscribe, Join-hand, Jot(tings), Journalese, Journalist, Journo, Kaleyard School, Kana, Kanji, Katakana, Keelivine, Keelyvine, Leader, Leetspeak, Lexigraphy, Lexis, Linear A, Lipogram, Littérateur, Longhand, Lucubrate, Marivaudage, Memoirist, Mimographer, Minoan, Mirror, Miscellany, Monodist, Monograph, Ms(s), Nesk(h), Nib, Notary, Notate, Novelese, →**NOVELIST**, Palaeography, Pamphleteer, Paragraphia, Pasigraphy, Pen, Pencil, Penmanship, Penne, Penny-a-liner, Pentel®, Phrasemonger, Picture, Pinyin, Planchette, →**POET**, Polemic, Polygraphy, Pot-hook, Prosaist, Proser, Pseudepigrapha, Psychogram, Psychography, Purana, Purple patch, Quill, Rhymer, Roundhand, Runic, Samizdat, Sanskrit, Scenarist, Sci-fi, Scissorer, Score, Scratch, Scrawl, Screed, Screeve, Scribble, Scribe, Scrip(t), Scripture, Scrivener, Scrow, Scytale, Secretary, Shaster, Shastra, Sign, Sing, Sling-ink, Small-hand, Space, Spirit, Stichometry, Style, Stylist, Stylography, Subscript, Superscribe, Sutra, Syllabary, Syllabic, Syllabism, Syngraph, Synoptist, Tantra, Telegraphese, Text, Tractarian, Transcribe, Treatise, Tushery, Type, Uncial, Varityper®, Wisdom, Wordsmith, Zend-Avesta

## WRITERS

| 3 letters: | Bolt | Loti | Shaw |
|---|---|---|---|
| APH | Buck | Lyly | Snow |
| Eco | Cary | Mahy | Ward |
| Lee | Dahl | Mann | West |
| Paz | Elia | More | Zola |
| Poe | Gide | Muir | |
| RLS | Grey | Nash | 5 letters: |
| Roy | Hope | Opie | Acton |
| | Hugo | Ovid | Adams |
| 4 letters: | Hunt | Pope | Aesop |
| Amis | King | Roth | Ahern |
| Asch | Lamb | Rudd | Aiken |
| Aymé | Lang | Saki | Albee |
| Bede | Lear | Sand | Alger |
| Behn | Loos | Seth | Asher |

| | | | |
|---|---|---|---|
| Auden | Niven | Braine | Miller |
| Awdry | Orczy | Brontë | Milton |
| Ayres | Ouida | Buchan | Morgan |
| Bacon | Paine | Bunyan | Morris |
| Bates | Pater | Butler | Nerval |
| Benet | Paton | Capote | Nesbit |
| Blair | Pliny | Cardus | O'Brien |
| Blake | Pound | Cather | Onions |
| Byatt | Powys | Cicero | Orwell |
| Caine | Reade | Clancy | Powell |
| Camus | Renan | Clarke | Proust |
| Capek | Rilke | Conrad | Racine |
| Corvo | Sagan | Cooper | Rankin |
| Crane | Scott | Cowper | Romaji |
| Crump | Seuss | Cronin | Runyon |
| Dante | Shute | Darwin | Ruskin |
| Defoe | Spark | Daudet | Sapper |
| Doyle | Stark | De Sade | Sappho |
| Dumas | Stead | Dexter | Sartre |
| Duras | Stein | Dryden | Sayers |
| Eliot | Stowe | Duggan | Sendac |
| Ellis | Swift | Engels | Seneca |
| Genet | Synge | Ennius | Sewell |
| Gogol | Twain | Forbes | Singer |
| Gorki | Verne | Fowles | Smiles |
| Gorky | Vidal | France | Sontag |
| Gosse | Waugh | George | Spring |
| Grass | Wells | Gibbon | Steele |
| Greer | White | Goethe | Sterne |
| Grimm | Wilde | Graves | Stoker |
| Hardy | Woolf | Greene | Storey |
| Harte | Yates | Harris | Tagore |
| Hecht | Yonge | Heller | Thiele |
| Hegel | | Hobbes | Thomas |
| Henry | **6 letters:** | Hoberg | Updike |
| Henty | Alcott | Hughes | Virgil |
| Hesse | Ambler | Huxley | Walker |
| Heyer | Aragon | Jekyll | Walton |
| Homer | Arnold | Jerome | Wilder |
| Hoyle | Arnott | Jonson | |
| Ibsen | Artaud | Keller | **7 letters:** |
| Innes | Asimov | Le Fanu | Addison |
| James | Atwood | Lennon | Aldrich |
| Joyce | Austen | Le Sage | Allende |
| Kafka | Balzac | London | Allston |
| Lewis | Baring | Lowell | Angelou |
| Lodge | Barrie | Lucian | Aretino |
| Lorca | Belloc | Ludlum | Bagehot |
| Marsh | Bellow | Lytton | Bagnold |
| Mason | Bierce | Mailer | Balchin |
| Milne | Binchy | Malory | Baldwin |
| Munro | Blyton | Mannin | Ballard |
| Musil | Borges | Masoch | Beckett |
| Nashe | Borrow | Mayhew | Bennett |

Bentley
Blunden
Boileau
Boswell
Burgess
Burnett
Carlyle
Chaucer
Chekhov
Claudel
Cobbett
Cocteau
Coetzee
Colette
Collins
Cookson
Coppard
Corelli
Cranmer
Deeping
Dickens
Diderot
Dinesen
Dodgson
Douglas
Drabble
Dreiser
Duhamel
Durrell
Emerson
Fenelon
Feydeau
Fleming
Forster
Forsyth
Fuentes
Gardner
Gaskell
Gissing
Golding
Grahame
Grisham
Haggard
Hammett
Hazlitt
Hazzard
Herbert
Herriot
Hichens
Holberg
Johnson
Kerouac
Kipling
Lardner

Leacock
Le Carre
Lessing
Malamud
Mallory
Marryat
Maugham
Mauriac
Mérimée
Mitford
Molière
Moravia
Murdoch
Nabokov
Naipaul
Narayan
Osborne
Peacock
Pushkin
Pynchon
Ransome
Rendell
Richter
Robbins
Rostand
Rowling
Rushdie
Saroyan
Sassoon
Shelley
Simenon
Sitwell
Spender
Surtees
Tennant
Terence
Theroux
Thoreau
Tolkien
Tolstoy
Travers
Ustinov
Wallace
Walpole
Walters
Wharton
Whitman
Wyndham

**8 letters:**
Anacreon
Andersen
Beaumont
Beerbohm

Benjamin
Bernanos
Bradbury
Brittain
Brookner
Browning
Caldwell
Cartland
Chandler
Childers
Christie
Congreve
Constant
Cornwell
Crompton
Deighton
De la Mare
Disraeli
Donleavy
Faulkner
Fielding
Flaubert
Forester
Goncourt
Gordimer
Ishiguro
Kingsley
Koestler
Langland
Lawrence
Lovelace
Mannheim
McCarthy
Melville
Meredith
Mitchell
Ondaatje
Perrault
Plutarch
Proudhon
Rabelais
Rattigan
Remarque
Rossetti
Rousseau
Salinger
Schiller
Shadbolt
Sheridan
Sherriff
Sillitoe
Smollett
Spillane
Stendhal

Strachey
Taffrail
Traherne
Trollope
Turgenev
Voltaire
Vonnegut
Williams
Xenophon

**9 letters:**
Aeschylus
Ainsworth
Aldington
Allingham
Blackmore
Boccaccio
Burroughs
Cervantes
Charteris
Corneille
Courtenay
De Quincey
Descartes
Dos Passos
Du Maurier
Edgeworth
Goldsmith
Hawthorne
Hemingway
Isherwood
La Bruyère
Lermontov
Linklater
Lovecraft
Mackenzie
Madariaga
Mansfield
Martineau
O'Flaherty
Oppenheim
Pasternak
Priestley
Santayana
Sholokhov
Sophocles
Steinbeck
Stevenson
Thackeray
Wodehouse

**10 letters:**
Ballantyne
Chesterton

| | 11 *letters:* | Robbe-Grillet | 15 *letters:* |
|---|---|---|---|
| De Beauvoir | Dostoyevsky | Saint-Exupéry | Somerset |
| Dostoevsky | Machiavelli | Solzhenitsyn | Maugham |
| Fitzgerald | Maeterlinck | | |
| Galsworthy | Shakespeare | 13 *letters:* | |
| Mandeville | | Chateaubriand | |
| Maupassant | 12 *letters:* | Sackville-West | |
| Pirandello | Aristophanes | | |
| Richardson | De Maupassant | 14 *letters:* | |
| Waterhouse | Quiller-Couch | Compton-Burnett | |
| Williamson | | | |

**Write-off** Amortise, Annul, Cancel, Scrap
**Writhe, Writhing** Athetosis, Contort, Curl, Scriggle, Squirm, Thraw, Twist, Wriggle
▷ **Writhing** *may indicate* an anagram
**Writing-case** Kalamdan
**Writing-room** Scriptorium
**Wrong(ful), Wrongdoer, Wrongdoing** Aggrieve, Agley, Amiss, Astray, Awry,
Bad, Bum, Chout, Defect, Delict, Disservice, Err, Fallacious, False, Falsism, Harm, Ill,
Immoral, Improper, Incorrect, Injury, Mischief, Misconduct, Misfaring, Misintelligence,
Misled, Mistake(n), Misuse, Nocent, Offbase, Offend, Pear-shaped, Peccadillo,
Perpetrator, Perverse, Private, Public, Sin(ful), Sinner, Tort, Tortious, Transgress,
Unethical, Unright, Unsuitable, Withershins, Wryly, X
▷ **Wrong** *may indicate* an anagram
**Wrong-headed** Perverse
**Wrong opinion** Cacodoxy
**Wrought (up)** Agitated, Beaten, Carved, Created, Excited, Filigree, Freestone, Shaped
**Wrung** Twisted, Withers
**Wry** Askew, Contrary, Devious, Distort, Droll, Grimace, Ironic
**Wryneck** Iynx, Jynx, Torticollis, Yunx
**Wycliffian** Lollard
**Wyoming** Wy

# Xx

**X(-shaped)** Buss, By, Chi, Christ, Cross, Decussate, Drawn, Generation, Kiss, Ten,
Times, Unknown, X-ray

**Xant(h)ippe** Battle-axe, Dragon

**Xenon** Xe

**Xenophobia** Insularism

**Xerophyte, Xerophytic** Cactus, Cereus, Mesquite, Tamaricaceae, Tamarisk

**Xhosan** Caffre, Kaf(f)ir

**Ximenes** Cardinal

▶ **Xmas** *see* CHRISTMAS(TIME)

**X-ray** Angiogram, Anticathode, Arthrogram, Characteristic, Cholangiography,
C(A)T-scanner, Emi-Scanner, Encephalogram, Encephalograph, Fermi, Grenz,
Mammogram, Plate, Pyelogram, Radiogram, Radioscopy, Rem, Roentgen, Sciagram,
Screening, Sigmatron, Skiagram, Skiagraph, Tomography, Venogram, X, Xeroradiography

**Xylophone** Marimba, Semantra, Sticcado, Sticcato

# Yy

**Y** Samian, Unknown, Yankee, Yard, Year, Yen, Yttrium

**Yabber** Convo

**Yacht** Britannia, Dragon, Ice, Keelboat, Ketch, Knockabout, Land, Maxi, Sailboat, Sand, Yngling

**Yachtsman, Yachtsmen** Chichester, Heath, RYS

**Yak** Gup, Natter, Talk

**Yale®** Key, Lock

**Yam** Adjigo, Batata, Breadroot, Camote, Dioscorea, Diosgenin, Kumara

**Yank(ee)** Bet, Carpetbagger, Hitch, Jerk, Jonathan, Lug, Northerner, Pluck, Pull, Rug, Schlep(p), So(o)le, Sowl(e), →**TUG**, Tweak, Twitch, Wrench, Wrest, Y

▷ **Yank** *may indicate* an anagram

**Yap** Bark, Yelp

**Yard(s)** Area, CID, Close, Court, Farm-toun, Garden, Hard, Haw, Hof, Junk, Kail, Knacker's, Lay, Main, Marshalling, Mast, Measure, Met, Navy, Patio, Poultry, Prison, Ree(d), Sail, Scotland, Show, Spar, Sprit, Steel, Stick, Stockyard, Stride, Switch, Tilt, Timber, Victualling, Y, Yd, Y-track

**Yarn(s)** Abb, Anecdote, Berlin, Bouclé, Caddice, Caddis, Chenille, Clew, Clue, Cop, Cord, Crewel, Fib, Fibroline, Fingering, Genappe, Gimp, Gingham, Guimp(e), Gymp, Homespun, Jaw, Knittle, Knot, Lay, Lea, Ley, Line, Lisle, Lurex®, Marl, Merino, Mohair, Nylon, Organzine, Orlon®, Ply, Rigmarole, Ripping, Rogue's, Rope, Saxony, Schappe, Sennit, Sinnet, Skein, Small stuff, Spun, Story, Strand, Tale, Taradiddle, Thread, Thrid, Thrum(my), Tram, Twice-laid, Warp, Water twist, Weft, Woof, Wool, Worsted, Zephyr

**Yarrow** Milfoil

**Yashmak** Veil

**Yaw(s)** Boba, Buba, Deviate, Framboesia, Lean, Morula, Tack, Veer

**Yawn(ing)** Boredom, Chasmy, Fissure, Gant, Gape, Gaunt, Greys, Hiant, Oscitation, Pandiculation, Rictus

**Yea** Certainly, Surely, Truly, Verily, Yes

**Year(ly), Years** A, Age, Anno, Annual, Anomalistic, Astronomical, AUC, Autumn, Calendar, Canicular, Civil, Common, Cosmic, Decennium, Donkey's, Dot, Ecclesiastical, Egyptian, Embolismic, Equinoctial, Financial, Fiscal, Gap, Grade, Great, Hebrew, Holy, Indiction, Julian, Leap, Legal, Light, Locust, Lunar, Lunisolar, Natural, PA, Perfect, Platonic, Prophetic week, Riper, Sabbatical, School, Sidereal, Solar, Sothic, Spring, Summer, Sun, Tax, Theban, Time, Towmon(d), Towmont, Tropical, Twelvemonth, Vintage, Wander(jahr), Winter, Zodiac

**Yearbook** Almanac, Annual

**Yearling** Colt, Hogget, Stirk, Teg

**Yearn(ing)** Ache, Ake, Aspire, Brame, Burn, Covet, Crave, Curdle, Desire, Erne, Greed, Green, Grein, Hanker, Hone, →**LONG**, Lust, Nostalgia, Pant, Pine, Sigh, Wistful

▷ **Yearning** *may indicate* an anagram

**Year's end** Dec

**Yeast** Barm, Bees, Brewer's, Ferment, Flor, Leaven, Saccharomycete, Torula, Vegemite®

**Yell** Bawl, Cry, Hue, Rant, Rebel, Screech, Shout, Shriek, Skelloch, Squall, Thunder, Tiger, Ululate, Waul, Yoick

**Yellow(ish)** Abram, Amber, Anthoclore, Auburn, Back, Beige, Bisque, Bistre, Buff, Butternut, Cadmium, Canary, Champagne, Chartreuse, Chicken, Chrome, Citrine, Clay-bank, Cowardly, Craven, Curcumin(e), Daffadowndilly, Daffodil, Eggshell, Etiolin, Fallow, Fever, Filemot, Flavescent, Flavin(e), Flavon, Flaxen, Fulvous, Gamboge, Gaudy-green, Gold, Icteric, Isabel(le), Isabella, Jack, Jaundiced, King's, Lammer, Lemon(y), Lupulin, Lurid, Lutein, Luteous, Lutescent, Maize, Mustard, Nankeen, Naples, Oaker, Ochery, Ochre(y), Ochroid, Or(eide), Oroide, Pages, Peach, Peril, Pink, Primrose, Queen's, River, Saffron, Sallow, Sand, Sear, Sherry, Spineless, Strae, Straw, Sulfur, Sulphur, Tawny, Topaz, Tow, Unheroic, Vitelline, Weld, Xanthous, Yolk

**Yellowhammer** Bunting, Yeldring, Yeldrock, Yite, Yoldring

**Yellow-wood** Gopher

**Yelp** Cry, Squeal, Whee, Ya(w)p

**Yemeni** Adeni, Saba, Sabean, Sheba

**Yen** Desire, Itch, Longing, Urge, Y, Yearn

**Yeoman** Beefeater, Exon, Farmer, Goodman, Goodwife, Salvation

**Yep** OK, Yes

**Yerd** Inter

**Yes** Agreed, Ay(e), Da, I, Indeed, Ja, Jokol, Nod, OK, Oke, Quite, Sure, Truly, Uh-huh, Whoopee, Wilco, Yah, Yea, Yokul, Yup

**Yesterday** Démodé, Eve, Hesternal, Pridian

**Yet** But, Even, How-be, Moreover, Nay, Nevertheless, Now, Still, Though

**Yeti** Abominable snowman, Sasquatch

**Yew** Podocarp(us), Taxus, Yvonne

**Yibbles** A(i)blins

**Yield(ing), Yielded** Abandon, Afford, Bear, Bend, Bow, Breed, Capitulate, Catch, Cede, Come, Comply, Concede, Crack, Crop, Defer, Dividend, Docile, Ductile, Easy, Elastic, Exert, Facile, Flaccid, Flexible, Give, Harvest, Interest, Knock under, Knuckle, Knuckle under, Meek, Meltith, Mess, Obtemper, Output, Pan, Pay, Pliant, Produce, Quantum, Redemption, Relent, Render, Return, Sag, Soft, Squashy, →**SUBMIT**, Succumb, Supple, Surrender, Susceptible, Sustained, Temporise, Tolerant, Truckle, Weak-kneed, Yold

**Yob** Lager lout, Lout, Oaf, Ted

**Yodel** Song, Warble

**Yog(h)urt** Dahi, Madzoon, Matzoon, Tzatziki

**Yoga, Yogi** As(h)tanga (vinyasa), Bear, Bhakti, Bikram, Fakir, Hatha, Hot, Maha, Power, Raja, Sid(d)ha, Sivananda

**Yoke** Bow, Cang(ue), Collar, Couple, Harness, Inspan, Jugal, Oxbow, Pair, Span, Square, Tucker

**Yokel** Boor, Bumpkin, Chaw(-bacon), Clumperton, Culchie, Hayseed, Hick, Jake, Jock, Joskin, Peasant, Rube, Rustic

**Yolk(ed)** Azygous, Isolecithal, Meroistic, Parablast, Vitellicle, Vitelline, Vitellus, Yelk, Yellow

**Yon(der)** Distant, Further, O'erby, Thae, There, Thether, Thither

**Yore** Agone, Olden, Past

**Yorick** Sterne

**York(shire), Yorkshireman** Batter, Bowl, Dales, Ebor, Pudding, Ridings, See, Tyke, White rose

**Yorker** Tice

**You** One, Second person, Sie, Thee, Thou, Usted, Wena, Ye

**Young (person), Youngster, Youth(ful)** Adolescent, Ageless, Amorino, Bairn, Bev(an), Bit, Bodgie, Boy, Boyhood, Brigham, Bub, Buckeen, Buckie, Buppie, Calf-time, Ch, Charver, Chick, Chicken, Chiel, Child, Chile, Cion, Cock(erel), Cockle, Colt, Comsomol, Cornstalk, Cub, Day-old, Dell, Dilling, DJ, Early, Ephebe, Ephebus, Esquire, Flapper, Fledgling, Foetus, Fox, Fresh, Fry, Gigolo, Gilded, Gillet, Girl, Gunsel, Halfling, Hebe, Hobbledehoy, Immature, Imp, Infant, Issue, Jeunesse d'orée, Junior, Juvenal,

Juvenesce, Juvenile, Keral, Kid, Kiddo, Kiddy, Kipper, Knave-bairn, Komsomol, Lad, Lamb, Latter-day, Leaping-time, Less, Litter, Little, Loretta, Middle, Minor, Misspent, Mod, Mormon, Mot, Muchacha, Nance, Narcissus, Neanic, Ned(ette), Neophyte, Nestling, New, New Romantic, Nipper, Nurs(e)ling, Nymph, Plant, Popsy, Poult, (Pre-)pubescent, Pre-teen, Progeny, Protégé(e), Punk, Pup, Rude boy, Salad days, Sapling, Scent, Scion, Screenager, Shaveling, Shaver, Sien(t), Skinhead, Slip, Small, Son, Spark, Spawn, Spide, Sprig, Springal(d), Stripling, Subteen, Swain, Syen, Ted, Teenager, Teens, Teenybopper, Tir na n'Og, Tit, Tot, Toyboy, Vernal, Waif, Well-preserved, Whelp, Whippersnapper, Widge, Wigga, Wigger, Wimp, Yippy, Yoof, Yopper, Younker, Yukon, Yumpie, Yuppie

**Younger, Youngest** Baby, Benjamin, Cadet, Last born, Less, Minimus, Seneca, Wallydrag, Wallydraigle, Yr

**Your(s)** Thee, Thine, Thy

▸ **Youth** *see* **YOUNG (PERSON)**

**Yo-yo** Bandalore

**Ytterbium** Yb

**Yttrium** Y

**Yucatan** Maya

**Yucca** Adam's needle

**Yuck(y)** Gooey, Grooly, Gross, Sickly, Sticky

**Yugoslav** Croat(ian), Serb, Slovene, Ustashi

**Yukon** YT

**Yuletide** Advent, Dec, Noel, Xmas

**Yummy** Delish

# Zz

**Z** Izzard, Izzet, Zambia, Zebra
**Zambia** .zm
**Zamenhof** Esperanto
**Zander** Fogash, Sander
**Zany** Barmy, Bor(r)el, Comic, Cuckoo, Idiotic, Mad, Offbeat
**Zanzibar** EAZ, Swahili
**Zap** Control, Nuke
**Zeal(ous)** Ardour, Bigotry, Devotion, Eager, Earnest, Enthusiasm, Evangelic, Fanatical, Fanaticism, Fervour, Fire, Hamas, Happy-clappy, Perfervid, Rabid, Study, Zest
**Zealot** Bigot, Crusader, Devotee, Essene, Extremist, Fan(atic), St Simon, Votary
**Zebra** Convict, Quagga, Z, Zeal
**Zebu** Brahmin bull, Brahmin cow
**Zenith** Acme, Apogee, Height, Pole, Summit, Vertex
**Zeno** Colonnade, Elea, Stoic
**Zeolite** Analcime, Analcite, Gmelinite
**Zephyr** Breeze, Wind
**Zeppelin** Airship, Balloon, Dirigible
**Zero** Absolute, Blob, Cipher, Circle, Donut, Double, Ground, Nil, Nilpotent, None, Nothing, Nought, O, Status, Year, Z
**Zest** Brio, Condiment, Crave, Élan, Enthusiasm, Gusto, Peel, Pep, Piquancy, Relish, Spark, Spice, Tang, Taste, Zap, Zing
**Ziegfeld** Flo
**Zigzag** Crémaillère, Crinkle-crankle, Dancette, Feather-stitch, Indent, Major Mitchell, Pink, Ric-rac, Slalom, Stagger, Switchback, Tack, Traverse, Vandyke, Yaw
**Zimbabwe** -.zw
**Zinc** Blende, Gahnite, Mossy, Sherardise, Spelter, Sphalerite, Tutenag, Tutty, Willemite, Wurtzite, Zn
**Zip(per)** Dart, Dash, Energy, Fastener, Fly, Go, Nada, O, Oomph, Pep, Presto, Slide fastener, Stingo, Verve, Vim, Vivacity, Whirry, Zero
**Zircon** Hyacinth, Jacinth, Jargo(o)n
**Zirconium** Baddeleyite, Zr
**Zither** Autoharp, Cithara, Kantela, Kantele, Koto
**Zodiac(al)** Aquarius, Archer, Aries, Bull, Cancer, Capricorn, Counter-glow, Crab, Fish, Gegenschein, Gemini, Goat, Horoscope, Leo, Libra, Lion, Ophiuchus, Pisces, Ram, Sagittarius, Scales, Scorpio(n), Taurus, Trigon, Twins, Virgin, Virgo, Watercarrier
**Zola** Budd, Emile, Nana, Realism
**Zombie** Catatonic, Dolt, Robot, Undead
**Zone(s)** Abyssal, Aerospace, Anacoustic, Area, Arid, Auroral, Band, Bathyal, Belt, Benioff, Buffer, Canal, Climate, Collision, Comfort, Convergence, Crumple, Dead, Demilitarized, District, Drop, Economic, Ecotone, End, Enterprise, Erogenous, Eruv, Euro, Exclusion, Exclusive, F layer, Fracture, Free(-fire), Fresnel, Frigid, Hadal, Home, Hot, Impact, Ionopause, Krumhole, Low velocity, Mix, Neutral, No-fly, Nuclear-free, Precinct, → REGION, Rift, Ring, Russian, Sahel, Saturation, Schlieren, Sector, Shear, Skip, Smokeless, Soviet, Stratopause, Strike, Subduction, T, Taiga, Temperate, Time, Tolerance, Torrid, Tundra, Twilight, Vadose, Z

**Zoo** Bedlam, Circus, Menagerie, Vivarium, Whipsnade
**Zoologist, Zoology** Biologist, Botanist, Cetology, Leisler, Lorenz, Naturalist, Primatology, Schneider
**Zoom** Close-up, Speed
**Zoroastrian** Avestan, Fire-worshipper, Gabar, Gheber, Ghebre, Gueber, Guebre, Magus, Mazdaist, Mazdean, Ormazd, Ormuzd, Parsee, Parsi
**Zulu** Chaka, Impi, Inkatha, Matabele, Niger, Shaka, Warrior, Z
**Zut** Crimini
**Zygote** Oospore